Quick Tax Facts—2004 Jobs Act Changes

Key Tax Breaks Added or Eliminated

The chart below provides a list of important tax breaks and incentives that have been added by the American Jobs Creation Act of 2004 and those benefits that have been eliminated or restricted. See the explanations in CCH's *American Jobs Creation Act of 2004: Law, Explanation and Analysis* for complete discussions of the changes, including effective dates and transitional rules.

TAX BREAKS AND INCENTIVES ADDED

✔ **Manufacturing deduction**—Businesses granted new deduction for domestic manufacturing and production activities. For 2005-2006, the deduction equals 3% of the lesser of qualified production activities income or taxable income. Percentage rises to 6% in 2007-2009 and to 9% in 2010 and after.

✔ **Sales tax deduction**—Individuals given option to deduct state and local *sales* taxes instead of state and local *income* taxes for 2004 and 2005.

✔ **Sec. 179 expensing**—Enhanced Code Sec. 179 expensing rules extended through 2007. Businesses can deduct up to $100,000 of qualifying property ($102,000 for 2004). Up to $400,000 of property can be placed in service ($410,000 for 2004) before the $100,000 deduction amount must be reduced. Indexing of amounts for inflation also extended through 2007.

✔ **S corporation reform**—Maximum number of S corporation shareholders increased from 75 to 100, and family members counted as one shareholder. Other S corporation rules simplified.

✔ **International tax**—Numerous changes permit companies to repatriate foreign earnings and also impact the foreign tax credit, FTC carryovers, sourcing rules and determination of subpart F income.

✔ **International shipping**—Shippers allowed to elect to compute tax on international shipping activities based on a per ton rate, instead of the corporate income tax rate.

✔ **VEETC (volumetric ethanol excise tax credit)**—New income and excise tax credits added for biodiesel fuel that is sold or used after September 30, 2004.

TAX BREAKS AND INCENTIVES ELIMINATED

✗ **ETI repeal**—U.S. exporters gradually lose the benefit of the exclusion from gross income for extraterritorial income (ETI), starting in 2005. Transitional relief delays complete repeal of the exclusion until 2007.

✗ **SUV loophole**—SUV loophole tightened, so that business owners can no longer deduct the full cost of sports utility vehicles under the Code Sec. 179 expensing rules. Deductible amount capped at $25,000 for property placed in service after the date of enactment.

✗ **Donations**—Deduction limited for car, boat or plane with claimed value $500 that is given to charity after 2004. Instead of "blue book" estimate deduction capped at the charity's proceeds from sale of the vehicle. Cl that keeps vehicle for its use must provide acknowledgment. Deductio limited for donations of patents and similar property.

✗ **Expatriation rules**—Individual and corporate expatriation rules tighter to prevent taxpayers from avoiding U.S. tax by giving up U.S. citizensh residency or by moving operations offshore.

✗ **Leasing**—Tax benefits of certain leasing arrangements with foreign en governments and tax-exempt organizations restricted.

✗ **Tax avoidance**—Penalties and disclosure requirements heightened f promoters and investors involved in tax shelters, listed transactions a reportable transactions.

✗ **Fuel tax evasion**—Rules added to combat fuel tax evasion, including new and enhanced dyed fuel penalties and tracking and recordkeeping requirements.

THE FSC - ETI EXPORT TAX BENEFIT CONTROVERSY

Here is a look at the long-running dispute between the United States and the European Union over U.S. export tax benefits. Key developments in the debate are shown below.

1971

1971 The Domestic International Sales Corporation (DISC) provisions were enacted as part of the Revenue Act of 1971 (P.L. 92-178). The DISC was an export incentive that allowed U.S. companies to defer tax on income from products sold abroad. Congress enacted DISC rules to combat an increase in trade competition from abroad.

1972 The DISC was challenged by the European Community as an impermissible export subsidy in violation of the General Agreement on Tariffs and Trade (GATT). The United States countered that the incentive balanced the effect of the "territorial" income system used by other trading partners.

1976 The GATT Panel sustained challenges made against the DISC, as well as U.S. challenges to export incentives provided by France, Belgium and the Netherlands.

1981 The United States agreed to adopt the general findings of the GATT Panel, subject to a 1981 GATT Counsel Decision (1981 Understanding), which qualified the findings. The 1981 Understanding held that the countries were not required to tax income from economic processes occurring outside their territory, arm's-length pricing applied to territorial system exports and the prevention of double taxation of fsi was permitted.

1984 The Foreign Sales Corporation (FSC) was added as part of the Deficit Reduction Act of 1984 (P.L. 98-369), replacing the DISC. The provisions were designed to comply with the 1981 Understanding. The FSC exempted a portion of export income from tax. Also enacted was the Interest-Charge Domestic International Sales Corporation (IC-DISC).

1997 **November** The European Union (EU) began to challenge the FSC provisions in the World Trade Organization (WTO) as a prohibited export subsidy. The IC-DISC was not challenged.

1998 **July** The EU requested that the WTO Dispute Settlement Panel determine whether the FSC provisions were consistent with the WTO rules.

1999 **October 8** The WTO Panel ruled that the FSC provisions did not comply with the United States' WTO obligation. The United States appealed the ruling, but was unsuccessful.

2000 **November 15** The FSC and Extraterritorial Income Exclusion Act (P.L. 106-519) was enacted to repeal the FSC provisions and prevent retaliatory measures. The EU challenged ETI in the WTO as a tax subsidy contingent on exporting.

2001 **August 20** The WTO Panel issued a report that found ETI in violation of WTO rules. The WTO Appellate body denied a U.S. appeal.

2001 **August 30** A WTO arbitration panel authorized the EU to impose $4 billion of tariffs on U.S. products.

2003 **November** The EU set a deadline of March 2004 for WTO compliance.

2004 **March 1** Tariffs started being imposed on U.S. products. The tariffs began at a rate of 5%, with 1% increases scheduled each month for a year, until the rate would reach a ceiling of 17% in March of 2005.

2004 **October** The American Jobs Creation Act of 2004 repeals ETI for transactions after 2004 and provides generous transitional relief. The changes are under study by the EU, according to a 10/11/04 press release.

TAX LEGISLATION 2004

American Jobs Creation Act of 2004

Law, Explanation and Analysis

CCH Editorial Staff Publication

CCH INCORPORATED
Chicago

A WoltersKluwer Company

This publication is designed to provide accurate and authoritative information in regard to the subject matter covered. It is sold with the understanding that the publisher is not engaged in rendering legal, accounting, or other professional service. If legal advice or other expert assistance is required, the services of a competent professional person should be sought.

ISBN 0-8080-1210-X

No claim is made to original government works; however, within this Product or Publication, the following are subject to CCH's copyright: (1) the gathering, compilation, and arrangement of such government materials; (2) the magnetic translation and digital conversion of data, if applicable; (3) the historical, statutory and other notes and references; and (4) the commentary and other materials.

American Jobs Creation Act of 2004

Not Just for Exporters: ETI Repeal and a Whole Lot More

Typically, election years are not marked by significant tax legislation. By that standard, 2004 is not a typical election year. Lest one believe that the 108th Congress is simply an overachiever, understand that the American Jobs Creation Act of 2004 comes after years of attempts to right what many perceived as a legislative wrong.

The 2004 Jobs Act is being termed the most significant reform of U.S. business taxation, in terms of both impact and number of provisions, since the U.S. Internal Revenue Code was overhauled back in 1986. The Act was passed by the House on October 7th, one day before its scheduled adjournment for the November 2004 election, by a vote of 280 to 141. And, it was passed by the Senate on October 11th, by a vote of 69-17, three days after the Senate's scheduled adjournment. As we go to press, the bill has been enrolled, but it has not been received by President Bush for his signature. The President, however, has indicated that he will sign the bill into law.

The impetus for the long awaited legislation was the repeal of the extraterritorial income (ETI) taxing regime. The ETI provisions had been deemed violative of international trade agreements by the World Trade Organization back in January of 2002, and the European Union started imposing multi-million dollar sanctions on the United States as of March of 2004. The U.S. Department of Commerce estimated that domestic manufacturers, businesses and farmers could pay over $475 million in tariffs by March of 2005 if the ETI rules were not effectively replaced. The American Jobs Creation Act of 2004 hopefully signals the end of the imposition of these sanctions. However, the European Commission has said it will lift trade sanctions only after it has fully analyzed the legislation. Some believe that the fact that the ETI regime is phased out over time, rather than immediately repealed, may result in sanctions being preserved as a bargaining tool in other trade disputes.

The bill began as an effort to compensate exporters for the repeal of the $50 billion tax-based trade subsidy, however, it ballooned into a $145 billion package of pre-election business tax breaks. The main impact of this mammoth legislation will be made by the broad-based corporate incentives and tax cuts originally intended to compensate U.S. businesses for the ETI repeal. U.S. manufacturers, multinational operations, agribusiness and energy companies will all greatly benefit from the legislation, although small businesses, farmers, partnerships, S corporations and real estate investors will reap some benefits as well.

Because the Act purports to be fully funded, however, it is not all tax breaks and benefits. In fact, the revenue-raising provisions of the Act will hit hard at both individuals and business taxpayers. These provisions, coupled with the ETI repeal, are expected to raise $145 billion for the Treasury—enough to fully offset the cost of the accompanying tax breaks and incentives. Many of the revenue raisers are aimed at thwarting tax shelters and other tax avoidance schemes. The revenue provisions, however, have been permanently enacted while many of the tax breaks are effective only for a temporary period. By giving the tax breaks a limited life, Congress significantly reduced the cost of the bill and was more easily able to craft and pass a fully funded piece of legislation. In reality, however, many of these tax breaks will likely be extended by future Congresses bringing the real cost of the legislation much higher.

In this Act, you will find a wide range of provisions primarily impacting U.S. manufacturing and international trade, but also affecting vastly different types of transactions and taxpayers. The effective dates of these provisions are equally as disparate. Some provisions are retroactive, some become effective on the date the President signs the bill, some take effect next year, and still others aren't implemented until 2006.

Among others, the more significant provisions of the *American Jobs Creation Act of 2004*:

- Repeal the controversial extraterritorial income (ETI) taxing regime;
- Create a new business deduction for U.S. manufacturers effectively reducing their income tax rate;
- Continue enhanced small business expensing for two more years;
- Significantly narrow the SUV loophole by capping the related deduction;
- Accelerate depreciation for leasehold and restaurant improvements;
- Reform S corporation taxation including expanding the permissible number of shareholders;
- Attempt to simplify international taxation in part by reducing the foreign tax credit baskets from nine to two;
- Provide tax relief to farmers and agricultural businesses;
- Crack down on tax shelters and other tax avoidance schemes including leasing transactions;
- Tighten the rules surrounding charitable deductions for vehicle donations;
- Allow deductions of state sales tax in lieu of deductions of state income tax.

And, what would a significant piece of legislation be if it didn't contain a nod towards special interests? This Act does not disappoint. It houses a $10.14 billion buyout of the federal tobacco subsidy and benefits such specialized groups as native Alaskan whalers, NASCAR race track groups and importers of Chinese ceiling fans. Even foreign gamblers are granted a concession as they are no longer subject to withholding on their race track winnings.

About This Work and CCH

CCH's *American Jobs Creation Act of 2004: Law, Explanation and Analysis* provides readers with a single integrated reference tool covering all tax aspects of the American Jobs Creation Act of 2004. (The structure of the tobacco buyout is such that it does not directly impact the Internal Revenue Code, so a discussion of the Act's tobacco-related provisions are not contained in this publication.)

Along with the relevant Internal Revenue Code provisions, as amended by the Act, and supporting committee reports, CCH editors, together with several leading tax practitioners and commentators, have put together the most timely and complete practical analysis of the new law. Tax professionals looking for the Conference Report, including the related bill text, can find it in a separate CCH publication. Other books and tax services relating to the new legislation can be found at our website http://tax.cchgroup.com.

As always, CCH remains dedicated to responding to the needs of tax professionals in helping them quickly understand and work with these new laws as they take effect.

Mark A. Luscombe

Principal Analyst

CCH Tax and Accounting

October 2004

Outside Contributors

Neal J. Block
Baker & McKenzie
Chicago, Illinois

Martin J. Collins
PricewaterhouseCoopers, LLP
Chicago, Illinois

Michael DiFronzo
McDermott Will & Emery
Chicago, Illinois

Michael J. Grace
Buchanan Ingersoll PC
Washington, D.C.

Sidney Kess
New York, New York

Michael R. Maryn
Sonnenschein Nath & Rosenthal LLP
Washington, D.C.

Prof. Gary L. Maydew
Iowa State University (Retired)
Ames, Iowa

Keith Nakamoto
PricewaterhouseCoopers, LLP
Chicago, Illinois

Vincent J. O'Brien
Vincent J. O'Brien, CPA, P.C.
Lynbrook, New York

Gregory G. Palmer
McDermott Will & Emery
Chicago, Illinois

Jeffrey H. Paravano
Baker & Hostetler LLP
Cleveland, Ohio

Michael Schlesinger
Schlesinger & Sussman
New York, New York

Katherine Stenander
McDermott Will & Emery
Chicago, Illinois

Sydney S. Traum, Esq.
Sydney S. Traum, P.A.
Coral Gables, Florida

Lowell D. Yoder
McDermott Will & Emery
Chicago, Illinois

CCH Tax and Accounting Publishing

EDITORIAL STAFF

Explanation and Analysis

¶ 1
Features of This Book

This publication is your complete guide to the American Jobs Creation Act of 2004 (H.R. 4520), as passed by the House and Senate. The core portion of this publication contains the CCH Explanations and Analysis of the Act. The CCH Explanations outline all of the law changes and what they mean for you and your clients. The explanations feature practical guidance, examples, planning opportunities and strategies, as well as pitfalls to be avoided as a result of the law changes. Insights supplied by expert tax practitioners are highlighted throughout our analysis.

The law text and committee reports are reproduced following the analysis. Any new or amended Internal Revenue Code sections appear here, with changes highlighted in italics. You will also see the law text for portions of the Act that did not amend the tax code. The legislative history of each provision follows the law text. Relevant portions of the House Committee Report, Senate Committee Report, or Conference Committee Report make up the legislative history for each law change.

The book also contains numerous other features designed to help you locate and understand the changes enacted in the 2004 Jobs Act. These features include highlight summaries of important provisions, cross references to related materials, detailed effective dates, and numerous finding tables and indexes. A more detailed description of these features appears below.

HIGHLIGHTS

Highlights are quick summaries of the major provisions of the 2004 Jobs Act. The Highlights are arranged by area of interest, such as individuals, businesses, or investments. At the end of each summary is a paragraph reference to the longer CCH Explanation on that topic, giving you an easy way to find the parts of the book that are of most interest to you. *Highlights start at ¶5.*

TAXPAYERS AFFECTED

The first chapter of the book, *Taxpayers Affected*, contains a detailed look at how the new law affects specific categories of taxpayers. This chapter provides a quick reference for readers who want to know the immediate result the law will have on their clients. Each section of this chapter highlights a different taxpayer type, noting the tax savings or costs that result from the 2004 Jobs Act changes. *Taxpayers Affected starts at ¶101.*

CCH EXPLANATIONS

CCH Explanations are designed to give you a complete, accessible understanding of the new law. Explanations are arranged by subject for ease of use. There are three main finding devices you can use to locate explanations on a given topic. These are:

- A detailed table of contents at the beginning of the publication listing all of the CCH Explanations on the new law;
- A table of contents preceding each chapter; and
- An extensive topical index covering all subjects under the 2004 Jobs Act.

Each CCH Explanation contains special features to aid in your complete understanding of the new law. These include:

- A background or prior law discussion that puts the law changes into perspective;
- Practitioner commentary incorporated throughout the explanations, identifying planning opportunities and strategies, as well as pitfalls to avoid;

- Editorial aids—examples, cautions, planning notes, elections, comments, compliance tips, and key rates and figures—that highlight the impact of the new law;
- Charts and examples illustrating the ramifications of specific law changes;
- Boldface captions at the end of each explanation identifying the Code sections added, amended or repealed, as well as the Act sections containing the changes;
- Cross references to the law and committee report paragraphs related to the explanation;
- A line highlighting the effective date of each law change, marked by a star symbol;
- References at the end of the discussion to related information in the Standard Federal Tax Reporter, Federal Tax Service, Federal Tax Guide, Federal Estate and Gift Tax Reporter and the Federal Excise Tax Reporter.

The CCH Explanations begin at ¶205.

AMENDED CODE PROVISIONS

Changes to the Internal Revenue Code made by the American Jobs Creation Act of 2004 appear under the heading "Code Sections Added, Amended or Repealed." *Any changed or added law text is set out in italics.* Deleted Code text, or the Code provision prior to amendment, appears in the Amendment Notes following each reconstructed Code provision. An effective date for each Code change is also provided.

The amendment notes contain cross references to the corresponding Committee Reports and the CCH Explanations that discuss the new law. *The text of the Code begins at ¶5001.*

Sections of the American Jobs Creation Act of 2004 that do not amend the Internal Revenue Code appear in full text following "Code Sections Added, Amended or Repealed." *The text of these provisions appears in Act Section order beginning at ¶7005.*

COMMITTEE REPORTS

The controlling Committee Reports explain the intent of Congress in enacting the provisions in the 2004 Jobs Act. Included in this publication are portions of the House Committee Report accompanying H.R. 4520 (H.R. Rep. No. 108-548), the Senate Report accompanying H.R. 4520 (S. Rep. No. 108-192) and the Conference Committee Report (H.R. Conf. Rep. No. 108-755) to the bill. At the end of each section of Committee Report text, you will find references to the corresponding explanation and Code provisions. *Committee Reports appear in Act Section order beginning at ¶10,001.*

EFFECTIVE DATES

A table listing the major effective dates provides you with a reference bridge between Code Sections and Act Sections and indicates the retroactive or prospective nature of the laws explained. *This effective date table begins at ¶20,001.*

SPECIAL FINDING DEVICES

Other special tables and finding devices in this book include:

- A table cross-referencing Code Sections to the CCH Explanations (*see ¶25,001*);
- A table showing all Code Sections added, amended or repealed (*see ¶25,005*);
- A table showing provisions of other acts that were amended (*see ¶25,010*);
- A table of Act Sections not amending the Internal Revenue Code (*see ¶25,015*); and
- An Act Section to Code Section table (*see ¶25,020*).

¶ 2
Table of Contents

¶ 3
Detailed Table of Contents

CHAPTER 1. TAXPAYERS AFFECTED

¶3

CHAPTER 2. ETI REPEAL AND MANUFACTURING ACTIVITY DEDUCTION

CHAPTER 3. BUSINESS DEDUCTIONS AND CREDITS

CHAPTER 4. INTERNATIONAL TRANSACTIONS: FOREIGN TAX CREDIT, SUBPART F AND CFCs

CHAPTER 5. INTERNATIONAL TRANSACTIONS: EXPATRIATION AND OTHER PROVISIONS

¶3

CHAPTER 6. TAX AVOIDANCE AND TAX SHELTERS

CHAPTER 7. SALES, EXCHANGES AND FINANCING TRANSACTIONS

¶3

CHAPTER 8. AGRICULTURE AND ENERGY RESOURCES

CHAPTER 9. S CORPORATIONS AND PARTNERSHIPS

CHAPTER 10. CORPORATIONS

¶3

CHAPTER 11. RICs, REITs, FASITs AND INSURANCE COMPANIES

CHAPTER 12. INDIVIDUALS

CHAPTER 13. EXEMPT ORGANIZATIONS, CHARITABLE DONATIONS AND COOPERATIVES

¶3

CHAPTER 16. PROCEDURE AND ADMINISTRATION

¶ 5
Highlights

ETI Repeal and Manufacturing Activity Deduction

Extraterritorial income (ETI). The ETI exclusion is repealed, but taxpayers retain 100 percent of their ETI benefits in 2004, 80 percent of their ETI benefits in 2005, and 60 percent of their ETI benefits in 2006. The repeal does not apply to a transaction in the ordinary course of a trade or business under a binding contract between unrelated persons that was in effect on September 17, 2003 . . . . . .   ¶ 205

Deduction related to U.S. production activities. The ETI regime is replaced by a phased-in deduction related to domestic production. The maximum deduction becomes effective in 2010, and is equal to nine percent of the lesser of an eligible taxpayer's taxable income or qualified production activities income. . . . .   ¶ 210

Business Deductions and Credits

Code Sec. 179 expensing limits. The temporary increase in expensing limits for qualified depreciable property and computer software, which was scheduled to expire after 2005, is extended through 2006 and 2007 . . . .   ¶ 305

"SUV loophole" limited. The cost of a heavy truck or sport utility vehicle that may be expensed under Code Sec. 179 is reduced from $100,000 to $25,000 . . . .   ¶ 310

MACRS recovery periods. The 15-year recovery period applies to qualified leasehold improvement property and qualified restaurant property placed in service before 2006. The recovery periods for initial land clearing and grading costs incurred by electric and gas utilities are increased. A seven-year recovery period applies to qualified automobile racetracks and Alaska natural gas pipelines . .   ¶ 315, ¶ 317, ¶ 335, ¶ 340, ¶ 345

Film and television. For purposes of the income forecast method of depreciation for films, recordings, books, and similar property, qualified participations and residuals may be included in adjusted basis when the property is placed in service. Qualified film and television production costs can be deducted, rather than capitalized   ¶ 320, ¶ 365

Bonus depreciation. Qualified noncommercial aircraft placed in service after September 10, 2001, is eligible for bonus deprecation and the extended January 1, 2006 placed-in-service date. For qualified property subject to multiple unit syndicated leasing transactions, the rules governing placed-in-service dates are modified . . . .   ¶ 325, ¶ 330

Start-up expenses. Up to $5,000 in start-up expenditures is deductible in the year a new trade or business begins. Additional expenses are amortized over 180 months . . . .   ¶ 350

International Transactions

Tax Avoidance and Tax Shelters

Sales, Exchanges and Financing Transactions

Agriculture and Energy Resources

Alcohol fuel and biodiesel. Certain excise taxes on fuel can be reduced by credits for alcohol fuels in 2005 through 2010, and biodiesel mixtures in 2005 and 2006. The general business income tax credit for 2005 and 2006 includes credits for biodiesel mixtures and biodiesel used or sold as fuel; and the alcohol fuel component of the credit is extended through 2010. These income and excise tax credits are coordinated. Taxpayers claiming certain fuel-related tax benefits must file quarterly information returns . . . .

Involuntary conversions of livestock. Drought, flood or other weather-related conditions are added to environmental contamination as events that can cause the involuntary conversion of livestock, and the replacement period is extended to four years. The provision applies to tax years for which returns were due after December 31, 2002 . . . .

Cooperatives. The cost of feeding farm animals in anticipation of a subsequent sale is a valid marketing expense for purposes of calculating a cooperative's net earnings. Federal courts can issue declaratory judgments regarding the qualifications of a farmers' cooperative. A cooperative can elect to pass through its small ethanol producer credit as a patronage dividend . . . .

Reforestation expenses. Certain taxpayers may deduct their first $10,000 in qualified reforestation expenditures and amortize the remainder. The reforestation credit component of the investment tax credit is repealed . . . .

Sulfur fuels. Small business refiners can elect to deduct 75 percent of qualified capital costs incurred after 2002 to comply with the Environmental Protection Agency's Highway Diesel Fuel Sulfur Control Requirements. They can also claim a general business credit for expenses incurred after 2002 in the production of qualifying low sulfur diesel fuel . . . .

Oil and gas production incentives. The general business credit includes a new credit for producing oil and natural gas from marginal domestic wells. Expenses incurred in constructing a qualified natural gas treatment plant in Alaska qualify for the enhanced oil recovery credit . . . .

Renewable electricity production credit. Geothermal energy, solar energy, small irrigation power, municipal solid waste, and refined coal are added to wind, closed-loop biomass and open-loop biomass (including poultry waste) as qualified energy resources (QERs) that can be produced at qualified facilities (QFs). The allowable credit for electricity produced at certain QFs is reduced . . . .

S Corporations and Partnerships

Corporations

RICs, REITs, FASITs and Insurance Companies

Individuals

Health professionals. Qualified student loan repayments made by federal and state programs on behalf of health care professionals are excluded from gross income and employment taxes . . . .   ¶1225

Exempt Organizations and Charitable Donations

Donated vehicles. Taxpayers must obtain a contemporaneous written acknowledgement for donations of qualified vehicles, including cars, boats, and aircraft, that have a claimed value of over $500. Exempt organizations can be penalized for failing to provide accurate receipts. . . . .   ¶1305

Noncash contributions. Charitable contributions of property made after June 3, 2004 and valued at more than $500 are not deductible unless the donor meet specific appraisal and documentations requirements . . . .   ¶1310

Intellectual property. For patents and most other intellectual property donated to a charitable organization after June 3, 2004, the donor's deduction is limited to the lesser of the donor's basis in the property or its fair market value . . . .   ¶1315

Bowhead whaling expenses. A charitable contribution deduction is available for certain expenses incurred by whaling captains recognized by the Alaska Eskimo Whaling Commission . . . .   ¶1320

SBIC debt. For purposes of an exempt organization's unrelated business income arising from debt-financed property transactions, qualified indebtedness of a small business investment company (SBIC) is excluded from the organization's acquisition indebtedness   ¶1325

Brownfield gain or loss. A qualified exempt organization's unrelated business taxable income (UBTI) excludes gain or loss from the qualified disposition of certain brownfield property . . . .   ¶1330

Rural electric cooperatives. A rural electric cooperative (REC) can exclude qualified receipts from income for purposes of the rule requiring a co-op to collect at least 85-percent of its income from members for the sole purpose of meeting losses and expenses . . . . .   ¶1335

Cooperative's dividends. Certain dividends paid by a cooperative on its capital stock or other proprietary capital interests do not reduce patronage income. . . . .   ¶1340

Compensation and Pension Plans

Nonqualified deferred compensation plans. Requirements for nonqualified deferred compensation plans are consolidated and supplemented. Deferrals are included in the employee's gross income and additional tax is imposed as a result of certain plan failures relating to distributions, accelerated benefits and elections .   ¶1405

ISOs and ESPP options. FICA wages do not include remuneration arising from the acquisition of stock under an incentive stock option (ISO) or employer stock purchase plan (ESPP) option, or from the disposition of such stock. Employers are not required to withhold income tax when an employee realizes gain on a disqualifying disposition of stock. When federal conflict-of-interest rules require a shareholder to divest stock, the stock is treated as meeting the holding period requirements for ISOs and ESPP options . . . .

Transfer of excess pension assets to retiree health plan. For purposes of the minimum cost requirement, applicable employer costs can be reduced by as much as the maximum permissible reduction of retiree health benefit costs . . . .

Retirement plan contributions for nonresident aliens. Certain nontaxable retirement plan contributions for nonresident aliens are not included in the plan participant's basis . . . .

Withholding on supplemental wage payments. An employee's annual supplemental wage payments that exceed $1,000,000 are subject to withholding at the highest income tax rate . . . .

Excise Taxes

Fuel tax liability. In a qualified two-party exchange, the delivering person is not liable for the tax on the removal of a taxable fuel from a terminal . . . .

Aviation fuel tax. Like gasoline, diesel fuel and kerosene, aviation fuel is taxed upon its removal from a refinery or terminal, or upon entry into the U.S. . . . .

Transmix. Transmix and diesel fuel blendstocks identified by the IRS are taxed as if they were diesel fuel, regardless of whether the mixture contains gasoline. Re-refining constitutes a nontaxable off-highway business use of the transmix . . . .

Diesel fuel. A repeal of the excise tax on diesel fuel used in trains and on fuels used in certain barges is phased in during 2005 and 2006, and becomes fully effective in 2007 . . . .

Dyed fuel. Terminals must use mechanical injection systems to dye diesel fuel and kerosene held for sale for a nontaxable purpose. More persons are subject to the dyed fuel rules, and only limited administrative review is available for penalties imposed on repeat offenders. . . . .

Registration and reporting. For a bulk transfer of taxable fuel to be exempt from the manufacturers level fuel tax, any pipeline or vessel operator that is a party to the bulk transfer must be registered. Registered vessel owners must also display proof of registration on each vessel used to transport the fuel. Any person who has 25 or more reportable ExSTARS transactions in a month must file a report in electronic format. Penalties for failing to register and make timely reports may be imposed . . . .

Foreign trade zone. Persons that operate a terminal or a refinery within a foreign trade zone or within a customs bonded storage facility, or hold an inventory position with respect to a taxable fuel in such a terminal, are required to register with the IRS . . . . ¶ 1535

IRS inspection authority The scope of the IRS inspection authority is expanded to include any books, records, or shipping papers pertaining to taxable fuel. An assessable penalty of $1,000 is imposed for refusal to admit or permit any action relating to an IRS inspection of sites and equipment . . . . ¶ 1539, ¶ 1541

Highway use tax. The annual use tax imposed on heavy highway vehicles cannot be paid in installments after June 30, 2005. Taxpayers with at least 25 vehicles must file their Forms 2290 electronically. The tax may be prorated if a vehicle is stolen, destroyed or sold. Reduced rates for Canadian and Mexican vehicles are repealed . . . . ¶ 1547

Mobile machinery exemption. A three-part test for the mobile machinery exemption is codified for purposes of the retail tax on heavy vehicles, the tax on tires, and the heavy vehicle use tax. For purposes of the nontaxable use exemption, mobile machinery must satisfy a design test and a use test . . . . ¶ 1549

Off-highway transportation vehicle and nontransportation trailers and semitrailers. The definitions of off-highway transportation vehicle, nontransportation trailers and semitrailers contained in the June 2002 proposed regulations are codified . . . . ¶ 1551

Tire taxes. The excise tax on tires is based on the load capacity of the tire, rather than the tire weight . . . . ¶ 1553

Archery and fishing equipment. An 11-percent excise tax is imposed on the sale of certain bows by a manufacturer, producer, or importer; a 12-percent excise tax is imposed on the sale of most finished arrows; a three percent excise tax is imposed on the sale of fishing tackle boxes; and the excise tax on sonar fish-finding devices is repealed . . . . ¶ 1557, ¶ 1559, ¶ 1561

Taxable vaccines. Taxable vaccines include vaccines against hepatitis A and trivalent vaccines against influenza . . . . ¶ 1565

Occupational taxes. The special occupational taxes on producers and marketers of alcoholic beverages is suspended for three years . . . . . ¶ 1569

Procedure and Administration

Tax collection. The IRS may use private debt collection agencies to collect some tax debts . . . . ¶ 1605

Partial payment agreements. The IRS can enter into partial payment agreements with delinquent taxpayers . . . . ¶ 1610

Cash deposits and potential underpayments. A taxpayer can suspend the accrual of interest on an underpayment by making a cash deposit with the IRS before the underpayment is assessed . . . . ¶ 1615

Levies. A continuous levy can attach to 100 percent of the federal payments owed to a delinquent vendor of goods or services sold or leased to the federal government . . . . ¶ 1625

Chapter 1

Taxpayers Affected

AMERICAN JOBS CREATION ACT OF 2004

¶ 101

Overview

The American Jobs Creation Act of 2004 is a very unusual piece of tax legislation. Although primarily a tax law affecting business, it contains a number of highly-publicized provisions affecting individuals. With projected total revenue outlays of $145 billion, it is not a record-breaking number. The Working Families Tax Relief Act of 2004 that passed Congress a couple of weeks before this legislation actually cost slightly more. Unlike that legislation, however, the American Jobs Creation Act of 2004 is projected to be fully paid for over the 10-year budget period.

The legislation actually has more revenue-raising provisions than tax cut provisions. That result was in part externally forced upon this Congress. The need to repeal the extraterritorial income provisions provided almost $58 billion in revenue that this Congress was not about to let go to waste. They spent that and more on a long series of business tax breaks that has special interest legislation written all over it. What is unusual is that Congress came up with all of the additional revenue raisers to pay for the rest of the tax breaks as well: anti-expatriation provisions, anti-tax shelter provisions, anti-fuel tax evasion provisions, user fee extensions, excise taxes, business and individual tax loophole closers. In all, Congress added about half a dozen more revenue-raising provisions than revenue-losing provisions.

Having just passed tax legislation focused on individuals that was not paid for at all, it was clear that this legislation was not going to pass this year unless it was paid for. As has been the case in recent years, however, there is a lot of budget gimmickry in achieving "paid-for status." Phase-ins and phase-outs have once again been used to achieve balance. In the years beyond the 10-year budget window, this legislation is likely to contribute further to the federal deficit. Many are predicting that it will add to the deficit even within the 10-year window with pressure to extend popular provisions.

Although there are some elements of simplification in this legislation, especially in the international area and relating to choice of business entities, no one will confuse this legislation with a simplification bill. There are 34 new Internal Revenue Code sections added by this legislation, with a total of 274 Code sections affected in some way. Like a poker game, the only way a taxpayer has won a dollar of tax cuts with this legislation is if another taxpayer has lost a dollar. Taxpayers will have to carefully scan the more than 120 provisions to see what kind of hand that they were dealt. With many provisions including retroactive effective dates and effective dates that correspond with enactment, the impact is likely to be felt on the 2004 tax return.

GENERAL BUSINESS AND CORPORATIONS

¶ 102

Overall Effect on Business

The American Jobs Creation Act of 2004 presents many opportunities along with some new worries for businesses. Domestic manufacturers have an opportunity for a new deduction (¶ 210).

On the negative side, the 2004 Jobs Act presents potential problems in the form of new restrictions on corporate inversions (¶ 506 and ¶ 508) and new tax-shelter rules (¶ 520 and ¶ 625).

Other provisions that affect business generally include the modification of the application of the income forecast method of accounting (¶ 320), the modification of the minimum cost requirement for the transfer of excess defined benefit assets (¶ 1420), the modification of the rules for charitable contributions of intellectual property (¶ 1315) and noncash contributions generally (¶ 1310), the disallowance of interest on certain convertible debt (¶ 715), the denial of installment sale treatment for readily tradable debt (¶ 710), the revision of the amortization period for start-up and organizational expenses (¶ 350), increased withholding on supplemental wage payments exceeding $1 million (¶ 1430), and new limitations on deductions for employee entertainment expenses and use of a company aircraft (¶ 360).

¶ 103

Effect on Corporations

Domestic manufacturers.—Corporations with domestic manufacturing or production will be able to take advantage of the new domestic manufacturing deduction (¶ 210). In fact, the manner in which employee wages are worked into the calculation of the deduction may encourage the use of the corporate format because of the potential for more favorable treatment of the compensation of owner/employees.

Nonqualified preferred stock.—When property is transferred to a corporation solely in exchange for stock of that corporation, no gain or loss is recognized if, immediately after the exchange, the transferor is in control of the corporation. In this type of exchange, nonqualified preferred stock is not treated as stock. Preferred stock is stock that is limited and preferred as to dividends and that does not participate in corporate growth to any significant extent. It is now clarified that not participating in corporate growth to any significant extent means that there must be no real and meaningful likelihood of the shareholder actually participating in the earnings and growth of the corporation (¶ 1005).

Reorganizations.—In a reorganization, no gain or loss is recognized when a transferor corporation contributes property to another participant corporation solely in exchange for stock or securities of the other corporation. If, instead, the transferor receives money or other property in addition to stock or securities, gain will be recognized unless the money or other property is distributed to shareholders or creditors of the transferor. There will now be a limit on the amount distributed to creditors without gain recognition. The limit is the basis of assets contributed by the transferor corporation. In addition, an acquisitive reorganization will no longer be subject to the rules involving assumption of liabilities (¶ 1015).

A new reporting requirement is imposed on an acquiring corporation where gain or loss is recognized by shareholders of a corporation by reason of a merger or acquisition (¶ 510).

Consolidated returns.—The 2004 Jobs Act affirms the authority of the IRS to issue consolidated return regulations that treat corporations in the consolidated filing differently from corporations filing separate returns. This is a response to the *Rite Aid* case; however, it does not change the outcome of that case (¶ 1635).

International tax implications.—Many of the international tax changes included in this legislation will have an impact on corporations. In particular, a domestic corporation will be entitled to claim a deemed-paid foreign tax credit with respect to a foreign corporation that is held indirectly through a foreign or domestic partnership (¶ 435). Under the controlled foreign corporation provisions, two items of property are excepted from the definition of what constitutes U.S. property for controlled foreign corporation purposes (¶ 460). The sale by a controlled foreign corporation of a partnership interest is treated as a sale of the proportionate share of partnership assets attributable to such interest for purposes of determining subpart F foreign personal holding company income (¶ 465).

Expatriations.—Under the expatriation provisions, two different corporate inversion transactions are addressed with separate consequences for each (¶ 506). An excise tax is imposed on the value of specified stock compensation held by or for a disqualified individual at any time during the 12-month period beginning six months before the corporation's expatriation date (¶ 508). If a gain or loss is recognized in whole or in part by shareholders of a corporation by reason of a second corporation's acquisition of the stock or assets of the first corporation, then the acquiring corporation is required to make a disclosure of certain information with respect to the transaction (¶ 510).

Tax shelters.—Under the tax shelter provisions, a net built-in loss is treated as imported into the United States only if the aggregate adjusted bases of property received by a transferee corporation exceeds the fair market value of the properties transferred (¶ 520). Corporations are denied a deduction for interest paid or accrued within a tax year on any portion of an underpayment of tax that is attributable to an understatement arising from an undisclosed listed transaction (¶ 625). Code Sec. 338(h)(13)is clarified to provide that the exception for estimated tax purposes with respect to tax attributable to a deemed asset sale does not apply with respect to a qualified stock purchase for which a Code Sec. 338(h)(10) election is in effect (¶ 1020).

¶ 103

Consolidated returns.—The new law confirms the Treasury's authority to issue consolidated return regulation treating corporations filing consolidated returns differently from corporations filing separate returns (¶1635).

The new law expands the disallowance of interest deductions on certain corporate convertible or equity-linked debt that is payable in, or by reference to, the value of equity (¶715).

The requirement that donors must obtain a qualified appraisal for donated noncash property valued at more than $5,000 is extended to C corporations, and, if the value exceeds $500,000, the appraisal must be attached to the donor's tax return (¶1310).

A distribution of earnings by a U.S. holding company to a foreign corporation in a complete liquidation, if the U.S. holding company was in existence for less than five years, is treated as a dividend (¶1010).

¶ 104

Effect on Controlled Groups of Corporations

Modified definition.—There are two types of controlled groups; the parent-subsidiary type and the brother-sister type. A brother-sister controlled group means two or more corporations where an ownership (actual or constructive) threshold exists. The threshold is where five or fewer persons (individuals, estates or trusts) own stock with (1) at least 80 percent of the total combined voting power of all classes of voting stock and at least 80 percent of the total value of all stock, and (2) with respect to identical ownership of each corporation, more than 50 percent of the total combined voting power of all classes of voting stock and more than 50 percent of the total value of all stock. Brother-sister groups will now need to meet the threshold only with respect to the 50-percent level of identical ownership. This modified definition will apply only for the purpose of tax brackets, the accumulated earnings credit, and the minimum tax (¶1025).

MULTI-NATIONAL BUSINESS

¶ 105

Overall Effect on Multi-National Businesses

Although ETI repeal could have been handled in isolation, Congress took the opportunity to address a number of perceived problems in the international tax area. ETI repeal itself is subject to phase-outs to help ease the impact on those multinational businesses that have relied most heavily on its provisions (¶205). One effect of the phase-outs is that it is not immediately clear whether the European Union will consider this legislation to be in compliance with the World Trade Organization ruling and remove its sanctions. Although the primary replacement for the repealed ETI exclusion is a new deduction for domestic manufacturers, the beneficiaries of the new deduction are not closely aligned with those companies that had benefited from the ETI exclusion (¶210).

Multi-national businesses will also be affected by a series of reform and simplification provisions targeted in the area of international taxation. These include more flexible interest expense allocation rules to reduce the risk of double taxation of cross-border income (¶405). A one-year window is created to repatriate offshore income at a reduced tax rate (¶535).

Several provisions relate to the foreign tax credit. The number of foreign tax credit baskets has been reduced from nine to two: a general basket and a passive basket (¶410). With the elimination of the 10/50 company basket with respect to noncontrolled Code Sec. 902 corporations, a new look-through approach is being applied to all dividends paid by a 10/50 company (¶430). Where an overall domestic loss has reduced a taxpayer's foreign tax credit limitation, the taxpayer will be permitted to recharacterize a portion of U.S.-source income as foreign-source income (¶420).

The foreign tax credit carryover period has been extended to 10 years, but the carryback period has been reduced to one year (¶415). The 90-percent limitation of the use of foreign tax credits for alternative minimum tax purposes has also been eliminated (¶455). The new law also extends the deemed paid concepts under Code Sec. 902 and Code Sec. 960 to partnerships, making foreign tax credits more readily available where the foreign stock is owned indirectly through a partnership (¶435). Deemed payments under Code Sec. 367(d) are to be treated as royalties for foreign tax credit purposes, making it possible for them to fall into the general basket (¶445).

The new law also modifies the treatment of gains and losses with respect to commodities as subpart F foreign personal holding company income (¶470). Rents and gains derived in the active conduct of an aircraft leasing business would not be treated as either subpart F personal holding company income or subpart F shipping income (¶475). The new law also delays the effective date of Treasury regulations addressing earnings of a foreign corporation derived from the international operation of ships and aircraft (¶552). The active financing income exceptions as to what constitutes subpart F foreign personal holding company income and foreign base company services income have been modified (¶480) as well.

The new law provides greater flexibility in determining the appropriate exchange rate for use in translating foreign income tax payments (¶450).

A potential for the imposition of a second withholding tax on dividend payments from certain foreign corporations has been eliminated (¶555). The withholding income tax rate on U.S.-source dividends paid to a Puerto Rican corporation has been reduced (¶585).

Another provision eliminating different treatment for partnerships treats interest paid by foreign partnerships in a manner similar to interest paid by foreign corporations (¶570). Foreign mutual fund holders are permitted to treat certain interest, gains and dividends payments in the same manner as if they had held directly the interest held by the mutual fund (¶560).

Some overlap in the international rules is reduced by eliminating the rules applicable to foreign personal holding companies and foreign investment companies, excluding foreign corporations from the application of the personal holding company rules, and including personal services contract income as subpart F foreign personal holding company income (¶490).

This legislation specifies conditions under which a real estate investment trust (REIT) capital gain distribution to a foreign investor from dispositions of U.S. real property interests is no longer treated as effectively connected with a U.S. trade or business (¶540).

Other provisions throughout the legislation also have an impact on international business. For example, corporations are permitted to elect a tonnage tax rather than the corporate income tax on taxable income from certain international shipping (¶545).

The new law also directs the Treasury to study the earnings stripping rules in order to better prevent the shifting of income outside the U.S. (¶525).

¶105

In contrast to these changes that are generally favorable to international businesses, there is also included in the legislation a package of anti-expatriation provisions. New anti-inversion provisions apply when a domestic corporation or partnership moves its headquarters overseas with at least 60-percent commonality of ownership (¶506). An excise tax is imposed on the stock compensation of corporate insiders involved in an inversion transaction (¶508).

The Treasury is given authority to reallocate and recharacterize items among parties to a reinsurance agreement (¶515).

A new reporting requirement is imposed on an acquiring corporation where gain or loss is recognized by shareholders of a corporation by reason of a merger or acquisition (¶510).

The Treasury is also directed to undertake three studies on the effectiveness of the transfer pricing rules, possible abuses as a result of provisions in income tax treaties, and the impact of this tax legislation on inversion transactions (¶530).

Also on the revenue-raising side of the ledger is a minimum holding period requirement imposed for the foreign tax credit on withholding taxes with respect to income other than dividends (¶440). A distribution by a U.S. holding company that has been in existence for less than five years to a foreign corporation in complete liquidation is treated as a dividend (¶1010). Categories of foreign source income effectively connected to a U.S. trade or business are expanded to include economic equivalents of such income (¶575). The special recapture rules that apply to overall foreign losses on the disposition of foreign trade or business assets is extended to apply to the disposition of controlled foreign corporation stock (¶425).

¶ 106

Effect on Controlled Foreign Corporations

Under the controlled foreign corporation (CFC) provisions, two items of property are excepted from the definition of what constitutes U.S. property for CFC purposes (¶460). The sale by a CFC of a partnership interest is treated as a sale of the proportionate share of partnership assets attributable to such interest for purposes of determining subpart F foreign personal holding company income (¶465). The new law provides that deductions for amounts accrued but unpaid to related CFCs are allowable only to the extent that accrued amounts are currently includible in the income of the U.S. owners (¶705). The special recapture rules that apply to overall foreign losses on the disposition of foreign trade or business assets is extended to apply to the disposition of CFC stock (¶425).

¶ 107

Effect on FPHCs, FICs, and PFICs

The rules applicable to Foreign Personal Holding Companies (FPHCs) and Foreign Investment Companies (FICs) are eliminated (¶490).

The new law provides that deductions for amounts accrued but unpaid to related FPHCs or Personal Foreign Investment Companies (PFICs) are allowable only to the extent that accrued amounts are currently includible in the income of the U.S. owners (¶705).

S CORPORATIONS AND PARTNERSHIPS

¶ 110

Overall Effect on S Corporations and Partnerships

The IRS estimates that almost 3.5 million returns using Form 1120S (U.S. Income Tax Return for S Corporations) will be filed for the 2004 tax year. Recognizing the popularity and importance of these pass-through entities to the country's economy, the American Jobs Creation Act of 2004 provides new rules pertaining to S corporations—most of which should be interpreted as beneficial (¶ 905 through ¶ 950). These include provisions that would increase the availability of S corporations generally, limit existing restrictions, and otherwise provide a more taxpayer-friendly environment for their use.

Partnerships were also the subject of this broad-reaching legislation. Partnership basis adjustments and loss transfers (¶ 960), recognition of cancellation-of-indebtedness income (¶ 720), attribution of foreign tax credits (¶ 435) were all addressed. In addition, the 2004 Jobs Act includes provisions relating to partnerships and controlled foreign corporations (¶ 460 and ¶ 465), partnerships participating in tax shelters (¶ 665), and the impact on partnerships of increased substantiation requirements for noncash charitable contribution (¶ 1310). Finally, the new deduction for qualified production activities income also applies to partnerships (¶ 210).

¶ 111

Effect on S Corporations

Rules liberalized.—S corporations and their shareholders were the recipients of some legislative largesse in the form of a number of small, but significant, changes to the S corporation rules. Among the changes made by the 2004 Jobs Act are the following:

(1) The number of permissible shareholders in an S corporation is increased from 75 to 100 (¶ 905);

(2) All members of a family will be treated as one shareholder for purposes of the rules limiting the number of permissible shareholders in an S corporation. The term "members of the family" includes the common ancestor and all lineal descendants of the common ancestor (not more than six generations removed), plus spouses (or former spouses) of these individuals (¶ 910);

(3) Suspended losses or deductions in connection with S corporation stock that are transferred to a shareholder's spouse, or an ex-spouse incident to a divorce, would be treated as if they were incurred by the S corporation in the tax year following the transfer (¶ 915);

(4) The waiver relief currently available with respect to invalid S corporation elections and terminations is expanded to include elections and terminations connected with qualified subchapter S subsidiaries (QSubs) (¶ 920);

(5) The beneficiary of a qualified subchapter S trust (QSST), rather than the trust itself, would be allowed to deduct suspended losses on the disposition of S corporation stock under the passive activity loss limitation rules and the "at risk" rules (¶ 925);

(6) Unexercised powers of appointment can be ignored in determining who is a potential current beneficiary of an electing small business trust (ESBT) and the period during which an ESBT can dispose of S corporation stock after an ineligible shareholder becomes a potential current beneficiary has been increased to one year (¶ 930);

(7) Effective for distributions after December 31, 1997, an S corporation's leveraged employee stock ownership plan (ESOP) will not jeopardize its qualified status or the exempt status of a loan used to purchase qualified employer securities if it uses distributions from S corporation stock purchased with the loan to make payments on the loan (¶935);

(8) IRAs and Roth IRAs could be shareholders in a bank that is an S corporation to the extent of bank stock held by the IRA (the IRA account owner is effectively treated as the shareholder and an exemption from the prohibited transaction rules is permitted) (¶940); and

(9) Interest income and dividends on assets required to be held by S corporation banks (e.g., stock in the Federal Reserve Bank, the Federal Home Loan Bank, or the Federal Agricultural Mortgage Bank) would be exempted from the passive investment income limitation (¶945).

Information returns and reporting of noncash charitable contributions.—Although most of the new provisions concerning S corporations would be considered liberalizations of current rules, the 2004 Jobs Act also includes some new limitations. For example, new requirements pertaining to increased substantiation of noncash charitable contributions also apply to S corporations (¶1310). In addition, the 2004 Jobs Act authorizes the IRS to promulgate new regulations concerning information returns for QSubs (¶950).

Impact of deduction relating to income from domestic production activities.— The new deduction for income attributable to qualified production activities income (QPAI) applies to S corporations at the shareholder level based on the entity's proportionate share of QPAI (¶210). A related rule creates a special test for applying the limitation that restricts the deduction, generally, to 50 percent of the wages paid by the taxpayer and reported on Form W-2. In applying this test to determine the deduction at the shareholder level, each person is treated as having been allocated wages from the entity in an amount equal to the lesser of (1) that person's allocable share of wages (as per the applicable regulations) or (2) *twice* the appropriate percentage of QPAI actually allocated to that person for the tax year.

¶ 112

Effect on Partnerships

Basis adjustments and loss transfers.—New rules designed to end the purported practice of shifting built-in losses to other partners upon the liquidation of an existing partner's interest are included in the American Jobs Creation Act of 2004. Accordingly, the 2004 Jobs Act provides that a built-in loss may only be taken into account by the contributing partner and not by others (¶960). Thus, after the transfer or liquidation of a contributing partner's interest, the partnership's adjusted basis in property is to be based on its fair market value at the time it was contributed and any built-in loss would be eliminated. The basis-adjustment rules of Code Sec. 743 would be mandatory if a partnership interest is transferred and the partnership's adjusted basis exceeds the property's fair market value by more than $250,000. Instead of a basis adjustment, different loss deferral rules apply in the case of an "electing investment partnership."

A basis adjustment under Code Sec. 734(b) will also be required for distributions that result in a "substantial basis reduction" (i.e., a downward adjustment of more than $250,000). A separate rule involving the Code Sec. 755 basis allocation rules, provides that, in the case of a liquidating distribution, there is no reduction in basis for stock held by a partnership in a corporate partner (¶965). Any basis decrease that would have otherwise been allocated to the stock is to be allocated to other partnership assets and any excess left after that allocation is to be recognized as gain by the partnership.

Cancellation-of-indebtedness income to be recognized.—The 2004 Jobs Act clears up an ambiguity with respect to whether a partnership must realize cancellation-of-indebtedness income when it transfers a capital or profits interest in the partnership to a creditor in satisfaction of a debt. (¶720). At least for cancellations of indebtedness after the 2004 Job Act's effective date, such income must be recognized. This new rule applies whether the debt is recourse or nonrecourse and the income so recognized is to be allocated only among the partners who held an interest in the partnership immediately before the debt was satisfied.

Net income of publicly traded partnerships considered income of RIC.— Income from publicly traded partnerships receives new status with respect to the operation of regulated investment companies (RICs). Income from these partnerships can now be used to meet the 90-percent-of-gross-income test for RIC qualification (¶1105). With respect to a partnership, the 2004 Jobs Act provision applies as if each partner had transferred their proportionate share of the partnership property.

Imported built-in losses limited.—The new basis limitation rule applicable to the transfer or importation of built-in losses in a tax-free reorganization or reorganization from persons who are not subject to U.S. tax also applies to partnerships (¶520). With respect to a partnership, the 2004 Jobs Act provision applies as if each partner had transferred their proportionate share of the partnership property.

Attribution for foreign tax credits.—Attribution rules pertaining to the ownership of stock through a partnership are liberalized by the 2004 Jobs Act. Under the 2004 Jobs Act, individual partners (as well as estate and trust beneficiaries) may now claim direct foreign tax credits with respect to their proportionate shares of such taxes paid or accrued by a partnership (or an estate or trust) (¶435).

Inversion transactions faced with new tax consequences.—Among the many provisions of the 2004 Jobs Act directed at limiting tax avoidance through expatriation is a provision directed at certain corporate inversion transactions that also has implications for partnerships (¶506). Specifically, under the 2004 Jobs Act, inversion transactions in tax years ending after March 4, 2003, include those in which a foreign-incorporated entity acquires substantially all of the trade or business property of a domestic partnership, if after the acquisition, at least 60 percent of the stock in the entity is held by former partners in the partnership.

Sales of partnership interests receive look-thorough treatment.—The sale of a partnership interest by a controlled foreign corporation (CFC) is treated by the 2004 Jobs Act as the sale of a proportionate share of partnership assets attributable to the interest for purposes of determining foreign personal holding company income under the subpart F rules of the Code (¶465). Partners must own at least a 25-percent direct, indirect, or constructive interest in the capital or profits of the partnership for the look-through rule to apply.

Exception to definition of U.S. property for some assets of a CFC.—The 2004 Jobs Act adds two new exceptions to the definition of U.S. property under Code Sec. 956 for purposes of determining the current income inclusion requirements for U.S. shareholders with a 10-percent or greater interest in a CFC (¶460). The first exception covers securities acquired and held by a CFC in the ordinary course of its trade or business as a securities dealer. The second exception impacts partnerships since it applies to the acquisition by a CFC of obligations issued by a U.S. person that is not a domestic corporation and is also not a U.S. 10-percent shareholder or a partnership, estate, or trust in which the CFC or a related person is a *partner*, beneficiary, or trustee immediately after the CFC's acquisition of the obligation.

Additional provisions affecting partnerships.—The 2004 Jobs Act also includes several other provisions that affect partnerships. For example, the new deduction for income attributable to qualified production activities income (QPAI) applies to partnerships at the partner level, based on the entity's proportionate share of QPAI and a separate rule governs application of the wage limitation requirement at the partner level (¶210). The new exclusion from unrelated business taxable income (UBTI) for gain or loss on the sale or exchange of certain brownfields properties is available to a "qualifying partnership" (¶1330). Partnerships participating in tax shelters will find the confidentiality of communications privilege applicable to federally authorized tax practitioners has been limited (¶665). Finally, several of the requirements pertaining to increased substantiation of noncash charitable contributions also apply to partnerships (¶1310).

REITS, RICS, FASITS AND REMICS

¶113

Overall Effect on REITs, RICs, FASITs and REMICs

The American Jobs Creation Act of 2004 contains a number of significant changes that affect the operation of real estate investment trusts (REITs) generally (¶1110) and provide special treatment for timber REITs (¶1115) and certain REIT distributions (¶540).

The 2004 Jobs Act also provides new rules that will allow income from publicly traded partnerships to be used to meet the 90-percent-of-gross-income test for qualification of regulated investment companies (RICs) (¶1105) and for the treatment of dividends from a RIC (¶560).

The 2004 Jobs Act prospectively repeals financial asset securitization trusts (FASITs), while real estate mortgage investment conduits (REMICs) will benefit from new liberalized rules (¶1120).

¶114

Effect on REITs

REITs receive major attention.—The American Jobs Creation Act of 2004 contains a number of favorable modifications to the rules governing real estate investment trusts (REITs) (¶1110). Included among these are the following items:

(1) Although a REIT is not allowed to hold more than 10 percent of the value of a single issuer, the 2004 Jobs Act modifies the definition of the term "straight debt" to provide more flexibility and, generally, straight debt will not be considered a security for purposes of this rule;

(2) The rule that required a REIT to own a 20-percent equity interest in a partnership in order for debt to qualify as straight debt is replaced with a look-through rule for determining a REIT partner's share of partnership securities;

(3) Safe-harbor dates are provided for purposes of applying the 90-percent test for rents from unrelated persons;

(4) The rules governing hedging by a REIT are liberalized so that they can take advantage of virtually any type of hedge to reduce interest rate risk;

(5) The failure to meet certain REIT requirements will not be fatal to the REIT's qualification if (a) such failure was due to reasonable cause, (b) the failure is corrected, and, generally, (c) a penalty amount is paid;

(6) Any taxes or penalties paid are to be deducted from the REIT's net income in determining the amount the REIT must distribute under the 90-percent requirement;

(7) Payments to a taxable REIT subsidiary (TRS) for customary services would be exempt from excise tax under a safe harbor for payments that represent at least 150 percent of the cost of the services to the TRS; and

(8) The circumstances under which a REIT may declare a deficiency dividend are expanded.

Safe-harbor for timber REITs.—A safe-harbor provision permits a REIT that owns timberland to make sales of timber property without being considered a dealer, provided a six-part test is met (¶ 1115).

REIT distributions resulting from sales or exchanges of U.S. property interests.—Capital gain distributions by a REIT to a foreign owner will no longer be treated as income connected with a trade or business within the United States (¶ 540). Provided the distribution is connected with a class of stock that is regularly traded on an established U.S. securities market and the foreign investor owns five percent or less of that class of stock, the distribution will be treated as a REIT dividend.

¶ 115

Effect on RICs

Net income of publicly traded partnerships considered income of RIC.—Income from publicly traded partnerships receives a new status with respect to the operation of regulated investment companies (RICs), commonly known as mutual funds. Income from these partnerships can now be used to meet the 90-percent-of-gross-income test for RIC qualification (¶ 1105). Effectively, this means mutual funds may now invest in publicly traded partnerships.

Dividends treatment.—The 2004 Jobs Act provides an exemption from U.S. basis tax for "interest-related dividends" and "short-term capital gain dividends" from a RIC. Interest-related dividends would be exempt from the 30-percent (or lower tax treaty rate) tax. Both types of dividends must be designated as such by a written notice mailed to shareholders no more than 60 days after the close of the RIC's tax year. This provision is effective for dividends with respect to tax years of RICs beginning after December 31, 2004, and before January 1, 2008 (¶ 560).

REIT rules extended to RICs.—Extending the present-law treatment applicable to distributions from real estate investment trusts (REITs), a distribution from a RIC to a foreign person will be considered as gain from the sale of a U.S. property interest to the extent the distribution is attributable to gain from the sale or exchange by the RIC of an asset that is considered a U.S. real property interest. Additional rules applicable to domestically controlled REITs are now available to domestically controlled RICs (¶ 564).

Holding stripped bonds and preferred stock.—The IRS is given authority to issue regulations addressing the tax treatment of stripped bonds and preferred stock held by a RIC (¶ 725).

¶ 116

Effect on FASITs and REMICs

FASITs repealed and REMICs liberalized.—Financial asset securitization trusts (FASITs) are repealed; however, the repeal does not apply, generally, to FASITs in existence on the date of enactment of the American Jobs Creation Act of 2004. Rules pertaining to real estate mortgage investment conduits (REMICs) are liberalized. These changes include beneficial changes in the definition of a REMIC qualified mortgage, reverse mortgage loans, and qualified reserve funds (¶1120).

AGRIBUSINESS

¶ 120

Overall Effect on Agribusiness

The broad reach of the American Jobs Creation Act of 2004 is certainly exemplified if one examines the category of agribusiness. Everything from timber (¶740) to tobacco received consideration, although in the case of tobacco it was not a tax break, but a reform of tobacco supports. Livestock sellers are granted relief in the form of tax deferral (¶820). Several different types of cooperatives will benefit from new more liberal rules (¶830, ¶835, and ¶1335). Farmers and fisherman also receive relief from the alternative minimum tax (¶825). Small producers of ethanol were not forgotten either, as they receive a new credit (¶845).

¶ 121

Effect on Farming and Ranching

Livestock conversion/replacement.—Certain sales of livestock qualify as involuntary conversions. The gain on the sale can be deferred by purchasing similar property within the applicable replacement period. Taxpayers now will be able to defer the gain by purchasing other farm property when it is not feasible to purchase similar livestock. Under some conditions, the replacement period will be extended to four years (or more) from two years. The initial extension will be available when drought, flood, or other weather-related conditions cause the area to be designated for federal assistance (¶820).

Relief for cash method taxpayers.—A taxpayer using the cash method of accounting can defer inclusion of gain only until the year following the sale of livestock. This elective deferral can now be extended until the replacement period expires (¶820).

The new deduction for domestic manufacturing includes qualifying production property grown in the United States. Special provision is also made in the deduction for agricultural and horticultural cooperatives (¶210).

A major section of the legislation titled Agricultural Tax Relief and Incentives increases the rate of excise tax that applies for most alcohol-blended fuels, but creates two new excise tax credits: an alcohol fuel mixture credit and a biodiesel mixture credit (¶805). In addition, a biodiesel income tax credit is created (¶810). The Secretary of the Treasury may impose information reporting requirements to insure the proper administration of these provisions (¶815).

Major beneficiaries of this legislation are tobacco farmers. Through provisions not related to the Internal Revenue Code, a Tobacco Trust Fund is set up with assessments from manufacturers and importers of tobacco products to terminate the federal tobacco support program and provide payments over a 10-year period to tobacco producers based on their quota allotments under the support program.

The legislation also provides alternative minimum tax protection for farmers utilizing income averaging (¶825). Also included in the legislation is a provision modifying the payment of interest of fuel tax refunds where the fuel is used for farming purposes (¶1511).

¶ 122

Effect on Cooperatives

Farmers' cooperatives declaratory judgment.—A declaratory judgment procedure is available to some taxpayers. This procedure permits a judicial review of an IRS determination prior to the issuance of a notice of deficiency. This procedure will now be available to a cooperative when the IRS makes a determination regarding the taxpayer's status as a farmers' cooperative (¶835).

Dividends paid by cooperatives.—Dividends paid by a cooperative on capital stock are allocated so that the amount related to patronage operations reduces net earnings available to pay patronage dividends. A special rule will now allow the cooperative to pay dividends on capital stock without reducing patronage income (¶830).

Rural electric cooperatives.—Income is tax exempt for a rural electric cooperative if it meets the 85-percent test. This test requires that 85 percent of the income comes from amounts collected from members for the sole purpose of meeting the expenses (or losses) of providing service to the members. The IRS also requires that the cooperative meet four fundamental principles of operating on a cooperative basis. Rural electric cooperatives will now be able to exclude certain kinds of income from the 85-percent test. Qualifying income from services provided on an open access basis will be excluded. Income from a nuclear decommissioning transaction will be excluded. Gain from a qualified exchange or conversion will be excluded. Income from a load loss transaction will be treated as member income in the 85-percent test and will also be excluded from the tax on unrelated trade or business income. A taxable electric cooperative will be able to treat income from load loss transactions as income from patrons who are members. Further, income from load loss transactions will not cause a taxable cooperative to fail the fundamental principles test (¶1335).

Dividends on capital stock of a cooperative can be set up in the organizational documents so as to not reduce patronage dividends and not prevent the cooperative from being treated as operating on a cooperative basis (¶1340). Cooperatives may also elect to pass-through the small ethanol producer credits to their patrons (¶845).

¶ 123

Effect on Timber Industry

Sale of timber by landowner.—Disposal of timber is eligible for capital gains treatment in several situations. A disposal of timber by the owner who retains an economic interest in the timber can receive capital gains treatment. It will now be possible for the owner of the land to make an outright sale of timber, not retaining an economic interest, to qualify for capital gains treatment (¶750).

The timber industry is benefited by several other provisions. Timber is included in the manufacturing activities eligible for the new manufacturing deduction (¶210). Real estate investment trusts (REITS) involved in the production of timber are allowed to sell property without being deemed a real estate dealer (¶1115). Also, the legislation provides a deduction for certain reforestation expenses (¶840).

¶ 124

Effect on Fishing and Whaling

Fishermen are extended the income averaging rights previously reserved for farmers, and fishermen are also afforded alternative minimum tax protection for income averaging (¶ 825). The legislation also reduces the excise tax on fishing tackle boxes and reduces the excise tax on fish-finding sonar devices (¶ 1559 and ¶ 1561). In addition, a new charitable deduction is created with respect to expenses in support of native Alaska subsistence whaling (¶ 1320).

¶ 125

Effect on Food and Drink Industry

Rehabilitation expenses for stand-alone restaurant properties qualify for 15-year depreciation (¶ 315). The occupational taxes relating to distilled spirits, wine, and beer are suspended for three years (¶ 1569).

¶ 126

Effect on Tobacco Industry

Reform of tobacco supports.—The tobacco program consists of supply management done through marketing quotas and price supports accomplished by nonrecourse loans. There is an assessment on the industry in connection with the nonrecourse loans. The 2004 Jobs Act repeals both components of the tobacco program. In its place, eligible quota holders and producers will receive payments over a 10-year period from the Tobacco Trust Fund. Manufacturers and importers of tobacco products will pay a quarterly assessment into the Trust to provide for the payments to quota holders and producers, and to meet any program losses incurred by the federal government. (As the details of the tobacco program are not tax related, they are not analyzed further in the explanatory section of this text.)

SMALL BUSINESSES

¶ 127

Effect on Small Business

Expensing of business investment.—A taxpayer may elect to deduct the cost of qualifying property not to exceed $100,000 in a given tax year. The $100,000 amount is reduced to the extent that qualified property placed in service during the tax year exceeds $400,000. The availability of this election is now extended to tax years beginning before 2008. Amounts will continue to be indexed for inflation. Also, qualifying property will include off-the-shelf computer software (¶ 305). The 2004 Jobs Act also imposes a limitation on the availability of this expensing election for heavy SUVs (¶ 310).

Expensing of EPA compliance costs.—A small business refiner will now be able to deduct up to 75 percent of the costs of complying with Environmental Protection Agency (EPA) regulations to control the sulfur content of highway diesel fuel (¶ 850).

SBIC.—An exempt organization is taxed on unrelated business income. Certain passive income is unrelated business income if the assets generating the income were acquired using indebtedness. The 2004 Jobs Act redefines acquisition indebtedness in the case of a newly formed small business investment company. In general, debt issued in connection with the Small Business Investment Act that is held or guaranteed by the Small Business Administration will not be considered acquisition indebtedness (¶ 1325).

BUSINESSES WITH DEPRECIABLE PROPERTY

¶128

Effect on Businesses with Depreciable Property

Leasehold improvements.—Leasehold improvements are generally depreciated using the MACRS system. Qualified leasehold improvement property is allowed an additional first-year depreciation deduction. Qualified leasehold improvement property will now have a 15-year recovery period using the straight-line method, if it is placed in service before January 1, 2006. In general, leasehold improvement property ceases to be qualified as to any subsequent owner of the improvement (¶315 and ¶317).

Restaurant improvements.—Improvements to nonresidential real property are depreciated over 39 years using the straight-line method. Qualified restaurant improvements placed in service before January 1, 2006, will now be depreciable over 15 years (¶315 and ¶317).

Bonus depreciation for aircraft.—Property eligible for the additional first-year depreciation allowance must meet several requirements including a placed in service date. Some property has an extended placed in service date. Certain noncommercial aircraft placed in service during 2005 will now be eligible for the extended placed in service date (¶325).

Sale-leaseback property.—Property that is sold and then leased back to the seller can qualify for the additional first-year allowance. This includes sale-leasebacks that are syndicated by the lessor. The placed in service date is now modified for leases having multiple units of property. In general, the placed in service date will be the date of sale (¶330).

Alaska natural gas pipeline.—Assets including pipelines are assigned a MACRS recovery period of 15 years. An Alaska natural gas pipeline will now have a 7-year recovery period (¶345).

Motorsports assets.—Nonresidential real property is depreciated over 39 years; however, assets in the theme and amusement park industry have a 7-year recovery period. Motorsports racetrack complexes will now be afforded the same treatment and will have a 7-year recovery period (¶340).

Utility clearing and grading.—The costs of initial clearing and grading relating to electric transmission and distribution lines is recovered over 7 years as property not having a class life under MACRS. Similarly, there is no class life for initial clearing and grading relating to gas utility trunk pipelines. These clearing and grading costs will now have a class life. The recovery period for these electric utility assets will be 20 years. For gas utilities, the recovery period will be 15 years (¶335).

Sport utility vehicles.—Passenger automobiles can be depreciated if they are used in a trade or business or for the production of income. There is a special limit on depreciation of luxury automobiles. On a small investment, a taxpayer can elect to expense the cost rather than capitalize and depreciate the amount. Although the Code Sec. 179 expensing limits generally were extended by the 2004 Jobs Act (¶305), the Act will limit the ability of a taxpayer to expense the cost of a sport utility vehicle that is not covered by the luxury automobile depreciation limitation. The maximum write-off will be $25,000; the balance would be depreciated as five-year recovery property (¶310).

OWNERS OF INTANGIBLES

¶ 129

Effect on Owners of Intangibles and Amortization

Sports franchises.—When a business acquires intangible assets, the amount allocated to these assets is generally capitalized and amortized over a 15-year period. In the case of a sports franchise, however, special rules applied and in some situations the assets may not be amortizable. The 15-year recovery period will now be available to professional sports franchises. The special rules are repealed, so the general rules for amortization of intangibles will now apply to a sports franchise (¶355).

Start-up and organizational expenditures.—A taxpayer could elect to amortize start-up expenditures and organizational expenditures over a period of not less than 60 months. Most acquired intangibles can be amortized over a 15-year period. Taxpayers will now be able, within limits, to deduct up to $5,000 of start-up expenditures and $5,000 of organizational expenditures in the first year, amortizing the remainder over a 15-year period (¶350).

Film and television productions.—Certain films and similar items are depreciated using the income forecast method. Qualifying film and television productions may now elect to deduct certain production expenditures in the year incurred. This election will be available to qualified productions having an aggregate cost not to exceed $15 million. The limit will be $20 million if a significant amount of costs are incurred in designated low-income or distressed areas (¶365).

Income forecast method.—The income forecast method of depreciation is used for certain intangible property. Under this method, the annual allowance is a function of the adjusted basis and estimated income for the forecast period. The 2004 Jobs Act clarifies several things. For example, participations and residuals may be included in adjusted basis. As an alternative, they may be deducted as paid. Also, it is gross income that is used for the computation and distribution costs are not taken into account (¶320).

BUSINESS OPERATIONS GENERALLY

¶ 130

Effect on Business Operations

Fuel excise tax—highway.—Excise tax is payable on motor fuels used in highway vehicles. By regulation, mobile machinery has been excluded from the definition of highway vehicle. The IRS proposed to eliminate the mobile machinery exception; however, the Code will now require this exception for qualified mobile machinery (¶1549).

Fuel excise tax—aviation.—Aviation fuel is taxed when sold by a producer or importer. A reduced tax rate applies to fuel used in commercial aviation. The tax will now apply when fuel is removed from a refinery or terminal when it enters the United States. The tax will now be imposed on the person receiving the fuel instead of the producer or importer. The qualifications for the reduced rate will be tightened in order to reduce the possibility of tax evasion. In addition, the IRS is given expanded authority to enforce the excise tax rules, including the imposition of penalties (¶1507).

Highway use tax—heavy vehicles.—A highway use tax is imposed on heavy highway vehicles based on weight. This tax will no longer be payable in installments.

In addition, Canadian and Mexican vehicles will no longer qualify for a reduced rate (¶1547).

Fuel excise tax—rail and barge.—A General Fund excise tax of 4.3 cents per gallon applies to rail diesel fuel and fuel used in designated inland waterway barges. The 2004 Jobs Act repeals this tax (¶1513).

Excise tax—bows and arrows.—There is an excise tax on bows with a draw weight of 10 pounds or more. A tax also applies to accessories, and some arrow components, but not finished arrows. The 2004 Jobs Act redefines a taxable bow as one with a peak draw weight of 30 pounds or more. The tax on arrows will be simplified and the tax rate on broadheads will be reduced (¶1557).

Excise tax—fishing tackle boxes.—There is a 10-percent excise tax on several types of sport fishing equipment. The 2004 Jobs Act reduces the excise tax on fishing tackle boxes to 3 percent (¶1559).

Excise tax—sonar.—There is a 3-percent excise tax on electric outboard motors and sonar devices suitable for finding fish. The 2004 Jobs Act repeals the tax on sonar devices (¶1561).

Alcoholic beverages.—A special occupational tax is imposed on producers and marketers of distilled spirits, wine, and beer. The 2004 Jobs Act suspends this tax from July 1, 2005, through June 30, 2008. Recordkeeping and registration requirements will remain in place (¶1569).

Business energy credits.—In general, business tax credits can be applied only to the excess of income tax liability over tentative minimum tax. The 2004 Jobs Act will allow the alcohol fuels credit and the renewable electricity production credit to be applied to income tax liability without reduction for tentative minimum tax (¶370).

Railroad track maintenance credit.—The 2004 Jobs Act adds a new business tax credit for 50 percent of the maintenance expenditures on railroad track. The annual credit is limited to $3,500 times the track mileage owned or leased (¶375).

Deduction—use of aircraft.—No deduction is allowed for entertainment, amusement, recreation, or facilities used in that connection unless the activity is directly related to business. One exception to the rule is allowed when costs are included in compensation or gross income of another person. With respect to employee nonbusiness use of company aircraft, it has been common to deduct expenses in excess of the amount included in compensation. This deduction will now be limited with respect to certain employees and nonemployees. There will be no deduction for nonbusiness activity and related facilities to the extent expenses exceed the amount treated as compensation or included in income (¶360).

Federal payments.—Federal payment to a vendor of goods and services is subject to a levy for unpaid internal revenue tax. This levy is now increased to 100 percent from the previous limit of 15 percent (¶1625).

IRS user fees.—Under statutory authority, the IRS generally charges a fee for a private letter ruling, a determination letter, and similar items. The 2004 Jobs Act extends the authority to charge fees through September 30, 2014 (¶1630).

Customs user fees.—The Treasury Department is authorized to collect fees for certain customs services. The authority for passenger and conveyance, and merchandise processing fees is extended through September 30, 2014 (¶597).

Whaling.—A charitable deduction is allowed for individuals who claim itemized deductions. The 2004 Jobs Act will allow a charitable deduction, up to $10,000, to a whaling captain recognized by the Alaska Eskimo Whaling Commission who is responsible for qualified subsistence bowhead whale hunting activities (¶ 1320).

Enhanced oil recovery credit.—A taxpayer is allowed to claim a credit for 15 percent of enhanced oil recovery costs, subject to a phaseout. The 2004 Jobs Act extends this credit to construction of qualifying plants for the processing of Alaska natural gas (¶ 865).

Shipbuilding contracts.—Certain ship construction contracts are accounted for using a method known as the 40/60 percentage-of-completion/capitalized cost method. The use of this method generally results in a reduction of tax liability when compared to the percentage-of-completion method. The 2004 Jobs Act will require shipbuilders (on new contracts) to include the tax reduction from the first five tax years of the contract as a tax liability in the sixth tax year (¶ 395).

Transfer of excess pension assets.—An employer's defined benefit plan may transfer excess assets to an account for payment of retiree health benefits. The transfer must meet several requirements including the minimum cost requirement. A reduction in retiree health coverage during a relevant period will not disqualify the transfer so long as the reduction is not significant. The 2004 Jobs Act will give the plan a qualifying alternative to reducing coverage. Applicable employer costs may be reduced up to the amount corresponding to the maximum permissible health coverage reduction without disqualifying the asset transfer (¶ 1420).

Ceiling fans.—There is a 4.7-percent ad valorem customs duty on the import of ceiling fans. The 2004 Jobs Act suspends this duty through December 31, 2006 (¶ 590).

Steam generators.—Currently, the duty on nuclear steam generators is suspended. The 2004 Jobs Act extends that suspension through December 31, 2008 (¶ 595).

Electric transmission property.—The 2004 Jobs Act will allow a taxpayer to recognize gain from a qualifying transaction over an 8-year period. A qualifying transaction is a sale (or other disposition) of electric transmission property to an independent transmission company. This election will be available only if the amount realized is reinvested in exempt utility property (¶ 890).

Marginal wells.—The 2004 Jobs Act creates a new credit for production from marginal wells. The credit is $3 per barrel for crude oil and 50 cents per 1000 cubic feet of natural gas, subject to limitations. The credit will be treated as part of the general business credit but with an extended carryback period (¶ 860).

TRANSPORTATION

¶ 131

Overall Effect on Transportation

Various segments of the transportation industry were the focus of many of the provisions in this legislation.

¶ 132

Effect on Automobiles

Two individual provisions will have an impact on automobiles. Vehicles donated to charity qualify for a charitable deduction limited to the sales price acknowledged to have been obtained by the charity (¶ 1305). Also, the ability of a small business owner to fully expense the cost of a heavy SUV has been curtailed (¶ 310).

¶133

Effect on Aircraft

The placed in service date for bonus depreciation of certain aircraft has been extended (¶325). The subpart F rules are modified to provide that the rents and gains derived in the active conduct of an aircraft leasing business would not be either subpart F personal holding company income or subpart F shipping income (¶475). The law also delays the effective date of final regulations governing the exclusion of income from the international operation of aircraft (¶552). The excise taxes on aviation-grade kerosene are revised (¶1507). Limits have been placed on the entertainment expense deduction available with respect to the use of company-provided aircraft by covered employees (¶360). Also, aircraft donated to charity qualify for a charitable deduction limited to the sales price acknowledged to have been obtained by the charity (¶1305).

¶134

Effect on Railroads

The excise tax on diesel fuel used in trains is phased out under this legislation (¶1513). A new temporary tax credit is provided for certain expenditures for maintaining railroad track (¶375).

¶135

Effect on Ships, Vessels, and Barges

The excise tax on diesel fuel used in barges is phased out under this legislation (¶1513). Corporations engaged in international shipping activities are allowed to elect a tonnage tax on their taxable income in lieu of the U.S. corporate income tax (¶545). The law also delays the effective date of final regulations governing the exclusion of income from the international operation of ships (¶552). The bulk transfer exemption from taxable fuels is extended to registered vessel operators; display of such registration is required (¶1527, ¶1529). Naval shipbuilders will be permitted to use a method of accounting that results in more favorable income tax treatment (¶395).

¶136

Effect on Buses

The ability of intercity buses to buy dyed fuel is terminated (¶1523).

¶137

Effect on Trucks and Tires

An exemption from certain excise taxes is provided for mobile machinery designed for non-highway functions (¶1549). The definition of what constitutes an off-road vehicle is modified (¶1551). The use tax on heavy highway vehicles is modified to eliminate installment payments and to eliminate the reduced rate for Canadian and Mexican vehicles (¶1547). Several of the penalties addressed in this legislation are dedicated as revenues of the Highway Trust Fund (¶1573). The heavy truck tire tax is also simplified (¶1553).

ENERGY AND FUELS

¶ 140

Overall Effect on Energy and Utilities

Although this legislation in the end picked up very few provisions from the energy legislation that had been included in the Senate version of the bill, energy-related provisions still figure prominently in both the tax break provisions and revenue-raising provisions. The provisions primarily impact the areas of utilities, oil and gas, and fuels. Domestic production gross receipts under the new domestic manufacturing deduction include the sale, exchange or other disposition of electricity, natural gas, or potable water produced by a taxpayer. Domestic production gross receipts do not include the transmission or distribution of electricity, natural gas, or potable water (¶210).

¶ 141

Effect on Oil and Gas

Small business refiners may claim an immediate deduction for a portion of the costs paid for the purpose of complying with highway diesel fuel sulfur control requirements of the EPA (¶850). Small business refiners may also claim a credit based on the gallons of low sulfur diesel fuel produced during the tax year that complies with the EPA's highway diesel fuel sulfur control requirements (¶855). A new credit is created for oil and gas production from marginal wells with a five-year carryback of unused credits (¶860). A reduced seven-year recovery period is provided for large Alaska natural gas pipelines (¶345). Qualified enhanced oil recovery costs eligible for the enhanced oil recovery credit include expenses incurred in connection with the construction of large natural gas processing plants capable of producing carbon dioxide for re-injection into a producing oil or gas field (¶865). The Code Sec. 40 alcohol fuels credit and the Code Sec. 45 credit for electricity produced from a facility during the first four years of production are allowed for alternative minimum tax purposes (¶370).

For a bulk transfer of fuel to be exempt from tax, pipeline or vessel operators party to the bulk transfer must be registered (¶1527). Failure to register and failure to display registration on a vessel subjects the operator to penalties (¶1529). Registration is also required for terminals or refineries within a foreign trade zone or a customs bonded storage facility (¶1535). Terminals and bulk transport carriers are subject to penalties for failure to file reports and furnish information required under the Excise Summary Terminal Activity Reporting System (ExSTARs) (¶1533). Persons with frequent reportable transactions under ExSTARs are required to report electronically (¶1531). The IRS is granted authority to inspect books, records and shipping papers pertaining to fuel kept at any terminal, fuel storage facility, retail fuel facility or designated inspection site (¶1539). The IRS can more easily assess penalties for refusal to allow an inspection (¶1541). Depreciable gas utility clearing and grading costs incurred to locate pipelines are assigned a class life based on the asset classes of the property to which the clearing and grading costs relate (¶335).

¶ 142

Effect on Fuel

Excise tax rates for alcohol-blended fuels are restored to their full rate and replaced with two new excise tax credits: the alcohol fuel mixture credit and the biodiesel mixture credit (¶805). Also, a new biodiesel fuels income tax credit is created (¶810). The Secretary of the Treasury is authorized to impose certain reporting requirements in connection with receiving the benefits of these fuel credits (¶815).

General fund excise taxes on diesel fuel used in trains and fuels used in barges are phased-out and repealed (¶1513).

Cooperatives are permitted under this legislation to elect to pass-through the small ethanol producer credit to the patrons of the cooperative (¶845).

Small business refiners may claim a deduction for costs incurred for the purpose of complying with the Highway Diesel Fuel Sulfur Control Requirements of the EPA and a credit for each gallon of low sulfur diesel fuel produced in compliance with those requirements (¶850 and ¶855).

The alcohol fuels credit is allowed for alternative minimum tax purposes (¶370).

A variety of provisions are included in the legislation to address a severe problem of fuel tax evasion. The fuel excise tax exemption for off-highway mobile machinery is codified (¶1549). The point of taxation for aviation fuel is changed (¶1507). Stiffer procedures and penalties are imposed for mechanically dyeing fuel (¶1517). Intercity buses are no longer permitted to buy dyed fuel (¶1523). Inspection authority is expanded, with related penalties for refusing entry to the inspectors (¶1539 and ¶1541). The exemption for bulk fuel transfers requires that the parties be registered (¶1527). Registrations are required to be displayed, with penalties for noncompliance (¶1529). Terminals and refineries in foreign trade zones are also required to register (¶1535). Penalties are imposed for failure to report under the Excise Summary Terminal Activity Reporting System (ExSTARS) (¶1533). Certain fuel information reports are required to be made electronically (¶1531). Refund procedures are identified for taxed sales of fuel to state and local governments or not-for-profit educational institutions (¶1511). Procedures are established for a tax-free transfer of fuel within a registered terminal (¶1505). Two new categories are added to the definition of diesel fuel, including transmix fuel and diesel fuel blend stocks (¶1509). Finally, the Treasury is directed to undertake a study of fuel tax compliance (¶1543).

¶ 143

Effect on Utilities

The production of electricity falls within the scope of the new domestic manufacturing deduction (¶210).

Class lives are assigned to depreciable electric and gas utility clearing and grading costs incurred to locate transmission and distribution lines and pipelines, effectively extending the allowed recovery periods (¶335). The legislation permits an election to recognize gain from a qualifying electric transmission transaction ratably over an eight-year period (¶890).

The credit for electricity produced from renewable resources is expanded to apply to certain closed-loop biomass facilities modified to use closed-loop biomass to co-fire with coal, to co-fire with other biomass, or to co-fire with coal and other biomass. New qualifying resources include open-loop biomass (including agricultural livestock waste nutrients), geothermal energy, solar energy, small irrigation power, refined coal and municipal solid waste. The latter may be used in landfill gas facilities or trash combustion facilities (¶870, ¶872 and ¶874). This credit is also allowed for alternative minimum tax purposes (¶370).

ENTERTAINMENT

¶ 145

Overall Effect on Entertainment

Certain aspects of the entertainment industry were singled out for tax breaks in this legislation, including the film, sound and television industry; the racing industry; and sports franchises.

¶ 146

Effect on Film, Videos, Sound, TV

Qualifying sound recordings, motion picture film and video tape are specifically included as qualifying production property under the new domestic manufacturing deduction (¶210). Participations and residuals, such as those associated with motion picture films, videos, and sound recordings may be included in the basis of property for purposes of computing the allowable deduction under the income forecast method of depreciation (¶320). An election is also provided to deduct the cost of qualifying film and television productions in the year the expenditure is incurred rather than through depreciation (¶365).

¶ 147

Effect on Sports Franchises

The 15-year recovery period for intangible assets is extended to franchises engaged in professional sports and related intangible assets such as player contracts (¶355).

¶ 148

Effect on Racing

An exclusion is created from gross income for the winnings of nonresident aliens on legal wagers placed outside of the U.S. on live U.S. horse and dog races (¶565). A seven-year recovery period is established for certain permanent motorsports race-track complexes (¶340).

BANKS AND FINANCE

¶ 150

Overall Effect on Banks and Finance

This new tax legislation includes provisions relevant to banks, insurance companies, the leasing industry, and the commodities and securities industry.

¶ 151

Effect on Banks

Several of the S Corporation reform provisions address banking operations. Grandfathered individual retirement accounts are allowed to be shareholders of a bank that is an S Corporation (¶940). Interest income and dividends on assets required to be held by a bank or bank holding company are not treated as passive investment income for purposes of the S Corporation excess net passive income rules (¶945).

Under the new interest expense allocation rules, taxpayers may apply the bank group rules to exclude certain financial institutions from the affiliated group for interest allocation purposes under the worldwide fungibility approach (¶407). The reduction of the foreign tax credit baskets to two will result in financial services income of a member of a financial services group being treated as general category income (¶410). The exceptions from subpart F foreign personal holding company income and foreign base company services income are modified for income derived in the active conduct of a banking, financing, or similar business (¶480).

The exception from the definition of U.S. property under Code Sec. 956 for deposits with persons carrying on a banking business is limited to certain specified deposits (¶485).

¶ 152

Effect on Leasing

For purposes of the domestic manufacturing deduction, domestic production gross receipts do not include any gross receipts derived from property that is leased, licensed or rented by the taxpayer for use by a related person (¶210).

Leasehold improvements are given a recovery period for depreciation of 15 years (¶315).

In cases of multiple units of property subject to the same lease, the property will qualify as placed in service on the date of sale if it is sold within three months after the final unit is placed in service, so long as all units are placed in service within 12 months (¶330).

A safe harbor is provided for rents derived from leasing an aircraft or vessel in foreign commerce under an exception to foreign personal holding company income (¶475).

The tax benefits associated with sale in/lease out transactions with tax-indifferent parties are restricted (¶670).

¶ 153

Effect on Insurance

The reduction of the foreign tax credit baskets to two will result in insurance income of a member of a financial services group being treated as general category income (¶410).

For a two-year period, the application of the rules imposing income tax on distributions to shareholders from the policyholders surplus account of a stock life insurance company is suspended and the order in which distributions reduce various accounts is reversed (¶1125).

Under the provisions addressing corporate expatriation, the authority of the Secretary of the Treasury to allocate items among the parties to a reinsurance agreement is clarified, authorizing such allocations, recharacterizations, or other adjustments, in order to reflect the proper source, character or amount of the item (¶515).

¶ 154

Effect on Securities and Commodities

Under the international tax reform provisions, a new exception from the definition of U.S. property, for purposes of determining current income inclusion by a U.S. 10-percent shareholder with respect to an investment in U.S. property by a controlled foreign corporation, is provided for securities acquired and held by a controlled foreign corporation in the ordinary course of its trade or business as a dealer in securities (¶460).

The requirements that must be satisfied for gains or losses from a commodities hedging transaction to qualify for exclusion from the definition of subpart F foreign personal holding company income are modified (¶470).

The Treasury is authorized to promulgate regulations that apply the stripped bonds and stripped preferred stock rules to direct or indirect interests in an entity or account substantially all of the assets of which consist of bonds, preferred stock, or any combination thereof (¶725). The Treasury is directed to conduct a study of earnings stripping rules (¶525).

The straddle rules are modified to permit taxpayers to identify offsetting positions of a straddle, to provide a special rule to clarify the treatment of certain physically settled positions of a straddle, and to repeal the stock exception (¶730).

MISCELLANEOUS BUSINESS CONCERNS

¶ 156

Effect on Construction

The construction industry was able to get construction activities performed in the U.S. included in the definition for domestic production gross receipts for purposes of the new domestic manufacturing deduction (¶210). The new legislation also clarifies the excise taxes applicable to off-highway vehicles and nontransportation trailers and semitrailers (¶1549, ¶1551). New qualified green exempt-facility bonds should promote the construction of "green" buildings and sustainable design projects (¶745).

¶ 157

Effect on Environment

A new category of exempt-financing bonds, labeled the qualified green building and sustainable design project bond ("qualified green bond") is created (¶745). An exclusion from unrelated business taxable income is provided for the gain or loss from the qualified sale, exchange, or other disposition of a qualifying brownsfield property (¶1330). A deduction is allowed for certain qualified reforestation costs (¶840).

¶ 158

Effect on Intellectual Property

Under the new domestic manufacturing deduction, the licensing of computer software to a related person for reproduction and sale, exchange, lease, rental or sublicense to an unrelated person for the ultimate use of the unrelated person is treated as property included in the definition of domestic production gross receipts (¶210). The extension of the Code Sec. 179 small business expensing provision specifically includes computer software as qualifying property (¶305).

If a taxpayer contributes a patent or other intellectual property (other than certain copyrights or inventory) to a charitable organization, the taxpayer's initial charitable deduction is limited to the lesser of the taxpayer's basis in the contributed property or its fair market value. Over time, additional deductions may be permitted based on the donee's income with respect to the contributed property (¶1315).

¶158

INDIVIDUALS

¶ 160

Overall Effect on Individual Taxpayers

Although the American Jobs Creation Act of 2004 is generally directed toward businesses, that is not to say that individuals were ignored. Perhaps the most interesting provision relating to individuals is one restoring the deduction for state and local sales taxes (¶ 1205). Other provisions of note concern charitable donations of vehicles (¶ 1305) and noncash items (¶ 1310). Investors will be impacted by new straddle rules (¶ 730) and investors in tax shelters should also be forewarned of tougher rules, as well (¶ 605, ¶ 610, ¶ 615 and ¶ 620). Certain nonresident aliens and citizens who become residents of U.S. possessions must consider the implications of revised rules concerning basis and income source (¶ 1425). Expatriates also come under scrutiny with respect to income taxes (¶ 502), as well as estate and gift taxes (¶ 504).

Persons dealing with the IRS should benefit from looser restrictions on installment payments and deposits, but will face the possibility of being pursued by private tax collectors (¶ 1605). Those who practice before the IRS also face new rules (¶ 660).

Finally, the 2004 Jobs Act also includes a number of miscellaneous provisions addressing a variety of issues of interest to individual taxpayers. Among these items are the following:

- Tax relief for recipients of judgments and settlements stemming from civil rights violations (¶ 1215);

- Limitations applicable to participants in certain nonqualified deferred compensation arrangements (¶ 1405);

- A break for recipients of stock options for FICA, FUTA, and withholding purposes (¶ 1410);

- A restriction applicable to sellers of a principal residence that was acquired in a like-kind exchange (¶ 1210); as well as

- New rules for rural letter carriers (¶ 1220), certain federal employees (¶ 1415), and participants in the National Health Service Corps Loan Repayment Program (¶ 1225).

¶ 161

Effect on Individual Taxpayers Who Itemize

Sales tax deduction.—A federal income tax deduction for sales taxes paid by individuals has not been available since the second term of President Ronald Reagan, when it was eliminated by the Tax Reform Act of 1986 (P.L. 99-514). That situation is about to change. Championed by representatives from states without an income tax, such as Texas and Florida, the deduction for state and local sales taxes returns, at least for tax years 2004 and 2005 (¶ 1205).

In this new incarnation, taxpayers can elect to claim an itemized deduction for state and local general sales taxes in lieu of taking an itemized deduction for state and local income taxes. One potential dilemma for taxpayers, particularly with respect to 2004, is that the new law gives taxpayers the option of (1) using tables prepared by the IRS or (2) accumulating receipts throughout the year to substantiate their deduction. For certain specified big-ticket items, such as automobiles and boats, taxpayers are allowed to add the sales tax paid on those items to the amounts specified in the tables for their particular taxpayer status.

In addition to the states that do not impose an income tax, there are several states in which the sales tax rate exceeds the highest individual income tax rate, as indicated in the following chart.

States with a Sales Tax Rate Exceeding Its Highest Individual Marginal Income Tax Rate (in Order of Descending Sales Tax Rates)

State	Sales Tax Rate %	Income Tax Rates %
Mississippi	7%	3—5%
Tennessee	7%	6% (interest and dividends only)
Nevada	6.5%	0%
Washington	6.5%	0%
Illinois	6.25%	3%
Texas	6.25%	0%
Connecticut	6%	3—5%
Florida	6%	0%
Indiana	6%	3.4%
Michigan	6%	3.9%
Pennsylvania	6%	3.07%
Arizona	5.6%	2.87—5.04%
Maryland	5%	2—4.75%
South Dakota	4%	0%
Wyoming	4%	0%
Alaska	"Local taxes"	0%

This sets up an interesting numbers game for taxpayers to play in doing their tax planning. Because of the special treatment of big-ticket items, this provision should be given particular scrutiny by those persons who may be contemplating the purchase of a new car, SUV, or boat before the end of 2005.

Opinions on the benefits of this particular provision vary. As might be expected, those who fought for reinstatement of the deduction herald its passage. For example, a press release from the office of Rep. Kevin Brady (R. Tex.) claims that the preliminary estimates from the Texas State Comptroller's office indicate that the deduction will put $1 billion back into the hands of his state's residents and result in over 16,000 jobs annually. On the other hand, watchdog groups, such as the Center on Budget and Policy Priorities (*www.cbpp.org*) suggest that the true cost of the measure is masked by the fact that it is being implemented for only two years and that its benefits will flow inordinately to high-income taxpayers since a relatively low percentage of taxpayers with incomes below $100,000 per year are able to itemize their deductions (the standard deduction for joint filers in 2004 is $9,700 and will go to $10,000 in 2005). Even the conservative Heritage Foundation (*www.heritage.org*) has indicated that the deduction for state and local sales taxes would effectively subsidize bigger government at the state level. It would also appear that the proponents of this particular provision did not take into account the potential adverse impact of the alternative minimum tax and the phase-out of itemized deductions for high-income taxpayers—two factors that should serve to limit the total number of individuals who will be able to claim this deduction.

Another point worth noting is the issue of tax simplification. Although Congress is currently holding hearings on possible scenarios for simplification of the tax system, it continues to add complexity to the existing structure. As pointed out in the portion of the Conference Committee Report (H.R. Conf. Rep. No. 108-755) explaining the sales tax deduction provision, the IRS is currently finalizing the 2004 income tax forms. Not only will the IRS have to take into account the new deduction on revised forms, it will also have to develop the tables necessary for taxpayers to compute their allowable deduction. This is a process that the conferees acknowledge will "require a significant amount of time and effort."

¶ 162

Effect on Charitable Donors

Vehicle donations.—Individuals making charitable donations will also face new requirements under the American Jobs Creation Act of 2004. One provision tightens up what has been a controversial issue for several years—the donation of motor vehicles to charity (¶1305). The IRS has consistently been after taxpayers and charitable organizations to "clean up" their procedures with respect to this type of charitable giving (IRS News Release IR-2004-84 and IRS Pub. 4303, "A Donor's Guide to Car Donations").

Effective for contributions made after 2004, a donor of a motor vehicle, the claimed value of which exceeds $500, will be required to substantiate the contribution with a contemporaneous written acknowledgement from the donee. The acknowledgement must contain certain specific information about the vehicle and the donor (i.e., vehicle identification number and name of donor). Further information is required if the donee sells the vehicle without using it or improving it. A penalty will be imposed for knowingly failing to furnish such an acknowledgement or for knowingly furnishing a false or fraudulent acknowledgement.

Noncash donations.—New rules also apply to other noncash donations (¶1310). For contributions made after June 3, 2004, a charitable donor of property other than cash, inventory, or publicly traded securities, that exceeds $500,000 in value will be *required to attach* a qualified appraisal to the donor's tax return. This requirement applies if the donor is an individual, a partnership, or a corporation. The present-law requirement that donors must obtain a qualified appraisal for donated property valued at more than $5,000 now applies to C corporations as well as to individuals, partnerships, S corporations, and closely held or personal service corporations.

Finally, a charitable deduction will be available for amounts of up to $10,000 per tax year for certain travel expenses incurred in sanctioned whaling activities (¶1320). These activities are limited to subsistence bowhead whale hunting activities conducted under a management plan of the Alaska Eskimo Whaling Commission and the deduction is available only to an individual recognized by the Commission as a whaling captain. The Commission was formed in 1977 as a tax-exempt organization to protect the related Eskimo culture, traditions, and activities connected with bowhead whales and subsistence whaling.

¶ 163

Effect on Investors

New rules on straddles.—Sophisticated investors have long realized the benefits of straddles (i.e., identical or substantially identical offsetting positions in actively traded personal property) as a means to recognize current losses while deferring gains, to extend holding periods, and to diminish the risk of loss. Under the American Jobs Creation Act of 2004, investors are affected by several modifications of the rules governing straddles (¶730). First, the 2004 Jobs Act now defines an "identified straddle" as a straddle only when the value of each position is not less than the basis of each position in the hands of the taxpayer at the time the strategy is created. The new law also allows taxpayers to identify offsetting positions of a straddle. If there is a loss in conjunction with a position of an identified straddle, the general loss deferral rules would not apply, but taxpayers would be required to make a basis adjustment.

A second change clarifies the present-law treatment of "physically settled straddle positions." This change effectively treats the physical settlement of straddle position as a two-step transaction, with the taxpayer treated as having terminated the position at its fair market value just before the settlement and then selling the property used to settle the position at fair market value. In addition, the stock exception to the straddle rules is repealed. The latter change reflects the fact that the exception had, over time, become increasingly narrow. However, the exception still remains intact for certain "covered call options."

Investors should also be aware that the 2004 Jobs Act also provides the authority for the issuance of future regulations on the proper method for identifying a straddle, application of the identified straddle rules if a taxpayer fails to properly identify the positions therein, and an ordering rule for dispositions of less than an entire position.

¶ 164
Effect on Persons Dealing With the IRS

Private tax collectors.—The American Jobs Creation Act of 2004 initiates a number of changes for taxpayers as well as their representatives in dealing with the IRS. Perhaps most significantly, the 2004 Jobs Act authorizes the IRS to use private debt collection companies to locate and contact taxpayers concerning *any type* of outstanding taxes and to arrange payment of those taxes (¶ 1605). Although a pilot program using private collectors was instituted in 1996 and 1997, it was later abandoned as unsuccessful. A proposal for private collection was included in the Administration's 2005 budget requests, but drew criticism from various individuals and consumer groups, such as the Consumer Federation of America, as well as the National Treasury Employees Union.

The Treasury Department's estimate suggests that the proposal will bring in $467 million during the five-year period ending in 2009. However, considering the relatively poor results obtained during the earlier pilot program, the 2004 Jobs Act calls for a biennial report to Congress on the program's success. Another important caveat noted in the Conference Committee Report (H.R. Conf. Rep. No. 108-755) is that the conferees expect that activities by private tax collectors will be in conformity with the Fair Debt Collection Practices Act (15 USC § 1692).

Suspension of interest and deposits.—The 18-month rule governing the suspension of interest and penalties where the IRS has not contacted the taxpayer is now made permanent (¶ 1620). The rule was to have reverted to one year for tax years beginning after December 31, 2003. However, the suspension-of-interest rules do not cover certain items such as "gross misstatements," as well as "listed" and "reportable avoidance transactions" (tax shelters).

Taxpayers will be allowed to deposit cash with the IRS that can later be used to pay income, estate, gift, generation-skipping transfer or certain excise taxes (¶ 1615). The amount on deposit may be used to pay an underpayment of tax that is subsequently assessed. Thus, except for any underpayment interest that accrues between the due date of the return and the date of the deposit, underpayment interest would only be charged on the difference between the amount of the deposit and the total underpayment. Taxpayers will also be allowed to withdraw any amount of the deposit upon request, assuming it has not already been used to pay tax owed or the

IRS determines that the collection of tax would somehow be in jeopardy. Interest is to be paid on withdrawn deposits based on the short-term applicable federal rate (AFR), however, interest would not be payable unless the deposit was attributable to a "disputable tax" (one for which the taxpayer believes that both the taxpayer and the IRS have a reasonable basis for their respective positions as to the treatment of the item).

Installment agreements.—Since 1998, IRS personnel have not been authorized to enter into installment payment agreements with delinquent taxpayers unless the agreement was for full payment of the taxpayer's full tax liability. The 2004 Jobs Act provides that the IRS is allowed to enter into installment agreements that provide for only partial payment of a taxpayer's liability (¶ 1610). However, such agreements are to be reviewed every two years to see if the financial condition of the taxpayer has improved sufficiently to warrant an increase in the amount of the installment payments.

User fees.—IRS user fees with respect to requests for a letter ruling, determination letter, or other rulings have been extended through 2014 (¶ 1630). Prior to passage of the 2004 Jobs Act, they were authorized only through the end of 2004.

Persons practicing before the IRS.—Two new sanctions have been added to those that can be imposed under the Circular 230 rules applicable to individuals practicing before the IRS (¶ 660). The 2004 Jobs Act permits censure as well as the imposition of a monetary fine. Under the new rules, a monetary penalty may be imposed on the representative individually as well as on his or her employer, if the employer reasonably should have known of the conduct. However, the amount of the penalties imposed should not exceed the amount of income derived by the practitioner as a result of the engagement that gave rise to the penalty.

¶ 165

Effect on Individuals With Foreign Financial Interests

Penalty for failure to disclose interest.—Several provisions affect taxpayers who have foreign financial interests. First, in an effort to gain greater compliance from taxpayers required to disclose their interests in foreign accounts or trusts (see Form 1040, Schedule B, Part III), the American Jobs Creation Act of 2004 imposes a new penalty and increases an existing penalty (¶ 655). The new penalty, of up to $10,000, is for *non-willful* violations of the disclosure rules. The 2004 Jobs Act also increases the existing penalty for *willful* violations to a maximum of $100,000 or 50 percent of the amount of the account or transaction.

Foreign tax credits.—Attribution rules pertaining to the ownership of stock through a partnership are liberalized by the 2004 Jobs Act. Individual partners (as well as estate and trust beneficiaries) may now claim direct foreign tax credits with respect to their proportionate shares of foreign taxes paid or accrued by a partnership (or an estate or trust) (¶ 435).

Translation of foreign taxes.—Under the 2004 Jobs Act provides that an election is now available to allow taxpayers to translate foreign income taxes into U.S. dollar amounts at the exchange rate applicable when the taxes are paid. To be eligible for the election, the foreign taxes must have been denominated in a currency other than the taxpayer's functional currency (¶ 450).

¶ 166

Effect on Nonresidents

Basis rules.—Certain nonresident aliens receiving retirement distributions and property in connection with the performance of services face new rules that change the treatment of various contributions and earnings as basis under the rules governing annuities. Specifically, employee or employer contributions will *not* be included in basis if: (1) the employee was a nonresident alien when the services related to the contribution were performed; (2) the contribution is connected to compensation for labor or personal services outside the United States; (3) the contribution was not subject to income tax (but would have been, if paid as compensation when the services were rendered) under U.S. law or that of any foreign country (¶1425). Earnings on employee or employer contributions will be treated under similar rules. However, the new rules do not apply to contributions or earnings while an employee is a U.S. resident and do not override other provisions of the Code or treaty agreements.

Wagers on dog/horse races.—A special provision of the 2004 Jobs Act carves out an exclusion from gross income for winnings paid to a nonresident alien stemming from a dog or horse race in the United States if the wager was initiated outside the United States (¶565). The exclusion applies regardless of whether the winnings come from an exclusively foreign betting pool or one that is considered a "merged pool" that combines pools from inside and outside the United States.

¶ 167

Effect on Expatriates

Income tax rules.—Concern over whether the current rules are adequate to prevent persons who relinquish their citizenship from effectively "gaming" the U.S. tax system has led to tighter standards for imposition of the so-called alternative tax regime applicable to nonresident aliens. The American Jobs Creation Act of 2004 includes new objective standards, relating to average income tax liability and net worth, for determining when tax avoidance is a principal purpose for an individual having relinquished citizenship or terminated residency (¶502). There are other exceptions, also based on objective standards, for dual citizens and minors with no substantial contact with the United States. Regardless of the exception, a certification of compliance with U.S. tax laws for the five preceding years, provided under penalty of perjury, will be required before the person can avoid the alternative tax regime. The new rules also call for actual notice of an act of expatriation or termination of residency. Taxpayers who are concerned with these rules should take special note of the *June 3, 2004*, effective date of the new provisions.

Estate tax ramifications.—Individuals who find themselves subject to the alternative tax regime should be concerned about the potential federal estate tax implications of the 2004 Jobs Act as well (¶504). For example, if a former citizen or long-term resident who is subject to the alternative tax regime dies within 10 years of relinquishing citizenship or residency, the estate tax is imposed on the transfer of U.S.-situs property, including the decedent's pro rata share of the U.S. property held by a foreign corporation. The estate tax is computed on the taxable estate, as determined under Code Sec. 2106, by applying the same estate tax rate schedule as used for the estate of a U.S. citizen or resident. However, depending on the existence of an applicable treaty, such individual's estate may only be entitled to an applicable credit amount of $13,000.

In addition, such individuals should also be concerned about the potential implications of being present in the United States for more than 30 days in any calendar year. An individual fitting this description would be treated as a U.S. citizen or resident for that tax year and his or her worldwide estate would be subject to U.S. estate tax. A physical presence test would determine the application of this rule; however, exceptions for certain individuals, such as professional athletes, persons receiving medical care in the United States, teachers, and students, may apply.

Gift tax ramifications.—Rules similar to those for estate tax will apply for gift tax purposes. Accordingly, individuals who exceed the 30-day limitation in any tax year will have to be wary of the application of U.S. gift taxes to any transfer from his or her worldwide assets during that year (¶504). In addition, former citizens or former long-term residents who are subject to the alternative tax regime and who make gifts of stock in closely held foreign corporations within the 10-year period following relinquishment of citizenship or termination of residency are subject to another new gift tax rule. Assuming the ownership thresholds of that rule are met, the donor's taxable gifts will include a percentage of the value of the foreign stock transferred based on the percentage of the foreign corporation's assets that are situated inside, as opposed to outside, the United States.

Information reporting.—The 2004 Jobs Act also imposes new reporting requirements on former citizens and long-term residents subject to the alternative tax regime (¶502). Specifically, an annual return that includes information on the individual's permanent home, country of residence, number of days present in the United States, details about his or her income and assets, as well as information required to comply with the estate and gift tax rules, must be filed regardless of whether any U.S. income tax is due.

¶ 168

Effect on Citizens Who Become Residents of U.S. Possessions

New tests for bona fide residents.—Fueled by recent publicity concerning perceived abuses surrounding the Virgin Islands Economic Development Program, the American Jobs Creation Act of 2004 creates new rules to prevent certain individuals from avoiding U.S. taxes by falsely claiming to be residents of the Virgin Islands or other U.S. possessions. This is accomplished by way of new tests to determine qualification as a "bona fide resident" (¶580).

Under the first part of the test, the individual must be physically present in the possession for at least 183 days in the tax year. In addition, the individual must not have a home outside of the possession and not have a closer connection to the United States or a foreign country during the tax year. Taxpayers will also be required to file a notice in the first tax year they claim to be bona fide residents of a possession, subject to a $1,000 fine for failure to do so.

¶ 169

Effect on Participants in Nonqualified Deferred Compensation Plans

Abuses curtailed.—The basic planning strategy behind nonqualified deferred compensation arrangements, typically involving executives and members of upper management, is to defer the inclusion of income until a time when the employee/participant is retired or otherwise in a lower tax bracket. In such arrangements, the object is (1) to avoid the constructive receipt of property by the employee, in the case of a funded arrangement and (2) not to inadvertently remove the risk of forfeiture with respect to a nonfunded arrangement, such as a so-called rabbi trust. One particular downside to the rabbi trust concept is that, if bankruptcy or other financial calamity should occur, the deferred compensation arrangement is subject to the general claims of the employer's creditors.

Although rabbi trusts and other forms of nonqualified deferred compensation have been used by compensation planners for many years, the American Jobs Creation Act of 2004 recognizes the need to close off some perceived abuses with respect to these arrangements. Specifically targeted are those attempts by some to protect the assets in a rabbi trust from creditors (by moving assets offshore, for example), regardless of the terms of the trust, and the practice of making deferred amounts available to the participants while claiming the plan still comes within the safe-harbor limitations imposed by the IRS (¶1405).

New provisions in the 2004 Jobs Act would mandate current income inclusion on deferred compensation that is not subject to a substantial risk of forfeiture and not previously included in income. Perhaps even more significant is the 2004 Job Act's imposition of a 20-percent additional tax and interest at the underpayment rate plus one percent on underpayments arising from compensation that should have been included in income when it was first deferred. In addition, the 2004 Jobs Act will allow distributions from a nonqualified deferred compensation plan only upon (1) separation from service, (2) death, (3) disability, (4) a specific time or according to a fixed schedule, (5) a change in corporate control, or (6) the occurrence of an unforeseen emergency. The 2004 Jobs Act also contains numerous definitions and limitations relevant to the operation of these new provisions.

Although these provisions are generally effective after December 31, 2004, a special rule applies to limit material modifications to plans after October 3, 2004. The Conference Committee Report (H.R. Conf. Rep. No. 108-755) specifically cites the following as examples that would be considered material modifications: (1) an attempt, after October 3, 2004, to accelerate vesting under a plan; and (2) the addition of a provision allowing distributions upon request if the participant is required to forfeit 10 percent of such distributions (often referred to as a "haircut"). However, the new rules do not apply to certain nonelective plans (Code Sec. 457(e)(12)) that were in existence on May 1, 2004, assuming no material modification in the plan occurs after that date. In addition, the provision contains a special exception for any plan "established or maintained by an organization incorporated on July 2, 1974, " which has been reported to be designed for the PGA Tour Inc. (WALL STREET JOURNAL, October 14, 2004, p. A1), but which could benefit any other corporation that happens to share the same incorporation date.

¶ 170

Effect on Recipients of Stock Options

No FICA or FUTA treatment.—Proposed regulations dealing with the tax treatment of incentive stock options (ISOs) and options under employee stock purchase plans (ESPPs), commonly referred to as statutory stock options, under the Federal Insurance Contribution Act (FICA) and Federal Unemployment Tax Act (FUTA) raised a firestorm among affected taxpayers. So much so that the IRS was forced to issue an administrative moratorium on employment taxes and withholding obligations with respect to the exercise of such an option or the disposition of the stock acquired by an employee pursuant to the exercise of the option (Notice 2002-47, IRB 2002-28, 97).

The American Jobs Creation Act of 2004 provides relief in that FICA and FUTA taxes will not apply to the exercise of a statutory stock option (¶1410). Additionally, any remuneration received in such a transaction will not be taken into account in determining Social Security benefits. Finally, withholding will not be required on a disqualifying disposition of stock acquired by exercising a statutory stock option or when compensation is recognized in connection an ESPP discount.

¶ 171

Effect on Recipients of Large Bonuses

Withholding at highest rate.—Particularly in good economic times, Wall Street brokers, fund managers, and other financial gurus are granted large bonuses in addition to their regular salaries. For those individuals talented enough or lucky enough to be paid supplemental wages (e.g., bonuses or commissions) in excess of $1 million for any tax year, the American Jobs Creation Act of 2004 imposes new withholding rules (¶1430). Accordingly, any supplemental wages in excess of $1 million will be subject to withholding at the highest current income tax rate of 35 percent rather than at the 25-percent rate.

¶ 172

Effect on Homeowners

No exclusion for certain like-kind exchanges.—Some homeowners may be adversely affected by new rules closing an apparent loophole by limiting the exclusion available for gain realized on the sale of a principal residence. The American Jobs Creation Act of 2004 provides that the $250,000 ($500,000 for married couples filing jointly) exclusion from gain on the sale of a principal residence is not allowed if the principal residence was acquired in a like-kind exchange within the prior five years and any gain on such exchange was not recognized (¶1210).

¶ 173

Effect on Civil Rights Litigants

New deduction for attorney's fees.—Litigants who receive a judgment or settlement pursuant to certain civil rights statutes will be pleased to find that the American Jobs Creation Act of 2004 has resolved a contentious point with respect to the treatment of attorney's fees incurred in connection with such cases. The 2004 Jobs Act provides an above-the-line deduction for attorney's fees and related costs incurred in the pursuit of these cases, thus ending a controversy that has led to several conflicting opinions from the U.S. Tax Court and the various federal circuit courts of appeal (¶1215). The deduction is limited to the amount of income actually includible in the recipient's income for the tax year as a result of the litigation. With respect to the laws covered by the new rule, the Conference Committee Report (H.R. Conf. Rep. No. 108-755) contains a litany of statutes that includes the Civil Rights Acts of 1964 and 1991, the National Labor Relations Act, the Age Discrimination in Employment Act of 1967, and the Americans with Disabilities Act of 1990.

¶ 174

Effect on Gamblers

Wagers on dog/horse races by nonresident aliens.—A special provision of the 2004 Jobs Act carves out an exclusion from gross income for winnings paid to a nonresident alien stemming from a dog or horse race in the United States if the wager was initiated outside the United States (¶565). The exclusion applies regardless of whether the betting pool that the winnings come from is an exclusively foreign pool or one that is considered a "merged pool" in which betting pools from inside and outside the United States are combined.

¶ 175

Effect on Federal Employees

More liberal conflict-of-interest rule.—In recognition of the sometimes onerous impact of various conflict-of-interest rules dealing with the ownership of stock by persons employed by the federal government, the American Jobs Creation Act of 2004 clears up at least one ambiguity. The 2004 Jobs Act provides that, if the federal conflict-of-interest rules require a person to sell stock that was acquired as a result of the exercise of a statutory stock option, he or she will be treated as having met the holding period requirements, no matter how long the stock was actually held (¶ 1415). Accordingly, the individual would be entitled to capital gains treatment on the sale and would be eligible for deferral under Code Sec. 1043. This provision would normally cover employees of the Executive Branch, as well members of that person's family under the attribution rules.

¶ 176

Effect on Rural Mail Carriers

Excess costs deductible.—Providing a clear example of how almost no taxpayer was left behind by the American Jobs Creation Act of 2004, rural mail carriers get a much-deserved tax break. The 2004 Jobs Act provides that, if reimbursements from the U.S. Postal Service received by a rural letter carrier are less than his or her actual automobile expenses incurred, the excess costs will qualify as a miscellaneous itemized deduction subject to the two-percent floor (¶ 1220). However, this change does not alter the present-law rule that if the carrier's reimbursement amount exceeds his or her actual costs, the excess is not required to be included in gross income.

¶ 177

Effect on Recipients of Payments Under NHSC Loan Repayment Program

Exclusion from gross income.—The National Health Service Corps (NHSC) Loan Repayment Program is one in which medical service providers pledge to work in certain geographic areas in return for having their education loans paid. The American Jobs Creation Act of 2004 provides that loan repayments under the program and similar state programs will be excluded from gross income and not subject to employment taxes (¶ 1225). However, the loan repayments will not be considered as wages in determining the computation of Social Security benefits.

¶ 178

Effect on Native Americans and Native Alaskans

Community revitalization.—The American Jobs Creation Act of 2004 modifies the Treasury Secretary's authority to designate targeted areas as low-income communities. Rather than designating targeted areas, the Secretary must issue regulations under which targeted populations may be designated as low-income communities (¶ 380). A "targeted population" is defined as individuals or an identifiable group of individuals, including an Indian tribe, who are low-income persons or otherwise lack adequate access to loans or equity investments. A targeted population is not required to be within any census tract. In addition, the regulations must include procedures for determining which entities are qualified active low-income community businesses with respect to targeted populations.

Whaling.—A charitable deduction will be available for amounts of up to $10,000 per tax year for certain travel expenses incurred in sanctioned whaling activities (¶ 1320). These activities are limited to subsistence bowhead whale hunting activities conducted under a management plan of the Alaska Eskimo Whaling Commission, and the deduction is available only to an individual recognized by the Commission as a whaling captain. The Commission was formed in 1977 as a tax-exempt organization to protect the Eskimo culture, traditions, and activities connected with bowhead whales and subsistence whaling associated with them.

TAX SHELTER PROMOTERS AND PARTICIPANTS

¶ 180

Overall Effect on Tax Shelter Promoters and Participants

Tax shelters targeted.—The American Jobs Creation Act of 2004 takes dead aim at tax shelters (¶ 605). The end results include new penalties (¶ 615 and ¶ 620), registration and reporting requirements (¶ 630, ¶ 635 and ¶ 640), an extended statute of limitations (¶ 610), and limitations on privileged communications (¶ 665). New restrictions are also imposed on certain leasing arrangements (¶ 675). New penalties with respect to recordkeeping and reporting requirements for persons with foreign financial accounts are also introduced (¶ 655).

¶ 181

Effect on Tax Shelter Promoters and Participants

Disclosure and penalties.—Among the tax-shelter related changes made by the American Jobs Creation Act of 2004 are new disclosure requirements (¶ 605) and a new penalty that applies to any person who fails to include with any tax return, information concerning a "reportable transaction," regardless of whether the transaction results in an understatement of tax (¶ 615). This penalty ($10,000 for a natural person and $50,000 in other cases) can be imposed in addition to the existing accuracy-related penalty, and it increases to $100,000 and $200,000, respectively, if the failure to provide information is in connection with a "listed transaction." The 2004 Jobs Act gives the Secretary of the Treasury authorization to define "reportable transaction" and "listed transaction." The IRS is also directed to take into account prior conduct and the taxpayer's intent or lack thereof in determining whether to rescind or abate the new penalty.

Accuracy-related penalty.—In conjunction with the changes noted above, the accuracy-related penalty has also been modified by replacing the former rules applicable to tax shelters with a new accuracy-related penalty (¶ 620) directed at "reportable avoidance transactions" (i.e., one that has a significant tax avoidance purpose). A related amendment makes it more difficult for taxpayers to avail themselves of the reasonable-cause exception to the penalty by relying on the opinion of a qualified professional. The new law effectively disqualifies opinions that fail to meet certain factual and legal tests. If a transaction is not adequately disclosed, there will be no reasonable cause exception and the penalty will increase from 20 to 30 percent.

Statute of limitations.—Tax shelter participants will also find it harder to escape the long arm of the IRS by simply running out the clock. The extended six-year statute of limitations will now apply if a taxpayer fails to include any required information about a listed transaction on a return or statement (¶ 610). A footnote to the Conference Committee Report (H.R. Conf. Rep. No. 108-755) describes the potential ramifications of this change if a transaction is listed in a year subsequent to the year the transaction was entered into and the year of entry is a closed tax year. Assuming the tax benefits of the transaction are recognized over multiple tax years, the extension of the statute of limitations will apply to tax years in which the statute had not closed before the transaction became a listed transaction.

Registration.—Under the law as it existed prior to passage of the 2004 Jobs Act, the organizer of a tax shelter was required to register the transaction and a failure to do so incurred a penalty of *the greater of* one percent of the amount invested in the shelter or $500. The 2004 Jobs Act replaces these rules with a stricter requirement for information returns and stiffer penalties for failure to furnish information on reportable transactions. Each material advisor in a reportable transaction will be required to file an information return. The failure to file or a filing with false or incomplete information incurs a penalty of $50,000. The penalty with respect to a listed transaction will be a minimum of $200,000 (¶630).

Investor lists.—An organizer or seller of a potentially abusive tax shelter is required to maintain a list of investors if the transaction is required to be registered. The penalty for failing to maintain the list is $50 per name up to a maximum of $100,000. The 2004 Jobs Act modifies the rule by making each material advisor in a reportable transaction responsible for maintaining the list. The penalty will now be $10,000 per day with no maximum (¶635).

Promoters.—There is a penalty on persons who participate in the organization or sale of tax shelters if they make a statement that qualifies as false, fraudulent, or a gross overvaluation. The penalty is $1,000 subject to reduction or waiver. The 2004 Jobs Act enhances the penalty on statements other than gross overvaluation statements. The penalty will now be 50 percent of the person's gross income from the transaction. The penalty will apply if the person makes a statement about the tax benefits while they know or should know that the statement is false or fraudulent in any material way (¶640).

Injunctions.—The 2004 Jobs Act extends the authority to obtain injunctions for various actions or inactions with respect to tax shelter activities. These activities include the reporting requirements and the maintenance of investor lists (¶650).

Foreign financial accounts.—There is a recordkeeping and reporting obligation for persons who engage in a transaction or maintain an account with a foreign financial entity. A willful violation of this requirement can result in a civil penalty up to $100,000 and a criminal penalty of a fine or imprisonment, or both. The 2004 Jobs Act adds a civil penalty for non-willful violations up to $10,000. In addition, the penalty for willful violations will be increased to the greater of $100,000 or 50 percent of the amount of the transaction or value of the account (¶655).

Confidentiality.—Prior to passage of the 2004 Jobs Act, corporate tax shelters provided an exception to the general rule that communications between a taxpayer and a federally authorized tax practitioner are entitled to the same privilege of confidentiality as those of an attorney and his or her client. The exception for corporate tax shelters has now been expanded to *all* tax shelters (¶665). Accordingly, individuals, partnerships, or other entities participating in tax shelters can no longer rely on the possibility of protecting communications about these transactions with their tax practitioner.

Lease to a tax-exempt entity.—Property leased to a tax-exempt entity is depreciated over a recovery period that is the longer of class life or 125 percent of the lease term. A special rule allows qualified technological equipment to be depreciated over five years. Except for short-term leases, qualified technological property will now be depreciated in the same manner as other property leased to a tax-exempt entity. In determining whether a lease is short term, renewals or extensions based on fair market value rents will not be included. Additional limits are placed on deductions from some lease transactions (¶675).

Suspension of interest and deposits.—In a provision that was not specifically included with the tax-shelter provisions but is related, the 18-month rule governing the suspension of interest and penalties where the IRS has not contacted the taxpayer is now made permanent (¶1620). The rule was to have reverted to one year for tax years beginning after December 31, 2003. However, the suspension-of-interest rules do not cover certain items such as "gross misstatements," as well as "listed" and "reportable avoidance transactions."

ESTATES AND TRUSTS

¶ 183

Overall Effect on Estates and Trusts

Provisions common to estates and trusts.—Although the main thrust of the American Jobs Creation Act of 2004 is certainly not directed toward estates and trusts, there are several significant provisions that do affect both estates and trusts. For one, the new deduction for income attributable to qualified production activities income (QPAI) applies to estates and trusts at the beneficiary level, based on the entity's proportionate share of QPAI, and a separate rule governs application of the wage limitation requirement at the beneficiary level (¶210). Plus, under the 2004 Jobs Act, estate and trust beneficiaries may now claim direct foreign tax credits with respect to their proportionate shares of foreign taxes paid or accrued by an estate or trust (¶435). In addition, the second of two exceptions to the definition of U.S. property under Code Sec. 956 for purposes of determining the current income inclusion requirements for U.S. shareholders with a 10-percent or greater interest in a controlled foreign corporation (CFC) has implications for estates and trusts (¶460). It applies to the acquisition by a CFC of obligations issued by a U.S. person that is not a domestic corporation and is also not a U.S. 10-percent shareholder or a partnership, estate, or trust in which the CFC or a related person is a partner, beneficiary, or trustee immediately after the CFC's acquisition of the obligation.

¶ 184

Effect on Estates

Estate exemption for RIC stock.—Included in conjunction with a provision dealing with the treatment of certain dividends of a regulated investment company (RIC) is one that provides a partial exemption from U.S. estate tax for the estate of a nonresident, noncitizen decedent (¶560). The exemption applies to that portion of stock in a RIC held by the estate at the end of the quarter preceding the decedent's death that is in proportion to the assets held by the RIC that are considered qualifying assets. Such assets include debt obligations, bank deposits, or other property that would generally be treated as *property situated outside the United States*, if held directly by the estate. This provision is limited to the estates of decedents dying after December 31, 2004, and before January 1, 2008.

Estates of expatriates hit with new limitations.—The 2004 Jobs Act also affects the estates of individuals who are subject to the alternative tax regime (¶504). For example, if a former citizen or long-term resident who is subject to the alternative tax regime dies within 10 years of relinquishing citizenship or residency, the estate tax is imposed on the transfer of U.S.-situs property, including the decedent's pro rata share of the U.S. property held by a foreign corporation.

Effective date of basis provision changed.—In conjunction with the repeal of the foreign personal holding company rules (¶490), the 2004 Jobs Act changes the effective date of the provision (Code Sec. 1014(b)(5)) that governs the basis of stock in a foreign personal holding company acquired from a decedent. The provision will expire for the estates of decedents dying after December 31, 2004.

¶ 185
Effect on Trusts

Electing small business trusts.—Unexercised powers of appointment can be ignored in determining who is a potential current beneficiary of an electing small business trust (ESBT). Also, the period during which an ESBT can dispose of S corporation stock after an ineligible shareholder becomes a potential current beneficiary is increased to one year (¶ 930).

Qualified subchapter S trusts.—The beneficiary of a qualified subchapter S trust (QSST), rather than the trust itself, is allowed to deduct suspended losses on the disposition of S corporation stock under the passive activity loss limitation rules and the "at risk" rules (¶ 925). Other provisions involving farm cooperatives relate to declarative judgments (¶ 835), dividends and patronage income (¶ 830), and pass-throughs of ethanol producer credits (¶ 845).

Rabbi trusts face new rules.—New provisions in the 2004 Jobs Act mandate current income inclusion on deferred amounts in certain "rabbi trusts" that are not subject to a substantial risk of forfeiture and were not previously included in income (¶ 1405). The provision is aimed at purported attempts to move rabbi trust assets outside of the United States to protect them from creditors while at the same time taking advantage of the income deferral rules applicable to such trusts.

TAX-EXEMPT ORGANIZATIONS

¶ 187
Overall Effect on Tax-Exempt Organizations

As a result of passage of the American Jobs Creation Act of 2004, tax-exempt organizations will confront significant new requirements with respect to dealing with donations of vehicles (¶ 1305), noncash items generally (¶ 1310), and patents and other items of intellectual property (¶ 1315). However, the 2004 Jobs Act also includes provisions dealing with unrelated business taxable income (¶ 1325 and ¶ 1330) and with the treatment of dividends paid by cooperatives. Certain "specialty" provisions also involve tax-exempt organizations, including those relating to subsistence whaling and (¶ 1320) and electric cooperatives (¶ 1335).

¶ 188
Effect on Tax-Exempt Organizations

Vehicle donations.—Charitable organizations participating in vehicle donation programs will have to provide donors with a contemporaneous written acknowledgement for any qualified vehicle donation if the claimed value of the vehicle exceeds $500 or face penalties (¶ 1305). Qualified vehicles would include motor vehicles, boats, and aircraft. The acknowledgement must include the name of the donor and the vehicle identification number of the vehicle along with other information depending upon whether the organization will be retaining the vehicle for its usage or selling the vehicle "as is."

Noncash contributions.—While there is no specific new requirement imposed on charitable organizations with respect to noncash contributions, newly enacted reporting requirements may limit the ability of donors to take a charitable deduction for these contributions and, thus, may have at least an indirect impact on charitable giving. These new provisions of the 2004 Jobs Act impose additional substantiation requirements on donors and are imposed on individual donors, partnerships, and corporations (¶ 1310).

Patents and similar property.—As a result of reported abusive transactions involving contributions of patents and other items of intellectual property, the 2004 Jobs Act targeted these types of contributions for specific consideration. This provision centers on assuring the proper valuation of the contributed property (¶ 1315). In addition, the donee organization is allowed a further charitable deduction in the year of contribution and later years based on a percentage of the qualified donee income received or accrued by the organization from the property. The 2004 Jobs Act also imposes a new notice requirement on donors and reporting requirements on donees.

Cooperatives.—Certain cooperatives, such as those established for farmers, will benefit from a new provision in the 2004 Jobs Act that involves the treatment of dividends. Under the provision, dividends paid by a cooperative on its capital stock or other proprietor interests will no longer reduce patronage income (¶ 1340).

In addition, rural electric cooperatives benefit from a new provision that excludes certain income for purposes of the 85-test that governs whether such organizations remain exempt from tax (¶ 1335). Income from services provided on an open access basis will be excluded as will income from a nuclear decommissioning transaction.

Additional provisions concerning tax-exempt entities.—The 2004 Jobs Act also includes what might be termed "specialty" provisions connected with tax-exempt organizations that have relatively limited applicability. For example, a charitable contribution deduction of up to $10,000 per tax year is now available for certain expenses incurred in connection with sanctioned whaling activities by individuals who are recognized as captains by the Alaska Eskimo Whaling Commission (¶ 1320).

STATE AND LOCAL GOVERNMENTS

¶ 190

Overall Effect on State and Local Governments

State and local governments also found themselves the recipients (or the "targets") of congressional action in the American Jobs Creation Act of 2004. Probably the most significant portion of the legislation affecting governmental units will be the new restrictions on certain leasing arrangements (¶ 670 and ¶ 675). These arrangements have recently been cited as abusive tax-avoidance schemes, but did provide needed benefits to cash-strapped municipalities and other governmental entities.

Other provisions of the 2004 Jobs Creation Act, such as those creating qualified green bonds (¶ 745), expanding the qualified small issue bond program (¶ 735), and allowing special tax treatment for recipients of the National Health Service Corps Loan Repayment Program (¶ 1225), should also prove beneficial to state and local governments and related entities.

¶ 191

Effect on State and Local Governments

Leasing deals hit.—Sale in, lease out (SILO) arrangements were a major target of the American Jobs Creation Act of 2004 (¶ 670 and ¶ 675). These arrangements involve the purchase of assets from a city or other government entity by a bank or an insurance company which then leases the property back to the municipality. The deals generated large deductions for investors and cash for municipalities looking for additional funds. The WALL STREET JOURNAL recently reported (October 7, 2004, p. A1) one such deal involving the city of Chicago in which the city received $140 million that was used for improvements to its 911 system.

The 2004 Jobs Act limits SILO arrangements in different ways. First, the new law makes adjustments to the modified accelerated cost recovery system (MACRS) rules for calculating deductions stemming from tax-exempt use property, so that certain intangible property is subject to an extended recovery period of not less than 125 percent of the lease term. In addition, a new provision is added to prohibit the deduction of tax-exempt losses if the lessor does not have sufficient ownership rights in the property. However, the final legislation was primarily based on the House version, rather than the somewhat more harsh Senate version, and does provide some transitional relief for arrangements already in the pipeline if an application for approval was submitted to the Federal Transit Administration (FTA) after June 30, 2003, and before March 13, 2004, and the FTA approves the arrangement before January 1, 2005.

"Green" bonds.—The 2004 Jobs Act includes provisions that create a new type of exempt-facility bond called a "qualified green bond." These bonds would be issued for projects designated by the Secretary of the Treasury and the Environmental Protection Agency as a "green" building and sustainable design project and would have to be nominated by a state or local government within 180 days of enactment of the 2004 Jobs Act (¶745).

Small issue bonds.—Provisions relating to "qualified small issue bonds" were amended to provide that the maximum amount of capital expenditures allowed for an eligible business in the same city or county during the applicable six-year period is increased from $10 million to $20 million (¶735).

Exclusion from gross income for NHSC loan repayments.—An exclusion from gross income and employment taxes for loan repayments under the National Health Service Corps (NHSC) Loan Repayment Program should provide at least an indirect benefit to states and municipalities trying to attract medical services personnel to their locales (¶1225).

Chapter 2

ETI Repeal and Manufacturing Activity Deduction

¶ 205

Extraterritorial Income (ETI) Regime Repealed

Background

United States taxpayers are taxed on their worldwide taxable income, regardless of its source. In contrast, most European taxpayers are taxed only on income earned in the country imposing the tax. For instance, an Irish taxpayer generally pays Irish taxes only on income it earns in Ireland while a U.S. taxpayer generally pays U.S. taxes on income earned in Ireland as well as income earned in the United States. This inequity, coupled with the relatively high U.S. corporate income tax rate (see the Background at ¶ 210) arguably places U.S. taxpayers at a competitive disadvantage in the international marketplace.

Congress is aware of this disadvantage, but efforts to correct it are complicated by the nation's commitment to free trade. The U.S. is bound by a number of international treaties and agreements that are intended to prevent one nation from discriminating against another in its trade policies, or even from favoring products produced within its borders over imported goods. The U.S. has enacted three tax regimes to try to level the international playing field for U.S. exporters, but all have been deemed to violate international trade agreements.

The first tax regime for U.S. exporters employed an entity called a domestic international sales corporation (DISC), which allowed U.S. firms to defer taxation on a percentage of their export profits (Code Secs. 991—997). In 1984, after U.S. trading partners complained that the DISC provisions constituted an improper export subsidy, the DISC rules were largely replaced by the foreign sales corporation (FSC) rules (Code Secs. 921-927, prior to repeal by the FSC Repeal and Extraterritorial Income Exclusion Act of 2000 (P.L. 106-519)). FSCs generally were foreign subsidiaries of U.S. companies that exported goods manufactured in the U.S. A portion of FSC income was attributed to the U.S. parent company, while a portion was exempt from U.S. taxation. The European Union (EU) alleged that the FSC rules were another prohibited export subsidy that unfairly favored goods produced in the U.S. The World Trade Organization (WTO), an international body that administers trade agreements and settles trade disputes, agreed, finding that the FSC rules violated the WTO Agreement on Subsidies and Countervailing Measures.

In response to the WTO finding, the U.S. enacted the FSC Repeal and Extraterritorial Income Exclusion Act (P.L. 106-519) in November 2000.

Background

> **Comment:** Since the extraterritorial income (ETI) rules replaced the FSC rules, many tax practitioners refer to the two sets of rules in combination as the FSC/ETI regime.

The ETI regime did not provide for a new entity like a DISC or an FSC. Instead, it excluded "extraterritorial income" from a U.S. exporter's gross income (Code Sec. 114, prior to repeal by the American Jobs Creation Act of 2004). Theoretically, the exclusion applied to all foreign trade income and, therefore, did not favor goods produced in the U.S. However, the EU challenged the ETI provisions on the grounds that they did not alter the substance of the FSC export subsidy. Once again, the WTO agreed and, in January of 2002, made a final determination that the ETI exclusion, like the FSC rules, constituted a prohibited export subsidy.

As a result, the WTO Dispute Settlement Body gave the EU final authorization in May, 2003, to impose more than $4 billion in sanctions on U.S. goods. In order to give the U.S. time to replace the ETI regime, the EU waited several months to impose any sanctions, and then did so only gradually. On March 1, 2004, the EU began imposing an additional import duty on over 1,600 U.S. products, equal to five- percent of an imported item's value. The duty was scheduled to automatically rise by one percentage point each month until it reached a ceiling of 17 percent in March 2005. The EU announced it would determine its next course of action at that time if the ETI regime was still in place.

> **Comment:** The U.S. Department of Commerce estimated that the potential sanctions imposed on U.S. products from March 1, 2004, through March 31, 2005, could total more than $475 million. However, the economic impact of the sanctions has been blunted by the weakness of the dollar against European currencies, because a weak dollar effectively lowers the cost of U.S. imports.

ETI regime. Under the ETI regime, a U.S. taxpayer's gross income does not include extraterritorial income (ETI) that is qualifying foreign trade income (Code Sec. 114(a) and (b), prior to repeal by the 2004 Jobs Act). *Qualifying foreign trade income* is defined by reference to an exclusion from income (Code Sec. 941(a), prior to repeal by 2004 Jobs Act). It is the amount of gross income which, if excluded, would reduce the taxpayer's taxable income by the greatest of:

(1) 1.2 percent of the taxpayer's foreign trading gross receipts. *Foreign trading gross receipts* are gross receipts from the sale, exchange, disposition, or leasing of qualifying foreign trade property (Code Sec. 942, prior to repeal by the 2004 Jobs Act). *Qualifying foreign trade property* is property manufactured, produced, grown or extracted inside or outside the U.S., that is held primarily for sale, lease or rental in the ordinary course of business for direct use, consumption or disposition outside the U.S. No more than 50 percent of the fair market value of the property may be attributable to the sum of (1) the fair market value of items manufactured outside the U.S., plus (2) the direct cost of labor performed outside the U.S. (Code Sec. 943(a), prior to repeal by the 2004 Jobs Act).

(2) 15 percent of the taxpayer's foreign trade income. *Foreign trade income* is the taxpayer's taxable income, including qualifying foreign trade income, that is attributable to foreign trading gross receipts (Code Sec. 941(b), prior to repeal by the 2004 Jobs Act).

(3) 30 percent of the taxpayer's foreign sale and leasing income. *Foreign sale and leasing income* includes three types of income: (a) foreign trade income allocable to certain activities performed outside the U.S.; (b) foreign trade income arising in connection with the lease or rental of qualifying foreign trade

property for use by the lessee outside the U.S.; and (c) income from the sale, exchange, or other disposition of qualifying foreign trade property that is or was subject to such a lease (Code Sec. 941(c), prior to repeal by the 2004 Jobs Act).

Comment: According to the EU, the formulas for determining qualifying foreign trade income were arithmetically calculated to produce the same tax benefits that had been produced by the FSC regime.

Domestication election. The ETI regime also allows certain foreign corporations to elect to be treated as domestic corporations for all tax purposes (Code Sec. 943(e), prior to repeal by the 2004 Jobs Act). A corporation that makes the election can no longer use the ETI rules to effectively defer U.S. taxation of its earnings, but it can treat some of its income as qualifying foreign trade income.

The election can be made by *applicable foreign corporations.* A foreign corporation can be an applicable foreign corporation if: (a) it manufactures, produces, grows, or extracts property in the ordinary course of the corporation's trade or business; or (b) substantially all of its gross receipts are foreign trading gross receipts (Code Sec. 943(e)(2), prior to repeal by the 2004 Jobs Act). The election results in a deemed inbound transfer of assets from a foreign corporation to a domestic corporation (Code Sec. 943(e)(4)(B)(i), prior to repeal by the 2004 Jobs Act). If the election is revoked or otherwise terminated, there is a deemed outbound transfer of assets from a domestic corporation to a foreign corporation (Code Sec. 943(e)(4)(B)(ii), prior to repeal by the 2004 Jobs Act). The corporation generally must recognize gain or loss on these deemed transfers (Code Sec. 367(a)).

Comment: The U.S. argued before the WTO that the domestication election illustrated that the ETI regime was not intended to subsidize U.S.-produced goods. Any applicable foreign corporation could make the election and, thus, become entitled to ETI tax benefits, regardless of where its goods were produced. However, the U.S. also admitted that the election was primarily intended to provide parity between U.S. corporations that manufacture abroad through branches that are not separate taxable entities, and U.S. corporations that manufacture abroad through foreign subsidiaries that are separate taxable entities. The tax treatment for goods manufactured by a branch and for goods manufactured by a domesticated foreign subsidiary is essentially the same. In both cases, the goods are effectively treated as being manufactured by the U.S. corporation and, thus, they give rise to extraterritorial income.

The EU argued that few, if any, foreign corporations would benefit from the domestication election. First, a corporation making the election must waive all benefits granted to it by any tax treaties. Second, the election results in a deemed inbound transfer of assets that immediately makes the foreign corporation's non-distributed profits subject to U.S. taxation. Third, and even worse, the termination of the election results in a deemed outbound transfer that imposes U.S. tax on all of the corporation's undistributed profits, as well as the unrealized capital gain in the value of its assets. Finally, the election could cause the corporation to be subject to reporting and compliance requirements that might conflict with its domestic law. Thus, according to the EU, the election was effectively limited to foreign corporations that are owned by U.S. corporations.

American Jobs Creation Act Impact

ETI exclusion repealed; transitional rules provided.—The extraterritorial income (ETI) regime is repealed (Act Sec. 101(a) of the American Jobs Creation Act of

2004). The repeal becomes fully effective in 2007. For transactions prior to 2005, taxpayers retain 100 percent of their ETI benefits. For transactions in 2005, taxpayers retain 80 percent of the benefits they would have been entitled to under the ETI provisions. For transactions in 2006, taxpayers retain 60 percent of the benefits they would have been entitled to under the ETI provisions (Act Sec. 101(d) of the 2004 Jobs Act).

Example: Under the ETI regime, $10 million would have been excluded from the gross income of XYZ Co. in 2005, 2006 and 2007. XYZ can exclude $8 million in 2005, and $6 million in 2006. It cannot exclude any of the $10 million in 2007.

An applicable foreign corporation that elected to be treated as a domestic corporation for federal tax purposes has one year from the date of enactment in which to revoke the election without recognizing gain or loss. The nonrecognition rule applies to all property deemed transferred because of the revocation, to the extent that (1) the property was deemed transferred because of the election, or (2) the property was acquired during the tax year to which the election applies and before May 1, 2003, in the ordinary course of the corporation's trade or business. The IRS may prescribe regulations as necessary to prevent abuse of these rules (Act Sec. 101(e) of the 2004 Jobs Act).

The ETI repeal does not apply to any transaction in the ordinary course of a trade or business that occurs under a binding contract between unrelated persons that was in effect on September 17, 2003, and at all times thereafter (Act Sec. 101(f) of the 2004 Jobs Act). Persons are related if they are members of a controlled group of corporations or an affiliated service group, or are other entities under common control (Act Sec. 101(f)(1) of the 2004 Jobs Act; Code Sec. 943(b)(3), prior to repeal by the 2004 Jobs Act). A binding contract includes a purchase option, renewal option, or replacement option that is included in the contract and is enforceable against the seller or lessor (Act Sec. 101(f) of the 2004 Jobs Act). A replacement option is considered enforceable against a lessor notwithstanding the fact that a lessor retained approval of the replacement lessee (Conference Committee Report (H.R. Conf. Rep. No. 108-755)).

Comment: See ¶210 for discussion of a new deduction relating to income attributable to U.S. production activities, which is intended to replace the ETI regime.

PRACTICAL ANALYSIS. Neal J. Block, Partner with Baker & McKenzie LLP in Chicago, Illinois, observes that the repeal of the extraterritorial income exclusion (ETI) ends Congressionally authorized tax relief for publicly held companies that sell U.S. origin property in large quantities outside the United States. The ETI benefit will be available for 2005 and 2006, but at a reduced rate of the prior benefit of 80 percent and 60 percent, respectively. While the phase-out will also be accompanied by a phase-in of the domestic production deduction, the domestic production deduction will not be available to exporters or other dealers who do not engage in manufacturing, production or extraction activities. It is important, however, to note that the domestic international sales corporation (DISC) remains in existence. The DISC provisions provide for reduced U.S. taxation of income from exports of U.S. manufactured, produced, grown or extracted property. The DISC provisions do not require that the exporters be the manufacturers. While there are certain limitations to the benefits under DISC on export gross receipts over $10 million, U.S. exporters generally may reduce their tax rate on qualifying exports to 20 percent or less.

For further information on this subject, consult any of the following CCH reporter explanations:

- Standard Federal Tax Reporter, 2004FED ¶7110.01, ¶28,406.01, ¶28,416.01, ¶28,426.01 and ¶29,033.01

- Federal Tax Service, FTS § M:16.20 and § M:16A.225

- Federal Tax Guide, 2004FTG ¶17,310

★ *Effective date.* The provision applies to transactions after December 31, 2004 (Act Sec. 101(c) of the American Jobs Creation Act of 2004).

Act Sec. 101(a) of the American Jobs Creation Act of 2004, repealing Code Sec. 114; Act Sec. 101(b)(1), repealing Code Secs. 941, 942 and 943; Act Sec. 101(b)(4), amending Code Sec. 56(g)(4)(B)(i); Act Sec. 101(b)(5), amending Code Sec. 275(a); Act Sec. 101(b)(6), amending Code Sec. 864(e)(3); Act Sec. 101(b)(7), amending Code Sec. 903; Act Sec. 101(b)(8), amending Code Sec. 999(c)(1); Act Secs. 101(d), 101(e), and 101(f); Act Sec. 101(c). Law at ¶5085, ¶5125, ¶5600, ¶5650, ¶5695, ¶5700, ¶5705 and ¶5750. Committee Report at ¶10,010.

¶ 210

Deduction Relating to U.S. Production Activities

Background

U.S. corporations are subject to a progressive tax on income, as follows (Code Sec. 11):

Marginal Federal Corporate Income Tax Rates for 2004

Taxable income	Income tax rate
$0-$50,000	15 percent of taxable income
$50,001-$75,000	25 percent of taxable income
$75,001-$10,000,000	34 percent of taxable income
Over $10,000,000	35 percent of taxable income

The 34-percent rate is phased out by an additional five-percent rate on income between $100,000 and $335,000. The 35-percent rate is phased out by an additional three-percent rate on income over $15 million, but this additional tax is limited to $100,000 (Code Sec. 11(b)(1)). As a result of these phase-outs and add-ons, a flat 35-percent tax rate applies to corporations with taxable income in excess of $18.33 million; and a flat 34-percent tax rate applies to corporations with taxable income in excess of $335,000, up to $10 million. The income tax is imposed on the corporation's taxable income, which is the corporation's gross income less allowable deductions (Code Sec. 63(a)). Many tax credits can be used to reduce the corporation's tax liability.

The corporate income tax rates in the United States are higher than the corporate tax rates in many other countries, which arguably puts U.S. corporations at a competitive disadvantage in the international marketplace. For instance, according to the Organization for Economic Cooperation and Development (OECD), the combined corporate income tax rate in the U.S. for 2003 is 39.4 percent, which is the third highest rate among the 40 nations surveyed. The United States also lacks a broad-based consumption tax, such as a value-added tax (VAT), which may make the U.S. more reliant than most countries on revenue from corporate income taxes.

Background

> **Comment:** The perceived corporate income tax burden may be worse than the reality. A study of 275 of America's largest and most profitable corporations determined that their aggregate effective federal income tax rate for 2002 and 2003 was only 17.2 percent (Corporate Income Taxes in the Bush Years, available at http://www.ctj.org/corpfed04an.pdf). Another study concluded that from fiscal 2000 through fiscal 2004, corporate income tax revenues in the United States declined by 12.5 percent, even though corporate profits rose by almost 40 percent (An Analysis of the Recent Deterioration in the Fiscal Condition of the U.S. Government, available at http://www.americanprogress.org).

The United States has attempted to correct these perceived disadvantages by enacting a series of tax benefits targeted at U.S. exporters, first utilizing domestic international sales corporations (DISCs), then foreign sales corporations (FSCs), and finally an extraterritorial income (ETI) exclusion. However, international trading bodies determined that all of these tax benefits constituted export subsidies that violated international trade agreements (see Background at ¶205).

American Jobs Creation Act Impact

New deduction provided for portion of income attributable to U.S. production activities.—Taxpayers now receive a deduction equal to the lesser of a phased-in percentage of taxable income (or an individual's adjusted gross income) or qualified production activities income (Code Sec. 199, as added by the American Jobs Creation Act of 2004). In applying these rules, only items that are attributable to the actual conduct of a trade or business are taken into account (Code Sec. 199(d)(5), as added by the 2004 Jobs Act).

> **Comment:** According to the Conference Committee Report to the 2004 Jobs Act, this new deduction replaces the benefits of the repealed exclusion for extraterritorial income (ETI) (see ¶205), and is intended to provide tax relief that is economically equivalent to a three-percent reduction in taxes applicable to U.S.-based manufacturing (H.R. Conf. Rep. No. 108-755). However, this new deduction is significantly more expensive, costing an estimated $76.5 billion over the next 10 years, as compared to the $49.2 billion estimated cost for the ETI exclusion over the same period. The new deduction also applies to a much broader group of activities, but it does not replace the ETI benefits lost by nonmanufacturing exporters, such as distributors and export agents.

Deduction amount. The maximum deduction is nine percent of the lesser of the taxpayer's taxable income or qualified production activities income (Code Sec. 199(a)(1), as added by the 2004 Jobs Act). The maximum amount is phased in over five years. For tax years beginning in 2005 and 2006, the deduction is equal to three percent of the lesser of the taxpayer's taxable income or qualified production activities income. For tax years beginning in 2007, 2008 and 2009, the deduction is equal to six percent of the taxpayer's taxable income or qualified production activities income. For tax years beginning in 2010 and thereafter, the deduction is equal to nine percent of the lesser of the taxpayer's taxable income or qualified production activities income (Code Sec. 199(a)(2), as added by the 2004 Jobs Act). If the taxpayer is an individual, these calculations use adjusted gross income, rather than taxable income (Code Sec. 199(d)(2), as added by the 2004 Jobs Act).

> **Comment:** The tax benefits that would have been realized under the ETI regime are phased out over 2005 and 2006 (see ¶205).

The amount of the deduction cannot exceed 50 percent of the W-2 wages paid by the taxpayer as an employer during the tax year (Code Sec. 199(b)(1), as added by the 2004 Jobs Act). W-2 wages are defined as the sum of the wages and elective deferrals that must be reported on Forms W-2 with respect to the taxpayer's employment of

¶210

employees during the calendar year ending during the taxpayer's tax year (Code Sec. 199(b)(2), as added by the 2004 Jobs Act). Elective deferrals include amounts defined in Code Sec. 402(g)(3) (employer contributions that are excluded from the employee's income); amounts deferred under Code Sec. 457 (deferral programs for employees of state and local governments and exempt organizations); and, for tax years beginning after 2005, designated Roth contributions as defined by Code Sec. 402A (H.R. Conf. Rep. No. 108-755). The Treasury is instructed to provide guidance for the application of the W-2 wages limitation to taxpayers that acquire or dispose of a major portion of a trade or business or a major portion of a separate unit of a trade or business during the tax year (Code Sec. 199(b)(3), as added by the 2004 Jobs Act).

AMT. The deduction is also allowed against the alternative minimum tax (AMT). For individual taxpayers, the calculation of the deduction is the same for both income tax and AMT liability. For other taxpayers, however, the deduction for AMT purposes is calculated as nine percent of the lesser of (1) the taxpayer's qualified production activities income (determined without regard to available tax credits), or (2) the taxpayer's alternative minimum taxable income (determined without regard to this deduction) (Code Sec. 199(d)(6), as added by the 2004 Jobs Act).

PRACTICAL ANALYSIS. Neal J. Block, Partner with Baker & McKenzie LLP in Chicago, Illinois, observes that the domestic production deduction eventually will result in a nine-percent deduction on income from U.S. manufactured, produced, grown or extracted property. The qualifying activities, in large part, track the qualifying U.S. activities under the DISC and the foreign sales corporation (FSC) rules for parties that actually engage in manufacturing, production and extraction activities in the United States. The production deduction, however, does not apply to parties who engage in solely sales activities. While many of the terms are not defined in the legislation, the same terms are, in some cases, identical to those found in the FSC and DISC Code provisions and regulations. Thus, the terms manufactured, produced, grown or extracted in the new provisions likely will have the same definition as those same terms in the regulations under Code Secs. 927(a) and 993(c) of the FSC and DISC regulations, respectively. The computation of income allocable to the domestic production activities basically tracks the FSC and DISC methodology under the regulations of Code Secs. 925 and 994, respectively. Similarly, the restrictions on imported goods being valued at fair market value, definition of the United States, definition of engineering or architectural services, and limitations on transactions between related persons should be basically covered in whole or in part by existing FSC and DISC regulations. The FSC regulations also address goods which are subject to further manufacture both inside and outside of the United States. The Code is unclear as to whether the production deduction must be computed on an item-by-item basis or requires an overall profit to be subject to the deduction. However, it is noted that the DISC, and former FSC provisions, do provide for item-by-item computations.

Companies whose products are primarily or are exclusively consumed in the United States will receive the greatest benefit under this legislation. Consequently, while companies which produce for export remain beneficiaries of the new legislation, the benefits are much broader and encompass more companies and products than the repealed FSC and ETI legislation.

¶210

Qualified production activities income is equal to the taxpayer's domestic production gross receipts, reduced by (1) the cost of goods sold that is allocable to those receipts; (2) other deductions, expenses and losses that are directly allocable to those receipts; and (3) a proper share of other deductions, expenses and losses that are not directly allocable to those receipts or another class of income (Code Sec. 199(c)(1), as added by the 2004 Jobs Act). The Treasury is given authority to prescribe rules for the proper allocation of items of income, deduction, expense and loss for purposes of determining income attributable to domestic production activities (Code Sec. 199(c)(2), as added by the 2004 Jobs Act). Where appropriate, these rules should be similar to and consistent with existing relevant rules, such as the Code Sec. 263A rules for determining cost of goods sold, and the Code Sec. 861 rules for determining the source of income. Directly allocable items include such things as selling and marketing expenses. Other items that are not directly allocable include such things as general and administrative expenses allocable to sales and marketing expenses (H.R. Conf. Rep. No. 108-755).

For purposes of determining cost of goods sold, any item or service brought into the United States is treated as acquired by purchase, and its cost is not less than its value immediately after it entered the United States (Code Sec. 199(c)(3)(A), as added by the 2004 Jobs Act). Except as provided otherwise by the Treasury, the value of property is its customs value (H.R. Conf. Rep. No. 108-755). Similar rules apply in determining the adjusted basis of leased or rented property where the lease or rental gives rise to domestic production gross receipts (Code Sec. 199(c)(3)(A), as added by the 2004 Jobs Act). These rules also apply if the item or service was imported into the United States without an arm's-length transfer price (H.R. Conf. Rep. No. 108-755). However, if the taxpayer had exported the property for further manufacture, the increase in cost or adjusted basis cannot exceed the difference between the property's value when it was exported, and its value when it was brought back into the United States (Code Sec. 199(c)(3)(B), as added by the 2004 Jobs Act).

Domestic production gross receipts are the taxpayer's gross receipts derived from one or more of the following:

(1) Any lease, rental, license, sale exchange or other disposition of qualifying production property that was manufactured, produced, grown, or extracted by the taxpayer in whole or in significant part within the Unites States (Code Sec. 199(c)(4)(A)(i)(I), as added by the 2004 Jobs Act). *Qualifying production property* is any tangible personal property, any computer software, and any sound recordings (Code Sec. 199(c)(5), as added by the 2004 Jobs Act).

(2) Any lease, rental, license, sale exchange or other disposition of any qualified film produced by the taxpayer (Code Sec. 199(c)(4)(A)(i)(II), as added by the 2004 Jobs Act). For a motion picture film or videotape to be a qualified film, it must not be pornographic, and at least 50 percent of the total compensation relating to the production must be compensation for services performed in the United States by actors, production personnel, directors and producers (Code Sec. 199(c)(6), as added by the 2004 Jobs Act). The medium and the means of distribution are irrelevant to the definition of a qualified film. Live or delayed television programming should be included in the material that can be a qualified film. The IRS should provide appropriate rules governing the determination of total compensation for services performed in the United States, including residuals and participations. If residuals and participations have been estimated for purposes of depreciation under the income forecast method, the same estimate must be used for determining total compensation (H.R. Conf. Rep. No. 108-755).

¶210

(3) Any lease, rental, license, sale exchange or other disposition of electricity, natural gas, or potable water produced by the taxpayer within the United States (Code Sec. 199(c)(4)(A)(i)(III), as added by the 2004 Jobs Act) (see *Gas, electricity and water*, below, for further discussion).

(4) Construction performed in the United States (Code Sec. 199(c)(4)(A)(ii), as added by the 2004 Jobs Act). This includes activities that are directly related to the erection or substantial renovation of residential and commercial buildings and infrastructure. Substantial renovation includes structural improvements, but not mere cosmetic changes, such as painting (H.R. Conf. Rep. No. 108-755).

(5) Engineering or architectural services performed in the United States for construction in the United States (Code Sec. 199(c)(4)(A)(iii), as added by the 2004 Jobs Act).

Domestic production gross receipts include gross receipts derived from the sale, exchange or other disposition of agricultural products only if (1) the taxpayer performs storage, handling or other processing activities (other than transportation activities) with respect to the products, and (2) the products are consumed in connection with, or incorporated into, the manufacturing, production, growth or extraction of qualifying production property, by the taxpayer or by some other party (H.R. Conf. Rep. No. 108-755).

Comment: These rules seem to suggest that many corporate farming operations will be able to claim the deduction because their daily operations will qualify as production activities. Small farms may be less likely to perform processing activities.

Exclusions. Domestic production gross receipts do not include gross receipts derived from:

(1) the sale of food and beverages prepared by the taxpayer at a retail establishment (Code Sec. 199(c)(4)(B)(i), as added by the 2004 Jobs Act) (see *Food processing*, below, for further discussion);

(2) the transmission or distribution of electricity, natural gas, or potable water (Code Sec. 199(c)(4)(B)(ii), as added by the 2004 Jobs Act) (see *Gas, electricity and water*, below, for further discussion); or

(3) property leased, licensed, or rented by the taxpayer for use by any related person (Code Sec. 199(c)(7)(A), as added by the 2004 Jobs Act) (see *Related persons*, below, for further discussion).

Food processing. Food processing generally is a qualified production activity, but the sale of food and beverages prepared by the taxpayer at a retail establishment is not. For instance, operations at a meat packing plant give rise to qualified domestic production gross receipts, but a chef's creation of a venison sausage for his or her restaurant does not (H.R. Conf. Rep. No. 108-755).

However, a single taxpayer may operate food processing facilities, as well as retail facilities that sell the produced goods and other foods and beverages. The IRS is instructed to provide guidance as to how these taxpayers can allocate gross receipts between qualified and nonqualified gross receipts. This guidance should draw on the principles of Code Sec. 482 for allocating income and deductions among commonly controlled taxpayers (H.R. Conf. Rep. No. 108-755).

Example: Moondollar, Inc. buys coffee beans, and roasts and packages them at its food processing facility. It then sells the packaged coffee to retailers. Moondollar also operates retail facilities that sell the packaged coffee, along with brewed coffee and other foods. The gross receipts from Moondollar's retail

¶210

operations are qualified domestic production gross receipts to the extent they represent receipts from the sale of Moondollar's roasted coffee beans, but they are generally nonqualified to the extent they represent receipts from the sale of food and brewed coffee. However, Moondollar may allocate part of the brewed coffee receipts to qualified receipts to the extent of the value of the roasted beans used to brew the coffee. Moondollar's sale of roasted beans to unrelated retailers provides a value for the beans it uses to brew a cup of coffee for retail sale (H.R. Conf. Rep. No. 108-755).

The exclusion of retail receipts should not be construed narrowly to apply only to establishments where customers dine on the premises. The exclusion also applies to facilities that prepare food and beverage solely for take-out service. Similarly, the exclusion is not limited to establishments that are primarily engaged in the dining trade. For instance, if a supermarket includes an in-store bakery, it must allocate its gross receipts between qualified and nonqualified domestic production gross receipts (H.R. Conf. Rep. No. 108-755).

> **Comment:** To illustrate the difficulty of defining manufacturing activity, the 2004 Economic Report of the President noted that mixing water and concentrate to produce soft drinks is generally classified as manufacturing, but when the activity is performed at a snack bar, it is considered a service. The report also asked a rhetorical question: "When a fast-food restaurant sells a hamburger, is it providing a service, or is it combining inputs to manufacture a product?"

Gas, electricity and water. Qualified domestic production gross receipts (QDPGR) include gross receipts from the production in the United States of electricity, gas and potable water, but exclude gross receipts from the transmission of these items. Thus, gross receipts from the production of electricity are QDPGR, whether the producing facility is part of a regulated utility or is an independent power facility. However, if the taxpayer is an integrated producer that generates electricity and delivers it to end users, its QDPGR does not include gross receipts that are properly attributable to the transmission of the electricity from the generating facility to the final customers or to a point of local distribution (H.R. Conf. Rep. No. 108-755).

> **Example:** PowerCo owns a wind turbine that generates electricity. UtilityCo owns a local distribution network. TransCo owns a high-voltage transmission line. PowerCo sells its turbine-produced electricity to UtilityCo, which uses its distribution network to sell the electricity to its customers. PowerCo contracts with TransCo to transmit the electricity to UtilityCo. PowerCo's receipts from the sale of the electricity to UtilityCo are QDPGR. TransCo's gross receipts from transporting the electricity from PowerCo to UtilityCo, and UtilityCo's receipts from distributing the electricity to its customers, are not QDPGR.
>
> Moreover, if PowerCo makes direct sales of electricity to customers in UtilityCo's service area and UtilityCo receives remuneration for the distribution of electricity, UtilityCo's receipts are not QDPGR. If PowerCo, UtilityCo and TransCo are related taxpayers, they must allocate their gross receipts among their production, distribution and transmission activities (H.R. Conf. Rep. No. 108-755).

These same principles apply to the natural gas and water supply industries. For natural gas, production activities that give rise to QDPGR generally include all activities involved in extracting natural gas from the ground and processing it into pipeline quality gas. QDPGR does not include receipts attributable to the transmission of pipeline quality gas from a natural gas field or processing plant to a local distribution company's citygate or any other customer. Similarly, gas purchased by a local gas distribution company and distributed from the citygate to local customers does not give rise to QDPGR (H.R. Conf. Rep. No. 108-755).

Activities included in the production of potable water include the acquisition, collection and storage of raw (untreated) water, as well as the transportation of raw water to, and the treatment of raw water at, a treatment facility. However, gross receipts attributable to the storage of potable water or the delivery of potable water to customers do not give rise to QDPGR. A taxpayer that both produces and distributes potable water must properly allocate gross receipts between qualifying and nonqualifying domestic production gross receipts (H.R. Conf. Rep. No. 108-755).

Related persons. For purposes of the exclusion from QDPGR of gross receipts derived from property leased, licensed, or rented by the taxpayer for use by a related person, persons are related if they are members of a controlled group of corporations or an affiliated service group, or are other entities under common control (Code Sec. 199(c)(7)(B), as added by the 2004 Jobs Act). These rules should be interpreted under principles similar to those applicable under the ETI regime, as expressed in Temporary Reg. §1.927(a)-1T(f)(2)(i). Thus, this exclusion from QDPGR does not apply to property leased by the taxpayer to a related person if the property is subleased or held for sublease by the related person to, and for the ultimate use of, an unrelated person. Similarly, the exclusion does not apply to the license of computer software to a related person for reproduction and sale, exchange, lease, rental or sublicense to, and for the ultimate use of, an unrelated person.

Affiliated groups. For purposes of the deduction, all members of an expanded affiliated group are treated as a single corporation (Code Sec. 199(d)(4)(A), as added by the 2004 Jobs Act). An expanded affiliated group is an affiliated group as defined for purposes of consolidated returns, except that the stock ownership threshold is reduced to 50 percent from 80 percent, and insurance companies and corporations that elect to use a possessions tax credit are not excluded (Code Sec. 199(d)(4)(B), as added by the 2004 Jobs Act). Except as provided in regulations, the qualified production activities deduction is allocated among the members of the group in proportion to the member's respective amount (if any) of qualified production activities income (Code Sec. 199(d)(4)(C)).

Passthrough entities. The deduction is available to pass-through entities, including S corporations, partnerships, estates and trusts (but see *Agricultural and horticultural cooperatives,* below for special rules applicable to certain cooperatives). The deduction is generally applied at the shareholder, partner, or similar level (Code Sec. 199(d)(1)(A)(i), as added by the 2004 Jobs Act). The IRS is instructed to prescribe rules for this purpose, especially relating to restrictions on the allocation of the deduction to taxpayers at the partner or similar level, and additional reporting requirements (Code Sec. 199(d)(1)(A)(ii), as added by the 2004 Jobs Act). The W-2 wages limitation on the amount of the credit is applied first at the entity level, but the deduction itself is determined at the shareholder, partner or similar level (H.R. Conf. Rep. No. 108-755). A shareholder, partner or similar person that is allocated qualified production activities income from a passthrough entity is treated as having been allocated W-2 wages from the entity in an amount equal to the lesser of (1) the person's allocable share of the wages, as determined under regulations, or (2) twice the qualified production activities income that is actually allocated to the person for the tax year (Code Sec. 199(d)(1)(B), as added by the 2004 Jobs Act).

Planning Note: The deduction does not affect the existing tax deferral benefits of interest charge domestic international sales corporations (IC-DISCs). Thus, a closely held exporter organized as an S corporation or LLC will probably prefer to maximize cash flow savings by continuing to use an IC-DISC.

¶210

PRACTICAL ANALYSIS. Michael J. Grace of Buchanan Ingersoll PC and Georgetown University Law Center, Washington, D.C., observes that in planning to take deductions with respect to qualified production activities in tax years beginning after December 31, 2004, business entities and individuals should heed numerous definitional issues and other unanswered questions under new Code Sec. 199. The Treasury Department and the IRS should consider promptly addressing these issues in published guidance.

Deduction Limited to Wages Paid. An employer's deduction annually will be limited to 50 percent of the amount of wages and elective deferrals the employer reports to employees on Forms W-2. Taxpayers using a tax year other than the calendar year should note that the 50-percent limitation applies to the wages and elective deferrals for the calendar year that ends during the tax year for which the deduction is sought. See Code Sec. 199(b)(2). This 50-percent limitation creates a new incentive to obtain services through employees rather than independent contractors and increases the importance of distinguishing between them. For qualifying businesses, the limitation could reverse the recent years' trend toward outsourcing work to contract or other temporary workers.

Acquisitions and Dispositions. For purposes of determining W-2 wages when a business changes hands during the year, what will constitute the "major portion" of a trade or business or separate unit thereof? *Compare* former Code Sec. 52(c)(1) (repealed in 1978), attributing to an employer the unemployment insurance wages paid by a predecessor when the employer acquires the major portion of a trade or business or the major portion of a separate unit of a trade or business.

Allocation of Items. Numerous issues will arise in allocating gross receipts, income, deductions, expenses, and losses in determining "qualified production activities income." Items will have to be allocated, for example, between domestic and foreign sources and between production activities and nonqualifying activities. The Conference Report directs that the allocation rules "shall be similar to and consistent with relevant present-law rules" (e.g., Code Secs. 263A and 861 and also refers to Code Sec. 482. On an interim basis, the Treasury and the IRS either should instruct taxpayers to apply particular existing allocation rules or provide that taxpayers may use "any reasonable method "until detailed allocation rules have been promulgated.

Domestic Production Gross Receipts (DPGRs). For purposes of determining domestic production gross receipts (DPGRs), under what circumstances is property manufactured, produced, grown, or extracted "in whole or in significant part" within the United States? Many items (for example, motor vehicles and aircraft) are assembled in stages both within and outside the United States. Will an item be treated as manufactured, etc., in the United States if its final assembly occurs here, or will the relative values of the components and their origins (both parts and labor) be considered? It would be helpful for the Treasury and the IRS to define "in whole or in significant part." Compare Code Sec. 199(c)(3), providing rules for determining cost of goods sold allocable to DPGRs when items or services are brought into the United States.

DPGRs will not include gross receipts from leasing, licensing, or renting property for use by a related person. Code Sec. 199(c)(7)(A). Apparently, however, DPGRs do include gross receipts from selling property to, or exchanging property with, a related person.

Passthrough Entities. Code Sec. 199 generally will be applied by looking through partnerships, estates, trusts, and other passthrough entities and applying the various rules and limitations at the owner level. Code Sec. 199(d)(1)(A)(i); *contrast* Code Sec. 179, which applies to partnerships and S corporations at both the entity level and the owner level. Code Sec. 199(d)(1)(A)(ii)(I) directs the Treasury Department to prescribe rules "relating to restrictions on the allocation of the deduction to taxpayers at the partner or similar level." This directive raises at least two questions. First, given that Code Sec. 199 is to be applied at the partner, etc., level, do deductions potentially allowable to partners, etc., under Code Sec. 199 arise at the entity level? In other words, are there any entity-level deductions under Code Sec. 199 to be allocated among owners, or does each owner determine the owner's deduction based on the owner's allocable share of the entity's qualified production activities income? Second, assuming that deductions under Code Sec. 199 arise at the entity level, what "restrictions" are needed? Instead of further complicating the tax law, why not rely on existing allowcation rules such as Code Secs. 704(b) (partnerships) and 1366 and 1367 (S corporations) and their extensive regulations?

In order to take deductions under Code Sec. 199, partners, S shareholders and owners of other passthrough entities apparently need not pay W-2 wages. Instead, an owner to whom the entity allocates qualified production activities income also will be allocated a share of the entity's W-2 wages. Code Sec. 199(d)(1)(B). However, may an owner also count W-2 wages that the owner itself pays employees? Stating that the wage limitation is applied "first" at the entity level, the Conference Report does not appear to preclude an owner's taking into account wages and elective deferrals that the owner actually pays. Items that an owner itself pays arguably should be included in the owner's wage base, at least to the extent that the owner conducts qualified production activities separately from such activities of any passthrough entity.

It would be helpful for regulations or other published guidance to define "other passthrough entity" under Code Sec. 199.

Individuals. Individual taxpayers' deductions under Code Sec. 199 will not be limited by the two-percent floor on miscellaneous itemized deductions. See Code Sec. 199(d)(2). Whether or not the deductions are subject to limitation by Code Sec. 469 requires clarification. Code Sec. 469 disallows an individual's "passive activity loss" for the tax year. Regulations define "passive activity loss" as the amount by which the passive activity deductions exceed the passive activity gross income for the tax year. Temporary Reg. §1.469-2T(b)(1). In general, a deduction is a passive activity deduction if and only if the deduction "arises in connection with the conduct of an activity that is a passive activity for the taxable year." Temporary Reg. §1.469-2T(d)(1)(i). Deductions under Code Sec. 199, however, equal a percentage (nine percent once fully phased in) of a taxpayer's qualified production activities income for the year, defined as the amount by which qualifying gross receipts exceed the sum of allocable deductions. The allocable deductions apparently arise in connection with some "activity" (within the meaning of Code Sec. 469), but can the same be said of the deduction allowable under Code Sec. 199? If so, and if the deduction arises in a trade or business activity in which an individual does not materially participate, then the deduction will be disallowed and suspended under Code Sec. 469. Individuals could be subject to this limitation with respect to either production activities conducted directly (or through a single-owner entity disregarded for federal tax purposes) or production activities owned through a partnership, S corporation or other passthrough entity. Once the deductions have been allowed under Code Sec. 469, they would become allowable under Code Sec. 199 subject to its limitations. See Temporary Reg. § 1.469-2T(d). Code Sec. 469 also disallows passive activity losses of estates, trusts, closely held C corporations and personal service corporations.

Trade or Business Requirement. Code Sec. 199 will be applied by taking into account only items attributable to the "actual conduct of a trade or business." Code Sec. 199(d)(5). Typically, provisions of the Code refer to the "active conduct" of a trade or business. See, for example, Code Secs. 179, 274 and 355. Query whether "actual" means anything different than "active."

Fundamental Tax Reform. In explaining Code Sec. 199, the Conference Report anticipates that Congressional tax-writing committees will explore the merits of a unified top corporate tax rate for all corporate taxpayers including manufacturers. Manufacturing and other activities increasingly are conducted through passthrough entities not subject to the corporate tax regime (for example, limited liability companies classified for tax purposes as partnerships). When evaluating corporate tax rates, the tax-writing committees also should consider the rates applicable to income taxable solely at the level of partners and S shareholders.

PRACTICAL ANALYSIS. Michael Schlesinger of Schlesinger & Sussman of New York, New York, notes that the IRS Statistics of Income Bulletin (Winter 2004) details that S corporations are a very popular vehicle, with 2004 projections indicating that the number of S corporations will grow at an average annual percentage of 3.45 percent for 2004 through 2010. In 2004, the projection is that there will be 3,486,400 Forms 1120S filed. However, Code Sec. 199's manufacturing deduction geared to income will probably cause more S corporations to be formed, for the simple reason that in an S corporation, income can be manipulated through shareholder employee salaries. *J. Radtke,* CA-7, 90-1 USTC ¶ 50,113, 895 F2d 1196 only requires that S corporation shareholder employees take a "reasonable salary." While there is a limit regarding the amount of Code Sec. 199 deduction geared to wages, it is obvious that calculators will be grinding to determine the maximum tax benefit for S corporate shareholder employees, keeping in mind that if a shareholder employee's wages are too low, this might affect retirement plan contributions and social security benefits. If it appears that this Code Sec. 199 deduction will yield a big deduction, then S corporations will probably aggressively reduce shareholder employees' salaries to a minimum to maximize this deduction, taking the balance of the profits as a distribution self-employment tax-free, as sustained in *P.B. Ding,* 74 TCM 708, Dec. 52,269(M), TC Memo. 1997-435, *aff'd,* CA-9, 2000-1 USTC ¶ 50,137, 200 F3d 587. If the Code Sec. 199 deduction has no effect, given the nebulous concept of the *Radtke* standard of "reasonable compensation," the S corporation still may keep shareholder employee salaries low to take advantage of profit distributions being self-employment tax-free.

While it is difficult to project from the IRS Statistics of Income Bulletin the number of S corporations who would be classified as manufacturers for § 199 purposes, it is probable that a significant amount exists, given the broad definition of "manufacturers" and "production activities." Consequently, given such a large number of S corporation returns, it is doubtful if IRS can effectively audit this "reasonable compensation" loophole generated in § 199.

Agricultural and horticultural cooperatives. Member-owned agricultural and horticultural cooperatives qualify for the deduction under the same rules applicable to other taxpayers. Thus, qualified production activities income can arise from agricultural or horticultural products that are manufactured, produced, grown or extracted by the cooperative (H.R. Conf. Rep. No. 108-755). A marketing cooperative is treated as having manufactured, produced, grown or extracted any qualifying production property that is manufactured, produced, grown or extracted by its members and marketed by the co-op (Code Sec. 199(d)(3)(B)(ii), as added by the 2004 Jobs Act). For this purpose, agricultural and horticultural products include fertilizer, diesel fuel, and other supplies used in agricultural or horticultural production that are manufactured, produced, grown or extracted by the cooperative (H.R. Conf. Rep. No. 108-755). In determining the co-op's taxable income for purposes of calculating the deduction, the co-op cannot take into account deductions related to patronage dividends, per-unit allocations, or nonpatronage dividends (Code Sec. 199(d)(3)(B)(i), as added by the 2004 Jobs Act).

Patronage dividends or per-unit retain allocations paid to a member are deductible by the member if they are allocable to the deductible portion of the cooperative's qualified production activities income, and the co-op designates them as such. This designation must be made via written notice mailed to co-op patrons during the payment period used with respect to the co-op's patronage dividends and per-unit allocations. These amounts are not deductible by the co-op as patronage dividends or per-unit allocations (Code Sec. 199(d)(3)(A), as added by the 2004 Jobs Act).

PRACTICAL ANALYSIS. Gary L. Maydew, retired accounting professor at Iowa State University and author of SMALL BUSINESS TAXATION— PLANNING AND PRACTICE and AGRIBUSINESS ACCOUNTING AND TAXATION, observes that the new deduction for domestic production activities cannot exceed 50 percent of the employer's W-2 wages paid during the tax year. This requirement may encourage sole proprietor farmers and ranchers to consider incorporating and paying themselves a salary. Sole proprietors and partnerships may also want to consider paying wages to a spouse.

Regulations. The IRS is authorized to prescribe regulations as necessary for purposes of the definitions and special rules applicable to passthrough entities, individual taxpayers, agricultural and horticultural cooperatives, affiliated groups, the trade or business requirement, and application to the AMT (Code Sec. 199(d)(7), as added by the 2004 Jobs Act).

Timber. If, for a tax year ending on or before the date of enactment, a taxpayer elected to treat timber cutting as a sale or exchange, the taxpayer may revoke the election without IRS consent for any tax year ending after the date of enactment. Thus, a taxpayer's historic election will not prevent it from claiming the production activities deduction. The prior election and revocation will be disregarded for purposes of making a subsequent election (Act Sec. 102(c) of the 2004 Jobs Act).

PRACTICAL ANALYSIS. Greg Palmer of McDermott Will & Emery, Chicago, Illinois, observes that the new domestic production activities deduction raises the stakes for 2004 with respect to normal year-end efforts to defer income and accelerate deductions. If the deductions or income relate to qualified production activities, there is an added benefit to the tune of the three-percent transition percentage. The same will be true as the percentage increases at the beginning of 2007 and 2010. So, for example, if a domestic entity has substantial sales to a foreign affiliate, it may want to delay some of those sales which would otherwise occur before year-end, to the beginning of the following year.

These planning opportunities can also take on a multi-year dimension. For example, taxpayers who have claimed bonus depreciation on manufacturing equipment deployed in domestic production activities will receive an indirect added benefit for the next several years because, to the extent such bonus depreciation found its way into the costing of inventory, that inventory (LIFO layer building aside) will already have been sold.

There could also be an interesting interaction with future liquidations of low cost LIFO layers. Although it is probably counterproductive to cause a LIFO liquidation to reduce cost of goods sold, thereby boosting the deduction for qualified production activities, at least the deduction helps to reduce the sting of a LIFO liquidation.

The interaction with LIFO points out another potential opportunity, or issue, concerning the impact of accounting method changes. Taxpayers should review how Code Sec. 481(a) adjustments from accounting method changes relating to revenue or expense items associated with domestic production activities could impact their calculations.

Taxpayers for whom labor costs represent a very low portion of the cost of production could run afoul of the limitation based on 50 percent of W-2 wages. Interestingly, particularly given the avowed purpose of the legislation to promote U.S. manufacturing jobs, this 50-percent limitation does not appear to be restricted to wages paid to employees involved with production. Furthermore, the special rules concerning affiliated groups suggest that it is perfectly acceptable to aggregate wages paid by affiliates operating service business with those of manufacturing affiliates, in order to boost the 50-percent limitation.

For further information on this subject, consult any of the following CCH reporter explanations:

- Standard Federal Tax Reporter, 2004FED ¶3375.01, ¶6005.01 and ¶29,033.01

- Federal Tax Service, FTS §G:4.20, §G:6.20, §I:1.141 and §M:16A.225

- Federal Tax Guide, 2004FTG ¶7001 and ¶12,045

★ *Effective date.* The provision applies to tax years beginning after December 31, 2004 (Act Sec. 102(e) of the American Jobs Creation Act of 2004).

Act Sec. 102(a) of the American Jobs Creation Act of 2004, adding Code Sec. 199; Act Sec. 102(b), amending Code Sec. 56(g)(4)(C); Act Sec. 102(c); Act Sec. 102(d)(1), amending Code Sec. 86(b)(2)(A), Code Sec. 135(c)(4)(A), Code Sec.

137(b)(3)(A) and Code Sec. 219(g)(3)(A)(ii); Act Sec. 102(d)(2), amending Code Sec. 221(b)(2)(C)(i); Act Sec. 102(d)(3), amending Code Sec. 222(b)(2)(C)(i); Act Sec. 102(d)(4), amending Code Sec. 246(b)(1); Act Sec. 102(d)(5), amending Code Sec. 469(i)(3)(F)(iii); Act Sec. 102(d)(6), amending Code Sec. 613(a); Act Sec. 102(d)(7), amending Code Sec. 1402(a); Act Sec. 102(d)(8); Act Sec. 102(e). Law at ¶5085, ¶5110, ¶5135, ¶5140,¶5230, ¶5235, ¶5240, ¶5245, ¶5255, ¶5390 and ¶5495. Committee Report at ¶10,020.

Chapter 3

Business Deductions and Credits

CODE SEC. 179 EXPENSING

¶ 305

Code Sec. 179 Expensing Limits Extended

Background

The Jobs and Growth Tax Relief Reconciliation Act of 2003 (JGTRRA) (P.L. 108-27) increased the maximum dollar amount that a taxpayer may expense under Code Sec. 179 from $25,000 to $100,000 for tax years beginning in 2003, 2004, and 2005 (Code Sec. 179(b)(1); Temporary Reg. § 1.179-2T(b)). The $100,000 limit is adjusted for inflation in 2004 and 2005 (Code Sec. 179(b)(5)). The inflation-adjusted limit for 2004 is $102,000 (Rev. Proc. 2003-85, I.R.B. 2003-49, 1184). The investment limitation was also increased from $200,000 to $400,000 for tax years beginning in 2003, 2004, and 2005 (Code Sec. 179(b)(2)). The investment limitation is adjusted for inflation in 2004

Background

and 2005 (Code Sec. 179(b)(5)). The inflation-adjusted limit for 2004 is $410,000 (Rev. Proc. 2003-85). In tax years beginning in 2006 and thereafter, the dollar limitation and investment limitation are scheduled to return to $25,000 and $200,000, respectively.

> **Comment:** Under the investment limitation, the applicable dollar limit for the tax year is reduced by the amount by which the cost of qualifying property placed in service during the tax year exceeds the applicable investment limitation. Amounts disallowed because of the investment limitation may not be carried forward.

> **Example:** Tolton Company purchased and placed in service in 2004, $500,000 of property of the type that qualifies for expensing under Code Sec. 179. The dollar limitation for 2004 is $102,000. This amount must be reduced by $90,000 ($500,000 − $410,000 investment limitation). The taxpayer may expense $12,000 ($102,000 − $90,000) assuming that the Tolton Company's taxable income is at least $12,000.

Generally, only new or used *tangible* Code Sec. 1245 property purchased for use in the active conduct of a trade or business and which is *depreciable under MACRS* (i.e., Code Sec. 168) qualifies for expensing under Code Sec. 179 (Code Sec. 179(d)(1)). JGTRRA, however, included a provision that treats certain computer software as qualifying property if it is placed in service in a tax year beginning in 2003, 2004, and 2005 (Code Sec. 179(d)(1)(A)(ii); Temporary Reg. § 1.179-4T(a)). In general, "off-the-shelf" computer software that is otherwise amortizable over three years under Code Sec. 167(f)(1) qualifies for expensing under this rule.

An additional change to the Code Sec. 179 expensing rules made by JGTRRA allows a taxpayer to revoke or modify a Code Sec. 179 election made with respect to property placed in service in a tax year beginning in 2003, 2004, or 2005 without IRS permission on an amended return (Code Sec. 179(c); Temporary Reg. § 1.179-5T(c)). Prior to JGTRRA, an expensing election could only be revoked or modified with IRS consent. This rule is also scheduled to expire for property placed in service in a tax year beginning after 2005.

American Jobs Creation Act Impact

Two-year extensions for increased Code Sec. 179 expensing limits, computer software expensing, and election revocations.—The American Jobs Creation Act of 2004 extends for an additional two years (i.e., for tax years beginning in 2006 and 2007) the changes made to the Code Sec. 179 expense allowance by the Jobs and Growth Tax Relief Reconciliation Act of 2003 (JGTRRA) (P.L. 108-27). Under JGTRRA these changes applied only to property placed in service in tax years beginning in 2003, 2004, and 2005.

Thus, for tax years beginning in 2003, 2004, 2005, 2006, and 2007, the Code Sec. 179 dollar limitation is $100,000 and the investment limitation is $400,000 (Code Sec. 179(b)(1), as amended by the 2004 Jobs Act). For tax years beginning in 2008, these limits return to the $25,000 and $200,000 levels, respectively.

> **Comment:** The $100,000 limitation and $400,000 investment limitation will be inflation-adjusted in 2006 and 2007 (as well as in 2004 and 2005, as provided for by JGTRRA) (Code Sec. 179(b)(5), as amended by the 2004 Jobs Act).

Off-the-shelf computer software purchased in a tax year beginning in 2003, 2004, 2005, 2006, and 2007 will qualify for expensing (Code Sec. 179(d)(1)(A)(ii), as amended by the 2004 Jobs Act).

¶305

Finally, a taxpayer may file an amended return to revoke or change a Code Sec. 179 election made with respect to property placed in service in a tax year that begins in 2003, 2004, 2005, 2006, or 2007 (Code Sec. 179(c)(2), as amended by the 2004 Jobs Act).

Comment: Another provision in the new law limits to $25,000 the expense deduction for the cost of a sports utility vehicle (SUV). This limitation applies to an SUV that is not subject to the luxury car depreciation caps because its gross vehicle weight rating exceeds 6,000 pounds. The provision is effective for vehicles placed in service after the date of enactment. See ¶310.

PRACTICAL ANALYSIS. Michael Schlesinger of Schlesinger & Sussman of New York, New York, notes that Congress extended Code Sec. 179 for two years by simply changing the expiration date from December 31, 2005, to December 31, 2007, keeping all the provisions of Code Sec. 179, including the indexing for inflation provision, as well as the asset category of "off-the-shelf computer software." However, to remove the "embarrassment," as Senator Grassley called it, Congress amended Code Sec. 179(b) by adding Code Sec. 179(b)(6) to limit the depreciation deduction of SUVs, with loaded vehicle ratings over 6,000 pounds. Before this amendment, buyers of these heavy SUVs could expense up to $102,000 of the cost in the year the SUV was purchased. Now, the deduction is capped at $25,000 for SUVs with loaded weights between 6,000 and 14,000 pounds. While Congress' intention was a good one, owners of these heavy SUVs still come out ahead, because the first-year depreciation deduction amounts for vehicles under 6,000 pounds is currently capped at $2,960.

When Congress increased the Code Sec. 179 expensing amount in 2003 to a maximum of $100,000, it was projected that the cost to the country would be $1 billion. Presumably, the same cost figure will apply for the two-year period ending December 31, 2007. Congress obviously feels that, notwithstanding the high cost, this high-cost deduction is necessary to stimulate the economy. Individuals, S corporations, partnerships, LLCs and C corporations have two more years to write off the purchase of new and used qualified property, provided they satisfy Code Sec. 179's various provisions, such as Code Sec. 179(b)(3)'s trade or business income limitation. Estates, trusts, and certain noncorporate lessors are precluded from this maximum $100,000 write-off.

It remains to be seen whether Congress will make permanent the changes it made to Code Sec. 179 in the Jobs and Growth Tax Relief Reconciliation Act of 2003. Notwithstanding, expensing up to $100,000 of qualified property in the year that the property is placed in service under Code Sec. 179 is a very good provision to help taxpayers (particularly the small ones) operate a business.

For further information on this subject, consult any of the following CCH reporter explanations:

- Standard Federal Tax Reporter, 2004FED ¶12,126.01 and ¶12,126.021
- Federal Tax Service, FTS §G:19.20
- Federal Tax Guide, 2004FTG ¶9130

★ *Effective date.* No specific effective date is provided by the Act. The provision is, therefore, considered effective on the date of enactment.

Act Sec. 201 of the American Jobs Creation Act of 2004, amending Code Sec. 179(b), (c), and (d). Law at ¶5195. Committee Report at ¶10,040.

¶ 310

$25,000 Code Sec. 179 Expensing Limit on SUVs

Background

A well-publicized tax break allows taxpayers who purchase a truck or van with a gross vehicle weight rating (GVWR) in excess of 6,000 pounds to deduct more than $100,000 of the vehicle's cost in the year of purchase assuming that the vehicle is used 100 percent for business purposes. A sport utility vehicle (SUV) built on a truck chassis is considered a truck for this purpose.

The "luxury car" rules of Code Sec. 280F place strict limits on the maximum amount of depreciation that may be claimed on passenger automobiles, including trucks and vans, during each year of a vehicle's recovery (depreciation) period. Depreciation includes any amount expensed under Code Sec. 179 and any amount claimed as bonus depreciation.

In general, the luxury car limits apply to vehicles primarily used on public streets with an unloaded gross vehicle weight of 6,000 pounds or less. However, a truck or van, including a sport utility vehicle built on a truck chassis, is not subject to the annual depreciation limitations if its gross vehicle weight rating (maximum loaded weight) is in excess of 6,000 pounds (Code Sec. 280F(d)(5)).

In the absence of the limitation, the purchaser of an exempt vehicle in 2004 may be able to expense up to $102,000 of the cost of the vehicle under Code Sec. 179 and, if the vehicle costs more than $102,000, claim a 50-percent bonus depreciation deduction on the excess. The regular depreciation deduction may then be claimed on the remaining cost.

> **Comment:** With the exception of the Hummer H-1, the cost of an SUV will not normally exceed $100,000. The practical impact of the tax break is that taxpayers purchasing a heavy SUV may write off the entire cost in the year of purchase under Code Sec. 179. The maximum amount that may be expensed under Code Sec. 179 (without regard to inflation adjustment) is $100,000. The $100,000 limit was scheduled to be reduced to $25,000 in tax years beginning in 2006, but it has been extended for two more years, through tax years beginning in 2007 (see ¶305). The $100,000 limit has been inflation adjusted to $102,000 for tax years beginning in 2004.

> **Example 1:** A salesman purchases a Hummer H-1 for $127,000 in September 2004. The Hummer is not subject to the depreciation limitations because it has a GVWR in excess of 6,000 pounds. Assuming that the salesman's taxable income is at least $102,000, he may expense $102,000 of the cost under Code Sec. 179 and claim a $12,500 bonus depreciation deduction ($127,000 − $102,000 × 50%). In addition, he may claim a $2,500 regular first-year depreciation deduction, assuming the half-year convention applies ($127,000 − $102,000 − $12,500 × 20% first-year table percentage). The total deductible amount is $117,000.

> **Example 2:** Assume the same facts except that the salesman purchases an expensive sports car costing $127,000. The first-year deduction under the luxury car depreciation limitations is limited to $10,610 (the applicable first-year cap on a car other than a truck or van if bonus depreciation is claimed). The second-year deduction is limited to $4,800, the third year deduction to $2,850, and the fourth, fifth, and sixth year deductions to $1,675 per year. The $103,715 unrecovered basis of the vehicle at the end of the regular recovery period ($127,000 − $10,610 −

Background

$4,800 – $2,850 – $1,675 – $1,675 – $1,675) may only be deducted at the rate of $1,675 per year.

Comment: The exemption from the luxury car depreciation limitations for vehicles over 6,000 pounds was intended to exclude working vehicles such as trucks used in farming and construction or heavy vans used by the self-employed. When Code Sec. 280F was originally enacted, SUVs represented a very small share of the new vehicle market and few SUVs had a GVWR in excess of 6,000 pounds. Now, however, about half of all new car purchases are trucks and SUVs.

American Jobs Creation Act Impact

Code Sec. 179 expense allowance for heavy sport utility vehicles limited to $25,000.—The American Jobs Creation Act of 2004 limits the cost of a sport utility vehicle (SUV) that may be expensed under Code Sec. 179 to $25,000 if the SUV is exempt from the Code Sec. 280F depreciation limitations. The provision is effective for vehicles placed in service after the date of enactment (Code Sec. 179(b)(6), as added by the 2004 Jobs Act).

Comment: The new law does not eliminate the exemption from the Code Sec. 280F luxury car depreciation limitations for sport utility vehicles that have a gross vehicle weight rating in excess of 6,000 pounds. It simply prevents a taxpayer from expensing the maximum amount otherwise allowable under Code Sec. 179 (i.e., $102,000 in 2004) if the vehicle is exempt. Consequently, owners of heavy sport utility vehicles will still be able to claim a significantly higher first-year depreciation deduction than owners of lighter vehicles that are not exempt from the limitations. Alternatively, a taxpayer may still purchase a pick-up truck with a GVWR in excess of 6,000 pounds and expense the entire cost, assuming 100 percent business use.

Caution Note: The Code Sec. 179 expense allowance and bonus depreciation deduction cannot be claimed on a vehicle that is used 50 percent or less for business purposes in the year that it is placed in service. Depreciation on the vehicle must be computed using the Modified Accelerated Cost Recovery System (MACRS) alternative depreciation system (ADS) whether or not it is subject to the luxury car depreciation rules (Code Sec. 280F(b)(1)). If the 50-percent test is satisfied in the year that the vehicle is placed in service but business use falls to 50 percent or less before the close of the vehicle's recovery period, depreciation recapture applies (Code Sec. 280F(b)(2)). The recapture amount is the excess of the depreciation claimed in the prior recovery years (including the Code Sec. 179 expense allowance and the bonus deduction) over the depreciation that would have been allowed using ADS computed as if no amount had been expensed under Code Sec. 179 or claimed as bonus depreciation.

The following example shows the deductions that are allowable under the new law on an SUV purchased in 2004 after the date of enactment and costing $100,000 when (1) the depreciation limitations apply and 50-percent bonus depreciation is claimed, (2) the depreciation limitations do not apply and 50-percent bonus depreciation is not claimed, and (3) the depreciation limitations do not apply and 50-percent bonus depreciation is claimed. Note that bonus depreciation is not available for vehicles placed in service after 2004. This example assumes that the half-year convention applies.

¶310

Tax Year	Deduction if limitations apply/bonus claimed	Deduction if limitations do not apply/no bonus	Deduction if limitations do not apply/bonus claimed
2004	$10,910	$40,000 ($25,000 + $15,000)	$70,000 ($25,000 + $37,500 + $7,500)
2005	5,300	24,000	12,000
2006	3,150	14,400	7,200
2007	1,875	8,640	4,320
2008	1,875	8,640	4,320
2009	1,875	4,320	2,160
Total	$24,985	$100,000	$100,000

Comment: The MACRS mid-quarter convention applies if more than 40 percent of the cost of all depreciable personal property placed in service by the taxpayer in the tax year is placed in service in the last three months of the tax year (October, November, and December for a calendar-year taxpayer). Any amount that a taxpayer elects to treat as an expense under Code Sec. 179 reduces the cost that is taken into account in applying the 40 percent test (Reg. § 1.168(d)-1(b)(4)). In the case of a vehicle subject to the mid-quarter convention and placed in service in the fourth quarter, the recovery percentages for each year of the six year recovery period are 5, 38, 22.8, 13.68, 10.94, and 9.58 percent, respectively. If the half-year convention applies, the recovery percentages are 20, 32, 19.2, 11.52. 11.52, and 5.76 percent, respectively.

The following example assumes the same facts as above except that the mid-month convention applies.

Tax Year	Deduction if limitations apply/bonus claimed	Deduction if limitations do not apply/no bonus	Deduction if limitations do not apply/bonus claimed
2004	$10,910	$28,750 ($25,000 + $3,750)	$64,375 ($25,000 + $37,500 + $1,875)
2005	5,300	28,500	14,250
2006	3,150	17,100	8,550
2007	1,875	10,260	5,130
2008	1,875	8,205	4,102.50
2009	1,875	7,185	3,592.50
Total	$24,985	$100,000	$100,000

Comment: The tax break associated with the purchase of heavy SUVs, trucks, and vans will still be significant even after the expense allowance is limited to $25,000 and bonus depreciation expires. For a vehicle costing $100,000 and subject to the half-year convention, 40-percent of the cost may be deducted in the first year, as opposed to about 3-percent of the cost of a lighter vehicle of the same price that is subject to the depreciation limitations (the first-year depreciation limitation on an SUV on which bonus depreciation is not claimed is $3,260 for 2004 (see Rev. Proc. 2004-20, Table 3)). A more typically priced heavy SUV will cost $50,000 or less. The first-year deduction on such an SUV would be 60-percent of the cost ($25,000 + ($50,000 − $25,000 × 20%) = $30,000 or 60-percent of $50,000). About 6-percent of the $50,000 cost ($3,260) would be deductible in the first year if the depreciation limitations applied.

¶310

Caution Note: The second example in the Conference Committee Report (¶11,820) shows bonus depreciation being claimed on a vehicle placed in service in *2005*. The example is wrong because bonus depreciation does not apply to property placed in service after *2004*.

Sport utility vehicle defined. A sport utility vehicle is any four-wheeled vehicle:

(1) primarily designed or which can be used to carry passengers over public streets, roads, or highways (except any vehicle operated exclusively on a rail or rails);

(2) which is not subject to the Code Sec. 280F depreciation caps (i.e., the vehicle has a GVWR in excess of 6,000 pounds or is otherwise exempt); and

(3) which has a GVWR of not more than 14,000 pounds (Code Sec. 179(b)(6)(B)(i), as added by the 2004 Jobs Act).

Because this definition would include heavy pickup trucks, vans, and small buses in addition to sport utility vehicles, the term "sport utility vehicle" is further defined to exclude any of the following vehicles:

(1) a vehicle designed to have a seating capacity of more than 9 persons behind the driver's seat;

(2) a vehicle equipped with a cargo area of at least 6 feet in interior length that is an open area and is not readily accessible directly from the passenger compartment;

(3) a vehicle equipped with a cargo area of at least 6 feet in interior length that is designed for use as an open area but is enclosed by a cap and is not readily accessible directly from the passenger compartment; or

(4) a vehicle with an integral enclosure, fully enclosing the driver compartment and load carrying device, does not have seating rearward of the driver's seat, and has no body section protruding more than 30 inches ahead of the leading edge of the windshield (Code Sec. 179(b)(6)(B)(ii), as added by the 2004 Jobs Act).

Comment: Although the definition of an SUV does not apply to SUVs that weigh 6,000 pounds or less and are subject to the depreciation caps, a taxpayer is already effectively prevented from claiming any expense allowance on such a vehicle in most cases because regular first-year depreciation exceeds the first year luxury car cap.

Planning Note: For purposes of determining whether the luxury car depreciation limitations apply, the IRS has defined a truck or van as a passenger automobile that is built on a truck chassis, including minivans and SUVs that are built on a truck chassis (Rev. Proc. 2004-20 (Section 2.01), I.R.B. 2004-13, setting forth 2004 depreciation limitations; Rev. Proc. 2003-75 (Section 2.01), I.R.B. 2003-45, setting forth 2003 depreciation limitations). (This definition first appeared in Rev. Proc. 2003-75.) Most vans and SUVs with a GVWR in excess of 6,000 pounds are built on a truck chassis and should be unaffected by this rule. The truck chassis issue, however, is also relevant in the case of lighter vehicles that are subject to the depreciation limitations. This is because in 2003 the IRS began issuing separate depreciation limitation amounts for "trucks and vans" that are subject to the limitations. These limitations are higher than those that apply to other vehicles. Many "crossover" or "hybrid" SUVs are built on a passenger car or unibody chassis, for example, the Ford Escape, Buick Rendezvous, Pontiac Aztek, Honda CR-V, Acura MDX, and Hyundai Sante Fe. Although these vehicles may be marketed as SUVs, under the IRS definition, they are subject to the lower annual depreciation limitations that apply to vehicles other than trucks and vans.

Planning Note: Although the $25,000 limit on expensing large SUVs is effective for SUVs placed in service after the date of enactment, the full amount of the 50-percent bonus depreciation deduction on large SUVs that are exempt from the luxury car limitations may still be claimed. The MACRS midquarter convention, if applicable, will not affect the amount of the bonus depreciation deduction or the section 179 expense deduction. However, the vehicle must be acquired and placed in service by the end of 2004 to claim bonus depreciation. The bonus deduction is *not* available for vehicles that are placed in service after December 31, 2004.

PRACTICAL ANALYSIS. Vincent O'Brien, President of Vincent J. O'Brien, CPA, PC, Lynbrook, New York, observes how the 2004 Jobs Act reduces the allowable Code Sec. 179 deduction for heavier vehicles; however, heavier vehicles still receive preferential tax treatment as compared to lighter ones.

A vehicle that weighs 6,000 pounds or less is defined as a passenger automobile and is subject to the strict dollar limits on annual deductions (i.e., depreciation plus Code Sec. 179). A vehicle that weighs over 6,000 pounds is exempt from the annual deduction limits.

Trucks (including SUVs) and vans have an easier time exceeding the weight limit, not just because they tend to weigh more, but also due to the definition of weight that applies to such vehicles. When applying the 6,000-pound test, taxpayers use the rated (also known as loaded) weight. For other vehicles, taxpayers must use the unloaded weight of the vehicle when applying the 6,000-pound test.

Beginning in 2003 and ending on the enactment date of the new law, eligible taxpayers were permitted to use the Code Sec. 179 deduction to expense the cost of vehicles that exceeded 6,000 pounds, up to $100,000. (The Code Sec. 179 limit increased to $102,000 for 2004.)

Comment: Some states impose limitations on the deductions for SUVs for the purpose of computing state income taxes.

Under the new law, the Code Sec. 179 deduction for an SUV is limited to $25,000. (There is no limit for other trucks and vans that exceed 6,000 pounds.)

Nevertheless, an SUV that weighs more than 6,000 pounds is still not subject to the annual dollar limits that apply to passenger vehicles. Therefore, after claiming a Code Sec. 179 deduction of up to $25,000, taxpayers can still depreciate the remaining cost over the normal MACRS recovery period, without a dollar limit. In addition, during the remainder of 2004, such a vehicle is generally also eligible for the 50-percent depreciation bonus. (Reminder: Used vehicles are not eligible for the bonus.)

Since the 50-percent bonus depreciation provision is still in effect for the remainder of 2004, taxpayers will not appreciate the full effects of the new law's provision until after 2004, when the bonus depreciation provision expires.

Example: John purchases a new SUV for $65,000 during 2004. The vehicle will be used solely in John's business. Assume that the business is eligible to use the Code Sec. 179 election and the half-year convention for MACRS. If he places the SUV into service before the enactment of the new law, the business is permitted to expense the entire $65,000 cost using the Code Sec. 179 election.

If he places the SUV into service after the new law is enacted, the business will be entitled to a first-year deduction of $49,000. This includes a Code Sec. 179 deduction of $25,000, a depreciation bonus of $20,000 (50% × ($65,000 – $25,000)), and a normal first-year depreciation amount of $4,000 (20% × $20,000).

While the new law prevented a deduction of the entire purchase price of the vehicle in its first year of service, the business is still able to deduct just over three-quarters of the cost in the first year.

If John waits until 2005 to purchase and place the vehicle into service, the first-year deduction will be limited to $33,000. This includes a Code Sec. 179 deduction of $25,000 and a normal first-year depreciation amount of $8,000 (20% × ($65,000 – $25,000)). Thus, the new law has reduced the recovery amount in the first year to just over half of the vehicle's cost.

PRACTICAL ANALYSIS. Gary L. Maydew, retired accounting professor at Iowa State University and author of SMALL BUSINESS TAXATION— PLANNING AND PRACTICE **and** AGRIBUSINESS ACCOUNTING AND TAXATION, **observes that farm pickups weighing in excess of 6,000 pounds will still be eligible for the $100,000 expensing allowance as they were specifically excluded from the new $25,000 yearly limit.**

For further information on this subject, consult any of the following CCH reporter explanations:

- Standard Federal Tax Reporter, 2004FED ¶ 12,126.01
- Federal Tax Service, FTS § G:19.62
- Federal Tax Guide, 2004FTG ¶ 8140 and ¶ 9130

★ *Effective date.* The provision applies to property placed in service after the date of enactment of the American Jobs Creation Act of 2004 (Act Sec. 910(b) of the 2004 Jobs Act).

Act Sec. 910(a) of the American Jobs Creation Act of 2004, adding Code Sec. 179(b)(6); Act Sec. 910(b). Law at ¶ 5195. Committee Report at ¶ 11,820.

DEPRECIATION AND AMORTIZATION

¶ 315

Leasehold Improvement Property

Background

A leasehold improvement made by either the lessor or lessee of a building is depreciated under MACRS (Code Sec. 168(i)(8)(A)). In most cases improvements will be considered structural components of the building. A structural component is section 1250 property. If such an improvement is made to nonresidential real property, the improvement is treated as MACRS 39-year nonresidential real property and depreciated over 39 years using the straight-line method beginning in the month the improvement is placed in service. If the improvement is made to residential rental property, it is depreciated as MACRS 27.5-year residential rental property over 27.5

years using the straight-line method beginning in the month it is placed in service. The mid-month convention applies.

> **Comment:** Certain improvements may be considered personal property (section 1245 property) rather than a structural component of a building (section 1250 property). These improvements are generally depreciated as MACRS 5- or 7-year property depending upon the lessee's business activity. The depreciation period is determined by reference to the lessee's business activity even if the lessor makes the improvements unless there is an asset guideline class in effect for the lessor (Reg. § 1.167(a)-11(e)(3)(iii)).

A lessee who makes and depreciates a leasehold improvement may generally claim a loss deduction equal to the remaining undepreciated basis of the improvement when the improvement is irrevocably disposed of or abandoned at the end of the lease. Similarly, if the lessor makes an improvement for the lessee and depreciates the improvement, a loss deduction equal to the remaining undepreciated basis may be claimed if the lessor irrevocably disposes of or abandons the improvement at the end of the lease (Code Sec. 168(i)(8)(B)).

Although the 30- or 50-percent bonus depreciation allowance (also referred to as the additional depreciation allowance) (Code Sec. 168(k)) is generally only available for MACRS property with a recovery period of 20 years or less, a limited exception applies to "qualified leasehold improvement property," (Code Sec. 168(k)(2)(A)(i)(IV); Code Sec. 168(k)(3); Temporary Reg. § 1.168(k)-1T(c)).

American Jobs Creation Act Impact

15-year MACRS recovery period for qualified leasehold improvement property.—The new law provides that "qualified leasehold improvement property" placed in service after the effective date of the Act and before January 1, 2006, is 15-year MACRS property with a 15-year recovery period (Code Sec. 168(e)(3)(E)(iv), as added by the American Jobs Creation Act of 2004). As explained below, the improvements must be made to the interior portion of nonresidential real property. The applicable depreciation method is the MACRS straight-line method (Code Sec. 168(b)(3)(G), as added by the 2004 Jobs Act). If the MACRS alternative depreciation system (ADS) is elected or otherwise applies, the recovery period is 39 years and the recovery method is the straight-line method (Code Sec. 168(g)(3)(B), as amended by the 2004 Jobs Act). Whether or not ADS is elected, the applicable convention is the half-year convention unless the midquarter convention applies.

> **Comment:** Under MACRS, 15-year property is generally depreciated using the 150-percent declining balance method unless the GDS straight-line or ADS election is made. The new law, however, requires taxpayers to use the straight-line method on qualified leasehold improvement property even though it is 15-year property (Code Sec. 168(b)(2)(A), as amended by the 2004 Jobs Act; Code Sec. 168(b)(3)(G), as added by the 2004 Jobs Act).

> **Planning Note:** This provision is not elective. If the requirements for qualification are met, then the improvement must be depreciated over 15 years using the straight-line method. A taxpayer, however, could effectively avoid the provision by electing ADS and depreciating the improvements over 39 years. However, the ADS election would also apply to any other MACRS 15-year property that the taxpayer happened to place in service in the same tax year (Code Sec. 168(g)(7)).

¶315

Qualified leasehold improvement property defined. "Qualified leasehold improvement property" is defined the same way as the term is defined in Code Sec. 168(k)(3) for purposes of the bonus depreciation deduction.

Qualified leasehold improvement property is any improvement to an interior portion of *nonresidential real property* if the following requirements are satisfied:

(1) The improvement is made under or pursuant to a lease by the lessee, any sublessee, or the lessor (a commitment to enter into a lease is treated as a lease for this purpose);

(2) the lease is not between related persons;

(3) the building (or portion that the improvement is made to) is occupied exclusively by the lessee or sublessee;

(4) the improvement is section 1250 property (i.e., a structural component); and

(5) the improvement is placed into service more than 3 years after the date that the building was first placed into service (Code Sec. 168(k)(3); Temporary Reg. § 1.168(k)-1T(c)).

Comment: Improvements to residential rental property do not qualify. The building must be nonresidential real property (section 1250 property with a class life of 27.5 years or greater that is not residential rental property (Code Sec. 168(e)(2)(B)), such as an office building, retail store, or industrial building.

A commitment to enter into a lease is treated as a lease, with the parties to the commitment treated as the lessor and lessee (Temporary Reg. § 1.168(k)-1T(c)(3)(vi)).

The lease may not be between related persons. Members of an affiliated group (as defined in Code Sec. 1504) are related persons. Persons with a relationship described in Code Sec. 267(b) are related persons. However, the phrase "80 percent or more" is substituted in each place that the phrase "more than 50 percent" appears (Temporary Reg. § 1.168(k)-1T(c)(3)(vi)).

Comment: The IRS has issued bonus depreciation regulations which provide guidance concerning the definition of qualified leasehold improvement property under Code Sec. 168(k)(3) (Temporary Reg. § 1.168(k)-1T(c)). These regulations should apply equally to the definition for purposes of the new 15-year recovery period.

Comment: A leasehold improvement which is section 1245 property may be separately depreciated over a shorter recovery period (usually 5 or 7 years depending upon the business activity in which the improvement is primarily used) under the MACRS cost segregation rules (Standard Federal Tax Reporter ¶ 11,279.051 et seq. and Federal Tax Service § G:17.44 et seq). Examples of section 1245 leasehold improvements include removable carpeting and removable partitions. Qualified section 1250 leasehold improvements to nonresidential real property would normally be considered structural components depreciable over 39 years in the absence of this new provision.

Expenditures for the following are not qualified leasehold improvement property:

(1) the enlargement (as defined in Reg. § 1.48-12(c)(10)) of the building;

(2) elevators and escalators;

(3) structural components (as defined in Reg. § 1.48-1(e)(2)) that benefit a common area; and

(4) internal structural framework (as defined in Reg. § 1.48-12(b)(3)(i)(D)).

¶315

The term "common area" generally refers to areas used by different lessees of a building, such as stairways, hallways, lobbies, common seating areas, interior and exterior pedestrian walkways and pedestrian bridges, loading docks and areas, and rest rooms (Temporary Reg. § 1.168(k)-1T(c)(3)(vi)).

Limitations on subsequent owners with respect to improvements placed in service by original lessor. An improvement made and depreciated by the lessor when the improvement is placed in service can be qualified leasehold improvement property only so long as the improvement is held by the lessor (Code Sec. 168(e)(6)(A), as added by the 2004 Jobs Act).

> **Planning Note:** This limitation prevents a subsequent purchaser of a building from using the 15-year depreciation period on leasehold improvements placed in service by the prior lessor-owner.

This limitation, however, is not triggered if the leasehold improvement is acquired from the original lessor by reason of the lessor's death (Code Sec. 168(e)(6)(B)(i), as added by the 2004 Jobs Act) or in any of the following types of transactions that qualify for nonrecognition treatment:

(1) transactions to which Code Sec. 381(a) applies (relating to corporate acquisitions in transactions involving the liquidation of subsidiaries or certain qualified reorganizations) (Code Sec. 168(e)(6)(B)(ii), as added by the 2004 Jobs Act);

(2) a mere change in the form of conducting the trade or business so long as the property is retained in the trade or business as qualified leasehold improvement property and the taxpayer retains a substantial interest in the trade or business (Code Sec. 168(e)(6)(B)(iii), as added by the 2004 Jobs Act);

(3) a like-kind exchange (Code Sec. 1031), involuntary conversion (Code Sec. 1033), or the sale of real estate which is reacquired in partial or full satisfaction of debt on the property (Code Sec. 1038) to the extent that the basis in the acquired leasehold improvement property is a carryover basis (Code Sec. 168(e)(6)(B)(iv), as added by the 2004 Jobs Act); and

(4) a transaction described in Code Sec. 332 (complete liquidation of a subsidiary), Code Sec. 351 (transfers to controlled corporations), Code Sec. 361 (exchanges of property solely for corporate stock in a reorganization), Code Sec. 721 (contributions of property in exchange for a partnership interest), and Code Sec. 731 (distributions of property by partnerships to partners) to the extent that the basis of the leasehold improvement property in the hands of the taxpayer is determined by reference to its basis in the hands of the transferor or distributor (Code Sec. 168(e)(6)(B)(v), as added by the 2004 Jobs Act).

> **Comment:** The acquisition of property by a taxpayer from a transferee or acquiring corporation in a Code Sec. 332, 351, 361, 721, or 731 transaction described above also does not cease to be leasehold improvement property to the extent that the basis of the property in the hands of the taxpayer is determined by reference to its basis in the hands of the transferor or distributor (Code Sec. 168(e)(6)(B)(v), as added by the 2004 Jobs Act).

PRACTICAL ANALYSIS. Michael J. Grace of Buchanan Ingersoll PC and Georgetown University Law Center, Washington, D.C., observes that taxpayers planning to depreciate leasehold improvements should pay close attention to the effective dates of both new and established rules. The 2004 Jobs Act amends Code Sec. 168(b)(3) and (e)(3) to provide that a lessor or lessee may recover the cost of qualified leasehold improvement property using the straight line method over a

recovery period of 15 years. To qualify, however, the property must be placed in service after the date of enactment of the Act (yet to be determined) and before January 1, 2006. Otherwise, the cost of the leasehold improvements must be recovered over the same recovery period and using the same method applicable to the improved property, even if that period exceeds the term of the lease. See Code Sec. 168(i)(6). Bonus depreciation also may be taken on qualified leasehold improvement property under Code Sec. 168(k). In fact, 50-percent bonus depreciation must be taken unless the taxpayer either elects out or instead elects a 30-percent bonus. See Code Sec. 168(k)(2)(C)(iii) and (k)(4)(E). For purposes of computing other allowable depreciation, the adjusted basis of the property must be reduced by the bonus depreciation taken. Code Sec. 168(k)(1)(B). However, bonus depreciation may be taken only with respect to leasehold improvements placed in service before January 1, 2005 (January 1, 2006, for certain self-constructed property subject to Code Sec. 263A). See Code Sec. 168(k)(2)(B).

For further information on this subject, consult any of the following CCH reporter explanations:

- Standard Federal Tax Reporter, 2004FED ¶11,011.021, ¶11,279.01, ¶11,279.023, ¶11,279.05 and ¶11,279.052

- Federal Tax Service, FTS §G:18.60

- Federal Tax Guide, 2004FTG ¶9015

★ *Effective date.* The provision applies to property placed in service after the date of enactment of the American Jobs Creation Act of 2004 (Act Sec. 211(f) of the American Jobs Creation Act of 2004).

Act Sec. 211(a)-(e) of the American Jobs Creation Act of 2004, adding Code Sec. 168(e)(3)(E)(iv), (e)(6), and (b)(3)(G) and amending Code Sec. 168(b)(2)(A) and (g)(3)(B); Act Sec. 211(f). Law at ¶5180. Committee Report at ¶10,050.

¶317

Qualified Restaurant Property

Background _____

Under the Modified Accelerated Cost Recovery System (MACRS), a restaurant building is considered 39-year nonresidential real property. Accordingly, it is depreciated over 39 years using the straight-line method. The depreciation treatment of an improvement made to an existing restaurant depends upon whether the improvement is a structural component (section 1250 property) or personal property (section 1245 property). An improvement which is personal property may be separately depreciated as five-year MACRS property. See Asset Class 57.0 of Rev. Proc. 87-56 which assigns a 5-year recovery period to section 1245 assets used in wholesale and retail trades. If the improvement is a structural component (section 1250 property), then it is depreciated beginning in the month of the year that it is placed in service as 39-year real property.

It is generally recognized that restaurants are subject to more wear and tear than other commercial buildings and that as a consequence restaurant owners are required to repair and upgrade their facilities more frequently than other taxpayers. The 39-year recovery period that applies to most capitalized repairs and upgrades does not accurately reflect the true economic life of the property.

American Jobs Creation Act Impact

Depreciation period of qualified restaurant property set at 15 years.—The new law assigns a 15-year MACRS recovery period to "qualified restaurant property" placed in service after the effective date of the American Jobs Creation Act of 2004 and before January 1, 2006 (Code Sec. 168(e)(3)(E)(v), as added by the 2004 Jobs Act). The straight-line method applies to such property (Code Sec. 168(b)(3)(H), as added by the 2004 Jobs Act). If the MACRS alternative depreciation system (ADS) is elected or otherwise applies, the applicable MACRS recovery period is 39 years and the straight-line method applies (Code Sec. 168(g)(3)(B), as amended by the 2004 Jobs Act). Whether or not ADS is elected, the applicable conventon is the half-year convention, unless the midquarter convention applies.

Planning Note: The 15-year recovery period is not elective. However, a taxpayer could effectively elect out by making an ADS election. An ADS election, however, would apply to all MACRS 15-year property placed in service by the taxpayer during the tax year.

Qualified restaurant property defined. Qualified restaurant property is any section 1250 property which is an improvement to a building if the improvement is placed in service more than three years after the date the building was first placed in service and more than 50 percent of the building's square footage is devoted to preparation of and seating for on-premises consumption of prepared meals (Code Sec. 168(e)(7), as added by the 2004 Jobs Act).

Comment: Fast-food restaurants with limited seating space should be able to qualify since the meal preparation area is taken into account in determining whether the more-than-50-percent test is satisfied. Note, also, that the three-year period is measured from the date that the building was originally placed in service, whether or not it was originally placed in service by the taxpayer. For example, improvements to a restaurant building that is at least three years old at the time the taxpayer buys the building may qualify.

Comment: Prior to enactment of the new law, a section 1250 improvement to a restaurant building would be depreciated over 39 years beginning in the month that it was placed in service using the mid-month convention. The new law does not change the current rule that allows an improvement to a restaurant that is section 1245 property (personal property) to be depreciated as MACRS five-year property (Asset Class 57.0) under the MACRS cost segregation rules.

The IRS issued an "Industry Directive" dated December 8, 2003 which, contains a detailed chart that categorizes various original restaurant components as section 1250 property (depreciable over 39 years) or section 1245 property (depreciable over five years under the cost segregation rules) (LMSB Directive on Cost Segregation in the Restaurant Industry reproduced at ¶11,279.0516 of the Standard Federal Tax Reporter; §G:17.46[1] of the Federal Tax Service and page 853 of the 2004 CCH U.S. Master Depreciation Tax Guide). Items listed in this chart as section 1250 property and placed in service after the effective date and before January 1, 2006, as an improvement to an existing restaurant building (but more than 3 years after the building was originally placed in service) should qualify for 15-year depreciation under the new law. Examples of such qualifying items include, electrical system components not dedicated to specific machinery or kitchen equipment, most interior and exterior lighting, elevators and escalators, fire protection systems, security systems, fireplaces, permanent floor coverings (other than carpeting), floors, most HVACs (heating ventilating and air conditioning units) unless dedicated solely to the kitchen, most plumbing unless dedicated to specific equipment, restroom accessories and partitions, walls, permanent wall coverings, and roofs.

Comment: The new law also assigns a 15-year recovery period and straight-line depreciation method to "qualified leasehold improvement property" placed in service after the date of enactment and before January 1, 2006 (Code Sec. 168(e)(6), as added by the 2004 Jobs Act). Qualified leasehold improvement property is generally defined as section 1250 leasehold improvements made to commercial property by a lessor or lessee pursuant to a lease more than three years after the commercial property was placed in service. In certain circumstances, an improvement made by a lessor or lessee of a restaurant building could apparently qualify for a 15-year recovery period either as "qualified leasehold improvement property" or as "qualified restaurant property." The provision for qualified restaurant property, however, is much broader in that it is not limited to leasehold improvements or by other restrictions that apply to "qualified leasehold improvement property." See ¶315 for a discussion of the new provision for qualified leasehold improvement property.

Planning Note: The requirement that qualified restaurant property must be placed in service more than three years after the building is placed in service may be a significant (albeit temporary) disincentive for the construction of new restaurants since only improvements to a building which is at least three years old (i.e., has been in service for three years) qualify for the 15-year recovery period. For example, the benefits of the provision could be obtained by a new restaurateur by purchasing an existing building and then making the improvements necessary to convert it to a restaurant or by buying an existing restaurant and remodeling or upgrading it. Note also that the requirement that qualified restaurant property must be placed in service before January 1, 2006, will also prevent a taxpayer who constructs a new restaurant from taking advantage of the 15-year recovery period by delaying nonessential improvements for the requisite three-year period.

Caution Note: The provision only applies to improvements "to a building." Improvements that are not part of or attached to the restaurant building, for example, a detached sign supported on a concrete foundation, sidewalk, or depreciable landscaping, would generally constitute separately depreciable land improvements which also have a 15-year recovery period but may be depreciated using the 150-percent declining balance method. Other unattached improvements may qualify for a shorter recovery period if not considered a land improvement.

Planning Note: Technically, the assignment of a 15-year recovery period to qualified restaurant property means that such property can qualify for the 50-percent bonus depreciation allowance (Code Sec. 168(k)). The allowance could not previously be claimed because it only applies to MACRS property with a recovery period of 20 years or less. However, since bonus depreciation generally does not apply to property placed in service after December 31, 2004, the window of opportunity for claiming this additional benefit is very limited. With respect to the Code Sec. 179 expense allowance, the shortened depreciation period does not change the status of qualified restaurant property as section 1250 property. Since the Code Sec. 179 expense allowance only applies to section 1245 property (Code Sec. 179(d)(1)), qualified restaurant property may not be expensed.

Comment: It appears that if qualified restaurant property is placed into service after the effective date and before January 1, 2006, and the building is later sold, the qualified restaurant property retains its status as such and the new owner may depreciate the property over 15 years. The new law only requires that the restaurant property be placed in service before January 1, 2006; it does not require that the "taxpayer" place the restaurant property in service before January 1, 2006 (Code Sec. 168(e)(3)(E)(v), as added by the 2004 Jobs Act). In this regard, note that the new provision allowing qualified leasehold improvements to be depreciated over 15 years (¶315) includes a specific rule which provides that a qualified leasehold improvement made by the lessor generally retains its status only so long as it is held by the lessor (Code Sec. 168(e)(6)(A), as added by the 2004 Jobs Act). No similar rule was included in the case of qualified restaurant property.

For further information on this subject, consult any of the following CCH reporter explanations:

- Standard Federal Tax Reporter, 2004FED ¶11,279.01, ¶11,279.023 and ¶11,279.05

- Federal Tax Service, FTS §G:16.83[5]

- Federal Tax Guide, 2004FTG ¶9110

★ *Effective date.* The provision applies to property placed in service after the date of enactment of the American Jobs Creation Act of 2004 (Act Sec. 211(f) of the American Jobs Creation Act of 2004).

Act Sec. 211(a)–(e) of the American Jobs Creation Act of 2004, adding Code Sec. 168(e)(3)(E)(v), Code Sec. 168(e)(6)–(7), Code Sec. 168(b)(3)(G)–(H), and amending Code Sec. 168(g)(3)(B); Act Sec. 211(f). Law at ¶5180. Committee Report at ¶10,060.

¶320

Income Forecast Depreciation Method

Background _____

The cost of motion picture films, sound recordings, copyrights, books, and patents may be recovered using the income forecast depreciation method described in Code Sec. 167(g).

Under the income forecast method, each year's deduction is determined by multiplying the adjusted basis of the property by a fraction, the numerator of which is the income generated by the property during the tax year and the denominator of which is the total forecasted or estimated income expected to be generated prior to the close of the tenth tax year after the tax year the property was placed in service.

Only amounts that satisfy the economic performance rule of Code Sec. 461(h) may be included in the adjusted basis (Code Sec. 167(g)(1)(B)).

Comment: In accordance with Code Sec. 167(g)(1)(B), proposed regulations provide that the economic performance requirement precludes the inclusion of contingent expenses in the basis of income forecast property until the year that the economic performance requirement is satisfied (Proposed Reg. §1.167(n)-2(a)(2)). The Ninth Circuit Court of Appeals has held that estimated percentages to be paid based on the forecasted future gross receipts and net profits from a motion picture (participations), as well as percentages to be paid stemming from forecasted future revenue received from the movie's television exhibition (residuals), were includible in the cost basis of the property for purposes of computing depreciation under the income forecast method. However, this case was decided before enactment of Code Sec. 461(h) and Code Sec. 167(g)(1)(B) (*Transamerica Corp.*, 93-2 USTC ¶50,388).

Background

Taxpayers that claim depreciation under the income forecast method are required to pay (or may be entitled to receive) interest based on the recalculation of deprecation using actual income figures. This look-back calculation is required during a "recomputation year." In general, a recomputation year is the third and tenth tax year beginning after the tax year in which the film or other property was placed in service (Code Sec. 167(g)(2)). The look-back rule does not apply to property that had a cost basis of $100,000 or less, or if the actual income from the property for the period before the close of the recomputation year was within 10 percent of the estimated income from the property for that period (Code Sec. 167(g)(3)).

American Jobs Creation Act Impact

Treatment of participations and residuals under income forecast method clarified.—The new law provides that a taxpayer may include participations and residuals in the adjusted basis of a property in the tax year that it is placed in service, but only to the extent that the participations and residuals relate to income estimated to be earned in connection with the property before the close of the tenth tax year after the tax year the property was placed in service (Code Sec. 167(g)(7)(A), as added by the American Jobs Creation Act of 2004).

As an alternative to including such participations and residuals in the adjusted basis of the property and recovering their cost over a 10-year period, a taxpayer may exclude the participations and residuals from the adjusted basis of the property and deduct them in full in the year that they are actually paid (Code Sec. 167(g)(7)(D)(i), as added by the 2004 Jobs Act). The Conference Committee Report (H.R. Conf. Rep. No. 108-755) states that the decision to currently deduct these expenses may be made on a property-by-property basis but must be applied consistently with respect to a given property thereafter.

> **Comment:** This rule allowing a current deduction in the year a participation or residual is actually paid codifies the holding in *Associated Patentees*, 4 TC 979, Dec. 14,440 (1945). The IRS position has been that these amounts must be capitalized into the basis of income forecast property in accordance with Reg. § 1.263A-1(e).

> **Comment:** The new law also includes a separate provision which allows the current deduction of up to $15 million of the costs of a qualifying film which does not cost more than $15 million to produce (Code Sec. 181, as added by the 2004 Jobs Act). See ¶ 365.

Participations and residuals are defined as costs the amount of which by contract varies with the amount of income earned in connection with the property (Code Sec. 167(g)(7)(B), as added by the 2004 Jobs Act).

> **Comment:** Generally, participations are fees paid to producers, directors, actors, and others in the form of a percentage of a film's future net profits or gross receipts. Residuals are fees paid by a producer, usually under a collective bargaining agreement, to the director and writer guilds (which represent writers, directors, actors and others), in the form of a percentage of revenues received from television exhibition.

Income from the property defined. The new law also clarifies that the term "income from the property" for purposes of computing depreciation under the income forecast method is the taxpayer's gross income from the property (Code Sec. 167(g)(5)(E), as added by the 2004 Jobs Act).

¶320

Comment: This definition precludes taxpayers from taking distribution costs into account for purposes of determining current and total forecasted income with respect to a property (Conference Committee Report (H.R. Conf. Rep. No. 108-755)).

Application of look-back rule. As noted in the *Background* section, the look-back rule does not apply in a recomputation year if the actual income from the property for the period before the close of the recomputation year was within 10 percent of the estimated income from the property "for such period" (Code Sec. 167(g)(3)). The new law provides that if the adjusted basis of the property is determined under this provision, the rule is applied by replacing the phase "for such period" with "for each taxable year in such period" (Code Sec. 167(g)(7)(C), as added by the 2004 Jobs Act).

Adjustments to basis. The IRS is required to prescribe appropriate adjustments to the basis of property and to the look-back method to reflect the additional deductions allowed solely by reason of new Code Sec. 167(g)(7) (Code Sec. 167(g)(7)(E), as added by the 2004 Jobs Act).

Coordination with other Code provision. Deductions computed in accordance with this provision are allowable notwithstanding certain other Code provisions that would require capitalization, delay the time of the deduction, or otherwise prevent or limit the deduction. These Code provisions are Code Secs. 263 (capitalization), 263A (uniform capitalization rules), 404 (contributions to employee's trust or annuity plan), 419 (welfare benefit funds), and 461(h) (economic performance rules).

Comment: Although the Conference Committee Report (H.R. Conf. Rep. No. 108-755) provides that no inference is intended to be drawn from the provision with respect to the treatment of property placed in service before the effective date, it encourages the IRS to take the principles of the provision into account in resolving open cases in a "balanced manner." The Committee Report further requests the IRS to expedite the resolution of all open cases.

For further information on this subject, consult any of the following CCH reporter explanations:

- Standard Federal Tax Reporter, 2004FED ¶ 11,037.036
- Federal Tax Service, FTS § G:20.243
- Federal Tax Guide, 2004FTG ¶ 9325

★ *Effective date.* The provision applies to property placed in service after the date of enactment (Act Sec. 242(c) of the American Jobs Creation Act of 2004).

Act Sec. 242(a) of the American Jobs Creation Act of 2004, adding Code Sec. 167(g)(7); Act Sec. 242(b), amending Code Sec. 167(g)(5)(F)–(G) and adding Code Sec. 167(g)(5)(E); Act Sec. 242(c). Law at ¶ 5175. Committee Report at ¶ 10,230.

¶ 325

Bonus Depreciation on Noncommercial Aircraft

Background _____

In general, property may qualify for the Code Sec. 168(k) bonus depreciation allowance only if it is acquired after September 10, 2001, and placed in service before January 1, 2005. However, the placed in service date is extended to January 1, 2006, for certain property that is subject to the uniform capitalization rules of Code Sec. 263A and either has an estimated production period exceeding two years or an estimated production period exceeding one year and a cost exceeding $1 million (Code Sec. 168(k)(2)(B)).

Background

To qualify under this exception the property:

(1) must have a Modified Accelerated Cost Recovery System (MACRS) recovery period of at least 10 years but not greater than 20 years, or

(2) be tangible personal property used in the trade or business of transporting persons or property, such as a commercial airplane.

In addition, to qualify for bonus depreciation and the extended placed-in-service date:

(1) the original use of the property must commence with the taxpayer after September 10, 2001 (i.e., property must be new and not be used); and

(2) either

(a) the property must be acquired after September 10, 2001, and before January 1, 2005, and no written binding contract for the acquisition of the property may be in effect before September 11, 2001, or

(b) the property must be acquired by the taxpayer pursuant to a written binding contract which was entered into after September 10, 2001, and before January 1, 2005 (Code Sec. 168(k)(2)(B)(i)(I)).

If a taxpayer manufactures, constructs, or produces property for use in the taxpayer's own business, requirement (2), above, is considered satisfied if the taxpayer began to manufacture, construct, or produce the property after September 10, 2001, and before January 1, 2005 (Code Sec. 168(k)(2)(D)(i), prior to redesignation as Code Sec. 168(k)(2)(E)(ii) by the American Jobs Creation Act of 2004). Temporary regulations provide that if property to be used in a taxpayer's own business is manufactured, produced, or constructed for the taxpayer by another person under a written binding contract entered into prior to the manufacture, production, or construction of the property, then the taxpayer is considered to have manufactured, constructed, or produced the property (Temporary Reg. § 1.168(k)-1T(b)(4)(iii)(A)). Thus, requirement (2) is satisfied if manufacture, construction, or production of the property on behalf of the taxpayer begins after September 10, 2001, and before January 1, 2005.

Although the placed-in-service date is extended (i.e., the property must be placed in service before January 1, 2006), the basis of property eligible for the bonus depreciation deduction is limited to pre-January 1, 2005 progress expenditures (Code Sec. 168(k)(2)(B)(ii); Temporary Reg. § 1.168(k)-1T(d)(1)(2)).

American Jobs Creation Act Impact

Extended placed-in-service date for bonus depreciation on noncommercial aircraft.—An aircraft that is *not* used in the trade or business of transporting persons or property (other than for agricultural or firefighting purposes) will qualify for bonus deprecation and the extended January 1, 2006, placed-in-service date if the following requirements are met:

(1) the original use of the aircraft commences with the taxpayer after September 10, 2001; and

(2) either;

(a) the aircraft was acquired by the taxpayer after September 10, 2001, and before January 1, 2005 and no written binding contract for the acquisition was in effect before September 11, 2001, or

(b) the aircraft was acquired pursuant to a written binding contract entered into after September 10, 2001, and before January 1, 2005;

(3) the aircraft is purchased and the at the time of the contract for purchase, the purchaser made a nonrefundable deposit at least equal to 10 percent of the cost or $100,000; and

(4) the aircraft has an estimated production period exceeding four months and a cost exceeding $200,000 (Code Sec. 168(k)(2)(A)(iv), as amended by the American Jobs Creation Act of 2004; Code Sec. 168(k)(2)(C), as added by the 2004 Jobs Act).

Comment: The restriction contained in Code Sec. 168(k)(2)(B)(ii) which limits the basis of property eligible for the bonus depreciation deduction to pre-January 1, 2005, progress expenditures does not apply to aircraft described in this new provision (Code Sec. 168(k)(2)(B)(iv), as added by the 2004 Jobs Act).

For purposes of requirement (3), the term "purchase" is intended to have the same meaning as used in Code Sec. 179(d)(2) (H.R. Conf. Rep. No. 108-755). See, also, Reg. § 1.179-4(c).

Example: ABC corporation enters into a binding contract to purchase a corporate jet on June 1, 2004. The purchase price is $2,000,000. A $100,000 nonrefundable deposit is made. Production begins on November 1, 2004. Assuming that the production period for the aircraft exceeds four months, the entire cost should qualify for 50-percent bonus depreciation if the plane is placed in service by ABC by the end of 2005.

Comment: Property described by the provision qualifies for bonus depreciation under present law if placed in service prior to January 1, 2005. Thus, the provision only modifies the treatment of property placed in service during calendar year 2005 (H.R. Conf. Rep. No. 108-755).

For further information on this subject, consult any of the following CCH reporter explanations:

- Standard Federal Tax Reporter, 2004FED ¶ 11,279.058
- Federal Tax Service, FTS § G:16.260
- Federal Tax Guide, 2004FTG ¶ 9131

★ *Effective date.* The provision is effective for property placed in service after September 10, 2001 (Act Sec. 336(c) of the American Jobs Creation Act of 2004 and Act Sec. 101(b) of the Job Creation and Worker Assistance Act of 2002 (P.L. 107-147)).

Act Sec. 336(a) of the American Jobs Creation Act of 2004, amending Code Sec. 168(k)(2)(D)–(G) and adding new subparagraph (C); Act Sec. 336(b), adding Code Sec. 168(k)(2)(B)(iv) and amending Code Sec. 168(k)(4)(A)(ii), Code Sec. 168(k)(4)(B)(iii), Code Sec. 168(k)(4)(C) and Code Sec. 168(k)(4)(D); Act Sec. 336(c). Law at ¶ 5180. Committee Report at ¶ 10,510.

¶ 330

Syndicated Leasing Transactions—Bonus Depreciation

Background _____

The Working Families Tax Relief Act of 2004 (P.L. 108-311) included a technical correction that clarified that investors in syndicated leasing transactions could qualify for the Modified Accelerated Cost Recovery System (MACRS) bonus depreciation allowance (Code Sec. 168(k)) if certain requirements were met.

Background _____

The technical correction provides that if:

(1) a lessor of property originally places the property in service after September 10, 2001 (or is considered to have originally placed it in service after September 10, 2001 by operation of the sale-leaseback rule described in Code Sec. 168(k)(2)(D)(ii));

(2) the property is sold by the lessor (or any subsequent purchaser) within three months after the lessor places the property in service; and

(3) the user of the property after the last sale during the three-month period remains the same as when the property was originally placed in service,

then the property is treated as originally placed in service not earlier than the date of the last sale within the three-month period (Code Sec. 168(k)(2)(D)(iii), as added by P.L. 108-311).

Comment: In order to claim bonus depreciation, the original use of the bonus depreciation property must commence with the taxpayer after September 10, 2001 (Code Sec. 168(k)(2)(A)(ii)). Without this provision, in the case of a syndicated leasing transaction, the original use of the property could be considered to have started with the syndicator who initially purchases and leases the property.

Example: SYN Inc. purchases and leases a new cargo container to ABC Corp. on March 1, 2004. If SYN resells the container to an investor within three months after March 1, 2004, and ABC continues to use the container, the investor is considered to have originally placed the container in service on the date of purchase from SYN and may be able to claim the bonus depreciation deduction.

Comment: This technical correction simply confirms rules previously provided in Temporary Regulations adopted by the IRS in T.D. 9091, filed with the Federal Register on September 5, 2003 (see Temporary Reg. § 1.168(k)-1T(b)(3)(iii)(B) and Temporary Reg. § 1.168(k)-1T(b)(5)(ii)(B)).

American Jobs Creation Act Impact

Treatment of multiple unit syndicated leasing transactions clarified.—The new law modifies the syndication rule enacted by the Working Families Tax Relief Act of 2004 (P.L. 108-311) to clarify that, in the case of multiple units subject to the same lease, property will qualify as originally placed in service on the date of sale if it is sold within three months after the final unit is placed in service, so long as the period between the time the first and last units are placed in service does not exceed 12 months (Code Sec. 168(k)(2)(E)(iii), as amended by the American Jobs Creation Act of 2004).

Caution Note: Prior to the 2004 Jobs Act, the special rule dealing with syndication had been in Code Sec. 168(k)(2)(D). This provision was redesignated as Code Sec. 168(k)(2)(E) by another provision in the 2004 Jobs Act (Act Sec. 336(a)(1) of the 2004 Jobs Act).

Comment: The IRS's Temporary Regulations dealing with syndicated leasing transactions do not address the treatment of multiple units subject to the same lease.

Code Sec. 168(k)(2)(E)(iii), as redesignated and amended by the 2004 Jobs Act, provides that if:

¶330

(1) a lessor of property originally places the property in service after September 10, 2001, (or is considered to have originally placed it in service after September 10, 2001 by operation of the sale-leaseback rule described in Code Sec. 168(k)(2)(E)(ii));

(2) the property is sold by the lessor (or any subsequent purchaser) within three months after the lessor places the property in service (*or, in the case of multiple units of property subject to the same lease, within three months after the date the final unit is placed in service, so long as the period between the time the first unit is placed in service and the time the last unit is placed in service does not exceed 12 months*); and

(3) the user of the property after the last sale during the three-month period remains the same as when the property was originally placed in service,

then the property is treated as originally placed in service not earlier than the date of the last sale within the three-month period (Code Sec. 168(k)(2)(E)(iii), as amended the 2004 Jobs Act).

Example: SYN Inc. is the syndicator of a leasing transaction involving 100 cargo containers which are to be leased to ABC. The first container is purchased by SYN and leased to ABC on November 1, 2003. The last container is purchased within the required one-year period and leased to ABC on June 10, 2004. A person who purchases interests in the containers from SYN (or a subsequent purchaser from SYN) within 3 months after June 10, 2004, is treated as having originally placed the containers in service on the date of purchase and may be able to claim the bonus depreciation deduction.

Comment: The provision only applies to property sold after June 4, 2004. Accordingly, interests in property purchased from a lessor on or before June 4, 2004, do not qualify for bonus depreciation under this provision.

For further information on this subject, consult any of the following CCH reporter explanations:

- Standard Federal Tax Reporter, 2004FED ¶ 11,279.058
- Federal Tax Service, FTS § G:16.261
- Federal Tax Guide, 2004FTG ¶ 9131

★ *Effective date.* The provision applies to property sold after June 4, 2004 (Act Sec. 337(b) of the American Jobs Creation Act of 2004).

Act Sec. 337(a) of the American Jobs Creation Act of 2004, amending Code Sec. 168(k)(2)(E)(iii), as redesignated by Act Sec. 336(a)(1); Act Sec. 337(b). Law at ¶ 5180. Committee Report at ¶ 10,520.

¶ 335

Clearing Costs for Gas and Electric Utility Property

Background

When determining the depreciable life of property under the modified accelerated cost recovery system (MACRS), in most situations, Code Sec. 168 provides the necessary information. However, for some types of property, the depreciable period is determined by reference to the property's class life as set forth in Rev. Proc. 87-56, 1987-2 CB 674, as clarified and modified by Rev. Proc. 88-22, 1988-1 CB 785.

Electric utility property. With regard to property that is used in the transmission and distribution of electricity that is for sale, the MACRS recovery period is 20 years (Rev. Proc. 88-22, Asset Class 49.14). However, under Rev. Proc. 88-22, the cost of the

Background

initial clearing and grading of the land that is related to the construction of electric transmission lines and/or electric distribution lines is specifically excluded from the 20-year period. These initial clearing and grading land improvements are described in Rev. Rul. 72-403, 1972-2 CB 102. Because these land improvement costs do not have a class life, the costs are depreciated over a seven-year period under MACRS.

Comment: *Electric transmission lines* can be generally described as the largest and most visible type of electric lines. Their function is to transmit electric power from the power plant to a substation or step-down transformer.

Electric distribution lines can be generally defined as those lines that carry electricity from substations or step-down transformers to the customer.

Gas utility property. The tax treatment of the costs of the initial clearing of land for gas utility property face the same situation as those costs incurred in the clearing of land for electric lines. Although Rev. Proc. 87-56, Asset Class 49.24, provides a 15-year MACRS recovery period for gas utility trunk lines and related storage facilities, initial land clearing costs are specifically excluded from this 15-year period. Rev. Proc. 87-56 cites to Rev. Rul. 72-403 for a description of these initial land improvement costs. Because the land improvement costs are not provided with a class life, they have a seven-year life under the MACRS system.

American Jobs Creation Act Impact

Longer recovery period for land clearing costs.—Under the new legislation, the recovery period for the initial land clearing costs for electric utilities and gas utilities has been more than doubled (Code Sec. 168(e)(3), as amended by the American Jobs Creation Act of 2004).

Electric utility property. The recovery period for the cost of the initial clearing and grading land improvements pertaining to any electric utility and distribution plant has been changed from seven years to *20 years* (Code Sec. 168(e)(3)(F), as added by the 2004 Jobs Act).

Gas utility property. The recovery period for the cost of the initial clearing and grading land improvements pertaining to any gas utility property changed from seven years to *15 years* (Code Sec. 168(e)(3)(E)(vi), as added by the 2004 Jobs Act).

Comment: This lengthening in the recovery period for land clearing costs brings their recovery periods into conformity with the recovery period for the electric utility and gas utility property to which the land clearing expenses relate (i.e., 20 years for electric utility property and 15 years for gas utility property).

For further information on this subject, consult any of the following CCH reporter explanations:

- Standard Federal Tax Reporter, 2004FED ¶11,279.01, ¶11,279.023 and ¶11,279.0518

- Federal Tax Service, FTS §G:16.83[5] and §G:16.83[6]

- Federal Tax Guide, 2004FTG ¶9140

★ *Effective date.* The changes in the respective recovery periods for electric utility property and gas utility property are effective for property placed in service after the date of enactment of the American Jobs Creation Act of 2004.

Act Sec. 901(a) of the American Jobs Creation Act of 2004, adding Code Sec. 168(e)(3)(E)(vi); Act Sec. 901(b), adding Code Sec. 168(e)(3)(F); Act Sec. 901(c),

amending Code Sec. 168(g)(3)(B); Act Sec. 901(d). Law at ¶ 5180. Committee Report at ¶ 11,730.

¶ 340

Depreciation Period for Motorsports Facilities Clarified

Background

Under the modified accelerated cost recovery system (MACRS), most types of property associated with theme parks and/or amusement parks are depreciated over a seven-year period (Code Sec. 168(e)(1)). This period of depreciation stems from the fact that under Rev. Proc. 87-56, 1987-2 CB 674, as clarified and modified by Rev. Proc. 88-22, 1988-1 CB 785, theme parks and amusement parks, as Asset Class 80.0, have a class life of 12.5 years.

> **Comment:** According to Senator Rick Santorum (R-PA), in an August 1, 2003, press release, auto race tracks (a.k.a, "motorsports facilities") were treated by the IRS the same as theme or amusement parks and were thus depreciated over a seven-year period. However, according to Senator Santorum, the IRS has recently started to challenge the seven-year period and begun to assign a depreciation period of 15 years or more.

> There does not appear to be any reported IRS ruling dealing with the question of the proper depreciation period for auto race tracks. Nor does there appear to be any reported court decision dealing with this issue. Therefore, it appears likely that Senator Santorum was notified of this change in the IRS position by interested constituents. As the Senator commented in his press release, "Pennsylvania is home to numerous motorsport facilities" and that "the long-standing treatment of motorsports facilities for depreciation purposes" should be codified as seven years.

American Jobs Creation Act Impact

Seven-year depreciation period for motorsports entertainment complex.—The new law has established a seven-year depreciation period for a motorsports entertainment complex and related ancillary and support facilities (Code Sec. 168(e)(3)(C)(ii), as added by the American Jobs Creation Act of 2004).

Motorsports entertainment complex. The term "motorsports entertainment complex" refers to a racing track facility that (Code Sec. 168(i)(15)(A), as added by the 2004 Jobs Act):

(1) is permanently situated on land,

(2) during the 36-month period following the first day of the month in which the facility is placed in service, hosts *at least one* racing event for cars of any type, trucks, or motorcycles, and

(3) is open to the public for an admission charge.

Example 1: On January 2, 2005, a motorsports entertainment complex is placed in service. During the next 36 months, it hosts one public event for which an admission is charged. The event was the "World-Wide Bicycle Racing Challenge Cup." The entertainment complex would not be eligible for the seven-year depreciation period as a motorsports entertainment complex because the one event it hosted did not involve cars, trucks, or motorcycles.

Example 2: Assume the same facts as Example 1, except that the complex also scheduled a public event for which an admission charge applied. This event was the "Intra-State Challenge for Pick-Up Truck Racing." Under these facts, the facility would be classified as a motorsports entertainment complex and the seven-year depreciation period would apply.

Ancillary and support facilities. Ancillary and support facilities, as well as certain appurtenances that are owned by the taxpayer who owns the motorsports entertainment complex, are generally covered by the same seven-year depreciation period (Code Sec. 168(i)(15)(B), as added by the 2004 Jobs Act). The ancillary and support facilities must be provided for the benefit of the customers of the complex. These facilities are as follows:

(1) *Ancillary facilities* include land improvements in support of the complex's activities (e.g., parking lots, sidewalks, waterways, bridges, fences and landscaping (Code Sec. 168(i)(15)(B)(i), as added by the 2004 Jobs Act).

(2) *Support facilities* include food and beverage retailing, souvenir vending and other nonlodging accommodations (Code Sec. 168(i)(15)(B)(ii), as added by the 2004 Jobs Act).

(3) *Appurtenances* that are associated with the facilities and related attractions and amusements (Code Sec. 168(i)(15)(B)(iii), as added by the 2004 Jobs Act) include such items as ticket booths, race track surfaces, suites and hospitality facilities, grandstands, walls, special purpose structures, and buildings.

Excluded property. The term "motorsports entertainment complex" does *not* include such items as transportation equipment, administrative services assets, warehouses, administrative buildings, hotels, or motels (Code Sec. 168(i)(15)(C), as added by the 2004 Jobs Act).

Comment: The Conference Committee Report (H.R. Conf. Rep. No. 108-755) notes that while these provisions do not affect property placed in service on or before the date of enactment of the 2004 Jobs Act, the conferees strongly urge the IRS to reach an expeditious resolution concerning any disputes with taxpayers as to whether Asset Class 80.0 of Rev. Proc. 87-56 applies to such facilities.

For further information on this subject, consult any of the following CCH reporter explanations:

- Standard Federal Tax Reporter, 2004FED ¶11,279.01 and ¶11,279.023
- Federal Tax Service, FTS § G:16.83[3]
- Federal Tax Guide, 2004FTG ¶9015

★ *Effective date.* The new law applies to property placed in service after the date of enactment of the American Jobs Creation Act of 2004 (Act Sec. 704(c)(1) of the 2004 Jobs Act). However, these changes will not apply to any property placed in service after December 31, 2007 (Code Sec. 168(i)(15)(D), as added by the 2004 Jobs Act). In addition, motorsports facilities placed in service after the date of enactment of the 2004 Jobs Act will *not* be classified as theme and amusement facilities that are classified as Asset Class 80.0 in Rev. Proc. 87-56 (Act Sec. 704(c)(2) of the 2004 Jobs Act). Nothing in these amendments is to be construed to affect the treatment of property placed in service on or before the date of enactment of the 2004 Jobs Act.

Act Sec. 704(a) of the American Jobs Creation Act of 2004, adding Code Sec. 168(e)(3)(C)(ii); Act Sec. 704(b), adding Code Sec. 168(i)(15); Act Sec. 704(c). Law at ¶5180. Committee Report at ¶10,860.

¶ 345

Alaska Natural Gas Pipeline Depreciation

Background _____

Assets used in the private, commercial, and contract carrying of petroleum, gas, and other products by means of pipes and conveyors are assigned a Modified Accelerated Cost Recovery System (MACRS) recovery period of 15 years and a MACRS alternative depreciation system (ADS) recovery period of 22 years (Asset Class 46.0 of Rev. Proc. 87-56, 1987-2 CB 674). MACRS 15-year property is depreciated using the 150-percent declining balance method unless a straight-line MACRS general depreciation system (GDS) or straight-line ADS election is made.

American Jobs Creation Act Impact

Certain Alaska natural gas pipeline qualifies as 7-year MACRS property.—The new law includes a provision that treats "Alaska natural gas pipeline" as 7-year MACRS property (Code Sec. 168(e)(3)(C)(iii), as added by the American Jobs Creation Act of 2004).

Comment: MACRS 7-year property is depreciated using the 200-percent declining balance method unless a straight-line GDS or ADS election is made.

Alaska natural gas pipeline is defined as a natural gas pipeline system located in the state of Alaska which:

(1) has a capacity of more than 500 billion Btu of natural gas per day; and

(2) is placed in service after December 31, 2013, or is treated as placed in service on January 1, 2014, if a taxpayer who places the system in service before January 1, 2014, elects this treatment (Code Sec. 168(i)(16), as added by the 2004 Jobs Act).

The term "Alaska natural gas pipeline" includes the pipe, trunk lines, related equipment, and appurtenances used to carry natural gas, but does not include any gas processing plant (Code Sec. 168(i)(16)(B), as added by the 2004 Jobs Act).

The alternative depreciation system (ADS) period for Alaska natural gas pipeline property is 22 years (Code Sec. 168(g)(3)(B), as amended by the 2004 Jobs Act). This is the same ADS period that currently applies to such property under Asset Class 46.0 of Rev. Proc. 87-56, 1987-2 CB 674.

For further information on this subject, consult any of the following CCH reporter explanations:

- Standard Federal Tax Reporter, 2004FED ¶ 11,279.01 and ¶ 11,279.023
- Federal Tax Service, FTS § G:16.83[3]
- Federal Tax Guide, 2004FTG ¶ 9110

★ *Effective date.* The provision applies to property placed in service after December 31, 2004 (Act Sec. 706(d) of the American Jobs Creation Act of 2004).

Act Sec. 706(a) of the American Jobs Creation Act of 2004, redesignating Code Sec. 168(e)(3)(C)(iii) as Code Sec. 168(e)(3)(C)(iv) and adding Code Sec. 168(e)(3)(C)(iii); Act Sec. 706(b) adding Code Sec. 168(i)(16); Act Sec. 706(c), amending Code Sec. 168(g)(3)(B); Act Sec. 706(d). Law at ¶ 5180. Committee Report at ¶ 10,880.

¶ 350

Deduction and Amortization of Start-Up and Organizational Expenditures

Background

Start-up and organizational expenditures incurred by taxpayers who subsequently engage in a trade or business may be amortized (Code Secs. 195, 248, and 708, prior to amendment by the American Jobs Creation Act of 2004). Taxpayers may elect to amortize these expenditures over a period of not less than 60 months, beginning with the month in which the trade or business began. Start-up expenditures are amounts that would have been deductible as trade or business expenses, had they not been paid or incurred before the business began. Organizational expenditures are those that are incident to the creation of a corporation (Code Sec. 248) or the organization of a partnership (Code Sec. 709), are chargeable to capital, and that would be eligible for amortization had they been paid or incurred in connection with the organization of a corporation or partnership with a limited or ascertainable life.

Reg. § 1.195-1 provides that a taxpayer must file an election to amortize start-up expenditures no later than the due date for the tax year in which the trade or business begins. The election must describe the trade or business, indicate the period of amortization (not less than 60 months), describe each start-up expenditure incurred, and indicate the month in which the trade or business began. Similar requirements apply to the election to amortize organizational expenditures. A revised statement may be filed to include start-up and organizational expenditures that were not included on the original statement, but a taxpayer may not include as a start-up expenditure any amount that was previously claimed as a deduction.

Most acquired intangible assets, such as goodwill, trademarks, franchises and patents, that are held in connection with the conduct of a trade or business or an activity for the production of income are to be amortized over 15 years beginning with the month in which the intangible was acquired (Code Sec. 197).

American Jobs Creation Act Impact

Deduction for $5,000 of start-up and organizational expenditures and 15-year amortization for excess.—Effective for amounts paid or incurred after the date of enactment, the new law allows taxpayers to elect to deduct up to $5,000 of start-up expenditures in the tax year in which their trade or business begins (Code Sec. 195(b), as amended by the American Jobs Creation Act of 2004). The $5,000 amount must be reduced (but not below zero) by the amount by which the start-up expenditures exceed $50,000. The remainder of any start-up expenditures, those that are not deductible in the year in which the trade or business begins, must be ratably amortized over the 180-month period (15 years) beginning with the month in which the active trade or business begins. Similarly, corporations may elect to deduct up to $5,000 (but not below zero) of organizational expenditures for the tax year in which the corporation begins business (Code Sec. 248(a), as amended by the 2004 Jobs Act). The $5,000 amount must also be reduced by the amount by which the organizational expenditures exceed $50,000. The corporation may deduct any remainder of organizational expenditures ratably over the 180-month period beginning with the month in which the corporation begins business.

Comment: The 15-year amortization period for the start-up expenditures and organizational expenditures that are not deductible in the year in which the trade or business begins is consistent with the amortization period for section 197 intangibles.

Partnerships may also elect to deduct up to $5,000 of their organizational expenditures, reduced by the amount by which such expenditures exceed $50,000, for the tax year in which the partnership begins business (Code Sec. 709(b), as amended by the 2004 Jobs Act). The remainder of any organizational expenses can be deducted ratably over the 180-month period beginning with the month in which the partnership begins business. If a partnership liquidates before the end of the 180-month period, any deferred expenses attributable to the partnership which were not allowed as a deduction may be deducted as a loss under Code Sec. 165.

Comment: The Conference Committee Report (H.R. Conf. Rep. No. 108-755) states that all start-up and organizational expenditures related to a particular trade or business, whether incurred before or after the date of enactment, are taken into account in determining whether the cumulative cost of start-up or organizational expenditures exceeds $50,000. The amended Code text does not address this issue.

Comment: The provision will benefit smaller businesses that have around $5,000 of start-up or organizational expenditures. Larger start-ups, however, will now be required to amortize most or all of these expenses over 15 years rather than the five-year period currently provided. The Joint Committee on Taxation (JCX-69-04) estimates that the provision will cost $3 billion in tax revenue through 2014.

For further information on this subject, consult any of the following CCH reporter explanations:

- Standard Federal Tax Reporter, 2004FED ¶12,371.01, ¶12,371.03, ¶13,352.01 and ¶25,223.01

- Federal Tax Service, FTS §G:22.160 and §G:22.180

- Federal Tax Guide, 2004FTG ¶9520 and ¶9905

★ *Effective date.* The provision applies to amounts paid or incurred after the date of enactment (Act Sec. 902(d) of the American Jobs Creation Act of 2004).

Act Sec. 902(a)(1) of the American Jobs Creation Act of 2004, amending Code Sec. 195(b)(1); Act Sec. 902(b), amending Code Sec. 248(a); Act Sec. 902(c)(1), amending Code Sec. 709(b)(1)–(3); Act Sec. 902(c)(2), amending Code Sec. 709(b); Act Sec. 902(d). Law at ¶5215, ¶5260 and ¶5510. Committee Report at ¶11,740.

¶355

Sports Franchises and Player Contracts

Background _____

Historically, there have been a number of Internal Revenue Code provisions that only apply to professional sports franchises and player contracts. These provisions are summarized in the following explanations.

Sports franchises excluded from amortization rules. As a general rule, the cost of certain types of intangibles that have been acquired in connection with a business, or an activity for the production of income, may be amortized over a 15-year period (Code Sec. 197(a)). Intangibles that are covered by this amortization provision include goodwill, licenses, and franchises (Code Sec. 197(d)). However, sports franchises have been specially excluded from these amortization rules (Code Sec. 197(e)(6)). The term "sports franchise" includes a franchise to engage in any professional sport (e.g., baseball, basketball, and football), as well as any item acquired in connection with the franchise.

Background

Basis in player contracts. When a sports franchise is sold or exchanged, and as part of the transaction, there is a transfer of a player's contract, a special rule applies in order to determine the buyer's basis in the contract (Code Sec. 1056(a)). Under the general rule, the buyer's basis cannot exceed the total of (1) the adjusted basis of the contract in the hands of the seller at the time of the sale, plus (2) the gain, if any, recognized by the seller on the transfer of the player's contract. This general rule is subject to the stipulation that in the case of any sale of any sports franchise, no more than 50 percent of the total consideration paid can be allocated to player contracts. However, this rule can be waived if the IRS is satisfied that the player contracts do account for more than 50 percent of the total consideration paid (Code Sec. 1056(d)).

Gain from sale of player contracts. When a sports franchise is sold or exchanged, and player contracts are part of the transaction, the seller must use special computations in order to determine his basis in the contracts for purposes of computing depreciation recapture (Code Sec. 1245(a)(4)). Under these computations, the seller's basis in a contract is his adjusted basis, increased by the *greater* of: (1) the previously unrecaptured depreciation with respect to player contracts acquired by the seller at the time he acquired the franchise (i.e., initial contracts), or (2) the previously unrecaptured depreciation with respect to the contracts involved in the sale (i.e., contracts transferred) (Code Sec. 1245(a)(4)(A)). The definitions concerning unrecaptured depreciation pertaining to initial contracts, and contracts transferred, are set forth in the Internal Revenue Code (Code Sec. 1245(a)(4)(B) and (C)).

Sale or exchange of sports franchises. As a general rule, the sale or exchange of a franchise is *not* treated as the sale or exchange of a capital asset, when the seller retains any significant power, right or continuing interest in the subject matter of the franchise (Code Sec. 1253(a)). However, professional sports franchises are not covered by this rule (Code Sec. 1253(e)). In other words, the transfer of a professional sports franchise is considered to be a sale or exchange of a capital asset.

American Jobs Creation Act Impact

Changes in amortization and sale rules.—The new law has made changes in the rules pertaining to the amortization of sports franchises, the sale of sports franchises and other related rules.

15-year amortization of sports franchise. The new law makes a professional sports franchise, and items acquired in connection with the franchise, subject to the 15-year amortization period provided for in Code Sec. 197(a) (Code Sec. 197(e)(6), before being stricken by the American Jobs Creation Act of 2004).

> **Comment:** The House Committee Report (H.R. Rep. No. 108-548) states that one of the reasons that it brought sports franchises under the rules governing the 15-year amortization period is that it believes that the amortization provisions should apply to all types of businesses regardless of the nature of their assets. As a result of this change, the same rules that cover the amortization of intangibles now apply to sports franchises.

Basis in player contracts. The new law repeals the Internal Revenue Code section that required that a buyer's basis in player contracts acquired as part of sports franchise be determined under special rules (Code Sec. 1056, before repeal by the 2004 Jobs Act).

> **Comment:** The Conference Committee Report (H.R. Conf. Rep. No. 108-755) is silent as to why the special rules were repealed. However, it seems safe to assume that Congress believed that the repeal was required because of the application of the 15-year amortization rules to sports franchises and related items. In short, the special basis rules had been rendered moot.

¶355

Gain from sale of player contracts. Under the new law, it is no longer necessary to use special rules to determine the seller's basis in player contracts when a sports franchise is sold or exchanged (Code Sec. 1245(a)(4), before being stricken by the 2004 Jobs Act).

> **Comment:** Again, the Conference Committee Report (H.R. Conf. Rep. No. 108-755) is silent as to why the special rules were repealed. However, as with the repeal of the basis rules mentioned above, it is likely that Congress considered them moot because of the inclusion of sports franchises into the 15-year amortization provisions.

Sale or exchange of sports franchises. Generally, the new law provides that the sale or exchange of a professional sports franchise will *not* be treated as the sale or exchange of a capital asset (Code Sec. 1253(e), before being stricken by the 2004 Jobs Act). However, as with other types of franchises, the sports franchise will not be treated as a capital asset, only if the seller retains any significant power, right, or continuing interest with respect to the franchise (Code Sec. 1253(a)).

> **Planning Note:** The Code provides a nonexclusive list of six specific powers, rights, or continuing interests that are considered to be "significant" (Code Sec. 1253(b)(2)). The list includes such items as the right to disapprove any assignment of the interest, and the right to terminate at will. Considering the favorable tax consequences (i.e., capital gain) that will result when a taxpayer can show that a sports franchise was sold without any significant power, rights or interests being retained, one can expect this to be a very active area of tax planning over the coming years.

For further information on this subject, consult any of the following CCH reporter explanations:

- Standard Federal Tax Reporter, 2004FED ¶12,455.01, ¶12,455.034, ¶29,961.01, ¶30,909.01, ¶30,909.026 and ¶31,044.01
- Federal Tax Service, FTS §G:22.42[7], §G:20.86[16] and §G:21.101[3]
- Federal Tax Guide, 2004FTG ¶5544, ¶5798 and ¶5846

★ *Effective date.* Generally, the new law is effective for property acquired after the date of enactment of the American Jobs Creation Act of 2004 (Act Sec. 886(c)(1)). However, the amendments pertaining to player contracts apply to franchises acquired after the date of enactment of the 2004 Jobs Act (Act Sec. 886(c)(2) of the 2004 Jobs Act).

Act Sec. 886(a) of the American Jobs Creation Act of 2004, amending Code Sec. 197(e)(6)–(8); Act Sec. 886(b)(1)(A), repealing Code Sec. 1056; Act Sec. 886(b)(2), striking Code Sec. 1245(a)(4); Act Sec. 886(b)(3), striking Code Sec. 1253(e); Act Sec. 886(c). Law at ¶5225, ¶5770, ¶5795 and ¶5815. Committee Report at ¶11,580.

ENTERTAINMENT AND FILM EXPENSES

¶ 360

Employer Deduction for Certain Entertainment Expenses Limited

Background _____

Business expense deductions are not allowed with respect to an activity generally considered to be entertainment, amusement or recreation, unless (1) the taxpayer establishes that the item was directly related (or in certain cases, associated with) the active conduct of the taxpayer's trade or business, or (2) the facility (e.g., an airplane) for which the deduction is claimed is used in connection with such activity (Code Sec.

Background

274(a)). An expenditure for entertainment for an employee does not have to meet the directly related or associated-with tests if the expenses are reported by the taxpayer as compensation and wages to the employee (Code Sec. 274(e)(2)). Likewise, the deduction disallowance rule does not apply to expenses paid or incurred by a taxpayer for goods, services or facilities to the extent that the expenses are includible in the gross income of a recipient who is not an employee (e.g., nonemployee director) as compensation for services rendered or as a prize or award (Code Sec. 274(e)(9)).

The employer's deduction generally is the cost of the benefit provided, and the amount reported as compensation to the employee generally is the value of the benefit received. However, the employer's deduction is not limited to the amount included in the employee's income as compensation. In the context of an employer providing an aircraft to employees for nonbusiness (vacation) flights, the exception for expenses treated as compensation has been interpreted as not limiting the company's deduction for operation of the aircraft to the amount of compensation reported to its employees. The taxpayer in the *Sutherland* case (*Sutherland Lumber Southwest, Inc.*, CA-8, 2001-2 USTC ¶ 50,503, 225 F3d 495) was entitled to deduct all of the expenses it incurred in providing personal flights on its planes.

> **Comment:** As noted in the Conference Committee Report (H.R. Conf. Rep. No. 108-755), the fact that the employer's deduction is not limited to the amount included in the employee's income can result in a deduction many times larger than the amount required to be included in income.

American Jobs Creation Act Impact

Deduction limited for certain entertainment expenses.—In the case of specified individuals, entertainment expenses for goods, services or facilities are deductible only to the extent that the expenses do not exceed the amount of the expenses which are treated by the taxpayer, with respect to the recipient, as compensation paid to an employee and as wages subject to withholding (Code Sec. 274(e)(2)(A), as amended by the American Jobs Creation Act of 2004). A deduction is also allowed for entertainment expenses paid or incurred by a taxpayer for an individual who is not an employee only to the extent the expenses do not exceed the amount includible in the gross income of the recipient of the entertainment, amusement or recreation as compensation for services rendered or as a prize or award under Code Sec. 274 (Code Sec. 274(e)(9), as amended by the 2004 Jobs Act).

Specified individuals A specified individual is one who is subject to the requirements of section 16(a) of the Securities Exchange Act of 1934 with respect to the taxpayer or would be subject to such requirements if the taxpayer were an issuer of equity securities (Code Sec. 274(e)(2)(B), as amended by the 2004 Jobs Act).

> **Comment:** According to the Conference Committee Report (H. R. Conf. Rep. No. 108-755), specified individuals generally include officers, directors and 10-percent-or-greater owners of private and publicly held companies. An officer is defined as the president, principal financial officer, principal accounting officer, any vice-president in charge of a principal business unit, division or function, any other officer who performs a policy-making function or any other person who performs similar policy-making functions. It can be said that the new law overturns the *Sutherland* case "for specified individuals" and closes a loophole in the use of company aircraft by executives.

¶360

PRACTICAL ANALYSIS. Michael Schlesinger of Schlesinger & Sussman of New York, New York, observes that as of the date of enactment, Congress has closed a major loophole for S corporations created by *Sutherland Lumber-Southwest, Inc.*, 114 TC 197, Dec. 53,817(2000), *aff'd,* CA-8, 2001-2 USTC ¶ 50,503, 255 F3d 495, *acq.,* I.R.B. 2002-6. CCA 200344008 applied the *Sutherland* case to S corporations. For the vigilant, who picked up *Sutherland Lumber-Southwest* when it was first decided, they had a good couple of years of write-offs, and if these taxpayers had write-offs like what occurred in *Sutherland,* they profited handsomely by their scrupulous reading of tax case law.

For further information on this subject, consult any of the following CCH reporter explanations:

- Standard Federal Tax Reporter, 2004FED ¶ 14,408A.01
- Federal Tax Service, FTS § G:8.246[2]
- Federal Tax Guide, 2004FTG ¶ 8170 and ¶ 8250

★ *Effective date.* The provision applies to expenses incurred after the date of enactment (Act Sec. 907(b) of the American Jobs Creation Act of 2004).

Act Sec. 907(a) of the American Jobs Creation Act of 2004, amending Code Sec. 274(e)(2); Act Sec. 907(b). Law at ¶ 5280. Committee Report at ¶ 11,790.

¶ 365
Special Rules for Certain Film and Television Productions

Background

The television and film industry faces special problems with respect to depreciation of production costs. The revenue stream of a film or television show exponentially decreases as viewer interest wanes after the production's first showing. Additional showings are worth even less. Furthermore, Code Sec. 168(f)(3) specifically excludes motion picture films and videotapes from Accelerated Cost Recovery System (ACRS), so it cannot be used to smooth out the income distortion present in the television and film industry.

In response, the Taxpayer Relief Act of 1997 (P.L. 105-34) made film and videotape property eligible for the income forecast method (straight-line depreciation), effective for property placed into service after August 5, 1997. Under the income forecast method, the cost of an asset (less any salvage value), is multiplied by a fraction, the numerator of which is the net income from the asset for the tax year, and the denominator of which is the forecasted total net income to be derived from the asset before the close of the 10th tax year after the year in which the property is placed in service (Code Sec. 167(g)(1)). The unrecovered adjusted basis of the property as of the beginning of the 10th tax year is claimed as a depreciation deduction in the 10th tax year after the year in which the property is placed in service.

The American Jobs Creation Act of 2004 addresses the issue for certain smaller productions by allowing the cost of any qualified film or television production to be taken as an immediate expense.

American Jobs Creation Act Impact

Allowance to immediately expense costs.—Under the new legislation, a taxpayer may elect to treat the cost of any "qualified" film or television production as a currently deductible expense which is not chargeable to a capital account (Code Sec. 181(a)(1), as added by the American Jobs Creation Act of 2004). If the taxpayer elects, it may not depreciate or amortize any assets which are expensed. For computation purposes, amortization rules similar to the control group rules (Code Sec. 194(b)(2)) and basis allocation rules (Code Sec. 194(c)(4)) apply.

Election: The election must be made by the due date (including extensions) for filing the taxpayer's tax return for the tax year in which costs of the production are first incurred. Once the election is made, the election may not be revoked without the IRS consent (Code Sec. 181(c), as added by the 2004 Jobs Act).

A production is a "qualified production" if 75 percent of the total compensation is qualified compensation and the production is property described in Code Sec. 168(f)(3) (prohibiting motion picture films and videotapes from ACRS). With respect to television series, only the first 44 episodes of such series may be taken into account (Code Sec. 181(d), as added by the 2004 Jobs Act).

Caution Note: A production is not qualified if records on any performer in the production are required to be maintained pursuant to 18 U.S.C. § 2257 (dealing with depictions of sexually explicit conduct) (Code Sec. 181(d)(2)(B), as added by the 2004 Jobs Act).

Qualified compensation expenses are restricted to compensation paid for services performed in the United States by actors, directors, producers, and other relevant production personnel.

Caution Note: Compensation does not include participations and residuals (Code Sec. 167(g)(7)(B)).

Dollar limitation. The election to expense costs applies only to small film productions with an aggregate cost that does not exceed $15,000,000 (Code Sec. 181(a)(2), as added by the 2004 Jobs Act). The dollar limitation increases to $20,000,000 if the production costs are significantly incurred in an area eligible for designation as a low-income community under Code Sec. 45D or a distressed county or isolated area of distress by the Delta Regional Authority established under 7 U.S.C. § 2009aa-1.

Example (1): Heidi Hamm is a recent graduate of the UCLA film school. While a student, Heidi developed the concept for a reality television show that depicts the antics of two young heiresses who move in with a family living in a rural community that qualifies as a distressed area by the Delta Regional Authority. Now out of school, she begins production and the aggregate costs amount to $16,500,000. Because the production is located in a qualified low-income community and the costs are less than $20,000,000, Heidi may expense the entire cost of the production in the first tax year.

Example (2): Steven Silverman is a member of Heidi's graduating class. During school, Steven also developed a concept for a reality television show. This particular show depicts various young professionals trying to win an apprenticeship with a prominent Hollywood movie studio. Production for the show took place in Los Angeles. Like Heidi's show, the aggregate costs of Steven's production amounted to $16,500,000. Because Los Angeles does not qualify as a low-income community, Steven may not expense any of the production's costs since they exceed the $15,000,000 limitation. However, Steven may depreciate the expenses using the income forecast method (i.e., straight-line depreciation).

Comment: The higher dollar limitation is targeted to low-income and distressed communities to attract film and television productions to these communities in an effort to boost the local economy. Other tax incentives for businesses doing business in low-income communities include: the new markets

¶365

tax credit enacted in the Community Renewal Tax Relief Act of 2000 (P.L. 106-554); tax-exempt financing for low-income communities enacted in the Omnibus Budget Reconciliation Act of 1993 (P.L. 103-66); and credits for construction of residential rental projects providing low-income housing enacted in the Tax Reform Act of 1986 (P.L. 99-514) and the Omnibus Budget Reconciliation Act of 1989 (P.L. 101-239).

Planning Note: This election will not be available for qualified film and television productions beginning after December 31, 2008 (Code Sec. 181(f), as added by the 2004 Jobs Act).

For further information on this subject, consult any of the following CCH reporter explanations:

- Standard Federal Tax Reporter, 2004FED ¶ 11,037.036
- Federal Tax Service, FTS § G:19.20
- Federal Tax Guide, 2004FTG ¶ 9325

★ *Effective date.* The provisions apply to qualified film and television productions, as defined by Code Sec. 181(d)(1), commencing after the date of the enactment of the 2004 Jobs Act (Act Sec. 244(c) of the American Jobs Creation Act of 2004).

Act Sec. 244(a) of the American Jobs Creation Act of 2004, adding Code Sec. 181; Act Sec. 244(b); Act Sec. 244(c). Law at ¶ 5205. Committee Report at ¶ 10,250.

CREDITS

¶ 370

Business Related Energy Credits Allowed Against Regular and Minimum Tax

Background _____

The alternative minimum tax (AMT) is imposed on individuals and corporations to insure that all taxpayers pay some tax. The AMT is an amount equal to the excess of the tentative minimum tax over the taxpayer's regular tax and is payable in addition to the regular tax. The tentative minimum tax is an amount equal to specified rates of tax imposed on the excess of the alternative minimum taxable income over an exemption amount (Code Sec. 55).

Generally, the only tax credit that may directly offset the AMT by reducing the tentative minimum tax is the AMT foreign tax credit (Code Secs. 55(b)(1)(A)(i), 55(b)(1)(B)(ii) and 55(c)(2)). Also, for purposes of computing AMT, the regular tax, against which the tentative minimum tax is compared, may not be offset by any tax credits except the foreign tax credit (Code Secs. 27(a) and 901), the possessions tax credit (Code Sec. 936), and the Puerto Rico economic activity credit (Code Secs. 30A and 55(c)(1)). There is no AMT if the regular tax exceeds the tentative minimum tax.

Even when there is no direct AMT liability because the regular tax exceeds the tentative minimum tax, most business credits cannot be used to completely reduce the regular tax liability. This assures that at least some tax will be paid by businesses. The general business credit allowed in computing regular tax liability for any tax year cannot exceed the excess (if any) of the taxpayer's net income tax over the greater of:

(1) the tentative minimum tax for the tax year, or

(2) 25 percent of so much of the taxpayer's net regular tax liability as exceeds $25,000 (Code Sec. 38(c)(1)).

For this purpose, the term "net income tax" means the sum of the regular tax liability and any AMT tax imposed, as reduced by any allowable nonrefundable personal

Background

credits and certain "other" credits. The term "net regular tax liability" means the regular tax liability reduced by the sum of the allowable nonrefundable personal credits and certain "other" credits. The "other" credits consist of the possessions tax credit, nonconventional fuels credit, electric vehicle credit and Puerto Rico economic activity credit (Code Secs. 38(c) and 55(c)(2)). Business credits in excess of this limit may be carried back one year and carried forward for up to 20 years (Code Sec. 39(a)(1)) with some exceptions (Code Sec. 39(d)).

American Jobs Creation Act Impact

Specified business energy credits offset regular tax liability and minimum tax.—The alcohol fuels and the electricity from renewable sources credits may be used against both the regular and minimum tax liability (Code Sec. 38(c)(4), as added by the American Jobs Creation Act of 2004). This is accomplished by modifying the general business credit limitation rules and related general business credit carryover rules (Code Secs. 38 and 39) used to compute the taxpayer's regular tax liability (Code Sec. 38(c)(4), as added by the 2004 Jobs Act).

> **Comment:** Under prior law, Congress believed that the alternative minimum tax limited the intended incentive effects of certain energy-related business credits. They felt that the incentive effects of business energy credits should be available to taxpayers regardless of their alternative minimum tax status. Thus, certain specified energy credits can be used to offset both the regular tax and the alternative minimum tax.

The specified energy credit that can be used to offset both the regular tax and the AMT are the following credits:

(1) the alcohol fuels credit (Code Sec. 40) for tax years beginning after December 31, 2004 (Code Sec. 38(c)(4)(B)(i), as added by the 2004 Jobs Act), and

(2) the credit for electricity or refined coal (Code Sec. 45, as amended by the 2004 Jobs Act) produced at a facility placed in service after the date of enactment, during the first four years of production beginning on the date the facility was originally placed in service (Code Sec. 38(c)(4)(B)(ii), as added by the 2004 Jobs Act).

Conforming changes were made to the general business credit limitation rules (Code Secs. 38(c)(2)(A)(ii)(II) and 38(c)(3)(A)(ii)(II), as amended by the 2004 Jobs Act).

For further information on this subject, consult any of the following CCH reporter explanations:

- Standard Federal Tax Reporter, 2004FED ¶ 4251.01

- Federal Tax Service, FTS § G:24.40

- Federal Tax Guide, 2004FTG ¶ 2825

★ *Effective date.* These provisions apply to tax years ending after the date of enactment (Act Sec. 711(c) of the American Jobs Creation Act of 2004).

Act Sec. 711(a) of the American Jobs Creation Act of 2004, redesignating Code Sec. 38(c)(4) as Code Sec. 38(c)(5) and adding new Code Sec. 38(c)(4); Act Sec. 711(b), amending Code Secs. 38(c)(2)(A)(ii)(II) and 38(c)(3)(A)(ii)(II); Act Sec. 711(c). Law at ¶ 5010. Committee Report at ¶ 10,924.

¶370

¶ 375

Railroad Track Maintenance Credit

Background

Over the years, the large railroad companies have consolidated and eliminated many of the smaller and shorter freight routes. To service the communities and businesses on the eliminated routes, numerous small and mid-sized railroad companies were formed and prospered. These small railroad companies have been able to maintain the existing infrastructure of track and bridges from their operating revenues.

Recently, technology has been able to significantly increase the load capacity of the average freight rail car. This has allowed the large railroad companies to haul larger quantities of goods at a significant cost saving; however, these heavier cars are taking their toll on the short haul railroad companies' infrastructure. The increased wear and tear of these newer, heavier freight cars is requiring the small railroad companies to invest additional revenue into maintenance. This results in lower profitability, which increases the difficulty of attracting outside investment. The reason for the need for outside investment is to upgrade and modernize the current rail infrastructure to handle the new cars and maintain or increase profitability. The difficulty in attracting outside investment has resulted in continued deterioration of the short haul rail lines.

Over the years, several bills have been introduced with the purpose of injecting federal funds into railroad infrastructure upgrading. The estimated cost of upgrading the rail infrastructure has been estimated at approximately $7 billion due to the years of neglect during the period of railroad consolidation. Of this estimated $7 billion, only approximately $2 billion is potentially available from the short haul railroad companies.

The argument goes that should these rail upgrades fail to be implemented, the short haul lines will become uncompetitive or eliminated, and the bulk of transporting goods will then fall to the trucking industry with its resulting wear and tear on the nation's highways. The small and mid-sized railroad companies estimate that approximately $10 billion of additional appropriations is needed to maintain the highways. If this money was made available to the railroad companies, they claim the result will be an improved rail system which will be able to haul greater quantities of goods at a lower cost. Additionally, the cost of maintenance of the modernized system will fall on the railroad companies and not the on the public as it would if the trucking industry were to become the primary hauler. Despite this argument, no special tax provisions, federal grants or federally guaranteed loans have been created by Congress.

American Jobs Creation Act Impact

Railroad track maintenance credit.—To address the need to update and modernize the railroad infrastructure used by small and mid-sized railroads, a new general business credit has been created (Code Sec. 45G, as added by the American Jobs Creation Act of 2004). The railroad track maintenance credit amount is equal to 50 percent of the qualified railroad track maintenance expenditures paid or incurred by eligible taxpayers during the tax year (Code Sec. 45G(a), as added by the 2004 Jobs Act).

Limitations. The maximum amount of credit that may be claimed cannot be greater that $3,500 multiplied by the number of miles of railroad track owned or leased by the eligible taxpayer as of the close of the tax year. Each mile of track may be taken into account only once. Thus, if the owner of the track assigns certain track mileage to another person for purposes of this credit, the owner cannot also claim the credit for the same miles (Code Sec. 45G(b), as added by the 2004 Jobs Act). As with many business credits, any basis the taxpayer may have in the track must be reduced by any credit amount claimed (Code Sec. 45G(e)(3), as added by the 2004 Jobs Act). Railroads that are considered a controlled group and file a consolidated return will be viewed as a single taxpayer. The credit amount, if any, is to be pro-rated among the group based on the proportion of the amount of qualified railroad track maintenance expenses each member incurred to the total qualified credit expenses for the controlled group. Rules similar to Code Sec. 41(f) are to be followed (Code Sec. 45G(e)(2), as added by the 2004 Jobs Act). Finally, only expenditures paid or incurred after December 31, 2004, and before January 1, 2008, will be considered qualified expenditures for the purpose of this credit (Code Sec. 45G(f), as added by the 2004 Jobs Act).

> **Comment:** If Congressional history is any indication of future events, there is a high probability that this credit will be extended, similar to the research expenses credit.

Qualified railroad track maintenance expenditures. Qualified railroad track maintenance expenditures are defined as expenditures for maintenance of railroad track owned or leased by a Class II or Class III railroad as of January 1, 2005. The expenditures will be considered qualified expenditures whether or not they are chargeable to capital accounts. Expenditures need not be only for track maintenance, but can include amounts paid or incurred for work on roadbeds, bridges and other related track structures (Code Sec. 45G(d), as added by the 2004 Jobs Act).

Eligible taxpayers. There are two categories of eligible taxpayers:

(1) Class II and Class III railroads, and

(2) any person:

　(a) who transports property using the rail facilities of a person described in item (1) above, or

　(b) who furnishes railroad-related property or services to such a person (Code Sec. 45G(c), as added by the 2004 Jobs Act).

Class II and Class III railroads are given the same meaning as these terms are given by the Surface Transportation Board. A Class II railroad is defined as a carrier with annual operating revenues of less than $250 million but more than $20 million after applying the railroad revenue deflator formula. A Class III railroad is defined as a carrier with annual operating revenues of $20 million or less after applying the railroad deflator formula (49 CFR Part 1201 1-1(a)) (Code Sec. 45G(e), as added by the 2004 Jobs Act). All switching and terminal companies, and electric railway carriers, regardless of operating revenue, are Class III carriers (49 CFR Part 1201 1-1(d) and (e)).

> **Comment:** Under the regulations that classify railroad carriers, each carrier must file an annual report showing operating revenues. Every three years, the Surface Transportation Board reviews these annual reports to ensure that the carrier is properly classified. As a consequence of this rolling review, it is possible that a mid-sized carrier, following the modernization of its track infrastructure with the help of this tax credit, could find possible fiscal improvement that results in reclassification as a Class I railroad and the subsequent loss of the ability to claim the credit.

General business credit implications. As part of the general business credit under Code Sec. 38, the railroad track maintenance credit is subject to the credit limitation and the carryback and carryforward rules. Specifically, this credit is placed in the ordering list after the credit for employer-provided child care. Any unused credit in a single tax year may be carried back one year and forward 20 years under Code Sec. 39. However, for the purposes of the railroad track maintenance credit, the credit may not be carried back to tax years beginning before January 1, 2005 (Code Sec. 39(d), as amended by the 2004 Jobs Act.)

> **Comment:** The amendment made by Act Sec. 245(b) of the 2004 Jobs Act to Code Sec. 39 replaces the current 10 subsections with one concise, universal statement. Basically, for any general business credit, the unused credit cannot be carried back to any year prior to the year the credit was first allowed. This amendment to Code Sec. 39(d) is effective for all tax years beginning after December 31, 2003. This effective date is harmless in the fact that the last business credit with a carryback limitation provision was the small employer pension plan startup cost credit which was enacted for tax year beginning after December 31, 2001 (Code Sec. 39(d)(10), as amended by Act Sec. 245(b)(2) of the 2004 Jobs Act.)

> **Planning Note:** Practitioners need to be aware that no provision was made for unused railroad track maintenance credit after the 20-year carryforward period under Code Sec. 196, Deduction for Certain Unused Business Credits. Thus, any unused credit carried forward and still unused after 20 years will be lost. The same result will happen if the taxpayer should cease to exist.

For further information on this subject, consult any of the following CCH reporter explanations:

- Standard Federal Tax Reporter, 2004FED ¶4251.021, ¶4301.01 and ¶29,412.01

- Federal Tax Service, FTS § G:24.20

- Federal Tax Guide, 2004FTG ¶2625

★ *Effective date.* The provision is effective for tax years beginning after December 31, 2004 (Act Sec. 245(e) of the American Job Creation Act of 2004).

Act Sec. 245(a) of the American Jobs Creation Act of 2004, adding Code Sec. 45G; Act Sec. 245(b), amending Code Sec. 39(d); Act Sec. 245(c)(1), adding Code Sec. 38(b)(16); Act Sec. 245(c)(2), adding Code Sec. 1016(a)(29); Act Sec. 245(d); Act Sec. 245(e). Law at ¶5010, ¶5015, ¶5045 and ¶5760. Committee Report at ¶10,260.

COMMUNITY RENEWAL

¶ 380

Modification of Targeted Areas and Low-Income Communities for New Markets Tax Credit

Background

The new markets tax credit (Code Sec. 45D) was created to encourage investment in low-income or economically disadvantaged areas. Under provisions of the credit, a low-income community is defined as any population census tract that (1) has a poverty rate of at least 20 percent, or (2) if not located within a metropolitan area, the median family income does not exceed 80 percent of the statewide median family income, or (3) if located within a metropolitan area, the median family income does not exceed 80 percent of the greater of the statewide median family income or the metropolitan area median family income.

Background _____

The provisions of the new market tax credit authorize the Secretary of the Treasury to designate any targeted area within any census tract as a low-income community as long as (1) the boundary of the area is continuous, (2) the area would satisfy either the poverty rate or median income requirements if it were a census tract, and (3) there is inadequate access to investment capital in the area.

The new markets tax credit makes no provision for treating census tracts with low populations as low-income communities.

_____

American Jobs Creation Act Impact

Targeted populations.—The American Jobs Creation Act of 2004 modifies the Secretary's authority to designate targeted areas as low-income communities (Code Sec. 45D(e)(2), as amended by Act Sec. 221(a) of the 2004 Jobs Act). Rather than designating targeted areas, the Secretary must issue regulations under which targeted populations may be designated as low-income communities. A "targeted population" is defined as individuals, or an identifiable group of individuals, including an Indian tribe, who are low-income persons or otherwise lack adequate access to loans or equity investments (Act Sec. 103(20) of the Riegle Community Development and Regulatory Improvement Act of 1994 (12 U.S.C. § 4702(20))). A targeted population is not required to be within any census tract. In addition, the regulations must include procedures for determining which entities are qualified active low-income community businesses with respect to targeted populations.

> **Comment:** For purposes of defining a targeted population, Act Sec. 103(17) of the Riegle Community Development and Regulatory Improvement Act of 1994 (12 U.S.C. § 4702(17)) defines "low-income" as having an income, adjusted for family size, of not more than 80 percent of the area median income for metropolitan areas; and not more than, for nonmetropolitan areas, the greater of 80 percent of the area median income, or 80 percent of the statewide nonmetropolitan area median income.

> **Comment:** An "Indian tribe" is defined as any Indian tribe, band, pueblo, nation or other organized group or community, including any Alaska Native village or regional or village corporation, as defined in or established pursuant to the Alaska Native Claims Settlement Act (43 U.S.C. § 1601 et seq.), which is recognized as eligible for the special programs and services provided by the United States to Indians because of their status as Indians (Act Sec. 103(12) of the Riegle Community Development and Regulatory Improvement Act of 1994 (12 U.S.C. § 4702(12)).

Tracts with low population.—The 2004 Jobs Act expands the definition of low-income community by providing that a population census tract with a low population may be treated as a low-income community if:

   (1) the tract has a population of less than 2,000;

   (2) the tract is within an empowerment zone, the designation of which is in effect under Code Sec. 1391; and

   (3) the tract is contiguous with one or more low-income communities (determined without regard to this provision) (Code Sec. 45D(e)(4), as added by Act Sec. 221(b) of the 2004 Jobs Act).

For further information on this subject, consult any of the following CCH reporter explanations:

   • Standard Federal Tax Reporter, 2004FED ¶ 4490.01 and ¶ 4490.021

¶380

- Federal Tax Service, FTS § G:24.383[3]
- Federal Tax Guide, 2004FTG ¶ 2490

★ *Effective date.* The provision requiring the Secretary to issue regulations with respect to targeted populations applies to designations made by the Secretary after the date of enactment (Act Sec. 221(c)(1) of the American Jobs Creation Act of 2004).

The provision allowing certain population census tracts with low population to be treated as low-income communities applies to investments made after the date of enactment (Act Sec. 221(c)(2) of the American Jobs Creation Act of 2004).

Act Sec. 221(a) of the American Jobs Creation Act of 2004, amending Code Sec. 45D(e)(2); Act Sec. 221(b), adding Code Sec. 45D(e)(4); Act Sec. 221(c). Law at ¶ 5040. Committee Report at ¶ 10,090.

¶ 385

Expansion of Designated Renewal Community Area Based on 2000 Census Data

Background

Code Sec. 1400E, added by Sec. 101(a) of the Community Renewal Tax Relief Act of 2000 (P.L. 106-554), provides for the designation of certain communities as renewal communities. Renewal communities are eligible for tax incentives including: (1) a zero-percent capital gains rate from the sale of qualifying assets; (2) expanded expensing of qualified renewal property under Code Sec. 179; (3) a wage credit for employers doing business in renewal communities; (4) a work opportunity tax credit for employers who hire youths living in a renewal community; and (5) a commercial revitalization deduction.

A nominated area was designated as a renewal community only if it exhibited certain characteristics relating to geographic area, population, and economic distress. With respect to geographic area, the area must be within the jurisdiction of one or more local governments, and have a continuous boundary. With respect to population, the area must have a maximum population of not more than 200,000. The area must have a minimum population of at least 4,000 if any portion of the area (other than a rural area with a population of less than 50,000) is located within a metropolitan statistical area that has a population of 50,000 or more, or at least 1,000 in any other case. An area that is entirely within an Indian reservation does not have to meet these population requirements.

The designations of renewal communities were required to be made by December 31, 2001, using 1990 census data to determine populations and poverty rates.

American Jobs Creation Act Impact

Expansion of renewal community area based on 2000 census.—The Secretary of Housing and Urban Development (HUD) is authorized, at the request of all the governments that nominated an area as a renewal community, to expand the area of the community to include any census tract under the following circumstances (Code Sec. 1400E(g)(1), as added by the American Jobs Creation Act of 2004):

(1) The renewal community, including the census tract to be added, would have satisfied the renewal community eligibility requirements using 1990 census data at the time the community was originally nominated, and the census tract to be added has a poverty rate using 2000 census data that exceeds the poverty rate using 1990 census data.

(2) A census tract may be added to a renewal community even if the addition of the tract to the community would have caused the community to fail

one or more of the eligibility requirements when originally nominated using 1990 census data provided that:

(a) the renewal community, including the census tract, does not have a population of more than 200,000 using either 1990 or 2000 census data;

(b) the census tract has a poverty rate of at least 20 percent using 2000 census data; and

(c) the census tract has a poverty rate using 2000 census data that exceeds the poverty rate of the tract using 1990 census data. (Any census tract that did not have a poverty rate determined by the Bureau of Census using 1990 data may be added to an existing renewal community without satisfying this requirement.)

(3) A census tract may be added to an existing renewal community if such tract has no population using 2000 census data or no poverty rate for the tract is determined by the Bureau of Census using 2000 census data; the tract is one of general distress; and the renewal community, including the census tract, is within the jurisdiction of one or more local governments and has a continuous boundary.

For further information on this subject, consult any of the following CCH reporter explanations:

- Standard Federal Tax Reporter, 2004FED ¶ 32,435.01 and ¶ 32,435.04
- Federal Tax Service, FTS § G:1.101
- Federal Tax Guide, 2004FTG ¶ 8600

★ *Effective date.* The provision is effective on December 21, 2000, as if included in the amendments made by Act Sec. 101 of the Community Renewal Tax Relief Act of 2000 (P.L. 106-554). (Act Sec. 222(b) of the American Jobs Creation Act of 2004).

Act Sec. 222(a) of the American Jobs Creation Act of 2004, adding Code Sec. 1400E(g); Act Sec. 222(b). Law at ¶ 5915. Committee Report at ¶ 10,100.

¶ 390

Modification of Income Requirement for Census Tracts Within High Migration Rural Counties

Background

The new markets tax credit was created to encourage investment in low-income or economically disadvantaged areas (Code Sec. 45D, as added by the Community Renewal Tax Relief Act of 2000 (P.L. 106-554). Under provisions of the credit, a low-income community is defined as any population census tract that (1) has a poverty rate of at least 20 percent, or (2) if not located within a metropolitan area, the median family income does not exceed 80 percent of the statewide median family income, or (3) if located within a metropolitan area, the median family income does not exceed 80 percent of the greater of the statewide median family income or the metropolitan area median family income.

The provisions of the new market tax credit authorize the Secretary of the Treasury to designate any targeted area within any census tract as a low-income community as long as (1) the boundary of the area is continuous, (2) the area would satisfy either the poverty rate or median income requirements if it were a census tract, and (3) there is inadequate access to investment capital in the area.

Background

The new markets tax credit makes no special provision for census tracts located within high migration rural counties.

American Jobs Creation Act Impact

Income requirement modified.—The low-income test for the new markets tax credit is modified for population census tracts located in high migration rural counties. If a population census tract is located in a high migration rural county, it will be considered a low-income community (1) if it has a poverty rate of at least 20 percent, or (2) if it is not located within a metropolitan area, the median family income does not exceed 85 percent (rather than 80 percent) of the statewide median family income, or (3) if located within a metropolitan area, the median family income does not exceed 80 percent of the greater of the statewide median family income or the metropolitan area median family income. (Code Sec. 45D(e)(5), as added by Act Sec. 223(a) of the American Jobs Creation Act of 2004).

A high migration rural county is any county that, during the 20-year period ending with the year in which the most recent census was conducted, lost 10 percent of its population (as of the beginning of the 20-year period) to migration out of the county (Code Sec. 45D(e)(5)(B), as added by Act Sec. 223(a) of the 2004 Jobs Act).

For further information on this subject, consult any of the following CCH reporter explanations:

- Standard Federal Tax Reporter, 2004FED ¶4490.01
- Federal Tax Service, FTS §G:1.101
- Federal Tax Guide, 2004FTG ¶2490

★ *Effective date.* The provision applies to investments made after December 31, 2000, as if included in the amendment made by Act Sec. 121(a) of the Community Renewal Tax Relief Act of 2000 (Act Sec. 223(b) of the American Jobs Creation Act of 2004).

Act Sec. 223(a) of the American Jobs Creation Act of 2004, adding Code Sec. 45D(e)(5); Act Sec. 223(b). Law at ¶5040. Committee Report at ¶10,110.

METHOD OF ACCOUNTING

¶ 395

Special Accounting Method for Naval Shipbuilders

Background

Generally, Code Sec. 460, requires taxpayers to use the percentage-of-completion method to determine taxable income from long-term contracts. However, an exception exists for certain ship construction contracts, which may be accounted for using the 40/60 percentage-of-completion/capitalized cost method (PCCM) (Act Sec. 10203 of the Omnibus Budget Reconciliation Act of 1987 (P.L. 100-203)). Under this method, 40 percent of the items are accounted for under the percentage-of-completion method and 60 percent are accounted for under the taxpayer's exempt contract method of accounting. Qualified ship construction contracts are contracts for the construction of no more than five ships that: (1) are constructed in the United States; (2) are under a contract that the taxpayer reasonably expects to complete within five years of the contract commencement date; and (3) are not constructed directly or indirectly for the federal government.

American Jobs Creation Act Impact

PCCM method extended to naval shipbuilders.—Shipbuilders may now use the percentage-of-completion/capitalized cost method (PCCM) of accounting for qualified *naval* ship contracts. The method may be used for the first five tax years of the contract beginning with the contract commencement year. A qualified naval ship contract is any contract, or portion thereof, for the construction of one ship or submarine: (1) within the United States; (2) for the federal government; (3) under which the taxpayer reasonably expects the acceptance date to occur no later than 9 years after the date on which the physical fabrication of any section or component of the ship or submarine begins in the taxpayer's shipyard (construction commencement date).

However, the taxpayer's use of PCCM is subject to a recapture provision in the sixth tax year. Thus, the taxpayer's income tax for the first tax year following the 5-year period is increased by the excess, if any, of (1) the amount of tax which would have been imposed during that period if this provision had not been enacted, over (2) the amount of tax that was actually imposed during that period.

For further information on this subject, consult any of the following CCH reporter explanations:

- Standard Federal Tax Reporter, 2004FED ¶ 21,560.027
- Federal Tax Service, FTS § K:12.81[2]
- Federal Tax Guide, 2004FTG ¶ 15,465

★ *Effective date.* This section shall apply to contracts for ships or submarines with respect to which the construction commencement date occurs after the date of enactment (Act Sec. 708(d) of the American Jobs Creation Act of 2004).

Act Sec. 708(a)–(c) of the American Jobs Creation Act of 2004, referencing Act Sec. 10203 of P.L. 100-203 (Omnibus Budget Reconciliation Act of 1987). Law at ¶ 7065. Committee Report at ¶ 10,900.

Chapter 4

International Transactions: Foreign Tax Credit, Subpart F and CFCs

FOREIGN TAX CREDIT

¶ 405

Interest Expense Sourcing for Worldwide Affiliated Groups

Background _____

A U.S. taxpayer is allowed a credit against U.S. income tax liability for taxes paid during the year to a foreign country or U.S. possession (alternatively, foreign taxes can be deducted). The foreign tax credit is subject to several limits, including an overall limit designed to prevent the taxpayer from using the credit to reduce U.S. tax liability on U.S. source income (Code Sec. 904(a)). This limit essentially caps the credit at the amount of U.S. tax that would have been paid on foreign-source taxable income. The calculation requires the taxpayer to determine its taxable income from foreign sources as a percentage of worldwide taxable income.

$$\text{Maximum credit} = \frac{\text{Taxable income from foreign sources}}{\text{Worldwide taxable income}} \times \frac{\text{U.S. income tax on}}{\text{worldwide income}}$$

Motivation to minimize foreign-source deductions. As the formula suggests, a taxpayer claiming foreign tax credits has a strong incentive to maximize the amount of income classified as foreign sourced. Foreign-source income increases the numerator of the limitation fraction, resulting in a higher percentage of U.S. tax that can be offset by foreign taxes paid. Maximizing foreign-source income is especially relevant for taxpayers in an excess credit position, that is, who have paid more in creditable foreign taxes than the Code Sec. 904(a) limitation allows them to claim as credits. The basic planning formula for increasing foreign source taxable income is to maximize the amount of gross income characterized as foreign source while minimizing deductions (such as interest expense) allocated to foreign source income. Every attempt is made to source deductions, including interest expense, as domestic.

> **Comment:** Prior to the American Jobs Creation Act of 2004, taxpayers were required to separate income and deductions into nine separate limitation "baskets" based on the nature of the item (passive, etc.). The baskets necessitated extensive juggling to make sure that foreign-source income fell within the same limitation basket as the foreign tax credits available to be used. The 2004 Jobs Act reduces the number of baskets from nine to two (general and passive income), eliminating much of this onerous step (see ¶ 410).

Affiliated group sourcing rules for interest expenses. The sourcing rules for interest expenses are based on the concept that money is fungible and interest expenses should be attributed to all business activities and property of a taxpayer regardless of any special purpose for borrowing. Interest allocations must be made based on the gross assets of an affiliated group of corporations; the assumption is that the source of the interest expense should match the source of the income generated by the group's overall assets. Domestic members of the group generally are treated as a single corporation (the "one-taxpayer" rule) and allocation must be made on the basis of the single corporation's assets rather than its gross income. Foreign affiliates (and thus their assets) are excluded from the interest allocation formula (Code Sec. 864(e)(5)).

> **Comment:** Exclusion of foreign affiliates from the interest allocation formula has been described as "water's edge fungibility" since the IRS theory that money flows indiscriminately among business functions does not seem to extend to overseas operations.

Each member of the affiliated group allocates its interest expense among foreign and U.S-source categories by referring to the total percentage of the group's worldwide assets that fall into that category. For example, if 60 percent of the affiliated group's assets produce general foreign-source income and 40 percent of the assets produce general U.S.-source income, then 60 percent of the member's interest expense must be allocated to foreign general-source interest expense (Temporary Reg. § 1.861-11T(c)).

Affiliated group under interest allocation rules. An affiliated group is treated as a single taxpayer for the interest allocation rules. An affiliated group is generally defined as a group of related corporations that are eligible to file a consolidated tax return (defined under Code Sec. 1504), whether or not a consolidated return is filed. Foreign affiliates are excluded from the group. Most financial corporations such as banks are also excluded from the affiliated group. However, a taxpayer (which must be a nonfinancial group) can elect to treat certain financial institutions that it owns (banks, savings and loans) as a separate group and can thus allocate the interest of these types of institutions separately (see ¶ 407 for a separate discussion of financial institution rules).

Problems associated with excluding foreign affiliates from interest allocation formulas. The current interest allocation formula has been criticized by many businesses and by the Treasury Department itself for ignoring foreign debt and overstating foreign assets, resulting in over-allocation of interest to foreign-source categories. The system has been cited as problematic because:

- foreign debt is ignored in the formula,

- foreign assets are overstated, resulting in over-allocation of company interest expense to foreign source income,

- formula results in overly restricted use of foreign tax credits, causing double taxation of foreign income,

- international double taxation violates the economic neutrality principle promoted by NAFTA,

- limits on ability to deduct interest expense (due to loss of foreign tax credits) places U.S. firms at a competitive disadvantage in global merger and acquisition activities, i.e. a U.S. firm must reduce its bid to offset double taxation, and

- competitive disadvantages cause limited growth, job expansion, etc.

American Jobs Creation Act Impact

Affiliated group may elect global interest expense allocation starting in 2009.—An affiliated group of corporations may make a one-time election to determine foreign-source taxable income of the group by allocating and apportioning interest expense of the domestic members of a worldwide affiliated group on a worldwide-group basis, as if all members of the worldwide group were a single corporation (Code Sec. 864(f)(1), as added by the American Jobs Creation Act of 2004). A group that makes this election will determine the taxable income of the domestic members of the group from sources outside the United States by allocating and apportioning the third-party interest expense of those domestic members to foreign-source income in an amount equal to the excess (if any) of:

(1) the worldwide affiliated group's worldwide third-party interest expense multiplied by the ratio which the foreign assets of the worldwide affiliated group bears to the total assets of the worldwide affiliated group, over

(2) the third-party interest expense incurred by foreign members of the group to the extent such interest would be allocated to foreign sources if the provision's principles were applied separately to the foreign members of the group (Code Sec. 864(f)(1)(B), as amended by the 2004 Jobs Act).

Worldwide affiliated group defined. A worldwide affiliated group eligible to elect global interest allocation consists of:

- all of the corporations in an affiliated group (as defined under present law for interest allocation purposes, under Code Sec. 1504(a), except that it includes insurance companies otherwise excluded under Code Sec. 1504(b)(2) and corporations subject to a possessions tax credit election otherwise excluded under Code Sec. 1504(b)(4)), plus

- all controlled foreign corporations that, in the aggregate, meet the consolidated group ownership requirements either directly or indirectly, and would be members of the affiliated group if foreign corporations were not excluded from the definition of includible corporation under Code Sec. 1504(b)(3) (i.e., in which at least 80 percent of the vote and value of the stock of such corporations is owned by one or more other corporations included in the affiliated group) (Code Sec. 864(f)(1)(C), as added by the 2004 Jobs Act).

Comment: Financial institutions are excluded from the worldwide affiliated group, as is the case if the worldwide allocation election is not made (under Code Sec. 864(e)(5)(B)). However, excluded financial institutions can be treated as a separate interest allocation subgroup, and the institutions eligible for the subgroup is expanded if the worldwide allocation election is made (Code Sec. 864(f)(4) and (5), as added by the 2004 Jobs Act). See ¶ 407 for a discussion of the worldwide financial institutions subgroup.

The election is available for tax years beginning after December 31, 2008 (Act Sec. 401(c) of the 2004 Jobs Act).

Planning Note: This allocation method is elective. A taxpayer is not required to apply the new global interest allocation and may continue to use Code Sec. 864(e) allocation rules if the taxpayer would receive a higher foreign tax credit limitation under the old rules.

Comment: The basic result of the worldwide interest allocation formula, if elected, is to increase the weight given to foreign assets in the allocation formula. This should in turn result in a greater proportion of the interest expense being allocated to U.S.-source income under the foreign tax credit formula.

Interest expense definition limited to third-party interest. The formula for allocating interest expense to domestic members of the worldwide group excludes interest that is not paid to a third party. Accordingly, related party interest is not treated as interest under the formula. Non-interest expenses (including related-party interest) that cannot be directly allocated to any specific income-producing activity are allocated and apportioned as if all members of the affiliated group were a single corporation (Code Sec. 864(f)(2), as added by the 2004 Jobs Act). Note that for these purposes, apportionment is made to members of the affiliated group, not to the worldwide affiliated group. A worldwide affiliated group includes foreign members while an affiliated group excludes foreign members. Here, therefore, the foreign members otherwise included for the worldwide interest expense allocation are excluded. Affiliated group retains its historic definition and includes only those members included in the Code Sec. 1504 definition (but including insurance companies otherwise excluded under Code Sec. 1504(b)(2) and corporations subject to a possessions tax credit election otherwise excluded under Code Sec. 1504(b)(4)).

Comment: The advantages of making the election to allocate interest on a worldwide basis are basically not available for related-party interest expenses.

Making the election. An election to allocate interest expense based on a worldwide group may be made only by the common parent of the domestic affiliated group (Code Sec. 864(f)(6), as added by the 2004 Jobs Act). The election may be made only for the first tax year of the worldwide group's existence beginning after December 31, 2008. The worldwide group is considered to exist for purposes of making the election once the group includes at least one foreign corporation that qualifies for inclusion in the worldwide group. Once made, the election will apply to the common parent and all other corporations which are members of the worldwide affiliated group for the tax year of the election and for all subsequent years unless the election is revoked with the consent of the IRS.

Caution Note: The worldwide group election may be made only for the first tax year of the group beginning after December 31, 2008. For existing multinationals, this means that by 2010 it may be too late to make the election. The election is irrevocable without IRS consent.

Tax-exempt assets. Assets that produce tax-exempt U.S. income may not be a factor in an interest expense apportionment or any other expense apportionment, and this is true whether or not the worldwide interest allocation election is made (Code Sec. 864(f)(3) and Code Sec. 864(e)(3)). The portion of any stock that produces dividends eligible for the dividends-received deduction is considered a tax-exempt asset. To the extent of any dividend benefits from the dividends received deduction under Code Sec. 243 (allowing a dividends-received deduction for certain dividends from U.S. corporations) or Code Sec. 245(a) (allowing a dividends-received deduction for the U.S.-source portion of certain dividends from foreign corporations), that portion of the dividend is treated as tax-exempt income for the purpose of the expense allocation rules and that portion of the related asset is treated as a tax-exempt asset (Code Sec. 864(e)(3)).

Nonaffiliated 10-percent owned corporations. A group making the worldwide group interest allocation election must apply the rules for nonaffiliated 10-percent owned corporations on a worldwide affiliated group basis (Code Sec. 864(f)(3) and Code Sec. 864(e)(4)). The nonaffiliated 10-percent corporation rules require that, when interest expenses are allocated according to the value of stock held in a corporation of this kind, the adjusted basis of the stock must either be (1) increased by the portion of the corporation's earnings that can be attributed to the stock during the period the stock is held by a taxpayer, or (2) reduced (but not below zero) by the portion of a deficit in corporate earnings that can be attributed to the stock.

The adjustment to asset value on a look-through basis is also applied to stock of foreign corporations that is indirectly 10-percent owned by the taxpayer's affiliated group. Stock owned directly or indirectly by a corporation, partnership, or trust is treated as being owned proportionately by its shareholders, partners, or beneficiaries. When a taxpayer is treated under this look-through rule as owning stock in a lower-tier corporation, the adjustment to the basis of the upper-tier corporation in which the taxpayer actually owns stock is to include an adjustment for the amount of the earnings and profits (or deficit in earnings and profits) of the lower-tier corporation which is attributable to the stock the taxpayer is treated as owning and to the period during which the taxpayer is treated as owning that stock. Moreover, the proper adjustment is to be made to the earnings and profits of any corporation for purposes of Code Sec. 864(e) to take into account any earnings and profits included in gross income under subpart F current inclusion rules (or under any other provision) that are reflected in the adjusted basis of the stock (Code Sec. 864(e)(4)(D)). Thus, a subpart F inclusion, which increases stock basis but does not decrease earnings and profits of a controlled foreign corporation, is not to result in double counting of earnings and profits (Code Sec. 864(e)).

Regulation authority. The IRS is authorized to issue regulations to carry out the new election rules, including providing for the direct allocation of interest expenses in circumstances where direct allocation would be appropriate to carry out the purposes of Code Sec. 864(f), and preventing assets or interest expense from being taken into account more than once (Code Sec. 864(e)(7), as amended by the 2004 Jobs Act).

For further information on this subject, consult any of the following CCH reporter explanations:

- Standard Federal Tax Reporter, 2004FED ¶ 27,189.04
- Federal Tax Service, FTS § M:2.64
- Federal Tax Guide, 2004FTG ¶ 17,235 and ¶ 17,240

★ *Effective date.* The provision applies to tax years beginning after December 31, 2008 (Act Sec. 401(c) of the American Jobs Creation Act of 2004).

Act Sec. 401(a) of the American Jobs Creation Act of 2004, redesignating former Code Sec. 864(f) as Code Sec. 864(g) and adding new Code Sec. 864(f); Act Sec. 401(b), amending Code Sec. 864(e)(7); Act Sec. 401(c). Law at ¶ 5600. Committee Report at ¶ 10,570.

¶ 407

Interest Allocation for Financial Institutions

Background _____

The general rule for determining the source of interest expense for an affiliated group is that interest is apportioned among the members according to the gross assets of the group, as if the group were a single taxpayer (Code Sec. 864(e)). Only domestic affiliates are included in the group; foreign affiliates are excluded. Financial institutions are also excluded from the affiliated group for interest allocation purposes (Code Sec. 864(e)(5)(B)) and Temporary Reg. § 1.861-11T(d)(4)). Excluded financial institutions include any taxpayer described in Code Sec. 581 or Code Sec. 591 (banks and savings and loans), the business of which is predominantly with persons other than related persons or their customers, and which is required by state or federal law to be operated separately from any other entity which is not a financial institution (Code Sec. 864(e)(5)(C)). This category of excluded financial corporations also includes bank holding companies (including financial holding companies), subsidiaries of banks and bank holding companies (including financial holding companies), and savings institutions predominantly engaged in the active conduct of a banking, financing, or similar business (Code Sec. 864(e)(5)(D)).

Financial institutions such as these that are owned by a nonfinancial affiliated group are permitted to calculate their interest expense based on the assets of the banking subgroup (Code Sec. 864(e)(5)(B) and Temporary Reg. § 1.861-11T(d)(4)). This provides a limited exception to the rule that all foreign affiliates are excluded from group allocation calculations. An institution that is excluded from the general one-taxpayer group may be treated as a member of the separate one-taxpayer group covering financial institutions only for purposes of allocating interest expense (Code Sec. 864(e)(5)(B)).

American Jobs Creation Act Impact

Election to expand financial institution subgroup in making interest expense allocations.—An affiliated group that makes the election to be treated as a worldwide affiliated group (¶ 405) for purposes of interest expense allocations must exclude certain financial institutions from the worldwide affiliated group, treating these financial institution members as a separate group for interest allocation purposes (Code Sec. 864(f)(5)(A), as added by the American Jobs Creation Act of 2004). The following members are eligible to be part of the financial institution subgroup of the worldwide affiliated group:

(1) all corporations that are part of the present-law bank group (Code Sec. 864(f)(4)(B), as added by the 2004 Jobs Act), and

(2) at the election of the taxpayer, all financial corporations (this new category includes any member that derives at least 80 percent of its gross income from financial services income (as described in Code Sec. 904(d)(2)(D)(i) (as designated by the 2004 Jobs Act) and Reg. § 1.904-4(e)(2)) from transactions with unrelated persons).

Comment: The categories of financial institutions that can be included in the financial institution subgroup are expanded from the prior law definition, and now include the additional "financial corporation" category. Finance companies and insurance companies that are primarily involved in financial services (generating 80% financial services income) but that do not meet the definition of a bank under Code Secs. 581 or 591 would be included in the expanded category. If the group parent does not elect to include them, these types of businesses are be treated as non-financial institutions.

Financial corporation defined. A corporation is a financial corporation if at least 80 percent of its gross income is financial services income that is derived from transactions with unrelated persons (within the meaning of Code Sec. 267(b) or Code Sec. 707(b)(1)). Financial services income retains its historic definition under the Code and related regulations, but is now found at Code Sec. 904(d)(2)(D)(ii), as redesignated by the 2004 Jobs Act. Financial services income is extensively defined in Reg. § 1.904-4(e)(2). Items of income or gain from a transaction or series of transactions are disregarded if a principal purpose for the transaction or transactions is to qualify any corporation as a financial corporation (Code Sec. 864(f)(5)(B), as added by the 2004 Jobs Act).

Making the election. The common parent of the pre-election worldwide affiliated group must make the election to include financial corporations for the first tax year beginning after December 31, 2008, in which a worldwide affiliated group includes a financial corporation (Code Sec. 864(f)(5)(D), as added by the 2004 Jobs Act). Once made, the election applies to the financial institution group for the tax year and all subsequent tax years.

Caution Note: The opportunity to include non-bank financial services corporations in the financial institutions subgroup for interest allocation purposes is available only if the election is made to allocate interest on a "worldwide affiliated group" basis (under Code Sec. 864(f), as added by the 2004 Jobs Act). If no worldwide allocation election is made, the financial institutions subgroup will continue to consist only of banks and bank holding companies as described in Code Sec. 864(e)(5)(C) and (D).

Anti-abuse rules. An anti-abuse rule is targeted at situations in which certain transfers from one member of a financial institution group to a member of the worldwide affiliated group outside of the financial institution group are treated as reducing the amount of indebtedness of the separate financial institution group (Code Sec. 864(f)(5)(C), as added by the 2004 Jobs Act). To the extent that a corporation which is a member of an electing financial institution group:

- distributes dividends or makes other distributions with respect to its stock after the date of the enactment to any member of the pre-election worldwide affiliated group (other than to a member of the electing financial institution group) in excess of the greater of (1) its average annual dividend (expressed as a percentage of current earnings and profits) during the five-tax-year period ending with the tax year preceding the tax year, or (2) 25 percent of its average annual earnings and profits for such five-tax-year period, or

- deals with any person in any manner not clearly reflecting the income of the corporation (as determined under principles similar to the principles of Code Sec. 482), then an amount of indebtedness of the electing financial institution group equal to the excess distribution or the understatement (or overstatement) of income will be recharacterized as indebtedness of the worldwide affiliated group (excluding the electing financial institution group) (Code Sec. 864(f)(5)(C), as added by the 2004 Jobs Act). If a corporation has not been in existence for five tax years, the rule will be applied with respect to the period it was in existence.

Regulation authority. The IRS is authorized to issue regulations to carry out the new election rules, including providing for the direct allocation of interest expense in other circumstances where such allocation would be appropriate. Regulatory topics may also include preventing assets or interest expense from being taken into account more than once and dealing with changes in members of any group (through acquisitions or otherwise) treated under this paragraph as an affiliated group for purposes of the Code Sec. 864(f)(5) election (Code Sec. 864(f)(5)(F), as added by the 2004 Jobs Act).

For further information on this subject, consult any of the following CCH reporter explanations:

- Standard Federal Tax Reporter, 2004FED ¶ 27,189.04
- Federal Tax Service, FTS § M:2.64[4]
- Federal Tax Guide, 2004FTG ¶ 17,235 and ¶ 17,255

★ *Effective date.* The provision applies to tax years beginning after December 31, 2008 (Act Sec. 401(c) of the American Jobs Creation Act of 2004).

Act Sec. 401(a) of the American Jobs Creation Act of 2004, adding Code Sec. 864(f)(5); Act Sec. 401(c). Law at ¶ 5600. Committee Report at ¶ 10,570.

¶ 410

Reduction to Two Foreign Tax Credit Baskets

Background ⎯⎯⎯⎯⎯⎯⎯⎯⎯⎯⎯⎯⎯⎯⎯⎯⎯⎯⎯⎯⎯⎯⎯⎯⎯⎯⎯⎯⎯⎯⎯

The United States taxes the worldwide income of U.S. citizens, resident aliens and domestic corporations without regard to whether the income arose from a transaction outside its geographic borders. To prevent double taxation—once by the foreign country where the income is earned and again by the United States—these taxpayers are allowed to reduce their U.S. tax liability on foreign-source income by the amount of foreign taxes paid on that income. The amount of credit that may be claimed is subject to an overall limitation under Code Sec. 904. This limitation operates so that the amount of foreign tax credit claimed by a taxpayer for the tax year cannot exceed the amount of U.S. tax imposed on its foreign-source income. The limitation is calculated by multiplying the taxpayer's pre-credit U.S. tax liability for the tax year by the ratio of the taxpayer's foreign-source taxable income to its worldwide taxable income for the year.

A taxpayer is required to compute its foreign tax credit limitation separately for various categories of income, generally known as "separate limitation categories" or "baskets." The significance of the basket system is that the total amount of foreign tax credit available to the taxpayer for the tax year in each basket is limited to its portion of U.S. tax liability allocated to that basket. Thus, an excess credit for the tax year in one basket cannot be used to offset U.S. tax liability in another basket. Code Sec. 904(d) outlines the nine separate baskets:

(1) passive income,

(2) high withholding tax interest,

(3) financial services income,

(4) shipping income,

(5) certain dividends received from noncontrolled section 902 foreign corporations ("10/50 companies"),

(6) certain dividends from a domestic international sales corporation (DISC) or former DISC,

(7) taxable income attributable to certain foreign trade income,

(8) certain distributions from a foreign sales corporation (FSC) or former FSC, and

(9) general basket income, which is other income not described in items (1) through (8).

Financial services income. The term "financial services income" includes certain types of income received or accrued by a person predominantly engaged in the active conduct of a banking, insurance, financing, or similar business (Code Sec. 904(d)(2)(C) and Reg. §1.904-4(e)(1)). It also includes income derived from an insurance company's investment of its unearned premiums or reserves, as well as subpart F "insurance income" as defined under Code Sec. 953(a), passive income, and export financing interest that is subject to at least a five percent foreign withholding tax. Financial services income does not include any high withholding tax interest, any dividend from a noncontrolled section 902 corporation out of earnings and profits accumulated before January 1, 2003, and any export financing interest that would also be high withholding tax interest.

Treasury regulations define a person as "predominantly engaged" in the active conduct of a banking, insurance, finance, or similar business if at least 80 percent of its gross income is "active financing income" (Reg. §§1.904-4(e)(2)(i) and (3)(i)). The regulations further provide that a corporation that is not predominantly engaged in such a business can derive financial services income as a member of an affiliated group that as a whole meets this test (Reg. §1.904-4(e)(3)(ii)). For this purpose, an affilated group is defined by Code Sec. 1504, but also includes foreign corporations. In determining whether an affiliated group meets the predominantly engaged test, only the income of members who are either U.S. corporations or controlled foreign corporations (CFCs) is counted. Furthermore, U.S. corporations must own at least 80 percent of the total voting power and stock value of the CFCs directly or indirectly.

"Base difference" items. Foreign taxes are allocated and apportioned to the same limitation categories as the income to which they relate (Reg. §1.904-6). However, so-called "base difference" items may arise in cases in which foreign law imposes tax on an item of income that does not constitute income under U.S. tax law. Under current law, the tax on this item is treated as allocated to the general limitation income category.

American Jobs Creation Act Impact

Reduction to two foreign tax credit baskets.—The number of foreign tax credit limitation categories or baskets has been reduced to two: passive category income and general category income (Code Sec. 904(d)(1), as amended by the American Jobs Creation Act of 2004). Passive category income is defined as passive income and specified passive category income, while the general category includes income other than passive category income. The specified passive category of income includes:

(1) dividends from a DISC or former DISC,

(2) taxable income attributable to foreign trade income under Code Sec. 923(b), and

(3) distributions from a FSC or former FSC, out of earnings and profits attributable to foreign trade income, or interest or carrying charges as defined in Code Sec. 927(d)(1), derived from a transaction which results in foreign trade income.

Other income which would have been included in one of the deleted categories will be included in one of the two remaining categories, as appropriate. For example, shipping income generally falls into the general category, whereas high withholding tax interest could fall into either one, depending upon the circumstances, as discussed later. According to the House Committee Report, the provision does not affect the separate computation of foreign tax credit limitations under special provisions such as the treaty-based sourcing rules or specified countries under Code Sec. 901(j) (House Committee Report (H.R. Rep. No. 108-548)).

Financial services income. Financial services income will be treated as general category income for members of a financial services group and any other person predominantly engaged in the active conduct of a banking, insurance, financing, or similar business (Code Sec. 904(d)(2), as amended by the 2004 Jobs Act). The new provision maintains the current definition of what it means to be "predominantly engaged." In addition, it incorporates some of the language from Reg. § 1.904-4(e)(3)(ii), by defining a financial services group as any affiliated group under Code Sec. 1504(a) which is predominantly engaged in the active conduct of a banking, insurance, financing, or similar business. For this purpose, an affiliated group is defined by Code Sec. 1504, but also includes foreign corporations and insurance companies subject to U.S. taxation.

As under present law, in determining whether an affiliated group meets this test, only the income of members who are either U.S. corporations or controlled foreign corporations (CFCs) is counted. Similarly, the U.S. corporations must own at least 80 percent of the total voting power and stock value of the CFCs directly or indirectly. The IRS may issue regulations specifying the treatment of financial services income received or accrued by partnerships and pass-thru entities which are not members of a financial services group.

Practical Analysis: As stated earlier, the present law interpretation of what it means to be "predominantly engaged" in the active conduct of a banking, insurance, financing, or similar business has not changed. Thus, other Code provisions that rely on this same concept are not affected. The House Committee Report presented the following illustrations for clarification:

• Under the "accumulated deficit rule" of Code Sec. 952(c)(1)(B), subpart F inclusions of a U.S. shareholder attributable to a "qualified activity" of a CFC may be reduced by the amount of the U.S. shareholder's pro rata share of certain prior year deficits attributable to the same qualified activity. For a qualified financial institution, qualified activity consists of any activity giving rise to foreign personal holding company income, but only if the CFC was "predominantly engaged" in the active conduct of a banking, financing, or similar business in both the year in which the corporation earned the income, and the year in which the corporation incurred the deficit.

• Similarly, in the case of a qualified insurance company, qualified activity consists of activity giving rise to insurance income or foreign personal holding company income, but only if the CFC was "predominantly engaged" in the active conduct of an insurance business in both the year in which the corporation earned the income and the year in which the corporation incurred the deficit (House Committee Report (H.R. Rep. No. 108-548)).

Base difference items. For tax years beginning after December 31, 2006, creditable foreign taxes that are imposed on amounts that do not constitute income under U.S. tax law are treated as imposed on general category income (Code Sec. 904(d)(2)(H), as amended by the 2004 Jobs Act). For tax years beginning after December 31, 2004, but before January 1, 2007, the taxpayer may elect the income category to which these foreign taxes would be treated as imposed upon. Once made, however, this election applies for the tax year it was made and for all subsequent tax years. It is only revocable with the consent of the IRS.

> **Caution Note:** According to the Conference Committee Report (H.R. Conf. Rep. No. 108-755), a taxpayer may choose to treat the foreign taxes as imposed on either "general limitation income" or "financial services income." At first glance, it appears that the text of the new provision conflicts with this statement. New Code Sec. 904(d)(2)(H)(ii)(I), which sets forth the special rule for years before 2007 with regard to the treatment of income tax base differences, refers to "... income described in subparagraph (C) or (I) of paragraph (1)" as the choices for the taxpayer's election. Subparagraph (C) refers to financial services income, while subparagraph (I) of paragraph (1), which refers to general limitation income under present law, has been stricken. However, this subparagraph has only been stricken for years after 2007; it remains applicable for this transitional period.

Look-through rules for CFCs. The look-through rules with regard to controlled foreign corporations (CFCs) have also been amended to reflect the income category changes beginning in 2007 (Code Sec. 904(d)(3), as amended by the 2004 Jobs Act). The general rule governing dividends, interest, rents and royalties received or accrued by a U.S. shareholder of a CFC has been changed so that they will be treated as general category income unless an exception applies. For example, subpart F inclusions under Code Sec. 951(a)(1)(A) will be treated as passive category income to the extent the inclusion can be attributed to that type of income. Likewise, interest, rents and royalties received from a CFC will be treated as passive category income to the extent the income is allocated to that type of income under the regulations. To the extent that dividends are paid out of the earnings and profits of a CFC in which the taxpayer is a U.S. shareholder, then they also will be treated as passive category income based on the ratio of earnings and profits attributable to passive category income to the total amount of earnings and profits.

> **Example:** S is a wholly-owned foreign subsidiary of P, a domestic corporation. S earns $200 of net income, of which $85 is foreign base company shipping income, $15 is foreign personal holding company income, and $100 is non-subpart F general category income. No foreign tax is imposed on the income. Half of S's income ($100) is subpart F income which must be included in the gross income of P under Code Sec. 951(a)(1)(A). Because $85 of the subpart F inclusion is attributable to shipping income of S, $85 of the subpart F inclusion is also shipping income to P, which is general category income. Because $15 of the subpart F inclusion is attributable to passive income of S, $15 of the subpart F inclusion is passive category income to P.

The look-through rules only apply where subpart F applies. Thus, if the CFC meets the "de minimis rule" under Code Sec. 954(b)(3)(A), then none of its Code Sec.

954(a) foreign base company income, and none of its Code Sec. 954(b)(3)(C) gross insurance income shall be treated as passive category income. However, the "de minimis rule" does not apply to financial services income.

The look-through rules override the high-taxed income exception to passive income (Code Sec. 904(d)(2)(B)(iii)(II), as amended by the 2004 Jobs Act). Thus, an analysis must first be made as to whether the income should be treated as passive category income before determining if the amount is high-taxed income. In addition, for purposes of these rules, the term "dividend" includes any inclusion under Code Sec. 951(a)(1)(B). However, the dividend gross-up amount under Code Sec. 78, to the extent attributable to a Code Sec. 951(a)(1)(A) inclusion, shall not be treated as a dividend, but as a Code Sec. 951(a)(1)(A) inclusion.

> **Caution Note:** The look-through rules applicable after December 31, 2006, also apply to the passive foreign investment company inclusion. However, the Bill text in Code Sec. 904(d)(3)(H), as amended by the 2004 Jobs Act, contains the present law reference to "income in a separate category." Most likely the intent was to change this reference to passive category income.

Transitional rules provide that taxes carried forward from any tax year beginning before January 1, 2007, to any tax year beginning on or after that date, shall be treated as either passive category income or general category income. In addition, the IRS may issue regulations that provide for the allocation of any carryback of taxes with respect to income from a tax year beginning on or after January 1, 2007, to a tax year beginning before such date, for purposes of allocating among the separate categories of income then in effect (Code Sec. 904(d)(2)(K), as added by the 2004 Jobs Act).

For further information on this subject, consult any of the following CCH reporter explanations:

- Standard Federal Tax Reporter, 2004FED ¶27,901.01, ¶27,901.024 and ¶27,901.0456
- Federal Tax Service, FTS §M:11.60
- Federal Tax Guide, 2004FTG ¶17,210

★ *Effective date.* In general, the amendments made by this section shall apply to tax years beginning after December 31, 2006. A transitional rule relating to income tax base differences under Code Sec. 904(d)(2)(H)(ii) shall apply to tax years beginning after December 31, 2004 (Act Sec. 404(g) of the American Jobs Creation Act of 2004).

Act Sec. 404(a) of the American Jobs Creation Act of 2004, amending Code Sec. 904(d)(1); Act Sec. 404(b), amending Code Secs. 904(d)(2)(A) and (B); Act Sec. 404(c), adding Code Sec. 904(d)(2)(B)(v); Act Sec. 404(d), amending Code Sec. 904(d)(2)(C)–(D); Act Sec. 404(e), amending Code Sec. 904(d)(2)(H)–(J); Act Sec. 404(f), amending Code Sec. 904(d)(2) and (j)(3)(A)(i); Act Sec. 404(g). Law at ¶5655. Committee Report at ¶10,600.

¶415

10-Year Foreign Tax Credit Carryover; One-Year Foreign Tax Credit Carryback

Background _____

U.S. taxpayers are allowed to reduce their U.S. tax liability on foreign-source income by the amount of foreign taxes paid on that income. The amount of credit that may be claimed is subject to an overall limitation under Code Sec. 904. This limitation operates so that the amount of foreign tax credit claimed by a taxpayer for the tax year cannot exceed the amount of U.S. tax imposed on its foreign-source income. The limitation is calculated by multiplying the taxpayer's pre-credit U.S. tax liability for

Background

the tax year by the ratio that the taxpayer's foreign-source taxable income has to its worldwide taxable income for the year. A taxpayer is required to compute its foreign tax credit limitation separately for various categories of income, generally known as "separate limitation categories" or "baskets" (Code Sec. 904(d)).

Where foreign taxes paid or accrued for any tax year are more than the amount allowed (whether calculated overall or for each basket), then the taxpayer winds up with an excess credit. This excess may be carried back to the two preceding tax years (first applied in the second preceding year) and then carried forward to the five succeeding tax years (Code Sec. 904(c) and Reg. § 1.904-2). The significance of the basket system is that the total amount of foreign tax credit available to the taxpayer for the tax year in each basket is limited to its portion of U.S. tax liability allocated to that basket. Thus, an excess credit for the tax year in one basket cannot be used to offset U.S. tax liability in another basket. The taxpayer may only carryback or carryforward the excess in that particular basket.

> **Comment:** A foreign tax credit may not be carried to a tax year in which a foreign tax deduction was claimed. If this happens, excess credits are used up as though the foreign tax credit was being claimed in the deduction year. In other words, the taxpayer must reduce the carryback or carryforward by the amount it would have chosen to claim as a credit rather than a deduction during the tax year without resulting in a refund. A taxpayer can avoid this by timely filing an amended return and electing to claim the credit instead of the deduction. For this purpose, a 10-year statute of limitations is available for filing the amended return (Code Sec. 6511(d)(3)(A)). However, the taxpayer will still be liable for interest on any deficiency that is eliminated by a carryback (Code Sec. 6601(d)).

Specific ordering rules apply, such that taxes actually paid within a basket in a given year are always credited before any excess credits carried back or forward to that year. When excess credits from different years are carried to the same year, taxes from earlier years are credited first. To the extent they are not used up, excess credits expire in the order in which they were originally paid.

Foreign oil and gas income. Because of industry-specific factors, the foreign tax credit limitation is calculated separately for foreign oil and gas extraction income (FOGEI) from other categories of foreign-source income (Code Sec. 907). For corporations, the credit for foreign oil and gas extraction taxes is limited to the product of the corporation's FOGEI for the tax year multiplied by the highest applicable U.S. corporate tax rate. For individuals, the credit is limited to the taxpayer's effective tax rate which is the ratio of the taxpayer's entire tax liability (calculated before application of the foreign tax credit for income taxes), over the individual's entire taxable income.

Where the amount of FOGEI taxes paid or accrued for the tax year exceeds these limitations, the taxpayer winds up with an amount of unused FOGEI taxes which may be carried back to the two preceding tax years (first applied in the second preceding year) and then forward to the five succeeding tax years (Code Sec. 907(f)). However, the unused taxes that may be carried back or forward is limited to the lesser of: (1) the excess extraction limitation; or (2) the excess of foreign income tax limitation for the carryback or carryover tax year.

American Jobs Creation Act Impact

Foreign tax credit carryover extended to 10 years; foreign tax credit carryback limited to one year.—The excess foreign tax credit carryforward period for both income taxes and foreign oil and gas extraction income has been extended to 10 years and limited to a carryback period of one year (Code Sec. 904(c) and 907(f)(1), as amended by the American Jobs Creation Act of 2004).

> **Comment:** As noted, the Code requires taxpayers to separately calculate their foreign tax credit for each basket of income. Currently there are nine separate baskets. However, Code Sec. 904(d)(1) has been amended by the 2004 Jobs Act to reduce the number of baskets to two for tax years beginning after December 31, 2006 (see ¶410). The change in the carryback and carryforward periods makes no reference to the change in the number of baskets or whether the calculation of the limit for each basket (and overall) is affected. It is anticipated that detailed guidance would be forthcoming to assist in this area.

For further information on this subject, consult any of the following CCH reporter explanations:

- Standard Federal Tax Reporter, 2004FED ¶27,901.0214 and ¶27,963.028
- Federal Tax Service, FTS §M:11.140 and §M:11.163
- Federal Tax Guide, 2004FTG ¶17,220

★ *Effective date.* The extension of the carryforward period applies to excess foreign tax credits that may be carried to any tax year ending after the date of enactment (Act Sec. 417(c)(2) of the American Jobs Creation Act of 2004). The limitation of the carryback period applies to excess foreign tax credits arising in tax years beginning after the date of enactment (Act Sec. 417(c)(1) of the 2004 Jobs Act).

Act Sec. 417(a) of the American Jobs Creation Act of 2004, amending Code Sec. 904(c); Act Sec. 417(b), amending Code Sec. 907(f)(1); Act Sec. 417(c). Law at ¶5655 and ¶5660. Committee Report at ¶10,730.

¶ 420

Recharacterization of Overall Domestic Loss

Background _____

U.S. persons and residents are taxed on their worldwide income. Congress enacted the foreign tax credit to prevent these taxpayers from being taxed twice— once by the foreign country where the income is earned and again by the United States. The foreign tax credit allows U.S. taxpayers to reduce their U.S. tax liability on foreign-source income by the amount of foreign taxes paid on the income, subject to limitation under Code Sec. 904. This overall limitation is designed so that a taxpayer's foreign tax credit cannot exceed the amount of U.S. tax imposed on foreign-source income. It is calculated by prorating a taxpayer's pre-credit U.S. tax on its worldwide income between its U.S.-source and foreign-source taxable income. The ratio (not exceeding 100 percent) of the taxpayer's foreign-source taxable income to worldwide taxable income is multiplied by its pre-credit U.S. tax to establish the amount of U.S. tax allocable to the taxpayer's foreign-source income. This calculation represents the upper limit on the foreign tax credit for the year.

Code Sec. 904 requires a taxpayer to compute its foreign tax credit limitation separately for nine various categories of income, or what are generally known as "baskets" or "separate limitation categories" (Code Sec. 904(d)). The significance of the basket system lies in this allocation of foreign taxes to separate limitation categories, because such an allocation gives rise to credits only within that basket. That is, the total amount of the foreign tax credit used to offset the U.S. tax on income in each separate limitation category may not exceed the proportion of the taxpayer's

Background _____

U.S. tax which the taxpayer's foreign-source taxable income in that category bears to its worldwide taxable income (Code Sec. 904(d)).

A taxpayer must generally track its losses on a basket-by-basket basis. If the taxpayer has a net loss in a basket, otherwise known as a "separate limitation loss" (SLL), that loss must first be allocated proportionately to reduce the taxpayer's income in other baskets with foreign-source income (Code Sec. 904(f)(5)(B)). To the extent the SLL for all limitation baskets exceeds the taxpayer's separate limitation income in all baskets with foreign-source income, the aggregate foreign loss reduces U.S.-source income (Code Sec. 904(f)(5)(A)). Such an offset of U.S.-source income reduces the effective rate of U.S. tax on U.S.-source income. In order to eliminate a double benefit (that is, the reduction of U.S. tax previously noted and, later, full allowance of a foreign tax credit with respect to foreign-source income), present law includes an overall foreign loss (OFL) recapture rule (Code Sec. 904(f)(2)).

Generally, an OFL for a year is the amount by which the gross income for the tax year from foreign sources for such year is exceeded by the sum of the deductions properly apportioned or allocated to that income, except that any net operating loss deduction, foreign expropriation loss, otherwise deductible casualty or theft loss, is not taken into account (Code Sec. 904(f)(2)). In such cases, the taxpayer is required to establish an OFL account for the applicable loss basket and to adjust it to account for any future OFL recaptures and additional overall foreign losses (Reg. §1.904(f)-(1)(b)). If, in a later year, the taxpayer earns foreign-source income in the same basket that created the OFL, the taxpayer is required to recapture as U.S.-source income, the lesser of the unrecaptured loss or 50 percent (or a higher percentage if the taxpayer so elects) of the foreign-source income (Code Sec. 904(f)(1) and Reg. §1.904(f)-2(a)). The effect of the recapture is to reduce the foreign tax credit limitation in one or more years following an OFL year, and therefore, the amount of U.S. tax that can be offset by foreign tax credits in those later years.

> **Comment:** Although foreign losses that reduce U.S.-source income are recaptured as domestic-source income, in the reverse situation, there is currently no mechanism for recharacterizing such domestic-source income as foreign-source income.

If viewed in a vacuum, a domestic loss reduces pre-credit U.S. tax on worldwide income to an amount less than the tax that would apply to the taxpayer's foreign-source income had there not been a domestic loss. However, the existence of foreign-source taxable income in the year of the domestic loss reduces or eliminates any net operating loss carryover that the U.S.-source loss would otherwise have generated, absent the foreign income. In addition, because the pre-credit U.S. tax on worldwide income is reduced, so is the foreign tax credit limitation. And, because any domestic loss must be apportioned proportionately among, and reduces the income in, the separate limitation categories of foreign income, some foreign tax credits may need to be carried over. Although tax on U.S.-source taxable income in a subsequent year may be offset by a net operating loss carryforward, it cannot be offset by a foreign tax credit carryforward.

> **Comment:** The treatment of losses under the foreign tax credit limitation rules of Code Sec. 904 has often produced a windfall for the U.S. Treasury. If a taxpayer has an overall loss from domestic sources and foreign-source income in the same year, the taxpayer reaps no foreign tax benefit, as the U.S. losses typically do not reduce the amount of foreign income taxes paid. In addition, if worldwide operations produce a gain overall, there is also no domestic net operating loss carryforward for U.S. tax purposes. Thus, the domestic loss may

produce no U.S. tax benefit, and future domestic-source income will effectively be overtaxed.

Example: Assume a calendar-year taxpayer generates a $100 U.S.-source loss and earns $100 of foreign-source income in 2004, and pays $30 of foreign tax on the $100 of foreign-source income. The U.S.-source loss is offset against the foreign-source income, thus, there is no U.S.-source loss to carry forward to future years. Furthermore, because the taxpayer has no net taxable income in 2004, no foreign tax credit can be claimed in 2004 with respect to the $30 of foreign taxes. If the taxpayer then earns $100 of U.S.-source income and $100 of foreign-source income in 2005, the taxpayer cannot recharacterize any portion of the $100 of U.S.-source income as foreign-source income to reflect the fact that the previous year's $100 U.S.-source loss reduced the taxpayer's ability to claim foreign tax credits or reap other tax benefits (House Committee Report (H.R. Rep. No. 108-548)).

American Jobs Creation Act Impact

Recharacterization of overall domestic loss as foreign-source.—For foreign tax credit limitation purposes as well as Puerto Rico and Possessions tax credit purposes, U.S.-source income may be re-sourced as foreign-source income where a taxpayer's foreign tax credit limitation has been reduced due to an overall domestic loss sustained in a post-2006 tax year (Code Sec. 904(g), as added by the American Jobs Creation Act of 2004). For foreign tax credit limitation purposes, a portion of the taxpayer's U.S.-source income for each succeeding tax year is recharacterized as foreign-source income in an amount equal to the lesser of: (1) the amount of the unrecharacterized overall domestic losses for years prior to such succeeding year, or (2) 50 percent of the taxpayer's U.S.-source income for such succeeding tax year (Code Sec. 904(g)(1), as added by the 2004 Jobs Act). This change also applies for purposes of computing the Puerto Rico and Possessions tax credit under Code Sec. 936 (Code Sec. 936(a)(2)(A), as amended by the 2004 Jobs Act).

Example: Assume a calendar-year taxpayer has a domestic loss of $1,000 and foreign-source income of $1,000 in 2007. In 2008, it has domestic income of $1,000 and foreign-source income of $1,000. Assume that all income and loss are in the general limitation basket, and that the U.S. and foreign income tax rates are both 25 percent. In 2007, the taxpayer pays $250 of tax to the foreign country, but can claim no foreign tax credit because worldwide taxable income is 0, leaving no U.S. tax to offset. In 2008, foreign income tax of $250 is paid, and the general credit limitation is $250. The Treasury collects $250 after the credit. The result in 2008 appears correct. Yet, upon examining the results in both years, the Treasury collects $250 of tax on total domestic-source income of 0, while the foreign government collects $500 of tax on $2,000 of foreign-source income.

Under prior law, unless the taxpayer could generate some low-taxed foreign-source income, the excess credit from 2007 may have simply carried over unused until it expired. Under the new law, however, a portion of this taxpayer's U.S.-source income for 2008 and each succeeding tax year is recharacterized as foreign-source income in an amount equal to the lesser of: (1) the amount of the unrecharacterized overall domestic losses for years prior to such succeeding year, or (2) 50 percent of the taxpayer's U.S.-source income for such succeeding tax year. Thus, under the new law, the taxpayer will have some foreign-source income to help boost his foreign tax credit limitation amount (Code Sec. 904(g), as amended by the 2004 Jobs Act).

¶420

Comment: The House Ways and Means Committee felt it was important to create parity in the treatment of overall foreign and domestic losses to prevent the double taxation of income. The Committee was concerned that such double taxation reduced the competitiveness of U.S. businesses and harmed export sales. It is their hope that this change will increase export sales, thereby increasing production and jobs in the United States (House Committee Report, H.R. Rep. No. 108-548).

Overall domestic loss is defined as any domestic loss to the extent it offsets foreign-source taxable income for the current tax year, or for any preceding tax year by reason of a loss carryback. Domestic loss is the amount by which U.S.-source gross income is exceeded by the sum of all properly apportioned or allocated deductions without regard to any loss carried back from a subsequent tax year. A loss can only be included as an "overall domestic loss" if the taxpayer elected the use of the foreign tax credit for the tax year (Code Sec. 904(g)(2), as added by the 2004 Jobs Act).

Similar to the recharacterization rules for separate limitation losses in Code Sec. 904(f)(5)(E)(i), any U.S.-source income that is recharacterized as foreign-source income is allocated among the various separate limitation categories in the same proportion that those categories were reduced by the prior overall domestic losses (Code Sec. 904(g)(3), as added by the 2004 Jobs Act). In addition, the Secretary has been given the authority to prescribe regulations needed to coordinate this new provision with the recapture of overall foreign losses (Code Sec. 904(f) and (g)(4), as added by the 2004 Jobs Act).

Caution Note: As noted, the Code requires taxpayers to separately calculate their foreign tax credit for each of the nine baskets of income. However, Code Sec. 904(d)(1) has been amended by the 2004 Jobs Act, reducing the number of baskets to two for tax years beginning after December 31, 2006 (see ¶410). The rules for recharacterizing overall domestic losses make no reference to the change in the number of baskets or whether the calculation of the limitation for each basket (and overall) is affected.

Although many other changes have been made by this legislation, two are particularly pertinent to this analysis. The interest expense allocation rules under Code Sec. 864 have been amended by the 2004 Jobs Act, whereby an affiliated group of corporations is now allowed to make a one-time election to allocate and apportion interest expense of the domestic members of a worldwide affiliated group on a worldwide-group basis (see ¶405 and ¶407). In addition, the special recapture rules for overall foreign losses that currently apply to dispositions of foreign trade or business assets, now apply to the disposition of a taxpayer's stock in a controlled foreign corporation (CFC) (Code Sec. 904(f)(3)(D)(ii), as added by the 2004 Jobs Act (see ¶425)). To the extent the application of the new interest allocation method decreases the amount of interest expense that must be allocated and apportioned to a taxpayer's foreign-source gross income, thus increasing the foreign tax credit limitation, the taxpayer's foreign loss position may be lessened, and the amount of loss that ultimately must be recaptured may be reduced.

For further information on this subject, consult any of the following CCH reporter explanations:

- Standard Federal Tax Reporter, 2004FED ¶23,045.05, ¶27,901.01 and ¶28,394.01
- Federal Tax Service, FTS §M:11.42[1] and §M:11.121[4]
- Federal Tax Guide, 2004FTG ¶17,250

¶420

★ *Effective date.* The recharacterization of overall domestic losses applies to losses for tax years beginning after December 31, 2006 (Act Sec. 402(c) of the American Jobs Creation Act of 2004).

Act Sec. 402(a) of the American Jobs Creation Act of 2004, redesignating Code Sec. 904(g)–(k) as Code Sec. 904(h)–(l) and adding new Code Sec. 904(g) and amending Code Sec. 904(h)–(l); Act Sec. 402(b)(1), amending Code Sec. 535(d)(2); Act Sec. 402(b)(2), amending Code Sec. 936(a)(2)(A); Act Sec. 402(c). Law at ¶ 5425, ¶ 5655 and ¶ 5685. Committee Report at ¶ 10,580.

¶ 425

Recapture of Overall Foreign Losses on Sale of Controlled Foreign Corporation

Background _____

U.S. taxpayers are allowed to claim a foreign tax credit to reduce their U.S. tax liability on foreign-source income by the amount of foreign taxes paid on that income. The amount of credit that may be claimed is subject to an overall limitation under Code Sec. 904(a). This limitation operates so that the amount of foreign tax credit claimed by a taxpayer for the year cannot exceed the amount of U.S. tax imposed on its foreign-source income (which would otherwise occur where the tax rate imposed by a foreign country exceeds the U.S. rate). The limitation is calculated by multiplying the taxpayer's pre-credit U.S. tax liability for the year, by the ratio of the taxpayer's foreign-source taxable income to worldwide taxable income. A taxpayer is required to compute its foreign tax credit limitation separately for the nine various categories of income, generally known as "baskets" or "separate limitation categories."

Likewise, a taxpayer must generally track its losses on a basket-by-basket basis. For example, if a taxpayer earns $100 of foreign-source income which consists of $200 of general limitation income and a passive loss of $100, the taxpayer is required to track the items of income and loss separately. When a taxpayer has a net loss in a basket, otherwise known as a "separate limitation loss" (SLL) (as defined under Code Sec. 904(f)(5)(E)(iii)), that loss must first be allocated proportionately to reduce the taxpayer's income in other baskets with foreign-source income (Code Sec. 904(f)(5)(B)). To the extent the SLL for a limitation basket exceeds the taxpayer's aggregate separate limitation income in all baskets, the loss reduces U.S.-source income (Code Sec. 904(f)(5)(A)). Such an offset of U.S.-source income reduces the effective rate of U.S. tax on U.S.-source income. In order to eliminate a double benefit (that is, the reduction of U.S. tax previously noted and, later, full allowance of a foreign tax credit with respect to foreign-source income), present law includes an overall foreign loss (OFL) recapture rule (Code Sec. 904(f)(2)).

The taxpayer is required to establish an OFL account for the applicable loss basket and to adjust it to account for any future OFL recaptures and any additional overall foreign losses (Reg. § 1.904(f)-1(b)). Special recapture rules apply, so that if the taxpayer earns foreign-source income in the same basket that created the OFL, the taxpayer is required to recapture 50 percent (or more if the taxpayer elects) of the foreign-source income as U.S.-source income (Reg. § 1.904(f)-2(a)). The effect of the recapture is to reduce the foreign tax credit limitation in one or more years following an OFL year, and therefore, the amount of U.S. tax that can be offset by foreign tax credits in those years (Code Sec. 904(f)(1)).

A special recapture rule applies where property predominantly used in a taxpayer's foreign trade or business is disposed of before the time for recapturing the loss (Code Sec. 904(f)(3)). A taxpayer who disposes of such property must recognize

Background

the gain as foreign-source income (Code Sec. 904(f)(3)(A)(i)), but only to the extent of any overall foreign losses not previously recaptured as U.S.-source gain (Code Sec. 904(f)(3)(A)(ii)). This foreign-source income is re-sourced entirely as U.S.-source income without regard to the 50 percent limit (Code Sec. 904(f)(3)(A)(ii)). Without this rule, taxpayers could transfer foreign business-use property to another entity before the overall foreign loss is recaptured.

Example: The Conference Committee Report (H.R. Conf. Rep. No. 108-755) provides further clarification: "For example, if a U.S. corporation transfers its foreign branch business assets to a foreign corporation in a nontaxable section 351 transaction, the taxpayer would be treated for purposes of the recapture rules as having recognized foreign-source income in the year of the transfer in an amount equal to the excess of the fair market value of the property disposed over its adjusted basis (or the amount of unrecaptured foreign losses, if smaller). Such income would be recaptured as U.S.-source income to the extent of any prior unrecaptured overall foreign losses."

Comment: It is not uncommon for profitable U.S. multinational corporations to be in a chronic foreign loss position. In a situation where a U.S. parent is highly leveraged, the rules under Code Sec. 864(e) and Temporary Reg. § 1.861-9T require that a portion of such interest expense be allocated to foreign-source income. An overall foreign loss results to the extent foreign-source interest expense exceeds the taxpayer's foreign-source income.

Comment: Taking this a step further, the Senate Committee noted that ownership of stock in a foreign subsidiary can also lead to or increase, an overall foreign loss because of the rules requiring the allocation of interest expense against foreign-source income. They were concerned that the recapture of foreign losses created by such interest expense allocations could be avoided if the stock of the foreign subsidiary was subsequently transferred to unaffiliated parties in nontaxable transactions (Senate Committee Report (S. Rep. No. 108-192)).

Detailed rules apply in allocating and apportioning deductions and losses for foreign tax credit limitation purposes. Accordingly, the allocation and apportionment of interest expense must be made on the basis of assets rather than gross income. Under the asset method, the taxpayer apportions interest expense to the various statutory groupings based on the average total value of assets within each grouping for the tax year, under the asset valuation rules and asset characterization rules of Temporary Reg. §§ 1.861-9T(g) and 1.861-12T. A statutory grouping of gross income refers to gross income from a specific source or activity that must be determined in order to calculate taxable income. Since Code Sec. 904 is the operative section, the statutory groupings are foreign-source income in each of the Code Sec. 904(d) separate categories, and the residual grouping is U.S. source income. Assets are characterized according to the source and type of income the assets generate or can reasonably be expected to generate (Temporary Reg. § 1.861-9T(g)(3)).

Taxpayers may elect to value assets based on either tax book value or fair market value (Temporary Reg. § 1.861-9T(g)(1)(ii)). Use of the adjusted tax basis for purposes of apportioning expenses under the tax book value method may cause disparities between the bases of domestic and foreign assets. Assets used primarily outside the United States are depreciated using the alternative depreciation system (ADS) under Code Sec. 168(g). This method results in slower depreciation than that allowed under the modified accelerated cost recovery system (MACRS), which is the applicable method for assets used within the United States (Code Sec. 168(d)). This timing

¶425

difference causes more interest expense to be allocated to foreign-source income, which reduces both foreign-source income and the taxpayer's foreign tax credit limitation.

In addition, another timing difference can result when a U.S. corporation owns a 10 percent or greater interest in a foreign subsidiary that holds tangible property. Each member of an affiliated group is required to apportion its interest expense according to apportionment fractions determined by reference to all assets of the affiliated group, defined to include only domestic corporations (Temporary Reg. §§ 1.861-9T(g), 1.861-11T and 1.861-12T). Stock in a foreign subsidiary, however, is treated as a foreign asset. As such, it may attract the allocation of U.S. interest expense for these purposes. If tax basis is elected to value assets, the adjusted basis of the stock of 10-percent or more owned foreign subsidiaries (or other non-affiliated corporations), for purposes of the interest apportionment, must be increased by the corporation's earnings and profits accumulated during the period the U.S. share-holder held the stock (Temporary Reg. § 1.861-12T(c)(2)).

American Jobs Creation Act Impact

Recapture of overall foreign losses applies to sale of CFC stock.—The special recapture rules for overall foreign losses that currently apply to dispositions of foreign trade or business assets has been extended to the disposition of a taxpayer's stock in a controlled foreign corporation (CFC) (Code Sec. 904(f)(3)(D)), as added by the American Jobs Creation Act of 2004). The provision does not apply unless the taxpayer owns more than 50 percent of the CFC's stock (by vote or value) before the disposition (Code Sec. 904(f)(3)(D)(ii), as added by the 2004 Jobs Act). Such a disposition results in the recognition of foreign-source income in an amount equal to the lesser of the fair market value of the stock over its adjusted basis, or the amount of prior unrecaptured overall foreign losses (Code Sec. 904(f)(3)(A)).

> **Caution Note:** The total amount of income is re-sourced as U.S.-source income for foreign tax credit limitation purposes without regard to the 50-percent limit under Code Sec. 904(f)(1)(B), since the new provision falls within the purview of the rules pertaining to foreign trade or business asset dispositions under Code Sec. 904(f)(3)(A)(ii).

> **Comment:** This change reflects the Senate Committee's belief that disposi-tions of a CFC's stock should be subject to the special recapture rules for overall foreign losses, regardless of whether such stock is disposed of in a nontaxable transaction. As noted in the Background, the Committee was concerned that the recapture of overall foreign losses could otherwise be avoided if the stock of a foreign subsidiary was subsequently transferred to unaffiliated parties in non-taxable transactions. (Senate Committee Report (S. Rep. No. 108-192)).

Although the provision generally extends to all dispositions of such stock, exceptions are made for certain internal restructurings where ownership percentages are retained. Thus tax-free contributions to corporations or partnerships under Code Secs. 351 and 721, where ownership percentages are retained, do not trigger the recapture of overall foreign losses (Code Sec. 904(f)(3)(D)(iii)(I), as added by the 2004 Jobs Act). Similarly excepted are transactions under which the transferor receives stock in a foreign corporation in exchange for the stock in the CFC and the stock received is exchanged basis property, where ownership percentages are retained (Code Sec. 7701(a)(44), also referred to as, substituted basis property) (Code Sec. 904(f)(3)(D)(iii)(I), as added by the 2004 Jobs Act).

¶425

Also excepted from these overall foreign loss recapture rules are transactions in which the taxpayer, or any member of a controlled group of corporations filing a consolidated return under Code Sec. 1501 which includes the taxpayer, acquires the assets of a CFC in exchange for the shares of the CFC in a Code Sec. 332 liquidation, or a Code Sec. 368(a)(1) reorganization (Code Sec. 904(f)(3)(D)(iii)(II), as added by the 2004 Jobs Act).

Although there are exceptions from the overall foreign loss recapture rules for these dispositions, any gain, such as boot, that is recognized in one of these excepted transactions triggers the recapture of overall foreign losses to the extent of such gain (Code Sec. 904(f)(3)(D)(ii), as added by the 2004 Jobs Act).

Comment: As noted, the Code requires taxpayers to separately calculate their foreign tax credit for each of the nine baskets of income. However, Code Sec. 904(d)(1) has been amended by the 2004 Jobs Act, reducing the number of baskets to two for tax years beginning after December 31, 2006 (see ¶410). The rules for recapturing overall foreign losses make no reference to the change in the number of baskets or whether the calculation of the limit for each basket (and overall) is affected.

In addition, the interest expense allocation rules under Code Sec. 864 have also been amended by the 2004 Jobs Act. An affiliated group of corporations is now allowed to make a one-time election to allocate and apportion interest expense of the domestic members of a worldwide affiliated group on a world-wide-group basis (see ¶405 and ¶407). To the extent the application of this new method decreases the amount of interest expense that must be allocated and apportioned to a taxpayer's foreign-source gross income, the taxpayer's foreign loss position may be lessened, thus potentially reducing the amount of loss that ultimately must be recaptured.

PRACTICAL ANALYSIS. Katherine Stenander of McDermott Will & Emery, Chicago, Illinois, notes that this legislation represents a substantial departure from current law related to overall foreign loss (OFL) recapture because it applies to stock of a foreign corporation. Although the legislation does not apply to certain nonrecognition transactions, there is OFL recapture if gain would otherwise be recognized in such a transaction. The example in the Statement of Conference Managers includes gain recognized as a result of boot in a Code Sec. 351 or a Code Sec. 368 transaction. It seems that OFL recapture would also be triggered by the recognition of gain in a Code Sec. 351 or Code Sec. 368(a)(1)(D) transaction that recognizes gain under Code Sec. 357(c)— i.e., gain on the transferor of liabilities in excess of the tax basis of assets transferred.

This provision appears to apply only to first-tier CFCs (as there is no reference to indirect or constructive ownership in the statutory language), and it should not apply, for example, if a second-tier CFC recognized Code Sec. 357(c) gain on the transfer of assets to a third-tier CFC. Such gain could generally be subpart F income to the U.S. shareholder and would be foreign source income that would only be recaptured subject to the 50-percent limitation rather than subject to full 100-percent recapture.

A taxpayer is required to compute an OFL for each of its Code Sec. 904(d) categories. Taxpayers should consider the impact of the reduction of foreign tax credit limitation categories to two on their OFL positions. For example, for tax years beginning after December 31, 2006, it appears

that a taxpayer with an existing OFL in the financial services category will be required to treat such OFL as either general or passive, with potentially unexpected foreign tax credit results.

For further information on this subject, consult any of the following CCH reporter explanations:

- Standard Federal Tax Reporter, 2004FED ¶ 27,901.035
- Federal Tax Service, FTS § M:11.121[3]
- Federal Tax Guide, 2004FTG ¶ 17,250

★ *Effective date.* The provision shall apply to dispositions after the date of enactment (Act Sec. 895(b) of the American Jobs Creation Act of 2004).

Act Sec. 895(a) of the American Jobs Creation Act of 2004, adding Code Sec. 904(f)(3)(D); Act Sec. 895(b). Law at ¶ 5655. Committee Report at ¶ 11,670.

¶ 430

Look-through Treatment for Dividends from Noncontrolled Section 902 (10/50) Companies

Background _____

The foreign tax credit is generally limited to the amount of U.S. tax that is paid on foreign source income. The limitation is necessary to prevent the erosion of U.S. tax on U.S.-source income that can occur when a taxpayer earns income in a high-tax country. Under Code Sec. 904(a), the actual limitation is the lesser of the foreign tax paid or:

$$\text{U.S. pre-credit tax} \times \frac{\text{Foreign source taxable income}}{\text{Worldwide taxable income}}$$

The foreign tax credit limitation is calculated separately for certain categories of income (Code Sec. 904(d)). Without the separate limitation, taxpayers could inflate the foreign tax credit by averaging low-tax income and high-tax income. There is a separate foreign tax credit limitation category or "basket" for the following types of income:

(1) passive income;

(2) high withholding tax interest;

(3) financial services income;

(4) shipping income;

(5) dividends from noncontrolled section 902 corporations paid from pre-2003 earnings and profits;

(6) dividends from a domestic international sales corporation (DISC) or former DISC;

(7) distributions from a foreign sales corporation (FSC) or former FSC out of earnings and profits attributable to foreign trade income;

(8) taxable income attributable to Code Sec. 923(b) foreign trade income; and

(9) income not assigned to any of the categories above.

A U.S. corporation owning at least 10-percent of the voting stock of a foreign corporation is treated as if it had paid a portion of the foreign corporation's taxes upon the receipt of a dividend distribution from the foreign corporation (i.e., indirect

Background

or deemed-paid credit) (Code Sec. 902). A separate basket for dividends from a noncontrolled section 902 corporation ("10/50 company or corporation") was added by the Tax Reform Act of 1986 (P.L. 99-514). A 10/50 corporation is a foreign corporation with at least 10-percent but not more than 50-percent U.S. ownership (Code Sec. 904(d)(2)(E)).

When first enacted, the limitation applied on a corporation-by-corporation basis. The Taxpayer Relief Act of 1997 (P.L. 105-34) eliminated the corporation-by-corporation requirement and required instead that the limitation be determined according to the underlying earnings and profits from which the dividend was paid (look-through treatment), for earnings and profits accumulated in post-2002 tax years. Dividends paid from pre-2003 earnings and profits are assigned to a single 10/50 dividend basket, unless paid by a passive foreign investment company (PFIC) (Code Sec. 904(d)(4)). Dividends paid by a PFIC from pre-2003 earnings and profits are assigned to a 10/50 dividend basket on a corporation-by-corporation basis.

Code Sec. 904(c) provides that foreign income taxes paid or accrued in any tax year that exceed the foreign tax credit limitation can be carried back two years and forward five years.

American Jobs Creation Act Impact

Separate foreign tax credit limitation basket for dividends from 10/50 companies eliminated.—The separate foreign tax credit limitation category or "basket" for dividends received from noncontrolled section 902 corporations ("10/50 companies or corporations") and paid from pre-2003 accumulated earnings and profits is eliminated, for tax years beginning after December 31, 2002. Thus, taxpayers will no longer be required to determine a separate limitation for dividends received from 10/50 companies based on when the earnings and profits arose. Under the look-through rule, the dividend income is assigned to the appropriate foreign tax credit limitation basket in proportion to the ratio of the corporation's (1) earnings and profits attributable to income in that basket, to (2) total earnings and profits. Thus, the foreign tax credit limitation basket that applies is based on the underlying earnings and profits from which the distribution is made (Code Sec. 904(d)(4)(A), as amended by the American Jobs Creation Act of 2004).

> **Example:** Jtventure is a foreign corporation that has a 40% U.S. owner and a 60% foreign owner. For the 2003 tax year, Jtventure has earnings and profits of $200,000. The earnings and profits consist of $150,000 from its business operations and $50,000 in interest income. Thus, 75% of its earnings and profits are in the general limitation category and 25% of its earnings and profits are in the passive income category. If an $80,000 dividend were paid to the U.S. owner, under the look-through rule, 75% of the dividend, or $60,000, would be treated as general limitation income and 25% of the dividend, or $20,000, would be treated as passive income for purposes of the foreign tax credit limitation.

Look-through treatment will also apply to dividends from a 10/50 company that are first received by a controlled foreign corporation (CFC) and then distributed to a U.S. shareholder. The applicable foreign tax credit limitation basket is determined based on the underlying earnings and profits of the 10/50 company, even though the distribution passes through a CFC (Code Sec. 904(d)(4)(B), as amended by the 2004 Jobs Act).

> **Comment:** The changes made by the 2004 Jobs Act are intended to reduce significant compliance burdens associated with dividends received from 10/50

companies. Prior to the change, dividends paid in tax years beginning after 2002 were subject to a single-basket approach if paid from pre-2003 earnings and profits or look-through treatment if paid from post-2002 earnings and profits. The change also appears to be consistent with the reason for enacting the look-through rule in 1997, which was to reduce the bias against U.S. participation in foreign joint venture and investment by U.S. companies with minority foreign ownership (see Joint Committee on Taxation Study of the Overall State of the Federal Tax System and Recommendations for Simplification Pursuant to Section 8022(3)(B) of the Internal Revenue Code of 1986, JCS-3-01). Interestingly, the General Explanation of the Tax Reform Act of 1986, Joint Committee on Taxation, cites the complexity of the look-through rules as one reason for enacting the separate limitation for dividends from each noncontrolled section 902 corporation.

Caution Note: The IRS issued Notice 2003-5, I.R.B. 2003-3, 294, to provide guidance with respect to the foreign tax credit limitation and dividends paid by 10/50 companies. Some of the rules, however, are based on distinctions in treatment between dividends from pre-2003 and post-2002 earnings. The notice states that it can be relied upon until new regulations are issued.

Inadequate substantiation. In order for the look-through rule to apply, the taxpayer must substantiate that the dividend was assigned to the proper limitation basket. If the IRS determines that there has not been substantiation, the dividend will be treated as attributable to passive income, for purposes of the foreign tax credit limitation categories (Code Sec. 904(d)(4)(C)(ii), as amended by the 2004 Jobs Act). The Conference Committee Report (H.R. Conf. Rep. No. 108-755) notes that regulations will need to be reconsidered to make sure the high-tax income rules apply appropriately to dividends treated as passive income because of the inadequate substantiation rule.

Coordination with other baskets. The separate limitation basket for dividends from noncontrolled section 902 corporations took priority over other limitation categories. With the elimination of the separate limitation basket for dividends from noncontrolled section 902 corporations, rules that preserved this priority with respect to financial services income and shipping income are no longer necessary (Code Sec. 904(d)(2)(C)(iii)(II), prior to being stricken by the 2004 Jobs Act and Code Sec. 904(d)(2)(D), prior to amendment by the 2004 Jobs Act). The special rule relating to the separate limitation for high withholding tax interest has also been eliminated. That rule restricted deemed-paid credits for high withholding taxes (i.e., those in excess of 5-percent on interest received by noncontrolled section 902 corporations. The restriction was enacted in 1986 in lieu of a look-through rule (Code Sec. 904(d)(2)(E)(ii), prior to being stricken by the 2004 Jobs Act).

Comment: Note that for tax years beginning after December 31, 2006, the 2004 Jobs Act has reduced the number of foreign tax credit limitation baskets to two, a passive category income basket and a general category income basket (Code Sec. 904(d)(1), as amended by the 2004 Jobs Act; see ¶410).

Look-through rules that remain unchanged. The following rules, which were enacted along with the look-through rules by the Taxpayer Relief Act of 1997 (P.L. 105-34), remain unchanged:

(1) Earnings and profits are defined under Code Sec. 316 so that distributions are treated as made from the most recently accumulated earnings and profits (Code Sec. 904(d)(4)(C)(i)(I), as amended by the 2004 Jobs Act);

¶430

(2) The CFC look-through rules of Code Sec. 904(d)(3)(F) are applicable when determining separate categories and coordinating the high-taxed income rules (Code Sec. 904(d)(4)(C)(iii), as amended by the 2004 Jobs Act); and

(3) The IRS is authorized to prescribe regulations for the treatment of distributions made out of earnings and profits accumulated before the taxpayer acquired the stock (Code Sec. 904(d)(4)(C)(i)(II), as amended by the 2004 Jobs Act).

Caution Note: Notice 2003-5, I.R.B. 2003-3, 294, describes the rules for treating distributions made out of earnings and profits accumulated before a taxpayer acquires stock. The rules in the notice, however, are based on the distinction in treatment between dividends from pre-2003 and post-2002 earnings. For example, the notice states that the regulations will provide look-through treatment for dividends paid to a new qualifying shareholder by a 10/50 corporation out of "post-2002 earnings and profits" accumulated during a period when the foreign corporation was either a 10/50 corporation with respect to any qualifying shareholder or a CFC, but before the recipient became a shareholder. If dividends are paid out of "post-2002" earnings accumulated when the 10/50 corporation was not a 10/50 corporation with respect to any qualifying shareholder or a CFC, the general rule for "pre-2003" earnings apply. Earnings and profits accumulated in a tax year when a corporation becomes a 10/50 corporation are considered accumulated after the corporation becomes a 10/50 corporation.

Transitional rules for credit carryforwards and carryback. A special transitional rule allows look-through treatment with respect to excess foreign taxes attributable to dividends (excess credits) that are carried over under Code Sec. 904(c) from a tax year beginning before 2003. The IRS is authorized to issue regulations covering the carryback of taxes attributable to dividends from 10/50 companies from a tax year beginning on or after January 1, 2003, to pre-2003 tax years (Code Sec. 904(d)(4)(C)(iv), as added by the 2004 Jobs Act).

Caution Note: The transitional rule for credit carryforwards conflicts with the rule in Notice 2003-5, I.R.B. 2003-3, 294. Notice 2003-5 provides that excess credits carried forward from a pre-2003 year are placed in a single 10/50 basket. Thus, look-through treatment is not allowed. The notice does allow post-2002 excess credits in a look-through basket to be carried back to a pre-2003 tax year in a look-through basket.

Comment: The 2004 Jobs Act has also changed the foreign tax credit carryforward and carryback periods. For excess foreign tax credits that may be carried to any tax year ending after the date of enactment of the 2004 Jobs Act, the carryforward period is extended to 10 years. The carryback period has been reduced to one year and is also effective for excess foreign tax credits arising in tax years beginning after the date of enactment of the 2004 Jobs Act (Code Sec. 904(d)(1), as amended by the 2004 Jobs Act; see ¶415).

Planning Note: Because the provision is effective for tax years beginning after December 31, 2002, taxpayers may be required to recalculate their foreign tax credit limitation for 2003. Taxpayers must complete a separate Form 1118, Foreign Tax Credit-Corporations, for each separate category of income limitation.

PRACTICAL ANALYSIS. Lowell D. Yoder of McDermott Will & Emery, Chicago, Illinois, observes that the deemed paid tax credit rules of current law literally apply to dividends received by a corporate share-

holder. There has been some uncertainty concerning whether deemed paid tax credits are available when the dividend is received by a partnership with corporate partners. This provision makes it clear that a partnership is looked through for this purpose, and a corporate partner is entitled to a deemed paid tax credit if it owns 10 percent of the stock indirectly through the partnership. This is a particularly important clarification when the entity is a foreign company that is classified as a partnership for U.S. tax purposes because in the past the government has only been willing to apply look through principles to domestic general partnerships. Nevertheless, many have taken the position that deemed paid foreign tax credits are already available for foreign entities classified as partnerships if properly structured, but this provision provides certainty.

For further information on this subject, consult any of the following CCH reporter explanations:

- Standard Federal Tax Reporter, 2004FED ¶ 27,189.04 and ¶ 27,901.0229
- Federal Tax Service, FTS § M:11.102
- Federal Tax Guide, 2004FTG ¶ 17,225

★ *Effective date.* The provision applies to tax years beginning after December 31, 2002 (Act Sec. 403(c) of the American Jobs Creation Act of 2004).

Act Sec. 403(a) of the American Jobs Creation Act of 2004, amending Code Sec. 904(d)(4); Act Sec. 403(b)(1), repealing Code Sec. 904(d)(1)(E); Act Sec. 403(b)(2), striking Code Sec. 904(d)(2)(C)(iii)(II), and redesignating (III) as (II); Act Sec. 403(b)(3), amending Code Sec. 904(d)(2)(D); Act Sec. 403(b)(4), amending Code Sec. 904(d)(2)(E); Act Sec. 403(b)(5), amending Code Sec. 904(d)(3)(F); Act Sec. 403(b)(6), amending Code Sec. 864(d)(5)(A)(i); Act Sec. 403(c). Law at ¶ 5600 and ¶ 5655. Committee Report at ¶ 10,590.

¶ 435

Attribution of Stock Ownership Through Partnerships for Purposes of Deemed-Paid Credits

Background _____

The foreign tax credit may be claimed for foreign taxes paid directly and in some cases indirectly. An indirect or deemed-paid foreign tax credit can be claimed by a U.S. corporation that owns 10 percent or more of the voting stock of a foreign corporation (Code Sec. 902). The U.S. corporation is treated as if it had paid a portion of the foreign corporation's taxes upon the receipt of a dividend distribution from the foreign corporation. The amount of tax "deemed paid" is based on the ratio of the amount of the dividend to the foreign corporation's post-1986 undistributed earnings and profits. The credit is equal to the foreign corporation's post-1986 foreign taxes multiplied by that ratio.

The deemed-paid credit may be claimed for foreign taxes paid by lower-tier foreign corporations (through the sixth tier). The foreign corporation must be a member of a *qualified group*, and the foreign corporation must own 10 percent or more of the voting stock of the member of the qualified group from which the dividend is received. The qualified group includes a chain of corporations, including the first-tier foreign corporation and the foreign corporations not below the sixth tier. Each corporation in the chain must own at least 10 percent of the voting stock of the lower-tier corporation, and the domestic shareholder must own at least five percent of the

Background

voting stock of the foreign corporation indirectly through the chain (Code Sec. 902(b)).

A domestic corporation that must include subpart F income in gross income under Code Sec. 951(a) can claim a deemed-paid credit for the foreign taxes paid or accrued on the subpart F income of the controlled foreign corporation (CFC) under the rules of Code Sec. 902 (Code Sec. 960).

Although Code Sec. 902 is silent as to whether a domestic corporation can claim a deemed-paid credit for dividends received from a partnership or other passthrough entity, the IRS addressed this issue in Rev. Rul. 71-141, 1971-1 CB 211. In Rev. Rul. 71-141, the IRS ruled that two 50-percent domestic corporate general partners in a domestic general partnership could claim a deemed-paid credit for dividends received through the partnership. Questions remained, however, as to whether the deemed-paid credit could be claimed in other circumstances involving partnerships and flow-through entities (e.g., by domestic corporations that are partners in domestic limited partnerships or foreign partnerships or that are shareholders in limited liability companies). The IRS issued final regulations under Code Sec. 902 that affirmed Rev. Rul. 71-141, but did not solve whether the ruling applied beyond the domestic general partnership situation. Commentators on the proposed regulations uniformly argued that the aggregate theory of partnerships should apply to allow domestic corporate partners to compute the deemed-paid credit with respect to dividends paid to any partnership by a foreign corporation, provided that partner owns at least 10 percent of the voting stock of the corporation through the partnership (T.D. 8708, 1997-1 CB 137).

Individual partners, as well as individual beneficiaries of an estate or trust may claim a *direct foreign tax credit* for the proportionate share of the foreign taxes paid or accrued by the partnership, estate or trust (Code Sec. 901(b)(5)). The rule does not specifically cover corporate partners or beneficiaries of an estate or trust, although the IRS ruled in Rev. Rul. 71-141, discussed above, that corporate partners could claim a foreign tax credit for foreign withholding taxes. The partnership rules also provide that each partner, whether corporate or individual, must take into account separately its distributive share of the partnership's foreign taxes paid or accrued (Code Sec. 702(a)(6) and Reg. § 1.702-1(a)(6)).

American Jobs Creation Act Impact

Deemed-paid credits allowed where stock is owned through a partnership.— The eligibility rules for claiming a deemed-paid foreign tax credit have been clarified with respect to stock owned through partnerships. A U.S. corporation may claim the deemed-paid credit with respect to the stock in a foreign corporation that is owned directly or indirectly, by or for a partnership, whether foreign or domestic. Each partner is considered to own the stock in proportion to its interest in the partnership (Code Sec. 902(c)(7), as added by the American Jobs Creation Act of 2004 and the Conference Committee Report (H.R. Conf. Rep. No. 108-755)).

> **Example:** Two U.S. corporations, Far and Near, form a domestic partnership to acquire 40% of the voting stock of a foreign corporation. Each partner owns 50% of all of the assets in the partnership. Each partner is treated as owning 20% of the stock in the foreign corporation, thus meeting the 10% ownership rule of Code Sec. 902.

The stock that is constructively owned by a person under this rule is considered as actually owned by that person (Code Sec. 902(c)(7), as added by the 2004 Jobs Act).

Although not specifically stated in the Code, the new rule also applies to the Code Sec. 960 credit because the credit is determined under the rules of Code Sec. 902 (Code Sec. 960(a)(1)).

The Conference Committee Report (H.R. Conf. Rep. No. 108-755) states that no inference can be drawn as to the application of prior law. The IRS may issue regulations where necessary to account for special partnership allocations of dividends, credits and other incidents of ownership of stock in determining proportionate ownership (Code Sec. 902(c)(7), as added by the 2004 Jobs Act).

Direct foreign tax credit for corporate partners. The rule under Code Sec. 901(b)(5) that attributes the foreign taxes paid by a partnership, trust or estate to the individual partners and beneficiaries in proportion to their ownership now applies to "persons" who are members of a partnership or beneficiaries of an estate or trust. The term "person" includes an individual, trust, estate, partnership, association, company or corporation. Thus, the rule covers both individual and corporate partners and is comparable to the partnership attribution rules in Code Sec. 702(a)(6).

For further information on this subject, consult any of the following CCH reporter explanations:

- Standard Federal Tax Reporter, 2004FED ¶27,826.026 and ¶27,843.021
- Federal Tax Service, FTS §M:10.101
- Federal Tax Guide, 2004FTG ¶17,225

★ *Effective date.* The provision applies to taxes of foreign corporations for tax years of such corporations beginning after the date of enactment (Act Sec. 405(c) of the American Jobs Creation Act of 2004).

Act Sec. 405(a) of the American Jobs Creation Act of 2004, redesignating Code Sec. 902(c)(7) as (c)(8), and adding new Code Sec. 902(c)(7); Act Sec. 405(b), amending Code Sec. 901(b)(5); Act Sec. 405(c). Law at ¶5640 and ¶5645. Committee Report at ¶10,610.

¶ 440

Minimum Holding Period for Foreign Tax Credit on Withholding Taxes on Income Other Than Dividends

Background

U.S. taxpayers are allowed to reduce their U.S. tax liability on foreign-source income by the amount of foreign taxes paid on that income (Code Sec. 901). The amount of credit that may be claimed is subject to an overall limitation (Code Sec. 904). This limitation operates so that the amount of foreign tax credit claimed by a taxpayer for the tax year cannot exceed the amount of U.S. tax imposed on its foreign-source income. However, under no circumstances is the credit available to U.S. shareholders for any foreign withholding tax on a dividend from a corporation unless certain minimum holding period requirements are met (Code Sec. 901(k)). For income other than dividends, no minimum holding period is required for any foreign withholding tax.

American Jobs Creation Act Impact

Minimum holding rule for income other than dividends.—The disallowance of the foreign tax credit for withholding taxes on dividends not held for a minimum period is expanded. Generally, no foreign tax credit will be allowed for any withholding tax on any item of income or gain with respect to *any property*: (1) if the property is held by the recipient for 15 days or less during the 31-day period beginning 15 days before the right to receive payment arises; or (2) to the extent that the recipient is under an obligation to make related payments with respect to positions in substantially similar or related property (Code Sec. 901(l), as added by the American Jobs Creation Act of 2004). This rule applies whether or not the obligation arises in connection with a short sale or otherwise. For this purpose, a withholding tax includes any tax determined on a gross basis but does not include any tax which is in the nature of a prepayment of tax imposed on a net basis (Code Sec. 901(k)(1)(B)).

Exception for taxes paid by dealers. The holding period requirement does not apply to any qualified tax for any property held in the active conduct in a foreign country of a business as a dealer of such property (Code Sec. 901(l)(2), as added by the 2004 Jobs Act). A qualified tax means a tax paid to a foreign country (other than the foreign country in which the business is conducted) if: (1) the item to which the tax is attributable is subject to tax on a net basis by the foreign country in which the business is conducted; and (2) the foreign country in which the business is conducted allows a credit against its net basis tax for the full amount of the tax paid to such other foreign country.

In the case of securities, a dealer is any person who is: (1) registered as a securities broker or dealer under Section 15 of the Securities and Exchange Act of 1934; (2) registered as a government securities broker or dealer under Section 15C(a) of such Act; or (3) licensed or authorized in a foreign country to conduct securities activities in a foreign country and is subject to bona fide regulation by a securities regulating authority in that country. In the case of other property, a dealer is any person with respect to whom such property is described under Code Sec. 1221(a)(1) as stock in trade, of a kind which would be included in inventory if on hand at the close of the tax year, or held primarily for sale to customers in the ordinary course of the person's trade or business.

IRS regulations. The IRS may provide regulations to prevent the abuse of the dealer exception and to treat other taxes as qualified taxes. In addition, the IRS may provide rules to prevent the application of the general minimum holding period rule where it determines that the application of the rule to property is not necessary to carry out the purpose of the rule (Code Sec. 901(l)(3), as added by the 2004 Jobs Act).

Holding period. Rules similar for determining a U.S. shareholder's holding period of stock for this purpose will apply for determining the holding period of other property (Code Sec. 901(l)(4), as added by the 2004 Jobs Act). Thus, the holding period of other property is determined by taking into account the day property is disposed, but not the day of acquisition (Code Sec. 246(c)(3)). The holding period of property under the wash sales rules will not be added on for this purpose. In addition, the holding period will be computed without regard to the holding period rules for sales and exchanges of patents (Code Sec. 901(l)(5), as added by the 2004 Jobs Act). A U.S. taxpayer's holding period will be reduced for periods when the risk of loss is diminished (Code Sec. 246(c)(4)). An exception from the risk reduction rule exists for bona fide contracts to sell the property. Under such circumstances, the determination of whether the holding period requirement is met is made on the date the contract is entered into (Code Sec. 901(k)(6)).

Foreign tax deduction. Generally, a U.S. taxpayer may elect to claim a deduction for foreign taxes in lieu of the credit. However, no deduction will be permitted for foreign withholding taxes that are disallowed under the minimum holding period requirements (Code Sec. 901(k)(7)).

For further information on this subject, consult any of the following CCH reporter explanations:

- Standard Federal Tax Reporter, 2004FED ¶ 27,826.01 and ¶ 27,826.036
- Federal Tax Service, FTS § M:10.101[8]
- Federal Tax Guide, 2004FTG ¶ 17,060

★ *Effective date.* The provisions apply to amounts paid or accrued more than 30 days after the date of enactment (Act Sec. 832(c) of the American Jobs Creation Act of 2004).

Act Sec. 832(a) of the American Jobs Creation Act of 2004, redesignating Code Sec. 901(l) as (m) and adding new Code Sec. 901(l); Act Sec. 832(b), amending Code Sec. 901(k); Act Sec. 832(c). Law at ¶ 5640. Committee Report at ¶ 11,150.

¶ 445

Clarification of Treatment of Transfers of Intangible Property

Background

In an effort to minimize U.S. income and maximize foreign-source income, domestic corporations may be tempted to transfer intangible property overseas to foreign corporations via outright contributions or other nontaxable transactions. In order to prevent such temptation, Code Sec. 367(d) dictates that the outbound transfer of intangible property be treated as a sale of the property for a stream of contingent payments. These payments constitute ordinary income to the U.S. corporation, and the earnings and profits of the foreign corporation are reduced to reflect these amounts (Code Sec. 367(d)(2)).

Historically, these payments had been deemed to constitute U.S.-source income for the domestic corporation. This characterization, however, impeded U.S. corporations' ability to claim foreign tax credits and the rule was repealed by the Taxpayer Relief Act of 1997. By repealing the provision, Congress intended to help alleviate the federal tax burden of domestic corporations and allow them to claim greater foreign tax credits. As a result of the repeal, the deemed payments are currently categorized as royalties under the general sourcing rules and give rise to foreign-source income as long as the intangible is located outside the United States (Code Secs. 862(a) and 865(d)).

Congress did not, however, address the question of which foreign tax credit baskets the payments should fall under. If the deemed payments are treated like royalties, they could fall into the general basket under various look-through rules (Code Sec. 904(d)(3)). If, on the other hand, the payments are treated as proceeds from the sale of an intangible, they most likely fall into the passive basket (Code Sec. 904(d)(1)(A)).

American Jobs Creation Act Impact

Deemed payments under Code Sec. 367(d) characterized as royalties.—For purposes of applying the separate limitation categories of the foreign tax credit, i.e., placing the payments in the proper basket, deemed payments under Code Sec. 367(d) are characterized as royalties (Code Sec. 367(d)(2)(C), as amended by the American Jobs Creation Act of 2004).

> **Comment:** This categorization allows for many payments to fall into the general basket under look-through rules applicable to payments of dividends, interest, rents and royalties from controlled foreign corporations. In most cases, U.S. multi-national corporations have excess credits in their general basket, i.e., they pay more in creditable foreign tax than they are able to offset. These credits yield no tax benefit if not used within a carryover period. Allocating foreign

source income to the general basket, therefore, is normally preferred as it yields more opportunity to use credits. In addition, the average tax rate applicable to the income in the general basket is normally higher, adding further incentive to offset general income as much as possible.

Caution Note: The new rule has a retroactive effect.

For further information on this subject, consult any of the following CCH reporter explanations:

- Standard Federal Tax Reporter, 2004FED ¶ 16,677.04
- Federal Tax Service, FTS § M:18.60
- Federal Tax Guide, 2004FTG ¶ 17,235

★ *Effective date.* This provision applies to amounts treated as received pursuant to Code Sec. 367(d)(2) on or after August 5, 1997 (Act Sec. 406(b) of the American Jobs Creation Act of 2004).

Act Sec. 406(a) of the American Jobs Creation Act of 2004, amending Code Sec. 367(d)(2)(C); Act Sec. 406(b). Law at ¶ 5340. Committee Report at ¶ 10,620.

¶ 450
Translation of Foreign Taxes

Background

The United States taxes the worldwide income of U.S. persons and resident aliens without regard to where the activity that generates the income occurs. To mitigate the potential for double taxation of income from foreign sources, a U.S. taxpayer may claim a credit for foreign income taxes paid or accrued on such income for the tax year (Code Sec. 901).

For taxpayers that account for foreign income taxes on an accrual basis, the amount of foreign tax credit available for a particular tax year is generally determined by translating the amount of foreign income taxes paid for the year into U.S. dollars using the average exchange rate for that year (Code Sec. 986(a)). This rule, however, does not apply if the foreign income taxes are paid:

- more than two years after the close of the tax year;
- in a tax year prior to the year to which they relate; or
- in inflationary currency.

Foreign income taxes that fall into one of these exceptions, or that are accounted for on the cash basis, are translated into U.S. dollars using the exchange rate at the time they are actually paid. For this purpose, the date taxes are withheld is generally considered the date payment is made. In addition, a domestic corporation's deemed share of foreign income taxes paid by a foreign corporation in which it owns at least 10 percent of the voting stock is considered as taxes paid by the domestic corporation (Code Secs. 902 and 960). The IRS is authorized to issue regulations allowing foreign income taxes paid (or deemed paid) to be translated into U.S. dollars using the average exchange rate for a specified period (Code Secs. 986(a)(3) and 989(c)(6)).

American Jobs Creation Act Impact

Election not to use the average exchange rate.—A taxpayer that is otherwise required to translate foreign income taxes into U.S. dollars using the average exchange rate for the tax year may elect to translate such taxes using the exchange rate at the time the taxes are paid (or deemed paid) (Code Sec. 986(a)(1)(D), as added by the American Jobs Creation Act of 2004). The election, however, can only be made for foreign income taxes that are denominated in a currency other than the taxpayer's functional currency. Once made, the election applies to the taxpayer's current tax year and all subsequent tax years unless revoked with the consent of the IRS.

Generally, the functional currency of U.S. taxpayers will be the U.S. dollar (Code Sec. 985(b)). However, in the case of a qualified business unit (QBU), the functional currency is the currency in which it does a significant part of its business operations and maintains its books and records. For this purpose, a QBU is any separate and clearly identified unit of a trade or business of the taxpayer that keeps separate books and records (e.g., foreign subsidiary of a U.S. corporation or a foreign corporation) (Code Sec. 989(a)). The IRS is authorized to issue regulations with respect to the election by QBUs to use the exchange rate at the time the foreign income taxes are paid.

Special rule for mutual funds. For regulated investment companies (i.e., mutual funds) that account for income on the accrual basis, a special rule applies. The amount of foreign tax credit available for a particular tax year will be determined by translating the amount of foreign income taxes paid or accrued for that year into U.S. dollars at the exchange rate on the date the income accrues (Code Sec. 986(a)(1)(E), as added by the 2004 Jobs Act). Thus, accrual basis mutual funds are not eligible to elect to translate foreign taxes at the exchange rate on the date the taxes are paid or to use the average exchange rate for the tax year.

> **Comment:** A mutual fund may elect to pass its foreign tax credit through to its shareholders instead of claiming it on its own return (Code Sec. 853). If the election is made, the mutual fund must send shareholders a written notice within 60 days of the end of its tax year of each shareholder's proportionate share of foreign income taxes paid. The change in the law to require mutual funds to translate foreign taxes paid or accrued at the exchange rate on the date income accrues is intended to ensure that mutual funds meet this notice requirement.

For further information on this subject, consult any of the following CCH reporter explanations:

- Standard Federal Tax Reporter, 2004FED ¶ 28,861.024
- Federal Tax Service, FTS § M:10.124
- Federal Tax Guide, 2004FTG ¶ 17,090

★ *Effective date.* The provision applies to tax years beginning after December 31, 2004 (Act Sec. 408(c) of the American Jobs Creation Act of 2004).

Act Sec. 408(a) of the American Jobs Creation Act of 2004, redesignating Code Sec. 986(a)(1)(D) as (E) and adding new Code Sec. 986(a)(1)(D); Act Sec. 408(b), redesignating Code Sec. 986(a)(1)(E) as (F) and adding new Code Sec. 986(a)(1)(E); Act Sec. 408(c). Law at ¶ 5740. Committee Report at ¶ 10,640.

¶ 455

Limit on AMT Foreign Tax Credit Repealed

Background _____

The alternative minimum tax (AMT) foreign tax credit (FTC) reduces the pre-credit tentative minimum tax to arrive at the tentative minimum tax (Code Secs. 55(b)(1)(A)(i) and 55(b)(1)(B)(ii)). The AMT-FTC is the foreign tax credit that would be determined under the regular tax rules (Code Sec. 27(a)) if: (1) the pre-credit tentative minimum tax was the tax against which such credit was taken for purposes

Background _____

of the regular tax FTC limitation rules (Code Sec. 904), (2) the regular tax FTC limitation rules were applied on the basis of alternative minimum taxable income (AMTI) instead of taxable income, and (3) the determination of whether any income is high-taxed income under the FTC limitation rules was made on the basis of the applicable AMT rate(s) (Code Sec. 59(a)(1)). The pre-credit tentative minimum tax is the product of the appropriate AMT rate and the excess of the AMTI over a phased-out exemption amount (Code Sec. 55(b)(1)(A)(i)(I) and (II), 55(b)(1)(B)(i) and 59(a)(3)).

The AMT-FTC may not offset more than 90 percent of gross AMT, computed without regard to the AMT net operating loss deduction and the excess intangible drilling costs tax preference exception for independent oil and gas producers (Code Secs. 57(a)(2)(E) and 59(a)(2)). The tentative minimum tax as offset by any AMT-FTC is then compared to the regular tax. If it exceeds the regular tax, the difference constitutes AMT liability (Code Sec. 55(a)).

American Jobs Creation Act Impact

90-percent limit on AMT foreign tax credit repealed.—The 90-percent limit on use of the alternative minimum tax foreign tax credit (AMT-FTC) to offset AMT is repealed (Act Sec. 421(a)(1) of the American Jobs Creation Act of 2004, striking Code Sec. 59(a)(2)). As a result, taxpayers now have full use of alternative minimum tax foreign tax credits in computing AMT.

> **Caution Note:** Taxpayers must still apply regular tax FTC limitations in computing the AMT-FTC, even though the AMT-FTC, as so computed, may fully offset AMT (Code Sec. 59(a)(1)).

For further information on this subject, consult any of the following CCH reporter explanations:

- Standard Federal Tax Reporter, 2004FED ¶5003.021 and ¶5411.021
- Federal Tax Service, FTS § M:11.44
- Federal Tax Guide, 2004FTG ¶1320 and ¶17,470

★ *Effective date.* The provision applies to tax years beginning after December 31, 2004 (Act Sec. 421(b) of the American Jobs Creation Act of 2004).

Act Sec. 421(a)(1) of the American Jobs Creation Act of 2004, striking Code Sec. 59(a)(2) and redesignating Code Sec. 59(a)(3) and Code Sec. 59(a)(4) as Code Sec. 59(a)(2) and Code Sec. 59(a)(3), respectively; Act Sec. 421(a)(2), amending Code Sec. 53(d)(1)(B)(i)(II); Act Sec. 421(b). Law at ¶5075 and ¶5090. Committee Report at ¶10,770.

SUBPART F AND CONTROLLED FOREIGN CORPORATIONS

¶ 460

New Exceptions to Definition of U.S. Property

Background _____

The Code requires U.S. shareholders of a controlled foreign corporation (CFC) to include in gross income their proportionate share of certain income of the CFC regardless of whether it is distributed (Code Secs. 951 and 957). For this purpose, a U.S. shareholder is any U.S. person or entity that owns 10 percent or more of the total combined voting power of the CFC either directly or indirectly on the last day of the CFC's tax year. A foreign corporation is a CFC if more than 50 percent of its total voting power or value is owned by U.S. shareholders for an uninterrupted period of 30 days or more during the tax year.

A U.S. shareholder's gross income includes earnings of the CFC deemed to be invested in "U.S. property" during the tax year. A U.S. shareholder's proportionate share of CFC earnings invested in U.S. property is the lesser of: (1) the CFC's average investment in U.S. property as of the close of each quarter of the tax year (to the extent that such investments have not been previously subject to U.S. taxation); or (2) the CFC's current or accumulated earnings (but not including a deficit), reduced by any distributions made during the tax year and by earnings previously subject to U.S. taxation (Code Secs. 956 and 959). In essence, these rules mean that U.S. shareholders are being taxed on foreign source earnings brought back into the United States on the theory that they are substantially the same as a dividend (see Notice 2004-70 regarding whether such inclusions are treated as "qualified dividend income" under Code Sec. 1(h)(11)).

The term "U.S. property" is broadly defined to include tangible property (personal or real) located in the United States; stock of a domestic corporation; an obligation of a U.S. person; or any right to the use in the United States of a patent, copyright, invention, model, design, secret formula or process, or any other similar property right (Code Sec. 956(c)). The term also includes any trade or service receivable if it is acquired (directly or indirectly) from a related U.S. person and the obligor under such receivable is a U.S. person.

A number of items are specifically excepted from being considered "U.S. property" including:

• obligations of the United States, money, or deposits with any bank or any corporation which is not a bank but in which a bank holding company or financial holding company owns more than 80 percent of the stock (see ¶485);

• certain trade or business obligations;

• property located in the United States that is purchased for export to, or use in, a foreign country;

• any aircraft, railroad rolling stock, vessel, motor vehicle, or container used in the transportation of persons or property in foreign commerce that is used predominantly outside the United States;

• certain insurance company reserves and unearned premiums related to insurance of foreign risks;

• the stock or obligations of certain unrelated U.S. corporations;

• moveable property (other than a vessel or aircraft) that is used for the purpose of exploring or developing resources from waters connected with the U.S. continental shelf;

• an amount of assets equal to the accumulated earnings and profits of the CFC attributable to income effectively connected with a U.S. trade or business;

• to the extent provided in regulations, property held by a foreign sales corporation (FSC) that is related to its export activities;

• certain deposits of cash or securities made or received on commercial terms in the ordinary course of a U.S. or foreign person's business as a dealer in securities or commodities; and

Background _____

> • an obligation of a U.S. person to the extent the principal amount of the obligation does not exceed fair market value of readily marketable securities sold or purchase pursuant to a sale and repurchase agreement.

American Jobs Creation Act Impact

U. S. property not to include certain assets of controlled foreign corporation.— Two additions have been added to the list of property excluded from the definition of "U.S. property" for purposes of the controlled foreign corporation (CFC) rules. First, securities will not be considered U.S. property if they are acquired and held by the CFC in the ordinary course of its trade or business of being a securities dealer (Code Sec. 956(c)(2)(L), as added by the American Jobs Creation Act of 2004). This exception will only apply, however, if the CFC-dealer:

> (1) accounts for the securities as property held primarily for sale to customers in the ordinary course of business; and

> (2) disposes of the securities (or the securities mature while held by the CFC) within a period consistent with holding of securities for sale to customers in the ordinary course of business.

Comment: For this purpose, a CFC will be considered a securities dealer if it regularly purchases and sells securities to customers in the ordinary course of a trade or business (Code Sec. 475(c)(1)). It will also be a securities dealer if it regularly offers to enter into, assumes, offsets, assigns or otherwise terminates positions in securities with customers in the ordinary course of a trade or business. A CFC whose sole business consists of "trading" securities is not considered a dealer in securities (Rev. Rul. 97-39, 1997-2 CB 62).

The second new exception applies to the acquisition by a CFC of an obligation issued by any U.S. person that is not a domestic corporation and is not:

> (1) a U.S. shareholder of the CFC (i.e., owns 10 percent or more of the combined voting power of the CFC); or

> (2) a partnership, estate or trust in which the CFC (or any related person) is a partner, beneficiary or trustee immediately following the CFC's acquisition of the entity's obligation (Code Sec. 956(c)(2)(M), as added by the 2004 Jobs Act).

A person is related if it controls the CFC, or is controlled by the CFC or another person who also controls the CFC (Code Sec. 954(d)(3)). For this purpose, "control" means with respect to a corporation, ownership (directly or indirectly) of more than 50 percent of the total voting power of all classes of stock or the total value of all stock of the corporation. In the case of a partnership, estate or trust, "control" means ownership (directly or indirectly) of more than 50 percent of the value of the beneficial interests of the partnership, estate or trust.

For further information on this subject, consult any of the following CCH reporter explanations:

> • Standard Federal Tax Reporter, 2004FED ¶ 28,576.025

> • Federal Tax Service, FTS § M:8.123

> • Federal Tax Guide, 2004FTG ¶ 17,460 and ¶ 17,475

★ *Effective date.* This provision shall apply to tax years of foreign corporations beginning after December 31, 2004, and to tax years of U.S. shareholders with or within which such tax years of foreign corporations end (Act Sec. 407(c) of the American Jobs Creation Act of 2004).

Act Sec. 407(a) of the American Jobs Creation Act of 2004, adding Code Secs. 956(c)(2)(L)–(M); Act Sec. 407(b), amending Code Sec. 956(c)(2); Act Sec. 407(c). Law at ¶5725. Committee Report at ¶10,630.

¶ 465

Look-through Treatment for Sales of Partnership Interests

Background

U.S. shareholders with a 10-percent or greater interest in a controlled foreign corporation (CFC) must include in gross income for U.S. tax purposes their pro rata share of the CFC's subpart F income, whether or not that income is actually distributed (Code Secs. 951 and 957). Subpart F income includes foreign personal holding company income which, in turn, includes dividends, interest, royalties, rents and annuities, as well as net gains from the disposition of property that gives rise to such types of income, property that does not give rise to any income, and interests in trusts, partnerships and real estate mortgage investment conduits (Code Sec. 954). Net gains from the disposition of property held by the CFC in the ordinary course of its trade or business is not considered foreign personal holding company income. Under these rules, if a CFC sells a partnership interest at a gain, then the gain generally constitutes foreign personal holding company income and must be included in the gross income of U.S. shareholders with a 10-percent or greater interest of the CFC as subpart F income.

American Jobs Creation Act Impact

Look-through treatment for sales of partnership interests.—For purposes of determining subpart F foreign personal holding company income, the sale of a partnership interest by a CFC is treated as a sale of the proportionate share of partnership assets attributable to that interest. Thus, the sale of a partnership interest by a CFC constitutes subpart F income only to the extent that a proportionate sale of the underlying partnership assets attributable to the partnership interest would constitute subpart F income (Code Sec. 954(c)(4)(A), as added by the American Jobs Creation Act of 2004). This rule, however, applies only to CFCs that own directly, indirectly or constructively, at least 25 percent of a capital or profits interest in the partnership (Code Sec. 954(c)(4)(B), as added by the 2004 Jobs Act).

> **Example:** Lettco is a controlled foreign corporation with a 40 percent capital interest in the AMZ partnership. Upon sale of its partnership interest, Lettco realizes a gain of $1,000,000. If a sale of AMZ's assets would result in subpart F income with respect to 60% of those assets, then 60%, or $600,000 of the gain Lettco realized, would be treated as subpart F income, and would be included in the income of Lettco's U.S. shareholders with a 10-percent or greater interest as subpart F income.

PRACTICAL ANALYSIS. Lowell D. Yoder of McDermott Will & Emery, Chicago, Illinois, notes that this is an important amendment that treats gain derived by a controlled foreign corporation from the sale of an interest in a partnership the same as gain from the sale of the interests in a disregarded entity. Therefore, if the partnership has only assets used in a trade or business, the gain on the sale of the interest in the partnership will not be subpart F income. Correspondingly, the CFC's resulting earnings should not be passive for purposes of the foreign tax credit rules. Note, however, that there must be a minimum ownership in the partnership of 25 percent and it does not appear that constructive

ownership rules apply for this purpose (i.e., only direct and down-stream ownership is counted).

For further information on this subject, consult any of the following CCH reporter explanations:

- Standard Federal Tax Reporter, 2004FED ¶ 28,543.025 and ¶ 28,543.04
- Federal Tax Service, FTS § M:11.100
- Federal Tax Guide, 2004FTG ¶ 17,445

★ *Effective date.* The amendment made by this section shall apply to tax years of foreign corporations beginning after December 31, 2004, and tax years of U.S. shareholders with or within which such tax years of such foreign corporations end (Act Sec. 412(b) of the American Jobs Creation Act of 2004).

Act Sec. 412(a) of the American Jobs Creation Act of 2004, adding Code Sec. 954(c)(4); Act Sec. 412(b). Law at ¶ 5720. Committee Report at ¶ 10,680.

¶ 470

Determination of Foreign Personal Holding Company Income With Respect to Transactions in Commodities

Background

U.S. shareholders with a 10-percent or greater interest in a controlled foreign corporation (CFC) must include in gross income for U.S. tax purposes their pro rata share of the CFC's subpart F income, whether or not that income is actually distributed (Code Secs. 951 and 957). Subpart F income includes foreign personal holding company (FPHC) income. FPHC income includes, among other things, dividends, interest, royalties, rents and annuities, as well as net gains from the disposition of property that gives rise to such types of income, property that does not give rise to any income, and interests in trusts, partnerships and real estate mortgage investment conduits (Code Sec. 954). Net gains from the disposition of property held by the CFC in the ordinary course of its trade or business is not considered foreign personal holding company income.

FPHC income does include net gains from commodities transactions (Code Sec. 954(c)(1)(C)). However, FPHC income will not consist of gains or losses which arise out of bona fide hedging transactions that are reasonably necessary to the conduct of any business by a producer, processor, merchant or handler of a commodity in the manner in which such business is customarily and usually conducted by others. In addition, if substantially all of a CFC's business is conducted as an active producer, processor, merchant, or handler of commodities, then gains or losses from the sale of commodities from that active business will not be considered FPHC income.

American Jobs Creation Act Impact

Determination of foreign personal holding company income with respect to transactions in commodities.—The requirements that must be satisfied for net gains from commodities transactions to qualify for the exclusion of subpart F FPHC income have been modified. Net gains from such transactions will not be included in FPHC income if they arise out of commodity hedging transactions (Code Sec. 954(c)(1)(C)(i), as amended by the American Jobs Creation Act of 2004). A commodity hedging transaction means a hedging transaction with respect to a commodity, entered into by a CFC in the normal course of its trade or business, primarily: (1) to manage the risk of price changes or currency fluctuations with respect to ordinary property or property used in a trade or business (Code Sec. 1231(b) property); or (2) to manage such other risks as the Secretary may prescribe in regulations (Code Sec. 954(c)(5), as added by the 2004 Jobs Act). For this exception to apply, a commodity hedging transaction must be clearly identified as such in accordance with Code Sec. 1221(a)(7).

> **Caution Note:** The 2004 Jobs Act amends Code Sec. 954(c)(1)(C)(i) to refer to Code Sec. 954(c)(4)(A) for the definition of a commodity hedging transaction. However, that Code section addresses look-through rules for sales of certain partnership interests. The definition of commodity hedging transactions is contained in Code Sec. 954(c)(5), as added by the 2004 Jobs Act.

Net gains from commodities transactions will also not be included in FPHC income if they are active business gains or losses from the sale of commodities (Code Sec. 954(c)(1)(C)(ii), as amended by the 2004 Jobs Act). However, this exception will only apply if substantially all of the CFC's commodities are:

- stock in trade of the CFC or other property of a kind which would properly be included in the inventory of the CFC or property held by the CFC primarily for sale to customers in the ordinary course of the CFC's trade or business (Code Sec. 1221(a)(1));

- property used in the trade or business of the CFC and of a character which is subject to the allowance for depreciation under Code Sec. 167, or real property used in the trade or business (Code Sec. 1221(a)(2)); or

- supplies of a type regularly used or consumed by the CFC in the ordinary course of a trade or business of the CFC (Code Sec. 1221(a)(8)).

For purposes of this provision, commodities with respect to which gains and losses will not be taken into account under Code Sec. 954(c)(2)(C) because the CFC is a regular dealer in forward contracts, option contracts, or other similar financial instruments, will not be taken into account for purposes of the "substantially all" test. Additionally, the dealer exception rule has been modified to exclude items of income, gain deduction or loss from transactions involving physical settlement when calculating FPHC income (Code Sec. 954(c)(2)(C)(i), as amended by the 2004 Jobs Act).

For further information on this subject, consult any of the following CCH reporter explanations:

- Standard Federal Tax Reporter, 2004FED ¶ 28,543.025 and ¶ 28,543.067
- Federal Tax Service, FTS § M:8.63
- Federal Tax Guide, 2004FTG ¶ 17,445

★ *Effective date.* The amendments made by this section apply to transactions entered into after December 31, 2004 (Act Sec. 414(d) of the American Jobs Creation Act of 2004).

Act Sec. 414(a) of the American Jobs Creation Act of 2004, amending Code Sec. 954(c)(1)(C); Act Sec. 414(b), adding Code Sec. 954(c)(5); Act Sec. 414(c), amending Code Sec. 954(c)(2)(C)(i); Act Sec. 414(d). Law at ¶ 5720. Committee Report at ¶ 10,700.

¶ 475

Modification of Treatment of Aircraft Leasing and Shipping Income

Background ⎯⎯⎯⎯⎯⎯⎯⎯⎯⎯⎯⎯⎯⎯⎯⎯⎯⎯⎯⎯⎯⎯⎯⎯⎯⎯⎯⎯⎯⎯⎯⎯⎯⎯⎯⎯⎯

The subpart F rules require that a U.S. shareholder of a controlled foreign corporation (CFC) include in income, a pro rata share of the CFC's subpart F income. One type of subpart F income is foreign base company shipping income (Code Sec. 954(f)). Foreign base company shipping income generally includes income from the

Background _____

use of an aircraft or vessel in foreign commerce. Foreign base company shipping income also includes income from the performance of services or the sale or disposition of the aircraft or vessel.

Another type of subpart F income is foreign personal holding company income (Code Sec. 954(c)). Foreign personal holding company income generally includes such income as dividends, rents, royalties and interest.

Rents and royalties that are received from unrelated persons and derived in the active conduct of a trade or business may be excluded from foreign personal holding company income (Code Sec. 954(c)(2)(A)).

Under the general rules of Reg. § 1.954-2(c), a lessor will qualify for the active trade or business exception if the rents are derived from property that is leased by the lessor as a result of marketing functions carried on by the lessor's officers or employees through an organization maintained in another country. The organization maintained and operated in the foreign country must regularly engage in the business of marketing, or marketing and servicing, the leased property. The business of marketing, or marketing and servicing, must be substantial in relation to the rents derived from the leased property.

The "substantial business" requirement can be met either under a facts and circumstances test or by complying with a safe harbor in the regulations. Under the safe harbor, an organization in a foreign country is substantial in relation to rents if the active leasing expenses equal at least 25 percent of the adjusted leasing profit (Reg. § 1.954-2(c)(2)(ii)).

"Active leasing expenses" include the Code Sec. 162 business expenses that are properly allocated to rental income. Deductions for employee and shareholder compensation, rent, depreciation and payments to independent contractors are excluded (Reg. § 1.965-2(c)(2)(iii)). "Adjusted leasing profit" means rental income less rent paid or accrued, depreciation and payments to independent contractors (Reg. § 1.954-2(c)(2)(iv)).

_____

American Jobs Creation Act Impact

Elimination of foreign base company shipping income as subpart F income, safe harbor for leasing income.—Foreign base company shipping income is no longer defined as subpart F income, effective for tax years of foreign corporations beginning after December 31, 2004, and for tax years of U.S. shareholders with or within which such tax years of foreign corporations end (Code Sec. 954(a)(4) and (f), repealed by the American Jobs Creation Act of 2004). Additionally, the exception from foreign personal holding company income for active rents is made more favorable with respect to income from leasing aircraft and vessels in foreign commerce (Code Sec. 954(c)(2)(A), as amended by the 2004 Jobs Act).

> **Comment:** The U.S. imposes an immediate U.S. tax on foreign shipping income; other countries do not. Removing shipping income from subpart F classification will provide U.S. shippers the opportunity to be competitive with their tax-advantaged foreign competitors. In addition, for the same competitive reasons, the exception from foreign base company income for rents and royalties received by a controlled foreign corporation (CFC) in the active conduct of a trade or business from related persons is too narrow in the context of the leasing of an aircraft or vessel in foreign commerce (House Committee Report (H.R. Rep. No. 108-548)).

¶475

Foreign personal holding company safe harbor for leasing activities. A new 10-percent safe-harbor rule applies for purposes of determining whether a lessor's income from leasing aircraft and vessels in foreign commerce may be excluded from foreign personal holding company income under the active trade or business test in Code Sec. 954(c)(2)(A). Specifically, the exception for rents received in the active conduct of a trade or business will apply if the active leasing expenses are not less than 10 percent of the profits on the lease. The regulations under Code Sec. 954(c)(2)(A) must be used when applying the safe harbor rule (Code Sec. 954(c)(2)(A), as amended by the 2004 Jobs Act and the House Committee Report (H.R. Rep. No. 108-548)).

Under the rules that now apply to the leasing of aircraft and vessels in foreign commerce, an organization will be considered substantial in relation to rents if the active leasing expenses equal at least 10 percent of the adjusted leasing profit (see Reg. § 1.954-2(c)(1)(iv) and Reg. § 1.954-2(c)(2)).

> **Comment:** The characterization of leasing income of aircraft and vessels in foreign commerce as subpart F income has been a recurring issue for many years. Such issues have surfaced, for example, in FSAs, as well as in comments from Congressional leaders. As discussed above, one measure of "active conduct of a trade or business" in IRS regulations focuses on the percentage of leasing expenses in relationship to profits, and specifies 25% as the threshold percentage. Many taxpayers would have preferred that the focus not be on a percentage of expenses at all but on the "degree of activity". It would appear that Congress settled somewhere "in the middle" at 10%. By lowering the threshold to 10%, taxpayers now need to incur fewer leasing expenses than before in order to avoid immediate taxation of leasing income under subpart F.

Facts and circumstances. A lessor may also demonstrate that it meets the active trade or business test under the facts and circumstances test. The requirements of Code Sec. 954(c)(2)(A) will be met if the lessor regularly and directly performs active and substantial marketing, remarketing, management, and operational functions with respect to the leasing of an aircraft or vessel (or component engines). The rule applies regardless of whether the marketing of the lease is a form of financing or whether the lease is classified as a financing lease or an operating lease for financial accounting purposes (House Committee Report (H.R. Rep. No. 108-548)).

Leased in foreign commerce. An aircraft or vessel is "leased in foreign commerce" if it is used for the transportation of property or passengers between:

(1) a U.S. port or airport and a foreign port or airport, or

(2) between foreign ports or airports.

In both cases, the aircraft or vessel must be predominately used outside of the United States. This means that more than 50 percent of the miles are traveled outside of the United States or the aircraft or vessel is located outside of the United States more than 50 percent of the time during the tax year (House Committee Report (H.R. Rep. No. 108-548)).

An aircraft or vessel includes engines that are leased separately from the aircraft or vessel (Conference Committee Report (H.R. Conf. Rep. No. 108-755)).

Future regulations. The regulations will be amended to reflect the changes made by the 2004 Jobs Act. Additional rules will provide that aircraft or leasing activity that meets the requirements of Code Sec. 954(c)(2)(A) will also be excluded from income under Code Sec. 956 (subpart F inclusion for CFC earnings invested in U.S. real property) and Code Sec. 367(a) (transfers by U.S. persons to foreign corporation) (House Committee Report (HR. Rep. No. 108-548)).

¶475

Lease acquisitions. A lessor may acquire from either a related or unrelated party an aircraft or vessel subject to an existing lease. The requirements of Code Sec. 954(c)(2)(A) will be met if the lessor performs active and substantial management, operational, and remarketing functions. The transfer of an existing FSC or ETI lease to a CFC lessor will terminate FSC or ETI benefits (Conference Committee Report (H.R. Rep. No. 108-755)).

Restructuring operations. The structuring or restructuring of operations for the purpose of adapting to the repeal of ETI or the FSC rules will be considered to serve a valid business purpose and not to constitute tax avoidance. As an example, the Conference Committee states that a restructuring undertaken to transfer aircraft subject to an existing FSC or ETI lease to a CFC lessor would not constitute tax avoidance. Thus, nonrecognition of gain could apply to the restructuring, and if applicable, the restructuring could meet the requirements of Code Sec. 368 (Conference Committee Report (H.R. Conf. Rep. No. 108-755)).

For further information on this subject, consult any of the following CCH reporter explanations:

- Standard Federal Tax Reporter, 2004FED ¶28,543.01, ¶28,543.025 and ¶28,543.028

- Federal Tax Service, FTS § M:8.63[1] and § M:8.66

- Federal Tax Guide, 2004FTG ¶17,445

★ *Effective date.* The amendments shall apply to tax years of foreign corporations beginning after December 31, 2004, and to tax years of U.S. shareholders with or within which such tax years of foreign corporations end (Act Sec. 415(d) of the American Jobs Creation Act of 2004).

Act Sec. 415(a) of the American Jobs Creation Act of 2004, striking Code Sec. 954(a)(4) and (f); Act Sec. 415(b), amending Code Sec. 954(c)(2)(A); Act Sec. 415(c), amending Code Secs. 952(c)(1)(B)(iii) and 954(b); Act Sec. 415(d). Law at ¶5720. Committee Report at ¶10,710.

¶ 480

Modification of the Subpart F Foreign Personal Holding Company Income Exception for Active Financing

Background ―――――――――――――――――――――――――――――

A U.S. shareholder of a controlled foreign corporation (CFC) must include in income the pro rata share of the CFC's subpart F income. Subpart F income includes both foreign personal holding company income and foreign base company services income (Code Sec. 954(a)). Under a temporary exception that extends through 2006, foreign personal holding company income and foreign base company services income do not include certain income derived in the active conduct of a banking, financing or similar business, or in the conduct of an insurance business (so-called active financing income) (Code Sec. 954(h), 954(e)(2) and 954(i)). For purposes of excluding the qualified banking, financing or similar business income of an eligible CFC, the income must be earned in the active conduct of the business by a CFC or its qualified business unit (QBU). Additionally, the income must be derived from transactions, substantially all of which are conducted *directly* by the CFC or QBU in the home country.

American Jobs Creation Act Impact

Active financing exception under subpart F modified.—The American Jobs Creation Act of 2004 eases the rules for applying the subpart F exception for income earned in the active conduct of a banking, financing or similar business.

> **Comment:** The rules for determining whether income earned by an eligible controlled foreign corporation (CFC) or qualified business unit (QBU) is active financing income are now more consistent with the rules for determining whether a CFC or QBU is eligible to earn active financing income (House Committee Report (H.R. Rep. No. 108-548)).

Code Sec. 954(h)(3)(A)(ii)(II) defines qualified banking or financing income as income of an eligible CFC which is derived from one or more transactions substantially all of the activities in connection with which are conducted directly by the CFC or QBU in its home country. For purposes of this definition, an activity will be treated as conducted directly by an eligible CFC or QBU in its home country if the activity is performed by employees of a related person and (1) the related person is an eligible CFC with the same home country as the CFC or QBU to which Code Sec. 954(h)(3)(A)(ii)(II) is being applied; (2) the activity is performed in the home country of the related person; and (3) the related person is compensated on an arm's-length basis for its employees' activities, and the compensation is treated as earned by the person in its home country for purposes of the home country's tax laws. For purposes of determining whether a CFC or QBU is eligible to earn active financing income, such activity may not be taken into account by any CFC or QBU (including the employer of the employees performing the activity) other than the CFC or QBU for which the activities are performed (House Committee Report (H.R. Rep. No. 108-548)).

For further information on this subject, consult any of the following CCH reporter explanations:

- Standard Federal Tax Reporter, 2004FED ¶28,543.0662 and ¶28,543.0666
- Federal Tax Service, FTS §M:8.63[6]
- Federal Tax Guide, 2004FTG ¶17,445

★ *Effective date.* This amendment applies to tax years of such foreign corporations beginning after December 31, 2004, and to tax years of U.S. shareholders with or within which such tax years of such foreign corporations end (Act Sec. 416(b) of the American Jobs Creation Act of 2004).

Act Sec. 416(a) of the American Jobs Creation Act of 2004, adding Code Sec. 954(h)(3)(E); Act Sec. 416(b). Law at ¶5720. Committee Report at ¶10,720.

¶485

Clarification of Items Not Considered U.S. Property

Background —————————————————————————————————

The Code requires U.S. shareholders of a controlled foreign corporation (CFC) to include in gross income their proportionate share of certain income of the CFC regardless of whether it is distributed (Code Secs. 951 and 957). For this purpose, a U.S. shareholder is any U.S. person or entity that owns 10 percent or more of the total combined voting power of the CFC either directly or indirectly on the last day of the CFC's tax year. A foreign corporation is a CFC if more than 50 percent of its total voting power or value is owned by U.S. shareholders for an uninterrupted period of 30 days or more during the tax year.

Background

A U.S. shareholder's gross income includes earnings of the CFC deemed to be invested in "U.S. property" during the tax year. A U.S. shareholder's proportionate share of CFC earnings invested in U.S. property is the lesser of: (1) the CFC's average investment in U.S. property as of the close of each quarter of the tax year (to the extent that such investments have not been previously subject to U.S. taxation); or (2) the CFC's current or accumulated earnings (but not including a deficit), reduced by any distributions made during the tax year and by earnings previously subject to U.S. taxation (Code Secs. 956 and 959). In essence, these rules mean that U.S. shareholders are being taxed on foreign source earnings brought back into the United States on the theory that they are substantially the same as a dividend (see Notice 2004-70 regarding whether such inclusions are treated as "qualified dividend income" under Code Sec. 1(h)(11)).

The term "U.S. property" is broadly defined to include tangible property (personal or real) located in the United States; stock of a domestic corporation; an obligation of a U.S. person; or any right to the use in the United States of a patent, copyright, invention, model, design, secret formula or process, or any other similar property right (Code Sec. 956(c)). The term also includes any trade or service receivable if it is acquired (directly or indirectly) from a related U.S. person and the obligor under such receivable is a U.S. person.

A number of items are specifically excepted from being considered "U.S. property" including obligations of the United States, money, or deposits with persons carrying on the banking business (Code Sec. 956(c)(2)(A)). The Code does not define what constitutes "carrying on the banking business" for this purpose. However, the U.S. Court of Appeals for the Sixth Circuit has ruled that the phrase refers to ordinary and natural banking services that may be provided by a taxpayer, as opposed to any particular form of banking business (*Limited, Inc.*, CA-6, 2002-1 USTC ¶ 50,353, 286 F3d 324, *rev'g*, 113 TC 169, Dec. 53,533. Thus, the exception for deposits with persons carrying on the banking business applied where the CFC of a consolidated manufacturer and retail sales group purchased (through its subsidiary) certificates of deposit from the group's affiliated domestic credit card company. The credit card company was a nationally chartered bank that issued credit cards, extended credit, received loan payments and accepted certain deposits.

American Jobs Creation Act Impact

Clarification of banking business for purposes of determining investment of earnings in U. S. property.—The exception from the definition of U.S. property for deposits under Code Sec. 956 is now based on definitions from the Bank Holding Company Act of 1956, rather than whether the deposits are made with persons carrying on the banking business. The phrase "carrying on the banking business" has been removed, and the Conference Committee Report states that no inference can be drawn as to the phrase's meaning under present law (H.R. Conf. Rep. No. 108-755). The exception is limited to deposits with: (1) any bank; or (2) any corporation which is not a bank, but in which a bank holding company or financial holding company, directly or indirectly owns more than 80 percent of vote or the value of the corporation's stock (Code Sec. 956(c)(2)(A), as amended by the American Jobs Creation Act of 2004).

For this purpose, a bank is generally defined as any institution organized under U.S. law (including state or territorial law) that accepts demand deposits and is engaged in the business of making commercial loans (12 U.S.C. § 1841(c)). It also includes any bank in which the deposits are insured under the Federal Deposit Insurance Act. A bank holding company is any company that:

(1) has control over any bank by directly or indirectly owning at least 25 percent of any class of securities of the bank;

(2) has control over any bank by controlling in any manner the election of a majority of the directors or trustees of the bank; or

(3) is determined to directly or indirectly exercise a controlling influence over the management or policies of the bank (12 U.S.C. § 1841(a)).

A financial holding company is any bank holding company that files an election with the Federal Reserve Board to be treated as a financial holding company, and that certifies that all of its depository institution subsidiaries are well capitalized and well managed (12 U.S.C. § § 1841(p) and 1843(l)(1)).

> **Comment:** In *Limited, Inc.*, the Court of Appeals specifically held that there was no legal basis for applying 12 U.S.C. § 1841(c)(2)(F), which excludes credit card companies from the definition of "bank." It appears that the changes made by the 2004 Jobs Act are intended not only to provide a clearer definition of deposits excepted from the definition of U.S. property, but also to prevent decisions like the one in *Limited, Inc.*

For further information on this subject, consult any of the following CCH reporter explanations:

- Standard Federal Tax Reporter, 2004FED ¶ 28,576.025
- Federal Tax Service, FTS § M:8.123
- Federal Tax Guide, 2004FTG ¶ 17,445

★ *Effective date.* The amendment made by this section shall take effect on the date of enactment (Act Sec. 837(b) of the American Jobs Creation Act of 2004).

Act Sec. 837(a) of the American Jobs Creation Act of 2004, amending Code Sec. 956(c)(2)(A); Act Sec. 837(b). Law at ¶ 5725. Committee Report at ¶ 11,200.

¶ 490

Repeal of Foreign Personal Holding Company and Foreign Investment Company Rules

Background _____

At present, several sets of anti-deferral rules impose current U.S. tax on certain income earned by a U.S. person through a foreign corporation. Detailed rules for coordination among the anti-deferral rules are provided to prevent the U.S. person from being subject to U.S. tax on the same item of income under multiple rules. These rules include the subpart F controlled foreign corporation (CFC) rules in Code Secs. 951–964, the passive foreign investment company (PFIC) rules in Code Secs. 1291–1298, the foreign personal holding company (FPHC) rules in Code Secs. 551–558, the accumulated earnings tax rules in Code Secs. 531–537 and the foreign investment company rules in Code Secs. 1246–1247.

> **Comment:** The Conference Committee Report indicates that the overlap among the various anti-deferral regimes results in significant complexity, usually with little or no ultimate tax consequences. The overlaps require the application of specific rules of priority for income inclusions among the regimes, as well as additional coordination provisions pertaining to other operational differences

among the various regimes (Conference Committee Report (H.R. Conf. Rep. No. 108-755)).

American Jobs Creation Act Impact

Repeal of foreign personal holding company and foreign investment company rules.—The American Jobs Creation Act of 2004 repeals Code Sec. 1246, relating to the gain on foreign investment company stock, Code Sec. 1247, relating to the election by foreign investment companies to distribute income currently, and most significantly, the foreign personal holding company (FPHC) rules under Code Secs. 551–558. The 2004 Jobs Act also excludes foreign corporations from the application of the personal holding company rules under Code Sec. 543, and expands the foreign base company income rules under subpart F to treat income from personal services contracts as FPHC income (Code Sec. 954(c)(1)(I), as added by the 2004 Jobs Act).

Under prior law, income that would have been taxable under the FPHC rules may also have been taxable under the subpart F rules governing controlled foreign corporations (CFCs). However, Code Sec. 951(d) coordinated the taxation of overlap situations by stating that amounts included in a U.S. shareholder's income under both provisions were considered to be included only under subpart F.

> **Comment:** This income was more likely to be taxed as subpart F income anyway, because of the more restrictive "de minimis" rule in Code Sec. 954(b)(3). Accordingly, taxation under subpart F can be avoided if the sum of foreign base company income and gross insurance income for the tax year is less than the lesser of 5 percent of gross income, or $1,000,000. However, according to Code Sec. 552(a)(1), a foreign corporation was able to avoid being taxed under the FPHC rules only if less than 50 percent of its gross income was foreign personal holding company income.

Code Sec. 954(c), which addresses FPHC income within the context of foreign base company income, has not only been retained, but expanded by the present legislation. In addition, Code Sec. 1293, which is unaffected by the 2004 Jobs Act, overlapped with Code Sec. 551 in the case of passive foreign investment companies. As already noted, Code Secs. 551–558 have been repealed by the 2004 Jobs Act.

Code Secs. 1246–1247 contained rules regarding gain on foreign investment company stock and the election by foreign investment companies to distribute income currently. A foreign investment company was a foreign corporation, where more than 50 percent of its stock (by vote or value) was held by U.S. persons, and the corporation was registered with the Securities and Exchange Commission as a management company or as a unit investment trust, or primarily engaged in (or held itself out as being primarily engaged in) the business of investing, reinvesting or trading in securities, commodities or any interest therein, including a futures or forward contract or option (Code Secs. 1246–1247, as repealed by the 2004 Jobs Act).

In addition to the repealed provisions, foreign corporations have been excluded from the definition of a personal holding company (Code Sec. 542(c)(5), as amended by the 2004 Jobs Act). Further, personal services contract income that was subject to the foreign personal holding company rules previously contained in Code Sec. 553(a)(5), is included as subpart F foreign personal holding company income (Code Sec. 954(c)(1)(I), as added by the 2004 Jobs Act).

> **PRACTICAL ANALYSIS. Michael DiFronzo of McDermott Will & Emery, Chicago, Illinois, notes that the repeal of the foreign personal holding company (FPHC) rules, formerly under Code Sec. 551–558, is a

welcome development. In addition to overlap problems with subpart F, the FPHC rules sometimes proved to be a trap for the unwary. This was certainly the case when an investment was made in a foreign corporation through a partnership that included individual U.S. partners. Under the FPHC rules, a U.S. individual partner in a partnership was treated as owning all of the interests of all of the other partners regardless of how small that partner's interest may have been. Therefore, if, for example, a private equity fund structured its investment in a foreign corporation through a foreign partnership and that partnership included a U.S. individual as a partner, the FPHC rules could have applied even though subpart F may not have applied.

In addition to removing the onerous attribution rules and the subpart F overlap issues, the repeal of the FPHC regime also removes issues encountered with dividend qualification under Code Sec. 1(h)(11) and the loss of a basis step-up under Code Sec. 1014.

For further information on this subject, consult any of the following CCH reporter explanations:

- Standard Federal Tax Reporter, 2004FED ¶23,195.01, ¶23,316.01, ¶23,337.01, ¶23,352.01, ¶23,372.01, ¶23,402.01, ¶23,414.01, ¶23,431.01, ¶28,543.025, ¶30,921.01, ¶30,946.01 and ¶35,485.01

- Federal Tax Service, FTS §M:17.20

- Federal Tax Guide, 2004FTG ¶17,445

- Federal Estate and Gift Tax Reporter, FEGT ¶15,138.05 and ¶17,675.011

★ *Effective date.* The provision applies to tax years of foreign corporations beginning after December 31, 2004, and tax years of U.S. shareholders with or within which such tax years of foreign corporations end (Act Sec. 413(d)(1) of the American Jobs Creation Act of 2004); the provision shall apply to disclosures of return or return information under Code Sec. 6103(e)(1)(D) for tax years beginning after December 31, 2004 (Act Sec. 413(d)(2) of the 2004 Jobs Act).

Act Sec. 413(a)(1) of the American Jobs Creation Act of 2004, repealing Code Secs. 551–558; Act Sec. 413(a)(2)–(3), repealing Code Secs. 1246 and 1247; Act Sec. 413(b)(1), amending Code Sec. 542(c); Act Sec. 413(b)(2), adding Code Sec. 954(c)(1)(I); Act Sec. 413(c), amending Code Secs. 1(h), 171(c)(2), 245(a)(2), 312(j), 312(m), 443(e), 465(c)(7)(B), 543(b)(1), 562(b)(1), 563, 751(d), 864(d)(2), 898(b), 898(c), 904(d)(2)(A)(ii), 904(h)(1)(A), 904(h)(2), 951, 989(b)(3), 1014(b)(5), 1016(a)(13), 1212(a)(3), 1223, 1248(d), 1260(c)(2), 1291(b)(3)(F), 1291(e) and 1294(a)(2); repealing Code Sec. 6035; amending Code Secs. 6103(e)(1)(D), 6501(e)(1)(B), 6679(a), 170(f)(10)(A), 508(d), 4947 and 4948(c)(4); Act Sec. 413(d). Law at ¶5430, ¶5440, ¶5445, ¶5450, ¶5455, ¶5460, ¶5465, ¶5470, ¶5475, ¶5720, ¶5800 and ¶5805. Committee Report at ¶10,690.

¶490

Chapter 5

International Transactions: Expatriation and Other Provisions

EXPATRIATION AND INTERNATIONAL TAX AVOIDANCE

¶ 502

Revision of Tax Rules on Expatriation of Individuals

Background _____

The present rules under Code Sec. 877 were designed to discourage U.S. citizens and long-term residents from giving up their U.S. citizenship or terminating residence to avoid U.S. taxation. An individual who relinquishes or terminates his or her U.S. citizenship or residency with such a purpose is subject to an alternative method of income taxation for the 10 years ending after the relinquishment or termination. The alternative tax regime is a hybrid of the tax treatment of a U.S. citizen and a noncitizen who is a nonresident. For the 10-year period following citizenship relinquishment, the former citizen is subject to tax only on U.S.-source income at the rates applicable to U.S. citizens, rather than the more favorable rates applicable to noncitizens who are nonresidents. Under this regime, U.S.-source income has a broader scope than it does for normal federal tax purposes, and includes, for example, gain from the sale of U.S. corporate stock or debt obligations. However, the alternative rules apply only if the result is a higher U.S. tax liability than would otherwise result had the individual been taxed as a nonresident noncitizen (Code Sec. 877(a)(1) and (b)). In addition, anti-abuse rules are provided to prevent the circumvention of this alternative tax regime.

> **Comment:** There is widespread concern that the current expatriation tax rules are difficult to administer and largely ineffective. The Joint Committee on Taxation in its February 2003 *Review of the Present-Law Tax and Immigration Treatment of Relinquishment of Citizenship and Termination of Long-Term Residency* (JCS-2-03), cited the GAO's 2000 report, finding that the IRS does not yet have a systematic compliance effort in place to enforce the present-law alternative tax regime. In addition, other than compiling a Certificate of Loss of Nationality (CLN) database and publishing their names in the Federal Register as required by Code Sec. 6039G, the Joint Committee concluded that the IRS has generally ceased all compliance efforts under the alternative tax regime. And, according to this same report, the INS and the Department of State have not denied re-entry into the United States to a single former citizen under these rules.

A tax-avoidance motive is presumed if the expatriating individual meets either a "tax liability" or "net worth" test (Code Sec. 877, prior to amendment by the American Jobs Creation Act of 2004). Under these rules, the presumption applies if: (1) the individual's average annual net income tax (as defined by Code Sec. 38(c)(1)) for the five years preceding the expatriation date exceeds $100,000 ("tax liability test"); or (2) the individual's net worth as of the expatriation date equals at least $500,000 ("net worth test"). For calendar years after December 31, 1996, these amounts are indexed for inflation (Code Sec. 877(a)), and stand at $124,000 and $622,000, respectively, for 2004 (Rev. Proc. 2003-85, I.R.B. 2003-49, 1184). Qualified dual residents and certain minors may avoid being deemed to have a tax avoidance motive by submitting and receiving a favorable IRS ruling request on their tax status.

Under the present rules, a U.S. citizen must provide a statement to the State Department or other designated government entity that includes his or her social security number, forwarding foreign address, new country of residence and citizenship, a balance sheet in the case of an individual having a net worth equal to the inflation-adjusted amount under Code Sec. 877(a)(2)(b) ($622,000 for 2004), and information detailing his or her assets and liabilities. Additionally, the individual

Background

must supply any other information deemed necessary by the Secretary (Code Sec. 6039G(b)).

American Jobs Creation Act Impact

Income tax rules with respect to expatriates.—The American Jobs Creation Act of 2004 reflects recommendations contained in the Joint Committee on Taxation, *Review of the Present Law Tax and Immigration Treatment of Relinquishment of Citizenship and Termination of Long-Term Residency* (JCS-2-03), February 2003, and according to the Conference Committee Report (H.R. Conf. Rep. No. 108-755) amends Code Sec. 877 in order to provide:

(1) objective standards for determining whether former citizens or long-term residents are subject to the alternative tax regime;

(2) tax-based, instead of immigration-based, rules for determining when an individual is no longer a U.S. citizen or long-term resident for U.S. tax purposes;

(3) the imposition of full U.S. taxation for individuals who are subject to the alternative tax regime and who return to the United States for extended periods; and

(4) an annual information return-filing requirement for individuals who are subject to the alternative tax regime, for each of the 10 years following citizenship relinquishment or residency termination.

Objective standards. The present law subjective determination of tax avoidance has been replaced with objective rules under Code Sec. 877(a) and (c), as amended by the 2004 Jobs Act. This alternative tax regime will apply to individuals who expatriate after June 3, 2004, if:

(1) the individual had average annual net income tax liability in excess of $124,000 for the five-year period preceding the date of the loss of U.S. citizenship. The $124,000 amount is increased by the cost-of-living adjustment determined under Code Sec. 1(f)(3), after calendar year 2004;

(2) the individual's net worth is $2 million or more on the date of the loss of U.S. citizenship; or

(3) the individual fails to certify under penalties of perjury, that he or she has complied with all U.S. tax obligations for the preceding five years and has provided evidence of compliance as required by the Secretary of the Treasury.

The "tax liability test" and a "net worth test" are retained but now are used to conclusively determine whether a former citizen or long-term resident is subject to the alternative tax regime. Use of the monetary thresholds eliminates the need to inquire into an individual's tax motivation, and no subsequent inquiry into the taxpayer's intent is required or permitted since the ruling process has been eliminated (House Committee Report, H.R. Rep. No. 108-548). Second, because this objective monetary standard is less flexible than present law, the amount for the net-worth threshold has been increased (Joint Committee on Taxation, *Review of the Present Law Tax and Immigration Treatment of Relinquishment of Citizenship and Termination of Long-Term Residency* (JCS-2-03), February 2003).

Exceptions. The monetary thresholds discussed above will not be applied to tax an expatriate under the alternative regime of Code Sec. 877 if, subject to the following rules, the expatriate is a dual citizen, or is a minor.

An expatriate will qualify as a dual citizen if he or she:

(1) became, at birth, both a citizen of the United States and of another country, and continues to be a citizen of that other country, and

(2) has no "substantial contacts" with the United States.

An individual will be deemed to have no substantial contacts with the United States only if he or she:

(1) never was a resident of the United States;

(2) never held a U.S. passport; and

(3) has not been present in the United States for more than 30 days during any calendar year that is one of the 10 calendar years preceding the individual's loss of U.S. citizenship (Code Sec. 877(c)(2)(B), as amended by the 2004 Jobs Act).

The $124,000 income and $2,000,000 threshold amount tests will also not apply to a minor if:

(1) the minor became a U.S. citizen at birth,

(2) neither of the minor's parents was a U.S. citizen at the time of the minor's birth,

(3) the minor's loss of U.S. citizenship occurred before the minor attains age 18 1/2, and

(4) the minor was not present in the United States for more than 30 days during any calendar year that is one of the 10 calendar years preceding the minor's loss of U.S. citizenship (Code Sec. 877(c)(3), as amended by the 2004 Jobs Act).

Tax-based rules for determining when an individual is no longer a citizen or resident. Despite the fact that an individual might otherwise qualify for treatment as a person who is no longer taxed as a U.S. citizen or resident, such an individual will continue to be taxed as such until he or she:

(1) gives notice of an expatriating act or termination of residency (with the requisite intent to relinquish citizenship or terminate residency) to the Secretary of State or the Secretary of Homeland Security, and

(2) provides the statement required under Code Sec. 6039G (as amended by the 2004 Jobs Act) which includes: the taxpayer's TIN and the mailing address of his or her principal foreign residence; the foreign country in which the taxpayer is residing; the foreign country of which the taxpayer is a citizen; information detailing the taxpayer's income, assets, and liabilities; the number of days (or portion of which) the taxpayer was physically present in the United States during the tax year; and any other information that the Secretary of the Treasury requires (Code Sec. 7701(n), as added by the 2004 Jobs Act).

The above statements required under Code Sec. 6039G must be filed by an individual in each tax year that Code Sec. 877(a) applies to the individual. Unless excused by a finding of reasonable cause, an individual who fails to file this statement for any tax year in which it was required, is subject to a $10,000 penalty (Code Sec. 6039G(d), as amended by the 2004 Jobs Act).

Physical presence in the United States. An individual's presence in the United States for more than 30 days in any calendar year during the 10-year period following citizenship or residency relinquishment or termination, will cause the alternative tax regime to no longer apply to that individual (Code Sec. 877(g), as added by the 2004 Jobs Act). He or she becomes subject to U.S. taxation as a U.S. resident for that tax year and is taxed on his or her worldwide income.

¶502

For purposes of these rules, an individual is treated as present in the United States on any day that he or she is physically present in the United States at any time during that day. However, under newly added Code Sec. 877(g)(2)(A), a day of physical presence in the United States is disregarded if the individual is performing services in the United States for his or her employer. This exception will not apply if the employer is related to the taxpayer within the meaning of Code Secs. 267 and 707(b), or if the employer fails to meet anti-avoidance regulations that may be prescribed by the Secretary of the Treasury. Under this newly added provision, not more than 30 days during any calendar year may be disregarded.

The alternative tax regime of Code Sec. 877 will also not apply to individuals with certain ties to countries other than the United States. To qualify under this exception, an individual, within a reasonable time period after he or she has lost U.S. citizenship or terminated residency, must become a citizen or resident in (and fully liable for income taxes of) the country in which:

(1) the individual was born;

(2) the individual's spouse was born; or

(3) either of the individual's parents were born (Code Sec. 877(g)(2)(B), as added by the 2004 Jobs Act).

An individual will also fall outside of the alternative tax regime of Code Sec. 877 if the individual had minimal prior physical presence in the United States, defined as less than 30 days of presence in the United States for each year in the 10-year period ending on the date that the individual lost U.S. citizenship or terminated residence. Under the rule of Code Sec. 7701(b)(3)(D)(ii), a day for which the person was not able to leave the United States because of a medical condition that arose while the person was present in the United States, will not be counted for purposes of the 30-day limit (Code Sec. 877(g)(2)(c), as added by the 2004 Jobs Act).

For further information on this subject, consult any of the following CCH reporter explanations:

- Standard Federal Tax Reporter, 2004FED ¶27,425.01, ¶27,425.027 and ¶35,696.01

- Federal Tax Service, FTS §M:3.140

- Federal Tax Guide, 2004FTG ¶17,055

★ *Effective date.* The provision applies to individuals who expatriate after June 3, 2004 (Act Sec. 804(f) of the American Jobs Creation Act of 2004).

Act Sec. 804(a)(1) of the American Jobs Creation Act of 2004, amending Code Sec. 877(a); Act Sec. 804(a)(2), amending Code Sec. 877(c); Act Sec. 804(b), adding new Code Sec. 7701(n); Act Sec. 804(c), adding Code Sec. 877(g); Act Sec. 804(e)(1), amending Code Sec. 6039G(a); Act Sec. 804(e)(2) amending Code Sec. 6039G(b); Act Sec. 804(e)(3), amending Code Sec. 6039G(d); Act Sec. 804(e)(4), striking Code Sec. 6039G(c), (f), and (g) and redesignating Code Sec. 6039G(d) and (e) as Code Sec. 6039G(c) and (d); Act Sec. 804(f). Law at ¶5615, ¶6135 and ¶6355. Committee Report at ¶11,000.

¶504

Estate and Gift Tax Rules of Expatriates Revised

Background

Estate tax.—Generally, a federal estate tax is imposed on the entire taxable estate of a decedent (Code Sec. 2001(a)). The taxable estate is determined by subtracting the deductions permitted under Code Sec. 2053 through Code Sec. 2057 from the gross estate. The gross estate includes all property owned by the decedent at death, whether the property is real or personal, tangible or intangible, and wherever located. The estate tax is then calculated by applying the estate tax rate schedule in Code Sec. 2001(c) to the sum of the taxable estate and adjusted taxable gifts. The tentative estate tax is then reduced by any applicable credits available to the decedent: (1) applicable credit amount ($555,800 for 2004 and 2005); (2) credit for state death tax (until the end of 2004, after which it becomes a deduction); (3) credit for gift tax; (4) credit for estate tax on prior transfers; and (5) credit for foreign death taxes paid.

The estate of a nonresident noncitizen is subject to the federal estate tax to the extent the gross estate contains property situated in the United States at the time of death. The estate tax on this portion of a nonresident noncitizen decedent's gross estate is computed by first determining the taxable estate under Code Sec. 2106 and applying the same estate tax rate schedule as for a U.S. citizen or resident. The tentative tax is then reduced by the applicable credit allowed an estate of a nonresident noncitizen in the amount of $13,000 (unless otherwise specified by treaty, then the estate is allowed a share of the unified credit that is proportionate to the decedent's U.S. estate (Code Sec. 2102(c)(3)(A)) as well as the credit for state death tax (through 2004), credit for gift tax, and credit for estate tax on prior transfers (Code Sec. 2102(a)). However, if the nonresident noncitizen is a former citizen or long-term resident who relinquished citizenship or residency with the principal purpose of tax avoidance and he or she dies within 10 years after relinquishment of citizenship or long-term residency, he or she is treated as owning his or her pro rata share of the U.S. property held by any foreign corporation (1) in which he or she alone owns a 10-percent or larger interest in the total combined voting power and (2) which he or she, directly or indirectly, owns over 50 percent of the total combined voting power or value of the stock (in the case of residents who terminate residency after February 6, 1995) (Code Sec. 2107(b)). In determining whether these tests are met, the former citizen or long-term resident is treated as owning stock that he or she transferred during his or her lifetime under circumstances that would not have removed the stock from his or her gross estate for federal estate tax purposes, i.e., under Code Sec. 2035–Code Sec. 2038. A former citizen or long-term resident is deemed to have tax avoidance as a principal motive for relinquishment if his or her: (1) average annual net income tax (as defined by Code Sec. 38(c)(1)) for the five years preceding the expatriation date exceeds $124,000 (as adjusted for 2004) (tax liability test) or (2) net worth, as of the expatriation date, equals at least $622,000 (as adjusted for 2004) (net worth test) (Code Sec. 877(a)(2)).

> **Comment:** The Joint Committee on Taxation concluded, in its *Review of the Present-Law Tax and Immigration Treatment of Relinquishment of Citizenship and Termination of Long-Term Residency* (JCS-2-03), that the enforcement of the alternative tax provisions for expatriates has been severely hindered. The key reason for the lack of enforcement is the inability of the IRS to obtain the necessary information from the former citizens to enforce the alternative tax scheme under Code Sec. 877(b), Code Sec. 2107, and Code Sec. 2501(a) and the inability of the Attorney General to access the minimal information collected by the IRS. Further, the Attorney General does not have an objective standard by which to determine whether a former citizen's principal motivation for relinquishment of citizenship is tax avoidance.

Gift tax.—In general, all transfers made by gift in any calendar year, whether outright or in trust, direct or indirect, of property, whether real or personal, tangible or intangible, are subject to the federal gift tax under Code Sec. 2501. The amount of

Background

the gift tax liability is computed on the net taxable gifts by subtracting any applicable annual exclusions under Code Sec. 2503 and deductions under Code Sec. 2522 (marital deduction) and Code Sec. 2523 (charitable deduction) from the value of the donor's gross gifts for that calendar year. The tentative tax is calculated by applying the gift tax rate schedule, with rates incrementally increasing to a top marginal rate of 48 percent (for 2004), to the net taxable gifts (Code Sec. 2502(a)(2)). The tentative tax is then reduced by the donor's unused applicable credit under Code Sec. 2505 ($1 million) to determine the net gift tax liability.

Only transfers of tangible property situated in the United States, including stock in a domestic corporation and debt obligations of a U.S. person or government entity, made by nonresident noncitizens, are subject to gift tax and computed using the same rates as U.S. citizens and residents (Code Sec. 2511(a)). However, transfers of U.S.-situs intangible property (such as stocks and bonds) are also subject to gift tax, if the nonresident noncitizen is treated as an expatriate for the purposes of Code Sec. 877(a)(2) (Code Sec. 2501(a) (2) and (3)). An individual is treated as an expatriate if he or she relinquished U.S. citizenship, or long-term U.S. residency, within 10 years preceding the transfer in question and is deemed, under Code Sec. 877(a)(2), to have tax avoidance as one of his or her principal purposes for the relinquishment by satisfying either the $124,000 tax liability test or the $2,000,000 net worth test. If a transfer is subject to foreign gift tax solely because of Code Sec. 2501(a)(3), the former citizen or long-term resident is entitled to a credit for any foreign gift tax actually paid with respect to this transfer (Code Sec. 2501(a)(3)(D)).

Although a former citizen or long-term resident satisfies the requirements to be treated as an expatriate, the expatriation gift tax provisions will not apply if he or she is a dual citizen or submits a request to the IRS within one year of relinquishment of citizenship or residency to determine whether tax avoidance was a principal purpose for such relinquishment. Further, even though a former citizen or long-term resident is not considered an expatriate, if the IRS can reasonably establish that relinquishment would result in a substantial reduction in gift tax liability, the former citizen or long-term resident bears the burden of proving that tax avoidance was not a principal purpose for relinquishment (Code Sec. 2501(a)(4)).

American Jobs Creation Act Impact

Expatriate alternative estate tax regime revised.—If a former citizen or long-term resident who is subject to the alternative tax regime of Code Sec. 877(b) dies within 10 years of relinquishment of citizenship or residency, an estate tax is imposed on the transfer of U.S.-situs property, including the decedent's pro rata share of the U.S. property held by a foreign corporation pursuant to Code Sec. 2107(b). The estate tax is computed on the taxable estate, as determined by Code Sec. 2106, using the same estate tax rate schedule used for the estate of a U.S. citizen or resident (Code Sec. 2107(a), as amended by the American Jobs Creation Act of 2004). A former citizen or long-term resident is subject to the alternative tax regime if the individual (1) has average annual net income tax for the five-year period preceding the loss of U.S. citizenship in excess of $124,000; (2) has a net worth on that date of $2,000,000 or more; or (3) fails to certify compliance with all federal tax obligations for the five-year period, unless he or she is a dual citizen or minor without substantial contact with the United States (Code Sec. 877(a), as amended by the 2004 Jobs Act) (see ¶502). However, if, pursuant to Code Sec. 877(g), as added by the 2004 Jobs Act, the former citizen or long-term resident is present in the United States for a period of 30 days or more in any calendar year that ends during the 10-year period following relinquish-

¶504

ment of citizenship or long-term residency and dies within that same calendar year, he or she is treated as a resident of the United States for federal estate tax purposes (see ¶502). Thus, all property in which the former citizen or long-term resident has an interest is includible in his or her gross estate, wherever located, including foreign assets.

> **Comment:** The estate of a former citizen or long-term resident decedent who dies within 10 years of relinquishment of citizenship or long-term residency and is subject to the alternative tax regime is still only entitled to an applicable credit in the amount of $13,000 (unless otherwise specified by treaty, then the estate is allowed a share of the unified credit that is proportionate to the decedent's U.S. estate (Code Sec. 2102(c)(3)(A))). However, it would seem to be the correct result that if a former citizen or long-term resident is treated as a U.S. resident for estate tax purposes under the new law, then the higher applicable credit amount used for U.S. residents ($555,800 in 2004 and 2005, sheltering $1.5 million) would apply.

Expatriate alternative gift tax regime revised.—Gratuitous transfers of tangible or intangible property situated in the United States by a former citizen or long-term resident who is subject to the alternative tax regime of Code Sec. 877(b) and made during the 10-year period following relinquishment of citizenship or long-term residency, are subject to federal gift tax (Code Sec. 2501(a), as amended by the 2004 Jobs Act). However, if, pursuant to Code Sec. 877(g), as added by the 2004 Jobs Act, such a former citizen or long-term resident is present in the United States for a period of 30 days or more in any calendar year that ends during the 10-year period following relinquishment of citizenship or long-term residency, he or she is treated as a resident of the United States for federal gift tax purposes (see ¶502). Thus, all gratuitous transfers, regardless of where the property is situated, made by such former citizen or long-term resident in that calendar year are subject to the federal gift tax under Code Sec. 2501.

Gift tax imposed on transfers of stock in certain closely held foreign corporations.—Gratuitous transfers of stock in certain closely held foreign corporations, regardless of where the stock is located, by a former citizen or long-term resident who is subject to the alternative tax regime of Code Sec. 877(b), are subject to the federal gift tax, if made during the 10-year period following relinquishment of citizenship or long-term residency (Code Sec. 2501(a)(5)(A), as added by the 2004 Jobs Act). A foreign corporation that is subject to this gift tax rule is one in which the former citizen or long-term resident (1) owns 10 percent or more of the total combined voting power of all classes of stock and (2) directly or indirectly owns over 50 percent of the total combined voting power of all classes of stock or total value of stock (Code Sec. 2501(a)(5)(B), as added by the 2004 Jobs Act). The value of the stock for gift tax purposes is the U.S.-asset value of the stock at the time of the transfer. The U.S.-asset value is equal to the proportionate share of the fair market value, at the time of the transfer, of the foreign stock transferred which the fair market value of any assets owned by the foreign corporation that are situated in the United States bears to the total fair market value of all assets owned by such foreign corporation (Code Sec. 2501(a)(5)(C), as added by the 2004 Jobs Act).

> **Example:** Marco Ferraro, owner of 75 percent of the voting stock in Black Inc., a Spanish closely held corporation, transfers his interest to his two children on October 15, 2004. Ferraro, who relinquished his U.S. citizenship five years before the transfer, recently spent 45 days in the United States visiting relatives and friends. Black Inc. at the time of the transfer, owned $2 million in assets, $500,000 of which were situated in the United States. On October 15, 2004, the fair market value of the transferred stock was $1.5 million. For purposes of

determining Ferraro's gift tax liability on the transfer, the value of the stock is computed by first determining the fraction or percentage that the fair market value of the U.S.-situated assets bears to the fair market value of all assets owned by Black Inc.: 500,000/2,000,000 which is ¼ or 25 percent. Then apply this same percentage to the fair market value of transferred stock to determine the U.S.-asset value of the stock: $1,500,000 × 25% = $375,000.

For further information on this subject, consult any of the following CCH reporter explanations:

- Federal Tax Service, FTS § N:22.120

- Federal Tax Guide, 2004FTG ¶5546 and ¶19,230

- Federal Estate and Gift Tax Reporter, FEGT ¶8175.05, ¶9340.08, ¶10,555.08 and ¶10,555.081

★ *Effective date.* This provision applies to individuals who expatriate after June 3, 2004 (Act Sec. 804(f) of the American Jobs Creation Act of 2004).

Act Sec. 804(a)(3) of the American Jobs Creation Act of 2004, amending Code Sec. 2107(a); Act Sec. 804(d), amending Code Sec. 2501(a); Act Sec. 804(f). Law at ¶5950 and ¶5955. Committee Report at ¶11,000.

¶ 506

Tax Treatment of Expatriated Entities and Their Foreign Parents

Background

The U.S. tax treatment of a multinational corporate group depends significantly on whether the parent corporation of the group is domestic or foreign. For purposes of U.S. tax law, a corporation is treated as domestic if it is incorporated under the law of the United States or of any state (Code Sec. 7701(a)(4)). All other corporations (i.e., those incorporated under the laws of foreign countries) are treated as foreign (Code Sec. 7701(a)(5)).

Generally, domestic corporations are taxed on worldwide income. However, they are allowed to offset that U.S. tax on worldwide income in part with a foreign tax credit for income taxes paid to foreign countries on foreign-source income. Domestic parent corporations are taxed on income from foreign operations when the income is distributed as a dividend to the domestic parent, unless an anti-deferral rule operates to cause current taxation (e.g., highly mobile income earned by a foreign subsidiary is subject to current U.S. taxation, regardless of whether it has been distributed to the domestic parent). A foreign tax credit is usually available to offset the U.S. tax on this foreign-source income of a domestic parent, whether repatriated as an actual dividend or included under one of the anti-deferral regimes.

Generally, a foreign corporation is subject to U.S. tax in the same manner as a domestic corporation, on net income that is effectively connected with a U.S. trade or business. At times, a treaty may limit the U.S. tax to business operations conducted through a permanent establishment in the United States. Foreign corporations are also subject to a flat 30-percent tax on the gross amount of interest, dividends, rents, royalties and similar periodic income derived from U.S. sources. This 30-percent gross withholding tax may be limited by treaty.

Comment: A foreign corporation is not usually subject to U.S. tax on purely foreign income.

A U.S. corporation may reincorporate in a foreign jurisdiction and thereby replace the U.S. parent corporation of a multinational corporate group with a foreign parent corporation. These transactions are commonly referred to as inversion transactions. Inversion transactions may take many different forms, including stock inversions, asset inversions, and various combinations of and variations on the two. Most of the transactions to date have been stock inversions. In one example of a stock inversion, a U.S. corporation forms a foreign corporation, which in turn forms a domestic merger subsidiary. The domestic merger subsidiary then merges into the U.S. corporation, with the U.S. corporation surviving, now as a subsidiary of the new foreign corporation. The U.S. corporation's shareholders receive shares of the foreign corporation and are treated as having exchanged their U.S. corporation shares for the foreign corporation shares.

An asset inversion reaches a result similar to a stock inversion, but through a direct merger of the top-tier U.S. corporation into a new foreign corporation, among other possible forms. An inversion transaction may be accompanied or followed by further restructuring of the corporate group. For example, in the case of a stock inversion, in order to remove income from foreign operations from the U.S. taxing jurisdiction, the U.S. corporation may transfer some or all of its foreign subsidiaries directly to the new foreign parent corporation or other related foreign corporations.

> **Comment:** In addition to removing foreign operations from the U.S. taxing jurisdiction, the corporate group may derive further advantage from the inverted structure by reducing U.S. tax on U.S. source income through various earnings stripping or other transactions, just like other multinational corporate groups with foreign parents and U.S. subsidiaries, but subject to the same limitations (e.g., Code Secs. 163(j) and 482) that apply to those multinational corporate groups.

Inversion transactions may give rise to immediate U.S. tax consequences at the shareholder and/or the corporate level, depending on the type of inversion. In stock inversions, the U.S. shareholders generally recognize gain (but not loss) under Code Sec. 367(a), based on the difference between the fair market value of the foreign corporation shares received and the adjusted basis of the domestic corporation stock exchanged. To the extent that a corporation's share value has declined, and/or it has many foreign or tax-exempt shareholders, the impact of this "toll charge" is reduced. The transfer of foreign subsidiaries or other assets to the foreign parent corporation also may give rise to U.S. tax consequences at the corporate level (e.g., gain recognition and earnings and profits inclusions under Code Secs. 1001, 311(b), 304, 367, 368, 1248 or other provisions). The tax on any income recognized as a result of these restructurings may be reduced or eliminated through the use of net operating losses, foreign tax credits, and other tax attributes. In asset inversions, the U.S. corporation generally recognizes gain (but not loss) under Code Sec. 367(a) as though it had sold all of its assets, but the shareholders generally do not recognize gain or loss, assuming the transaction meets the requirements of a reorganization under Code Sec. 368.

American Jobs Creation Act Impact

Benefits of corporate inversion transactions limited.—The tax benefits of corporate inversion transactions have been limited (Code Sec. 7874, as added by the American Jobs Creation Act of 2004). The manner in which the benefits are limited depends upon whether the inversion transaction involves at least 80-percent identity of stock ownership or whether the transaction involves at least 60-percent but less than 80-percent identity of stock ownership. Generally, in the "80-percent identity" transactions, the tax benefits of inversion are limited by treating the top-tier foreign corporation as a domestic corporation for U.S. tax purposes (Code Sec. 7874(b), as added by the 2004 Jobs Act). In the "60-80 percent identity" transactions, the benefits of inversion are limited by barring corporate-level "toll charges" from being offset by tax attributes (Code Sec. 7874(a)(1), as added by the 2004 Jobs Act).

Comment: Congress believed that corporate inversion transactions were a symptom of larger problems with our current uncompetitive system for taxing U.S.-based global businesses (House Committee Report, H.R. Rep. No. 108-548). It also believed that inversion transactions were indicative of the unfair advantages that our tax laws provide to foreign ownership. The 2004 Jobs Act addresses the underlying problems with the U.S. system of taxing U.S.-based global businesses and contains provisions to remove the incentives for entering into inversion transactions.

Inversion transaction defined. An inversion is a transaction in which, pursuant to a plan or a series of related transactions:

(1) a U.S. corporation or partnership becomes a subsidiary of a foreign-incorporated entity or otherwise transfers substantially all of its properties to such an entity after March 4, 2003,

(2) the former shareholders of the U.S. corporation hold (by reason of holding stock in the U.S. corporation) 60 percent or more (by vote or value) of the stock of the foreign incorporated entity after the transaction, and

(3) the foreign incorporated entity, considered together with all companies connected to it by a chain of greater than 50-percent ownership (i.e., the "expanded affiliated group" as defined in Code Sec. 7874(c)(1)) does not conduct substantial business activities in the entity's country of incorporation compared to the total worldwide business activities of the expanded affiliated group (Code Sec. 7874(a)(2), as added by the 2004 Jobs Act).

Comment: Acquisitions with respect to a domestic corporation or partnership are deemed to be pursuant to a plan if they occur within the four-year period beginning on the date which is two years before the ownership threshold is met (Code Sec. 7874(c)(3), as added by the 2004 Jobs Act, and Conference Committee Report, H.R. Conf. Rep. No. 108-755).

Inversion transactions can also include certain partnership transactions (Code Sec. 7874(a)(2), as added by the 2004 Jobs Act). Transactions in which a foreign-incorporated entity acquires substantially all of the properties constituting a trade or business of a domestic partnership is an inversion transaction, if after the acquisition, at least 60 percent of the stock of the entity is held by former partners of the partnership (by reason of holding their partnership interests), assuming the other conditions itemized above exist. For these purposes, all partnerships that are under common control (see Code Sec. 482 and Code Sec. 7874(c)(5), as added by the 2004 Jobs Act) are treated as one partnership, except as otherwise provided in regulations. Toll charges are applied at the partner level (Conference Committee Report, H.R. Conf. Rep. No. 108-755).

Caution Note: A transaction will not be treated as a corporate inversion transaction if, on or before March 4, 2003, the foreign incorporated entity has acquired directly or indirectly more than half of the properties held directly or indirectly by the domestic corporation, or more than half of the properties constituting the domestic partnership's trade or business (Code Sec. 7874(a)(2)(B), as added by the 2004 Jobs Act).

80-percent identity transactions. In an inversion transaction in which the former shareholders of the U.S. corporation hold (by reason of holding stock in the U.S.

corporation) 80 percent or more (by vote or value) of the stock of the foreign incorporated entity after the transaction, the foreign corporation is treated as a domestic corporation for U.S. tax purposes (Code Secs. 7874(a)(3) and (b), as added by the 2004 Jobs Act). Thus, the incentives for entering into a corporate inversion transaction are eliminated in this situation.

> **Caution Note:** Since the top-tier foreign corporation is treated for all purposes of the Code as a domestic corporation in these 80-percent identity transactions, the shareholder-level toll charge imposed on outbound transactions (Code Sec. 367(a)) does not apply to these transactions (Code Sec. 7874(d)(2), as added by the 2004 Jobs Act, and Conference Committee Report, H.R. Conf. Rep. No. 108-755).

60-80 percent identity transactions. In corporate inversion transactions in which the former shareholders of the U.S. corporation hold (by reason of holding stock in the U.S. corporation) at least 60 percent but less than 80 percent (by vote or value) of the stock of the foreign incorporated entity after the transaction, the benefits of inversion are limited by barring corporate-level "toll charges" from being offset by tax attributes (Code Sec. 7874(a)(1), as added by the 2004 Jobs Act). This is accomplished by imposing a corporate inversion "tax" on the inversion gain of expatriated entities. Specifically, the taxable income of an expatriated entity for any tax year that includes any portion of the "applicable period," generally the 10-year period that begins with a corporate inversion transaction, cannot be less than the inversion gain of the entity for that tax year (Code Secs. 7874(a) and (d), as added by the 2004 Jobs Act). This tax on inversion gain cannot be offset by foreign tax credits or other tax attributes (Code Sec. 7874(e)(1), as added by the 2004 Jobs Act).

The term "applicable period" means the period that begins on the first date properties are acquired as part of the direct or indirect acquisition of substantially all of the properties held directly or indirectly by a domestic corporation or substantially all of the properties constituting a trade or business of a domestic partnership (Code Sec. 7874(d)(1), as added by the 2004 Jobs Act). The "applicable period" ends on the date which is 10 years after the last date properties are acquired as part of such acquisition.

Generally, the inversion gain is (1) the income or gain recognized by reason of the transfer during the applicable period of stock or other properties by an expatriated entity, and (2) any income received or accrued during the applicable period by reason of a license of any property by an expatriated entity as part of the direct or indirect acquisition of substantially all of the properties held directly or indirectly by a domestic corporation or substantially all of the properties constituting a trade or business of a domestic partnership (Code Sec. 7874(d)(2), as added by the 2004 Jobs Act). Income or gain recognized after such acquisition is also inversion gain if the transfer or license is to a foreign related person, unless the property is inventory in the hands of the expatriated entity (Code Sec. 7874(d)(2)(B), as added by the 2004 Jobs Act). A foreign related person is a foreign person who is related (within the meaning of Code Secs. 267(b) or 707(b)(1)) to the expatriated entity, or is under the same common control (within the meaning of Code Sec. 482) as such expatriated entity (Code Sec. 7874(d)(3), as added by the 2004 Jobs Act).

> **Comment:** In essence, under these inversion transaction rules, any applicable corporate-level "toll charges" for establishing the inverted structure cannot be offset by tax attributes such as net operating losses or foreign tax credits. Specifically, any applicable corporate-level income or gain otherwise required to be recognized under Code Secs. 304, 311(b), 367, 1001, 1248, or any other provision with respect to the transfer of controlled foreign corporation stock or

¶506

the transfer or license of other assets by a U.S. corporation as part of the inversion transaction, or after such transaction to a related foreign person, is taxable. Furthermore, that tax cannot be offset by any tax attributes (e.g., net operating losses or foreign tax credits). As previously noted, this rule does not apply to certain transfers of inventory and similar property (House Committee Report, H.R. Rep. No. 108-548).

An "expatriated entity" is:

(1) the domestic corporation or partnership with respect to which a foreign corporation is a surrogate foreign corporation, and

(2) any U. S. person who is related (as determined under Code Secs. 267(b) or 707(b)(1)) to such a domestic corporation or partnership (Code Sec. 7874(a)(2)(A), as added by the 2004 Jobs Act).

A foreign corporation is treated as a surrogate foreign corporation if, pursuant to a plan (or a series of related transactions):

(1) the entity completes, after March 4, 2003, the direct or indirect acquisition of substantially all of the properties held directly or indirectly by a domestic corporation or substantially all of the properties constituting a trade or business of a domestic partnership,

(2) after the acquisition, at least 60 percent of the stock (by vote or value) of the entity is held by former shareholders or partners of the acquired corporation or partnership, respectively, by reason of holding stock in the domestic corporation or capital or profits interest in the domestic partnership, and

(3) after the acquisition, the expanded affiliated group which includes the entity does not have substantial business activities in the foreign country in which, or under the law of which, the entity is created or organized, when compared to the total business activities of such expanded affiliated group (Code Sec. 7874(a)(2)(B), as added by the 2004 Jobs Act).

The term "expanded affiliated group" includes the foreign-incorporated entity and all companies connected to it by a chain of greater than 50-percent ownership (Code Sec. 7874(c)(1), as added by the 2004 Jobs Act).

Comment: An entity will not be treated as a surrogate foreign corporation if, on or before March 4, 2003, such entity acquired more than half of the properties held by such corporation or more than half of the properties constituting such partnership trade or business, as the case may be (Code Sec. 7874(a)(2)(B), as added by the 2004 Jobs Act).

In determining whether after the acquisition at least 60 percent of the stock (by vote or value) of the entity is held by former shareholders or partners of the acquired corporation or partnership, certain stock is excluded (Code Sec. 7874(c)(2), as added by the 2004 Jobs Act). Stock held by members of the expanded affiliated group which includes the foreign corporation, or stock of such foreign corporation which is sold in a public offering related to the acquisition is excluded when making this determination.

Example: A former top-tier U.S. corporation received stock of a foreign incorporated entity. This so-called "hook" stock is not considered in determining whether the transaction meets the inversion transaction definition (House Committee Report, H.R. Rep. No. 108-548).

Example: A U.S. parent corporation converted an existing wholly owned U.S. subsidiary into a new wholly owned controlled foreign corporation. The stock of the new foreign corporation is disregarded in determining if the transac-

¶506

tion is an inversion transaction (House Committee Report, H.R. Rep. No. 108-548).

A prohibited acquisition plan will be deemed in certain cases (Code Sec. 7874(c)(3), as added by the 2004 Jobs Act). If a foreign corporation acquires substantially all of the properties of a domestic corporation or partnership, either directly or indirectly, during the four-year period beginning on the date that is two years before the requisite 60-percent ownership requirement is met, those actions shall be treated as pursuant to such a plan. Furthermore, the transfer of properties or liabilities (including by contribution or distribution) shall be disregarded if such transfers are part of a plan a principal purpose of which is to avoid the purposes of these inversion transaction rules (Code Sec. 7874(c)(4), as added by the 2004 Jobs Act). Finally, for purposes of applying the 60-percent ownership rule to the acquisition of a trade or business of a domestic partnership, except as provided in regulations, all partnerships which are under common control (Code Sec. 482) are treated as one partnership (Code Sec. 7874(c)(5), as added by the 2004 Jobs Act). The Treasury has specific authority to prescribe whatever regulations that may be appropriate to determine whether a corporation is a surrogate foreign corporation, including regulations: (1) to treat warrants, options, contracts to acquire stock, convertible debt interests, and other similar interests as stock, and (2) to treat stock as not stock (Code Sec. 7874(c)(6), as added by the 2004 Jobs Act).

Credits are not allowed to offset the tax on inversion gain (Code Sec. 7874(e)(1), as added by the 2004 Jobs Act). Credits (other than the direct foreign tax credit of Code Sec. 901) are allowed against the tax on an expatriated entity for any tax year during the "applicable period" only to the extent such tax exceeds the product of the amount of the inversion gain for the tax year, and the highest rate of corporate tax (Code Sec. 11(b)(1)). For purposes of determining the direct foreign tax credit, inversion gain is treated as U.S. source income.

In the case of an expatriated entity which is a partnership, this prohibition on credits applies at the partner rather than the partnership level (Code Sec. 7874(e)(2), as added by the 2004 Jobs Act). Also, the inversion gain of any partner for any tax year is equal to the sum of the partner's distributive share of inversion gain of the partnership for such tax year plus gain recognized for the tax year by the partner by reason of the transfer during the applicable period of any partnership interest of the partner in such partnership to the surrogate foreign corporation. Moreover, the highest rate of tax applicable to the partner is substituted for the highest rate of corporate tax.

Coordination with AMT and NOL rules. Rules similar to those under Code Sec. 860E(a)(3) and (4) that apply to the holders of a residual interest in a real estate mortgage investment conduit (REMIC) will apply for purposes of determining the tax on inversion gain of expatriated entities (Code Sec. 7874(e)(3), as added by the 2004 Jobs Act). Under these REMIC rules, the taxable income of any holder of a residual interest in a REMIC for any tax year is not less than the "excess inclusion" for such tax year. Under these REMIC rules, any excess inclusion for any tax year is not taken into account in determining the amount of any net operating loss for the tax year, and in determining net operating loss carrybacks and carryovers. Taxable income, for purposes of computing alternative minimum tax income (AMTI) is treated as taxable income determined without regard to these REMIC rules. Also, the alternative minimum taxable income of any holder of a residual interest in a REMIC for any tax year is not less than the excess inclusion for such tax year, and any excess inclusion is disregarded for purposes of computing the alternative tax net operating loss deduction.

¶506

Limitations period. The statutory period for the assessment of any deficiency attributable to the inversion gain of any taxpayer for any pre-inversion year stays open for three years from the date the Secretary is notified by the taxpayer (in such manner as the Secretary may prescribe) of the acquisition of substantially all of the properties held by a domestic corporation or constituting a trade or business of a domestic partnership to which such gain relates (Code Sec. 7874(e)(4)(A), as added by the 2004 Jobs Act). The deficiency may be assessed before the expiration of the three-year period notwithstanding the provisions of any other law or rule of law which would otherwise prevent such assessment. The term "pre-inversion year" means any tax year if any portion of the applicable period is included in such tax year, and such year ends before the tax year in which the acquisition is completed (Code Sec. 7874(e)(4)(B)).

Treaties inapplicable. Nothing in Code Sec. 894 or 7852(d) or in any other provision of law shall be construed as permitting an exemption, by reason of any treaty obligation of the United States from the provisions of this tax on the inversion gain of expatriated entities (Code Sec. 7874(f), as added by the 2004 Jobs Act).

Regulatory authority. The Secretary of the Treasury will issue regulations necessary to carry out the tax on inversion gain of expatriated entities, including regulations necessary to prevent avoidance of these rules (Code Sec. 7874(g), as added by the 2004 Jobs Act). Regulations may prevent the avoidance through the use of related persons, passthrough or other noncorporate entities, or other intermediaries, or through transactions designed to have persons cease to be (or not become) members of expanded affiliated groups or related persons.

> **PRACTICAL ANALYSIS.** Michael DiFronzo of McDermott Will & Emery, Chicago, Illinois, observes that the inversion legislation is extremely broad and could apply to transactions outside of what most people would consider to be an inversion transaction. These arguably unintended results occur because the legislation does not include a nonpublicly traded exception (which existed in an earlier Senate version of the legislation) or a non-U.S. shareholder exception.
>
> For example, assume UKCo, a UK corporation, and GermanCo, a German corporation, are unrelated corporations. UKCo and GermanCo each hold 50 percent of a joint venture interest in USCo, a U.S. corporation. Assume further that UKCo and GermanCo also hold joint venture corporations in Canada and Mexico. In order to consolidate those various joint interests into a single joint venture holding company, UKCo and GermanCo form LuxCo, a Luxembourg corporation. Neither UKCo nor GermanCo have substantial business activity in Luxembourg. UKCo and GermanCo contribute all of their USCo stock to LuxCo solely in exchange for stock of LuxCo. Although the contribution would not be subject to tax under Code Sec. 367 (the U.S. outbound transfer rule) because there is no exchanging U.S. shareholder, the acquisition of USCo by LuxCo seems subject to the new inversion legislation and LuxCo would be a "surrogate foreign corporation." Although new Code Sec. 7874(c)(2)(A) seems to turn the legislation off for the transfer of a greater than 50 percent owned interest, inversion treatment could result in this scenario because Code Sec. 7874(c)(2)(A) is not satisfied. Here, because the former shareholders of USCo would receive 100 percent of the shares of LuxCo in equal portions (i.e., 50 percent each), it appears that LuxCo would be treated as a U.S. corporation for all purposes of the Code. Thus, if UKCo and GermanCo also contribute the stock of their Canadian and Mexico joint venture corporations, those entities

would arguably become controlled foreign corporations of LuxCo, a U.S. corporation for all purposes of the Code. This result would occur even if USCo only represented a small portion of the resulting value of LuxCo. In other words, a small transaction subject to the inversion rule could taint a much larger restructuring with unwelcome consequences.

Hopefully, the above possible unintended result, and others like it, will be addressed by a technical correction that would remove application of Code Sec. 7874 from nonpublic companies (as existed in an earlier Senate version of the legislation) or the Treasury will use its regulatory authority to narrow the possible broad application of this provision to the types of transactions that the legislation was intended to cover.

In addition to possible unintended results, the legislation does not define "substantial business activity." Moreover, the legislation is more than 18 months retroactive. Therefore, companies that suddenly find themselves subject to this legislation will have to struggle with the meaning of substantial business activity and possibly file for withholding tax refunds for the period prior to enactment of the legislation.

For further information on this subject, consult any of the following CCH reporter explanations:

- Standard Federal Tax Reporter, 2004FED ¶35,888.01
- Federal Tax Service, FTS §M:18.40
- Federal Tax Guide, 2004FTG ¶17,055

★ *Effective date.* These corporate inversion transaction rules apply to tax years ending after March 4, 2003 (Act Sec. 801(c) of the American Jobs Creation Act of 2004).

Act Sec. 801(a) of the American Jobs Creation Act of 2004, adding Code Sec. 7874; Act Sec. 801(b) and (c). Law at ¶6375. Committee Report at ¶10,970.

¶ 508

Excise Tax on Stock Compensation of Insiders in Expatriated Corporations

Background

The income taxation of a nonstatutory compensatory stock option is determined under the rules that apply to property transferred in connection with the performance of services (Code Sec. 83). Generally, nonstatutory stock options refer to stock options other than incentive stock options and employee stock purchase plans (see Code Secs. 421–424). If a nonstatutory stock option does not have a readily ascertainable fair market value at the time of grant, which is generally the case unless the option is actively traded on an established market, no amount is included in the gross income of the recipient with respect to the option until the recipient exercises the option (Code Sec. 83(f)(3)). If an individual receives a grant of a nonstatutory option that has a readily ascertainable fair market value at the time the option is granted, the excess of the fair market value of the option over the amount paid for the option is included in the recipient's gross income as ordinary income in the first tax year in which the option is either transferable or not subject to a substantial risk of forfeiture (Code Sec. 83(a)).

Upon exercise of such a nonstatutory stock option, the excess of the fair market value of the stock purchased over the option price is generally included in the recipient's gross income as ordinary income. Generally, such amount is includible in

Background _____

gross income in the first tax year in which the rights to the stock are transferable or are not subject to substantial risk of forfeiture (Code Sec. 83(a)).

The tax treatment of other forms of stock-based compensation (e.g., restricted stock and stock appreciation rights) is also determined under the rules that apply to property transferred in connection with the performance of services. The excess of the fair market value over the amount paid (if any) for such property is generally includible in gross income in the first tax year in which the rights to the property are transferable or are not subject to substantial risk of forfeiture.

Shareholders are generally required to recognize gain from corporate inversion transactions. An inversion transaction is generally not a taxable event for holders of stock options and other stock-based compensation (House Committee Report, H.R. Rep. No. 108-548).

_____

American Jobs Creation Act Impact

Excise tax on stock compensation of expatriated corporations' insiders.—The stock compensation of certain insiders in some expatriated corporations is subject to an excise tax (Code Sec. 4985, as added by the American Jobs Creation Act of 2004). Generally, the excise tax will apply only if any of the expatriated corporation's shareholders recognize gains (if any) on any stock in the corporation by reason of the corporate inversion transaction that caused the expatriation (Code Sec. 7874(a)(2)(B)(i), as added by the 2004 Jobs Act) (see ¶506 for a discussion of corporate inversion transactions) (Code Sec. 4985(c), as added by the 2004 Jobs Act). It will not apply in certain circumstances where stock option or specified stock compensation gain is recognized (Code Sec. 4985(d), as added by the 2004 Jobs Act).

> **Comment:** Congress believed that certain inversion transactions are a means of avoiding U.S. tax and should be curtailed. It was concerned that, while shareholders are generally required to recognize gain upon stock inversion transactions, executives holding stock options and certain stock-based compensation are not taxed upon such transactions. Since such executives are often instrumental in deciding whether to engage in inversion transactions, Congress believed that, upon certain inversion transactions, it is appropriate to impose an excise tax on certain executives holding stock options and stock-based compensation. Because shareholders are taxed at the capital gains rate upon inversion transactions, Congress believed that it is appropriate to impose the excise tax at an equivalent rate (House Committee Report, H.R. Rep. No. 108-548).

A corporation's payment of this excise tax on the stock compensation of insiders in expatriated corporations is not deductible by the corporation. Furthermore, the $1 million limit on deductible compensation is reduced by payment of this excise tax (Code Sec. 275(a)(6), as amended by the 2004 Jobs Act, and Code Sec. 162(m)(4)(G), as added by the 2004 Jobs Act). See further "Deductions Denied", below.

Excise tax imposed. An excise tax is imposed on and payable by an individual who is a disqualified individual with respect to any expatriated corporation (Code Sec. 4985(a), as added by the 2004 Jobs Act). The tax is equal to a percentage of the value of specified stock compensation held (directly or indirectly) by or for the benefit of a disqualified individual with respect to an expatriated corporation, or held by a member of such individual's family (Code Sec. 267) at any time during the 12-month period beginning on the date which is six months before the expatriation date.

> **Caution Note:** Specified stock compensation previously granted to a disqualified individual but cancelled or cashed-out within the six-month period

¶508

ending with the expatriation date, and any specified stock compensation awarded in the six-month period beginning with the expatriation date is subject to the excise tax. As a result, for example, if a corporation cancels outstanding options three months before the inversion transaction and then reissues comparable options three months after the transaction, the tax applies both to the cancelled options and the newly granted options. It is intended that the Secretary issue guidance to avoid double counting with respect to specified stock compensation that is cancelled and then regranted during the applicable 12-month period (House Committee Report, H.R. Rep. No. 108-548).

The tax rate is tied to the maximum rate of tax on the adjusted net capital gain of an individual (Code Sec. 1(h)(1)(C)). Thus, a 15-percent excise tax rate applies for the 2005 through 2008 tax years, but a 20-percent rate applies for tax years beginning after 2008 (Conference Committee Report, H.R. Conf. Rep. No. 108-755).

Value determined. The value of the specified stock compensation on which the excise tax is imposed is the fair value in the case of stock options (including warrants or other similar rights to acquire stock) and stock appreciation rights and the fair market value for all other forms of such compensation. The determination of value is made on the expatriation date in the case of specified stock compensation held on the expatriation date. In the case of compensation that is canceled during the six months before the expatriation date, determination of value is made on the day before the cancellation. In the case of compensation that is granted after the expatriation date, the determination of value is made on the date such compensation is granted (Code Sec. 4985(b), as added by the 2004 Jobs Act). Under these rules, the cancellation of a nonlapse restriction is treated as a grant (Code Sec. 4985(f)(1), as added by the 2004 Jobs Act). Whether there is specified stock compensation, and its value, is determined without regard to any restriction other than a restriction which by its terms will never lapse (Code Sec. 4985(f)(3), as added by the 2004 Jobs Act).

For purposes of this excise tax, the fair value of an option (or a warrant or other similar right to acquire stock) or a stock appreciation right is determined using an appropriate option-pricing model, as specified or permitted by the Secretary, that takes into account the following items:

(1) the stock price at the valuation date;

(2) the exercise price under the option;

(3) the remaining term of the option;

(4) the volatility of the underlying stock and the expected dividends on it; and

(5) the risk-free interest rate over the remaining term of the option.

Options that have no intrinsic value (or "spread") because the exercise price under the option equals or exceeds the fair market value of the stock at valuation nevertheless have a fair value and are subject to tax under the provision. The value of other forms of compensation, such as phantom stock or restricted stock, is the fair market value of the stock as of the date of the expatriation transaction. The value of any deferred compensation that can be valued by reference to stock is the amount that the disqualified individual would receive if the plan were to distribute all such deferred compensation in a single sum on the date of the expatriation transaction (or the date of cancellation or grant, if applicable) (House Committee Report, H.R. Rep. No. 108-548).

Comment: It is expected that the Secretary will issue guidance on valuation of specified stock compensation, including guidance similar to that issued under the "golden parachute" rules of Code Sec. 280G, except that the guidance would not permit the use of a term other than the full remaining term and would be modified as necessary or appropriate to carry out the purposes of the provision. Pending the issuance of guidance, it is intended that taxpayers can rely on the guidance issued under the "golden parachute" rules of Code Sec. 280G (except that the full remaining term must be used and recalculation is not permitted) (House Committee Report, H.R. Rep. No. 108-548).

Qualifications and exceptions. The excise tax is imposed on any disqualified individual with respect to an expatriated corporation only if shareholder gain, if any, is recognized in whole or in part by reason of the acquisition referred to in the corporate inversion transaction rules (Code Sec. 7874(a)(2)(B)(i), as added by the 2004 Jobs Act) (See ¶506 for further information on corporate inversion transactions) (Code Sec. 4985(c), as added by the 2004 Jobs Act).

The excise tax will not apply to any stock option which is exercised on the expatriation date or during the six-month period before that date and to the stock acquired in such exercise, if income is recognized under the usual restricted property transfer compensation rules (Code Sec. 83) on or before the expatriation date with respect to the stock acquired from such exercise (Code Sec. 4985(d)(1), as added by the 2004 Jobs Act). Also, the excise tax will not apply to any other specified stock compensation which is exercised, sold, exchanged, distributed, cashed-out, or otherwise paid during such period in a transaction in which income, gain, or loss is recognized in full (Code Sec. 4985(d)(2), as added by the 2004 Jobs Act).

Disqualified individual defined. A "disqualified individual" is any individual who, at any time during the 12-month period beginning on the date that is six months before the expatriation date, is subject to Section 16(a) of the Securities Exchange Act of 1934 with respect to a corporation or any member of the expanded affiliated group which includes such corporation. Similarly, a disqualified individual includes an individual who would be subject to Section 16(a) of the Securities Exchange Act of 1934 if the corporation or member were an issuer of equity securities referred to in Section 16(a) of the Securities Exchange Act of 1934 (Code Sec. 4985(e)(1), as added by the 2004 Jobs Act).

> **Comment:** Disqualified individuals include officers, directors, and 10-percent-or-greater owners of private and publicly held corporations. An officer is defined as the president, principal financial officer, principal accounting officer or controller. An officer also includes any vice-president in charge of a principal business unit, division or function such as sales, administration or finance. Furthermore, an officer includes any other officer who performs a policy-making function, or any other person who performs similar policy-making functions (House Committee Report (H. R. Rept. No. 108-548)).

Expatriated corporation defined. The term "expatriated corporation" means any corporation which is an expatriated entity (as defined in Code Sec. 7874(a)(2), as added by the 2004 Jobs Act). Generally, an expatriated entity is a domestic corporation or partnership or related U.S. person with respect to which a foreign corporation is a surrogate foreign corporation. Generally, a foreign corporation is a surrogate foreign corporation if, after March 4, 2003, that foreign entity completes an acquisition of substantially all of the properties held by the domestic corporation or constituting a trade or business of the partnership, respectively, and after the acquisition at least 60 percent of the stock by vote or value of the foreign corporation is held by former shareholders or partners of the domestic corporation or partnership, respectively (See ¶506 for further guidance on corporate inversion transactions). The term "expatriated corporation" includes any predecessor or successor of such a corporation. The term "expatriation date" means, with respect to a corporation, the

¶508

date on which the corporation first becomes an expatriated corporation (Code Sec. 4985(e)(2), as added by the 2004 Jobs Act).

Specified stock compensation defined. The term "specified stock compensation" means payment (or right to payment) granted by the expatriated corporation (or by any member of the expanded affiliated group which includes such corporation) to any person in connection with the performance of services by a disqualified individual for such corporation or member if the value of such payment or right is based on (or determined by reference to) the value (or change in value) of stock in such corporation (or any affiliated group member) (Code Sec. 4985(e)(3), as added by the 2004 Jobs Act). The term "expanded affiliated group" means any affiliated group (Code Sec. 1504(a)), except that the group is determined without regard to the exceptions for foreign corporations, and a "50-percent" vote and value ownership test is used instead of an "80-percent" vote and value ownership test (Code Sec. 4985(e)(4) as added by the 2004 Jobs Act). A payment includes a transfer of property, and any right to a transfer of property is treated as a right to a payment (Code Sec. 4985(f)(4), as added by the 2004 Jobs Act, and House Committee Report, H.R. Rep. No. 108-548). The term "specified stock compensation" does not include certain statutory stock options (see Code Secs. 421– 424), or any payment or right to payment from certain qualified plans (see Code Sec. 280G(b)(6)) (Code Sec. 4985(e)(3)(B), as added by the 2004 Jobs Act). Such qualified plans include a qualified retirement plan or annuity, tax-sheltered annuity, simplified employee pension, or SIMPLE (House Committee Report, H.R. Rep. No. 108-548).

> **Comment:** In determining whether specified stock compensation exists, and in valuing such compensation, all restrictions, other than nonlapse restrictions are ignored. Thus, the excise tax applies, and the value subject to tax is determined without regard to whether the specified stock compensation is subject to a substantial risk of forfeiture or is exercisable at the time of the inversion transaction (House Committee Report, H.R. Rep. No. 108-548).

Specified stock compensation includes compensatory stock and restricted stock grants, compensatory stock options, and other forms of stock-based compensation, including stock appreciation rights, phantom stock, and phantom stock options. Specified stock compensation also includes nonqualified deferred compensation that is treated as though it were invested in stock or stock options of the expatriating corporation (or member). For example, the provision applies to a disqualified individual's deferred compensation if company stock is one of the actual or deemed investment options under the nonqualified deferred compensation plan (House Committee Report, H.R. Rep. No. 108-548).

Specified stock compensation includes a compensation arrangement that gives the disqualified individual an economic stake substantially similar to that of a corporate shareholder. A payment directly tied to the value of the stock is specified stock compensation. The excise tax does not apply if a payment is simply triggered by a target value of the corporation's stock or where a payment depends on a performance measure other than the value of the corporation's stock. Similarly, the tax does not apply if the amount of the payment is not directly measured by the value of the stock or an increase in the value of the stock (House Committee Report, H.R. Rep. No. 108-548).

> **Example:** Expat Co. has an arrangement under which its CEO, a disqualified individual, would be paid a cash bonus equal to $10,000 for every $1 increase in the share price of the corporation's stock. The CEO is subject to the excise tax because the direct connection between the compensation amount and the value of the corporation's stock gives the CEO, a disqualified individual, an

economic stake substantially similar to that of a shareholder. By contrast, an arrangement under which the CEO would be paid a cash bonus of $500,000 if the corporation's stock increased in value by 25 percent over two years or $1,000,000 if the stock increased by 33 percent over two years is not specified stock compensation, even though the amount of the bonus generally is tied to an increase in the value of the stock (House Committee Report, H.R. Rep. No. 108-548).

Any payment of this excise tax directly or indirectly by the expatriated corporation or by any member of the expanded affiliated group which includes such corporation is treated as specified stock compensation, and is not allowed as an income tax deduction (Code Sec. 4985(f)(2), as added by the 2004 Jobs Act). Whether there is specified stock compensation, and its value, is determined without regard to any restriction other than a restriction which by its terms will never lapse (Code Sec. 4985(f)(3), as added by the 2004 Jobs Act).

Special rules. Certain special rules apply. The cancellation of a restriction which by its terms will never lapse is treated as a grant. Whether there is specified stock compensation, and its value, is determined without regard to any restriction other than a restriction which by its terms will never lapse. Moreover, any transfer of property is treated as a payment and any right to a transfer of property is treated as a right to a payment. For purposes of exempt organization rules, any excise tax imposed by these rules will be treated as an income tax (Code Sec. 4985(f), as added the 2004 Jobs Act).

The rule that any amount deferred under a nonqualified deferred compensation plan will be taken into account for purposes of the FICA rules as of the later of when the services are performed, or when there is no substantial risk of forfeiture of the rights to such amount does not apply to any specified stock compensation on which this excise tax is imposed (Code Sec. 3121(v)(2)(A), as amended by the 2004 Jobs Act).

Deductions denied. Not only is an excise tax imposed on the stock compensation of certain insiders of expatriated corporations, but deductions related to the compensation are denied (Code Sec. 275(a) and 162(m)(4), as amended by the 2004 Jobs Act). First, the payment of this excise tax is not deductible as a tax (Code Secs. 275(a), as amended by the 2004 Jobs Act). Also, as previously noted, the payment of this excise tax directly or indirectly (e.g., through reimbursement of the disqualified individual's payment) by the expatriated corporation or by any member of the expanded affiliated group is both treated as specified stock compensation and is not allowed as any type of deduction in computing income taxes (Code Sec. 4985(f)(2), as added by the 2004 Jobs Act). Second, the $1,000,000 limit on deductible compensation is reduced (but not below zero) by the payment of this excise tax directly or indirectly by the expatriated corporation or by any member of the expanded affiliated group (Code Sec. 162(m)(4), as amended by the 2004 Jobs Act).

Regulatory authority. The Treasury Secretary can issue whatever regulations are necessary or appropriate to carry out the purposes of these rules (Code Sec. 4985(g), as added by the 2004 Jobs Act).

For further information on this subject, consult any of the following CCH reporter explanations:

- Standard Federal Tax Reporter, 2004FED ¶ 8520.01 and ¶ 14,502.01
- Federal Tax Service, FTS § B:6.40 and § B:8.40
- Federal Tax Guide, 2004FTG ¶ 11,810 and ¶ 17,055

★ *Effective date.* The amendments made by these rules take effect retroactively on March 4, 2003. However, periods before March 4, 2003, will not be taken into account in determining the "12-month period that is six months before the expatriation date" referred to in the rule described above imposing this excise tax and in defining a disqualified individual (see Code Sec. 4985(a) and (e)(1), as added by the American Jobs Creation Act of 2004 (Act Sec. 802(d) of the 2004 Jobs Act).

Act Sec. 802(a) of the American Jobs Creation Act of 2004, adding Code Sec. 4985; Act Sec. 802(b)(1), amending Code Sec. 275(a)(6); Act Sec. 802(b)(2), adding Code Sec. 162(m)(4)(G); Act Sec. 802(c), amending Code Sec. 3121(v)(2)(A); Act Sec. 802(d). Law at ¶ 5160, ¶ 5285, ¶ 5960, ¶ 6105. Committee Report at ¶ 10,980.

¶ 510

Reporting of Taxable Mergers and Acquisitions

Background ————————————————————————

Brokers (defined to include stock transfer agents) are required to make information returns and provide corresponding payee statements with regard to sales made on behalf of their customers (Code Sec. 6045). Failure to do so will subject a broker to penalties. This requirement generally does not apply with respect to taxable transactions other than exchanges for cash, such as, for example, stock inversion transactions taxable to shareholders by reason of Code Sec. 367(a) (Temporary Reg. § 1.6045-3T(b)). However, recently issued temporary regulations under Code Sec. 6043 (relating to information reporting with respect to liquidations, recapitalizations, and changes in control) impose information reporting requirements with respect to certain taxable inversion transactions (see Temporary Reg. § 1.6043-4T, as amended by T.D. 9101, 12/29/2003). Furthermore, proposed regulations would expand these requirements more generally to taxable transactions occurring after the proposed regulations are finalized (Proposed Reg. § 1.6043-4).

American Jobs Creation Act Impact

Taxable merger and acquisition reporting rules modified.—If gain or loss is recognized in whole or in part by shareholders of a corporation by reason of a second corporation's acquisition of the stock or assets of the first corporation, then the acquiring corporation is required to make a return. The acquiring corporation in any taxable acquisition must make a return setting forth:

(1) a description of the acquisition,

(2) the name and address of each shareholder of the acquired corporation who is required to recognize gain (if any) as a result of the acquisition,

(3) the amount of money and the fair market value of other property transferred to each such shareholder as part of such acquisition, and

(4) such other information as the Secretary may prescribe (Code Sec. 6043A, as added by the American Jobs Creation Act of 2004).

Comment: Congress believed that administration of the tax laws would be improved by greater information reporting with respect to taxable non-cash transactions. Congress believed that the Treasury Secretary's authority to require such enhanced reporting should be made explicit in the Code.

Caution Note: The IRS has not yet released the form that will be used to report these taxable acquisitions. However, to the extent provided by the Secretary, the reporting requirements applicable to the acquiring corporation will be applicable to the acquired corporation instead of the acquiring corporation.

Comment: According to the House Committee Report to the 2004 Jobs Act (H. Rept. 108-548), a stock transfer agent who records transfers of stock in these transactions may make this information return instead of the second acquiring corporation.

Statement for shareholders. According to the forms or regulations prescribed by the Secretary, every person required to make one of these information returns will give to each shareholder whose name is required to be set forth in such return a written statement showing:

(1) the name, address, and phone number of the information contact of the person required to make such return,

(2) the information required to be shown on such return with respect to such shareholder, and

(3) such other information as the Secretary may prescribe.

This written statement must be given to the shareholder on or before January 31 of the year following the calendar year during which the taxable acquisition occurred (Code Sec. 6043A(d), as added by the 2004 Jobs Act).

Nominees. Any person who holds stock as a nominee for another person will give the other person the information that must be provided by the corporation to the shareholders. In the case of stock held by any person as a nominee, references to a shareholder shall be treated as a reference to the nominee (other than when defining a taxable acquisition under these rules) (Code Sec. 6043A(b), as added by the 2004 Jobs Act).

Taxable acquisition. For purposes of these rules, the term "taxable acquisition" means any acquisition by a corporation of stock in or property of another corporation if any shareholder of the acquired corporation is required to recognize gain (if any) as a result of such acquisition (Code Sec. 6043A(c), as added by the 2004 Jobs Act).

Penalties. Any failure to file an information return with the Secretary on or before the required filing date, and any failure to include all of the information required to be shown on the return or the inclusion of incorrect information is subject to existing information reporting requirement penalties (Code Sec. 6721 and Code Sec. 6724(d), as amended by the 2004 Jobs Act). Similarly, any failure to furnish a payee statement on or before the appropriate date to the person to whom such statement is required to be furnished, and any failure to include all of the information required to be shown on the payee statement or the inclusion of incorrect information is subject to existing penalties (Code Sec. 6722).

For further information on this subject, consult any of the following CCH reporter explanations:

- Standard Federal Tax Reporter, 2004FED ¶35,888.01 and ¶40,285.01
- Federal Tax Service, FTS §I:3.184 and §P:3.161
- Federal Tax Guide, 2004FTG ¶22,037

★ *Effective date.* The amendments made by these provisions apply to acquisitions after the date of the enactment (Act Sec. 805(d) of the American Jobs Creation Act of 2004).

Act Sec. 805(a) of the American Jobs Creation Act of 2004, adding Code Sec. 6043A; Act Sec. 805(b)(1), amending Code Sec. 6724(d)(1)(B); Act Sec. 805(b)(2), amending Code Sec. 6724(d)(2); Act Sec. 805(c); Act Sec. 805(d). Law at ¶6145 and ¶6310. Committee Report at ¶11,010.

¶ 515

Reinsurance of United States Risks in Foreign Jurisdictions

Background

In the case of a reinsurance agreement between two or more related persons, the IRS has the authority to allocate among the parties or recharacterize income (whether investment income, premium or otherwise), deductions, assets, reserves, credits and any other items related to the reinsurance agreement, or make any other adjustment, in order to reflect the proper source and character of the items for each party (Code Sec. 845(a)). Persons are related if they are organizations, trades or businesses (whether or not incorporated, whether or not organized in the United States, and whether or not affiliated) that are owned or controlled directly or indirectly by the same interests (Code Sec. 482). The provision may apply to a contract even if one of the related parties is not a domestic company. In addition, the provision also permits such allocation, recharacterization, or other adjustments in a case in which one of the parties to a reinsurance agreement is, with respect to any contract covered by the agreement, in effect an agent of another party to the agreement, or a conduit between related persons.

American Jobs Creation Act Impact

IRS power to reallocate items among the parties to a reinsurance agreement expanded.—In the case of two or more related persons who are parties to a reinsurance agreement, the IRS may reallocate certain items (Code Sec. 482). These rules also apply where one of the parties to a reinsurance agreement is, with respect to any contract covered by the agreement, in effect an agent of another party to such agreement or a conduit between related persons. In such cases, the IRS may allocate between or among such person's income (whether investment income, premium, or otherwise), deductions, assets, reserves, credits, and other items related to such agreement. The IRS may also recharacterize any such items. Further, the IRS may make any other adjustment, if it determines that such allocation, recharacterization, or adjustment is necessary to reflect the proper *amount*, source, and character of the taxable income (or any item relating to such taxable income) of each such person (Code Sec. 845(a), as amended by the American Jobs Creation Act of 2004).

> **Comment:** Congress was concerned that reinsurance transactions were being used to allocate income, deductions, or other items inappropriately among U.S. and foreign related persons. Congress was concerned that foreign related-party reinsurance arrangements may be a technique for eroding the U.S. tax base. Congress believed that the rules permitting the IRS to allocate or recharacterize items related to a reinsurance agreement should be applied to prevent misallocation and improper characterization, or to make any other adjustment in the case of such reinsurance transactions between U.S. and foreign related persons (or agents or conduits). Congress also wished to clarify that, in applying the authority with respect to reinsurance agreements, the *amount*, source or character of the items may be allocated, recharacterized or adjusted (House Committee Report to the 2004 Jobs Act, H.R. Rept. No. 108-548).

> **Caution Note:** It is intended that this reallocation authority be exercised in a manner similar to the authority under the rules (Code Sec. 482) that allow the IRS to make adjustments between related parties. It is also intended that this authority be applied in situations in which the related persons (or agents or conduits) are engaged in cross-border transactions that require allocation, recharacterization, or other adjustments in order to reflect the proper source,

character or amount of the item or items. However, it cannot be inferred that prior law did not provide this authority with respect to reinsurance agreements.

Comment: According to the House Committee Report, this authority to allocate, recharacterize or make other adjustments was granted in connection with the repeal of provisions relating to modified coinsurance transactions (House Committee Report to the 2004 Jobs Act, H. R. Rept. No. 108-548). No regulations have yet been issued under these rules. It is expected that regulations will be issued under these rules that will address effectively the allocation of income (whether investment income, premium or otherwise) and other items, the recharacterization of such items, or any other adjustment necessary to reflect the proper amount, source or character of the item.

For further information on this subject, consult any of the following CCH reporter explanations:

- Standard Federal Tax Reporter, 2004FED ¶26,311.01

- Federal Tax Service, FTS §M:8.61

- Federal Tax Guide, 2004FTG ¶17,445

★ *Effective date.* These changes to the IRS reallocation powers apply to any risk reinsured after the date of enactment (Act Sec. 803(b) of the American Jobs Creation Act of 2004).

Act Sec. 803(a) of the American Jobs Creation Act of 2004, amending Code Sec. 845(a); Act Sec. 803(b). Law at ¶5540. Committee Report at ¶10,990.

¶ 520

Limitation on Transfer or Importation of Built-In Losses

Background ——————————————————————————

Under Code Sec. 362, a corporation's basis in assets received in a tax-free transfer is the same as the adjusted basis of the assets in the hands of the transferor, increased by the amount of any gain recognized by the transferor in the transaction. The basis of the transferred assets is also replicated in the basis of the stock received by the transferor in the exchange, adjusted for any gain or loss recognized by the transferor, and for the amount of any money or property received in the exchange (Code Sec. 358). After a complete liquidation of a subsidiary, a parent company usually holds the distributed assets with the same basis that the assets formerly had in the hands of the subsidiary. However, if the subsidiary recognizes gain or loss in the liquidation, the parent's basis in the assets is their fair market value (Code Sec. 334(b)).

The above basis rules apply whether or not the transferee of the assets is a domestic or foreign person. In the latter case, however, there is a tax avoidance potential where assets with foreign-generated built-in losses are imported into the U.S. and used to shelter U.S. income that would otherwise be taxed. The current tax rules, particularly Code Secs. 367, 897 and 1291, deal only with the expatriation of built-in gain property intended to shelter the inherent gain from U.S. taxation. These rules do not address the importation of built-in losses into the U.S.

The same tax avoidance potential exists when built-in loss property is transferred by domestic persons and the transaction is governed by Code Sec. 351. Since Code Sec. 362 basis rules apply to Code Sec. 351 transactions, such transfers may also result in the duplication of built-in loss.

American Jobs Creation Act Impact

Transfer or importation of built-in losses limited in tax-free transactions.—If a net built-in loss is imported into the U.S. in a tax-free transfer by persons not subject to U.S. tax, the corporate transferee's basis in the property transferred by such persons is its fair market value (Code Secs. 362(e)(1)(A) and 362(e)(1)(B), as added by the American Jobs Creation Act of 2004). A net built-in loss is treated as imported if the corporate transferee's aggregate adjusted basis in the property transferred is greater than the fair market value of such property immediately after the transaction (Code Sec. 362(e)(1)(C), as added by the 2004 Jobs Act). If the transferor is a partnership, either domestic or foreign, the built-in loss limitation rules apply as if the property had been transferred by each of the partners in proportion to their interests in the partnership (Code Sec. 362(e)(1)(B), as added by the 2004 Jobs Act).

Similarly, a domestic corporation's basis in the property distributed in a tax-free liquidation of a foreign subsidiary is limited to the fair market value of the property if the parent's aggregate adjusted basis in such property exceeds its fair market value immediately after the liquidation (Code Sec. 334(b)(1), as amended by the 2004 Jobs Act).

> **Comment:** The new provisions prevent taxpayers from using foreign-generated losses to offset U.S. taxable income by requiring corporate transferees to step-up or step-down the basis of the transferred assets to their fair market value. The new rules apply in the cases where the transferors are persons exempt from U.S. tax, such as foreign corporations that do not have a Code Sec. 902 U.S. shareholder and nonresident alien individuals. The limitation on built-in loss importation also applies to transfers of property from a Code Sec. 501 tax-exempt organization where gain or loss would not be subject to tax if the property were sold by the organization (Senate Committee Report, S. Rep. No. 108-192).

In addition, if persons subject to U.S. tax transfer property in a Code Sec. 351 transaction and the aggregate adjusted basis of the transferred property exceeds its aggregate fair market value, the corporate transferee's aggregate basis in the transferred property is generally limited to its aggregate fair market value immediately after the transaction (Code Sec. 362(e)(2)(A), as added by the 2004 Jobs Act). As a result of the limitation, any required aggregate basis reduction is allocated among the transferred properties in proportion to their built-in loss immediately before the transaction (Code Sec. 362(e)(2)(B), as added by the 2004 Jobs Act). The transferor and transferee are allowed, instead of limiting the basis of the transferred property, to make an irrevocable election to limit the basis in the stock received by the transferor to the aggregate fair market value of the transferred property (Code Sec. 362(e)(2)(C), as added by the 2004 Jobs Act). The election must be included with the tax returns of the transferor and transferee for the tax year in which the Code Sec. 351 transaction occurs.

> **Comment:** This provision will prevent the economic loss inherent in the transferred assets from being replicated both in the transferor's basis in the stock and the assets' basis in the hands of the corporate transferee, i.e. the loss can no longer be deducted more than once.

PRACTICAL ANALYSIS. Jeffrey Paravano of Baker & Hostetler and former Treasury official observes that the limitation on transfer and importation of built-in losses has been scaled back substantially compared to the Senate version. The Senate proposal would have eliminated duplication of losses without taking into account gain duplication.

For further information on this subject, consult any of the following CCH reporter explanations:

- Standard Federal Tax Reporter, 2004FED ¶ 16,152.01 and ¶ 16,612.01
- Federal Tax Service, FTS § I:12.140
- Federal Tax Guide, 2004FTG ¶ 12,390 and ¶ 17,085

★ *Effective date.* The provisions apply to transactions after the date of enactment (Act Sec. 836(c) of the American Jobs Creation Act of 2004).

Act Sec. 836(a) of the American Jobs Creation Act of 2004, adding Code Sec. 362(e); Act. Sec. 836(b) amending Code Sec. 334(b)(1); Act Sec. 836(c). Law at ¶ 5310 and ¶ 5335. Committee Report at ¶ 11,190.

¶ 525
Study on Effect of Earnings Stripping Rules

Background

"Earnings stripping" occurs when a U.S. corporation pays deductible expenses to a related non-U.S. corporation, thus reducing or "stripping" the U.S. company of its U.S. taxable income. The company receiving the interest typically pays little or no U.S. tax on the interest income (Joint Committee on Taxation Report on the U.S. International Tax Rules: Background, Data, and Selected Issues Relating to the Competitiveness of U.S.-Based Operations, JCX-67-03, July 9, 2003).

The Code currently contains rules to restrict earnings stripping through interest payments. Interest payments to certain related parties are not deductible if the payor's debt-equity ratio exceeds 1.5 to 1 and the payor's net interest expense exceeds 50 percent of its adjusted taxable income (computed without certain expenses such as interest, depreciation, and losses) (Code Sec. 163(j)). Disallowed interest deductions can be carried forward indefinitely. Excess limitation amounts (the amount by which the company's interest expense is less than the 50 percent limit) can be carried forward three years.

Earnings stripping and noncorporate entities. The earnings stripping provision in Code Sec. 163(j) does not apply to partnerships or S corporations. It is thus possible for a partnership or S corporation to deduct interest payments that would be disallowed to a C corporation under the earnings stripping rule. As one step toward reforming this loophole, the IRS has issued proposed regulations attributing partnership debt to a corporate partner (Proposed Reg. § 1.163(j)-3(b)(3)) for purposes of determining the corporation's debt-equity ratio and providing that interest paid or accrued by a partnership is treated as interest expense of a corporate partner (Proposed Reg. § 1.163(j)-2(e)(4)), with the result that a deduction for the interest expense may be disallowed if that expense would be disallowed under the earnings stripping rules if paid by the corporate partner itself. A proposed Senate amendment to the American Jobs Creation Act of 2004 would have attributed partnership debt to a corporate partner for purposes of applying the earnings stripping rules, but this amendment was not adopted (Conference Committee Report, H.R. Rep. No. 108-755).

Enron Corporation was among the companies that have made extensive use of the entity loopholes in the earnings stripping rules. The Joint Committee on Taxation's report on Enron specifically recommended strengthening the earnings stripping rules to disregard or limit the creation of business entities formed with the specific purpose of evading the earnings stripping rules (Report of Investigation of Enron Corporation and Related Entities Regarding Federal Tax and Compensation Issues, and Policy Recommendations, Volume I, JCS-3-03, February 2003).

Background

Earnings stripping and inversions. The lure of earnings stripping encourages corporate inversions. Corporate inversion occurs when a U.S. company sets up a foreign incorporated firm to become the parent corporation, while the U.S. firm becomes the subsidiary of the foreign corporation. Inversion offers two main tax advantages: avoiding U.S. tax on foreign earnings and earnings stripping. The inverted business form facilitates earnings stripping because the U.S. subsidiary can reduce its taxable domestic earnings by making deductible interest payments to a foreign parent company that is not subject to U.S. income tax on the interest income.

The foreign parent may have to recognize the interest payments as income, but will likely avoid U.S. tax on the income. A withholding provision designed to prevent earnings stripping requires the U.S. interest payer to withhold 30% of interest payments to the foreign parent; however, the withholding tax may be reduced or eliminated through tax treaty provisions. An inversion transaction may be set up with the foreign parent in a nontreaty country (such as a tax haven with no corporate income tax) in order to avoid corporate income tax, while a subsidiary in a treaty country is set up to receive the interest payments and thus avoid the withholding obligation (see Congressional Research Service Report for Congress: Firms That Incorporate Abroad for Tax Purposes: Corporate "Inversions" and "Expatriation," June 24, 2004).

Treasury Department proposals to reform earnings stripping. The Treasury Department issued a report on corporate inversions in 2002 in which it recommended tightening the earnings stripping rules. The report also noted that further work is needed to address income shifting in areas apart from related-party debt (U.S. Department of the Treasury, Office of Tax Policy, Corporate Inversion Transactions: Tax Policy Implications, May 2002).

The Treasury Department's recommended changes to the earnings stripping rules include replacing the safe harbor debt-equity test with a test that measures the extent to which a corporate group's level of indebtedness in the United States exceeds its worldwide level of indebtedness. The worldwide test would compare (i) the ratio of indebtedness incurred by the U.S. members of the corporate group to their assets, with (ii) the ratio of the entire corporate group's worldwide indebtedness (excluding related party debt) to its worldwide assets. It also proposed changing the definition of adjusted taxable income for the 50-percent-of-income test so that depreciation, amortization and depletion are not added back, in order to focus the test on interest as a percentage of net income rather than net cash flow. The Treasury report also suggests limiting the carryforward of disallowed deductions to five years. For a summary of the 2004 Budget and other proposals related to earnings stripping, see the Joint Committee on Taxation Report on the U.S. International Tax Rules: Background, Data, and Selected Issues Relating to the Competitiveness of U.S.-Based Operations, JCX-67-03, July 9, 2003.

American Jobs Creation Act Impact

Treasury Department required to conduct study of earnings stripping rules.— The Treasury Department is required to conduct a study of the earnings stripping rules, including:

(1) the effectiveness of earnings stripping rules under Code Sec. 163(j) in preventing the shifting of income outside the United States;

(2) whether any deficiencies in the earnings stripping rules have the effect of placing U.S.-based businesses at a competitive disadvantage relative to foreign-based businesses;

(3) the impact of earnings stripping activities on the U.S. tax base;

(4) whether laws of foreign countries facilitate the stripping of earnings out of the United States; and

(5) whether changes to the earnings stripping rules would affect jobs in the United States.

This study is to include specific recommendations for improving these rules and is to be submitted to Congress not later than June 30, 2005.

For further information on this subject, consult any of the following CCH reporter explanations:

- Standard Federal Tax Reporter, 2004FED ¶9406N.01
- Federal Tax Service, FTS § G:7.105
- Federal Tax Guide, 2004FTG ¶17,395 and ¶17,460

★ *Effective date.* The provision is effective on the date of enactment. The study required by the provision is to be submitted to Congress no later than June 30, 2005.

Act Sec. 424 of the American Jobs Creation Act of 2004. Law at ¶7030. Committee Report at ¶10,800.

¶ 530
Studies

Background

Tax rates and tax systems vary among countries. As a consequence, a multinational enterprise, whether U.S.-based or foreign-based, may have an incentive to shift income, deductions, or tax credits in order to arrive at a reduced overall tax burden. Such a shifting of items could be accomplished by establishing artificial, non-arm's-length prices for transactions between group members.

The Treasury Secretary is authorized to reallocate income, deductions, or credits between or among two or more organizations, trades, or businesses under common control if he determines that such a reallocation is necessary to prevent tax evasion or to clearly reflect income (Code Sec. 482). The arm's-length standard is the standard for determining whether such reallocations are appropriate. Transactions involving intangible property and certain services may present particular challenges to the administration of the arm's-length standard, because the nature of these transactions may make it difficult or impossible to compare them with third-party transactions.

In addition to the statutory rules governing the taxation of foreign income of U.S. persons and U.S. income of foreign persons, bilateral income tax treaties limit the amount of income tax that may be imposed by one treaty partner on residents of the other treaty partner. This may present opportunities for artificially lowering the overall tax burden of a multinational enterprise.

Inversion transactions may present an opportunity to shift income, deductions, or tax credits in order to arrive at a reduced overall tax burden. Under present law, a U.S. corporation may reincorporate in a foreign jurisdiction and thereby replace the U.S. parent corporation of a multinational corporate group with a foreign parent corporation. These transactions are commonly referred to as inversion transactions.

American Jobs Creation Act Impact

Treasury to study foreign income tax rules.—The Secretary of the Treasury or the Secretary's delegate is empowered to conduct studies on transfer pricing, income tax treaties and the impact of corporate expatriation rules (Act Sec. 806 of the American Jobs Creation Act of 2004). Congress believes that it is important to evaluate the effectiveness of the current transfer pricing rules and compliance efforts with respect to related-party transactions to ensure that income is not being shifted outside of the United States (House Committee Report, H.R. Rep. No. 108-548). Congress also believes that it is necessary to review current U.S. income tax treaties to identify any inappropriate reductions in withholding tax rates that may create opportunities for shifting income outside the United States. In addition, Congress believes that the impact of the provisions of the 2004 Jobs Act on inversion transactions (Act Sec. 801 of the 2004 Jobs Act, see ¶506) should be studied.

Transfer pricing study. The Secretary of the Treasury or the Secretary's delegate will conduct a study regarding the effectiveness of current transfer pricing rules and compliance efforts in ensuring that cross-border transfers and other related-party transactions, particularly transactions involving intangible assets, service contracts, or leases, cannot be used improperly to shift income out of the United States. The study must include a review of the contemporaneous documentation and penalty rules under Code Sec. 6662. It must also include a review of the regulatory and administrative guidance implementing the principles of Code Sec. 482 to transactions involving intangible property and services and to cost-sharing arrangements. The study will also include an examination of whether increased disclosure of cross-border transactions should be required. The study will provide specific recommendations to address all abuses identified in the study. The Secretary or delegate must submit a report of such study to Congress not later than June 30, 2005.

Income tax treaties study. The Secretary of the Treasury or the Secretary's delegate must conduct a study of U. S. income tax treaties to identify any inappropriate reductions in U. S. withholding tax that provide opportunities for shifting income out of the United States. The study must also evaluate whether existing anti-abuse mechanisms are operating properly. The study will include specific recommendations to address all inappropriate uses of tax treaties. The Secretary or delegate must submit a report of such study to Congress not later than June 30, 2005.

Inversion transactions study. The Secretary of the Treasury or the Secretary's delegate shall conduct a study of the impact of the provisions of this title on corporate expatriation. The study shall include such recommendations as such Secretary or delegate may have to improve the impact of such provisions in carrying out the purposes of this title. The Secretary or delegate must submit a report of such study to Congress not later than December 31, 2005.

For further information on this subject, consult any of the following CCH reporter explanations:

- Standard Federal Tax Reporter, 2004FED ¶22,283.01, ¶27,642.01, ¶35,888.01, ¶39,490.01 and ¶39,651D.01
  - Federal Tax Service, FTS §M:5.20 and §M:6.20
  - Federal Tax Guide, 2004FTG ¶17,020

★ *Effective date.* No specific effective date is provided by the Act. The provision is, therefore, considered effective on the date of enactment.

Act Sec. 806 of the American Jobs Creation Act of 2004. Law at ¶7090. Committee Report at ¶11,020.

¶530

INVESTMENT IN THE UNITED STATES

¶ 535

Temporary Dividends Received Deduction

Background

The general rule with respect to the U.S. taxation of dividends earned by foreign corporation subsidiaries is that the income is not taxed until the dividends are repatriated back to the parent corporation (with exceptions for various anti-deferral provisions like subpart F income). This residual U.S. tax on repatriated dividends can serve as a disincentive to repatriate these earnings. Indeed, U.S. companies have reinvested billions of dollars overseas as a result of this policy. It is intended that a temporary reduction in the U.S. tax on repatriated dividends will stimulate the U.S. domestic economy by triggering the repatriation of earnings that otherwise would have remained abroad.

American Jobs Creation Act Impact

Temporary dividend deduction allowed.—In the case of a corporation that is a U.S. shareholder and for which an election is in effect for the tax year, there is allowed a deduction equal to 85 percent of the cash dividends received during the tax year by the shareholder from controlled foreign corporations and invested in the United States (Code Sec. 965(a), as added by the American Jobs Creation Act of 2004).

Election. The taxpayer may elect to apply the temporary dividends-received deduction to either:

(1) the taxpayer's last tax year that begins before the date of enactment or

(2) the taxpayer's first tax year that begins during the one-year period beginning on that date.

The election may be made for a tax year only if made before the due date (including extensions) for filing the tax return for the tax year (Code Sec. 965(f), as added by the 2004 Jobs Act).

> **Comment:** The Conferees emphasized the temporary nature of this dividends-received deduction and stated explicitly that there is no intent to make this tax break permanent, or to extend or enact it again in the future (H.R. Conf. Rep. No. 108-755). This means that taxpayers will have to act quickly to elect the benefits under this temporary provision, paying special attention to effective dates, as well as the timing and manner of making the election.

Dividends paid indirectly from CFCs. If, within the tax year for which an election is in effect, a U.S. shareholder receives a cash distribution from a controlled foreign corporation (CFC) that is excluded from gross income under the previously taxed income (PTI) provisions of Code Sec. 959(a), the distribution is treated as a cash dividend to the extent of any amount included in income by the U.S. shareholder under Code Sec. 951(a)(1)(A) (subpart F income) as a result of any cash dividend paid during the tax year to:

(1) the CFC from another CFC that is in a chain of ownership described in Code Sec. 958(a) (direct or indirect stock ownership), or

(2) any other CFC in the chain of ownership, but only to the extent of cash distributions described under Code Sec. 959(b) that are made during the tax year to the CFC from which the U.S. shareholder received the distribution (Code Sec. 965(a)(2), as added by the 2004 Jobs Act).

This exception enables multinational corporate groups to qualify for the deduction in connection with the repatriation of earnings from lower-tier controlled foreign corporations (H.R. Conf. Rep. No. 108-755).

> PRACTICAL ANALYSIS. Lowell D. Yoder of McDermott Will & Emery, Chicago, Illinois, notes that this new section provides a one-year window to U.S. corporations to receive low-taxed dividends from their controlled foreign corporations (CFCs) with only a 5.25-percent tax rate. Under certain circumstances, the rate may be reduced to zero with excess foreign tax credits.
>
> This provision is elective and is available for cash dividends in excess of a base period amount. The base period amount is determined as the annual average amount of certain actual and deemed distributions received from CFCs during three of the prior five years. The amounts include actual dividends, Code Sec. 956 investments in U.S. property and distributions of previously taxed income resulting from subpart F income inclusions.
>
> This dividends received deduction (DRD) benefits a company with low-taxed earnings offshore, which can distribute the earnings and reduce the tax rate from 35 percent to 5.25 percent. Applying this provision to high-taxed foreign earnings also can be beneficial to a company with net operating losses (it preserves the losses) or a company with overall foreign losses.
>
> It is critical that the provisions be applied correctly. If they are not, the full amount of the dividend is subject to taxation (i.e., as much as a 35-percent tax rate on low-taxed dividends). In particular, it is essential that the dividend be properly invested in the United States and this should be carefully documented and the proper authorizations should be obtained.
>
> Unfortunately, the legislation does not allow investments in U.S. property included in gross income under subpart F (e.g., a loan from a CFC to its U.S. parent) to qualify for the DRD (yet such amounts are included in the base period calculation). Only actual cash dividends qualify. Dividends paid by lower-tier CFCs, however, qualify if they are included in the gross income of the U.S. company under subpart F and the cash is distributed to the U.S. shareholder during the tax year.
>
> Since cash has to be distributed to the U.S. shareholder, it is important to minimize foreign withholding taxes. Under the provision, 85 percent of such withholding taxes cannot be claimed as a credit or deduction. Recently, the U.K. treaty provided for zero withholding taxes on dividends and the Dutch treaty may provide for no withholding taxes in 2005. In addition, various holding company structures may be used to minimize withholding taxes as well as Code Sec. 304 related party sale transactions (and deemed dividends under that section qualify for the DRD).
>
> It is critical to carefully apply all of the computational rules to a company's particular circumstances to determine the full U.S. tax costs of a qualifying dividend. One aspect of the legislation is that the gross-up amount for deemed paid taxes is excluded from dividends that qualify for the 85-percent deduction, and only deemed paid taxes associated with the 15-percent amount included in income can be claimed as

a credit (but there may be some uncertainty concerning whether the noncreditable amount is included in income under Code Sec. 78). In this regard, the base amount should be satisfied with high-taxed earnings (and the foreign tax credits used in full) and low-taxed earnings used for the 85-percent DRD. In addition, expenses allocable and apportionable to the deductible amount may not be claimed as a deduction. State income taxes also must be considered.

Limitations on the dividend deduction.—In general, the amount of dividends taken into account may not exceed the greater of: or

(1) $500,000,000,

(2) the amount shown on the applicable financial statement as earnings permanently reinvested outside the U.S.,

(3) in the case of an applicable financial statement that fails to show a specific amount of earnings permanently reinvested outside the United States and that shows a specific amount of tax liability attributable to such earnings, the amount of the liability divided by 0.35.

The effect of this mathematical operation is to produce an earnings amount by effectively "grossing up" the tax liability at a 35-percent rate.

However, if there is no applicable financial statement or if that statement fails to show a specific amount of earnings or tax liability upon which a computation of earnings can be made, the earnings amount is deemed to be zero for limitation purposes and therefore, the limitation amount is, in effect, $500,000,000 (Code Sec. 965(b)(1), as added by the 2004 Jobs Act).

Dividends must be extraordinary. The deduction applies only to repatriations in excess of the taxpayer's base period amount (discussed below) of past repatriations. The amount of dividends taken into account cannot exceed the excess (if any) of (1) the dividends received during the tax year by the shareholder from CFCs, over (2) the annual average for the base period years of: (i) the dividends received during each base period year by the shareholder from CFCs, (ii) the amounts includible in the shareholder's gross income for each base period year under Code Sec. 951(a)(1)(B) (investment of earnings in U.S. property) with respect to CFCs and (iii) the amounts that would have been included for each base period year but for the previously taxed earnings and profits exclusion provisions of Code Sec. 959(a) (PTI) with respect to CFCs. The amount taken into account under (iii) above (PTI), for any base period must not include any amount that is not includable in gross income by reason of an amount described in (ii) above (investment of earnings in U.S. property) with respect to a prior tax year. The dividends used in computing the annual average for the base period for any base period year are the amounts reported on the most recent return filed for that year, except that amended returns filed after June 30, 2003, do not count for this purpose (Code Sec. 965(b)(2), as added by the 2004 Jobs Act).

General rule for computing base period years. The deduction is allowed only for repatriations in excess of the base period average computed in a specified manner over a specified number of years. The base period years are the three tax years (1) that are among the five most recent tax years ending on or before June 30, 2003, and (2) that are determined by disregarding the highest and lowest repatriation years. (Code Sec. 965(c)(2)(A), as added by the 2004 Jobs Act).

If the taxpayer has fewer than five tax years ending on or before June 30, 2003, then in lieu of applying the general rule above, the base period years includes all of the tax years of the taxpayer ending on or before June 30, 2003 (Code Sec. 965(c)(2)(B), as added by the 2004 Jobs Act).

Special base period rule for mergers, acquisitions and spin-offs. In general, rules similar to the tax credit rules for increasing research activities under Code Secs. 41(f)(3)(A) and 41(f)(3)(B) apply for purposes of computing the base period years. These credit rules relate to adjustments to the amount of qualified research expenses for certain acquisitions and dispositions of a major portion of a trade or business.

With respect to spin-offs, if there is a distribution to which Code Sec. 355 (distributions of stock and securities of a controlled corporation), or so much of Code Sec. 356 (receipt of additional consideration in certain distributions and reorganizations) as relates to Code Sec. 355 applies during the five-year base period and the controlled corporation is a U.S. shareholder, then the following rules apply: (1) the controlled corporation is treated as being in existence during the period that the distributing corporation is in existence and (2) for purposes of applying the base period years rules to the controlled corporation and the distributing corporations, the amounts that are received or includible by the distributing corporation or controlled corporation before the distribution from a CFC is allocated between the corporations in proportion to their respective interests as U.S. shareholders of the CFC immediately after the distribution. The above allocation rule does not apply if neither the controlled corporation nor the distributing corporation is a U.S. shareholder of the CFC immediately after the distribution (Code Sec. 965(c)(2)(C), as added by the 2004 Jobs Act).

Reduction of benefit for increases in related party indebtedness. The dividend deduction amount otherwise allowable is reduced by the excess (if any) of: (1) the amount of indebtedness of the CFC to any related person as defined under Code Sec. 954(d)(3) as of the close of the tax year for which the election is in effect, over (2) the amount of indebtedness of the CFC to any related person as of the close of October 3, 2004. For purposes of this related party indebtedness rule, all CFCs with respect to which the taxpayer is a U.S. shareholder are treated as one CFC (Code Sec. 965(b)(3), as added by the 2004 Jobs Act).

> **Comment:** This rule is intended to prevent a deduction from being claimed in cases in which the U.S. shareholder directly or indirectly finances the payment of a dividend from a CFC. In such a case, there may be no net repatriation of funds, and thus, it would be inappropriate to provide the deduction (Conference Committee Report (H.R. Conf. Rep. No. 108-755)).

Domestic reinvestment plan requirement to invest in U.S. The deduction is not allowed for any dividend received by a U.S. shareholder unless the amount of the dividend is invested in the U.S. pursuant to a domestic reinvestment plan that: (1) is approved by the taxpayer's president, chief executive officer, or comparable official before the payment of the dividend and subsequently approved by the taxpayer's board of directors, management committee, executive committee or similar body and of such shareholder, and (2) provides for the reinvestment of the dividend in the U.S. (other than as payment for executive compensation), including as a source for the funding of worker hiring and training, infrastructure, research and development, capital investments, or the financial stabilization of the corporation for the purposes of job retention or creation (Code Sec. 965(b)(4), as added by the 2004 Jobs Act).

> **Comment:** The Conferees note that this list of permitted uses is not exclusive (H.R. Conf. Rep. No. 108-755).

> **PRACTICAL ANALYSIS. Martin J. Collins of PricewaterhouseCoopers LLP, in Chicago, Illinois,** notes that the 2004 Jobs Act creates a temporary incentive for U.S. multinationals to repatriate accumulated foreign earnings by providing an 85-percent dividends received deduction for certain dividends from controlled foreign corporations (commonly

known as the Homeland Investment Act, or HIA). The deduction is subject to a number of limitations. It applies only to repatriations in excess of the average repatriation level over three of the five most recent tax years ending on or before June 30, 2003 (the base period amount).

The HIA dividend is the actual cash dividend and does not include the Code Sec. 78 gross-up. The Code Sec. 78 gross-up relating to the HIA dividend should generally represent 15 percent of the normal underlying deemed paid foreign tax credits, but this provision is not entirely clear. Companies will need to look at their controlled foreign corporations' tax pools related to the HIA dividend to determine the true cost of the HIA dividend.

The amount of eligible dividends is limited to the greater of (1) $500 million, (2) the amount shown on the company's financial statement (certified on or before June 30, 2003) as permanently reinvested outside the United States, or (3) in the case of an applicable financial statement which fails to show a specific amount of earnings permanently reinvested outside the United States and which shows a specific amount of tax liability attributable to such earnings, the amount equal to the amount of such liability divided by 0.35. Unfortunately, companies that have stated an "incremental tax" liability amount in their financial statement may be unfairly disadvantaged as an "incremental tax" liability amount divided by 0.35 produces a smaller amount than intended and an amount that has no relationship to the relevant underlying earnings amount, particularly where the underlying earnings were subject to a high foreign tax rate. For companies that have a calendar year end, the applicable financial statements will be for their year-ended December 31, 2002.

The reinvestment plan requirements are generally vague. The Act requires a reinvestment plan to be approved by the CEO prior to the payment of the HIA dividend. Care should be exercised to make certain this requirement is not overlooked. Board of Director approval of the plan is also required, but that can be done after the HIA dividend.

The Act provides an election to apply the deduction to dividends received either during the first tax year beginning on or after the date of enactment, or during the last tax year beginning before the date of enactment. Thus, calendar year taxpayers may chose either to receive HIA benefits for either their 2004 or 2005 tax year. If a calendar year taxpayer elects to receive the HIA benefits for its 2004 tax year, an interesting question arises as to whether such a taxpayer will be able to satisfy the CEO pre-approval requirement with respect to its reinvestment plan. For additional coverage of Act Sec. 422, see Michael F. Urse, Tadd A. Fowler and Martin J. Collins, *Utilizing the Homeland Investment/Invest in USA Acts*, J. TAX'N GLOBAL TRANS., Fall 2004, at 39.

Applicable financial statement.—Under this provision, the term "applicable financial statement" means, with respect to a U.S. shareholder, the most recently audited financial statement (including notes and other documents which accompany the statement) that includes the shareholder: (1) that is certified on or before June 30, 2003, as being prepared in accordance with generally accepted accounting principles (GAAP); and (2) that is used for the purposes of a statement or report to creditors and shareholders, or for any other substantial nontax purpose. In the case of a corporation required to file a financial statement with the SEC, the term means the most recent statement filed on or before June 30, 2004 (Code Sec. 965(c)(1), as added by the 2004 Jobs Act).

Dividends.—The term "dividend" does not include amounts includible in gross income as a dividend under Code Sec. 78 (relating to dividends received from certain foreign corporations by domestic corporations choosing a foreign tax credit), Code Sec. 367 (relating to certain transfers of property from the U.S. to foreign corporations) or Code Sec. 1248 (relating to gain from certain sales or exchanges of stock in certain foreign corporations). However, this rule does not apply in the case of a liquidation under Code Sec. 332, to which Code Sec. 367(b) applies (relating to other transfers with respect to foreign corporations) to the extent that the U.S. shareholder actually receives cash as part of the liquidation (Code Sec. 965(c)(3), as added by the 2004 Jobs Act).

Coordination with dividends received deduction.—No deduction is allowed under Code Secs. 243 or 245 (dividends received deduction for domestic and foreign corporations) for any dividend for which a deduction is allowed under the new rule (Code Sec. 965(c)(4), as added by the 2004 Jobs Act).

Controlled groups. In general, all U.S. shareholders that are members of an affiliated group filing a consolidated return under Code Sec. 1501 are treated as one U.S. shareholder. In applying the $500,000,000 limit, all corporations that are treated as a single employer under Code Sec. 52(a) are limited to one $500,000,000 amount, and that amount is divided among the corporations according to regulations (Code Sec. 965(c)(5), as added by the 2004 Jobs Act). With respect to permanently reinvested earnings, if a financial statement is an applicable financial statement for more than one U.S. shareholder, the amount is divided among the shareholders under IRS regulations (Code Sec. 965(c)(5)(C), as added by the 2004 Jobs Act).

Denial of foreign tax credit and certain expenses.—In general, no foreign tax credit is allowed for any taxes paid or accrued (or treated as paid or accrued) with respect to the deductible portion of any dividend or of any amount described in Code Sec. 965(a)(2) (PTI) that is included in income under subpart F. In addition, no deduction is allowed for any tax for which the credit is not allowable under this rule (Code Sec. 965(d), as added by the 2004 Jobs Act).

Expenses. No deduction is allowed for expenses properly allocated and apportioned to the deduction portion of any dividend. Unless the taxpayer specifies otherwise, the deductible portion of any dividend or other amount is the amount that bears the same ratio to the amount of such dividend or other amount as the amount allowed as a deduction under this new provision for the tax year bears to the amount described in Code Sec. 965(b)(2)(A) for the year (the dividends received during the taxable year by the shareholder from CFCs) (Code Sec. 965(d), as added by the 2004 Jobs Act).

Increase in tax on included amounts not reduced by credits and other items.— For purposes of Internal Revenue Code provisions under Chapter 1, Normal Taxes and Surtaxes, any tax imposed by reason of nondeductible CFC dividends is not treated as a tax for purposes of determining: (1) the amount of any credit allowable (except for the credit for prior year minimum tax liability under Code Sec. 53 or the foreign tax credit under Code Secs. 27(a) and 901) or (2) the alternative minimum tax (Code Sec. 965(e)(1), as added by the 2004 Jobs Act).

Limitations on reduction in taxable income and other items. In general, the taxable income of any U.S. shareholder for any tax year can not be less than the amount of nondeductible CFC dividends received during such year. For purposes of coordination with the net operating loss provisions (NOLs) of Code Sec. 172, the nondeduct-

¶535

ible CFC dividends for any tax year is not taken into account: (1) in determining under the net operating loss provisions (NOL) of Code Sec. 172, the amount of any NOL for such tax year, and (2) in determining taxable income for such tax year for purposes of determining the amount of NOL carryback loss that may be carried to years other than the earliest carryback year under Code Sec. 172(b)(2)(Code Sec. 965(e)(2), as added by the 2004 Jobs Act).

Nondeductible CFC dividends. The term "nondeductible CFC dividends" means the excess of the amount of dividends taken into account over the dividend deduction allowed under the new provision.

Special alternative minimum tax rule for certain distributions from CFCs.— The alternative minimum tax adjusted current earnings (ACE) preference adjustment rule under Code Sec. 56(g)(4)(C)(i), which provides that no deduction is allowed for any item if the item would not be deductible in computing earnings and profits, does not apply to any of the dividend deduction allowable under this new provision (Code Sec. 56(g)(4)(C)(vi), as amended by the 2004 Jobs Act).

For further information on this subject, consult any of the following CCH reporter explanations:

- Standard Federal Tax Reporter, 2004FED ¶5201.01, ¶13,057.01, ¶13,152.01 and ¶28,474.01

- Federal Tax Service, FTS §I:2.20 and §M:15A.66

- Federal Tax Guide, 2004FTG ¶17,440 and ¶17,460

★ *Effective date.* The amendments apply to tax years ending on or after the date of enactment (Act Sec. 422(d) of the American Jobs Creation Act of 2004).

Act Sec. 422(a) of the American Jobs Creation Act of 2004, adding Code Sec. 965; Act Sec. 422(b), adding Code Sec. 56(g)(4)(C)(vi); Act Sec. 422(c); Act Sec. 422(d). Law at ¶5085 and ¶5735. Committee Report at ¶10,780.

¶540

FIRPTA Rules Modified for REITs

Background ——————————————————————————————————————

A real estate investment trust (REIT) is a U.S. corporation, or a trust or association taxable as a corporation, that invests in real estate, mortgages and similar assets and that elects to be treated as a REIT. To be eligible for a REIT election and to maintain REIT status, a REIT must satisfy numerous requirements on an annual basis relating to organizational structure, source of income, nature of assets, distribution of income, and recordkeeping. If an electing entity meets the requirements for REIT status, the portion of its income that is distributed to its investors each year generally is treated as a dividend deductible by the REIT, and includible in income by its investors. In this manner, the distributed income of the REIT is not taxed at the entity level. The distributed income is taxed only at the investor level. A REIT generally is required to distribute 90 percent of its income to its investors before the end of its tax year.

U.S. tax rules apply to gains of foreign persons attributable to dispositions of interests in U.S. real property, including certain transactions involving REITs. The rules governing the imposition and collection of tax on such dispositions are contained in a series of provisions that were enacted in 1980 and that are collectively referred to as the Foreign Investment in Real Property Tax Act (FIRPTA).

Background

In general, FIRPTA provides that gain or loss derived by a nonresident individual or a foreign corporation from the disposition of a U.S. real property interest is treated as gain or loss that is effectively connected with the conduct of a U.S. trade or business (Code Sec. 897(a)(1)). This provision applies to both gains and losses and to dispositions (rather than only sales or exchanges), so that the provision is invoked on any transfer of a U.S. real property interest. A U.S. real property interest includes not only a real property interest as defined by general law, but also personal property associated with the use of real property and holdings in a domestic U.S. real property holding corporation (Code Sec. 897(c)(6)(B)).

For these purposes, the receipt of a distribution from a REIT is treated as a disposition of a U.S. real property interest by the recipient to the extent that it is attributable to a sale or exchange of a U.S. real property interest by the REIT. These capital gains distributions from REITs generally are subject to withholding tax at a rate of 35 percent (or a lower treaty rate).

If a REIT made an actual designation of a prior distribution, in whole or in part, as a capital gain dividend, that prior distribution is not subject to withholding under FIRPTA. Instead, the REIT must characterize and treat as a capital gain dividend distribution (solely for purposes of FIRPTA withholding) each distribution, determined for each share or certificate of beneficial interest, made on the day of, or any time after, the designation of the prior distribution as a capital gain dividend until the characterized amounts equal the amount of the prior distribution that was designated as a capital gains dividend (Reg. § 1.1445-8(c)(2)(ii)(C)).

Since the recipients of these capital gains distributions are treated as earning income effectively connected with a U.S. trade or business, they are required to file U.S. income tax returns.

In addition, foreign corporations that have effectively connected income generally are subject to the branch profits tax at a 30-percent rate (or a lower treaty rate).

> **Comment:** Treaties negotiated by the United States after 1988 contain specific rules excluding REIT dividends from the reduced rates of withholding tax generally applicable to dividends. Accordingly, under such treaties, REIT dividends may be subject to U.S. withholding tax at the full statutory rate of 30 percent. The exclusion of REIT dividends from the reduced rates of withholding tax generally applicable to dividends reflects the view that REIT dividends should be treated in a manner that generally is comparable to the treatment of rental income earned on a direct investment in real property.

American Jobs Creation Act Impact

Certain distributions from REITs no longer treated as effectively connected income.—Under the new law, a capital gain distribution from a REIT is removed from treatment as effectively connected income for a foreign investor provided that:

(1) the distribution is received with respect to a class of stock that is regularly traded on an established securities market located in the United States and

(2) the foreign investor does not own more than five percent of the class of stock at any time during the tax year within which the distribution is received (Code Sec. 897(h)(1), as amended by the American Jobs Creation Act of 2004).

¶540

The distribution is to be treated as a REIT dividend to that investor, taxed as a REIT dividend that is not a capital gain (Code Sec. 857(b)(3)(F), as added by the 2004 Jobs Act).

Planning Note: Thus, a foreign investor is not required to file a U.S. Federal income tax return by reason of receiving such a distribution and the branch profits tax no longer applies to such a distribution.

Practical Analysis: This provision eliminates a major barrier to foreign investment in publicly traded REITs that had treated portfolio investors as doing business in the United States merely because they received REIT capital gain distributions. This change parallels the existing rule for a foreign person's sale of a publicly traded REIT stock under which gains on the sale of REIT shares are not subject to tax under FIRPTA, unless the majority of the shares are held by foreign persons. Prior to these new provisions, foreign persons could avoid FIRPTA by selling qualifying shares prior to receiving the distribution from the REIT. Now such steps may be unnecessary.

Caution Note: Numerous other provisions concerning REITs have been modified by the 2004 Jobs Act; see ¶1105.

See ¶564 for a discussion of the extension of the REIT rules under Code Sec. 897 to RICs.

For further information on this subject, consult any of the following CCH reporter explanations:

- Standard Federal Tax Reporter, 2004FED ¶26,533.01, ¶26,533.025 and ¶27,711.01
- Federal Tax Service, FTS § M:14.66[4] and § F:9.53[4]
- Federal Tax Guide, 2004FTG ¶16,650 and ¶17,065

★ *Effective date.* This provision applies to tax years beginning after the date of enactment (Act Sec. 418(c) of the American Jobs Creation Act of 2004).

Act Sec. 418(a) of the American Jobs Creation Act of 2004, amending Code Sec. 897(h)(1); Act Sec. 418(b), adding Code Sec. 857(b)(3)(F); Act Sec. 418(c). Law at ¶5555 and ¶5630. Committee Report at ¶10,740.

INTERNATIONAL SHIPPING

¶ 545

Election to Determine Taxable Income from Certain International Shipping Activities

Background _____

Businesses engaged in international shipping activities are particularly vulnerable to double taxation, given the nature of the activities involved. Typically, these firms either have operations or operate in many countries. Under our "worldwide taxation" regime, U.S. domestic corporations are generally subject to tax on all income (including that from shipping activities) from domestic or foreign operations. The potential for double taxation is addressed through foreign tax credits that off-set income taxes paid to foreign countries by reducing or eliminating (with some limitations) U.S. taxes owed on that income. Foreign corporations are generally subject to U.S. taxation on income that meets the Code Sec. 882 criteria for income "effectively connected" with the conduct of a trade or business within the United States at the same rates as income from a U.S. corporation.

Background

Under Code Sec. 887, a foreign corporation is subject to a four-percent tax on its U.S.-source gross transportation income, subject to certain exceptions. One such exception is U.S. gross transportation income that falls under Code Sec. 882 and is treated as income "effectively connected" with the conduct of a U.S. trade or business because the taxpayer has a fixed place of business in the United States that is involved in the earning of the income and substantially all of that income is attributable to regularly-scheduled transportation. Transportation income includes income from the use, hire or lease of a vessel, as well as income from services directly associated with the use of the vessel. U.S.-source gross transportation income includes 50 percent of the transportation income attributable to transportation that either begins or ends in the United States.

Taxes on income from international shipping activities under Code Secs. 882 and 887 may be limited if: (1) a foreign corporation's country grants an equivalent exemption to corporations organized in the United States, consistent with Code Sec. 883(a)(1); or (2) a U.S. bilateral income tax treaty applies. Article 8 (Shipping and Air Transport) of the U.S. Model Income Tax Convention (1996) provides guidelines for the taxation of profits from the operation of ships and aircraft in international traffic.

American Jobs Creation Act Impact

Alternative tax on qualifying shipping activities.—The American Jobs Creation Act of 2004 provides an alternative to application of the corporate income tax for certain shipping activity income. It allows a corporation to elect the application of a "tonnage tax" instead of the corporate tax on income from qualifying shipping activities. Qualifying shipping activity income is not included in an electing corporation's gross income. The qualifying shipping activities of an electing corporation are treated as a separate trade or business activity distinct from all other activities conducted by the corporation. An electing corporation is subject to tax on income from qualifying shipping activities at the maximum corporate income tax rate on its notional shipping income. The corporation's notional shipping income is derived from the net tonnage of the corporation's qualifying vessels.

The electing corporation's tax, therefore, is the "tonnage tax" (which is equal to the maximum corporate rate multiplied by the notional shipping income for the tax year) plus the corporate tax on nonqualifying activity income (Code Sec. 1352).

Notional shipping income. The electing corporation's notional shipping income for the tax year is calculated by multiplying: (1) the daily notional shipping income from the operation of qualifying vessels that it operates in U.S. foreign trade (meaning, 40 cents for each 100 tons of the net tonnage of the vessel, for the first 25,000 net tons, and 20 cents for each 100 tons of the net tonnage of the vessel, in excess of 25,000 net tons); by (2) the total days during that tax year that the corporation operated the vessel as a qualifying vessel in U.S. foreign trade (Code Sec. 1353(a), (b) and (c)). If, for any period, two or more persons are operators of a qualifying vessel, the notional shipping income from the operation of the vessel for that period is allocated among those persons on the basis of their respective ownership and charter interests in the vessel or on some other basis as regulations may provide (Code Sec. 1353(d)).

With respect to income from a qualifying vessel that is not otherwise subject to tax, either by reason of Code Sec. 883 or otherwise, the amount of notional shipping income from that vessel for the tax year will be the amount that bears the same ratio to such shipping income as the gross income from the operation of the vessel in U.S. foreign trade bears to the sum of such gross income and the income so excluded (Code Sec. 1353(b)(2)).

¶545

Alternative tax election and termination. In general, any qualifying vessel operator may elect application of the "tonnage tax" (Code Sec. 1354(a)). Such election must be made in the form prescribed by the Secretary of the Treasury and is effective only if made before the due date (including extensions) for filing the corporation's return for a given tax year. The election is effective for the tax year in which it was made and all succeeding tax years until the election is terminated (Code Sec. 1354(b)). If a qualifying vessel operator is a member of a controlled group, the election by one member of that group into the "tonnage tax" regime will apply to all qualifying vessel operators who are members of that controlled group (Code Sec. 1354(c)).

An election into the tonnage tax regime may be terminated by revocation. If the revocation is made during the tax year, on or before the fifteenth day of the third month of that tax year, it will be considered effective on the first day of that tax year; if the revocation is made after the fifteenth day of the third month but during the tax year, it will be effective on the first day of the following tax year. If the revocation specifies a date for revocation that is on or after the date the revocation was made, the revocation will be effective for tax years beginning on or after the date that was specified (Code Sec. 1354(d)).

An election may also be terminated if, at any time on or after the first day of the first tax year that the corporation is an electing corporation, that corporation ceases to be a qualifying vessel operator. In this case, the termination will be effective on and after the date of such cessation. Annualization and other rules that apply to terminations of this type will be prescribed by the Secretary of the Treasury.

If a qualifying vessel operator has made an election and the election has been terminated, that operator, and any successor operator, will be ineligible to make an election back into the "tonnage tax" regime for any tax year before the fifth tax year after the termination was effective, unless the Secretary of the Treasury consents to this election (Code Sec. 1354(e)).

Definitions and special rules. "U.S. foreign trade" is defined as transportation of goods or passengers between a place in the United States and a foreign place or between foreign places. A "qualifying vessel," under this Act, is a self-propelled (or combination self-propelled and non-self-propelled) United States flag vessel of not less than 10,000 deadweight tons used exclusively in the U. S. foreign trade during the period that the election under this subchapter is in effect. A "United States flag vessel" means any vessel documented under the laws of the United States. A "qualifying vessel operator" is any corporation that operates one or more qualifying vessels and meets the shipping activity requirement. The term "U.S. domestic trade" refers to the transportation of goods or passengers between places in the United States. The term "charter" includes an operating agreement.

An "electing corporation" is any corporation for which an election is in effect under this Act. An "electing group" is a controlled group of which one or more members is an electing corporation. A "controlled group" means any group which would be treated as a single employer under Code Sec. 52(a) or (b) if paragraphs (1) and (2) of Code Sec. 52(a) did not apply (Code Sec. 1355(a)).

For purposes of this subchapter, a person is treated as "operating a vessel," (any vessel during any period) if the vessel is owned by or chartered to (including a time charter) the person and is in use as a qualifying vessel during this period. A person is treated as operating and using a vessel that it has chartered out on bareboat charter terms only (i.e., without crew) if the vessel is temporarily surplus to the person's requirements and and: (1) the charter term does not exceed three years; or (2) the vessel is bareboat chartered to a member of a controlled group that includes that person or to an unrelated person who sub-bareboats or time charters the vessel to a member (which could include the owner of the vessel) and the vessel is used as a qualifying vessel by the person who ultimately chartered it (Code Sec. 1355(b)).

In general, a corporation meets the shipping activity requirement, for purposes of this subchapter, for any tax year only if an aggregate tonnage requirement is met for each of the two preceding tax years. To meet the aggregate tonnage requirement, at least 25 percent, on average during a given tax year, of the aggregate tonnage of qualifying vessels used by the corporation must have been owned by the corporation or chartered to the corporation on bareboat charter terms. A special rule applies for the first year of an election into the tonnage tax regime. A corporation meets the shipping activity requirement for the first tax year in which the election is in effect only if the above aggregate tonnage requirement is met for the preceding tax year. A special rule also applies to corporations that are members of a controlled group. Such corporations will meet the shipping activity requirement only if the requirement is met while treating all members of the group as one person and by disregarding vessel charters between members of that group (Code Sec. 1355(c)).

Partnerships are also subject to special rules. Each partner is treated as operating vessels that are operated by the partnership and as conducting the activities that are conducted by the partnership. A partner's interest in the partnership is the basis upon which his ownership or charter interest in any vessel owned by or chartered by the partnership is determined. A similar rule is applied to other pass-through entities (Code Sec. 1355(d)).

For purposes of meeting the "operating a vessel" and "shipping activity" requirements, an electing corporation will be considered to be continuing to use a qualifying vessel during any period of temporary cessation if the corporation gives timely notice to the Secretary of the Treasury. This notice must state: (1) that the electing corporation has temporarily ceased to operate the qualifying vessel; and (2) its intention to resume operating the qualifying vessel. The notice will be deemed timely if it is given by the due date (including extensions) for the corporation's tax return for the tax year in which the temporary cessation began. The period of temporary cessation will continue until the earlier of the date on which the corporation abandons its intention to resume operation of the qualifying vessel or the corporation resumes operation of the vessel (Code Sec. 1355(e)).

An electing corporation will be treated as continuing to use a qualifying vessel in U.S. foreign trade during any period of temporary use in U.S. domestic trade (not exceeding 30 days during the tax year) if the corporation gives timely notice to the Secretary of the Treasury. The notice must state: (1) that the electing corporation temporarily operates or has operated a qualifying vessel in U.S. domestic trade which had been used in U.S. foreign trade; and (2) its intention to resume operation of the qualifying vessel in U.S. foreign trade. The notice will be deemed timely if it is given by the due date (including extensions) for the corporation's tax return for the tax year in which the temporary cessation began. The temporary use period (for qualifying vessels used in U.S. domestic trade) continues until the earlier of the date on which: (1) an electing corporation abandons its intention to resume operations of the vessel in U.S. foreign trade; or (2) the corporation resumes operation of the vessel in U.S. foreign trade (Code Sec. 1355(f)). Regulations, as may be necessary or appropriate, will be issued by the Secretary of the Treasury (Code Sec. 1355(g)).

Qualifying shipping activities. Under the 2004 Jobs Act, qualifying shipping activities are broken down into three categories: (1) core qualifying activities; (2) qualifying secondary activities; and (3) qualifying incidental activities. The Act defines "core qualifying activities" as activities in operating qualifying vessels in United States foreign trade. All of an electing corporation's core qualifying activities are excluded from gross income. "Qualifying secondary activities" include managing and operating nonqualifying vessels in U.S. foreign trade; providing vessel, barge, container and cargo-related facilities and services; and other activities that form an integral part of the electing corporation's or group's business of operating qualifying vessels in U.S. foreign trade. The 2004 Jobs Act clarifies that secondary activities do not include core qualifying activities and, with respect to a nonelecting corporation that is a member of an electing group, any activities of that corporation that would otherwise constitute core qualifying activities will be treated as qualifying secondary activities. Finally, "incidental activities" are shipping-related activities that are incidental to core qualifying activities and are not qualifying secondary activities. Only a portion of an electing corporation's secondary and incidental activities are considered qualifying income and, thereby, excluded from gross income (Code Sec. 1356).

Credits, income and deductions. As previously noted, gross income of an electing corporation does not include its income from qualifying shipping activities (Code Sec. 1357(a), as added by the 2004 Jobs Act). Under the 2004 Jobs Act, each item of loss, deduction (other than for income expense) or credit of any taxpayer is disallowed with respect to the income that is excluded from gross income. The interest expense of an electing corporation is disallowed in the ratio that the fair market value of the corporation's qualifying vessels bear to the fair market value of the corporation's total assets; special rules apply for electing groups (Code Sec. 1357).

No deductions are allowed against the notional shipping income of an electing corporation and no credit is allowed against the tax imposed. No deduction is allowed for any net operating loss attributable to qualifying shipping activities to the extent that the loss is carried forward from a tax year preceding the first tax year for which it was an electing corporation (Code Sec. 1358(b))) Code Sec. 482 allocations may apply to certain transactions that are not at arm's length (Code Sec. 1358(c)).

> **Caution Note:** Despite the general disallowance of losses or expenses, the adjusted basis for purposes of determining gain of any qualifying vessel is determined as if depreciation were allowed (Code Sec. 1357(c)(2)(A), as added by the 2004 Jobs Act).

Disposition of qualifying vessels. At the election of a qualifying vessel operator, no gain will be recognized if the operator sells or disposes of a qualifying vessel in an otherwise taxable transaction and a replacement qualifying vessel is acquired during a limited replacement time period except to the extent that the amount realized from the sale or disposition exceeds the cost of the replacement vessel. If a replacement results in the nonrecognition of any part of the gain, the basis is the cost of the replacement qualifying vessel decreased in the amount of gain not recognized (Code Sec. 1359). A special limitations period applies to the assessment of a deficiency attributable to such gain realized (Code Sec. 1359(d)).

For further information on this subject, consult any of the following CCH reporter explanations:

- Standard Federal Tax Reporter, 2004FED ¶ 5210.01, ¶ 27,503.01, ¶ 27,522.01 and ¶ 27,585.01
- Federal Tax Service, FTS § M:1.261 and § M:8.66
- Federal Tax Guide, 2004FTG ¶ 17,140 and ¶ 17,440

★ *Effective date.* This provision is effective for tax years beginning after the date of enactment (Act Sec. 248(c) of the American Jobs Creation Act of 2004).

Act Sec. 248(a) of the American Jobs Creation Act of 2004, adding new Code Secs. 1352, 1353, 1354, 1355, 1356, 1357, 1358 and 1359; Act Sec. 248(b), amending

Code Sec. 56(g)(4)(B)(i); Act Sec. 248(c). Law at ¶5085, ¶5850, ¶5855, ¶5860, ¶5865, ¶5870, ¶5875, ¶5880 and ¶5885. Committee Report at ¶10,290.

¶ 552

Delay in Effective Date of Final Regulations Governing Exclusion of Income from International Operation of Ships or Aircraft

Background

The general rule of Code Sec. 883 provides that gross income derived by a corporation organized in a foreign country from the international operation of a ship or aircraft is not included in gross income of the foreign corporation and is exempt from U.S. taxation if such foreign country grants an equivalent exemption to corporations organized in the United States (Code Sec. 883(a)). Final regulations implementing the rules of Code Sec. 883 are effective for tax years of foreign corporations seeking qualified foreign corporation status beginning 30 days or more after August 26, 2003 (Reg. § 1.883-5(a)). These regulations (Reg. § 1.883-1 through Reg. § 1.883-5) generally provide that qualified income derived by a qualified foreign corporation from its international operation of ships or aircraft is excluded from gross income and exempt from U.S. federal income tax (Reg. § 1.883-1(a)).

American Jobs Creation Act Impact

Delay in effective date of final regulations governing exclusion of income from international operation of ships or aircraft.—The effective date of the final regulations under Code Sec. 883 has been delayed. Reg. § § 1.883-1 through 1.883-5 apply to tax years of a foreign corporation seeking qualified foreign corporation status beginning after September 24, 2004 (Act Sec. 423 of the American Jobs Creation Act of 2004). This delay applies notwithstanding the effective date noted in Reg. § 1.883-5.

For further information on this subject, consult any of the following CCH reporter explanations:

- Standard Federal Tax Reporter, 2004FED ¶27,522.01 and ¶27,522.021
- Federal Tax Service, FTS § M:1.262
- Federal Tax Guide, 2004FTG ¶17,140

★ *Effective date.* No specific effective date is provided by the Act. The provision is, therefore, considered effective on the date of enactment.

Act Sec. 423 of the American Jobs Creation Act of 2004. Law at ¶7025. Committee Report at ¶10,790.

NONRESIDENT ALIENS

¶ 555

Tax on Dividends from Certain Foreign Corporations

Background

Nonresident aliens and foreign corporations (i.e., foreign persons) are generally taxed in the same manner as U.S. citizens and domestic corporations on all income effectively connected with the conduct of a U.S. trade or business (Code Secs. 871(b) and 882). Generally, any U.S.-source income of a foreign person which is not effectively connected with a U.S. trade or business, is taxed at a flat 30-percent rate, unless a lower rate applies pursuant to an income tax treaty (Code Secs. 871(a) and

881). The 30-percent tax is collected through certain withholding procedures (Code Secs. 1441 and 1442). Foreign persons will generally not be subject to U.S. tax on any foreign-source income they receive which is not effectively connected with a U.S. trade or business.

> **Comment:** A nonresident alien is any individual who is not a U.S. citizen and does not qualify for U.S. residency under either the lawful permanent residence test or the substantial presence test, or who has not elected resident status (Code Sec. 7701(b)(1)).

Dividend income is considered to be fixed and determinable income not effectively connected with a U.S. trade or business. As such, dividends paid to foreign persons are subject to the 30-percent withholding rate if considered U.S.-source income. The residence of the payor generally determines the source of any dividend payment (Code Secs. 861(a)(2) and 862(a)(2)). Thus, dividends paid by a domestic corporation are U.S.-source income and dividends paid by a foreign corporation are generally foreign-source income.

However, a portion of the dividends paid by a foreign corporation will be considered U.S.-source income if 25 percent of more of the corporation's total gross income for the three-year period ending with the close of the tax year preceding the dividend declaration date was effectively connected (or treated as effectively connected) with a trade or business in the United States (Code Sec. 861(a)(2)(B)). If this requirement is met, then the amount of dividends paid by the foreign corporation that will be treated as U.S.-source income is the portion of dividends paid that bears the same ratio that the corporation's gross income that was effectively connected income bears to its gross income from all sources. Dividends paid by foreign corporations that do not meet the 25-percent test are treated as entirely foreign-source income.

> **Example:** In the three years preceding its dividend declaration date for 2004, a foreign corporation has $10 million of gross income, 80 percent of which is income effectively connected with a U.S. trade or business. Thus, for every $1 of dividends paid by the corporation for 2004, 80 cents will be considered dividends income from a U.S. source. This exposes dividends paid by the corporation to foreign persons to the 30-percent withholding tax. This rule is sometimes known as the "secondary withholding tax."

The 30-percent withholding tax will not apply against dividends paid by a foreign corporation to foreign persons if the corporation is subject to the branch profits tax (Code Sec. 884(e)(3)(A)). Under the branch profits rules, a foreign corporation with branches in the United States will be subject to a tax on its "dividend equivalent amount" (Code Sec. 884). In essence, this is the deemed amount of dividends a U.S. branch office of the foreign corporation could remit (or is deemed to remit) to the corporation's head office during the tax year, based on its earnings and profits. The "dividend equivalent amount" is the foreign corporation's effectively connected earnings and profits for the tax year, with certain adjustments (Code Sec. 884(b)).

The rate of the branch profits tax is 30 percent unless the corporation is subject to a reduced rate under an applicable tax treaty (Code Sec. 884(a)). The tax is not in lieu of, but in addition to, regular U.S. corporate income taxes that apply to a foreign corporation with income effectively connected with a U.S. trade or business. A foreign corporation may be exempt from the branch profits tax if it is qualified resident of a foreign country with which the United States has an income tax treaty

_____

that exempts it from the tax. However, if a foreign corporation is exempt from the branch profits tax under an applicable treaty, then the secondary withholding tax would apply with respect to dividends it pays to its shareholders.

American Jobs Creation Act Impact

Repeal of secondary withholding tax.—The new law effectively repeals the secondary withholding tax. For dividend payments after 2004, the 30-percent withholding tax will not apply to the portion of dividends of a foreign corporation which are treated as U.S.-source income under the 25-percent source rule and paid to nonresident aliens and foreign corporations (i.e., foreign persons) (Code Sec. 871(i)(2)(D), as added by the American Jobs Creation Act of 2004; see also Code Sec. 881(d)).

> **Caution Note:** The new legislation does not repeal the 25-percent source rule for dividends from foreign corporations. It merely provides an exemption to the application of the 30-percent withholding tax to dividends of a foreign corporation paid to foreign persons. The treatment of some portion of dividends from a foreign corporation as U.S.-source income is still relevant to the amount of foreign tax credit available to U.S. shareholders of a foreign corporation.

> **Comment:** In practical terms, the branch profits tax has supplanted the secondary withholding tax except in limited circumstances (e.g., a foreign corporation is exempt from the branch profits tax under an income tax treaty) (Code Sec. 884(e)(3)). Consequently, repeal of the secondary withholding tax should have no effect on most taxpayers.

For further information on this subject, consult any of the following CCH reporter explanations:

- Standard Federal Tax Reporter, 2004FED ¶ 27,343.01
- Federal Tax Service, FTS § M:13.80 and § M:13A.40
- Federal Tax Guide, 2004FTG ¶ 17,030 and ¶ 17,050

★ *Effective date.* The amendment made by this section shall apply to payments made after December 31, 2004 (Act Sec. 409(b) of the American Jobs Creation Act of 2004).

Act Sec. 409(a) of the American Jobs Creation Act of 2004, amending Code Sec. 871(i)(2); Act Sec. 409(b). Law at ¶ 5605. Committee Report at ¶ 10,650.

¶ 560

Treatment of Certain Dividends of Regulated Investment Companies

Background _____

A regulated investment company (RIC), commonly known as a mutual fund, is a domestic corporation or common trust fund that invests in stocks and securities. RICs must satisfy a number of complex tests relating to income, assets, and other matters (Code Sec. 851(a)). A RIC does not generally pay income tax because it is allowed to deduct dividends paid to shareholders when it computes its taxable income. RICs also pass through the character of their long-term capital gains to their shareholders, by designating any dividends paid as a capital gain dividend to the extent that the RIC has net capital gains available (Code Sec. 852). Shareholders treat these gains as long-term capital gains.

Background

Taxation of nonresident aliens, non-U.S. citizens. The taxation of income earned by non-U.S. citizens depends on whether the individual is classified as a resident alien or a nonresident alien. Resident aliens are taxed on their worldwide income, as are U.S. citizens. A nonresident alien is generally subject to tax on U.S.-source income and on foreign-source gross income effectively connected with a U.S. trade or business. Generally, U.S.-source income received by a nonresident non-U.S. citizen that is not "effectively connected with a U.S. trade or business" is subject to a flat 30-percent withholding tax (or lower tax rate provided by treaty), while U.S. source net income that is "effectively connected" to a trade or business is subject to tax in the same manner as income earned by U.S. citizens (Code Sec. 871(a) and (b)). The 30-percent (or lower treaty rate) tax is imposed on payments of U.S.-source interest that is not effectively connected with a U.S. trade or business. However,

(1) interest from certain bank deposits is exempt from tax (Code Secs. 871(i)(2)(A) and 881(d));

(2) original issue discount obligations that mature within 183 days or less from the original issue date are exempt from tax (Code Sec. 871(g)); and

(3) interest paid on portfolio obligation is exempt from tax (Code Secs. 871(h) and 881(c)).

Portfolio interest includes interest from any U.S.-source interest, including original issue discount, that is not effectively connected to a U.S. trade or business. The obligation must satisfy certain registration requirements and not be received by a 10-percent shareholder of the entity issuing the obligation (Code Sec. 871(h)(2) and (h)(5) and Code Sec. 881(c)(2)).

Capital gains. Foreign persons are generally not subject to tax on gain realized when they dispose of stock or securities issued by a U.S. entity, unless the gain is effectively connected with the conduct of a U.S. trade or business. This exception does not apply, however, in the case of a nonresident alien who is present in the United States for more than 183 aggregated days in a tax year (Code Sec. 871(a)(2)). A RIC may elect to withhold tax on a distribution, representing a capital gain dividend, to a foreign person (Reg. § 1.1441-3(c)(2)(i)(D)).

American Jobs Creation Act Impact

Tax treatment of certain dividends of regulated investment companies.—The American Jobs Creation Act of 2004 exempts interest-related dividends and short-term capital gains dividends from a regulated investment company (RIC) from U.S. tax under certain circumstances.

Interest-related dividends.—Interest-related dividends received from a RIC are exempt from the 30-percent tax (Code Secs. 871(k)(1)(A) and 881(e)(1)(A), as added by 2004 Jobs Act). However, the exemption does not apply to any interest-related dividend:

(1) paid to a controlled foreign corporation to the extent the dividends are attributable to income received by the RIC on a debt obligation of a person to whom the recipient (i.e., the controlled foreign corporation) is considered to be a related person (Code Sec. 881(e)(1)(B)(ii), as added by the 2004 Jobs Act);

(2) attributable to income (other than short-term original issue discount or bank deposit interest) received by the RIC on indebtedness issued by the RIC dividend recipient or an entity in which the recipient of the RIC dividend is a 10-percent shareholder within the meaning of Code Sec. 871(h)(3)(B) (Code Secs. 871(k)(1)(B)(i) and 881(e)(1)(B)(i), as added by the 2004 Jobs Act);

(3) on shares of RIC stock if the withholding agent does not receive a statement, similar to that required under the Code Sec. 871(h)(5) portfolio interest rules, that the beneficial owner of the shares is not a U.S. person (Code Secs. 871(k)(1)(B)(ii) and 881(e)(1)(B)(i), as added by the 2004 Jobs Act); and

(4) paid to any person within a foreign country (or dividends addressed to, or for the account of, persons within the foreign country) with respect to which the IRS has determined, under the Code Sec. 871(h)(6) portfolio interest rules, that exchange of information is inadequate to prevent evasion of U.S. income tax by U.S. persons. However, this exception does not apply to any dividend with respect to any stock that was acquired on or before the publication date of the IRS's determination (Code Secs. 871(k)(1)(B)(iii) and 881(e)(1)(B)(i), as added by the 2004 Jobs Act).

However, the exemption still applies with respect to exceptions (1) and (2) and the RIC remains exempt from its withholding obligation, unless the RIC has knowledge that the controlled foreign corporation or the 10-percent shareholder is the dividend recipient (Code Sec. 1441(c)(12), as added by the 2004 Jobs Act, and Code Sec. 1442(a), as amended by the 2004 Jobs Act).

An "interest-related dividend" is any dividend (or portion thereof) that is designated by a RIC as an interest-related dividend in a written notice mailed to its shareholders no later than 60 days after the close of its tax year (Code Sec. 871(k)(1)(C), as added by the 2004 Jobs Act).

Caution Note: Interest-related dividends do not include any dividends with respect to any tax year of a RIC beginning after December 31, 2007.

The aggregate amount designated as interest-related dividends for a tax year is limited to the RIC's qualified net interest income for the tax year. Qualified net interest income is the excess of:

(1) the amount of qualified interest income of the RIC; over

(2) the amount of the expenses of the RIC allocable to the interest income (Code Sec. 871(k)(1)(D), as added by the 2004 Jobs Act).

Qualified interest income. Qualified interest income is equal to the sum of the RIC's U.S.-source income with respect to:

(1) bank deposit interest;

(2) short-term original issue discount that is currently exempt from tax under Code Sec. 871;

(3) any interest (including amounts recognized as ordinary income in respect of original issue discount, market discount, or acquisition discount, and any other such amounts that may be prescribed by regulations) on an obligation that is in registered form (unless the interest was earned on an obligation issued by a corporation or partnership in which the RIC is a 10-percent shareholder or is contingent interest not treated as portfolio interest under Code Sec. 871(h)(4); and

(4) any interest-related dividend from another RIC (Code Sec. 871(k)(1)(E), as added by the 2004 Jobs Act).

Foreign corporations. The 2004 Jobs Act also provides that interest-related dividends received by a foreign corporation are generally exempt from U.S. gross basis tax under Code Sec. 881 (tax on income of foreign corporations not connected with a U.S. business) (Code Sec. 881(e)(1)(A), as added by the 2004 Jobs Act) and from the withholding rules applicable to such tax (Code Sec. 1441(c)(12)(A), as added by the 2004 Jobs Act, and Code Sec. 1442(a), as amended by the 2004 Jobs Act), under the interest-related dividend rules described above. To the extent that an interest-related dividend received by a controlled foreign corporation is attributable to the interest income of a RIC that would be portfolio interest if received by a foreign corporation, the dividend is treated as portfolio interest for purposes of the Code Sec. 881(c)(5)(A)*de minimis* rules, high-tax exception, and the same-country exception (Code Sec. 881(e)(1)(C), as added by the 2004 Jobs Act).

Short-term capital gain dividends.—A RIC is permitted to designate all or a portion of a dividend as a "short-term capital gain dividend" by written notice mailed to its shareholders no later than 60 days after the close of its tax year (Code Sec. 871(k)(2)(C), as added by the 2004 Jobs Act). A short-term capital gain dividend received by a nonresident alien not a citizen is generally exempt from the 30-percent tax on U.S.-source income that is not connected with a U.S. trade or business. This exemption does not apply when the nonresident alien is present in the U.S. 183 days or more during the tax year (Code Sec. 871(k)(2)(A) and (B), as added by the 2004 Jobs Act). If the exemption is inapplicable, the RIC, nevertheless, remains exempt from its withholding obligation, unless it knows that the dividend recipient has been present in the United States for such period (Code Sec. 1441(c)(12)(B), as added by the 2004 Jobs Act).

> **Caution Note:** Short-term capital gain dividends do not include any dividends with respect to any tax year of a RIC beginning after December 31, 2007 (Code Sec. 871(k)(2)(C), as added by the 2004 Jobs Act).

If the amount designated as short-term capital gain dividends exceeds the qualified short-term capital gain, the portion of the distribution that constitutes a short-term capital gain dividend is equal to that proportion of the designated amount that the qualified short-term gain bears to the aggregate amount designated. The amount qualified to be designated as short-term capital gain dividends for the RIC's tax year is equal to the excess of the RIC's net short-term capital gains over net long-term capital losses. Short-term capital gain includes short-term capital gain dividends from another RIC. Net short-term capital gain is determined without regard to any net capital loss or net short-term capital loss attributable to transactions occurring after October 31 of the tax year. Such loss is treated as arising on the first day of the next tax year. To the extent provided in regulations, this rule will apply for purposes of computing the RIC's taxable income (Code Sec. 871(k)(2)(D), as added by the 2004 Jobs Act). In computing the short-term capital gain dividend for a particular year, the RIC is not allowed to deduct the amount of expenses allocable to such net gains (House Committee Report (H.R. Rep. No. 108-548)).

Foreign corporations. The 2004 Jobs Act also provides that short-term capital gain dividends received by a foreign corporation are generally exempt from U.S. gross basis tax under Code Sec. 881 (tax on income of foreign corporations not connected with a U.S. business) (Code Sec. 881(e)(2), as added by the 2004 Jobs Act) and from the withholding rules applicable to such tax (Code Sec. 1441(c)(12)(A), as added by the 2004 Jobs Act, and Code Sec. 1442(a), as amended by the 2004 Jobs Act), under the short-term capital gain rules described above apply.

For further information on this subject, consult any of the following CCH reporter explanations:

- Standard Federal Tax Reporter, 2004FED ¶ 26,408.01, ¶ 27,343.01, ¶ 27,484.01, ¶ 32,716.01 and ¶ 32,723.01

- Federal Tax Service, FTS § M:13A.62

- Federal Tax Guide, 2004FTG ¶ 17,050 and ¶ 17,240

★ *Effective date.* The provision generally applies to dividends with respect to tax years of RICs beginning after December 31, 2004 (Act Sec. 411(d)(1) of the American Jobs Creation Act of 2004).

Act Sec. 411(a)(1) of the American Jobs Creation Act of 2004, redesignating Code Sec. 871(k) as Code Sec. 871(l) and adding new Code Sec. 871(k); Act Sec. 411(a)(2), redesignating Code Sec. 881(e) as Code Sec. 881(f) and adding new Code Sec. 881(e); Act Sec. 411(a)(3), adding Code Sec. 1441(c)(12) and amending Code Sec. 1442(a); Act Sec. 411(d)(1). Law at ¶5605, ¶5620, ¶5925 and ¶5930. Committee Report at ¶10,670.

¶ 562
Estate Tax Treatment of Stock in Regulated Investment Companies

Background _____

Decedents who are nonresidents and are not U.S. citizens are generally subject to federal estate tax only on property that is located in the United States (Code Sec. 2105). Property within the United States includes debt obligations of U.S. persons, but does not include either bank deposits or portfolio obligations where the interest earned would be exempt from U.S. income tax under Code Sec. 871. Stock owned and held by a nonresident who is not a U.S. citizen is treated as property within the United States only if the stock was issued by a domestic corporation. Tax treaties with various countries may reduce the amount of U.S. taxation on transfers by estates of nonresident, non-U.S. citizen decedents. Some treaties have eliminated U.S. taxation except when transferred property includes U.S. real or business property of a U.S. entity.

American Jobs Creation Act Impact

Estate tax treatment of stock in regulated investment companies.—A portion of stock in a regulated investment company (RIC) owned by a nonresident, non U.S. citizen will be treated as property without the United States (Code Sec. 2105(d)(1), as added by the American Jobs Creation Act of 2004) and will not be includible in the estate of such shareholder for federal estate tax purposes. The portion that is exempt from taxation is determined at the end of the quarter of the RIC's tax year immediately preceding the decedent's date of death or other time to be prescribed by regulation. The exempt amount is the proportion of the RIC's assets that were qualifying assets with respect to the decedent in relation to the total assets of the RIC. Qualifying assets are those assets that, if owned by the decedent, would have been:

    (1) bank deposits that are exempt from income tax;

    (2) portfolio debt obligations;

    (3) certain original issue discount obligations;

    (4) debt obligations of a U.S. corporation that are treated as giving rise to foreign source income; and

    (5) other property not within the United States (Code Sec. 2105(d)(2), as added by the 2004 Jobs Act).

Caution Note: This provision applies to the estates of nonresident, non-U.S. citizens dying after December 31, 2004, and before January 1, 2008 (Act Sec. 411(d)(2) of the 2004 Jobs Act and Code Sec. 2105(d)(3), as added by the 2004 Jobs Act).

For further information on this subject, consult any of the following CCH reporter explanations:

- Federal Tax Service, FTS § N:7.80
- Federal Tax Guide, 2004FTG ¶17,240 and ¶20,390
- Federal Estate and Gift Tax Reporter, FEGT ¶7975.05

★ *Effective date.* This provision applies to the estates of decedents dying after December 31, 2004 (Act Sec. 411(d)(2) of the American Jobs Creation Act of 2004).

Act Sec. 411(b) of the American Jobs Creation Act of 2004, adding Code Sec. 2105(d); Act Sec. 411(d)(2). Law at ¶ 5945. Committee Report at ¶ 10,670.

¶ 564

Investment in U.S. Real Property by RICs

Background

Nonresident aliens and foreign corporations are taxed on the net gain from dispositions of U.S. real property interests. This rule applies regardless of whether the gain was effectively connected with a U.S. trade or business or the seller was present in the United States (Code Sec. 897(a)). A U.S. real property interest includes real property located in the United States or the Virgin Islands (Code Sec. 897(c)(1)(A)(i) and Reg. § 1.897-1(b)). A U.S. real property interest also includes any interest in a domestic corporation, unless the taxpayer establishes that the corporation was not, during the five-year period ending on the date of disposition of the interest, a U.S. real property holding corporation. A corporation will be considered a U.S. real property holding corporation if the fair market value of its real property interests equals or exceeds 50 percent of the sum of the fair market values of its real property interests within the United States and outside of the United States and any other assets used or held for use in a trade or business (Code Sec. 897(c)(1)(A)(ii)).

A look-through rule applies to distributions made by real estate investment trusts (REITs) to a nonresident alien or foreign corporation, to the extent that the gain distributed is attributable to gain from the sale by the REIT of a U.S. property interest (Code Sec. 897(h)(1)). With respect to sales of REIT stock, a U.S. real property interest does *not* include any interest in a domestically controlled REIT (Code Sec. 897(h)(2) and Reg. § 1.897-1(c)(2)). A domestically controlled REIT is a REIT in which at all times during the testing period less than 50 percent of the value of stock was held directly or indirectly by foreign persons. For such purposes, the "testing period" is the shorter of: (1) the period beginning June 19, 1980, and ending on the date of distribution or disposition; (2) the five-year period ending on the date of the distribution or disposition; or (3) the period in which the REIT was in existence (Code Sec. 897(h)(3) and (h)(4) and Reg. § 1.897-1(c)(2)).

American Jobs Creation Act Impact

REIT treatment extended to RICs.—The American Jobs Creation Act of 2004 extends current law regarding the treatment of gain from the exchange of real property interests by REITs to regulated investment companies (RICs). Any distribution by a qualified investment entity to a foreign person will, to the extent attributable to gain from the sale or exchange of a U.S. real property interest, be treated as gain recognized from the sale or exchange of a U.S. real property interest (Code Sec. 897(h)(1), as amended by the 2004 Jobs Act). A "qualified investment entity" includes REITs and RICs (Code Sec. 897(h)(4), as amended by the 2004 Jobs Act).

> **Caution Note:** The term "qualified investment entity" will not include a RIC after December 31, 2007 (Code Sec. 897(h)(4)(A)(ii), as amended by the 2004 Jobs Act).

Domestically controlled qualified investment entities. U.S. real property interests do not include any interest in a domestically controlled qualified investment entity (Code Sec. 897(h)(2), as amended by the 2004 Jobs Act). A "domestically controlled qualified investment entity" is any qualified investment entity in which at all times during the testing period less than 50 percent of the value of stock is held directly or indirectly by foreign persons (Code Sec. 897(h)(4)(B), as amended by the 2004 Jobs Act).

For additional rules that apply to REITs under Code Sec. 897, see ¶ 540.

For further information on this subject, consult any of the following CCH reporter explanations:

- Standard Federal Tax Reporter, 2004FED ¶ 27,711.01 and ¶ 27,711.03
- Federal Tax Service, FTS § F:9.53[4] and § M:1.220
- Federal Tax Guide, 2004FTG ¶ 3205 and ¶ 17,240

★ *Effective date.* The provision is generally effective after December 31, 2004 (Act Sec. 411(d)(3) of the American Jobs Creation Act of 2004).

Act Sec. 411(c) of the American Jobs Creation Act of 2004, amending Code Sec. 897(h); Act Sec. 411(d)(3). Law at ¶ 5630. Committee Report at ¶ 10,670.

¶ 565

Exclusion of Income Derived from Certain Wagers on Horse Races and Dog Races from Gross Income of Nonresident Alien Individuals

Background

The general rule of Code Sec. 872 is that the gross income of a nonresident alien includes income which is derived from sources within the United States that is not connected with the conduct of a trade or business in the United States and income that is connected with the conduct of a trade or business in the United States. Code Sec. 872(b) provides specific exclusions from the gross income of a nonresident alien. Income derived from wagers on horse races and dog races is not specifically excluded from gross income under Code Sec. 872(b), although certain gambling winnings of nonresident aliens are exempt from gross income (Code Sec. 871(j), Reg. § 1.872-2(c)). Horse racing and dog racing involve pari-mutuel betting pools in which those who bet on competitors finishing in the first three places share the total amount bet. If the payout to the nonresident alien is made from a separate foreign pool, a pool containing funds derived from sources outside the United States, the payout will not be subject to withholding because the amounts received would not be U.S.-source income, even though the actual event, horse or dog race, was taking place in the United States. However, if the funds for payout have been commingled and consist of funds contributed by foreign sources as well as sources within the United States, at least some of the income derived by a nonresident alien resulting from a winning bet is U.S.-source income, requiring withholding of 30 percent of the amount received that came from sources within the United States (Code Sec. 871(a)).

American Jobs Creation Act Impact

Exclusion of certain horse-racing and dog-racing gambling winnings from the income of nonresident alien individuals.—The provision exempts from a nonresident alien's gross income any income derived from a legal wager transaction initiated outside of the United States in a pari-mutuel pool with respect to a live horse race or dog race taking place in the United States (Code Sec. 872(b)(5), as amended by the American Jobs Creation Act of 2004). As a result, no withholding will be required and no tax due on any winnings of a nonresident alien resulting from a legal bet placed outside of the United States on a horse or dog race occurring within the United States.

Comment: This exclusion applies even if some of the winnings are derived from wagers placed within the United States.

For further information on this subject, consult any of the following CCH reporter explanations:

- Standard Federal Tax Reporter, 2004FED ¶27,348.01 and ¶27,522.01
- Federal Tax Service, FTS §M:13A.65[2]
- Federal Tax Guide, 2004FTG ¶17,050

★ *Effective date.* The provision is effective for wagers made after the date of enactment (Act Sec. 419(c) of the 2004 Jobs Act).

Act Sec. 419(a) of the American Jobs Creation Act of 2004, amending Code Sec. 872(b); Act Sec. 419(b), amending Code Sec. 883(a)(4); Act Sec. 419(c). Law at ¶5610 and ¶5625. Committee Report at ¶10,750.

SOURCE OF INCOME

¶ 570

Interest Paid by Foreign Partnerships

Background

In order to apply certain federal income tax provisions, it is necessary to determine whether income is derived from sources within or without the United States. The source of interest income is generally determined by the residence or place of incorporation of the person who issued the interest-bearing obligation. Interest received from an obligation issued by a U.S. resident or a domestic corporation is treated as U.S.-source income (Code Sec. 861(a)(1)). For this purpose, a foreign corporation or foreign partnership will be treated as a U.S. resident if at any time during its tax year it is engaged in trade or business in the United States (Reg. §1.861-2(a)(2)). Thus, *any* interest received from such foreign corporations or foreign partnerships will be treated as U.S.-source income.

However, in the case of a foreign corporation engaged in a U.S. trade or business (or having gross income that is treated as effectively connected with the conduct of a U.S. trade or business), interest paid by the corporation will be treated as U.S.-source income *only* if it is paid by a U.S. trade or business of the corporation (or allocable to income that is treated as effectively connected with the conduct of a U.S. trade or business) (Code Sec. 884(f)(1)). Interest paid by a foreign trade or business of the corporation (or allocable to income not treated as effectively connected with a U.S. trade or business) remains foreign-source income. No similar exception applies to the interest paid by a foreign partnership. If a foreign partnership is engaged in trade or business in the United States, then all interest it pays on its obligations will be considered U.S.-source income, regardless of whether it is paid by a U.S. trade or business of the partnership or not.

American Jobs Creation Act Impact

Equal treatment for foreign partnerships.—Interest paid by a foreign partnership will be treated in a similar manner to the interest paid by a foreign corporation for purposes of the income sourcing rules. Interest paid by a foreign partnership with trade or business in the U.S. will be considered U.S.-source income *only* if it is paid by a U.S. trade or business of the partnership (or allocable to income that is effectively connected or is treated as effectively connected with the conduct of a U.S. trade or business) (Code Sec. 861(a)(1), as amended by the American Jobs Creation Act of 2004). However, to be eligible for this treatment, the foreign partnership must be predominantly engaged in the active conduct of a trade or business outside the United States. If the partnership is not predominantly engaged in the active conduct of a foreign trade or business, then *all* interest paid by the partnership will be treated as U.S.-source income.

> **Comment:** No definition is provided in the legislation when a foreign partnership will be considered "predominantly engaged" in a foreign trade or business. Any definition would most likely turn on the facts and circumstances of each case. However, other provisions of the Code do provide a definition of what it means to be "predominantly engaged" in a particular type of business. For example, under the foreign tax credit rules, a taxpayer is considered "predominantly engaged" in the active conduct of a banking, insurance, financing or similar business if at least 80 percent of its gross income for the tax year is derived from such a business (Code Sec. 904(d)(2)(C); Reg. § 1.904-4(e)(3)(i)). Under the subpart F rules, a controlled foreign corporation may be considered "predominantly engaged" in the active conduct of banking, insurance, financing or similar business if at least 70 percent of its gross income for the tax year is derived from such a business (Code Sec. 954(h)(2)(B)).

For further information on this subject, consult any of the following CCH reporter explanations:

- Standard Federal Tax Reporter, 2004FED ¶ 27,125.01
- Federal Tax Service, FTS § M:1.66
- Federal Tax Guide, 2004FTG ¶ 17,070

★ *Effective date.* The amendments made by this section shall apply to tax years beginning after December 31, 2003 (Act Sec. 410(b) of the American Jobs Creation Act of 2004).

Act Sec. 410(a) of the American Jobs Creation Act of 2004, amending Code Sec. 861(a)(1); Act Sec. 410(b). Law at ¶ 5595. Committee Report at ¶ 10,660.

¶ 575

Effectively Connected Income

Background ——

Nonresident aliens and foreign corporations (i.e., foreign persons) are subject to U.S. taxation in the same manner as U.S. persons on income effectively connected with the conduct of a U.S. trade or business (Code Secs. 871(b) and 882(a)). Foreign persons are also subject to a flat 30-percent rate (unless a lower rate applies by treaty) on the amount of fixed or determinable annual or periodical (FDAP) income derived from U.S. sources not effectively connected with a U.S. trade or business (Code Secs. 871(a) and 881)). Foreign persons are generally not taxed on foreign-source income not effectively connected with a U.S. trade or business.

FDAP income generally includes interest, dividends, rents, salaries, wages, premiums, annuities, compensation, remunerations, emoluments and any other item of periodical gain, profit or income from U.S. sources. It also includes royalties for timber, coal and iron ore, and the use of patents, copyrights, secret processes formulas and other like property. Substitute interest and dividend payments from U.S. sources will be treated as FDAP income for this purpose (Reg. § § 1.871-7(b)(2) and 1.881-2(b)(2)).

Whether income of a foreign person is treated as effectively connected with a U.S. trade or business (i.e., effectively-connected income) depends on its source. Generally, all U.S.-source income of a foreign person is treated as effectively con-

_____

nected income (Code Sec. 864(c)(1)). However, FDAP income of a foreign person from U.S. sources (as well as U.S.-source capital gains) will be treated as effectively connected income only if:

> (1) the income or gain is derived from assets used or held for use in the conduct of a U.S. trade or business; or

> (2) the activities of a U.S. trade or business are a material factor in the realization of the income or gain (Code Sec. 864(c)(2)).

Whether a foreign taxpayer is engaged in the conduct of a "U.S. trade or business" is determined based on the facts and circumstances of each case. Neither the Code or regulations specifically define the term. However, the conduct of a U.S. trade or business generally denotes considerable, continuous and regular course of activity by the taxpayer, or through an agent, partnership, estate or trust. The taxpayer need not be present in the United States to be engaged in a U.S. trade or business.

All foreign-source income of a foreign person is generally treated as *not* effectively connected with a U.S. trade or business (Code Sec. 864(c)(4)). However, certain foreign-source income will be treated as effectively connected income if it is attributable to an office or other fixed place of business in the United States of the foreign person. Income is attributable to an office or other fixed placed of business in the United States if the office is a material factor in the realization of the income and the income is derived in the ordinary course of a trade or business carried on through the office (Code Sec. 864(c)(5)). Thus, the activities of the U.S. office must provide a significant contribution to the realization of the income.

Foreign-source income which may be treated as effectively connected income includes:

> (1) rents and royalties derived from the use of intangible property outside the United States such as patents, copyrights, goodwill, or other similar property (gains or losses from the sale of such property are also included);

> (2) dividends or interest derived from the active conduct of a banking, financial or similar business within the United States or received by a corporation which has the principal business of trading of stocks and securities for its own account; or

> (3) income from the disposition of inventory or personal property held for sale in the normal course of business and sold outside the United States through the U.S. office of the foreign person (this does not include property disposed of for use, consumption or disposition outside the United States if a foreign office of the foreign person materially participated in the sale).

Foreign-source dividends, interest or royalties paid by a foreign corporation will not be treated as effectively connected income under this rule if the foreign person owns directly or indirectly more than 50 percent of the total combined voting power of all classes of voting stock of the corporation (Code Sec. 864(c)(4)(D)). Foreign-source income will also not be treated as effectively connected income if it is subpart F income of a controlled foreign corporation.

For these purposes, the determination of whether income is derived from U.S. or foreign sources is made by applying rules for certain types of income (Code Secs. 861 through 865). For example, sourcing rules apply to income such as interest, dividends, rents or royalties, gains from the sale of real property and inventory, and income from personal services.

¶575

Background —————————————————————————————————

The Code's sourcing rules are limited to only a few major types of income. Thus, the determination of the source of income not specifically governed by these rules proceeds by analogy with income of a known source. For example, alimony is not specifically mentioned in the source rules, but alimony payments may generally be sourced under principles analogous to the payment of interest (i.e., residence of the payor) (Rev. Rul. 69-108, 1969-1 CB 192). Similarly, fees for accepting letters of credit are sourced under principles analogous to interest (i.e., residence of the payor) (*Bank of America*, CtCls, 82-1 USTC ¶9415, 680 F. 2d 142).

American Jobs Creation Act Impact

Effectively connected income to include certain foreign-source income.—The new law expands on the types of foreign-source income that may be treated as effectively connected income. Foreign-source income which is the economic equivalent of rents or royalties derived from intangible property, dividends or interest derived from the active conduct of financial business, and income from the disposition of inventory or personal property held for sale in the normal course of business, will be treated as effectively connected with the conduct of a U.S. trade or business (Code Sec. 864(c)(4)(B), as amended by the American Jobs Creation Act of 2004).

Example: ABL is a foreign corporation engaged in the conduct of a U.S. trade or business. ABL has an office in Seattle, Washington, where new computer software is developed. ABL enters into an agreement allowing BKR, a foreign corporation with no U.S. office, to use the software. BKR, however, will not pay ABL any fee for the use of the software. Instead, BKR will forgive a portion of a loan owed to it by ABL. The cancellation of indebtedness is income which is the economic equivalent of rent or royalties paid for the use of intangible property outside the United States. Thus, ABL must treat such income as effectively connected with the conduct of a U.S. trade or business because it is attributable to its office in the United States.

For further information on this subject, consult any of the following CCH reporter explanations:

- Standard Federal Tax Reporter, 2004FED ¶27,189.01 and ¶27,189.021
- Federal Tax Service, FTS §M:13.20
- Federal Tax Guide, 2004FTG ¶17,095

★ *Effective date.* The amendment made by this section applies to tax years beginning after the date of enactment (Act Sec. 894(b) of the American Job Creation Act of 2004).

Act Sec. 894(a) of the American Jobs Creation Act of 2004, amending Code Sec. 864(c)(4)(B); Act Sec. 894(b). Law at ¶5600. Committee Report at ¶11,660.

POSSESSIONS

¶ 580

U.S. Possessions' Residence and Income Source Rules

Background —————————————————————————————————

U.S. citizens are subject to U.S. income tax on their worldwide income, regardless of the source. Aliens are subject to U.S. income tax according to different rules, depending on whether they are residents or nonresidents of the United States. In addition, special U.S. income tax rules apply to U.S. persons who are bona fide

Background

residents of certain U.S. possessions and have possession source income or income effectively connected to the conduct of a trade or business within a possession.

Resident aliens. A resident alien is generally taxed by the U.S. in the same manner as a U.S. citizen—on worldwide income, regardless of the source. An alien is a U.S. resident for U.S. income tax purposes if the individual:

(1) is a lawful permanent resident of the U.S. at any time during the year (Reg. § 301.7701(b)-1(b));

(2) is present in the U.S. for a substantial period of time (Reg. § 301.7701(b)-1(c)); or

(3) elects to be treated as a resident of the U.S. (Code Sec. 7701(b)(1)(A)).

An alien who has been lawfully given the privilege of residing permanently in the United States as an immigrant is deemed to be a lawful permanent resident of the United States unless the status has been revoked or judicially or administratively determined to have been abandoned. This is also referred to as the *green card test* (Reg. § 301.7701(b)-1(b)).

An alien who is physically present in the United States for at least 31 days during the calendar year and a total of at least 183 days during the last three years meets the *substantial presence test.* For purposes of the 183-day requirement, each day present in the U.S. during the current calendar year counts as a full day, each day in the first preceding year as one-third of a day, and each day in the second preceding year as one-sixth of a day (Code Sec. 7701(b)(3)(A); Reg. § 301.7701(b)-1(c)(1)). An individual is present in the U.S. for a particular day if he or she is physically present in the U.S. during any time during such day (Code Sec. 7701(b)(7)(A)).

Exception to substantial presence. An alien individual who otherwise meets the substantial presence test will be deemed to be a *nonresident* if the person:

(1) is present in the U.S. for fewer than 183 days during the current calendar year;

(2) has a tax home (as defined in Code Sec. 911(d)(3)) in a foreign country during the year; and

(3) has a closer connection to that foreign country than to the U.S. (Reg. § 301.7701(b)-2).

An individual alien who moves to the United States too late in the year to meet the substantial presence test, and does not otherwise qualify as a resident, may elect to be a resident for that year. This election is effective for the calendar year, referred to as the election year, if the requirements of Code Sec. 7701(b)(4) are satisfied.

Nonresident aliens. A nonresident alien is generally subject to U.S. income tax at a flat 30-percent rate on certain U.S. source income *and* at the same graduated rates applicable to U.S. citizens and residents on net income that is effectively connected with the conduct of a trade or business in the U.S. (Code Sec. 871). The rate of U.S. tax, or the amount of a nonresident alien individual's income subject to U.S. tax, can be limited by treaty (Reg. § 1.871-1(b)(2); Reg. § 1.871-12). An alien who fails to satisfy either the green card test or the substantial presence test and does not elect to be treated as a resident of the U.S. pursuant to Code Sec. 7701(b)(1)(A)(iii) is treated as a nonresident alien for U.S. income tax purposes.

¶580

Background

For purposes of determining resident alien and nonresident alien status under Code Sec. 7701(b), the United States includes the states and the District of Columbia, but does not include U.S. possessions (Reg. § 301.7701(b)-1(c)(2)(ii)).

Bona fide residents of U.S. possessions. Special U.S. income tax rules apply to *U.S. persons* who are bona fide residents of certain U.S. possessions and have possession source income, or income effectively connected with the conduct of a trade or business within a possession. *U.S. persons* are citizens or residents of the U.S. (Code Sec. 7701(a)(30).

A bona fide resident of a U.S. possession is determined by using the subjective facts-and-circumstances test set forth in the regulations under Code Sec. 871 and the individual's intentions as to length and nature of the stay in the possession. However, the basis for determining whether an alien individual is a resident of a U.S. possession with a mirror income tax code (tax laws that are identical to those in the U.S.) is Code Sec. 7701(b).

Income sourcing rules. The same rules that apply in determining income from sources within and without the U.S. generally apply in determining source of income within and without a U.S. possession (Reg. § 1.863-6). The U.S. income tax rules and regulations are silent regarding the determination of whether income is effectively connected with the conduct of a trade or business within a U.S. possession. However, Code Sec. 864(c) provides rules for determining whether income is effectively connected to a trade or business conducted within the U.S.

Information reporting and penalty. Information reporting on Form 5074 is required to determine the amount of U.S. taxes paid by bona fide residents of Guam and the Northern Mariana Islands that must be paid over to the treasuries of the respective possessions under Code Sec. 7654(a) (Code Sec. 7654(e)). A penalty of $100 is imposed for each failure to report (Code Sec. 6688).

Comment: Notice 2004-45, released on June 24, 2004, specifically describes a tax avoidance scheme involving U.S. citizens and residents who purport to establish residency in the Virgin Islands and, therefore, become subject to the Virgin Island's income tax laws. They then invoke significant tax reductions under the Economic Development Program (EDP) of the Virgin Islands. The EDP was actually established to encourage economic development in the Virgin Islands through tax incentives, not create windfall gains to taxpayers who live and work in the U.S. and have minimal contact with the Virgin Islands.

American Jobs Creation Act Impact

Codification of U.S. possessions' income sourcing and bona fide residence rules.—The requirements necessary to establish bona fide residence in the U.S. possessions of American Samoa, Guam, the Northern Mariana Islands, Puerto Rico, or the Virgin Islands are now provided by statute. In addition, the statute clarifies that the same rules used to determine income sourcing within the U.S., including income effectively connected with the conduct of a trade or business in the U.S. (Code Sec. 864(c), as amended by the American Jobs Creation Act of 2004), apply to determine income sourcing within American Samoa, Guam, the Northern Mariana Islands, Puerto Rico, or the Virgin Islands, including income effectively connected with a trade or business conducted within these possessions.

Comment: The conference agreement, at the outset, very clearly enunciates concern over the Virgin Islands tax avoidance scheme described in Notice 2004-45 (Conference Committee Report (H.R. Conf. Rep. No. 108-755)). Statutorily providing a definition of the term "bona fide resident" (applicable to American Samoa, Guam, the Northern Mariana Islands, Puerto Rico, and the Virgin Islands) that contains a 183-day rule similar to that of the substantial presence test, and including income sourcing rules, as well, appears to be a direct response to the Virgin Islands-type tax avoidance schemes.

Bona fide residence in a U.S. possession. The term "bona fide resident" means a person who:

(1) is present for at least 183 days during the tax year in American Samoa, Guam, the Northern Mariana Islands, Puerto Rico, or the Virgin Islands; and

(2) does not have a tax home outside the possession during the tax year *and* does not have a closer connection to the U.S. or a foreign country than to the possession (Code Sec. 937(a), as added by the 2004 Jobs Act).

An individual is present in the possession for a particular day if he or she is physically present in the possession during any time during such day (Code Sec. 7701(b)(7)(A)). A person's absence from a possession due to a medical emergency or other specified circumstance is ignored.

Comment: The 183-day rule applicable in determining bona fide residence in any of these five U.S. possessions is a modified version of the substantial presence test used to determine U.S. resident alien status. The tax home principles of Code Sec. 911(d)(3) apply (applied without regard to the second sentence of (d)(3)) in determining bona fide residence in any of the five possessions. The rules of Code Sec. 7701(b)(3)(B)(ii) apply to determine whether the person has a closer connection to a foreign country or the U.S., than to the possession.

Caution Note: Although the application of Code Sec. 937 is generally effective for tax years *ending* after the date of enactment of the 2004 Jobs Act, the 183-day rule applies to tax years *beginning* after the date of enactment.

Generally, a person's tax home is in the area where his primary place of business or duty post is located, regardless of where he maintains a family home. The location of a person's tax home often depends on whether a work assignment is temporary or indefinite. If the taxpayer is temporarily absent from a tax home in the U.S. on business, the taxpayer may be able to deduct certain travel, meal and lodging expenses. If, however, a new work assignment is for an indefinite period, the new place of employment may be the tax home and, therefore, associated expenses would not be considered deductible "away from home" expenses (Code Sec. 911(d)(3); Reg. § 1.911-2(b)).

Comment: Applying a uniform definition of bona fide residence in the possessions of American Samoa, Guam, the Northern Mariana Islands, Puerto Rico, and the Virgin Islands is intended to address the problem of U.S. citizens and residents who claim exemption from U.S. tax on worldwide income on the basis of being residents in a possession, although they continue to live and work in the U.S. (Conference Committee Report (H.R. Conf. Rep. No. 108-755)).

The statutory definition of bona fide resident specifically applies, except as provided in regulations, for purposes of:

(1) the application of the U.S. possessions Code sections (Code Secs. 931–937);

(2) stock sales by bona fide residents of Puerto Rico under Code Sec. 865(g)(3);

(3) alien individuals who are bona fide residents of American Samoa, Guam, the Northern Mariana Islands, or Puerto Rico that are subject to U.S. tax on worldwide income under Code Sec. 876;

(4) the exception to the 30-percent tax rate for possessions corporations receiving U.S. source income under Code Sec. 881(b), as amended by the 2004 Jobs Act;

(5) claiming the foreign tax credit for taxes paid to U.S. possessions by bona fide residents of Puerto Rico and for taxes paid to a foreign country by alien individuals who are bona fide residents of Puerto Rico under Code Sec. 901(b), as amended by the 2004 Jobs Act;

(6) excluding bona fide residents of Puerto Rico and American Samoa (Northern Mariana Islands and Guam, as well, when implementing agreements with the U.S. are effective) from the definition of U.S. person under Code Sec. 957(c), as amended by the 2004 Jobs Act;

(7) excluding remuneration paid to a U.S. citizen within Puerto Rico from the definition of "wages" under Code Sec. 3401(a)(8)(C) because he or she is expected to be a bona fide resident of Puerto Rico for the entire calendar year; and

(8) the payment to the treasuries of American Samoa, Guam, the Northern Mariana Islands and the Virgin Islands, pursuant to Code Sec. 7654(a), of U.S. tax paid by bona fide residents of these possessions (Code Sec. 937(a), as added by the 2004 Jobs Act).

Comment: The IRS is granted authority to create exceptions to the bona fide residence rules. The conference committee indicated that such exceptions should cover persons whose presence outside a possession for extended periods of time lacks a tax avoidance purpose, such as military personnel, workers in the fisheries trade, or retirees who travel outside the possession for certain personal reasons (Conference Committee Report (H.R. Conf. Rep. No. 108-755)).

Reporting requirement. An individual must file a notice in the first tax year that he or she takes the position that, for U.S. income tax reporting purposes, he or she became (or ceased to be) a bona fide resident of American Samoa, Guam, the Northern Mariana Islands, Puerto Rico, or the Virgin Islands. The notice of the position must be filed as prescribed by the IRS (Code Sec. 937(c)(1), as added by the 2004 Jobs Act). A transition rule provides that if an individual claimed to be a bona fide resident (or ceased to be a bona fide resident) of a possession for any of the three tax years ending before the individual's first tax year that ends after the date of enactment of the 2004 Jobs Act, the individual must also file a notice (Code Sec. 937(c)(2), as added by the 2004 Jobs Act).

Compliance Tip: The transition rule requires taxpayers to disclose their previous claims to have been a bona fide resident of a possession. This appears aimed at identifying participants in tax avoidance schemes for purposes of enforcement.

Penalty. The penalty for failure to file the required notice is $1,000 for each failure (Code Sec. 6688, as amended by the 2004 Jobs Act).

Comment: The penalty under Code Sec. 6688, as amended by the 2004 Jobs Act, also applies for failure to comply with the information reporting requirements of Code Sec. 7654 pertaining to the duty of the U.S. to pay over to the treasuries of American Samoa, Guam, the Northern Mariana Islands, or the Virgin Islands, the U.S. income tax paid by a bona fide resident of the respective possession. The penalty for failure to meet the Code Sec. 7654 reporting requirements, which was $100 prior to amendment by the 2004 Jobs Act, is increased to $1,000.

Income sourcing rules for U.S. possessions. For purposes of determining whether income, including income that is effectively connected to a trade or business conducted in a possession, is sourced within American Samoa, Guam, the Northern Mariana Islands, Puerto Rico, or the Virgin Islands, rules similar to those for determining the sourcing of income within the U.S. will apply, including the rules sourcing income that is effectively connected with the conduct of a trade or business in the U.S. (Code Sec. 937(b)(1), as added by the 2004 Jobs Act). The provision also provides that income treated as U.S. source income, or treated as income effectively connected with the conduct of a trade or business within the U.S., is not treated as income from within any of the possessions, or as income effectively connected with the conduct of a trade or business within any of the possessions (Code Sec. 937(b)(2), as added by the 2004 Jobs Act). These income sourcing rules apply to income earned after the date of enactment of the 2004 Jobs Act. Authority is granted to the IRS to create exceptions to these sourcing rules.

It is anticipated that the IRS authority to create exceptions will be used to continue "the existing treatment of income from the sale of goods manufactured in a possession." Furthermore, it is intended that exceptions will be used to prevent tax avoidance, for example to prevent U.S. persons from avoiding U.S. tax on the disposition of appreciated property by establishing possession residency prior to the disposition (Conference Committee Report (H.R. Conf. Rep. No. 108-755)).

Comment: Although Reg. § 1.863-6 had previously provided that the same rules used to determine whether income was from sources within or without the U.S. generally applied to determine the source of income within or without U.S. possessions, this rule is now specifically stated in Code Sec. 937(b), as added by the 2004 Jobs Act. The U.S. income sourcing rules are provided in Code Secs. 861 through 865 and now apply, by statute, to the five U.S. possessions as a result of the addition of Code Sec. 937 to the Internal Revenue Code.

Comment: U.S. citizens and residents have erroneously sourced their U.S. income to various U.S. possessions offering favorable tax regimes, including income that is actually effectively connected with the conduct of a trade or business in the U.S. In order to combat this erosion of the U.S. tax base, the conference committee expressed the need to establish uniform rules sourcing income within American Samoa, Guam, the Northern Mariana Islands, Puerto Rico, and the Virgin Islands. Residents of U.S. possessions who continue to live and work in the U.S. should not have the benefit of exemptions from U.S. tax provided to residents of possessions (Conference Committee Report (H.R. Conf. Rep. No. 108-755)).

The Conference Report notes that no inference is intended as to the current-law rules for determining (1) bona fide residence in a possession, (2) whether income is possession source, and (3) whether income is effectively connected with the conduct of a trade or business within a possession (Conference Committee Report, (H.R. Conf. Rep. No. 108-755)).

Conforming amendments. Certain conforming amendments to various Code sections were required to reflect the strengthened residency requirements for possessions and the tightened income sourcing rules for U.S. citizens who become residents of American Samoa, Guam, the Northern Mariana Islands, Puerto Rico, and the Virgin Islands:

¶580

- The special sourcing and residency rules for bona fide residents of American Samoa, Guam, and the Northern Mariana Islands have been removed (Code Sec. 931(d), as amended by the 2004 Jobs Act).

- In order to report all worldwide income on a Virgin Islands income tax return, rather than a U.S. tax return, the Virgin Islands bona fide resident must have bona fide residency status *during the entire tax year*, not just as of the last day of the tax year (Code Sec. 932, as amended by the 2004 Jobs Act).

- For purposes of the Virgin Islands' authority to reduce certain tax liabilities, the regulations under Code Sec. 934 do not determine whether income is sourced in the Virgin Islands (Code Sec. 934(b)(4), as amended by the 2004 Jobs Act).

- Application of the coordination rules between Guam and the U.S. require a resident of Guam to be a bona fide resident, and the status of an individual subject to the coordination rules must be the same during the entire tax year (Code Sec. 935, as amended by the 2004 Jobs Act).

- Regulations under Code Sec. 957 may only prescribe rules to determine whether income was derived from the *active* conduct of a trade or business within a possession, not rules to determine whether the source of income was from within a possession, or rules to determine whether income was effectively connected with the conduct of a trade or business in a possession (Code Sec. 957(c), as amended by the 2004 Jobs Act).

For further information on this subject, consult any of the following CCH reporter explanations:

- Standard Federal Tax Reporter, 2004FED ¶27,189.01, ¶28,245.01, ¶28,281.01, ¶28,322.01 and¶28,596.01

- Federal Tax Service, FTS §M:15.20

- Federal Tax Guide, 2004FTG ¶17,045

★ *Effective date.* In general, these provisions apply to tax years ending after the date of enactment (Act Sec. 908(d)(1) of the American Jobs Creation Act of 2004). However, the 183-day rule applicable to the residency test of Code Sec. 937(a)(1) applies to tax years beginning after the date of enactment, and the income sourcing rules of Code Sec. 937(b)(2) apply to income earned after the date of enactment (Act Sec. 908(d)(2) and (3) of the 2004 Jobs Act).

Act Sec. 908(a) of the American Jobs Creation Act of 2004, adding Code Sec. 937; Act Sec. 908(b), amending Code Sec. 6688; Act Sec. 908(c)(1), amending Code Sec. 931(d); Act Sec. 908(c)(2), amending Code Sec. 932; Act Sec. 908(c)(3), amending Code Sec. 934(b)(4); Act Sec. 908(c)(4), amending Code Sec. 935; Act Sec. 908(c)(5), amending Code Sec. 957(c); Act Sec. 908(d). Law at ¶5665, ¶5670, ¶5675, ¶5680, ¶5690, ¶5730, and ¶6255. Committee Report at ¶11,800.

¶ 585

U.S. Source Dividends Paid to Puerto Rico Corporations Subject to Reduced Tax and Withholding

Background ⎯⎯⎯⎯⎯⎯⎯⎯⎯⎯⎯⎯⎯⎯⎯⎯⎯⎯⎯⎯⎯⎯⎯⎯⎯⎯⎯⎯

Generally, dividends paid by U.S. corporations to non-U.S. corporations are subject to 30 percent U.S. income tax withholding, unless reduced or eliminated pursuant to a tax treaty (Code Sec. 1442(a)). Different rules apply when dividends are paid by U.S. corporations to corporations organized in U.S. possessions. Furthermore, no mitigation of tax laws through treaty benefits applies between a U.S. corporation

Background ———

and a U.S. possessions corporation (Senate Report No. 1707, Foreign Investors Tax Act of 1966 (P.L. 89-809)).

Dividends paid by U.S. corporations to corporations organized in the U.S. possessions of American Samoa, Guam, the Northern Mariana Islands or the Virgin Islands are not subject to U.S. withholding, if specific local ownership and activity requirements are met (Code Sec. 1442(c)). There is a zero rate of withholding on dividends paid by corporations organized in any of these U.S. possessions to U.S. corporations, pursuant to internal revenue codes adopted in each of the four possessions.

Dividends paid by a corporation organized in the Commonwealth of Puerto Rico, a U.S. possession, to non-Puerto Rico corporations are subject to 10 percent withholding by Puerto Rico (Sec. 1150 of the Puerto Rico IRC). If the dividend is paid out of income that is subject to certain Puerto Rico tax incentives, the 10 percent withholding rate may be subject to exemption or elimination. A reduction of the underlying Puerto Rico corporate tax rate to between two and seven percent may result from these incentives, as well.

Dividends paid by U.S. corporations to Puerto Rico corporations are subject to a 30 percent U.S. tax and a 30 percent U.S. withholding rate (Code Secs. 881(a) and 1442(a)). Puerto Rico corporations may credit their U.S. income taxes (the 30 percent withholding and the underlying U.S. tax attributable to the dividends) against their Puerto Rico income taxes (Sec. 1131 of the Puerto Rico IRC). Generally, however, the sum of the U.S. creditable taxes exceeds the amount of Puerto Rico corporate income tax imposed on the dividend, thereby limiting the credit. Thus, Puerto Rico corporations with subsidiaries organized in the U.S. may be subject to some level of double taxation on their U.S. subsidiaries' earnings.

American Jobs Creation Act Impact

U.S. tax and withholding rates decrease to 10 percent.—U.S. source dividends paid to a Puerto Rico corporation are subject to U.S. taxation and withholding at a 10 percent rate (Code Secs. 881(b)(2)(A) and 1442(c)(2)(A), as added by the American Jobs Creation Act of 2004). This provision applies to dividends paid after the date of enactment of the 2004 Jobs Act. The 10 percent tax and withholding rate for U.S. source dividends paid to Puerto Rico corporations applies if:

(1) at all times during the tax year less than 25 percent in value of the Puerto Rico corporation's stock is beneficially owned (directly or indirectly) by foreign persons;

(2) at least 65 percent of the Puerto Rico corporation's gross income is shown to the satisfaction of the IRS to be effectively connected with the conduct of a trade or business in Puerto Rico or in the U.S. for the three-year period ending with the close of the tax year of the corporation; and

(3) no substantial part of the income of the Puerto Rico corporation is used (either directly or indirectly) to satisfy obligations to persons who are not bona fide residents of Puerto Rico or the U.S. (Code Secs. 881(b)(2)(A) and 1442(c)(2)(A), as added by the 2004 Jobs Act; Code Sec. 881(b)(1), as amended by the 2004 Jobs Act).

Comment: The reduction in the U.S. tax and withholding rates from 30 percent to 10 percent on U.S. source dividends paid to a Puerto Rico corporation creates parity with the generally applicable Puerto Rico 10 percent withholding tax imposed on dividends paid by Puerto Rico corporations to U.S. corporations.

The potential for double taxation of Puerto Rico corporations with U.S. subsidiaries is minimized because the credit for U.S. taxes (10 percent withholding and U.S. tax attributable to the dividends) more closely approximates the amount of Puerto Rico corporate income tax imposed on the dividends. The Senate Committee believed that creating and maintaining parity between U.S. and Puerto Rico dividend withholding tax rates would place Puerto Rico corporations on a more level playing field with corporations organized in treaty countries and other possessions (Senate Committee Report, S. Rep. No. 108-192).

Dividends paid by U.S. corporations to Puerto Rico corporations may again be subject to the 30 percent U.S. tax and withholding rates under certain circumstances. If at any time, on or after the date of enactment of the 2004 Jobs Act, the Puerto Rico withholding tax rate on dividends paid by a Puerto Rico corporation to a U.S. corporation, not engaged in a trade or business in Puerto Rico, increases to greater than 10 percent, the 30 percent U.S. tax and withholding rates will become effective (Code Secs. 881(b)(2)(B) and 1442(c)(2)(B), as added by the 2004 Jobs Act). The U.S. tax and withholding rates return to 30 percent for dividends received on or after the date that the Puerto Rico increased withholding rate becomes effective.

> **Caution Note:** The 30 percent U.S. tax and withholding rates will apply to U.S. source dividends paid to Puerto Rico corporations any time the Puerto Rico withholding rate on dividends paid by Puerto Rico corporations to U.S. corporations increases to greater than 10 percent.

For further information on this subject, consult any of the following CCH reporter explanations:

- Standard Federal Tax Reporter, 2004FED ¶ 27,484.01 and ¶ 32,723.01
- Federal Tax Service, FTS § M:15.42
- Federal Tax Guide, 2004FTG ¶ 17,120

★ *Effective date.* The provision applies to dividends paid after the date of enactment (Act Sec. 420(d) of the American Jobs Creation Act of 2004).

Act Sec. 420(a) of the American Jobs Creation Act of 2004, redesignating Code Sec. 881(b)(2) as Code Sec. 881(b)(3) and adding new Code Sec. 881(b)(2); Act Sec. 420(b), amending Code Sec. 1442(c) and adding Code Sec. 1442(c)(2); Act Sec. 420(c), amending Code Sec. 881(b) and Code Sec. 881(b)(1); Act Sec. 420(d). Law at ¶ 5620 and ¶ 5930. Committee Report at ¶ 10,760.

CUSTOMS AND TRADE

¶ 590

Ceiling Fans

Background _____

The Harmonized Tariff Schedule of the United States (HTSUS) is a comprehensive classification of products that sets forth a description for each product and specifies the rate of duty that U.S. Customs authorities will apply to imports of the products upon entry into the United States. It is maintained and published by the United States International Trade Commission (USITC). The HTSUS is organized by section, chapter, subchapter, heading, and subheading which progressively define products into various categories based on function, use or level of processing.

Products are assigned tariff numbers that reflect this breakdown. The first six digits of a tariff number are standardized throughout the world. They are set by the World Customs Organization, an international organization based in Brussels. Coun-

Background _____

tries are permitted to assign up to four more digits to the tariff number (for a total of 10 digits) to more precisely describe the product for duty or quota purposes. These additional digits differ between countries. Interpretation of the classifications can be problematic because international and national rules of interpretation apply.

Ceiling fans imported into the United States from all sources are subject to a 4.7-percent *ad valorem* customs duty on entry.

American Jobs Creation Act Impact

Duty-free imports.—This provision of the American Jobs Creation Act of 2004 amends subchapter II of chapter 99 of the Harmonized Tariff Schedule of the United States (HTSUS) by inserting a new heading for ceiling fans for permanent installation (provided for in subheading 8414.51.00). Imports classified under this new heading, 9902.84.14, will enter the United States duty-free, generally, suspending the prior duty rate through December 31, 2006.

★ *Effective date.* This provision applies to goods entered, or withdrawn from warehouse, for consumption on or after the fifteenth day after the date of enactment (Act Sec. 713(b) of the American Jobs Creation Act of 2004).

Act Sec. 713(a) of the American Jobs Creation Act of 2004, amending subchapter II of chapter 99 of the Harmonized Tariff Schedule of the United States; Act Sec. 713(b). Law at ¶ 7080. Committee Report at ¶ 10,940.

¶ 595

Certain Steam Generators, Certain Reactor Vessel Heads and Pressurizers Used in Nuclear Facilities

Background _____

The Harmonized Tariff Schedule of the United States (HTSUS) is a comprehensive product classification system that sets forth a description and specifies a rate of duty that U.S. Customs authorities will apply to imports of products upon entry into the United States. Prior to January 1, 1989, the United States used the Tariff Schedules of the United States for these purposes. The HTSUS was created to conform the U.S. system to the Harmonized Commodity Description and Coding System, also known as the "Harmonized System," which was developed by the Customs Cooperation Council to facilitate international trade.

Imports of certain steam generators classified under heading 9902.84.02 of subchapter II of chapter 99 of the HTSUS are, generally, accorded duty-free treatment upon entry. Such duty-free treatment, however, will expire on December 31, 2006. After that date, imports falling under this heading will be subject to the general rate of duty (column 1) of 5.2 percent under subheading 8402.11.00 of the HTSUS. Imports of certain reactor vessel heads used in nuclear facilities (falling under subheading 8401.40.00) are currently subject to a general rate of duty (column 1) of 3.3 percent.

American Jobs Creation Act Impact

Suspension of duties.—This provision of the American Jobs Creation Act of 2004 amends heading 9902.84.02 of subchapter II of chapter 99 of the Harmonized Tariff Schedule of the United States (HTSUS) by striking "12/31/2006" and inserting "12/31/2008." Accordingly, the effective period for the suspension of duty rates for certain steam generators is extended until December 31, 2008.

The provision further amends subchapter II of chapter 99 of the HTSUS by inserting a new heading, 9902.84.03, for reactor vessel heads and pressurizers for nuclear reactors (provided for in subheading 8401.40.00). The provision temporarily suspends the present customs duty applicable to reactor vessel heads for column 1 countries through December 31, 2008. Consistent with the Conference Committee Report (H.R. Conf. Rep. No. 108-755), the customs duty applicable to nuclear reactor pressurizers is also temporarily suspended.

★ *Effective date.* This provision is effective with respect to steam generators on the date of enactment of the American Jobs Creation Act of 2004; the provision applies to nuclear reactor vessel heads and pressurizers entered, or withdrawn from warehouse for consumption, on or after the fifteenth day after the date of enactment (Act Sec. 714(c) of the 2004 Jobs Act).

Act Sec. 714(a) and (b) of the American Jobs Creation Act of 2004, amending subchapter II of chapter 99 of the Harmonized Tariff Schedule of the United States; Act Sec. 714(c). Law at ¶ 7085. Committee Report at ¶ 10,950 and ¶ 10,960.

¶ 597

Customs User Fees

Background

Customs user fees are, essentially, processing fees imposed by the United States on merchandise, passengers, and conveyances that enter the United States. They were first authorized by Congress with the intent that they would be used to offset costs associated with the commercial operations of the U.S. Customs Service. These commercial operations primarily include inspection and clearance services performed by the U.S. Customs Service, but also extend to other activities performed by U.S. Customs personnel.

Under Title 19 U.S.C. §58c, the fees for certain customs services specifically include processing fees for air and sea passengers, commercial trucks, rail cars, private aircraft and vessels, commercial vessels, dutiable mail packages, barges and bulk carriers, merchandise, and customs broker permits. In order for the collection of these fees to continue, periodic reauthorization is required. The Secretary of the Treasury was authorized to collect "service fees" under Sec. 13031 of the Consolidated Omnibus Budget Reconciliation Act of 1985 ("COBRA") (19 U.S.C. §58c) (P.L. 99-272) and to delegate this authority to the Secretary of Homeland Security under Sec. 412 of the Homeland Security Act of 2002 (P.L. 107-296). COBRA has been amended several times, most recently by the Military Family Tax Relief Act of 2003 (P.L. 108-121); that reauthorization for collection of these fees extends through March 1, 2005.

American Jobs Creation Act Impact

Extension of customs user fees.—The American Jobs Creation Act of 2004 extends the authorization to collect merchandise processing fees and passenger and conveyance processing fees, originally authorized under COBRA, through September 30, 2014. Beginning in fiscal year 2006, the Secretary of the Treasury is to charge fees that are reasonably related to the costs of providing customs services in connection with the item or activity for which the fee was charged.

It is the sense of Congress that the fees are reasonably related to the cost of providing the customs services and are not excessive. The Secretary of the Treasury is directed to conduct a study of all fees collected by the Department of Homeland

Security and to submit that report to Congress with recommendations no later than September 30, 2005.

★ *Effective date.* No specific effective date is provided by the Act. The provision is, therefore, considered effective on the date of enactment.

Act Sec. 892 of the American Jobs Creation Act of 2004, amending Sec. 13031(f) of the Consolidated Omnibus Budget Act of 1985 (19 U.S.C. § 58c(f)). Law at ¶ 7150. Committee Report at ¶ 11,640.

Chapter 6

Tax Avoidance and Tax Shelters

REPORTING AND DISCLOSURE

¶ 605

Disclosure of Reportable Transactions

Background _____

An organizer of a tax shelter is required to register the shelter with the IRS on or before the date it is offered for sale (Code Sec. 6111(a), prior to amendment by the American Jobs Creation Act of 2004). Registration was made on Form 8264, Application for Registration of a Tax Shelter. A tax shelter was defined as an investment, from which a person could reasonably infer, from the representations made or to be made regarding the investment, that the tax benefits of investing in the shelter exceed the amount of the investment by a ratio of two to one at the end of any of the first five tax years ending after the date the investment is offered for sale that is: (1) required to be registered under federal or state securities laws; (2) sold pursuant to an exemption from registration requiring the filing of a notice with a federal or state securities agency; or (3) a substantial investment (greater than $250,000 and involving at least five investors) (Code Sec. 6111(c), prior to amendment by the 2004 Jobs Act).

Additional promoted arrangements were treated as tax shelters for registration purposes if: (1) a significant purpose of the arrangement was the avoidance or evasion of federal income tax by a corporate participant; (2) the arrangement was offered under conditions of confidentiality; and (3) the promoter could have received fees in excess of $100,000 in the aggregate (Code Sec. 6111(d), prior to amendment by the 2004 Jobs Act). Generally, a transaction was defined as having a "significant purpose of avoiding or evading federal income tax" if the transaction: (1) was the same as or substantially similar to a listed transaction, or (2) was structured to produce tax benefits that constitute an important part of the intended results of the arrangement and the promoter reasonably expected to present the arrangement to more than one taxpayer. Certain exceptions were provided with respect to the second category of transactions. An arrangement was considered offered under conditions of confidentiality if an offeree had an understanding or agreement to limit the disclosure of the transaction or any significant tax features of the transaction or the promoter knew, or had reason to know, that the offeree's use or disclosure of information relating to the transaction was limited in any other manner.

American Jobs Creation Act of 2004 Impact

New reporting requirements for material advisors.—A material advisor with respect to any reportable transaction (including any listed transaction) is required to file a new information return. The information return must include: (1) information identifying and describing the transaction, (2) information describing any potential tax benefits expected to result from the transaction, and (3) any other information sought by the IRS (Code Sec. 6111(a), as amended by the American Jobs Creation Act of 2004). See ¶630 for discussion of the penalty for failing to furnish this requested information.

> **Compliance Tip:** The IRS will now have to develop the new information return form and provide filing details.

Material advisor. A material advisor is any person who: (1) provides any material aid, assistance, or advice with respect to organizing, managing, promoting, selling, implementing, insuring, or carrying out any reportable transaction; and (2) directly or indirectly derives gross income for the advice or assistance in excess of an established threshold amount (or other amount that may be provided by the IRS). The threshold amount is $50,000 in the case of a reportable transaction where substantially all of the tax benefits are provided to natural persons and $250,000 in any other case (Code Sec. 6111(b)(1), as amended by the 2004 Jobs Act).

Reportable transaction. A reportable transaction is one in which information is required to be included with a return or statement because the transaction is of a type that has been determined as having a potential for tax avoidance or evasion under regulations prescribed under Code Sec. 6011 (Code Sec. 6111(b)(2), as amended by the 2004 Jobs Act, referencing Code Sec. 6707A(c), as added by the 2004 Jobs Act).

Regulations. Regulations may be issued that provide: (1) that only one person will be required to meet the reporting and disclosure requirements of Code Sec. 6111(a) in cases in which two or more persons would otherwise be required to meet the requirements, (2) exemptions from these requirements, and (3) the rules that may be necessary to carry out the purposes of this section (Code Sec. 6111(c), as amended by the 2004 Jobs Act).

Lists of advisees.—Each material advisor with respect to any reportable transaction must maintain a list (in a manner prescribed by regulations) that: (1) identifies each person to whom the advisor acted as a material advisor with respect to the reportable transaction, and (2) contains any other information that may be required in regulations. The requirement to maintain the lists applies whether or not the material advisor is required to file a return under Code Sec. 6111 with respect to the transaction. Any person required to maintain a list also is required to make the list available for inspection upon written request by the I.R.S. (Code Sec. 6112(a) and (b), as amended by the 2004 Jobs Act).

> **Comment:** According to the House Committee Report (H.R. Rep. No. 108-548), requiring material advisors to maintain a list of advisees with respect to each reportable transaction, coupled with more meaningful penalties for failing to maintain an investor list, are important tools in the ongoing efforts to curb the use of abusive tax avoidance transactions.

> **PRACTICAL ANALYSIS. Jeffrey Paravano of Baker & Hostetler and former Treasury official observes that what is most interesting about the tax shelter legislation is what it does not include.The Conference Committee dropped Senate provisions that would have codified the economic substance doctrine, required CEO declarations to be attached to tax returns and denied deductions for certain fines and penalties. The Conference Committee also generally adopted House bill effective dates and grandfather provisions, which cushion the harm to taxpayers of many of the new provisions. The House had previously adopted many provisions that first appeared in the Senate, but additional movement toward Senate positions did not occur.**

For further information on this subject, consult any of the following CCH reporter explanations:

- Standard Federal Tax Reporter, 2004FED ¶35,141.06, ¶37,002.01, ¶37,022.01 and ¶40,100.01

- Federal Tax Service, FTS §P:3.180

- Federal Tax Guide, 2004FTG ¶22,237 and ¶22,240

★ *Effective date.* The amendments made by this provision apply to transactions with respect to which material aid, assistance, or advice under Code Sec. 6111(b)(1)(a)(i) is provided after the date of enactment (Act Sec. 815(c) of the American Jobs Creation Act of 2004).

Act Sec. 815(a) of the American Jobs Creation Act of 2004, amending Code Sec. 6111; Act Sec. 815(b)(2), amending Code Sec. 6112(a) and (b); Act Sec. 815(b)(3)(B), amending Code Sec. 6112(b)(1); Act Sec. 815(b)(3)(C), amending Code Sec. 6112(b)(2); Act Sec. 815(b)(5)(A), amending Code Sec. 6708; Act Sec. 815(c). Law at ¶6165, ¶6170 and ¶6275. Committee Report at ¶11,070.

¶610

Extended Statute of Limitations for Unreported Listed Transactions

Background

As a general rule, a three-year statute of limitations applies to most tax returns. Thus, once three years has passed after the taxpayer has filed the return, the IRS can no longer assess and collect deficiencies related to that return. However, there are exceptions to this three-year statute of limitations. A six-year limit applies if there has been a substantial omission of income, defined as more than 25 percent of the gross income reported on the return. Further, an unlimited period of time for assessment and collection applies in situations where the taxpayer has filed a false or fraudulent return with intent to evade tax. The IRS also gets the benefit of this unlimited period if the taxpayer does not file a return at all.

American Jobs Creation Act Impact

Extended statute of limitations for listed transactions.—Some taxpayers and tax advisors have been known to use delaying tactics and other forms of noncooperation with the IRS in hopes of "waiting out" the three-year statute of limitations, and thereby forestalling IRS assessment and collection of tax deficiencies. The American Jobs Creation Act of 2004 aims to eliminate this possibility with respect to certain listed transactions, as defined in Code Sec. 6707A(c)(2) (as added by the 2004 Jobs Act; see ¶615).

Effective for tax years that are still open on the date of enactment, if a taxpayer fails to include any information required by Code Sec. 6011 on a tax return or statement relating to a listed transaction, the statute of limitations with respect to that transaction will not expire before one year after the earlier of:

(1) the date on which the information is furnished to the IRS, or

(2) the date that a material advisor (see ¶605) satisfies the list maintenance requirements of Code Sec. 6112 (as amended by the 2004 Jobs Act) with respect to the IRS's request relating to the taxpayer's transaction.

Example: Stacy Hollard engaged in a 2005 transaction that becomes a listed transaction in 2007. If Hollard fails to disclose the transaction as required by Treasury regulations, the transaction will be subject to the extended statute of limitations.

The Conference Committee Report (H.R. Rep. No. 108-755) states that the 2004 Jobs Act provision will not extend the statute of limitations with respect to a transaction for a tax year that has previously been closed before the transaction was designated as a listed transaction. However, if a transaction has provided tax benefits for multiple tax years, only some of which were closed for assessment and collection before the transaction becomes a listed transaction, the extended statute of limitations will apply to the tax years that are still open.

Example: Rupert Rolander entered into a transaction that gives rise to tax benefits reported on his income tax returns that were filed on April 15th of 2005, 2006, and 2007. In December 2009, the IRS determines that the transaction reported on Rolander's returns is a listed transaction. Rolander's 2007 return will be subject to the extended statute of limitations if the return does not include the information required under Treasury regulations. The 2005 and 2006 returns, which were closed before the IRS designated the transaction as a listed transaction, will not be subject to the extended statute of limitations.

For further information on this subject, consult any of the following CCH reporter explanations:

• Standard Federal Tax Reporter, 2004FED ¶38,963.01, ¶38,963.021 and ¶38,963.023

• Federal Tax Service, FTS §P:3.180 and §P:17.41

• Federal Tax Guide, 2004FTG ¶22,240 and ¶22,465

★ *Effective date.* The provision extending the statute of limitations with respect to failure to include required information relating to listed transactions applies to tax years with respect to which the period for assessing a deficiency did not expire before the date of enactment (Act Sec. 814(b) of the American Jobs Creation Act of 2004).

Act Sec. 814(a) of the American Jobs Creation Act of 2004, adding Code Sec. 6501(c)(10); Act Sec. 814(b). Law at ¶ 6225. Committee Report at ¶ 11,060.

PENALTIES AND SANCTIONS

¶ 615

Penalty for Failing to Disclose Tax Shelters

Background

An abusive tax shelter is most broadly defined as an entity, plan or arrangement with a significant purpose of avoiding or evading federal income tax (Code Sec. 6662(d)(2)(C)(iii)). Tax shelters are varied, complex, and difficult to detect because they generally involve multiple steps and manipulate several sections of the Internal Revenue Code. The IRS Office of Tax Shelter Analysis has identified several common shelter characteristics, including promotion or marketing, confidentiality, high transaction costs, a lack of meaningful economic risk or potential for gain, and unnecessary steps or novel investments.

In 1986, when statutory changes made individual participation in tax shelters more difficult, the focus of tax shelter development shifted to the corporate sector. Corporate tax shelters received additional impetus during the 1990s, when many companies transformed their tax departments from compliance centers to profit centers. During this same period, many accountants and lawyers spent less time offering individualized tax advice, and more time developing and marketing shelters. IRS data suggest that, from 1993 through 2003, known tax shelters resulted in more than $33 billion in lost federal tax revenues, with another $52 billion lost in transactions that were similar to the known shelters. The "Son of Boss" shelter alone resulted in more than $6 billion in tax understatements, according to IRS estimates. The lost revenue is not limited to the federal level. The Multistate Tax Commission estimates that in 2001, corporate tax shelters cost the states more than $12 billion, representing one-third of total state corporate tax revenues.

The IRS has promulgated regulations describing tax shelter transactions as reportable transactions that must be disclosed by taxpayers who enter into them on or after February 28, 2003 (Reg. § 1.6011-4). The regulations identify six types of reportable transactions:

(1) Listed transactions, which are (a) abusive transactions that the IRS has identified by notice, regulation, or other published guidance; or (b) transactions that are expected to obtain the same or substantially similar tax consequences.

(2) Confidential transactions, which are transactions in which a paid advisor limits the taxpayer's disclosure of the tax treatment or tax structure of the transaction.

(3) Transactions with contractual protection, in which (a) the taxpayer's fees are contingent on achieving the intended tax consequences, or (b) the taxpayer has a right to a full or partial refund of fees if the expected tax consequences are not sustained.

(4) Excessive loss transactions, which are transactions that (a) are not included in the "angel list" of acceptable transactions in Rev. Proc. 2003-24, and (b) result in a deductible loss exceeding:

- $10 million in a single tax year (or $20 million in any combination of tax years) if the taxpayer is a corporation or a partnership having only corporations as partners;

- $2 million in a single tax year (or $4 million in any combination of tax years) if the taxpayer is a partnership, S corporation, individual or trust; or

- $50,000 in a single tax year if the loss arises from certain foreign currency transactions and the taxpayer is an individual or a trust.

(5) Transactions with significant book-tax differences, in which (a) the taxpayer is governed by the Securities and Exchange Commission or is a business entity with assets of at least $250 million; (b) the transaction is not included on the "angel list" of acceptable transactions in Rev. Proc. 2003-25; and (c) the tax treatment of the transaction differs by more than $10 million from its book treatment using generally accepted accounting principles.

(6) Transactions involving assets with brief holding periods (45 days or less) that produce a tax credit exceeding $250,000.

Compliance Tip: Reportable transactions are reported on Form 8886, Reportable Transaction Disclosure Statement, which must be attached to each year's tax return that includes the transaction. In the first year of the transaction, a copy of the Form 8886 must also be filed with the IRS Office of Tax Shelter Analysis.

Although these mandatory disclosure rules are a principal tool in the battle against shelters, there is no independent penalty for failing to disclose a reportable transaction. A failure to disclose has an impact only if the taxpayer has an understatement of tax attributable to the undisclosed transaction. In that case, the failure to disclose limits the taxpayer's defense to accuracy-related penalties that can be imposed on the understatement, because the failure precludes the taxpayer from claiming that the understatement was due to reasonable cause and that the taxpayer acted in good faith (see Background at ¶620).

Example: XYZ Corp. participated in a listed transaction that it failed to disclose. However, the transaction did not produce any tax benefits and, thus, did not cause XYZ to understate its tax liabilities. No penalty can be imposed on XYZ for failing to disclose the transaction.

American Jobs Creation Act Impact

Separate penalty imposed for failing to disclose reportable transactions.—A new, independent penalty is imposed on taxpayers who fail to disclose a reportable transaction (Code Sec. 6707A(a), as added by the American Jobs Creation Act of 2004). The amount of the penalty is (Code Sec. 6707A(b), as added by the 2004 Jobs Act):

	Reportable Transactions	Listed Transactions
Natural persons	$10,000	$100,000
All other taxpayers	$50,000	$200,000

The penalty is in addition to any other accuracy-related penalties that may be imposed on the taxpayer (Code Sec. 6707A(f), as added by the 2004 Jobs Act).

The statute does not describe the necessary disclosure, or define a reportable transaction or a listed transaction. Instead, a *reportable transaction* is any transaction with respect to which information must be included with the taxpayer's return because the Treasury Department has determined, under regulations prescribed under Code Sec. 6011, that the transaction is of the type that has the potential for tax avoidance or evasion (Code Sec. 6707A(c)(1), as added by the 2004 Jobs Act). Similarly, a *listed transaction* is a reportable transaction that is the same as or substantially similar to a transaction that has been specifically identified by the Treasury as a tax avoidance transaction (Code Sec. 6707A(c)(2), as added by the 2004 Jobs Act).

> **Comment:** The American Institute of Certified Public Accountants (AICPA) has criticized the absence of any reasonable cause exception to the penalty, especially in light of the magnitude of the penalty, the discretion given to the IRS to determine when a transaction is similar to a listed one, and the restrictions placed on rescission of the penalty.

Rescission of penalty. The penalty may be abated or rescinded, in whole or in part, by the IRS, but only if the transaction at issue was not a listed transaction and the rescission would promote compliance with the tax laws and effective tax administration (Code Sec. 6707A(d)(1), as added by the 2004 Jobs Act). If a decision is made to rescind a penalty, the IRS must provide an opinion that includes a statement of the facts and circumstances relating to the violation, the reasons for the rescission, and the amount of the penalty rescinded. This opinion must be placed in the file in the Office of the Commissioner (Code Sec. 6707A(d)(3), as added by the 2004 Jobs Act). In determining whether to rescind a penalty, the IRS should consider whether (1) the taxpayer has a history of complying with the tax laws, (2) the violation was due to an unintentional mistake of fact, and (3) imposing the penalty would be against equity and good conscience (Conference Committee Report to the 2004 Jobs Act, H.R. Conf. Rep. No. 108-755).

A decision regarding the rescission of a penalty is not subject to judicial review (Code Sec. 6707A(d)(2), as added by the 2004 Jobs Act). However, a taxpayer may litigate the issue of whether the transaction was reportable and thus, whether the penalty should have been imposed at all (H.R. Conf. Rep. No. 108-755).

> **Example:** XYZ Corp. fails to disclose its participation in a listed transaction, a confidential transaction, and a transaction with contractual protection. The listed transaction and the confidential transaction did not result in any tax understatement. XYZ is subject to three penalties, even though two of the transactions did not produce an understatement.
>
> The IRS rescinds the entire penalty imposed with respect to the confidential transaction and a portion of the penalty imposed with respect to the contractual protection transaction. The IRS cannot rescind the penalty imposed with respect to the listed transaction.
>
> XYZ files a Tax Court petition challenging its deficiency assessment, which includes the penalties. The court cannot review the IRS rescission determinations. However, if the issue is properly raised, the court can review whether any of the transactions were reportable.

The IRS must provide an annual report to the House Ways and Means Committee and the Senate Finance Committee that summarizes the total number and aggregate amount of penalties imposed and rescinded, describes the penalties rescinded, and provides the reasons for the rescissions (Act Sec. 811(d) of the 2004 Jobs Act).

Public entities. Public entities, which are entities that are required to file certain reports with the Securities and Exchange Commission (SEC), are subject to additional disclosure requirements (Code Sec. 6707A(e)(1), as added by the 2004 Jobs Act). These requirements apply if the entity:

- is required to pay the Code Sec. 6707A penalty for failing to disclose a listed transaction;

- is required to pay the 30-percent accuracy-related penalty imposed by new Code Sec. 6662A on understatements attributable to undisclosed reportable transactions (see ¶620); or

- would have had to pay the new 30-percent accuracy-related penalty with respect to an undisclosed reportable transaction, but was subject instead to the Code Sec. 6662(h) penalty for gross valuation understatements (Code Sec. 6707A(e)(2), as added by the 2004 Jobs Act).

Comment: Thus, these additional disclosure requirements do not apply if the penalty is imposed for an undisclosed reportable transaction that was not a listed transaction, and did not result in a tax understatement.

The entity must disclose the penalty in SEC reports for periods specified by the Treasury. Any failure to do so is treated as an additional failure to disclose a listed transaction and, thus, is subject to an additional failure-to-disclose penalty (Code Sec. 6707A(e)(2), as added by the 2004 Jobs Act). This disclosure requirement applies once the taxpayer has exhausted its administrative and judicial remedies with respect to the penalty or, if earlier, once the taxpayer has paid the penalty. The penalty must be reported only once, but it must be disclosed regardless of whether the taxpayer determines that the amount of the penalty is material to the reports in which it must appear (Conference Committee Report to the 2004 Jobs Act, H.R. Conf. Rep. No. 108-755).

For further information on this subject, consult any of the following CCH reporter explanations:

- Standard Federal Tax Reporter, 2004FED ¶35,141.05 and ¶39,651D.01

- Federal Tax Service, FTS §P:24.121

- Federal Tax Guide, 2004FTG ¶22,595

★ *Effective date.* The provision is effective for returns and statements the due date for which is after the date of enactment (Act Sec. 811(c) of the American Jobs Creation Act of 2004).

Act Sec. 811(a) of the American Jobs Creation Act of 2004, adding Code Sec. 6707A; Act Sec. 811(c); Act Sec. 811(d). Law at ¶6270 and ¶7095. Committee Report at ¶11,030.

¶620

Accuracy-Related Penalty for Listed and Reportable Transactions

Background _____

An accuracy-related penalty applies to any tax underpayment arising from:

- negligence or disregard of the rules and regulations;

- a substantial understatement of tax (an understatement equal to the greater of 10 percent of the proper tax liability, or $5,000 for individual taxpayers and $10 million for corporate taxpayers);

- a substantial overstatement of pension liabilities;

- substantial valuation misstatements; or

- a substantial estate or gift tax valuation understatement (Code Sec. 6662(b)).

Background

The penalty is equal to 20 percent of the underpayment. Generally, however, the amount of an understatement is reduced by the amount attributable to an item if (1) the taxpayer's treatment of the item was supported by substantial authority, or (2) the taxpayer disclosed the item to the IRS and there was a reasonable basis for its tax treatment (Code Sec. 6662(d)(2)(B)).

The penalty is stricter if part of the taxpayer's understatement is attributable to an abusive tax shelter. Amounts attributable to a tax shelter are included in an individual taxpayer's understatement unless the taxpayer can show that: (1) the tax treatment of the tax shelter item was, or is, supported by substantial authority, and (2) the taxpayer reasonably believed that the treatment was more likely than not proper (Code Sec. 6662(d)(2)(C); Reg. § 1.6662-4(g)(1)(i)). Disclosure of a tax shelter item does not mitigate the penalty for individuals or corporations (Reg. § 1.6662-4(g)(1)(iii)). A corporate taxpayer cannot reduce the amount of an understatement attributable to a tax shelter, because the substantial authority/reasonable basis test does not apply to corporations (Code Sec. 6662(d)(2)(C)(ii)).

However, the penalty may be abated for both individual and corporate taxpayers if the taxpayer can show that there was a reasonable cause for an underpayment attributable to a tax shelter, and the taxpayer acted in good faith (Code Sec. 6664(c)). Reasonable cause exists where the taxpayer reasonably relied in good faith on an opinion based on a professional tax advisor's analysis of the transaction that unambiguously concluded that the taxpayer's treatment of the item had more than a 50-percent chance of being upheld if it was challenged by the IRS (Reg. § § 1.6662-4(g)(4)(i)(B) and 1.6664-4(c)).

An abusive tax shelter is most broadly defined as an entity, plan or arrangement with a significant purpose of avoiding or evading federal income tax (Code Sec. 6662(d)(2)(C)(iii)). Regulations describe tax shelter transactions that must be disclosed by taxpayers who enter into them on or after February 28, 2003 (Reg. § 1.6011-4). The regulations identify six types of reportable transactions: listed transactions, confidential transactions, transactions with contractual protections, excessive loss transactions, transactions with significant book-tax differences, and transactions involving assets with brief holding periods (see Background at ¶ 615).

American Jobs Creation Act Impact

New accuracy-related penalty applies to understatements arising from listed and reportable transactions.—A new accuracy-related penalty is provided for understatements resulting from listed and reportable transactions (Code Sec. 6662A, as added by the American Jobs Creation Act of 2004). The penalty applies to understatements attributable to (1) any listed transaction, and (2) any reportable transaction with a significant tax avoidance purpose (Code Sec. 6662A(b)(2), as added by the 2004 Jobs Act). "Listed transaction" and "reportable transaction" are defined by reference to new Code Sec. 6707A(c) which, in turn, defines those terms by reference to applicable regulations under Code Sec. 6011 (Code Sec. 6662A(d), as added by the 2004 Jobs Act) (See ¶ 615).

Penalty amount. The penalty is generally 20 percent of the understatement if the taxpayer disclosed the transaction, and 30 percent if the transaction was not disclosed (Code Sec. 6662A(a) and (c), as added by the 2004 Jobs Act). The penalty applies only to the amount of the understatement that is attributable to the listed and/or reportable transaction, without regard to other items on the taxpayer's return. The amount of the reportable transaction understatement is determined as follows:

(1) Calculate the difference in taxable income that results from the proper treatment of the item and from the taxpayer's treatment of the item. Any reductions of the taxpayer's excess deductions over gross income, and any reductions in the taxpayer's capital losses (without regard to the Code Sec. 1211 limitations), are treated as an increase in taxable income.

(2) Multiply the amount from (1), above, by the highest individual tax rate (or the highest corporate tax rate, if applicable).

(3) Add the result from (2), above, to the amount of any decrease in the aggregate amount of credits that results from the difference between the taxpayer's treatment of the item and the proper treatment of the item (Code Sec. 6662A(b)(1), as added by the 2004 Jobs Act).

Except as provided in the regulations, the taxpayer's treatment of an item does not take into account any amendment or supplement to the taxpayer's return filed after the taxpayer is first contacted regarding an examination of the return or, if earlier, such other date as is specified by the IRS (Code Sec. 6662A(e)(3), as added by the 2004 Jobs Act).

Penalty coordination. The listed and reportable transactions penalty is coordinated with three other penalties:

(1) *Code Sec. 6662 accuracy-related penalty.* The understatement attributable to listed and reportable transactions is included in the amount of the taxpayer's total understatement for purposes of determining whether the taxpayer has a substantial understatement of tax. However, the understatement attributable to a listed or reportable transaction is not included in the taxpayer's total understatement for purposes of calculating the amount of the accuracy-related penalty under Code Sec. 6662 (Code Sec. 6662A(e)(1), as added by the 2004 Jobs Act, and Code Sec. 6662(d)(2)(A), as amended by the 2004 Jobs Act). The general exceptions to the penalty for a taxpayer who had substantial authority for the tax treatment of an item, or who disclosed the item and had a reasonable basis for its treatment, are inapplicable to any item attributable to a tax shelter (Code Sec. 6662(d)(2)(C), as amended by the 2004 Jobs Act).

(2) *Code Sec. 6663 fraud penalty.* An underpayment for purposes of the fraud penalty includes understatements attributable to listed and reportable transactions (Code Sec. 6662A(e)(2)(A), as added by the 2004 Jobs Act). However, a double penalty is avoided because the listed and reportable transactions penalty is not imposed on any portion of the underpayment on which the 75-percent fraud penalty was imposed (Code Sec. 6662A(e)(2)(B), as added by the 2004 Jobs Act).

(3) *The valuation misstatement penalties under Code Sec. 6662(e) and Code Sec. 6662(h).* These valuation misstatement penalties do not apply to any portion of an understatement on which the listed and reportable avoidance transaction penalty was imposed (Code Sec. 6662A(e)(2)(C), as added by the 2004 Jobs Act).

Reasonable cause exception. The accuracy-related penalty applicable to listed and reportable transactions can be avoided with respect to any portion of an understatement if:

(1) it is shown that there was reasonable cause for that portion of the understatement and the taxpayer acted in good faith (Code Sec. 6664(d)(1), as added by the 2004 Jobs Act);

(2) the relevant facts affecting the taxpayer's tax treatment of the item are adequately disclosed in accordance with the Code Sec. 6011 regulations (Code Sec. 6664(d)(2)(A), as added by the 2004 Jobs Act); or the new Code Sec. 6707A

penalty for failing to disclose the item was rescinded by the IRS (see ¶615) (Code Sec. 6664(d)(2), as added by the 2004 Jobs Act);

(3) there is, or was, substantial authority for the taxpayer's treatment of the item (Code Sec. 6664(d)(2)(B), as added by the 2004 Jobs Act); and

(4) the taxpayer reasonably believed that the treatment of the item on the return was more likely than not proper (Code Sec. 6664(d)(2)(C), as added by the 2004 Jobs Act).

Caution Note: This test is more demanding than the reasonable-cause exception to the accuracy-related (Code Sec. 6662) and fraud (Code Sec. 6663) penalties (Code Sec. 6664(c)).

Reasonable belief. For purposes of item (4), above, the taxpayer's reasonable belief must be based on the facts and law that existed when the return was filed; and it must relate solely to the taxpayer's success on the merits of the issue, without considering the possibility that the return will not be audited or, if the return is audited, that the treatment of the item will not be raised or will be resolved through settlement (Code Sec. 6664(d)(3)(A), as added by 2004 Jobs Act). A taxpayer may rely on a qualified tax advisor, but is not required to do so (Conference Committee Report (H.R. Conf. Rep. No. 108-755)).

To establish reasonable belief, the taxpayer may not rely on a disqualified tax advisor or a disqualified opinion (Code Sec. 6664(d)(3)(B), as added by 2004 Jobs Act). A *disqualified opinion* is one that (1) is based on unreasonable factual or legal assumptions, including assumptions as to future events; (2) unreasonably relies on representations, statements, findings or agreements of the taxpayer or any other person; (3) does not identify and consider all relevant facts; or (4) fails to meet any other requirements that the IRS may prescribe (Code Sec. 6664(d)(3)(B)(iii), as amended by the 2004 Jobs Act).

A *disqualified tax advisor* is someone who:

• is a material advisor who (1) participates in the organization, management, promotion or sale of the transaction; or (2) is related, under the rules of Code Secs. 267(b) and 707(b)(1), to a person who does so;

• is compensated directly or indirectly by a material advisor with respect to the reportable avoidance transaction (as when, for instance, an advisor arranges to have a shelter organizer refer potential participants to the advisor for an opinion regarding the transaction) (H.R. Conf. Rep. No. 108-755);

• has a fee agreement with respect to the transaction that is contingent on all or part of its intended tax benefits being sustained; or

• is determined, under IRS regulations, to have a disqualifying financial interest with respect to the transaction (Code Sec. 6664(d)(3)(B)(ii), as added by the 2004 Jobs Act).

A material advisor is defined by reference to Code Sec. 6111(b)(1), as amended by the 2004 Jobs Act (see¶605). An advisor does not participate in the organization of a transaction merely by rendering an opinion regarding its tax consequences. However, a qualified tax advisor can become disqualified if the IRS determines that the advisor has a continuing financial interest with respect to the transaction (H.R. Conf. Rep. No. 108-755).

A material advisor participates in the organization of a reportable transaction by performing acts related to its development, such as preparing documents that: (1) establish a partnership agreement or other structure used in the transaction, (2) describe the transaction, or (3) relate to the registration of the transaction with any government body. Participation in the management of the transaction means involvement in the decision-making process regarding any business activity with respect to the transaction. Participation in the promotion or sale means involvement in the marketing or solicitation of the transaction, such as providing information about the transaction or recommending it to a participant (H.R. Conf. Rep. No. 108-755).

For further information on this subject, consult any of the following CCH reporter explanations:

- Standard Federal Tax Reporter, 2004FED ¶35,141.06, ¶39,651D.01, ¶39,658.01 and ¶39,661.022

- Federal Tax Service, FTS § P:24.64[4]

- Federal Tax Guide, 2004FTG ¶22,527

★ *Effective date.* The provision applies to tax years ending after the date of enactment (Act Sec. 812(f) of the American Jobs Creation Act of 2004).

Act Sec. 812(a) of the American Job Creation Act of 2004, adding Code Sec. 6662A; Act. Sec. 812(b), amending Code Sec. 6662(d)(2)(A); Act Sec. 812(c)(1), adding Code Sec. 6664(d); Act Sec. 812(c)(2), amending Code Sec. 6664(c); Act Sec. 812(d), amending Code Sec. 6662(d)(2)(C); Act Sec. 812(f). Law at ¶6235, ¶6240 and ¶6245. Committee Report at ¶11,040.

¶ 625

Denial of Interest on Underpayments Attributable to Nondisclosed Reportable Transactions

Background

For individuals, interest paid or accrued on delinquent federal, state or local taxes and on indebtedness used to pay such taxes is considered nondeductible personal interest. Corporations, however can deduct such interest as an ordinary and necessary business expense.

American Jobs Creation Act of 2004 Impact

Denial of deduction for interest on underpayment attributable to nondisclosed reportable transactions.—Taxpayers may not deduct any interest paid or accrued on any underpayment of tax that is attributable to an understatement arising from an undisclosed listed transaction or from an undisclosed reportable avoidance transaction (Code Sec. 163(m), as added by the American Jobs Creation Act of 2004).

A reportable transaction understatement is determined, under Code Sec. 6662A(b) (¶620), by adding the following amounts:

(1) the product of (a) the highest corporate or individual tax rate, and (b) any increase in taxable income resulting from the difference between the taxpayer's treatment of the item as shown on the taxpayer's tax return and the proper tax treatment of such item, and

(2) the amount of any decrease in the aggregate amount of credits that results from the difference between the taxpayer's treatment of an item as shown on the taxpayer's tax return and the proper treatment of such item.

Comment: For purposes of (1) above, any reduction in the excess of deductions allowed for the tax year over gross income for such year, and any reduction in the amount of capital loss that would (without regard to the capital loss limitation rules of Code Sec. 1211) be allowed for such year, shall be treated as an increase in taxable income.

For further information on this subject, consult any of the following CCH reporter explanations:

- Standard Federal Tax Reporter, 2004FED ¶9104.01
- Federal Tax Service, FTS §G:7.160
- Federal Tax Guide, 2004FTG ¶6555

★ *Effective date.* The provision applies to transactions in tax years beginning after the date of enactment (Act Sec. 838(b) of the American Jobs Creation Act of 2004).

Act Sec. 838 of the American Jobs Creation Act of 2004, redesignating Code Sec. 163(m) as Code Sec. 163(n) and adding new Code Sec. 163(m); Act Sec. 838(b). Law at ¶5165. Committee Report at ¶11,210.

¶ 630
Failure to Furnish Information on Reportable Transactions

Background

An organizer of a tax shelter is required to register the tax shelter with the IRS on the first day that it is offered for sale. Among other things, the organizer must provide information identifying and describing the tax shelter, information describing the tax benefits that are represented to the investors in the tax shelter, and other information required by Treasury regulations (Code Sec. 6111, prior to amendment by the American Jobs Creation Act of 2004).

A variety of penalties may apply to a failure to register a tax shelter, or for providing false information in the registration. The general penalty is computed as the greater of one percent of the aggregate amount invested, or $500. If, however, the tax shelter is offered under a confidential arrangement and the shelter promoters may receive aggregate fees in excess of $100,000, the penalty is the greater of $10,000 or 50 percent of the fees payable to all of the shelter promoters for offerings made before the shelter was registered. If a promoter intentionally disregards the registration requirements, the penalty is increased to 75 percent of the applicable fees. Additionally, a tax shelter promoter can be assessed a $100 penalty for each failure to furnish investors with the required tax shelter identification number, and a $250 penalty can be assessed on an investor for each failure to include the tax shelter identification number on a return (Code Sec. 6707, prior to amendment by the American Jobs Creation Act of 2004).

American Jobs Creation Act Impact

Penalty for failure to provide tax shelter information.—Individuals who are required to file an information return with respect to a reportable transaction under newly enacted Code Sec. 6111(a) (see ¶605), but fail to do so, will be subject to a new penalty (Code Sec. 6707, amended by the American Jobs Creation Act of 2004). The penalty applies to a failure to file a required return by the due date, and also to a filed return that includes false or incomplete information.

Computation of penalty. In order to encourage compliance with the disclosure requirements of the new reportable transaction rules of Code Sec. 6707, the 2004 Jobs Act provides penalty provisions that are intended to be clearer and more meaningful than the tax shelter registration penalties that they replace. Under this new penalty regime, a $50,000 penalty is generally assessed for failure to furnish required information with respect to a reportable transaction (Code Sec. 6707(a), as amended by the 2004 Jobs Act). A much stiffer penalty applies to the failure to file a return regarding listed transactions (see ¶615). In such cases, the penalty assessed will be *the greater of*:

(1) $200,000, or

(2) 50 percent of the gross income derived by the person required to file the return with respect to aid, assistance, or advice that is provided with respect to the listed transaction.

The 50-percent limit in (2), above, is raised to 75 percent in cases involving an intentional failure or act (Code Sec. 6707(b), as amended by the 2004 Jobs Act).

IRS rescission authority. Pursuant to newly enacted Code Sec. 6707A(d), the IRS will have the power to rescind penalties assessed with respect to failures to provide information relating to reportable transactions, but not those relating to listed transactions (see ¶ 615).

For further information on this subject, consult any of the following CCH reporter explanations:

- Standard Federal Tax Reporter, 2004FED ¶ 40,100.01
- Federal Tax Service, FTS § P:24.121
- Federal Tax Guide, 2004FTG ¶ 22,595

★ *Effective date.* The penalty for failure to furnish information regarding reportable transactions applies to returns the due date of which is after the date of enactment (Act Sec. 816(c) of the American Jobs Creation Act of 2004).

Act Sec. 816 of the American Jobs Creation Act of 2004, amending Code Sec. 6707; Act Sec. 816(c). Law at ¶ 6265. Committee Report at ¶ 11,070.

¶ 635

Modified Penalty for Failure to Maintain Investor Lists

Background

The list maintenance rules require organizers and sellers of potentially abusive tax shelters to maintain a list identifying each person who purchases an interest in the tax shelter and any additional information required by the IRS in regulations (Code Sec. 6112(a)). A potentially abusive tax shelter is defined to include any tax shelter for which registration is required under Code Sec. 6111, as well as any other entity, investment plan or arrangement that is specified in the regulations as having a potential for tax avoidance or evasion (Code Sec. 6112(b)). The organizer or seller is also required to make the list available for inspection upon request by the IRS (Code Sec. 6112(c)). An organizer or seller who fails to comply with the Code Sec. 6112 requirements will be subject to the penalty imposed by Code Sec. 6708 for failure to maintain investor lists.

The penalty for failing to maintain an investor list, as required by Code Sec. 6112, is $50 per name omitted from the list. The maximum penalty that can be imposed is $100,000 per year (Code Sec. 6708).

Citing the refusal of some tax shelter promoters to provide the IRS with investor lists when requested, the House Committee Report (H.R. Rep. No. 108-548) states that this penalty was not meaningful and more effective tools for curbing the use of abusive tax avoidance transactions were needed.

American Jobs Creation Act Impact

Penalty for failure to maintain investor lists.—The new law modifies the penalty for failing to maintain the required list identifying tax shelter investors by making the penalty time-sensitive. Any person required to maintain investor lists with respect to reportable transactions, who receives a written request from the IRS and fails to make the lists available within 20 business days, may be assessed a $10,000 penalty for each day of failure after the 20th business day (Code Sec. 6708(a)(1), as amended by the American Jobs Creation Act of 2004). The penalty will be applied to persons required to maintain lists who fail to maintain required lists, maintain incomplete lists, or maintain complete lists, but do not make them available to the IRS upon a written request (Conference Committee Report (H.R. Conf. Rep. No. 108-755)).

No penalty is to be imposed if the failure to reproduce the lists is due to reasonable cause (Code Sec. 6708(a)(2), as amended by the 2004 Jobs Act).

> **Caution Note:** The House Committee Report (H.R. Rep. No. 108-548) makes it clear that in no event will the failure to maintain a list be considered reasonable cause for failing to make a list available.

Other provisions of the 2004 Jobs Act change the definition of a person required to maintain a list and reportable transactions. The person required to maintain lists is referred to as a "material advisor." A "material advisor" is any person who: (1) provides any material aid, assistance, or advice with respect to organizing, managing, promoting, selling, implementing, insuring, or carrying out any reportable transaction, and (2) directly or indirectly derives gross income for the advice or assistance in excess of an established threshold amount (or other amount that may be provided by the IRS). The threshold amount is $50,000 in the case of a reportable transaction where substantially all of the tax benefits are provided to natural persons and $250,000 in any other case (Code Sec. 6111(b)(1), as amended by the 2004 Jobs Act). See ¶605.

A *reportable transaction* is any transaction with respect to which information must be included with the taxpayer's return because the IRS has determined, under regulations prescribed under Code Sec. 6011, that the transaction is of the type that has the potential for tax avoidance or evasion (Code Sec. 6707A(c)(1), as added by the 2004 Jobs Act). See ¶615.

For further information on this subject, consult any of the following CCH reporter explanations:

- Standard Federal Tax Reporter, 2004FED ¶40,100.01
- Federal Tax Service, FTS § P:24.122
- Federal Tax Guide, 2004FTG ¶22,597

★ *Effective date.* The penalty provision for failure to maintain a list of investors applies to requests made after the date of enactment (Act Sec. 817(b) of the American Jobs Creation Act of 2004).

Act Sec. 817(a) of the American Jobs Creation Act of 2004, amending Code Sec. 6708(a); Act Sec. 817(b). Law at ¶6275. Committee Report at ¶11,080.

¶ 640

Penalty Increased on Tax Shelter Promoters

Background _____

Over 20 years ago, a civil penalty was added to the Internal Revenue Code that applies specifically to promoters of abusive tax shelters. The penalty is imposed on any person who engages in the organization of, or sale of any interest in, a partnership or other entity, an investment plan or arrangement, or any other plan or arrangement, if the person makes or furnishes, or causes another to make or furnish:

(1) a false or fraudulent tax benefit statement as to a material matter; or

(2) a gross valuation overstatement as to a material matter (Code Sec. 6700, added by the Tax Equity and Fiscal Responsibility Act of 1982 (P.L. 97-248)).

In 1982, the penalty for promoting an abusive tax shelter under Code Sec. 6700 was equal to the greater of $1,000 or 10 percent of the gross income derived, or to be derived, from the tax shelter activity.

Any matter is material to the plan or arrangement if it would have a substantial impact on the decision-making process of a reasonably prudent investor (Conference Committee Report, Deficit Reduction Act of 1984 (P.L. 98-369)). Statements regarding whether any deduction or credit is allowable, the excludability of any income, or the securing of any other tax benefit by participating in a plan or arrangement are considered tax benefit statements. The term *gross valuation overstatement* means a statement or representation of the value of property or services that exceeds 200 percent of the correct value and is directly related to the amount of any income tax deduction or credit allowable to any tax shelter plan or arrangement participant. A penalty based on a gross valuation overstatement may be waived if it is shown that there was a reasonable basis for the valuation and it was made in good faith (Code Sec. 6700(b)(2)).

In 1984, the promoter penalty was increased to the greater of $1,000 or 20 percent of the gross income derived, or to be derived, from the abusive tax shelter activity. Although the percentage of gross income was increased, the $1,000 provision was not increased. From the inception of Code Sec. 6700, the $1,000 penalty provision was intended to be a minimum penalty on small promoters reaping small profits (Conference Committee Report, Deficit Reduction Act of 1984 (P.L. 98-369)).

The current penalty for tax shelter promoters is the lesser of $1,000 or 100 percent of the gross income derived, or to be derived, by the person from the activity (Code Sec. 6700(a)). For purposes of computing this penalty, the organization of an entity, plan or arrangement and the sale of each interest in an entity, plan or arrangement are separate activities subject to penalty (Conference Committee Report, Omnibus Budget Reconciliation Act of 1989 (P.L. 101-239)). This penalty level was established in 1989 and no modifications have been made since that time.

American Jobs Creation Act Impact

Penalty increased to 50 percent of gross income.—The penalty applicable to a person who knowingly makes, or causes another to make, a false or fraudulent tax benefit statement as to any material matter pertaining to a tax shelter plan or arrangement is increased to 50 percent of the gross income derived, or to be derived, from the abusive plan or arrangement (Code Sec. 6700(a), as amended by the American Jobs Creation Act of 2004). The enhanced penalty applies to activities engaged in after the date of enactment of the 2004 Jobs Act.

Comment: Prior to this amendment, the penalty for a false or fraudulent statement was the same as that applicable to gross valuation overstatements, i.e., the lesser of $1,000 or 100 percent of the gross income derived by the person from the activity. In computing the $1,000 or 100-percent penalty, the organization of an entity, plan or arrangement and the sale of each interest in an entity, plan or arrangement were considered separate activities subject to a penalty (Code Sec. 6700(a)). The separate activities rule has no relevance to the enhanced 50-percent penalty applicable to false or fraudulent statements since the penalty amount is the same whether the 50 percent is applied to each separate activity or to the total gross income from all activities.

Example: In December 2004, Jeremy Jones received $35,000 in gross income for establishing a cattle breeding tax shelter arrangement premised on a false statement regarding an income tax deduction. During the last two weeks of December 2004, Jeremy also sold 25 separate interests in the breeding arrangement at $10,000 per interest using the same false income tax deduction statement. His total gross income from the breeding arrangement was $285,000 ($35,000 + (25 × $10,000)). Subsequently, the breeding arrangement was determined to be an abusive tax shelter. Applying the enhanced penalty rate of 50 percent of gross income yields a total penalty of $142,500 (.50 × $285,000). If all of Jeremy's activities with regard to the abusive tax shelter had taken place in 2003, his penalty would have been the lesser of $1,000 or 100 percent of gross income from each separate activity. The total penalty would have been $26,000 ($1,000 + (25 × $1,000)).

Comment: The penalty level as to false or fraudulent statements in effect since 1989 was ineffectual in deterring tax shelter activities. The newly enhanced penalty rate results in a meaningful increase in the penalty. This significantly higher penalty is just one of several provisions of the 2004 Jobs Act aimed at deterring tax shelter abuses. A new penalty for failure to disclose a reportable transaction has been created. See ¶615. Information reporting replaces tax shelter registration and the applicable penalty is increased. See ¶605 and ¶630. The penalty for failure to maintain and disclose investor lists is now a time-sensitive penalty. See ¶605 and ¶635. The authority to seek injunctions against tax shelter material advisors has been expanded. See ¶650.

The enhanced penalty does not apply to *gross valuation overstatements*. Any person who makes, or causes another to make, a gross valuation overstatement as to any material matter pertaining to a tax shelter plan or arrangement continues to be subject to a penalty equal to the lesser of $1,000 or 100 percent of the gross income derived, or to be derived, by the person from such activity (Code Sec. 6700(a)). For purposes of computing this penalty, the organization of an entity, plan or arrangement and the sale of each interest in an entity, plan or arrangement also continue to be separate activities subject to penalty. The $1,000 or 100-percent penalty for gross valuation overstatements may be waived if a reasonable basis for the valuation is shown and the statement was made in good faith (Code Sec. 6700(b)(2)).

Comment: There is no provision for the waiver of the enhanced (50 percent of gross income) penalty applicable to any person who makes, or causes another to make, a false or fraudulent tax benefit statement as to any material matter pertaining to a tax shelter plan or arrangement.

For further information on this subject, consult any of the following CCH reporter explanations:

- Standard Federal Tax Reporter, 2004FED ¶40,030.01 and ¶40,030.03

- Federal Tax Service, FTS § P:24.123

- Federal Tax Guide, 2004FTG ¶22,587

★ *Effective date.* The provision applies to activities after the date of enactment (Act Sec. 818(b) of the American Jobs Creation Act of 2004).

Act Sec. 818(a) of the American Jobs Creation Act of 2004, amending Code Sec. 6700(a); Act Sec. 818(b). Law at ¶6260. Committee Report at ¶11,090.

¶640

¶ 645

Substantial Understatements by Corporations; Substantial Authority for Return Positions

Background _____

Taxpayers are subject to an accuracy-related penalty on any tax underpayments attributable to a substantial understatement of tax (see Background at ¶ 620). For most taxpayers, a substantial understatement is equal to the lesser of 10 percent of the proper tax liability or $5,000. For a corporation (other than an S corporation, or a personal holding company as defined in Code Sec. 542), a substantial understatement is equal to the lesser of 10 percent of the proper tax liability or $10,000 (Code Sec. 6662(d)(1)). Generally, the amount of the penalty is equal to 20 percent of the understatement (Code Sec. 6662(a)).

The amount of an understatement is reduced by the amount attributable to an item if (1) the taxpayer's treatment of the item was supported by substantial authority, or (2) the taxpayer disclosed the item to the IRS and there was a reasonable basis for its tax treatment (Code Sec. 6662(d)(2)(B)).

An income tax return preparer is subject to a $250 penalty if:

• any part of an understatement or refund claim is due to a position for which there was not a realistic possibility of being sustained on the merits,

• the preparer knew or reasonably should have known of the position, and

• the position was not disclosed in the return or refund claim (or in an attached statement), or was frivolous.

The penalty is imposed automatically unless it is shown that there was reasonable cause for the understatement and the return preparer acted in good faith (Code Sec. 6694(a)).

_____

American Jobs Creation Act Impact

Substantial understatement threshold increased for corporate taxpayers; IRS can list frivolous positions.—The threshold for a corporate taxpayer's substantial understatement is increased. A corporate taxpayer has a substantial understatement of tax if the amount of the understatement exceeds the lesser of:

(1) 10 percent of the taxpayer's proper tax liability (or, if greater, $10,000); or

(2) $10 million (Code Sec. 6662(d)(1)(B), as amended by the American Jobs Creation Act of 2004).

Comment: Effectively, a substantial understatement for a corporate taxpayer is any understatement that equals or exceeds $10,000. An understatement of less than $10,000 is no longer substantial, even if it exceeds 10 percent of the taxpayer's proper tax liability.

The IRS is authorized, but not required, to prescribe a list of positions that it believes fail to meet one or more of the standards for:

(1) substantial authority for a taxpayer's position for purposes of reducing an understatement subject to the substantial understatement penalty (Code Sec. 6662(d)(2)(B)(i));

(2) substantial authority for a taxpayer's position for purposes of the reasonable cause exception to the new penalty for understatements attributable to

listed and reportable transactions (Code Sec. 6664(d)(2), as added by the 2004 Jobs Act) (see ¶620); or

(3) a position for which there was not a realistic possibility of being sustained on the merits for purposes of the exception to the return preparer penalty (Code Sec. 6694(a)(1)).

Any such list, plus revisions, must be published in the Federal Register or the Internal Revenue Bulletin (Code Sec. 6662(d)(3), as amended by the 2004 Jobs Act).

Comment: Currently, the IRS uses a variety of facts sheets, news releases and other materials to describe some of the most common frivolous positions. The authorized list could provide a single source for taxpayers and return preparers to check before taking a position that might result in an understatement.

For further information on this subject, consult any of the following CCH reporter explanations:

- Standard Federal Tax Reporter, 2004FED ¶39,652.01 and ¶39,652.024
- Federal Tax Service, FTS § P:24.64[1]
- Federal Tax Guide, 2004FTG ¶22,527

★ *Effective date.* The amendments apply to tax years beginning after the date of enactment (Act Sec. 819(c) of the American Jobs Creation Act of 2004).

Act Sec. 819(a) of the American Jobs Creation Act of 2004, amending Code Sec. 6662(d)(1)(B); Act Sec. 819(b)(1), adding Code Sec. 6662(d)(3); Act Sec. 819(b)(2), striking Code Sec. 6662(d)(2)(D); Act Sec. 819(c). Law at ¶6235. Committee Report at ¶11,100.

¶ 650
Authority to Enjoin Tax Shelter Material Advisors Expanded

Background _____

In conjunction with the establishment of the civil penalty for organizing or selling abusive tax investments under Code Sec. 6700, a provision was added to the Internal Revenue Code to prevent the recurrence of such activities. The United States may seek injunctive relief against any person from further engaging in any conduct subject to the penalty for organizing or selling abusive tax investments (Code Sec. 7408, added by the Tax Equity and Fiscal Responsibility Act of 1982 (P.L. 97-248)). Two years later, government injunctive relief was extended to activities subject to the Code Sec. 6701 aiding and abetting understatements penalty. The government may seek an injunction against any person who knowingly aids and abets in the understatement of the tax liability of another person from further engaging in such activities (Code Sec. 7408, as amended by the Deficit Reduction Act of 1984 (P.L. 98-369)).

In an effort to combat abusive tax avoidance transactions, additional tax shelter requirements were added to the Internal Revenue Code in 1984. Tax shelter organizations are required to register tax shelters with the IRS by the day on which the offering for sale of the interests in the tax shelter occurs (Code Sec. 6111(a)). The definition of tax shelter includes confidential arrangements known as confidential corporate tax shelters (Code Sec. 6111(d)). The penalties applicable to persons who fail to comply with the tax shelter registration rules are stated in Code Sec. 6707 and differ depending on whether the tax shelter is a confidential corporate tax shelter or not.

Organizers and sellers of tax shelters that are subject to the registration requirements of Code Sec. 6111 must also keep a list of investors and furnish the list to the IRS upon request (Code Sec. 6112(a) and (c)). An organizer or seller of a potentially abusive tax shelter who must maintain lists of investors is any person qualifying as a material advisor with respect to the transaction. A material advisor is a person who is either required to register the transaction, or makes a tax statement and receives a minimum fee (Reg. § 301.6112-1(c)).

When these registration and list-maintenance rules, and the applicable penalties, were added to the Internal Revenue Code, however, no provision was made to prevent any person from engaging in further violations of the tax shelter registration rules or the tax shelter list-maintenance requirements.

American Jobs Creation Act Impact

Injunctive relief may be sought against material advisors responsible for tax shelter information reporting and maintenance of investor lists.—Under the new law, the United States, at the request of the Treasury, may seek injunctive relief against tax shelter material advisors from further engaging in the following conduct:

(1) failure to file an information return with respect to a reportable tax shelter transaction as required by Code Sec. 6111, as amended by the American Jobs Creation Act of 2004, and subject to penalty under Code Sec. 6707, as amended by the 2004 Jobs Act; and

(2) failure to maintain, or to timely furnish upon written request by the IRS, a list of investors with respect to each reportable tax shelter transaction as required by Code Sec. 6112, as amended by the 2004 Jobs Act, and subject to penalty under Code Sec. 6708, as amended by the 2004 Jobs Act (Code Sec. 7408(a) and (c)(1), as added by the 2004 Jobs Act).

Furthermore, injunctive relief may be sought for violations of any rules under Treasury Department Circular 230, "Regulations Governing the Practice of Attorneys, Certified Public Accountants, Enrolled Agents, Enrolled Actuaries, and Appraisers before the Internal Revenue Service" (Code Sec. 7408(c)(2), as added by the 2004 Jobs Act). Circular 230 is issued pursuant to section 330 of title 31 of the United States Code, which regulates practice before the Department of the Treasury.

Comment: This expansion of injunctive authority is in addition to the existing authority to seek injunctive relief against any person for organizing or selling abusive tax investments, subject to penalty under Code Sec. 6700, or for knowingly aiding and abetting in the understatement of the tax liability of another person, subject to penalty under Code Sec. 6701. The penalty for promoting abusive tax shelters has been increased to 50 percent of gross income derived from the activity (Code Sec. 6700(a), as amended by the 2004 Jobs Act). See ¶640 for more information.

Comment: Material advisors are now required to timely file an information return instead of registering a tax shelter, and the penalty for failure to comply is increased (Code Secs. 6111 and 6707, as amended by the 2004 Jobs Act). See ¶605 and ¶630 for more information. The penalty applicable to material advisors who fail to maintain or timely furnish investor lists is now a time-sensitive penalty (Code Secs. 6112 and 6708, as amended by the 2004 Jobs Act). See ¶605 and ¶635 for more information.

If the court finds that injunctive relief is appropriate because a person has promoted an abusive tax shelter, aided and abetted the understatement of a tax liability, failed to comply with tax shelter information reporting, failed to keep lists of investors in a potentially abusive tax shelter, or violated any rules regulating practice before the Treasury Department, the court may enjoin the person from further engaging in the prohibited conduct, *or in any other activity subject to penalty under the Internal Revenue Code* (Code Sec. 7408(b), as added by the 2004 Jobs Act).

Comment: Prior to the 2004 Jobs Act, the court's injunction power was limited to enjoining the promotion of abusive tax shelters or the aiding and abetting of the understatement of tax liability. The provision allowing a court to not only enjoin the activity for which is has determined injunctive relief is appropriate, but also any other activity subject to penalty under the Code seems to be a broad allowance for a court to extend its power to enjoin conduct.

Comment: The purpose of expanding the authority to obtain injunctions is to discourage abusive tax avoidance activity and encourage compliance with the tax shelter disclosure requirements. The tax shelter disclosures required by the reporting rules and the list-maintenance requirements are intended to increase the transparency of questionable transactions so that the IRS can evaluate these transactions as early as possible.

For further information on this subject, consult any of the following CCH reporter explanations:

- Standard Federal Tax Reporter, 2004FED ¶ 41,673.01
- Federal Tax Service, FTS § P:24.124
- Federal Tax Guide, 2004FTG ¶ 22,597

★ *Effective date.* The provision is effective on the day after the date of enactment (Act Sec. 820(c) of the American Jobs Creation Act of 2004).

Act Sec. 820(a) of the American Jobs Creation Act of 2004, striking Code Sec. 7408(a) and (b), adding Code Sec. 7408(a) and (b), redesignating Code Sec. 7408(c) as Code Sec. 7408(d), and adding Code Sec. 7408(c); Act Sec. 820(c). Law at ¶ 6330. Committee Report at ¶ 11,110.

¶ 655

Penalty for Failure to Report Interest in Foreign Financial Accounts

Background

Currently, citizens, residents, or persons doing business in the United States, who maintain an account with a foreign financial entity, must keep records and file reports regarding that account with the Treasury Department (31 U.S.C. § 5314). The Treasury Department imposes a civil penalty for willful violations of these foreign financial account reporting requirements under 31 U.S.C. § 5321(a)(5). The civil penalty for a *willful* violation is the amount of the transaction or the value of the account, up to a maximum of $100,000; the minimum penalty is $25,000. Additionally, a willful violation may subject the taxpayer to a criminal penalty of a maximum $25,000 fine or imprisonment for not more than five years (or both). If the violation is part of a pattern of illegal activity, the maximum fine increases to $500,000 and the maximum length of imprisonment to 10 years (31 U.S.C. § 5322).

American Jobs Creation Act Impact

New civil penalty for failure to report interest in foreign financial accounts.— In order to increase voluntary compliance, a new civil penalty has been added for a taxpayer's violation of the foreign financial account reporting requirements, whether or not the violation was willful (31 U.S.C. § 5321(a)(5)(A), as amended by the

American Jobs Creation Act of 2004). The penalty, which may be up to $10,000 (31 U.S.C. § 5321(a)(5)(B)(i), as amended by the 2004 Jobs Act), may be waived if there is a reasonable cause for the failure to report, and if any income from the transaction was properly reported (31 U.S.C. § 5321(a)(5)(B)(ii), as amended by the 2004 Jobs Act). The penalty for willful violations is also increased to the greater of $100,000 or 50 percent of the amount of the transaction or the balance in the account at the time of the violation (31 U.S.C. § 5321(a)(5)(C), as amended by the 2004 Jobs Act).

> **Compliance Tip:** Individuals usually fulfill the foreign financial account reporting requirements by answering the questions regarding foreign accounts or foreign trusts in Part III of Schedule B of Form 1040. A taxpayer who answer "yes" in response to those questions must then also file Form TD F-90-22.1 with the Treasury Department, which is filed separately from the taxpayer's federal income tax return.

For further information on this subject, consult any of the following CCH reporter explanations:

- Federal Tax Service, FTS § P:3.62
- Federal Tax Guide, 2004FTG ¶ 17,060

★ *Effective date.* The amendment shall apply to violations occurring after the date of the enactment (Act Sec. 821(b) of the American Jobs Creation Act of 2004).

Act Sec. 821 of the American Jobs Creation Act of 2004, amending 31 U.S.C. § 5321(a)(5); Act Sec. 821(b). Law at ¶ 7100. Committee Report at ¶ 11,120.

STANDARDS OF PRACTICE AND PROFESSIONAL CONDUCT

¶ 660

Regulation of Individuals Practicing Before Department of Treasury

Background

Attorneys, certified public accountants, enrolled agents, and enrolled actuaries who practice before the IRS are subject to regulation by the Secretary of Treasury, as authorized under 31 U.S.C. § 330. The rules promulgated by the Secretary pursuant to this provision are found in Circular 230 (31 CFR § 10, et al.) In general, these rules govern who may represent taxpayers before the IRS, the duties and restrictions to which they are subject, the sanctions for any violation, and disciplinary proceedings. In particular, Circular 230 provides requirements that representatives must follow when issuing tax shelter opinions, i.e., written advice regarding the federal tax aspects of a tax shelter. Representatives who violate any of these rules of practice, are incompetent, engage in disreputable conduct or, with the intent to defraud, willfully and knowingly mislead or threaten the taxpayer that they are representing or may be representing, may have suspension or disbarment proceedings initiated against them (31 U.S.C. § 330(b)).

> **Comment:** In response to the recent flurry of highly publicized tax shelter abuses, the IRS has proposed changes to Circular 230 that would revise the ethical standards for representatives to include a "highest quality representation" requirement and modify the standards for tax shelter opinions, including the definition of a tax shelter (NPRM REG-122379-02). These proposed changes, which have been met with much comment and debate, have yet to be finalized.

American Jobs Creation Act Impact

Representatives practicing before the Department of Treasury may be subject to censure as well as monetary penalties for violations.—Attorneys, certified public accountants, enrolled agents and enrolled actuaries who violate the rules of practice before the Department of Treasury, as promulgated by the Secretary of Treasury in Circular 230, may, in addition to disbarment or suspension, be subject to censure (31 U.S.C. § 330(b), as amended by the American Jobs Creation Act of 2004). The Secretary may also impose monetary penalties for such violations in addition to, or in lieu of, suspension, disbarment or censure. Employers, firms and entities on behalf of which a representative may be acting may also be subject to separate monetary penalties if such employer, firm or entity knew, or reasonably should have known, of the representative's conduct. The amount of the monetary penalty imposed, however, cannot exceed the gross income derived from such conduct (31 U.S.C. § 330(b), as amended by the 2004 Jobs Act).

> **Comment:** The Senate Finance Committee, in Senate Report 108-192, stated that it is critical that the Secretary have the authority to censure tax advisors as well as to impose monetary penalties because of the important role tax advisors have in our tax system. Use of these sanctions is expected to curb the participation of tax advisors in both tax shelter activity and any other activity that is contrary to Circular 230 standards.

Secretary authorized to regulate tax shelter opinions.—The authority of the Secretary of the Treasury to impose standards applicable to tax shelter opinions has been codified (31 U.S.C. § 330(d), as added by the 2004 Jobs Act). No provision of 31 U.S.C. § 330 or any other law is to be construed so as to limit this authority.

For further information on this subject, consult any of the following CCH reporter explanations:

- Standard Federal Tax Reporter, 2004FED ¶ 43,499.01, ¶ 43,808.051, ¶ 43,808.052 and ¶ 43,808.055
- Federal Tax Service, FTS § P:8.121
- Federal Tax Guide, 2004FTG ¶ 24,301

★ *Effective date.* The amendments made by Act Sec. 822(a) apply to violations occurring after the date of enactment (Act Sec. 822(a)(2) of the American Jobs Creation Act of 2004).

Act Sec. 822(a)(1) of the American Jobs Creation Act of 2004, amending 31 U.S.C. § 330(b); Act Sec. 822(b), adding 31 U.S.C. § 330(d); Act Sec. 822(a)(2). Law at ¶ 7105. Committee Report at ¶ 11,130.

¶ 665

Tax Shelter Exception to Confidentiality Privileges Relating to Taxpayer Communications

Background _____

In certain circumstances, taxpayers are entitled to treat communications with their tax professionals as confidential and privileged. A common law privilege of confidentiality exists for communications between an attorney and client with respect to the legal advice given to the client. A limited confidentiality privilege with respect to tax advice in noncriminal tax matters, similar to the attorney-client privilege, applies to federally authorized tax practitioners (Code Sec. 7525, as added by the IRS Restructuring and Reform Act of 1998 (P.L. 105-206)). Federally authorized tax practitioners include nonattorneys authorized to practice before the IRS, such as

Background

certified public accountants, enrolled agents and enrolled actuaries. The privilege applies only in noncriminal tax matters before the IRS and the federal courts. The Code Sec. 7525 tax practitioner privilege does not apply to written communications between a federally authorized tax practitioner and a director, shareholder, officer, employee, agent, or representative of a corporation in connection with the promotion of the direct or indirect participation of the corporation in any tax shelter as defined in Code Sec. 6662(d)(2)(C)(iii).

American Jobs Creation Act Impact

Tax practitioner privilege not to apply to any tax shelter communications.— The federally authorized tax practitioner privilege does not apply to any written communication between a taxpayer and a federally authorized tax practitioner if the communication is with respect to any tax shelter (Code Sec. 7525(b), as amended by the American Jobs Creation Act of 2004). Prior to the 2004 Jobs Act, this rule applied only to communications regarding corporate tax shelters. Now the tax practitioner privilege does not apply to written communications between a federally authorized tax practitioner and:

- any person,
- any director, officer, employee, agent or representative of the person, or
- any other person holding a capital or profits interest in the person

in connection with the promotion of the direct or indirect participation of the person in any tax shelter. This rule limiting application of the privilege applies to tax shelters whether entered into by corporations, individuals, partnerships, tax-exempt entities, or any other entity.

> **Comment:** The provision does not clarify the overall wording of the exception, wording that commentators have found to be vague and ambiguous.

For further information on this subject, consult any of the following CCH reporter explanations:

- Standard Federal Tax Reporter, 2004FED ¶ 42,816F.01
- Federal Tax Service, FTS § P:13.181[7]
- Federal Tax Guide, 2004FTG ¶ 22,237 and ¶ 22,309

★ *Effective date.* The provision applies to communications made on or after the date of enactment (Act Sec. 813(b) of the American Jobs Creation Act of 2004).

Act Sec. 813(a) of the American Jobs Creation Act of 2004, amending Code Sec. 7525(b); Act Sec. 813(b). Law at ¶ 6345. Committee Report at ¶ 11,050.

LEASING

¶ 670

Limits on Deductions for Property Leased to Tax-Exempt Entities (SILOs)

Background

Deductions for depreciation and other expenses are generally available to property owners. If the owner of property is a tax-exempt or tax-indifferent entity, such as a charitable organization, governmental unit, or foreign person or entity, those deductions go to waste. Enterprising lawyers have developed lease arrangements that effectively transfer those unwanted deductions to taxpayers who can make use

Background _____

of them. In a sale-in, lease-out (SILO) arrangement, a taxpayer can purchase property, such as subways, buses or sewers, from a municipality and immediately lease it back to the original owner. The taxpayer claims the tax deductions associated with owning the property, and the tax savings are apportioned between the taxpayer and the municipality according to their agreement. In some cases, the agreement requires the municipality to provide security for its lease payments and perhaps to repurchase the assets for a set price at the end of the lease. In such cases, the taxpayer can, to a great extent, avoid the risks of ownership.

> **Comment:** Estimates of the value of SILO transactions that occur every year range from $15 billion to $190 billion (CRS Report for Congress—Tax Implications of SILOs, QTEs and Other Leasing Transactions with Tax-Exempt Entities, July 20, 2004). In testimony before the House Ways and Means Committee in February 2004, Pamela F. Olson, Assistant Treasury Secretary (Tax Policy), stated that "SILOs represent a threat to the viability of the corporate tax base. They present a ready-made tool for self-help tax relief for large corporations and consortiums of smaller ones. Indeed, the magnitude of SILO transactions is such that the Treasury Department had to re-estimate and reduce its baseline estimate of corporate tax receipts over the ten-year budget window."

Certain depreciation rules apply that make some SILO arrangements less attractive than they would otherwise be. Tangible property that is leased to a tax-exempt entity ("tax-exempt use property") must be depreciated on a straight-line basis over an extended recovery period equal to the longer of the property's class life or 125 percent of the lease term (Code Sec. 168(g)(3)(A)). This period is generally significantly longer than the normal recovery periods under the modified accelerated cost recovery system (MACRS). Excluded from the definition of tax-exempt use property is property used by the taxpayer to provide a service to the tax-exempt entity, property leased for only a short term, and certain qualified technological equipment (Code Sec. 168(h)(1) and (3)). Computer software is excluded because it is intangible.

American Jobs Creation Act Impact

Limits on deductions allocable to property leased to tax-exempt entities expanded.—Sale-in, lease-out transactions (SILOs) involving purchases of municipal property are restricted by making certain types of intangible property subject to the existing extended MACRS recovery period rules and by the addition of new Code Sec. 470, which prohibits the deduction of tax-exempt use losses if the lessor does not have sufficient ownership rights in the property.

Leased intangibles made subject to the extended MACRS recovery period rule.—Certain intangible property must be amortized over an extended recovery period of not less than 125 percent of the lease term (as defined in Code Sec. 168(i)(3)(A)) if it is leased to a tax-exempt entity and would otherwise be considered tax-exempt use property under Code Sec. 168(h) (Code Sec. 167(f), as amended by the American Jobs Creation Act of 2004). Intangible property now subject to the extended recovery period includes:

> (1) computer software, as described in Code Sec. 167(f)(1)(B) and otherwise amortizable over 36 months (Code Sec. 167(f)(1)(C), as added by the 2004 Jobs Act);

> (2) the following separately acquired interests and rights which are specifically excluded by Code Sec. 197(e)(4) from the definition of a section 197 intangible:

¶670

(a) patent or copyright interests, as described in Code Sec. 197(e)(4)(C),

(b) a right held under a contract or granted by a governmental unit to receive tangible property or services, as described in Code Sec. 197(e)(4)(B), and

(c) a right held under a contract or granted by a governmental unit that has a fixed duration of less than 15 years, or that is fixed as to amount and recoverable under a method similar to the unit-of-production method, as described in Code Sec. 197(e)(4)(D) (Code Sec. 167(f)(2), as amended by the 2004 Jobs Act); and

(3) Code Sec. 197 intangibles (Code Sec. 197(f)(10), as added by the 2004 Jobs Act).

Comment: The useful life or amortization period for these intangibles is set under the new law as *not less* than 125 percent of the lease term (Code Secs. 167(f)(1)(C), as added by the 2004 Jobs Act; 167(f)(2), as amended by the 2004 Jobs Act; and 197(f)(10), as added by the 2004 Jobs Act). Thus, for example, if 125 percent of the lease term of a section 197 intangible is less than the regular 15-year amortization period that applies to the intangible under Code Sec. 197, the 15-year amortization period continues to apply.

Prohibition of loss deductions related to property leased to tax-exempt entities.—A taxpayer leasing property to a government or other tax-exempt entity is prohibited from claiming deductions related to the property to the extent that they exceed the taxpayer's income from the lease payments (a tax-exempt use loss), subject to some exceptions (Code Sec. 470, as added by the 2004 Jobs Act). Amounts disallowed as a tax-exempt use loss are carried over to the next year and treated as a deduction with respect to the property (Code Sec. 470(b), as added by the 2004 Jobs Act).

A tax-exempt use loss is defined as the amount by which the sum of the aggregate deductions (other than interest) directly allocable to the property plus interest properly allocable to the property exceeds the taxpayer's aggregate income from the tax-exempt use property (Code Sec. 470(c)(1), as added by the 2004 Jobs Act).

Comment: The deductions related to a lease of tax-exempt property commonly include depreciation or amortization, maintenance expenses, taxes, the cost of acquiring the property and interest.

Tax-exempt use property. The existing definition of tax-exempt use property in Code Sec. 168(h) is incorporated by reference in new Code Sec. 470, with certain adjustments.

Under the existing definition, tangible property other than nonresidential real property is tax-exempt use property if leased to a tax-exempt entity (Code Sec. 168(h)(1)(A)). The term "nonresidential real property" includes residential rental property (Code Sec. 168(h)(1)(E)). Nonresidential real property is tax-exempt use property to the extent that it is leased to tax-exempt entities in disqualified leases, if the disqualified leases cover more than 35 percent of the property. A lease of nonresidential real estate to a tax-exempt entity is a disqualified lease if:

(1) part or all of the subject property was financed directly or indirectly by tax-exempt bonds and the entity or a related entity participated in the financing,

(2) under the lease, there is a purchase or sale option that upon exercise allows (or requires) the entity or a related entity to purchase the property for a fixed or determinable price,

(3) the lease term is in excess of 20 years, or

(4) the lease occurs after a sale of the property by, or lease from the entity or a related entity, and the property was previously used for more than three months by the entity or a related entity (Code Sec. 168(h)(1)(B)).

Property predominantly used by a tax-exempt entity in an unrelated trade or business is *not* tax-exempt use property (Code Sec. 168(h)(1)(D)).

Property leased to a tax-exempt entity in a short-term lease is included in the definition of tax-exempt use property under Code Sec. 470, in contrast to the Code Sec. 168(h)(3) rule. In addition, the exclusion of certain leased high technology equipment from the definition of tax-exempt use property in Code Sec. 168(h)(3) does not apply for Code Sec. 470 purposes (Code Sec. 470(c)(2)(A), as added by the 2004 Jobs Act).

The following types of intangible property are treated as tangible property, and thus can be tax-exempt use property, for Code Sec. 470 purposes (and are also newly subject to extended recovery periods of no less than 125 percent of the lease term as explained above) (Code Secs. 167(f)(1)(C), 167(f)(2) and 197(f)(10)):

(1) computer software, as described in Code Sec. 167(f)(1)(B) and otherwise amortizable over 36 months (Code Sec. 167(f)(1)(C), as added by the 2004 Jobs Act);

(2) the following separately acquired interests and rights which are specifically excluded by Code Sec. 197(e)(4) from the definition of a section 197 intangible:

(a) patent or copyright interests, as described in Code Sec. 197(e)(4)(C),

(b) a right held under a contract or granted by a governmental unit to receive tangible property or services, as described in Code Sec. 197(e)(4)(B), and

(c) a right held under a contract or granted by a governmental unit that has a fixed duration of less than 15 years, or that is fixed as to amount and recoverable under a method similar to the unit-of-production method, as described in Code Sec. 197(e)(4)(D) (Code Sec. 167(f)(2), as amended by the 2004 Jobs Act); and

(3) Code Sec. 197 intangibles (Code Sec. 197(f)(10), as added by the 2004 Jobs Act).

Comment: Most of the provisions of Code Sec. 470 apply to leases entered into after March 12, 2004. However, the intangibles listed in items (2) and (3) above are only considered to be tangible property for leases entered into after October 3, 2004 (Act Sec. 849(b)(4) of the 2004 Jobs Act).

Under existing law, a property is also treated as tax-exempt use property if it is owned by a partnership which has at least one tax-exempt partner and the allocations of partnership items attempt to inappropriately transfer the deductions from the tax-exempt partner to taxable partners (Code Sec. 168(h)(6)). Such property, however, will not be treated as tax-exempt use property for Code Sec. 470 purposes if the low income housing credit or the rehabilitation credit is claimed on the property (Code Sec. 470(c)(2), as added by the 2004 Jobs Act).

Tax-exempt entity. Under existing law, a tax-exempt entity is a tax-exempt organization, governmental unit, or foreign person or entity. For leases entered into after October 3, 2004, the definition of tax-exempt entity for purposes of Code Sec. 168 and new Code Sec. 470 is expanded to include Indian tribal governments (Code Sec. 168(h)(2)(A), as amended by the 2004 Jobs Act).

Current deduction of tax-exempt use losses allowed if certain requirements are met.—Tax-exempt use losses will not be disallowed if the transaction meets a number of specific conditions (Code Sec. 470(d), as added by the 2004 Jobs Act). These conditions attempt to distinguish legitimate lease transactions from those which are entered into solely for tax avoidance purposes. The conditions are:

(1) the amount of funds subject to an arrangement protecting the lessor's interest or otherwise set aside to pay the lease must not exceed an allowable amount generally equal to 20 percent of the lessor's adjusted basis in the property at the time the lease is entered into (Code Sec. 470(d)(1), as added by the 2004 Jobs Act);

(2) if the lease is for a term longer than five years, the lessor must have a substantial equity investment, equal to at least 20 percent of its adjusted basis, in the property at the inception and throughout the term of the lease (Code Sec. 470(d)(2), as added by the 2004 Jobs Act);

(3) if the lease is for a term longer than five years, the lessee must not bear more than a minimal risk of loss (Code Sec. 470(d)(3), as added by the 2004 Jobs Act); and

(4) in the case of property with a class life of more than seven years (other than fixed-wing aircraft and vessels), if the lease includes an option for the lessee to purchase the property, the purchase price under the option must be the fair market value of the property at the time of the option exercise (Code Sec. 470(d)(4), as added by the 2004 Jobs Act).

Limit on degree of security for lessor. The amount of funds subject to an arrangement protecting the lessor's interest or otherwise set aside to pay the lease must not exceed an allowable amount generally equal to 20 percent of the lessor's adjusted basis in the property at the time the lease is entered into (Code Sec. 470(d)(1), as added by the 2004 Jobs Act). The types of arrangements restricted include defeasance arrangements, a loan by the lessee to the lessor or a lender, a deposit arrangement, a letter of credit collateralized with cash or cash equivalents, a payment undertaking agreement, prepaid rent, a sinking fund arrangement, a guaranteed investment contract, financial guaranty insurance, and any similar arrangement.

Comment: Maintenance of any of these types of security arrangements reduces the credit risk assumed by the lessor, and moves the transaction away from characterization as a financing lease.

Allowable amount of lease security. The IRS is authorized to issue regulations providing an increase in the 20-percent of basis allowable amount to not more than 50 percent of the lessor's adjusted basis where it is necessary because of the creditworthiness of the lessee (Code Sec. 470(d)(1)(C)(ii), as added by the 2004 Jobs Act). If under the lease the lessee has the option to purchase the property for a fixed price or for other than the fair market value at the time of exercise, the allowable amount at the time of exercise may not exceed 50 percent of the option price (Code Sec. 470(d)(1)(C)(iii), as added by the 2004 Jobs Act). The allowable amount is zero with respect to any arrangement that involves a loan from the lessee to the lessor or a lender; any deposit received, letter of credit issued, or payment undertaking agreement entered into by a lender otherwise involved in the transaction; or in the case of a transaction that involves a lender, any credit support made available to the lessor in which any such lender does not have a claim that is senior to the claim of the lessor (Code Sec. 470(d)(1)(C)(iv), as added by the 2004 Jobs Act).

¶670

Lender defined. A lender, with respect to any lease, means a person that makes a loan to the lessor which is secured by the lease or the leased property (Code Sec. 470(f)(3), as added by the 2004 Jobs Act).

Equity investment required by lessor. If the lease is for a term longer than five years, the lessor must have a substantial equity investment, equal to at least 20 percent of its adjusted basis, in the property at the inception and throughout the term of the lease (Code Sec. 470(d)(2), as added by the 2004 Jobs Act). In addition, the fair market value of the property at the end of the lease must reasonably be expected to be equal to at least 20 percent of the lessor's adjusted basis in the property. That fair market value is reduced to the extent that a person other than the lessor bears the risk of loss in value of the property.

Lessor's basis defined. For purposes of these rules, if the lessor acquired the property in a like-kind exchange or involuntary conversion transaction occurring after the date of enactment of the 2004 Jobs Act, the lessor's basis is the lesser of the property's fair market value as of the beginning of the lease term or the amount which would be the lessor's adjusted basis if Code Secs. 1031 or 1033 did not apply to the acquisition transaction (Code Sec. 470(e)(4)(B), as added by the 2004 Jobs Act).

Limits on lessee risk of loss. If the lease is for a term longer than five years, the lessee must not bear more than a minimal risk of loss (Code Sec. 470(d)(3), as added by the 2004 Jobs Act). The lessee cannot be required to bear any portion of the loss that would occur if the fair market value of the property were 25 percent less than its expected fair market value at the time the lease is terminated, or more than 50 percent of the loss that would occur if the fair market value of the property at the time the lease is terminated were zero.

Option price must be fair market value. In the case of property with a class life of more than seven years (other than fixed-wing aircraft and vessels), if the lease includes an option for the lessee to purchase the property, the purchase price under the option must be the fair market value of the property at the time of the option exercise (Code Sec. 470(d)(4), as added by the 2004 Jobs Act).

Comment: Property with a class life of more than seven years includes buses, railroad cars, and land improvements.

Former tax-exempt use property and dispositions of tax-exempt use property.—Previously disallowed tax-exempt use losses are carried over to succeeding years, subject to the limitation that they cannot be deducted unless there is income from the property (Code Sec. 470(b), as added by the 2004 Jobs Act). Even when the property is no longer tax-exempt use property, the deduction is still limited to the amount of net income from the property (Code Sec. 470(e)(1), as added by the 2004 Jobs Act). When the taxpayer disposes of its entire interest in the property, the previously disallowed losses are generally available, under rules similar to those applicable to passive activity losses (Code Sec. 470(e)(2), as added by the 2004 Jobs Act, referring to Code Sec. 469(g)).

Lease term defined.—The lease term includes the periods of any options to renew for a rental other than fair market value at the time of the renewal, the term of successive leases that are part of the same transaction, and the term of any service contract or similar agreement with respect to the lease property that is made as part of the same transaction or series of related transactions (Code Sec. 470(f)(2), as added by the 2004 Jobs Act, incorporating Code Sec. 168(i)(3), as amended by the 2004 Jobs Act).

As previously noted, under existing law, certain leased qualified technological equipment is excluded from the definition of tax-exempt use property if the lease term is five years or less. The new law provides that a renewal period (up to 24 months) under a lessee's option to renew at a fair market value rent is not treated as extending the term of the lease for such property (Code Sec. 168(h)(3)(A), as amended by the 2004 Jobs Act).

Coordination with passive loss, like-kind exchange, and involuntary conversion rules.—The rules limiting deductions for property leased to tax-exempt entities are applied before the passive activity loss limitations (Code Sec. 470(e)(3)).

Neither the like-kind exchange nor the involuntary conversion rules apply to property exchanged or converted after the date of enactment of the 2004 Jobs Act if either:

(1) the exchanged or converted property was tax-exempt use property subject to a lease entered into before March 13, 2004, and which would not have met the requirements under new Code Sec. 470 for current deduction of tax-exempt use losses if Code Sec. 470 had been in effect at that time, or

(2) the replacement property is tax-exempt use property subject to a lease which does not meet those requirements (Code Sec. 470(e)(4)(A)).

Regulations.—The IRS is authorized to prescribe regulations necessary and appropriate to carry out the purposes of new Code Sec. 470, including regulations to allow the aggregation of property subject to a single lease and provide for the allocation of interest expense (Code Sec. 470(g), as added by the 2004 Jobs Act).

PRACTICAL ANALYSIS. Jeffrey Paravano of Baker & Hostetler and former Treasury official observes that there are at least three interesting aspects of the leasing provisions: (1) the revenue score, (2) the prospective effective date, and (3) the grandfather rules. The hefty revenue score (raising nearly $27 billion over 10 years) suggests a significant change in the law—meaning that the targeted lease transactions must be viewed by Congress, the Joint Committee on Taxation and the Treasury Department (which performed its own revenue score before the legislation was forwarded to the White House for signature) as acceptable tax planning under prior law. The prospective effective date—which follows the House bill and provides that the new rules generally apply to leases entered into after March 12, 2004—suggests continuing tax benefits from existing leases should continue. The grandfather rules send a similar message. There are 15 or 16 transactions that potentially qualify under the grandfather rules and a number of municipalities pushed for this transition relief. The Federal Transit Administration (FTA) suspended at the Treasury's request its approval of certain municipal transportation leases. Under the legislation, municipalities now have until January 1, 2006, to obtain FTA approval for applications submitted by March 13, 2004. It seems as though Congress anticipates such approval would be forthcoming. On the enforcement side, the existence of the prospective effective date, the grandfather rules and the high revenue score strengthen taxpayers' arguments that targeted leases delivered tax benefits under prior law. I would not want to be in the IRS's shoes arguing that a transaction "grandfathered" by Congress never worked in the first place; and if the grandfathered leases deliver tax benefits, leases entered into before the effective date should similarly be protected. That said, IRS agents around the country are making clear they intend to challenge prior transactions. This litigation likely will continue for years, and Congress just gave taxpayers a significant head start *vis-a-vis* the IRS.

¶670

For further information on this subject, consult any of the following CCH reporter explanations:

- Standard Federal Tax Reporter, 2004FED ¶11,004.01, ¶11,278.01, ¶11,278.027, ¶11,278.049 and ¶12,455.023
- Federal Tax Service, FTS §G:18.80
- Federal Tax Guide, 2004FTG ¶9015

★ *Effective date.* The new rules limiting the availability of deductions related to property leased to tax-exempt entities generally apply to leases entered into after March 12, 2004 (Act Sec. 849(a) of the American Jobs Creation Act of 2004). However, the rules do not apply to "qualified transportation property" (Act Sec. 849(b)(1) of the 2004 Jobs Act). Qualified transportation property is domestic property subject to a lease with respect to which a formal application:

(1) was submitted to the Federal Transit Administration after June 30, 2003, and before March 13, 2004,

(2) is approved by the Federal Transit Administration before January 1, 2006, and

(3) includes a description and statement of the value of the property.

The restrictions on the applicability of the like-kind exchange and involuntary conversion rules to tax-exempt use property (Code Sec. 470(e)(4)(A), as added by the 2004 Jobs Act), and the special rule for determining the basis of property acquired in a like-kind exchange or involuntary conversion transaction (Code Sec. 470(e)(4)(B), as added by the 2004 Jobs Act) apply to property exchanged or converted after the date of enactment of the 2004 Jobs Act (Act Sec. 849(b)(3) of the 2004 Jobs Act).

The provisions treating intangibles described in Code Sec. 167(f)(2) and Code Sec. 197 intangibles as tangible property for purposes of the definition of tax-exempt use property and subjecting those intangibles to the extended useful life rules apply only for leases entered into after October 3, 2004 (Act Sec. 849(b)(4) of the 2004 Jobs Act).

Act Sec. 847(a) of the American Jobs Creation Act of 2004, amending Code Sec. 168(g)(3)(A); Act Sec. 847(b), adding Code Sec. 167(f)(1)(C), amending Code Sec. 167(f)(2), adding Code Sec. 197(f)(10); Act Sec. 847(c), amending Code Sec. 168(i)(3)(A); Act Sec. 847(d), amending Code Sec. 168(h)(3)(A); Act Sec. 847(e), amending Code Sec. 168(h)(2)(A); Act Sec. 848(a), adding Code Sec. 470; Act Sec. 849. Law at ¶5175, ¶5180, ¶5225, and ¶5395. Committee Report at ¶11,290.

Chapter 7

Sales, Exchanges, Financing and Investment

DEBT TRANSACTIONS

¶705

OID and Interest Deductions and Income Inclusions When Debt Is Held by Related Foreign Persons

Background

Original Issue Discount (OID). Under the OID rules, the holder of a debt instrument that is issued at a discount is required to accrue daily portions of the discount and include such amounts in income (Code Sec. 1272). The total of these daily accruals of OID for the year are included in the debt holder's gross income regardless of the holder's method of accounting (Reg. §1.1272-1(a)(1)). For the issuer of the debt instrument, the total of the daily accruals of OID for the year is generally deductible as interest (Code Sec. 163(e)(1)).

Limitations on the deduction of OID by the issuer apply when the debt instrument is held by a foreign person who is related to the issuer within the meaning of Code Sec. 267(b) (Code Sec. 163(e)(3)(B)). In that situation, the accrued OID is not deductible by the issuer until it is paid to the related foreign person (Code Sec.

163(e)(3)(A)). By requiring payment, this essentially puts the issuer on the cash method of accounting with respect to the deduction of OID owed to the related foreign person (Reg. §1.163-12(a)). However, the issuer can deduct accrued but unpaid OID to the extent that the OID is effectively connected with the conduct by the foreign related person of a trade or business within the United States, unless the OID that is includible in the related foreign person's income is exempt from taxation or is subject to a reduced rate of tax pursuant to a treaty obligation of the United States (Code Sec. 163(e)(3)(A); Reg. §1.163-12(b)). Thus, accrued OID that is owed to a related foreign person can be deducted before it is paid as long as it is effectively connected income for the related foreign person and is fully subject to U.S. tax.

If the OID is owed to a related person that is a controlled foreign corporation (CFC) or a passive foreign investment company (PFIC), the amount is deductible on the day that the amount is includible in the income of the CFC or PFIC. For a CFC, the day on which the amount is includible in income is determined under the accounting method that the CFC uses to compute its taxable income and earnings and profits (Reg. §1.163-12(b)(3)(ii)). For a PFIC, the day on which the amount is includible in income is determined under the accounting method that the PFIC uses to compute its earnings and profits (Reg. §1.163-12(b)(3)(iii)). However, the person that owes the amount at issue must have a Code Sec. 1295 election in effect that treats the PFIC to which the amount is owed as a qualified electing fund (QEF). Under a QEF election, the electing U.S. shareholder of the QEF is taxed currently on a share of the QEF's income.

Unpaid interest. In the case of unpaid interest incurred in transactions between related persons, Code Sec. 267 generally requires application of a matching principle so that the deduction for interest is not allowed until the interest is includible in the income of the person receiving it (Code Sec. 267(a)(2)). Thus, if the payor of the interest is on the accrual method but the recipient of the interest is on the cash method, the payor cannot claim the deduction until the interest is includible in the recipient's income, which would be when the interest is paid. The Treasury Department was instructed to issue regulations that apply this matching principle in situations in which the person to whom the interest payment is made is not a U.S. person (Code Sec. 267(a)(3)). These regulations provide a parallel rule to the related foreign person rule for OID under Code Sec. 163(e). Under the regulations, amounts are deductible on the day that the amount is includible in income of the related foreign person as effectively connected income, unless the related foreign person is exempt from U.S. tax on the amount owed or is subject to a reduced rate of tax pursuant to a treaty obligation of the United States (Reg. §1.267(a)-3(c)).

If an amount is owed to a related person that is a CFC or a PFIC, the amount is deductible on the day that the amount is includible in the income of the CFC or PFIC. For a CFC, the day on which the amount is includible in income is determined under the accounting method that the CFC uses to compute its taxable income and earnings and profits (Reg. §1.267(a)-3(c)(4)(ii)). For a PFIC, the day on which the amount is includible in income is determined under the accounting method that the PFIC uses to compute its earnings and profits (Reg. §1.267(a)-3(c)(4)(iii)). However, the person that owes the amount at issue must have a Code Sec. 1295 election in effect that treats the PFIC to which the amount is owed as a QEF. Under a QEF election, the electing U.S. shareholder of the QEF is taxed currently on a share of the QEF's income.

Comment: A U.S. person that conducts foreign operations through a foreign corporation generally is subject to U.S. tax when the income is repatriated to the United States through a dividend distribution to the U.S. person. Thus, amounts owed to a related foreign corporation could be included in the income of the related foreign corporation and deductible by the payor under the accrual method before the amounts are included in the income of the foreign corporation's U.S. shareholders (House Committee Report (H.R. Rep. No. 108-548)).

American Jobs Creation Act Impact

Matching of deductions and income inclusions.—In debt or lending transactions with certain related foreign corporations, a matching principle will be applied. Accrued but unpaid interest or original issue discount (OID) is deductible by the payor when the interest is includible in the income of the direct or indirect U.S. owners of the related foreign corporation under the appropriate income inclusion rule (Code Sec. 163(e)(3)(B)(i), as amended by the American Jobs Creation Act of 2004; House Committee Report (H.R. Rep. No. 108-548)).

Original Issue Discount (OID). A special rule on the proper time for deducting OID has been added where the debt instrument is held by a related foreign person that is a controlled foreign corporation (CFC) or a passive foreign investment company (PFIC). In the case of any debt instrument having OID that is held by a related CFC or a PFIC, the deduction for OID is allowable to the issuer for a tax year before the tax year in which the OID is paid, but only to the extent that the OID is includible during that prior tax year in the gross income of the U.S. person who owns stock in the CFC or PFIC (Code Sec. 163(e)(3)(B)(i), as added by the 2004 Jobs Act). In determining whether a U.S. person owns stock in the CFC or PFIC, both stock of the CFC or PFIC that is owned directly by the U.S. person and stock owned indirectly through a foreign corporation, partnership, estate or trust are considered (Code Sec. 958(a)). The new rule on deduction of OID applies to payments accrued on or after the date of enactment (Act Sec. 841(c) of the 2004 Jobs Act).

> **Comment:** The focus of when the OID deduction is allowed shifts from when the CFC or PFIC includes the OID in income to when the U.S. owners of the CFC or PFIC include the OID in income. One commentator has noted that it is unclear how to determine when the OID would be includible in income of the CFC's or PFIC's U.S. owners and deductible by the issuer if the ownership of the CFC or PFIC is in the hands of foreign shareholders.

> **Comment:** Personal foreign holding companies (PFHCs) are not mentioned because they are repealed by another provision of the 2004 Jobs Act (see ¶490).

The determination of whether OID is includible in the gross income of the U.S. shareholder of the CFC or PFIC is made without regard to properly allocable deductions under Code Sec. 954(b)(5) and qualified deficits under Code Sec. 952(c)(1)(B) (accumulated deficit rule). Qualified deficits are prior-year deficits in the earnings and profits of a CFC that are attributable to activities that give rise to certain types of income, such as foreign base company shipping, sales, services or oil-related income. These qualified deficits normally reduce the CFC shareholders' taxable inclusion by their pro rata share of the deficits, and the subpart F income that is eliminated by these deficits is deferred until a later year. When the CFC later has non-subpart F earnings and profits, a portion of them is recharacterized as subpart F income and is taxed.

> **Comment:** The Treasury Department is authorized to issue regulations that would exempt transactions from the new deduction limitation rule for OID owed to a CFC or PFIC. An exempt transaction could include one that is entered into by the payor in the ordinary course of a trade or business in which the

payor is predominantly engaged (Code Sec. 163(e)(3)(B)(i), as added by the 2004 Jobs Act).

Unpaid interest. A special rule has been added on the proper time for deducting payments owed to a related foreign person that is a CFC or a PFIC, effective for payments accrued on or after the date of enactment. This rule is a parallel rule to the OID deduction rule described above. In the case of any item payable to a CFC or to a PFIC, a deduction is allowable to the payor for a tax year before the tax year in which the item is paid, but only to the extent that an amount attributable to the item is includible during that prior tax year in the gross income of the U.S. person who owns stock in the CFC or PFIC (Code Sec. 267(a)(3)(B)(i), as added by the 2004 Jobs Act). In determining whether a U.S. person owns stock in the CFC or PFIC, both stock of the CFC or PFIC that is owned directly by the U.S. person and stock owned indirectly through a foreign corporation, partnership, estate or trust are considered (Code Sec. 958(a)). The determination of whether an amount is includible in the gross income of the U.S. shareholder of the CFC or PFIC is made without regard to properly allocable deductions under Code Sec. 954(b)(5) and qualified deficits under Code Sec. 952(c)(1)(B), as described above.

> **Example:** Americo Corp., a U.S. corporation, owns 60 percent of the stock of a CFC, and an unrelated foreign corporation owns the remaining 40 percent. The U.S. parent accrues an interest expense of $100 owed to the CFC that is not paid by the end of the tax year. The CFC counts the $100 as foreign base company income, but also incurs $60 in deductions that are properly allocated to the foreign base company income under Code Sec. 954(b)(5), resulting in only $40 of net foreign base company income counted as subpart F income for the tax year (assuming that the CFC's earnings and profits for the year are $40). Americo's includible share of the subpart F income is $24 ($40 × its 60% interest in the CFC). Americo is allowed a deduction of $60 for the tax year ($100 × its 60% ownership interest in the CFC). Under prior law, Americo would have been able to deduct the $100 unpaid interest obligation (Conference Committee Report (H.R. Conf. Rep. No. 108-755)).

The Treasury Department is authorized to issue regulations that would exempt transactions from the new deduction limitation rule for payments owed to a CFC or PFIC. An exempt transaction could include one that is entered into by the payor in the ordinary course of a trade or business in which the payor is predominantly engaged and in which the payment of the accrued amounts occurs within 8 ½ months after accrual or within such other period as may be prescribed in the regulations (Code Sec. 267(a)(3)(B)(ii), as added by the 2004 Jobs Act).

> **Comment:** The 8 ½ month rule that the Treasury Department is instructed to include in the regulation on exempt transactions mimics the recurring items exception to the economic performance rule for deduction of liabilities (Code Sec. 461(h)(3)(A)).

For further information on this subject, consult any of the following CCH reporter explanations:

- Standard Federal Tax Reporter, 2004FED ¶9303.04 and ¶14,161.044
- Federal Tax Service, FTS § G:7.85, § K:5.82 and § K:13.112[4]
- Federal Tax Guide, 2004FTG ¶5822, ¶6573, ¶17,445 and ¶17,485

★ *Effective date.* The amendments made by this provision apply to payments accrued on or after the date of enactment (Act Sec. 841(c) of the American Jobs Creation Act of 2004).

¶705

Act Sec. 841(a) of the American Jobs Creation Act of 2004, redesignating Code Sec. 163(e)(3)(B) as (C) and adding Code Sec. 163(e)(3)(B); Act Sec. 841(b)(1), amending Code Sec. 267(a)(3); Act Sec. 841(b)(2), adding Code Sec. 267(a)(3)(B); Act Sec. 841(c). Law at ¶5165 and ¶5275. Committee Report at ¶11,240.

¶710

Denial of Installment Sale Treatment for Readily Tradable Debt

Background

Currently, taxpayers are permitted to recognize gain on the disposition of property under the installment method. Under the installment method, the amount of income reported by a taxpayer is the amount of any payment multiplied by the gross profit ratio. The gross profit ratio is the gross profit realized from the sale over the total contract price.

> **Compliance Tip:** Form 6252, "Installment Sale Income," is used to report an installment sale in the year that it occurs and to report any payments received in later years.

A payment is any amount actually or constructively received under an installment obligation. Payments include amounts received in the form of cash or other property, including foreign currency, marketable securities, and the receipt of "non-purchaser" debt. However, receipt of indebtedness of the purchaser is not a payment unless it is payable on demand or readily tradable debt *that is issued by a corporation or a government* (or a political subdivision thereof).

American Jobs Creation Act Impact

Installment treatment denied for all sales in exchange for readily tradable debt, regardless of the issuer.—Installment sale treatment is denied for any sale in which the taxpayer receives readily tradable debt, even if the debt was issued by a party other than a corporation or political subdivision. The provision removes the qualifying language (issued by a corporation or a government (or political subdivision thereof)) regarding readily tradable debt from Code Sec. 453(f)(4)(B) (Code Sec. 453(f)(4)(B), as amended by the American Jobs Creation Act of 2004). Thus, debt that is payable on demand or is readily tradable, regardless of the nature of the issuer, is considered a payment for purposes of the installment method.

> **Comment:** For example, if the taxpayer receives readily tradable debt of a partnership or an individual in a sale, the debt is treated as a payment on the installment note.

For further information on this subject, consult any of the following CCH reporter explanations:

- Standard Federal Tax Reporter, 2004FED ¶21,406.01 and ¶21,406.028
- Federal Tax Service, FTS § E:12.61[2]
- Federal Tax Guide, 2004FTG ¶15,365

★ *Effective date.* The provision is effective for sales occurring after the date of enactment (Act Sec. 897(b) of the American Jobs Creation Act of 2004).

Act Sec. 897(a) of the American Jobs Creation Act of 2004, amending Code Sec. 453(f)(4)(B); Act Sec. 897(b). Law at ¶5380. Committee Report at ¶11,690.

¶715

Disallowed Deduction for Interest on Convertible Debt

Background

Convertible or "equity-linked" debt is basically debt issued by a corporation that is payable in stock of the corporation on maturity. As a general rule, interest paid or accrued during the year on straight debt is deductible by the issuer of the debt (Code Sec. 163(a)) and is includible in income by the holder of the debt (Code Sec. 61(a)(4)). In contrast, interest paid or accrued on convertible debt is not deductible by the issuer (Code Sec. 163(l)) because such debt does not represent a true borrowing transaction. The issuer received cash upon issuance of the debt but is giving up an ownership interest when the debt matures, rather than paying back the amount of the debt in cash.

Under the Internal Revenue Code, the denial of the deduction for interest on convertible debt applies to a "disqualified debt instrument." A "disqualified debt instrument" is defined as debt of a corporation that is payable in equity of the issuer or a related party (Code Sec. 163(l)(1) and (2)). Debt is treated as payable in equity of the issuer or a related party under the following three circumstances:

(1) Debt is treated as payable in equity of the issuer or a related party if a substantial amount of the principal or interest is required to be paid or converted into such equity (mandatory conversion feature) or is payable in or is convertible into such equity at the option of the issuer or a related party (Code Sec. 163(l)(3)(A)).

(2) Debt is treatable as payable in equity of the issuer or a related party if a substantial amount of the principal or interest is required to be determined, or is determined at the option of the issuer or a related party, by reference to the value of such equity (Code Sec. 163(l)(3)(B)).

(3) Debt is treatable as payable in equity of the issuer or a related party if the debt is part of an arrangement that is reasonably expected to result in the payment of the debt instrument with such equity or by reference to the value of such equity (Code Sec. 163(l)(3)(C)). Some examples include the issuance of a forward contract in connection with the issuance of debt, nonrecourse debt that is secured principally by such equity, and debt instruments that are paid in, converted to, or determined by reference to the value of equity if it is at the option of the holder or related party and there is a substantial certainty that the option will be exercised (Senate Finance Committee Report (S. Rep. No. 108-192)).

A related party is a person who bears a relationship to the other person that is described in Code Sec. 267(b) or 707(b) (Code Sec. 163(l)(4)). Among the numerous relationships described in Code Secs. 267(b) and 707(b) are two corporations that are members of the same controlled group. In applying the control test, however, the threshold is 50-percent control, rather than 80-percent control (Code Secs. 267(b)(2) and (f) and 1563).

Comment: Companies attempted to skirt the interest deduction disallowance rule by issuing debt that was payable on maturity in stock of an affiliate that was slightly less than 50-percent owned by the company. The debt did not fall within the definition of a "disqualified debt instrument" because the debt was convertible into equity of a company that was not related to the issuer under the 50-percent control test. In economic terms, however, the transaction was virtually the same as one in which debt was convertible into stock of a

Background

related party that was slightly more than 50-percent owned by the issuer (Senate Finance Committee Report (S. Rep. No. 108-192)).

American Jobs Creation Act Impact

Debt convertible into equity of another party.—The definition of a "disqualified debt instrument" has been expanded for debt instruments issued after October 3, 2004. A "disqualified debt instrument" is now defined as debt of a corporation that is payable in equity of the issuer or a related party *or* that is payable in equity held by the issuer or any related party in any other person (Code Sec. 163(l)(2), as amended by the American Jobs Creation Act of 2004). Thus, a corporation that issues a debt instrument after October 3, 2004, that is convertible into an equity interest that it holds or that a related party holds in another person, cannot deduct the interest paid or accrued on the debt. The interest deduction is denied whether or not the issuer of the debt or a related party holds more than a 50-percent ownership interest in the other person (Senate Finance Committee Report (S. Rep. No. 108-192)).

> **Planning Note:** The IRS has previously ruled that a convertible debt instrument that provides for *contingent* interest payments is not a disqualified debt instrument under Code Sec. 163(l) because it is not substantially certain that a substantial amount of principal or interest will be required to be paid in stock (Rev. Rul. 2002-31, 2002-1 CB 1023). This exception for contingent convertible securities remains intact.

Issuers who lose their interest deduction due to the expansion of the definition of a "disqualified debt instrument" are allowed to increase the basis of the equity that the debt will be converted into at maturity. Thus, if the issuer's debt is convertible into equity held by the issuer in a person other than the issuer or a person related to the issuer, the issuer can increase the basis of such equity by the amount of the interest deduction that was denied with respect to the debt (Code Sec. 163(l)(4), as added by the 2004 Jobs Act).

> **Comment:** A comparable capitalization rule for interest tied to straddles is outlined in Proposed Reg. § 1.263(g)-4.

Exception for dealers in securities. For debt instruments issued after October 3, 2004, an exception to the rule that denies a deduction for interest paid or accrued on convertible debt applies to dealers in securities. Debt issued by a dealer in securities or by a related party that is payable in or by reference to equity other than equity of the issuer or a related party that is held by such dealer in its capacity as a dealer in securities is not treated as a "disqualified debt instrument." Thus, interest paid or accrued on such debt is deductible by the dealer. A "dealer in securities" is a taxpayer who regularly purchases securities from or sells securities to customers in the ordinary course of a trade or business or who regularly offers to enter into, assume, offset, assign or otherwise terminate positions in securities with customers in the ordinary course of business (Code Sec. 163(l)(5), as added by the 2004 Jobs Act; Code Sec. 475(c)(1)).

For further information on this subject, consult any of the following CCH reporter explanations:

- Standard Federal Tax Reporter, 2004FED ¶9104.0314, ¶9104.062 and ¶9303.0662
- Federal Tax Service, FTS § G:7.108
- Federal Tax Guide, 2004FTG ¶6555

★ *Effective date.* The amendments made by this provision apply to debt instruments issued after October 3, 2004 (Act Sec. 845(e) of the American Jobs Creation Act of 2004).

Act Sec. 845(a) of the American Jobs Creation Act of 2004, amending Code Sec. 163(l)(2); Act Sec. 845(b), redesignating Code Sec. 163(l)(4) and (5) as Code Sec. 163(l)(5) and (6) and adding new Code Sec. 163(l)(4); Act Sec. 845(c), redesignating Code Sec. 163(l)(5) and (6) as Code Sec. 163(l)(6) and (7) and adding new Code Sec. 163(l)(5); Act Sec. 845(d), amending Code Sec. 163(l)(3); Act Sec. 845(e). Law at ¶ 5165. Committee Report at ¶ 11,280.

¶ 720

Income on Cancellation of Corporate or Partnership Debt

Background ———————————————————————————————————

Subject to certain exceptions, a creditor's cancellation of a debt can give rise to gross income to a debtor. Accordingly, a corporation that transfers shares of its stock to a creditor in satisfaction of debt must recognize cancellation of indebtedness income. The amount of income will equal that which would have been realized if the debt were satisfied with money equal to the fair market value of the stock transferred (Code Sec. 108(e)(8)). Prior to enactment of the American Jobs Creation Act of 2004, there was no provision of the Code, and no clear case law, that would similarly require a partnership to treat a transfer of a capital or profits interest in the partnership as giving rise to cancellation of indebtedness income. It was also unclear if any requirement to recognize cancellation of indebtedness income was affected by whether the debt was recourse or nonrecourse.

When cancellation of indebtedness income is realized by a partnership, it is generally allocated among partners by reference to the partnership agreement, provided the allocations under the agreement have substantial economic effect.

American Jobs Creation Act Impact

Cancellation of indebtedness income to corporation or partnership.—Effective for cancellations of indebtedness occurring on or after the date of enactment, the 2004 Jobs Act provides that a debtor that satisfies an indebtedness by transferring its stock (if the debtor is a corporation) or a capital or profits interest in itself (if the debtor is a partnership) will recognize cancellation of indebtedness income from such a transfer to a creditor (Code Sec. 108(e)(8), as amended by the 2004 Jobs Act). In determining the amount of income recognized upon cancellation of the debt, the corporation or partnership will be deemed to have transferred money in an amount equal to the fair market value of the stock or partnership interest transferred to the creditor. Thus, a partnership will have income from the discharge of indebtedness to the extent that the principal of the debt exceeds the value of the partnership interest transferred.

> **Example:** Bandit LLC transfers a 10 percent interest in the partnership to Nu-Loan Finance Company in cancellation of a $500,000 debt to Nu-Loan. At the time of this transfer, the 10 percent interest had a total value of $380,000. Bandit will recognize cancellation of indebtedness income of $120,000 ($500,000 value of cancelled debt – $380,000 value of the interest transferred).

Recourse or nonrecourse debt. Determination of a corporation's or partnership's cancellation of indebtedness income under the new law is unaffected by the status of the cancelled debt as recourse or nonrecourse. Both recourse and nonrecourse debt cancelled in exchange for corporate stock or partnership interests will give rise to income to the corporation, or to the partnership, respectively.

Effect on partners. Discharge of indebtedness income of a partnership that is recognized under Code Sec. 108(e)(8) is to be included in the distributive share of taxpayers who were partners in the partnership immediately before the debt was discharged.

According to the Senate Conference Report (S. Rep. No. 108-192), the amendment of Code Sec. 108(e)(8) by the 2004 Jobs Act is not intended to give rise to any inference as to the correct tax treatment under prior law of a transfer of a partnership interest in satisfaction of a partnership debt.

> **PRACTICAL ANALYSIS. Michael J. Grace of Buchanan Ingersoll PC and Georgetown University Law Center, Washington, D.C., observes that the 2004 Jobs Act's repeal of the "partnership debt for equity" exception to cancellation of indebtedness (COD) income, effective with respect to cancellations occurring on or after the date of enactment, increases the importance of strategically allocating COD income among partners. New Code Sec. 108(e)(8)(B) and the Conference Report direct that any COD income recognized (i.e., taken into account at the partnership level on account of the Act's amendment) be allocated solely among the partners who held interests in the partnership immediately before the debt was discharged. However, the Conference Report also acknowledges that the availability of the various exclusions of COD income from gross income under Code Sec. 108(e) apply at the partner level rather than the partnership level; see also Code Sec. 108(d)(6). Accordingly, subject to the constraints imposed by Code Sec. 704(b) and its regulations, partnerships generally should attempt to allocate COD income to those partners able to exclude it from their gross income. See, in particular, Rev. Rul. 92-97, 1992-2 CB 124.**

For further information on this subject, consult any of the following CCH reporter explanations:

- Standard Federal Tax Reporter, 2004FED ¶7010.01 and ¶7010.052
- Federal Tax Service, FTS §G:7.108
- Federal Tax Guide, 2004FTG ¶4203, ¶4215 and ¶4218

★ *Effective date.* The provision is effective for cancellations of indebtedness occurring on or after the date of enactment (Act Sec. 896(b) of the American Jobs Creation Act of 2004).

Act Sec. 896(a) of the American Jobs Creation Act of 2004, amending Code Sec. 108(e)(8); Act Sec. 896(b). Law at ¶5120. Committee Report at ¶11,680.

INVESTMENT

¶725

Stripped Income Rules Expanded to Bond and Preferred Stock Funds

Background

Special tax rules control the taxation of financial instruments that are commonly known as "stripped bonds" and "stripped preferred stock." The definitions of these instruments appear immediately below.

Stripped bond defined. A "stripped bond" is a debt instrument where there has been a separation in ownership between the bond and coupon interest that has not yet become payable (Code Sec. 1286(e)(2)). Under this definition, the term "bond" is broadly defined and includes debentures, notes, and other evidences of debt (e.g., certificates) (Code Sec. 1286(e)(1)). The term "stripped coupon" refers to any coupon that relates to the stripped bond (Code Sec. 1286(e)(3)).

Stripped preferred stock defined. The term "stripped preferred stock" is defined to mean preferred stock where there has been a separation in ownership between the stock and dividends that have not yet become payable (Code Sec. 305(e)(5)(A)). The term "preferred stock" refers to stock that: (1) is limited and preferred as to dividends paid by the corporation, (2) does not participate in corporate growth to any significant extent, and (3) has a fixed redemption price (Code Sec. 305(e)(5)(B)).

> **Comment:** Due to the characteristics of preferred stock (e.g., preference as to the payment of dividends, fixed redemption price and generally a fixed dividend rate), it has many similarities to a long-term corporate bond. It was this similarity in characteristics that prompted Congress to bring stripped preferred stock under the same general tax rules that apply to stripped bonds.

Tax treatment of stripped instruments. The basic income tax aspects of stripped instruments are as follows:

(1) *Stripped bonds and coupons.* After a bond has been stripped, the seller of the stripped bond has the right to receive the principal (redemption price) payment. The buyer of the stripped coupon has the right to receive interest on the bond. The seller must include in income the interest that accrued while he held the bond before the date of sale to the extent that the interest was not reported as income. Also, the seller must generally include the market discount that accrued before the date of sale of the stripped bond (or coupon) (Code Sec. 1286(b)). The interest and market discount included in income is added to the basis of the bond and coupons. This adjusted basis is then allocated between the items kept (e.g., bonds) and the items sold (e.g., coupons), based on the fair market value of the items. The difference between the sale price of the bond (or coupon) and the allocated basis of the bond (or coupon) is the seller's gain or loss from the sale. The bond kept by the seller is treated as an original issue discount (OID) bond. The tax treatment of OID bonds is provided by Code Sec. 1272.

The buyer of a stripped bond or stripped coupon is required to treat it as if it were originally issued on the date of purchase. In the case of a stripped bond, the excess of the stated redemption price at maturity over the purchase price is treated as OID. In the case of a stripped coupon, any excess of the amount payable on the due date of the coupon over the purchase price is treated as OID (Code Sec. 1286(a)).

> **Comment:** As a general rule, the OID rules do not apply to stripped tax-exempt bonds (Code Sec. 1286(d)).

(2) *Stripped preferred stock.* When the dividend rights are stripped from preferred stock, generally, the buyer of the stripped preferred stock may have to include amounts in income equal to the amounts that would have been included if the stock were a bond with OID (Code Sec. 305(e)). The person who strips the dividends and retains the stock is treated as having purchased the stock on the date that the dividend rights were sold (Code Sec. 305(e)(3)). The seller's adjusted basis in the stripped preferred stock is treated as the purchase price.

American Jobs Creation Act Impact

IRS regulations to address stripped bonds and/or preferred stock held by funds.—The new provision gives the IRS authority to write regulations that will address the tax treatment of stripped bonds and preferred stock that are held by a fund, an account or other type of entity. The regulations will only apply to those funds or accounts when *substantially all* of the entity's assets consist of bonds and/or preferred stock (Code Sec. 1286(f), as added by the American Jobs Creation Act of 2004). The Conference Committee Report (H.R. Conf. Rep. No. 108-755) states that the regulations are to deal with those situations when current law and regulations do not address the tax treatment of bonds or preferred stock.

Comment: The House Conference Report (H.R. Rep. No. 108-548) states that giving this regulatory authority to the IRS was warranted in order to address tax avoidance transactions that taxpayers may be entering into. The Report specifically mentions transactions involving the buying or selling of bonds and/or preferred stock when the transactions act to generate artificial losses, or defer the recognition of ordinary income and convert the income into capital gains.

Planning Note: The IRS regulations will address situations involving funds or accounts when *substantially all* the fund's or entity's assets are in bonds and/or preferred stock. At this point, how the IRS will define the term *substantially all* is unknown. However, in situations involving the determination of how the term should be defined, the IRS and the courts have sometimes held that it can range from 80 percent to 90 percent (e.g., see Reg. §1.41-2(d)(2) and Rev. Proc. 86-42, 1986-2 CB 722). It must be noted that these cited references do not involve bonds and/or preferred stock. However, it is clear that the term *substantially all* is meant to encompass more than a simple majority (i.e., 51 percent) of a fund's assets, but it does not require that 100 percent of the fund's assets consist of these types of assets.

Committee's example. In considering what types of transactions the IRS will address in its future regulations, the Conference Committee Report (H.R. Conf. Rep. No. 108-755) does provide one example of a situation where the IRS regulations could apply. According to the Report, the regulations could apply to a transaction that involves a person who effectively strips future dividends from money market shares held by a mutual fund and then contributes the shares and future dividends to a custodial account. Acting through the custodial account, another person would then purchase the right to either the stripped shares or the stripped future shares.

Planning Note: The Conference Committee Report (H.R. Conf. Rep. No. 108-755) makes clear that the IRS regulations *will not* apply to transactions involving direct or indirect interests in a fund where substantially all of its assets are held in tax-exempt obligations as defined by Code Sec. 1275(a)(3). The Report specifically mentions that a tax-exempt bond partnership that is described in Rev. Proc. 2002-68, I.R.B. 2002-43, 753, is an example of the type of fund that will *not* be covered by the future IRS regulations. (However, see Caution Note below.) The basic structure of a tax-exempt bond partnership is as follows: The partnership receives a tax-exempt obligation from a sponsor. The partnership then issues two classes of equity interests: (1) interests that are entitled to a preferred variable return on its capital (variable-rate interests), and (2) interests that are entitled to all of the remaining income of the partnership (inverse interest). As a result of the partnership's structure, the partner that holds a variable-rate interest receives a return that is equivalent to the return on a variable-rate tax-exempt bond.

Caution Note: The Conference Committee Report (H.R. Conf. Rep. No. 108-755) states that Rev. Proc. 2002-68 should be consulted in order to establish the type of tax-exempt bond partnership that might be exempt from the new law. However, Rev. Proc. 2003-84, I.R.B. 2003-48, has modified and superseded

Rev. Proc. 2002-68. In addition, the House Committee Report (H.R. Rep. No. 108-548) states that it is Rev. Proc. 2003-84 that should be consulted. Based upon these facts, it appears that Rev. Proc. 2003-84 is the valid document to use as a reference.

Future regulations. According to the Conference Committee Report (H.R. Conf. Rep. No. 108-755), the IRS regulations will, as a general rule, be applied prospectively. However, a proviso concludes that the regulations may be applied retrospectively in order to prevent abuse of the tax provisions.

Caution Note: The Conference Committee Report (H.R. Conf. Rep. No. 108-755) comments that the new regulatory authority that has been given to the IRS is not intended to infer anything with regard to the current tax treatment of bonds and/or preferred stock held by a fund when substantially all the fund's assets consist of these assets.

For further information on this subject, consult any of the following CCH reporter explanations:

- Standard Federal Tax Reporter, 2004FED ¶15,402.042, ¶31,481.01 and ¶31,481.021

- Federal Tax Service, FTS § E:5.122, § E:8.204 and § K:13.160

- Federal Tax Guide, 2004FTG ¶5854

★ *Effective date.* This provision applies to purchases and dispositions made after the date of enactment (Act Sec. 831(c) of the American Jobs Creation Act of 2004).

Act Sec. 831(a) of the American Jobs Creation Act of 2004, redesignating Code Sec. 1286(f) as Code Sec. 1286(g) and adding new Code Sec. 1286(f); Act Sec. 831(b), adding Code Sec. 305(e)(7); Act Sec. 831(c). Law at ¶5295 and ¶5830. Committee Report at ¶11,140.

¶730

Straddle Rules Modified

Background _____

A "straddle" can be generally defined as a type of financial transaction whereby an investor holds offsetting positions in personal property. By engaging in these offsetting positions, the investor seeks to diminish the risk of loss. The tax consequences to a taxpayer who uses a straddle as an investment technique are determined under the rules established by Code Sec. 1092.

The use of straddles as an investment tool can be exceedingly complex. As a result, the tax rules governing the treatment of straddles has grown in complexity. Some of these rules are discussed in the following material.

Straddle losses. One of the main purposes of Code Sec. 1092 is to establish a loss deferral rule. This rule provides that any realized loss with respect to certain straddle positions (known as "unidentified straddles") is allowed only to the extent that the realized loss exceeds the taxpayer's unrealized gain (i.e., paper profit) in the offsetting positions (Code Sec. 1092(a)(1)(A)). The amount of the unallowed realized loss is carried forward to the next year and its deductibility is subject to the same deferral provision (Code Sec. 1092(a)(1)(B)). However, in the case of "identified straddles," realized losses are not subject to this deferral rule. Instead, realized losses are netted against realized gains when all the positions in the identified straddle are closed (Code Sec. 1092(a)(2)(A)).

Background _____

Identified straddle defined. Basically, the term "identified straddle" is defined as a straddle: (1) that is identified in the taxpayer's records before the close of the day it was acquired (Code Sec. 1092(a)(2(B)(i)), (2) where all of the positions are acquired on the same day, and (a) all of the positions are disposed of on the same day, or (b) none of the positions were disposed of as of the close of the tax year (Code Sec. 1092(a)(2)(B)(ii)), and (3) that is not part of a larger straddle (Code Sec. 1092(a)(2(B)(iii)).

Unbalanced straddles. In a perfect financial world, one position of a straddle would exactly offset the other position (i.e., a balanced straddle). However, on occasion one position will only offset a portion of one or more other positions (i.e., an unbalanced straddle). On other occasions, the taxpayer may hold identical property in various accounts, and it may be unclear which of the properties is the offsetting position in the straddle. In order to avoid confusion in situations involving unbalanced straddles, in 1981, Congress directed the IRS to issue regulations that would determine how the rules are to be applied to these unbalanced straddles (Code Sec. 1092(c)(2)(B)). Although the IRS never provided the needed regulations, it did provide some insight into its thinking on this subject in a private letter ruling (IRS Letter Ruling 199925044, Feb. 3, 1999). In this private letter ruling, the IRS stated that in the absence of regulations, it was permissible for the taxpayer who was involved in the unbalanced straddle to use the identification procedures contained in Reg. § 1.1012-1(c)(2) and (3), or Temporary Reg. § 1.1092(b)-3T(d)(4). In essence, both of these regulations require the taxpayer to take definitive steps to identify the property involved in the transaction, and in some situations to receive corroboration from a third party (e.g., a broker). Of course, the holding of this private letter ruling cannot be used as a legal authority by any other taxpayer. As a result, in the absence of regulations, no firm identification procedures have ever been established for unbalanced straddles.

Stock excluded from straddle rules. Stock may be *excluded* from the type of personal property that is subject to the straddle rules (Code Sec. 1092(d)(3)(A)). However, an offsetting position in stock will come under the straddle rules if the other offsetting position involves a stock option, security futures contracts, or substantially similar property (Code Sec. 1092(d)(3)(B)(i)). Also, stock in a corporation formed or used to take offsetting positions to positions established by any shareholder comes under the straddle rules (Code Sec. 1092(d)(3)(B)(i)).

> **Comment:** As a practical matter, the exclusion of stock from the straddle rules has been becoming exceedingly narrow. For example, under an IRS proposed regulation, the exclusion for stock would, in most situations, be limited to offsetting positions involving direct ownership of stock, or short sales of stock (Proposed Reg. § 1.1092(d)-2(c)).

Unrecognized gain defined. In situations involving "unidentified straddles," the taxpayer must be able to determine the amount of the unrecognized gain at the end of the tax year. This is necessary because any realized loss on the offsetting position may only be claimed to the extent of unrecognized loss.

> **Example:** On July 1, 2004, Tom Adams enters into an unidentified straddle. On December 16, 2004, he closed one position of the straddle at a loss of $15,000. On December 31, 2004, the end of his tax year, Tom has an unrecognized gain of $12,750 in the offsetting open position. On his 2004 return, Tom's deductible loss on the position he closed is limited to $2,250 ($15,000 realized loss minus $12,750 unrecognized gain). He must carry his excess realized loss of $12,750 ($15,000 total realized loss minus $2,250 deductible loss in 2004) forward to 2005.

¶730

Background

> **Comment:** Although a straddle transaction has many of the same character-istics as a hedging transaction, these two types of transactions are treated differently under the tax law. A hedging transaction is defined as a transaction that is entered into in the normal course of the taxpayer's business, and used primarily to manage certain business risks (e.g., price changes, interest rate changes and/or currency fluctuations) (Code Sec. 1221(b)(2)(A)). Gain or loss from hedging transactions is generally classified as ordinary because it arises from a business activity. Conversely, gain or loss from straddle transactions is generally treated as capital because it arises from an investment activity.

American Jobs Creation Act Impact

Modified rules pertain to identified straddles and other provisions.—The modified rules have brought about the following changes:

(1) a required basis adjustment in situations involving identified straddles (Code Sec. 1092(a)(2)(A), as amended by the American Jobs Creation Act of 2004);

(2) a change in the definition of identified straddles (Code Sec. 1092(a)(2)(B), as amended by the 2004 Jobs Act);

(3) a method of computing the amount of unrecognized gain in an identi-fied straddle (Code Sec. 1092(a)(3)(B), as added by the 2004 Jobs Act);

(4) a clarification pertaining to situations when the taxpayer settles a position by the delivery of property (Code Sec. 1092(d)(8), as added by the 2004 Jobs Act);

(5) the inclusion of stock within the definition of personal property (Code Sec. 1092(d)(3), as amended by the 2004 Jobs Act); and

(6) the manner of calculating whether stock offered by a qualified covered call option has been held the requisite number of days for the dividend exclusion to apply (Code Sec. 246(c), as amended by the 2004 Jobs Act).

These changes are discussed in the following explanations.

> **Comment:** The House Committee Report (H.R. Rep. No. 108-548) comments that one of the reasons for this modification of the straddle rules is that while the IRS has had the authority to issue regulations pertaining to "unbalanced strad-dles" (Code Sec. 1092(c)(2)(B)), before repeal by the 2004 Jobs Act), the needed regulations have never been issued. Therefore, the Committee believed it was time to issue the needed guidance by amending the Code. The Committee also noted that additional modifications were needed due to prior changes in the law, and the need for clarification in certain tax aspects of straddles.

Identified straddles—Basis adjustment. Under the new provisions, the deferral of loss rules that apply to identified straddles applies only to "identified positions" that make up the "identified straddle" (Code Sec. 1092(a)(2)(A)(i), as amended by the 2004 Jobs Act). When there is a loss with respect to any identified position in the identified straddle, the taxpayer's basis in each of the offsetting positions of the straddle must be increased by a certain amount. The amount of the required increase bears the same ratio to the loss as the "unrecognized gain" for the offsetting position bears to the total "unrecognized gain" for all the offsetting positions (Code Sec. 1092(a)(2)(A)(ii), as amended by the 2004 Jobs Act). (See, *"Computing unrecognized gain in identified straddles,"* below, for information concerning the determination of "unrecognized gain.") The loss determined under this rule may only be taken into account by

¶730

adjusting the taxpayer's basis in the offsetting positions (Code Sec. 1092(a)(2)(A)(iii), as amended by the 2004 Jobs Act).

Computing unrecognized gain in identified straddles. When a taxpayer is required to make an adjustment to basis in an identified straddle (see *"Identified straddles—Basis adjustment,"* above), the amount of unrecognized gain must be computed (Code Sec. 1092(a)(2)(A)(ii), as amended by the 2004 Jobs Act). The term "unrecognized gain" is defined as the amount that is equal to the excess of the fair market value of the identified offsetting position (i.e., Gain Position) at the time the taxpayer incurs a loss on another identified position (i.e., Loss Position), over the fair market value of the Gain Position at the time it was identified as being part of the identified straddle (i.e., Gain Position and Loss Position) (Code Sec. 1092(a)(3)(B), as amended by the 2004 Jobs Act).

Example 1: On January 4, 2005, Jim Burr enters into an identified straddle that consists of Position A and Position B. At the time the straddle was created, Jim's basis in Position A was $2,200 and its fair market value was $2,400. At the same time, his basis in Position B was $2,000 and its fair market value was $2,600. On May 5, 2005, Jim terminates Position A for $1,800 and as a result has a realized loss of $400 ($2,200 basis minus $1,800 amount received). At the same time, the fair market value of Position B is $2,700. Under the new rules that pertain to identified straddles, Jim must adjust his basis in Position B by the ratio of the loss on Position A that is equal to the ratio of his unrecognized gain in Position B to the total unrecognized gain in all the offsetting positions. (In this example, Jim only had one offsetting position to his loss position.) His unrecognized gain on Position B is equal to the fair market value of the position at the time Position A was terminated ($2,700) minus the fair market value of Position B at the time the straddle was created ($2,600). Thus, Jim's unrecognized gain for Position B was $100 ($2,700 minus $2,600) at the time Position A was terminated. Because Jim only held one offsetting position, the full amount of the realized loss of $400 on Position A is added to Jim's basis in Position B. His adjusted basis in Position B is now $2,400 ($2,000 original basis plus $400 realized loss from Position A).

Identified straddle defined. The new provision modifies the definition of an "identified straddle" by providing that the term refers to straddles only when the *value* of each position is *not less* than the *basis* of each position in the hands of the taxpayer at the time the straddle is created (Code Sec. 1092(a)(2)(B)(ii), as amended by the 2004 Jobs Act). The value of each position is determined in the hands of the taxpayer immediately before the creation of the straddle. The IRS is to provide regulations providing the details how such values will be determined.

Example 2: On January 5, 2005, Mark Madison enters into a straddle transaction that consists of Position A and Position B. At the time the straddle is created, the value of Position A is $3,000 and Mark's basis in the position is $2,800. At the same time, the value of Position B is $3,200 and Mark's basis in the position is $2,900. Based on these facts, the straddle can qualify as an "identified straddle" because the value of each position immediately before the creation of the straddle is not less than Mark's basis in each position.

Planning Note: The IRS is given the task of providing regulations that specify the proper methods to be used for identifying an identified straddle and the positions that make up the straddle. The regulations are to address such issues as the consequences of not properly identifying the positions in the straddle and the ordering rules that will apply when a taxpayer only disposes a portion of the identified straddle (Code Sec. 1092(a)(2)(B), flush sentence at the

¶730

end, as added by the 2004 Jobs Act). This mandate that directs the IRS to provide regulations that will provide rules for the adequate identification of offsetting positions is Congress's attempt to end the problems and confusion that have occurred in "unbalanced straddles" where identification guidelines have been lacking. With regard to situations when the future regulations will provide guidance concerning proper identification of positions, the Committee Report observes that it may be necessary to establish rules that require all balanced offsetting positions to be included in an identified straddle. The Committee noted that this rule would be called for when a taxpayer elects to identify any of the offsetting positions as an identified straddle.

Comment: Although some rules covering identified straddles have been modified, many fundamental rules remain unchanged. For example, if a position is not identified as being part of an identified straddle, it may not offset any position that is part of the identified straddle (Code Sec. 1092(c)(2)(B), as redesignated by the 2004 Jobs Act).

Physically settled positions. A new provision clarifies the tax treatment of a straddle when a taxpayer settles a position by the physical delivery of property to which the position pertained (Code Sec. 1092(d)(8), as added by the 2004 Jobs Act). The clarification applies to those situations in which the taxpayer would have realized a loss if the position had been terminated, as opposed to settled by the physical delivery of property. For purposes of determining the taxpayer's realized loss, the taxpayer will be treated as if he had: (1) terminated the position for its fair market value immediately before settlement, and (2) sold the delivered property at its fair market value.

Stock covered by straddle rules. The term "personal property" has been broadened to include stock (Code Sec. 1092(d)(3), as amended by the 2004 Jobs Act).

Planning Note: As a result of this change, the former rule that generally excluded stock from the straddle rules is no longer in effect. However, certain qualified covered call options are still *not* classified as straddles (Code Sec. 1092(c)(4)).

Stock is treated as personal property, and thus subject to the straddle rules under Code Sec. 1092(d)(1), when it is:

(1) any stock that is part of a straddle and at least one of the offsetting positions is with respect to the stock or substantially similar or substantially related property (Code Sec. 1092(d)(3)(A)(i), as amended by the 2004 Jobs Act), or

(2) any stock of a corporation that was formed or used to take positions in personal property that are used to offset positions taken by a shareholder (Code Sec. 1092(d)(3)(A)(ii), as amended by the 2004 Jobs Act).

Planning Note: Certain hedging transactions are not covered by the straddle rules (Code Sec. 1092(e)). In making the determination of whether stock is part of a hedging transaction, all "affiliated group corporations" (as that term is defined under the provisions of Code Sec. 1504(a)) are treated as one taxpayer (Code Sec. 1092(d)(3)(B), as amended by the 2004 Jobs Act).

Planning Note: With regard to making the determination whether a position in stock is offset by a position in "substantially similar or related property," the House Ways and Means Committee Report states that it is their intent that the current IRS regulations will apply when making the determination. At present, Reg. § 1.1092(d)-2(a) refers to the definition contained in Reg. § 1.246-5 (with the exception of Reg. § 1.246-5(b)(3)) in order to make the determination.

Basically, Reg. § 1.246-5(b)(1) provides that the determination of whether property is substantially similar or related to stock is made on a facts-and-circumstances basis. However, the test will generally be satisfied when the fair market value of the property and the stock primarily reflect the performance of: (1) a single firm or enterprise; (2) the same industry or industries; or (3) the same economic factors (e.g., interest rates, foreign exchange rates, or commodity prices).

Holding period for dividend exclusion. When a corporation grants certain covered call options that are covered by the rules of Code Sec. 1092(f), it may not include the period of time it was protected from loss when determining if it met the holding period requirement for the exclusion of corporate dividends it has received (Code Sec. 246(c), last sentence, as added by the 2004 Jobs Act). As a result of this change, a corporation, when making the calculation to determine if it held the stock for at least 46 days (at least 91 days for preferred stock), and thus qualifying for the dividend exclusion, may not count the days during which it was the grantor of the option (Code Sec. 1092(f)(2)).

> **Comment:** The Code uses the term "qualified covered call option" in Code Sec. 1092(f), whereas the Committee Report in describing the new provision refers to an " in-the-money call option." According to a definition provided by the Chicago Board Options Exchange (CBOE), a call option is "in-the-money" when the underlying security is higher than the striking price of the call. Similarly, the Code requires that the qualified covered call option rules apply when "the stock has a strike price less than the applicable stock price" (Code Sec. 1092(f)). In short, both terms refer to the same type of financial transaction.

For further information on this subject, consult any of the following CCH reporter explanations:

- Standard Federal Tax Reporter, 2004FED ¶ 30,206.01 and ¶ 30,206.023
- Federal Tax Service, FTS § E:16.80
- Federal Tax Guide, 2004FTG ¶ 5496, ¶ 5498 and ¶ 5849

★ *Effective date.* These amendments are effective for positions established on or after the date of enactment (Act Sec. 888(e) of the American Jobs Creation Act of 2004).

Act Sec. 888(a)(1) of the American Jobs Creation Act of 2004, amending Code Sec. 1092(a)(2)(A); Act Sec. 888(a)(2)(A)-(B), amending Code Sec. 1092(a)(2)(B); Act Sec. 888(a)(3), redesignating Code Sec. 1092(a)(3)(B) as Code Sec. 1092(a)(3)(C) and adding Code Sec. 1092(a)(3)(B); Act Sec. 888(a)(4), redesignating Code Sec. 1092(c)(2)(B) as Code Sec. 1092(c)(2)(C); Act Sec. 888(b), adding Code Sec. 1092(d)(8); Act Sec. 888(c)(1), amending Code Sec. 1092(d)(3); Act Sec. 888(c)(2), amending Code Sec. 1258(d)(1); Act Sec. 888(d), amending Code Sec. 246(c), the last sentence; Act Sec. 888(e). Law at ¶ 5255, ¶ 5775 and ¶ 5820. Committee Report at ¶ 11,600.

BOND ISSUES

¶ 735

Expansion of Qualified Small-Issue Bond Program

Background _____

Interest on certain small issues of private activity bonds is excludable from gross income if at least 95 percent of the bond proceeds is to be used to finance manufactur-

Background

ing facilities or the acquisition of certain agricultural land or equipment. These bond issues are "qualified small-issue bonds" if they have an aggregate authorized face amount of $1,000,000 or less. At the election of the issuer, the aggregate face amount of qualified small issue bonds may be increased to $10,000,000. If the election is made, the face amount of the bonds includes specified capital expenditures made during the six-year period beginning three years before the date of issue and ending three years after the date of issue.

American Jobs Creation Act Impact

Cap increased.—The American Jobs Creation Act of 2004 increases the cap on the amount of financing for small businesses to qualify for industrial development bonds with respect to bonds issued after September 30, 2009. Under the cap increase, capital expenditures of $10,000,000 or less, in addition to any capital expenditure described in Code Sec. 144(a)(4)(C), will not be taken into account for purposes of applying the rules in Code Sec. 144(a)(4)(A)(ii) for determining the aggregate face amount of the issue for bond issuers that elect to issue bonds under the higher $10,000,000 threshold (Code Sec. 144(a)(4)(G), as added by the 2004 Jobs Act). Thus, the maximum allowable amount of total capital expenditures by an eligible business or related party in the same municipality or county increases from $10,000,000 to $20,000,000.

> **Comment:** Qualified small-issue bonds, like most other private activity bonds, are subject to annual state private activity bond volume limitations. Therefore, the limitation that prohibits more than $10,000,000 of bond financing to be outstanding at any time for property of an eligible business located in the same locality and the $40,000,000 per borrower limitation continue to apply.

> **Caution Note:** The cap increase will not apply to bonds issued after September 30, 2009, for capital expenditures used to provide facilities where an urban development action grant has been made under Section 119 of the Housing and Community Development Act of 1974 (Code Sec. 144(a)(4)(F), as amended by the 2004 Jobs Act).

For further information on this subject, consult any of the following CCH reporter explanations:

- Standard Federal Tax Reporter, 2004FED ¶7814.01 and ¶7814.04
- Federal Tax Service, FTS § E:17.140
- Federal Tax Guide, 2004FTG ¶4793

★ *Effective date.* No specific effective date is provided by the 2004 Jobs Act. The provision is, therefore, considered effective on the date of enactment.

Act Sec. 340(a) of the American Jobs Creation Act of 2004, adding Code Sec. 144(a)(4)(G); Act Sec. 340(b), amending Code Sec. 144(a)(4)(F). Law at ¶5150. Committee Report at ¶10,550.

¶745

Qualified Green Building and Sustainable Design Project Bonds

Background

States or local governments may provide tax-exempt financing for private activities by issuing private activity bonds (PABs) (Code Secs. 103 and 141). Interest on PABs is tax-exempt only if the PABs are classified as exempt facility bonds, qualified small issue bonds, qualified redevelopment bonds, qualified Code Sec. 501(c)(3) bonds, qualified mortgage bonds, qualified veterans' mortgage bonds, qualified student loan bonds, and eligible empowerment zone and enterprise community businesses (Code Sec. 141(e)).

To qualify as an exempt facility bond, at least 95 percent of the net proceeds of the bond must be used to finance one of the following exempt facilities:

    (1) airports,

    (2) docks and wharves,

    (3) mass commuting facilities,

    (4) facilities for the furnishing of water,

    (5) sewage facilities,

    (6) solid waste disposal facilities,

    (7) qualified residential rental projects,

    (8) facilities for the local furnishing of electric energy or gas,

    (9) local district heating or cooling facilities,

    (10) qualified hazardous waste facilities,

    (11) high-speed intercity rail facilities,

    (12) environmental enhancements of hydroelectric generating facilities, or

    (13) qualified public educational facilities (Code Sec. 142(a)).

Many types of PABs are taxable if the aggregate face value of the bonds, when added to the total amount of PABs issued during the calendar year, exceeds the volume cap (Code Sec. 146(a)). For calendar years beginning in 2003, the amounts used to calculate the state ceiling for the PAB volume cap is the greater of $75 multiplied by the state population or $228,580,000 (Code Sec. 146(d)). Generally, the volume cap is divided, with one-half allocated to all state agencies, which are treated as a single unit, and the remainder allocated to all other issuers.

A volume cap applies to all private activity bonds issued after August 15, 1986, with the following exceptions:

    (1) qualified veterans' mortgage bonds;

    (2) qualified Code Sec. 501(c)(3) bonds, which are subject to their own volume caps;

    (3) exempt facility bonds that are part of an issue of which at least 95 percent of the net bond proceeds are used to finance airports, docks and wharves, environmental enhancements of hydroelectric generating facilities, or qualified public educational facilities;

    (4) 75 percent of any exempt facility bonds issued to finance high-speed intercity rail facilities, if the bond-financed property is privately owned, and 100 percent for such bonds issued after 1993, if all of the property is owned by a governmental unit; or

    (5) exempt facility bonds for solid waste disposal facilities that are government-owned (privately owned solid waste disposal facilities will be treated as being government-owned, if they are subject to leases of not more than 20 years) (Code Sec. 146(g) and (h)).

Brownfield redevelopment sites and green buildings. A brownfield site is real property, the expansion, redevelopment, or reuse of which may be complicated by

Background

the presence or potential presence of a hazardous substance, pollutant, or contaminant (Section 101 of the Comprehensive Environmental Response, Compensation, and Liability Act of 1980 (42 U.S.C. §9601)). Brownfield sites are dangerous to neighboring areas from both a safety and health perspective. Usually, brownfield sites are identifiable by their appearance—abandoned or neglected properties with or without some type of industrial structure.

> **Comment:** Brownfield redevelopment is beneficial to the community. However, there is a reluctance to undertake brownfield redevelopment due to a lack of funding for cleanup, concerns regarding liability, the need for environmental assessments of the properties, uncertainty as to cleanup standards, unfavorable neighborhood and market conditions, land-assembly issues, and a reluctance to invest in distressed communities due to concerns with urban socioeconomic conditions.

The Taxpayer Relief Act of 1997 (P.L. 105-34) and the Community Renewal Tax Relief Act of 2000 (P.L. 106-554) provided for tax incentives intended to facilitate cleanup and reuse of contaminated property. Brownfield redevelopment was encouraged by allowing taxpayers to immediately reduce their taxable income by the cost of their eligible cleanup expenses (Code Sec. 198). This created an immediate tax advantage, helping to offset short-term cleanup costs.

Green buildings. The U.S. Green Building Council created the Leadership in Energy and Environmental Design (LEED) rating system, a voluntary, consensus-based national standard, for developing high-performance sustainable buildings. Various levels of certification are available, depending upon the number of LEED criteria that are satisfied by the structure. The LEED certification rating level is determined based on how environmentally sound and resource-efficient the structure proves to be. Buildings eligible for certification include, but are not limited to, offices, retail and service establishments, hotels, residential buildings of four or more habitable stories, and institutional buildings, such as libraries, schools, museums, and churches (H.R. Conf. Rep. No. 108-755).

> **Comment:** Green building promotes resource conservation, including energy efficiency, renewable energy, and water conservation. It considers environmental impact issues and waste minimization, while striving to reduce operation and maintenance costs. In addition, it addresses issues of historical preservation, access to public transportation, and other community infrastructures.

American Jobs Creation Act Impact

Qualified green building and sustainable design project bonds.—Qualified green building and sustainable design projects have been added to the list of facilities that can be financed by exempt facility bonds while continuing to maintain tax-exempt status (Code Sec. 142(a)(14), as added by the American Jobs Creation Act of 2004). This designation applies with respect to bonds issued before October 1, 2009 (Code Sec. 142(l)(8), as added by the 2004 Jobs Act). A qualified green bond is any bond issued as part of an issue that finances a project designated as a qualified green building and sustainable design project by the Treasury Secretary, after consultation with the Administrator of the Environmental Protection Agency (EPA).

Project designation process. Each project must be nominated by a state or local government within 180 days of enactment of the 2004 Jobs Act, and the state or local government must provide written assurances that the project will satisfy the eligibility criteria of Code Sec. 142(l)(4), as added by the 2004 Jobs Act (Code Sec. 142(l)(3), as added by the 2004 Jobs Act). The seven eligibility criteria are listed under the *Application process* section, below.

Within 60 days after the end of the application period, the Treasury Secretary, after consulting with the EPA Administrator, will designate qualified green building and sustainable design projects that meet the following criteria:

• at least 75 percent of the square footage of the commercial buildings that are part of the project is registered for LEED certification and is reasonably expected, at the time of designation, to receive certification (projects using wood, renewable wood, and composite wood products are credited points in determining certification);

• the project includes a brownfield site;

• the project receives support of at least $5 million in state or local government resources that may include tax abatement benefits and contributions in kind; and

• the project includes either one million square feet of building or at least 20 acres (Code Sec. 142(l)(1), as added by the 2004 Jobs Act).

No more than one project will be designated in a state, and designation will not be given to any project that includes a stadium or arena for professional sports exhibitions or games. At least one of the projects designated must be located in, or within a 10-mile radius of, an empowerment zone, as defined in Code Sec. 1391, and at least one designated project must be located in a rural state (Code Sec. 142(l)(2)(A), as added by the 2004 Jobs Act). A "rural state" is one that has a population of less than 4.5 million and a population density of less than 150 people per square mile according to the 2000 census, and has increased in population by less than half the rate of the national increase between the 1990 and 2000 censuses (Code Sec. 142(l)(6)(A), as added by the 2004 Jobs Act).

> **Comment:** Since 1994, areas in economically depressed sections of the country have been designated as empowerment zones. A number of tax incentives are available to taxpayers operating businesses in those areas. The tax breaks include a wage-based employment credit that motivates employers to hire workers living in the community (Code Sec. 51, as amended by the Working Families Tax Relief Act of 2004 (P.L. 108-311)), increased Code Sec. 179 deductions to boost investment in assets used in the targeted areas, and tax-exempt bond financing benefits.

The Treasury Secretary, after consultation with the EPA Administrator, must ensure that, in the aggregate, the projects designated will:

(1) reduce electric consumption by more than 150 megawatts annually, as compared to conventional construction;

(2) reduce daily sulfur dioxide emissions by at least 10 tons, compared to coal generation power;

(3) expand by 75 percent the domestic solar photovoltaic market in the United States (measured in megawatts), as compared to the expansion of that market from 2001 to 2002; and

(4) use at least 25 megawatts of fuel cell energy generation (Code Sec. 142(l)(2)(B), as added by the 2004 Jobs Act).

Application process. The application for each project must include a project proposal that describes the energy efficiency, renewable energy, and sustainable design features of the project, specifically:

- the amount of electric consumption reduced, as compared to conventional construction;

- the amount of sulfur dioxide daily emissions reduced, compared to coal generation;

- the amount of the gross installed capacity of the project's solar photovoltaic capacity measured in megawatts; and

- the amount of the project's fuel cell energy generation, measured in megawatts (Code Sec. 142(l)(4)(B), as added by the 2004 Jobs Act).

Each project application must also demonstrate that the project satisfies the following eligibility criteria:

(1) at least 75 percent of the square footage of the commercial buildings that are part of the project is registered for LEED certification and is reasonably expected, at the time of designation, to receive certification (projects using wood, renewable wood, and composite wood products are credited points in determining certification);

(2) the project includes a brownfield site;

(3) the project receives support of at least $5 million in state or local government resources that may include tax abatement benefits and contributions in kind;

(4) the project includes either one million square feet of building or at least 20 acres;

(5) the project is expected to provide permanent employment of at least 1,500 full-time equivalents (150 full-time equivalents in rural states) when completed, and construction employment of at least 1,000 full-time equivalents (100 full-time equivalents in rural states);

(6) the net benefit of the qualified green building and sustainable design project tax-exempt financing provided will be allocated for financing one or more of the following:

(a) the purchase, construction, integration, or other use of energy efficiency, renewable energy, and sustainable design features of the project;

(b) compliance with LEED certification standards; or

(c) the purchase, remediation, and foundation construction and preparation of the brownfield site; and

(7) the issue of exempt facility bonds will not be used for any facility that sells food or alcoholic beverages for consumption on the premises as its principal business (Code Sec. 142(l)(4)(A)(i) through (vii), as amended by the 2004 Jobs Act).

Additionally, the application must include an independent analysis describing the project's economic impact, including the amount of projected employment (Code Sec. 142(l)(4)(A), as added by the 2004 Jobs Act).

Comment: To further encourage the cleanup and reuse of contaminated property, the 2004 Jobs Act expands the list of properties that qualify for use of exempt facility bonds to finance brownfield redevelopment projects to include qualified green building and sustainable design projects.

Certification. Each project, within 30 days of the completion, must certify that the net benefit of the tax-exempt financing was used as described in the application process (item (6), above) (Code Sec. 142(l)(5), as added by the 2004 Jobs Act). The net benefit of the tax-exempt financing is the present value of the interest savings from the tax-exempt bonds (Code Sec. 142(l)(6)(C), as added by the 2004 Jobs Act).

Bond volume limitations. Qualified green bonds are *not* subject to the state bond volume limitations. There is a national qualified green bond limitation of $2 billion. The Treasury Secretary may allocate, in the aggregate, no more than $2 billion of bonds to qualified green building and sustainable design projects (Code Sec. 142(l)(7), as added by the 2004 Jobs Act). Further, qualified green building and sustainable design project bonds have been added to the list of bonds to which the state volume cap does not apply (Code Sec. 146(g)(3), as amended by the 2004 Jobs Act).

Treatment of current refunding bonds. Qualified green bonds may be currently refunded if certain conditions are met, but they cannot be advance refunded. The bond volume limitations and the termination of the exempt facility bond designation does not apply to any bond or series of bonds issued to refund a qualified green bond issued before October 1, 2009, if:

(1) the average maturity date of the issue of which the refunding bond is a part is no later than the average maturity date of the bonds that are to be refunded;

(2) the amount of the refunding bond does not exceed the outstanding amount of the refunded bond; and

(3) the net proceeds of the refunding bond are used to redeem the refunded bond no later than 90 days after the issuance date of the refunding bond (Code Sec. 142(l)(9), as added by the 2004 Jobs Act).

Accountability. Issuers must maintain an interest-bearing reserve account, on behalf of each project, in an amount equal to one percent of the net proceeds of any qualified green bond issued for the project. Within five years after the issuance date, the Treasury Secretary is to consult with the EPA Administrator to determine whether the project has substantially complied with the requirements described in the project application for designation, including certification. If the project is found to have substantially complied with those requirements, the funds in the reserve account, including interest, will be released to the project. If substantial compliance is lacking, the funds in the reserve account, including interest, will be forfeited to the U.S. Treasury (Act Sec. 701(d) of the 2004 Jobs Act).

For further information on this subject, consult any of the following CCH reporter explanations:

- Standard Federal Tax Reporter, 2004FED ¶7752.01 and ¶7752.021

- Federal Tax Service, FTS § E:17.100 and § E:17.101

- Federal Tax Guide, 2004FTG ¶4781

★ *Effective date.* These changes apply to qualified green bonds issued after December 31, 2004, and before October 1, 2009 (Act Sec. 701(e) of the American Jobs Creation Act of 2004).

Act Sec. 701(a) of the American Jobs Creation Act of 2004, adding Code Sec. 142(a)(14); Act Sec. 701(b), adding Code Sec. 142(l); Act Sec. 701(c), amending Code Sec. 146(g)(3); Act Sec. 701(d); Act Sec. 701(e). Law at ¶5145, ¶5155 and ¶7055. Committee Report at ¶10,830.

TIMBER SALES

¶ 750

Capital Gain Treatment Accorded to Outright Timber Sales

Background

Standing timber is a uniquely renewable resource that has been recognized as a capital asset by state real property laws. Standing timber that is neither used in a trade or business, nor held primarily for sale to customers in the ordinary course of a trade or business, is also a capital asset under federal income tax laws. Several factors determine the type of gain or loss incurred upon disposition of standing timber: ownership purpose; type of timber related activities in which the owner is normally engaged; manner of disposition; and the length of ownership. A timber owner making an outright sale of the timber (purchaser comes on the land and cuts) for a lump sum is disposing of a capital asset if the timber is not used in the owner's business, nor held primarily for sale in the ordinary course of a trade or business. Assuming the timber is held for the appropriate time period, the owner reports any gain realized as capital gain.

Historically, ordinary income treatment applied if the owner cut the timber for sale or use in his business. For example, a sawmill operator who owned standing timber and cut it for use in the mill was subject to ordinary income treatment on the difference between the basis of the standing timber and the value of the cut timber. If the sawmill operator had sold the standing timber outright, any gain would have been capital gain. The mill operator could then enter into a cutting contract with another standing timber owner (purchaser pays an amount per board foot of timber when he cuts and removes it), as needed. This, however, proved problematic to timber owners because the IRS treated cutting contract payments as royalty payments not subject to capital gain treatment. Therefore, standing timber owners preferred outright sales to cutting contract sale arrangements and frequently small sawmill operators had difficulty finding sellers willing to negotiate a cutting contract. In addition, forest management was generally ignored due to the high percentage of outright sales and some form of stimulation was needed to encourage growth of forest resources.

The predecessor to Code Sec. 631, Code Sec. 117(k), was enacted in 1943 to introduce some equity to the standing timber income tax dilemma. The adoption of an election to treat the cutting of timber as a sale or exchange eligible for capital gain treatment equalized the tax playing field for those who managed their timber properties and cut timber for use in their businesses. Additionally, in certain situations capital gain treatment was accorded to the gain realized from timber sales if specified requirements were met. More favorable tax treatment across the timber industry resulted in a stimulation of timber growth, as well as the development of scientific forestry.

Code Sec. 631(a) provides an election to treat the cutting of timber as a sale or exchange of the timber and, therefore, eligible for capital gain treatment. The election applies to the cutting of timber for sale or for use in the taxpayer's trade or business. The election is limited to standing timber owners or to holders of a contract right to cut the timber. Specific holding period requirements must also be met. See ¶ 210 for changes made to this election provision by the American Jobs Creation Act of 2004.

A standing timber owner who disposes of timber, while retaining an economic interest in the timber, is entitled to capital gains treatment on any gain realized from the disposition, assuming compliance with the applicable holding requirements

Background

(Code Sec. 631(b)). For purposes of Code Sec. 631(b), the term owner includes a sublessor and a holder of a contract to cut timber. A standing timber owner who enters into a cutting contract retains an economic interest in the timber. Although cutting contracts are advantageous to the owner from a capital gain standpoint, the risk of physical loss rests with the owner until title passes to the buyer upon severance of the timber and payment. Cutting contracts also create an environment for possible purchaser fraud in the scaling (measurement) of the cut timber, or even removal with no scaling. Furthermore, purchasers may be less cautious in their cutting procedures, since they only pay for good quality timber. If they brake off trees while cutting, they pay nothing for them.

The essence of a retained economic interest is that the consideration paid must depend upon, or be directly related to, the severance of the timber. Only payments made to the owner that depend on the severance of the timber provide the owner with a retained economic interest. Owners do not retain any economic interest when receiving lump sum payments in an outright sale transaction. The buyer takes immediate title and assumes all risk of loss from the date of the sale until the felling of the timber.

American Jobs Creation Act Impact

Retained economic interest requirement does not apply to outright sales of timber.—Outright sales of standing timber after December 31, 2004, will qualify for capital gain treatment (Code Sec. 631(b), as amended by the 2004 Jobs Act). The requirement that the owner of timber must retain an economic interest in the timber in order to obtain capital gain treatment does not apply to outright sales of timber (Code Sec. 631(b), as amended by the 2004 Jobs Act).

> **Comment:** Small timber owners who essentially hold the standing timber as an investment and enter into infrequent sales transactions are entitled to capital gain treatment for any gain realized on the outright sale of timber. Historically, owners who periodically sold timber in outright transactions were often classified as dealers by the IRS because of the number of sales transactions. The preferential capital gain treatment was lost because their multiple transactions were treated as a business. Small standing timber owners tended to restrict their sales to cutting contract arrangements, with the attendant retained economic interest, to receive capital gain treatment under Code Sec. 631(b). Now, these same small timber owners can enter into multiple outright sales transactions and still receive the benefits of capital gain treatment under Code Sec. 631(b), as amended by the 2004 Jobs Act.

> **Planning:** In the current timber industry, outright sales offer timber owners the ability to get the best possible price for their timber through the use of sealed bids. Small standing timber owners can participate in the search for the best possible price, as well as shift the timber liability risks to the buyers, through the use of outright sales transactions without suffering adverse income tax ramifications.

> **Comment:** Although outright sales of timber pre-1943 resulted in poor timber management because of the cut and run mentality, this is no longer the case. Timber management is equally effective where cutting contracts predominate or where outright sales transactions are favored. However, the standing timber is subject to more abuse when a cutting contract is used. The buyer's focus is not on careful cutting, since he only pays for good quality timber. Broken trees do not economically impact buyers, nor does the trampling

of young trees. Providing for capital gain treatment in outright sales transactions, just as in the cutting contract situations, should result in less timber abuse generally across the timber industry as more timber owners choose outright sales.

Date of disposal. General tax rules as to the timing of income from a sale apply to outright sales of standing timber that receive capital gain treatment pursuant to Code Sec. 631(b). The special date of disposal rules enumerated in Code Sec. 631(b) apply to timber dispositions with a retained economic interest only (Code Sec. 631(b), as amended by the 2004 Jobs Act).

For further information on this subject, consult any of the following CCH reporter explanations:

- Standard Federal Tax Reporter, 2004FED ¶ 24,154.01

- Federal Tax Service, FTS § L:7.100

- Federal Tax Guide, 2004FTG ¶ 5520

★ *Effective date.* The provision is effective for sales of timber after December 31, 2004 (Act Sec. 315(c) of the American Jobs Creation Act of 2004).

Act Sec. 315(a) and (b) of the American Jobs Creation Act of 2004, amending Code Sec. 631(b); Act Sec. 315(c). Law at ¶ 5500. Committee Report at ¶ 10,380.

Chapter 8

Agriculture and Energy Resources

BIODIESEL CREDITS

¶ 805

Alcohol Fuel and Biodiesel Mixtures Excise Tax Credit

Background _____

An excise tax is imposed on the removal of any taxable fuel from a refinery or terminal, the entry of any taxable fuel into the United States, or the sale of any taxable fuel. Taxable fuels include gasoline, kerosene, and diesel fuel. The tax is equal to 18.4 cents per gallon for gasoline and 24.4 cents per gallon for kerosene and diesel fuel (Code Sec. 4081). A retail back-up tax is imposed on these fuels if the sale was not taxed under Code Sec. 4081 or if the tax was credited or refunded (Code Sec. 4041).

To encourage fossil fuel conservation, alcohol and gasoline mixtures are taxed at lower rates. Although the rates vary depending on the type and volume of alcohol used (ethanol or methanol), the lowest rates generally apply to mixtures with higher percentages of alcohol. For 2004 the following rates apply:

(1) 15.436 cents per gallon for mixtures that contain 5.7-percent ethanol (or 16.369 cents per gallon for mixtures that contain 5.7-percent methanol)

(2) 14.396 cents per gallon for mixtures that contain 7.7-percent ethanol (or 15.596 cents per gallon for mixtures that contain 7.7-percent methanol)

(3) 13.200 cents per gallon for mixtures that contain 10-percent ethanol (or 14.666 cents per gallon for mixtures that contain 10-percent methanol)

For 2005 the following rates apply:

(1) 15.493 cents per gallon for mixtures that contain 5.7-percent ethanol (or 16.429 cents per gallon for mixtures that contain 5.7-percent methanol)

(2) 14.473 cents per gallon for mixtures that contain 7.7-percent ethanol (or 15.680 cents per gallon for mixtures that contain 7.7-percent methanol)

(3) 13.300 cents per gallon for mixtures that contain 10-percent ethanol (or 14.778 cents per gallon for mixtures that contain 10-percent methanol)

Even lower rates apply to qualified ethanol and methanol. Qualified ethanol and methanol is any liquid that contains at least 85-percent ethanol or methanol. For 2004, qualified ethanol is taxed at 13.15 cents per gallon and qualified methanol is taxed at 12.35 cents per gallon. From January 1, 2005, through September 30, 2007, the rate of tax on qualified ethanol is 13.25 cents-per-gallon. (Code Sec. 4041(b)(2)).

Biodiesel. Biodiesel is a liquid composed of monoalkyl esters of long chain fatty acids derived from vegetable oils or animal fat. Biodiesel is suitable for use as fuel in a diesel-powered highway vehicle, but is not treated as a taxable diesel fuel because it contains less that four percent normal paraffins. However, it is subject to the Code Sec. 4041 retail tax if it is sold for use or used as a fuel in a diesel-powered highway vehicle or a diesel-powered train. If biodiesel is used in the production of a blended fuel, then an excise tax is imposed on the removal or sale of the blended taxable fuel (Rev. Rul. 2002-76, IRB 2002-46, 840). There is no reduced tax rate for biodiesel fuel.

Highway Trust Fund. The excise taxes imposed on gasoline, diesel fuel, and kerosene, with certain exceptions, are credited to the Highway Trust Fund (HTF). The HTF was created by the Highway Revenue Act of 1956 (P.L. 84-627) to fund the creation and maintenance of federal highways. The taxes are collected and deposited into the HTF, except that one-tenth of a cent per gallon is deducted for the Leaking Underground Storage Tank Trust Fund (LUST), and 2.86 cents are transferred into the Mass Transit Fund (MTF). The result is that for each gallon of gasoline, 15.44 cents is deposited into the HTF (18.4 cents/gallon excise tax − .1 cent − 2.86 cents).

For alcohol fuel blends, an additional 2.5 cents per gallon stays in the Treasury's general fund. Because alcohol fuel blends are taxed at lower rates and 2.5 cents is retained by the general fund, a significantly reduced dollar amount is contributed to the HTF from alcohol fuel blends. In the case of a mixture that contains 10-percent ethanol, only 7.74 cents per gallon is credited to the HTF (13.2 cents/gallon excise tax − .1 cent − 2.86 cents − 2.5 cents) (Code Sec. 9503).

Refund of tax on fuels used for nontaxable purpose. A credit or refund is available where taxable fuel is used to produce an alcohol and gasoline mixture. The amount of the credit or refund is the difference between the gasoline, diesel or kerosene excise tax paid and the excise tax that would have been paid on the production of the fuel mixture. Taxpayers can apply for a "quick refund" if $200 or more is payable for the time period for which the refund is claimed and the period is not less than one week. In the case of a quick refund, interest accrues on the refund amount if not paid within 20 days of the date the claim is filed (Code Sec. 6427(i)(3)).

¶805

Background

Registration requirement. Blenders, enterers, refiners, terminal operators, position holders, pipeline and vessel operators must register with IRS by filing Form 637, Application for Registration (For Certain Excise Tax Activities) before engaging in certain excise tax activities (Code Sec. 4101(a) and Reg. § 48.4101-1).

Alcohol fuels credit. A nonrefundable credit for alcohol fuels is available under Code Sec. 40. The amount of the credit is equal to the sum of the alcohol mixture credit, alcohol credit and small ethanol producer credit (Code Sec. 40(b) and (d)). The credit is computed as follows:

> (1) 60 cents per gallon on alcohol at least 190 proof used to produce a qualified alcohol mixture (45 cents per gallon on alcohol between 150 and 190 proof); plus

> (2) 60 cents per gallon on alcohol that is at least 190 proof and is not a mixture with gas or special fuel (45 cents per gallon on alcohol between 150 and 190 proof); plus

> (3) 10 cents per gallon of qualified ethanol fuel produced by a small ethanol producer (a taxpayer whose ethanol production does not exceed 30 million gallons a year).

The total credit amount is reduced by the amount of any benefit derived from the lower excise tax rates that apply to alcohol and gasoline mixtures (Code Sec. 40(c)).

The credit for alcohol fuels applies to any sale or use of alcohol fuels for any period before January 1, 2008. The credit will not apply for any period before January 1, 2008, that the excise tax imposed by Code Sec. 4081 is 4.3 cents per gallon (Code Sec. 40(e)(1)).

Lower alcohol mixture and alcohol credit amounts apply to taxpayers who mix ethanol and gasoline ("ethanol blenders"). For blenders of ethanol, the credit amounts equal 52 cents per gallon of ethanol used for 2004 (38.52 cents for low-proof blends) and 51 cents for 2005 through 2007 (37.78 cents for low-proof blends). The credit applies to the sale or use of ethanol blended fuels through 2007. Alternatively, registered ethanol blenders can forgo the credit and opt to pay the reduced rates of tax on gasoline purchased for blending with ethanol or methanol.

American Jobs Creation Act Impact

Alcohol fuel and biodiesel mixtures excise tax credit.—The new law eliminates reduced rates of excise tax for most alcohol-blended fuels and imposes the full rate of tax on the blends. In their place, the new law creates a credit for alcohol fuel and biodiesel mixtures that is claimed against the excise tax imposed by Code Sec. 4081 on certain removals, entries and sales of taxable fuels. The total credit amount is the sum of two components: the alcohol fuel mixture credit and the biodiesel mixture credit (Code Sec. 6426, as added by the American Jobs Creation Act of 2004).

> **Caution Note:** While the alcohol fuel and biodiesel mixture credits apply to fuel sold or used after December 31, 2004, they terminate on different dates. The alcohol fuel mixture credit does not apply to any sale, use, or removal for any period after December 31, 2010. Whereas, the biodiesel mixture credit does not apply to any sale, use, or removal for any period after December 31, 2006 (Code Sec. 6426(b)(5) and (c)(6), as added by the 2004 Jobs Act).

Alcohol fuel mixture credit. The amount of the alcohol fuel mixture credit is determined by multiplying the number of gallons of alcohol used by the taxpayer to produce any alcohol fuel mixture for sale in the taxpayer's trade or business by the applicable amount. The applicable amount is:

(1) 51 cents, or

(2) 60 cents if none of the alcohol in the alcohol fuel mixture consists of ethanol.

An "alcohol fuel mixture" is any mixture of alcohol and a taxable fuel that is sold by the producer to any person for use as a fuel or used as a fuel by the producer. A mixture produced by any refinery prior to a taxable event, which includes ethyl tertiary butyl ether or other ethers produced from alcohol is treated as sold at the time of its removal from the refinery *and only at such time* to another person for use as a fuel. The term "alcohol" includes methanol, ethanol, and the alcohol gallon equivalent of ethyl tertiary butyl ether or other ethers produced from alcohol. It does not include alcohol produced from petroleum, natural gas, coal (including peat), or alcohol with a proof of less than 190. The proof of alcohol is determined without regard to any added denaturants. The term "taxable fuel" means gasoline, diesel fuel, and kerosene as provided in Code Sec. 4083(a)(1) (Code Sec. 6426(b), as added by the 2004 Jobs Act).

> **Example:** Energy Corporation is a fuel supplier that sells a mixture of 85-percent ethanol and 15-percent unleaded gasoline (E85) to various carriers for distribution to retail gas stations. In 2005, Energy Corporation sells 1,000,000 gallons of E85. It used 850,000 gallons of ethanol in the production of the 1,000,000 gallons of E85 sold. Energy Corporation's excise tax liability under Code Sec. 4081 is $132,500 (13.25 cents/gallon × 1,000,000 gallons of E85). Under the new law, they are entitled to an alcohol fuel mixture credit of $43,350 (51 cents/gallon of ethanol × 850,000 gallons of ethanol used in 2005).

Biodiesel mixture credit. The amount of the biodiesel mixture credit is determined by multiplying the number of gallons of biodiesel used by the taxpayer to produce any biodiesel mixture for sale or use in the taxpayer's trade or business, by the applicable amount. The applicable amount is:

(1) 50 cents, or

(2) $1.00 in the case of any biodiesel that is agri-biodiesel.

"Biodiesel mixture" is any mixture of a biodiesel and diesel fuel determined without regard to any use of kerosene that is sold by the producer to any person for use as a fuel or used as a fuel by the producer. "Agri-biodiesel" means biodiesel derived solely from virgin oils, including esters derived from virgin vegetable oils from corn, soybeans, sunflower seeds, cottonseeds, canola, crambe, rapeseeds, safflowers, flaxseeds, rice bran and mustard seeds, and from animal fats (Code Secs. 40A(d)(2) and 6426(c)(5)), as added by the 2004 Jobs Act).

To claim the biodiesel mixture credit, the taxpayer must obtain certification from the producer of the biodiesel. The certification must specify the product produced and the percentages of biodiesel and agri-biodiesel in the product. The IRS is to prescribe the form and the manner of certification (Code Sec. 6426(c)(4), as added by the 2004 Jobs Act).

> **Example:** Bio-Tech Coop is a fuel blender that produces B20. B20 is an agri-biodiesel mixture of a 20-percent soybean source and 80-percent petroleum diesel. In 2005, Bio-Tech sells 1,000,000 gallons of B20. They use 200,000 gallons of soy biodiesel in producing the total quantity of the agri-biodiesel mixture sold. Their excise tax liability for 2005 is $244,000 (1,000,000 gallons of agri-biodiesel × 24.4 cents). They may claim a credit of $200,000 (200,000 gallons × $1.00).

Caution Note: After September 30, 2005, the 24.4 cents per gallon excise tax, used in the above example, is scheduled to drop to 4.3 cents per gallon (Code Sec. 4081(d)(1)). In all likelihood, however, the rate will not drop, because Congress will extend it as part of comprehensive highway reauthorization legislation that it is slated to consider in 2005.

A tax is imposed if the alcohol or biodiesel mixture credits are claimed and the alcohol or biodiesel is separated from the mixture or, without separation, the mixture is not used as fuel. The amount of the tax imposed is equal to the applicable amount multiplied by the number of gallons of alcohol or biodiesel (Code Sec. 6426(d), as added by the 2004 Jobs Act).

Coordination with other excise tax benefits. Taxpayers may not take the full benefit of both the alcohol fuel credit under Code Sec. 40 and the new alcohol fuel and biodiesel mixture credit. Under regulations to be prescribed, the amount of the alcohol fuel credit must be reduced by any amount claimed as a credit for alcohol fuel or biodiesel mixtures (Code Sec. 40(c), as amended by the 2004 Jobs Act and Code Sec. 6426(e), as added by the 2004 Jobs Act).

Refund claims. For claims filed after December 31, 2004, the new law distinguishes between electronic and paper claims for a refund of taxes paid by any person who used fully taxed gasoline, diesel or kerosene fuel to produce a qualified alcohol mixture. For paper refund claims, the time period within which the blender's claim must be paid before interest starts to accrue is extended from 20 to 45 days. However, for claims filed electronically, the time period remains the same and interest begins to accrue if the claim is not paid within 20 days. Additionally, taxpayers may claim a refund of less than $200 if the claim is filed electronically (Code Sec. 6427(i)(3), as amended by the 2004 Jobs Act). The IRS is required to prescribe the electronic format for filing such claims no later than December 31, 2004 (Act Sec. 301(e) of the 2004 Jobs Act).

Registration requirements. The new law extends the registration requirements of Code Sec. 4101 to producers and importers of biodiesel and alcohol effective on April 1, 2005 (Code Sec. 4101(a)(1), as amended by the 2004 Jobs Act). Information reporting is also required (see ¶815).

Highway Trust Fund. The portion of excises taxes on gasoline and other fuels paid into the Highway Trust Fund (HTF) is determined without a reduction for the alcohol fuel and biodiesel mixtures credit (Code Sec. 9503(b)(1), as amended by the 2004 Jobs Act). In addition, the new law provides that the full amount of the alcohol fuels tax will be appropriated to the HTF applicable to fuel sold or used after September 30, 2004 (Code Sec. 9503(b)(4), as amended by the 2004 Jobs Act). Finally, the HTF is no longer required to reimburse the Treasury's General Fund for credits or payments made with respect to qualified alcohol and biodiesel fuel mixtures (Code Sec. 9503(c)(2)(A), as amended by the 2004 Jobs Act).

Extension of alcohol fuels credit. The credit for alcohol fuels under Code Sec. 40 is extended to any sale or use of alcohol fuels for any period before January 1, 2011. The credit will not apply for any period before January 1, 2011, that the excise tax imposed by Code Sec. 4081 is 4.3 cents per gallon (Code Sec. 40(e)(1), as amended by the 2004 Jobs Act). For ethanol blended fuels, the alcohol fuel credit is extended to the sale or use of the fuel through 2010 (Code Secs. 40(e)(1) and (h), as amended by the 2004 Jobs Act).

For further information on this subject, consult any of the following CCH reporter explanations:

- Standard Federal Tax Reporter, 2004FED ¶4304.01, ¶4304.021 and ¶4304.025

  - Federal Tax Service, FTS §G:24.60

  - Federal Tax Guide, 2004FTG ¶2400

  - Federal Excise Tax Reporter, ETR ¶2215.01, ¶2215.02, ¶8915.04 and ¶49,685.10

★ *Effective date.* The provisions generally apply to fuel sold or used after December 31, 2004. However, as provided in Code Sec. 6426(b)(5) and (c)(6), the alcohol fuel mixture excise tax credit shall not apply to any sale, use, or removal for any period after December 31, 2010, and the biodiesel mixture excise tax credit shall not apply to any sale, use, or removal for any period after December 31, 2006. The repeal of the General Fund retention of the 2.5/2.8 cents per gallon regarding alcohol fuels is effective for fuel sold or used after September 30, 2004. The requirement that producers and importers of alcohol and biodiesel be registered is effective on April 1, 2005. The amendments with respect to claims for a refund of taxes paid related to nontaxable use of gasoline, diesel and kerosene fuel apply to claims filed after December 31, 2004 (Act Sec. 301(d) of the American Jobs Creation Act of 2004).

Act Sec. 301(a) of the American Jobs Creation Act of 2004, adding Code Sec. 6426; Act Sec. 301(b), amending Code Sec. 4101(a)(1); Act Sec. 301(c)(1)-(3), amending Code Sec. 40(c), (d)(4), and (e)(1); Act Sec. 301(c)(4), amending Code Sec. 40(h); Act Sec. 301(c)(5)-(6), amending Code Sec. 4041; Act Sec. 301(c)(7), striking Code Sec. 4081(c); Act Sec. 301(c)(8), amending Code Sec. 4083(a)(2); Act Sec. 301(c)(9), adding Code Sec. 6427(e); Act Sec. 301(c)(10), amending Code Sec. 6427(i)(3); Act Sec. 301(c)(11)-(13), amending Code Sec. 9503; Act Sec. 301(d); Act Sec. 301(e). Law at ¶5020, ¶5980, ¶6010, ¶6020, ¶6040, ¶6215, ¶6220,¶6385 and ¶7020. Committee Report at ¶10,320.

¶810

Incentives for Biodiesel

Background _____

The concept of renewable and alternative energy sources has gained prominence in the news recently, particularly in light of America's interest in freeing itself from dependence on foreign oil. One promising alternative involves "biodiesel" fuel. In layman's terms, "biodiesel" refers to a fuel mix made from vegetable oils and animal fats, combined with diesel. A popular fuel mix is sometimes referred to as B20 (i.e., 20-percent biodiesel and 80-percent diesel). Advocates such as the National Biodiesel Board tout biodiesel fuels as safer than petroleum diesel, less polluting, and representing a significant improvement in domestic energy security.

Current law does not provide any tax incentives for biodiesel fuel. However, other alternative fuel mixtures such as ethanol and methanol do qualify for special treatment. For example, an income tax credit (the alcohol fuels credit) is allowed for ethanol and methanol (Code Sec. 40, prior to amendment by the American Jobs Creation Act of 2004). That provision actually encompasses three credits, including a 52 cents per gallon (38.52 cents per gallon, in some cases) income tax credit in 2004 to businesses that sell ethanol at retail as vehicle fuel or use it themselves as fuel in their trade or business. The other credits available under that provision include those for small ethanol producers and for ethanol blenders who produce qualified mixtures of alcohol and gasoline.

American Jobs Creation Act Impact

Income tax credit for biodiesel.—A new income tax credit is provided for certain biodiesel fuels (Code Sec. 40A, as added by the American Jobs Creation Act of 2004). The biodiesel fuels income tax credit is actually the sum of two credits—the "biodiesel mixture credit" and the "biodiesel credit"—and is treated as a general business credit.

The biodiesel mixture credit is 50 cents for each gallon of biodiesel used by the taxpayer in the production of a qualified biodiesel mixture (Code Sec. 40A(b)(1)(A), as added by the 2004 Jobs Act). A qualified biodiesel mixture is a mixture of biodiesel and diesel fuel (as defined in Code Sec. 4083(a)(3)), determined without regard to any use of kerosene, that is sold by the taxpayer producing such mixture to any person for use as fuel or used as a fuel by the taxpayer producing the mixture. In order to qualify for the credit, the sale or use must be in a trade or business of the taxpayer, and the biodiesel must be taken into account for the tax year in which the sale or use occurs (Code Sec. 40A(b)(1)(C), as added by the 2004 Jobs Act). Casual off-farm production of a biodiesel mixture is not eligible for the credit (Code Sec. 40A(b)(1)(D), as added by the 2004 Jobs Act).

The second credit, the biodiesel credit, is 50 cents for each gallon of biodiesel (but see special rule for agri-biodiesel, below) that is *not* in a mixture with diesel fuel and during the tax year is either (1) used by the taxpayer as a fuel in a trade or business, or (2) sold by the taxpayer at retail to a person and placed in the fuel tank of the retail purchaser's vehicle (Code Sec. 40A(b)(2)(A), as added by the 2004 Jobs Act). However, no user credit is allowed for any biodiesel that was sold in a retail sale (Code Sec. 40A(b)(2)(B), as added by the 2004 Jobs Act).

In order to claim the biodiesel credit or the biodiesel mixture credit, the taxpayer must obtain a certification from the producer or importer of the biodiesel identifying the product produced and the percentage of biodiesel and agri-biodiesel in the product. The form and manner of the certification will be prescribed by the IRS (Code Sec. 40A(b)(4), as added by the 2004 Jobs Act).

Special rules for agri-biodiesel and for estates and trusts. A special rule applies for agri-biodiesel. In that case, the biodiesel mixture credit or the biodiesel credit is increased to $1 per gallon (instead of 50 cents per gallon) (Code Sec. 40A(b)(3), as added by the 2004 Jobs Act). A separate provision provides that, under regulations to be prescribed by the IRS, passthrough rules similar to those found in Code Sec. 52(d) will apply to apportion the biodiesel fuels credit between an estate or trust and its beneficiaries (Code Sec. 40A(d)(4), as added by the 2004 Jobs Act).

Definitions. The terms "biodiesel" and "agri-biodiesel" are specifically defined by the new law. For purposes of the "biodiesel" credit and the biodiesel mixture credit, biodiesel is defined as "monoalkyl esters of long chain fatty acids derived from plant or animal matter" that meet the registration requirements for fuels and fuel additives imposed by the Environmental Protection Agency under Section 211 of the Clean Air Act (42 U.S.C. 7545) and the requirements of the American Society of Testing and Materials D6751 (Code Sec. 40A(d)(1), as added by the 2004 Jobs Act). The term "agri-biodiesel" means biodiesel derived solely from virgin oils, including esters derived from virgin vegetable oils from corn, soybeans, sunflower seeds, cottonseeds, canola, crambe, rapeseeds, safflowers, flaxseeds, rice bran, and mustard seeds, and from animal fats (Code Sec. 40A(d)(2), as added by the 2004 Jobs Act).

Tax imposed on later separation or failure to use as fuel. If a biodiesel fuels credit has been claimed with respect to biodiesel used in the production of a biodiesel mixture and any person subsequently separates the biodiesel from the mixture or, without separation, uses the biodiesel mixture for a reason other than as a fuel, a tax is imposed on that person in an amount necessary to recover the credit. The amount of the tax is equal to the per-gallon rate originally used to compute the biodiesel mixture credit multiplied by the number of gallons of the biodiesel in the mixture (Code Sec. 40A(d)(3)(A), as added by the 2004 Jobs Act). Similar rules apply if a biodiesel credit was claimed with respect to the retail sale of biodiesel. If any person mixes such biodiesel or uses the biodiesel other than as a fuel, a tax is imposed on such person. The amount of the tax is equal to the per-gallon rate originally used to compute the biodiesel credit multiplied by the number of gallons of biodiesel (Code Sec. 40A(d)(3)(B), as added by the 2004 Jobs Act). This tax is to be treated for all purposes, including penalties, as if it was imposed under Code Sec. 4081 (Code Sec. 40A(d)(3)(C), as added by the 2004 Jobs Act).

General provisions. The biodiesel fuels credit is part of the general business credit (Code Sec. 38(b)(17), as added by the 2004 Jobs Act) and is added to the list of qualified business credits that qualify for a deduction if they remain unused at the end of the applicable carryforward period (Code Sec. 196(c), as amended by the 2004 Jobs Act). In addition, the biodiesel fuels credit is included in gross income (Code Sec. 87, as amended by the 2004 Jobs Act).

Coordination with excise tax credit. The biodiesel fuels credit is also coordinated with the excise tax credit allowed under new Code Sec. 6426 and Code Sec. 6427(e), as added by the 2004 Jobs Act. The amount of the biodiesel fuels credit determined with respect to any biodiesel will be reduced to take into account any benefit claimed with respect to such biodiesel under the excise tax credit provision (Code Sec. 40A(c), as added by the 2004 Jobs Act).

Termination of credit. The biodiesel fuels credit is set to expire for any sale or use after December 31, 2006 (Code Sec. 40A(e), as added by the 2004 Jobs Act).

For further information on this subject, consult any of the following CCH reporter explanations:

- Standard Federal Tax Reporter, 2004FED ¶4251.021, ¶6431.01 and ¶12,430.01
- Federal Tax Service, FTS §G:24.20
- Federal Tax Guide, 2004FTG ¶2400
- Federal Excise Tax Reporter, ETR ¶2215.01 and ¶2215.015

★ *Effective date.* The biodiesel fuel income tax credit provision applies to fuel produced, and sold or used, after December 31, 2004, in tax years ending after that date (Act Sec. 302(d) of the American Jobs Creation Act of 2004).

Act Sec. 302(a) of the American Jobs Creation Act of 2004, adding Code Sec. 40A; Act Sec. 302(b), amending Code Sec. 38(b); Act Sec. 302(c)(1), amending Code Sec. 87; Act Sec. 302(c)(2), amending Code Sec. 196(c); Act Sec. 302(d). Law at ¶5010, ¶5025, ¶5115 and ¶5220. Committee Report at ¶10,324.

¶815

Information Reporting for Persons Claiming Certain Fuel Tax Benefits

Background ——————————————————————————————

Blenders, enterers, refiners, terminal operators, position holders, pipeline and vessel operators must register with the IRS by filing Form 637, Application for Registration (For Certain Excise Tax Activities) before engaging in certain excise tax activities (Code Sec. 4101(a) and Reg. §48.4101-1). In addition to the activities currently requiring registration, persons who produce or import biodiesel or alcohol

Background ——————————————————————————————————————

are required to register with the IRS (Code Sec. 4101(a), as amended by the American Jobs Creation Act of 2004).

———

American Jobs Creation Act Impact

Information reporting for persons claiming certain fuel tax credits.—The new law requires taxpayers claiming certain tax benefits related to alcohol and biodiesel fuel to file quarterly tax returns (Code Sec. 4104, as added by the American Jobs Creation Act of 2004). The quarterly return will provide information related to such benefits and the coordination of such benefits as required by the IRS to ensure the proper administration and use of the benefits. The benefits for which a quarterly return is required include the:

(1) income tax credit for gasoline and special fuels used for farming or off-highway business purposes, local or school bus use, or for a nontaxable purpose (Code Sec. 34);

(2) alcohol fuels credit (Code Sec. 40);

(3) biodiesel fuels credit (Code Sec. 40A, as added by the 2004 Jobs Act);

(4) reduced retail excise tax on qualified ethanol and methanol (Code Sec. 4041(b)(2));

(5) credit for alcohol fuels and biodiesel mixtures (Code Sec. 6426, as added by the 2004 Jobs Act; and

(6) credit or refund for the difference between the excise tax imposed on gasoline, diesel fuel or kerosene and the reduced rates for alcohol or biodiesel mixtures (Code Sec. 6427(e), as added by the 2004 Jobs Act.

The IRS has the authority to prescribe the manner in which taxpayers are required to file a quarterly return. The IRS may deny, revoke, or suspend a taxpayer's registration for failure to comply with the reporting requirements (Code Sec. 4104(c)as added by the 2004 Jobs Act.

For further information on this subject, consult any of the following CCH reporter explanations:

- Standard Federal Tax Reporter, 2004FED ¶4151.075 and ¶4304.075
- Federal Tax Guide, 2004FTG ¶2400
- Federal Excise Tax Reporter, ETR ¶2075.01, ¶2215.01 and ¶5700.065

★ *Effective date.* The amendments will take effect on January 1, 2005 (Act Sec. 303(c) of the American Jobs Creation Act of 2004).

Act Sec. 303(a) of the American Jobs Creation Act of 2004, adding Code Sec. 4104; Act Sec. 303(b); Act Sec. 303(c). Law at ¶6050. Committee Report at ¶10,330.

AGRICULTURE

¶ 820

Special Rules for Livestock Sold on Account of Weather-Related Conditions

Background ——————————————————————————————————

If soil contamination or other environmental contamination renders it infeasible for a taxpayer to reinvest the proceeds, from involuntarily converted livestock that was sold on account of drought, flood or other weather-related conditions, in property that is similar or related in use to the property that was involuntarily converted, other property, including real property used for farming purposes, shall be treated as property similar or related in use to the livestock that was involuntarily converted. (Code Sec. 1033(f)).

If livestock, not including poultry, held by the taxpayer for draft, breeding or dairy purposes, is sold or exchanged as a result of drought, flood or other weather-related conditions, and the number of livestock sold exceeds the number that would be sold in the farmer's usual course of business, this is an involuntary conversion and the farmer may defer recognition of the gain (Code Sec. 1033(e)). The period during which replacement property may be obtained without gain recognition is two years after the close of the first tax year in which any part of the gain upon the conversion is realized (Code Sec. 1033(a)(2)(B)(i)) or subject to such terms and conditions as may be prescribed by the IRS upon application of the taxpayer.

If livestock is sold on account of drought, flood or other weather-related conditions in numbers that exceed the number the taxpayer would ordinarily sell in his usual course of business, a taxpayer reporting on the cash receipts and disbursements method of accounting may elect to include such income in the tax year following the tax year in which such sale or exchange occurs. This deferral is permitted if the taxpayer establishes that the conditions requiring the sale of livestock resulted in the area being designated as eligible for assistance by the federal government. This deferral provision applies only for taxpayers whose principal trade or business is farming (Code Sec. 451(e)).

American Jobs Creation Act Impact

Special rules for livestock sold on account of weather-related conditions.—The provision expands the events that may precipitate the involuntary conversion of livestock to include not only soil contamination or other environmental contamination but also drought, flood or other weather-related conditions. The provision also preserves the ability of the taxpayer to replace the involuntarily converted livestock with property similar or related in use to the livestock so converted, or if that is not feasible, to replace the converted property with other property used for farming purposes including real property, but real property will be considered replacement property only in the case of soil contamination or other environmental contamination (Code Sec. 1033(f), as amended by the American Jobs Creation Act of 2004).

The provision extends the replacement period during which the proceeds from involuntarily converted livestock under 1033(e) may be used to obtain replacement property that is similar or related in use without the recognition of gain. The provision extends from two years to four years the time period during which the taxpayer may purchase replacement property (Code Sec. 1033(e)(2)(A), as amended by the 2004 Jobs Act). In addition, the provision expands the IRS's authority to extend on a regional basis the period for replacement under the section for such additional time as the IRS determines appropriate if the weather-related conditions resulting in such application continue for more than three years (Code Sec. 1033(e)(2)(B), as amended by the 2004 Jobs Act).

The provision also revises the income inclusion rule indicating that if livestock has been involuntarily converted as determined under Code Sec. 1033(e)(2), a special election to defer reporting of gain from the involuntary conversion to the year after the year of conversion is deemed valid if made during the replacement period described in that section, which is four years after the end of the tax year during which the involuntary conversion was made (Code Sec. 451(e)(3), as amended by the 2004 Jobs Act).

¶820

PRACTICAL ANALYSIS. Gary L. Maydew, retired accounting professor at Iowa State University and author of SMALL BUSINESS TAXATION— PLANNING AND PRACTICE and AGRIBUSINESS ACCOUNTING AND TAXATION, observes that the new involuntary conversions for livestock sold on account of weather-related conditions will give much more flexibility to farmers and ranchers. Extension of the replacement time period from two to four years will be especially helpful in areas experiencing extended droughts. In addition, if it is impractical for the rancher to replace the livestock sold (e.g., loss of grazing land), the farmer or rancher can now defer gain recognition by investing the proceeds in other property used for farming purposes, including machinery and equipment.

For further information on this subject, consult any of the following CCH reporter explanations:

- Standard Federal Tax Reporter, 2004FED ¶21,021.0733 and ¶29,650.01
- Federal Tax Service, FTS § L:1.102 and § L:1.103
- Federal Tax Guide, 2004FTG ¶25,390A

★ *Effective date.* The provision applies to any tax year for which the due date (without regard to extensions) for the return is after December 31, 2002 (Act Sec. 311(d) of the American Jobs Creation Act of 2004).

Act Sec. 311(a) of the American Jobs Creation Act of 2004 , amending Code Sec. 1033(f); Act Sec. 311(b) amending Code Sec. 1033(e); Act Sec. 311(c) amending Code Sec. 451(e). Law at ¶5375 and ¶5765. Committee Report at ¶10,340.

¶ 825

Farmers' and Fishermen's Income Averaging and Alternative Minimum Tax Coordination

Background

An individual engaged in a farming business may elect to average farm income (Code Sec. 1301) and allocate all or part of the income from the election year over the three prior years. The tax imposed for that election tax year will equal (1) the tax computed on taxable income for the year, as reduced by the amount of farm income elected for averaging, plus (2) the increase in tax that would result if taxable income for each of the three prior tax years (base years) were increased by an amount equal to one-third of the elected farm income. By reducing farm income for a high-income year and spreading the amount of the reduction over the three prior years, the taxpayer may be able to stay within the lower tax brackets and reduce the overall amount of tax for the period.

A taxpayer's alternative minimum tax (AMT) for a tax year is the excess of the taxpayer's tentative minimum tax over his or her regular tax. AMT must be paid in addition to the regular tax liability (Code Sec. 55(a)). The "regular tax," for purposes of computing AMT, is based on the taxpayer's regular tax liability decreased by certain credits and computed without increases for certain taxes.

A farm income averaging election does not apply in determining AMT for any base year or the tentative minimum tax for the election year or any base year (Reg. § 1.1301-1(f)(4)). The election to use income averaging does, however, apply in determining the regular tax for the election year when computing AMT (Reg. § 1.1301-1(f)(4)).

American Jobs Creation Act Impact

Coordination of farmers' and fishermen's income averaging and AMT.— Commercial fishermen are now able to elect to use income averaging, just like farmers engaged in a farming business (Code Sec. 1301(a) and (b), as amended by the American Jobs Creation Act of 2004). Futhermore, both fishermen and farmers may receive the full benefit of income averaging, even if they are otherwise subject to the alternative minimum tax (AMT) (Code Sec. 55(c), as amended by the 2004 Jobs Act).

> **Election:** The use of income averaging is elective, not mandatory. Currently, farmers use Form 1040, Schedule J, "Farm Income Averaging," to make the election and figure their tax under income averaging. In all likelihood, fishermen will also use Schedule J to make the income averaging election, but the IRS will need to update the schedule so that it applies to both businesses.

The availability of income averaging for fishermen applies to individuals engaged in a fishing business, not recreational fishermen (Code Sec. 1301(a), as amended by the 2004 Jobs Act). A fishing business is defined as the conduct of commercial fishing (Code Sec. 1301(b)(4), as added by the 2004 Jobs Act), where the harvested fish enter commerce or are intended to enter commerce through sale, barter or trade (16 U.S.C. 1802).

The same mechanical rules that have been applied to average income from farming businesses will now apply to fishing businesses. Thus, the definition of "elected farm income," which is the amount of income that the taxpayer elects to spread over the prior three tax years, has been broadened to include income attributable to both a farming business and a fishing business (Code Sec. 1301(b)(1)(A), as amended by the 2004 Jobs Act).

> **Compliance Tip:** Commercial fishermen who elect income averaging for their 2004 tax year will need to track down copies of their tax returns for 2001–2003 to be sure that they have all the right figures for determining the tax under the election.

Alternative minimum tax (AMT). Both a farmer and a fisherman may choose to use the income averaging rules to reduce their regular tax liability. Since the amount of a taxpayer's AMT is equal to the excess of the taxpayer's tentative minimum tax over his or her regular tax, such a reduction in the taxpayer's regular tax could end up leading to a higher AMT liability. Thus, solely for purposes of computing any AMT liability, the regular tax is determined without regard to averaging of farm and fishing income (Code Sec. 55(c)(2), as added by the 2004 Jobs Act). Consequently, the AMT, that is, the excess of that taxpayer's tentative minimum tax over the regular tax, will be smaller by not applying the income averaging rules when computing AMT.

> **Comment:** A farmer or fisherman will receive the full benefit of income averaging under these rules because income averaging can be used to reduce the regular tax, while the AMT rules ignore the tax reduction resulting from income averaging when determining AMT liability.

> **Example:** In each of years 2001, 2002, and 2003, Farmer Jones, a single taxpayer, had taxable income of $20,000. In 2004, Farmer Jones had taxable income of $30,000 (prior to any farm income averaging election) and electable farm income of $10,000. Assume the regular tax on $30,000 in 2004 for Farmer Jones is $4,238.In order to lower his tax bill, Farmer Jones decides to makes a farm income averaging election with respect to $9,000 of his electable farm income for 2004. Thus, $3,000 of elected farm income is allocated to each of years

2001, 2002, and 2003. Farmer Jones' 2004 regular tax liability is the sum of the tax on (1) $21,000 (2004 taxable income of $30,000 minus $9,000 of elected farm income), plus (2) for each of years 2001, 2002, and 2003, the tax on $23,000 minus the tax on $20,000 (the amount by which the tax would be increased if one-third of elected farm income were allocated to such year). Assume that for 2004 Farmer Jones has a tentative minimum tax of $7,800. Also assume that Farmer Jones' 2004 regular tax computed using income averaging is $4,142. Farmer Jones' 2004 AMT is equal to $3,562, the excess of his tentative minimum tax of $7,800 less his regular tax, computed without income averaging, of $4,238. Under prior law, Farmer Jones' AMT would have been $3,658, which is equal to the excess of his $7,800 tentative minimum tax over his $4,142 regular tax computed using income averaging.

PRACTICAL ANALYSIS. Gary L. Maydew, retired accounting professor at Iowa State University and author of SMALL BUSINESS TAXATION— PLANNING AND PRACTICE and AGRIBUSINESS ACCOUNTING AND TAXATION, observes that the more generous rule for computing AMT during a year in which income averaging is elected will help farmers and ranchers who have several dependents; have substantial capital gains; live in a high state income tax state; or have other AMT tax attributes.

For further information on this subject, consult any of the following CCH reporter explanations:

- Standard Federal Tax Reporter, 2004FED ¶5101.03, ¶31,791.01 and ¶31,791.033

- Federal Tax Service, FTS § A:1.42[6] and § L:1.140

- Federal Tax Guide, 2004FTG ¶1320 and ¶25,337

★ *Effective date.* The coordination of farmers' and fishermen's income averaging and the change in AMT apply to tax years beginning after December 31, 2003 (Act Sec. 314(c) of the American Jobs Creation Act of 2004).

Act Sec. 314(a) of the American Jobs Creation Act of 2004, amending Code Sec. 55(c); Act Sec. 314(b)(1), amending Code Sec. 1301(a); Act Sec. 314(b)(2)-(3), amending Code Sec. 1301(b); Act Sec. 314(c). Law at ¶5080 and ¶5845. Committee Report at ¶10,370.

¶ 830

Cooperative Marketing and Livestock Expenses

Background

A cooperative (or federation of cooperatives) of farmers, fruit growers, and persons engaged in similar pursuits may qualify for tax-exempt status if it is organized and operated for the purpose of marketing the products of members and returning to them net proceeds or purchasing supplies and equipment for the use of members at cost plus expenses (Code Sec. 521). Entities that qualify as cooperatives, however, are subject to special rules of taxation such as the allowance of certain deductions from gross income in addition to other deductions permitted to corporations (Code Secs. 1381–1388). Corporations to which these special rules do not apply include organizations exempt from taxation (other than as a cooperative), mutual savings banks, cooperative banks, domestic building and loan associations, insurance companies, or any corporation that furnishes electric energy or provides telephone service to persons in rural areas.

Background _____

One of the special rules permitted to farmers' cooperatives is that they are allowed to deduct any patronage dividends made during the tax year. Patronage dividends are paid by the cooperative to its patrons based on the quantity or value of the business which is done with or for the patron. The amount paid must be determined by reference to the cooperative's net earnings from the business that the cooperative has done with or for its patrons. Since cooperative marketing is a key service that cooperatives perform for their patrons, marketing expenses are a key element used in calculating a cooperative's net earnings.

The IRS takes the position that an organization is not operated on a cooperative basis unless its stock is owned by the producers who market their products or purchase their supplies through the association. The IRS, however, has also taken the position that a cooperative is not marketing the products of its members if it "adds value" to a farmer's products while in the cooperative's care. For example, the cooperative is not marketing the corn of its members when it purchases and uses corn to feed livestock, which it then sells.

_____

American Jobs Creation Act Impact

Feeding livestock is an element of marketing.—The cost of feeding farm animals in anticipation of a subsequent sale of either the animals or products derived from these animals is a valid marketing expense to use in calculating the net earnings of a cooperative. Consequently, such costs are included in calculating the appropriate amount of the patronage dividends to be paid out by the cooperative (Code Sec. 1388(k), as added by the American Jobs Creation Act of 2004). This rule is applicable to both nonexempt cooperatives and farmers' cooperatives exempt under Code Sec. 521. The process of feeding the animals while in the care of the cooperative is termed "value-added processing involving animals" (Act Sec. 316(a) of the 2004 Jobs Act).

For further information on this subject, consult any of the following CCH reporter explanations:

- Standard Federal Tax Reporter, 2004FED ¶22,882.01, ¶32,328.01 and ¶32,328.05

- Federal Tax Service, FTS § L:3.60

- Federal Tax Guide, 2004FTG ¶16,755 and ¶25,355

★ *Effective date.* This amendment applies in tax years beginning after the date of enactment of the American Jobs Creation Act of 2004 (Act Sec. 316(c) of the 2004 Jobs Act).

Act Sec. 316(a) of the American Jobs Creation Act of 2004, amending Code Sec. 1388; Act Sec. 316(b), amending Code Sec. 521(b); Act Sec. 316(c). Law at ¶5420 and ¶5910. Committee Report at ¶10,390.

¶ 835
Farmers' Cooperatives and Declaratory Judgments

Background _____

Under Code Sec. 7428, the U.S. Court of Federal Claims, the U.S. District Court for the District of Columbia, and the U.S. Tax Court have jurisdiction to issue declaratory judgments in cases which involve a controversy as to a determination or failure to make a determination by the IRS in connection with either the initial qualification or continuing qualification of any of the following types of organizations:

Background ___

(1) a charitable, educational, etc., organization (Code Sec. 501(c)(3));

(2) qualified charitable contribution donee (Code Sec. 170(c)(2));

(3) a private foundation (Code Sec. 509(a)); or

(4) a private operating foundation (Code Sec. 4942(j)(3)).

A declaratory judgment action is available only when the organization has exhausted all administrative remedies available to it within the IRS, but in no event will an organization be deemed to have exhausted its administrative remedies until 270 days have passed after the organization files its request for a determination (Code Sec. 7428(b)(2)). After the 270-day period has elapsed without an IRS determination, the organization may bring a declaratory judgment action.

If the IRS makes a determination during the 270-day period, the organization may file an immediate action and does not have to wait for the 270-day period to end. An action for a declaratory judgment must be brought within 90 days after the date that the IRS mails its notice of determination on the organization's status (Code Sec. 7428(b)(3)).

In addition, the U.S. District Court for the District of Columbia has authority to issue subpoenas throughout the nation to require witnesses to attend trials or hearings concerning declaratory judgment actions (Code Sec. 7428(d)).

American Jobs Creation Act Impact

Declaratory judgment actions extended to farmers' cooperatives.—The new provision extends the jurisdiction to issue declaratory judgments under Code Sec. 7428 to include determining the initial or continuing classification of farmers' cooperatives under Code Sec. 521 (Code Sec. 7428(a)(1)(D), as added by the American Jobs Creation Act of 2004).

For further information on this subject, consult any of the following CCH reporter explanations:

- Standard Federal Tax Reporter, 2004FED ¶41,723.01
- Federal Tax Service, FTS §P:35.74
- Federal Tax Guide, 2004FTG ¶16,470

★ *Effective date.* This provision is applicable to pleadings filed after the date of enactment (Act Sec. 317(b) of the American Jobs Creation Act of 2004).

Act Sec. 317(a) of the American Jobs Creation Act of 2004, amending Code Sec. 7428(a)(1); Act Sec. 317(b). Law at ¶6335. Committee Report at ¶10,400.

¶840

Reforestation Expenses

Background ___

A taxpayer could elect to claim an amortization deduction on up to $10,000 of reforestation expenses each year ($5,000 in the case of a separate return by a married individual). Such expenditures can be amortized over an 84-month period (Code Sec. 194(b), prior to amendment by the American Jobs Creation Act of 2004). No carryover or carryback of expenditures in excess of $10,000 is permitted.

The direct costs of forestation or reforestation by planting or seeding are qualifying expenditures. These direct costs include costs for preparation of the site, for seeds or seedlings, and for labor and tools (including depreciation on equipment used in these activities).

In addition to the amortization for reforestation expenses, Code Sec. 48(b), prior to amendment by the 2004 Jobs Act, provided a 10-percent credit on up to $10,000 of qualified amortizable basis in timber property. When a taxpayer claimed the benefit of both rapid amortization and this credit, the amount amortized under Code Sec. 194 had to be reduced by one-half of the amount of the credit claimed under Code Sec. 48(b).

American Jobs Creation Act Impact

Reforestation deduction increased; credit repealed.—The new law provides that up to $10,000 ($5,000 for married taxpayers filing separately) in qualified reforestation expenditures may be currently deducted in the year paid or incurred (Code Sec. 194(b), as amended by the Amercan Jobs Creation Act of 2004). The amendment is effective for expenditures paid or incurred after the date of enactment. The Conference Committee Report states that qualified reforestation expenditures in excess of this $10,000 annual amount may be capitalized and amortized over 84 months under Code Sec. 194(a), which was not amended by the 2004 Jobs Act.

> **Example:** Angela Broward incurs qualified reforestation expenses of $20,000 on January 1, 2005. On her 2005 tax return, she may claim a $10,000 deduction under newly amended Code Sec. 194(b). Under Code Sec. 194(a), Angela can also elect to charge the remaining $10,000 of expenditures to a capital account and amortize them over an 84-month period. Under this 84-month schedule, the amortization deduction for the first month would be computed as $10,000 ÷ 84 months, or $119.05 per month. The deduction for the second month would also equal $119.05 (($10,000 – $119.05) ÷ 83).

> **Comment:** The 84-month amortization period of Code Sec. 194(a) is deemed to begin on the first day of the first month of the second half of the tax year in which the amortizable basis is acquired. Thus, expenditures can be amortized only for a half year in the tax year the expenditures are incurred, regardless of whether they were incurred in the first or second half of the year. Accordingly, in the above example, the total amortization deduction for reforestation expenditures in 2005 would be limited to $714.30 ($119.05 × 6 months).

If a deduction for reforestation expenses is allowed under Code Sec. 194, no deduction for the same expenditure will be allowed under any other provision of Chapter 1 of the Internal Revenue Code (Code Secs. 1 through 1400L).

Prior to amendment by the 2004 Jobs Act, amortization of reforestation expenditures was denied to trusts but was available to estates (Code Sec. 194(b)(3) and (4), prior to repeal by the 2004 Jobs Act). This rule still applies under Code Sec. 194, as amended by the new law. However, while the benefits of Code Sec. 194 generally have been expanded to include a new current deduction for up to $10,000 in annual reforestation expenditures (in addition to the amortization deduction allowed for expenditures exceeding this limit), a strict reading of Code Sec. 194(c)(4)(B) (as added by the 2004 Jobs Act) could lead to the conclusion that estates will be allowed the benefits of Code Sec. 194(a) amortization but not the benefits of the new current deduction (Code Sec. 194(b), as amended by the 2004 Jobs Act). Nothing in the Conference Committee Report (H.R. Conf. Rep. No. 108-755) or the Senate Committee Report (S. Rep. No. 108-192) appears to support the conclusion that this is the intended result.

¶840

As was the case prior to changes made by the new law, any amortization deduction allowed to an estate must be apportioned between an income beneficiary and the estate fiduciary under regulations to be prescribed. Any amount apportioned to a beneficiary must be taken into account for purposes of determining amortization allowable to the beneficiary under Code Sec. 194(a) (Code Sec. 194(c)(4)(B), as amended by the 2004 Jobs Act).

Repeal of reforestation credit. The reforestation tax credit (Code Sec. 48(b)), which was a component of the investment tax credit (Code Sec. 46) has been repealed, effective for expenditures paid or incurred after date of enactment.

For further information on this subject, consult any of the following CCH reporter explanations:

- Standard Federal Tax Reporter, 2004FED ¶4580.01, ¶4671.052 and ¶12,335.01

- Federal Tax Service, FTS § L:7.60 and § G:23.100

- Federal Tax Guide, 2004FTG ¶25,368A

★ *Effective date.* The amendments with respect to the deduction of qualified reforestation expenditures, and with respect the repeal of the reforestation tax credit, are effective for expenditures paid or incurred after the date of enactment (Act Sec. 322(e) of the American Jobs Creation Act of 2004).

Act Sec. 322(a) of the American Jobs Creation Act of 2004, amending Code Sec. 194(b); Act Sec. 322(b), amending Code Sec. 194(c)(2); Act Sec. 322(c), amending Code Sec. 194(b)(2), striking Code Sec. 194(b)(3)-(4), and adding Code Sec. 194(c)(4) -(5); Act Sec. 322(d)(1), amending Code Sec. 46; Act Sec. 322(d)(2), amending Code Secs. 48 and 50(c)(3); Act Sec. 322(e). Law at ¶5060, ¶5065, ¶5070 and ¶5210. Committee Report at ¶10,450.

ENERGY RESOURCES

¶ 845

Election to Passthrough Small Ethanol Producer Credit to Co-op Patrons

Background

A number of tax benefits are available for ethanol and methanol produced from renewable sources that are used as motor fuel or that are blended with other fuels for such use. One such benefit is the income tax credit for small ethanol producers (Code Sec. 40(b)(4)). A small ethanol producer is a person whose ethanol production capacity does not exceed 30 million gallons per year (Code Sec. 40(g)(1)). The credit is 10 cents per gallon of ethanol produced during the tax year for up to a maximum of 15 million gallons (Code Sec. 40(b)(4)(A)). The credits that comprise the alcohol fuels tax credit are includible in income (Code Sec. 87), and like tax credits generally, are subject to limitations and cannot be used to offset alternative minimum tax liability. Under coordination rules with the federal excise tax exemptions for gasohol, the alcohol fuels credit is subject to reduction to take into account any benefit the taxpayer received with respect to the same alcohol for which the taxpayer received an excise tax exemption (Code Sec. 40(c)).

Cooperatives are generally treated as pass-through entities to the extent they distribute their profits to their patrons in the form of patronage dividends (Code Secs. 1381, 1382, and 1385). The small ethanol producer credit has not been among the credits that cooperatives are allowed to passthrough to their patrons.

American Jobs Creation Act Impact

Cooperatives can elect to passthrough credit to their patrons.—The American Jobs Creation Act of 2004 allows a cooperative to elect to apportion the small ethanol producers credit pro rata among its patrons on the basis of the quantity or value of business done with or for such patrons for the tax year (Code Sec. 40(g)(6)(A)(i), as added by the 2004 Job Act). Such amounts are included in the patron's gross income as patronage dividends (Code Secs. 1385(a) and 1388(a)). The patron rather than the cooperative claims the benefit of the credit to the extent the patron includes patronage dividends derived from such credit in the patron's income for the tax year (Code Sec. 40(g)(6)(B), as added by the 2004 Jobs Act).

Under a special rule, if the amount of a credit apportioned to any patron is decreased for any reason, the amount shall not increase the tax imposed on such patron, and the tax imposed on the cooperative will increase by that amount. This increase is not treated as tax for purposes of determining the amount of any tax credit or for purposes of the alternative minimum tax under Code Sec. 55 (Code Sec. 40(g)(6)(B)(iii), as added by the 2004 Jobs Act). For information concerning business related energy credits that are allowed against the regular income tax and the alternative minimum tax, see ¶ 370.

> **Comment:** This rule ensures that patrons who have to reduce their credit due to operation of the coordination rules with respect to the federal excise tax on fuels will not be taxed on the reduced amount.

> **Election:** Passthrough treatment for cooperative patrons must be elected on a timely filed return for the relevant tax year. Once made, the election is irrevocable for that tax year (Code Sec. 40(g)(6)(A)(ii), as added by the 2004 Jobs Act). Form 6478, Credit for Alcohol Used as Fuel, is used to claim the credit.

> **Planning Note:** The new legislation does not contain any information concerning how a cooperative notifies the IRS that it has made the election to pass through the credit to its patrons. Nor is there any information as to whether the cooperative and/or the patron has to file the Form 6478, Credit for Alcohol Used as Fuel.

For further information on this subject, consult any of the following CCH reporter explanations:

- Standard Federal Tax Reporter, 2004FED ¶ 4304.01 and ¶ 4304.03
- Federal Tax Service, FTS § L:3.61 and § G:24.70
- Federal Tax Guide, 2004FTG ¶ 2400 and ¶ 16,755

★ *Effective date.* These amendments apply to tax years ending after the date of enactment (Act Sec. 313(b) of the American Jobs Creation Act of 2004).

Act Sec. 313(a) of the American Jobs Creation Act of 2004, adding Code Sec. 40(g)(6); Act Sec. 313(b). Law at ¶ 5020. Committee Report at ¶ 10,360.

¶ 850

Deduction for Capital Costs Incurred in Complying with Environmental Protection Agency Sulfur Regulations

Background _____

The Environmental Protection Agency (EPA), in consultation with the Office of Advocacy, environmental groups, and industry representatives, recently issued rules to limit the amount of sulfur in gasoline and highway diesel fuel. The EPA has allowed small refiners to stagger compliance with these two major regulations; yet, even with a staggered phase-in, small refiners face substantially increased costs when the grace period ends.

No election for expensing capital costs incurred in complying with the sulfur regulations is currently available. Taxpayers are generally allowed annual depreciation deductions for property used in a trade or business, which would include investments in refinery property. These allowances take into account the exhaustion, wear and tear of the underlying asset (Code Sec. 167(a)). However, under limited circumstances, a taxpayer may elect to expense immediately the cost of certain depreciable business assets (Code Sec. 179). Property eligible for this election is defined as tangible section 1245 property which is acquired for use in the active conduct of a trade or business, to which Code Sec. 168 applies (Code Sec. 179(d)).

> **Comment:** According to Chief Counsel for Advocacy, Thomas M. Sullivan, in a March 19, 2002, letter to Senators Daschle and Lott, many refiners will need to invest in expensive hydro-treater technology for desulfurization, while fuel transporters and retailers most likely will need to purchase segregated tanks. According to Sullivan, this provision will provide welcome relief to small business refiners faced with this added burden by allowing them to expense 75 percent of the equipment costs. He noted that this provision helps to address the concerns of small refiners that do not have the production volumes over which to spread the costs of regulation or the buying power of many larger refineries to keep costs down. Thus, by extending relief to the small refiners, the new provision helps to maintain as much domestic refining capacity as possible while protecting human health and the environment.

American Jobs Creation Act Impact

Election to deduct qualified capital costs.—The new law allows a small business refiner to make an election to deduct 75 percent of qualified capital costs paid or incurred during the tax year. To be deductible, the costs must be paid or incurred for the purpose of complying with the Highway Diesel Fuel Sulfur Control Requirements of the EPA (Code Sec. 179B(a), as added by the American Jobs Creation Act of 2004). See ¶855 for the definitions of "small business refiner" and "qualified capital costs."

Reduced percentage. The number of percentage points of qualified costs is to be reduced, but not below zero, for small business refiners with average daily domestic refinery runs in excess of 155,000 barrels for the one-year period ending on December 31, 2002 (Code Sec. 179B(b), as added by the 2004 Jobs Act). The percentage is reduced by the product of that number and the ratio of such excess to 50,000 barrels.

Basis reductions. The property's basis is to be reduced by the portion of the cost that was expensed. For purposes of Code Sec. 1245, the amount of the deduction allowable is to be treated as a depreciation deduction allowed under Code Sec. 167 (Code Sec. 179B(c), as added by the 2004 Jobs Act).

Coordination with other provisions. Code Sec. 280B, which specifies that no deduction is allowable for amounts expended for the demolition of structures, does not apply to amounts which are expensed under this section (Code Sec. 179B(d), as added by the 2004 Jobs Act).

For further information on this subject, consult any of the following CCH reporter explanations:

- Standard Federal Tax Reporter, 2004FED ¶13,709.01, ¶13,822.01 and ¶30,909.01
  - Federal Tax Service, FTS §G:19.20 and §G:19.100
  - Federal Tax Guide, 2004FTG ¶2625 and ¶9800

★ *Effective date.* This amendment applies to expenses paid or incurred after December 31, 2002, in tax years ending after that date (Act Sec. 338(c) of the American Jobs Creation Act of 2004).

Act Sec. 338(a) of the American Jobs Creation Act of 2004, adding Code Sec. 179B; Act Sec. 338(b)(1), amending Code Sec. 263(a)(1)(G)-(I); Act Sec. 338(b)(2), amending Code Sec. 263A(c)(3); Act Sec. 338(b)(3), amending Code Sec. 312(k)(3)(B); Act Sec. 338(b)(4), amending Code Sec. 1016(a)(28)–(30); Act Sec. 338(b)(5), amending Code Sec. 1245(a)(2)(C) and Code Sec. 1245(a)(3)(C); Act Sec. 338(c). Law at ¶5200, ¶5265, ¶5270, ¶5300, ¶5760 and ¶5795. Committee Report at ¶10,530.

¶855

Low Sulfur Diesel Fuel Production Credit

Background

No business-related credit is available under current law to small business refiners of low sulfur diesel fuel. Pursuant to a comprehensive national control program established by the U.S. Environmental Protection Agency (EPA) to regulate heavy duty vehicles and their fuel as a single system, the level of sulfur in highway diesel fuel is being reduced by 97 percent.

The EPA final rule, which was published in the *Federal Register* on January 18, 2001, requires refiners to start producing diesel fuel with a sulfur content of no more than 15 parts per million (ppm) beginning on June 1, 2006. At the terminal level, highway diesel fuel sold as low sulfur fuel must meet the sulfur standard as of July 15, 2006. The program provides substantial flexibility for refiners, especially for small refiners.

American Jobs Creation Act Impact

Credit for production of low sulfur diesel fuel.—Small business refiners can claim a general business credit for the production of low sulfur diesel fuel (with a sulfur content of 15 parts per million or less) in an amount equal to five cents for each gallon of low sulfur diesel fuel produced during the tax year at any of their facilities. The fuel must be in compliance with the EPA's Highway Diesel Fuel Sulfur Control Requirements. The aggregate production credit is limited to 25 percent of the qualified capital costs incurred by a small business refiner to achieve compliance with the EPA rules, reduced by the aggregate credits determined under new Code Sec. 45H for all prior tax years with respect to its facility (Code Sec. 45H(b)(1), as added by the American Jobs Creation Act of 2004).

A refiner with average daily domestic refinery runs for the one-year period ending on December 31, 2002, that exceed 155,000 barrels is subject to a reduction in the available credit. The number of percentage points of qualified capital costs is to be reduced, but not below zero, by the product of that number and the ratio of such excess to 50,000 barrels (Code Sec. 45H(b)(2), as added by the 2004 Jobs Act).

For purposes of Code Sec. 45H(e) and 179B(b), in the calculation of average daily domestic refinery runs or retained production, only those refineries that on April 1, 2003, were refineries of the refiner or a related person (within the meaning of Code

Sec. 613A(d)(3)), are to be taken into account (Code Sec. 45H(e), as added by the 2004 Jobs Act).

Qualified capital costs of small business refiners. A refiner of crude oil satisfies the definition of "small business refiner" if:

(1) no more than 1,500 individuals are engaged in the refinery operations on any day during the tax year, and

(2) the average daily domestic refinery run or average retained production of which for all of the taxpayer's facilities for the one-year period ending on December 31, 2002, did not exceed 205,000 barrels (Code Sec. 45H(c)(1), as added by the 2004 Jobs Act).

"Qualified capital costs" are those paid or incurred during the applicable period for compliance with the EPA regulations regarding a facility. These amounts include:

(1) expenditures for the construction of new process operation units;

(2) expenditures for the dismantling and reconstruction of existing process units to be used in the production of low sulfur diesel fuel;

(3) costs of associated adjacent or offsite equipment (such as tankage, catalyst, and power supply); and

(4) engineering, construction period interest, and sitework expenses (Code Sec. 45H(c)(2), as added by the 2004 Jobs Act).

Applicable period. Qualifying capital costs are those costs paid or incurred with respect to a facility beginning January 1, 2003, and ending on the earlier of the date that is one year after the date on which the taxpayer must comply with the EPA regulations or December 31, 2009. (Code Sec. 45H(c)(4), as added by the 2004 Jobs Act).

Certification. Small business refiners must obtain certification from the Treasury Secretary, following consultation with the Administrator of the EPA, that their qualified capital costs for a facility will result in compliance with the EPA regulations. In order to be eligible for the credit, the certification must be obtained no later than 30 months after the first day of the first tax year in which the low sulfur diesel fuel production credit is allowed for a facility.

Applications for certification must include relevant information regarding unit capacities and operating characteristics that is sufficient to support a determination that the qualified capital costs are necessary for compliance with the EPA regulations. The Treasury is required to issue a notice of certification, if applicable, within 60 days of receiving a small business refiner's application; if notification is not timely made, the refiner can presume the certification to be issued until so notified.

The statutory period for assessing a deficiency attributable to the low sulfur diesel fuel production credit is three years, ending on the date when the 60-day review period ends with respect to the small business refiner. However, a deficiency can be assessed prior to the expiration of the three-year period (Code Sec. 45H(f), as added by the 2004 Jobs Act).

Reduction in basis. If a low sulfur diesel fuel production credit is determined under Code Sec. 45H for any expenditure with respect to a small business refiner's property, the taxpayer's basis in that property is to be reduced by the amount of the credit claimed (Code Sec. 45H(d), as added by the 2004 Jobs Act).

Apportionment of credit for cooperative organizations. In circumstances where a qualifying small business refiner is owned by a cooperative organization described in Code Sec. 1381(a), the cooperative can elect to pass any low sulfur diesel fuel production credits to its patrons who are eligible to share in patronage dividends. The apportionment is based on the quantity or value of business done with or for such patrons for the tax year.

Election: The cooperative must make the apportionment election on a timely filed return for the applicable tax year. Once made, the election is irrevocable for that year (Code Sec. 45H(g)(1), as added by the 2004 Jobs Act).

The amount of the production credit that is not apportioned to patrons is includible in the credit amount determined under Code Sec. 45H(a) for the cooperative's tax year. The credit amount apportioned to the patrons is includible in the amount determined under Code Sec. 45H(a) for the first tax year of the patron ending on or after the last day of the Code Sec. 1382(d) payment period for the organization's tax year or, if earlier, for the tax year of each patron ending on or after the date on which they receive notice of the apportionment from the cooperative (Code Sec. 45H(g)(2), as added by the 2004 Jobs Act).

If the amount of a credit that has been apportioned to any patron is decreased for any reason, that amount will not increase the tax imposed on the patron. Also, the tax imposed on the cooperative is to be increased by that amount; such increase is not to be treated as tax imposed for purposes of determining the amount of any credit or for Code Sec. 55 alternative minimum tax purposes (Code Sec. 45H(g)(3), as added by the 2004 Jobs Act).

Denial of double tax benefit. No deduction can be claimed for that portion of a refiner's expenditures that are otherwise deductible for the tax year which is equal to the amount of the production credit determined for such year under Code Sec. 45H(a) (Code Sec. 280C(d), as added by the 2004 Jobs Act).

For further information on this subject, consult any of the following CCH reporter explanations:

- Standard Federal Tax Reporter, 2004FED ¶4251.01, ¶12,430.01, ¶14,954.01 and ¶29,412.01

- Federal Tax Service, FTS §G:24.41

- Federal Tax Guide, 2004FTG ¶2025 and ¶2625

★ *Effective date.* These amendments apply to expenses paid or incurred after December 31, 2002, in tax years ending after that date (Act Sec. 339(f) of the American Jobs Creation Act of 2004).

Act Sec. 339(a) of the American Jobs Creation Act of 2004, adding Code Sec. 45H; Act Sec. 339(b), amending Code Sec. 38(b); Act Sec. 339(c), adding Code Sec. 280C(d); Act Sec. 339(d), amending Code Sec. 1016(a); Act Sec. 339(e), amending Code Sec. 196(c); Act Sec. 339(f). Law at ¶5010, ¶5050, ¶5220, ¶5290 and ¶5760. Committee Report at ¶10,540.

¶ 860

Credit for Producing Oil and Gas from Marginal Wells

Background _____

Prior to enactment of the American Jobs Creation Act of 2004, production costs associated with marginal oil and natural gas wells could be recovered through the application of depreciation and depletion rules. In other cases, these production costs could be taken as a deduction of ordinary and necessary business expenses. No credit existed for the production of oil and gas from marginal wells.

American Jobs Creation Act Impact

Production incentives for marginal wells.—A tax credit is available for producing oil and natural gas from qualified marginal wells (Code Sec. 45I, as added by the American Jobs Creation Act of 2004). The credit is effective for qualifying production occurring in tax years beginning after December 31, 2004 (Act Sec. 341(e) of the 2004 Jobs Act). This credit is a component of the general business credit (Code Sec. 38(b)(19), as added by the 2004 Jobs Act).

Subject to the details and limitations noted below, the marginal well production credit is equal to $3 per barrel of qualified crude oil production, and 50 cents per 1,000 cubic feet of qualified natural gas production. If triggered by the required crude oil reference price (see "Reduction of credit as oil and gas prices increase," below), this credit will, in effect, allow for much faster recovery of production expenses than was previously available.

General rules for qualification. In order for a well to be a qualified marginal well, both of the following requirements must be met:

(1) the well must be a domestic well, and produce either qualified crude oil or qualified natural gas, and

(2) the production must be treated as marginal production under Code Sec. 613A(c)(6), or during the tax year, the well must have an average daily production of not more than 25 barrel-of-oil equivalents and must produce water at a rate of not less than 95 percent of its total fluid output (Code Sec. 45I(c)(3)(A), as added by the 2004 Jobs Act).

Computation of the credit. Subject to several reductions and limitations discussed below, the marginal well production credit for any tax year is computed as follows:

(1) a *credit amount* ($3 per barrel of qualified crude oil production and 50 cents per 1,000 cubic feet of qualified natural gas production), *is multiplied by*

(2) the amount of the qualified oil or gas production that is *attributable to the taxpayer* (Code Secs. 45I(a) and (b), as added by the 2004 Jobs Act).

The second requirement, above, will ensure that where more than one taxpayer has an interest in a qualified well, the aggregate of their credits claimed will not exceed the credit limitation for the well.

Example: In 2005, a qualified marginal well produces 1,095 barrels of crude oil. Jake owns a 40-percent operating interest in the well; Stan and Irving each own 30-percent interests. Jake's credit would be $1,314 (1095 × $3 × .40). Stan and Irving each would have a credit of $985.50 (1095 × $3 × .30). (For purposes of this example, any cut-down of the credit based on a crude oil price that exceeds the applicable reference price (discussed below) is ignored.)

Only the owners of operating interests in a well can claim a credit for oil and gas production from a marginal well (Code Sec. 45I(d)(2), as added by the 2004 Jobs Act).

Reduction of credit as oil and gas prices increase. The amount of the marginal well production credit is reduced once the applicable reference price of crude oil exceeds $15, and the applicable reference price of natural gas exceeds $1.67 (Code Sec. 45I(b)(2), as added by the 2004 Jobs Act). These reductions are computed as follows:

• Crude oil: The $3-per-barrel credit amount is reduced (but not below zero), by an amount that bears the same ratio to $3 as the excess of the applicable reference price over $15 bears to $3.

- Natural gas: The 50-cents-per-1,000-cubic-feet credit amount is reduced (but not below zero), by an amount that bears the same ratio to 50 cents as the excess of the applicable reference price over $1.67 bears to 33 cents.

Comment: The Conference Committee Report (H.R. Conf. Rep. No. 108-755) states that the credit for crude oil is not available if the reference price of crude oil exceeds $18, and that the credit is reduced proportionately with respect to crude oil reference prices between $15 and $18. The Report states that the credit for natural gas is not available if the reference price of natural gas exceeds $2, and that the credit is reduced proportionately with respect to natural gas reference prices between $1.67 and $2.

In light of the elevated crude oil prices for the first 10 months of 2004, it is virtually certain that the reference price for this commodity for 2004 will not be under the $18 amount necessary for marginal well producers to qualify for at least a portion of the $3-per-barrel credit under new Code Sec. 45I. Based on crude oil prices for the last several years, the outlook for the credit to be available in the immediate future is uncertain. The last year that the crude oil reference price was under $18 per barrel was 1999, and the last published reference price, for 2003, was $27.56 (Notice 2004-33, I.R.B. 2004-18, 847).

The method for determining the reference price for purposes of Code Sec. 45I differs for crude oil and for natural gas production. For qualified crude oil production, the reference price is determined under Code Sec. 29(d)(2)(C). In other words, this reference price is determined according to the Secretary of the Treasury's estimate of the annual wellhead price per barrel for all domestic (unregulated) crude oil. For qualified natural gas production, the reference price is determined with respect to the Secretary's estimate of the annual average wellhead price per 1,000 cubic feet for all domestic natural gas (Code Sec. 45I(b)(2)(C), as added by the 2004 Jobs Act).

The applicable reference price for a tax year is the reference price for the calendar year preceding the calendar year in which the tax year begins (Code Sec. 45I(b)(2)(A), as added by the 2004 Jobs Act). Thus, if the taxpayer's tax year begins on January 1, 2006, the reference price for 2005 will be the applicable reference price.

Inflation-based adjustments. For tax years beginning after 2005, each of the dollar amounts contained in Code Sec. 45I(b)(2)(A) (as added by the 2004 Jobs Act), relating to the reduction of the credit as crude oil and natural gas prices increase is increased by the inflation adjustment factor for the calendar year. This inflation adjustment factor is determined under the rules of Code Sec. 43(b)(3)(B), substituting 2004 (for 1990) as the base year (Code Sec. 45I(b)(2)(B), as added by the 2004 Jobs Act).

Limitations on production qualifying for the credit. The operation of several rules may serve to limit the amount of crude oil or natural gas production that a taxpayer can use to compute the marginal well production credit in a tax year.

The definitions of *qualified crude oil production* and *qualified natural gas production* are limited to production of oil and gas from a *qualified marginal well* (Code Sec. 45I(c)(1), as added by the 2004 Jobs Act). Because a qualified marginal well must be a domestic well, as indicated by Code Sec. 45I(c)(3)(A) (as added by the 2004 Jobs Act), qualified crude oil production and qualified natural gas production are limited to production from domestic wells.

If a well is not capable of production during each day of a tax year, the limitations under Code Sec. 45I(c)(2) must be proportionately reduced to reflect the ratio that the number of days of production bears to 365 (Code Sec. 45I(c)(2)(B)(ii), as added by the 2004 Jobs Act).

In determining the marginal well production credit that is available for a tax year, only the first 1,095 barrels or barrels-of-oil equivalents produced from a marginal well will be considered (Code Sec. 45I(c)(2)(A), as added by the 2004 Jobs Act). The barrel-of-oil equivalent is defined in Code Sec. 29(d)(5).

If a taxpayer claims a marginal well production credit in a short tax year, the 1,095 barrel and barrel-of-oil equivalent amounts will be proportionately reduced to reflect the ratio that the number of days in such short tax year bears to 365 (Code Sec. 45I(c)(2)(B)(i), as added by the 2004 Jobs Act).

If more than one individual owns operating interests in a qualified marginal well that produces crude oil or natural gas which exceeds the 1,095 barrel or barrel-of-oil equivalent limitation in the tax year, each such owner will compute his or her share of the 1,095 barrel limit based on the ratio that the owner's revenue interest in the production bears to the aggregate of the revenue interest of all operating interest owners in the production (Code Sec. 45I(d)(1), as added by the 2004 Jobs Act).

> **Example:** John Knox and Kay Johnson own the operating interest in a qualified marginal well that produces 1,200 barrels of oil in the tax year. John's revenue interest in the production is 65 percent; Kay's is 35 percent. The production that is attributable to John is 712 barrels (1,095 × .65). Kay's production is computed as 383 barrels (1,095 × .35).

Definitions. For purposes of the new rules for the Code Sec. 45I marginal well production credit, the terms "crude oil", "natural gas", "domestic" and "barrels", have the same definitions as contained in Code Sec. 613A(e), relating to limitations on percentage depletion for oil and gas wells (Code Sec. 45I(c)(3)(B), as added by the 2004 Jobs Act).

Production from nonconventional sources excluded. If production from a well could qualify for both a credit under Code Sec. 45I (oil and gas production from marginal wells) and under Code Sec. 29 (production from nonconventional sources), the credit under Code Sec. 45I cannot be claimed unless the taxpayer elects not to claim a Code Sec. 29 credit with respect to the well (Code Sec. 45I(d)(3), as added by the 2004 Jobs Act).

Component of general business credit. The new credit for oil and gas produced from a qualified marginal well is a component of the general business credit (Code Sec. 38(b)(19), as added by the 2004 Jobs Act). As such, the rules of Code Sec. 38 govern the claiming of the marginal well production credit, including the carryback and carryforward of any credit amounts that cannot be utilized in the tax year in which they were generated (Code Sec. 38(a)).

Carryback and carryforward of unused credit extended. The general rule is that Code Sec. 38 general business credits that cannot be used in a single tax year can be carried back one tax year and carried forward for 20 tax years. However, unused marginal well production credits can be carried back five years and carried forward for 20 tax years (Code Sec. 39(a), as amended by the 2004 Jobs Act).

For further information on this subject, consult any of the following CCH reporter explanations:

- Standard Federal Tax Reporter, 2004FED ¶4251.01 and ¶4301.01
- Federal Tax Service, FTS §G:24.41 and §L:6.80
- Federal Tax Guide, 2004FTG ¶9645

★ *Effective date.* The provision applies to production of oil and natural gas in tax years beginning after December 31, 2004 (Act Sec. 341(e) of the American Jobs Creation Act of 2004).

Act Sec. 341(a) of the American Jobs Creation Act of 2004, adding Code Sec. 45I; Act Sec. 341(b), amending Code Sec. 38(b) and adding Code Sec. 38(b)(19); Act Sec. 341(c), amending Code Sec. 39(a); Act Sec. 341(d); Act Sec. 341(e). Law at ¶ 5010, ¶ 5015 and ¶ 5055. Committee Report at ¶ 10,560.

¶ 865

Extension of Enhanced Oil Recovery Credit to Certain Alaska Facilities

Background

A taxpayer who owns an operating mineral interest in a property qualifying as an enhanced oil recovery (EOR) project is entitled to claim a credit for the qualified EOR costs paid or incurred during the year. The credit amount is equal to 15 percent of the qualified EOR costs attributable to a certified EOR project located within the United States (Code Sec. 43(a)). Qualified EOR costs include the following costs paid or incurred with respect to a qualified EOR project:

- the cost of tangible property that is an integral part of the project and which is subject to a deduction for depreciation or amortization;

- intangible drilling and development costs that may be deducted by the taxpayer; and

- qualified tertiary injectant expenses that may be deducted by the taxpayer (Code Sec. 43(c)(1)).

A project is a qualified EOR project if it involves the application of a qualifying tertiary recovery method that is reasonably expected to increase crude oil production by more than an insignificant degree. To remain a qualified EOR project, each year the project must be certified by a state-registered petroleum engineer that the project meets all the requirements imposed under the Code (Code Sec. 43(c)(2); Reg. § 1.43-2(a)).

Qualified tertiary methods include:

Thermal recovery methods:

- Steam drive injection,

- Cyclis team injection, and

- In situ combustion.

Gas flood recovery methods:

- Miscible fluid displacement,

- Carbon dioxide augmented waterflooding,

- Immiscible carbon dioxide displacement, and

- Immiscible nonhydrocarbon gas displacement.

Chemical flood recovery methods:

- Microemulsion flooding,

- Caustic flooding, and

- Mobility control recovery method-polymer augmented waterflooding (Reg. § 1.43-2(e)(3)).

This credit is claimed as one of the components of the general business credit, making it subject to the tax liability limitation and the carryback and carryforward rules imposed on the general business credits. Taxpayers have an option of electing out of claiming the credit and claiming a deduction for the cost of tertiary injectants. The amount of any credit claimed will reduce the basis of the property as well as any

Background

deductible amount. Finally, the amount of EOR credit is subject to a phase-out rule. The credit phases out by the ratio that the reference price of oil for the preceding year exceeds $28 (adjusted for inflation) over $6. Currently, there is no phase out of the credit since the reference price is less than $28 adjusted for inflation.

American Jobs Creation Act Impact

Enhanced oil recovery credit extended to high volume Alaska natural gas facility.—The qualified costs for purposes of claiming the enhanced oil recovery credit have been expanded to include the cost of constructing a gas treatment plant in Alaska (Code Sec. 43(c)(1)(D), as added by the American Jobs Creation Act of 2004). The construction costs must be incurred in building a gas treatment plant that:

(1) is north of 64 degrees latitude within the United States (Code Sec. 43(c)(1)(D)(i), as added by the 2004 Jobs Act);

(2) can process Alaska natural gas for transportation through a pipeline at a minimum capacity of two trillion Btus per day (Code Sec. 43(c)(1)(D)(ii), as added by the 2004 Jobs Act); and

(3) produces carbon dioxide to be injected into hydrocarbon-bearing geological formations (Code Sec. 43(c)(1)(D)(iii), as added by the 2004 Jobs Act).

The term "Alaska natural gas" is defined to mean natural gas entering the Alaska natural gas pipeline that is produced from wells north of 64 degrees latitude including wells located on the continental shelf but excluding the Alaska National Wildlife Refuge (Code Sec. 43(c)(5), as added by the 2004 Jobs Act).

Comment: The enhanced oil recovery (EOR) credit was enacted as part of the Omnibus Revenue Reconciliation Act of 1990 (P.L. 101-508). The credit was intended to increase the domestic supply of crude oil, to reduce the demand for imported oil, and thus to make the United States less dependent upon Persian Gulf producers and other unstable foreign oil producers. It was also intended to further enhance the energy security of the United States. At the time, the supplies of natural gas were considered abundant and need to increase products was deemed unnecessary.

Planning Note: The enhanced oil recovery credit is claimed on Form 8830 and, as mentioned above, is a part of the general business credits. If the taxpayer is claiming more than one general business credit, Form 3800 will also need to be completed. The EOR credit is subject to the tax liability rules of Code Sec. 38 and the carryback and carryforward rules of Code Sec. 39, as amended by the 2004 Jobs Act. Practitioners should note that the EOR credit is not included in Code Sec. 196 and, thus, any unused credit at the end of the carryforward period or the cessation of the taxpayer is lost.

Planning Note: Practitioners need to remember that taxpayers may elect out of taking the EOR credit and use the cost as a deduction against income. The IRS allows a taxpayer to either make or revoke an election at any time within three years after the last day prescribed by law for the filing of the tax return for the tax year involved (Code Sec. 43(e)(2); Reg. § 1.43-6(a)).

Caution Note: It is not clear whether this new provision will be subject to the year certification process under Code Sec. 43(c)(2)(B) that is required of EOR projects.

For further information on this subject, consult any of the following CCH reporter explanations:

- Standard Federal Tax Reporter, 2004FED ¶4387.035
- Federal Tax Service, FTS §G:24.140 and §L:6.80
- Federal Tax Guide, 2004FTG ¶2500

★ *Effective date.* The provision applies to costs paid or incurred in tax years beginning after December 31, 2004 (Act Sec. 707(c) of the American Jobs Creation Act of 2004).

Act Sec. 707(a) of the American Jobs Creation Act of 2004, adding Code Sec. 43(c)(1)(D); Act Sec. 707(b), adding Code Sec. 43(c)(5); Act Sec. 707(c). Law at ¶5030. Committee Report at ¶10,890.

¶ 870

Qualified Energy Resources

Background

A nonrefundable tax credit is available for the domestic production of electricity from certain "qualified energy resources" (QERs) (Code Sec. 45(a)). The three types of QERs are: (1) wind, (2) closed-loop biomass, and (3) poultry waste. The Code provides the following definitions for two QERs:

(1) *Closed-loop biomass.* The term "closed-loop biomass" means any organic material from a plant which is planted exclusively for purposes of being used at a qualified facility to produce electricity (Code Sec. 45(c)(2)).

(2) *Poultry waste.* The term "poultry waste" means poultry manure and litter, including wood shavings, straw, rice hulls, and other bedding material for the disposition of manure (Code Sec. 45(c)(4)).

Comment: With regard to *wind energy facilities* and the type of property (e.g., wind turbines) that will qualify for the credit, the IRS has provided helpful information in Rev. Rul. 94-31, 1994-1 CB 16.

The electricity from the QER must be produced at a qualified facility. See ¶872 for information concerning qualified facilities.

For 2004, the renewable electricity production credit is 1.8 cents multiplied by the kilowatt hours of electricity sold by the taxpayer during the tax year and produced from qualified energy resources at a qualified facility. See ¶874 for information concerning the computation of the renewable electricity production credit.

Only sales of electricity that is produced in the United States or a U.S. possession are taken into account. When a facility has more than one owner, production must be allocated in proportion to the respective ownership interest in gross sales from the facility (Code Sec. 45(d)(3)).

Planning Note: Recent tax legislation extended the "placed in service" date for these three qualified facilities to December 31, 2005 (Code Sec. 45(c)(3)(A), (B) and (C), as amended by the Working Families Tax Relief Act of 2004). Without this extension, the facilities would have had to be placed in service before January 1, 2004.

American Jobs Creation Act Impact

Expansion in types of "qualified energy resources."— Under the new legislation, the types of "qualified energy resources" (QERs) that produce electricity that is eligible for the renewable electricity production credit have been *expanded from three to eight resources* (Code Sec. 45(c)(1), as amended by the American Jobs Creation Act of 2004).

Planning Note: Wind and closed-loop biomass are resources that remain from the original QERs. However, poultry waste has been eliminated as a separate QER, but is included in the new type of qualified resource called "open-loop biomass."

New types of qualified energy resources. The newly added QERs are (Code Sec. 45(c)(1), as amended by the 2004 Jobs Act):

    (1) open-loop biomass,

    (2) geothermal energy,

    (3) solar energy,

    (4) small irrigation power,

    (5) municipal solid waste, and

    (6) refined coal.

Comment: Definitions of six of the eight QERs appear in the following material. The Code does not define "solar energy" probably because Congress did not think a definition was necessary. The IRS has provided information concerning wind energy facilities and the type of property (e.g., wind turbines) that will qualify for the credit in Rev. Rul. 94-31, 1994-1 CB 16.

Closed-loop biomass. The term "closed-loop biomass" means any organic material from a plant which is planted *exclusively* for purposes of being used at a qualified facility to produce electricity (Code Sec. 45(c)(2), as amended by the 2004 Jobs Act). The definition of this QER was not changed by the new legislation.

Planning Note: The organic material must be planted exclusively for the purpose of producing electricity. Under this limitation, residual organic material that is left over from another activity (e.g., logging) does not qualify as closed-loop biomass, even if it is ultimately used to produce electricity. However, this type of organic material may qualify as open-loop biomass QER (see, immediately below).

Open-loop biomass. The term "open-loop biomass" is defined to mean (Code Sec. 45(c)(3), as amended by the 2004 Jobs Act):

    (1) Any agricultural livestock waste nutrients. The term "agricultural livestock waste nutrients" is defined to include agricultural livestock manure, as well as litter and other bedding material for the disposing of manure (e.g., wood shavings, straw, rice hulls, etc.). Included in the term "agricultural livestock" are bovine (e.g., cows), swine (e.g., pigs and hogs), poultry, and sheep (Code Sec. 45(c)(3)(B), as amended by the 2004 Jobs Act).

    (2) Any solid, nonhazardous, cellulosic waste material that is segregated from other waste materials (Code Sec. 45(c)(3)(A)(ii), as amended by the 2004 Jobs Act). (Note: In this context, cellulose can be generally defined as the woody portion of a plant.) To qualify, the cellulosic waste material must be derived from: (a) certain forest-related resources (e.g., mill and harvesting residues, precommercial thinnings, slash, and brush), (b) certain solid wood waste materials (e.g., waste pallets, crates, dunnage, manufacturing and construction wood wastes), and landscape or right-of-way tree trimmings, or (c) agriculture sources, including orchard tree crops, vineyard, grain, legumes, sugar, and other crop by-products or residues.

Planning Note: The Code states that the term "agricultural livestock" *includes* bovine, swine, poultry and sheep. It does not state that the term "agricultural livestock" is limited to these species of animals. Thus, it appears that agricultural livestock waste nutrients obtained from other species (e.g., horses, goats, bison, or llamas) may qualify as open-loop biomass resources.

Caution Note: Not all solid wood waste materials qualify as cellulosic waste. Excluded are pressure-treated, chemically treated, or painted wood wastes, municipal solid waste, gas derived from the biogradation of solid waste, or paper that is commonly recycled (Code Sec. 45(c)(3)(A)(ii)(II), as amended by the 2004 Jobs Act). In addition, if organic material qualifies as a closed-loop biomass resource, the material cannot be classified as an open-loop biomass resource, except for certain ancillary uses (e.g., startup and flame stabilization).

Geothermal energy. "Geothermal energy" means energy derived from a geothermal deposit (Code Sec. 45(c)(4), as amended by the 2004 Jobs Act). The term "geothermal deposit" means a geothermal reservoir consisting of natural heat that is stored in rocks or in an aqueous liquid or vapor. The vapor need not be under pressure in order to qualify (Code Sec. 613(e)(2)).

Small irrigation power. The term "small irrigation power" means power generated without any dam or impoundment of water through an irrigation system canal or ditch. The nameplate or installed capacity rating cannot be less than 150 kilowatts but must be less than five megawatts (Code Sec. 45(c)(5), as amended by the 2004 Jobs Act).

Municipal solid waste. The term "municipal solid waste" includes any garbage, refuse, sludge from a waste treatment plant, water supply treatment plant, or air pollution control facility (Code Sec. 45(c)(6), as amended by the 2004 Jobs Act). Also included are other discarded material, including solid, liquid, semisolid, or contained gaseous material resulting from industrial, commercial, mining, and agricultural operations, and from community activities (Section 2(27) of the Solid Waste Disposal Act (42 U.S.C. 6903)). The term does *not* include solid or dissolved material in domestic sewage, or solid or dissolved materials in irrigation return flows or industrial discharges that are subject to special permits, or certain materials defined by the Atomic Energy Act of 1954.

Refined coal. The term "refined coal" means a fuel that is (Code Sec. 45(c)(7)(A), as amended by the 2004 Jobs Act):

(1) a liquid, gaseous, or solid synthetic fuel produced from coal, including lignite, or high carbon fly ash (e.g., fuel used as feedstock),

(2) sold by the taxpayer with the reasonable expectation that it will be used to produce steam,

(3) certified by the taxpayer as resulting in a "qualified emission reduction" when the fuel is used to produce steam, and

(4) produced in a manner that results in at least a 50 percent increase in the market value of the refined coal, when compared to the value of the feedstock coal. (Note: The 50 percent increase in market value, does not include any increase that results from the addition of any materials during the production process.)

As noted above, the taxpayer must certify that the use of the refined coal to produce steam resulted in a qualified emission reduction (QER). The QER must be a reduction of at least 20 percent of the emissions of nitrogen oxide, and either sulfur dioxide or mercury released during the burning of the refined coal, when compared to feedstock or comparable coal that was predominantly available in the marketplace on January 1, 2003 (Code Sec. 45(c)(7)(B), as amended by the 2004 Jobs Act). The reduction of emissions excludes any dilution caused by material added during the production process of the refined coal.

¶870

For further information on this subject, consult any of the following CCH reporter explanations:

- Standard Federal Tax Reporter, 2004FED ¶4415.01 and ¶4415.04
- Federal Tax Service, FTS §G:24.240
- Federal Tax Guide, 2004FTG ¶2575

★ *Effective date.* Generally, these provisions apply to electricity produced and sold after the date of enactment of the American Jobs Creation Act of 2004, in tax years ending after that date (Act Sec. 710(g)(1) of the 2004 Jobs Act). However, with regard to *certain open-loop biomass facilities* placed in service before January 1, 2006 and described in Code Sec. 45(d)(3)(A)(ii), as amended by the 2004 Jobs Act, the new law applies to electricity produced and sold after December 31, 2004, in tax year ending after that date (Act Sec. 710(g)(2) of the 2004 Jobs Act). With regard to *refined coal production facilities*, the new provisions apply to refined coal produced and sold after the date of enactment of the 2004 Jobs Act (Act Sec. 710(g)(5) of the 2004 Jobs Act). The new law does not apply to *poultry waste facilities* that were placed in service before January 1, 2004 (Act Sec. 710(g)(4) of the 2004 Jobs Act). New rules concerning the credit rate and period for new facilities apply to electricity produced and sold after December 31, 2004, in tax years ending after that date (Act Sec. 710(g)(3) of the 2004 Jobs Act). (See ¶874 for information concerning the credit rate.)

Act Sec. 710(a) of the American Jobs Creation Act of 2004, amending Code Sec. 45(c); Act Sec. 710(b)(3), amending Code Sec. 45(e); Act Sec. 710(g). Law at ¶5035. Committee Report at ¶10,920.

¶872

Qualified Facilities Used for Production

Background ───

In order to be eligible for the renewable electricity production credit, the electricity must be produced from a qualified energy resource (QER) and it must be produced at a "qualified facility" (QF). The three types of QFs are (Code Sec. 45(c)(3)):

(1) closed-loop biomass facilities placed in service after 1992 and before January 1, 2006,

(2) wind energy facilities placed in service after 1993 and before January 1, 2006, and

(3) poultry waste facilities placed in service after 1999 and before January 1, 2006.

───

American Jobs Creation Act Impact

New types of qualified facilities.—The new law expands the types of qualified facilities (QFs) that may be used to produce electricity from qualified energy resources (QERs) (Code Sec. 45(d), as added by the American Jobs Creation Act of 2004). This expansion is a necessary corollary to the expansion in the types of resources that qualify as QERs (see ¶870). The rules pertaining to each QF are discussed in the following material.

Wind facility. When a facility uses wind to produce electricity, a qualified facility is defined to mean any facility owned by the taxpayer and that is originally placed in service after December 31, 1993, and before January 1, 2006 (Code Sec. 45(d)(1), as added by the 2004 Jobs Act).

Closed-loop biomass facility. When a facility uses closed-loop biomass (i.e., organic material planted exclusively to produce electricity), a qualified facility generally refers to a facility owned by the taxpayer and that is originally placed in service after December 31, 1992, and before January 1, 2006 (Code Sec. 45(d)(2)(A)(i), as added by the 2004 Jobs Act). A QF may also include a facility owned by the taxpayer which before January 1, 2006, is originally placed in service and modified to use closed-loop biomass to co-fire with coal, with other biomass, or with both. However, this modified closed-loop biomass facility must have its modification approved under the Biomass Power for Rural Development Programs or be part of a pilot project of the Commodity Credit Corporation (Code Sec. 45(d)(2)(A)(ii), as added by the 2004 Jobs Act).

> **Caution:** Special rules apply to these modified closed-loop biomass QFs. One special rule provides that the 10-year period during which electricity produced at the modified closed-loop QF is eligible for the tax credit begins no earlier than the date of enactment of the 2004 Jobs Act (Code Sec. 45(d)(2)(B)(i), as added by the 2004 Jobs Act). Another special rule provides that if the owner of the modified closed-loop biomass QF is not the producer of the electricity, the taxpayer eligible for the credit is the lessee or operator of the facility (Code Sec. 45(d)(2)(B)(iii), as added by the 2004 Jobs Act). This rule is an exception to the general requirement that only the owner of the QF may claim the credit. In addition, special computations apply when calculating the allowable credit for electricity produced from a modified closed-loop biomass QF (Code Sec. 45(d)(2)(B)(ii), as added by the 2004 Jobs Act). See ¶ 874 for information concerning the computation of the allowable credit.

> **Planning Note:** No credit reduction is required by certain modified closed-loop biomass facilities that have received grants and other types of subsidized financing (Code Sec. 45(b)(3), last sentence, as added by the 2004 Jobs Act).

Open-loop biomass facility. When a facility uses agricultural livestock waste nutrients as an open-loop biomass to produce electricity, the term "qualified facility" means any facility owned by the taxpayer that: (1) is originally placed in service after the date of the enactment of the 2004 Jobs Act and before January 1, 2006, and (2) its nameplate capacity rating is at least 150 kilowatts (Code Sec. 45(d)(3)(A)(i), as added by the 2004 Jobs Act). However, if the open-loop biomass facility uses material other than agricultural livestock waste nutrients (e.g., certain wood waste or waste from agriculture sources), the facility is qualified if it is originally placed in service before January 1, 2006 (Code Sec. 45(d)(3)(A)(ii), as added by the 2004 Jobs Act).

> **Comment:** If the owner of the open-loop biomass facility is not the producer of the electricity, the lessee or operator of the facility is eligible to claim the credit (Code Sec. 45(d)(3)(B), as added by the 2004 Jobs Act). This is an exception to the general rule that only the owner of the QF may claim the tax credit.

Geothermal or solar energy facility. When a facility uses geothermal or solar energy to produce electricity, the term "qualified facility" means any facility owned by the taxpayer that is originally placed in service after the date of the enactment of the 2004 Jobs Act and before January 1, 2006 (Code Sec. 45(d)(4), as added by the 2004 Jobs Act). However, the term does not include certain energy property described in Code Sec. 48(a)(3) (e.g., certain solar energy or geothermal equipment), the basis of which is taken into account by the taxpayer for purposes of determining the allowable energy credit under Code Sec. 48.

> **Caution Note:** According to the Conference Committee Report (H.R. Conf. Rep. No. 108-755), when a solar energy or geothermal facility claims a credit

under Code Sec. 45, the facility may not claim any investment credit under Code Sec. 48 in the future.

Small irrigation power facility. When a facility uses small irrigation power to produce electricity, a qualified facility is any facility owned by the taxpayer that is originally placed in service after the date of the enactment of the 2004 Jobs Act and before January 1, 2006 (Code Sec. 45(d)(5), as added by the 2004 Jobs Act).

Comment: With regard to small irrigation power facilities, the Conference Agreement defines this type of facility as one that generates electric power by means of an irrigation system or ditch, without any dam or impoundment of water. In addition, the installed capacity of a qualified facility cannot be less than 150 kilowatts and must be less than five megawatts.

Landfill gas facility. When a facility produces electricity from methane gas derived from the biodegradation of municipal solid waste, a qualified facility is any facility owned by the taxpayer that is originally placed in service after the date of the enactment of the 2004 Jobs Act and before January 1, 2006 (Code Sec. 45(d)(6), as added by the 2004 Jobs Act).

Trash combustion facilities. When a facility burns municipal solid waste to produce electricity, a qualified facility is any facility owned by the taxpayer that is originally placed in service after the date of the enactment of the 2004 Jobs Act and before January 1, 2006 (Code Sec. 45(d)(7), as added by the 2004 Jobs Act).

Comment: According to the Conference Agreement, the burning of the municipal solid waste (garbage) must be used to produce steam that will drive a turbine that produces electricity.

Refined coal production facility. A refined coal production facility must be placed in service after the date of enactment of the 2004 Jobs Act and before January 1, 2009 (Code Sec. 45(d)(8), as added by the 2004 Jobs Act). The allowable credit from this type of facility is subject to special computations (Code Sec. 45(e)(8), as added by the 2004 Jobs Act). For information concerning the credit computation, see ¶874.

Poultry waste facilities. Under a grandfather provision, poultry waste facilities, as defined by Code Sec. 45(c)(3)(C), before enactment of the 2004 Jobs Act, are not subject to the amendments of the 2004 Jobs Act. In order for this grandfather provision to apply, the poultry waste facility must have been placed in service before January 1, 2004 (Act Sec. 710(g)(4) of the 2004 Jobs Act). As a result of this grandfather provision, these poultry waste facilities are not subject to the tax credit reduction that open-loop biomass facilities must contend with. The credit reduction is discussed at ¶874.

Caution Note: A "qualified facility" for purposes of the renewable electricity production credit, cannot include any facility that produces fuel from a nonconventional source that is eligible for the tax credit under Code Sec. 29 for the current tax year, or any prior tax year (Code Sec. 45(e)(9), as added by the 2004 Jobs Act).

Planning Note: The energy credit provided for under Code Sec. 48 cannot be claimed for any property that is part of a facility that produces electricity for which the renewable electricity production credit is allowed (Code Sec. 48(a)(3), last sentence, as added by the 2004 Jobs Act).

For further information on this subject, consult any of the following CCH reporter explanations:

- Standard Federal Tax Reporter, 2004FED ¶4415.01 and ¶4415.04

- Federal Tax Service, FTS § G:24.241
- Federal Tax Guide, 2004FTG ¶ 2575

★ *Effective date.* Generally, these provisions apply to qualified facilities placed in service after the date of enactment of the American Jobs Act of 2004 (Act Sec. 710(g)(1) of the 2004 Jobs Act). However, wind facilities originally placed in service after December 31, 1993, and closed-loop biomass facilities originally placed in service after December 31, 1992, are subject to the 2004 Jobs Act amendments. The Conference Agreement notes that the provisions that apply to modified closed-loop biomass facilities include any facility originally placed in service *before* December 31, 1992.

Act Sec. 710(b)(1) of the American Jobs Creation Act of 2004, redesignating Code Sec. 45(d) as Code Sec. 45(e), and adding new Code Sec. 45(d); Act Sec. 710(b)(2), adding Code Sec. 45(e)(8); Act Sec. 710(d), adding Code Sec. 45(e)(9); Act Sec. 710(e), amending Code Sec. 48(a)(3); Act Sec. 710(g). Law at ¶ 5035 and ¶ 5065. Committee Report at ¶ 10,920.

¶ 874

Computation of Renewable Electricity Production Tax Credit

Background ————————————————————————————

For 2004, the renewable electricity production credit is 1.8 cents (as adjusted for inflation) per kilowatt hour of electricity produced from a qualified energy resource at a qualified facility during the 10-year period beginning on the date the facility is placed in service (Code Sec. 45(a) and Notice 2004-29, IRB 2004-17, 828). The electricity must be sold during the tax year by the taxpayer to an unrelated person. The credit is subject to certain limit and phaseout rules (Code Sec. 45(b)).

No credit for electricity produced from a renewable resource is allowed for that portion of capital determined at the close of the tax year that was financed by: (1) government grants, (2) tax-exempt bonds, (3) direct or indirect subsidized financing through government programs, or (4) any other credit allowable with respect to the property (e.g., the business energy investment credit). The reduction is computed by means of a fraction, the numerator of which is the total of various grants and subsidies, and the denominator of which is the total capital account for the project for the tax year and all prior tax years (Code Sec. 45(b)).

American Jobs Creation Act Impact

Reduced credit rate for electricity produced at certain qualified facilities.—The new law reduces the allowable credit for electricity produced at certain qualified facilities (Code Sec. 45(b)(4)(A), as added by the American Jobs Creation Act of 2004). In addition, special rate computation rules are introduced for refined coal production facilities (Code Sec. 45(e)(8), as added by the 2004 Jobs Act). Both the rate reduction and the special computations are discussed in the following material.

Reduced credit rate. For electricity produced and sold in any calendar year after 2003, the credit allowed for electricity produced by certain facilities is one-half of the rate that is generally used. For 2004, the general rate is 1.8 cents (Notice 2004-29, IRB 2004-17, 82). Thus, under the new law, the rate is 9/10 of a cent for these facilities. The inflation adjusted general rate for 2005 has not been announced as of this date. The qualified facilities that must use this reduced rate are (Code Sec. 45(b)(4)(A), as added by the 2004 Jobs Act):

    (1) open-loop biomass facilities,

    (2) small irrigation power facilities,

(3) landfill gas facilities, and

(4) trash combustion facilities.

Caution Note: When determining the allowable credit and the time period over which the credit may be claimed, it is important to keep in mind that special rules apply to certain modified closed-loop biomass facilities. These special rules, which are in the areas of credit computation and the amount of the allowable credit, are highlighted below under the heading "Modified closed-loop biomass facilities."

Credit reduction. The new law has changed the formula that must generally be used when computing the reduced credit when the facility has been financed with grants, tax-exempt bonds, certain subsidized financing and other credits (Code Sec. 45(b)(3), as amended by the 2004 Jobs Act). Under the new formula, the allowable credit is reduced by *the lesser of:* one-half of the credit before the required reduction, *or* a fraction, the numerator of which is the total of various grants and subsidies, and the denominator of which is the total capital account for the project for the tax year and all prior tax years.

Planning Note: No credit reduction is required by certain modified closed-loop biomass facilities that are described in Code Sec. 45(d)(2)(A)(ii) and that have received grants and other types of subsidized financing (Code Sec. 45(b)(3), last sentence, as added by the 2004 Jobs Act).

Credit period reduction. The time period over which the renewable electricity production credit may be claimed is reduced from 10 years to five years when electricity is produced at certain facilities. The five-year period begins on the date the qualified facility was originally place in service. The facilities subject to the five-year rule are (Code Sec. 45(b)(4)(B)(i), as added by the 2004 Jobs Act):

(1) open-loop biomass facilities,

(2) geothermal or solar energy facilities,

(3) small irrigation power facilities,

(4) landfill gas facilities, and

(5) trash combustion facilities.

Planning Note: The 10-year credit period applies to the following facilities: (1) wind, (2) closed-loop biomass, and (3) refined coal. Under a special rule, a five-year credit period that begins on the date of enactment of the 2004 Jobs Act, applies to certain open-loop biomass facilities that were placed in service before the date of enactment of the 2004 Jobs Act (Code Sec. 45(b)(4)(B)(ii), as added by the 2004 Jobs Act). These open-loop biomass facilities are those that use material other than agricultural livestock waste nutrients (Code Sec. 45(d)(3)(A)(ii), as added by the 2004 Jobs Act).

Modified closed-loop biomass facilities. A modified closed-loop biomass facility is one that has been modified to use coal and/or other biomass to generate electricity. The modification must have been approved by the Biomass Power for Rural Development Programs, or be part of a pilot project of the Commodity Credit Corporation (Code Sec. 45(d)(2)(A)(ii), as added by the 2004 Jobs Act). The following special rules apply when determining the allowable renewable electricity production credit for electricity produced from these facilities:

(1) The allowable tax credit does not have to be reduced when the modified facility has received grants and other types of subsidized financing (Code Sec. 45(b)(3), last sentence, as added by the 2004 Jobs Act).

(2) The 10-year credit period begins no earlier than the date of enactment of the 2004 Jobs Act (Code Sec. 45(d)(2)(b)(i), as added by the 2004 Jobs Act).

(3) The amount of the allowable credit for electricity produced from a modified facility is computed by multiplying the credit determined under the general formula contained in Code Sec. 45(a) by a ratio of the thermal content of the closed-loop biomass used at the modified facility to the thermal content of all fuels used at the modified facility (Code Sec. 45(d)(2)(B)(ii), as added by the 2004 Jobs Act).

Example: Newpower, Inc. produces electricity at its qualified closed-loop biomass facility. For 2005, Newpower determines that its allowable renewable electricity production credit, as computed under the general formula, is $50,000. However, because the corporation uses a combination of coal, closed-loop biomass and open-loop biomass to produce the electricity, it must use a ratio to compute its allowable tax credit. Assume that during 2005, the thermal content of the closed-loop biomass resources used at the facility was 25x and that the thermal content of all fuels used at the facility was 100x. In applying this ratio to its generally allowable tax credit of $50,000, Newpower determines that its allowable tax credit is $12,500 ($50,000 x 25%).

Refined coal production facilities. The credit for refined coal production is computed under its own set of rules (Code Sec. 45(e)(8), as added by the 2004 Jobs Act). (See ¶870 for information pertaining to the definition of "refined coal.") The producer of refined coal is generally entitled to claim a credit at a rate of $4.375 per ton of qualified refined coal that is: (1) produced by the producer at a refined coal production facility during the 10-year period that begins on the date the facility was originally placed in service, and (2) sold by the producer to an unrelated person during the 10-year period.

Comment: The Conference Committee Report (H.R. Conf. Rep. No. 108-755) states that the $4.375 credit rate is indexed for inflation after 1992. This is the same base year that is used to determine the inflation adjustment for the renewable electricity credit (Code Sec. 45(e)(2)(B), as redesignated by the 2004 Jobs Act).

The refined coal credit is subject to a phaseout (Code Sec. 45(e)(8)(B), as added by the 2004 Jobs Act). Under this phaseout, the otherwise allowable credit is reduced by an amount that bears the same ratio to the amount of the increase as: (1) the amount by which the reference price of fuel used as feedstock for the calendar year in which the sale occurs, exceeds an amount equal to 1.7 multiplied by the reference price for such fuel in 2002, bears to (2) $8.75.

Comment: According the Conference Committee Report (H.R. Conf. Rep. No. 108-755), the phaseout rule provides that as the market price of refined coal exceeds certain threshold levels, the otherwise allowable credit will be reduced. The threshold is geared to the price of the feedstock fuel used to produce the refined coal. As examples, the Committee Report states that if a producer of refined coal uses Powder River Basin coal as a feedstock, the threshold price is determined by reference to the price of Powder River Basin coal. Conversely, if the producer uses Appalachian coal as feedstock, the threshold price is determined by Appalachian coal.

When determining the allowable credit for a refined coal facility, many of the same rules that apply to the renewable electricity credit also apply (e.g.,Code Sec. 45(e), as redesignated by the 2004 Jobs Act). For example, the credit is reduced if certain subsidies are received, the production must be in the United States and production must be attributable to the taxpayer (Code Sec. 45(e)(8)(C), as added by the 2004 Jobs Act).

For further information on this subject, consult any of the following CCH reporter explanations:

- Standard Federal Tax Reporter, 2004FED ¶4415.01, ¶4415.021 and ¶4415.07

- Federal Tax Service, FTS §G:24.242

- Federal Tax Guide, 2004FTG ¶2575

★ *Effective date.* Generally, the new provisions apply to electricity produced and sold after the date of enactment of the American Jobs Creation Act of 2004, in tax years ending after such date (Act Sec. 710(g)(1) of the 2004 Jobs Act). With regard to modified open-loop biomass facilities placed in service before the date of enactment of the 2004 Jobs Act, the provisions apply to electricity produced and sold after December 31, 2004, in tax years ending after that date (Act Sec. 710(g)(2) of the 2004 Jobs Act). The five-year credit period that applies to open-loop biomass facilities, geothermal or solar energy facilities, small irrigation power facilities, landfill gas facilities, and trash combustion facilities starts on the date the facility is placed in service. The reduced credit rate that applies to these facilities applies to electricity produced and sold after December 31, 2004, in tax years ending after that date (Act Sec. 710(g)(3) of the 2004 Jobs Act). The 10-year credit period for certain modified closed-loop biomass facilities begins no earlier than the date of enactment of the 2004 Jobs Act (Code Sec. 45(d)(2)(B)(i), as added by the 2004 Jobs Act). The provisions that apply to refined coal production facilities apply to refined coal produced and sold after the date of enactment of the 2004 Jobs Act (Act Sec. 710(g)(5) of the 2004 Jobs Act).

Act Sec. 710(c) of the American Jobs Creation Act of 2004, adding new Code Sec. 45(b)(4); Act Sec. 710(f), amending Code Sec. 45(b)(3); Act Sec. 710(g). Law at ¶5035. Committee Report at ¶10,920.

¶ 890

Sales or Dispositions to Implement FERC or State Electric Restructuring Policy

Background

Gains, profits, and income are included in gross income for the tax year in which they are received by the taxpayer, unless they are included in a different period in accordance with an approved method of accounting followed by the taxpayer (Code Sec. 451(a)). Gain or loss is included in taxable income if realized and recognized. Realization occurs when property is transferred by a sale or other disposition. All realized gains and losses are currently recognized unless the Internal Revenue Code provides an exemption or allows a deferral. Gain equals the excess of the amount realized in a transaction over the adjusted basis of property given up.

American Jobs Creation Act Impact

Tax deferral allowed for gains on electric transmission assets.—A taxpayer can elect to recognize qualified gain from a qualifying electric transmission transaction over an eight-year period (Code Sec. 451(i), as added by the American Jobs Creation

Act of 2004). The qualified gain is recognized beginning in the tax year of the transaction.

The election can be made for qualified gain. Qualified gain is immediately recognized to the extent the amount realized from the transaction exceeds:

(1) the cost of exempt utility property that is purchased by the taxpayer during the four-year period beginning on the date of the transaction, reduced by

(2) any portion of the cost previously taken into account under these gain deferral rules (Code Sec. 451(i)(1)(A), as added by the 2004 Jobs Act).

The cost of exempt utility property taken into account under this formula cannot be reduced below zero. Any remaining qualified gain would be recognized ratably over eight years (Code Sec. 451(i)(1)(B), as added by the 2004 Jobs Act).

Comment: The provision is intended to encourage transmission infrastructure reinvestment and assist those in the industry who are restructuring.

Qualified gain. Qualified gain is:

(1) any ordinary income derived from a qualifying electric transmission transaction that would be required to be recognized under Code Sec. 1245 or Code Sec. 1250, and

(2) any income from a transaction in excess of the amount that is required to be included in gross income for the tax year (Code Sec. 451(i)(2), as added by the 2004 Jobs Act).

Qualifying electric transmission transaction. A qualifying electric transmission transaction is any sale or other disposition to an independent transmission company of (1) property used in the trade or business of providing electric transmission services or, (2) an ownership interest in a corporation or partnership whose principal trade or business consists of providing such services. The sale or disposition must be made before January 1, 2007 (Code Sec. 451(i)(3), as added by the 2004 Jobs Act).

Independent transmission company. An independent transmission company is:

(1) an independent transmission provider approved by the Federal Energy Regulatory Commission (FERC);

(2) a person:

(a) who FERC determines under Section 203 of the Federal Power Act (16 U.S.C. 824b) is not a "market participant," and

(b) whose transmission facilities to which the deferral election applies are under the operational control of a FERC-approved independent transmission provider within a specified time frame; or

(3) in the case of facilities subject to the jurisdiction of the Public Utility Commission of Texas, (a) a person approved by that commission as consistent with Texas state law regarding an independent transmission organization, or (b) a political subdivision or affiliate whose transmission facilities are controlled by that person (Code Sec. 451(i)(4), as added by the 2004 Jobs Act).

In the case of item (2) above, the transmission facilities must be under the control of the independent transmission provider before the close of the period specified in the FERC authorization of the transaction (Code Sec. 451(i)(4)(B)(ii)). In any event, control cannot occur later than January 1, 2007 (Code Sec. 451(i)(4)(B)(ii); Conference Committee Report, H.R. Conf. Rep. No. 108-755).

Exempt utility property. Exempt utility property is property used in the trade or business of:

¶890

(1) generating, transmitting, distributing, or selling electricity; or

(2) producing, transmitting, distributing, or selling natural gas.

Stock in a controlled corporation can be exempt utility property. However, acquisition of control of a corporation is taken into account in a qualifying electric transmission transaction only if one of these activities is the principal trade or business of the corporation (Code Sec. 451(i)(5), as added by the 2004 Jobs Act).

Consolidated groups. If a corporation is a member of an affiliated group filing a consolidated return, any exempt utility property purchased by another member of the group is treated as purchased by the corporation (Code Sec. 451(i)(6), as added by the 2004 Jobs Act).

Purchase. A taxpayer is considered to have purchased any property if the unadjusted basis of the property is its cost under Code Sec. 1012 (Code Sec. 451(i)(8), as added by the 2004 Jobs Act).

Time for assessment of deficiencies. The period for assessing any deficiency on gain recognized under this gain deferral election will not expire prior to three years from the date the taxpayer notifies the IRS of the purchase of exempt utility property or its intention not to purchase such property. The provision overrides any other rule or law that would prevent a deficiency from being assessed before the expiration of the three-year period (Code Sec. 451(i)(7), as added by the 2004 Jobs Act).

Installment sales. The installment sales rules of Code Sec. 453 will not apply to any qualifying transmission transaction if this gain deferral election is made (Code Sec. 451(i)(10), as added by the 2004 Jobs Act).

Election: The election, which is irrevocable, will be binding for the tax year made and all later tax years (Code Sec. 451(i)(9), as added by the 2004 Jobs Act). The electing taxpayer is to attach a statement that the election is being made to the return for the tax year in which the transaction takes place and in the manner to be prescribed by regulations. In addition, the taxpayer must attach a statement identifying the reinvestment property in the manner to be prescribed by the IRS (Conference Committee Report, H.R. Conf. Rep. No. 108-755).

For further information on this subject, consult any of the following CCH reporter explanations:

- Standard Federal Tax Reporter, 2004FED ¶21,005.01
- Federal Tax Service, FTS § K:4.40
- Federal Tax Guide, 2004FTG ¶5070 and ¶5580

★ *Effective date.* The provision applies to transactions occurring after the date of enactment of the American Jobs Creation Act of 2004, in tax years ending after such date (Act Sec. 909(b) of the 2004 Jobs Act).

Act Sec. 909(a) of the American Jobs Creation Act of 2004, adding Code Sec. 451(i); Act Sec. 909(b). Law at ¶5375. Committee Report at ¶11,810.

Chapter 9

S Corporations and Partnerships

S CORPORATIONS

¶ 905

S Corporation Shareholder Limit Increased

Background

The decision to elect S corporation status is popular with closely held businesses because it offers both the limited liability protection of the corporation and the ability to pass through corporate income to shareholders where it is taxed only once at individual rates. One of the requirements for an S corporation is that it may not have more than 75 shareholders (Code Sec. 1361(b)). When the S corporation rules were first enacted, this number was only 10; it has grown over the years. Most recently, the limit was increased to 75 from 35 in 1996 (Small Business Job Protection Act of 1996, P.L. 104-188).

American Jobs Creation Act Impact

Shareholder limit increased from 75 to 100.—The maximum number of eligible S corporation shareholders is increased from 75 to 100 (Code Sec. 1361(b)(1)(A), as amended by the American Jobs Creation Act of 2004).

> **Comment:** While it seems like a fairly basic provision, this increase in eligible shareholder limit is an attempt to modernize the S corporation rules and

eliminate undue restrictions. The intent is to expand the application of the S corporation provisions so that more corporations and shareholders will be able to enjoy the benefits of subchapter S status. This increase in the number of shareholders that an S corporation may have, in conjunction with the new provision allowing members of a family to be treated as one shareholder (discussed in ¶910), will make it easier for investors to utilize the subchapter S corporate structure.

PRACTICAL ANALYSIS. Michael Schlesinger of Schlesinger & Sussman of New York, New York, observes that the IRS Statistics of Income Bulletin (Winter 2004) detailed that fewer than 20,000 returns for 2001 had more than 10 shareholders. Notwithstanding, Congress' increase of the shareholder limit to 100 is helpful for S corporations looking to diversify investors to withstand business fluctuations. In the case of S corporations that will exceed 100 shareholders, shareholders may consider doing an "end run" around Code Sec. 1361(b)(1)(A)'s 100-shareholder limit by forming a partnership of S corporations. Rev. Rul. 94-43, I.R.B. 1994-27, 8, approved such a procedure. In Rev. Rul. 94-43, the IRS sustained a partnership of three S corporations where each S corporation had the maximum number of shareholders permitted. So if 300 shareholders wanted to operate as a single business, they could form three S corporations comprised of 100 shareholders each, and have these three S corporations enter into a partnership to do business. Partnerships can also be used by S corporations where a nonresident alien wants to be part of the business venture (see Reg. §1.701-2(d), Example 2).

For further information on this subject, consult any of the following CCH reporter explanations:

- Standard Federal Tax Reporter, 2004FED ¶32,026.022
- Federal Tax Service, FTS §I:18.43
- Federal Tax Guide, 2004FTG ¶13,005 and ¶13,015

★ *Effective date.* The provision is effective for tax years beginning after December 31, 2004 (Act Sec. 232(b) of the American Jobs Creation Act of 2004).

Act Sec. 232(a) of the American Jobs Creation Act of 2004, amending Code Sec. 1361(b)(1)(A); Act Sec. 232(b). Law at ¶5890. Committee Report at ¶10,130.

¶910

S Corporation Family Members Treated as One Shareholder

Background

Many small businesses are organized as S corporations, which pass through income and loss to shareholders. The shareholders then report their allocable portion of these items on their individual tax returns. Both the number and type of shareholders are limited. One historic requirement of an S corporation is that it have no more than 75 shareholders, all of whom are individual (and certain trusts, estates, charities, and qualified retirement plans) citizens or residents of the United States (Code Sec. 1361(b)). For purposes of the 75-shareholder limitation, a husband and wife (and their estates) are treated as one shareholder (Code Sec. 1361(c)).

American Jobs Creation Act Impact

Family members may be treated as one shareholder.—The number of eligible S corporation shareholders has been increased from 75 to 100 (see ¶ 905) For purposes of counting the number of shareholders to determine if this 100-shareholder limit is exceeded, all family members can elect to be treated as one shareholder. The term "members of the family" is defined as the common ancestor, the lineal descendants of the common ancestor, and the spouses (or former spouses) of the lineal descendants or common ancestor. Note that the common ancestor cannot be more than six generations removed from the youngest generation of shareholders at the time the S election is made (or the effective date of this provision, if later). A spouse (or former spouse) will be treated as being of the same generation as the individual to which he or she is (or was) married (Code Sec. 1361(c)(1), as amended by the American Jobs Creation Act of 2004).

The members of a family may be treated as one shareholder, for the purposes of determining the number of shareholders, whether a family member holds stock directly or is treated as a shareholder by reason of being a beneficiary of an electing small business trust or qualified subchapter S trust (under Code Sec. 1361(c)(2)(B)).

Historically, a legally adopted child, a child who is lawfully placed with a household for legal adoption and a foster child were considered a "child" when it came to determining "member of family" relationships. This has not changed with the 2004 Jobs Act.

> **Comment:** Allowing members of a family to be treated as one shareholder is an attempt to simplify and modernize the S corporation rules. Because family members will not have to be treated as separate shareholders, the small business will be better able to diversify its investors and withstand business fluctuations. Allowing members of a family to be treated as one shareholder, in conjunction with the new provision increasing the number of shareholders that an S corporation may have (discussed in ¶ 905), will make it easier for investors to utilize the subchapter S corporate structure.

> **Comment:** Large family businesses (especially those that have a number of generations) will now be able to obtain or retain S corporation status without precluding employees or others from having an equity stake. Some multi-generational family-owned businesses have been denied the benefit of S corporation status simply because there are too many family members.

PRACTICAL ANALYSIS. Sydney S. Traum, of Sydney S. Traum, P.A., which is "of counsel" to Levey, Airan, Brownstein, Shevin, Friedman, Roen & Kelso, LLP, in Coral Gables, Florida applauds the S Corporation Reform and Simplification provisions of Subtitle D of the 2004 Jobs Act. The increase in the number of permitted shareholders to 100 and the treatment of a family group as one shareholder will enable extended families to continue their S corporations without the need to resort to partnerships of S corporations when the number of owners increases as their families expand. Prior to the effective date of the new provision, when the family expanded so that the number of shareholders test would be violated, it was necessary for the business to be transferred to a partnership of several family-owned S corporations, as permitted in Rev. Rul. 94-43, 1994-2 CB 198.

Except as provided by future regulations, the election may be made by any family member and will remain in effect until terminated.

¶910

PRACTICAL ANALYSIS. Michael Schlesinger of Schlesinger & Sussman of New York, New York, notes that Senator Grassley considers S corporations as the "nation's chief job-creating force." As such, he made a number of changes for S corporations. One change was to amend Code Sec. 1361(c)(1) to allow all members of a family to elect to be treated as one shareholder, limiting this election to six generations. The purpose of this amendment was to allow an S corporation to "diversify its investors and therefore better withstand business fluctuation," especially for community and independent banks. Senator Grassley feels that allowing diversified ownership will make these community and independent banks "stronger for the rural economy." Regulations will be issued by the IRS to prescribe how to terminate the election. Notwithstanding, to protect family members and the S corporation from one family member electing termination, provisions should be inserted in the S corporate shareholders agreement mandating that all family members vote to maintain the election, with the provision that if a family member wants to break the election, leave the corporation, etc., the corporation and/or the remaining shareholders must purchase this shareholder's interest.

For further information on this subject, consult any of the following CCH reporter explanations:

- Standard Federal Tax Reporter, 2004FED ¶ 32,026.022 and ¶ 32,053.054
- Federal Tax Service, FTS § I:18.43
- Federal Tax Guide, 2004FTG ¶ 13,015

★ *Effective date.* The provision is effective for tax years beginning after December 31, 2004 (Act Sec. 231(c) of the American Jobs Creation Act of 2004).

Act Sec. 231(a) of the American Jobs Creation Act of 2004, amending Code Sec. 1361(c)(1); Act Sec. 231(b), amending Code Sec. 1362(f); Act Sec. 231(c). Law at ¶ 5890 and ¶ 5895. Committee Report at ¶ 10,120.

¶ 915

Transfer of Suspended Losses to Spouse or Incident to Divorce

Background

Losses and deductions that are disallowed because a shareholder has insufficient basis in the stock and debt of an S corporation are carried over to a subsequent year only with respect to that shareholder. Once a shareholder transfers all of his or her shares to another person, the suspended losses and deductions are irretrievably disallowed and are no longer available to any shareholder.

American Jobs Creation Act Impact

Transfer of suspended losses to spouse or former spouse incident to divorce.— An exception is provided to the rule that suspended losses and deductions are irretrievably disallowed and are not available to anyone once an S corporation shareholder transfers all of his or her shares to another person. If a shareholder's stock is transferred to his or her spouse, or to a former spouse incident to divorce (as described in Code Sec. 1041(a)), any suspended loss or deduction with respect to that stock will be treated as incurred by the S corporation in the succeeding tax year with respect to the transferee (Code Sec. 1366(d)(2), as amended by the American Jobs Creation Act of 2004).

Caution Note: If all of a spouse's S corporation shares are transferred to his or her spouse, or to a former spouse incident to divorce, the suspended losses and deductions attributable to the shares would be included in the transfer. Arguably, if a shareholder transferred some shares to his or her spouse, or to a former spouse incident to divorce, a portion (*pro rata* amount) of the suspended losses and deductions would become available to the transferee, and the remaining amount of suspended losses would remain with the transferor. However, the treatment of a transfer of some but not all of the shareholder's stock is not clearly spelled out in the new provision.

PRACTICAL ANALYSIS. Michael J. Grace of Buchanan Ingersoll PC and Georgetown University Law Center, Washington, D.C., observes that the 2004 Jobs Act's amendment of Code Sec. 1366(d)(2), concerning carryovers of losses and deductions exceeding basis in an S corporation, answers some but certainly not all questions that arise when one spouse transfers stock to another spouse. Code Sec. 1041(a) characterizes the transaction as a gift, with the transferor's basis in the stock carrying over to the transferee. Overriding Reg. §1.1366-2(a)(5) in the case of interspousal transfers, the Act sensibly provides that the transferor's losses (if any) suspended under Code Sec. 1366(d) also transfer to the transferee spouse. As a result, the losses will become allowable under Code Sec. 1366(d)(1) once the transferee obtains basis in stock or indebtedness of the S corporation. At that point, however, the losses become subject to other limitations that apply after Code Sec. 1366. In order to deduct the losses freed under Code Sec. 1366(d), the transferee will have to be at risk for the losses (under Code Sec. 465) and will have to overcome the limitation on passive activity losses (Code Sec. 469). Both limitations may "trap" the losses for one or more years after the losses become allowable under Code Sec. 1366(d), but disallowed losses carry over indefinitely under the other two limitations, respectively. See Temporary Reg. §1.469-2T(d)(6), which coordinates the limitations under Code Secs. 1366(d), 465 and 469.

Note that the Act's amendment of Code Sec. 1366(d)(2) applies to tax years beginning after December 31, 2004. Spouses or former spouses contemplating transfers of S corporation stock having suspended losses should consider deferring such transfers until the amendment takes effect.

The Act's amendment of Code Sec. 1366 does not resolve the similar issue of how losses suspended under Code Sec. 469 are treated when a spouse transfers an interest in an activity to a spouse or former spouse. Code Sec. 1041(a) treats an interspousal transfer as a gift regardless of the transaction's form. See Temporary Reg. §1.1041-1T, Q&A 2. If the transaction also is characterized as a gift under Code Sec. 469, then any suspended passive losses allocable to the transferred activity should be added to its basis under Code Sec. 469(j)(6). If, however, the transaction is characterized as a "disposition" of the activity to a related party, then the losses remain with the transferor under Code Sec. 469(g)(1)(B) until the activity is acquired in a "fully taxable transaction" by a person not related to the transferor. It would be helpful for future legislation or administrative guidance to resolve this issue.

PRACTICAL ANALYSIS. Michael Schlesinger of Schlesinger & Sussman of New York, New York, observes that the amendment to Code Sec. 1366(d)(2) provides clarification for purposes of dividing marital property under Code Sec. 1041, so that if S corporate stock is transferred to a spouse, any suspended losses can be utilized by the spouse when basis is restored, such as when the S corporation has undistributed profits. Hopefully, Congress, the IRS or both will detail what occurs when a spouse only transfers a portion of S corporate stock under Code Sec. 1041, keeping the balance.

For further information on this subject, consult any of the following CCH reporter explanations:

- Standard Federal Tax Reporter, 2004FED ¶ 32,084.027
- Federal Tax Service, FTS § I:18.142
- Federal Tax Guide, 2004FTG ¶ 13,205

★ *Effective date.* The provision applies to tax years beginning after December 31, 2004 (Act Sec. 235(b) of the American Jobs Creation Act of 2004).

Act Sec. 235(a) of the American Jobs Creation Act of 2004, amending Code Sec. 1366(d)(2); Act Sec. 235(b). Law at ¶ 5900. Committee Report at ¶ 10,160.

¶ 920

Relief from Inadvertently Invalid Qualified S Subsidiary Elections and Terminations

Background

Code Sec. 1362(f) authorizes the IRS to provide relief for inadvertent invalid S corporation elections and terminations. Inadvertent elections and terminations frequently occur because S corporations and their shareholders are unfamiliar with the technical or procedural requirements for making or terminating S corporation elections. Taxpayers usually seek relief for inadvertent elections and terminations through the letter ruling process.

American Jobs Creation Act Impact

Relief from inadvertently invalid qualified S subsidiary (QSub) elections and terminations.—The IRS is empowered with the authority to grant relief for inadvertent QSub elections and terminations in the same manner that it does for inadvertent S corporation elections and terminations (Code Sec. 1362(f), as amended by the American Jobs Creation Act of 2004).

Comment: The IRS had provided for inadvertently invalid QSub election and termination relief in proposed QSub regulations, but did not include them in the final regulations because of concern that Congress needed to grant the IRS the authority to provide this type of relief.

Example: A QSub election would be terminated if an S corporation inadvertently transferred a share of stock to another person. The subsidiary is not eligible to have a QSub election in effect during the period the parent does not own 100 percent of its stock. The QSub would no longer be solely owned by the parent S corporation and generally it would no longer be eligible to elect to be a QSub for at least another five years. Prior to the enactment of this new provision, the IRS did not have the authority to grant relief from this type of inadvertent QSub termination.

PRACTICAL ANALYSIS. Michael Schlesinger of Schlesinger & Sussman of New York, New York, notes that the amendment of Code Sec. 1362(f)—while missing conjunctions in two statutory definitions—pro-

vides needed relief to cover inadvertent invalid qualified subchapter S subsidiary elections and terminations.

For further information on this subject, consult any of the following CCH reporter explanations:

- Standard Federal Tax Reporter, 2004FED ¶32,053.027, ¶32,053.034 and ¶32,053.054

- Federal Tax Service, FTS §I:18.202 and §I:18.203

- Federal Tax Guide, 2004FTG ¶13,005 and ¶13,125

★ *Effective date.* The provision applies to elections and terminations made after December 31, 2004 (Act Sec. 238(b) of the American Jobs Creation Act of 2004).

Act Sec. 238(a) of the American Jobs Creation Act of 2004, amending Code Sec. 1362(f); Act Sec. 238(b). Law at ¶5895. Committee Report at ¶10,190.

¶925

Use of Passive Activity Loss and At-Risk Amounts by Qualified Subchapter S Trusts

Background

A qualified subchapter S trust (QSST) may qualify as a shareholder of an S corporation. A QSST generally is a trust with one individual income beneficiary for the life of the beneficiary. The share of income of an S corporation whose stock is held by a QSST, with respect to which the beneficiary makes an election, is taxed to the beneficiary (Code Sec. 1361(d)(1)).

Although the QSST beneficiary is taxed on all of the items of income, loss, deduction and credit attributable to the ownership of S stock by the QSST, the trust, and not the beneficiary, is treated as the owner of the S corporation stock for purposes of determining the tax consequences on the disposition of the S corporation stock by the trust (see Reg. §1.1361-1(j)(8)).

In general, the at-risk rules of Code Sec. 465 limit a taxpayer's loss to the amount that the taxpayer has at risk and could actually lose from an activity. The at-risk rules applicable to losses apply at the shareholder level rather than at the corporate level for S corporations. Any gain recognized on the transfer or disposition of an interest in an activity is treated as income from the activity, thus generally permitting disallowed losses from previous years to be taken in the year of disposition.

Deductions from a passive trade or business activity, including expenses such as interest attributable to acquiring or carrying an interest in a passive activity, generally may not be deducted from other income for the tax year to the extent that the deductions exceed income from all such passive activities (i.e., the loss is "suspended."). Suspended losses may be used to offset passive income in future years or may be recognized upon the taxpayer's entire disposition of his interest in an activity to which a suspended loss is allocated (Code Sec. 469(g)).

Due to the operation of Reg. §1.1361-1(j)(8), it is not clear how to treat such suspended losses when S corporation stock is sold by a QSST.

American Jobs Creation Act Impact

Disposition of S corporation stock by QSST treated as disposition by the QSST beneficiary.—The disposition of S corporation stock by a trust electing QSST status is treated as a disposition of the stock by the QSST beneficiary for purposes of applying the passive activity loss and the at-risk limitations of Code Sec. 465 and Code Sec. 469(g). Therefore, the beneficiary of a qualified subchapter S trust is generally allowed to deduct suspended losses under the at-risk rules and the passive loss rules when the trust disposes of the S corporation stock (Code Sec. 1361(d)(1), as amended by the American Jobs Creation Act of 2004.)

> **Caution Note:** This change is made only with respect to the passive activity loss and the at-risk limitations of Code Sec. 465 and Code Sec. 469(g). Thus, upon the disposition of Subchapter S stock, the QSST election terminates as to the stock sold and any gain or loss recognized on the sale will continue to be that of the trust, not the income beneficiary.

> **Comment:** Another provision of the 2004 Jobs Act concerns the transfer of suspended losses incident to divorce, see ¶915. However, proposals to amend Code Sec. 1371(b) to permit the carryover of suspended passive activity losses from a year in which a corporation was a C corporation to a year in which the corporation is an S corporation were not included in the final version of the 2004 Jobs Act.

For further information on this subject, consult any of the following CCH reporter explanations:

- Standard Federal Tax Reporter, 2004FED ¶21,893.01, ¶21,966.01 and ¶32,026.026

- Federal Tax Service, FTS §I:18.45

- Federal Tax Guide, 2004FTG ¶13,015

★ *Effective date.* The provision is applicable to transfers made after December 31, 2004 (Act Sec. 236(b) of the American Jobs Creation Act of 2004).

Act Sec. 236(a) of the American Jobs Creation Act of 2004, amending Code Sec. 1361(d)(1); Act Sec. 236(b). Law at ¶5890. Committee Report at ¶10,170.

¶930

Disregard of Unexercised Powers of Appointment in Determining Potential Current Beneficiaries of ESBT

Background

An electing small business trust (ESBT) may be a shareholder in an S corporation. Potential current beneficiaries of such a trust are counted as shareholders of the S corporation for purposes of determining whether the corporation qualifies for the S corporation election. Accordingly, it is important that potential current beneficiaries qualify as S corporation shareholders both in terms of who they are (for example, a nonresident alien would not qualify), and in terms of number (for example, not being so great in number that they cause the S corporation to exceed the maximum number of permissible shareholders).

A "potential current beneficiary" is any person who, with respect to any period, is entitled to, or at the discretion of any person may receive, a distribution from the principal or income of the trust (Code Sec. 1361(e)(2)). The IRS construes this definition broadly to include all those who may benefit from a power of appointment, whether that power has been exercised or not (Reg. §1.1361-1(m)(4)(vi)). Thus, for example, if the trust provides a beneficiary with a power to appoint income or principal to any of her six grandchildren, those six grandchildren are potential current beneficiaries regardless of whether the beneficiary has exercised her power in their favor.

If current potential beneficiaries of an ESBT disqualify a corporation in which the ESBT holds stock from S corporation status, the ESBT can remedy the situation by disposing of the offending shares within 60 days. In the event of such a disposition, any person who first met the requirements for being a potential current beneficiary during the 60-day period ending with the disposition of the stock is not treated as a potential current beneficiary (Code Sec. 1361(e)(2)).

American Jobs Creation Act Impact

Current potential beneficiaries no longer include those who might benefit from an unexercised power of appointment.—The definition of potential current beneficiary for ESBT purposes has been clarified. Powers of appointment, to the extent they are not exercised, are disregarded in determining the potential current beneficiaries of an ESBT. Thus, a potential current beneficiary does not include anyone by virtue of a power of appointment that remained unexercised during the relevant period (Code Sec. 1361(e)(2), as amended by the American Jobs Creation Act of 2004). The 2004 Jobs Act also extends the remedial period from 60 days to one year (Code Sec. 1361(e)(2), as amended by the 2004 Jobs Act).

> **PRACTICAL ANALYSIS. Sydney S. Traum, of Sydney S. Traum, P.A., which is "of counsel" to Levey, Airan, Brownstein, Shevin, Friedman, Roen & Kelso, LLP, in Coral Gables, Florida** notes that the provision changing the definition of a potential current beneficiary of an electing small business trust (ESBT) to exclude persons who may be named under a power of appointment until they are actually named is very helpful. It gives greater flexibility to those wishing to give a discretionary power for someone to name future beneficiaries. Thus, a trust which permits someone to name which charities will benefit from a certain provision will no longer need to limit the choices to a limited number of specifically named charities. But the provision does not go far enough. Since an ESBT pays tax on its S corporation income at the highest income tax rates, there seems to be no fiscal reason for limiting the number of potential current beneficiaries, or even the requirement that the potential beneficiaries must meet the stringent S corporation shareholder tests. Perhaps future legislation will change these requirements and allow even greater flexibility for the S corporation form of doing business.

> **PRACTICAL ANALYSIS. Michael Schlesinger of Schlesinger & Sussman of New York, New York,** notes that the amendment of Code Sec. 1361(e)(2) is helpful in extending the period of time from 60 days to one year to allow for more time for action, reducing the need for a ruling request to be made due to inadvertence. Also, the provision regarding defining potential current beneficiaries is helpful, because the rules have been eased for determining these individuals.

Example 1: Martha and Arnold Morgan are calendar-year taxpayers. On January 1, 2004, Martha creates an ESBT for the benefit of Arnold into which she puts S corporation stock. The trust provides Arnold with a currently exercisable power to appoint income and principal to anyone except Arnold himself, his creditors, his estate, and the creditors of his estate (a common provision allowing Arnold to "spray" the benefits of the trust while keeping Arnold's creditors away from the trust assets). The potential current beneficiaries of the trust will be Arnold and all other persons, except for his creditors, his estate, and the creditors of his estate. As a result, the number of potential current beneficiaries will exceed the maximum number of shareholders for an S corporation (Code

Sec. 1361(b)(1)(A)). Under the IRS's regulatory construal of "potential current beneficiary," the corporation's S election would terminate (Reg. § 1.1361-1(m)(8), Ex. 7) unless the trust disposed of all of the stock within 60 days.

Example 2: Assume the same facts in Example 1, except that Martha creates the ESBT on January 1, 2005. In that case, the potential beneficiaries of the unexercised power of appointment are disregarded for purposes of identifying potential current beneficiaries of the trust. Accordingly, the unexercised power of appointment would not cause the corporation's S election to terminate.

Example 3: Assume the same facts in Example 1, except that Martha created the ESBT on January 1, 2005, and Arnold is a nonresident alien. Arnold is a potential current beneficiary who will cause the corporation to lose its S election because nonresident aliens are not permissible S corporation shareholders. The trust has until December 31, 2005, to dispose of all of the S corporation stock in order to avoid termination of the corporation's S election.

For further information on this subject, consult any of the following CCH reporter explanations:

- Standard Federal Tax Reporter, 2004FED ¶ 32,026.028
- Federal Tax Service, FTS § I:18.48[1]
- Federal Tax Guide, 2004FTG ¶ 13,015

★ *Effective date.* The provision applies to tax years beginning after December 31, 2004 (Act Sec. 234(b) of the American Jobs Creation Act of 2004).

Act Sec. 234(a) of the American Jobs Creation Act of 2004, amending Code Sec. 1361(e)(2); Act Sec. 234(b). Law at ¶ 5890. Committee Report at ¶ 10,150.

¶ 935

ESOP Repayment of Exempt Loans with Distributions from S Corporation Stock

Background _____

An employee stock ownership plan (ESOP) is a contribution plan subject to special qualification requirements that invests primarily in qualifying employer securities (Code Sec. 409(a)). An ESOP can be funded by employer contributions in the same manner as other defined contribution plans. ESOPs, however, typically also borrow funds to purchase employer securities. Such ESOPs are called leveraged ESOPs. Employers get a limited break on contribution limits to the extent contributions are used to pay back the loan (Code Sec. 404(a)(9)).

The source of a leveraged ESOP's borrowed funds is usually the employer. Ordinarily, such a loan would be a prohibited transaction subject to a special tax (Code Sec. 4975). However, an exemption from this special tax applies to a loan to a leveraged ESOP if certain conditions are met (Code Sec. 4975(d)(3) and (e)(7)). Loans that qualify for this exception are typically called exempt loans.

Exempt loans are secured by the purchased qualifying employer securities, which the ESOP holds in a separate suspense account. As the debt is paid, the appropriate number of shares are released and allocated to individual employee accounts on a yearly basis (Reg. § 54.4975-11(c) and (d)).

Income with respect to securities acquired with the proceeds of an exempt loan must be allocated as income of the plan except to the extent that the ESOP provides for the use of income from such securities to repay the loan (Reg. § 54.4975-11(d)(3)).

In the case of C corporations, dividends used to make payments on an exempt loan are deductible (Code Sec. 404(k)(1) and (k)(2)). Furthermore, the Code specifically provides that the ESOP of a C corporation can, in accordance with the plan provisions, use stock dividends generated by the qualified employer securities to pay interest and principal on the exempt loan without threatening the loan's exempt status or the plan's qualified status (Code Sec. 404(k)(5)(B)). This rule does not apply to dividends paid on stock that has been allocated to an employee's account, unless the plan provides that employer securities with a fair market value of not less than the amount of the dividend is allocated to the employee's account for the year in which the dividend would have been so allocated (Code Sec. 404(k)(2)(B) and (5)(B)).

American Jobs Creation Act Impact

ESOPs can repay exempt loan from S corporation stock distributions.—The American Jobs Creation Act of 2004 clarifies how ESOPs of S corporations are to be treated with respect to distributions from S corporation stock used to pay off an exempt loan. The 2004 Jobs Act provides rules similar to those applicable to C corporations so that an ESOP does not jeopardize its status as an ESOP or the loan's status as exempt merely because it uses distributions from the S corporation stock purchased with the loan proceeds to pay down the loan. This rule does not apply to distributions paid on stock that has been allocated to an employee's account, unless the plan provides that employer securities with a fair market value of not less than the amount of the dividend is allocated to the employee's account for the year in which the dividend would have been so allocated (Code Sec. 4975(f)(7), as added by the 2004 Jobs Act).

Planning Note: Using distributions from qualified employee securities held in a suspense account to pay down the exempt loan rather than allocating such distributions to employee accounts may enable the ESOP to avoid contribution limits for annual additions under Code Sec. 415. Suppose C corporation stock in a suspense account generates $1,000 in distributions in the tax year. In a series of private rulings, the IRS has taken the position that if the $1,000 is allocated to employee accounts it is considered compensation for purposes of the annual addition limits, but if it is used to pay off the exempt loan it is considered a distribution of earnings to shareholders and avoids the annual addition limit (see, e.g., IRS Letter Ruling 200243055, Aug. 1, 2002).

Comment: S corporation stock held by any tax-exempt entities or account is generally subject to unrelated business income tax on the theory its earnings must be taxed at least once, but the unrelated business income tax does not apply with respect to S corporation stock held by an ESOP (Code Sec. 512(e)(3)).

For further information on this subject, consult any of the following CCH reporter explanations:

- Standard Federal Tax Reporter, 2004FED ¶34,410.03 and ¶34,410.031
- Federal Tax Service, FTS §C:25.141
- Federal Tax Guide, 2004FTG ¶11,850 and ¶13,015

★ *Effective date.* This amendment applies to distributions with respect to S corporation stock made after December 31, 1997 (Act Sec. 240(b) of the American Jobs Creation Act of 2004).

Act Sec. 240(a) of the American Jobs Creation Act of 2004, adding Code Sec. 4975(f)(7); Act Sec. 240(b). Law at ¶6100. Committee Report at ¶10,210.

¶ 940

Expansion of Bank S Corporation Eligible Shareholders to Include IRAs

Background

Banks have been able to elect S corporation status since 1997, but some have encountered a problem. S corporation shareholders have to be individuals, but bank employees often own bank stock in their individual retirement accounts (IRAs). Although there are exceptions to the rule that only individuals can be S corporation shareholders, IRAs are not among the exceptions (Code Sec. 1361(b)(1)(B)). Therefore, banks have had to somehow get those shares out of their employees' IRAs if they wanted to be treated as S corporations. Redemption by the bank is a legal possibility, but not always a practical one. IRA beneficiaries might be willing to buy the shares from their IRAs, but such transactions between an IRA and beneficiaries are not allowed (Code Sec. 4975(c)(1)(A)).

American Jobs Creation Act Impact

Banks can now elect S corporation status despite ownership of bank stock by IRAs.—The American Jobs Creation Act of 2004 allows a bank with stock held in IRAs to make an S corporation election without first having to redeem those shares. The 2004 Jobs Act does this in two ways. First, it allows a transaction between IRAs and their beneficiaries in which bank stock held in the IRA on the date of enactment of the 2004 Jobs Act is sold to the employee no later than 120 days after the S corporation election (Code Sec. 4975(d)(16), as added by the 2004 Jobs Act). Second, IRA and Roth IRA ownership of bank S corporation stock is allowed to the extent such stock is held by the IRA or Roth IRA on the date of enactment of the 2004 Jobs Act (Code Sec. 1361(c)(2)(A)(vi), as added by the 2004 Jobs Act).

> **PRACTICAL ANALYSIS. Michael Schlesinger of Schlesinger & Sussman of New York, New York, notes that the amendment to Code Sec. 1361(c)(2)(A) and (B) permitting an IRA, including a Roth IRA, to be a shareholder of a bank that is an S corporation, but only to the extent of bank stock held by the IRA on the date of enactment of this amendment, smacks of special interest legislation, because of the limitation on a date for application of this rule. Hopefully Congress will decide to expand this provision to allow IRAs to hold stock in all S corporations, since they already allow ESOPs to be shareholders in S corporations.**

Sale of bank stock by IRA to beneficiary. Under certain conditions, an IRA holding bank stock can sell the stock to the beneficiary (Code Sec. 4975(d)(16), as added by the 2004 Jobs Act). To qualify, these conditions must be satisfied:

- the stock is in a bank as defined in Code Sec. 581;
- the stock is held by the IRA on the date of enactment of the 2004 Jobs Act;
- the sale is pursuant to an S corporation election by the bank;
- the sale is for fair market value at the time of sale (as established by an independent appraiser) and is on terms at least as favorable to the IRA as the terms would be on a sale to an unrelated party;
- the IRA incurs no commissions, costs, or other expenses in connection with the sale; and
- the stock is sold in a single transaction for cash no later than 120 days after the S corporation election is made.

PRACTICAL ANALYSIS. Sydney S. Traum, of Sydney S. Traum, P.A., which is "of counsel" to Levey, Airan, Brownstein, Shevin, Friedman, Roen & Kelso, LLP, in Coral Gables, Florida observes that the expansion of bank S corporation eligible shareholders to include IRAs may be a trap for the unwary. That is because the provision applies only to stock held by an IRA on the date that President Bush signs the legislation (the date of enactment). It will not apply to future acquisitions of stock by IRAs. Similarly, the exemption from the prohibited transaction rules which will permit an IRA to sell S corporation bank stock to the owner of the IRA will also apply only to stock held by the IRA on the date of enactment.

IRAs as bank S corporation shareholders. The beneficiary of an IRA holding bank S corporation stock is to be treated as a shareholder of the bank (Code Sec. 1361(c)(2)(B)(vi), as added by the 2004 Jobs Act). Since IRA beneficiaries are individuals and individuals are allowed to be S corporation shareholders, this rule does not pose a problem unless the individual is a nonresident alien and therefore not qualified to be an S corporation shareholder (Code Sec. 1361(b)(1)(C)). The beneficiary will be counted for purposes of determining whether the number of shareholders exceeds the maximum permitted for an S corporation (Code Sec. 1361(b)(1)(B)).

Taxation of bank S corporation shares held in an IRA. Although income accumulated in an IRA is ordinarily tax-exempt, IRAs are subject to taxation for unrelated business income (Code Sec. 408(e)(1)). The unrelated business income tax is applicable to tax-exempt entities and is aimed at taxing businesses regularly carried on by such entities that are not substantially related to the exempt purpose (Code Secs. 511 and 512). As applied to charitable trusts or trusts in connection with a qualified pension, profit-sharing, or stock bonus plan, a membership in a partnership that conducts an unrelated business counts as an unrelated business interest (Code Sec. 513(b)). Although the Code is less than clear on this point, the IRS applies this rule to IRAs (see, e.g., IRS Letter Ruling 9703026, Oct. 29, 1996).

S corporation stock is generally treated the same way as partnership interests for purposes of unrelated business taxable income. There are no historic situations involving IRA ownership of S corporation stock, but looking to the analogous case of Code Sec. 401(a) qualified plans is instructive. Qualified plans (unlike IRAs) have historically been allowed to own S corporation stock (Code Sec. 1361(c)(6)). S corporation stock held in such plans is treated as an interest in an unrelated business, and all items of income, loss, or deduction, as well as gain or loss on the disposition of the stock in the S corporation are taken into account in computing the unrelated business taxable income of the organization (Code Secs. 511(a) and 512(e)). An exception is specifically carved out for S corporation stock held by employee stock ownership plans (ESOPs) (Code Sec. 512(e)(3)). But no such exception was carved out for IRAs either in the past or by the 2004 Jobs Act, so one can conclude that S corporation stock owned in an IRA will be treated as an interest in an unrelated business.

Comment: The Conference Committee Report indicates that Congress intended the unrelated business income tax to apply to S corporation stock held in an IRA (H. R. Conf Rep. No. 108-755). However, some clarification in the Code would have been welcome. The reasoning supporting the imposition of the unrelated business income tax on IRA-held S corporation stock relies to a large extent on the failure of Congress to carve out an exception (as it did for ESOPs) for treating something (S corporation stock as an unrelated business interest) that was never straightforwardly promulgated with respect to IRAs in the first place. (Compare the clear treatment of Code Sec. 401(a) qualified pension plans in Code Secs. 511 to 515 —including the rule treating S corporation stock in a qualified plan as an unrelated business interest—to the lack of any reference to IRAs in those sections.)

For further information on this subject, consult any of the following CCH reporter explanations:

- Standard Federal Tax Reporter, 2004FED ¶ 32,026.024 and ¶ 34,410.03
- Federal Tax Service, FTS § I:18.44[7] and § C:22.240
- Federal Tax Guide, 2004FTG ¶ 13,005 and ¶ 13,015

★ *Effective date.* These provisions take effect on the date of the enactment of the American Jobs Creation Act of 2004 (Act Sec. 233(e) of the American Jobs Creation Act of 2004).

Act Sec. 233(a) of the American Jobs Creation Act of 2004, adding Code Sec. 1361(c)(2)(A)(vi); Act Sec. 233(b) adding Code Sec. 1361(c)(2)(B)(vi); Act Sec. 233(c), adding Code Sec. 4975(d)(16); Act Sec. 233(d), amending Code Sec. 512(e)(1); Act Sec. 233(e). Law at ¶ 5410, ¶ 5890 and ¶ 6100. Committee Report at ¶ 10,140.

¶ 945

Investment Securities Income Excluded from Passive Income Test for Bank S Corporations

Background

An S corporation is subject to corporate-level tax, at the highest corporate tax rate, on its excess net passive income if the corporation has (1) accumulated earnings and profits at the close of the tax year, and (2) gross receipts more than 25 percent of which are passive investment income. In addition, an S corporation election is terminated whenever the S corporation has accumulated earnings and profits at the close of three consecutive tax years and has gross receipts for each of those years more than 25 percent of which are passive investment income.

Excess net passive income is the net passive income for a tax year multiplied by a fraction, the numerator of which is the amount of passive investment income in excess of 25 percent of gross receipts and the denominator of which is the passive investment income for the year. Net passive income is defined as passive investment income reduced by the allowable deductions that are directly connected with the production of that income. Passive investment income generally means gross receipts derived from royalties, rents, dividends, interest, annuities, and sales or exchanges of stock or securities (to the extent of gains).

Passive investment income generally does not include interest on accounts receivable, gross receipts that are derived directly from the active and regular conduct of a lending or finance business, gross receipts from certain liquidations, or gain or loss from any Code Sec. 1256 contract (or related property) of an options or commodities dealer.

Notice 97-5, 1997-1 CB 352 generally provides that gross receipts directly derived in the ordinary course of a banking business are not passive investment income for purposes of the passive investment income tax. Income from the following assets are considered part of the active and regular conduct of a banking business:

- loan, participations, or REMIC regular interests;
- equity investments needed to conduct business (such as Federal Reserve Bank, Federal Home Loan Bank, or Federal Agricultural Mortgage Bank stock or participation certificates issued by a Federal Intermediate Credit Bank which represent nonvoting stock in the bank);

- assets pledged to a third party to secure deposits or business (such as assets pledged to qualify as a depository for federal taxes or state funds); and

- investment assets needed for liquidity or loan demand.

The amount of investment assets needed for liquidity or loan demand can be very subjective, with most banks not wanting to gamble that an IRS agent may disagree with their estimates. Banks find this uncertainty regarding the possible application of the passive investment income tax (and possible S corporation termination) to be problematic and many have delayed or discarded their decision to make the S corporation election.

American Jobs Creation Act Impact

Investment securities income excluded from passive income test for bank S corporations—For purposes of applying the excess net passive income rules, passive investment income does not include interest income and certain dividends on assets required to be held by:

(1) a bank, as defined in Code Sec. 581;

(2) a bank holding company, as defined in Section 2(a) of the Bank Holding Company Act of 1956; or

(3) a financial holding company, as defined in Section 2(p) of that Act (Code Sec. 1362(d)(3)(F), as added by the American Jobs Creation Act of 2004).

The exclusion relates to interest income earned by the bank or holding company (Code Sec. 1362(d)(3)(F)(i), as added by the 2004 Jobs Act). The dividends on assets required to be held include stock in the Federal Reserve Bank, the Federal Home Loan Bank, or the Federal Agricultural Mortgage Bank or participation certificates issued by a Federal Intermediate Credit Bank (Code Sec. 1362(d)(3)(F)(ii), as added by the 2004 Jobs Act).

> **Comment:** In Notice 97-5, 1997-1 CB 352, the IRS excluded interest income on investments necessary to meet "reasonable liquidity needs (including funds needed to meet anticipated loan demands)," but did not provide the unqualified exclusion that the new provision provides.

For an institution to qualify as a "bank," it must be incorporated and doing business under state or federal law, with a substantial part of its business consisting of either: receiving deposits and making loans, or exercising fiduciary powers similar to those permitted to national banks under the authority of the Comptroller of the Currency (Code Sec. 581).

A "bank holding company" is a company which has control over any bank or over any company that is or becomes a bank holding company. Any company has control over a bank or over any company if it directly or indirectly or acting through one or more other persons owns, controls, or has power to vote 25 percent or more of any class of voting securities of the bank or company (see Section 2(a) of the Bank Holding Company Act of 1956).

The term "financial holding company" means a bank holding company that satisfies certain requirements (see Section 1843(l)(1) of the Bank Holding Company Act of 1956).

> **Caution Note:** This new provision only applies to specific banking institutions. The IRS believes that special bank treatment of items should not apply to nonbanks, even if the nonbank is affiliated with a bank and the parent makes the

qualified subchapter S subsidiary (QSSS) election with respect to all of its subsidiaries.

For further information on this subject, consult any of the following CCH reporter explanations:

- Standard Federal Tax Reporter, 2004FED ¶ 32,053.047
- Federal Tax Service, FTS § I:18.103[1]
- Federal Tax Guide, 2004FTG ¶ 13,220 and ¶ 13,235

★ *Effective date.* The provision applies to tax years beginning after December 31, 2004 (Act Sec. 237(b) of the American Jobs Creation Act of 2004).

Act Sec. 237(a) of the American Jobs Creation Act of 2004, adding Code Sec. 1362(d)(3)(F); Act Sec. 237(b). Law at ¶ 5895. Committee Report at ¶ 10,180.

¶ 950
Information Returns for Qualified Subchapter S Subsidiaries

Background

An S corporation is permitted to own a qualified subchapter S subsidiary (QSub). A QSub includes any domestic corporation that qualifies as an S corporation and is 100 percent owned by an S corporation parent that elects to treat it as a QSub (Code Sec. 1361(b)(3)(B)). All of the assets, liabilities, and items of income, deduction, and credit of the QSub are treated as the assets, liabilities, and items of the parent S corporation. The IRS has authority to provide exceptions to the general rule that a QSub is not treated as a separate corporation, but as a subsidiary or division of the parent S corporation (Code Sec. 1361(b)(3)(A)).

American Jobs Creation Act Impact

Information returns for qualified subchapter S corporations.—The IRS is authorized to provide guidance regarding information returns of qualified subchapter S subsidiaries (QSub) (Code Sec. 1361(b)(3)(A), as amended by the American Jobs Creation Act of 2004).

Comment: The IRS was already authorized to provide regulations regarding the treatment of QSubs. This provision merely adds that the IRS may also provide regulations regarding the information returns required to be filed by QSubs.

Comment: The Section of Taxation of the American Bar Association submitted a statement to the House Committee on Ways and Means that questioned the need for this provision. Instead, the Section on Taxation recommended that information returns required under present law be filed by the S corporation parent because the existence of the QSub is usually disregarded for federal tax purposes, except to the extent provided by IRS regulations (comments on behalf of the American Bar Association, Section of Taxation, to the House Subcommittee on Select Revenue Measures of the House Ways and Means Committee on the subject of the Subchapter S Modernization Act of 2003, July 1, 2003).

For further information on this subject, consult any of the following CCH reporter explanations:

- Standard Federal Tax Reporter, 2004FED ¶ 32,026.035, ¶ 32,026.036 and ¶ 32,026.075
- Federal Tax Service, FTS § I:18.200

- Federal Tax Guide, 2004FTG ¶13,015

★ *Effective date.* The provision is effective for tax years beginning after December 31, 2004 (Act Sec. 239(b) of the American Jobs Creation Act of 2004).

Act Sec. 239(a) of the American Jobs Creation Act of 2004, amending Code Sec. 1361(b)(3)(A); Act Sec. 239(b). Law at ¶5890. Committee Report at ¶10,200.

PARTNERSHIPS

¶960

Disallowance of Partnership Loss Duplication

Background

Partnerships are flexible business entities that allow members a large degree of choice in how to allocate gains and losses from the business. This flexibility, plus the tradition of nonrecognition when property is contributed to or taken out of a partnership, has created opportunities for taxpayers to use partnerships to inappropriately transfer or duplicate losses.

Loss duplication transactions depend on nonrecognition when property goes in or out of a partnership and on the elective basis adjustment rules for partnerships. At the contribution end, contributions of property to a partnership typically do not result in gain or loss to the contributing partner or the partnership (Code Sec. 721). The contributed property's basis carries over from the partner to the partnership (Code Sec. 723), and the contributing partner records its property contribution by increasing its basis in the partnership by the adjusted basis of the contributed property (Code Sec. 722). For distributions, partners may receive distributions of partnership property without recognition of gain or loss by either the partner or the partnership (Code Sec. 731(a) and (b)). At the election of the partnership, basis adjustments to partnership property may be made following a distribution of property (Code Sec. 754).

Adjustments to partnership property basis following transfer of interest. The default rule is that no basis adjustments to partnership property are made following the transfer of a partnership interest by sale or death of a partner. A partnership can make an election to adjust the basis of partnership property following each time a partnership interest is transferred (Code Sec. 743(a)). The amount of the adjustment is the difference between the transferee partner's proportionate share of the adjusted basis of the partnership property, and the transferee's basis in its partnership interest (Code Sec. 743(b)). These adjustments are intended to approximate the result of a direct purchase of the property by the transferee partner. Based on these rules, if a partner purchases an interest in a partnership with an existing built-in loss, and no election under Code Sec. 754 is in effect, the transferee partner may be allocated a share of the loss when the partnership disposes of the property. In a gain situation with no partnership basis adjustment election in effect, a partner who purchased an interest within the last two years could avoid the unwanted gain allocation by unilaterally electing to adjust his share of the inside basis (Code Sec. 732(d)).

Adjustments to partnership property basis following distributions of partnership property. In the case of a distribution in liquidation of a partner's interest, the basis of the property distributed in the liquidation is equal to the partner's adjusted basis in its partnership interest (reduced by any money distributed in the transaction) (Code Sec. 732(b)). In a distribution other than in liquidation of a partner's interest, the distributee partner's basis in the distributed property is equal to the partnership's adjusted basis in the property immediately before the distribution, not to exceed the partner's adjusted basis in the partnership interest (reduced by any money distributed in the same transaction) (Code Sec. 734(a)).

Adjustments to the basis of the partnership's undistributed properties are not required unless the partnership has made the election under section 754 to make basis adjustments (Code Sec. 734(a)).

Opportunities for abuse through failure to make Code Sec. 754 election. The basis adjustment rules can be manipulated in loss situations to transfer or duplicate losses among partners. The following examples illustrate how this is done.

Example 1: Caymen Corp. owns equipment with a basis of $1,000,000 and a fair market value of $600,000. Anron Corp. wishes to purchase the equipment. Instead of conducting the sale directly, Caymen forms a partnership with two of its subsidiaries, Triton and Venilia, whose cash contributions ($600,000) are used to purchase an investment asset. Caymen transfers the equipment to the new CTV partnership. CTV leases the land to Anron for 3 years with an option to buy at the end of the lease term. After 3 years, Caymen's interest is liquidated, and it receives the investment property in satisfaction of its interest. Caymen's basis in the investment property is $1,000,000 (under Code Sec. 723 and Code Sec. 732(b)), and Caymen recognizes a $400,000 loss immediately upon selling the investment (the corporation's economic loss from the equipment).

CTV does not make a Code Sec. 754 election, and accordingly its basis in the equipment remains $1,000,000 (under the general Code Sec. 723 carryover basis rule). After Caymen liquidates its interest in CTV, the remaining partners sell the equipment to Anron for its fair market value, $600,000. CTV recognizes a $400,000 loss on the sale which is allocated equally between Triton and Venilia. Triton and Venilia have remaining basis in their partnership interests of $100,000 following the loss distribution (under Code Sec. 705). Their interests are worth $300,000 each, representing in total the $600,000 cash from the equipment sale. Each subsidiary has the potential to recognize $200,000 of gain if the cash is distributed (and reverse the $200,000 loss that was claimed); however, this gain can be deferred indefinitely assuming the continued existence of CTV.

Example 2: Caymen Corp. and its subsidiaries, Triton and Venilia, each contribute $500,000 to newly formed Seaside LLC. Seaside purchases a hurricane alley motel for $1.5 million. If a hurricane hits and the property declines in value to $900,000, Caymen could sell its interest to Ursula for $300,000 and recognize a loss of $200,000. Assuming no Code Sec. 754 election is made by Seaside, if Seaside then sells the motel for $900,000, Ursula would also be allocated a loss of $200,000 (its share of the $600,000 partnership loss).

Comment: The partnership rules include an extensive anti-abuse regulation (Reg. § 1.701-2) that describes failure to make the Code Sec. 754 election with the intention of duplicating losses as an abuse of the partnership rules (Reg. § 1.701-2(d), Example 8). The anti-abuse rule apparently has not been sufficient to deter taxpayers from using partnerships in this manner.

Allocations of partnership items. Partners can generally allocate partnership items to any partner as long as the allocation is reflected in the capital accounts. Without a special rule, however, it would be possible for a contributing partner to shift unrecognized gain or loss inherent in contributed property to the other partners. The partnership could simply allocate items attributable to the property to the noncontributing partners based on their distributive shares, and allocate the remainder to the contributing partner. To prevent this result, items of partnership income, gain, loss and deduction with respect to contributed property must be allocated to the contributing partner to the extent of any built-in gain or loss at the time of the contribution (Code Sec. 704(c)(1)(A)).

If the contributing partner transfers its partnership interest, the built-in gain or loss will be allocated to the transferee partner as it would have been allocated to the contributing partner (Reg. § 1.704-3(a)(7)). Thus, it appears that even though losses cannot be shifted to existing partners at the time of contribution, they can be shifted to other partners if the contributing partner ceases to be a partner.

American Jobs Creation Act Impact

Partnership basis and allocation rules revised to prevent transfer of partnership losses.—The new law places limits on the use of partnerships to shift or duplicate losses by restricting partnership allocations traceable to built-in loss property and by limiting opportunistic elections not to make partnership basis adjustments under Code Secs. 743 and 734 in "substantial" loss situations. There are some exceptions to these rules for investment and securitization partnerships. The law changes designed to achieve these results are:

- built-in loss may be taken into account only by the contributing partner, and not by other partners (Code Sec. 704(c)(1)(C)(i), as added by the American Jobs Creation Act of 2004);

- allocations to non-contributing partners are made by assuming that the basis of contributed property is its fair market value at the time of contribution (Code Sec. 704(c)(1)(C)(ii), as amended by the 2004 Jobs Act);

- the partnership must make Code Sec. 743 basis adjustments following a transfer of a partnership interest if the *partnership* has a substantial built-in loss (over $250,000), whether or not a Code Sec. 754 election is in effect;

- property with a substantial built-in loss (over $250,000) is adjusted downward to its fair market value if the contributing partner's partnership interest is transferred or liquidated, whether or not a Code Sec. 754 election is in effect; and

- the partnership must make a Code Sec. 734(b) basis adjustment with respect to any distribution of partnership property with respect to which there is a substantial basis reduction (a downward adjustment of more than $250,000) (Code Sec. 734(b) and (d), as amended by the 2004 Jobs Act).

PRACTICAL ANALYSIS. Jeffrey Paravano of Baker & Hostetler and former Treasury official notes that the substantive changes to partnership tax law are among the most striking changes in the legislation. Section 833 requires a partnership to reduce basis in its assets even in situations where no built-in loss exists. Many gain deferral techniques are now history given the breadth of this provision.

Allocations with respect to built-in loss property limited to contributing partner.—A built-in loss may be taken into account only in determining partnership items allocated to the contributing partner, and not by other partners (Code Sec. 704(c)(1)(C), as added by the 2004 Jobs Act). The basis of the contributed property in the hands of the partnership will be treated as equal to fair market value at the time of contribution for purposes of determining the amounts of items allocated to other partners (Code Sec. 704(c)(1)(C)(ii), as amended by the 2004 Jobs Act). The IRS is given authority to refine this basis rule in the regulations.

Comment: The fair market value basis rule means that if the contributing partner's interest is transferred or liquidated, the partnership's adjusted basis in the property for future allocations will be based on its fair market value at the date of contribution, and the built-in loss will be eliminated. The basis step-up eliminates the prior law trick of obtaining double loss deductions by passing along loss property through a partnership intermediary.

For the contributed property allocation rule, built-in loss is defined as any excess of the adjusted basis of the property over its fair market value at the time of contribution (Code Sec. 704(c)(1)(C)(ii), as amended by the 2004 Jobs Act). The restriction on allocating built-in loss to noncontributing partners is not subject to any minimum dollar safe harbor for which alternative built-in loss allocations would be permissible.

Comment: The Conference Committee Report states that a corporation succeeding to attributes of the contributing corporate partner under Code Sec. 381 should be treated in the same manner as the contributing partner (H.R. Conf. Rep. No. 108-755). This carves out a slight exception to the "same taxpayer" rule.

Mandatory Code Sec. 743 adjustment to basis of partnership property following transfer of interest if substantial built-in loss exists immediately following transfer.—A partnership is required to adjust the basis of partnership property following a transfer of a partnership interest to reflect differences in the transferee partner's basis in its partnership interest and its proportionate share of the adjusted basis of partnership property in any situation in which the partnership has a substantial built-in loss immediately after the transfer (Code Sec. 743(a) and (b), as amended by the 2004 Jobs Act). The Code Sec. 743 adjustment is thus mandatory in any situation in which a partnership interest is transferred at a time when the partnership's adjusted basis in the partnership property exceeds the property's fair market value by more than $250,000 (Code Sec. 743(d), as added by the 2004 Jobs Act). An alternative basis adjustment rule is provided for electing investment partnerships, described below, and an exception is also provided for securitization partnerships in the sole business of issuing securities.

Example: Caymen Corp. sells its partnership interest to Ursula for $400,000 at a time when the partnership property has an adjusted basis of $1.5 million and a fair market value of $1.2 million. The 1/3 share of the partnership loss allocable to Caymen's interest is $100,000; however, the partnership as a whole has a $300,000 loss. Immediately following the transfer, there is a substantial built-in loss with respect to the interest because the partnership's adjusted basis in its property ($1.5 million) exceeds its fair market value ($1.2 million) by more than $250,000. The partnership will be required to make an adjustment to the adjusted basis of the partnership property with respect to Ursula. As a result of the Code Sec. 743 adjustment, Ursula will recognize no gain or loss if the partnership immediately sells its property for fair market value.

The $250,000 threshold for measuring a substantial built-in loss applies regardless of the dollar value of the partnership property. There is no alternative percentage-based safe harbor in the definition of substantial built-in loss.

Comment: The mandatory basis adjustment for transfers in cases involving a substantial built-in loss applies even in cases where a partnership interest is transferred due to the death of the partner, a situation which does not suggest opportunistic loss duplication.

Substantial built-in loss defined. A substantial built-in loss exists if the partnership's adjusted basis in the property exceeds its fair market value by more than

$250,000 (Code Sec. 743(d)(1), as added by the 2004 Jobs Act). The IRS is given the authority to further define this limit, including issuing regulations requiring aggregation of related partnerships and providing that property acquired by the partnership in an attempt to avoid the loss threshold will be disregarded (Code Sec. 743(d)(2), as added by the 2004 Jobs Act).

Comment: Prior versions of this definition, which were not adopted, defined a substantial loss as any situation where the contributing partner's proportionate share of basis in the partnership property exceeded its fair market value by 10 percent. The 10 percent threshold would have meant a larger safe harbor for transactions involving multi-million dollar properties. This alternative percentage definition of a substantial built-in loss was not adopted in the final version of the 2004 Jobs Act.

Comment: The $250,000 threshold may be easily met since the value of many large buildings handled by real estate partnerships can be tens or hundreds of millions of dollars.

Alternative rules for electing investment partnerships. An "electing investment partnership" (defined below) is not treated as having a substantial built-in loss, and thus is not required to make basis adjustments to partnership property in the case of a transfer of a partnership interest (Code Sec. 743(e)(1), as added by the 2004 Jobs Act).

Comment: It is possible for a new partner to make a unilateral election to adjust inside basis with respect to itself, thus perhaps forcing the partnership to make basis adjustment calculations despite the absence of a Code Sec. 754 election (Code Sec. 732(d)). An investment partnership may be able to avoid this possibility by requiring partners to waive their rights under Code Sec. 732(d).

In place of the partnership level basis adjustment, the electing investment partnership members must apply a partner-level loss limitation rule. The partner-level loss limitation disallows the transferee partner's distributive share of losses from the sale or exchange of partnership property, except to the extent it can be established that the transferee's share of losses exceeds the loss recognized by the transferor partner (i.e., that the loss has not been duplicated by transferring the partnership interest) (Code Sec. 743(e)(2), as added by the 2004 Jobs Act). The amount of the loss is reduced by the amount of any basis reduction required to be taken under Code Sec. 732(a)(2) (Code Sec. 743(e)(5), as added by the 2004 Jobs Act). Under Code Sec. 732(a)(2), the basis of the property in the hands of the distributee partner cannot exceed the adjusted basis of his partnership interest, reduced by any money distributed in the same transaction.

The disallowance applies even if the partnership is terminated under Code Sec. 708 (Code Sec. 743(e)(4), as added by the 2004 Jobs Act).

Comment: Examples of investment partnerships include venture capital funds, buyout funds, or funds of funds.

The partner-level loss limitation also restricts the ability of the transferee to transfer any losses through successive transfers of the partnership interest (except to the extent that the losses are not duplicated losses or losses offset by a prior disallowance) (Code Sec. 743(e)(2), as added by the 2004 Jobs Act). Investment partnership losses disallowed under the partner-level loss limitation rule do not decrease the transferee partner's basis in its partnership interest (Code Sec. 743(e)(3), as added by the 2004 Jobs Act).

Comment: When a transferee subsequently disposes of its partnership interest, any gain realized will be reduced (or loss increased) to the extent of any disallowed losses that did not reduce the partner's basis.

Electing investment partnership defined. An electing investment partnership:

(1) makes an election to have this subsection apply;

(2) would be an investment company under section 3(a)(1)(A) of the Investment Company Act of 1940 but for an exemption under paragraph (1) or (7) of section 3(c) of such Act;

(3) has never been engaged in a trade or business;

(4) holds substantially all of its assets for investment;

(5) has contributed assets at least 95 percent of which consist of money;

(6) allows no assets contributed to the partnership to have an adjusted basis in excess of fair market value at the time of contribution;

(7) issues all partnership interests of the partnership pursuant to a private offering before the date which is 24 months after the date of the first capital contribution to the partnership;

(8) has a partnership agreement that provides for substantive restrictions on each partner's ability to cause a redemption of the partner's interest; and

(9) has a partnership agreement that provides for a term that is not in excess of 15 years (Code Sec. 743(e)(6), as added by the 2004 Jobs Act).

Caution Note: This election, once made, is irrevocable except with the consent of the IRS.

Comment: The requirement that all partnership interests be issued pursuant to a private offering prior to the date that is 24 months after the date of the first capital contribution to the partnership was a relatively recent addition to the definition of electing investment partnership (i.e., it was not contained in previous proposals of the amendment). The Conference Committee Report states that "dry" closings in which partnership interests are issued without the contribution of capital should not start the running of the 24-month period (H. R. Conf. Rep. No. 108-755).

Comment: Regulations are expected to outline the application of the investment partnership election in the case of tiered partnerships (Code Sec. 743(e)(7), as added by the 2004 Jobs Act).

Compliance Tip: An investment partnership that makes an election under this provision must furnish to any transferee partner the information necessary to enable the partner to compute the amount of losses disallowed under Code Sec. 743(e)(2).

An electing investment partnership is required to place substantive restrictions on each partner's ability to cause a redemption (Code Sec. 743(e)(6)(H), as added by the 2004 Jobs Act). As examples of substantive restrictions, the Conference Committee Report cites a violation of federal or state law (such as ERISA or the Bank Holding Company Act) or an imposition of a federal excise tax on, or a change in the federal tax-exempt status of, a tax-exempt partner (H. R. Conf. Rep. No. 108-755).

Furnishing information to transferee partners. An electing investment partnership is required to furnish information to any partner subject to the loss limitation rule of Code Sec. 743(e)(2) sufficient to enable the partner to compute the amount of disallowed losses (Code Sec. 6031(f), as added by the 2004 Jobs Act).

Compliance Tip: In some cases, it may be permissible for the transferor of the partnership interest to furnish the information relating to the amount of its loss to the transferee partner, according to the Conference Committee Report. The Conference Committee Report indicates that it expects the IRS to administer the requirement to furnish information in a manner that minimizes the need for the partnership to furnish information to the transferee partner that duplicates information that the transferee partner has obtained from the transferor (H.R. Conf. Rep. No. 108-755).

Exception for securitization partnerships. A securitization partnership is not treated as having a substantial built-in loss with respect to any transfers, and thus does not need to make any basis adjustments under Code Sec. 743 (Code Sec. 743(f), as added by the 2004 Jobs Act). A securitization partnership is defined as any partnership the sole business activity of which is to issue securities which provide for a fixed principal (or similar) amount and which are primarily serviced by the cash flows of a discrete pool (either fixed or revolving) of receivables or other financial assets. These receivables or other financial assets must, by their terms, convert into cash in a finite period, but only if the sponsor of the pool reasonably believes that the receivables and other financial assets comprising the pool are not acquired to be disposed of.

> **Comment:** There are no "alternative" required basis adjustments or limitations (such as partner-level loss limitations) for securitization partnerships.

Failure to continue to meet the definition of electing investment partnership or securitization partnership. An electing investment partnership or securitization partnership that subsequently fails to meet the definition of an electing investment partnership or securitization partnership will be subject to the regular partnership basis adjustment rules (including mandatory basis adjustments in cases where there is a substantial built-in loss) as of the first transfer of a partnership interest that occurs after the partnership ceases to meet the applicable definition (Conference Committee Report, H.R. Conf. Rep. No. 108-755).

> **Comment:** The Senate version of the bill (S. 1637) would have repealed Code Sec. 754 altogether and made basis adjustments mandatory any time there was a sale of a partnership interest or a partner redemption. Real estate organizations, among others, complained that this requirement was too harsh and that tracking property basis adjustments for all partnership transfers would add costly administrative burdens for entities with numerous partners. The real estate industry was also disappointed in the House version of the bill (H.R. 4520) which provided the exception for investment partnerships, but not for real estate partnerships which might face the same administrative difficulties in tracking basis.

Mandatory Code Sec. 734 adjustment to basis of partnership property following distribution of property with respect to which there is a substantial basis reduction.—A partnership is required to make downward basis adjustments to the basis of partnership assets under Code Sec. 734 in the case of a distribution with respect to which there is a substantial basis reduction (Code Sec. 734(b) and (d), as added by the 2004 Jobs Act). A substantial basis reduction means a downward adjustment of more than $250,000 that would be made to the basis of partnership assets if a Code Sec. 754 election were in effect. There is no percentage-of-assets alternative to the definition of a substantial basis reduction. As with the Code Sec. 743 rule, there is an exception for securitization partnerships.

> **Comment:** Prior to the 2004 Jobs Act, when property was distributed by a partnership, the partnership was not required to make an adjustment to the basis of the partnership property to reflect any differences in the distributees' basis in its partnership interest and the basis of the property. This could mean that when property was distributed to other partners later, a portion of losses recognized by the distributee could be duplicated by the other partners. This provision disallows that outcome.

¶960

Example: Anron Inc. and Benron Inc. each contributed $2.5 million to a newly formed partnership, while Caymen contributes $5 million. The partnership purchases LMN stock for $3 million and XYZ stock for $7 million. The value of each stock declines to $1 million. LMN stock is distributed to Caymen in liquidation of its partnership interest. As under present law, the basis of LMN stock in Caymen's hands is $5 million. Caymen would recognize a loss of $4 million if the LMN stock were sold for $1 million. There is a substantial basis adjustment because the $2 million increase in the adjusted basis of LMN stock is greater than $250,000. The partnership would thus be required to decrease the basis of XYZ stock (under Code Sec. 734(b)(2)) by $2 million (the amount by which the basis LMN stock was increased), leaving a basis of $5 million. If the XYZ stock were then sold by the partnership for $1 million, Anron and Benron would each recognize a loss of $2 million (rather than duplicating Caymen's loss with a $6 million loss to split between them).

Exception for securitization partnerships. A securitization partnership is not treated as having a substantial basis reduction in the case of a partnership distribution, and thus is not required to make basis adjustments to partnership property (Code Sec. 734(e), as added by the 2004 Jobs Act). The definition of a securitization partnership under this rule is identical to the exception under Code Sec. 743(f). As mentioned above, a securitization partnership is any partnership the sole business activity of which is to issue securities that provide for a fixed principal (or similar) amount and that are primarily serviced by the cash flows of a discrete pool (either fixed or revolving) of receivables or other financial assets. These receivables or other financial asset must, by their terms, convert into cash in a finite period, but only if the sponsor of the pool reasonably believes that the receivables and other financial assets comprising the pool are not acquired to be disposed of.

Comment: The Conference Committee Report states that rules similar to those applicable to sponsors of REMICs apply in determining whether the sponsor's belief is reasonable (under Reg. § 1.860G-2(a)(3)). A sponsor's belief is not reasonable if the sponsor actually knows or has reason to know that the requirement is not met, or if the requirement is later discovered not to have been met.

For further information on this subject, consult any of the following CCH reporter explanations:

- Standard Federal Tax Reporter, 2004FED ¶ 25,124.03, ¶ 25,135.01, ¶ 25,383.01, ¶ 25,482.01 and ¶ 35,389.01

- Federal Tax Service, FTS § H:3.80

- Federal Tax Guide, 2004FTG ¶ 14,210 and ¶ 14,465

★ *Effective date.* The provision limiting allocations with respect to contributed property with a built-in loss under Code Sec. 704(c)(1)(C)) applies to contributions made after the date of the enactment of this Act (Act Sec. 833(d)(1) of the American Jobs Creation Act of 2004). The rules for transfers of partnership interests if there is a substantial built-in loss apply to transfers after the date of the enactment (Act Sec. 833(d)(2)), subject to a transition rule for electing investment partnerships. In the case of an electing investment partnership which is in existence on June 4, 2004, Code Sec. 743(e)(6)(H) shall not apply to such partnership and Code Sec. 743(e)(6)(I) shall be applied by substituting "20 years" for "15 years". The rules for adjustments to basis if there is a substantial basis reduction apply to distributions after the date of the enactment (Act Sec. 833(d)(3) of the 2004 Jobs Act).

¶960

Act Sec. 833(a) of the American Jobs Creation Act of 2004, adding Code Sec. 704(c)(1)(C); Act Sec. 833(b), amending Code Sec. 743(a) and (b) and adding Code Sec. 743(d), (e) and (f) and Code Sec. 6031(f); Act Sec. 833(c), amending Code Sec. 734(a) and (b) and adding Code Sec. 734(d) and (e); Act Sec. 833(d). Law at ¶5505, ¶5515, ¶5520, and ¶6125. Committee Report at ¶11,160.

¶965

Basis Decreases Related to Stock of a Corporate Partner

Background

Distributions of partnership property do not generally result in recognition of gain or loss by the partner or the partnership (Code Sec. 731). Property distributed by the partnership in liquidation of a partner's interest takes a basis equal to the partner's tax basis in its partnership interest (reduced by any cash received in the liquidation) (Code Sec. 732). A partnership that distributes property in liquidation of a partner's interest is not required to adjust the basis of partnership property to reflect the effects of the transfer. However, the partnership may make an election to adjust the basis of partnership property to reflect any basis adjustments made to the distributed property by the distributee partner (the Code Sec. 754 election).

A partnership that distributes partnership property and that has a Code Sec. 754 election in effect makes an adjustment to the basis of the remaining partnership property (Code Sec. 755). The partnership increases the basis of partnership property by (1) any gain recognized by the distributee partner, and (2) the excess of the adjusted basis of the distributed property to the partnership immediately before its distribution over the basis of the property to the distributee partner. The partnership decreases the basis of partnership property by (1) any loss recognized by the distributee partner, and (2) the excess of the basis of the property to the distributee partner over the adjusted basis of the distributed property to the partnership immediately before the distribution. The allocation of the increase or decrease in basis of partnership property should reduce the difference between the fair market value and the adjusted basis of partnership properties and should be allocated to property similar in character to the distributed property (Code Sec. 755(a)).

> **Comment:** The grouping rules for making Code Sec. 755 basis allocations are flexible enough to allow a partnership to reduce the basis of stock and increase the basis of physical assets, such as depreciable buildings or equipment. This basis allocation benefits corporate partners in cases in which the basis of their own stock in the hands of the partnership is adjusted. When the stock is distributed to the corporate partner and sold, the corporation is not required to recognize cash income from the sale of its own stock. Enron Corporations was among the companies that have made use of this technique.

A partnership with no Code Sec. 754 election in effect is able to distribute property with an adjusted basis lower than the distributee partner's proportionate share of the adjusted basis of all partnership property. This leaves the remaining partners with a smaller net built-in gain or a larger net built-in loss than before the distribution.

American Jobs Creation Act Impact

No basis decrease under Code Sec. 734 in stock held by the partnership in a corporate partner.—When a distribution of property is made in liquidation of a partner's interest, a partnership may not decrease the basis of stock it owns in a corporate partner or other related party when it allocates basis adjustments to partnership property under Code Sec. 734 (Code Sec. 755(c), as amended by the American Jobs Creation Act of 2004). Any basis decrease that would have been allocated to a corporate partner's stock is allocated to other partnership assets. If the decrease in basis exceeds the basis of the other partnership assets, then gain is recognized by the partnership in the amount of the excess.

Stock in a corporate partner or any person related to such corporation. The partnership is prohibited from adjusting the basis of stock in a corporation or any related person, as defined in Code Secs. 267(b) and 707(b)(1) (Code Sec. 755(c)(1), as added by the 2004 Jobs Act). A person who could be related to a corporation within the meaning of Code Sec. 267(b) would include:

(1) An individual and a corporation of which more than 50 percent in value of the outstanding stock is owned, directly or indirectly, by or for that individual;

(2) Two corporations that are members of the same controlled group;

(3) A trust fiduciary and a corporation of which more than 50 percent in value of the outstanding stock is owned, directly or indirectly, by or for the trust, or by or for the grantor of the trust;

(4) A corporation and a partnership if the same persons own more than 50 percent in value of the outstanding stock of the corporation and more than 50 percent of the capital or profit interest in the partnership;

(5) An S corporation and another S corporation if the same persons own more than 50 percent of the value in the outstanding stock of each corporation; and

(6) An S corporation and a regular corporation if the same persons own more than 50 percent in value of the outstanding stock of each corporation.

Additional related parties, defined in Code Sec. 707(b)(1), include:

(1) A partnership and a person owning, directly or indirectly, more than 50 percent of the capital interest, or the profits interest, in the partnership, or

(2) two partnerships in which the same persons own, directly or indirectly, more than 50 percent of the capital interests or profits interests.

For further information on this subject, consult any of the following CCH reporter explanations:

- Standard Federal Tax Reporter, 2004FED ¶ 25,583.022

- Federal Tax Service, FTS § H:18.80

- Federal Tax Guide, 2004FTG ¶ 14,310 and ¶ 14,460

★ *Effective date.* The provision applies to distributions after the date of enactment of the American Jobs Creation Act of 2004.

Act Sec. 834(a) of the American Jobs Creation Act of 2004, adding Code Sec. 755(c); Act Sec. 834(b). Law at ¶ 5530. Committee Report at ¶ 11,170.

Chapter 10

Corporations

¶ 1005

Nonqualified Preferred Stock

Background ————————————————————————————

When property is transferred to a corporation solely in exchange for stock of that corporation, no gain or loss is recognized if, immediately after the exchange, the transferor is in control of the corporation (Code Sec. 351(a)). In this type of exchange, nonqualified preferred stock is not treated as stock transferred for property (Code Sec. 351(g)(1)).

Preferred stock is nonqualified if (Code Sec. 351(g)(2)):

(1) the holder of the stock can require the issuer (or a related person) to redeem or purchase the stock,

(2) the issuer (or a related person) is required to redeem or purchase the stock,

(3) the issuer (or a related person) has a right to redeem or purchase the stock and that right, as of the issue date, is more likely than not to be exercised, or

(4) the dividend rate on the stock is set with reference to interest rates, commodity prices, or other similar measures.

Preferred stock is stock that is limited and preferred as to dividends and that does not participate in corporate growth to any significant extent (Code Sec. 351(g)(3)(A)).

American Jobs Creation Act Impact

Nonqualified preferred stock definition clarified.—In order for stock to be treated as participating in corporate growth to any significant extent (and, thus, avoid being classified as "preferred stock" for purposes of Code Sec. 351), there must be a real and meaningful likelihood that the shareholder will actually participate in the earnings and growth of the corporation (Code Sec. 351(g)(3)(A), as amended by the American Jobs Creation Act of 2004). This clarification has been added, effective for transactions after May 14, 2003, to thwart possible attempts by some taxpayers to avoid characterization of an instrument as nonqualified preferred stock by including illusory participation rights or including terms that the taxpayers could argue create an "unlimited" dividend.

> **Example (1):** Ashwood Lumber Corp. has two classes of stock: Class A Common and Class A Preferred. The preferred stock has preferential rights on liquidation and is entitled to the same dividends as may be declared on the common stock. If Ashwood Corp. pays no dividends to holders of the common and preferred stock, Class A Preferred will be classified as nonqualified preferred stock.

> **Example (2):** The preferred stock of Furless Coats, Inc., entitles shareholders to a dividend equal to the greater of 7 percent or the dividends that common stock shareholders receive. If the common stock shareholders are not expected to receive dividends greater than 7 percent, the Furless Coats' preferred stock will be classified as nonqualified preferred stock.

The Conference Committee Report (H.R. Conf. Rep. No. 108-755) states that no inference is intended with respect the present law treatment (that is, prior to the effective date of the 2004 Jobs Act) of stock that has stated unlimited dividends or participation rights but, based on all the facts and circumstances, is limited and preferred as to dividends, and does not participate in corporate growth to any significant extent.

For further information on this subject, consult any of the following CCH reporter explanations:

- Standard Federal Tax Reporter, 2004FED ¶ 16,405.043
- Federal Tax Service, FTS § I:12.122[4]
- Federal Tax Guide, 2004FTG ¶ 12,003

★ *Effective date.* The provision applies to transactions after May 14, 2003 (Act Sec. 899(b) of the American Jobs Creation Act of 2004).

Act Sec. 899(a) of the American Jobs Creation Act of 2004, amending Code Sec. 351(g)(3)(A); Act Sec. 899(b). Law at ¶ 5320. Committee Report at ¶ 11,710.

¶ 1010

Gain Recognition Upon Holding Company Liquidation

Background

A U.S. corporation owned by foreign persons is subject to U.S. income tax on its net income (Code Sec. 11). In addition, the earnings of a U.S. corporation are subject to a second tax when dividends are paid to the corporation's shareholders (Code Secs. 301 and 316). In general, dividends paid by a U.S. corporation to nonresident alien individuals and foreign corporations that are not effectively connected with a U.S. trade or business are subject to a U.S. withholding tax on the gross amount of

Background

such income at a rate of 30 percent, unless reduced by treaty (Code Secs. 871(a) and 881(a)).

In addition, the United States imposes a branch profits tax on U.S. earnings of a foreign corporation that are shifted out of a U.S. branch of the foreign corporation (Code Sec. 884(a)). The branch profits tax is comparable to the second-level taxes imposed on dividends paid by a U.S. corporation to foreign shareholders. The branch profits tax is designed to achieve parity in tax treatment between a foreign corporation that conducts business in the United States through a branch and a foreign corporation that operates in the United States by establishing a U.S. subsidiary. The branch profits tax equals 30 percent (subject to possible income tax treaty reduction) of a foreign corporation's dividend equivalent amount. Generally, the "dividend equivalent amount" is the earnings and profits of a U.S. branch of a foreign corporation attributable to its income effectively connected with a U.S. trade or business (Code Sec. 884(a)).

U.S. withholding tax is not usually imposed with respect to a distribution of a U.S. corporation's earnings to a foreign corporation in complete liquidation of the subsidiary, because the distribution is treated as made in exchange for stock and not as a dividend. In addition, detailed rules apply for purposes of exempting foreign corporations from the branch profits tax for the year in which it completely terminates its U.S. business conducted in branch form.

The exemption from the branch profits tax generally applies if, among other things, for three years after the termination of the U.S. branch, the foreign corporation has no income effectively connected with a U.S. trade or business and the U.S. assets of the terminated branch are not used by the foreign corporation or a related corporation in a U.S. trade or business.

The IRS may require a domestic liquidating corporation to recognize gain on distributions in liquidation made to a foreign corporation if a principal purpose of the liquidation is the avoidance of U.S. tax (Reg. § 1.367(e)-2(d)). Avoidance of U.S. tax for this purpose includes, but is not limited to, the distribution of a liquidating corporation's earnings and profits with a principal purpose of avoiding U.S. tax.

American Jobs Creation Act Impact

Holding company liquidation triggering gain recognition.—Generally, a distribution of earnings by an applicable U.S. holding company to a foreign corporation in a complete liquidation will be treated as a dividend if the U.S. holding company was in existence for less than five years (Code Sec. 332(d), as added by the American Jobs Creation Act of 2004). Thus, in the case of any distribution to a foreign corporation in complete liquidation of an applicable holding company, the usual liquidation gain or loss nonrecognition rules of Code Secs. 331 and 332(a) do not apply. Instead, the distribution is treated as a distribution of property to which Code Sec. 301 applies and is taxable as a dividend.

An applicable holding company is any domestic corporation that is a common parent of an affiliated group, the stock of which is directly owned by the distributee foreign corporation. Furthermore, substantially all of the assets of the domestic corporation must consist of stock in other members of the affiliated group, and the domestic corporation must not have been in existence at all times during the five years immediately preceding the date of the liquidation (Code Sec. 332(d)(2), as added by the 2004 Jobs Act). The term "affiliated group" generally retains its historic definition for these purposes; however, insurance companies and corporations with respect to which a possessions tax credit election is in effect may be members of the group (Code Sec. 332(d)(2)(B), as added by the 2004 Jobs Act).

In the case of a distribution to a foreign corporation in complete liquidation of an applicable holding company, if the distributee is a controlled foreign corporation, then the distribution will instead be treated as a distribution made in full payment in exchange for the stock to which Code Sec. 331 applies (Code Sec. 332(d)(3), as added by the 2004 Jobs Act).

Regulations authorized. The IRS is specifically authorized to issue regulations to prevent the abuse of these rules, including regulations which provide, for the purposes of determining whether a corporation has been in existence at all times during the five years before the liquidation, that a corporation is not in existence for any period unless it is engaged in the active conduct of a trade or business or owns a significant ownership interest in another corporation that is engaged in the active conduct of a trade or business (Code Sec. 332(d)(4), as added by the 2004 Jobs Act).

For further information on this subject, consult any of the following CCH reporter explanations:

- Standard Federal Tax Reporter, 2004FED ¶ 16,052.021
- Federal Tax Service, FTS § I:10.70
- Federal Tax Guide, 2004FTG ¶ 12,480

★ *Effective date.* These rules apply to distributions in complete liquidation occurring on or after the date of enactment (Act Sec. 893(b) of the American Jobs Creation Act of 2004).

Act Sec. 893(a) of the American Jobs Creation Act of 2004, adding Code Sec. 332(d); Act Sec. 893(b). Law at ¶ 5305. Committee Report at ¶ 11,650.

¶ 1015

Tax-Free Transfers and Liability Assumption Rules Limited in Type "D" Reorganizations

Background _____

Code Sec. 355 provides rules for divisive transactions in which corporations may separate their businesses tax-free. Under these rules, a corporation may distribute the stock or securities of a controlled subsidiary to its shareholders without recognizing gain or loss, provided the distribution satisfies the requirements set forth in Code Sec. 355. If, as part of a complete liquidation, a corporation transfers substantially all of its assets to a controlled subsidiary solely for the stock or securities of the subsidiary, and then distributes such stock or securities to its shareholders under Code Sec. 354 or 356, the transaction qualifies as an *acquisitive* type "D" reorganization under Code Sec. 368(a)(1)(D). As such, the corporate transferor recognizes no gain or loss pursuant to Code Sec. 361(a)(1). When a corporation transfers part of its assets to a controlled subsidiary for its stock and distributes that stock to its shareholders in a divisive spin-off, split-off or split-up reorganization under Code Sec. 355, the transaction qualifies as a tax-free *divisive* type "D" reorganization (Code Sec. 368(a)(1)(D)).

A corporate transferor in both acquisitive and divisive type "D" reorganizations may receive other property or money in addition to the permitted stock or securities, but it must distribute the property or money to its shareholders or creditors as part of the plan of the reorganization to avoid recognition of gain (Code Sec. 361(b)). There are currently no restrictions on the amount of property that may be distributed without gain recognition. On the other hand, if the controlled subsidiary in a Code Sec. 368(a)(1)(D) reorganization, whether acquisitive or divisive, assumes the trans-

Background

feror's liabilities that exceed the adjusted basis of the transferred properties, the corporate transferor recognizes gain in the amount of the excess (Code Sec. 357(c)(1)(B)).

American Jobs Creation Act Impact

Tax-free transfers to creditors limited in divisive type "D" reorganizations and liability assumption rules inapplicable to acquisitive type "D" reorganizations.—A corporate transferor that receives money or other property in addition to permitted stock or securities in a divisive type "D" reorganization involving a Code Sec. 355 distribution, recognizes gain to the extent the amount of money plus the fair market value of the other property distributed to creditors is greater than the basis of the transferred assets (Code Sec. 361(b)(3), as amended by the American Jobs Creation Act of 2004).

> **Comment:** The new rule prevents taxpayers who engage in divisive type "D" reorganizations involving Code Sec. 355 distributions from avoiding the gain recognition rules under Code Sec. 357(c). Previously, because there was no limitation on the amount of money that a corporate transferor could receive and distribute tax free to creditors, the transferor could, in effect, pay off its debt without tax consequences. At the same time, the assumption of the transferor's debt by the subsidiary may result in gain recognition under Code Sec. 357(c). As a result, two economically similar transactions had different tax consequences because there was no limitation on the amount that could be distributed tax free to creditors.

> **Comment:** The new rule does not apply to acquisitive type "D" reorganizations, because, unlike the divisive type "D" reorganizations, the former results in a complete liquidation of the corporate transferor. Since the transferor's liabilities are limited to its assets, which are transferred to the subsidiary corporation in the transaction and the transferor then ceases to exist, the transfer of money or other property, as well as the assumption of liabilities, may not enrich the transferor in any way.

In addition, the rule that requires a corporate transferor to recognize gain in the cases when the liabilities assumed by the transferee exceed the adjusted basis of the transferred properties applies only with respect to divisive type "D" reorganizations that involve Code Sec. 355 distributions (Code Sec. 357(c)(1)(B), as amended by the 2004 Jobs Act).

> **Comment:** The same rationale that stands behind the inapplicability of Code Sec. 361(b)(3)) to acquisitive type "D" reorganizations, explains the rule that excludes those transactions from the application of Code Sec. 357(c). As mentioned above, because the transferor contributes substantially all of its assets to the subsidiary corporation and goes out of existence in an acquisitive type "D" reorganization, the assumption of liabilities does not result in any enrichment to the transferor. The new rule conforms the treatment of acquisitive type "D" reorganization to that of other acquisitive reorganizations (Conference Committee Report (H.R. Conf. Rep. No. 108-755)).

For further information on this subject, consult any of the following CCH reporter explanations:

- Standard Federal Tax Reporter, 2004FED ¶ 16,522.04 and ¶ 16,582.01
- Federal Tax Service, FTS § I:14.105

¶1015

- Federal Tax Guide, 2004FTG ¶ 12,343

★ *Effective date.* These provisions apply to transfers of money or other property, or liabilities assumed in connection with a reorganization occurring on or after the date of enactment (Act Sec. 898(c) of the American Jobs Creation Act of 2004).

Act Sec. 898(a) of the American Jobs Creation Act of 2004, amending Code Sec. 361(b)(3); Act Sec. 898(b), amending Code Sec. 357(c)(1)(B); Act Sec. 898(c). Law at ¶ 5325 and ¶ 5330. Committee Report at ¶ 11,700.

¶ 1020

Clarification of Rules for Estimated Tax Payments on Deemed Asset Sales

Background

Corporate acquisitions are often accomplished via a large stock purchase. To effect the acquisition, the acquiring corporation buys enough stock in the target corporation to secure a controlling interest. While this method can be direct and effective from a legal and economic standpoint, it is not always the ideal structure from a federal tax perspective. Had the acquiring corporation purchased the assets, rather than the stock, of the target corporation, it could have taken those assets with a fair market value, or stepped-up basis. By purchasing the stock of the corporation, it is, instead, forced to take a carryover basis in the assets of its new subsidiary. The purchase of the stock of a corporation, therefore, can lead to remarkably different tax consequences than the economic equivalent of the purchase of the assets of a corporation.

In response to this disparate treatment, the Code allows certain parties to a qualified stock purchase to make a joint election under Code Sec. 338(h)(10) to treat the stock sale as an asset sale for federal tax purposes. The election is generally available when a corporation purchases 80 percent of the stock of a target corporation from a member of an affiliated group. If both parties consent to the election, the basis in the target assets is stepped up upon the sale and the gain inherent in those assets is recognized immediately by the target rather than down the line by the buyer.

If both parties do not agree to, or do not qualify for, an election under Code Sec. 338(h)(10), the buyer may make a unilateral election under Code Sec. 338(a) to treat the stock purchase as an asset acquisition. The seller recognizes gain or loss on the stock sale and the target corporation recognizes gain or loss on the deemed asset sale. In this case, the seller must account for any estimated tax payments due upon the stock sale under Code Sec. 6655. The buyer, however, is specifically directed by the Code to disregard the tax attributable to the deemed asset sale for estimated tax purposes (Code Sec. 338(h)(13)).

The Code has been historically silent, however, as to how the tax attributable to a deemed asset sale under Code Sec. 338(h)(10) should be treated for estimated tax purposes. This has encouraged some taxpayers to claim that estimated tax applies neither to the stock sale nor to the asset sale in the case of a Code Sec. 338(h)(10) election.

American Jobs Creation Act Impact

Estimated tax payments due despite Code Sec. 338(h)(10) election.—The exception, which allows a corporation to disregard tax attributable to a deemed asset sale for estimated tax purposes, is limited to deemed assets sales under Code Sec. 338(a) and does not apply to deemed asset sales stemming from Code Sec. 338(h)(10) elections (Code Sec. 338(h)(13), as amended by the American Jobs Creation Act of 2004).

When a qualified stock purchase eligible for a Code Sec. 338(h)(10) election is made, estimated tax is determined based on the stock sale until an agreement to make the election is reached. If, at the time of the qualified stock purchase, there is an agreement between the parties to make a Code Sec. 338(h)(10) election, the estimated tax is determined based on the asset sale and is computed from the date of the sale. In the case where the parties agree to make a Code Sec. 338(h)(10) election *after* the stock sale, but within the statutory time period for the election, the estimated tax is initially determined based on the stock sale and is later recomputed based on the asset sale election (House Committee Report (H.R. Rep. No. 108-548)).

For further information on this subject, consult any of the following CCH reporter explanations:

- Standard Federal Tax Reporter, 2004FED ¶ 16,288.048
- Federal Tax Service, FTS § I:24.282
- Federal Tax Guide, 2004FTG ¶ 12,270

★ *Effective date.* The provision is effective for qualified stock purchase transactions occurring after the date of enactment (Act Sec. 839(b) of the American Jobs Creation Act of 2004).

Act Sec. 839(a) of the American Jobs Creation Act of 2004, amending Code Sec. 338(h)(13); Act Sec. 839(b). Law at ¶ 5315. Committee Report at ¶ 11,220.

¶ 1025

Definition of Brother-Sister Controlled Group of Corporations Modified

Background _____

In general, the Code treats every corporation as a separate taxable entity and imposes a tax on the income of every corporation at graduated tax rates under Code Sec. 11. However, by dividing a single business into two or more related corporations under common control, taxpayers may exploit the progressive tax rates and avoid the dollar limitations on various tax allowances to their advantage. To prevent members of controlled groups from obtaining multiple tax benefits, Code Sec. 1561 departs from the separate-entity approach and limits the component members of these controlled groups to only one amount in each of the taxable income brackets, one alternative minimum tax exemption, and one accumulated earnings credit (Code Sec. 1561(a)). Thus, the component members must divide these tax benefits among themselves as if the entire group were only one corporation. In addition, if a member cannot use its allocable share of any of the benefits, the amount is not reallocated to other members of the group.

Controlled groups of corporations are subject to the Code Sec. 1561 limitations only if they are connected through either a parent-subsidiary or a brother-sister relationship described in Code Sec. 1563. A parent-subsidiary controlled group includes one or more chains of corporations connected to a common parent through stock ownership, provided that: (1) at least 80 percent of the total voting power or value of each of the corporations (excluding the parent corporation) is owned by one or more of the other corporations, and (2) the common parent owns at least 80 percent of the total voting power or value of at least one of the other corporations, provided the stock owned directly by such other corporation is excluded from the computation of the voting power and value (Code Sec. 1563(a)(1)).

Background

A brother-sister controlled group means two or more corporations owned by five or fewer persons who are individuals, estates or trusts and possess: (1) at least 80 percent of the total combined voting power or value of each corporation, and (2) more than 50 percent of the total combined voting power and value of all stock, taking into account the stock owned by each person only if such person owns stock in each corporation (Code Sec. 1563(a)(2)).

Taxpayers are sometimes able to avoid the limitations of Code Sec. 1561 and obtain multiple tax benefits when the 80-percent test of Code Sec. 1563(a)(2) is technically not met, but related corporations are effectively under common control. If taxpayers effectively control a group of related corporations, they can shift some of the activities of the business enterprise to the members of the group who enjoy a more favorable tax regime.

American Jobs Creation Act Impact

Modified definition of a brother-sister controlled group.—Under the new provision, a "brother-sister controlled group" means two or more corporations if five or fewer persons who are individuals, trusts or estates own stock possessing more than 50 percent of the total combined voting power of all classes of stock entitled to vote, or more than 50 percent of the total value of all stock, taking into account the stock ownership of each person only to the extent the person owns stock in each corporation (Code Sec. 1563(a)(2), as amended by the American Jobs Creation Act of 2004).

> **Comment:** This change broadens the historic definition of a brother-sister corporation in which the owners had to satisfy an 80-percent ownership test as well as the 50-percent test (see Background, above). By broadening the definition, Congress has widened the application of Code Sec. 1561, thereby preventing related corporations from otherwise circumventing its limitations.

This new definition applies only for purposes of Code Sec. 1561 and does not affect other Code provisions that incorporate or refer to the Code Sec. 1563 definition of a brother-sister corporation controlled group. For purposes of these Code provisions, the historic definition still must be met. This means that a brother-sister corporation exists if the stock owned by five or fewer persons who are individuals, estates or trusts possess at least 80 percent of the total combined voting power, or at least 80 percent of the total value, of each corporation and more than 50 percent of the total combined voting power, or more than 50 percent of the total value, of each corporation, taking into account the stock ownership of each person only if the person owns stock in each corporation (Code Sec. 1563(f)(5), as added by the 2004 Jobs Act).

For further information on this subject, consult any of the following CCH reporter explanations:

- Standard Federal Tax Reporter, 2004FED ¶ 33,382.032
- Federal Tax Service, FTS § I:23.60
- Federal Tax Guide, 2004FTG ¶ 12,698

★ *Effective date.* The provision applies to tax years beginning after the date of enactment (Act Sec. 900(c) of the American Jobs Creation Act of 2004).

Act Sec. 900(a) of the American Jobs Creation Act of 2004, amending Code Sec. 1563(a)(2); Act Sec. 900(b), adding Code Sec. 1563(f)(5); Act Sec. 900(c). Law at ¶ 5940. Committee Report at ¶ 11,720.

¶1025

Chapter 11

RICs, REITs, FASITs and Insurance Companies

¶ 1105

Mutual Funds Permitted to Invest in Publicly Traded Partnerships

Background

A mutual fund is taxed under the rules for regulated investment companies (RICs). RICs that meet a 90-percent distribution requirement generally only pay tax on undistributed investment company income and net undistributed capital gains. In order to meet the definition of a RIC, a mutual fund must derive at least 90 percent of its income from qualifying sources (Code Sec. 851(b)(2)). Permissible sources are enumerated in the Code and include dividends, interest, gains from stock, securities, or currency transactions, and assorted options, futures, and forwards. Partnerships, however, are not listed as a permissible investment. A partnership interest held by a mutual fund, therefore, is judged the same as other investments. The partnership interest is a permissible investment only if its income consists of interest, dividends, capital gains, and other income that the fund would be permitted to realize directly (this is known as the look-through rule).

> **Comment:** The absence of publicly traded partnerships from the list of permissible mutual fund investments should not necessarily be construed as an historic public policy statement. Rather, the publicly traded partnership as an entity did not exist at the time the list of permissible mutual fund investments was drafted in 1936.

A publicly traded partnership (PTP) is a partnership whose interests are traded on a public exchange. An interest in a PTP, therefore, is a liquid investment. A PTP is required to register the same information with the Securities and Exchange Commission as a publicly traded corporation. There are currently about 50 publicly traded partnerships (also known as master limited partnerships (MLPs)). About half of the existing publicly traded partnerships are in the oil and gas business, investing in pipelines for transporting oil and gas. Other PTPs invest in timber, real estate, or mortgage securities, plus the miscellaneous horse racing operation or nut farm.

Background

Except for certain PTPs grandfathered in as of 1987, PTPs must limit themselves to passive investments to avoid paying a corporate-level tax (Code Sec. 7704).

Distributions of earnings to PTP unitholders are not taxed upon receipt. Instead, the distribution is treated as a tax-free reduction in basis until basis is exhausted. This differs from corporate dividends, which are immediately included in income. Another big difference is that PTP investors are responsible for paying tax on their share of the partnership's taxable income, if any. This is because a PTP is a passthrough entity and does not pay an entity-level tax. Unitholders are also allocated shares of partnership depreciation, losses, and credits. A loss from a PTP is considered a passive loss and cannot be used to offset any income other than income from the same PTP. The combined impact of the treatment of PTP distributions and this passthrough reporting makes PTP investments considerably more complicated than ordinary mutual fund investments.

Proposals to add PTPs to the list of allowable regulated investment company investments have been made in numerous previous bills, including the vetoed 1999 Taxpayer Refund and Relief Act and the proposed Energy Tax Policy Act of 2003 (which ultimately did not pass Congress).

> **Comment:** Proposals to allow mutual funds to invest in PTPs are squarely aimed at benefitting oil and gas businesses. Mutual funds have the potential to invest large sums in pipeline partnerships, allowing expansion of profitable oil and gas activities (and incidentally raising the value of units for existing PTP unitholders). Proponents of the law change have argued that the influx of capital into pipeline projects would help create valuable energy infrastructure, thereby increasing U.S. capacity to move oil and gas from remote areas to extraction facilities and refiners and to consumers in other regions of the country. The creation of construction jobs to build these pipelines would be an added bonus.

American Jobs Creation Act Impact

Mutual funds allowed to invest in publicly traded partnerships.—Mutual funds may now derive income from qualified publicly traded partnerships (PTPs) and still qualify as regulated investment companies (RICs) for tax purposes (Code Sec. 851(b)(2)(B), as added by the American Jobs Creation Act of 2004). The list of income sources which must make up 90 percent of a mutual fund's income has been revised to include distributions or other income derived from any interest in a qualified publicly traded partnership. The RIC asset tests (see below) have likewise been revised to account for qualified PTP investments.

Qualified publicly traded partnership. A qualified publicly traded partnership is any partnership that is traded on an established securities market or readily tradable on a secondary market (as defined in Code Sec. 7704(b)) other than a partnership that derives 90 percent of its income from interest, dividends, capital gains, and other traditional permitted mutual fund income (Code Sec. 851(h), as added by the 2004 Jobs Act). The definition excludes partnerships that invest solely in traditional mutual fund intangible assets (stocks, bonds, currencies, and other securities).

> **Comment:** Any of the publicly traded partnerships involved in energy production or transportation should meet this definition.

RIC income and asset tests. As noted earlier, the 90-percent income test for regulated investment companies has been expanded to allow mutual funds to treat distributions and other income from qualified publicly traded partnerships as income from a qualifying source. Corresponding changes were made to the 50-percent asset test and the 25-percent asset test to account for qualifying PTP investments.

Under the 50-percent asset test, at least 50 percent of the value of a mutual fund's total assets at the end of each quarter must consist of:

(1) cash and cash items, government securities, and securities of other RICs; and

(2) other securities, subject to additional limitations as to each issuer (Code Sec. 851(b)(3)(A)).

The amount of other securities referenced in item (2), above, is limited. Securities from a single issuer, other than the government or other RICs, are limited to a maximum of 5 percent of the value of the taxpayer's total assets and to a maximum of 10 percent of the issuer's outstanding voting securities. In applying the 10-percent ownership test, equity securities of a qualified PTP are treated as outstanding voting securities (Code Sec. 851(b)(3)(a)(ii); Code Sec. 851(c)(5), as added by the 2004 Jobs Act).

Under the 25-percent asset test, a maximum of 25 percent of a mutual fund's total assets at the end of each quarter can consist of:

(1) securities of any one issuer, other than government securities or securities of other RICs;

(2) securities of two or more issuers that the taxpayer controls and that are engaged in the same or similar or related trades or businesses; or

(3) securities of one or more qualified PTPs (Code Sec. 851(b)(3)(B), as amended by the 2004 Jobs Act).

Look-through rule not to apply to investments in publicly traded partnerships. The source flow-through rule does not apply to investments in publicly traded partnerships (Code Sec. 851(b), as amended by the 2004 Jobs Act). This means that a mutual fund may invest in a PTP regardless of the type of business the partnership operates (for example, building oil and gas pipelines). Before this amendment, all partnership income of a mutual fund was judged under the usual permitted-income categories. Income that did not consist of traditional interest, dividends, capital gains, etc., i.e., income from pipeline activities, could prevent the mutual fund from qualifying as a RIC.

Passive activity rules for PTP held by a mutual fund. A mutual fund holding a PTP interest is treated as the taxpayer under the passive activity rules (Code Sec. 469(k)(4), as added by the 2004 Jobs Act). This means that the income from the PTP is passive activity income, and losses from the PTP are passive losses that cannot be used to offset any income other than income from the same PTP. Deductions passed through by the PTP also cannot be used to offset income from other sources. Unused deductions and credits from the PTP are carried over to future years to offset income from the PTP. Losses and deductions that remain unused may be recaptured only when the mutual fund disposes of its entire interest in the PTP (Code Sec. 469(k)(1)).

Comment: Mutual fund investors whose funds hold publicly traded partnerships are not required to track passive activity items.

Publicly traded partnership items not to flow through to mutual fund investors. Unlike direct holders of PTP units, mutual fund investors whose funds hold PTP units will not need to tangle with Schedule K-1s, passive losses, depreciation recapture, or passive loss limitations associated with publicly traded partnerships. The partnership's passed-through items will be used in calculating the fund's earnings and profits. Earnings and profits are paid to fund investors as dividends. It is not yet clear to what extent, if any, mutual fund investors will be required to separately account for PTP items.

Comment: The freedom from partnership reporting is a significant advantage to investing in PTPs via a mutual fund.

Comment: The Conference Committee Report directs the IRS to develop ways to prevent mutual funds from being used by shareholders to avoid paying tax on otherwise owed PTP income or to avoid backup withholding. Shareholders who would owe unrelated business tax and foreign shareholders are mentioned as particular concerns.

For further information on this subject, consult any of the following CCH reporter explanations:

- Standard Federal Tax Reporter, 2004FED ¶21,966.059, ¶26,408.03, ¶26,408.04 and ¶43,182.01
- Federal Tax Service, FTS §I:21.41
- Federal Tax Guide, 2004FTG ¶16,600

★ *Effective date.* The provision applies to tax years beginning after the date of enactment (Act Sec. 331(h) of the American Jobs Creation Act of 2004).

Act Sec. 331(a) of the American Jobs Creation Act of 2004, amending Code Sec. 851(b)(2); Act Sec. 331(b), amending Code Sec. 851(b); Act Sec. 331(c), adding new Code Sec. 851(c)(5) and redesignating former Code Sec. 851(c)(5) as Code Sec. 851(c)(6); Act Sec. 331(d), adding Code Sec. 851(h); Act Sec. 331(e), amending Code Sec. 7704(d)(4); Act Sec. 331(f), amending Code Sec. 851(b)(3)(B); Act Sec. 331(g), adding Code Sec. 469(k)(4); Act Sec. 331(h). Law at ¶5390, ¶5545, and¶6360. Committee Report at ¶10,460.

¶1110

Improvements Related to Real Estate Investment Trusts

Background _____

A real estate investment trust (REIT) holds passive investments in real property equity and mortgages. To qualify to elect REIT status, an entity must satisfy detailed organizational requirements, source of income tests, asset holding tests, distribution requirements and recordkeeping requirements.

A REIT is subject to tax at the highest corporate rate on its net income from foreclosure property. A 100-percent tax is imposed on a REIT's net income from prohibited transactions. A four-percent excise tax is imposed on undistributed income. If an entity qualifies as a REIT, income that is distributed to its investors is taxed directly to them without first being taxed at the REIT level. The REIT is taxed as a corporation on its REIT taxable income. It calculates its income as if it were a regular corporation, except that certain adjustments apply, the most important of which is the deduction for dividends paid. If a REIT has net capital gain for the year, its tax can be computed under an alternative method. Alternatively, it can elect passthrough treatment of its net long-term capital gain.

Organizational structure requirements. A qualified REIT must satisfy requirements regarding its structure ownership and management. A REIT must:

(1) be managed by one or more trustees or directors;

(2) have its beneficial ownership evidenced by transferable shares or by transferable certificates of beneficial interest;

Background

    (3) be taxable as a domestic corporation;

    (4) not be a bank, insurance company, state-chartered business development corporation or a building and loan association;

    (5) have its beneficial ownership held by at least 100 persons; and

    (6) not be closely held within the meaning of the rules that apply to personal holding corporations (Code Sec. 856(a)).

The first four conditions must be met during the entire tax year (Code Sec. 856(b)). The 100-shareholder requirement and the requirement that a REIT not be closely held are waived for the first tax year for which an entity elects REIT status (Code Sec. 856(h)(2)).

A REIT is disqualified for any year in which it does not comply with regulations to ascertain the actual ownership of the REIT's outstanding shares.

Income requirements. A REIT must satisfy two source-of-income tests. For each tax year, the REIT must derive:

    • at least 75 percent of its gross income from real property-related source and

    • at least 95 percent of its gross income from real property-related sources, dividends, interest and securities (Code Sec. 856(c)(2) and (3)).

A REIT failing to meet these tests for any tax year generally loses its REIT status. However, a REIT that fails to meet the 75- or 95-percent test, or both, for any tax year may continue to qualify as a REIT under a good faith exception (Code Sec. 856(c)(6)). For purposes of determining a REIT's income, a REIT that is a partner in a partnership owns its proportionate share of income and assets of the partnership (Reg. § 1.856-3(g)).

Tenant services income. Charges for services customarily furnished or rendered in connection with the rental of real property are treated as rents from real property for purposes of the 75-percent and 95-percent income tests (Code Sec. 856(d)(1)(B)). Rents from property do not include any amount received or accrued directly or indirectly by a REIT if the REIT receives or accrues more than a *de minimis* amount for furnishing or rendering other services to the tenants of the property, or managing or operating the property (Code Sec. 856(d)(2)(C), (7)(B)). Amounts are *de minimis* if they do not exceed one percent of the amounts received or accrued during the tax year directly or indirectly by the REIT with respect to the property. The services cannot be valued at less than 150 percent of the REIT's direct costs for the services of furnishing the management or operation (Code Sec. 856(d)(7)).

A REIT is not treated as providing services that produce impermissible tenant services income if the services are provided by an independent contractor from whom the REIT does not derive or receive any income. An independent contractor is defined as a person who does not own, directly or indirectly, more than 35 percent of the shares of the REIT. Also, no more than 35 percent of the total shares of stock of an independent contractor (or of the interests in net assets or net profits, if not a corporation) can be owned directly or indirectly by persons owning 35 percent or more of the interests in the REIT (Code Sec. 856(d)(7)(C)(i)); Reg. § 1.856-4(b)(5)(iii)).

Rents for certain personal property leased in connection with the rental of real property are treated as rents from real property if the fair market value of the personal property does not exceed 15 percent of the aggregate fair market values of the real and personal property (Code Sec. 856(d)(1)(C)).

Example: A REIT forms a taxable REIT subsidiary (TRS) to perform noncustomary services to tenants of the REIT. No service charges are separately stated from the rents paid by the tenants to the REIT. The primary issue in determining the treatment of the REIT's income from the services is whether they are considered to be rendered by the REIT or by the TRS for purposes of Code Sec. 856(d)(7). In Rev. Rul. 2002-38 (I.R.B. 2002-26, 4), the IRS determined that services that are rendered by the TRS under a facts and circumstances analysis do not give rise to impermissible tenant service income.

For purposes of the income requirements, income from real property-related sources can also include amounts received from certain "foreclosure property," if it was treated as foreclosure property for three years after it was acquired by the REIT in foreclosure after a default (or imminent default) on a lease of such property or an indebtedness that such property secured (Code Sec. 856(e)).

Rents from real property, for purposes of the 95-percent and 75-percent income tests, generally do not include any amount received or accrued from any person in which the REIT owns, directly or indirectly, 10 percent or more of the vote or value (Code Sec. 856(d)(2)(B)). An exception applies to rents received from a taxable REIT subsidiary (TRS) (described further below) if at least 90 percent of the leased space of the property is rented to persons other than a TRS or certain related persons, and if the rents from the TRS are substantially comparable to unrelated party rents (Code Sec. 856(d)(8)).

Certain hedging instruments. A payment to a REIT under an interest rate swap or cap agreement, option, futures contract, forward rate agreement, or any similar financial instrument, entered into by the trust in a transaction to reduce the interest rate risks with respect to any indebtedness incurred or to be incurred by the REIT to acquire or carry real estate assets, and any gain from the sale or disposition of any such investment, is treated as income qualifying for the 95-percent income test (Code Sec. 856(c)(5)(G)).

Comment: Thus, a REIT can take advantage of any type of hedge that reduces the risk associated with fluctuating interest rates and be assured that payments under the hedging agreement will be treated as qualifying passive income.

Tax if qualified income tests not met. A REIT that fails to meet the 95-percent or 75-percent income test, can still retain its qualified status under a good faith exception. This exception applies if: a schedule is attached to its income tax return for the tax year that sets forth the nature and amount of each item of gross income qualifying under the income tests; any incorrect information included in the schedule is not due to fraud with intent to evade tax; and the failure to meet the tests is due to reasonable cause and not willful neglect (Code Sec. 856(c)(6)).

If these requirements are satisfied the REIT does not lose its REIT status but instead pays a tax measured by the greater of (1) the amount by which 90 percent of the REIT's gross income exceeds the amount of items subject to the 95-percent test, or (2) the amount by which 75 percent of the REIT's gross income exceeds the amount of items subject to the 75-percent test. The ratio of the REIT's net to gross income is applied to the excess amount to determine the amount of tax (disregarding certain items otherwise subject to a 100-percent tax). In effect, the formula seeks to require that all of the REIT net income attributable to the failure of the income tests will be paid as tax (Code Sec. 857(b)(5)).

Background

Asset requirements. A qualified REIT must concentrate its investments in real estate assets. Its investments outside of real estate assets must meet limits on diversification and size. The REIT must satisfy the following requirements at the close of each quarter of the tax year:

- at least 75 percent of the value of the REIT's total assets must consist of real estate assets, cash and cash items, including receivables and government securities;

- not more than 25 percent of the value of the REIT's total assets can be invested in securities other than those constituting real estate assets and government securities (see below);

- not more than 20 percent of the value of the REIT's total assets may be composed of securities of taxable REIT subsidiaries;

- except for government securities and securities of taxable REIT subsidiaries, not more than five percent of the value of the REIT's total assets can be invested in the securities of any one issuer;

- except for government securities and securities of taxable REIT subsidiaries, a REIT's investment in the securities of one issuer cannot exceed 10 percent of the voting power of the outstanding securities of that issuer; and

- except for government securities and securities of taxable REIT subsidiaries, a REIT's investment in the securities of one issuer cannot exceed 10 percent of the total value of the outstanding securities of that issuer (Code Sec. 856(c)(4)).

The term "real estate assets" is defined to mean real property (including interests in real property and mortgages on real property) and interests in REITs (Code Sec. 856(c)(5)(B)).

Under an exception to the rule limiting a REIT's securities holdings to no more than 10 percent of the vote or value of a single issuer, a REIT can own 100 percent of the stock of a corporation, but in that case the income and assets of such corporation are treated as income and assets of the REIT (Code Sec. 856(i)).

"Straight debt" exception. Securities of an issuer that are within a safe-harbor definition of "straight debt" are not taken into account in applying the limitation that a REIT may not hold more than 10 percent of the value of outstanding securities of a single issuer, if:

(1) the issuer is an individual,

(2) the only securities of such issuer held by the REIT or a taxable REIT subsidiary of the REIT are straight debt, or

(3) the issuer is a partnership and the trust holds at least a 20-percent profits interest in the partnership (Code Sec. 856(c)(7); Code Sec. 1361(c)(5), without regard to paragraph (B)(iii)).

Straight debt for purposes of the REIT provision is defined as a written or unconditional promise to pay on demand or on a specified date a sum certain in money if the interest rate (and interest payment dates) are not contingent on profits, the borrower's discretion, or similar factors, and there is no convertibility (directly or indirectly) into stock (Code Sec. 856(c)(7); Code Sec. 1361(c)(5)(B)).

Comment: Although the straight debt rules were intended to prevent REITs from owning more than 10 percent of the value of the equity of another corporation, the rules potentially apply to many situations when individuals and businesses owe some sort of debt to a REIT. There are many situations in which

REITs make non-abusive, ordinary loans in the course of business for which they could face loss of REIT status because the loans do not qualify as straight debt.

Special rules for taxable REIT subsidiaries. Under an exception to the general rule limiting REIT securities ownership of other entities, a REIT can own stock of a taxable REIT subsidiary (TRS), which is generally a corporation other than a REIT with which the REIT makes a joint election to be subject to special rules. A TRS can engage in active business operations that would produce income that would not be qualified income for purposes of the 95- percent or 75-percent income tests for a REIT, and that income is not attributed to the REIT. For example, a TRS can provide noncustomary services to REIT tenants, or it can engage directly in the active operation and management of real estate (without use of an independent contractor); and the income the TRS derived from these nonqualified activities is not treated as disqualified REIT income.

> **Caution Note:** Certain corporations are not eligible to be a TRS, such as a corporation that directly or indirectly operates or manages a lodging facility or a health care facility, or directly or indirectly provides to any other person rights to a brand name under which any lodging facility or health care facility is operated (Code Sec. 856(l)(3)).

Transactions between a TRS and a REIT are subject to a number of specific rules that are intended to prevent the TRS (taxable as a separate corporate entity) from shifting taxable income from its activities to the passthrough entity REIT or from absorbing more than its share of expenses. Under one rule, a 100-percent excise tax is imposed on rents, deductions, or interest paid by the TRS to the REIT to the extent such items would exceed an arm's length amount as determined under Code Sec. 482. If the excise tax applies, then the item is not reallocated back to the TRS under Code Sec. 482 (Code Sec. 857(b)(7)).

Rents subject to the 100-percent excise tax do not include rents for services of a TRS that are for services customarily furnished or rendered in connection with the rental of real property. They also do not include rents from a TRS that are for real property or from incidental personal property provided with such real property (Code Sec. 857(b)(7)(B)(ii)).

Income distribution requirements. A REIT is generally required to distribute:

- 90 percent of its REIT taxable income, determined without deducting the dividends paid, and by excluding the net capital gain and making the other adjustments to regular taxable income; and

- 90 percent of its after-tax net income from foreclosure property; reduced by

- any excess noncash income (Code Sec. 857(a)(1)(A)).

This rule is similar to a rule for a regulated investment company (RIC) that requires distribution of 90 percent of income (Code Sec. 852(a)).

If a REIT declares certain dividends after the end of its tax year but before the time prescribed for filing its return for that year and distributes those amounts to shareholders within the 12 months following the close of that tax year, such distributions are treated as made during such tax year for this purpose (Code Sec. 858). As described further below, a REIT can also make certain "deficiency dividends" after the close of the tax year after a determination that it has not distributed the correct amount for qualification as a REIT.

Background

Consequences of failure to meet requirements. A REIT loses its status as a REIT, and becomes subject to tax as a C corporation, if it fails to meet specified tests regarding the sources of its income, the nature and amount of its assets, its structure, and the amount of its income distributed to shareholders.

In the case of a failure to meet the source of income requirements, if the failure is due to reasonable cause and not to willful neglect, the REIT may continue its REIT status if it pays the disallowed income as a tax (Code Secs. 856(c)(6) and 857(b)(5)). There is no similar provision that allows a REIT to pay a penalty and avoid disqualification in the case of other qualification failures.

A REIT that does not distribute the correct amount of its income can avoid disqualification by making a deficiency dividend. The Code provides only for determinations involving a controversy with the IRS and does not provide for a REIT to make such a distribution on its own initiative. Deficiency dividends may be declared on or after the date of "determination" (Code Sec. 860(f)). A determination includes only:

(1) a final decision by the Tax Court or other court of competent jurisdiction,

(2) a closing agreement under Code Sec. 7121, or

(3) under IRS regulations, an agreement signed by the IRS and the REIT (Code Sec. 860(e); Reg. § 1.860-2(b)(1)).

Comment: Because publicly-held REITs have to report quarterly to the SEC that they are in compliance with the specialized income and asset tests discussed above, the uncertain application of these tax rules creates greater difficulties in REIT business operators than unclear tax rules do for other corporations.

American Jobs Creation Act Impact

REIT rules clarified and improved.—The American Jobs Creation Act of 2004 makes numerous improvements to the real estate investment trust (REIT) rules. The key provisions modify and broaden the definition of "straight debt" securities, permit a REIT to declare a correcting deficiency dividend without awaiting an IRS or court determination and expand the straight debt safe harbor. The consequences of a failure to meet REIT requirements are also modified.

Straight debt modification. For purposes of the limitation that a REIT may not hold more than 10 percent of the value of the outstanding securities of a single issuer, the definition of "straight debt" is modified to provide more flexibility than existed under the prior rules. In addition, except as provided in regulations, neither straight debt nor certain other types of securities are considered "securities" for purposes of this rule.

PRACTICAL ANALYSIS. Keith Nakamoto of PricewaterhouseCoopers, LLP, Chicago, Illinois, notes that the original straight debt safe harbor rules were enacted to allow REITs to exclude true debt instruments in determining if they owned 10 percent or more of the value of an issuer. For the purposes of the 10-percent ownership test, the rules were intended to include loans which had some of the characteristics of equity. However, REITs found that many nonabusive loans in the ordinary course of business did not qualify as "straight debt." The modifications to the "straight debt" safe harbor are intended to expand the types of loans which qualify for the safe harbor. Examples of loans

which will now qualify under the rules are loans to individuals, loans to governments, any obligation of a tenant to pay rent, and contingent payment obligations which are within specified parameters.

As under former law, "straight-debt" is still defined by reference to Code Sec. 1361(c)(5), without regard to Code Sec. 1361(c)(5)(B)(iii), which limits the nature of the creditor (Code Sec. 856(m)(2)(A), as added by the 2004 Jobs Act). Thus, straight debt is debt payable on demand or at a date certain where the interest rate and interest payment dates are not contingent on profits, the borrower's discretion, or similar factors, and there is no convertibility, directly or indirectly, into stock.

Special rules are provided permitting certain contingencies for purposes of the straight debt provision. Any interest or principal will not be treated as failing to satisfy Code Sec. 1361(c)(5)(B)(i) solely by reason of the fact that the time of payment of such interest or principal is subject to a contingency, but only if one of several factors applies. The first type of contingency that is permitted is one that does not have the effect of changing the effective yield to maturity, as determined under Code Sec. 1272, other than a change in the annual yield to maturity, but only if:

(1) any such contingency does not exceed the greater of $\frac{1}{4}$ of one percent or five percent of the annual yield to maturity, or

(2) neither the aggregate issue price nor the aggregate face amount of the debt instruments held by the REIT exceeds $1,000,000 and not more than 12 months of unaccrued interest can be required to be prepaid (Code Sec. 856(m)(2)(B)(i), as added by the 2004 Jobs Act).

A second type of permitted contingency is one where the time or amount of any payment is subject to a contingency upon a default or the exercise of a prepayment right by the issuer of the debt, provided that such contingency is consistent with customary commercial practice (Code Sec. 856(m)(2)(B)(ii), as added by the 2004 Jobs Act).

Caution Note: Rules that limit qualified interest income to amounts the determination of which do not depend, in whole or in part, on the income or profits of any person, continue to apply to a contingent interest. See, e.g., Code Sec. 856(c)(2)(G), (c)(3)(G) and (f).

The former rule requiring a REIT to own a 20-percent equity interest in a partnership in order for debt to qualify as "straight debt" has been eliminated (Act Sec. 243(a)(1) of the 2004 Jobs Act, striking Code Sec. 856(c)(7)(C)).

A new "look-through" rule is provided for determining a REIT partner's share of partnership securities, which generally treats debt to the REIT as part of the REIT's partnership interest for this purpose, except in the case of otherwise qualifying debt of the partnership (Code Sec. 856(m)(3), as added by the 2004 Jobs Act).

Certain securities of corporate or partnership issuers that otherwise would be permitted to be held without limitation under the special straight debt rules described above will not be so permitted if the REIT holding the securities, and any of the REIT's taxable REIT subsidiaries, holds any securities of the issuer that are not permitted securities (prior to the application of this rule) and that have an aggregate value greater than one percent of the issuer's outstanding securities (Code Sec. 856(m)(2)(C), as added by the 2004 Jobs Act).

Except as provided in regulations, the following also are **not** considered "securities" for purposes of the rule that a REIT cannot own more than 10 percent of the value of the outstanding securities of a single issuer:

(1) any loan to an individual or an estate,

(2) any Code Sec. 467 rental agreement, (as defined in Code Sec. 467(d)), other than with a person described in Code Sec. 856(d)(2)(B),

(3) any obligation to pay rents from real property,

(4) any security issued by a state or any political subdivision thereof, the District of Columbia, a foreign government, or any political subdivision thereof, or the Commonwealth of Puerto Rico, but only if the determination of any payment received or accrued under such security does not depend in whole or in part on the profits of any entity not described in this category, or payments on any obligation issued by such an entity,

(5) any security issued by a REIT, and

(6) any other arrangement that, as determined by the IRS, is excepted from the definition of a security (Code Sec. 856(m)(1), as added by the 2004 Jobs Act).

Example: A REIT lends a tenant money for leasehold improvements. Under prior law, in some circumstances, even a small loan could represent more than 10 percent of the tenant's total debt obligation and could lead to REIT disqualification. Under the new rules, certain categories of debt are non-abusive and present little or no opportunity for the REIT to participate in the profits of the issuer's business. These types of debt include any loan from a REIT to an individual or to a governmental entity and any debt arising from a real property rent arrangement.

In addition any debt issued by a partnership, and not described above, is not considered a security:

- to the extent of the REIT's interest as a partner in the partnership, and

- if at least 75 percent of the partnership's gross income (excluding income from prohibited transactions) is derived from sources referred to in Code Sec. 856(c)(3), such as rents, dividends, interest, etc. (Code Sec. 856(m)(4), as added by the 2004 Jobs Act).

Caution Note: The IRS is authorized to issue guidance that a certain arrangement will not be considered a security even though it qualifies under these rules (Code Sec. 856(m)(5), as added by the 2004 Jobs Act).

Limited rental exception. Rents from real property, for purposes of the 90-percent and 75-percent income tests, generally do not include any amount received or accrued from any person in which the REIT owns, directly or indirectly, 10 percent or more of the vote or value (see Code Sec. 856(d)(2)(B)). An exception applies to rents received from a taxable REIT subsidiary (TRS) if at least 90 percent of the leased space of the property is rented to persons other than a TRS or certain related persons, and if the rents from the TRS are substantially comparable to unrelated party rents (Code Sec. 856(d)(8)(A)). New safe-harbor rules provide dates for testing whether 90 percent of a REIT property is rented to unrelated persons and whether the rents paid by related persons are substantially comparable to unrelated party rents. These testing rules apply solely for purposes of the special provision permitting rents received from a TRS to be treated as qualified rental income for the income tests.

PRACTICAL ANALYSIS. Keith Nakamoto of PricewaterhouseCoopers, LLP, Chicago, Illinois, notes that the REIT Modernization Act of 1999 allowed a REIT to lease space to its taxable REIT subsidiary as long as unrelated parties leased at least 90 percent of the property and the taxable REIT subsidiary paid rent which was comparable to rent paid by unrelated parties. The practical problem of applying the rule was that it did not contain a measurement date, so that a conservative

application of the rule required continuous testing, i.e., any new tenant vacancy required a testing of the 90 percent of leased space and any new tenant lease required a testing of comparable rents. The clarification of the rule now applies the testing at the execution of the lease, the extension of the lease, any modification which increases the rent, and any increase in leased space to the taxable REIT subsidiary.

The limited rental exception applies only to the extent that the amounts paid to the trust as rents are substantially comparable to rents paid by the other tenants of the trust's property for comparable space (Code Sec. 856(d)(8)(A)(ii), as amended by the 2004 Jobs Act).

The substantial comparability requirement must be met:

(1) at the time such lease is entered into,

(2) at the time of each extension of the lease, including a failure to exercise a right to terminate, and

(3) at the time of any modification of the lease between the trust and the TRS if the rent under such lease is effectively increased pursuant to the modification (Code Sec. 856(d)(8)(A)(iii), as amended by the 2004 Jobs Act).

With respect to item (3), above, if the TRS is a controlled TRS, rents from real property do not in any event include rent under the lease to the extent of the increase in rent on account of the modification (Code Sec. 856(d)(8)(A)(iii), as amended by the 2004 Jobs Act). For these purposes, the term "controlled TRS subsidiary" means any TRS if a REIT owns directly or indirectly:

- stock possessing more than 50 percent of the total voting power of the outstanding stock of the subsidiary, or

- stock having a value of more than 50 percent of the total value of the outstanding stock of the subsidiary (Code Sec. 856(d)(8)(A)(iv), as amended by the 2004 Jobs Act).

If the requirements of the limited rental exception are met at a time referred to above, the requirements continue to be treated as met so long as there is no increase in the space leased to any TRS (or to any person described in Code Sec. 856(d)(2)(B)) (Code Sec. 856(d)(8)(A)(v), as amended by the 2004 Jobs Act). If there is an increase in the space leased to any TRS during any calendar quarter with respect to any property, the substantial comparability requirements are treated as met during the quarter and the succeeding quarter if such requirements are met at the close of such succeeding quarter (Code Sec. 856(d)(8)(A)(vi), as amended by the 2004 Jobs Act).

Caution Note: These provisions do not modify any of the standards of Code Sec. 482 as they apply to REITs and to TRSs. Under that code section the IRS may reallocate income, deductions, allowances, or credits among two or more organizations, that are controlled or owned by the same interests.

Customary services exception. The 2004 Jobs Act prospectively eliminates the safe harbor allowing rents received by a REIT to be exempt from the 100-percent excise tax if the rents are for customary services performed by the TRS or are from a TRS and are for the provision of certain incidental personal property. Instead, such payments would be free of the excise tax if they satisfy the existing safe harbor that applies if the REIT pays the TRS at least 150 percent of the cost to the TRS of providing any services (Code Sec. 857(b)(7)(B), as amended by the 2004 Jobs Act).

Comment: Although a REIT could provide such services itself and receive the income without receiving any disqualified income, the REIT would be bearing the cost of providing the service. Under the former exception for a TRS providing such service, there was no explicit requirement that the TRS be reimbursed for the full cost of the service.

> **PRACTICAL ANALYSIS.** Keith Nakamoto of PricewaterhouseCoopers, LLP, Chicago, Illinois, notes that the REIT Modernization Act of 1999 (RMA) included a drafting omission in imposing a 100-percent excise tax on income or deductions which are improperly shifted between a REIT and its taxable REIT subsidiary. The RMA provided a safe harbor for customary services provided by the taxable REIT subsidiary to or on behalf of the REIT. However, the safe harbor applied only when the REIT directly or indirectly recognized the income from the services. The safe harbor did not include customary services provided by the taxable REIT subsidiary to the REIT's tenants when the taxable REIT subsidiary recognized the income from the services. The modification deletes the previous safe harbor. In the absence of this safe harbor, a REIT and its taxable REIT subsidiary must rely upon the general REIT safe harbor which requires income from customary services to equal at least 150 percent of the direct costs of providing the service.

Hedging rules. The rules governing the tax treatment of arrangements engaged in by a REIT to reduce interest rate risks are prospectively conformed to the rules included in Code Sec. 1221.

For these purposes, the term "hedging transaction" means any transaction entered into by the REIT in the normal course of the business primarily to manage the risk of interest rate or price changes or currency fluctuations with respect to borrowings made or to be made, or ordinary obligations incurred or to be incurred, by the REIT (Code Sec. 1221(b)(2)(A)(ii)), or to manage such other risks as the IRS may prescribe in regulations (Code Sec. 1221(b)(2)(A)(iii)). Any hedging transaction must be clearly identified as such before the close of the day on which it was acquired, originated, or entered into (Code Sec. 1221(a)(7)). Any gain from such a hedging transaction is not gross income to the extent the transaction hedges any indebtedness incurred to acquire or carry real estate assets (Code Sec. 856(c)(5)(G), as amended by the 2004 Jobs Act).

> **PRACTICAL ANALYSIS.** Keith Nakamoto of PricewaterhouseCoopers, LLP, Chicago, Illinois, notes that gross income from specified hedging instruments to reduce interest rate risks on real estate debt has histori-cally qualified as gross income for purposes of the 95-percent gross income test. However, the hedging instruments which are defined in the REIT rules do not cover all of the types of hedging instruments which are currently available. The modification updates the REIT hedg-ing rules to conform to the general hedging rules of Code Sec. 1221 and provides that any income under a hedging transaction to reduce interest rate risk on real estate debt is disregarded for purposes of the REIT income tests.

95-percent gross income requirement. In determining the tax liability owed by the REIT when it fails to meet the 95-percent of gross income test, a taxable fraction based on 95 percent is applied, rather than on 90 percent, of the REIT's gross income (Code Sec. 857(b)(5)(A), as amended by the 2004 Jobs Act). This change applies prospectively.

> **Comment:** The rule now conforms with the rule provided for regulated investment companies (RICs) (see Code Sec. 854(b)(1)(B)).

¶1110

Consequences of failure to meet requirements. A REIT may avoid disqualification in the event of certain failures of the requirements for REIT status, provided that:

(1) the failure was due to reasonable cause and not willful neglect,

(2) the failure is corrected, and

(3) except for certain failures not exceeding a specified *de minimis* amount, a penalty amount is paid (House Committee Report (H.R. Rep. No. 108-548)).

PRACTICAL ANALYSIS. Keith Nakamoto of PricewaterhouseCoopers, LLP, Chicago, Illinois, notes that the imposition of tax under Code Sec. 857(b)(5)(A) for failure to meet the 95-percent REIT income test was previously assessed on a REIT only if it failed the test and qualifying income was less than 90 percent of gross income. Therefore, a failure to meet the 95-percent REIT income test did not result in a tax unless the failure was greater than five percentage points. The modification conforms the base for calculating the tax to the base for measuring the 95-percent REIT income test, i.e., any failure to meet the 95-percent REIT income test will now result in a tax.

De minimis failures of 5-percent or 10-percent asset tests. Under current law, with certain exceptions, not more than 5 percent of the value of total REIT assets may be represented by securities of one issuer, and a REIT may not hold securities possessing more than 10 percent of the total voting power or 10 percent of the total value of the outstanding securities of any one issuer (Code Sec. 856(c)(4)(B)(iii)). The requirements must be satisfied each quarter.

Comment: These rules do not apply to securities of a TRS or to securities that qualify for the 75-percent asset test of Code Sec. 856(c)(4)(A), such as real estate assets, cash items (including receivables), or government securities.

Under the new rules, a REIT will not lose its REIT status for failing to satisfy the 5-percent or 10-percent asset tests in a quarter if the failure is due to the ownership of assets the total value of which does not exceed the lesser of one percent of the total value of the REIT's assets at the end of the quarter for which such measurement is done, or 10 million dollars. However, in either case, the REIT must either dispose of the assets within six months after the last day of the quarter in which the REIT identifies the failure (or other time period prescribed by the IRS), or otherwise meet the requirements of those rules by the end of that time period (Code Sec. 856(c)(7)(A), as added by the 2004 Jobs Act).

Planning Note: A REIT might satisfy the requirements without a disposition, for example, by increasing its other assets in the case of the 5-percent rule, or by the issuer modifying the amount or value of its total securities outstanding in the case of the 10-percent rule.

PRACTICAL ANALYSIS. Keith Nakamoto of PricewaterhouseCoopers, LLP, Chicago, Illinois, notes that the inadvertent failure of a REIT to meet the income tests could subject the REIT to tax, as opposed to the loss of REIT status. However, there was not a similar provision for any failure of a REIT to meet the asset tests. Therefore, any failure of a REIT asset test would cause a loss of REIT status. The modification establishes rules for an inadvertent failure of asset tests which are similar to the existing rules for a failure to meet the income tests.

Larger asset test failures. If a REIT fails to meet any of the asset test requirements for a particular quarter and the failure exceeds the *de minimis* threshold described above, the REIT will still be deemed to have satisfied the requirements if:

(1) following the REIT's identification of the failure, the REIT files a schedule that provides a description of each asset that caused the failure, in accordance with IRS regulations;

(2) the failure to meet the requirements was due to reasonable cause and not to willful neglect;

(3) the REIT disposes of the assets within six months after the last day of the quarter in which the identification of the failure occurred or such other time period as prescribed by the IRS (or the requirements of the rules are otherwise met within such period); and

(4) the REIT pays a tax on its failure to meet the requirements (Code Sec. 856(c)(7)(B), as added by the 2004 Jobs Act).

The tax that the REIT must pay on the failure is the greater of $50,000, or an amount determined (pursuant to regulations) by multiplying the highest corporate tax rate under Code Sec. 11, by the net income generated by the assets for the period beginning on the first date of the failure to meet the requirements and ending on the date the REIT disposed of the assets (or otherwise satisfied the requirements) (Code Sec. 856(c)(7)(C), as added by the 2004 Jobs Act).

Comment: The potential of the loss of REIT status could be a catastrophic occurrence that the management of a REIT tries to avoid at all costs, so much so that they expend significant resources to put compliance measures in place to avoid such a result. The assessment of a $50,000 penalty under the new rules is more reasonable than the disqualification from REIT status under prior rules. These changes are similar to the intermediate sanctions legislation in the nonprofit organization area. The intermediate sanctions legislation, like the current changes to REIT sanctions, make it more likely that an entity will be penalized monetarily then under draconian rules that disqualify the organization.

These taxes are treated as excise taxes, for which the deficiency provisions of the excise tax subtitle of the Code (subtitle F) apply (Code Sec. 856(c)(7)(C)(iv), as amended by the 2004 Jobs Act).

Other provisions. The reporting and reasonable cause standards for failure to meet the income tests is conformed to the new asset test standards. After determining a failure to meet the income requirements, the REIT must now file a schedule in accordance with IRS regulations. Former law required the schedule to be attached to the REIT's income tax return (Code Sec. 856(c)(6), as amended by the 2004 Jobs Act).

If a REIT fails to satisfy one or more requirements for REIT qualification, other than the 95-percent and 75-percent gross income tests and other than the new rules provided for failures of the asset tests, the REIT may retain its REIT qualification if the failures are due to reasonable cause and not willful neglect, and if the REIT pays a penalty of $50,000 for each such failure (Code Sec. 856(g)(5), as added by the 2004 Jobs Act).

Any taxes or penalties paid under the provision are deducted from the net income of the REIT in determining the amount that the REIT must distribute under the 90-percent distribution requirement (Code Sec. 857(b)(2), as amended by the 2004 Jobs Act).

The circumstances in which a REIT may declare a deficiency dividend is expanded by allowing such a declaration to occur after the REIT has unilaterally identified a failure to pay the relevant amount (Code Sec. 860(e), as amended by the 2004 Jobs Act).

Planning Note: Thus, the declaration need no longer wait for a decision of the Tax Court, a closing agreement, or an agreement signed by the IRS.

Caution Note: Other provisions concerning REITs have been impacted by the 2004 Jobs Act. See ¶540 for the modification of FIRPTA rules for REITs and ¶1115 for a modified safe harbor rule for timber REITs.

For further information on this subject, consult any of the following CCH reporter explanations:

- Standard Federal Tax Reporter, 2004FED ¶26,512.024, ¶26,533.068 and ¶26,586.01

- Federal Tax Service, FTS § F:9.40, § F:9.43 and § F:9.51

- Federal Tax Guide, 2004FTG ¶13,220, ¶16,665 and ¶25,278

★ *Effective date.* These provisions are generally effective for tax years beginning after December 31, 2000. However, the new "look through" rules, the change in the gross income reference from 90 percent to 95 percent, the new hedging definition, the rule modifying the treatment of rents with respect to customary services, and the new rules for correction of certain failures to satisfy the REIT requirements are effective for tax years beginning after the date of enactment (Act Sec. 243(g) of the American Jobs Creation Act of 2004).

Act Sec. 243(a) of the American Jobs Creation Act of 2004, striking Code Sec. 856(c)(7) and adding new Code Sec. 856(m); Act Sec. 243(b), amending Code Sec. 856(d)(8)(A); Act Sec. 243(c), striking Code Sec. 857(b)(7)(B)(ii) and redesignating Code Sec. 857(b)(7)(B)(iii)-(vii) as (ii) -(vi); Act Sec. 243(d), amending Code Sec. 856(c)(5)(G); Act Sec. 243(e), amending Code Sec. 857(b)(5)(A)(i); Act Sec. 243(f)(1), adding Code Sec. 856(c)(7); Act Sec. 243(f)(2), amending Code Sec. 856(c)(6)(A)-(B); Act Sec. 243(f)(3), amending Code Sec. 856(g)(1) and adding new (g)(5); Act Sec. 243(f)(4), amending Code Sec. 857(b)(2)(E); Act Sec. 243(f)(5), amending Code Sec. 860(e); Act Sec. 243(g). Law at ¶5550, ¶5555 and ¶5560. Committee Report at ¶10,240.

¶1115

Modified Safe Harbor Rule for Timber REITs

Background ——————————————————————————————

A real estate investment trust (REIT) is an entity that derives most of its income from passive real-estate-related investments. A REIT must satisfy a number of tests on an annual basis that relate to the entity's organizational structure, the source of its income, and the nature of its assets. If an electing entity meets the requirements for REIT status, the portion of its income that is distributed to its investors each year generally is treated as a dividend deductible by the REIT, and includible in income by its investors. In this manner, the distributed income of the REIT is not taxed at the entity level. The distributed income is taxed only at the investor level. A REIT generally is required to distribute 90 percent of its income to its investors before the end of its tax year. To qualify as a REIT, a corporation must satisfy a number of requirements, among which are four tests: organizational structure, source of income, nature of assets, and distribution of income (Code Sec. 856).

A REIT must satisfy two source-of-income tests. For each tax year, the REIT must derive at least 75 percent of its gross income from real-property-related sources and at least 95 percent of its gross income from real-property-related sources, dividends, interest and securities. Income from prohibited transactions does not count towards meeting the 75-percent or 95-percent gross income tests (Code Sec. 856(c)(2) and (3)).

Background _____

A prohibited transaction is a sale or other disposition of property held primarily for sale to customers in the ordinary course of a trade or business that is not foreclosure property (Code Sec. 857(b)(6)(B)(iii)). The IRS has privately ruled that income from timber cutting is not a prohibited transaction income if the rules on timber cutting agreements are met (e.g., I.R.S. Private Letter Ruling 200052021).

If a safe harbor test is met, the term "prohibited transaction" does not include the sale of property that is foreclosure property (Code Sec. 857(b)(6)(B)(iii)) or a real estate asset (Code Sec. 857(b)(6)(C)). Income and gain from property that the REIT elects to treat as foreclosure property are specifically included in the income counted towards meeting the 75-percent and 95-percent gross income tests (Code Sec. 856(c)(2)(F) and (3)(F)).

Under the safe harbor test, the sale of property that is held for sale to customers is not a prohibited transaction if:

(1) the property has not been held by the REIT for at least four years;

(2) total expenditures made by the REIT, or any partner of the REIT, during the four years before the property is sold that are included in the basis of the property do not exceed 30 percent of the net selling price;

(3) during the year either:

(a) the REIT does not make more than seven sales of property, other than sales of foreclosure property or sales of property covered by the involuntary conversion rules, or

(b) the aggregate adjusted bases of property in transactions, other than sales of foreclosure property or sales of property covered by the involuntary conversion rules, sold during the year does not exceed 10 percent of the aggregate bases of all the REIT's assets as of the beginning of the tax year, but substantially all of the marketing and development expenditures for the property sold must have been made through a qualified independent contractor; and

(4) in the case of property consisting of land or improvements not acquired through foreclosure or lease termination, the REIT has held the property for not less than four years for the production of rental income (Code Sec. 857(b)(6)(C)(i) through (v)).

Some REITs have been formed to hold land on which trees are grown. Upon maturity of the trees, the standing trees are sold by the REIT. The IRS has issued private letter rulings stating that the income from the sale of the trees can qualify as REIT real property income because the uncut timber and the timberland on which the timber grew is considered real property and the sale of uncut trees can qualify as capital gain derived from the sale of real property (IRS Private Letter Rulings 200052021, 199945055 and 8838016).

_____

American Jobs Creation Act Impact

Modified safe harbor rule for timber REITs provided.—A safe harbor is provided under which certain sales of REIT timber property will not be considered sales of property held for sale in the ordinary course of business. Under this safe harbor, a sale of a real estate asset by a REIT will not be a prohibited transaction if the following six requirements are met:

(1) The asset must have been held for at least four years in connection with the trade or business of producing timber;

(2) The aggregate expenditures made by the REIT (or a partner of the REIT) during the four-year period preceding the date of sale that (a) are includible in the basis of the property (other than timberland acquisition expenditures), and (b) are directly related to the operation of the property for the production of timber or for the preservation of the property for use as timberland, must not exceed 30 percent of the net selling price of the property;

(3) The aggregate expenditures made by the REIT (or a partner of the REIT) during the four-year period preceding the date of sale (a) that are includible in the basis of the property and (b) that are *not* directly related to the operation of the property for the production of timber or the preservation of the property for use as timberland must not exceed five percent of the net selling price of the property;

(4) The REIT either:

(a) does not make more than seven sales of property (other than sales of foreclosure property or sales covered by the involuntary conversion rules) during the tax year; or

(b) the aggregate adjusted bases (as determined for purposes of computing earnings and profits) of property sold during the year (other than sales of foreclosure property or sales covered by the involuntary conversion rules) do not exceed 10 percent of the aggregate bases (as determined for purposes of computing earnings and profits) of all assets of the REIT as of the beginning of the tax year;

(5) If the requirement of 4(a), above, is not satisfied, substantially all of the marketing expenditures with respect to the property must be made by persons who are independent contractors (as defined by Code Sec. 856(d)(3)) with respect to the REIT and from whom the REIT does not derive any income; and

(6) The sales price on the sale of the property cannot be based in whole or in part on income or profits of any person, including income or profits derived from the sale of such properties (Code Sec. 857(b)(6)(D), as amended by the American Jobs Creation Act of 2004).

Comment: The purpose of this safe harbor is to permit a REIT that holds timberland to make sales of timber property without being considered a dealer, provided there has not been significant development of the property. A similar provision already exists for rental properties.

Planning Note: The timberland acquisition expenditures referred to in 2(a), above, are those expenditures that are related to timberland other than the specific timberland that is being sold under the safe harbor, but costs of which may be combined with costs of such property in the same "management block" (under Reg. § 1.611-3(d)). Any specific timberland being sold must meet the requirement that it has been held for at least four years by the REIT in order to qualify for the safe harbor (see H.R. Conf. Rep. No. 108-755).

According to the Conference Committee Report (H.R. Conf. Rep. No. 108-755), capital expenditures counted towards the 30-percent limit are those expenditures that are includible in the basis of the property (other than timberland acquisition expenditures), and that are directly related to operation of the property for the production of timber, or for the preservation of the property for use as timberland. These capital expenditures are those incurred directly in the operation of raising timber (i.e., silviculture), as opposed to capital expenditures incurred in the ownership of undeveloped land. In general, these capital expenditures incurred directly in the operation of raising timber include capital expenditures incurred by the REIT to create an established stand of growing trees. A stand of trees is considered established when a target stand exhibits the expected growing rate and is free of nontarget competition (e.g., hardwoods, grasses, brush, etc.) that may significantly inhibit or threaten the target stand survival. The costs commonly incurred during stand establishment are:

(1) site preparation including manual or mechanical scarification, manual or mechanical cutting, disking, bedding, shearing, raking, piling, broadcast and windrow/pile burning (including slash disposal costs as required for stand establishment);

(2) site regeneration including manual or mechanical hardwood coppice;

(3) chemical application via aerial or ground to eliminate or reduce vegetation;

(4) nursery operating costs including personnel salaries and benefits, facilities costs, cone collection and seed extraction, and other costs directly attributable to the nursery operations (to the extent such costs are allocable to seedlings used by the REIT);

(5) seedlings, including their storage, transportation and handling equipment;

(6) direct planting of seedlings; and

(7) initial stand fertilization, up through stand establishment.

Other examples of capital expenditures incurred directly in the operation of raising timber include construction costs of roads to be used for managing the timberland (including removal of logs or fire protection), environmental costs (i.e., habitat conservation plans), and any other post-stand establishment capital costs (e.g., mid-term fertilization costs).

The Conference Committee Report also explains that capital expenditures counted towards the five-percent limit are those capital expenditures incurred in the ownership of undeveloped land that are not incurred in the direct operation of raising timber. This category of capital expenditures includes:

(1) expenditures to separate the REIT's holdings of land into separate parcels;

(2) costs of granting leases or easements to cable, cellular or similar companies;

(3) costs in determining the presence or quality of minerals located on the land;

(4) costs incurred to defend changes in law that would limit future use of the land by the REIT or a purchaser from the REIT;

(5) costs incurred to determine alternative uses of the land (e.g., recreational use);

(6) development costs of the property incurred by the REIT (e.g., engineering, surveying, legal, permit, consulting, road construction, utilities, and other development costs for use other than to grow timber).

Costs that are not includible in the basis of the property are not counted towards either the 30-percent or five-percent requirements.

For further information on this subject, consult any of the following CCH reporter explanations:

- Standard Federal Tax Reporter, 2004FED ¶ 26,553.0682
- Federal Tax Service, FTS § F:9.50

- Federal Tax Guide, 2004FTG ¶16,665

★ *Effective date.* The provision is applicable to tax years beginning after the date of enactment (Act Sec. 321(b) of the American Jobs Creation Act of 2004).

Act Sec. 321(a) of the American Jobs Creation Act of 2004, amending Code Sec. 857(b)(6); Act Sec. 321(b). Law at ¶5555. Committee Report at ¶10,440.

¶1120

FASITs and REMICs

Background _____

In 1996, Congress created a new statutory entity called a financial asset securitization investment trust (FASIT). A FASIT pools revolving, nonmortgage consumer debt and then issues its own debt obligations with terms, such as interest rates and maturities, that differ from the underlying debts. FASITs were intended to facilitate the securitization of consumer debt obligations like credit card receivables, home equity loans and auto loans, much as mortgage loans had been securitized. By combining loans and remarketing them as securities, debt securitization effectively spreads the risk of any individual loan among multiple investors and, ideally, equalizes the availability and cost of loans across a broader market.

However, Congress concluded that FASITs have not been used as they were intended and are particularly prone to abuse. In fact, they have been used most commonly to facilitate tax avoidance transactions. For instance, Enron Corporation used a FASIT in an arrangement called Project Apache, which increased the company's financial net income by more than $50 million over three years even though the company was essentially loaning money to itself. Enron also participated as an accommodation party in another circular financing transaction called Project Renegade, which used a FASIT to yield significant tax benefits to another participant. FASITs have also been used to facilitate cross-border hybrid instruments that are treated as debt by the United States, and as equity in the foreign country where the holder of the instrument resides (Joint Committee on Taxation, Report of Investigation of Enron Corporation and Related Entities Regarding Federal Tax and Compensation Issues, and Policy Recommendations, Volume I, JCS-3-03, February 2003).

FASIT qualifications. Any entity, including corporations, partnerships, trusts, or segregated asset pools, may qualify as a FASIT by meeting several requirements (Code Sec. 860L):

(1) The entity must make an election to be treated as a FASIT for the year of the election and all subsequent years.

(2) Substantially all of the entity's assets must be permitted assets. Permitted assets are cash and cash equivalents; certain specified debt instruments, foreclosure properties, and instruments or contracts representing a hedge or guarantee of debt held or issued by the FASIT; contract rights to acquire permitted debt instruments or hedges; and regular interests in another FASIT.

(3) The entity's nonownership interests must be limited to specific types of debt instruments called "regular interests." A regular interest generally must have fixed terms, unconditionally entitle the holder to receive the principal amount, pay interest based on fixed rates or permitted variable rates, mature within 30 years, be issued to the public at no more than a 25-percent premium, and have a yield to maturity of less than five percentage points above the applicable federal rate (AFR) for its date of issue. Interests that do not meet these requirements can still qualify as regular interests if they are held by a domestic taxable C corporation that is not a regulated investment company (RIC), real

Background

estate investment trust (REIT), FASIT, or cooperative. A regular interest is taxed like any other debt instrument to the holder, except that the holder must use the accrual method to account for income related to the interest.

(4) The entity must have a single ownership interest that is held by an eligible holder. A FASIT can be owned only by a C corporation that does not qualify as a RIC, REIT, real estate mortgage investment conduit (REMIC) or cooperative. An entity ceases to be a FASIT if its owner ceases to be an eligible corporation. Loss of FASIT status is treated as if all the FASIT's regular interests were retired and then reissued, without the application of the rule that deems regular interests of a FASIT to be debt.

Tax treatment of FASITs. A FASIT is a passthrough entity that is not subject to tax. Instead, all of the FASIT's income, gains, deductions and losses pass through to the FASIT owner which thereby becomes subject to the tax rules applicable to FASITs. The FASIT's taxable income must be calculated under the accrual method of accounting. In calculating a FASIT's interest and discount income, and premium deductions or adjustments, the taxpayer must use the constant yield method and the principles used to determine the accrual of original issue discount (OID) on debt obligations whose principal is subject to acceleration (Code Sec. 860H).

The character of the income to the owner is the same as its character to the FASIT, except a FASIT's tax-exempt interest is ordinary, nonexempt income for the owner. The owner cannot recognize loss upon the contribution of assets to a FASIT, but the owner can recognize loss upon the FASIT's disposition of the assets. Generally, the value of FASIT assets is the fair market value, but special valuation rules apply to the calculation of gain or loss on the transfer to a FASIT of debt instruments that are not traded on an established securities market. The owner cannot offset taxable FASIT income with other losses. A FASIT owner's net operating loss carryovers must be computed without regard for any income arising from a disallowed loss (Code Secs. 860H and 860J).

REMICs. A real estate mortgage investment conduit (REMIC) is a self-liquidating passthrough entity that holds a fixed pool of mortgages and issues several classes of investor interests. An entity can qualify as a REMIC if substantially all of its assets consist of qualified mortgages and permitted investments within three months after the entity's startup date (Code Sec. 860D).

A *qualified mortgage* is an obligation that is principally secured by an interest in real property, and (1) is transferred to the REMIC within three months of the entity's start-up date under a contract in place on the start-up date; or (2) is purchased by the REMIC within the three-month period beginning on the start-up day if, except as provided in the regulations, the purchase is pursuant to a fixed price contract in effect on the start-up day. Qualified mortgages also include qualified replacement mortgages and certain regular interests in a REMIC or a FASIT. A *regular interest* in a REMIC must be identified as such, must be issued for a fixed term, and must unconditionally entitle the holder to receive a specified principal amount along with interest payments based on fixed or permitted variable rates. A REMIC may also establish one class of residual interests, for which only pro rata distributions (if any) are allowed. Holders of a residual interest are taxed on REMIC income that is not allocated to the holders of regular interests (Code Sec. 860D and Code Sec. 860G).

Qualified mortgages do not include *reverse mortgages.* The primary purpose of a reverse mortgage loan is to enable elderly persons with limited incomes to remain in their homes by withdrawing some of the equity. The mortgage lender commits itself to a principal amount equal to a percentage of the appraised value of the home, which is paid to the borrower in installments over a period of months or years. Generally, repayment of the loan is due when the principal amount has been fully paid to the borrower, the property that secures the loan is sold, the borrower dies, or the property ceases to be the borrower's principal residence. A reverse mortgage has the following characteristics:

(1) it must be secured by an interest in real property;

(2) it must provide for advances of principal to the obligor that are principally secured by an interest in the same real property and that increase the balance due on the loan;

(3) it may provide for a contingent payment at maturity based upon the value or appreciation in value of the real property;

(4) it must provide for an amount due at maturity that cannot exceed the value, or a specified fraction of the value, of the real property;

(5) it must provide that all payments under the loan are due only upon the maturity of the loan; and

(6) it must mature after a fixed term or at the time the obligor ceases to use the real property as a personal residence (H.R. Conf. Rep. No. 108-755).

A *permitted investment* includes intangible property held for investment to pay certain expenses of the REMIC. Permitted investments also include qualified reserve assets. A qualified reserve asset is any intangible asset held for investment as part of a qualified reserve fund. A *qualified reserve fund* is any reasonably required reserve to provide for full payment of expenses of the REMIC or amounts due on regular interests in the event of defaults on qualified mortgages or lower-than-expected returns on cash-flow investments. The amount of a qualified reserve fund must be reduced as payments of qualified mortgages are received. A reserve is not a qualified reserve fund if more than 30 percent of the gross income from the fund assets is derived from the sale or other disposition of property held for less than three months. However, gain on the disposition of a qualified reserve asset is not taken into account if the disposition is required to prevent default on a regular interest where the threatened default results from a default on one or more qualified mortgages (Code Sec. 860G(a)(7)).

American Jobs Creation Act Impact

FASITs repealed, and REMICs liberalized.—The American Jobs Creation Act of 2004 repeals the rules that permit FASITs (Act. Sec. 835(a) of the 2004 Jobs Act, repealing Code Secs. 860H through 860L). However, the repeal does not apply to any FASIT in existence on the date of enactment, to the extent that regular interests already issued by the FASIT remain outstanding in accordance with their original terms (Act Sec. 835(c)(2) of the 2004 Jobs Act).

Rules applicable to REMICs are also liberalized by modifying the definitions of regular interests, reverse mortgages, qualified mortgages, and permitted investments, so that certain types of real estate loans and loan pools can be transferred to or purchased by a REMIC. The definition of a REMIC *regular interest* is modified to permit the principal amount of a regular interest (or the interest accrued on a regular interest) to be reduced as a result of the nonoccurrence of one or more contingent payments with respect to one or more reverse mortgage loans held by the REMIC, provided that on the start-up day for the REMIC, the REMIC sponsor reasonably believes that all principal and interest due under the regular interest will be paid at or prior to the liquidation of the REMIC (Code Sec. 860G(a)(1), as amended by the 2004

Jobs Act). A sponsor is presumed to have a reasonable belief concerning the ultimate payment of amounts due under an interest if, as of the start-up day, the interest receives an investment grade rating from at least one nationally recognized statistical rating agency (House Committee Report (H.R. Conf. Rep. No. 108-755).

The definition of a REMIC *qualified mortgage* is also modified to include an obligation principally secured by real property that represents an increase in the principal amount under the original terms of an obligation, provided that the increase (1) is attributable to an advance made to the obligor pursuant to the original terms of the obligation, (2) occurs after the REMIC start-up day, and (3) is purchased by the REMIC pursuant to a fixed price contract in effect on the start-up day (Code Sec. 860G(a)(3)(A)(iii), as amended by the 2004 Jobs Act).

Similarly, *reverse mortgage loans* and the periodic advances made to their obligors that meet this same test are considered obligations secured by an interest in real property (Code Sec. 860G(a)(3), as amended by the 2004 Jobs Act). Obligations secured by an interest in real property also include each obligation transferred to or purchased by a REMIC, if more than 50 percent of the obligations transferred to or purchased by the REMIC are principally secured by an interest in real property and originated by the United States or any state, or any political subdivision, agency, or instrumentality of the United States or any state (Code Sec. 860G(a)(3), as amended by the 2004 Jobs Act).

The definition of a *qualified reserve fund* is modified to include any reasonably required reserve to provide a source of funds for the purchase of obligations that (1) are transferred to the REMIC on the start-up day in exchange for regular or residual interests in the REMIC, or (2) are purchased by the REMIC within the three-month period beginning on the start-up day if, except as provided in regulations, the purchase is pursuant to a fixed price contract in effect on the start-up day. The amount held in the reserve fund must be promptly and appropriately reduced as amounts are no longer required for these purposes. Also, the aggregate fair market value of assets held in a reserve fund must not exceed 50 percent of the aggregate fair market value of all of the REMIC's assets on the start-up day (Code Sec. 860G(a)(7)(B), as amended by the 2004 Jobs Act).

For further information on this subject, consult any of the following CCH reporter explanations:

- Standard Federal Tax Reporter, 2004FED ¶26,721.01, ¶26,731.01, ¶26,733.01, ¶26,737.01 and ¶26,739.01

- Federal Tax Service, FTS §F:10.40 and §I:21A.40

- Federal Tax Guide, 2004FTG ¶16,705 and ¶16,746

★ *Effective date.* The amendments take effect on January 1, 2005, but they do not apply to a FASIT in existence on the date of enactment to the extent that regular interests issued by the FASIT before the date of enactment continue to remain outstanding in accordance with the original terms of issuance (Act Sec. 835(c) of the American Jobs Creation Act of 2004).

Act Sec. 835(a) of the American Jobs Creation Act of 2004, repealing Code Secs. 860H, 860I, 860J, 860K and 860L; Act Sec. 835(b)(1), amending Code Sec. 56(g)(6); Act Sec. 835(b)(2), amending Code Sec. 382(l)(4)(B); Act Sec. 835(b)(3), amending Code Sec. 582(c); Act Sec. 835(b)(4), amending Code Sec. 856(c)(5)(E); Act Secs. 835(b)(5) through (b)(8), amending Code Sec. 860G(a); Act Sec. 835(b)(9), amending Code Sec. 1202(e)(4)(C); Act Sec. 835(b)(10), amending Code Sec. 7701(a)(19)(C)(xi); Act Sec. 835(b)(11), amending Code Sec. 7701(i)(2)(A); Act Sec. 835(b)(12); Act Sec.

835(c). Law at ¶5085, ¶5345, ¶5490, ¶5550, ¶5565, ¶5570, ¶5575, ¶5580, ¶5590, ¶5780, ¶5585 and ¶6355. Committee Report at ¶11,180.

¶ 1125

Distributions to Shareholders From Policyholders Surplus Account of a Life Insurance Company

Background

Prior to 1984, a life insurance company was subject to a three-phase taxable income computation under which it was taxed on the lesser of its gain from operations or its taxable investment income and, if its gain from operations exceeded its taxable investment income, 50 percent of the excess. Federal income tax on the other 50 percent of the gain was deferred, becoming a part of a policyholders surplus account and generally taxed only when distributed to stockholders or upon corporate dissolution. The company also maintained a shareholders surplus account, which generally included the company's previously taxed income that would be available for distribution to shareholders. Distributions to the shareholders were treated as being first out of the shareholders surplus account, then out of the policyholders surplus account, and, finally, out of other accounts.

With the enactment of the Deficit Reduction Act of 1984 (P.L. 98-369), this regime of tax deferral has been eliminated, and stock life insurance companies are not permitted to add such deferred income to existing policyholder surplus accounts. The companies may not enlarge their policyholders surplus account, but are still not taxed on previously deferred amounts until those amounts are treated as distributed to shareholders or subtracted from the policyholders surplus accounts.

The taxable income of a stock life insurance company that has an existing policyholders surplus account must be increased by direct or indirect distributions to shareholders from the account. The company is then taxed under Code Sec. 801 on the sum of the life insurance company taxable income for the year, plus the amount of direct and indirect distributions during the year to shareholders from such account (Code Sec. 815(a)). Distributions to shareholders are made pursuant to the ordering rule found in Code Sec. 815(b), which is the same as it was under pre-1984 law: first out of the shareholders surplus account, then out of the policyholders surplus account, and, finally, out of other accounts.

American Jobs Creation Act Impact

Distributions to shareholders from policyholders surplus account of a stock life insurance company.—For tax years beginning in 2005 and 2006, the amount of direct and indirect distributions to shareholders from an existing policyholders surplus account (the amount described in Code Sec. 815(a)(2)) will be treated as zero (Code Sec. 815(g)(1), as added by the American Jobs Creation Act of 2004). In effect, tax will be imposed only on actual life insurance company taxable income for those years under Code Sec. 815(a)(1).

Furthermore, in determining any subtractions from an account under Code Sec. 815(c)(3) and (d)(3), the order in which distributions reduce the various accounts is changed. Any distribution to shareholders during the tax year will be treated as made first out of the policyholders surplus account, then out of the shareholders surplus account, and, finally, out of other accounts (Code Sec. 815(g)(2), as added by the 2004 Jobs Act).

For further information on this subject, consult any of the following CCH reporter explanations:

- Standard Federal Tax Reporter, 2004FED ¶25,977.01
- Federal Tax Service, FTS §I:5.163
- Federal Tax Guide, 2004FTG ¶3205 and ¶4028

★ *Effective date.* The amendment made by this section shall apply to tax years beginning after December 31, 2004 (Act Sec. 705(b) of the American Jobs Creation Act of 2004).

Act Sec. 705(a) of the American Jobs Creation Act of 2004, adding Code Sec. 815(g); Act Sec. 705(b). Law at ¶5535. Committee Report at ¶10,870.

Chapter 12

Individuals

¶ 1205

Deduction of State and Local General Sales Taxes

Background

Prior to 1987, taxpayers were allowed to deduct not only their state and local income taxes paid but also the amount of state and local *general sales taxes* paid. These amounts were deducted as itemized deductions on Schedule A of Form 1040. Taxpayers could either claim the actual amount of sales taxes paid or take a deduction based upon IRS-generated tables. The tables contained state-by-state estimates of tax liability for individuals at different income levels and the deductible amount was based on adjusted gross income and the number of individuals in a taxpayer's household (the taxpayer, his or her spouse, and dependents). To be deductible, the tax had to be imposed on sales at the retail level and generally had to apply at one rate to a broad range of items. Sales taxes imposed at lower rates on certain items were deductible as were sales taxes imposed at higher rates on motor vehicles.

As part of the Tax Reform Act of 1986 (P.L. 99-514), the deduction for state and local general sales taxes was repealed for tax years after 1986. In repealing the deduction, Congress maintained that repeal was appropriate in light of its approach to reduce tax rates and simplify the tax system. It cited the following as support for its decision: (1) general sales taxes were not uniformly imposed in all states and, since the amount of sales tax paid reflected more of a personal consumption choice, repeal would lead to more consistent application of federal tax policy; (2) only a small percentage of the general sales taxes paid were claimed as a deduction and, thus, repeal would have little or no economic impact on those states with only a general sales tax and no income tax; and (3) substantial recordkeeping was required by taxpayers who did not use the IRS tables and often resulted in tax controversies with the IRS over the actual general sales tax percentage. (Senate Finance Committee Report on the Tax Reform Act of 1986 (S. Rep. No. 99-313)).

American Jobs Creation Act Impact

Election to deduct state and local general sales taxes in lieu of state and local income taxes.—For tax years beginning after 2003 and before 2006, individual taxpayers may now elect to deduct *either* state and local income taxes *or* state and local general sales taxes as an itemized deduction on their federal income tax returns (Code Sec. 164(b)(5), as added by the American Jobs Creation Act of 2004). The amount to be deducted is *either* (1) the total of actual general sales taxes paid as substantiated by accumulated receipts *or* (2) an amount from IRS-generated tables plus, if any, the amount of general sales taxes paid in the purchase of a motor vehicle, boat, or other items as prescribed by the Secretary. The deduction is subject to the phase-out limitation on itemized deductions for taxpayers with adjusted gross income over specified amounts.

> **Comment:** The statutory language of new Code Sec. 164(b)(5) is substantially identical to the language that was repealed in 1986.

General sales taxes. For purposes of the deduction, "general sales tax" means a tax imposed at one rate on the sales at retail of a broad range of items (Code Sec. 164(b)(5)(B), as added by the 2004 Jobs Act). Except in the case of a lower rate of tax applicable to food, clothing, medical supplies, and motor vehicles, no deduction is allowed for general sales tax at a rate other than the general rate of tax (Code Secs. 164(b)(5)(C) and (D), as added by the 2004 Jobs Act). If the sales tax rate for motor vehicles exceeds the general rate of tax, the excess is disregarded and the general sales tax rate is treated as the rate of tax. Thus, only the amount of tax that is equal to the general sales taxes will be allowed as a deduction (Code Sec. 164(b)(5)(F), as added by the 2004 Jobs Act). If the amount of the general sales tax is separately stated, to the extent it is paid by the consumer, other than in connection with the consumer's trade or business, the amount will be treated as a tax imposed on, and paid by, the consumer (Code Sec. 164(b)(5)(G), as added by the 2004 Jobs Act). Finally, a compensating use tax will be treated as a general sales tax provided (1) such a tax is complimentary to a general sales tax and (2) a deduction for sales tax is allowed with respect to similar items sold at retail in the taxing jurisdiction. The tax must be imposed on the use, storage, or consumption of an item (Code Sec. 164(b)(5)(E), as added by the 2004 Jobs Act).

Deductible amount. Taxpayers may elect to deduct the actual amount of general sales taxes paid by *either* accumulating receipts showing general sales tax paid *or* using the amount from IRS-generated tables (Code Sec. 164(b)(5)(H)(i), as added by the 2004 Jobs Act). Taxpayers who elect to use the tables, are allowed, in addition to the table amount, to include any general sale taxes paid during the tax year for the purchase of a motor vehicle, boat, or other items to be prescribed by the IRS. The tables are to reflect average consumption by taxpayers and to take into account filing status, the number of dependents, adjusted gross income, and rates of state and local sales taxes (Code Sec. 164(b)(5)(H)(ii), as added by the 2004 Jobs Act). The tables do not reflect items, such as motor vehicles, boats, or other items specified by the IRS. The tables need only be generated for up to the threshold amount for the phase-out of itemized deductions (Code Sec. 164(b)(5)(i)(III), as added by the 2004 Jobs Act).

> **Planning Note:** The table for 2004 will only need to be generated for up to $142,700, the adjusted gross income amount at which the phase-out of itemized deductions begins (see Rev. Proc. 2003-85, I.R.B. 2003-49, 1184) (in 2005, as projected by CCH, the table will need to be generated for up to $145,950).

> **Comment:** The election to deduct either state and local income taxes or state and local general sales taxes applies only for 2004 and 2005. The sponsors of the bill are probably counting on the fact that, like so many other tax benefits

available for a limited number of years, this deduction will be extended in the next Congress.

PRACTICAL ANALYSIS. Michael J. Grace of Buchanan Ingersoll PC and Georgetown University Law Center, Washington, D.C., notes that new Code Sec. 164(b)(5), providing an election to deduct state and local sales taxes in lieu of state and local income taxes, closely resembles the text of Code Sec. 164(b), before its amendment by the Tax Reform Act of 1986. Former Code Sec. 164(b)(2) and (5) allowed itemized deductions for state and local sales taxes. In general, taxpayers could deduct either the actual amount of sales taxes they paid or an amount determined under optional sales tax tables. Like its pre-1986 Act predecessor, new Code Sec. 164(b)(5) directs the Treasury Department to provide tables. As under the prior law, even taxpayers who use the tables will be able to deduct—in addition to the amount provided by the table—sales taxes on purchases of motor vehicles, boats, and other items specified by the Treasury Department. Because the prior and new laws so closely resemble one another, tax advisors should consult Reg. §1.164-3, which was never amended to reflect the Tax Reform Act of 1986. New Code Sec. 164(b)(5) adds to the Code yet another rule requiring taxpayers to "run the numbers" in completing their annual income tax returns, in that most individuals will strive to deduct the higher of their state and local sales taxes (actual or table amount) or their state and local income taxes. The election first may be made for tax years beginning after December 31, 2003. Consequently, for example, individual taxpayers will consider making this election on their returns for calendar year 2004. Many taxpayers who have not been maintaining receipts of their expenditures may find, at least for 2004, that the forthcoming tables provide them a more generous deduction than the actual method. The election is made "for the taxable year." Code Sec. 164(b)(5)(A)(i). Thus, each year, taxpayers should consider whether to make the election, depending on their relative amounts of state/local income taxes compared to sales taxes for that particular year. Reversing the decision reflected in the Tax Reform Act of 1986, the 2004 Jobs Act creates a significant incentive for taxpayers to retain receipts of all their expenditures during the year. However, under the Act, the election may be made only for tax years beginning after December 31, 2003, and before January 1, 2006 (e.g., taxable calendar years 2004 and 2005).

Planning Note: Practitioners need to be aware that the Conference Committee acknowledged that the IRS was currently finalizing the 2004 forms but that it fully expected the IRS to implement this provision and to generate the necessary tables for the filing of 2004 income tax returns (H.R. Conf. Rep. No. 108-755). When these instructions and tables are released will affect the number of last-minute filers and the number of requests for filing extensions. Practitioners need to remember that the extension for additional time to file is *only* applicable for the filing of the income tax return and not the payment of any tax liability.

Caution Note: State and local income taxes are an alternative minimum tax (AMT) adjustment to the alternative minimum taxable income (AMTI). Since taxpayers are electing to substitute state and local general sales taxes for state and local income taxes, and since new Code Sec. 164(b)(5) is silent regarding the AMT, one must assume that, if the deduction for general sales taxes is elected, this amount will need to be added back to adjusted gross income to determine AMTI. Taxpayers in states with no state-wide income tax (Alaska, Florida, New

Hampshire, Nevada, South Dakota, Tennessee, Texas, Washington, and Wyoming) who elect to deduct the general sales taxes paid may now become subject to the AMT.

PRACTICAL ANALYSIS. Sidney Kess, New York, CCH consulting editor and lecturer, observes that the sales tax break benefits those in states with no income tax (Florida, Nevada, South Dakota, Alaska, Texas, Washington and Wyoming) and those in low-income tax states (including Tennessee and New Hampshire that only tax interest and dividends).

Since individuals can opt to deduct sales tax instead of income tax, those in low tax states, especially who make a big-ticket purchase (such as a car), may receive a larger benefit from deducting sales tax rather than income tax. The deduction is based on IRS-provided tables, which may not be ready by the due date of the 2004 return, requiring individuals to obtain filing extensions if they plan to use the new deduction. Since only taxpayers who itemize rather than use the standard deduction can use the new deduction, the deduction benefits would be limited to a small group of taxpayers.

Like state and local income and property taxes, individuals cannot deduct sales tax for purposes of the alternative minimum tax (AMT) and may lose the benefit of the write-off if they are subject to the AMT.

Planning Note: Practitioners will need to do comparison calculations to determine which tax deduction will result in the lowest possible tax liability. For those individuals in states with no income taxes, one need only to check if claiming the deduction for general sales taxes paid will cause a taxpayer to become liable for the AMT. The net result may be that, although a taxpayer's regular tax liability may be lowered, if the taxpayer must pay the AMT, he or she may lose most or all of the advantage of taking the sales tax deduction. Practitioners in states with a state income tax that is less than or equal to the general sales tax rate (Alaska (some local sales taxes), Arizona, Connecticut, Illinois, Indiana, Maryland, Michigan, Mississippi, Pennsylvania, and Tennessee (see Taxpayers Affected, ¶161)) will need to compare the amount of income tax paid to the amount of sales tax paid to determine the greatest deduction, especially if the taxpayer purchased a new motor vehicle or boat during the year. But, once again, practitioners must watch out for the AMT effect. Finally, in those states where the income tax is greater than the general sales tax rate, it would appear to be easy, except if the taxpayer has during the tax year purchased an automobile, boat or other item prescribed by the IRS. Such a purchase may generate an amount of sales tax greater than the income tax. And, as always, practitioners need to watch out for the effect of the AMT.

For further information on this subject, consult any of the following CCH reporter explanations:

- Standard Federal Tax Reporter, 2004FED ¶9502.0365 and ¶9602.024
- Federal Tax Service, FTS § A:15.60
- Federal Tax Guide, 2004FTG ¶6523

★ *Effective date.* These provisions are effective for tax years beginning after December 31, 2003 (Act Sec. 501(b) of the American Jobs Creation Act of 2004).

Act Sec. 501(a) of the American Jobs Creation Act of 2004, adding Code Sec. 164(b)(5); Act Sec. 501(b). Law at ¶5170. Committee Report at ¶10,810.

¶1205

¶ 1210

Exclusion of Gain from Sale of Principal Residence

Background _____

An individual may exclude from income up to $250,000 of gain ($500,000 on a joint return in most situations) realized on the sale or exchange of a principal residence (Code Sec. 121(b)). Ownership and use tests must be met (see "Ownership and Use," below). The exclusion may not be used more frequently than once every two years (Code Sec. 121(b)(3)).

Ownership and use. Gain may only be excluded if, during the five-year period that ends on the date of the sale or exchange, the individual owned and used the property as a principal residence for periods aggregating two years or more. Short temporary absences for vacations or seasonal absences are counted as periods of use, even if the individual rents out the property during these periods of absence. However, an absence of an entire year is not considered a short temporary absence. The ownership and use tests may be met during nonconcurrent periods, provided that both tests are met during the five-year period that ends on the date of sale (Reg. § 1.121-1(c)). Military and foreign service personnel who are called to active duty away from home may elect to suspend the five-year test period (Code Sec. 121(d)(9)). The maximum length of the suspension is five years and it may only be made with respect to one property.

Reduced exclusion. An individual who fails to meet the ownership and use requirements for claiming the full exclusion (i.e., $250,000 or $500,000), may still be eligible for a reduced exclusion when the primary reason for sale of the home is due to: (1) a change in place of employment, (2) health reasons, or (3) unforeseen circumstances (Code Sec. 121(c)(2) and Reg. § 1.121-3(b)).

American Jobs Creation Act Impact

Period of ownership for home acquired in like-kind exchange.—When an individual acquires a principal residence in a like-kind exchange, the new law requires that the individual own the property for at least five years prior to its sale or exchange in order for the exclusion of gain rule to apply (Code Sec. 121(d)(10), as added by the American Jobs Creation Act of 2004).

> **Comment:** This new requirement is a substantial lengthening in the period of time that an individual is required to own the principal residence. Formerly, if the principal residence was acquired in a like-kind exchange, the individual need only own the property for two years before the exclusion provision generally became available. The ownership period must now be at least five years, dating from the day that the property was acquired. The two-year ownership rule continues to apply to other types of acquisitions (e.g., purchase).

> **Example 1:** Hank Bosch, a single individual, has had his principal residence in Gallup, New Mexico for a number of years. He has also owned residential rental property in Las Vegas, Nevada for the past 10 years. On February 2, 2001, he exchanged his Las Vegas property for a single family rental home in Santa Fe, New Mexico. At the time of the exchange, Hank's Las Vegas property had a fair market value of $150,000 and a basis of $50,000. The Santa Fe property also had a fair market value of $150,000. The exchange did not involve any cash or assumptions of mortgage. Assume that the exchange satisfied all the requirements for a tax-deferred like-kind exchange of property. As a result, Hank's realized gain on the Las Vegas property ($100,000) is not recognized and his basis in the Santa Fe property is $50,000.

Hank rents out the Santa Fe property for six months. On August 1, 2001, he decides to retire and sell his home in Gallup and make the home in Santa Fe his principal residence. His realized gain on his Gallup principal residence was $200,000 and he was able to exclude 100% of this gain because he satisfied all the necessary requirements for exclusion. On September 1, 2001, Hank moves into the Santa Fe home and establishes it as his new principal residence. During the period from September 1, 2001, through February 3, 2004, he satisfies the ownership and use requirements. On February 3, 2004, he sells his Santa Fe home for $320,000. Assume that Hank did not claim depreciation during the six months he held the Santa Fe home as rental property. Based on these facts, Hank would be eligible to exclude $250,000 of his realized gain from the sale of his home. His recognized gain, which would be taxed as a long-term capital gain, would be $20,000 (i.e., $320,000 sales price less $50,000 basis less $250,000 exclusion).

Example 2: Assume the same basic facts as in Example 1, except that Hank does not exchange his Las Vegas property for the Santa Fe property until February 2, 2005 (i.e., after the date of enactment of the 2004 Jobs Act). Also, assume he established the Santa Fe home as his principal residence on September 1, 2005. Under these changed facts, Hank would *not* be eligible to exclude any portion of his realized gain from his Santa Fe personal residence before February 3, 2010 because he would not satisfy the five-year ownership requirement until that date. As a result, if he sold the Santa Fe home before February 3, 2010, his realized and recognized gain would be $270,000 (i.e., $320,000 sales price less $50,000 basis less $0 exclusion).

Planning Note: This new rule *only* applies to homes acquired in like-kind exchanges. In addition, it does not extend the minimum requirement that the individual use the property as a principal residence for at least two years. As a general rule, if the two-year "use rule" is met, the individual will still be eligible for the maximum exclusion (e.g., $250,000) when the home is owned for a minimum for five years. Thus, the law change does not prohibit the ability to claim the exclusion; it only delays the ultimate use of the exclusion.

Caution Note: Under current law, an individual may qualify for a reduced exclusion if the ownership and use tests (i.e., two years) are not met due to special circumstances (e.g., health reasons, change of place of employment, or unforeseen circumstances) (Code Sec. 121(c)). At this point, it is not clear if this reduced exclusion applies when an individual who acquired the home in a like-kind exchange does not satisfy the five-year ownership period due to one of these special circumstances. The House Committee Report (H.R. Rep. No. 108-548) states that the purpose of the new rule is to reduce "tax shelter concerns" in situations when an individual converts a home acquired in a like-kind exchange into a personal residence. The Committee did not provide any insight into whether the partial exclusion will apply to such homes when they are sold due to special circumstances. Until this important issue is clarified by Congress and/or the IRS, caution must be the watchword.

For further information on this subject, consult any of the following CCH reporter explanations:

- Standard Federal Tax Reporter, 2004FED ¶7266.01
- Federal Tax Service, FTS § F:8.83[1]
- Federal Tax Guide, 2004FTG ¶4426

¶1210

★ *Effective date.* This new provision applies to sales and exchanges after the date of enactment of the American Jobs Creation Act of 2004 (Act Sec. 840(b) of the American Jobs Creation Act of 2004).

Act Sec. 840(a) of the American Jobs Creation Act of 2004, adding Code Sec. 121(d)(10); Act Sec. 840(b). Law at ¶ 5130. Committee Report at ¶ 11,230.

¶ 1215

"Above-the-Line" Deduction for Costs Incurred in Civil Rights Actions

Background

Amounts received as damages (other than punitive damages) in a suit or settlement of a claim for personal physical injuries or physical sickness are generally excludable from gross income (Code Sec. 104(a)(2)). In order to prevent what would, in effect, be a double deduction, expenses relating to the recovery of such tax-exempt damages are not deductible (Code Sec. 265(a)(1)).

Damages received on account of a nonphysical injury or sickness, such as actions based on age, race or sex discrimination, are generally includible in gross income. Related expenses, however, are not treated as "above-the-line" deductions (i.e., deductible from gross income). Instead, they are deductible as miscellaneous itemized deductions, which are allowed only to the extent that their total (aggregated with other categories of miscellaneous itemized deductions) exceeds two percent of the individual's adjusted gross income (AGI) (Code Sec. 67(a)). As miscellaneous itemized deductions, these expenses (1) are subject to the reduction of deductible itemized deductions applicable to high-income individuals whose AGI exceeds a designated threshold amount (Code Sec. 68), and (2) cannot be claimed for alternative minimum tax (AMT) purposes.

In recent years, a judicial split has arisen as to whether amounts paid to an attorney representing a claimant in a suit for nonphysical injuries are taxable income to the claimant where paid under a contingent fee arrangement. In a contingent fee arrangement, the attorney is paid a prearranged percentage of any recovered damages. In the event that no damages are recovered, the attorney does not receive a fee. Several federal appellate courts (the U.S. Courts of Appeals for Fifth, Sixth, Ninth and Eleventh Circuits), have held that, depending on state law, a claimant may be able to exclude from income fees paid from a recovery directly to an attorney. Other appellate courts (U.S. Courts of Appeals for the Fourth, Seventh, Tenth and Federal Circuits) require contingent attorneys' fees to be included in the claimant's income.

> **Comment:** This issue may soon be resolved by the U.S. Supreme Court, which, earlier this year, agreed to review two decisions (*J.W. Banks II*, CA-6, 2003-2 USTC ¶ 50,675, SCt, cert. granted, March 29, 2004, and *S.J. Banaitis*, CA-9, 2003-2 USTC ¶ 50,638, SCt, cert. granted, March 29, 2004) allowing taxpayers to exclude attorneys' contingency fees from income.

American Jobs Creation Act Impact

"Above-the-line" deduction provided for attorneys' fees and court costs incurred in civil rights suits.—The new law establishes a deduction from gross income for attorneys' fees and court costs incurred by, or on behalf of, an individual in connection with any action involving:

(1) a claim of unlawful discrimination;

(2) claims against the federal government under subchapter III of chapter 37 of Title 31, United States Code; or

(3) a private cause of action under the Medicare Secondary Payer statute.

The above-the-line deduction is limited to the amount includible in the individual's gross income for the tax year (whether paid in a lump sum or in periodic payments) on account of a judgment or settlement (whether by suit or agreement) resulting from the claim.

Comment: Because a deduction that qualifies under the new provision is above-the-line, affected attorneys' fees and court costs (1) are no longer subject to the reduction in itemized deductions for high-income individuals, and (2) can be claimed for alternative minimum tax (AMT) purposes.

Unlawful discrimination. "Unlawful discrimination" is defined in Code Sec. 62(e), as an act that is illegal under any of the following:

(1) section 302 of the Civil Rights Act of 1991;

(2) section 201, 202, 203, 204, 205, 206 or 207 of the Congressional Accountability Act of 1995;

(3) the National Labor Relations Act;

(4) the Fair Labor Standards Act of 1938;

(5) section 4 or 15 of the Age Discrimination in Employment Act of 1967;

(6) section 501 or 504 of the Rehabilitation Act of 1973;

(7) section 510 of the Employee Retirement Income Security Act of 1974 (P.L. 93-406);

(8) Title IX of the Education Amendments of 1972;

(9) the Employee Polygraph Protection Act of 1988;

(10) the Worker Adjustment and Retraining Notification Act;

(11) section 105 of the Family and Medical Leave Act of 1993;

(12) chapter 43 of Title 38 of the United States Code;

(13) section 1977, 1979 or 1980 of the Revised Statutes;

(14) section 703, 704 or 717 of the Civil Rights Act of 1964;

(15) section 804, 805, 806, 808 or 818 of the Fair Housing Act;

(16) section 102, 202, 302 or 503 of the Americans with Disabilities Act of 1990;

(17) any provision of federal law prohibiting any form of retaliation or reprisal against an employee for asserting rights or taking other actions permitted under federal law (commonly referred to as whistle-blower protection provisions) ; or

(18) any provision of federal, state or local law, or common law claims permitted under federal, state, or local law providing for the enforcement of civil rights or regulating any aspect of the employment relationship, or prohibiting any form of retaliation or reprisal against an employee for asserting rights or taking other actions permitted by law.

For further information on this subject, consult any of the following CCH reporter explanations:

- Standard Federal Tax Reporter, 2004FED ¶ 6005.01
- Federal Tax Service, FTS § A:10.40
- Federal Tax Guide, 2004FTG ¶ 4106

★ *Effective date.* The provision is applicable to fees and costs paid after the date of enactment with regard to any judgment or settlement occurring after that date (Act Sec. 703(c) of the American Jobs Creation Act of 2004).

¶1215

Act Sec. 703(a) of the American Jobs Creation Act of 2004, adding Code Sec. 62(a)(19)[20]; Act Sec. 703(b), adding Code Sec. 62(e); Act Sec. 703(c). Law at ¶ 5095. Committee Report at ¶ 10,850.

¶ 1220

Rural Letter Carriers

Background

U. S. Postal Service employees who provided their own automobiles for the collection and delivery of the mail on rural routes were, prior to 1998, allowed a business expense deduction for the cost of operating their automobiles. The allowable amount of the deduction was determined by multiplying the number of miles driven in collecting and delivering the mail by 150 percent of the applicable standard business mileage rate for the year. Rural letter carriers covered by collective bargaining agreements were paid an equipment maintenance allowance (EMA) to compensate them for the use of their personal automobiles. When claiming the deduction for their automotive expenses on their income tax returns, these carriers had to reduce the amount of their allowable automobile expense deduction by the amount of the EMA payment. If the EMA payment exceeded the allowable automobile expenses, the excess payment amount was includible in gross income. In the event that the EMA payment was less than the allowable automobile expense deduction, the excess allowable automobile deduction amount could be claimed as an itemized deduction, subject to the two percent of adjusted gross income limitation.

The Tax Relief Act of 1997 (P.L. 105-34) changed the method for calculating the allowable automobile expense deduction for Postal Service employees on rural routes. The Act repealed the 150 percent of the standard business mileage calculation and modified the treatment of the EMA payment. For tax years beginning after December 31, 1997, the allowable amount of deductible automobile expenses was considered equal to the amount of qualified reimbursement received by the rural letter carrier. Qualified reimbursements are defined as the EMA payments as determined under the 1991 collective bargaining agreement between the United States Postal Service and the National Rural Letter Carriers' Association, adjusted for inflation. The payments were treated as if received as reimbursement for business expenses under an accountable plan and, thus, were excludible from gross income. Rural mail carriers could not claim itemized deductions for costs in excess of reimbursement nor were they required to include in income reimbursements in excess of their actual costs. The resulting tax treatment for rural letter carriers was that their allowable automobile expenses could only equal their qualified reimbursements regardless of their actual expenses.

American Jobs Creation Act Impact

Clarification of certain expenses of rural mail carriers.—United States Postal Service employees who perform services involving the collection and delivery of mail on rural routes and who receive qualified reimbursements for automobile expenses incurred in performing these services may deduct their actual automobile expenses that exceed the qualified reimbursement amount. The deduction is claimed as a miscellaneous itemized deduction, subject to the two percent of adjusted gross income limitation (Code Sec. 162(o), as amended by the American Jobs Creation Act of 2004).

Comment: This is a solid tax break for rural letter carriers. Since their EMA payment is inflation adjusted from the 1991 levels, their current actual automobile expenses probably exceed their qualified reimbursement payment, especially in light of the steady increase in the cost of gasoline.

Comment: According to the Conference Committee Report (H.R. Conf. Rep. No. 108-755), reimbursements in excess of the mail carrier's actual costs do not have be included in gross income.

Planning Note: Practitioners need to make sure that their rural letter carrier clients are maintaining records of their automobile expenses.

For further information on this subject, consult any of the following CCH reporter explanations:

- Standard Federal Tax Reporter, 2004FED ¶ 8590.022
- Federal Tax Service, FTS § G:8.223[3]
- Federal Tax Guide, 2004FTG ¶ 8110

★ *Effective date.* The amendments are effective for tax years beginning after December 31, 2003 (Act Sec. 318(c) of the American Jobs Creation Act of 2004).

Act Sec. 318(a) of the American Jobs Creation Act of 2004, redesignating Code Sec. 162(o)(2) as Code Sec. 162(o)(3) and adding new Code Sec. 162(o)(2); Act Sec. 318(b), amending Code Sec. 162(o); Act Sec. 318(c). Law at ¶ 5160. Committee Report at ¶ 10,410.

¶ 1225

National Health Services Corps Loan Repayments

Background _____

Under the National Health Service Corps (NHSC) Loan Program, health care professionals participating in the program may receive repayment of their educational loans. To qualify for payment of up to $35,000 per year, plus a tax assistance payment of 39 percent of the repayment amount, the participant is required to provide medical services in a geographic area identified by the Public Health Service as having a shortage of health care professionals.

Loan repayment amounts received under the NHSC Loan Repayment Program are taxable income to the recipient, and are also subject to employment taxes (FICA and FUTA).

American Jobs Creation Act Impact

Income and Employment Tax Exclusions.—The American Jobs Creation Act of 2004 provides that National Health Service Corps Loan Program repayments made to health care professionals are excluded from gross income and employment taxes. Loan repayments received under similar state programs eligible for funds under the Public Health Service Act are also excluded from income and employment taxes. Repayment amounts excluded will not be taken into account as wages for purposes of determining a recipient's Social Security benefits.

For further information on this subject, consult any of the following CCH reporter explanations:

- Standard Federal Tax Reporter, 2004FED ¶ 7010.049 and ¶ 33,506.01
- Federal Tax Service, FTS § A:5.40
- Federal Tax Guide, 2004FTG ¶ 25,808

★ *Effective date.* The provision applies to amounts received by an individual in tax years beginning after December 31, 2003.

Act Sec. 320(a) of the American Jobs Creation Act of 2004, adding Code Sec. 108(f)(4); Act Sec. 320(b), amending Code Secs. 3121(a)(20), 3231(e)(5), 3306(b)(16) and 3401(a)(19) and Sec. 209(a)(17) of the Social Security Act; Act Sec. 320(c). Law at ¶5120, ¶5960, ¶5965, ¶5970, ¶5975 and ¶7021. Committee Report at ¶10,430.

¶1230

Prevention and Treatment of Sickle Cell Disease

Background _____

Sickle cell disease is a blood disorder involving abnormally shaped hemoglobin cells. The sickle shape prevents the blood from circulating properly, causing severe pain, strokes and other deadly complications. There is no cure. The disease is transmitted genetically. An individual receives genes for the shape of hemoglobin cells from both parents. Like color blindness, an individual may be a "carrier" of the abnormal gene, the "sickle cell trait," without having the disease. An individual who receives the sickle cell trait from one parent will be a carrier; one who receives it from both parents will have the disease.

Medicaid programs are operated by the states, in part with federal matching funds. Medicaid law requires states to provide certain services including, among others, inpatient hospital, outpatient hospital, X-ray, laboratory, and physician services. States may choose to cover certain additional optional services. Within federal guidelines, states may limit the amount and duration of any Medicaid service.

The federal government matches states' Medicaid expenditures through a statutory formula, the Federal Medical Assistance Percentage (FMAP), that pays a higher rate to states with lower per capita incomes. For some Medicaid services and activities, the FMAP is set by statute. Because Medicaid is an individual entitlement, there is no annual ceiling on federal expenditures; however, states must expend their own funds to receive federal payments.

Under present law, states should have covered diagnosis and treatment of sickle cell disease to the extent that those services were covered for Medicaid beneficiaries with other diagnoses. However, some services for sickle cell disease, such as genetic testing and counseling, may not have been covered because they were not specifically listed in the Medicaid statute as either mandatory or optional services.

_____

American Jobs Creation Act Impact

New optional Medicaid services.—The American Jobs Creation Act of 2004 amends Section 1905(a) of the Social Security Act to add a new category of optional Medicaid services. Primary and secondary medical strategies, treatment, and services for individuals with sickle cell disease are now specifically included. The available strategies, treatment, and services include: (1) chronic blood transfusion (with deferoxamine chelation) to prevent stroke in individuals with sickle cell disease at high risk for stroke; (2) genetic counseling, testing, and treatment for individuals with sickle cell disease or the sickle cell trait; and (3) other treatment and services to prevent individuals who have sickle cell disease from having a second stroke.

The amendment sets a 50-percent FMAP for costs attributable to: (1) identifying and educating likely Medicaid enrollees who have or are carriers of sickle cell disease; or (2) education regarding the risks and prevention of stroke and other complications for likely Medicaid enrollees with sickle cell disease. These educational services directed toward likely, rather than actual, Medicaid beneficiaries, would not otherwise have been covered.

Sickle cell preventive care demonstration program grants. The 2004 Jobs Act authorizes an appropriation of $10,000,000 for each of fiscal years 2005 through 2009 for a demonstration program. Grants will be available to up to 40 eligible entities to develop and establish systemic mechanisms for the prevention and treatment of sickle cell disease. These mechanisms include: (1) coordination of service delivery; (2) genetic counseling and testing; (3) bundling of technical services related to the prevention and treatment of the disease; (4) training health professionals; and (5) identifying and establishing efforts to expand and coordinate education, treatment, and continuity of care programs for individuals with the disease.

The Administrator of the Health Resources and Services Administration will award and administer the grants through the Bureau of Primary Health Care and the Maternal Child Health Bureau. Eligible entities include federally qualified health centers, as defined in the Medicaid statute, nonprofit hospitals or clinics, or university health centers that provide primary health care that: (1) have a collaborative agreement with a community-based or nonprofit entity with experience working with individuals with sickle cell disease; and (2) demonstrate that either they or the entity with which they collaborated has at least five years of experience in working with individuals who have sickle cell disease.

In awarding the grants, the Administrator must consider geographic diversity and give priority to federally qualified health centers that either have or plan to have a partnership or other arrangement with a comprehensive sickle cell disease treatment center that does not receive funds from the National Institutes of Health. Grant recipients must use the funds for the following activities: (1) to facilitate and coordinate the delivery of education, treatment, and continuity of care through (a) the entity's collaborative agreement with the community-based sickle cell disease organization or nonprofit entity described above, (b) the state's newborn sickle cell screening program, and (c) the state's Maternal and Child Health program; (2) to train nursing and other health staff who provide care for individuals with sickle cell disease; (3) to enter into a partnership with area hematologists and other regional experts in sickle cell disease at tertiary or academic health centers and at state and county health offices; and (4) to identify and secure resources for ensuring reimbursement from Medicaid, the state children's health insurance program, and other health programs.

Section 712(c)(3) of the 2004 Jobs Act directs the Administrator to contract with an entity to serve as the National Coordinating Center for the demonstration projects. The Center must collect, compile, and publish data, findings, and best practices from the grant projects and develop educational materials on and a model protocol for the prevention and treatment of sickle cell disease. The Center must also make a final report to Congress detailing the number and type of health care services used, such as hospital visits and length of stay, and specifying the number of individuals who underwent testing and received genetic counseling.

For further information on this subject, consult the following CCH reporter explanation:

- Federal Tax Guide, 2004FTG ¶3265

★ *Effective date.* The amendments to the Social Security Act take effect on the date of enactment of the American Jobs Creation Act of 2004 and apply to medical assistance and services provided under Medicaid on or after that date. The provision authorizing grants for preventive care demonstration programs is effective on the date of enactment (Act Sec. 712(d) of the American Jobs Creation Act of 2004).

Act Sec. 712(a) of the American Jobs Creation Act of 2004, amending Act Sec. 1905(a) of the Social Security Act; Act Sec. 712(b), amending Act Sec. 1903(a) of the Social Security Act; Act Sec. 712(c); Act Sec. 712(d). Law at ¶7075. Committee Report at ¶10,930.

¶1230

Chapter 13

Exempt Organizations, Charitable Donations and Cooperatives

CHARITABLE DONATIONS

¶ 1305

Substantiating Vehicle Donations

Background

Charitable contributions of noncash property pose special problems, primarily because the amount of the deduction is generally the fair market value of the contributed property on the date of contribution. The fair market value of noncash property generally is the price for which the property would sell on the open market (Reg. § 1.170A-1(c)(2)). It is the price that would be agreed upon between a willing seller and a willing buyer when neither is required to act and both possess a reasonable knowledge and understanding of the facts.

The burden of establishing the fair market value of a donated item is on the taxpayer seeking to take the deduction. Generally, the minimum requirements for substantiation are dependent upon the value of the donation and require the taxpayer to (1) maintain a written record, and (2) account for some amount of depreciation due to the physical condition and relative obsolescence of the donated item. For items valued at $5,000 or more, generally a qualified appraisal is necessary.

American Jobs Creation Act Impact

Donations of motor vehicles, boats and aircraft.—The reporting requirements for charitable contributions of most vehicles have been increased. A charitable deduction under Code Sec. 170(a) will be denied to any taxpayer that fails to obtain a contemporaneous written acknowledgement for any "qualified vehicle" donation if the claimed value of the vehicle exceeds $500 (Code Sec. 170(f)(12)(A), as added by the American Jobs Creation Act of 2004).

> **Comment:** Once the claimed value of the vehicle donation exceeds $500, the new substantiation requirements supplant the substantiation requirements of Code Sec. 170(f)(8), which apply to contributions with claimed values of $250 or more.

For this purpose, a "qualified vehicle" includes any:

(1) motor vehicle that is manufactured primarily for use on public streets, roads or highways,

(2) boat, or

(3) aircraft (Code Sec. 170(f)(12)(E), as added by the 2004 Jobs Act).

The term "qualified vehicle" does not include any inventory property, as described by Code Sec. 1221(a)(1).

> **Caution Note:** The new substantiation provision bifurcates the tax treatment based on whether the donee organization merely sells the donated vehicle or uses the vehicle in support of its exempt purposes.

To be considered contemporaneous, the written acknowledgement must be provided to the donor by the donee organization within 30 days of:

(1) the contribution of the qualified vehicle, or

(2) the date of sale of the qualified vehicle by the donee organization if it sells the vehicle without any significant intervening use or material improvement.

The acknowledgement must contain the name and taxpayer identification number of the donor and the vehicle identification (or similar) number. It must also include:

- if the donee organization sells the qualified vehicle without any significant intervening use or material improvement:

    (a) a certification that the vehicle was sold in an arm's-length transaction between unrelated parties;

    (b) the gross proceeds of the sale; and

    (c) a statement that the deductible amount may not exceed the gross proceeds.

or

- if the donee organization retains the qualified vehicle for its usage:

    (a) a certification stating the intended use of the vehicle or any material improvement intended for the vehicle, and the intended duration of such use; and

    (b) a certification that the vehicle will not be transferred in exchange for money, property or services prior to completion of the intended use or improvement.

If the donee organization sells the qualified vehicle without any significant intervening use or material improvement, the maximum deduction the taxpayer will be allowed under Code Sec. 170(a) will be equal to the gross proceeds received by the donee organization from the sale of that qualified vehicle (Code Sec. 170(f)(12)(A)(ii), as added by the 2004 Jobs Act).

The taxpayer is required to submit the acknowledgment with the taxpayer's return that includes the deduction (Code Sec. 170(F)(12)(A)(i), as added by the 2004

Jobs Act). In addition, the donee organization is also required to provide the IRS with a copy of the acknowledgement (Code Sec. 170(f)(12)(D), as added by the 2004 Jobs Act). However, the details of how and when the donee organization is to submit such copies are left up to the IRS to specify. The IRS is also authorized to issue regulations as necessary to exempt donee organizations from two limitations in situations where sales of the qualified vehicles are in direct furtherance of the organization's charitable purpose. The limitations from which a donee organization could be exempted include:

(1) the limitation on the donor's deduction not exceeding the gross proceeds that the organization receives from selling the qualified vehicle; and

(2) when the organization retains the vehicle, the requirement of certification that the vehicle will not be transferred in exchange for money, property or services prior to completion of the intended use or improvement.

Comment: In June 2004, the IRS released two new publications addressing the donation of a motor vehicle to charitable organizations: Pub. 4302, "A Charity's Guide to Car Donations," and Pub. 4303, "A Donor's Guide to Car Donations." The publications are aimed at educating donors and charities about the rules for donating cars and consequences for breaking those rules. It is expected that the IRS will update the publications to reflect the changes made by the 2004 Jobs Act.

PRACTICAL ANALYSIS. Sidney Kess, New York, CCH consulting editor, author and lecturer, points out the change in the charitable contribution deduction rules for car donations is designed to clamp down on excessive write-offs. If the charity does not use the car and it or its agent (if the charity uses a third party) sells the car, the charitable contribution deduction is limited to the gross sales proceeds.

Donors will have to rely on information provided from the charity about any sales. This change applies to contributions made after December 31, 2004. However, it is not clear how charities will adapt to this change. Also starting next year, charities are required to give a copy of written acknowledgments of such donations to the IRS. Presumably, the IRS will use this information to cross-check claimed deductions.

It is also important to bear in mind that many charities utilize car donations as a valuable source of funds. For charities that have been legitimate, the new rules should not change the use of this method of receiving contributions.

New penalties. A donee organization that knowingly provides a false or fraudulent acknowledgment, or that fails to provide a contemporaneous written acknowledgement containing the required information within the prescribed time frame, will be penalized for each such act or failure (Code Sec. 6720, as added by the 2004 Jobs Act). Those penalties are as follows:

(1) if the donee organization sells the qualified vehicle without any significant intervening use or material improvement, the penalty is the greater of:

(a) the product of the highest rate of tax specified in Code Sec. 1 and the sales price stated on the acknowledgement, or

(b) the gross proceeds from the sale of the qualified vehicle;

(2) with respect to any other qualified vehicle to which Code Sec. 170(f)(12) applies, the penalty is the greater of:

(a) the product of the highest rate of tax specified in Code Sec. 1 and the claimed value of the vehicle; or

(b) $5,000.

PRACTICAL ANALYSIS. Vincent O'Brien, President of Vincent J. O'Brien, CPA, PC, Lynbrook, New York, observes that, in recent years, Congress and the IRS have suggested that unreasonably high values have been used by taxpayers who donate vehicles. In addition, many organizations have aggressively marketed vehicle-donation programs, fueling an increase in such donations. For example, during the 2000 tax year, vehicle donations accounted for $2.5 billion of charitable deductions.

The 2004 Jobs Act places an increased compliance burden on organizations that receive vehicle donations, and they are threatened with significant penalties for violations of the new rules. In addition, the new rules generally limit the amount of a taxpayer's donation to the true disposal value of the vehicle. As a result, interest in vehicle donation programs could rapidly decline both for organizations that would receive and taxpayers that would donate vehicles.

Since the provision is not effective until after December 31, 2004, practitioners have time to inform their clients about the new rules. In the meantime, even though the old rules still apply for 2004, taxpayers and practitioners should approach vehicle donations with caution, since it is likely to remain a hot-button topic with the IRS.

For 2004, for deductions of $500 or more, simply using the value from a used-car pricing guide is not sufficient to establish the value of the vehicle if the taxpayer is audited. The taxpayer must also be able to prove that the value matches the condition of the vehicle at the time of the donation. Therefore, taxpayers should maintain extra documentation, such as pictures of the vehicle and a statement from a mechanic as to its condition.

For further information on this subject, consult any of the following CCH reporter explanations:

- Standard Federal Tax Reporter, 2004FED ¶11,700.01, ¶11,700.027, ¶11,700.033 and ¶11,700.038

- Federal Tax Service, FTS § A:17.203

- Federal Tax Guide, 2004FTG ¶6594

★ *Effective date.* These amendments are applicable to contributions made after December 31, 2004 (Act Sec. 884(c) of the American Jobs Creation Act of 2004).

Act Sec. 884(a) of the American Jobs Creation Act of 2004, adding Code Sec. 170(f)(12); Act Sec. 884(b), adding Code Sec. 6720; Act Sec. 884(c). Law at ¶5185 and ¶6305. Committee Report at ¶11,560.

¶ 1310

Noncash Donations and Reporting Requirements

Background ———————————————————————————

Charitable contributions of noncash property pose special problems because the amount of the charitable deduction associated with the contribution is generally the fair market value of the property on the date of contribution. The fair market value of

Background

noncash property generally is the price for which the property would sell on the open market (Reg. § 1.170A-1(c)(2)). It is the price that would be agreed upon between a willing seller and a willing buyer when neither is required to act and both possess a reasonable knowledge and understanding of the facts.

The burden of establishing the fair market value of a donated item is on the taxpayer seeking to take the deduction. In the case of minor items, the taxpayer may either estimate the value at the time of the donation based on recent sales of similar items, or may determine the amount it would cost to replace the donated item on the valuation date. In either case, the taxpayer must account for some amount of depreciation due to the physical condition and relative obsolescence of the donated item. In the case of items of significant value, an appraisal is generally the best method for establishing an item's fair market value. If the donated item exceeds $5,000 in value, the taxpayer is required to obtain a qualified appraisal of the item and attach a summary of the appraisal to the tax return (Reg. § 1.170A-13(c)).

In addition, for any property donation exceeding $500 in value, the taxpayer must maintain a written record containing: (1) the approximate date and manner of acquisition of the property (or the date of completion if the taxpayer created the property); and (2) the cost or other basis of property held for less than 12 months immediately preceding the date of contribution (Reg. § 1.170-13(b)(3)).

American Jobs Creation Act Impact

Increased reporting for noncash charitable contributions.—The reporting requirements for noncash charitable contributions have been increased. A charitable deduction under Code Sec. 170(a) will be denied to any individual, partnership or corporation that fails to meet specific appraisal and documentation requirements (Code Sec. 170(f)(11), as added by the American Jobs Creation Act of 2004). An exception exists if the taxpayer fails to meet these requirements due to reasonable cause, and not because of willful neglect (Code Sec. 170(f)(11)(A)(ii)(II), as added by the 2004 Jobs Act). For purposes of determining the threshold values for the various reporting requirements, all similar items of noncash property, whether donated to a single donee or multiple donees, shall be aggregated and treated as a single property donation (Code Sec. 170(f)(11)(F), as added by the 2004 Jobs Act).

For property valued at more than $500, the taxpayer (other than a personal service corporation or closely held C corporation) must include with its return for the tax year in which the contribution is made a written description of the donated property (Code Sec. 170(f)(11)(B), as added by the 2004 Jobs Act) and such other required information as the IRS may prescribe by regulation (Code Sec. 170(f)(11)(H), as added by the 2004 Jobs Act).

For property valued at more than $5,000, the taxpayer must include with its return for the tax year in which the contribution is made whatever information about the property and about the qualified appraisal of that property that the IRS prescribes by regulations (Code Sec. 170(f)(11)(C), as added by the 2004 Jobs Act). If the contributions are valued at $500,000 or more, then the qualified appraisal must be attached to the return when filed (Code Sec. 170(f)(11)(D), as added by the 2004 Jobs Act).

> **Comment:** For property valued at $5,000 or more but less than $500,000, there is no change in the reporting requirements from those currently established under Reg. § 1.170A-13(c), but the door is left open for the IRS to amend this regulation and these reporting requirements.

¶1310

These substantiation requirements for properties exceeding the $5,000 and $500,000 levels do not apply to donations of:

(1) cash;

(2) publicly-traded securities (as defined in Code Sec. 6050L(a)(2)(B));

(3) inventory (as defined in Code Sec. 1221(a)(1)); and

(4) any qualified vehicles sold by a donee organization without any significant intervening use or material improvement and for which an acknowledgment is provided (see ¶1305) (Code Sec. 170(f)(11)(A)(ii)(I), as added by the 2004 Jobs Act).

PRACTICAL ANALYSIS. Vincent O'Brien, President of Vincent J. O'Brien, CPA, PC, Lynbrook, New York, notes how the 2004 Jobs Act affects C corporations making noncash charitable donations. Previously, when a C corporation made a contribution of an item valued at more than $5,000, it was required to attach Form 8283, *Noncash Charitable Contributions,* **to its return, but it was generally not required to obtain a written appraisal of such property, unless the property was a piece of art valued at $20,000 or more.**

Now, noncash contributions made by C corporations of items valued at more than $5,000 will generally require a written appraisal. This increases the compliance burden on donors and may act as a disincentive to certain C corporations, especially smaller ones, that are contemplating a charitable contribution of noncash property.

Comment: **Practitioners should warn affected clients about the new provision as soon as possible, since it is retroactively effective for contributions made after June 3, 2004.**

For partnerships and S corporations, these new requirements are applied at the entity level. However, if the entities fail to meet these new requirements, the denial of the deduction will be made at the partner and shareholder level (Code Sec. 170(f)(11)(G), as added by the 2004 Jobs Act).

For further information on this subject, consult any of the following CCH reporter explanations:

• Standard Federal Tax Reporter, 2004FED ¶11,700.01, ¶11,700.033 and ¶11,700.038

• Federal Tax Service, FTS § A:17.203

• Federal Tax Guide, 2004FTG ¶6597

★ *Effective date.* This amendment is applicable to contributions made after June 3, 2004 (Act Sec. 883(b) of the American Jobs Creation Act of 2004).

Act Sec. 883(a) of the American Jobs Creation Act of 2004, adding Code Sec. 170(f)(11); Act Sec. 883(b). Law at ¶5185. Committee Report at ¶11,550.

¶1315
Charitable Contributions of Patents and Similar Property

Background _____

The amount of a taxpayer's charitable contribution generally is the amount of money or the fair market value of the property contributed. The amount of the charitable contribution may be reduced by the amount of gain that would have resulted if the donor had sold the contributed property for its fair market value at the

Background _____

time of the contribution, depending upon both the type of property contributed and the nature of the donee. If a sale of the contributed property would have produced ordinary income or short-term capital gain, the amount of the taxpayer's contribution, the fair market value of the contributed property, must be reduced by the amount of ordinary income or short-term capital gain (Code Sec. 170(e)(1)(A)).

Contributions of appreciated property, other than qualified appreciated stock made to private non-operating foundations, and contributions of tangible personal property when the donee's use of the property is unrelated to its tax-exempt purposes or functions, must be reduced by the amount of long-term capital gain that the donor would have recognized had the contributed property been sold for its fair market value on the contribution date. Both the ordinary income and long-term capital gain reduction rules may apply to a contribution if the sale of the property would have produced both ordinary income, including short-term capital gain, and long-term capital gain (Code Sec. 170(e)(1)).

In 2003, the IRS announced that they were cracking down on inflated deductions for charitable contributions of patents and other intellectual property (IRS News Release IR-2003-141, December 22, 2003). The plan included a multi-pronged attack on taxpayers, promoters, and appraisers. IRS audit activity was to focus on disallowing inflated deductions and applying penalties. To find the promoters and appraisers who facilitated this abuse, the IRS planned to review promotions of transactions involving improper deductions and aggressively sought penalties against both promoters and appraisers.

> **Comment:** In 2004 testimony before the Senate Committee on Finance, IRS Commissioner Mark Everson stated, "A key issue in intellectual property donations, as in all other property donations, is whether the property has been appropriately valued. In the case of patent and other intellectual property donations in particular, we have concerns about overvaluation, whether consideration has been received in return, and whether only a partial interest of property is being transferred." (IRS News Release IR-2004-81, June 23, 2004).

If the donee of charitable deduction property sells, exchanges, or otherwise disposes of the donated property within two years of receipt, the donee must file Form 8282, Donee Information Return, with the IRS and also furnish the donor with a copy of the return (Code Sec. 6050L(a) and (c)). "Charitable deduction property" is property (other than money or publicly traded securities) for which a donee must sign a Form 8283, Noncash Charitable Contributions, appraisal summary because the claimed value of the charitable contribution exceeds $5,000 (Code Sec. 6050L(b)). The reporting requirements also apply to successor donees that receive charitable deduction property that was transferred by the original donee and who dispose of the property within two years after the original donation (Reg. § 1.6050L-1(c)).

Form 8282 must be filed with the IRS within 125 days of the disposition, and a copy must be supplied to the donor (Code Sec. 6050L(c); Reg. § 1.6050L-1(f)(2)).

> **Comment:** "Charitable contributions of intellectual property offer research universities and other nonprofits the opportunity to develop potential new technologies while providing businesses with a tax deduction," said Sheldon Steinbach, vice president and general counsel at the American Council on Education, in a press release (Higher Education & National Affairs, June 10, 2004). "If Congress acts too aggressively to limit the valuation of intellectual property donations, it could cause a significant disincentive for donors and the country could lose a vital technology transfer tool."

¶1315

American Jobs Creation Act Impact

Deduction for donation of patents and other intellectual property limited to basis.—The amount of a patent or other intellectual property (other than certain copyrights or inventory) contributed to a charitable organization is limited to the lesser of the taxpayer's basis in the property or the fair market value of the property (Code Sec. 170(e)(1)(B), as amended by the American Jobs Creation Act of 2004). This limitation applies to contributions of patents, certain copyrights, trademarks, trade name, trade secret, know-how, certain software, or similar intellectual property or applications or registrations of such property.

> **Comment:** An earlier, similar version of the provision was criticized by the Intellectual Property Owners Association (IPO) in a March 22, 2004, letter to Charles Grassley, Chairman of the Senate Finance Committee. IPO wrote that the provision "would effectively end the opportunity for academic and scientific professionals at non-profit research institutions and universities to develop valuable technologies acquired through patent donations from U.S. companies for which the technology is no longer a part of their strategic business plans."

Donee income from intellectual property. A donor is also allowed an additional charitable deduction for certain amounts in the year of contribution and in later tax years based on a specified percentage of the "qualified donee income" received or accrued by the charity from the donated property (Code Sec. 170(m)(3), as added by the 2004 Jobs Act). Qualified donee income is any net income received or accrued to the donee that is allocable to qualified intellectual property. For purposes of this additional deduction, "qualified intellectual property" includes patents, certain copyrights, trademarks, trade name, trade secret, know-how, certain software, or similar intellectual property or applications or registrations of such property but does not include such property donated to a private foundation, other than a private operating foundation or certain other foundations described in Code Sec. 170(b)(1)(E) (Code Sec. 170(m)(9), as added by the 2004 Jobs Act).

The amount of any additional charitable deduction is calculated as a sliding-scale percentage of qualified donee income received or accrued by the charitable donee that is allocable to the property to the applicable tax year of the donor (Code Sec. 170(m)(1) and Code Sec. 170 (m)(7), as added by the 2004 Jobs Act).

Taxable Year of Donor Ending on or After Date of Contribution	Applicable Percentage
1st	100
2nd	100
3rd	90
4th	80
5th	70
6th	60
7th	50
8th	40
9th	30
10th	20
11th	10
12th	10

The additional charitable deduction is allowed only to the extent that the aggregate of the amounts that are calculated with the sliding scale exceed the amount

¶1315

of the deduction claimed upon the contribution of the patent or intellectual property (Code Sec. 170(m)(2), as added by the 2004 Jobs Act). If the donor's tax year differs from the donee's tax year, the donor bases its additional charitable deduction on the qualified donee income of the charitable donee allocable to the donee's tax year that ends within the donor's tax year (Code Sec. 170(m)(4), as amended by the 2004 Jobs Act).

Caution Note: The deduction is limited to 12 years and cannot be taken after the donor's 12th tax year ending on or after the date of the contribution, unless regulations are prescribed regarding short tax years (Code Sec. 170(m)(10)(C) and Code Sec. 170(m)(10)(D), as added by the 2004 Jobs Act). This 12-year limitation under Code Sec. 170(m)(7) appears to conflict with the 10-year limitation under Code Sec. 170(m)(5). (See below).

The taxpayer is required to inform the donee at the time of the contribution that the taxpayer intends to treat the contribution as a qualified intellectual property contribution (Code Sec. 170(m)(8)(B), as added by the 2004 Jobs Act).

No charitable deduction is permitted for any revenues or income received or accrued by a charitable donee after:

(1) the 10-year period beginning on the date of contribution of the property (Code Sec. 170(m)(5), as added by the 2004 Jobs Act); or

(2) the expiration of the legal life of the property (Code Sec. 170(m)(6), as added by the 2004 Jobs Act).

Practical Analysis: A contribution may end up costing the donor money. This would occur if the valuation of the property is less than the related costs made to ensure that the donee has the resources to further the technology.

Reporting requirements. The taxpayer must obtain written substantiation from the donee of the amount of any qualified intellectual property contributions properly allocable to the contributed property during the charity's tax year (Code Sec. 6050L(b), as amended by the 2004 Jobs Act). The donee is required to file an annual information return that reports the qualified intellectual property contribution and other information (such as the donor's name, address, and taxpayer identification number (TIN)) relating to the contribution.

Anti-abuse rules. The Secretary of the Treasury may issue regulations or other guidance to prevent avoidance of the provision's purposes, including preventing:

- the circumvention of the reduction in the amount of the charitable deduction by embedding or bundling the patent or similar property;

- the manipulation of the property's basis through the use of related parties, passthrough entities, or other intermediaries or through the use of any other law or regulation, including the consolidated return regulations; and

- a donor from changing the form of the property to escape the reduction rules (Act Sec. 882(e) of the 2004 Jobs Act).

For further information on this subject, consult any of the following CCH reporter explanations:

- Standard Federal Tax Reporter, 2004FED ¶11,660.01 and ¶36,262.01
- Federal Tax Service, FTS § A:17.80
- Federal Tax Guide, 2004FTG ¶6587 and ¶6597

★ *Effective date.* The provisions apply to contributions made after June 3, 2004 (Act Sec. 882(f) of the American Jobs Creation Act of 2004).

Act Sec. 882(a) of the American Jobs Creation Act of 2004, amending Code Sec. 170(e)(1)(B); Act Sec. 882(b), redesignating Code Sec. 170(m) as Code Sec. 170(n) and adding new Code Sec. 170(m); Act Sec. 882(c), amending Code Sec. 6050L; Act Sec. 882(d), amending Code Sec. 170(f)(11)(A)(ii)(I); Act Sec. 882(e); Act Sec. 882(f). Law at ¶5185, ¶6150 and ¶7140. Committee Report at ¶11,540.

¶1320

Charitable Deduction for Expenses in Support of Native Alaskan Subsistence Whaling

Background

The Alaska Eskimo Whaling Commission was formed to represent whaling communities and coordinate activities with agencies responsible for subsistence whaling. Its primary responsibilities include monitoring the spring and fall subsistence bowhead whale hunt and enforcing the quota established for each hunt. The Commission's operations are funded by a federal grant from the National Marine Fisheries Service.

American Jobs Creation Act Impact

Charitable contribution deduction for bowhead whaling expenses.—Individuals can claim a charitable contribution deduction of up to $10,000 per tax year for certain expenses incurred in carrying out sanctioned whaling activities. The individual claiming the deduction must be recognized by the Alaska Eskimo Whaling Commission as a whaling captain charged with the responsibility of maintaining and carrying out sanctioned whaling activities (Code Sec. 170(n)(1), as added by the American Jobs Creation Act of 2004). The deduction is limited to the aggregate of the reasonable and necessary whaling expenses paid by the taxpayer during the tax year in carrying out sanctioned whaling activities.

For purposes of the deduction, the term "whaling expenses" includes expenses for:

- the acquisition and maintenance of whaling boats, weapons, and gear used in sanctioned whaling activities;
- the supplying of food for the crew and other provisions for carrying out such activities; and
- storage and distribution of the catch from such activities.

Furthermore, "subsistence whaling activities" are limited to subsistence bowhead whale hunting activities conducted pursuant to the management plan of the Alaska Eskimo Whaling Commission (Code Sec. 170(n)(2)(B), as added by the 2004 Jobs Act).

Compliance Tip: To claim the deduction, taxpayers will need to substantiate their expenses. Compliance guidance will be issued by the Secretary of the Treasury. However, until guidance is issued, taxpayers should maintain appropriate written records with respect to the time, place, date, amount, and nature of the expense, as well as any other documentation that supports the taxpayer's eligibility for the deduction.

For further information on this subject, consult any of the following CCH reporter explanations:

- Standard Federal Tax Reporter, 2004FED ¶11,620.01 and ¶11,620.034
- Federal Tax Service, FTS § A:17.40
- Federal Tax Guide, 2004FTG ¶6577

★ *Effective date.* This provision applies to contributions made after December 31, 2004 (Act Sec. 335(b) of the American Jobs Creation Act of 2004).

Act Sec. 335(a) of the American Jobs Creation Act of 2004, redesignating Code Sec. 170(n) as Code Sec. 170(o) and adding new Code Sec. 170(n); Act Sec. 335(b). Law at ¶ 5185. Committee Report at ¶ 10,500.

UNRELATED BUSINESS INCOME

¶ 1325

Unrelated Business Income Limitation Modified

Background

A percentage of the unrelated debt-financed income of an exempt organization is taxed as unrelated business taxable income. The percentage of total gross income from the debt-financed property to be included in unrelated business income is the same percentage (but not more than 100 percent) as the "average acquisition indebtedness" for the tax year is of the "average amount of the adjusted basis" of the property during the period it is held in the tax year. Debt-financed property includes any income-producing property (other than some exempt types) on which there is an acquisition indebtedness at any time during the tax year (or during the preceding 12 months, if the property is disposed of during the year).

An acquisition indebtedness is the unpaid amount of any indebtedness:

(1) incurred in acquiring or improving the property;

(2) incurred before the acquisition or improvement, provided the indebtedness would not have been incurred but for the acquisition or improvement; or

(3) incurred after the acquisition or improvement, provided the indebtedness would not have been incurred but for the acquisition or improvement and the incurring of indebtedness was reasonably foreseeable at the time of acquisition or improvement.

Excluded from the "acquisition indebtedness" classification are certain annuities and obligations insured by the Federal Housing Administration to purchase, rehabilitate, or construct low- or moderate-income housing (Code Sec. 514(c)(6)).

American Jobs Creation Act Impact

Acquisition indebtedness definition modified for certain federal financing.— For purposes of unrelated business income from debt-financed property transactions, the American Jobs Creation Act of 2004 excludes from the definition of "acquisition indebtedness" certain indebtedness incurred by a small business investment company (Code Sec. 514(c)(6), as amended by the 2004 Jobs Act).

To be excluded from the acquisition indebtedness rules:

(1) the small business investment company must be licensed after the date of enactment of the 2004 Jobs Act under the Small Business Investment Act of 1958 (SBIA); *and*

(2) the indebtedness must be evidenced by a debenture:

(a) issued by the company under Section 303(a) of the SBIA; *and*

(b) held or guaranteed by the Small Business Administration.

Comment: This provision was proposed in 2001 by the National Association of Small Business Investment Companies (NASBIC) in testimony before a subcommittee of the U.S. House of Representatives Committee on Small Business. NASBIC President Lee W. Mercer stated that, to increase the size of the Small Business Investment Companies (SBICs) program and the amount of capital available to small businesses, the above provision should be enacted. According to Mercer, debenture SBICs are important sources of subordinated debt capital for small businesses, making investments that currently average $435,000 in size, with the median size at $150,000. "The amendment to the IRC would benefit all Debenture SBICs, including the minority oriented Specialized SBICs, in their private fund-raising activities, thus helping to increase the size of the Debenture SBIC program and, therefore, the amount of important subordinated debt capital available to small businesses."

However, the exclusion does not apply during any period:

(1) that any exempt organization (other than a governmental unit) owns more than 25 percent of the capital or profits interest in the small business investment company; or

(2) that exempt organizations (including governmental units other than any agency or instrumentality of the United States) own, in the aggregate, 50 percent or more of the capital or profits interest in the company.

Comment: Tax-exempt organizations that invest in small business investment companies that are treated as partnerships and that incur indebtedness that is held or guaranteed by the Small Business Administration may be subject to unrelated business income tax on their distributive shares of income from the small business investment company. The House Committee Report to the 2004 Jobs Act stated, as a reason for making the change, that committee members believe that the imposition of unrelated business income tax in such cases creates a disincentive for tax-exempt organizations to invest in small business investment companies, thereby reducing the amount of investment capital that may be provided by small business investment companies to the nation's small businesses.

For further information on this subject, consult any of the following CCH reporter explanations:

- Standard Federal Tax Reporter, 2004FED ¶ 22,859.01
- Federal Tax Service, FTS § J:6.106
- Federal Tax Guide, 2004FTG ¶ 16,250

★ *Effective date.* The amendment applies to indebtedness incurred after the date of enactment of the American Jobs Creation Act of 2004 by a small business investment company licensed after the date of the enactment (Act Sec. 247(b) of the 2004 Jobs Act).

Act Sec. 247(a) of the American Jobs Creation Act of 2004, amending Code Sec. 514(c)(6); Act Sec. 247(b). Law at ¶ 5415. Committee Report at ¶ 10,280.

¶ 1330

Brownfield Remediation and the Tax on Unrelated Business

Background _____

Although an organization may be granted tax-exempt status under Code Sec. 501, it may, nevertheless, be subject to tax on its unrelated business income (Code Sec. 511). Unrelated business taxable income (UBTI) is income from a trade or business regularly carried on by an exempt organization if the trade or business is not substantially related to the organization's exempt purpose (Code Sec. 512). The unrelated business income tax (UBIT) extends to almost all exempt organizations. Generally, the only exempt organizations that are untouched by UBIT are government instrumentalities, other than colleges and universities (Code Sec. 511(a)(2)).

The UBTI of an organization that is regularly carrying on two or more unrelated businesses is the aggregate of its gross income from all unrelated businesses, less the aggregate of the deductions allowed with respect to all such unrelated businesses.

Income that a tax-exempt organization derives from property that is debt-financed is generally considered unrelated business income in the same percentage as the property is debt-financed (Code Sec. 514(a)(1)). Acquisition indebtedness is generally the amount of unpaid funds borrowed by an organization for the purpose of acquiring or improving a property that otherwise would not have been incurred by the organization. There are four situations in which acquisition indebtedness specifically does not result in the acquired property meeting the definition of debt-financed property:

(1) substantially all use of the property is substantially related to the exercise or performance of the organization's exempt purpose or function;

(2) the property's income is already subject to tax as income from the conduct of an unrelated trade or business;

(3) the property's income is derived from research activities specifically excluded from treatment as unrelated income by Code Sec. 512(b)(7), (8) and (9); and

(4) the property is used in a trade or business described in Code Sec. 513(a)(1), (2) or (3).

American Jobs Creation Act Impact

Brownfield gain or loss excluded from UBTI.—Any gain or loss from the qualified sale, exchange, or other disposition of any qualifying brownfield property acquired by an eligible taxpayer after December 31, 2004, and before January 1, 2010, is excluded from unrelated business taxable income (UBTI) (Code Sec. 512(b)(18)[(19)](A), as amended by the American Jobs Creation Act of 2004).

Brownfield property. A "qualifying brownfield property" is any real property that has been certified as a brownfield site within the meaning of Act Sec. 101(39) of the Comprehensive Environmental Response, Compensation, and Liability Act of 1980 (CERCLA, 42 U.S.C. 9601), as in effect on the date of enactment of the 2004 Jobs Act (Code Sec. 512(b)(18)[(19)](C)(i), as added by the 2004 Jobs Act). Certification must be made by an appropriate state agency (as defined by Code Sec. 198(c)(4)) in the state in which the property is located, and must be made before the taxpayer incurs any eligible remediations expenditures (other than to obtain a Phase I environmental site assessment). Requests for certification should include supporting documentation showing the presence of hazardous substances, pollutants or contaminants on the property, including a Phase I environmental site assessment, any other environmental assessments prepared or obtained by the taxpayer, and evidence of the property's listing on any federal, state, or local inventory of brownfields and/or contaminated properties (Code Sec. 512(b)(18)[(19)](C)(ii), as added by the 2004 Jobs Act).

Eligible taxpayers. An "eligible taxpayer" is any organization that is exempt from taxation under Code Sec. 501(a) that:

(1) acquires a qualifying brownfield property from an unrelated person, and

(2) pays or incurs eligible remediation expenses related to that property in an amount exceeding the greater of $550,000 or 12 percent of the fair market value of the property at the time the property was acquired by the eligible taxpayer.

The fair market value of the property as determined for this purpose is calculated as if the property contained no hazardous substance, pollutant or contaminant complicating the expansion, redevelopment or reuse of the property (Code Sec. 512(b)(18)[(19)](B)(i), as added by the 2004 Jobs Act).

No organization will be considered an eligible taxpayer that is:

(1) potentially liable under CERCLA Sec. 107 with respect to the qualifying brownfield property;

(2) affiliated with any person potentially liable under CERCLA Sec. 107 because of either:

(a) any direct or indirect familial relationship, or

(b) any financial, contractual, or corporate relationship (other than an instrument by which title to the brownfield property is transferred to the eligible taxpayer, or a contract for the sale of goods or services);

or

(3) an organization that was potentially liable under CERCLA Sec. 107 prior to reorganization (Code Sec. 512(b)(18)[(19)](B)(ii), as added by the 2004 Jobs Act).

Comment: Generally, a person is potentially liable under CERCLA Sec. 107 if: (1) it is the owner and operator of a vessel or a facility; (2) at the time of disposal of any hazardous substance, it owned or operated any facility at which hazardous substances were disposed; (3) by contract or agreement, it arranged for disposal or treatment, or arranged for transport for disposal or treatment of hazardous substances; or (4) it accepts or accepted any hazardous substances for transport to disposal or treatment facilities, incineration vessels or sites, from which there is a release or threatened release that causes the incurrence of response costs of a hazardous substance (42 U.S.C. 9607).

A related person is, for these purposes, defined by either Code Sec. 267(b) (excepting 267(b)(9)) or Code Sec. 707(b)(1), substituting 25 percent for 50 percent. In addition, if the other person is a nonprofit organization that controls, directly or indirectly, more than 25 percent of the governing body of the taxpayer, such other person will be considered to be a related person (Code Sec. 512(b)(18)[(19)](J), as added by the 2004 Jobs Act).

If an eligible taxpayer is a partner in a "qualifying partnership" that acquires, remediates, and sells, exchanges or otherwise disposes of a qualifying brownfield property, the exclusion of gains and losses from qualified dispositions of qualifying brownfield properties is applied to the eligible taxpayer's distributive share of the qualifying partnership's gain or loss from the disposition (Code Sec. 512(b)(18)[(19)](G), as added by the 2004 Jobs Act). A qualifying partnership is a partnership that:

(1) has a partnership agreement meeting the Code Sec. 514(c)(9)(B)(vi) requirements on the date the first certification is received by the partnership and at all times thereafter during the property's ownership;

(2) satisfies all of the requirements that apply to eligible taxpayers (except the requirement to file copies of both certification requests with their tax return under Code Sec. 512(b)(18)[(19)](D)(iii); see below); and

(3) is not an organization that would have been barred from being an eligible taxpayer because it or an affiliate was potentially liable under CERCLA Sec. 107 regarding the property (Code Sec. 512(b)(18)[(19)](B)(ii), as added by the 2004 Jobs Act).

In addition, this provision is only applicable if the eligible taxpayer/partner was a partner in the qualifying partnership on the date the first certification (that the property is a qualifying brownfield property) is received by the partnership, and remains a partner at all times through the date of the disposition of the property by the partnership (Code Sec. 512(b)(18)[(19)](G)(iii), as added by the 2004 Jobs Act).

> **Comment:** The Secretary of the Treasury is authorized to issue regulations to prevent abuses, including abuse through the special allocations of gains or losses, or changes in ownership of partnership interests held by eligible taxpayers (Code Sec. 512(b)(18)[(19)](G)(iv), as added by the 2004 Jobs Act).

Eligible remediation expenditures. For purposes of this provision, the term "eligible remediation expenditures" includes any amounts paid or incurred to unrelated third persons:

(1) to obtain a Phase I environmental site assessment of the property, and

(2) for goods and services necessary for the remediation, paid or incurred after the date the property is certified as being qualifying brownfield property, in order to obtain certification that the property will no longer be considered a qualifying brownfield property, including expenditures to:

> (a) remove, contain or otherwise remediate pollutants, contaminants, or hazardous substances on the property;

> (b) obtain a Phase II environmental assessment of the property, including expenditures to monitor, sample or otherwise evaluate the presence or threat of release of pollutants, contaminants or hazardous substances on the property;

> (c) obtain environmental regulatory approvals and certifications required to manage the remediation and monitoring of the pollutants, contaminants, or hazardous substances on the property; and

> (d) obtain remediation cost-cap or stop-loss coverage, re-opener or regulatory action coverage, or similar coverage under environmental insurance policies, or financial guarantees required to manage such remediation and monitoring, *regardless of whether these expenditures are necessary for obtaining a certification that the property will no longer be considered a qualifying brownfield property.*

However, eligible remediation expenditures do *not* include:

(1) any part of the purchase price of the qualifying brownfield property;

(2) environmental insurance costs that are paid or incurred for legal defense coverage, owner/operator liability coverage, lender liability coverage, professional liability coverage, or similar forms of insurance coverage;

(3) any amounts that are funded, reimbursed or subsidized by grants from the federal or state governments or a political subdivision thereof for use in connection with the property;

(4) any amounts that are the proceeds from the issuance of tax-exempt state or local government obligations;

(5) any amounts constituting subsidized financing of the remediation of the property provided, directly or indirectly, under a federal, state, or local program; or

(6) any expenditures paid or incurred prior to the date of enactment of this provision (Code Sec. 512(b)(18)[(19)](E), as added by the 2004 Jobs Act).

Multiple-properties election. An eligible taxpayer (or a qualifying partnership of which the eligible taxpayer is a partner) may make a one-time election to apply this provision to multiple brownfield properties. If such election is made, it applies to all qualified sales, exchanges and dispositions of qualifying brownfield properties that are acquired and transferred during the period in which the election is effective. During this period, all eligible remediation expenditures for all qualifying brownfield properties acquired during the period will be averaged (Code Sec. 512(b)(18)[(19)](H)(i), as added by the 2004 Jobs Act).

The election is made with the eligible taxpayer's or qualifying partnership's timely-filed tax return (including extensions) for the first tax year to which the election is intended to be applicable. The election is effective beginning on the first day of the tax year to which the accompanying return applies, or such later day in that tax year that the eligible taxpayer or qualifying partnership specifies. The election ends on the earliest of the following dates:

(1) a date of revocation selected by the eligible taxpayer or qualifying partnership;

(2) the date eight years after the date on which the election became effective; or

(3) the date of the termination of the qualifying partnership, if the election was made by a qualifying partnership.

An election may be revoked by filing a statement of revocation with a timely-filed tax return (including extensions). The revocation is effective beginning on the first day of the tax year to which the accompanying return applies, or such later day in that tax year that the eligible taxpayer or qualifying partnership specifies. Once an election is revoked, it may never again be made with respect to that qualifying brownfield property by that eligible taxpayer or qualifying partnership (Code Sec. 512(b)(18)[(19)](H)(iii), as added by the 2004 Jobs Act).

Qualified sale. A sale, exchange or other disposition is qualified if:

(1) the real property is transferred by the eligible taxpayer to an unrelated person; and

(2) within one year of the property transfer, the taxpayer receives a certification from the Environmental Protection Agency (or other appropriate state agency, within the meaning of Code Sec. 198(c)(4)) in the state in which the property is located stating that, as a result of the eligible taxpayer's remediation actions, the property will not be treated as a qualifying brownfield property in the hands of the transferee.

Caution Note: This is a second certification that is required to substantiate the exclusion of gain or loss on the transfer of a brownfield property. The first, discussed above, certifies that the site is a qualifying brownfield property. This second certification states that the property will no longer be considered as a qualifying brownfield property following the property's transfer to an unrelated person.

Public notice and an opportunity for public commentary on the certification request is required and must follow the form and manner prescribed by CERCLA

Sec. 117(a) as in effect on the date of enactment. The actual request for certification must be made no later than the date on which the property is transferred to an unrelated person, and must include a sworn statement by the eligible taxpayer certifying that:

(1) remedial actions on the property have been substantially completed such that no pollutants, contaminants, or hazardous substances remain on the property that complicate the expansion, redevelopment or reuse of the property, and such remedial actions complied with all requirements consistent with CER-CLA Sec. 121(d) given the property's reasonably anticipated future land uses or capacity for use (42 U.S.C. 9621);

(2) the future uses or capacity for uses of the property can reasonably be anticipated to be *either*—

- more economically productive, *or*
- more environmentally friendly

than the property was prior to the remediation expenditures (use as a landfill or other hazardous waste facility will *not* be considered more economically productive or environmentally friendly);

(3) the remediation plan being implemented brought the property into compliance with all applicable federal, state, and local environmental laws, regulations and standards, and protects both human health and the environment;

(4) the remediation plan has either been completed or substantially completed and, if not completed, that sufficient controls, monitoring, funding and financing have been established prior to making the certification request to ensure the remediation of the property is completed in accordance with the plan as rapidly as possible following the property transfer; and

(5) the public notice and opportunity for public comment (as described above) was completed prior to the date of the request for certification. At a minimum, public notice requires publication in a major local newspaper of general circulation (Code Sec. 512(b)(18)[(19)](D)(ii), as added by the 2004 Jobs Act).

For these purposes, a remedial action is substantially complete when any necessary physical construction has been completed, all immediate threats have been eliminated, and all long-term threats are under control (Code Sec. 512(b)(18)[(19)](D)(iv), as added by the 2004 Jobs Act).

Prior to issuing such certification, the issuing state agency is required to respond to the public comments it received in the same form and manner as required under CERCLA Sec. 117(b) as in effect on the date of enactment (Code Sec. 512(b)(18)[(19)](D)(i), as added by the 2004 Jobs Act).

The eligible taxpayer (and, if applicable, the qualifying partnership) must include copies of each of the certification requests (for the property to be certified a qualifying brownfield property, *and* for the property to no longer be a qualifying brownfield property in the hands of the transferee) with the tax return filed for the tax year in which the transfer to an unrelated person occurs (Code Sec. 512(b)(18)[(19)](D)(iii), as added by the 2004 Jobs Act).

Gain, loss and recapture. For purposes of this provision, gain and loss does not include any amounts that are recaptured as ordinary income under Code Secs. 1245 or 1250, including amounts deducted under Code Sec. 198 as remediation costs subject to recapture under Code Sec. 198(e), if the taxpayer had deducted such amounts in calculating its UBTI (Code Sec. 512(b)(18)[(19)](F), as added by the 2004 Jobs Act).

If an eligible taxpayer excludes gain or loss from the disposition of a property included in a multiple-properties election, and that property subsequently fails to meet the requirements of this provision, the taxpayer must, when calculating its UBTI for the year in which the failure occurred, include any previously excluded gain or loss from such property disposition allocable to the taxpayer. Interest must also be included for the period beginning with the due date of the return for the tax year during which the property disposition occurred and ending on the date of payment, determined at the interest rate in effect as specified under Code Sec. 6621 (Code Sec. 512(b)(18)[(19)](I)), as added by the 2004 Jobs Act).

Caution Note: This provision will not apply to any property acquired after December 31, 2009, except for the purpose of calculating the average eligible remediation expenditures for properties acquired during a period in which a multiple-properties election is effective (Code Sec. 512(b)(18)[(19)](K), as added by the 2004 Jobs Act). Properties acquired during the five-year acquisition period (January 1, 2005, through December 31, 2009) do not have to be disposed of by December 31, 2009, to qualify for the exclusion. Also, for purposes of the multiple-properties election, properties acquired after the five-year acquisition period expires but during a multiple-properties election period are included for purposes of calculating the average eligible remediation expenditures.

Debt-financed property. The definition of "debt-financed property" specifically excludes the gain or loss on disposition of any property covered by Code Sec. 512(b)(18)[(19)] (Code Sec. 514(b)(1)(E), as added by the 2004 Jobs Act). Therefore, any gain or loss resulting from the disposition of a qualifying brownfield property that otherwise satisfies the requirements of this provision will not be subject to the tax on unrelated business income merely because the eligible taxpayer incurred debt to acquire and/or improve the property.

Savings clause. The 2004 Jobs Act clarifies that nothing in Act Sec. 702 of the 2004 Jobs Act changes any duty, liability or other requirement imposed under federal or state law. A certification provided by the U.S. Environmental Protection Agency, a state environmental protection agency, or an otherwise appropriate state agency (as defined in Code Sec. 198(c)(4)) will not affect the liability of any person under Act Sec. 107(a) of CERCLA, notwithstanding Act Sec. 128(b) of CERCLA (Act Sec. 702(c) of the 2004 Jobs Act).

For further information on this subject, consult any of the following CCH reporter explanations:

- Standard Federal Tax Reporter, 2004FED ¶ 22,837.01 and ¶ 22,859.01

- Federal Tax Service, FTS § J:5.140

- Federal Tax Guide, 2004FTG ¶ 7402 and ¶ 16,250

★ *Effective date.* The provisions apply to any gain or loss on the sale, exchange, or other disposition of any property acquired by the taxpayer after December 31, 2004 (Act Sec. 702(d) of the American Jobs Creation Act of 2004).

Act Sec. 702(a) of the American Jobs Creation Act of 2004, adding Code Sec. 512(b)(18)[(19)]; Act Sec. 702(b), amending Code Sec. 514(b)(1); Act Sec. 702(c); Act Sec. 702(d). Law at ¶ 5410, ¶ 5415 and ¶ 7060. Committee Report at ¶ 10,840.

¶1330

COOPERATIVES

¶ 1335

Treatment of Certain Income of Electric Cooperatives

Background _____

Local benevolent life insurance associations, mutual ditch or irrigation companies, mutual or cooperative telephone companies and like organizations (not defined in the Internal Revenue Code or regulations, but including mutual or cooperative electric companies) are exempt from tax under Code Sec. 501(c)(12)(A) if at least 85 percent of the income of the organization consist of amounts collected from members for the sole purpose of meeting losses and expenses.

The 85-percent test is applied annually so that an electric cooperative could be taxable one year and tax-exempt the next year. Code Sec. 501(c)(12) and the regulations thereunder do not define income. However, Rev. Rul. 74-362, 1974-2 CB 170, states that the term means "gross income" for purposes of the 85-percent member-income test.

An organization must satisfy three requirements to qualify for exemption under Code Sec. 501(c)(12). First, it must be organized and operated as a cooperative. Second, it must conduct activities described in Code Sec. 501(c)(12) and its regulations. Third, it must derive 85 percent or more of its income from members (*IRS Technical Instruction Program for Fiscal Year 2002*, Topic E, "General Survey of I.R.C. 501(c)(12) Cooperatives and Examination of Current Issues").

In determining whether a mutual or cooperative electric company satisfies the 85-percent member-income test of Code Sec. 501(c)(12)(A), any income from qualified pole rentals is disregarded (Code Sec. 501(c)(12)(B)). In applying the 85-percent member-income test to a mutual or cooperative telephone company, any income received under a reciprocal call-completion arrangement (whereby the mutual or cooperative telephone company completes calls to its members made by customers of another company) from a nonmember telephone company is to be disregarded. Also, the income from the sale of display listings in a telephone directory furnished to members of the company or from the discharge of indebtedness arising from the prepayment of a loan under Section 306A, 306B, or 311 of the Rural Electrification Act of 1936, as in effect on January 1, 1987, is to be disregarded in applying the 85-percent member-income test to a mutual or cooperative telephone company.

Code Sec. 501(c)(12) organizations are subject to the tax on unrelated business income.

American Jobs Creation Act Impact

Cooperative income from certain transactions excluded from 85-percent test.— Income received or accrued by a rural electric cooperative is excluded for purposes of the 85-percent test for exemption under Code Sec. 501(c)(12) if the income is from:

(1) the provision or sale of electric energy transmission services or ancillary services on a nondiscriminatory open-access basis under an open access transmission tariff approved or accepted by the Federal Energy Regulatory Commission (FERC) or under an independent transmission provider agreement approved or accepted by FERC;

(2) the provision or sale of electric energy distribution services or ancillary services, as long as the services are provided on a nondiscriminatory open-access basis to distribute electric energy not owned by the cooperative:

(a) to end-users who are served by distribution facilities not owned by the cooperative or any of its members, or

(b) that is generated by a generation facility that is not owned or leased by the cooperative or any of its members and that is directly connected to distribution facilities owned by the cooperative or any of its members;

(3) a nuclear decommissioning transaction; or

(4) an asset exchange or conversion transaction (Code Sec. 501(c)(12)(C), as amended by the American Jobs Creation Act of 2004).

FERC. Under this provision, FERC includes the Federal Energy Regulatory Commission and the Public Utility Commission of Texas (Code Sec. 501(c)(12)(E), as added by the 2004 Jobs Act).

Nuclear decommissioning transaction. A nuclear decommissioning transaction is:

(1) any transfer into a trust, fund, or instrument established to pay any nuclear decommissioning costs if the transfer is in connection with the transfer of the mutual or cooperative electric company's interest in a nuclear power plant or nuclear power plant unit;

(2) any distribution from a trust, fund, or instrument established to pay any nuclear decommissioning costs; or

(3) any earnings from any trust, fund, or instrument established to pay any nuclear decommissioning costs (Code Sec. 501(c)(12)(F), as added by the 2004 Jobs Act).

Asset exchange or conversion transaction. An asset exchange or conversion transaction is defined as a voluntary exchange or involuntary conversion by a mutual or cooperative electric company of property that is related to generating, transmitting, distributing or selling electric energy. In addition:

(1) the gain from the transaction must qualify for deferred recognition under Code Sec. 1031 (exchanges of property held for productive use or investment) or Code Sec. 1033 (involuntary conversions), and

(2) the replacement property acquired by the company must be used for:

(a) generating, transmitting, distributing, or selling electric energy, or

(b) producing, transmitting, distributing, or selling natural gas (Code Sec. 501(c)(12)(G), as added by the 2004 Jobs Act).

Load loss transaction. Receipt or accrual of income from load loss transactions, by mutual or cooperative electric companies, is treated as income from patrons who are members of the cooperative. A load loss transaction is any wholesale or retail sale of electric energy to the extent that the aggregate amount of the sales during a seven-year period beginning with the start-up year does not exceed the limit placed on such sales. That limit is the sum for all seven years of the amount by which sales to members in each year is less than the amount of sales to members in the "base" year. The "base" year is the year before the start-up year or, at the company's election, the second or third year before the start-up year. Load loss transactions do not include sales to cooperative members (Code Sec. 501(c)(12)(H), as added by the 2004 Jobs Act).

Start-up year. The start-up year is the first year that a cooperative offers nondiscriminatory open access or, if later and at the election of the cooperative, the calendar year that includes the enactment of this provision (Code Sec. 501(c)(12)(H)(vii), as added by the 2004 Jobs Act).

Unrelated business taxable income. Income received or accrued by mutual or cooperative electric companies from load loss transactions is excluded from the tax on unrelated trade or business income (Code Sec. 512(b)(18), as added by the 2004 Jobs Act).

> **Comment:** The tax provisions in the 2004 Jobs Act "provide additional certainty for electric cooperatives in an evolving utility marketplace," according to the National Rural Electric Cooperative Association.

For further information on this subject, consult any of the following CCH reporter explanations:

- Standard Federal Tax Reporter, 2004FED ¶22,634.01
- Federal Tax Service, FTS §J:3.200
- Federal Tax Guide, 2004FTG ¶16,755

★ *Effective date.* The provision is effective for tax years beginning after the date of enactment. Amendments made to Code Sec. 501(c)(12)(C) and (H) cease to apply for tax years beginning after 2006 (Act Sec. 319(a)(1), (b) and (e) of the American Jobs Creation Act of 2004).

Act Sec. 319(a)(1) of the American Jobs Creation Act of 2004, amending Code Sec. 501(c)(12)(C); Act Sec. 319(a)(2), adding Code Sec. 501(c)(12)(E), (F) and (G); Act Sec. 319(b), adding Code Sec. 501(c)(12)(H); Act Sec. 319(c), adding Code Sec. 512(b)(18); Act Sec. 319(d), adding Code Sec. 1381(c); Act Sec. 319(e). Law at ¶5400, ¶5410 and ¶5905. Committee Report at ¶10,420.

¶1340

Payment of Dividends on Stock of Cooperatives

Background

A cooperative is not taxed as long as any patronage income is distributed to its members. A cooperative may deduct dividends paid to patrons from taxable income, but generally only to the extent of net income derived from transactions with its members. Members may have income from the cooperative in the form of patronage dividends. Patronage dividends are amounts paid by the cooperative to its patrons under the following circumstances:

(1) the amount must be based on quantity or the value of the business that is done with or for the patron;

(2) the cooperative must have been under an obligation to pay this amount and the obligation must have existed before the cooperative received the amount that is paid to the patron; and

(3) the amount paid must be determined by reference to the cooperative's net earnings from the business that it has done with or for its patrons (Code Sec. 1388(a)).

Under the dividend allocation rule, dividends paid on capital stock and other proprietary interests of the cooperative are allocated between patronage and nonpatronage business. The amounts allocated to patronage business then reduce net earnings from which patronage dividends are paid (Conference Committee Report (H.R. Conf. Rep. No. 108-755) and Reg. §1.1388-1(a)(1)).

The effect of this rule is to reduce the amount of earnings that a cooperative can treat as patronage income. This reduces the amount that the cooperative can pay back to their patrons as patronage dividends. By returning money to nonmembers, it loses its corporate deduction, which in turn reduces the return of earnings that the patron has already paid taxes on. Thus, cooperatives pay an additional layer of tax if they pay a dividend on capital stock or other proprietary interests.

> **Comment:** The dividend allocation rule penalizes co-ops that issue and pay dividends on capital stock, according to the National Cooperative Business Association (/www.ncba.coop/serv_pubp_tripletax_fact.cfm). The rule "discourages co-ops from issuing non-voting stock as a means to raise capital—one of the few equity-generation options available to them."

American Jobs Creation Act Impact

Special rule for dividends paid on capital stock of a cooperative.—Certain dividends paid by a cooperative on its capital stock or other proprietary capital interests will no longer reduce patronage income (Code Sec. 1388(a), as amended by the American Jobs Creation Act of 2004). Dividends will not reduce net earnings to the extent the cooperative's articles of incorporation, bylaws or other contracts with patrons provide that the dividends are in addition to the amounts otherwise paid to the patrons in connection with patronage business.

> **Comment:** The National Milk Producers Federation (www.nmpf.org/govIssues/Index.cfm) states that the rule clarifies the dividend allocation rule for farmer cooperatives, eliminates triple tax on cooperative dividends, promotes tax fairness for cooperatives, and provides improved access to capital, which is a major challenge for cooperatives.

> **Planning Note:** Cooperatives can create a class of preferred stock or other proprietary capital interest to pay out dividends. Cooperatives may have to amend their articles of incorporation, bylaws, or other contracts to take advantage of this provision.

For further information on this subject, consult any of the following CCH reporter explanations:

- Standard Federal Tax Reporter, 2004FED ¶ 32,328.01 and ¶ 32,328.04

- Federal Tax Service, FTS § L:3.62

- Federal Tax Guide, 2004FTG ¶ 16,765

★ *Effective date.* The provision applies to distributions in tax years beginning after the date of enactment (Act Sec. 312(b) of the American Jobs Creation Act of 2004).

Act Sec. 312(a) of the American Jobs Creation Act of 2004, amending Code Sec. 1388(a); Act Sec. 312(b). Law at ¶ 5910. Committee Report at ¶ 10,350.

¶1340

Chapter 14

Compensation and Pension Plans

¶ 1405

Treatment of Nonqualified Deferred Compensation Plans

Background

Nonqualified plans are deferred compensation arrangements that do not meet the tax qualification requirements of Code Sec. 401 and so do not receive favored treatment under the tax law. Nonqualified plans are nevertheless useful, typically as part of a compensation package designed to provide executive and middle management employees with special incentives in excess of those allowed under the qualified plan rules. According to the ERISA Industry Committee, approximately 92 percent of Fortune 1000 companies maintain nonqualified deferred compensation plans.

If a plan is qualified, the employer is permitted to immediately deduct contributions to the plan's trust, but the employees are not currently taxed on the amounts contributed on their behalf by the employer, and the trust's earnings are exempt from tax. Employees are taxed when they receive distributions. If a plan is nonqualified, its tax consequences may be governed by a number of different provisions, depending on the nature of the plan. Income inclusion generally depends on whether the plan is funded or unfunded.

Unfunded arrangements are the employer's unsecured promise to pay the deferred compensation. If the arrangement is unfunded, the compensation is includible in income in the year it is actually or constructively received (Code Sec. 451). Income is constructively received when it is credited to an individual's account, set aside, or otherwise made available to be drawn on by the employee. Until that time, the employee is dependent on the employer's willingness to live up to its promise.

If the plan is funded or secured (that is, when there has been a transfer of property), income is includible in the year in which the individual's rights to the property are transferable and not subject to a "substantial risk of forfeiture" (Code Secs. 83(a) and 402(b)). These rules apply if the employer sets aside funds outside of the reach of its creditors to meet its promises to the employee under the plan.

In order to avoid immediate taxation of the employee but still provide some assurance that the compensation will be paid, "rabbi trusts" are used. (The arrangement is called a rabbi trust because a rabbi received the first favorable letter ruling.)

Background

In a rabbi trust, an irrevocable trust is set up for the benefit of employees, but remains subject to the claims of the employer's creditors. Thus, the employer is considered the owner of the trust, and the employee is not subject to tax on deferred amounts until he or she receives the payouts. The IRS has issued a model form for rabbi trusts (Rev. Proc. 92-64).

American Jobs Creation Act Impact

Nonqualified deferred compensation plans.—The American Jobs Creation Act of 2004 consolidates and supplements the existing requirements for deferral of recognition of amounts paid under nonqualified deferred compensation plans, provides for interest and an increase in the tax when the requirements are not met, and makes additional related clarifications regarding wage reporting and withholding. It also requires the IRS to issue certain necessary guidance within 60 and 90 days after the enactment of the 2004 Jobs Act.

If certain operational or design failures occur in a nonqualified deferred compensation plan, the deferred amounts, including compensation deferred under the plan in prior years and notional or actual income attributable to the deferred compensation, will be included in the affected plan participants' gross income immediately unless it is still subject to a substantial risk of forfeiture (Code Sec. 409A(a)(1)(A), as added by the 2004 Jobs Act). The tax on the compensation required to be included is increased by interest on the portion of the compensation that was deferred in prior years and by an amount equal to 20 percent of the compensation required to be included. The interest is the amount of interest at the underpayment rate plus one percentage point on the underpayments that would have occurred had the deferred compensation been includible in gross income for the tax year in which it was deferred, or if later, the first tax year in which it was not subject to a substantial risk of forfeiture (Code Sec. 409A(a)(1)(B), as added by the 2004 Jobs Act).

The plan failures that a nonqualified plan must avoid include those having to do with distributions, the acceleration of benefits, and the timing and nature of the election to defer compensation and other elections allowed under the plan.

Distribution rules.—Compensation deferred under the plan must not be distributed earlier than:

(1) the date of the participant's separation from service (or in the case of a specified employee, six months after the date of the employee's separation from service), becoming disabled, or dying,

(2) a time specified in the plan at the time of the deferral election,

(3) the time of a change in the ownership or effective control of the employer or in the ownership of a substantial portion of the assets of the employer (to the extent provided by the IRS), or

(4) the occurrence of an unforeseeable emergency (Code Sec. 409A(a)(2)(A), as added by the 2004 Jobs Act).

Specified employees. Distributions to a specified employee relating to the employee's separation from service cannot be made until six months after the specified employee's separation from service (or if earlier, the specified employee's death). A specified employee is an employee of any corporation with publicly traded stock who is an officer of the corporation having annual compensation in excess of $130,000, is a five-percent owner of the corporation, or is a one percent owner of the corporation and has annual compensation in excess of $150,000. The tests for specified employee status are borrowed from the definition of "key employee" in Code Sec. 416(i) (Code Sec. 409A(a)(2)(B)(i), as added by the 2004 Jobs Act).

Unforeseeable emergencies. Distributions upon the occurrence of an unforeseeable emergency are allowed. An unforeseeable emergency is a severe financial hardship to the participant resulting from an illness or accident of the participant, the participant's spouse or a dependent of the participant; a loss of the participant's property due to casualty; or other similar extraordinary and unforeseeable circumstances beyond the control of the participant. The amount of a distribution made because of an unforeseeable emergency cannot exceed the amount necessary to satisfy the emergency plus the amount necessary to pay taxes reasonably anticipated as a result of the distribution. The amount necessary to satisfy the emergency must be reduced to take into account the extent to which the hardship can be relieved through reimbursement or compensation by insurance or otherwise or by liquidation of the participant's other assets (Code Sec. 409A(a)(2)(B)(ii), as added by the 2004 Jobs Act).

Comment: In regulations regarding allowable distributions of deferrals under eligible governmental plans, it is stated that: "the imminent foreclosure of or eviction from the participant's or beneficiary's primary residence may constitute an unforeseeable emergency. In addition, the need to pay for medical expenses, including nonrefundable deductibles, as well as for the cost of prescription drug medication, may constitute an unforeseeable emergency. Finally, the need to pay for the funeral expenses of a spouse or a dependent . . . may also constitute an unforeseeable emergency. Except as otherwise specifically provided . . . the purchase of a home and the payment of college tuition are not unforeseeable emergencies . . . " (Reg. § 1.457-6(c)(2)).

Disability. Distributions upon the participant's disability are allowed. A participant is disabled if the participant is unable to engage in any substantial gainful activity by reason of any medically determinable physical or mental impairment which can reasonably be expected to result in death or can be expected to last for a continuous period of at least 12 months. A participant is also considered disabled if the participant is, by reason of any medically determinable physical or mental impairment which can be expected to result in death or can be expected to last for at least 12 months, receiving income replacement benefits for a period of at least three months from an accident or health plan covering employees of the employer (Code Sec. 409A(a)(2)(C), as added by the 2004 Jobs Act).

Comment: The IRS has issued regulations on the very similar definition of "disabled" in Code Sec. 72(m) (see Reg. § 1.72-17A(f)).

Acceleration of benefits rule.—A nonqualified deferred compensation plan cannot permit the acceleration of the time or schedule of any payment under the plan, except as permitted by regulations (Code Sec. 409A(a)(3), as added by the 2004 Jobs Act).

Election rules.—A nonqualified deferred compensation plan must meet certain requirements regarding the participants' elections to defer compensation and to receive distributions (Code Sec. 409A(a)(4), as added by the 2004 Jobs Act).

Initial deferral decisions. A plan must provide that compensation for services performed during a tax year can be deferred only if the participant's election to defer is made before the close of the preceding tax year. In the case of the first year in which a participant becomes eligible to participate in the plan, the election may be made within 30 days after the date the participant becomes eligible to participate. That election is effective only for compensation with respect to services performed after the election is made. In the case of any performance-based compensation that is based on services performed over a period of at least 12 months, the election may be made no later than six months before the end of the period (Code Sec. 409A(a)(4)(B), as added by the 2004 Jobs Act).

Subsequent elections. A plan may permit subsequent elections to delay or change the form of payments under the plan. If it does permit such elections, a plan must require that the new election cannot take effect until at least 12 months after it is made. A subsequent election to further defer a distribution to be made after the participant's separation from service, on a predetermined date or schedule, or upon a change of ownership of the employer must defer the payment for at least an additional five years. A subsequent election relating to a payment to be made on a predetermined date or schedule cannot be made less than 12 months prior to the first scheduled payment (Code Sec. 409A(a)(4)(C), as added by the 2004 Jobs Act).

> **Comment:** Requiring lead times before a new election takes effect will presumably reduce the opportunities for taxpayers to shift the receipt of deferred income to years in which the taxpayer expects to have a lower marginal tax rate.

Funding rules.—In certain situations, the setting aside of assets to fund a nonqualified deferred compensation plan will be treated as constituting a Code Sec. 83 transfer, even if the assets are nominally available to satisfy the claims of creditors (Code Sec. 409A(b), as added by the 2004 Jobs Act). Any increase in the value of or earnings on assets set aside under these circumstances is treated as an additional transfer of property (Code Sec. 409A(b)(3), as added by the 2004 Jobs Act). In such cases, the employee will be taxed on the compensation at the time of the deemed transfer. Assets set aside to pay deferred compensation under a nonqualified plan will be treated as property transferred in connection with the performance of services for purposes of Code Sec. 83, whether or not they are available to satisfy the claims of the employer's general creditors, if the assets of the trust or other arrangement in which they are held is located outside of the United States, or if the assets or trust or arrangement are transferred out of the United States. This rule does not apply if substantially all of the services to which the deferred compensation relates were performed in the foreign jurisdiction in which the assets are located (Code Sec. 409A(b)(1), as added by the 2004 Jobs Act).

> **Comment:** Offshore rabbi trusts may be more difficult for an employer's general creditors to reach, even if by their terms they satisfy the requirement that trust assets be available to pay the employer's debts.

Setting aside assets to pay promised deferred compensation is also considered to be a transfer of property if the plan provides that the assets will become restricted to the payment of benefits under the plan if there is a change in the employer's financial health, or if the assets actually become so restricted (Code Sec. 409A(b)(2), as added by the 2004 Jobs Act).

The tax on an amount required to be included in income because it is located in a foreign jurisdiction or because it is subject to restrictions upon a change in the employer's financial health is increased for interest and by an amount equal to 20 percent of the amount required to be included. The interest is the amount of interest at the underpayment rate plus one percentage point on the underpayments that would have occurred had the amount been includible in gross income for the tax year in which it was deferred, or if later, the first tax year in which it was not subject to a substantial risk of forfeiture (Code Sec. 409A(b)(4), as added by the 2004 Jobs Act).

Interaction with other provisions.—These new rules should not delay the earlier inclusion of amounts in income if earlier inclusion is otherwise required under the law, and amounts included in income by reason of the new rules are not to be included in income again under any other provision (Code Sec. 409A(c), as added by the 2004 Jobs Act).

Definitions and special rules.—A "nonqualified deferred compensation plan" means any plan that provides for deferral of compensation except a qualified employer plan or a bona fide vacation leave, sick leave, compensatory time, disability pay, or death benefit plan (Code Sec. 409A(d)(1), as added by the 2004 Jobs Act). A "plan" includes any agreement or arrangement, including an agreement or arrangement that includes just one person (Code Sec. 409A(d)(3), as added by the 2004 Jobs Act).

A "qualified employer plan" generally includes any plan funded by a trust and qualified under Code Sec. 401(a), a qualified annuity plan (Code Sec. 403(a)), a Code Sec. 403(b) annuity contract, a simplified employee pension (Code Sec. 408(k)), a SIMPLE retirement account (Code Sec. 408(p)), an eligible deferred compensation plan of a state or local government or tax-exempt organization (Code Sec. 457(b)), or a qualified governmental excess benefit arrangement (Code Sec. 415(m)) (Code Sec. 409A(d)(2), as added by the 2004 Jobs Act).

The law does not provide a complete definition of "substantial risk of forfeiture." However, it does state that the rights of a person to compensation are subject to a "substantial risk of forfeiture" if those rights are conditioned upon the future performance of substantial services by any person (Code Sec. 409A(d)(4), as added by the 2004 Jobs Act).

Aggregation rules. Employees of corporations that are part of a controlled group and employees of partnerships or other entities under common control are treated as employees of a single employer, except as provided by the IRS (Code Sec. 409A(d)(6), as added by the 2004 Jobs Act). The Conference Committee Report suggests that aggregation rules should apply in cases of separation from service, so that a participant who separates from service with one member of a controlled group but continues service with another member of the group would not be eligible to receive a distribution. However, aggregation would not be appropriate in the case of a change in control of one member of a group. Such a change should not be a permissible distribution event for participants in plans of other members of the group (H.R. Conf. Rep. No. 108-755).

Regulations and mandated IRS guidance.—The 2004 Jobs Act requires the IRS to issue guidance, not later than 60 days after its enactment, setting out a limited remedial amendment period to allow existing plans to be modified to meet the new requirements with regard to amounts deferred after December 31, 2004, or to allow participants to withdraw from participation in the plan or cancel an existing deferral election with regard to amounts deferred after December 31, 2004. Amounts subject to the termination or cancellation must be included in the participant's income as they are earned, or if later, when they are no longer subject to a substantial risk of forfeiture (Act Sec. 885(f) of the 2004 Jobs Act).

Not later than 90 days after the 2004 Jobs Act's enactment, the IRS is required to issue guidance on what constitutes a change in ownership or effective control for purposes of Code Sec. 409A (Act Sec. 885(e) of the 2004 Jobs Act).

Comment: The IRS has issued regulations under Code Sec. 280G, regarding golden parachute payments, describing when a change in the ownership of a corporation occurs, when a change in the effective control of a corporation occurs, and when a change in the ownership of a substantial portion of the

¶1405

corporation's assets occurs (Reg. § 1.280G-1). Presumably, guidance issued under Code Sec. 409A would be quite similar.

The IRS is authorized to prescribe the regulations necessary and appropriate to carry out the purposes of Code Sec. 409A, including regulations:

(1) providing for the determination of amounts deferred in the case of a defined benefit plan,

(2) relating to changes in the ownership and control of the employer or the assets of the employer,

(3) exempting from the funding rules arrangements that do not improperly defer taxation and do not place assets effectively beyond the reach of creditors,

(4) defining financial health for purposes of the funding rules, and

(5) disregarding a substantial risk of forfeiture where necessary (Code Sec. 409A(e), as added by the 2004 Jobs Act).

Reporting and withholding implications.—*W-2 Forms.* The total amount of deferrals under a nonqualified deferred compensation plan for the year must be shown on the Form W-2 provided to employees and the IRS. The IRS is authorized to issue regulations establishing a minimum threshold for reporting of deferrals (Code Sec. 6051(a)(13), as added by the 2004 Jobs Act).

Withholding. For withholding purposes, any amount includible in the gross income of an employee under Code Sec. 409A is included in the employee's wages for the year of inclusion (Code Sec. 3401(a), as amended by the 2004 Jobs Act).

Reporting of deferred compensation for nonemployees. Amounts deferred by nonemployees are reported on a Form 1099, rather than Form W-2. Any amount includible in gross income under Code Sec. 409A that is not treated as wages also must be reported on a Form 1099 (Code Sec. 6041(g), as added by the 2004 Jobs Act).

> **Comment:** A special provision in the 2004 Jobs Act carves out an exclusion from the new rules for any nonqualified deferred compensation plan which was in existence and was providing nonelective deferred compensation (as described in Code Sec. 457(e)(12)) on May 1, 2004, and which was established or maintained by an organization incorporated on July 2, 1974 (Act Sec. 885(d)(3) of the 2004 Jobs Act). The Wall Street Journal has reported that this exclusion was included for the benefit of the plan maintained by the PGA to provide deferred compensation benefits to professional golfers.

PRACTICAL ANALYSIS. Michael Maryn of Sonnenschein Nath & Rosenthal, Washington, D.C., notes that Congress enacted sweeping changes to the tax treatment of nonqualified deferred compensation in Section 885 of the 2004 Jobs Act. This provision imposes new restrictions and limitations on the timing of an individual's election to defer the receipt of compensation and when nonqualified deferred compensation may be distributed. The new law also imposes substantial taxes and penalties on individuals whose deferred compensation fails to comply with the new restrictions. The new law is effective for amounts deferred on or after January 1, 2005. Amounts deferred prior to January 1, 2005, are exempt from the new law if (1) such amounts are fully vested prior to January 1, 2005, and (2) there is no material modification to the deferral arrangement after October 3, 2004.

While many questions concerning the new law remain unanswered, employers and other service recipients should immediately undertake a thorough review of all compensation arrangements that may result in

the deferred payment of compensation to employees and other persons. Note that certain types of retirement plans are exempt from the legislation including qualified retirement plans, 403(b) annuities, SEPs, SIMPLEs, 457(b) plans and *bona fide* vacation leave, sick leave, compensatory time, disability pay, and death benefit plans. Among the arrangements that may be subject to the new law are equity incentive plans that provide for grants of deferred stock units, restricted stock units, stock appreciation rights and/or discounted stock options. In addition, employers should review their executive employment and consulting agreements to determine whether such agreements provide for the deferral of compensation.

After identifying its nonqualified deferred compensation arrangements, employers should prepare to take immediate action to modify such plans to conform with the new law or to discontinue future deferrals under such arrangements. In making decisions involving the future of their nonqualified deferred compensation arrangements, employers will need to pay close attention to recordkeeping requirements to ensure that pre-2005 and post-2004 deferrals can be accounted for separately. In addition, employers with 401(k) excess arrangements will need to examine those plans very carefully to ensure that such arrangements conform with the timing restrictions on the deferral of bonuses. In general, 401(k) excess plans will need to be amended either to exclude bonuses from the amounts subject to the deferral election or require irrevocable deferral elections to be made as much as six months or a year prior to the first day of the year for which the election is made.

Finally, while employers should start the planning process, they should refrain from acting too precipitously in amending existing arrangements. Congress has directed the Department of Treasury to issue guidance within 60 days after enactment of the 2004 Jobs Act to allow employers to amend existing nonqualified deferred compensation arrangements to conform with the new requirements or to discontinue deferrals under such arrangements. There remains considerable uncertainty as to the application of new law to existing deferral arrangements, and rash action taken before the Treasury issues such guidance could result in adverse tax consequences with respect to amounts previously deferred.

For further information on this subject, consult any of the following CCH reporter explanations:

- Standard Federal Tax Reporter, 2004FED ¶18,209.01, ¶33,506.053, ¶35,836.075 and ¶36,425.01

- Federal Tax Service, FTS §B:5.47

- Federal Tax Guide, 2004FTG ¶11,720

★ *Effective date.* The new rules governing nonqualified deferred compensation plans and the associated reporting and withholding rules apply to amounts deferred after December 31, 2004, and the earnings on those amounts. The rules generally do not apply to amounts deferred before January 1, 2005, or the earnings on those amounts. However, if a plan is materially modified after October 3, 2004, in a way that is not pursuant to the mandated guidance to be issued within 60 days after the enactment of the American Jobs Creation Act of 2004, amounts previously deferred under the plan will be subject to the new rules (Act Sec. 885(d) of the 2004 Jobs Act).

¶1405

Act Sec. 885(a) of the American Jobs Creation Act of 2004, adding Code Sec. 409A; Act Sec. 885(b)(1), amending Code Sec. 6051(a); Act Sec. 885(b)(2), amending Code Sec. 3401(a); Act Sec. 885(b)(3), adding Code Sec. 6041(g); Act Sec. 885(d). Law at ¶5350, ¶5975, ¶6140, ¶6155, and ¶7145. Committee Report at ¶11,570.

¶1410

Employment Taxes and Income Tax Withholding Not Applicable to Qualified Stock Options

Background

The IRS has waffled on whether to impose withholding requirements on employers in the context of qualified stock options.

Qualified stock options (sometimes called statutory stock options) offer tax advantages over nonqualifed options. Nonqualified stock options provided to an employee are generally treated as compensation to the employee when the employee exercises the option (unless the value of the option is ascertainable on the date of transfer, in which case that value is treated as income as of the transfer date). In contrast, an employee who receives a qualified option has no taxable income either upon receipt or exercise of the option, and the employee recognizes capital gain income when the stock is sold.

Qualified stock options include incentive stock options (ISOs) and options received under an employer stock purchase plan (ESPP options). Both kinds of qualified options are subject to a variety of definitional requirements (Code Secs. 422(b) and 423(b)), as well as requirements regarding holding periods and employment requirements (Code Secs. 422(a) and 423(a)). If the definitional requirements are satisfied, but the holding periods and employment requirements are not satisfied, sale of the stock will be treated as a disqualifying disposition. As a result, the employee recognizes a gain in the tax year of disposition that will be treated as compensation (Code Sec. 421(b)).

Taxation of ESPP options provides an additional twist in the form of the 85/100-percent rule. Unlike ISOs, which must have an exercise price at least equal to the fair market value of the stock when the option is granted, options granted under an ESPP can have an exercise price as low as 85 percent of the fair market value of the stock. The difference between the option price and 100 percent of the actual value of the stock at the time the option was granted (or the amount received in a disposition, if lower) is treated as compensation upon disposition of the stock. The balance of any gain is treated as capital gain (Code Sec. 423(c)).

Wage compensation is generally subject to employment taxes as well as income tax, and it is the employer's job to withhold such amounts. In 2001, the IRS issued proposed regulations providing that Federal Insurance Contributions Act (FICA) tax and Federal Unemployment Tax Act (FUTA) tax are triggered when an individual exercises an ISO or ESPP option (Notice of Proposed Rulemaking REG-142686-01 (Nov. 13, 2001)). The proposed regulations were to become effective for exercises occurring on or after January 1, 2003. In Notice 2002-47, however, the IRS stated that it would neither impose withholding obligations nor assess FICA or FUTA taxes upon the exercise of a statutory stock option or the disposition of stock so acquired until after final guidance is issued. No final guidance has been forthcoming.

American Jobs Creation Act Impact

Employment taxes do not apply to qualified stock options.—The American Jobs Creation Act of 2004 changes the definition of wages for FICA tax purposes to exclude from wages remuneration on account of a transfer of a share of stock pursuant to an exercise of an ISO or ESPP option, or on account of a disposition of stock acquired through such an exercise (Code Sec. 3121(a), as amended by Act Sec. 251(a) of the 2004 Jobs Act). Similar changes are made with respect to Railroad Retirement Act and FUTA taxes (Code Sec. 3231(e), as amended by Act Sec. 251(a)(2) of the 2004 Jobs Act; Code Sec. 3306(b), as amended by Act Sec. 251(a)(3) of the 2004 Jobs Act).

No income tax withholding. Gains resulting from a disqualifying disposition of stock acquired through exercise of a qualified stock option or reportable under the 85/100-percent ESPP option rule are subject to income tax at ordinary rates. However, the 2004 Jobs Act makes it clear that the employer is not required to withhold income tax in the event of a disqualifying disposition of stock (Code Sec. 421(b), as amended by Act Sec. 251(b) of the 2004 Jobs Act). Furthermore, withholding is not required with respect to amounts taxable under the 85/100-percent rule (Code Sec. 423(c), as amended by Act Sec. 251(c) of the 2004 Jobs Act).

Compliance Tip: The IRS has taken the position that compensation may have to be reported on Form W-2 whether or not income tax is withheld, and has specifically stated that income realized from a disqualifying disposition of statutory stock (whether through an ESPP or ISO) must be reported as compensation on Form W-2 (Reg. § 1.6041-2(a)(1); Notice 2002-47).

PRACTICAL ANALYSIS. Mark Luscombe, Principal Analyst, CCH Tax and Accounting, observes that this provision basically preserves current law with respect to the taxation of incentive stock options and employee stock purchase plan stock options, as reflected in the projection that it has a negligible effect of revenue. Many companies that utilize stock options, particularly technology companies, have not been shy about approaching Congress when suggestions for taxation of or accounting for stock options are not to their liking. The introduction of the proposed regulations was one of those occasions. Even though Treasury clearly presented those regulations as proposals that were open to comment and followed up with a statement that they were not to be effective in any case until such time as regulations were made final, opponents did not want to chance an outcome that followed the proposed rules. This action was deemed necessary out of concern that the IRS had not tabled the proposals after the initial wave of criticism and had plans to work toward final regulations.

On another front, the Financial Accounting Standards Board (FASB) is again reviving efforts to require expensing of stock options on financial statements. Although there is a split in the business community on the merits of this idea, those that oppose expensing treatment have again gone to Congress in an effort to head off the efforts of the FASB. Although in the past the FASB had buckled to industry pressure to back away from expensing of stock options, in a post-Enron environment the FASB is less likely to be willing to succumb to industry pressure, and the industry probably does not want to be seen as pressuring its standard setting body. In spite of the creation of the Public Company Accounting Oversight Board by the Sarbanes-Oxley Act of 2002 as an independent voice in accounting standard setting, many in Congress appear to be all too willing to continue to meddle in setting accounting standards, just as they have shown a willingness to derail Treasury regulatory projects that an interest group opposes.

For further information on this subject, consult any of the following CCH reporter explanations:

- Standard Federal Tax Reporter, 2004FED ¶19,611.03, ¶19,611.034, ¶19,611.035 and ¶19,903.042
- Federal Tax Service, FTS §B:17.83
- Federal Tax Guide, 2004FTG ¶18,019

★ *Effective date.* These amendments apply to stock acquired pursuant to options exercised after date of enactment (Act Sec. 251(d) of the American Jobs Creation Act of 2004).

Act Sec. 251(a)(1) of the American Jobs Creation Act of 2004, amending Code Sec. 3121(a); Act Sec. 251(a)(2), amending Code Sec. 3231(e); Act Sec. 251(a)(3), amending Code Sec. 3306(b); Act Sec. 251(b), amending Code Sec. 421(b); Act Sec. 251(c), amending Code Sec. 423(c); Act Sec. 251(d). Law at ¶5360, ¶5365, ¶5960, ¶5965, and ¶5970. Committee Report at ¶10,310.

¶1415

Conflict of Interest Divestiture Reconciled with Holding Period for Stock Acquired Through Qualified Stock Option

Background

Officers and employees of the executive branch of the federal government are sometimes required to divest themselves of certain property that might cause a conflict of interest. In such cases, the President or the Director of the Office of Government Ethics will issue a Certificate of Divestiture that identifies the property to be disposed. Because favorable tax treatment of qualified stock options depends on the employee satisfying certain holding period requirements, a divestiture can cause the employee to lose the benefits normally associated with qualified stock options.

A qualified stock option granted to an employee is not taxed on receipt or exercise of the option. Tax applies when the employee sells the stock and the gain is treated as capital gain (Code Sec. 421(a)).

Qualified stock options include incentive stock options (ISOs) and options received under an employer stock purchase plan (ESPP options). Both kinds of qualified options are subject to holding period requirements. In order to receive favorable treatment, the stock cannot be disposed of within two years from the grant of the option or one year of the transfer of the stock to the employee. (Code Secs. 422(a)(1) and 423(a)(1)). If these requirements are not satisfied, sale of the stock will be treated as a disqualifying disposition which results in the employee recognizing income in the tax year of the disposition (Code Sec. 421(b)).

Individuals who divest themselves of property to avoid a conflict of interest can elect to recognize gain from the sale of the property only to the extent the amount realized from the sale exceeds the cost of replacement U.S. obligations or diversified investment fund shares purchased within 60 days from the date of the sale. This election is available only to an "eligible person," that is, an officer or employee of the executive branch, or to the employee's spouse or minor or dependent child (Code Sec. 1043(b)(1)). The election also requires a certificate of divestiture (Code Sec. 1043(b)(2)).

American Jobs Creation Act Impact

Divestiture for conflict of interest does not cause loss of qualified stock option benefits.—If a share of stock is transferred to an eligible person (as defined in Code

Sec. 1043(b)(1)) pursuant to exercise of a qualified stock option, and that person disposes of the share pursuant to a certificate of divestiture (as defined in Code Sec. 1043(b)(2)), such disposition will be treated as meeting the holding period requirements for ISOs (Code Sec. 422(a)) and ESPP options (Code Sec. 423(a)) (Code Sec. 421(d), as added by Act Sec. 905(a) of the American Jobs Creation Act of 2004).

According to the Conference Committee Report, the employer granting the option is not allowed a deduction upon the sale of the stock by the individual.

> **Comment:** Although the new rule borrows definitions from Code Sec. 1043, it does not require the employee to elect Code Sec. 1043 treatment.

For further information on this subject, consult any of the following CCH reporter explanations:

- Standard Federal Tax Reporter, 2004FED ¶ 19,611.035 and ¶ 19,806.021
- Federal Tax Service, FTS § B:7.42 and § B:8.43
- Federal Tax Guide, 2004FTG ¶ 5664 and ¶ 11,830

★ *Effective date.* The provision applies to sales after the date of enactment (Act Sec. 905(b) of the American Jobs Creation Act of 2004).

Act Sec. 905(a) of the American Jobs Creation Act of 2004, adding Code Sec. 421(d); Act Sec. 905(b). Law at ¶ 5360. Committee Report at ¶ 11,770.

¶ 1420
Transfer of Excess Pension Assets

Background _____

An employer is permitted to transfer the excess assets of a defined benefit (DB) pension plan to a retiree health benefits account without incurring a penalty or tax (Code Sec. 420(a)). In order for the transfer to be permitted, the employer must meet certain vesting, use, and cost requirements.

Vesting requirement. All accrued benefits in the DB pension plan must be fully vested, pursuant to the plan terms, as though the plan had been terminated immediately before the transfer (Code Sec. 420(c)(2)(A)). Generally, a participant's accrued benefits under a DB pension plan are pension or retirement benefits only (Code Sec. 411(a)(7)). They do not include ancillary benefits such as healthcare benefits, disability benefits, etc.

Use requirement. The transferred assets may only be used to pay for current retiree health benefits coverage (Code Sec. 420(c)(1)(A)). As a result, the employer must reasonably estimate the amount of money needed to pay for these liabilities in the year of the transfer (Code Sec. 420(b)(3)). Only an amount equal to this estimate may be transferred (Code Sec. 420(c)(1)(A)). The projection cannot include expenses for key employees.

> **Comment:** Any transferred assets that are not used to pay for current retiree health benefits must be transferred back to the DB pension plan. In addition, the amount is subject to a 20 percent excise tax as an employer reversion from a qualified plan (Code Sec. 420(c)(1)(B) and Code Sec. 4980(a)).

Cost requirement. The employer must provide a minimum dollar level of health benefits coverage to its retirees (and spouses and dependents of retirees) for five years. This five-year period is known as the "cost maintenance period" and begins with the year of the transfer (Code Sec. 420(c)(3)(D)). In order to determine the minimum amount of coverage that needs to be given, the employer must compare its applicable expenses in the two years immediately before the transfer. The coverage level must be at least as much as the higher of these two years (Code Sec.

420(c)(3)(A)). The two-year comparison period is known as the "minimum cost requirements" period.

If an employer significantly reduces retiree health benefits during the cost mantenance period (the five-year period), the transfer is prohibited and subject to excise tax (Code Sec. 420(c)(3)(E)). A significant reduction is one that exceeds a 10 percent decrease in any year of the cost maintenance period, or a total reduction of 20 percent during the entire cost maintenance period (Reg. § 1.420-1(b)).

American Jobs Creation Act Impact

Insignificant cost reductions permitted.—The new law provides that an eligible employer will not fail the minimum cost requirement if, in lieu of any reduction of retiree health coverage during the cost maintenance period, the employer reduces its applicable employer cost by an amount that does not exceed the maximum permissible reduction of retiree health benefit costs (Code Sec. 420(c)(3)(E)(ii)(I), as added by the American Jobs Creation Act of 2004).

> **Comment:** Generally, the "applicable employer cost" is calculated by (1) dividing the employer's "qualified current retiree health liabilities" for the tax year by (2) the number of retirees, spouses of retirees, and dependents of retirees who received coverage during the tax year (Code Sec. 420(c)(3)(B)).

The new law specifies that an employer is an eligible employer for any tax year if, in the preceding year, the qualified current retiree health liabilities were at least five percent of the employer's gross receipts (Code Sec. 420(c)(3)(E)(ii)(II), as added by the 2004 Jobs Act).

For further information on this subject, consult any of the following CCH reporter explanations:

- Standard Federal Tax Reporter, 2004FED ¶ 19,303.029
- Federal Tax Service, FTS § C:16.84[2]
- Federal Tax Guide, 2004FTG ¶ 11,050

★ *Effective date.* The provisions relating to insignificant cost reductions apply to tax years ending after the date of enactment of the American Jobs Creation Act of 2004 (Act. Sec. 709(b)(3) of the 2004 Jobs Act).

Act Sec. 709(a)(1) of the American Jobs Creation Act of 2004, amending Sec. 101(e)(3) of the Employee Retirement Income Security Act of 1974 (ERISA); Act Sec. 709(a)(2), amending Sec. 403(c)(1) of ERISA; Act Sec. 709(a)(3), amending Sec. 408(b) of ERISA; Act Sec. 709(b)(1), adding Code Sec. 420(c)(3)(E)(ii); Act Sec. 709(b)(2) amending Code Sec. 420(c)(3)(E); Act Sec. 709(b)(3). Law at ¶ 5355 and ¶ 7070. Committee Report at ¶ 10,910.

¶ 1425

Application of Annuity Basis Rules to Nonresident Aliens

Distributions from pension plans are taxed under the same rules that apply to annuity contracts (Code Secs. 72 and 402). As such, whether or not a pension distribution is included in a participant's gross income depends on the "participant's investment in the annuity contract." The investment, which generally consists of the premiums paid for an annuity, is referred to as "basis" (Code Sec. 72(f)).

A participant's basis in pension plan distributions is excluded from his or her gross income. The basis includes after-tax contributions made by the participant and

Background _____

the employer (as well as earnings on the contributions), less any previous distributions that were excluded from the participant's gross income. By the same token, an employer's basis in a pension plan is the employer's contributions to the plan, including any purchase of retirement annuities.

If an employer purchases a pension annuity for a participant, and pays the annuity premiums, the payments become basis for the employer. When the participant begins to receive retirement distributions from the annuity, each distribution will be taxed as income, since the participant made no investment in the annuity contract (Code Secs. 402(a) and 72(f)). Additionally, employer contributions that could have been excluded from the participant's gross income because they were paid directly to the participant are also part of basis.

An employer's contributions to a pension plan relating to services performed outside of the United States by a nonresident alien are not considered U.S.-based income and are taxed in the individual's country of residence. However, this rule is limited to amounts that were not previously included as income in the country of residence. Any employer contributions relating to services performed by a nonresident alien within the United States are subject to U.S. tax (Code Sec. 871).

Under certain circumstances, property transferred in connection with the performance of services by a nonresident alien may be considered income. If, in connection with a performance of services, property is transferred to anyone other than the person receiving the services, a portion of the property's value is included in the gross income of the nonresident alien in the year that the property was transferred (Code Sec. 83(a)). The amount included is calculated as follows: (1) fair market value of the property, over (2) any price paid for the property. Any amount included as income is also considered basis.

American Jobs Creation Act Impact

Application of basis rules to nonresident aliens.—The new law provides that contributions are not part of basis if: (1) if contribution is made regarding compensation for labor or services by an employee who was a nonresident alien at the time the labor or services were performed (Code Sec. 72(w)(2)(A)(i), as added by the American Jobs Creation Act of 2004); (2) the compensation was for work treated as from sources outside of the United States (Code Sec. 72(w)(2)(A)(ii), as added by the 2004 Jobs Act); and (3) the contribution is not subject to tax by the United States or a foreign country (and would have been subject to tax if paid in cash) (Code Sec. 72(w)(2)(B), as added by the 2004 Jobs Act). Thus, distributions from a foreign pension plan are included in the calculation of the participant's basis only if the nonresident alien has been subject to tax on the distribution by the United States or a foreign country.

> **Comment:** According to the Conference Committee Report (H.R. Conf. Rep. No. 108-755), the provision does not change the rules relating to the calculation of basis for contributions made while the alien was a resident of the United States.

> *Basis in transferred property.* The new law provides that, for determining basis in property that is transferred in connection with the performance of services, basis does not include amounts that are not subject to tax (and would have been taxed if paid as cash compensation when the services were performed) under U.S. laws or any foreign jurisdiction (Code Sec. 72(w)(3), as added by the 2004 Jobs Act).

IRS regulations. The IRS is given the authority to issue the regulations necessary to carry out the provisions of the new law (Code Sec. 72(w)(4), as added by the 2004 Jobs Act).

For further information on this subject, consult any of the following CCH reporter explanations:

- Standard Federal Tax Reporter, 2004FED ¶6114.0305, ¶6114.0455 and ¶6390.01
- Federal Tax Service, FTS §C:14.140
- Federal Tax Guide, 2004FTG ¶11,060

★ *Effective date.* These provisions are effective for distributions made on or after the date of enactment of the American Jobs Creation Act of 2004 (Act. Sec. 906(c) of the 2004 Jobs Act).

Act Sec. 906(a) of the American Jobs Creation Act of 2004, redesignating Code Sec. 72(w) as Code Sec. 72(x) and adding Code Sec. 72(w); Act Sec. 906(b), adding Code Sec. 83(c)(4); Act Sec. 906(c). Law at ¶5100 and ¶5105. Committee Report at ¶11,780.

¶ 1430

Withholding Increased for Large Supplemental Wage Payments

Background

Income tax must generally be withheld by employers on wages paid to employees. Special computation methods may be required to determine the proper amount of income tax withholding when an extra payment, or supplemental wage payment, is made to an employee in the same calendar year in which regular wages are received (Code Sec. 3402(g)). A supplemental wage payment may be in the form of a Christmas bonus, a commission, dismissal pay, a backpay award, overtime pay or vacation pay. The supplemental payment must be made in the same calendar year as the regular wage payments in order for the special computation methods to apply.

If supplemental wages are paid at the same time as regular wages, the two are added together and the withholding tax is computed on the total as a single wage payment. If the supplemental wages are not paid at the same time as the regular wages, the supplemental wages may be added either to the regular wages for the preceding payroll period or for the current payroll period within the same calendar year.

Under an alternative method, the employer may treat the supplemental wages as wholly separate from regular wages and withhold at a flat rate on the supplemental wage payment without any allowance for exemptions and without reference to any regular payment of wages (Reg. §31.3402(g)-1). The flat rate cannot be less than the third lowest rate of tax applicable to single filers (25 percent for tax years beginning in 2005) (Act Sec. 101(c)(11) of the Economic Growth and Tax Releif Reconciliation Act of 2001 (EGTRRA) (P.L. 107-16)).

American Jobs Creation Act Impact

Withholding increased for supplemental wage payments in excess of $1,000,000.—If an employer elects to treat supplemental wages as separate from regular wages and withhold at a flat rate (under Reg. §31.3402(g)-1), the flat rate shall not be less than 28% (or the rate under Code Sec. 1(i)(2) for the year in which the payment is made) (Act Sec. 904(a) of the American Jobs Creation Act of 2004).The new law also provides that, once the total of supplemental wage payments made to an employee, within a calendar year, exceeds $1,000,000, the excess will be subject to withholding at the highest income tax rate (35 percent for tax years beginning in 2005) (Act Sec. 904(b)(1) of the 2004 Jobs Act). This rule applies regardless of the method otherwise used to withhold supplemental wages paid to the employee.

> **Comment:** The Conference Committee Report ((H.R. Conf. Rep. No. 108-755) notes that the new provision does not apply for any purpose other than wage withholding. Thus, for example, it does not apply to pension or backup withholding.

Any controlled group of corporations or commonly controlled trades or businesses (for example, partnerships and proprietorships) that are treated as a single employer under Code Sec. 52(a) or (b) are treated as a single employer for purposes of the new supplemental withholding rule (Act Sec. 904(b)(2) of the 2004 Jobs Act).

For further information on this subject, consult any of the following CCH reporter explanations:

- Standard Federal Tax Reporter, 2004FED ¶4860.021
- Federal Tax Service, FTS § B:18.48[3]
- Federal Tax Guide, 2004FTG ¶18,061

★ *Effective date.* The new provision is effective with respect to payments made after December 31, 2004 (Act Sec. 904(d) of the American Jobs Creation Act of 2004.).

Act Sec. 904 of the American Jobs Creation Act of 2004; Act Sec. 904(c), repealing Act Sec. 13273 of the Revenue Reconciliation Act of 1993 (P.L. 103-66); Act Sec. 904(d). Law at ¶7155. Committee Report at ¶11,760.

Chapter 15

Excise Taxes

FUELS

¶ 1505

Two-Party Exchanges

Background _____

Generally, gasoline, diesel fuel, and kerosene are taxed upon removal of the fuel from a terminal rack (Code Sec. 4081(a)(1)(A)(ii)). A terminal is a storage and distribution facility that is supplied by a pipeline or vessel. A rack is a mechanism used to deliver taxable fuel into a means of transport other than a vessel or pipeline (e.g., a tanker truck or rail car) (Reg. § 48.4081-1(b)).

A position holder is the party responsible for payment of the tax on the gasoline, diesel fuel, and kerosene when removed from the terminal rack. The position holder is a person who holds the inventory position in fuel, as reflected by the records of the terminal operator. A person holds the inventory position if the person has a contractual agreement with the terminal operator for the use of the storage facilities and for services at a terminal with respect to the fuel. The position holder may include a terminal operator if that person owns fuel in its terminal.

As a practical matter, fuel companies often enter into exchange agreements in which one fuel company will service the needs of a second fuel company's clients in an effort to minimize transportation and distribution costs. For example, when the wholesale or retail customers of Company B obtain fuel from Company A's more conveniently located terminal, Company B (the exchange agreement party) is treated as owning the fuel when it is removed from A's terminal and sold to B's customer. However, Company A is liable for the federal excise tax on the fuel removed from its terminal because it is the position holder.

American Jobs Creation Act Impact

Two-party exchanges.—Under the new law, two-party exchanges are now recognized. Thus, the position holder at the terminal that delivers the fuel is not liable for the tax on the removal of the fuel from the terminal rack (Code Sec. 4105(a), as added by the American Jobs Creation Act of 2004). A two-party exchange is defined as a transaction, other than a sale, in which a registered delivering person transfers taxable fuel to a registered receiving person and all of the following occur:

(1) the transaction includes a transfer from the delivering person, who holds the inventory position for taxable fuel in the terminal as recorded in the terminal operator's books;

(2) the exchange transaction occurs before or at the same time as completion of removal across the rack from the terminal by the receiving person;

(3) in its books and records, the terminal operator treats the receiving person as the person who removes the fuel across the terminal rack for purposes of reporting the transaction to the IRS; and

(4) the transaction is the subject of a written contract (Code Sec. 4105(b), as added by the 2004 Jobs Act).

Comment: A two-party exchange allows two registered parties to switch position holder status in fuel within a registered terminal, thus relieving the delivering person of tax liability.

Comment: Many states already recognize two-party exchanges. This provision will come as a relief for many in the fuel industry as it provides parity on this issue with many state fuel tax rules.

For further information on this subject, consult any of the following CCH reporter explanations:

- Federal Excise Tax Reporter, ETR ¶ 8925.02

- Federal Tax Guide, 2004FTG ¶ 21,005

¶1505

★ *Effective date.* The provision allowing two-party exchanges takes effect on the date of enactment (Act Sec. 866(c) of the American Jobs Creation Act of 2004).

Act Sec. 866(a) of the American Jobs Creation Act of 2004, adding Code Sec. 4105; Act Sec. 866(b); Act Sec. 866(c). Law at ¶ 6055. Committee Report at ¶ 11,470.

¶ 1507

Aviation Fuel Taxed at Terminal Rack

Background

Most fuels are taxed upon their removal from the terminal rack. Aviation fuel, however, is taxed upon sale by a producer or importer (Code Sec. 4091(a)(1)) at a rate of 21.8 cents per gallon (Code Sec. 4091(b)(1)). In addition, a 0.1-cent-per-gallon Leaking Underground Storage Tank (LUST) tax is imposed on aviation fuel (Code Sec. 4091(b)(2)), providing for a total tax rate of 21.9 cents per gallon. Aviation fuel is defined as kerosene and any other liquid that is suitable for use as fuel in an aircraft provided that the fuel was not taxed under Code Sec. 4081 (Code Sec. 4093(a)).

Because a "ticket tax" is imposed on commercial airline flights under Code Sec. 4261, aviation fuel sold for use or used in commercial aviation is taxed at a reduced rate of 4.4 cents per gallon (Code Sec. 4092(b)). In order to qualify for the reduced rate, persons engaged in commercial aviation must be registered with the IRS and must provide the seller of aviation fuel with a written exemption certificate.

Certain uses of aviation fuel are exempt from tax. These uses include:

(1) use other than fuel in an aircraft;

(2) use on a farm for farming purposes;

(3) use in a military aircraft owned by the United States or foreign country;

(4) use in a domestic air carrier or foreign air carrier engaged in foreign trade or trade between the United States and it possessions;

(5) exclusive use by a state or local government;

(6) sales for export or shipment to a U.S. possession;

(7) exclusive use by a nonprofit educational organization;

(8) use by an aircraft museum operated exclusively for the procurement, care and exhibition of World War II type aircraft; and

(9) use as fuel in a helicopter or a fixed-wing aircraft under certain circumstances.

In order to qualify for these exemptions, the buyer of the fuel must provide the seller with a written exemption certificate. In addition, a producer that is registered with the IRS may sell aviation fuel tax-free to another registered producer (Code Sec. 4092(c)).

A registered aviation fuel producer may claim a credit or refund of tax (without interest) if: (1) the fuel tax was paid by an importer or producer and the tax has not otherwise been credited or refunded; (2) the fuel was acquired by a registered aviation fuel producer after the tax was paid; (3) the second producer files a timely refund claim with the proper information; and (4) the first producer and any other person who owns the fuel after its sale by the first producer and before its purchase by the second producer have met the requisite reporting requirements (Reg. § 48.4091-3(b)).

American Jobs Creation Act Impact

Jet fuel taxed at the terminal rack.—Aviation fuel is now taxed upon its removal from a refinery or terminal, or upon entry into the United States, similar to gasoline, diesel fuel and kerosene (Code Sec. 4081(a)(2)(A)(iv), as added by the American Jobs Creation Act of 2004). The 2004 Jobs Act did not change the rate of tax on aviation fuel (21.9 cents per gallon for use in noncommercial aviation and 4.4 cents per gallon for use in commercial aviation). Sales of aviation fuel to an unregistered person are also subject to tax.

> **Comment:** By moving the incidence of taxation to the terminal rack, Congress is trying to alleviate the actions of deceitful persons who were removing fuel tax-free, purportedly for aviation use, but then reselling the fuel for highway use and keeping the amount of the tax.

Certain refueling vehicles treated as terminal. Certain refueler trucks, tankers and wagons are treated as a terminal under the new law if the vehicle:

(1) is located within a secure area of an airport;

(2) contains aviation fuel that is for delivery only into aircraft at the airport in which the vehicle is located;

(3) has a storage tank, hose and coupling equipment designed and used for fueling aircraft;

(4) is not registered for highway use; and

(5) is operated by the terminal operator of the terminal or by a person that makes a daily accounting to the terminal operator of each fuel delivery from the vehicle (Code Sec. 4081(a)(3), as added by the 2004 Jobs Act).

In addition to the daily accounting noted at (5), above, the IRS also requires that the person report any similar information maintained by the terminal operator (Code Sec. 4081(a)(3)(C), as amended by the 2004 Jobs Act).

No later than December 15, 2004, the IRS is required to publish and maintain a list of airports that include a secure area in which a terminal is located (Act. Sec. 853(a)(3)(B) of the 2004 Jobs Act). The Conference Committee Report (H.R. Conf. Rep. No. 108-755) includes a list of airports that the conferees believe should be included on the IRS's initial list (see ¶ 11,340). The Conference Committee Report also notes that the IRS has the discretion to add or remove airports from the list.

Liability for tax. The 4.4-cents aviation fuel tax on commercial aviation is imposed upon the person using the fuel. Fuel is treated as "used" when it is removed into the fuel tank of an aircraft (Code Sec. 4081(a)(4), as amended by the 2004 Jobs Act). Commercial aviation is defined as any use of an aircraft in the business of transporting persons or property for compensation or hire by air. It does not include aircraft used for skydiving, small aircraft on nonestablished lines, or transportation for affiliated group members (Code Sec. 4083(b), as added by the 2004 Jobs Act).

> **Compliance Tip:** According to the Conference Committee Report, the IRS is expected to delay the due date of Form 720, Quarterly Federal Excise Tax Return, with respect to aviation fuel for the quarter beginning January 1, 2005. Semimonthly deposits of taxes, however, will remain unaffected by the delayed filing requirement.

Refunds of tax. The 2004 Jobs Act does not change the present-law nontaxable uses of aviation fuel. If previously taxed fuel is used for a nontaxable purpose, the user may claim a refund for the tax previously paid (Code Sec. 6427(l)(1), as amended by the 2004 Jobs Act). If the previously taxed fuel is used for a taxable nonaircraft use, the fuel is subject to the 24.4-cents-per-gallon tax on kerosene and a refund of the previously paid aviation fuel tax is allowed (Code Sec. 4041(a)(1)(B), as amended by the 2004 Jobs Act). Claims by the ultimate vendor or the purchaser that are not taken as a refund claim may be allowable as an income tax credit.

Under the 2004 Jobs Act, a refund is allowable to the ultimate vendor of aviation fuel if the vendor pays the tax on fuel it purchases and subsequently sells the fuel to a person qualified to purchase at a reduced rate (Code Sec. 6427(l)(5)(B), as amended by the 2004 Jobs Act). In this case, the ultimate vendor can make refund claims against any excise tax liability for the difference in the tax, similar to the current law treatment of ultimate purchase payment claims.

> **Example (1):** Assume an airport is not served by a pipeline, and aviation fuel is removed from a terminal and transported to an airport storage facility. Upon its removal from the terminal, the fuel was taxed at 21.9 cents per gallon. At the airport, the fuel is purchased for 4.4 cents per gallon by John Doe Airlines, which is registered with the IRS. The ultimate vendor may claim a refund for 17.5 cents per gallon (the difference between the taxable price and the purchase price).

> **Example (2):** Assume the same facts as in Example (1), except that the fuel purchased will be used by John Doe Airlines on an international flight, and thus, it expects to pay zero tax on the purchased fuel. In order for John Doe Airlines to obtain a zero rate of tax on the purchase, it must certify to the vendor that the fuel is to be used on an international flight. If John Doe Airlines fails to provide this certification, it must pay the 4.4-cents-per-gallon tax and file a refund claim with the IRS.

Floor stocks tax. A floor stocks tax applies to aviation fuel held on January 1, 2005, by a person if: (1) the aviation fuel has not been paid with respect to the fuel; and (2) the fuel would have been subject to the aviation fuel tax upon a prior removal, entry or sale if the new rules had been in effect at the time of such removal, entry or sale (Act Sec. 853(f)(1) of the 2004 Jobs Act). The floor stocks tax does not apply to aviation fuel actually held in the fuel tank of an aircraft on January 1, 2005 (Act Sec. 853(f)(2) of the 2004 Jobs Act).

The rate of tax is 4.4 cents per gallon for fuel held for use or sale in commercial aviation and 21.9 cents per gallon for any other use. Of the collected floor stocks tax, 0.1 cent will be transferred to the Leaking Underground Storage Tank (LUST) Trust Fund and the remaining tax will be transferred to the Airport and Airway Trust Fund.

For further information on this subject, consult any of the following CCH reporter explanations:

- Federal Excise Tax Reporter, ETR ¶ 8975.01, ¶ 8975.03 and ¶ 8975.08
- Federal Tax Guide, 2004FTG ¶ 21,050

★ *Effective date.* The provisions apply to aviation-grade kerosene removed, entered or sold after December 31, 2004 (Act Sec. 853(e) of the American Jobs Creation Act of 2004).

Act Sec. 853(a)(1) of the American Jobs Creation Act of 2004, amending Code Sec. 4081(a)(2)(A); Act Sec. 853(a)(2), adding Code Sec. 4081(a)(2)(C); Act Sec. 853(a)(3)(A), adding Code Sec. 4081(a)(3); Act Sec. 853(a)(3)(B); Act Sec. 853(a)(4), adding Code Sec. 4081(a)(4); Act Sec. 853(a)(5)(A), adding Code Sec. 4082(e); Act Sec. 853(a)(5)(B)(i), amending Code Sec. 4082(b); Act Sec. 853(a)(5)(B)(ii), striking Code Sec. 4082(d)(1); Act Sec. 853(a)(6), amending Code Sec. 4041(a)(1); Act Sec. 853(b), adding Code Sec. 4083(b); Act Sec. 853(c)(1), amending Code Sec. 6427(l)(4);

Act Sec. 853(c)(2), amending Code Sec. 6427(i)(4)(A); Act Sec. 853(c)(3), amending Code Sec. 6427(l)(2)(B); Act Sec. 853(d)(1), striking Code Secs. 4091, 4092 and 4093; Act Sec. 853(d)(2)(A), amending Code Sec. 4041(c); Act Sec. 853(d)(2)(B), amending Code Sec. 4041(d)(2); Act Sec. 853(d)(2)(C)-(D), striking Code Secs. 4041(e) and 4041(i); Act Sec. 853(d)(2)(E), amending Code Sec. 4041(m)(1); Act Sec. 853(d)(2)(F), amending Code Secs. 4101(a), 4103, 4221(a) and 6206; Act Sec. 853(d)(2)(G)-(I), amending Code Sec. 6416; Act Sec. 853(d)(2)(J), amending Code Sec. 6427(j)(1); Act Sec. 853(d)(2)(K), amending Code Sec. 6427(l); Act Sec. 853(d)(2)(L)-(M), amending Code Sec. 6724(d); Act Sec. 853(d)(2)(N)-(O), amending Code Sec. 9502(b): Act Sec. 853(d)(2)(P)-(Q), amending Code Sec. 9508; Act Sec. 853(e); Act Sec. 853(f). Law at ¶5980, ¶6010, ¶6015, ¶6020, ¶6025, ¶6030, ¶6035, ¶6040, ¶6045, ¶6075, ¶6185, ¶6205, ¶6220, ¶6310, ¶6380, ¶6390 and ¶7115. Committee Report at ¶11,340.

¶1509

Transmix and Diesel Blendstocks Considered Taxable Fuel

Background

Taxable fuels include gasoline, diesel fuel and kerosene (Code Sec. 4083(a)(1)). Diesel fuel includes any fuel that is suitable for use as a fuel in a diesel-powered highway vehicle or a diesel-powered train (Code Sec. 4083(a)(3)). Under Reg. §48.4081-1(c)(2)(i), a liquid is suitable for this use if it has practical and commercial fitness for the use in the train's or vehicle's propulsion engine. Excluded from the definition of diesel fuel is gasoline, kerosene, No. 5 and No. 6 fuel oils covered by ASTM specification D 396, F-76 (Fuel Navel Distillate) covered by military specification MIL-F-16884, any liquid that contains less than four percent normal paraffins, or liquid that has a distillation range of 125° F. or less, has a sulfur content of 10 ppm or less and has a minimum color of +27 Saybolt (Reg. §48.4081-1(b) and (c)(2)(ii)).

Much of the fuel that is delivered throughout the United States and Canada is delivered from a refinery via a pipeline to a terminal facility where the fuel is stored and then further distributed to other storage facilities or even to the local fuel retailer. Pipelines in the United States transport many different fuel types to an array of terminals. Transmix is the by-product that results from the mixture of two fuels in the pipeline system during pipeline transportation.

> **Example:** Bob's Terminal orders diesel fuel #2 from its distributor. Karen's Terminal orders gasoline from the same distributor. The distributor first sends the diesel fuel #2 down the pipeline to Bob's Terminal. Immediately following the diesel #2 shipment, the distributor sends the gasoline ordered by Karen's Terminal. The portion of the fuel that is mixed from the last of the diesel fuel #2 and the beginning of the gasoline is considered transmix. In this case, the transmix fuel is neither all gasoline nor all diesel fuel, but a combination of the two fuels.

Generally, transmix is stored at a terminal and is disposed of in three ways: (1) blended into a large tank of gasoline, (2) returned to the refinery for more refining or (3) sold to a refinery for further refining.

American Jobs Creation Act Impact

Transmix is taxed as diesel fuel.—Under the new law, transmix and diesel fuel blendstocks identified by the IRS will be taxed as if they were diesel fuel, regardless of whether the mixture contains gasoline (Code Sec. 4083(a)(3), as amended by the American Jobs Creation Act of 2004). "Transmix" means a by-product of refined products created by the mixing of different specification products during the pipeline transportation.

The re-refining of tax-paid transmix into gasoline, diesel fuel or kerosene qualifies as a nontaxable off-highway business use of the transmix (Conference Committee Report (H.R. Conf. Rep. No. 108-755)). As a result, the refund and payment provisions of Code Sec. 6427 relating to nontaxable uses of diesel fuel apply. Specifically, the IRS will credit or refund the aggregate tax paid (without interest) on a diesel fuel blendstock if the user establishes that the ultimate use of the removed diesel blendstock will not be used to produce diesel fuel (Code Sec. 6427(h)(2), as amended by the 2004 Jobs Act).

For further information on this subject, consult any of the following CCH reporter explanations:

- Federal Excise Tax Reporter, ETR ¶ 9310.03
- Federal Tax Guide, 2004FTG ¶ 21,030

★ *Effective date.* The provisions apply to fuel removed, sold or used after December 31, 2004 (Act Sec. 870(c) of the American Jobs Creation Act of 2004).

Act Sec. 870(a) of the American Jobs Creation Act of 2004, amending Code Sec. 4083(a)(3); Act Sec. 870(b), amending Code Sec. 6427(h); Act Sec. 870(c). Law at ¶ 6020 and ¶ 6220. Committee Report at ¶ 11,510.

¶ 1511

Taxable Fuel Refunds for Certain Ultimate Vendors

Background

If a wholesale distributor purchases gasoline on which tax was previously paid and sells the gasoline to its ultimate purchaser for use in certain exempt purposes, the wholesale distributor is treated as the person who paid the tax and is therefore authorized to file a claim for a credit or refund of the tax paid (Code Sec. 6416(a)(4)(A)). An exempt purpose includes sale to a state or local government, to a nonprofit educational organization, for supplies for vessels or aircraft, for export, or for the production of special fuels. For undyed diesel fuel or kerosene used on a farm for farming purposes or by a state or local government, only the ultimate registered vendors are allowed a credit or payment.

Refunds of taxes are generally paid without interest. However, the IRS is required to pay interest on certain refunds of overpayments of tax on gasoline, diesel fuel or kerosene that is used to produce a qualified alcohol mixture, and on refunds due ultimate vendors of diesel fuel or kerosene used on a farm for farming purposes or by a state or local government. The IRS must pay interest on refunds of $200 or more ($100 or more for kerosene) arising from sales over any period of a week or more if payment of the refund is not made within 20 days.

American Jobs Creation Act Impact

Gasoline tax credits and refunds to be claimed by ultimate vendors.—The ultimate vendor is the proper party to claim a refund of taxes imposed on the sale of gasoline to a state or local government for its exclusive use or to a nonprofit educational organization for its exclusive use, so long as the ultimate vendor is registered under Code Sec. 4101 (Code Sec. 6416(a)(4), as amended by the American Jobs Creation Act of 2004). The Act conforms the payment of refunds on gasoline sales with the procedure established under current law for diesel fuel and kerosene sales, where the ultimate vendor makes the claims for refund.

The procedure and timing of any claim by an ultimate vendor are the same as that for vendor refunds under Code Sec. 6427(i)(4). However, the rules regarding electronic claims under Code Sec. 6427(i)(3)(B) will not apply unless the ultimate vendor has certified to the IRS for the most recent quarter of the tax year that all of the vendor's ultimate purchasers are state or local governments or nonprofit educational organizations.

For further information on this subject, consult any of the following CCH reporter explanations:

- Federal Excise Tax Reporter, ETR ¶48,215.02
- Federal Tax Guide, 2004FTG ¶21,015

★ *Effective date.* The provision is effective on January 1, 2005 (Act. Sec. 865(b) of the American Jobs Creation Act of 2004).

Act Sec. 865(a) of the American Jobs Creation Act of 2004, amending Code Sec. 6416(a)(4); Act Sec. 865(b). Law at ¶6205. Committee Report at ¶11,460.

¶1513

Repeal of 4.3-Cents Excise Tax on Rail Diesel Fuel and Inland Waterway Barge Fuel

Background

Diesel fuel used in diesel-powered trains is subject to a 4.4-cents-per-gallon excise tax. Of this amount, 4.3 cents are deposited in the General Fund of the Treasury, while 0.1 cent is deposited in the Leaking Underground Storage Tank (LUST) Trust Fund (Code Sec. 4041(a)(1) and (d)).

Fuel used in barges operating on the designated inland waterway system is subject to a 4.3-cents-per-gallon excise tax which is deposited to the Treasury's General Fund (Code Sec. 4042(b)(1)(C)). This excise tax is in addition to the 20.1-cents-per-gallon excise taxes that are collected with respect to the fuel used in barges to fund the Inland Waterways Trust Fund and the LUST Trust Fund.

The permanent 4.3-cents-per-gallon excise tax on motor fuels was originally enacted as a deficit reduction measure, with the receipts payable to the General Fund. Since then, nearly all of the amounts paid as excise taxes on fuels have been diverted by Congress to specified trust funds that provide specific benefits for the motor fuel users who pay the excise taxes. Rail and barge operators are the only group of transportation service providers subject to the 4.3-cents-per-gallon excise tax who receive no benefits from a dedicated trust fund, but whose payments are instead deposited into the General Fund.

The LUST Trust Fund excise tax is scheduled to expire after March 31, 2005.

American Jobs Creation Act Impact

Repeal of tax on diesel fuel used in trains and on fuels used by inland waterway barges.—The American Jobs Creation Act of 2004 repeals the 4.3-cents-per-gallon excise tax imposed on diesel fuel used in trains and on fuels used in barges operating on the designated inland waterway system over the course of a prescribed phase-out period. The tax is reduced to 3.3 cents per gallon for the first six months of calendar year 2005 (January 1, 2005, through June 30, 2005) to 2.3 cents per gallon from July 1, 2005, through December 31, 2006 (Code Sec. 4041(a)(1)(C)(ii)(II), as added by the 2004 Jobs Act), and is completely eliminated beginning on January 1, 2007 (Code Sec. 4041(a)(1)(C)(ii), as added by the 2004 Jobs Act). The imposition of the

0.1-cent-per-gallon LUST tax on diesel fuel used in trains and on fuels used in barges operating on the inland waterway system remains unchanged.

For further information on this subject, consult any of the following CCH reporter explanations:

- Federal Excise Tax Reporter, ETR ¶5700.027 and ¶5835.02
- Federal Tax Guide, 2004FTG ¶21,020 and ¶21,080

★ *Effective date.* The provision is effective on January 1, 2005 (Act Sec. 241(c) of the American Jobs Creation Act of 2004).

Act Sec. 241(a)(1) of the American Jobs Creation Act of 2004, amending Code Sec. 4041(a)(1)(C)(ii); Act Sec. 241(a)(2)(A), adding Code Sec. 4041(d)(3); Act Sec. 241(a)(2)(B), amending Code Sec. 4082(f); Act Sec. 241(a)(2)(C), amending Code Sec. 6421(f)(3)(B); Act Sec. 241(a)(2)(D), amending Code Sec. 6427(l)(3)(B); Act Sec. 241(b), amending Code Sec. 4042(b)(2)(C); Act Sec. 241(c). Law at ¶5980, ¶5985, ¶6015, ¶6210, and ¶6220. Committee Report at ¶10,220.

DYED FUELS

¶1517

Mechanical Dye Injection Equipment

Background

Diesel fuel and kerosene are generally taxed upon their removal from a terminal rack (Code Sec. 4081). However, diesel fuel and kerosene removed or sold for certain uses are exempt from excise tax if: (1) the IRS determines that the fuel is destined for a nontaxable use; (2) the fuel is indelibly dyed; and (3) the marking requirements are met (Code Sec. 4082(a)). If these three requirements are met, dyed diesel fuel and kerosene may be removed at the terminal rack with no federal tax charged. Exempt uses of diesel fuel and kerosene include:

(1) use on a farm for farming purposes;

(2) exclusive use by a state or local government in the operation of an essential government function;

(3) use in a vehicle owned by an aircraft museum;

(4) use in a school bus while the bus is engaged in the transportation of students and school employees;

(5) use in a qualified local bus;

(6) use in a highway vehicle that is not registered (and is not required to be registered) for highway use under the laws of any state or foreign country and is used in the operator's trade or business;

(7) exclusive use by a nonprofit educational organization;

(8) use in a vehicle owned by the United States that is not used on a highway;

(9) fuel that is exported;

(10) use other than as a fuel in a propulsion engine of a diesel-powered highway vehicle;

(11) use as fuel in a propulsion engine of a diesel-powered train; and

(12) use in a scheduled mass transit bus.

Background

Because diesel fuel and kerosene can be removed without the payment of federal tax, it can be very attractive to sell nontaxed diesel fuel and kerosene for a taxable purpose in order to increase one's profits. As a result, the IRS mandated that nontaxed diesel fuel and kerosene be dyed so that it will not be mistaken for taxable fuel. Fuel is usually dyed at a terminal rack by means of mechanical injection, although there is no requirement that mechanical injection be used.

Diesel fuel and kerosene, regardless of sulphur content, satisfies the dyeing requirements if it: (1) contains the dye Solvent Red 164 at a concentration spectrally equivalent to 3.9 pounds of the solid dye standard Solvent Red 26 per thousand barrels of diesel fuel; or (2) contains any dye of a type and in a concentration approved by the IRS (Reg. § 48.4082-1(b)). To date, the IRS has not issued any marking requirements. Furthermore, the IRS announced in March 2000 that it had no immediate plans to issue final regulations relating to dye injection systems.

Despite the mandated dyeing requirements, every year, countless gallons of dyed diesel fuel and kerosene are sold and/or used for a taxable purpose. This causes the federal government to lose revenue that could be used to repair and build roads and maintain the federal highway system.

A penalty is imposed on any person who sells (or holds for sale) dyed fuel for any use that he or she knows or has reason to know is for a taxable use (Code Sec. 6715(a)). Anyone who willfully alters or attempts to alter the strength or composition of the dye is also subject to a penalty (Code Sec. 6715). The penalty is the greater of $1,000 per act or $10 per gallon of dyed fuel. In the case of repeated violations, the penalty is multiplied by the number of prior penalties that had been imposed (Code Sec. 6715(b)(2)). Finally, if the penalty is imposed on a business entity, any officer, employee or agent of the entity who willfully participated in any act giving rise to the penalty will be jointly and severally liable with the entity for the penalty (Code Sec. 6715(d)).

American Jobs Creation Act Impact

Mechanical dye injections systems required.—Terminals that offer dyed fuel are required to dye diesel fuel and kerosene held for sale for a nontaxable purpose by use of a mechanical injection system (Code Sec. 4082(a)(2), as amended by the American Jobs Creation Act of 2004). No later than 180 days after the 2004 Jobs Act's enactment date, the IRS is to issue regulations establishing standards for tamper-resistant mechanical injector dyeing (Act Sec. 854(b) of the 2004 Jobs Act).

> **Comment:** As a practical matter, most terminals already have a mechanical mechanism for dyeing fuel at the rack. Consequently, most terminals have already complied with the first part of the new rules. Until the IRS issues the regulations on tamper resistance, it is unclear how much the new rules will cost terminals in increased compliance costs.

A penalty equal to the greater of $25,000 or $10 for each gallon of fuel involved applies to each act of tampering with a mechanical dye injection system (Code Sec. 6715A(a)(1) and (b)(1), as added by the 2004 Jobs Act). In addition, a $1,000 penalty is imposed for each failure to maintain security for mechanical dye injection systems. An extra $1,000 penalty is imposed for each day any violation remains uncorrected after the first day the violation was discovered (or should have been discovered) (Code Sec. 6715A(b)(2), as added by the 2004 Jobs Act).

¶1517

Comment: For purposes of the $1,000 per day penalty, a violation can be corrected if the portion of the system causing the violation is shut down, according to the Conference Committee Report (H.R. Conf. Rep. No. 108-755).

If any of the penalties are imposed on a business entity, each officer, employee, or agent of the entity, or other contracting party who willfully participated in any act giving rise to the penalty, will be jointly and severally liable with the entity for the new penalty (Code Sec. 6715A(c), as added by the 2004 Jobs Act). The parent corporation of an offending business entity that is a member of an affiliated group is also jointly and severally liable for the penalty (Code Sec. 6715A(c)(2), as added by the 2004 Jobs Act).

For further information on this subject, consult any of the following CCH reporter explanations:

- Federal Excise Tax Reporter, ETR ¶9215 and ¶51,750.01
- Federal Tax Guide, 2004FTG ¶21,035

★ *Effective date.* The IRS has 180 days from the date of enactment to issue regulations regarding mechanical dye injection systems, including standards for making the systems tamper resistant (Act Sec. 854(b) of the American Jobs Creation Act of 2004). The provision requiring mechanical dying and the new penalty for tampering with a mechanical system take effect 180 days after the IRS issues regulations setting forth the standards for the mechanical dyeing systems (Act Sec. 854(d) of the 2004 Jobs Act).

Act Sec. 854(a) of the American Jobs Creation Act of 2004, amending Code Sec. 4082(a)(2); Act Sec. 854(b); Act Sec. 854(c)(1) adding Code Sec. 6715A; Act Sec. 854(d). Law at ¶6015, ¶6285 and ¶7120. Committee Report at ¶11,350.

¶1519

Administrative Review for Dyed Fuel Violations

Background

Diesel fuel and kerosene are generally taxed upon their removal from a terminal rack (Code Sec. 4081). However, diesel fuel and kerosene removed or sold for certain uses are exempt from excise tax if: (1) the IRS determines that the fuel is destined for a nontaxable use; (2) the fuel is indelibly dyed; and (3) the marking requirements are met (Code Sec. 4082(a)).

A penalty is imposed on any person who sells (or holds for sale) dyed fuel for any use that he or she knows or has reason to know is for a taxable use (Code Sec. 6715(a)). Anyone who willfully alters or attempts to alter the strength or composition of the dye is also subject to a penalty under Code Sec. 6715. The penalty is the greater of $1,000 per act or $10 per gallon of dyed fuel. In the case of repeated violations, the penalty is multiplied by the number of prior penalties that had been imposed (Code Sec. 6715(b)(2)).

In Rev. Proc. 2001-33, IRB 2001-23, 1322, the IRS provided guidance on how taxpayers should request an administrative appeal of this penalty. Basically, the IRS notifies the taxpayer in writing that it intends to impose the Code Sec. 6715 penalty. Within 30 days from the date of the notification, a taxpayer can contest the penalty by completing Form 12009, Request for an Informal Conference and Appeals Review. If, after the conference, the IRS still proposes to assert the penalty and the taxpayer still disagrees with the penalty's imposition, the taxpayer can request an Appeals review of the case.

American Jobs Creation Act Impact

No administrative appeal for dyed fuel violations.—The American Jobs Creation Act of 2004 limits certain remedies for repeat offenders of the dyed fuel rules. Specifically, any person who is found to be subject to the Code Sec. 6715 penalty at least twice will be denied the right to an administrative appeal or review. An appeal or review, however, will be allowed if the claim asserts fraud or mistakes in the chemical analysis or in the mathematical calculation in the amount of the penalty (Code Sec. 6715(e), as added by the 2004 Jobs Act).

For further information on this subject, consult any of the following CCH reporter explanations:

- Federal Excise Tax Reporter, ETR ¶9215.01, ¶9215.02 and ¶51,750.01
- Federal Tax Guide, 2004FTG ¶22,569

★ *Effective date.* The provision applies to penalties assessed after the date of enactment of the Act (Act Sec. 855(b) of the American Jobs Creation Act of 2004).

Act Sec. 855(a) of the American Jobs Creation Act of 2004, adding Code Sec. 6715(e); Act Sec. 855(b). Law at ¶6280. Committee Report at ¶11,350.

¶1521

Altered Dyed Fuel

Background ————————————————————————————————

Diesel fuel and kerosene are generally taxed upon their removal from a terminal rack (Code Sec. 4081). However, diesel fuel and kerosene removed or sold for certain uses are exempt from excise tax if: (1) the IRS determines that the fuel is destined for a nontaxable use; (2) the fuel is indelibly dyed; and (3) the marking requirements are met (Code Sec. 4082(a)). See ¶1517 for the exempt uses of diesel fuel and kerosene.

Currently, a penalty is imposed on any person who sells (or holds for sale) dyed fuel for any use that he or she knows or has reason to know is for a taxable use (Code Sec. 6715(a)). Anyone who willfully alters or attempts to alter the strength or composition of the dye is also subject to the penalty. The penalty is the greater of $1,000 per act or $10 per gallon of dyed fuel (Code Sec. 6715(b)).

American Jobs Creation Act Impact

Extension of penalty for sales of chemically altered dyed fuel.—The new law extends the Code Sec. 6715 penalty to any persons who willfully alter dyed fuel chemically or by another means (Code Sec. 6715(a)(3), as amended by the American Jobs Creation Act of 2004). Thus, for example, if someone removes fuel that purports to be dyed at the terminal rack and is able to do so without the dye being added, he or she will now be subject to the penalty.

In addition, the penalty now applies to any person: (1) who has knowledge that untaxed or partially taxed dyed fuel has been chemically or otherwise altered; and (2) who sells or holds for sale the fuel for a purpose that the person knows is a taxable use (Code Sec. 6715(a)(4), as added by the 2004 Jobs Act).

For further information on this subject, consult any of the following CCH reporter explanations:

- Federal Excise Tax Reporter, ETR ¶9215.01, ¶9215.02 and ¶51,750.01
- Federal Tax Guide, 2004FTG ¶22,569

★ *Effective date.* The provision is effective on the date of the enactment of the Act (Act Sec. 856(c) of the American Jobs Creation Act of 2004).

Act Sec. 856(a) of the American Jobs Creation Act of 2004, adding Code Sec. 6715(a)(4); Act Sec. 856(b), amending Code Sec. 6715(a)(3); Act Sec. 856(c). Law at ¶ 6280. Committee Report at ¶ 11,350.

¶ 1523

Termination of Dyed Diesel Fuel Use by Intercity Buses

Background

If a tax has been imposed on the sale of diesel fuel, kerosene or special motor fuel and the purchaser uses the fuel for a nontaxable or exempt purpose, or resells the fuel, then the purchaser is entitled to either an income tax credit or refund equal to the amount of the excise tax paid. If the purchaser has used part of the fuel for a taxable use, the credit or refund is reduced by the amount of the taxable use (Code Sec. 6427(a)).

A reduced tax of 7.4 cents per gallon is imposed on dyed fuel delivered into the fuel supply tank of an intercity or local bus (Code Sec. 6427(b)(2)(A)). However, a bus furnishing intracity passenger land transportation for compensation is eligible for a full refund of, or credit for, the excise tax if the bus:

(1) is available to the general public;

(2) has scheduled and regular routes;

(3) has a seating capacity of 20 or more adults (excluding the driver); and

(4) is under contract with or receives more than a nominal subsidy from any state or local government to furnish such transportation (Code Sec. 6427(b)(2)(C)).

Certain persons must register with the IRS regarding fuel taxes imposed by Code Secs. 4041(a)(1), 4081 and 4091 (Code Sec. 4101(a)). Registration is accomplished by filing Form 637, Application for Registration (For Certain Excise Tax Activities) (Reg. § 48.4101-1(e)). A letter of registration will be sent to the taxpayer upon the IRS's approval of an application. A person is registered only upon receipt of the letter of registration (and if the registration has not been revoked or suspended) (Reg. § 48.4101-1(a)(2)).

American Jobs Creation Act Impact

Ultimate vendor refund.—For diesel fuel used on an intercity or local bus, if the ultimate *purchaser* of the fuel waives the right to payment of the refund under Code Sec. 6427(b)(1) and assigns the right to the ultimate *vendor*, then the IRS may pay the amount to the vendor (Code Sec. 6427(b)(4), as added by the American Jobs Creation Act of 2004). However, to receive the refund, the vendor must:

(1) be registered under Code Sec. 4101;

(2) not have included the tax in the price of the article with respect to which the tax was imposed, and not collected the amount of the tax from the person who purchased the fuel;

(3) have repaid the amount of the tax to the ultimate purchaser; and

(4) have filed with the IRS the written consent of the ultimate purchaser to the allowance of the refund.

A refund claim may only be filed for any period that is less than one week and, generally, for amounts of $200 or more (Code Sec. 6427(i)(4)(A), as amended by the 2004 Jobs Act).

For further information on this subject, consult any of the following CCH reporter explanations:

- Federal Excise Tax Reporter, ETR ¶10,945.01, ¶49,685.01 and ¶49,685.02
- Federal Tax Guide, 2004FTG ¶21,035

★ *Effective date.* The provisions apply to fuel sold after December 31, 2004 (Act Sec. 857(d) of the American Jobs Creation Act of 2004).

Act Sec. 857(a) of the American Jobs Creation Act of 2004, amending Code Sec. 4082(b)(3); Act Sec. 857(b), adding Code Sec. 6427(b)(4); Act Sec. 857(c), amending Code Sec. 6427(i)(4)(A); Act Sec. 857(d). Law at ¶6015 and ¶6220. Committee Report at ¶11,350.

REGISTRATION AND REPORTING

¶1527

Registration of Pipeline and Vessel Operators in Bulk Transfers

Background

Code Sec. 4081 imposes a fuel tax at the manufacturers level. The tax is triggered in several ways, including when taxable fuel (1) is removed from any refinery, (2) is removed from any terminal, or (3) enters into the United States (Code Sec. 4081(a)(1)(A)). There is an exemption, however, for bulk transfers of taxable fuel. For purposes of the exemption, "bulk transfer" means any transfer of taxable fuel by pipeline or vessel (Reg. § 48.4081-1(b)). The exemption applies if the person removing the fuel from a terminal or refinery, or bringing it into the United States, and the operator of the terminal or refinery to which it is being transferred, are both registered under Code Sec. 4101 (Code Sec. 4081(a)(1)(B)).

An unregistered vessel or pipeline that transfers fuel as part of a bulk transfer does not disqualify the bulk transfer from the exemption. For example, a registered refiner may transfer fuel to an unregistered vessel or pipeline operator who in turn transfers it to a registered terminal operator. So long as the person initially removing the fuel and the terminal operator receiving it are registered, the transfer is exempt, despite the intermediate transfer to the unregistered vessel or pipeline operator.

American Jobs Creation Act Impact

Exemption from fuel tax requires pipeline and vessel operators to register.— For a bulk transfer of taxable fuel to be exempt from the Code Sec. 4081 manufacturers level fuel tax, any pipeline or vessel operator that is a party to the bulk transfer must be registered under Code Sec. 4101. Transfer to an unregistered party will trigger the tax. Beginning on January 1, 2005, the Treasury will periodically publish under Code Sec. 6103(k)(7) a current list of persons who are registered and are required to be registered under Code Sec. 4101 (Act Sec. 860(c) of the 2004 Jobs Act).

> **Comment:** This provision is aimed at curbing unregistered pipeline and vessel operators who are receiving bulk transfers of taxable fuel and then diverting the fuel to retailers or end users without the tax ever being paid. By requiring that a pipeline or vessel operator be registered with the IRS in order to claim a bulk transfer exemption, Congress is trying to ensure that bulk transfers

of fuel are delivered as intended to approved refineries and terminals and taxed appropriately.

For further information on this subject, consult any of the following CCH reporter explanations:

- Federal Excise Tax Reporter, ETR ¶8915.018 and ¶10,945.02
- Federal Tax Guide, 2004FTG ¶21,010

★ *Effective date.* The provision is effective on March 1, 2005 (Act Sec. 860(b) of the American Jobs Creation Act of 2004).

Act Sec. 860 of the American Jobs Creation Act of 2004, amending Code Sec. 4081(a)(1)(B); Act Sec. 860(b); Act Sec. 860(c). Law at ¶6010 and ¶7125. Committee Report at ¶11,410.

¶1529

Proof of Registration Displayed on Vessel

Background

Vessel operators are among the persons who must register in connection with the fuel taxes imposed by Code Secs. 4041(a)(1), 4081, and 4091 (Reg. §48.4101-1(c)(1)(vii)). Any person who is required to register with the IRS and fails to do so is liable for a $50 penalty (Code Sec. 7272(a)). A $5,000 criminal penalty or imprisonment of not more than five years, or both, may also apply to those who fail to register (Code Sec. 7232).

American Jobs Creation Act Impact

Vessel operators must display proof of registration or face penalty.—Every vessel operator that is required to register under Code Sec. 4101 must display proof of registration through an identification device prescribed by the IRS on each vessel the operator uses to transport taxable fuel (Code Sec. 4101(a)(2), as added by Act Sec. 861(a)(2) of the American Jobs Creation Act of 2004).

In connection with this, a $500 penalty is imposed on a vessel operator's failure to display the proof of registration, with a limit of one penalty per vessel per month (Code Sec. 6718(a), as added by the 2004 Jobs Act). For multiple violations, $500 multiplied by the number of penalties imposed on the vessel operator in prior months is added to the $500 penalty for the new violation (Code Sec. 6718(b), as added by the 2004 Jobs Act). If, however, the vessel operator shows a reasonable cause for failing to display proof of registration, the penalty does not apply (Code Sec. 6718(c), as added by the 2004 Jobs Act).

For further information on this subject, consult any of the following CCH reporter explanations:

- Federal Excise Tax Reporter, ETR ¶10,945.02, ¶54,375.01 and ¶55,275.01
- Federal Tax Guide, 2004FTG ¶21,065

★ *Effective date.* The provision requiring the display of registration takes effect on January 1, 2005. The provisions relating to penalties for failure to display registration on vessels apply to penalties imposed after December 31, 2004 (Act Sec. 861(c) of the American Jobs Creation Act of 2004).

Act Sec. 861(a) of the American Jobs Creation Act of 2004, amending Code Sec. 4101(a); Act Sec. 861(b), adding Code Sec. 6718; Act Sec. 861(c). Law at ¶6040 and ¶6295. Committee Report at ¶11,420.

¶ 1531

Electronic Reporting Under ExSTARS

Background ———————————————————————————————

The Excise Summary Terminal Activity Reporting System, or ExSTARS, is the IRS's fuel information reporting system under Code Sec. 4101(d). Terminal operators use Form 720-TO (Terminal Operator Report) to report all bulk and nonbulk receipts of liquid products into an approved terminal and all disbursements by position holders from an approved terminal, as well as monthly inventory reconciliation by product. Terminal operators file a separate form for each approved terminal. Bulk transport carriers (barge, pipeline, and vessel operators) who receive liquid product from or deliver liquid product to an approved terminal report that movement on Form 720-CS (Carrier Summary Report) (IRS Pub. 510, *Excise Taxes for 2004*, and IRS Pub. 3536, *Motor Fuel Excise Tax EDI Guide*). Each report covers a one-month period and must be filed by the end of the month following the month to which it relates (Reg. § 48.4101-2(a)).

Forms 720-TO and 720-CS can be filed on paper or electronically. Electronic filings are transmitted in Electronic Data Interchange (EDI) format using an Internet connection, a browser, and secure communications protocol. (See IRS Pub. 3536 for instructions and EDI data record and file formats.)

American Jobs Creation Act Impact

Electronic filing required for 25 or more reportable transactions in a month.— Any person who must report under ExSTARS and who has 25 or more reportable transactions in a month must file the report in electronic format (Code Sec. 4101(d), as amended by the American Jobs Creation Act of 2004).

For further information on this subject, consult any of the following CCH reporter explanations:

- Federal Excise Tax Reporter, ETR ¶ 10,945.10
- Federal Tax Guide, 2004FTG ¶ 21,065

★ *Effective date.* The provision applies on January 1, 2006 (Act Sec. 864(b) of the American Jobs Creation Act of 2004).

Act Sec. 864(a) of the American Jobs Creation Act of 2004, amending Code Sec. 4101(d); Act Sec. 864(b). Law at ¶ 6040. Committee Report at ¶ 11,450.

¶ 1533

Penalties for Failing to Register and Failing to Report Under Code Sec. 4101

Background ———————————————————————————————

Code Sec. 4101(a) requires various persons to register in connection with the fuel taxes imposed by Code Secs. 4041(a)(1), 4081, and 4091. Under Code Sec. 4101(d), the IRS may require information reporting by registered persons and others.

Penalties for failure to register. There is a general nonassessable penalty of $50 for failing to register as required by the Tax Code (Code Sec. 7272). This general penalty, therefore, applies to the failure to register under Code Sec. 4101(a).

> **Comment:** Civil penalties are either *assessable* penalties and are assessed in the same manner as taxes, or are *nonassessable* penalties that require the taxpayer be given notice and an opportunity to respond before assessment.

Background

In addition, there is a $5,000 criminal penalty and a possible five-year prison term for someone who fails the Code Sec. 4101 registration requirement, falsely represents himself to be registered, or willfully makes any false statement in an application for registration (Code Sec. 7232).

Reporting requirements and penalties. The Excise Summary Terminal Activity Reporting System (ExSTARS) is the IRS's fuel information reporting system under Code Sec. 4101(d). It requires terminal operators and bulk transport carriers (barge, pipeline, and vessel operators) to report on the movement of any liquid product into or out of an approved terminal. Each report covers a one-month period and must be filed by the end of the month following the month to which it relates (Reg. § 48.4101-2(a)).

Terminal operators use Form 720-TO (Terminal Operator Report) to report the receipt and disbursement of all liquid product to and from approved terminals, filing a separate form for each approved terminal. Bulk transport carriers who receive liquid product from or deliver liquid product to an approved terminal report that movement on Form 720-CS (Carrier Summary Report). Forms 720-TO and 720-CS can be filed on paper or submitted electronically through the Internet. (See ¶ 1531 for further discussion of electronic reporting, including when it is required.)

Under Code Sec. 6721(a), the penalty for failing to report—including failing to file a timely information return, failing to include all required information, or including incorrect information—is $50 for each return.

American Jobs Creation Act Impact

New penalties for failing to register and failing to report.—The American Jobs Creation Act of 2004 increases the burden of both civil and criminal penalties for failing to register and introduces a new penalty for failing to make timely reports under ExSTARS.

New penalties and larger penalties for failing to register. Failing to register as required by Code Sec. 4101 now carries its own nonassessable civil penalty of $10,000 (Code Sec. 7272, as amended by the 2004 Jobs Act). In addition, the criminal penalty has increased to $10,000 (Code Sec. 7232, as amended by the 2004 Jobs Act). Also, there is a new assessable civil penalty for failing to register: $10,000 for each initial failure and $1,000 for each day that the failure to register continues. This penalty does not apply if the taxpayer shows reasonable cause (Code Sec. 6719, as added by the 2004 Jobs Act).

New assessable penalty for failing to report. There is now an assessable penalty of $10,000 for failing to make a timely report as required by ExSTARS under Code Sec. 4101(d), or for failing to include all the required information, or for including incorrect information (Code Sec. 6725, as added by the 2004 Jobs Act). The penalty applies to each failure concerning a vessel or a facility for which information is required. If the taxpayer can show reasonable cause, however, the penalty does not apply.

For further information on this subject, consult any of the following CCH reporter explanations:

- Federal Excise Tax Reporter, ETR ¶ 10,945.042
- Federal Tax Guide, 2004FTG ¶ 21,065

★ *Effective date.* The provision applies to penalties imposed after December 31, 2004 (Act Sec. 863(e) of the American Jobs Creation Act of 2004).

Act Sec. 863(a) of the American Jobs Creation Act of 2004, amending Code Sec. 7272(a); Act Sec. 863(b), amending Code Sec. 7232; Act Sec. 863(c), adding Code Sec. 6719; Act Sec. 863(d), adding Code Sec. 6725; Act Sec. 863(e). Law at ¶6300, ¶6315, ¶6320 and ¶6325. Committee Report at ¶11,440.

¶1535

Registration of Persons Within Foreign Trade Zones

Background _____

Foreign trade zones are located in or near U.S. Customs ports of entry and provide an advantage to U.S. companies doing business in a worldwide market by, among other things, allowing duty-free export and deferral of customs duty payments. Although terminal and refinery operators are generally required to register with the IRS in connection with fuel taxes imposed by Code Secs. 4041(a)(1) and 4081, terminal and refinery operators within a foreign trade zone or within a customs bonded storage facility have not been required to register.

American Jobs Creation Act Impact

Registration of persons within an FTZ.—Any person that operates a terminal or refinery within a foreign trade zone or within a customs bonded storage facility, or that holds an inventory position with respect to a taxable fuel in such a terminal, is required to register with the IRS in connection with fuel taxes (Code Sec. 4101(a)(2), as added by the American Jobs Creation Act of 2004). The Conference Committee intends for the IRS to establish a date by which persons required to register must be registered (Conference Committee Report, H.R. Conf. Rep. No. 108-755).

For further information on this subject, consult any of the following CCH reporter explanations:

- Federal Excise Tax Reporter, ETR ¶10,945.02
- Federal Tax Guide, 2004FTG ¶21,065

★ *Effective date.* The provision takes effect on January 1, 2005 (Act Sec. 862(c) of the American Jobs Creation Act of 2004).

Act Sec. 862(a) of the American Jobs Creation Act of 2004, adding new Code Sec. 4101(a)(2); Act Sec. 862(b), amending Code Sec. 6718(a); Act Sec. 862(c). Law at ¶6040 and ¶6295. Committee Report at ¶11,430.

ENFORCEMENT

¶1539

Expanded IRS Recordkeeping Inspection Authority

Background _____

In order to ensure compliance with the excise tax laws, the IRS is authorized to inspect any place where taxable fuel (or fuel dyes or fuel markers) is produced or is stored (or may be stored). The inspection is authorized to:

(1) examine the equipment used to determine the amount or composition of the taxable fuel and the equipment used to store the fuel (including equipment used for dyeing or marking fuel); and

(2) take and remove samples of taxable fuel (Code Sec. 4083(c)(1)(A)).

Background

Places of inspection include, but are not limited to, terminals, fuel storage facilities, retail fuel facilities or any designated inspection site (Code Sec. 4083(c) and Reg. §48.4083-1(b)(1)). Concerning that, the IRS is authorized to establish inspection sites (Code Sec. 4083(c)(2)). A designated inspection site is any state highway inspection station, weigh station, agricultural inspection station, mobile station or other location designated by the IRS (Reg. §48.4083-1(b)(2)).

American Jobs Creation Act Impact

Authority to inspect expanded.—The scope of the IRS's inspection authority is expanded to include any books, records, or shipping papers pertaining to taxable fuel, located in any authorized inspection location (Code Sec. 4083(d)(1)(A), as amended by the American Jobs Creation Act of 2004).

For further information on this subject, consult any of the following CCH reporter explanations:

- Federal Excise Tax Reporter, ETR ¶9310.04
- Federal Tax Guide, 2004FTG ¶21,070

★ *Effective date.* The provision is effective on the date of enactment (Act Sec. 858(b) of the American Jobs Creation Act of 2004).

Act Sec. 858(a) of the American Jobs Creation Act of 2004, amending Code Sec. 4083(d)(1)(A); Act Sec. 858(b). Law at ¶6020. Committee Report at ¶11,390.

¶1541

Assessable Penalty for Refusal of Entry

Background

In order to ensure compliance with the excise tax laws, the IRS is authorized to inspect any place where taxable fuel (or fuel dyes or fuel markers) is produced or is stored (or may be stored). The inspection is authorized to:

(1) examine the equipment used to determine the amount or composition of the taxable fuel and the equipment used to store the fuel (including equipment used for dyeing or marking fuel); and

(2) take and remove samples of taxable fuel (Code Sec. 4083(c)(1)(A)).

Places of inspection include, but are not limited to, terminals, fuel storage facilities, retail fuel facilities, or any designated inspection site (Code Sec. 4083(c) and Reg. §48.4083-1(b)(1)). Concerning that, the IRS is authorized to establish inspection sites (Code Sec. 4083(c)(2)). A designated inspection site is any state highway inspection station, weigh station, agricultural inspection station, mobile station, or other location designated by the IRS (Reg. §48.4083-1(b)(2)).

To conduct the inspection, the IRS may detain any receptacle that contains or may contain any taxable fuel (Code Sec. 4083(c)(1)(B)). The IRS may detain any vehicle or train to inspect its fuel tanks and storage tanks (Reg. §48.4083-1(c)(2)). The scope of the inspection includes the books and records kept to determine excise tax liability under Code Sec. 4081 (Reg. §48.4083-1(c)(1)). Any person that refuses to allow an inspection is subject to a fine of $1,000 for each refusal (Code Sec. 4083(c)(3)). This penalty is separate and in addition to any taxes that may be imposed and any penalty for misuse of dyed fuel under Code Sec. 6715 (Reg. §48.4083-1(d)). The IRS is not able to assess this penalty in the same manner as it would a tax. It must first seek

Background _____

the assistance of the Department of Justice to obtain a judgment (H.R. Conf. Rep. No. 108-755).

American Jobs Creation Act Impact

Refusal of entry penalty.—In addition to the $1,000 penalty under Code Sec. 4083 for refusal to allow an inspection, an assessable penalty is imposed on any person for the refusal to admit entry or permit any other action relating to the IRS's Code Sec. 4083 authority to inspect sites and equipment (Code Sec. 6717(a), as added by the American Jobs Creation Act of 2004). The assessable penalty is $1,000 for the refusal.

Joint and several liability. If the penalty is imposed on a business entity, then there is joint and several liability for each officer, employee or agent of the entity or other contracting party who willfully participated in the act giving rise to the penalty (Code Sec. 6717(b), as added by the 2004 Jobs Act). If the business entity is part of an affiliated group, the parent corporation of the entity will be jointly and severally liable for the penalty.

Reasonable cause exception. The penalty will not apply if it is shown that the refusal of entry was due to reasonable cause (Code Sec. 6717(c), as added by the 2004 Jobs Act).

For further information on this subject, consult any of the following CCH reporter explanations:

- Federal Excise Tax Reporter, ETR ¶ 9310.04
- Federal Tax Guide, 2004FTG ¶ 21,070

★ *Effective date.* The provision is effective on January 1, 2005 (Act Sec. 859(c) of the American Jobs Creation Act of 2004).

Act Sec. 859(a) of the American Jobs Creation Act of 2004, adding Code Sec. 6717; Act Sec. 859(b), amending Code Sec. 4083(d)(3); Act Sec. 859(c). Law at ¶ 6020 and ¶ 6290. Committee Report at ¶ 11,400.

¶ 1543

Fuel Tax Compliance Study

Background _____

The fuel tax imposed on manufacturers by Code Sec. 4081 applies to gasoline blendstocks in addition to gasoline. Gasoline blendstocks are defined in the regulations (Reg. § 48.4081-1(c)(3)(i)).

The retail excise tax on diesel fuel, special motor fuel, compressed natural gas and aircraft fuel does not apply to sales for the exclusive use of a state, a political subdivision, or the District of Columbia, or to the use by a state, a political subdivision, or the District of Columbia of fuel for a motor vehicle, motorboat or aircraft (Code Sec. 4041(g)(2)). In order to claim the exemption, the vendor must produce evidence of orders or contracts, or in the absence of these, an exemption certificate in the form specified in Reg. § 48.4041-15(b).

American Jobs Creation Act Impact

Study on fuel tax compliance.—The American Jobs Creation Act of 2004 requires the Secretary of the Treasury to submit a report regarding fuel tax compliance to the Senate Committee on Finance and the House of Representatives Ways and

Means Committee (Act Sec. 871 of the 2004 Jobs Act). The report is to include information, analysis, and recommendations in three areas:

(1) *Taxable fuel blendstocks.* The Secretary is required to identify chemical products to be added to the list of blendstocks from lab analysis of fuel samples collected by the IRS that have been blended with taxable fuel but are not treated as blendstocks. Statistics should be included on the frequency in which a chemical product has been collected, and whether the sample contained a concentration of the chemical product that was above normal.

(2) *Waste products added to taxable fuels.* The report must include a discussion of IRS findings on the addition of waste products to taxable fuel and recommendations to address taxation of these products.

(3) *Erroneous claims of fuel tax exemption.* The report will include a discussion of IRS findings on sales of taxable fuel to entities claiming exempt status as a state or local government, and the frequency of erroneous certification of tax-exempt status. The report will include recommendations, after consultation with state and local governments, to address erroneous claims, including recommendations on the feasibility of a state-maintained list of exempt governmental entities within the state.

The study is to be completed no later than January 31, 2005.

For further information on this subject, consult any of the following CCH reporter explanations:

- Federal Excise Tax Reporter, ETR ¶5700.105 and ¶8915.015
- Federal Tax Guide, 2004FTG ¶21,020

★ *Effective date.* No specific effective date is provided by the Act. The provision is, therefore, considered effective on the date of enactment.

Act Sec. 871 of the American Jobs Creation Act of 2004. Law at ¶7130. Committee Report at ¶11,510.

VEHICLES AND TIRES

¶1547

Modification of Heavy Vehicle Use Tax

Background

An annual heavy vehical use tax (HVUT) is imposed on certain trucks, truck tractors, and buses that have a taxable gross weight of 55,000 pounds or more (Code Sec. 4481(a)). The tax is imposed for a taxable period of July 1 through June 30. A taxpayer may pay the HVUT in installments if the return is filed on or before the due date (Code Sec. 6156(a)). If a taxpayer does not timely pay an installment, all of the unpaid tax is due upon notice and demand by the IRS (Code Sec. 6156(d)).

The heavy vehicle use tax may be prorated if a vehicle is stolen, or destroyed to the point that it is not economical to rebuild, before the first day of the last month of a tax period (Code Sec. 4481(c)(2)). The tax is prorated from the first day of the first month in which the vehicle was used to the last day of the month the vehicle was destroyed or stolen (Reg. §41.4481-1(c)(5)).

Exemptions and reduced rates are provided for certain highway vehicles. Any highway motor vehicle that is issued a base plate by Canada or Mexico and is operated on U.S. highways is subject to the heavy vehicle use tax whether or not it is

Background —————————————————————————————————————

required to be registered in the United States. The tax rate is reduced by 25 percent for Canadian and Mexican vehicles (Code Sec. 4483(f); Reg. § 41.4483-7).

American Jobs Creation Act Impact

Use tax on certain vehicles modified.—The ability to pay the annual use tax imposed on heavy highway vehicles in installments has been repealed for tax periods beginning after the date of enactment (Act Sec. 867(b) of the American Jobs Creation Act of 2004, repealing Code Sec. 6156). Thus, installment payments are still allowed for the tax period July 1, 2004, through June 30, 2005.

Electronic filing. Taxpayers with 25 or more vehicles for any tax period must file their Forms 2290, Heavy Highway Vehicle Use Tax Return, electronically (Code Sec. 4481(e), as added by the 2004 Jobs Act).

Proration of tax. The heavy vehicle use tax may now be prorated if a vehicle is stolen, destroyed, *or* sold (Code Sec. 4481(c)(2)(A), as amended by the 2004 Jobs Act).

Canadian and Mexican vehicles. The 2004 Jobs Act repeals the reduced use rates for Canadian and Mexican vehicles (Code Sec. 4483, as amended by the 2004 Jobs Act).

For further information on this subject, consult any of the following CCH reporter explanations:

- Federal Excise Tax Reporter, ETR ¶ 29,545.01, ¶ 29,975.07 and ¶ 42,725.01
- Federal Tax Guide, 2004FTG ¶ 21,120

★ *Effective date.* The provision applies to tax periods beginning after the date of enactment (Act Sec. 867(e) of the American Jobs Creation Act of 2004).

Act Sec. 867(a) of the American Jobs Creation Act of 2004, amending Code Sec. 4481(c)(2); Act Sec. 867(b), repealing Code Sec. 6156; Act Sec. 867(c), redesignating Code Sec. 4481(e) as Code Sec. 4481(f) and adding new Code Sec. 4481(e); Act Sec. 867(d), striking Code Sec. 4483(f); Act Sec. 867(e). Law at ¶ 6080, ¶ 6085 and ¶ 6175. Committee Report at ¶ 11,480.

¶ 1549

Mobile Machinery Exemption Codified

Background —————————————————————————————————————

The definition of "highway vehicle" affects the application of the following excise taxes:

- The Code Sec. 4051(a)(1) tax on the first retail sale of heavy trucks and trailers, which is 12 percent of the retail price.
- The Code Sec. 4481 tax on highway vehicles above a certain weight.
- The Code Sec. 4071 tax on tires of the type used on highway vehicles, by weight of the tire.
- The Code Sec. 4081 tax on fuels at the manufacturers level (and the related refunds for fuel used in an off-highway business use).
- The Code Sec. 4041 retail excise tax on fuels used in diesel-powered highway vehicles and various other fuels (and the related refund for fuel not used for taxable purposes).

For purposes of these taxes, Treasury regulations define a highway vehicle as any self-propelled vehicle, trailer, or semitrailer designed to perform a function of

Background

transporting a load over the public highway (Reg. § 48.4061(a)-1(d)). The regulations, however, exclude from the definition of "highway vehicle" (1) certain vehicles specially designed for off-highway transportation; (2) certain vehicles that function as enclosed stationary shelters; and (3) certain specially designed mobile machinery vehicles for nontransportation functions. This last exclusion is referred to as the "mobile machinery exemption."

Three tests must be satisfied for the mobile machinery exemption to apply: (1) the vehicle consists of a chassis to which jobsite machinery (not related to transportation) has been permanently attached; (2) the chassis is specially designed to serve only as a mobile carriage and mount for the particular machinery; and (3) due to its special design, the chassis could not be used to transport a load other than the particular machinery without substantial structural modification. A commonly cited example of a mobile machinery vehicle is a crane mounted on a truck chassis.

In proposed regulations issued in 2002, the IRS sought to remove the mobile machinery exemption. Thus, the chassis of a mobile machinery vehicle would be subject to the retail sales tax on heavy vehicles (unless it qualified for the off-highway transportation vehicle exception); could be subject to the heavy vehicle use tax; and the tax credits, refunds and exemptions from tax might not be available for the fuel used in these vehicles. The IRS commented that "it has become apparent that the assumption that most mobile machinery vehicles would make minimal use of the public highway is incorrect" (NPRM REG-103829-99).

American Jobs Creation Act Impact

Mobile machinery exemption codified.—The mobile machinery exemption—with its three-part test—is codified for the retail tax on heavy vehicles, the tax on tires, and the heavy vehicle use tax. Specifically, Code Sec. 4053, covering exemptions to the retail tax on heavy vehicles, is amended to include an eighth exemption for mobile machinery, defined as any vehicle that consists of a chassis—

(1) to which there has been permanently mounted (by welding, bolting, riveting, or other means) machinery or equipment to perform a construction, manufacturing, processing, farming, mining, drilling, timbering, or similar operation if the operation of the machinery or equipment is unrelated to transportation on or off the public highways;

(2) which has been specially designed to serve only as a mobile carriage and mount (and a power source, where applicable) for the particular machinery or equipment involved, whether or not such machinery or equipment is in operation; and

(3) which, by reason of such special design, could not, without substantial structural modification, be used as a component of a vehicle designed to perform a function of transporting any load other than that particular machinery or equipment or similar machinery or equipment requiring such a specially designed chassis (Code Sec. 4053(8), as added by the American Jobs Creation Act of 2004).

Code Sec. 4483, covering exemptions to the heavy vehicle use tax, now incorporates the mobile machinery exemption by reference to Code Sec. 4053(8), as does Code Sec. 4072(b)(2), which provides definitions for the Code Sec. 4071 tax on tires.

Satisfying the three-part mobile machinery test alone, however, does not enable a taxpayer to obtain a refund of the manufacturers level tax on fuel for highway vehicles under Code Sec. 4081. That is, it does not result in a "nontaxable use" exemption under Code Sec. 4082(b) (Code Sec. 4082(b)(3), as amended by the 2004 Jobs Act). However, if a vehicle passes both the design test—the three-part test discussed above—*and* the "use test," it qualifies as mobile machinery under Code Sec. 6421(e)(2)(C), which constitutes an "off-highway business use" and results in a refund of the Code Sec. 4081 tax. The use-based test requires that the vehicle's use on public highways be less than 7,500 miles during the taxpayer's tax year.

Comment: Vehicles owned by a tax-exempt Code Sec. 501(c) organization, however, need only satisfy the three-part design test to qualify for a refund of fuel taxes under Code Sec. 6421 (Code Sec. 6421(e)(2)(C)(iv), as added by the 2004 Jobs Act).

Finally, Code Sec. 6427(i)(2), which provides exceptions to the general "one claim" rule of Code Sec. 6427(i)(1), does not apply to any fuel used in an off-highway business use described in Code Sec. 6421(e)(2)(C).

For further information on this subject, consult any of the following CCH reporter explanations:

- Federal Excise Tax Reporter, ETR ¶6325.04
- Federal Tax Guide, 2004FTG ¶21,120

★ *Effective date.* The amendments generally take effect on the day after the date of the enactment of the Act (Act Sec. 851(a)(2), (b)(2) and (c)(2) of the American Jobs Creation Act of 2004); except that the rules relating to the refunds of fuel taxes apply to tax years beginning after the date of the enactment of the Act (Act Sec. 851(d)(4) of the 2004 Jobs Act).

Act Sec. 851(a)(1) of the American Jobs Creation Act of 2004, adding Code Sec. 4053(8); Act Sec. 851(b)(1), amending Code Sec. 4483; Act Sec. 851(c), amending Code Sec. 4072(b)(2); Act Sec. 851(d)(1), amending Code Sec. 6421(e)(2); Act Sec. 851(d)(2), amending Code Sec. 4082(b); Act Sec. 851(d)(3), amending Code Sec. 6427(i)(2); Act Sec. 851(a)(2), (b)(2), (c)(2) and (d)(4). Law at ¶5990, ¶6000, ¶6015, ¶6085, ¶6210 and ¶6220. Committee Report at ¶11,320.

¶ 1551

Definition of Off-Highway Vehicle and Nontransportation Trailers and Semitrailers Codified

Background

The definition of "highway vehicle" affects the application of the following excise taxes:

- The Code Sec. 4051(a)(1) tax on the first retail sale of heavy trucks and trailers, which is 12 percent of the retail price.
- The Code Sec. 4481 tax on highway vehicles above a certain weight.
- The Code Sec. 4071 tax on tires of the type used on highway vehicles, by weight of the tire.
- The Code Sec. 4081 tax on fuels at the manufacturers level (and the related refunds for fuel used in an off-highway business use).
- The Code Sec. 4041 retail excise tax on fuels used in diesel-powered highway vehicles and various other fuels (and the related refund for fuel not used for taxable purposes).

For purposes of these taxes, Treasury regulations define a highway vehicle as any self-propelled vehicle, trailer, or semitrailer designed to perform a function of transporting a load over the public highway (Reg. § 48.4061(a)-1(d)). The regulations, however, exclude from the definition of "highway vehicle" certain (1) specially designed mobile machinery vehicles for nontransportation functions (see ¶1549, which discusses the codification of the "mobile machinery exemption"); (2) trailers and semitrailers that function as enclosed stationary shelters; and (3) vehicles specially designed for off-highway transportation.

Proposed regulations issued on June 6, 2002, provided definitions for both off-highway transportation vehicles and nontransportation trailers and semitrailers (Proposed Reg. §§48.4051-1(a)(2)(i) and 48.4051-1(a)(2)(ii)).

American Jobs Creation Act Impact

Off-highway transportation vehicle and nontransportation trailers and semitrailers defined.—The American Jobs Creation Act of 2004 adopts the definition of off-highway transportation vehicle contained in the June 2002 proposed regulations (Code Sec. 7701(a)(48)(A), as added by the 2004 Jobs Act). Therefore, a vehicle is treated as an off-highway transportation vehicle if it satisfies the following requirements:

(1) It is specially designed for the primary function of transporting a particular type of load *other than* over the public highway; and

(2) Because of this special design, its capability to transport a load over the public highway is substantially limited or impaired.

For purposes of the first requirement, a vehicle's design is determined based solely on its physical characteristics. For purposes of the second requirement, in determining whether a vehicle's ability to transport a load over the public highway is substantially limited or impaired, the following factors are taken in account:

- the size of the vehicle;

- whether the vehicle is subject to the licensing, safety, and other requirements applicable to highway vehicles; and

- whether the vehicle can transport a load at a sustained speed of at least 25 miles per hour.

Note, however, that whether a vehicle can transport a greater load off the public highway than it is permitted to transport over the public highway is immaterial.

The proposed regulations provide an example of a vehicle that meets the definition of an off-highway transportation vehicle (Proposed Reg. §48.4051-1(c), Example 3). That example is reproduced with minor changes in the Conference Committee Report for the 2004 Jobs Act (H.R. Conf. Rep. No. 108-755). The report's version is as follows:

Example: Vehicle C consists of a truck chassis on which an oversize body designed to transport and apply liquid agricultural chemicals on farms has been installed. It is capable of transporting a load over the public highway. It is 132 inches in width, which is considerably in excess of standard highway vehicle width. For travel on uneven and soft terrain, it is equipped with oversize wheels with high-flotation tires, and nonstandard axles, brakes, and transmission. It has a special fuel and carburetor air filtration system that enable [sic] it to perform efficiently in an environment of dirt and dust. It is not able to maintain a speed of 25 miles per hour for more than one mile while fully loaded. Because Vehicle C is a self-propelled vehicle capable of transporting a load over the public highway, it would meet the general definition of a highway vehicle. However, its considerable physical characteristics for transporting its load other than over the public highway, when compared with its physical characteristics for transporting the load over the public highway, establish that it is specially designed for the primary function of transporting its load other than over the public highway. Further, the physical characteristics for transporting its load other than over the public highway substantially limit its capability to transport a load over the public highway. Therefore, Vehicle C is an offhighway vehicle and is not treated as a highway vehicle.

The 2004 Jobs Act also adopts the definition of nontransportation trailers and semitrailers contained in the June 2002 proposed regulations (Proposed Reg. § 48.4051-1(a)(2)(ii)). A trailer or semitrailer is not treated as a highway vehicle if it is specially designed to function only as an enclosed stationary shelter used to perform an off-highway function at an off-highway site (Code Sec. 7701(a)(48)(B), as added by the 2004 Jobs Act). A trailer that is capable of functioning only as an office for an off-highway construction operation is cited by the proposed regulations as an example of a vehicle that is not a highway vehicle.

For further information on this subject, consult any of the following CCH reporter explanations:

- Federal Excise Tax Reporter, ETR ¶ 6325.04
- Federal Tax Guide, 2004FTG ¶ 21,120

★ *Effective date.* The provisions are generally effective on the date of enactment of the Act, except with respect to the fuel taxes imposed by Code Secs. 4041, 4042, 4081 and 4091, the provision applies to tax periods beginning after the date of enactment (Act Sec. 852(c) of the American Jobs Creation Act of 2004).

Act Sec. 852(a) of the American Jobs Creation Act of 2004, adding Code Sec. 7701(a)(48); Act Sec. 852(c). Law at ¶ 6355. Committee Report at ¶ 11,320.

¶ 1553
Simplification of Tax on Tires

Background

A graduated excise tax is imposed upon the sale by a manufacturer, producer, or importer of tires of the type used on highway vehicles, made wholly or partially of rubber (Code Sec. 4071). The rates are based on the weight of the tire. Certain tires are not subject to the tax, including tires of extruded tiring with an internal wire fastening agent and recapped tires that were previously taxed (Code Sec. 4073). The tax is scheduled to expire on October 1, 2005.

American Jobs Creation Act Impact

Tires taxed based on load capacity.—The excise tax on tires based on tire weight is replaced with rates based on the load capacity of a tire. The tax is imposed on taxable tires sold by a manufacturer, producer, or importer at the rate of 9.45 cents for each 10 pounds of tire load capacity in excess of 3,500 pounds. The rate of tax for super single or biasply tires is 4.725 cents for each 10 pounds of tire load capacity in excess of 3,500 pounds (Code Sec. 4071(a), as amended by the American Jobs Creation Act of 2004).

> **Comment:** Rather than basing the excise tax on the weight of the tire, the tax will now be based on the tire load capacity that is stamped on the side of highway tires as required by the Department of Transportation. This will simplify administration of the tax because the tire manufacturers and the IRS will no longer have to weigh sample batches of tires.

A taxable tire means any tire of the type used on highway vehicles if wholly or in part made of rubber and marked for highway use pursuant to federal regulations (Code Sec. 4072(a), as added by the 2004 Jobs Act). A super single tire is defined as a tire greater than 13 inches in cross section width and designed to replace two tires in a dual fitment (Code Sec. 4072(e), as added by the 2004 Jobs Act). A biasply tire is defined as a pneumatic tire on which the ply cords that extend to the beads are laid at alternate angles substantially less than 90 degrees to the centerline of the tread (Code Sec. 4072(d), as added by the 2004 Jobs Act).

Any tires sold for exclusive use of the Department of Defense or the Coast Guard are exempt from the excise tax. The former exemption for tires with an internal wire fastening agent was removed.

The Conference Committee Report notes that nothing in these provisions is to be construed to have any effect on the existing rules dealing with recapped and retreaded tires under Reg. § 48.4071-1(d). This regulation provides that no tax is imposed on the recapping or retreading of a tire that was previously taxed, and the conferees intend that regulations implementing the new provisions will not affect this existing regulation (Conference Committee Report, H.R. Conf. Rep. No. 108-755).

For further information on this subject, consult any of the following CCH reporter explanations:

- Federal Excise Tax Reporter, ETR ¶ 8045.01, ¶ 8045.05 and ¶ 8215.02
- Federal Tax Guide, 2004FTG ¶ 21,130

★ *Effective date.* These provisions apply to sales in calendar years beginning more than 30 days after the date of enactment (Act Sec. 869(e)[(f)] of the American Jobs Creation Act of 2004).

Act Sec. 869(a) of the American Jobs Creation Act of 2004, amending Code Sec. 4071(a); Act Sec. 869(b), adding Code Secs. 4072(c) and (d); Act Sec. 869(b)[(c)], redesignating Code Sec. 4072(a)-(d) as Code Sec. 4072(b) -(e) and adding new Code Sec. 4072(a); Act Sec. 869(c)[(d)], amending Code Sec. 4073; Act Sec. 869(d)[(e)], striking Code Sec. 4071(c) and redesignating Code Sec. 4073(e) as Code Sec. 4073(c); Act Sec. 869(e)[(f)]). Law at ¶ 5995, ¶ 6000 and ¶ 6005. Committee Report at ¶ 11,500.

SPORTING GOODS

¶ 1557

Simplification of Excise Tax Imposed on Bows and Arrows

Background

The Code imposes on the sale by a manufacturer, producer or importer of bows with a draw weight of 10 pounds or more, a tax equal to 11 percent of the price for which it was sold. The Code also imposes on the sale by a manufacturer, producer, or importer of any shaft, point, nock, or vane designed for use as part of an arrow that after assembly is (1) over 18 inches long, or (2) designed for use with a taxable bow, a tax equal to 12.4 percent of the price for which it was sold.

Finished arrows are not subject to the excise tax. Because the tax is imposed on the arrow components, foreign manufacturers and importers of arrows avoid the 12.4-percent excise tax paid by domestic manufacturers. Thus, arrows assembled outside the United States have a price advantage over domestically manufactured arrows. Accessories for taxable bows and certain quivers for use with arrows over 18 inches long, or designed to be used with a taxable bow, are also subject to an 11-percent excise tax.

American Jobs Creation Act Impact

Bows and archery equipment.—The draw weight for a taxable bow is increased from 10 pounds or more to a peak draw weight of 30 pounds or more. An 11-percent excise tax is imposed on the sale by a manufacturer, producer, or importer of any bow with a peak draw weight of 30 pounds or more (Code Sec. 4161(b)(1), as amended by the American Jobs Creation Act of 2004). The lower draw weight bows used for instructional purposes are no longer subject to the excise tax. The 11-percent excise tax continues to apply to archery equipment (parts and accessories for bows), and now includes broadheads (a type of arrow point).

Arrows. An excise tax is imposed on the sale by a manufacturer, producer, or importer of any arrow, a tax equal to 12 percent of the price for which it was sold (Code Sec. 4161(b)(3)(A), as added by the 2004 Jobs Act). The existing 12.4-percent excise tax on arrow components remains the same and does not apply to broadheads since they are taxed as archery equipment. An arrow is defined, for purposes of the arrow tax, as any shaft (described in Code Sec. 4161(b)(2)) to which additional components are attached (Code Sec. 4161(b)(3)(C), as added by the 2004 Jobs Act).

The manufacturer, producer or importer that sells finished arrows composed of shafts or arrow components previously taxed under Code Sec. 4161(b)(1) or (b)(2) is permitted to reduce the tax due on the finished arrows in lieu of claiming a refund of the tax paid on the components. For any arrow composed of a shaft or other component upon which tax was imposed, the amount of the arrow tax is equal to the excess of (1) the arrow tax that would have been imposed but for the exception, over (2) the amount of tax paid with respect to such components (Code Sec. 4161(b)(3)(B), as added by the 2004 Jobs Act).

For further information on this subject, consult any of the following CCH reporter explanations:

- Federal Excise Tax Reporter, ETR ¶ 13,105.05
- Federal Tax Guide, 2004FTG ¶ 21,725

★ *Effective date.* The provisions apply to articles sold by the manufacturer, producer, or importer after the date which is 30 days after the date of enactment (Act Sec. 332(d) of the American Jobs Creation Act of 2004).

Act Sec. 332(a) of the American Jobs Creation Act of 2004, amending Code Sec. 4161(b)(1); Act Sec. 332(b), redesignating Code Sec. 4161(b)(3) as Code Sec. 4161(b)(4) and adding a new Code Sec. 4161(b)(3); Act Sec. 332(c), amending Code Sec. 4161(b)(2); Act Sec. 332(d). Law at ¶ 6065. Committee Report at ¶ 10,470.

¶ 1559

Reduction of Excise Tax on Fishing Tackle Boxes

A 10-percent manufacturer's excise tax applies to certain sport fishing equipment, including fishing tackle boxes. The excise tax imposed on sport fishing equipment is deposited into the Sport Fishing Account of the Aquatic Resources Trust Fund. Fund monies are spent to support federal-state sport fishing enhancement and safety programs.

American Jobs Creation Act Impact

Excise tax rate reduced.—The excise tax imposed on the sale of fishing tackle boxes by the manufacturer, producer or importer is reduced from 10 to three percent (Code Sec. 4161(a), as amended by the American Jobs Creation Act of 2004).

For further information on this subject, consult any of the following CCH reporter explanations:

- Federal Excise Tax Reporter, ETR ¶ 13,105.02
- Federal Tax Guide, 2004FTG ¶ 21,720

★ *Effective date.* This provision applies to articles sold by the manufacturer, producer or importer after December 31, 2004 (Act Sec. 333(b) of the American Jobs Creation Act of 2004).

Act Sec. 333(a) of the American Jobs Creation Act of 2004, amending Code Sec. 4161(a); Act Sec. 333(b). Law at ¶ 6065. Committee Report at ¶ 10,480.

¶ 1561

Repeal of Excise Tax on Sonar Devices Suitable for Finding Fish

Background _____

A three-percent excise tax is imposed on the sale, by a manufacturer, producer or importer, of sonar devices suitable for finding fish. The current exemption from the three-percent tax for certain sonar devices has the effect of exempting almost all devices currently on the market, except those utilizing light-emitting diode (LED) technology.

American Jobs Creation Act Impact

Excise tax on sonar fish-finding devices repealed. — The three-percent excise tax that applied to the sale of sonar devices suitable for finding fish is repealed (Code Sec. 4162(a), as amended by the American Jobs Creation Act of 2004).

For further information on this subject, consult any of the following CCH reporter explanations:

- Federal Excise Tax Reporter, ETR ¶ 13,275.07
- Federal Tax Guide, 2004FTG ¶ 21,720

★ *Effective date.* The provision applies to articles sold by the manufacturer, producer, or importer after December 31, 2004 (Act Sec. 334(c) of the American Jobs Creation Act of 2004).

Act Sec. 334(a) of the American Jobs Creation Act of 2004, amending Code Sec. 4162(a); Act Sec. 334(b), striking Code Sec. 4162(b); Act Sec. 334(c). Law at ¶ 6070. Committee Report at ¶ 10,490.

VACCINES

¶ 1565

Vaccines Against Hepatitis A and Influenza Now Taxable

Background _____

To provide funding for the Vaccine Trust Fund under the National Vaccine Injury Compensation Program, a 75-cents-per-dose manufacturer's excise tax is imposed on the sale of the following vaccines routinely recommended for administration to

Background _____

children: diphtheria, pertussis, tetanus, measles, mumps, rubella, polio, haemophilus influenza type B (HIB), hepatitis B, chicken pox, rotavirus gastroenteritis, and streptococcus pneumoniae. Vaccines containing more than one taxable vaccine component are taxed at a rate of 75 cents multiplied by the number of components.

The National Vaccine Injury Compensation Program is a no-fault federal insurance system created to compensate individuals who are injured or die due to the administration of these vaccines. Individuals who suffer injuries following the administration of taxable vaccines after September 30, 1988, must pursue their claims under the compensation program before bringing civil tort actions under State law.

American Jobs Creation Act Impact

Addition of vaccines to taxable list.—Any vaccine against hepatitis A and any trivalent vaccine against influenza is added to the list of taxable vaccines (Code Sec. 4132(a)(1), as amended by the American Jobs Creation Act of 2004).

For further information on this subject, consult any of the following CCH reporter explanations:

- Federal Excise Tax Reporter, ETR ¶ 12,575.01
- Federal Tax Guide, 2004FTG ¶ 21,710

★ *Effective date.* With respect to the addition of any hepatitis A vaccine, the amendments apply to sales and uses on or after the first day of the first month which begins more than four weeks after the date of enactment (Act Sec. 889(b)(1) of the American Jobs Creation Act of 2004).

With respect to the addition of any trivalent vaccine against influenza, the amendment applies to sales and uses on or after the later of: the first day of the first month which begins more than four weeks after the date of enactment, or the date on which the Secretary of Health and Human Services lists any vaccine against influenza for purposes of compensation for any vaccine-related injury or death through the Vaccine Injury Compensation Trust Fund (Act Sec. 890(b)(1) of the 2004 Jobs Act).

Deliveries. With respect to any hepatitis A vaccine, for purposes of the effective date and Code Sec. 4131, in the case of sales on or before the effective date for which delivery is made after that date, the delivery date is considered the sale date (Act Sec. 889(b)(2) of the 2004 Jobs Act). With respect to any trivalent vaccine against influenza, for purposes of the effective date and Code Sec. 4131, in the case of sales on or before the effective date for which delivery is made after that date, the delivery date is considered the sale date (Act Sec. 890(b)(2) of the 2004 Jobs Act).

Act Sec. 889(a) and Act Sec. 890(a) of the American Jobs Creation Act of 2004, amending Code Sec. 4132(a)(1); Act Sec. 889(b); Act Sec. 890(b). Law at ¶ 6060. Committee Report at ¶ 11,610 and ¶ 11,620.

OCCUPATIONAL TAXES ON ALCOHOL

¶ 1569

Suspension of Occupational Taxes on Producers and Marketers of Alcoholic Beverages

Background _____

Federal liquor taxes are both regulatory and revenue producing. They are of two classes: (1) excise taxes on distilled spirits, wines and fermented malt liquors (beer)

Background

(Code Secs. 5001–5067), and (2) so-called special taxes (occupational taxes) imposed on certain manufacturers and on retail and wholesale dealers (Code Secs. 5081–5148). The special occupational taxes are due on July 1 of each year.

Producers of distilled spirits and wines and brewers must pay a special occupational tax of $1,000 per year, per premises (Code Secs. 5081 and 5091). A reduced tax rate of $500 is imposed on small proprietors. Wholesale dealers of liquors, wines, or beer are required to pay a special occupational tax of $500 per year (Code Sec. 5111), and retail dealers are required to pay $250 per year (Code Sec. 5121).

A manufacturer who has used distilled spirits for nonbeverage purposes and has paid the special tax of $500 on such use is eligible for a refund, referred to as a drawback (Code Sec. 5131).

Wholesale or retail dealers in liquors, wine or beer are required to keep records of their transactions (Code Secs. 5114 and 5124). Industrial users of distilled spirits and proprietors of distilled spirits plants are also subject to recordkeeping requirements (Code Secs. 5207 and 5275). There are penalties for failing to comply with the recordkeeping requirements (Code Sec. 5603).

A dealer may only purchase its liquor stock intended for resale from:

(1) a wholesale dealer in liquors who has paid the special occupational tax to cover the place where the purchase is made;

(2) a wholesale dealer who is exempt, at the place where the purchase is made, from payment of the tax under any provision of Chapter 51 of the Code; or

(3) a person who is not required to pay special occupational tax as a wholesale dealer in liquors.

American Jobs Creation Act Impact

Special occupational taxes suspended.—The new law suspends for a three-year period the special occupational taxes on producers and marketers of alcoholic beverages under Code Secs. 5081, 5091, 5111, 5121 and 5131 (Code Sec. 5148(a), as added by American Jobs Creation Act of 2004). The suspension period begins on July 1, 2005, and ends on June 30, 2008 (Code Sec. 5148(b), as added by the 2004 Jobs Act).

During the suspension period, the recordkeeping and registration requirements and the related penalties continue to apply to persons engaged in or carrying on a trade or business covered by the occupational taxes. During the suspension period, except as provided by regulations, it is unlawful for any dealer to purchase distilled spirits for resale from any person other than a wholesale dealer in liquors who is subject to the recordkeeping requirements under Code Sec. 5114 (Code Sec. 5117(d), as added by the 2004 Jobs Act). However, the current exception that allows limited retail dealers to purchase distilled spirits for resale from a retail dealer in liquor continues to apply under Code Sec. 5117(b).

For further information on this subject, consult the following CCH reporter explanation:

- Federal Tax Guide, 2004FTG ¶ 21,740

★ *Effective date.* The provision takes effect on the date of enactment, and the three-year suspension period is July 1, 2005, through June 30, 2008 (Act Sec. 246(d) of the American Jobs Creation Act of 2004).

Act Sec. 246(a) of the American Jobs Creation Act of 2004, redesignating Code Sec. 5148 as Code Sec. 5149 and adding new Code Sec. 5148; Act Sec. 246(b), adding Code Sec. 5117(d); Act Sec. 246(d). Law at ¶6110, ¶6115 and ¶6120. Committee Report at ¶10,270.

APPROPRIATIONS

¶1573

Penalties Revenue Dedicated to Highway Trust Fund

Background

The Highway Trust Fund is funded by excise taxes on heavy trucks and trailers, on tires, gasoline, diesel fuels, special motor fuels and kerosene, and on the use of certain vehicles (Code Sec. 9503(b)(1)). In addition, interest on, and proceeds from the sale or redemption of, obligations held by the Fund are credited to the Fund (Code Sec. 9602(b)(3)).

However, no amounts from penalties related to the excise taxes supporting the Highway Trust Fund are dedicated to the Fund.

American Jobs Creation Act Impact

Revenues from certain penalties dedicated to Highway Trust Fund.—Amounts equivalent to the penalties paid under the following provisions are dedicated to the Highway Trust Fund (Code Sec. 9503(b)(5), as added by the American Jobs Creation Act of 2004):

(1) the penalty for improper use of dyed fuel (Code Sec. 6715, as amended by the 2004 Jobs Act);

(2) the penalty for tampering with or failing to maintain security requirements for mechanical dye injection systems (Code Sec. 6715A, as added by the 2004 Jobs Act);

(3) the penalty for the refusal of entry (Code Sec. 6717, as added by the 2004 Jobs Act);

(4) the penalty for failing to display tax registration on vessels (Code Sec. 6718, as added by the 2004 Jobs Act);

(5) the assessable penalty for failing to register under Code Sec. 4101 (Code Sec. 6719, as added by the 2004 Jobs Act);

(6) the penalty for failing to report required information under Code Sec. 4101 (Code Sec. 6725, as added by the 2004 Jobs Act);

(7) the criminal penalty for failing to register under Code Sec. 4101 (Code Sec. 7232, as amended by the 2004 Jobs Act); and

(8) the penalty related to failing to register under Code Sec. 4101 (Code Sec. 7272, as amended by the 2004 Jobs Act).

For further information on this subject, consult the following CCH reporter explanation:

- Federal Tax Guide, 2004FTG ¶21,120

★ *Effective date.* The provision applies to penalties assessed on or after the date of enactment (Act Sec. 868(c) of the American Jobs Creation Act of 2004).

Act Sec. 868(a) of the American Jobs Creation Act of 2004, amending Code Sec. 9503(b)(5) and (6); Act Sec. 868(c). Law at ¶6385. Committee Report at ¶11,490.

Chapter 16

Procedure and Administration

¶ 1605

Qualified Tax Collection Contracts

Background

In 1996 and 1997, the IRS experimented with the use of private debt collection (PDC) agencies. The PDCs were used to help the IRS locate and contact taxpayers and to suggest payment options. However, once a taxpayer agreed to pay, the case was transferred back to the IRS since only IRS employees were permitted to collect the taxes. The PDCs were paid a flat fee for their services and, therefore, the amount ultimately collected by the IRS was not taken into account in the payment structure. This resulted in the IRS paying out in collection fees as much as was collected. This pilot program was discontinued because of the disappointing results, which were attributed to the limitations on the scope of work the PDCs were permitted to do, the number and type of cases referred, and the ability of the IRS's computer system to identify, select, and transmit collection cases to the PDCs.

American Jobs Creation Act Impact

Contracts authorized with private debt collection agencies.—This provision allows the IRS, like other federal agencies, to use private debt collection (PDC) agencies to recover federal debts while providing safeguards for taxpayers' rights and privacy. PDCs may be used to locate and contact taxpayers owing outstanding tax liabilities of any type and to arrange payment of those taxes. In order to refer a taxpayer's account, the IRS must have made an assessment pursuant to Code Sec. 6201.

Comment: Since the amount reported as due on the taxpayer's tax return is self-assessed, taxpayers who have filed a return showing a balance due, but who have failed to pay that balance, are likely to have collection efforts transferred to a PDC.

PDCs are authorized to offer taxpayers who cannot pay in full an installment agreement providing for full payment of the taxes over a five-year period. If the taxpayer is unable to pay the outstanding tax liability in full over a five-year period, the PDC would obtain specific financial information from the taxpayer and provide that information to the IRS for further processing.

In order to protect taxpayers, there are several restrictions on a PDC's operations. First, provisions of the Fair Debt Collection Practices Act apply to the PDCs. Second, taxpayer protections applicable to the IRS and its employees are also specifically applicable to the PDCs. Third, a PDC may not use subcontractors to contact taxpayers, provide quality assurance services, or compose debt collection notices, and the IRS must approve any other service provided by a subcontractor. Fourth, PDCs are required to inform every taxpayer contacted of the availability of assistance from the Taxpayer Advocate, whose orders would apply to the PDC in the same manner and to the same extent as to the IRS. Finally, the IRS must process all payments.

The provision creates a revolving fund from the amounts collected by the PDCs from which the PDCs will be paid, and payment of fees for all services is capped at 25 percent of the amount collected under a tax collection contract. In addition, the IRS is allowed to keep up to 25 percent of amounts collected by a PDC for collection enforcement activities. The provision also absolves the IRS from liability for damages for the acts or omissions of persons performing services under a qualified tax collection contract. However, the PDCs will be liable for unauthorized collection activities in the same manner and to the same extent as the IRS and its employees. Additionally, if the Secretary of the Treasury determines that a PDC or an individual has engaged in unauthorized collection activities, they can be barred form performing services under any qualified tax collection contract.

> **Comment:** Although allowing the IRS to "outsource" tax debt collection will require the IRS to disclose confidential taxpayer information, Code Sec. 6103 has not been amended because Code Sec. 6103(n) permits the disclosure of taxpayer information for "the providing of other services . . . for purposes of tax administration."

PRACTICAL ANALYSIS. George Jones of CCH Tax and Accounting, Washington, D.C., points out that the role of the tax advisor in running interference for the taxpayer in the case of third-party tax collectors is not made entirely clear under the new law. The new law leaves unanswered what obligation a third-party qualified tax collector has to notify a properly designated representative of the taxpayer under a filed Form 2848, Power of Attorney and Declaration of Representative. Reg. § 601.506, Statement of Procedural Rules, requires that any notice or other written communication given to a taxpayer in any matter before the IRS must be given to the taxpayer and, unless restricted by the taxpayer, to the taxpayer's representative. Telephone calls by the third-party collector apparently are not covered by this rule. And while this regulation requires notice, it further provides that failure to give notice or other written communication to the recognized representative of a taxpayer will not affect the validity of any notice or other written communication delivered to a taxpayer.

Reg. § 601.506(b), on the other hand, provides that if a representative fails to furnish, after repeated request, nonprivileged information necessary to an examination, collection or investigation, the IRS may contact the taxpayer directly for the information. This latter rule implies that the IRS first must contact the representative. The new law imposes upon the third-party collector the same rules of conduct required of IRS employees.

To complicate matters, the new law also makes private debt collectors answerable to The Fair Debt Collection Practices Act. Section 805 of that Act states that without prior written consent, a debt collector is not allowed to communicate or otherwise deal with the consumer (taxpayer) if the collector knows the consumer is represented by an attorney with respect to such debt and has knowledge of, or can readily ascertain, the attorney's name and address and the attorney responds within a reasonable time to communications. Unfortunately, this rule muddles things further in the tax collection area since it does not answer the extent to which notice must be given to a nonattorney licensed to practice before the IRS who is representing the taxpayer.

In the end, the IRS most likely will find itself facing the type of collection matter allowed to be outsourced under the new law only in those cases in which the taxpayer remains unresponsive to its correspondence. If the representative takes the initiative in following up promptly with the IRS on any matter that may trigger collection, the inclination of the IRS to give the matter to an outside contactor hopefully will be removed and the issues on what notification must be given under the new third-party collection provisions will be avoided entirely.

For further information on this subject, consult any of the following CCH reporter explanations:

- Standard Federal Tax Reporter, 2004FED ¶38,079F.01, ¶38,089.01 and ¶43,312.01
- Federal Tax Service, FTS §P:25.20
- Federal Tax Guide, 2004FTG ¶28,829

★ *Effective date.* The provision is effective on the date of enactment (Act Sec. 881(f) of the American Jobs Creation Act of 2004).

Act Sec. 881(a)(1) of the American Jobs Creation Act of 2004, adding Code Sec. 6306; Act Sec. 881(a)(2)(A), amending Code Sec. 7809(a); Act Sec. 881(b)(1), adding Code Sec. 7433A; Act. Sec. 881(c), adding Code Sec. 7811(g); Act Sec. 881(d), amending Act Sec. 1203 of the IRS Restructuring and Reform Act of 1998 (P.L. 105-206); Act Sec. 881(e); Act. Sec. 881(f). Law at ¶6190, ¶6340, ¶6365, ¶6370 and ¶7135. Committee Report at ¶11,530.

¶ 1610

Part Pay Agreements Permitted

Background

When a taxpayer cannot pay the full amount of tax due, the IRS has the authority to enter into a written agreement with the taxpayer that allows the tax liability to be paid in monthly installments (Code Sec. 6159(a) and Reg. §301.6159-1(a)). The taxpayer makes the request for installment payments on Form 9465 (Installment Agreement Request). In most situations, the IRS has complete authority to accept or reject the taxpayer's request. However, if certain conditions are met, the IRS is *required* to grant the taxpayer's request to make installment payments (see "Required acceptance of installment offer," below). As a general rule, the taxpayer may have up to 60 months in which to fully pay the liability (Form 9465, Instructions for Installment Agreement Request). However, in some situations, the time period for an individual's full payment of the liability may not exceed 36 months (see "Required acceptance of installment offer," below).

Background

Required acceptance of installment offer. An individual's offer of an installment agreement pertaining to an income tax liability must be accepted by the IRS when the tax due is not more than $10,000 and all three of the following requirements are satisfied (Code Sec. 6159(c)):

(1) during the past five tax years, the individual (and the individual's spouse, in the case of a joint tax liability) timely filed all income tax returns, paid any income tax due, and did not enter into an installment agreement for the payment of income tax;

(2) the IRS determines that the individual cannot pay the tax owed in full when it is due and the individual provides the IRS with any information that it needs to make the determination; and

(3) the individual agrees to pay the full amount of the tax liability within three years and to comply with the tax laws while the agreement is in effect.

American Jobs Creation Act Impact

Part payment allowed in most situations.—The IRS is now authorized, in most situations, to enter into a partial payment agreement with a delinquent taxpayer. (However, see "Full payment still required in some situations," below, for an explanation of when partial payment agreements are not permissible.) Under the new rule, the IRS is no longer restricted to seeking a payment agreement that will "satisfy the liability." Instead, the goal of the agreement is to have the taxpayer "make payments" in "full or partial" satisfaction of the liability (Code Sec. 6159(a), as amended by the American Jobs Creation Act of 2004).

> **Comment:** A House Committee Report (H.R. Rep. No. 108-548) noted that, according to figures supplied by the Treasury Department, at the end of fiscal year 2003, the IRS had not pursued 2.25 million cases, representing more than $16.5 billion in delinquent taxes. By enacting this "part pay" provision, it is clear that Congress is seeking to provide the IRS with a new collection tool that will reduce the amount of outstanding delinquent taxes. The new provision is only effective for agreements entered into on or after the date the 2004 Jobs Act is signed into law. However, this effective date does not prevent the IRS from contacting taxpayers involved in prior collection cases that have been written off as uncollectible. The goal of such contacts will be to secure partial payment agreements and thereby reduce the amount of outstanding delinquent taxes.

Mandatory review. When the IRS enters into a partial payment agreement with a taxpayer, the agreement must be reviewed by the IRS *at least* every two years (Code Sec. 6159(d), as added by the 2004 Jobs Act). Although the legislation does not spell out the details of the IRS review, it appears reasonable to assume that the IRS will be looking at those factors that would enable the taxpayer to pay the liability in full, or that would support an increase in the amount of the payments under a revised part payment agreement. On the other hand, if the review finds that the taxpayer's financial situation has deteriorated, the IRS would then be in a position to suspend collection activity instead of wasting time and manpower on further fruitless collection efforts.

> **Planning Note:** A *part payment agreement* should not be confused with an *offer in compromise.* An offer in compromise is a contractual agreement between the IRS and a taxpayer under which the taxpayer agrees to pay a specified amount in full settlement of assessed tax liabilities, including interest and most penalties (Code Sec. 7122(a)). On the other hand, a part payment agreement does

not provide a method by which the taxpayer's liability is compromised for a lesser amount. Currently, the compromise process is used by taxpayers who are experiencing financial difficulties. The offer in compromise provides a means by which they can have their tax liability reduced and settled. It appears that the new part payment provision will allow financially strapped taxpayers to achieve almost the same goal without having to go through the more rigorous process of making an offer in compromise.

Also, a *part payment agreement* should not be confused with a *closing agreement*. A closing agreement is a written agreement between the IRS and a taxpayer pertaining to the taxpayer's total tax liability or to specific issues affecting that liability for any specified tax period (Code Sec. 7121(a)). Closing agreements are generally used when there appears to be an advantage in having a tax matter permanently and conclusively closed, or when the taxpayer shows good and sufficient reasons for desiring the agreement and the IRS determines that no disadvantage to the government will result. Closing agreements are final, conclusive, and binding upon both parties. They cannot be reopened or modified except upon a showing of fraud or malfeasance or the misrepresentation of a material fact (Code Sec. 7121(b)).

Full payment still required in some situations. As explained above (see, "Required acceptance of installment offer"), the IRS has been required to accept an individual's offer to make installment payments for the full payment of income taxes if certain conditions are satisfied (e.g., the total tax liability does not exceed $10,000 and full payment is made within three years) (Code Sec. 6159(c)(1) through Code Sec. 6159(c)(5)). Even under the new law, full payment is still required and the part payment option does *not* apply if full payment can be made in three years (Code Sec. 6159(c), first paragraph, as amended by the 2004 Jobs Act).

Comment: The amendment appears to have been drafted for the purpose of reinforcing the "full-payment-within-three-years" requirement that is already imposed by Code Sec. 6159(c)(4). This amendment also helps highlight the fact that, while part payment agreements may be allowed, when it comes to an individual's income tax liability, if certain requirements are satisfied, the IRS is only required to enter into the agreement if *full payment* is the goal of the agreement.

For further information on this subject, consult any of the following CCH reporter explanations:

- Standard Federal Tax Reporter, 2004FED ¶ 37,181.01 and ¶ 37,181.022

- Federal Tax Service, FTS § P:25.66[3]

- Federal Tax Guide, 2004FTG ¶ 22,639 and ¶ 28,411

- Federal Estate and Gift Tax Reporter, FEGT ¶ 15,193.01 and ¶ 15,193.05

★ *Effective date.* These provisions apply to payment agreements entered into on or after the date of enactment (Act Sec. 843(c) of the American Jobs Creation Act of 2004).

Act Sec. 843(a)(1) of the American Jobs Creation Act of 2004, amending Code Sec. 6159(a); Act Sec. 843(a)(2), amending Code Sec. 6159(c); Act Sec. 843(b), redesignating Code Secs. 6159(d) and (e), respectively, as Code Sec. 6159(e) and Code Sec. 6159(f), and adding a new Code Sec. 6159(d); Act Sec. 843(c). Law at ¶ 6180. Committee Report at ¶ 11,260.

¶ 1615

Suspension of Interest on Underpayments

Background _____

A taxpayer currently or potentially facing a tax liability dispute with the IRS has two options to mitigate the interest charges that will be due if the dispute is lost. The interest liability can be significant, particularly in the case of a protracted dispute involving a large disputed tax liability.

> **Comment:** The interest rate on tax underpayments is generally equal to the federal short-term rate plus three percentage points and is imposed from the original due date of the return to the date of payment (Code Sec. 6621). For the calendar quarter beginning October 1, 2004, the underpayment rate is five percent (seven percent for corporate underpayments in excess of $100,000) (Rev. Rul. 2004-92, I.R.B. 2004-37). The interest is compounded daily (Code Sec. 6622).

In order to avoid the accrual of underpayment interest, a taxpayer may:

(1) pay the disputed amount (i.e., pay the tax) and file a claim for refund; or

(2) make a deposit in the nature of a cash bond pursuant to the procedures of Rev. Proc. 84-58, 1984-2 CB 501.

Each of these choices has significant downsides. The first option prevents a taxpayer from bringing suit in the Tax Court, which could be a more favorable forum. Further, once the disputed amount is paid, it generally cannot be recovered by the taxpayer on demand. Instead, the taxpayer must await final determination of its tax liability. Moreover, even if the determination is in the taxpayer's favor, the overpaid amount and interest payable on it may be used to offset other liabilities of the taxpayer.

Although a payment in the nature of a cash bond will not bar access to the Tax Court and will stop the accrual of interest on an amount of underpayment equal to the deposit if the taxpayer loses its dispute, no interest is earned on the deposit if the taxpayer wins its dispute. In addition, if a taxpayer withdraws its deposit prior to a final determination and a deficiency is later determined, the taxpayer will still owe underpayment interest on the portion of the underpayment period that the cash was on deposit. No credit is received for the period that the funds were held as a deposit. In addition, the cash bond will not be returned if the IRS assesses a tax liability, determines that collection of the tax is in jeopardy, or determines that the cash bond should be applied against another tax liability.

American Jobs Creation Act Impact

Deposits may be made to suspend interest on potential underpayments.—The new law allows a taxpayer to make a cash deposit with the IRS for future application against an underpayment of income, gift, estate, or generation-skipping tax which has not been assessed at the time of the deposit. Deposits may also be made for future application against underpayments of excise taxes imposed by Internal Revenue Code Chapters 41 (Public Charities), 42 (Private Foundations, Black Lung Benefit Trusts, Section 501(c)(3) organizations, Excess Benefit Transactions), 43 (Pension Plans), or 44 (Qualified Investment Entities) (Code Sec. 6603, as added by the American Jobs Creation Act of 2004).

To the extent that a deposit is used by the IRS to pay a tax liability, the tax is treated as paid when the deposit is made and no interest underpayment is imposed

(Code Sec. 6603(b), as added by the 2004 Jobs Act). Furthermore, if the dispute is resolved in favor of the taxpayer or the taxpayer withdraws the deposited money before resolution of the dispute, interest is payable on the deposit at the federal short-term rate (Code Sec. 6603(d), as added by the 2004 Jobs Act).

Example: John Jacobs, a calendar-year taxpayer, deposits $50,000 on June 15, 2005, with respect to his 2004 income tax return. On July 1, 2007, the IRS and the taxpayer agree that Jacobs underpaid his 2004 tax liability by $60,000. The $50,000 deposit is applied toward the $60,000 underpayment and Jacobs pays the remaining $10,000 of the underpayment on that date. Jacobs will owe underpayment interest on $10,000 from the due date of the 2004 return (April 15, 2005) through July 1, 2007. He will owe underpayment interest on $50,000 from the due date of the original return (April 15, 2005) to June 15, 2005, the date that the $50,000 was deposited.

Caution Note: In order to stop the accrual of interest on both underpaid tax and interest that has accrued up to the time of a deposit, a taxpayer must make a deposit that is sufficient to cover both the tax and the accrued interest as of the date of the deposit. Under the compounding rules, interest will accrue on accrued interest, even if the underlying tax has been paid.

The IRS is required to return any amount of a deposit that a taxpayer requests in writing unless it determines that the collection of tax is in jeopardy (Code Sec. 6603(c), as added by the 2004 Jobs Act). A taxpayer may request the withdrawal of any amount of the deposit at any time.

Comment: Apparently, a taxpayer will need to make a formal written request to obtain the return of a deposit even if the taxpayer has won its tax dispute in a final determination. The law contains no specific requirement for the automatic return of the deposit in such a situation.

Caution Note: If a taxpayer does not request the return of a deposit, no interest will be earned on the deposit for any period during which there is no disputable tax liability.

Interest payable on deposits. A taxpayer is entitled to receive interest on a returned deposit at the federal short-term rate determined under Code Sec. 6621(b), compounded daily, if the deposit was made with respect to a "disputable tax." Interest is payable only for the period that the tax was disputable (Code Sec. 6603(d)(1) and (4), as added by the 2004 Jobs Act).

Comment: A taxpayer who withdraws a deposit prior to the resolution of a tax dispute will be entitled to interest for the period of the deposit that the tax was disputable. In contrast, no interest is payable on a Rev. Proc. 84-58 deposit in the nature of a cash bond whether or not it is withdrawn prior to resolution of the disputed liability.

Caution Note: The interest payable on a section 6603 deposit is limited to the federal short-term rate as determined under Code Sec. 6621(b), compounded daily. For example, for the calendar quarter beginning in October 2004, the federal short-term rate based on daily compounding is two percent (Rev. Rul. 2004-92, I.R.B. 2004-37). The overpayment rate, which can be significantly higher, is not applicable. For noncorporate taxpayers, the interest rate on overpayments is equal to the federal short-term rate plus three percentage points. For corporate taxpayers, the overpayment rate is the federal short-term rate plus two percentage points (0.5 percentage points if the overpayment exceeds $10,000) (Code Sec. 6621). These interest rate increases do not apply to section 6603 deposits.

Planning Note: With the exception of corporate overpayments that exceeds $10,000, the federal short-term interest rate payable on returned section 6603 deposits is significantly less than the overpayment rate in the current interest rate climate. Taxpayers should have no trouble safely achieving a rate of return in excess of the federal short-term rate that is payable on section 6603 deposits. However, it could be considerably more difficult to find a safe investment that pays a rate equivalent to the interest underpayment rate which can be avoided by making a section 6603 deposit. This is particularly true in the case of a corporation with a dispute involving an underpayment in excess of $100,000. As indicated previously, the underpayment rate in such a case is the federal short-term rate plus five percentage points (e.g., seven percent for the calendar quarter beginning in October 2004).

Disputable tax defined. A disputable tax is the amount of tax specified by the taxpayer at the time of the deposit as the taxpayer's reasonable estimate of the maximum amount of tax attributable to "disputable items" (Code Sec. 6603(d)(2), as added by the 2004 Jobs Act).

A disputable item is any item of income, gain, loss, deduction, or credit for which a taxpayer:

(1) has a reasonable basis for the treatment used on its return, and

(2) reasonably believes that the IRS also has a reasonable basis for disallowing the taxpayer's treatment of such item (Code Sec. 6603(d)(3)(A), as added by the 2004 Jobs Act).

Example: XYZ Corporation, which is located within the Second Circuit Court of Appeals' jurisdiction, takes a position on its 2004 return with respect to a deduction which is supported by a decision of the First Circuit but is contrary to a decision of the Seventh Circuit. The deduction is a disputable item. XYZ will be entitled to an interest payment with respect to a section 6603 deposit that is withdrawn prior to a final determination or which is withdrawn after a final determination in its favor.

All items included in a 30-day letter are considered "disputable" (Code Sec. 6603(d)(2)(B), as added by the 2004 Jobs Act).

A 30-day letter is the first letter of a proposed deficiency that allows a taxpayer the opportunity for administrative review in the IRS Office of Appeals (Code Sec. 6603(d)(3)(B), as added by the 2004 Jobs Act).

Comment: The rule treating all items set forth in a 30-day letter as disputable is intended as a safe harbor. Once a 30-day letter has been issued, the disputable amount cannot be less than the amount of the deficiency shown in the 30-day letter.

Comment: The IRS is required to issue regulations which prescribe rules similar to Code Sec. 6611(b)(2) (Code Sec. 6603(d)(1), as added by the 2004 Jobs Act). Code Sec. 6611(b) provides for the payment of interest on an overpayment from the date of the overpayment to a date that precedes the refund check by no more than 30 days. Thus, in determining the amount of interest payable to a taxpayer with respect to a returned section 6603 deposit, the IRS must pay interest from the date of the deposit to a date no more than 30 days preceding the date of the check paying the withdrawn deposit.

Example: John Jacobs received a 30-day letter showing a $30,000 deficiency for the 2003 tax year. Jacobs makes a $30,000 Code Sec. 6603 deposit on May 15, 2005. On April 15, 2006, the IRS and Jacobs agree that the actual underpayment is $20,000. Jacobs requests a return of the $10,000 excess deposit on that date. Jacobs will owe underpayment interest on $20,000 from April 15, 2004 (due date of 2003 return) to May 15, 2005 (the date of the $30,000 deposit). Jacobs is entitled to receive interest (determined at the short-term applicable federal rate) on $10,000 from May 15, 2005, to a date not more than 30 days preceding the date of the check repaying the $10,000 excess deposit.

Comment: According to the Conference Committee Report (H.R. Conf. Rep. No. 108-755), a deposit is not treated as a tax overpayment for purposes of the interest netting provisions of Code Sec. 6621(d). Thus, withdrawal of a deposit will not establish a period for which interest was allowable at the short-term applicable federal rate for the purpose of establishing a net zero interest rate on a similar amount of underpayment for the same period. Also, interest earned on a withdrawn deposit is included in a taxpayer's income.

Comment: The Joint Committee on Taxation recommended enactment of a provision similar to new Code Sec. 6603 in its 1999 study of penalties and interest (JCT Study of Present-Law Penalty and Interest Provisions (JCS-3-99)). Under that proposal, taxpayers would make deposits into an interest bearing "dispute reserve account" within the U.S. Treasury. The account could not be maintained beyond the period for which an underpayment of tax could be determined for the year the account was established. It appears that under the enacted provision, deposits may be maintained even if there is no current dispute with the IRS. However, no interest would be paid in the absence of a disputable tax.

Use of deposits. If a taxpayer makes multiple deposits, they are considered used for the payment of a tax in the order of the deposits unless a taxpayer specifies otherwise (Code Sec. 6603(e)(1), as added by the 2004 Jobs Act).

Return of deposits. If a taxpayer makes multiple deposits, deposits are considered returned on a last-in, first-out (LIFO) basis (Code Sec. 6603(e)(2), as added by the 2004 Jobs Act).

Example: XYZ Corporation makes a $10,000 section 6603 deposit on January 1, 2005, and a $7,000 section 6603 deposit on July 1, 2005. It withdraws $7,000 on January 1, 2006. Under the LIFO rule, XYZ is treated as having withdrawn the July 1, 2005, deposit and is entitled to interest at the federal short-term rate on $7,000 from July 1, 2005, through December 31, 2005. If XYZ loses its tax dispute, it is not liable for an interest underpayment charge (federal short-term rate plus 5%) with respect to $10,000 of its underpayment for the period beginning January 1, 2005, to the date of payment.

Planning Note: A section 6603 deposit is not permissible with respect to a tax that has been assessed (Code Sec. 6603(a), as added by the 2004 Jobs Act). Thus, the deposit must be made prior to the issuance of a notice of deficiency. Once a notice of deficiency has been issued, however, a taxpayer may stop an interest charge on the potential tax underpayment by paying the assessment. The payment of the assessment after a notice of deficiency has been issued does not preclude the taxpayer from obtaining Tax Court jurisdiction (Reg. § 301.6213-1(b)(3)). Of course, the taxpayer may also pay the assessment and file a claim for refund in a U.S. District Court or the U.S. Court of Federal Claims.

Planning Note: If a taxpayer has made a section 6603 deposit prior to an assessment and decides to pay the assessment prior to proceeding to court, the section 6603 deposit should be withdrawn since it is no longer necessary to stop the accrual of interest on the potential underpayment. Furthermore, the payment of an assessment has a distinct advantage in that the overpayment rate will apply if the taxpayer wins its case. The overpayment rate, as explained above, is generally substantially higher than the section 6603 interest rate unless the taxpayer is a corporation with a potential overpayment in excess of $100,000.

Example: Sam Jones wants to claim a deduction that reduces his 2004 tax liability by $100,000 but also wants to avoid the imposition of an underpayment penalty if the deduction (a disputable item) is disallowed. One option for Sam is to pay his tax without regard to the deduction and file a claim for credit or refund. If the IRS denies the claim, he may pursue his case in District Court or the U.S. Court of Federal Claims. In this situation, no section 6603 deposit is necessary because the tax has been paid and there is no underpayment involved. Alternatively, Sam may claim the deduction. In this situation, Sam may want to make a $100,000 section 6603 deposit on April 15, 2005, in order to protect against any underpayment interest charge. If the IRS issues a notice of deficiency, Sam should withdraw the section 6603 deposit (and receive interest at the federal short-term rate), pay the assessment, and file suit in the Tax Court, District Court, or U.S. Court of Federal Claims. By paying the assessment, Sam continues to protect himself against an underpayment charge and will be eligible for the higher overpayment interest rate if he wins his suit.

Planning Note: By making the section 6603 deposit, Sam will be able to obtain Tax Court jurisdiction. Tax Court jurisdiction is unavailable if Sam pays the tax with his return and files a claim for refund.

Coordination with Rev. Proc. 84-58. Taxpayers who, pursuant to Rev. Proc. 84-58, have made a deposit in the nature of a cash bond with the IRS, may redesignate a portion or all of such deposits held by the IRS on the date of enactment as a section 6603 deposit. The amount treated as a cash bond under Rev. Proc. 84-58 is treated as deposited for purposes of Code Sec. 6603 on the date that the taxpayer identifies the amount as a deposit made pursuant to Code Sec. 6603 (Act Sec. 842(c)(2) of the 2004 Jobs Act).

Planning Note: Generally, taxpayers will want to make this redesignation. A section 6603 deposit and a deposit in the nature of a cash bond made pursuant to the procedures contained in Rev. Proc. 84-58 both stop the running of interest on an amount of underpayment equal to the deposit. However, unlike a section 6603 deposit, the cash bond deposit does not earn interest if the taxpayer wins its dispute or withdraws the deposit prior to the resolution of the dispute. Further, if the taxpayer requests the return of its cash bond deposit and a deficiency is later determined, no credit is received for the period that the funds were held as a deposit.

For further information on this subject, consult any of the following CCH reporter explanations:

- Standard Federal Tax Reporter, 2004FED ¶ 39,415.01

- Federal Tax Service, FTS § P:23.44

- Federal Tax Guide, 2004FTG ¶ 22,494

★ *Effective date.* The provision applies to deposits made after the date of enactment (Act Sec. 842(c)(1) of the American Jobs Creation Act of 2004).

Act Sec. 842(a) of the American Jobs Creation Act of 2004, adding Code Sec. 6603; Act Sec. 842(c)(1); Act Sec. 843(c)(2). Law at ¶ 6230. Committee Report at ¶ 11,250.

¶1615

¶ 1620

Freeze of Provision Regarding Suspension of Interest Where Taxpayer Not Notified

Background

Generally, interest and penalties accrue during periods for which taxes are unpaid, regardless of whether the taxpayer is aware that there is a tax due. Interest and penalties can quickly increase a tax debt to the point that it can cause a severe financial hardship for certain taxpayers to pay off the debt. To address this problem, the IRS Restructuring and Reform Act of 1998 (P.L. 105-206) added a special rule for abating interest and penalties that accrue unknown to the taxpayer, applicable for tax years ending after July 22, 1998.

Under the rule added by P.L. 105-206, the accrual of interest and penalties is suspended after 18 months, unless the IRS provides the taxpayer a notice within 18 months following the later of: (1) the original due date of the return (without regard to extensions), or (2) the date on which a timely return is filed (Code Sec. 6404(g)). For tax years beginning on or after January 1, 2004, the 18-month period is shortened to one year.

The suspension of interest and penalties is available only for individuals. Further, the suspension pertains only to tax related to timely filed returns (i.e., returns filed by the original due date or by the extended due date).

The suspension is applied separately with respect to each item or adjustment. Additionally, the provision does not apply where the taxpayer has self-assessed the tax.

In order for the IRS to continue the accrual of interest and penalties, the notice it provides to the taxpayer must specifically state the taxpayer's liability and the basis for the liability. Interest and penalties resume 21 days after the IRS sends notice that meets these criteria.

The suspension does not stop the accrual of:

(1) the failure to pay and failure to file penalties (any penalty imposed by Code Sec. 6651);

(2) any interest, penalty or other addition to tax in a case involving fraud (including, but not limited to, Code Sec. 6663);

(3) any interest, penalty, addition to tax, or additional amount with respect to any tax liability shown on the return; or

(4) any criminal penalty.

American Jobs Creation Act Impact

18-month suspension period made permanent.—The American Jobs Creation Act of 2004 makes the 18-month suspension period permanent (Code Sec. 6404(g), as amended by the 2004 Jobs Act). The Code provision that established the 12-month period, which began as of January 1, 2004, is retroactively repealed. Because the due date for returns for the tax period beginning January 1, 2004, is generally April 15, 2005, the latter is the earliest date from which calculation of the 18-month suspension period can begin. As a result, suspension of interest cannot begin until October 16, 2006.

Example: Sam Goodwin gets an automatic extension to file his 2004 return, and timely files on August 15, 2005. Goodwin inadvertently fails to include his receipt of $5,000 of interest on the return. The IRS sends Goodwin the required notice on July 1, 2007, and Goodwin pays the deficiency on September 1, 2007. Goodwin owes interest on the deficiency from April 15, 2005 (since a filing extension does not prevent the accrual of interest from the original filing date) through February 15, 2007. Interest is suspended from February 16, 2007, through July 21, 2007 (21 days after the notice was sent). Interest again runs from July 22, 2007, until Goodwin pays the deficiency on September 1, 2007.

In addition, the new law adds "gross misstatements" and "listed and reportable avoidance transactions" to the list of provisions to which the suspension of interest does not apply Code Sec. 6404(g)(2), as amended by the 2004 Jobs Act).

The Senate Committee Report (S. Rep. No. 108-192) defines "gross misstatements" to include (1) any substantial omission of items to which the six-year statute of limitations under Code Sec. 6051(e) applies, (2) gross valuation misstatements under Code Sec. 6662(h) and (3) similar provisions.

According to the Conference Committee Report (H.R. Conf. Rep. No. 108-755), "reportable avoidance transactions" are "reportable transactions" with a significance tax avoidance purpose. Under new Code Sec. 6707A(e), as added by the 2004 Jobs Act (see ¶615), the definition of a "reportable transaction" is to be determined by the Treasury Department. The definition of a "listed transaction" is also to be determined by the Treasury Department.

> **PRACTICAL ANALYSIS. Mark Luscombe, Principal Analyst, CCH Tax and Accounting, points out that, although this provision of the 2004 Jobs Act is not included with the anti-tax shelter provisions, it could be a very effective tool in combating individual tax shelters. Frequently, the IRS has been able to identify a shelter transaction it does not like long before it has been able to identify and bring under audit all of the participants in that shelter. Therefore, many participants in a transaction that has been identified as an abusive tax shelter by the IRS are aware of the IRS attack but have not received any notice from the IRS concerning their particular use of that transaction. By adding gross misstatements and listed and reportable avoidance transactions to the list of provisions to which the suspension of interest does not apply, there is a much increased financial detriment to taxpayers if they just sit back and wait for the IRS to find them. This provision, especially when combined with the continued accrual of the stiffer tax-shelter related penalties under the new law, could well create financial pressure to encourage taxpayers to come forward voluntarily, which is probably just what it was designed to do.**

For further information on this subject, consult any of the following CCH reporter explanations:

- Standard Federal Tax Reporter, 2004FED ¶38,580.01 and ¶38,580.037
- Federal Tax Service, FTS § P:23.43[5]
- Federal Tax Guide, 2004FTG ¶22,495 and ¶22,545
- Federal Estate and Gift Tax Reporter, FEGT ¶15,513.01

★ *Effective date.* This provision is effective for tax years beginning after December 31, 2003, except that the addition of listed and reportable avoidance transactions is applicable to interest accruing after October 3, 2004.

Act Sec. 903(a) of the American Jobs Creation Act of 2004, amending Code Sec. 6404(g); Act Sec. 903(b), redesignating Code Sec. 6404(g)(2)(D) as Code Sec.

6404(g)(2)(E) and adding new Code Sec. 6404(g)(2)(D); Act Sec. 903(c), redesignating Code Sec. 6404(g)(2)(E) as Code Sec. 6404(g)(2)(F) and adding new Code Sec. 6404(g)(2)(E); Act Sec. 903(d). Law at ¶6200. Committee Report at ¶11,750.

¶1625

Modification of Continuing Levy on Payments to Federal Vendors

Background

If a person is liable for taxes and refuses to pay within 10 days after notice and demand, the IRS may seek collection of the taxes by levy (Code Sec. 6331(a)). A levy may be made upon the salary or wages or other property of any person after the IRS has notified the delinquent taxpayer of his intention to make such a levy. The effect of a levy on salary or wages is continuous from the date such levy is first made until the levy is released (Code Sec. 6331(h)). Property subject to a continuous levy that is otherwise exempt from levy under Code Sec. 6334, is not exempt if the IRS approves the levy. Specified payments under Code Sec. 6331(h) to which a continuous levy may attach include certain federal payments not based on the payee's eligibility, unemployment benefits, worker's compensation payments, minimum exemptions for wages, salary and other income and certain public assistance payments, any annuity or pension under the Railroad Retirement Act or benefit under the Railroad Unemployment Insurance Act. Under existing law, a continuous levy may attach to these specified payments in an amount up to 15 percent of the payment due to the taxpayer (Code Sec. 6331(h)(1)).

American Jobs Creation Act Impact

Modification of continuing levy on payments to federal vendors.—The current law is amended to provide that in the case of any specified payment due to a vendor of goods or services sold or leased to the federal government, a continuous levy may be attached of up to 100 percent of the amount of the payment until the tax levy is released. This increases the previous 15 percent limit as it is applied specifically to payments due to a vendor of goods or services sold or leased to the federal government (Code Sec. 6331(h)(1), as amended by the American Jobs Creation Act of 2004).

For further information on this subject, consult any of the following CCH reporter explanations:

- Standard Federal Tax Reporter, 2004FED ¶38,187.021

- Federal Tax Service, FTS § P:27.45[7]

- Federal Tax Guide, 2004FTG ¶22,384

- Federal Estate and Gift Tax Reporter, FEGT ¶15,456.05

★ *Effective date.* This provision is effective on the date of the enactment (Act Sec. 887(b) of the American Jobs Creation Act of 2004).

Act Sec. 887(a) of the American Jobs Creation Act of 2004, amending Code Sec. 6331(h); Act. Sec. 887(b). Law at ¶6195. Committee Report at ¶11,590.

¶ 1630

Extension of IRS User Fees

Background _____

Taxpayers that require written determinations or rulings from the IRS with respect to their inquiries concerning their tax status or the tax effects of particular transactions may be subject to fees. These user fees are payable in advance of the request and they vary based on the request category.

American Jobs Creation Act Impact

User fees extended.—The American Jobs Creation Act of 2004 extends the statutory authorization for the IRS to charge fees related to requests for letter rulings, determination letters, opinion letters, or other similar rulings or determinations. The authority to charge these user fees has been extended to September 30, 2014, from the original termination date of December 31, 2004 (Code Sec. 7528(c), as amended by the 2004 Jobs Act).

For further information on this subject, consult any of the following CCH reporter explanations:

- Standard Federal Tax Reporter, 2004FED ¶ 42,816Y.01
- Federal Tax Service, FTS § P:10.110[12]
- Federal Tax Guide, 2004FTG ¶ 28,039

★ *Effective date.* The provision applies to requests after date of the enactment (Act Sec. 891(b) of the American Jobs Creation Act of 2004).

Act Sec. 891(a) of the American Jobs Creation Act of 2004, amending Code Sec. 7528(c); Act Sec. 891(b). Law at ¶ 6350. Committee Report at ¶ 11,630.

¶ 1635

Authority to Issue Consolidated Return Regulations Affirmed

Background _____

An affiliated group of corporations may elect to file a consolidated return in lieu of separate returns, provided all members of the group consent to the consolidated return regulations under Code Sec. 1502 (Code Sec. 1501). Code Sec. 1502 grants the Treasury Department authority to issue such regulations as it deems necessary to determine and clearly reflect the tax liability of the group and each of its members, and to prevent the avoidance of tax liability.

Under this statutory authority, the Treasury Department has issued lengthy consolidated return regulations which generally adopt a single-entity approach to the tax treatment of an affiliated group of corporations. The consolidated return regulations are generally considered to be "legislative" rather than "interpretive" in character. As such, the courts have given them greater deference than regulations in other areas in cases involving challenges (Conference Committee Report (H.R. Conf. Rept. 108-755)). Despite the advantages that the filing of a consolidated return can provide (such as gain deferral on intercompany transactions, tax-free intercompany distributions, or offsetting of losses of one member against profits of another member of the group), taxpayers often challenge the consolidated return regulations on the basis that the tax results under these regulations are different from the results for taxpayers filing separate returns.

Background

In *Rite Aid Corp.*, CA-FC, 2001-2 USTC ¶ 50,516, 255 F3d 1357, the Federal Circuit Court of Appeals invalidated the duplicated loss provision of Reg. § 1.1502-20(c)(1)(iii), which disallows loss on a disposition of subsidiary's stock to the amount of the duplicated loss in that stock. In this case, the duplicated loss provision would have denied a loss on the sale of subsidiary's stock by a parent corporation that had filed a consolidated return with the subsidiary, to the extent the subsidiary had assets that had a built-in loss, or had a net operating loss, that could be recognized or used later outside the group. The court stated that the duplicated loss problem is not a result of the filing of a consolidated return and that the same issue can arise on the sale of the stock of a nonconsolidated subsidiary. However, in the case where the stock of a nonconsolidated subsidiary is sold, the duplicated loss issue is addressed by limiting the subsidiary's potential future deduction under Code Secs. 382 and 383, not the parent's loss on the sale of stock. Therefore, the duplicated loss regulation produced a different result for the consolidated corporations than the result the same corporations would have obtained if they had filed separate returns. Because the Code Sec. 1502 regulations are generally limited to instances in which the filing of consolidated returns could distort the tax liability of the consolidated group and may not tax income that would not otherwise be taxed, the court invalidated Reg. § 1.1502-20(c)(1)(iii).

Following the *Rite Aid Corp.* decision, the Treasury Department announced that it will not continue to litigate the validity of the duplicated loss provision under Reg. § 1.1502-20(c)(1)(iii) and issued temporary regulations under Temporary Reg. § 1.1502-20T(i)(2), Temporary Reg. § 1.337(d)-2T and Temporary Reg. § 1.1502-35T to provide taxpayers with the choice to elect a different treatment for all years or apply the duplicated loss provision for the past.

American Jobs Creation Act Impact

Treasury Department's authority to issue consolidated return regulations affirmed.—In exercising its authority to issue consolidated return regulations under Code Sec. 1502, the Treasury Department may prescribe rules that treat corporations filing consolidated returns differently from corporations filing separate returns (Code Sec. 1502, as amended by the American Jobs Creation Act of 2004).

The amendment affirms the statutory authority of the Treasury Department to issue consolidated return regulations that may adopt either the single taxpayer or separate taxpayer approach or a combination of the two approaches and modify the application of the Code provisions with respect to members of a consolidated group (Conference Committee Report (H.R. Conf. Rep. No. 108-755)). Thus, taxpayers may not successfully challenge the consolidated return regulations solely on the basis that they produce tax results different from the results under the separate returns regime.

The 2004 Jobs Act further provides that Reg. § 1.1502-20(c)(1)(iii) is inapplicable to the factual situation of the *Rite Aid Corp.* case (Act Sec. 844(b) of the 2004 Jobs Act).

Comment: The Conference Committee Report (H.R. Conf. Rep. No. 108-755) clarifies that the amendment to Code Sec. 1502 overrules *Rite Aid Corp.* to the extent it suggests that the Treasury Department is required to identify a problem created from the filing of consolidated returns in order to issue regulations that change the application of a Code provision. However, the new rule does not overturn the result in *Rite Aid Corp.* with respect to the specific facts presented in the case. Moreover, the override of the application of Reg. § 1.1502-20(c)(1)(iii) to "*Rite Aid Corp.*" type factual situations does not prevent or invalidate other approaches that the Treasury Department may use in lieu of the approach of this regulation. Nor does it overrule Temporary Reg. § 1.1502-20T(i)(2), which allows taxpayers to apply Reg. § 1.1502-20(c)(1)(iii) to past transactions under certain circumstances.

PRACTICAL ANALYSIS. Jeffrey Paravano of Baker & Hostetler and former Treasury official notes that the most interesting effective date provision of the legislation appears in Section 844. That provision affirms Treasury's consolidated return regulatory authority and applies to "taxable years beginning before, on, or after the date of enactment." The Treasury Department has worked tirelessly in recent years cleaning up the most problematic consolidated return regulation provisions. This legislation sends a signal to the courts that the Treasury is entitled to wide latitude when making difficult choices in the consolidated return context.

For further information on this subject, consult any of the following CCH reporter explanations:

- Standard Federal Tax Reporter, 2004FED ¶ 33,168.01 and ¶ 33,168.028
- Federal Tax Service, FTS § I:24.185
- Federal Tax Guide, 2004FTG ¶ 12,650

★ *Effective date.* The provision is effective for all tax years beginning before, on or after the date of enactment (Act Sec. 844(c) of the American Jobs Creation Act of 2004).

Act Sec. 844(a) of the American Jobs Creation Act of 2004, amending Code Sec. 1502; Act Sec. 844(b); Act Sec. 844(c). Law at ¶ 5935 and ¶ 7110 . Committee Report at ¶ 11,270.

CODE SECTIONS ADDED, AMENDED OR REPEALED

[¶ 5001]
INTRODUCTION.

The Internal Revenue Code provisions amended by the American Jobs Creation Act of 2004 (H.R. 4520), as passed by the House and Senate, are shown in the following paragraphs. Deleted Code material or the text of the Code Section prior to amendment appears in the amendment notes following each amended Code provision. *Any changed or added material is set out in italics.*

[¶ 5005] CODE SEC. 1. TAX IMPOSED.

* * *

(h) MAXIMUM CAPITAL GAINS RATE.—

* * *

(10) PASS-THRU ENTITY DEFINED.—For purposes of this subsection, the term "pass-thru entity" means—

(A) a regulated investment company;

(B) a real estate investment trust;

(C) an S corporation;

(D) a partnership;

(E) an estate or trust;

(F) a common trust fund; *and*

(G) a qualified electing fund (as defined in section 1295).

(11) DIVIDENDS TAXED AS NET CAPITAL GAIN.—

* * *

(C) QUALIFIED FOREIGN CORPORATIONS.—

* * *

(iii) EXCLUSION OF DIVIDENDS OF CERTAIN FOREIGN CORPORATIONS.—Such term shall not include any foreign corporation which for the taxable year of the corporation in which the dividend was paid, or the preceding taxable year, is a passive foreign investment company (as defined in section 1297).

* * *

[CCH Explanation at ¶ 490. Committee Reports at ¶ 10,690.]

Amendments

• 2004, American Jobs Creation Act of 2004 (H.R. 4520)

H.R. 4520, § 413(c)(1)(A):

Amended Code Sec. 1(h)(10) by inserting "and" at the end of subparagraph (F), by striking subparagraph (G), and by redesignating subparagraph (H) as subparagraph (G). **Effective** for tax years of foreign corporations beginning after 12-31-2004, and for tax years of United States shareholders with or within which such tax years of foreign corporations end. Prior to being stricken, Code Sec. 1(h)(10)(G) read as follows:

(G) a foreign investment company which is described in section 1246(b)(1) and for which an election is in effect under section 1247; and

H.R. 4520, § 413(c)(1)(B):

Amended Code Sec. 1(h)(11)(C)(iii) by striking "a holding company (as defined in section 552), a foreign investment company (as defined in section 1246(b)), or" immediately preceding "a passive foreign investment company". **Effective** for tax years of foreign corporations beginning after 12-31-2004, and for tax years of United States shareholders with or within which such tax years of foreign corporations end.

[¶ 5010] CODE SEC. 38. GENERAL BUSINESS CREDIT.

* * *

(b) CURRENT YEAR BUSINESS CREDIT.—For purposes of this subpart, the amount of the current year business credit is the sum of the following credits determined for the taxable year:

* * *

(14) in the case of an eligible employer (as defined in section 45E(c)), the small employer pension plan startup cost credit determined under section 45E(a),

(15) the employer-provided child care credit determined under section 45F(a),

(16) *the railroad track maintenance credit determined under section 45G(a),*

(17) *the biodiesel fuels credit determined under section 40A(a),*

(18) *the low sulfur diesel fuel production credit determined under section 45H(a), plus*

(19) *the marginal oil and gas well production credit determined under section 45I(a).*

[CCH Explanation at ¶375, ¶810, ¶855 and ¶860. Committee Reports at ¶10,260, ¶10,324, ¶10,540 and ¶10,560.

Amendments

• **2004, American Jobs Creation Act of 2004 (H.R. 4520)**

H.R. 4520, §245(c)(1):

Amended Code Sec. 38(b) by striking "plus" at the end of paragraph (14), by striking the period at the end of paragraph (15) and inserting ", plus", and by adding at the end a new paragraph (16). **Effective** for tax years beginning after 12-31-2004.

H.R. 4520, §302(b):

Amended Code Sec. 38(b), as amended by this Act, by striking "plus" at the end of paragraph (15), by striking the period at the end of paragraph (16) and inserting ", plus", and by inserting after paragraph (16) a new paragraph (17). **Effective** for fuel produced, and sold or used, after 12-31-2004, in tax years ending after such date.

H.R. 4520, §339(b):

Amended Code Sec. 38(b), as amended by this Act, by striking "plus" at the end of paragraph (16), by striking the period at the end of paragraph (17) and inserting ", plus", and by inserting after paragraph (17) a new paragraph (18). **Effective** for expenses paid or incurred after 12-31-2002, in tax years ending after such date.

H.R. 4520, §341(b):

Amended Code Sec. 38(b), as amended by this Act, by striking "plus" at the end of paragraph (17), by striking the period at the end of paragraph (18) and inserting ", plus", and by inserting after paragraph (18) a new paragraph (19). **Effective** for production in tax years beginning after 12-31-2004.

(c) LIMITATION BASED ON AMOUNT OF TAX.—

* * *

(2) EMPOWERMENT ZONE EMPLOYMENT CREDIT MAY OFFSET 25 PERCENT OF MINIMUM TAX.—

(A) IN GENERAL.—In the case of the empowerment zone employment credit credit—

(i) this section and section 39 shall be applied separately with respect to such credit, and

(ii) for purposes of applying paragraph (1) to such credit—

(I) 75 percent of the tentative minimum tax shall be substituted for the tentative minimum tax under subparagraph (A) thereof, and

(II) the limitation under paragraph (1) (as modified by subclause (I)) shall be reduced by the credit allowed under subsection (a) for the taxable year (other than the empowerment zone employment credit or the New York Liberty Zone business employee credit *or the specified credits*).

* * *

(3) SPECIAL RULES FOR NEW YORK LIBERTY ZONE BUSINESS EMPLOYEE CREDIT.—

(A) IN GENERAL.—In the case of the New York Liberty Zone business employee credit—

(i) this section and section 39 shall be applied separately with respect to such credit, and

(ii) in applying paragraph (1) to such credit—

(I) the tentative minimum tax shall be treated as being zero, and

(II) the limitation under paragraph (1) (as modified by subclause (I)) shall be reduced by the credit allowed under subsection (a) for the taxable year (other than the New York Liberty Zone business employee credit *or the specified credits*).

* * *

(4) *SPECIAL RULES FOR SPECIFIED CREDITS.—*

(A) *IN GENERAL.—In the case of specified credits—*

(i) *this section and section 39 shall be applied separately with respect to such credits, and*

(ii) *in applying paragraph (1) to such credits—*

(I) the tentative minimum tax shall be treated as being zero, and

(II) the limitation under paragraph (1) (as modified by subclause (I)) shall be reduced by the credit allowed under subsection (a) for the taxable year (other than the specified credits).

(B) SPECIFIED CREDITS.—For purposes of this subsection, the term "specified credits" includes—

(i) for taxable years beginning after December 31, 2004, the credit determined under section 40,

(ii) the credit determined under section 45 to the extent that such credit is attributable to electricity or refined coal produced—

(I) at a facility which is originally placed in service after the date of the enactment of this paragraph, and

(II) during the 4-year period beginning on the date that such facility was originally placed in service.

(5) SPECIAL RULES.—

* * *

[CCH Explanation at ¶ 370. Committee Reports at ¶ 10,924.]

Amendments

• **2004, American Jobs Creation Act of 2004 (H.R. 4520)**

H.R. 4520, § 711(a):

Amended Code Sec. 38(c) by redesignating paragraph (4) as paragraph (5) and by inserting after paragraph (3) a new paragraph (4). **Effective** for tax years ending after the date of the enactment of this Act.

H.R. 4520, § 711(b):

Amended Code Sec. 38(c)(2)(A)(ii)(II) and (3)(A)(ii)(II) by inserting "or the specified credits" after "employee credit". **Effective** for tax years ending after the date of the enactment of this Act.

[¶ 5015] CODE SEC. 39. CARRYBACK AND CARRYFORWARD OF UNUSED CREDITS.

(a) IN GENERAL.—

* * *

(3) 5-YEAR CARRYBACK FOR MARGINAL OIL AND GAS WELL PRODUCTION CREDIT.—Notwithstanding subsection (d), in the case of the marginal oil and gas well production credit—

(A) this section shall be applied separately from the business credit (other than the marginal oil and gas well production credit),

(B) paragraph (1) shall be applied by substituting "5 taxable years" for "1 taxable years" in subparagraph (A) thereof, and

(C) paragraph (2) shall be applied—

(i) by substituting "25 taxable years" for "21 taxable years" in subparagraph (A) thereof, and

(ii) by substituting "24 taxable years" for "20 taxable years" in subparagraph (B) thereof.

* * *

[CCH Explanation at ¶ 860. Committee Reports at ¶ 10,560.]

Amendments

• **2004, American Jobs Creation Act of 2004 (H.R. 4520)**

H.R. 4520, § 341(c):

Amended Code Sec. 39(a) by adding at the end a new paragraph (3). **Effective** for production in tax years beginning after 12-31-2004.

(d) TRANSITIONAL RULE.—No portion of the unused business credit for any taxable year which is attributable to a credit specified in section 38(b) or any portion thereof may be carried back to any taxable year before the first taxable year for which such specified credit or such portion is allowable (without regard to subsection (a)).

[CCH Explanation at ¶ 375. Committee Reports at ¶ 10,260.]

Amendments

• 2004, American Jobs Creation Act of 2004 (H.R. 4520)

H.R. 4520, § 245(b)(1):

Amended Code Sec. 39(d). **Effective** with respect to tax years ending after 12-31-2003. Prior to amendment, Code Sec. 39(d) read as follows:

(d) TRANSITIONAL RULES.—

(1) NO CARRYBACK OF ENHANCED OIL RECOVERY CREDIT BEFORE 1991.— No portion of the unused business credit for any taxable year which is attributable to the credit determined under section 43(a) (relating to enhanced oil recovery credit) may be carried to a taxable year beginning before January 1, 1991.

(2) NO CARRYBACK OF SECTION 44 CREDIT BEFORE ENACT-MENT.—No portion of the unused business credit for any taxable year which is attributable to the disabled access credit determined under section 44 may be carried to a taxable year ending before the date of the enactment of section 44.

(3) NO CARRYBACK OF RENEWABLE ELECTRICITY PRODUCTION CREDIT BEFORE EFFECTIVE DATE.—No portion of the unused business credit for any taxable year which is attributable to the credit determined under section 45 (relating to electricity produced from certain renewable resources) may be carried back to any taxable year ending before January 1, 1993 (before January 1, 1994, to the extent such credit is attributable to wind as a qualified energy resource).

(4) EMPOWERMENT ZONE EMPLOYMENT CREDIT.—No portion of the unused business credit which is attributable to the credit determined under section 1396 (relating to empowerment zone employment credit) may be carried to any taxable year ending before January 1, 1994.

(5) NO CARRYBACK OF section 45A CREDIT BEFORE ENACT-MENT.—No portion of the unused business credit for any taxable year which is attributable to the Indian employment credit determined under section 45A may be carried to a taxable year ending before the date of the enactment of section 45A.

(6) NO CARRYBACK OF section 45B CREDIT BEFORE ENACT-MENT.—No portion of the unused business credit for any taxable year which is attributable to the employer social security credit determined under section 45B may be carried back to a taxable year ending before the date of the enactment of section 45B.

(7) No carryback of SECTION 45C CREDIT BEFORE JULY 1, 1996.—No portion of the unused business credit for any taxable year which is attributable to the orphan drug credit determined under section 45C may be carried back to a taxable year ending before July 1, 1996.

(8) NO CARRYBACK OF DC ZONE CREDITS BEFORE EFFECTIVE DATE.—No portion of the unused business credit for any taxable year which is attributable to the credits allowable under subchapter U by reason of section 1400 may be carried back to a taxable year ending before the date of the enactment of section 1400.

(9) NO CARRYBACK OF NEW MARKETS TAX CREDIT BEFORE JANU-ARY 1, 2001.—No portion of the unused business credit for any taxable year which is attributable to the credit under section 45D may be carried back to a taxable year ending before January 1, 2001.

(10) NO CARRYBACK OF SMALL EMPLOYER PENSION PLAN STARTUP COST CREDIT BEFORE JANUARY 1, 2002.—No portion of the unused business credit for any taxable year which is attributable to the small employer pension plan startup cost credit determined under section 45E may be carried back to a taxable year beginning before January 1, 2002.

[¶ 5020] CODE SEC. 40. ALCOHOL USED AS FUEL.

* * *

(c) COORDINATION WITH EXEMPTION FROM EXCISE TAX.—The amount of the credit determined under this section with respect to any alcohol shall, under regulations prescribed by the Secretary, be properly reduced to take into account any benefit provided with respect to such alcohol solely by reason of the application of *section 4041(b)(2), section 6426, or section 6427(e)*.

[CCH Explanation at ¶ 805. Committee Reports at ¶ 10,320.]

Amendments

• 2004, American Jobs Creation Act of 2004 (H.R. 4520)

H.R. 4520, § 301(c)(1):

Amended Code Sec. 40(c) by striking "subsection (b)(2), (k), or (m) of section 4041, section 4081(c), or section

4091(c)" and inserting "section 4041(b)(2), section 6426, or section 6427(e)". **Effective** for fuel sold or used after 12-31-2004.

(d) DEFINITIONS AND SPECIAL RULES.—For purposes of this section—

* * *

(4) *VOLUME OF ALCOHOL.—For purposes of determining under subsection (a) the number of gallons of alcohol with respect to which a credit is allowable under subsection (a), the volume of alcohol shall include the volume of any denaturant (including gasoline) which is added under any formulas approved by the Secretary to the extent that such denaturants do not exceed 5 percent of the volume of such alcohol (including denaturants).*

* * *

[CCH Explanation at ¶805. Committee Reports at ¶10,320.]

Amendments

• **2004, American Jobs Creation Act of 2004 (H.R. 4520)**

H.R. 4520, §301(c)(2):

Amended Code Sec. 40(d)(4). **Effective** for fuel sold or used after 12-31-2004. Prior to amendment, Code Sec. 40(d)(4) read as follows:

(4) VOLUME OF ALCOHOL.—For purposes of determining—

(A) under subsection (a) the number of gallons of alcohol with respect to which a credit is allowable under subsection (a), or

(B) under section 4041(k) or 4081(c) the percentage of any mixture which consists of alcohol,

the volume of alcohol shall include the volume of any denaturant (including gasoline) which is added under any formulas approved by the Secretary to the extent that such denaturants do not exceed 5 percent of the volume of such alcohol (including denaturants).

(e) TERMINATION.—

(1) IN GENERAL.—This section shall not apply to any sale or use—

(A) for any period after December 31, *2010*, or

(B) for any period before January 1, *2011*, during which the rates of tax under section 4081(a)(2)(A) are 4.3 cents per gallon.

* * *

[CCH Explanation at ¶805. Committee Reports at ¶10,320.]

Amendments

• **2004, American Jobs Creation Act of 2004 (H.R. 4520)**

H.R. 4520, §301(c)(3)(A)-(B):

Amended Code Sec. 40(e)(1) by striking "2007" in subparagraph (A) and inserting "2010", and by striking "2008" in

subparagraph (B) and inserting "2011". **Effective** on the date of the enactment of this Act.

(g) DEFINITIONS AND SPECIAL RULES FOR ELIGIBLE SMALL ETHANOL PRODUCER CREDIT.—For purposes of this section—

* * *

(6) ALLOCATION OF SMALL ETHANOL PRODUCER CREDIT TO PATRONS OF COOPERATIVE.—

(A) ELECTION TO ALLOCATE.—

(i) IN GENERAL.—In the case of a cooperative organization described in section 1381(a), any portion of the credit determined under subsection (a)(3) for the taxable year may, at the election of the organization, be apportioned pro rata among patrons of the organization on the basis of the quantity or value of business done with or for such patrons for the taxable year.

(ii) FORM AND EFFECT OF ELECTION.—An election under clause (i) for any taxable year shall be made on a timely filed return for such year. Such election, once made, shall be irrevocable for such taxable year.

(B) TREATMENT OF ORGANIZATIONS AND PATRONS.—

(i) ORGANIZATIONS.—The amount of the credit not apportioned to patrons pursuant to subparagraph (A) shall be included in the amount determined under subsection (a)(3) for the taxable year of the organization.

(ii) PATRONS.—The amount of the credit apportioned to patrons pursuant to subparagraph (A) shall be included in the amount determined under such subsection for the first taxable year of each patron ending on or after the last day of the payment period (as defined in section 1382(d)) for the taxable year of the organization or, if earlier, for the taxable year of each patron ending on or after the date on which the patron receives notice from the cooperative of the apportionment.

(iii) SPECIAL RULES FOR DECREASE IN CREDITS FOR TAXABLE YEAR.—If the amount of the credit of the organization determined under such subsection for a taxable year is less than the amount of such credit shown on the return of the organization for such year, an amount equal to the excess of—

(I) such reduction, over

(II) *the amount not apportioned to such patrons under subparagraph (A) for the taxable year,*

shall be treated as an increase in tax imposed by this chapter on the organization. Such increase shall not be treated as tax imposed by this chapter for purposes of determining the amount of any credit under this chapter or for purposes of section 55.

[CCH Explanation at ¶845. Committee Reports at ¶10,360.]
Amendments
• **2004, American Jobs Creation Act of 2004 (H.R. 4520)**

H.R. 4520, §313(a):

Amended Code Sec. 40(g) by adding at the end a new paragraph (6). **Effective** for tax years ending after the date of the enactment of this Act.

(h) REDUCED CREDIT FOR ETHANOL BLENDERS.—

(1) IN GENERAL.—In the case of any alcohol mixture credit or alcohol credit with respect to any sale or use of alcohol which is ethanol during calendar years 2001 through *2010* —

(A) subsections (b)(1)(A) and (b)(2)(A) shall be applied by substituting "the blender amount" for "60 cents",

(B) subsection (b)(3) shall be applied by substituting "the low-proof blender amount" for "45 cents" and "the blender amount" for "60 cents", and

(C) subparagraphs (A) and (B) of subsection (d)(3) shall be applied by substituting "the blender amount" for "60 cents" and "the low-proof blender amount" for "45 cents".

(2) AMOUNTS.—For purposes of paragraph (1), the blender amount and the low-proof blender amount shall be determined in accordance with the following table:

In the case of any sale or use during calendar year:	The blender amount is:	The low-proof blender amount is:
2001 or 2002	53 cents	39.26 cents
2003 or 2004	52 cents	38.52 cents
2005 *through 2010*	51 cents	37.78 cents

[CCH Explanation at ¶805. Committee Reports at ¶10,320.]
Amendments
• **2004, American Jobs Creation Act of 2004 (H.R. 4520)**

H.R. 4520, §301(c)(4)(A)-(B):

Amended Code Sec. 40(h) by striking "2007" in paragraph (1) and inserting "2010", and by striking ", 2006, or 2007" in the table contained in paragraph (2) and inserting "through 2010" **Effective** on the date of the enactment of this Act.

[¶5025] *CODE SEC. 40A. BIODIESEL USED AS FUEL.*

(a) GENERAL RULE.—*For purposes of section 38, the biodiesel fuels credit determined under this section for the taxable year is an amount equal to the sum of—*

(1) *the biodiesel mixture credit, plus*

(2) *the biodiesel credit.*

(b) DEFINITION OF BIODIESEL MIXTURE CREDIT AND BIODIESEL CREDIT.—*For purposes of this section—*

(1) BIODIESEL MIXTURE CREDIT.—

(A) IN GENERAL.—*The biodiesel mixture credit of any taxpayer for any taxable year is 50 cents for each gallon of biodiesel used by the taxpayer in the production of a qualified biodiesel mixture.*

(B) QUALIFIED BIODIESEL MIXTURE.—*The term "qualified biodiesel mixture" means a mixture of biodiesel and diesel fuel (as defined in section 4083(a)(3)), determined without regard to any use of kerosene, which—*

(i) *is sold by the taxpayer producing such mixture to any person for use as a fuel, or*

(ii) *is used as a fuel by the taxpayer producing such mixture.*

(C) SALE OR USE MUST BE IN TRADE OR BUSINESS, ETC..—Biodiesel used in the production of a qualified biodiesel mixture shall be taken into account—

(i) only if the sale or use described in subparagraph (B) is in a trade or business of the taxpayer, and

(ii) for the taxable year in which such sale or use occurs.

(D) CASUAL OFF-FARM PRODUCTION NOT ELIGIBLE.—No credit shall be allowed under this section with respect to any casual off-farm production of a qualified biodiesel mixture.

(2) BIODIESEL CREDIT.—

(A) IN GENERAL.—The biodiesel credit of any taxpayer for any taxable year is 50 cents for each gallon of biodiesel which is not in a mixture with diesel fuel and which during the taxable year—

(i) is used by the taxpayer as a fuel in a trade or business, or

(ii) is sold by the taxpayer at retail to a person and placed in the fuel tank of such person's vehicle.

(B) USER CREDIT NOT TO APPLY TO BIODIESEL SOLD AT RETAIL.—No credit shall be allowed under subparagraph (A)(i) with respect to any biodiesel which was sold in a retail sale described in subparagraph (A)(ii).

(3) CREDIT FOR AGRI-BIODIESEL.—In the case of any biodiesel which is agri-biodiesel, paragraphs (1)(A) and (2)(A) shall be applied by substituting "$1.00" for "50 cents".

(4) CERTIFICATION FOR BIODIESEL.—No credit shall be allowed under this section unless the taxpayer obtains a certification (in such form and manner as prescribed by the Secretary) from the producer or importer of the biodiesel which identifies the product produced and the percentage of biodiesel and agri-biodiesel in the product.

(c) COORDINATION WITH CREDIT AGAINST EXCISE TAX.—The amount of the credit determined under this section with respect to any biodiesel shall be properly reduced to take into account any benefit provided with respect to such biodiesel solely by reason of the application of section 6426 or 6427(e).

(d) DEFINITIONS AND SPECIAL RULES.—For purposes of this section—

(1) BIODIESEL.—The term "biodiesel" means the monoalkyl esters of long chain fatty acids derived from plant or animal matter which meet—

(A) the registration requirements for fuels and fuel additives established by the Environmental Protection Agency under section 211 of the Clean Air Act (42 U.S.C. 7545), and

(B) the requirements of the American Society of Testing and Materials D6751.

(2) AGRI-BIODIESEL.—The term "agri-biodiesel" means biodiesel derived solely from virgin oils, including esters derived from virgin vegetable oils from corn, soybeans, sunflower seeds, cottonseeds, canola, crambe, rapeseeds, safflowers, flaxseeds, rice bran, and mustard seeds, and from animal fats.

(3) MIXTURE OR BIODIESEL NOT USED AS A FUEL, ETC.—

(A) MIXTURES.—If—

(i) any credit was determined under this section with respect to biodiesel used in the production of any qualified biodiesel mixture, and

(ii) any person—

(I) separates the biodiesel from the mixture, or

(II) without separation, uses the mixture other than as a fuel,

then there is hereby imposed on such person a tax equal to the product of the rate applicable under subsection (b)(1)(A) and the number of gallons of such biodiesel in such mixture.

(B) BIODIESEL.—If—

(i) any credit was determined under this section with respect to the retail sale of any biodiesel, and

(ii) any person mixes such biodiesel or uses such biodiesel other than as a fuel,

then there is hereby imposed on such person a tax equal to the product of the rate applicable under subsection (b)(2)(A) and the number of gallons of such biodiesel.

(C) Applicable laws.—All provisions of law, including penalties, shall, insofar as applicable and not inconsistent with this section, apply in respect of any tax imposed under subparagraph (A) or (B) as if such tax were imposed by section 4081 and not by this chapter.

(4) Pass-thru in the case of estates and trusts.—Under regulations prescribed by the Secretary, rules similar to the rules of subsection (d) of section 52 shall apply.

(e) Termination.—This section shall not apply to any sale or use after December 31, 2006.

[CCH Explanation at ¶ 810. Committee Reports at ¶ 10,324.]

Amendments

• **2004, American Jobs Creation Act of 2004 (H.R. 4520)**

H.R. 4520, § 302(a):

Amended subpart D of part IV of subchapter A of chapter 1 by inserting after Code Sec. 40 a new Code Sec. 40A.

Effective for fuel produced, and sold or used, after 12-31-2004, in tax years ending after such date.

[¶ 5030] CODE SEC. 43. ENHANCED OIL RECOVERY CREDIT.

* * *

(c) Qualified Enhanced Oil Recovery Costs.—For purposes of this section—

(1) In general.—The term "qualified enhanced oil recovery costs" means any of the following:

* * *

(D) Any amount which is paid or incurred during the taxable year to construct a gas treatment plant which—

(i) is located in the area of the United States (within the meaning of section 638(1)) lying north of 64 degrees North latitude,

(ii) prepares Alaska natural gas for transportation through a pipeline with a capacity of at least 2,000,000,000,000 Btu of natural gas per day, and

(iii) produces carbon dioxide which is injected into hydrocarbon-bearing geological formations.

* * *

(5) Alaska Natural Gas.—For purposes of paragraph (1)(D)—

(1) In general.—The term "Alaska natural gas" means natural gas entering the Alaska natural gas pipeline (as defined in section 168(i)(16) (determined without regard to subparagraph (B) thereof)) which is produced from a well—

(A) located in the area of the State of Alaska lying north of 64 degrees North latitude, determined by excluding the area of the Alaska National Wildlife Refuge (including the continental shelf thereof within the meaning of section 638(1)), and

(B) pursuant to the applicable State and Federal pollution prevention, control, and permit requirements from such area (including the continental shelf thereof within the meaning of section 638(1)).

(2) Natural gas.—The term "natural gas" has the meaning given such term by section 613A(e)(2).

* * *

[CCH Explanation at ¶ 707. Committee Reports at ¶ 10,890.]

Amendments

• **2004, American Jobs Creation Act of 2004 (H.R. 4520)**

H.R. 4520, § 707(a):

Amended Code Sec. 43(c)(1) by adding at the end a new subparagraph (D). **Effective** for costs paid or incurred in tax years beginning after 12-31-2004.

H.R. 4520, § 707(b):

Amended Code Sec. 43(c) by adding at the end a new paragraph (5). **Effective** for costs paid or incurred in tax years beginning after 12-31-2004.

[¶ 5035] CODE SEC. 45. ELECTRICITY PRODUCED FROM CERTAIN RENEWABLE RESOURCES, *etc.* [*sic*]

* * *

(b) LIMITATIONS AND ADJUSTMENTS.—

* * *

(2) CREDIT AND PHASEOUT ADJUSTMENT BASED ON INFLATION.—*The 1.5 cent amount in subsection (a), the 8 cent amount in paragraph (1), the $4.375 amount in subsection (e)(8)(A), and in subsection (e)(8)(B)(i) the reference price of fuel used as a feedstock (within the meaning of subsection (c)(7)(A)) in 2002* shall each be adjusted by multiplying such amount by the inflation adjustment factor for the calendar year in which the sale occurs. If any amount as increased under the preceding sentence is not a multiple of 0.1 cent, such amount shall be rounded to the nearest multiple of 0.1 cent.

(3) CREDIT REDUCED FOR GRANTS, TAX-EXEMPT BONDS, SUBSIDIZED ENERGY FINANCING, AND OTHER CREDITS.—The amount of the credit determined under subsection (a) with respect to any project for any taxable year (determined after the application of paragraphs (1) and (2)) shall be reduced by the amount which is the product of the amount so determined for such year and *the lesser of ½ or* a fraction—

(A) the numerator of which is the sum, for the taxable year and all prior taxable years, of—

(i) grants provided by the United States, a State, or a political subdivision of a State for use in connection with the project,

(ii) proceeds of an issue of State or local government obligations used to provide financing for the project the interest on which is exempt from tax under section 103,

(iii) the aggregate amount of subsidized energy financing provided (directly or indirectly) under a Federal, State, or local program provided in connection with the project, and

(iv) the amount of any other credit allowable with respect to any property which is part of the project, and

(B) the denominator of which is the aggregate amount of additions to the capital account for the project for the taxable year and all prior taxable years.

The amounts under the preceding sentence for any taxable year shall be determined as of the close of the taxable year. *This paragraph shall not apply with respect to any facility described in subsection (d)(2)(A)(ii).*

(4) CREDIT RATE AND PERIOD FOR ELECTRICITY PRODUCED AND SOLD FROM CERTAIN FACILITIES.—

(A) CREDIT RATE.—In the case of electricity produced and sold in any calendar year after 2003 at any qualified facility described in paragraph (3), (5), (6), or (7) of subsection (d), the amount in effect under subsection (a)(1) for such calendar year (determined before the application of the last sentence of paragraph (2) of this subsection) shall be reduced by one-half.

(B) CREDIT PERIOD.—

(i) IN GENERAL.—Except as provided in clause (ii), in the case of any facility described in paragraph (3), (4), (5), (6), or (7) of subsection (d), the 5-year period beginning on the date the facility was originally placed in service shall be substituted for the 10-year period in subsection (a)(2)(A)(ii).

(ii) CERTAIN OPEN-LOOP BIOMASS FACILITIES.—In the case of any facility described in subsection (d)(3)(A)(ii) placed in service before the date of the enactment of this paragraph, the 5-year period beginning on the date of the enactment of this Act shall be substituted for the 10-year period in subsection (a)(2)(A)(ii).

[CCH Explanation at ¶ 874. Committee Reports at ¶ 10,920.]

Amendments

• **2004, American Jobs Creation Act of 2004 (H.R. 4520)**

H.R. 4520, § 710(b)(3)(B):

Amended the heading of Code Sec. 45 by inserting before the period at the end ", etc". **Effective** for electricity produced and sold after the date of the enactment of this Act, in tax years ending after such date. For a special rule, see Act Sec. 710(g)(4), below.

H.R. 4520, § 710(b)(3)(C):

Amended Code Sec. 45(b)(2) by striking "The 1.5 cent amount" and all that follows through "paragraph (1)" and inserting "The 1.5 cent amount in subsection (a), the 8 cent amount in paragraph (1), the $4.375 amount in subsection (e)(8)(A), and in subsection (e)(8)(B)(i) the reference price of fuel used as a feedstock (within the meaning of subsection (c)(7)(A)) in 2002". **Effective** generally for electricity produced and sold after the date of the enactment of this Act, in tax years ending after such date. For a special rule, see Act Sec. 710(g)(4), below. Prior to amendment, Code Sec. 45(b)(2) read as follows:

(2) CREDIT AND PHASEOUT ADJUSTMENT BASED ON INFLATION.—The 1.5 cent amount in subsection (a) and the 8 cent amount in paragraph (1) shall each be adjusted by multiplying such amount by the inflation adjustment factor for the calendar year in which the sale occurs. If any amount as increased under the preceding sentence is not a multiple of 0.1 cent, such amount shall be rounded to the nearest multiple of 0.1 cent.

H.R. 4520, § 710(c):

Amended Code Sec. 45(b) by adding at the end a new paragraph (4). **Effective** for electricity produced and sold after 12-31-2004, in tax years ending after such date. For a special rule, see Act Sec. 710(g)(4), below.

H.R. 4520, § 710(f)(1)-(2):

Amended Code Sec. 45(b)(3) by inserting "the lesser of ½ or" before "a fraction" in the matter preceding subparagraph (A), and by adding at the end a new sentence. **Effective** generally for electricity produced and sold after the date of the enactment of this Act, in tax years ending after such date. For a special rule, see Act Sec. 710(g)(4), below.

H.R. 4520, § 710(g)(4), provides:

(4) NONAPPLICATION OF AMENDMENTS TO PREEFFECTIVE DATE POULTRY WASTE FACILITIES.—The amendments made by this section shall not apply with respect to any poultry waste facility (within the meaning of section 45(c)(3)(C), as in effect on the day before the date of the enactment of this Act) placed in service before January 1, 2004.

(c) QUALIFIED ENERGY RESOURCES AND REFINED COAL.—For purposes of this section:

    (1) IN GENERAL.—The term "qualified energy resources" means—

        (A) wind,

        (B) closed-loop biomass,

        (C) open-loop biomass,

        (D) geothermal energy,

        (E) solar energy,

        (F) small irrigation power, and

        (G) municipal solid waste.

    (2) CLOSED-LOOP BIOMASS.—The term "closed-loop biomass" means any organic material from a plant which is planted exclusively for purposes of being used at a qualified facility to produce electricity.

    (3) OPEN-LOOP BIOMASS.—

        (A) IN GENERAL.—The term "open-loop biomass" means—

            (i) any agricultural livestock waste nutrients, or

            (ii) any solid, nonhazardous, cellulosic waste material which is segregated from other waste materials and which is derived from—

                (I) any of the following forest-related resources: mill and harvesting residues, precommercial thinnings, slash, and brush, or

                (II) solid wood waste materials, including waste pallets, crates, dunnage, manufacturing and construction wood wastes (other than pressure-treated, chemically-treated, or painted wood wastes), and landscape or right-of-way tree trimmings, but not including municipal solid waste, gas derived from the biodegradation of solid waste, or paper which is commonly recycled, or

                (III) agriculture sources, including orchard tree crops, vineyard, grain, legumes, sugar, and other crop by-products or residues.

    Such term shall not include closed-loop biomass or biomass burned in conjunction with fossil fuel (cofiring) beyond such fossil fuel required for startup and flame stabilization.

(B) AGRICULTURAL LIVESTOCK WASTE NUTRIENTS.—

　　(i) IN GENERAL.—The term "agricultural livestock waste nutrients" means agricultural livestock manure and litter, including wood shavings, straw, rice hulls, and other bedding material for the disposition of manure.

　　(ii) AGRICULTURAL LIVESTOCK.—The term "agricultural livestock" includes bovine, swine, poultry, and sheep.

(4) GEOTHERMAL ENERGY.—The term "geothermal energy" means energy derived from a geothermal deposit (within the meaning of section 613(e)(2)).

(5) SMALL IRRIGATION POWER.—The term "small irrigation power" means power—

　　(A) generated without any dam or impoundment of water through an irrigation system canal or ditch, and

　　(B) the nameplate capacity rating of which is not less than 150 kilowatts but is less than 5 megawatts.

(6) MUNICIPAL SOLID WASTE.—The term "municipal solid waste" has the meaning given the term "solid waste" under section 2(27) of the Solid Waste Disposal Act (42 U.S.C. 6903).

(7) REFINED COAL.—

　　(A) IN GENERAL.—The term "refined coal" means a fuel which—

　　　　(i) is a liquid, gaseous, or solid synthetic fuel produced from coal (including lignite) or high carbon fly ash, including such fuel used as a feedstock,

　　　　(ii) is sold by the taxpayer with the reasonable expectation that it will be used for purpose of producing steam,

　　　　(iii) is certified by the taxpayer as resulting (when used in the production of steam) in a qualified emission reduction, and

　　　　(iv) is produced in such a manner as to result in an increase of at least 50 percent in the market value of the refined coal (excluding any increase caused by materials combined or added during the production process), as compared to the value of the feedstock coal.

　　(B) QUALIFIED EMISSION REDUCTION.—The term "qualified emission reduction" means a reduction of at least 20 percent of the emissions of nitrogen oxide and either sulfur dioxide or mercury released when burning the refined coal (excluding any dilution caused by materials combined or added during the production process), as compared to the emissions released when burning the feedstock coal or comparable coal predominantly available in the marketplace as of January 1, 2003.

[CCH Explanation at ¶870. Committee Reports at ¶10,920.]

Amendments

• 2004, American Jobs Creation Act of 2004 (H.R. 4520)

H.R. 4520, §710(a):

Amended Code Sec. 45(c). **Effective** generally for electricity produced and sold after the date of the enactment of this Act, in tax years ending after such date. For a special rule, see Act Sec. 710(g)(4), below. Prior to amendment, Code Sec. 45(c) read as follows:

(c) DEFINITIONS.—For purposes of this section—

(1) QUALIFIED ENERGY RESOURCES.—The term "qualified energy resources" means—

(A) wind,

(B) closed-loop biomass, and

(C) poultry waste.

(2) CLOSED-LOOP BIOMASS.—The term "closed-loop biomass" means any organic material from a plant which is planted exclusively for purposes of being used at a qualified facility to produce electricity.

(3) QUALIFIED FACILITY.—

(A) WIND FACILITY.—In the case of a facility using wind to produce electricity, the term "qualified facility" means any facility owned by the taxpayer which is originally placed in service after December 31, 1993, and before January 1, 2006.

(B) CLOSED-LOOP BIOMASS FACILITY.—In the case of a facility using closed-loop biomass to produce electricity, the term "qualified facility" means any facility owned by the taxpayer which is originally placed in service after December 31, 1992, and before January 1, 2006.

(C) POULTRY WASTE FACILITY.—In the case of a facility using poultry waste to produce electricity, the term "qualified facility" means any facility of the taxpayer which is originally placed in service after December 31, 1999, and before January 1, 2006.

(4) POULTRY WASTE.—The term "poultry waste" means poultry manure and litter, including wood shavings, straw, rice hulls, and other bedding material for the disposition of manure.

H.R. 4520, §710(g)(4), provides:

(4) NONAPPLICATION OF AMENDMENTS TO PREEFFECTIVE DATE POULTRY WASTE FACILITIES.—The amendments made by this section shall not apply with respect to any poultry waste facility (within the meaning of section 45(c)(3)(C), as in effect on the day before the date of the enactment of this Act) placed in service before January 1, 2004.

Code Sec. 45(c)(7)(B)　　**¶5035**

(d) QUALIFIED FACILITIES.—*For purposes of this section:*

(1) WIND FACILITY.—*In the case of a facility using wind to produce electricity, the term "qualified facility" means any facility owned by the taxpayer which is originally placed in service after December 31, 1993, and before January 1, 2006.*

(2) CLOSED-LOOP BIOMASS FACILITY.—

(A) IN GENERAL.—*In the case of a facility using closed-loop biomass to produce electricity, the term "qualified facility" means any facility—*

(i) owned by the taxpayer which is originally placed in service after December 31, 1992, and before January 1, 2006, or

(ii) owned by the taxpayer which before January 1, 2006, is originally placed in service and modified to use closed-loop biomass to co-fire with coal, with other biomass, or with both, but only if the modification is approved under the Biomass Power for Rural Development Programs or is part of a pilot project of the Commodity Credit Corporation as described in 65 Fed. Reg. 63052.

(B) SPECIAL RULES.—*In the case of a qualified facility described in subparagraph (A)(ii)—*

(i) the 10-year period referred to in subsection (a) shall be treated as beginning no earlier than the date of the enactment of this clause,

(ii) the amount of the credit determined under subsection (a) with respect to the facility shall be an amount equal to the amount determined without regard to this clause multiplied by the ratio of the thermal content of the closed-loop biomass used in such facility to the thermal content of all fuels used in such facility, and

(iii) if the owner of such facility is not the producer of the electricity, the person eligible for the credit allowable under subsection (a) shall be the lessee or the operator of such facility.

(3) OPEN-LOOP BIOMASS FACILITIES.—

(A) IN GENERAL.—*In the case of a facility using open-loop biomass to produce electricity, the term "qualified facility" means any facility owned by the taxpayer which—*

(i) in the case of a facility using agricultural livestock waste nutrients—

(I) is originally placed in service after the date of the enactment of this subclause and before January 1, 2006, and

(II) the nameplate capacity rating of which is not less than 150 kilowatts, and

(ii) in the case of any other facility, is originally placed in service before January 1, 2006.

(B) CREDIT ELIGIBILITY.—*In the case of any facility described in subparagraph (A), if the owner of such facility is not the producer of the electricity, the person eligible for the credit allowable under subsection (a) shall be the lessee or the operator of such facility.*

(4) GEOTHERMAL OR SOLAR ENERGY FACILITY.—*In the case of a facility using geothermal or solar energy to produce electricity, the term "qualified facility" means any facility owned by the taxpayer which is originally placed in service after the date of the enactment of this paragraph and before January 1, 2006. Such term shall not include any property described in section 48(a)(3) the basis of which is taken into account by the taxpayer for purposes of determining the energy credit under section 48.*

(5) SMALL IRRIGATION POWER FACILITY.—*In the case of a facility using small irrigation power to produce electricity, the term "qualified facility" means any facility owned by the taxpayer which is originally placed in service after the date of the enactment of this paragraph and before January 1, 2006.*

(6) LANDFILL GAS FACILITIES.—*In the case of a facility producing electricity from gas derived from the biodegradation of municipal solid waste, the term "qualified facility" means any facility owned by the taxpayer which is originally placed in service after the date of the enactment of this paragraph and before January 1, 2006.*

(7) TRASH COMBUSTION FACILITIES.—*In the case of a facility which burns municipal solid waste to produce electricity, the term "qualified facility" means any facility owned by the taxpayer which is originally placed in service after the date of the enactment of this paragraph and before January 1, 2006.*

(8) REFINED COAL PRODUCTION FACILITY.—*The term "refined coal production facility" means a facility which is placed in service after the date of the enactment of this paragraph and before January 1, 2009.*

[CCH Explanation at ¶872. Committee Reports at ¶10,920.]

Amendments

• 2004, American Jobs Creation Act of 2004 (H.R. 4520)

H.R. 4520, §710(b)(1):

Amended Code Sec. 45 by redesignating subsection (d) as subsection (e) and by inserting after subsection (c) a new subsection (d). **Effective** generally for electricity produced and sold after the date of the enactment of this Act, in tax years ending after such date. For special rules, see Act Sec. 710(g)(2) and (4), below.

H.R. 4520, §710(g)(2), provides:

(2) CERTAIN BIOMASS FACILITIES.—With respect to any facility described in section 45(d)(3)(A)(ii) of the Internal Revenue

Code of 1986, as added by subsection (b)(1), which is placed in service before the date of the enactment of this Act, the amendments made by this section shall apply to electricity produced and sold after December 31, 2004, in taxable years ending after such date.

H.R. 4520, §710(g)(4), provides:

(4) NONAPPLICATION OF AMENDMENTS TO PREEFFECTIVE DATE POULTRY WASTE FACILITIES.—The amendments made by this section shall not apply with respect to any poultry waste facility (within the meaning of section 45(c)(3)(C), as in effect on the day before the date of the enactment of this Act) placed in service before January 1, 2004.

(e) DEFINITIONS AND SPECIAL RULES.—For purposes of this section—

* * *

(7) CREDIT NOT TO APPLY TO ELECTRICITY SOLD TO UTILITIES UNDER CERTAIN CONTRACTS.—

(A) IN GENERAL.—The credit determined under subsection (a) shall not apply to electricity—

(i) produced at a qualified facility described in *subsection (d)(1)* which is placed in service by the taxpayer after June 30, 1999, and

(ii) sold to a utility pursuant to a contract originally entered into before January 1, 1987 (whether or not amended or restated after that date).

* * *

(8) REFINED COAL PRODUCTION FACILITIES.—

(A) DETERMINATION OF CREDIT AMOUNT.—*In the case of a producer of refined coal, the credit determined under this section (without regard to this paragraph) for any taxable year shall be increased by an amount equal to $4.375 per ton of qualified refined coal—*

(i) produced by the taxpayer at a refined coal production facility during the 10-year period beginning on the date the facility was originally placed in service, and

(ii) sold by the taxpayer—

(I) to an unrelated person, and

(II) during such 10-year period and such taxable year.

(B) PHASEOUT OF CREDIT.—*The amount of the increase determined under subparagraph (A) shall be reduced by an amount which bears the same ratio to the amount of the increase (determined without regard to this subparagraph) as—*

(i) the amount by which the reference price of fuel used as a feedstock (within the meaning of subsection (c)(7)(A)) for the calendar year in which the sale occurs exceeds an amount equal to 1.7 multiplied by the reference price for such fuel in 2002, bears to

(ii) $8.75.

(C) APPLICATION OF RULES.—*Rules similar to the rules of the subsection (b)(3) and paragraphs (1) through (5) and (9) of this subsection shall apply for purposes of determining the amount of any increase under this paragraph.*

(9) COORDINATION WITH CREDIT FOR PRODUCING FUEL FROM A NONCONVENTIONAL SOURCE.—*The term "qualified facility" shall not include any facility the production from which is allowed as a credit under section 29 for the taxable year or any prior taxable year.*

* * *

[CCH Explanation at ¶872. Committee Reports at ¶10,920.]

Amendments

• **2004, American Jobs Creation Act of 2004 (H.R. 4520)**

H.R. 4520, §710(b)(1):

Amended Code Sec. 45 by redesignating subsection (d) as subsection (e). **Effective** generally for electricity produced and sold after the date of the enactment of this Act, in tax years ending after such date. For special rules, see Act Sec. 710(g)(2) and (4), below.

H.R. 4520, §710(b)(2):

Amended Code Sec. 45(e), as so redesignated, by adding at the end a new paragraph (8). **Effective** for refined coal produced and sold after the date of the enactment of this Act. For a special rule, see Act Sec. 710(g)(4), below.

H.R. 4520, §710(b)(3)(A):

Amended Code Sec. 45(e), as so redesignated, by striking "subsection (c)(3)(A)" in paragraph (7)(A)(i) and inserting "subsection (d)(1)". **Effective** generally for electricity produced and sold after the date of the enactment of this Act, in tax years ending after such date. For a special rule, see Act Sec. 710(g)(4), below.

H.R. 4520, §710(d):

Amended Code Sec. 45(e), as redesignated and amended by this section, by inserting after paragraph (8) a new paragraph (9). **Effective** generally for electricity produced and sold after the date of the enactment of this Act, in tax years ending after such date. For a special rule, see Act Sec. 710(g)(4), below.

H.R. 4520, §710(g)(2), provides:

(2) CERTAIN BIOMASS FACILITIES.—With respect to any facility described in section 45(d)(3)(A)(ii) of the Internal Revenue Code of 1986, as added by subsection (b)(1), which is placed in service before the date of the enactment of this Act, the amendments made by this section shall apply to electricity produced and sold after December 31, 2004, in taxable years ending after such date.

H.R. 4520, §710(g)(4), provides:

(4) NONAPPLICATION OF AMENDMENTS TO PREEFFECTIVE DATE POULTRY WASTE FACILITIES.—The amendments made by this section shall not apply with respect to any poultry waste facility (within the meaning of section 45(c)(3)(C), as in effect on the day before the date of the enactment of this Act) placed in service before January 1, 2004.

[¶5040] CODE SEC. 45D. NEW MARKETS TAX CREDIT.

* * *

(e) LOW-INCOME COMMUNITY.—For purposes of this section—

* * *

(2) TARGETED POPULATIONS.—The Secretary shall prescribe regulations under which 1 or more targeted populations (within the meaning of section 103(20) of the Riegle Community Development and Regulatory Improvement Act of 1994 (12 U.S.C. 4702(20))) may be treated as low-income communities. Such regulations shall include procedures for determining which entities are qualified active low-income community businesses with respect to such populations.

* * *

(4) TRACTS WITH LOW POPULATION.—A population census tract with a population of less than 2,000 shall be treated as a low-income community for purposes of this section if such tract—

(A) is within an empowerment zone the designation of which is in effect under section 1391, and

(B) is contiguous to 1 or more low-income communities (determined without regard to this paragraph).

(5) MODIFICATION OF INCOME REQUIREMENT FOR CENSUS TRACTS WITHIN HIGH MIGRATION RURAL COUNTIES.—

(A) IN GENERAL.—In the case of a population census tract located within a high migration rural county, paragraph (1)(B)(i) shall be applied by substituting "85 percent" for "80 percent".

(B) HIGH MIGRATION RURAL COUNTY.—For purposes of this paragraph, the term "high migration rural county" means any county which, during the 20-year period ending with the year in which the most recent census was conducted, has a net out-migration of inhabitants from the county of at least 10 percent of the population of the county at the beginning of such period.

* * *

[CCH Explanation at ¶380 and ¶390. Committee Reports at ¶10,090 and ¶10,110.]

Amendments

• **2004, American Jobs Creation Act of 2004 (H.R. 4520)**

H.R. 4520, §221(a):

Amended Code Sec. 45D(e)(2). **Effective** for designations made by the Secretary of the Treasury after the date of the enactment of this Act. Prior to amendment, Code Sec. 45D(e)(2) read as follows:

(2) TARGETED AREAS.—The Secretary may designate any area within any census tract as a low-income community if—

(A) the boundary of such area is continuous,

(B) the area would satisfy the requirements of paragraph (1) if it were a census tract, and

(C) an inadequate access to investment capital exists in such area.

H.R. 4520, §221(b):

Amended Code Sec. 45D(e) by adding at the end a new paragraph (4). **Effective** for investments made after the date of the enactment of this Act.

H.R. 4520, §223(a):

Amended Code Sec. 45D(e), as amended by this Act, by inserting after paragraph (4) a new paragraph (5). **Effective**

as if included in the amendment made by section 121(a) of the Community Renewal Tax Relief Act of 2000 [**effective** for investments made after 12-31-2000.—CCH].

[¶5045] *CODE SEC. 45G. RAILROAD TRACK MAINTENANCE CREDIT.*

(a) GENERAL RULE.—For purposes of section 38, the railroad track maintenance credit determined under this section for the taxable year is an amount equal to 50 percent of the qualified railroad track maintenance expenditures paid or incurred by an eligible taxpayer during the taxable year.

(b) LIMITATION.—The credit allowed under subsection (a) for any taxable year shall not exceed the product of—

(1) $3,500, and

(2) the number of miles of railroad track owned or leased by the eligible taxpayer as of the close of the taxable year.

A mile of railroad track may be taken into account by a person other than the owner only if such mile is assigned to such person by the owner for purposes of this subsection. Any mile which is so assigned may not be taken into account by the owner for purposes of this subsection.

(c) ELIGIBLE TAXPAYER.—For purposes of this section, the term "eligible taxpayer" means—

(1) any Class II or Class III railroad, and

(2) any person who transports property using the rail facilities of a person described in paragraph (1) or who furnishes railroad-related property or services to such a person.

(d) QUALIFIED RAILROAD TRACK MAINTENANCE EXPENDITURES.—For purposes of this section, the term "qualified railroad track maintenance expenditures" means expenditures (whether or not otherwise chargeable to capital account) for maintaining railroad track (including roadbed, bridges, and related track structures) owned or leased as of January 1, 2005, by a Class II or Class III railroad.

(e) OTHER DEFINITIONS AND SPECIAL RULES.—

(1) CLASS II OR CLASS III RAILROAD.—For purposes of this section, the terms "Class II railroad" and "Class III railroad" have the respective meanings given such terms by the Surface Transportation Board.

(2) CONTROLLED GROUPS.—Rules similar to the rules of paragraph (1) of section 41(f) shall apply for purposes of this section.

(3) BASIS ADJUSTMENT.—For purposes of this subtitle, if a credit is allowed under this section with respect to any railroad track, the basis of such track shall be reduced by the amount of the credit so allowed.

(f) APPLICATION OF SECTION.—This section shall apply to qualified railroad track maintenance expenditures paid or incurred during taxable years beginning after December 31, 2004, and before January 1, 2008.

[CCH Explanation at ¶375. Committee Reports at ¶10,260.]
Amendments
• **2004, American Jobs Creation Act of 2004 (H.R. 4520)**

H.R. 4520, §245(a):

Amended subpart D of part IV of subchapter A of chapter 1 by adding at the end a new Code Sec. 45G. **Effective** for tax years beginning after 12-31-2004.

[¶5050] *CODE SEC. 45H. CREDIT FOR PRODUCTION OF LOW SULFUR DIESEL FUEL.*

(a) IN GENERAL.—For purposes of section 38, the amount of the low sulfur diesel fuel production credit determined under this section with respect to any facility of a small business refiner is an amount equal to 5 cents for each gallon of low sulfur diesel fuel produced during the taxable year by such small business refiner at such facility.

(b) Maximum Credit.—

(1) In general.—The aggregate credit determined under subsection (a) for any taxable year with respect to any facility shall not exceed—

(A) 25 percent of the qualified capital costs incurred by the small business refiner with respect to such facility, reduced by

(B) the aggregate credits determined under this section for all prior taxable years with respect to such facility.

(2) Reduced percentage.—In the case of a small business refiner with average daily domestic refinery runs for the 1-year period ending on December 31, 2002, in excess of 155,000 barrels, the number of percentage points described in paragraph (1) shall be reduced (not below zero) by the product of such number (before the application of this paragraph) and the ratio of such excess to 50,000 barrels.

(c) Definitions and Special Rule.—For purposes of this section—

(1) Small business refiner.—The term "small business refiner" means, with respect to any taxable year, a refiner of crude oil—

(A) with respect to which not more than 1,500 individuals are engaged in the refinery operations of the business on any day during such taxable year, and

(B) the average daily domestic refinery run or average retained production of which for all facilities of the taxpayer for the 1-year period ending on December 31, 2002, did not exceed 205,000 barrels.

(2) Qualified capital costs.—The term "qualified capital costs" means, with respect to any facility, those costs paid or incurred during the applicable period for compliance with the applicable EPA regulations with respect to such facility, including expenditures for the construction of new process operation units or the dismantling and reconstruction of existing process units to be used in the production of low sulfur diesel fuel, associated adjacent or offsite equipment (including tankage, catalyst, and power supply), engineering, construction period interest, and sitework.

(3) Applicable epa regulations.—The term "applicable EPA regulations" means the Highway Diesel Fuel Sulfur Control Requirements of the Environmental Protection Agency.

(4) Applicable period.—The term "applicable period" means, with respect to any facility, the period beginning on January 1, 2003, and ending on the earlier of the date which is 1 year after the date on which the taxpayer must comply with the applicable EPA regulations with respect to such facility or December 31, 2009.

(5) Low sulfur diesel fuel.—The term "low sulfur diesel fuel" means diesel fuel with a sulfur content of 15 parts per million or less.

(d) Reduction in Basis.—For purposes of this subtitle, if a credit is determined under this section for any expenditure with respect to any property, the increase in basis of such property which would (but for this subsection) result from such expenditure shall be reduced by the amount of the credit so determined.

(e) Special Rule for Determination of Refinery Runs.—For purposes this section and section 179B(b), in the calculation of average daily domestic refinery run or retained production, only refineries which on April 1, 2003, were refineries of the refiner or a related person (within the meaning of section 613A(d)(3)), shall be taken into account.

(f) Certification.—

(1) Required.—No credit shall be allowed unless, not later than the date which is 30 months after the first day of the first taxable year in which the low sulfur diesel fuel production credit is determined with respect to a facility, the small business refiner obtains certification from the Secretary, after consultation with the Administrator of the Environmental Protection Agency, that the taxpayer's qualified capital costs with respect to such facility will result in compliance with the applicable EPA regulations.

(2) Contents of application.—An application for certification shall include relevant information regarding unit capacities and operating characteristics sufficient for the Secretary, after consultation with the Administrator of the Environmental Protection Agency, to determine that such qualified capital costs are necessary for compliance with the applicable EPA regulations.

(3) REVIEW PERIOD.—*Any application shall be reviewed and notice of certification, if applicable, shall be made within 60 days of receipt of such application. In the event the Secretary does not notify the taxpayer of the results of such certification within such period, the taxpayer may presume the certification to be issued until so notified.*

(4) STATUTE OF LIMITATIONS.—*With respect to the credit allowed under this section—*

(A) *the statutory period for the assessment of any deficiency attributable to such credit shall not expire before the end of the 3-year period ending on the date that the review period described in paragraph (3) ends with respect to the taxpayer, and*

(B) *such deficiency may be assessed before the expiration of such 3-year period notwithstanding the provisions of any other law or rule of law which would otherwise prevent such assessment.*

(g) COOPERATIVE ORGANIZATIONS.—

(1) APPORTIONMENT OF CREDIT.—

(A) IN GENERAL.—*In the case of a cooperative organization described in section 1381(a), any portion of the credit determined under subsection (a) for the taxable year may, at the election of the organization, be apportioned among patrons eligible to share in patronage dividends on the basis of the quantity or value of business done with or for such patrons for the taxable year.*

(B) FORM AND EFFECT OF ELECTION.—*An election under subparagraph (A) for any taxable year shall be made on a timely filed return for such year. Such election, once made, shall be irrevocable for such taxable year.*

(2) TREATMENT OF ORGANIZATIONS AND PATRONS.—

(A) ORGANIZATIONS.—*The amount of the credit not apportioned to patrons pursuant to paragraph (1) shall be included in the amount determined under subsection (a) for the taxable year of the organization.*

(B) PATRONS.—*The amount of the credit apportioned to patrons pursuant to paragraph (1) shall be included in the amount determined under subsection (a) for the first taxable year of each patron ending on or after the last day of the payment period (as defined in section 1382(d)) for the taxable year of the organization or, if earlier, for the taxable year of each patron ending on or after the date on which the patron receives notice from the cooperative of the apportionment.*

(3) SPECIAL RULE.—*If the amount of a credit which has been apportioned to any patron under this subsection is decreased for any reason—*

(A) *such amount shall not increase the tax imposed on such patron, and*

(B) *the tax imposed by this chapter on such organization shall be increased by such amount.*

The increase under subparagraph (B) shall not be treated as tax imposed by this chapter for purposes of determining the amount of any credit under this chapter or for purposes of section 55.

[CCH Explanation at ¶ 855. Committee Reports at ¶ 10,540.]

Amendments

• **2004, American Jobs Creation Act of 2004 (H.R. 4520)**

H.R. 4520, § 339(a):

Amended subpart D of part IV of subchapter A of chapter 1, as amended by this Act, by inserting after Code Sec. 45G a

new Code Sec. 45H. **Effective** for expenses paid or incurred after 12-31-2002, in tax years ending after such date.

[¶ 5055] *CODE SEC. 45I. CREDIT FOR PRODUCING OIL AND GAS FROM MARGINAL WELLS.*

(a) GENERAL RULE.—*For purposes of section 38, the marginal well production credit for any taxable year is an amount equal to the product of—*

(1) *the credit amount, and*

(2) *the qualified credit oil production and the qualified natural gas production which is attributable to the taxpayer.*

(b) CREDIT AMOUNT.—*For purposes of this section—*

(1) IN GENERAL.—The credit amount is—

(A) $3 per barrel of qualified crude oil production, and

(B) 50 cents per 1,000 cubic feet of qualified natural gas production.

(2) REDUCTION AS OIL AND GAS PRICES INCREASE.—

(A) IN GENERAL.—The $3 and 50 cents amounts under paragraph (1) shall each be reduced (but not below zero) by an amount which bears the same ratio to such amount (determined without regard to this paragraph) as—

(i) the excess (if any) of the applicable reference price over $15 ($1.67 for qualified natural gas production), bears to

(ii) $3 ($0.33 for qualified natural gas production).

The applicable reference price for a taxable year is the reference price of the calendar year preceding the calendar year in which the taxable year begins.

(B) INFLATION ADJUSTMENT.—In the case of any taxable year beginning in a calendar year after 2005, each of the dollar amounts contained in subparagraph (A) shall be increased to an amount equal to such dollar amount multiplied by the inflation adjustment factor for such calendar year (determined under section 43(b)(3)(B) by substituting "2004" for "1990").

(C) REFERENCE PRICE.—For purposes of this paragraph, the term "reference price" means, with respect to any calendar year—

(i) in the case of qualified crude oil production, the reference price determined under section 29(d)(2)(C), and

(ii) in the case of qualified natural gas production, the Secretary's estimate of the annual average wellhead price per 1,000 cubic feet for all domestic natural gas.

(c) QUALIFIED CRUDE OIL AND NATURAL GAS PRODUCTION.—For purposes of this section—

(1) IN GENERAL.—The terms "qualified crude oil production" and "qualified natural gas production" mean domestic crude oil or natural gas which is produced from a qualified marginal well.

(2) LIMITATION ON AMOUNT OF PRODUCTION WHICH MAY QUALIFY.—

(A) IN GENERAL.—Crude oil or natural gas produced during any taxable year from any well shall not be treated as qualified crude oil production or qualified natural gas production to the extent production from the well during the taxable year exceeds 1,095 barrels or barrel-of-oil equivalents (as defined in section 29(d)(5)).

(B) PROPORTIONATE REDUCTIONS.—

(i) SHORT TAXABLE YEARS.—In the case of a short taxable year, the limitations under this paragraph shall be proportionately reduced to reflect the ratio which the number of days in such taxable year bears to 365.

(ii) WELLS NOT IN PRODUCTION ENTIRE YEAR.—In the case of a well which is not capable of production during each day of a taxable year, the limitations under this paragraph applicable to the well shall be proportionately reduced to reflect the ratio which the number of days of production bears to the total number of days in the taxable year.

(3) DEFINITIONS.—

(A) QUALIFIED MARGINAL WELL.—The term "qualified marginal well" means a domestic well—

(i) the production from which during the taxable year is treated as marginal production under section 613A(c)(6), or

(ii) which, during the taxable year—

(I) has average daily production of not more than 25 barrel-of-oil equivalents (as so defined), and

(II) produces water at a rate not less than 95 percent of total well effluent.

(B) CRUDE OIL, ETC.—The terms "crude oil", "natural gas", "domestic", and "barrel" have the meanings given such terms by section 613A(e).

(d) Other Rules

(1) *Production attributable to the taxpayer.*—In the case of a qualified marginal well in which there is more than one owner of operating interests in the well and the crude oil or natural gas production exceeds the limitation under subsection (c)(2), qualifying crude oil production or qualifying natural gas production attributable to the taxpayer shall be determined on the basis of the ratio which taxpayer's revenue interest in the production bears to the aggregate of the revenue interests of all operating interest owners in the production.

(2) *Operating interest required.*—Any credit under this section may be claimed only on production which is attributable to the holder of an operating interest.

(3) *Production from nonconventional sources excluded.*—In the case of production from a qualified marginal well which is eligible for the credit allowed under section 29 for the taxable year, no credit shall be allowable under this section unless the taxpayer elects not to claim the credit under section 29 with respect to the well.

[CCH Explanation at ¶ 860. Committee Reports at ¶ 10,560.]

Amendments

• **2004, American Jobs Creation Act of 2004 (H.R. 4520)**

H.R. 4520, § 341(a):

Amended subpart D of part IV of subchapter A of chapter 1, as amended by this Act, by inserting after Code Sec. 45H

a new Code Sec. 45I. **Effective** for production in tax years beginning after 12-31-2004.

[¶ 5060] CODE SEC. 46. AMOUNT OF CREDIT.

For purposes of section 38, the amount of the investment credit determined under this section for any taxable year shall be the sum of—

(1) the rehabilitation credit, *and*

(2) the energy credit.

* * *

[CCH Explanation at ¶ 840. Committee Reports at ¶ 10,450.]

Amendments

• **2004, American Jobs Creation Act of 2004 (H.R. 4520)**

H.R. 4520, § 322(d)(1)(A)-(C):

Amended Code Sec. 46 by adding "and" at the end of paragraph (1), by striking ", and" at the end of paragraph

(2) and inserting a period, and by striking paragraph (3). **Effective** with respect to expenditures paid or incurred after the date of the enactment of this Act. Prior to being stricken, Code Sec. 46(3) read as follows:

(3) the reforestation credit.

[¶ 5065] CODE SEC. 48. ENERGY CREDIT.

(a) *Energy Credit.*—

* * *

(3) *Energy property.*—For purposes of this subpart, the term "energy property" means any property—

(A) which is—

(i) equipment which uses solar energy to generate electricity, to heat or cool (or provide hot water for use in) a structure, or to provide solar process heat, or

(ii) equipment used to produce, distribute, or use energy derived from a geothermal deposit (within the meaning of section 613(e)(2)), but only, in the case of electricity generated by geothermal power, up to (but not including) the electrical transmission stage,

(B)(i) the construction, reconstruction, or erection of which is completed by the taxpayer, or

(ii) which is acquired by the taxpayer if the original use of such property commences with the taxpayer,

(C) with respect to which depreciation (or amortization in lieu of depreciation) is allowable, and

(D) which meets the performance and quality standards (if any) which—

(i) have been prescribed by the Secretary by regulations (after consultation with the Secretary of Energy), and

(ii) are in effect at the time of the acquisition of the property.

The term "energy property" shall not include any property which is public utility property (as defined in section 46(f)(5) as in effect on the day before the date of the enactment of the Revenue Reconciliation Act of 1990). *Such term shall not include any property which is part of a facility the production from which is allowed as a credit under section 45 for the taxable year or any prior taxable year.*

* * *

[CCH Explanation at ¶ 840 and ¶ 872. Committee Reports at ¶ 10,450 and ¶ 10,920.]

Amendments

• **2004, American Jobs Creation Act of 2004 (H.R. 4520)**

H.R. 4520, § 322(d)(2)(B):

Amended Code Sec. 48 by striking "; REFORESTATION CREDIT" following "ENERGY CREDIT" in the heading. **Effective** with respect to expenditures paid or incurred after the date of the enactment of this Act.

H.R. 4520, § 710(e):

Amended Code Sec. 48(a)(3) by adding at the end a new sentence. **Effective** generally for electricity produced and sold after the date of the enactment of this Act, in tax years ending after such date.

(b) CERTAIN PROGRESS EXPENDITURE RULES MADE APPLICABLE.—Rules similar to the rules of subsections (c)(4) and (d) of section 46 (as in effect on the day before the date of the enactment of the Revenue Reconciliation Act of 1990) shall apply for purposes of *subsection (a)*.

[CCH Explanation at ¶ 840. Committee Reports at ¶ 10,450.]

Amendments

• **2004, American Jobs Creation Act of 2004 (H.R. 4520)**

H.R. 4520, § 322(d)(2)(A)(i)-(iii):

Amended Code Sec. 48 by striking subsection (b), by striking "this subsection" in paragraph (5) of subsection (a) and inserting "subsection (a)", and by redesignating such paragraph (5) as subsection (b). **Effective** with respect to expenditures paid or incurred after the date of the enactment of this Act. Prior to amendment, Code Sec. 48(b) read as follows:

(b) REFORESTATION CREDIT.—

(1) IN GENERAL.—For purposes of section 46, the reforestation credit for any taxable year is 10 percent of the portion of the amortizable basis of any qualified timber property which was acquired during such taxable year and which is taken into account under section 194 (after the application of section 194(b)(1)).

(2) DEFINITIONS.—For purposes of this subpart, the terms "amortizable basis" and "qualified timber property" have the respective meanings given to such terms by section 194.

[¶ 5070] CODE SEC. 50. OTHER SPECIAL RULES.

* * *

(c) BASIS ADJUSTMENT TO INVESTMENT CREDIT PROPERTY.—

* * *

(3) SPECIAL RULE.—In the case of any energy credit—

(A) only 50 percent of such credit shall be taken into account under paragraph (1), and

(B) only 50 percent of any recapture amount attributable to such credit shall be taken into account under paragraph (2).

* * *

[CCH Explanation at ¶ 840. Committee Reports at ¶ 10,450.]

Amendments

• **2004, American Jobs Creation Act of 2004 (H.R. 4520)**

H.R. 4520, § 322(d)(2)(D):

Amended Code Sec. 50(c)(3) by striking "or reforestation credit" following "energy credit". **Effective** with respect to

expenditures paid or incurred after the date of the enactment of this Act.

[¶ 5075] CODE SEC. 53. CREDIT FOR PRIOR YEAR MINIMUM TAX LIABILITY.

* * *

(d) DEFINITIONS.—For purposes of this section—

(1) NET MINIMUM TAX.—

* * *

(B) CREDIT NOT ALLOWED FOR EXCLUSION PREFERENCES.—

(i) ADJUSTED NET MINIMUM TAX.—The adjusted net minimum tax for any taxable year is—

* * *

(II) the amount which would be the net minimum tax for such taxable year if the only adjustments and items of tax preference taken into account were those specified in clause (ii).

* * *

[CCH Explanation at ¶ 455. Committee Reports at ¶ 10,770.]
Amendments
• **2004, American Jobs Creation Act of 2004 (H.R. 4520)**

H.R. 4520, § 421(a)(2):

Amended Code Sec. 53(d)(1)(B)(i)(II) by striking "and if section 59(a)(2) did not apply" before the period at the end. **Effective** for tax years beginning after 12-31-2004.

[¶ 5080] CODE SEC. 55. ALTERNATIVE MINIMUM TAX IMPOSED.

* * *

(c) REGULAR TAX.—

* * *

(2) COORDINATION WITH INCOME AVERAGING FOR FARMERS AND FISHERMEN.—Solely for purposes of this section, section 1301 (relating to averaging of farm and fishing income) shall not apply in computing the regular tax.

(3) CROSS REFERENCES.—

For provisions providing that certain credits are not allowable against the tax imposed by this section, see sections 26(a), 29(b)(6), 30(b)(3), and 38(c).

[CCH Explanation at ¶ 825. Committee Reports at ¶ 10,370.]
Amendments
• **2004, American Jobs Creation Act of 2004 (H.R. 4520)**

H.R. 4520, § 314(a):

Amended Code Sec. 55(c) by redesignating paragraph (2) as paragraph (3) and by inserting after paragraph (1) a new paragraph (2). **Effective** for tax years beginning after 12-31-2003.

[¶ 5085] CODE SEC. 56. ADJUSTMENTS IN COMPUTING ALTERNATIVE MINIMUM TAXABLE INCOME.

* * *

(g) ADJUSTMENTS BASED ON ADJUSTED CURRENT EARNINGS.—

* * *

(4) ADJUSTMENTS.—In determining adjusted current earnings, the following adjustments shall apply:

* * *

(B) INCLUSION OF ITEMS INCLUDED FOR PURPOSES OF COMPUTING EARNINGS AND PROFITS.—

(i) IN GENERAL.—In the case of any amount which is excluded from gross income for purposes of computing alternative minimum taxable income but is taken into account in determining the amount of earnings and profits—

(I) such amount shall be included in income in the same manner as if such amount were includible in gross income for purposes of computing alternative minimum taxable income, and

(II) the amount of such income shall be reduced by any deduction which would have been allowable in computing alternative minimum taxable income if such amount were includible in gross income.

The preceding sentence shall not apply in the case of any amount excluded from gross income under section 108 (or the corresponding provisions of prior law) or under section 139A *or 1357*. In the case of any insurance company taxable under section 831(b), this clause shall not apply to any amount not described in section 834(b).

* * *

(C) DISALLOWANCE OF ITEMS NOT DEDUCTIBLE IN COMPUTING EARNINGS AND PROFITS.—

* * *

(iv) SPECIAL RULE FOR CERTAIN DIVIDENDS RECEIVED BY CERTAIN COOPERATIVES.—In the case of a cooperative described in section 927(a)(4), clause (i) shall not apply to any amount allowable as a deduction under section 245(c).

(v) DEDUCTION FOR DOMESTIC PRODUCTION.—*Clause (i) shall not apply to any amount allowable as a deduction under section 199.*

(vi) SPECIAL RULE FOR CERTAIN DISTRIBUTIONS FROM CONTROLLED FOREIGN CORPORATIONS.— *Clause (i) shall not apply to any deduction allowable under section 965.*

* * *

(6) EXCEPTION FOR CERTAIN CORPORATIONS.—This subsection shall not apply to any S corporation, regulated investment company, real estate investment trust, *or REMIC.*

* * *

[CCH Explanation at ¶205, ¶210, ¶535, ¶545 and ¶1120. Committee Reports at ¶10,010, ¶10,020, ¶10,290, ¶10,780 and ¶11,180.]

Amendments

• 2004, American Jobs Creation Act of 2004 (H.R. 4520)

H.R. 4520, §101(b)(4):

Amended Code Sec. 56(g)(4)(B)(i) by striking "114 or" after "law) or under" in the second sentence. **Effective** for transactions after 12-31-2004. For transitional and special rules, see Act Sec. 101(d)-(f), below.

H.R. 4520, §101(d)-(f), provides:

(d) TRANSITIONAL RULE FOR 2005 AND 2006.—

(1) IN GENERAL.—In the case of transactions during 2005 or 2006, the amount includible in gross income by reason of the amendments made by this section shall not exceed the applicable percentage of the amount which would have been so included but for this subsection.

(2) APPLICABLE PERCENTAGE.—For purposes of paragraph (1), the applicable percentage shall be as follows:

(A) For 2005, the applicable percentage shall be 20 percent.

(B) For 2006, the applicable percentage shall be 40 percent.

(e) REVOCATION OF ELECTION TO BE TREATED AS DOMESTIC CORPORATION.—If, during the 1-year period beginning on the date of the enactment of this Act, a corporation for which an election is in effect under section 943(e) of the Internal Revenue Code of 1986 revokes such election, no gain or loss shall be recognized with respect to property treated as transferred under clause (ii) of section 943(e)(4)(B) of such Code to the extent such property—

(1) was treated as transferred under clause (i) thereof, or

(2) was acquired during a taxable year to which such election applies and before May 1, 2003, in the ordinary course of its trade or business.

The Secretary of the Treasury (or such Secretary's delegate) may prescribe such regulations as may be necessary to prevent the abuse of the purposes of this subsection.

(f) BINDING CONTRACTS.—The amendments made by this section shall not apply to any transaction in the ordinary course of a trade or business which occurs pursuant to a binding contract—

(1) which is between the taxpayer and a person who is not a related person (as defined in section 943(b)(3) of such Code, as in effect on the day before the date of the enactment of this Act), and

(2) which is in effect on September 17, 2003, and at all times thereafter.

For purposes of this subsection, a binding contract shall include a purchase option, renewal option, or replacement option which is included in such contract and which is enforceable against the seller or lessor.

H.R. 4520, §102(b):

Amended Code Sec. 56(g)(4)(C) by adding at the end a new clause (v). **Effective** for tax years beginning after 12-31-2004.

H.R. 4520, §248(b)(1):

Amended the second sentence of Code Sec. 56(g)(4)(B)(i), as amended by this Act, by inserting "or 1357" after "section 139A". **Effective** for tax years beginning after the date of the enactment of this Act.

H.R. 4520, §422(b):

Amended Code Sec. 56(g)(4)(C) by inserting after clause (v) a new clause (vi). **Effective** for tax years ending on or after the date of the enactment of this Act.

H.R. 4520, § 835(b)(1):

Amended Code Sec. 56(g)(6) by striking "REMIC, or FASIT" and inserting "or REMIC". **Effective** 1-1-2005. For an exception, see Act Sec. 835(c)(2), below.

H.R. 4520, § 835(c)(2), provides:

(2) EXCEPTION FOR EXISTING FASITS.—Paragraph (1) shall not apply to any FASIT in existence on the date of the enactment

of this Act to the extent that regular interests issued by the FASIT before such date continue to remain outstanding in accordance with the original terms of issuance.

[¶ 5090] CODE SEC. 59. OTHER DEFINITIONS AND SPECIAL RULES.

(a) ALTERNATIVE MINIMUM TAX FOREIGN TAX CREDIT.—For purposes of this part—

* * *

(2) PRE-CREDIT TENTATIVE MINIMUM TAX.—For purposes of this subsection, the term "pre-credit tentative minimum tax" means—

(A) in the case of a taxpayer other than a corporation, the amount determined under the first sentence of section 55(b)(1)(A)(i), or

(B) in the case of a corporation, the amount determined under section 55(b)(1)(B)(i).

(3) ELECTION TO USE SIMPLIFIED SECTION 904 LIMITATION.—

* * *

[CCH Explanation at ¶ 455. Committee Reports at ¶ 10,770.]

Amendments

• **2004, American Jobs Creation Act of 2004 (H.R. 4520)**

H.R. 4520, § 421(a)(1):

Amended Code Sec. 59(a) by striking paragraph (2) and by redesignating paragraphs (3) and (4) as paragraphs (2) and (3), respectively. **Effective** for tax years beginning after 12-31-2004. Prior to being stricken, Code Sec. 59(a)(2) read as follows:

(2) LIMITATION TO 90 PERCENT OF TAX.—

(A) IN GENERAL.—The alternative minimum tax foreign tax credit for any taxable year shall not exceed the excess (if any) of—

(i) the pre-credit tentative minimum tax for the taxable year, over

(ii) 10 percent of the amount which would be the pre-credit tentative minimum tax without regard to the alternative tax net operating loss deduction and section 57(a)(2)(E).

(B) CARRYBACK AND CARRYFORWARD.—If the alternative minimum tax foreign tax credit exceeds the amount determined under subparagraph (A), such excess shall, for purposes of this part, be treated as an amount to which section 904(c) applies.

[¶ 5095] CODE SEC. 62. ADJUSTED GROSS INCOME DEFINED.

(a) GENERAL RULE.—For purposes of this subtitle, the term "adjusted gross income" means, in the case of an individual, gross income minus the following deductions:

* * *

(19)[(20)] COSTS INVOLVING DISCRIMINATION SUITS, ETC.—*Any deduction allowable under this chapter for attorney fees and court costs paid by, or on behalf of, the taxpayer in connection with any action involving a claim of unlawful discrimination (as defined in subsection (e)) or a claim of a violation of subchapter III of chapter 37 of title 31, United States Code or a claim made under section 1862(b)(3)(A) of the Social Security Act (42 U.S.C. 1395y(b)(3)(A)). The preceding sentence shall not apply to any deduction in excess of the amount includible in the taxpayer's gross income for the taxable year on account of a judgment or settlement (whether by suit or agreement and whether as lump sum or periodic payments) resulting from such claim.*

Nothing in this section shall permit the same item to be deducted more than once.

* * *

[CCH Explanation at ¶ 1215. Committee Reports at ¶ 10,850.]

Amendments

• **2004, American Jobs Creation Act of 2004 (H.R. 4520)**

H.R. 4520, § 703(a):

Amended Code Sec. 62(a) by inserting after paragraph (18)[(19)] a new paragraph (19)[(20)]. **Effective** for fees and

costs paid after the date of the enactment of this Act with respect to any judgment or settlement occurring after such date.

(e) UNLAWFUL DISCRIMINATION DEFINED.—For purposes of subsection (a)(19), the term "unlawful discrimi-nation" means an act that is unlawful under any of the following:

(1) Section 302 of the Civil Rights Act of 1991 (2 U.S.C. 1202).

(2) Section 201, 202, 203, 204, 205, 206, or 207 of the Congressional Accountability Act of 1995 (2 U.S.C. 1311, 1312, 1313, 1314, 1315, 1316, or 1317).

(3) The National Labor Relations Act (29 U.S.C. 151 et seq.).

(4) The Fair Labor Standards Act of 1938 (29 U.S.C. 201 et seq.).

(5) Section 4 or 15 of the Age Discrimination in Employment Act of 1967 (29 U.S.C. 623 or 633a).

(6) Section 501 or 504 of the Rehabilitation Act of 1973 (29 U.S.C. 791 or 794).

(7) Section 510 of the Employee Retirement Income Security Act of 1974 (29 U.S.C. 1140).

(8) Title IX of the Education Amendments of 1972 (20 U.S.C. 1681 et seq.).

(9) The Employee Polygraph Protection Act of 1988 (29 U.S.C. 2001 et seq.).

(10) The Worker Adjustment and Retraining Notification Act (29 U.S.C. 2102 et seq.).

(11) Section 105 of the Family and Medical Leave Act of 1993 (29 U.S.C. 2615).

(12) Chapter 43 of title 38, United States Code (relating to employment and reemployment rights of members of the uniformed services).

(13) Section 1977, 1979, or 1980 of the Revised Statutes (42 U.S.C. 1981, 1983, or 1985).

(14) Section 703, 704, or 717 of the Civil Rights Act of 1964 (42 U.S.C. 2000e-2, 2000e-3, or 2000e-16).

(15) Section 804, 805, 806, 808, or 818 of the Fair Housing Act (42 U.S.C. 3604, 3605, 3606, 3608, or 3617).

(16) Section 102, 202, 302, or 503 of the Americans with Disabilities Act of 1990 (42 U.S.C. 12112, 12132, 12182, or 12203).

(17) Any provision of Federal law (popularly known as whistleblower protection provisions) prohibit-ing the discharge of an employee, the discrimination against an employee, or any other form of retaliation or reprisal against an employee for asserting rights or taking other actions permitted under Federal law.

(18) Any provision of Federal, State, or local law, or common law claims permitted under Federal, State, or local law—

(i) providing for the enforcement of civil rights, or

(ii) regulating any aspect of the employment relationship, including claims for wages, compen-sation, or benefits, or prohibiting the discharge of an employee, the discrimination against an employee, or any other form of retaliation or reprisal against an employee for asserting rights or taking other actions permitted by law.

* * *

[CCH Explanation at ¶1215. Committee Reports at ¶10,850.]

Amendments

• **2004, American Jobs Creation Act of 2004 (H.R. 4520)**

H.R. 4520, §703(b):

Amended Code Sec. 62 by adding at the end a new subsection (e). **Effective** for fees and costs paid after the date of the enactment of this Act with respect to any judg-ment or settlement occurring after such date.

[¶5100] CODE SEC. 72. ANNUITIES; CERTAIN PROCEEDS OF ENDOWMENT AND LIFE INSURANCE CONTRACTS.

* * *

(w) APPLICATION OF BASIS RULES TO NONRESIDENT ALIENS.—

(1) IN GENERAL.—Notwithstanding any other provision of this section, for purposes of determining the portion of any distribution which is includible in gross income of a distributee who is a citizen or resident of the United States, the investment in the contract shall not include any applicable nontaxable contributions or applicable nontaxable earnings.

(2) APPLICABLE NONTAXABLE CONTRIBUTION.—For purposes of this subsection, the term "applicable nontaxable contribution" means any employer or employee contribution—

(A) which was made with respect to compensation—

(i) for labor or personal services performed by an employee who, at the time the labor or services were performed, was a nonresident alien for purposes of the laws of the United States in effect at such time, and

(ii) which is treated as from sources without the United States, and

(B) which was not subject to income tax (and would have been subject to income tax if paid as cash compensation when the services were rendered) under the laws of the United States or any foreign country.

(3) APPLICABLE NONTAXABLE EARNINGS.—For purposes of this subsection, the term "applicable nontaxable earnings" means earnings—

(A) which are paid or accrued with respect to any employer or employee contribution which was made with respect to compensation for labor or personal services performed by an employee,

(B) with respect to which the employee was at the time the earnings were paid or accrued a nonresident alien for purposes of the laws of the United States, and

(C) which were not subject to income tax under the laws of the United States or any foreign country.

(4) REGULATIONS.—The Secretary shall prescribe such regulations as may be necessary to carry out the provisions of this subsection, including regulations treating contributions and earnings as not subject to tax under the laws of any foreign country where appropriate to carry out the purposes of this subsection.

[CCH Explanation at ¶1425. Committee Reports at ¶11,780.]

Amendments

• **2004, American Jobs Creation Act of 2004 (H.R. 4520)**

H.R. 4520, § 906(a):

Amended Code Sec. 72 by redesignating subsection (w) as subsection (x) and by inserting after subsection (v) a new subsection (w). **Effective** for distributions on or after the date of the enactment of this Act.

(x) CROSS REFERENCE.—

For limitation on adjustments to basis of annuity contracts sold, see section 1021.

* * *

[CCH Explanation at ¶1425. Committee Reports at ¶11,780.]

Amendments

• **2004, American Jobs Creation Act of 2004 (H.R. 4520)**

H.R. 4520, § 906(a):

Amended Code Sec. 72 by redesignating subsection (w) as subsection (x). **Effective** for distributions on or after the date of the enactment of this Act.

[¶5105] CODE SEC. 83. PROPERTY TRANSFERRED IN CONNECTION WITH PERFORMANCE OF SERVICES.

* * *

(c) SPECIAL RULES.—For purposes of this section—

* * *

(4) For purposes of determining an individual's basis in property transferred in connection with the performance of services, rules similar to the rules of section 72(w) shall apply.

* * *

[CCH Explanation at ¶1425. Committee Reports at ¶11,780.]

Amendments

• 2004, American Jobs Creation Act of 2004 (H.R. 4520)

H.R. 4520, §906(b):

Amended Code Sec. 83(c) by adding after paragraph (3) a new paragraph (4). **Effective** for distributions on or after the date of the enactment of this Act.

[¶5110] CODE SEC. 86. SOCIAL SECURITY AND TIER 1 RAILROAD RETIREMENT BENEFITS.

* * *

(b) TAXPAYERS TO WHOM SUBSECTION (a) APPLIES.—

* * *

(2) MODIFIED ADJUSTED GROSS INCOME.—For purposes of this subsection, the term "modified adjusted gross income" means adjusted gross income—

(A) determined without regard to this section and sections 135, 137, *199*, 221, 222, 911, 931, and 933, and

* * *

[CCH Explanation at ¶210. Committee Reports at ¶10,020.]

Amendments

• 2004, American Jobs Creation Act of 2004 (H.R. 4520)

H.R. 4520, §102(d)(1):

Amended Code Sec. 86(b)(2)(A) by inserting "199," before "221". **Effective** for tax years beginning after 12-31-2004.

[¶5115] CODE SEC. 87. *ALCOHOL AND BIODIESEL FUELS CREDITS.*

Gross income includes—

(1) the amount of the alcohol fuel credit determined with respect to the taxpayer for the taxable year under section 40(a), and

(2) the biodiesel fuels credit determined with respect to the taxpayer for the taxable year under section 40A(a).

* * *

[CCH Explanation at ¶810. Committee Reports at ¶10,324.]

Amendments

• 2004, American Jobs Creation Act of 2004 (H.R. 4520)

H.R. 4520, §302(c)(1)(A):

Amended Code Sec. 87. **Effective** for fuel produced, and sold or used, after 12-31-2004, in tax years ending after such date. Prior to amendment, Code Sec. 87 read as follows:

SEC. 87. ALCOHOL FUEL CREDIT.

Gross income includes the amount of the alcohol fuel credit determined with respect to the taxpayer for the taxable year under section 40(a).

[¶5120] CODE SEC. 108. INCOME FROM DISCHARGE OF INDEBTEDNESS.

* * *

(e) GENERAL RULES FOR DISCHARGE OF INDEBTEDNESS (INCLUDING DISCHARGES NOT IN TITLE 11 CASES OR INSOLVENCY).—For purposes of this title—

* * *

(8) INDEBTEDNESS SATISFIED BY CORPORATE STOCK OR PARTNERSHIP INTEREST.—For purposes of determining income of a debtor from discharge of indebtedness, if—

(A) a debtor corporation transfers stock, or

(B) a debtor partnership transfers a capital or profits interest in such partnership,

to a creditor in satisfaction of its recourse or nonrecourse indebtedness, such corporation or partnership shall be treated as having satisfied the indebtedness with an amount of money equal to the fair market value of the stock or interest. In the case of any partnership, any discharge of indebtedness income recognized under this paragraph shall be included in the distributive shares of taxpayers which were the partners in the partnership immediately before such discharge.

* * *

[CCH Explanation at ¶720. Committee Reports at ¶11,680.]

Amendments

• **2004, American Jobs Creation Act of 2004 (H.R. 4520)**

H.R. 4520, §896(a):

Amended Code Sec. 108(e)(8). **Effective** with respect to cancellations of indebtedness occurring on or after the date of the enactment of this Act. Prior to amendment, Code Sec. 108(e)(8) read as follows:

(f) STUDENT LOANS.—

(8) INDEBTEDNESS SATISFIED BY CORPORATION'S STOCK.—For purposes of determining income of a debtor from discharge of indebtedness, if a debtor corporation transfers stock to a creditor in satisfaction of its indebtedness, such corporation shall be treated as having satisfied the indebtedness with an amount of money equal to the fair market value of the stock.

* * *

(4) PAYMENTS UNDER NATIONAL HEALTH SERVICE CORPS LOAN REPAYMENT PROGRAM AND CERTAIN STATE LOAN REPAYMENT PROGRAMS.—In the case of an individual, gross income shall not include any amount received under section 338B(g) of the Public Health Service Act or under a State program described in section 338I of such Act.

* * *

[CCH Explanation at ¶1225. Committee Reports at ¶10,430.]

Amendments

• **2004, American Jobs Creation Act of 2004 (H.R. 4520)**

H.R. 4520, §320(a):

Amended Code Sec. 108(f) by adding at the end new paragraph (4). **Effective** for amounts received by an individual in tax years beginning after 12-31-2003.

[¶5125] CODE SEC. 114. EXTRATERRITORIAL INCOME. [*Repealed.*]

* * *

[CCH Explanation at ¶205. Committee Reports at ¶10,010.]

Amendments

• **2004, American Jobs Creation Act of 2004 (H.R. 4520)**

H.R. 4520, §101(a):

Repealed Code Sec. 114. **Effective** for transactions after 12-31-2004. For transitional and special rules, see Act Sec. 101(d)-(f), below. Prior to repeal, Code Sec. 114 read as follows:

SEC. 114. EXTRATERRITORIAL INCOME.

(a) EXCLUSION.—Gross income does not include extraterritorial income.

(b) EXCEPTION.—Subsection (a) shall not apply to extraterritorial income which is not qualifying foreign trade income as determined under subpart E of part III of subchapter N.

(c) DISALLOWANCE OF DEDUCTIONS.—

(1) IN GENERAL.—Any deduction of a taxpayer allocated under paragraph (2) to extraterritorial income of the taxpayer excluded from gross income under subsection (a) shall not be allowed.

(2) ALLOCATION.—Any deduction of the taxpayer properly apportioned and allocated to the extraterritorial income derived by the taxpayer from any transaction shall be allocated on a proportionate basis between—

(A) the extraterritorial income derived from such transaction which is excluded from gross income under subsection (a), and

(B) the extraterritorial income derived from such transaction which is not so excluded.

(d) DENIAL OF CREDITS FOR CERTAIN FOREIGN TAXES.—Notwithstanding any other provision of this chapter, no credit shall be allowed under this chapter for any income, war profits, and excess profits taxes paid or accrued to any foreign country or possession of the United States with respect to extraterritorial income which is excluded from gross income under subsection (a).

(e) EXTRATERRITORIAL INCOME.—For purposes of this section, the term "extraterritorial income" means the gross income of the taxpayer attributable to foreign trading gross receipts (as defined in section 942) of the taxpayer.

H.R. 4520, §101(d)-(f), provides:

(d) TRANSITIONAL RULE FOR 2005 AND 2006.—

(1) IN GENERAL.—In the case of transactions during 2005 or 2006, the amount includible in gross income by reason of the amendments made by this section shall not exceed the applicable percentage of the amount which would have been so included but for this subsection.

(2) APPLICABLE PERCENTAGE.—For purposes of paragraph (1), the applicable percentage shall be as follows:

(A) For 2005, the applicable percentage shall be 20 percent.

(B) For 2006, the applicable percentage shall be 40 percent.

(e) REVOCATION OF ELECTION TO BE TREATED AS DOMESTIC CORPORATION.—If, during the 1-year period beginning on the date of the enactment of this Act, a corporation for which an election is in effect under section 943(e) of the Internal Revenue Code of 1986 revokes such election, no gain or loss shall be recognized with respect to property treated as transferred under clause (ii) of section 943(e)(4)(B) of such Code to the extent such property—

(1) was treated as transferred under clause (i) thereof, or

(2) was acquired during a taxable year to which such election applies and before May 1, 2003, in the ordinary course of its trade or business.

The Secretary of the Treasury (or such Secretary's delegate) may prescribe such regulations as may be necessary to prevent the abuse of the purposes of this subsection.

(f) BINDING CONTRACTS.—The amendments made by this section shall not apply to any transaction in the ordinary course of a trade or business which occurs pursuant to a binding contract—

(1) which is between the taxpayer and a person who is not a related person (as defined in section 943(b)(3) of such Code, as in effect on the day before the date of the enactment of this Act), and

(2) which is in effect on September 17, 2003, and at all times thereafter.

For purposes of this subsection, a binding contract shall include a purchase option, renewal option, or replacement option which is included in such contract and which is enforceable against the seller or lessor.

[¶5130] CODE SEC. 121. EXCLUSION OF GAIN FROM SALE OF PRINCIPAL RESIDENCE.

* * *

(d) SPECIAL RULES.—

* * *

(10)[(11)] PROPERTY ACQUIRED IN LIKE-KIND EXCHANGE.—If a taxpayer acquired property in an exchange to which section 1031 applied, subsection (a) shall not apply to the sale or exchange of such property if it occurs during the 5-year period beginning with the date of the acquisition of such property.

* * *

[CCH Explanation at ¶1210. Committee Reports at ¶11,230.]

Amendments

• 2004, American Jobs Creation Act of 2004 (H.R. 4520)

H.R. 4520, §840(a):

Amended Code Sec. 121(d) by adding at the end a new paragraph (10)[(11)]. **Effective** for sales or exchanges after the date of the enactment of this Act.

[¶5135] CODE SEC. 135. INCOME FROM UNITED STATES SAVINGS BONDS USED TO PAY HIGHER EDUCATION TUITION AND FEES.

* * *

(c) DEFINITIONS.—For purposes of this section—

* * *

(4) MODIFIED ADJUSTED GROSS INCOME.—The term "modified adjusted gross income" means the adjusted gross income of the taxpayer for the taxable year determined—

(A) without regard to this section and sections 137, 199, 221, 222, 911, 931, and 933, and

* * *

[CCH Explanation at ¶210.]

Amendments

• 2004, American Jobs Creation Act of 2004 (H.R. 4520)

H.R. 4520, §102(d)(1):

Amended Code Sec. 135(c)(4)(A) by inserting "199," before "221". **Effective** for tax years beginning after 12-31-2004.

[¶ 5140] CODE SEC. 137. ADOPTION ASSISTANCE PROGRAMS.

* * *

(b) LIMITATIONS.—

* * *

(3) DETERMINATION OF ADJUSTED GROSS INCOME.—For purposes of paragraph (2), adjusted gross income shall be determined—

(A) without regard to this section and sections *199,* 221, 222, 911, 931, and 933, and

* * *

[CCH Explanation at ¶ 210.]

Amendments

• **2004, American Jobs Creation Act of 2004 (H.R. 4520)**

H.R. 4520, § 102(d)(1):

Amended Code Sec. 137(b)(3)(A) by inserting "199," before "221". **Effective** for tax years beginning after 12-31-2004.

[¶ 5145] CODE SEC. 142. EXEMPT FACILITY BOND.

(a) GENERAL RULE.—For purposes of this part, the term "exempt facility bond" means any bond issued as part of an issue 95 percent or more of the net proceeds of which are to be used to provide—

* * *

(12) environmental enhancements of hydroelectric generating facilities,

(13) qualified public educational facilities, *or*

(14) *qualified green building and sustainable design projects.*

* * *

[CCH Explanation at ¶ 745. Committee Reports at ¶ 10,830.]

Amendments

• **2004, American Jobs Creation Act of 2004 (H.R. 4520)**

H.R. 4520, § 701(a):

Amended Code Sec. 142(a) by striking "or" at the end of paragraph (12), by striking the period at the end of para-graph (13) and inserting ", or", and by inserting at the end a new paragraph (14). **Effective** for bonds issued after 12-31-2004.

(l) QUALIFIED GREEN BUILDING AND SUSTAINABLE DESIGN PROJECTS.—

(1) IN GENERAL.—For purposes of subsection (a)(14), the term "qualified green building and sustainable design project" means any project which is designated by the Secretary, after consultation with the Administrator of the Environmental Protection Agency, as a qualified green building and sustainable design project and which meets the requirements of clauses (i), (ii), (iii), and (iv) of paragraph (4)(A).

(2) DESIGNATIONS.—

(A) IN GENERAL.—Within 60 days after the end of the application period described in paragraph (3)(A), the Secretary, after consultation with the Administrator of the Environmental Protection Agency, shall designate qualified green building and sustainable design projects. At least one of the projects designated shall be located in, or within a 10-mile radius of, an empowerment zone as designated pursuant to section 1391, and at least one of the projects designated shall be located in a rural State. No more than one project shall be designated in a State. A project shall not be designated if such project includes a stadium or arena for professional sports exhibitions or games.

(B) MINIMUM CONSERVATION AND TECHNOLOGY INNOVATION OBJECTIVES.—The Secretary, after consultation with the Administrator of the Environmental Protection Agency, shall ensure that, in the aggregate, the projects designated shall—

(i) reduce electric consumption by more than 150 megawatts annually as compared to conventional generation,

(ii) reduce daily sulfur dioxide emissions by at least 10 tons compared to coal generation power,

(iii) expand by 75 percent the domestic solar photovoltaic market in the United States (measured in megawatts) as compared to the expansion of that market from 2001 to 2002, and

(iv) use at least 25 megawatts of fuel cell energy generation.

(3) LIMITED DESIGNATIONS.—*A project may not be designated under this subsection unless—*

(A) the project is nominated by a State or local government within 180 days of the enactment of this subsection, and

(B) such State or local government provides written assurances that the project will satisfy the eligibility criteria described in paragraph (4).

(4) APPLICATION.—

(A) IN GENERAL.—*A project may not be designated under this subsection unless the application for such designation includes a project proposal which describes the energy efficiency, renewable energy, and sustainable design features of the project and demonstrates that the project satisfies the following eligibility criteria:*

(i) GREEN BUILDING AND SUSTAINABLE DESIGN.—*At least 75 percent of the square footage of commercial buildings which are part of the project is registered for United States Green Building Council's LEED certification and is reasonably expected (at the time of the designation) to receive such certification. For purposes of determining LEED certification as required under this clause, points shall be credited by using the following:*

(I) For wood products, certification under the Sustainable Forestry Initiative Program and the American Tree Farm System.

(II) For renewable wood products, as credited for recycled content otherwise provided under LEED certification.

(III) For composite wood products, certification under standards established by the American National Standards Institute, or such other voluntary standards as published in the Federal Register by the Administrator of the Environmental Protection Agency.

(ii) BROWNFIELD REDEVELOPMENT.—*The project includes a brownfield site as defined by section 101(39) of the Comprehensive Environmental Response, Compensation, and Liability Act of 1980 (42 U.S.C. 9601), including a site described in subparagraph (D)(ii)(II)(aa) thereof.*

(iii) STATE AND LOCAL SUPPORT.—*The project receives specific State or local government resources which will support the project in an amount equal to at least $5,000,000. For purposes of the preceding sentence, the term "resources" includes tax abatement benefits and contributions in kind.*

(iv) SIZE.—*The project includes at least one of the following:*

(I) At least 1,000,000 square feet of building.

(II) At least 20 acres.

(v) USE OF TAX BENEFIT.—*The project proposal includes a description of the net benefit of the tax-exempt financing provided under this subsection which will be allocated for financing of one or more of the following:*

(I) The purchase, construction, integration, or other use of energy efficiency, renewable energy, and sustainable design features of the project.

(II) Compliance with certification standards cited under clause (i).

(III) The purchase, remediation, and foundation construction and preparation of the brownfields site.

(vi) PROHIBITED FACILITIES.—*An issue shall not be treated as an issue described in subsection (a)(14) if any proceeds of such issue are used to provide any facility the principal business of which is the sale of food or alcoholic beverages for consumption on the premises.*

(vii) EMPLOYMENT.—*The project is projected to provide permanent employment of at least 1,500 full time equivalents (150 full time equivalents in rural States) when completed and construction employment of at least 1,000 full time equivalents (100 full time equivalents in rural States).*

The application shall include an independent analysis which describes the project's economic impact, including the amount of projected employment.

(B) PROJECT DESCRIPTION.—Each application described in subparagraph (A) shall contain for each project a description of—

(i) the amount of electric consumption reduced as compared to conventional construction,

(ii) the amount of sulfur dioxide daily emissions reduced compared to coal generation,

(iii) the amount of the gross installed capacity of the project's solar photovoltaic capacity measured in megawatts, and

(iv) the amount, in megawatts, of the project's fuel cell energy generation.

(5) CERTIFICATION OF USE OF TAX BENEFIT.—No later than 30 days after the completion of the project, each project must certify to the Secretary that the net benefit of the tax-exempt financing was used for the purposes described in paragraph (4).

(6) DEFINITIONS.—For purposes of this subsection—

(A) RURAL STATE.—The term "rural State" means any State which has—

(i) a population of less than 4,500,000 according to the 2000 census,

(ii) a population density of less than 150 people per square mile according to the 2000 census, and

(iii) increased in population by less than half the rate of the national increase between the 1990 and 2000 censuses.

(B) LOCAL GOVERNMENT.—The term "local government" has the meaning given such term by section 1393(a)(5).

(C) NET BENEFIT OF TAX-EXEMPT FINANCING.—The term "net benefit of tax-exempt financing" means the present value of the interest savings (determined by a calculation established by the Secretary) which result from the tax-exempt status of the bonds.

(7) AGGREGATE FACE AMOUNT OF TAX-EXEMPT FINANCING.—

(A) IN GENERAL.—An issue shall not be treated as an issue described in subsection (a)(14) if the aggregate face amount of bonds issued by the State or local government pursuant thereto for a project (when added to the aggregate face amount of bonds previously so issued for such project) exceeds an amount designated by the Secretary as part of the designation.

(B) LIMITATION ON AMOUNT OF BONDS.—The Secretary may not allocate authority to issue qualified green building and sustainable design project bonds in an aggregate face amount exceeding $2,000,000,000.

(8) TERMINATION.—Subsection (a)(14) shall not apply with respect to any bond issued after September 30, 2009.

(9) TREATMENT OF CURRENT REFUNDING BONDS.—Paragraphs (7)(B) and (8) shall not apply to any bond (or series of bonds) issued to refund a bond issued under subsection (a)(14) before October 1, 2009, if—

(A) the average maturity date of the issue of which the refunding bond is a part is not later than the average maturity date of the bonds to be refunded by such issue,

(B) the amount of the refunding bond does not exceed the outstanding amount of the refunded bond, and

(C) the net proceeds of the refunding bond are used to redeem the refunded bond not later than 90 days after the date of the issuance of the refunding bond.

For purposes of subparagraph (A), average maturity shall be determined in accordance with section 147(b)(2)(A).

* * *

[CCH Explanation at ¶745. Committee Reports at ¶10,830.]

Amendments

• 2004, American Jobs Creation Act of 2004 (H.R. 4520)

H.R. 4520, §701(b):

Amended Code Sec. 142 by adding at the end a new subsection (l). **Effective** for bonds issued after 12-31-2004.

[¶5150] CODE SEC. 144. QUALIFIED SMALL ISSUE BOND; QUALIFIED STUDENT LOAN BOND; QUALIFIED REDEVELOPMENT BOND.

(a) QUALIFIED SMALL ISSUE BOND.—

* * *

(4) $10,000,000 LIMIT IN CERTAIN CASES.—

* * *

(F) AGGREGATE AMOUNT OF CAPITAL EXPENDITURES WHERE THERE IS URBAN DEVELOPMENT ACTION GRANT.—In the case of any issue 95 percent or more of the net proceeds of which are to be used to provide facilities with respect to which an urban development action grant has been made under section 119 of the Housing and Community Development Act of 1974, capital expenditures of not to exceed $10,000,000 shall not be taken into account for purposes of applying subparagraph (A)(ii). *This subparagraph shall not apply to bonds issued after September 30, 2009.*

(G) ADDITIONAL CAPITAL EXPENDITURES NOT TAKEN INTO ACCOUNT.—With respect to bonds issued after September 30, 2009, in addition to any capital expenditure described in subparagraph (C), capital expenditures of not to exceed $10,000,000 shall not be taken into account for purposes of applying subparagraph (A)(ii).

* * *

[CCH Explanation at ¶735. Committee Reports at ¶10,550.]

Amendments

• 2004, American Jobs Creation Act of 2004 (H.R. 4520)

H.R. 4520, §340(a):

Amended Code Sec. 144(a)(4) by adding at the end a new subparagraph (G). **Effective** on the date of the enactment of this Act.

H.R. 4520, §340(b):

Amended Code Sec. 144(a)(4)(F) by adding at the end a new sentence. **Effective** on the date of the enactment of this Act.

[¶5155] CODE SEC. 146. VOLUME CAP.

* * *

(g) EXCEPTION FOR CERTAIN BONDS.—Only for purposes of this section, the term "private activity bond" shall not include—

* * *

(3) any exempt facility bond issued as part of an issue described in paragraph (1), (2), (12), *(13), or (14)* of section 142(a) (relating to airports, docks and wharves, environmental enhancements of hydroelectric generating facilities, *qualified public educational facilities, and qualified green building and sustainable design projects*), and

* * *

[CCH Explanation at ¶745. Committee Reports at ¶10,830.]

Amendments

• 2004, American Jobs Creation Act of 2004 (H.R. 4520)

H.R. 4520, §701(c)(1)-(2):

Amended Code Sec. 146(g)(3) by striking "or (13)" and inserting "(13), or (14)", and by striking "and qualified public educational facilities" and inserting "qualified public educational facilities, and qualified green building and sustainable design projects". **Effective** for bonds issued after 12-31-2004.

[¶ 5160] CODE SEC. 162. TRADE OR BUSINESS EXPENSES.

* * *

(m) CERTAIN EXCESSIVE EMPLOYEE REMUNERATION.—

* * *

(4) APPLICABLE EMPLOYEE REMUNERATION.—For purposes of this subsection—

* * *

(G) COORDINATION WITH EXCISE TAX ON SPECIFIED STOCK COMPENSATION.—The dollar limitation contained in paragraph (1) with respect to any covered employee shall be reduced (but not below zero) by the amount of any payment (with respect to such employee) of the tax imposed by section 4985 directly or indirectly by the expatriated corporation (as defined in such section) or by any member of the expanded affiliated group (as defined in such section) which includes such corporation.

* * *

[CCH Explanation at ¶ 508. Committee Reports at ¶ 10,980.]

Amendments

• **2004, American Jobs Creation Act of 2004 (H.R. 4520)**

H.R. 4520, § 802(b)(2):

Amended Code Sec. 162(m)(4) by adding at the end a new subparagraph (G). **Effective** on 3-4-2003; except that periods before such date shall not be taken into account in applying the periods in Code Sec. 4985(a) and (e)(1), as added by this Act.

(o) TREATMENT OF CERTAIN EXPENSES OF RURAL MAIL CARRIERS.—

* * *

(2) SPECIAL RULE WHERE EXPENSES EXCEED REIMBURSEMENTS.—Notwithstanding paragraph (1)(A), if the expenses incurred by an employee for the use of a vehicle in performing services described in paragraph (1) exceed the qualified reimbursements for such expenses, such excess shall be taken into account in computing the miscellaneous itemized deductions of the employee under section 67.

(3) DEFINITION OF QUALIFIED REIMBURSEMENTS.—For purposes of this subsection, the term "qualified reimbursements" means the amounts paid by the United States Postal Service to employees as an equipment maintenance allowance under the 1991 collective bargaining agreement between the United States Postal Service and the National Rural Letter Carriers' Association. Amounts paid as an equipment maintenance allowance by such Postal Service under later collective bargaining agreements that supersede the 1991 agreement shall be considered qualified reimbursements if such amounts do not exceed the amounts that would have been paid under the 1991 agreement, adjusted for changes in the Consumer Price Index (as defined in section 1(f)(5)) since 1991.

* * *

[CCH Explanation at ¶ 1220. Committee Reports at ¶ 10,410.]

Amendments

• **2004, American Jobs Creation Act of 2004 (H.R. 4520)**

H.R. 4520, § 318(a):

Amended Code Sec. 162(o) by redesignating paragraph (2) as paragraph (3) and by inserting after paragraph (1) new paragraph (2). **Effective** for tax years beginning after 12-31-2003.

H.R. 4520, § 318(b):

Amended Code Sec. 162(o) by striking "REIMBURSED" in the heading before "EXPENSES". **Effective** for tax years beginning after 12-31-2003.

[¶ 5165] CODE SEC. 163. INTEREST.

* * *

(e) ORIGINAL ISSUE DISCOUNT.—

* * *

(3) SPECIAL RULE FOR ORIGINAL ISSUE DISCOUNT ON OBLIGATION HELD BY RELATED FOREIGN PERSON.—

* * *

(B) SPECIAL RULE FOR CERTAIN FOREIGN ENTITIES.—

(i) IN GENERAL.—In the case of any debt instrument having original issue discount which is held by a related foreign person which is a controlled foreign corporation (as defined in section 957) or a passive foreign investment company (as defined in section 1297), a deduction shall be allowable to the issuer with respect to such original issue discount for any taxable year before the taxable year in which paid only to the extent such original issue discount is includible (determined without regard to properly allocable deductions and qualified deficits under section 952(c)(1)(B)) during such prior taxable year in the gross income of a United States person who owns (within the meaning of section 958(a)) stock in such corporation.

(ii) SECRETARIAL AUTHORITY.—The Secretary may by regulation exempt transactions from the application of clause (i), including any transaction which is entered into by a payor in the ordinary course of a trade or business in which the payor is predominantly engaged.

(C) RELATED FOREIGN PERSON.—For purposes of subparagraph (A), the term "related foreign person" means any person—

(i) who is not a United States person, and

(ii) who is related (within the meaning of section 267(b)) to the issuer.

* * *

[CCH Explanation at ¶705. Committee Reports at ¶11,240.]

Amendments

• **2004, American Jobs Creation Act of 2004 (H.R. 4520)**

H.R. 4520, § 841(a):

Amended Code Sec. 163(e)(3) by redesignating subparagraph (B) as subparagraph (C) and by inserting after sub-

paragraph (A) a new subparagraph (B). **Effective** for payments accrued on or after the date of the enactment of this Act.

(l) DISALLOWANCE OF DEDUCTION ON CERTAIN DEBT INSTRUMENTS OF CORPORATIONS.—

* * *

(2) DISQUALIFIED DEBT INSTRUMENT.—For purposes of this subsection, the term "disqualified debt instrument" means any indebtedness of a corporation which is payable in equity of the issuer or a related party *or equity held by the issuer (or any related party) in any other person.*

(3) SPECIAL RULES FOR AMOUNTS PAYABLE IN EQUITY.—For purposes of paragraph (2), indebtedness shall be treated as payable in equity of the issuer *or any other person* only if—

(A) a substantial amount of the principal or interest is required to be paid or converted, or at the option of the issuer or a related party is payable in, or convertible into, such equity,

(B) a substantial amount of the principal or interest is required to be determined, or at the option of the issuer or a related party is determined, by reference to the value of such equity, or

(C) the indebtedness is part of an arrangement which is reasonably expected to result in a transaction described in subparagraph (A) or (B).

For purposes of this paragraph, principal or interest shall be treated as required to be so paid, converted, or determined if it may be required at the option of the holder or a related party and there is a substantial certainty the option will be exercised.

(4) CAPITALIZATION ALLOWED WITH RESPECT TO EQUITY OF PERSONS OTHER THAN ISSUER AND RELATED PARTIES.—If the disqualified debt instrument of a corporation is payable in equity held by the issuer (or any related party) in any other person (other than a related party), the basis of such equity shall be increased by the amount not allowed as a deduction by reason of paragraph (1) with respect to the instrument.

(5) EXCEPTION FOR CERTAIN INSTRUMENTS ISSUED BY DEALERS IN SECURITIES.—For purposes of this subsection, the term "disqualified debt instrument" does not include indebtedness issued by a dealer in securities (or a related party) which is payable in, or by reference to, equity (other than equity of the issuer or a related party) held by such dealer in its capacity as a dealer in securities. For purposes of this paragraph, the term "dealer in securities" has the meaning given such term by section 475.

(6) RELATED PARTY.—For purposes of this subsection, a person is a related party with respect to another person if such person bears a relationship to such other person described in section 267(b) or 707(b).

(7) REGULATIONS.—The Secretary shall prescribe such regulations as may be necessary or appropriate to carry out the purposes of this subsection, including regulations preventing avoidance of this subsection through the use of an issuer other than a corporation.

[CCH Explanation at ¶715. Committee Reports at ¶11,280.]

Amendments

• **2004, American Jobs Creation Act of 2004 (H.R. 4520)**

H.R. 4520, §845(a):

Amended Code Sec. 163(l)(2) by inserting "or equity held by the issuer (or any related party) in any other person" after "or a related party". **Effective** for debt instruments issued after 10-3-2004.

H.R. 4520, §845(b):

Amended Code Sec. 163(l) by redesignating paragraphs (4) and (5) as paragraphs (5) and (6) and by inserting after paragraph (3) a new paragraph (4). **Effective** for debt instruments issued after 10-3-2004.

H.R. 4520, §845(c):

Amended Code Sec. 163(l), as amended by Act Sec. 845(b), by redesignating paragraphs (5) and (6) as paragraphs (6) and (7) and by inserting after paragraph (4) a new paragraph (5). **Effective** for debt instruments issued after 10-3-2004.

H.R. 4520, §845(d):

Amended Code Sec. 163(l)(3) by striking "or a related party" in the material preceding subparagraph (A) and inserting "or any other person". **Effective** for debt instruments issued after 10-3-2004.

(m) INTEREST ON UNPAID TAXES ATTRIBUTABLE TO NONDISCLOSED REPORTABLE TRANSACTIONS.—*No deduction shall be allowed under this chapter for any interest paid or accrued under section 6601 on any underpayment of tax which is attributable to the portion of any reportable transaction understatement (as defined in section 6662A(b)) with respect to which the requirement of section 6664(d)(2)(A) is not met.*

[CCH Explanation at ¶625. Committee Reports at ¶11,210.]

Amendments

• **2004, American Jobs Creation Act of 2004 (H.R. 4520)**

H.R. 4520, §838(a):

Amended Code Sec. 163 by redesignating subsection (m) as subsection (n) and by inserting after subsection (l) a new

(n) CROSS REFERENCES.—

subsection (m). **Effective** for transactions in tax years beginning after the date of the enactment of this Act.

* * *

[CCH Explanation at ¶625. Committee Reports at ¶11,210.]

Amendments

• **2004, American Jobs Creation Act of 2004 (H.R. 4520)**

H.R. 4520, §838(a):

Amended Code Sec. 163 by redesignating subsection (m) as subsection (n). **Effective** for transactions in tax years beginning after the date of the enactment of this Act.

[¶5170] CODE SEC. 164. TAXES.

* * *

(b) DEFINITIONS AND SPECIAL RULES.—For purposes of this section—

* * *

(5) GENERAL SALES TAXES.—*For purposes of subsection (a)—*

(A) ELECTION TO DEDUCT STATE AND LOCAL SALES TAXES IN LIEU OF STATE AND LOCAL INCOME TAXES.—

(i) IN GENERAL.—*At the election of the taxpayer for the taxable year, subsection (a) shall be applied—*

(I) without regard to the reference to State and local income taxes, and

(II) as if State and local general sales taxes were referred to in a paragraph thereof.

(B) Definition of general sales tax.—The term "general sales tax" means a tax imposed at one rate with respect to the sale at retail of a broad range of classes of items.

(C) Special rules for food, etc.—In the case of items of food, clothing, medical supplies, and motor vehicles—

(i) the fact that the tax does not apply with respect to some or all of such items shall not be taken into account in determining whether the tax applies with respect to a broad range of classes of items, and

(ii) the fact that the rate of tax applicable with respect to some or all of such items is lower than the general rate of tax shall not be taken into account in determining whether the tax is imposed at one rate.

(D) Items taxed at different rates.—Except in the case of a lower rate of tax applicable with respect to an item described in subparagraph (C), no deduction shall be allowed under this paragraph for any general sales tax imposed with respect to an item at a rate other than the general rate of tax.

(E) Compensating use taxes.—A compensating use tax with respect to an item shall be treated as a general sales tax. For purposes of the preceding sentence, the term "compensating use tax" means, with respect to any item, a tax which—

(i) is imposed on the use, storage, or consumption of such item, and

(ii) is complementary to a general sales tax, but only if a deduction is allowable under this paragraph with respect to items sold at retail in the taxing jurisdiction which are similar to such item.

(F) Special rule for motor vehicles.—In the case of motor vehicles, if the rate of tax exceeds the general rate, such excess shall be disregarded and the general rate shall be treated as the rate of tax.

(G) Separately stated general sales taxes.—If the amount of any general sales tax is separately stated, then, to the extent that the amount so stated is paid by the consumer (other than in connection with the consumer's trade or business) to the seller, such amount shall be treated as a tax imposed on, and paid by, such consumer.

(H) Amount of deduction may be determined under tables.—

(i) In general.—At the election of the taxpayer for the taxable year, the amount of the deduction allowed under this paragraph for such year shall be—

(I) the amount determined under this paragraph (without regard to this subparagraph) with respect to motor vehicles, boats, and other items specified by the Secretary, and

(II) the amount determined under tables prescribed by the Secretary with respect to items to which subclause (I) does not apply.

(ii) Requirements for tables.—The tables prescribed under clause (i)—

(I) shall reflect the provisions of this paragraph,

(II) shall be based on the average consumption by taxpayers on a State-by-State basis (as determined by the Secretary) of items to which clause (i)(I) does not apply, taking into account filing status, number of dependents, adjusted gross income, and rates of State and local general sales taxation, and

(III) need only be determined with respect to adjusted gross incomes up to the applicable amount (as determined under section 68(b)).

(I) Application of paragraph.—This paragraph shall apply to taxable years beginning after December 31, 2003, and before January 1, 2006.

* * *

[CCH Explanation at ¶1205. Committee Reports at ¶10,810.]

Amendments

• **2004, American Jobs Creation Act of 2004 (H.R. 4520)**

H.R. 4520, §501(a):

Amended Code Sec. 164(b) by adding at the end a new paragraph (5). **Effective** for tax years beginning after 12-31-2003.

[¶5175] CODE SEC. 167. DEPRECIATION.

* * *

  (f) TREATMENT OF CERTAIN PROPERTY EXCLUDED FROM SECTION 197.—

    (1) COMPUTER SOFTWARE.—

* * *

      (C) TAX-EXEMPT USE PROPERTY SUBJECT TO LEASE.—In the case of computer software which would be tax-exempt use property as defined in subsection (h) of section 168 if such section applied to computer software, the useful life under subparagraph (A) shall not be less than 125 percent of the lease term (within the meaning of section 168(i)(3)).

    (2) CERTAIN INTERESTS OR RIGHTS ACQUIRED SEPARATELY.—If a depreciation deduction is allowable under subsection (a) with respect to any property described in subparagraph (B), (C), or (D) of section 197(e)(4), such deduction shall be computed in accordance with regulations prescribed by the Secretary. *If such property would be tax-exempt use property as defined in subsection (h) of section 168 if such section applied to such property, the useful life under such regulations shall not be less than 125 percent of the lease term (within the meaning of section 168(i)(3)).*

* * *

[CCH Explanation at ¶670. Committee Reports at ¶11,290.]

Amendments

• **2004, American Jobs Creation Act of 2004 (H.R. 4520)**

H.R. 4520, §847(b)(1):

Amended Code Sec. 167(f)(1) by adding at the end a new subparagraph (C). **Effective** generally for leases entered into after 3-12-2004. For an exception, see Act Sec. 849(b)(1)-(2), below.

H.R. 4520, §847(b)(2):

Amended Code Sec. 167(f)(2) by adding at the end a new sentence. **Effective** for leases entered into after 10-3-2004.

H.R. 4520, §849(b)(1)-(2), provides:

(b) EXCEPTION.—

(1) IN GENERAL.—The amendments made by this part shall not apply to qualified transportation property.

(2) QUALIFIED TRANSPORTATION PROPERTY.—For purposes of paragraph (1), the term "qualified transportation property" means domestic property subject to a lease with respect to which a formal application—

(A) was submitted for approval to the Federal Transit Administration (an agency of the Department of Transportation) after June 30, 2003, and before March 13, 2004,

(B) is approved by the Federal Transit Administration before January 1, 2006, and

(C) includes a description of such property and the value of such property.

  (g) DEPRECIATION UNDER INCOME FORECAST METHOD.—

* * *

    (5) SPECIAL RULES.—

* * *

      (E) TREATMENT OF DISTRIBUTION COSTS.—For purposes of this subsection, the income with respect to any property shall be the taxpayer's gross income from such property.

      (F) DETERMINATIONS.—For purposes of paragraph (2), determinations of the amount of income earned in connection with any property shall be made in the same manner as for purposes of applying the income forecast method; except that any income from the disposition of such property shall be taken into account.

      (G) TREATMENT OF PASS-THRU ENTITIES.—Rules similar to the rules of section 460(b)(4) shall apply for purposes of this subsection.

* * *

(7) TREATMENT OF PARTICIPATIONS AND RESIDUALS.—

(A) IN GENERAL.—For purposes of determining the depreciation deduction allowable with respect to a property under this subsection, the taxpayer may include participations and residuals with respect to such property in the adjusted basis of such property for the taxable year in which the property is placed in service, but only to the extent that such participations and residuals relate to income estimated (for purposes of this subsection) to be earned in connection with the property before the close of the 10th taxable year referred to in paragraph (1)(A).

(B) PARTICIPATIONS AND RESIDUALS.—For purposes of this paragraph, the term "participations and residuals" means, with respect to any property, costs the amount of which by contract varies with the amount of income earned in connection with such property.

(C) SPECIAL RULES RELATING TO RECOMPUTATION YEARS.—If the adjusted basis of any property is determined under this paragraph, paragraph (4) shall be applied by substituting "for each taxable year in such period" for "for such period".

(D) OTHER SPECIAL RULES.—

(i) PARTICIPATIONS AND RESIDUALS.—Notwithstanding subparagraph (A), the taxpayer may exclude participations and residuals from the adjusted basis of such property and deduct such participations and residuals in the taxable year that such participations and residuals are paid.

(ii) COORDINATION WITH OTHER RULES.—Deductions computed in accordance with this paragraph shall be allowable notwithstanding paragraph (1)(B), section 263, 263A, 404, 419, or 461(h).

(E) AUTHORITY TO MAKE ADJUSTMENTS.—The Secretary shall prescribe appropriate adjustments to the basis of property and to the look-back method for the additional amounts allowable as a deduction solely by reason of this paragraph.

* * *

[CCH Explanation at ¶ 320. Committee Reports at ¶ 10,230.]

Amendments

• 2004, American Jobs Creation Act of 2004 (H.R. 4520)

H.R. 4520, § 242(a):

Amended Code Sec. 167(g) by adding at the end a new paragraph (7). **Effective** for property placed in service after the date of the enactment of this Act.

H.R. 4520, § 242(b):

Amended Code Sec. 167(g)(5) by redesignating subparagraphs (E) and (F) as subparagraphs (F) and (G), respectively, and inserting after subparagraph (D) a new subparagraph (E). **Effective** for property placed in service after the date of the enactment of this Act.

[¶ 5180] CODE SEC. 168. ACCELERATED COST RECOVERY SYSTEM.

* * *

(b) APPLICABLE DEPRECIATION METHOD.—For purposes of this section—

* * *

(2) 150 PERCENT DECLINING BALANCE METHOD IN CERTAIN CASES.—Paragraph (1) shall be applied by substituting "150 percent" for "200 percent" in the case of—

(A) any 15-year or 20-year property *not referred to in paragraph (3)*,

(B) any property used in a farming business (within the meaning of section 263A(e)(4)), or

(C) any property (other than property described in paragraph (3)) with respect to which the taxpayer elects under paragraph (5) to have the provisions of this paragraph apply.

(3) PROPERTY TO WHICH STRAIGHT LINE METHOD APPLIES.—The applicable depreciation method shall be the straight line method in the case of the following property:

(A) Nonresidential real property.

(B) Residential rental property.

(C) Any railroad grading or tunnel bore.

(D) Property with respect to which the taxpayer elects under paragraph (5) to have the provisions of this paragraph apply.

(E) Property described in subsection (e)(3)(D)(ii).

(F) Water utility property described in subsection (e)(5).

(G) Qualified leasehold improvement property described in subsection (e)(6).

(H) Qualified restaurant property described in subsection (e)(7).

* * *

[CCH Explanation at ¶315 and ¶317. Committee Reports at ¶10,050.]

Amendments

• **2004, American Jobs Creation Act of 2004 (H.R. 4520)**

H.R. 4520, §211(d)(1):

Amended Code Sec. 168(b)(3) by adding at the end new subparagraphs (G) and (H). **Effective** for property placed in service after the date of the enactment of this Act.

H.R. 4520, §211(d)(2):

Amended Code Sec. 168(b)(2)(A) by inserting before the comma "not referred to in paragraph (3)". **Effective** for property placed in service after the date of the enactment of this Act.

(e) Classification of Property.—For purposes of this section—

* * *

(3) Classification of certain property.—

* * *

(C) 7-year property.—The term "7-year property" includes—

(i) any railroad track,

(ii) any motorsports entertainment complex,

(iii) any Alaska natural gas pipeline, and

(iv) any property which—

(I) does not have a class life, and

(II) is not otherwise classified under paragraph (2) or this paragraph.

* * *

(E) 15-year property.—The term "15-year property" includes—

(i) any municipal wastewater treatment plant,

(ii) any telephone distribution plant and comparable equipment used for 2-way exchange of voice and data communications,

(iii) any section 1250 property which is a retail motor fuels outlet (whether or not food or other convenience items are sold at the outlet),

(iv) any qualified leasehold improvement property placed in service before January 1, 2006,

(v) any qualified restaurant property placed in service before January 1, 2006, and

(vi) initial clearing and grading land improvements with respect to gas utility property.

(F) 20-year property.—The term "20-year property" means initial clearing and grading land improvements with respect to any electric utility transmission and distribution plant.

* * *

(6) Qualified leasehold improvement property.—The term "qualified leasehold improvement property" has the meaning given such term in section 168(k)(3) except that the following special rules shall apply:

(A) Improvements made by lessor.—In the case of an improvement made by the person who was the lessor of such improvement when such improvement was placed in service, such improvement shall be qualified leasehold improvement property (if at all) only so long as such improvement is held by such person.

(B) Exception for changes in form of business.—Property shall not cease to be qualified leasehold improvement property under subparagraph (A) by reason of—

(i) death,

(ii) a transaction to which section 381(a) applies,

(iii) a mere change in the form of conducting the trade or business so long as the property is retained in such trade or business as qualified leasehold improvement property and the taxpayer retains a substantial interest in such trade or business,

(iv) the acquisition of such property in an exchange described in section 1031, 1033, or 1038 to the extent that the basis of such property includes an amount representing the adjusted basis of other property owned by the taxpayer or a related person, or

(v) the acquisition of such property by the taxpayer in a transaction described in section 332, 351, 361, 721, or 731 (or the acquisition of such property by the taxpayer from the transferee or acquiring corporation in a transaction described in such section), to the extent that the basis of the property in the hands of the taxpayer is determined by reference to its basis in the hands of the transferor or distributor.

(7) QUALIFIED RESTAURANT PROPERTY.—The term "qualified restaurant property" means any section 1250 property which is an improvement to a building if—

(A) such improvement is placed in service more than 3 years after the date such building was first placed in service, and

(B) more than 50 percent of the building's square footage is devoted to preparation of, and seating for on-premises consumption of, prepared meals.

* * *

[CCH Explanation at ¶315, ¶317, ¶335, ¶340 and ¶345. Committee Reports at ¶10,050, ¶10,860, ¶10,880 and ¶11,730.]

Amendments

• **2004, American Jobs Creation Act of 2004 (H.R. 4520)**

H.R. 4520, §211(a):

Amended Code Sec. 168(e)(3)(E) by striking "and" at the end of clause (ii), by striking the period at the end of clause (iii) and inserting a comma, and by adding at the end new clauses (iv) and (v). **Effective** for property placed in service after the date of the enactment of this Act.

H.R. 4520, §211(b):

Amended Code Sec. 168(e) by adding at the end a new paragraph (6). **Effective** for property placed in service after the date of the enactment of this Act.

H.R. 4520, §211(c):

Amended Code Sec. 168(e), as amended by Act Sec. 211(b), by adding at the end a new paragraph (7). **Effective** for property placed in service after the date of the enactment of this Act.

H.R. 4520, §704(a):

Amended Code Sec. 168(e)(3)(C) by redesignating clause (ii) as clause (iii) and by inserting after clause (i) a new clause (ii). **Effective** generally for property placed in service after the date of the enactment of this Act. For special rules, see Act Secs. 704(c)(2)-(3), below.

H.R. 4520, §704(c)(2)-(3), provides:

(2) SPECIAL RULE FOR ASSET CLASS 80.0.—In the case of race track facilities placed in service after the date of the enact-

ment of this Act, such facilities shall not be treated as theme and amusement facilities classified under asset class 80.0.

(3) NO INFERENCE.—Nothing in this section or the amendments made by this section shall be construed to affect the treatment of property placed in service on or before the date of the enactment of this Act.

H.R. 4520, §706(a):

Amended Code Sec. 168(e)(3)(C), as amended by this Act, by striking "and" at the end of clause (ii), by redesignating clause (iii) as clause (iv), and by inserting after clause (ii) a new clause (iii). **Effective** for property placed in service after 12-31-2004.

H.R. 4520, §901(a):

Amended Code Sec. 168(e)(3)(E), as amended by this Act, by striking "and" at the end of clause (iv), by striking the period at the end of clause (v) and inserting ", and", and by adding at the end a new clause (vi). **Effective** for property placed in service after the date of the enactment of this Act.

H.R. 4520, §901(b):

Amended Code Sec. 168(e)(3) by adding at the end a new subparagraph (F). **Effective** for property placed in service after the date of the enactment of this Act.

(g) ALTERNATIVE DEPRECIATION SYSTEM FOR CERTAIN PROPERTY.—

* * *

(3) SPECIAL RULES FOR DETERMINING CLASS LIFE.—

(A) TAX-EXEMPT USE PROPERTY SUBJECT TO LEASE.—In the case of any tax-exempt use property subject to a lease, the recovery period used for purposes of paragraph (2) shall (*notwithstanding any other subparagraph of this paragraph*) in no event be less than 125 percent of the lease term.

(B) Special rule for certain property assigned to classes.—For purposes of paragraph (2), in the case of property described in any of the following subparagraphs of subsection (e)(3), the class life shall be determined as follows:

If property is described in subparagraph:	The class life is:
(A)(iii)	4
(B)(ii)	5
(B)(iii)	9.5
(C)(i)	10
(C)(iii)	22
(D)(i)	15
(D)(ii)	20
(E)(i)	24
(E)(ii)	24
(E)(iii)	20
(E)(iv)	39
(E)(v)	39
(E)(vi)	20
(F)	25

* * *

[CCH Explanation at ¶315, ¶317, ¶345 and ¶670. Committee Reports at ¶10,050, ¶10,880, ¶11,290 and ¶11,730.]

Amendments

• **2004, American Jobs Creation Act of 2004 (H.R. 4520)**

H.R. 4520, §211(e):

Amended the table contained in Code Sec. 168(g)(3)(B) by adding at the end two new items. **Effective** for property placed in service after the date of the enactment of this Act.

H.R. 4520, §706(c):

Amended the table contained in Code Sec. 168(g)(3)(B) by inserting after the item relating to subparagraph (C)(ii)[(i)] a new item. **Effective** for property placed in service after 12-31-2004.

H.R. 4520, §847(a):

Amended Code Sec. 168(g)(3)(A) by inserting "(notwithstanding any other subparagraph of this paragraph)" after "shall". **Effective** generally for leases entered into after 3-12-2004. For an exception, see Act Sec. 849(b)(1)-(2), below.

H.R. 4520, §849(b)(1)-(2), provides:

(b) Exception.—

(1) In general.—The amendments made by this part shall not apply to qualified transportation property.

(2) Qualified transportation property.—For purposes of paragraph (1), the term "qualified transportation property" means domestic property subject to a lease with respect to which a formal application—

(A) was submitted for approval to the Federal Transit Administration (an agency of the Department of Transportation) after June 30, 2003, and before March 13, 2004,

(B) is approved by the Federal Transit Administration before January 1, 2006, and

(C) includes a description of such property and the value of such property.

H.R. 4520, §901(c):

Amended the table contained in Code Sec. 168(g)(3)(B), as amended by this Act, by inserting after the item relating to subparagraph (E)(v) two new items. **Effective** for property placed in service after the date of the enactment of this Act.

(h) Tax-Exempt Use Property.—

* * *

(2) Tax-exempt entity.—

(A) In general.—For purposes of this subsection, the term "tax-exempt entity" means—

(i) the United States, any State or political subdivision thereof, any possession of the United States, or any agency or instrumentality of any of the foregoing,

(ii) an organization (other than a cooperative described in section 521) which is exempt from tax imposed by this chapter,

(iii) any foreign person or entity, *and*

(iv) *any Indian tribal government described in section 7701(a)(40).*

For purposes of applying this subsection, any Indian tribal government referred to in clause (iv) shall be treated in the same manner as a State.

* * *

(3) Special rules for certain high technology equipment.—

(A) Exemption where lease term is 5 years or less.—For purposes of this section, the term "tax-exempt use property" shall not include any qualified technological equipment if the lease to the tax-exempt entity has a lease term of 5 years or less. *Notwithstanding subsection (i)(3)(A)(i), in determining a lease term for purposes of the preceding sentence, there shall not be taken into account any option of the lessee to renew at the fair market value rent determined at the time of renewal; except that the aggregate period not taken into account by reason of this sentence shall not exceed 24 months.*

* * *

[CCH Explanation at ¶ 670. Committee Reports at ¶ 11,290.]

Amendments

• **2004, American Jobs Creation Act of 2004 (H.R. 4520)**

H.R. 4520, § 847(d):

Amended Code Sec. 168(h)(3)(A) by adding at the end a new sentence. **Effective** generally for leases entered into after 3-12-2004. For an exception, see Act Sec. 849(b)(1)-(2), below.

H.R. 4520, § 847(e):

Amended Code Sec. 168(h)(2)(A) by striking "and" at the end of clause (ii), by striking the period at the end of clause (iii) and inserting ", and" and by inserting at the end a new clause (iv) and a flush sentence that follows clause (iv). **Effective** generally for leases entered into after 10-3-2004. For an exception, see Act Sec. 849(b)(1)-(2), below.

H.R. 4520, § 849(b)(1)-(2), provides:

(b) Exception.—

(1) In general.—The amendments made by this part shall not apply to qualified transportation property.

(2) Qualified transportation property.—For purposes of paragraph (1), the term "qualified transportation property" means domestic property subject to a lease with respect to which a formal application—

(A) was submitted for approval to the Federal Transit Administration (an agency of the Department of Transportation) after June 30, 2003, and before March 13, 2004,

(B) is approved by the Federal Transit Administration before January 1, 2006, and

(C) includes a description of such property and the value of such property.

(i) Definitions and Special Rules.—For purposes of this section—

* * *

(3) Lease term.—

(A) In general.—In determining a lease term—

(i) there shall be taken into account options to renew,

(ii) *the term of a lease shall include the term of any service contract or similar arrangement (whether or not treated as a lease under section 7701(e))—*

(I) *which is part of the same transaction (or series of related transactions) which includes the lease, and*

(II) *which is with respect to the property subject to the lease or substantially similar property,*

(iii) 2 or more successive leases which are part of the same transaction (or a series of related transactions) with respect to the same or substantially similar property shall be treated as 1 lease.

* * *

(15) *Motorsports entertainment complex.—*

(A) *In general.—The term "motorsports entertainment complex" means a racing track facility which—*

(i) *is permanently situated on land, and*

(ii) *during the 36-month period following the first day of the month in which the asset is placed in service, hosts 1 or more racing events for automobiles (of any type), trucks, or motorcycles which are open to the public for the price of admission.*

(B) *Ancillary and support facilities.—Such term shall include, if owned by the taxpayer who owns the complex and provided for the benefit of patrons of the complex—*

(i) *ancillary facilities and land improvements in support of the complex's activities (including parking lots, sidewalks, waterways, bridges, fences, and landscaping),*

(ii) *support facilities (including food and beverage retailing, souvenir vending, and other nonlodging accommodations), and*

(iii) *appurtenances associated with such facilities and related attractions and amusements (including ticket booths, race track surfaces, suites and hospitality facilities, grandstands and viewing structures, props, walls, facilities that support the delivery of entertainment services, other special purpose structures, facades, shop interiors, and buildings).*

(C) EXCEPTION.—*Such term shall not include any transportation equipment, administrative services assets, warehouses, administrative buildings, hotels, or motels.*

(D) TERMINATION.—*This paragraph shall not apply to any property placed in service after December 31, 2007.*

(16) ALASKA NATURAL GAS PIPELINE.—*The term "Alaska natural gas pipeline" means the natural gas pipeline system located in the State of Alaska which—*

(A) *has a capacity of more than 500,000,000,000 Btu of natural gas per day, and*

(B) *is—*

(i) *placed in service after December 31, 2013, or*

(ii) *treated as placed in service on January 1, 2014, if the taxpayer who places such system in service before January 1, 2014, elects such treatment.*

Such term includes the pipe, trunk lines, related equipment, and appurtenances used to carry natural gas, but does not include any gas processing plant.

* * *

[CCH Explanation at ¶340, ¶345 and ¶670. Committee Reports at ¶10,860, ¶10,880 and ¶11,290.]

Amendments

• **2004, American Jobs Creation Act of 2004 (H.R. 4520)**

H.R. 4520, §704(b):

Amended Code Sec. 168(i) by adding at the end a new paragraph (15). **Effective** generally for any property placed in service after the date of the enactment of this Act. For special rules, see Act Secs. 704(c)(2)-(3), below.

H.R. 4520, §704(c)(2)-(3), provides:

(2) SPECIAL RULE FOR ASSET CLASS 80.0.—In the case of race track facilities placed in service after the date of the enactment of this Act, such facilities shall not be treated as theme and amusement facilities classified under asset class 80.0.

(3) NO INFERENCE.—Nothing in this section or the amendments made by this section shall be construed to affect the treatment of property placed in service on or before the date of the enactment of this Act.

H.R. 4520, §706(b):

Amended Code Sec. 168(i), as amended by this Act, by inserting after paragraph (15) a new paragraph (16). **Effective** for property placed in service after 12-31-2004.

H.R. 4520, §847(c):

Amended Code Sec. 168(i)(3)(A) by striking "and" at the end of clause (i), by redesignating clause (ii) as clause (iii) and by inserting after clause (i) a new clause (ii). **Effective** generally for leases entered into after 3-12-2004. For an exception, see Act Sec. 849(b)(1)-(2), below.

H.R. 4520, §849(b)(1)-(2), provides:

(b) EXCEPTION.—

(1) IN GENERAL.—The amendments made by this part shall not apply to qualified transportation property.

(2) QUALIFIED TRANSPORTATION PROPERTY.—For purposes of paragraph (1), the term "qualified transportation property" means domestic property subject to a lease with respect to which a formal application—

(A) was submitted for approval to the Federal Transit Administration (an agency of the Department of Transportation) after June 30, 2003, and before March 13, 2004,

(B) is approved by the Federal Transit Administration before January 1, 2006, and

(C) includes a description of such property and the value of such property.

(k) SPECIAL ALLOWANCE FOR CERTAIN PROPERTY ACQUIRED AFTER SEPTEMBER 10, 2001, AND BEFORE JANUARY 1, 2005.—

* * *

(2) QUALIFIED PROPERTY.—For purposes of this subsection—

(A) IN GENERAL.—The term "qualified property" means property—

(i)(I) to which this section applies which has a recovery period of 20 years or less,

(II) which is computer software (as defined in section 167(f)(1)(B)) for which a deduction is allowable under section 167(a) without regard to this subsection,

(III) which is water utility property, or

(IV) which is qualified leasehold improvement property,

(ii) the original use of which commences with the taxpayer after September 10, 2001,

(iii) which is—

(I) acquired by the taxpayer after September 10, 2001, and before January 1, 2005, but only if no written binding contract for the acquisition was in effect before September 11, 2001, or

(II) acquired by the taxpayer pursuant to a written binding contract which was entered into after September 10, 2001, and before January 1, 2005, and

(iv) which is placed in service by the taxpayer before January 1, 2005, or, in the case of property described in *subparagraphs (B) and (C)*, before January 1, 2006.

(B) Certain property having longer production periods treated as qualified property.—

* * *

(iv) Application of subparagraph.—This subparagraph shall not apply to any property which is described in subparagraph (C).

(C) Certain aircraft.—The term "qualified property" includes property—

(i) which meets the requirements of clauses (ii) and (iii) of subparagraph (A),

(ii) which is an aircraft which is not a transportation property (as defined in subparagraph (B)(iii)) other than for agricultural or firefighting purposes,

(iii) which is purchased and on which such purchaser, at the time of the contract for purchase, has made a nonrefundable deposit of the lesser of—

(I) 10 percent of the cost, or

(II) $100,000, and

(iv) which has—

(I) an estimated production period exceeding 4 months, and

(II) a cost exceeding $200,000.

(D) Exceptions.—

* * *

(E) Special rules.—

* * *

(iii) Syndication.—For purposes of subparagraph (A)(ii), if—

(I) property is originally placed in service after September 10, 2001, by the lessor of such property,

(II) such property is sold by such lessor or any subsequent purchaser within 3 months after the date such property was originally placed in service *(or, in the case of multiple units of property subject to the same lease, within 3 months after the date the final unit is placed in service, so long as the period between the time the first unit is placed in service and the time the last unit is placed in service does not exceed 12 months)*, and

(III) the user of such property after the last sale during such 3-month period remains the same as when such property was originally placed in service,

such property shall be treated as originally placed in service not earlier than the date of such last sale.

* * *

(F) Coordination with Section 280F.—For purposes of section 280F—

(i) Automobiles.—In the case of a passenger automobile (as defined in section 280F(d)(5)) which is qualified property, the Secretary shall increase the limitation under section 280F(a)(1)(A)(i) by $4,600.

(ii) Listed property.—The deduction allowable under paragraph (1) shall be taken into account in computing any recapture amount under section 280F(b)(2).

(G) Deduction allowed in computing minimum tax.—For purposes of determining alternative minimum taxable income under section 55, the deduction under subsection (a) for qualified property shall be determined under this section without regard to any adjustment under section 56.

* * *

(4) 50-percent bonus depreciation for certain property.—

(A) In general.—In the case of 50-percent bonus depreciation property—

(i) paragraph (1)(A) shall be applied by substituting "50 percent" for "30 percent", and

(ii) except as provided in *paragraph (2)(D)*, such property shall be treated as qualified property for purposes of this subsection.

(B) 50-percent bonus depreciation property.—For purposes of this subsection, the term "50-percent bonus depreciation property" means property described in paragraph (2)(A)(i)—

(i) the original use of which commences with the taxpayer after May 5, 2003,

(ii) which is acquired by the taxpayer after May 5, 2003, and before January 1, 2005, but only if no written binding contract for the acquisition was in effect before May 6, 2003, and

(iii) which is placed in service by the taxpayer before January 1, 2005, or, in the case of property described in paragraph (2)(B) (as modified by subparagraph (C) of this paragraph) *and paragraph (2)(C)*, before January 1, 2006.

(C) Special rules.—Rules similar to the rules of *subparagraphs (B), (C), and (E)* of paragraph (2) shall apply for purposes of this paragraph; except that references to September 10, 2001, shall be treated as references to May 5, 2003.

(D) Automobiles.—*Paragraph (2)(F)* shall be applied by substituting "$7,650" for "$4,600" in the case of 50-percent bonus depreciation property.

* * *

[CCH Explanation at ¶325 and ¶330. Committee Reports at ¶10,510 and ¶10,520.]

Amendments

• **2004, American Jobs Creation Act of 2004 (H.R. 4520)**

H.R. 4520, §336(a)(1):

Amended Code Sec. 168(k)(2) by redesignating subparagraphs (C) through (F) as subparagraphs (D) through (G), respectively, and by inserting after subparagraph (B) a new subparagraph (C). **Effective** as if included in the amendments made by section 101 of the Job Creation and Worker Assistance Act of 2002 (P.L. 107-147) [**effective** for property placed in service after 9-10-2001, in tax years ending after such date.—CCH].

H.R. 4520, §336(a)(2):

Amended Code Sec. 168(k)(2)(A)(iv) by striking "subparagraph (B)" and inserting "subparagraphs (B) and (C)". **Effective** as if included in the amendments made by section 101 of the Job Creation and Worker Assistance Act of 2002 (P.L. 107-147) [**effective** for property placed in service after 9-10-2001, in tax years ending after such date.—CCH].

H.R. 4520, §336(b)(1):

Amended Code Sec. 168(k)(2)(B) by adding at the end a new clause (iv). **Effective** as if included in the amendments made by section 101 of the Job Creation and Worker Assistance Act of 2002 (P.L. 107-147) [**effective** for property placed in service after 9-10-2001, in tax years ending after such date.—CCH].

H.R. 4520, §336(b)(2):

Amended Code Sec. 168(k)(4)(A)(ii) by striking "paragraph (2)(C)" and inserting "paragraph (2)(D)". **Effective** as if included in the amendments made by section 101 of the

Job Creation and Worker Assistance Act of 2002 (P.L. 107-147) [**effective** for property placed in service after 9-10-2001, in tax years ending after such date.—CCH].

H.R. 4520, §336(b)(3):

Amended Code Sec. 168(k)(4)(B)(iii) by inserting "and paragraph (2)(C)" after "of this paragraph)". **Effective** as if included in the amendments made by section 101 of the Job Creation and Worker Assistance Act of 2002 (P.L. 107-147) [**effective** for property placed in service after 9-10-2001, in tax years ending after such date.—CCH].

H.R. 4520, §336(b)(4):

Amended Code Sec. 168(k)(4)(C) by striking "subparagraphs (B) and (D)" and inserting "subparagraphs (B), (C), and (E)". **Effective** as if included in the amendments made by section 101 of the Job Creation and Worker Assistance Act of 2002 (P.L. 107-147) [**effective** for property placed in service after 9-10-2001, in tax years ending after such date.—CCH].

H.R. 4520, §336(b)(5):

Amended Code Sec. 168(k)(4)(D) by striking "Paragraph (2)(E)" and inserting "Paragraph (2)(F)". **Effective** as if included in the amendments made by section 101 of the Job Creation and Worker Assistance Act of 2002 (P.L. 107-147) [**effective** for property placed in service after 9-10-2001, in tax years ending after such date.—CCH].

H.R. 4520, §337(a):

Amended Code Sec. 168(k)(2)(E)(iii)(II), as amended by the Working Families Tax Relief Act of 2004 (P.L. 108-311) and as redesignated by Act Sec. 336(a)(1), by inserting before the comma at the end the following: "(or, in the case of multiple units of property subject to the same lease, within 3 months after the date the final unit is placed in service, so long as the period between the time the first unit is placed in service and the time the last unit is placed in service does not exceed 12 months)". **Effective** for property sold after 6-4-2004.

[¶5185] CODE SEC. 170. CHARITABLE, ETC., CONTRIBUTIONS AND GIFTS.

* * *

(e) CERTAIN CONTRIBUTIONS OF ORDINARY INCOME AND CAPITAL GAIN PROPERTY.—

(1) GENERAL RULE.—The amount of any charitable contribution of property otherwise taken into account under this section shall be reduced by the sum of—

(A) the amount of gain which would not have been long-term capital gain if the property contributed had been sold by the taxpayer at its fair market value (determined at the time of such contribution), and

(B) in the case of a charitable contribution—

(i) of tangible personal property, if the use by the donee is unrelated to the purpose or function constituting the basis for its exemption under section 501 (or, in the case of a governmental unit, to any purpose or function described in subsection (c)),

(ii) to or for the use of a private foundation (as defined in section 509(a)), other than a private foundation described in subsection (b)(1)(E), *or*

(iii) *of any patent, copyright (other than a copyright described in section 1221(a)(3) or 1231(b)(1)(C)), trademark, trade name, trade secret, know-how, software (other than software described in section 197(e)(3)(A)(i)), or similar property, or applications or registrations of such property,*

the amount of gain which would have been long-term capital gain if the property contributed had been sold by the taxpayer at its fair market value (determined at the time of such contribution).

For purposes of applying this paragraph (other than in the case of gain to which section 617(d)(1), 1245(a), 1250(a), 1252(a), or 1254(a) applies), property which is property used in the trade or business (as defined in section 1231(b)) shall be treated as a capital asset. For purposes of applying this paragraph in the case of a charitable contribution of stock in an S corporation, rules similar to the rules of section 751 shall apply in determining whether gain on such stock would have been long-term capital gain if such stock were sold by the taxpayer.

* * *

[CCH Explanation at ¶1315. Committee Reports at ¶11,540.]

Amendments

• **2004, American Jobs Creation Act of 2004 (H.R. 4520)**

H.R. 4520, §882(a):

Amended Code Sec. 170(e)(1)(B) by striking "or" at the end of clause (i), by adding "or" at the end of clause (ii), and by inserting after clause (ii) a new clause (iii). **Effective** for contributions made after 6-3-2004.

(f) DISALLOWANCE OF DEDUCTION IN CERTAIN CASES AND SPECIAL RULES.—

* * *

(10) SPLIT-DOLLAR LIFE INSURANCE, ANNUITY, AND ENDOWMENT CONTRACTS.—

(A) IN GENERAL.—Nothing in this section or in section 545(b)(2), 642(c), 2055, 2106(a)(2), or 2522 shall be construed to allow a deduction, and no deduction shall be allowed, for any transfer to or for the use of an organization described in subsection (c) if in connection with such transfer—

(i) the organization directly or indirectly pays, or has previously paid, any premium on any personal benefit contract with respect to the transferor, or

(ii) there is an understanding or expectation that any person will directly or indirectly pay any premium on any personal benefit contract with respect to the transferor.

* * *

(11) QUALIFIED APPRAISAL AND OTHER DOCUMENTATION FOR CERTAIN CONTRIBUTIONS.—

(A) IN GENERAL.—

(i) DENIAL OF DEDUCTION.—In the case of an individual, partnership, or corporation, no deduction shall be allowed under subsection (a) for any contribution of property for which a deduction of more than $500 is claimed unless such person meets the requirements of subparagraphs (B), (C), and (D), as the case may be, with respect to such contribution.

(ii) EXCEPTIONS.—

(I) READILY VALUED PROPERTY.—Subparagraphs (C) and (D) shall not apply to cash, property described in subsection (e)(1)(B)(iii) or section 1221(a)(1), publicly traded securities (as defined in section 6050L(a)(2)(B)), and any qualified vehicle described in paragraph (12)(A)(ii) for which an acknowledgement under paragraph (12)(B)(iii) is provided.

(II) REASONABLE CAUSE.—Clause (i) shall not apply if it is shown that the failure to meet such requirements is due to reasonable cause and not to willful neglect.

(B) PROPERTY DESCRIPTION FOR CONTRIBUTIONS OF MORE THAN $500.—In the case of contributions of property for which a deduction of more than $500 is claimed, the requirements of this subparagraph are met if the individual, partnership or corporation includes with the return for the taxable year in which the contribution is made a description of such property and such other information as the Secretary may require. The requirements of this subparagraph shall not apply to a C corporation which is not a personal service corporation or a closely held C corporation.

(C) QUALIFIED APPRAISAL FOR CONTRIBUTIONS OF MORE THAN $5,000.—In the case of contributions of property for which a deduction of more than $5,000 is claimed, the requirements of this subparagraph are met if the individual, partnership, or corporation obtains a qualified appraisal of such property and attaches to the return for the taxable year in which such contribution is made such information regarding such property and such appraisal as the Secretary may require.

(D) SUBSTANTIATION FOR CONTRIBUTIONS OF MORE THAN $500,000.—In the case of contributions of property for which a deduction of more than $500,000 is claimed, the requirements of this subparagraph are met if the individual, partnership, or corporation attaches to the return for the taxable year a qualified appraisal of such property.

(E) QUALIFIED APPRAISAL.—For purposes of this paragraph, the term "qualified appraisal" means, with respect to any property, an appraisal of such property which is treated for purposes of this paragraph as a qualified appraisal under regulations or other guidance prescribed by the Secretary.

(F) AGGREGATION OF SIMILAR ITEMS OF PROPERTY.—For purposes of determining thresholds under this paragraph, property and all similar items of property donated to 1 or more donees shall be treated as 1 property.

(G) SPECIAL RULE FOR PASS-THRU ENTITIES.—In the case of a partnership or S corporation, this paragraph shall be applied at the entity level, except that the deduction shall be denied at the partner or shareholder level.

(H) REGULATIONS.—The Secretary may prescribe such regulations as may be necessary or appropriate to carry out the purposes of this paragraph, including regulations that may provide that some or all of the requirements of this paragraph do not apply in appropriate cases.

(12) CONTRIBUTIONS OF USED MOTOR VEHICLES, BOATS, AND AIRPLANES.—

(A) IN GENERAL.—In the case of a contribution of a qualified vehicle the claimed value of which exceeds $500—

(i) paragraph (8) shall not apply and no deduction shall be allowed under subsection (a) for such contribution unless the taxpayer substantiates the contribution by a contemporaneous written acknowledgement of the contribution by the donee organization that meets the requirements of subparagraph (B) and includes the acknowledgement with the taxpayer's return of tax which includes the deduction, and

(ii) if the organization sells the vehicle without any significant intervening use or material improvement of such vehicle by the organization, the amount of the deduction allowed under subsection (a) shall not exceed the gross proceeds received from such sale.

Code Sec. 170(f)(12)(A)(ii) ¶5185

(B) CONTENT OF ACKNOWLEDGEMENT.—*An acknowledgement meets the requirements of this subparagraph if it includes the following information:*

(i) *The name and taxpayer identification number of the donor.*

(ii) *The vehicle identification number or similar number.*

(iii) *In the case of a qualified vehicle to which subparagraph (A)(ii) applies—*

(I) *a certification that the vehicle was sold in an arm's length transaction between unrelated parties,*

(II) *the gross proceeds from the sale, and*

(III) *a statement that the deductible amount may not exceed the amount of such gross proceeds.*

(iv) *In the case of a qualified vehicle to which subparagraph (A)(ii) does not apply—*

(I) *a certification of the intended use or material improvement of the vehicle and the intended duration of such use, and*

(II) *a certification that the vehicle would not be transferred in exchange for money, other property, or services before completion of such use or improvement.*

(C) CONTEMPORANEOUS.—*For purposes of subparagraph (A), an acknowledgement shall be considered to be contemporaneous if the donee organization provides it within 30 days of—*

(i) *the sale of the qualified vehicle, or*

(ii) *in the case of an acknowledgement including a certification described in subparagraph (B)(iv), the contribution of the qualified vehicle.*

(D) INFORMATION TO SECRETARY.—*A donee organization required to provide an acknowledgement under this paragraph shall provide to the Secretary the information contained in the acknowledgement. Such information shall be provided at such time and in such manner as the Secretary may prescribe.*

(E) QUALIFIED VEHICLE.—*For purposes of this paragraph, the term "qualified vehicle" means any—*

(i) *motor vehicle manufactured primarily for use on public streets, roads, and highways,*

(ii) *boat, or*

(iii) *airplane.*

Such term shall not include any property which is described in section 1221(a)(1).

(F) REGULATIONS OR OTHER GUIDANCE.—*The Secretary shall prescribe such regulations or other guidance as may be necessary to carry out the purposes of this paragraph. The Secretary may prescribe regulations or other guidance which exempts sales by the donee organization which are in direct furtherance of such organization's charitable purpose from the requirements of subparagraphs (A)(ii) and (B)(iv)(II).*

* * *

[CCH Explanation at ¶ 490, ¶ 1305, ¶ 1310 and ¶ 1315. Committee Reports at ¶ 10,690, ¶ 11,540, ¶ 11,550 and ¶ 11,560.]

Amendments

• **2004, American Jobs Creation Act of 2004 (H.R. 4520)**

H.R. 4520, § 413(c)(30):

Amended Code Sec. 170(f)(10)(A) by striking "556(b)(2)," immediately preceding "642(c)". **Effective** for tax years of foreign corporations beginning after 12-31-2004, and for tax years of United States shareholders with or within which such tax years of foreign corporations end.

H.R. 4520, § 882(d):

Amended Code Sec. 170(f)(11)(A)(ii)(I), as added by this Act, by inserting "subsection (e)(1)(B)(iii) or" before "section 1221(a)(1)" **Effective** for contributions made after 6-3-2004.

H.R. 4520, § 883(a):

Amended Code Sec. 170(f) by adding after paragraph (10) a new paragraph (11). **Effective** for contributions made after 6-3-2004.

H.R. 4520, § 884(a):

Amended Code Sec. 170(f), as amended by this Act, by inserting after paragraph (11) a new paragraph (12). **Effective** for contributions made after 12-31-2004.

(m) CERTAIN DONEE INCOME FROM INTELLECTUAL PROPERTY TREATED AS AN ADDITIONAL CHARITABLE CONTRIBUTION.—

(1) TREATMENT AS ADDITIONAL CONTRIBUTION.—*In the case of a taxpayer who makes a qualified intellectual property contribution, the deduction allowed under subsection (a) for each taxable year of the taxpayer ending on or after the date of such contribution shall be increased (subject to the limitations under subsection (b)) by the applicable percentage of qualified donee income with respect to such contribution which is properly allocable to such year under this subsection.*

(2) REDUCTION IN ADDITIONAL DEDUCTIONS TO EXTENT OF INITIAL DEDUCTION.—*With respect to any qualified intellectual property contribution, the deduction allowed under subsection (a) shall be increased under paragraph (1) only to the extent that the aggregate amount of such increases with respect to such contribution exceed the amount allowed as a deduction under subsection (a) with respect to such contribution determined without regard to this subsection.*

(3) QUALIFIED DONEE INCOME.—*For purposes of this subsection, the term "qualified donee income" means any net income received by or accrued to the donee which is properly allocable to the qualified intellectual property.*

(4) ALLOCATION OF QUALIFIED DONEE INCOME TO TAXABLE YEARS OF DONOR.—*For purposes of this subsection, qualified donee income shall be treated as properly allocable to a taxable year of the donor if such income is received by or accrued to the donee for the taxable year of the donee which ends within or with such taxable year of the donor.*

(5) 10-YEAR LIMITATION.—*Income shall not be treated as properly allocable to qualified intellectual property for purposes of this subsection if such income is received by or accrued to the donee after the 10-year period beginning on the date of the contribution of such property.*

(6) BENEFIT LIMITED TO LIFE OF INTELLECTUAL PROPERTY.—*Income shall not be treated as properly allocable to qualified intellectual property for purposes of this subsection if such income is received by or accrued to the donee after the expiration of the legal life of such property.*

(7) APPLICABLE PERCENTAGE.—*For purposes of this subsection, the term "applicable percentage" means the percentage determined under the following table which corresponds to a taxable year of the donor ending on or after the date of the qualified intellectual property contribution:*

Taxable Year of Donor Ending on or After Date of Contribution:	Applicable Percentage:
1st	100
2nd	100
3rd	90
4th	80
5th	70
6th	60
7th	50
8th	40
9th	30
10th	20
11th	10
12th	10 .

(8) QUALIFIED INTELLECTUAL PROPERTY CONTRIBUTION.—*For purposes of this subsection, the term "qualified intellectual property contribution" means any charitable contribution of qualified intellectual property—*

(A) the amount of which taken into account under this section is reduced by reason of subsection (e)(1), and

(B) with respect to which the donor informs the donee at the time of such contribution that the donor intends to treat such contribution as a qualified intellectual property contribution for purposes of this subsection and section 6050L.

Code Sec. 170(m)(8)(B)   ¶5185

(9) QUALIFIED INTELLECTUAL PROPERTY.—*For purposes of this subsection, the term "qualified intellectual property" means property described in subsection (e)(1)(B)(iii) (other than property contributed to or for the use of an organization described in subsection (e)(1)(B)(ii)).*

(10) OTHER SPECIAL RULES.—

(A) APPLICATION OF LIMITATIONS ON CHARITABLE CONTRIBUTIONS.—*Any increase under this subsection of the deduction provided under subsection (a) shall be treated for purposes of subsection (b) as a deduction which is attributable to a charitable contribution to the donee to which such increase relates.*

(B) NET INCOME DETERMINED BY DONEE.—*The net income taken into account under paragraph (3) shall not exceed the amount of such income reported under section 6050L(b)(1).*

(C) DEDUCTION LIMITED TO 12 TAXABLE YEARS.—*Except as may be provided under subparagraph (D)(i), this subsection shall not apply with respect to any qualified intellectual property contribution for any taxable year of the donor after the 12th taxable year of the donor which ends on or after the date of such contribution.*

(D) REGULATIONS.—*The Secretary may issue regulations or other guidance to carry out the purposes of this subsection, including regulations or guidance—*

(i) *modifying the application of this subsection in the case of a donor or donee with a short taxable year, and*

(ii) *providing for the determination of an amount to be treated as net income of the donee which is properly allocable to qualified intellectual property in the case of a donee who uses such property to further a purpose or function constituting the basis of the donee's exemption under section 501 (or, in the case of a governmental unit, any purpose described in section 170(c)) and does not possess a right to receive any payment from a third party with respect to such property.*

[CCH Explanation at ¶ 1315. Committee Reports at ¶ 11,540.]

Amendments

• **2004, American Jobs Creation Act of 2004 (H.R. 4520)**

H.R. 4520, § 882(b):

Amended Code Sec. 170 by redesignating subsection (m) as subsection (n) and by inserting after subsection (l) a new

subsection (m). **Effective** for contributions made after 6-3-2004.

(n) EXPENSES PAID BY CERTAIN WHALING CAPTAINS IN SUPPORT OF NATIVE ALASKAN SUBSISTENCE WHALING.—

(1) IN GENERAL.—*In the case of an individual who is recognized by the Alaska Eskimo Whaling Commission as a whaling captain charged with the responsibility of maintaining and carrying out sanctioned whaling activities and who engages in such activities during the taxable year, the amount described in paragraph (2) (to the extent such amount does not exceed $10,000 for the taxable year) shall be treated for purposes of this section as a charitable contribution.*

(2) AMOUNT DESCRIBED.—

(A) IN GENERAL.—*The amount described in this paragraph is the aggregate of the reasonable and necessary whaling expenses paid by the taxpayer during the taxable year in carrying out sanctioned whaling activities.*

(B) WHALING EXPENSES.—*For purposes of subparagraph (A), the term "whaling expenses" includes expenses for—*

(i) *the acquisition and maintenance of whaling boats, weapons, and gear used in sanctioned whaling activities,*

(ii) *the supplying of food for the crew and other provisions for carrying out such activities, and*

(iii) *storage and distribution of the catch from such activities.*

(3) SANCTIONED WHALING ACTIVITIES.—*For purposes of this subsection, the term "sanctioned whaling activities" means subsistence bowhead whale hunting activities conducted pursuant to the management plan of the Alaska Eskimo Whaling Commission.*

(4) Substantiation of Expenses.—*The Secretary shall issue guidance requiring that the taxpayer substantiate the whaling expenses for which a deduction is claimed under this subsection, including by maintaining appropriate written records with respect to the time, place, date, amount, and nature of the expense, as well as the taxpayer's eligibility for such deduction, and that (to the extent provided by the Secretary) such substantiation be provided as part of the taxpayer's return of tax.*

[CCH Explanation at ¶1320. Committee Reports at ¶10,500.]

Amendments

• **2004, American Jobs Creation Act of 2004 (H.R. 4520)**

H.R. 4520, §335(a):

Amended Code Sec. 170, as amended by this Act, by redesignating subsection (n) as subsection (o) and by in-

serting after subsection (m) a new subsection (n). **Effective** for contributions made after 12-31-2004.

(o) Other Cross References.—

* * *

[CCH Explanation at ¶1320. Committee Reports at ¶10,500 and ¶11,540.]

Amendments

• **2004, American Jobs Creation Act of 2004 (H.R. 4520)**

H.R. 4520, §335(a):

Amended Code Sec. 170, as amended by this Act, by redesignating subsection (n) as subsection (o). **Effective** for contributions made after 12-31-2004.

H.R. 4520, §882(b):

Amended Code Sec. 170 by redesignating subsection (m) as subsection (n). **Effective** for contributions made after 6-3-2004.

[¶5190] CODE SEC. 171. AMORTIZABLE BOND PREMIUM.

* * *

(c) Election as to Taxable Bonds.—

* * *

(2) Manner and effect of election.—The election authorized under this subsection shall be made in accordance with such regulations as the Secretary shall prescribe. If such election is made with respect to any bond (described in paragraph (1)) of the taxpayer, it shall also apply to all such bonds held by the taxpayer at the beginning of the first taxable year to which the election applies and to all such bonds thereafter acquired by him and shall be binding for all subsequent taxable years with respect to all such bonds of the taxpayer, unless, on application by the taxpayer, the Secretary permits him, subject to such conditions as the Secretary deems necessary, to revoke such election. In the case of bonds held by a common trust fund, as defined in section 584(a), the election authorized under this subsection shall be exercisable with respect to such bonds only by the common trust fund. In case of bonds held by an estate or trust, the election authorized under this subsection shall be exercisable with respect to such bonds only by the fiduciary.

* * *

[CCH Explanation at ¶490. Committee Reports at ¶10,690.]

Amendments

• **2004, American Jobs Creation Act of 2004 (H.R. 4520)**

H.R. 4520, §413(c)(2)(A)-(B):

Amended Code Sec. 171(c)(2) by striking ", or by a foreign personal holding company, as defined in section 552" im-

mediately following "as defined in section 584(a),", and by striking ", or foreign personal holding company" before the period at the end of the third sentence. **Effective** for tax years of foreign corporations beginning after 12-31-2004, and for tax years of United States shareholders with or within which such tax years of foreign corporations end.

[¶5195] CODE SEC. 179. ELECTION TO EXPENSE CERTAIN DEPRECIABLE BUSINESS ASSETS.

* * *

(b) LIMITATIONS.—

(1) DOLLAR LIMITATION.—The aggregate cost which may be taken into account under subsection (a) for any taxable year shall not exceed $25,000 ($100,000 in the case of taxable years beginning after 2002 and before *2008*).

(2) REDUCTION IN LIMITATION.—The limitation under paragraph (1) for any taxable year shall be reduced (but not below zero) by the amount by which the cost of section 179 property placed in service during such taxable year exceeds $200,000 ($400,000 in the case of taxable years beginning after 2002 and before *2008*).

* * *

(5) INFLATION ADJUSTMENTS.—

(A) IN GENERAL.—In the case of any taxable year beginning in a calendar year after 2003 and before *2008*, the $100,000 and $400,000 amounts in paragraphs (1) and (2) shall each be increased by an amount equal to—

(i) such dollar amount, multiplied by

(ii) the cost-of-living adjustment determined under section 1(f)(3) for the calendar year in which the taxable year begins, by substituting "calendar year 2002" for "calendar year 1992" in subparagraph (B) thereof.

* * *

(6) LIMITATION ON COST TAKEN INTO ACCOUNT FOR CERTAIN PASSENGER VEHICLES.—

(A) IN GENERAL.—The cost of any sport utility vehicle for any taxable year which may be taken into account under this section shall not exceed $25,000.

(B) SPORT UTILITY VEHICLE.—For purposes of subparagraph (A)—

(i) IN GENERAL.—The term "sport utility vehicle" means any 4-wheeled vehicle—

(I) which is primarily designed or which can be used to carry passengers over public streets, roads, or highways (except any vehicle operated exclusively on a rail or rails),

(II) which is not subject to section 280F, and

(III) which is rated at not more than 14,000 pounds gross vehicle weight.

(ii) CERTAIN VEHICLES EXCLUDED.—Such term does not include any vehicle which—

(I) is designed to have a seating capacity of more than 9 persons behind the driver's seat,

(II) is equipped with a cargo area of at least 6 feet in interior length which is an open area or is designed for use as an open area but is enclosed by a cap and is not readily accessible directly from the passenger compartment, or

(III) has an integral enclosure, fully enclosing the driver compartment and load carrying device, does not have seating rearward of the driver's seat, and has no body section protruding more than 30 inches ahead of the leading edge of the windshield.

[CCH Explanation at ¶305 and ¶310. Committee Reports at ¶10,040 and ¶11,820.]

Amendments

• **2004, American Jobs Creation Act of 2004 (H.R. 4520)**

H.R. 4520, §201:

Amended Code Sec. 179(b) by striking "2006" each place it appears and inserting "2008". **Effective** on the date of the enactment of this Act.

H.R. 4520, §910(a):

Amended Code Sec. 179(b) by adding at the end a new paragraph (6). **Effective** for property placed in service after the date of the enactment of this Act.

(c) ELECTION.—

(1) IN GENERAL.—An election under this section for any taxable year shall—

(A) specify the items of section 179 property to which the election applies and the portion of the cost of each of such items which is to be taken into account under subsection (a), and

(B) be made on the taxpayer's return of the tax imposed by this chapter for the taxable year.

Such election shall be made in such manner as the Secretary may by regulations prescribe.

(2) ELECTION IRREVOCABLE.—Any election made under this section, and any specification contained in any such election, may not be revoked except with the consent of the Secretary. Any such election or specification with respect to any taxable year beginning after 2002 and before 2008 may be revoked by the taxpayer with respect to any property, and such revocation, once made, shall be irrevocable.

[CCH Explanation at ¶ 305. Committee Reports at ¶ 10,040.]

Amendments

• **2004, American Jobs Creation Act of 2004 (H.R. 4520)**

H.R. 4520, § 201:

Amended Code Sec. 179(c) by striking "2006" and inserting "2008". **Effective** on the date of the enactment of this Act.

(d) DEFINITIONS AND SPECIAL RULES.—

(1) SECTION 179 PROPERTY.—For purposes of this section, the term "section 179 property" means property—

(A) which is—

(i) tangible property (to which section 168 applies), or

(ii) computer software (as defined in section 197(e)(3)(B) which is described in section 197(e)(3)(A)(i), to which section 167 applies, and which is placed in service in a taxable year beginning after 2002 and before 2008,

(B) which is section 1245 property (as defined in section 1245(a)(3)), and

(C) which is acquired by purchase for use in the active conduct of a trade or business.

Such term shall not include any property described in section 50(b) and shall not include air conditioning or heating units.

* * *

[CCH Explanation at ¶ 305. Committee Reports at ¶ 10,040.]

Amendments

• **2004, American Jobs Creation Act of 2004 (H.R. 4520)**

H.R. 4520, § 201:

Amended Code Sec. 179(d) by striking "2006" and inserting "2008". **Effective** on the date of the enactment of this Act.

[¶ 5200] *CODE SEC. 179B. DEDUCTION FOR CAPITAL COSTS INCURRED IN COMPLYING WITH ENVIRONMENTAL PROTECTION AGENCY SULFUR REGULATIONS.*

(a) ALLOWANCE OF DEDUCTION.—In the case of a small business refiner (as defined in section 45H(c)(1)) which elects the application of this section, there shall be allowed as a deduction an amount equal to 75 percent of qualified capital costs (as defined in section 45H(c)(2)) which are paid or incurred by the taxpayer during the taxable year.

(b) REDUCED PERCENTAGE.—In the case of a small business refiner with average daily domestic refinery runs for the 1-year period ending on December 31, 2002, in excess of 155,000 barrels, the number of percentage points described in subsection (a) shall be reduced (not below zero) by the product of such number (before the application of this subsection) and the ratio of such excess to 50,000 barrels.

(c) BASIS REDUCTION.—

(1) IN GENERAL.—For purposes of this title, the basis of any property shall be reduced by the portion of the cost of such property taken into account under subsection (a).

(2) ORDINARY INCOME RECAPTURE.—For purposes of section 1245, the amount of the deduction allowable under subsection (a) with respect to any property which is of a character subject to the allowance for depreciation shall be treated as a deduction allowed for depreciation under section 167.

(d) COORDINATION WITH OTHER PROVISIONS.—Section 280B shall not apply to amounts which are treated as expenses under this section.

* * *

[CCH Explanation at ¶ 850. Committee Reports at ¶ 10,530.]

Amendments
• **2004, American Jobs Creation Act of 2004 (H.R. 4520)**

H.R. 4520, § 338(a):

Amended part VI of subchapter B of chapter 1 by inserting after Code Sec. 179A a new Code Sec. 179B. **Effective**

for expenses paid or incurred after 12-31-2002 in tax years ending after such date.

[¶ 5205] *CODE SEC. 181. TREATMENT OF CERTAIN QUALIFIED FILM AND TELEVISION PRODUCTIONS.*

(a) ELECTION TO TREAT COSTS AS EXPENSES.—

(1) IN GENERAL.—A taxpayer may elect to treat the cost of any qualified film or television production as an expense which is not chargeable to capital account. Any cost so treated shall be allowed as a deduction.

(2) DOLLAR LIMITATION.—

(A) IN GENERAL.—Paragraph (1) shall not apply to any qualified film or television production the aggregate cost of which exceeds $15,000,000.

(B) HIGHER DOLLAR LIMITATION FOR PRODUCTIONS IN CERTAIN AREAS.—In the case of any qualified film or television production the aggregate cost of which is significantly incurred in an area eligible for designation as—

(i) a low-income community under section 45D, or

(ii) a distressed county or isolated area of distress by the Delta Regional Authority established under section 2009aa-1 of title 7, United States Code,

subparagraph (A) shall be applied by substituting " $20,000,000" for "$15,000,000".

(b) NO OTHER DEDUCTION OR AMORTIZATION DEDUCTION ALLOWABLE.—With respect to the basis of any qualified film or television production to which an election is made under subsection (a), no other depreciation or amortization deduction shall be allowable.

(c) ELECTION.—

(1) IN GENERAL.—An election under this section with respect to any qualified film or television production shall be made in such manner as prescribed by the Secretary and by the due date (including extensions) for filing the taxpayer's return of tax under this chapter for the taxable year in which costs of the production are first incurred.

(2) REVOCATION OF ELECTION.—Any election made under this section may not be revoked without the consent of the Secretary.

(d) QUALIFIED FILM OR TELEVISION PRODUCTION.—For purposes of this section—

(1) IN GENERAL.—The term "qualified film or television production" means any production described in paragraph (2) if 75 percent of the total compensation of the production is qualified compensation.

(2) PRODUCTION.—

(A) IN GENERAL.—A production is described in this paragraph if such production is property described in section 168(f)(3). For purposes of a television series, only the first 44 episodes of such series may be taken into account.

(B) EXCEPTION.—*A production is not described in this paragraph if records are required under section 2257 of title 18, United States Code, to be maintained with respect to any performer in such production.*

(3) QUALIFIED COMPENSATION.—*For purposes of paragraph (1)—*

(A) IN GENERAL.—*The term "qualified compensation" means compensation for services performed in the United States by actors, directors, producers, and other relevant production personnel.*

(B) PARTICIPATIONS AND RESIDUALS EXCLUDED.—*The term "compensation" does not include participations and residuals (as defined in section 167(g)(7)(B)).*

(e) APPLICATION OF CERTAIN OTHER RULES.—*For purposes of this section, rules similar to the rules of subsections (b)(2) and (c)(4) of section 194 shall apply.*

(f) TERMINATION.—*This section shall not apply to qualified film and television productions commencing after December 31, 2008.*

* * *

[CCH Explanation at ¶ 365. Committee Reports at ¶ 10,250.]

Amendments

• **2004, American Jobs Creation Act of 2004 (H.R. 4520)**

H.R. 4520, § 244(a):

Amended part VI of subchapter B of chapter 1 by inserting after Code Sec. 180 a new Code Sec. 181. **Effective** for qualified film and television productions commencing after the date of the enactment of this Act.

[¶ 5210] CODE SEC. 194. *TREATMENT* OF REFORESTATION EXPENDITURES.

* * *

(b) TREATMENT AS EXPENSES.—

(1) ELECTION TO TREAT CERTAIN REFORESTATION EXPENDITURES AS EXPENSES.—

(A) IN GENERAL.—*In the case of any qualified timber property with respect to which the taxpayer has made (in accordance with regulations prescribed by the Secretary) an election under this subsection, the taxpayer shall treat reforestation expenditures which are paid or incurred during the taxable year with respect to such property as an expense which is not chargeable to capital account. The reforestation expenditures so treated shall be allowed as a deduction.*

(B) DOLLAR LIMITATION.—*The aggregate amount of reforestation expenditures which may be taken into account under subparagraph (A) with respect to each qualified timber property for any taxable year shall not exceed $10,000 ($5,000 in the case of a separate return by a married individual (as defined in section 7703)).*

(2) ALLOCATION OF DOLLAR LIMIT.—

(A) CONTROLLED GROUP.—For purposes of applying the dollar limitation under *paragraph (1)(B)* —

(i) all component members of a controlled group shall be treated as one taxpayer, and

(ii) the Secretary shall, under regulations prescribed by him, apportion such dollar limitation among the component members of such controlled group.

For purposes of the preceding sentence, the term "controlled group" has the meaning assigned to it by section 1563(a), except that the phrase "more than 50 percent" shall be substituted for the phrase "at least 80 percent" each place it appears in section 1563(a)(1).

(B) PARTNERSHIPS AND S CORPORATIONS.—In the case of a partnership, the dollar limitation contained in *paragraph (1)(B)* shall apply with respect to the partnership and with respect to each partner. A similar rule shall apply in the case of an S corporation and its shareholders.

[CCH Explanation at ¶ 840. Committee Reports at ¶ 10,450.]

Amendments

• **2004, American Jobs Creation Act of 2004 (H.R. 4520)**

H.R. 4520, § 322(a):

Amended so much of Code Sec. 194(b) as precedes paragraph (2). **Effective** with respect to expenditures paid or incurred after the date of the enactment of this Act. Prior to amendment, so much of Code Sec. 194(b) as precedes paragraph (2) read as follows:

(b) LIMITATIONS.—

(1) MAXIMUM DOLLAR AMOUNT.—The aggregate amount of amortizable basis acquired during the taxable year which may be taken into account under subsection (a) for such taxable year shall not exceed $10,000 ($5,000 in the case of a separate return by a married individual (as defined in section 7703)).

H.R. 4520, § 322(c)(1):

Amended Code Sec. 194(b) by striking paragraphs (3) and (4). **Effective** with respect to expenditures paid or incurred

after the date of the enactment of this Act. Prior to amendment Code Sec. 194(b)(3) and (4) read as follows:

(3) SECTION NOT TO APPLY TO TRUSTS.—This section shall not apply to trusts.

(4) ESTATES.—The benefit of the deduction for amortization provided by this section shall be allowed to estates in the same manner as in the case of an individual. The allowable deduction shall be apportioned between the income beneficiary and the fiduciary under regulations prescribed by the Secretary. Any amount so apportioned to a beneficiary shall be taken into account for purposes of determining the amount allowable as a deduction under this section to such beneficiary.

H.R. 4520, § 322(c)(2):

Amended Code Sec. 194(b)(2) by striking "paragraph (1)" both places it appears and inserting "paragraph (1)(B)". **Effective** with respect to expenditures paid or incurred after the date of the enactment of this Act.

(c) DEFINITIONS AND SPECIAL RULE.—For purposes of this section—

* * *

(2) AMORTIZABLE BASIS.—The term "amortizable basis" means that portion of the basis of the qualified timber property attributable to reforestation expenditures *which have not been taken into account under subsection (b).*

* * *

(4) TREATMENT OF TRUSTS AND ESTATES.—

(A) IN GENERAL.—*Except as provided in subparagraph (B), this section shall not apply to trusts and estates.*

(B) AMORTIZATION DEDUCTION ALLOWED TO ESTATES.—*The benefit of the deduction for amortization provided by subsection (a) shall be allowed to estates in the same manner as in the case of an individual. The allowable deduction shall be apportioned between the income beneficiary and the fiduciary under regulations prescribed by the Secretary. Any amount so apportioned to a beneficiary shall be taken into account for purposes of determining the amount allowable as a deduction under subsection (a) to such beneficiary.*

(5) APPLICATION WITH OTHER DEDUCTIONS.—*No deduction shall be allowed under any other provision of this chapter with respect to any expenditure with respect to which a deduction is allowed or allowable under this section to the taxpayer.*

* * *

[CCH Explanation at ¶ 840. Committee Reports at ¶ 10,450.]

Amendments

• **2004, American Jobs Creation Act of 2004 (H.R. 4520)**

H.R. 4520, § 322(b):

Amended Code Sec. 194(c)(2) by inserting "which have not been taken into account under subsection (b)" after "expenditures". **Effective** with respect to expenditures paid or incurred after the date of the enactment of this Act.

H.R. 4520, § 322(c)(3):

Amended Code Sec. 194(c) by striking paragraph (4) and inserting new paragraphs (4) and (5). **Effective** with respect to expenditures paid or incurred after the date of the enactment of this Act. Prior to being stricken, Code Sec. 194(c)(4) read as follows:

(4) BASIS ALLOCATION.—If the amount of the amortizable basis acquired during the taxable year of all qualified timber property with respect to which the taxpayer has made an election under subsection (a) exceeds the amount of the limitation under subsection (b)(1), the taxpayer shall allocate that portion of such amortizable basis with respect to which a deduction is allowable under subsection (a) to each such qualified timber property in such manner as the Secretary may by regulations prescribe.

H.R. 4520, § 322(c)(4):

Amended the heading for Code Sec. 194 by striking "**AMORTIZATION**" and inserting "**TREATMENT**". **Effective** with respect to expenditures paid or incurred after the date of the enactment of this Act.

[¶5215] CODE SEC. 195. START-UP EXPENDITURES.

* * *

(b) ELECTION TO DEDUCT.—

(1) ALLOWANCE OF DEDUCTION.—*If a taxpayer elects the application of this subsection with respect to any start-up expenditures—*

(A) *the taxpayer shall be allowed a deduction for the taxable year in which the active trade or business begins in an amount equal to the lesser of—*

(i) *the amount of start-up expenditures with respect to the active trade or business, or*

(ii) *$5,000, reduced (but not below zero) by the amount by which such start-up expenditures exceed $50,000, and*

(B) *the remainder of such start-up expenditures shall be allowed as a deduction ratably over the 180-month period beginning with the month in which the active trade or business begins.*

* * *

[CCH Explanation at ¶350. Committee Reports at ¶11,740.]

Amendments

• **2004, American Jobs Creation Act of 2004 (H.R. 4520)**

H.R. 4520, §902(a)(1):

Amended Code Sec. 195(b)(1). **Effective** for amounts paid or incurred after the date of the enactment of this Act. Prior to amendment, Code Sec. 195(b)(1) read as follows:

(1) IN GENERAL.—Start-up expenditures may, at the election of the taxpayer, be treated as deferred expenses. Such

deferred expenses shall be allowed as a deduction prorated equally over such period of not less than 60 months as may be selected by the taxpayer (beginning with the month in which the active trade or business begins).

H.R. 4520, §902(a)(2):

Amended Code Sec. 195(b) by striking "AMORTIZE" and inserting "DEDUCT" in the heading. **Effective** for amounts paid or incurred after the date of the enactment of this Act.

[¶5220] CODE SEC. 196. DEDUCTION FOR CERTAIN UNUSED BUSINESS CREDITS.

* * *

(c) QUALIFIED BUSINESS CREDITS.—For purposes of this section, the term "qualified business credits" means—

(1) the investment credit determined under section 46 (but only to the extent attributable to property the basis of which is reduced by section 50(c)),

(2) the work opportunity credit determined under section 51(a),

(3) the alcohol fuels credit determined under section 40(a),

(4) the research credit determined under section 41(a) (other than such credit determined under section 280C(c)(3)) for taxable years beginning after December 31, 1988,

(5) the enhanced oil recovery credit determined under section 43(a),

(6) the empowerment zone employment credit determined under section 1396(a),

(7) the Indian employment credit determined under section 45A(a),

(8) the employer Social Security credit determined under section 45B(a),

(9) the new markets tax credit determined under section 45D(a),

(10) the small employer pension plan startup cost credit determined under section 45E(a),

(11) *the biodiesel fuels credit determined under section 40A(a), and*

(12) *the low sulfur diesel fuel production credit determined under section 45H(a).*

* * *

[CCH Explanation at ¶810 and ¶855. Committee Reports at ¶10,324 and ¶10,540.]

Amendments

• **2004, American Jobs Creation Act of 2004 (H.R. 4520)**

H.R. 4520, §302(c)(2):

Amended Code Sec. 196(c) by striking "and" at the end of paragraph (9), by striking the period at the end of paragraph (10) and inserting ", and", and by adding at the end a new paragraph (11). **Effective** for fuel produced, and sold or used, after 12-31-2004, in tax years ending after such date.

H.R. 4520, §339(e):

Amended Code Sec. 196(c), as amended by Act Sec. 302(c)(2), by striking "and" at the end of paragraph (10), by striking the period at the end of paragraph (11) and inserting ", and", and by adding after paragraph (11) a new paragraph (12). **Effective** for expenses paid or incurred after 12-31-2002, in tax years ending after such date.

[¶ 5225] CODE SEC. 197. AMORTIZATION OF GOODWILL AND CERTAIN OTHER INTANGIBLES.

* * *

(e) Exceptions.—For purposes of this section, the term "section 197 intangible" shall not include any of the following:

* * *

(6) Mortgage servicing.—Any right to service indebtedness which is secured by residential real property unless such right is acquired in a transaction (or series of related transactions) involving the acquisition of assests (other than rights described in this paragraph) constituting a trade or business or substantial portion thereof.

(7) Certain transaction costs.—Any fees for professional services, and any transaction costs, incurred by parties to a transaction with respect to which any portion of the gain or loss is not recognized under part III of subchapter C.

[CCH Explanation at ¶ 355. Committee Reports at ¶ 11,580.]

Amendments

• **2004, American Jobs Creation Act of 2004 (H.R. 4520)**

H.R. 4520, § 886(a):

Amended Code Sec. 197(e) by striking paragraph (6) and by redesignating paragraphs (7) and (8) as paragraphs (6)

and (7), respectively. **Effective** for property acquired after the date of the enactment of this Act. Prior to being stricken, Code Sec. 197(e)(6) read as follows:

(6) Treatment of sports franchises.—A franchise to engage in professional football, basketball, baseball, or other professional sport, and any item acquired in connection with such a franchise.

(f) Special Rules.—

* * *

(10) Tax-exempt use property subject to lease.—*In the case of any section 197 intangible which would be tax-exempt use property as defined in subsection (h) of section 168 if such section applied to such intangible, the amortization period under this section shall not be less than 125 percent of the lease term (within the meaning of section 168(i)(3)).*

* * *

[CCH Explanation at ¶ 670. Committee Reports at ¶ 11,290.]

Amendments

• **2004, American Jobs Creation Act of 2004 (H.R. 4520)**

H.R. 4520, § 847(b)(3):

Amended Code Sec. 197(f) by adding at the end a new paragraph (10). **Effective** for leases entered into after 10-3-2004. For an exception, see Act Sec. 849(b)(1)-(2) below.

H.R. 4520, § 849(b)(1)-(2), provides:

(b) Exception.—

(1) In general.—The amendments made by this part shall not apply to qualified transportation property.

(2) Qualified Transportation Property.—For purposes of paragraph (1), the term "qualified transportation property" means domestic property subject to a lease with respect to which a formal application—

(A) was submitted for approval to the Federal Transit Administration (an agency of the Department of Transportation) after June 30, 2003, and before March 13, 2004,

(B) is approved by the Federal Transit Administration before January 1, 2006, and

(C) includes a description of such property and the value of such property.

[¶ 5230] *CODE SEC. 199. INCOME ATTRIBUTABLE TO DOMESTIC PRODUCTION ACTIVITIES.*

(a) *Allowance of Deduction.*—

(1) *In general.*—*There shall be allowed as a deduction an amount equal to 9 percent of the lesser of*—

(A) *the qualified production activities income of the taxpayer for the taxable year, or*

(B) *taxable income (determined without regard to this section) for the taxable year.*

(2) *Phasein.*—*In the case of any taxable year beginning after 2004 and before 2010, paragraph (1) and subsections (d)(1) and (d)(6) shall be applied by substituting for the percentage contained therein the transition percentage determined under the following table:*

For taxable years beginning in:	The transition percentage is:
2005 or 2006	3
2007, 2008, or 2009	6.

(b) DEDUCTION LIMITED TO WAGES PAID.—

(1) IN GENERAL.—The amount of the deduction allowable under subsection (a) for any taxable year shall not exceed 50 percent of the W-2 wages of the employer for the taxable year.

(2) W-2 WAGES.—For purposes of paragraph (1), the term "W-2 wages" means the sum of the aggregate amounts the taxpayer is required to include on statements under paragraphs (3) and (8) of section 6051(a) with respect to employment of employees of the taxpayer during the calendar year ending during the taxpayer's taxable year.

(3) ACQUISITIONS AND DISPOSITIONS.—The Secretary shall provide for the application of this subsection in cases where the taxpayer acquires, or disposes of, the major portion of a trade or business or the major portion of a separate unit of a trade or business during the taxable year.

(c) QUALIFIED PRODUCTION ACTIVITIES INCOME.—For purposes of this section—

(1) IN GENERAL.—The term "qualified production activities income" for any taxable year means an amount equal to the excess (if any) of—

(A) the taxpayer's domestic production gross receipts for such taxable year, over

(B) the sum of—

(i) the cost of goods sold that are allocable to such receipts,

(ii) other deductions, expenses, or losses directly allocable to such receipts, and

(iii) a ratable portion of other deductions, expenses, and losses that are not directly allocable to such receipts or another class of income.

(2) ALLOCATION METHOD.—The Secretary shall prescribe rules for the proper allocation of items of income, deduction, expense, and loss for purposes of determining income attributable to domestic production activities.

(3) SPECIAL RULES FOR DETERMINING COSTS.—

(A) IN GENERAL.—For purposes of determining costs under clause (i) of paragraph (1)(B), any item or service brought into the United States shall be treated as acquired by purchase, and its cost shall be treated as not less than its value immediately after it entered the United States. A similar rule shall apply in determining the adjusted basis of leased or rented property where the lease or rental gives rise to domestic production gross receipts.

(B) EXPORTS FOR FURTHER MANUFACTURE.—In the case of any property described in subparagraph (A) that had been exported by the taxpayer for further manufacture, the increase in cost or adjusted basis under subparagraph (A) shall not exceed the difference between the value of the property when exported and the value of the property when brought back into the United States after the further manufacture.

(4) DOMESTIC PRODUCTION GROSS RECEIPTS.—

(A) IN GENERAL.—The term "domestic production gross receipts" means the gross receipts of the taxpayer which are derived from—

(i) any lease, rental, license, sale, exchange, or other disposition of—

(I) qualifying production property which was manufactured, produced, grown, or extracted by the taxpayer in whole or in significant part within the United States,

(II) any qualified film produced by the taxpayer, or

(III) electricity, natural gas, or potable water produced by the taxpayer in the United States,

(ii) construction performed in the United States, or

(iii) engineering or architectural services performed in the United States for construction projects in the United States.

Code Sec. 199(c)(4)(A)(iii) ¶5230

(B) EXCEPTIONS.—*Such term shall not include gross receipts of the taxpayer which are derived from—*

    (i) *the sale of food and beverages prepared by the taxpayer at a retail establishment, and*

    (ii) *the transmission or distribution of electricity, natural gas, or potable water.*

(5) QUALIFYING PRODUCTION PROPERTY.—*The term "qualifying production property" means—*

    (A) *tangible personal property,*

    (B) *any computer software, and*

    (C) *any property described in section 168(f)(4).*

(6) QUALIFIED FILM.—*The term "qualified film" means any property described in section 168(f)(3) if not less than 50 percent of the total compensation relating to the production of such property is compensation for services performed in the United States by actors, production personnel, directors, and producers. Such term does not include property with respect to which records are required to be maintained under section 2257 of title 18, United States Code.*

(7) RELATED PERSONS.—

    (A) IN GENERAL.—*The term "domestic production gross receipts" shall not include any gross receipts of the taxpayer derived from property leased, licensed, or rented by the taxpayer for use by any related person.*

    (B) RELATED PERSON.—*For purposes of subparagraph (A), a person shall be treated as related to another person if such persons are treated as a single employer under subsection (a) or (b) of section 52 or subsection (m) or (o) of section 414, except that determinations under subsections (a) and (b) of section 52 shall be made without regard to section 1563(b).*

(d) DEFINITIONS AND SPECIAL RULES.—

(1) APPLICATION OF SECTION TO PASS-THRU ENTITIES.—

    (A) IN GENERAL.—*In the case of an S corporation, partnership, estate or trust, or other pass-thru entity—*

        (i) *subject to the provisions of paragraphs (2) and (3), this section shall be applied at the shareholder, partner, or similar level, and*

        (ii) *the Secretary shall prescribe rules for the application of this section, including rules relating to—*

            (I) *restrictions on the allocation of the deduction to taxpayers at the partner or similar level, and*

            (II) *additional reporting requirements.*

    (B) APPLICATION OF WAGE LIMITATION.—*Notwithstanding subparagraph (A)(i), for purposes of applying subsection (b), a shareholder, partner, or similar person which is allocated qualified production activities income from an S corporation, partnership, estate, trust, or other pass-thru entity shall also be treated as having been allocated W-2 wages from such entity in an amount equal to the lesser of—*

        (i) *such person's allocable share of such wages (without regard to this subparagraph), as determined under regulations prescribed by the Secretary, or*

        (ii) *2 times 9 percent of the qualified production activities income allocated to such person for the taxable year.*

(2) APPLICATION TO INDIVIDUALS.—*In the case of an individual, subsection (a)(1)(B) shall be applied by substituting "adjusted gross income" for "taxable income". For purposes of the preceding sentence, adjusted gross income shall be determined—*

    (A) *after application of sections 86, 135, 137, 219, 221, 222, and 469, and*

    (B) *without regard to this section.*

(3) PATRONS OF AGRICULTURAL AND HORTICULTURAL COOPERATIVES.—

    (A) IN GENERAL.—*If any amount described in paragraph (1) or (3) of section 1385(a)—*

(i) is received by a person from an organization to which part I of subchapter T applies which is engaged—

(I) in the manufacturing, production, growth, or extraction in whole or significant part of any agricultural or horticultural product, or

(II) in the marketing of agricultural or horticultural products, and

(ii) is allocable to the portion of the qualified production activities income of the organization which, but for this paragraph, would be deductible under subsection (a) by the organization and is designated as such by the organization in a written notice mailed to its patrons during the payment period described in section 1382(d),

then such person shall be allowed a deduction under subsection (a) with respect to such amount. The taxable income of the organization shall not be reduced under section 1382 by reason of any amount to which the preceding sentence applies.

(B) SPECIAL RULES.—For purposes of applying subparagraph (A), in determining the qualified production activities income which would be deductible by the organization under subsection (a)—

(i) there shall not be taken into account in computing the organization's taxable income any deduction allowable under subsection (b) or (c) of section 1382 (relating to patronage dividends, per-unit retain allocations, and nonpatronage distributions), and

(ii) in the case of an organization described in subparagraph (A)(i)(II), the organization shall be treated as having manufactured, produced, grown, or extracted in whole or significant part any qualifying production property marketed by the organization which its patrons have so manufactured, produced, grown, or extracted.

(4) SPECIAL RULE FOR AFFILIATED GROUPS.—

(A) IN GENERAL.—All members of an expanded affiliated group shall be treated as a single corporation for purposes of this section.

(B) EXPANDED AFFILIATED GROUP.—For purposes of this section, the term "expanded affiliated group" means an affiliated group as defined in section 1504(a), determined—

(i) by substituting "50 percent" for "80 percent" each place it appears, and

(ii) without regard to paragraphs (2) and (4) of section 1504(b).

(C) ALLOCATION OF DEDUCTION.—Except as provided in regulations, the deduction under subsection (a) shall be allocated among the members of the expanded affiliated group in proportion to each member's respective amount (if any) of qualified production activities income.

(5) TRADE OR BUSINESS REQUIREMENT.—This section shall be applied by only taking into account items which are attributable to the actual conduct of a trade or business.

(6) COORDINATION WITH MINIMUM TAX.—The deduction under this section shall be allowed for purposes of the tax imposed by section 55; except that for purposes of section 55, the deduction under subsection (a) shall be 9 percent of the lesser of—

(A) qualified production activities income (determined without regard to part IV of subchapter A), or

(B) alternative minimum taxable income (determined without regard to this section) for the taxable year.

In the case of an individual, subparagraph (B) shall be applied by substituting "adjusted gross income" for "alternative minimum taxable income". For purposes of the preceding sentence, adjusted gross income shall be determined in the same manner as provided in paragraph (2).

(7) REGULATIONS.—The Secretary shall prescribe such regulations as are necessary to carry out the purposes of this section.

* * *

[CCH Explanation at ¶ 210. Committee Reports at ¶ 10,020.]

Amendments

• **2004, American Jobs Creation Act of 2004 (H.R. 4520)**

H.R. 4520, § 102(a):

Amended part VI of subchapter B of chapter 1 by adding at the end a new Code Sec. 199. **Effective** for tax years beginning after 12-31-2004.

[¶ 5235] CODE SEC. 219. RETIREMENT SAVINGS.

* * *

(g) LIMITATION ON DEDUCTION FOR ACTIVE PARTICIPANTS IN CERTAIN PENSION PLANS.—

* * *

(3) ADJUSTED GROSS INCOME; APPLICABLE DOLLAR AMOUNT.—For purposes of this subsection—

(A) ADJUSTED GROSS INCOME.—Adjusted gross income of any taxpayer shall be determined—

* * *

(ii) without regard to sections 135, 137, *199* , 221, 222, and 911 or the deduction allowable under this section.

* * *

[CCH Explanation at ¶ 210.]

Amendments

• **2004, American Jobs Creation Act of 2004 (H.R. 4520)**

H.R. 4520, § 102(d)(1):

Amended Code Sec. 219(g)(3)(A)(ii) by inserting "199," before "221". **Effective** for tax years beginning after 12-31-2004.

[¶ 5240] CODE SEC. 221. INTEREST ON EDUCATION LOANS.

* * *

(b) MAXIMUM DEDUCTION.—

* * *

(2) LIMITATION BASED ON MODIFIED ADJUSTED GROSS INCOME.—

* * *

(C) MODIFIED ADJUSTED GROSS INCOME.—The term "modified adjusted gross income" means adjusted gross income determined—

(i) without regard to this section and sections *199* , 222, 911, 931, and 933, and

* * *

[CCH Explanation at ¶ 210.]

Amendments

• **2004, American Jobs Creation Act of 2004 (H.R. 4520)**

H.R. 4520, § 102(d)(2):

Amended Code Sec. 221(b)(2)(C)(i) by inserting "199," before "222". **Effective** for tax years beginning after 12-31-2004.

[¶ 5245] CODE SEC. 222. QUALIFIED TUITION AND RELATED EXPENSES.

* * *

(b) DOLLAR LIMITATIONS.—

* * *

(2) APPLICABLE DOLLAR LIMIT.—

* * *

(C) ADJUSTED GROSS INCOME.—For purposes of this paragraph, adjusted gross income shall be determined—

(i) without regard to this section and sections *199*, 911, 931, and 933, and

* * *

[CCH Explanation at ¶ 210.]

Amendments

• **2004, American Jobs Creation Act of 2004 (H.R. 4520)**

H.R. 4520, § 102(d)(3):

Amended Code Sec. 222(b)(2)(C)(i) by inserting "199," before "911". **Effective** for tax years beginning after 12-31-2004.

[¶ 5250] CODE SEC. 245. DIVIDENDS RECEIVED FROM CERTAIN FOREIGN CORPORATIONS.

(a) DIVIDENDS FROM 10-PERCENT OWNED FOREIGN CORPORATIONS.—

* * *

(2) QUALIFIED 10-PERCENT OWNED FOREIGN CORPORATION.—For purposes of this subsection, the term "qualified 10-percent owned foreign corporation" means any foreign corporation (other than a passive foreign investment company) if at least 10 percent of the stock of such corporation (by vote and value) is owned by the taxpayer.

* * *

[CCH Explanation at ¶ 490. Committee Reports at ¶ 10,690.]

Amendments

• **2004, American Jobs Creation Act of 2004 (H.R. 4520)**

H.R. 4520, § 413(c)(3):

Amended Code Sec. 245(a)(2) by striking "foreign personal holding company or" immediately preceding "passive foreign investment company". **Effective** for tax years of foreign corporations beginning after 12-31-2004, and for tax years of United States shareholders with or within which such tax years of foreign corporations end.

[¶ 5255] CODE SEC. 246. RULES APPLYING TO DEDUCTIONS FOR DIVIDENDS RECEIVED.

* * *

(b) LIMITATION ON AGGREGATE AMOUNT OF DEDUCTIONS.—

(1) GENERAL RULE.—Except as provided in paragraph (2), the aggregate amount of the deductions allowed by sections 243(a)(1), 244(a), and subsection (a) or (b) of section 245 shall not exceed the percentage determined under paragraph (3) of the taxable income computed without regard to the deductions allowed by sections 172, *199*, 243(a)(1), 244(a), subsection (a) or (b) of section 245, and 247, without regard to any adjustment under section 1059, and without regard to any capital loss carryback to the taxable year under section 1212(a)(1).

* * *

[CCH Explanation at ¶ 210.]

Amendments

• **2004, American Jobs Creation Act of 2004 (H.R. 4520)**

H.R. 4520, § 102(d)(4):

Amended Code Sec. 246(b)(1) by inserting "199," after"172,". **Effective** for tax years beginning after 12-31-2004.

(c) EXCLUSION OF CERTAIN DIVIDENDS.—

* * *

(4) HOLDING PERIOD REDUCED FOR PERIODS WHERE RISK OF LOSS DIMINISHED.—The holding periods determined for purposes of this subsection shall be appropriately reduced (in the manner provided in regulations prescribed by the Secretary) for any period (during such periods) in which—

(A) the taxpayer has an option to sell, is under a contractual obligation to sell, or has made (and not closed) a short sale of, substantially identical stock or securities,

(B) the taxpayer is the grantor of an option to buy substantially identical stock or securities, or

(C) under regulations prescribed by the Secretary, a taxpayer has diminished his risk of loss by holding 1 or more other positions with respect to substantially similar or related property.

The preceding sentence shall not apply in the case of any qualified covered call (as defined in section 1092(c)(4) but without regard to the requirement that gain or loss with respect to the option not be ordinary income or loss), *other than a qualified covered call option to which section 1092(f) applies.*

* * *

[CCH Explanation at ¶ 730. Committee Reports at ¶ 11,600.]

Amendments

• **2004, American Jobs Creation Act of 2004 (H.R. 4520)**

H.R. 4520, § 888(d):

Amended Code Sec. 246(c) by inserting ", other than a qualified covered call option to which section 1092(f) ap-

plies" in the last sentence before the period at the end. **Effective** for positions established on or after the date of the enactment of this Act.

[¶ 5260] CODE SEC. 248. ORGANIZATIONAL EXPENDITURES.

(a) ELECTION TO DEDUCT.—If a corporation elects the application of this subsection (in accordance with regulations prescribed by the Secretary) with respect to any organizational expenditures—

(1) the corporation shall be allowed a deduction for the taxable year in which the corporation begins business in an amount equal to the lesser of—

(A) the amount of organizational expenditures with respect to the taxpayer, or

(B) $5,000, reduced (but not below zero) by the amount by which such organizational expenditures exceed $50,000, and

(2) the remainder of such organizational expenditures shall be allowed as a deduction ratably over the 180-month period beginning with the month in which the corporation begins business.

* * *

[CCH Explanation at ¶ 350. Committee Reports at ¶ 11,740.]

Amendments

• **2004, American Jobs Creation Act of 2004 (H.R. 4520)**

H.R. 4520, § 902(b):

Amended Code Sec. 248(a). **Effective** for amounts paid or incurred after the date of the enactment of this Act. Prior to amendment, Code Sec. 248(a) read as follows:

(a) ELECTION TO AMORTIZE.—The organizational expenditures of a corporation may, at the election of the corporation (made in accordance with regulations prescribed by the Secretary), be treated as deferred expenses. In computing taxable income, such deferred expenses shall be allowed as a deduction ratably over such period of not less than 60 months as may be selected by the corporation (beginning with the month in which the corporation begins business).

[¶ 5265] CODE SEC. 263. CAPITAL EXPENDITURES.

(a) General Rule.—No deduction shall be allowed for—

(1) Any amount paid out for new buildings or for permanent improvements or betterments made to increase the value of any property or estate. This paragraph shall not apply to—

(A) expenditures for the development of mines or deposits deductible under section 616,

(B) research and experimental expenditures deductible under section 174,

(C) soil and water conservation expenditures deductible under section 175,

(D) expenditures by farmers for fertilizer, etc., deductible under section 180,

(E) expenditures for removal of architectural and transportation barriers to the handicapped and elderly which the taxpayer elects to deduct under section 190,

(F) expenditures for tertiary injectants with respect to which a deduction is allowed under section 193;

(G) expenditures for which a deduction is allowed under section 179;

(H) expenditures for which a deduction is allowed under section 179A, *or*

(I) *expenditures for which a deduction is allowed under section 179B.*

* * *

[CCH Explanation at ¶ 850. Committee Reports at ¶ 10,530.]

Amendments

• **2004, American Jobs Creation Act of 2004 (H.R. 4520)**

H.R. 4520, § 338(b)(1):

Amended Code Sec. 263(a)(1), as amended by this Act, by striking "or" at the end of subparagraph (G), by striking the period at the end of subparagraph (H) and inserting ", or", and by adding at the end a new subparagraph (I). **Effective** for expenses paid or incurred after 12-31-2002, in tax years ending after such date.

[¶ 5270] CODE SEC. 263A. CAPITALIZATION AND INCLUSION IN INVENTORY COSTS OF CERTAIN EXPENSES.

* * *

(c) General Exceptions.—

* * *

(3) Certain development and other costs of oil and gas wells or other mineral property.— This section shall not apply to any cost allowable as a deduction under section *179B*, 263(c), 263(i), 291(b)(2), 616, or 617.

* * *

[CCH Explanation at ¶ 850. Committee Reports at ¶ 10,530.]

Amendments

• **2004, American Jobs Creation Act of 2004 (H.R. 4520)**

H.R. 4520, § 338(b)(2):

Amended Code Sec. 263A(c)(3) by inserting "179B," after "section". **Effective** for expenses paid or incurred after 12-31-2002, in tax years ending after such date.

[¶ 5275] CODE SEC. 267. LOSSES, EXPENSES, AND INTEREST WITH RESPECT TO TRANSACTIONS BETWEEN RELATED TAXPAYERS.

(a) In General.—

* * *

(3) PAYMENTS TO FOREIGN PERSONS.—

(A) IN GENERAL.—The Secretary shall by regulations apply the matching principle of paragraph (2) in cases in which the person to whom the payment is to be made is not a United States person.

(B) SPECIAL RULE FOR CERTAIN FOREIGN ENTITIES.—

(i) IN GENERAL.—Notwithstanding subparagraph (A), in the case of any item payable to a controlled foreign corporation (as defined in section 957) or a passive foreign investment company (as defined in section 1297), a deduction shall be allowable to the payor with respect to such amount for any taxable year before the taxable year in which paid only to the extent that an amount attributable to such item is includible (determined without regard to properly allocable deductions and qualified deficits under section 952(c)(1)(B)) during such prior taxable year in the gross income of a United States person who owns (within the meaning of section 958(a)) stock in such corporation.

(ii) SECRETARIAL AUTHORITY.—The Secretary may by regulation exempt transactions from the application of clause (i), including any transaction which is entered into by a payor in the ordinary course of a trade or business in which the payor is predominantly engaged and in which the payment of the accrued amounts occurs within 8½ months after accrual or within such other period as the Secretary may prescribe.

* * *

[CCH Explanation at ¶705. Committee Reports at ¶11,240.]

Amendments

• **2004, American Jobs Creation Act of 2004 (H.R. 4520)**

H.R. 4520, §841(b)(1)-(2):

Amended Code Sec. 267(a)(3) by striking "The Secretary" and inserting "(A) IN GENERAL.—The Secretary", and by adding at the end a new subparagraph (B). **Effective** for payments accrued on or after the date of the enactment of this Act.

[¶5280] CODE SEC. 274. DISALLOWANCE OF CERTAIN ENTERTAINMENT, ETC., EXPENSES.

* * *

(e) SPECIFIC EXCEPTIONS TO APPLICATION OF SUBSECTION (a).—Subsection (a) shall not apply to—

* * *

(2) EXPENSES TREATED AS COMPENSATION.—

(A) IN GENERAL.—Except as provided in subparagraph (B), expenses for goods, services, and facilities, to the extent that the expenses are treated by the taxpayer, with respect to the recipient of the entertainment, amusement, or recreation, as compensation to an employee on the taxpayer's return of tax under this chapter and as wages to such employee for purposes of chapter 24 (relating to withholding of income tax at source on wages).

(B) SPECIFIED INDIVIDUALS.—

(i) IN GENERAL.—In the case of a recipient who is a specified individual, subparagraph (A) and paragraph (9) shall each be applied by substituting "to the extent that the expenses do not exceed the amount of the expenses which" for "to the extent that the expenses".

(ii) SPECIFIED INDIVIDUAL.—For purposes of clause (i), the term "specified individual" means any individual who—

(I) is subject to the requirements of section 16(a) of the Securities Exchange Act of 1934 with respect to the taxpayer, or

(II) would be subject to such requirements if the taxpayer were an issuer of equity securities referred to in such section.

* * *

[CCH Explanation at ¶ 360. Committee Reports at ¶ 11,790.]

Amendments

• **2004, American Jobs Creation Act of 2004 (H.R. 4520)**

H.R. 4520, § 907(a):

Amended Code Sec. 274(e)(2). **Effective** for expenses incurred after the date of the enactment of this Act. Prior to amendment, Code Sec. 274(e)(2) read as follows:

(2) EXPENSES TREATED AS COMPENSATION.—Expenses for goods, services, and facilities, to the extent that the expenses are treated by the taxpayer, with respect to the recipient of the entertainment, amusement, or recreation, as compensation to an employee on the taxpayer's return of tax under this chapter and as wages to such employee for purposes of chapter 24 (relating to withholding of income tax at source on wages).

[¶ 5285] CODE SEC. 275. CERTAIN TAXES.

(a) GENERAL RULE.—No deduction shall be allowed for the following taxes:

(1) Federal income taxes, including—

(A) the tax imposed by section 3101 (relating to the tax on employees under the Federal Insurance Contributions Act);

(B) the taxes imposed by sections 3201 and 3211 (relating to the taxes on railroad employees and railroad employee representatives); and

(C) the tax withheld at source on wages under section 3402.

(2) Federal war profits and excess profits taxes.

(3) Estate, inheritance, legacy, succession, and gift taxes.

(4) Income, war profits, and excess profits taxes imposed by the authority of any foreign country or possession of the United States if—

(A) the taxpayer chooses to take to any extent the benefits of section 901, *or*

(B) such taxes are paid or accrued with respect to foreign trade income (within the meaning of section 923(b)) of a FSC.

(5) Taxes on real property, to the extent that section 164(d) requires such taxes to be treated as imposed on another taxpayer.

(6) Taxes imposed by chapters 41, 42, 43, 44, *45*, 46, and 54.

Paragraph (1) shall not apply to any taxes to the extent such taxes are allowable as a deduction under section 164(f). Paragraph (1) shall not apply to the tax imposed by section 59A.

* * *

[CCH Explanation at ¶ 205 and ¶ 508. Committee Reports at ¶ 10,010 and ¶ 10,980.]

Amendments

• **2004, American Jobs Creation Act of 2004 (H.R. 4520)**

H.R. 4520, § 101(b)(5)(A):

Amended Code Sec. 275(a) by inserting "or" at the end of paragraph (4)(A), by striking "or" at the end of paragraph (4)(B) and inserting a period, and by striking subparagraph (C). **Effective** for transactions after 12-31-2004. For transitional and special rules, see Act Sec. 101(d)-(f), below. Prior to being stricken, Code Sec. 275(a)(4)(C) read as follows:

(C) such taxes are paid or accrued with respect to qualifying foreign trade income (as defined in section 941).

H.R. 4520, § 101(b)(5)(B):

Amended Code Sec. 275(a) by striking the last sentence. **Effective** for transactions after 12-31-2004. For transitional and special rules, see Act Sec. 101(d)-(f), below. Prior to being stricken, the last sentence of Code Sec. 275(a) read as follows:

A rule similar to the rule of section 943(d) shall apply for purposes of paragraph (4)(C).

H.R. 4520, § 101(d)-(f), provides:

(d) TRANSITIONAL RULE FOR 2005 AND 2006.—

(1) IN GENERAL.—In the case of transactions during 2005 or 2006, the amount includible in gross income by reason of the amendments made by this section shall not exceed the applicable percentage of the amount which would have been so included but for this subsection.

(2) APPLICABLE PERCENTAGE.—For purposes of paragraph (1), the applicable percentage shall be as follows:

(A) For 2005, the applicable percentage shall be 20 percent.

(B) For 2006, the applicable percentage shall be 40 percent.

(e) REVOCATION OF ELECTION TO BE TREATED AS DOMESTIC CORPORATION.—If, during the 1-year period beginning on the date of the enactment of this Act, a corporation for which an election is in effect under section 943(e) of the Internal Revenue Code of 1986 revokes such election, no gain or loss shall be recognized with respect to property treated as transferred under clause (ii) of section 943(e)(4)(B) of such Code to the extent such property—

(1) was treated as transferred under clause (i) thereof, or

(2) was acquired during a taxable year to which such election applies and before May 1, 2003, in the ordinary course of its trade or business.

The Secretary of the Treasury (or such Secretary's delegate) may prescribe such regulations as may be necessary to prevent the abuse of the purposes of this subsection.

(f) BINDING CONTRACTS.—The amendments made by this section shall not apply to any transaction in the ordinary course of a trade or business which occurs pursuant to a binding contract—

(1) which is between the taxpayer and a person who is not a related person (as defined in section 943(b)(3) of such Code, as in effect on the day before the date of the enactment of this Act), and

(2) which is in effect on September 17, 2003, and at all times thereafter.

For purposes of this subsection, a binding contract shall include a purchase option, renewal option, or replacement option which is included in such contract and which is enforceable against the seller or lessor.

H.R. 4520, § 802(b)(1):

Amended Code Sec. 275(a)(6) by inserting "45," before "46,". **Effective** on 3-4-2003; except that periods before such date shall not be taken into account in applying the periods in Code Sec. 4985(a) and (e)(1), as added by Act Sec. 802(a).

[¶ 5290] CODE SEC. 280C. CERTAIN EXPENSES FOR WHICH CREDITS ARE ALLOWABLE.

* * *

(d) LOW SULFUR DIESEL FUEL PRODUCTION CREDIT.—*No deduction shall be allowed for that portion of the expenses otherwise allowable as a deduction for the taxable year which is equal to the amount of the credit determined for the taxable year under section 45H(a).*

* * *

[CCH Explanation at ¶ 855. Committee Reports at ¶ 10,540.]
Amendments
• **2004, American Jobs Creation Act of 2004 (H.R. 4520)**

H.R. 4520, § 339(c):

Amended Code Sec. 280C by adding at the end a new subsection (d). **Effective** for expenses paid or incurred after 12-31-2002, in tax years ending after such date.

[¶ 5295] CODE SEC. 305. DISTRIBUTIONS OF STOCK AND STOCK RIGHTS.

* * *

(e) TREATMENT OF PURCHASER OF STRIPPED PREFERRED STOCK.—

* * *

(7) CROSS REFERENCE.—

For treatment of stripped interests in certain accounts or entities holding preferred stock, see section 1286(f).

* * *

[CCH Explanation at ¶ 725. Committee Reports at ¶ 11,140.]
Amendments
• **2004, American Jobs Creation Act of 2004 (H.R. 4520)**

H.R. 4520, § 831(b):

Amended Code Sec. 305(e) by adding at the end a new paragraph (7). **Effective** for purchases and dispositions after the date of the enactment of this Act.

[¶ 5300] CODE SEC. 312. EFFECT ON EARNINGS AND PROFITS.

* * *

(j) [*Stricken.*]

[CCH Explanation at ¶ 490. Committee Reports at ¶ 10,690.]
Amendments
• **2004, American Jobs Creation Act of 2004 (H.R. 4520)**

H.R. 4520, § 413(c)(4):

Amended Code Sec. 312 by striking subsection (j). **Effective** for tax years of foreign corporations beginning after 12-31-2004, and for tax years of United States shareholders with or within which such tax years of foreign corporations end. Prior to being stricken, Code Sec. 312(j) read as follows:

(j) EARNINGS AND PROFITS OF FOREIGN INVESTMENT COMPANIES.—

(1) ALLOCATION WITHIN AFFILIATED GROUP.—In the case of a sale or exchange of stock in a foreign investment company (as defined in section 1246(b)) by a United States person (as defined in section 7701(a)(30)), if such company is a member of an affiliated group, then the accumulated earnings and profits of all members of such affiliated group shall be allocated, under regulations prescribed by the Secretary, in

such manner as is proper to carry out the purposes of section 1246.

(2) AFFILIATED GROUP DEFINED.—For purposes of paragraph (1) of this subsection, the term "affiliated group" has the meaning assigned to such term by section 1504(a); except that (A) "more than 50 percent" shall be substituted for "80 percent or more", and (B) all corporations shall be treated as includible corporations (without regard to the provisions of section 1504(b)).

(k) EFFECT OF DEPRECIATION ON EARNINGS AND PROFITS.—

* * *

(3) EXCEPTION FOR TANGIBLE PROPERTY.—

* * *

(B) TREATMENT OF AMOUNTS DEDUCTIBLE UNDER SECTION 179[,] *179A, OR 179B.*—For purposes of computing the earnings and profits of a corporation, any amount deductible under section 179[,] *179A, or 179B* shall be allowed as a deduction ratably over the period of 5 taxable years (beginning with the taxable year for which such amount is deductible under section 179[,] *179A, or 179B*, as the case may be).

* * *

[CCH Explanation at ¶ 850. Committee Reports at ¶ 10,530.]

Amendments

• **2004, American Jobs Creation Act of 2004 (H.R. 4520)**

H.R. 4520, § 338(b)(3):

Amended Code Sec. 312(k)(3)(B) by striking "or 179A" each place it appears in the heading and text and inserting

"[,] 179A, or 179B". **Effective** for expenses paid or incurred after 12-31-2002, in tax years ending after such date.

(m) NO ADJUSTMENT FOR INTEREST PAID ON CERTAIN REGISTRATION-REQUIRED OBLIGATIONS NOT IN REGISTERED FORM.—The earnings and profits of any corporation shall not be decreased by any interest with respect to which a deduction is not or would not be allowable by reason of section 163(f), unless at the time of issuance the issuer is a foreign corporation that is not a controlled foreign corporation (within the meaning of section 957), and the issuance did not have as a purpose the avoidance of section 163(f) of this subsection.

* * *

[CCH Explanation at ¶ 490. Committee Reports at ¶ 10,690.]

Amendments

• **2004, American Jobs Creation Act of 2004 (H.R. 4520)**

H.R. 4520, § 413(c)(5):

Amended Code Sec. 312(m) by striking ", a foreign investment company (within the meaning of section 1246(b)), or a

foreign personal holding company (within the meaning of section 552)" immediately following "(within the meaning of section 957),". **Effective** for tax years of foreign corporations beginning after 12-31-2004, and for tax years of United States shareholders with or within which such tax years of foreign corporations end.

[¶ 5305] CODE SEC. 332. COMPLETE LIQUIDATIONS OF SUBSIDIARIES.

* * *

(d) *RECOGNITION OF GAIN ON LIQUIDATION OF CERTAIN HOLDING COMPANIES.*—

(1) *IN GENERAL.—In the case of any distribution to a foreign corporation in complete liquidation of an applicable holding company—*

(A) *subsection (a) and section 331 shall not apply to such distribution, and*

(B) *such distribution shall be treated as a distribution to which section 301 applies.*

(2) *APPLICABLE HOLDING COMPANY.—For purposes of this subsection:*

(A) *IN GENERAL.—The term "applicable holding company" means any domestic corporation—*

(i) *which is a common parent of an affiliated group,*

(ii) *stock of which is directly owned by the distributee foreign corporation,*

(iii) *substantially all of the assets of which consist of stock in other members of such affiliated group, and*

(iv) which has not been in existence at all times during the 5 years immediately preceding the date of the liquidation.

(B) AFFILIATED GROUP.—For purposes of this subsection, the term "affiliated group" has the meaning given such term by section 1504(a) (without regard to paragraphs (2) and (4) of section 1504(b)).

(3) COORDINATION WITH SUBPART F.—If the distributee of a distribution described in paragraph (1) is a controlled foreign corporation (as defined in section 957), then notwithstanding paragraph (1) or subsection (a), such distribution shall be treated as a distribution to which section 331 applies.

(4) REGULATIONS.—The Secretary shall provide such regulations as appropriate to prevent the abuse of this subsection, including regulations which provide, for the purposes of clause (iv) of paragraph (2)(A), that a corporation is not in existence for any period unless it is engaged in the active conduct of a trade or business or owns a significant ownership interest in another corporation so engaged.

* * *

[CCH Explanation at ¶ 1010. Committee Reports at ¶ 11,650.]

Amendments

• **2004, American Jobs Creation Act of 2004 (H.R. 4520)**

H.R. 4520, § 893(a):

Amended Code Sec. 332 by adding at the end a new subsection (d). **Effective** for distributions in complete liqui-dation occurring on or after the date of the enactment of this Act.

[¶ 5310] CODE SEC. 334. BASIS OF PROPERTY RECEIVED IN LIQUIDATIONS.

* * *

(b) LIQUIDATION OF SUBSIDIARY.—

(1) IN GENERAL.—If property is received by a corporate distributee in a distribution in a complete liquidation to which section 332 applies (or in a transfer described in section 337(b)(1)), the basis of such property in the hands of such distributee shall be the same as it would be in the hands of the transferor; except that the basis of such property in the hands of such distributee shall be the fair market value of the property at the time of the distribution—

(A) in any case in which gain or loss is recognized by the liquidating corporation with respect to such property, or

(B) in any case in which the liquidating corporation is a foreign corporation, the corporate distributee is a domestic corporation, and the corporate distributee's aggregate adjusted bases of property described in section 362(e)(1)(B) which is distributed in such liquidation would (but for this subparagraph) exceed the fair market value of such property immediately after such liquidation.

* * *

[CCH Explanation at ¶ 520. Committee Reports at ¶ 11,190.]

Amendments

• **2004, American Jobs Creation Act of 2004 (H.R. 4520)**

H.R. 4520, § 836(b):

Amended Code Sec. 334(b)(1). **Effective** for liquidations after the date of the enactment of this Act. Prior to amendment, Code Sec. 334(b)(1) read as follows:

(1) IN GENERAL.—If property is received by a corporate distributee in a distribution in a complete liquidation to which section 332 applies (or in a transfer described in section 337(b)(1)), the basis of such property in the hands of such distributee shall be the same as it would be in the hands of the transferor; except that, in any case in which gain or loss is recognized by the liquidating corporation with respect to such property, the basis of such property in the hands of such distributee shall be the fair market value of the property at the time of the distribution.

[¶ 5315] CODE SEC. 338. CERTAIN STOCK PURCHASES TREATED AS ASSET ACQUISITIONS.

* * *

(h) DEFINITIONS AND SPECIAL RULES.—For purposes of this section—

* * *

(13) Tax on deemed sale not taken into account for estimated tax purposes.—For purposes of section 6655, tax attributable to the sale described in subsection (a)(1) shall not be taken into account. *The preceding sentence shall not apply with respect to a qualified stock purchase for which an election is made under paragraph (10).*

* * *

[CCH Explanation at ¶ 1020. Committee Reports at ¶ 11,220.]

Amendments

• 2004, American Jobs Creation Act of 2004 (H.R. 4520)

H.R. 4520, § 839(a):

Amended Code Sec. 338(h)(13) by adding at the end a new sentence. **Effective** for transactions occurring after the date of the enactment of this Act.

[¶ 5320] CODE SEC. 351. TRANSFER TO CORPORATION CONTROLLED BY TRANSFEROR.

* * *

(g) Nonqualified Preferred Stock Not Treated as Stock.—

* * *

(3) Definitions.—For purposes of this subsection—

(A) Preferred stock.—The term "preferred stock" means stock which is limited and preferred as to dividends and does not participate in corporate growth to any significant extent. *Stock shall not be treated as participating in corporate growth to any significant extent unless there is a real and meaningful likelihood of the shareholder actually participating in the earnings and growth of the corporation.*

* * *

[CCH Explanation at ¶ 1005. Committee Reports at ¶ 11,710.]

Amendments

• 2004, American Jobs Creation Act of 2004 (H.R. 4520)

H.R. 4520, § 899(a):

Amended Code Sec. 351(g)(3)(A) by adding at the end a new sentence. **Effective** for transactions after 5-14-2003.

[¶ 5325] CODE SEC. 357. ASSUMPTION OF LIABILITY.

* * *

(c) Liabilities in Excess of Basis.—

(1) In General.—In the case of an exchange—

* * *

(B) to which section 361 applies by reason of a plan of reorganization within the meaning of section 368(a)(1)(D) *with respect to which stock or securities of the corporation to which the assets are transferred are distributed in a transaction which qualifies under section 355,*

* * *

[CCH Explanation at ¶ 1015. Committee Reports at ¶ 11,700.]

Amendments

• 2004, American Jobs Creation Act of 2004 (H.R. 4520)

H.R. 4520, § 898(b):

Amended Code Sec. 357(c)(1)(B) by inserting "with respect to which stock or securities of the corporation to which the assets are transferred are distributed in a transaction which qualifies under section 355" after "section 368(a)(1)(D)". **Effective** for transfers of money or other property, or liabilities assumed, in connection with a reorganization occurring on or after the date of the enactment of this Act.

[¶5330] CODE SEC. 361. NONRECOGNITION OF GAIN OR LOSS TO CORPORATIONS; TREATMENT OF DISTRIBUTIONS.

* * *

(b) EXCHANGES NOT SOLELY IN KIND.—

* * *

(3) TREATMENT OF TRANSFERS TO CREDITORS.—For purposes of paragraph (1), any transfer of the other property or money received in the exchange by the corporation to its creditors in connection with the reorganization shall be treated as a distribution in pursuance of the plan of reorganization. The Secretary may prescribe such regulations as may be necessary to prevent avoidance of tax through abuse of the preceding sentence or subsection (c)(3). *In the case of a reorganization described in section 368(a)(1)(D) with respect to which stock or securities of the corporation to which the assets are transferred are distributed in a transaction which qualifies under section 355, this paragraph shall apply only to the extent that the sum of the money and the fair market value of other property transferred to such creditors does not exceed the adjusted bases of such assets transferred.*

* * *

[CCH Explanation at ¶1015. Committee Reports at ¶11,700.]

Amendments

• **2004, American Jobs Creation Act of 2004 (H.R. 4520)**

H.R. 4520, §898(a):

Amended Code Sec. 361(b)(3) by adding at the end a new sentence. **Effective** for transfers of money or other property,

or liabilities assumed, in connection with a reorganization occurring on or after the date of the enactment of this Act.

[¶5335] CODE SEC. 362. BASIS TO CORPORATIONS.

* * *

(e) LIMITATIONS ON BUILT-IN LOSSES.—

(1) LIMITATION ON IMPORTATION OF BUILT-IN LOSSES.—

(A) IN GENERAL.—*If in any transaction described in subsection (a) or (b) there would (but for this subsection) be an importation of a net built-in loss, the basis of each property described in subparagraph (B) which is acquired in such transaction shall (notwithstanding subsections (a) and (b)) be its fair market value immediately after such transaction.*

(B) PROPERTY DESCRIBED.—*For purposes of subparagraph (A), property is described in this subparagraph if—*

(i) *gain or loss with respect to such property is not subject to tax under this subtitle in the hands of the transferor immediately before the transfer, and*

(ii) *gain or loss with respect to such property is subject to such tax in the hands of the transferee immediately after such transfer.*

In any case in which the transferor is a partnership, the preceding sentence shall be applied by treating each partner in such partnership as holding such partner's proportionate share of the property of such partnership.

(C) IMPORTATION OF NET BUILT-IN LOSS.—*For purposes of subparagraph (A), there is an importation of a net built-in loss in a transaction if the transferee's aggregate adjusted bases of property described in subparagraph (B) which is transferred in such transaction would (but for this paragraph) exceed the fair market value of such property immediately after such transaction.*

(2) LIMITATION ON TRANSFER OF BUILT-IN LOSSES IN SECTION 351 TRANSACTIONS.—

(A) IN GENERAL.—*If—*

(i) *property is transferred by a transferor in any transaction which is described in subsection (a) and which is not described in paragraph (1) of this subsection, and*

(ii) *the transferee's aggregate adjusted bases of such property so transferred would (but for this paragraph) exceed the fair market value of such property immediately after such transaction, then, notwithstanding subsection (a), the transferee's aggregate adjusted bases of the property so transferred shall not exceed the fair market value of such property immediately after such transaction.*

(B) Allocation of basis reduction.—*The aggregate reduction in basis by reason of subparagraph (A) shall be allocated among the property so transferred in proportion to their respective built-in losses immediately before the transaction.*

(C) Election to apply limitation to transferor's stock basis.—

(i) In general.—*If the transferor and transferee of a transaction described in subparagraph (A) both elect the application of this subparagraph—*

(I) *subparagraph (A) shall not apply, and*

(II) *the transferor's basis in the stock received for property to which subparagraph (A) does not apply by reason of the election shall not exceed its fair market value immediately after the transfer.*

(ii) Election.—*An election under clause (i) shall be included with the return of tax for the taxable year in which the transaction occurred, shall be in such form and manner as the Secretary may prescribe, and, once made, shall be irrevocable.*

* * *

[CCH Explanation at ¶ 520. Committee Reports at ¶ 11,190.]
Amendments

• **2004, American Jobs Creation Act of 2004 (H.R. 4520)**

H.R. 4520, § 836(a):

Amended Code Sec. 362 by adding at the end a new subsection (e). **Effective** for transactions after the date of the enactment of this Act.

[¶ 5340] CODE SEC. 367. FOREIGN CORPORATIONS.

* * *

(d) Special Rules Relating to Transfers of Intangibles.—

* * *

(2) Transfer of intangibles treated as transfer pursuant to sale of contingent payments.—

* * *

(C) Amounts received treated as ordinary income.—For purposes of this chapter, any amount included in gross income by reason of this subsection shall be treated as ordinary income. *For purposes of applying section 904(d), any such amount shall be treated in the same manner as if such amount were a royalty.*

* * *

[CCH Explanation at ¶ 445. Committee Reports at ¶ 10,620.]
Amendments

• **2004, American Jobs Creation Act of 2004 (H.R. 4520)**

H.R. 4520, § 406(a):

Amended Code Sec. 367(d)(2)(C) by adding at the end a new sentence. **Effective** for amounts treated as received pursuant to Code Sec. 367(d)(2) on or after 8-5-97.

[¶ 5345] CODE SEC. 382. LIMITATION ON NET OPERATING LOSS CARRYFORWARDS AND CERTAIN BUILT-IN LOSSES FOLLOWING OWNERSHIP CHANGE.

* * *

(l) Certain Additional Operating Rules.—For purposes of this section—

* * *

(4) REDUCTION IN VALUE WHERE SUBSTANTIAL NONBUSINESS ASSETS.—

* * *

(B) CORPORATION HAVING SUBSTANTIAL NONBUSINESS ASSETS.—For purposes of subparagraph (A)—

* * *

(ii) EXCEPTION FOR CERTAIN INVESTMENT ENTITIES.—A regulated investment company to which part I of subchapter M applies, a real estate investment trust to which part II of subchapter M applies, *or a REMIC to which part IV of subchapter M applies,* shall not be treated as a new loss corporation having substantial nonbusiness assets.

* * *

[CCH Explanation at ¶1120. Committee Reports at ¶11,180.]

Amendments

• 2004, American Jobs Creation Act of 2004 (H.R. 4520)

H.R. 4520, §835(b)(2):

Amended Code Sec. 382(l)(4)(B)(ii) by striking "a REMIC to which part IV of subchapter M applies, or a FASIT to which part V of subchapter M applies," and inserting "or a REMIC to which part IV of subchapter M applies,". **Effective** 1-1-2005. For an exception, see Act Sec. 835(c)(2), below.

H.R. 4520, §835(c)(2), provides:

(2) EXCEPTION FOR EXISTING FASITS.—Paragraph (1) shall not apply to any FASIT in existence on the date of the enactment of this Act to the extent that regular interests issued by the FASIT before such date continue to remain outstanding in accordance with the original terms of issuance.

[¶5350] *CODE SEC. 409A. INCLUSION IN GROSS INCOME OF DEFERRED COMPENSATION UNDER NONQUALIFIED DEFERRED COMPENSATION PLANS.*

(a) RULES RELATING TO CONSTRUCTIVE RECEIPT.—

(1) PLAN FAILURES.—

(A) GROSS INCOME INCLUSION.—

(i) IN GENERAL.—*If at any time during a taxable year a nonqualified deferred compensation plan—*

(I) *fails to meet the requirements of paragraphs (2), (3), and (4), or*

(II) *is not operated in accordance with such requirements,*

all compensation deferred under the plan for the taxable year and all preceding taxable years shall be includible in gross income for the taxable year to the extent not subject to a substantial risk of forfeiture and not previously included in gross income.

(ii) APPLICATION ONLY TO AFFECTED PARTICIPANTS.—*Clause (i) shall only apply with respect to all compensation deferred under the plan for participants with respect to whom the failure relates.*

(B) INTEREST AND ADDITIONAL TAX PAYABLE WITH RESPECT TO PREVIOUSLY DEFERRED COMPENSATION.—

(i) IN GENERAL.—*If compensation is required to be included in gross income under subparagraph (A) for a taxable year, the tax imposed by this chapter for the taxable year shall be increased by the sum of—*

(I) *the amount of interest determined under clause (ii), and*

(II) *an amount equal to 20 percent of the compensation which is required to be included in gross income.*

(ii) INTEREST.—*For purposes of clause (i), the interest determined under this clause for any taxable year is the amount of interest at the underpayment rate plus 1 percentage point on the underpayments that would have occurred had the deferred compensation been includible in gross income for the taxable year in which first deferred or, if later, the first taxable year in which such deferred compensation is not subject to a substantial risk of forfeiture.*

(2) Distributions.—

(A) In general.—The requirements of this paragraph are met if the plan provides that compensation deferred under the plan may not be distributed earlier than—

(i) separation from service as determined by the Secretary (except as provided in subparagraph (B)(i)),

(ii) the date the participant becomes disabled (within the meaning of subparagraph (C)),

(iii) death,

(iv) a specified time (or pursuant to a fixed schedule) specified under the plan at the date of the deferral of such compensation,

(v) to the extent provided by the Secretary, a change in the ownership or effective control of the corporation, or in the ownership of a substantial portion of the assets of the corporation, or

(vi) the occurrence of an unforeseeable emergency.

(B) Special rules.—

(i) Specified employees.—In the case of any specified employee, the requirement of subparagraph (A)(i) is met only if distributions may not be made before the date which is 6 months after the date of separation from service (or, if earlier, the date of death of the employee). For purposes of the preceding sentence, a specified employee is a key employee (as defined in section 416(i) without regard to paragraph (5) thereof) of a corporation any stock in which is publicly traded on an established securities market or otherwise.

(ii) Unforeseeable emergency.—For purposes of subparagraph (A)(vi)—

(I) In general.—The term "unforeseeable emergency" means a severe financial hardship to the participant resulting from an illness or accident of the participant, the participant's spouse, or a dependent (as defined in section 152(a)) of the participant, loss of the participant's property due to casualty, or other similar extraordinary and unforeseeable circumstances arising as a result of events beyond the control of the participant.

(II) Limitation on distributions.—The requirement of subparagraph (A)(vi) is met only if, as determined under regulations of the Secretary, the amounts distributed with respect to an emergency do not exceed the amounts necessary to satisfy such emergency plus amounts necessary to pay taxes reasonably anticipated as a result of the distribution, after taking into account the extent to which such hardship is or may be relieved through reimbursement or compensation by insurance or otherwise or by liquidation of the participant's assets (to the extent the liquidation of such assets would not itself cause severe financial hardship).

(C) Disabled.—For purposes of subparagraph (A)(ii), a participant shall be considered disabled if the participant—

(i) is unable to engage in any substantial gainful activity by reason of any medically determinable physical or mental impairment which can be expected to result in death or can be expected to last for a continuous period of not less than 12 months, or

(ii) is, by reason of any medically determinable physical or mental impairment which can be expected to result in death or can be expected to last for a continuous period of not less than 12 months, receiving income replacement benefits for a period of not less than 3 months under an accident and health plan covering employees of the participant's employer.

(3) Acceleration of benefits.—The requirements of this paragraph are met if the plan does not permit the acceleration of the time or schedule of any payment under the plan, except as provided in regulations by the Secretary.

(4) Elections.—

(A) In general.—The requirements of this paragraph are met if the requirements of subparagraphs (B) and (C) are met.

(B) Initial deferral decision.—

(i) In general.—The requirements of this subparagraph are met if the plan provides that compensation for services performed during a taxable year may be deferred at the participant's

election only if the election to defer such compensation is made not later than the close of the preceding taxable year or at such other time as provided in regulations.

(ii) FIRST YEAR OF ELIGIBILITY.—In the case of the first year in which a participant becomes eligible to participate in the plan, such election may be made with respect to services to be performed subsequent to the election within 30 days after the date the participant becomes eligible to participate in such plan.

(iii) PERFORMANCE-BASED COMPENSATION.—In the case of any performance-based compensation based on services performed over a period of at least 12 months, such election may be made no later than 6 months before the end of the period.

(C) CHANGES IN TIME AND FORM OF DISTRIBUTION.—The requirements of this subparagraph are met if, in the case of a plan which permits under a subsequent election a delay in a payment or a change in the form of payment—

(i) the plan requires that such election may not take effect until at least 12 months after the date on which the election is made,

(ii) in the case of an election related to a payment not described in clause (ii), (iii), or (vi) of paragraph (2)(A), the plan requires that the first payment with respect to which such election is made be deferred for a period of not less than 5 years from the date such payment would otherwise have been made, and

(iii) the plan requires that any election related to a payment described in paragraph (2)(A)(iv) may not be made less than 12 months prior to the date of the first scheduled payment under such paragraph.

(b) RULES RELATING TO FUNDING.—

(1) OFFSHORE PROPERTY IN A TRUST.—In the case of assets set aside (directly or indirectly) in a trust (or other arrangement determined by the Secretary) for purposes of paying deferred compensation under a nonqualified deferred compensation plan, for purposes of section 83 such assets shall be treated as property transferred in connection with the performance of services whether or not such assets are available to satisfy claims of general creditors—

(A) at the time set aside if such assets (or such trust or other arrangement) are located outside of the United States, or

(B) at the time transferred if such assets (or such trust or other arrangement) are subsequently transferred outside of the United States.

This paragraph shall not apply to assets located in a foreign jurisdiction if substantially all of the services to which the nonqualified deferred compensation relates are performed in such jurisdiction.

(2) EMPLOYER'S FINANCIAL HEALTH.—In the case of compensation deferred under a nonqualified deferred compensation plan, there is a transfer of property within the meaning of section 83 with respect to such compensation as of the earlier of—

(A) the date on which the plan first provides that assets will become restricted to the provision of benefits under the plan in connection with a change in the employer's financial health, or

(B) the date on which assets are so restricted,

whether or not such assets are available to satisfy claims of general creditors.

(3) INCOME INCLUSION FOR OFFSHORE TRUSTS AND EMPLOYER'S FINANCIAL HEALTH.—For each taxable year that assets treated as transferred under this subsection remain set aside in a trust or other arrangement subject to paragraph (1) or (2), any increase in value in, or earnings with respect to, such assets shall be treated as an additional transfer of property under this subsection (to the extent not previously included in income).

(4) INTEREST ON TAX LIABILITY PAYABLE WITH RESPECT TO TRANSFERRED PROPERTY.—

(A) IN GENERAL.—If amounts are required to be included in gross income by reason of paragraph (1) or (2) for a taxable year, the tax imposed by this chapter for such taxable year shall be increased by the sum of—

(i) the amount of interest determined under subparagraph (B), and

(ii) an amount equal to 20 percent of the amounts required to be included in gross income.

(B) INTEREST.—For purposes of subparagraph (A), the interest determined under this subparagraph for any taxable year is the amount of interest at the underpayment rate plus 1 percentage point on the underpayments that would have occurred had the amounts so required to be included in gross income by paragraph (1) or (2) been includible in gross income for the taxable year in which first deferred or, if later, the first taxable year in which such amounts are not subject to a substantial risk of forfeiture.

(c) NO INFERENCE ON EARLIER INCOME INCLUSION OR REQUIREMENT OF LATER INCLUSION.—Nothing in this section shall be construed to prevent the inclusion of amounts in gross income under any other provision of this chapter or any other rule of law earlier than the time provided in this section. Any amount included in gross income under this section shall not be required to be included in gross income under any other provision of this chapter or any other rule of law later than the time provided in this section.

(d) OTHER DEFINITIONS AND SPECIAL RULES.—For purposes of this section:

(1) NONQUALIFIED DEFERRED COMPENSATION PLAN.—The term "nonqualified deferred compensation plan" means any plan that provides for the deferral of compensation, other than—

(A) a qualified employer plan, and

(B) any bona fide vacation leave, sick leave, compensatory time, disability pay, or death benefit plan.

(2) QUALIFIED EMPLOYER PLAN.—The term "qualified employer plan" means—

(A) any plan, contract, pension, account, or trust described in subparagraph (A) or (B) of section 219(g)(5) (without regard to subparagraph (A)(iii)),

(B) any eligible deferred compensation plan (within the meaning of section 457(b)), and

(C) any plan described in section 415(m).

(3) PLAN INCLUDES ARRANGEMENTS, ETC.—The term "plan" includes any agreement or arrangement, including an agreement or arrangement that includes one person.

(4) SUBSTANTIAL RISK OF FORFEITURE.—The rights of a person to compensation are subject to a substantial risk of forfeiture if such person's rights to such compensation are conditioned upon the future performance of substantial services by any individual.

(5) TREATMENT OF EARNINGS.—References to deferred compensation shall be treated as including references to income (whether actual or notional) attributable to such compensation or such income.

(6) AGGREGATION RULES.—Except as provided by the Secretary, rules similar to the rules of subsections (b) and (c) of section 414 shall apply.

(e) REGULATIONS.—The Secretary shall prescribe such regulations as may be necessary or appropriate to carry out the purposes of this section, including regulations—

(1) providing for the determination of amounts of deferral in the case of a nonqualified deferred compensation plan which is a defined benefit plan,

(2) relating to changes in the ownership and control of a corporation or assets of a corporation for purposes of subsection (a)(2)(A)(v),

(3) exempting arrangements from the application of subsection (b) if such arrangements will not result in an improper deferral of United States tax and will not result in assets being effectively beyond the reach of creditors,

(4) defining financial health for purposes of subsection (b)(2), and

(5) disregarding a substantial risk of forfeiture in cases where necessary to carry out the purposes of this section.

* * *

[CCH Explanation at ¶1405. Committee Reports at ¶11,570.]

Amendments

• 2004, American Jobs Creation Act of 2004 (H.R. 4520)

H.R. 4520, §885(a):

Amended subpart A of part I of subchapter D of chapter 1 part I, subpart A by adding at the end a new Code Sec.

409A. **Effective** generally for amounts deferred after 12-31-2004. For special rules, see Act Sec. 885(d)(2)-(3), 885(e), and 885(f), below.

H.R. 4520, §885(d)(2)-(3), provides:

(2) SPECIAL RULES.—

(A) EARNINGS.—The amendments made by this section shall apply to earnings on deferred compensation only to the extent that such amendments apply to such compensation.

(B) MATERIAL MODIFICATIONS.—For purposes of this subsection, amounts deferred in taxable years beginning before January 1, 2005, shall be treated as amounts deferred in a taxable year beginning on or after such date if the plan under which the deferral is made is materially modified after October 3, 2004, unless such modification is pursuant to the guidance issued under subsection (f).

(3) EXCEPTION FOR NONELECTIVE DEFERRED COMPENSATION.— The amendments made by this section shall not apply to any nonelective deferred compensation to which section 457 of the Internal Revenue Code of 1986 does not apply by reason of section 457(e)(12) of such Code, but only if such compensation is provided under a nonqualified deferred compensation plan—

(A) which was in existence on May 1, 2004,

(B) which was providing nonelective deferred compensation described in such section 457(e)(12) on such date, and

(C) which is established or maintained by an organization incorporated on July 2, 1974.

If, after May 1, 2004, a plan described in the preceding sentence adopts a plan amendment which provides a material change in the classes of individuals eligible to participate in the plan, this paragraph shall not apply to any nonelective deferred compensation provided under the plan on or after the date of the adoption of the amendment.

H.R. 4520, §885(e), provides:

(e) GUIDANCE RELATING TO CHANGE OF OWNERSHIP OR CONTROL.—Not later than 90 days after the date of the enactment of this Act, the Secretary of the Treasury shall issue guidance on what constitutes a change in ownership or effective control for purposes of section 409A of the Internal Revenue Code of 1986, as added by this section.

H.R. 4520, §885(f), provides:

(f) GUIDANCE RELATING TO TERMINATION OF CERTAIN EXISTING ARRANGEMENTS.—Not later than 60 days after the date of the enactment of this Act, the Secretary of the Treasury shall issue guidance providing a limited period during which a nonqualified deferred compensation plan adopted before December 31, 2004, may, without violating the requirements of paragraphs (2), (3), and (4) of section 409A(a) of the Internal Revenue Code of 1986 (as added by this section), be amended—

(1) to provide that a participant may terminate participation in the plan, or cancel an outstanding deferral election with regard to amounts deferred after December 31, 2004, but only if amounts subject to the termination or cancellation are includible in income of the participant as earned (or, if later, when no longer subject to substantial risk of forfeiture), and

(2) to conform to the requirements of such section 409A with regard to amounts deferred after December 31, 2004.

[¶5355] CODE SEC. 420. TRANSFERS OF EXCESS PENSION ASSETS TO RETIREE HEALTH ACCOUNTS.

* * *

(c) REQUIREMENTS OF PLANS TRANSFERRING ASSETS.—

* * *

(3) MINIMUM COST REQUIREMENTS.—

* * *

(E) REGULATIONS.—

(i) IN GENERAL.—*The Secretary* shall prescribe such regulations as may be necessary to prevent an employer who significantly reduces retiree health coverage during the cost maintenance period from being treated as satisfying the minimum cost requirement of this subsection.

(ii) INSIGNIFICANT COST REDUCTIONS PERMITTED.—

(I) IN GENERAL.—*An eligible employer shall not be treated as failing to meet the requirements of this paragraph for any taxable year if, in lieu of any reduction of retiree health coverage permitted under the regulations prescribed under clause (i), the employer reduces applicable employer cost by an amount not in excess of the reduction in costs which would have occurred if the employer had made the maximum permissible reduction in retiree health coverage under such regulations. In applying such regulations to any subsequent taxable year, any reduction in applicable employer cost under this clause shall be treated as if it were an equivalent reduction in retiree health coverage.*

(II) ELIGIBLE EMPLOYER.—*For purposes of subclause (I), an employer shall be treated as an eligible employer for any taxable year if, for the preceding taxable year, the qualified current retiree health liabilities of the employer were at least 5 percent of the gross receipts of the employer. For purposes of this subclause, the rules of paragraphs (2), (3)(B), and (3)(C) of section 448(c) shall apply in determining the amount of an employer's gross receipts.*

[CCH Explanation at ¶1420. Committee Reports at ¶10,910.]

Amendments

• **2004, American Jobs Creation Act of 2004 (H.R. 4520)**

H.R. 4520, §709(b)(1):

Amended Code Sec. 420(c)(3)(E) by adding at the end a new clause (ii). **Effective** for tax years ending after the date of the enactment of this Act.

H.R. 4520, §709(b)(2):

Amended Code Sec. 420(c)(3)(E) by striking "The Secretary" and inserting "(i) IN GENERAL.—The Secretary". **Effective** for tax years ending after the date of the enactment of this Act.

[¶5360] CODE SEC. 421. GENERAL RULES.

* * *

(b) EFFECT OF DISQUALIFYING DISPOSITION.—If the transfer of a share of stock to an individual pursuant to his exercise of an option would otherwise meet the requirements of section 422(a) or 423(a) except that there is a failure to meet any of the holding period requirements of section 422(a)(1) or 423(a)(1), then any increase in the income of such individual or deduction from the income of his employer corporation for the taxable year in which such exercise occurred attributable to such disposition, shall be treated as an increase in income or a deduction from income in the taxable year of such individual or of such employer corporation in which such disposition occurred. *No amount shall be required to be deducted and withheld under chapter 24 with respect to any increase in income attributable to a disposition described in the preceding sentence.*

* * *

[CCH Explanation at ¶1410. Committee Reports at ¶10,310.]

Amendments

• **2004, American Jobs Creation Act of 2004 (H.R. 4520)**

H.R. 4520, §251(b):

Amended Code Sec. 421(b) by adding at the end a new sentence. **Effective** for stock acquired pursuant to options exercised after the date of the enactment of this Act.

(d) *CERTAIN SALES TO COMPLY WITH CONFLICT-OF-INTEREST REQUIREMENTS.—If—*

(1) *a share of stock is transferred to an eligible person (as defined in section 1043(b)(1)) pursuant to such person's exercise of an option to which this part applies, and*

(2) *such share is disposed of by such person pursuant to a certificate of divestiture (as defined in section 1043(b)(2)),*

such disposition shall be treated as meeting the requirements of section 422(a)(1) or 423(a)(1), whichever is applicable.

* * *

[CCH Explanation at ¶1415. Committee Reports at ¶11,770.]

Amendments

• **2004, American Jobs Creation Act of 2004 (H.R. 4520)**

H.R. 4520, §905(a):

Amended Code Sec. 421 by adding at the end new subsection (d). **Effective** for sales after the date of the enactment of this Act.

[¶5365] CODE SEC. 423. EMPLOYEE STOCK PURCHASE PLANS.

* * *

(c) SPECIAL RULE WHERE OPTION PRICE IS BETWEEN 85 PERCENT AND 100 PERCENT OF VALUE OF STOCK.—If the option price of a share of stock acquired by an individual pursuant to a transfer to which subsection (a) applies was less than 100 percent of the fair market value of such share at the time such option was granted, then, in the event of any disposition of such share by him which meets the holding period requirements of subsection (a), or in the event of his death (whenever occurring) while owning such share, there shall be included as compensation (and not as gain upon the sale or exchange of a capital asset) in his gross income, for the taxable year in which falls the date of such disposition or for the taxable year closing with his death, whichever applies, an amount equal to the lesser of—

(1) the excess of the fair market value of the share at the time of such disposition or death over the amount paid for the share under the option, or

(2) the excess of the fair market value of the share at the time the option was granted over the option price.

If the option price is not fixed or determinable at the time the option is granted, then for purposes of this subsection, the option price shall be determined as if the option were exercised at such time. In the case of the disposition of such share by the individual, the basis of the share in his hands at the time of such disposition shall be increased by an amount equal to the amount so includible in his gross income. *No amount shall be required to be deducted and withheld under chapter 24 with respect to any amount treated as compensation under this subsection.*

* * *

[CCH Explanation at ¶ 1410. Committee Reports at ¶ 10,310.]

Amendments

• **2004, American Jobs Creation Act of 2004 (H.R. 4520)**

H.R. 4520, § 251(c):

Amended Code Sec. 423(c) by adding at the end a new sentence. **Effective** for stock acquired pursuant to options exercised after the date of the enactment of this Act.

[¶ 5370] CODE SEC. 443. RETURNS FOR A PERIOD OF LESS THAN 12 MONTHS.

* * *

(e) CROSS REFERENCES.—

For inapplicability of subsection (b) in computing—

* * *

(3) The taxable income of a regulated investment company, see section 852(b)(2)(E).

(4) The taxable income of a real estate investment trust, see section 857(b)(2)(C).

* * *

[CCH Explanation at ¶ 490. Committee Reports at ¶ 10,690.]

Amendments

• **2004, American Jobs Creation Act of 2004 (H.R. 4520)**

H.R. 4520, § 413(c)(6):

Amended Code Sec. 443(e) by striking paragraph (3) and by redesignating paragraphs (4) and (5) as paragraphs (3) and (4), respectively. **Effective** for tax years of foreign corporations beginning after 12-31-2004, and for tax years of United States shareholders with or within which such tax years of foreign corporations end. Prior to being stricken, Code Sec. 443(e)(3) read as follows:

(3) Undistributed foreign personal holding company income, see section 557.

[¶ 5375] CODE SEC. 451. GENERAL RULE FOR TAXABLE YEAR OF INCLUSION.

* * *

(e) SPECIAL RULE FOR PROCEEDS FROM LIVESTOCK SOLD ON ACCOUNT OF DROUGHT, FLOOD, OR OTHER WEATHER-RELATED CONDITIONS.—

* * *

(3) SPECIAL ELECTION RULES.—If section 1033(e)(2) applies to a sale or exchange of livestock described in paragraph (1), the election under paragraph (1) shall be deemed valid if made during the replacement period described in such section.

* * *

[CCH Explanation at ¶ 820. Committee Reports at ¶ 10,340.]

Amendments

• **2004, American Jobs Creation Act of 2004 (H.R. 4520)**

H.R. 4520, § 311(c):

Amended Code Sec. 451(e) by adding at the end a new paragraph (3). **Effective** for any tax year with respect to

which the due date (without regard to extensions) for the return is after 12-31-2002.

(i) SPECIAL RULE FOR SALES OR DISPOSITIONS TO IMPLEMENT FEDERAL ENERGY REGULATORY COMMISSION OR STATE ELECTRIC RESTRUCTURING POLICY.—

(1) IN GENERAL.—In the case of any qualifying electric transmission transaction for which the taxpayer elects the application of this section, qualified gain from such transaction shall be recognized—

(A) in the taxable year which includes the date of such transaction to the extent the amount realized from such transaction exceeds—

(i) the cost of exempt utility property which is purchased by the taxpayer during the 4-year period beginning on such date, reduced (but not below zero) by

(ii) any portion of such cost previously taken into account under this subsection, and

(B) ratably over the 8-taxable year period beginning with the taxable year which includes the date of such transaction, in the case of any such gain not recognized under subparagraph (A).

(2) QUALIFIED GAIN.—For purposes of this subsection, the term "qualified gain" means, with respect to any qualifying electric transmission transaction in any taxable year—

(A) any ordinary income derived from such transaction which would be required to be recognized under section 1245 or 1250 for such taxable year (determined without regard to this subsection), and

(B) any income derived from such transaction in excess of the amount described in subparagraph (A) which is required to be included in gross income for such taxable year (determined without regard to this subsection).

(3) QUALIFYING ELECTRIC TRANSMISSION TRANSACTION.—For purposes of this subsection, the term "qualifying electric transmission transaction" means any sale or other disposition before January 1, 2007, of—

(A) property used in the trade or business of providing electric transmission services, or

(B) any stock or partnership interest in a corporation or partnership, as the case may be, whose principal trade or business consists of providing electric transmission services,

but only if such sale or disposition is to an independent transmission company.

(4) INDEPENDENT TRANSMISSION COMPANY.—For purposes of this subsection, the term "independent transmission company" means—

(A) an independent transmission provider approved by the Federal Energy Regulatory Commission,

(B) a person—

(i) who the Federal Energy Regulatory Commission determines in its authorization of the transaction under section 203 of the Federal Power Act (16 U.S.C. 824b) or by declaratory order is not a market participant within the meaning of such Commission's rules applicable to independent transmission providers, and

(ii) whose transmission facilities to which the election under this subsection applies are under the operational control of a Federal Energy Regulatory Commissionapproved independent transmission provider before the close of the period specified in such authorization, but not later than the close of the period applicable under subsection (a)(2)(B) as extended under paragraph (2), or

(C) in the case of facilities subject to the jurisdiction of the Public Utility Commission of Texas—

(i) a person which is approved by that Commission as consistent with Texas State law regarding an independent transmission provider, or

(ii) a political subdivision or affiliate thereof whose transmission facilities are under the operational control of a person described in clause (i).

(5) EXEMPT UTILITY PROPERTY.—*For purposes of this subsection:*

(A) IN GENERAL.—*The term "exempt utility property" means property used in the trade or business of—*

(i) *generating, transmitting, distributing, or selling electricity, or*

(ii) *producing, transmitting, distributing, or selling natural gas.*

(B) NONRECOGNITION OF GAIN BY REASON OF ACQUISITION OF STOCK.—*Acquisition of control of a corporation shall be taken into account under this subsection with respect to a qualifying electric transmission transaction only if the principal trade or business of such corporation is a trade or business referred to in subparagraph (A).*

(6) SPECIAL RULE FOR CONSOLIDATED GROUPS.—*In the case of a corporation which is a member of an affiliated group filing a consolidated return, any exempt utility property purchased by another member of such group shall be treated as purchased by such corporation for purposes of applying paragraph (1)(A).*

(7) TIME FOR ASSESSMENT OF DEFICIENCIES.—*If the taxpayer has made the election under paragraph (1) and any gain is recognized by such taxpayer as provided in paragraph (1)(B), then—*

(A) *the statutory period for the assessment of any deficiency, for any taxable year in which any part of the gain on the transaction is realized, attributable to such gain shall not expire prior to the expiration of 3 years from the date the Secretary is notified by the taxpayer (in such manner as the Secretary may by regulations prescribe) of the purchase of exempt utility property or of an intention not to purchase such property, and*

(B) *such deficiency may be assessed before the expiration of such 3-year period notwithstanding any law or rule of law which would otherwise prevent such assessment.*

(8) PURCHASE.—*For purposes of this subsection, the taxpayer shall be considered to have purchased any property if the unadjusted basis of such property is its cost within the meaning of section 1012.*

(9) ELECTION.—*An election under paragraph (1) shall be made at such time and in such manner as the Secretary may require and, once made, shall be irrevocable.*

(10) NONAPPLICATION OF INSTALLMENT SALES TREATMENT.—*Section 453 shall not apply to any qualifying electric transmission transaction with respect to which an election to apply this subsection is made.*

[CCH Explanation at ¶890. Committee Reports at ¶11,810.]

Amendments

• 2004, American Jobs Creation Act of 2004 (H.R. 4520)

H.R. 4520, §909(a):

Amended Code Sec. 451 by adding at the end a new subsection (i). **Effective** for transactions occurring after the date of the enactment of this Act, in tax years ending after such date.

[¶5380] CODE SEC. 453. INSTALLMENT METHOD.

* * *

(f) DEFINITIONS AND SPECIAL RULES.—For purposes of this section—

* * *

(4) PURCHASER EVIDENCES OF INDEBTEDNESS PAYABLE ON DEMAND OR READILY TRADABLE.—Receipt of a bond or other evidence of indebtedness which—

* * *

(B)   is readily tradable,

* * *

[CCH Explanation at ¶710. Committee Reports at ¶11,690.]

Amendments

• **2004, American Jobs Creation Act of 2004 (H.R. 4520)**

H.R. 4520, §897(a):

Amended Code Sec. 453(f)(4)(B) by striking "is issued by a corporation or a government or political subdivision thereof and" following "(B)". **Effective** for sales occurring on or after the date of the enactment of this Act.

[¶5385] CODE SEC. 465. DEDUCTIONS LIMITED TO AMOUNT AT RISK.

* * *

(c) ACTIVITIES TO WHICH SECTION APPLIES.—

* * *

(7) EXCLUSION OF ACTIVE BUSINESSES OF QUALIFIED C CORPORATIONS.—

* * *

(B) QUALIFIED C CORPORATION.—For purposes of subparagraph (A), the term "qualified C corporation" means any corporation described in subparagraph (B) of subsection (a)(1) which is not—

(i) a personal holding company (as defined in section 542(a)), *or*

(ii) a personal service corporation (as defined in section 269A(b) but determined by substituting "5 percent" for "10 percent" in section 269A(b)(2)).

* * *

[CCH Explanation at ¶490. Committee Reports at ¶10,690.]

Amendments

• **2004, American Jobs Creation Act of 2004 (H.R. 4520)**

H.R. 4520, §413(c)(7):

Amended Code Sec. 465(c)(7)(B) by adding "or" at the end of clause (i), by striking clause (ii), and by redesignating clause (iii) as clause (ii). **Effective** for tax years of foreign corporations beginning after 12-31-2004, and for tax years of United States shareholders with or within which such tax years of foreign corporations end. Prior to being stricken, Code Sec. 465(c)(7)(B)(ii) read as follows:

(ii) a foreign personal holding company (as defined in section 552(a)), or

[¶5390] CODE SEC. 469. PASSIVE ACTIVITY LOSSES AND CREDITS LIMITED.

* * *

(i) $25,000 OFFSET FOR RENTAL REAL ESTATE ACTIVITIES.—

* * *

(3) PHASE-OUT OF EXEMPTION.—

* * *

(F) ADJUSTED GROSS INCOME.—For purposes of this paragraph, adjusted gross income shall be determined without regard to—

(i) any amount includible in gross income under section 86,

(ii) the amounts excludable from gross income under sections 135 and 137,

(iii) the amounts allowable as a deduction under sections *199,* 219, 221, and 222 and

(iv) any passive activity loss or any loss allowable by reason of subsection (c)(7).

* * *

[CCH Explanation at ¶210.]

Amendments

• **2004, American Jobs Creation Act of 2004 (H.R. 4520)**

H.R. 4520, §102(d)(5):

Amended Code Sec. 469(i)(3)(F)(iii) by inserting "199," before"219,". **Effective** for tax years beginning after 12-31-2004.

(k) SEPARATE APPLICATION OF SECTION IN CASE OF PUBLICLY TRADED PARTNERSHIPS.—

* * *

(4) APPLICATION TO REGULATED INVESTMENT COMPANIES.—For purposes of this section, a regulated investment company (as defined in section 851) holding an interest in a qualified publicly traded partnership (as defined in section 851(h)) shall be treated as a taxpayer described in subsection (a)(2) with respect to items attributable to such interest.

* * *

[CCH Explanation at ¶ 1105. Committee Reports at ¶ 10,460.]

Amendments

• **2004, American Jobs Creation Act of 2004 (H.R. 4520)**

H.R. 4520, § 331(g):

Amended Code Sec. 469(k) by adding at the end a new paragraph (4). **Effective** for tax years beginning after the date of the enactment of this Act.

[¶ 5395] *CODE SEC. 470. LIMITATION ON DEDUCTIONS ALLOCABLE TO PROPERTY USED BY GOVERNMENTS OR OTHER TAX-EXEMPT ENTITIES.*

(a) LIMITATION ON LOSSES.—Except as otherwise provided in this section, a tax-exempt use loss for any taxable year shall not be allowed.

(b) DISALLOWED LOSS CARRIED TO NEXT YEAR.—Any tax-exempt use loss with respect to any tax-exempt use property which is disallowed under subsection (a) for any taxable year shall be treated as a deduction with respect to such property in the next taxable year.

(c) DEFINITIONS.—For purposes of this section—

(1) TAX-EXEMPT USE LOSS.—The term "tax-exempt use loss" means, with respect to any taxable year, the amount (if any) by which—

(A) the sum of—

(i) the aggregate deductions (other than interest) directly allocable to a tax-exempt use property, plus

(ii) the aggregate deductions for interest properly allocable to such property, exceed

(B) the aggregate income from such property.

(2) TAX-EXEMPT USE PROPERTY.—The term "tax-exempt use property" has the meaning given to such term by section 168(h), except that such section shall be applied—

(A) without regard to paragraphs (1)(C) and (3) thereof, and

(B) as if property described in—

(i) section 167(f)(1)(B),

(ii) section 167(f)(2), and

(iii) section 197 intangible,

were tangible property.

Such term shall not include property which would (but for this sentence) be tax-exempt use property solely by reason of section 168(h)(6) if any credit is allowable under section 42 or 47 with respect to such property.

(d) EXCEPTION FOR CERTAIN LEASES.—This section shall not apply to any lease of property which meets the requirements of all of the following paragraphs:

(1) AVAILABILITY OF FUNDS

(A) IN GENERAL.—A lease of property meets the requirements of this paragraph if (at any time during the lease term) not more than an allowable amount of funds are—

(i) subject to any arrangement referred to in subparagraph (B), or

(ii) set aside or expected to be set aside,

to or for the benefit of the lessor or any lender, or to or for the benefit of the lessee to satisfy the lessee's obligations or options under the lease. For purposes of clause (ii), funds shall be treated as set aside or expected to be set aside only if a reasonable person would conclude, based on the facts and circumstances, that such funds are set aside or expected to be set aside.

(B) ARRANGEMENTS.—The arrangements referred to in this subparagraph include a defeasance arrangement, a loan by the lessee to the lessor or any lender, a deposit arrangement, a letter of credit collateralized with cash or cash equivalents, a payment undertaking agreement, prepaid rent (within the meaning of the regulations under section 467), a sinking fund arrangement, a guaranteed investment contract, financial guaranty insurance, and any similar arrangement (whether or not such arrangement provides credit support).

(C) ALLOWABLE AMOUNT.—

(i) IN GENERAL.—Except as otherwise provided in this subparagraph, the term "allowable amount" means an amount equal to 20 percent of the lessor's adjusted basis in the property at the time the lease is entered into.

(ii) HIGHER AMOUNT PERMITTED IN CERTAIN CASES.—To the extent provided in regulations, a higher percentage shall be permitted under clause (i) where necessary because of the credit-worthiness of the lessee. In no event may such regulations permit a percentage of more than 50 percent.

(iii) OPTION TO PURCHASE.—If under the lease the lessee has the option to purchase the property for a fixed price or for other than the fair market value of the property (determined at the time of exercise), the allowable amount at the time such option may be exercised may not exceed 50 percent of the price at which such option may be exercised.

(iv) NO ALLOWABLE AMOUNT FOR CERTAIN ARRANGEMENTS.—The allowable amount shall be zero with respect to any arrangement which involves—

(I) a loan from the lessee to the lessor or a lender,

(II) any deposit received, letter of credit issued, or payment undertaking agreement entered into by a lender otherwise involved in the transaction, or

(III) in the case of a transaction which involves a lender, any credit support made available to the lessor in which any such lender does not have a claim that is senior to the lessor.

For purposes of subclause (I), the term "loan" shall not include any amount treated as a loan under section 467 with respect to a section 467 rental agreement.

(2) LESSOR MUST MAKE SUBSTANTIAL EQUITY INVESTMENT.—

(A) IN GENERAL.—A lease of property meets the requirements of this paragraph if—

(i) the lessor—

(I) has at the time the lease is entered into an unconditional at-risk equity investment (as determined by the Secretary) in the property of at least 20 percent of the lessor's adjusted basis in the property as of that time, and

(II) maintains such investment throughout the term of the lease, and

(ii) the fair market value of the property at the end of the lease term is reasonably expected to be equal to at least 20 percent of such basis.

(B) RISK OF LOSS.—For purposes of clause (ii), the fair market value at the end of the lease term shall be reduced to the extent that a person other than the lessor bears a risk of loss in the value of the property.

(C) PARAGRAPH NOT TO APPLY TO SHORT-TERM LEASES.—This paragraph shall not apply to any lease with a lease term of 5 years or less.

(3) LESSEE MAY NOT BEAR MORE THAN MINIMAL RISK OF LOSS.—

(A) IN GENERAL.—A lease of property meets the requirements of this paragraph if there is no arrangement under which the lessee bears—

(i) any portion of the loss that would occur if the fair market value of the leased property were 25 percent less than its reasonably expected fair market value at the time the lease is terminated, or

(ii) more than 50 percent of the loss that would occur if the fair market value of the leased property at the time the lease is terminated were zero.

(B) EXCEPTION.—The Secretary may by regulations provide that the requirements of this paragraph are not met where the lessee bears more than a minimal risk of loss.

(C) PARAGRAPH NOT TO APPLY TO SHORT-TERM LEASES.—This paragraph shall not apply to any lease with a lease term of 5 years or less.

(4) PROPERTY WITH MORE THAN 7-YEAR CLASS LIFE.—In the case of a lease—

(A) of property with a class life (as defined in section 168(i)(1)) of more than 7 years, other than fixed-wing aircraft and vessels, and

(B) under which the lessee has the option to purchase the property,

the lease meets the requirements of this paragraph only if the purchase price under the option equals the fair market value of the property (determined at the time of exercise).

(e) SPECIAL RULES.—

(1) TREATMENT OF FORMER TAX-EXEMPT USE PROPERTY.—

(A) IN GENERAL.—In the case of any former tax-exempt use property—

(i) any deduction allowable under subsection (b) with respect to such property for any taxable year shall be allowed only to the extent of any net income (without regard to such deduction) from such property for such taxable year, and

(ii) any portion of such unused deduction remaining after application of clause (i) shall be treated as a deduction allowable under subsection (b) with respect to such property in the next taxable year.

(B) FORMER TAX-EXEMPT USE PROPERTY.—For purposes of this subsection, the term "former tax-exempt use property" means any property which—

(i) is not tax-exempt use property for the taxable year, but

(ii) was tax-exempt use property for any prior taxable year.

(2) DISPOSITION OF ENTIRE INTEREST IN PROPERTY.—If during the taxable year a taxpayer disposes of the taxpayer's entire interest in tax-exempt use property (or former tax-exempt use property), rules similar to the rules of section 469(g) shall apply for purposes of this section.

(3) COORDINATION WITH SECTION 469.—This section shall be applied before the application of section 469.

(4) COORDINATION WITH SECTIONS 1031 AND 1033.—

(A) IN GENERAL.—Sections 1031(a) and 1033(a) shall not apply if—

(i) the exchanged or converted property is tax-exempt use property subject to a lease which was entered into before March 13, 2004, and which would not have met the requirements of subsection (d) had such requirements been in effect when the lease was entered into, or

(ii) the replacement property is tax-exempt use property subject to a lease which does not meet the requirements of subsection (d).

(B) ADJUSTED BASIS.—In the case of property acquired by the lessor in a transaction to which section 1031 or 1033 applies, the adjusted basis of such property for purposes of this section shall be equal to the lesser of—

(i) the fair market value of the property as of the beginning of the lease term, or

(ii) the amount which would be the lessor's adjusted basis if such sections did not apply to such transaction.

(f) OTHER DEFINITIONS.—For purposes of this section—

(1) RELATED PARTIES.—The terms "lessor", "lessee", and "lender" each include any related party (within the meaning of section 197(f)(9)(C)(i)).

(2) LEASE TERM.—*The term "lease term" has the meaning given to such term by section 168(i)(3).*

(3) LENDER.—*The term "lender" means, with respect to any lease, a person that makes a loan to the lessor which is secured (or economically similar to being secured) by the lease or the leased property.*

(4) LOAN.—*The term "loan" includes any similar arrangement.*

(g) REGULATIONS.—*The Secretary shall prescribe such regulations as may be necessary or appropriate to carry out the purposes of this section, including regulations which—*

(1) *allow in appropriate cases the aggregation of property subject to the same lease, and*

(2) *provide for the determination of the allocation of interest expense for purposes of this section.*

* * *

[CCH Explanation at ¶ 670. Committee Reports at ¶ 11,290.]

Amendments

• **2004, American Jobs Creation Act of 2004 (H.R. 4520)**

H.R. 4520, § 848(a):

Amended subpart C of part II of subchapter E of chapter 1 by adding at the end a new Code Sec. 470. **Effective** generally for leases entered into after 3-12-2004. For an exception, see Act Sec. 849(b), below.

H.R. 4520, § 849(b), provides:

(b) EXCEPTION.—

(1) IN GENERAL.—The amendments made by this part shall not apply to qualified transportation property.

(2) QUALIFIED TRANSPORTATION PROPERTY.—For purposes of paragraph (1), the term "qualified transportation property" means domestic property subject to a lease with respect to which a formal application—

(A) was submitted for approval to the Federal Transit Administration (an agency of the Department of Transportation) after June 30, 2003, and before March 13, 2004,

(B) is approved by the Federal Transit Administration before January 1, 2006, and

(C) includes a description of such property and the value of such property.

(3) EXCHANGES AND CONVERSION OF TAX-EXEMPT USE PROPERTY.—Section 470(e)(4) of the Internal Revenue Code of 1986, as added by section 848, shall apply to property exchanged or converted after the date of the enactment of this Act.

(4) INTANGIBLES AND INDIAN TRIBAL GOVERNMENTS.—The amendments made subsections (b)(2), (b)(3), and (e) of section 847, and the treatment of property described in clauses (ii) and (iii) of section 470(c)(2)(B) of the Internal Revenue Code of 1986 (as added by section 848) as tangible property, shall apply to leases entered into after October 3, 2004.

[¶ 5400] CODE SEC. 501. EXEMPTION FROM TAX ON CORPORATIONS, CERTAIN TRUSTS, ETC.

* * *

(c) LIST OF EXEMPT ORGANIZATIONS.—The following organizations are referred to in subsection (a):

* * *

(12)(A) Benevolent life insurance associations of a purely local character, mutual ditch or irrigation companies, mutual or cooperative telephone companies, or like organizations; but only if 85 percent or more of the income consists of amounts collected from members for the sole purpose of meeting losses and expenses.

* * *

(C) In the case of a mutual or cooperative electric company, subparagraph (A) shall be applied without taking into account any income received or accrued—

(i) from qualified pole rentals, or

(ii) *from any provision or sale of electric energy transmission services or ancillary services if such services are provided on a nondiscriminatory open access basis under an open access transmission tariff approved or accepted by FERC or under an independent transmission provider agreement approved or accepted by FERC (other than income received or accrued directly or indirectly from a member),*

(iii) *from the provision or sale of electric energy distribution services or ancillary services if such services are provided on a nondiscriminatory open access basis to distribute electric energy not owned by the mutual or electric cooperative company—*

(I) *to end-users who are served by distribution facilities not owned by such company or any of its members (other than income received or accrued directly or indirectly from a member), or*

(II) *generated by a generation facility not owned or leased by such company or any of its members and which is directly connected to distribution facilities owned by such* company or any of its members (other than income received or accrued directly or indirectly from a member),

(iv) from any nuclear decommissioning transaction, or

(v) from any asset exchange or conversion transaction.

Clauses (ii) through (v) shall not apply to taxable years beginning after December 31, 2006.

* * *

(E) For purposes of subparagraph (C)(ii), the term "FERC" means the Federal Energy Regulatory Commission and references to such term shall be treated as including the Public Utility Commission of Texas with respect to any ERCOT utility (as defined in section 212(k)(2)(B) of the Federal Power Act (16 U.S.C. 824k(k)(2)(B))).

(F) For purposes of subparagraph (C)(iii), the term "nuclear decommissioning transaction" means—

(i) any transfer into a trust, fund, or instrument established to pay any nuclear decommissioning costs if the transfer is in connection with the transfer of the mutual or cooperative electric company's interest in a nuclear power plant or nuclear power plant unit,

(ii) any distribution from any trust, fund, or instrument established to pay any nuclear decommissioning costs, or

(iii) any earnings from any trust, fund, or instrument established to pay any nuclear decommissioning costs.

(G) For purposes of subparagraph (C)(iv), the term "asset exchange or conversion transaction" means any voluntary exchange or involuntary conversion of any property related to generating, transmitting, distributing, or selling electric energy by a mutual or cooperative electric company, the gain from which qualifies for deferred recognition under section 1031 or 1033, but only if the replacement property acquired by such company pursuant to such section constitutes property which is used, or to be used, for—

(i) generating, transmitting, distributing, or selling electric energy, or

(ii) producing, transmitting, distributing, or selling natural gas.

(H)(i) In the case of a mutual or cooperative electric company described in this paragraph or an organization described in section 1381(a)(2)(C), income received or accrued from a load loss transaction shall be treated as an amount collected from members for the sole purpose of meeting losses and expenses.

(ii) For purposes of clause (i), the term "load loss transaction" means any wholesale or retail sale of electric energy (other than to members) to the extent that the aggregate sales during the recovery period do not exceed the load loss mitigation sales limit for such period.

(iii) For purposes of clause (ii), the load loss mitigation sales limit for the recovery period is the sum of the annual load losses for each year of such period.

(iv) For purposes of clause (iii), a mutual or cooperative electric company's annual load loss for each year of the recovery period is the amount (if any) by which—

(I) the megawatt hours of electric energy sold during such year to members of such electric company are less than

(II) the megawatt hours of electric energy sold during the base year to such members.

(v) For purposes of clause (iv)(II), the term "base year" means—

(I) the calendar year preceding the start-up year, or

(II) at the election of the mutual or cooperative electric company, the second or third calendar years preceding the start-up year.

(vi) For purposes of this subparagraph, the recovery period is the 7-year period beginning with the start-up year.

(vii) For purposes of this subparagraph, the start-up year is the first year that the mutual or cooperative electric company offers nondiscriminatory open access or the calendar year which includes the date of the enactment of this subparagraph, if later, at the election of such company.

(viii) A company shall not fail to be treated as a mutual or cooperative electric company for purposes of this paragraph or as a corporation operating on a cooperative basis for purposes of section 1381(a)(2)(C) by reason of the treatment under clause (i).

(ix) For purposes of subparagraph (A), in the case of a mutual or cooperative electric company, income received, or accrued, indirectly from a member shall be treated as an amount collected from members for the sole purpose of meeting losses and expenses.

(x) This subparagraph shall not apply to taxable years beginning after December 31, 2006.

* * *

[CCH Explanation at ¶1335. Committee Reports at ¶10,420.]

Amendments

• **2004, American Jobs Creation Act of 2004 (H.R. 4520)**

H.R. 4520, §319(a)(1):

Amended Code Sec. 501(c)(12)(C) by striking clause (ii) and adding at the end new clauses (ii)-(v) and a new flush sentence. **Effective** for tax years beginning after the date of the enactment of this Act. Prior to being striken, Code Sec 501(c)(12)(C)(ii) read as follows:

(ii) from the prepayment of a loan under section 306A, 306B, or 311 of the Rural Electrification Act of 1936 (as in effect on January 1, 1987).

H.R. 4520, §319(a)(2):

Amended Code Sec. 501(c)(12) by adding at the end new subparagraphs (E)-(G). **Effective** for tax years beginning after the date of the enactment of this Act.

H.R. 4520, §319(b):

Amended Code Sec. 501(c)(12), as amended by Act Sec. 319(a)(2), by adding after subparagraph (G) new subparagraph (H). **Effective** for tax years beginning after the date of the enactment of this Act.

[¶5405] CODE SEC. 508. SPECIAL RULES WITH RESPECT TO SECTION 501(c)(3) ORGANIZATIONS.

* * *

(d) DISALLOWANCE OF CERTAIN CHARITABLE, ETC., DEDUCTIONS.—

(1) GIFT OR BEQUEST TO ORGANIZATIONS SUBJECT TO SECTION 507(c) TAX.—No gift or bequest made to an organization upon which the tax provided by section 507(c) has been imposed shall be allowed as a deduction under section 170, 545(b)(2), 642(c), 2055, 2106(a)(2), or 2522, if such gift or bequest is made—

(A) by any person after notification is made under section 507(a), or

(B) by a substantial contributor (as defined in section 507(d)(2)) in his taxable year which includes the first day on which action is taken by such organization which culminates in the imposition of tax under section 507(c) and any subsequent taxable year.

(2) GIFT OR BEQUEST TO TAXABLE PRIVATE FOUNDATION, SECTION 4947 TRUST, ETC.—No gift or bequest made to an organization shall be allowed as a deduction under section 170, 545(b)(2), 642(c), 2055, 2106(a)(2), or 2522, if such gift or bequest is made—

(A) to a private foundation or a trust described in section 4947 in a taxable year for which it fails to meet the requirements of subsection (e) (determined without regard to subsection (e)(2)), or

(B) to any organization in a period for which it is not treated as an organization described in section 501(c)(3) by reason of subsection (a).

* * *

[CCH Explanation at ¶490. Committee Reports at ¶10,690.]

Amendments

• **2004, American Jobs Creation Act of 2004 (H.R. 4520)**

H.R. 4520, §413(c)(30):

Amended Code Sec. 508(d) by striking "556(b)(2)," each place it occurs immediately preceding "642(c), 2055". **Effec**-

tive for tax years of foreign corporations beginning after 12-31-2004 and for tax years of United States shareholders with or within which such tax years of foreign corporations end.

[¶5410] CODE SEC. 512. UNRELATED BUSINESS TAXABLE INCOME.

* * *

(b) MODIFICATIONS.—The modifications referred to in subsection (a) are the following:

* * *

(18) TREATMENT OF MUTUAL OR COOPERATIVE ELECTRIC COMPANIES.—In the case of a mutual or cooperative electric company described in section 501(c)(12), there shall be excluded income which is treated as member income under subparagraph (H) thereof.

(18)[(19)] TREATMENT OF GAIN OR LOSS ON SALE OR EXCHANGE OF CERTAIN BROWNFIELD SITES.—

(A) IN GENERAL.—Notwithstanding paragraph (5)(B), there shall be excluded any gain or loss from the qualified sale, exchange, or other disposition of any qualifying brownfield property by an eligible taxpayer.

(B) ELIGIBLE TAXPAYER.—For purposes of this paragraph—

(i) IN GENERAL.—The term "eligible taxpayer" means, with respect to a property, any organization exempt from tax under section 501(a) which—

(I) acquires from an unrelated person a qualifying brownfield property, and

(II) pays or incurs eligible remediation expenditures with respect to such property in an amount which exceeds the greater of $550,000 or 12 percent of the fair market value of the property at the time such property was acquired by the eligible taxpayer, determined as if there was not a presence of a hazardous substance, pollutant, or contaminant on the property which is complicating the expansion, redevelopment, or reuse of the property.

(ii) EXCEPTION.—Such term shall not include any organization which is—

(I) potentially liable under section 107 of the Comprehensive Environmental Response, Compensation, and Liability Act of 1980 with respect to the qualifying brownfield property,

(II) affiliated with any other person which is so potentially liable through any direct or indirect familial relationship or any contractual, corporate, or financial relationship (other than a contractual, corporate, or financial relationship which is created by the instruments by which title to any qualifying brownfield property is conveyed or financed or by a contract of sale of goods or services), or

(III) the result of a reorganization of a business entity which was so potentially liable.

(C) QUALIFYING BROWNFIELD PROPERTY.—For purposes of this paragraph—

(i) IN GENERAL.—The term "qualifying brownfield property" means any real property which is certified, before the taxpayer incurs any eligible remediation expenditures (other than to obtain a Phase I environmental site assessment), by an appropriate State agency (within the meaning of section 198(c)(4)) in the State in which such property is located as a brownfield site within the meaning of section 101(39) of the Comprehensive Environmental Response, Compensation, and Liability Act of 1980 (as in effect on the date of the enactment of this paragraph).

(ii) REQUEST FOR CERTIFICATION.—Any request by an eligible taxpayer for a certification described in clause (i) shall include a sworn statement by the eligible taxpayer and supporting documentation of the presence of a hazardous substance, pollutant, or contaminant on the property which is complicating the expansion, redevelopment, or reuse of the property given the property's reasonably anticipated future land uses or capacity for uses of the property (including a Phase I environmental site assessment and, if applicable, evidence of the property's presence on a local, State, or Federal list of brownfields or contaminated property) and other environmental assessments prepared or obtained by the taxpayer.

(D) QUALIFIED SALE, EXCHANGE, OR OTHER DISPOSITION.—For purposes of this paragraph—

(i) IN GENERAL.—A sale, exchange, or other disposition of property shall be considered as qualified if—

(I) such property is transferred by the eligible taxpayer to an unrelated person, and

(II) within 1 year of such transfer the eligible taxpayer has received a certification from the Environmental Protection Agency or an appropriate State agency (within the meaning of section 198(c)(4)) in the State in which such property is located that, as a result of the eligible taxpayer's remediation actions, such property would not be treated as a qualifying brownfield property in the hands of the transferee.

For purposes of subclause (II), before issuing such certification, the Environmental Protection Agency or appropriate State agency shall respond to comments received pursuant to clause (ii)(V) in the same form and manner as required under section 117(b) of the Comprehensive

Environmental Response, Compensation, and Liability Act of 1980 (as in effect on the date of the enactment of this paragraph).

(ii) REQUEST FOR CERTIFICATION.—Any request by an eligible taxpayer for a certification described in clause (i) shall be made not later than the date of the transfer and shall include a sworn statement by the eligible taxpayer certifying the following:

(I) Remedial actions which comply with all applicable or relevant and appropriate requirements (consistent with section 121(d) of the Comprehensive Environmental Response, Compensation, and Liability Act of 1980) have been substantially completed, such that there are no hazardous substances, pollutants, or contaminants which complicate the expansion, redevelopment, or reuse of the property given the property's reasonably anticipated future land uses or capacity for uses of the property.

(II) The reasonably anticipated future land uses or capacity for uses of the property are more economically productive or environmentally beneficial than the uses of the property in existence on the date of the certification described in subparagraph (C)(i). For purposes of the preceding sentence, use of property as a landfill or other hazardous waste facility shall not be considered more economically productive or environmentally beneficial.

(III) A remediation plan has been implemented to bring the property into compliance with all applicable local, State, and Federal environmental laws, regulations, and standards and to ensure that the remediation protects human health and the environment.

(IV) The remediation plan described in subclause (III), including any physical improvements required to remediate the property, is either complete or substantially complete, and, if substantially complete, sufficient monitoring, funding, institutional controls, and financial assurances have been put in place to ensure the complete remediation of the property in accordance with the remediation plan as soon as is reasonably practicable after the sale, exchange, or other disposition of such property.

(V) Public notice and the opportunity for comment on the request for certification was completed before the date of such request. Such notice and opportunity for comment shall be in the same form and manner as required for public participation required under section 117(a) of the Comprehensive Environmental Response, Compensation, and Liability Act of 1980 (as in effect on the date of the enactment of this paragraph). For purposes of this subclause, public notice shall include, at a minimum, publication in a major local newspaper of general circulation.

(iii) ATTACHMENT TO TAX RETURNS.—A copy of each of the requests for certification described in clause (ii) of subparagraph (C) and this subparagraph shall be included in the tax return of the eligible taxpayer (and, where applicable, of the qualifying partnership) for the taxable year during which the transfer occurs.

(iv) SUBSTANTIAL COMPLETION.—For purposes of this subparagraph, a remedial action is substantially complete when any necessary physical construction is complete, all immediate threats have been eliminated, and all long-term threats are under control.

(E) ELIGIBLE REMEDIATION EXPENDITURES.—For purposes of this paragraph—

(i) IN GENERAL.—The term "eligible remediation expenditures" means, with respect to any qualifying brownfield property, any amount paid or incurred by the eligible taxpayer to an unrelated third person to obtain a Phase I environmental site assessment of the property, and any amount so paid or incurred after the date of the certification described in subparagraph (C)(i) for goods and services necessary to obtain a certification described in subparagraph (D)(i) with respect to such property, including expenditures—

(I) to manage, remove, control, contain, abate, or otherwise remediate a hazardous substance, pollutant, or contaminant on the property,

(II) to obtain a Phase II environmental site assessment of the property, including any expenditure to monitor, sample, study, assess, or otherwise evaluate the release, threat of release, or presence of a hazardous substance, pollutant, or contaminant on the property,

(III) to obtain environmental regulatory certifications and approvals required to manage the remediation and monitoring of the hazardous substance, pollutant, or contaminant on the property, and

(IV) regardless of whether it is necessary to obtain a certification described in subparagraph (D)(i)(II), to obtain remediation cost-cap or stoploss coverage, re-opener or

Code Sec. 512(b)(18)[(19)](E)(i)(IV)   ¶5410

regulatory action coverage, or similar coverage under environmental insurance policies, or financial guarantees required to manage such remediation and monitoring.

(ii) EXCEPTIONS.—*Such term shall not include—*

(I) *any portion of the purchase price paid or incurred by the eligible taxpayer to acquire the qualifying brownfield property,*

(II) *environmental insurance costs paid or incurred to obtain legal defense coverage, owner/operator liability coverage, lender liability coverage, professional liability coverage, or similar types of coverage,*

(III) *any amount paid or incurred to the extent such amount is reimbursed, funded, or otherwise subsidized by grants provided by the United States, a State, or a political subdivision of a State for use in connection with the property, proceeds of an issue of State or local government obligations used to provide financing for the property the interest of which is exempt from tax under section 103, or subsidized financing provided (directly or indirectly) under a Federal, State, or local program provided in connection with the property, or*

(IV) *any expenditure paid or incurred before the date of the enactment of this paragraph.*

For purposes of subclause (III), the Secretary may issue guidance regarding the treatment of government-provided funds for purposes of determining eligible remediation expenditures.

(F) DETERMINATION OF GAIN OR LOSS.—*For purposes of this paragraph, the determination of gain or loss shall not include an amount treated as gain which is ordinary income with respect to section 1245 or section 1250 property, including amounts deducted as section 198 expenses which are subject to the recapture rules of section 198(e), if the taxpayer had deducted such amounts in the computation of its unrelated business taxable income.*

(G) SPECIAL RULES FOR PARTNERSHIPS.—

(i) IN GENERAL.—*In the case of an eligible taxpayer which is a partner of a qualifying partnership which acquires, remediates, and sells, exchanges, or otherwise disposes of a qualifying brownfield property, this paragraph shall apply to the eligible taxpayer's distributive share of the qualifying partnership's gain or loss from the sale, exchange, or other disposition of such property.*

(ii) QUALIFYING PARTNERSHIP.—*The term "qualifying partnership" means a partnership which—*

(I) *has a partnership agreement which satisfies the requirements of section 514(c)(9)(B)(vi) at all times beginning on the date of the first certification received by the partnership under subparagraph (C)(i),*

(II) *satisfies the requirements of subparagraphs (B)(i), (C), (D), and (E), if "qualified partnership" is substituted for "eligible taxpayer" each place it appears therein (except subparagraph (D)(iii)), and*

(III) *is not an organization which would be prevented from constituting an eligible taxpayer by reason of subparagraph (B)(ii).*

(iii) REQUIREMENT THAT TAX-EXEMPT PARTNER BE A PARTNER SINCE FIRST CERTIFICATION.—*This paragraph shall apply with respect to any eligible taxpayer which is a partner of a partnership which acquires, remediates, and sells, exchanges, or otherwise disposes of a qualifying brownfield property only if such eligible taxpayer was a partner of the qualifying partnership at all times beginning on the date of the first certification received by the partnership under subparagraph (C)(i) and ending on the date of the sale, exchange, or other disposition of the property by the partnership.*

(iv) REGULATIONS.—*The Secretary shall prescribe such regulations as are necessary to prevent abuse of the requirements of this subparagraph, including abuse through—*

(I) *the use of special allocations of gains or losses, or*

(II) *changes in ownership of partnership interests held by eligible taxpayers.*

(H) SPECIAL RULES FOR MULTIPLE PROPERTIES.—

(i) IN GENERAL.—*An eligible taxpayer or a qualifying partnership of which the eligible taxpayer is a partner may make a 1-time election to apply this paragraph to more than 1 qualifying brownfield property by averaging the eligible remediation expenditures for all such properties acquired during the election period. If the eligible taxpayer or qualifying partnership makes such an election, the election shall apply to all qualified sales, exchanges, or other dispositions of qualifying brownfield properties the acquisition and transfer of which occur during the period for which the election remains in effect.*

(ii) ELECTION.—*An election under clause (i) shall be made with the eligible taxpayer's or qualifying partnership's timely filed tax return (including extensions) for the first taxable year for which the taxpayer or qualifying partnership intends to have the election apply. An election under clause (i) is effective for the period—*

(I) *beginning on the date which is the first day of the taxable year of the return in which the election is included or a later day in such taxable year selected by the eligible taxpayer or qualifying partnership, and*

(II) *ending on the date which is the earliest of a date of revocation selected by the eligible taxpayer or qualifying partnership, the date which is 8 years after the date described in subclause (I), or, in the case of an election by a qualifying partnership of which the eligible taxpayer is a partner, the date of the termination of the qualifying partnership.*

(iii) REVOCATION.—*An eligible taxpayer or qualifying partnership may revoke an election under clause (i)(II) by filing a statement of revocation with a timely filed tax return (including extensions). A revocation is effective as of the first day of the taxable year of the return in which the revocation is included or a later day in such taxable year selected by the eligible taxpayer or qualifying partnership. Once an eligible taxpayer or qualifying partnership revokes the election, the eligible taxpayer or qualifying partnership is ineligible to make another election under clause (i) with respect to any qualifying brownfield property subject to the revoked election.*

(I) RECAPTURE.—*If an eligible taxpayer excludes gain or loss from a sale, exchange, or other disposition of property to which an election under subparagraph (H) applies, and such property fails to satisfy the requirements of this paragraph, the unrelated business taxable income of the eligible taxpayer for the taxable year in which such failure occurs shall be determined by including any previously excluded gain or loss from such sale, exchange, or other disposition allocable to such taxpayer, and interest shall be determined at the overpayment rate established under section 6621 on any resulting tax for the period beginning with the due date of the return for the taxable year during which such sale, exchange, or other disposition occurred, and ending on the date of payment of the tax.*

(J) RELATED PERSONS.—*For purposes of this paragraph, a person shall be treated as related to another person if—*

(i) *such person bears a relationship to such other person described in section 267(b) (determined without regard to paragraph (9) thereof), or section 707(b)(1), determined by substituting '25 percent' for 50 "percent" each place it appears therein, and*

(ii) *in the case such other person is a nonprofit organization, if such person controls directly or indirectly more than 25 percent of the governing body of such organization.*

(K) TERMINATION.—*Except for purposes of determining the average eligible remediation expenditures for properties acquired during the election period under subparagraph (H), this paragraph shall not apply to any property acquired by the eligible taxpayer or qualifying partnership after December 31, 2009.*

* * *

[CCH Explanation at ¶1330 and ¶1335. Committee Reports at ¶10,420 and ¶10,840.]

Amendments

• **2004, American Jobs Creation Act of 2004 (H.R. 4520)**

H.R. 4520, §319(c):

Amended Code Sec. 512(b) by adding at the end new paragraph (18). **Effective** for tax years beginning after the date of the enactment of this Act.

H.R. 4520, §702(a):

Amended Code Sec. 512(b) by adding at the end new paragraph (18)[(19)]. **Effective** for any gain or loss on the sale, exchange, or other disposition of any property acquired by the taxpayer after 12-31-2004.

(e) Special Rules Applicable to S corporations.—

(1) In general.—If an organization described in section *1361(c)(2)(A)(vi) or* 1361(c)(6) holds stock in an S corporation—

(A) such interest shall be treated as an interest in an unrelated trade or business; and

(B) notwithstanding any other provision of this part—

(i) all items of income, loss, or deduction taken into account under section 1366(a), and

(ii) any gain or loss on the disposition of the stock in the S corporation

shall be taken into account in computing the unrelated business taxable income of such organization.

* * *

[CCH Explanation at ¶1330. Committee Reports at ¶10,140.]

Amendments

• **2004, American Jobs Creation Act of 2004 (H.R. 4520)**

H.R. 4520, § 233(d):

Amended Code Sec. 512(e)(1) by inserting "1361(c)(2)(A)(vi) or" before "1361(c)(6)". **Effective** on the date of the enactment of this Act.

[¶5415] CODE SEC. 514. UNRELATED DEBT-FINANCED INCOME.

* * *

(b) Definition of Debt-Financed Property.—

(1) In general.—For purposes of this section, the term "debt-financed property" means any property which is held to produce income and with respect to which there is an acquisition indebtedness (as defined in subsection (c)) at any time during the taxable year (or, if the property was disposed of during the taxable year, with respect to which there was an acquisition indebtedness at any time during the 12-month period ending with the date of such disposition), except that such term does not include—

* * *

(C) any property to the extent that the income from such property is excluded by reason of the provisions of paragraph (7), (8), or (9) of section 512(b) in computing the gross income of any unrelated trade or business;

(D) any property to the extent that it is used in any trade or business described in paragraph (1), (2), or (3) of section 513(a); *or*

(E) *any property the gain or loss from the sale, exchange, or other disposition of which would be excluded by reason of the provisions of section 512(b)(18) in computing the gross income of any unrelated trade or business.*

For purposes of subparagraph (A), substantially all the use of a property shall be considered to be substantially related to the exercise or performance by an organization of its charitable, educational, or other purpose or function constituting the basis for its exemption under section 501 if such property is real property subject to a lease to a medical clinic entered into primarily for purposes which are substantially related (aside from the need of such organization for income or funds or the use it makes of the rents derived) to the exercise or performance by such organization of its charitable, educational, or other purpose or function constituting the basis for its exemption under section 501.

* * *

[CCH Explanation at ¶ 1330. Committee Reports at ¶ 10,840.]

Amendments

• **2004, American Jobs Creation Act of 2004 (H.R. 4520)**

H.R. 4520, § 702(b):

Amended Code Sec. 514(b)(1) by striking "or" at the end of subparagraph (C), by striking the period at the end of subparagraph (D) and inserting "; or", and by inserting after subparagraph (D) a new subparagraph (E). **Effective** for any gain or loss on the sale, exchange, or other disposition of any property acquired by the taxpayer after 12-31-2004. For a special rule, see Act Sec. 702(c), below.

(c) ACQUISITION INDEBTEDNESS.—

* * *

(6) CERTAIN FEDERAL FINANCING.—

(A) IN GENERAL.—For purposes of this section, the term "acquisition indebtedness" does not include—

(i) an obligation, to the extent that it is insured by the Federal Housing Administration, to finance the purchase, rehabilitation, or construction of housing for low and moderate income persons, or

(ii) indebtedness incurred by a small business investment company licensed after the date of the enactment of the American Jobs Creation Act of 2004 under the Small Business Investment Act of 1958 if such indebtedness is evidenced by a debenture—

(I) issued by such company under section 303(a) of such Act, and

(II) held or guaranteed by the Small Business Administration.

(B) LIMITATION.—Subparagraph (A)(ii) shall not apply with respect to any small business investment company during any period that—

(i) any organization which is exempt from tax under this title (other than a governmental unit) owns more than 25 percent of the capital or profits interest in such company, or

(ii) organizations which are exempt from tax under this title (including governmental units other than any agency or instrumentality of the United States) own, in the aggregate, 50 percent or more of the capital or profits interest in such company.

* * *

H.R. 4520, § 702(c), provides:

(c) SAVINGS CLAUSE.—Nothing in the amendments made by this section shall affect any duty, liability, or other requirement imposed under any other Federal or State law. Notwithstanding section 128(b) of the Comprehensive Environmental Response, Compensation, and Liability Act of 1980, a certification provided by the Environmental Protection Agency or an appropriate State agency (within the meaning of section 198(c)(4) of the Internal Revenue Code of 1986) shall not affect the liability of any person under section 107(a) of such Act.

[CCH Explanation at ¶ 1325. Committee Reports at ¶ 10,280.]

Amendments

• **2004, American Jobs Creation Act of 2004 (H.R. 4520)**

H.R. 4520, § 247(a):

Amended Code Sec. 514(c)(6). **Effective** for indebtedness incurred after the date of the enactment of this Act by a small business investment company licensed after the date of the enactment of this Act. Prior to amendment, Code Sec. 514(c)(6) read as follows:

(6) CERTAIN FEDERAL FINANCING.—For purposes of this section, the term "acquisition indebtedness" does not include an obligation, to the extent that it is insured by the Federal Housing Administration, to finance the purchase, rehabilitation, or construction of housing for low and moderate income persons.

[¶ 5420] CODE SEC. 521. EXEMPTION OF FARMERS' COOPERATIVES FROM TAX.

* * *

(b) APPLICABLE RULES.—

* * *

(7) CROSS REFERENCE.—

For treatment of value-added processing involving animals, see section 1388(k).

* * *

[CCH Explanation at ¶ 830. Committee Reports at ¶ 10,390.]

Amendments

• 2004, American Jobs Creation Act of 2004 (H.R. 4520)

H.R. 4520, §316(b):

Amended Code Sec. 521(b) by adding at the end a new paragraph (7). **Effective** for tax years beginning after the date of the enactment of this Act.

[¶ 5425] CODE SEC. 535. ACCUMULATED TAXABLE INCOME.

* * *

(d) INCOME DISTRIBUTED TO UNITED STATES-OWNED FOREIGN CORPORATION RETAINS UNITED STATES CONNECTION.—

* * *

⟫⟶ *Caution: Code Sec. 535(d)(2), below, as amended by H.R. 4520, §402(b)(1), applies to losses for tax years beginning after December 31, 2006.*

(2) UNITED STATES-OWNED FOREIGN CORPORATION.—The term "United States-owned foreign corporation" has the meaning given to such term by *section 904(h)(6)*.

* * *

[CCH Explanation at ¶ 420. Committee Reports at ¶ 10,580.]

Amendments

• 2004, American Jobs Creation Act of 2004 (H.R. 4520)

H.R. 4520, §402(b)(1):

Amended Code Sec. 535(d)(2) by striking "section 904(g)(6)" and inserting "section 904(h)(6)". **Effective** for losses for tax years beginning after 12-31-2006.

[¶ 5430] CODE SEC. 542. DEFINITION OF PERSONAL HOLDING COMPANY.

* * *

(c) EXCEPTIONS.—The term "personal holding company" as defined in subsection (a) does not include—

(1) a corporation exempt from tax under subchapter F (sec. 501 and following);

(2) a bank as defined in section 581, or a domestic building and loan association within the meaning of section 7701(a)(19);

(3) a life insurance company;

(4) a surety company;

(5) *a foreign corporation,* [;]

(6) a lending or finance company if—

(A) 60 percent or more of its ordinary gross income (as defined in section 543(b)(1)) is derived directly from the active and regular conduct of a lending or finance business;

(B) the personal holding company income for the taxable year (computed without regard to income described in subsection (d)(3) and income derived directly from the active and regular conduct of a lending or finance business, and computed by including as personal holding company income the entire amount of the gross income from rents, royalties, produced film rents, and compensation for use of corporate property by shareholders) is not more than 20 percent of the ordinary gross income;

(C) the sum of the deductions which are directly allocable to the active and regular conduct of its lending or finance business equals or exceeds the sum of—

(i) 15 percent of so much of the ordinary gross income derived therefrom as does not exceed $500,000, plus

(ii) 5 percent of so much of the ordinary gross income derived therefrom as exceeds $500,000; and

(D) the loans to a person who is a shareholder in such company during the taxable year by or for whom 10 percent or more in value of its outstanding stock is owned directly or indirectly (including, in the case of an individual, stock owned by members of his family as defined in section 544(a)(2)), outstanding at any time during such year do not exceed $5,000 in principal amount;

(7) a small business investment company which is licensed by the Small Business Administration and operating under the Small Business Investment Act of 1958 (15 U.S.C. 661 and following) and which is actively engaged in the business of providing funds to small business concerns under that Act. This paragraph shall not apply if any shareholder of the small business investment company owns at any time during the taxable year directly or indirectly (including, in the case of an individual, ownership by the members of his family as defined in section 544(a)(2)) a 5 per centum or more proprietary interest in a small business concern to which funds are provided by the investment company or 5 per centum or more in value of the outstanding stock of such concern; *and*

(8) a corporation which is subject to the jurisdiction of the court in a title 11 or similar case (within the meaning of section 368(a)(3)(A)) unless a major purpose of instituting or continuing such case is the avoidance of the tax imposed by section 541.

* * *

[CCH Explanation at ¶ 490. Committee Reports at ¶ 10,690.]

Amendments

• **2004, American Jobs Creation Act of 2004 (H.R. 4520)**

H.R. 4520, § 413(b)(1)(A)-(D):

Amended Code Sec. 542(c) by striking paragraph (5) and inserting "(5) a foreign corporation,", by striking paragraphs (7) and (10) and redesignating paragraphs (8) and (9) as paragraphs (7) and (8), respectively, by inserting "and" at the end of paragraph (7) (as so redesignated), and by striking "; and" at the end of paragraph (8) (as so redesignated) and inserting a period. **Effective** for tax years of foreign corporations beginning after 12-31-2004 and for tax years of United States shareholders with or within which such tax

years of foreign corporations end. Prior to being stricken, Code Sec. 542(c)(5), (7) and (10) read as follows:

(5) a foreign personal holding company as defined in section 552;

(7) a foreign corporation (other than a corporation which has income to which section 543(a)(7) applies for the taxable year), if all of its stock outstanding during the last half of the taxable year is owned by nonresident alien individuals, whether directly or indirectly through foreign estates, foreign trusts, foreign partnerships, or other foreign corporations;

(10) a passive foreign investment company (as defined in section 1297).

[¶ 5435] CODE SEC. 543. PERSONAL HOLDING COMPANY INCOME.

* * *

(b) Definitions.—For purposes of this part—

(1) Ordinary gross income.—The term "ordinary gross income" means the gross income determined by excluding—

(A) all gains from the sale or other disposition of capital assets, *and*

(B) all gains (other than those referred to in subparagraph (A)) from the sale or other disposition of property described in section 1231(b).

* * *

[CCH Explanation at ¶ 490. Committee Reports at ¶ 10,690.]

Amendments

• **2004, American Jobs Creation Act of 2004 (H.R. 4520)**

H.R. 4520, § 413(c)(8):

Amended Code Sec. 543(b)(1) by inserting "and" at the end of subparagraph (A), by striking ", and" at the end of subparagraph (B) and inserting a period, and by striking subparagraph (C). **Effective** for tax years of foreign corporations beginning after 12-31-2004 and for tax years of United States shareholders with or within which such tax years of

foreign corporations end. Prior to being stricken, Code Sec. 543(b)(1)(C) read as follows:

(C) in the case of a foreign corporation all of the outstanding stock of which during the last half of the taxable year is owned by nonresident alien individuals (whether directly or indirectly through foreign estates, foreign trusts, foreign partnerships, or other foreign corporations), all items of income which would, but for this subparagraph, constitute personal holding company income under any paragraph of subsection (a) other than paragraph (7) thereof.

[¶ 5440] CODE SEC. 551. FOREIGN PERSONAL HOLDING COMPANY INCOME TAXED TO UNITED STATES SHAREHOLDERS. [*Repealed.*]

* * *

[CCH Explanation at ¶ 490. Committee Reports at ¶ 10,690.]

Amendments

• 2004, American Jobs Creation Act of 2004 (H.R. 4520)

H.R. 4520, § 413(a)(1):

Repealed part III of subchapter G of chapter 1 (Code Secs. 551-558). **Effective** for tax years of foreign corporations beginning after 12-31-2004, and for tax years of United States shareholders with or within which such tax years of foreign corporations end. Prior to repeal, Code Sec. 551 read as follows:

SEC. 551. FOREIGN PERSONAL HOLDING COMPANY INCOME TAXED TO UNITED STATES SHAREHOLDERS.

(a) GENERAL RULE.—The undistributed foreign personal holding company income of a foreign personal holding company shall be included in the gross income of the citizens or residents of the United States, domestic corporations, domestic partnerships, and estates or trusts (other than foreign estates or trusts), who are shareholders in such foreign personal holding company (hereinafter called "United States shareholders") in the manner and to the extent set forth in this part.

(b) AMOUNT INCLUDED IN GROSS INCOME.—Each United States shareholder, who was a shareholder on the day in the taxable year of the company which was the last day on which a United States group (as defined in section 552(a)(2)) existed with respect to the company, shall include in his gross income, as a dividend, for the taxable year in which or with which the taxable year of the company ends, the amount he would have received as a dividend (determined as if any distribution in liquidation actually made in such taxable year had not been made) if on such last day there had been distributed by the company, and received by the shareholders, an amount which bears the same ratio to the undistributed foreign personal holding company income of the company for the taxable year as the portion of such taxable year up to and including such last day bears to the entire taxable year.

(c) INFORMATION IN RETURN.—Every United States shareholder who is required under subsection (b) to include in his gross income any amount with respect to the undistributed foreign personal holding company income of a foreign personal holding company and who, on the last day on which a United States group existed with respect to the company, owned 5 percent or more in value of the outstanding stock of such company, shall set forth in his return in complete detail the gross income, deductions and credits, taxable income, foreign personal holding company income, and undistributed foreign personal holding company income of such company.

(d) EFFECT ON CAPITAL ACCOUNT OF FOREIGN PERSONAL HOLDING COMPANY.—An amount which bears the same ratio to the undistributed foreign personal holding company income of the foreign personal holding company for its taxable year as the portion of such taxable year up to and including the last day on which a United States group existed with respect to the company bears to the entire taxable year, shall, for the purpose of determining the effect of distributions in subsequent taxable years by the corporation, be considered as paid-in surplus or as a contribution to capital, and the accumulated earnings and profits as of the close of the taxable year shall be correspondingly reduced, if such amount or any portion thereof is required to be included as a dividend, directly or indirectly, in the gross income of United States shareholders.

(e) BASIS OF STOCK IN HANDS OF SHAREHOLDERS.—The amount required to be included in the gross income of a United States shareholder under subsection (b) shall, for the purpose of adjusting the basis of his stock with respect to which the distribution would have been made (if it had been made), be treated as having been reinvested by the shareholder as a contribution to the capital of the corporation; but only to the extent to which such amount is included in his gross income in his return, increased or decreased by any adjustment of such amount in the last determination of the shareholder's tax liability, made before the expiration of 6 years after the date prescribed by law for filing the return.

(f) STOCK HELD THROUGH FOREIGN ENTITY.—For purposes of this section, stock of a foreign personal holding company owned (directly or through the application of this subsection) by—

(1) a foreign partnership or an estate or trust which is a foreign estate or trust, or

(2) a foreign corporation which is not a foreign personal holding company, shall be considered as being owned proportionately by its partners, beneficiaries, or shareholders.

In any case to which the preceding sentence applies, the Secretary may by regulations provide that rules similar to the rules of section 1298(b)(5) shall apply, and provide for such other adjustments in the application of this subchapter as may be necessary to carry out the purposes of this subsection.

(g) COORDINATION WITH PASSIVE FOREIGN INVESTMENT COMPANY PROVISIONS.—If, but for this subsection, an amount would be included in the gross income of any person under subsection (a) and under section 1293 (relating to current taxation of income from certain passive foreign investment companies), such amount shall be included in the gross income of such person only under subsection (a).

(h) CROSS REFERENCES.—

(1) For basis of stock or securities in a foreign personal holding company acquired from a decedent, see section 1014(b)(5).

(2) For period of limitation on assessment and collection without assessment, in case of failure to include in gross income the amount properly includible therein under subsection (b), see section 6501.

[¶ 5445] CODE SEC. 552. DEFINITION OF FOREIGN PERSONAL HOLDING COMPANY. [*Repealed.*]

* * *

[CCH Explanation at ¶ 490. Committee Reports at ¶ 10,690.]

Amendments

• 2004, American Jobs Creation Act of 2004 (H.R. 4520)

H.R. 4520, § 413(a)(1):

Repealed part III of subchapter G of chapter 1 (Code Secs. 551-558). **Effective** for tax years of foreign corporations beginning after 12-31-2004, and for tax years of United States shareholders with or within which such tax years of foreign corporations end. Prior to repeal, Code Sec. 552 read as follows:

SEC. 552. DEFINITION OF FOREIGN PERSONAL HOLDING COMPANY.

(a) GENERAL RULE.—For purposes of this subtitle, the term "foreign personal holding company" means any foreign corporation if—

(1) GROSS INCOME REQUIREMENT.—At least 60 percent of its gross income (as defined in section 555(a)) for the taxable year is foreign personal holding company income as defined in section 553; but if the corporation is a foreign personal holding company with respect to any taxable year ending after August 26, 1937, then, for each subsequent taxable year, the minimum percentage shall be 50 percent in lieu of 60 percent, until a taxable year during the whole of which the stock ownership required by paragraph (2) does not exist, or until the expiration of three consecutive taxable years in each of which less than 50 percent of the gross income is foreign personal holding company income. For purposes of this paragraph, there shall be included in the gross income the amount includible therein as a dividend by reason of the application of section 555(c)(2); and

(2) STOCK OWNERSHIP REQUIREMENT.—At any time during the taxable year more than 50 percent of—

(A) the total combined voting power of all classes of stock of such corporation entitled to vote, or

(B) the total value of the stock of such corporation,

is owned (directly or indirectly) by or for not more than 5 individuals who are citizens or residents of the United States (hereinafter in this part referred to as the "United States group").

(b) EXCEPTIONS.—The term "foreign personal holding company" does not include—

(1) a corporation exempt from tax under subchapter F (sec. 501 and following); and

(2) a corporation organized and doing business under the banking and credit laws of a foreign country if it is established (annually or at other periodic intervals) to the satisfaction of the Secretary that such corporation is not formed or availed of for the purpose of evading or avoiding United States income taxes which would otherwise be imposed upon its shareholders. If the Secretary is satisfied that such corporation is not so formed or availed of, he shall issue to such corporation annually or at other periodic intervals a certification that the corporation is not a foreign personal holding company.

Each United States shareholder of a foreign corporation which would, except for the provisions of paragraph (2), be a foreign personal holding company, shall attach to and file with his income tax return for the taxable year a copy of the certification by the Secretary made pursuant to paragraph (2). Such copy shall be filed with the taxpayer's return for the taxable year if he has been a shareholder of such corporation for any part of such year.

(c) LOOK-THRU FOR CERTAIN DIVIDENDS AND INTEREST.—

(1) IN GENERAL.—For purposes of this part, any related person dividend or interest shall be treated as foreign personal holding company income only to the extent such dividend or interest is attributable (determined under rules similar to the rules of subparagraphs (C) and (D) of section 904(d)(3)) to income of the related person which would be foreign personal holding company income.

(2) RELATED PERSON DIVIDEND OR INTEREST.—For purposes of paragraph (1), the term "related person dividend or interest" means any dividend or interest which—

(A) is described in subparagraph (A) of section 954(c)(3), and

(B) is received from a related person which is not a foreign personal holding company (determined without regard to this subsection).

For purposes of the preceding sentence, the term "related person" has the meaning given such term by section 954(d)(3) (determined by substituting "foreign personal holding company" for "controlled foreign corporation" each place it appears).

[¶5450] CODE SEC. 553. FOREIGN PERSONAL HOLDING COMPANY INCOME. [*Repealed.*]

* * *

[CCH Explanation at ¶490. Committee Reports at ¶10,690.]

Amendments

• 2004, American Jobs Creation Act of 2004 (H.R. 4520)

H.R. 4520, §413(a)(1):

Repealed part III of subchapter G of chapter 1 (Code Secs. 551-558). **Effective** for tax years of foreign corporations beginning after 12-31-2004, and for tax years of United States shareholders with or within which such tax years of foreign corporations end. Prior to repeal, Code Sec. 553 read as follows:

SEC. 553. FOREIGN PERSONAL HOLDING COMPANY INCOME.

(a) FOREIGN PERSONAL HOLDING COMPANY INCOME.—For purposes of this subtitle, the term "foreign personal holding company income" means that portion of the gross income, determined for purposes of section 552, which consists of:

(1) DIVIDENDS, ETC.—Dividends, interest, royalties, and annuities. This paragraph shall not apply to active business computer software royalties (as defined in section 543(d)).

(2) STOCK AND SECURITIES TRANSACTIONS.—Except in the case of regular dealers in stock or securities, gains from the sale or exchange of stock or securities.

(3) COMMODITIES TRANSACTIONS.—Gains from futures transactions in any commodity on or subject to the rules of a board of trade or commodity exchange. This paragraph shall not apply to gains by a producer, processor, merchant, or handler of the commodity which arise out of bona fide hedging transactions reasonably necessary to the conduct of its business in the manner in which such business is customarily and usually conducted by others.

(4) ESTATES AND TRUSTS.—Amounts includible in computing the taxable income of the corporation under part I of subchapter J (sec. 641 and following, relating to estates, trusts, and beneficiaries); and gains from the sale or other disposition of any interest in an estate or trust.

(5) PERSONAL SERVICE CONTRACTS.—

(A) Amounts received under a contract under which the corporation is to furnish personal services; if some person other than the corporation has the right to designate (by name or by description) the individual who is to perform the services, or if the individual who is to perform the services is designated (by name or by description) in the contract; and

(B) amounts received from the sale or other disposition of such a contract.

This paragraph shall apply with respect to amounts received for services under a particular contract only if at some time during the taxable year 25 percent or more in value of the outstanding stock of the corporation is owned, directly or indirectly, by or for the individual who has performed, is to perform, or may be designated (by name or by description) as the one to perform, such services.

(6) USE OF CORPORATION PROPERTY BY SHAREHOLDER.—Amounts received as compensation (however designated and from whomsoever received) for the use of, or right to

use, property of the corporation in any case where, at any time during the taxable year, 25 percent or more in value of the outstanding stock of the corporation is owned, directly or indirectly, by or for an individual entitled to the use of the property; whether such right is obtained directly from the corporation or by means of a sublease or other arrangement. This paragraph shall apply only to a corporation which has foreign personal holding company income for the taxable year, computed without regard to this paragraph and paragraph (7), in excess of 10 percent of its gross income.

(7) RENTS.—Rents, unless constituting 50 percent or more of the gross income. For purposes of this paragraph, the term "rents" means compensation, however designated, for the use of, or right to use, property; but does not include

amounts constituting foreign personal holding company income under paragraph (6).

(b) LIMITATION ON GROSS INCOME IN CERTAIN TRANSACTIONS.—For purposes of this part—

(1) gross income and foreign personal holding company income determined with respect to transactions described in subsection (a)(2) (relating to gains from stock and security transactions) shall include only the excess of gains over losses from such transactions, and

(2) gross income and foreign personal holding company income determined with respect to transactions described in subsection (a)(3) (relating to gains from commodity transactions) shall include only the excess of gains over losses from such transactions.

[¶ 5455] CODE SEC. 554. STOCK OWNERSHIP. [*Repealed.*]

* * *

[CCH Explanation at ¶ 490. Committee Reports at ¶ 10,690.]

Amendments

• **2004, American Jobs Creation Act of 2004 (H.R. 4520)**

H.R. 4520, § 413(a)(1):

Repealed part III of subchapter G of chapter 1 (Code Secs. 551-558). **Effective** for tax years of foreign corporations beginning after 12-31-2004, and for tax years of United States shareholders with or within which such tax years of foreign corporations end. Prior to repeal, Code Sec. 554 read as follows:

SEC. 554. STOCK OWNERSHIP.

(a) CONSTRUCTIVE OWNERSHIP.—For purposes of determining whether a corporation is a foreign personal holding company, insofar as such determination is based on stock ownership under section 552(a)(2), section 553(a)(5), or section 553(a)(6)—

(1) STOCK NOT OWNED BY INDIVIDUAL.—Stock owned, directly or indirectly, by or for a corporation, partnership, estate, or trust shall be considered as being owned proportionately by its shareholders, partners, or beneficiaries.

(2) FAMILY AND PARTNERSHIP OWNERSHIP.—An individual shall be considered as owning the stock owned, directly or indirectly, by or for his family or by or for his partner. For purposes of this paragraph, the family of an individual includes only his brothers and sisters (whether by the whole or half blood), spouse, ancestors, and lineal descendants.

(3) OPTIONS.—If any person has an option to acquire stock, such stock shall be considered as owned by such person. For purposes of this paragraph, an option to acquire such an option, and each one of a series of such options, shall be considered as an option to acquire such stock.

(4) APPLICATION OF FAMILY-PARTNERSHIP AND OPTION RULES.—Paragraphs (2) and (3) shall be applied—

(A) for purposes of the stock ownership requirement provided in section 552(a)(2), if, but only if, the effect is to make the corporation a foreign personal holding company;

(B) for purposes of section 553(a)(5) (relating to personal service contracts) or of section 553(a)(6) (relating to the use of property by shareholders), if, but only if, the effect is to make the amounts therein referred to includible under such paragraph as foreign personal holding company income.

(5) CONSTRUCTIVE OWNERSHIP AS ACTUAL OWNERSHIP.—Stock constructively owned by a person by reason of the application of paragraph (1) or (3) shall, for purposes of applying paragraph (1) or (2), be treated as actually owned by such person; but stock constructively owned by an individual by reason of the application of paragraph (2) shall not be treated as owned by him for purposes of again applying such paragraph in order to make another the constructive owner of such stock.

(6) OPTION RULE IN LIEU OF FAMILY AND PARTNERSHIP RULE.—If stock may be considered as owned by an individual under either paragraph (2) or (3) it shall be considered as owned by him under paragraph (3).

(b) CONVERTIBLE SECURITIES.—Outstanding securities convertible into stock (whether or not convertible during the taxable year) shall be considered as outstanding stock—

(1) for purposes of the stock ownership requirement provided in section 552(a)(2), but only if the effect of the inclusion of all such securities is to make the corporation a foreign personal holding company;

(2) for purposes of section 553(a)(5) (relating to personal service contracts), but only if the effect of the inclusion of all such securities is to make the amounts therein referred to includible under such paragraph as foreign personal holding company income; and

(3) for purposes of section 553(a)(6) (relating to the use of property by shareholders), but only if the effect of the inclusion of all such securities is to make the amounts therein referred to includible under such paragraph as foreign personal holding company income.

The requirement in paragraphs (1), (2), and (3) that all convertible securities must be included if any are to be included shall be subject to the exception that, where some of the outstanding securities are convertible only after a later date than in the case of others, the class having the earlier conversion date may be included although the others are not included, but no convertible securities shall be included unless all outstanding securities having a prior conversion date are also included.

(c) SPECIAL RULES FOR APPLICATION OF SUBSECTION (a)(2).—For purposes of the stock ownership requirement provided in section 552(a)(2)—

(1) stock owned by a nonresident alien individual (other than a foreign trust or foreign estate) shall not be considered by reason of so much of subsection (a)(2) as relates to attribution through family membership as owned by a citizen or by a resident alien individual who is not the spouse of the nonresident individual and who does not otherwise own stock in such corporation (determined after the application of subsection (a), other than attribution through family membership), and

(2) stock of a corporation owned by any foreign person shall not be considered by reason of so much of subsection (a)(2) as relates to attribution through partners as owned by a citizen or resident of the United States who does not otherwise own stock in such corporation (determined after application of subsection (a) and paragraph (1), other than attribution through partners).

[¶ 5460] CODE SEC. 555. GROSS INCOME OF FOREIGN PERSONAL HOLDING COMPANIES. [*Repealed.*]

* * *

[CCH Explanation at ¶ 490. Committee Reports at ¶ 10,690.]

Amendments

• **2004, American Jobs Creation Act of 2004 (H.R. 4520)**

H.R. 4520, § 413(a)(1):

Repealed part III of subchapter G of chapter 1 (Code Secs. 551-558). **Effective** for tax years of foreign corporations beginning after 12-31-2004, and for tax years of United States shareholders with or within which such tax years of foreign corporations end. Prior to repeal, Code Sec. 555 read as follows:

SEC. 555. GROSS INCOME OF FOREIGN PERSONAL HOLDING COMPANIES.

(a) GENERAL RULE.—For purposes of this part, the term "gross income" means, with respect to a foreign corporation, gross income computed (without regard to the provisions of subchapter N (and following)) as if the foreign corporation were a domestic corporation which is a personal holding company.

(b) ADDITIONS TO GROSS INCOME.—In the case of a foreign personal holding company (whether or not a United States group, as defined in, existed with respect to such company on the last day of its taxable year) which was a shareholder in another foreign personal holding company on the day in the taxable year of the second company which was the last

day on which a United States group existed with respect to the second company, there shall be included, as a dividend, in the gross income of the first company, for the taxable year in which or with which the taxable year of the second company ends, the amount the first company would have received as a dividend if on such last day there had been distributed by the second company, and received by the shareholders, an amount which bears the same ratio to the undistributed foreign personal holding company income of the second company for its taxable year as the portion of such taxable year up to and including such last day bears to the entire taxable year.

(c) APPLICATION OF SUBSECTION (b).—The rule provided in subsection (b)—

(1) shall be applied in the case of a foreign personal holding company for the purpose of determining its undistributed foreign personal holding company income which, or a part of which, is to be included in the gross income of its shareholders, whether United States shareholders or other foreign personal holding companies;

(2) shall be applied in the case of every foreign corporation with respect to which a United States group exists on some day of its taxable year, for the purpose of determining whether such corporation meets the gross income requirements of section 552(a)(1).

[¶ 5465] CODE SEC. 556. UNDISTRIBUTED FOREIGN PERSONAL HOLDING COMPANY INCOME. [*Repealed.*]

* * *

[CCH Explanation at ¶ 490. Committee Reports at ¶ 10,690.]

Amendments

• **2004, American Jobs Creation Act of 2004 (H.R. 4520)**

H.R. 4520, § 413(a)(1):

Repealed part III of subchapter G of chapter 1 (Code Secs. 551-558). **Effective** for tax years of foreign corporations beginning after 12-31-2004, and for tax years of United States shareholders with or within which such tax years of foreign corporations end. Prior to repeal, Code Sec. 556 read as follows:

SEC. 556. UNDISTRIBUTED FOREIGN PERSONAL HOLDING COMPANY INCOME.

(a) DEFINITION.—For purposes of this part, the term "undistributed foreign personal holding company income" means the taxable income of a foreign personal holding company adjusted in the manner provided in subsection (b), minus the dividends paid deduction (as defined in section 561).

(b) ADJUSTMENTS TO TAXABLE INCOME.—For the purposes of subsection (a), the taxable income shall be adjusted as follows:

(1) TAXES.—There shall be allowed as a deduction Federal income and excess profits taxes and income, war profits, and excess profits taxes of foreign countries and possessions of the United States (to the extent not allowable as a deduction under section 275(a)(4)), accrued during the taxable year, but not including the accumulated earnings tax imposed by section 531, the personal holding company tax imposed by section 541, or the taxes imposed by corresponding sections of a prior income tax law.

(2) CHARITABLE CONTRIBUTIONS.—The deduction for charitable contributions provided under section 170 shall be allowed, but in computing such deduction the limitations in section 170(b)(1)(A), (B), and (D) shall apply, and section 170(b)(2) and (d)(1) shall not apply. For purposes of this paragraph, the term "contribution base" when used in sec-

tion 170(b)(1) means the taxable income computed with the adjustments (other than the 10-percent limitation) provided in section 170(b)(2) and (d)(1) and without the deduction of the amounts disallowed under paragraphs (5) and (6) of this subsection or the inclusion in gross income of the amounts includible therein as dividends by reason of the application of the provisions of section 555(b) (relating to the inclusion in gross income of a foreign personal holding company of its distributive share of the undistributed foreign personal holding company income of another company in which it is a shareholder).

(3) SPECIAL DEDUCTIONS DISALLOWED.—The special deductions for corporations provided in part VIII (except section 248 of subchapter B (section 241 and following, relating to the deduction for dividends received by corporations, etc.) shall not be allowed.

(4) NET OPERATING LOSS.—The net operating loss deduction provided in section 172 shall not be allowed, but there shall be allowed as a deduction the amount of the net operating loss (as defined in section 172(c)) for the preceding taxable year computed without the deductions provided in part VIII (except section 248) of subchapter B.

(5) EXPENSES AND DEPRECIATION APPLICABLE TO PROPERTY OF THE TAXPAYER.—The aggregate of the deductions allowed under section 162 (relating to trade or business expenses) and section 167 (relating to depreciation) which are allocable to the operation and maintenance of property owned or operated by the company, shall be allowed only in an amount equal to the rent or other compensation received for the use of, or the right to use, the property, unless it is established (under regulations prescribed by the Secretary) to the satisfaction of the Secretary—

(A) that the rent or other compensation received was the highest obtainable, or, if none was received, that none was obtainable;

(B) that the property was held in the course of a business carried on bona fide for profit; and

(C) either that there was reasonable expectation that the operation of the property would result in a profit, or that the property was necessary to the conduct of the business.

(6) TAXES AND CONTRIBUTIONS TO PENSION TRUSTS.—The deductions provided in section 164(e) (relating to taxes of a shareholder paid by the corporation) and in section 404 (relating to pension, etc., trusts) shall not be allowed.

[¶5470] CODE SEC. 557. INCOME NOT PLACED ON ANNUAL BASIS. [*Repealed.*]

* * *

[CCH Explanation at ¶490. Committee Reports at ¶10,690.]

Amendments

• **2004, American Jobs Creation Act of 2004 (H.R. 4520)**

H.R. 4520, §413(a)(1):

Repealed part III of subchapter G of chapter 1 (Code Secs. 551-558). **Effective** for tax years of foreign corporations beginning after 12-31-2004, and for tax years of United States shareholders with or within which such tax years of foreign

corporations end. Prior to repeal, Code Sec. 557 read as follows:

SEC. 557. INCOME NOT PLACED ON ANNUAL BASIS.

Section 443(b) (relating to computation of tax on change of annual accounting period) shall not apply in the computation of the undistributed foreign personal holding company income under section 556.

[¶5475] CODE SEC. 558. RETURNS OF OFFICERS, DIRECTORS, AND SHAREHOLDERS OF FOREIGN PERSONAL HOLDING COMPANIES. [*Repealed.*]

* * *

[CCH Explanation at ¶490. Committee Reports at ¶10,690.]

Amendments

• **2004, American Jobs Creation Act of 2004 (H.R. 4520)**

H.R. 4520, §413(a)(1):

Repealed part III of subchapter G of chapter 1 (Code Secs. 551-558). **Effective** for tax years of foreign corporations beginning after 12-31-2004, and for tax years of United States shareholders with or within which such tax years of foreign

corporations end. Prior to repeal, Code Sec. 558 read as follows:

SEC. 558. RETURNS OF OFFICERS, DIRECTORS, AND SHAREHOLDERS OF FOREIGN PERSONAL HOLDING COMPANIES.

For provisions relating to returns of officers, directors, and shareholders of foreign personal holding companies, see section 6035.

[¶5480] CODE SEC. 562. RULES APPLICABLE IN DETERMINING DIVIDENDS ELIGIBLE FOR DIVIDENDS PAID DEDUCTION.

* * *

(b) DISTRIBUTIONS IN LIQUIDATION.—

(1) Except in the case of a personal holding company described in section 542—

(A) in the case of amounts distributed in liquidation, the part of such distribution which is properly chargeable to earnings and profits accumulated after February 28, 1913, shall be treated as a dividend for purposes of computing the dividends paid deduction, and

(B) in the case of a complete liquidation occurring within 24 months after the adoption of a plan of liquidation, any distribution within such period pursuant to such plan shall, to the extent of the earnings and profits (computed without regard to capital losses) of the corporation for the taxable year in which such distribution is made, be treated as a dividend for purposes of computing the dividends paid deduction.

For purposes of subparagraph (A), a liquidation includes a redemption of stock to which section 302 applies. Except to the extent provided in regulations, the preceding sentence shall not apply in the case of any mere holding or investment company which is not a regulated investment company.

* * *

[CCH Explanation at ¶490. Committee Reports at ¶10,690.]

Amendments

• **2004, American Jobs Creation Act of 2004 (H.R. 4520)**

H.R. 4520, §413(c)(9):

Amended Code Sec. 562(b)(1) by striking "or a foreign personal holding company described in section 552" imme-

diately following "section 542". **Effective** for tax years of foreign corporations beginning after 12-31-2004, and for tax years of United States shareholders with or within which such tax years of foreign corporations end.

[¶ 5485] CODE SEC. 563. RULES RELATING TO DIVIDENDS PAID AFTER CLOSE OF TAXABLE YEAR.

* * *

(c) DIVIDENDS CONSIDERED AS PAID ON LAST DAY OF TAXABLE YEAR.—For the purpose of applying section 562(a), with respect to distributions under *subsection (a) or (b)* of this section, a distribution made after the close of a taxable year and on or before the 15th day of the third month following the close of the taxable year shall be considered as made on the last day of such taxable year.

* * *

[CCH Explanation at ¶ 490. Committee Reports at ¶ 10,690.]

Amendments

● **2004, American Jobs Creation Act of 2004 (H.R. 4520)**

H.R. 4520, § 413(c)(10)(A)-(C):

Amended Code Sec. 563 by striking subsection (c), by redesignating subsection (d) as subsection (c), and by striking "subsection (a), (b), or (c)" in subsection (c) (as so redesignated) and inserting "subsection (a) or (b)". **Effective** for tax years of foreign corporations beginning after 12-31-2004, and for tax years of United States shareholders with or within which such tax years of foreign corporations end. Prior to being stricken, Code Sec. 563(c) read as follows:

(c) FOREIGN PERSONAL HOLDING COMPANY TAX.—

(1) IN GENERAL.—In the determination of the dividends paid deduction for purposes of part III, a dividend paid after the close of any taxable year and on or before the 15th day of the 3rd month following the close of such taxable year shall, to the extent the company designates such dividend as being taken into account under this subsection, be considered as paid during such taxable year. The amount allowed as a deduction by reason of the application of this subsection with respect to any taxable year shall not exceed the undistributed foreign personal holding company income of the corporation for the taxable year computed without regard to this subsection.

(2) SPECIAL RULES.—In the case of any distribution referred to in paragraph (1)—

(A) paragraph (1) shall apply only if such distribution is to the person who was the shareholder of record (as of the last day of the taxable year of the foreign personal holding company) with respect to the stock for which such distribution is made,

(B) the determination of the person required to include such distribution in gross income shall be made under the principles of section 551(f), and

(C) any person required to include such distribution in gross or distributable net income shall include such distribution in income for such person's taxable year in which the taxable year of the foreign personal holding company ends.

[¶ 5490] CODE SEC. 582. BAD DEBTS, LOSSES, AND GAINS WITH RESPECT TO SECURITIES HELD BY FINANCIAL INSTITUTIONS.

* * *

(c) BOND, ETC., LOSSES AND GAINS OF FINANCIAL INSTITUTIONS.—

(1) GENERAL RULE.—For purposes of this subtitle, in the case of a financial institution referred to in paragraph (2), the sale or exchange of a bond, debenture, note, or certificate or other evidence of indebtedness shall not be considered a sale or exchange of a capital asset. For purposes of the preceding sentence, any regular or residual interest in a REMIC shall be treated as an evidence of indebtedness.

* * *

[CCH Explanation at ¶ 1120. Committee Reports at ¶ 11,180.]

Amendments

● **2004, American Jobs Creation Act of 2004 (H.R. 4520)**

H.R. 4520, § 835(b)(3):

Amended Code Sec. 582(c)(1) by striking ", and any regular interest in a FASIT," after "in a REMIC". **Effective** 1-1-2005. For an exception, see Act Sec. 835(c)(2), below.

H.R. 4520, § 835(c)(2), provides:

(2) EXCEPTION FOR EXISTING FASITS.—Paragraph (1) shall not apply to any FASIT in existence on the date of the enactment of this Act to the extent that regular interests issued by the FASIT before such date continue to remain outstanding in accordance with the original terms of issuance.

[¶ 5495] CODE SEC. 613. PERCENTAGE DEPLETION.

(a) GENERAL RULE.—In the case of the mines, wells, and other natural deposits listed in subsection (b), the allowance for depletion under section 611 shall be the percentage, specified in subsection (b), of the gross income from the property excluding from such gross income an amount equal to any rents or royalties paid or incurred by the taxpayer in respect of the property. Such allowance shall not exceed 50 percent (100 percent in the case of oil and gas properties) of the taxpayer's taxable income from the property (computed without allowances for depletion *and without the deduction under section 199*). For purposes of the preceding sentence, the allowable deductions taken into account with respect to expenses of mining in computing the taxable income from the property shall be decreased by an amount equal to so much of any gain which (1) is treated under section 1245 (relating to gain from disposition of certain depreciable property) as ordinary income, and (2) is properly allocable to the property. In no case shall the allowance for depletion under section 611 be less than it would be if computed without reference to this section.

* * *

[CCH Explanation at ¶210.]

Amendments

• **2004, American Jobs Creation Act of 2004 (H.R. 4520)**

H.R. 4520, §102(d)(6):

Amended Code Sec. 613(a) by inserting "and without the deduction under section 199" after "without allowances for

depletion". **Effective** for tax years beginning after 12-31-2004.

[¶5500] CODE SEC. 631. GAIN OR LOSS IN THE CASE OF TIMBER, COAL, OR DOMESTIC IRON ORE.

* * *

(b) DISPOSAL OF TIMBER.—In the case of the disposal of timber held for more than 1 year before such disposal, by the owner thereof under any form or type of contract by virtue of which such owner *either retains an economic interest in such timber or makes an outright sale of such timber*, the difference between the amount realized from the disposal of such timber and the adjusted depletion basis thereof, shall be considered as though it were a gain or loss, as the case may be, on the sale of such timber. In determining the gross income, the adjusted gross income, or the taxable income of the lessee, the deductions allowable with respect to rents and royalties shall be determined without regard to the provisions of this subsection. *In the case of disposal of timber with a retained economic interest, the date of disposal* of such timber shall be deemed to be the date such timber is cut, but if payment is made to the owner under the contract before such timber is cut the owner may elect to treat the date of such payment as the date of disposal of such timber. For purposes of this subsection, the term "owner" means any person who owns an interest in such timber, including a sublessor and a holder of a contract to cut timber.

* * *

[CCH Explanation at ¶750. Committee Reports at ¶10,380.]

Amendments

• **2004, American Jobs Creation Act of 2004 (H.R. 4520)**

H.R. 4520, §315(a):

Amended Code Sec. 631(b) by striking "retains an economic interest in such timber" and inserting "either retains an economic interest in such timber or makes an outright sale of such timber". **Effective** for sales after 12-31-2004.

H.R. 4520, §315(b)(1):

Amended Code Sec. 631(b) by striking "The date of disposal" in the third sentence and inserting "In the case of

disposal of timber with a retained economic interest, the date of disposal". **Effective** for sales after 12-31-2004.

H.R. 4520, §315(b)(2):

Amended Code Sec. 631(b) by striking "WITH A RETAINED ECONOMIC INTEREST" after "DISPOSAL OF TIMBER" in the heading. **Effective** for sales after 12-31-2004.

[¶5505] CODE SEC. 704. PARTNER'S DISTRIBUTIVE SHARE.

* * *

(c) CONTRIBUTED PROPERTY.—

(1) IN GENERAL.—Under regulations prescribed by the Secretary—

(A) income, gain, loss, and deduction with respect to property contributed to the partnership by a partner shall be shared among the partners so as to take account of the variation between the basis of the property to the partnership and its fair market value at the time of contribution,

(B) if any property so contributed is distributed (directly or indirectly) by the partnership (other than to the contributing partner) within 7 years of being contributed—

(i) the contributing partner shall be treated as recognizing gain or loss (as the case may be) from the sale of such property in an amount equal to the gain or loss which would have been allocated to such partner under subparagraph (A) by reason of the variation described in subparagraph (A) if the property had been sold at its fair market value at the time of the distribution,

(ii) the character of such gain or loss shall be determined by reference to the character of the gain or loss which would have resulted if such property had been sold by the partnership to the distributee, and

(iii) appropriate adjustments shall be made to the adjusted basis of the contributing partner's interest in the partnership and to the adjusted basis of the property distributed to reflect any gain or loss recognized under this subparagraph, *and*

(C) if any property so contributed has a built-in loss—

(i) such built-in loss shall be taken into account only in determining the amount of items allocated to the contributing partner, and

(ii) except as provided in regulations, in determining the amount of items allocated to other partners, the basis of the contributed property in the hands of the partnership shall be treated as being equal to its fair market value at the time of contribution.

For purposes of subparagraph (C), the term "built-in loss" means the excess of the adjusted basis of the property (determined without regard to subparagraph (C)(ii)) over its fair market value at the time of contribution.

* * *

[CCH Explanation at ¶ 960. Committee Reports at ¶ 11,160.]

Amendments

• **2004, American Jobs Creation Act of 2004 (H.R. 4520)**

H.R. 4520, § 833(a):

Amended Code Sec. 704(c)(1) by striking "and" at the end of subparagraph (A), by striking the period at the end of subparagraph (B) and inserting ", and", and by adding at the end a new subparagraph (C). **Effective** for contributions made after the date of the enactment of this Act.

[¶ 5510] CODE SEC. 709. TREATMENT OF ORGANIZATION AND SYNDICATION FEES.

* * *

(b) DEDUCTION OF ORGANIZATION FEES.—

(1) ALLOWANCE OF DEDUCTION.—If a taxpayer elects the application of this subsection (in accordance with regulations prescribed by the Secretary) with respect to any organizational expenses—

(A) the taxpayer shall be allowed a deduction for the taxable year in which the partnership begins business in an amount equal to the lesser of—

(i) the amount of organizational expenses with respect to the partnership, or

(ii) $5,000, reduced (but not below zero) by the amount by which such organizational expenses exceed $50,000, and

(B) the remainder of such organizational expenses shall be allowed as a deduction ratably over the 180-month period beginning with the month in which the partnership begins business.

(2) DISPOSITIONS BEFORE CLOSE OF AMORTIZATION PERIOD.—In any case in which a partnership is liquidated before the end of the period to which paragraph (1)(B) applies, any deferred expenses attributable to the partnership which were not allowed as a deduction by reason of this section may be deducted to the extent allowable under section 165.

*(3) ORGANIZATIONAL EXPENSES DEFINED.—*The organizational expenses to which paragraph (1) applies, are expenditures which—

(A) are incident to the creation of the partnership;

(B) are chargeable to capital account; and

(C) are of a character which, if expended incident to the creation of a partnership having an ascertainable life, would be amortized over such life.

* * *

[CCH Explanation at ¶ 350. Committee Reports at ¶ 11,740.]

Amendments

• **2004, American Jobs Creation Act of 2004 (H.R. 4520)**

H.R. 4520, § 902(c)(1):

Amended Code Sec. 709(b) by redesignating paragraph (2) as paragraph (3) and by amending paragraph (1) [and inserting a new paragraph (2)]. **Effective** for amounts paid or incurred after the date of the enactment of this Act. Prior to amendment, Code Sec. 709(b)(1) read as follows:

(1) DEDUCTION.—Amounts paid or incurred to organize a partnership may, at the election of the partnership (made in accordance with regulations prescribed by the Secretary), be

treated as deferred expenses. Such deferred expenses shall be allowed as a deduction ratably over such period of not less than 60 months as may be selected by the partnership (beginning with the month in which the partnership begins business), or if the partnership is liquidated before the end of such 60-month period, such deferred expenses (to the extent not deducted under this section) may be deducted to the extent provided in section 165.

H.R. 4520, § 902(c)(2):

Amended Code Sec. 709(b) by striking "AMORTIZATION" and inserting "DEDUCTION" in the heading. **Effective** for amounts paid or incurred after the date of the enactment of this Act.

[¶ 5515] CODE SEC. 734. *ADJUSTMENT TO BASIS OF UNDISTRIBUTED PARTNERSHIP PROPERTY WHERE SECTION 754 ELECTION OR SUBSTANTIAL BASIS REDUCTION.*

(a) GENERAL RULE.—The basis of partnership property shall not be adjusted as the result of a distribution of property to a partner unless the election, provided in section 754 (relating to optional adjustment to basis of partnership property), is in effect with respect to such partnership *or unless there is a substantial basis reduction.*

[CCH Explanation at ¶ 960. Committee Reports at ¶ 11,160.]

Amendments

• **2004, American Jobs Creation Act of 2004 (H.R. 4520)**

H.R. 4520, § 833(c)(1):

Amended Code Sec. 734(a) by inserting before the period "or unless there is a substantial basis reduction". **Effective** for distributions after the date of the enactment of this Act.

H.R. 4520, § 833(c)(5)(A):

Amended the heading for Code Sec. 734. **Effective** for distributions after the date of the enactment of this Act. Prior to amendment, the heading for Code Sec. 734 read as follows:

SEC. 734. OPTIONAL ADJUSTMENT TO BASIS OF UN-DISTRIBUTED PARTNERSHIP PROPERTY.

(b) METHOD OF ADJUSTMENT.—In the case of a distribution of property to a partner, a partnership, with respect to which the election provided in section 754 is in effect *or unless there is a substantial basis reduction,* shall—

(1) increase the adjusted basis of partnership property by—

(A) the amount of any gain recognized to the distributee partner with respect to such distribution under section 731(a)(1), and

(B) in the case of distributed property to which section 732(a)(2) or (b) applies, the excess of the adjusted basis of the distributed property to the partnership immediately before the distribution (as adjusted by section 732(d)) over the basis of the distributed property to the distributee, as determined under section 732, or

(2) decrease the adjusted basis of partnership property by—

(A) the amount of any loss recognized to the distributee partner with respect to such distribution under section 731(a)(2), and

(B) in the case of distributed property to which section 732(b) applies, the excess of the basis of the distributed property to the distributee, as determined under section 732, over the adjusted basis of the distributed property to the partnership immediately before such distribution (as adjusted by section 732(d)).

Paragraph (1)(B) shall not apply to any distributed property which is an interest in another partnership with respect to which the election provided in section 754 is not in effect.

* * *

[CCH Explanation at ¶ 960. Committee Reports at ¶ 11,160.]

Amendments

• **2004, American Jobs Creation Act of 2004 (H.R. 4520)**

H.R. 4520, § 833(c)(2):

Amended Code Sec. 734(b) by inserting "or unless there is a substantial basis reduction" after "section 754 is in effect".

Effective for distributions after the date of the enactment of this Act.

(d) SUBSTANTIAL BASIS REDUCTION.—

(1) IN GENERAL.—*For purposes of this section, there is a substantial basis reduction with respect to a distribution if the sum of the amounts described in subparagraphs (A) and (B) of subsection (b)(2) exceeds $250,000.*

(2) REGULATIONS.—

For regulations to carry out this subsection, see section 743(d)(2).

[CCH Explanation at ¶ 960. Committee Reports at ¶ 11,160.]
Amendments
• **2004, American Jobs Creation Act of 2004 (H.R. 4520)**

H.R. 4520, § 833(c)(3):

Amended Code Sec. 734 by adding at the end a new subsection (d). **Effective** for distributions after the date of the enactment of this Act.

(e) EXCEPTION FOR SECURITIZATION PARTNERSHIPS.—*For purposes of this section, a securitization partnership (as defined in section 743(f)) shall not be treated as having a substantial basis reduction with respect to any distribution of property to a partner.*

* * *

[CCH Explanation at ¶ 960. Committee Reports at ¶ 11,160.]
Amendments
• **2004, American Jobs Creation Act of 2004 (H.R. 4520)**

H.R. 4520, § 833(c)(4):

Amended Code Sec. 734 by inserting after subsection (d) a new subsection (e). **Effective** for distributions after the date of the enactment of this Act.

[¶ 5520] CODE SEC. 743. *SPECIAL RULES WHERE SECTION 754 ELECTION OR SUBSTANTIAL BUILT-IN LOSS.*

(a) GENERAL RULE.—The basis of partnership property shall not be adjusted as the result of a transfer of an interest in a partnership by sale or exchange or on the death of a partner unless the election provided by section 754 (relating to optional adjustment to basis of partnership property) is in effect with respect to such partnership *or unless the partnership has a substantial built-in loss immediately after such transfer.*

[CCH Explanation at ¶ 960. Committee Reports at ¶ 11,160.]
Amendments
• **2004, American Jobs Creation Act of 2004 (H.R. 4520)**

H.R. 4520, § 833(b)(1):

Amended Code Sec. 743(a) by inserting before the period "or unless the partnership has a substantial built-in loss immediately after such transfer". **Effective** for transfers after the date of the enactment of this Act. For a transition rule, see Act Sec. 833(d)(2)(B), below.

H.R. 4520, § 833(b)(6)(A):

Amended the heading for Code Sec. 743. **Effective** for transfers after the date of the enactment of this Act. For a transition rule, see Act Sec. 833(d)(2)(B), below. Prior to amendment, the heading for Code Sec. 743 read as follows:

SEC. 743. OPTIONAL ADJUSTMENT TO BASIS OF PARTNERSHIP PROPERTY.

H.R. 4520, § 833(d)(2)(B), provides:

(B) TRANSITION RULE.—In the case of an electing investment partnership which is in existence on June 4, 2004, section 743(e)(6)(H) of the Internal Revenue Code of 1986, as added by this section, shall not apply to such partnership and section 743(e)(6)(I) of such Code, as so added, shall be applied by substituting "20 years" for "15 years".

(b) ADJUSTMENT TO BASIS OF PARTNERSHIP PROPERTY.—In the case of a transfer of an interest in a partnership by sale or exchange or upon the death of a partner, a partnership with respect to which the election provided in section 754 is in effect *or which has a substantial built-in loss immediately after such transfer* shall—

(1) increase the adjusted basis of the partnership property by the excess of the basis to the transferee partner of his interest in the partnership over his proportionate share of the adjusted basis of the partnership property, or

(2) decrease the adjusted basis of the partnership property by the excess of the transferee partner's proportionate share of the adjusted basis of the partnership property over the basis of his interest in the partnership.

Under regulations prescribed by the Secretary, such increase or decrease shall constitute an adjustment to the basis of partnership property with respect to the transferee partner only. A partner's proportionate share of the adjusted basis of partnership property shall be determined in accordance with his interest in partnership capital and, in the case of property contributed to the partnership by a partner, section 704(c) (relating to contributed property) shall apply in determining such share. In the case of an adjustment under this subsection to the basis of partnership property subject to depletion, any depletion allowable shall be determined separately for the transferee partner with respect to his interest in such property.

* * *

[CCH Explanation at ¶ 960. Committee Reports at ¶ 11,160.]

Amendments

• **2004, American Jobs Creation Act of 2004 (H.R. 4520)**

H.R. 4520, § 833(b)(2):

Amended Code Sec. 743(b) by inserting "or which has a substantial built-in loss immediately after such transfer" after "section 754 is in effect". **Effective** for transfers after the date of the enactment of this Act. For a transition rule, see Act Sec. 833(d)(2)(B), below.

H.R. 4520, § 833(d)(2)(B), provides:

(B) TRANSITION RULE.—In the case of an electing investment partnership which is in existence on June 4, 2004, section 743(e)(6)(H) of the Internal Revenue Code of 1986, as added by this section, shall not apply to such partnership and section 743(e)(6)(I) of such Code, as so added, shall be applied by substituting "20 years" for "15 years".

(d) SUBSTANTIAL BUILT-IN LOSS.—

(1) IN GENERAL.—For purposes of this section, a partnership has a substantial built-in loss with respect to a transfer of an interest in a partnership if the partnership's adjusted basis in the partnership property exceeds by more than $250,000 the fair market value of such property.

(2) REGULATIONS.—The Secretary shall prescribe such regulations as may be appropriate to carry out the purposes of paragraph (1) and section 734(d), including regulations aggregating related partnerships and disregarding property acquired by the partnership in an attempt to avoid such purposes.

[CCH Explanation at ¶ 960. Committee Reports at ¶ 11,160.]

Amendments

• **2004, American Jobs Creation Act of 2004 (H.R. 4520)**

H.R. 4520, § 833(b)(3):

Amended Code Sec. 743 by adding at the end a new subsection (d). **Effective** for transfers after the date of the enactment of this Act. For a transition rule, see Act Sec. 833(d)(2)(B), below.

H.R. 4520, § 833(d)(2)(B), provides:

(B) TRANSITION RULE.—In the case of an electing investment partnership which is in existence on June 4, 2004, section 743(e)(6)(H) of the Internal Revenue Code of 1986, as added by this section, shall not apply to such partnership and section 743(e)(6)(I) of such Code, as so added, shall be applied by substituting "20 years" for "15 years".

(e) ALTERNATIVE RULES FOR ELECTING INVESTMENT PARTNERSHIPS.—

(1) NO ADJUSTMENT OF PARTNERSHIP BASIS.—For purposes of this section, an electing investment partnership shall not be treated as having a substantial built-in loss with respect to any transfer occurring while the election under paragraph (6)(A) is in effect.

(2) LOSS DEFERRAL FOR TRANSFEREE PARTNER.—In the case of a transfer of an interest in an electing investment partnership, the transferee partner's distributive share of losses (without regard to gains) from the sale or exchange of partnership property shall not be allowed except to the extent that it is established that such losses exceed the loss (if any) recognized by the transferor (or any prior transferor to the extent not fully offset by a prior disallowance under this paragraph) on the transfer of the partnership interest.

(3) NO REDUCTION IN PARTNERSHIP BASIS.—Losses disallowed under paragraph (2) shall not decrease the transferee partner's basis in the partnership interest.

(4) EFFECT OF TERMINATION OF PARTNERSHIP.—This subsection shall be applied without regard to any termination of a partnership under section 708(b)(1)(B).

(5) CERTAIN BASIS REDUCTIONS TREATED AS LOSSES.—In the case of a transferee partner whose basis in property distributed by the partnership is reduced under section 732(a)(2), the amount of the loss

recognized by the transferor on the transfer of the partnership interest which is taken into account under paragraph (2) shall be reduced by the amount of such basis reduction.

(6) ELECTING INVESTMENT PARTNERSHIP.—*For purposes of this subsection, the term "electing investment partnership" means any partnership if—*

(A) *the partnership makes an election to have this subsection apply,*

(B) *the partnership would be an investment company under section 3(a)(1)(A) of the Investment Company Act of 1940 but for an exemption under paragraph (1) or (7) of section 3(c) of such Act,*

(C) *such partnership has never been engaged in a trade or business,*

(D) *substantially all of the assets of such partnership are held for investment,*

(E) *at least 95 percent of the assets contributed to such partnership consist of money,*

(F) *no assets contributed to such partnership had an adjusted basis in excess of fair market value at the time of contribution,*

(G) *all partnership interests of such partnership are issued by such partnership pursuant to a private offering before the date which is 24 months after the date of the first capital contribution to such partnership,*

(H) *the partnership agreement of such partnership has substantive restrictions on each partner's ability to cause a redemption of the partner's interest, and*

(I) *the partnership agreement of such partnership provides for a term that is not in excess of 15 years.*

The election described in subparagraph (A), once made, shall be irrevocable except with the consent of the Secretary.

(7) REGULATIONS.—*The Secretary shall prescribe such regulations as may be appropriate to carry out the purposes of this subsection, including regulations for applying this subsection to tiered partnerships.*

[CCH Explanation at ¶ 960. Committee Reports at ¶ 11,160.]

Amendments

• **2004, American Jobs Creation Act of 2004 (H.R. 4520)**

H.R. 4520, § 833(b)(4)(A):

Amended Code Sec. 743 by adding after subsection (d) a new subsection (e). **Effective** for transfers after the date of the enactment of this Act. For a transition rule, see Act Sec. 833(d)(2)(B), below.

H.R. 4520, § 833(d)(2)(B), provides:

(B) TRANSITION RULE.—In the case of an electing investment partnership which is in existence on June 4, 2004, section 743(e)(6)(H) of the Internal Revenue Code of 1986, as added by this section, shall not apply to such partnership and section 743(e)(6)(I) of such Code, as so added, shall be applied by substituting "20 years" for "15 years".

(f) EXCEPTION FOR SECURITIZATION PARTNERSHIPS.—

(1) NO ADJUSTMENT OF PARTNERSHIP BASIS.—*For purposes of this section, a securitization partnership shall not be treated as having a substantial built-in loss with respect to any transfer.*

(2) SECURITIZATION PARTNERSHIP.—*For purposes of paragraph (1), the term "securitization partnership" means any partnership the sole business activity of which is to issue securities which provide for a fixed principal (or similar) amount and which are primarily serviced by the cash flows of a discrete pool (either fixed or revolving) of receivables or other financial assets that by their terms convert into cash in a finite period, but only if the sponsor of the pool reasonably believes that the receivables and other financial assets comprising the pool are not acquired so as to be disposed of.*

[CCH Explanation at ¶ 960. Committee Reports at ¶ 11,160.]

Amendments

• **2004, American Jobs Creation Act of 2004 (H.R. 4520)**

H.R. 4520, § 833(b)(5):

Amended Code Sec. 743 by adding after subsection (e) a new subsection (f). **Effective** for transfers after the date of the enactment of this Act. For a transition rule, see Act Sec. 833(d)(2)(B), below.

H.R. 4520, § 833(d)(2)(B), provides:

(B) TRANSITION RULE.—In the case of an electing investment partnership which is in existence on June 4, 2004, section 743(e)(6)(H) of the Internal Revenue Code of 1986, as added by this section, shall not apply to such partnership and section 743(e)(6)(I) of such Code, as so added, shall be applied by substituting "20 years" for "15 years".

[¶ 5525] CODE SEC. 751. UNREALIZED RECEIVABLES AND INVENTORY ITEMS.

* * *

(d) INVENTORY ITEMS.—For purposes of this subchapter, the term "inventory items" means—

(1) property of the partnership of the kind described in section 1221(a)(1),

(2) any other property of the partnership which, on sale or exchange by the partnership, would be considered property other than a capital asset and other than property described in section 1231, *and*

(3) any other property held by the partnership which, if held by the selling or distributee partner, would be considered property of the type described in *paragraph (1) or (2)*.

* * *

[CCH Explanation at ¶ 490. Committee Reports at ¶ 10,690.]

Amendments

• **2004, American Jobs Creation Act of 2004 (H.R. 4520)**

H.R. 4520, § 413(c)(11):

Amended Code Sec. 751(d) by adding "and" at the end of paragraph (2), by striking paragraph (3), by redesignating paragraph (4) as paragraph (3), and by striking "paragraph (1), (2), or (3)" in paragraph (3) (as so redesignated) and

inserting "paragraph (1) or (2)". **Effective** for tax years of foreign corporations beginning after 12-31-2004, and for tax years of United States shareholders with or within which such tax years of foreign corporations end. Prior to being stricken, Code Sec. 751(d)(3) read as follows:

(3) any other property of the partnership which, if sold or exchanged by the partnership, would result in a gain taxable under subsection (a) of section 1246 (relating to gain on foreign investment company stock), and

[¶ 5530] CODE SEC. 755. RULES FOR ALLOCATION OF BASIS.

* * *

(c) NO ALLOCATION OF BASIS DECREASE TO STOCK OF CORPORATE PARTNER.—In making an allocation under subsection (a) of any decrease in the adjusted basis of partnership property under section 734(b)—

(1) no allocation may be made to stock in a corporation (or any person related (within the meaning of sections 267(b) and 707(b)(1)) to such corporation) which is a partner in the partnership, and

(2) any amount not allocable to stock by reason of paragraph (1) shall be allocated under subsection (a) to other partnership property.

Gain shall be recognized to the partnership to the extent that the amount required to be allocated under paragraph (2) to other partnership property exceeds the aggregate adjusted basis of such other property immediately before the allocation required by paragraph (2).

* * *

[CCH Explanation at ¶ 965. Committee Reports at ¶ 11,170.]

Amendments

• **2004, American Jobs Creation Act of 2004 (H.R. 4520)**

H.R. 4520, § 834(a):

Amended Code Sec. 755 by adding at the end a new subsection (c). **Effective** for distributions after the date of the enactment of this Act.

[¶ 5535] CODE SEC. 815. DISTRIBUTIONS TO SHAREHOLDERS FROM PRE-1984 POLICYHOLDERS SURPLUS ACCOUNT.

* * *

(g) SPECIAL RULES APPLICABLE DURING 2005 AND 2006.—In the case of any taxable year of a stock life insurance company beginning after December 31, 2004, and before January 1, 2007—

(1) the amount under subsection (a)(2) for such taxable year shall be treated as zero, and

(2) notwithstanding subsection (b), in determining any subtractions from an account under subsections (c)(3) and (d)(3), any distribution to shareholders during such taxable year shall be treated as made first out of the policyholders surplus account, then out of the shareholders surplus account, and finally out of other accounts.

* * *

[CCH Explanation at ¶1125. Committee Reports at ¶10,870.]

Amendments

• 2004, American Jobs Creation Act of 2004 (H.R. 4520)

H.R. 4520, §705(a):

Amended Code Sec. 815 by adding at the end a new subsection (g). **Effective** for tax years beginning after 12-31-2004.

[¶5540] CODE SEC. 845. CERTAIN REINSURANCE AGREEMENTS.

(a) ALLOCATION IN CASE OF REINSURANCE AGREEMENT INVOLVING TAX AVOIDANCE OR EVASION.—In the case of 2 or more related persons (within the meaning of section 482) who are parties to a reinsurance agreement (or where one of the parties to a reinsurance agreement is, with respect to any contract covered by the agreement, in effect an agent of another party to such agreement or a conduit between related persons), the Secretary may—

(1) allocate between or among such persons income (whether investment income, premium, or otherwise), deductions, assets, reserves, credits, and other items related to such agreement,

(2) recharacterize any such items, or

(3) make any other adjustment,

if he determines that such allocation, recharacterization, or adjustment is necessary to reflect the proper *amount, source, or character* of the taxable income (or any item described in paragraph (1) relating to such taxable income) of each such person.

* * *

[CCH Explanation at ¶515. Committee Reports at ¶10,990.]

Amendments

• 2004, American Jobs Creation Act of 2004 (H.R. 4520)

H.R. 4520, §803(a):

Amended Code Sec. 845(a) by striking "source and character" and inserting "amount, source, or character". **Effec**-tive for any risk reinsured after the date of the enactment of this Act.

[¶5545] CODE SEC. 851. DEFINITION OF REGULATED INVESTMENT COMPANY.

* * *

(b) LIMITATIONS.—A corporation shall not be considered a regulated investment company for any taxable year unless—

(1) it files with its return for the taxable year an election to be a regulated investment company or has made such election for a previous taxable year;

(2) *at least 90 percent of its gross income is derived from—*

(A) dividends, interest, payments with respect to securities loans (as defined in section 512(a)(5)), and gains from the sale or other disposition of stock or securities (as defined in section 2(a)(36) of the Investment Company Act of 1940, as amended) or foreign currencies, or other income (including but not limited to gains from options, futures or forward contracts) derived with respect to its business of investing in such stock, securities, or currencies, and

(B) net income derived from an interest in a qualified publicly traded partnership (as defined in subsection (h)); and

(3) at the close of each quarter of the taxable year—

(A) at least 50 percent of the value of its total assets is represented by—

(i) cash and cash items (including receivables), Government securities and securities of other regulated investment companies, and

(ii) other securities for purposes of this calculation limited, except and to the extent provided in subsection (e), in respect of any one issuer to an amount not greater in value than 5 percent of the value of the total assets of the taxpayer and to not more than 10 percent of the outstanding voting securities of such issuer, and

(B) *not more than 25 percent of the value of its total assets is invested in—*

(i) the securities (other than Government securities or the securities of other regulated investment companies) of any one issuer,

(ii) the securities (other than the securities of other regulated investment companies) of two or more issuers which the taxpayer controls and which are determined, under regulations prescribed by the Secretary, to be engaged in the same or similar trades or businesses or related trades or businesses, or

(iii) the securities of one or more qualified publicly traded partnerships (as defined in subsection (h)).

For purposes of paragraph (2), the Secretary may by regulation exclude from qualifying income foreign currency gains which are not directly related to the company's principal business of investing in stock or securities (or options and futures with respect to stock or securities). For purposes of paragraph (2), there shall be treated as dividends amounts included in gross income under section 951(a)(1)(A)(i) or 1293(a) for the taxable year to the extent that, under section 959(a)(1) or 1293(c) (as the case may be), there is a distribution out of the earnings and profits of the taxable year which are attributable to the amounts so included. For purposes of paragraph (2), amounts excludable from gross income under section 103(a) shall be treated as included in gross income. Income derived from a partnership *(other than a qualified publicly traded partnership as defined in subsection (h))* or trust shall be treated as described in paragraph (2) only to the extent such income is attributable to items of income of the partnership or trust (as the case may be) which would be described in paragraph (2) if realized by the regulated investment company in the same manner as realized by the partnership or trust.

[CCH Explanation at ¶1105. Committee Reports at ¶10,460.]

Amendments

• **2004, American Jobs Creation Act of 2004 (H.R. 4520)**

H.R. 4520, §331(a):

Amended Code Sec. 851(b)(2). **Effective** for tax years beginning after the date of the enactment of this Act. Prior to amendment, Code Sec. 851(b)(2) read as follows:

(2) at least 90 percent of its gross income is derived from dividends, interest, payments with respect to securities loans (as defined in section 512(a)(5)), and gains from the sale or other disposition of stock or securities (as defined in section 2(a)(36) of the Investment Company Act of 1940, as amended) or foreign currencies, or other income (including but not limited to gains from options, futures, or forward contracts) derived with respect to its business of investing in such stock, securities, or currencies; and

H.R. 4520, §331(b):

Amended Code Sec. 851(b) by inserting "(other than a qualified publicly traded partnership as defined in subsec-

tion (h))" after "derived from a partnership" in the last sentence. **Effective** for tax years beginning after the date of the enactment of this Act.

H.R. 4520, §331(f):

Amended Code Sec. 851(b)(3)(B). **Effective** for tax years beginning after the date of the enactment of this Act. Prior to amendment, Code Sec. 851(b)(3)(B) read as follows:

(B) not more than 25 percent of the value of its total assets is invested in the securities (other than Government securities or the securities of other regulated investment companies) of any one issuer, or of two or more issuers which the taxpayer controls and which are determined, under regulations prescribed by the Secretary, to be engaged in the same or similar trades or businesses or related trades or businesses.

(c) RULES APPLICABLE TO SUBSECTION (b)(3).—For purposes of subsection (b)(3) and this subsection—

* * *

(5) The term "outstanding voting securities of such issuer" shall include the equity securities of a qualified publicly traded partnership (as defined in subsection (h)).

(6) All other terms shall have the same meaning as when used in the Investment Company Act of 1940, as amended.

* * *

[CCH Explanation at ¶1105. Committee Reports at ¶10,460.]

Amendments

• **2004, American Jobs Creation Act of 2004 (H.R. 4520)**

H.R. 4520, §331(c):

Amended Code Sec. 851(c) by redesignating paragraph (5) as paragraph (6) and inserting after paragraph (4) a new

paragraph (5). **Effective** for tax years beginning after the date of the enactment of this Act.

(h) QUALIFIED PUBLICLY TRADED PARTNERSHIP.—For purposes of this section, the term "qualified publicly traded partnership" means a publicly traded partnership described in section 7704(b) other than a partnership which would satisfy the gross income requirements of section 7704(c)(2) if qualifying income included only income described in subsection (b)(2)(A).

* * *

[CCH Explanation at ¶ 1105. Committee Reports at ¶ 10,460.]
Amendments
• **2004, American Jobs Creation Act of 2004 (H.R. 4520)**

H.R. 4520, § 331(d):

Amended Code Sec. 851 by adding at the end a new subsection (h). **Effective** for tax years beginning after the date of the enactment of this Act.

[¶ 5550] CODE SEC. 856. DEFINITION OF REAL ESTATE INVESTMENT TRUST.

* * *

(c) LIMITATIONS.—A corporation, trust, or association shall not be considered a real estate investment trust for any taxable year unless—

* * *

(5) For purposes of this part—

* * *

(E) A regular or residual interest in a REMIC shall be treated as a real estate asset, and any amount includible in gross income with respect to such an interest shall be treated as interest on an obligation secured by a mortgage on real property; except that, if less than 95 percent of the assets of such REMIC are real estate assets (determined as if the real estate investment trust held such assets), such real estate investment trust shall be treated as holding directly (and as receiving directly) its proportionate share of the assets and income of the REMIC. For purposes of determining whether any interest in a REMIC qualifies under the preceding sentence, any interest held by such REMIC in another REMIC shall be treated as a real estate asset under principles similar to the principles of the preceding sentence, except that, if such REMIC's are part of a tiered structure, they shall be treated as one REMIC for purposes of this subparagraph.

* * *

(G) TREATMENT OF CERTAIN HEDGING INSTRUMENTS.—Except to the extent provided by regulations, any income of a real estate investment trust from a hedging transaction (as defined in clause (ii) or (iii) of section 1221(b)(2)(A)) which is clearly identified pursuant to section 1221(a)(7), including gain from the sale or disposition of such a transaction, shall not constitute gross income under paragraph (2) to the extent that the transaction hedges any indebtedness incurred or to be incurred by the trust to acquire or carry real estate assets.

(6) A corporation, trust, or association which fails to meet the requirements of paragraph (2) or (3), or of both such paragraphs, for any taxable year shall nevertheless be considered to have satisfied the requirements of such paragraphs for such taxable year if—

(A) following the corporation, trust, or association's identification of the failure to meet the requirements of paragraph (2) or (3), or of both such paragraphs, for any taxable year, a description of each item of its gross income described in such paragraphs is set forth in a schedule for such taxable year filed in accordance with regulations prescribed by the Secretary, and

(B) the failure to meet the requirements of paragraph (2) or (3), or of both such paragraphs, is due to reasonable cause and not due to willful neglect.

(7) RULES OF APPLICATION FOR FAILURE TO SATISFY PARAGRAPH (4).—

(A) DE MINIMIS FAILURE.—A corporation, trust, or association that fails to meet the requirements of paragraph (4)(B)(iii) for a particular quarter shall nevertheless be considered to have satisfied the requirements of such paragraph for such quarter if—

(i) such failure is due to the ownership of assets the total value of which does not exceed the lesser of—

(I) 1 percent of the total value of the trust's assets at the end of the quarter for which such measurement is done, and

(II) $10,000,000, and

(ii)(I) the corporation, trust, or association, following the identification of such failure, disposes of assets in order to meet the requirements of such paragraph within 6 months after the last day of the quarter in which the corporation, trust or association's identification of the failure to satisfy the requirements of such paragraph occurred or such other time period prescribed by the Secretary and in the manner prescribed by the Secretary, or

(II) the requirements of such paragraph are otherwise met within the time period specified in subclause (I).

(B) FAILURES EXCEEDING DE MINIMIS AMOUNT.—A corporation, trust, or association that fails to meet the requirements of paragraph (4) for a particular quarter shall nevertheless be considered to have satisfied the requirements of such paragraph for such quarter if—

(i) such failure involves the ownership of assets the total value of which exceeds the de minimis standard described in subparagraph (A)(i) at the end of the quarter for which such measurement is done,

(ii) following the corporation, trust, or association's identification of the failure to satisfy the requirements of such paragraph for a particular quarter, a description of each asset that causes the corporation, trust, or association to fail to satisfy the requirements of such paragraph at the close of such quarter of any taxable year is set forth in a schedule for such quarter filed in accordance with regulations prescribed by the Secretary,

(iii) the failure to meet the requirements of such paragraph for a particular quarter is due to reasonable cause and not due to willful neglect,

(iv) the corporation, trust, or association pays a tax computed under subparagraph (C), and

(v)(I) the corporation, trust, or association disposes of the assets set forth on the schedule specified in clause (ii) within 6 months after the last day of the quarter in which the corporation, trust or association's identification of the failure to satisfy the requirements of such paragraph occurred or such other time period prescribed by the Secretary and in the manner prescribed by the Secretary, or

(II) the requirements of such paragraph are otherwise met within the time period specified in subclause (I).

(C) TAX.—For purposes of subparagraph (B)(iv)—

(i) TAX IMPOSED.—If a corporation, trust, or association elects the application of this subparagraph, there is hereby imposed a tax on the failure described in subparagraph (B) of such corporation, trust, or association. Such tax shall be paid by the corporation, trust, or association.

(ii) TAX COMPUTED.—The amount of the tax imposed by clause (i) shall be the greater of—

(I) $50,000, or

(II) the amount determined (pursuant to regulations promulgated by the Secretary) by multiplying the net income generated by the assets described in the schedule specified in subparagraph (B)(ii) for the period specified in clause (iii) by the highest rate of tax specified in section 11.

(iii) PERIOD.—For purposes of clause (ii)(II), the period described in this clause is the period beginning on the first date that the failure to satisfy the requirements of such paragraph (4) occurs as a result of the ownership of such assets and ending on the earlier of the date on which the trust disposes of such assets or the end of the first quarter when there is no longer a failure to satisfy such paragraph (4).

(iv) ADMINISTRATIVE PROVISIONS.—For purposes of subtitle F, the taxes imposed by this subparagraph shall be treated as excise taxes with respect to which the deficiency procedures of such subtitle apply.

[CCH Explanation at ¶ 1110 and ¶ 1120. Committee Reports at ¶ 10,240 and ¶ 11,180.]

Amendments

• **2004, American Jobs Creation Act of 2004 (H.R. 4520)**

H.R. 4520, § 243(a)(1):

Amended Code Sec. 856(c) by striking paragraph (7). **Effective** for tax years beginning after 12-31-2000. Prior to being stricken, Code Sec. 856(c)(7) read as follows:

(7) STRAIGHT DEBT SAFE HARBOR IN APPLYING PARAGRAPH (4).—Securities of an issuer which are straight debt (as defined in section 1361(c)(5) without regard to subparagraph (B)(iii) thereof) shall not be taken into account in applying paragraph (4)(B)(iii)(III) if—

(A) the issuer is an individual, or

(B) the only securities of such issuer which are held by the trust or a taxable REIT subsidiary of the trust are straight debt (as so defined), or

(C) the issuer is a partnership and the trust holds at least a 20 percent profits interest in the partnership.

H.R. 4520, § 243(d):

Amended Code Sec. 856(c)(5)(G). **Effective** for tax years beginning after the date of the enactment of this Act. Prior to amendment, Code Sec. 856(c)(5)(G) read as follows:

(G) TREATMENT OF CERTAIN HEDGING INSTRUMENTS.—Except to the extent provided by regulations, any—

(i) payment to a real estate investment trust under an interest rate swap or cap agreement, option, futures contract, forward rate agreement, or any similar financial instrument, entered into by the trust in a transaction to reduce the interest rate risks with respect to any indebtedness incurred or to be incurred by the trust to acquire or carry real estate assets, and

(ii) gain from the sale or other disposition of any such investment,

(d) RENTS FROM REAL PROPERTY DEFINED.—

shall be treated as income qualifying under paragraph (2).

H.R. 4520, § 243(f)(1):

Amended Code Sec. 856(c) by inserting after paragraph (6) a new paragraph (7). **Effective** for tax years beginning after the date of the enactment of this Act.

H.R. 4520, § 243(f)(2):

Amended Code Sec. 856(c)(6) by striking subparagraphs (A) and (B), by redesignating subparagraph (C) as subparagraph (B), and by inserting before subparagraph (B) (as so redesignated) a new subparagraph (A). **Effective** for tax years beginning after the date of the enactment of this Act. Prior to being stricken, Code Sec. 856(c)(6)(A)-(B) read as follows:

(A) the nature and amount of each item of its gross income described in such paragraphs is set forth in a schedule attached to its income tax return for such taxable year;

(B) the inclusion of any incorrect information in the schedule referred to in subparagraph (A) is not due to fraud with intent to evade tax; and

H.R. 4520, § 835(b)(4):

Amended Code Sec. 856(c)(5)(E) by striking the last sentence. **Effective** 1-1-2005. For an exception, see Act Sec. 835(c)(2), below. Prior to being stricken, the last sentence of Code Sec. 856(c)(5)(E) read as follows:

The principles of the preceding provisions of this subparagraph shall apply to regular interests in a FASIT.

H.R. 4520, § 835(c)(2), provides:

(2) EXCEPTION FOR EXISTING FASITS.—Paragraph (1) shall not apply to any FASIT in existence on the date of the enactment of this Act to the extent that regular interests issued by the FASIT before such date continue to remain outstanding in accordance with the original terms of issuance.

* * *

(8) SPECIAL RULE FOR TAXABLE REIT SUBSIDIARIES.—For purposes of this subsection, amounts paid to a real estate investment trust by a taxable REIT subsidiary of such trust shall not be excluded from rents from real property by reason of paragraph (2)(B) if the requirements of either of the following subparagraphs are met:

(A) LIMITED RENTAL EXCEPTION.—

(i) IN GENERAL.—The requirements of this subparagraph are met with respect to any property if at least 90 percent of the leased space of the property is rented to persons other than taxable REIT subsidiaries of such trust and other than persons described in paragraph (2)(B).

(ii) RENTS MUST BE SUBSTANTIALLY COMPARABLE.—Clause (i) shall apply only to the extent that the amounts paid to the trust as rents from real property (as defined in paragraph (1) without regard to paragraph (2)(B)) from such property are substantially comparable to such rents paid by the other tenants of the trust's property for comparable space.

(iii) TIMES FOR TESTING RENT COMPARABILITY.—The substantial comparability requirement of clause (ii) shall be treated as met with respect to a lease to a taxable REIT subsidiary of the trust if such requirement is met under the terms of the lease—

(I) at the time such lease is entered into,

(II) at the time of each extension of the lease, including a failure to exercise a right to terminate, and

(III) at the time of any modification of the lease between the trust and the taxable REIT subsidiary if the rent under such lease is effectively increased pursuant to such modification.

Code Sec. 856(d)(8)(A)(iii)(III) **¶ 5550**

With respect to subclause (III), if the taxable REIT subsidiary of the trust is a controlled taxable REIT subsidiary of the trust, the term "rents from real property" shall not in any event include rent under such lease to the extent of the increase in such rent on account of such modification.

(iv) CONTROLLED TAXABLE REIT SUBSIDIARY.—For purposes of clause (iii), the term "controlled taxable REIT subsidiary" means, with respect to any real estate investment trust, any taxable REIT subsidiary of such trust if such trust owns directly or indirectly—

(I) stock possessing more than 50 percent of the total voting power of the outstanding stock of such subsidiary, or

(II) stock having a value of more than 50 percent of the total value of the outstanding stock of such subsidiary.

(v) CONTINUING QUALIFICATION BASED ON THIRD PARTY ACTIONS.—If the requirements of clause (i) are met at a time referred to in clause (iii), such requirements shall continue to be treated as met so long as there is no increase in the space leased to any taxable REIT subsidiary of such trust or to any person described in paragraph (2)(B).

(vi) CORRECTION PERIOD.—If there is an increase referred to in clause (v) during any calendar quarter with respect to any property, the requirements of clause (iii) shall be treated as met during the quarter and the succeeding quarter if such requirements are met at the close of such succeeding quarter.

* * *

[CCH Explanation at ¶1110. Committee Reports at ¶10,240.]

Amendments

• **2004, American Jobs Creation Act of 2004 (H.R. 4520)**

H.R. 4520, §243(b):

Amended Code Sec. 856(d)(8)(A). **Effective** for tax years beginning after 12-31-2000. Prior to amendment, Code Sec. 856(d)(8)(A) read as follows:

(A) LIMITED RENTAL EXCEPTION.—The requirements of this subparagraph are met with respect to any property if at least 90 percent of the leased space of the property is rented to persons other than taxable REIT subsidiaries of such trust and other than persons described in section 856(d)(2)(B). The preceding sentence shall apply only to the extent that the amounts paid to the trust as rents from real property (as defined in paragraph (1) without regard to paragraph (2)(B)) from such property are substantially comparable to such rents made by the other tenants of the trust's property for comparable space.

(g) TERMINATION OF ELECTION.—

(1) FAILURE TO QUALIFY.—An election under subsection (c)(1) made by a corporation, trust, or association shall terminate if the corporation, trust, or association is not a real estate investment trust to which the provisions of this part apply for the taxable year with respect to which the election is made, or for any succeeding taxable year *unless paragraph (5) applies.* Such termination shall be effective for the taxable year for which the corporation, trust, or association is not a real estate investment trust to which the provisions of this part apply, and for all succeeding taxable years.

* * *

(5) ENTITIES TO WHICH PARAGRAPH APPLIES.—This paragraph applies to a corporation, trust, or association—

(A) which is not a real estate investment trust to which the provisions of this part apply for the taxable year due to one or more failures to comply with one or more of the provisions of this part (other than subsection (c)(6) or (c)(7) of section 856),

(B) such failures are due to reasonable cause and not due to willful neglect, and

(C) if such corporation, trust, or association pays (as prescribed by the Secretary in regulations and in the same manner as tax) a penalty of $50,000 for each failure to satisfy a provision of this part due to reasonable cause and not willful neglect.

* * *

[CCH Explanation at ¶ 1110. Committee Reports at ¶ 10,240.]

Amendments

• **2004, American Jobs Creation Act of 2004 (H.R. 4520)**

H.R. 4520, § 243(f)(3)(A):

Amended Code Sec. 856(g)(1) by inserting "unless paragraph (5) applies" before the period at the end of the first sentence. **Effective** for tax years beginning after the date of the enactment of this Act.

H.R. 4520, § 243(f)(3)(B):

Amended Code Sec. 856(g) by adding at the end a new paragraph (5). **Effective** for tax years beginning after the date of the enactment of this Act.

(m) SAFE HARBOR IN APPLYING SUBSECTION (c)(4).—

(1) IN GENERAL.—In applying subclause (III) of subsection (c)(4)(B)(iii), except as otherwise determined by the Secretary in regulations, the following shall not be considered securities held by the trust:

(A) Straight debt securities of an issuer which meet the requirements of paragraph (2).

(B) Any loan to an individual or an estate.

(C) Any section 467 rental agreement (as defined in section 467(d)), other than with a person described in subsection (d)(2)(B).

(D) Any obligation to pay rents from real property (as defined in subsection (d)(1)).

(E) Any security issued by a State or any political subdivision thereof, the District of Columbia, a foreign government or any political subdivision thereof, or the Commonwealth of Puerto Rico, but only if the determination of any payment received or accrued under such security does not depend in whole or in part on the profits of any entity not described in this subparagraph or payments on any obligation issued by such an entity,

(F) Any security issued by a real estate investment trust.

(G) Any other arrangement as determined by the Secretary.

(2) SPECIAL RULES RELATING TO STRAIGHT DEBT SECURITIES.—

(A) IN GENERAL.—For purposes of paragraph (1)(A), securities meet the requirements of this paragraph if such securities are straight debt, as defined in section 1361(c)(5) (without regard to subparagraph (B)(iii) thereof).

(B) SPECIAL RULES RELATING TO CERTAIN CONTINGENCIES.—For purposes of subparagraph (A), any interest or principal shall not be treated as failing to satisfy section 1361(c)(5)(B)(i) solely by reason of the fact that—

(i) the time of payment of such interest or principal is subject to a contingency, but only if—

(I) any such contingency does not have the effect of changing the effective yield to maturity, as determined under section 1272, other than a change in the annual yield to maturity which does not exceed the greater of ¼ of 1 percent or 5 percent of the annual yield to maturity, or

(II) neither the aggregate issue price nor the aggregate face amount of the issuer's debt instruments held by the trust exceeds $1,000,000 and not more than 12 months of unaccrued interest can be required to be prepaid thereunder, or

(ii) the time or amount of payment is subject to a contingency upon a default or the exercise of a prepayment right by the issuer of the debt, but only if such contingency is consistent with customary commercial practice.

(C) SPECIAL RULES RELATING TO CORPORATE OR PARTNERSHIP ISSUERS.—In the case of an issuer which is a corporation or a partnership, securities that otherwise would be described in paragraph (1)(A) shall be considered not to be so described if the trust holding such securities and any of its controlled taxable REIT subsidiaries (as defined in subsection (d)(8)(A)(iv)) hold any securities of the issuer which—

(i) are not described in paragraph (1) (prior to the application of this subparagraph), and

(ii) have an aggregate value greater than 1 percent of the issuer's outstanding securities determined without regard to paragraph (3)(A)(i).

(3) LOOK-THROUGH RULE FOR PARTNERSHIP SECURITIES.—

(A) IN GENERAL.—For purposes of applying subclause (III) of subsection (c)(4)(B)(iii)—

Code Sec. 856(m)(3)(A)   ¶5550

(i) a trust's interest as a partner in a partnership (as defined in section 7701(a)(2)) shall not be considered a security, and

(ii) the trust shall be deemed to own its proportionate share of each of the assets of the partnership.

(B) DETERMINATION OF TRUST'S INTEREST IN PARTNERSHIP ASSETS.—For purposes of subparagraph (A), with respect to any taxable year beginning after the date of the enactment of this subparagraph—

(i) the trust's interest in the partnership assets shall be the trust's proportionate interest in any securities issued by the partnership (determined without regard to subparagraph (A)(i) and paragraph (4), but not including securities described in paragraph (1)), and

(ii) the value of any debt instrument shall be the adjusted issue price thereof, as defined in section 1272(a)(4).

(4) CERTAIN PARTNERSHIP DEBT INSTRUMENTS NOT TREATED AS A SECURITY.—For purposes of applying subclause (III) of subsection (c)(4)(B)(iii)—

(A) any debt instrument issued by a partnership and not described in paragraph (1) shall not be considered a security to the extent of the trust's interest as a partner in the partnership, and

(B) any debt instrument issued by a partnership and not described in paragraph (1) shall not be considered a security if at least 75 percent of the partnership's gross income (excluding gross income from prohibited transactions) is derived from sources referred to in subsection (c)(3).

(5) SECRETARIAL GUIDANCE.—The Secretary is authorized to provide guidance (including through the issuance of a written determination, as defined in section 6110(b)) that an arrangement shall not be considered a security held by the trust for purposes of applying subclause (III) of subsection (c)(4)(B)(iii) notwithstanding that such arrangement otherwise could be considered a security under subparagraph (F) of subsection (c)(5).

[CCH Explanation at ¶ 1110. Committee Reports at ¶ 10,240.]

Amendments

• **2004, American Jobs Creation Act of 2004 (H.R. 4520)**

H.R. 4520, § 243(a)(2):

Amended Code Sec. 856 by adding at the end a new subsection (m). **Effective** for tax years beginning after 12-31-2000.

[¶ 5555] CODE SEC. 857. TAXATION OF REAL ESTATE INVESTMENT TRUSTS AND THEIR BENEFICIARIES.

* * *

(b) METHOD OF TAXATION OF REAL ESTATE INVESTMENT TRUSTS AND HOLDERS OF SHARES OR CERTIFICATES OF BENEFICIAL INTEREST.—

* * *

(2) REAL ESTATE INVESTMENT TRUST TAXABLE INCOME.—For purposes of this part, the term "real estate investment trust taxable income" means the taxable income of the real estate investment trust, adjusted as follows:

* * *

(E) There shall be deducted an amount equal to the tax imposed by paragraphs (5) and (7) of this subsection, section 856(c)(7)(B)(iii), and section 856(g)(1). [sic] for the taxable year.

* * *

(3) CAPITAL GAINS.—

* * *

(F) CERTAIN DISTRIBUTIONS.—In the case of a shareholder of a real estate investment trust to whom section 897 does not apply by reason of the second sentence of section 897(h)(1), the amount which would be included in computing long-term capital gains for such shareholder under subparagraph (B) or (D) (without regard to this subparagraph)—

(i) shall not be included in computing such shareholder's long-term capital gains, and

(ii) *shall be included in such shareholder's gross income as a dividend from the real estate investment trust.*

* * *

(5) IMPOSITION OF TAX IN CASE OF FAILURE TO MEET CERTAIN REQUIREMENTS.—If section 856(c)(6) applies to a real estate investment trust for any taxable year, there is hereby imposed on such trust a tax in an amount equal to the greater of—

(A) the excess of—

(i) *95 percent* of the gross income (excluding gross income from prohibited transactions) of the real estate investment trust, over

* * *

(6) INCOME FROM PROHIBITED TRANSACTIONS.—

* * *

(D) CERTAIN SALES NOT TO CONSTITUTE PROHIBITED TRANSACTIONS.—*For purposes of this part, the term "prohibited transaction" does not include a sale of property which is a real estate asset (as defined in section 856(c)(5)(B)) if—*

(i) *the trust held the property for not less than 4 years in connection with the trade or business of producing timber,*

(ii) *the aggregate expenditures made by the trust, or a partner of the trust, during the 4-year period preceding the date of sale which—*

(I) *are includible in the basis of the property (other than timberland acquisition expenditures), and*

(II) *are directly related to operation of the property for the production of timber or for the preservation of the property for use as timberland,*

do not exceed 30 percent of the net selling price of the property,

(iii) *the aggregate expenditures made by the trust, or a partner of the trust, during the 4-year period preceding the date of sale which—*

(I) *are includible in the basis of the property (other than timberland acquisition expenditures), and*

(II) *are not directly related to operation of the property for the production of timber, or for the preservation of the property for use as timberland,*

do not exceed 5 percent of the net selling price of the property,

(iv)(I) *during the taxable year the trust does not make more than 7 sales of property (other than sales of foreclosure property or sales to which section 1033 applies), or*

(II) *the aggregate adjusted bases (as determined for purposes of computing earnings and profits) of property (other than sales of foreclosure property or sales to which section 1033 applies) sold during the taxable year does not exceed 10 percent of the aggregate bases (as so determined) of all of the assets of the trust as of the beginning of the taxable year,*

(v) *in the case that the requirement of clause (iv)(I) is not satisfied, substantially all of the marketing expenditures with respect to the property were made through an independent contractor (as defined in section 856(d)(3)) from whom the trust itself does not derive or receive any income, and*

(vi) *the sales price of the property sold by the trust is not based in whole or in part on income or profits, including income or profits derived from the sale or operation of such property.*

(E) SPECIAL RULES.—In applying subparagraph (C) the following special rules apply:

(i) The holding period of property acquired through foreclosure (or deed in lieu of foreclosure), or termination of the lease, includes the period for which the trust held the loan which such property secured, or the lease of such property.

(ii) In the case of a property acquired through foreclosure (or deed in lieu of foreclosure), or termination of a lease, expenditures made by, or for the account of, the mortgagor or lessee after default became imminent will be regarded as made by the trust.

(iii) Expenditures (including expenditures regarded as made directly by the trust, or indirectly by any partner of the trust, under clause (ii)) will not be taken into account if they relate to foreclosure property and did not cause the property to lose its status as foreclosure property.

(iv) Expenditures will not be taken into account if they are made solely to comply with standards or requirements of any government or governmental authority having relevant jurisdiction, or if they are made to restore the property as a result of losses arising from fire, storm or other casualty.

(v) The term "expenditures" does not include advances on a loan made by the trust.

(vi) The sale of more than one property to one buyer as part of one transaction constitutes one sale.

(vii) The term "sale" does not include any transaction in which the net selling price is less than $10,000.

(F) SALES NOT MEETING REQUIREMENTS.—In determining whether or not any sale constitutes a "prohibited transaction" for purposes of subparagraph (A), the fact that such sale does not meet the requirements of subparagraph (C) of this paragraph shall not be taken into account; and such determination, in the case of a sale not meeting such requirements, shall be made as if subparagraphs (C) and (D) had not been enacted.

(7) INCOME FROM REDETERMINED RENTS, REDETERMINED DEDUCTIONS, AND EXCESS INTEREST.—

* * *

(B) REDETERMINED RENTS.—

* * *

(ii) EXCEPTION FOR DE MINIMIS AMOUNTS.—Clause (i) shall not apply to amounts described in section 856(d)(7)(A) with respect to a property to the extent such amounts do not exceed the one percent threshold described in section 856(d)(7)(B) with respect to such property.

(iii) EXCEPTION FOR COMPARABLY PRICED SERVICES.—Clause (i) shall not apply to any service rendered by a taxable REIT subsidiary of a real estate investment trust to a tenant of such trust if—

(I) such subsidiary renders a significant amount of similar services to persons other than such trust and tenants of such trust who are unrelated (within the meaning of section 856(d)(8)(F)) to such subsidiary, trust, and tenants, but

(II) only to the extent the charge for such service so rendered is substantially comparable to the charge for the similar services rendered to persons referred to in subclause (I).

(iv) EXCEPTION FOR CERTAIN SEPARATELY CHARGED SERVICES.—Clause (i) shall not apply to any service rendered by a taxable REIT subsidiary of a real estate investment trust to a tenant of such trust if—

(I) the rents paid to the trust by tenants (leasing at least 25 percent of the net leasable space in the trust's property) who are not receiving such service from such subsidiary are substantially comparable to the rents paid by tenants leasing comparable space who are receiving such service from such subsidiary, and

(II) the charge for such service from such subsidiary is separately stated.

(v) EXCEPTION FOR CERTAIN SERVICES BASED ON SUBSIDIARY'S INCOME FROM THE SERVICES.—Clause (i) shall not apply to any service rendered by a taxable REIT subsidiary of a real estate investment trust to a tenant of such trust if the gross income of such subsidiary from such service is not less than 150 percent of such subsidiary's direct cost in furnishing or rendering the service.

(vi) EXCEPTIONS GRANTED BY SECRETARY.—The Secretary may waive the tax otherwise imposed by subparagraph (A) if the trust establishes to the satisfaction of the Secretary that rents charged to tenants were established on an arms' length basis even though a taxable REIT subsidiary of the trust provided services to such tenants.

* * *

[CCH Explanation at ¶540, ¶1110 and ¶1115. Committee Reports at ¶10,240, ¶10,440 and ¶10,740.]

Amendments

• **2004, American Jobs Creation Act of 2004 (H.R. 4520)**

H.R. 4520, §243(c):

Amended Code Sec. 857(b)(7)(B) by striking clause (ii) and by redesignating clauses (iii), (iv), (v), (vi), and (vii) as clauses (ii), (iii), (iv), (v), and (vi), respectively. **Effective** for tax years beginning after the date of the enactment of this Act. Prior to being stricken, Code Sec. 857(b)(7)(B)(ii) read as follows:

(ii) EXCEPTION FOR CERTAIN AMOUNTS.—Clause (i) shall not apply to amounts received directly or indirectly by a real estate investment trust—

(I) for services furnished or rendered by a taxable REIT subsidiary that are described in paragraph (1)(B) of section 856(d), or

(II) from a taxable REIT subsidiary that are described in paragraph (7)(C)(ii) of such section.

H.R. 4520, §243(e):

Amended Code Sec. 857(b)(5)(A)(i) by striking "90 percent" and inserting "95 percent". **Effective** for tax years beginning after the date of the enactment of this Act.

H.R. 4520, §243(f)(4):

Amended Code Sec. 857(b)(2)(E) by striking "(7)" and inserting "(7) of this subsection, section 856(c)(7)(B)(iii), and section 856(g)(1).". **Effective** for tax years beginning after the date of the enactment of this Act.

H.R. 4520, §321(a):

Amended Code Sec. 857(b)(6) by redesignating subparagraphs (D) and (E) as subparagraphs (E) and (F), respectively, and by inserting after subparagraph (C) a new subparagraph (D). **Effective** for tax years beginning after the date of the enactment of this Act.

H.R. 4520, §418(b):

Amended Code Sec. 857(b)(3) by adding at the end a new subparagraph (F). **Effective** for tax years beginning after the date of the enactment of this Act.

[¶5560] CODE SEC. 860. DEDUCTION FOR DEFICIENCY DIVIDENDS.

* * *

(e) DETERMINATION.—For purposes of this section, the term "determination" means—

(1) a decision by the Tax Court, or a judgment, decree, or other order by any court of competent jurisdiction, which has become final;

(2) a closing agreement made under section 7121;

(3) under regulations prescribed by the Secretary, an agreement signed by the Secretary and by, or on behalf of, the qualified investment entity relating to the liability of such entity for tax; *or*

(4) *a statement by the taxpayer attached to its amendment or supplement to a return of tax for the relevant tax year.*

* * *

[CCH Explanation at ¶1110. Committee Reports at ¶10,240.]

Amendments

• **2004, American Jobs Creation Act of 2004 (H.R. 4520)**

H.R. 4520, §243(f)(5):

Amended Code Sec. 860(e) by striking "or" at the end of paragraph (2), by striking the period at the end of paragraph (3) and inserting "; or", and by adding at the end a new paragraph (4). **Effective** for tax years beginning after the date of the enactment of this Act.

[¶5565] CODE SEC. 860G. OTHER DEFINITIONS AND SPECIAL RULES.

(a) DEFINITIONS.—For purposes of this part—

(1) REGULAR INTEREST.—The term "regular interest" means any interest in a REMIC which is issued on the startup day with fixed terms and which is designated as a regular interest if—

(A) such interest unconditionally entitles the holder to receive a specified principal amount (or other similar amount), and

(B) interest payments (or other similar amount), if any, with respect to such interest at or before maturity—

(i) are payable based on a fixed rate (or to the extent provided in regulations, at a variable rate), or

(ii) consist of a specified portion of the interest payments on qualified mortgages and such portion does not vary during the period such interest is outstanding.

The interest shall not fail to meet the requirements of subparagraph (A) merely because the timing (but not the amount) of the principal payments (or other similar amounts) may be contingent on the extent of prepayments on qualified mortgages and the amount of income from permitted investments. *An interest shall not fail to qualify as a regular interest solely because the specified principal amount of the regular interest (or the amount of interest accrued on the regular interest) can be reduced as a result of the nonoccurrence of 1 or more contingent payments with respect to any reverse mortgage loan held by the REMIC if, on the startup day for the REMIC, the sponsor reasonably believes that all principal and interest due under the regular interest will be paid at or prior to the liquidation of the REMIC.*

* * *

(3) QUALIFIED MORTGAGE.—The term "qualified mortgage" means—

(A) any obligation (including any participation or certificate of beneficial ownership therein) which is principally secured by an interest in real property and which—

(i) is transferred to the REMIC on the startup day in exchange for regular or residual interests in the REMIC,

(ii) is purchased by the REMIC within the 3-month period beginning on the startup day if, except as provided in the regulations, such purchase is pursuant to a fixed price contract in effect on the startup day, *or*

(iii) represents an increase in the principal amount under the original terms of an obligation described in clause (i) or (ii) if such increase—

(I) is attributable to an advance made to the obligor pursuant to the original terms of the obligation,

(II) occurs after the startup day, and

(III) is purchased by the REMIC pursuant to a fixed price contract in effect on the startup day.

(B) any qualified replacement mortgage, *and*

(C) any regular interest in another REMIC transferred to the REMIC on the startup day in exchange for regular or residual interests in the REMIC.

For purposes of subparagraph (A) any obligation secured by stock held by a person as a tenant-stockholder (as defined in section 216) in a cooperative housing corporation (as so defined) shall be treated as secured by an interest in real property, *and any reverse mortgage loan (and each balance increase on such loan meeting the requirements of subparagraph (A)(iii)) shall be treated as an obligation secured by an interest in real property. For purposes of subparagraph (A), if more than 50 percent of the obligations transferred to, or purchased by, the REMIC are originated by the United States or any State (or any political subdivision, agency, or instrumentality of the United States or any State) and are principally secured by an interest in real property, then each obligation transferred to, or purchased by, the REMIC shall be treated as secured by an interest in real property.*

* * *

(7) QUALIFIED RESERVE ASSET.—

* * *

(B) QUALIFIED RESERVE FUND.—For purposes of subparagraph (A), the term "qualified reserve fund" means any reasonably required reserve to—

(i) provide for full payment of expenses of the REMIC or amounts due on regular interests in the event of defaults on qualified mortgages or lower than expected returns on cash flow investments, or

(ii) provide a source of funds for the purchase of obligations described in clause (ii) or (iii) of paragraph (3)(A).

The aggregate fair market value of the assets held in any such reserve shall not exceed 50 percent of the aggregate fair market value of all of the assets of the REMIC on the startup day, and the amount of any such reserve shall be promptly and appropriately reduced to the extent the amount held in such reserve is no longer reasonably required for purposes specified in clause (i) or (ii) of this subparagraph.

* * *

[CCH Explanation at ¶1120. Committee Reports at ¶11,180.]

Amendments

• 2004, American Jobs Creation Act of 2004 (H.R. 4520)

H.R. 4520, §835(b)(5)(A):

Amended Code Sec. 860G(a)(1) by adding at the end a new sentence. **Effective** 1-1-2005. For an exception, see Act Sec. 835(c)(2), below.

H.R. 4520, §835(b)(5)(B):

Amended the last sentence of Code Sec. 860G(a)(3) by inserting ", and any reverse mortgage loan (and each balance increase on such loan meeting the requirements of subparagraph (A)(iii)) shall be treated as an obligation secured by an interest in real property" before the period at the end. **Effective** 1-1-2005. For an exception, see Act Sec. 835(c)(2), below.

H.R. 4520, §835(b)(6):

Amended Code Sec. 860G(a)(3) by adding "and" at the end of subparagraph (B), by striking ", and" at the end of subparagraph (C) and inserting a period, and by striking subparagraph (D). **Effective** 1-1-2005. For an exception, see Act Sec. 835(c)(2), below. Prior to being stricken, Code Sec. 860G(a)(3)(D) read as follows:

(D) any regular interest in a FASIT which is transferred to, or purchased by, the REMIC as described in clauses (i) and (ii) of subparagraph (A) but only if 95 percent or more of the value of the assets of such FASIT is at all times attributable to obligations described in subparagraph (A) (without regard to such clauses).

H.R. 4520, §835(b)(7):

Amended Code Sec. 860G(a)(3), as amended by paragraph (6)[(5)], by adding at the end a new sentence. **Effective** 1-1-2005. For an exception, see Act Sec. 835(c)(2), below.

H.R. 4520, §835(b)(8)(A):

Amended Code Sec. 860G(a)(3)(A) by striking "or" at the end of clause (i), by inserting "or" at the end of clause (ii), and by inserting after clause (ii) a new clause (iii). **Effective** 1-1-2005. For an exception, see Act Sec. 835(c)(2), below.

H.R. 4520, §835(b)(8)(B):

Amended Code Sec. 860G(a)(7)(B). **Effective** 1-1-2005. For an exception, see Act Sec. 835(c)(2), below. Prior to amendment, Code Sec. 860G(a)(7)(B) read as follows:

(B) QUALIFIED RESERVE FUND.—For purposes of subparagraph (A), the term "qualified reserve fund" means any reasonably required reserve to provide for full payment of expenses of the REMIC or amounts due on regular interests in the event of defaults on qualified mortgages or lower than expected returns on cash-flow investments. The amount of any such reserve shall be promptly and appropriately reduced as payments of qualified mortgages are received.

H.R. 4520, §835(c)(2), provides:

(2) EXCEPTION FOR EXISTING FASITS.—Paragraph (1) shall not apply to any FASIT in existence on the date of the enactment of this Act to the extent that regular interests issued by the FASIT before such date continue to remain outstanding in accordance with the original terms of issuance.

[¶5570] CODE SEC. 860H. TAXATION OF A FASIT; OTHER GENERAL RULES. *[Repealed.]*

* * *

[CCH Explanation at ¶1120. Committee Reports at ¶11,180.]

Amendments

• 2004, American Jobs Creation Act of 2004 (H.R. 4520)

H.R. 4520, §835(a):

Repealed part V of subchapter M of chapter 1 (Code Secs. 860H-860L). **Effective** generally 1-1-2005. For an exception, see Act Sec. 835(c)(2), below. Prior to repeal, Code Sec. 860H read as follows:

SEC. 860H. TAXATION OF A FASIT; OTHER GENERAL RULES.

(a) TAXATION OF FASIT.—A FASIT as such shall not be subject to taxation under this subtitle (and shall not be treated as a trust, partnership, corporation, or taxable mortgage pool).

(b) TAXATION OF HOLDER OF OWNERSHIP INTEREST.—In determining the taxable income of the holder of the ownership interest in a FASIT—

(1) all assets, liabilities, and items of income, gain, deduction, loss, and credit of a FASIT shall be treated as assets, liabilities, and such items (as the case may be) of such holder,

(2) the constant yield method (including the rules of section 1272(a)(6)) shall be applied under an accrual method of accounting in determining all interest, acquisition discount,

original issue discount, and market discount and all premium deductions or adjustments with respect to each debt instrument of the FASIT,

(3) there shall not be taken into account any item of income, gain, or deduction allocable to a prohibited transaction, and

(4) interest accrued by the FASIT which is exempt from tax imposed by this subtitle shall, when taken into account by such holder, be treated as ordinary income.

(c) TREATMENT OF REGULAR INTERESTS.—For purposes of this title—

(1) a regular interest in a FASIT, if not otherwise a debt instrument, shall be treated as a debt instrument,

(2) section 163(e)(5) shall not apply to such an interest, and

(3) amounts includible in gross income with respect to such an interest shall be determined under an accrual method of accounting.

H.R. 4520, §835(c)(2), provides:

(2) EXCEPTION FOR EXISTING FASITS.—Paragraph (1) shall not apply to any FASIT in existence on the date of the enactment of this Act to the extent that regular interests issued by the FASIT before such date continue to remain outstanding in accordance with the original terms of issuance.

[¶ 5575] CODE SEC. 860I. GAIN RECOGNITION ON CONTRIBUTIONS TO A FASIT AND IN OTHER CASES. [*Repealed.*]

* * *

[CCH Explanation at ¶ 1120. Committee Reports at ¶ 11,180.]

Amendments

• 2004, American Jobs Creation Act of 2004 (H.R. 4520)

H.R. 4520, § 835(a):

Repealed part V of subchapter M of chapter 1 (Code Secs. 860H-860L). **Effective** generally 1-1-2005. For an exception, see Act Sec. 835(c)(2), below. Prior to repeal, Code Sec. 860I read as follows:

SEC. 860I. GAIN RECOGNITION ON CONTRIBUTIONS TO A FASIT AND IN OTHER CASES.

(a) TREATMENT OF PROPERTY ACQUIRED BY FASIT.—

(1) PROPERTY ACQUIRED FROM HOLDER OF OWNERSHIP INTEREST OR RELATED PERSON.—If property is sold or contributed to a FASIT by the holder of the ownership interest in such FASIT (or by a related person) gain (if any) shall be recognized to such holder (or person) in an amount equal to the excess (if any) of such property's value under subsection (d) on the date of such sale or contribution over its adjusted basis on such date.

(2) PROPERTY ACQUIRED OTHER THAN FROM HOLDER OF OWNERSHIP INTEREST OR RELATED PERSON.—Property which is acquired by a FASIT other than in a transaction to which paragraph (1) applies shall be treated—

(A) as having been acquired by the holder of the ownership interest in the FASIT for an amount equal to the FASIT's cost of acquiring such property, and

(B) as having been sold by such holder to the FASIT at its value under subsection (d) on such date.

(b) GAIN RECOGNITION ON PROPERTY OUTSIDE FASIT WHICH SUPPORTS REGULAR INTERESTS.—If property held by the holder of the ownership interest in a FASIT (or by any person related to such holder) supports any regular interest in such FASIT—

(1) gain shall be recognized to such holder (or person) in the same manner as if such holder (or person) had sold such property at its value under subsection (d) on the earliest date such property supports such an interest, and

(2) such property shall be treated as held by such FASIT for purposes of this part.

(c) DEFERRAL OF GAIN RECOGNITION.—The Secretary may prescribe regulations which—

(1) provide that gain otherwise recognized under subsection (a) or (b) shall not be recognized before the earliest date

on which such property supports any regular interest in such FASIT or any indebtedness of the holder of the ownership interest (or of any person related to such holder), and

(2) provide such adjustments to the other provisions of this part to the extent appropriate in the context of the treatment provided under paragraph (1).

(d) VALUATION.—For purposes of this section—

(1) IN GENERAL.—The value of any property under this subsection shall be—

(A) in the case of a debt instrument which is not traded on an established securities market, the sum of the present values of the reasonably expected payments under such instrument determined (in the manner provided by regulations prescribed by the Secretary)—

(i) as of the date of the event resulting in the gain recognition under this section, and

(ii) by using a discount rate equal to 120 percent of the applicable Federal rate (as defined in section 1274(d)), or such other discount rate specified in such regulations, compounded semiannually, and

(B) in the case of any other property, its fair market value.

(2) SPECIAL RULE FOR REVOLVING LOAN ACCOUNTS.—For purposes of paragraph (1)—

(A) each extension of credit (other than the accrual of interest) on a revolving loan account shall be treated as a separate debt instrument, and

(B) payments on such extensions of credit having substantially the same terms shall be applied to such extensions beginning with the earliest such extension.

(e) SPECIAL RULES.—

(1) NONRECOGNITION RULES NOT TO APPLY.—Gain required to be recognized under this section shall be recognized notwithstanding any other provision of this subtitle.

(2) BASIS ADJUSTMENTS.—The basis of any property on which gain is recognized under this section shall be increased by the amount of gain so recognized.

H.R. 4520, § 835(c)(2), provides:

(2) EXCEPTION FOR EXISTING FASITs.—Paragraph (1) shall not apply to any FASIT in existence on the date of the enactment of this Act to the extent that regular interests issued by the FASIT before such date continue to remain outstanding in accordance with the original terms of issuance.

[¶ 5580] CODE SEC. 860J. NON-FASIT LOSSES NOT TO OFFSET CERTAIN FASIT INCLUSIONS. [*Repealed.*]

* * *

[CCH Explanation at ¶ 1120. Committee Reports at ¶ 11,180.]

Amendments

• 2004, American Jobs Creation Act of 2004 (H.R. 4520)

H.R. 4520, § 835(a):

Repealed part V of subchapter M of chapter 1 (Code Secs. 860H-860L). **Effective** generally 1-1-2005. For an exception, see Act Sec. 835(c)(2), below. Prior to repeal, Code Sec. 860J read as follows:

SEC. 860J. NON-FASIT LOSSES NOT TO OFFSET CERTAIN FASIT INCLUSIONS.

(a) IN GENERAL.—The taxable income of the holder of the ownership interest or any high-yield interest in a FASIT for any taxable year shall in no event be less than the sum of—

(1) such holder's taxable income determined solely with respect to such interests (including gains and losses from sales and exchanges of such interests), and

(2) the excess inclusion (if any) under section 860E(a)(1) for such taxable year.

(b) COORDINATION WITH SECTION 172.—Any increase in the taxable income of any holder of the ownership interest or a high-yield interest in a FASIT for any taxable year by reason of subsection (a) shall be disregarded—

(1) in determining under section 172 the amount of any net operating loss for such taxable year, and

(2) in determining taxable income for such taxable year for purposes of the second sentence of section 172(b)(2).

(c) COORDINATION WITH MINIMUM TAX.—For purposes of part VI of subchapter A of this chapter—

(1) the reference in section 55(b)(2) to taxable income shall be treated as a reference to taxable income determined without regard to this section,

(2) the alternative minimum taxable income of any holder of the ownership interest or a high-yield interest in a FASIT

for any taxable year shall in no event be less than such holder's taxable income determined solely with respect to such interests, and

(3) any increase in taxable income under this section shall be disregarded for purposes of computing the alternative tax net operating loss deduction.

(d) AFFILIATED GROUPS.—All members of an affiliated group filing a consolidated return shall be treated as one taxpayer for purposes of this section.

H.R. 4520, § 835(c)(2), provides:

(2) EXCEPTION FOR EXISTING FASITS.—Paragraph (1) shall not apply to any FASIT in existence on the date of the enactment of this Act to the extent that regular interests issued by the FASIT before such date continue to remain outstanding in accordance with the original terms of issuance.

[¶ 5585] CODE SEC. 860K. TREATMENT OF TRANSFERS OF HIGH-YIELD INTERESTS TO DISQUALIFIED HOLDERS. [*Repealed.*]

* * *

[CCH Explanation at ¶ 1120. Committee Reports at ¶ 11,180.]

Amendments

• **2004, American Jobs Creation Act of 2004 (H.R. 4520)**

H.R. 4520, § 835(a):

Repealed part V of subchapter M of chapter 1 (Code Secs. 860H-860L). **Effective** generally 1-1-2005. For an exception, see Act Sec. 835(c)(2), below. Prior to repeal, Code Sec. 860K read as follows:

SEC. 860K. TREATMENT OF TRANSFERS OF HIGH-YIELD INTERESTS TO DISQUALIFIED HOLDERS.

(a) GENERAL RULE.—In the case of any high-yield interest which is held by a disqualified holder—

(1) the gross income of such holder shall not include any income (other than gain) attributable to such interest, and

(2) amounts not includible in the gross income of such holder by reason of paragraph (1) shall be included (at the time otherwise includible under paragraph (1)) in the gross income of the most recent holder of such interest which is not a disqualified holder.

(b) EXCEPTIONS.—Rules similar to the rules of paragraphs (4) and (7) of section 860E(e) shall apply to the tax imposed by reason of the inclusion in gross income under subsection (a).

(c) DISQUALIFIED HOLDER.—For purposes of this section, the term "disqualified holder" means any holder other than—

(1) an eligible corporation (as defined in section 860L(a)(2)), or

(2) a FASIT.

(d) TREATMENT OF INTERESTS HELD BY SECURITIES DEALERS.—

(1) IN GENERAL.—Subsection (a) shall not apply to any high-yield interest held by a disqualified holder if such holder is a dealer in securities who acquired such interest exclusively for sale to customers in the ordinary course of business (and not for investment).

(2) CHANGE IN DEALER STATUS.—

(A) IN GENERAL.—In the case of a dealer in securities which is not an eligible corporation (as defined in section 860L(a)(2)), if—

(i) such dealer ceases to be a dealer in securities, or

(ii) such dealer commences holding the high-yield interest for investment,

there is hereby imposed (in addition to other taxes) an excise tax equal to the product of the highest rate of tax specified

in section 11(b)(1) and the income of such dealer attributable to such interest for periods after the date of such cessation or commencement.

(B) HOLDING FOR 31 DAYS OR LESS.—For purposes of subparagraph (A)(ii), a dealer shall not be treated as holding an interest for investment before the thirty-second day after the date such dealer acquired such interest unless such interest is so held as part of a plan to avoid the purposes of this paragraph.

(C) ADMINISTRATIVE PROVISIONS.—The deficiency procedures of subtitle F shall apply to the tax imposed by this paragraph.

(e) TREATMENT OF HIGH-YIELD INTERESTS IN PASS-THRU ENTITIES.—

(1) IN GENERAL.—If a pass-thru entity (as defined in section 860E(e)(6)) issues a debt or equity interest—

(A) which is supported by any regular interest in a FASIT, and

(B) which has an original yield to maturity which is greater than each of—

(i) the sum determined under clauses (i) and (ii) of section 163(i)(1)(B) with respect to such debt or equity interest, and

(ii) the yield to maturity to such entity on such regular interest (determined as of the date such entity acquired such interest),

there is hereby imposed on the pass-thru entity a tax (in addition to other taxes) equal to the product of the highest rate of tax specified in section 11(b)(1) and the income of the holder of such debt or equity interest which is properly attributable to such regular interest. For purposes of the preceding sentence, the yield to maturity of any equity interest shall be determined under regulations prescribed by the Secretary.

(2) EXCEPTION.—Paragraph (1) shall not apply to arrangements not having as a principal purpose the avoidance of the purposes of this subsection.

H.R. 4520, § 835(c)(2), provides:

(2) EXCEPTION FOR EXISTING FASITS.—Paragraph (1) shall not apply to any FASIT in existence on the date of the enactment of this Act to the extent that regular interests issued by the FASIT before such date continue to remain outstanding in accordance with the original terms of issuance.

[¶5590] CODE SEC. 860L. DEFINITIONS AND OTHER SPECIAL RULES. [*Repealed.*]

* * *

[CCH Explanation at ¶1120. Committee Reports at ¶11,180.]

Amendments

• **2004, American Jobs Creation Act of 2004 (H.R. 4520)**

H.R. 4520, §835(a):

Repealed part V of subchapter M of chapter 1 (Code Secs. 860H-860L). **Effective** generally 1-1-2005. For an exception, see Act Sec. 835(c)(2), below. Prior to repeal, Code Sec. 860L read as follows:

SEC. 860L. DEFINITIONS AND OTHER SPECIAL RULES.

(a) FASIT.—

(1) IN GENERAL.—For purposes of this title, the terms "financial asset securitization investment trust" and "FASIT" mean any entity—

(A) for which an election to be treated as a FASIT applies for the taxable year,

(B) all of the interests in which are regular interests or the ownership interest,

(C) which has only one ownership interest and such ownership interest is held directly by an eligible corporation,

(D) as of the close of the third month beginning after the day of its formation and at all times thereafter, substantially all of the assets of which (including assets treated as held by the entity under section 860I(b)(2)) consist of permitted assets, and

(E) which is not described in section 851(a).

A rule similar to the rule of the last sentence of section 860D(a) shall apply for purposes of this paragraph.

(2) ELIGIBLE CORPORATION.—For purposes of paragraph (1)(C), the term "eligible corporation" means any domestic C corporation other than—

(A) a corporation which is exempt from, or is not subject to, tax under this chapter,

(B) an entity described in section 851(a) or 856(a),

(C) a REMIC, and

(D) an organization to which part I of subchapter T applies.

(3) ELECTION.—An entity (otherwise meeting the requirements of paragraph (1)) may elect to be treated as a FASIT. Except as provided in paragraph (5), such an election shall apply to the taxable year for which made and all subsequent taxable years unless revoked with the consent of the Secretary.

(4) TERMINATION.—If any entity ceases to be a FASIT at any time during the taxable year, such entity shall not be treated as a FASIT after the date of such cessation.

(5) INADVERTENT TERMINATIONS, ETC.—Rules similar to the rules of section 860D(b)(2)(B) shall apply to inadvertent failures to qualify or remain qualified as a FASIT.

(6) PERMITTED ASSETS NOT TREATED AS INTEREST IN FASIT.— Except as provided in regulations prescribed by the Secretary, any asset which is a permitted asset at the time acquired by a FASIT shall not be treated at any time as an interest in such FASIT.

(b) INTERESTS IN FASIT.—For purposes of this part—

(1) REGULAR INTEREST.—

(A) IN GENERAL.—The term "regular interest" means any interest which is issued by a FASIT on or after the startup date with fixed terms and which is designated as a regular interest if—

(i) such interest unconditionally entitles the holder to receive a specified principal amount (or other similar amount),

(ii) interest payments (or other similar amounts), if any, with respect to such interest are determined based on a fixed rate, or, except as otherwise provided by the Secretary, at a variable rate permitted under section 860G(a)(1)(B)(i),

(iii) such interest does not have a stated maturity (including options to renew) greater than 30 years (or such longer period as may be permitted by regulations),

(iv) the issue price of such interest does not exceed 125 percent of its stated principal amount, and

(v) the yield to maturity on such interest is less than the sum determined under section 163(i)(1)(B) with respect to such interest.

An interest shall not fail to meet the requirements of clause (i) merely because the timing (but not the amount) of the principal payments (or other similar amounts) may be contingent on the extent that payments on debt instruments held by the FASIT are made in advance of anticipated payments and on the amount of income from permitted assets.

(B) HIGH-YIELD INTERESTS.—

(i) IN GENERAL.—The term "regular interest" includes any high-yield interest.

(ii) HIGH-YIELD INTEREST.—The term "high-yield interest" means any interest which would be described in subparagraph (A) but for—

(I) failing to meet the requirements of one or more of clauses (i), (iv), or (v) thereof, or

(II) failing to meet the requirement of clause (ii) thereof but only if interest payments (or other similar amounts), if any, with respect to such interest consist of a specified portion of the interest payments on permitted assets and such portion does not vary during the period such interest is outstanding.

(2) OWNERSHIP INTEREST.—The term "ownership interest" means the interest issued by a FASIT after the startup day which is designated as an ownership interest and which is not a regular interest.

(c) PERMITTED ASSETS.—For purposes of this part—

(1) IN GENERAL.—The term "permitted asset" means—

(A) cash or cash equivalents,

(B) any debt instrument (as defined in section 1275(a)(1)) under which interest payments (or other similar amounts), if any, at or before maturity meet the requirements applicable under clause (i) or (ii) of section 860G(a)(1)(B),

(C) foreclosure property,

(D) any asset—

(i) which is an interest rate or foreign currency notional principal contract, letter of credit, insurance, guarantee against payment defaults, or other similar instrument permitted by the Secretary, and

(ii) which is reasonably required to guarantee or hedge against the FASIT's risks associated with being the obligor on interests issued by the FASIT,

(E) contract rights to acquire debt instruments described in subparagraph (B) or assets described in subparagraph (D),

(F) any regular interest in another FASIT, and

(G) any regular interest in a REMIC.

(2) DEBT ISSUED BY HOLDER OF OWNERSHIP INTEREST NOT PERMITTED ASSET.—The term "permitted asset" shall not include any debt instrument issued by the holder of the ownership interest in the FASIT or by any person related to such holder or any direct or indirect interest in such a debt instrument. The preceding sentence shall not apply to cash equivalents and to any other investment specified in regulations prescribed by the Secretary.

(3) FORECLOSURE PROPERTY.—

(A) IN GENERAL.—The term "foreclosure property" means property—

(i) which would be foreclosure property under section 856(e) (determined without regard to paragraph (5) thereof) if such property were real property acquired by a real estate investment trust, and

(ii) which is acquired in connection with the default or imminent default of a debt instrument held by the FASIT unless the security interest in such property was created for the principal purpose of permitting the FASIT to invest in such property.

Solely for purposes of subsection (a)(1), the determination of whether any property is foreclosure property shall be made without regard to section 856(e)(4).

(B) AUTHORITY TO REDUCE GRACE PERIOD.—In the case of property other than real property and other than personal property incident to real property, the Secretary may by regulation reduce for purposes of subparagraph (A) the periods otherwise applicable under paragraphs (2) and (3) of section 856(e).

(d) STARTUP DAY.—For purposes of this part—

(1) IN GENERAL.—The term "startup day" means the date designated in the election under subsection (a)(3) as the startup day of the FASIT. Such day shall be the beginning of the first taxable year of the FASIT.

(2) TREATMENT OF PROPERTY HELD ON STARTUP DAY.—All property held (or treated as held under section 860I(b)(2)) by an entity as of the startup day shall be treated as contributed to such entity on such day by the holder of the ownership interest in such entity.

(e) TAX ON PROHIBITED TRANSACTIONS.—

(1) IN GENERAL.—There is hereby imposed for each taxable year of a FASIT a tax equal to 100 percent of the net income derived from prohibited transactions. Such tax shall be paid by the holder of the ownership interest in the FASIT.

(2) PROHIBITED TRANSACTIONS.—For purposes of this part, the term "prohibited transaction" means—

(A) except as provided in paragraph (3), the receipt of any income derived from any asset that is not a permitted asset,

(B) except as provided in paragraph (3), the disposition of any permitted asset other than foreclosure property,

(C) the receipt of any income derived from any loan originated by the FASIT, and

(D) the receipt of any income representing a fee or other compensation for services (other than any fee received as compensation for a waiver, amendment, or consent under permitted assets (other than foreclosure property) held by the FASIT).

(3) EXCEPTION FOR INCOME FROM CERTAIN DISPOSITIONS.—

(A) IN GENERAL.—Paragraph (2)(B) shall not apply to a disposition which would not be a prohibited transaction (as defined in section 860F(a)(2)) by reason of—

(i) clause (ii), (iii), or (iv) of section 860F(a)(2)(A), or

(ii) section 860F(a)(5),

if the FASIT were treated as a REMIC and permitted assets (other than cash or cash equivalents) were treated as qualified mortgages.

(B) SUBSTITUTION OF DEBT INSTRUMENTS; REDUCTION OF OVER-COLLATERALIZATION.—Paragraph (2)(B) shall not apply to—

(i) the substitution of a debt instrument described in subsection (c)(1)(B) for another debt instrument which is a permitted asset, or

(ii) the distribution of a debt instrument contributed by the holder of the ownership interest to such holder in order to reduce over-collateralization of the FASIT,

but only if a principal purpose of acquiring the debt instrument which is disposed of was not the recognition of gain (or the reduction of a loss) as a result of an increase in the market value of the debt instrument after its acquisition by the FASIT.

(C) LIQUIDATION OF CLASS OF REGULAR INTERESTS.—Paragraph (2)(B) shall not apply to the complete liquidation of any class of regular interests.

(D) INCOME FROM DISPOSITIONS OF FORMER HEDGE ASSETS.—Paragraph (2)(A) shall not apply to income derived from the disposition of—

(i) an asset which was described in subsection (c)(1)(D) when first acquired by the FASIT but on the date of such disposition was no longer described in subsection (c)(1)(D)(ii), or

(ii) a contract right to acquire an asset described in clause (i).

(4) NET INCOME.—For purposes of this subsection, net income shall be determined in accordance with section 860F(a)(3).

(f) COORDINATION WITH OTHER PROVISIONS.—

(1) WASH SALES RULES.—Rules similar to the rules of section 860F(d) shall apply to the ownership interest in a FASIT.

(2) SECTION 475.—Except as provided by the Secretary by regulations, if any security which is sold or contributed to a FASIT by the holder of the ownership interest in such FASIT was required to be marked-to-market under section 475 by such holder, section 475 shall continue to apply to such security; except that in applying section 475 while such security is held by the FASIT, the fair market value of such security for purposes of section 475 shall not be less than its value under section 860I(d).

(g) RELATED PERSON.—For purposes of this part, a person (hereinafter in this subsection referred to as the "related person") is related to any person if—

(1) the related person bears a relationship to such person specified in section 267(b) or section 707(b)(1), or

(2) the related person and such person are engaged in trades or businesses under common control (within the meaning of subsections (a) and (b) of section 52).

For purposes of paragraph (1), in applying section 267(b) or 707(b)(1), "20 percent" shall be substituted for "50 percent".

(h) REGULATIONS.—The Secretary shall prescribe such regulations as may be necessary or appropriate to carry out the purposes of this part, including regulations to prevent the abuse of the purposes of this part through transactions which are not primarily related to securitization of debt instruments by a FASIT.

H.R. 4520, § 835(c)(2), provides:

(2) EXCEPTION FOR EXISTING FASITS.—Paragraph (1) shall not apply to any FASIT in existence on the date of the enactment of this Act to the extent that regular interests issued by the FASIT before such date continue to remain outstanding in accordance with the original terms of issuance.

[¶ 5595] CODE SEC. 861. INCOME FROM SOURCES WITHIN THE UNITED STATES.

(a) GROSS INCOME FROM SOURCES WITHIN UNITED STATES.—The following items of gross income shall be treated as income from sources within the United States:

(1) INTEREST.—Interest from the United States or the District of Columbia, and interest on bonds, notes, or other interest-bearing obligations of noncorporate residents or domestic corporations, not including—

(A) interest from a resident alien individual or domestic corporation, if such individual or corporation meets the 80-percent foreign business requirements of subsection (c)(1),

(B) interest—

(i) on deposits with a foreign branch of a domestic corporation or a domestic partnership if such branch is engaged in the commercial banking business, and

(ii) on amounts satisfying the requirements of subparagraph (B) of section 871(i)(3) which are paid by a foreign branch of a domestic corporation or a domestic partnership, and

(C) in the case of a foreign partnership, which is predominantly engaged in the active conduct of a trade or business outside the United States, any interest not paid by a trade or business engaged in by the partnership in the United States and not allocable to income which is effectively connected (or treated as effectively connected) with the conduct of a trade or business in the United States.

* * *

[CCH Explanation at ¶ 570. Committee Reports at ¶ 10,660.]

Amendments

• 2004, American Jobs Creation Act of 2004 (H.R. 4520)

H.R. 4520, § 410(a):

Amended Code Sec. 861(a)(1) by striking "and" at the end of subparagraph (A), by striking the period at the end of subparagraph (B) and inserting ", and," and by adding at the end a new subparagraph (C). **Effective** for tax years beginning after 12-31-2003.

[¶ 5600] CODE SEC. 864. DEFINITIONS AND SPECIAL RULES.

* * *

(c) EFFECTIVELY CONNECTED INCOME, ETC.—

* * *

(4) INCOME FROM SOURCES WITHOUT UNITED STATES.—

* * *

(B) Income, gain, or loss from sources without the United States shall be treated as effectively connected with the conduct of a trade or business within the United States by a nonresident alien individual or a foreign corporation if such person has an office or other fixed place of business within the United States to which such income, gain, or loss is attributable and such income, gain, or loss—

(i) consists of rents or royalties for the use of or for the privilege of using intangible property described in section 862(a)(4) derived in the active conduct of such trade or business;

(ii) consists of dividends or interest, and either is derived in the active conduct of a banking, financing, or similar business within the United States or is received by a corporation the principal business of which is trading in stocks or securities for its own account; or

(iii) is derived from the sale or exchange (outside the United States) through such office or other fixed place of business of personal property described in section 1221(a)(1), except that this clause shall not apply if the property is sold or exchanged for use, consumption, or disposition outside the United States and an office or other fixed place of business of the taxpayer in a foreign country participated materially in such sale.

Any income or gain which is equivalent to any item of income or gain described in clause (i), (ii), or (iii) shall be treated in the same manner as such item for purposes of this subparagraph.

* * *

[CCH Explanation at ¶ 575. Committee Reports at ¶ 11,660.]

Amendments

• **2004, American Jobs Creation Act of 2004 (H.R. 4520)**

H.R. 4520, § 894(a):

Amended Code Sec. 864(c)(4)(B) by adding at the end a new flush sentence. **Effective** for tax years beginning after the date of the enactment of this Act.

(d) TREATMENT OF RELATED PERSON FACTORING INCOME.—

* * *

(2) PROVISIONS TO WHICH PARAGRAPH (1) APPLIES.—The provisions set forth in this paragraph are as follows:

(A) Section 904 (relating to limitation on foreign tax credit).

(B) Subpart F of part III of this subchapter (relating to controlled foreign corporations).

* * *

(5) CERTAIN PROVISIONS NOT TO APPLY.—

(A) CERTAIN EXCEPTIONS.—The following provisions shall not apply to any amount treated as interest under paragraph (1) or (6):

(i) Subparagraph (A)(iii)(II), (B)(ii), and *(C)(iii)(II)* of section 904(d)(2) (relating to exceptions for export financing interest).

(ii) Subparagraph (A) of section 954(b)(3) (relating to exception where foreign base company income is less than 5 percent or $1,000,000).

(iii) Subparagraph (B) of section 954(c)(2) (relating to certain export financing).

(iv) Clause (i) of section 954(c)(3)(A) (relating to certain income received from related persons).

* * *

[CCH Explanation at ¶ 430 and ¶ 490. Committee Reports at ¶ 10,590 and ¶ 10,690.]

Amendments

• **2004, American Jobs Creation Act of 2004 (H.R. 4520)**

H.R. 4520, § 403(b)(6):

Amended Code Sec. 864(d)(5)(A)(i) by striking "(C)(iii)(III)" and inserting "(C)(iii)(II)". **Effective** for tax years beginning after 12-31-2002.

H.R. 4520, § 413(c)(12):

Amended Code Sec. 864(d)(2) by striking subparagraph (A) and by redesignating subparagraphs (B) and (C) as subparagraphs (A) and (B), respectively. **Effective** for tax years of foreign corporations beginning after 12-31-2004, and for tax years of United States shareholders with or within which such tax years of foreign corporations end. Prior to being stricken, Code Sec. 864(d)(2)(A) read as follows:

(A) Part III of subchapter G of this chapter (relating to foreign personal holding companies).

(e) RULES FOR ALLOCATING INTEREST, ETC.—For purposes of this subchapter—

* * *

(3) TAX-EXEMPT ASSETS NOT TAKEN INTO ACCOUNT.—For purposes of allocating and apportioning any deductible expense, any tax-exempt asset (and any income from such an asset) shall not be taken into account. A similar rule shall apply in the case of the portion of any dividend (other than a qualifying dividend as defined in section 243(b)) equal to the deduction allowable under section 243 or 245(a) with respect to such dividend and in the case of a like portion of any stock the dividends on which would be so deductible and would not be qualifying dividends (as so defined).

* * *

>>→ *Caution: Code Sec. 864(e)(7), below, as amended by H.R. 4520, is effective for tax years beginning after December 31, 2008.*

(7) REGULATIONS.—The Secretary shall prescribe such regulations as may be necessary or appropriate to carry out the purposes of this section, including regulations providing—

(A) for the resourcing of income of any member of an affiliated group or modifications to the consolidated return regulations to the extent such resourcing or modification is necessary to carry out the purposes of this section,

(B) for direct allocation of interest expense incurred to carry out an integrated financial transaction to any interest (or interest-type income) derived from such transaction *and in other circumstances where such allocation would be appropriate to carry out the purposes of this subsection,*

(C) for the apportionment of expenses allocated to foreign source income among the members of the affiliated group and various categories of income described in section 904(d)(1),

(D) for direct allocation of interest expense in the case of indebtedness resulting in a disallowance under section 246A,

(E) for appropriate adjustments in the application of paragraph (3) in the case of an insurance company,

(F) preventing assets or interest expense from being taken into account more than once, and

(G) that this subsection shall not apply for purposes of any provision of this subchapter to the extent the Secretary determines that the application of this subsection for such purposes would not be appropriate.

[CCH Explanation at ¶205 and ¶405. Committee Reports at ¶10,010 and ¶10,570.]

Amendments

• 2004, American Jobs Creation Act of 2004 (H.R. 4520)

H.R. 4520, §101(b)(6)(A)-(B):

Amended Code Sec. 864(e)(3) by striking "(3) TAX-EXEMPT ASSETS NOT TAKEN INTO ACCOUNT.—(A) IN GENERAL.—For purposes of" and inserting "(3) TAX-EXEMPT ASSETS NOT TAKEN INTO ACCOUNT.—For purposes of", and by striking subparagraph (B). **Effective** for transactions after 12-31-2004. For transitional and special rules, see Act Secs. 101(d)-(f), below. Prior to being stricken, Code Sec. 864(e)(3)(B) read as follows:

(B) ASSETS PRODUCING EXEMPT EXTRATERRITORIAL INCOME.—For purposes of allocating and apportioning any interest expense, there shall not be taken into account any qualifying foreign trade property (as defined in section 943(a)) which is held by the taxpayer for lease or rental in the ordinary course of trade or business for use by the lessee outside the United States (as defined in section 943(b)(2)).

H.R. 4520, §101(d)-(f), provides:

(d) TRANSITIONAL RULE FOR 2005 AND 2006.—

(1) IN GENERAL.—In the case of transactions during 2005 or 2006, the amount includible in gross income by reason of the amendments made by this section shall not exceed the applicable percentage of the amount which would have been so included but for this subsection.

(2) APPLICABLE PERCENTAGE.—For purposes of paragraph (1), the applicable percentage shall be as follows:

(A) For 2005, the applicable percentage shall be 20 percent.

(B) For 2006, the applicable percentage shall be 40 percent.

(e) REVOCATION OF ELECTION TO BE TREATED AS DOMESTIC CORPORATION.—If, during the 1-year period beginning on the date of the enactment of this Act, a corporation for which an election is in effect under section 943(e) of the Internal Revenue Code of 1986 revokes such election, no gain or loss shall be recognized with respect to property treated as transferred under clause (ii) of section 943(e)(4)(B) of such Code to the extent such property—

(1) was treated as transferred under clause (i) thereof, or

(2) was acquired during a taxable year to which such election applies and before May 1, 2003, in the ordinary course of its trade or business.

The Secretary of the Treasury (or such Secretary's delegate) may prescribe such regulations as may be necessary to prevent the abuse of the purposes of this subsection.

(f) BINDING CONTRACTS.—The amendments made by this section shall not apply to any transaction in the ordinary course of a trade or business which occurs pursuant to a binding contract—

(1) which is between the taxpayer and a person who is not a related person (as defined in section 943(b)(3) of such Code, as in effect on the day before the date of the enactment of this Act), and

(2) which is in effect on September 17, 2003, and at all times thereafter.

For purposes of this subsection, a binding contract shall include a purchase option, renewal option, or replacement option which is included in such contract and which is enforceable against the seller or lessor.

H.R. 4520, §401(b)(1)-(2):

Amended Code Sec. 864(e)(7) by inserting before the comma at the end of subparagraph (B) "and in other circumstances where such allocation would be appropriate to carry out the purposes of this subsection", and by striking "and" at the end of subparagraph (E), by redesignating subparagraph (F) as subparagraph (G), and by inserting after subparagraph (E) a new subparagraph (F). **Effective** for tax years beginning after 12-31-2008.

>>> *Caution: Code Sec. 864(f), below, as added by H.R. 4520, is effective for tax years beginning after December 31, 2008.*

(f) ELECTION TO ALLOCATE INTEREST, ETC. ON WORLDWIDE BASIS.—*For purposes of this subchapter, at the election of the worldwide affiliated group—*

(1) ALLOCATION AND APPORTIONMENT OF INTEREST EXPENSE.—

(A) IN GENERAL.—*The taxable income of each domestic corporation which is a member of a worldwide affiliated group shall be determined by allocating and apportioning interest expense of each member as if all members of such group were a single corporation.*

(B) TREATMENT OF WORLDWIDE AFFILIATED GROUP.—*The taxable income of the domestic members of a worldwide affiliated group from sources outside the United States shall be determined by allocating and apportioning the interest expense of such domestic members to such income in an amount equal to the excess (if any) of—*

(i) *the total interest expense of the worldwide affiliated group multiplied by the ratio which the foreign assets of the worldwide affiliated group bears to all the assets of the worldwide affiliated group, over*

(ii) *the interest expense of all foreign corporations which are members of the worldwide affiliated group to the extent such interest expense of such foreign corporations would have been allocated and apportioned to foreign source income if this subsection were applied to a group consisting of all the foreign corporations in such worldwide affiliated group.*

(C) WORLDWIDE AFFILIATED GROUP.—*For purposes of this paragraph, the term "worldwide affiliated group" means a group consisting of—*

(i) *the includible members of an affiliated group (as defined in section 1504(a), determined without regard to paragraphs (2) and (4) of section 1504(b)), and*

(ii) *all controlled foreign corporations in which such members in the aggregate meet the ownership requirements of section 1504(a)(2) either directly or indirectly through applying paragraph (2) of section 958(a) or through applying rules similar to the rules of such paragraph to stock owned directly or indirectly by domestic partnerships, trusts, or estates.*

(2) ALLOCATION AND APPORTIONMENT OF OTHER EXPENSES.—*Expenses other than interest which are not directly allocable or apportioned to any specific income producing activity shall be allocated and apportioned as if all members of the affiliated group were a single corporation. For purposes of the preceding sentence, the term "affiliated group" has the meaning given such term by section 1504 (determined without regard to paragraph (4) of section 1504(b)).*

(3) TREATMENT OF TAX-EXEMPT ASSETS; BASIS OF STOCK IN NONAFFILIATED 10-PERCENT OWNED CORPORATIONS.—*The rules of paragraphs (3) and (4) of subsection (e) shall apply for purposes of this subsection, except that paragraph (4) shall be applied on a worldwide affiliated group basis.*

(4) TREATMENT OF CERTAIN FINANCIAL INSTITUTIONS.—

(A) IN GENERAL.—*For purposes of paragraph (1), any corporation described in subparagraph (B) shall be treated as an includible corporation for purposes of section 1504 only for purposes of applying this subsection separately to corporations so described.*

(B) DESCRIPTION.—*A corporation is described in this subparagraph if—*

(i) *such corporation is a financial institution described in section 581 or 591,*

(ii) *the business of such financial institution is predominantly with persons other than related persons (within the meaning of subsection (d)(4)) or their customers, and*

(iii) *such financial institution is required by State or Federal law to be operated separately from any other entity which is not such an institution.*

(C) TREATMENT OF BANK AND FINANCIAL HOLDING COMPANIES.—*To the extent provided in regulations—*

(i) *a bank holding company (within the meaning of section 2(a) of the Bank Holding Company Act of 1956 (12 U.S.C. 1841(a)),*

(ii) *a financial holding company (within the meaning of section 2(p) of the Bank Holding Company Act of 1956 (12 U.S.C. 1841(p)), and*

Code Sec. 864(f)(4)(C)(ii) ¶5600

(iii) any subsidiary of a financial institution described in section 581 or 591, or of any such bank or financial holding company, if such subsidiary is predominantly engaged (directly or indirectly) in the active conduct of a banking, financing, or similar business,

shall be treated as a corporation described in subparagraph (B).

(5) ELECTION TO EXPAND FINANCIAL INSTITUTION GROUP OF WORLDWIDE GROUP.—

(A) IN GENERAL.—*If a worldwide affiliated group elects the application of this subsection, all financial corporations which—*

(i) are members of such worldwide affiliated group, but

(ii) are not corporations described in paragraph (4)(B),

shall be treated as described in paragraph (4)(B) for purposes of applying paragraph (4)(A). This subsection (other than this paragraph) shall apply to any such group in the same manner as this subsection (other than this paragraph) applies to the pre-election worldwide affiliated group of which such group is a part.

(B) FINANCIAL CORPORATION.—*For purposes of this paragraph, the term "financial corporation" means any corporation if at least 80 percent of its gross income is income described in section 904(d)(2)(D)(ii) and the regulations thereunder which is derived from transactions with persons who are not related (within the meaning of section 267(b) or 707(b)(1)) to the corporation. For purposes of the preceding sentence, there shall be disregarded any item of income or gain from a transaction or series of transactions a principal purpose of which is the qualification of any corporation as a financial corporation.*

(C) ANTI-ABUSE RULES.—*In the case of a corporation which is a member of an electing financial institution group, to the extent that such corporation—*

(i) distributes dividends or makes other distributions with respect to its stock after the date of the enactment of this paragraph to any member of the pre-election worldwide affiliated group (other than to a member of the electing financial institution group) in excess of the greater of—

(I) its average annual dividend (expressed as a percentage of current earnings and profits) during the 5-taxable-year period ending with the taxable year preceding the taxable year, or

(II) 25 percent of its average annual earnings and profits for such 5-taxable-year period, or

(ii) deals with any person in any manner not clearly reflecting the income of the corporation (as determined under principles similar to the principles of section 482),

an amount of indebtedness of the electing financial institution group equal to the excess distribution or the understatement or overstatement of income, as the case may be, shall be recharacterized (for the taxable year and subsequent taxable years) for purposes of this paragraph as indebtedness of the worldwide affiliated group (excluding the electing financial institution group). If a corporation has not been in existence for 5 taxable years, this subparagraph shall be applied with respect to the period it was in existence.

(D) ELECTION.—*An election under this paragraph with respect to any financial institution group may be made only by the common parent of the pre-election worldwide affiliated group and may be made only for the first taxable year beginning after December 31, 2008, in which such affiliated group includes 1 or more financial corporations. Such an election, once made, shall apply to all financial corporations which are members of the electing financial institution group for such taxable year and all subsequent years unless revoked with the consent of the Secretary.*

(E) DEFINITIONS RELATING TO GROUPS.—*For purposes of this paragraph—*

(i) PRE-ELECTION WORLDWIDE AFFILIATED GROUP.—*The term "pre-election worldwide affiliated group" means, with respect to a corporation, the worldwide affiliated group of which such corporation would (but for an election under this paragraph) be a member for purposes of applying paragraph (1).*

(ii) ELECTING FINANCIAL INSTITUTION GROUP.—*The term "electing financial institution group" means the group of corporations to which this subsection applies separately by reason of the application of paragraph (4)(A) and which includes financial corporations by reason of an election under subparagraph (A).*

(F) REGULATIONS.—*The Secretary shall prescribe such regulations as may be appropriate to carry out this subsection, including regulations—*

(i) providing for the direct allocation of interest expense in other circumstances where such allocation would be appropriate to carry out the purposes of this subsection,

(ii) preventing assets or interest expense from being taken into account more than once, and

(iii) dealing with changes in members of any group (through acquisitions or otherwise) treated under this paragraph as an affiliated group for purposes of this subsection.

(6) ELECTION.—*An election to have this subsection apply with respect to any worldwide affiliated group may be made only by the common parent of the domestic affiliated group referred to in paragraph (1)(C) and may be made only for the first taxable year beginning after December 31, 2008, in which a worldwide affiliated group exists which includes such affiliated group and at least 1 foreign corporation. Such an election, once made, shall apply to such common parent and all other corporations which are members of such worldwide affiliated group for such taxable year and all subsequent years unless revoked with the consent of the Secretary.*

[CCH Explanation at ¶ 405 and ¶ 407. Committee Reports at ¶ 10,570.]

Amendments

• **2004, American Jobs Creation Act of 2004 (H.R. 4520)**

H.R. 4520, § 401(a):

Amended Code Sec. 864 by redesignating subsection (f) as subsection (g) and by inserting after subsection (e) a new

subsection (f). **Effective** for tax years beginning after 12-31-2008.

➽→ *Caution: Former Code Sec. 864(f), below, is redesignated as Code Sec. 864(g) by H.R. 4520, effective for tax years beginning after December 31, 2008.*

(g) ALLOCATION OF RESEARCH AND EXPERIMENTAL EXPENDITURES.—

* * *

[CCH Explanation at ¶ 405. Committee Reports at ¶ 10,570.]

Amendments

• **2004, American Jobs Creation Act of 2004 (H.R. 4520)**

H.R. 4520, § 401(a):

Amended Code Sec. 864 by redesignating subsection (f) as subsection (g). **Effective** for tax years beginning after 12-31-2008.

[¶ 5605] CODE SEC. 871. TAX ON NONRESIDENT ALIEN INDIVIDUALS.

* * *

(i) TAX NOT TO APPLY TO CERTAIN INTEREST AND DIVIDENDS.—

* * *

(2) AMOUNTS TO WHICH PARAGRAPH (1) APPLIES.—The amounts described in this paragraph are as follows:

* * *

(D) Dividends paid by a foreign corporation which are treated under section 861(a)(2)(B) as income from sources within the United States.

* * *

[CCH Explanation at ¶ 555. Committee Reports at ¶ 10,650.]

Amendments

• **2004, American Jobs Creation Act of 2004 (H.R. 4520)**

H.R. 4520, § 409(a):

Amended Code Sec. 871(i)(2) by adding at the end a new subparagraph (D). **Effective** for payments made after 12-31-2004.

(k) EXEMPTION FOR CERTAIN DIVIDENDS OF REGULATED INVESTMENT COMPANIES.—

(1) INTEREST-RELATED DIVIDENDS.—

(A) IN GENERAL.—*Except as provided in subparagraph (B), no tax shall be imposed under paragraph (1)(A) of subsection (a) on any interest-related dividend received from a regulated investment company.*

(B) EXCEPTIONS.—*Subparagraph (A) shall not apply—*

(i) to any interest-related dividend received from a regulated investment company by a person to the extent such dividend is attributable to interest (other than interest described in subparagraph (E) (i) or (iii)) received by such company on indebtedness issued by such person or by any corporation or partnership with respect to which such person is a 10-percent shareholder,

(ii) to any interest-related dividend with respect to stock of a regulated investment company unless the person who would otherwise be required to deduct and withhold tax from such dividend under chapter 3 receives a statement (which meets requirements similar to the requirements of subsection (h)(5)) that the beneficial owner of such stock is not a United States person, and

(iii) to any interest-related dividend paid to any person within a foreign country (or any interest-related dividend payment addressed to, or for the account of, persons within such foreign country) during any period described in subsection (h)(6) with respect to such country.

Clause (iii) shall not apply to any dividend with respect to any stock which was acquired on or before the date of the publication of the Secretary's determination under subsection (h)(6).

(C) INTEREST-RELATED DIVIDEND.—*For purposes of this paragraph, the term "interest-related dividend" means any dividend (or part thereof) which is designated by the regulated investment company as an interest-related dividend in a written notice mailed to its shareholders not later than 60 days after the close of its taxable year. If the aggregate amount so designated with respect to a taxable year of the company (including amounts so designated with respect to dividends paid after the close of the taxable year described in section 855) is greater than the qualified net interest income of the company for such taxable year, the portion of each distribution which shall be an interest-related dividend shall be only that portion of the amounts so designated which such qualified net interest income bears to the aggregate amount so designated. Such term shall not include any dividend with respect to any taxable year of the company beginning after December 31, 2007.*

(D) QUALIFIED NET INTEREST INCOME.—*For purposes of subparagraph (C), the term "qualified net interest income" means the qualified interest income of the regulated investment company reduced by the deductions properly allocable to such income.*

(E) QUALIFIED INTEREST INCOME.—*For purposes of subparagraph (D), the term "qualified interest income" means the sum of the following amounts derived by the regulated investment company from sources within the United States:*

(i) Any amount includible in gross income as original issue discount (within the meaning of section 1273) on an obligation payable 183 days or less from the date of original issue (without regard to the period held by the company).

(ii) Any interest includible in gross income (including amounts recognized as ordinary income in respect of original issue discount or market discount or acquisition discount under part V of subchapter P and such other amounts as regulations may provide) on an obligation which is in registered form; except that this clause shall not apply to—

(I) any interest on an obligation issued by a corporation or partnership if the regulated investment company is a 10-percent shareholder in such corporation or partnership, and

(II) any interest which is treated as not being portfolio interest under the rules of subsection (h)(4).

(iii) Any interest referred to in subsection (i)(2)(A) (without regard to the trade or business of the regulated investment company).

(iv) Any interest-related dividend includable in gross income with respect to stock of another regulated investment company.

(F) 10-PERCENT SHAREHOLDER.—*For purposes of this paragraph, the term "10-percent shareholder" has the meaning given such term by subsection (h)(3)(B).*

(2) Short-term capital gain dividends.—

(A) In general.—Except as provided in subparagraph (B), no tax shall be imposed under paragraph (1)(A) of subsection (a) on any short-term capital gain dividend received from a regulated investment company.

(B) Exception for aliens taxable under subsection (a)(2).—Subparagraph (A) shall not apply in the case of any nonresident alien individual subject to tax under subsection (a)(2).

(C) Short-term capital gain dividend.—For purposes of this paragraph, the term "short-term capital gain dividend" means any dividend (or part thereof) which is designated by the regulated investment company as a short-term capital gain dividend in a written notice mailed to its shareholders not later than 60 days after the close of its taxable year. If the aggregate amount so designated with respect to a taxable year of the company (including amounts so designated with respect to dividends paid after the close of the taxable year described in section 855) is greater than the qualified short-term gain of the company for such taxable year, the portion of each distribution which shall be a short-term capital gain dividend shall be only that portion of the amounts so designated which such qualified short-term gain bears to the aggregate amount so designated. Such term shall not include any dividend with respect to any taxable year of the company beginning after December 31, 2007.

(D) Qualified short-term gain.—For purposes of subparagraph (C), the term "qualified short-term gain" means the excess of the net short-term capital gain of the regulated investment company for the taxable year over the net long-term capital loss (if any) of such company for such taxable year. For purposes of this subparagraph—

(i) the net short-term capital gain of the regulated investment company shall be computed by treating any short-term capital gain dividend includible in gross income with respect to stock of another regulated investment company as a short-term capital gain, and

(ii) the excess of the net short-term capital gain for a taxable year over the net long-term capital loss for a taxable year (to which an election under section 4982(e)(4) does not apply) shall be determined without regard to any net capital loss or net short-term capital loss attributable to transactions after October 31 of such year, and any such net capital loss or net short-term capital loss shall be treated as arising on the 1st day of the next taxable year.

To the extent provided in regulations, clause (ii) shall apply also for purposes of computing the taxable income of the regulated investment company.

[CCH Explanation at ¶560. Committee Reports at ¶10,670.]
Amendments

• **2004, American Jobs Creation Act of 2004 (H.R. 4520)**

H.R. 4520, §411(a)(1):

Amended Code Sec. 871 by redesignating subsection (k) as subsection (l) and by inserting after subsection (j) a new

(l) Cross References.—

subsection (k). **Effective** for dividends with respect to tax years of regulated investment companies beginning after 12-31-2004.

* * *

[CCH Explanation at ¶560. Committee Reports at ¶10,670.]
Amendments

• **2004, American Jobs Creation Act of 2004 (H.R. 4520)**

H.R. 4520, §411(a)(1):

Amended Code Sec. 871 by redesignating subsection (k) as subsection (l). **Effective** for dividends with respect to tax

years of regulated investment companies beginning after 12-31-2004.

[¶5610] CODE SEC. 872. GROSS INCOME.

* * *

(b) Exclusions.—The following items shall not be included in gross income of a nonresident alien individual, and shall be exempt from taxation under this subtitle:

* * *

(5) INCOME DERIVED FROM WAGERING TRANSACTIONS IN CERTAIN PARIMUTUEL POOLS.—Gross income derived by a nonresident alien individual from a legal wagering transaction initiated outside the United States in a parimutuel pool with respect to a live horse race or dog race in the United States.

(6) CERTAIN RENTAL INCOME.—Income to which paragraphs (1) and (2) apply shall include income which is derived from the rental on a full or bareboat basis of a ship or ships or aircraft, as the case may be.

(7) APPLICATION TO DIFFERENT TYPES OF TRANSPORTATION.—The Secretary may provide that this subsection be applied separately with respect to income from different types of transportation.

(8) TREATMENT OF POSSESSIONS.—To the extent provided in regulations, a possession of the United States shall be treated as a foreign country for purposes of this subsection.

[CCH Explanation at ¶ 565. Committee Reports at ¶ 10,750.]

Amendments

• **2004, American Jobs Creation Act of 2004 (H.R. 4520)**

H.R. 4520, § 419(a):

Amended Code Sec. 872(b) by redesignating paragraphs (5), (6), and (7) as paragraphs (6), (7), and (8), respectively,

and inserting after paragraph (4) a new paragraph (5). **Effective** for wagers made after the date of the enactment of this Act.

[¶ 5615] CODE SEC. 877. EXPATRIATION TO AVOID TAX.

(a) TREATMENT OF EXPATRIATES.—

(1) IN GENERAL.—Every nonresident alien individual to whom this section applies and who, within the 10-year period immediately preceding the close of the taxable year, lost United States citizenship shall be taxable for such taxable year in the manner provided in subsection (b) if the tax imposed pursuant to such subsection (after any reduction in such tax under the last sentence of such subsection) exceeds the tax which, without regard to this section, is imposed pursuant to section 871.

(2) INDIVIDUALS SUBJECT TO THIS SECTION.—This section shall apply to any individual if—

(A) the average annual net income tax (as defined in section 38(c)(1)) of such individual for the period of 5 taxable years ending before the date of the loss of United States citizenship is greater than $124,000,

(B) the net worth of the individual as of such date is $2,000,000 or more, or

(C) such individual fails to certify under penalty of perjury that he has met the requirements of this title for the 5 preceding taxable years or fails to submit such evidence of such compliance as the Secretary may require.

In the case of the loss of United States citizenship in any calendar year after 2004, such $124,000 amount shall be increased by an amount equal to such dollar amount multiplied by the cost-of-living adjustment determined under section 1(f)(3) for such calendar year by substituting "2003" for "1992" in subparagraph (B) thereof. Any increase under the preceding sentence shall be rounded to the nearest multiple of $1,000.

* * *

[CCH Explanation at ¶ 502. Committee Reports at ¶ 11,000.]

Amendments

• **2004, American Jobs Creation Act of 2004 (H.R. 4520)**

H.R. 4520, § 804(a)(1):

Amended Code Sec. 877(a). **Effective** for individuals who expatriate after 6-3-2004. Prior to amendment, Code Sec. 877(a) read as follows:

(a) TREATMENT OF EXPATRIATES.—

(1) IN GENERAL.—Every nonresident alien individual who, within the 10-year period immediately preceding the close of the taxable year, lost United States citizenship, unless such loss did not have for one of its principal purposes the avoidance of taxes under this subtitle or subtitle B, shall be taxable for such taxable year in the manner provided in subsection (b) if the tax imposed pursuant to such subsec-

tion (after any reduction in such tax under the last sentence of such subsection) exceeds the tax which, without regard to this section, is imposed pursuant to section 871.

(2) CERTAIN INDIVIDUALS TREATED AS HAVING TAX AVOIDANCE PURPOSE.—For purposes of paragraph (1), an individual shall be treated as having a principal purpose to avoid such taxes if—

(A) the average annual net income tax (as defined in section 38(c)(1)) of such individual for the period of 5 taxable years ending before the date of the loss of United States citizenship is greater than $100,000, or

(B) the net worth of the individual as of such date is $500,000 or more.

In the case of the loss of United States citizenship in any calendar year after 1996, such $100,000 and $500,000 amounts shall be increased by an amount equal to such dollar amount multiplied by the cost-of-living adjustment determined under section 1(f)(3) for such calendar year by substituting "1994" for "1992" in subparagraph (B) thereof.

Any increase under the preceding sentence shall be rounded to the nearest multiple of $1,000.

(c) EXCEPTIONS.—

(1) IN GENERAL.—Subparagraphs (A) and (B) of subsection (a)(2) shall not apply to an individual described in paragraph (2) or (3).

(2) DUAL CITIZENS.—

(A) IN GENERAL.—An individual is described in this paragraph if—

(i) the individual became at birth a citizen of the United States and a citizen of another country and continues to be a citizen of such other country, and

(ii) the individual has had no substantial contacts with the United States.

(B) SUBSTANTIAL CONTACTS.—An individual shall be treated as having no substantial contacts with the United States only if the individual—

(i) was never a resident of the United States (as defined in section 7701(b)),

(ii) has never held a United States passport, and

(iii) was not present in the United States for more than 30 days during any calendar year which is 1 of the 10 calendar years preceding the individual's loss of United States citizenship.

(3) CERTAIN MINORS.—An individual is described in this paragraph if—

(A) the individual became at birth a citizen of the United States,

(B) neither parent of such individual was a citizen of the United States at the time of such birth,

(C) the individual's loss of United States citizenship occurs before such individual attains age 18½, and

(D) the individual was not present in the United States for more than 30 days during any calendar year which is 1 of the 10 calendar years preceding the individual's loss of United States citizenship.

* * *

[CCH Explanation at ¶ 502. Committee Reports at ¶ 11,000.]

Amendments

• **2004, American Jobs Creation Act of 2004 (H.R. 4520)**

H.R. 4520, § 804(a)(2):

Amended Code Sec. 877(c). **Effective** for individuals who expatriate after 6-3-2004. Prior to amendment, Code Sec. 877(c) read as follows:

(c) TAX AVOIDANCE NOT PRESUMED IN CERTAIN CASES.—

(1) IN GENERAL.—Subsection (a)(2) shall not apply to an individual if—

(A) such individual is described in a subparagraph of paragraph (2) of this subsection, and

(B) within the 1-year period beginning on the date of the loss of United States citizenship, such individual submits a ruling request for the Secretary's determination as to whether such loss has for one of its principal purposes the avoidance of taxes under this subtitle or subtitle B.

(2) INDIVIDUALS DESCRIBED.—

(A) DUAL CITIZENSHIP, ETC.—An individual is described in this subparagraph if—

(i) the individual became at birth a citizen of the United States and a citizen of another country and continues to be a citizen of such other country, or

(ii) the individual becomes (not later than the close of a reasonable period after loss of United States citizenship) a citizen of the country in which—

(I) such individual was born,

(II) if such individual is married, such individual's spouse was born, or

(III) either of such individual's parents were born.

(B) LONG-TERM FOREIGN RESIDENTS.—An individual is described in this subparagraph if, for each year in the 10-year period ending on the date of loss of United States citizenship, the individual was present in the United States for 30 days or less. The rule of section 7701(b)(3)(D)(ii) shall apply for purposes of this subparagraph.

(C) RENUNCIATION UPON REACHING AGE OF MAJORITY.—An individual is described in this subparagraph if the individual's loss of United States citizenship occurs before such individual attains age 18½.

(D) INDIVIDUALS SPECIFIED IN REGULATIONS.—An individual is described in this subparagraph if the individual is described in a category of individuals prescribed by regulation by the Secretary.

(g) PHYSICAL PRESENCE.—

(1) IN GENERAL.—This section shall not apply to any individual to whom this section would otherwise apply for any taxable year during the 10-year period referred to in subsection (a) in which such individual is physically present in the United States at any time on more than 30 days in the calendar year

ending in such taxable year, and such individual shall be treated for purposes of this title as a citizen or resident of the United States, as the case may be, for such taxable year.

(2) EXCEPTION.—

(A) IN GENERAL.—*In the case of an individual described in any of the following subparagraphs of this paragraph, a day of physical presence in the United States shall be disregarded if the individual is performing services in the United States on such day for an employer. The preceding sentence shall not apply if—*

(i) *such employer is related (within the meaning of section 267 and 707) to such individual,* or

(ii) *such employer fails to meet such requirements as the Secretary may prescribe by regulations to prevent the avoidance of the purposes of this paragraph.*

Not more than 30 days during any calendar year may be disregarded under this subparagraph.

(B) INDIVIDUALS WITH TIES TO OTHER COUNTRIES.—*An individual is described in this subparagraph if—*

(i) *the individual becomes (not later than the close of a reasonable period after loss of United States citizenship or termination of residency) a citizen or resident of the country in which—*

(I) *such individual was born,*

(II) *if such individual is married, such individual's spouse was born, or*

(III) *either of such individual's parents were born, and*

(ii) *the individual becomes fully liable for income tax in such country.*

(C) MINIMAL PRIOR PHYSICAL PRESENCE IN THE UNITED STATES.—*An individual is described in this subparagraph if, for each year in the 10-year period ending on the date of loss of United States citizenship or termination of residency, the individual was physically present in the United States for 30 days or less. The rule of section 7701(b)(3)(D)(ii) shall apply for purposes of this subparagraph.*

[CCH Explanation at ¶ 502. Committee Reports at ¶ 11,000.]

Amendments

• **2004, American Jobs Creation Act of 2004 (H.R. 4520)**

H.R. 4520, § 804(c):

Amended Code Sec. 877 by adding at the end a new subsection (g). **Effective** for individuals who expatriate after 6-3-2004.

[¶ 5620] CODE SEC. 881. TAX ON INCOME OF FOREIGN CORPORATIONS NOT CONNECTED WITH UNITED STATES BUSINESS.

* * *

(b) EXCEPTION FOR CERTAIN POSSESSIONS.—

(1) GUAM, AMERICAN SAMOA, THE NORTHERN MARIANA ISLANDS, AND THE VIRGIN ISLANDS.—For purposes of this section and section 884, a corporation created or organized in Guam, American Samoa, the Northern Mariana Islands, or the Virgin Islands or under the law of any such possession shall not be treated as a foreign corporation for any taxable year if—

(A) at all times during such taxable year less than 25 percent in value of the stock of such corporation is beneficially owned (directly or indirectly) by foreign persons,

(B) at least 65 percent of the gross income of such corporation is shown to the satisfaction of the Secretary to be effectively connected with the conduct of a trade or business in such a possession or the United States for the 3-year period ending with the close of the taxable year of such corporation (or for such part of such period as the corporation or any predecessor had been in existence), and

(C) no substantial part of the income of such corporation is used (directly or indirectly) to satisfy obligations to persons who are not bona fide residents of such a possession or the United States.

(2) COMMONWEALTH OF PUERTO RICO.—

    (A) IN GENERAL.—*If dividends are received during a taxable year by a corporation—*

        (i) created or organized in, or under the law of, the Commonwealth of Puerto Rico, and

        (ii) with respect to which the requirements of subparagraphs (A), (B), and (C) of paragraph (1) are met for the taxable year,

subsection (a) shall be applied for such taxable year by substituting "10 percent" for "30 percent".

    (B) APPLICABILITY.—*If, on or after the date of the enactment of this paragraph, an increase in the rate of the Commonwealth of Puerto Rico's withholding tax which is generally applicable to dividends paid to United States corporations not engaged in a trade or business in the Commonwealth to a rate greater than 10 percent takes effect, this paragraph shall not apply to dividends received on or after the effective date of the increase.*

(3) DEFINITIONS.—

* * *

[CCH Explanation at ¶ 585. Committee Reports at ¶ 10,760.]

Amendments

• 2004, American Jobs Creation Act of 2004 (H.R. 4520)

H.R. 4520, § 420(a):

Amended Code Sec. 881(b) by redesignating paragraph (2) as paragraph (3) and by inserting after paragraph (1) a new paragraph (2). **Effective** for dividends paid after the date of the enactment of this Act.

H.R. 4520, § 420(c)(1):

Amended the heading of Code Sec. 881(b) by striking "GUAM AND VIRGIN ISLANDS CORPORATIONS" and inserting

"POSSESSIONS". **Effective** for dividends paid after the date of the enactment of this Act.

H.R. 4520, § 420(c)(2):

Amended the heading of Code Sec. 881(b)(1) by striking "IN GENERAL" and inserting "GUAM, AMERICAN SAMOA, THE NORTHERN MARIANA ISLANDS, AND THE VIRGIN ISLANDS". **Effective** for dividends paid after the date of the enactment of this Act.

(e) TAX NOT TO APPLY TO CERTAIN DIVIDENDS OF REGULATED INVESTMENT COMPANIES.—

    (1) INTEREST-RELATED DIVIDENDS.—

        (A) IN GENERAL.—*Except as provided in subparagraph (B), no tax shall be imposed under paragraph (1) of subsection (a) on any interest-related dividend (as defined in section 871(k)(1)) received from a regulated investment company.*

        (B) EXCEPTION.—*Subparagraph (A) shall not apply—*

            (i) to any dividend referred to in section 871(k)(1)(B), and

            (ii) to any interest-related dividend received by a controlled foreign corporation (within the meaning of section 957(a)) to the extent such dividend is attributable to interest received by the regulated investment company from a person who is a related person (within the meaning of section 864(d)(4)) with respect to such controlled foreign corporation.

        (C) TREATMENT OF DIVIDENDS RECEIVED BY CONTROLLED FOREIGN CORPORATIONS.—*The rules of subsection (c)(5)(A) shall apply to any (within the meaning of section 957(a)) to the extent such dividend is attributable to interest received by the regulated investment company which is described in clause (ii) of section 871(k)(1)(E) (and not described in clause (i) or (iii) of such section).*

    (2) SHORT-TERM CAPITAL GAIN DIVIDENDS.—*No tax shall be imposed under paragraph (1) of subsection (a) on any short-term capital gain dividend (as defined in section 871(k)(2)) received from a regulated investment company.*

[CCH Explanation at ¶ 560. Committee Reports at ¶ 10,670.]

Amendments

• 2004, American Jobs Creation Act of 2004 (H.R. 4520)

H.R. 4520, § 411(a)(2):

Amended Code Sec. 881 by redesignating subsection (e) as subsection (f) and by inserting after subsection (d) a new

subsection (e). **Effective** for dividends with respect to tax years of regulated investment companies beginning after 12-31-2004.

(f) CROSS REFERENCE.—

* * *

[CCH Explanation at ¶ 560. Committee Reports at ¶ 10,670.]

Amendments

• **2004, American Jobs Creation Act of 2004 (H.R. 4520)**

H.R. 4520, § 411(a)(2):

Amended Code Sec. 881 by redesignating subsection (e) as subsection (f). **Effective** for dividends with respect to tax years of regulated investment companies beginning after 12-31-2004.

[¶ 5625] CODE SEC. 883. EXCLUSIONS FROM GROSS INCOME.

(a) INCOME OF FOREIGN CORPORATIONS FROM SHIPS AND AIRCRAFT.—The following items shall not be included in gross income of a foreign corporation, and shall be exempt from taxation under this subtitle:

* * *

(4) SPECIAL RULES.—The rules of paragraphs *(6), (7), and (8)* of section 872(b) shall apply for purposes of this subsection.

* * *

[CCH Explanation at ¶ 565. Committee Reports at ¶ 10,750.]

Amendments

• **2004, American Jobs Creation Act of 2004 (H.R. 4520)**

H.R. 4520, § 419(b):

Amended Code Sec. 883(a)(4) by striking "(5), (6), and (7)" and inserting "(6), (7), and (8)". **Effective** for wagers made after the date of the enactment of this Act.

[¶ 5630] CODE SEC. 897. DISPOSITION OF INVESTMENT IN UNITED STATES REAL PROPERTY.

* * *

(h) SPECIAL RULES FOR CERTAIN INVESTMENT ENTITIES.—For purposes of this section—

(1) LOOK-THROUGH OF DISTRIBUTIONS.—Any distribution by a *qualified investment entity* to a nonresident alien individual or a foreign corporation shall, to the extent attributable to gain from sales or exchanges by the *qualified investment entity* of United States real property interests, be treated as gain recognized by such nonresident alien individual or foreign corporation from the sale or exchange of a United States real property interest. *Notwithstanding the preceding sentence, any distribution by a REIT with respect to any class of stock which is regularly traded on an established securities market located in the United States shall not be treated as gain recognized from the sale or exchange of a United States real property interest if the shareholder did not own more than 5 percent of such class of stock at any time during the taxable year.*

(2) *SALE OF STOCK IN DOMESTICALLY CONTROLLED ENTITY NOT TAXED.—The term "United States real property interest" does not include any interest in a domestically controlled qualified investment entity.*

(3) *DISTRIBUTIONS BY DOMESTICALLY CONTROLLED QUALIFIED INVESTMENT ENTITIES.—In the case of a domestically controlled qualified investment entity, rules similar to the rules of subsection (d) shall apply to the foreign ownership percentage of any gain.*

(4) DEFINITIONS.—

(A) *QUALIFIED INVESTMENT ENTITY.—*

(i) *IN GENERAL.—The term "qualified investment entity" means—*

(I) *any real estate investment trust, and*

(II) *any regulated investment company.*

(ii) *TERMINATION.—Clause (i)(II) shall not apply after December 31, 2007.*

(B) Domestically controlled.—*The term "domestically controlled qualified investment entity" means any qualified investment entity in which at all times during the testing period less than 50 percent in value of the stock was held directly or indirectly by foreign persons.*

(C) Foreign ownership percentage.—The term "foreign ownership percentage" means that percentage of the stock of the *qualified investment entity* which was held (directly or indirectly) by foreign persons at the time during the testing period during which the direct and indirect ownership of stock by foreign persons was greatest.

(D) Testing period.—The term "testing period" means whichever of the following periods is the shortest:

(i) the period beginning on June 19, 1980, and ending on the date of the disposition or of the distribution, as the case may be,

(ii) the 5-year period ending on the date of the disposition or of the distribution, as the case may be, or

(iii) the period during which the *qualified investment entity* was in existence.

[CCH Explanation at ¶ 540 and ¶ 564. Committee Reports at ¶ 10,670 and ¶ 10,740.]

Amendments

• 2004, American Jobs Creation Act of 2004 (H.R. 4520)

H.R. 4520, § 411(c)(1):

Amended Code Sec. 897(h)(1) by striking "REIT" each place it appears and inserting "qualified investment entity". **Effective** for dividends with respect to tax years of regulated investment companies beginning after 12-31-2004.

H.R. 4520, § 411(c)(2):

Amended Code Sec. 897(h)(2) and (3). **Effective** after 12-31-2004. Prior to amendment, Code Sec. 897(h)(2) and (3) read as follows:

(2) Sale of stock in domestically-controlled REIT not taxed.—The term "United States real property interest" does not include any interest in a domestically-controlled REIT.

(3) Distributions by domestically-controlled REITs.—In the case of a domestically-controlled REIT, rules similar to the rules of subsection (d) shall apply to the foreign ownership percentage of any gain.

H.R. 4520, § 411(c)(3):

Amended Code Sec. 897(h)(4)(A) and (B). **Effective** after 12-31-2004. Prior to amendment, Code Sec. 897(h)(4)(A) and (B) read as follows:

(A) REIT.—The term "REIT" means a real estate investment trust.

(B) Domestically-controlled REIT.—The term "domestically-controlled REIT" means a REIT in which at all times during the testing period less than 50 percent in value of the stock was held directly or indirectly by foreign persons.

H.R. 4520, § 411(c)(4):

Amended Code Sec. 897(h)(4)(C) and (D) by striking "REIT" and inserting "qualified investment entity". **Effective** after 12-31-2004.

H.R. 4520, § 411(c)(5):

Amended the heading for Code Sec. 897(h) by striking "REITS" and inserting "Certain Investment Entities". **Effective** after 12-31-2004.

H.R. 4520, § 418(a):

Amended Code Sec. 897(h)(1) by adding at the end a new sentence. **Effective** for tax years beginning after the date of the enactment of this Act.

[¶ 5635] CODE SEC. 898. TAXABLE YEAR OF CERTAIN FOREIGN CORPORATIONS.

* * *

(b) Specified Foreign Corporation.—For purposes of this section—

(1) In general.—The term "specified foreign corporation" means any foreign corporation—

(A) which is treated as a controlled foreign corporation for any purpose under subpart F of part III of this subchapter, and

(B) with respect to which the ownership requirements of paragraph (2) are met.

(2) Ownership requirements.—

(A) In general.—The ownership requirements of this paragraph are met with respect to any foreign corporation if a United States shareholder owns, on each testing day, more than 50 percent of—

(i) the total voting power of all classes of stock of such corporation entitled to vote, or

(ii) the total value of all classes of stock of such corporation.

(B) OWNERSHIP.—For purposes of subparagraph (A), the rules of subsections (a) and (b) of section 958 shall apply in determining ownership.

(3) UNITED STATES SHAREHOLDER.—The term "United States shareholder" has the meaning given to such term by section 951(b), except that, in the case of a foreign corporation having related person insurance income (as defined in section 953(c)(2)), the Secretary may treat any person as a United States shareholder for purposes of this section if such person is treated as a United States shareholder under section 953(c)(1).

[CCH Explanation at ¶ 490. Committee Reports at ¶ 10,690.]

Amendments

• 2004, American Jobs Creation Act of 2004 (H.R. 4520)

H.R. 4520, § 413(c)(13)(A):

Amended Code Sec. 898(b)(1)(A). **Effective** for tax years of foreign corporations beginning after 12-31-2004, and for tax years of United States shareholders with or within which such tax years of foreign corporations end. Prior to amendment, Code Sec. 898(b)(1)(A) read as follows:

(A) which is—

(i) treated as a controlled foreign corporation for any purpose under subpart F of part III of this subchapter, or

(ii) a foreign personal holding company (as defined in section 552), and

H.R. 4520, § 413(c)(13)(B):

Amended Code Sec. 898(b)(2)(B) by striking "and sections 551(f) and 554, whichever are applicable," immediately following "section 958". **Effective** for tax years of foreign corporations beginning after 12-31-2004, and for tax years of United States shareholders with or within which such tax years of foreign corporations end.

H.R. 4520, § 413(c)(13)(C):

Amended Code Sec. 898(b)(3). **Effective** for tax years of foreign corporations beginning after 12-31-2004, and for tax years of United States shareholders with or within which such tax years of foreign corporations end. Prior to amendment, Code Sec. 898(b)(3) read as follows:

(3) UNITED STATES SHAREHOLDER.—

(A) IN GENERAL.—The term "United States shareholder" has the meaning given to such term by section 951(b), except that, in the case of a foreign corporation having related person insurance income (as defined in section 953(c)(2)), the Secretary may treat any person as a United States shareholder for purposes of this section if such person is treated as a United States shareholder under section 953(c)(1).

(B) FOREIGN PERSONAL HOLDING COMPANIES.—In the case of any foreign personal holding company (as defined in section 552) which is not a specified foreign corporation by reason of paragraph (1)(A)(i), the term "United States shareholder" means any person who is treated as a United States shareholder under section 551.

(c) DETERMINATION OF REQUIRED YEAR.—

(1) IN GENERAL.—The required year is—

(A) the majority U.S. shareholder year, or

(B) if there is no majority U.S. shareholder year, the taxable year prescribed under regulations.

(2) 1-MONTH DEFERRAL ALLOWED.—A specified foreign corporation may elect, in lieu of the taxable year under paragraph (1)(A), a taxable year beginning 1 month earlier than the majority U.S. shareholder year.

(3) MAJORITY U.S. SHAREHOLDER YEAR.—

(A) IN GENERAL.—For purposes of this subsection, the term "majority U.S. shareholder year" means the taxable year (if any) which, on each testing day, constituted the taxable year of—

(i) each United States shareholder described in subsection (b)(2)(A), and

(ii) each United States shareholder not described in clause (i) whose stock was treated as owned under subsection (b)(2)(B) by any shareholder described in such clause.

(B) TESTING DAY.—The testing days shall be—

(i) the first day of the corporation's taxable year (determined without regard to this section), or

(ii) the days during such representative period as the Secretary may prescribe.

[CCH Explanation at ¶ 490. Committee Reports at ¶ 10,690.]

Amendments

• 2004, American Jobs Creation Act of 2004 (H.R. 4520)

H.R. 4520, § 413(c)(13)(D):

Amended Code Sec. 898(c). **Effective** for tax years of foreign corporations beginning after 12-31-2004, and for tax years of United States shareholders with or within which

such tax years of foreign corporations end. Prior to amendment, Code Sec. 898(c) read as follows:

(c) DETERMINATION OF REQUIRED YEAR.—

(1) CONTROLLED FOREIGN CORPORATIONS.—

(A) IN GENERAL.—In the case of a specified foreign corporation described in subsection (b)(1)(A)(i), the required year is—

(i) the majority U.S. shareholder year, or

(ii) if there is no majority U.S. shareholder year, the taxable year prescribed under regulations.

(B) 1-MONTH DEFERRAL ALLOWED.—A specified foreign corporation may elect, in lieu of the taxable year under subparagraph (A)(i), a taxable year beginning 1 month earlier than the majority U.S. shareholder year.

(C) MAJORITY U.S. SHAREHOLDER YEAR.—

(i) IN GENERAL.—For purposes of this subsection, the term "majority U.S. shareholder year" means the taxable year (if any) which, on each testing day, constituted the taxable year of—

(I) each United States shareholder described in subsection (b)(2)(A), and

(II) each United States shareholder not described in subclause (I) whose stock was treated as owned under subsection (b)(2)(B) by any shareholder described in such subclause.

(ii) TESTING DAY.—The testing days shall be—

(I) the first day of the corporation's taxable year (determined without regard to this section), or

(II) the days during such representative period as the Secretary may prescribe.

(2) FOREIGN PERSONAL HOLDING COMPANIES.—In the case of a foreign personal holding company described in subsection (b)(3)(B), the required year shall be determined under paragraph (1), except that subparagraph (B) of paragraph (1) shall not apply.

[¶5640] CODE SEC. 901. TAXES OF FOREIGN COUNTRIES AND OF POSSESSIONS OF UNITED STATES.

* * *

(b) AMOUNT ALLOWED.—Subject to the limitation of section 904, the following amounts shall be allowed as the credit under subsection (a):

* * *

(5) PARTNERSHIPS AND ESTATES.—In the case of *any person* described in paragraph (1), (2), (3), or (4), who is a member of a partnership or a beneficiary of an estate or trust, the amount of his proportionate share of the taxes (described in such paragraph) of the partnership or the estate or trust paid or accrued during the taxable year to a foreign country or to any possession of the United States, as the case may be. Under rules or regulations prescribed by the Secretary, in the case of any foreign trust of which the settlor or another person would be treated as owner of any portion of the trust under subpart E but for section 672(f), [the term "taxes imposed on the trust" includes] the allocable amount of any income, war profits, and excess profits taxes imposed by any foreign country or possession of the United States on the settlor or such other person in respect of trust income.

* * *

[CCH Explanation at ¶435. Committee Reports at ¶10,610.]
Amendments
• **2004, American Jobs Creation Act of 2004 (H.R. 4520)**

H.R. 4520, §405(b):

Amended Code Sec. 901(b)(5) by striking "any individual" and inserting "any person". **Effective** for taxes of for-

eign corporations for tax years of such corporations beginning after the date of the enactment of this Act.

(k) MINIMUM HOLDING PERIOD FOR CERTAIN TAXES *ON DIVIDENDS*.—

* * *

[CCH Explanation at ¶440. Committee Reports at ¶11,150.]
Amendments
• **2004, American Jobs Creation Act of 2004 (H.R. 4520)**

H.R. 4520, §832(b):

Amended the heading of Code Sec. 901(k) by inserting "ON DIVIDENDS" after "TAXES". **Effective** for amounts paid or

accrued more than 30 days after the date of the enactment of this Act.

(*l*) MINIMUM HOLDING PERIOD FOR WITHHOLDING TAXES ON GAIN AND INCOME OTHER THAN DIVIDENDS ETC.—

(1) IN GENERAL.—In no event shall a credit be allowed under subsection (a) for any withholding tax (as defined in subsection (k)) on any item of income or gain with respect to any property if—

(A) such property is held by the recipient of the item for 15 days or less during the 31-day period beginning on the date which is 15 days before the date on which the right to receive payment of such item arises, or

(B) to the extent that the recipient of the item is under an obligation (whether pursuant to a short sale or otherwise) to make related payments with respect to positions in substantially similar or related property.

This paragraph shall not apply to any dividend to which subsection (k) applies.

(2) EXCEPTION FOR TAXES PAID BY DEALERS.—

(A) IN GENERAL.—Paragraph (1) shall not apply to any qualified tax with respect to any property held in the active conduct in a foreign country of a business as a dealer in such property.

(B) QUALIFIED TAX.—For purposes of subparagraph (A), the term "qualified tax" means a tax paid to a foreign country (other than the foreign country referred to in subparagraph (A)) if—

(i) the item to which such tax is attributable is subject to taxation on a net basis by the country referred to in subparagraph (A), and

(ii) such country allows a credit against its net basis tax for the full amount of the tax paid to such other foreign country.

(C) DEALER.—For purposes of subparagraph (A), the term "dealer" means—

(i) with respect to a security, any person to whom paragraphs (1) and (2) of subsection (k) would not apply by reason of paragraph (4) thereof if such security were stock, and

(ii) with respect to any other property, any person with respect to whom such property is described in section 1221(a)(1).

(D) REGULATIONS.—The Secretary may prescribe such regulations as may be appropriate to carry out this paragraph, including regulations to prevent the abuse of the exception provided by this paragraph and to treat other taxes as qualified taxes.

(3) EXCEPTIONS.—The Secretary may by regulation provide that paragraph (1) shall not apply to property where the Secretary determines that the application of paragraph (1) to such property is not necessary to carry out the purposes of this subsection.

(4) CERTAIN RULES TO APPLY.—Rules similar to the rules of paragraphs (5), (6), and (7) of subsection (k) shall apply for purposes of this subsection.

(5) DETERMINATION OF HOLDING PERIOD.—Holding periods shall be determined for purposes of this subsection without regard to section 1235 or any similar rule.

[CCH Explanation at ¶440. Committee Reports at ¶11,150.]

Amendments

• **2004, American Jobs Creation Act of 2004 (H.R. 4520)**

H.R. 4520, §832(a):

Amended Code Sec. 901 by redesignating subsection (l) as subsection (m) and by inserting after subsection (k) a new

subsection (l). **Effective** for amounts paid or accrued more than 30 days after the date of the enactment of this Act.

(m) CROSS REFERENCE.—

* * *

[CCH Explanation at ¶440. Committee Reports at ¶11,150.]

Amendments

• **2004, American Jobs Creation Act of 2004 (H.R. 4520)**

H.R. 4520, §832(a):

Amended Code Sec. 901 by redesignating subsection (l) as subsection (m). **Effective** for amounts paid or accrued more than 30 days after the date of the enactment of this Act.

[¶ 5645] CODE SEC. 902. DEEMED PAID CREDIT WHERE DOMESTIC CORPORATION OWNS 10 PERCENT OR MORE OF VOTING STOCK OF FOREIGN CORPORATION.

* * *

(c) DEFINITIONS AND SPECIAL RULES.—For purposes of this section—

* * *

(7) CONSTRUCTIVE OWNERSHIP THROUGH PARTNERSHIPS.—Stock owned, directly or indirectly, by or for a partnership shall be considered as being owned proportionately by its partners. Stock considered to be owned by a person by reason of the preceding sentence shall, for purposes of applying such sentence, be treated as actually owned by such person. The Secretary may prescribe such regulations as may be necessary to carry out the purposes of this paragraph, including rules to account for special partnership allocations of dividends, credits, and other incidents of ownership of stock in determining proportionate ownership.

(8) REGULATIONS.—The Secretary shall provide such regulations as may be necessary or appropriate to carry out the provisions of this section and section 960, including provisions which provide for the separate application of this section and section 960 to reflect the separate application of section 904 to separate types of income and loss.

[CCH Explanation at ¶ 435. Committee Reports at ¶ 10,610.]

Amendments

• **2004, American Jobs Creation Act of 2004 (H.R. 4520)**

H.R. 4520, § 405(a):

Amended Code Sec. 902(c) by redesignating paragraph (7) as paragraph (8) and by inserting after paragraph (6) a

new paragraph (7). **Effective** for taxes of foreign corporations for tax years of such corporations beginning after the date of the enactment of this Act.

[¶ 5650] CODE SEC. 903. CREDIT FOR TAXES IN LIEU OF INCOME, ETC., TAXES.

For purposes of this part and of sections *164(a)* and 275(a), the term "income, war profits, and excess profits taxes" shall include a tax paid in lieu of a tax on income, war profits, or excess profits otherwise generally imposed by any foreign country or by any possession of the United States.

[CCH Explanation at ¶ 205. Committee Reports at ¶ 10,010.]

Amendments

• **2004, American Jobs Creation Act of 2004 (H.R. 4520)**

H.R. 4520, § 101(b)(7):

Amended Code Sec. 903 by striking "114, 164(a)," and inserting "164(a)". **Effective** for transactions after 12-31-2004. For transitional and special rules, see Act Secs. 101(d)-(f), below.

H.R. 4520, § 101(d)-(f), provides:

(d) TRANSITIONAL RULE FOR 2005 AND 2006.—

(1) IN GENERAL.—In the case of transactions during 2005 or 2006, the amount includible in gross income by reason of the amendments made by this section shall not exceed the applicable percentage of the amount which would have been so included but for this subsection.

(2) APPLICABLE PERCENTAGE.—For purposes of paragraph (1), the applicable percentage shall be as follows:

(A) For 2005, the applicable percentage shall be 20 percent.

(B) For 2006, the applicable percentage shall be 40 percent.

(e) REVOCATION OF ELECTION TO BE TREATED AS DOMESTIC CORPORATION.—If, during the 1-year period beginning on the date of the enactment of this Act, a corporation for which an election is in effect under section 943(e) of the Internal

Revenue Code of 1986 revokes such election, no gain or loss shall be recognized with respect to property treated as transferred under clause (ii) of section 943(e)(4)(B) of such Code to the extent such property—

(1) was treated as transferred under clause (i) thereof, or

(2) was acquired during a taxable year to which such election applies and before May 1, 2003, in the ordinary course of its trade or business.

The Secretary of the Treasury (or such Secretary's delegate) may prescribe such regulations as may be necessary to prevent the abuse of the purposes of this subsection.

(f) BINDING CONTRACTS.—The amendments made by this section shall not apply to any transaction in the ordinary course of a trade or business which occurs pursuant to a binding contract—

(1) which is between the taxpayer and a person who is not a related person (as defined in section 943(b)(3) of such Code, as in effect on the day before the date of the enactment of this Act), and

(2) which is in effect on September 17, 2003, and at all times thereafter.

For purposes of this subsection, a binding contract shall include a purchase option, renewal option, or replacement option which is included in such contract and which is enforceable against the seller or lessor.

[¶ 5655] CODE SEC. 904. LIMITATION ON CREDIT.

* * *

(c) CARRYBACK AND CARRYOVER OF EXCESS TAX PAID.—Any amount by which all taxes paid or accrued to foreign countries or possessions of the United States for any taxable year for which the taxpayer chooses to have the benefits of this subpart exceed the limitation under subsection (a) shall be deemed taxes paid or accrued to foreign countries or possessions of the United States in the first preceding taxable year, *and in any of the first 10* succeeding taxable years, in that order and to the extent not deemed taxes paid or accrued in a prior taxable year, in the amount by which the limitation under subsection (a) for such preceding or succeeding taxable year exceeds the sum of the taxes paid or accrued to foreign countries or possessions of the United States for such preceding or succeeding taxable year and the amount of the taxes for any taxable year earlier than the current taxable year which shall be deemed to have been paid or accrued in such preceding or subsequent taxable year (whether or not the taxpayer chooses to have the benefits of this subpart with respect to such earlier taxable year). Such amount deemed paid or accrued in any year may be availed of only as a tax credit and not as a deduction and only if the taxpayer for such year chooses to have the benefits of this subpart as to taxes paid or accrued for that year to foreign countries or possessions of the United States.

[CCH Explanation at ¶410 and ¶415. Committee Reports at ¶10,730.]

Amendments

• **2004, American Jobs Creation Act of 2004 (H.R. 4520)**

H.R. 4520, §417(a)(1):

Amended Code Sec. 904(c) by striking "in the second preceding taxable year," immediately preceding "in the first preceding taxable year". **Effective** for excess foreign taxes arising in tax years beginning after the date of the enactment of this Act.

H.R. 4520, §417(a)(2):

Amended Code Sec. 904(c) by striking ", and in the first, second, third, fourth, or fifth" and inserting "and in any of the first 10". **Effective** for excess foreign taxes which (without regard to the amendments made by Act Sec. 417) may be carried to any tax year ending after the date of the enactment of this Act.

(d) Separate Application of Section with Respect to Certain Categories of Income.—

⮞ *Caution: Code Sec. 904(d)(1), below, as amended by H.R. 4520, Act Sec. 403(b)(1), but prior to amendment by H.R. 4520, Act Sec. 404(a), applies to tax years beginning on or before December 31, 2006.*

(1) In General.—The provisions of subsections (a), (b), and (c) and sections 902, 907, and 960 shall be applied separately with respect to each of the following items of income:

(A) passive income,

(B) high withholding tax interest,

(C) financial services income,

(D) shipping income,

(E) [*Repealed.*]

(F) dividends from a DISC or former DISC (as defined in section 992(a)) to the extent such dividends are treated as income from sources without the United States,

(G) taxable income attributable to foreign trade income (within the meaning of section 923(b)),

(H) distributions from a FSC (or former FSC) out of earnings and profits attributable to foreign trade income (within the meaning of section 923(b) or interest or carrying charges (as defined in section 927(d)(1)) derived from a transaction which results in foreign trade income (as defined in section 923(b)), and

(I) income other than income described in any of the preceding subparagraphs.

⮞ *Caution: Code Sec. 904(d)(1), below, as amended by H.R. 4520, Act Sec. 404(a), applies to tax years beginning after December 31, 2006.*

(1) *In General.—The provisions of subsections (a), (b), and (c) and sections 902, 907, and 960 shall be applied separately with respect to—*

(A) *passive category income, and*

(B) *general category income.*

➤➤➤ *Caution: Code Sec. 904(d)(2), below, as amended by H.R. 4520, Act Sec. 403(b)(2)-(4) and 413(c)(14), but prior to amendment by H.R. 4520, Act Sec. 404(b)-(f), applies to tax years beginning on or before December 31, 2006.*

(2) DEFINITIONS AND SPECIAL RULES.—For purposes of this subsection—

(A) PASSIVE INCOME.—

(i) IN GENERAL.—Except as otherwise provided in this subparagraph, the term "passive income" means any income received or accrued by any person which is of a kind which would be foreign personal holding company income (as defined in section 954(c)).

(ii) CERTAIN AMOUNTS INCLUDED.—Except as provided in clause (iii), the term "passive income" includes, except as provided in subparagraph (E)(iii) or paragraph (3)(I), any amount includible in gross income under section 1293 (relating to certain passive foreign investment companies).

(iii) EXCEPTIONS.—The term "passive income" shall not include—

(I) any income described in a subparagraph of paragraph (1) other than subparagraph (A),

(II) any export financing interest, and

(III) any high-taxed income.

(iv) CLARIFICATION OF APPLICATION OF SECTION 864(d)(6).—In determining whether any income is of a kind which would be foreign personal holding company income, the rules of section 864(d)(6) shall apply only in the case of income of a controlled foreign corporation.

(B) HIGH WITHHOLDING TAX INTEREST.—

(i) IN GENERAL.—Except as otherwise provided in this subparagraph, the term "high withholding tax interest" means any interest if—

(I) such interest is subject to a withholding tax of a foreign country or possession of the United States (or other tax determined on a gross basis), and

(II) the rate of such tax applicable to such interest is at least 5 percent.

(ii) EXCEPTION FOR EXPORT FINANCING.—The term "high withholding tax interest" shall not include any export financing interest.

(iii) REGULATIONS.—The Secretary may by regulations provide that—

(I) amounts (not otherwise high withholding tax interest) shall be treated as high withholding tax interest where necessary to prevent avoidance of the purposes of this subparagraph, and

(II) a tax shall not be treated as a withholding tax or other tax imposed on a gross basis if such tax is in the nature of a prepayment of a tax imposed on a net basis.

(C) FINANCIAL SERVICES INCOME.—

(i) IN GENERAL.—Except as otherwise provided in this subparagraph, the term "financial services income" means any income which is received or accrued by any person predominantly engaged in the active conduct of a banking, insurance, financing, or similar business, and which is—

(I) described in clause (ii),

(II) passive income (determined without regard to subclauses (I) and (III) of subparagraph (A)(iii)), or

(III) export financing interest which (but for subparagraph (B)(ii)) would be high withholding tax interest.

(ii) GENERAL DESCRIPTION OF FINANCIAL SERVICES INCOME.—Income is described in this clause if such income is—

(I) derived in the active conduct of a banking, financing, or similar business,

(II) derived from the investment by an insurance company of its unearned premiums or reserves ordinary and necessary for the proper conduct of its insurance business, or

(III) of a kind which would be insurance income as defined in section 953(a) determined without regard to those provisions of paragraph (1)(A) of such section which limit insurance income to income from countries other than the country in which the corporation was created or organized.

(iii) EXCEPTIONS.—The term "financial services income" does not include—

(I) any high withholding tax interest, *and*

(II) any export financing interest not described in clause (i)(III).

(D) SHIPPING INCOME.—The term "shipping income" means any income received or accrued by any person which is of a kind which would be foreign base company shipping income (as defined in section 954(f)). *Such term does not include any financial services income.*

(E) NONCONTROLLED SECTION 902 CORPORATION.—

(i) IN GENERAL.—The term "noncontrolled section 902 corporation" means any foreign corporation with respect to which the taxpayer meets the stock ownership requirements of section 902(a) (or, for purposes of applying paragraph (3) *or (4)*, the requirements of section 902(b)). A controlled foreign corporation shall not be treated as a noncontrolled section 902 corporation with respect to any distribution out of its earnings and profits for periods during which it was a controlled foreign corporation.

(ii) TREATMENT OF INCLUSIONS UNDER SECTION 1293.—If any foreign corporation is a non-controlled section 902 corporation with respect to the taxpayer, any inclusion under section 1293 with respect to such corporation shall be treated as a dividend from such corporation.

(F) HIGH-TAXED INCOME.—The term "high-taxed income" means any income which (but for this subparagraph) would be passive income if the sum of—

(i) the foreign income taxes paid or accrued by the taxpayer with respect to such income, and

(ii) the foreign income taxes deemed paid by the taxpayer with respect to such income under section 902 or 960,

exceeds the highest rate of tax specified in section 1 or 11 (whichever applies) multiplied by the amount of such income (determined with regard to section 78). For purposes of the preceding sentence, the term "foreign income taxes" means any income, war profits, or excess profits tax imposed by any foreign country or possession of the United States.

(G) EXPORT FINANCING INTEREST.—For purposes of this paragraph, the term "export financing interest" means any interest derived from financing the sale (or other disposition) for use or consumption outside the United States of any property—

(i) which is manufactured, produced, grown, or extracted in the United States by the taxpayer or a related person, and

(ii) not more than 50 percent of the fair market value of which is attributable to products imported into the United States.

For purposes of clause (ii), the fair market value of any property imported into the United States shall be its appraised value, as determined by the Secretary under section 402 of the Tariff Act of 1930 (19 U.S.C. 1401a) in connection with its importation.

(H) RELATED PERSON.—For purposes of this paragraph, the term "related person" has the meaning given such term by section 954(d)(3), except that such section shall be applied by substituting "the person with respect to whom the determination is being made" for "controlled foreign corporation" each place it appears.

(I) TRANSITIONAL RULE.—For purposes of paragraph (1)—

(i) taxes paid or accrued in a taxable year beginning before January 1, 1987, with respect to income which was described in subparagraph (A) of paragraph (1) (as in effect on the day before the date of the enactment of the Tax Reform Act of 1986) shall be treated as taxes paid or accrued with respect to income described in subparagraph (A) of paragraph (1) (as in effect after such date),

(ii) taxes paid or accrued in a taxable year beginning before January 1, 1987, with respect to income which was described in subparagraph (E) of paragraph (1) (as in effect on the day before the date of the enactment of the Tax Reform Act of 1986) shall be treated as taxes paid or accrued with respect to income described in subparagraph (I) of paragraph (1) (as in effect after such date) except that

(I) such taxes shall be treated as paid or accrued with respect to shipping income to the extent the taxpayer establishes to the satisfaction of the Secretary that such taxes were paid or accrued with respect to such income,

(II) in the case of a person described in subparagraph (C)(i), such taxes shall be treated as paid or accrued with respect to financial services income to the extent the taxpayer establishes to the satisfaction of the Secretary that such taxes were paid or accrued with respect to such income, and

(III) such taxes shall be treated as paid or accrued with respect to high withholding tax interest to the extent the taxpayer establishes to the satisfaction of the Secretary that such taxes were paid or accrued with respect to such income, and

(iii) taxes paid or accrued in a taxable year beginning before January 1, 1987, with respect to income described in any other subparagraph of paragraph (1) (as so in effect before such date) shall be treated as taxes paid or accrued with respect to income described in the corresponding subparagraph of paragraph (1) (as so in effect after such date).

➤ *Caution: Code Sec. 904(d)(2), below, as amended by H.R. 4520, Act Sec. 403(b)(2)-(4), 404(b)-(f), and 413(c)(14), applies to tax years beginning after December 31, 2006.*

(2) DEFINITIONS AND SPECIAL RULES.—For purposes of this subsection—

(A) CATEGORIES.—

(i) PASSIVE CATEGORY INCOME.—The term "passive category income" means passive income and specified passive category income.

(ii) GENERAL CATEGORY INCOME.—The term "general category income" means income other than passive category income.

(B) PASSIVE INCOME.—

(i) IN GENERAL.—Except as otherwise provided in this subparagraph, the term "passive income" means any income received or accrued by any person which is of a kind which would be foreign personal holding company income (as defined in section 954(c)).

(ii) CERTAIN AMOUNTS INCLUDED.—Except as provided in clause (iii), the term "passive income" includes, except as provided in subparagraph (E)(iii) or paragraph (3)(I), any amount includible in gross income under section 1293 (relating to certain passive foreign investment companies).

(iii) EXCEPTIONS.—The term "passive income" shall not include—

(I) any export financing interest, and

(II) any high-taxed income.

(iv) CLARIFICATION OF APPLICATION OF SECTION 864(d)(6).—In determining whether any income is of a kind which would be foreign personal holding company income, the rules of section 864(d)(6) shall apply only in the case of income of a controlled foreign corporation.

(v) SPECIFIED PASSIVE CATEGORY INCOME.—The term "specified passive category income" means—

(I) dividends from a DISC or former DISC (as defined in section 992(a)) to the extent such dividends are treated as income from sources without the United States,

(II) taxable income attributable to foreign trade income (within the meaning of section 923(b)), and

(III) *distributions from a FSC (or a former FSC) out of earnings and profits attributable to foreign trade income (within the meaning of section 923(b)) or interest or carrying charges (as defined in section 927(d)(1)) derived from a transaction which results in foreign trade income (as defined in section 923(b)).*

(C) TREATMENT OF FINANCIAL SERVICES INCOME AND COMPANIES.—

(i) IN GENERAL.—*Financial services income shall be treated as general category income in the case of*—

(I) *a member of a financial services group,*

(II) *any other person if such person is predominantly engaged in the active conduct of a banking, insurance, financing, or similar business.*

(ii) FINANCIAL SERVICES GROUP.—*The term "financial services group" means any affiliated group (as defined in section 1504(a) without regard to paragraphs (2) and (3) of section 1504(b)) which is predominantly engaged in the active conduct of a banking, insurance, financing, or similar business. In determining whether such a group is so engaged, there shall be taken into account only the income of members of the group that are—*

(I) *United States corporations, or*

(II) *controlled foreign corporations in which such United States corporations own, directly or indirectly, at least 80 percent of the total voting power and value of the stock.*

(iii) PASS-THRU ENTITIES.—*The Secretary shall by regulation specify for purposes of this subparagraph the treatment of financial services income received or accrued by partnerships and by other pass-thru entities which are not members of a financial services group.*

(D) FINANCIAL SERVICES INCOME.—

(i) IN GENERAL.—Except as otherwise provided in this subparagraph, the term "financial services income" means any income which is received or accrued by any person predominantly engaged in the active conduct of a banking, insurance, financing, or similar business, and which is—

(I) described in clause (ii), *or*

(II) *passive income (determined without regard to subparagraph (B)(iii)(II)).*

(ii) GENERAL DESCRIPTION OF FINANCIAL SERVICES INCOME.—Income is described in this clause if such income is—

(I) derived in the active conduct of a banking, financing, or similar business,

(II) derived from the investment by an insurance company of its unearned premiums or reserves ordinary and necessary for the proper conduct of its insurance business, or

(III) of a kind which would be insurance income as defined in section 953(a) determined without regard to those provisions of paragraph (1)(A) of such section which limit insurance income to income from countries other than the country in which the corporation was created or organized.

(iii) [*Stricken.*]

(E) NONCONTROLLED SECTION 902 CORPORATION.—

(i) IN GENERAL.—The term "noncontrolled section 902 corporation" means any foreign corporation with respect to which the taxpayer meets the stock ownership requirements of section 902(a) (or, for purposes of applying paragraph (3) *or (4)*, the requirements of section 902(b)). A controlled foreign corporation shall not be treated as a noncontrolled section 902 corporation with respect to any distribution out of its earnings and profits for periods during which it was a controlled foreign corporation.

(ii) TREATMENT OF INCLUSIONS UNDER SECTION 1293.—If any foreign corporation is a non-controlled section 902 corporation with respect to the taxpayer, any inclusion under section 1293 with respect to such corporation shall be treated as a dividend from such corporation.

(F) HIGH-TAXED INCOME.—The term "high-taxed income" means any income which (but for this subparagraph) would be passive income if the sum of—

(i) the foreign income taxes paid or accrued by the taxpayer with respect to such income, and

(ii) the foreign income taxes deemed paid by the taxpayer with respect to such income under section 902 or 960,

exceeds the highest rate of tax specified in section 1 or 11 (whichever applies) multiplied by the amount of such income (determined with regard to section 78). For purposes of the preceding sentence, the term "foreign income taxes" means any income, war profits, or excess profits tax imposed by any foreign country or possession of the United States.

(G) EXPORT FINANCING INTEREST.—For purposes of this paragraph, the term "export financing interest" means any interest derived from financing the sale (or other disposition) for use or consumption outside the United States of any property—

(i) which is manufactured, produced, grown, or extracted in the United States by the taxpayer or a related person, and

(ii) not more than 50 percent of the fair market value of which is attributable to products imported into the United States.

For purposes of clause (ii), the fair market value of any property imported into the United States shall be its appraised value, as determined by the Secretary under section 402 of the Tariff Act of 1930 (19 U.S.C. 1401a) in connection with its importation.

(H) *TREATMENT OF INCOME TAX BASE DIFFERENCES.—*

(i) *IN GENERAL.—In the case of taxable years beginning after December 31, 2006, tax imposed under the law of a foreign country or possession of the United States on an amount which does not constitute income under United States tax principles shall be treated as imposed on income described in paragraph (1)(B).*

(ii) *SPECIAL RULE FOR YEARS BEFORE 2007.—*

(I) *IN GENERAL.—In the case of taxes paid or accrued in taxable years beginning after December 31, 2004, and before January 1, 2007, a taxpayer may elect to treat tax imposed under the law of a foreign country or possession of the United States on an amount which does not constitute income under United States tax principles as tax imposed on income described in subparagraph (C) or (I) of paragraph (1).*

(II) *ELECTION IRREVOCABLE.—Any such election shall apply to the taxable year for which made and all subsequent taxable years described in subclause (I) unless revoked with the consent of the Secretary.*

(I) RELATED PERSON.—For purposes of this paragraph, the term "related person" has the meaning given such term by section 954(d)(3), except that such section shall be applied by substituting "the person with respect to whom the determination is being made" for "controlled foreign corporation" each place it appears.

(J) TRANSITIONAL RULE.—For purposes of paragraph (1)—

(i) taxes paid or accrued in a taxable year beginning before January 1, 1987, with respect to income which was described in subparagraph (A) of paragraph (1) (as in effect on the day before the date of the enactment of the Tax Reform Act of 1986) shall be treated as taxes paid or accrued with respect to income described in subparagraph (A) of paragraph (1) (as in effect after such date),

(ii) taxes paid or accrued in a taxable year beginning before January 1, 1987, with respect to income which was described in subparagraph (E) of paragraph (1) (as in effect on the day before the date of the enactment of the Tax Reform Act of 1986) shall be treated as taxes paid or accrued with respect to income described in subparagraph (I) of paragraph (1) (as in effect after such date) except that

(I) such taxes shall be treated as paid or accrued with respect to shipping income to the extent the taxpayer establishes to the satisfaction of the Secretary that such taxes were paid or accrued with respect to such income,

(II) in the case of a person described in subparagraph (C)(i), such taxes shall be treated as paid or accrued with respect to financial services income to the extent the taxpayer establishes to the satisfaction of the Secretary that such taxes were paid or accrued with respect to such income, and

(III) such taxes shall be treated as paid or accrued with respect to high withholding tax interest to the extent the taxpayer establishes to the satisfaction of the Secretary that such taxes were paid or accrued with respect to such income, and

(iii) taxes paid or accrued in a taxable year beginning before January 1, 1987, with respect to income described in any other subparagraph of paragraph (1) (as so in effect before such date) shall be treated as taxes paid or accrued with respect to income described in the corresponding subparagraph of paragraph (1) (as so in effect after such date).

(K) TRANSITIONAL RULES FOR 2007 CHANGES.—*For purposes of paragraph (1)—*

(i) taxes carried from any taxable year beginning before January 1, 2007, to any taxable year beginning on or after such date, with respect to any item of income, shall be treated as described in the subparagraph of paragraph (1) in which such income would be described were such taxes paid or accrued in a taxable year beginning on or after such date, and

(ii) the Secretary may by regulations provide for the allocation of any carryback of taxes with respect to income from a taxable year beginning on or after January 1, 2007, to a taxable year beginning before such date for purposes of allocating such income among the separate categories in effect for the taxable year to which carried.

⨠→ *Caution: Code Sec. 904(d)(3), below, as amended by H.R. 4520, Act Sec. 403(b)(5), but prior to amendment by H.R. 4520, Act Sec. 404(f)(4), applies to tax years beginning on or before December 31, 2006.*

(3) LOOK-THRU IN CASE OF CONTROLLED FOREIGN CORPORATIONS.—

(A) IN GENERAL.—Except as otherwise provided in this paragraph, dividends, interest, rents, and royalties received or accrued by the taxpayer from a controlled foreign corporation in which the taxpayer is a United States shareholder shall not be treated as income in a separate category.

(B) SUBPART F INCLUSIONS.—Any amount included in gross income under section 951(a)(1)(A) shall be treated as income in a separate category to the extent the amount so included is attributable to income in such category.

(C) INTEREST, RENTS, AND ROYALTIES.—Any interest, rent, or royalty which is received or accrued from a controlled foreign corporation in which the taxpayer is a United States shareholder shall be treated as income in a separate category to the extent it is properly allocable (under regulations prescribed by the Secretary) to income of the controlled foreign corporation in such category.

(D) DIVIDENDS.—Any dividend paid out of the earnings and profits of any controlled foreign corporation in which the taxpayer is a United States shareholder shall be treated as income in a separate category in proportion to the ratio of—

(i) the portion of the earnings and profits attributable to income in such category, to

(ii) the total amount of earnings and profits.

(E) LOOK-THRU APPLIES ONLY WHERE SUBPART F APPLIES.—If a controlled foreign corporation meets the requirements of section 954(b)(3)(A) (relating to de minimis rule) for any taxable year, for purposes of this paragraph, none of its foreign base company income (as defined in section 954(a) without regard to section 954(b)(5)) and none of its gross insurance income (as defined in section 954(b)(3)(C)) for such taxable year shall be treated as income in a separate category, except that this sentence shall not apply to any income which (without regard to this sentence) would be treated as financial services income. Solely for purposes of applying subparagraph (D), passive income of a controlled foreign corporation shall not be treated as income in a separate category if the requirements of section 954(b)(4) are met with respect to such income.

(F) SEPARATE CATEGORY.—For purposes of this paragraph—

(i) IN GENERAL.—Except as provided in clause (ii), the term "separate category" means any category of income described in subparagraph (A), (B), (C), or (D) of paragraph (1).

(ii) COORDINATION WITH HIGH-TAXED INCOME PROVISIONS.—

(I) In determining whether any income of a controlled foreign corporation is in a separate category, subclause (III) of paragraph (2)(A)(iii) shall not apply.

(II) Any income of the taxpayer which is treated as income in a separate category under this paragraph shall be so treated notwithstanding any provision of paragraph (2); except that the determination of whether any amount is high-taxed income shall be made after the application of this paragraph.

(G) DIVIDEND.—For purposes of this paragraph, the term "dividend" includes any amount included in gross income in section 951(a)(1)(B). Any amount included in gross income under section 78 to the extent attributable to amounts included in gross income in section 951(a)(1)(A) shall not be treated as a dividend but shall be treated as included in gross income under section 951(a)(1)(A).

(H) EXCEPTION FOR CERTAIN HIGH WITHHOLDING TAX INTEREST.—This paragraph shall not apply to any amount which—

(i) without regard to this paragraph, is high withholding tax interest (including any amount treated as high withholding tax interest under paragraph (2)(B)(iii)), and

(ii) would (but for this subparagraph) be treated as financial services income under this paragraph.

The amount to which this paragraph does not apply by reason of the preceding sentence shall not exceed the interest or equivalent income of the controlled foreign corporation taken into account in determining financial services income without regard to this subparagraph.

(I) LOOK-THRU APPLIES TO PASSIVE FOREIGN INVESTMENT COMPANY INCLUSION.—If—

(i) a passive foreign investment company is a controlled foreign corporation, and

(ii) the taxpayer is a United States shareholder in such controlled foreign corporation,

any amount included in gross income under section 1293 shall be treated as income in a separate category to the extent such amount is attributable to income in such category.

⟫⟫→ *Caution: Code Sec. 904(d)(3), below, as amended by H.R. 4520, applies to tax years beginning after December 31, 2006.*

(3) LOOK-THRU IN CASE OF CONTROLLED FOREIGN CORPORATIONS.—

(A) IN GENERAL.—Except as otherwise provided in this paragraph, dividends, interest, rents, and royalties received or accrued by the taxpayer from a controlled foreign corporation in which the taxpayer is a United States shareholder shall not be treated as passive category income.

(B) SUBPART F INCLUSIONS.—Any amount included in gross income under section 951(a)(1)(A) shall be treated as passive category income to the extent the amount so included is attributable to passive category income.

(C) INTEREST, RENTS, AND ROYALTIES.—Any interest, rent, or royalty which is received or accrued from a controlled foreign corporation in which the taxpayer is a United States shareholder shall be treated as passive category income to the extent it is properly allocable (under regulations prescribed by the Secretary) to passive category income of the controlled foreign corporation.

(D) DIVIDENDS.—Any dividend paid out of the earnings and profits of any controlled foreign corporation in which the taxpayer is a United States shareholder shall be treated as passive category income in proportion to the ratio of—

(i) the portion of the earnings and profits attributable to passive category income, to

(ii) the total amount of earnings and profits.

(E) LOOK-THRU APPLIES ONLY WHERE SUBPART F APPLIES.—If a controlled foreign corporation meets the requirements of section 954(b)(3)(A) (relating to de minimis rule) for any taxable year, for purposes of this paragraph, none of its foreign base company income (as defined in section 954(a) without regard to section 954(b)(5)) and none of its gross insurance income (as defined in section

954(b)(3)(C)) for such taxable year shall be treated as passive category income, except that this sentence shall not apply to any income which (without regard to this sentence) would be treated as financial services income. Solely for purposes of applying subparagraph (D), passive income of a controlled foreign corporation shall not be treated as passive category income if the requirements of section 954(b)(4) are met with respect to such income.

(F) COORDINATION WITH HIGH-TAXED INCOME PROVISIONS.—

(i) In determining whether any income of a controlled foreign corporation is passive category income, subclause (II) of paragraph (2)(B)(iii) shall not apply.

(ii) Any income of the taxpayer which is treated as passive category income under this paragraph shall be so treated notwithstanding any provision of paragraph (2); except that the determination of whether any amount is high-taxed income shall be made after the application of this paragraph.

(G) DIVIDEND.—For purposes of this paragraph, the term "dividend" includes any amount included in gross income in section 951(a)(1)(B). Any amount included in gross income under section 78 to the extent attributable to amounts included in gross income in section 951(a)(1)(A) shall not be treated as a dividend but shall be treated as included in gross income under section 951(a)(1)(A).

(H) LOOK-THRU APPLIES TO PASSIVE FOREIGN INVESTMENT COMPANY INCLUSION.—If—

(i) a passive foreign investment company is a controlled foreign corporation, and

(ii) the taxpayer is a United States shareholder in such controlled foreign corporation,

any amount included in gross income under section 1293 shall be treated as income in a separate category to the extent such amount is attributable to income in such category.

(4) LOOK-THRU APPLIES TO DIVIDENDS FROM NONCONTROLLED SECTION 902 CORPORATIONS.—

(A) IN GENERAL.—For purposes of this subsection, any dividend from a noncontrolled section 902 corporation with respect to the taxpayer shall be treated as income described in a subparagraph of paragraph (1) in proportion to the ratio of—

(i) the portion of earnings and profits attributable to income described in such subparagraph, to

(ii) the total amount of earnings and profits.

(B) EARNINGS AND PROFITS OF CONTROLLED FOREIGN CORPORATIONS.—In the case of any distribution from a controlled foreign corporation to a United States shareholder, rules similar to the rules of subparagraph (A) shall apply in determining the extent to which earnings and profits of the controlled foreign corporation which are attributable to dividends received from a noncontrolled section 902 corporation may be treated as income in a separate category.

(C) SPECIAL RULES.—For purposes of this paragraph—

(i) EARNINGS AND PROFITS.—

(I) IN GENERAL.—The rules of section 316 shall apply.

(II) REGULATIONS.—The Secretary may prescribe regulations regarding the treatment of distributions out of earnings and profits for periods before the taxpayer's acquisition of the stock to which the distributions relate.

(ii) INADEQUATE SUBSTANTIATION.—If the Secretary determines that the proper subparagraph of paragraph (1) in which a dividend is described has not been substantiated, such dividend shall be treated as income described in paragraph (1)(A).

(iii) COORDINATION WITH HIGH-TAXED INCOME PROVISIONS.—Rules similar to the rules of paragraph (3)(F) shall apply for purposes of this paragraph.

(iv) LOOK-THRU WITH RESPECT TO CARRYOVER OF CREDIT.—Rules similar to subparagraph (A) also shall apply to any carryforward under subsection (c) from a taxable year beginning before January 1, 2003, of tax allocable to a dividend from a noncontrolled section 902 corporation with respect to the taxpayer. The Secretary may by regulations provide for the allocation of any carryback of tax allocable to a dividend from a noncontrolled section 902 corporation from a taxable year beginning on or after January 1, 2003, to a taxable year

beginning before such date for purposes of allocating such dividend among the separate categories in effect for the taxable year to which carried.

(5) CONTROLLED FOREIGN CORPORATION; UNITED STATES SHAREHOLDER.—For purposes of this subsection—

(A) CONTROLLED FOREIGN CORPORATION.—The term "controlled foreign corporation" has the meaning given such term by section 957 (taking into account section 953(c)).

(B) UNITED STATES SHAREHOLDER.—The term "United States shareholder" has the meaning given such term by section 951(b) (taking into account section 953(c)).

(6) REGULATIONS.—The Secretary shall prescribe such regulations as may be necessary or appropriate for the purposes of this subsection, including regulations—

(A) for the application of paragraph (3) and subsection (f)(5) in the case of income paid (or loans made) through 1 or more entities or between 2 or more chains of entities,

(B) preventing the manipulation of the character of income the effect of which is to avoid the purposes of this subsection, and

(C) providing that rules similar to the rules of paragraph (3)(C) shall apply to interest, rents, and royalties received or accrued from entities which would be controlled foreign corporations if they were foreign corporations.

* * *

[CCH Explanation at ¶430 and ¶490. Committee Reports at ¶10,590, ¶10,600 and ¶10,690.]

Amendments

- 2004, American Jobs Creation Act of 2004 (H.R. 4520)

H.R. 4520, §403(a):

Amended Code Sec. 904(d)(4). **Effective** for tax years beginning after 12-31-2002. Prior to amendment, Code Sec. 904(d)(4) read as follows:

(4) LOOK-THRU APPLIES TO DIVIDENDS FROM NONCONTROLLED SECTION 902 CORPORATIONS.—

(A) IN GENERAL.—For purposes of this subsection, any applicable dividend shall be treated as income in a separate category in proportion to the ratio of—

(i) the portion of the earnings and profits described in subparagraph (B)(ii) attributable to income in such category, to

(ii) the total amount of such earnings and profits.

(B) APPLICABLE DIVIDEND.—For purposes of subparagraph (A), the term "applicable dividend" means any dividend—

(i) from a noncontrolled section 902 corporation with respect to the taxpayer, and

(ii) paid out of earnings and profits accumulated in taxable years beginning after December 31, 2002.

(C) SPECIAL RULES.—

(i) IN GENERAL.—Rules similar to the rules of paragraph (3)(F) shall apply for purposes of this paragraph.

(ii) EARNINGS AND PROFITS.—For purposes of this paragraph and paragraph (1)(E)—

(I) IN GENERAL.—The rules of section 316 shall apply.

(II) REGULATIONS.—The Secretary may prescribe regulations regarding the treatment of distributions out of earnings and profits for periods prior to the taxpayer's acquisition of such stock.

H.R. 4520, §403(b)(1):

Repealed Code Sec. 904(d)(1)(E). **Effective** for tax years beginning after 12-31-2002. Prior to repeal, Code Sec. 904(d)(1)(E) read as follows:

(E) in the case of a corporation, dividends from noncontrolled section 902 corporations out of earnings and profits accumulated in taxable years beginning before January 1, 2003,

H.R. 4520, §403(b)(2):

Amended Code Sec. 904(d)(2)(C)(iii) by adding "and" at the end of subclause (I), by striking subclause (II), and by redesignating subclause (III) as subclause (II). **Effective** for tax years beginning after 12-31-2002. Prior to being stricken, Code Sec. 904(d)(2)(C)(iii)(II) read as follows:

(II) any dividend from a noncontrolled section 902 corporation out of earnings and profits accumulated in taxable years beginning before January 1, 2003, and

H.R. 4520, §403(b)(3):

Amended the last sentence of Code Sec. 904(d)(2)(D). **Effective** for tax years beginning after 12-31-2002. Prior to amendment, the last sentence of Code Sec. 904(d)(2)(D) read as follows:

Such term does not include any dividend from a noncontrolled section 902 corporation out of earnings and profits accumulated in taxable years beginning before January 1, 2003 and does not include any financial services income.

H.R. 4520, §403(b)(4)(A)-(B):

Amended Code Sec. 904(d)(2)(E) by inserting "or (4)" after "paragraph (3)" in clause (i), and by striking clauses (ii) and (iv), and by redesignating clause (iii) as clause (ii). **Effective** for tax years beginning after 12-31-2002. Prior to being stricken, Code Sec. 904(d)(2)(E)(ii) and (iv) read as follows:

(ii) SPECIAL RULE FOR TAXES ON HIGH-WITHHOLDING TAX INTEREST.—If a foreign corporation is a noncontrolled section 902 corporation with respect to the taxpayer, taxes on high withholding tax interest (to the extent imposed at a rate in excess of 5 percent) shall not be treated as foreign taxes for purposes of determining the amount of foreign taxes deemed paid by the taxpayer under section 902.

* * *

(iv) ALL NON-PFICS TREATED AS ONE.—All noncontrolled section 902 corporations which are not passive foreign investment companies (as defined in section 1297) shall be treated as one noncontrolled section 902 corporation for purposes of paragraph (1).

H.R. 4520, § 403(b)(5):

Amended Code Sec. 904(d)(3)(F) by striking "(D), or (E)" and inserting "or (D)". **Effective** for tax years beginning after 12-31-2002.

H.R. 4520, § 404(a):

Amended Code Sec. 904(d)(1). **Effective** for tax years beginning after 12-31-2006. Prior to amendment, but as amended by Act Sec. 403(b)(1), Code Sec. 904(d)(1) read as follows:

(1) IN GENERAL.—The provisions of subsections (a), (b), and (c) and sections 902, 907, and 960 shall be applied separately with respect to each of the following items of income:

(A) passive income,

(B) high withholding tax interest,

(C) financial services income,

(D) shipping income,

(E) [*Repealed.*]

(F) dividends from a DISC or former DISC (as defined in section 992(a)) to the extent such dividends are treated as income from sources without the United States,

(G) taxable income attributable to foreign trade income (within the meaning of section 923(b)),

(H) distributions from a FSC (or former FSC) out of earnings and profits attributable to foreign trade income (within the meaning of section 923(b)) or interest or carrying charges (as defined in section 927(d)(1)) derived from a transaction which results in foreign trade income (as defined in section 923(b)), and

(I) income other than income described in any of the preceding subparagraphs.

H.R. 4520, § 404(b):

Amended Code Sec. 904(d)(2) by striking subparagraph (B), by redesignating subparagraph (A) as subparagraph (B), and by inserting before subparagraph (B) (as so redesignated) a new subparagraph (A). **Effective** for tax years beginning after 12-31-2006. Prior to being stricken, Code Sec. 904(d)(2)(B) read as follows:

(B) HIGH WITHHOLDING TAX INTEREST.—

(i) IN GENERAL.—Except as otherwise provided in this subparagraph, the term "high withholding tax interest" means any interest if—

(I) such interest is subject to a withholding tax of a foreign country or possession of the United States (or other tax determined on a gross basis), and

(II) the rate of such tax applicable to such interest is at least 5 percent.

(ii) EXCEPTION FOR EXPORT FINANCING.—The term "high withholding tax interest" shall not include any export financing interest.

(iii) REGULATIONS.—The Secretary may by regulations provide that—

(I) amounts (not otherwise high withholding tax interest) shall be treated as high withholding tax interest where necessary to prevent avoidance of the purposes of this subparagraph, and

(II) a tax shall not be treated as a withholding tax or other tax imposed on a gross basis if such tax is in the nature of a prepayment of a tax imposed on a net basis.

H.R. 4520, § 404(c):

Amended Code Sec. 904(d)(2)(B), as so redesignated, by adding at the end a new clause (v). **Effective** for tax years beginning after 12-31-2006.

H.R. 4520, § 404(d):

Amended Code Sec. 904(d)(2), as amended by Act Sec. 403(b)(3), by striking subparagraph (D), by redesignating subparagraph (C) as subparagraph (D), and by inserting

before subparagraph (D) (as so redesignated) a new subparagraph (C). **Effective** for tax years beginning after 12-31-2006. Prior to being stricken, but as amended by Act Sec. 403(b)(3), Code Sec. 904(d)(2)(D) read as follows:

(D) SHIPPING INCOME.—The term "shipping income" means any income received or accrued by any person which is of a kind which would be foreign base company shipping income (as defined in section 954(f)). *Such term does not include any financial services income.*

H.R. 4520, § 404(e):

Amended Code Sec. 904(d)(2) by redesignating subparagraphs (H) and (I) as subparagraphs (I) and (J), respectively, and by inserting after subparagraph (G) a new subparagraph (H). **Effective** generally for tax years beginning after 12-31-2006. For a transitional rule, see Act Sec. 404(g)(2), below.

H.R. 4520, § 404(f)(1):

Amended Code Sec. 904(d)(2)(B)(iii), as so redesignated, by striking subclause (I) and by redesignating subclauses (II) and (III) as subclauses (I) and (II), respectively. **Effective** for tax years beginning after 12-31-2006. Prior to being stricken, but as redesignated by Act Sec. 404(b), Code Sec. 904(d)(2)(B)(iii)(I) read as follows:

(I) any income described in a subparagraph of paragraph (1) other than subparagraph (A),

H.R. 4520, § 404(f)(2):

Amended Code Sec. 904(d)(2)(D)(i), as so redesignated, by adding "or" at the end of subclause (I) and by striking subclauses (II) and (III) and inserting a new subclause (II). **Effective** for tax years beginning after 12-31-2006. Prior to being stricken, but as redesignated by Act Sec. 404(d), Code Sec. 904(d)(2)(D)(i)(II) and (III) read as follows:

(II) passive income (determined without regard to subclauses (I) and (III) of subparagraph (A)(iii)), or

(III) export financing interest which (but for subparagraph (B)(ii)) would be high withholding tax interest.

H.R. 4520, § 404(f)(3):

Amended Code Sec. 904(d)(2)(D), as so redesignated and amended by Act Sec. 403(b)(3)[403(b)(2)], by striking clause (iii). **Effective** for tax years beginning after 12-31-2006. Prior to being stricken, but as amended by Act Sec. 403(b)(2) and redesignated by Act Sec. 404(d), Code Sec. 904(d)(2)(D)(iii) read as follows:

(iii) EXCEPTIONS.—The term "financial services income" does not include—

(I) any high withholding tax interest, and

(II) any export financing interest not described in clause (i)(III).

H.R. 4520, § 404(f)(4):

Amended Code Sec. 904(d)(3). **Effective** for tax years beginning after 12-31-2006. Prior to amendment, Code Sec. 904(d)(3) read as follows:

(3) LOOK-THRU IN CASE OF CONTROLLED FOREIGN CORPORATIONS.—

(A) IN GENERAL.—Except as otherwise provided in this paragraph, dividends, interest, rents, and royalties received or accrued by the taxpayer from a controlled foreign corporation in which the taxpayer is a United States shareholder shall not be treated as income in a separate category.

(B) SUBPART F INCLUSIONS.—Any amount included in gross income under section 951(a)(1)(A) shall be treated as income in a separate category to the extent the amount so included is attributable to income in such category.

(C) INTEREST, RENTS, AND ROYALTIES.—Any interest, rent, or royalty which is received or accrued from a controlled foreign corporation in which the taxpayer is a United States shareholder shall be treated as income in a separate category to the extent it is properly allocable (under regulations prescribed by the Secretary) to income of the controlled foreign corporation in such category.

(D) DIVIDENDS.—Any dividend paid out of the earnings and profits of any controlled foreign corporation in which the taxpayer is a United States shareholder shall be treated as income in a separate category in proportion to the ratio of—

(i) the portion of the earnings and profits attributable to income in such category, to

(ii) the total amount of earnings and profits.

(E) LOOK-THRU APPLIES ONLY WHERE SUBPART F APPLIES.—If a controlled foreign corporation meets the requirements of section 954(b)(3)(A) (relating to de minimis rule) for any taxable year, for purposes of this paragraph, none of its foreign base company income (as defined in section 954(a) without regard to section 954(b)(5)) and none of its gross insurance income (as defined in section 954(b)(3)(C)) for such taxable year shall be treated as income in a separate category, except that this sentence shall not apply to any income which (without regard to this sentence) would be treated as financial services income. Solely for purposes of applying subparagraph (D), passive income of a controlled foreign corporation shall not be treated as income in a separate category if the requirements of section 954(b)(4) are met with respect to such income.

(F) SEPARATE CATEGORY.—For purposes of this paragraph—

(i) IN GENERAL.—Except as provided in clause (ii), the term "separate category" means any category of income described in subparagraph (A), (B), (C), or (D) of paragraph (1).

(ii) COORDINATION WITH HIGH-TAXED INCOME PROVISIONS.—

(I) In determining whether any income of a controlled foreign corporation is in a separate category, subclause (III) of paragraph (2)(A)(iii) shall not apply.

(II) Any income of the taxpayer which is treated as income in a separate category under this paragraph shall be so treated notwithstanding any provision of paragraph (2); except that the determination of whether any amount is high-taxed income shall be made after the application of this paragraph.

(G) DIVIDEND.—For purposes of this paragraph, the term "dividend" includes any amount included in gross income in section 951(a)(1)(B). Any amount included in gross income under section 78 to the extent attributable to amounts included in gross income in section 951(a)(1)(A) shall not be treated as a dividend but shall be treated as included in gross income under section 951(a)(1)(A).

(f) RECAPTURE OF OVERALL FOREIGN LOSS.—

* * *

(3) DISPOSITIONS.—

* * *

(H) EXCEPTION FOR CERTAIN HIGH WITHHOLDING TAX INTEREST.—This paragraph shall not apply to any amount which—

(i) without regard to this paragraph, is high withholding tax interest (including any amount treated as high withholding tax interest under paragraph (2)(B)(iii)), and

(ii) would (but for this subparagraph) be treated as financial services income under this paragraph.

The amount to which this paragraph does not apply by reason of the preceding sentence shall not exceed the interest or equivalent income of the controlled foreign corporation taken into account in determining financial services income without regard to this subparagraph.

(I) LOOK-THRU APPLIES TO PASSIVE FOREIGN INVESTMENT COMPANY INCLUSION.—If—

(i) a passive foreign investment company is a controlled foreign corporation, and

(ii) the taxpayer is a United States shareholder in such controlled foreign corporation,

any amount included in gross income under section 1293 shall be treated as income in a separate category to the extent such amount is attributable to income in such category.

H.R. 4520, § 404(f)(5):

Amended Code Sec. 904(d)(2) by adding at the end a new subparagraph (K). **Effective** for tax years beginning after 12-31-2006.

H.R. 4520, § 404(g)(2), provides:

(2) TRANSITIONAL RULE RELATING TO INCOME TAX BASE DIFFERENCE.—Section 904(d)(2)(H)(ii) of the Internal Revenue Code of 1986, as added by subsection (e), shall apply to taxable years beginning after December 31, 2004.

H.R. 4520, § 413(c)(14):

Amended Code Sec. 904(d)(2)(A)(ii), prior to redesignation by Act Sec. 404(b). **Effective** for tax years of foreign corporations beginning after 12-31-2004, and for tax years of United States shareholders with or within which such tax years of foreign corporations end. Prior to amendment and redesignation, Code Sec. 904(d)(2)(A)(ii) read as follows:

(ii) CERTAIN AMOUNTS INCLUDED.—Except as provided in clause (iii), the term "passive income" includes any amount includible in gross income under section 551 or, except as provided in subparagraph (E)(iii) or paragraph (3)(I), section 1293 (relating to certain passive foreign investment companies).

(D) APPLICATION TO CERTAIN DISPOSITIONS OF STOCK IN CONTROLLED FOREIGN CORPORATION.—

(i) IN GENERAL.—This paragraph shall apply to an applicable disposition in the same manner as if it were a disposition of property described in subparagraph (A), except that the exception contained in subparagraph (C)(i) shall not apply.

(ii) APPLICABLE DISPOSITION.—For purposes of clause (i), the term "applicable disposition" means any disposition of any share of stock in a controlled foreign corporation in a transaction or series of transactions if, immediately before such transaction or series of transactions, the taxpayer owned more than 50 percent (by vote or value) of the stock of the controlled foreign corporation. Such term shall not include a disposition described in clause (iii) or (iv), except that clause (i) shall apply to any gain recognized on any such disposition.

(iii) EXCEPTION FOR CERTAIN EXCHANGES WHERE OWNERSHIP PERCENTAGE RETAINED.—A disposition shall not be treated as an applicable disposition under clause (ii) if it is part of a transaction or series of transactions—

(I) to which section 351 or 721 applies, or under which the transferor receives stock in a foreign corporation in exchange for the stock in the controlled foreign corporation and the stock received is exchanged basis property (as defined in section 7701(a)(44)), and

(II) immediately after which, the transferor owns (by vote or value) at least the same percentage of stock in the controlled foreign corporation (or, if the controlled foreign corporation is not in existence after such transaction or series of transactions, in another foreign corporation stock in which was received by the transferor in exchange for stock in the controlled foreign corporation) as the percentage of stock in the controlled foreign corporation which the taxpayer owned immediately before such transaction or series of transactions.

(iv) EXCEPTION FOR CERTAIN ASSET ACQUISITIONS.—A disposition shall not be treated as an applicable disposition under clause (ii) if it is part of a transaction or series of transactions in which the taxpayer (or any member of a controlled group of corporations filing a consolidated return under section 1501 which includes the taxpayer) acquires the assets of a controlled foreign corporation in exchange for the shares of the controlled foreign corporation in a liquidation described in section 332 or a reorganization described in section 368(a)(1).

(v) CONTROLLED FOREIGN CORPORATION.—For purposes of this subparagraph, the term "controlled foreign corporation" has the meaning given such term by section 957.

(vi) STOCK OWNERSHIP.—For purposes of this subparagraph, ownership of stock shall be determined under the rules of subsections (a) and (b) of section 958.

* * *

[CCH Explanation at ¶ 425. Committee Reports at ¶ 11,670.]

Amendments

• **2004, American Jobs Creation Act of 2004 (H.R. 4520)**

H.R. 4520, § 895(a):

Amended Code Sec. 904(f)(3) by adding at the end new subparagraph (D). **Effective** for dispositions after the date of the enactment of this Act.

⫸→ *Caution: Code Sec. 904(g), below, as added by H.R. 4520, is effective for tax years beginning after December 31, 2006.*

(g) RECHARACTERIZATION OF OVERALL DOMESTIC LOSS.—

(1) GENERAL RULE.—For purposes of this subpart and section 936, in the case of any taxpayer who sustains an overall domestic loss for any taxable year beginning after December 31, 2006, that portion of the taxpayer's taxable income from sources within the United States for each succeeding taxable year which is equal to the lesser of—

(A) the amount of such loss (to the extent not used under this paragraph in prior taxable years), or

(B) 50 percent of the taxpayer's taxable income from sources within the United States for such succeeding taxable year,

shall be treated as income from sources without the United States (and not as income from sources within the United States).

(2) OVERALL DOMESTIC LOSS DEFINED.—For purposes of this subsection—

(A) IN GENERAL.—The term "overall domestic loss" means any domestic loss to the extent such loss offsets taxable income from sources without the United States for the taxable year or for any preceding taxable year by reason of a carryback. For purposes of the preceding sentence, the term "domestic loss" means the amount by which the gross income for the taxable year from sources within the United States is exceeded by the sum of the deductions properly apportioned or allocated thereto (determined without regard to any carryback from a subsequent taxable year).

(B) TAXPAYER MUST HAVE ELECTED FOREIGN TAX CREDIT FOR YEAR OF LOSS.—The term "overall domestic loss" shall not include any loss for any taxable year unless the taxpayer chose the benefits of this subpart for such taxable year.

(3) CHARACTERIZATION OF SUBSEQUENT INCOME.—

(A) IN GENERAL.—Any income from sources within the United States that is treated as income from sources without the United States under paragraph (1) shall be allocated among and increase the income categories in proportion to the loss from sources within the United States previously allocated to those income categories.

(B) INCOME CATEGORY.—For purposes of this paragraph, the term "income category" has the meaning given such term by subsection (f)(5)(E)(i).

(4) COORDINATION WITH SUBSECTION (f).—The Secretary shall prescribe such regulations as may be necessary to coordinate the provisions of this subsection with the provisions of subsection (f).

[CCH Explanation at ¶ 420. Committee Reports at ¶ 10,580.]

Amendments

• **2004, American Jobs Creation Act of 2004 (H.R. 4520)**

H.R. 4520, § 402(a):

Amended Code Sec. 904 by redesignating subsections (g), (h), (i), (j), and (k) as subsections (h), (i), (j), (k), and (l)

respectively, and by inserting after subsection (f) a new subsection (g). **Effective** for losses for tax years beginning after 12-31-2006.

⋙→ Caution: Former Code Sec. 904(g), below, was redesignated as Code Sec. 904(h) by H.R. 4520, applicable to losses for tax years beginning after December 31, 2006.

(h) SOURCE RULES IN CASE OF UNITED STATES-OWNED FOREIGN CORPORATIONS.—

(1) IN GENERAL.—The following amounts which are derived from a United States-owned foreign corporation and which would be treated as derived from sources outside the United States without regard to this subsection shall, for purposes of this section, be treated as derived from sources within the United States to the extent provided in this subsection:

(A) Any amount included in gross income under—

(i) section 951(a) (relating to amounts included in gross income of United States shareholders), *or*

(ii) section 1293 (relating to current taxation of income from qualified funds).

(B) Interest.

(C) Dividends.

(2) SUBPART F AND PASSIVE FOREIGN INVESTMENT COMPANY INCLUSIONS.—Any amount described in subparagraph (A) of paragraph (1) shall be treated as derived from sources within the United States to the extent such amount is attributable to income of the United States-owned foreign corporation from sources within the United States.

* * *

[CCH Explanation at ¶ 420 and ¶ 490. Committee Reports at ¶ 10,580 and ¶ 10,690.]

Amendments

• **2004, American Jobs Creation Act of 2004 (H.R. 4520)**

H.R. 4520, § 402(a):

Amended Code Sec. 904 by redesignating subsection (g) as subsection (h). **Effective** for losses for tax years beginning after 12-31-2006.

H.R. 4520, § 413(c)(15)(A):

Amended Code Sec. 904(h)(1)(A), as redesignated by Act Sec. 402(a), by adding "or" at the end of clause (i), by striking clause (ii), and by redesignating clause (iii) as clause (ii). **Effective** for tax years of foreign corporations beginning after 12-31-2004, and for tax years of United States share-

holders with or within which such tax years of foreign corporations end. Prior to being stricken, Code Sec. 904(h)(1)(A)(ii) read as follows:

(ii) section 551 (relating to foreign personal holding company income taxed to United States shareholders), or

H.R. 4520, § 413(c)(15)(B):

Amended the heading of Code Sec. 904(h)(2), as redesignated by Act Sec. 402(a), by striking "FOREIGN PERSONAL HOLDING OR" immediately preceding "PASSIVE FOREIGN INVESTMENT". **Effective** for tax years of foreign corporations beginning after 12-31-2004, and for tax years of United States shareholders with or within which such tax years of foreign corporations end.

>>>→ *Caution: Former Code Sec. 904(h), below, was redesignated as Code Sec. 904(i) by H.R. 4520, applicable to losses for tax years beginning after December 31, 2006.*

(i) COORDINATION WITH NONREFUNDABLE PERSONAL CREDITS.—In the case of an individual, for purposes of subsection (a), the tax against which the credit is taken is such tax reduced by the sum of the credits allowable under subpart A of part IV of subchapter A of this chapter (other than sections 23, 24, and 25B). This subsection shall not apply to taxable years beginning during 2000, 2001, 2002, 2003, 2004, or 2005.

[CCH Explanation at ¶ 420. Committee Reports at ¶ 10,580.]

Amendments
• **2004, American Jobs Creation Act of 2004 (H.R. 4520)**

H.R. 4520, § 402(a):

Amended Code Sec. 904 by redesignating subsection (h) as subsection (i). **Effective** for losses for tax years beginning after 12-31-2006.

>>>→ *Caution: Former Code Sec. 904(i), below, was redesignated as Code Sec. 904(j) by H.R. 4520, applicable to losses for tax years beginning after December 31, 2006.*

(j) LIMITATION ON USE OF DECONSOLIDATION TO AVOID FOREIGN TAX CREDIT LIMITATIONS.—If 2 or more domestic corporations would be members of the same affiliated group if—

    (1) section 1504(b) were applied without regard to the exceptions contained therein, and

    (2) the constructive ownership rules of section 1563(e) applied for purposes of section 1504(a),

the Secretary may by regulations provide for resourcing the income of any of such corporations or for modifications to the consolidated return regulations to the extent that such resourcing or modifications are necessary to prevent the avoidance of the provisions of this subpart.

[CCH Explanation at ¶ 420. Committee Reports at ¶ 10,580.]

Amendments
• **2004, American Jobs Creation Act of 2004 (H.R. 4520)**

H.R. 4520, § 402(a):

Amended Code Sec. 904 by redesignating subsection (i) as subsection (j). **Effective** for losses for tax years beginning after 12-31-2006.

>>>→ *Caution: Former Code Sec. 904(j), below, was redesignated as Code Sec. 904(k) by H.R. 4520, applicable to losses for tax years beginning after December 31, 2006.*

(k) CERTAIN INDIVIDUALS EXEMPT.—

* * *

    (3) DEFINITIONS.—For purposes of this subsection—

        (A) QUALIFIED PASSIVE INCOME.—The term "qualified passive income" means any item of gross income if—

            (i) such item of income is passive income (as defined in *subsection (d)(2)(B)* without regard to clause (iii) thereof), and

            (ii) such item of income is shown on a payee statement furnished to the individual.

* * *

[CCH Explanation at ¶ 420. Committee Reports at ¶ 10,580.]

Amendments

• **2004, American Jobs Creation Act of 2004 (H.R. 4520)**

H.R. 4520, § 402(a):

Amended Code Sec. 904 by redesignating subsection (j) as subsection (k). **Effective** for losses for tax years beginning after 12-31-2006.

H.R. 4520, § 404(f)(6):

Amended Code Sec. 904(j)(3)(A)(i) [prior to redesignation by § 402(a)] by striking "subsection (d)(2)(A)" and inserting

"subsection (d)(2)(B)". **Effective** generally for tax years beginning after 12-31-2006. For a transitional rule, see Act Sec. 404(g)(2), below.

H.R. 4520, § 404(g)(2), provides:

(2) TRANSITIONAL RULE RELATING TO INCOME TAX BASE DIFFERENCE.—Section 904(d)(2)(H)(ii) of the Internal Revenue Code of 1986, as added by subsection (e), shall apply to taxable years beginning after December 31, 2004.

>>>→ *Caution: Former Code Sec. 904(k), below, was redesignated as Code Sec. 904(l) by H.R. 4520, applicable to losses for tax years beginning after December 31, 2006.*

(l) CROSS REFERENCES.—

* * *

[CCH Explanation at ¶ 420. Committee Reports at ¶ 10,580.]

• **2004, American Jobs Creation Act of 2004 (H.R. 4520)**

H.R. 4520, § 402(a):

Amended Code Sec. 904 by redesignating subsection (k) as subsection (l). **Effective** for losses for tax years beginning after 12-31-2006.

[¶ 5660] CODE SEC. 907. SPECIAL RULES IN CASE OF FOREIGN OIL AND GAS INCOME.

* * *

(f) CARRYBACK AND CARRYOVER OF DISALLOWED CREDITS.—

(1) IN GENERAL.—If the amount of the oil and gas extraction taxes paid or accrued during any taxable year exceeds the limitation provided by subsection (a) for such taxable year (hereinafter in this subsection referred to as the "unused credit year"), such excess shall be deemed to be oil and gas extraction taxes paid or accrued in the first preceding taxable year, *and in any of the first 10* succeeding taxable year, in that order and to the extent not deemed tax paid or accrued in a prior taxable year by reason of the limitation imposed by paragraph (2). Such amount deemed paid or accrued in any taxable year may be availed of only as a tax credit and not as a deduction and only if the taxpayer for such year chooses to have the benefits of this subpart as to taxes paid or accrued for that year to foreign countries or possessions.

* * *

[CCH Explanation at ¶ 415. Committee Reports at ¶ 10,730.]

Amendments

• **2004, American Jobs Creation Act of 2004 (H.R. 4520)**

H.R. 4520, § 417(b)(1):

Amended Code Sec. 907(f)(1) by striking "in the second preceding taxable year," immediately preceding "in the first preceding taxable year". **Effective** for excess foreign taxes arising in tax years beginning after the date of the enactment of this Act.

H.R. 4520, § 417(b)(2):

Amended Code Sec. 907(f)(1) by striking ", and in the first, second, third, fourth, or fifth" and inserting "and in

any of the first 10". **Effective** for excess foreign taxes which (without regard to the amendments made by this section) may be carried to any tax year ending after the date of the enactment of this Act.

H.R. 4520, § 417(b)(3):

Amended Code Sec. 907(f)(1) by striking the last sentence. **Effective** on the date of enactment of this Act. Prior to amendment, the last sentence of Code Sec. 907(f)(1) read as follows:

For purposes of this subsection, the terms "second preceding taxable year", and "first preceding taxable year" do not include any taxable year ending before January 1, 1975.

[¶5665] CODE SEC. 931. INCOME FROM SOURCES WITHIN GUAM, AMERICAN SAMOA, OR THE NORTHERN MARIANA ISLANDS.

* * *

(d) EMPLOYEES OF THE UNITED STATES.—Amounts paid for services performed as an employee of the United States (or any agency thereof) shall be treated as not described in paragraph (1) or (2) of subsection (a).

[CCH Explanation at ¶580. Committee Reports at ¶11,800.]

Amendments

• 2004, American Jobs Creation Act of 2004 (H.R. 4520)

H.R. 4520, §908(c)(1):

Amended Code Sec. 931(d). **Effective** for tax years ending after the date of the enactment of this Act. Prior to amendment, Code. Sec. 931(d) read as follows:

(d) SPECIAL RULES.—For purposes of this section—

(1) EMPLOYEES OF THE UNITED STATES.—Amounts paid for services performed as an employee of the United States (or

any agency thereof) shall be treated as not described in paragraph (1) or (2) of subsection (a).

(2) DETERMINATION OF SOURCE, ETC.—The determination as to whether income is described in paragraph (1) or (2) of subsection (a) shall be made under regulations prescribed by the Secretary.

(3) DETERMINATION OF RESIDENCY.—For purposes of this section and section 876, the determination of whether an individual is a bona fide resident of Guam, American Samoa, or the Northern Marina Islands shall be made under regulations prescribed by the Secretary.

[¶5670] CODE SEC. 932. COORDINATION OF UNITED STATES AND VIRGIN ISLANDS INCOME TAXES.

(a) TREATMENT OF UNITED STATES RESIDENTS.—

(1) APPLICATION OF SUBSECTION.—This subsection shall apply to an individual for the taxable year if—

(A) such individual—

(i) is a citizen or resident of the United States (other than a bona fide resident of the Virgin Islands *during the entire taxable year*), and

(ii) has income derived from sources within the Virgin Islands, or effectively connected with the conduct of a trade or business within such possession, for the taxable year, or

(B) such individual files a joint return for the taxable year with an individual described in subparagraph (A).

* * *

[CCH Explanation at ¶580. Committee Reports at ¶11,800.]

Amendments

• 2004, American Jobs Creation Act of 2004 (H.R. 4520)

H.R. 4520, §908(c)(2):

Amended Code Sec. 932 by striking "at the close of the taxable year" and inserting "during the entire taxable year"

each place it appears. **Effective** for tax years ending after the date of the enactment of this Act.

(c) TREATMENT OF VIRGIN ISLANDS RESIDENTS.—

(1) APPLICATION OF SUBSECTION.—This subsection shall apply to an individual for the taxable year if—

(A) such individual is a bona fide resident of the Virgin Islands *during the entire taxable year*, or

(B) such individual files a joint return for the taxable year with an individual described in subparagraph (A).

(2) FILING REQUIREMENT.—Each individual to whom this subsection applies for the taxable year shall file an income tax return for the taxable year with the Virgin Islands.

(3) EXTENT OF INCOME TAX LIABILITY.—In the case of an individual to whom this subsection applies in a taxable year for purposes of so much of this title (other than this section and section 7654) as relates to the taxes imposed by this chapter, the Virgin Islands shall be treated as including the United States.

(4) RESIDENTS OF THE VIRGIN ISLANDS.—In the case of an individual—

(A) who is a bona fide resident of the Virgin Islands *during the entire taxable year*,

(B) who, on his return of income tax to the Virgin Islands, reports income from all sources and identifies the source of each item shown on such return, and

(C) who fully pays his tax liability referred to in section 934(a) to the Virgin Islands with respect to such income,

for purposes of calculating income tax liability to the United States, gross income shall not include any amount included in gross income on such return, and allocable deductions and credits shall not be taken into account.

* * *

[CCH Explanation at ¶ 580. Committee Reports at ¶ 11,800.]

Amendments

• **2004, American Jobs Creation Act of 2004 (H.R. 4520)**

H.R. 4520, § 908(c)(2):

Amended Code Sec. 932 by striking "at the close of the taxable year" and inserting "during the entire taxable year"

each place it appears. **Effective** for tax years ending after the date of the enactment of this Act.

[¶ 5675] CODE SEC. 934. LIMITATION ON REDUCTION IN INCOME TAX LIABILITY INCURRED TO THE VIRGIN ISLANDS.

* * *

(b) REDUCTIONS PERMITTED WITH RESPECT TO CERTAIN INCOME.—

* * *

(4) DETERMINATION OF INCOME SOURCE, ETC.—The determination as to whether income is derived from sources within the United States or is effectively connected with the conduct of a trade or business within the United States shall be made under regulations prescribed by the Secretary.

[CCH Explanation at ¶ 580. Committee Reports at ¶ 11,800.]

Amendments

• **2004, American Jobs Creation Act of 2004 (H.R. 4520)**

H.R. 4520, § 908(c)(3):

Amended Code Sec. 934(b)(4) by striking "the Virgin Islands or" each place it appears after "within". **Effective** for tax years ending after the date of the enactment of this Act.

»»→ *Caution: Code Sec. 935, below, was repealed by P.L. 99-514 but remains effective until an implementing agreement between the U.S. and Guam is entered into.*

[¶ 5680] CODE SEC. 935. COORDINATION OF UNITED STATES AND GUAM INDIVIDUAL INCOME TAXES.

(a) APPLICATION OF SECTION.—This section shall apply to any individual *who, during the entire taxable year—*

(1) is a *bona fide* resident of Guam,

(2) is a citizen of Guam but not otherwise a citizen of the United States,

(3) has income derived from Guam for the taxable year and is a citizen or resident of the United States, or

(4) files a joint return for the taxable year with an individual who satisfies paragraph (1), (2), or (3) for the taxable year.

[CCH Explanation at ¶ 580. Committee Reports at ¶ 11,800.]

Amendments

• **2004, American Jobs Creation Act of 2004 (H.R. 4520)**

H.R. 4520, § 908(c)(4)(A)-(B):

Amended Code Sec. 935, as in effect before the effective date of its repeal, by striking "for the taxable year who" in

subsection (a) and inserting "who, during the entire taxable year", and by inserting "bona fide" before "resident" in subsection (a)(1). **Effective** for tax years ending after the date of the enactment of this Act.

(b) FILING REQUIREMENT.—

(1) IN GENERAL.—Each individual to whom this section applies for the taxable year shall file his income tax return for the taxable year—

(A) with the United States *(other than a bona fide resident of Guam during the entire taxable year)*, if he is a resident of the United States,

(B) with Guam, if he is a *bona fide* resident of Guam, and

(C) if neither subparagraph (A) nor subparagraph (B) applies—

(i) with Guam, if he is a citizen of Guam but not otherwise a citizen of the United States, or

(ii) with the United States, if clause (i) does not apply.

(2) DETERMINATION DATE.—For purposes of this section, determinations of citizenship for the taxable year shall be made as of the close of the taxable year.

* * *

[CCH Explanation at ¶ 580. Committee Reports at ¶ 11,800.]

Amendments

• **2004, American Jobs Creation Act of 2004 (H.R. 4520)**

H.R. 4520, § 908(c)(4)(C)(i)-(ii):

Amended Code Sec. 935(b)(1), as in effect before the effective date of its repeal, by inserting "(other a bona fide resident of Guam during the entire taxable year)" after "United States" in subparagraph (A), and by inserting "bona fide" before "resident" in subparagraph (B). **Effective** for tax years ending after the date of the enactment of this Act.

H.R. 4520, § 908(c)(4)(D):

Amended Code Sec. 935(b)(2), as in effect before the effective date of its repeal, by striking "residence and" before "citizenship". **Effective** for tax years ending after the date of the enactment of this Act.

[¶ 5685] CODE SEC. 936. PUERTO RICO AND POSSESSION TAX CREDIT.

(a) ALLOWANCE OF CREDIT.—

* * *

(2) CONDITIONS WHICH MUST BE SATISFIED.—The conditions referred to in paragraph (1) are:

»»→ *Caution: Code Sec. 936(a)(2)(A), below, as amended by H.R. 4520, applies to losses for tax years beginning after December 31, 2006.*

(A) 3-YEAR PERIOD.—If 80 percent or more of the gross income of such domestic corporation for the 3-year period immediately preceding the close of the taxable year (or for such part of such period immediately preceding the close of such taxable year as may be applicable) was derived from sources within a possession of the United States (determined without regard to *subsections (f) and (g) of section 904*); and

* * *

[CCH Explanation at ¶ 420. Committee Reports at ¶ 10,580.]

Amendments

• **2004, American Jobs Creation Act of 2004 (H.R. 4520)**

H.R. 4520, § 402(b)(2):

Amended Code Sec. 936(a)(2)(A) by striking "section 904(f)" and inserting "subsections (f) and (g) of section 904". **Effective** for losses for tax years beginning after 12-31-2006.

[¶ 5690] *CODE SEC. 937. RESIDENCE AND SOURCE RULES INVOLVING POSSESSIONS.*

(a) BONA FIDE RESIDENT.—For purposes of this subpart, section 865(g)(3), section 876, section 881(b), paragraphs (2) and (3) of section 901(b), section 957(c), section 3401(a)(8)(C), and section 7654(a), except as provided in regulations, the term "bona fide resident" means a person—

(1) who is present for at least 183 days during the taxable year in Guam, American Samoa, the Northern Mariana Islands, Puerto Rico, or the Virgin Islands, as the case may be, and

(2) who does not have a tax home (determined under the principles of section 911(d)(3) without regard to the second sentence thereof) outside such specified possession during the taxable year and does not have a closer connection (determined under the principles of section 7701(b)(3)(B)(ii)) to the United States or a foreign country than to such specified possession.

For purposes of paragraph (1), the determination as to whether a person is present for any day shall be made under the principles of section 7701(b).

(b) SOURCE RULES.—Except as provided in regulations, for purposes of this title—

(1) except as provided in paragraph (2), rules similar to the rules for determining whether income is income from sources within the United States or is effectively connected with the conduct of a trade or business within the United States shall apply for purposes of determining whether income is from sources within a possession specified in subsection (a)(1) or effectively connected with the conduct of a trade or business within any such possession, and

(2) any income treated as income from sources within the United States or as effectively connected with the conduct of a trade or business within the United States shall not be treated as income from sources within any such possession or as effectively connected with the conduct of a trade or business within any such possession.

(c) REPORTING REQUIREMENT.—

(1) IN GENERAL.—If, for any taxable year, an individual takes the position for United States income tax reporting purposes that the individual became, or ceases to be, a bona fide resident of a possession specified in subsection (a)(1), such individual shall file with the Secretary, at such time and in such manner as the Secretary may prescribe, notice of such position.

(2) TRANSITION RULE.—If, for any of an individual's 3 taxable years ending before the individual's first taxable year ending after the date of the enactment of this subsection, the individual took a position described in paragraph (1), the individual shall file with the Secretary, at such time and in such manner as the Secretary may prescribe, notice of such position.

* * *

[CCH Explanation at ¶ 580. Committee Reports at ¶ 11,800.]

Amendments

• **2004, American Jobs Creation Act of 2004 (H.R. 4520)**

H.R. 4520, § 908(a):

Amended subpart D of part III of subchapter N of chapter 1 by adding at the end new Code Sec. 937. **Effective** generally for tax years ending after the date of the enactment of this Act. For special rules, see Act Sec. 908(d)(2)-(3), below.

H.R. 4520, § 908(d)(2)-(3), provides:

(2) 183-DAY RULE.—Section 937(a)(1) of the Internal Revenue Code of 1986 (as added by this section) shall apply to taxable years beginning after the date of the enactment of this Act.

(3) SOURCING.—Section 937(b)(2) of such Code (as so added) shall apply to income earned after the date of the enactment of this Act.

[¶ 5695] CODE SEC. 941. QUALIFYING FOREIGN TRADE INCOME. [*Repealed.*]

* * *

[CCH Explanation at ¶ 205. Committee Reports at ¶ 10,010.]

Amendments

• **2004, American Jobs Creation Act of 2004 (H.R. 4520)**

H.R. 4520, § 101(b)(1):

Repealed subpart E of part III of subchapter N of chapter 1 (Code Secs. 941-943). **Effective** for transactions after 12-31-2004. For transitional and special rules, see Act Secs. 101(d)-(f), below. Prior to repeal, Code Sec. 941 read as follows:

SEC. 941. QUALIFYING FOREIGN TRADE INCOME.

(a) QUALIFYING FOREIGN TRADE INCOME.—For purposes of this subpart and section 114—

(1) IN GENERAL.—The term "qualifying foreign trade income" means, with respect to any transaction, the amount of gross income which, if excluded, will result in a reduction of the taxable income of the taxpayer from such transaction equal to the greatest of—

(A) 30 percent of the foreign sale and leasing income derived by the taxpayer from such transaction,

(B) 1.2 percent of the foreign trading gross receipts derived by the taxpayer from the transaction, or

(C) 15 percent of the foreign trade income derived by the taxpayer from the transaction.

In no event shall the amount determined under subparagraph (B) exceed 200 percent of the amount determined under subparagraph (C).

(2) ALTERNATIVE COMPUTATION.—A taxpayer may compute its qualifying foreign trade income under a subparagraph of paragraph (1) other than the subparagraph which results in the greatest amount of such income.

(3) LIMITATION ON USE OF FOREIGN TRADING GROSS RECEIPTS METHOD.—If any person computes its qualifying foreign trade income from any transaction with respect to any property under paragraph (1)(B), the qualifying foreign trade income of such person (or any related person) with respect

to any other transaction involving such property shall be zero.

(4) RULES FOR MARGINAL COSTING.—The Secretary shall prescribe regulations setting forth rules for the allocation of expenditures in computing foreign trade income under paragraph (1)(C) in those cases where a taxpayer is seeking to establish or maintain a market for qualifying foreign trade property.

(5) PARTICIPATION IN INTERNATIONAL BOYCOTTS, ETC.—Under regulations prescribed by the Secretary, the qualifying foreign trade income of a taxpayer for any taxable year shall be reduced (but not below zero) by the sum of—

(A) an amount equal to such income multiplied by the international boycott factor determined under section 999, and

(B) any illegal bribe, kickback, or other payment (within the meaning of section 162(c)) paid by or on behalf of the taxpayer directly or indirectly to an official, employee, or agent in fact of a government.

(b) FOREIGN TRADE INCOME.—For purposes of this subpart—

(1) IN GENERAL.—The term "foreign trade income" means the taxable income of the taxpayer attributable to foreign trading gross receipts of the taxpayer.

(2) SPECIAL RULE FOR COOPERATIVES.—In any case in which an organization to which part I of subchapter T applies which is engaged in the marketing of agricultural or horticultural products sells qualifying foreign trade property, in computing the taxable income of such cooperative, there shall not be taken into account any deduction allowable under subsection (b) or (c) of section 1382 (relating to patronage dividends, per-unit retain allocations, and nonpatronage distributions).

(c) FOREIGN SALE AND LEASING INCOME.—For purposes of this section—

(1) IN GENERAL.—The term "foreign sale and leasing income" means, with respect to any transaction—

(A) foreign trade income properly allocable to activities which—

(i) are described in paragraph (2)(A)(i) or (3) of section 942(b), and

(ii) are performed by the taxpayer (or any person acting under a contract with such taxpayer) outside the United States, or

(B) foreign trade income derived by the taxpayer in connection with the lease or rental of qualifying foreign trade property for use by the lessee outside the United States.

(2) SPECIAL RULES FOR LEASED PROPERTY.—

(A) SALES INCOME.—The term "foreign sale and leasing income" includes any foreign trade income derived by the taxpayer from the sale of property described in paragraph (1)(B).

(B) LIMITATION IN CERTAIN CASES.—Except as provided in regulations, in the case of property which—

(i) was manufactured, produced, grown, or extracted by the taxpayer, or

(ii) was acquired by the taxpayer from a related person for a price which was not determined in accordance with the rules of section 482,

the amount of foreign trade income which may be treated as foreign sale and leasing income under paragraph (1)(B) or subparagraph (A) of this paragraph with respect to any transaction involving such property shall not exceed the amount which would have been determined if the taxpayer had acquired such property for the price determined in accordance with the rules of section 482.

(3) SPECIAL RULES.—

(A) EXCLUDED PROPERTY.—Foreign sale and leasing income shall not include any income properly allocable to excluded property described in subparagraph (B) of section 943(a)(3) (relating to intangibles).

(B) ONLY DIRECT EXPENSES TAKEN INTO ACCOUNT.—For purposes of this subsection, any expense other than a directly allocable expense shall not be taken into account in computing foreign trade income.

H.R. 4520, § 101(d)-(f), provides:

(d) TRANSITIONAL RULE FOR 2005 AND 2006.—

(1) IN GENERAL.—In the case of transactions during 2005 or 2006, the amount includible in gross income by reason of the amendments made by this section shall not exceed the applicable percentage of the amount which would have been so included but for this subsection.

(2) APPLICABLE PERCENTAGE.—For purposes of paragraph (1), the applicable percentage shall be as follows:

(A) For 2005, the applicable percentage shall be 20 percent.

(B) For 2006, the applicable percentage shall be 40 percent.

(e) REVOCATION OF ELECTION TO BE TREATED AS DOMESTIC CORPORATION.—If, during the 1-year period beginning on the date of the enactment of this Act, a corporation for which an election is in effect under section 943(e) of the Internal Revenue Code of 1986 revokes such election, no gain or loss shall be recognized with respect to property treated as transferred under clause (ii) of section 943(e)(4)(B) of such Code to the extent such property—

(1) was treated as transferred under clause (i) thereof, or

(2) was acquired during a taxable year to which such election applies and before May 1, 2003, in the ordinary course of its trade or business.

The Secretary of the Treasury (or such Secretary's delegate) may prescribe such regulations as may be necessary to prevent the abuse of the purposes of this subsection.

(f) BINDING CONTRACTS.—The amendments made by this section shall not apply to any transaction in the ordinary course of a trade or business which occurs pursuant to a binding contract—

(1) which is between the taxpayer and a person who is not a related person (as defined in section 943(b)(3) of such Code, as in effect on the day before the date of the enactment of this Act), and

(2) which is in effect on September 17, 2003, and at all times thereafter.

For purposes of this subsection, a binding contract shall include a purchase option, renewal option, or replacement option which is included in such contract and which is enforceable against the seller or lessor.

[¶ 5700] CODE SEC. 942. FOREIGN TRADING GROSS RECEIPTS. [*Repealed.*]

* * *

[CCH Explanation at ¶ 205. Committee Reports at ¶ 10,010.]

Amendments

• 2004, American Jobs Creation Act of 2004 (H.R. 4520)

H.R. 4520, § 101(b)(1):

Repealed subpart E of part III of subchapter N of chapter 1 (Code Sec. 942). **Effective** for transactions after 12-31-2004. For transitional and special rules, see Act Secs. 101(d)-(f), below. Prior to repeal, Code Sec. 942 read as follows:

SEC. 942. FOREIGN TRADING GROSS RECEIPTS.

(a) FOREIGN TRADING GROSS RECEIPTS.—

(1) IN GENERAL.—Except as otherwise provided in this section, for purposes of this subpart, the term "foreign trading gross receipts" means the gross receipts of the taxpayer which are—

(A) from the sale, exchange, or other disposition of qualifying foreign trade property,

(B) from the lease or rental of qualifying foreign trade property for use by the lessee outside the United States,

(C) for services which are related and subsidiary to—

(i) any sale, exchange, or other disposition of qualifying foreign trade property by such taxpayer, or

(ii) any lease or rental of qualifying foreign trade property described in subparagraph (B) by such taxpayer,

(D) for engineering or architectural services for construction projects located (or proposed for location) outside the United States, or

(E) for the performance of managerial services for a person other than a related person in furtherance of the production of foreign trading gross receipts described in subparagraph (A), (B), or (C).

Subparagraph (E) shall not apply to a taxpayer for any taxable year unless at least 50 percent of its foreign trading gross receipts (determined without regard to this sentence) for such taxable year is derived from activities described in subparagraph (A), (B), or (C).

(2) CERTAIN RECEIPTS EXCLUDED ON BASIS OF USE; SUBSIDIZED RECEIPTS EXCLUDED.—The term "foreign trading gross receipts" shall not include receipts of a taxpayer from a transaction if—

(A) the qualifying foreign trade property or services—

(i) are for ultimate use in the United States, or

(ii) are for use by the United States or any instrumentality thereof and such use of qualifying foreign trade property or services is required by law or regulation, or

(B) such transaction is accomplished by a subsidy granted by the government (or any instrumentality thereof) of the country or possession in which the property is manufactured, produced, grown, or extracted.

(3) ELECTION TO EXCLUDE CERTAIN RECEIPTS.—The term "foreign trading gross receipts" shall not include gross receipts of a taxpayer from a transaction if the taxpayer elects not to have such receipts taken into account for purposes of this subpart.

(b) FOREIGN ECONOMIC PROCESS REQUIREMENTS.—

(1) IN GENERAL.—Except as provided in subsection (c), a taxpayer shall be treated as having foreign trading gross receipts from any transaction only if economic processes with respect to such transaction take place outside the United States as required by paragraph (2).

(2) REQUIREMENT.—

(A) IN GENERAL.—The requirements of this paragraph are met with respect to the gross receipts of a taxpayer derived from any transaction if—

(i) such taxpayer (or any person acting under a contract with such taxpayer) has participated outside the United States in the solicitation (other than advertising), the negotiation, or the making of the contract relating to such transaction, and

(ii) the foreign direct costs incurred by the taxpayer attributable to the transaction equal or exceed 50 percent of the total direct costs attributable to the transaction.

(B) ALTERNATIVE 85-PERCENT TEST.—A taxpayer shall be treated as satisfying the requirements of subparagraph (A)(ii) with respect to any transaction if, with respect to each of at least 2 subparagraphs of paragraph (3), the foreign direct costs incurred by such taxpayer attributable to activities described in such subparagraph equal or exceed 85 percent of the total direct costs attributable to activities described in such subparagraph.

(C) DEFINITIONS.—For purposes of this paragraph—

(i) TOTAL DIRECT COSTS.—The term "total direct costs" means, with respect to any transaction, the total direct costs incurred by the taxpayer attributable to activities described in paragraph (3) performed at any location by the taxpayer or any person acting under a contract with such taxpayer.

(ii) FOREIGN DIRECT COSTS.—The term "foreign direct costs" means, with respect to any transaction, the portion of the total direct costs which are attributable to activities performed outside the United States.

(3) ACTIVITIES RELATING TO QUALIFYING FOREIGN TRADE PROPERTY.—The activities described in this paragraph are any of the following with respect to qualifying foreign trade property—

(A) advertising and sales promotion,

(B) the processing of customer orders and the arranging for delivery,

(C) transportation outside the United States in connection with delivery to the customer,

(D) the determination and transmittal of a final invoice or statement of account or the receipt of payment, and

(E) the assumption of credit risk.

(4) ECONOMIC PROCESSES PERFORMED BY RELATED PERSONS.—A taxpayer shall be treated as meeting the requirements of this subsection with respect to any sales transaction involving any property if any related person has met such requirements in such transaction or any other sales transaction involving such property.

(c) EXCEPTION FROM FOREIGN ECONOMIC PROCESS REQUIREMENT.—

(1) IN GENERAL.—The requirements of subsection (b) shall be treated as met for any taxable year if the foreign trading gross receipts of the taxpayer for such year do not exceed $5,000,000.

(2) RECEIPTS OF RELATED PERSONS AGGREGATED.—All related persons shall be treated as one person for purposes of paragraph (1), and the limitation under paragraph (1) shall be allocated among such persons in a manner provided in regulations prescribed by the Secretary.

(3) SPECIAL RULE FOR PASS-THRU ENTITIES.—In the case of a partnership, S corporation, or other pass-thru entity, the limitation under paragraph (1) shall apply with respect to the partnership, S corporation, or entity and with respect to each partner, shareholder, or other owner.

H.R. 4520, § 101(d)-(f), provides:

(d) TRANSITIONAL RULE FOR 2005 AND 2006.—

(1) IN GENERAL.—In the case of transactions during 2005 or 2006, the amount includible in gross income by reason of the amendments made by this section shall not exceed the

applicable percentage of the amount which would have been so included but for this subsection.

(2) APPLICABLE PERCENTAGE.—For purposes of paragraph (1), the applicable percentage shall be as follows:

(A) For 2005, the applicable percentage shall be 20 percent.

(B) For 2006, the applicable percentage shall be 40 percent.

(e) REVOCATION OF ELECTION TO BE TREATED AS DOMESTIC CORPORATION.—If, during the 1-year period beginning on the date of the enactment of this Act, a corporation for which an election is in effect under section 943(e) of the Internal Revenue Code of 1986 revokes such election, no gain or loss shall be recognized with respect to property treated as transferred under clause (ii) of section 943(e)(4)(B) of such Code to the extent such property—

(1) was treated as transferred under clause (i) thereof, or

(2) was acquired during a taxable year to which such election applies and before May 1, 2003, in the ordinary course of its trade or business.

The Secretary of the Treasury (or such Secretary's delegate) may prescribe such regulations as may be necessary to prevent the abuse of the purposes of this subsection.

(f) BINDING CONTRACTS.—The amendments made by this section shall not apply to any transaction in the ordinary course of a trade or business which occurs pursuant to a binding contract—

(1) which is between the taxpayer and a person who is not a related person (as defined in section 943(b)(3) of such Code, as in effect on the day before the date of the enactment of this Act), and

(2) which is in effect on September 17, 2003, and at all times thereafter.

For purposes of this subsection, a binding contract shall include a purchase option, renewal option, or replacement option which is included in such contract and which is enforceable against the seller or lessor.

[¶ 5705] CODE SEC. 943. OTHER DEFINITIONS AND SPECIAL RULES. [*Repealed.*]

* * *

[CCH Explanation at ¶ 205. Committee Reports at ¶ 10,010.]

Amendments

• **2004, American Jobs Creation Act of 2004 (H.R. 4520)**

H.R. 4520, § 101(b)(1):

Repealed subpart E of part III of subchapter N of chapter 1 (Code Sec. 943). **Effective** for transactions after 12-31-2004. For transitional and special rules, see Act Secs. 101(d)-(f), below. Prior to repeal, Code Sec. 943 read as follows:

SEC. 943. OTHER DEFINITIONS AND SPECIAL RULES.

(a) QUALIFYING FOREIGN TRADE PROPERTY.—For purposes of this subpart—

(1) IN GENERAL.—The term "qualifying foreign trade property" means property—

(A) manufactured, produced, grown, or extracted within or outside the United States,

(B) held primarily for sale, lease, or rental, in the ordinary course of trade or business for direct use, consumption, or disposition outside the United States, and

(C) not more than 50 percent of the fair market value of which is attributable to—

(i) articles manufactured, produced, grown, or extracted outside the United States, and

(ii) direct costs for labor (determined under the principles of section 263A) performed outside the United States.

For purposes of subparagraph (C), the fair market value of any article imported into the United States shall be its appraised value, as determined by the Secretary under section 402 of the Tariff Act of 1930 (19 U.S.C. 1401a) in connection with its importation, and the direct costs for labor under clause (ii) do not include costs that would be treated under the principles of section 263A as direct labor costs attributable to articles described in clause (i).

(2) U.S. TAXATION TO ENSURE CONSISTENT TREATMENT.—Property which (without regard to this paragraph) is qualifying foreign trade property and which is manufactured, produced, grown, or extracted outside the United States shall be treated as qualifying foreign trade property only if it is manufactured, produced, grown, or extracted by—

(A) a domestic corporation,

(B) an individual who is a citizen or resident of the United States,

(C) a foreign corporation with respect to which an election under subsection (e) (relating to foreign corporations electing to be subject to United States taxation) is in effect, or

(D) a partnership or other pass-thru entity all of the partners or owners of which are described in subparagraph (A), (B), or (C).

Except as otherwise provided by the Secretary, tiered partnerships or pass-thru entities shall be treated as described in subparagraph (D) if each of the partnerships or entities is directly or indirectly wholly owned by persons described in subparagraph (A), (B), or (C).

(3) EXCLUDED PROPERTY.—The term "qualifying foreign trade property" shall not include—

(A) property leased or rented by the taxpayer for use by any related person,

(B) patents, inventions, models, designs, formulas, or processes whether or not patented, copyrights (other than films, tapes, records, or similar reproductions, and other than computer software (whether or not patented), for commercial or home use), goodwill, trademarks, trade brands, franchises, or other like property,

(C) oil or gas (or any primary product thereof),

(D) products the transfer of which is prohibited or curtailed to effectuate the policy set forth in paragraph (2)(C) of section 3 of Public Law 96-72, or

(E) any unprocessed timber which is a softwood.

For purposes of subparagraph (E), the term "unprocessed timber" means any log, cant, or similar form of timber.

(4) PROPERTY IN SHORT SUPPLY.—If the President determines that the supply of any property described in paragraph (1) is insufficient to meet the requirements of the domestic economy, the President may by Executive order designate the property as in short supply. Any property so designated shall not be treated as qualifying foreign trade property during the period beginning with the date specified in the Executive order and ending with the date specified in an Executive order setting forth the President's determination that the property is no longer in short supply.

(b) OTHER DEFINITIONS AND RULES.—For purposes of this subpart—

(1) TRANSACTION.—

(A) IN GENERAL.—The term "transaction" means—

(i) any sale, exchange, or other disposition,

(ii) any lease or rental, and

(iii) any furnishing of services.

(B) GROUPING OF TRANSACTIONS.—To the extent provided in regulations, any provision of this subpart which, but for this subparagraph, would be applied on a transaction-by-transaction basis may be applied by the taxpayer on the basis of groups of transactions based on product lines or recognized industry or trade usage. Such regulations may permit different groupings for different purposes.

(2) UNITED STATES DEFINED.—The term "United States" includes the Commonwealth of Puerto Rico. The preceding sentence shall not apply for purposes of determining whether a corporation is a domestic corporation.

(3) RELATED PERSON.—A person shall be related to another person if such persons are treated as a single employer under subsection (a) or (b) of section 52 or subsection (m) or (o) of section 414, except that determinations under subsections (a) and (b) of section 52 shall be made without regard to section 1563(b).

(4) GROSS AND TAXABLE INCOME.—Section 114 shall not be taken into account in determining the amount of gross income or foreign trade income from any transaction.

(c) SOURCE RULE.—Under regulations, in the case of qualifying foreign trade property manufactured, produced, grown, or extracted within the United States, the amount of income of a taxpayer from any sales transaction with respect to such property which is treated as from sources without the United States shall not exceed—

(1) in the case of a taxpayer computing its qualifying foreign trade income under section 941(a)(1)(B), the amount of the taxpayer's foreign trade income which would (but for this subsection) be treated as from sources without the United States if the foreign trade income were reduced by an amount equal to 4 percent of the foreign trading gross receipts with respect to the transaction, and

(2) in the case of a taxpayer computing its qualifying foreign trade income under section 941(a)(1)(C), 50 percent of the amount of the taxpayer's foreign trade income which would (but for this subsection) be treated as from sources without the United States.

(d) TREATMENT OF WITHHOLDING TAXES.—

(1) IN GENERAL.—For purposes of section 114(d), any withholding tax shall not be treated as paid or accrued with respect to extraterritorial income which is excluded from gross income under section 114(a). For purposes of this paragraph, the term "withholding tax" means any tax which is imposed on a basis other than residence and for which credit is allowable under section 901 or 903.

(2) EXCEPTION.—Paragraph (1) shall not apply to any taxpayer with respect to extraterritorial income from any transaction if the taxpayer computes its qualifying foreign trade income with respect to the transaction under section 941(a)(1)(A).

(e) ELECTION TO BE TREATED AS DOMESTIC CORPORATION.—

(1) IN GENERAL.—An applicable foreign corporation may elect to be treated as a domestic corporation for all purposes of this title if such corporation waives all benefits to such corporation granted by the United States under any treaty. No election under section 1362(a) may be made with respect to such corporation.

(2) APPLICABLE FOREIGN CORPORATION.—For purposes of paragraph (1), the term "applicable foreign corporation" means any foreign corporation if—

(A) such corporation manufactures, produces, grows, or extracts property in the ordinary course of such corporation's trade or business, or

(B) substantially all of the gross receipts of such corporation are foreign trading gross receipts.

(3) PERIOD OF ELECTION.—

(A) IN GENERAL.—Except as otherwise provided in this paragraph, an election under paragraph (1) shall apply to the taxable year for which made and all subsequent taxable years unless revoked by the taxpayer. Any revocation of such election shall apply to taxable years beginning after such revocation.

(B) TERMINATION.—If a corporation which made an election under paragraph (1) for any taxable year fails to meet the requirements of subparagraph (A) or (B) of paragraph (2) for any subsequent taxable year, such election shall not apply to any taxable year beginning after such subsequent taxable year.

(C) EFFECT OF REVOCATION OR TERMINATION.—If a corporation which made an election under paragraph (1) revokes such election or such election is terminated under subparagraph (B), such corporation (and any successor corporation) may not make such election for any of the 5 taxable years beginning with the first taxable year for which such election is not in effect as a result of such revocation or termination.

(4) SPECIAL RULES.—

(A) REQUIREMENTS.—This subsection shall not apply to an applicable foreign corporation if such corporation fails to meet the requirements (if any) which the Secretary may prescribe to ensure that the taxes imposed by this chapter on such corporation are paid.

(B) EFFECT OF ELECTION, REVOCATION, AND TERMINATION.—

(i) ELECTION.—For purposes of section 367, a foreign corporation making an election under this subsection shall be treated as transferring (as of the first day of the first taxable year to which the election applies) all of its assets to a domestic corporation in connection with an exchange to which section 354 applies.

(ii) REVOCATION AND TERMINATION.—For purposes of section 367, if—

(I) an election is made by a corporation under paragraph (1) for any taxable year, and

(II) such election ceases to apply for any subsequent taxable year,

such corporation shall be treated as a domestic corporation transferring (as of the 1st day of the first such subsequent taxable year to which such election ceases to apply) all of its property to a foreign corporation in connection with an exchange to which section 354 applies.

(C) ELIGIBILITY FOR ELECTION.—The Secretary may by regulation designate one or more classes of corporations which may not make the election under this subsection.

(f) RULES RELATING TO ALLOCATIONS OF QUALIFYING FOREIGN TRADE INCOME FROM SHARED PARTNERSHIPS.—

(1) IN GENERAL.—If—

(A) a partnership maintains a separate account for transactions (to which this subpart applies) with each partner,

(B) distributions to each partner with respect to such transactions are based on the amounts in the separate account maintained with respect to such partner, and

(C) such partnership meets such other requirements as the Secretary may by regulations prescribe,

then such partnership shall allocate to each partner items of income, gain, loss, and deduction (including qualifying foreign trade income) from any transaction to which this subpart applies on the basis of such separate account.

(2) SPECIAL RULES.—For purposes of this subpart, in the case of a partnership to which paragraph (1) applies—

(A) any partner's interest in the partnership shall not be taken into account in determining whether such partner is a related person with respect to any other partner, and

(B) the election under section 942(a)(3) shall be made separately by each partner with respect to any transaction for which the partnership maintains separate accounts for each partner.

(g) EXCLUSION FOR PATRONS OF AGRICULTURAL AND HORTICULTURAL COOPERATIVES.—Any amount described in paragraph (1) or (3) of section 1385(a)—

(1) which is received by a person from an organization to which part I of subchapter T applies which is engaged in the marketing of agricultural or horticultural products, and

(2) which is allocable to qualifying foreign trade income and designated as such by the organization in a written

notice mailed to its patrons during the payment period described in section 1382(d),

shall be treated as qualifying foreign trade income of such person for purposes of section 114. The taxable income of the organization shall not be reduced under section 1382 by reason of any amount to which the preceding sentence applies.

(h) SPECIAL RULE FOR DISCs.—Section 114 shall not apply to any taxpayer for any taxable year if, at any time during the taxable year, the taxpayer is a member of any controlled group of corporations (as defined in section 927(d)(4), as in effect before the date of the enactment of this subsection) of which a DISC is a member.

H.R. 4520, § 101(d)-(f), provides:

(d) TRANSITIONAL RULE FOR 2005 AND 2006.—

(1) IN GENERAL.—In the case of transactions during 2005 or 2006, the amount includible in gross income by reason of the amendments made by this section shall not exceed the applicable percentage of the amount which would have been so included but for this subsection.

(2) APPLICABLE PERCENTAGE.—For purposes of paragraph (1), the applicable percentage shall be as follows:

(A) For 2005, the applicable percentage shall be 20 percent.

(B) For 2006, the applicable percentage shall be 40 percent.

(e) REVOCATION OF ELECTION TO BE TREATED AS DOMESTIC CORPORATION.—If, during the 1-year period beginning on the date of the enactment of this Act, a corporation for which an election is in effect under section 943(e) of the Internal Revenue Code of 1986 revokes such election, no gain or loss shall be recognized with respect to property treated as transferred under clause (ii) of section 943(e)(4)(B) of such Code to the extent such property—

(1) was treated as transferred under clause (i) thereof, or

(2) was acquired during a taxable year to which such election applies and before May 1, 2003, in the ordinary course of its trade or business.

The Secretary of the Treasury (or such Secretary's delegate) may prescribe such regulations as may be necessary to prevent the abuse of the purposes of this subsection.

(f) BINDING CONTRACTS.—The amendments made by this section shall not apply to any transaction in the ordinary course of a trade or business which occurs pursuant to a binding contract—

(1) which is between the taxpayer and a person who is not a related person (as defined in section 943(b)(3) of such Code, as in effect on the day before the date of the enactment of this Act), and

(2) which is in effect on September 17, 2003, and at all times thereafter.

For purposes of this subsection, a binding contract shall include a purchase option, renewal option, or replacement option which is included in such contract and which is enforceable against the seller or lessor.

[¶ 5710] CODE SEC. 951. AMOUNTS INCLUDED IN GROSS INCOME OF UNITED STATES SHAREHOLDERS.

* * *

(c) [*Stricken.*]

[CCH Explanation at ¶ 490. Committee Reports at ¶ 10,690.]

Amendments

• **2004, American Jobs Creation Act of 2004 (H.R. 4520)**

H.R. 4520, § 413(c)(16):

Amended Code Sec. 951 by striking subsections (c) and (d) and by redesignating subsections (e) and (f) as subsections (c) and (d), respectively. **Effective** for tax years of foreign corporations beginning after 12-31-2004, and for tax years of United States shareholders with or within which

such tax years of foreign corporations end. Prior to being stricken, Code Sec. 951(c) read as follows:

(c) COORDINATION WITH ELECTION OF A FOREIGN INVESTMENT COMPANY TO DISTRIBUTE INCOME.—A United States shareholder who, for his taxable year, is a qualified shareholder (within the meaning of section 1247(c)) of a foreign investment company with respect to which an election under section 1247 is in effect shall not be required to include in gross income, for such taxable year, any amount under subsection (a) with respect to such company.

(c) FOREIGN TRADE INCOME NOT TAKEN INTO ACCOUNT.—

* * *

[CCH Explanation at ¶ 490. Committee Reports at ¶ 10,690.]

Amendments

• **2004, American Jobs Creation Act of 2004 (H.R. 4520)**

H.R. 4520, § 413(c)(16):

Amended Code Sec. 951 by redesignating subsection (e) as subsection (c). **Effective** for tax years of foreign corpora-

tions beginning after 12-31-2004, and for tax years of United States shareholders with or within which such tax years of foreign corporations end.

(d) [*Stricken.*]

[CCH Explanation at ¶ 490. Committee Reports at ¶ 10,690.]

Amendments

• **2004, American Jobs Creation Act of 2004 (H.R. 4520)**

H.R. 4520, § 413(c)(16):

Amended Code Sec. 951 by striking subsection (d). **Effective** for tax years of foreign corporations beginning after 12-31-2004, and for tax years of United States shareholders with or within which such tax years of foreign corporations

end. Prior to being stricken, Code Sec. 951(d) read as follows:

(d) COORDINATION WITH FOREIGN PERSONAL HOLDING COMPANY PROVISIONS.—If, but for this subsection, an amount would be included in the gross income of a United States shareholder for any taxable year both under subsection (a)(1)(A)(i) and under section 551(b) (relating to foreign personal holding company income included in gross income of United States shareholder), such amount shall be included in the gross income of such shareholder only under subsection (a)(1)(A).

(d) COORDINATION WITH PASSIVE FOREIGN INVESTMENT COMPANY PROVISIONS.—If, but for this subsection, an amount would be included in the gross income of a United States shareholder for any taxable year both under subsection (a)(1)(A)(i) and under section 1293 (relating to current taxation of income from certain passive foreign investment companies), such amount shall be included in the gross income of such shareholder only under subsection (a)(1)(A).

[CCH Explanation at ¶ 490. Committee Reports at ¶ 10,690.]

Amendments

• **2004, American Jobs Creation Act of 2004 (H.R. 4520)**

H.R. 4520, § 413(c)(16):

Amended Code Sec. 951 by redesignating subsection (f) as subsection (d). **Effective** for tax years of foreign corpora-

tions beginning after 12-31-2004, and for tax years of United States shareholders with or within which such tax years of foreign corporations end.

[¶ 5715] CODE SEC. 952. SUBPART F INCOME DEFINED.

* * *

(c) LIMITATION.—

(1) IN GENERAL.—

* * *

(B) CERTAIN PRIOR YEAR DEFICITS MAY BE TAKEN INTO ACCOUNT.—

* * *

(iii) QUALIFIED ACTIVITY.—For purposes of this paragraph, the term "qualified activity" means any activity giving rise to—

(I) foreign base company oil related income,

(II) foreign base company sales income,

(III) foreign base company services income,

(IV) in the case of a qualified insurance company, insurance income or foreign personal holding company income, or

(V) in the case of a qualified financial institution, foreign personal holding company income.

* * *

[CCH Explanation at ¶ 475. Committee Reports at ¶ 10,710.]

Amendments

• **2004, American Jobs Creation Act of 2004 (H.R. 4520)**

H.R. 4520, § 415(c)(1):

Amended Code Sec. 952(c)(1)(B)(iii) by striking subclause (I) and redesignating subclauses (II) through (VI) as sub-

clauses (I) through (V), respectively. **Effective** for tax years of foreign corporations beginning after 12-31-2004, and for tax years of United States shareholders with or within which such tax years of foreign corporations end. Prior to being stricken, Code Sec. 952(c)(1)(B)(iii)(I) read as follows:

(I) foreign base company shipping income,

[¶ 5720] CODE SEC. 954. FOREIGN BASE COMPANY INCOME.

(a) FOREIGN BASE COMPANY INCOME.—For purposes of section 952(a)(2), the term "foreign base company income" means for any taxable year the sum of—

(1) the foreign personal holding company income for the taxable year (determined under subsection (c) and reduced as provided in subsection (b)(5)),

(2) the foreign base company sales income for the taxable year (determined under subsection (d) and reduced as provided in subsection (b)(5)),

(3) the foreign base company services income for the taxable year (determined under subsection (e) and reduced as provided in subsection (b)(5)),

(4) *[Stricken.]*

(5) the foreign base company oil related income for the taxable year (determined under subsection (g) and reduced as provided in subsection (b)(5)).

[CCH Explanation at ¶475. Committee Reports at ¶10,710.]

Amendments

• **2004, American Jobs Creation Act of 2004 (H.R. 4520)**

H.R. 4520, §415(a)(1):

Amended Code Sec. 954(a) by striking paragraph (4). **Effective** for tax years of foreign corporations beginning after 12-31-2004 and for tax years of United States shareholders with or within which such tax years of foreign corporations end. Prior to being stricken, Code Sec. 954(a)(4) read as follows:

(4) the foreign base company shipping income for the taxable year (determined under subsection (f) and reduced as provided in subsection (b)(5)), and

(b) EXCLUSIONS AND SPECIAL RULES.—

* * *

(5) DEDUCTIONS TO BE TAKEN INTO ACCOUNT.—For purposes of subsection (a), the foreign personal holding company income, the foreign base company sales income, the foreign base company services income, and the foreign base company oil related income shall be reduced, under regulations prescribed by the Secretary, so as to take into account deductions (including taxes) properly allocable to such income. Except to the extent provided in regulations prescribed by the Secretary, any interest which is paid or accrued by the controlled foreign corporation to any United States shareholder in such corporation (or any controlled foreign corporation related to such a shareholder) shall be allocated first to foreign personal holding company income which is passive income (within the meaning of section 904(d)(2)) of such corporation to the extent thereof. The Secretary may, by regulations, provide that the preceding sentence shall apply also to interest paid or accrued to other persons.

(6) FOREIGN BASE COMPANY OIL RELATED INCOME NOT TREATED AS ANOTHER KIND OF BASE COMPANY INCOME.—Income of a corporation which is foreign base company oil related income shall not be considered foreign base company income of such corporation under paragraph (2), or (3) of subsection (a).

[CCH Explanation at ¶475. Committee Reports at ¶10,710.]

Amendments

• **2004, American Jobs Creation Act of 2004 (H.R. 4520)**

H.R. 4520, §415(c)(2)(A):

Amended Code Sec. 954(b)(5) by striking "the foreign base company shipping income," immediately following "the foreign base company services income,". **Effective** for tax years of foreign corporations beginning after 12-31-2004 and for tax years of United States shareholders with or within which such tax years of foreign corporations end.

H.R. 4520, §415(c)(2)(B)-(C):

Amended Code Sec. 954(b) by striking paragraphs (6) and (7) and by redesignating paragraph (8) as paragraph (6). **Effective** for tax years of foreign corporations beginning after 12-31-2004 and for tax years of United States shareholders with or within which such tax years of foreign corporations end. Prior to being stricken, Code Sec. 954(b)(6)-(7) read as follows:

(6) SPECIAL RULES FOR FOREIGN BASE COMPANY SHIPPING INCOME.—Income of a corporation which is foreign base company shipping income under paragraph (4) of subsection (a)—

(A) shall not be considered foreign base company income of such corporation under any other paragraph of subsection (a) and

(B) if distributed through a chain of ownership described under section 958(a), shall not be included in foreign base company income of another controlled foreign corporation in such chain.

(7) SPECIAL EXCLUSION FOR FOREIGN BASE COMPANY SHIPPING INCOME.—Income of a corporation which is foreign base company shipping income under paragraph (4) of subsection (a) shall be excluded from foreign base company income if derived by a controlled foreign corporation from, or in connection with, the use (or hiring or leasing for use) of an aircraft or vessel in foreign commerce between two points within the foreign country in which such corporation is created or organized and such aircraft or vessel is registered.

(c) FOREIGN PERSONAL HOLDING COMPANY INCOME.—

(1) IN GENERAL.—For purposes of subsection (a)(1), the term "foreign personal holding company income" means the portion of the gross income which consists of:

(A) DIVIDENDS, ETC.—Dividends, interest, royalties, rents, and annuities.

* * *

(C) COMMODITIES TRANSACTIONS.—The excess of gains over losses from transactions (including futures, forward, and similar transactions) in any commodities. This subparagraph shall not apply to gains or losses which—

    (i) arise out of commodity hedging transactions (as defined in paragraph (4)(A)),

(ii) *are active business gains or losses from the sale of commodities, but only if substantially all of the controlled foreign corporation's commodities are property described in paragraph (1), (2), or (8) of section 1221(a), or*

(iii) are foreign currency gains or losses (as defined in section 988(b)) attributable to any section 988 transactions.

* * *

(I)[(H)] PERSONAL SERVICE CONTRACTS.—

(i) *Amounts received under a contract under which the corporation is to furnish personal services if—*

(I) *some person other than the corporation has the right to designate (by name or by description) the individual who is to perform the services, or*

(II) *the individual who is to perform the services is designated (by name or by description) in the contract, and*

(ii) *amounts received from the sale or other disposition of such a contract.*

This subparagraph shall apply with respect to amounts received for services under a particular contract only if at some time during the taxable year 25 percent or more in value of the outstanding stock of the corporation is owned, directly or indirectly, by or for the individual who has performed, is to perform, or may be designated (by name or by description) as the one to perform, such services.

(2) EXCEPTION FOR CERTAIN AMOUNTS.—

(A) RENTS AND ROYALTIES DERIVED IN ACTIVE BUSINESS.—Foreign personal holding company income shall not include rents and royalties which are derived in the active conduct of a trade or business and which are received from a person other than a related person (within the meaning of subsection (d)(3)). *For purposes of the preceding sentence, rents derived from leasing an aircraft or vessel in foreign commerce shall not fail to be treated as derived in the active conduct of a trade or business if, as determined under regulations prescribed by the Secretary, the active leasing expenses are not less than 10 percent of the profit on the lease.*

* * *

(C) EXCEPTION FOR DEALERS.—Except as provided by regulations, in the case of a regular dealer in property which is property described in paragraph (1)(B), forward contracts, option contracts, or similar financial instruments (including notional principal contracts and all instruments referenced to commodities), there shall not be taken into account in computing foreign personal holding company income—

(i) any item of income, gain, deduction, or loss (other than any item described in subparagraph (A), (E), or (G) of paragraph (1)) from any transaction (including hedging transactions *and transactions involving physical settlement*) entered into in the ordinary course of such dealer's trade or business as such a dealer, and

(ii) if such dealer is a dealer in securities (within the meaning of section 475), any interest or dividend or equivalent amount described in subparagraph (E) or (G) of paragraph (1) from any transaction (including any hedging transaction or transaction described in section 956(c)(2)(J)) entered into in the ordinary course of such dealer's trade or business as such a dealer in securities, but only if the income from the transaction is attributable to activities of the dealer in the country under the laws of which the dealer is created or organized (or in the case of a qualified business unit described in section 989(a), is attributable to activities of the unit in the country in which the unit both maintains its principal office and conducts substantial business activity).

* * *

(4) *LOOK-THRU RULE FOR CERTAIN PARTNERSHIP SALES.—*

(A) IN GENERAL.—*In the case of any sale by a controlled foreign corporation of an interest in a partnership with respect to which such corporation is a 25-percent owner, such corporation shall be treated for purposes of this subsection as selling the proportionate share of the assets of the partnership attributable to such interest. The Secretary shall prescribe such regulations as may be appropriate to prevent abuse of the purposes of this paragraph, including regulations providing for coordination of this paragraph with the provisions of subchapter K.*

(B) 25-PERCENT OWNER.—*For purposes of this paragraph, the term "25-percent owner" means a controlled foreign corporation which owns directly 25 percent or more of the capital or profits interest in a partnership. For purposes of the preceding sentence, if a controlled foreign corporation is a shareholder or partner of a corporation or partnership, the controlled foreign corporation shall be treated as owning directly its proportionate share of any such capital or profits interest held directly or indirectly by such corporation or partnership.*

(5) DEFINITION AND SPECIAL RULES RELATING TO COMMODITY TRANSACTIONS.—

(A) COMMODITY HEDGING TRANSACTIONS.—*For purposes of paragraph (1)(C)(i), the term "commodity hedging transaction" means any transaction with respect to a commodity if such transaction—*

(i) *is a hedging transaction as defined in section 1221(b)(2), determined—*

(I) *without regard to subparagraph (A)(ii) thereof,*

(II) *by applying subparagraph (A)(i) thereof by substituting "ordinary property or property described in section 1231(b)" for "ordinary property", and*

(III) *by substituting "controlled foreign corporation" for "taxpayer" each place it appears, and*

(ii) *is clearly identified as such in accordance with section 1221(a)(7).*

(B) TREATMENT OF DEALER ACTIVITIES UNDER PARAGRAPH (1)(C).—*Commodities with respect to which gains and losses are not taken into account under paragraph (2)(C) in computing a controlled foreign corporation's foreign personal holding company income shall not be taken into account in applying the substantially all test under paragraph (1)(C)(ii) to such corporation.*

(C) REGULATIONS.—*The Secretary shall prescribe such regulations as are appropriate to carry out the purposes of paragraph (1)(C) in the case of transactions involving related parties.*

* * *

[CCH Explanation at ¶465, ¶470, ¶475 and ¶490. Committee Reports at ¶10,680, ¶10,690, ¶10,700 and ¶10,710.]

Amendments

• **2004, American Jobs Creation Act of 2004 (H.R. 4520)**

H.R. 4520, §412(a):

Amended Code Sec. 954(c) by adding after paragraph (3) a new paragraph (4). **Effective** for tax years of foreign corporations beginning after 12-31-2004, and for tax years of United States shareholders with or within which such tax years of foreign corporations end.

H.R. 4520, §413(b)(2):

Amended Code Sec. 954(c)(1) by adding at the end a new subparagraph (I)[H]. **Effective** for tax years of foreign corporations beginning after 12-31-2004, and for tax years of United States shareholders with or within which such tax years of foreign corporations end.

H.R. 4520, §414(a):

Amended Code Sec. 954(c)(1)(C)(i)-(ii). **Effective** for transactions entered into after 12-31-2004. Prior to amendment, Code Sec. 954(c)(1)(C)(i)-(ii) read as follows:

(i) arise out of bona fide hedging transactions reasonably necessary to the conduct of any business by a producer, processor, merchant, or handler of a commodity in the

manner in which such business is customarily and usually conducted by others,

(ii) are active business gains or losses from the sale of commodities, but only if substantially all of the controlled foreign corporation's business is as an active producer, processor, merchant, or handler of commodities, or

H.R. 4520, §414(b):

Amended Code Sec. 954(c) by adding after paragraph (4), as amended by this Act, a new paragraph (5). **Effective** for transactions entered into after 12-31-2004.

H.R. 4520, §414(c):

Amended Code Sec. 954(c)(2)(C)(i) by inserting "and transactions involving physical settlement" after "(including hedging transactions)". **Effective** for transactions entered into after 12-31-2004.

H.R. 4520, §415(b):

Amended Code Sec. 954(c)(2)(A) by adding at the end a new sentence. **Effective** for tax years of foreign corporations beginning after 12-31-2004 and for tax years of United States shareholders with or within which such tax years of foreign corporations end.

(f) [*Stricken.*]

[CCH Explanation at ¶475. Committee Reports at ¶10,710.]

Amendments

• 2004, American Jobs Creation Act of 2004 (H.R. 4520)

H.R. 4520, §415(a)(2):

Amended Code Sec. 954 by striking subsection (f). **Effective** for tax years of foreign corporations beginning after 12-31-2004 and for tax years of United States shareholders with or within which such tax years of foreign corporations end. Prior to being stricken, Code Sec. 954(f) read as follows:

(f) FOREIGN BASE COMPANY SHIPPING INCOME.—For purposes of subsection (a)(4), the term "foreign base company shipping income" means income derived from, or in connection with, the use (or hiring or leasing for use) of any aircraft or vessel in foreign commerce, or from, or in connection with, the performance of services directly related to the use of any such aircraft, or vessel, or from the sale, ex-

change, or other disposition of any such aircraft or vessel. Such term includes, but is not limited to—

(1) dividends and interest received from a foreign corporation in respect of which taxes are deemed paid under section 902, and gain from the sale, exchange, or other disposition of stock or obligations of such a foreign corporation to the extent that such dividends, interest, and gains are attributable to foreign base company shipping income, and

(2) that portion of the distributive share of the income of a partnership attributable to foreign base company shipping income.

Such term includes any income derived from a space or ocean activity (as defined in section 863(d)(2)). Except as provided in paragraph (1), such term shall not include any dividend or interest income which is foreign personal holding company income (as defined in subsection (c)).

(h) SPECIAL RULE FOR INCOME DERIVED IN THE ACTIVE CONDUCT OF BANKING, FINANCING, OR SIMILAR BUSINESSES.—

* * *

(3) QUALIFIED BANKING OR FINANCING INCOME.—For purposes of this subsection—

* * *

(E) DIRECT CONDUCT OF ACTIVITIES.—For purposes of subparagraph (A)(ii)(II), an activity shall be treated as conducted directly by an eligible controlled foreign corporation or qualified business unit in its home country if the activity is performed by employees of a related person and—

(i) the related person is an eligible controlled foreign corporation the home country of which is the same as the home country of the corporation or unit to which subparagraph (A)(ii)(II) is being applied,

(ii) the activity is performed in the home country of the related person, and

(iii) the related person is compensated on an arm's-length basis for the performance of the activity by its employees and such compensation is treated as earned by such person in its home country for purposes of the home country's tax laws.

* * *

[CCH Explanation at ¶480. Committee Reports at ¶10,720.]

Amendments

• 2004, American Jobs Creation Act of 2004 (H.R. 4520)

H.R. 4520, §416(a):

Amended Code Sec. 954(h)(3) by adding at the end a new paragraph (E). **Effective** for tax years of such foreign corpo-

rations beginning after 12-31-2004 and for tax years of United States shareholders with or within which such tax years of such foreign corporations end.

[¶5725] CODE SEC. 956. INVESTMENT OF EARNINGS IN UNITED STATES PROPERTY.

* * *

(c) UNITED STATES PROPERTY DEFINED.—

* * *

(2) EXCEPTIONS.—For purposes of subsection (a), the term "United States property" does not include—

(A) obligations of the United States, money, or deposits with—

(i) any bank (as defined by section 2(c) of the Bank Holding Company Act of 1956 (12 U.S.C. 1841(c)), without regard to subparagraphs (C) and (G) of paragraph (2) of such section), or

(ii) any corporation not described in clause (i) with respect to which a bank holding company (as defined by section 2(a) of such Act) or financial holding company (as defined by section 2(p) of such Act) owns directly or indirectly more than 80 percent by vote or value of the stock of such corporation;

(B) property located in the United States which is purchased in the United States for export to, or use in, foreign countries;

(C) any obligation of a United States person arising in connection with the sale or processing of property if the amount of such obligation outstanding at no time during the taxable year exceeds the amount which would be ordinary and necessary to carry on the trade or business of both the other party to the sale or processing transaction and the United States person had the sale or processing transaction been made between unrelated persons;

(D) any aircraft, railroad rolling stock, vessel, motor vehicle, or container used in the transportation of persons or property in foreign commerce and used predominantly outside the United States;

(E) an amount of assets of an insurance company equivalent to the unearned premiums or reserves ordinary and necessary for the proper conduct of its insurance business attributable to contracts which are not contracts described in section 953(a)(1);

(F) the stock or obligations of a domestic corporation which is neither a United States shareholder (as defined in section 951(b)) of the controlled foreign corporation, nor a domestic corporation, 25 percent or more of the total combined voting power of which, immediately after the acquisition of any stock in such domestic corporation by the controlled foreign corporation, is owned, or is considered as being owned, by such United States shareholders in the aggregate;

(G) any movable property (other than a vessel or aircraft) which is used for the purpose of exploring for, developing, removing, or transporting resources from ocean waters or under such waters when used on the Continental Shelf of the United States;

(H) an amount of assets of the controlled foreign corporation equal to the earnings and profits accumulated after December 31, 1962, and excluded from subpart F income under section 952(b);

(I) to the extent provided in regulations prescribed by the Secretary, property which is otherwise United States property which is held by a FSC and which is related to the export activities of such FSC;

(J) deposits of cash or securities made or received on commercial terms in the ordinary course of a United States or foreign person's business as a dealer in securities or in commodities, but only to the extent such deposits are made or received as collateral or margin for (i) a securities loan, notional principal contract, options contract, forward contract, or futures contract, or (ii) any other financial transaction in which the Secretary determines that it is customary to post collateral or margin;

(K) an obligation of a United States person to the extent the principal amount of the obligation does not exceed the fair market value of readily marketable securities sold or purchased pursuant to a sale and repurchase agreement or otherwise posted or received as collateral for the obligation in the ordinary course of its business by a United States or foreign person which is a dealer in securities or commodities;

(L) securities acquired and held by a controlled foreign corporation in the ordinary course of its business as a dealer in securities if—

(i) the dealer accounts for the securities as securities held primarily for sale to customers in the ordinary course of business, and

(ii) the dealer disposes of the securities (or such securities mature while held by the dealer) within a period consistent with the holding of securities for sale to customers in the ordinary course of business; and

(M) an obligation of a United States person which—

(i) is not a domestic corporation, and

(ii) is not—

(I) a United States shareholder (as defined in section 951(b)) of the controlled foreign corporation, or

(II) a partnership, estate, or trust in which the controlled foreign corporation, or any related person (as defined in section 954(d)(3)), is a partner, beneficiary, or trustee *immediately after the acquisition of any obligation of such partnership, estate, or trust by the controlled foreign corporation.*

For purposes of subparagraphs (J), *(K), and (L),* the term "dealer in securities" has the meaning given such term by section 475(c)(1), and the term "dealer in commodities" has the meaning given such term by section 475(e), except that such term shall include a futures commission merchant.

* * *

[CCH Explanation at ¶ 460 and ¶ 485. Committee Reports at ¶ 10,630 and ¶ 11,200.]

Amendments

• **2004, American Jobs Creation Act of 2004 (H.R. 4520)**

H.R. 4520, § 407(a):

Amended Code Sec. 956(c)(2) by striking "and" at the end of subparagraph (J), by striking the period at the end of subparagraph (K) and inserting a semicolon, and by adding at the end new subparagraphs (L) and (M). **Effective** for tax years of foreign corporations beginning after 12-31-2004, and for tax years of United States shareholders with or within which such tax years of foreign corporations end.

H.R. 4520, § 407(b):

Amended Code Sec. 956(c)(2) by striking "and (K)" in the last sentence and inserting ", (K), and (L)". **Effective** for tax

years of foreign corporations beginning after 12-31-2004, and for tax years of United States shareholders with or within which such tax years of foreign corporations end.

H.R. 4520, § 837(a):

Amended Code Sec. 956(c)(2)(A). **Effective** on the date of the enactment of this Act. Prior to amendment, Code Sec. 956(c)(2)(A) read as follows:

(A) obligations of the United States, money, or deposits with persons carrying on the banking business;

[¶ 5730] CODE SEC. 957. CONTROLLED FOREIGN CORPORATIONS; UNITED STATES PERSONS.

* * *

(c) UNITED STATES PERSON.—For purposes of this subpart, the term "United States person" has the meaning assigned to it by section 7701(a)(30) except that—

(1) with respect to a corporation organized under the laws of the Commonwealth of Puerto Rico, such term does not include an individual who is a bona fide resident of Puerto Rico, if a dividend received by such individual during the taxable year from such corporation would, for purposes of section 933(1), be treated as income derived from sources within Puerto Rico, and

(2) with respect to a corporation organized under the laws of Guam, American Samoa, or the Northern Mariana Islands—

(A) 80 percent or more of the gross income of which for the 3-year period ending at the close of the taxable year (or for such part of such period as such corporation or any predecessor has been in existence) was derived from sources within such a possession or was effectively connected with the conduct of a trade or business in such a possession, and

(B) 50 percent or more of the gross income of which for such period (or part) was derived from the *active conduct of a* trade or business within such a possession,

such term does not include an individual who is a bona fide resident of Guam, American Samoa, or the Northern Mariana Islands.

For purposes of subparagraph (A) and (B) of paragraph (2), the determination as to whether income was derived from the active conduct of a trade or business within a possession shall be made under regulations prescribed by the Secretary.

* * *

[CCH Explanation at ¶ 580. Committee Reports at ¶ 11,800.]

Amendments

• **2004, American Jobs Creation Act of 2004 (H.R. 4520)**

H.R. 4520, § 908(c)(5)(A)-(B):

Amended Code Sec. 957(c) by striking "conduct of an active" in paragraph (2)(B) and inserting "active conduct of

a", and by striking "derived from sources within a possession, was effectively connected with the conduct of a trade or business within a possession, or" after "whether income was" in the last sentence. **Effective** for tax years ending after the date of the enactment of this Act.

[¶ 5735] *CODE SEC. 965. TEMPORARY DIVIDENDS RECEIVED DEDUCTION.*

(a) Deduction.—

(1) In General.—In the case of a corporation which is a United States shareholder and for which the election under this section is in effect for the taxable year, there shall be allowed as a deduction an amount equal to 85 percent of the cash dividends which are received during such taxable year by such shareholder from controlled foreign corporations.

(2) Dividends paid indirectly from controlled foreign corporations.—If, within the taxable year for which the election under this section is in effect, a United States shareholder receives a cash distribution from a controlled foreign corporation which is excluded from gross income under section 959(a), such distribution shall be treated for purposes of this section as a cash dividend to the extent of any amount included in income by such United States shareholder under section 951(a)(1)(A) as a result of any cash dividend during such taxable year to—

> *(A) such controlled foreign corporation from another controlled foreign corporation that is in a chain of ownership described in section 958(a), or*

> *(B) any other controlled foreign corporation in such chain of ownership, but only to the extent of cash distributions described in section 959(b) which are made during such taxable year to the controlled foreign corporation from which such United States shareholder received such distribution.*

(b) Limitations.—

(1) In general.—The amount of dividends taken into account under subsection (a) shall not exceed the greater of—

> *(A) $500,000,000,*

> *(B) the amount shown on the applicable financial statement as earnings permanently reinvested outside the United States, or*

> *(C) in the case of an applicable financial statement which fails to show a specific amount of earnings permanently reinvested outside the United States and which shows a specific amount of tax liability attributable to such earnings, the amount equal to the amount of such liability divided by 0.35.*

The amounts described in subparagraphs (B) and (C) shall be treated as being zero if there is no such statement or such statement fails to show a specific amount of such earnings or liability, as the case may be.

(2) Dividends must be extraordinary.—The amount of dividends taken into account under subsection (a) shall not exceed the excess (if any) of—

> *(A) the dividends received during the taxable year by such shareholder from controlled foreign corporations, over*

> *(B) the annual average for the base period years of—*

>> *(i) the dividends received during each base period year by such shareholder from controlled foreign corporations,*

>> *(ii) the amounts includible in such shareholder's gross income for each base period year under section 951(a)(1)(B) with respect to controlled foreign corporations, and*

>> *(iii) the amounts that would have been included for each base period year but for section 959(a) with respect to controlled foreign corporations.*

The amount taken into account under clause (iii) for any base period year shall not include any amount which is not includible in gross income by reason of an amount described in clause (ii) with respect to a prior taxable year. Amounts described in subparagraph (B) for any base period year shall be such amounts as shown on the most recent return filed for such year; except that amended returns filed after June 30, 2003, shall not be taken into account.

(3) Reduction of benefit if increase in related party indebtedness.—The amount of dividends which would (but for this paragraph) be taken into account under subsection (a) shall be reduced by the excess (if any) of—

> *(A) the amount of indebtedness of the controlled foreign corporation to any related person (as defined in section 954(d)(3)) as of the close of the taxable year for which the election under this section is in effect, over*

(B) *the amount of indebtedness of the controlled foreign corporation to any related person (as so defined) as of the close of October 3, 2004.*

All controlled foreign corporations with respect to which the taxpayer is a United States shareholder shall be treated as 1 controlled foreign corporation for purposes of this paragraph.

(4) REQUIREMENT TO INVEST IN UNITED STATES.—*Subsection (a) shall not apply to any dividend received by a United States shareholder unless the amount of the dividend is invested in the United States pursuant to a domestic reinvestment plan which—*

(A) *is approved by the taxpayer's president, chief executive officer, or comparable official before the payment of such dividend and subsequently approved by the taxpayer's board of directors, management committee, executive committee, or similar body, and*

(B) *provides for the reinvestment of such dividend in the United States (other than as payment for executive compensation), including as a source for the funding of worker hiring and training, infrastructure, research and development, capital investments, or the financial stabilization of the corporation for the purposes of job retention or creation.*

(c) DEFINITIONS AND SPECIAL RULES.—*For purposes of this section—*

(1) APPLICABLE FINANCIAL STATEMENT.—*The term "applicable financial statement" means, with respect to a United States shareholder, the most recently audited financial statement (including notes and other documents which accompany such statement) which includes such shareholder—*

(A) *which is certified on or before June 30, 2003, as being prepared in accordance with generally accepted accounting principles, and*

(B) *which is used for the purposes of a statement or report—*

(i) *to creditors,*

(ii) *to shareholders, or*

(iii) *for any other substantial nontax purpose.*

In the case of a corporation required to file a financial statement with the Securities and Exchange Commission, such term means the most recent such statement filed on or before June 30, 2003.

(2) BASE PERIOD YEARS.—

(A) IN GENERAL.—*The base period years are the 3 taxable years—*

(i) *which are among the 5 most recent taxable years ending on or before June 30, 2003, and*

(ii) *which are determined by disregarding—*

(I) *1 taxable year for which the sum of the amounts described in clauses (i), (ii), and (iii) of subsection (b)(2)(B) is the largest, and*

(II) *1 taxable year for which such sum is the smallest.*

(B) SHORTER PERIOD.—*If the taxpayer has fewer than 5 taxable years ending on or before June 30, 2003, then in lieu of applying subparagraph (A), the base period years shall include all the taxable years of the taxpayer ending on or before June 30, 2003.*

(C) MERGERS, ACQUISITIONS, ETC.—

(i) IN GENERAL.—*Rules similar to the rules of subparagraphs (A) and (B) of section 41(f)(3) shall apply for purposes of this paragraph.*

(ii) SPIN-OFFS, ETC.—*If there is a distribution to which section 355 (or so much of section 356 as relates to section 355) applies during the 5-year period referred to in subparagraph (A)(i) and the controlled corporation (within the meaning of section 355) is a United States shareholder—*

(I) *the controlled corporation shall be treated as being in existence during the period that the distributing corporation (within the meaning of section 355) is in existence, and*

(II) *for purposes of applying subsection (b)(2) to the controlled corporation and the distributing corporation, amounts described in subsection (b)(2)(B) which are received or includible by the distributing corporation or controlled corporation (as the case may be) before the distribution referred to in subclause (I) from a controlled foreign corporation shall be allocated between such corporations in proportion to their respective interests as United*

States shareholders of such controlled foreign corporation immediately after such distribution.

Subclause (II) shall not apply if neither the controlled corporation nor the distributing corporation is a United States shareholder of such controlled foreign corporation immediately after such distribution.

(3) DIVIDEND.—The term "dividend" shall not include amounts includible in gross income as a dividend under section 78, 367, or 1248. In the case of a liquidation under section 332 to which section 367(b) applies, the preceding sentence shall not apply to the extent the United States shareholder actually receives cash as part of the liquidation.

(4) COORDINATION WITH DIVIDENDS RECEIVED DEDUCTION.—No deduction shall be allowed under section 243 or 245 for any dividend for which a deduction is allowed under this section.

(5) CONTROLLED GROUPS.—

(A) IN GENERAL.—All United States shareholders which are members of an affiliated group filing a consolidated return under section 1501 shall be treated as one United States shareholder.

(B) APPLICATION OF $500,000,000 LIMIT.—All corporations which are treated as a single employer under section 52(a) shall be limited to one $500,000,000 amount in subsection (b)(1)(A), and such amount shall be divided among such corporations under regulations prescribed by the Secretary.

(C) PERMANENTLY REINVESTED EARNINGS.—If a financial statement is an applicable financial statement for more than 1 United States shareholder, the amount applicable under subparagraph (B) or (C) of subsection (b)(1) shall be divided among such shareholders under regulations prescribed by the Secretary.

(d) DENIAL OF FOREIGN TAX CREDIT; DENIAL OF CERTAIN EXPENSES.—

(1) FOREIGN TAX CREDIT.—No credit shall be allowed under section 901 for any taxes paid or accrued (or treated as paid or accrued) with respect to the deductible portion of—

(A) any dividend, or

(B) any amount described in subsection (a)(2) which is included in income under section 951(a)(1)(A).

No deduction shall be allowed under this chapter for any tax for which credit is not allowable by reason of the preceding sentence.

(2) EXPENSES.—No deduction shall be allowed for expenses properly allocated and apportioned to the deductible portion described in paragraph (1).

(3) DEDUCTIBLE PORTION.—For purposes of paragraph (1), unless the taxpayer otherwise specifies, the deductible portion of any dividend or other amount is the amount which bears the same ratio to the amount of such dividend or other amount as the amount allowed as a deduction under subsection (a) for the taxable year bears to the amount described in subsection (b)(2)(A) for such year.

(e) INCREASE IN TAX ON INCLUDED AMOUNTS NOT REDUCED BY CREDITS, ETC.—

(1) IN GENERAL.—Any tax under this chapter by reason of nondeductible CFC dividends shall not be treated as tax imposed by this chapter for purposes of determining—

(A) the amount of any credit allowable under this chapter, or

(B) the amount of the tax imposed by section 55.

Subparagraph (A) shall not apply to the credit under section 53 or to the credit under section 27(a) with respect to taxes attributable to such dividends.

(2) LIMITATION ON REDUCTION IN TAXABLE INCOME, ETC.—

(A) IN GENERAL.—The taxable income of any United States shareholder for any taxable year shall in no event be less than the amount of nondeductible CFC dividends received during such year.

(B) COORDINATION WITH SECTION 172.—The nondeductible CFC dividends for any taxable year shall not be taken into account—

(i) in determining under section 172 the amount of any net operating loss for such taxable year, and

(ii) *in determining taxable income for such taxable year for purposes of the 2nd sentence of section 172(b)(2).*

(3) NONDEDUCTIBLE CFC DIVIDENDS.—*For purposes of this subsection, the term "nondeductible CFC dividends" means the excess of the amount of dividends taken into account under subsection (a) over the deduction allowed under subsection (a) for such dividends.*

(f) ELECTION.—*The taxpayer may elect to apply this section to—*

(1) *the taxpayer's last taxable year which begins before the date of the enactment of this section, or*

(2) *the taxpayer's first taxable year which begins during the 1-year period beginning on such date.*

Such election may be made for a taxable year only if made before the due date (including extensions) for filing the return of tax for such taxable year.

* * *

[CCH Explanation at ¶ 535. Committee Reports at ¶ 10,780.]

Amendments

• **2004, American Jobs Creation Act of 2004 (H.R. 4520)**

H.R. 4520, § 422(a):

Amended subpart F of part III of subchapter N of chapter 1 by adding at the end a new Code Sec. 965. **Effective** for tax years ending on or after the date of the enactment of this Act.

[¶ 5740] CODE SEC. 986. DETERMINATION OF FOREIGN TAXES AND FOREIGN CORPORATION'S EARNINGS AND PROFITS.

(a) FOREIGN INCOME TAXES.—

(1) TRANSLATION OF ACCRUED TAXES.—

* * *

(D) ELECTIVE EXCEPTION FOR TAXES PAID OTHER THAN IN FUNCTIONAL CURRENCY.—

(i) IN GENERAL.—*At the election of the taxpayer, subparagraph (A) shall not apply to any foreign income taxes the liability for which is denominated in any currency other than in the taxpayer's functional currency.*

(ii) APPLICATION TO QUALIFIED BUSINESS UNITS.—*An election under this subparagraph may apply to foreign income taxes attributable to a qualified business unit in accordance with regulations prescribed by the Secretary.*

(iii) ELECTION.—*Any such election shall apply to the taxable year for which made and all subsequent taxable years unless revoked with the consent of the Secretary.*

(E) SPECIAL RULE FOR REGULATED INVESTMENT COMPANIES.—*In the case of a regulated investment company which takes into account income on an accrual basis, subparagraphs (A) through (D) shall not apply and foreign income taxes paid or accrued with respect to such income shall be translated into dollars using the exchange rate as of the date the income accrues.*

(F) CROSS REFERENCE.—

For adjustments where tax is not paid within 2 years, see section 905(c).

(2) TRANSLATION OF TAXES TO WHICH PARAGRAPH (1) DOES NOT APPLY.—For purposes of determining the amount of the foreign tax credit, in the case of any foreign income taxes to which subparagraph (A) *or (E)* of paragraph (1) does not apply—

(A) such taxes shall be translated into dollars using the exchange rates as of the time such taxes were paid to the foreign country or possession of the United States, and

(B) any adjustment to the amount of such taxes shall be translated into dollars using—

(i) except as provided in clause (ii), the exchange rate as of the time when such adjustment is paid to the foreign country or possession, or

(ii) in the case of any refund or credit of foreign income taxes, using the exchange rate as of the time of the original payment of such foreign income taxes.

* * *

[CCH Explanation at ¶ 450. Committee Reports at ¶ 10,640.]

Amendments

• 2004, American Jobs Creation Act of 2004 (H.R. 4520)

H.R. 4520, § 408(a):

Amended Code Sec. 986(a)(1) by redesignating subparagraph (D) as subparagraph (E) and by inserting after subparagraph (C) a new subparagraph (D). **Effective** for tax years beginning after 12-31-2004.

H.R. 4520, § 408(b)(1):

Amended Code Sec. 986(a)(1), as amended by Act Sec. 408(a), by redesignating subparagraph (E) as subparagraph

(F) and by inserting after subparagraph (D) a new subparagraph (E). **Effective** for tax years beginning after 12-31-2004.

H.R. 4520, § 408(b)(2):

Amended Code Sec. 986(a)(2) by inserting "or (E)" after "subparagraph (A)". **Effective** for tax years beginning after 12-31-2004.

[¶ 5745] CODE SEC. 989. OTHER DEFINITIONS AND SPECIAL RULES.

* * *

(b) APPROPRIATE EXCHANGE RATE.—Except as provided in regulations, for purposes of this subpart, the term "appropriate exchange rate" means—

* * *

(3) in the case of any amounts included in income under section 951(a)(1)(A) or 1293(a), the averaged exchange rate for the taxable year of the foreign corporation, or

* * *

[CCH Explanation at ¶ 490. Committee Reports at ¶ 10,690.]

Amendments

• 2004, American Jobs Creation Act of 2004 (H.R. 4520)

H.R. 4520, § 413(c)(17):

Amended Code Sec. 989(b)(3) by striking ", 551(a)," immediately preceding "or 1293(a)". **Effective** for tax years of

foreign corporations beginning after 12-31-2004, and for tax years of United States shareholders with or within which such tax years of foreign corporations end.

[¶ 5750] CODE SEC. 999. REPORTS BY TAXPAYERS; DETERMINATIONS.

* * *

(c) INTERNATIONAL BOYCOTT FACTOR.—

(1) INTERNATIONAL BOYCOTT FACTOR.—For purposes of sections 908(a), 952(a)(3), and 995(b)(1)(F)(ii), the international boycott factor is a fraction, determined under regulations prescribed by the Secretary, the numerator of which reflects the world-wide operations of a person (or, in the case of a controlled group (within the meaning of section 993(a)(3)) which includes that person, of the group) which are operations in or related to a group of countries associated in carrying out an international boycott in or with which that person or a member of that controlled group has participated or cooperated in the taxable year, and the denominator of which reflects the world-wide operations of that person or group.

* * *

[CCH Explanation at ¶ 205. Committee Reports at ¶ 10,010.]

Amendments

• 2004, American Jobs Creation Act of 2004 (H.R. 4520)

H.R. 4520, § 101(b)(8):

Amended Code Sec. 999(c)(1) by striking "941(a)(5)," immediately following "908(a),". **Effective** for transactions after 12-31-2004. For transitional and special rules, see Act Secs. 101(d)-(f), below.

H.R. 4520, § 101(d)-(f), provides:

(d) TRANSITIONAL RULE FOR 2005 AND 2006.—

(1) IN GENERAL.—In the case of transactions during 2005 or 2006, the amount includible in gross income by reason of the amendments made by this section shall not exceed the

applicable percentage of the amount which would have been so included but for this subsection.

(2) APPLICABLE PERCENTAGE.—For purposes of paragraph (1), the applicable percentage shall be as follows:

(A) For 2005, the applicable percentage shall be 20 percent.

(B) For 2006, the applicable percentage shall be 40 percent.

(e) REVOCATION OF ELECTION TO BE TREATED AS DOMESTIC CORPORATION.—If, during the 1-year period beginning on the date of the enactment of this Act, a corporation for which an election is in effect under section 943(e) of the Internal Revenue Code of 1986 revokes such election, no gain or loss shall be recognized with respect to property treated as transferred under clause (ii) of section 943(e)(4)(B) of such Code to the extent such property—

(1) was treated as transferred under clause (i) thereof, or

(2) was acquired during a taxable year to which such election applies and before May 1, 2003, in the ordinary course of its trade or business.

The Secretary of the Treasury (or such Secretary's delegate) may prescribe such regulations as may be necessary to prevent the abuse of the purposes of this subsection.

(f) BINDING CONTRACTS.—The amendments made by this section shall not apply to any transaction in the ordinary course of a trade or business which occurs pursuant to a binding contract—

(1) which is between the taxpayer and a person who is not a related person (as defined in section 943(b)(3) of such Code, as in effect on the day before the date of the enactment of this Act), and

(2) which is in effect on September 17, 2003, and at all times thereafter.

For purposes of this subsection, a binding contract shall include a purchase option, renewal option, or replacement option which is included in such contract and which is enforceable against the seller or lessor.

[¶5755] CODE SEC. 1014. BASIS OF PROPERTY ACQUIRED FROM A DECEDENT.

* * *

(b) PROPERTY ACQUIRED FROM THE DECEDENT.—For purposes of subsection (a), the following property shall be considered to have been acquired from or to have passed from the decedent:

* * *

(5) In the case of decedents dying after August 26, 1937, *and before January 1, 2005,* property acquired by bequest, devise, or inheritance or by the decedent's estate from the decedent, if the property consists of stock or securities of a foreign corporation, which with respect to its taxable year next preceding the date of the decedent's death was, under the law applicable to such year, a foreign personal holding company. In such case, the basis shall be the fair market value of such property at the date of the decedent's death or the basis in the hands of the decedent, whichever is lower;

* * *

[CCH Explanation at ¶490. Committee Reports at ¶10,690.]

Amendments

• **2004, American Jobs Creation Act of 2004 (H.R. 4520)**

H.R. 4520, §413(c)(18):

Amended Code Sec. 1014(b)(5) by inserting "and before January 1, 2005," after "August 26, 1937,". **Effective** for tax years of foreign corporations beginning after 12-31-2004, and for tax years of United States shareholders with or within which such tax years of foreign corporations end.

[¶5760] CODE SEC. 1016. ADJUSTMENTS TO BASIS.

(a) GENERAL RULE.—Proper adjustment in respect of the property shall in all cases be made—

* * *

(13) *[Stricken.]*

* * *

(27) in the case of a residence with respect to which a credit was allowed under section 1400C, to the extent provided in section 1400C(h),

(28) in the case of a facility with respect to which a credit was allowed under section 45F, to the extent provided in section 45F(f)(1) ,

(29) *in the case of railroad track with respect to which a credit was allowed under section 45G, to the extent provided in section 45G(e)(3),*

(30) *to the extent provided in section 179B(c), and*

(31) *in the case of a facility with respect to which a credit was allowed under section 45H, to the extent provided in section 45H(d).*

* * *

[CCH Explanation at ¶375, ¶490, ¶850 and ¶855. Committee Reports at ¶10,260, ¶10,530, ¶10,540 and ¶10,690.]

Amendments

• 2004, American Jobs Creation Act of 2004 (H.R. 4520)

H.R. 4520, §245(c)(2):

Amended Code Sec. 1016(a) by striking "and" at the end of paragraph (27), by striking the period at the end of paragraph (28) and inserting ", and", and by inserting after paragraph (28) a new paragraph (29). **Effective** for tax years beginning after 12-31-2004.

H.R. 4520, §338(b)(4):

Amended Code Sec. 1016(a) by striking "and" at the end of paragraph (28), by striking the period at the end of paragraph (29) and inserting ", and", and by inserting after paragraph (29) a new paragraph (30). **Effective** for expenses paid or incurred after 12-31-2002 in tax years ending after such date.

H.R. 4520, §339(d):

Amended Code Sec. 1016(a), as amended by this Act, by striking "and" at the end of paragraph (29), by striking the period at the end of paragraph (30) and inserting ", and", and by inserting after paragraph (30) a new paragraph (31). **Effective** for expenses paid or incurred after 12-31-2002, in tax years ending after such date.

H.R. 4520, §413(c)(19):

Amended Code Sec. 1016(a) by striking paragraph (13). **Effective** for tax years of foreign corporations beginning after 12-31-2004, and for tax years of United States shareholders with or within which such tax years of foreign corporations end. Prior to being stricken, Code Sec. 1016(a)(13) read as follows:

(13) to the extent provided in section 551(e) in the case of the stock of United States shareholders in a foreign personal holding company;

[¶5765] CODE SEC. 1033. INVOLUNTARY CONVERSIONS.

* * *

(e) LIVESTOCK SOLD ON ACCOUNT OF DROUGHT, FLOOD, OR OTHER WEATHER-RELATED *CONDITIONS.*—

(1) IN GENERAL.— *For purposes* of this subtitle, the sale or exchange of livestock (other than poultry) held by a taxpayer for draft, breeding, or dairy purposes in excess of the number the taxpayer would sell if he followed his usual business practices shall be treated as an involuntary conversion to which this section applies if such livestock are sold or exchanged by the taxpayer solely on account of drought, flood, or other weather-related conditions.

(2) EXTENSION OF REPLACEMENT PERIOD.—

(A) IN GENERAL.—*In the case of drought, flood, or other weather-related conditions described in paragraph (1) which result in the area being designated as eligible for assistance by the Federal Government, subsection (a)(2)(B) shall be applied with respect to any converted property by substituting "4 years" for "2 years".*

(B) FURTHER EXTENSION BY SECRETARY.—*The Secretary may extend on a regional basis the period for replacement under this section (after the application of subparagraph (A)) for such additional time as the Secretary determines appropriate if the weather-related conditions which resulted in such application continue for more than 3 years.*

[CCH Explanation at ¶820. Committee Reports at ¶10,340.]

Amendments

• 2004, American Jobs Creation Act of 2004 (H.R. 4520)

H.R. 4520, §311(b)(1)-(2):

Amended Code Sec. 1033(e) by striking "CONDITIONS.— For purposes" and inserting "CONDITIONS.—"followed by "(1) IN GENERAL.—For purposes", and by adding at the end a new paragraph (2). **Effective** for any tax year with respect to which the due date (without regard to extensions) for the return is after 12-31-2002.

(f) REPLACEMENT OF LIVESTOCK WITH OTHER FARM PROPERTY IN CERTAIN CASES.—For purposes of subsection (a), if, because of *drought, flood, or other weather-related conditions, or* soil contamination or other environmental contamination, it is not feasible for the taxpayer to reinvest the proceeds from compulsorily or involuntarily converted livestock in property similar or related in use to the livestock so converted, other property (including real property *in the case of soil contamination or other environmental contamination*) used for farming purposes shall be treated as property similar or related in service or use to the livestock so converted.

* * *

[CCH Explanation at ¶ 820. Committee Reports at ¶ 10,340.]

Amendments

• **2004, American Jobs Creation Act of 2004 (H.R. 4520)**

H.R. 4520, § 311(a)(1)-(3):

Amended Code Sec. 1033(f) by inserting "drought, flood, or other weather-related conditions, or" after "because of",

by inserting "in the case of soil contamination or other environmental contamination" after "including real property", and by striking "WHERE THERE HAS BEEN ENVIRONMENTAL CONTAMINATION" in the heading and inserting "IN CERTAIN CASES". **Effective** for any tax year with respect to which the due date (without regard to extensions) for the return is after 12-31-2002.

[¶ 5770] CODE SEC. 1056. BASIS LIMITATION FOR PLAYER CONTRACTS TRANSFERRED IN CONNECTION WITH THE SALE OF A FRANCHISE. [*Repealed.*]

* * *

[CCH Explanation at ¶ 355. Committee Reports at ¶ 11,580.]

Amendments

• **2004, American Jobs Creation Act of 2004 (H.R. 4520)**

H.R. 4520, § 886(b)(1)(A):

Repealed Code Sec. 1056. **Effective** for property acquired after the date of the enactment of this Act. Prior to repeal, Code Sec. 1056 read as follows:

SEC. 1056. BASIS LIMITATION FOR PLAYER CONTRACTS TRANSFERRED IN CONNECTION WITH THE SALE OF A FRANCHISE.

(a) GENERAL RULE.—If a franchise to conduct any sports enterprise is sold or exchanged, and if, in connection with such sale or exchange, there is a transfer of a contract for the services of an athlete, the basis of such contract in the hands of the transferee shall not exceed the sum of—

(1) the adjusted basis of such contract in the hands of the transferor immediately before the transfer, plus

(2) the gain (if any) recognized by the transferor on the transfer of such contract.

(b) EXCEPTIONS.—Subsection (a) shall not apply—

(1) to an exchange described in section 1031 (relating to exchange of property held for productive use or investment), and

(2) to property in the hands of a person acquiring the property from a decedent or to whom the property passed from a decedent (within the meaning of section 1014(a)).

(c) TRANSFEROR REQUIRED TO FURNISH CERTAIN INFORMATION.—Under regulations prescribed by the Secretary, the transfer[or] shall, at the times and in the manner provided in such regulations, furnish to the Secretary and to the transferee the following information:

(1) the amount which the transferor believes to be the adjusted basis referred to in paragraph (1) of subsection (a),

(2) the amount which the transferor believes to be the gain referred to in paragraph (2) of subsection (a), and

(3) any subsequent modification of either such amount.

To the extent provided in such regulations, the amounts furnished pursuant to the preceding sentence shall be binding on the transferor and on the transferee.

(d) PRESUMPTION AS TO AMOUNT ALLOCABLE TO PLAYER CONTRACTS.—In the case of any sale or exchange described in subsection (a), it shall be presumed that not more than 50 percent of the consideration is allocable to contracts for the services of athletes unless it is established to the satisfaction of the Secretary that a specified amount in excess of 50 percent is properly allocable to such contracts. Nothing in the preceding sentence shall give rise to a presumption that an allocation of less than 50 percent of the consideration to contracts for the services of athletes is a proper allocation.

[¶ 5775] CODE SEC. 1092. STRADDLES.

(a) RECOGNITION OF LOSS IN CASE OF STRADDLES, ETC.—

* * *

(2) SPECIAL RULE FOR IDENTIFIED STRADDLES.—

(A) IN GENERAL.—*In the case of any straddle which is an identified straddle—*

(i) *paragraph (1) shall not apply with respect to identified positions comprising the identified straddle,*

(ii) *if there is any loss with respect to any identified position of the identified straddle, the basis of each of the identified offsetting positions in the identified straddle shall be increased by an amount which bears the same ratio to the loss as the unrecognized gain with respect to such offsetting position bears to the aggregate unrecognized gain with respect to all such offsetting positions, and*

(iii) *any loss described in clause (ii) shall not otherwise be taken into account for purposes of this title.*

(B) IDENTIFIED STRADDLE.—The term "identified straddle" means any straddle—

(i) which is clearly identified on the taxpayer's records as an identified straddle before the earlier of—

(I) the close of the day on which the straddle is acquired, or

(II) such time as the Secretary may prescribe by regulations.

(ii) to the extent provided by regulations, the value of each position of which (in the hands of the taxpayer immediately before the creation of the straddle) is not less than the basis of such position in the hands of the taxpayer at the time the straddle is created, and

(iii) which is not part of a larger straddle.

The Secretary shall prescribe regulations which specify the proper methods for clearly identifying a straddle as an identified straddle (and the positions comprising such straddle), which specify the rules for the application of this section for a taxpayer which fails to properly identify the positions of an identified straddle, and which specify the ordering rules in cases where a taxpayer disposes of less than an entire position which is part of an identified straddle.

(3) UNRECOGNIZED GAIN.—For purposes of this subsection—

* * *

(B) SPECIAL RULE FOR IDENTIFIED STRADDLES.—For purposes of paragraph (2)(A)(ii), the unrecognized gain with respect to any identified offsetting position shall be the excess of the fair market value of the position at the time of the determination over the fair market value of the position at the time the taxpayer identified the position as a position in an identified straddle.

(C) REPORTING OF GAIN.—

(i) IN GENERAL.—Each taxpayer shall disclose to the Secretary, at such time and in such manner and form as the Secretary may prescribe by regulations—

(I) each position (whether or not part of a straddle) with respect to which, as of the close of the taxable year, there is unrecognized gain, and

(II) the amount of such unrecognized gain.

(ii) REPORTS NOT REQUIRED IN CERTAIN CASES.—Clause (i) shall not apply—

(I) to any position which is part of an identified straddle,

(II) to any position which, with respect to the taxpayer, is property described in paragraph (1) or (2) of section 1221(a) or to any position which is part of a hedging transaction (as defined in section 1256(e)), or

(III) with respect to any taxable year if no loss on a position (including a regulated futures contract) has been sustained during such taxable year or if the only loss sustained on such position is a loss described in subclause (II).

* * *

[CCH Explanation at ¶ 730. Committee Reports at ¶ 11,600.]

Amendments

• **2004, American Jobs Creation Act of 2004 (H.R. 4520)**

H.R. 4520, § 888(a)(1):

Amended Code Sec. 1092(a)(2)(A). **Effective** for positions established on or after the date of the enactment of this Act. Prior to amendment Code Sec. 1092(a)(2)(A) read as follows:

(A) IN GENERAL.—In the case of any straddle which is an identified straddle as of the close of any taxable year—

(i) paragraph (1) shall not apply for such taxable year, and

(ii) any loss with respect to such straddle shall be treated as sustained not earlier than the day on which all of the positions making up the straddle are disposed of.

H.R. 4520, § 888(a)(2)(A)-(B):

Amended Code Sec. 1092(a)(2)(B) by striking clause (ii) and inserting a new clause (ii), and by adding at the end a

new flush sentence. **Effective** for positions established on or after the date of the enactment of this Act. Prior to amendment, Code Sec. 1092(a)(2)(B)(ii) read as follows:

(ii) all of the original positions of which (as identified by the taxpayer) are acquired on the same day and with respect to which—

(I) all of such positions are disposed of on the same day during the taxable year, or

(II) none of such positions has been disposed of as of the close of the taxable year, and

H.R. 4520, § 888(a)(3):

Amended Code Sec. 1092(a)(3) by redesignating subparagraph (B) as subparagraph (C) and by inserting after subparagraph (A) new subparagraph (B). **Effective** for positions established on or after the date of the enactment of this Act.

(c) STRADDLE DEFINED.—For purposes of this section—

* * *

(2) Offsetting positions.—

* * *

(B) Special rule for identified straddles.—In the case of any position which is not part of an identified straddle (within the meaning of subsection (a)(2)(B)), such position shall not be treated as offsetting with respect to any position which is part of an identifed straddle.

* * *

[CCH Explanation at ¶730. Committee Reports at ¶11,600.]

Amendments

• **2004, American Jobs Creation Act of 2004 (H.R. 4520)**

H.R. 4520, §888(a)(4):

Amended Code Sec. 1092(c)(2) by striking subparagraph (B) and by redesignating subparagraph (C) as subparagraph (B). **Effective** for positions established on or after the date of

the enactment of this Act. Prior to being striken, Code Sec. 1092(c)(2)(B) read as follows:

(B) One side larger than other side.—If 1 or more positions offset only a portion of 1 or more other positions, the Secretary shall by regulations prescribe the method for determining the portion of such other positions which is to be taken into account for purposes of this section.

(d) Definitions and Special Rules.—*For purposes of this section—*

* * *

(3) Special rules for stock.—*For purposes of paragraph (1)—*

(A) In general.—*In the case of stock, the term 'personal property' includes stock only if—*

(i) such stock is of a type which is actively traded and at least 1 of the positions offsetting such stock is a position with respect to such stock or substantially similar or related property, or

(ii) such stock is of a corporation formed or availed of to take positions in personal property which offset positions taken by any shareholder.

(B) Rule for application.—*For purposes of determining whether subsection (e) applies to any transaction with respect to stock described in subparagraph (A)(ii), all includible corporations of an affiliated group (within the meaning of section 1504(a)) shall be treated as 1 taxpayer.*

* * *

(8) Special rules for physically settled positions.—*For purposes of subsection (a), if a taxpayer settles a position which is part of a straddle by delivering property to which the position relates (and such position, if terminated, would result in a realization of a loss), then such taxpayer shall be treated as if such taxpayer—*

(A) terminated the position for its fair market value immediately before the settlement, and

(B) sold the property so delivered by the taxpayer at its fair market value.

* * *

[CCH Explanation at ¶730. Committee Reports at ¶11,600.]

Amendments

• **2004, American Jobs Creation Act of 2004 (H.R. 4520)**

H.R. 4520, §888(b):

Amended Code Sec. 1092(d) by adding at the end a new paragraph (8). **Effective** for positions established on or after the date of the enactment of this Act.

H.R. 4520, §888(c)(1):

Amended Code Sec. 1092(d)(3). **Effective** for positions established on or after the date of the enactment of this Act. Prior to amendment, Code Sec. 1092(d)(3) read as follows:

(3) Special rules for stock.—For purposes of paragraph (1)—

(A) In general.—Except as provided in subparagraph (B), the term "personal property" does not include stock. The preceding sentence shall not apply to any interest in stock.

(B) Exceptions.—The term "personal property" includes—

(i) any stock which is part of a straddle at least 1 of the offsetting positions of which is—

(I) an option with respect to such stock or substantially identical stock or securities,

(II) a securities futures contract (as defined in section 1234B) with respect to such stock or substantially identical stock or securities, or

(III) under regulations, a position with respect to substantially similar or related property (other than stock), and

(ii) any stock of a corporation formed or availed of to take positions in personal property which offset positions taken by any shareholder.

(C) Special rules.—

(i) For purposes of subparagraph (B), subsection (c) and paragraph (4) shall be applied as if stock described in clause (i) or (ii) of subparagraph (B) were personal property.

(ii) For purposes of determining whether subsection (e) applies to any transaction with respect to stock described in clause (ii) of subparagraph (B), all includible corporations of an affiliated group (within the meaning of section 1504(a)) shall be treated as 1 taxpayer.

[¶5780] CODE SEC. 1202. PARTIAL EXCLUSION FOR GAIN FROM CERTAIN SMALL BUSINESS STOCK.

* * *

(e) ACTIVE BUSINESS REQUIREMENT.—

* * *

(4) ELIGIBLE CORPORATION.—For purposes of this subsection, the term "eligible corporation" means any domestic corporation; except that such term shall not include—

* * *

(C) a regulated investment company, real estate investment trust, *or REMIC,* and

* * *

[CCH Explanation at ¶1120. Committee Reports at ¶11,180.]

Amendments

• **2004, American Jobs Creation Act of 2004 (H.R. 4520)**

H.R. 4520, §835(b)(9):

Amended Code Sec. 1202(e)(4)(C) by striking "REMIC, or FASIT" and inserting "or REMIC". **Effective** 1-1-2005. For an exception, see Act Sec. 835(c)(2), below.

H.R. 4520, §835(c)(2), provides:

(2) EXCEPTION FOR EXISTING FASITS.—Paragraph (1) shall not apply to any FASIT in existence on the date of the enactment of this Act to the extent that regular interests issued by the FASIT before such date continue to remain outstanding in accordance with the original terms of issuance.

[¶5785] CODE SEC. 1212. CAPITAL LOSS CARRYBACKS AND CARRYOVERS.

(a) CORPORATIONS.—

* * *

(3) SPECIAL RULES ON CARRYBACKS.—*A net capital loss of a corporation shall not be carried back under paragraph (1)(A) to a taxable year—*

(A) for which it is a regulated investment company (as defined in section 851), or

(B) for which it is a real estate investment trust (as defined in section 856).

* * *

[CCH Explanation at ¶490. Committee Reports at ¶10,690.]

Amendments

• **2004, American Jobs Creation Act of 2004 (H.R. 4520)**

H.R. 4520, §413(c)(20)(A):

Amended Code Sec. 1212(a)(3). **Effective** for tax years beginning after 12-31-2004. Prior to amendment, Code Sec. 1212(a)(3) read as follows:

(3) SPECIAL RULES ON CARRYBACKS.—A net capital loss of a corporation shall not be carried back under paragraph (1)(A) to a taxable year—

(A) for which it is a foreign personal holding company (as defined in section 552);

(B) for which it is a regulated investment company (as defined in section 851);

(C) for which it is a real estate investment trust (as defined in section 856); or

(D) for which an election made by it under section 1247 is applicable (relating to election by foreign investment companies to distribute income currently).

[¶5790] CODE SEC. 1223. HOLDING PERIOD OF PROPERTY.

For purposes of this subtitle—

* * *

(10) In the case of a person acquiring property from a decedent or to whom property passed from a decedent (within the meaning of section 1014(b)), if—

(A) the basis of such property in the hands of such person is determined under section 1014, and

(B) such property is sold or otherwise disposed of by such person within 1 year after the decedent's death,

then such person shall be considered to have held such property for more than 1 year.

(11) If—

(A) property is acquired by any person in a transfer to which section 1040 applies,

(B) such property is sold or otherwise disposed of by such person within 1 year after the decedent's death, and

(C) such sale or disposition is to a person who is a qualified heir (as defined in section 2032A(e)(1)) with respect to the decedent,

then the person making such sale or other disposition shall be considered to have held such property for more than 1 year.

(12) In determining the period for which the taxpayer has held qualified replacement property (within the meaning of section 1042(b)) the acquisition of which resulted under section 1042 in the nonrecognition of any part of the gain realized on the sale of qualified securities (within the meaning of section 1042(b)), there shall be included the period for which such qualified securities had been held by the taxpayer.

(13) In determining the period for which the taxpayer has held property the acquisition of which resulted under section 1043 in the nonrecognition of any part of the gain realized on the sale of other property, there shall be included the period for which such other property had been held as of the date of such sale.

(14) Except for purposes of sections 1202(a)(2), 1202(c)(2)(A), 1400B(b), and 1400F(b), in determining the period for which the taxpayer has held property the acquisition of which resulted under section 1045 or 1397B in the nonrecognition of any part of the gain realized on the sale of other property, there shall be included the period for which such other property has been held as of the date of such sale.

(15) If the security to which a securities futures contract (as defined in section 1234B) relates (other than a contract to which section 1256 applies) is acquired in satisfaction of such contract, in determining the period for which the taxpayer has held such security, there shall be included the period for which the taxpayer held such contract if such contract was a capital asset in the hands of the taxpayer.

(16) CROSS REFERENCE.—

For special holding period provision relating to certain partnership distributions, see section 735(b).

* * *

[CCH Explanation at ¶490. Committee Reports at ¶10,690.]

Amendments

• **2004, American Jobs Creation Act of 2004 (H.R. 4520)**

H.R. 4520, §413(c)(21):

Amended Code Sec. 1223 by striking paragraph (10) and by redesignating the following paragraphs accordingly. **Effective** for tax years of foreign corporations beginning after 12-31-2004, and for tax years of United States shareholders with or within which such tax years of foreign corporations

end. Prior to being stricken, Code Sec. 1223(10) read as follows:

(10) In determining the period for which the taxpayer has held trust certificates of a trust to which subsection (d) of section 1246 applies, or the period for which the taxpayer has held stock in a corporation to which subsection (d) of section 1246 applies, there shall be included the period for which the trust or corporation (as the case may be) held the stock of foreign investment companies.

[¶5795] CODE SEC. 1245. GAIN FROM DISPOSITIONS OF CERTAIN DEPRECIABLE PROPERTY.

(a) GENERAL RULE.—

* * *

(2) RECOMPUTED BASIS.—For purposes of this section—

* * *

(C) CERTAIN DEDUCTIONS TREATED AS AMORTIZATION.—Any deduction allowable under section 179, 179A, *179B*, 190, or 193 shall be treated as if it were a deduction allowable for amortization.

(3) SECTION 1245 PROPERTY.—For purposes of this section, the term "section 1245 property" means any property which is or has been property of a character subject to the allowance for depreciation provided in section 167 and is either—

(A) personal property,

(B) other property (not including a building or its structural components) but only if such other property is tangible and has an adjusted basis in which there are reflected adjustments described in paragraph (2) for a period in which such property (or other property)—

(i) was used as an integral part of manufacturing, production, or extraction or of furnishing transportation, communications, electrical energy, gas, water, or sewage disposal services, or

(ii) constituted a research facility used in connection with any of the activities referred to in clause (i), or

(iii) constituted a facility used in connection with any of the activities referred to in clause (i) for the bulk storage of fungible commodities (including commodities in a liquid or gaseous state),

(C) so much of any real property (other than any property described in subparagraph B)) which has an adjusted basis in which there are reflected adjustments for amortization under section 169, 179, 179A, *179B*, 185, 188 (as in effect before its repeal by the Revenue Reconciliation Act of 1990), 190, 193, or 194,

(D) a single purpose agricultural or horticultural structure (as defined in section 168(i)(13)),

(E) a storage facility (not including a building or its structural components) used in connection with the distribution of petroleum or any primary product of petroleum, or

(F) any railroad grading or tunnel bore (as defined in section 168(e)(4)).

(4) [*Stricken.*]

* * *

[CCH Explanation at ¶ 355 and ¶ 850. Committee Reports at ¶ 10,530 and ¶ 11,580.]

Amendments

• **2004, American Jobs Creation Act of 2004 (H.R. 4520)**

H.R. 4520, § 338(b)(5):

Amended Code Sec. 1245(a)(2)(C) and (3)(C) by inserting "179B," after "179A,". **Effective** for expenses paid or incurred after 12-31-2002, in tax years ending after such date.

H.R. 4520, § 886(b)(2):

Amended Code Sec. 1245(a) by striking paragraph (4). **Effective** for franchises acquired after the date of the enactment of this Act. Prior to being stricken, Code Sec. 1245(a)(4) read as follows:

(4) SPECIAL RULE FOR PLAYER CONTRACTS.—

(A) IN GENERAL.—For purposes of this section, if a franchise to conduct any sports enterprise is sold or exchanged, and if, in connection with such sale or exchange, there is a transfer of any player contracts, the recomputed basis of such player contracts in the hands of the transferor shall be the adjusted basis of such contracts increased by the greater of—

(i) the previously unrecaptured depreciation with respect to player contracts acquired by the transferor at the time of acquisition of such franchise, or

(ii) the previously unrecaptured depreciation with respect to the player contracts involved in such transfer.

(B) PREVIOUSLY UNRECAPTURED DEPRECIATION WITH RESPECT TO INITIAL CONTRACTS.—For purposes of subparagraph (A)(i), the term "previously unrecaptured depreciation" means the excess (if any) of—

(i) the sum of the deduction allowed or allowable to the taxpayer transferor for the depreciation attributable to periods after December 31, 1975, of any player contracts acquired by him at the time of acquisition of such franchise, plus the deduction allowed or allowable for losses incurred after December 31, 1975, with respect to such player contracts acquired at the time of such acquisition, over

(ii) the aggregate of the amounts described in clause (i) treated as ordinary income by reason of this section with respect to prior dispositions of such player contracts acquired upon acquisition of the franchise.

(C) PREVIOUSLY UNRECAPTURED DEPRECIATION WITH RESPECT TO CONTRACTS TRANSFERRED.—For purposes of subparagraph (A)(ii), the term "previously unrecaptured depreciation" means the amount of any deduction allowed or allowable to the taxpayer transferor for the depreciation of any contracts involved in such transfer.

(D) PLAYER CONTRACT.—For purposes of this paragraph, the term "player contract" means any contract for the services of an athlete which, in the hands of the taxpayer, is of a character subject to the allowance for depreciation provided in section 167.

¶5795 Code Sec. 1245(a)(3)(B)

[¶5800] CODE SEC. 1246. GAIN ON FOREIGN INVESTMENT COMPANY STOCK.
[*Repealed.*]

* * *

[CCH Explanation at ¶490. Committee Reports at ¶10,690.]

Amendments

• **2004, American Jobs Creation Act of 2004 (H.R. 4520)**

H.R. 4520, §413(a)(2):

Repealed Code Sec. 1246. **Effective** for tax years of foreign corporations beginning after 12-31-2004, and for tax years of United States shareholders with or within which such tax years of foreign corporations end. Prior to repeal, Code Sec. 1246 read as follows:

SEC. 1246. GAIN ON FOREIGN INVESTMENT COMPANY STOCK.

(a) TREATMENT OF GAIN AS ORDINARY INCOME.—

(1) GENERAL RULE.—In the case of a sale or exchange (or a distribution which, under section 302 or 331, is treated as an exchange of stock) after December 31, 1962, of stock in a foreign corporation which was a foreign investment company (as defined in subsection (b)) at any time during the period during which the taxpayer held such stock, any gain shall be treated as ordinary income, to the extent of the taxpayer's ratable share of the earnings and profits of such corporation accumulated for taxable years beginning after December 31, 1962.

(2) RATABLE SHARE.—For purposes of this section, the taxpayer's ratable share shall be determined under regulations prescribed by the Secretary, but shall include only his ratable share of the accumulated earnings and profits of such corporation—

(A) for the period during which the taxpayer held such stock, but

(B) excluding such earnings and profits attributable to—

(i) any amount previously included in the gross income of such taxpayer under section 951 (but only to the extent the inclusion of such amount did not result in an exclusion of any other amount from gross income under section 959), or

(ii) any taxable year during which such corporation was not a foreign investment company but only if—

(I) such corporation was not a foreign investment company at any time before such taxable year, and

(II) such corporation was treated as a foreign investment company solely by reason of subsection (b)(2).

(3) TAXPAYER TO ESTABLISH EARNINGS AND PROFITS.—Unless the taxpayer establishes the amount of the accumulated earnings and profits of the foreign investment company and the ratable share thereof for the period during which the taxpayer held such stock, all the gain from the sale or exchange of stock in such company shall be considered as ordinary income.

(4) HOLDING PERIOD OF STOCK MUST BE MORE THAN 1 YEAR.— This section shall not apply with respect to the sale or exchange of stock where the holding period of such stock as of the date of such sale or exchange is 1 year or less.

(b) DEFINITION OF FOREIGN INVESTMENT COMPANY.—For purposes of this section, the term "foreign investment company" means any foreign corporation which, for any taxable year beginning after December 31, 1962, is—

(1) registered under the Investment Company Act of 1940, as amended (15 U. S. C. 80a-1 to 80b-2), either as a management company or as a unit investment trust, or

(2) engaged (or holding itself out as being engaged) primarily in the business of investing, reinvesting, or trading in—

(A) securities (as defined in section 2(a)(36) of the Investment Company Act of 1940, as amended),

(B) commodities, or

(C) any interest (including a futures or forward contract or option) in property described in subparagraph (A) or (B),

at a time when 50 percent or more of the total combined voting power of all classes of stock entitled to vote, or the total value of all classes of stock, was held directly (or indirectly through applying paragraphs (2) and (3) of section 958(a) and paragraph (4) of section 318(a)) by United States persons (as defined in section 7701(a)(30)).

(c) STOCK HAVING TRANSFERRED OR SUBSTITUTED BASIS.—To the extent provided in regulations prescribed by the Secretary, stock in a foreign corporation, the basis of which (in the hands of the taxpayer selling or exchanging such stock) is determined by reference to the basis (in the hands of such taxpayer or any other person) of stock in a foreign investment company, shall be treated as stock of a foreign investment company and held by the taxpayer throughout the holding period for such stock (determined under section 1223).

(d) RULES RELATING TO ENTITIES HOLDING FOREIGN INVESTMENT COMPANY STOCK.—To the extent provided in regulations prescribed by the Secretary—

(1) trust certificates of a trust to which section 677 (relating to income for benefit of grantor) applies, and

(2) stock of a domestic corporation,

shall be treated as stock of a foreign investment company and held by the taxpayer throughout the holding period for such certificates or stock (determined under section 1223) in the same proportion that the investment in stock in a foreign investment company by the trust or domestic corporation bears to the total assets of such trust or corporation.

➤➤➤ *Caution: Code Sec. 1246(e), below, was stricken by P.L. 107-16, applicable to estates of decedents dying after December 31, 2009.*

(e) RULES RELATING TO STOCK ACQUIRED FROM A DECEDENT.—

(1) BASIS.—In the case of stock of a foreign investment company acquired by bequest, devise, or inheritance (or by the decedent's estate) from a decedent dying after December 31, 1962, the basis determined under section 1014 shall be reduced (but not below the adjusted basis of such stock in the hands of the decedent immediately before his death) by the amount of the decedent's ratable share of the earnings and profits of such company accumulated after December 31, 1962. Any stock so acquired shall be treated as stock described in subsection (c).

(2) DEDUCTION FOR ESTATE TAX.—If stock to which subsection (a) applies is acquired from a decedent, the taxpayer shall, under regulations prescribed by the Secretary or his delegate, be allowed (for the taxable year of the sale or exchange) a deduction from gross income equal to that portion of the decedent's estate tax deemed paid which is attributable to the excess of (A) the value at which such stock was taken into account for purposes of determining the value of the decedent's gross estate, over (B) the value at which it would have been so taken into account if such value had been reduced by the amount described in paragraph (1).

(f) INFORMATION WITH RESPECT TO CERTAIN FOREIGN INVESTMENT COMPANIES.—Every United States person who, on the last day of the taxable year of a foreign investment company, owns 5 percent or more in value of the stock of such company shall furnish with respect to such company such information as the Secretary shall by regulations prescribe.

(g) COORDINATION WITH Section 1248.—This section shall not apply to any gain to the extent such gain is treated as ordinary income under section 1248 (determined without regard to section 1248(g)(2)).

(h) CROSS REFERENCE.—

For special rules relating to the earnings and profits of foreign investment companies, see section 312(j).

[¶ 5805] CODE SEC. 1247. ELECTION BY FOREIGN INVESTMENT COMPANIES TO DISTRIBUTE INCOME CURRENTLY. [*Repealed.*]

*   *   *

[CCH Explanation at ¶ 490. Committee Reports at ¶ 10,690.]

Amendments

• **2004, American Jobs Creation Act of 2004 (H.R. 4520)**

H.R. 4520, § 413(a)(3):

Repealed Code Sec. 1247. **Effective** for tax years of foreign corporations beginning after 12-31-2004, and for tax years of United States shareholders with or within which such tax years of foreign corporations end. Prior to repeal, Code Sec. 1247 read as follows:

SEC. 1247. ELECTION BY FOREIGN INVESTMENT COMPANIES TO DISTRIBUTE INCOME CURRENTLY.

(a) ELECTION BY FOREIGN INVESTMENT COMPANY.—

(1) IN GENERAL.—If a foreign investment company which is described in section 1246(b)(1) elects (in the manner provided in regulations prescribed by the Secretary) on or before December 31, 1962, with respect to each taxable year beginning after December 31, 1962, to—

(A) distribute to its shareholders 90 percent or more of what its taxable income would be if it were a domestic corporation;

(B) designate in a written notice mailed to its shareholders at any time before the expiration of 45 days after the close of its taxable year the pro rata amount of the amount (determined as if such corporation were a domestic corporation) of the net capital gain of the taxable year; and the portion thereof which is being distributed; and

(C) provide such information as the Secretary deems necessary to carry out the purposes of this section,

then section 1246 shall not apply with respect to the qualified shareholders of such company during any taxable year to which such election applies.

(2) SPECIAL RULES.—

(A) COMPUTATION OF TAXABLE INCOME.—For purposes of paragraph (1)(A), the taxable income of the company shall be computed without regard to—

(i) the net capital gain referred to in paragraph (1)(B),

(ii) section 172 (relating to net operating losses), and

(iii) any deduction provided by part VIII of subchapter B (other than the deduction provided by section 248, relating to organizational expenditures).

(B) DISTRIBUTIONS AFTER THE CLOSE OF THE TAXABLE YEAR.— For purposes of paragraph (1)(A), a distribution made after the close of the taxable year and on or before the 15th day of the third month of the next taxable year shall be treated as distributed during the taxable year to the extent elected by the company (in accordance with regulations prescribed by the Secretary) on or before the 15th day of such third month.

(C) CARRYOVER OF CAPITAL LOSSES FROM NONELECTION YEARS DENIED.—In computing the net capital gain referred to in paragraph (1)(B), section 1212 shall not apply to losses incurred in or with respect to taxable years before the first taxable year to which the election applies.

(b) YEARS TO WHICH ELECTION APPLIES.—The election of any foreign investment company under this section shall terminate as of the close of the taxable year preceding its first taxable year in which any of the following occurs:

(1) the company fails to comply with the provisions of subparagraph (A), (B), or (C) of subsection (a)(1), unless it is shown that such failure is due to reasonable cause and not due to willful neglect,

(2) the company is a foreign personal holding company, or

(3) the company is not a foreign investment company which is described in section 1246(b)(1).

(c) QUALIFIED SHAREHOLDERS.—For purposes of this section—

(1) IN GENERAL.—The term "qualified shareholder" means any shareholder who United States person (as defined in section 7701(a)(30)), other than a shareholder described in paragraph (2).

(2) CERTAIN UNITED STATES PERSONS EXCLUDED FROM DEFINITION.—A United States person shall not be treated as a qualified shareholder for the taxable year if for such taxable year (or for any prior taxable year) he did not include, in computing his long-term capital gains in his return for such taxable year, the amount designated by such company pursuant to subsection (a)(1)(B) as his share of the undistributed capital gains of such company for its taxable year ending within or with such taxable year of the taxpayer. The preceding sentence shall not apply with respect to any failure by the taxpayer to treat an amount as provided therein if the taxpayer shows that such failure was due to reasonable cause and not due to willful neglect.

(d) TREATMENT OF DISTRIBUTED AND UNDISTRIBUTED CAPITAL GAINS BY A QUALIFIED SHAREHOLDER.—Every qualified shareholder of a foreign investment company for any taxable year of such company with respect to which an election pursuant to subsection (a) is in effect shall include, in computing his long-term capital gains—

(1) for his taxable year in which received, his pro rata share of the distributed portion of the net capital gain for such taxable year of such company, and

(2) for his taxable year in which or with which the taxable year of such company ends, his pro rata share of the undistributed portion of the net capital gain for such taxable year of such company.

(e) ADJUSTMENTS.—Under regulations prescribed by the Secretary, proper adjustment shall be made—

(1) in the earnings and profits of the electing foreign investment company and a qualified shareholder's ratable share thereof, and

(2) in the adjusted basis of stock of such company held by such shareholder,

to reflect such shareholder's inclusion in gross income of undistributed capital gains.

(f) ELECTION BY FOREIGN INVESTMENT COMPANY WITH RESPECT TO FOREIGN TAX CREDIT.—A foreign investment company with respect to which an election pursuant to subsection (a) is in effect and more than 50 percent of the value (as defined in section 851(c)(4)) of whose total assets at the close of the taxable year consists of stock or securities in foreign corporations may, for such taxable year, elect the application of this subsection with respect to income, war profits, and excess profits taxes described in section 901(b)(1) which are paid by the foreign investment company during such taxable year to foreign countries and possessions of the United States. If such election is made—

(1) the foreign investment company—

(A) shall compute its taxable income, for purposes of subsection (a)(1)(A), without any deductions for income, war profits, or excess profits taxes paid to foreign countries or possessions of the United States, and

(B) shall treat the amount of such taxes, for purposes of subsection (a)(1)(A), as distributed to its shareholders;

(2) each qualified shareholder of such foreign investment company—

(A) shall include in gross income and treat as paid by him his proportionate share of such taxes, and

(B) shall treat, for purposes of applying subpart A of part III of subchapter N, his proportionate share of such taxes as having been paid to the country in which the foreign investment company is incorporated, and

(C) shall treat as gross income from sources within the country in which the foreign investment company is incorporated, for purposes of applying subpart A of part III of subchapter N, the sum of his proportionate share of such taxes and any dividend paid to him by such foreign investment company.

(g) NOTICE TO SHAREHOLDERS.—The amounts to be treated by qualified shareholders, for purposes of subsection (f)(2), as their proportionate share of the taxes described in subsection (f)(1)(A) paid by a foreign investment company shall not exceed the amounts so designated by the foreign investment company in a written notice mailed to its shareholders not later than 45 days after the close of its taxable year.

(h) MANNER OF MAKING ELECTION AND NOTIFYING SHAREHOLDERS.—The election provided in subsection (f) and the notice to shareholders required by subsection (g) shall be made in such manner as the Secretary may prescribe by regulations.

(i) LOSS ON SALE OR EXCHANGE OF CERTAIN STOCK HELD LESS THAN 1 YEAR.—If—

(1) under this section, any qualified shareholder treats any amount designated under subsection (a)(1)(B) with respect to a share of stock as long-term capital gain, and

(2) such share is held by the taxpayer for less than 1 year

then any loss on the sale or exchange of such share shall, to the extent of the amount described in paragraph (1), be treated as loss from the sale or exchange of a capital asset held for more than 1 year.

[¶ 5810] CODE SEC. 1248. GAIN FROM CERTAIN SALES OR EXCHANGES OF STOCK IN CERTAIN FOREIGN CORPORATIONS.

* * *

(d) EXCLUSIONS FROM EARNINGS AND PROFITS.—For purposes of this section, the following amounts shall be excluded, with respect to any United States person, from the earnings and profits of a foreign corporation:

* * *

(5) FOREIGN TRADE INCOME.—Earnings and profits of the foreign corporation attributable to foreign trade income of a FSC other than foreign trade income which—

(A) is section 923(a)(2) non-exempt income (within the meaning of section 927(d)(6)), or

(B) would not (but for section 923(a)(4)) be treated as exempt foreign trade income.

For purposes of the preceding sentence, the terms "foreign trade income" and "exempt foreign trade income" have the respective meanings given such terms by section 923.

(6) AMOUNTS INCLUDED IN GROSS INCOME UNDER SECTION 1293.—Earnings and profits of the foreign corporation attributable to any amount previously included in the gross income of such person under section 1293 with respect to the stock sold or exchanged, but only to the extent the inclusion of such amount did not result in an exclusion of an amount under section 1293(c).

* * *

[CCH Explanation at ¶ 490. Committee Reports at ¶ 10,690.]

Amendments

• **2004, American Jobs Creation Act of 2004 (H.R. 4520)**

H.R. 4520, § 413(c)(22):

Amended Code Sec. 1248(d) by striking paragraph (5) and by redesignating paragraphs (6) and (7) as paragraphs (5) and (6), respectively. **Effective** for tax years of foreign corporations beginning after 12-31-2004, and for tax years of United States shareholders with or within which such tax

years of foreign corporations end. Prior to being stricken, Code Sec. 1248(d)(5) read as follows:

(5) AMOUNTS INCLUDED IN GROSS INCOME UNDER SECTION 1247.—If the United States person whose stock is sold or exchanged was a qualified shareholder (as defined in section 1247(c)) of a foreign corporation which was a foreign investment company (as described in section 1246(b)(1)), the earnings and profits of the foreign corporation for taxable years in which such person was a qualified shareholder.

[¶ 5815] CODE SEC. 1253. TRANSFERS OF FRANCHISES, TRADEMARKS, AND TRADE NAMES.

* * *

(e) [*Stricken.*]

* * *

[CCH Explanation at ¶355. Committee Reports at ¶11,580.]

Amendments

• **2004, American Jobs Creation Act of 2004 (H.R. 4520)**

H.R. 4520, §886(b)(3):

Amended Code Sec. 1253 by striking subsection (e). **Effective** for property acquired after the date of the enactment of

this Act. Prior to being stricken, Code Sec. 1253(e) read as follows:

(e) EXCEPTION.—This section shall not apply to the transfer of a franchise to engage in professional football, basketball, baseball, or other professional sport.

[¶5820] CODE SEC. 1258. RECHARACTERIZATION OF GAIN FROM CERTAIN FINANCIAL TRANSACTIONS.

* * *

(d) DEFINITIONS AND SPECIAL RULES.—For purposes of this section—

(1) APPLICABLE STRADDLE.—The term "applicable straddle" means any straddle (within the meaning of section 1092(c)).

* * *

[CCH Explanation at ¶730. Committee Reports at ¶11,600.]

Amendments

• **2004, American Jobs Creation Act of 2004 (H.R. 4520)**

H.R. 4520, §888(c)(2):

Amended Code Sec. 1258(d)(1) by striking "; except that the term 'personal property' shall include stock" immedi-

ately after "section 1092(c))". **Effective** for positions established on or after the date of the enactment of this Act.

[¶5825] CODE SEC. 1260. GAINS FROM CONSTRUCTIVE OWNERSHIP TRANSACTIONS.

* * *

(c) FINANCIAL ASSET.—For purposes of this section—

* * *

(2) PASS-THRU ENTITY.—For purposes of paragraph (1), the term "pass-thru entity" means—

(A) a regulated investment company,

(B) a real estate investment trust,

(C) an S corporation,

(D) a partnership,

(E) a trust,

(F) a common trust fund,

(G) a passive foreign investment company (as defined in section 1297 without regard to subsection (e) thereof), [*and*]

(H) a REMIC.

* * *

[CCH Explanation at ¶490. Committee Reports at ¶10,690.]

Amendments

• **2004, American Jobs Creation Act of 2004 (H.R. 4520)**

H.R. 4520, §413(c)(23):

Amended Code Sec. 1260(c)(2) by striking subparagraphs (H) and (I) and by redesignating subparagraph (J) as subparagraph (H). **Effective** for tax years of foreign corpora-

tions beginning after 12-31-2004, and for tax years of United States shareholders with or within which such tax years of foreign corporations end. Prior to being stricken, Code Sec. 1260(c)(2)(H)-(I) read as follows:

(H) a foreign personal holding company,

(I) a foreign investment company (as defined in section 1246(b)), and

[¶5830] CODE SEC. 1286. TAX TREATMENT OF STRIPPED BONDS.

* * *

(f) TREATMENT OF STRIPPED INTERESTS IN BOND AND PREFERRED STOCK FUNDS, ETC.—In the case of an account or entity substantially all of the assets of which consist of bonds, preferred stock, or a combination thereof, the Secretary may by regulations provide that rules similar to the rules of this section and 305(e), as appropriate, shall apply to interests in such account or entity to which (but for this subsection) this section or section 305(e), as the case may be, would not apply.

[CCH Explanation at ¶725. Committee Reports at ¶11,140.]

Amendments

• **2004, American Jobs Creation Act of 2004 (H.R. 4520)**

H.R. 4520, §831(a):

Amended Code Sec. 1286 by redesignating subsection (f) as subsection (g) and by inserting after subsection (e) a new

subsection (f). **Effective** for purchases and dispositions after the date of the enactment of this Act.

(g) REGULATION AUTHORITY.—The Secretary may prescribe regulations providing that where, by reason of varying rates of interest, put or call options, or other circumstances, the tax treatment under this section does not accurately reflect the income of the holder of a stripped coupon or stripped bond, or of the person disposing of such bond or coupon, as the case may be, for any period, such treatment shall be modified to require that the proper amount of income be included for such period.

* * *

[CCH Explanation at ¶725. Committee Reports at ¶11,140.]

Amendments

• **2004, American Jobs Creation Act of 2004 (H.R. 4520)**

H.R. 4520, §831(a):

Amended Code Sec. 1286 by redesignating subsection (f) as subsection (g). **Effective** for purchases and dispositions after the date of the enactment of this Act.

[¶5835] CODE SEC. 1291. INTEREST ON TAX DEFERRAL.

* * *

(b) EXCESS DISTRIBUTION.—

* * *

(3) ADJUSTMENTS.—Under regulations prescribed by the Secretary—

* * *

(F) proper adjustment shall be made for amounts not includible in gross income by reason of section *959(a)* or 1293(c), and

* * *

[CCH Explanation at ¶490. Committee Reports at ¶10,690.]

Amendments

• **2004, American Jobs Creation Act of 2004 (H.R. 4520)**

H.R. 4520, §413(c)(24)(A):

Amended Code Sec. 1291(b)(3)(F) by striking "551(d), 959(a)," and inserting "959(a)". **Effective** for tax years of

foreign corporations beginning after 12-31-2004, and for tax years of United States shareholders with or within which such tax years of foreign corporations end.

⫸→ *Caution: Code Sec. 1291(e), below, prior to amendment by P.L. 107-16, but as amended by H.R. 4520, applies to estates of decedents dying on or before December 31, 2009.*

(e) CERTAIN BASIS, ETC., RULES MADE APPLICABLE.—Except to the extent inconsistent with the regulations prescribed under subsection (f), rules similar to the rules of subsections (c), (d), (e), and (f) of section 1246 *(as in effect on the day before the date of the enactment of the American Jobs Creation Act of 2004)* shall apply for purposes of this section; except that—

(1) the reduction under subsection (e) of such section shall be the excess of the basis determined under section 1014 over the adjusted basis of the stock immediately before the decedent's death, and

(2) such a reduction shall not apply in the case of a decedent who was a nonresident alien at all times during his holding period in the stock.

⟫⟫→ *Caution: Code Sec. 1291(e), below, as amended by P.L. 107-16 and H.R. 4520, applies to estates of decedents dying after December 31, 2009.*

(e) CERTAIN BASIS, ETC., RULES MADE APPLICABLE.—Except to the extent inconsistent with the regulations prescribed under subsection (f), rules similar to the rules of subsections (c), (d), and (f) of section 1246 *(as in effect on the day before the date of the enactment of the American Jobs Creation Act of 2004)* shall apply for purposes of this section.

* * *

[CCH Explanation at ¶ 490. Committee Reports at ¶ 10,690.]

Amendments

• 2004, American Jobs Creation Act of 2004 (H.R. 4520)

H.R. 4520, § 413(c)(24)(B):

Amended Code Sec. 1291(e) by inserting "(as in effect on the day before the date of the enactment of the American

Jobs Creation Act of 2004)" after "section 1246". **Effective** for tax years of foreign corporations beginning after 12-31-2004, and for tax years of United States shareholders with or within which such tax years of foreign corporations end.

[¶ 5840] CODE SEC. 1294. ELECTION TO EXTEND TIME FOR PAYMENT OF TAX ON UNDISTRIBUTED EARNINGS.

(a) EXTENSION ALLOWED BY ELECTION.—

* * *

(2) ELECTION NOT PERMITTED WHERE AMOUNTS OTHERWISE INCLUDIBLE UNDER SECTION 951.—The taxpayer may not make an election under paragraph (1) with respect to the undistributed PFIC earnings tax liability attributable to a qualified electing fund for the taxable year if any amount is includible in the gross income of the taxpayer under section 951 with respect to such fund for such taxable year.

* * *

[CCH Explanation at ¶ 490. Committee Reports at ¶ 10,690.]

Amendments

• 2004, American Jobs Creation Act of 2004 (H.R. 4520)

H.R. 4520, § 413(c)(25):

Amended Code Sec. 1294(a)(2). **Effective** for tax years of foreign corporations beginning after 12-31-2004, and for tax years of United States shareholders with or within which such tax years of foreign corporations end. Prior to amendment, Code Sec. 1294(a)(2) read as follows:

(2) ELECTION NOT PERMITTED WHERE AMOUNTS OTHERWISE INCLUDIBLE UNDER SECTION 551 OR 951.—The taxpayer may not

make an election under paragraph (1) with respect to the undistributed PFIC earnings tax liability attributable to a qualified electing fund for the taxable year if—

(A) any amount is includible in the gross income of the taxpayer under section 551 with respect to such fund for such taxable year, or

(B) any amount is includible in the gross income of the taxpayer under section 951 with respect to such fund for such taxable year.

[¶ 5845] CODE SEC. 1301. AVERAGING OF FARM INCOME.

(a) IN GENERAL.—At the election of an individual engaged in a *farming business or fishing business*, the tax imposed by section 1 for such taxable year shall be equal to the sum of—

(1) a tax computed under such section on taxable income reduced by elected farm income, plus

(2) the increase in tax imposed by section 1 which would result if taxable income for each of the 3 prior taxable years were increased by an amount equal to one-third of the elected farm income.

Any adjustment under this section for any taxable year shall be taken into account in applying this section for any subsequent taxable year.

[CCH Explanation at ¶ 825. Committee Reports at ¶ 10,370.]

Amendments

• 2004, American Jobs Creation Act of 2004 (H.R. 4520)

H.R. 4520, § 314(b)(1):

Amended Code Sec. 1301(a) by striking "farming business" and inserting "farming business or fishing business". **Effective** for tax years beginning after 12-31-2003.

(b) DEFINITIONS.—In this section—

(1) ELECTED FARM INCOME.—

(A) IN GENERAL.—The term "elected farm income" means so much of the taxable income for the taxable year—

(i) which is attributable to any farming business *or fishing business*; and

(ii) which is specified in the election under subsection (a).

(B) TREATMENT OF GAINS.—For purposes of subparagraph (A), gain from the sale or other disposition of property (other than land) regularly used by the taxpayer in such a farming business *or fishing business* for a substantial period shall be treated as attributable to such a farming business *or fishing business*.

* * *

(4) *FISHING BUSINESS.—The term "fishing business" means the conduct of commercial fishing as defined in section 3 of the Magnuson-Stevens Fishery Conservation and Management Act (16 U.S.C. 1802).*

* * *

[CCH Explanation at ¶ 825. Committee Reports at ¶ 10,370.]

Amendments

• 2004, American Jobs Creation Act of 2004 (H.R. 4520)

H.R. 4520, § 314(b)(2)(A):

Amended Code Sec. 1301(b)(1)(A)(i) by inserting "or fishing business" before the semicolon. **Effective** for tax years beginning after 12-31-2003.

H.R. 4520, § 314(b)(2)(B):

Amended Code Sec. 1301(b)(1)(B) by inserting "or fishing business" after "farming business" both places it occurs. **Effective** for tax years beginning after 12-31-2003.

H.R. 4520, § 314(b)(3):

Amended Code Sec. 1301(b) by adding at the end new paragraph (4). **Effective** for tax years beginning after 12-31-2003.

[¶ 5850] *CODE SEC. 1352. ALTERNATIVE TAX ON QUALIFYING SHIPPING ACTIVITIES.*

In the case of an electing corporation, the tax imposed by section 11 shall be the amount equal to the sum of—

(1) the tax imposed by section 11 determined after the application of this subchapter, and

(2) a tax equal to—

(A) the highest rate of tax specified in section 11, multiplied by

(B) the notional shipping income for the taxable year.

[CCH Explanation at ¶ 545. Committee Reports at ¶ 10,290.]

Amendments

• 2004, American Jobs Creation Act of 2004 (H.R. 4520)

H.R. 4520, § 248(a):

Amended chapter 1 by inserting after subchapter Q a new subchapter R (Code Secs. 1352-1359). **Effective** for tax years beginning after the date of the enactment of this Act.

[¶5855] CODE SEC. 1353. NOTIONAL SHIPPING INCOME.

(a) IN GENERAL.—For purposes of this subchapter, the notional shipping income of an electing corporation shall be the sum of the amounts determined under subsection (b) for each qualifying vessel operated by such electing corporation.

(b) AMOUNTS.—

(1) IN GENERAL.—For purposes of subsection (a), the amount of notional shipping income of an electing corporation for each qualifying vessel for the taxable year shall equal the product of—

(A) the daily notional shipping income, and

(B) the number of days during the taxable year that the electing corporation operated such vessel as a qualifying vessel in United States foreign trade.

(2) TREATMENT OF VESSELS THE INCOME FROM WHICH IS NOT OTHERWISE SUBJECT TO TAX.—In the case of a qualifying vessel any of the income from which is not included in gross income by reason of section 883 or otherwise, the amount of notional shipping income from such vessel for the taxable year shall be the amount which bears the same ratio to such shipping income (determined without regard to this paragraph) as the gross income from the operation of such vessel in the United States foreign trade bears to the sum of such gross income and the income so excluded.

(c) DAILY NOTIONAL SHIPPING INCOME.—For purposes of subsection (b), the daily notional shipping income from the operation of a qualifying vessel is—

(1) 40 cents for each 100 tons of so much of the net tonnage of the vessel as does not exceed 25,000 net tons, and

(2) 20 cents for each 100 tons of so much of the net tonnage of the vessel as exceeds 25,000 net tons.

(d) MULTIPLE OPERATORS OF VESSEL.—If for any period 2 or more persons are operators of a qualifying vessel, the notional shipping income from the operation of such vessel for such period shall be allocated among such persons on the basis of their respective ownership and charter interests in such vessel or on such other basis as the Secretary may prescribe by regulations.

[CCH Explanation at ¶545. Committee Reports at ¶10,290.]
Amendments
• **2004, American Jobs Creation Act of 2004 (H.R. 4520)**

H.R. 4520, §248(a):

Amended chapter 1 by inserting after subchapter Q a new subchapter R (Code Secs. 1352-1359). **Effective** for tax years beginning after the date of the enactment of this Act.

[¶5860] CODE SEC. 1354. ALTERNATIVE TAX ELECTION; REVOCATION; TERMINATION.

(a) IN GENERAL.—A qualifying vessel operator may elect the application of this subchapter.

(b) TIME AND MANNER; YEARS FOR WHICH EFFECTIVE.—An election under this subchapter—

(1) shall be made in such form as prescribed by the Secretary, and

(2) shall be effective for the taxable year for which made and all succeeding taxable years until terminated under subsection (d).

Such election may be effective for any taxable year only if made before the due date (including extensions) for filing the corporation's return for such taxable year.

(c) CONSISTENT ELECTIONS BY MEMBERS OF CONTROLLED GROUPS.—An election under subsection (a) by a member of a controlled group shall apply to all qualifying vessel operators that are members of such group.

(d) TERMINATION.—

(1) BY REVOCATION.—

(A) IN GENERAL.—An election under subsection (a) may be terminated by revocation.

(B) WHEN EFFECTIVE.—Except as provided in subparagraph (C)—

(i) *a revocation made during the taxable year and on or before the 15th day of the 3d month thereof shall be effective on the 1st day of such taxable year, and*

(ii) *a revocation made during the taxable year but after such 15th day shall be effective on the 1st day of the following taxable year.*

(C) REVOCATION MAY SPECIFY PROSPECTIVE DATE.—*If the revocation specifies a date for revocation which is on or after the day on which the revocation is made, the revocation shall be effective for taxable years beginning on and after the date so specified.*

(2) BY PERSON CEASING TO BE QUALIFYING VESSEL OPERATOR.—

(A) IN GENERAL.—*An election under subsection (a) shall be terminated whenever (at any time on or after the 1st day of the 1st taxable year for which the corporation is an electing corporation) such corporation ceases to be a qualifying vessel operator.*

(B) WHEN EFFECTIVE.—*Any termination under this paragraph shall be effective on and after the date of cessation.*

(C) ANNUALIZATION.—*The Secretary shall prescribe such annualization and other rules as are appropriate in the case of a termination under this paragraph.*

(e) ELECTION AFTER TERMINATION.—*If a qualifying vessel operator has made an election under subsection (a) and if such election has been terminated under subsection (d), such operator (and any successor operator) shall not be eligible to make an election under subsection (a) for any taxable year before its 5th taxable year which begins after the 1st taxable year for which such termination is effective, unless the Secretary consents to such election.*

[CCH Explanation at ¶ 545. Committee Reports at ¶ 10,290.]

Amendments

• 2004, American Jobs Creation Act of 2004 (H.R. 4520)

H.R. 4520, § 248(a):

Amended chapter 1 by inserting after subchapter Q a new subchapter R (Code Secs. 1352-1359). **Effective** for tax years beginning after the date of the enactment of this Act.

[¶ 5865] *CODE SEC. 1355. DEFINITIONS AND SPECIAL RULES.*

(a) DEFINITIONS.—*For purposes of this subchapter—*

(1) ELECTING CORPORATION.—*The term "electing corporation" means any corporation for which an election is in effect under this subchapter.*

(2) ELECTING GROUP; CONTROLLED GROUP.—

(A) ELECTING GROUP.—*The term "electing group" means a controlled group of which one or more members is an electing corporation.*

(B) CONTROLLED GROUP.—*The term "controlled group" means any group which would be treated as a single employer under subsection (a) or (b) of section 52 if paragraphs (1) and (2) of section 52(a) did not apply.*

(3) QUALIFYING VESSEL OPERATOR.—*The term "qualifying vessel operator" means any corporation—*

(A) *who operates one or more qualifying vessels, and*

(B) *who meets the shipping activity requirement in subsection (c).*

(4) QUALIFYING VESSEL.—*The term "qualifying vessel" means a self-propelled (or a combination self-propelled and non-self-propelled) United States flag vessel of not less than 10,000 deadweight tons used exclusively in the United States foreign trade during the period that the election under this subchapter is in effect.*

(5) UNITED STATES FLAG VESSEL.—*The term "United States flag vessel" means any vessel documented under the laws of the United States.*

(6) UNITED STATES DOMESTIC TRADE.—*The term "United States domestic trade" means the transportation of goods or passengers between places in the United States.*

(7) UNITED STATES FOREIGN TRADE.—The term "United States foreign trade" means the transportation of goods or passengers between a place in the United States and a foreign place or between foreign places.

(8) CHARTER.—The term "charter" includes an operating agreement.

(b) OPERATING A VESSEL.—For purposes of this subchapter—

(1) IN GENERAL.—Except as provided in paragraph (2), a person is treated as operating any vessel during any period if such vessel is—

(A) owned by, or chartered (including a time charter) to, the person, and

(B) is in use as a qualifying vessel during such period.

(2) BAREBOAT CHARTERS.—A person is treated as operating and using a vessel that it has chartered out on bareboat charter terms only if—

(A)(i) the vessel is temporarily surplus to the person's requirements and the term of the charter does not exceed 3 years, or

(ii) the vessel is bareboat chartered to a member of a controlled group which includes such person or to an unrelated person who subbareboats or time charters the vessel to such a member (including the owner of the vessel), and

(B) the vessel is used as a qualifying vessel by the person to whom ultimately chartered.

(c) SHIPPING ACTIVITY REQUIREMENT.—For purposes of this section—

(1) IN GENERAL.—Except as otherwise provided in this subsection, a corporation meets the shipping activity requirement of this subsection for any taxable year only if the requirement of paragraph (4) is met for each of the 2 preceding taxable years.

(2) SPECIAL RULE FOR 1ST YEAR OF ELECTION.—A corporation meets the shipping activity requirement of this subsection for the first taxable year for which the election under section 1354(a) is in effect only if the requirement of paragraph (4) is met for the preceding taxable year.

(3) CONTROLLED GROUPS.—A corporation who is a member of a controlled group meets the shipping activity requirement of this subsection only if such requirement is met determined—

(A) by treating all members of such group as 1 person, and

(B) by disregarding vessel charters between members of such group.

(4) REQUIREMENT.—The requirement of this paragraph is met for any taxable year if, on average during such year, at least 25 percent of the aggregate tonnage of qualifying vessels used by the corporation were owned by such corporation or chartered to such corporation on bareboat charter terms.

(d) ACTIVITIES CARRIED ON [BY] PARTNERSHIPS, ETC.—In applying this subchapter to a partner in a partnership—

(1) each partner shall be treated as operating vessels operated by the partnership,

(2) each partner shall be treated as conducting the activities conducted by the partnership, and

(3) the extent of a partner's ownership or charter interest in any vessel owned by or chartered to the partnership shall be determined on the basis of the partner's interest in the partnership.

A similar rule shall apply with respect to other pass-thru entities.

(e) EFFECT OF TEMPORARILY CEASING TO OPERATE A QUALIFYING VESSEL.—

(1) IN GENERAL.—For purposes of subsections (b) and (c), an electing corporation shall be treated as continuing to use a qualifying vessel during any period of temporary cessation if the electing corporation gives timely notice to the Secretary stating—

(A) that it has temporarily ceased to operate the qualifying vessel, and

(B) its intention to resume operating the qualifying vessel.

(2) NOTICE.—Notice shall be deemed timely if given not later than the due date (including extensions) for the corporation's tax return for the taxable year in which the temporary cessation begins.

(3) PERIOD DISREGARD IN EFFECT.—The period of temporary cessation under paragraph (1) shall continue until the earlier of the date on which—

(A) the electing corporation abandons its intention to resume operation of the qualifying vessel, or

(B) the electing corporation resumes operation of the qualifying vessel.

(f) EFFECT OF TEMPORARILY OPERATING A QUALIFYING VESSEL IN THE UNITED STATES DOMESTIC TRADE.—

(1) IN GENERAL.—For purposes of this subchapter, an electing corporation shall be treated as continuing to use a qualifying vessel in the United States foreign trade during any period of temporary use in the United States domestic trade if the electing corporation gives timely notice to the Secretary stating—

(A) that it temporarily operates or has operated in the United States domestic trade a qualifying vessel which had been used in the United States foreign trade, and

(B) its intention to resume operation of the vessel in the United States foreign trade.

(2) NOTICE.—Notice shall be deemed timely if given not later than the due date (including extensions) for the corporation's tax return for the taxable year in which the temporary cessation begins.

(3) PERIOD DISREGARD IN EFFECT.—The period of temporary use under paragraph (1) continues until the earlier of the date of which—

(A) the electing corporation abandons its intention to resume operations of the vessel in the United States foreign trade, or

(B) the electing corporation resumes operation of the vessel in the United States foreign trade.

(4) NO DISREGARD IF DOMESTIC TRADE USE EXCEEDS 30 DAYS.—Paragraph (1) shall not apply to any qualifying vessel which is operated in the United States domestic trade for more than 30 days during the taxable year.

(g) REGULATIONS.—The Secretary shall prescribe such regulations as may be necessary or appropriate to carry out the purposes of this section.

[CCH Explanation at ¶ 545. Committee Reports at ¶ 10,290.]
Amendments
• **2004, American Jobs Creation Act of 2004 (H.R. 4520)**

H.R. 4520, § 248(a):

Amended chapter 1 by inserting after subchapter Q a new subchapter R (Code Secs. 1352-1359). **Effective** for tax years beginning after the date of the enactment of this Act.

[¶ 5870] *CODE SEC. 1356. QUALIFYING SHIPPING ACTIVITIES.*

(a) QUALIFYING SHIPPING ACTIVITIES.—For purposes of this subchapter, the term "qualifying shipping activities" means—

(1) core qualifying activities,

(2) qualifying secondary activities, and

(3) qualifying incidental activities.

(b) CORE QUALIFYING ACTIVITIES.—For purposes of this subchapter, the term "core qualifying activities" means activities in operating qualifying vessels in United States foreign trade.

(c) QUALIFYING SECONDARY ACTIVITIES.—For purposes of this section—

(1) IN GENERAL.—The term "qualifying secondary activities" means secondary activities but only to the extent that, without regard to this subchapter, the gross income derived by such corporation from such activities does not exceed 20 percent of the gross income derived by the corporation from its core qualifying activities.

(2) SECONDARY ACTIVITIES.—The term "secondary activities" means—

(A) the active management or operation of vessels other than qualifying vessels in the United States foreign trade,

(B) the provision of vessel, barge, container, or cargo-related facilities or services to any person,

(C) other activities of the electing corporation and other members of its electing group that are an integral part of its business of operating qualifying vessels in United States foreign trade, including—

(i) ownership or operation of barges, containers, chassis, and other equipment that are the complement of, or used in connection with, a qualifying vessel in United States foreign trade,

(ii) the inland haulage of cargo shipped, or to be shipped, on qualifying vessels in United States foreign trade, and

(iii) the provision of terminal, maintenance, repair, logistical, or other vessel, barge, container, or cargo-related services that are an integral part of operating qualifying vessels in United States foreign trade, and

(D) such other activities as may be prescribed by the Secretary pursuant to regulations.

(3) COORDINATION WITH CORE ACTIVITIES.—

(A) IN GENERAL.—Such term shall not include any core qualifying activities.

(B) NONELECTING CORPORATIONS.—In the case of a corporation (other than an electing corporation) which is a member of an electing group, any core qualifying activities of the corporation shall be treated as qualifying secondary activities (and not as core qualifying activities).

(d) QUALIFYING INCIDENTAL ACTIVITIES.—For purposes of this section, the term "qualified incidental activities" means shipping-related activities if—

(1) they are incidental to the corporation's core qualifying activities,

(2) they are not qualifying secondary activities, and

(3) without regard to this subchapter, the gross income derived by such corporation from such activities does not exceed 0.1 percent of the corporation's gross income from its core qualifying activities.

(e) APPLICATION OF GROSS INCOME TESTS IN CASE OF ELECTING GROUP.—In the case of an electing group, subsections (c)(1) and (d)(3) shall be applied as if such group were 1 entity, and the limitations under such subsections shall be allocated among the corporations in such group.

[CCH Explanation at ¶ 545. Committee Reports at ¶ 10,290.]

Amendments

• 2004, American Jobs Creation Act of 2004 (H.R. 4520)

H.R. 4520, § 248(a):

Amended chapter 1 by inserting after subchapter Q a new subchapter R (Code Secs. 1352-1359). **Effective** for tax years beginning after the date of the enactment of this Act.

[¶ 5875] CODE SEC. 1357. ITEMS NOT SUBJECT TO REGULAR TAX; DEPRECIATION; INTEREST.

(a) EXCLUSION FROM GROSS INCOME.—Gross income of an electing corporation shall not include its income from qualifying shipping activities.

(b) ELECTING GROUP MEMBER.—Gross income of a corporation (other than an electing corporation) which is a member of an electing group shall not include its income from qualifying shipping activities conducted by such member.

(c) DENIAL OF LOSSES, DEDUCTIONS, AND CREDITS.—

(1) GENERAL RULE.—Subject to paragraph (2), each item of loss, deduction (other than for interest expense), or credit of any taxpayer with respect to any activity the income from which is excluded from gross income under this section shall be disallowed.

(2) DEPRECIATION.—

(A) IN GENERAL.—Notwithstanding paragraph (1), the adjusted basis (for purposes of determining gain) of any qualifying vessel shall be determined as if the deduction for depreciation had been allowed.

(B) METHOD.—

(i) IN GENERAL.—Except as provided in clause (ii), the straight-line method of depreciation shall apply to qualifying vessels the income from operation of which is excluded from gross income under this section.

(ii) EXCEPTION.—Clause (i) shall not apply to any qualifying vessel which is subject to a charter entered into before the date of the enactment of this subchapter.

(3) INTEREST.—

(A) IN GENERAL.—Except as provided in subparagraph (B), the interest expense of an electing corporation shall be disallowed in the ratio that the fair market value of such corporation's qualifying vessels bears to the fair market value of such corporation's total assets.

(B) ELECTING GROUP.—In the case of a corporation which is a member of an electing group, the interest expense of such corporation shall be disallowed in the ratio that the fair market value of such corporation's qualifying vessels bears to the fair market value of the electing groups total assets.

[CCH Explanation at ¶ 545. Committee Reports at ¶ 10,290.]
Amendments
• **2004, American Jobs Creation Act of 2004 (H.R. 4520)**

H.R. 4520, § 248(a):

Amended chapter 1 by inserting after subchapter Q a new subchapter R (Code Secs. 1352-1359). **Effective** for tax years beginning after the date of the enactment of this Act.

[¶ 5880] *CODE SEC. 1358. ALLOCATION OF CREDITS, INCOME, AND DEDUCTIONS.*

(a) QUALIFYING SHIPPING ACTIVITIES.—For purposes of this chapter, the qualifying shipping activities of an electing corporation shall be treated as a separate trade or business activity distinct from all other activities conducted by such corporation.

(b) EXCLUSION OF CREDITS OR DEDUCTIONS.—

(1) No deduction shall be allowed against the notional shipping income of an electing corporation, and no credit shall be allowed against the tax imposed by section 1352(a)(2).

(2) No deduction shall be allowed for any net operating loss attributable to the qualifying shipping activities of any person to the extent that such loss is carried forward by such person from a taxable year preceding the first taxable year for which such person was an electing corporation.

(c) TRANSACTIONS NOT AT ARM'S LENGTH.—Section 482 applies in accordance with this subsection to a transaction or series of transactions—

(1) as between an electing corporation and another person, or

(2) as between an person's qualifying shipping activities and other activities carried on by it.

[CCH Explanation at ¶ 545. Committee Reports at ¶ 10,290.]
Amendments
• **2004, American Jobs Creation Act of 2004 (H.R. 4520)**

H.R. 4520, § 248(a):

Amended chapter 1 by inserting after subchapter Q a new subchapter R (Code Secs. 1352-1359). **Effective** for tax years beginning after the date of the enactment of this Act.

[¶ 5885] *CODE SEC. 1359. DISPOSITION OF QUALIFYING VESSELS.*

(a) IN GENERAL.—If any qualifying vessel operator sells or disposes of any qualifying vessel in an otherwise taxable transaction, at the election of such operator, no gain shall be recognized if any replacement qualifying vessel is acquired during the period specified in subsection (b), except to the extent that the amount realized upon such sale or disposition exceeds the cost of the replacement qualifying vessel.

(b) PERIOD WITHIN WHICH PROPERTY MUST BE REPLACED.—The period referred to in subsection (a) shall be the period beginning one year prior to the disposition of the qualifying vessel and ending—

(1) 3 years after the close of the first taxable year in which the gain is realized, or

(2) subject to such terms and conditions as may be specified by the Secretary, on such later date as the Secretary may designate on application by the taxpayer.

Such application shall be made at such time and in such manner as the Secretary may by regulations prescribe.

(c) APPLICATION OF SECTION TO NONCORPORATE OPERATORS.—For purposes of this section, the term "qualifying vessel operator" includes any person who would be a qualifying vessel operator were such person a corporation.

(d) TIME FOR ASSESSMENT OF DEFICIENCY ATTRIBUTABLE TO GAIN.—If a qualifying vessel operator has made the election provided in subsection (a), then—

(1) the statutory period for the assessment of any deficiency, for any taxable year in which any part of the gain is realized, attributable to such gain shall not expire prior to the expiration of 3 years from the date the Secretary is notified by such operator (in such manner as the Secretary may by regulations prescribe) of the replacement qualifying vessel or of an intention not to replace, and

(2) such deficiency may be assessed before the expiration of such 3-year period notwithstanding the provisions of section 6212(c) or the provisions of any other law or rule of law which would otherwise prevent such assessment.

(e) BASIS OF REPLACEMENT QUALIFYING VESSEL.—In the case of any replacement qualifying vessel purchased by the qualifying vessel operator which resulted in the nonrecognition of any part of the gain realized as the result of a sale or other disposition of a qualifying vessel, the basis shall be the cost of the replacement qualifying vessel decreased in the amount of the gain not so recognized; and if the property purchased consists of more than one piece of property, the basis determined under this sentence shall be allocated to the purchased properties in proportion to their respective costs.

[CCH Explanation at ¶ 545. Committee Reports at ¶ 10,290.]

Amendments

• 2004, American Jobs Creation Act of 2004 (H.R. 4520)

H.R. 4520, § 248(a):

Amended chapter 1 by inserting after subchapter Q a new subchapter R (Code Secs. 1352-1359). **Effective** for tax years beginning after the date of the enactment of this Act.

[¶ 5890] CODE SEC. 1361. S CORPORATION DEFINED.

* * *

(b) SMALL BUSINESS CORPORATION.—

(1) IN GENERAL.—For purposes of this subchapter, the term "small business corporation" means a domestic corporation which is not an ineligible corporation and which does not—

(A) have more than *100* shareholders,

* * *

(3) TREATMENT OF CERTAIN WHOLLY OWNED SUBSIDIARIES.—

(A) IN GENERAL.—Except as provided in regulations prescribed by the Secretary *and in the case of information returns required under part III of subchapter A of chapter 61*, for purposes of this title—

(i) a corporation which is a qualified subchapter S subsidiary shall not be treated as a separate corporation, and

(ii) all assets, liabilities, and items of income, deduction, and credit of a qualified subchapter S subsidiary shall be treated as assets, liabilities, and such items (as the case may be) of the S corporation.

* * *

[CCH Explanation at ¶905 and ¶950. Committee Reports at ¶10,130 and ¶10,200.]

Amendments

• **2004, American Jobs Creation Act of 2004 (H.R. 4520)**

H.R. 4520, §232(a):

Amended Code Sec. 1361(b)(1)(A) by striking "75" and inserting "100". **Effective** for tax years beginning after 12-31-2004.

H.R. 4520, §239(a):

Amended Code Sec. 1361(b)(3)(A) by inserting "and in the case of information returns required under part III of subchapter A of chapter 61" after "Secretary". **Effective** for tax years beginning after 12-31-2004.

(c) SPECIAL RULES FOR APPLYING SUBSECTION (b).—

(1) MEMBERS OF FAMILY TREATED AS 1 SHAREHOLDER.—

(A) IN GENERAL.—*For purpose of subsection (b)(1)(A)—*

(i) except as provided in clause (ii), a husband and wife (and their estates) shall be treated as 1 shareholder, and

(ii) in the case of a family with respect to which an election is in effect under subparagraph (D), all members of the family shall be treated as 1 shareholder.

(B) MEMBERS OF THE FAMILY.—*For purpose of subparagraph (A)(ii)—*

(i) IN GENERAL.—*The term "members of the family" means the common ancestor, lineal descendants of the common ancestor, and the spouses (or former spouses) of such lineal descendants or common ancestor.*

(ii) COMMON ANCESTOR.—*For purposes of this paragraph, an individual shall not be considered a common ancestor if, as of the later of the effective date of this paragraph or the time the election under section 1362(a) is made, the individual is more than 6 generations removed from the youngest generation of shareholders who would (but for this clause) be members of the family. For purposes of the preceding sentence, a spouse (or former spouse) shall be treated as being of the same generation as the individual to which such spouse is (or was) married.*

(C) EFFECT OF ADOPTION, ETC.—*In determining whether any relationship specified in subparagraph (B) exists, the rules of section 152(b)(2) shall apply.*

(D) ELECTION.—*An election under subparagraph (A)(ii)—*

(i) may, except as otherwise provided in regulations prescribed by the Secretary, be made by any member of the family, and

(ii) shall remain in effect until terminated as provided in regulations prescribed by the Secretary.

(2) CERTAIN TRUSTS PERMITTED AS SHAREHOLDERS.—

(A) IN GENERAL.—For purposes of subsection (b)(1)(B), the following trusts may be shareholders:

* * *

(vi) In the case of a corporation which is a bank (as defined in section 581), a trust which constitutes an individual retirement account under section 408(a), including one designated as a Roth IRA under section 408A, but only to the extent of the stock held by such trust in such bank as of the date of the enactment of this clause.

This subparagraph shall not apply to any foreign trust.

(B) TREATMENT AS SHAREHOLDERS.—For purposes of subsection (b)(1)—

* * *

(vi) In the case of a trust described in clause (vi) of subparagraph (A), the individual for whose benefit the trust was created shall be treated as a shareholder.

* * *

[CCH Explanation at ¶910 and ¶940. Committee Reports at ¶10,120 and ¶10,140.]

Amendments

• **2004, American Jobs Creation Act of 2004 (H.R. 4520)**

H.R. 4520, §231(a):

Amended Code Sec. 1361(c)(1). **Effective** for tax years beginning after 12-31-2004. Prior to amendment, Code Sec. 1361(c)(1) read as follows:

(1) HUSBAND AND WIFE TREATED AS 1 SHAREHOLDER.—For purposes of subsection (b)(1)(A), a husband and wife (and their estates) shall be treated as 1 shareholder.

H.R. 4520, §233(a):

Amended Code Sec. 1361(c)(2)(A) by inserting after clause (v) a new clause (vi). **Effective** on the date of the enactment of this Act.

H.R. 4520, §233(b):

Amended Code Sec. 1361(c)(2)(B) by adding at the end a new clause (vi). **Effective** on the date of the enactment of this Act.

(d) SPECIAL RULE FOR QUALIFIED SUBCHAPTER S TRUST.—

(1) IN GENERAL.—In the case of a qualified subchapter S trust with respect to which a beneficiary makes an election under paragraph (2)—

(A) such trust shall be treated as a trust described in subsection (c)(2)(A)(i),

(B) for purposes of section 678(a), the beneficiary of such trust shall be treated as the owner of that portion of the trust which consists of stock in an S corporation with respect to which the election under paragraph (2) is made, *and*

(C) *for purposes of applying sections 465 and 469 to the beneficiary of the trust, the disposition of the S corporation stock by the trust shall be treated as a disposition by such beneficiary.*

* * *

[CCH Explanation at ¶925. Committee Reports at ¶10,170.]

Amendments

• **2004, American Jobs Creation Act of 2004 (H.R. 4520)**

H.R. 4520, §236(a)(1)-(3):

Amended Code Sec. 1361(d)(1) by striking "and" at the end of subparagraph (A), by striking the period at the end

of subparagraph (B) and inserting ", and", and by adding at the end a new subparagraph (C). **Effective** for transfers made after 12-31-2004.

(e) ELECTING SMALL BUSINESS TRUST DEFINED.—

* * *

(2) POTENTIAL CURRENT BENEFICIARY.—For purposes of this section, the term "potential current beneficiary" means, with respect to any period, any person who at any time during such period is entitled to, or at the discretion of any person may receive, a distribution from the principal or income of the trust *(determined without regard to any power of appointment to the extent such power remains unexercised at the end of such period)*. If a trust disposes of all of the stock which it holds in an S corporation, then, with respect to such corporation, the term "potential current beneficiary" does not include any person who first met the requirements of the preceding sentence during the *1-year* period ending on the date of such disposition.

* * *

[CCH Explanation at ¶930. Committee Reports at ¶10,150.]

Amendments

• **2004, American Jobs Creation Act of 2004 (H.R. 4520)**

H.R. 4520, §234(a)(1)-(2):

Amended Code Sec. 1361(e)(2) by inserting "(determined without regard to any power of appointment to the extent

such power remains unexercised at the end of such period)" after "of the trust" in the first sentence, and by striking "60-day" and inserting "1-year" in the second sentence. **Effective** for tax years beginning after 12-31-2004.

[¶5895] CODE SEC. 1362. ELECTION; REVOCATION; TERMINATION.

* * *

(d) TERMINATION.—

* * *

(3) WHERE PASSIVE INVESTMENT INCOME EXCEEDS 25 PERCENT OF GROSS RECEIPTS FOR 3 CONSECUTIVE TAXABLE YEARS AND CORPORATION HAS ACCUMULATED EARNINGS AND PROFITS.—

* * *

(F) EXCEPTION FOR BANKS; ETC.—In the case of a bank (as defined in section 581), a bank holding company (within the meaning of section 2(a) of the Bank Holding Company Act of 1956 (12 U.S.C. 1841(a))), or a financial holding company (within the meaning of section 2(p) of such Act), the term "passive investment income" shall not include—

(i) interest income earned by such bank or company, or

(ii) dividends on assets required to be held by such bank or company, including stock in the Federal Reserve Bank, the Federal Home Loan Bank, or the Federal Agricultural Mortgage Bank or participation certificates issued by a Federal Intermediate Credit Bank.

* * *

[CCH Explanation at ¶945. Committee Reports at ¶10,180.]
Amendments
• **2004, American Jobs Creation Act of 2004 (H.R. 4520)**

H.R. 4520, §237(a):

Amended Code Sec. 1362(d)(3) by adding at the end a new subparagraph (F). **Effective** for tax years beginning after 12-31-2004.

(f) INADVERTENT INVALID ELECTIONS OR TERMINATIONS.—If—

(1) an election under subsection (a), *section 1361(b)(3)(B)(ii), or section 1361(c)(1)(A)(ii)* by any corporation—

(A) was not effective for the taxable year for which made (determined without regard to subsection (b)(2)) by reason of a failure to meet the requirements of section 1361(b) or to obtain shareholder consents, or

(B) was terminated under paragraph (2) or (3) of subsection (d), *section 1361(b)(3)(C), or section 1361(c)(1)(D)(iii),*

(2) the Secretary determines that the circumstances resulting in such ineffectiveness or termination were inadvertent,

(3) no later than a reasonable period of time after discovery of the circumstances resulting in such ineffectiveness or termination, steps were taken—

(A) so that the corporation for which the election was made or the termination occurred is a small business corporation or a qualified subchapter S subsidiary, as the case may be, or

(B) to acquire the required shareholder consents, and

(4) the corporation for which the election was made or the termination occurred, and each person who was a shareholder in such corporation at any time during the period specified pursuant to this subsection, agrees to make such adjustments (consistent with the treatment of such corporation as an S corporation or a qualified subchapter S subsidiary, as the case may be) as may be required by the Secretary with respect to such period,

then, notwithstanding the circumstances resulting in such ineffectiveness or termination, such corporation shall be treated as an S corporation *or a qualified subchapter S subsidiary, as the case may be* during the period specified by the Secretary.

* * *

[CCH Explanation at ¶910 and ¶920. Committee Reports at ¶10,120 and ¶10,190.]
Amendments
• **2004, American Jobs Creation Act of 2004 (H.R. 4520)**

H.R. 4520, §231(b)(1):

Amended Code Sec. 1362(f)(1), as amended by this Act, by inserting "or section 1361(c)(1)(A)(ii)" after "section 1361(b)(3)(B)(ii),". **Effective** for elections and terminations made after 12-31-2004.

H.R. 4520, §231(b)(2):

Amended Code Sec. 1362(f)(1)(B), as amended by this Act, by inserting "or section 1361(c)(1)(D)(iii)" after "section 1361(b)(3)(C),". **Effective** for elections and terminations made after 12-31-2004.

H.R. 4520, §238(a)(1):

Amended Code Sec. 1362(f)(1) by inserting ", section 1361(b)(3)(B)(ii)," after "subsection (a)". **Effective** for elections made and terminations made after 12-31-2004.

H.R. 4520, §238(a)(2):

Amended Code Sec. 1362(f)(1)(B) by inserting ", section 1361(b)(3)(C)," after "subsection (d)". **Effective** for elections made and terminations made after 12-31-2004.

H.R. 4520, §238(a)(3):

Amended Code Sec. 1362(f)(3)(A). **Effective** for elections made and terminations made after 12-31-2004. Prior to amendment, Code Sec. 1362(f)(3)(A) read as follows:

(A) so that the corporation is a small business corporation, or

H.R. 4520, §238(a)(4):

Amended Code Sec. 1362(f)(4). **Effective** for elections made and terminations made after 12-31-2004. Prior to amendment, Code Sec. 1362(f)(4) read as follows:

(4) the corporation, and each person who was a shareholder in the corporation at any time during the period specified pursuant to this subsection, agrees to make such adjustments (consistent with the treatment of the corporation as an S corporation) as may be required by the Secretary with respect to such period,

H.R. 4520, §238(a)(5):

Amended Code Sec. 1362(f) by inserting "or a qualified subchapter S subsidiary, as the case may be" after "S corporation" in the matter following paragraph (4). **Effective** for elections made and terminations made after 12-31-2004.

[¶5900] CODE SEC. 1366. PASS-THRU OF ITEMS TO SHAREHOLDERS.

* * *

(d) SPECIAL RULES FOR LOSSES AND DEDUCTIONS.—

* * *

(2) INDEFINITE CARRYOVER OF DISALLOWED LOSSES AND DEDUCTIONS.—

(A) IN GENERAL.—*Except as provided in subparagraph (B), any loss or deduction which is disallowed for any taxable year by reason of paragraph (1) shall be treated as incurred by the corporation in the succeeding taxable year with respect to that shareholder.*

(B) TRANSFERS OF STOCK BETWEEN SPOUSES OR INCIDENT TO DIVORCE.—*In the case of any transfer described in section 1041(a) of stock of an S corporation, any loss or deduction described in subparagraph (A) with respect [to] such stock shall be treated as incurred by the corporation in the succeeding taxable year with respect to the transferee.*

* * *

[CCH Explanation at ¶915. Committee Reports at ¶10,160.]

Amendments

• **2004, American Jobs Creation Act of 2004 (H.R. 4520)**

H.R. 4520, §235(a):

Amended Code Sec. 1366(d)(2). **Effective** for tax years beginning after 12-31-2004. Prior to amendment, Code Sec. 1366(d)(2) read as follows:

(2) INDEFINITE CARRYOVER OF DISALLOWED LOSSES AND DEDUCTIONS.—Any loss or deduction which is disallowed for any taxable year by reason of paragraph (1) shall be treated as incurred by the corporation in the succeeding taxable year with respect to that shareholder.

[¶5905] CODE SEC. 1381. ORGANIZATIONS TO WHICH PART APPLIES.

* * *

(c) CROSS REFERENCE.—

For treatment of income from load loss transactions of organizations described in subsection (a)(2)(C), see section 501(c)(12)(H).

[CCH Explanation at ¶1335. Committee Reports at ¶10,420.]

Amendments

• **2004, American Jobs Creation Act of 2004 (H.R. 4520)**

H.R. 4520, §319(d):

Amended Code Sec. 1381 by adding at the end a new subsection (c). **Effective** for tax years beginning after the date of the enactment of this Act.

[¶5910] CODE SEC. 1388. DEFINITIONS; SPECIAL RULES.

(a) PATRONAGE DIVIDEND.—For purposes of this subchapter, the term "patronage dividend" means an amount paid to a patron by an organization to which part I of this subchapter applies—

(1) on the basis of quantity or value of business done with or for such patron,

(2) under an obligation of such organization to pay such amount, which obligation existed before the organization received the amount so paid, and

(3) which is determined by reference to the net earnings of the organization from business done with or for its patrons.

Such term does not include any amount paid to a patron to the extent that (A) such amount is out of earnings other than from business done with or for patrons, or (B) such amount is out of earnings from business done with or for other patrons to whom no amounts are paid, or to whom smaller amounts are paid, with respect to substantially identical transactions. *For purposes of paragraph (3), net earnings shall not be reduced by amounts paid during the year as dividends on capital stock or other proprietary capital interests of the organization to the extent that the articles of incorporation or bylaws of such organization or other contract with patrons provide that such dividends are in addition to amounts otherwise payable to patrons which are derived from business done with or for patrons during the taxable year.*

* * *

[CCH Explanation at ¶ 1340. Committee Reports at ¶ 10,350.]

Amendments

• **2004, American Jobs Creation Act of 2004 (H.R. 4520)**

H.R. 4520, § 312(a):

Amended Code Sec. 1388(a) by adding at the end a new sentence. **Effective** for distributions in tax years beginning after the date of the enactment of this Act.

(k) Cooperative Marketing Includes Value Added Processing Involving Animals.—For purposes of section 521 and this subchapter, the marketing of the products of members or other producers shall include the feeding of such products to cattle, hogs, fish, chickens, or other animals and the sale of the resulting animals or animal products.

[CCH Explanation at ¶ 830. Committee Reports at ¶ 10,390.]

Amendments

• **2004, American Jobs Creation Act of 2004 (H.R. 4520)**

H.R. 4520, § 316(a):

Amended Code Sec. 1388 by adding at the end a new subsection (k). **Effective** for tax years beginning after the date of the enactment of this Act.

[¶ 5915] CODE SEC. 1400E. DESIGNATION OF RENEWAL COMMUNITIES.

* * *

(g) Expansion of Designated Area Based on 2000 Census.—

(1) In general.—At the request of all governments which nominated an area as a renewal community, the Secretary of Housing and Urban Development may expand the area of such community to include any census tract if—

(A)(i) at the time such community was nominated, such community would have met the requirements of this section using 1990 census data even if such tract had been included in such community, and

(ii) such tract has a poverty rate using 2000 census data which exceeds the poverty rate for such tract using 1990 census data, or

(B)(i) such community would be described in subparagraph (A)(i) but for the failure to meet one or more of the requirements of paragraphs (2)(C)(i), (3)(C), and (3)(D) of subsection (c) using 1990 census data,

(ii) such community, including such tract, has a population of not more than 200,000 using either 1990 census data or 2000 census data,

(iii) such tract meets the requirement of subsection (c)(3)(C) using 2000 census data, and

(iv) such tract meets the requirement of subparagraph (A)(ii).

(2) EXCEPTION FOR CERTAIN CENSUS TRACTS WITH LOW POPULATION IN 1990.—*In the case of any census tract which did not have a poverty rate determined by the Bureau of the Census using 1990 census data, paragraph (1)(B) shall be applied without regard to clause (iv) thereof.*

(3) SPECIAL RULE FOR CERTAIN CENSUS TRACTS WITH LOW POPULATION IN 2000.—*At the request of all governments which nominated an area as a renewal community, the Secretary of Housing and Urban Development may expand the area of such community to include any census tract if—*

(A) *either—*

(i) *such tract has no population using 2000 census data, or*

(ii) *no poverty rate for such tract is determined by the Bureau of the Census using 2000 census data,*

(B) *such tract is one of general distress, and*

(C) *such community, including such tract, meets the requirements of subparagraphs (A) and (B) of subsection (c)(2).*

(4) PERIOD IN EFFECT.—*Any expansion under this subsection shall take effect as provided in subsection (b).*

* * *

[CCH Explanation at ¶ 385. Committee Reports at ¶ 10,100.]

Amendments

• **2004, American Jobs Creation Act of 2004 (H.R. 4520)**

H.R. 4520, § 222(a):

Amended Code Sec. 1400E by adding at the end a new subsection (g). **Effective** as if included in the amendments made by section 101 of the Community Renewal Tax Relief Act of 2000 [**effective** 12-21-2000.—CCH].

[¶ 5920] CODE SEC. 1402. DEFINITIONS.

(a) NET EARNINGS FROM SELF-EMPLOYMENT.—The term "net earnings from self-employment" means the gross income derived by an individual from any trade or business carried on by such individual, less the deductions allowed by this subtitle which are attributable to such trade or business, plus his distributive share (whether or not distributed) of income or loss described in section 702(a)(8) from any trade or business carried on by a partnership of which he is a member; except that in computing such gross income and deductions and such distributive share of partnership ordinary income or loss—

* * *

(14) in the case of church employee income, the special rules of subsection (j)(1) shall apply;

(15) in the case of a member of an Indian tribe, the special rules of section 7873 (relating to income derived by Indians from exercise of fishing rights) shall apply, *and*

(16) *the deduction provided by section 199 shall not be allowed.*

* * *

[CCH Explanation at ¶ 210.]

Amendments

• **2004, American Jobs Creation Act of 2004 (H.R. 4520)**

H.R. 4520, § 102(d)(7):

Amended Code Sec. 1402(a) by striking "and" at the end of paragraph (14), by striking the period at the end of paragraph (15) and inserting ", and", and by inserting after paragraph (15) a new paragraph (16). **Effective** for tax years beginning after 12-31-2004.

[¶ 5925] CODE SEC. 1441. WITHHOLDING OF TAX ON NONRESIDENT ALIENS.

* * *

(c) EXCEPTIONS.—

* * *

(12) CERTAIN DIVIDENDS RECEIVED FROM REGULATED INVESTMENT COMPANIES.—

(A) IN GENERAL.—No tax shall be required to be deducted and withheld under subsection (a) from any amount exempt from the tax imposed by section 871(a)(1)(A) by reason of section 871(k).

(B) SPECIAL RULE.—For purposes of subparagraph (A), clause (i) of section 871(k)(1)(B) shall not apply to any dividend unless the regulated investment company knows that such dividend is a dividend referred to in such clause. A similar rule shall apply with respect to the exception contained in section 871(k)(2)(B).

* * *

[CCH Explanation at ¶560. Committee Reports at ¶10,670.]

Amendments

• **2004, American Jobs Creation Act of 2004 (H.R. 4520)**

H.R. 4520, §411(a)(3)(A):

Amended Code Sec. 1441(c) by adding at the end a new paragraph (12). **Effective** for dividends with respect to tax years of regulated investment companies beginning after 12-31-2004.

[¶5930] CODE SEC. 1442. WITHHOLDING OF TAX ON FOREIGN CORPORATIONS.

(a) GENERAL RULE.—In the case of foreign corporations subject to taxation under this subtitle, there shall be deducted and withheld at the source in the same manner and on the same items of income as is provided in section 1441 a tax equal to 30 percent thereof. For purposes of the preceding sentence, the references in section 1441(b) to sections 871(a)(1)(C) and (D) shall be treated as referring to sections 881(a)(3) and (4), the reference in section 1441(c)(1) to section 871(b)(2) shall be treated as referring to section 842 or section 882(a)(2), as the case may be, the reference in section 1441(c)(5) to section 871(a)(1)(D) shall be treated as referring to section 881(a)(4), the reference in section 1441(c)(8) to section 871(a)(1)(C) shall be treated as referring to section 881(a)(3), the references in section 1441(c)(9) to sections 871(h) and 871(h)(3) or (4) shall be treated as referring to sections 881(c) and 881(c)(3) or (4), *the reference in section 1441(c)(10)* to section 871(i)(2) shall be treated as referring to section 881(d), *and the references in section 1441(c)(12) to sections 871(a) and 871(k) shall be treated as referring to sections 881(a) and 881(e) (except that for purposes of applying subparagraph (A) of section 1441(c)(12), as so modified, clause (ii) of section 881(e)(1)(B) shall not apply to any dividend unless the regulated investment company knows that such dividend is a dividend referred to in such clause).*

* * *

[CCH Explanation at ¶560. Committee Reports at ¶10,670.]

Amendments

• **2004, American Jobs Creation Act of 2004 (H.R. 4520)**

H.R. 4520, §411(a)(3)(B)(i)-(ii):

Amended Code Sec. 1442(a) by striking "and the reference[s] in section 1441(c)(10)" and inserting "the reference in section 1441(c)(10)", and by inserting before the period at the end the following: ", and the references in section 1441(c)(12) to sections 871(a) and 871(k) shall be treated as referring to sections 881(a) and 881(e) (except that for purposes of applying subparagraph (A) of section 1441(c)(12), as so modified, clause (ii) of section 881(e)(1)(B) shall not apply to any dividend unless the regulated investment company knows that such dividend is a dividend referred to in such clause)". **Effective** for dividends with respect to tax years of regulated investment companies beginning after 12-31-2004.

(c) EXCEPTION FOR CERTAIN POSSESSIONS CORPORATIONS.—

(1) GUAM, AMERICAN SAMOA, THE NORTHERN MARIANA ISLANDS, AND THE VIRGIN ISLANDS.—For purposes of this section, the term "foreign corporation" does not include a corporation created or organized in Guam, American Samoa, the Northern Mariana Islands, or the Virgin Islands or under the law of any such possession if the requirements of subparagraphs (A), (B), and (C) of section 881(b)(1) are met with respect to such corporation.

(2) COMMONWEALTH OF PUERTO RICO.—

(A) IN GENERAL.—If dividends are received during a taxable year by a corporation—

(i) created or organized in, or under the law of, the Commonwealth of Puerto Rico, and

(ii) with respect to which the requirements of subparagraphs (A), (B), and (C) of section 881(b)(1) are met for the taxable year,

subsection (a) shall be applied for such taxable year by substituting "10 percent" for "30 percent".

(B) APPLICABILITY.—If, on or after the date of the enactment of this paragraph, an increase in the rate of the Commonwealth of Puerto Rico's withholding tax which is generally applicable to dividends paid to United States corporations not engaged in a trade or business in the Commonwealth to a rate greater than 10 percent takes effect, this paragraph shall not apply to dividends received on or after the effective date of the increase.

[CCH Explanation at ¶585. Committee Reports at ¶10,760.]

Amendments

• **2004, American Jobs Creation Act of 2004 (H.R. 4520)**

H.R. 4520, §420(b)(1)-(2):

Amended Code Sec. 1442(c) by striking "For purposes" and inserting "(1) GUAM, AMERICAN SAMOA, THE NORTHERN MARIANA ISLANDS, AND THE VIRGIN ISLANDS.—For purposes", and by adding at the end a new paragraph (2). **Effective** for dividends paid after the date of the enactment of this Act.

[¶5935] CODE SEC. 1502. REGULATIONS.

The Secretary shall prescribe such regulations as he may deem necessary in order that the tax liability of any affiliated group of corporations making a consolidated return and of each corporation in the group, both during and after the period of affiliation, may be returned, determined, computed, assessed, collected, and adjusted, in such manner as clearly to reflect the income tax liability and the various factors necessary for the determination of such liability, and in order to prevent avoidance of such tax liability. *In carrying out the preceding sentence, the Secretary may prescribe rules that are different from the provisions of chapter 1 that would apply if such corporations filed separate returns.*

[CCH Explanation at ¶1635. Committee Reports at ¶11,270.]

Amendments

• **2004, American Jobs Creation Act of 2004 (H.R. 4520)**

H.R. 4520, §844(a):

Amended Code Sec. 1502 by adding at the end a new sentence. **Effective** for tax years beginning before, on, or after the date of the enactment of this Act. For a special rule, see Act Sec. 844(b), below.

H.R. 4520, §844(b), provides:

(b) RESULT NOT OVERTURNED.—Notwithstanding the amendment made by subsection (a), the Internal Revenue Code of 1986 shall be construed by treating Treasury Regulation §1.1502-20(c)(1)(iii) (as in effect on January 1, 2001) as being inapplicable to the factual situation in Rite Aid Corporation and Subsidiary Corporations v. United States, 255 F.3d 1357 (Fed. Cir. 2001).

[¶5940] CODE SEC. 1563. DEFINITIONS AND SPECIAL RULES.

(a) CONTROLLED GROUP OF CORPORATIONS.—For purposes of this part, the term "controlled group of corporations" means any group of—

* * *

(2) BROTHER-SISTER CONTROLLED GROUP.—Two or more corporations if 5 or fewer persons who are individuals, estates, or trusts own (within the meaning of subsection (d)(2)) stock *possessing* more than 50 percent of the total combined voting power of all classes of stock entitled to vote or more than 50 percent of the total value of shares of all classes of stock of each corporation, taking into account the stock ownership of each such person only to the extent such stock ownership is identical with respect to each such corporation.

* * *

[CCH Explanation at ¶1025. Committee Reports at ¶11,720.]

Amendments

• **2004, American Jobs Creation Act of 2004 (H.R. 4520)**

H.R. 4520, §900(a):

Amended Code Sec. 1563(a)(2) by striking "possessing—" and all that follows through "(B)" and inserting "possessing". **Effective** for tax years beginning after the date of the enactment of this Act. Prior to amendment, Code Sec. 1563(a)(2) read as follows:

(2) BROTHER-SISTER CONTROLLED GROUP.—Two or more corporations if 5 or fewer persons who are individuals, estates, or trusts own (within the meaning of subsection (d)(2)) stock possessing—

(A) at least 80 percent of the total combined voting power of all classes of stock entitled to vote or at least 80 percent of the total value of shares of all classes of the stock of each corporation, and

(B) more than 50 percent of the total combined voting power of all classes of stock entitled to vote or more than 50 percent of the total value of shares of all classes of stock of each corporation, taking into account the stock ownership of each such person only to the extent such stock ownership is identical with respect to each such corporation.

(f) OTHER DEFINITIONS AND RULES.—

* * *

(5) BROTHER-SISTER CONTROLLED GROUP DEFINITION FOR PROVISIONS OTHER THAN THIS PART.—

(A) IN GENERAL.—*Except as specifically provided in an applicable provision, subsection (a)(2) shall be applied to an applicable provision as if it read as follows:*

(2) "BROTHER-SISTER CONTROLLED GROUP.—*Two or more corporations if 5 or fewer persons who are individuals, estates, or trusts own (within the meaning of subsection (d)(2) stock possessing—*

(A) "*at least 80 percent of the total combined voting power of all classes of stock entitled to vote, or at least 80 percent of the total value of shares of all classes of stock, of each corporation, and*

(B) "*more than 50 percent of the total combined voting power of all classes of stock entitled to vote or more than 50 percent of the total value of shares of all classes of stock of each corporation, taking into account the stock ownership of each such person only to the extent such stock ownership is identical with respect to each such corporation.*"

(B) APPLICABLE PROVISION.—*For purposes of this paragraph, an applicable provision is any provision of law (other than this part) which incorporates the definition of controlled group of corporations under subsection (a).*

[CCH Explanation at ¶1025. Committee Reports at ¶11,720.]

Amendments

• **2004, American Jobs Creation Act of 2004 (H.R. 4520)**

H.R. 4520, §900(b):

Amended Code Sec. 1563(f) by adding at the end a new paragraph (5). **Effective** for tax years beginning after the date of the enactment of this Act.

[¶5945] CODE SEC. 2105. PROPERTY WITHOUT THE UNITED STATES.

* * *

(d) STOCK IN A RIC.—

(1) IN GENERAL.—*For purposes of this subchapter, stock in a regulated investment company (as defined in section 851) owned by a nonresident not a citizen of the United States shall not be deemed property within the United States in the proportion that, at the end of the quarter of such investment company's taxable year immediately preceding a decedent's date of death (or at such other time as the Secretary may designate in regulations), the assets of the investment company that were qualifying assets with respect to the decedent bore to the total assets of the investment company.*

(2) QUALIFYING ASSETS.—*For purposes of this subsection, qualifying assets with respect to a decedent are assets that, if owned directly by the decedent, would have been—*

(A) *amounts, deposits, or debt obligations described in subsection (b) of this section,*

(B) *debt obligations described in the last sentence of section 2104(c), or*

(C) *other property not within the United States.*

(3) TERMINATION.—*This subsection shall not apply to estates of decedents dying after December 31, 2007.*

[CCH Explanation at ¶562. Committee Reports at ¶10,670.]

Amendments

• **2004, American Jobs Creation Act of 2004 (H.R. 4520)**

H.R. 4520, §411(b):

Amended Code Sec. 2105 by adding at the end a new subsection (d). **Effective** for estates of decedents dying after 12-31-2004.

[¶ 5950] CODE SEC. 2107. EXPATRIATION TO AVOID TAX.

(a) TREATMENT OF EXPATRIATES.—*A tax computed in accordance with the table contained in section 2001 is hereby imposed on the transfer of the taxable estate, determined as provided in section 2106, of every decedent nonresident not a citizen of the United States if the date of death occurs during a taxable year with respect to which the decedent is subject to tax under section 877(b).*

* * *

[CCH Explanation at ¶ 504. Committee Reports at ¶ 11,000.]

Amendments

• **2004, American Jobs Creation Act of 2004 (H.R. 4520)**

H.R. 4520, § 804(a)(3):

Amended Code Sec. 2107(a). **Effective** for individuals who expatriate after 6-3-2004. Prior to amendment, Code Sec. 2107(a) read as follows:

(a) TREATMENT OF EXPATRIATES.—

(1) RATE OF TAX.—A tax computed in accordance with the table contained in section 2001 is hereby imposed on the transfer of the taxable estate, determined as provided in section 2106, of every decedent nonresident not a citizen of the United States if, within the 10-year period ending with the date of death, such decedent lost United States citizenship, unless such loss did not have for 1 of its principal purposes the avoidance of taxes under this subtitle or subtitle A.

(2) CERTAIN INDIVIDUALS TREATED AS HAVING TAX AVOIDANCE PURPOSE.—

(A) IN GENERAL.—For purposes of paragraph (1), an individual shall be treated as having a principal purpose to avoid such taxes if such individual is so treated under section 877(a)(2).

(B) EXCEPTION.—Subparagraph (A) shall not apply to a decedent meeting the requirements of section 877(c)(1).

[¶ 5955] CODE SEC. 2501. IMPOSITION OF TAX.

(a) TAXABLE TRANSFERS.—

* * *

(3) EXCEPTION.—

(A) CERTAIN INDIVIDUALS.—*Paragraph (2) shall not apply in the case of a donor to whom section 877(b) applies for the taxable year which includes the date of the transfer.*

(B) CREDIT FOR FOREIGN GIFT TAXES.—*The tax imposed by this section solely by reason of this paragraph shall be credited with the amount of any gift tax actually paid to any foreign country in respect of any gift which is taxable under this section solely by reason of this paragraph.*

(4) TRANSFERS TO POLITICAL ORGANIZATIONS.—Paragraph (1) shall not apply to the transfer of money or other property to a political organization (within the meaning of section 527(e)(1)) for the use of such organization.

(5) TRANSFERS OF CERTAIN STOCK.—

(A) IN GENERAL.—*In the case of a transfer of stock in a foreign corporation described in subparagraph (B) by a donor to whom section 877(b) applies for the taxable year which includes the date of the transfer—*

(i) section 2511(a) shall be applied without regard to whether such stock is situated within the United States, and

(ii) the value of such stock for purposes of this chapter shall be its U.S.-asset value determined under subparagraph (C).

(B) FOREIGN CORPORATION DESCRIBED.—*A foreign corporation is described in this subparagraph with respect to a donor if—*

(i) the donor owned (within the meaning of section 958(a)) at the time of such transfer 10 percent or more of the total combined voting power of all classes of stock entitled to vote of the foreign corporation, and

(ii) such donor owned (within the meaning of section 958(a)), or is considered to have owned (by applying the ownership rules of section 958(b)), at the time of such transfer, more than 50 percent of—

(I) the total combined voting power of all classes of stock entitled to vote of such corporation, or

(II) the total value of the stock of such corporation.

(C) U.S.-ASSET VALUE.—*For purposes of subparagraph (A), the U.S.-asset value of stock shall be the amount which bears the same ratio to the fair market value of such stock at the time of transfer as—*

(i) *the fair market value (at such time) of the assets owned by such foreign corporation and situated in the United States, bears to*

(ii) *the total fair market value (at such time) of all assets owned by such foreign corporation.*

* * *

[CCH Explanation at ¶ 504. Committee Reports at ¶ 11,000.]

Amendments

• **2004, American Jobs Creation Act of 2004 (H.R. 4520)**

H.R. 4520, § 804(d)(1):

Amended Code Sec. 2501(a) by striking paragraph (4), by redesignating paragraph (5) as paragraph (4), and by striking paragraph (3) and inserting a new paragraph (3). **Effective** for individuals who expatriate after 6-3-2004. Prior to being stricken, Code Sec. 2501(a)(3)-(4) read as follows:

(3) EXCEPTION.—

(A) CERTAIN INDIVIDUALS.—Paragraph (2) shall not apply in the case of a donor who, within the 10-year period ending with the date of transfer, lost United States citizenship, unless such loss did not have for 1 of its principal purposes the avoidance of taxes under this subtitle or subtitle A.

(B) CERTAIN INDIVIDUALS TREATED AS HAVING TAX AVOIDANCE PURPOSE.—For purposes of subparagraph (A), an individual shall be treated as having a principal purpose to avoid such taxes if such individual is so treated under section 877(a)(2).

(C) EXCEPTION FOR CERTAIN INDIVIDUALS.—Subparagraph (B) shall not apply to a donor meeting the requirements of section 877(c)(1).

(D) CREDIT FOR FOREIGN GIFT TAXES.—The tax imposed by this section solely by reason of this paragraph shall be credited with the amount of any gift tax actually paid to any foreign country in respect of any gift which is taxable under this section solely by reason of this paragraph.

(E) CROSS REFERENCE.—For comparable treatment of long-term lawful permanent residents who ceased to be taxed as residents, see section 877(e).

(4) BURDEN OF PROOF.—If the Secretary establishes that it is reasonable to believe that an individual's loss of United States citizenship would, but for paragraph (3), result in a substantial reduction for the calendar year in the taxes on the transfer of property by gift, the burden of proving that such loss of citizenship did not have for one of its principal purposes the avoidance of taxes under this subtitle or subtitle A shall be on such individual.

H.R. 4520, § 804(d)(2):

Amended Code Sec. 2501(a) by adding at the end a new paragraph (5). **Effective** for individuals who expatriate after 6-3-2004.

[¶ 5960] CODE SEC. 3121. DEFINITIONS.

(a) WAGES.—For purposes of this chapter, the term "wages" means all remuneration for employment, including the cash value of all remuneration (including benefits) paid in any medium other than cash; except that such term shall not include—

* * *

(20) any benefit provided to or on behalf of an employee if at the time such benefit is provided it is reasonable to believe that the employee will be able to exclude such benefit from income under section 74(c), *108(f)(4),* 117, or 132;

(21) in the case of a member of an Indian tribe, any remuneration on which no tax is imposed by this chapter by reason of section 7873 (relating to income derived by Indians from exercise of fishing rights)*; or*

(22) *remuneration on account of—*

(A) *a transfer of a share of stock to any individual pursuant to an exercise of an incentive stock option (as defined in section 422(b)) or under an employee stock purchase plan (as defined in section 423(b)), or*

(B) *any disposition by the individual of such stock.*

Nothing in the regulations prescribed for purposes of chapter 24 (relating to income tax withholding) which provides an exclusion from "wages" as used in such chapter shall be construed to require a similar exclusion from "wages" in the regulations prescribed for purposes of this chapter.

Except as otherwise provided in regulations prescribed by the Secretary, any third party which makes a payment included in wages solely by reason of the parenthetical matter contained in subparagraph (A) of paragraph (2) shall be treated for purposes of this chapter and chapter 22 as the employer with respect to such wages.

* * *

[CCH Explanation at ¶ 1225 and ¶ 1410. Committee Reports at ¶ 10,310 and ¶ 10,430.]

Amendments

• **2004, American Jobs Creation Act of 2004 (H.R. 4520)**

H.R. 4520, § 251(a)(1)(A):

Amended Code Sec. 3121(a) by striking "or" at the end of paragraph (20), by striking the period at the end of paragraph (21) and inserting "; or", and by inserting after paragraph (21) a new paragraph (22). **Effective** for stock acquired pursuant to options exercised after the date of the enactment of this Act.

H.R. 4520, § 320(b)(1):

Amended Code Sec. 3121(a)(20) by inserting "108(f)(4)," after "74(c),". **Effective** for amounts received by an individual in tax years beginning after 12-31-2003.

(v) Treatment of Certain Deferred Compensation and Salary Reduction Arrangements.—

* * *

(2) Treatment of certain nonqualified deferred compensation plans.—

(A) In general.—Any amount deferred under a nonqualified deferred compensation plan shall be taken into account for purposes of this chapter as of the later of—

(i) when the services are performed, or

(ii) when there is no substantial risk of forfeiture of the rights to such amount.

The preceding sentence shall not apply to any excess parachute payment (as defined in section 280G(b)) *or to any specified stock compensation (as defined in section 4985) on which tax is imposed by section 4985.*

* * *

[CCH Explanation at ¶ 508. Committee Reports at ¶ 10,980.]

Amendments

• **2004, American Jobs Creation Act of 2004 (H.R. 4520)**

H.R. 4520, § 802(c)(1):

Amended the last sentence of Code Sec. 3121(v)(2)(A) by inserting before the period "or to any specified stock compensation (as defined in section 4985) on which tax is imposed by section 4985". For the **effective** date, see Act Sec. 802(d), below.

H.R. 4520, § 802(d), provides:

(d) Effective Date.—The amendments made by this section shall take effect on March 4, 2003; except that periods before such date shall not be taken into account in applying the periods in subsections (a) and (e)(1) of section 4985 of the Internal Revenue Code of 1986, as added by this section.

[¶ 5965] CODE SEC. 3231. DEFINITIONS.

* * *

(e) Compensation.—For purposes of this chapter—

* * *

(5) The term "compensation" shall not include any benefit provided to or on behalf of an employee if at the time such benefit is provided it is reasonable to believe that the employee will be able to exclude such benefit from income under section 74(c), *108(f)(4),* 117, or 132.

* * *

(12) Qualified stock options.—The term "compensation" shall not include any remuneration on account of—

(A) a transfer of a share of stock to any individual pursuant to an exercise of an incentive stock option (as defined in section 422(b)) or under an employee stock purchase plan (as defined in section 423(b)), or

(B) any disposition by the individual of such stock.

* * *

[CCH Explanation at ¶ 1225 and ¶ 1410. Committee Reports at ¶ 10,310 and ¶ 10,430.]

Amendments

• **2004, American Jobs Creation Act of 2004 (H.R. 4520)**

H.R. 4520, § 251(a)(2):

Amended Code Sec. 3231(e) by adding at the end a new paragraph (12). **Effective** for stock acquired pursuant to options exercised after the date of the enactment of this Act.

H.R. 4520, § 320(b)(2):

Amended Code Sec. 3231(e)(5) by inserting "108(f)(4)," after "74(c),". **Effective** for amounts received by an individual in tax years beginning after 12-31-2003.

[¶5970] CODE SEC. 3306. DEFINITIONS.

* * *

(b) WAGES.—For purposes of this chapter, the term "wages" means all remuneration for employment, including the cash value of all remuneration (including benefits) paid in any medium other than cash; except that such term shall not include—

* * *

(16) any benefit provided to or on behalf of an employee if at the time such benefit is provided it is reasonable to believe that the employee will be able to exclude such benefit from income under section 74(c), *108(f)(4)*, 117 or 132;

(17) any payment made to or for the benefit of an employee if at the time of such payment it is reasonable to believe that the employee will be able to exclude such payment from income under section 106(b);

(18) any payment made to or for the benefit of an employee if at the time of such payment it is reasonable to believe that the employee will be able to exclude such payment from income under section 106(d); *or*

(19) remuneration on account of—

(A) a transfer of a share of stock to any individual pursuant to an exercise of an incentive stock option (as defined in section 422(b)) or under an employee stock purchase plan (as defined in section 423(b)), or

(B) any disposition by the individual of such stock.

Except as otherwise provided in regulations prescribed by the Secretary, any third party which makes a payment included in wages solely by reason of the parenthetical matter contained in subparagraph (A) of paragraph (2) shall be treated for purposes of this chapter and chapter 22 as the employer with respect to such wages. Nothing in the regulations prescribed for purposes of chapter 24 (relating to income tax withholding) which provides an exclusion from "wages" as used in such chapter shall be construed to require a similar exclusion from "wages" in the regulations prescribed for purposes of this chapter.

* * *

[CCH Explanation at ¶1225 and ¶1410. Committee Reports at ¶10,310 and ¶10,430.]

Amendments

• **2004, American Jobs Creation Act of 2004 (H.R. 4520)**

H.R. 4520, §251(a)(3):

Amended Code Sec. 3306(b) by striking "or" at the end of paragraph (17), by striking the period at the end of paragraph (18) and inserting "; or", and by inserting after paragraph (18) a new paragraph (19). **Effective** for stock acquired pursuant to options exercised after the date of the enactment of this Act.

H.R. 4520, §320(b)(3):

Amended Code Sec. 3306(b)(16) by inserting "108(f)(4)," after "74(c),". **Effective** for amounts received by an individual in tax years beginning after 12-31-2003.

[¶5975] CODE SEC. 3401. DEFINITIONS.

(a) WAGES.—For purposes of this chapter, the term "wages" means all remuneration (other than fees paid to a public official) for services performed by an employee for his employer, including the cash value of all remuneration (including benefits) paid in any medium other than cash; except that such term shall not include remuneration paid—

* * *

(19) for any benefit provided to or on behalf of an employee if at the time such benefit is provided it is reasonable to believe that the employee will be able to exclude such benefit from income under section 74(c), *108(f)(4)*, 117 or 132;

* * *

The term "wages" includes any amount includible in gross income of an employee under section 409A and payment of such amount shall be treated as having been made in the taxable year in which the amount is so includible.

* * *

[CCH Explanation at ¶ 1225 and ¶ 1405. Committee Reports at ¶ 10,430 and ¶ 11,570.]

Amendments

• **2004, American Jobs Creation Act of 2004 (H.R. 4520)**

H.R. 4520, §320(b)(4):

Amended Code Sec. 3401(a)(19) by inserting "108(f)(4)," after "74(c),". **Effective** for amounts received by an individual in tax years beginning after 12-31-2003.

H.R. 4520, §885(b)(2):

Amended Code Sec. 3401(a) by adding at the end a new flush sentence. **Effective** generally for amounts deferred after 12-31-2004. For special rules, see Act Sec. 885(d)(2)-(3) and (f), below.

H.R. 4520, §885(d)(2)-(3), provides:

(2) SPECIAL RULES.—

(A) EARNINGS.—The amendments made by this section shall apply to earnings on deferred compensation only to the extent that such amendments apply to such compensation.

(B) MATERIAL MODIFICATIONS.—For purposes of this subsection, amounts deferred in taxable years beginning before January 1, 2005, shall be treated as amounts deferred in a taxable year beginning on or after such date if the plan under which the deferral is made is materially modified after October 3, 2004, unless such modification is pursuant to the guidance issued under subsection (f).

(3) EXCEPTION FOR NONELECTIVE DEFERRED COMPENSATION.— The amendments made by this section shall not apply to any nonelective deferred compensation to which section 457 of the Internal Revenue Code of 1986 does not apply by reason of section 457(e)(12) of such Code, but only if such compensation is provided under a nonqualified deferred compensation plan—

(A) which was in existence on May 1, 2004,

(B) which was providing nonelective deferred compensation described in such section 457(e)(12) on such date, and

(C) which is established or maintained by an organization incorporated on July 2, 1974.

If, after May 1, 2004, a plan described in the preceding sentence adopts a plan amendment which provides a material change in the classes of individuals eligible to participate in the plan, this paragraph shall not apply to any nonelective deferred compensation provided under the plan on or after the date of the adoption of the amendment.

H.R. 4520, §885(f), provides:

(f) GUIDANCE RELATING TO TERMINATION OF CERTAIN EXISTING ARRANGEMENTS.—Not later than 60 days after the date of the enactment of this Act, the Secretary of the Treasury shall issue guidance providing a limited period during which a nonqualified deferred compensation plan adopted before December 31, 2004, may, without violating the requirements of paragraphs (2), (3), and (4) of section 409A(a) of the Internal Revenue Code of 1986 (as added by this section), be amended—

(1) to provide that a participant may terminate participation in the plan, or cancel an outstanding deferral election with regard to amounts deferred after December 31, 2004, but only if amounts subject to the termination or cancellation are includible in income of the participant as earned (or, if later, when no longer subject to substantial risk of forfeiture), and

(2) to conform to the requirements of such section 409A with regard to amounts deferred after December 31, 2004.

[¶ 5980] CODE SEC. 4041. IMPOSITION OF TAX.

(a) DIESEL FUEL AND SPECIAL MOTOR FUELS.—

(1) TAX ON DIESEL FUEL *AND KEROSENE* IN CERTAIN CASES.—

* * *

(B) EXEMPTION FOR PREVIOUSLY TAXED FUEL.—No tax shall be imposed by this paragraph on the sale or use of any liquid if tax was imposed on such liquid under section 4081 and the tax thereon was not credited or refunded. *This subparagraph shall not apply to aviation-grade kerosene.*

(C) RATE OF TAX.—

* * *

(ii) RATE OF TAX ON TRAINS.—In the case of any sale for use, or use, of diesel fuel in a train, the rate of tax imposed by this paragraph shall be—

(I) *3.3 cents per gallon after December 31, 2004, and before July 1, 2005,*

(II) *2.3 cents per gallon after June 30, 2005, and before January 1, 2007, and*

(III) *0 after December 31, 2006.*

* * *

[CCH Explanation at ¶ 1507 and ¶ 1513. Committee Reports at ¶ 10,220 and ¶ 11,340.]

Amendments

• **2004, American Jobs Creation Act of 2004 (H.R. 4520)**

H.R. 4520, §241(a)(1):

Amended Code Sec. 4041(a)(1)(C)(ii) by striking subclauses (I), (II), and (III) and inserting new subclauses (I), (II) and (III). **Effective** on 1-1-2005. Prior to amendment, Code Sec. 4041(a)(1)(C)(ii)(I)-(III) read as follows:

(I) 6.8 cents per gallon after September 30, 1993, and before October 1, 1995,

(II) 5.55 cents per gallon after September 30, 1995, and before November 1, 1998, and

(III) 4.3 cents per gallon after October 31, 1998.

H.R. 4520, § 853(a)(6)(A):

Amended Code Sec. 4041(a)(1)(B) by adding at the end a new sentence. **Effective** for aviation-grade kerosene removed, entered, or sold after 12-31-2004. For special rules, see Act Sec. 853(f), in the amendment notes following Code Sec. 4041(c), below.

H.R. 4520, § 853(a)(6)(B):

Amended the heading for Code Sec. 4041(a)(1) by inserting "AND KEROSENE" after "DIESEL FUEL". **Effective** for aviation-grade kerosene removed, entered, or sold after 12-31-2004. For special rules, see Act Sec. 853(f), in the amendment notes following Code Sec. 4041(c), below.

(b) EXEMPTION FOR OFF-HIGHWAY BUSINESS USE; REDUCTION IN TAX FOR QUALIFIED METHANOL AND ETHANOL FUEL.—

* * *

(2) QUALIFIED METHANOL AND ETHANOL FUEL.—

* * *

(B) QUALIFIED METHANOL OR ETHANOL FUEL.—The term "qualified methanol or ethanol fuel" means any liquid at least 85 percent of which consists of methanol, ethanol, or other alcohol produced from *coal (including peat)*.

* * *

[CCH Explanation at ¶ 805. Committee Reports at ¶ 10,320.]

Amendments

• **2004, American Jobs Creation Act of 2004 (H.R. 4520)**

H.R. 4520, § 301(c)(5):

Amended Code Sec. 4041(b)(2)(B) by striking "a substance other than petroleum or natural gas" and inserting "coal

(including peat)". **Effective** for fuel sold or used after 12-31-2004.

(c) AVIATION-GRADE KEROSENE.—

(1) IN GENERAL.—*There is hereby imposed a tax upon aviation-grade kerosene—*

(A) *sold by any person to an owner, lessee, or other operator of an aircraft for use in such aircraft, or*

(B) *used by any person in an aircraft unless there was a taxable sale of such fuel under subparagraph (A).*

(2) EXEMPTION FOR PREVIOUSLY TAXED FUEL.—*No tax shall be imposed by this subsection on the sale or use of any aviation-grade kerosene if tax was imposed on such liquid under section 4081 and the tax thereon was not credited or refunded.*

(3) RATE OF TAX.—*The rate of tax imposed by this subsection shall be the rate of tax applicable under section 4081(a)(2)(A)(iv) which is in effect at the time of such sale or use.*

[CCH Explanation at ¶ 1507. Committee Reports at ¶ 11,340.]

Amendments

• **2004, American Jobs Creation Act of 2004 (H.R. 4520)**

H.R. 4520, § 853(d)(2)(A):

Amended Code Sec. 4041(c). **Effective** for aviation-grade kerosene removed, entered, or sold after 12-31-2004. For special rules, see Act Sec. 853(f), below. Prior to amendment, Code Sec. 4041(c) read as follows:

(c) NONCOMMERCIAL AVIATION.—

(1) TAX ON NONGASOLINE FUELS WHERE NO TAX IMPOSED ON FUEL UNDER SECTION 4091.—There is hereby imposed a tax upon kerosene and any other liquid (other than any product taxable under section 4081)—

(A) sold by any person to an owner, lessee, or other operator of an aircraft, for use as a fuel in such aircraft in noncommercial aviation; or

(B) used by any person as a fuel in an aircraft in noncommercial aviation, unless there was a taxable sale of such liquid under this section.

The rate of the tax imposed by this paragraph shall be the rate of tax specified in section 4091(b)(1) which is in effect at

the time of such sale or use. No tax shall be imposed by this paragraph on the sale or use of kerosene and any other liquid if there was a taxable sale of such liquid under section 4091.

(2) DEFINITION OF NONCOMMERCIAL AVIATION.—For purposes of this chapter, the term "noncommercial aviation" means any use of an aircraft, other than use in a business of transporting persons or property for compensation or hire by air. The term also includes any use of an aircraft, in a business described in the preceding sentence, which is properly allocable to any transportation exempt from the taxes imposed by sections 4261 and 4271 by reason of section 4281 or 4282 or by reason of section 4261(h).

(3) TERMINATION.—The rate of the taxes imposed by paragraph (1) shall be 4.3 cents per gallon—

(A) after December 31, 1996, and before the date which is 7 days after the date of the enactment of the Airport and Airway Trust Fund Tax Reinstatement Act of 1997, and

(B) after September 30, 2007.

H.R. 4520, § 853(f), provides:

(f) FLOOR STOCKS TAX.—

Code Sec. 4041(c)(3)   ¶ 5980

(1) IN GENERAL.—There is hereby imposed on aviation-grade kerosene held on January 1, 2005, by any person a tax equal to—

(A) the tax which would have been imposed before such date on such kerosene had the amendments made by this section been in effect at all times before such date, reduced by

(B) the sum of—

(i) the tax imposed before such date on such kerosene under section 4091 of the Internal Revenue Code of 1986, as in effect on such date, and

(ii) in the case of kerosene held exclusively for such person's own use, the amount which such person would (but for this clause) reasonably expect (as of such date) to be paid as a refund under section 6427(l) of such Code with respect to such kerosene.

(2) EXCEPTION FOR FUEL HELD IN AIRCRAFT FUEL TANK.—Paragraph (1) shall not apply to kerosene held in the fuel tank of an aircraft on January 1, 2005.

(3) LIABILITY FOR TAX AND METHOD OF PAYMENT.—

(A) LIABILITY FOR TAX.—The person holding the kerosene on January 1, 2005, to which the tax imposed by paragraph (1) applies shall be liable for such tax.

(B) METHOD AND TIME FOR PAYMENT.—The tax imposed by paragraph (1) shall be paid at such time and in such manner

as the Secretary of the Treasury (or the Secretary's delegate) shall prescribe, including the nonapplication of such tax on de minimis amounts of kerosene.

(4) TRANSFER OF FLOOR STOCK TAX REVENUES TO TRUST FUNDS.—For purposes of determining the amount transferred to any trust fund, the tax imposed by this subsection shall be treated as imposed by section 4081 of the Internal Revenue Code of 1986—

(A) in any case in which tax was not imposed by section 4091 of such Code, at the Leaking Underground Storage Tank Trust Fund financing rate under such section to the extent of 0.1 cents per gallon, and

(B) at the rate under section 4081(a)(2)(A)(iv) of such Code to the extent of the remainder.

(5) HELD BY A PERSON.—For purposes of this subsection, kerosene shall be considered as held by a person if title thereto has passed to such person (whether or not delivery to the person has been made).

(6) OTHER LAWS APPLICABLE.—All provisions of law, including penalties, applicable with respect to the tax imposed by section 4081 of such Code shall, insofar as applicable and not inconsistent with the provisions of this subsection, apply with respect to the floor stock tax imposed by paragraph (1) to the same extent as if such tax were imposed by such section.

(d) ADDITIONAL TAXES TO FUND LEAKING UNDERGROUND STORAGE TANK TRUST FUND.—

* * *

(2) LIQUIDS USED IN AVIATION.—In addition to the taxes imposed by subsection (c), there is hereby imposed a tax of 0.1 cent a gallon on any liquid (other than gasoline (as defined in section 4083))—

(A) sold by any person to an owner, lessee, or other operator of an aircraft for use as a fuel in such aircraft, or

(B) used by any person as a fuel in an aircraft unless there was a taxable sale of such liquid under subparagraph (A).

No tax shall be imposed by this paragraph on the sale or use of any liquid if there was a taxable sale of such liquid under *section 4081*.

(3) DIESEL FUEL USED IN TRAINS.—*In the case of any sale for use or use after December 31, 2006, there is hereby imposed a tax of 0.1 cent per gallon on any liquid other than gasoline (as defined in section 4083)—*

(A) *sold by any person to an owner, lessee, or other operator of a diesel-powered train for use as a fuel in such train, or*

(B) *used by any person as a fuel in a diesel-powered train unless there was a taxable sale of such fuel under subparagraph (A).*

No tax shall be imposed by this paragraph on the sale or use of any liquid if tax was imposed on such liquid under section 4081.

(4) TERMINATION.—The taxes imposed by this subsection shall not apply during any period during which the Leaking Underground Storage Tank Trust Fund financing rate under section 4081 does not apply.

[CCH Explanation at ¶1507 and ¶1513. Committee Reports at ¶10,220 and ¶11,340.]

Amendments

• 2004, American Jobs Creation Act of 2004 (H.R. 4520)

H.R. 4520, §241(a)(2)(A):

Amended Code Sec. 4041(d) by redesignating paragraph (3) as paragraph (4) and by inserting after paragraph (2) a new paragraph (3). **Effective** on 1-1-2005.

H.R. 4520, §853(d)(2)(B):

Amended Code Sec. 4041(d)(2) by striking "section 4091" and inserting "section 4081". **Effective** for aviation-grade kerosene removed, entered, or sold after 12-31-2004. For special rules, see Act Sec. 853(f), in the amendment notes following Code Sec. 4041(c), above.

(e) [*Stricken.*]

* * *

[CCH Explanation at ¶1507. Committee Reports at ¶11,340.]

Amendments

• **2004, American Jobs Creation Act of 2004 (H.R. 4520)**

H.R. 4520, § 853(d)(2)(C):

Amended Code Sec. 4041 by striking subsection (e). **Effective** for aviation-grade kerosene removed, entered, or sold after 12-31-2004. For special rules, see Act Sec. 853(f), in the amendment notes following Code Sec. 4041(c), above. Prior to being stricken, Code Sec. 4041(e) read as follows:

(e) ADDITIONAL TAX.—If a liquid on which tax was imposed on the sale thereof is taxable at a higher rate under subsection (c)(1) of this section on the use thereof, there is hereby imposed a tax equal to the difference between the tax so imposed and the tax payable at such higher rate.

(i) [*Stricken.*]

* * *

[CCH Explanation at ¶1507. Committee Reports at ¶11,340.]

Amendments

• **2004, American Jobs Creation Act of 2004 (H.R. 4520)**

H.R. 4520, § 853(d)(2)(D):

Amended Code Sec. 4041 by striking subsection (i). **Effective** for aviation-grade kerosene removed, entered, or sold after 12-31-2004. For special rules, see Act Sec 853(f), in the amendment notes following Code Sec. 4041(c), above. Prior to being stricken, Code Sec. 4041(i) read as follows:

(i) REGISTRATION.—If any liquid is sold by any person for use as a fuel in an aircraft, it shall be presumed for purposes of this section that a tax imposed by this section applies to the sale of such liquid unless the purchaser is registered in such manner (and furnishes such information in respect of the use of the liquid) as the Secretary shall by regulations provide.

(k) [*Stricken.*]

* * *

[CCH Explanation at ¶805. Committee Reports at ¶10,320.]

Amendments

• **2004, American Jobs Creation Act of 2004 (H.R. 4520)**

H.R. 4520, § 301(c)(6):

Amended Code Sec. 4041 by striking subsection (k). **Effective** for fuel sold or used after 12-31-2004. Prior to being stricken, Code Sec. 4041(k) read as follows:

(k) FUELS CONTAINING ALCOHOL.—

(1) IN GENERAL.—Under regulations prescribed by the Secretary, in the case of the sale or use of any liquid at least 10 percent of which consists of alcohol (as defined in section 4081(c)(3))—

(A) the rates under paragraphs (1) and (2) of subsection (a) shall be the comparable rates under section 4081(c), and

(B) the rate of the tax imposed by subsection (c)(1) shall be the comparable rate under section 4091(c).

(2) LATER SEPARATION.—If any person separates the liquid fuel from a mixture of the liquid fuel and alcohol to which paragraph (1) applied, such separation shall be treated as a sale of the liquid fuel. Any tax imposed on such sale shall be reduced by the amount (if any) of the tax imposed on the sale of such mixture.

(3) TERMINATION.—Paragraph (1) shall not apply to any sale or use after September 30, 2007.

(m) CERTAIN ALCOHOL FUELS.—

(1) IN GENERAL.—In the case of the sale or use of any partially exempt methanol or ethanol fuel the rate of the tax imposed by subsection (a)(2) shall be—

(A) after September 30, 1997, and before October 1, 2005—

(i) in the case of fuel none of the alcohol in which consists of ethanol, 9.15 cents per gallon, and

(ii) in any other case, 11.3 cents per gallon, and

(B) after September 30, 2005—

(i) in the case of fuel none of the alcohol in which consists of ethanol, 2.15 cents per gallon, and

(ii) in any other case, 4.3 cents per gallon.

* * *

Code Sec. 4041(m)(1)(B)(ii) **¶5980**

[CCH Explanation at ¶1507. Committee Reports at ¶11,340.]

Amendments

• **2004, American Jobs Creation Act of 2004 (H.R. 4520)**

H.R. 4520, §853(d)(2)(E):

Amended Code Sec. 4041(m)(1). **Effective** for aviation-grade kerosene removed, entered, or sold after 12-31-2004. For special rules, see Act Sec. 853(f), in the amendment notes following Code Sec. 4041(c), above. Prior to amendment, Code Sec. 4041(m)(1) read as follows:

(1) IN GENERAL.—In the case of the sale or use of any partially exempt methanol or ethanol fuel—

(A) the rate of the tax imposed by subsection (a)(2) shall be—

(i) after September 30, 1997, and before October 1, 2005—

(I) in the case of fuel none of the alcohol in which consists of ethanol, 9.15 cents per gallon, and

(II) in any other case, 11.3 cents per gallon, and

(ii) after September 30, 2005—

(I) in the case of fuel none of the alcohol in which consists of ethanol, 2.15 cents per gallon, and

(II) in any other case, 4.3 cents per gallon, and

(B) the rate of the tax imposed by subsection (c)(1) shall be the comparable rate under section 4091(c)(1).

[¶5985] CODE SEC. 4042. TAX ON FUEL USED IN COMMERCIAL TRANSPORTATION ON INLAND WATERWAYS.

* * *

(b) AMOUNT OF TAX.—

* * *

(2) RATES.—For purposes of paragraph (1)—

* * *

(C) *The deficit reduction rate is—*

(i) *3.3 cents per gallon after December 31, 2004, and before July 1, 2005,*

(ii) *2.3 cents per gallon after June 30, 2005, and before January 1, 2007, and*

(iii) *0 after December 31, 2006.*

* * *

[CCH Explanation at ¶1513. Committee Reports at ¶10,220.]

Amendments

• **2004, American Jobs Creation Act of 2004 (H.R. 4520)**

H.R. 4520, §241(b):

Amended Code Sec. 4042(b)(2)(C). **Effective** on 1-1-2005. Prior to amendment, Code Sec. 4042(b)(2)(C) read as follows:

(C) The deficit reduction rate is 4.3 cents per gallon.

[¶5990] CODE SEC. 4053. EXEMPTIONS.

No tax shall be imposed by section 4051 on any of the following articles:

* * *

(8) *MOBILE MACHINERY.—Any vehicle which consists of a chassis—*

(A) *to which there has been permanently mounted (by welding, bolting, riveting, or other means) machinery or equipment to perform a construction, manufacturing, processing, farming, mining, drilling, timbering, or similar operation if the operation of the machinery or equipment is unrelated to transportation on or off the public highways,*

(B) *which has been specially designed to serve only as a mobile carriage and mount (and a power source, where applicable) for the particular machinery or equipment involved, whether or not such machinery or equipment is in operation, and*

(C) *which, by reason of such special design, could not, without substantial structural modification, be used as a component of a vehicle designed to perform a function of transporting any load other than that particular machinery or equipment or similar machinery or equipment requiring such a specially designed chassis.*

[CCH Explanation at ¶1549. Committee Reports at ¶11,320.]
Amendments
• 2004, American Jobs Creation Act of 2004 (H.R. 4520)

H.R. 4520, §851(a)(1):

Amended Code Sec. 4053 by adding at the end a new paragraph (8). **Effective** on the day after the date of the enactment of this Act.

[¶5995] CODE SEC. 4071. IMPOSITION OF TAX.

(a) IMPOSITION AND RATE OF TAX.—*There is hereby imposed on taxable tires sold by the manufacturer, producer, or importer thereof a tax at the rate of 9.45 cents (4.725 cents in the case of a biasply tire or super single tire) for each 10 pounds so much of the maximum rated load capacity thereof as exceeds 3,500 pounds.*

* * *

[CCH Explanation at ¶1553. Committee Reports at ¶11,500.]
Amendments
• 2004, American Jobs Creation Act of 2004 (H.R. 4520)

H.R. 4520, §869(a):

Amended Code Sec. 4071(a). **Effective** for sales in calendar years beginning more than 30 days after the date of the enactment of this Act. Prior to amendment, Code Sec. 4071(a) read as follows:

(a) IMPOSITION AND RATE OF TAX.—There is hereby imposed on tires of the type used on highway vehicles, if wholly or in part made of rubber, sold by the manufacturer, producer, or importer a tax at the following rates:

If the tire weighs:	The rate of tax is:
Not more than 40 lbs.	No tax.
More than 40 lbs. but not more than 70 lbs.	15 cents per lb. in excess of 40 lbs.
More than 70 lbs. but not more than 90 lbs.	$4.50 plus 30 cents per lb. in excess of 70 lbs.
More than 90 lbs.	$10.50 plus 50 cents per lb. in excess of 90 lbs.

(c) TIRES ON IMPORTED ARTICLES.—For the purposes of subsection (a), if an article imported into the United States is equipped with tires—

(1) the importer of the article shall be treated as the importer of the tires with which such article is equipped, and

(2) the sale of the article by the importer thereof shall be treated as the sale of the tires with which such article is equipped.

This subsection shall not apply with respect to the sale of an automobile bus chassis or an automobile bus body.

* * *

[CCH Explanation at ¶1553. Committee Reports at ¶11,500.]
Amendments
• 2004, American Jobs Creation Act of 2004 (H.R. 4520)

H.R. 4520, §869(d)(1)[(e)(1)]:

Amended Code Sec. 4071 by striking subsection (c) and by moving subsection (e) after subsection (b) and redesignating subsection (e) as subsection (c). **Effective** for sales in calendar years beginning more than 30 days after the date of the enactment of this Act. Prior to being stricken, Code Sec. 4071(c) read as follows:

(c) DETERMINATION OF WEIGHT.—For purposes of this section, weight shall be based on total weight exclusive of metal rims or rim bases. Total weight of the articles shall be determined under regulations prescribed by the Secretary.

[¶6000] CODE SEC. 4072. DEFINITIONS.

(a) TAXABLE TIRE.—*For purposes of this chapter, the term "taxable tire" means any tire of the type used on highway vehicles if wholly or in part made of rubber and if marked pursuant to Federal regulations for highway use.*

[CCH Explanation at ¶1553. Committee Reports at ¶11,500.]
Amendments
• 2004, American Jobs Creation Act of 2004 (H.R. 4520)

H.R. 4520, §869(b)[(c)]:

Amended Code Sec. 4072, as amended by Act Sec. 869(a) [Act Sec. 869(b)], by redesignating subsections (a), (b), (c), and (d) as subsections (b), (c), (d), and (e), respectively, and by inserting before subsection (b) (as so redesignated) a new subsection (a). **Effective** for sales in calendar years beginning more than 30 days after the date of the enactment of this Act.

(b) RUBBER.—For purposes of this chapter, the term "rubber" includes synthetic and substitute rubber.

[CCH Explanation at ¶ 1553. Committee Reports at ¶ 11,500.]

Amendments

• 2004, American Jobs Creation Act of 2004 (H.R. 4520)

H.R. 4520, § 869(b)[(c)]:

Amended Code Sec. 4072, as amended by Act Sec. 869(a) [Act Sec. 869(b)], by redesignating subsection (a) as subsec-

tion (b). **Effective** for sales in calendar years beginning more than 30 days after the date of the enactment of this Act.

(c) TIRES OF THE TYPE USED ON HIGHWAY VEHICLES.—For purposes of this part, the term "tires of the type used on highway vehicles" means tires of the type used on—

(1) motor vehicles which are highway vehicles, or

(2) vehicles of the type used in connection with motor vehicles which are highway vehicles.

Such term shall not include tires of a type used exclusively on vehicles described in section 4053(8).

[CCH Explanation at ¶ 1549 and ¶ 1553. Committee Reports at ¶ 11,320 and ¶ 11,500.]

Amendments

• 2004, American Jobs Creation Act of 2004 (H.R. 4520)

H.R. 4520, § 851(c)(1):

Amended Code Sec. 4072(b)(2), prior to redesignation, by adding at the end a flush sentence. **Effective** on the day after the date of the enactment of this Act.

H.R. 4520, § 869(b)[(c)]:

Amended Code Sec. 4072, as amended by Act Sec. 869(a) [Act Sec. 869(b)], by redesignating subsection (b) as subsection (c). **Effective** for sales in calendar years beginning more than 30 days after the date of the enactment of this Act.

(d) BIASPLY.—*For purposes of this part, the term "biasply tire" means a pneumatic tire on which the ply cords that extend to the beads are laid at alternate angles substantially less than 90 degrees to the centerline of the tread.*

[CCH Explanation at ¶ 1553. Committee Reports at ¶ 11,500.]

Amendments

• 2004, American Jobs Creation Act of 2004 (H.R. 4520)

H.R. 4520, § 869(b):

Amended Code Sec. 4072 by adding at the end a new subsection (c). **Effective** for sales in calendar years beginning more than 30 days after the date of the enactment of this Act.

H.R. 4520, § 869(b)[(c)]:

Amended Code Sec. 4072, as amended by Act Sec. 869(a) [Act Sec. 869(b)], by redesignating subsection (c) as subsection (d). **Effective** for sales in calendar years beginning more than 30 days after the date of the enactment of this Act.

(e) SUPER SINGLE TIRE.—*For purposes of this part, the term "super single tire" means a single tire greater than 13 inches in cross section width designed to replace 2 tires in a dual fitment.*

[CCH Explanation at ¶ 1553. Committee Reports at ¶ 11,500.]

Amendments

• 2004, American Jobs Creation Act of 2004 (H.R. 4520)

H.R. 4520, § 869(b):

Amended Code Sec. 4072 by adding at the end a new subsection (d). **Effective** for sales in calendar years beginning more than 30 days after the date of the enactment of this Act.

H.R. 4520, § 869(b)[(c)]:

Amended Code Sec. 4072, as amended by Act Sec. 869(a) [Act Sec. 869(b)], by redesignating subsection (d) as subsection (e). **Effective** for sales in calendar years beginning more than 30 days after the date of the enactment of this Act.

[¶ 6005] *CODE SEC. 4073. EXEMPTIONS.*

The tax imposed by section 4071 shall not apply to tires sold for the exclusive use of the Department of Defense or the Coast Guard.

[CCH Explanation at ¶ 1553. Committee Reports at ¶ 11,500.]

Amendments

• 2004, American Jobs Creation Act of 2004 (H.R. 4520)

H.R. 4520, § 869(c)[(d)]:

Amended Code Sec. 4073. **Effective** for sales in calendar years beginning more than 30 days after the date of the

enactment of this Act. Prior to amendment, Code Sec. 4073 read as follows:

SEC. 4073. EXEMPTION FOR TIRES WITH INTERNAL WIRE FASTENING.

The tax imposed by section 4071 shall not apply to tires of extruded tiring with an internal wire fastening agent.

[¶6010] CODE SEC. 4081. IMPOSITION OF TAX.

(a) TAX IMPOSED.—

(1) TAX ON REMOVAL, ENTRY, OR SALE.—

* * *

➤➤➤ *Caution: Code Sec. 4081(a)(1)(B), below, as amended by H.R. 4520, is effective March 1, 2005.*

(B) EXEMPTION FOR BULK TRANSFERS TO REGISTERED TERMINALS OR REFINERIES.—The tax imposed by this paragraph shall not apply to any removal or entry of a taxable fuel transferred in bulk *by pipeline or vessel* to a terminal or refinery if the person removing or entering the taxable fuel, *the operator of such pipeline or vessel*, and the operator of such terminal or refinery are registered under section 4101.

(2) RATES OF TAX.—

(A) IN GENERAL.—The rate of the tax imposed by this section is—

(i) in the case of gasoline other than aviation gasoline, 18.3 cents per gallon,

(ii) in the case of aviation gasoline, 19.3 cents per gallon,

(iii) in the case of diesel fuel or kerosene, 24.3 cents per gallon , *and*

(iv) in the case of aviation-grade kerosene, 21.8 cents per gallon.

* * *

(C) TAXES IMPOSED ON FUEL USED IN COMMERCIAL AVIATION.—In the case of aviation-grade kerosene which is removed from any refinery or terminal directly into the fuel tank of an aircraft for use in commercial aviation, the rate of tax under subparagraph (A)(iv) shall be 4.3 cents per gallon.

(3) CERTAIN REFUELER TRUCKS, TANKERS, AND TANK WAGONS TREATED AS TERMINAL.—

(A) IN GENERAL.—For purposes of paragraph (2)(C), a refueler truck, tanker, or tank wagon shall be treated as part of a terminal if—

(i) such terminal is located within a secured area of an airport,

(ii) any aviation-grade kerosene which is loaded in such truck, tanker, or wagon at such terminal is for delivery only into aircraft at the airport in which such terminal is located,

(iii) such truck, tanker, or wagon meets the requirements of subparagraph (B) with respect to such terminal, and

(iv) except in the case of exigent circumstances identified by the Secretary in regulations, no vehicle registered for highway use is loaded with aviation-grade kerosene at such terminal.

(B) REQUIREMENTS.—A refueler truck, tanker, or tank wagon meets the requirements of this subparagraph with respect to a terminal if such truck, tanker, or wagon—

(i) has storage tanks, hose, and coupling equipment designed and used for the purposes of fueling aircraft,

(ii) is not registered for highway use, and

(iii) is operated by—

(I) the terminal operator of such terminal, or

(II) a person that makes a daily accounting to such terminal operator of each delivery of fuel from such truck, tanker, or wagon.

(C) REPORTING.—The Secretary shall require under section 4101(d) reporting by such terminal operator of—

(i) any information obtained under subparagraph (B)(iii)(II), and

(ii) any similar information maintained by such terminal operator with respect to deliveries of fuel made by trucks, tankers, or wagons operated by such terminal operator.

(4) LIABILITY FOR TAX ON AVIATION-GRADE KEROSENE USED IN COMMERCIAL AVIATION.—For purposes of paragraph (2)(C), the person who uses the fuel for commercial aviation shall pay the tax imposed under such paragraph. For purposes of the preceding sentence, fuel shall be treated as used when such fuel is removed into the fuel tank.

* * *

[CCH Explanation at ¶ 1507 and ¶ 1527. Committee Reports at ¶ 10,340 and ¶ 11,410.]

Amendments

- **2004, American Jobs Creation Act of 2004 (H.R. 4520)**

H.R. 4520, § 853(a)(1):

Amended Code Sec. 4081(a)(2)(A) by striking "and" at the end of clause (ii), by striking the period at the end of clause (iii) and inserting ", and", and by adding at the end a new clause (iv). **Effective** for aviation-grade kerosene removed, entered, or sold after 12-31-2004. For special rules, see Act Sec. 853(f), below.

H.R. 4520, § 853(a)(2):

Amended Code Sec. 4081(a)(2) by adding at the end a new subparagraph (C). **Effective** for aviation-grade kerosene removed, entered, or sold after 12-31-2004. For special rules, see Act Sec. 853(f), below.

H.R. 4520, § 853(a)(3)(A):

Amended Code Sec. 4081(a) by adding at the end a new paragraph (3). **Effective** for aviation-grade kerosene removed, entered, or sold after 12-31-2004. For special rules, see Act Sec. 853(f), below.

H.R. 4520, § 853(a)(3)(B), provides:

(B) LIST OF AIRPORTS WITH SECURED TERMINALS.—Not later than December 15, 2004, the Secretary of the Treasury shall publish and maintain a list of airports which include a secured area in which a terminal is located (within the meaning of section 4081(a)(3)(A)(i) of the Internal Revenue Code of 1986, as added by this paragraph).

H.R. 4520, § 853(a)(4):

Amended Code Sec. 4081(a) by adding at the end a new paragraph (4). **Effective** for aviation-grade kerosene removed, entered, or sold after 12-31-2004. For special rules, see Act Sec. 853(f), below.

H.R. 4520, § 853(f), provides:

(f) FLOOR STOCKS TAX.—

(1) IN GENERAL.—There is hereby imposed on aviation-grade kerosene held on January 1, 2005, by any person a tax equal to—

(A) the tax which would have been imposed before such date on such kerosene had the amendments made by this section been in effect at all times before such date, reduced by

(B) the sum of—

(i) the tax imposed before such date on such kerosene under section 4091 of the Internal Revenue Code of 1986, as in effect on such date, and

(ii) in the case of kerosene held exclusively for such person's own use, the amount which such person would (but for this clause) reasonably expect (as of such date) to be paid as a refund under section 6427(l) of such Code with respect to such kerosene.

(2) EXCEPTION FOR FUEL HELD IN AIRCRAFT FUEL TANK.—Paragraph (1) shall not apply to kerosene held in the fuel tank of an aircraft on January 1, 2005.

(3) LIABILITY FOR TAX AND METHOD OF PAYMENT.—

(A) LIABILITY FOR TAX.—The person holding the kerosene on January 1, 2005, to which the tax imposed by paragraph (1) applies shall be liable for such tax.

(B) METHOD AND TIME FOR PAYMENT.—The tax imposed by paragraph (1) shall be paid at such time and in such manner as the Secretary of the Treasury (or the Secretary's delegate) shall prescribe, including the nonapplication of such tax on de minimis amounts of kerosene.

(4) TRANSFER OF FLOOR STOCK TAX REVENUES TO TRUST FUNDS.—For purposes of determining the amount transferred to any trust fund, the tax imposed by this subsection shall be treated as imposed by section 4081 of the Internal Revenue Code of 1986—

(A) in any case in which tax was not imposed by section 4091 of such Code, at the Leaking Underground Storage Tank Trust Fund financing rate under such section to the extent of 0.1 cents per gallon, and

(B) at the rate under section 4081(a)(2)(A)(iv) of such Code to the extent of the remainder.

(5) HELD BY A PERSON.—For purposes of this subsection, kerosene shall be considered as held by a person if title thereto has passed to such person (whether or not delivery to the person has been made).

(6) OTHER LAWS APPLICABLE.—All provisions of law, including penalties, applicable with respect to the tax imposed by section 4081 of such Code shall, insofar as applicable and not inconsistent with the provisions of this subsection, apply with respect to the floor stock tax imposed by paragraph (1) to the same extent as if such tax were imposed by such section.

H.R. 4520, § 860(a)(1)-(2):

Amended Code Sec. 4081(a)(1)(B) by inserting "by pipeline or vessel" after "transferred in bulk", and by inserting ", the operator of such pipeline or vessel," after "the taxable fuel". **Effective** 3-1-2005.

(c) [*Stricken.*]

[CCH Explanation at ¶ 805. Committee Reports at ¶ 10,320.]

Amendments

- **2004, American Jobs Creation Act of 2004 (H.R. 4520)**

H.R. 4520, § 301(c)(7):

Amended Code Sec. 4081 by striking subsection (c). **Effective** for fuel sold or used after 12-31-2004. Prior to being stricken, Code Sec. 4081(c) read as follows:

(c) TAXABLE FUELS MIXED WITH ALCOHOL.—Under regulations prescribed by the Secretary—

(1) IN GENERAL.—The rate of tax under subsection (a) shall be the alcohol mixture rate in the case of the removal or entry of any qualified alcohol mixture.

(2) TAX PRIOR TO MIXING.—

(A) IN GENERAL.—In the case of the removal or entry of any taxable fuel for use in producing at the time of such removal or entry a qualified alcohol mixture, the rate of tax under subsection (a) shall be the applicable fraction of the alcohol mixture rate. Subject to such terms and conditions as the Secretary may prescribe (including the application of section 4101), the treatment under the preceding sentence also shall apply to sue in producing a qualified alcohol mixture after the time of such removal or entry.

(B) APPLICABLE FRACTION.—For purposes of subparagraph (A), the applicable fraction is—

(i) in the case of a qualified alcohol mixture which contains gasoline, the fraction the numerator of which is 10 and the denominator of which is—

(I) 9 in the case of 10 percent gasohol,

(II) 9.23 in the case of 7.7 percent gasohol, and

(III) 9.43 in the case of 5.7 percent gasohol, and

(ii) in the case of a qualified alcohol mixture which does not contain gasoline, $^{10}/_9$.

(3) ALCOHOL; QUALIFIED ALCOHOL MIXTURE.—For purposes of this subsection—

(A) ALCOHOL.—The term "alcohol" includes methanol and ethanol but does not include alcohol produced from petroleum, natural gas, or coal (including peat). Such term does not include alcohol with a proof of less than 190 (determined without regard to any added denaturants).

(B) QUALIFIED ALCOHOL MIXTURE.—The term "qualified alcohol mixture" means—

(i) any mixture of gasoline with alcohol if at least 5.7 percent of such mixture is alcohol, and

(ii) any mixture of diesel fuel with alcohol if at least 10 percent of such mixture is alcohol.

(4) ALCOHOL MIXTURE RATES FOR GASOLINE MIXTURES.—For purposes of this subsection—

(A) GENERAL RULES.—

(i) MIXTURES CONTAINING ETHANOL.—Except as provided in clause (ii), in the case of a qualified alcohol mixture which contains gasoline, the alcohol mixture rate is the excess of the rate which would (but for this paragraph) be determined under subsection (a) over—

(I) in the case of 10 percent gasohol, the applicable blender rate (as defined in section 4041(b)(2)(C)) per gallon,

(II) in the case of 7.7 percent gasohol, the number of cents per gallon equal to 77 percent of such applicable blender rate, and

(III) in the case of 5.7 percent gasohol, the number of cents per gallon equal to 57 percent of such applicable blender rate.

(ii) MIXTURES NOT CONTAINING ETHANOL.—In the case of a qualified alcohol mixture which contains gasoline and none of the alcohol in which consists of ethanol, the alcohol mixture rate is the excess of the rate which would (but for this paragraph) be determined under subsection (a) over—

(I) in the case of 10 percent gasohol, 6 cents per gallon,

(II) in the case of 7.7 percent gasohol, 4.62 cents per gallon, and

(III) in the case of 5.7 percent gasohol, 3.42 cents per gallon.

(B) 10 PERCENT GASOHOL.—The term "10 percent gasohol" means any mixture of gasoline with alcohol if at least 10 percent of such mixture is alcohol.

(C) 7.7 PERCENT GASOHOL.—The term "7.7 percent gasohol" means any mixture of gasoline with alcohol if at least 7.7 percent, but not 10 percent or more, of such mixture is alcohol.

(D) 5.7 PERCENT GASOHOL.—The term "5.7 percent gasohol" means any mixture of gasoline with alcohol if at least 5.7 percent, but not 7.7 percent or more, of such mixture is alcohol.

(5) ALCOHOL MIXTURE RATE FOR DIESEL FUEL MIXTURES.—The alcohol mixture rate for a qualified alcohol mixture which does not contain gasoline is the excess of the rate which would (but for this paragraph) be determined under subsection (a) over the applicable blender rate (as defined in section 4041(b)(2)(C)) per gallon (6 cents per gallon in the case of a qualified alcohol mixture none of the alcohol in which consists of ethanol).

(6) LIMITATION.—In no event shall any alcohol mixture rate determined under this subsection be less than 4.3 cents per gallon.

(7) LATER SEPARATION OF FUEL FROM QUALIFIED ALCOHOL MIXTURE.—If any person separates the taxable fuel from a qualified alcohol mixture on which tax was imposed under subsection (a) at a rate determined under paragraph (1) or (2) (or with respect to which a credit or payment was allowed or made by reason of section 6427(f)(1)), such person shall be treated as the refiner of such taxable fuel. The amount of tax imposed on any removal of such fuel by such person shall be reduced by the amount of tax imposed (and not credited or refunded) on any prior removal or entry of such fuel.

(8) TERMINATION.—Paragraphs (1) and (2) shall not apply to any removal, entry, or sale after September 30, 2007.

[¶6015] CODE SEC. 4082. EXEMPTIONS FOR DIESEL FUEL AND KEROSENE.

(a) IN GENERAL.—The tax imposed by section 4081 shall not apply to diesel fuel and kerosene—

(1) which the Secretary determines is destined for a nontaxable use,

⟫→ *Caution: Code Sec. 4082(a)(2), below, as amended by H.R. 4520, Act Sec. 854(a), is effective on the 180th day after the date on which the Secretary issues the regulations described in Act Sec. 854(b).*

(2) which is indelibly dyed *by mechanical injection* in accordance with regulations which the Secretary shall prescribe, and

(3) which meets such marking requirements (if any) as may be prescribed by the Secretary in regulations.

Such regulations shall allow an individual choice of dye color approved by the Secretary or chosen from any list of approved dye colors that the Secretary may publish.

[CCH Explanation at ¶1517. Committee Reports at ¶11,350.]

Amendments

• **2004, American Jobs Creation Act of 2004 (H.R. 4520)**

H.R. 4520, §854(a):

Amended Code Sec. 4082(a)(2) by inserting "by mechanical injection" after "indelibly dyed". **Effective** on the 180th day after the date on which the Secretary issues the regulations described in Act Sec. 854(b), below.

H.R. 4520, §854(b), provides:

(b) DYE INJECTOR SECURITY.—Not later than 180 days after the date of the enactment of this Act, the Secretary of the Treasury shall issue regulations regarding mechanical dye injection systems described in the amendment made by subsection (a), and such regulations shall include standards for making such systems tamper resistant.

(b) NONTAXABLE USE.—For purposes of this section, the term "nontaxable use" means—

(1) any use which is exempt from the tax imposed by section 4041(a)(1) other than by reason of a prior imposition of tax,

(2) any use in a train, and

(3) *any use described in section 4041(a)(1)(C)(iii)(II).*

The term "nontaxable use" does not include the use of aviation-grade kerosene in an aircraft and such term shall not include any use described in section 6421(e)(2)(C).

* * *

[CCH Explanation at ¶1507, ¶1523 and ¶1549. Committee Reports at ¶11,320, ¶11,340 and ¶11,350.]

Amendments

• **2004, American Jobs Creation Act of 2004 (H.R. 4520)**

H.R. 4520, §851(d)(2):

Amended Code Sec. 4082(b) [as amended by Act Sec. 853(a)(5)(B)(i)] by inserting before the period at the end "and such term shall not include any use described in section 6421(e)(2)(C)". **Effective** for tax years beginning after the date of the enactment of this Act.

H.R. 4520, §853(a)(5)(B)(i):

Amended Code Sec. 4082(b) by adding at the end a new flush sentence. **Effective** for aviation-grade kerosene re-

moved, entered, or sold after 12-31-2004. For special rules, see Act Sec. 853(f) in the amendment notes following Code Sec. 4082(e), below.

H.R. 4520, §857(a):

Amended Code Sec. 4082(b)(3). **Effective** for fuel sold after 12-31-2004. Prior to amendment, Code Sec. 4082(b)(3) read as follows:

(3) any use described in section 6427(b)(1) (after the application of section 6427(b)(3)).

(d) ADDITIONAL EXCEPTIONS TO DYEING REQUIREMENTS FOR KEROSENE.—

(1) USE FOR NON-FUEL FEEDSTOCK PURPOSES.—Subsection (a)(2) shall not apply to kerosene—

(A) received by pipeline or vessel for use by the person receiving the kerosene in the manufacture or production of any substance (other than gasoline, diesel fuel, or special fuels referred to in section 4041), or

(B) to the extent provided in regulations, removed or entered—

(i) for such a use by the person removing or entering the kerosene, or

(ii) for resale by such person for such a use by the purchaser, but only if the person receiving, removing, or entering the kerosene and such purchaser (if any) are registered under section 4101 with respect to the tax imposed by section 4081.

(2) WHOLESALE DISTRIBUTORS.—To the extent provided in regulations, subsection (a)(2) shall not apply to kerosene received by a wholesale distributor of kerosene if such distributor—

(A) is registered under section 4101 with respect to the tax imposed by section 4081 on kerosene, and

(B) sells kerosene exclusively to ultimate vendors described in section 6427(l)(5)(B) with respect to kerosene.

[CCH Explanation at ¶1507. Committee Reports at ¶11,340.]

Amendments

• **2004, American Jobs Creation Act of 2004 (H.R. 4520)**

H.R. 4520, §853(a)(5)(B)(ii):

Amended Code Sec. 4082(d) by striking paragraph (1) and by redesignating paragraphs (2) and (3) as paragraphs (1) and (2), respectively. **Effective** for aviation-grade kerosene

removed, entered, or sold after 12-31-2004. For special rules, see Act Sec. 853(f) in the amendment notes following Code Sec. 4082(e), below. Prior to being stricken, Code Sec. 4082(d)(1) read as follows:

(1) AVIATION-GRADE KEROSENE.—Subsection (a)(2) shall not apply to aviation-grade kerosene (as determined under regulations prescribed by the Secretary) which the Secretary determines is destined for use as a fuel in an aircraft.

(e) AVIATION-GRADE KEROSENE.—*In the case of aviation-grade kerosene which is exempt from the tax imposed by section 4041(c) (other than by reason of a prior imposition of tax) and which is removed from any refinery or terminal directly into the fuel tank of an aircraft, the rate of tax under section 4081(a)(2)(A)(iv) shall be zero.*

[CCH Explanation at ¶1507. Committee Reports at ¶11,340.]

Amendments

• **2004, American Jobs Creation Act of 2004 (H.R. 4520)**

H.R. 4520, § 853(a)(5)(A):

Amended Code Sec. 4082 by redesignating subsections (e) and (f) as subsections (f) and (g), respectively, and by inserting after subsection (d) a new subsection (e). **Effective** for aviation-grade kerosene removed, entered, or sold after 12-31-2004. For special rules, see Act Sec. 853(f), below.

H.R. 4520, § 853(f), provides:

(f) FLOOR STOCKS TAX.—

(1) IN GENERAL.—There is hereby imposed on aviation-grade kerosene held on January 1, 2005, by any person a tax equal to—

(A) the tax which would have been imposed before such date on such kerosene had the amendments made by this section been in effect at all times before such date, reduced by

(B) the sum of—

(i) the tax imposed before such date on such kerosene under section 4091 of the Internal Revenue Code of 1986, as in effect on such date, and

(ii) in the case of kerosene held exclusively for such person's own use, the amount which such person would (but for this clause) reasonably expect (as of such date) to be paid as a refund under section 6427(l) of such Code with respect to such kerosene.

(2) EXCEPTION FOR FUEL HELD IN AIRCRAFT FUEL TANK.—Paragraph (1) shall not apply to kerosene held in the fuel tank of an aircraft on January 1, 2005.

(3) LIABILITY FOR TAX AND METHOD OF PAYMENT.—

(A) LIABILITY FOR TAX.—The person holding the kerosene on January 1, 2005, to which the tax imposed by paragraph (1) applies shall be liable for such tax.

(B) METHOD AND TIME FOR PAYMENT.—The tax imposed by paragraph (1) shall be paid at such time and in such manner as the Secretary of the Treasury (or the Secretary's delegate) shall prescribe, including the nonapplication of such tax on de minimis amounts of kerosene.

(4) TRANSFER OF FLOOR STOCK TAX REVENUES TO TRUST FUNDS.—For purposes of determining the amount transferred to any trust fund, the tax imposed by this subsection shall be treated as imposed by section 4081 of the Internal Revenue Code of 1986—

(A) in any case in which tax was not imposed by section 4091 of such Code, at the Leaking Underground Storage Tank Trust Fund financing rate under such section to the extent of 0.1 cents per gallon, and

(B) at the rate under section 4081(a)(2)(A)(iv) of such Code to the extent of the remainder.

(5) HELD BY A PERSON.—For purposes of this subsection, kerosene shall be considered as held by a person if title thereto has passed to such person (whether or not delivery to the person has been made).

(6) OTHER LAWS APPLICABLE.—All provisions of law, including penalties, applicable with respect to the tax imposed by section 4081 of such Code shall, insofar as applicable and not inconsistent with the provisions of this subsection, apply with respect to the floor stock tax imposed by paragraph (1) to the same extent as if such tax were imposed by such section.

(f) REGULATIONS.—The Secretary shall prescribe such regulations as may be necessary to carry out this section, including regulations requiring the conspicuous labeling of retail diesel fuel and kerosene pumps and other delivery facilities to assure that persons are aware of which fuel is available only for nontaxable uses.

[CCH Explanation at ¶1507. Committee Reports at ¶11,340.]

Amendments

• **2004, American Jobs Creation Act of 2004 (H.R. 4520)**

H.R. 4520, § 853(a)(5)(A):

Amended Code Sec. 4082 by redesignating subsection (e) as subsection (f). **Effective** for aviation-grade kerosene re-

moved, entered, or sold after 12-31-2004. For special rules, see Act Sec. 853(f) in the amendment notes following Code Sec. 4082(e), above.

(g) CROSS REFERENCE.—

For tax on train and certain bus uses of fuel purchased tax-free, see *subsections (a)(1) and (d)(3) of section 4041.*

[CCH Explanation at ¶1507 and ¶1513. Committee Reports at ¶10,220 and ¶11,340.]

Amendments

• **2004, American Jobs Creation Act of 2004 (H.R. 4520)**

H.R. 4520, § 241(a)(2)(B):

Amended Code Sec. 4082(f) by striking "section 4041(a)(1)" and inserting "subsections (a)(1) and (d)(3) of section 4041". **Effective** on 1-1-2005.

H.R. 4520, § 853(a)(5)(A):

Amended Code Sec. 4082 by redesignating subsection (f) as subsection (g). **Effective** for aviation-grade kerosene removed, entered, or sold after 12-31-2004. For special rules, see Act Sec. 853(f) in the amendment notes following Code Sec. 4082(e), above.

[¶6020] CODE SEC. 4083. DEFINITIONS; SPECIAL RULE; ADMINISTRATIVE AUTHORITY.

(a) TAXABLE FUEL.—For purposes of this subpart—

* * *

(2) GASOLINE.—The term "gasoline"—

(A) includes any gasoline blend, other than qualified methanol or ethanol fuel (as defined in section 4041(b)(2)(B)), partially exempt methanol or ethanol fuel (as defined in section 4041(m)(2)), or a denatured alcohol, and

(B) includes, to the extent prescribed in regulations—

(i) any gasoline blend stock, and

(ii) any product commonly used as an additive in gasoline (other than alcohol).

(3) DIESEL FUEL.—

(A) IN GENERAL.—The term "diesel fuel" means—

(i) any liquid (other than gasoline) which is suitable for use as a fuel in a diesel-powered highway vehicle, or a diesel-powered train,

(ii) transmix, and

(iii) diesel fuel blend stocks identified by the Secretary.

(B) TRANSMIX.—For purposes of subparagraph (A), the term "transmix" means a byproduct of refined products pipeline operations created by the mixing of different specification products during pipeline transportation.

[CCH Explanation at ¶805 and ¶1509. Committee Reports at ¶10,320 and ¶11,510.]

Amendments

• **2004, American Jobs Creation Act of 2004 (H.R. 4520)**

H.R. 4520, §301(c)(8):

Amended Code Sec. 4083(a)(2). **Effective** for fuel sold or used after 12-31-2004. Prior to amendment, Code Sec. 4083(a)(2) read as follows:

(2) GASOLINE.—The term "gasoline" includes, to the extent prescribed in regulations—

(A) gasoline blend stocks, and

(B) products commonly used as additives in gasoline.

For purposes of subparagraph (A), the term "gasoline blend stock" means any petroleum product component of gasoline.

H.R. 4520, §870(a):

Amended Code Sec. 4083(a)(3). **Effective** for fuel removed, sold, or used after 12-31-2004. Prior to amendment, Code Sec. 4083(a)(3) read as follows:

(3) DIESEL FUEL.—The term "diesel fuel" means any liquid (other than gasoline) which is suitable for use as a fuel in a diesel-powered highway vehicle or a diesel-powered train.

(b) COMMERCIAL AVIATION.—For purposes of this subpart, the term "commercial aviation" means any use of an aircraft in a business of transporting persons or property for compensation or hire by air, unless properly allocable to any transportation exempt from the taxes imposed by sections 4261 and 4271 by reason of section 4281 or 4282 or by reason of section 4261(h).

[CCH Explanation at ¶1507. Committee Reports at ¶11,340.]

Amendments

• **2004, American Jobs Creation Act of 2004 (H.R. 4520)**

H.R. 4520, §853(b):

Amended Code Sec. 4083 by redesignating subsections (b) and (c) as subsections (c) and (d), respectively, and by inserting after subsection (a) a new subsection (b). **Effective** for aviation-grade kerosene removed, entered, or sold after 12-31-2004. For special rules, see Act Sec. 853(f), below.

H.R. 4520, §853(f), provides:

(f) FLOOR STOCKS TAX.—

(1) IN GENERAL.—There is hereby imposed on aviation-grade kerosene held on January 1, 2005, by any person a tax equal to—

(A) the tax which would have been imposed before such date on such kerosene had the amendments made by this section been in effect at all times before such date, reduced by

(B) the sum of—

(i) the tax imposed before such date on such kerosene under section 4091 of the Internal Revenue Code of 1986, as in effect on such date, and

(ii) in the case of kerosene held exclusively for such person's own use, the amount which such person would (but for this clause) reasonably expect (as of such date) to be paid as a refund under section 6427(l) of such Code with respect to such kerosene.

(2) EXCEPTION FOR FUEL HELD IN AIRCRAFT FUEL TANK.—Paragraph (1) shall not apply to kerosene held in the fuel tank of an aircraft on January 1, 2005.

(3) LIABILITY FOR TAX AND METHOD OF PAYMENT.—

(A) LIABILITY FOR TAX.—The person holding the kerosene on January 1, 2005, to which the tax imposed by paragraph (1) applies shall be liable for such tax.

(B) METHOD AND TIME FOR PAYMENT.—The tax imposed by paragraph (1) shall be paid at such time and in such manner as the Secretary of the Treasury (or the Secretary's delegate) shall prescribe, including the nonapplication of such tax on de minimis amounts of kerosene.

(4) TRANSFER OF FLOOR STOCK TAX REVENUES TO TRUST FUNDS.—For purposes of determining the amount transferred to any trust fund, the tax imposed by this subsection shall be treated as imposed by section 4081 of the Internal Revenue Code of 1986—

(A) in any case in which tax was not imposed by section 4091 of such Code, at the Leaking Underground Storage

Tank Trust Fund financing rate under such section to the extent of 0.1 cents per gallon, and

(B) at the rate under section 4081(a)(2)(A)(iv) of such Code to the extent of the remainder.

(5) HELD BY A PERSON.—For purposes of this subsection, kerosene shall be considered as held by a person if title thereto has passed to such person (whether or not delivery to the person has been made).

(6) OTHER LAWS APPLICABLE.—All provisions of law, including penalties, applicable with respect to the tax imposed by section 4081 of such Code shall, insofar as applicable and not inconsistent with the provisions of this subsection, apply with respect to the floor stock tax imposed by paragraph (1) to the same extent as if such tax were imposed by such section.

(c) CERTAIN USES DEFINED AS REMOVAL.—If any person uses taxable fuel (other than in the production of taxable fuels or special fuels referred to in section 4041), such use shall for the purposes of this chapter be considered a removal.

[CCH Explanation at ¶ 1507. Committee Reports at ¶ 11,340.]

Amendments

• **2004, American Jobs Creation Act of 2004 (H.R. 4520)**

H.R. 4520, § 853(b):

Amended Code Sec. 4083 by redesignating subsection (b) as subsection (c). **Effective** for aviation-grade kerosene re-

moved, entered, or sold after 12-31-2004. For special rules, see Act Sec. 853(f) in the amendment notes following Code Sec. 4083(b), above.

(d) ADMINISTRATIVE AUTHORITY.—

(1) IN GENERAL.—In addition to the authority otherwise granted by this title, the Secretary may in administering compliance with this subpart, section 4041, and penalties and other administrative provisions related thereto—

(A) enter any place at which taxable fuel is produced or is stored (or may be stored) for purposes of—

(i) examining the equipment used to determine the amount or composition of such fuel and the equipment used to store such fuel,

(ii) taking and removing samples of such fuel, and

(iii) inspecting any books and records and any shipping papers pertaining to such fuel, and

(B) detain, for the purposes referred in subparagraph (A), any container which contains or may contain any taxable fuel.

(2) INSPECTION SITES.—The Secretary may establish inspection sites for purposes of carrying out the Secretary's authority under paragraph (1)(B).

(3) PENALTY FOR REFUSAL OF *ENTRY*.—

(A) FORFEITURE.—The penalty provided by section 7342 shall apply to any refusal to admit entry or other refusal to permit an action by the Secretary authorized by paragraph (1), except that section 7342 shall be applied by substitution "$1,000" for "$500" for each such refusal.

(B) ASSESSABLE PENALTY.—For additional assessable penalty for the refusal to admit entry or other refusal to permit an action by the Secretary authorized by paragraph (1), see section 6717.

[CCH Explanation at ¶ 1539 and ¶ 1541. Committee Reports at ¶ 11,340, ¶ 11,390 and ¶ 11,400.]

Amendments

• **2004, American Jobs Creation Act of 2004 (H.R. 4520)**

H.R. 4520, § 853(b):

Amended Code Sec. 4083 by redesignating subsection (c) as subsection (d). **Effective** for aviation-grade kerosene removed, entered, or sold after 12-31-2004. For special rules, see Act Sec. 853(f) in the amendment notes following Code Sec. 4083(b), above.

H.R. 4520, § 858(a):

Amended Code Sec. 4083(d)(1)(A), as amended by Act Sec. 853(b), by striking "and" at the end of clause (i) and by

inserting after clause (ii) a new clause (iii). **Effective** on the date of the enactment of this Act.

H.R. 4520, § 859(b)(1)(A)-(B):

Amended Code Sec. 4083(d)(3), as amended by Act Sec. 853(b), by striking "ENTRY.—The penalty" and inserting: "ENTRY.—(A) FORFEITURE.—The penalty", and by adding at the end a new subparagraph (B). **Effective** 1-1-2005.

[¶ 6025] CODE SEC. 4091. IMPOSITION OF TAX. [*Stricken.*]

[CCH Explanation at ¶ 1507. Committee Reports at ¶ 11,340.]

Amendments

• 2004, American Jobs Creation Act of 2004 (H.R. 4520)

H.R. 4520, § 853(d)(1):

Amended part III of subchapter A of chapter 32 by striking subpart B (Code Secs. 4091-4093) and by redesignating subpart C as subpart B. **Effective** for aviation-grade kerosene removed, entered, or sold after 12-31-2004. Prior to being stricken, Code Sec. 4091 read as follows:

SEC. 4091. IMPOSITION OF TAX.

(a) TAX ON SALE.—

(1) IN GENERAL.—There is hereby imposed a tax on the sale of aviation fuel by the producer or the importer thereof or by any producer of aviation fuel.

(2) USE TREATED AS SALE.—For purposes of paragraph (1), if any producer uses aviation fuel (other than for a nontaxable use as defined in section 6427(l)(2)(B)) on which no tax has been imposed under such paragraph or on which tax has been credited or refunded, then such use shall be considered a sale.

(b) RATE OF TAX.—

(1) IN GENERAL.—The rate of the tax imposed by subsection (a) shall be 21.8 cents per gallon.

(2) LEAKING UNDERGROUND STORAGE TANK TRUST FUND TAX.—The rate of tax specified in paragraph (1) shall be increased by 0.1 cent per gallon. The increase in tax under this paragraph shall in this title be referred to as the Leaking Underground Storage Tank Trust Fund financing rate.

(3) TERMINATION.—

(A) The rate of tax specified in paragraph (1) shall be 4.3 cents per gallon—

(i) after December 31, 1996, and before the date which is 7 days after the date of the enactment of the Airport and Airway Trust Fund Tax Reinstatement Act of 1997, and

(ii) after September 30, 2007.

(B) The Leaking Underground Storage Tank Fund financing rate shall not apply during any period during which the Leaking Underground Storage Tank Trust Fund financing rate under section 4081 does not apply.

(c) REDUCED RATE OF TAX FOR AVIATION FUEL IN ALCOHOL MIXTURE, ETC.—Under regulations prescribed by the Secretary—

(1) IN GENERAL.—The rate of tax under subsection (a) shall be reduced by the applicable blender amount per gallon in the case of the sale of any mixture of aviation fuel if—

(A) at least 10 percent of such mixture consists of alcohol (as defined in section 4081(c)(3)), and

(B) the aviation fuel in such mixture was not taxed under paragraph (2).

In the case of such a mixture none of the alcohol in which is ethanol, the preceding sentence shall be applied by substituting "14 cents" for "the applicable blender amount". For purposes of this paragraph, the term "applicable blender amount" means 13.3 cents in the case of any sale or use during 2001 or 2002, 13.2 cents in the case of any sale or use during 2003 or 2004, 13.1 cents in the case of any sale or use during 2005, 2006, or 2007, and 13.4 cents in the case of any sale or use during 2008 or thereafter.

(2) TAX PRIOR TO MIXING.—In the case of the sale of aviation fuel for use (at the time of such sale) in producing a mixture described in paragraph (1), the rate of tax under subsection (a) shall be $^{10}/_9$ of the rate which would (but for this paragraph) have been applicable to such mixture had such mixture been created prior to such sale.

(3) LATER SEPARATION.—If any person separates the aviation fuel from a mixture of the aviation fuel and alcohol on which tax was imposed under subsection (a) at a rate determined under paragraph (1) or (2) (or with respect to which a credit or payment was allowed or made by reason of section 6427(f)(1)), such person shall be treated as the producer of such aviation fuel. The amount of tax imposed on any sale of such aviation fuel by such person shall be reduced by the amount of tax imposed (and not credited or refunded) on any prior sale of such fuel.

(4) LIMITATION.—In no event shall any rate determined under paragraph (1) be less than 4.3 cents per gallon.

(5) TERMINATION.—Paragraphs (1) and (2) shall not apply to any sale after September 30, 2007.

(d) REFUND OF TAX-PAID AVIATION FUEL TO REGISTERED PRODUCER OF FUEL.—If—

(1) a producer of aviation fuel is registered under section 4101, and

(2) such producer establishes to the satisfaction of the Secretary that a prior tax was paid (and not credited or refunded) on aviation fuel held by such producer,

then an amount equal to the tax so paid shall be allowed as a refund (without interest) to such producer in the same manner as if it were an overpayment of tax imposed by this section.

[¶ 6030] CODE SEC. 4092. EXEMPTIONS. [*Stricken.*]

[CCH Explanation at ¶ 1507. Committee Reports at ¶ 11,340.]

Amendments

• 2004, American Jobs Creation Act of 2004 (H.R. 4520)

H.R. 4520, § 853(d)(1):

Amended part III of subchapter A of chapter 32 by striking subpart B (Code Secs. 4091-4093) and by redesignating subpart C as subpart B. **Effective** for aviation-grade kerosene removed, entered, or sold after 12-31-2004. Prior to being stricken, Code Sec. 4092 read as follows:

SEC. 4092. EXEMPTIONS.

(a) NONTAXABLE USES.—No tax shall be imposed by section 4091 on aviation fuel sold by a producer or importer for use by the purchaser in a nontaxable use (as defined in section 6427(l)(2)(B)).

(b) NO EXEMPTION FROM CERTAIN TAXES ON FUEL USED IN COMMERCIAL AVIATION.—In the case of fuel sold for use in commercial aviation (other than supplies for vessels or aircraft within the meaning of section 4221(d)(3)), subsection (a) shall not apply to so much of the tax imposed by section 4091 as is attributable to—

(1) the Leaking Underground Storage Tank Trust Fund financing rate imposed by such section, and

(2) in the case of fuel sold after September 30, 1995, 4.3 cents per gallon of the rate specified in section 4091(b)(1).

For purposes of the preceding sentence, the term "commercial aviation" means any use of an aircraft other than in noncommercial aviation (as defined in section 4041(c)(2)).

(c) Sales to Producer.—Under regulations prescribed by the Secretary, the tax imposed by section 4091 shall not apply to aviation fuel sold to a producer of such fuel.

[¶6035] CODE SEC. 4093. DEFINITIONS. [*Stricken.*]

[CCH Explanation at ¶1507. Committee Reports at ¶11,340.]

Amendments

• **2004, American Jobs Creation Act of 2004 (H.R. 4520)**

H.R. 4520, §853(d)(1):

Amended part III of subchapter A of chapter 32 by striking subpart B (Code Secs. 4091-4093) and by redesignating subpart C as subpart B. **Effective** for aviation-grade kerosene removed, entered, or sold after 12-31-2004. Prior to being stricken, Code Sec. 4093 read as follows:

SEC. 4093. DEFINITIONS.

(a) Aviation Fuel.—For purposes of this subpart, the term "aviation fuel" means kerosene and any other liquid (other than any product taxable under section 4081) which is suitable for use as a fuel in an aircraft.

(b) Producer.—For purposes of this subpart—

(1) Certain persons treated as producers.—

(A) In general.—The term "producer" includes any person described in subparagraph (B) and registered under section 4101 with respect to the tax imposed by section 4091.

(B) Persons described.—A person is described in this subparagraph if such person is—

(i) a refiner, blender, or wholesale distributor of aviation fuel, or

(ii) a dealer selling aviation fuel exclusively to producers of aviation fuel.

(C) Reduced rate purchasers treated as producers.—Any person to whom aviation fuel is sold at a reduced rate under this subpart shall be treated as the producer of such fuel.

(2) Wholesale distributor.—For purposes of paragraph (1), the term "wholesale distributor" includes any person who sells aviation fuel to producers, retailers, or to users who purchase in bulk quantities and accept delivery into bulk storage tanks. Such term does not include any person who (excluding the term "wholesale distributor" from paragraph (1)) is a producer or importer.

[¶6040] CODE SEC. 4101. REGISTRATION AND BOND.

⟫⟶ *Caution: Code Sec. 4101(a), below, as amended by H.R. 4520, Act Secs. 853(d)(2)(F), 861(a)(1)-(2), and 862(a), but prior to amendment by Act Sec. 301(b), is effective January 1, 2005, through March 31, 2005.*

(a) Registration.—

(1) In General.—Every person required by the Secretary to register under this section with respect to the tax imposed by section 4041(a)(1)*or 4081* shall register with the Secretary at such time, in such form and manner, and subject to such terms and conditions, as the Secretary may by regulations prescribe. A registration under this section may be used only in accordance with regulations prescribed under this section.

(2) Registration of persons within foreign trade zones, etc.—The Secretary shall require registration by any person which—

(A) operates a terminal or refinery within a foreign trade zone or within a customs bonded storage facility, or

(B) holds an inventory position with respect to a taxable fuel in such a terminal.

(3) Display of registration.—Every operator of a vessel required by the Secretary to register under this section shall display proof of registration through an identification device prescribed by the Secretary on each vessel used by such operator to transport any taxable fuel.

⟫⟶ *Caution: Code Sec. 4101(a), below, as amended by H.R. 4520, Act Secs. 853(d)(2)(F), 861(a)(1)-(2), and 862(a), and as further amended by Act Sec. 301(b), is effective April 1, 2005.*

(a) Registration .—

(1) In General.—Every person required by the Secretary to register under this section with respect to the tax imposed by section 4041(a)(1)*or 4081 and every person producing or importing biodiesel (as defined in section 40A(d)(1)) or alcohol (as defined in section 6426(b)(4)(A))* shall register with the Secretary at such time, in such form and manner, and subject to such terms and conditions, as the Secretary may by regulations prescribe. A registration under this section may be used only in accordance with regulations prescribed under this section.

(2) Registration of persons within foreign trade zones, etc.—The Secretary shall require registration by any person which—

(A) operates a terminal or refinery within a foreign trade zone or within a customs bonded storage facility, or

(B) holds an inventory position with respect to a taxable fuel in such a terminal.

(3) DISPLAY OF REGISTRATION.—Every operator of a vessel required by the Secretary to register under this section shall display proof of registration through an identification device prescribed by the Secretary on each vessel used by such operator to transport any taxable fuel.

* * *

[CCH Explanation at ¶805, ¶1507, ¶1529 and ¶1535. Committee Reports at ¶10,320, ¶11,340, ¶11,420 and ¶11,430.]

Amendments

• **2004, American Jobs Creation Act of 2004 (H.R. 4520)**

H.R. 4520, §301(b):

Amended Code Sec. 4101(a)(1), as amended by Act Sec. 861, by inserting "and every person producing or importing biodiesel (as defined in section 40A(d)(1)) or alcohol (as defined in section 6426(b)(4)(A))" before "shall register with the Secretary". **Effective** 4-1-2005.

H.R. 4520, §853(d)(2)(F):

Amended Code Sec. 4101(a) by striking ", 4081, or 4091" and inserting "or 4081". **Effective** for aviation-grade kerosene removed, entered, or sold after 12-31-2004. For special rules, see Act Sec. 853(f), below.

H.R. 4520, §853(f), provides:

(f) FLOOR STOCKS TAX.—

(1) IN GENERAL.—There is hereby imposed on aviation-grade kerosene held on January 1, 2005, by any person a tax equal to—

(A) the tax which would have been imposed before such date on such kerosene had the amendments made by this section been in effect at all times before such date, reduced by

(B) the sum of—

(i) the tax imposed before such date on such kerosene under section 4091 of the Internal Revenue Code of 1986, as in effect on such date, and

(ii) in the case of kerosene held exclusively for such person's own use, the amount which such person would (but for this clause) reasonably expect (as of such date) to be paid as a refund under section 6427(l) of such Code with respect to such kerosene.

(2) EXCEPTION FOR FUEL HELD IN AIRCRAFT FUEL TANK.—Paragraph (1) shall not apply to kerosene held in the fuel tank of an aircraft on January 1, 2005.

(3) LIABILITY FOR TAX AND METHOD OF PAYMENT.—

(A) LIABILITY FOR TAX.—The person holding the kerosene on January 1, 2005, to which the tax imposed by paragraph (1) applies shall be liable for such tax.

(B) METHOD AND TIME FOR PAYMENT.—The tax imposed by paragraph (1) shall be paid at such time and in such manner as the Secretary of the Treasury (or the Secretary's delegate) shall prescribe, including the nonapplication of such tax on de minimis amounts of kerosene.

(4) TRANSFER OF FLOOR STOCK TAX REVENUES TO TRUST FUNDS.—For purposes of determining the amount transferred to any trust fund, the tax imposed by this subsection shall be treated as imposed by section 4081 of the Internal Revenue Code of 1986—

(A) in any case in which tax was not imposed by section 4091 of such Code, at the Leaking Underground Storage Tank Trust Fund financing rate under such section to the extent of 0.1 cents per gallon, and

(B) at the rate under section 4081(a)(2)(A)(iv) of such Code to the extent of the remainder.

(5) HELD BY A PERSON.—For purposes of this subsection, kerosene shall be considered as held by a person if title thereto has passed to such person (whether or not delivery to the person has been made).

(6) OTHER LAWS APPLICABLE.—All provisions of law, including penalties, applicable with respect to the tax imposed by section 4081 of such Code shall, insofar as applicable and not inconsistent with the provisions of this subsection, apply with respect to the floor stock tax imposed by paragraph (1) to the same extent as if such tax were imposed by such section.

H.R. 4520, §861(a)(1)-(2):

Amended Code Sec. 4101(a) by striking "Every" and inserting "(1) IN GENERAL.—Every", and by adding at the end a new paragraph (2). **Effective** 1-1-2005.

H.R. 4520, §862(a):

Amended Code Sec. 4101(a), as amended by this Act, by redesignating paragraph (2) as paragraph (3), and by inserting after paragraph (1) a new paragraph (2). **Effective** 1-1-2005.

⯈⯈⯈ *Caution: Code Sec. 4101(d), below, as amended by H.R. 4520, is effective on January 1, 2006.*

(d) INFORMATION REPORTING.—The Secretary may require—

(1) information reporting by any person registered under this section, and

(2) information reporting by such other persons as the Secretary deems necessary to carry out this part.

Any person who is required to report under this subsection and who has 25 or more reportable transactions in a month shall file such report in electronic format.

¶6040   Code Sec. 4101(a)(2)(A)

[CCH Explanation at ¶1531. Committee Reports at ¶11,450.]

Amendments

• **2004, American Jobs Creation Act of 2004 (H.R. 4520)**

H.R. 4520, §864(a):

Amended Code Sec. 4101(d) by adding at the end a new flush sentence. **Effective** 1-1-2006.

[¶6045] CODE SEC. 4103. CERTAIN ADDITIONAL PERSONS LIABLE FOR TAX WHERE WILLFUL FAILURE TO PAY.

In any case in which there is a willful failure to pay the tax imposed by section 4041(a)(1)*or 4081*, each person—

(1) who is an officer, employee, or agent of the taxpayer who is under a duty to assure the payment of such tax and who willfully fails to perform such duty, or

(2) who willfully causes the taxpayer to fail to pay such tax,

shall be jointly and severally liable with the taxpayer for the tax to which such failure relates.

[CCH Explanation at ¶1507. Committee Reports at ¶11,340.]

Amendments

• **2004, American Jobs Creation Act of 2004 (H.R. 4520)**

H.R. 4520, §853(d)(2)(F):

Amended Code Sec. 4103 by striking ", 4081, or 4091" and inserting "or 4081". **Effective** for aviation-grade kerosene removed, entered, or sold after 12-31-2004.

[¶6050] CODE SEC. 4104. INFORMATION REPORTING FOR PERSONS CLAIMING CERTAIN TAX BENEFITS.

(a) *In General.—The Secretary shall require any person claiming tax benefits—*

(1) *under the provisions of section 34, 40, and 40A, to file a return at the time such person claims such benefits (in such manner as the Secretary may prescribe), and*

(2) *under the provisions of section 4041(b)(2), 6426, or 6427(e) to file a quarterly return (in such manner as the Secretary may prescribe).*

(b) *Contents of Return.—Any return filed under this section shall provide such information relating to such benefits and the coordination of such benefits as the Secretary may require to ensure the proper administration and use of such benefits.*

(c) *Enforcement.—With respect to any person described in subsection (a) and subject to registration requirements under this title, rules similar to rules of section 4222(c) shall apply with respect to any requirement under this section.*

[CCH Explanation at ¶815. Committee Reports at ¶10,330.]

Amendments

• **2004, American Jobs Creation Act of 2004 (H.R. 4520)**

H.R. 4520, §303(a):

Amended subpart C of part III of subchapter A of chapter 32 by adding at the end a new Code Sec. 4104. **Effective** 1-1-2005.

[¶6055] CODE SEC. 4105. TWO-PARTY EXCHANGES.

(a) *In General.—In a two-party exchange, the delivering person shall not be liable for the tax imposed under of [sic] section 4081(a)(1)(A)(ii).*

(b) *Two-Party Exchange.—The term "two-party exchange" means a transaction, other than a sale, in which taxable fuel is transferred from a delivering person registered under section 4101 as a taxable fuel registrant to a receiving person who is so registered where all of the following occur:*

(1) The transaction includes a transfer from the delivering person, who holds the inventory position for taxable fuel in the terminal as reflected in the records of the terminal operator.

(2) The exchange transaction occurs before or contemporaneous with completion of removal across the rack from the terminal by the receiving person.

(3) The terminal operator in its books and records treats the receiving person as the person that removes the product across the terminal rack for purposes of reporting the transaction to the Secretary.

(4) The transaction is the subject of a written contract.

* * *

[CCH Explanation at ¶1505. Committee Reports at ¶11,470.]

Amendments

• **2004, American Jobs Creation Act of 2004 (H.R. 4520)**

H.R. 4520, § 866(a):

Amended subpart C of part III of subchapter A of chapter 32, as amended by this Act, by inserting after Code Sec. 4104 a new Code Sec. 4105. **Effective** on the date of the enactment of this Act.

[¶6060] CODE SEC. 4132. DEFINITIONS AND SPECIAL RULES.

(a) Definitions Relating to Taxable Vaccines.—For purposes of this subchapter—

(1) Taxable vaccine.—The term "taxable vaccine" means any of the following vaccines which are manufactured or produced in the United States or entered into the United States for consumption, use, or warehousing:

(A) Any vaccine containing diphtheria toxoid.

(B) Any vaccine containing tetanus toxoid.

(C) Any vaccine containing pertussis bacteria, extracted or partial cell bacteria, or specific pertussis antigens.

(D) Any vaccine against measles.

(E) Any vaccine against mumps.

(F) Any vaccine against rubella.

(G) Any vaccine containing polio virus.

(H) Any HIB vaccine.

(I) Any vaccine against hepatitis A.

(J) Any vaccine against hepatitis B.

(K) Any vaccine against chicken pox.

(L) Any vaccine against rotavirus gastroenteritis.

(M) Any conjugate vaccine against streptococcus pneumoniae.

(N) Any trivalent vaccine against influenza.

* * *

[CCH Explanation at ¶1565. Committee Reports at ¶11,610 and ¶11,620.]

Amendments

• **2004, American Jobs Creation Act of 2004 (H.R. 4520)**

H.R. 4520, § 889(a):

Amended Code Sec. 4132(a)(1) by redesignating subparagraphs (I), (J), (K), and (L) as subparagraphs (J), (K), (L), and (M), respectively, and by inserting after subparagraph (H) a new subparagraph (I). For the **effective** date, see Act Sec. 889(b)(1)-(2), below.

H.R. 4520, § 889(b)(1)-(2), provides:

(b) Effective Date.—

(1) Sales, etc.—The amendments made by subsection (a) shall apply to sales and uses on or after the first day of the first month which begins more than 4 weeks after the date of the enactment of this Act.

(2) Deliveries.—For purposes of paragraph (1) and section 4131 of the Internal Revenue Code of 1986, in the case of sales on or before the effective date described in such paragraph for which delivery is made after such date, the delivery date shall be considered the sale date.

H.R. 4520, § 890(a):

Amended Code Sec. 4132(a)(1), as amended by Act Sec. 889(a), by adding at the end a new subparagraph (N). For the **effective** date, see Act Sec. 890(b)(1)-(2), below.

H.R. 4520, § 890(b)(1)-(2), provides:

(b) Effective Date.—

(1) SALES, ETC.—The amendment made by this section shall apply to sales and uses on or after the later of—

(A) the first day of the first month which begins more than 4 weeks after the date of the enactment of this Act, or

(B) the date on which the Secretary of Health and Human Services lists any vaccine against influenza for purposes of compensation for any vaccine-related injury or death through the Vaccine Injury Compensation Trust Fund.

(2) DELIVERIES.—For purposes of paragraph (1) and section 4131 of the Internal Revenue Code of 1986, in the case of sales on or before the effective date described in such paragraph for which delivery is made after such date, the delivery date shall be considered the sale date.

[¶ 6065] CODE SEC. 4161. IMPOSITION OF TAX.

(a) SPORT FISHING EQUIPMENT.—

* * *

(3) 3 PERCENT RATE OF TAX FOR TACKLE BOXES.—*In the case of fishing tackle boxes, paragraph (1) shall be applied by substituting "3 percent" for "10 percent".*

(4) PARTS OR ACCESSORIES SOLD IN CONNECTION WITH TAXABLE SALE.—In the case of any sale by the manufacturer, producer, or importer of any article of sport fishing equipment, such article shall be treated as including any parts or accessories of such article sold on or in connection therewith or with the sale thereof.

[CCH Explanation at ¶ 1559. Committee Reports at ¶ 10,480.]

Amendments

• **2004, American Jobs Creation Act of 2004 (H.R. 4520)**

H.R. 4520, § 333(a):

Amended Code Sec. 4161(a) by redesignating paragraph (3) as paragraph (4) and by inserting after paragraph (2) a

new paragraph (3). **Effective** for articles sold by the manufacturer, producer, or importer after 12-31-2004.

(b) BOWS AND ARROWS, ETC.—

(1) BOWS.—

(A) IN GENERAL.—*There is hereby imposed on the sale by the manufacturer, producer, or importer of any bow which has a peak draw weight of 30 pounds or more, a tax equal to 11 percent of the price for which so sold.*

(B) ARCHERY EQUIPMENT.—*There is hereby imposed on the sale by the manufacturer, producer, or importer—*

(i) *of any part or accessory suitable for inclusion in or attachment to a bow described in subparagraph (A), and*

(ii) *of any quiver or broadhead suitable for use with an arrow described in paragraph (2),*

a tax equal to 11 percent of the price for which so sold.

(2) ARROW COMPONENTS.—There is hereby imposed on the sale by the manufacturer, producer, or importer of any shaft, point *(other than broadheads)*, nock, or vane of a type used in the manufacture of any arrow which after its assembly—

(A) measures 18 inches overall or more in length, or

(B) measures less than 18 inches overall in length but is suitable for use with a bow described in paragraph (1)(A),

a tax equal to 12.4 percent of the price for which so sold.

(3) ARROWS.—

(A) IN GENERAL.—*There is hereby imposed on the sale by the manufacturer, producer, or importer of any arrow, a tax equal to 12 percent of the price for which so sold.*

(B) EXCEPTION.—*In the case of any arrow of which the shaft or any other component has been previously taxed under paragraph (1) or (2)—*

(i) *section 6416(b)(3) shall not apply, and*

(ii) *the tax imposed by subparagraph (A) shall be an amount equal to the excess (if any) of—*

(I) *the amount of tax imposed by this paragraph (determined without regard to this subparagraph), over*

(II) *the amount of tax paid with respect to the tax imposed under paragraph (1) or (2) on such shaft or component.*

(C) ARROW.—*For purposes of this paragraph, the term "arrow" means any shaft described in paragraph (2) to which additional components are attached.*

(4) COORDINATION WITH SUBSECTION (a).—No tax shall be imposed under this subsection with respect to any article taxable under subsection (a).

[CCH Explanation at ¶1557. Committee Reports at ¶10,470.]

Amendments

• **2004, American Jobs Creation Act of 2004 (H.R. 4520)**

H.R. 4520, §332(a):

Amended Code Sec. 4161(b)(1). **Effective** for articles sold by the manufacturer, producer, or importer after the date which is 30 days after the date of the enactment of this Act. Prior to amendment, Code Sec. 4161(b)(1) read as follows:

(1) BOWS.—

(A) IN GENERAL.—There is hereby imposed on the sale by the manufacturer, producer, or importer of any bow which has a draw weight of 10 pounds or more, a tax equal to 11 percent of the price for which so sold.

(B) PARTS AND ACCESSORIES.—There is hereby imposed upon the sale by the manufacturer, producer, or importer—

(i) of any part of accessory suitable for inclusion in or attachment to a bow described in subparagraph (A), and

(ii) of any quiver suitable for use with arrows described in paragraph (2), a tax equivalent to 11 percent of the price for which so sold.

H.R. 4520, §332(b):

Amended Code Sec. 4161(b) by redesignating paragraph (3) as paragraph (4) and inserting after paragraph (2) a new paragraph (3). **Effective** for articles sold by the manufacturer, producer, or importer after the date which is 30 days after the date of the enactment of this Act.

H.R. 4520, §332(c)(1)-(2):

Amended Code Sec. 4161(b)(2) by inserting "(other than broadheads)" after "point", and by striking "ARROWS.—"in the heading and inserting "ARROW COMPONENTS.—". **Effective** for articles sold by the manufacturer, producer, or importer after the date which is 30 days after the date of the enactment of this Act.

[¶6070] CODE SEC. 4162. DEFINITIONS; TREATMENT OF CERTAIN RESALES.

(a) SPORT FISHING EQUIPMENT DEFINED.—For purposes of this part, the term "sport fishing equipment" means—

* * *

(8) fishing rod belts, fishing rodholders, fishing harnesses, fish fighting chairs, fishing outriggers, and fishing downriggers, *and*

(9) electric outboard boat motors.

(10) [*Stricken.*]

[CCH Explanation at ¶1561. Committee Reports at ¶10,490.]

Amendments

• **2004, American Jobs Creation Act of 2004 (H.R. 4520)**

H.R. 4520, §334(a):

Amended Code Sec. 4162(a) by inserting "and" at the end of paragraph (8), by striking ", and" at the end of paragraph

(9) and inserting a period, and by striking paragraph (10). **Effective** for articles sold by the manufacturer, producer, or importer after 12-31-2004. Prior to being stricken, Code Sec. 4162(a)(10) read as follows:

(10) sonar devices suitable for finding fish.

(b) TREATMENT OF CERTAIN RESALES.—

* * *

[CCH Explanation at ¶1561. Committee Reports at ¶10,490.]

Amendments

• **2004, American Jobs Creation Act of 2004 (H.R. 4520)**

H.R. 4520, §334(b):

Amended Code Sec. 4162 by striking subsection (b) and by redesignating subsection (c) as subsection (b). **Effective** for articles sold by the manufacturer, producer, or importer after 12-31-2004. Prior to being stricken, Code Sec. 4162(b) read as follows:

(b) SONAR DEVICE SUITABLE FOR FINDING FISH.—For purposes of this part, the term "sonar device suitable for finding fish" shall not include any sonar device which is—

(1) a graph recorder,

(2) a digital type,

(3) a meter readout, or

(4) a combination graph recorder or combination meter readout.

[¶ 6075] CODE SEC. 4221. CERTAIN TAX-FREE SALES.

(a) GENERAL RULE.—Under regulations prescribed by the Secretary, no tax shall be imposed under this chapter (other than under section 4121 *or 4081*) on the sale by the manufacturer (or under subchapter A or C of chapter 31 on the first retail sale) of an article—

(1) for use by the purchaser for further manufacture, or for resale by the purchaser to a second purchaser for use by such second purchaser in further manufacture,

(2) for export, or for resale by the purchaser to a second purchaser for export,

(3) for use by the purchaser as supplies for vessels or aircraft,

(4) to a State or local government for the exclusive use of a State or local government, or

(5) to a nonprofit educational organization for its exclusive use,

but only if such exportation or use is to occur before any other use. Paragraphs (4) and (5) shall not apply to the tax imposed by section 4064. In the case of taxes imposed by section 4051 or 4071, paragraphs (4) and (5) shall not apply on and after October 1, 2005. In the case of the tax imposed by section 4131, paragraphs (3), (4), and (5) shall not apply and paragraph (2) shall apply only if the use of the exported vaccine meets such requirements as the Secretary may by regulations prescribe. In the case of taxes imposed by subchapter A of chapter 31, paragraphs (1), (3), (4), and (5) shall not apply.

* * *

[CCH Explanation at ¶ 1507. Committee Reports at ¶ 11,340.]

Amendments

• **2004, American Jobs Creation Act of 2004 (H.R. 4520)**

H.R. 4520, § 853(d)(2)(F):

Amended Code Sec. 4221(a) by striking ", 4081, or 4091" and inserting "or 4081". **Effective** for aviation-grade kerosene removed, entered, or sold after 12-31-2004.

[¶ 6080] CODE SEC. 4481. IMPOSITION OF TAX.

* * *

(c) PRORATION OF TAX.—

* * *

(2) WHERE VEHICLE *SOLD, DESTROYED, OR STOLEN.*—

(A) IN GENERAL.—If in any taxable period a highway motor vehicle is *sold, destroyed, or stolen* before the first day of the last month in such period and not subsequently used during such taxable period, the tax shall be reckoned proportionately from the first day of the month in such period in which the first use of such highway motor vehicle occurs to and including the last day of the month in which such highway motor vehicle was *sold, destroyed, or stolen.*

(B) DESTROYED.—For purposes of subparagraph (A), a highway motor vehicle is destroyed if such vehicle is damaged by reason of an accident or other casualty to such an extent that it is not economic to rebuild.

* * *

[CCH Explanation at ¶ 1547. Committee Reports at ¶ 11,480.]

Amendments

• **2004, American Jobs Creation Act of 2004 (H.R. 4520)**

H.R. 4520, § 867(a)(1):

Amended Code Sec. 4481(c)(2)(A) by striking "destroyed or stolen" both places it appears and inserting "sold, destroyed, or stolen". **Effective** for tax periods beginning after the date of the enactment of this Act.

H.R. 4520, § 867(a)(2):

Amended the heading for Code Sec. 4481(c)(2) by striking "DESTROYED OR STOLEN" and inserting "SOLD, DESTROYED, OR STOLEN". **Effective** for tax periods beginning after the date of the enactment of this Act.

(e) ELECTRONIC FILING.—*Any taxpayer who files a return under this section with respect to 25 or more vehicles for any taxable period shall file such return electronically.*

[CCH Explanation at ¶ 1547. Committee Reports at ¶ 11,480.]

Amendments

• 2004, American Jobs Creation Act of 2004 (H.R. 4520)

H.R. 4520, § 867(c):

Amended Code Sec. 4481 by redesignating subsection (e) as subsection (f) and by inserting after subsection (d) a new

(f) PERIOD TAX IN EFFECT.—The tax imposed by this section shall apply only to use before October 1, 2005.

* * *

subsection (e). **Effective** for tax periods beginning after the date of the enactment of this Act.

[CCH Explanation at ¶ 1547. Committee Reports at ¶ 11,480.]

Amendments

• 2004, American Jobs Creation Act of 2004 (H.R. 4520)

H.R. 4520, § 867(c):

Amended Code Sec. 4481 by redesignating subsection (e) as subsection (f). **Effective** for tax periods beginning after the date of the enactment of this Act.

[¶ 6085] CODE SEC. 4483. EXEMPTIONS.

* * *

(f) [*Stricken.*]

[CCH Explanation at ¶ 1547. Committee Reports at ¶ 11,480.]

Amendments

• 2004, American Jobs Creation Act of 2004 (H.R. 4520)

H.R. 4520, § 867(d):

Amended Code Sec. 4483 by striking subsection (f). **Effective** for tax periods beginning after the date of the enactment of this Act. Prior to being stricken, Code Sec. 4483(f) read as follows:

(f) REDUCTION IN TAX FOR TRUCKS BASE-PLATED IN A CONTIGUOUS FOREIGN COUNTRY.—If the base for registration purposes of any highway motor vehicle is in a contiguous foreign country for any taxable period, the tax imposed by section 4481 for such period shall be 75 percent of the tax which would (but for this subsection) be imposed by section 4481 for such period.

(g) EXEMPTION FOR MOBILE MACHINERY.—No tax shall be imposed by section 4481 on the use of any vehicle described in section 4053(8).

[CCH Explanation at ¶ 1549. Committee Reports at ¶ 11,320.]

Amendments

• 2004, American Jobs Creation Act of 2004 (H.R. 4520)

H.R. 4520, § 851(b)(1):

Amended Code Sec. 4483 by redesignating subsection (g) as subsection (h) and by inserting after subsection (f) a new

(h) TERMINATION OF EXEMPTIONS.—Subsections (a) and (c) shall not apply on and after October 1, 2005.

* * *

subsection (g). **Effective** on the day after the date of the enactment of this Act.

[CCH Explanation at ¶ 1549. Committee Reports at ¶ 11,320.]

Amendments

• 2004, American Jobs Creation Act of 2004 (H.R. 4520)

H.R. 4520, § 851(b)(1):

Amended Code Sec. 4483 by redesignating subsection (g) as subsection (h). **Effective** on the day after the date of the enactment of this Act.

[¶6090] CODE SEC. 4947. APPLICATION OF TAXES TO CERTAIN NONEXEMPT TRUSTS.

(a) APPLICATION OF TAX.—

(1) CHARITABLE TRUSTS.—For purposes of part II of subchapter F of chapter 1 (other than section 508(a), (b), and (c)) and for purposes of this chapter, a trust which is not exempt from taxation under section 501(a), all of the unexpired interests in which are devoted to one or more of the purposes described in section 170(c)(2)(B), and for which a deduction was allowed under section 170, 545(b)(2), 642(c), 2055, 2106(a)(2), or 2522 (or the corresponding provisions of prior law), shall be treated as an organization described in section 501(c)(3). For purposes of section 509(a)(3)(A), such a trust shall be treated as if organized on the day on which it first becomes subject to this paragraph.

(2) SPLIT-INTEREST TRUSTS.—In the case of a trust which is not exempt from tax under section 501(a), not all of the unexpired interests in which are devoted to one or more of the purposes described in section 170(c)(2)(B), and which has amounts in trust for which a deduction was allowed under section 170, 545(b)(2), 642(c), 2055, 2106(a)(2), or 2522, section 507 (relating to termination of private foundation status), section 508(e) (relating to governing instruments) to the extent applicable to a trust described in this paragraph, section 4941 (relating to taxes on self-dealing), section 4943 (relating to taxes on excess business holdings) except as provided in subsection (b)(3), section 4944 (relating to investments which jeopardize charitable purpose) except as provided in subsection (b)(3), and section 4945 (relating to taxes on taxable expenditures) shall apply as if such trust were a private foundation. This paragraph shall not apply with respect to—

(A) any amounts payable under the terms of such trust to income beneficiaries, unless a deduction was allowed under section 170(f)(2)(B), 2055(e)(2)(B), or 2522(c)(2)(B),

(B) any amounts in trust other than amounts for which a deduction was allowed under section 170, 545(b)(2), 642(c), 2055, 2106(a)(2), or 2522, if such other amounts are segregated from amounts for which no deduction was allowable, or

(C) any amounts transferred in trust before May 27, 1969.

* * *

[CCH Explanation at ¶490. Committee Reports at ¶10,690.]

Amendments

• 2004, American Jobs Creation Act of 2004 (H.R. 4520)

H.R. 4520, §413(c)(30):

Amended Code Sec. 4947 by striking "556(b)(2)," immediately preceding "642(c), 2055," each place it appears. Effective for tax years of foreign corporations beginning after 12-31-2004, and for tax years of United States shareholders with or within which such tax years of foreign corporations end.

(b) SPECIAL RULES.—

* * *

(3) SECTIONS 4943 AND 4944 .—Sections 4943 and 4944 shall not apply to a trust which is described in subsection (a)(2) if—

(A) all the income interest (and none of the remainder interest) of such trust is devoted solely to one or more of the purposes described in section 170(c)(2)(B), and all amounts in such trust for which a deduction was allowed under section 170, 545(b)(2), 642(c), 2055, 2106(a)(2), or 2522 have an aggregate value not more than 60 percent of the aggregate fair market value of all amounts in such trusts, or

(B) a deduction was allowed under section 170, 545(b)(2), 642(c), 2055, 2106(a)(2), or 2522 for amounts payable under the terms of such trust to every remainder beneficiary but not to any income beneficiary.

* * *

[CCH Explanation at ¶ 490. Committee Reports at ¶ 10,690.]

Amendments

• **2004, American Jobs Creation Act of 2004 (H.R. 4520)**

H.R. 4520, § 413(c)(30):

Amended Code Sec. 4947 by striking "556(b)(2)," immediately preceding "642(c), 2055," each place it appears. **Effec-** tive for tax years of foreign corporations beginning after 12-31-2004, and for tax years of United States shareholders with or within which such tax years of foreign corporations end.

[¶ 6095] CODE SEC. 4948. APPLICATION OF TAXES AND DENIAL OF EXEMPTION WITH RESPECT TO CERTAIN FOREIGN ORGANIZATIONS.

* * *

(c) DENIAL OF EXEMPTION TO FOREIGN ORGANIZATIONS ENGAGED IN PROHIBITED TRANSACTIONS.—

* * *

(4) DISALLOWANCE OF CERTAIN CHARITABLE DEDUCTIONS.—No gift or bequest shall be allowed as a deduction under section 170, 545(b)(2), 642(c), 2055, 2106(a)(2), or 2522, if made—

(A) to a foreign organization described in subsection (b) after the date on which the Secretary publishes notice under paragraph (3)(A) that he has notified such organization that it has engaged in a prohibited transaction, and

(B) in a taxable year of such organization for which it is not exempt from taxation under section 501(a) by reason of paragraph (1).

* * *

[CCH Explanation at ¶ 490. Committee Reports at ¶ 10,690.]

Amendments

• **2004, American Jobs Creation Act of 2004 (H.R. 4520)**

H.R. 4520, § 413(c)(30):

Amended Code Sec. 4948(c)(4) by striking "556(b)(2)," immediately preceding "642(c), 2055,". **Effective** for tax years of foreign corporations beginning after 12-31-2004, and for tax years of United States shareholders with or within which such tax years of foreign corporations end.

[¶ 6100] CODE SEC. 4975. TAX ON PROHIBITED TRANSACTIONS.

* * *

(d) EXEMPTIONS.—Except as provided in subsection (f)(6), the prohibitions provided in subsection (c) shall not apply to—

* * *

(14) any transaction required or permitted under part 1 of subtitle E of title IV or section 4223 of the Employee Retirement Income Security Act of 1974, but this paragraph shall not apply with respect to the application of subsection (c)(1)(E) or (F);

(15) a merger of multiemployer plans, or the transfer of assets or liabilities between multiemployer plans, determined by the Pension Benefit Guaranty Corporation to meet the requirements of section 4231 of such Act, but this paragraph shall not apply with respect to the application of subsection (c)(1)(E) or (F); or

(16) a sale of stock held by a trust which constitutes an individual retirement account under section 408(a) to the individual for whose benefit such account is established if—

(A) such stock is in a bank (as defined in section 581),

(B) such stock is held by such trust as of the date of the enactment of this paragraph,

(C) such sale is pursuant to an election under section 1362(a) by such bank,

(D) such sale is for fair market value at the time of sale (as established by an independent appraiser) and the terms of the sale are otherwise at least as favorable to such trust as the terms that would apply on a sale to an unrelated party,

(E) such trust does not pay any commissions, costs, or other expenses in connection with the sale, and

(F) the stock is sold in a single transaction for cash not later than 120 days after the S corporation election is made.

* * *

[CCH Explanation at ¶940. Committee Reports at ¶10,140.]
Amendments
• **2004, American Jobs Creation Act of 2004 (H.R. 4520)**

H.R. 4520, §233(c):

Amended Code Sec. 4975(d) by striking "or" at the end of paragraph (14), by striking the period at the end of para-graph (15) and inserting "; or", and by adding at the end a new paragraph (16). **Effective** on the date of the enactment of this Act.

(f) OTHER DEFINITIONS AND SPECIAL RULES.—For purposes of this section—

* * *

(7) S CORPORATION REPAYMENT OF LOANS FOR QUALIFYING EMPLOYER SECURITIES.—A plan shall not be treated as violating the requirements of section 401 or 409 or subsection (e)(7), or as engaging in a prohibited transaction for purposes of subsection (d)(3), merely by reason of any distribution (as described in section 1368(a)) with respect to S corporation stock that constitutes qualifying employer securities, which in accordance with the plan provisions is used to make payments on a loan described in subsection (d)(3) the proceeds of which were used to acquire such qualifying employer securities (whether or not allocated to participants). The preceding sentence shall not apply in the case of a distribution which is paid with respect to any employer security which is allocated to a participant unless the plan provides that employer securities with a fair market value of not less than the amount of such distribution are allocated to such participant for the year which (but for the preceding sentence) such distribution would have been allocated to such participant.

* * *

[CCH Explanation at ¶935. Committee Reports at ¶10,210.]
Amendments
• **2004, American Jobs Creation Act of 2004 (H.R. 4520)**

H.R. 4520, §240(a):

Amended Code Sec. 4975(f) by adding at the end a new paragraph (7). **Effective** for distributions with respect to S corporation stock made after 12-31-97.

[¶6105] *CODE SEC. 4985. STOCK COMPENSATION OF INSIDERS IN EXPATRIATED CORPORATIONS.*

(a) IMPOSITION OF TAX.—In the case of an individual who is a disqualified individual with respect to any expatriated corporation, there is hereby imposed on such person a tax equal to—

(1) the rate of tax specified in section 1(h)(1)(C), multiplied by

(2) the value (determined under subsection (b)) of the specified stock compensation held (directly or indirectly) by or for the benefit of such individual or a member of such individual's family (as defined in section 267) at any time during the 12-month period beginning on the date which is 6 months before the expatriation date.

(b) VALUE.—For purposes of subsection (a)—

(1) IN GENERAL.—The value of specified stock compensation shall be—

(A) in the case of a stock option (or other similar right) or a stock appreciation right, the fair value of such option or right, and

(B) in any other case, the fair market value of such compensation.

(2) DATE FOR DETERMINING VALUE.—The determination of value shall be made—

(A) in the case of specified stock compensation held on the expatriation date, on such date,

(B) in the case of such compensation which is canceled during the 6 months before the expatriation date, on the day before such cancellation, and

(C) in the case of such compensation which is granted after the expatriation date, on the date such compensation is granted.

(c) Tax To Apply Only if Shareholder Gain Recognized.—Subsection (a) shall apply to any disqualified individual with respect to an expatriated corporation only if gain (if any) on any stock in such corporation is recognized in whole or part by any shareholder by reason of the acquisition referred to in section 7874(a)(2)(B)(i) with respect to such corporation.

(d) Exception Where Gain Recognized on Compensation.—Subsection (a) shall not apply to—

(1) any stock option which is exercised on the expatriation date or during the 6-month period before such date and to the stock acquired in such exercise, if income is recognized under section 83 on or before the expatriation date with respect to the stock acquired pursuant to such exercise, and

(2) any other specified stock compensation which is exercised, sold, exchanged, distributed, cashed-out, or otherwise paid during such period in a transaction in which income, gain, or loss is recognized in full.

(e) Definitions.—For purposes of this section—

(1) Disqualified individual.—The term "disqualified individual" means, with respect to a corporation, any individual who, at any time during the 12-month period beginning on the date which is 6 months before the expatriation date—

(A) is subject to the requirements of section 16(a) of the Securities Exchange Act of 1934 with respect to such corporation or any member of the expanded affiliated group which includes such corporation, or

(B) would be subject to such requirements if such corporation or member were an issuer of equity securities referred to in such section.

(2) Expatriated corporation; expatriation date.—

(A) Expatriated corporation.—The term "expatriated corporation" means any corporation which is an expatriated entity (as defined in section 7874(a)(2)). Such term includes any predecessor or successor of such a corporation.

(B) Expatriation date.—The term "expatriation date" means, with respect to a corporation, the date on which the corporation first becomes an expatriated corporation.

(3) Specified stock compensation.—

(A) In general.—The term "specified stock compensation" means payment (or right to payment) granted by the expatriated corporation (or by any member of the expanded affiliated group which includes such corporation) to any person in connection with the performance of services by a disqualified individual for such corporation or member if the value of such payment or right is based on (or determined by reference to) the value (or change in value) of stock in such corporation (or any such member).

(B) Exceptions.—Such term shall not include—

(i) any option to which part II of subchapter D of chapter 1 applies, or

(ii) any payment or right to payment from a plan referred to in section 280G(b)(6).

(4) Expanded affiliated group.—The term "expanded affiliated group" means an affiliated group (as defined in section 1504(a) without regard to section 1504(b)(3)); except that section 1504(a) shall be applied by substituting "more than 50 percent" for "at least 80 percent" each place it appears.

(f) Special Rules.—For purposes of this section—

(1) Cancellation of restriction.—The cancellation of a restriction which by its terms will never lapse shall be treated as a grant.

(2) Payment or reimbursement of tax by corporation treated as specified stock compensation.—Any payment of the tax imposed by this section directly or indirectly by the expatriated corporation or by any member of the expanded affiliated group which includes such corporation—

(A) shall be treated as specified stock compensation, and

(B) shall not be allowed as a deduction under any provision of chapter 1.

(3) Certain restrictions ignored.—Whether there is specified stock compensation, and the value thereof, shall be determined without regard to any restriction other than a restriction which by its terms will never lapse.

(4) PROPERTY TRANSFERS.—Any transfer of property shall be treated as a payment and any right to a transfer of property shall be treated as a right to a payment.

(5) OTHER ADMINISTRATIVE PROVISIONS.—For purposes of subtitle F, any tax imposed by this section shall be treated as a tax imposed by subtitle A.

(g) REGULATIONS.—The Secretary shall prescribe such regulations as may be necessary or appropriate to carry out the purposes of this section.

* * *

[CCH Explanation at ¶508. Committee Reports at ¶10,980.]

Amendments

• **2004, American Jobs Creation Act of 2004 (H.R. 4520)**

H.R. 4520, §802(a):

Amended subtitle D by inserting after chapter 44 a new chapter 45 (Code Sec. 4985). **Effective** on 3-4-2003; except

that periods before such date shall not be taken into account in applying the periods in Code Sec. 4985(a) and (e)(1), as added by Act Sec. 802(a).

[¶6110] CODE SEC. 5117. PROHIBITED PURCHASES BY DEALERS.

* * *

(d) SPECIAL RULE DURING SUSPENSION PERIOD.—Except as provided in subsection (b) or by the Secretary, during the suspension period (as defined in section 5148) it shall be unlawful for any dealer to purchase distilled spirits for resale from any person other than a wholesale dealer in liquors who is required to keep records under section 5114.

* * *

[CCH Explanation at ¶1569. Committee Reports at ¶10,270.]

Amendments

• **2004, American Jobs Creation Act of 2004 (H.R. 4520)**

H.R. 4520, §246(b):

Amended Code Sec. 5117 by adding at the end a new subsection (d). **Effective** on the date of the enactment of this Act.

[¶6115] *CODE SEC. 5148. SUSPENSION OF OCCUPATIONAL TAX.*

(a) IN GENERAL.—Notwithstanding sections 5081, 5091, 5111, 5121, and 5131, the rate of tax imposed under such sections for the suspension period shall be zero. During such period, persons engaged in or carrying on a trade or business covered by such sections shall register under section 5141 and shall comply with the recordkeeping requirements under this part.

(b) SUSPENSION PERIOD.—For purposes of subsection (a), the suspension period is the period beginning on July 1, 2005, and ending on June 30, 2008.

[CCH Explanation at ¶1569. Committee Reports at ¶10,270.]

Amendments

• **2004, American Jobs Creation Act of 2004 (H.R. 4520)**

H.R. 4520, §246(a):

Amended subpart G of part II of subchapter A of chapter 51 by redesignating Code Sec. 5148 as Code Sec. 5149 and by

inserting after Code Sec. 5147 a new Code Sec. 5148. **Effective** on the date of the enactment of this Act.

756 American Jobs Creation Act of 2004

[¶6120] CODE SEC. 5149. CROSS REFERENCES.

* * *

[CCH Explanation at ¶1569. Committee Reports at ¶10,270.]
Amendments
• **2004, American Jobs Creation Act of 2004 (H.R. 4520)**

H.R. 4520, §246(a):

Amended subpart G of part II of subchapter A of chapter 51 by redesignating Code Sec. 5148 as Code Sec. 5149. **Effective** on the date of the enactment of this Act.

[¶6125] CODE SEC. 6031. RETURN OF PARTNERSHIP INCOME.

* * *

(f) ELECTING INVESTMENT PARTNERSHIPS.—In the case of any electing investment partnership (as defined in section 743(e)(6)), the information required under subsection (b) to be furnished to any partner to whom section 743(e)(2) applies shall include such information as is necessary to enable the partner to compute the amount of losses disallowed under section 743(e).

[CCH Explanation at ¶960. Committee Reports at ¶11,160.]
Amendments
• **2004, American Jobs Creation Act of 2004 (H.R. 4520)**

H.R. 4520, §833(b)(4)(B):

Amended Code Sec. 6031 by adding at the end a new subsection (f). **Effective** for transfers after the date of the enactment of this Act. For a transition rule, see Act Sec. 833(d)(2)(B), below.

H.R. 4520, §833(d)(2)(B), provides:

(B) TRANSITION RULE.—In the case of an electing investment partnership which is in existence on June 4, 2004, section 743(e)(6)(H) of the Internal Revenue Code of 1986, as added by this section, shall not apply to such partnership and section 743(e)(6)(I) of such Code, as so added, shall be applied by substituting "20 years" for "15 years".

[¶6130] CODE SEC. 6035. RETURNS OF OFFICERS, DIRECTORS, AND SHAREHOLDERS OF FOREIGN PERSONAL HOLDING COMPANIES. [Repealed.]

* * *

[CCH Explanation at ¶490. Committee Reports at ¶10,690.]
Amendments
• **2004, American Jobs Creation Act of 2004 (H.R. 4520)**

H.R. 4520, §413(c)(26):

Repealed Code Sec. 6035. **Effective** for tax years of foreign corporations beginning after 12-31-2004 and for tax years of United States shareholders with or within which such tax years of foreign corporations end. Prior to repeal, Code Sec. 6035 read as follows:

SEC. 6035. RETURNS OF OFFICERS, DIRECTORS, AND SHAREHOLDERS OF FOREIGN PERSONAL HOLDING COMPANIES.

(a) GENERAL RULE.—Each United States citizen or resident who is an officer, director, or 10-percent shareholder of a corporation which was a foreign personal holding company (as defined in section 552) for any taxable year shall file a return with respect to such taxable year setting forth—

(1) the shareholder information required by subsection (b),

(2) the income information required by subsection (c), and

(3) such other information with respect to such corporation as the Secretary shall by forms or regulations prescribe as necessary for carrying out the purposes of this title.

(b) SHAREHOLDER INFORMATION.—The shareholder information required by this subsection with respect to any taxable year shall be—

(1) the name and address of each person who at any time during such taxable year held any share in the corporation,

(2) a description of each class of shares and the total number of shares of such class outstanding at the close of the taxable year,

(3) the number of shares of each class held by each person, and

(4) any changes in the holdings of shares during the taxable year.

For purposes of paragraphs (1), (3), and (4), the term "share" includes any security convertible into a share in the corporation and any option granted by the corporation with respect to any share in the corporation.

(c) INCOME INFORMATION.—The income information required by this subsection for any taxable year shall be the gross income, deductions, credits, taxable income, and undistributed foreign personal holding company income of the corporation for the taxable year.

(d) TIME AND MANNER FOR FURNISHING INFORMATION.—The information required under subsection (a) shall be furnished at such time and in such manner as the Secretary shall by forms and regulations prescribe.

(e) DEFINITION AND SPECIAL RULES.—

(1) 10-PERCENT SHAREHOLDER.—For purposes of this section, the term "10-percent shareholder" means any individual who owns directly or indirectly (within the meaning of section 554) 10 percent or more in value of the outstanding stock of a foreign corporation.

(2) TIME FOR MAKING DETERMINATIONS.—

(A) IN GENERAL.—Except as provided in subparagraph (B), the determination of whether any person is an officer, director, or 10-percent shareholder with respect to any foreign

¶6120   Code Sec. 5149

corporation shall be made as of the date on which the return is required to be filed.

(B) SPECIAL RULE.—If after the application of subparagraph (A) no person is required to file a return under subsection (a) with respect to any foreign corporation for any taxable year, the determination of whether any person is an officer, director, or 10-percent shareholder with respect to such foreign corporation shall be made on the last day of such taxable year on which there was such a person who was a United States citizen or resident.

(3) 2 OR MORE PERSONS REQUIRED TO FURNISH INFORMATION WITH RESPECT TO SAME FOREIGN CORPORATION.—If, but for this paragraph, 2 or more persons would be required to furnish information under subsection (a) with respect to the same foreign corporation for the same taxable year, the Secretary may by regulations provide that such information shall be required only from 1 person.

[¶ 6135] CODE SEC. 6039G. INFORMATION ON INDIVIDUALS LOSING UNITED STATES CITIZENSHIP.

(a) IN GENERAL.—Notwithstanding any other provision of law, any individual to whom section 877(b) applies for any taxable year shall provide a statement for such taxable year which includes the information described in subsection (b).

[CCH Explanation at ¶ 502. Committee Reports at ¶ 11,000.]
Amendments

• **2004, American Jobs Creation Act of 2004 (H.R. 4520)**

H.R. 4520, § 804(e)(1):

Amended Code Sec. 6039G(a). **Effective** for individuals who expatriate after 6-3-2004. Prior to amendment, Code Sec. 6039G(a) read as follows:

(a) IN GENERAL.—Notwithstanding any other provision of law, any individual who loses United States citizenship

(within the meaning of section 877(a)) shall provide a statement which includes the information described in subsection (b). Such statement shall be—

(1) provided not later than the earliest date of any act referred to in subsection (c), and

(2) provided to the person or court referred to in subsection (c) with respect to such act.

(b) INFORMATION TO BE PROVIDED.—Information required under subsection (a) shall include—

(1) the taxpayer's TIN,

(2) the mailing address of such individual's principal foreign residence,

(3) the foreign country in which such individual is residing,

(4) the foreign country of which such individual is a citizen,

(5) information detailing the income, assets, and liabilities of such individual,

(6) the number of days during any portion of which that the individual was physically present in the United States during the taxable year, and

(7) such other information as the Secretary may prescribe.

[CCH Explanation at ¶ 502. Committee Reports at ¶ 11,000.]
Amendments

• **2004, American Jobs Creation Act of 2004 (H.R. 4520)**

H.R. 4520, § 804(e)(2):

Amended Code Sec. 6039G(b). **Effective** for individuals who expatriate after 6-3-2004. Prior to amendment, Code Sec. 6039G(b) read as follows:

(b) INFORMATION TO BE PROVIDED.—Information required under subsection (a) shall include—

(1) the taxpayer's TIN,

(2) the mailing address of such individual's principal foreign residence,

(3) the foreign country in which such individual is residing,

(4) the foreign country of which such individual is a citizen,

(5) in the case of an individual having a net worth of at least the dollar amount applicable under section 877(a)(2)(B), information detailing the assets and liabilities of such individual, and

(6) such other information as the Secretary may prescribe.

(c) [Stricken.]

[CCH Explanation at ¶ 502. Committee Reports at ¶ 11,000.]
Amendments

• **2004, American Jobs Creation Act of 2004 (H.R. 4520)**

H.R. 4520, § 804(e)(4):

Amended Code Sec. 6039G by striking subsections (c), (f), and (g) and by redesignating subsections (d) and (e) as subsections (c) and (d), respectively. **Effective** for individuals who expatriate after 6-3-2004. Prior to being stricken, Code Sec. 6039G(c) read as follows:

(c) ACTS DESCRIBED.—For purposes of this section, the acts referred to in this subsection are—

(1) the individual's renunciation of his United States nationality before a diplomatic or consular officer of the United States pursuant to paragraph (5) of section 349(a) of the Immigration and Nationality Act (8 U.S.C. 1481(a)(5)),

(2) the individual's furnishing to the United States Department of State a signed statement of voluntary relinquishment of United States nationality confirming the performance of an act of expatriation specified in paragraph

(1), (2), (3), or (4) of section 349(a) of the Immigration and Nationality Act (8 U.S.C. 1481(a)(1)-(4)),

(3) the issuance by the United States Department of State of a certificate of loss of nationality to the individual, or

(4) the cancellation by a court of the United States of a naturalized citizen's certificate of naturalization.

(c) PENALTY.—If—

(1) an individual is required to file a statement under subsection (a) for any taxable year, and

(2) fails to file such a statement with the Secretary on or before the date such statement is required to be filed or fails to include all the information required to be shown on the statement or includes incorrect information,

such individual shall pay a penalty of $10,000 unless it is shown that such failure is due to reasonable cause and not to willful neglect.

[CCH Explanation at ¶ 502. Committee Reports at ¶ 11,000.]

Amendments

• 2004, American Jobs Creation Act of 2004 (H.R. 4520)

H.R. 4520, § 804(e)(3):

Amended Code Sec. 6039G(d). **Effective** for individuals who expatriate after 6-3-2004. Prior to amendment, Code Sec. 6039G(d) read as follows:

(d) PENALTY.—Any individual failing to provide a statement required under subsection (a) shall be subject to a penalty for each year (of the 10-year period beginning on the date of loss of United States citizenship) during any portion of which such failure continues in an amount equal to the greater of—

(1) 5 percent of the tax required to be paid under section 877 for the taxable year ending during such year, or

(2) $1,000,

unless it is shown that such failure is due to reasonable cause and not to willful neglect.

H.R. 4520, § 804(e)(4):

Amended Code Sec. 6039G by redesignating subsection (d) as subsection (c). **Effective** for individuals who expatriate after 6-3-2004.

(d) INFORMATION TO BE PROVIDED TO SECRETARY.—

* * *

[CCH Explanation at ¶ 502. Committee Reports at ¶ 11,000.]

Amendments

• 2004, American Jobs Creation Act of 2004 (H.R. 4520)

H.R. 4520, § 804(e)(4):

Amended Code Sec. 6039G by redesignating subsection (e) as subsection (d). **Effective** for individuals who expatriate after 6-3-2004.

(f) [Stricken.]

[CCH Explanation at ¶ 502. Committee Reports at ¶ 11,000.]

Amendments

• 2004, American Jobs Creation Act of 2004 (H.R. 4520)

H.R. 4520, § 804(e)(4):

Amended Code Sec. 6039G by striking subsection (f). **Effective** for individuals who expatriate after 6-3-2004. Prior to being stricken, Code Sec. 6039G(f) read as follows:

(f) REPORTING BY LONG-TERM LAWFUL PERMANENT RESIDENTS WHO CEASE TO BE TAXED AS RESIDENTS.—In lieu of applying the last sentence of subsection (a), any individual who is required to provide a statement under this section by reason of section 877(e)(1) shall provide such statement with the return of tax imposed by chapter 1 for the taxable year during which the event described in such section occurs.

(g) [Stricken.]

[CCH Explanation at ¶ 502. Committee Reports at ¶ 11,000.]

Amendments

• 2004, American Jobs Creation Act of 2004 (H.R. 4520)

H.R. 4520, § 804(e)(4):

Amended Code Sec. 6039G by striking subsection (g). **Effective** for individuals who expatriate after 6-3-2004. Prior to being stricken, Code Sec. 6039G(g) read as follows:

(g) EXEMPTION.—The Secretary may by regulations exempt any class of individuals from the requirements of this section if he determines that applying this section to such individuals is not necessary to carry out the purposes of this section.

[¶6140] CODE SEC. 6041. INFORMATION AT SOURCE.

* * *

(g) NONQUALIFIED DEFERRED COMPENSATION.—*Subsection (a) shall apply to—*

(1) any deferrals for the year under a nonqualified deferred compensation plan (within the meaning of section 409A(d)), whether or not paid, except that this paragraph shall not apply to deferrals which are required to be reported under section 6051(a)(13) (without regard to any de minimis exception), and

(2) any amount includible under section 409A and which is not treated as wages under section 3401(a).

* * *

[CCH Explanation at ¶1405. Committee Reports at ¶11,570.]

Amendments

• **2004, American Jobs Creation Act of 2004 (H.R. 4520)**

H.R. 4520, §885(b)(3):

Amended Code Sec. 6041 by adding at the end a new subsection (g). **Effective** generally for amounts deferred after 12-31-2004. For special rules, see Act Sec. 885(d)(2)-(3), below.

H.R. 4520, §885(d)(2)-(3), provides:

(2) SPECIAL RULES.—

(A) EARNINGS.—The amendments made by this section shall apply to earnings on deferred compensation only to the extent that such amendments apply to such compensation.

(B) MATERIAL MODIFICATIONS.—For purposes of this subsection, amounts deferred in taxable years beginning before January 1, 2005, shall be treated as amounts deferred in a taxable year beginning on or after such date if the plan under which the deferral is made is materially modified

after October 3, 2004, unless such modification is pursuant to the guidance issued under subsection (f).

(3) EXCEPTION FOR NONELECTIVE DEFERRED COMPENSATION.— The amendments made by this section shall not apply to any nonelective deferred compensation to which section 457 of the Internal Revenue Code of 1986 does not apply by reason of section 457(e)(12) of such Code, but only if such compensation is provided under a nonqualified deferred compensation plan—

(A) which was in existence on May 1, 2004,

(B) which was providing nonelective deferred compensation described in such section 457(e)(12) on such date, and

(C) which is established or maintained by an organization incorporated on July 2, 1974.

If, after May 1, 2004, a plan described in the preceding sentence adopts a plan amendment which provides a material change in the classes of individuals eligible to participate in the plan, this paragraph shall not apply to any nonelective deferred compensation provided under the plan on or after the date of the adoption of the amendment.

[¶6145] *CODE SEC. 6043A. RETURNS RELATING TO TAXABLE MERGERS AND ACQUISITIONS.*

(a) IN GENERAL.—*According to the forms or regulations prescribed by the Secretary, the acquiring corporation in any taxable acquisition shall make a return setting forth—*

(1) a description of the acquisition,

(2) the name and address of each shareholder of the acquired corporation who is required to recognize gain (if any) as a result of the acquisition,

(3) the amount of money and the fair market value of other property transferred to each such shareholder as part of such acquisition, and

(4) such other information as the Secretary may prescribe.

To the extent provided by the Secretary, the requirements of this section applicable to the acquiring corporation shall be applicable to the acquired corporation and not to the acquiring corporation.

(b) NOMINEES.—*According to the forms or regulations prescribed by the Secretary:*

(1) REPORTING.—*Any person who holds stock as a nominee for another person shall furnish in the manner prescribed by the Secretary to such other person the information provided by the corporation under subsection (d).*

(2) REPORTING TO NOMINEES.—*In the case of stock held by any person as a nominee, references in this section (other than in subsection (c)) to a shareholder shall be treated as a reference to the nominee.*

(c) TAXABLE ACQUISITION.—*For purposes of this section, the term "taxable acquisition" means any acquisition by a corporation of stock in or property of another corporation if any shareholder of the acquired corporation is required to recognize gain (if any) as a result of such acquisition.*

(d) STATEMENTS TO BE FURNISHED TO SHAREHOLDERS.—*According to the forms or regulations prescribed by the Secretary, every person required to make a return under subsection (a) shall furnish to each shareholder whose name is required to be set forth in such return a written statement showing—*

(1) *the name, address, and phone number of the information contact of the person required to make such return,*

(2) *the information required to be shown on such return with respect to such shareholder, and*

(3) *such other information as the Secretary may prescribe.*

The written statement required under the preceding sentence shall be furnished to the shareholder on or before January 31 of the year following the calendar year during which the taxable acquisition occurred.

* * *

[CCH Explanation at ¶ 510. Committee Reports at ¶ 11,010.]

Amendments

• **2004, American Jobs Creation Act of 2004 (H.R. 4520)**

Effective for acquisitions after the date of the enactment of this Act.

H.R. 4520, § 805(a):

Amended subpart B of part III of subchapter A of chapter 61 by inserting after Code Sec. 6043 a new Code Sec. 6043A.

[¶ 6150] CODE SEC. 6050L. *RETURNS RELATING TO CERTAIN DONATED PROPERTY.*

(a) DISPOSITIONS OF DONATED PROPERTY.—

(1) IN GENERAL.—*If the donee of any charitable deduction property sells, exchanges, or otherwise disposes of such property within 2 years after its receipt, the donee shall make a return (in accordance with forms and regulations prescribed by the Secretary) showing—*

(A) *the name, address, and TIN of the donor,*

(B) *a description of the property,*

(C) *the date of the contribution,*

(D) *the amount received on the disposition, and*

(E) *the date of such disposition.*

(2) DEFINITIONS.—*For purposes of this subsection:*

(A) CHARITABLE DEDUCTION PROPERTY.—*The term "charitable deduction property" means any property (other than publicly traded securities) contributed in a contribution for which a deduction was claimed under section 170 if the claimed value of such property (plus the claimed value of all similar items of property donated by the donor to 1 or more donees) exceeds $5,000.*

(B) PUBLICLY TRADED SECURITIES.—*The term "publicly traded securities" means securities for which (as of the date of the contribution) market quotations are readily available on an established securities market.*

(b) QUALIFIED INTELLECTUAL PROPERTY CONTRIBUTIONS.—

(1) IN GENERAL.—*Each donee with respect to a qualified intellectual property contribution shall make a return (at such time and in such form and manner as the Secretary may by regulations prescribe) with respect to each specified taxable year of the donee showing—*

(A) *the name, address, and TIN of the donor,*

(B) *a description of the qualified intellectual property contributed,*

(C) *the date of the contribution, and*

(D) *the amount of net income of the donee for the taxable year which is properly allocable to the qualified intellectual property (determined without regard to paragraph (10)(B) of section 170(m) and with the modifications described in paragraphs (5) and (6) of such section).*

(2) DEFINITIONS.—*For purposes of this subsection:*

(A) IN GENERAL.—*Terms used in this subsection which are also used in section 170(m) have the respective meanings given such terms in such section.*

(B) SPECIFIED TAXABLE YEAR.—*The term "specified taxable year" means, with respect to any qualified intellectual property contribution, any taxable year of the donee any portion of which is part of the 10-year period beginning on the date of such contribution.*

(c) STATEMENT TO BE FURNISHED TO DONORS.—Every person making a return under subsection (a) or (b) shall furnish a copy of such return to the donor at such time and in such manner as the Secretary may by regulations prescribe.

* * *

[CCH Explanation at ¶1315. Committee Reports at ¶11,540.]

Amendments

• **2004, American Jobs Creation Act of 2004 (H.R. 4520)**

H.R. 4520, § 882(c)(1):

Amended Code Sec. 6050L. **Effective** for contributions made after 6-3-2004. Prior to amendment, Code Sec. 6050L read as follows:

SEC. 6050L. RETURNS RELATING TO CERTAIN DISPOSITIONS OF DONATED PROPERTY.

(a) GENERAL RULE.—If the donee of any charitable deduction property sells, exchanges, or otherwise disposes of such property within 2 years after its receipt, the donee shall make a return (in accordance with forms and regulations prescribed by the Secretary) showing—

(1) the name, address, and TIN of the donor,

(2) a description of the property,

(3) the date of the contribution,

(4) the amount received on the disposition, and

(5) the date of such disposition.

(b) CHARITABLE DEDUCTION PROPERTY.—For purposes of this section, the term "charitable deduction property" means any property (other than publicly traded securities) contributed in a contribution for which a deduction was claimed under section 170 if the claimed value of such property (plus the claimed value of all similar items of property donated by the donor to 1 or more donees) exceeds $5,000.

(c) STATEMENT TO BE FURNISHED TO DONORS.—Every person making a return under subsection (a) shall furnish a copy of such return to the donor at such time and in such manner as the Secretary may by regulations prescribe.

(d) DEFINITION OF PUBLICLY TRADED SECURITIES.—The term "publicly traded securities" means securities for which (as of the date of the contribution) market quotations are readily available on an established securities market.

[¶6155] CODE SEC. 6051. RECEIPTS FOR EMPLOYEES.

(a) REQUIREMENT.—Every person required to deduct and withhold from an employee a tax under section 3101 or 3402, or who would have been required to deduct and withhold a tax under section 3402 (determined without regard to subsection (n)) if the employee had claimed no more than one withholding exemption, or every employer engaged in a trade or business who pays remuneration for services performed by an employee, including the cash value of such remuneration paid in any medium other than cash, shall furnish to each such employee in respect of the remuneration paid by such person to such employee during the calendar year, on or before January 31 of the succeeding year, or, if his employment is terminated before the close of such calendar year, within 30 days after the date of receipt of a written request from the employee if such 30-day period ends before January 31, a written statement showing the following:

* * *

(11) the amount contributed to any Archer MSA (as defined in section 220(d)) of such employee or such employee's spouse,

(12) the amount contributed to any health savings account (as defined in section 223(d)) of such employee or such employee's spouse, *and*

(13) the total amount of deferrals for the year under a nonqualified deferred compensation plan (within the meaning of section 409A(d)).

In the case of compensation paid for service as a member of a uniformed service, the statement shall show, in lieu of the amount required to be shown by paragraph (5), the total amount of wages as defined in section 3121(a), computed in accordance with such section and section 3121(i)(2). In the case of compensation paid for service as a volunteer or volunteer leader within the meaning of the Peace Corps Act, the statement shall show, in lieu of the amount required to be shown by paragraph (5), the total amount of wages as defined in section 3121(a), computed in accordance with such section and section 3121(i)(3). In the case of tips received by an employee in the course of his employment, the amounts required to be shown by paragraphs (3) and (5) shall include only such tips as are included in statements furnished to the employer pursuant to section 6053(a). The amounts required to be shown by paragraph (5) shall not include wages which are exempted pursuant to sections 3101(c) and 3111(c) from the taxes imposed by section 3101 and 3111. *In the case of the amounts required to be shown by paragraph (13), the Secretary may (by regulation) establish a minimum amount of deferrals below which paragraph (13) does not apply.*

* * *

[CCH Explanation at ¶ 1405. Committee Reports at ¶ 11,570.]

Amendments

• 2004, American Jobs Creation Act of 2004 (H.R. 4520)

H.R. 4520, § 885(b)(1)(A):

Amended Code Sec. 6051(a) by striking "and" at the end of paragraph (11), by striking the period at the end of paragraph (12) and inserting ", and", and by inserting after paragraph (12) a new paragraph (13). **Effective** for amounts deferred after 12-31-2004. For special rules, see Act Sec. 885(d)(2)-(3), (e)-(f), below.

H.R. 4520, § 885(b)(1)(B):

Amended Code Sec. 6051(a) by adding at the end a new sentence. **Effective** for amounts deferred after 12-31-2004. For special rules, see Act Sec. 885(d)(2)-(3), (e)-(f), below.

H.R. 4520, § 885(d)(2)-(3), (e)-(f), provides:

(2) SPECIAL RULES.—

(A) EARNINGS.—The amendments made by this section shall apply to earnings on deferred compensation only to the extent that such amendments apply to such compensation.

(B) MATERIAL MODIFICATIONS.—For purposes of this subsection, amounts deferred in taxable years beginning before January 1, 2005, shall be treated as amounts deferred in a taxable year beginning on or after such date if the plan under which the deferral is made is materially modified after October 3, 2004, unless such modification is pursuant to the guidance issued under subsection (f).

(3) EXCEPTION FOR NONELECTIVE DEFERRED COMPENSATION.—The amendments made by this section shall not apply to any nonelective deferred compensation to which section 457 of the Internal Revenue Code of 1986 does not apply by reason of section 457(e)(12) of such Code, but only if such compensation is provided under a nonqualified deferred compensation plan—

(A) which was in existence on May 1, 2004,

(B) which was providing nonelective deferred compensation described in such section 457(e)(12) on such date, and

(C) which is established or maintained by an organization incorporated on July 2, 1974.

If, after May 1, 2004, a plan described in the preceding sentence adopts a plan amendment which provides a material change in the classes of individuals eligible to participate in the plan, this paragraph shall not apply to any nonelective deferred compensation provided under the plan on or after the date of the adoption of the amendment.

(e) GUIDANCE RELATING TO CHANGE OF OWNERSHIP OR CONTROL.—Not later than 90 days after the date of the enactment of this Act, the Secretary of the Treasury shall issue guidance on what constitutes a change in ownership or effective control for purposes of section 409A of the Internal Revenue Code of 1986, as added by this section.

(f) GUIDANCE RELATING TO TERMINATION OF CERTAIN EXISTING ARRANGEMENTS.—Not later than 60 days after the date of the enactment of this Act, the Secretary of the Treasury shall issue guidance providing a limited period during which a nonqualified deferred compensation plan adopted before December 31, 2004, may, without violating the requirements of paragraphs (2), (3), and (4) of section 409A(a) of the Internal Revenue Code of 1986 (as added by this section), be amended—

(1) to provide that a participant may terminate participation in the plan, or cancel an outstanding deferral election with regard to amounts deferred after December 31, 2004, but only if amounts subject to the termination or cancellation are includible in income of the participant as earned (or, if later, when no longer subject to substantial risk of forfeiture), and

(2) to conform to the requirements of such section 409A with regard to amounts deferred after December 31, 2004.

[¶ 6160] CODE SEC. 6103. CONFIDENTIALITY AND DISCLOSURE OF RETURNS AND RETURN INFORMATION.

* * *

(e) DISCLOSURE TO PERSONS HAVING MATERIAL INTEREST.—

(1) IN GENERAL.—The return of a person shall, upon written request, be open to inspection by or disclosure to—

* * *

(D) in the case of the return of a corporation or a subsidiary thereof—

(i) any person designated by resolution of its board of directors or other similar governing body,

(ii) any officer or employee of such corporation upon written request signed by any principal officer and attested to by the secretary or other officer,

(iii) any bona fide shareholder of record owning 1 percent or more of the outstanding stock of such corporation,

(iv) if the corporation was an S corporation, any person who was a shareholder during any part of the period covered by such return during which an election under section 1362(a) was in effect, or

(v) if the corporation has been dissolved, any person authorized by applicable State law to act for the corporation or any person who the Secretary finds to have a material interest which will be affected by information contained therein;

* * *

[CCH Explanation at ¶490. Committee Reports at ¶10,690.]

Amendments

• 2004, American Jobs Creation Act of 2004 (H.R. 4520)

H.R. 4520, §413(c)(27):

Amended Code Sec. 6103(e)(1)(D) by striking clause (iv) and redesignating clauses (v) and (vi) as clauses (iv) and (v), respectively. **Effective** for disclosures of return or return information with respect to tax years beginning after

12-31-2004. Prior to being stricken, Code Sec. 6103(e)(1)(D)(iv) read as follows:

(iv) if the corporation was a foreign personal holding company, as defined by section 552, any person who was a shareholder during any part of a period covered by such return if with respect to that period, or any part thereof, such shareholder was required under section 551 to include in his gross income undistributed foreign personal holding company income of such company,

[¶6165] CODE SEC. 6111. *DISCLOSURE OF REPORTABLE TRANSACTIONS.*

(a) IN GENERAL.—*Each material advisor with respect to any reportable transaction shall make a return (in such form as the Secretary may prescribe) setting forth—*

(1) *information identifying and describing the transaction,*

(2) *information describing any potential tax benefits expected to result from the transaction, and*

(3) *such other information as the Secretary may prescribe.*

Such return shall be filed not later than the date specified by the Secretary.

(b) DEFINITIONS.—*For purposes of this section—*

(1) MATERIAL ADVISOR.—

(A) IN GENERAL.—*The term "material advisor" means any person—*

(i) *who provides any material aid, assistance, or advice with respect to organizing, managing, promoting, selling, implementing, insuring, or carrying out any reportable transaction, and*

(ii) *who directly or indirectly derives gross income in excess of the threshold amount (or such other amount as may be prescribed by the Secretary) for such advice or assistance.*

(B) THRESHOLD AMOUNT.—*For purposes of subparagraph (A), the threshold amount is—*

(i) *$50,000 in the case of a reportable transaction substantially all of the tax benefits from which are provided to natural persons, and*

(ii) *$250,000 in any other case.*

(2) REPORTABLE TRANSACTION.—*The term "reportable transaction" has the meaning given to such term by section 6707A(c).*

(c) REGULATIONS.—*The Secretary may prescribe regulations which provide—*

(1) *that only 1 person shall be required to meet the requirements of subsection (a) in cases in which 2 or more persons would otherwise be required to meet such requirements,*

(2) *exemptions from the requirements of this section, and*

(3) *such rules as may be necessary or appropriate to carry out the purposes of this section.*

[CCH Explanation at ¶605. Committee Reports at ¶11,070.]

Amendments

• 2004, American Jobs Creation Act of 2004 (H.R. 4520)

H.R. 4520, §815(a):

Amended Code Sec. 6111. **Effective** for transactions with respect to which material aid, assistance, or advice referred to in Code Sec. 6111(b)(1)(A)(i) (as added by this section) is provided after the date of the enactment of this Act. Prior to amendment, Code Sec. 6111 read as follows:

SEC. 6111. REGISTRATION OF TAX SHELTERS.

(a) REGISTRATION.—

(1) IN GENERAL.—Any tax shelter organizer shall register the tax shelter with the Secretary (in such form and in such manner as the Secretary may prescribe) not later than the day on which the first offering for sale of interests in such tax shelter occurs.

(2) INFORMATION INCLUDED IN REGISTRATION.—Any registration under paragraph (1) shall include—

(A) information identifying and describing the tax shelter,

(B) information describing the tax benefits of the tax shelter represented (or to be represented) to investors, and

(C) such other information as the Secretary may prescribe.

(b) FURNISHING OF TAX SHELTER IDENTIFICATION NUMBER; INCLUSION ON RETURN.—

(1) SELLERS, ETC.—Any person who sells (or otherwise transfers) an interest in a tax shelter shall (at such times and in such manner as the Secretary shall prescribe) furnish to each investor who purchases (or otherwise acquires) an interest in such tax shelter from such person the identification number assigned by the Secretary to such tax shelter.

(2) INCLUSION OF NUMBER ON RETURN.—Any person claiming any deduction, credit, or other tax benefit by reason of a tax shelter shall include (in such manner as the Secretary may prescribe) on the return of tax on which such deduction, credit, or other benefit is claimed the identification number assigned by the Secretary to such tax shelter.

(c) TAX SHELTER.—For purposes of this section—

(1) IN GENERAL.—The term "tax shelter" means any investment—

(A) with respect to which any person could reasonably infer from the representations made, or to be made, in connection with the offering for sale of interests in the investment that the tax shelter ratio for any investor as of the close of any of the first 5 years ending after the date on which such investment is offered for sale may be greater than 2 to 1, and

(B) which is—

(i) required to be registered under a Federal or State law regulating securities,

(ii) sold pursuant to an exemption from registration requiring the filing of a notice with a Federal or State agency regulating the offering or sale of securities, or

(iii) a substantial investment.

(2) TAX SHELTER RATIO DEFINED.—For purposes of this subsection, the term "tax shelter ratio" means, with respect to any year, the ratio which—

(A) the aggregate amount of the deductions and 350 percent of the credits which are represented to be potentially allowable to any investor under subtitle A for all periods up to (and including) the close of such year, bears to

(B) the investment base as of the close of such year.

(3) INVESTMENT BASE.—

(A) IN GENERAL.—Except as provided in this paragraph, the term "investment base" means, with respect to any year, the amount of money and the adjusted basis of other property (reduced by any liability to which such other property is subject) contributed by the investor as of the close of such year.

(B) CERTAIN BORROWED AMOUNTS EXCLUDED.—For purposes of subparagraph (A), there shall not be taken into account any amount borrowed from any person—

(i) who participated in the organization, sale, or management of the investment, or

(ii) who is a related person (as defined in section 465(b)(3)(C)) to any person described in clause (i),

unless such amount is unconditionally required to be repaid by the investor before the close of the year for which the determination is being made.

(C) CERTAIN OTHER AMOUNTS INCLUDED OR EXCLUDED.—

(i) AMOUNTS HELD IN CASH EQUIVALENTS, ETC.—No amount shall be taken into account under subparagraph (A) which is to be held in cash equivalent or marketable securities.

(ii) AMOUNTS INCLUDED OR EXCLUDED BY SECRETARY.—The Secretary may by regulation—

(I) exclude from the investment base any amount described in subparagraph (A), or

(II) include in the investment base any amount not described in subparagraph (A),

if the Secretary determines that such exclusion or inclusion is necessary to carry out the purposes of this section.

(4) SUBSTANTIAL INVESTMENT.—An investment is a substantial investment if—

(A) the aggregate amount which may be offered for sale exceeds $250,000, and

(B) there are expected to be 5 or more investors.

(d) CERTAIN CONFIDENTIAL ARRANGEMENTS TREATED AS TAX SHELTERS.—

(1) IN GENERAL.—For purposes of this section, the term "tax shelter" includes any entity, plan, arrangement, or transaction—

(A) a significant purpose of the structure of which is the avoidance or evasion of Federal income tax for a direct or indirect participant which is a corporation,

(B) which is offered to any potential participant under conditions of confidentiality, and

(C) for which the tax shelter promoters may receive fees in excess of $100,000 in the aggregate.

(2) CONDITIONS OF CONFIDENTIALITY.—For purposes of paragraph (1)(B), an offer is under conditions of confidentiality if—

(A) the potential participant to whom the offer is made (or any other person acting on behalf of such participant) has an understanding or agreement with or for the benefit of any promoter of the tax shelter that such participant (or such other person) will limit disclosure of the tax shelter or any significant tax features of the tax shelter, or

(B) any promoter of the tax shelter—

(i) claims, knows, or has reason to know,

(ii) knows or has reason to know that any other person (other than the potential participant) claims, or

(iii) causes another person to claim, that the tax shelter (or any aspect thereof) is proprietary to any person other than the potential participant or is otherwise protected from disclosure to or use by others.

For purposes of this subsection, the term "promoter" means any person or any related person (within the meaning of section 267 or 707) who participates in the organization, management, or sale of the tax shelter.

(3) PERSONS OTHER THAN PROMOTER REQUIRED TO REGISTER IN CERTAIN CASES.—

(A) IN GENERAL.—If—

(i) the requirements of subsection (a) are not met with respect to any tax shelter (as defined in paragraph (1)) by any tax shelter promoter, and

(ii) no tax shelter promoter is a United States person,

then each United States person who discussed participation in such shelter shall register such shelter under subsection (a).

(B) EXCEPTION.—Subparagraph (A) shall not apply to a United States person who discussed participation in a tax shelter if—

(i) such person notified the promoter in writing (not later than the close of the 90th day after the day on which such discussions began) that such person would not participate in such shelter, and

(ii) such person does not participate in such shelter.

(4) OFFER TO PARTICIPATE TREATED AS OFFER FOR SALE.—For purposes of subsections (a) and (b), an offer to participate in a tax shelter (as defined in paragraph (1)) shall be treated as an offer for sale.

(e) OTHER DEFINITIONS.—For purposes of this section—

(1) TAX SHELTER ORGANIZER.—The term "tax shelter organizer" means—

(A) the person principally responsible for organizing the tax shelter,

(B) if the requirements of subsection (a) are not met by a person described in subparagraph (A) at the time prescribed therefor, any other person who participated in the organization of the tax shelter, and

(C) if the requirements of subsection (a) are not met by a person described in subparagraph (A) or (B) at the time prescribed therefor, any person participating in the sale or management of the investment at a time when the tax shelter was not registered under subsection (a).

(2) YEAR.—The term "year" means—

(A) the taxable year of the tax shelter, or

(B) if the tax shelter has no taxable year, the calendar year.

(f) REGULATIONS.—The Secretary may prescribe regulations which provide—

(1) rules for the aggregation of similar investments offered by the same person or persons for purposes of applying subsection (c)(4),

(2) that only 1 person shall be required to meet the requirements of subsection (a) in cases in which 2 or more persons would otherwise be required to meet such requirements,

(3) exemptions from the requirements of this section, and

(4) such rules as may be necessary or appropriate to carry out the purposes of this section in the case of foreign tax shelters.

[¶6170] CODE SEC. 6112. *MATERIAL ADVISORS OF REPORTABLE TRANSACTIONS MUST KEEP LISTS OF ADVISEES, ETC.*

(a) IN GENERAL.—*Each material advisor (as defined in section 6111) with respect to any reportable transaction (as defined in section 6707A(c)) shall (whether or not required to file a return under section 6111 with respect to such transaction) maintain (in such manner as the Secretary may by regulations prescribe) a list—*

(1) *identifying each person with respect to whom such advisor acted as a material advisor with respect to such transaction, and*

(2) *containing such other information as the Secretary may by regulations require.*

[CCH Explanation at ¶605. Committee Reports at ¶11,070.]

Amendments

• **2004, American Jobs Creation Act of 2004 (H.R. 4520)**

H.R. 4520, §815(b)(2):

Amended so much of Code Sec. 6112 as precedes subsection (c). **Effective** for transactions with respect to which material aid, assistance, or advice referred to in Code Sec. 6111(b)(1)(A)(i), as added by Act Sec. 815, is provided after the date of the enactment of this Act. Prior to amendment, so much of Code Sec. 6112 as precedes subsection (c) read as follows:

SEC. 6112. ORGANIZERS AND SELLERS OF POTENTIALLY ABUSIVE TAX SHELTERS MUST KEEP LISTS OF INVESTORS.

(a) IN GENERAL.—Any person who—

(1) organizes any potentially abusive tax shelter, or

(2) sells any interest in such a shelter,

shall maintain (in such manner as the Secretary may by regulations prescribe) a list identifying each person who was sold an interest in such shelter and containing such other information as the Secretary may by regulations require.

(b) POTENTIALLY ABUSIVE TAX SHELTER.—For purposes of this section, the term "potentially abusive tax shelter" means—

(1) any tax shelter (as defined in section 6111) with respect to which registration is required under section 6111, and

(2) any entity, investment plan or arrangement, or other plan or arrangement which is of a type which the Secretary determines by regulations as having a potential for tax avoidance or evasion.

(b) SPECIAL RULES.—

(1) AVAILABILITY FOR INSPECTION; RETENTION OF INFORMATION ON LIST.—Any person who is required to maintain a list under subsection (a)—

(A) shall make such list available to the Secretary for inspection upon *written* request by the Secretary, and

(B) except as otherwise provided under regulations prescribed by the Secretary, shall retain any information which is required to be included on such list for 7 years.

(2) LISTS WHICH WOULD BE REQUIRED TO BE MAINTAINED BY 2 OR MORE PERSONS.—The Secretary *may prescribe* regulations which provide that, in cases in which 2 or more persons are required under subsection (a) to maintain the same list (or portion thereof), only 1 person shall be required to maintain such list (or portion).

* * *

[CCH Explanation at ¶605. Committee Reports at ¶11,070.]

Amendments

• **2004, American Jobs Creation Act of 2004 (H.R. 4520)**

H.R. 4520, §815(b)(3)(A)-(C):

Amended Code Sec. 6112 by redesignating subsection (c) as subsection (b), by inserting "written" before "request" in

subsection (b)(1) (as so redesignated), and by striking "shall prescribe" in subsection (b)(2) (as so redesignated) and inserting "may prescribe". **Effective** for transactions with respect to which material aid, assistance, or advice referred to in Code Sec. 6111(b)(1)(A)(i), as added by Act Sec. 815, is provided after the date of the enactment of this Act.

[¶ 6175] CODE SEC. 6156. INSTALLMENT PAYMENTS OF TAX ON USE OF HIGHWAY MOTOR VEHICLES. [Repealed.]

* * *

[CCH Explanation at ¶ 1547. Committee Reports at ¶ 11,480.]

Amendments

• **2004, American Jobs Creation Act of 2004 (H.R. 4520)**

H.R. 4520, § 867(b)(1):

Repealed Code Sec. 6156. **Effective** for tax periods beginning after the date of the enactment of this Act. Prior to repeal, Code Sec. 6156 read as follows:

SEC. 6156. INSTALLMENT PAYMENTS OF TAX ON USE OF HIGHWAY MOTOR VEHICLES.

(a) PRIVILEGE TO PAY TAX IN INSTALLMENTS.—If the taxpayer files a return of the tax imposed by section 4481 on or before the date prescribed for the filing of such return, he may elect to pay the tax shown on such return in equal installments in accordance with the following table:

If liability is incurred in—	The number of installments shall be—
July, August, or September	4
October, November, or December	3
January, February, or March	2

(b) DATES FOR PAYING INSTALLMENTS.—In the case of any tax payable in installments by reason of an election under subsection (a)—

(1) the first installment shall be paid on the date prescribed for payment of the tax,

(2) the second installment shall be paid on or before the last day of the third month following the calendar quarter in which the liability was incurred,

(3) the third installment (if any) shall be paid on or before the last day of the sixth month following the calendar quarter in which the liability was incurred, and

(4) the fourth installment (if any) shall be paid on or before the last day of the ninth month following the calendar quarter in which the liability was incurred.

(c) PRORATION OF ADDITIONAL TAX TO INSTALLMENTS.—If an election has been made under subsection (a) in respect of tax reported on a return filed by the taxpayer and tax required to be shown but not shown on such return is assessed before the date prescribed for payment of the last installment, the additional tax shall be prorated equally to the installments for which the election was made. That part of the additional tax so prorated to any installment the date for payment of which has not arrived shall be collected at the same time as and as part of such installment. That part of the additional tax so prorated to any installment the date for payment of which has arrived shall be paid upon notice and demand from the Secretary.

(d) ACCELERATION OF PAYMENTS.—If the taxpayer does not pay any installment under this section on or before the date prescribed for its payment, the whole of the unpaid tax shall be paid upon notice and demand from the Secretary.

(e) SECTION INAPPLICABLE TO CERTAIN LIABILITIES.—This section shall not apply to any liability for tax incurred in—

(1) April, May, or June of any year, or

(2) July, August, or September of 2005.

[¶ 6180] CODE SEC. 6159. AGREEMENTS FOR PAYMENT OF TAX LIABILITY IN INSTALLMENTS.

(a) AUTHORIZATION OF AGREEMENTS.—The Secretary is authorized to enter into written agreements with any taxpayer under which such taxpayer is allowed to *make payment on* any tax in installment payments if the Secretary determines that such agreement will facilitate *full or partial* collection of such liability.

* * *

[CCH Explanation at ¶ 1610. Committee Reports at ¶ 11,260.]

Amendments

• **2004, American Jobs Creation Act of 2004 (H.R. 4520)**

H.R. 4520, § 843(a)(1)(A)-(B):

Amended Code Sec. 6159(a) by striking "satisfy liability for payment of" and inserting "make payment on", and by

inserting "full or partial" after "facilitate". **Effective** for agreements entered into on or after the date of the enactment of this Act.

(c) SECRETARY REQUIRED TO ENTER INTO INSTALLMENT AGREEMENTS IN CERTAIN CASES.—In the case of a liability for tax of an individual under subtitle A, the Secretary shall enter into an agreement to accept the *full* payment of such tax in installments if, as of the date the individual offers to enter into the agreement—

(1) the aggregate amount of such liability (determined without regard to interest, penalties, additions to the tax, and additional amounts) does not exceed $10,000;

(2) the taxpayer (and, if such liability relates to a joint return, the taxpayer's spouse) has not, during any of the preceding 5 taxable years—

(A) failed to file any return of tax imposed by subtitle A;

(B) failed to pay any tax required to be shown on any such return; or

(C) entered into an installment agreement under this section for payment of any tax imposed by subtitle A,

(3) the Secretary determines that the taxpayer is financially unable to pay such liability in full when due (and the taxpayer submits such information as the Secretary may require to make such determination);

(4) the agreement requires full payment of such liability within 3 years; and

(5) the taxpayer agrees to comply with the provisions of this title for the period such agreement is in effect.

[CCH Explanation at ¶1610. Committee Reports at ¶11,260.]

Amendments
• **2004, American Jobs Creation Act of 2004 (H.R. 4520)**

H.R. 4520, §843(a)(2):

Amended the matter preceding paragraph (1) of Code Sec. 6159(c) by inserting "full" before "payment". **Effective** for agreements entered into on or after the date of the enactment of this Act.

(d) *SECRETARY REQUIRED TO REVIEW INSTALLMENT AGREEMENTS FOR PARTIAL COLLECTION EVERY TWO YEARS.—In the case of an agreement entered into by the Secretary under subsection (a) for partial collection of a tax liability, the Secretary shall review the agreement at least once every 2 years.*

[CCH Explanation at ¶1610. Committee Reports at ¶11,260.]

Amendments
• **2004, American Jobs Creation Act of 2004 (H.R. 4520)**

H.R. 4520, §843(b):

Amended Code Sec. 6159 by redesignating subsections (d) and (e) as subsections (e) and (f), respectively, and inserting after subsection (c) a new subsection (d). **Effective** for agreements entered into on or after the date of the enactment of this Act.

(e) *ADMINISTRATIVE REVIEW.*—The Secretary shall establish procedures for an independent administrative review of terminations of installment agreements under this section for taxpayers who request such a review.

[CCH Explanation at ¶1610. Committee Reports at ¶11,260.]

Amendments
• **2004, American Jobs Creation Act of 2004 (H.R. 4520)**

H.R. 4520, §843(b):

Amended Code Sec. 6159 by redesignating subsection (d) as subsection (e). **Effective** for agreements entered into on or after the date of the enactment of this Act.

(f) *CROSS REFERENCE.*—

For rights to administrative review and appeal, see section 7122(d).

* * *

[CCH Explanation at ¶1610. Committee Reports at ¶11,260.]

Amendments
• **2004, American Jobs Creation Act of 2004 (H.R. 4520)**

H.R. 4520, §843(b):

Amended Code Sec. 6159 by redesignating subsection (e) as subsection (f). **Effective** for agreements entered into on or after the date of the enactment of this Act.

[¶ 6185] CODE SEC. 6206. SPECIAL RULES APPLICABLE TO EXCESSIVE CLAIMS UNDER SECTIONS 6420, 6421, AND 6427.

Any portion of a payment made under section 6420, 6421, or 6427 which constitutes an excessive amount (as defined in section 6675(b)), and any civil penalty provided by section 6675, may be assessed and collected as if it were a tax imposed by section 4081 (with respect to payments under sections 6420 and 6421), or 4041 *or 4081* (with respect to payments under section 6427) and as if the person who made the claim were liable for such tax. The period for assessing any such portion, and for assessing any such penalty, shall be 3 years from the last day prescribed for the filing of the claim under section 6420, 6421, or 6427 as the case may be.

* * *

[CCH Explanation at ¶ 1507. Committee Reports at ¶ 11,340.]

Amendments

• 2004, American Jobs Creation Act of 2004 (H.R. 4520)

H.R. 4520, § 853(d)(2)(F):

Amended Code Sec. 6206 by striking ", 4081, or 4091" and inserting "or 4081". **Effective** for aviation-grade kerosene removed, entered, or sold after 12-31-2004.

[¶ 6190] *CODE SEC. 6306. QUALIFIED TAX COLLECTION CONTRACTS.*

(a) In General.—Nothing in any provision of law shall be construed to prevent the Secretary from entering into a qualified tax collection contract.

(b) Qualified Tax Collection Contract.—For purposes of this section, the term "qualified tax collection contract" means any contract which—

(1) is for the services of any person (other than an officer or employee of the Treasury Department)—

(A) to locate and contact any taxpayer specified by the Secretary,

(B) to request full payment from such taxpayer of an amount of Federal tax specified by the Secretary and, if such request cannot be met by the taxpayer, to offer the taxpayer an installment agreement providing for full payment of such amount during a period not to exceed 5 years, and

(C) to obtain financial information specified by the Secretary with respect to such taxpayer,

(2) prohibits each person providing such services under such contract from committing any act or omission which employees of the Internal Revenue Service are prohibited from committing in the performance of similar services,

(3) prohibits subcontractors from—

(A) having contacts with taxpayers,

(B) providing quality assurance services, and

(C) composing debt collection notices, and

(4) permits subcontractors to perform other services only with the approval of the Secretary.

(c) Fees.—The Secretary may retain and use—

(1) an amount not in excess of 25 percent of the amount collected under any qualified tax collection contract for the costs of services performed under such contract, and

(2) an amount not in excess of 25 percent of such amount collected for collection enforcement activities of the Internal Revenue Service.

The Secretary shall keep adequate records regarding amounts so retained and used. The amount credited as paid by any taxpayer shall be determined without regard to this subsection.

(d) No Federal Liability.—The United States shall not be liable for any act or omission of any person performing services under a qualified tax collection contract.

(e) Application of Fair Debt Collection Practices Act.—The provisions of the Fair Debt Collection Practices Act (15 U.S.C. 1692 et seq.) shall apply to any qualified tax collection contract, except to the extent superseded by section 6304, section 7602(c), or by any other provision of this title.

(f) CROSS REFERENCES.—

(1) For damages for certain unauthorized collection actions by persons performing services under a qualified tax collection contract, see section 7433A.

(2) For application of Taxpayer Assistance Orders to persons performing services under a qualified tax collection contract, see section 7811(g).

* * *

[CCH Explanation at ¶ 1605. Committee Reports at ¶ 11,530.]
Amendments
• **2004, American Jobs Creation Act of 2004 (H.R. 4520)**

H.R. 4520, § 881(a)(1):

Amended subchapter A of chapter 64 by adding at the end a new Code Sec. 6306. **Effective** on the date of the enactment of this Act.

[¶ 6195] CODE SEC. 6331. LEVY AND DISTRAINT.

* * *

(h) CONTINUING LEVY ON CERTAIN PAYMENTS.—

* * *

(3) INCREASE IN LEVY FOR CERTAIN PAYMENTS.—*Paragraph (1) shall be applied by substituting "100 percent" for "15 percent" in the case of any specified payment due to a vendor of goods or services sold or leased to the Federal Government.*

* * *

[CCH Explanation at ¶ 1625. Committee Reports at ¶ 11,590.]
Amendments
• **2004, American Jobs Creation Act of 2004 (H.R. 4520)**

H.R. 4520, § 887(a):

Amended Code Sec. 6331(h) by adding at the end a new paragraph (3). **Effective** on the date of the enactment of this Act.

[¶ 6200] CODE SEC. 6404. ABATEMENTS.

* * *

(g) SUSPENSION OF INTEREST AND CERTAIN PENALTIES WHERE SECRETARY FAILS TO CONTACT TAXPAYER.—

(1) SUSPENSION.—

(A) IN GENERAL.—In the case of an individual who files a return of tax imposed by subtitle A for a taxable year on or before the due date for the return (including extensions), if the Secretary does not provide a notice to the taxpayer specifically stating the taxpayer's liability and the basis for the liability before the close of the *18-month period* beginning on the later of—

   (i) the date on which the return is filed; or

   (ii) the due date of the return without regard to extensions,

the Secretary shall suspend the imposition of any interest, penalty, addition to tax, or additional amount with respect to any failure relating to the return which is computed by reference to the period of time the failure continues to exist and which is properly allocable to the suspension period.

* * *

(2) EXCEPTIONS.—Paragraph (1) shall not apply to—

   (A) any penalty imposed by section 6651;

   (B) any interest, penalty, addition to tax, or additional amount in a case involving fraud;

(C) any interest, penalty, addition to tax, or additional amount with respect to any tax liability shown on the return;

(D) any interest, penalty, addition to tax, or additional amount with respect to any gross misstatement;

(E) any interest, penalty, addition to tax, or additional amount with respect to any reportable transaction with respect to which the requirement of section 6664(d)(2)(A) is not met and any listed transaction (as defined in 6707A(c)); or

(F) any criminal penalty.

(3) SUSPENSION PERIOD.—For purposes of this subsection, the term "suspension period" means the period—

(A) beginning on the day after the close of the *18-month period* under paragraph (1); and

* * *

[CCH Explanation at ¶ 1620. Committee Reports at ¶ 11,750.]

Amendments

• **2004, American Jobs Creation Act of 2004 (H.R. 4520)**

H.R. 4520, § 903(a):

Amended Code Sec. 6404(g) by striking "1-year period (18-month period in the case of taxable years beginning before January 1, 2004)" both places it appears and inserting "18-month period". **Effective** for tax years beginning after 12-31-2003.

H.R. 4520, § 903(b):

Amended Code Sec. 6404(g)(2) by striking "or" at the end of subparagraph (C), by redesignating subparagraph (D) as

subparagraph (E), and by inserting after subparagraph (C) a new subparagraph (D). **Effective** for tax years beginning after 12-31-2003.

H.R. 4520, § 903(c):

Amended Code Sec. 6404(g)(2), as amended by Act Sec. 903(b), by striking "or" at the end of subparagraph (D), by redesignating subparagraph (E) as subparagraph (F), and by inserting after subparagraph (D) a new subparagraph (E). **Effective** with respect to interest accruing after 10-3-2004.

[¶ 6205] CODE SEC. 6416. CERTAIN TAXES ON SALES AND SERVICES.

(a) CONDITION TO ALLOWANCE.—

* * *

(4) REGISTERED ULTIMATE VENDOR TO ADMINISTER CREDITS AND REFUNDS OF GASOLINE TAX.—

(A) IN GENERAL.—For purposes of this subsection, if an ultimate vendor purchases any gasoline on which tax imposed by section 4081 has been paid and sells such gasoline to an ultimate purchaser described in subparagraph (C) or (D) of subsection (b)(2) (and such gasoline is for a use described in such subparagraph), such ultimate vendor shall be treated as the person (and the only person) who paid such tax, but only if such ultimate vendor is registered under section 4101.

(B) TIMING OF CLAIMS.—The procedure and timing of any claim under subparagraph (A) shall be the same as for claims under section 6427(i)(4), except that the rules of section 6427(i)(3)(B) regarding electronic claims shall not apply unless the ultimate vendor has certified to the Secretary for the most recent quarter of the taxable year that all ultimate purchasers of the vendor are certified and entitled to a refund under subparagraph (C) or (D) of subsection (b)(2).

[CCH Explanation at ¶ 1511. Committee Reports at ¶ 11,460.]

Amendments

• **2004, American Jobs Creation Act of 2004 (H.R. 4520)**

H.R. 4520, § 865(a):

Amended Code Sec. 6416(a)(4). **Effective** 1-1-2005. Prior to amendment, Code Sec. 6416(a)(4) read as follows:

(4) WHOLESALE DISTRIBUTORS TO ADMINISTER CREDITS AND REFUNDS OF GASOLINE TAX.—

(A) IN GENERAL.—For purposes of this subsection, a wholesale distributor who purchases any gasoline on which

tax imposed by section 4081 has been paid and who sells the gasoline to its ultimate purchaser shall be treated as the person (and the only person) who paid such tax.

(B) WHOLESALE DISTRIBUTOR.—For purposes of subparagraph (A), the term "wholesale distributor" has the meaning given such term by section 4093(b)(2) (determined by substituting "any gasoline taxable under section 4081" for "aviation fuel" therein). Such term includes any person who makes retail sales of gasoline at 10 or more retail motor fuel outlets.

(b) SPECIAL CASES IN WHICH TAX PAYMENTS CONSIDERED OVERPAYMENTS.—Under regulations prescribed by the Secretary, credit or refund (without interest) shall be allowed or made in respect of the overpayments determined under the following paragraphs:

* * *

(2) SPECIFIED USES AND RESALES.—The tax paid under chapter 32 (or under subsection (a) or (d) of section 4041 in respect of sales or under section 4051) in respect of any article shall be deemed to be an overpayment if such article was, by any person—

(A) exported;

(B) used or sold for use as supplies for vessels or aircraft;

(C) sold to a State or local government for the exclusive use of a State or local government;

(D) sold to a nonprofit educational organization for its exclusive use;

(E) in the case of any tire taxable under section 4071(a), sold to any person for use as described in section 4221(e)(3); or

(F) in the case of gasoline, used or sold for use in the production of special fuels referred to in section 4041.

Subparagraphs (C) and (D) shall not apply in the case of any tax paid under section 4064. This paragraph shall not apply in the case of any tax imposed under section 4041(a)(1) or 4081 on diesel fuel or kerosene and any tax paid under section 4121. In the case of the tax imposed by section 4131, subparagraphs (B), (C), and (D) shall not apply and subparagraph (A) shall apply only if the use of the exported vaccine meets such requirements as the Secretary may by regulations prescribe.

(3) TAX-PAID ARTICLES USED FOR FURTHER MANUFACTURE, ETC.—If the tax imposed by chapter 32 has been paid with respect to the sale of any article (other than coal taxable under section 4121) by the manufacturer, producer, or importer thereof and such article is sold to a subsequent manufacturer or producer before being used, such tax shall be deemed to be an overpayment by such subsequent manufacturer or producer if—

(A) in the case of any article other than any fuel taxable under section 4081, such article is used by the subsequent manufacturer or producer as material in the manufacture or production of, or as a component part of—

(i) another article taxable under chapter 32, or

(ii) an automobile bus chassis or an automobile bus body, manufactured or produced by him; or

(B) in the case of any fuel taxable under section 4081, such fuel is used by the subsequent manufacturer or producer, for nonfuel purposes, as a material in the manufacture or production of any other article manufactured or produced by him.

* * *

[CCH Explanation at ¶1507. Committee Reports at ¶11,340.]

Amendments

• **2004, American Jobs Creation Act of 2004 (H.R. 4520)**

H.R. 4520, §853(d)(2)(G):

Amended Code Sec. 6416(b)(2) by striking "4091 or" immediately preceding "4121". **Effective** for aviation-grade kerosene removed, entered, or sold after 12-31-2004.

H.R. 4520, §853(d)(2)(H):

Amended Code Sec. 6416(b)(3) by striking "or 4091" after "section 4081" each place it appears. **Effective** for aviation-grade kerosene removed, entered, or sold after 12-31-2004.

(d) CREDIT ON RETURNS.—Any person entitled to a refund of tax imposed by chapter 31 or 32, paid to the Secretary may, instead of filing a claim for refund, take credit therefor against taxes imposed by such chapter due on any subsequent return. The preceding sentence shall not apply to the tax imposed by section 4081 in the case of refunds described in section 4081(e).

* * *

[CCH Explanation at ¶ 1507. Committee Reports at ¶ 11,340.]
Amendments

• 2004, American Jobs Creation Act of 2004 (H.R. 4520)

H.R. 4520, § 853(d)(2)(I):

Amended Code Sec. 6416(d) by striking "or to the tax imposed by section 4091 in the case of refunds described in section 4091(d)" immediately preceding the period at the end of the last sentence. **Effective** for aviation-grade kerosene removed, entered, or sold after 12-31-2004.

[¶ 6210] CODE SEC. 6421. GASOLINE USED FOR CERTAIN NONHIGHWAY PURPOSES, USED BY LOCAL TRANSIT SYSTEMS, OR SOLD FOR CERTAIN EXEMPT PURPOSES.

* * *

(e) DEFINITIONS.—For purposes of this section—

* * *

(2) OFF-HIGHWAY BUSINESS USE.—

* * *

(C) USES IN MOBILE MACHINERY.—

(i) IN GENERAL.—*The term "off-highway business use" shall include any use in a vehicle which meets the requirements described in clause (ii).*

(ii) REQUIREMENTS FOR MOBILE MACHINERY.—*The requirements described in this clause are—*

(I) *the design-based test, and*

(II) *the use-based test.*

(iii) DESIGN-BASED TEST.—*For purposes of clause (ii)(I), the design-based test is met if the vehicle consists of a chassis—*

(I) *to which there has been permanently mounted (by welding, bolting, riveting, or other means) machinery or equipment to perform a construction, manufacturing, processing, farming, mining, drilling, timbering, or similar operation if the operation of the machinery or equipment is unrelated to transportation on or off the public highways,*

(II) *which has been specially designed to serve only as a mobile carriage and mount (and a power source, where applicable) for the particular machinery or equipment involved, whether or not such machinery or equipment is in operation, and*

(III) *which, by reason of such special design, could not, without substantial structural modification, be used as a component of a vehicle designed to perform a function of transporting any load other than that particular machinery or equipment or similar machinery or equipment requiring such a specially designed chassis.*

(iv) USE-BASED TEST.—*For purposes of clause (ii)(II), the use-based test is met if the use of the vehicle on public highways was less than 7,500 miles during the taxpayer's taxable year. This clause shall be applied without regard to use of the vehicle by any organization which is described in section 501(c) and exempt from tax under section 501(a).*

[CCH Explanation at ¶ 1549. Committee Reports at ¶ 11,320.]
Amendments

• 2004, American Jobs Creation Act of 2004 (H.R. 4520)

H.R. 4520, § 851(d)(1):

Amended Code Sec. 6421(e)(2) by adding at the end a new subparagraph (C). **Effective** for tax years beginning after the date of the enactment of this Act.

(f) EXEMPT SALES; OTHER PAYMENTS OR REFUNDS AVAILABLE.—

* * *

(3) GASOLINE USED IN TRAINS.—In the case of gasoline used as a fuel in a train, this section shall not apply with respect to—

(A) the Leaking Underground Storage Tank Trust Fund financing rate under section 4081, and

(B) *so much of the rate specified in section 4081(a)(2)(A) as does not exceed the rate applicable under section 4041(a)(1)(C)(ii).*

* * *

[CCH Explanation at ¶ 1513. Committee Reports at ¶ 10,220.]

Amendments

• **2004, American Jobs Creation Act of 2004 (H.R. 4520)**

H.R. 4520, § 241(a)(2)(C):

Amended Code Sec. 6421(f)(3)(B). **Effective** on 1-1-2005. Prior to amendment, Code Sec. 6421(f)(3)(B) read as follows:

(B) so much of the rate specified in section 4081(a)(2)(A) as does not exceed—

(i) 6.8 cents per gallon after September 30, 1993, and before October 1, 1995,

(ii) 5.55 cents per gallon after September 30, 1995, and before November 1, 1998, and

(iii) 4.3 cents per gallon after October 31, 1998.

[¶ 6215] *CODE SEC. 6426. CREDIT FOR ALCOHOL FUEL AND BIODIESEL MIXTURES.*

(a) ALLOWANCE OF CREDITS.—There shall be allowed as a credit against the tax imposed by section 4081 an amount equal to the sum of—

(1) the alcohol fuel mixture credit, plus

(2) the biodiesel mixture credit.

(b) ALCOHOL FUEL MIXTURE CREDIT.—

(1) IN GENERAL.—For purposes of this section, the alcohol fuel mixture credit is the product of the applicable amount and the number of gallons of alcohol used by the taxpayer in producing any alcohol fuel mixture for sale or use in a trade or business of the taxpayer.

(2) APPLICABLE AMOUNT.—For purposes of this subsection—

(A) IN GENERAL.—Except as provided in subparagraph (B), the applicable amount is 51 cents.

(B) MIXTURES NOT CONTAINING ETHANOL.—In the case of an alcohol fuel mixture in which none of the alcohol consists of ethanol, the applicable amount is 60 cents.

(3) ALCOHOL FUEL MIXTURE.—For purposes of this subsection, the term "alcohol fuel mixture" means a mixture of alcohol and a taxable fuel which—

(A) is sold by the taxpayer producing such mixture to any person for use as a fuel, or

(B) is used as a fuel by the taxpayer producing such mixture.

For purposes of subparagraph (A), a mixture produced by any person at a refinery prior to a taxable event which includes ethyl tertiary butyl ether or other ethers produced from alcohol shall be treated as sold at the time of its removal from the refinery (and only at such time) to another person for use as a fuel.

(4) OTHER DEFINITIONS.—For purposes of this subsection—

(A) ALCOHOL.—The term "alcohol" includes methanol and ethanol but does not include—

(i) alcohol produced from petroleum, natural gas, or coal (including peat), or

(ii) alcohol with a proof of less than 190 (determined without regard to any added denaturants).

Such term also includes an alcohol gallon equivalent of ethyl tertiary butyl ether or other ethers produced from such alcohol.

(B) TAXABLE FUEL.—The term "taxable fuel" has the meaning given such term by section 4083(a)(1).

(5) TERMINATION.—This subsection shall not apply to any sale, use, or removal for any period after December 31, 2010.

(c) BIODIESEL MIXTURE CREDIT.—

(1) IN GENERAL.—*For purposes of this section, the biodiesel mixture credit is the product of the applicable amount and the number of gallons of biodiesel used by the taxpayer in producing any biodiesel mixture for sale or use in a trade or business of the taxpayer.*

(2) APPLICABLE AMOUNT.—*For purposes of this subsection—*

(A) IN GENERAL.—*Except as provided in subparagraph (B), the applicable amount is 50 cents.*

(B) AMOUNT FOR AGRI–BIODIESEL.—*In the case of any biodiesel which is agri-biodiesel, the applicable amount is $1.00.*

(3) BIODIESEL MIXTURE.—*For purposes of this section, the term "biodiesel mixture" means a mixture of biodiesel and diesel fuel (as defined in section 4083(a)(3)), determined without regard to any use of kerosene, which—*

(A) is sold by the taxpayer producing such mixture to any person for use as a fuel, or

(B) is used as a fuel by the taxpayer producing such mixture.

(4) CERTIFICATION FOR BIODIESEL.—*No credit shall be allowed under this subsection unless the taxpayer obtains a certification (in such form and manner as prescribed by the Secretary) from the producer of the biodiesel which identifies the product produced and the percentage of biodiesel and agri-biodiesel in the product.*

(5) OTHER DEFINITIONS.—*Any term used in this subsection which is also used in section 40A shall have the meaning given such term by section 40A.*

(6) TERMINATION.—*This subsection shall not apply to any sale, use, or removal for any period after December 31, 2006.*

(d) MIXTURE NOT USED AS A FUEL, ETC.—

(1) IMPOSITION OF TAX.—*If—*

(A) any credit was determined under this section with respect to alcohol or biodiesel used in the production of any alcohol fuel mixture or biodiesel mixture, respectively, and

(B) any person—

(i) separates the alcohol or biodiesel from the mixture, or

(ii) without separation, uses the mixture other than as a fuel,

then there is hereby imposed on such person a tax equal to the product of the applicable amount and the number of gallons of such alcohol or biodiesel.

(2) APPLICABLE LAWS.—*All provisions of law, including penalties, shall, insofar as applicable and not inconsistent with this section, apply in respect of any tax imposed under paragraph (1) as if such tax were imposed by section 4081 and not by this section.*

(e) COORDINATION WITH EXEMPTION FROM EXCISE TAX.—*Rules similar to the rules under section 40(c) shall apply for purposes of this section.*

[CCH Explanation at ¶ 805. Committee Reports at ¶ 10,320.]

Amendments

• **2004, American Jobs Creation Act of 2004 (H.R. 4520)**

H.R. 4520, § 301(a):

Amended subchapter B of chapter 65 by inserting after Code Sec. 6425 a new Code Sec. 6426. **Effective** for fuel sold or used after 12-31-2004.

[¶ 6220] CODE SEC. 6427. FUELS NOT USED FOR TAXABLE PURPOSES.

* * *

(b) INTERCITY, LOCAL OR SCHOOL BUSES.

* * *

(4) REFUNDS FOR USE OF DIESEL FUEL IN CERTAIN INTERCITY BUSES.—With respect to any fuel to which paragraph (2)(A) applies, if the ultimate purchaser of such fuel waives (at such time and in such form and manner as the Secretary shall prescribe) the right to payment under paragraph (1) and assigns such right to the ultimate vendor, then the Secretary shall pay the amount which would be paid under paragraph (1) to such ultimate vendor, but only if such ultimate vendor—

(A) is registered under section 4101, and

(B) meets the requirements of subparagraph (A), (B), or (D) of section 6416(a)(1).

* * *

[CCH Explanation at ¶ 1523. Committee Reports at ¶ 11,350.]

Amendments

• **2004, American Jobs Creation Act of 2004 (H.R. 4520)**

H.R. 4520, § 857(b):

Amended Code Sec. 6427(b) by adding at the end a new paragraph (4). **Effective** for fuel sold after 12-31-2004.

(e) ALCOHOL OR BIODIESEL USED TO PRODUCE ALCOHOL FUEL AND BIODIESEL MIXTURES.—Except as provided in subsection (k)—

(1) USED TO PRODUCE A MIXTURE.—If any person produces a mixture described in section 6426 in such person's trade or business, the Secretary shall pay (without interest) to such person an amount equal to the alcohol fuel mixture credit or the biodiesel mixture credit with respect to such mixture.

(2) COORDINATION WITH OTHER REPAYMENT PROVISIONS.—No amount shall be payable under paragraph (1) with respect to any mixture with respect to which an amount is allowed as a credit under section 6426.

(3) TERMINATION.—This subsection shall not apply with respect to—

(A) any alcohol fuel mixture (as defined in section 6426(b)(3)) sold or used after December 31, 2010, and

(B) any biodiesel mixture (as defined in section 6426(c)(3)) sold or used after December 31, 2006.

* * *

[CCH Explanation at ¶ 805. Committee Reports at ¶ 10,320.]

Amendments

• **2004, American Jobs Creation Act of 2004 (H.R. 4520)**

H.R. 4520, § 301(c)(9):

Amended Code Sec. 6427 by inserting after subsection (d) a new subsection (e). **Effective** for fuel sold or used after 12-31-2004.

(h) BLEND STOCKS NOT USED FOR PRODUCING TAXABLE FUEL.—

(1) GASOLINE BLEND STOCKS OR ADDITIVES NOT USED FOR PRODUCING GASOLINE.—Except as provided in subsection (k), if any gasoline blend stock or additive (within the meaning of section 4083(a)(2)) is not used by any person to produce gasoline and such person establishes that the ultimate use of such gasoline blend stock or additive is not to produce gasoline, the Secretary shall pay (without interest) to such person an amount equal to the aggregate amount of the tax imposed on such person with respect to such gasoline blend stock or additive.

(2) DIESEL FUEL BLEND STOCKS OR ADDITIVES NOT USED FOR PRODUCING DIESEL.—Except as provided in subsection (k), if any diesel fuel blend stock is not used by any person to produce diesel fuel and such person establishes that the ultimate use of such diesel fuel blend stock is not to produce diesel fuel, the Secretary shall pay (without interest) to such person an amount equal to the aggregate amount of the tax imposed on such person with respect to such diesel fuel blend stock.

[CCH Explanation at ¶1509. Committee Reports at ¶11,510.]

Amendments

• **2004, American Jobs Creation Act of 2004 (H.R. 4520)**

H.R. 4520, §870(b):

Amended Code Sec. 6427(h). **Effective** for fuel removed, sold, or used after 12-31-2004. Prior to amendment, Code Sec. 6427(h) read as follows:

(h) GASOLINE BLEND STOCKS OR ADDITIVES NOT USED FOR PRODUCING GASOLINE.—Except as provided in subsection (k), if any gasoline blend stock or additive (within the meaning of section 4083(a)(2)) is not used by any person to produce gasoline and such person establishes that the ultimate use of such gasoline blend stock or additive is not to produce gasoline, the Secretary shall pay (without interest) to such person an amount equal to the aggregate amount of the tax imposed on such person with respect to such gasoline blend stock or additive.

(i) TIME FOR FILING CLAIMS; PERIOD COVERED.—

* * *

(2) EXCEPTIONS.—

* * *

(C) NONAPPLICATION OF PARAGRAPH.—*This paragraph shall not apply to any fuel used solely in any off-highway business use described in section 6421(e)(2)(C).*

(3) SPECIAL RULE FOR *ALCOHOL FUEL AND BIODIESEL MIXTURE* CREDIT.—

(A) IN GENERAL.—A claim may be filed under *subsection (e)(1)* by any person with respect to *a mixture described in section 6426* for any period—

(i) for which $200 or more is payable under such *subsection (e)(1)*, and

(ii) which is not less than 1 week.

In the case of an electronic claim, this subparagraph shall be applied without regard to clause (i).

(B) PAYMENT OF CLAIM.—Notwithstanding *subsection (e)(1)*, if the Secretary has not paid pursuant to a claim filed under this section within *45 days of the date of the filing of such claim (20 days in the case of an electronic claim)*, the claim shall be paid with interest from such date determined by using the overpayment rate and method under section 6621.

(C) TIME FOR FILING CLAIM.—No claim filed under this paragraph shall be allowed unless filed on or before the last day of the first quarter following the earliest quarter included in the claim.

(4) SPECIAL RULE FOR VENDOR REFUNDS.—

(A) IN GENERAL.—A claim may be filed under *subsections (b)(4) and paragraph (4)(B) or (5) of subsection (l)* by any person with respect to fuel sold by such person for any period—

(i) for which $200 or more ($100 or more in the case of kerosene) is payable under *paragraph (4)(B) or (5) of subsection (l)*, and

(ii) which is not less than 1 week.

Notwithstanding subsection (l)(1), paragraph (3)(B) shall apply to claims filed under *subsections (b)(4) and subsection (l)(5).*

* * *

[CCH Explanation at ¶805, ¶1507, ¶1523 and ¶1549. Committee Reports at ¶10,320, ¶11,320, ¶11,340 and ¶11,350.]

Amendments

• **2004, American Jobs Creation Act of 2004 (H.R. 4520)**

H.R. 4520, §301(c)(10)(A)-(F):

Amended Code Sec. 6427(i)(3) by striking "subsection (f)" both places it appears in subparagraph (A) and inserting "subsection (e)(1)", by striking "gasoline, diesel fuel, or kerosene used to produce a qualified alcohol mixture (as defined in section 4081(c)(3))" in subparagraph (A) and inserting "a mixture described in section 6426", by adding at the end of subparagraph (A) a new flush sentence, by striking "subsection (f)(1)" in subparagraph (B) and inserting "subsection (e)(1)", by striking "20 days of the date of the filing of such claim" in subparagraph (B) and inserting "45 days of the date of the filing of such claim (20 days in the case of an electronic claim)", and by striking "ALCOHOL MIXTURE" in the heading and inserting "ALCOHOL FUEL AND BIODIESEL MIXTURE". **Effective** for fuel sold or used after 12-31-2004. For a special rule, see Act Sec. 301(e), below. Prior to amendment, Code Sec. 6427(i)(3) read as follows:

(3) SPECIAL RULE FOR ALCOHOL MIXTURE CREDIT.—

(A) IN GENERAL.—A claim may be filed under subsection (f) by any person with respect to gasoline, diesel fuel, or kerosene used to produce a qualified alcohol mixture (as defined in section 4081(c)(3)) for any period—

(i) for which $200 or more is payable under such subsection (f), and

(ii) which is not less than 1 week.

(B) PAYMENT OF CLAIM.—Notwithstanding subsection (f)(1), if the Secretary has not paid pursuant to a claim filed under this section within 20 days of the date of the filing of such claim, the claim shall be paid with interest from such date determined by using the overpayment rate and method under section 6621.

(C) TIME FOR FILING CLAIM.—No claim filed under this paragraph shall be allowed unless filed on or before the last day of the first quarter following the earliest quarter included in the claim.

H.R. 4520, § 301(e), provides:

(e) FORMAT FOR FILING.—The Secretary of the Treasury shall describe the electronic format for filing claims described in section 6427(i)(3)(B) of the Internal Revenue Code of 1986 (as amended by subsection (c)(10)(C)) not later than December 31, 2004.

H.R. 4520, § 851(d)(3):

Amended Code Sec. 6427(i)(2) by adding at the end a new subparagraph (C). **Effective** for tax years beginning after the date of the enactment of this Act.

H.R. 4520, § 853(c)(2)(A)-(B):

Amended Code Sec. 6427(i)(4)(A) by striking "subsection (l)(5)" both places it appears and inserting "paragraph (4)(B) or (5) of subsection (l)", and by striking "the preceding sentence" and inserting "subsection (l)(5)". **Effective** for aviation-grade kerosene removed, entered, or sold after 12-31-2004. For special rules, see Act Sec. 853(f), below.

H.R. 4520, § 853(f), provides:

(f) FLOOR STOCKS TAX.—

(1) IN GENERAL.—There is hereby imposed on aviation-grade kerosene held on January 1, 2005, by any person a tax equal to—

(A) the tax which would have been imposed before such date on such kerosene had the amendments made by this section been in effect at all times before such date, reduced by

(B) the sum of—

(i) the tax imposed before such date on such kerosene under section 4091 of the Internal Revenue Code of 1986, as in effect on such date, and

(j) APPLICABLE LAWS.—

(ii) in the case of kerosene held exclusively for such person's own use, the amount which such person would (but for this clause) reasonably expect (as of such date) to be paid as a refund under section 6427(l) of such Code with respect to such kerosene.

(2) EXCEPTION FOR FUEL HELD IN AIRCRAFT FUEL TANK.—Paragraph (1) shall not apply to kerosene held in the fuel tank of an aircraft on January 1, 2005.

(3) LIABILITY FOR TAX AND METHOD OF PAYMENT.—

(A) LIABILITY FOR TAX.—The person holding the kerosene on January 1, 2005, to which the tax imposed by paragraph (1) applies shall be liable for such tax.

(B) METHOD AND TIME FOR PAYMENT.—The tax imposed by paragraph (1) shall be paid at such time and in such manner as the Secretary of the Treasury (or the Secretary's delegate) shall prescribe, including the nonapplication of such tax on de minimis amounts of kerosene.

(4) TRANSFER OF FLOOR STOCK TAX REVENUES TO TRUST FUNDS.—For purposes of determining the amount transferred to any trust fund, the tax imposed by this subsection shall be treated as imposed by section 4081 of the Internal Revenue Code of 1986—

(A) in any case in which tax was not imposed by section 4091 of such Code, at the Leaking Underground Storage Tank Trust Fund financing rate under such section to the extent of 0.1 cents per gallon, and

(B) at the rate under section 4081(a)(2)(A)(iv) of such Code to the extent of the remainder.

(5) HELD BY A PERSON.—For purposes of this subsection, kerosene shall be considered as held by a person if title thereto has passed to such person (whether or not delivery to the person has been made).

(6) OTHER LAWS APPLICABLE.—All provisions of law, including penalties, applicable with respect to the tax imposed by section 4081 of such Code shall, insofar as applicable and not inconsistent with the provisions of this subsection, apply with respect to the floor stock tax imposed by paragraph (1) to the same extent as if such tax were imposed by such section.

H.R. 4520, § 857(c):

Amended Code Sec. 6427(i)(4)(A), as amended by this Act, by inserting "subsections (b)(4) and" after "filed under". **Effective** for fuel sold after 12-31-2004.

(1) IN GENERAL.—All provisions of law, including penalties, applicable in respect of the taxes imposed by sections 4041 *and 4081* shall, insofar as applicable and not inconsistent with this section, apply in respect of the payments provided for in this section to the same extent as if such payments constituted refunds of overpayments of the tax so imposed.

* * *

[CCH Explanation at ¶ 1507. Committee Reports at ¶ 11,340.]

Amendments

• **2004, American Jobs Creation Act of 2004 (H.R. 4520)**

H.R. 4520, § 853(d)(2)(J):

Amended Code Sec. 6427(j)(1) by striking ", 4081, and 4091" and inserting "and 4081". **Effective** for aviation-grade

kerosene removed, entered, or sold after 12-31-2004. For special rules, see Act Sec. 853(f) in the amendment notes following Code Sec. 6427(i).

(l) NONTAXABLE USES OF DIESEL FUEL, KEROSENE AND AVIATION FUEL.—

(1) IN GENERAL.—Except as otherwise provided in this subsection and in subsection (k), if any diesel fuel or kerosene on which tax has been imposed by section 4041 or 4081 is used by any person in a nontaxable use, the Secretary shall pay (without interest) to the ultimate purchaser of such fuel an amount equal to the aggregate amount of tax imposed on such fuel under section 4041 or 4081, as the case may be, reduced by any payment made to the ultimate vendor under paragraph (4)(B).

(2) NONTAXABLE USE.—For purposes of this subsection, the term "nontaxable use" means—

(A) in the case of diesel fuel or kerosene, any use which is exempt from the tax imposed by section 4041(a)(1) other than by reason of a prior imposition of tax, and

(B) *in the case of aviation-grade kerosene—*

(i) *any use which is exempt from the tax imposed by section 4041(c) other than by reason of a prior imposition of tax, or*

(ii) *any use in commercial aviation (within the meaning of section 4083(b)).*

(3) REFUND OF CERTAIN TAXES ON FUEL USED IN DIESEL-POWERED TRAINS.—For purposes of this subsection, the term "nontaxable use" includes fuel used in a diesel-powered train. The preceding sentence shall not apply with respect to—

(A) the Leaking Underground Storage Tank Trust Fund financing rate under sections 4041 and 4081, and

(B) *so much of the rate specified in section 4081(a)(2)(A) as does not exceed the rate applicable under section 4041(a)(1)(C)(ii).*

The preceding sentence shall not apply in the case of fuel sold for exclusive use by a State or any political subdivision thereof.

(4) *REFUNDS FOR AVIATION-GRADE KEROSENE.—*

(A) *NO REFUND OF CERTAIN TAXES ON FUEL USED IN COMMERCIAL AVIATION.—In the case of aviation-grade kerosene used in commercial aviation (as defined in section 4083(b)) (other than supplies for vessels or aircraft within the meaning of section 4221(d)(3)), paragraph (1) shall not apply to so much of the tax imposed by section 4081 as is attributable to—*

(i) *the Leaking Underground Storage Tank Trust Fund financing rate imposed by such section, and*

(ii) *so much of the rate of tax specified in section 4081(a)(2)(A)(iv) as does not exceed 4.3 cents per gallon.*

(B) *PAYMENT TO ULTIMATE, REGISTERED VENDOR.—With respect to aviationgrade kerosene, if the ultimate purchaser of such kerosene waives (at such time and in such form and manner as the Secretary shall prescribe) the right to payment under paragraph (1) and assigns such right to the ultimate vendor, then the Secretary shall pay the amount which would be paid under paragraph (1) to such ultimate vendor, but only if such ultimate vendor—*

(i) *is registered under section 4101, and*

(ii) *meets the requirements of subparagraph (A), (B), or (D) of section 6416(a)(1).*

(5) REGISTERED VENDORS TO ADMINISTER CLAIMS FOR REFUND OF DIESEL FUEL OR KEROSENE SOLD TO FARMERS AND STATE AND LOCAL GOVERNMENTS.—

* * *

(B) SALES OF KEROSENE NOT FOR USE IN MOTOR FUEL.— *Paragraph (1) shall not apply to kerosene (other than aviation-grade kerosene) sold by a vendor—*

(i) for any use if such sale is from a pump which (as determined under regulations prescribed by the Secretary) is not suitable for use in fueling any diesel-powered highway vehicle or train, or

(ii) to the extent provided by the Secretary, for blending with heating oil to be used during periods of extreme or unseasonable cold.

* * *

[CCH Explanation at ¶1507 and ¶1513. Committee Reports at ¶10,220 and ¶11,340.]

Amendments

• **2004, American Jobs Creation Act of 2004 (H.R. 4520)**

H.R. 4520, §241(a)(2)(D):

Amended Code Sec. 6427(l)(3)(B). **Effective** on 1-1-2005. Prior to amendment, Code Sec. 6427(l)(3)(B) read as follows:

(B) so much of the rate specified in section 4081(a)(2)(A) as does not exceed—

(i) 6.8 cents per gallon after September 30, 1993, and before October 1, 1995,

(ii) 5.55 cents per gallon after September 30, 1995, and before November 1, 1998, and

(iii) 4.3 cents per gallon after October 31, 1998.

H.R. 4520, §853(c)(1):

Amended Code Sec. 6427(l)(4). **Effective** for aviation-grade kerosene removed, entered, or sold after 12-31-2004.

For special rules, see Act Sec. 853(f) in the amendment notes following Code Sec. 6427(i). Prior to amendment, Code Sec. 6427(l)(4) read as follows:

(4) No REFUND OF CERTAIN TAXES ON FUEL USED IN COMMERCIALAVIATION.—In the case of fuel used in commercial aviation (as defined in section 4092(b)) (other than supplies for vessels or aircraft within the meaning of section 4221(d)(3)), paragraph (1) shall not apply to so much of the tax imposed by section 4091 as is attributable to—

(A) the Leaking Underground Storage Tank Trust Fund financing rate imposed by such section, and

(B) in the case of fuel purchased after September 30, 1995, so much of the rate of tax specified in section 4091(b)(1) as does not exceed 4.3 cents per gallon.

H.R. 4520, § 853(c)(3):

Amended Code Sec. 6427(l)(2)(B). **Effective** for aviation-grade kerosene removed, entered, or sold after 12-31-2004. For special rules, see Act Sec. 853(f) in the amendment notes following Code Sec. 6427(i). Prior to amendment, Code Sec. 6427(l)(2)(B) read as follows:

(B) in the case of aviation fuel, any use which is exempt from the tax imposed by section 4041(c)(1) other than by reason of a prior imposition of tax.

H.R. 4520, § 853(d)(2)(K)(i):

Amended Code Sec. 6427(l)(1). **Effective** for aviation-grade kerosene removed, entered, or sold after 12-31-2004.

For special rules, see Act Sec. 853(f) in the amendment notes following Code Sec. 6427(i). Prior to amendment, Code Sec. 6427(l)(1) read as follows:

(1) IN GENERAL.—Except as otherwise provided in this subsection and in subsection (k), if—

(A) any diesel fuel or kerosene on which tax has been imposed by section 4041 or 4081, or

(B) any aviation fuel on which tax has been imposed by section 4091,

is used by any person in a nontaxable use, the Secretary shall pay (without interest) to the ultimate purchaser of such fuel an amount equal to the aggregate amount of tax imposed on such fuel under section 4041, 4081, or 4091, as the case may be.

H.R. 4520, § 853(d)(2)(K)(ii):

Amended Code Sec. 6427(l)(5)(B) by striking "Paragraph (1)(A) shall not apply to kerosene" and inserting "Paragraph (1) shall not apply to kerosene (other than aviation-grade kerosene)". **Effective** for aviation-grade kerosene removed, entered, or sold after 12-31-2004. For special rules, see Act Sec. 853(f) in the amendment notes following Code Sec. 6427(i).

[¶ 6225] CODE SEC. 6501. LIMITATIONS ON ASSESSMENT AND COLLECTION.

* * *

(c) EXCEPTIONS.—

* * *

(10) LISTED TRANSACTIONS.—*If a taxpayer fails to include on any return or statement for any taxable year any information with respect to a listed transaction (as defined in section 6707A(c)(2)) which is required under section 6011 to be included with such return or statement, the time for assessment of any tax imposed by this title with respect to such transaction shall not expire before the date which is 1 year after the earlier of—*

(A) the date on which the Secretary is furnished the information so required, or

(B) the date that a material advisor (as defined in section 6111) meets the requirements of section 6112 with respect to a request by the Secretary under section 6112(b) relating to such transaction with respect to such taxpayer.

* * *

[CCH Explanation at ¶ 610. Committee Reports at ¶ 11,060.]

Amendments

• **2004, American Jobs Creation Act of 2004 (H.R. 4520)**

H.R. 4520, § 814(a):

Amended Code Sec. 6501(c) by adding at the end a new paragraph (10). **Effective** for tax years with respect to which

the period for assessing a deficiency did not expire before the date of the enactment of this Act.

(e) SUBSTANTIAL OMISSION OF ITEMS.—Except as otherwise provided in subsection (c)—

(1) INCOME TAXES.—In the case of any tax imposed by subtitle A—

* * *

(B) CONSTRUCTIVE DIVIDENDS.—If the taxpayer omits from gross income an amount properly includible therein under section 951(a), the tax may be assessed, or a proceeding in court for the collection of such tax may be done without assessing, at any time within 6 years after the return was filed.

* * *

[CCH Explanation at ¶490. Committee Reports at ¶10,690.]

Amendments

• **2004, American Jobs Creation Act of 2004 (H.R. 4520)**

H.R. 4520, §413(c)(28):

Amended Code Sec. 6501(e)(1)(B). **Effective** for tax years of foreign corporations beginning after 12-31-2004, and for tax years of United States shareholders with or within which such tax years of foreign corporations end. Prior to amendment, Code Sec. 6501(e)(1)(B) read as follows:

(B) CONSTRUCTIVE DIVIDENDS.—If the taxpayer omits from gross income an amount properly includible therein under section 551(b) (relating to the inclusion in the gross income of United States shareholders of their distributive shares of the undistributed foreign personal holding company income), the tax may be assessed, or a proceeding in court for the collection of such tax may be begun without assessment, at any time within 6 years after the return was filed.

[¶6230] *CODE SEC. 6603. DEPOSITS MADE TO SUSPEND RUNNING OF INTEREST ON POTENTIAL UNDERPAYMENTS, ETC.*

(a) AUTHORITY TO MAKE DEPOSITS OTHER THAN AS PAYMENT OF TAX.—*A taxpayer may make a cash deposit with the Secretary which may be used by the Secretary to pay any tax imposed under subtitle A or B or chapter 41, 42, 43, or 44 which has not been assessed at the time of the deposit. Such a deposit shall be made in such manner as the Secretary shall prescribe.*

(b) NO INTEREST IMPOSED.—*To the extent that such deposit is used by the Secretary to pay tax, for purposes of section 6601 (relating to interest on underpayments), the tax shall be treated as paid when the deposit is made.*

(c) RETURN OF DEPOSIT.—*Except in a case where the Secretary determines that collection of tax is in jeopardy, the Secretary shall return to the taxpayer any amount of the deposit (to the extent not used for a payment of tax) which the taxpayer requests in writing.*

(d) PAYMENT OF INTEREST.—

(1) IN GENERAL.—*For purposes of section 6611 (relating to interest on overpayments), except as provided in paragraph (4), a deposit which is returned to a taxpayer shall be treated as a payment of tax for any period to the extent (and only to the extent) attributable to a disputable tax for such period. Under regulations prescribed by the Secretary, rules similar to the rules of section 6611(b)(2) shall apply.*

(2) DISPUTABLE TAX.—

(A) IN GENERAL.—*For purposes of this section, the term "disputable tax" means the amount of tax specified at the time of the deposit as the taxpayer's reasonable estimate of the maximum amount of any tax attributable to disputable items.*

(B) SAFE HARBOR BASED ON 30-DAY LETTER.—*In the case of a taxpayer who has been issued a 30-day letter, the maximum amount of tax under subparagraph (A) shall not be less than the amount of the proposed deficiency specified in such letter.*

(3) OTHER DEFINITIONS.—*For purposes of paragraph (2)—*

(A) DISPUTABLE ITEM.—*The term "disputable item" means any item of income, gain, loss, deduction, or credit if the taxpayer—*

(i) *has a reasonable basis for its treatment of such item, and*

(ii) *reasonably believes that the Secretary also has a reasonable basis for disallowing the taxpayer's treatment of such item.*

(B) 30-DAY LETTER.—*The term "30-day letter" means the first letter of proposed deficiency which allows the taxpayer an opportunity for administrative review in the Internal Revenue Service Office of Appeals.*

(4) RATE OF INTEREST.—*The rate of interest under this subsection shall be the Federal short-term rate determined under section 6621(b), compounded daily.*

(e) USE OF DEPOSITS.—

(1) PAYMENT OF TAX.—*Except as otherwise provided by the taxpayer, deposits shall be treated as used for the payment of tax in the order deposited.*

(2) RETURNS OF DEPOSITS.—*Deposits shall be treated as returned to the taxpayer on a last-in, first-out basis.*

* * *

[CCH Explanation at ¶ 1615. Committee Reports at ¶ 11,250.]

Amendments

• **2004, American Jobs Creation Act of 2004 (H.R. 4520)**

H.R. 4520, § 842(a):

Amended subchapter A of chapter 67 by adding at the end a new Code Sec. 6603. **Effective** generally for deposits made after the date of enactment of this Act. For a special rule, see Act Sec. 842(c)(2), below.

H.R. 4520, § 842(c)(2), provides:

(2) COORDINATION WITH DEPOSITS MADE UNDER REVENUE PROCEDURE 84-58.—In the case of an amount held by the Secre-

tary of the Treasury or his delegate on the date of the enactment of this Act as a deposit in the nature of a cash bond deposit pursuant to Revenue Procedure 84-58, the date that the taxpayer identifies such amount as a deposit made pursuant to section 6603 of the Internal Revenue Code (as added by this Act) shall be treated as the date such amount is deposited for purposes of such section 6603.

[¶ 6235] CODE SEC. 6662. *IMPOSITION OF ACCURACY-RELATED PENALTY ON UNDERPAYMENTS.*

* * *

(d) SUBSTANTIAL UNDERSTATEMENT OF INCOME TAX.—

(1) SUBSTANTIAL UNDERSTATEMENT.—

(A) IN GENERAL.—For purposes of this section, there is a substantial understatement of income tax for any taxable year if the amount of the understatement for the taxable year exceeds the greater of—

(i) 10 percent of the tax required to be shown on the return for the taxable year, or

(ii) $5,000.

(B) SPECIAL RULE FOR CORPORATIONS.—*In the case of a corporation other than an S corporation or a personal holding company (as defined in section 542), there is a substantial understatement of income tax for any taxable year if the amount of the understatement for the taxable year exceeds the lesser of—*

(i) 10 percent of the tax required to be shown on the return for the taxable year (or, if greater, $10,000), or

(ii) $10,000,000.

(2) UNDERSTATEMENT.—

(A) IN GENERAL.—For purposes of paragraph (1), the term "understatement" means the excess of—

(i) the amount of the tax required to be shown on the return for the taxable year, over

(ii) the amount of the tax imposed which is shown on the return, reduced by any rebate (within the meaning of section 6211(b)(2)).

The excess under the preceding sentence shall be determined without regard to items to which section 6662A applies.

* * *

(C) REDUCTION NOT TO APPLY TO TAX SHELTERS.—

(i) IN GENERAL.—Subparagraph (B) shall not apply to any item attributable to a tax shelter.

(ii) TAX SHELTER.—For purposes of clause (i), the term "tax shelter" means—

(I) a partnership or other entity,

(II) any investment plan or arrangement, or

(III) any other plan or arrangement,

if a significant purpose of such partnership, entity, plan, or arrangement is the avoidance or evasion of Federal income tax.

(3) SECRETARIAL LIST.—The Secretary may prescribe a list of positions which the Secretary believes do not meet the 1 or more of the standards specified in paragraph (2)(B)(i), section 6664(d)(2), and section 6694(a)(1). Such list (and any revisions thereof) shall be published in the Federal Register or the Internal Revenue Bulletin.

* * *

[CCH Explanation at ¶ 620 and ¶ 645. Committee Reports at ¶ 11,040 and ¶ 11,100.]

Amendments

- **2004, American Jobs Creation Act of 2004 (H.R. 4520)**

H.R. 4520, § 812(b):

Amended Code Sec. 6662(d)(2)(A) by adding at the end a flush sentence. **Effective** for tax years ending after the date of the enactment of this Act.

H.R. 4520, § 812(d):

Amended Code Sec. 6662(d)(2)(C). **Effective** for tax years ending after the date of the enactment of this Act. Prior to amendment, Code Sec. 6662(d)(2)(C) read as follows:

(C) SPECIAL RULES IN CASES INVOLVING TAX SHELTERS.—

(i) IN GENERAL.—In the case of any item of a taxpayer other than a corporation which is attributable to a tax shelter—

(I) subparagraph (B)(ii) shall not apply, and

(II) subparagraph (B)(i) shall not apply unless (in addition to meeting the requirements of such subparagraph) the taxpayer reasonably believed that the tax treatment of such item by the taxpayer was more likely than not the proper treatment.

(ii) SUBPARAGRAPH (B) NOT TO APPLY TO CORPORATIONS.—Subparagraph (B) shall not apply to any item of a corporation which is attributable to a tax shelter.

(iii) TAX SHELTER.—For purposes of this subparagraph, the term "tax shelter" means—

(I) a partnership or other entity,

(II) any investment plan or arrangement, or

(III) any other plan or arrangement,

if a significant purpose of such partnership, entity, plan, or arrangement is the avoidance or evasion of Federal income tax.

H.R. 4520, § 812(e)(1):

Amended the heading for Code Sec. 6662. **Effective** for tax years ending after the date of the enactment of this Act. Prior to amendment, the heading for Code Sec. 6662 read as follows:

SEC. 6662. IMPOSITION OF ACCURACY-RELATED PENALTY.

H.R. 4520, § 819(a):

Amended Code Sec. 6662(d)(1)(B). **Effective** for tax years beginning after the date of the enactment of this Act. Prior to amendment, Code Sec. 6662(d)(1)(B) read as follows:

(B) SPECIAL RULE FOR CORPORATIONS.—In the case of a corporation other than an S corporation or a personal holding company (as defined in section 542), paragraph (1) shall be applied by substituting "$10,000" for "$5,000".

H.R. 4520, § 819(b)(1):

Amended Code Sec. 6662(d) by adding at the end a new paragraph (3). **Effective** for tax years beginning after the date of the enactment of this Act.

H.R. 4520, § 819(b)(2):

Amended Code Sec. 6662(d)(2) by striking subparagraph (D). **Effective** for tax years beginning after the date of the enactment of this Act. Prior to being stricken, Code Sec. 6662(d)(2)(D) read as follows:

(D) SECRETARIAL LIST.—The Secretary shall prescribe (and revise not less frequently than annually) a list of positions—

(i) for which the Secretary believes there is not substantial authority, and

(ii) which affect a significant number of taxpayers.

Such list (and any revision thereof) shall be published in the Federal Register.

[¶ 6240] CODE SEC. 6662A. IMPOSITION OF ACCURACTY-RELATED PENALTY ON UNDERSTATEMENTS WITH RESPECT TO REPORTABLE TRANSACTIONS.

(a) IMPOSITION OF PENALTY.—If a taxpayer has a reportable transaction understatement for any taxable year, there shall be added to the tax an amount equal to 20 percent of the amount of such understatement.

(b) REPORTABLE TRANSACTION UNDERSTATEMENT.—For purposes of this section—

(1) IN GENERAL.—The term "reportable transaction understatement" means the sum of—

(A) the product of—

(i) the amount of the increase (if any) in taxable income which results from a difference between the proper tax treatment of an item to which this section applies and the taxpayer's treatment of such item (as shown on the taxpayer's return of tax), and

(ii) the highest rate of tax imposed by section 1 (section 11 in the case of a taxpayer which is a corporation), and

(B) the amount of the decrease (if any) in the aggregate amount of credits determined under subtitle A which results from a difference between the taxpayer's treatment of an item to which this section applies (as shown on the taxpayer's return of tax) and the proper tax treatment of such item.

For purposes of subparagraph (A), any reduction of the excess of deductions allowed for the taxable year over gross income for such year, and any reduction in the amount of capital losses which would (without regard to section 1211) be allowed for such year, shall be treated as an increase in taxable income.

(2) ITEMS TO WHICH SECTION APPLIES.—This section shall apply to any item which is attributable to—

(A) any listed transaction, and

(B) any reportable transaction (other than a listed transaction) if a significant purpose of such transaction is the avoidance or evasion of Federal income tax.

(c) HIGHER PENALTY FOR NONDISCLOSED LISTED AND OTHER AVOIDANCE TRANSACTIONS.—Subsection (a) shall be applied by substituting "30 percent" for "20 percent" with respect to the portion of any reportable transaction understatement with respect to which the requirement of section 6664(d)(2)(A) is not met.

(d) DEFINITIONS OF REPORTABLE AND LISTED TRANSACTIONS.—For purposes of this section, the terms "reportable transaction" and "listed transaction" have the respective meanings given to such terms by section 6707A(c).

(e) SPECIAL RULES.—

(1) COORDINATION WITH PENALTIES, ETC., ON OTHER UNDERSTATEMENTS.—In the case of an understatement (as defined in section 6662(d)(2))—

(A) the amount of such understatement (determined without regard to this paragraph) shall be increased by the aggregate amount of reportable transaction understatements for purposes of determining whether such understatement is a substantial understatement under section 6662(d)(1), and

(B) the addition to tax under section 6662(a) shall apply only to the excess of the amount of the substantial understatement (if any) after the application of subparagraph (A) over the aggregate amount of reportable transaction understatements.

(2) COORDINATION WITH OTHER PENALTIES.—

(A) APPLICATION OF FRAUD PENALTY.—References to an underpayment in section 6663 shall be treated as including references to a reportable transaction understatement.

(B) NO DOUBLE PENALTY.—This section shall not apply to any portion of an understatement on which a penalty is imposed under section 6663.

(C) COORDINATION WITH VALUATION PENALTIES.—

(i) SECTION 6662(e) .—Section 6662(e) shall not apply to any portion of an understatement on which a penalty is imposed under this section.

(ii) SECTION 6662(h) .—This section shall not apply to any portion of an understatement on which a penalty is imposed under section 6662(h).

(3) SPECIAL RULE FOR AMENDED RETURNS.—Except as provided in regulations, in no event shall any tax treatment included with an amendment or supplement to a return of tax be taken into account in determining the amount of any reportable transaction understatement if the amendment or supplement is filed after the earlier of the date the taxpayer is first contacted by the Secretary regarding the examination of the return or such other date as is specified by the Secretary.

* * *

[CCH Explanation at ¶ 620. Committee Reports at ¶ 11,040.]

Amendments

• **2004, American Jobs Creation Act of 2004 (H.R. 4520)**

H.R. 4520, § 812(a):

Amended [part II of] subchapter A of chapter 68 by inserting after Code Sec. 6662 a new Code Sec. 6662A.

Effective for tax years ending after the date of the enactment of this Act.

[¶ 6245] CODE SEC 6664. DEFINITIONS AND SPECIAL RULES.

* * *

(c) REASONABLE CAUSE EXCEPTION FOR UNDERPAYMENTS.—

(1) IN GENERAL.—No penalty shall be imposed under *section 6662 or 6663* with respect to any portion of an underpayment if it is shown that there was a reasonable cause for such portion and that the taxpayer acted in good faith with respect to such portion.

* * *

[CCH Explanation at ¶ 620. Committee Reports at ¶ 11,040.]

Amendments

• **2004, American Jobs Creation Act of 2004 (H.R. 4520)**

H.R. 4520, § 812(c)(2)(A):

Amended Code Sec. 6664(c)(1) by striking "this part" and inserting "section 6662 or 6663". **Effective** for tax years ending after the date of the enactment of this Act.

H.R. 4520, § 812(c)(2)(B):

Amended the heading of Code Sec. 6664(c) by inserting "FOR UNDERPAYMENTS" after "EXCEPTION". **Effective** for tax years ending after the date of the enactment of this Act.

(d) REASONABLE CAUSE EXCEPTION FOR REPORTABLE TRANSACTION UNDERSTATEMENTS.—

(1) IN GENERAL.—No penalty shall be imposed under section 6662A with respect to any portion of a reportable transaction understatement if it is shown that there was a reasonable cause for such portion and that the taxpayer acted in good faith with respect to such portion.

(2) SPECIAL RULES.—Paragraph (1) shall not apply to any reportable transaction understatement unless—

(A) the relevant facts affecting the tax treatment of the item are adequately disclosed in accordance with the regulations prescribed under section 6011,

(B) there is or was substantial authority for such treatment, and

(C) the taxpayer reasonably believed that such treatment was more likely than not the proper treatment.

A taxpayer failing to adequately disclose in accordance with section 6011 shall be treated as meeting the requirements of subparagraph (A) if the penalty for such failure was rescinded under section 6707A(d).

(3) RULES RELATING TO REASONABLE BELIEF.—For purposes of paragraph (2)(C)—

(A) IN GENERAL.—A taxpayer shall be treated as having a reasonable belief with respect to the tax treatment of an item only if such belief—

(i) is based on the facts and law that exist at the time the return of tax which includes such tax treatment is filed, and

(ii) relates solely to the taxpayer's chances of success on the merits of such treatment and does not take into account the possibility that a return will not be audited, such treatment will not be raised on audit, or such treatment will be resolved through settlement if it is raised.

(B) CERTAIN OPINIONS MAY NOT BE RELIED UPON.—

(i) IN GENERAL.—An opinion of a tax advisor may not be relied upon to establish the reasonable belief of a taxpayer if—

(I) the tax advisor is described in clause (ii), or

(II) the opinion is described in clause (iii).

(ii) DISQUALIFIED TAX ADVISORS.—A tax advisor is described in this clause if the tax advisor—

(I) is a material advisor (within the meaning of section 6111(b)(1)) and participates in the organization, management, promotion, or sale of the transaction or is related (within the meaning of section 267(b) or 707(b)(1)) to any person who so participates,

(II) is compensated directly or indirectly by a material advisor with respect to the transaction,

(III) has a fee arrangement with respect to the transaction which is contingent on all or part of the intended tax benefits from the transaction being sustained, or

(IV) as determined under regulations prescribed by the Secretary, has a disqualifying financial interest with respect to the transaction.

(iii) DISQUALIFIED OPINIONS.—For purposes of clause (i), an opinion is disqualified if the opinion—

(I) is based on unreasonable factual or legal assumptions (including assumptions as to future events),

(II) unreasonably relies on representations, statements, findings, or agreements of the taxpayer or any other person,

(III) *does not identify and consider all relevant facts, or*

(IV) *fails to meet any other requirement as the Secretary may prescribe.*

* * *

[CCH Explanation at ¶ 620. Committee Reports at ¶ 11,040.]

Amendments

• **2004, American Jobs Creation Act of 2004 (H.R. 4520)**

H.R. 4520, § 812(c)(1):

Amended Code Sec. 6664 by adding at the end a new subsection (d). **Effective** for tax years ending after the date of the enactment of this Act.

[¶ 6250] CODE SEC. 6679. FAILURE TO FILE RETURNS, ETC., WITH RESPECT TO FOREIGN CORPORATIONS OR FOREIGN PARTNERSHIPS.

(a) CIVIL PENALTY.—

(1) IN GENERAL.—In addition to any criminal penalty provided by law, any person required to file a return under section *6046 and[or] 6046A* who fails to file such return at the time provided in such section, or who files a return which does not show the information required pursuant to such section, shall pay a penalty of $10,000, unless it is shown that such failure is due to reasonable cause.

* * *

(3) *[Stricken]*

* * *

[CCH Explanation at ¶ 490. Committee Reports at ¶ 10,690.]

Amendments

• **2004, American Jobs Creation Act of 2004 (H.R. 4520)**

H.R. 4520, § 413(c)(29)(A)-(B):

Amended Code Sec. 6679(a) by striking "6035, 6046, and[or] 6046A" in paragraph (1) and inserting "6046 and[or] 6046A", and by striking paragraph (3). **Effective** for tax years of foreign corporations beginning after 12-31-2004, and for tax years of United States shareholders with or within which such tax years of foreign corporations end. Prior to being stricken, Code Sec. 6679(a)(3) read as follows:

(3) REDUCED PENALTY FOR RETURNS RELATING TO FOREIGN PERSONAL HOLDING COMPANIES.—In the case of a return required under section 6035, paragraph (1) shall be applied by substituting "$1,000" for "$10,000", and paragraph (2) shall not apply.

[¶ 6255] CODE SEC. 6688. ASSESSABLE PENALTIES WITH RESPECT TO INFORMATION REQUIRED TO BE FURNISHED UNDER SECTION 7654.

In addition to any criminal penalty provided by law, any person described in section 7654(a) who is required *under section 937(c) or* by regulations prescribed under section 7654 to furnish information and who fails to comply with such requirement at the time prescribed by such regulations, unless it is shown that such failure is due to reasonable cause and not to willful neglect, shall pay (upon notice and demand by the Secretary and in the same manner as tax) a penalty of *$1,000* for each such failure.

* * *

[CCH Explanation at ¶ 580. Committee Reports at ¶ 11,800.]

Amendments

• **2004, American Jobs Creation Act of 2004 (H.R. 4520)**

H.R. 4520, § 908(b)(1)-(2):

Amended Code Sec. 6688 by inserting "under section 937(c) or" before "by regulations", and by striking "$100" and inserting "$1,000". **Effective** for tax years ending after the date of the enactment of this Act.

[¶ 6260] CODE SEC. 6700. PROMOTING ABUSIVE TAX SHELTERS, ETC.

(a) IMPOSITION OF PENALTY.—Any person who—

(1)(A) organizes (or assists in the organization of)—

(i) a partnership or other entity,

(ii) any investment plan or arrangement, or

(iii) any other plan or arrangement, or

(B) participates (directly or indirectly) in the sale of any interest in an entity or plan or arrangement referred to in subparagraph (A), and

(2) makes or furnishes or causes another person to make or furnish (in connection with such organization or sale)—

(A) a statement with respect to the allowability of any deduction or credit, the excludability of any income, or the securing of any other tax benefit by reason of holding an interest in the entity or participating in the plan or arrangement which the person knows or has reason to know is false or fraudulent as to any material matter, or

(B) a gross valuation overstatement as to any material matter,

shall pay, with respect to each activity described in paragraph (1), a penalty equal to the $1,000 or, if the person establishes that it is lesser, 100 percent of the gross income derived (or to be derived) by such person from such activity. For purposes of the preceding sentence, activities described in paragraph (1)(A) with respect to each entity or arrangement shall be treated as a separate activity and participation in each sale described in paragraph (1)(B) shall be so treated. *Notwithstanding the first sentence, if an activity with respect to which a penalty imposed under this subsection involves a statement described in paragraph (2)(A), the amount of the penalty shall be equal to 50 percent of the gross income derived (or to be derived) from such activity by the person on which the penalty is imposed.*

* * *

[CCH Explanation at ¶ 640. Committee Reports at ¶ 11,090.]

Amendments

• **2004, American Jobs Creation Act of 2004 (H.R. 4520)**

H.R. 4520, § 818(a):

Amended Code Sec. 6700(a) by adding at the end a new sentence. **Effective** for activities after the date of the enactment of this Act.

[¶ 6265] CODE SEC. 6707. *FAILURE TO FURNISH INFORMATION REGARDING REPORTABLE TRANSACTIONS.*

(a) In General.—If a person who is required to file a return under section 6111(a) with respect to any reportable transaction—

(1) fails to file such return on or before the date prescribed therefor, or

(2) files false or incomplete information with the Secretary with respect to such transaction,

such person shall pay a penalty with respect to such return in the amount determined under subsection (b).

(b) Amount of Penalty.—

(1) In general.—Except as provided in paragraph (2), the penalty imposed under subsection (a) with respect to any failure shall be $50,000.

(2) Listed transactions.—The penalty imposed under subsection (a) with respect to any listed transaction shall be an amount equal to the greater of—

(A) $200,000, or

(B) 50 percent of the gross income derived by such person with respect to aid, assistance, or advice which is provided with respect to the listed transaction before the date the return is filed under section 6111.

Subparagraph (B) shall be applied by substituting "75 percent" for "50 percent" in the case of an intentional failure or act described in subsection (a).

(c) Rescission Authority.—The provisions of section 6707A(d) (relating to authority of Commissioner to rescind penalty) shall apply to any penalty imposed under this section.

(d) Reportable and Listed Transactions.—For purposes of this section, the terms "reportable transaction" and "listed transaction" have the respective meanings given to such terms by section 6707A(c).

[CCH Explanation at ¶ 630. Committee Reports at ¶ 11,070.]

Amendments

• 2004, American Jobs Creation Act of 2004 (H.R. 4520)

H.R. 4520, § 816(a):

Amended Code Sec. 6707. **Effective** for returns the due date for which is after the date of the enactment of this Act. Prior to amendment, Code Sec. 6707 read as follows:

SEC. 6707. FAILURE TO FURNISH INFORMATION REGARDING TAX SHELTERS.

(a) FAILURE TO REGISTER TAX SHELTER.—

(1) IMPOSITION OF PENALTY.—If a person who is required to register a tax shelter under section 6111(a)—

(A) fails to register such tax shelter on or before the date described in section 6111(a)(1), or

(B) files false or incomplete information with the Secretary with respect to such registration,

such person shall pay a penalty with respect to such registration in the amount determined under paragraph (2) or (3), as the case may be. No penalty shall be imposed under the preceding sentence with respect to any failure which is due to reasonable cause.

(2) AMOUNT OF PENALTY.—Except as provided in paragraph (3), the penalty imposed under paragraph (1) with respect to any tax shelter shall be an amount equal to the greater of—

(A) 1 percent of the aggregate amount invested in such tax shelter, or

(B) $500.

(3) CONFIDENTIAL ARRANGEMENTS.—

(A) IN GENERAL.—In the case of a tax shelter (as defined in section 6111(d)), the penalty imposed under paragraph (1) shall be an amount equal to the greater of—

(i) 50 percent of the fees paid to all promoters of the tax shelter with respect to offerings made before the date such shelter is registered under section 6111, or

(ii) $10,000.

Clause (i) shall be applied by substituting "75 percent" for "50 percent" in the case of an intentional failure or act described in paragraph (1).

(B) SPECIAL RULE FOR PARTICIPANTS REQUIRED TO REGISTER SHELTER.—In the case of a person required to register such a tax shelter by reason of section 6111(d)(3)—

(i) such person shall be required to pay the penalty under paragraph (1) only if such person actually participated in such shelter,

(ii) the amount of such penalty shall be determined by taking into account under subparagraph (A)(i) only the fees paid by such person, and

(iii) such penalty shall be in addition to the penalty imposed on any other person for failing to register such shelter.

(b) FAILURE TO FURNISH TAX SHELTER IDENTIFICATION NUMBER.—

(1) SELLERS, ETC.—Any person who fails to furnish the identification number of a tax shelter which such person is required to furnish under section 6111(b)(1) shall pay a penalty of $100 for each such failure.

(2) FAILURE TO INCLUDE NUMBER ON RETURN.—Any person who fails to include an identification number on a return on which such number is required to be included under section 6111(b)(2) shall pay a penalty of $250 for each such failure, unless such failure is due to reasonable cause.

[¶ 6270] CODE SEC. 6707A. PENALTY FOR FAILURE TO INCLUDE REPORTABLE TRANSACTION INFORMATION WITH RETURN.

(a) IMPOSITION OF PENALTY.—Any person who fails to include on any return or statement any information with respect to a reportable transaction which is required under section 6011 to be included with such return or statement shall pay a penalty in the amount determined under subsection (b).

(b) AMOUNT OF PENALTY.—

(1) IN GENERAL.—Except as provided in paragraph (2), the amount of the penalty under subsection (a) shall be—

(A) $10,000 in the case of a natural person, and

(B) $50,000 in any other case.

(2) LISTED TRANSACTION.—The amount of the penalty under subsection (a) with respect to a listed transaction shall be—

(A) $100,000 in the case of a natural person, and

(B) $200,000 in any other case.

(c) DEFINITIONS.—For purposes of this section:

(1) REPORTABLE TRANSACTION.—The term "reportable transaction" means any transaction with respect to which information is required to be included with a return or statement because, as determined under regulations prescribed under section 6011, such transaction is of a type which the Secretary determines as having a potential for tax avoidance or evasion.

(2) LISTED TRANSACTION.—The term "listed transaction" means a reportable transaction which is the same as, or substantially similar to, a transaction specifically identified by the Secretary as a tax avoidance transaction for purposes of section 6011.

(d) AUTHORITY TO RESCIND PENALTY.—

(1) IN GENERAL.—The Commissioner of Internal Revenue may rescind all or any portion of any penalty imposed by this section with respect to any violation if—

(A) the violation is with respect to a reportable transaction other than a listed transaction, and

(B) rescinding the penalty would promote compliance with the requirements of this title and effective tax administration.

(2) NO JUDICIAL APPEAL.—Notwithstanding any other provision of law, any determination under this subsection may not be reviewed in any judicial proceeding.

(3) RECORDS.—If a penalty is rescinded under paragraph (1), the Commissioner shall place in the file in the Office of the Commissioner the opinion of the Commissioner with respect to the determination, including—

(A) a statement of the facts and circumstances relating to the violation,

(B) the reasons for the rescission, and

(C) the amount of the penalty rescinded.

(e) PENALTY REPORTED TO SEC.—In the case of a person—

(1) which is required to file periodic reports under section 13 or 15(d) of the Securities Exchange Act of 1934 or is required to be consolidated with another person for purposes of such reports, and

(2) which—

(A) is required to pay a penalty under this section with respect to a listed transaction,

(B) is required to pay a penalty under section 6662A with respect to any reportable transaction at a rate prescribed under section 6662A(c), or

(C) is required to pay a penalty under section 6662(h) with respect to any reportable transaction and would (but for section 6662A(e)(2)(C)) have been subject to penalty under section 6662A at a rate prescribed under section 6662A(c),

the requirement to pay such penalty shall be disclosed in such reports filed by such person for such periods as the Secretary shall specify. Failure to make a disclosure in accordance with the preceding sentence shall be treated as a failure to which the penalty under subsection (b)(2) applies.

(f) COORDINATION WITH OTHER PENALTIES.—The penalty imposed by this section shall be in addition to any other penalty imposed by this title.

[CCH Explanation at ¶615. Committee Reports at ¶11,030.]

Amendments

• **2004, American Jobs Creation Act of 2004 (H.R. 4520)**

H.R. 4520, §811(a):

Amended part I of subchapter B of chapter 68 by inserting after Code Sec. 6707A a new Code Sec. 6707A. **Effective** for

returns and statements the due date for which is after the date of the enactment of this Act.

[¶6275] CODE SEC. 6708. *FAILURE TO MAINTAIN LISTS OF ADVISEES WITH RESPECT TO REPORTABLE TRANSACTIONS.*

(a) IMPOSITION OF PENALTY.—

(1) IN GENERAL.—If any person who is required to maintain a list under section 6112(a) fails to make such list available upon written request to the Secretary in accordance with section 6112(b) within 20 business days after the date of such request, such person shall pay a penalty of $10,000 for each day of such failure after such 20th day.

(2) REASONABLE CAUSE EXCEPTION.—No penalty shall be imposed by paragraph (1) with respect to the failure on any day if such failure is due to reasonable cause.

* * *

[CCH Explanation at ¶605 and ¶635. Committee Reports at ¶11,070 and ¶ 11,080.]

Amendments

• **2004, American Jobs Creation Act of 2004 (H.R. 4520)**

H.R. 4520, §815(b)(5)(A):

Amended the heading for Code Sec. 6708. **Effective** for transactions with respect to which material aid, assistance, or advice referred to in Code Sec. 6111(b)(1)(A)(i) (as added by this section) is provided after the date of the enactment of this Act. Prior to amendment, the heading for Code Sec. 6708 read as follows:

SEC. 6708. FAILURE TO MAINTAIN LISTS OF INVESTORS IN POTENTIALLY ABUSIVE TAX SHELTERS.

H.R. 4520, §817(a):

Amended Code Sec. 6708(a). **Effective** for requests made after the date of the enactment of this Act. Prior to amendment, Code Sec. 6708(a) read as follows:

(a) IN GENERAL.—Any person who fails to meet any requirement imposed by section 6112 shall pay a penalty of $50 for each person with respect to whom there is such a failure, unless it is shown that such failure is due to reasonable cause and not due to willful neglect. The maximum penalty imposed under this subsection for any calendar year shall not exceed $100,000.

[¶6280] CODE SEC. 6715. DYED FUEL SOLD FOR USE OR USED IN TAXABLE USE, ETC.

(a) IMPOSITION OF PENALTY.—If—

(1) any dyed fuel is sold or held for sale by any person for any use which such person knows or has reason to know is not a nontaxable use of such fuel,

(2) any dyed fuel is held for use or used by any person for a use other than a nontaxable use and such person knew, or had reason to know, that such fuel was so dyed,

(3) any person willfully *alters, chemically or otherwise, or attempts to so alter,* the strength or composition of any dye or marking done pursuant to section 4082 in any dyed fuel, *or*

(4) *any person who has knowledge that a dyed fuel which has been altered as described in paragraph (3) sells or holds for sale such fuel for any use which the person knows or has reason to know is not a nontaxable use of such fuel,*

then such person shall pay a penalty in addition to the tax (if any).

* * *

[CCH Explanation at ¶1521. Committee Reports at ¶11,350.]

Amendments

• **2004, American Jobs Creation Act of 2004 (H.R. 4520)**

H.R. 4520, §856(a):

Amended Code Sec. 6715(a) by striking "or" in paragraph (2), by inserting "or" at the end of paragraph (3), and by inserting after paragraph (3) a new paragraph (4). **Effective** on the date of the enactment of this Act.

H.R. 4520, §856(b):

Amended Code Sec. 6715(a)(3) by striking "alters, or attempts to alter," and inserting "alters, chemically or otherwise, or attempts to so alter,". **Effective** on the date of the enactment of this Act.

(e) *NO ADMINISTRATIVE APPEAL FOR THIRD AND SUBSEQUENT VIOLATIONS.—In the case of any person who is found to be subject to the penalty under this section after a chemical analysis of such fuel and who has been penalized under this section at least twice after the date of the enactment of this subsection, no administrative appeal or review shall be allowed with respect to such finding except in the case of a claim regarding—*

(1) *fraud or mistake in the chemical analysis, or*

(2) *mathematical calculation of the amount of the penalty.*

[CCH Explanation at ¶1519. Committee Reports at ¶11,350.]

Amendments

• **2004, American Jobs Creation Act of 2004 (H.R. 4520)**

H.R. 4520, §855(a):

Amended Code Sec. 6715 by inserting at the end a new subsection (e). **Effective** for penalties assessed after the date of the enactment of this Act.

[¶ 6285] CODE SEC. 6715A. TAMPERING WITH OR FAILING TO MAINTAIN SECURITY REQUIREMENTS FOR MECHANICAL DYE INJECTION SYSTEMS.

(a) IMPOSITION OF PENALTY—

(1) TAMPERING.—If any person tampers with a mechanical dye injection system used to indelibly dye fuel for purposes of section 4082, such person shall pay a penalty in addition to the tax (if any).

(2) FAILURE TO MAINTAIN SECURITY REQUIREMENTS.—If any operator of a mechanical dye injection system used to indelibly dye fuel for purposes of section 4082 fails to maintain the security standards for such system as established by the Secretary, then such operator shall pay a penalty in addition to the tax (if any).

(b) AMOUNT OF PENALTY.—The amount of the penalty under subsection (a) shall be—

(1) for each violation described in paragraph (1), the greater of—

(A) $25,000, or

(B) $10 for each gallon of fuel involved, and

(2) for each—

(A) failure to maintain security standards described in paragraph (2), $1,000, and

(B) failure to correct a violation described in paragraph (2), $1,000 per day for each day after which such violation was discovered or such person should have reasonably known of such violation.

(c) JOINT AND SEVERAL LIABILITY.—

(1) IN GENERAL.—If a penalty is imposed under this section on any business entity, each officer, employee, or agent of such entity or other contracting party who willfully participated in any act giving rise to such penalty shall be jointly and severally liable with such entity for such penalty.

(2) AFFILIATED GROUPS.—If a business entity described in paragraph (1) is part of an affiliated group (as defined in section 1504(a)), the parent corporation of such entity shall be jointly and severally liable with such entity for the penalty imposed under this section.

* * *

[CCH Explanation at ¶ 1517. Committee Reports at ¶ 11,350.]

Amendments

• **2004, American Jobs Creation Act of 2004 (H.R. 4520)**

H.R. 4520, § 854(b), provides:

(b) DYE INJECTOR SECURITY.—Not later than 180 days after the date of the enactment of this Act, the Secretary of the Treasury shall issue regulations regarding mechanical dye injection systems described in the amendment made by subsection (a), and such regulations shall include standards for making such systems tamper resistant.

H.R. 4520, § 854(c)(1):

Amended part I of subchapter B of chapter 68 by adding after Code Sec. 6715 a new Code Sec. 6715A. **Effective** on the 180th day after the date on which the Secretary issues the regulations described in subsection (b), above.

[¶ 6290] CODE SEC. 6717. REFUSAL OF ENTRY.

(a) IN GENERAL.—In addition to any other penalty provided by law, any person who refuses to admit entry or refuses to permit any other action by the Secretary authorized by section 4083(d)(1) shall pay a penalty of $1,000 for such refusal.

(b) JOINT AND SEVERAL LIABILITY.—

(1) IN GENERAL.—If a penalty is imposed under this section on any business entity, each officer, employee, or agent of such entity or other contracting party who willfully participated in any act giving rise to such penalty shall be jointly and severally liable with such entity for such penalty.

(2) AFFILIATED GROUPS.—If a business entity described in paragraph (1) is part of an affiliated group (as defined in section 1504(a)), the parent corporation of such entity shall be jointly and severally liable with such entity for the penalty imposed under this section.

(c) REASONABLE CAUSE EXCEPTION.—No penalty shall be imposed under this section with respect to any failure if it is shown that such failure is due to reasonable cause.

[CCH Explanation at ¶1541. Committee Reports at ¶11,400.]

Amendments

• 2004, American Jobs Creation Act of 2004 (H.R. 4520)

H.R. 4520, §859(a):

Amended part I of subchapter B of chapter 68, as amended by this Act, by inserting after Code Sec. 6716 a new Code Sec. 6717. **Effective** 1-1-2005.

[¶6295] *CODE SEC. 6718. FAILURE TO DISPLAY TAX REGISTRATION ON VESSELS.*

(a) FAILURE TO DISPLAY REGISTRATION.—*Every operator of a vessel who fails to display proof of registration pursuant to section 4101(a)(3) shall pay a penalty of $500 for each such failure. With respect to any vessel, only one penalty shall be imposed by this section during any calendar month.*

[CCH Explanation at ¶1535. Committee Reports at ¶11,430.]

Amendments

• 2004, American Jobs Creation Act of 2004 (H.R. 4520)

H.R. 4520, §862(b):

Amended Code Sec. 6718(a), as added by this Act, by striking "section 4101(a)(2)" and inserting "section 4101(a)(3)". **Effective** 1-1-2005.

(b) MULTIPLE VIOLATIONS.—*In determining the penalty under subsection (a) on any person, subsection (a) shall be applied by increasing the amount in subsection (a) by the product of such amount and the aggregate number of penalties (if any) imposed with respect to prior months by this section on such person (or a related person or any predecessor of such person or related person).*

(c) REASONABLE CAUSE EXCEPTION.—*No penalty shall be imposed under this section with respect to any failure if it is shown that such failure is due to reasonable cause.*

[CCH Explanation at ¶1529. Committee Reports at ¶11,420.]

Amendments

• 2004, American Jobs Creation Act of 2004 (H.R. 4520)

H.R. 4520, §861(b)(1):

Amended part I of subchapter B of chapter 68, as amended by this Act, by inserting after Code Sec. 6717 a new Code Sec. 6718. **Effective** for penalties imposed after 12-31-2004.

[¶6300] *CODE SEC. 6719. FAILURE TO REGISTER.*

(a) FAILURE TO REGISTER.—*Every person who is required to register under section 4101 and fails to do so shall pay a penalty in addition to the tax (if any).*

(b) AMOUNT OF PENALTY.—*The amount of the penalty under subsection (a) shall be—*

(1) *$10,000 for each initial failure to register, and*

(2) *$1,000 for each day thereafter such person fails to register.*

(c) REASONABLE CAUSE EXCEPTION.—*No penalty shall be imposed under this section with respect to any failure if it is shown that such failure is due to reasonable cause.*

[CCH Explanation at ¶1533. Committee Reports at ¶11,440.]

Amendments

• 2004, American Jobs Creation Act of 2004 (H.R. 4520)

H.R. 4520, §863(c)(1):

Amended part I of subchapter B of chapter 68, as amended by this Act, by inserting after Code Sec. 6718 a new Code Sec. 6719. **Effective** for penalties imposed after 12-31-2004.

[¶ 6305] *CODE SEC. 6720. FRAUDULENT ACKNOWLEDGMENTS WITH RESPECT TO DONATIONS OF MOTOR VEHICLES, BOATS, AND AIRPLANES.*

Any donee organization required under section 170(f)(12)(A) to furnish a contemporaneous written acknowledgment to a donor which knowingly furnishes a false or fraudulent acknowledgment, or which knowingly fails to furnish such acknowledgment in the manner, at the time, and showing the information required under section 170(f)(12), or regulations prescribed thereunder, shall for each such act, or for each such failure, be subject to a penalty equal to—

(1) in the case of an acknowledgment with respect to a qualified vehicle to which section 170(f)(12)(A)(ii) applies, the greater of—

(A) the product of the highest rate of tax specified in section 1 and the sales price stated on the acknowledgment, or

(B) the gross proceeds from the sale of such vehicle, and

(2) in the case of an acknowledgment with respect to any other qualified vehicle to which section 170(f)(12) applies, the greater of—

(A) the product of the highest rate of tax specified in section 1 and the claimed value of the vehicle, or

(B) $5,000.

* * *

[CCH Explanation at ¶ 1305. Committee Reports at ¶ 11,560.]

Amendments

• **2004, American Jobs Creation Act of 2004 (H.R. 4520)**

H.R. 4520, § 884(b)(1):

Amended part I of subchapter B of chapter 68, as amended by this Act, by inserting after Code Sec. 6719 a

new Code Sec. 6720. **Effective** for contributions made after 12-31-2004.

[¶ 6310] CODE SEC. 6724. WAIVER; DEFINITIONS AND SPECIAL RULES.

* * *

(d) DEFINITIONS.—For purposes of this part—

(1) INFORMATION RETURN.—The term "information return" means—

* * *

(B) any return required by—

(i) section 6041A(a) or (b) (relating to returns of direct sellers),

(ii) section 6043A(a) (relating to returns relating to taxable mergers and acquisitions),

(iii) section 6045(a) or (d) (relating to returns of brokers),

(iv) section 6050H(a) (relating to mortgage interest received in trade or business from individuals),

(v) section 6050I(a) or (g)(1) (relating to cash received in trade or business, etc.),

(vi) section 6050J(a) (relating to foreclosures and abandonments of security),

(vii) section 6050K(a) (relating to exchanges of certain partnership interests),

(viii) section 6050L(a) (relating to returns relating to certain dispositions of donated property),

(ix) section 6050P (relating to returns relating to the cancellation of indebtedness by certain financial entities),

(x) section 6050Q (relating to certain long-term care benefits),

(xi) section 6050S (relating to returns relating to payments for qualified tuition and related expenses),

(xii) section 6050T (relating to returns relating to credit for health insurance costs of eligible individuals),

(xiii) section 6052(a) (relating to reporting payment of wages in the form of group-life insurance),

(xiv) section 6053(c)(1) (relating to reporting with respect to certain tips),

(xv) subsection (b) or (e) of section 1060 (relating to reporting requirements of transferors and transferees in certain asset acquisitions),

(xvi) section 4101(d) (relating to information reporting with respect to fuels taxes),

(xvii) subparagraph (C) of section 338(h)(10) (relating to information required to be furnished to the Secretary in case of elective recognition of gain or loss), or

(xviii) section 264(f)(5)(A)(iv) (relating to reporting with respect to certain life insurance and annuity contracts), and

* * *

(2) PAYEE STATEMENT.—The term "payee statement" means any statement required to be furnished under—

(A) section 6031(b) or (c), 6034A, or 6037(b) (relating to statements furnished by certain pass-thru entities),

(B) section 6039(a) (relating to information required in connection with certian options),

(C) section 6041(d) (relating to information at source),

(D) section 6041A(e) (relating to returns regarding payments of remuneration for services and direct sales),

(E) section 6042(c) (relating to returns regarding payments of dividends and corporate earnings and profits),

(F) subsections (b) and (d) of section 6043A (relating to returns relating to taxable mergers and acquisitions).[,]

(G) section 6044(e) (relating to returns regarding payments of patronage dividends),

(H) section 6045(b) or (d) (relating to returns of brokers),

(I) section 6049(c) (relating to returns regarding payments of interest),

(J) section 6050A(b) (relating to reporting requirements of certain fishing boat operators),

(K) section 6050H(d) (relating to returns relating to mortgage interest received in trade or business from individuals),

(L) section 6050I(e) or paragraph (4) or (5) of section 6050I(g) (relating to cash received in trade or business, etc.),

(M) section 6050J(e) (relating to returns relating to foreclosures and abandonments of security),

(N) section 6050K(b) (relating to returns relating to exchanges of certain partnership interests),

(O) section 6050L(c) (relating to returns relating to certain dispositions of donated property),

(P) section 6050N(b) (relating to returns regarding payments of royalties),

(Q) section 6050P(d) (relating to returns relating to the cancellation of indebtedness by certain financial entities),

(R) section 6050Q(b) (relating to certain long-term care benefits),

(S) section 6050R(c) (relating to returns relating to certain purchases of fish),

(T) section 6051 (relating to receipts for employees),

(U) section 6052(b) (relating to returns regarding payment of wages in the form of group-term life insurance),

(V) section 6053(b) or (c) (relating to reports of tips),

(W) section 6048(b)(1)(B) (relating to foreign trust reporting requirements),

(X) section 408(i) (relating to reports with respect to individual retirement plans) to any person other than the Secretary with respect to the amount of payments made to such person,

(Y) section 6047(d) (relating to reports by plan administrators) to any person other than the Secretary with respect to the amount of payments made to such person,

(Z) section 6050S(d) (relating to returns relating to qualified tuition and related expenses),

(AA) section 264(f)(5)(A)(iv) (relating to reporting with respect to certain life insurance and annuity contracts), or

(BB) section 6050T (relating to returns relating to credit for health insurance costs of eligible individuals).

Such term also includes any form, statement, or schedule required to be furnished to the recipient of any amount from which tax was required to be deducted and withheld under chapter 3 (or from which tax would be required to be so deducted and withheld but for an exemption under this title or any treaty obligation of the United States).

* * *

[CCH Explanation at ¶510 and ¶1507. Committee Reports at ¶11,010 and ¶11,340.]

Amendments

• 2004, American Jobs Creation Act of 2004 (H.R. 4520)

H.R. 4520, §805(b)(1):

Amended Code Sec. 6724(d)(1)(B) by redesignating clauses (ii) through (xviii) as clauses (iii) through (xix), respectively, and by inserting after clause (i) a new clause (ii). **Effective** for acquisitions after the date of the enactment of this Act.

H.R. 4520, §805(b)(2):

Amended Code Sec. 6724(d)(2) by redesignating subparagraphs (F) through (BB) as subparagraphs (G) through (CC), respectively, and by inserting after subparagraph (E) a new subparagraph (F). **Effective** for acquisitions after the date of the enactment of this Act.

H.R. 4520, §853(d)(2)(L):

Amended Code Sec. 6724(d)(1)(B), as amended by Act Sec. 805(b)(1), by striking clause (xvi) and by redesignating

the succeeding clauses accordingly. **Effective** for aviation-grade kerosene removed, entered, or sold after 12-31-2004. Prior to being stricken, Code Sec. 6724(d)(1)(b)(xvi), as redesignated by Act Sec. 805(b)(1), read as follows:

(xvi) subparagraph (A) or (C) of subsection (c)(4) of section 4093 (relating to information reporting with respect to tax on diesel and aviation fuels),

H.R. 4520, §853(d)(2)(M):

Amended Code Sec. 6724(d)(2), as amended by Act Sec. 805(b)(2), by striking subparagraph (X) and by redesignating the succeeding subparagraphs accordingly. **Effective** for aviation-grade kerosene removed, entered, or sold after 12-31-2004. Prior to being stricken, Code Sec. 6724(d)(2)(X), as redesignated by Act Sec. 805(b)(2), read as follows:

(X) section 4093(c)(4)(B) (relating to certain purchasers of diesel and aviation fuels),

[¶6315] *CODE SEC. 6725. FAILURE TO REPORT INFORMATION UNDER SECTION 4101.*

(a) IN GENERAL.—In the case of each failure described in subsection (b) by any person with respect to a vessel or facility, such person shall pay a penalty of $10,000 in addition to the tax (if any).

(b) FAILURES SUBJECT TO PENALTY.—For purposes of subsection (a), the failures described in this subsection are—

(1) any failure to make a report under section 4101(d) on or before the date prescribed therefor, and

(2) any failure to include all of the information required to be shown on such report or the inclusion of incorrect information.

(c) REASONABLE CAUSE EXCEPTION.—No penalty shall be imposed under this section with respect to any failure if it is shown that such failure is due to reasonable cause.

* * *

[CCH Explanation at ¶1533. Committee Reports at ¶11,440.]

Amendments

• 2004, American Jobs Creation Act of 2004 (H.R. 4520)

H.R. 4520, §863(d)(1):

Amended part II of subchapter B of chapter 68 by adding at the end a new Code Sec. 6725. **Effective** for penalties imposed after 12-31-2004.

[¶6320] CODE SEC. 7232. FAILURE TO REGISTER UNDER SECTION 4101, FALSE REPRESENTATIONS OF REGISTRATION STATUS, ETC.

Every person who fails to register as required by section 4101, or who in connection with any purchase of any taxable fuel (as defined in section 4083), or aviation fuel falsely represents himself to be registered as provided by section 4101, or who willfully makes any false statement in an application for registration under section 4101, shall, upon conviction thereof, be fined not more than $10,000, or imprisoned not more than 5 years, or both, together with the costs of prosecution.

* * *

[CCH Explanation at ¶ 1533. Committee Reports at ¶ 11,440.]

Amendments

• **2004, American Jobs Creation Act of 2004 (H.R. 4520)**

H.R. 4520, § 863(b):

Amended Code Sec. 7232 by striking "$5,000" and inserting "$10,000". **Effective** for penalties imposed after 12-31-2004.

[¶ 6325] CODE SEC. 7272. PENALTY FOR FAILURE TO REGISTER.

(a) IN GENERAL.—Any person (other than persons required to register under subtitle E, or persons engaging in a trade or business on which a special tax is imposed by such subtitle) who fails to register with the Secretary as required by this title or by regulations issued thereunder shall be liable to a penalty of $50 (*$10,000 in the case of a failure to register under section 4101*).

* * *

[CCH Explanation at ¶ 1533. Committee Reports at ¶ 11,440.]

Amendments

• **2004, American Jobs Creation Act of 2004 (H.R. 4520)**

H.R. 4520, § 863(a):

Amended Code Sec. 7272(a) by inserting "($10,000 in the case of a failure to register under section 4101)" after "$50". **Effective** for penalties imposed after 12-31-2004.

[¶ 6330] CODE SEC. 7408. *ACTIONS TO ENJOIN SPECIFIED CONDUCT RELATED TO TAX SHELTERS AND REPORTABLE TRANSACTIONS.*

(a) AUTHORITY TO SEEK INJUNCTION.—A civil action in the name of the United States to enjoin any person from further engaging in specified conduct may be commenced at the request of the Secretary. Any action under this section shall be brought in the district court of the United States for the district in which such person resides, has his principal place of business, or has engaged in specified conduct. The court may exercise its jurisdiction over such action (as provided in section 7402(a)) separate and apart from any other action brought by the United States against such person.

[CCH Explanation at ¶ 650. Committee Reports at ¶ 11,110.]

Amendments

• **2004, American Jobs Creation Act of 2004 (H.R. 4520)**

H.R. 4520, § 820(a):

Amended Code Sec. 7408 by redesignating subsection (c) as subsection (d) and by striking subsections (a) and (b) and inserting new subsections (a), (b), and (c). **Effective** on the day after the date of the enactment of this Act. Prior to being stricken, Code Sec. 7408(a) read as follows:

(a) AUTHORITY TO SEEK INJUNCTION.—A civil action in the name of the United States to enjoin any person from further engaging in conduct subject to penalty under section 6700 (relating to penalty for promoting abusive tax shelters, etc.) or section 6701 (relating to penalties for aiding and abetting understatement of tax liability) may be commenced at the

request of the Secretary. Any action under this section shall be brought in the district court of the United States for the district in which such person resides, has his principal place of business, or has engaged in conduct subject to penalty under section 6700 or section 6701. The court may exercise its jurisdiction over such action (as provided in section 7402(a)) separate and apart from any other action brought by the United States against such person.

H.R. 4520, § 820(b)(1):

Amended the heading of Code Sec. 7408. **Effective** on the day after the date of the enactment of this Act. Prior to amendment, the heading of Code Sec. 7408 read as follows:

SEC. 7408. ACTION TO ENJOIN PROMOTERS OF ABUSIVE TAX SHELTERS, ETC.

(b) ADJUDICATION AND DECREE.—In any action under subsection (a), if the court finds—

(1) that the person has engaged in any specified conduct, and

(2) that injunctive relief is appropriate to prevent recurrence of such conduct,

the court may enjoin such person from engaging in such conduct or in any other activity subject to penalty under this title.

[CCH Explanation at ¶ 650. Committee Reports at ¶ 11,110.]

Amendments

• **2004, American Jobs Creation Act of 2004 (H.R. 4520)**

H.R. 4520, § 820(a):

Amended Code Sec. 7408 by redesignating subsection (c) as subsection (d) and by striking subsections (a) and (b) and inserting new subsections (a), (b), and (c). **Effective** on the day after the date of the enactment of this Act. Prior to being stricken, Code Sec. 7408(b) read as follows:

(b) ADJUDICATION AND DECREE.—In any action under subsection (a), if the court finds—

(1) that the person has engaged in any conduct subject to penalty under section 6700 (relating to penalty for promoting abusive tax shelters, etc.) or section 6701 (relating to penalties for aiding and abetting understatement of tax liability), and

(2) that injunctive relief is appropriate to prevent recurrence of such conduct,

the court may enjoin such person from engaging in such conduct or in any other activity subject to penalty under section 6700 or section 6701.

(c) SPECIFIED CONDUCT.—*For purposes of this section, the term "specified conduct" means any action, or failure to take action, which is—*

(1) *subject to penalty under section 6700, 6701, 6707, or 6708, or*

(2) *in violation of any requirement under regulations issued under section 330 of title 31, United States Code.*

[CCH Explanation at ¶ 650. Committee Reports at ¶ 11,110.]

Amendments

• **2004, American Jobs Creation Act of 2004 (H.R. 4520)**

H.R. 4520, § 820(a):

Amended Code Sec. 7408 by redesignating subsection (c) as subsection (d) and by striking subsections (a) and (b) and inserting new subsections (a), (b), and (c). **Effective** on the day after the date of the enactment of this Act.

(d) CITIZENS AND RESIDENTS OUTSIDE THE UNITED STATES.—If any citizen or resident of the United States does not reside in, and does not have his principal place of business in, any United States judicial district, such citizen or resident shall be treated for purposes of this section as residing in the District of Columbia.

* * *

[CCH Explanation at ¶ 650. Committee Reports at ¶ 11,110.]

Amendments

• **2004, American Jobs Creation Act of 2004 (H.R. 4520)**

H.R. 4520, § 820(a):

Amended Code Sec. 7408 by redesignating subsection (c) as subsection (d). **Effective** on the day after the date of the enactment of this Act.

[¶ 6335] CODE SEC. 7428. DECLARATORY JUDGMENTS RELATING TO STATUS AND CLASSIFICATION OF ORGANIZATIONS UNDER SECTION 501(c)(3), ETC.

(a) CREATION OF REMEDY.—In a case of actual controversy involving—

(1) a determination by the Secretary—

(A) with respect to the initial qualification or continuing qualification of an organization as an organization described in section 501(c)(3) which is exempt from tax under section 501(a) or as an organization described in section 170(c)(2),

(B) with respect to the initial classification or continuing classification of an organization as a private foundation (as defined in section 509(a)),

(C) with respect to the initial classification or continuing classification of an organization as a private operating foundation (as defined in section 4942(j)(3)), or

(D) *with respect to the initial classification or continuing classification of a cooperative as an organization described in section 521(b) which is exempt from tax under section 521(a), or*

(2) a failure by the Secretary to make a determination with respect to an issue referred to in paragraph (1),

upon the filing of an appropriate pleading, the United States Tax Court, the United States Claims Court, or the district court of the United States for the District of Columbia may make a declaration with respect to such initial qualification or continuing qualification or with respect to such initial classification or continuing classification. Any such declaration shall have the force and effect of a decision of the Tax Court or a final judgment or decree of the district court or the Claims Court, as the case may be, and shall be reviewable as such. For purposes of this section, a determination with respect to a continuing qualification or continuing classification includes any revocation of or other change in a qualification or classification.

* * *

[CCH Explanation at ¶835. Committee Reports at ¶10,400.]

Amendments

• **2004, American Jobs Creation Act of 2004 (H.R. 4520)**

H.R. 4520, §317(a):

Amended Code Sec. 7428(a)(1) by striking "or" at the end of subparagraph (B) and by adding at the end a new subpar-agraph (D). **Effective** for pleadings filed after the date of the enactment of this Act.

[¶6340] CODE SEC. 7433A. CIVIL DAMAGES FOR CERTAIN UNAUTHORIZED COLLECTION ACTIONS BY PERSONS PERFORMING SERVICES UNDER QUALIFIED TAX COLLECTION CONTRACTS.

(a) IN GENERAL.—*Subject to the modifications provided by subsection (b), section 7433 shall apply to the acts and omissions of any person performing services under a qualified tax collection contract (as defined in section 6306(b)) to the same extent and in the same manner as if such person were an employee of the Internal Revenue Service.*

(b) MODIFICATIONS.—*For purposes of subsection (a):*

(1) *Any civil action brought under section 7433 by reason of this section shall be brought against the person who entered into the qualified tax collection contract with the Secretary and shall not be brought against the United States.*

(2) *Such person and not the United States shall be liable for any damages and costs determined in such civil action.*

(3) *Such civil action shall not be an exclusive remedy with respect to such person.*

(4) *Subsections (c), (d)(1), and (e) of section 7433 shall not apply.*

* * *

[CCH Explanation at ¶1605. Committee Reports at ¶11,530.]

Amendments

• **2004, American Jobs Creation Act of 2004 (H.R. 4520)**

H.R. 4520, §881(b)(1):

Amended subchapter B of chapter 76 by inserting after Code Sec. 7433 a new Code Sec. 7433A. **Effective** on the date of the enactment of this Act.

[¶6345] CODE SEC. 7525. CONFIDENTIALITY PRIVILEGES RELATING TO TAXPAYER COMMUNICATIONS.

* * *

(b) SECTION NOT TO APPLY TO COMMUNICATIONS REGARDING TAX SHELTERS.—*The privilege under subsection (a) shall not apply to any written communication which is—*

(1) *between a federally authorized tax practitioner and—*

(A) *any person,*

(B) *any director, officer, employee, agent, or representative of the person, or*

(C) *any other person holding a capital or profits interest in the person, and*

(2) in connection with the promotion of the direct or indirect participation of the person in any tax shelter (as defined in section 6662(d)(2)(C)(ii)).

* * *

[CCH Explanation at ¶665. Committee Reports at ¶11,050.]

Amendments

• **2004, American Jobs Creation Act of 2004 (H.R. 4520)**

H.R. 4520, § 813(a):

Amended Code Sec. 7525(b). **Effective** for communications made on or after the date of the enactment of this Act. Prior to amendment, Code Sec. 7525(b) read as follows:

(b) SECTION NOT TO APPLY TO COMMUNICATIONS REGARDING CORPORATE TAX SHELTERS.—The privilege under subsection (a) shall not apply to any written communication between a federally authorized tax practitioner and a director, shareholder, officer, or employee, agent, or representative of a corporation in connection with the promotion of the direct or indirect participation of such corporation in any tax shelter (as defined in section 6662(d)(2)(C)(iii)).

[¶6350] CODE SEC. 7528. INTERNAL REVENUE SERVICE USER FEES.

* * *

(c) TERMINATION.—No fee shall be imposed under this section with respect to requests made after *September 30, 2014.*

* * *

[CCH Explanation at ¶1630. Committee Reports at ¶11,630.]

Amendments

• **2004, American Jobs Creation Act of 2004 (H.R. 4520)**

H.R. 4520, § 891(a):

Amended Code Sec. 7528(c) by striking "December 31, 2004" and inserting "September 30, 2014". **Effective** for requests after the date of the enactment of this Act.

[¶6355] CODE SEC. 7701. DEFINITIONS.

(a) When used in this title, where not otherwise distinctly expressed or manifestly incompatible with the intent thereof—

* * *

(19) DOMESTIC BUILDING AND LOAN ASSOCIATION.—The term "domestic building and loan association" means a domestic building and loan association, a domestic savings and loan association, and a Federal savings and loan association—

(A) which either (i) is an insured institution within the meaning of section 401(a) of the National Housing Act (12 U. S. C. sec. 1724(a)), or (ii) is subject by law to supervision and examination by State or Federal authority having supervision over such associations;

(B) the business of which consists principally of acquiring the savings of the public and investing in loans; and

(C) at least 60 percent of the amount of the total assets of which (at the close of the taxable year) consists of—

(i) cash,

(ii) obligations of the United States or of a State or political subdivision thereof, and stock or obligations of a corporation which is an instrumentality of the United States or of a State or political subdivision thereof, but not including obligations the interest on which is excludable from gross income under section 103,

(iii) certificates of deposit in, or obligations of, a corporation organized under a State law which specifically authorizes such corporation to insure the deposits or share accounts of member associations,

(iv) loans secured by a deposit or share of a member,

(v) loans (including redeemable ground rents, as defined in section 1055) secured by an interest in real property which is (or, from the proceeds of the loan, will become) residential real property or real property used primarily for church purposes, loans made for the improvement of residential real property or real property used primarily for church purposes, provided that for purposes of this clause, residential real property shall include single or multifamily dwellings, facilities in residential developments dedicated to public use or property used on a nonprofit basis for residents, and mobile homes not used on a transient basis,

(vi) loans secured by an interest in real property located within an urban renewal area to be developed for predominantly residential use under an urban renewal plan approved by the Secretary of Housing and Urban Development under part A or part B of title I of the Housing Act of 1949, as amended, or located within any area covered by a program eligible for assistance under section 103 of the Demonstration Cities and Metropolitan Development Act of 1966, as amended, and loans made for the improvement of any such real property,

(vii) loans secured by an interest in educational, health, or welfare institutions or facilities, including structures designed or used primarily for residential purposes for students, residents, and persons under care, employees, or members of the staff of such institutions or facilities,

(viii) property acquired through the liquidation of defaulted loans described in clause (v), (vi), or (vii),

(ix) loans made for the payment of expenses of college or university education or vocational training, in accordance with such regulations as may be prescribed by the Secretary,

(x) property used by the association in the conduct of the business described in subparagraph (B), and,

(xi) any regular or residual interest in a REMIC, but only in the proportion which the assets of such REMIC consist of property described in any of the preceding clauses of this subparagraph; except that if 95 percent or more of the assets of such REMIC are assets described in clauses (i) through (x), the entire interest in the REMIC shall qualify.

At the election of the taxpayer, the percentage specified in this subparagraph shall be applied on the basis of the average assets outstanding during the taxable year, in lieu of the close of the taxable year, computed under regulations prescribed by the Secretary. For purposes of clause (v), if a multifamily structure securing a loan is used in part for nonresidential purposes, the entire loan is deemed a residential real property loan if the planned residential use exceeds 80 percent of the property's planned use (determined as of the time the loan is made). For purposes of clause (v), loans made to finance the acquisition or development of land shall be deemed to be loans secured by an interest in residential real property if, under regulations prescribed by the Secretary, there is reasonable assurance that the property will become residential real property within a period of 3 years from the date of acquisition of such land; but this sentence shall not apply for any taxable year unless, within such 3-year period, such land becomes residential real property. For purposes of determining whether any interest in a REMIC qualifies under clause (xi), any regular interest in another REMIC held by such REMIC shall be treated as a loan described in a preceding clause under principles similar to the principles of clause (xi); except that, if such REMIC's are part of a tiered structure, they shall be treated as 1 REMIC for purposes of clause (xi).

* * *

[CCH Explanation at ¶1120. Committee Reports at ¶11,180.]

Amendments

• 2004, American Jobs Creation Act of 2004 (H.R. 4520)

H.R. 4520, §835(b)(10)(A)-(B):

Amended Code Sec. 7701(a)(19)(C)(xi) by striking "and any regular interest in a FASIT,", and by striking "or FASIT" each place it appears. **Effective** 1-1-2005. For an exception, see Act Sec. 835(c)(2), below. Prior to amendment, Code Sec. 7701(a)(19)(C)(xi) read as follows:

(xi) any regular or residual interest in a REMIC, and any regular interest in a FASIT, but only in the proportion which

the assets of such REMIC or FASIT consist of property described in any of the preceding clauses of this subparagraph; except that if 95 percent or more of the assets of such REMIC or FASIT are assets described in clauses (i) through (x), the entire interest in the REMIC or FASIT shall qualify.

H.R. 4520, §835(c)(2), provides:

(2) EXCEPTION FOR EXISTING FASITS.—Paragraph (1) shall not apply to any FASIT in existence on the date of the enactment of this Act to the extent that regular interests issued by the FASIT before such date continue to remain outstanding in accordance with the original terms of issuance.

(48) OFF-HIGHWAY VEHICLES.—

(A) OFF-HIGHWAY TRANSPORTATION VEHICLES.—

(i) IN GENERAL.—A vehicle shall not be treated as a highway vehicle if such vehicle is specially designed for the primary function of transporting a particular type of load other than over the public highway and because of this special design such vehicle's capability to transport a load over the public highway is substantially limited or impaired.

(ii) DETERMINATION OF VEHICLE'S DESIGN.—For purposes of clause (i), a vehicle's design is determined solely on the basis of its physical characteristics.

(iii) DETERMINATION OF SUBSTANTIAL LIMITATION OR IMPAIRMENT.—For purposes of clause (i), in determining whether substantial limitation or impairment exists, account may be taken of factors such as the size of the vehicle, whether such vehicle is subject to the licensing, safety, and other requirements applicable to highway vehicles, and whether such vehicle can transport a load at a sustained speed of at least 25 miles per hour. It is immaterial that a vehicle can transport a greater load off the public highway than such vehicle is permitted to transport over the public highway.

(B) NONTRANSPORTATION TRAILERS AND SEMITRAILERS.—A trailer or semitrailer shall not be treated as a highway vehicle if it is specially designed to function only as an enclosed stationary shelter for the carrying on of an offhighway function at an off-highway site.

* * *

[CCH Explanation at ¶ 1551. Committee Reports at ¶ 11,320.]

Amendments

• **2004, American Jobs Creation Act of 2004 (H.R. 4520)**

H.R. 4520, § 852(a):

Amended Code Sec. 7701(a) by adding at the end a new paragraph (48). **Effective** on the date of the enactment of this Act. For a special rule, see Act Sec. 852(c)(2), below.

H.R. 4520, § 852(c)(2), provides:

(2) FUEL TAXES.—With respect to taxes imposed under subchapter B of chapter 31 and part III of subchapter A of chapter 32, the amendment made by this section shall apply to taxable periods beginning after the date of the enactment of this Act.

(i) TAXABLE MORTGAGE POOLS.—

* * *

(2) TAXABLE MORTGAGE POOL DEFINED.—For purposes of this title—

(A) IN GENERAL.—Except as otherwise provided in this paragraph, a taxable mortgage pool is any entity (other than a REMIC) if—

(i) substantially all of the assets of such entity consists of debt obligations (or interests therein) and more than 50 percent of such debt obligations (or interests) consists of real estate mortgages (or interests therein),

(ii) such entity is the obligor under debt obligations with 2 or more maturities, and

(iii) under the terms of the debt obligations referred to in clause (ii) (or underlying arrangement), payments on such debt obligations bear a relationship to payments on the debt obligations (or interests) referred to in clause (i).

* * *

[CCH Explanation at ¶ 1120. Committee Reports at ¶ 11,180.]

Amendments

• **2004, American Jobs Creation Act of 2004 (H.R. 4520)**

H.R. 4520, § 835(b)(11):

Amended Code Sec. 7701(i)(2)(A) by striking "or a FASIT" after "REMIC". **Effective** generally 1-1-2005. For an exception, see Act Sec. 835(c)(2), below.

H.R. 4520, § 835(c)(2), provides:

(2) EXCEPTION FOR EXISTING FASITS.—Paragraph (1) shall not apply to any FASIT in existence on the date of the enactment of this Act to the extent that regular interests issued by the FASIT before such date continue to remain outstanding in accordance with the original terms of issuance.

(n) SPECIAL RULES FOR DETERMINING WHEN AN INDIVIDUAL IS NO LONGER A UNITED STATES CITIZEN OR LONG-TERM RESIDENT.—An individual who would (but for this subsection) cease to be treated as a citizen or resident of the United States shall continue to be treated as a citizen or resident of the United States, as the case may be, until such individual—

(1) gives notice of an expatriating act or termination of residency (with the requisite intent to relinquish citizenship or terminate residency) to the Secretary of State or the Secretary of Homeland Security, and

(2) provides a statement in accordance with section 6039G.

[CCH Explanation at ¶502. Committee Reports at ¶11,000.]

Amendments
• **2004, American Jobs Creation Act of 2004 (H.R. 4520)**

subsection (n). **Effective** for individuals who expatriate after 6-3-2004.

H.R. 4520, §804(b):

Amended Code Sec. 7701 by redesignating subsection (n) as subsection (o) and by inserting after subsection (m) a new

(o) CROSS REFERENCES.—

* * *

[CCH Explanation at ¶502. Committee Reports at ¶11,000.]

Amendments
• **2004, American Jobs Creation Act of 2004 (H.R. 4520)**

H.R. 4520, §804(b):

Amended Code Sec. 7701 by redesignating subsection (n) as subsection (o). **Effective** for individuals who expatriate after 6-3-2004.

[¶6360] CODE SEC. 7704. CERTAIN PUBLICLY TRADED PARTNERSHIPS TREATED AS CORPORATIONS.

* * *

(d) QUALIFYING INCOME.—For purposes of this section—

* * *

(4) CERTAIN INCOME QUALIFYING UNDER REGULATED INVESTMENT COMPANY OR REAL ESTATE TRUST PROVISIONS.—The term "qualifying income" also includes any income which would qualify under *section 851(b)(2)(A) or 856(c)(2).*

* * *

[CCH Explanation at ¶1105. Committee Reports at ¶10,460.]

Amendments
• **2004, American Jobs Creation Act of 2004 (H.R. 4520)**

tax years beginning after the date of the enactment of this Act.

H.R. 4520, §331(e):

Amended Code Sec. 7704(d)(4) by striking "section 851(b)(2)" and inserting "section 851(b)(2)(A)". **Effective** for

[¶6365] CODE SEC. 7809. DEPOSIT OF COLLECTIONS.

(a) GENERAL RULE.—Except as provided in subsections (b) and (c) and in sections *6306,* 7651, 7652, 7654, and 7810, the gross amount of all taxes and revenues received under the provisions of this title, and collections of whatever nature received or collected by authority of any internal revenue law, shall be paid daily into the Treasury of the United States under instructions of the Secretary as internal revenue collections, by the officer or employee receiving or collecting the same, without any abatement or deduction on account of salary, compensation, fees, costs, charges, expenses, or claims of any description. A certificate of such payment, stating the name of the depositor and the specific account on which the deposit was made, signed by the Treasurer of the United States, designated depositary, or proper officer of a deposit bank, shall be transmitted to the Secretary.

* * *

[CCH Explanation at ¶ 1605. Committee Reports at ¶ 11,530.]

Amendments

• 2004, American Jobs Creation Act of 2004 (H.R. 4520)

H.R. 4520, § 881(a)(2)(A):

Amended Code Sec. 7809(a) by inserting "6306," before "7651". **Effective** on the date of the enactment of this Act.

[¶ 6370]　CODE SEC. 7811.　TAXPAYER ASSISTANCE ORDERS.

* * *

(g) APPLICATION TO PERSONS PERFORMING SERVICES UNDER A QUALIFIED TAX COLLECTION CONTRACT.—Any order issued or action taken by the National Taxpayer Advocate pursuant to this section shall apply to persons performing services under a qualified tax collection contract (as defined in section 6306(b)) to the same extent and in the same manner as such order or action applies to the Secretary.

* * *

[CCH Explanation at ¶ 1605. Committee Reports at ¶ 11,530.]

Amendments

• 2004, American Jobs Creation Act of 2004 (H.R. 4520)

H.R. 4520, § 881(c):

Amended Code Sec. 7811 by adding at the end a new subsection (g). **Effective** on the date of the enactment of this Act.

[¶ 6375]　*CODE SEC. 7874.　RULES RELATING TO EXPATRIATED ENTITIES AND THEIR FOREIGN PARENTS.*

(a) TAX ON INVERSION GAIN OF EXPATRIATED ENTITIES.—

(1) IN GENERAL.—The taxable income of an expatriated entity for any taxable year which includes any portion of the applicable period shall in no event be less than the inversion gain of the entity for the taxable year.

(2) EXPATRIATED ENTITY.—For purposes of this subsection—

(A) IN GENERAL.—The term "expatriated entity" means—

(i) the domestic corporation or partnership referred to in subparagraph (B)(i) with respect to which a foreign corporation is a surrogate foreign corporation, and

(ii) any United States person who is related (within the meaning of section 267(b) or 707(b)(1)) to a domestic corporation or partnership described in clause (i).

(B) SURROGATE FOREIGN CORPORATION.—A foreign corporation shall be treated as a surrogate foreign corporation if, pursuant to a plan (or a series of related transactions)—

(i) the entity completes after March 4, 2003, the direct or indirect acquisition of substantially all of the properties held directly or indirectly by a domestic corporation or substantially all of the properties constituting a trade or business of a domestic partnership,

(ii) after the acquisition at least 60 percent of the stock (by vote or value) of the entity is held—

(I) in the case of an acquisition with respect to a domestic corporation, by former shareholders of the domestic corporation by reason of holding stock in the domestic corporation, or

(II) in the case of an acquisition with respect to a domestic partnership, by former partners of the domestic partnership by reason of holding a capital or profits interest in the domestic partnership, and

(iii) after the acquisition the expanded affiliated group which includes the entity does not have substantial business activities in the foreign country in which, or under the law of which, the entity is created or organized, when compared to the total business activities of such expanded affiliated group.

An entity otherwise described in clause (i) with respect to any domestic corporation or partnership trade or business shall be treated as not so described if, on or before March 4, 2003, such entity acquired directly or indirectly more than half of the properties held directly or indirectly by such corporation or more than half of the properties constituting such partnership trade or business, as the case may be.

(3) COORDINATION WITH SUBSECTION (b).—Paragraph (1) shall not apply to any entity which is treated as a domestic corporation under subsection (b).

(b) INVERTED CORPORATIONS TREATED AS DOMESTIC CORPORATIONS.—Notwithstanding section 7701(a)(4), a foreign corporation shall be treated for purposes of this title as a domestic corporation if such corporation would be a surrogate foreign corporation if subsection (a)(2) were applied by substituting "80 percent" for "60 percent".

(c) DEFINITIONS AND SPECIAL RULES.—

(1) EXPANDED AFFILIATED GROUP.—The term "expanded affiliated group" means an affiliated group as defined in section 1504(a) but without regard to section 1504(b)(3), except that section 1504(a) shall be applied by substituting "more than 50 percent" for "at least 80 percent" each place it appears.

(2) CERTAIN STOCK DISREGARDED.—There shall not be taken into account in determining ownership under subsection (a)(2)(B)(ii)—

(A) stock held by members of the expanded affiliated group which includes the foreign corporation, or

(B) stock of such foreign corporation which is sold in a public offering related to the acquisition described in subsection (a)(2)(B)(i).

(3) PLAN DEEMED IN CERTAIN CASES.—If a foreign corporation acquires directly or indirectly substantially all of the properties of a domestic corporation or partnership during the 4-year period beginning on the date which is 2 years before the ownership requirements of subsection (a)(2)(B)(ii) are met, such actions shall be treated as pursuant to a plan.

(4) CERTAIN TRANSFERS DISREGARDED.—The transfer of properties or liabilities (including by contribution or distribution) shall be disregarded if such transfers are part of a plan a principal purpose of which is to avoid the purposes of this section.

(5) SPECIAL RULE FOR RELATED PARTNERSHIPS.—For purposes of applying subsection (a)(2)(B)(ii) to the acquisition of a trade or business of a domestic partnership, except as provided in regulations, all partnerships which are under common control (within the meaning of section 482) shall be treated as 1 partnership.

(6) REGULATIONS.—The Secretary shall prescribe such regulations as may be appropriate to determine whether a corporation is a surrogate foreign corporation, including regulations—

(A) to treat warrants, options, contracts to acquire stock, convertible debt interests, and other similar interests as stock, and

(B) to treat stock as not stock.

(d) OTHER DEFINITIONS.—For purposes of this section—

(1) APPLICABLE PERIOD.—The term "applicable period" means the period—

(A) beginning on the first date properties are acquired as part of the acquisition described in subsection (a)(2)(B)(i), and

(B) ending on the date which is 10 years after the last date properties are acquired as part of such acquisition.

(2) INVERSION GAIN.—The term "inversion gain" means the income or gain recognized by reason of the transfer during the applicable period of stock or other properties by an expatriated entity, and any income received or accrued during the applicable period by reason of a license of any property by an expatriated entity—

(A) as part of the acquisition described in subsection (a)(2)(B)(i), or

(B) after such acquisition if the transfer or license is to a foreign related person.

Subparagraph (B) shall not apply to property described in section 1221(a)(1) in the hands of the expatriated entity.

(3) F*OREIGN* *RELATED* *PERSON*.—The term "foreign related person" means, with respect to any expatriated entity, a foreign person which—

(A) is related (within the meaning of section 267(b) or 707(b)(1)) to such entity, or

(B) is under the same common control (within the meaning of section 482) as such entity.

(e) S*PECIAL* R*ULES*.—

(1) C*REDITS* *NOT* *ALLOWED* *AGAINST* *TAX* *ON* *INVERSION* *GAIN*.—Credits (other than the credit allowed by section 901) shall be allowed against the tax imposed by this chapter on an expatriated entity for any taxable year described in subsection (a) only to the extent such tax exceeds the product of—

(A) the amount of the inversion gain for the taxable year, and

(B) the highest rate of tax specified in section 11(b)(1).

For purposes of determining the credit allowed by section 901, inversion gain shall be treated as from sources within the United States.

(2) S*PECIAL* *RULES* *FOR* *PARTNERSHIPS*.—In the case of an expatriated entity which is a partnership—

(A) subsection (a)(1) shall apply at the partner rather than the partnership level,

(B) the inversion gain of any partner for any taxable year shall be equal to the sum of—

(i) the partner's distributive share of inversion gain of the partnership for such taxable year, plus

(ii) gain recognized for the taxable year by the partner by reason of the transfer during the applicable period of any partnership interest of the partner in such partnership to the surrogate foreign corporation, and

(C) the highest rate of tax specified in the rate schedule applicable to the partner under this chapter shall be substituted for the rate of tax referred to in paragraph (1).

(3) C*OORDINATION* *WITH* *SECTION* 172 *AND* *MINIMUM* *TAX*.—Rules similar to the rules of paragraphs (3) and (4) of section 860E(a) shall apply for purposes of subsection (a).

(4) S*TATUTE* *OF* *LIMITATIONS*.—

(A) I*N* G*ENERAL*.—The statutory period for the assessment of any deficiency attributable to the inversion gain of any taxpayer for any pre-inversion year shall not expire before the expiration of 3 years from the date the Secretary is notified by the taxpayer (in such manner as the Secretary may prescribe) of the acquisition described in subsection (a)(2)(B)(i) to which such gain relates and such deficiency may be assessed before the expiration of such 3-year period notwithstanding the provisions of any other law or rule of law which would otherwise prevent such assessment.

(B) P*RE-INVERSION* *YEAR*.—For purposes of subparagraph (A), the term "pre-inversion year" means any taxable year if—

(i) any portion of the applicable period is included in such taxable year, and

(ii) such year ends before the taxable year in which the acquisition described in subsection (a)(2)(B)(i) is completed.

(f) S*PECIAL* R*ULE* *FOR* T*REATIES*.—Nothing in section 894 or 7852(d) or in any other provision of law shall be construed as permitting an exemption, by reason of any treaty obligation of the United States heretofore or hereafter entered into, from the provisions of this section.

(g) R*EGULATIONS*.—The Secretary shall provide such regulations as are necessary to carry out this section, including regulations providing for such adjustments to the application of this section as are necessary to prevent the avoidance of the purposes of this section, including the avoidance of such purposes through—

(1) the use of related persons, pass-through or other noncorporate entities, or other intermediaries, or

(2) transactions designed to have persons cease to be (or not become) members of expanded affiliated groups or related persons.

* * *

[CCH Explanation at ¶ 506. Committee Reports at ¶ 10,970.]

Amendments

• 2004, American Jobs Creation Act of 2004 (H.R. 4520)

H.R. 4520, § 801(a):

Amended subchapter C of chapter 80 by adding at the end a new Code Sec. 7874. **Effective** for tax years ending after 3-4-2003.

[¶ 6380] CODE SEC. 9502. AIRPORT AND AIRWAY TRUST FUND.

* * *

(b) TRANSFERS TO AIRPORT AND AIRWAY TRUST FUND.—There are hereby appropriated to the Airport and Airway Trust Fund amounts equivalent to—

(1) the taxes received in the Treasury under—

(A) subsections (c) and (e) of section 4041 (relating to aviation fuels),

(B) sections 4261 and 4271 (relating to transportation by air), *and*

(C) *section 4081 with respect to aviation gasoline and aviation-grade kerosene, and*

(2) the amounts determined by the Secretary of the Treasury to be equivalent to the amounts of civil penalties collected under section 47107(n) of title 49, United States Code.

There shall not be taken into account under paragraph (1) so much of the taxes imposed by section 4081 as are determined at the rate specified in section 4081(a)(2)(B).

* * *

[CCH Explanation at ¶ 1507. Committee Reports at ¶ 11,340.]

Amendments

• 2004, American Jobs Creation Act of 2004 (H.R. 4520)

H.R. 4520, § 853(d)(2)(N):

Amended Code Sec. 9502(b)(1) by adding "and" at the end of subparagraph (B) and by striking subparagraphs (C) and (D) and inserting a new subparagraph (C). **Effective** for aviation-grade kerosene removed, entered, or sold after 12-31-2004. Prior to being stricken, Code Sec. 9502(b)(1)(C)-(D) read as follows:

(C) section 4081 (relating to gasoline) with respect to aviation gasoline, and

(D) section 4091 (relating to aviation fuel), and

H.R. 4520, § 853(d)(2)(O):

Amended the last sentence of Code Sec. 9502(b). **Effective** for aviation-grade kerosene removed, entered, or sold after 12-31-2004. Prior to amendment, the last sentence of Code Sec. 9502(b) read as follows:

There shall not be taken into account under paragraph (1) so much of the taxes imposed by sections 4081 and 4091 as are determined at the rates specified in section 4081(a)(2)(B) or 4091(b)(2).

[¶ 6385] CODE SEC. 9503. HIGHWAY TRUST FUND.

* * *

(b) TRANSFER TO HIGHWAY TRUST FUND OF AMOUNTS EQUIVALENT TO CERTAIN TAXES *AND PENALTIES.*—

(1) *CERTAIN TAXES.*—There are hereby appropriated to the Highway Trust Fund amounts equivalent to the taxes received in the Treasury before October 1, 2005, under the following provisions—

(A) section 4041 (relating to taxes on diesel fuels and special motor fuels),

(B) section 4051 (relating to retail tax on heavy trucks and trailers),

(C) section 4071 (relating to tax on tires),

(D) section 4081 (relating to tax on gasoline, diesel fuel, and kerosene), and

(E) section 4481 (relating to tax on use of certain vehicles).

For purposes of this paragraph, taxes received under sections 4041 and 4081 shall be determined without reduction for credits under section 6426.

* * *

(4) CERTAIN TAXES NOT TRANSFERRED TO HIGHWAY TRUST FUND.—For purposes of paragraphs (1) and (2), there shall not be taken into account the taxes imposed by—

(A) section 4041(d),

(B) section 4081 to the extent attributable to the rate specified in section 4081(a)(2)(B),

(C) section 4041 or 4081 to the extent attributable to fuel used in a train, *or*

(D) in the case of gasoline and special motor fuels used as described in paragraph (4)(D) or (5)((B) of subsection (c), section 4041 or 4081 with respect to so much of the rate of tax as exceeds—

(i) 11.5 cents per gallon with respect to taxes imposed before October 1, 2001,

(ii) 13 cents per gallon with respect to taxes imposed after September 30, 2001, and before October 1, 2003, and

(iii) 13.5 cents per gallon with respect to taxes imposed after September 30, 2003, and before October 1, 2005.

(5) CERTAIN PENALTIES.—There are hereby appropriated to the Highway Trust Fund amounts equivalent to the penalties paid under sections 6715, 6715A, 6717, 6718, 6719, 6725, 7232, and 7272 (but only with regard to penalties under such section related to failure to register under section 4101).

(6) LIMITATION ON TRANSFERS TO HIGHWAY TRUST FUND.—

* * *

[CCH Explanation at ¶ 805 and ¶ 1573. Committee Reports at ¶ 10,320 and ¶ 11,490.]

Amendments

• **2004, American Jobs Creation Act of 2004 (H.R. 4520)**

H.R. 4520, § 301(c)(11):

Amended Code Sec. 9503(b)(1) by adding at the end a new flush sentence. **Effective** for fuel sold or used after 12-31-2004.

H.R. 4520, § 301(c)(12)(A)-(C):

Amended Code Sec. 9503(b)(4) by adding "or" at the end of subparagraph (C), by striking the comma at the end of subparagraph (D)(iii) and inserting a period, and by striking subparagraphs (E) and (F). **Effective** for fuel sold or used after 9-30-2004. Prior to being stricken, Code Sec. 9503(b)(4)(E) and (F) read as follows:

(E) in the case of fuels described in section 4041(b)(2)(A), 4041(k), or 4081(c), section 4041 or 4081 before October 1, 2003, and for the period beginning after September 30, 2004, and before October 1, 2005, with respect to a rate equal to 2.5 cents per gallon, or

(F) in the case of fuels described in section 4081(c)(2), such section before October 1, 2003, and for the period beginning after September 30, 2004, and before October 1, 2005, with respect to a rate equal to 2.8 cents per gallon.

H.R. 4520, § 868(a):

Amended Code Sec. 9503(b) by redesignating paragraph (5) as paragraph (6) and inserting after paragraph (4) a new paragraph (5). **Effective** for penalties assessed on or after the date of the enactment of this Act.

H.R. 4520, § 868(b)(1):

Amended the heading of Code Sec. 9503(b) by inserting "AND PENALTIES" after "TAXES". **Effective** for penalties assessed on or after the date of the enactment of this Act.

H.R. 4520, § 868(b)(2):

Amended the heading of Code Sec. 9503(b)(1) by striking "IN GENERAL" and inserting "CERTAIN TAXES". **Effective** for penalties assessed on or after the date of the enactment of this Act.

(c) EXPENDITURES FROM HIGHWAY TRUST FUND.—

* * *

(2) TRANSFERS FROM HIGHWAY TRUST FUND FOR CERTAIN REPAYMENTS AND CREDITS.—

(A) IN GENERAL.—The Secretary shall pay from time to time from the Highway Trust Fund into the general fund of the Treasury amounts equivalent to—

(i) the amounts paid before July 1, 2006, under—

(I) section 6420 (relating to amounts paid in respect of gasoline used on farms),

(II) section 6421 (relating to amounts paid in respect of gasoline used for certain nonhighway purposes or by local transit systems), and

(III) section 6427 (relating to fuels not used for taxable purposes), on the basis of claims filed for periods ending before October 1, 2005, and

(ii) the credits allowed under section 34 (relating to credit for certain uses of fuel) with respect to fuel used before October 1, 2005.

The amounts payable from the Highway Trust Fund under this subparagraph or paragraph (3) shall be determined by taking into account only the portion of the taxes which are deposited into the Highway Trust Fund. *Clauses (i)(III) and (ii) shall not apply to claims under section 6427(e).*

* * *

[CCH Explanation at ¶805. Committee Reports at ¶10,320.]

Amendments

• **2004, American Jobs Creation Act of 2004 (H.R. 4520)**

H.R. 4520, §301(c)(13):

Amended Code Sec. 9503(c)(2)(A) by adding at the end a new sentence. **Effective** for fuel sold or used after 12-31-2004.

[¶6390] CODE SEC. 9508. LEAKING UNDERGROUND STORAGE TANK TRUST FUND.

* * *

(b) TRANSFER TO TRUST FUND.—There are hereby appropriated to the Leaking Underground Storage Tank Trust Fund amounts equivalent to—

(1) taxes received in the Treasury under section 4041(d) (relating to additional taxes on motor fuels),

(2) taxes received in the Treasury under section 4081 (relating to tax on gasoline, diesel fuel, and kerosene) to the extent attributable to the Leaking Underground Storage Tax Trust Fund financing rate under such section,

(3) taxes received in the Treasury under section 4042 (relating to tax on fuel used in commercial transportation on inland waterways) to the extent attributable to the Leaking Underground Storage Tank Trust Fund financing rate under such section, and

(4) amounts received in the Treasury and collected under section 9003(h)(6) of the Solid Waste Disposal Act.

For purposes of this subsection, there shall not be taken into account the taxes imposed by sections 4041 and 4081 on diesel fuel sold for use or used as fuel in a diesel-powered boat.

[CCH Explanation at ¶1507. Committee Reports at ¶11,340.]

Amendments

• **2004, American Jobs Creation Act of 2004 (H.R. 4520)**

H.R. 4520, §853(d)(2)(P):

Amended Code Sec. 9508(b) by striking paragraph (3) and by redesignating paragraphs (4) and (5) as paragraphs (3) and (4), respectively. **Effective** for aviation-grade kerosene removed, entered, or sold after 12-31-2004. For special rules, see Act Sec. 853(f), below. Prior to being stricken, Code Sec. 9508(b)(3) read as follows:

(3) taxes received in the Treasury under section 4091 (relating to tax on aviation fuel) to the extent attributable to the Leaking Underground Storage Tank Trust Fund financing rate under such section,

H.R. 4520, §853(f), provides:

(f) FLOOR STOCKS TAX.—

(1) IN GENERAL.—There is hereby imposed on aviation-grade kerosene held on January 1, 2005, by any person a tax equal to—

(A) the tax which would have been imposed before such date on such kerosene had the amendments made by this section been in effect at all times before such date, reduced by

(B) the sum of—

(i) the tax imposed before such date on such kerosene under section 4091 of the Internal Revenue Code of 1986, as in effect on such date, and

(ii) in the case of kerosene held exclusively for such person's own use, the amount which such person would (but for this clause) reasonably expect (as of such date) to be paid as a refund under section 6427(l) of such Code with respect to such kerosene.

(2) EXCEPTION FOR FUEL HELD IN AIRCRAFT FUEL TANK.—Paragraph (1) shall not apply to kerosene held in the fuel tank of an aircraft on January 1, 2005.

(3) LIABILITY FOR TAX AND METHOD OF PAYMENT.—

(A) LIABILITY FOR TAX.—The person holding the kerosene on January 1, 2005, to which the tax imposed by paragraph (1) applies shall be liable for such tax.

(B) METHOD AND TIME FOR PAYMENT.—The tax imposed by paragraph (1) shall be paid at such time and in such manner as the Secretary of the Treasury (or the Secretary's delegate) shall prescribe, including the nonapplication of such tax on de minimis amounts of kerosene.

(4) TRANSFER OF FLOOR STOCK TAX REVENUES TO TRUST FUNDS.—For purposes of determining the amount transferred to any trust fund, the tax imposed by this subsection shall be treated as imposed by section 4081 of the Internal Revenue Code of 1986—

(A) in any case in which tax was not imposed by section 4091 of such Code, at the Leaking Underground Storage Tank Trust Fund financing rate under such section to the extent of 0.1 cents per gallon, and

(B) at the rate under section 4081(a)(2)(A)(iv) of such Code to the extent of the remainder.

(5) HELD BY A PERSON.—For purposes of this subsection, kerosene shall be considered as held by a person if title thereto has passed to such person (whether or not delivery to the person has been made).

(6) OTHER LAWS APPLICABLE.—All provisions of law, including penalties, applicable with respect to the tax imposed by section 4081 of such Code shall, insofar as applicable and not inconsistent with the provisions of this subsection, apply with respect to the floor stock tax imposed by paragraph (1) to the same extent as if such tax were imposed by such section.

(c) Expenditures.—

* * *

(2) Transfers from Trust Fund for Certain Repayments and Credits.—

(A) In General.—The Secretary shall pay from time to time from the Leaking Underground Storage Tank Trust Fund into the general fund of the Treasury amounts equivalent to—

* * *

(ii) credits allowed under section 34, with respect to the taxes imposed by section 4041(d) or by *section 4081* (to the extent attributable to the Leaking Underground Storage Tank Trust Fund financing rate under such sections).

* * *

[CCH Explanation at ¶1507. Committee Reports at ¶11,340.]

Amendments

• **2004, American Jobs Creation Act of 2004 (H.R. 4520)**

H.R. 4520, § 853(d)(2)(Q):

Amended Code Sec. 9508(c)(2)(A) by striking "sections 4081 and 4091" and inserting "section 4081". **Effective** for aviation-grade kerosene removed, entered, or sold after 12-31-2004. For special rules, see Act Sec. 853(f), below.

H.R. 4520, § 853(f), provides:

(f) Floor Stocks Tax.—

(1) In general.—There is hereby imposed on aviation-grade kerosene held on January 1, 2005, by any person a tax equal to—

(A) the tax which would have been imposed before such date on such kerosene had the amendments made by this section been in effect at all times before such date, reduced by

(B) the sum of—

(i) the tax imposed before such date on such kerosene under section 4091 of the Internal Revenue Code of 1986, as in effect on such date, and

(ii) in the case of kerosene held exclusively for such person's own use, the amount which such person would (but for this clause) reasonably expect (as of such date) to be paid as a refund under section 6427(l) of such Code with respect to such kerosene.

(2) Exception for fuel held in aircraft fuel tank.—Paragraph (1) shall not apply to kerosene held in the fuel tank of an aircraft on January 1, 2005.

(3) Liability for tax and method of payment.—

(A) Liability for tax.—The person holding the kerosene on January 1, 2005, to which the tax imposed by paragraph (1) applies shall be liable for such tax.

(B) Method and time for payment.—The tax imposed by paragraph (1) shall be paid at such time and in such manner as the Secretary of the Treasury (or the Secretary's delegate) shall prescribe, including the nonapplication of such tax on de minimis amounts of kerosene.

(4) Transfer of floor stock tax revenues to trust funds.—For purposes of determining the amount transferred to any trust fund, the tax imposed by this subsection shall be treated as imposed by section 4081 of the Internal Revenue Code of 1986—

(A) in any case in which tax was not imposed by section 4091 of such Code, at the Leaking Underground Storage Tank Trust Fund financing rate under such section to the extent of 0.1 cents per gallon, and

(B) at the rate under section 4081(a)(2)(A)(iv) of such Code to the extent of the remainder.

(5) Held by a person.—For purposes of this subsection, kerosene shall be considered as held by a person if title thereto has passed to such person (whether or not delivery to the person has been made).

(6) Other laws applicable.—All provisions of law, including penalties, applicable with respect to the tax imposed by section 4081 of such Code shall, insofar as applicable and not inconsistent with the provisions of this subsection, apply with respect to the floor stock tax imposed by paragraph (1) to the same extent as if such tax were imposed by such section.

ACT SECTIONS NOT AMENDING CODE SECTIONS

AMERICAN JOBS CREATION ACT OF 2004

[¶7005] ACT SEC. 1. SHORT TITLE; ETC.

(a) SHORT TITLE.—This Act may be cited as the "American Jobs Creation Act of 2004".

(b) AMENDMENT OF 1986 CODE.—Except as otherwise expressly provided, whenever in this Act an amendment or repeal is expressed in terms of an amendment to, or repeal of, a section or other provision, the reference shall be considered to be made to a section or other provision of the Internal Revenue Code of 1986.

* * *

TITLE I—PROVISIONS RELATING TO REPEAL OF EXCLUSION FOR EXTRATERRITORIAL INCOME

[¶7010] ACT SEC. 101. REPEAL OF EXCLUSION FOR EXTRATERRITORIAL INCOME.

* * *

(d) TRANSITIONAL RULE FOR 2005 AND 2006.—

(1) IN GENERAL.—In the case of transactions during 2005 or 2006, the amount includible in gross income by reason of the amendments made by this section shall not exceed the applicable percentage of the amount which would have been so included but for this subsection.

(2) APPLICABLE PERCENTAGE.—For purposes of paragraph (1), the applicable percentage shall be as follows:

(A) For 2005, the applicable percentage shall be 20 percent.

(B) For 2006, the applicable percentage shall be 40 percent.

(e) REVOCATION OF ELECTION TO BE TREATED AS DOMESTIC CORPORATION.—If, during the 1-year period beginning on the date of the enactment of this Act, a corporation for which an election is in effect under section 943(e) of the Internal Revenue Code of 1986 revokes such election, no gain or loss shall be recognized with respect to property treated as transferred under clause (ii) of section 943(e)(4)(B) of such Code to the extent such property—

(1) was treated as transferred under clause (i) thereof, or

(2) was acquired during a taxable year to which such election applies and before May 1, 2003, in the ordinary course of its trade or business.

The Secretary of the Treasury (or such Secretary's delegate) may prescribe such regulations as may be necessary to prevent the abuse of the purposes of this subsection.

(f) BINDING CONTRACTS.—The amendments made by this section shall not apply to any transaction in the ordinary course of a trade or business which occurs pursuant to a binding contract—

(1) which is between the taxpayer and a person who is not a related person (as defined in section 943(b)(3) of such Code, as in effect on the day before the date of the enactment of this Act), and

(2) which is in effect on September 17, 2003, and at all times thereafter.

For purposes of this subsection, a binding contract shall include a purchase option, renewal option, or replacement option which is included in such contract and which is enforceable against the seller or lessor.

[CCH Explanation at ¶205. Committee Reports at ¶10,010.]

[¶7015] ACT SEC. 102. DEDUCTION RELATING TO INCOME ATTRIBUTABLE TO DOMESTIC PRODUCTION ACTIVITIES.

* * *

(c) SPECIAL RULE RELATING TO ELECTION TO TREAT CUTTING OF TIMBER AS A SALE OR EXCHANGE.—Any election under section 631(a) of the Internal Revenue Code of 1986 made for a taxable year ending on or before the date of the enactment of this Act may be revoked by the taxpayer for any taxable year ending after such date. For purposes of determining whether such taxpayer may make a further election under such section, such election (and any revocation under this section) shall not be taken into account.

* * *

[CCH Explanation at ¶210. Committee Reports at ¶10,030.]

TITLE II—BUSINESS TAX INCENTIVES
* * *

Subtitle F—Stock Options and Employee Stock Purchase Plan Stock Options

[¶7018] ACT SEC. 251. EXCLUSION OF INCENTIVE STOCK OPTIONS AND EMPLOYEE STOCK PURCHASE PLAN STOCK OPTIONS FROM WAGES.

(a) EXCLUSION FROM EMPLOYMENT TAXES.—

(1) SOCIAL SECURITY TAXES.—

* * *

(B) Section 209(a) of the Social Security Act is amended by striking "or" at the end of paragraph (17), by striking the period at the end of paragraph (18) and inserting "; or", and by inserting after paragraph (18) the following new paragraph:

"(19) Remuneration on account of—

"(A) a transfer of a share of stock to any individual pursuant to an exercise of an incentive stock option (as defined in section 422(b) of the Internal Revenue Code of 1986) or under an employee stock purchase plan (as defined in section 423(b) of such Code), or

"(B) any disposition by the individual of such stock.".

* * *

[CCH Explanation at ¶1410. Committee Reports at ¶10,310.]

TITLE III—TAX RELIEF FOR AGRICULTURE AND SMALL MANUFACTURERS

Subtitle A—Volumetric Ethanol Excise Tax Credit

[¶7020] ACT SEC. 301. ALCOHOL AND BIODIESEL EXCISE TAX CREDIT AND EXTENSION OF ALCOHOL FUELS INCOME TAX CREDIT.

* * *

(e) FORMAT FOR FILING.—The Secretary of the Treasury shall describe the electronic format for filing claims described in section 6427(i)(3)(B) of the Internal Revenue Code of 1986 (as amended by subsection (c)(10)(C)) not later than December 31, 2004.

* * *

[CCH Explanation at ¶805. Committee Reports at ¶10,320.]

Subtitle B—Agricultural Incentives

* * *

[¶7021] ACT SEC. 320. EXCLUSION FOR PAYMENTS TO INDIVIDUALS UNDER NATIONAL HEALTH SERVICE CORPS LOAN REPAYMENT PROGRAM AND CERTAIN STATE LOAN REPAYMENT PROGRAMS.

* * *

(b) Treatment for Purposes of Employment Taxes.—Each of the following provisions is amended by inserting "108(f)(4)," after "74(c),":

* * *

(5) Section 209(a)(17) of the Social Security Act.

* * *

[CCH Explanation at ¶1225. Committee Reports at ¶10,430.]

TITLE IV—TAX REFORM AND SIMPLIFICATION FOR UNITED STATES BUSINESSES

* * *

[¶7025] ACT SEC. 423. DELAY IN EFFECTIVE DATE OF FINAL REGULATIONS GOVERNING EXCLUSION OF INCOME FROM INTERNATIONAL OPERATION OF SHIPS OR AIRCRAFT.

Notwithstanding the provisions of Treasury regulation § 1.883-5, the final regulations issued by the Secretary of the Treasury relating to income derived by foreign corporations from the international operation of ships or aircraft (Treasury regulations § 1.883-1 through § 1.883-5) shall apply to taxable years of a foreign corporation seeking qualified foreign corporation status beginning after September 24, 2004.

[CCH Explanation at ¶550. Committee Reports at ¶10,790.]

[¶7030] ACT SEC. 424. STUDY OF EARNINGS STRIPPING PROVISIONS.

(a) In General.—The Secretary of the Treasury or the Secretary's delegate shall conduct a study of the effectiveness of the provisions of the Internal Revenue Code of 1986 applicable to earnings stripping, including a study of—

(1) the effectiveness of section 163(j) of such Code in preventing the shifting of income outside the United States,

(2) whether any deficiencies of such provisions place United States-based businesses at a competitive disadvantage relative to foreign-based businesses,

(3) the impact of earnings stripping activities on the United States tax base,

(4) whether laws of foreign countries facilitate stripping of earnings out of the United States, and

(5) whether changes to the earning stripping rules would affect jobs in the United States.

(b) Report.—Not later than June 30, 2005, the Secretary shall submit to the Congress a report of the study conducted under this section, including specific recommendations as to how to improve the provisions of such Code applicable to earnings stripping.

* * *

[CCH Explanation at ¶525. Committee Reports at ¶10,800.]

TITLE VII—MISCELLANEOUS PROVISIONS

[¶7055] ACT SEC. 701. BROWNFIELDS DEMONSTRATION PROGRAM FOR QUALIFIED GREEN BUILDING AND SUSTAINABLE DESIGN PROJECTS.

* * *

(d) Accountability.—Each issuer shall maintain, on behalf of each project, an interest bearing reserve account equal to 1 percent of the net proceeds of any bond issued under this section for such project. Not later than 5 years after the date of issuance, the Secretary of the Treasury, after consultation with the Administrator of the Environmental Protection Agency, shall determine whether the project financed with such bonds has substantially complied with the terms and conditions described in section 142(l)(4) of the Internal Revenue Code of 1986 (as added by this section). If the Secretary, after such consultation, certifies that the project has substantially complied with such terms and conditions and meets the commitments set forth in the application for such project described in section 142(l)(4) of such Code, amounts in the reserve account, including all interest, shall be released to the project. If the Secretary determines that the project has not substantially complied with such terms and conditions, amounts in the reserve account, including all interest, shall be paid to the United States Treasury.

* * *

[CCH Explanation at ¶745. Committee Reports at ¶10,830.]

[¶7060] ACT SEC. 702. EXCLUSION OF GAIN OR LOSS ON SALE OR EXCHANGE OF CERTAIN BROWNFIELD SITES FROM UNRELATED BUSINESS TAXABLE INCOME.

* * *

(c) SAVINGS CLAUSE.—Nothing in the amendments made by this section shall affect any duty, liability, or other requirement imposed under any other Federal or State law. Notwithstanding section 128(b) of the Comprehensive Environmental Response, Compensation, and Liability Act of 1980, a certification provided by the Environmental Protection Agency or an appropriate State agency (within the meaning of section 198(c)(4) of the Internal Revenue Code of 1986) shall not affect the liability of any person under section 107(a) of such Act.

* * *

[CCH Explanation at ¶1330. Committee Reports at ¶10,840.]

[¶7065] ACT SEC. 708. METHOD OF ACCOUNTING FOR NAVAL SHIPBUILDERS.

(a) IN GENERAL.—In the case of a qualified naval ship contract, the taxable income of such contract during the 5-taxable year period beginning with the taxable year in which the contract commencement date occurs shall be determined under a method identical to the method used in the case of a qualified ship contract (as defined in section 10203(b)(2)(B) of the Revenue Act of 1987).

(b) RECAPTURE OF TAX BENEFIT.—In the case of a qualified naval ship contract to which subsection (a) applies, the taxpayer's tax imposed by chapter 1 of the Internal Revenue Code of 1986 for the first taxable year following the 5-taxable year period described in subsection (a) shall be increased by the excess (if any) of—

(1) the amount of tax which would have been imposed during such period if this section had not been enacted, over

(2) the amount of tax so imposed during such period.

(c) QUALIFIED NAVAL SHIP CONTRACT.—For purposes of this section—

(1) IN GENERAL.—The term "qualified naval ship contract" means any contract or portion thereof that is for the construction in the United States of 1 ship or submarine for the Federal Government if the taxpayer reasonably expects the acceptance date will occur no later than 9 years after the construction commencement date.

(2) ACCEPTANCE DATE.—The term "acceptance date" means the date 1 year after the date on which the Federal Government issues a letter of acceptance or other similar document for the ship or submarine.

(3) CONSTRUCTION COMMENCEMENT DATE.—The term "construction commencement date" means the date on which the physical fabrication of any section or component of the ship or submarine begins in the taxpayer's shipyard.

(d) EFFECTIVE DATE.—This section shall apply to contracts for ships or submarines with respect to which the construction commencement date occurs after the date of the enactment of this Act.

[CCH Explanation at ¶395. Committee Reports at ¶10,900.]

[¶7070] ACT SEC. 709. MODIFICATION OF MINIMUM COST REQUIREMENT FOR TRANSFER OF EXCESS PENSION ASSETS.

(a) AMENDMENTS OF ERISA.—

(1) Section 101(e)(3) of the Employee Retirement Income Security Act of 1974 (29 U.S.C. 1021(e)(3)) is amended by striking "Pension Funding Equity Act of 2004" and inserting "American Jobs Creation Act of 2004".

(2) Section 403(c)(1) of such Act (29 U.S.C. 1103(c)(1)) is amended by striking "Pension Funding Equity Act of 2004" and inserting "American Jobs Creation Act of 2004".

(3) Paragraph (13) of section 408(b) of such Act (29 U.S.C. 1108(b)(3)) is amended by striking "Pension Funding Equity Act of 2004" and inserting "American Jobs Creation Act of 2004".

* * *

[CCH Explanation at ¶1420. Committee Reports at ¶10,910.]

[¶7075] ACT SEC. 712. INCLUSION OF PRIMARY AND SECONDARY MEDICAL STRATEGIES FOR CHILDREN AND ADULTS WITH SICKLE CELL DISEASE AS MEDICAL ASSISTANCE UNDER THE MEDICAID PROGRAM.

(a) OPTIONAL MEDICAL ASSISTANCE.—

(1) IN GENERAL.—Section 1905 of the Social Security Act (42 U.S.C. 1396d) is amended—

(A) in subsection (a)—

(i) by striking "and" at the end of paragraph (26);

(ii) by redesignating paragraph (27) as paragraph (28); and

(iii) by inserting after paragraph (26), the following:

"(27) subject to subsection (x), primary and secondary medical strategies and treatment and services for individuals who have Sickle Cell Disease; and"; and

(B) by adding at the end the following:

"(x) For purposes of subsection (a)(27), the strategies, treatment, and services described in that subsection include the following:

"(1) Chronic blood transfusion (with deferoxamine chelation) to prevent stroke in individuals with Sickle Cell Disease who have been identified as being at high risk for stroke.

"(2) Genetic counseling and testing for individuals with Sickle Cell Disease or the sickle cell trait to allow health care professionals to treat such individuals and to prevent symptoms of Sickle Cell Disease.

"(3) Other treatment and services to prevent individuals who have Sickle Cell Disease and who have had a stroke from having another stroke.".

(2) RULE OF CONSTRUCTION.—Nothing in subsections (a)(27) or (x) of section 1905 of the Social Security Act (42 U.S.C. 1396d), as added by paragraph (1), shall be construed as implying that a State medicaid program under title XIX of such Act could not have treated, prior to the date of enactment of this Act, any of the primary and secondary medical strategies and treatment and services described in such subsections as medical assistance under such program, including as early and periodic screening, diagnostic, and treatment services under section 1905(r) of such Act.

(b) FEDERAL REIMBURSEMENT FOR EDUCATION AND OTHER SERVICES RELATED TO THE PREVENTION AND TREATMENT OF SICKLE CELL DISEASE.—Section 1903(a)(3) of the Social Security Act (42 U.S.C. 1396b(a)(3)) is amended—

(1) in subparagraph (D), by striking "plus" at the end and inserting "and"; and

(2) by adding at the end the following:

"(E) 50 percent of the sums expended with respect to costs incurred during such quarter as are attributable to providing—

"(i) services to identify and educate individuals who are likely to be eligible for medical assistance under this title and who have Sickle Cell Disease or who are carriers of the sickle cell gene, including education regarding how to identify such individuals; or

"(ii) education regarding the risks of stroke and other complications, as well as the prevention of stroke and other complications, in individuals who are likely to be eligible for medical assistance under this title and who have Sickle Cell Disease; plus".

(c) Demonstration Program for the Development and Establishment of Systemic Mechanisms for the Prevention and Treatment of Sickle Cell Disease.—

(1) Authority to conduct demonstration program.—

(A) In general.—The Administrator, through the Bureau of Primary Health Care and the Maternal and Child Health Bureau, shall conduct a demonstration program by making grants to up to 40 eligible entities for each fiscal year in which the program is conducted under this section for the purpose of developing and establishing systemic mechanisms to improve the prevention and treatment of Sickle Cell Disease, including through—

(i) the coordination of service delivery for individuals with Sickle Cell Disease;

(ii) genetic counseling and testing;

(iii) bundling of technical services related to the prevention and treatment of Sickle Cell Disease;

(iv) training of health professionals; and

(v) identifying and establishing other efforts related to the expansion and coordination of education, treatment, and continuity of care programs for individuals with Sickle Cell Disease.

(B) Grant award requirements.—

(i) Geographic diversity.—The Administrator shall, to the extent practicable, award grants under this section to eligible entities located in different regions of the United States.

(ii) Priority.—In awarding grants under this subsection, the Administrator shall give priority to awarding grants to eligible entities that are—

(I) Federally-qualified health centers that have a partnership or other arrangement with a comprehensive Sickle Cell Disease treatment center that does not receive funds from the National Institutes of Health; or

(II) Federally-qualified health centers that intend to develop a partnership or other arrangement with a comprehensive Sickle Cell Disease treatment center that does not receive funds from the National Institutes of Health.

(2) Additional requirements.—An eligible entity awarded a grant under this subsection shall use funds made available under the grant to carry out, in addition to the activities described in paragraph (1)(A), the following activities:

(A) To facilitate and coordinate the delivery of education, treatment, and continuity of care for individuals with Sickle Cell Disease under—

(i) the entity's collaborative agreement with a community-based Sickle Cell Disease organization or a nonprofit entity that works with individuals who have Sickle Cell Disease;

(ii) the Sickle Cell Disease newborn screening program for the State in which the entity is located; and

(iii) the maternal and child health program under title V of the Social Security Act (42 U.S.C. 701 et seq.) for the State in which the entity is located.

(B) To train nursing and other health staff who provide care for individuals with Sickle Cell Disease.

(C) To enter into a partnership with adult or pediatric hematologists in the region and other regional experts in Sickle Cell Disease at tertiary and academic health centers and State and county health offices.

(D) To identify and secure resources for ensuring reimbursement under the medicaid program, State children's health insurance program, and other health programs for the prevention and treatment of Sickle Cell Disease.

(3) NATIONAL COORDINATING CENTER.—

(A) ESTABLISHMENT.—The Administrator shall enter into a contract with an entity to serve as the National Coordinating Center for the demonstration program conducted under this subsection.

(B) ACTIVITIES DESCRIBED.—The National Coordinating Center shall—

(i) collect, coordinate, monitor, and distribute data, best practices, and findings regarding the activities funded under grants made to eligible entities under the demonstration program;

(ii) develop a model protocol for eligible entities with respect to the prevention and treatment of Sickle Cell Disease;

(iii) develop educational materials regarding the prevention and treatment of Sickle Cell Disease; and

(iv) prepare and submit to Congress a final report that includes recommendations regarding the effectiveness of the demonstration program conducted under this subsection and such direct outcome measures as—

(I) the number and type of health care resources utilized (such as emergency room visits, hospital visits, length of stay, and physician visits for individuals with Sickle Cell Disease); and

(II) the number of individuals that were tested and subsequently received genetic counseling for the sickle cell trait.

(4) APPLICATION.—An eligible entity desiring a grant under this subsection shall submit an application to the Administrator at such time, in such manner, and containing such information as the Administrator may require.

(5) DEFINITIONS.—In this subsection:

(A) ADMINISTRATOR.—The term "Administrator" means the Administrator of the Health Resources and Services Administration.

(B) ELIGIBLE ENTITY.—The term "eligible entity" means a Federally-qualified health center, a nonprofit hospital or clinic, or a university health center that provides primary health care, that—

(i) has a collaborative agreement with a community-based Sickle Cell Disease organization or a nonprofit entity with experience in working with individuals who have Sickle Cell Disease; and

(ii) demonstrates to the Administrator that either the Federally-qualified health center, the nonprofit hospital or clinic, the university health center, the organization or entity described in clause (i), or the experts described in paragraph (2)(C), has at least 5 years of experience in working with individuals who have Sickle Cell Disease.

(C) FEDERALLY-QUALIFIED HEALTH CENTER.—The term "Federally-qualified health center" has the meaning given that term in section 1905(l)(2)(B) of the Social Security Act (42 U.S.C. 1396d(l)(2)(B)).

(6) AUTHORIZATION OF APPROPRIATIONS.—There is authorized to be appropriated to carry out this subsection, $10,000,000 for each of fiscal years 2005 through 2009.

(d) EFFECTIVE DATE.—The amendments made by subsections (a) and (b) take effect on the date of enactment of this Act and apply to medical assistance and services provided under title XIX of the Social Security Act (42 U.S.C. 1396 et seq.) on or after that date.

Act Sec. 712(d) **¶7075**

[CCH Explanation at ¶1230. Committee Reports at ¶10,930.]

[¶7080] ACT SEC. 713. CEILING FANS.

(a) IN GENERAL.—Subchapter II of chapter 99 of the Harmonized Tariff Schedule of the United States is amended by inserting in numerical sequence the following new heading:

| " 9902.84.14 | Ceiling fans for permanent installation (provided for in subheading 8414.51.00) | Free | No change | No change | On or before 12/31/2006 | ". |

(b) EFFECTIVE DATE.—The amendment made by this section applies to goods entered, or withdrawn from warehouse, for consumption on or after the 15th day after the date of enactment of this Act.

[CCH Explanation at ¶590. Committee Reports at ¶10,940.]

[¶7085] ACT SEC. 714. CERTAIN STEAM GENERATORS, AND CERTAIN REACTOR VESSEL HEADS AND PRESSURIZERS, USED IN NUCLEAR FACILITIES.

(a) CERTAIN STEAM GENERATORS.—Heading 9902.84.02 of the Harmonized Tariff Schedule of the United States is amended by striking "12/31/2006" and inserting "12/31/2008".

(b) CERTAIN REACTOR VESSEL HEADS AND PRESSURIZERS.—Subchapter II of chapter 99 of the Harmonized Tariff Schedule of the United States is amended by inserting in numerical sequence the following new heading:

| " 9902.84.03 | Reactor vessel heads and pressurizers for nuclear reactors (provided for in subheading 8401.40.00) . . . | Free | No change | No change | On or before 12/31/2008 | ". |

(c) EFFECTIVE DATE.—

(1) SUBSECTION (a).—The amendment made by subsection (a) shall take effect on the date of the enactment of this Act.

(2) SUBSECTION (b).—The amendment made subsection (b) shall apply to goods entered, or withdrawn from warehouse, for consumption on or after the 15th day after the date of the enactment of this Act.

[CCH Explanation at ¶595. Committee Reports at ¶10,950 and ¶10,960.]

TITLE VIII—REVENUE PROVISIONS

Subtitle A—Provisions to Reduce Tax Avoidance Through Individual and Corporate Expatriation

* * *

[¶7090] ACT SEC. 806. STUDIES.

(a) TRANSFER PRICING RULES.—The Secretary of the Treasury or the Secretary's delegate shall conduct a study regarding the effectiveness of current transfer pricing rules and compliance efforts in ensuring that cross-border transfers and other related-party transactions, particularly transactions involving intangible assets, service contracts, or leases cannot be used improperly to shift income out of the United States. The study shall include a review of the contemporaneous documentation and penalty rules under section 6662 of the Internal Revenue Code of 1986, a review of the regulatory and administrative guidance implementing the principles of section 482 of such Code to transactions involving intangible property and services and to cost-sharing arrangements, and an examination of whether increased disclosure of cross-border transactions should be required. The study shall set forth specific recommendations to address all abuses identified in the study. Not later than June 30, 2005, such Secretary or delegate shall submit to the Congress a report of such study.

(b) INCOME TAX TREATIES.—The Secretary of the Treasury or the Secretary's delegate shall conduct a study of United States income tax treaties to identify any inappropriate reductions in United States withholding tax that provide opportunities for shifting income out of the United States, and to evaluate whether existing anti-abuse mechanisms are operating properly. The study shall include specific recommendations to address all inappropriate uses of tax treaties. Not later than June 30, 2005, such Secretary or delegate shall submit to the Congress a report of such study.

(c) EFFECTIVENESS OF CORPORATE EXPATRIATION PROVISIONS.—The Secretary of the Treasury or the Secretary's delegate shall conduct a study of the effectiveness of the provisions of this title on corporate expatriation. The study shall include such recommendations as such Secretary or delegate may have to improve the effectiveness of such provisions in carrying out the purposes of this title. Not later than December 31, 2006, such Secretary or delegate shall submit to the Congress a report of such study.

[CCH Explanation at ¶ 530. Committee Reports at ¶ 11,020.]

Subtitle B—Provisions Relating to Tax Shelters

Part I—Taxpayer-Related Provisions

[¶ 7095] ACT SEC. 811. PENALTY FOR FAILING TO DISCLOSE REPORTABLE TRANSACTIONS.

* * *

(d) REPORT.—The Commissioner of Internal Revenue shall annually report to the Committee on Ways and Means of the House of Representatives and the Committee on Finance of the Senate—

(1) a summary of the total number and aggregate amount of penalties imposed, and rescinded, under section 6707A of the Internal Revenue Code of 1986, and

(2) a description of each penalty rescinded under section 6707(c) of such Code and the reasons therefor.

* * *

[CCH Explanation at ¶ 615. Committee Reports at ¶ 11,030.]

[¶ 7100] ACT SEC. 821. PENALTY ON FAILURE TO REPORT INTERESTS IN FOREIGN FINANCIAL ACCOUNTS.

(a) IN GENERAL.—Section 5321(a)(5) of title 31, United States Code, is amended to read as follows:

"(5) FOREIGN FINANCIAL AGENCY TRANSACTION VIOLATION.—

"(A) PENALTY AUTHORIZED.—The Secretary of the Treasury may impose a civil money penalty on any person who violates, or causes any violation of, any provision of section 5314.

"(B) AMOUNT OF PENALTY.—

"(i) IN GENERAL.—Except as provided in subparagraph (C), the amount of any civil penalty imposed under subparagraph (A) shall not exceed $10,000.

"(ii) REASONABLE CAUSE EXCEPTION.—No penalty shall be imposed under subparagraph (A) with respect to any violation if—

"(I) such violation was due to reasonable cause, and

"(II) the amount of the transaction or the balance in the account at the time of the transaction was properly reported.

"(C) WILLFUL VIOLATIONS.—In the case of any person willfully violating, or willfully causing any violation of, any provision of section 5314—

"(i) the maximum penalty under subparagraph (B)(i) shall be increased to the greater of—

"(I) $100,000, or

"(II) 50 percent of the amount determined under subparagraph (D), and

"(ii) subparagraph (B)(ii) shall not apply.

"(D) AMOUNT.—The amount determined under this subparagraph is—

"(i) in the case of a violation involving a transaction, the amount of the transaction, or

"(ii) in the case of a violation involving a failure to report the existence of an account or any identifying information required to be provided with respect to an account, the balance in the account at the time of the violation.".

(b) EFFECTIVE DATE.—The amendment made by this section shall apply to violations occurring after the date of the enactment of this Act.

[CCH Explanation at ¶ 655. Committee Reports at ¶ 11,120.]

[¶ 7105] ACT SEC. 822. REGULATION OF INDIVIDUALS PRACTICING BEFORE THE DEPARTMENT OF TREASURY.

(a) CENSURE; IMPOSITION OF PENALTY.—

(1) IN GENERAL.—Section 330(b) of title 31, United States Code, is amended—

(A) by inserting ", or censure," after "Department", and

(B) by adding at the end the following new flush sentence:

"The Secretary may impose a monetary penalty on any representative described in the preceding sentence. If the representative was acting on behalf of an employer or any firm or other entity in connection with the conduct giving rise to such penalty, the Secretary may impose a monetary penalty on such employer, firm, or entity if it knew, or reasonably should have known, of such conduct. Such penalty shall not exceed the gross income derived (or to be derived) from the conduct giving rise to the penalty and may be in addition to, or in lieu of, any suspension, disbarment, or censure of the representative.".

(2) EFFECTIVE DATE.—The amendments made by this subsection shall apply to actions taken after the date of the enactment of this Act.

(b) TAX SHELTER OPINIONS, ETC.—Section 330 of such title 31 is amended by adding at the end the following new subsection:

"(d) Nothing in this section or in any other provision of law shall be construed to limit the authority of the Secretary of the Treasury to impose standards applicable to the rendering of written advice with respect to any entity, transaction plan or arrangement, or other plan or arrangement, which is of a type which the Secretary determines as having a potential for tax avoidance or evasion.".

[CCH Explanation at ¶ 660. Committee Reports at ¶ 11,130.]

Part II—Other Provisions

* * *

[¶ 7110] ACT SEC. 844. AFFIRMATION OF CONSOLIDATED RETURN REGULATION AUTHORITY.

* * *

(b) RESULT NOT OVERTURNED.—Notwithstanding the amendment made by subsection (a), the Internal Revenue Code of 1986 shall be construed by treating Treasury Regulation § 1.1502-20(c)(1)(iii) (as in effect on January 1, 2001) as being inapplicable to the factual situation in Rite Aid Corporation and Subsidiary Corporations v. United States, 255 F.3d 1357 (Fed. Cir. 2001).

(c) EFFECTIVE DATE.—This section, and the amendment made by this section, shall apply to taxable years beginning before, on, or after the date of the enactment of this Act.

* * *

[CCH Explanation at ¶1635. Committee Reports at ¶11,270.]

Subtitle C—Reduction of Fuel Tax Evasion

* * *

[¶7115] ACT SEC. 853. TAXATION OF AVIATION-GRADE KEROSENE.

(a) RATE OF TAX.—

* * *

(3) CERTAIN REFUELER TRUCKS, TANKERS, AND TANK WAGONS TREATED AS TERMINAL.—

* * *

(B) LIST OF AIRPORTS WITH SECURED TERMINALS.—Not later than December 15, 2004, the Secretary of the Treasury shall publish and maintain a list of airports which include a secured area in which a terminal is located (within the meaning of section 4081(a)(3)(A)(i) of the Internal Revenue Code of 1986, as added by this paragraph).

* * *

(f) FLOOR STOCKS TAX.—

(1) IN GENERAL.—There is hereby imposed on aviation-grade kerosene held on January 1, 2005, by any person a tax equal to—

(A) the tax which would have been imposed before such date on such kerosene had the amendments made by this section been in effect at all times before such date, reduced by

(B) the sum of—

(i) the tax imposed before such date on such kerosene under section 4091 of the Internal Revenue Code of 1986, as in effect on such date, and

(ii) in the case of kerosene held exclusively for such person's own use, the amount which such person would (but for this clause) reasonably expect (as of such date) to be paid as a refund under section 6427(l) of such Code with respect to such kerosene.

(2) EXCEPTION FOR FUEL HELD IN AIRCRAFT FUEL TANK.—Paragraph (1) shall not apply to kerosene held in the fuel tank of an aircraft on January 1, 2005.

(3) LIABILITY FOR TAX AND METHOD OF PAYMENT.—

(A) LIABILITY FOR TAX.—The person holding the kerosene on January 1, 2005, to which the tax imposed by paragraph (1) applies shall be liable for such tax.

(B) METHOD AND TIME FOR PAYMENT.—The tax imposed by paragraph (1) shall be paid at such time and in such manner as the Secretary of the Treasury (or the Secretary's delegate) shall prescribe, including the nonapplication of such tax on de minimis amounts of kerosene.

(4) TRANSFER OF FLOOR STOCK TAX REVENUES TO TRUST FUNDS.—For purposes of determining the amount transferred to any trust fund, the tax imposed by this subsection shall be treated as imposed by section 4081 of the Internal Revenue Code of 1986—

(A) in any case in which tax was not imposed by section 4091 of such Code, at the Leaking Underground Storage Tank Trust Fund financing rate under such section to the extent of 0.1 cents per gallon, and

(B) at the rate under section 4081(a)(2)(A)(iv) of such Code to the extent of the remainder.

(5) HELD BY A PERSON.—For purposes of this subsection, kerosene shall be considered as held by a person if title thereto has passed to such person (whether or not delivery to the person has been made).

(6) OTHER LAWS APPLICABLE.—All provisions of law, including penalties, applicable with respect to the tax imposed by section 4081 of such Code shall, insofar as applicable and not inconsistent with the provisions of this subsection, apply with respect to the floor stock tax imposed by paragraph (1) to the same extent as if such tax were imposed by such section.

[CCH Explanation at ¶1507. Committee Reports at ¶11,340.]

[¶7120] ACT SEC. 854. DYE INJECTION EQUIPMENT.

* * *

(b) DYE INJECTOR SECURITY.—Not later than 180 days after the date of the enactment of this Act, the Secretary of the Treasury shall issue regulations regarding mechanical dye injection systems described in the amendment made by subsection (a), and such regulations shall include standards for making such systems tamper resistant.

* * *

[CCH Explanation at ¶1517. Committee Reports at ¶11,350.]

[¶7125] ACT SEC. 860. REGISTRATION OF PIPELINE OR VESSEL OPERATORS REQUIRED FOR EXEMPTION OF BULK TRANSFERS TO REGISTERED TERMINALS OR REFINERIES.

* * *

(c) PUBLICATION OF REGISTERED PERSONS.—Beginning on January 1, 2005, the Secretary of the Treasury (or the Secretary's delegate) shall periodically publish under section 6103(k)(7) of the Internal Revenue Code of 1986 a current list of persons registered under section 4101 of such Code who are required to register under such section.

* * *

[CCH Explanation at ¶1527. Committee Reports at ¶11,410.]

[¶7130] ACT SEC. 871. STUDY REGARDING FUEL TAX COMPLIANCE.

(a) IN GENERAL.—Not later than January 31, 2005, the Secretary of the Treasury shall submit to the Committee on Finance of the Senate and the Committee on Ways and Means of the House of Representatives a report regarding compliance with the tax imposed under subchapter B of chapter 31 and part III of subchapter A of chapter 32 of the Internal Revenue Code of 1986. Such report shall include the information, analysis, and recommendations specified in subsections (b), (c), and (d).

(b) TAXABLE FUEL BLENDSTOCKS.—The Secretary shall identify chemical products to be added to the list of blendstocks from lab analysis of fuel samples collected by the Internal Revenue Service which have been blended with taxable fuel but are not treated as blendstocks. The Secretary shall include statistics regarding the frequency in which a chemical product has been collected, and whether the sample contained an above normal concentration of the chemical product.

(c) WASTE PRODUCTS ADDED TO TAXABLE FUELS.—The report shall include a discussion of Internal Revenue Service findings regarding the addition of waste products to taxable fuel and any recommendations to address the taxation of such products.

(d) ERRONEOUS CLAIMS OF FUEL TAX EXEMPTIONS.—The report shall include a discussion of Internal Revenue Service findings regarding sales of taxable fuel to entities claiming exempt status as a State or local government and the frequency of erroneous certifications of tax exempt status. The Secretary, in consultation with representatives of State and local governments, shall provide recommendations to address such erroneous claims, including recommendations on the feasibility of a State maintained list of exempt governmental entities within the State.

[CCH Explanation at ¶1543. Committee Reports at ¶11,510.]

Subtitle D—Other Revenue Provisions

[¶7135] ACT SEC. 881. QUALIFIED TAX COLLECTION CONTRACTS.

* * *

(d) INELIGIBILITY OF INDIVIDUALS WHO COMMIT MISCONDUCT TO PERFORM UNDER CONTRACT.—Section 1203 of the Internal Revenue Service Restructuring Act of 1998 (relating to termination of employment for misconduct) is amended by adding at the end the following new subsection:

"(e) Individuals Performing Services Under a Qualified Tax Collection Contract. An individual shall cease to be permitted to perform any services under any qualified tax collection contract (as defined in section 6306(b) of the Internal Revenue Code of 1986) if there is a final determination by the Secretary of the Treasury under such contract that such individual committed any act or omission described under subsection (b) in connection with the performance of such services.".

(e) Biennial Report.—The Secretary of the Treasury shall biennially submit (beginning in 2005) to the Committee on Finance of the Senate and the Committee on Ways and Means of the House of Representatives a report with respect to qualified tax collection contracts under section 6306 of the Internal Revenue Code of 1986 (as added by this section) which includes—

(1) a complete cost benefit analysis,

(2) the impact of such contracts on collection enforcement staff levels in the Internal Revenue Service,

(3) the impact of such contracts on the total number and amount of unpaid assessments, and on the number and amount of assessments collected by Internal Revenue Service personnel after initial contact by a contractor,

(4) the amounts collected and the collection costs incurred (directly and indirectly) by the Internal Revenue Service,

(5) an evaluation of contractor performance,

(6) a disclosure safeguard report in a form similar to that required under section 6103(p)(5) of such Code, and

(7) a measurement plan which includes a comparison of the best practices used by the private collectors with the Internal Revenue Service's own collection techniques and mechanisms to identify and capture information on successful collection techniques used by the contractors which could be adopted by the Internal Revenue Service.

(f) Effective Date.—The amendments made to this section shall take effect on the date of the enactment of this Act.

[CCH Explanation at ¶1605. Committee Reports at ¶11,530.]

[¶7140] ACT SEC. 882. TREATMENT OF CHARITABLE CONTRIBUTIONS OF PATENTS AND SIMILAR PROPERTY.

* * *

(e) Anti-Abuse Rules.—The Secretary of the Treasury may prescribe such regulations or other guidance as may be necessary or appropriate to prevent the avoidance of the purposes of section 170(e)(1)(B)(iii) of the Internal Revenue Code of 1986 (as added by subsection (a)), including preventing—

(1) the circumvention of the reduction of the charitable deduction by embedding or bundling the patent or similar property as part of a charitable contribution of property that includes the patent or similar property,

(2) the manipulation of the basis of the property to increase the amount of the charitable deduction through the use of related persons, pass-thru entities, or other intermediaries, or through the use of any provision of law or regulation (including the consolidated return regulations), and

(3) a donor from changing the form of the patent or similar property to property of a form for which different deduction rules would apply.

* * *

[CCH Explanation at ¶1315. Committee Reports at ¶11,540.]

[¶7145] ACT SEC. 885. TREATMENT OF NONQUALIFIED DEFERRED COMPENSATION PLANS.

* * *

(e) Guidance Relating to Change of Ownership or Control.—Not later than 90 days after the date of the enactment of this Act, the Secretary of the Treasury shall issue guidance on what constitutes a change in ownership or effective control for purposes of section 409A of the Internal Revenue Code of 1986, as added by this section.

(f) GUIDANCE RELATING TO TERMINATION OF CERTAIN EXISTING ARRANGEMENTS.—Not later than 60 days after the date of the enactment of this Act, the Secretary of the Treasury shall issue guidance providing a limited period during which a nonqualified deferred compensation plan adopted before December 31, 2004, may, without violating the requirements of paragraphs (2), (3), and (4) of section 409A(a) of the Internal Revenue Code of 1986 (as added by this section), be amended—

(1) to provide that a participant may terminate participation in the plan, or cancel an outstanding deferral election with regard to amounts deferred after December 31, 2004, but only if amounts subject to the termination or cancellation are includible in income of the participant as earned (or, if later, when no longer subject to substantial risk of forfeiture), and

(2) to conform to the requirements of such section 409A with regard to amounts deferred after December 31, 2004.

* * *

[CCH Explanation at ¶1405. Committee Reports at ¶11,570.]

[¶7150] ACT SEC. 892. COBRA FEES.

(a) USE OF MERCHANDISE PROCESSING FEE.—Section 13031(f) of the Consolidated Omnibus Budget Reconciliation Act of 1985 (19 U.S.C. 58c(f)) is amended—

(1) in paragraph (1), by aligning subparagraph (B) with subparagraph (A); and

(2) in paragraph (2), by striking "commercial operations" and all that follows through "processing." and inserting "customs revenue functions as defined in section 415 of the Homeland Security Act of 2002 (other than functions performed by the Office of International Affairs referred to in section 415(8) of that Act), and for automation (including the Automation Commercial Environment computer system), and for no other purpose. To the extent that funds in the Customs User Fee Account are insufficient to pay the costs of such customs revenue functions, customs duties in an amount equal to the amount of such insufficiency shall be available, to the extent provided for in appropriations Acts, to pay the costs of such customs revenue functions in the amount of such insufficiency, and shall be available for no other purpose. The provisions of the first and second sentences of this paragraph specifying the purposes for which amounts in the Customs User Fee Account may be made available shall not be superseded except by a provision of law which specifically modifies or supersedes such provisions.".

• • *COBRA OF 1985 ACT SEC. 13031(f)(2) [as last amended by P.L. 101-382, §111(c)(1)] BEFORE AMENDMENT*———

ACT SEC. 13031. FEES FOR CERTAIN CUSTOMS SERVICES.

* * *

(f) DISPOSITION OF FEES.—

* * *

(2) Except as otherwise provided in this subsection, all funds in the Customs User Fee Account shall be available, to the extent provided for in appropriations Acts, to pay the costs (other than costs for which direct reimbursement under paragraph (3) is required) incurred by the United States Customs Service in conducting commercial operations, including, but not limited to, all costs associated with commercial passenger, vessel, vehicle, aircraft, and cargo processing. So long as there is a surplus of funds in the Customs User Fee Account, the Secretary of the Treasury may not reduce personnel staffing levels for providing commercial clearance and preclearance services.

(b) REIMBURSEMENT OF APPROPRIATIONS FROM COBRA FEES.—Section 13031(f)(3) of the Consolidated Omnibus Budget Reconciliation Act of 1985 (19 U.S.C. 58c(f)(3)) is amended by adding at the end the following:

"(E) Nothing in this paragraph shall be construed to preclude the use of appropriated funds, from sources other than the fees collected under subsection (a), to pay the costs set forth in clauses (i), (ii), and (iii) of subparagraph (A).".

(c) Sense of Congress; Effective Period for Collecting Fees; Standard for Setting Fees.—

(1) Sense of congress.—The Congress finds that—

(A) the fees set forth in paragraphs (1) through (8) of subsection (a) of section 13031 of the Consolidated Omnibus Budget Reconciliation Act of 1985 have been reasonably related to the costs of providing customs services in connection with the activities or items for which the fees have been charged under such paragraphs; and

(B) the fees collected under such paragraphs have not exceeded, in the aggregate, the amounts paid for the costs described in subsection (f)(3)(A) incurred in providing customs services in connection with the activities or items for which the fees were charged under such paragraphs.

(2) Effective period; standard for setting fees.—Section 13031(j)(3) of the Consolidated Omnibus Budget Reconciliation Act of 1985 is amended to read as follows:

"(3)(A) Fees may not be charged under paragraphs (9) and (10) of subsection (a) after September 30, 2014.

"(B)(i) Subject to clause (ii), Fees may not be charged under paragraphs (1) through (8) of subsection (a) after September 30, 2014.

"(ii) In fiscal year 2006 and in each succeeding fiscal year for which fees under paragraphs (1) through (8) of subsection (a) are authorized—

"(I) the Secretary of the Treasury shall charge fees under each such paragraph in amounts that are reasonably related to the costs of providing customs services in connection with the activity or item for which the fee is charged under such paragraph, except that in no case may the fee charged under any such paragraph exceed by more than 10 percent the amount otherwise prescribed by such paragraph;

"(II) the amount of fees collected under such paragraphs may not exceed, in the aggregate, the amounts paid in that fiscal year for the costs described in subsection (f)(3)(A) incurred in providing customs services in connection with the activity or item for which the fees are charged under such paragraphs;

"(III) a fee may not be collected under any such paragraph except to the extent such fee will be expended to pay the costs described in subsection (f)(3)(A) incurred in providing customs services in connection with the activity or item for which the fee is charged under such paragraph; and

"(IV) any fee collected under any such paragraph shall be available for expenditure only to pay the costs described in subsection (f)(3)(A) incurred in providing customs services in connection with the activity or item for which the fee is charged under such paragraph.".

• • *COBRA OF 1985 ACT SEC. 13031(j)(3) [as last amended by P.L. 108-121, §201]* *BEFORE AMENDMENT*——

ACT SEC. 13031. FEES FOR CERTAIN CUSTOMS SERVICES.

* * *

(j) Effective Dates.—

* * *

(3) Fees may not be charged under subsection (a) of this section after March 1, 2005.

——

(d) Clerical Amendments.—Section 13031 of the Consolidated Omnibus Budget Reconciliation Act of 1985 is amended—

(1) in subsection (a)(5)(B), by striking "$1.75" and inserting "$1.75.";

(2) in subsection (b)—

(A) in paragraph (1)(A), by aligning clause (iii) with clause (ii);

(B) in paragraph (7), by striking "paragraphs" and inserting "paragraph"; and

(C) in paragraph (9), by aligning subparagraph (B) with subparagraph (A); and

(3) in subsection (e)(2), by aligning subparagraph (B) with subparagraph (A).

• • *COBRA OF 1985 ACT SEC. 13031(a)(5)(B) AND (b)(7) AS AMENDED*————————

ACT SEC. 13031. FEES FOR CERTAIN CUSTOMS SERVICES.

(a) SCHEDULE OF FEES.—

* * *

(5) * * *

* * *

(B) For the arrival of each passenger aboard a commercial vessel from a place referred to in subsection (b)(1)(A)(i) of this section, *$1.75.*

* * *

(b) LIMITATIONS ON FEES.—

* * *

(7) No fee may be charged under *paragraph* (2), (3), or (4) of subsection (a) of this section for the arrival of any—

(A) commercial truck,

(B) railroad car, or

(C) private vessel,

that is being transported, at the time of the arrival, by any vessel that is not a ferry.

———————————————————————————————————————

(e) STUDY OF ALL FEES COLLECTED BY DEPARTMENT OF HOMELAND SECURITY.—The Secretary of the Treasury shall conduct a study of all the fees collected by the Department of Homeland Security, and shall submit to the Congress, not later than September 30, 2005, a report containing the recommendations of the Secretary on—

(1) what fees should be eliminated;

(2) what the rate of fees retained should be; and

(3) any other recommendations with respect to the fees that the Secretary considers appropriate.

* * *

[CCH Explanation at ¶ 597. Committee Reports at ¶ 11,640.]

[¶ 7155] ACT SEC. 904. INCREASE IN WITHHOLDING FROM SUPPLEMENTAL WAGE PAYMENTS IN EXCESS OF $1,000,000.

(a) IN GENERAL.—If an employer elects under Treasury Regulation 31.3402(g)-1 to determine the amount to be deducted and withheld from any supplemental wage payment by using a flat percentage rate, the rate to be used in determining the amount to be so deducted and withheld shall not be less than 28 percent (or the corresponding rate in effect under section 1(i)(2) of the Internal Revenue Code of 1986 for taxable years beginning in the calendar year in which the payment is made).

(b) SPECIAL RULE FOR LARGE PAYMENTS.—

(1) IN GENERAL.—Notwithstanding subsection (a), if the supplemental wage payment, when added to all such payments previously made by the employer to the employee during the calendar year, exceeds $1,000,000, the rate used with respect to such excess shall be equal to the maximum rate of tax in effect under section 1 of such Code for taxable years beginning in such calendar year.

(2) AGGREGATION.—All persons treated as a single employer under subsection (a) or (b) of section 52 of the Internal Revenue Code of 1986 shall be treated as a single employer for purposes of this subsection.

(c) CONFORMING AMENDMENT.—Section 13273 of the Revenue Reconciliation Act of 1993 (Public Law 103-66) is repealed.

• • *RRA of 1993 ACT SEC. 13273 [as amended by P.L. 107-16, §101(c)(11)] BEFORE REPEAL*——

ACT SEC. 13273. INCREASE IN WITHHOLDING FROM SUPPLEMENTAL WAGE PAYMENTS.

If an employee elects under Treasury Regulation 31.3402(g)-1 to determine the amount to be deducted and withheld from any supplemental wage payment by using a flat percentage rate, the rate to be used in determining the amount to be so deducted and withheld shall not be less than the third lowest rate of tax applicable under section 1(c) of the Internal Revenue Code of 1986. The preceding sentence shall apply to payments made after December 31, 1993.

———

(d) EFFECTIVE DATE.—The provisions of, and the amendment made by, this section shall apply to payments made after December 31, 2004.

* * *

[CCH Explanation at ¶1430. Committee Reports at ¶11,760.]

Committee Reports
American Jobs Creation Act of 2004

¶ 10,001
Introduction

The committee reports accompanying the American Jobs Creation Act of 2004 (H.R. 4520) explain the intent of Congress regarding the revenue-related provisions of the Act. At the end of each committee reports section, references are provided to the corresponding CCH explanations and Internal Revenue Code provisions. Subscribers to the electronic version can link from these references to the corresponding material. *The pertinent sections of the committee reports appear in Act Section order beginning at ¶10,010.*

¶ 10,005
Background

The American Jobs Creation Act of 2004 (H.R. 4520) was introduced in the House of Representatives on June 4, 2004. On June 16, 2004, the House Ways and Means Committee favorably reported the bill with an amendment (H.R. REP. NO. 108-548, pt. 1). The next day, the House passed H.R. 4520, as further amended, by a vote of 251 to 178.

On September 18, 2003, the Jumpstart Our Business Strength (JOBS) Act was introduced in the Senate as S. 1637. The Senate Finance Committee reported favorably on S. 1637 with an amendment in the nature of a substitute on November 7, 2003 (S. REP. NO. 108-192). The Senate passed S. 1637, as further amended, on May 11, 2004, by a vote of 92 to 5.

On July 15, 2004, after H.R. 4520 had passed the House and was received in the Senate, the Senate included the text of S. 1637 in a substitute amendment to H.R. 4520. That same day, the Senate passed H.R. 4520, as further amended, by voice vote, insisted on its amendment, and requested a conference. On September 29, 2004, the House by voice vote disagreed to the Senate amendment and agreed to a conference.

A conference report on H.R. 4520 was filed on October 7, 2004 (H.R. CONF. REP. NO. 108-755). The House agreed to the conference report that same day by a vote of 280 to 141. On October 11, 2004, the Senate agreed to the conference report by a vote of 69 to 17.

The following material includes the pertinent texts of the committee reports that explain the revenue-related changes made by H.R. 4520, the American Jobs Creation Act of 2004. The sections include the text of the relevant House, Senate and Conference Committee Reports, as released by the Congressional committees. Headings have been added for convenience. Omissions of text are indicated by asterisks (* * *). References are to the following reports:

• The American Jobs Creation Act of 2004 (H.R. 4520), House Ways and Means Committee Report, as reported on June 16, 2004, is referred to as House Committee Report (H.R. REP. NO. 108-548, pt. 1).

• The **Jumpstart Our Business Strength (JOBS) Act (S. 1637), Senate Finance Committee Report**, as reported November 7, 2003, is referred to as **Senate Committee Report (S. Rep. No. 108-192).**

• The **Conference Committee Report on the American Jobs Creation Act of 2004**, as released on October 7, 2004, is referred to as **Conference Committee Report (H.R. Conf. Rep. No. 108-755).**

[¶ 10,010] Act Sec. 101. Repeal of extraterritorial income regime

House Committee Report (H.R. Rep. No. 108-548, pt. 1)

[Code Secs. 114, 275, 864, 903, 941, 942, 943 and 999(c)]

Present Law

The United States has long provided export-related benefits under a series of tax regimes, including the domestic international sales corporation ("DISC") regime, the foreign sales corporation ("FSC") regime, and the extraterritorial income ("ETI") regime. Each of these regimes has been found to violate U.S. obligations under international trade agreements. In 2000, the European Union ("EU") succeeded in having the FSC regime declared a prohibited export subsidy by the WTO. In response to this WTO ruling, the United States repealed the FSC rules and enacted a new regime under the FSC Repeal and Extraterritorial Income Exclusion Act of 2000. The EU immediately challenged the ETI regime in the WTO, and in January of 2002 a WTO Appellate Body held that the ETI regime also constituted a prohibited export subsidy under the relevant trade agreements.

Under the ETI regime, an exclusion from gross income applies with respect to "extraterritorial income," which is a taxpayer's gross income attributable to "foreign trading gross receipts." This income is eligible for the exclusion to the extent that it is "qualifying foreign trade income." Qualifying foreign trade income is the amount of gross income that, if excluded, would result in a reduction of taxable income by the greatest of: (1) 1.2 percent of the foreign trading gross receipts derived by the taxpayer from the transaction; (2) 15 percent of the "foreign trade income" derived by the taxpayer from the transaction[2] ; or (3) 30 percent of the "foreign sale and leasing income" derived by the taxpayer from the transaction.[3]

Foreign trading gross receipts are gross receipts derived from certain activities in connection with "qualifying foreign trade property" with respect to which certain economic processes take place outside of the United States. Specifically, the gross receipts must be: (1) from the sale, exchange, or other disposition of qualifying foreign trade property; (2) from the lease or rental of qualifying foreign trade property for use by the lessee outside the United States; (3) for services which are related and subsidiary to the sale, exchange, disposition, lease, or rental of qualifying foreign trade property (as described above); (4) for engineering or architectural services for construction projects located outside the United States; or (5) for the performance of certain managerial services for unrelated persons. A taxpayer may elect to treat gross receipts from a transaction as not foreign trading gross receipts. As a result of such an election, a taxpayer may use any related foreign tax credits in lieu of the exclusion.

Qualifying foreign trade property generally is property manufactured, produced, grown, or extracted within or outside the United States that is held primarily for sale, lease, or rental in the ordinary course of a trade or business for direct use, consumption, or disposition outside the United States. No more than 50 percent of the fair market value of such property can be attributable to the sum of: (1) the fair market value of articles manufactured outside the United States; and (2) the direct costs of labor performed outside the United States. With respect to property that is manufactured outside the United States, certain rules are provided to ensure consistent U.S. tax treatment with respect to manufacturers.

Reasons for Change

The Committee believes it is important that the United States, and all members of the WTO, comply with WTO decisions and honor their

---

[2] "Foreign trade income" is the taxable income of the taxpayer (determined without regard to the exclusion of qualifying foreign trade income) attributable to foreign trading gross receipts.

[3] "Foreign sale and leasing income" is the amount of the taxpayer's foreign trade income (with respect to a transac-

tion) that is properly allocable to activities that constitute foreign economic processes. Foreign sale and leasing income also includes foreign trade income derived by the taxpayer in connection with the lease or rental of qualifying foreign trade property for use by the lessee outside the United States.

obligations under WTO agreements. Therefore, the Committee believes that the ETI regime should be repealed. The Committee believes that it is necessary and appropriate to provide transition relief comparable to that which has been included in the past in measures taken by WTO members to bring their laws into compliance with WTO decisions and obligations.

The Committee also believes that it is important to use the opportunity afforded by the repeal of the ETI regime to reform the U.S. tax system in a manner that makes U.S. businesses and workers more productive and competitive than they are today. To this end, the Committee believes that it is important to provide tax cuts to U.S. domestic manufacturers and to update the U.S. international tax rules, which are over 40 years old and make U.S. companies uncompetitive in the United States and abroad.

Explanation of Provision

The provision repeals the ETI exclusion. For transactions prior to 2005, taxpayers retain 100 percent of their ETI benefits. For transactions after 2004, the provision provides taxpayers with 80 percent of their otherwise-applicable ETI benefits for transactions during 2005 and 60 percent of their otherwise-applicable ETI benefits for transactions during 2006. However, the provision provides that the ETI exclusion provisions remain in effect for transactions in the ordinary course of a trade or business if such transactions are pursuant to a binding contract[4] between the taxpayer and an unrelated person and such contract is in effect on January 14, 2002, and at all times thereafter.

In addition, foreign corporations that elected to be treated for all Federal tax purposes as domestic corporations in order to facilitate the claiming of ETI benefits are allowed to revoke such elections within one year of the date of enactment of the provision without recognition of gain or loss, subject to anti-abuse rules.

Effective Date

The provision is effective for transactions after December 31, 2004.

Conference Committee Report (H.R. CONF. REP. NO. 108-755)

The conference agreement follows the House bill, except that under the conference agreement the ETI exclusion provisions remain in effect for transactions in the ordinary course of a trade or business if such transactions are pursuant to a binding contract[7] between the taxpayer and an unrelated person and such contract is in effect on September 17, 2003, and at all times thereafter.

Effective Date

The effective date is the same as the House bill.

[**Law at ¶5085, ¶5125, ¶5285, ¶5600, ¶5650, ¶5695, ¶5700, ¶5705, ¶5750 and ¶7010. CCH Explanation at ¶205.]**

[¶ 10,020] Act Secs. 102(a) and (b). Deduction relating to income attributable to United States production activities

Conference Committee Report (H.R. CONF. REP. NO. 108-755)

[Code Secs. 11 and 56(g)(4)(c) and New Code Sec. 199]

Present Law

A corporation's regular income tax liability is determined by applying the following tax rate schedule to its taxable income.

---

[4] This rule also applies to a purchase option, renewal option, or replacement option that is included in such contract and that is enforceable against the sellor or lessor. For this purpose, a replacement option will be considered enforceable against a lessor notwithstanding the fact that a lessor retained approval of the replacement lessee.

[7] This rule also applies to a purchase option, renewal option, or replacement option that is included in such contract. For this purpose, a replacement option will be considered enforceable against a lessor notwithstanding the fact that a lessor retained approval of the replacement lessee.

Table 1.—Marginal Federal Corporate Income Tax Rates for 2004

Taxable income:	Income tax rate:
$0 - $50,000 . . .	15 percent of taxable income
$50,001 -$75,000	25 percent of taxable income
$75,001 - $10,000,000 . . .	34 percent of taxable income
Over $10,000,000	35 percent of taxable income

The benefit of the first two graduated rates described above is phased out by a five-percent surcharge for corporations with taxable income between $100,000 and $335,000. Also, the benefit of the 34-percent rate is phased out by a three-percent surcharge for corporations with taxable income between $15 million and $18,333,333; a corporation with taxable income of $18,333,333 or more effectively is subject to a flat rate of 35 percent.

Under present law, there is no provision that reduces the corporate income tax for taxable income attributable to domestic production activities.

House Bill

In general

The House bill provides that the corporate tax rate applicable to qualified production activities income may not exceed 32 percent (34 percent for taxable years beginning before 2007) of the qualified production activities income.

Qualified production activities income

"Qualified production activities income" is the income attributable to domestic production gross receipts, reduced by the sum of: (1) costs of goods sold that are allocable to such receipts; (2) other deductions, expenses, or losses that are directly allocable to such receipts; and (3) a proper share of other deductions, expenses,

and losses that are not directly allocable to such receipts or another class of income.[8]

Domestic production gross receipts

Under the House bill, "domestic production gross receipts" generally are gross receipts of a corporation that are derived from: (1) any sale, exchange or other disposition, or any lease, rental or license, of qualifying production property that was manufactured, produced, grown or extracted (in whole or in significant part) by the corporation within the United States;[9] (2) any sale, exchange or other disposition, or any lease, rental or license, of qualified film produced by the taxpayer; or (3) construction, engineering or architectural services performed in the United States for construction projects located in the United States. However, domestic production gross receipts do not include any gross receipts of the taxpayer derived from property that is leased, licensed or rented by the taxpayer for use by any related person.[10]

"Qualifying production property" under the House bill generally is any tangible personal property, computer software, or property described in section 168(f)(4) of the Code. "Qualified film" is any property described in section 168(f)(3) of the Code (other than certain sexually explicit productions) if 50 percent or more of the total compensation relating to the production of such film (other than compensation in the form of residuals and participations) constitutes compensation for services performed in the United States by actors, production personnel, directors, and producers.

Under the House bill, an election under section 631(a) made by a corporate taxpayer for a taxable year ending on or before the date of enactment to treat the cutting of timber as a sale or exchange, may be revoked by the taxpayer without the consent of the IRS for any taxable year ending after that date. The prior election

---

[8] The House bill provides that Secretary shall prescribe rules for the proper allocation of items of income, deduction, expense, and loss for purposes of determining income attributable to domestic production activities. Where appropriate, such rules shall be similar to and consistent with relevant present-law rules (e.g., secs. 263A and 861).

[9] Domestic production gross receipts under the House bill include gross receipts of a taxpayer derived from any sale, exchange or other disposition of agricultural products with respect to which the taxpayer performs storage, handling or other processing activities (other than transportation activities) within the United States, provided such products are consumed in connection with, or incorporated into, the manufacturing, production, growth or extraction of qualifying production property (whether or not by the taxpayer). Domestic production gross receipts also include gross receipts of a taxpayer derived from any sale, exchange or

other disposition of food products with respect to which the taxpayer performs processing activities (in whole or in significant part) within the United States.

[10] It is intended under the House bill that principles similar to those under the present-law extraterritorial income regime apply for this purpose. *See* Temp. Treas. Reg. sec. 1.927(a)-1T(f)(2)(i). For example, this exclusion generally does not apply to property leased by the taxpayer to a related person if the property is held for sublease, or is subleased, by the related person to an unrelated person for the ultimate use of such unrelated person. Similarly, the license of computer software to a related person for reproduction and sale, exchange, lease, rental or sublicense to an unrelated person for the ultimate use of such unrelated person is not treated as excluded property by reason of the license to the related person.

(and revocation) is disregarded for purposes of making a subsequent election.

Effective Date

The House bill provision is effective for taxable years beginning after December 31, 2004.

Senate Amendment

In general

The Senate amendment provides a deduction equal to a portion of the taxpayer's qualified production activities income. For taxable years beginning after 2008, the Senate amendment deduction is nine percent of such income. For taxable years beginning in 2004, 2005, 2006, 2007 and 2008, the deduction is five, five, five, six, and seven percent of income, respectively. However, the deduction for a taxable year is limited to 50 percent of the wages paid by the taxpayer during such taxable year.[11] In the case of corporate taxpayers that are members of certain affiliated groups, the deduction is determined by treating all members of such groups as a single taxpayer.

Qualified production activities income

In general, "qualified production activities income" under the Senate amendment is the modified taxable income[12] of a taxpayer that is attributable to domestic production activities. Income attributable to domestic production activities generally is equal to domestic production gross receipts, reduced by the sum of: (1) the costs of goods sold that are allocable to such receipts;[13] (2) other deductions, expenses, or losses that are directly allocable to such receipts; and (3) a proper share of other deductions, expenses, and losses that are not directly allocable to such receipts or another class of income.[14]

For taxable years beginning before 2013, the Senate amendment provides that qualified production activities income is reduced by virtue of a fraction (not to exceed one), the numerator of which is the value of the domestic production of the taxpayer and the denominator of which is the value of the worldwide production of the taxpayer (the "domestic/worldwide fraction").[15] For taxable years beginning in 2010, 2011, and 2012, the reduction in qualified production activities income by virtue of this fraction is reduced by 25, 50, and 75 percent, respectively. For taxable years beginning after 2012, there is no reduction in qualified production activities income by virtue of this fraction.

Domestic production gross receipts

Under the Senate amendment, "domestic production gross receipts" are gross receipts of a taxpayer that are derived in the actual conduct of a trade or business from any sale, exchange or other disposition, or any lease, rental or license, of qualifying production property that was manufactured, produced, grown or extracted (in whole or in significant part) by the taxpayer within the United States or any possession of the

---

[11] For purposes of the Senate amendment, "wages" include the sum of the aggregate amounts of wages (as defined in section 3401(a) without regard to exclusions for remuneration paid for services performed in possessions of the United States) and elective deferrals that the taxpayer is required to include on statements with respect to the employment of employees of the taxpayer during the taxpayer's taxable year. Elective deferrals include elective deferrals as defined in section 402(g)(3), amounts deferred under section 457, and, for taxable years beginning after December 31, 2005, designated Roth contributions (as defined in section 402A). Any wages taken into account for purposes of determining the wage limitation under the Senate amendment cannot also be taken into account for purposes of determining any credit allowable under sections 30A or 936.

[12] "Modified taxable income" under the Senate amendment is taxable income of the taxpayer computed without regard to the deduction provided by the Senate amendment. Qualified production activities income is limited to the modified taxable income of the taxpayer.

[13] For purposes of determining such costs under the Senate amendment, any item or service that is imported into the United States without an arm's length transfer price shall be treated as acquired by purchase, and its cost shall be treated as not less than its fair market value when it entered the United States. A similar rule shall apply in determining the adjusted basis of leased or rented property where the lease or rental gives rise to domestic production gross receipts. With regard to property previously exported by the tax-

payer for further manufacture, the increase in cost or adjusted basis shall not exceed the difference between the fair market value of the property when exported and the fair market value of the property when re-imported into the United States after further manufacture.

[14] The Senate amendment provides that the Secretary shall prescribe rules for the proper allocation of items of income, deduction, expense, and loss for purposes of determining income attributable to domestic production activities. Where appropriate, such rules shall be similar to and consistent with relevant present-law rules (e.g., secs. 263A and 861).

[15] For purposes of the domestic/worldwide fraction under the Senate amendment, the value of domestic production is the excess of domestic production gross receipts (as defined below) over the cost of deductible purchased inputs that are allocable to such receipts. Similarly, the value of worldwide production is the excess of worldwide production gross receipts over the cost of deductible purchased inputs that are allocable to such receipts. For purposes of determining the domestic/worldwide fraction, purchased inputs include: purchased services (other than employees) used in manufacture, production, growth, or extraction activities; purchased items consumed in connection with such activities; and purchased items incorporated as part of the property being manufactured, produced, grown, or extracted. In the case of corporate taxpayers that are members of certain affiliated groups, the domestic/worldwide fraction is determined by treating all members of such groups as a single taxpayer.

United States.[16] Such term also includes a percentage of gross receipts derived from engineering or architectural services performed in the United States for construction projects in the United States.[17] Finally, such term includes gross receipts derived by the taxpayer from the use of film and videotape property produced in whole or in significant part by the taxpayer within the United States. "Qualifying production property" generally is any tangible personal property, computer software, or property described in section 168(f)(3) or (4) of the Code.[18] However, qualifying production property does not include: (1) consumable property that is sold, leased or licensed as an integral part of the provision of services; (2) oil or gas (other than certain primary products thereof);[19] (3) electricity; (4) water supplied by pipeline to the consumer; (5) utility services; and (6) any film, tape, recording, book, magazine, newspaper or similar property the market for which is primarily topical or otherwise essentially transitory in nature.[20]

Other rules

Qualified production activities income of passthrough entities (other than cooperatives)

With respect to domestic production activities of an S corporation, partnership, estate, trust or other passthrough entity (other than an agricultural or horticultural cooperative), the deduction under the Senate amendment generally is determined at the shareholder, partner or similar level by taking into account at such level the proportionate share of qualified production activities income of the entity.[21] The Senate amendment directs the Secretary to prescribe rules for the application of the deduction to passthrough entities, including reporting requirements and rules relating to restrictions on the allocation of the deduction to taxpayers at the partner or similar level.

Qualified production activities income of agricultural and horticultural cooperatives

With regard to member-owned agricultural and horticultural cooperatives formed under Subchapter T of the Code, the Senate amendment provides the same treatment of qualified production activities income derived from products marketed through cooperatives as it provides for qualified production activities income of other taxpayers (i.e., the cooperative may claim a deduction from qualified production activities income). In addition, the Senate amendment provides that the amount of any patronage dividends or per-unit retain allocations paid to a member of an agricultural or horticultural cooperative (to which Part I of Subchapter T applies), which is allocable to the portion of qualified production activities income of the cooperative that is deductible under the Senate amendment, is excludible from the gross income of the member. In order to qualify, such amount must be designated by the organization as allocable to the deductible portion of qualified production activities income in a written notice mailed to its patrons not later than the payment period described in section 1382(d). The cooperative cannot reduce its income under section 1382 (e.g., cannot claim a dividends-paid deduction) for such amounts.

---

[16] Under the Senate amendment, domestic production gross receipts include gross receipts of a taxpayer derived from any sale, exchange or other disposition of agricultural products with respect to which the taxpayer performs storage, handling or other processing activities (but not transportation activities) within the United States, provided such products are consumed in connection with, or incorporated into, the manufacturing, production, growth or extraction of qualifying production property (whether or not by the taxpayer).

[17] For taxable years beginning in 2004 through 2008, the applicable percentage is 25%. For taxable years beginning in 2009 through 2012, the applicable percentage is 50%. For taxable years beginning after 2012, the applicable percentage is 100%.

[18] For purposes of the definition of qualified production property under the Senate amendment, property described in section 168(f)(3) or (4) of the Code includes underlying copyrights and trademarks. In addition, gross receipts from the sale, exchange, lease, rental, license or other disposition of property described in section 168(f)(3) or (4) are treated as domestic production gross receipts if more than 50 percent of the aggregate development and production costs of such property are incurred by the taxpayer within the United States. For this purpose, property that is acquired by the taxpayer after development or production has commenced, but before such property generates substantial gross receipts, shall be treated as developed or produced by the taxpayer.

[19] Under the Senate amendment, qualifying production property does not include extracted but unrefined oil or gas, but generally includes primary products of oil and gas that are produced by the taxpayer. Examples of primary products for this purpose include motor fuels, chemical feedstocks and fertilizer. However, primary products do not include the output of a natural gas processing plant. Natural gas processing plants generally are located at or near the producing gas field that supplies the facility, and the facility serves to separate impurities from the natural gas liquids recovered from the field for the purpose of selling the liquids for future production and preparation of the natural gas for pipeline transportation.

[20] The topical and transitory exclusion does not apply to the extent of the gross receipts from the use of film and videotape property produced in whole or in significant part by the taxpayer within the United States.

[21] However, the wage limitation described above is determined at the entity level in computing the deduction with respect to qualified production activities income of a passthrough entity.

Separate application to films and videotape

Under the Senate amendment, the deduction provided by this provision with respect to films and videotape is determined separately with respect to qualified production activities income of the taxpayer allocable to each of three markets: theatrical, broadcast television, and home video. The Senate amendment provides rules for making a separate determination of qualified production activities allocable to each market.

Alternative minimum tax

The deduction provided by the Senate amendment is allowed for purposes of the alternative minimum tax (including adjusted current earnings). The deduction is determined by reference to modified alternative minimum taxable income.

Coordination with ETI repeal

For purposes of the Senate amendment, domestic production gross receipts does not include gross receipts from any transaction that produces excluded extraterritorial income pursuant to the binding contract exception to the ETI repeal provisions of the Senate amendment.

Qualified production activities income is determined without regard to any deduction provided by the ETI repeal provisions of the Senate amendment.

Effective Date

The Senate amendment provision is effective for taxable years ending after the date of enactment.

Conference Agreement

In general

The conference agreement provides a deduction from taxable income (or, in the case of an individual, adjusted gross income) that is equal to a portion of the taxpayer's qualified production activities income. For taxable years beginning after 2009, the deduction is equal to nine percent of the lesser of (1) the qualified production activities income of the taxpayer for the taxable year, or (2) taxable income (determined without regard to this provision) for the taxable year. For taxable years beginning in 2005 and 2006, the deduction is three percent of income and, for taxable years beginning in 2007, 2008 and 2009, the deduction is six percent of income. However, the deduction for a taxable year is limited to 50 percent of the wages paid by the taxpayer during the calendar year that ends in such taxable year.[22] In the case of corporate taxpayers that are members of certain affiliated groups, the deduction is determined by treating all members of such groups as a single taxpayer and the deduction is allocated among such members in proportion to each member's respective amount (if any) of qualified production activities income.

Qualified production activities income

In general, "qualified production activities income" is equal to domestic production gross receipts, reduced by the sum of: (1) the costs of goods sold that are allocable to such receipts;[23] (2) other deductions, expenses, or losses that are directly allocable to such receipts; and (3) a proper share of other deductions, expenses, and losses that are not directly allocable to such receipts or another class of income.[24]

Domestic production gross receipts

"Domestic production gross receipts" generally are gross receipts of a taxpayer that are derived from: (1) any sale, exchange or other disposition, or any lease, rental or license, of qualifying production property that was manufactured, produced, grown or extracted by the taxpayer in whole or in significant part within

---

[22] For purposes of the conference agreement, "wages" include the sum of the aggregate amounts of wages and elective deferrals that the taxpayer is required to include on statements with respect to the employment of employees of the taxpayer during the taxpayer's taxable year. Elective deferrals include elective deferrals as defined in section 402(g)(3), amounts deferred under section 457, and, for taxable years beginning after December 31, 2005, designated Roth contributions (as defined in section 402A).

[23] For purposes of determining such costs, any item or service that is imported into the United States without an arm's length transfer price shall be treated as acquired by purchase, and its cost shall be treated as not less than its value when it entered the United States. A similar rule shall apply in determining the adjusted basis of leased or rented property where the lease or rental gives rise to domestic production gross receipts. With regard to property previously exported by the taxpayer for further manufacture, the increase in cost or adjusted basis shall not exceed the differ-

ence between the value of the property when exported and the value of the property when re-imported into the United States after further manufacture. Except as provided by the Secretary, the value of property for this purpose shall be its customs value (as defined in section 1059A(b)(1)).

[24] The Secretary shall prescribe rules for the proper allocation of items of income, deduction, expense, and loss for purposes of determining income attributable to domestic production activities. Where appropriate, such rules shall be similar to and consistent with relevant present-law rules (e.g., sec. 263A, in determining the cost of goods sold, and sec. 861, in determining the source of such items). Other deductions, expenses or losses that are directly allocable to such receipts include, for example, selling and marketing expenses. A proper share of other deductions, expenses, and losses that are not directly allocable to such receipts or another class of income include, for example, general and administrative expenses allocable to selling and marketing expenses.

the United States;[25] (2) any sale, exchange or other disposition, or any lease, rental or license, of qualified film produced by the taxpayer; (3) any sale, exchange or other disposition electricity, natural gas, or potable water produced by the taxpayer in the United States; (4) construction activities performed in the United States;[26] or (5) engineering or architectural services performed in the United States for construction projects located in the United States.

However, domestic production gross receipts do not include any gross receipts of the taxpayer that are derived from (1) the sale of food or beverages prepared by the taxpayer at a retail establishment,[27] or (2) the transmission or distribution of electricity, natural gas, or potable water.[28] In addition, domestic production gross receipts do not include any gross receipts of the taxpayer derived from property that is leased,

---

[25] Domestic production gross receipts include gross receipts of a taxpayer derived from any sale, exchange or other disposition of agricultural products with respect to which the taxpayer performs storage, handling or other processing activities (other than transportation activities) within the United States, provided such products are consumed in connection with, or incorporated into, the manufacturing, production, growth or extraction of qualifying production property (whether or not by the taxpayer).

[26] For this purpose, construction activities include activities that are directly related to the erection or substantial renovation of residential and commercial buildings and infrastructure. Substantial renovation would include structural improvements, but not mere cosmetic changes, such as painting.

[27] The conferees intend that food processing, which generally is a qualified production activity under the conference agreement, does not include activities carried out at retail establishment. Thus, under the conference agreement while the gross receipts of a meat packing establishment are qualified domestic production gross receipts, the activities of a master chef who creates a venison sausage for his or her restaurant menu cannot be construed as a qualified production activity.

The conferees recognize that some taxpayers may own facilities at which the predominant activity is domestic production as defined in the conference agreement and other facilities at which they engage in the retail sale of the taxpayer's produced goods and also sell food and beverages. For example, assume that the taxpayer buys coffee beans and roasts those beans at a facility, the primary activity of which is the roasting and packaging of roasted coffee. The taxpayer sells the roasted coffee through a variety of unrelated third-party vendors and also sells roasted coffee at the taxpayer's own retail establishments. In addition, at the taxpayer's retail establishments, the taxpayer prepares brewed coffee and other foods. The conferees intend that to the extent that the gross receipts of the taxpayer's retail establishment represent receipts from the sale of its roasted coffee beans to customers, the receipts are qualified domestic production gross receipts, but to the extent that the gross receipts of the taxpayer's retail establishment represent receipts from the sale of brewed coffee or food prepared at the retail establishment, the receipts are not qualified domestic production gross receipts. However, the conferees intend that, in this case, the taxpayer may allocate part of the receipts from the sale of the brewed coffee as qualified domestic production gross receipts to the extent of the value of the roasted coffee beans used to brew the coffee. The conferees intend that the Secretary provide guidance drawing on the principles of section 482 by which such a taxpayer can allocate gross receipts between qualified and nonqualified gross receipts. The conferees observe that in this example, the taxpayer's sales of roasted coffee beans to unrelated third parties would provide a value for the beans used in brewing a cup of coffee for retail sale.

The conferees intend that the disqualification of gross receipts derived from the sale of food and beverage prepared by the taxpayer at a retail establishment not be construed narrowly to apply only to establishments at which

customers dine on premises. The receipts of a facility that prepares food and beverage solely for take out service would not be qualified production gross receipts. Likewise, the conferees intend that the disqualification of gross receipts derived from the sale of food and beverages prepared by the taxpayer need not be limited to retail establishments primarily engaged in the dining trade. For example, if a taxpayer operates a supermarket and as part of the supermarket the taxpayer operates an in-store bakery, the same allocation described above would apply to determine the extent to which the taxpayer's gross receipts represent qualified domestic production gross receipts.

[28] The conference agreement provides that domestic production gross receipts include the gross receipts from the production in the United States of electricity, gas, and potable water, but excludes the gross receipts from the transmission or distribution of electricity, gas, and potable water. Thus, in the case of a taxpayer who owns a facility for the production of electricity, whether the taxpayer's facility is part of a regulated utility or an independent power facility, the taxpayer's gross receipts from the production of electricity at that facility are qualified domestic production gross receipts. However, to the extent that the taxpayer is an integrated producer that generates electricity and delivers electricity to end users, any gross receipts properly attributable to the transmission of electricity from the generating facility to a point of local distribution and any gross receipts properly attributable to the distribution of electricity to final customers are not qualified domestic production gross receipts. For example, assume taxpayer A owns a wind turbine that generates electricity and taxpayer B owns a high-voltage transmission line that passes near taxpayer A's wind turbine and ends near the system of local distribution lines of taxpayer C. Taxpayer A sells the electricity produced at the wind turbine to taxpayer C and contracts with taxpayer B to transmit the electricity produced at the wind turbine to taxpayer C who sells the electricity to his or her customers using taxpayer C's distribution network. The gross receipts received by taxpayer A for the sale of electricity produced at the wind turbine constitute qualifying domestic production gross receipts. The gross receipts of taxpayer B from transporting taxpayer A's electricity to taxpayer C are not qualifying domestic production gross receipts. Likewise the gross receipts of taxpayer C from distributing the electricity are not qualifying domestic production gross receipts. Also, if taxpayer A made direct sales of electricity to customers in taxpayer C's service area and taxpayer C receives remuneration for the distribution of electricity, the gross receipts of taxpayer C are not qualifying domestic production gross receipts. If taxpayers A, B, and C are all related taxpayer, then taxpayers A, B, and C must allocate gross receipts to production activities, transmission activities, and distribution activities in a manner consistent with the preceding example.

The conference agreement provides that the same principles apply in the case of the natural gas and water supply industries. In the case of natural gas, production activities generally are all activities involved in extracting natural gas from the ground and processing the gas into pipeline quality gas. Such activities would produce qualifying domestic

licensed or rented by the taxpayer for use by any related person.[29]

"Qualifying production property" generally includes any tangible personal property, computer software, or sound recordings. "Qualified film" includes any motion picture film or videotape[30] (including live or delayed television programming, but not including certain sexually explicit productions) if 50 percent or more of the total compensation relating to the production of such film (including compensation in the form of residuals and participations[31]) constitutes compensation for services performed in the United States by actors, production personnel, directors, and producers.[32]

Other rules

Qualified production activities income of passthrough entities (other than cooperatives)

With respect to domestic production activities of an S corporation, partnership, estate, trust or other passthrough entity (other than an agricultural or horticultural cooperative), although the wage limitation is applied first at the entity level, the deduction under the conference agreement generally is determined at the shareholder, partner or similar level by taking into account at such level the proportionate share of qualified production activities income of the entity. The Secretary is directed to prescribe rules for the application of the conference agreement to passthrough entities, including reporting requirements and rules relating to restrictions on the allocation of the deduction to taxpayers at the partner or similar level.

For purposes of applying the wage limitation at the level of a shareholder, partner, or similar person, each person who is allocated qualified production activities income from a passthrough entity also is treated as having been allocated wages from such entity in an amount that is equal to the lesser of: (1) such person's allocable share of wages, as determined under regulations prescribed by the Secretary; or (2) twice the appropriate deductible percentage of qualified production activities income that actually is allocated to such person for the taxable year.

Qualified production activities income of agricultural and horticultural cooperatives

With regard to member-owned agricultural and horticultural cooperatives formed under Subchapter T of the Code, the conference agreement provides the same treatment of qualified production activities income derived from agricultural or horticultural products that are manufactured, produced, grown, or extracted by cooperatives,[33] or that are marketed through cooperatives, as it provides for qualified production activities income of other taxpayers (i.e., the cooperative may claim a deduction from qualified production activities income).

In addition, the conference agreement provides that the amount of any patronage dividends or per-unit retain allocations paid to a member of an agricultural or horticultural cooperative (to which Part I of Subchapter T applies), which is allocable to the portion of qualified production activities income of the cooperative

---

(Footnote Continued)

production gross receipts. However gross receipts of a taxpayer attributable to transmission of pipeline quality gas from a natural gas field (or from a natural gas processing plant) to a local distribution company's citygate (or to another customer) are not qualified domestic production gross receipts. Likewise gas purchased by a local gas distribution company and distributed from the citygate to the local customers does not give rise to domestic production gross receipts.

In the case of the production of potable water the conferees intend that activities involved in the production of potable water include the acquisition, collection, and storage of raw water (untreated water). It also includes the transportation of raw water to a water treatment facility and treatment of raw water at such a facility. However, any gross receipts from the storage of potable water after the water treatment facility or delivery of potable water to customers does not give rise to qualifying domestic production gross receipts. The conferees intend that a taxpayer that both produces potable water and distributes potable water will properly allocate gross receipts across qualifying and non-qualifying activities.

[29] It is intended that principles similar to those under the present-law extraterritorial income regime apply for this purpose. *See* Temp. Treas. Reg. sec. 1.927(a)-1T(f)(2)(i). For example, this exclusion generally does not apply to property

leased by the taxpayer to a related person if the property is held for sublease, or is subleased, by the related person to an unrelated person for the ultimate use of such unrelated person. Similarly, the license of computer software to a related person for reproduction and sale, exchange, lease, rental or sublicense to an unrelated person for the ultimate use of such unrelated person is not treated as excluded property by reason of the license to the related person.

[30] The conferees intend that the nature of the material on which properties described in section 168(f)(3) are embodied and the methods and means of distribution of such properties shall not affect their qualification under this provision.

[31] To the extent that a taxpayer has included an estimate of participations and/or residuals in its income forecast calculation under section 167(g), such taxpayer must use the same estimate of participations and/or residuals for purposes of determining total compensation.

[32] It is intended that the Secretary will provide appropriate rules governing the determination of total compensation for services performed in the United States.

[33] For this purpose, agricultural or horticultural products also include fertilizer, diesel fuel and other supplies used in agricultural or horticultural production that are manufactured, produced, grown, or extracted by the cooperative.

Act Sec. 102   ¶10,020

that is deductible under the conference agreement, is deductible from the gross income of the member. In order to qualify, such amount must be designated by the organization as allocable to the deductible portion of qualified production activities income in a written notice mailed to its patrons not later than the payment period described in section 1382(d). The cooperative cannot reduce its income under section 1382 (e.g., cannot claim a dividends-paid deduction) for such amounts.

Alternative minimum tax

The deduction provided by the conference agreement is allowed for purposes of computing alternative minimum taxable income (including adjusted current earnings). The deduction in computing alternative minimum taxable income is determined by reference to the lesser of the qualified production activities income (as determined for the regular tax) or the alternative minimum taxable income (in the case of an individual, adjusted gross income as determined for the regular tax) without regard to this deduction.

Timber cutting

Under the conference agreement, an election made for a taxable year ending on or before the date of enactment, to treat the cutting of timber as a sale or exchange, may be revoked by the taxpayer without the consent of the IRS for any taxable year ending after that date. The prior election (and revocation) is disregarded for purposes of making a subsequent election.

Exploration of fundamental tax reform

The conferees acknowledge that Congress has not reduced the statutory corporate income tax rate since 1986. According to the Organisation of Economic Cooperation and Development ("OECD"), the combined corporate income tax

rate, as defined by the OECD, in most instances is lower than the U.S. corporate income tax rate.[34] Higher corporate tax rates factor into the United States' ability to attract and retain economically vibrant industries, which create good jobs and contribute to overall economic growth.

This legislation was crafted to repeal an export tax benefit that was deemed inconsistent with obligations of the United States under the Agreement on Subsidies and Countervailing Measures and other international trade agreements. This legislation replaces the benefit with tax relief specifically designed to be economically equivalent to a 3-percentage point reduction in U.S.-based manufacturing.

The conferees recognize that manufacturers are a segment of the economy that has faced significant challenges during the nation's recent economic slowdown. The conferees recognize that trading partners of the United States retain subsidies for domestic manufacturers and exports through their indirect tax systems. The conferees are concerned about the adverse competitive impact of these subsidies on U.S. manufacturers.

These concerns should be considered in the context of the benefits of a unified top tax rate for all corporate taxpayers, including manufacturing, in terms of efficiency and fairness. The conferees also expect that the tax-writing committees will explore a unified top corporate tax rate in the context of fundamental tax reform.

Effective Date

The conference agreement is effective for taxable years beginning after December 31, 2004.

[Law at ¶5085, ¶5110, ¶5135, ¶5140, ¶5230, ¶5235, ¶5240, ¶5245, ¶5255, ¶5390, ¶5495 and ¶5920. CCH Explanation at ¶210.]

[¶10,030] Act Sec. 102(c). Election to treat cutting of timber as a sale or exchange

Senate Committee Report (S. REP. NO. 108-192)

[Act Sec. 102(c)]

Present Law

Under present law, a taxpayer may elect to treat the cutting of timber as a sale or exchange of the timber. If an election is made, the gain or loss is recognized in an amount equal to the difference between the fair market value of the

timber and the basis of the timber. An election, once made, is effective for the taxable year and all subsequent taxable years, unless the IRS, upon a showing of undue hardship by the taxpayer, permits the revocation of the election. If an election is revoked, a new election may be made only with the consent of the IRS.

---

[34] Organisation of Economic Cooperation and Development, Table 1.5, Tax Data Base Statistics, Tax Policy and Administration, Summary Tables (2003).

Reasons for Change

The Committee believes that changes made in the tax law should allow a taxpayer to revoke its election to treat the cutting of timber as a sale or exchange.

Explanation of Provision

Under the provision, an election made for a taxable year ending on or before the date of enactment, to treat the cutting of timber as a sale or exchange, may be revoked by the taxpayer without the consent of the IRS for any taxable year ending after that date. The prior election (and revocation) is disregarded for purposes of making a subsequent election.[100]

* * *

Conference Committee Report (H.R. CONF. REP. NO. 108-755)

Senate Amendment

The provision is the same as the House bill, except the provision applies to all taxpayers.

Effective Date

The provision applies to taxable years ending after the date of enactment.

Conference Agreement

The conference agreement includes the provision in the Senate amendment.

[Law at ¶7015. CCH Explanation at ¶210.]

[¶ 10,040] Act Sec. 201. Section 179 expensing

House Committee Report (H.R. REP. NO. 108-548, pt. 1)

[Code Sec. 179]

Present Law

Present law provides that, in lieu of depreciation, a taxpayer with a sufficiently small amount of annual investment may elect to deduct such costs. The Jobs and Growth Tax Relief Reconciliation Act (JGTRRA) of 2003[8] increased the amount a taxpayer may deduct, for taxable years beginning in 2003 through 2005, to $100,000 of the cost of qualifying property placed in service for the taxable year.[9] In general, qualifying property is defined as depreciable tangible personal property (and certain computer software) that is purchased for use in the active conduct of a trade or business. The $100,000 amount is reduced (but not below zero) by the amount by which the cost of qualifying property placed in service during the taxable year exceeds $400,000. The $100,000 and $400,000 amounts are indexed for inflation.

Prior to the enactment of JGTRRA (and for taxable years beginning in 2006 and thereafter) a taxpayer with a sufficiently small amount of annual investment could elect to deduct up to $25,000 of the cost of qualifying property placed in service for the taxable year. The $25,000 amount was reduced (but not below zero) by the amount by which the cost of qualifying property placed in service during the taxable year exceeds $200,000. In general, qualifying property is defined as depreciable tangible personal property that is purchased for use in the active conduct of a trade or business.

The amount eligible to be expensed for a taxable year may not exceed the taxable income for a taxable year that is derived from the active conduct of a trade or business (determined without regard to this provision). Any amount that is not allowed as a deduction because of the taxable income limitation may be carried forward to succeeding taxable years (subject to similar limitations). No general business credit under section 38 is allowed with respect to any amount for which a deduction is allowed under section 179.

Under present law, an expensing election is made under rules prescribed by the Secretary.[10] Applicable Treasury regulations provide that an expensing election generally is made on the taxpayer's original return for the taxable year to which the election relates.[11]

Prior to the enactment of JGTRRA (and for taxable years beginning in 2006 and thereafter),

---

[100] The present-law rules of section 631(a) apply to any subsequent election.

[8] Pub. L. No. 108-27, sec. 202 (2003).

[9] Additional section 179 incentives are provided with respect to a qualified property used by a business in the New York Liberty Zone (sec. 1400L(f)), an empowerment zone (sec. 1397A), or a renewal community (sec. 1400J).

[10] Sec. 179(c)(1).

[11] Treas. Reg. sec. 1.179-5. Under these regulations, a taxpayer may make the election on the original return (whether or not the return is timely), or on an amended return filed by the due date (including extensions) for filing the return for the tax year the property was placed in service. If the taxpayer timely filed an original return without making the election, the taxpayer may still make the election by filing

an expensing election may be revoked only with consent of the Commissioner.[12] JGTRRA permits taxpayers to revoke expensing elections on amended returns without the consent of the Commissioner with respect to a taxable year beginning after 2002 and before 2006.[13]

Reasons for Change

The Committee believes that section 179 expensing provides two important benefits for small businesses. First, it lowers the cost of capital for property used in a trade or business. With a lower cost of capital, the Committee believes small businesses will invest in more equipment and employ more workers. Second, it eliminates depreciation recordkeeping requirements with respect to expensed property. In JGTRRA, Congress acted to increase the value of these benefits and to increase the number of taxpayers eligible for taxable years through 2005. The Committee believes that these changes to section 179 expensing will continue to provide important benefits if extended, and the bill therefore extends these changes for an additional two years.

Explanation of Provision

The provision extends the increased amount that a taxpayer may deduct, and other changes

that were made by JGTRRA, for an additional two years. Thus, the provision provides that the maximum dollar amount that may be deducted under section 179 is $100,000 for property placed in service in taxable years beginning before 2008 ($25,000 for taxable years beginning in 2008 and thereafter). In addition, the $400,000 amount applies for property placed in service in taxable years beginning before 2008 ($200,000 for taxable years beginning in 2008 and thereafter). The provision extends, through 2007 (from 2005), the indexing for inflation of both the maximum dollar amount that may be deducted and the $400,000 amount. The provision also includes off-the-shelf computer software placed in service in taxable years beginning before 2008 as qualifying property. The provision permits taxpayers to revoke expensing elections on amended returns without the consent of the Commissioner with respect to a taxable year beginning before 2008. The Committee expects that the Secretary will prescribe regulations to permit a taxpayer to make an expensing election on an amended return without the consent of the Commissioner.

Effective Date

The provision is effective on the date of enactment.

Conference Committee Report (H.R. CONF. REP. NO. 108-755)

The conference agreement follows the House bill.

[Law at ¶ 5195. CCH Explanation at ¶ 305.]

[¶ 10,050] Act Sec. 211. Recovery period for depreciation of certain leasehold improvements

House Committee Report (H.R. REP. NO. 108-548, pt. 1)

[Code Sec. 168(e)]

Present Law

A taxpayer generally must capitalize the cost of property used in a trade or business and recover such cost over time through annual deductions for depreciation or amortization. Tangible property generally is depreciated under the modified accelerated cost recovery system ("MACRS"), which determines depreciation by applying specific recovery periods, placed-in-service conventions, and depreciation methods to the cost of various types of depreciable property (sec. 168). The cost of nonresidential real property is recovered using the straight-line method of depreciation and a recovery period of

39 years. Nonresidential real property is subject to the mid-month placed-in-service convention. Under the mid-month convention, the depreciation allowance for the first year property is placed in service is based on the number of months the property was in service, and property placed in service at any time during a month is treated as having been placed in service in the middle of the month.

Depreciation of leasehold improvements

Depreciation allowances for improvements made on leased property are determined under MACRS, even if the MACRS recovery period assigned to the property is longer than the term of the lease (sec. 168(i)(8)).[14] This rule applies

---

(Footnote Continued)

an amended return within six months of the due date of the return (excluding extensions).

[12] Sec. 179(c)(2).

[13] Id.

[14] The Tax Reform Act of 1986 modified the Accelerated Cost Recovery System ("ACRS") to institute MACRS. Prior

regardless of whether the lessor or the lessee places the leasehold improvements in service.[15] If a leasehold improvement constitutes an addition or improvement to nonresidential real property already placed in service, the improvement is depreciated using the straight-line method over a 39-year recovery period, beginning in the month the addition or improvement was placed in service (secs. 168(b)(3), (c), (d)(2), and (i)(6)).[16]

Qualified leasehold improvement property

The Job Creation and Worker Assistance Act of 2002[17] ("JCWAA"), as amended by JGTRRA, generally provides an additional first-year depreciation deduction equal to either 30 percent or 50 percent of the adjusted basis of qualified property placed in service before January 1, 2005. Qualified property includes qualified leasehold improvement property. For this purpose, qualified leasehold improvement property is any improvement to an interior portion of a building that is nonresidential real property, provided certain requirements are met. The improvement must be made under or pursuant to a lease either by the lessee (or sublessee), or by the lessor, of that portion of the building to be occupied exclusively by the lessee (or sublessee). The improvement must be placed in service more than three years after the date the building was first placed in service. Qualified leasehold improvement property does not include any improvement for which the expenditure is attributable to the enlargement of the building, any elevator or escalator, any structural component benefiting a common area, or the internal structural framework of the building.

Treatment of dispositions of leasehold improvements

A lessor of leased property that disposes of a leasehold improvement that was made by the lessor for the lessee of the property may take the adjusted basis of the improvement into account for purposes of determining gain or loss if the improvement is irrevocably disposed of or abandoned by the lessor at the termination of the lease. This rule conforms the treatment of lessors and lessees with respect to leasehold improvements disposed of at the end of a term of lease.

Reasons for Change

The Committee believes that taxpayers should not be required to recover the costs of certain leasehold improvements beyond the useful life of the investment. The present law 39-year recovery period for leasehold improvements extends well beyond the useful life of such investments. Although lease terms differ, the Committee believes that lease terms for commercial real estate typically are shorter than the present-law 39-year recovery period. In the interests of simplicity and administrability, a uniform period for recovery of leasehold improvements is desirable. The Committee bill therefore shortens the recovery period for leasehold improvements to a more realistic 15 years.

The Committee also believes that unlike other commercial buildings, restaurant buildings generally are more specialized structures. Restaurants also experience considerably more traffic, and remain open longer than most retail properties. This daily assault causes rapid deterioration of restaurant properties and forces restaurateurs to constantly repair and upgrade their facilities. As such, restaurant facilities have a much shorter life span than other commercial establishments. The Committee bill reduces the 39-year recovery period for improvements made to restaurant buildings and more accurately reflects the true economic life of the properties by reducing the recovery period to 15 years.

Explanation of Provision

The provision provides a statutory 15-year recovery period for qualified leasehold improvement property placed in service before January 1, 2006.[18] The provision requires that qualified leasehold improvement property be recovered using the straight-line method.

(Footnote Continued)

to the adoption of ACRS by the Economic Recovery Tax Act of 1981, taxpayers were allowed to depreciate the various components of a building as separate assets with separate useful lives. The use of component depreciation was repealed upon the adoption of ACRS. The Tax Reform Act of 1986 also denied the use of component depreciation under MACRS.

[15] Former sections 168(f)(6) and 178 provided that, in certain circumstances, a lessee could recover the cost of leasehold improvements made over the remaining term of the lease. The Tax Reform Act of 1986 repealed these provisions.

[16] If the improvement is characterized as tangible personal property, ACRS or MACRS depreciation is calculated using the shorter recovery periods, accelerated methods,

and conventions applicable to such property. The determination of whether improvements are characterized as tangible personal property or as nonresidential real property often depends on whether or not the improvements constitute a "structural component" of a building (as defined by Treas. Reg. sec. 1.48-1(e)(1)). *See, e.g., Metro National Corp* v. *Commissioner*, 52 TCM (CCH) 1440 (1987); *King Radio Corp Inc.* v. *U.S.*, 486 F.2d 1091 (10th Cir. 1973); *Mallinckrodt, Inc.* v. *Commissioner*, 778 F.2d 402 (8th Cir. 1985) (with respect to various leasehold improvements).

[17] Pub. L. No. 107-147, sec. 101 (2002), as amended by Pub. L. No. 108-27, sec. 201 (2003).

[18] Qualified leasehold improvement property continues to be eligible for the additional first-year depreciation deduction under sec. 168(k).

Qualified leasehold improvement property is defined as under present law for purposes of the additional first-year depreciation deduction (sec. 168(k)), with the following modification. If a lessor makes an improvement that qualifies as qualified leasehold improvement property such improvement shall not qualify as qualified leasehold improvement property to any subsequent owner of such improvement. An exception to the rule applies in the case of death and certain transfers of property that qualify for non-recognition treatment.

The provision also provides a statutory 15-year recovery period for qualified restaurant property placed in service before January 1, 2006.[19] For purposes of the provision, qualified restaurant property means any improvement to a building if such improvement is placed in service more than three years after the date such building was first placed in service and more than 50 percent of the building's square footage is devoted to the preparation of, and seating for, on-premises consumption of prepared meals. The provision requires that qualified restaurant property be recovered using the straight-line method.

Effective Date

The provision is effective for property placed in service after the date of enactment.

Conference Committee Report (H.R. CONF. REP. NO. 108-755)

Senate Amendment

No provision.

[Law at ¶ 5180. CCH Explanation at ¶ 315.]

Conference Agreement

The conference agreement follows the House bill.

[¶ 10,060] Act Sec. 211. Recovery period for depreciation of certain restaurant improvements

House Committee Report (H.R. REP. NO. 108-548, pt. 1)

[Code Sec. 168(e)]

Present Law

A taxpayer generally must capitalize the cost of property used in a trade or business and recover such cost over time through annual deductions for depreciation or amortization. Tangible property generally is depreciated under the modified accelerated cost recovery system ("MACRS"), which determines depreciation by applying specific recovery periods, placed-in-service conventions, and depreciation methods to the cost of various types of depreciable property (sec. 168). The cost of nonresidential real property is recovered using the straight-line method of depreciation and a recovery period of 39 years. Nonresidential real property is subject to the mid-month placed-in-service convention. Under the mid-month convention, the depreciation allowance for the first year property is placed in service is based on the number of months the property was in service, and property placed in service at any time during a month is treated as having been placed in service in the middle of the month.

Depreciation of leasehold improvements

Depreciation allowances for improvements made on leased property are determined under MACRS, even if the MACRS recovery period assigned to the property is longer than the term of the lease (sec. 168(i)(8)).[14] This rule applies regardless of whether the lessor or the lessee places the leasehold improvements in service.[15] If a leasehold improvement constitutes an addition or improvement to nonresidential real property already placed in service, the improvement is depreciated using the straight-line method over a 39-year recovery period, beginning in the

---

[19] Qualified restaurant property would become eligible for the additional first-year depreciation deduction under sec. 168(k) by virtue of the assigned 15-year recovery period.

[14] The Tax Reform Act of 1986 modified the Accelerated Cost Recovery System ("ACRS") to institute MACRS. Prior to the adoption of ACRS by the Economic Recovery Tax Act of 1981, taxpayers were allowed to depreciate the various components of a building as separate assets with separate useful lives. The use of component depreciation was repealed upon the adoption of ACRS. The Tax Reform Act of 1986 also denied the use of component depreciation under MACRS.

[15] Former sections 168(f)(6) and 178 provided that, in certain circumstances, a lessee could recover the cost of leasehold improvements made over the remaining term of the lease. The Tax Reform Act of 1986 repealed these provisions.

month the addition or improvement was placed in service (secs. 168(b)(3), (c), (d)(2), and (i)(6)).[16]

Qualified leasehold improvement property

The Job Creation and Worker Assistance Act of 2002[17] ("JCWAA"), as amended by JGTRRA, generally provides an additional first-year depreciation deduction equal to either 30 percent or 50 percent of the adjusted basis of qualified property placed in service before January 1, 2005. Qualified property includes qualified leasehold improvement property. For this purpose, qualified leasehold improvement property is any improvement to an interior portion of a building that is nonresidential real property, provided certain requirements are met. The improvement must be made under or pursuant to a lease either by the lessee (or sublessee), or by the lessor, of that portion of the building to be occupied exclusively by the lessee (or sublessee). The improvement must be placed in service more than three years after the date the building was first placed in service. Qualified leasehold improvement property does not include any improvement for which the expenditure is attributable to the enlargement of the building, any elevator or escalator, any structural component benefiting a common area, or the internal structural framework of the building.

Treatment of dispositions of leasehold improvements

A lessor of leased property that disposes of a leasehold improvement that was made by the lessor for the lessee of the property may take the adjusted basis of the improvement into account for purposes of determining gain or loss if the improvement is irrevocably disposed of or abandoned by the lessor at the termination of the lease. This rule conforms the treatment of lessors and lessees with respect to leasehold improvements disposed of at the end of a term of lease.

Reasons for Change

The Committee believes that taxpayers should not be required to recover the costs of certain leasehold improvements beyond the useful life of the investment. The present law 39-year recovery period for leasehold improvements extends well beyond the useful life of

such investments. Although lease terms differ, the Committee believes that lease terms for commercial real estate typically are shorter than the present-law 39-year recovery period. In the interests of simplicity and administrability, a uniform period for recovery of leasehold improvements is desirable. The Committee bill therefore shortens the recovery period for leasehold improvements to a more realistic 15 years.

The Committee also believes that unlike other commercial buildings, restaurant buildings generally are more specialized structures. Restaurants also experience considerably more traffic, and remain open longer than most retail properties. This daily assault causes rapid deterioration of restaurant properties and forces restaurateurs to constantly repair and upgrade their facilities. As such, restaurant facilities have a much shorter life span than other commercial establishments. The Committee bill reduces the 39-year recovery period for improvements made to restaurant buildings and more accurately reflects the true economic life of the properties by reducing the recovery period to 15 years.

Explanation of Provision

The provision provides a statutory 15-year recovery period for qualified leasehold improvement property placed in service before January 1, 2006.[18] The provision requires that qualified leasehold improvement property be recovered using the straight-line method.

Qualified leasehold improvement property is defined as under present law for purposes of the additional first-year depreciation deduction (sec. 168(k)), with the following modification. If a lessor makes an improvement that qualifies as qualified leasehold improvement property such improvement shall not qualify as qualified leasehold improvement property to any subsequent owner of such improvement. An exception to the rule applies in the case of death and certain transfers of property that qualify for non-recognition treatment.

The provision also provides a statutory 15-year recovery period for qualified restaurant property placed in service before January 1, 2006.[19] For purposes of the provision, qualified restaurant property means any improvement to a building if such improvement is placed in ser-

---

[16] If the improvement is characterized as tangible personal property, ACRS or MACRS depreciation is calculated using the shorter recovery periods, accelerated methods, and conventions applicable to such property. The determination of whether improvements are characterized as tangible personal property or as nonresidential real property often depends on whether or not the improvements constitute a "structural component" of a building (as defined by Treas. Reg. sec. 1.48-1(e)(1)). *See, e.g., Metro National Corp v. Commissioner*, 52 TCM (CCH) 1440 (1987); *King Radio Corp Inc. v. U.S.*, 486 F.2d 1091 (10th Cir. 1973); *Mallinckrodt, Inc.*

v. *Commissioner*, 778 F.2d 402 (8th Cir. 1985) (with respect to various leasehold improvements).

[17] Pub. L. No. 107-147, sec. 101 (2002), as amended by Pub. L. No. 108-27, sec. 201 (2003).

[18] Qualified leasehold improvement property continues to be eligible for the additional first-year depreciation deduction under sec. 168(k).

[19] Qualified restaurant property would become eligible for the additional first-year depreciation deduction under sec. 168(k) by virtue of the assigned 15-year recovery period.

vice more than three years after the date such building was first placed in service and more than 50 percent of the building's square footage is devoted to the preparation of, and seating for, on-premises consumption of prepared meals. The provision requires that qualified restaurant property be recovered using the straight-line method.

Effective Date

The provision is effective for property placed in service after the date of enactment.

Conference Committee Report (H.R. CONF. REP. NO. 108-755)

Senate Amendment

No provision.

Conference Agreement

The conference agreement follows the House bill.

[Law at ¶5180. CCH Explanation at ¶317.]

[¶ 10,090] Act Sec. 221. Modification of targeted areas and low-income communities designated for new markets tax credit

Conference Committee Report (H.R. CONF. REP. NO. 108-755)

[Code Sec. 45D]

Present Law

Section 45D provides a new markets tax credit for qualified equity investments made to acquire stock in a corporation, or a capital interest in a partnership, that is a qualified community development entity ("CDE").[340] The amount of the credit allowable to the investor (either the original purchaser or a subsequent holder) is (1) a five-percent credit for the year in which the equity interest is purchased from the CDE and for each of the following two years, and (2) a six-percent credit for each of the following four years. The credit is determined by applying the applicable percentage (five or six percent) to the amount paid to the CDE for the investment at its original issue, and is available for a taxable year to the taxpayer who holds the qualified equity investment on the date of the initial investment or on the respective anniversary date that occurs during the taxable year. The credit is recaptured if at any time during the seven-year period that begins on the date of the original issue of the investment the entity ceases to be a qualified CDE, the proceeds of the investment cease to be used as required, or the equity investment is redeemed.

A qualified CDE is any domestic corporation or partnership: (1) whose primary mission is serving or providing investment capital for low-income communities or low-income persons; (2) that maintains accountability to residents of low-income communities by their representation on any governing board of or any advisory board to

the CDE; and (3) that is certified by the Secretary as being a qualified CDE. A qualified equity investment means stock (other than nonqualified preferred stock) in a corporation or a capital interest in a partnership that is acquired directly from a CDE for cash, and includes an investment of a subsequent purchaser if such investment was a qualified equity investment in the hands of the prior holder. Substantially all of the investment proceeds must be used by the CDE to make qualified low-income community investments. For this purpose, qualified low-income community investments include: (1) capital or equity investments in, or loans to, qualified active low-income community businesses; (2) certain financial counseling and other services to businesses and residents in low-income communities; (3) the purchase from another CDE of any loan made by such entity that is a qualified low-income community investment; or (4) an equity investment in, or loan to, another CDE.

A "low-income community" is defined as a population census tract with either (1) a poverty rate of at least 20 percent or (2) median family income which does not exceed 80 percent of the greater of metropolitan area median family income or statewide median family income (for a non-metropolitan census tract, does not exceed 80 percent of statewide median family income). The Secretary may designate any area within any census tract as a low-income community provided that (1) the boundary is continuous, (2) the area (if it were a census tract) would otherwise satisfy the poverty rate or median income re-

---

[340] Section 45D was added by section 121(a) of the Community Renewal Tax Relief Act of 2000, P.L. No. 106-554 (December 21, 2000).

quirements, and (3) an inadequate access to investment capital exists in the area.

A qualified active low-income community business is defined as a business that satisfies, with respect to a taxable year, the following requirements: (1) at least 50 percent of the total gross income of the business is derived from the active conduct of trade or business activities in any low-income community; (2) a substantial portion of the tangible property of such business is used in a low-income community; (3) a substantial portion of the services performed for such business by its employees is performed in a low-income community; and (4) less than five percent of the average of the aggregate unadjusted bases of the property of such business is attributable to certain financial property or to certain collectibles.

The maximum annual amount of qualified equity investments is capped at $2.0 billion per year for calendar years 2004 and 2005, and at $3.5 billion per year for calendar years 2006 and 2007.

House Bill

No provision.

Senate Amendment

The Senate amendment modifies the Secretary's authority to designate certain areas as low-income communities to provide that the Secretary shall prescribe regulations to designate "targeted populations" as low-income communities for purposes of the new markets tax credit. For this purpose, a "targeted population" is defined by reference to section 103(20) of the Riegle Community Development and Regulatory Improvement Act of 1994 (12 U.S.C. 4702(20)) to mean individuals, or an identifiable group of individuals, including an Indian tribe, who (A) are low-income persons; or (B) otherwise lack adequate access to loans or equity investments. Under the Senate amendment, "low-income" means (1) for a targeted population within a metropolitan area, less than 80 percent of the area median family income; and (2) for a targeted population within a non-metropolitan area, less than the greater of 80 percent of the area median family income or 80 percent of the statewide non-metropolitan area median family income.[341] Under the Senate amendment, a targeted population is not required to be within any census tract.

Effective Date

The provision is effective for designations made after the date of enactment.

Conference Agreement

The conference agreement follows the Senate amendment with respect to targeted population designations, modified to provide that a population census tract with a population of less than 2,000 shall be treated as a low-income community for purposes of the credit if such tract is within an empowerment zone, the designation of which is in effect under section 1391, and is contiguous to one or more low-income communities.

Effective Date

The targeted population provision is effective for designations made after the date of enactment. The low-population provision is effective for investments made after the date of enactment.

[Law at ¶ 5040. CCH Explanation at ¶ 380.]

[¶ 10,100] Act Sec. 222. Expansion of designated renewal community area based on 2000 census data

Conference Committee Report (H.R. Conf. Rep. No. 108-755)

[Code Sec. 1400E]

Present Law

Section 1400E provides for the designation of certain communities as renewal communities.[368] An area designated as a renewal community is eligible for the following tax incentives: (1) a zero-percent rate for capital gain from the sale of qualifying assets; (2) a 15-percent wage credit to employers for the first $10,000 of qualified wages; (3) a "commercial revitalization deduction" that allows taxpayers (to the extent allocated by the appropriate State agency) to deduct either (a) 50 percent of qualifying expenditures for the taxable year in which a qualified building is placed in service, or (b) all of the

---

[341] 12. U.S.C. 4702(17) (used to define "low-income" for purposes of 12. U.S.C. 4702(20)).

[368] Section 1400E was added by section 101(a) of the Community Renewal Tax Relief Act of 2000, P.L. No. 106-554 (December 21, 2000).

qualifying expenditures ratably over a 10-year period beginning with the month in which such building is placed in service; (4) an additional $35,000 of section 179 expensing for qualified property; and (5) an expansion of the work opportunity tax credit with respect to individuals who live in a renewal community.

To be designated as a renewal community, a nominated area was required to meet the following criteria: (1) each census tract must have a poverty rate of at least 20 percent; (2) in the case of an urban area, at least 70 percent of the households have incomes below 80 percent of the median income of households within the local government jurisdiction; (3) the unemployment rate is at least 1.5 times the national unemployment rate; and (4) the area is one of pervasive poverty, unemployment, and general distress. There are no geographic size limitations placed on renewal communities. Instead, the boundary of a renewal community must be continuous. In addition, the renewal community must have a minimum population of 4,000 if the community is located within a metropolitan statistical area (at least 1,000 in all other cases), and a maximum population of not more than 200,000. The population limitations do not apply to any renewal community that is entirely within an Indian reservation.

The designations of renewal communities were required to be made by December 31, 2001, using 1990 census data to determine relevant populations and poverty rates.

House Bill

No provision.

Senate Amendment

The Senate amendment permits the Secretary of Housing and Urban Development to expand a renewal community to include: (1) any census tract that at the time such community was nominated, satisfied the requirements for inclusion in such community but for the failure of such tract to satisfy one or more of the population and poverty rate requirements using 1990 census data, and that satisfies all failed population and poverty rate requirements using 2000 census data; or (2) an area that is adjacent to at least one other area designated as a renewal community and that has a population less than the generally applicable population requirement, if the area is one of pervasive poverty, unemployment, and general distress that is within the jurisdiction of one or more local governments and the boundary of the area is continuous, or

the area contains a population of less than 100 people.

Effective Date

The provision is effective as if included in the amendments made by section 101 of the Community Renewal Tax Relief Act of 2000.

Conference Agreement

The conference agreement modifies the Senate amendment to authorize the Secretary of Housing and Urban Development, at the request of all of the governments that nominated a renewal community, to add a contiguous census tract to a renewal community in the following circumstances. First, the renewal community, including any tract to be added, would have met the renewal community eligibility requirements at the time of the community's original nomination, and any tract to be added has a poverty rate using 2000 census data that exceeds the poverty rate of such tract using 1990 census data. Second, a tract may be added to a renewal community even if the addition of such tract to such community would have caused the community to fail one or more eligibility requirements when originally nominated using 1990 census data, provided that: (1) the renewal community after the inclusion of such tract does not have a population that exceeds 200,000 using either 1990 or 2000 census data; (2) such tract has a poverty rate of at least 20 percent using 2000 census data; and (3) such tract has a poverty rate using 2000 census data that exceeds the poverty rate of such tract using 1990 census data. Census tracts that did not have a poverty rate determined by the Bureau of the Census using 1990 data may be added to an existing renewal community without satisfying requirement (3) above. Third, a tract may be added to an existing renewal community if such tract: (1) has no population using 2000 census data or no poverty rate for such tract is determined by the Bureau of the Census using 2000 census data; (2) such tract is one of general distress; and (3) the renewal community, including such tract, is within the jurisdiction of one or more local governments and has a continuous boundary.

Effective Date

The conference agreement provision is effective as if included in the amendments made by section 101 of the Community Renewal Tax Relief Act of 2000.

[Law at ¶ 5915. CCH Explanation at ¶ 385.]

[¶ 10,110] Act Sec. 223. Modification of income requirement for census tracts within high migration rural counties for new markets tax credit

Conference Committee Report (H.R. CONF. REP. NO. 108-755)

[Code Sec. 45D]

Present Law

Section 45D provides a new markets tax credit for qualified equity investments made to acquire stock in a corporation, or a capital interest in a partnership, that is a qualified community development entity ("CDE").[342] The amount of the credit allowable to the investor (either the original purchaser or a subsequent holder) is (1) a five-percent credit for the year in which the equity interest is purchased from the CDE and for each of the following two years, and (2) a six-percent credit for each of the following four years. The credit is determined by applying the applicable percentage (five or six percent) to the amount paid to the CDE for the investment at its original issue, and is available for the taxable year to the taxpayer who holds the qualified equity investment on the date of the initial investment or on the respective anniversary date that occurs during the taxable year. The credit is recaptured if at any time during the seven-year period that begins on the date of the original issue of the investment the entity ceases to be a qualified CDE, the proceeds of the investment cease to be used as required, or the equity investment is redeemed.

A qualified CDE is any domestic corporation or partnership: (1) whose primary mission is serving or providing investment capital for low-income communities or low-income persons; (2) that maintains accountability to residents of low-income communities by their representation on any governing board of or any advisory board to the CDE; and (3) that is certified by the Secretary as being a qualified CDE. A qualified equity investment means stock (other than nonqualified preferred stock) in a corporation or a capital interest in a partnership that is acquired directly from a CDE for cash, and includes an investment of a subsequent purchaser if such investment was a qualified equity investment in the hands of the prior holder. Substantially all of the investment proceeds must be used by the CDE to make qualified low-income community investments. For this purpose, qualified low-income community investments include: (1) capital or equity investments in, or loans to, qualified active low-income community businesses; (2) certain financial counseling and other services to businesses and residents in low-income communities; (3) the purchase from another CDE of any

loan made by such entity that is a qualified low-income community investment; or (4) an equity investment in, or loan to, another CDE.

A "low-income community" is defined as a population census tract with either (1) a poverty rate of at least 20 percent or (2) median family income which does not exceed 80 percent of the greater of metropolitan area median family income or statewide median family income (for a non-metropolitan census tract, does not exceed 80 percent of statewide median family income). The Secretary may designate any area within any census tract as a low-income community provided that (1) the boundary is continuous, (2) the area (if it were a census tract) would otherwise satisfy the poverty rate or median income requirements, and (3) an inadequate access to investment capital exists in the area.

A qualified active low-income community business is defined as a business that satisfies, with respect to a taxable year, the following requirements: (1) at least 50 percent of the total gross income of the business is derived from the active conduct of trade or business activities in any low-income community; (2) a substantial portion of the tangible property of such business is used in a low-income community; (3) a substantial portion of the services performed for such business by its employees is performed in a low-income community; and (4) less than five percent of the average of the aggregate unadjusted bases of the property of such business is attributable to certain financial property or to certain collectibles.

The maximum annual amount of qualified equity investments is capped at $2.0 billion per year for calendar years 2004 and 2005, and at $3.5 billion per year for calendar years 2006 and 2007.

House Bill

No provision.

Senate Amendment

The Senate amendment modifies the low-income test for high migration rural counties. Under the Senate amendment, in the case of a population census tract located within a high migration rural county, low-income is defined by reference to 85 percent (rather than 80 percent) of statewide median family income. For this purpose, a high migration rural county is

---

[342] Section 45D was added by section 121(a) of the Community Renewal Tax Relief Act of 2000, P.L. No. 106-554 (December 21, 2000).

any county that, during the 20-year period ending with the year in which the most recent census was conducted, has a net out-migration of inhabitants from the county of at least 10 percent of the population of the county at the beginning of such period.

Effective Date

The provision is effective as if included in the amendment made by section 121(a) of the Community Renewal Tax Relief Act of 2000.

Conference Agreement

The conference agreement follows the Senate amendment.

[Law at ¶ 5040. CCH Explanation at ¶ 390.]

[¶ 10,120] Act Sec. 231. S corporation reform and simplification: Members of family treated as one shareholder

House Committee Report (H.R. REP. NO. 108-548, pt. 1)

[Code Secs. 1361, 1362, 1363, 1366, 1367, 1368, 1371, 1372, 1373, 1374, 1375, 1377, 1378, 1379 and 4975]

Overview

In general, an S corporation is not subject to corporate-level income tax on its items of income and loss. Instead, an S corporation passes through its items of income and loss to its shareholders. The shareholders take into account separately their shares of these items on their individual income tax returns. To prevent double taxation of these items when the stock is later disposed of, each shareholder's basis in the stock of the S corporation is increased by the amount included in income (including tax-exempt income) and is decreased by the amount of any losses (including nondeductible losses) taken into account. A shareholder's loss may be deducted only to the extent of his or her basis in the stock or debt of the S corporation. To the extent a loss is not allowed due to this limitation, the loss generally is carried forward with respect to the shareholder.

Present Law

A small business corporation may elect to be an S corporation with the consent of all its shareholders, and may terminate its election with the consent of shareholders holding more than 50 percent of the stock. A "small business corporation" is defined as a domestic corporation which is not an ineligible corporation and which has (1) no more than 75 shareholders, all of whom are individuals (and certain trusts, estates, charities, and qualified retirement plans)[32] who are citizens or residents of the United States, and (2) only one class of stock. For purposes of the 75-shareholder limitation, a husband and wife are treated as one shareholder. An "ineligible

corporation" means a corporation that is a financial institution using the reserve method of accounting for bad debts, an insurance company, a corporation electing the benefits of the Puerto Rico and possessions tax credit, or a Domestic International Sales Corporation ("DISC") or former DISC.

Reasons for Change

The bill contains a number of general provisions relating to S corporations. The Committee adopted these provisions that modernize the S corporation rules and eliminate undue restrictions on S corporations in order to expand the application of the S corporation provisions so that more corporations and their shareholders will be able to enjoy the benefits of subchapter S status.

* * *

Explanation of Provision

The bill provides that all family members can elect to be treated as one shareholder for purposes of determining the number of shareholders in the corporation. A family is defined as the lineal descendants (and their spouses) of a common ancestor. The common ancestor cannot be more than three generations removed from the youngest generation of shareholder at the time the S election is made (or the effective date of this provision, if later). Except as provided by Treasury regulations, the election may be made by any family member and the election remains in effect until terminated.

* * *

Effective Date

The provision applies to taxable years beginning after December 31, 2004.

---

[32] If a qualified retirement plan (other than an employee stock ownership plan) or a charity holds stock in an S corporation, the interest held is treated as an interest in an unrelated trade or business, and the plan or charity's share of the S corporation's items of income, loss, or deduction, and gain or loss on the disposition of the S corporation stock, are taken into account in computing unrelated business taxable income.

Conference Committee Report (H.R. CONF. REP. NO. 108-755)

Senate Amendment

No provision.

Conference Agreement

The conference agreement includes the provision in the House bill, except that the number of generations is increased from three to six.

The conferees wish to clarify that members of a family may be treated as one shareholder, for the purpose of determining the number of shareholders, whether a family member holds stock directly or is treated as a shareholder (under section 1361(c)(2)(B)) by reason being a beneficiary of an electing small business trust or qualified subchapter S trust.

[Law at ¶ 5890 and ¶ 5895. CCH Explanation at ¶ 910.]

[¶ 10, 130] Act Sec. 232. S corporation reform and simplification: Increase in number of eligible shareholders to 100

House Committee Report (H.R. REP. NO. 108-548, pt. 1)

[Code Secs. 1361, 1362, 1363, 1366, 1367, 1368, 1371, 1372, 1373, 1374, 1375, 1377, 1378, 1379 and 4975]

Overview

In general, an S corporation is not subject to corporate-level income tax on its items of income and loss. Instead, an S corporation passes through its items of income and loss to its shareholders. The shareholders take into account separately their shares of these items on their individual income tax returns. To prevent double taxation of these items when the stock is later disposed of, each shareholder's basis in the stock of the S corporation is increased by the amount included in income (including tax-exempt income) and is decreased by the amount of any losses (including nondeductible losses) taken into account. A shareholder's loss may be deducted only to the extent of his or her basis in the stock or debt of the S corporation. To the extent a loss is not allowed due to this limitation, the loss generally is carried forward with respect to the shareholder.

Present Law

A small business corporation may elect to be an S corporation with the consent of all its shareholders, and may terminate its election with the consent of shareholders holding more than 50 percent of the stock. A "small business corporation" is defined as a domestic corporation which is not an ineligible corporation and which has (1) no more than 75 shareholders, all of whom are individuals (and certain trusts, estates, charities, and qualified retirement plans)[33] who are citizens or residents of the United States, and (2) only one class of stock. For purposes of the 75-shareholder limitation, a husband and wife are treated as one shareholder. An "ineligible corporation" means a corporation that is a financial institution using the reserve method of accounting for bad debts, an insurance company, a corporation electing the benefits of the Puerto Rico and possessions tax credit, or a Domestic International Sales Corporation ("DISC") or former DISC.

Reasons for Change

The bill contains a number of general provisions relating to S corporations. The Committee adopted these provisions that modernize the S corporation rules and eliminate undue restrictions on S corporations in order to expand the application of the S corporation provisions so that more corporations and their shareholders will be able to enjoy the benefits of subchapter S status.

* * *

Explanation of Provision

* * *

The bill increases the maximum number of eligible shareholders from 75 to 100.

Effective Date

The provision applies to taxable years beginning after December 31, 2004.

---

[33] If a qualified retirement plan (other than an employee stock ownership plan) or a charity holds stock in an S corporation, the interest held is treated as an interest in an unrelated trade or business, and the plan or charity's share of the S corporation's items of income, loss, or deduction, and gain or loss on the disposition of the S corporation stock, are taken into account in computing unrelated business taxable income.

Conference Committee Report (H.R. CONF. REP. NO. 108-755)

Senate Amendment   [Law at ¶ 5890. CCH Explanation at ¶ 905.]

No provision.

Conference Agreement

The conference agreement includes the provision in the House bill.

[¶ 10,140] Act Sec. 233. S corporation reform and simplification: Expansion of bank S corporation eligible shareholders to include IRAs

House Committee Report (H.R. REP. NO. 108-548, pt. 1)

[Code Secs. 1361, 1362, 1363, 1366, 1367, 1368, 1371, 1372, 1373, 1374, 1375, 1377, 1378, 1379 and 4975]

Overview

In general, an S corporation is not subject to corporate-level income tax on its items of income and loss. Instead, an S corporation passes through its items of income and loss to its shareholders. The shareholders take into account separately their shares of these items on their individual income tax returns. To prevent double taxation of these items when the stock is later disposed of, each shareholder's basis in the stock of the S corporation is increased by the amount included in income (including tax-exempt income) and is decreased by the amount of any losses (including nondeductible losses) taken into account. A shareholder's loss may be deducted only to the extent of his or her basis in the stock or debt of the S corporation. To the extent a loss is not allowed due to this limitation, the loss generally is carried forward with respect to the shareholder.

Present Law

An individual retirement account ("IRA") is a trust or account established for the exclusive benefit of an individual and his or her beneficiaries. There are two general types of IRAs: traditional IRAs, to which both deductible and nondeductible contributions may be made, and Roth IRAs, contributions to which are not deductible. Amounts held in a traditional IRA are includible in income when withdrawn (except to the extent the withdrawal is a return of nondeductible contributions). Amounts held in a Roth IRA that are withdrawn as a qualified distribution are not includible in income; distributions from a Roth IRA that are not qualified distributions are includible in income to the extent attributable to earnings. A qualified distribution is a

distribution that (1) is made after the five-taxable year period beginning with the first taxable year for which the individual made a contribution to a Roth IRA, and (2) is made after attainment of age 59½, on account of death or disability, or is made for first-time homebuyer expenses of up to $10,000.

Under present law, an IRA cannot be a shareholder of an S corporation.

Certain transactions are prohibited between an IRA and the individual for whose benefit the IRA is established, including a sale of property by the IRA to the individual. If a prohibited transaction occurs between an IRA and the IRA beneficiary, the account ceases to be an IRA, and an amount equal to the fair market value of the assets held in the IRA is deemed distributed to the beneficiary.

Reasons for Change

The bill contains a number of general provisions relating to S corporations. The Committee adopted these provisions that modernize the S corporation rules and eliminate undue restrictions on S corporations in order to expand the application of the S corporation provisions so that more corporations and their shareholders will be able to enjoy the benefits of subchapter S status.

The Committee is aware of obstacles that have prevented banks from electing subchapter S status.[31] The bill contains provisions that apply specifically to banks in order to remove these obstacles and make S corporation status more readily available to banks.

* * *

Explanation of Provision

The bill allows an IRA (including a Roth IRA) to be a shareholder of a bank that is an S

---

[31] See, for example, GAO/GGD-00-159, Banking Taxation, Implications of Proposed Revisions Governing S-Corporations on Community Banks (June 23, 2000).

corporation, but only to the extent of bank stock held by the IRA on the date of enactment of the provision.[33]

The bill also provides an exemption from prohibited transaction treatment for the sale by an IRA to the IRA beneficiary of bank stock held by the IRA on the date of enactment of the provision. Under the bill, a sale is not a prohibited transaction if: (1) the sale is pursuant to an S corporation election by the bank; (2) the sale is for fair market value (as established by an inde-

pendent appraiser) and is on terms at least as favorable to the IRA as the terms would be on a sale to an unrelated party; (3) the IRA incurs no commissions, costs, or other expenses in connection with the sale; and (4) the stock is sold in a single transaction for cash not later than 120 days after the S corporation election is made.

Effective Date

The provision takes effect on the date of enactment of the bill.

Conference Committee Report (H.R. CONF. REP. NO. 108-755)

Senate Amendment

No provision.

Conference Agreement

The conference agreement includes the provision in the House bill.

[Law at ¶ 5410, ¶ 5890 and ¶ 6100. CCH Explanation at ¶ 940.]

[¶ 10,150] Act Sec. 234. S corporation reform and simplification: Disregard of unexercised powers of appointment in determining potential current beneficiaries of ESBT

House Committee Report (H.R. REP. NO. 108-548, pt. 1)

[Code Secs. 1361, 1362, 1363, 1366, 1367, 1368, 1371, 1372, 1373, 1374, 1375, 1377, 1378, 1379 and 4975]

Overview

In general, an S corporation is not subject to corporate-level income tax on its items of income and loss. Instead, an S corporation passes through its items of income and loss to its shareholders. The shareholders take into account separately their shares of these items on their individual income tax returns. To prevent double taxation of these items when the stock is later disposed of, each shareholder's basis in the stock of the S corporation is increased by the amount included in income (including tax-exempt income) and is decreased by the amount of any losses (including nondeductible losses) taken into account. A shareholder's loss may be deducted only to the extent of his or her basis in the stock or debt of the S corporation. To the extent a loss is not allowed due to this limitation, the loss generally is carried forward with respect to the shareholder.

Present Law

An electing small business trust ("ESBT") holding stock in an S corporation is taxed at the

maximum individual tax rate on its ratable share of items of income, deduction, gain, or loss passing through from the S corporation. An ESBT generally is an electing trust all of whose beneficiaries are eligible S corporation shareholders. For purposes of determining the maximum number of shareholders, each person who is entitled to receive a distribution from the trust ("potential current beneficiary") is treated as a shareholder during the period the person may receive a distribution from the trust.

An ESBT has 60 days to dispose of the S corporation stock after an ineligible shareholder becomes a potential current beneficiary to avoid disqualification.

Reasons for Change

The bill contains a number of general provisions relating to S corporations. The Committee adopted these provisions that modernize the S corporation rules and eliminate undue restrictions on S corporations in order to expand the application of the S corporation provisions so that more corporations and their shareholders will be able to enjoy the benefits of subchapter S status.

* * *

---

[33] Under the bill, the present-law rules treating S corporation stock held by a qualified retirement plan (other than an employee stock ownership plan) or a charity as an interest

in an unrelated trade or business apply to an IRA holding S corporation stock of a bank.

Explanation of Provision

Under the bill, powers of appointment to the extent not exercised are disregarded in determining the potential current beneficiaries of an electing small business trust.

The bill increases the period during which an ESBT can dispose of S corporation stock, after an ineligible shareholder becomes a potential current beneficiary, from 60 days to one year.

Effective Date

The provision applies to taxable years beginning after December 31, 2004.

Conference Committee Report (H.R. CONF. REP. NO. 108-755)

Senate Amendment

No provision.

Conference Agreement

The conference agreement includes the provision in the House bill.

[Law at ¶ 5890. CCH Explanation at ¶ 930.]

[¶ 10,160] Act Sec. 235. S corporation reform and simplification: Transfers of suspended losses incident to divorce, etc.

House Committee Report (H.R. REP. NO. 108-548, pt. 1)

[Code Secs. 1361, 1362, 1363, 1366, 1367, 1368, 1371, 1372, 1373, 1374, 1375, 1377, 1378, 1379 and 4975]

Overview

In general, an S corporation is not subject to corporate-level income tax on its items of income and loss. Instead, an S corporation passes through its items of income and loss to its shareholders. The shareholders take into account separately their shares of these items on their individual income tax returns. To prevent double taxation of these items when the stock is later disposed of, each shareholder's basis in the stock of the S corporation is increased by the amount included in income (including tax-exempt income) and is decreased by the amount of any losses (including nondeductible losses) taken into account. A shareholder's loss may be deducted only to the extent of his or her basis in the stock or debt of the S corporation. To the extent a loss is not allowed due to this limitation, the loss generally is carried forward with respect to the shareholder.

Present Law

Under present law, any loss or deduction that is not allowed to a shareholder of an S corporation, because the loss exceeds the shareholder's basis in stock and debt of the corpora-tion, is treated as incurred by the S corporation with respect to that shareholder in the subsequent taxable year.

Reasons for Change

The bill contains a number of general provisions relating to S corporations. The Committee adopted these provisions that modernize the S corporation rules and eliminate undue restrictions on S corporations in order to expand the application of the S corporation provisions so that more corporations and their shareholders will be able to enjoy the benefits of subchapter S status.

* * *

Explanation of Provision

Under the bill, if a shareholder's stock in an S corporation is transferred to a spouse, or to a former spouse incident to a divorce, any suspended loss or deduction with respect to that stock is treated as incurred by the corporation with respect to the transferee in the subsequent taxable year.

Effective Date

The provision applies to taxable years beginning after December 31, 2004.

Conference Committee Report (H.R. CONF. REP. NO. 108-755)

Senate Amendment

No provision.

Conference Agreement

The conference agreement includes the provision in the House bill.

[Law at ¶ 5900. CCH Explanation at ¶ 915.]

[¶ 10,170] Act Sec. 236. S corporation reform and simplification: Use of passive activity loss and at-risk amounts by qualified subchapter S trust income beneficiaries

House Committee Report (H.R. Rep. No. 108-548, pt. 1)

[Code Secs. 1361, 1362, 1363, 1366, 1367, 1368, 1371, 1372, 1373, 1374, 1375, 1377, 1378, 1379 and 4975]

Overview

In general, an S corporation is not subject to corporate-level income tax on its items of income and loss. Instead, an S corporation passes through its items of income and loss to its shareholders. The shareholders take into account separately their shares of these items on their individual income tax returns. To prevent double taxation of these items when the stock is later disposed of, each shareholder's basis in the stock of the S corporation is increased by the amount included in income (including tax-exempt income) and is decreased by the amount of any losses (including nondeductible losses) taken into account. A shareholder's loss may be deducted only to the extent of his or her basis in the stock or debt of the S corporation. To the extent a loss is not allowed due to this limitation, the loss generally is carried forward with respect to the shareholder.

Present Law

Under present law, the share of income of an S corporation whose stock is held by a qualified subchapter S trust ("QSST"), with respect to which the beneficiary makes an election, is taxed to the beneficiary. However, the trust, and not the beneficiary, is treated as the owner of the S corporation stock for purposes of determining the tax consequences of the disposition of the S corporation stock by the trust. A QSST generally is a trust with one individual income beneficiary for the life of the beneficiary.

Reasons for Change

The bill contains a number of general provisions relating to S corporations. The Committee adopted these provisions that modernize the S corporation rules and eliminate undue restrictions on S corporations in order to expand the application of the S corporation provisions so that more corporations and their shareholders will be able to enjoy the benefits of subchapter S status.

* * *

Explanation of Provision

Under the bill, the beneficiary of a qualified subchapter S trust is generally allowed to deduct suspended losses under the at-risk rules and the passive loss rules when the trust disposes of the S corporation stock.

Effective Date

The provision applies to transfers made after December 31, 2004.

Conference Committee Report (H.R. Conf. Rep. No. 108-755)

Senate Amendment

No provision.

Conference Agreement

The conference agreement includes the provision in the House bill.

[Law at ¶ 5890. CCH Explanation at ¶ 925.]

[¶ 10,180] Act Sec. 237. S corporation reform and simplification: Exclusion of investment securities income from passive investment income test for bank S corporations

House Committee Report (H.R. REP. NO. 108-548, pt. 1)

[Code Secs. 1361, 1362, 1363, 1366, 1367, 1368, 1371, 1372, 1373, 1374, 1375, 1377, 1378, 1379 and 4975]

Overview

In general, an S corporation is not subject to corporate-level income tax on its items of income and loss. Instead, an S corporation passes through its items of income and loss to its shareholders. The shareholders take into account separately their shares of these items on their individual income tax returns. To prevent double taxation of these items when the stock is later disposed of, each shareholder's basis in the stock of the S corporation is increased by the amount included in income (including tax-exempt income) and is decreased by the amount of any losses (including nondeductible losses) taken into account. A shareholder's loss may be deducted only to the extent of his or her basis in the stock or debt of the S corporation. To the extent a loss is not allowed due to this limitation, the loss generally is carried forward with respect to the shareholder.

Present Law

An S corporation is subject to corporate-level tax, at the highest corporate tax rate, on its excess net passive income if the corporation has (1) accumulated earnings and profits at the close of the taxable year and (2) gross receipts more than 25 percent of which are passive investment income.

Excess net passive income is the net passive income for a taxable year multiplied by a fraction, the numerator of which is the amount of passive investment income in excess of 25 percent of gross receipts and the denominator of which is the passive investment income for the year. Net passive income is defined as passive investment income reduced by the allowable deductions that are directly connected with the production of that income. Passive investment income generally means gross receipts derived from royalties, rents, dividends, interest, annuities, and sales or exchanges of stock or securities

(to the extent of gains). Passive investment income generally does not include interest on accounts receivable, gross receipts that are derived directly from the active and regular conduct of a lending or finance business, gross receipts from certain liquidations, or gain or loss from any section 1256 contract (or related property) of an options or commodities dealer.[34]

In addition, an S corporation election is terminated whenever the S corporation has accumulated earnings and profits at the close of each of three consecutive taxable years and has gross receipts for each of those years more than 25 percent of which are passive investment income.

Reasons for Change

The bill contains a number of general provisions relating to S corporations. The Committee adopted these provisions that modernize the S corporation rules and eliminate undue restrictions on S corporations in order to expand the application of the S corporation provisions so that more corporations and their shareholders will be able to enjoy the benefits of subchapter S status.

The Committee is aware of obstacles that have prevented banks from electing subchapter S status.[31] The bill contains provisions that apply specifically to banks in order to remove these obstacles and make S corporation status more readily available to banks.

* * *

Explanation of Provision

The bill provides that, in the case of a bank (as defined in section 581), a bank holding company (as defined in section 2(a) of the Bank Holding Company Act of 1956), or a financial holding company (as defined in section 2(p) of that Act), interest income and dividends on assets required to be held by the bank or holding company are not treated as passive investment income for purposes of the S corporation passive investment income rules.

---

[34] Notice 97-5, 1997-1 C.B. 352, sets forth guidance relating to passive investment income on banking assets.

[31] See, for example, GAO/GGD-00-159, Banking Taxation, Implications of Proposed Revisions Governing S-Corporations on Community Banks (June 23, 2000).

Effective Date

The provision applies to taxable years beginning after December 31, 2004.

Conference Committee Report (H.R. Conf. Rep. No. 108-755)

Senate Amendment

[Law at ¶ 5895. CCH Explanation at ¶ 945.]

No provision.

Conference Agreement

The conference agreement includes the provision in the House bill.

[¶ 10,190] Act Sec. 238. S corporation reform and simplification: Relief from inadvertently invalid qualified subchapter S subsidiary elections and terminations

House Committee Report (H.R. Rep. No. 108-548, pt. 1)

[Code Secs. 1361, 1362, 1363, 1366, 1367, 1368, 1371, 1372, 1373, 1374, 1375, 1377, 1378, 1379 and 4975]

Overview

In general, an S corporation is not subject to corporate-level income tax on its items of income and loss. Instead, an S corporation passes through its items of income and loss to its shareholders. The shareholders take into account separately their shares of these items on their individual income tax returns. To prevent double taxation of these items when the stock is later disposed of, each shareholder's basis in the stock of the S corporation is increased by the amount included in income (including tax-exempt income) and is decreased by the amount of any losses (including nondeductible losses) taken into account. A shareholder's loss may be deducted only to the extent of his or her basis in the stock or debt of the S corporation. To the extent a loss is not allowed due to this limitation, the loss generally is carried forward with respect to the shareholder.

Present Law

Under present law, inadvertent invalid subchapter S elections and terminations may be waived.

Reasons for Change

The bill contains a number of general provisions relating to S corporations. The Committee adopted these provisions that modernize the S corporation rules and eliminate undue restrictions on S corporations in order to expand the application of the S corporation provisions so that more corporations and their shareholders will be able to enjoy the benefits of subchapter S status.

* * *

Explanation of Provision

The bill allows inadvertent invalid qualified subchapter S subsidiary elections and terminations to be waived by the IRS.

Conference Committee Report (H.R. Conf. Rep. No. 108-755)

Senate Amendment

[Law at ¶ 5895. CCH Explanation at ¶ 920.]

No provision.

Conference Agreement

The conference agreement includes the provision in the House bill, effective for elections and terminations after December 31, 2004.

[¶ 10,200] Act Sec. 239. S corporation reform and simplification: Information returns for qualified subchapter S subsidiaries

House Committee Report (H.R. REP. NO. 108-548, pt. 1)

[Code Secs. 1361, 1362, 1363, 1366, 1367, 1368, 1371, 1372, 1373, 1374, 1375, 1377, 1378, 1379 and 4975]

Overview

In general, an S corporation is not subject to corporate-level income tax on its items of income and loss. Instead, an S corporation passes through its items of income and loss to its shareholders. The shareholders take into account separately their shares of these items on their individual income tax returns. To prevent double taxation of these items when the stock is later disposed of, each shareholder's basis in the stock of the S corporation is increased by the amount included in income (including tax-exempt income) and is decreased by the amount of any losses (including nondeductible losses) taken into account. A shareholder's loss may be deducted only to the extent of his or her basis in the stock or debt of the S corporation. To the extent a loss is not allowed due to this limitation, the loss generally is carried forward with respect to the shareholder.

Present Law

Under present law, a corporation all of whose stock is held by an S corporation is treated as a qualified subchapter S subsidiary if the S corporation so elects. The assets, liabilities, and items of income, deduction, and credit of the subsidiary are treated as assets, liabilities, and items of income of the parent S corporation.

Reasons for Change

The bill contains a number of general provisions relating to S corporations. The Committee adopted these provisions that modernize the S corporation rules and eliminate undue restrictions on S corporations in order to expand the application of the S corporation provisions so that more corporations and their shareholders will be able to enjoy the benefits of subchapter S status.

* * *

Explanation of Provision

The bill provides authority to the Secretary to provide guidance regarding information returns of qualified subchapter S subsidiaries.

Effective Date

The provision applies to taxable years beginning after December 31, 2004.

Conference Committee Report (H.R. CONF. REP. NO. 108-755)

Senate Amendment

No provision.

Conference Agreement

The conference agreement includes the provision in the House bill.

[Law at ¶ 5890. CCH Explanation at ¶ 950.]

[¶ 10,210] Act Sec. 240. S corporation reform and simplification: Repayment of loans for qualifying employer securities

House Committee Report (H.R. REP. NO. 108-548, pt. 1)

[Code Secs. 1361, 1362, 1363, 1366, 1367, 1368, 1371, 1372, 1373, 1374, 1375, 1377, 1378, 1379 and 4975]

Overview

In general, an S corporation is not subject to corporate-level income tax on its items of income and loss. Instead, an S corporation passes through its items of income and loss to its shareholders. The shareholders take into account sep-

arately their shares of these items on their individual income tax returns. To prevent double taxation of these items when the stock is later disposed of, each shareholder's basis in the stock of the S corporation is increased by the amount included in income (including tax-exempt income) and is decreased by the amount of any losses (including nondeductible losses) taken into account. A shareholder's loss may be deducted only to the extent of his or her basis in the stock or debt of the S corporation. To the extent a loss is not allowed due to this limitation, the loss generally is carried forward with respect to the shareholder.

Present Law

An employee stock ownership plan (an "ESOP") is a defined contribution plan that is designated as an ESOP and is designed to invest primarily in qualifying employer securities. For purposes of ESOP investments, a "qualifying employer security" is defined as: (1) publicly traded common stock of the employer or a member of the same controlled group; (2) if there is no such publicly traded common stock, common stock of the employer (or member of the same controlled group) that has both voting power and dividend rights at least as great as any other class of common stock; or (3) noncallable preferred stock that is convertible into common stock described in (1) or (2) and that meets certain requirements. In some cases, an employer may design a class of preferred stock that meets these requirements and that is held only by the ESOP. Special rules apply to ESOPs that do not apply to other types of qualified retirement plans, including a special exemption from the prohibited transaction rules.

Certain transactions between an employee benefit plan and a disqualified person, including the employer maintaining the plan, are prohibited transactions that result in the imposition of an excise tax.[40] Prohibited transactions include, among other transactions, (1) the sale, exchange or leasing of property between a plan and a disqualified person, (2) the lending of money or other extension of credit between a plan and a disqualified person, and (3) the transfer to, or use by or for the benefit of, a disqualified person of the income or assets of the plan. However, certain transactions are exempt from prohibited transaction treatment, including certain loans to enable an ESOP to purchase qualifying employer securities.[41] In such a case, the employer securities purchased with the loan proceeds are generally pledged as security for the loan. Contributions to the ESOP and dividends paid on employer securities held by the ESOP are used to repay the loan. The employer securities are held in a suspense account and released for allocation to participants' accounts as the loan is repaid.

A loan to an ESOP is exempt from prohibited transaction treatment if the loan is primarily for the benefit of the participants and their bene-

ficiaries, the loan is at a reasonable rate of interest, and the collateral given to a disqualified person consists of only qualifying employer securities. No person entitled to payments under the loan can have the right to any assets of the ESOP other than (1) collateral given for the loan, (2) contributions made to the ESOP to meet its obligations on the loan, and (3) earnings attributable to the collateral and the investment of contributions described in (2).[42] In addition, the payments made on the loan by the ESOP during a plan year cannot exceed the sum of those contributions and earnings during the current and prior years, less loan payments made in prior years.

An ESOP of a C corporation is not treated as violating the qualification requirements of the Code or as engaging in a prohibited transaction merely because, in accordance with plan provisions, a dividend paid with respect to qualifying employer securities held by the ESOP is used to make payments on a loan (including payments of interest as well as principal) that was used to acquire the employer securities (whether or not allocated to participants).[43] In the case of a dividend paid with respect to any employer security that is allocated to a participant, this relief does not apply unless the plan provides that employer securities with a fair market value of not less than the amount of the dividend is allocated to the participant for the year which the dividend would have been allocated to the participant.[44]

Reasons for Change

The bill contains a number of general provisions relating to S corporations. The Committee adopted these provisions that modernize the S corporation rules and eliminate undue restrictions on S corporations in order to expand the application of the S corporation provisions so that more corporations and their shareholders will be able to enjoy the benefits of subchapter S status.

* * *

The bill also revises the prohibited transaction rules applicable to employee stock ownership plans ("ESOPs") maintained by S corporations in order to expand the ability to use distributions made with respect to S corporation stock held by an ESOP to repay a loan used to purchase the stock, subject to the same conditions that apply to C corporation dividends used to repay such a loan.

---

[40] Sec. 4975.

[41] Sec. 4975(d)(3). An ESOP that borrows money to purchase employer stock is referred to as a "leveraged" ESOP.

[42] Treas. Reg. sec. 54.4975-7(b)(5).

[43] Sec. 404(k)(5)(B).

[44] Sec. 404(k)(2)(B).

Explanation of Provision

Under the provision, an ESOP maintained by an S corporation is not treated as violating the qualification requirements of the Code or as engaging in a prohibited transaction merely because, in accordance with plan provisions, a distribution made with respect to S corporation stock that constitutes qualifying employer securities held by the ESOP is used to repay a loan that was used to acquire the securities (whether or not allocated to participants). This relief does not apply in the case of a distribution with re-spect to S corporation stock that is allocated to a participant unless the plan provides that stock with a fair market value of not less than the amount of such distribution is allocated to the participant for the year which the distribution would have been allocated to the participant.

Effective Date

The provision is effective for distributions made with respect to S corporation stock after December 31, 2004.

Conference Committee Report (H.R. CONF. REP. NO. 108-755)

Present Law

* * *

Effective for taxable years beginning after December 31, 1997, a qualified retirement plan (including an ESOP) may be a shareholder of an S corporation.[75] As a result, an S corporation may maintain an ESOP.

Senate Amendment

The Senate amendment is the same as House bill (other than the effective date).

* * *

Conference Agreement

The conference agreement contains the pro-vision in the House bill and Senate amendment, with a modification of the effective date. Thus, an ESOP maintained by an S corporation is not treated as violating the qualification require-ments of the Code or as engaging in a prohibited transaction merely because, in accordance with plan provisions, a distribution made with respect to S corporation stock that constitutes qualifying employer securities held by the ESOP is used to make payments on a loan (including payments of interest as well as principal) that was used to acquire the securities (whether or not allocated to participants). This relief does not apply in the case of a distribution with respect to S corpora-tion stock that is allocated to a participant unless the plan provides that stock with a fair market value of not less than the amount of such distri-bution is allocated to the participant for the year which the distribution would have been allo-cated to the participant.

Effective Date

The provision is effective for distributions made with respect to S corporation stock after December 31, 1997.

[Law at ¶ 5890 and ¶ 6100. CCH Explanation at ¶ 935.]

[¶ 10,220] Act Sec. 241. Repeal certain excise taxes on rail diesel fuel and inland waterway barge fuels

Conference Committee Report (H.R. CONF. REP. NO. 108-755)

[Code Secs. 4041, 4042, 6421 and 6427]

Present Law

Under present law, diesel fuel used in trains is subject to a 4.4-cents-per gallon excise tax. Revenues from 4.3 cents per gallon of this excise tax are retained in the General Fund of the Trea-sury. The remaining 0.1 cent per gallon is depos-ited in the Leaking Underground Storage Tank ("LUST") Trust Fund.

Similarly, fuels used in barges operating on the designated inland waterways system are subject to a 4.3-cents-per-gallon General Fund excise tax. This tax is in addition to the 20.1-cents-per-gallon tax rates that are imposed on fuels used in these barges to fund the Inland Waterways Trust Fund and the Leaking Under-ground Storage Tank Trust Fund.

In both cases, the 4.3-cents-per-gallon excise tax rates are permanent. The LUST Trust Fund tax is scheduled to expire after March 31, 2005.

House Bill

No provision.

Senate Amendment

The 4.3-cents-per-gallon General Fund ex-cise tax rate on diesel fuel used in trains and

---

[75] Sec. 1361(c)(6).

fuels used in barges operating on the designated inland waterways system is repealed. The 0.1 cent per gallon tax for the LUST Trust Fund is unchanged by the provision.

Conference Agreement

The conference agreement repeals the 4.3-cents-per-gallon General Fund excise tax rates on diesel fuel used in trains and fuels used in barges operating on the designated inland waterways system over a prescribed phase-out period. The 4.3-cent-per-gallon tax is reduced by 1 cent per gallon for the first six months of

calendar year 2005 (January 1, 2005 through June 30, 2005). The reduction is 2 cents per gallon from July 1, 2005 through December 31, 2006, and 4.3 cents/gallon thereafter. Thus, the tax would be fully repealed effective January 1, 2007. The 0.1 cent per gallon tax for the LUST Trust Fund is unchanged by the provision.

Effective Date

The provision is effective on January 1, 2005.

[Law at ¶ 5980, ¶ 5985, ¶ 6015, ¶ 6210 and ¶ 6220. CCH Explanation at ¶ 1513.]

[¶ 10,230] Act Sec. 242. Modification of application of income forecast method of depreciation

Senate Committee Report (S. REP. NO. 108-192)

[Code Sec. 167(g)]

Income forecast method of depreciation

Present Law

Depreciation

The modified Accelerated Cost Recovery System ("MACRS") does not apply to certain property, including any motion picture film, video tape, or sound recording, or to any other property if the taxpayer elects to exclude such property from MACRS and the taxpayer properly applies a unit-of-production method or other method of depreciation not expressed in a term of years. Section 197 does not apply to certain intangible property, including property produced by the taxpayer or any interest in a film, sound recording, video tape, book or similar property not acquired in a transaction (or a series of related transactions) involving the acquisition of assets constituting a trade or business or substantial portion thereof. Thus, the recovery of the cost of a film, video tape, or similar property that is produced by the taxpayer or is acquired on a "stand-alone" basis by the taxpayer may not be determined under either the MACRS depreciation provisions or under the section 197 amortization provisions. The cost recovery of such property may be determined under section 167, which allows a depreciation deduction for the reasonable allowance for the exhaustion, wear and tear, or obsolescence of the property. A taxpayer is allowed to recover, through annual depreciation deductions, the cost of certain property used in a trade or business or for the production of income. Section 167(g) provides that the cost of motion picture films, sound recordings, copyrights, books, and patents are eligible to be recovered using the income forecast method of depreciation.

Under the income forecast method, a property's depreciation deduction for a taxable year is determined by multiplying the adjusted basis of the property by a fraction, the numerator of which is the income generated by the property during the year and the denominator of which is the total forecasted or estimated income expected to be generated prior to the close of the tenth taxable year after the year the property was placed in service. Any costs that are not recovered by the end of the tenth taxable year after the property was placed in service may be taken into account as depreciation in such year.

The adjusted basis of property that may be taken into account under the income forecast method only includes amounts that satisfy the economic performance standard of section 461(h). In addition, taxpayers that claim depreciation deductions under the income forecast method are required to pay (or receive) interest based on a recalculation of depreciation under a "look-back" method.

The "look-back" method is applied in any "recomputation year" by: (1) comparing depreciation deductions that had been claimed in prior periods to depreciation deductions that would have been claimed had the taxpayer used actual, rather than estimated, total income from the property; (2) determining the hypothetical overpayment or underpayment of tax based on this recalculated depreciation; and (3) applying the overpayment rate of section 6621 of the Code. Except as provided in Treasury regulations, a "recomputation year" is the third and tenth taxable year after the taxable year the property was placed in service, unless the actual income from the property for each taxable year ending with or

Act Sec. 242   ¶10,230

before the close of such years was within 10-percent of the estimated income from the property for such years.

Reasons for Change

The Committee is aware that taxpayers and the IRS have expended significant resources in auditing and litigating disputes regarding the proper treatment of participations and residuals for purposes of computing depreciation under the income forecast method of depreciation. The Committee understands that these issues relate solely to the timing of deductions and not to whether such costs are valid deductions. In addition, the Committee is aware of other disagreements between taxpayers and the Treasury Department regarding the mechanics of the income forecast formula. The Committee believes expending taxpayer and government resources disputing these items is an unproductive use of economic resources. As such, the provision addresses the issues and eliminates any uncertainty as to the proper tax treatment of these items.

Explanation of Provision

The provision clarifies that, solely for purposes of computing the allowable deduction for property under the income forecast method of depreciation, participations and residuals may be included in the adjusted basis of the property beginning in the year such property is placed in service, but only if such participations and residuals relate to income to be derived from the property before the close of the tenth taxable year following the year the property is placed in service (as defined in section 167(g)(1)(A)). For purposes of the provision, participations and residuals are defined as costs the amount of which, by contract, varies with the amount of income earned in connection with such property. The provision also clarifies that the income from the property to be taken into account under the income forecast method is the gross income from such property.

The provision also grants authority to the Treasury Department to prescribe appropriate adjustments to the basis of property (and the look-back method) to reflect the treatment of participations and residuals under the provision.

In addition, the provision clarifies that, in the case of property eligible for the income forecast method that the holding in the *Associated Patentees*[98] decision will continue to constitute a valid method. Thus, rather than accounting for participations and residuals as a cost of the property under the income forecast method of depreciation, the taxpayer may deduct those payments as they are paid as under the *Associated Patentees* decision. This may be done on a property-by-property basis and shall be applied consistently with respect to a given property thereafter. The provision also clarifies that distribution costs are not taken into account for purposes of determining the taxpayer's current and total forecasted income with respect to a property.

Effective Date

The provision applies to property placed in service after date of enactment. No inference is intended as to the appropriate treatment under present law. It is intended that the Treasury Department and the IRS expedite the resolution of open cases. In resolving these cases in an expedited and balanced manner, the Treasury Department and IRS are encouraged to take into account the principles of the provision.

Conference Committee Report (H.R. CONF. REP. NO. 108-755)

House Bill

No provision.

Conference Agreement

The conference agreement follows the Senate amendment.

[Law at ¶ 5175. CCH Explanation at ¶ 320.]

---

[98] *Associated Patentees, Inc.* v. *Commissioner,* 4 T.C. 979 (1945).

[¶ 10,240] Act Sec. 243. Improvements related to real estate investment trusts

House Committee Report (H.R. REP. NO. 108-548, pt. 1)

[Code Secs. 856, 857 and 860]

Present Law

In general

Real estate investment trusts ("REITs") are treated, in substance, as pass-through entities under present law. Pass-through status is achieved by allowing the REIT a deduction for dividends paid to its shareholders. REITs are generally restricted to investing in passive investments primarily in real estate and securities.

A REIT must satisfy four tests on a year-by-year basis: organizational structure, source of income, nature of assets, and distribution of income. Whether the REIT meets the asset tests is generally measured each quarter.

Organizational structure requirements

To qualify as a REIT, an entity must be for its entire taxable year a corporation or an unincorporated trust or association that would be taxable as a domestic corporation but for the REIT provisions, and must be managed by one or more trustees. The beneficial ownership of the entity must be evidenced by transferable shares or certificates of ownership. Except for the first taxable year for which an entity elects to be a REIT, the beneficial ownership of the entity must be held by 100 or more persons, and the entity may not be so closely held by individuals that it would be treated as a personal holding company if all its adjusted gross income constituted personal holding company income. A REIT is required to comply with regulations to ascertain the actual ownership of the REIT's outstanding shares.

Income requirements

In order for an entity to qualify as a REIT, at least 95 percent of its gross income generally must be derived from certain passive sources (the "95-percent income test"). In addition, at least 75 percent of its income generally must be

derived from certain real estate sources (the "75-percent income test"), including rents from real property (as defined) and gain from the sale or other disposition of real property.

Qualified rental income

Amounts received as impermissible "tenant services income" are not treated as rents from real property.[72] In general, such amounts are for services rendered to tenants that are not "customarily furnished" in connection with the rental of real property.[73] Special rules also permit amounts to be received from certain "foreclosure property" treated as such for three years after the property is acquired by the REIT in foreclosure after a default (or imminent default) on a lease of such property or an indebtedness which such property secured.

Rents from real property, for purposes of the 95-percent and 75-percent income tests, generally do not include any amount received or accrued from any person in which the REIT owns, directly or indirectly, 10 percent or more of the vote or value.[74] An exception applies to rents received from a taxable REIT subsidiary ("TRS") (described further below) if at least 90 percent of the leased space of the property is rented to persons other than a TRS or certain related persons, and if the rents from the TRS are substantially comparable to unrelated party rents.[75]

Certain hedging instruments

Except as provided in regulations, a payment to a REIT under an interest rate swap or cap agreement, option, futures contract, forward rate agreement, or any similar financial instrument, entered into by the trust in a transaction to reduce the interest rate risks with respect to any indebtedness incurred or to be incurred by the REIT to acquire or carry real estate assets, and any gain from the sale or disposition of any such

---

[72] A REIT is not treated as providing services that produce impermissible tenant services income if such services are provided by an independent contractor from whom the REIT does not derive or receive any income. An independent contractor is defined as a person who does not own, directly or indirectly, more than 35 percent of the shares of the REIT. Also, no more than 35 percent of the total shares of stock of an independent contractor (or of the interests in net assets or net profits, if not a corporation) can be owned directly or indirectly by persons owning 35 percent or more of the interests in the REIT.

[73] Rents for certain personal property leased in connection with the rental of real property are treated as rents from real property if the fair market value of the personal property does not exceed 15 percent of the aggregate fair market values of the real and personal property.

[74] Sec. 856(d)(2)(B).

[75] Sec. 856(d)(8).

investment, is treated as income qualifying for the 95-percent income test.

Tax if qualified income tests not met

If a REIT fails to meet the 95-percent or 75-percent income tests but has set out the income it did receive in a schedule and any error in the schedule is due to reasonable cause and not willful neglect, then the REIT does not lose its REIT status but instead pays a tax measured by the greater of the amount by which 90 percent[76] of the REIT's gross income exceeds the amount of items subject to the 95-percent test, or the amount by which 75 percent of the REIT's gross income exceeds the amount of items subject to the 75-percent test.[77]

Asset requirements

75-percent asset test

To satisfy the asset requirements to qualify for treatment as a REIT, at the close of each quarter of its taxable year, an entity must have at least 75 percent of the value of its assets invested in real estate assets, cash and cash items, and government securities (the "75-percent asset test"). The term real estate asset is defined to mean real property (including interests in real property and mortgages on real property) and interests in REITs.

Limitation on investment in other entities

A REIT is limited in the amount that it can own in other corporations. Specifically, a REIT cannot own securities (other than Government securities and certain real estate assets) in an amount greater than 25 percent of the value of REIT assets. In addition, it cannot own such securities of any one issuer representing more than 5 percent of the total value of REIT assets or more than 10 percent of the voting securities or 10 percent of the value of the outstanding securities of any one issuer. Securities for purposes of these rules are defined by reference to the Investment Company Act of 1940.

"Straight debt" exception

Securities of an issuer that are within a safe-harbor definition of "straight debt" (as defined for purposes of subchapter S)[78] are not taken into account in applying the limitation that a REIT may not hold more than 10 percent of the value of outstanding securities of a single issuer, if: (1) the issuer is an individual, (2) the only securities of such issuer held by the REIT or a taxable REIT subsidiary of the REIT are straight debt, or (3) the issuer is a partnership and the trust holds at least a 20 percent profits interest in the partnership.

Straight debt for purposes of the REIT provision[79] is defined as a written or unconditional promise to pay on demand or on a specified date a sum certain in money if (i) the interest rate (and interest payment dates) are not contingent on profits, the borrower's discretion, or similar factors, and (ii) there is no convertibility (directly or indirectly) into stock.

Certain subsidiary ownership permitted with income treated as income of the REIT

Under one exception to the rule limiting a REIT's securities holdings to no more than 10 percent of the vote or value of a single issuer, a REIT can own 100 percent of the stock of a corporation, but in that case the income and assets of such corporation are treated as income and assets of the REIT.

Special rules for Taxable REIT subsidiaries

Under another exception to the general rule limiting REIT securities ownership of other entities, a REIT can own stock of a taxable REIT subsidiary ("TRS"), generally, a corporation other than a real estate investment trust[80] with which the REIT makes a joint election to be subject to special rules. A TRS can engage in active business operations that would produce income that would not be qualified income for purposes of the 95-percent or 75-percent income tests for a REIT, and that income is not attributed to the REIT. For example a TRS could provide noncustomary services to REIT tenants, or it could engage directly in the active operation and management of real estate (without use of an independent contractor); and the income the TRS derived from these nonqualified activities would not be treated as disqualified REIT income. Transactions between a TRS and a REIT are subject to a number of specified rules that are intended to prevent the TRS (taxable as a separate corporate entity) from shifting taxable income

---

[76] Prior to 1999, the rule had applied to the amount by which 95 percent of the income exceeded the items subject to the 95 percent test.

[77] The ratio of the REIT's net to gross income is applied to the excess amount, to determine the amount of tax (disregarding certain items otherwise subject to a 100-percent tax). In effect, the formula seeks to require that all of the REIT net income attributable to the failure of the income tests will be paid as tax. Sec. 857(b)(5).

[78] Sec. 1361(c)(5), without regard to paragraph (B)(iii) thereof.

[79] Sec. 856(c)(7).

[80] Certain corporations are not eligible to be a TRS, such as a corporation which directly or indirectly operates or manages a lodging facility or a health care facility, or directly or indirectly provides to any other person rights to a brand name under which any lodging facility or health care facility is operated. Sec. 856(l)(3).

from its activities to the pass-through entity REIT or from absorbing more than its share of expenses. Under one rule, a 100-percent excise tax is imposed on rents, deductions, or interest paid by the TRS to the REIT to the extent such items would exceed an arm's length amount as determined under section 482.[81]

Rents subject to the 100 percent excise tax do not include rents for services of a TRS that are for services customarily furnished or rendered in connection with the rental of real property.

They also do not include rents from a TRS that are for real property or from incidental personal property provided with such real property.

Income distribution requirements

A REIT is generally required to distribute 90 percent of its income before the end of its taxable year, as deductible dividends paid to shareholders. This rule is similar to a rule for regulated investment companies ("RICs") that requires distribution of 90 percent of income. If a REIT declares certain dividends after the end of its taxable year but before the time prescribed for filing its return for that year and distributes those amounts to shareholders within the 12 months following the close of that taxable year, such distributions are treated as made during such taxable year for this purpose. As described further below, a REIT can also make certain "deficiency dividends" after the close of the taxable year after a determination that it has not distributed the correct amount for qualification as a REIT.

Consequences of failure to meet requirements

A REIT loses its status as a REIT, and becomes subject to tax as a C corporation, if it fails to meet specified tests regarding the sources of its income, the nature and amount of its assets, its structure, and the amount of its income distributed to shareholders.

In the case of a failure to meet the source of income requirements, if the failure is due to reasonable cause and not to willful neglect, the REIT may continue its REIT status if it pays the disallowed income as a tax to the Treasury.[82]

There is no similar provision that allows a REIT to pay a penalty and avoid disqualification in the case of other qualification failures.

A REIT may make a deficiency dividend after a determination is made that it has not distributed the correct amount of its income, and avoid disqualification. The Code provides only for determinations involving a controversy with

the IRS and does not provide for a REIT to make such a distribution on its own initiative. Deficiency dividends may be declared on or after the date of "determination". A determination is defined to include only (i) a final decision by the Tax Court or other court of competent jurisdiction, (ii) a closing agreement under section 7121, or (iii) under Treasury regulations, an agreement signed by the Secretary and the REIT.

Reasons for Change

The Committee believes that a number of simplifying and conforming changes should be made to the "straight debt" provisions that exempt certain securities from the rule that a REIT may not hold more than 10 percent of the value of securities of a single issuer, as well as to the TRS rules, the rules relating to certain hedging arrangements, and the computation of tax liability when the 95-percent gross income test is not met.

The Committee also believes it is desirable to provide rules under which a REIT that inadvertently fails to meet certain REIT qualification requirements can correct such failure without losing REIT status.

Explanation of Provision

The provision makes a number of modifications to the REIT rules.

Straight debt modification

The provision modifies the definition of "straight debt" for purposes of the limitation that a REIT may not hold more than 10 percent of the value of the outstanding securities of a single issuer, to provide more flexibility than the present law rule. In addition, except as provided in regulations, neither such straight debt nor certain other types of securities are considered "securities" for purposes of this rule.

Straight debt securities

As under present law, "straight-debt" is still defined by reference to section 1361(c)(5), without regard to subparagraph (B)(iii) thereof (limiting the nature of the creditor).

Special rules are provided permitting certain contingencies for purposes of the REIT provision. Any interest or principal shall not be treated as failing to satisfy section 1361(c)(5)(B)(i) solely by reason of the fact that the time of payment of such interest or principal is subject to a contingency, but only if one of several factors applies. The first type of contingency that is permitted is one that does not have the effect of changing the effective yield to maturity, as deter-

---

[81] If the excise tax applies, then the item is not reallocated back to the TRS under section 482.

[82] Secs. 856(c)(6) and 857(b)(5).

mined under section 1272, other than a change in the annual yield to maturity, but only if (i) any such contingency does not exceed the greater of $1/4$ of one percent or five percent of the annual yield to maturity, or (ii) neither the aggregate issue price nor the aggregate face amount of the debt instruments held by the REIT exceeds $1,000,000 and not more than 12 months of unaccrued interest can be required to be prepaid thereunder.

Also, the time or amount of any payment is permitted to be subject to a contingency upon a default or the exercise of a prepayment right by the issuer of the debt, provided that such contingency is consistent with customary commercial practice.[83]

The provision eliminates the present law rule requiring a REIT to own a 20 percent equity interest in a partnership in order for debt to qualify as "straight debt". The bill instead provides new "look-through" rules determining a REIT partner's share of partnership securities, generally treating debt to the REIT as part of the REIT's partnership interest for this purpose, except in the case of otherwise qualifying debt of the partnership.

Certain corporate or partnership issues that otherwise would be permitted to be held without limitation under the special straight debt rules described above will not be so permitted if the REIT holding such securities, and any of its taxable REIT subsidiaries, holds any securities of the issuer which are not permitted securities (prior to the application of this rule) and have an aggregate value greater than one percent of the issuer's outstanding securities.

Other securities

Except as provided in regulations, the following also are not considered "securities" for purposes of the rule that a REIT cannot own more than 10 percent of the value of the outstanding securities of a single issuer: (i) any loan to an individual or an estate, (ii) any section 467 rental agreement, (as defined in section 467(d)), other than with a person described in section 856(d)(2)(B), (iii) any obligation to pay rents from real property, (iv) any security issued by a State or any political subdivision thereof, the District of Columbia, a foreign government, or any political subdivision thereof, or the Commonwealth

of Puerto Rico, but only if the determination of any payment received or accrued under such security does not depend in whole or in part on the profits of any entity not described in this category, or payments on any obligation issued by such an entity, (v) any security issued by a real estate investment trust; and (vi) any other arrangement that, as determined by the Secretary, is excepted from the definition of a security.

Safe harbor testing date for certain rents

The provision provides specific safe-harbor rules regarding the dates for testing whether 90 percent of a REIT property is rented to unrelated persons and whether the rents paid by related persons are substantially comparable to unrelated party rents. These testing rules are provided solely for purposes of the special provision permitting rents received from a TRS to be treated as qualified rental income for purposes of the income tests.[84]

Customary services exception

The provision prospectively eliminates the safe harbor allowing rents received by a REIT to be exempt from the 100 percent excise tax if the rents are for customary services performed by the TRS[85] or are from a TRS and are for the provision of certain incidental personal property. Instead, such payments are free of the excise tax if they satisfy the present law safe-harbor that applies if the REIT pays the TRS at least 150 percent of the cost to the TRS of providing any services.

Hedging rules

The rules governing the tax treatment of arrangements engaged in by a REIT to reduce certain interest rate risks are prospectively generally conformed to the rules included in section 1221. Also, the defined income of a REIT from such a hedging transaction is excluded from gross income for purposes of the 95-percent of gross income requirement.

95-percent of gross income requirement

The provision prospectively amends the tax liability owed by the REIT when it fails to meet the 95-percent of gross income test by applying a taxable fraction based on 95 percent, rather than 90 percent, of the REIT's gross income.

---

[83] The present law rules that limit qualified interest income to amounts the determination of which do not depend, in whole or in part, on the income or profits of any person, continue to apply to such contingent interest. See, e.g., secs. 856(c)(2)(G), 856(c)(3)(G) and 856(f).

[84] The provision does not modify any of the standards of section 482 as they apply to REITs and to TRSs.

[85] Although a REIT could itself provide such service and receive the income without receiving any disqualified income, in that case the REIT itself would be bearing the cost of providing the service. Under the present law exception for a TRS providing such service, there is no explicit requirement that the TRS be reimbursed for the full cost of the service.

Consequences of failure to meet REIT requirements

Under the provision, a REIT may avoid disqualification in the event of certain failures of the requirements for REIT status, provided that (1) the failure was due to reasonable cause and not willful neglect, (2) the failure is corrected, and (3) except for certain failures not exceeding a specified de minimis amount, a penalty amount is paid.

Certain de minimis asset failures of 5-percent or 10-percent tests

One requirement of present law is that, with certain exceptions, (i) not more than 5 percent of the value of total REIT assets may be represented by securities of one issuer, and (ii) a REIT may not hold securities possessing more than 10 percent of the total voting power or 10 percent of the total value of the outstanding securities of any one issuer.[86] The requirements must be satisfied each quarter.

The provision provides that a REIT will not lose its REIT status for failing to satisfy these requirements in a quarter if the failure is due to the ownership of assets the total value of which does not exceed the lesser of (i) one percent of the total value of the REIT's assets at the end of the quarter for which such measurement is done or (ii) 10 million dollars; provided in either case that the REIT either disposes of the assets within six months after the last day of the quarter in which the REIT identifies the failure (or such other time period prescribed by the Treasury), or otherwise meets the requirements of those rules by the end of such time period.[87]

Larger asset test failures (whether of 5-percent or 10-percent tests, or of 75-percent or other asset tests)

Under the provision, if a REIT fails to meet any of the asset test requirements for a particular quarter and the failure exceeds the de minimis threshold described above, then the REIT still will be deemed to have satisfied the requirements if: (i) following the REIT's identification of the failure, the REIT files a schedule with a description of each asset that caused the failure, in accordance with regulations prescribed by the Treasury; (ii) the failure was due to reasonable cause and not to willful neglect; (iii) the REIT disposes of the assets within 6 months after the last day of the quarter in which the identification occurred or such other time period as is pre-scribed by the Treasury (or the requirements of the rules are otherwise met within such period), and (iv) the REIT pays a tax on the failure.

The tax that the REIT must pay on the failure is the greater of (i) $50,000, or (ii) an amount determined (pursuant to regulations) by multiplying the highest rate of tax for corporations under section 11, times the net income generated by the assets for the period beginning on the first date of the failure and ending on the date the REIT has disposed of the assets (or otherwise satisfies the requirements).

Such taxes are treated as excise taxes, for which the deficiency provisions of the excise tax subtitle of the Code (subtitle F) apply.

Conforming reasonable cause and reporting standard for failures of income tests

The provision conforms the reporting and reasonable cause standards for failure to meet the income tests to the new asset test standards. However, the provision does not change the rule under section 857(b)(5) that for income test failures, all of the net income attributed to the disqualified gross income is paid as tax.

Other failures

The bill adds a provision under which, if a REIT fails to satisfy one or more requirements for REIT qualification, other than the 95-percent and 75-percent gross income tests and other than the new rules provided for failures of the asset tests, the REIT may retain its REIT qualification if the failures are due to reasonable cause and not willful neglect, and if the REIT pays a penalty of $50,000 for each such failure.

Taxes and penalties paid deducted from amount required to be distributed

Any taxes or penalties paid under the provision are deducted from the net income of the REIT in determining the amount the REIT must distribute under the 90-percent distribution requirement.

Expansion of deficiency dividend procedure

The provision expands the circumstances in which a REIT may declare a deficiency dividend, by allowing such a declaration to occur after the REIT unilaterally has identified a failure to pay the relevant amount. Thus, the declaration need not await a decision of the Tax Court, a closing agreement, or an agreement signed by the Secretary of the Treasury.

---

[86] Sec. 856(c)(4)(B)(iii). These rules do not apply to securities of a TRS, or to securities that qualify for the 75 percent asset test of section 856(c)(4)(A), such as real estate assets, cash items (including receivables), or Government securities.

[87] A REIT might satisfy the requirements without a disposition, for example, by increasing its other assets in the case of the 5 percent rule; or by the issuer modifying the amount or value of its total securities outstanding in the case of the 10 percent rule.

Effective Date

The provision is generally effective for taxable years beginning after December 31, 2000.

However, some of the provisions are effective for taxable years beginning after the date of enactment. These are: the new "look through" rules determining a REIT partner's share of partnership securities for purposes of the "straight debt" rules; the provision changing the 90-percent of gross income reference to 95 percent, for purposes of the tax liability if a REIT fails to meet the 95-percent of gross income test; the new hedging definition; the rule modifying the treatment of rents with respect to customary services; and the new rules for correction of certain failures to satisfy the REIT requirements.

Conference Committee Report (H.R. CONF. REP. NO. 108-755)

Present Law

* * *

Special rules for taxable REIT subsidiaries

* * *

The 100 percent excise tax does not apply to amounts received directly or indirectly by a REIT from a TRS that would be excluded from unrelated taxable income if received by an organization described in section 511(a)(2). Such amounts are defined in section 512(b)(3).

Rents paid by a TRS to a REIT generally are treated as rents from real property if at least 90 percent of the leased space of the property is rented to persons other than the REIT's TRSs and other than persons related to the REIT. In such a case, the rent paid by the TRS to the REIT is treated as rent from real property only to the extent that it is substantially comparable to rents from other tenants of the REIT's property for comparable space.

* * *

Consequences of failure to meet requirements

* * *

If a REIT fails to meet the source of income requirements, but has set out the income it did receive in a schedule and any error in the schedule is not due to fraud with intent to evade tax, then the REIT does not lose its REIT status, provided that the failure to meet the 95-percent or 75-percent test is due to reasonable cause and not to willful neglect. If the REIT qualifies for this relief, the REIT must pay the disallowed income as a tax to the Treasury.[142]

Failure to satisfy the asset test is excused if the REIT eliminates the discrepancy within 30 days. Failure to meet distribution requirements may also be excused if the REIT was unable to meet such requirement by reason of distributions previously made to meet the requirements of section 4981.

* * *

Senate Amendment

No provision.

Conference Agreement

The conference agreement follows the House bill.

[Law at ¶ 5550, ¶ 5555, ¶ 5560 and ¶ 5980. CCH Explanation at ¶ 1110.]

[¶ 10,250] Act Sec. 244. Special rules for certain film and television production

Senate Committee Report (S. REP. NO. 108-192)

[New Code Sec. 181]

Present Law

The modified Accelerated Cost Recovery System ("MACRS") does not apply to certain property, including any motion picture film, video tape, or sound recording, or to any other property if the taxpayer elects to exclude such property from MACRS and the taxpayer properly applies a unit-of-production method or other method of depreciation not expressed in a term of years. Section 197 does not apply to certain intangible property, including property produced by the taxpayer or any interest in a film, sound recording, video tape, book or similar property not acquired in a transaction (or a series of related transactions) involving the acquisition of assets constituting a trade or busi-

---

[142] Secs. 856(c)(6) and 857(b)(5).

ness or substantial portion thereof. Thus, the recovery of the cost of a film, video tape, or similar property that is produced by the taxpayer or is acquired on a "stand-alone" basis by the taxpayer may not be determined under either the MACRS depreciation provisions or under the section 197 amortization provisions. The cost recovery of such property may be determined under section 167, which allows a depreciation deduction for the reasonable allowance for the exhaustion, wear and tear, or obsolescence of the property. A taxpayer is allowed to recover, through annual depreciation deductions, the cost of certain property used in a trade or business or for the production of income. Section 167(g) provides that the cost of motion picture films, sound recordings, copyrights, books, and patents are eligible to be recovered using the income forecast method of depreciation.

Reasons for Change

The Committee understands that over the past decade, production of American film projects has moved to foreign locations. Specifically, in recent years, a number of foreign governments have offered tax and other incentives designed to entice production of U.S. motion pictures and television programs to their countries. These governments have recognized that the benefits of hosting such productions do not flow only to the film and television industry. These productions create broader economic effects, with revenues and jobs generated in a variety of other local businesses. Hotels, restaurants, catering companies, equipment rental facilities, transportation vendors, and many others benefit from these productions.

This has become a significant trend affecting the film and television industry as well as the small businesses that they support. The Committee understands that a recent report by the U.S. Department of Commerce estimated that runaway production drains as much as $10 billion per year from the U.S. economy. These losses have been most pronounced in made-for-television movies and miniseries productions. According to the report, out of the 308 U.S.-developed television movies produced in 1998, 139 were produced abroad. This is a significant increase from the 30 produced abroad in 1990.

The Committee believes the report makes a compelling case that runaway film and television production has eroded important segments of a vital American industry. According to official labor statistics, more than 270,000 jobs in the U.S. are directly involved in film production. By industry estimates, 70 to 80 percent of these workers are hired at the location where the production is filmed.

The Committee believes this legislation will encourage producers to bring feature film and television production projects to cities and towns across the United States, thereby decreasing the runaway production problem.

Explanation of Provision

The provision permits qualifying film and television productions to elect to deduct certain production expenditures in the year the expenditure is incurred in lieu of capitalizing the cost and recovering it through depreciation allowances.[95]

The provision limits the amount of production expenditures that may be expensed to $15 million for each qualifying production.[96] An additional $5 million of production expenditures may be deducted (up to $20 million in total) if a significant amount of the production expenditures are incurred in areas eligible for designation as a low-income community or eligible for designation by the Delta Regional Authority as a distressed county or isolated area of distress. Expenditures in excess of $15 million ($20 million in distressed areas) are required to be recovered over a three-year period using the straight-line method beginning in the month such property is placed in service.

The provision defines a qualified film or television production as any production of a motion picture (whether released theatrically or directly to video cassette or any other format); miniseries; scripted, dramatic television episode; or movie of the week if at least 75 percent of the total compensation expended on the production are for services performed in the United States.[97] With respect to property which is one or more episodes in a television series, only the first 44 episodes qualify under the proposal. Qualified property does not include sexually explicit pro-

---

[95] An election to deduct such costs shall be made in such manner as prescribed by the Secretary and by the due date (including extensions of time) for filing the taxpayer's return of tax for the taxable year in which production costs of such property are first incurred. An election may not be revoked without the consent of the Secretary. The Committee intends that, in the absence of specific guidance by the Secretary, deducting qualifying costs on the appropriate tax return shall constitute a valid election.

[96] Thus, a qualifying film that is co-produced is limited to $15 million of deduction. The benefits of this provision shall be allocated among the owners of a film in a manner that reasonably reflects each owner's proportionate investment in and economic interest in the film.

[97] The term compensation does not include participations and residuals.

ductions as defined by section 2257 of title 18 of the U.S. Code.

The provision also requires the Commerce Department to report on whether the provision materially aided in retaining film production in the U.S. The report is required to be submitted to the Senate Committee on Finance and the House Committee on Ways and Means no later than December 31, 2006.

Conference Committee Report (H.R. CONF. REP. NO. 108-755)

The conference agreement follows the Senate amendment, except that the provision does not apply to qualified productions the aggregate cost of which exceeds the $15 million threshold. The threshold is increased to $20 million if a significant amount of the production expenditures are incurred in areas eligible for designation as a low-income community or eligible for designation by the Delta Regional Authority as a distressed county or isolated area of distress.

Effective Date

The provision is effective for qualified productions commencing after the date of enactment and before January 1, 2009.[203]

[Law at ¶ 5205. CCH Explanation at ¶ 365.]

[¶ 10,260] Act Sec. 245. Provide a tax credit for maintenance of railroad track

Conference Committee Report (H.R. CONF. REP. NO. 108-755)

[New Code Sec. 45G]

Present Law

There is no provision that provides for a railroad track maintenance tax credit.

House Bill

No provision.

Senate Amendment

The Senate amendment provides a 30-percent business tax credit for qualified railroad track maintenance expenditures paid or incurred in a taxable year by eligible taxpayers. The credit is limited to the product of $3,500 times the number of miles of railroad track owned or leased by an eligible taxpayer as of the close of its taxable year. Qualified railroad track maintenance expenditures are defined as amounts expended (whether or not chargeable to a capital account) for maintaining railroad track (including roadbed, bridges, and related track structures) owned or leased as of January 1, 2005, by a Class II or Class III railroad. An eligible taxpayer is defined as: (1) any Class II or Class III railroad; and (2) any person who transports property using the rail facilities of a Class II or Class III railroad or who furnishes railroad-related property or services to such person. The taxpayer's basis in railroad track is reduced by the amount of the credit allowed. No portion of the credit may be carried back to any taxable year beginning before January 1, 2005. Other rules apply.

This credit applies to qualified railroad track maintenance expenditures paid or incurred during taxable years beginning after December 31, 2004, and before January 1, 2008.

Effective Date

The Senate amendment is effective for taxable years beginning after December 31, 2004.

Conference Agreement

The conference agreement follows the Senate amendment provision with the following modification. The conference agreement increases the credit percentage from 30-percent to 50-percent. In addition, the conference agreement clarifies that each mile of railroad track may be taken into account only once, either by the owner of such mile or by the owner's assignee, in computing the per-mile limitation.

[Law at ¶ 5010, ¶ 5015, ¶ 5045 and ¶ 5760. CCH Explanation at ¶ 375.]

---

[203] For this purpose, a production is treated as commencing on the first date of principal photography.

[¶ 10,270] Act Sec. 246. Suspension of occupational taxes relating to distilled spirits, wine, and beer

House Committee Report (H.R. REP. NO. 108-548, pt. 1)

[Code Sec. 5117 and New Code Sec. 5148]

Present Law

Under present law, special occupational taxes are imposed on producers and others engaged in the marketing of distilled spirits, wine, and beer. These excise taxes are imposed as part of a broader Federal tax and regulatory engine governing the production and marketing of alcoholic beverages. The special occupational taxes are payable annually, on July 1 of each year. The present tax rates are as follows:

Producers:[99]

Distilled spirits and wines (sec. 5081)	$1,000 per year, per premise.
Brewers (sec. 5091)	$1,000 per year, per premise.
Wholesale dealers (sec. 5111):	
Liquors, wines, or beer	$500 per year.
Retail dealers (sec. 5121):	
Liquors, wines, or beer	$250 per year.
Nonbeverage use of distilled spirits (sec. 5131)	$500 per year.
Industrial use of distilled spirits (sec. 5276)	$250 per year.

The Code requires every wholesale or retail dealer in liquors, wine or beer to keep records of their transactions.[100] A delegate of the Secretary of the Treasury is authorized to inspect the records of any dealer during business hours.[101] There are penalties for failing to comply with the recordkeeping requirements.[102]

The Code limits the persons from whom dealers may purchase their liquor stock intended for resale. Under the Code, a dealer may only purchase from:

(1) a wholesale dealer in liquors who has paid the special occupational tax as such dealer to cover the place where such purchase is made; or

(2) a wholesale dealer in liquors who is exempt, at the place where such purchase is made, from payment of such tax under any provision chapter 51 of the Code; or

(3) a person who is not required to pay special occupational tax as a wholesale dealer in liquors.[103]

In addition, a limited retail dealer (such as a charitable organization selling liquor at a picnic) may lawfully purchase distilled spirits for resale from a retail dealer in liquors.[104]

Violation of this restriction is punishable by $1,000 fine, imprisonment of one year, or both.[105] A violation also makes the alcohol subject to seizure and forfeiture.[106]

Reasons for Change

The special occupational tax is not a tax on alcoholic products but rather operates as a license fee on businesses. The Committee believes that this tax places an unfair burden on business owners. However, the Committee recognizes that the recordkeeping and registration authorities applicable to wholesalers and retailers engaged in such businesses are necessary enforcement tools to ensure the protection of the revenue arising from the excise taxes on these products. Thus, the Committee believes it appropriate to suspend the tax for a three-year period, while retaining present-law recordkeeping and registration requirements.

Explanation of Provision

Under the provision, the special occupational taxes on producers and marketers of alcoholic beverages are suspended for a three-year period, July 1, 2004 through June 30, 2007. Present law recordkeeping and registration requirements will continue to apply, notwithstanding the suspension of the special occupation taxes. In addition, during the suspension period, it shall be unlawful for any dealer to purchase distilled spirits for resale from any person other than a wholesale dealer in liquors who is subject to the recordkeeping requirements, except that a limited retail dealer may purchase distilled spirits

---

[99] A reduced rate of tax in the amount of $500 is imposed on small proprietors. Secs. 5081(b), 5091(b).

[100] Secs. 5114, 5124.

[101] Sec. 5146.

[102] Sec. 5603.

[103] Sec. 5117. For example, purchases from a proprietor of a distilled spirits plant at his principal business office would

be covered under item (2) since such a proprietor is not subject to the special occupational tax on account of sales at his principal business office. Sec. 5113(a). Purchases from a State-operated liquor store would be covered under item (3). Sec. 5113(b).

for resale from a retail dealer in liquors, as permitted under present law.

Effective Date

The provision is effective on the date of enactment.

Conference Committee Report (H.R. CONF. REP. NO. 108-755)

Senate Amendment

No provision.

Conference Agreement

The conference agreement follows the House bill except as follows. Under the provi-

sion as modified, the three-year suspension period is July 1, 2005 through June 30, 2008.

[Law at ¶ 6110, ¶ 6115 and ¶ 6120. CCH Explanation at ¶ 1569.]

[¶ 10,280] Act Sec. 247. Modification of unrelated business income limitation on investment in certain small business investment companies

House Committee Report (H.R. REP. NO. 108-548, pt. 1)

[Code Sec. 514]

Present Law

In general, an organization that is otherwise exempt from Federal income tax is taxed on income from a trade or business that is unrelated to the organization's exempt purposes. Certain types of income, such as rents, royalties, dividends, and interest, generally are excluded from unrelated business taxable income except when such income is derived from "debt-financed property." Debt-financed property generally means any property that is held to produce income and with respect to which there is acquisition indebtedness at any time during the taxable year.

In general, income of a tax-exempt organization that is produced by debt-financed property is treated as unrelated business income in proportion to the acquisition indebtedness on the income-producing property. Acquisition indebtedness generally means the amount of unpaid indebtedness incurred by an organization to acquire or improve the property and indebtedness that would not have been incurred but for the acquisition or improvement of the property. Acquisition indebtedness does not include, however, (1) certain indebtedness incurred in the performance or exercise of a purpose or function constituting the basis of the organization's exemption, (2) obligations to pay certain types of annuities, (3) an obligation, to the extent it is insured by the Federal Housing Administration, to finance the purchase, rehabilitation, or construction of housing for low and moderate income persons, or (4) indebtedness incurred by certain qualified organizations to acquire or improve real property. An extension, renewal, or refinancing of an obligation evidencing a pre-

existing indebtedness is not treated as the creation of a new indebtedness.

Special rules apply in the case of an exempt organization that owns a partnership interest in a partnership that holds debt-financed income-producing property. An exempt organization's share of partnership income that is derived from such debt-financed property generally is taxed as debt-financed income unless an exception provides otherwise.

Reasons for Change

Small business investment companies obtain financial assistance from the Small Business Administration in the form of equity or by incurring indebtedness that is held or guaranteed by the Small Business Administration pursuant to the Small Business Investment Act of 1958. Tax-exempt organizations that invest in small business investment companies who are treated as partnerships and who incur indebtedness that is held or guaranteed by the Small Business Administration may be subject to unrelated business income tax on their distributive shares of income from the small business investment company. The Committee believes that the imposition of unrelated business income tax in such cases creates a disincentive for tax-exempt organizations to invest in small business investment companies, thereby reducing the amount of investment capital that may be provided by small business investment companies to the nation's small businesses. The Committee believes, however, that ownership limitations on the percentage interests that may be held by exempt organizations are appropriate to prevent all or most of a small business investment company's income from escaping Federal income tax.

Explanation of Provision

The provision modifies the debt-financed property provisions by excluding from the definition of acquisition indebtedness any indebtedness incurred by a small business investment company licensed under the Small Business Investment Act of 1958 that is evidenced by a debenture (1) issued by such company under section 303(a) of said Act, and (2) held or guaranteed by the Small Business Administration. The exclusion shall not apply during any period that any exempt organization (other than a governmental unit) owns more than 25 percent of the capital or profits interest in the small business investment company, or exempt organizations (including governmental units other than any agency or instrumentality of the United States) own, in the aggregate, 50 percent or more of the capital or profits interest in such company.

Conference Committee Report (H.R. CONF. REP. NO. 108-755)

Conference Agreement

The conference agreement follows the House bill, modified to apply to small business investment companies licensed after (rather than formed after) the date of enactment.

by small business investment companies licensed after the date of enactment.

[Law at ¶ 5415. CCH Explanation at ¶ 1325.]

Effective Date

The conference agreement provision is effective for debt incurred after the date of enactment

[¶ 10,290] Act Sec. 248. Election to determine taxable income from certain international shipping activities using per ton rate

House Committee Report (H.R. REP. NO. 108-548, pt. 1)

[New Code Secs. 1352,1353, 1354, 1355, 1356, 1357, 1358 and 1359]

Present Law

The United States employs a "worldwide" tax system, under which domestic corporations generally are taxed on all income, including income from shipping operations, whether derived in the United States or abroad. In order to mitigate double taxation, a foreign tax credit for income taxes paid to foreign countries is provided to reduce or eliminate the U.S. tax owed on such income, subject to certain limitations.

Generally, the United States taxes foreign corporations only on income that has a sufficient nexus to the United States. Thus, a foreign corporation is generally subject to U.S. tax only on income, including income from shipping operations, which is "effectively connected" with the conduct of a trade or business in the United States (sec. 882). Such "effectively connected income" generally is taxed in the same manner and at the same rates as the income of a U.S. corporation.

The United States imposes a four percent tax on the amount of a foreign corporation's U.S. gross transportation income (sec. 887). Transportation income includes income from the use (or hiring or leasing for use) of a vessel and income from services directly related to the use of a vessel. Fifty percent of the transportation income attributable to transportation that either begins or ends (but not both) in the United States is treated as U.S. source gross transportation income. The tax does not apply, however, to U.S. gross transportation income that is treated as income effectively connected with the conduct of a U.S. trade or business. U.S. gross transportation income is not treated as effectively connected income unless (1) the taxpayer has a fixed place of business in the United States involved in earning the income, and (2) substantially all the income is attributable to regularly scheduled transportation.

The taxes imposed by sections 882 and 887 on income from shipping operations may be limited by an applicable U.S. income tax treaty or by an exemption of a foreign corporation's international shipping operations income in instances where a foreign country grants an equivalent exemption (sec. 883).

Under present law, there is no provision that provides an alternative to the corporate income tax for taxable income attributable to international shipping activities.

Reasons for Change

In general, operators of U.S.-flag vessels in international trade are subject to higher taxes than their foreign-based competition. The uncompetitive U.S. taxation of shipping income has caused a steady and substantial decline of the

Act Sec. 248   ¶10,290

U.S. shipping industry. The Committee believes that this provision will provide operators of U.S.-flag vessels in international trade the opportunity to be competitive with their tax-advantaged foreign competitors.

Explanation of Provision

In general

The provision generally allows corporations to elect a "tonnage tax" on their taxable income from certain shipping activities in lieu of the U.S. corporate income tax. Accordingly, a corporation's income from qualifying shipping activities is no longer taxable under sections 11, 55, 882, 887 or 1201(a) under the regime, and electing entities are only subject to tax at the maximum corporate income tax rate on a notional amount based on the net tonnage of a corporation's qualifying vessels. However, a foreign corporation is not subject to tax under the tonnage tax regime to the extent its income from qualifying shipping activities is subject to an exclusion for certain shipping operations by foreign corporations pursuant to section 883(a)(1) or pursuant to a treaty obligation of the United States.

Taxable income from qualifying shipping activities

Generally, the taxable income of an electing corporation from qualifying shipping activities is the corporate income percentage[107] of the sum of the taxable income from each of its qualifying vessels. The taxable income from each qualifying vessel is the product of (1) the daily notional taxable income[108] from the operation of the qualifying vessel in United States foreign trade,[109] and (2) the number of days during the taxable year that the electing entity operated such vessel as a qualifying vessel in U.S. foreign trade.[110] A "qualifying vessel" is described as a self-propelled U.S.-flag vessel of not less than 10,000 deadweight tons used in U.S. foreign trade.

An entity's qualifying shipping activities consist of its (1) core qualifying activities, (2) qualifying secondary activities, and (3) qualifying incidental activities. Generally, core qualifying activities are activities from operating vessels in U.S. foreign trade and other activities of an electing entity and an electing group that are an integral part of the business of operating qualifying vessels in U.S. foreign trade. Qualifying secondary activities generally consist of the active management or operation of vessels in U.S. foreign trade and provisions for vessel, container and cargo-related facilities or such other activities as may be prescribed by the Secretary (which are not core activities), and may not exceed 20 percent of the aggregate gross income derived from electing entities and other members of its electing group from their core qualifying activities. Qualifying incidental activities are activities that are incidental to core qualifying activities and are not qualifying secondary activities. The aggregate gross income from qualifying incidental activities cannot exceed one-tenth of one percent of the aggregate gross income from the core qualifying activities of the electing entities and other members of its electing group.

Items not subject to corporate income tax

Generally, gross income from an electing entity does not include the corporate income percentage of an entity's (1) income from qualifying shipping activities in U.S. foreign trade, (2) income from money, bank deposits and other temporary investments which are reasonably necessary to meet the working capital requirements of its qualifying shipping activities, and (3) income from money or other intangible assets accumulated pursuant to a plan to purchase qualifying shipping assets.[111] Generally, the corporate loss percentage[112] of each item of loss, deduction, or credit is disallowed with respect to any activity the income from which is excluded

---

[107] The "corporate income percentage" is the least aggregate share, expressed as a percentage, of any item of income or gain of an electing corporation, or an electing group (i.e., a controlled group of which one or more members is an electing entity) of which such corporation is a member from qualifying shipping activities that would otherwise be required to be reported on the U.S. Federal income tax return of an electing corporation during any taxable period. A "controlled group" is any group of trusts and business entities whose members would be treated as a single employer under the rules of section 52(a) (without regard to paragraphs (1) and (2) and section 52(b)(1)).

[108] The "daily notional taxable income" from the operation of a qualifying vessel is 40 cents for each 100 tons of the net tonnage of the vessel (up to 25,000 net tons), and 20 cents for each 100 tons of the net tonnage of the vessel, in excess of 25,000 net tons.

[109] "U.S. foreign trade" means the transportation of goods or passengers between a place in the United States and a foreign place or between foreign places. As a general

rule, the temporary operation in the U.S. domestic trade (i.e., the transportation of goods or passengers between places in the United States) of any qualifying vessel is disregarded. However, a vessel that is no longer used for operations in U.S. foreign trade (unless such non-use is on a temporary basis) ceases to be a qualifying vessel when such non-use begins.

[110] If there are multiple operators of a vessel, the taxable income of such vessel must be allocated among such persons on the basis of their ownership and charter interests or another basis that Treasury may prescribe in regulations.

[111] "Qualifying shipping assets" means any qualifying vessel and other assets which are used in core qualifying activities.

[112] "Corporate loss percentage" means the greatest aggregate share, expressed as a percentage, of any item of loss, deduction or credit of an electing corporation or electing group of which such corporation is a member from qualifying shipping activities that would otherwise be required to

from gross income under the provision. The corporate loss percentage of an electing entity's interest expense is disallowed in the ratio that the fair market value of its qualifying shipping assets bears to the fair market value of its total assets.

Allocation of credits, income and deductions

No deductions are allowed against the taxable income of an electing corporation from qualifying shipping activities, and no credit is allowed against the tax imposed under the tonnage tax regime. No deduction is allowed for any net operating loss attributable to the qualifying shipping activities of a corporation to the extent that such loss is carried forward by the corporation from a taxable year preceding the first taxable year for which such corporation was an electing corporation. For purposes of the provision, section 482 applies to a transaction or series of transactions between an electing entity and another person or between an entity's qualifying shipping activities and other activities carried on by it. The qualifying shipping activities of an electing entity shall be treated as a separate trade or business activity from all other activities conducted by the entity.

Qualifying shipping assets

If an electing entity sells or disposes of qualifying shipping assets in an otherwise taxable transaction, at the election of the entity no gain is recognized if replacement qualifying shipping assets are acquired during a limited replacement period except to the extent that the amount realized upon such sale or disposition exceeds the cost of the replacement qualifying shipping assets. In the case of replacement qualifying shipping assets purchased by an electing entity which results in the nonrecognition of any part of the gain realized as the result of a sale or other disposition of qualifying shipping assets, the basis is the cost of such replacement property decreased in the amount of gain not recognized. If the property purchased consists of more than one piece of property, the basis is allocated to the purchased properties in proportion to their respective costs.

The election not to recognize gain on the disposition and replacement of qualifying shipping assets is not available if the replacement qualifying shipping assets are acquired from a related person except to the extent that the related person (as defined under section 267(b) or 707(b)(1)) acquired the replacement qualifying shipping assets from an unrelated person during a limited replacement period.

Election

Generally, any qualifying entity may elect into the tonnage tax regime by filing an election with the qualifying entity's income tax return for the first taxable year to which the election applies. However, a qualifying entity, which is a member of a controlled group, may only make an election into the tonnage tax regime if all qualifying entities that are members of the controlled group make such an election. Once made, an election is effective for the taxable year in which it was made and for all succeeding taxable years of the entity until the election is terminated. An election may be terminated if the entity ceases to be a qualifying entity or if the election is revoked. In the event that a qualifying entity elects into the tonnage tax regime and subsequently revokes the election, such entity is barred from electing back into the regime until the fifth taxable year after the termination is effective, unless the Secretary of the Treasury consents to the election.

A qualifying entity means a trust or business entity that (1) operates one or more qualifying vessels and (2) meets the "shipping activity requirement."[113] The shipping activity requirement is met for a taxable year only by an entity that meets one of the following requirements: (1) in the first taxable year of its election into the tonnage tax regime, for the preceding taxable year on average at least 25 percent of the aggregate tonnage of the qualifying vessels which were operated by the entity were owned by the entity or bareboat chartered to the entity; (2) in the second or any subsequent taxable year of its election into the tonnage tax regime, in each of the two preceding taxable years on average at least 25 percent of the aggregate tonnage of the qualifying vessels which were operated by the entity were owned by the entity or bareboat chartered to the entity; or (3) requirements (1) or (2) above would be met if the 25 percent average tonnage requirement was applied on an aggregate basis to the controlled group of which such entity is a member, and vessel charters between members of the controlled group were disregarded.

(Footnote Continued)

be reported on the U.S. Federal income tax return of an electing corporation during any taxable period.

[113] An entity is generally treated as operating any vessel owned by or chartered to the entity. However, an entity is treated as operating a vessel that it has chartered out on bareboat basis only if: (1) the vessel is temporarily surplus to the entity's requirements and the term of the charter does

not exceed three years or (2) the vessel is bareboat chartered to a member of a controlled group which includes such entity or to an unrelated third party that sub-bareboats or time charters the vessel to a member of such controlled group (including the owner). Special rules apply in an instance in which an electing entity temporarily ceases to operate a qualifying vessel.

Act Sec. 248   ¶10,290

Effective Date

The provision is effective for taxable years beginning after the date of enactment.

Conference Committee Report (H.R. CONF. REP. NO. 108-755)

Senate Amendment

No provision.

Conference Agreement

The conference agreement follows the House bill with modifications.

In general

The proposal generally allows corporations to elect a "tonnage tax" in lieu of the corporate income tax on taxable income from certain shipping activities. Accordingly, an electing corporation's gross income does not include its income from qualifying shipping activities, and electing corporations are only subject to tax on these activities at the maximum corporate income tax rate on their notional shipping income, which is based on the net tonnage of the corporation's qualifying vessels. An electing corporation is treated as a separate trade or business activity distinct from all other activities conducted by such corporation.

Notional shipping income

An electing corporation's notional shipping income for the taxable year is the sum of the following amounts for each of the qualifying vessels it operates: (1) the daily notional shipping income[173] from the operation of the qualifying vessel in United States foreign trade,[174] and (2) the number of days during the taxable year that the electing corporation operated such vessel as a qualifying vessel in United States foreign trade.[175] However, in the case of a qualifying vessel any of the income of which is not included in gross income, the amount of notional shipping income from such vessel is equal to the notional shipping income from such vessel (determined without regard to this provision) that bears the same ratio as the gross income from the operation of such vessel in the United States foreign trade bears to the sum of such gross income and

the income so excluded. Generally, a "qualifying vessel" is described as a self-propelled U.S.-flag vessel of not less than 10,000 deadweight tons used exclusively in U.S. foreign trade.

Items not subject to corporate income tax

Generally, a corporate member of an electing group[176] does not include in gross income its income from qualifying shipping activities. Qualifying shipping activities consist of (1) core qualifying activities, (2) qualifying secondary activities, and (3) qualifying incidental activities. All of an electing entity's core qualifying activities are excluded from gross income. However, only a portion of an electing corporation's secondary and incidental activities are treated as qualifying income and thus, are excluded from gross income.

Core qualifying activities consist of the operation of qualifying vessels.[177] Secondary activities generally consist of (1) the active management or operation of vessels in U.S. foreign trade; (2) the provision of vessels, barge, container or cargo-related facilities or services; and (3) other activities of the electing corporation and other members of its electing group that are an integral part of its business of operating qualifying vessels in United States foreign trade. Secondary activities do not include any core qualifying activities. In addition, any activities that would otherwise constitute core qualifying activities of a corporation, who is a member of an electing group but is not an electing corporation, are treated as qualifying secondary activities. Incidental activities are activities that are incidental to core qualifying activities and are not qualifying secondary activities.

Denial of credits, income and deductions

Each item of loss, deduction, or credit of any taxpayer is disallowed with respect to the income that is excluded from gross income under

---

[173] The daily notional shipping income from the operation of a qualifying vessel is 40 cents for each 100 tons of the net tonnage of the vessel (up to 25,000 net tons), and 20 cents for each 100 tons of the net tonnage of the vessel, in excess of 25,000 net tons.

[174] "United States foreign trade" means the transportation of goods or passengers between a place in the United States and a foreign place or between foreign places. The temporary use in the United States domestic trade (i.e., the transportation of goods or passengers between places in the United States) of any qualifying vessel is deemed to be the use in the United States foreign trade of such vessel, if such use does not exceed 30 days in a taxable year.

[175] Special rules apply in the case of multiple operators of a vessel.

[176] An electing group means any group that would be treated as a single employer under subsection (a) or (b) of section 52 if paragraphs (1) and (2) of section 52(a) did not apply.

[177] It is intended that the operation of a lighter-aboard-ship be treated as the operation of a vessel and not the operation of a barge.

the proposal. An electing corporation's interest expense is disallowed in the ratio that the fair market value of its qualifying vessels bears to the fair market value of its total assets; special rules apply for disallowing interest expense in the context of an electing group.

No deductions are allowed against the notional shipping income of an electing corporation, and no credit is allowed against the notional tax imposed under the tonnage tax regime. No deduction is allowed for any net operating loss attributable to the qualifying shipping activities of a corporation to the extent that such loss is carried forward by the corporation from a taxable year preceding the first taxable year for which such corporation was an electing corporation.

Dispositions of qualifying vessels

Generally, if an qualifying vessel operator sells or disposes of a qualifying vessel in an otherwise taxable transaction, at the election of the operator no gain is recognized if a replacement qualifying vessel is acquired during a limited replacement period except to the extent that the amount realized upon such sale or disposition exceeds the cost of the replacement qualifying vessels. Generally, in the case of the replacement of a qualifying vessel that results in the nonrecognition of any part of the gain under the rule above, the basis of the replacement vessel is the cost of such replacement property decreased in the amount of gain not recognized.

Generally, a qualifying vessel operator is a corporation that (1) operates one or more qualifying vessels and (2) meets certain requirements with respect to its shipping activities.[178] Special rules apply in determining whether corporate partners in pass-through entities are treated as qualifying vessel operators.

Election

Generally, any qualifying vessel operator may elect into the tonnage tax regime and such election is made in the form prescribed by Treasury. An election is only effective if made before the due date (including extensions) for filing the corporation's return for such taxable year. However, a qualifying vessel operator, which is a member of a controlled group, may only make an election into the tonnage tax regime if all qualifying vessel operators that are members of the controlled group make such an election. Once made, an election is effective for the taxable year in which it was made and for all succeeding taxable years of the entity until the election is terminated.

[Law at ¶ 5085, ¶ 5850, ¶ 5855, ¶ 5860, ¶ 5865, ¶ 5870, ¶ 5875, ¶ 5880 and ¶ 5885. CCH Explanation at ¶ 545.]

[¶ 10,310] Act Sec. 251. Exclusion of incentive stock options and employee stock purchase plan stock options from wages

House Committee Report (H.R. Rep. No. 108-548, pt. 1)

[Code Secs. 421(b), 423(c), 3121(a), 3231 and 3306(b)]

Present Law

Generally, when an employee exercises a compensatory option on employer stock, the difference between the option price and the fair market value of the stock (i.e., the "spread") is includible in income as compensation. In the case of an incentive stock option or an option to purchase stock under an employee stock purchase plan (collectively referred to as "statutory stock options"), the spread is not included in income at the time of exercise.[61]

If the statutory holding period requirements are satisfied with respect to stock acquired through the exercise of a statutory stock option, the spread, and any additional appreciation, will be taxed as capital gain upon disposition of such stock. Compensation income is recognized, however, if there is a disqualifying disposition (i.e., if the statutory holding period is not satisfied) of stock acquired pursuant to the exercise of a statutory stock option.

Federal Insurance Contribution Act ("FICA") and Federal Unemployment Tax Act ("FUTA") taxes (collectively referred to as "em-

---

[178] A person is generally treated as operating and using any vessel owned by or chartered to it and that is used as a qualifying vessel during such period. Special rules apply in the case of pass-through entities, and special rules apply in an instance in which an electing entity temporarily ceases to operate a qualifying vessel due to dry-docking, surveying, inspection, repairs and the like.

[61] Sec. 421. For purposes of the individual alternative minimum tax, the transfer of stock pursuant to an incentive stock option is generally treated as the transfer of stock pursuant to a nonstatutory option. Sec. 56(b)(3).

ployment taxes") are generally imposed in an amount equal to a percentage of wages paid by the employer with respect to employment.[62] The applicable Code provisions[63] do not provide an exception from FICA and FUTA taxes for wages paid to an employee arising from the exercise of a statutory stock option.

There has been uncertainty in the past as to employer withholding obligations upon the exercise of statutory stock options. On June 25, 2002, the IRS announced that until further guidance is issued, it would not assess FICA or FUTA taxes, or impose Federal income tax withholding obligations, upon either the exercise of a statutory stock option or the disposition of stock acquired pursuant to the exercise of a statutory stock option.[64]

Reasons for Change

To provide taxpayers certainty, the Committee believes that it is appropriate to clarify the treatment of statutory stock options for employment tax and income tax withholding purposes. The Committee believes that in the past, the IRS has been inconsistent in its treatment of taxpayers with respect to this issue and did not uniformly challenge taxpayers who did not collect employment taxes and withhold income taxes on statutory stock options.

Until January 2001, the IRS had not published guidance with respect to the imposition of employment taxes and income tax withholding on statutory stock options. Many taxpayers relied on guidance published with respect to qualified stock options (the predecessor to incentive stock options) to take the position that no employment taxes or income tax withholding were required with respect to statutory stock options. It is the Committee's belief that a majority of taxpayers did not withhold employment and income taxes with respect to statutory stock options. Thus, proposed IRS regulations, if implemented, would have altered the treatment of statutory stock options for most employers.

Because there is a specific income tax exclusion with respect to statutory stock options, the

Committee believes it is appropriate to clarify that there is a conforming exclusion for employment taxes and income tax withholding. Statutory stock options are required to meet certain Code requirements that do not apply to nonqualified stock options. The Committee believes that such requirements are intended to make statutory stock options a tool of employee ownership rather than a form of compensation subject to employment taxes. Furthermore, this clarification will ensure that, if further IRS guidance is issued, employees will not be faced with a tax increase that will reduce their net paychecks even though their total compensation has not changed.

The clarification will also eliminate the administrative burden and cost to employers who, in the absence of the Committee bill, could be required to modify their payroll systems to provide for the withholding of income and employment taxes on statutory stock options that they are not currently required to withhold.

Explanation of Provision

The provision provides specific exclusions from FICA and FUTA wages for remuneration on account of the transfer of stock pursuant to the exercise of an incentive stock option or under an employee stock purchase plan, or any disposition of such stock. Thus, under the provision, FICA and FUTA taxes do not apply upon the exercise of a statutory stock option.[65] The provision also provides that such remuneration is not taken into account for purposes of determining Social Security benefits.

Additionally, the provision provides that Federal income tax withholding is not required on a disqualifying disposition, nor when compensation is recognized in connection with an employee stock purchase plan discount. Present law reporting requirements continue to apply.

Effective Date

The provision is effective for stock acquired pursuant to options exercised after the date of enactment.

Conference Committee Report (H.R. CONF. REP. NO. 108-755)

Senate Amendment

No provision.

Conference Agreement

The conference agreement follows the House bill.

[Law at ¶ 5360, ¶ 5365, ¶ 5960, ¶ 5965, ¶ 5970 and ¶ 7018. CCH Explanation at ¶ 1410.]

---

[62] Secs. 3101, 3111 and 3301.

[63] Secs. 3121 and 3306.

[64] Notice 2002-47, 2002-28 I.R.B. 97.

[65] The provision also provides a similar exclusion under the Railroad Retirement Tax Act.

[¶ 10,320] Act Sec. 301. Incentives for alcohol and biodiesel fuels

Conference Committee Report (H.R. CONF. REP. NO. 108-755)

[Code Secs. 40, 4041, 4081, 4083, 4101, 6427, 9503 and New Code Sec. 6426]

Present Law

Alcohol fuels income tax credit

The alcohol fuels credit is the sum of three credits: the alcohol mixture credit, the alcohol credit, and the small ethanol producer credit. Generally, the alcohol fuels credit expires after December 31, 2007.[76]

A taxpayer (generally a petroleum refiner, distributor, or marketer) who mixes ethanol with gasoline (or a special fuel[77]) is an "ethanol blender." Ethanol blenders are eligible for an income tax credit of 52 cents per gallon of ethanol used in the production of a qualified mixture (the "alcohol mixture credit"). A qualified mixture means a mixture of alcohol and gasoline (or of alcohol and a special fuel) sold by the blender as fuel or used as fuel by the blender in producing the mixture. The term alcohol includes methanol and ethanol but does not include (1) alcohol produced from petroleum, natural gas, or coal (including peat), or (2) alcohol with a proof of less than 150. Businesses also may reduce their income taxes by 52 cents for each gallon of ethanol (not mixed with gasoline or other special fuel) that they sell at the retail level as vehicle fuel or use themselves as a fuel in their trade or business ("the alcohol credit"). The 52-cents-per-gallon income tax credit rate is scheduled to decline to 51 cents per gallon during the period 2005 through 2007. For blenders using an alcohol other than ethanol, the rate is 60 cents per gallon.[78]

A separate income tax credit is available for small ethanol producers (the "small ethanol producer credit"). A small ethanol producer is defined as a person whose ethanol production capacity does not exceed 30 million gallons per year. The small ethanol producer credit is 10 cents per gallon of ethanol produced during the taxable year for up to a maximum of 15 million gallons.

The credits that comprise the alcohol fuels tax credit are includible in income. The credit may not be used to offset alternative minimum tax liability. The credit is treated as a general business credit, subject to the ordering rules and carryforward/carryback rules that apply to business credits generally.

Excise tax reductions for alcohol mixture fuels

In general

Generally, motor fuels tax rates are as follows:[79]

Gasoline	18.3 cents per gallon
Diesel fuel and kerosene	24.3 cents per gallon
Special motor fuels	18.3 cents per gallon generally

Alcohol-blended fuels are subject to a reduced rate of tax. The benefits provided by the alcohol fuels income tax credit and the excise tax reduction are integrated such that the alcohol fuels credit is reduced to take into account the benefit of any excise tax reduction.

Gasohol

Registered ethanol blenders may forgo the full income tax credit and instead pay reduced rates of excise tax on gasoline that they purchase for blending with ethanol. Most of the benefit of the alcohol fuels credit is claimed through the excise tax system.

The reduced excise tax rates apply to gasohol upon its removal or entry. Gasohol is defined as a gasoline/ethanol blend that contains 5.7 percent ethanol, 7.7 percent ethanol, or 10 percent ethanol. For the calendar year 2004, the following reduced rates apply to gasohol:[80]

5.7 percent ethanol	15.436 cents per gallon

---

[76] The alcohol fuels credit is unavailable when, for any period before January 1, 2008, the tax rates for gasoline and diesel fuels drop to 4.3 cents per gallon.

[77] A special fuel includes any liquid (other than gasoline) that is suitable for use in an internal combustion engine.

[78] In the case of any alcohol (other than ethanol) with a proof that is at least 150 but less than 190, the credit is 45 cents per gallon (the "low-proof blender amount"). For ethanol with a proof that is at least 150 but less than 190, the low-proof blender amount is 38.52 cents for sales or uses

during calendar year 2004, and 37.78 cents for calendar years 2005, 2006, and 2007.

[79] These fuels are also subject to an additional 0.1 cent-per-gallon excise tax to fund the Leaking Underground Storage Tank Trust Fund. See secs. 4041(d) and 4081(a)(2)(B). In addition, the basic fuel tax rate will drop to 4.3 cents per gallon beginning on October 1, 2005.

[80] These rates include the additional 0.1 cent-per-gallon excise tax to fund the Leaking Underground Storage Tank

7.7 percent ethanol	14.396 cents per gallon
10.0 percent ethanol	13.200 cents per gallon

Reduced excise tax rates also apply when gasoline is purchased for the production of "gasohol." When gasoline is purchased for blending into gasohol, the rates above are multiplied by a fraction (e.g., 10/9 for 10-percent gasohol) so that the increased volume of motor fuel will be subject to tax. The reduced tax rates apply if the person liable for the tax is registered with the IRS and (1) produces gasohol with gasoline within 24 hours of removing or entering the gasoline or (2) gasoline is sold upon its removal or entry and such person has an unexpired certificate from the buyer and has no reason to believe the certificate is false.[81]

Qualified methanol and ethanol fuels

Qualified methanol or ethanol fuel is any liquid that contains at least 85 percent methanol or ethanol or other alcohol produced from a substance other than petroleum or natural gas. These fuels are taxed at reduced rates.[82] The rate of tax on qualified methanol is 12.35 cents per gallon. The rate on qualified ethanol in 2004 is 13.15 cents. From January 1, 2005, through September 30, 2007, the rate of tax on qualified ethanol is 13.25 cents.

Alcohol produced from natural gas

A mixture of methanol, ethanol, or other alcohol produced from natural gas that consists of at least 85 percent alcohol is also taxed at reduced rates.[83] For mixtures not containing ethanol, the applicable rate of tax is 9.25 cents per gallon before October 1, 2005. In all other cases, the rate is 11.4 cents per gallon. After September 30, 2005, the rate is reduced to 2.15 cents per gallon when the mixture does not contain ethanol and 4.3 cents per gallon in all other cases.

Blends of alcohol and diesel fuel or special motor fuels

A reduced rate of tax applies to diesel fuel or kerosene that is combined with alcohol as long as at least 10 percent of the finished mixture is alcohol. If none of the alcohol in the mixture is ethanol, the rate of tax is 18.4 cents per gallon. For alcohol mixtures containing ethanol, the rate of tax in 2004 is 19.2 cents per gallon and 19.3 cents per gallon for 2005 through September 30, 2007. Fuel removed or entered for use in producing a 10 percent diesel-alcohol fuel mixture (without ethanol), is subject to a tax of 20.44 cents per gallon. The rate of tax for fuel removed or entered for use to produce a 10 percent diesel-ethanol fuel mixture is 21.333 cents per gallon for 2004 and 21.444 cents per gallon for the period January 1, 2005, through September 30, 2007.[84]

Special motor fuel (nongasoline) mixtures with alcohol also are taxed at reduced rates.

Aviation fuel

Noncommercial aviation fuel is subject to a tax of 21.9 cents per gallon.[85] Fuel mixtures containing at least 10 percent alcohol are taxed at lower rates.[86] In the case of 10 percent ethanol mixtures, for any sale or use during 2004, the 21.9 cents is reduced by 13.2 cents (for a tax of 8.7 cents per gallon), for 2005, 2006, and 2007 the reduction is 13.1 cents (for a tax of 8.8 cents per gallon) and is reduced by 13.4 cents in the case of any sale during 2008 or thereafter. For mixtures not containing ethanol, the 21.9 cents is reduced by 14 cents for a tax of 7.9 cents. These reduced rates expire after September 30, 2007.[87]

When aviation fuel is purchased for blending with alcohol, the rates above are multiplied by a fraction (10/9) so that the increased volume of aviation fuel will be subject to tax.

Refunds and payments

If fully taxed gasoline (or other taxable fuel) is used to produce a qualified alcohol mixture, the Code permits the blender to file a claim for a quick excise tax refund. The refund is equal to the difference between the gasoline (or other taxable fuel) excise tax that was paid and the tax that would have been paid by a registered blender on the alcohol fuel mixture being produced. Generally, the IRS pays these quick refunds within 20 days. Interest accrues if the refund is paid more than 20 days after filing. A

(Footnote Continued)

Trust Fund. These special rates will terminate after September 30, 2007 (sec. 4081(c)(8)).

[81] Treas. Reg. sec. 48.4081-6(c). A certificate from the buyer assures that the gasoline will be used to produce gasohol within 24 hours after purchase. A copy of the registrant's letter of registration cannot be used as a gasohol blender's certificate.

[82] These reduced rates terminate after September 30, 2007. Included in these rates is the 0.05-cent-per-gallon Leaking Underground Storage Tank Trust Fund tax imposed on such fuel. (sec. 4041(b)(2)).

[83] These rates include the additional 0.1 cent-per-gallon excise tax to fund the Leaking Underground Storage Tank Trust Fund (sec. 4041(d)(1)).

[84] These rates include the additional 0.1 cent-per-gallon excise tax to fund the Leaking Underground Storage Tank Trust Fund.

[85] This rate includes the additional 0.1 cent-per-gallon tax for the Leaking Underground Storage Tank Trust fund.

[86] Secs. 4041(k)(1) and 4091(c).

[87] Sec. 4091(c)(1).

claim may be filed by any person with respect to gasoline, diesel fuel, or kerosene used to produce a qualified alcohol fuel mixture for any period for which $200 or more is payable and which is not less than one week.

Ethyl tertiary butyl ether (ETBE)

Ethyl tertiary butyl ether ("ETBE") is an ether that is manufactured using ethanol. Unlike ethanol, ETBE can be blended with gasoline before the gasoline enters a pipeline because ETBE does not result in contamination of fuel with water while in transport. Treasury regulations provide that gasohol blenders may claim the income tax credit and excise tax rate reductions for ethanol used in the production of ETBE. The regulations also provide a special election allowing refiners to claim the benefit of the excise tax rate reduction even though the fuel being removed from terminals does not contain the requisite percentages of ethanol for claiming the excise tax rate reduction.

Highway trust fund

With certain exceptions, the taxes imposed by section 4041 (relating to retail taxes on diesel fuels and special motor fuels) and section 4081 (relating to tax on gasoline, diesel fuel and kerosene) are credited to the Highway Trust Fund. In the case of alcohol fuels, 2.5 cents per gallon of the tax imposed is retained in the General Fund.[88] In the case of a taxable fuel taxed at a reduced rate upon removal or entry prior to mixing with alcohol, 2.8 cents of the reduced rate is retained in the General Fund.[89]

Biodiesel

If biodiesel is used in the production of blended taxable fuel, the Code imposes tax on the removal or sale of the blended taxable fuel.[90] In addition, the Code imposes tax on any liquid other than gasoline sold for use or used as a fuel in a diesel-powered highway vehicle or diesel-powered train unless tax was previously imposed and not refunded or credited.[91] If biodiesel that was not previously taxed or exempt is sold for use or used as a fuel in a diesel-powered highway vehicle or a diesel-powered train, tax is imposed.[92] There are no reduced excise tax rates for biodiesel.

Taxes from gasoline and special motor fuels used in motorboats and gasoline used in the nonbusiness use of small-engine outdoor power equipment

The Aquatic Resources Trust Fund is funded by a portion of the receipts from the excise tax imposed on motorboat gasoline and special motor fuels, as well as small-engine fuel taxes, that are first deposited into the Highway Trust Fund. As a result, transfers to the Aquatic Resources Trust Fund are governed in part by Highway Trust Fund provisions.[93]

A total tax rate of 18.4 cents per gallon is imposed on gasoline and special motor fuels used in motorboats. Of this rate, 0.1 cent per gallon is dedicated to the Leaking Underground Storage Tank Trust Fund. Of the remaining 18.3 cents per gallon, the Code currently transfers 13.5 cents per gallon from the Highway Trust Fund to the Aquatics Resources Trust Fund and Land and Water Conservation Fund. The remainder, 4.8 cents per gallon, is retained in the General Fund. In addition, the Sport Fish Restoration Account of the Aquatics Resources Trust Fund receives 13.5 cents per gallon of the revenues from the tax imposed on gasoline used as a fuel in the nonbusiness use of small-engine outdoor power equipment. The balance of 4.8 cents per gallon is retained in the General Fund.[94]

House Bill

Overview

The provision eliminates reduced rates of excise tax for alcohol-blended fuels and imposes the full rate of excise tax on alcohol-blended fuels (18.4 cents per gallon on gasoline blends and 24.4 cents per gallon of diesel blended fuel). In place of reduced rates, the provision permits the section 40 alcohol mixture credit, with certain modifications, to be applied against excise tax liability. The credit may be taken against the tax imposed on taxable fuels (by section 4081). To the extent a person does not have section 4081 liability, the provision allows taxpayers to file a claim for payment equal to the amount of the credit for the alcohol used to produce an eligible mixture. Under certain circumstances, a tax is imposed if an alcohol fuel mixture credit is

---

[88] Sec. 9503(b)(4)(E).

[89] Sec. 9503(b)(4)(F).

[90] Sec. 4081(b); Rev. Rul. 2002-76, 2002-46 I.R.B. 841 (2002). "Taxable fuels" are gasoline, diesel and kerosene (sec. 4083). Biodiesel, although suitable for use as a fuel in a diesel-powered highway vehicle or diesel-powered train, contains four percent normal paraffins and, therefore, is not treated as diesel fuel under the applicable Treasury regulations. Treas. Reg. secs. 48.4081-1(c)(2)(i) and (ii), and 48.4081-1(b); Rev. Rul. 2002-76, 2002-46 I.R.B. 841 (2002). As a result, biodiesel alone is not a taxable fuel for purposes

of section 4081. As noted above, however, tax is imposed upon the removal or entry of blended taxable fuel made with biodiesel.

[91] Sec. 4041. The tax imposed under section 4041 also will not apply if an exemption from tax applies.

[92] Rev. Rul. 2002-76, 2002-46 I.R.B. 841 (2002).

[93] Sec. 9503(c)(4) and 9503(c)(5).

[94] The Sport Fish Restoration Account also is funded with receipts from an *ad valorem* manufacturers excise tax on sport fishing equipment.

Act Sec. 301   ¶10,320

claimed with respect to alcohol used in the production of any alcohol mixture, which is subsequently used for a purpose for which the credit is not allowed or changed into a substance that does not qualify for the credit. The provision eliminates the General Fund retention of certain taxes on alcohol fuels, and credits these taxes to the Highway Trust Fund.

Alcohol fuel mixture excise tax credit and payment provisions

Alcohol fuel mixture excise tax credit

The provision eliminates the reduced rates of excise tax for alcohol-blended fuels and taxable fuels used to produce an alcohol fuel mixture. Under the provision, the full rate of tax for taxable fuels is imposed on both alcohol fuel mixtures and the taxable fuel used to produce an alcohol fuel mixture.

In lieu of the reduced excise tax rates, the provision provides that the alcohol mixture credit provided under section 40 may be applied against section 4081 excise tax liability (hereinafter referred to as "the alcohol fuel mixture credit"). The credit is treated as a payment of the taxpayer's tax liability received at the time of the taxable event. The alcohol fuel mixture credit is 52 cents for each gallon of alcohol used by a person in producing an alcohol fuel mixture for sale or use in a trade or business of the taxpayer. The credit declines to 51 cents per gallon after calendar year 2004. For mixtures not containing ethanol (renewable source methanol), the credit is 60 cents per gallon. As discussed further below, the excise tax credit is refundable in order to provide a benefit equivalent to the reduced tax rates, which are being repealed under the provision.

For purposes of the alcohol fuel mixture credit, an "alcohol fuel mixture" is a mixture of alcohol and gasoline or alcohol and a special fuel which is sold for use or used as a fuel by the taxpayer producing the mixture. Alcohol for this purpose includes methanol, ethanol, and alcohol gallon equivalents of ETBE or other ethers produced from such alcohol. It does not include alcohol produced from petroleum, natural gas, or coal (including peat), or alcohol with a proof of less than 190 (determined without regard to any added denaturants). Special fuel is any liquid fuel (other than gasoline) which is suitable for use in an internal combustion engine. The benefit obtained from the excise tax credit is coordinated with the alcohol fuels income tax credit. For refiners making an alcohol fuel mixture with ETBE, the mixture is treated as sold to another person for use as a fuel only upon removal from the refinery. The excise tax credit is available through December 31, 2010.

Payments with respect to qualified alcohol fuel mixtures

To the extent the alcohol fuel mixture credit exceeds any section 4081 liability of a person, the Secretary is to pay such person an amount equal to the alcohol fuel mixture credit with respect to such mixture. These payments are intended to provide an equivalent benefit to replace the partial exemption for fuels to be blended with alcohol and alcohol fuels being repealed by the provision. If claims for payment are not paid within 45 days, the claim is to be paid with interest. The provision also provides that in the case of an electronic claim, if such claim is not paid within 20 days, the claim is to be paid with interest. If claims are filed electronically, the claimant may make a claim for less than $200.

The provision does not apply with respect to alcohol fuel mixtures sold after December 31, 2010.

Alcohol fuel subsidies borne by General Fund

The provision eliminates the requirement that 2.5 and 2.8 cents per gallon of excise taxes be retained in the General Fund with the result that the full amount of tax on alcohol fuels is credited to the Highway Trust Fund. The provision also authorizes the full amount of fuel taxes to be appropriated to the Highway Trust Fund without reduction for amounts equivalent to the excise tax credits allowed for alcohol fuel mixtures, and the Trust Fund is not required to reimburse any payments with respect to qualified alcohol fuel mixtures.

Motorboat and small engine fuel taxes

The provision eliminates the General Fund retention of the 4.8 cents per gallon of the taxes imposed on gasoline and special motor fuels used in motorboats and gasoline used as a fuel in the nonbusiness use of small-engine outdoor power equipment.

Effective Dates

The provisions generally are effective for fuel sold or used after September 30, 2004. The repeal of the General Fund retention of the 2.5/2.8 cents per gallon of tax regarding alcohol fuels is effective for taxes imposed after September 30, 2003. The repeal of the 4.8 cents per gallon General Fund retention of the taxes imposed on fuels used in motorboats and small engine equipment is effective for taxes imposed after September 30, 2006. The provision regarding the crediting of the full amount of tax to the Highway Trust Fund without regard to credits and payments is effective for taxes received after

September 30, 2004, and payments made after September 30, 2004.

Senate Amendment

Alcohol fuels

The Senate amendment is similar to the House bill with respect to alcohol fuels, except that it also provides that outlay payments are available for neat alcohol used as fuel. In addition, the Senate amendment also extends the alcohol fuels income tax credit (sec. 40) through December 31, 2010. The Senate amendment requires importers and producers of alcohol to be registered with the Secretary. Finally, the provision extends the temporary additional duty on ethanol through January 1, 2011.

Biodiesel fuels

The Senate amendment creates a refundable excise tax credit for biodiesel fuel mixtures similar to that created for alcohol fuel mixtures. The excise tax credit for biodiesel mixtures is 50 cents for each gallon of biodiesel used by the taxpayer in producing a qualified biodiesel mixture for sale or use in a trade or business of the taxpayer. A qualified biodiesel mixture is a mixture of biodiesel and diesel fuel (determined without regard to any use of kerosene) that is (1) sold for use or used by the taxpayer producing such mixture as a fuel, or (2) removed from the refinery by a person producing the mixture. In the case of agri-biodiesel, the credit is $1.00 per gallon. No credit is allowed unless the taxpayer obtains a certification (in such form and manner as prescribed by the Secretary) from the producer of the biodiesel that identifies the product produced and the percentage of biodiesel and agri-biodiesel in the product. The Senate amendment also provides for outlay payments for biodiesel, not in a mixture, used as a fuel.

The credit is not available for any sale or use for any period after December 31, 2006. Credits and outlay payments are paid out of the General Fund, rather than the Highway Trust Fund. The excise tax credit is coordinated with the income tax credit for biodiesel such that credit for the same biodiesel cannot be claimed for both income and excise tax purposes.

The Senate amendment requires importers and producers of biodiesel to be registered with the Secretary.

Motorboat and small engine fuel taxes

The Senate amendment does not change the General Fund's retention of the 4.8 cents per gallon imposed on motorboat and small engine fuel.

Effective Date

The provisions generally are effective for fuel sold or used after September 30, 2004. The repeal of the General Fund retention of the 2.5/2.8 cents per gallon regarding alcohol fuels is effective for fuel sold or used after September 30, 2003. The Secretary is to provide electronic filing instructions by September 30, 2004. The extension of the section 40 alcohol fuels credit is effective on the date of enactment. The requirement that producers and importers of alcohol and biodiesel be registered is effective April 1, 2005.

Conference Agreement

Overview

The conference agreement generally follows the Senate amendment. The conference agreement does not include outlay payments for neat alcohol and 100 percent biodiesel fuels. The conference agreement does not change the temporary duty on ethanol. In addition, the conference agreement does not change the General Fund's retention of the 4.8 cents per gallon imposed on motorboat and small engine fuel.

The conference agreement eliminates reduced rates of excise tax for most alcohol-blended fuels and imposes the full rate of excise tax on most alcohol-blended fuels (18.3 cents per gallon on gasoline blends and 24.3 cents per gallon of diesel blended fuel). In place of reduced rates, the conference agreement creates two new excise tax credits: the alcohol fuel mixture credit and the biodiesel mixture credit. The sum of these credits may be taken against the tax imposed on taxable fuels (by section 4081). The conference agreement allows taxpayers to file a claim for payment equal to the amount of these credits for biodiesel or alcohol used to produce an eligible mixture.

Under certain circumstances, a tax is imposed if an alcohol fuel mixture credit or biodiesel fuel mixture credit is claimed with respect to alcohol or biodiesel used in the production of any alcohol or biodiesel mixture, which is subsequently used for a purpose for which the credit is not allowed or changed into a substance that does not qualify for the credit.

The conference agreement eliminates the General Fund retention of certain taxes on alcohol fuels, and credits these taxes to the Highway Trust Fund. The Highway Trust Fund is credited with the full amount of tax imposed on alcohol and biodiesel fuel mixtures.

Act Sec. 301   ¶10,320

The conference agreement also extends the present-law alcohol fuels income tax credit through December 31, 2010.

Alcohol fuel mixture excise tax credit

The provision eliminates the reduced rates of excise tax for most alcohol-blended fuels.[95] Under the provision, the full rate of tax for taxable fuels is imposed on both alcohol fuel mixtures and the taxable fuel used to produce an alcohol fuel mixture.

In lieu of the reduced excise tax rates, the provision provides for an excise tax credit, the alcohol fuel mixture credit. The alcohol fuel mixture credit is 51 cents for each gallon of alcohol used by a person in producing an alcohol fuel mixture for sale or use in a trade or business of the taxpayer. For mixtures not containing ethanol (renewable source methanol), the credit is 60 cents per gallon.

For purposes of the alcohol fuel mixture credit, an "alcohol fuel mixture" is a mixture of alcohol and a taxable fuel that (1) is sold by the taxpayer producing such mixture to any person for use as a fuel or (2) is used as a fuel by the taxpayer producing the mixture. Alcohol for this purpose includes methanol, ethanol, and alcohol gallon equivalents of ETBE or other ethers produced from such alcohol. It does not include alcohol produced from petroleum, natural gas, or coal (including peat), or alcohol with a proof of less than 190 (determined without regard to any added denaturants). Taxable fuel is gasoline, diesel, and kerosene.[96] A mixture that includes ETBE or other ethers produced from alcohol produced by any person at a refinery prior to a taxable event is treated as sold at the time of its removal from the refinery (and only at such time) to another person for use as a fuel.

The excise tax credit is coordinated with the alcohol fuels income tax credit and is available through December 31, 2010.

Biodiesel mixture excise tax credit

The provision provides an excise tax credit for biodiesel mixtures.[97] The credit is 50 cents for each gallon of biodiesel used by the taxpayer in producing a qualified biodiesel mixture for sale or use in a trade or business of the taxpayer. A qualified biodiesel mixture is a mixture of biodiesel and diesel fuel that (1) is sold by the taxpayer producing such mixture to any person for use as a fuel, or (2) is used as a fuel by the taxpayer producing such mixture. In the case of

agri-biodiesel, the credit is $1.00 per gallon. No credit is allowed unless the taxpayer obtains a certification (in such form and manner as prescribed by the Secretary) from the producer of the biodiesel that identifies the product produced and the percentage of biodiesel and agri-biodiesel in the product.

The credit is not available for any sale or use for any period after December 31, 2006. This excise tax credit is coordinated with the income tax credit for biodiesel such that credit for the same biodiesel cannot be claimed for both income and excise tax purposes.

Payments with respect to qualified alcohol and biodiesel fuel mixtures

To the extent the alcohol fuel mixture credit exceeds any section 4081 liability of a person, the Secretary is to pay such person an amount equal to the alcohol fuel mixture credit with respect to such mixture. Thus, if the person has no section 4081 liability, the credit is totally refundable. These payments are intended to provide an equivalent benefit to replace the partial exemption for fuels to be blended with alcohol and alcohol fuels being repealed by the provision. Similar rules apply to the biodiesel fuel mixture credit.

If claims for payment are not paid within 45 days, the claim is to be paid with interest. The provision also provides that in the case of an electronic claim, if such claim is not paid within 20 days, the claim is to be paid with interest. If claims are filed electronically, the claimant may make a claim for less than $200. The Secretary is to describe the electronic format for filing claims by December 31, 2004.

The payment provision does not apply with respect to alcohol fuel mixtures sold after December 31, 2010, and biodiesel fuel mixtures sold after December 31, 2006.

Alcohol and biodiesel fuel subsidies borne by General Fund

The provision eliminates the requirement that 2.5 and 2.8 cents per gallon of excise taxes be retained in the General Fund with the result that the full amount of tax on alcohol fuels is credited to the Highway Trust Fund. The provision also authorizes the full amount of fuel taxes to be appropriated to the Highway Trust Fund without reduction for amounts equivalent to the excise tax credits allowed for alcohol or biodiesel

---

[95] The provision does not change the present-law treatment of fuels blended with alcohol derived from natural gas (under sec. 4041(m)), or alcohol derived from coal or peat (under sec. 4041(b)(2)). The provision does not change the taxes imposed to fund the Leaking Underground Storage Tank Trust Fund.

[96] Sec. 4083(a)(1). Under present law, dyed fuels are taxable fuels that have been exempted from tax.

[97] The excise tax credit uses the same definitions as the biodiesel fuels income tax credit.

fuel mixtures and the Highway Trust Fund is not required to reimburse the General Fund for any credits or payments taken or made with respect to qualified alcohol fuel mixtures or biodiesel fuel mixtures.

Registration requirement

Every person producing or importing biodiesel or alcohol is required to register with the Secretary.

Alcohol fuels income tax credit

The provision extends the alcohol fuels credit (sec. 40) through December 31, 2010.

Effective Dates

The provisions generally are effective for fuel sold or used after December 31, 2004. The repeal of the General Fund retention of the 2.5/2.8 cents per gallon regarding alcohol fuels is effective for fuel sold or used after September 30, 2004. The Secretary is to provide electronic filing instructions by December 31, 2004. The registration requirement is effective April 1, 2005.

[Law at ¶5020, ¶5980, ¶6010, ¶6020, ¶6040, ¶6215, ¶6220, ¶6385 and ¶7020. CCH Explanation at ¶805.]

[¶ 10,324] Act Sec. 302. Biodiesel income tax credit

Conference Committee Report (H.R. CONF. REP. NO. 108-755)

[Code Secs. 38(b), 87, 196(c) and New Code Sec. 40A]

Present Law

No income tax credit or excise tax rate reduction is provided for biodiesel fuels under present law. However, a 52-cents-per-gallon income tax credit (the "alcohol fuels credit") is allowed for ethanol and methanol (derived from renewable sources) when the alcohol is used as a highway motor fuel. Registered blenders may forgo the full income tax credit and instead pay reduced rates of excise tax on gasoline that they purchase for blending with alcohol. These present law provisions are scheduled to expire in 2007.

House Bill

No provision.

Senate Amendment

In general

The Senate amendment provides a new income tax credit for biodiesel and qualified biodiesel mixtures, the biodiesel fuels credit. The biodiesel fuels credit is the sum of the biodiesel mixture credit plus the biodiesel credit and is treated as a general business credit. The amount of the biodiesel fuels credit is includable in gross income. The biodiesel fuels credit is coordinated to take into account benefits from the biodiesel excise tax credit and payment provisions discussed above. The credit may not be carried back to a taxable year ending before or on September 30, 2004. The provision does not apply to fuel sold or used after December 31, 2006.

Biodiesel is monoalkyl esters of long chain fatty acids derived from plant or animal matter that meet (1) the registration requirements established by the Environmental Protection Agency

under section 211 of the Clean Air Act and (2) the requirements of the American Society of Testing and Materials D6751. Agri-biodiesel is biodiesel derived solely from virgin oils including oils from corn, soybeans, sunflower seeds, cottonseeds, canola, crambe, rapeseeds, safflowers, flaxseeds, rice bran, mustard seeds, or animal fats.

Biodiesel may be taken into account for purposes of the credit only if the taxpayer obtains a certification (in such form and manner as prescribed by the Secretary) from the producer or importer of the biodiesel which identifies the product produced and the percentage of the biodiesel and agri-biodiesel in the product.

Biodiesel mixture credit

The biodiesel mixture credit is 50 cents for each gallon of biodiesel used by the taxpayer in the production of a qualified biodiesel mixture. For agri-biodiesel, the credit is $1.00 per gallon. A qualified biodiesel mixture is a mixture of biodiesel and diesel fuel that is (1) sold by the taxpayer producing such mixture to any person for use as a fuel, or (2) is used as a fuel by the taxpayer producing such mixture. The sale or use must be in the trade or business of the taxpayer and is to be taken into account for the taxable year in which such sale or use occurs. No credit is allowed with respect to any casual off-farm production of a qualified biodiesel mixture.

Biodiesel credit

The biodiesel credit is 50 cents for each gallon of 100 percent biodiesel which is not in a mixture with diesel fuel and which during the taxable year is (1) used by the taxpayer as a fuel in a trade or business or (2) sold by the taxpayer at retail to a person and placed in the fuel tank of such person's vehicle. For agri-biodiesel, the credit is $1.00 per gallon.

Later separation or failure to use as fuel

In a manner similar to the treatment of alcohol fuels, a tax is imposed if a biodiesel fuels credit is claimed with respect to biodiesel that is subsequently used for a purpose for which the credit is not allowed or that is changed into a substance that does not qualify for the credit.

Effective Date

The biodiesel fuel income tax credit provision is effective for fuel produced, and sold or used after September 30, 2004, in taxable years ending after such date.

Conference Agreement

The conference agreement generally follows the Senate amendment, except for the effective date.

Effective Date

The provision is effective for fuel produced, and sold or used after December 31, 2004, in taxable years ending after such date

[Law at ¶ 5010, ¶ 5025, ¶ 5115, ¶ 5220 and ¶ 6215. CCH Explanation at ¶ 810.]

[¶ 10,330] Act Sec. 303. Information reporting for persons claiming certain tax benefits

Conference Committee Report (H.R. CONF. REP. NO. 108-755)

[New Code Sec. 4104]

Present Law

The Code provides an income tax credit for each gallon of ethanol and methanol derived from renewable sources (*e.g.*, biomass) used or sold as a fuel, or used to produce a qualified alcohol fuel mixture, such as gasohol. The amount of the credit is equal to 52 cents per gallon (ethanol)[760] and 60 cents per gallon (methanol).[761] This tax credit is provided to blenders of the alcohols with other taxable fuels, or to the retail sellers of unblended alcohol fuels. Part or all of the benefits of the income tax credit may be claimed through reduced excise taxes paid, either in reduced-tax sales or by expedited blender refunds on fully taxed sales of gasoline to obtain the benefit of the reduced rates. The amount of the income tax credit determined with respect to any alcohol is reduced to take into account any benefit provided by the reduced excise tax rates. To obtain a partial refund on fully taxed gasoline, the following requirements apply: (1) the claim must be for gasohol sold or used during a period of at least one week, (2) the claim must be for at least $200, and (3) the claim must be filed by the last day of the first quarter following the earliest quarter included in the claim. If the

blender cannot meet these requirements, the blender must claim a credit on the blender's income tax return.

House Bill

No provision.

Senate Amendment

The Senate amendment requires persons claiming the Code benefits related to alcohol fuels and biodiesel fuels to provide such information related to such benefits and the coordination of such benefits as the Secretary may require to ensure the proper administration and use of such benefits. The Secretary may deny, revoke or suspend the registration of any person to enforce this requirement.

Conference Agreement

The conference agreement follows the Senate amendment. Persons claiming excise tax benefits are to file quarterly information returns, rather than monthly.

Effective Date

The provision is effective January 1, 2004.

[Law at ¶ 6050. CCH Explanation at ¶ 815.]

[¶ 10,340] Act Sec. 311. Special rules for livestock sold on account of weather-related conditions

---

[760] The 52-cents-per-gallon credit is scheduled to decline to 51 cents per gallon beginning in calendar year 2005. The credit is scheduled to expire after the earlier of (1) expiration of the Highway Trust Fund excise taxes or (2) December 31, 2007.

[761] Ethanol produced by certain "small producers" is eligible for an additional producer tax credit of 10 cents per

gallon. Eligible small producers are defined as persons whose production capacity does not exceed 30 million gallons and whose annual production does not exceed 15 million gallons.

Conference Committee Report (H.R. CONF. REP. NO. 108-755)

[Code Sec. 451(e)]

Present Law

Generally, a taxpayer realizes gain to the extent the sales price (and any other consideration received) exceeds the taxpayer's basis in the property. The realized gain is subject to current income tax unless the gain is deferred or not recognized under a special tax provision.

Under section 1033, gain realized by a taxpayer from an involuntary conversion of property is deferred to the extent the taxpayer purchases property similar or related in service or use to the converted property within the applicable period. The taxpayer's basis in the replacement property generally is the cost of such property reduced by the amount of gain not recognized.

The applicable period for the taxpayer to replace the converted property begins with the date of the disposition of the converted property (or if earlier, the earliest date of the threat or imminence of requisition or condemnation of the converted property) and ends two years after the close of the first taxable year in which any part of the gain upon conversion is realized (the "replacement period"). Special rules extend the replacement period for certain real property and principal residences damaged by a Presidentially declared disaster to three years and four years, respectively, after the close of the first taxable year in which gain is realized.

Section 1033(e) provides that the sale of livestock (other than poultry) that is held for draft, breeding, or dairy purposes in excess of the number of livestock that would have been sold but for drought, flood, or other weather-related conditions is treated as an involuntary conversion. Consequently, gain from the sale of such livestock could be deferred by reinvesting the proceeds of the sale in similar property within a two-year period.

In general, cash-method taxpayers report income in the year it is actually or constructively received. However, section 451(e) provides that a cash-method taxpayer whose principal trade or business is farming who is forced to sell livestock due to drought, flood, or other weather-related conditions may elect to include income from the sale of the livestock in the taxable year following the taxable year of the sale. This elective deferral of income is available only if the taxpayer establishes that, under the taxpayer's usual business practices, the sale would not have occurred but for drought, flood, or weather-related conditions that resulted in the area being designated as eligible for Federal assistance. This exception is generally intended to put taxpayers who receive an unusually high amount of income in one year in the position they would have been in absent the weather-related condition.

House Bill

The House bill extends the applicable period for a taxpayer to replace livestock sold on account of drought, flood, or other weather-related conditions from two years to four years after the close of the first taxable year in which any part of the gain on conversion is realized. The extension is only available if the taxpayer establishes that, under the taxpayer's usual business practices, the sale would not have occurred but for drought, flood, or weather-related conditions that resulted in the area being designated as eligible for Federal assistance. In addition, the Secretary of the Treasury is granted authority to further extend the replacement period on a regional basis should the weather-related conditions continue longer than three years. Also, for property eligible for the provision's extended replacement period, the provision provides that the taxpayer can make an election under section 451(e) until the period for reinvestment of such property under section 1033 expires.

Effective Date

The House bill provision is effective for any taxable year with respect to which the due date (without regard to extensions) for the return is after December 31, 2002.

Senate Amendment

The Senate amendment is the same as the House bill, except that it also permits the taxpayer to replace compulsorily or involuntarily converted livestock with other farm property if, due to drought, flood, or other weather-related conditions, it is not feasible for the taxpayer to reinvest the proceeds in property similar or related in use to the livestock so converted.

Effective Date

The Senate amendment provision is effective for taxable years beginning after December 31, 2001.

Conference Agreement

The conference agreement follows the Senate amendment, except for the effective date.

Effective Date

The conference agreement provision is effective for any taxable year with respect to which the due date (without regard to extensions) for the return is after December 31, 2002.

[Law at ¶ 5375 and ¶ 5765. CCH Explanation at ¶ 820.]

Act Sec. 311   ¶ 10,340

[¶ 10,350] Act Sec. 312. Payment of dividends on stock of cooperatives without reducing patronage dividends

House Committee Report (H.R. Rep. No. 108-548, pt. 1)

[Code Sec. 1388]

Present Law

Under present law, cooperatives generally are entitled to deduct or exclude amounts distributed as patronage dividends in accordance with Subchapter T of the Code. In general, patronage dividends are comprised of amounts that are paid to patrons (1) on the basis of the quantity or value of business done with or for patrons, (2) under a valid and enforceable obligation to pay such amounts that was in existence before the cooperative received the amounts paid, and (3) which are determined by reference to the net earnings of the cooperative from business done with or for patrons.

Treasury Regulations provide that net earnings are reduced by dividends paid on capital stock or other proprietary capital interests (referred to as the "dividend allocation rule").[69] The dividend allocation rule has been interpreted to require that such dividends be allocated between a cooperative's patronage and nonpatronage operations, with the amount allocated to the patronage operations reducing the net earnings available for the payment of patronage dividends.

Reasons for Change

The Committee believes that the dividend allocation rule should not apply to the extent that the organizational documents of a cooperative provide that capital stock dividends do not reduce the amounts owed to patrons as patronage dividends. To the extent that capital stock dividends are in addition to amounts paid under the cooperative's organizational documents to patrons as patronage dividends, the Committee believes that those capital stock dividends are not being paid from earnings from patronage business.

In addition, the Committee believes cooperatives should be able to raise needed equity capital by issuing capital stock without dividends paid on such stock causing the cooperative to be taxed on a portion of its patronage income, and without preventing the cooperative from being treated as operating on a cooperative basis.

Explanation of Provision

The provision provides a special rule for dividends on capital stock of a cooperative. To the extent provided in organizational documents of the cooperative, dividends on capital stock do not reduce patronage income and do not prevent the cooperative from being treated as operating on a cooperative basis.

Effective Date

The provision is effective for distributions made in taxable years ending after the date of enactment.

Conference Committee Report (H.R. Conf. Rep. No. 108-755)

Senate Amendment

The Senate amendment is the same as the House bill.

* * *

Conference Agreement

The conference agreement follows the House bill and the Senate amendment.

[Law at ¶ 5910. CCH Explanation at ¶ 1340.]

---

[69] Treas. Reg. sec. 1.1388-1(a)(1).

[¶ 10,360] Act Sec. 313. Small ethanol producer credit

Conference Committee Report (H.R. Conf. Rep. No. 108-755)

[Code Sec. 40]

Present Law

Small ethanol producer credit

Present law provides several tax benefits for ethanol and methanol produced from renewable sources (e.g., biomass) that are used as a motor fuel or that are blended with other fuels (e.g., gasoline) for such a use. In the case of ethanol, a separate 10-cents-per-gallon credit is provided for small producers, defined generally as persons whose production does not exceed 15 million gallons per year and whose production capacity does not exceed 30 million gallons per year. The small producer credit is part of the alcohol fuels tax credit under section 40 of the Code. The alcohol fuels tax credits are includible in income. This credit, like tax credits generally, may not be used to offset alternative minimum tax liability. The credit is treated as a general business credit, subject to the ordering rules and carryforward/carryback rules that apply to business credits generally. The alcohol fuels tax credit is scheduled to expire after December 31, 2007.

Taxation of cooperatives and their patrons

Under present law, cooperatives in essence are treated as pass-through entities in that the cooperative is not subject to corporate income tax to the extent the cooperative timely pays patronage dividends. Under present law (sec. 38(d)(4)), the only excess credits that may be passed through to cooperative patrons are the rehabilitation credit (sec. 47), the energy property credit (sec. 48(a)), and the reforestation credit (sec. 48(b)).

House Bill

No provision.

Senate Amendment

The Senate amendment makes several modifications to the rules governing the small producer ethanol credit. First, the provision liberalizes the definition of an eligible small producer to include persons whose production capacity does not exceed 60 million gallons. Second, the provision allows cooperatives to elect to pass through the small ethanol producer credits to its patrons. The credit is apportioned pro rata among patrons of the cooperative on the basis of the quantity or value of the business done with or for such patrons for the taxable year. An election to pass through the credit is made on a timely filed return for the taxable year and is irrevocable for such taxable year.

Third, the provision repeals the rule that includes the small producer credit in income of taxpayers claiming it. Finally, the provision provides that the small producer ethanol credit is not treated as derived from a passive activity under the Code rules restricting credits and deductions attributable to such activities.

Effective Date

The provision is effective for taxable years ending after date of enactment.

Conference Agreement

The conference agreement allows cooperatives to elect to pass the small ethanol producer credit through to their patrons. Specifically, the credit is to be apportioned among patrons eligible to share in patronage dividends on the basis of the quantity or value of business done with or for such patrons for the taxable year. The election must be made on a timely filed return for the taxable year, and once made, is irrevocable for such taxable year.

The amount of the credit not apportioned to patrons is included in the organization's credit for the taxable year of the organization. The amount of the credit apportioned to patrons is to be included in the patron's credit for the first taxable year of each patron ending on or after the last day of the payment period for the taxable year of the organization, or, if earlier, for the taxable year of each patron ending on or after the date on which the patron receives notice from the cooperative of the apportionment.

If the amount of the credit shown on the cooperative's return for a taxable year is in excess of the actual amount of the credit for that year, an amount equal to the excess of the reduction in the credit over the amount not apportioned to patrons for the taxable year is treated as an increase in the cooperative's tax. The increase is not treated as tax imposed for purposes of determining the amount of any tax credit or for purposes of the alternative minimum tax.

The conference agreement does not contain any of the other modifications from the Senate amendment.

Effective Date

The provision is effective for taxable years ending after date of enactment.

[Law at ¶ 5020. CCH Explanation at ¶ 845.]

[¶ 10,370] Act Sec. 314. Alternative minimum tax relief: Coordinate farmer and fisherman income averaging and the alternative minimum tax

House Committee Report (H.R. REP. NO. 108-548, pt. 1)

[Code Secs. 55 and 1301]

Present Law

In general

Under present law, taxpayers are subject to an alternative minimum tax ("AMT"), which is payable, in addition to all other tax liabilities, to the extent that it exceeds the taxpayer's regular income tax liability. The tax is imposed at a flat rate of 20 percent, in the case of corporate taxpayers, on alternative minimum taxable income ("AMTI") in excess of a phased-out exemption amount. AMTI is the taxpayer's taxable income increased for certain tax preferences and adjusted by determining the tax treatment of certain items in a manner that limits the tax benefits resulting from the regular tax treatment of such items.

* * *

Farmer income averaging

An individual taxpayer engaged in a farming business (as defined by section 263A(e)(4)) may elect to compute his or her current year regular tax liability by averaging, over the prior three-year period, all or portion of his or her taxable income from the trade or business of farming. Because farmer income averaging reduces the regular tax liability, the AMT may be increased. Thus, the benefits of farmer income averaging may be reduced or eliminated for farmers subject to the AMT.

Reasons for Change

* * * The Committee believes that farmers should be allowed the full benefits of income averaging without incurring liability under the AMT.

Explanation of Provision

* * *

The provision provides that, in computing AMT, a farmer's regular tax liability is determined without regard to farmer income averaging. Thus, a farmer receives the full benefit of income averaging because averaging reduces the regular tax while the AMT (if any) remains unchanged.

Conference Committee Report (H.R. CONF. REP. NO. 108-755)

Senate Amendment

No provision.

Conference Agreement

The conference agreement extends the benefits of income averaging to fishermen. The provision also includes the provision in the House bill relating to the AMT, applicable to both farmers and fishermen.

Effective Date

Taxable years beginning after December 31, 2003.

[Law at ¶ 5080 and ¶ 5845. CCH Explanation at ¶ 825.]

[¶ 10,380] Act Sec. 315. Capital gains treatment to apply to outright sales of timber by landowner

House Committee Report (H.R. REP. NO. 108-548, pt. 1)

[Code Sec. 631(b)]

Present Law

Under present law, a taxpayer disposing of timber held for more than one year is eligible for capital gains treatment in three situations. First, if the taxpayer sells or exchanges timber that is a capital asset (sec. 1221) or property used in the trade or business (sec. 1231), the gain generally is long-term capital gain; however, if the timber is held for sale to customers in the taxpayer's business, the gain will be ordinary income. Second, if the taxpayer disposes of the timber with a retained economic interest, the gain is eligible for capital gain treatment (sec. 631(b)). Third, if the taxpayer cuts standing timber, the taxpayer may elect to treat the cutting as a sale or exchange eligible for capital gains treatment (sec. 631(a)).

Reasons for Change

The Committee believes that the requirement that the owner of timber retain an economic interest in the timber in order to obtain capital gain treatment under section 631(b) results in poor timber management. Under present law, the buyer, when cutting and removing timber, has no incentive to protect young or other uncut trees because the buyer only pays for the timber that is cut and removed. Therefore, the Committee bill eliminates this requirement and provides for capital gain treatment under section 631(b) in the case of outright sales of timber.

Explanation of Provision

Under the provision, in the case of a sale of timber by the owner of the land from which the timber is cut, the requirement that a taxpayer retain an economic interest in the timber in order to treat gains as capital gain under section 631(b) does not apply. Outright sales of timber by the landowner will qualify for capital gains treatment in the same manner as sales with a retained economic interest qualify under present law, except that the usual tax rules relating to the timing of the income from the sale of the timber will apply (rather than the special rule of section 631(b) treating the disposal as occurring on the date the timber is cut).

Effective Date

The provision is effective for sales of timber after December 31, 2004.

Conference Committee Report (H.R. CONF. REP. NO. 108-755)

Senate Amendment

The provision in the Senate amendment is the same as House bill.

Conference Agreement

The conference agreement includes the provision in the House bill and Senate amendment.

[Law at ¶5500. CCH Explanation at ¶740 and ¶750.]

[¶10,390] Act Sec. 316. Modification to cooperative marketing rules to include value-added processing involving animals

Senate Committee Report (S. REP. NO. 108-192)

[Code Sec. 1388]

Present Law

Under present law, cooperatives generally are treated similarly to pass-through entities in that the cooperative is not subject to corporate income tax to the extent the cooperative timely pays patronage dividends. Farmers' cooperatives are tax-exempt and include cooperatives of farmers, fruit growers, and like organizations that are organized and operated on a cooperative basis for the purpose of marketing the products of members or other producers and remitting the proceeds of sales, less necessary marketing expenses, on the basis of either the quantity or the value of products furnished by them (sec. 521). Farmers' cooperatives may claim a limited amount of additional deductions for dividends on capital stock and patronage-based distributions of nonpatronage income.

In determining whether a cooperative qualifies as a tax-exempt farmers' cooperative, the IRS has apparently taken the position that a cooperative is not marketing certain products of members or other producers if the cooperative adds value through the use of animals (e.g., farmers sell corn to a cooperative which is fed to chickens that produce eggs sold by the cooperative).

Reasons for Change

The Committee disagrees with the apparent IRS position concerning the marketing of certain products by cooperatives after the cooperative has added value to the products through the use of animals. Therefore, the Committee believes that the tax rules should be modified to clarify that cooperatives are permitted to market such products.

Explanation of Provision

The provision provides that marketing products of members or other producers includes feeding products of members or other producers to cattle, hogs, fish, chickens, or other animals and selling the resulting animals or animal products.

Effective Date

The provision is effective for taxable years beginning after the date of enactment.

Conference Committee Report (H.R. CONF. REP. NO. 108-755)

House Bill

No provision.

Conference Agreement

The conference agreement follows the Senate amendment.

[Law at ¶ 5420 and ¶ 5910. CCH Explanation at ¶ 830.]

[¶ 10,400] Act Sec. 317. Extension of declaratory judgment procedures to farmers' cooperative organizations

Senate Committee Report (S. REP. NO. 108-192)

[Code Sec. 7428]

Present Law

In limited circumstances, the Code provide declaratory judgment procedures, which generally permit a taxpayer to seek judicial review of an IRS determination prior to the issuance of a notice of deficiency and prior to payment of tax. Examples of declaratory judgment procedures that are available include disputes involving the initial or continuing classification of a tax-exempt organization described in section 501(c)(3), a private foundation described in section 509(a), or a private operating foundation described in section 4942(j)(3), the qualification of retirement plans, the value of gifts, the status of certain governmental obligations, or eligibility of an estate to pay tax in installments under section 6166.[82] In such cases, taxpayers may challenge adverse determinations by commencing a declaratory judgment action. For example, where the IRS denies an organization's application for recognition of exemption under section 501(c)(3) or fails to act on such application, or where the IRS informs a section 501(c)(3) organization that it is considering revoking or adversely modifying its tax-exempt status, present law authorizes the organization to seek a declaratory judgment regarding its tax exempt status.

Declaratory judgment procedures are not available under present law to a cooperative with respect to an IRS determination regarding its status as a farmers' cooperative under section 521.

Reasons for Change

The Committee believes that declaratory judgment procedures currently available to other organizations and in other situations also should be available to farmers' cooperative organizations with respect to an IRS determination regarding the status of an organization as a farmers' cooperative under section 521.

Explanation of Provision

The provision extends the declaratory judgment procedures to cooperatives. Such a case may be commenced in the U.S. Tax Court, a U.S. district court, or the U.S. Court of Federal Claims, and such court would have jurisdiction to determine a cooperative's initial or continuing qualification as a farmers' cooperative described in section 521.

Effective Date

The provision is effective for pleadings filed after the date of enactment.

Conference Committee Report (H.R. CONF. REP. NO. 108-755)

House Bill

No provision.

Conference Agreement

The conference agreement follows the Senate amendment.

[Law at ¶ 6335. CCH Explanation at ¶ 835.]

---

[82] For disputes involving the initial or continuing qualification of an organization described in sections 501(c)(3), 509(a), or 4942(j)(3), declaratory judgment actions may be brought in the U.S. Tax Court, a U.S. district court, or the U.S. Court of Federal Claims. For all other Federal tax declaratory judgment actions, proceedings may be brought only in the U.S. Tax Court.

[¶ 10,410] Act Sec. 318. Certain expenses of rural letter carriers

Conference Committee Report (H.R. CONF. REP. NO. 108-755)

[Code Sec. 162]

Present Law

The deductible automobile expenses of rural letter carriers equal the reimbursements that such carriers receive from the U.S. Postal Service. Carriers are not allowed to document their actual costs and claim itemized deductions for costs in excess of reimbursements,[363] nor are carriers required to include in income reimbursements in excess of their actual costs.

House Bill

No provision.

Senate Amendment

Under the Senate amendment, if the reimbursements a rural letter carrier receives from the U.S. Postal Service fall short of the carrier's actual costs, the costs in excess of reimbursements qualify as a miscellaneous itemized deduction subject to the two-percent floor. Reimbursements in excess of their actual costs continue not to be required to be included in gross income.

Effective Date

The provisions is effective for taxable years beginning after December 31, 2003.

Conference Agreement

The conference agreement follows the Senate amendment.

[Law at ¶ 5160. CCH Explanation at ¶ 1220.]

[¶ 10,420] Act Sec. 319. Treatment of certain income of electric cooperatives

Conference Committee Report (H.R. CONF. REP. NO. 108-755)

[Code Sec. 501]

Present Law

In general

Under present law, an entity must be operated on a cooperative basis in order to be treated as a cooperative for Federal income tax purposes. Although not defined by statute or regulation, the two principal criteria for determining whether an entity is operating on a cooperative basis are: (1) ownership of the cooperative by persons who patronize the cooperative; and (2) return of earnings to patrons in proportion to their patronage. The Internal Revenue Service requires that cooperatives must operate under the following principles: (1) subordination of capital in control over the cooperative undertaking and in ownership of the financial benefits from ownership; (2) democratic control by the members of the cooperative; (3) vesting in and allocation among the members of all excess of operating revenues over the expenses incurred to generate revenues in proportion to their participation in the cooperative (patronage); and (4) operation at cost (not operating for profit or below cost).[417]

In general, cooperative members are those who participate in the management of the coop-erative and who share in patronage capital. As described below, income from the sale of electric energy by an electric cooperative may be member or non-member income to the cooperative, depending on the membership status of the purchaser. A municipal corporation may be a member of a cooperative.

For Federal income tax purposes, a cooperative generally computes its income as if it were a taxable corporation, with one exception-the cooperative may exclude from its taxable income distributions of patronage dividends. In general, patronage dividends are the profits of the cooperative that are rebated to its patrons pursuant to a pre-existing obligation of the cooperative to do so. The rebate must be made in some equitable fashion on the basis of the quantity or value of business done with the cooperative.

Except for tax-exempt farmers' cooperatives, cooperatives that are subject to the cooperative tax rules of subchapter T of the Code (sec. 1381, et seq.) are permitted a deduction for patronage dividends from their taxable income only to the extent of net income that is derived from transactions with patrons who are members of the cooperative (sec. 1382). The availability of such deductions from taxable income has the effect of allowing the cooperative to be treated like a

---

[363] Section 162(o).

[417] Announcement 96-24, "Proposed Examination Guidelines Regarding Rural Electric Cooperatives," 1996-16 I.R.B. 35.

conduit with respect to profits derived from transactions with patrons who are members of the cooperative.

Cooperatives that qualify as tax-exempt farmers' cooperatives are permitted to exclude patronage dividends from their taxable income to the extent of all net income, including net income that is derived from transactions with patrons who are not members of the cooperative, provided the value of transactions with patrons who are not members of the cooperative does not exceed the value of transactions with patrons who are members of the cooperative (sec. 521).

Taxation of electric cooperatives exempt from subchapter T

In general, the cooperative tax rules of subchapter T apply to any corporation operating on a cooperative basis (except mutual savings banks, insurance companies, other tax-exempt organizations, and certain utilities), including tax-exempt farmers' cooperatives (described in sec. 521(b)). However, subchapter T does not apply to an organization that is "engaged in furnishing electric energy, or providing telephone service, to persons in rural areas" (sec. 1381(a)(2)(C)). Instead, electric cooperatives are taxed under rules that were generally applicable to cooperatives prior to the enactment of subchapter T in 1962. Under these rules, an electric cooperative can exclude patronage dividends from taxable income to the extent of all net income of the cooperative, including net income derived from transactions with patrons who are not members of the cooperative.[418]

Tax exemption of rural electric cooperatives

Section 501(c)(12) provides an income tax exemption for rural electric cooperatives if at least 85 percent of the cooperative's income consists of amounts collected from members for the sole purpose of meeting losses and expenses of providing service to its members. The IRS takes the position that rural electric cooperatives also must comply with the fundamental cooperative principles described above in order to qualify for tax exemption under section 501(c)(12).[419] The 85-percent test is determined without taking into account any income from qualified pole rentals and cancellation of indebtedness income from the prepayment of a loan under sections 306A, 306B, or 311 of the Rural Electrification Act of 1936 (as in effect on January 1, 1987). The exclusion for cancellation of indebtedness income ap-

plies to such income arising in 1987, 1988, or 1989 on debt that either originated with, or is guaranteed by, the Federal Government.

The receipt by a rural electric cooperative of contributions in aid of construction and connection charges is taken into account for purposes of applying the 85-percent test.

Rural electric cooperatives generally are subject to the tax on unrelated trade or business income under section 511.

House Bill

No provision.

Senate Amendment

Treatment of income from open access transactions

The Senate amendment provides that income received or accrued by a rural electric cooperative from any "open access transaction" (other than income received or accrued directly or indirectly from a member of the cooperative) is excluded in determining whether a rural electric cooperative satisfies the 85-percent test for tax exemption under section 501(c)(12). The term "open access transaction" is defined as

(1) the provision or sale of electric energy transmission services or ancillary services on a nondiscriminatory open access basis: (i) pursuant to an open access transmission tariff filed with and approved by the Federal Energy Regulatory Commission ("FERC") (including acceptable reciprocity tariffs), but only if (in the case of a voluntarily filed tariff) the cooperative files a report with FERC within 90 days of enactment of this provision relating to whether or not the cooperative will join a regional transmission organization ("RTO"); or (ii) under an RTO agreement approved by FERC (including an agreement providing for the transfer of control-but not ownership-of transmission facilities);[420]

(2) the provision or sale of electric energy distribution services or ancillary services on a nondiscriminatory open access basis to end-users served by distribution facilities owned by the cooperative or its members; or

(3) the delivery or sale of electric energy on a nondiscriminatory open access basis, provided that such electric energy is generated by a generation facility that is directly connected to distribution facilities owned by the coopera-

---

[418] See Rev. Rul. 83-135, 1983-2 C.B. 149.

[419] Rev. Rul. 72-36, 1972-1 C.B. 151.

[420] Under the Senate amendment, references to FERC are treated as including references to the Public Utility Commission of Texas or the Rural Utilities Service.

tive (or its members) which owns the generation facility.

For purposes of the 85-percent test, the Senate amendment also provides that income received or accrued by a rural electric cooperative from any "open access transaction" is treated as an amount collected from members for the sole purpose of meeting losses and expenses if the income is received or accrued indirectly from a member of the cooperative.

Treatment of income from nuclear decommissioning transactions

The Senate amendment provides that income received or accrued by a rural electric cooperative from any "nuclear decommissioning transaction" also is excluded in determining whether a rural electric cooperative satisfies the 85-percent test for tax exemption under section 501(c)(12). The term "nuclear decommissioning transaction" is defined as—

(1) any transfer into a trust, fund, or instrument established to pay any nuclear decommissioning costs if the transfer is in connection with the transfer of the cooperative's interest in a nuclear powerplant or nuclear powerplant unit;

(2) any distribution from a trust, fund, or instrument established to pay any nuclear decommissioning costs; or

(3) any earnings from a trust, fund, or instrument established to pay any nuclear decommissioning costs.

Treatment of income from asset exchange or conversion transactions

The Senate amendment provides that gain realized by a tax-exempt rural electric cooperative from a voluntary exchange or involuntary conversion of certain property is excluded in determining whether a rural electric cooperative satisfies the 85-percent test for tax exemption under section 501(c)(12). This provision only applies to the extent that: (1) the gain would qualify for deferred recognition under section 1031 (relating to exchanges of property held for productive use or investment) or section 1033 (relating to involuntary conversions); and (2) the replacement property that is acquired by the cooperative pursuant to section 1031 or section 1033 (as the case may be) constitutes property that is used, or to be used, for the purpose of generating, transmitting, distributing, or selling electricity or natural gas.

Treatment of cancellation of indebtedness income from prepayment of certain loans

The Senate amendment provides that income from the prepayment of any loan, debt, or obligation of a tax-exempt rural electric coopera-

tive that is originated, insured, or guaranteed by the Federal Government under the Rural Electrification Act of 1936 is excluded in determining whether the cooperative satisfies the 85-percent test for tax exemption under section 501(c)(12).

Treatment of income from load loss transactions

Tax-exempt rural electric cooperatives—The Senate amendment provides that income received or accrued by a tax-exempt rural electric cooperative from a "load loss transaction" is treated under 501(c)(12) as income collected from members for the sole purpose of meeting losses and expenses of providing service to its members. Therefore, income from load loss transactions is treated as member income in determining whether a rural electric cooperative satisfies the 85-percent test for tax exemption under section 501(c)(12). The bill also provides that income from load loss transactions does not cause a tax-exempt electric cooperative to fail to be treated for Federal income tax purposes as a mutual or cooperative company under the fundamental cooperative principles described above.

The term "load loss transaction" is generally defined as any wholesale or retail sale of electric energy (other than to a member of the cooperative) to the extent that the aggregate amount of such sales during a seven-year period beginning with the "start-up year" does not exceed the reduction in the amount of sales of electric energy during such period by the cooperative to members. The "start-up year" is defined as the calendar year which includes the date of enactment of this provision or, if later, at the election of the cooperative: (1) the first year that the cooperative offers nondiscriminatory open access; or (2) the first year in which at least 10 percent of the cooperative's sales of electric energy are to patrons who are not members of the cooperative.

The Senate amendment also excludes income received or accrued by rural electric cooperatives from load loss transactions from the tax on unrelated trade or business income.

Taxable electric cooperatives—The Senate amendment provides that the receipt or accrual of income from load loss transactions by taxable electric cooperatives is treated as income from patrons who are members of the cooperative. Thus, income from a load loss transaction is excludible from the taxable income of a taxable electric cooperative if the cooperative distributes such income pursuant to a pre-existing contract to distribute the income to a patron who is not a member of the cooperative. The Senate amendment also provides that income from load loss transactions does not cause a taxable electric cooperative to fail to be treated for Federal income tax purposes as a mutual or cooperative company under the fundamental cooperative principles described above.

Effective date

The senate amendment provision is effective for taxable years beginning after the date of enactment.

Conference Agreement

The conference agreement follows the Senate amendment with the following modifications.

Treatment of income from open access transactions

Income received or accrued by a rural electric cooperative (other than income received or accrued directly or indirectly from a member of the cooperative) from the provision or sale of electric energy transmission services or ancillary services on a nondiscriminatory open access basis under an open access transmission tariff approved or accepted by FERC or under an independent transmission provider agreement approved or accepted by FERC (including an agreement providing for the transfer of control—but not ownership—of transmission facilities)[421] is excluded in determining whether a rural electric cooperative satisfies the 85-percent test for tax exemption under section 501(c)(12).

In addition, income is excluded for purposes of the 85-percent test if it is received or accrued by a rural electric cooperative (other than income received or accrued directly or indirectly from a member of the cooperative) from the provision or sale of electric energy distribution services or ancillary services, provided such services are provided on a nondiscriminatory open access basis to distribute electric energy not owned by the cooperative: (1) to end-users who are served by distribution facilities not owned by the cooperative or any of its members; or (2) generated by a generation facility that is not owned or leased by the cooperative or any of its members and that is directly connected to distribution facilities owned by the cooperative or any of its members.

Treatment of cancellation of indebtedness income from prepayment of certain loans

The conference agreement does not include this provision.

Treatment of income from load loss transactions

For purposes of this provision, the "start-up year" is defined in the conference agreement as the first year that the cooperative offers nondiscriminatory open access or, if later and at the election of the cooperative, the calendar year that includes the date of enactment of this provision.

Effective date

The conference agreement provision is effective for taxable years beginning after the date of enactment and before January 1, 2007.

[Law at ¶ 5400, ¶ 5410 and ¶ 5905. CCH Explanation at ¶ 1335.]

[¶ 10,430] Act Sec. 320. Exclusion from gross income for amounts paid under National Health Service Corps loan repayment program

Conference Committee Report (H.R. CONF. REP. NO. 108-755)

[Code Sec. 108]

Present Law

The National Health Service Corps Loan Repayment Program (the "NHSC Loan Repayment Program") provides education loan repayments to participants on condition that the participants provide certain services. In the case of the NHSC Loan Repayment Program, the recipient of the loan repayment is obligated to provide medical services in a geographic area identified by the Public Health Service as having a shortage of health-care professionals. Loan repayments may be as much as $35,000 per year of service plus a tax assistance payment of 39 percent of the repayment amount.

States may also provide for education loan repayment programs for persons who agree to provide primary health services in health professional shortage areas. Under the Public Health Service Act, such programs may receive Federal grants with respect to such repayment programs if certain requirements are satisfied.

Generally, gross income means all income from whatever source derived including income for the discharge of indebtedness. However, gross income does not include discharge of in-

---

[421] Under the conference agreement, references to FERC are treated as including references to the Public Utility Commission of Texas.

debtedness income if: (1) the discharge occurs in a Title 11 case; (2) the discharge occurs when the taxpayer is insolvent; (3) the indebtedness discharged is qualified farm indebtedness; or (4) except in the case of a C corporation, the indebtedness discharged is qualified real property business indebtedness.

Because the loan repayments provided under the NHSC Loan Repayment Program or similar State programs under the Public Health Service Act are not specifically excluded from gross income, they are gross income to the recipient. There is also no exception from employment taxes (FICA and FUTA) for such loan repayments.

House Bill

No provision.

Senate Amendment

The provision excludes from gross income and employment taxes education loan repay-

ments provided under the NHSC Loan Repayment Program and State programs eligible for funds under the Public Health Service Act. The provision also provides that such repayments are not taken into account as wages in determining benefits under the Social Security Act.

Effective Date

The provision is effective with respect to amounts received in taxable years beginning after December 31, 2003.

Conference Agreement

The conference agreement follows the Senate amendment.

[Law at ¶ 5120, ¶ 5960, ¶ 5965, ¶ 5970, ¶ 5975 and ¶ 7021. CCH Explanation at ¶ 1225.]

[¶ 10,440] Act Sec. 321. Modified safe harbor rules for timber REITs

Senate Committee Report (S. REP. NO. 108-192)

[Code Sec. 857]

Present Law

In general

Under present law, real estate investment trusts ("REITs") are subject to a special taxation regime. Under this regime, a REIT is allowed a deduction for dividends paid to its shareholders. As a result, REITs generally do not pay tax on distributed income. REITs are generally restricted to earning certain types of passive income, primarily rents from real property and interests on mortgages secured by real property.

To qualify as a REIT, a corporation must satisfy a number of requirements, among which are four tests: organizational structure, source of income, nature of assets, and distribution of income.

Income or loss from prohibited transactions

A 100-percent tax is imposed on the net income of a REIT from "prohibited transactions". A prohibited transaction is the sale or other disposition of property held for sale in the ordinary course of a trade or business,[101] other than foreclosure property.[102] A safe harbor is provided for

certain sales of rent producing real property. To qualify for the safe harbor, three criteria generally must be met. First, the REIT must have held the property for at least four years for rental purposes. Second, the aggregate expenditures made by the REIT during the four-year period prior to the date of the sale must not exceed 30 percent of the net selling price of the property. Third, either (i) the REIT must make 7 or fewer sales of property during the taxable year or (ii) the aggregate adjusted basis of the property sold must not exceed 10 percent of the aggregate bases of all the REIT's assets at the beginning of the REIT's taxable year. In the latter case, substantially all of the marketing and development expenditures with respect to the property must be made through an independent contractor.

Certain timber income

Some REITs have been formed to hold land on which trees are grown. Upon maturity of the trees, the standing trees are sold by the REIT. The Internal Revenue Service has issued private letter rulings in particular instances stating that the income from the sale of the trees can qualify as REIT real property income because the uncut timber and the timberland on which the timber grew is considered real property and the sale of

---

[101] Sec. 1221(a)(l).

[102] Thus, the 100-percent tax on prohibited transactions helps to ensure that the REIT is a passive entity and may not

engage in ordinary retailing activities such as sales to customers of condominium units or subdivided lots in a development project.

uncut trees can qualify as capital gain derived from the sale of real property.[103]

Limitation on investment in other entities

A REIT is limited in the amount that it can own in other corporations. Specifically, a REIT cannot own securities (other than Government securities and certain real estate assets) in an amount greater than 25 percent of the value of REIT assets. In addition, it cannot own such securities of any one issuer representing more than five percent of the total value of REIT assets or more than 10 percent of the voting securities or 10 percent of the value of the outstanding securities of any one issuer. Securities for purposes of these rules are defined by reference to the Investment Company Act of 1940.[104]

Special rules for Taxable REIT subsidiaries

Under an exception to the general rule limiting REIT securities ownership of other entities, a REIT can own stock of a taxable REIT subsidiary ("TRS"), generally, a corporation other than a REIT[105] with which the REIT makes a joint election to be subject to special rules. A TRS can engage in active business operations that would produce income that would not be qualified income for purposes of the 95-percent or 75-percent income tests for a REIT, and that income is not attributed to the REIT. Transactions between a TRS and a REIT are subject to a number of specified rules that are intended to prevent the TRS (taxable as a separate corporate entity) from shifting taxable income from its activities to the pass through entity REIT or from absorbing more than its share of expenses. Under one rule, a 100-percent excise tax is imposed on rents, deductions, or interest paid by the TRS to the REIT to the extent such items would exceed an arm's length amount as determined under section 482.[106]

Reasons for Change

The Committee believes it is appropriate to provide a safe harbor from the prohibited transactions rules, to permit a REIT that holds timberland to make sales of timber property, provided there is not significant development of the prop-erty. A similar provision already exists for rental properties.

Explanation of Provision

Under the provision, a sale of a real estate asset by a REIT will not be a prohibited transaction if the following six requirements are met:

(1) The asset must have been held for at least four years in the trade or business of producing timber;

(2) The aggregate expenditures made by the REIT (or a partner of the REIT) during the four-year period preceding the date of sale that are includible in the basis of the property (other than timberland acquisition expenditures[107]) and that are directly related to the operation of the property for the production of timber or for the preservation of the property for use as timberland must not exceed 30 percent of the net selling price of the property;

(3) The aggregate expenditures made by the REIT (or a partner of the REIT) during the four-year period preceding the date of sale that are includible in the basis of the property and that are not directly related to the operation of the property for the production of timber or the preservation of the property for use as timberland must not exceed five percent of the net selling price of the property;

(4) The REIT either (a) does not make more than seven sales of property (other than sales of foreclosure property or sales to which 1033 applies) or (b) the aggregate adjusted bases (as determined for purposes of computing earnings and profits) of property sold during the year (other than sales of foreclosure property or sales to which 1033 applies) does not exceed 10 percent of the aggregate bases (as determined for purposes of computing earnings and profits) of property of all assets of the REIT as of the beginning of the year;

(5) Substantially all of the marketing expenditures with respect to the property are made by persons who are independent contractors (as defined by section 856(d)(3)) with respect to the REIT and from whom the REIT does not derive any income; and

---

[103] See, e.g., PLR 200052021, PLR 199945055, PLR 19927021, PLR 8838016. A private letter ruling may be relied upon only by the taxpayer to which the ruling is issued. However, such rulings provide an indication of administrative practice.

[104] Certain securities that are within a safe-harbor definition of "straight debt" are not taken into account for purposes of the limitation to no more than 10 percent of the value of an issuer's outstanding securities.

[105] Certain corporations are not eligible to be a TRS, such as a corporation which directly or indirectly operates or manages a lodging facility or a health care facility or directly or indirectly provides to any other person rights to a brand name under which any lodging facility or health care facility is operated. Sec. 856(l)(3).

[106] If the excise tax applies, the item is not also reallocated back to the TRS under section 482.

[107] The timberland acquisition expenditures that are excluded for this purpose are those expenditures that are related to timberland other than the specific timberland that is being sold under the safe harbor, but costs of which may be combined with costs of such property in the same "management block" under Treasury regulations section 1.611-3(d). Any specific timberland being sold must meet the requirement that it has been held for at least four years by the REIT in order to qualify for the safe harbor.

(6) The sales price on the sale of the property cannot be based in whole or in part on income or profits of any person, including income or profits derived from the sale of such properties.

Capital expenditures counted towards the 30-percent limit are those expenditures that are includible in the basis of the property (other than timberland acquisition expenditures), and that are directly related to operation of the property for the production of timber, or for the preservation of the property for use as timberland. These capital expenditures are those incurred directly in the operation of raising timber (i.e., silviculture), as opposed to capital expenditures incurred in the ownership of undeveloped land. In general, these capital expenditures incurred directly in the operation of raising timber include capital expenditures incurred by the REIT to create an established stand of growing trees. A stand of trees is considered established when a target stand exhibits the expected growing rate and is free of non-target competition (e.g., hardwoods, grasses, brush, etc.) that may significantly inhibit or threaten the target stand survival. The costs commonly incurred during stand establishment are: (1) site preparation including manual or mechanical scarification, manual or mechanical cutting, disking, bedding, shearing, raking, piling, broadcast and windrow/pile burning (including slash disposal costs as required for stand establishment); (2) site regeneration including manual or mechanical hardwood coppice; (3) chemical application via aerial or ground to eliminate or reduce vegetation; (4) nursery operating costs including personnel salaries and benefits, facilities costs, cone collection and seed extraction, and other costs directly attributable to the nursery operations (to the extent such costs are allocable to seedlings used by the REIT); (5) seedlings including storage, transportation and handling equipment; (6) direct planting of seedlings; and (7) initial stand fertilization, up through stand establishment. Other examples of capital expenditures incurred directly in the operation of raising timber include construction cost of road to be used for managing the timber land (including for removal of logs or fire protection), environmental costs (i.e., habitat conservation plans), and any other post stand establishment capital costs (e.g., "mid-term fertilization costs."

Capital expenditures counted towards the 5-percent limit are those capital expenditures incurred in the ownership of undeveloped land that are not incurred in the direct operation of raising timber (i.e., silviculture). This category of capital expenditures includes: (1) expenditures to separate the REIT's holdings of land into separate parcels; (2) costs of granting leases or easements to cable, cellular or similar companies; (3) costs in determining the presence or quality of minerals located on the land; (4) costs incurred to defend changes in law that would limit future use of the land by the REIT or a purchaser from the REIT; (5) costs incurred to determine alternative uses of the land (e.g., recreational use); and (6) development costs of the property incurred by the REIT (e.g., engineering, surveying, legal, permit, consulting, road construction, utilities, and other development costs for use other than to grow timber).

Costs that are not includible in the basis of the property are not counted towards either the 30-percent or five-percent requirements.

Effective Date

The provision is effective for taxable years beginning after the date of enactment.

Conference Committee Report (H.R. CONF. REP. NO. 108-755)

House Bill   [Law at ¶ 5555. CCH Explanation at ¶ 1115.]

No provision.

Conference Agreement

The conference agreement follows the Senate amendment.

[¶ 10,450] Act Sec. 322. Expensing of reforestation expenditures

Senate Committee Report (S. Rep. No. 108-192)

[Code Sec. 194]

Present Law

Amortization of reforestation costs (sec. 194)

A taxpayer may elect to amortize up to $10,000 ($5,000 in the case of a separate return by a married individual) of qualifying reforestation expenditures incurred during the taxable year with respect to qualifying timber property. Amortization is taken over 84 months (seven years) and is subject to a mandatory half-year convention. In the case of an individual, the amortization deduction is allowed in determining adjusted gross income (i.e., an "above-the-line deduction") rather than as an itemized deduction.

Qualifying reforestation expenditures are the direct costs a taxpayer incurs in connection with the forestation or reforestation of a site by planting or seeding, and include costs for the preparation of the site, the cost of the seed or seedlings, and the cost of the labor and tools (including depreciation of long lived assets such as tractors and other machines) used in the reforestation activity. Qualifying reforestation expenditures do not include expenditures that would otherwise be deductible and do not include costs for which the taxpayer has been reimbursed under a governmental cost sharing program, unless the amount of the reimbursement is also included in the taxpayer's gross income.

The amount amortized is reduced by one half of the amount of reforestation credit claimed under section 48(b) (see below). Reforestation amortization is subject to recapture as ordinary income on sale of qualifying timber property within 10 years of the year in which the qualifying reforestation expenditures were incurred.

Reforestation tax credit (sec. 48(b))

A tax credit is allowed equal to 10 percent of the reforestation expenditures incurred during the year that are properly elected to be amortized. An amount allowed as a credit is subject to recapture if the qualifying timber property to which the expenditure relates is disposed of within five years.

Reasons for Change

The Committee believes it is important to encourage taxpayers to make investments in reforestation. The Committee believes that by shortening the recovery period of such outlays taxpayers will find a greater investment return to investments in reforestation. In addition, the Committee observes that elimination of the overlapping amortization and credit provisions of present law will simplify tax computation, record keeping, and tax return filing for taxpayers.[99]

Explanation of Provision

The bill permits taxpayers to elect to deduct (i.e., expense) up to $10,000 ($5,000 in the case of a separate return by a married individual) of qualifying reforestation expenditures incurred during the taxable year with respect to qualifying timber property. Any expenses above $10,000 ($5,000) would be amortized over a seven-year period.

The provision replaces the credit provisions of present law.

Effective Date

The provision is effective for expenditures paid or incurred after date of enactment.

Conference Committee Report (H.R. Conf. Rep. No. 108-755)

House Bill

No provision.

Conference Agreement

The conference agreement follows the Senate amendment provision.

[Law at ¶5060, ¶5065, ¶5070 and ¶5210. CCH Explanation at ¶840.]

---

[99] The Committee notes that the staff of the Joint Committee on Taxation identified the overlap of amortization of reforestation expenses and the credit for reforestation expenses as an area of complexity and recommended that the overlapping provisions be replaced with expensing of quali-

fying expenses. Joint Committee on Taxation, Study of the Overall State of the Federal Tax System and Recommendations for Simplification, Pursuant to Section 8022(3)(B) of the Internal Revenue Code of 1986 (JCS-3-01), April 2001, Volume II, p. 463.

[¶ 10,460] Act Sec. 331. Net income from publicly traded partnerships treated as qualifying income of regulated investment company

House Committee Report (H.R. Rep. No. 108-548, pt. 1)

[Code Secs. 469(k) and 851]

Present Law

Treatment of RICs

A regulated investment company ("RIC") generally is treated as a conduit for Federal income tax purposes. In computing its taxable income, a RIC deducts dividends paid to its shareholders to achieve conduit treatment (sec. 852(b)). In order to qualify for conduit treatment, a RIC must be a domestic corporation that, at all times during the taxable year, is registered under the Investment Company Act of 1940 as a management company or as a unit investment trust, or has elected to be treated as a business development company under that Act (sec. 851(a)). In addition, the corporation must elect RIC status, and must satisfy certain other requirements (sec. 851(b)).

One of the RIC qualification requirements is that at least 90 percent of the RIC's gross income is derived from dividends, interest, payments with respect to securities loans, and gains from the sale or other disposition of stock or securities or foreign currencies, or other income (including but not limited to gains from options, futures, or forward contracts) derived with respect to its business of investing in such stock, securities, or currencies (sec. 851(b)(2)). Income derived from a partnership is treated as meeting this requirement only to the extent such income is attributable to items of income of the partnership that would meet the requirement if realized by the RIC in the same manner as realized by the partnership (the "look-through" rule for partnership income) (sec. 851(b)). Under present law, no distinction is made under this rule between a publicly traded partnership and any other partnership.

The RIC qualification rules include limitations on the ownership of assets and on the composition of the RIC's assets (sec. 851(b)(3)). Under the ownership limitation, at least 50 percent of the value of the RIC's total assets must be represented by cash, government securities, and securities of other RICs, and other securities; however, in the case of such other securities, the RIC may invest no more than five percent of the value of the total assets of the RIC in the securities of any one issuer, and may hold no more than 10 percent of the outstanding voting securi-

ties of any one issuer. Under the limitation on the composition of the RIC's assets, no more than 25 percent of the value of the RIC's total assets may be invested in the securities of any one issuer (other than Government securities), or in securities of two or more controlled issuers in the same or similar trades or businesses. These limitations generally are applied at the end of each quarter (sec. 851(d)).

Treatment of publicly traded partnerships

Present law provides that a publicly traded partnership means a partnership, interests in which are traded on an established securities market, or are readily tradable on a secondary market (or the substantial equivalent thereof). In general, a publicly traded partnership is treated as a corporation (sec. 7704(a)), but an exception to corporate treatment is provided if 90 percent or more of its gross income is interest, dividends, real property rents, or certain other types of qualifying income (sec. 7704(c) and (d)).

A special rule for publicly traded partnerships applies under the passive loss rules. The passive loss rules limit deductions and credits from passive trade or business activities (sec. 469). Deductions attributable to passive activities, to the extent they exceed income from passive activities, generally may not be deducted against other income. Deductions and credits that are suspended under these rules are carried forward and treated as deductions and credits from passive activities in the next year. The suspended losses from a passive activity are allowed in full when a taxpayer disposes of his entire interest in the passive activity to an unrelated person. The special rule for publicly traded partnerships provides that the passive loss rules are applied separately with respect to items attributable to each publicly traded partnership (sec. 469(k)). Thus, income or loss from the publicly traded partnership is treated as separate from income or loss from other passive activities.

Reasons for Change

The Committee understands that publicly traded partnerships generally are treated as corporations under rules enacted to address Congress' view that publicly traded partnerships resemble corporations in important respects.[70] Publicly traded partnerships with specified types of income are not treated as corporations,

---

[70] H.R. Rep. No. 100-391, pt. 2 of 2, at 1066 (1987).

however, for the reason that if the income is from sources that are commonly considered to be passive investments, then there is less reason to treat the publicly traded partnership as a corporation.[71] The Committee understands that these types of publicly traded partnerships may have improved access to capital markets if their interests were permitted investments of mutual funds. Therefore, the bill treats publicly traded partnership interests as permitted investments for mutual funds ("RICs").

Nevertheless, the Committee believes that permitting mutual funds to hold interests in a publicly traded partnership should not give rise to avoidance of unrelated business income tax or withholding of income tax that would apply if tax-exempt organizations or foreign persons held publicly traded partnership interests directly rather than through a mutual fund. Therefore, the Committee bill requires that present-law limitations on ownership and composition of assets of mutual funds apply to any investment in a publicly traded partnership by a mutual fund. The Committee believes that these limitations will serve to limit the use of mutual funds as conduits for avoidance of unrelated business income tax or withholding rules that would otherwise apply with respect to publicly traded partnership income.

Explanation of Provision

The provision modifies the 90-percent test with respect to income of a RIC to include income derived from an interest in a publicly traded partnership. The provision also modifies the lookthrough rule for partnership income of a RIC so that it applies only to income from a partnership other than a publicly traded partnership.

The provision provides that the limitation on ownership and the limitation on composition of assets that apply to other investments of a RIC also apply to RIC investments in publicly traded partnership interests.

The provision provides that the special rule for publicly traded partnerships under the passive loss rules (requiring separate treatment) applies to a RIC holding an interest in a publicly traded partnership, with respect to items attributable to the interest in the publicly traded partnership.

Effective Date

The provision is effective for taxable years beginning after the date of enactment.

Conference Committee Report (H.R. CONF. REP. NO. 108-755)

Senate Amendment

The Senate amendment is the same as the House bill.

Conference Agreement

The conference agreement follows the House bill and Senate amendment. In addition, the conference agreement provides that net income from an interest in a publicly traded partnership is used for purposes of both the numerator and denominator of the 90-percent test. As under present law, the conference agreement also provides that gains from the sale or other disposition of interests in publicly traded partnerships constitute qualifying income of regulated investment companies.

[Law at ¶ 5390, ¶ 5545 and ¶ 6360. CCH Explanation at ¶ 1105.]

[¶ 10,470] Act Sec. 332. Simplification of excise tax imposed on bows and arrows

House Committee Report (H.R. REP. NO. 108-548, pt. 1)

[Code Sec. 4161]

Present Law

The Code imposes an excise tax of 11 percent on the sale by a manufacturer, producer or importer of any bow with a draw weight of 10 pounds or more.[89] An excise tax of 12.4 percent is imposed on the sale by a manufacturer or importer of any shaft, point, nock, or vane designed for use as part of an arrow which after its assembly (1) is over 18 inches long, or (2) is designed for use with a taxable bow (if shorter than 18 inches).[90] No tax is imposed on finished arrows. An 11-percent excise tax also is imposed on any part of an accessory for taxable bows and on quivers for use with arrows (1) over 18 inches long or (2) designed for use with a taxable bow (if shorter than 18 inches).[91]

---

[71] Id.
[89] Sec. 4161(b)(1)(A).

[90] Sec. 4161(b)(2).
[91] Sec. 4161(b)(1)(B).

Reasons for Change

Under present law, foreign manufacturers and importers of arrows avoid the 12.4 percent excise tax paid by domestic manufacturers because the tax is placed on arrow components rather than finished arrows. As a result, arrows assembled outside of the United States have a price advantage over domestically manufactured arrows. The Committee believes it is appropriate to close this loophole. The Committee also believes that adjusting the minimum draw weight for taxable bows from 10 pounds to 30 pounds will better target the excise tax to actual hunting use by eliminating the excise tax on instructional ("youth") bows.

Explanation of Provision

The provision increases the draw weight for a taxable bow from 10 pounds or more to a peak draw weight of 30 pounds or more.[92] The provision also imposes an excise tax of 12 percent on arrows generally. An arrow for this purpose is defined as a taxable arrow shaft to which additional components are attached. The present law 12.4-percent excise tax on certain arrow components is unchanged by the bill. In the case of any arrow comprised of a shaft or any other component upon which tax has been imposed, the amount of the arrow tax is equal to the excess of (1) the arrow tax that would have been imposed but for this exception, over (2) the amount of tax paid with respect to such components.[93] Finally, the provision subjects certain broadheads (a type of arrow point) to an excise tax equal to 11 percent of the sales price instead of 12.4 percent.

Conference Committee Report (H.R. CONF. REP. NO. 108-755)

Senate Amendment

The Senate amendment is the same as the House bill.

Conference Agreement

The conference agreement follows the House bill and Senate amendment with the effective date of the Senate amendment.

Effective Date

The provision is effective for articles sold by the manufacturer, producer or importer 30 days after the date of enactment.

Effective Date

The conference agreement follows the Senate amendment.

[Law at ¶ 6065. CCH Explanation at ¶ 1557.]

[¶ 10,480] Act Sec. 333. Reduce rate of excise tax on fishing tackle boxes to three percent

House Committee Report (H.R. REP. NO. 108-548, pt. 1)

[Code Sec. 4161]

Present Law

Under present law, a 10-percent manufacturer's excise tax is imposed on specified sport fishing equipment. Examples of taxable equipment include fishing rods and poles, fishing reels, artificial bait, fishing lures, line and hooks, and fishing tackle boxes. Revenues from the excise tax on sport fishing equipment are deposited in the Sport Fishing Account of the Aquatic Resources Trust Fund. Monies in the fund are spent, subject to an existing permanent appropri-

ation, to support Federal-State sport fish enhancement and safety programs.

Reasons for Change

The Committee observes that fishing "tackle boxes" are little different in design and appearance from "tool boxes," yet the former are subject to a Federal excise tax at a rate of 10-percent, while the latter are not subject to Federal excise tax. This excise tax can create a sufficiently large price difference that some fishermen will choose to use a "tool box" to hold their hooks and lures rather than a traditional "tackle box." The Com-

---

[92] Draw weight is the maximum force required to bring the bowstring to a full-draw position not less than 26¼-inches, measured from the pressure point of the hand grip to the nocking position on the bowstring.

[93] A credit or refund may be obtained when an item was taxed and it is used in the manufacture or production of another taxable item. Sec. 6416(b)(3). As arrow components

and finished arrows are both taxable, in lieu of a refund of the tax paid on components, the provision suspends the application of sec. 6416(b)(3) and permits the taxpayer to reduce the tax due on the finished arrow by the amount of the previous tax paid on the components used in the manufacture of such arrow.

mittee finds that such a distortion of consumer choice places an inappropriate burden on the manufacturers and purchasers of traditional tackle boxes, particularly in comparison to the modest amount of revenue raised by the present-law provision, and that this burden warrants repeal of the tax. The excise tax also adds unwarranted complexity to the Code, by requiring taxpayers and the IRS to make highly factual determinations as to which similar-use items are subject to tax and which are not.[94]

Explanation of Provision

The provision repeals the excise tax on fishing tackle boxes.

Effective Date

The provision is effective for articles sold by the manufacturer, producer, or importer after December 31, 2004.

Conference Committee Report (H.R. CONF. REP. NO. 108-755)

Senate Amendment

No provision.

Conference Agreement

The conference agreement follows the House bill with modifications. Under the provi-

sion as modified, the rate of excise tax imposed on fishing tackle boxes is reduced to three percent.

[Law at ¶ 6065. CCH Explanation at ¶ 1559.]

[¶ 10,490] Act Sec. 334. Repeal of excise tax on sonar devices suitable for finding fish

House Committee Report (H.R. REP. NO. 108-548, pt. 1)

[Code Sec. 4162]

Present Law

In general, the Code imposes a 10 percent tax on the sale by the manufacturer, producer, or importer of specified sport fishing equipment.[95] A three percent rate, however, applies to the sale of electric outboard motors and sonar devices suitable for finding fish.[96] Further, the tax imposed on the sale of sonar devices suitable for finding fish is limited to $30. A sonar device suitable for finding fish does not include any device that is a graph recorder, a digital type, a meter readout, a combination graph recorder or combination meter readout.[97]

Revenues from the excise tax on sport fishing equipment are deposited in the Sport Fishing Account of the Aquatic Resources Trust Fund. Monies in the fund are spent, subject to an existing permanent appropriation, to support Federal-State sport fish enhancement and safety programs.

Reasons for Change

The Committee observes that the current exemption for certain forms of sonar devices has

the effect of exempting almost all of the devices currently on the market. The Committee understands that only one form of sonar device is not exempt from the tax, those units utilizing light-emitting diode ("LED") display technology. The Committee understands that LED devices are currently not exempt from the tax because the technology was developed after the exemption for the other technologies was enacted. In the Committee's view, the application of the tax to LED display devices, and not to devices performing the same function with a different technology, creates an unfair advantage for the exempt devices. Because most of the devices on the market already are exempt, the Committee believes it is appropriate to level the playing field by repealing the tax imposed on all sonar devices suitable for finding fish. The Committee believes this is a more suitable solution than exempting a device from the tax based on the type of technology used.

Explanation of Provision

The provision repeals the excise tax on all sonar devices suitable for finding fish.

---

[94] The Joint Committee on Taxation has cited the tackle box issue as an example of the complexity of the sport fishing excise tax, and has recommended the elimination of the sport fishing equipment excise tax. See Joint Committee on Taxation, Study of the Overall State of the Federal Tax System and Recommendations for Simplification, Pursuant to Section 8022(3)(B) of the Internal Revenue Code of 1986,

(JCS-3-01), Vol. II, Recommendations of the Staff of the Joint Committee on Taxation to Simplify the Federal Tax System, at 499-500, April 2001.

[95] Sec. 4161(a)(1).

[96] Sec. 4161(a)(2).

[97] Sec. 4162(b).

Effective Date

The provision is effective for articles sold by the manufacturer, producer, or importer after December 31, 2004.

Conference Committee Report (H.R. CONF. REP. NO. 108-755)

Senate Amendment [Law at ¶ 6070. CCH Explanation at ¶ 1561.]

No provision.

Conference Agreement

The conference agreement follows the House bill.

[¶ 10,500] Act Sec. 335. Charitable contribution deduction for certain expenses in support of Native Alaskan subsistence whaling

House Committee Report (H.R. REP. NO. 108-548, pt. 1)

[Code Sec. 170]

Present Law

In computing taxable income, individuals who do not elect the standard deduction may claim itemized deductions, including a deduction (subject to certain limitations) for charitable contributions or gifts made during the taxable year to a qualified charitable organization or governmental entity. Individuals who elect the standard deduction may not claim a deduction for charitable contributions made during the taxable year.

No charitable contribution deduction is allowed for a contribution of services. However, unreimbursed expenditures made incident to the rendition of services to an organization, contributions to which are deductible, may constitute a deductible contribution.[114] Specifically, section 170(j) provides that no charitable contribution deduction is allowed for traveling expenses (including amounts expended for meals and lodging) while away from home, whether paid directly or by reimbursement, unless there is no significant element of personal pleasure, recreation, or vacation in such travel.

Reasons for Change

The Committee believes that subsistence bowhead whale hunting activities are important to certain native peoples of Alaska and further charitable purposes. The Committee believes that certain expenses paid by individuals recognized as whaling captains by the Alaska Eskimo Whaling Commission in the conduct of sanctioned whaling activities conducted pursuant to the management plan of that Commission should be deductible expenses.

Explanation of Provision

The provision allows individuals to claim a deduction under section 170 not exceeding $10,000 per taxable year for certain expenses incurred in carrying out sanctioned whaling activities. The deduction is available only to an individual who is recognized by the Alaska Eskimo Whaling Commission as a whaling captain charged with the responsibility of maintaining and carrying out sanctioned whaling activities. The deduction is available for reasonable and necessary expenses paid by the taxpayer during the taxable year for: (1) the acquisition and maintenance of whaling boats, weapons, and gear used in sanctioned whaling activities; (2) the supplying of food for the crew and other provisions for carrying out such activities; and (3) the storage and distribution of the catch from such activities. The Committee intends that the Secretary shall require that the taxpayer substantiate deductible expenses by maintaining appropriate written records that show, for example, the time, place, date, amount, and nature of the expense, as well as the taxpayer's eligibility for the deduction, and that such substantiation be provided as part of the taxpayer's income tax return, to the extent provided by the Secretary.

For purposes of the provision, the term "sanctioned whaling activities" means subsistence bowhead whale hunting activities conducted pursuant to the management plan of the Alaska Eskimo Whaling Commission.

Effective Date

The provision is effective for contributions made after December 31, 2004.

---

[114] Treas. Reg. sec. 1.170A-1(g).

Conference Committee Report (H.R. Conf. Rep. No. 108-755)

Senate Amendment

No provision.

Conference Agreement

The conference agreement includes the House bill provision, modified to provide that

the Secretary shall issue guidance regarding substantiation of amounts claimed as deductible whaling expenses.

[Law at ¶ 5185. CCH Explanation at ¶ 1320.]

[¶ 10,510] Act Sec. 336. Extended placed in service date for bonus depreciation for certain aircraft (excluding aircraft used in the transportation industry)

House Committee Report (H.R. Rep. No. 108-548, pt. 1)

[Code Sec. 168]

Present Law

In general

A taxpayer is allowed to recover, through annual depreciation deductions, the cost of certain property used in a trade or business or for the production of income. The amount of the depreciation deduction allowed with respect to tangible property for a taxable year is determined under the modified accelerated cost recovery system ("MACRS"). Under MACRS, different types of property generally are assigned applicable recovery periods and depreciation methods. The recovery periods applicable to most tangible personal property range from 3 to 25 years. The depreciation methods generally applicable to tangible personal property are the 200-percent and 150-percent declining balance methods, switching to the straight-line method for the taxable year in which the depreciation deduction would be maximized.

Thirty-percent additional first year depreciation deduction

JCWAA allows an additional first-year depreciation deduction equal to 30 percent of the adjusted basis of qualified property.[20] The amount of the additional first-year depreciation deduction is not affected by a short taxable year.

The additional first-year depreciation deduction is allowed for both regular tax and alternative minimum tax purposes for the taxable year in which the property is placed in service.[21] The basis of the property and the depreciation allowances in the year of purchase and later years are appropriately adjusted to reflect the additional first-year depreciation deduction. In addition, there are generally no adjustments to the allowable amount of depreciation for purposes of computing a taxpayer's alternative minimum taxable income with respect to property to which the provision applies. A taxpayer is allowed to elect out of the additional first-year depreciation for any class of property for any taxable year.[22]

In order for property to qualify for the additional first-year depreciation deduction, it must meet all of the following requirements. First, the property must be (1) property to which MACRS applies with an applicable recovery period of 20 years or less, (2) water utility property (as defined in section 168(e)(5)), (3) computer software other than computer software covered by section 197, or (4) qualified leasehold improvement property (as defined in section 168(k)(3)).[23] Second, the original use[24] of the property must commence with the taxpayer on or after September 11, 2001. Third, the taxpayer must acquire the property within the applicable time period. Fi-

---

[20] The additional first-year depreciation deduction is subject to the general rules regarding whether an item is deductible under section 162 or subject to capitalization under section 263 or section 263A.

[21] However, the additional first-year depreciation deduction is not allowed for purposes of computing earnings and profits.

[22] A taxpayer may elect out of the 50-percent additional first-year depreciation (discussed below) for any class of property and still be eligible for the 30-percent additional first-year depreciation.

[23] A special rule precludes the additional first-year depreciation deduction for any property that is required to be

depreciated under the alternative depreciation system of MACRS.

[24] The term "original use" means the first use to which the property is put, whether or not such use corresponds to the use of such property by the taxpayer. If, in the normal course of its business, a taxpayer sells fractional interests in property to unrelated third parties, then the original use of such property begins with the first user of each fractional interest (i.e., each fractional owner is considered the original user of its proportionate share of the property).

nally, the property must be placed in service before January 1, 2005.

An extension of the placed-in-service date of one year (i.e., January 1, 2006) is provided for certain property with a recovery period of ten years or longer and certain transportation property.[25] Transportation property is defined as tangible personal property used in the trade or business of transporting persons or property.

The applicable time period for acquired property is (1) after September 10, 2001 and before January 1, 2005, but only if no binding written contract for the acquisition is in effect before September 11, 2001, or (2) pursuant to a binding written contract which was entered into after September 10, 2001, and before January 1, 2005.[26] For property eligible for the extended placed-in-service date, a special rule limits the amount of costs eligible for the additional first year depreciation. With respect to such property, only the portion of the basis that is properly attributable to the costs incurred before January 1, 2005 ("progress expenditures") is eligible for the additional first-year depreciation.[27]

Fifty-percent additional first year depreciation

JGTRRA provides an additional first-year depreciation deduction equal to 50 percent of the adjusted basis of qualified property. Qualified property is defined in the same manner as for purposes of the 30-percent additional first-year depreciation deduction provided by the JCWAA except that the applicable time period for acquisition (or self construction) of the property is modified. Property eligible for the 50-percent additional first-year depreciation deduction is not eligible for the 30-percent additional first-year depreciation deduction.

In order to qualify, the property must be acquired after May 5, 2003, and before January 1, 2005, and no binding written contract for the acquisition can be in effect before May 6, 2003.[28] With respect to property that is manufactured, constructed, or produced by the taxpayer for use

by the taxpayer, the taxpayer must begin the manufacture, construction, or production of the property after May 5, 2003. For property eligible for the extended placed-in-service date (i.e., certain property with a recovery period of ten years or longer and certain transportation property), a special rule limits the amount of costs eligible for the additional first-year depreciation. With respect to such property, only progress expenditures properly attributable to the costs incurred before January 1, 2005 are eligible for the additional first-year depreciation.[29]

Reasons for Change

The Committee believes that certain non-commercial aircraft represent property having characteristics that should qualify for the extended placed-in-service date accorded under present law for property having long production periods. This treatment should be available only if the purchaser makes a substantial deposit, the expected cost exceeds certain thresholds, and the production period is sufficiently long.

Explanation of Provision

Due to the extended production period, the provision provides criteria under which certain non-commercial aircraft can qualify for the extended placed-in-service date. Qualifying aircraft would be eligible for the additional first-year depreciation deduction if placed in service before January 1, 2006. In order to qualify, the aircraft must:

(a) Be acquired by the taxpayer during the applicable time period as under present law;

(b) Meet the appropriate placed-in-service date requirements;

(c) Not be tangible personal property used in the trade or business of transporting persons or property (except for agricultural or firefighting purposes);

(d) Be purchased[30] by a purchaser who, at the time of the contract for purchase, has made a nonrefundable deposit of the lesser of ten percent of the cost or $100,000; and

---

[25] In order for property to qualify for the extended placed-in-service date, the property must be subject to section 263A by reason of having a production period exceeding two years or an estimated production period exceeding one year and a cost exceeding $1 million.

[26] Property does not fail to qualify for the additional first-year depreciation merely because a binding written contract to acquire a component of the property is in effect prior to September 11, 2001.

[27] For purposes of determining the amount of eligible progress expenditures, it is intended that rules similar to sec. 46(d)(3) as in effect prior to the Tax Reform Act of 1986 shall apply.

[28] Property does not fail to qualify for the additional first-year depreciation merely because a binding written contract

to acquire a component of the property is in effect prior to May 6, 2003. However, no 50-percent additional first-year depreciation is permitted on any such component. No inference is intended as to the proper treatment of components placed in service under the 30-percent additional first-year depreciation provided by the JCWAA.

[29] For purposes of determining the amount of eligible progress expenditures, it is intended that rules similar to sec. 46(d)(3) as in effect prior to the Tax Reform Act of 1986 shall apply.

[30] For this purpose, the Committee intends that the term "purchase" be interpreted as it is defined in sec. 179(d)(2).

(e) Have an estimated production period exceeding four months and a cost exceeding $200,000.

Effective Date

The provision is effective as if included in the amendments made by section 101 of JCWAA, which applies to property placed in service after September 10, 2001. However, because the property described by the provision qualifies for the additional first-year depreciation deduction under present law if placed in service prior to January 1, 2005, the provision will modify the treatment only of property placed in service during calendar year 2005.

Conference Committee Report (H.R. CONF. REP. NO. 108-755)

The conference agreement follows the House bill.

[Law at ¶ 5180. CCH Explanation at ¶ 325.]

[¶ 10,520] Act Sec. 337. Special placed in service rule for bonus depreciation for certain property subject to syndication

House Committee Report (H.R. REP. NO. 108-548, pt. 1)

[Code Sec. 168]

Present Law

Section 101 of JCWAA provides generally for 30-percent additional first-year depreciation, and provides a binding contract rule in determining property that qualifies for it. The requirements that must be satisfied in order for property to qualify include that (1) the original use of the property must commence with the taxpayer on or after September 11, 2001, (2) the taxpayer must acquire the property after September 10, 2001 and before September 11, 2004, and (3) no binding written contract for the acquisition of the property is in effect before September 11, 2001 (or, in the case of self-constructed property, manufacture, construction, or production of the property does not begin before September 11, 2001). In addition, JCWAA provides a special rule in the case of certain leased property. In the case of any property that is originally placed in service by a person and that is sold to the taxpayer and leased back to such person by the taxpayer within three months after the date that the property was placed in service, the property is treated as originally placed in service by the taxpayer not earlier than the date that the property is used under the leaseback. JCWAA did not specifically address the syndication of a lease by the lessor.

JGTRRA provides an additional first-year depreciation deduction equal to 50 percent of the adjusted basis of qualified property. Qualified property is defined in the same manner as for purposes of the 30-percent additional first-year depreciation deduction provided by the JCWAA except that the applicable time period for acquisition (or self construction) of the property is modified. Property with respect to which the 50-percent additional first-year depreciation deduction is claimed is not also eligible for the 30-percent additional first-year depreciation deduction. In order to qualify, the property must be acquired after May 5, 2003 and before January 1, 2005, and no binding written contract for the acquisition can be in effect before May 6, 2003. With respect to property that is manufactured, constructed, or produced by the taxpayer for use by the taxpayer, the taxpayer must begin the manufacture, construction, or production of the property after May 5, 2003.

Reasons for Change

The Committee believes that the rules relating to 30-percent additional first-year depreciation should be clarified to reflect the legislative intent that syndicated property, if sold within three months of the date it was originally placed in service, be eligible for the additional first-year depreciation deduction. Further, the Committee is aware that certain syndication arrangements are entered into with respect to multiple units of property (such as rail cars) that, for logistical reasons, must be placed in service over a period of time that exceeds three months. In such cases, it would be impractical for the sale of the earlier produced units to occur within three months of its placed-in-service date. Thus, the Committee deems it appropriate to provide a special rule with respect to the syndication of multiple units of property that will be placed in service over a period of up to twelve months.

Explanation of Provision

The provision provides that if property is originally placed in service by a lessor (including by operation of the special rule for self-constructed property), such property is sold within three months after the date that the property was placed in service, and the user of such property does not change, then the property is treated as originally placed in service by the taxpayer not earlier than the date of such sale. The provision also provides a special rule in the case of multiple units of property subject to the same lease. In such cases, property will qualify as placed in service on the date of sale if it is sold within three months after the final unit is placed in service, so long as the period between the time the first and last units are placed in service does not exceed 12 months.

Effective Date

The provision is generally effective as if included in the amendments made by section 101 of JCWAA (i.e., generally for property placed in service after September 10, 2001, in taxable years ending after that date). However, the special rule in the case of multiple units of property subject to the same lease applies to property sold after June 4, 2004.

Conference Committee Report (H.R. CONF. REP. NO. 108-755)

Present Law

Section 101 of JCWAA provides generally for 30-percent additional first-year depreciation, and provides a binding contract rule in determining property that qualifies for it. The requirements that must be satisfied in order for property to qualify include that (1) the original use of the property must commence with the taxpayer on or after September 11, 2001, and (2) the taxpayer must acquire the property (i) after September 10, 2001, and before January 1, 2005, but only if no binding written contract for the acquisition is in effect before September 11, 2001, or (ii) pursuant to a binding contract which was entered into after September 10, 2001, and before January 1, 2005. In addition, JCWAA provides a special rule in the case of certain leased property. In the case of any property that is originally placed in service by a person and that is sold to the taxpayer and leased back to such person by the taxpayer within three months after the date that the property was placed in service, the property is treated as originally placed in service by the taxpayer not earlier than the date that the property is used under the leaseback. JCWAA did not specifically address the syndication of a lease by the lessor.

The Working Families Tax Relief Act of 2004 ("H.R. 1308") included a technical correction regarding the syndication of a lease by the lessor. The technical correction provides that if property is originally placed in service by a lessor (including by operation of the special rule for self-constructed property), such property is sold within three months after the date that the property was placed in service, and the user of such property does not change, then the property is treated as originally placed in service by the taxpayer not earlier than the date of such sale.

JGTRRA provides an additional first-year depreciation deduction equal to 50 percent of the adjusted basis of qualified property. Qualified property is defined in the same manner as for purposes of the 30-percent additional first-year depreciation deduction provided by the JCWAA except that the applicable time period for acquisition (or self construction) of the property is modified. Property with respect to which the 50-percent additional first-year depreciation deduction is claimed is not also eligible for the 30-percent additional first-year depreciation deduction. In order to qualify, the property must be acquired after May 5, 2003 and before January 1, 2005, and no binding written contract for the acquisition can be in effect before May 6, 2003. With respect to property that is manufactured, constructed, or produced by the taxpayer for use by the taxpayer, the taxpayer must begin the manufacture, construction, or production of the property after May 5, 2003.

House Bill[60]

* * * The provision also provides a special rule in the case of multiple units of property subject to the same lease. In such cases, property will qualify as placed in service on the date of sale if it is sold within three months after the final unit is placed in service, so long as the period between the time the first and last units are placed in service does not exceed 12 months.

* * *

Conference Agreement

The conference agreement follows the House bill with the following modification. The clauses that were duplicative of the provisions enacted as part of H.R. 1308 were removed. Thus, the conference agreement provision provides only for the special rule in the case of multiple units of property subject to the same lease.

[Law at ¶ 5180. CCH Explanation at ¶ 330.]

---

[60] The House bill predated the enactment of H.R. 1308, Pub. L. No. 108-311 (the "Working Families Tax Relief Act of 2004"), which included a number of technical corrections.

[¶ 10,530] Act Sec. 338. Expensing of capital costs incurred for production in complying with Environmental Protection Agency sulfur regulations for small refiners

Conference Committee Report (H.R. CONF. REP. NO. 108-755)

[New Code Sec. 179B]

Present Law

Taxpayers generally may recover the costs of investments in refinery property through annual depreciation deductions.

House Bill

No provision.

Senate Amendment

The Senate amendment permits small business refiners to immediately deduct as an expense up to 75 percent of the costs paid or incurred for the purpose of complying with the Highway Diesel Fuel Sulfur Control Requirements of the Environmental Protection Agency ("EPA"). Costs qualifying for the deduction are those costs paid or incurred with respect to any facility of a small business refiner during the period beginning on January 1, 2003 and ending on the earlier of the date that is one year after the date on which the taxpayer must comply with the applicable EPA regulations or December 31, 2009.

For these purposes a small business refiner is a taxpayer who is in the business of refining petroleum products and employs not more than 1,500 employees directly in refining and has less than 205,000 barrels per day (average) of total refinery capacity. The deduction is reduced, *pro rata*, for taxpayers with capacity in excess of 155,000 barrels per day.

Effective Date

The Senate amendment is effective for expenses paid or incurred after December 31, 2002, in taxable years ending after that date.

Conference Agreement

The conference agreement includes the Senate amendment provision. With respect to the definition of a small business refiner, the conferees intend that, in any case in which refinery through-put or retained production of the refinery differs substantially from its average daily output or refined product, capacity be measured by reference to the average daily output of refined product.

[Law at ¶ 5200, ¶ 5265, ¶ 5270, ¶ 5300, ¶ 5760 and ¶ 5795. CCH Explanation at ¶ 850.]

[¶ 10,540] Act Sec. 339. Credit for small refiners for production of diesel fuel in compliance with Environmental Protection Agency sulfur regulations for small refiners

Conference Committee Report (H.R. CONF. REP. NO. 108-755)

[New Code Sec. 45H]

Present Law

Present law does not provide a credit for the production of low-sulfur diesel fuel.

House Bill

No provision.

Senate Amendment

The Senate amendment provides that a small business refiner may claim credit equal to five cents per gallon for each gallon of low sulfur diesel fuel produced during the taxable year that is in compliance with the Highway Diesel Fuel Sulfur Control Requirements of the Environmental Protection Agency ("EPA"). The total produc-

tion credit claimed by the taxpayer is limited to 25 percent of the capital costs incurred to come into compliance with the EPA diesel fuel requirements. Costs qualifying for the credit are those costs paid or incurred with respect to any facility of a small business refiner during the period beginning on January 1, 2003 and ending on the earlier of the date that is one year after the date on which the taxpayer must comply with the applicable EPA regulations or December 31, 2009. The taxpayer's basis in property with respect to which the credit applies is reduced by the amount of production credit claimed.

In the case of a qualifying small business refiner that is owned by a cooperative, the cooperative is allowed to elect to pass any production credits to patrons of the organization.

For these purposes a small business refiner is a taxpayer who is in the business of refining petroleum products, employs not more than 1,500 employees directly in refining, and has less than 205,000 barrels per day (average) of total refinery capacity. The credit is reduced, *pro rata*, for taxpayers with capacity in excess of 155,000 barrels per day.

Effective Date

The Senate amendment is effective for expenses paid or incurred after December 31, 2002, in taxable years ending after that date.

Conference Agreement

The conference agreement includes the Senate amendment provision with modification as follows. The conference agreement makes the low sulfur diesel fuel credit a qualified business credit under section 169(c). Therefore, if any portion of the credit has not been allowed to the taxpayer as a general business credit (sec. 38) for any taxable year, an amount equal to that portion may be deducted by the taxpayer in the first taxable year following the last taxable year for which such portion could have been allowed as a credit under the carryback and carryforward rules (sec. 39). With respect to the definition of a small business refiner, the conferees intend that, in any case where refinery through-put or retained production of the refinery differs substantially from its average daily output of refined product, capacity be measured by reference to the average daily output of refined product.

[Law at ¶ 5010, ¶ 5050, ¶ 5220, ¶ 5290 and ¶ 5760. CCH Explanation at ¶ 855.]

[¶ 10,550] Act Sec. 340. Modification to qualified small issue bonds

Senate Committee Report (S. REP. NO. 108-192)

[Code Sec. 144]

Present Law

Qualified small-issue bonds are tax-exempt State and local government bonds used to finance private business manufacturing facilities (including certain directly related and ancillary facilities) or the acquisition of land and equipment by certain farmers. In both instances, these bonds are subject to limits on the amount of financing that may be provided, both for a single borrowing and in the aggregate. In general, no more than $1 million of small-issue bond financing may be outstanding at any time for property of a business (including related parties) located in the same municipality or county. Generally, this $1 million limit may be increased to $10 million if all other capital expenditures of the business in the same municipality or county over a six-year period are counted toward the limit. Outstanding aggregate borrowing is limited to $40 million per borrower (including related parties) regardless of where the property is located. No more than $250,000 per borrower ($62,500 for used property) may be used to finance eligible farm property.

Property and businesses eligible for this financing are specified. For example, only depreciable property (and related real property) used in the production of tangible personal property is eligible for financing as a manufacturing facility. Storage and distribution of products generally is not treated as production under this provision. Agricultural land and equipment may only be financed for first-time farmers, defined as individuals who have not at any prior time owned farmland in excess of: (1) 30 percent of the median size of a farm in the same county; or (2) $125,000 in value.

Before 1987, qualified small-issue bonds also could be used to finance commercial facilities. In addition to general prohibitions on the tax-exempt private activity bond financing of certain facilities, Federal law precludes the use of qualified small-issue bonds to finance a broader list of facilities. For example, no more than 25 percent of a bond issue can be used to finance restaurants, bars, automobile sales and service facilities, or entertainment facilities. No portion of these bond proceeds can be used to finance golf courses, country clubs, massage parlors, tennis clubs or other racquet sport facilities, skating facilities, hot tub facilities, or racetracks.

Reasons for Change

The Committee believes that the class of facilities eligible for qualified small-issue bond financing should be expanded to include otherwise eligible facilities with total capital expenditures of less than $20 million. The present-law capital expenditures limit of $10 million has not been adjusted in many years.

Explanation of Provision

The bill increases the maximum allowable amount of total capital expenditures by an eligible business in the same municipality or county during the six-year period from $10 million to $20 million. As under present-law, no more than $10 million of bond financing may be outstanding at any time for property of an eligible business (including related parties) located in the same municipality or county. Other present-law limits (e.g., the $40 million per borrower limit) continue to apply.

Conference Committee Report (H.R. CONF. REP. NO. 108-755)

House Bill

No provision.

Conference Agreement

The conference agreement follows the Senate amendment, except with respect to the effective date. The conference agreement increases the maximum allowable amount of total capital expenditures by an eligible business (or related

party) in the same municipality or county from $10 million to $20 million for bonds issued after September 30, 2009.

Effective Date

The provision is effective for bonds issued after September 30, 2009.

[Law at ¶ 5150. CCH Explanation at ¶ 735.]

[¶ 10,560] Act Sec. 341. Oil and gas production from marginal wells

Conference Committee Report (H.R. CONF. REP. NO. 108-755)

[New Code Sec. 45I]

Present Law

There is no credit for the production of oil and gas from marginal wells. The costs of such production may be recovered under the Code's depreciation and depletion rules and in other cases as a deduction for ordinary and necessary business expenses.

House Bill

No provision.

Senate Amendment

The Senate amendment would create a new, $3-per-barrel credit for the production of crude oil and a $0.50 credit per 1,000 cubic feet of qualified natural gas production. In both cases, the credit is available only for production from a "qualified marginal well." A qualified marginal well is defined as domestic well: (1) production from which is treated as marginal production for purposes of the Code percentage depletion rules; or (2) that during the taxable year had average daily production of not more than 25 barrel equivalents and produces water at a rate of not less than 95 percent of total well effluent. Production from any well during any period in which such well is not in compliance with applicable Federal pollution prevention, control, and permit requirements is not considered a qualified marginal well during such period. The maximum amount of production on which credit could be claimed is 1,095 barrels or barrel equivalents.

The credit is not available to production occurring if the reference price of oil exceeds $18

($2.00 for natural gas). The credit is reduced proportionately as for reference prices between $15 and $18 ($1.67 and $2.00 for natural gas). Reference prices are determined on a one-year look-back basis.

In the case of production from a qualified marginal well which is eligible for the credit allowed under section 29 for the taxable year, no marginal well credit is allowable unless the taxpayer elects not to claim the credit under section 29 with respect to the well. The credit is treated as a general business credit.

Effective Date

The Senate amendment is effective for production in taxable years beginning after December 31, 2004.

Conference Agreement

The conference agreement modifies the Senate amendment. The conference agreement does not include the Federal pollution prevention, control, and permit requirement provisions of the Senate amendment. The conference agreement treats the credit as part of the general business credit; however, unused credits can be carried back for up to five years rather than the generally applicable carryback period of one year. The credit is indexed for inflation for taxable years beginning in a calendar year after 2005.

Effective Date

The provision is effective for production in taxable years beginning after December 31, 2004.

[Law at ¶ 5010, ¶ 5015 and ¶ 5055. CCH Explanation at ¶ 860.]

[¶ 10,570] Act Sec. 401. Interest expense allocation rules

House Committee Report (H.R. REP. NO. 108-548, pt. 1)

[Code Sec. 864]

Present Law

In general

In order to compute the foreign tax credit limitation, a taxpayer must determine the amount of its taxable income from foreign sources. Thus, the taxpayer must allocate and apportion deductions between items of U.S.-source gross income, on the one hand, and items of foreign-source gross income, on the other.

In the case of interest expense, the rules generally are based on the approach that money is fungible and that interest expense is properly attributable to all business activities and property of a taxpayer, regardless of any specific purpose for incurring an obligation on which interest is paid.[115] For interest allocation purposes, the Code provides that all members of an affiliated group of corporations generally are treated as a single corporation (the so-called "one-taxpayer rule") and allocation must be made on the basis of assets rather than gross income.

Affiliated group

In general

The term "affiliated group" in this context generally is defined by reference to the rules for determining whether corporations are eligible to file consolidated returns. However, some groups of corporations are eligible to file consolidated returns yet are not treated as affiliated for interest allocation purposes, and other groups of corporations are treated as affiliated for interest allocation purposes even though they are not eligible to file consolidated returns. Thus, under the one-taxpayer rule, the factors affecting the allocation of interest expense of one corporation may affect the sourcing of taxable income of another, related corporation even if the two corporations do not elect to file, or are ineligible to file, consolidated returns.

Definition of affiliated group—consolidated return rules

For consolidation purposes, the term "affiliated group" means one or more chains of includible corporations connected through stock ownership with a common parent corporation which is an includible corporation, but only if:

(1) the common parent owns directly stock possessing at least 80 percent of the total voting power and at least 80 percent of the total value of at least one other includible corporation; and (2) stock meeting the same voting power and value standards with respect to each includible corporation (excluding the common parent) is directly owned by one or more other includible corporations.

Generally, the term "includible corporation" means any domestic corporation except certain corporations exempt from tax under section 501 (for example, corporations organized and operated exclusively for charitable or educational purposes), certain life insurance companies, corporations electing application of the possession tax credit, regulated investment companies, real estate investment trusts, and domestic international sales corporations. A foreign corporation generally is not an includible corporation.

Definition of affiliated group—special interest allocation rules

Subject to exceptions, the consolidated return and interest allocation definitions of affiliation generally are consistent with each other.[116] For example, both definitions generally exclude all foreign corporations from the affiliated group. Thus, while debt generally is considered fungible among the assets of a group of domestic affiliated corporations, the same rules do not apply as between the domestic and foreign members of a group with the same degree of common control as the domestic affiliated group.

Banks, savings institutions, and other financial affiliates

The affiliated group for interest allocation purposes generally excludes what are referred to in the Treasury regulations as "financial corporations" (Treas. Reg. sec. 1.861-11T(d)(4)). These include any corporation, otherwise a member of the affiliated group for consolidation purposes, that is a financial institution (described in section 581 or section 591), the business of which is predominantly with persons other than related persons or their customers, and which is required by State or Federal law to be operated separately from any other entity which is not a financial institution (sec. 864(e)(5)(C)). The category of financial corporations also includes, to the extent provided in regulations, bank holding

---

[115] However, exceptions to the fungibility principle are provided in particular cases, some of which are described below.

[116] One such exception is that the affiliated group for interest allocation purposes includes section 936 corporations that are excluded from the consolidated group.

companies (including financial holding companies), subsidiaries of banks and bank holding companies (including financial holding companies), and savings institutions predominantly engaged in the active conduct of a banking, financing, or similar business (sec. 864(e)(5)(D)).

A financial corporation is not treated as a member of the regular affiliated group for purposes of applying the one-taxpayer rule to other non-financial members of that group. Instead, all such financial corporations that would be so affiliated are treated as a separate single corporation for interest allocation purposes.

Reasons for Change

The Committee observes that the United States is the only country that currently imposes harsh and anti-competitive interest expense allocation rules on its businesses and workers. The present-law interest expense allocation rules result in U.S. companies allocating a portion of their U.S. interest expense against foreign-source income, even when the foreign operation has its own debt. The tax effect of this rule is that U.S. companies end up paying double tax. The practical effect is that the cost for U.S. companies to borrow in the United States is increased and it becomes more expensive to invest in the United States. The Committee believes that these rules should be modified so that U.S. companies are not discouraged from investing in the United States. To this end, U.S. companies should not be required to allocate U.S. interest expense against foreign-source income (and thereby incur double taxation) unless their debt-to-asset ratio is higher in the United States than in foreign countries.

Explanation of Provision

In general

The provision modifies the present-law interest expense allocation rules (which generally apply for purposes of computing the foreign tax credit limitation) by providing a one-time election under which the taxable income of the domestic members of an affiliated group from sources outside the United States generally is determined by allocating and apportioning inter-est expense of the domestic members of a worldwide affiliated group on a worldwide-group basis (i.e., as if all members of the worldwide group were a single corporation). If a group makes this election, the taxable income of the domestic members of a worldwide affiliated group from sources outside the United States is determined by allocating and apportioning third-party interest expense of those domestic members to foreign-source income in an amount equal to the excess (if any) of (1) the worldwide affiliated group's worldwide third-party interest expense multiplied by the ratio which the foreign assets of the worldwide affiliated group bears to the total assets of the worldwide affiliated group,[117] over (2) the third-party interest expense incurred by foreign members of the group to the extent such interest would be allocated to foreign sources if the provision's principles were applied separately to the foreign members of the group.[118]

For purposes of the new elective rules based on worldwide fungibility, the worldwide affiliated group means all corporations in an affiliated group (as that term is defined under present law for interest allocation purposes)[119] as well as all controlled foreign corporations that, in the aggregate, either directly or indirectly,[120] would be members of such an affiliated group if section 1504(b)(3) did not apply (i.e., in which at least 80 percent of the vote and value of the stock of such corporations is owned by one or more other corporations included in the affiliated group). Thus, if an affiliated group makes this election, the taxable income from sources outside the United States of domestic group members generally is determined by allocating and apportioning interest expense of the domestic members of the worldwide affiliated group as if all of the interest expense and assets of 80-percent or greater owned domestic corporations (i.e., corporations that are part of the affiliated group under present-law section 864(e)(5)(A) as modified to include insurance companies) and certain controlled foreign corporations were attributable to a single corporation.

---

[117] For purposes of determining the assets of the worldwide affiliated group, neither stock in corporations within the group nor indebtedness (including receivables) between members of the group is taken into account. It is anticipated that the Treasury Secretary will adopt regulations addressing the allocation and apportionment of interest expense on such indebtedness that follow principles analogous to those of existing regulations. Income from holding stock or indebtedness of another group member is taken into account for all purposes under the present-law rules of the Code, including the foreign tax credit provisions.

[118] Although the interest expense of a foreign subsidiary is taken into account for purposes of allocating the interest expense of the domestic members of the electing worldwide

affiliated group for foreign tax credit limitation purposes, the interest expense incurred by a foreign subsidiary is not deductible on a U.S. return.

[119] The provision expands the definition of an affiliated group for interest expense allocation purposes to include certain insurance companies that are generally excluded from an affiliated group under section 1504(b)(2) (without regard to whether such companies are covered by an election under section 1504(c)(2)).

[120] Indirect ownership is determined under the rules of section 958(a)(2) or through applying rules similar to those of section 958(a)(2) to stock owned directly or indirectly by domestic partnerships, trusts, or estates.

In addition, if an affiliated group elects to apply the new elective rules based on worldwide fungibility, the present-law rules regarding the treatment of tax-exempt assets and the basis of stock in nonaffiliated ten-percent owned corporations apply on a worldwide affiliated group basis.

The common parent of the domestic affiliated group must make the worldwide affiliated group election. It must be made for the first taxable year beginning after December 31, 2008, in which a worldwide affiliated group exists that includes at least one foreign corporation that meets the requirements for inclusion in a worldwide affiliated group. Once made, the election applies to the common parent and all other members of the worldwide affiliated group for the taxable year for which the election was made and all subsequent taxable years, unless revoked with the consent of the Secretary of the Treasury.

Financial institution group election

The provision allows taxpayers to apply the present-law bank group rules to exclude certain financial institutions from the affiliated group for interest allocation purposes under the worldwide fungibility approach. The provision also provides a one-time "financial institution group" election that expands the present-law bank group. Under the provision, at the election of the common parent of the pre-election worldwide affiliated group, the interest expense allocation rules are applied separately to a subgroup of the worldwide affiliated group that consists of (1) all corporations that are part of the present-law bank group, and (2) all "financial corporations." For this purpose, a corporation is a financial corporation if at least 80 percent of its gross income is financial services income (as described in section 904(d)(2)(C)(i) and the regulations thereunder) that is derived from transactions with unrelated persons.[121] For these purposes, items of income or gain from a transaction or series of transactions are disregarded if a principal purpose for the transaction or transactions is to qualify any corporation as a financial corporation.

The common parent of the pre-election worldwide affiliated group must make the election for the first taxable year beginning after December 31, 2008, in which a worldwide affiliated group includes a financial corporation. Once made, the election applies to the financial institution group for the taxable year and all subsequent taxable years. In addition, the provision provides anti-abuse rules under which certain transfers from one member of a financial institution group to a member of the worldwide affiliated group outside of the financial institution group are treated as reducing the amount of indebtedness of the separate financial institution group. The provision provides regulatory authority with respect to the election to provide for the direct allocation of interest expense in circumstances in which such allocation is appropriate to carry out the purposes of the provision, prevent assets or interest expense from being taken into account more than once, or address changes in members of any group (through acquisitions or otherwise) treated as affiliated under this provision.

Effective Date

The provision is effective for taxable years beginning after December 31, 2008.

Conference Committee Report (H.R. CONF. REP. NO. 108-755)

Senate Amendment

The Senate amendment is the same as the House bill.

[Law at ¶ 5600. CCH Explanation at ¶ 405 and ¶ 407.]

Conference Agreement

The conference agreement follows the House bill and the Senate amendment.

[¶ 10,580] Act Sec. 402. Recharacterize overall domestic loss

House Committee Report (H.R. REP. NO. 108-548, pt. 1)

[Code Sec. 904]

Present Law

The United States provides a credit for foreign income taxes paid or accrued. The foreign tax credit generally is limited to the U.S. tax liability on a taxpayer's foreign-source income, in order to ensure that the credit serves the purpose of mitigating double taxation of foreign-source income without offsetting the U.S. tax on

---

[121] See Treas. Reg. sec. 1.904-4(e)(2).

U.S.-source income. This overall limitation is calculated by prorating a taxpayer's pre-credit U.S. tax on its worldwide income between its U.S.-source and foreign-source taxable income. The ratio (not exceeding 100 percent) of the taxpayer's foreign-source taxable income to worldwide taxable income is multiplied by its pre-credit U.S. tax to establish the amount of U.S. tax allocable to the taxpayer's foreign-source income and, thus, the upper limit on the foreign tax credit for the year.

In addition, this limitation is calculated separately for various categories of income, generally referred to as "separate limitation categories." The total amount of the foreign tax credit used to offset the U.S. tax on income in each separate limitation category may not exceed the proportion of the taxpayer's U.S. tax which the taxpayer's foreign-source taxable income in that category bears to its worldwide taxable income.

If a taxpayer's losses from foreign sources exceed its foreign-source income, the excess ("overall foreign loss," or "OFL") may offset U.S.-source income. Such an offset reduces the effective rate of U.S. tax on U.S.-source income.

In order to eliminate a double benefit (that is, the reduction of U.S. tax previously noted and, later, full allowance of a foreign tax credit with respect to foreign-source income), present law includes an OFL recapture rule. Under this rule, a portion of foreign-source taxable income earned after an OFL year is recharacterized as U.S.-source taxable income for foreign tax credit purposes (and for purposes of the possessions tax credit). Unless a taxpayer elects a higher percentage, however, generally no more than 50 percent of the foreign-source taxable income earned in any particular taxable year is recharacterized as U.S.-source taxable income. The effect of the recapture is to reduce the foreign tax credit limitation in one or more years following an OFL year and, therefore, the amount of U.S. tax that can be offset by foreign tax credits in the later year or years.

Losses for any taxable year in separate foreign limitation categories (to the extent that they do not exceed foreign income for the year) are apportioned on a proportionate basis among (and operate to reduce) the foreign income categories in which the entity earns income in the loss year. A separate limitation loss recharacterization rule applies to foreign losses apportioned to foreign income pursuant to the above rule. If a separate limitation loss was apportioned to income subject to another separate limitation category and the loss category has income for a subsequent taxable year, then that income (to the extent that it does not exceed the aggregate separate limitation losses in the loss category not

previously recharacterized) must be recharacterized as income in the separate limitation category that was previously offset by the loss. Such recharacterization must be made in proportion to the prior loss apportionment not previously taken into account.

A U.S.-source loss reduces pre-credit U.S. tax on worldwide income to an amount less than the hypothetical tax that would apply to the taxpayer's foreign-source income if viewed in isolation. The existence of foreign-source taxable income in the year of the U.S.-source loss reduces or eliminates any net operating loss carryover that the U.S.-source loss would otherwise have generated absent the foreign income. In addition, as the pre-credit U.S. tax on worldwide income is reduced, so is the foreign tax credit limitation. Moreover, any U.S.-source loss for any taxable year is apportioned among (and operates to reduce) foreign income in the separate limitation categories on a proportionate basis. As a result, some foreign tax credits in the year of the U.S.-source loss must be credited, if at all, in a carryover year. Tax on U.S.-source taxable income in a subsequent year may be offset by a net operating loss carryforward, but not by a foreign tax credit carryforward. There is currently no mechanism for recharacterizing such subsequent U.S.-source income as foreign-source income.

For example, suppose a taxpayer generates a $100 U.S.-source loss and earns $100 of foreign-source income in Year 1, and pays $30 of foreign tax on the $100 of foreign-source income. Because the taxpayer has no net taxable income in Year 1, no foreign tax credit can be claimed in Year 1 with respect to the $30 of foreign taxes. If the taxpayer then earns $100 of U.S.-source income and $100 of foreign-source income in Year 2, present law does not recharacterize any portion of the $100 of U.S.-source income as foreign-source income to reflect the fact that the previous year's $100 U.S.-source loss reduced the taxpayer's ability to claim foreign tax credits.

Reasons for Change

The Committee believes that it is important to create parity in the treatment of overall foreign losses and overall domestic losses in order to prevent the double taxation of income. The Committee believes that preventing double taxation will make U.S. businesses more competitive and will lead to increased export sales. The Committee believes that this increase in export sales will increase production in the United States and increase jobs in the United States to support the increased exports.

Explanation of Provision

The provision applies a re-sourcing rule to U.S.-source income in cases in which a taxpayer's foreign tax credit limitation has been reduced as a result of an overall domestic loss. Under the provision, a portion of the taxpayer's U.S.-source income for each succeeding taxable year is recharacterized as foreign-source income in an amount equal to the lesser of: (1) the amount of the unrecharacterized overall domestic losses for years prior to such succeeding taxable year, and (2) 50 percent of the taxpayer's U.S.-source income for such succeeding taxable year.

The provision defines an overall domestic loss for this purpose as any domestic loss to the extent it offsets foreign-source taxable income for the current taxable year or for any preceding taxable year by reason of a loss carryback. For this purpose, a domestic loss means the amount by which the U.S.-source gross income for the taxable year is exceeded by the sum of the deductions properly apportioned or allocated thereto, determined without regard to any loss carried back from a subsequent taxable year. Under the provision, an overall domestic loss does not include any loss for any taxable year unless the taxpayer elected the use of the foreign tax credit for such taxable year.

Any U.S.-source income recharacterized under the provision is allocated among and increases the various foreign tax credit separate limitation categories in the same proportion that those categories were reduced by the prior overall domestic losses, in a manner similar to the recharacterization rules for separate limitation losses.

It is anticipated that situations may arise in which a taxpayer generates an overall domestic loss in a year following a year in which it had an overall foreign loss, or vice versa. In such a case, it would be necessary for ordering and other coordination rules to be developed for purposes of computing the foreign tax credit limitation in subsequent taxable years. The provision grants the Secretary of the Treasury authority to prescribe such regulations as may be necessary to coordinate the operation of the OFL recapture rules with the operation of the overall domestic loss recapture rules added by the provision.

Effective Date

The provision applies to losses incurred in taxable years beginning after December 31, 2006.

Conference Committee Report (H.R. CONF. REP. NO. 108-755)

Senate Amendment

The Senate amendment is the same as the House bill.

Conference Agreement

The conference agreement follows the House bill and the Senate amendment.

[Law at ¶ 5425, ¶ 5655 and ¶ 5685. CCH Explanation at ¶ 420.]

[¶ 10,590] Act Sec. 403. Apply look-through rules for dividends from noncontrolled section 902 corporations

House Committee Report (H.R. REP. NO. 108-548, pt. 1)

[Code Sec. 904(d)]

Present Law

U.S. persons may credit foreign taxes against U.S. tax on foreign-source income. In general, the amount of foreign tax credits that may be claimed in a year is subject to a limitation that prevents taxpayers from using foreign tax credits to offset U.S. tax on U.S.-source income. Separate limitations are also applied to specific categories of income.

Special foreign tax credit limitations apply in the case of dividends received from a foreign

corporation in which the taxpayer owns at least 10 percent of the stock by vote and which is not a controlled foreign corporation (a so-called "10/50 company"). Dividends paid by a 10/50 company that is not a passive foreign investment company out of earnings and profits accumulated in taxable years beginning before January 1, 2003 are subject to a single foreign tax credit limitation for all 10/50 companies (other than passive foreign investment companies).[130] Dividends paid by a 10/50 company that is a passive foreign investment company out of earnings and profits accumulated in taxable years beginning

---

[130] Dividends paid by a 10/50 company in taxable years beginning before January 1, 2003 are subject to a separate foreign tax credit limitation for each 10/50 company.

before January 1, 2003, continue to be subject to a separate foreign tax credit limitation for each such 10/50 company. Dividends paid by a 10/50 company out of earnings and profits accumulated in taxable years after December 31, 2002 are treated as income in a foreign tax credit limitation category in proportion to the ratio of the 10/50 company's earnings and profits attributable to income in such foreign tax credit limitation category to its total earnings and profits (a "look-through" approach).

For these purposes, distributions are treated as made from the most recently accumulated earnings and profits. Regulatory authority is granted to provide rules regarding the treatment of distributions out of earnings and profits for periods prior to the taxpayer's acquisition of such stock.

Reasons for Change

The Committee believes that significant simplification can be achieved by eliminating the requirement that taxpayers segregate the earnings and profits of 10/50 companies on the basis of when such earnings and profits arose.

Explanation of Provision

The provision generally applies the look-through approach to dividends paid by a 10/50 company regardless of the year in which the earnings and profits out of which the dividend is paid were accumulated.[131] If the Treasury Secretary determines that a taxpayer has inadequately substantiated that it assigned a dividend from a 10/50 company to the proper foreign tax credit limitation category, the dividend is treated as passive category income for foreign tax credit basketing purposes.[132]

Effective Date

The provision is effective for taxable years beginning after December 31, 2002.

The provision also provides transition rules regarding the use of pre-effective-date foreign tax credits associated with a 10/50 company separate limitation category in post-effective-date years. Look-through principles similar to those applicable to post-effective-date dividends from a 10/50 company apply to determine the appropriate foreign tax credit limitation category or categories with respect to carrying forward foreign tax credits into future years. The provision allows the Treasury Secretary to issue regulations addressing the carryback of foreign tax credits associated with a dividend from a 10/50 company to pre-effective-date years.

Conference Committee Report (H.R. CONF. REP. NO. 108-755)

Senate Amendment

The Senate amendment is the same as the House bill.

Conference Agreement

The conference agreement follows the House bill and the Senate amendment.

[Law at ¶ 5600 and ¶ 5655. CCH Explanation at ¶ 430.]

[¶ 10,600] Act Sec. 404. Foreign tax credit baskets and "base differences"

House Committee Report (H.R. REP. NO. 108-548, pt. 1)

[Code Sec. 904(d)]

Present Law

In general

The United States taxes its citizens and residents on their worldwide income. Because the countries in which income is earned also may assert their jurisdiction to tax the same income on the basis of source, foreign-source income earned by U.S. persons may be subject to double taxation. In order to mitigate this possibility, the United States provides a credit against U.S. tax liability for foreign income taxes paid, subject to a number of limitations. The foreign tax credit generally is limited to the U.S. tax liability on a taxpayer's foreign-source income, in order to en-

---

[131] This look-through treatment also applies to dividends that a controlled foreign corporation receives from a 10/50 company and then distributes to a U.S. shareholder.

[132] It is anticipated that the Treasury Secretary will reconsider the operation of the foreign tax credit regulations to

ensure that the high-tax income rules apply appropriately to dividends treated as passive category income because of inadequate substantiation.

sure that the credit serves its purpose of mitigating double taxation of cross-border income without offsetting the U.S. tax on U.S.-source income.

The foreign tax credit limitation is applied separately to the following categories of income: (1) passive income, (2) high withholding tax interest, (3) financial services income, (4) shipping income, (5) certain dividends received from noncontrolled section 902 foreign corporations ("10/50 companies"),[122] (6) certain dividends from a domestic international sales corporation or former domestic international sales corporation, (7) taxable income attributable to certain foreign trade income, (8) certain distributions from a foreign sales corporation or former foreign sales corporation, and (9) any other income not described in items (1) through (8) (so-called "general basket" income). In addition, a number of other provisions of the Code and U.S. tax treaties effectively create additional separate limitations in certain circumstances.[123]

Financial services income

In general, the term "financial services income" includes income received or accrued by a person predominantly engaged in the active conduct of a banking, insurance, financing, or similar business, if the income is derived in the active conduct of a banking, financing or similar business, or is derived from the investment by an insurance company of its unearned premiums or reserves ordinary and necessary for the proper conduct of its insurance business (sec. 904(d)(2)(C)). The Code also provides that financial services income includes income, received or accrued by a person predominantly engaged in the active conduct of a banking, insurance, financing, or similar business, of a kind which would generally be insurance income (as defined in section 953(a)), among other items.

Treasury regulations provide that a person is predominantly engaged in the active conduct of a banking, insurance, financing, or similar business for any year if for that year at least 80 percent of its gross income is "active financing income."[124] The regulations further provide that

a corporation that is not predominantly engaged in the active conduct of a banking, insurance, financing, or similar business under the preceding definition can derive financial services income if the corporation is a member of an affiliated group (as defined in section 1504(a), but expanded to include foreign corporations) that, as a whole, meets the regulatory test of being "predominantly engaged."[125] In determining whether an affiliated group is "predominantly engaged," only the income of members of the group that are U.S. corporations, or controlled foreign corporations in which such U.S. corporations own (directly or indirectly) at least 80 percent of the total voting power and value of the stock, are counted.

"Base difference" items

Under Treasury regulations, foreign taxes are allocated and apportioned to the same limitation categories as the income to which they relate.[126] In cases in which foreign law imposes tax on an item of income that does not constitute income under U.S. tax principles (a "base difference" item), the tax is treated as imposed on income in the general limitation category.[127]

Reasons for Change

The Committee believes that requiring taxpayers to separate income and tax credits into nine separate tax baskets creates some of the most complex tax reporting and compliance issues in the Code. Reducing the number of foreign tax credit baskets to two will greatly simplify the Code and undo much of the complexity created by the Tax Reform Act of 1986. The Committee believes that simplifying these rules will reduce double taxation, make U.S. businesses more competitive, and create jobs in the United States.

Explanation of Provision

In general

The provision generally reduces the number of foreign tax credit limitation categories to two: passive category income and general category income. Other income is included in one of the

---

[122] Subject to certain exceptions, dividends paid by a 10/50 company in taxable years beginning after December 31, 2002 are subject to either a look-through approach in which the dividend is attributed to a particular limitation category based on the underlying earnings which gave rise to the dividend (for post-2002 earnings and profits), or a single-basket limitation approach for dividends from all 10/50 companies that are not passive foreign investment companies (for pre-2003 earnings and profits). Under section 304 of the bill, these dividends are subject to a look-through approach, irrespective of when the underlying earnings and profits arose.

[123] See, e.g., sec. 56(g)(4)(C)(iii)(IV) (relating to certain dividends from corporations eligible for the sec. 936 credit);

sec. 245(a)(10) (relating to certain dividends treated as foreign source under treaties); sec. 865(h)(1)(B) (relating to certain gains from stock and intangibles treated as foreign source under treaties); sec. 901(j)(1)(B) (relating to income from certain specified countries); and sec. 904(g)(10)(A) (relating to interest, dividends, and certain other amounts derived from U.S.-owned foreign corporations and treated as foreign source under treaties).

[124] Treas. Reg. sec. 1.904-4(e)(3)(i) and (2)(i).

[125] Treas. Reg. sec. 1.904-4(e)(3)(ii).

[126] Treas. Reg. sec. 1.904-6.

[127] Treas. Reg. sec. 1.904-6(a)(1)(iv).

Act Sec. 404 ¶10,600

two categories, as appropriate. For example, shipping income generally falls into the general limitation category, whereas high withholding tax interest generally could fall into the passive income or the general limitation category, depending on the circumstances. Dividends from a domestic international sales corporation or former domestic international sales corporation, income attributable to certain foreign trade income, and certain distributions from a foreign sales corporation or former foreign sales corporation all are assigned to the passive income limitation category. The provision does not affect the separate computation of foreign tax credit limitations under special provisions of the Code relating to, for example, treaty-based sourcing rules or specified countries under section 901(j).

Financial services income

In the case of a member of a financial services group or any other person predominantly engaged in the active conduct of a banking, insurance, financing or similar business, the provision treats income meeting the definition of financial services income as general category income. Under the provision, a financial services group is an affiliated group that is predominantly engaged in the active conduct of a banking, insurance, financing or similar business. For this purpose, the definition of an affiliated group under section 1504(a) is applied, but expanded to include certain insurance companies (without regard to whether such companies are covered by an election under section 1504(c)(2)) and foreign corporations. In determining whether such a group is predominantly engaged in the active conduct of a banking, insurance, financing, or similar business, only the income of members of the group that are U.S. corporations or controlled foreign corporations in which such U.S. corporations own (directly or indirectly) at least 80 percent of total voting power and value of the stock are taken into account.

The provision does not alter the present law interpretation of what it means to be a "person predominantly engaged in the active conduct of a banking, insurance, financing, or similar business."[128] Thus, other provisions of the Code that rely on this same concept of a "person predominantly engaged in the active conduct of a banking, insurance, financing, or similar business" are not affected by the provision. For example, under the "accumulated deficit rule" of section 952(c)(1)(B), subpart F income inclusions of a U.S. shareholder attributable to a "qualified activity" of a controlled foreign corporation may be reduced by the amount of the U.S. share-

holder's pro rata share of certain prior year deficits attributable to the same qualified activity. In the case of a qualified financial institution, qualified activity consists of any activity giving rise to foreign personal holding company income, but only if the controlled foreign corporation was predominantly engaged in the active conduct of a banking, financing, or similar business in both the year in which the corporation earned the income and the year in which the corporation incurred the deficit. Similarly, in the case of a qualified insurance company, qualified activity consists of activity giving rise to insurance income or foreign personal holding company income, but only if the controlled foreign corporation was predominantly engaged in the active conduct of an insurance business in both the year in which the corporation earned the income and the year in which the corporation incurred the deficit. For this purpose, "predominantly engaged in the active conduct of a banking, insurance, financing, or similar business" is defined under present law by reference to the use of the term for purposes of the separate foreign tax credit limitations.[129] The present-law meaning of "predominantly engaged" for purposes of section 952(c)(1)(B) remains unchanged under the provision.

The provision requires the Treasury Secretary to specify the treatment of financial services income received or accrued by passthrough entities that are not members of a financial services group. The Committee expects these regulations to be generally consistent with regulations currently in effect.

"Base difference" items

Creditable foreign taxes that are imposed on amounts that do not constitute income under U.S. tax principles are treated as imposed on general limitation income.

Effective Date

The provision is effective for taxable years beginning after December 31, 2006.

Taxes paid or accrued in a taxable year beginning before January 1, 2007, and carried to any subsequent taxable year are treated as if this provision were in effect on the date such taxes were paid or accrued. Thus, such taxes are assigned to one of the two foreign tax credit limitation categories, as appropriate.

The Treasury Secretary is given authority to provide by regulations for the allocation of income with respect to taxes carried back to pre-

---

[128] See Treas. Reg. sec. 1.904-4(e).

[129] See H.R. Rep. No. 99-841, 99th Cong., 2d Sess. II-621 (1986); Staff of the Joint Committee on Taxation, 100th

Cong., 1st Sess., General Explanation of the Tax Reform Act of 1986, at 984 (1987).

effective-date years (in which more than two limitation categories are in effect).

Conference Committee Report (H.R. CONF. REP. NO. 108-755)

The conference agreement follows the House bill, with a modification relating to base differences. As in the House bill, creditable foreign taxes that are imposed on amounts that do not constitute income under U.S. tax principles are treated as imposed on general limitation income, as of the general effective date of the House bill provision. The conference agreement adds a provision under which any such taxes arising in taxable years beginning after Decem-

ber 31, 2004, but before January 1, 2007 (when the number of limitation categories is reduced to two), are treated as imposed on either general limitation income or financial services income, at the taxpayer's election. Once made, this election applies to all such taxes for the taxable years described above and is revocable only with the consent of the Treasury Secretary.

[Law at ¶ 5655. CCH Explanation at ¶ 410.]

[¶ 10,610] Act Sec. 405. Attribution of stock ownership through partnerships in determining section 902 and 960 credits

House Committee Report (H.R. REP. NO. 108-548, pt. 1)

[Code Secs. 901(b), 902(c) and 960]

Present Law

Under section 902, a domestic corporation that receives a dividend from a foreign corporation in which it owns ten percent or more of the voting stock is deemed to have paid a portion of the foreign taxes paid by such foreign corporation. Thus, such a domestic corporation is eligible to claim a foreign tax credit with respect to such deemed-paid taxes. The domestic corporation that receives a dividend is deemed to have paid a portion of the foreign corporation's post-1986 foreign income taxes based on the ratio of the amount of the dividend to the foreign corporation's post-1986 undistributed earnings and profits.

Foreign income taxes paid or accrued by lower-tier foreign corporations also are eligible for the deemed-paid credit if the foreign corporation falls within a qualified group (sec. 902(b)). A "qualified group" includes certain foreign corporations within the first six tiers of a chain of foreign corporations if, among other things, the product of the percentage ownership of voting stock at each level of the chain (beginning from the domestic corporation) equals at least five percent. In addition, in order to claim indirect credits for foreign taxes paid by certain fourth-, fifth-, and sixth-tier corporations, such corporations must be controlled foreign corporations

(within the meaning of sec. 957) and the shareholder claiming the indirect credit must be a U.S. shareholder (as defined in sec. 951(b)) with respect to the controlled foreign corporations. The application of the indirect foreign tax credit below the third tier is limited to taxes paid in taxable years during which the payor is a controlled foreign corporation. Foreign taxes paid below the sixth tier of foreign corporations are ineligible for the indirect foreign tax credit.

Section 960 similarly permits a domestic corporation with subpart F inclusions from a controlled foreign corporation to claim deemed-paid foreign tax credits with respect to foreign taxes paid or accrued by the controlled foreign corporation on its subpart F income.

The foreign tax credit provisions in the Code do not specifically address whether a domestic corporation owning ten percent or more of the voting stock of a foreign corporation through a partnership is entitled to a deemed-paid foreign tax credit.[133] In Rev. Rul. 71-141,[134] the IRS held that a foreign corporation's stock held indirectly by two domestic corporations through their interests in a domestic general partnership is attributed to such domestic corporations for purposes of determining the domestic corporations' eligibility to claim a deemed-paid foreign tax credit with respect to the foreign taxes paid by such foreign corporation. Accordingly, a gen-

---

[133] Under section 901(b)(5), an individual member of a partnership or a beneficiary of an estate or trust generally may claim a direct foreign tax credit with respect to the amount of his or her proportionate share of the foreign taxes paid or accrued by the partnership, estate, or trust. This rule does not specifically apply to corporations that are either members of a partnership or beneficiaries of an estate or trust. However, section 702(a)(6) provides that each partner

(including individuals or corporations) of a partnership must take into account separately its distributive share of the partnership's foreign taxes paid or accrued. In addition, under section 703(b)(3), the election under section 901 (whether to credit the foreign taxes) is made by each partner separately.

[134] 1971-1 C.B. 211.

eral partner of a domestic general partnership is permitted to claim deemed-paid foreign tax credits with respect to a dividend distribution from the foreign corporation to the partnership.

However, in 1997, the Treasury Department issued final regulations under section 902, and the preamble to the regulations states that "[t]he final regulations do not resolve under what circumstances a domestic corporate partner may compute an amount of foreign taxes deemed paid with respect to dividends received from a foreign corporation by a partnership or other pass-through entity."[135] In recognition of the holding in Rev. Rul. 71-141, the preamble to the final regulations under section 902 states that a "domestic shareholder" for purposes of section 902 is a domestic corporation that "owns" the requisite voting stock in a foreign corporation rather than one that "owns directly" the voting stock. At the same time, the preamble states that the IRS is still considering under what other circumstances Rev. Rul. 71-141 should apply. Consequently, uncertainty remains regarding whether a domestic corporation owning ten percent or more of the voting stock of a foreign corporation through a partnership is entitled to a deemed-paid foreign tax credit (other than through a domestic general partnership).

Reasons for Change

The Committee believes that a clarification is appropriate regarding the ability of a domestic

corporation owning ten percent or more of the voting stock of a foreign corporation through a partnership to claim a deemed-paid foreign tax credit.

Explanation of Provision

The provision clarifies that a domestic corporation is entitled to claim deemed-paid foreign tax credits with respect to a foreign corporation that is held indirectly through a foreign or domestic partnership, provided that the domestic corporation owns (indirectly through the partnership) ten percent or more of the foreign corporation's voting stock. No inference is intended as to the treatment of such deemed-paid foreign tax credits under present law. The provision also clarifies that both individual and corporate partners (or estate or trust beneficiaries) may claim direct foreign tax credits with respect to their proportionate shares of taxes paid or accrued by a partnership (or estate or trust).

Effective Date

The provision applies to taxes of foreign corporations for taxable years of such corporations beginning after the date of enactment.

Conference Committee Report (H.R. CONF. REP. No. 108-755)

Senate Amendment

The Senate amendment is the same as the House bill.

Conference Agreement

The conference agreement follows the House bill and the Senate amendment.

[Law at ¶ 5640 and ¶ 5645. CCH Explanation at ¶ 435.]

[¶ 10,620] Act Sec. 406. Foreign tax credit treatment of deemed payments under section 367(d) of the Code

House Committee Report (H.R. REP. No. 108-548, pt. 1)

[Code Sec. 367(d)]

Present Law

In the case of transfers of intangible property to foreign corporations by means of contributions and certain other nonrecognition transactions, special rules apply that are designed to mitigate the tax avoidance that may arise from shifting the income attributable to

intangible property offshore. Under section 367(d), the outbound transfer of intangible property is treated as a sale of the intangible for a stream of contingent payments. The amounts of these deemed payments must be commensurate with the income attributable to the intangible. The deemed payments are included in gross income of the U.S. transferor as ordinary income, and the earnings and profits of the foreign cor-

---

[135] T.D. 8708, 1997-1 C.B. 137.

poration to which the intangible was transferred are reduced by such amounts.

The Taxpayer Relief Act of 1997 (the "1997 Act") repealed a rule that treated all such deemed payments as giving rise to U.S.-source income. Because the foreign tax credit is generally limited to the U.S. tax imposed on foreign-source income, the prior-law rule reduced the taxpayer's ability to claim foreign tax credits. As a result of the repeal of the rule, the source of payments deemed received under section 367(d) is determined under general sourcing rules. These rules treat income from sales of intangible property for contingent payments the same as royalties, with the result that the deemed payments may give rise to foreign-source income.[136]

The 1997 Act did not address the characterization of the deemed payments for purposes of applying the foreign tax credit separate limitation categories.[137] If the deemed payments are treated like proceeds of a sale, then they could fall into the passive category; if the deemed payments are treated like royalties, then in many cases they could fall into the general category (under look-through rules applicable to payments of dividends, interest, rents, and royalties received from controlled foreign corporations).[138]

Reasons for Change

The Committee believes that it is appropriate to characterize deemed payments under section 367(d) as royalties for purposes of applying the separate limitation categories of the foreign tax credit, and that this treatment should be effective for all transactions subject to the underlying provision of the 1997 Act.

Explanation of Provision

The provision specifies that deemed payments under section 367(d) are treated as royalties for purposes of applying the separate limitation categories of the foreign tax credit.

Effective Date

The provision is effective for amounts treated as received on or after August 5, 1997 (the effective date of the relevant provision of the 1997 Act).

Conference Committee Report (H.R. CONF. REP. NO. 108-755)

Senate Amendment

The Senate amendment is the same as the House bill.

[Law at ¶ 5340. CCH Explanation at ¶ 445.]

Conference Agreement

The conference agreement follows the House bill and the Senate amendment.

[¶ 10,630] Act Sec. 407. United States property not to include certain assets of controlled foreign corporations

House Committee Report (H.R. REP. NO. 108-548, pt. 1)

[Code Sec. 956]

Present Law

In general, the subpart F rules[139] require U.S. shareholders with a 10-percent or greater interest in a controlled foreign corporation ("U.S. 10-percent shareholders") to include in taxable income their pro rata shares of certain income of the controlled foreign corporation (referred to as "subpart F income") when such income is earned, whether or not the earnings are distributed currently to the shareholders. In addition, the U.S. 10-percent shareholders of a controlled foreign corporation are subject to U.S. tax on their pro rata shares of the controlled foreign corporation's earnings to the extent invested by the controlled foreign corporation in certain U.S. property in a taxable year.[140]

A shareholder's income inclusion with respect to a controlled foreign corporation's investment in U.S. property for a taxable year is based on the controlled foreign corporation's average investment in U.S. property for such year. For this purpose, the U.S. property held (directly or indirectly) by the controlled foreign corporation must be measured as of the close of each quarter in the taxable year.[141] The amount taken into

---

[136] Secs. 865(d), 862(a).
[137] Sec. 904(d).
[138] Sec. 904(d)(3).

[139] Secs. 951-964.
[140] Sec. 951(a)(1)(B).
[141] Sec. 956(a).

account with respect to any property is the property's adjusted basis as determined for purposes of reporting the controlled foreign corporation's earnings and profits, reduced by any liability to which the property is subject. The amount determined for inclusion in each taxable year is the shareholder's pro rata share of an amount equal to the lesser of: (1) the controlled foreign corporation's average investment in U.S. property as of the end of each quarter of such taxable year, to the extent that such investment exceeds the foreign corporation's earnings and profits that were previously taxed on that basis; or (2) the controlled foreign corporation's current or accumulated earnings and profits (but not including a deficit), reduced by distributions during the year and by earnings that have been taxed previously as earnings invested in U.S. property.[142] An income inclusion is required only to the extent that the amount so calculated exceeds the amount of the controlled foreign corporation's earnings that have been previously taxed as subpart F income.[143]

For purposes of section 956, U.S. property generally is defined to include tangible property located in the United States, stock of a U.S. corporation, an obligation of a U.S. person, and certain intangible assets including a patent or copyright, an invention, model or design, a secret formula or process or similar property right which is acquired or developed by the controlled foreign corporation for use in the United States.[144]

Specified exceptions from the definition of U.S. property are provided for: (1) obligations of the United States, money, or deposits with persons carrying on the banking business; (2) certain export property; (3) certain trade or business obligations; (4) aircraft, railroad rolling stock, vessels, motor vehicles or containers used in transportation in foreign commerce and used predominantly outside of the United States; (5) certain insurance company reserves and unearned premiums related to insurance of foreign risks; (6) stock or debt of certain unrelated U.S. corporations; (7) moveable property (other than a vessel or aircraft) used for the purpose of exploring, developing, or certain other activities in connection with the ocean waters of the U.S. Continental Shelf; (8) an amount of assets equal to the controlled foreign corporation's accumulated earnings and profits attributable to income effectively connected with a U.S. trade or business; (9) property (to the extent provided in regulations) held by a foreign sales corporation and related to its export activities; (10) certain deposits or receipts of collateral or margin by a securities or commodities dealer, if such deposit is

made or received on commercial terms in the ordinary course of the dealer's business as a securities or commodities dealer; and (11) certain repurchase and reverse repurchase agreement transactions entered into by or with a dealer in securities or commodities in the ordinary course of its business as a securities or commodities dealer.[145]

Reasons for Change

The Committee believes that the acquisition of securities by a controlled foreign corporation in the ordinary course of its business as a securities dealer generally should not give rise to an income inclusion as an investment in U.S. property under the provisions of subpart F. Similarly, the Committee believes that the acquisition by a controlled foreign corporation of obligations issued by unrelated U.S. noncorporate persons generally should not give rise to an income inclusion as an investment in U.S. property.

Explanation of Provision

The provision adds two new exceptions from the definition of U.S. property for determining current income inclusion by a U.S. 10-percent shareholder with respect to an investment in U.S. property by a controlled foreign corporation.

The first exception generally applies to securities acquired and held by a controlled foreign corporation in the ordinary course of its trade or business as a dealer in securities. The exception applies only if the controlled foreign corporation dealer: (1) accounts for the securities as securities held primarily for sale to customers in the ordinary course of business; and (2) disposes of such securities (or such securities mature while being held by the dealer) within a period consistent with the holding of securities for sale to customers in the ordinary course of business.

The second exception generally applies to the acquisition by a controlled foreign corporation of obligations issued by a U.S. person that is not a domestic corporation and that is not (1) a U.S. 10-percent shareholder of the controlled foreign corporation, or (2) a partnership, estate or trust in which the controlled foreign corporation or any related person is a partner, beneficiary or trustee immediately after the acquisition by the controlled foreign corporation of such obligation.

Effective Date

The provision is effective for taxable years of foreign corporations beginning after December 31, 2004, and for taxable years of United States

---

[142] Secs. 956 and 959.
[143] Secs. 951(a)(1)(B) and 959.

[144] Sec. 956(c)(1).
[145] Sec. 956(c)(2).

shareholders with or within which such taxable years of such foreign corporations end.

Conference Committee Report (H.R. CONF. REP. NO. 108-755)

Senate Amendment   [Law at ¶5725. CCH Explanation at ¶460.]

The Senate amendment is the same as the House bill.

Conference Agreement

The conference agreement follows the House bill and the Senate amendment.

[¶10,640] Act Sec. 408. Election not to use average exchange rate for foreign tax paid other than in functional currency

House Committee Report (H.R. REP. NO. 108-548, pt. 1)

[Code Sec. 986]

Present Law

For taxpayers that take foreign income taxes into account when accrued, present law provides that the amount of the foreign tax credit generally is determined by translating the amount of foreign taxes paid in foreign currencies into a U.S. dollar amount at the average exchange rate for the taxable year to which such taxes relate.[146] This rule applies to foreign taxes paid directly by U.S. taxpayers, which taxes are creditable in the year paid or accrued, and to foreign taxes paid by foreign corporations that are deemed paid by a U.S. corporation that is a shareholder of the foreign corporation, and hence creditable in the year that the U.S. corporation receives a dividend or has an income inclusion from the foreign corporation. This rule does not apply to any foreign income tax: (1) that is paid after the date that is two years after the close of the taxable year to which such taxes relate; (2) of an accrual-basis taxpayer that is actually paid in a taxable year prior to the year to which the tax relates; or (3) that is denominated in an inflationary currency (as defined by regulations).

Foreign taxes that are not eligible for translation at the average exchange rate generally are translated into U.S. dollar amounts using the exchange rates as of the time such taxes are paid. However, the Secretary is authorized to issue regulations that would allow foreign tax payments to be translated into U.S. dollar amounts using an average exchange rate for a specified period.[147]

Reasons for Change

The Committee believes that taxpayers generally should be permitted to elect whether to translate foreign income tax payments using an average exchange rate for the taxable year or the exchange rate when the taxes are paid, provided the elected method continues to be applied consistently unless revoked with the consent of the Treasury Secretary.

Explanation of Provision

For taxpayers that are required under present law to translate foreign income tax payments at the average exchange rate, the provision provides an election to translate such taxes into U.S. dollar amounts using the exchange rates as of the time such taxes are paid, provided the foreign income taxes are denominated in a currency other than the taxpayer's functional currency.[148] Any election under the provision applies to the taxable year for which the election is made and to all subsequent taxable years unless revoked with the consent of the Secretary. The provision authorizes the Secretary to issue regulations that apply the election to foreign income taxes attributable to a qualified business unit.

Effective Date

The provision is effective with respect to taxable years beginning after December 31, 2004.

---

[146] Sec. 986(a)(1).
[147] Sec. 986(a)(2).
[148] Electing taxpayers translate foreign income tax payments pursuant to the same present-law rules that apply to

taxpayers that are required to translate foreign income taxes using the exchange rates as of the time such taxes are paid.

Conference Committee Report (H.R. CONF. REP. NO. 108-755)

Senate Amendment

The Senate amendment is the same as the House bill.

Conference Agreement

The conference agreement follows the House bill and the Senate amendment. In addition, the conference agreement provides that the election does not apply to regulated investment companies that take into account income on an accrual basis. Instead, the conference agreement provides that foreign income taxes paid or accrued by a regulated investment company with respect to such income are translated into U.S. dollar amounts using the exchange rate as of the date the income accrues.

[Law at ¶ 5740. CCH Explanation at ¶ 450.]

[¶ 10,650] Act Sec. 409. Eliminate secondary withholding tax with respect to dividends paid by certain foreign corporations

House Committee Report (H.R. REP. NO. 108-548, pt. 1)

[Code Sec. 871]

Present Law

Nonresident individuals who are not U.S. citizens and foreign corporations (collectively, foreign persons) are subject to U.S. tax on income that is effectively connected with the conduct of a U.S. trade or business; the U.S. tax on such income is calculated in the same manner and at the same graduated rates as the tax on U.S. persons (secs. 871(b) and 882). Foreign persons also are subject to a 30-percent gross basis tax, collected by withholding, on certain U.S.-source passive income (e.g., interest and dividends) that is not effectively connected with a U.S. trade or business. This 30-percent withholding tax may be reduced or eliminated pursuant to an applicable tax treaty. Foreign persons generally are not subject to U.S. tax on foreign-source income that is not effectively connected with a U.S. trade or business.

In general, dividends paid by a domestic corporation are treated as being from U.S. sources and dividends paid by a foreign corporation are treated as being from foreign sources. Thus, dividends paid by foreign corporations to foreign persons generally are not subject to withholding tax because such income generally is treated as foreign-source income.

An exception from this general rule applies in the case of dividends paid by certain foreign corporations. If a foreign corporation derives 25 percent or more of its gross income as income effectively connected with a U.S. trade or business for the three-year period ending with the close of the taxable year preceding the declaration of a dividend, then a portion of any dividend paid by the foreign corporation to its shareholders will be treated as U.S.-source income and, in the case of dividends paid to foreign shareholders, will be subject to the 30-percent withholding tax (sec. 861(a)(2)(B)). This rule is sometimes referred to as the "secondary withholding tax." The portion of the dividend treated as U.S.-source income is equal to the ratio of the gross income of the foreign corporation that was effectively connected with its U.S. trade or business over the total gross income of the foreign corporation during the three-year period ending with the close of the preceding taxable year. The U.S.-source portion of the dividend paid by the foreign corporation to its foreign shareholders is subject to the 30-percent withholding tax.

Under the branch profits tax provisions, the United States taxes foreign corporations engaged in a U.S. trade or business on amounts of U.S. earnings and profits that are shifted out of the U.S. branch of the foreign corporation. The branch profits tax is comparable to the second-level taxes imposed on dividends paid by a domestic corporation to its foreign shareholders. The branch profits tax is 30 percent of the foreign corporation's "dividend equivalent amount," which generally is the earnings and profits of a U.S. branch of a foreign corporation attributable to its income effectively connected with a U.S. trade or business (secs. 884(a) and (b)).

If a foreign corporation is subject to the branch profits tax, then no secondary withholding tax is imposed on dividends paid by the foreign corporation to its shareholders (sec. 884(e)(3)(A)). If a foreign corporation is a qualified resident of a tax treaty country and claims an exemption from the branch profits tax pursuant to the treaty, the secondary withholding tax could apply with respect to dividends it pays to its shareholders. Several tax treaties (including treaties that prevent imposition of the branch profits tax), however, exempt dividends paid by the foreign corporation from the secondary withholding tax.

Reasons for Change

The Committee observes that the secondary withholding tax with respect to dividends paid by certain foreign corporations has been largely superseded by the branch profits tax and applicable income tax treaties. Accordingly, the Committee believes that the tax should be repealed in the interest of simplification.

Explanation of Provision

The provision eliminates the secondary withholding tax with respect to dividends paid by certain foreign corporations.

Effective Date

The provision is effective for payments made after December 31, 2004.

Conference Committee Report (H.R. CONF. REP. NO. 108-755)

Senate Amendment

The Senate amendment is the same as the House bill.

[Law at ¶ 5605. CCH Explanation at ¶ 555.]

Conference Agreement

The conference agreement follows the House bill and the Senate amendment.

[¶ 10,660] Act Sec. 410. Equal treatment for interest paid by foreign partnerships and foreign corporations

House Committee Report (H.R. REP. NO. 108-548, pt. 1)

[Code Sec. 861]

Present Law

In general, interest income from bonds, notes or other interest-bearing obligations of noncorporate U.S. residents or domestic corporations is treated as U.S.-source income.[149] Other interest (e.g., interest on obligations of foreign corporations and foreign partnerships) generally is treated as foreign-source income. However, Treasury regulations provide that a foreign partnership is a U.S. resident for purposes of this rule if at any time during its taxable year it is engaged in a trade or business in the United States.[150] Therefore, any interest received from such a foreign partnership is U.S.-source income.

Notwithstanding the general rule described above, in the case of a foreign corporation engaged in a U.S. trade or business (or having gross income that is treated as effectively connected with the conduct of a U.S. trade or business), interest paid by such U.S. trade or business is treated as if it were paid by a domestic corporation (i.e., such interest is treated as U.S.-source income).[151]

Reasons for Change

The Committee believes that the source of interest income received from a foreign partner-

ship or foreign corporation should be consistent. The Committee believes that interest payments from a foreign partnership engaged in a trade or business in the United States should be sourced in the same manner as interest payments from a foreign corporation engaged in a trade or business in the United States.

Explanation of Provision

The provision treats interest paid by foreign partnerships in a manner similar to the treatment of interest paid by foreign corporations. Thus, interest paid by a foreign partnership is treated as U.S.-source income only if the interest is paid by a U.S. trade or business conducted by the partnership or is allocable to income that is treated as effectively connected with the conduct of a U.S. trade or business. The provision applies only to foreign partnerships that are predominantly engaged in the active conduct of a trade or business outside the United States.

Effective Date

This provision is effective for taxable years beginning after December 31, 2003.

---

[149] Sec. 861(a)(1).
[150] Treas. Reg. sec. 1.861-2(a)(2).

[151] Sec. 884(f)(1).

Conference Committee Report (H.R. CONF. REP. NO. 108-755)

Senate Amendment

[Law at ¶ 5595. CCH Explanation at ¶ 570.]

The Senate amendment is the same as the House bill.

Conference Agreement

The conference agreement follows the House bill and the Senate amendment.

[¶ 10,670] Act Sec. 411. Treatment of certain dividends of regulated investment companies

House Committee Report (H.R. REP. NO. 108-548, pt. 1)

[Code Secs. 871, 881, Code Sec. 897(h) and Code Sec. 2105]

Present Law

Regulated investment companies

A regulated investment company ("RIC") is a domestic corporation that, at all times during the taxable year, is registered under the Investment Company Act of 1940 as a management company or as a unit investment trust, or has elected to be treated as a business development company under that Act (sec. 851(a)).

In addition, to qualify as a RIC, a corporation must elect such status and must satisfy certain tests (sec. 851(b)). These tests include a requirement that the corporation derive at least 90 percent of its gross income from dividends, interest, payments with respect to certain securities loans, and gains on the sale or other disposition of stock or securities or foreign currencies, or other income derived with respect to its business of investment in such stock, securities, or currencies.

Generally, a RIC pays no income tax because it is permitted to deduct dividends paid to its shareholders in computing its taxable income. The amount of any distribution generally is not considered as a dividend for purposes of computing the dividends paid deduction unless the distribution is pro rata, with no preference to any share of stock as compared with other shares of the same class (sec. 562(c)). For distributions by RICs to shareholders who made initial investments of at least $10,000,000, however, the distribution is not treated as non-pro rata or preferential solely by reason of an increase in the distribution due to reductions in administrative expenses of the company.

A RIC generally may pass through to its shareholders the character of its long-term capital gains. It does this by designating a dividend it pays as a capital gain dividend to the extent that the RIC has net capital gain (i.e., net long-term capital gain over net short-term capital loss). These capital gain dividends are treated as long-term capital gain by the shareholders. A RIC generally also can pass through to its shareholders the character of tax-exempt interest from State and local bonds, but only if, at the close of each quarter of its taxable year, at least 50 percent of the value of the total assets of the RIC consists of these obligations. In this case, the RIC generally may designate a dividend it pays as an exempt-interest dividend to the extent that the RIC has tax-exempt interest income. These exempt-interest dividends are treated as interest excludable from gross income by the shareholders.

U.S. source investment income of foreign persons

In general

The United States generally imposes a flat 30-percent tax, collected by withholding, on the gross amount of U.S.-source investment income payments, such as interest, dividends, rents, royalties or similar types of income, to nonresident alien individuals and foreign corporations ("foreign persons") (secs. 871(a), 881, 1441, and 1442). Under treaties, the United States may reduce or eliminate such taxes. Even taking into account U.S. treaties, however, the tax on a dividend generally is not entirely eliminated. Instead, U.S.-source portfolio investment dividends received by foreign persons generally are subject to U.S. withholding tax at a rate of at least 15 percent.

Interest

Although payments of U.S.-source interest that is not effectively connected with a U.S. trade or business generally are subject to the 30-percent withholding tax, there are exceptions to that rule. For example, interest from certain deposits with banks and other financial institutions is exempt from tax (secs. 871(i)(2)(A) and 881(d)). Original issue discount on obligations maturing in 183 days or less from the date of original issue (without regard to the period held by the taxpayer) is also exempt from tax (sec. 871(g)). An additional exception is provided for certain interest paid on portfolio obligations (secs. 871(h) and 881(c)). "Portfolio interest" generally is defined as any U.S.-source interest (including original issue discount), not effectively connected with the conduct of a U.S. trade or business, (i) on an obligation that satisfies certain registration requirements or specified exceptions thereto (i.e., the obligation is "foreign targeted"), and (ii) that is not received by a 10-percent shareholder (secs. 871(h)(3) and 881(c)(3)). With respect to a registered obligation, a statement that the beneficial owner is not a U.S. person is required (secs. 871(h)(2), (5) and 881(c)(2)). This exception is not available for any interest received either by a bank on a loan extended in the ordinary course of its business (except in the case of interest paid on an obligation of the United States), or by a controlled foreign corporation from a related person (sec. 881(c)(3)). Moreover, this exception is not available for certain contingent interest payments (secs. 871(h)(4) and 881(c)(4)).

Capital gains

Foreign persons generally are not subject to U.S. tax on gain realized on the disposition of stock or securities issued by a U.S. person (other than a "U.S. real property holding corporation," as described below), unless the gain is effectively connected with the conduct of a trade or business in the United States. This exemption does not apply, however, if the foreign person is a nonresident alien individual present in the United States for a period or periods aggregating 183 days or more during the taxable year (sec. 871(a)(2)). A RIC may elect not to withhold on a distribution to a foreign person representing a capital gain dividend. (Treas. Reg. sec. 1.1441-3(c)(2)(D)).

Gain or loss of a foreign person from the disposition of a U.S. real property interest is subject to net basis tax as if the taxpayer were engaged in a trade or business within the United States and the gain or loss were effectively connected with such trade or business (sec. 897). In addition to an interest in real property located in the United States or the Virgin Islands, U.S. real property interests include (among other things) any interest in a domestic corporation unless the taxpayer establishes that the corporation was not, during a 5-year period ending on the date of the disposition of the interest, a U.S. real property holding corporation (which is defined generally to mean a corporation the fair market value of whose U.S. real property interests equals or exceeds 50 percent of the sum of the fair market values of its real property interests and any other of its assets used or held for use in a trade or business).

Estate taxation

Decedents who were citizens or residents of the United States are generally subject to Federal estate tax on all property, wherever situated.[88] Nonresidents who are not U.S. citizens, however, are subject to estate tax only on their property which is within the United States. Property within the United States generally includes debt obligations of U.S. persons, including the Federal government and State and local governments (sec. 2104(c)), but does not include either bank deposits or portfolio obligations, the interest on which would be exempt from U.S. income tax under section 871 (sec. 2105(b)). Stock owned and held by a nonresident who is not a U.S. citizen is treated as property within the United States only if the stock was issued by a domestic corporation (sec. 2104(a); Treas. Reg. sec. 20.2104-1(a)(5)).

Treaties may reduce U.S. taxation on transfers by estates of nonresident decedents who are not U.S. citizens. Under recent treaties, for example, U.S. tax may generally be eliminated except insofar as the property transferred includes U.S. real property or business property of a U.S. permanent establishment.

Reasons for Change

Under present law, a disparity exists between foreign persons who invest directly in certain interest-bearing and other securities and a foreign person who invests in such securities indirectly through U.S. mutual funds. In general, certain amounts received by the direct foreign investor (or a foreign investor through a foreign fund) may be exempt from the U.S. gross-basis withholding tax. In contrast, distributions from a RIC generally are treated as dividends subject to the withholding tax, notwithstanding that the distributions may be attributable to amounts that otherwise could qualify for an exemption from withholding tax. U.S. financial institutions often respond to this disparate treatment by forming "mirror funds" outside the United States. The Committee believes that such disparate treatment should be eliminated so that U.S. financial institutions will be encouraged to form and operate their mutual funds within the United States rather than outside the United States.

---

[88] The Economic Growth and Tax Relief Reconciliation Act of 2001 ("EGTRRA") repealed the estate tax for estates of decedents dying after December 31, 2009. However, EGT- RRA included a "sunset" provision, pursuant to which EGTRRA's provisions (including estate tax repeal) do not apply to estates of decedents dying after December 31, 2010.

Therefore, the Committee believes that, to the extent a RIC distributes to a foreign person a dividend attributable to amounts that would have been exempt from U.S. withholding tax had the foreign person received it directly (such as portfolio interest and capital gains, including short-term capital gains), such dividend similarly should be exempt from the U.S. gross-basis withholding tax. The Committee also believes that comparable treatment should be afforded for estate tax purposes to foreign persons who invest in certain assets through a RIC to the extent that such assets would not be subject to the estate tax if held directly.

Explanation of Provision

In general

Under the bill, a RIC that earns certain interest income that would not be subject to U.S. tax if earned by a foreign person directly may, to the extent of such income, designate a dividend it pays as derived from such interest income. A foreign person who is a shareholder in the RIC generally would treat such a dividend as exempt from gross-basis U.S. tax, as if the foreign person had earned the interest directly. Similarly, a RIC that earns an excess of net short-term capital gains over net long-term capital losses, which excess would not be subject to U.S. tax if earned by a foreign person, generally may, to the extent of such excess, designate a dividend it pays as derived from such excess. A foreign person who is a shareholder in the RIC generally would treat such a dividend as exempt from gross-basis U.S. tax, as if the foreign person had realized the excess directly. The bill also provides that the estate of a foreign decedent is exempt from U.S. estate tax on a transfer of stock in the RIC in the proportion that the assets held by the RIC are debt obligations, deposits, or other property that would generally be treated as situated outside the United States if held directly by the estate.

Interest-related dividends

Under the bill, a RIC may, under certain circumstances, designate all or a portion of a dividend as an "interest-related dividend," by written notice mailed to its shareholders not later than 60 days after the close of its taxable year. In addition, an interest-related dividend received by a foreign person generally is exempt from U.S. gross-basis tax under sections 871(a), 881, 1441 and 1442.

However, this exemption does not apply to a dividend on shares of RIC stock if the withholding agent does not receive a statement, similar to that required under the portfolio interest rules, that the beneficial owner of the shares is not a U.S. person. The exemption does not apply to a dividend paid to any person within a foreign country (or dividends addressed to, or for

the account of, persons within such foreign country) with respect to which the Treasury Secretary has determined, under the portfolio interest rules, that exchange of information is inadequate to prevent evasion of U.S. income tax by U.S. persons.

In addition, the exemption generally does not apply to dividends paid to a controlled foreign corporation to the extent such dividends are attributable to income received by the RIC on a debt obligation of a person with respect to which the recipient of the dividend (i.e., the controlled foreign corporation) is a related person. Nor does the exemption generally apply to dividends to the extent such dividends are attributable to income (other than short-term original issue discount or bank deposit interest) received by the RIC on indebtedness issued by the RIC-dividend recipient or by any corporation or partnership with respect to which the recipient of the RIC dividend is a 10-percent shareholder. However, in these two circumstances the RIC remains exempt from its withholding obligation unless the RIC knows that the dividend recipient is such a controlled foreign corporation or 10-percent shareholder. To the extent that an interest-related dividend received by a controlled foreign corporation is attributable to interest income of the RIC that would be portfolio interest if received by a foreign corporation, the dividend is treated as portfolio interest for purposes of the de minimis rules, the high-tax exception, and the same country exceptions of subpart F (see sec. 881(c)(5)(A)).

The aggregate amount designated as interest-related dividends for the RIC's taxable year (including dividends so designated that are paid after the close of the taxable year but treated as paid during that year as described in section 855) generally is limited to the qualified net interest income of the RIC for the taxable year. The qualified net interest income of the RIC equals the excess of: (1) the amount of qualified interest income of the RIC; over (2) the amount of expenses of the RIC properly allocable to such interest income.

Qualified interest income of the RIC is equal to the sum of its U.S.-source income with respect to: (1) bank deposit interest; (2) short term original issue discount that is currently exempt from the gross-basis tax under section 871; (3) any interest (including amounts recognized as ordinary income in respect of original issue discount, market discount, or acquisition discount under the provisions of sections 1271-1288, and such other amounts as regulations may provide) on an obligation which is in registered form, unless it is earned on an obligation issued by a corporation or partnership in which the RIC is a 10-percent shareholder or is contingent interest not treated as portfolio interest under section

871(h)(4); and (4) any interest-related dividend from another RIC.

If the amount designated as an interest-related dividend is greater than the qualified net interest income described above, the portion of the distribution so designated which constitutes an interest-related dividend will be only that proportion of the amount so designated as the amount of the qualified net interest income bears to the amount so designated.

Short-term capital gain dividends

Under the bill, a RIC also may, under certain circumstances, designate all or a portion of a dividend as a "short-term capital gain dividend," by written notice mailed to its shareholders not later than 60 days after the close of its taxable year. For purposes of the U.S. gross-basis tax, a short-term capital gain dividend received by a foreign person generally is exempt from U.S. gross-basis tax under sections 871(a), 881, 1441 and 1442. This exemption does not apply to the extent that the foreign person is a nonresident alien individual present in the United States for a period or periods aggregating 183 days or more during the taxable year. However, in this circumstance the RIC remains exempt from its withholding obligation unless the RIC knows that the dividend recipient has been present in the United States for such period.

The aggregate amount qualified to be designated as short-term capital gain dividends for the RIC's taxable year (including dividends so designated that are paid after the close of the taxable year but treated as paid during that year as described in sec. 855) is equal to the excess of the RIC's net short-term capital gains over net long-term capital losses. The short-term capital gain includes short-term capital gain dividends from another RIC. As provided under present law for purposes of computing the amount of a capital gain dividend, the amount is determined (except in the case where an election under sec. 4982(e)(4) applies) without regard to any net capital loss or net short-term capital loss attribu-

table to transactions after October 31 of the year. Instead, that loss is treated as arising on the first day of the next taxable year. To the extent provided in regulations, this rule also applies for purposes of computing the taxable income of the RIC.

In computing the amount of short-term capital gain dividends for the year, no reduction is made for the amount of expenses of the RIC allocable to such net gains. In addition, if the amount designated as short-term capital gain dividends is greater than the amount of qualified short-term capital gain, the portion of the distribution so designated which constitutes a short-term capital gain dividend is only that proportion of the amount so designated as the amount of the excess bears to the amount so designated.

As under present law for distributions from REITs, the bill provides that any distribution by a RIC to a foreign person shall, to the extent attributable to gains from sales or exchanges by the RIC of an asset that is considered a U.S. real property interest, be treated as gain recognized by the foreign person from the sale or exchange of a U.S. real property interest. The bill also extends the special rules for domestically-controlled REITs to domestically-controlled RICs.

Estate tax treatment

Under the bill, a portion of the stock in a RIC held by the estate of a nonresident decedent who is not a U.S. citizen is treated as property without the United States. The portion so treated is based upon the proportion of the assets held by the RIC at the end of the quarter immediately preceding the decedent's death (or such other time as the Secretary may designate in regulations) that are "qualifying assets". Qualifying assets for this purpose are bank deposits of the type that are exempt from gross-basis income tax, portfolio debt obligations, certain original issue discount obligations, debt obligations of a domestic corporation that are treated as giving rise to foreign source income, and other property not within the United States.

Conference Committee Report (H.R. CONF. REP. NO. 108-755)

Senate Amendment

No provision.

Conference Agreement

The conference agreement follows the House bill, except the conference agreement only applies: (1) to dividends with respect to taxable years of RICs beginning after December 31, 2004 and before January 1, 2008; (2) with respect to

the treatment of a RIC for estate tax purposes, to estates of decedents dying after December 31, 2004 and before January 1, 2008; and (3) with respect to the treatment of RICs under section 897 (relating to U.S. real property interests), after December 31, 2004 and before January 1, 2008.

[**Law at ¶ 5605, ¶ 5620, ¶ 5630, ¶ 5925, ¶ 5930 and ¶ 5945. CCH Explanation at ¶ 560, ¶ 562 and ¶ 564.]**

[¶ 10,680] Act Sec. 412. Look-through treatment under subpart F for sales of partnership interests

House Committee Report (H.R. REP. NO. 108-548, pt. 1)

[Code Sec. 954]

Present Law

In general, the subpart F rules (secs. 951-964) require U.S. shareholders with a 10-percent or greater interest in a controlled foreign corporation to include in income currently for U.S. tax purposes certain types of income of the controlled foreign corporation, whether or not such income is actually distributed currently to the shareholders (referred to as "subpart F income"). Subpart F income includes foreign personal holding company income. Foreign personal holding company income generally consists of the following: (1) dividends, interest, royalties, rents, and annuities; (2) net gains from the sale or exchange of (a) property that gives rise to the preceding types of income, (b) property that does not give rise to income, and (c) interests in trusts, partnerships, and REMICs; (3) net gains from commodities transactions; (4) net gains from foreign currency transactions; (5) income that is equivalent to interest; (6) income from notional principal contracts; and (7) payments in lieu of dividends. Thus, if a controlled foreign corporation sells a partnership interest at a gain, the gain generally constitutes foreign personal holding company income and is included in the income of 10-percent U.S. shareholders of the controlled foreign corporation as subpart F income.

Reasons for Change

The Committee believes that the sale of a partnership interest by a controlled foreign cor-

poration that owns a significant interest in the partnership should constitute subpart F income only to the extent that a proportionate sale of the underlying partnership assets attributable to the partnership interest would constitute subpart F income.

Explanation of Provision

The provision treats the sale by a controlled foreign corporation of a partnership interest as a sale of the proportionate share of partnership assets attributable to such interest for purposes of determining subpart F foreign personal holding company income. This rule applies only to partners owning directly, indirectly, or constructively at least 25 percent of a capital or profits interest in the partnership. Thus, the sale of a partnership interest by a controlled foreign corporation that meets this ownership threshold constitutes subpart F income under the provision only to the extent that a proportionate sale of the underlying partnership assets attributable to the partnership interest would constitute subpart F income. The Treasury Secretary is directed to prescribe such regulations as may be appropriate to prevent the abuse of this provision.

Effective Date

The provision is effective for taxable years of foreign corporations beginning after December 31, 2004, and taxable years of U.S. shareholders with or within which such taxable years of such foreign corporations end.

Conference Committee Report (H.R. CONF. REP. NO. 108-755)

Senate Amendment

The Senate amendment is the same as the House bill.

Conference Agreement

The conference agreement follows the House bill and the Senate amendment.

[Law at ¶ 5720. CCH Explanation at ¶ 465.]

[¶ 10,690] Act Sec. 413. Repeal of foreign personal holding company rules and foreign investment company rules

House Committee Report (H.R. REP. NO. 108-548, pt. 1)

[Code Secs. 542, 551, 552, 553, 554, 555, 556, 557, 558, 898, 904, 954, 1246 and 1247]

Present Law

Income earned by a foreign corporation from its foreign operations generally is subject to U.S. tax only when such income is distributed to any U.S. persons that hold stock in such corporation. Accordingly, a U.S. person that conducts foreign operations through a foreign corporation generally is subject to U.S. tax on the income from those operations when the income is repatriated to the United States through a dividend distribution to the U.S. person. The income is reported on the U.S. person's tax return for the year the distribution is received, and the United States imposes tax on such income at that time. The foreign tax credit may reduce the U.S. tax imposed on such income.

Several sets of anti-deferral rules impose current U.S. tax on certain income earned by a U.S. person through a foreign corporation. Detailed rules for coordination among the anti-deferral rules are provided to prevent the U.S. person from being subject to U.S. tax on the same item of income under multiple rules.

The Code sets forth the following anti-deferral rules: the controlled foreign corporation rules of subpart F (secs. 951-964); the passive foreign investment company rules (secs. 1291-1298); the foreign personal holding company rules (secs. 551-558); the personal holding company rules (secs. 541-547); the accumulated earnings tax

rules (secs. 531-537); and the foreign investment company rules (secs. 1246-1247).

Reasons for Change

The Committee believes that the overlap among the various antideferral regimes results in significant complexity usually with little or no ultimate tax consequences. These overlaps require the application of specific rules of priority for income inclusions among the regimes, as well as additional coordination provisions pertaining to other operational differences among the various regimes. The Committee believes that significant simplification will be achieved by streamlining these rules.

Explanation of Provision

The provision: (1) eliminates the rules applicable to foreign personal holding companies and foreign investment companies; (2) excludes foreign corporations from the application of the personal holding company rules; and (3) includes as subpart F foreign personal holding company income personal services contract income that is subject to the present-law foreign personal holding company rules.

Effective Date

The provision is effective for taxable years of foreign corporations beginning after December 31, 2004, and taxable years of U.S. shareholders with or within which such taxable years of foreign corporations end.

Conference Committee Report (H.R. CONF. REP. NO. 108-755)

Senate Amendment

The Senate amendment provision is the same as the House bill provision.

Conference Agreement

The conference agreement follows the House bill and the Senate amendment.

[Law at ¶ 5005, ¶ 5185, ¶ 5190, ¶ 5250, ¶ 5300, ¶ 5370, ¶ 5385, ¶ 5405, ¶ 5430, ¶ 5435, ¶ 5440,

¶ 5445, ¶ 5450, ¶ 5455, ¶ 5460, ¶ 5465, ¶ 5470, ¶ 5475, ¶ 5480, ¶ 5485, ¶ 5525, ¶ 5600, ¶ 5635, ¶ 5655, ¶ 5710, ¶ 5720, ¶ 5745, ¶ 5755, ¶ 5760, ¶ 5785, ¶ 5790, ¶ 5800, ¶ 5805, ¶ 5810, ¶ 5825, ¶ 5835, ¶ 5840, ¶ 6090, ¶ 6095, ¶ 6125, ¶ 6130, ¶ 6160, ¶ 6225 and ¶ 6250. CCH **Explanation at** ¶ 490.]

[¶ 10,700] Act Sec. 414. Determination of foreign personal holding company income with respect to transactions in commodities

House Committee Report (H.R. REP. NO. 108-548, pt. 1)

[Code Sec. 954]
Present Law

Subpart F foreign personal holding company income

Under the subpart F rules, U.S. shareholders with a 10-percent or greater interest in a controlled foreign corporation ("U.S. 10-percent shareholders") are subject to U.S. tax currently on certain income earned by the controlled foreign corporation, whether or not such income is distributed to the shareholders. The income subject to current inclusion under the subpart F rules includes, among other things, "foreign personal holding company income."

Foreign personal holding company income generally consists of the following: dividends, interest, royalties, rents and annuities; net gains from sales or exchanges of (1) property that gives rise to the foregoing types of income, (2) property that does not give rise to income, and (3) interests in trusts, partnerships, and real estate mortgage investment conduits ("REMICs"); net gains from commodities transactions; net gains from foreign currency transactions; income that is equivalent to interest; income from notional principal contracts; and payments in lieu of dividends.

With respect to transactions in commodities, foreign personal holding company income does not consist of gains or losses which arise out of bona fide hedging transactions that are reasonably necessary to the conduct of any business by a producer, processor, merchant, or handler of a commodity in the manner in which such business is customarily and usually conducted by others.[152] In addition, foreign personal holding company income does not consist of gains or losses which are comprised of active business gains or losses from the sale of commodities, but only if substantially all of the controlled foreign corporation's business is as an active producer, processor, merchant, or handler of commodities.[153]

Hedging transactions

Under present law, the term "capital asset" does not include any hedging transaction which is clearly identified as such before the close of the day on which it was acquired, originated, or entered into (or such other time as the Secretary may by regulations prescribe).[154] The term "hedging transaction" means any transaction entered into by the taxpayer in the normal course of the taxpayer's trade or business primarily: (1) to manage risk of price changes or currency fluctuations with respect to ordinary property which is held or to be held by the taxpayer; (2) to manage risk of interest rate or price changes or currency fluctuations with respect to borrowings made or to be made, or ordinary obligations incurred or to be incurred, by the taxpayer; or (3) to manage such other risks as the Secretary may prescribe in regulations.[155]

Reasons for Change

The Committee believes that exceptions from subpart F foreign personal holding company income for commodities hedging transactions and active business sales of commodities should be modified to better reflect current active business practices and, in the case of hedging transactions, to conform to recent tax law changes concerning hedging transactions generally.

Explanation of Provision

The provision modifies the requirements that must be satisfied for gains or losses from a

---

[152] For hedging transactions entered into on or after January 31, 2003, Treasury regulations provide that gains or losses from a commodities hedging transaction generally are excluded from the definition of foreign personal holding company income if the transaction is with respect to the controlled foreign corporation's business as a producer, processor, merchant or handler of commodities, regardless of whether the transaction is a hedge with respect to a sale of commodities in the active conduct of a commodities business by the controlled foreign corporation. The regulations also provide that, for purposes of satisfying the requirements for exclusion from the definition of foreign personal holding company income, a producer, processor, merchant or handler of commodities includes a controlled foreign corporation that regularly uses commodities in a manufacturing, construction, utilities, or transportation business (Treas. Reg. sec. 1.954-2(f)(2)(v)). However, the regulations provide that a controlled foreign corporation is not a

producer, processor, merchant or handler of commodities (and therefore would not satisfy the requirements for exclusion) if its business is primarily financial (Treas. Reg. sec. 1.954-2(f)(2)(v)).

[153] Treasury regulations provide that substantially all of a controlled foreign corporation's business is as an active producer, processor, merchant or handler of commodities if: (1) the sum of its gross receipts from all of its active sales of commodities in such capacity and its gross receipts from all of its commodities hedging transactions that qualify for exclusion from the definition of foreign personal holding company income, equals or exceeds (2) 85 percent of its total receipts for the taxable year (computed as though the controlled foreign corporation was a domestic corporation) (Treas. Reg. sec. 1.954-2(f)(2)(iii)(C)).

[154] Sec. 1221(a)(7).

[155] Sec. 1221(b)(2)(A).

commodities hedging transaction to qualify for exclusion from the definition of subpart F foreign personal holding company income. Under the provision, gains or losses from a transaction with respect to a commodity are not treated as foreign personal holding company income if the transaction satisfies the general definition of a hedging transaction under section 1221(b)(2). For purposes of this provision, the general definition of a hedging transaction under section 1221(b)(2) is modified to include any transaction with respect to a commodity entered into by a controlled foreign corporation in the normal course of the controlled foreign corporation's trade or business primarily: (1) to manage risk of price changes or currency fluctuations with respect to ordinary property or property described in section 1231(b) which is held or to be held by the controlled foreign corporation; or (2) to manage such other risks as the Secretary may prescribe in regulations. Gains or losses from a transaction that satisfies the modified definition of a hedging transaction are excluded from the definition of foreign personal holding company income only if the transaction is clearly identified as a hedging transaction in accordance with the hedge identification requirements that apply generally to hedging transactions under section 1221(b)(2).[156]

The provision also changes the requirements that must be satisfied for active business gains or losses from the sale of commodities to qualify for exclusion from the definition of foreign personal holding company income. Under the provision, such gains or losses are not treated as foreign personal holding company income if substan-

tially all of the controlled foreign corporation's commodities are comprised of: (1) stock in trade of the controlled foreign corporation or other property of a kind which would properly be included in the inventory of the controlled foreign corporation if on hand at the close of the taxable year, or property held by the controlled foreign corporation primarily for sale to customers in the ordinary course of the controlled foreign corporation's trade or business; (2) property that is used in the trade or business of the controlled foreign corporation and is of a character which is subject to the allowance for depreciation under section 167; or (3) supplies of a type regularly used or consumed by the controlled foreign corporation in the ordinary course of a trade or business of the controlled foreign corporation.[157]

For purposes of applying the requirements for active business gains or losses from commodities sales to qualify for exclusion from the definition of foreign personal holding company income, the provision also provides that commodities with respect to which gains or losses are not taken into account as foreign personal holding company income by a regular dealer in commodities (or financial instruments referenced to commodities) are not taken into account in determining whether substantially all of the dealer's commodities are comprised of the property described above.

Effective Date

The provision is effective with respect to transactions entered into after December 31, 2004.

Conference Committee Report (H.R. CONF. REP. No. 108-755)

Senate Amendment

The Senate amendment is the same as the House bill.

Conference Agreement

The conference agreement follows the House bill and the Senate amendment.

[Law at ¶ 5720. CCH Explanation at ¶ 470.]

[¶ 10,710] Act Sec. 415. Modifications to treatment of aircraft leasing and shipping income

House Committee Report (H.R. REP. No. 108-548, pt. 1)

[Code Sec. 954]

Present Law

In general, the subpart F rules (secs. 951-964) require U.S. shareholders with a 10-percent or

greater interest in a controlled foreign corporation ("CFC") to include currently in income for U.S. tax purposes certain income of the CFC (referred to as "subpart F income"), without regard to whether the income is distributed to the

---

[156] Sec. 1221(a)(7) and (b)(2)(B).

[157] For purposes of determining whether substantially all of the controlled foreign corporation's commodities are comprised of such property, it is intended that the 85-per-

cent requirement provided in the current Treasury regulations (as modified to reflect the changes made by the provision) continue to apply.

shareholders (sec. 951(a)(1)(A)). In effect, the Code treats the U.S. 10-percent shareholders of a CFC as having received a current distribution of their pro rata shares of the CFC's subpart F income. The amounts included in income by the CFC's U.S. 10-percent shareholders under these rules are subject to U.S. tax currently. The U.S. tax on such amounts may be reduced through foreign tax credits.

Subpart F income includes foreign base company shipping income (sec. 954(f)). Foreign base company shipping income generally includes income derived from the use of an aircraft or vessel in foreign commerce, the performance of services directly related to the use of any such aircraft or vessel, the sale or other disposition of any such aircraft or vessel, and certain space or ocean activities (e.g., leasing of satellites for use in space). Foreign commerce generally involves the transportation of property or passengers between a port (or airport) in the U.S. and a port (or airport) in a foreign country, two ports (or airports) within the same foreign country, or two ports (or airports) in different foreign countries. In addition, foreign base company shipping income includes dividends and interest that a CFC receives from certain foreign corporations and any gains from the disposition of stock in certain foreign corporations, to the extent the dividends, interest, or gains are attributable to foreign base company shipping income. Foreign base company shipping income also includes incidental income derived in the course of active foreign base company shipping operations (e.g., income from temporary investments in or sales of related shipping assets), foreign exchange gain or loss attributable to foreign base company shipping operations, and a CFC's distributive share of gross income of any partnership and gross income received from certain trusts to the extent that the income would have been foreign base company shipping income had it been realized directly by the corporation.

Subpart F income also includes foreign personal holding company income (sec. 954(c)). For subpart F purposes, foreign personal holding company income generally consists of the following: (1) dividends, interest, royalties, rents and annuities; (2) net gains from the sale or exchange of (a) property that gives rise to the preceding types of income, (b) property that does not give rise to income, and (c) interests in trusts, partnerships, and REMICS; (3) net gains from commodities transactions; (4) net gains from foreign currency transactions; (5) income that is equivalent to interest; (6) income from

notional principal contracts; and (7) payments in lieu of dividends.

Subpart F foreign personal holding company income does not include rents and royalties received by a CFC in the active conduct of a trade or business from unrelated persons (sec. 954(c)(2)(A)). The determination of whether rents or royalties are derived in the active conduct of a trade or business is based on all the facts and circumstances. However, the Treasury regulations provide certain types of rents are treated as derived in the active conduct of a trade or business. These include rents derived from property that is leased as a result of the performance of marketing functions by the lessor if the lessor (through its own officers or employees located in a foreign country) maintains and operates an organization in such country that regularly engages in the business of marketing, or marketing and servicing, the leased property and that is substantial in relation to the amount of rents derived from the leasing of such property. An organization in a foreign country is substantial in relation to rents if the active leasing expenses[158] equal at least 25 percent of the adjusted leasing profit.[159]

Also generally excluded from subpart F foreign personal holding company income are rents and royalties received by the CFC from a related corporation for the use of property within the country in which the CFC was organized (sec. 954(c)(3)). However, rent, and royalty payments do not qualify for this exclusion to the extent that such payments reduce subpart F income of the payor.

Reasons for Change

In general, other countries do not tax foreign shipping income, whereas the United States imposes immediate U.S. tax on such income. The uncompetitive U.S. taxation of shipping income has directly caused a steady and substantial decline of the U.S. shipping industry. The Committee believes that this provision will provide U.S. shippers the opportunity to be competitive with their tax-advantaged foreign competitors.

In addition, the Committee believes that the current-law exception from foreign base company income for rents and royalties received by a CFC in the active conduct of a trade or business from unrelated persons is too narrow in the context of the leasing of an aircraft or vessel in foreign commerce. The Committee believes the provision of the safe harbor under the bill will

---

[158] "Active-leasing expenses" are section 162 expenses properly allocable to rental income other than (1) deductions for compensation for personal services rendered by the lessor's shareholders or a related person, (2) deductions for rents, (3) section 167 and 168 expenses, and (4) deductions for payments to independent contractors with respect to leased property. Treas. Reg. sec. 1.954-2(c)(2)(iii).

[159] Generally, "adjusted leasing profit" is rental income less the sum of (1) rents paid or incurred by the CFC with respect to such rental income; (2) section 167 and 168 expenses with respect to such rental income; and (3) payments to independent contractors with respect to such rental income. Treas. Reg. sec. 1.954-2(c)(2)(iv).

improve the competitiveness of U.S.-based multinationals engaging in these activities.

Explanation of Provision

The provision repeals the subpart F rules relating to foreign base company shipping income. The bill also amends the exception from foreign personal holding company income applicable to rents or royalties derived from unrelated persons in an active trade or business, by providing a safe harbor for rents derived from leasing an aircraft or vessel in foreign commerce. Such rents are excluded from foreign personal holding company income if the active leasing expenses comprise at least 10 percent of the profit on the lease. This provision is to be applied in accordance with existing regulations under sec. 954(c)(2)(A) by comparing the lessor's "active leasing expenses" for its pool of leased assets to its "adjusted leasing profit."

The safe harbor will not prevent a lessor from otherwise showing that it actively carries on a trade or business. In this regard, the requirements of section 954(c)(2)(A) will be met if a lessor regularly and directly performs active and substantial marketing, remarketing, management and operational functions with respect to the leasing of an aircraft or vessel (or component engines). This will be the case regardless of whether the lessor engages in marketing of the lease as a form of financing (versus marketing the property as such) or whether the lease is classified as a finance lease or operating lease for financial accounting purposes. If a lessor acquires, from an unrelated or related party, a ship or aircraft subject to an existing FSC or ETI lease, the requirements of section 954(c)(2)(A) will be satisfied if, following the acquisition, the lessor performs active and substantial management, operational, and remarketing functions with respect to the leased property. If such a lease is transferred to a CFC lessor, it will no longer be eligible for FSC or ETI benefits.

An aircraft or vessel will be considered to be leased in foreign commerce if it is used for the transportation of property or passengers between a port (or airport) in the United States and one in a foreign country or between foreign ports (or airports), provided the aircraft or vessel is used predominantly outside the United States. An aircraft or vessel will be considered used predominantly outside the United States if more than 50 percent of the miles during the taxable year are traversed outside the United States or

the aircraft or vessel is located outside the United States more than 50 percent of the time during such taxable year.

The Committee expects that the Secretary of the Treasury will issue timely guidance to make conforming changes to existing regulations, including guidance that aircraft or vessel leasing activity that satisfies the requirements of section 954(c)(2)(A) shall also satisfy the requirements for avoiding income inclusion under section 956 and section 367(a).

The Committee anticipates that taxpayers now eligible for the benefits of the ETI exclusion (or the FSC provisions pursuant to the FSC Repeal and Extraterritorial Income Exclusion Act of 2000), will find it appropriate, as a matter of sound business judgment, to restructure their business operations to take into account the tax law changes brought about by the bill. The Committee notes that courts have recognized the validity of structuring operations for the purpose of obtaining the benefit of tax regimes expressly intended by Congress. The Committee intends that structuring or restructuring of operations for the purposes of adapting to the repeal of the ETI exclusion (or the FSC regime) will be considered to serve a valid business purpose and will not constitute tax avoidance, where the restructured operations conform to the requirements expressly mandated by Congress for obtaining tax benefits that remain available. For example, the Committee intends that a restructuring undertaken to transfer aircraft subject to existing FSC or ETI leases to a CFC lessor, to take advantange [sic—CCH.] of the amendments made by this bill, would serve as a valid business purpose and would not constitute tax avoidance, for purposes of determining whether a particular tax treatment (such as nonrecognition of gain) applies to such restructuring. The Committee intends, for example, that if such a restructuring meets the other requirements necessary to qualify as a "reorganization" under section 368, the transaction will also be deemed to meet the "business purpose" requirements under section 368, and thus, qualify as a reorganization under that section.

Effective Date

The provision is effective for taxable years of foreign corporations beginning after December 31, 2004, and taxable years of U.S. shareholders with or within which such taxable years of foreign corporations end.

Conference Committee Report (H.R. CONF. REP. NO. 108-755)

The conference agreement follows the House bill with the following clarifications. First, the terms "aircraft or vessels" include engines that are leased separately from an aircraft or vessel. Second, if a lessor acquires (from a related or unrelated party) or aircraft or vessel subject to an existing lease, the requirements of section 954(c)(2)(A) are satisfied if, following the acquisi-

tion, the lessor performs active and substantial management, operational, and remarketing functions with respect to the leased property. However, if an existing FSC or ETI lease is transferred to a CFC lessor, the lease will no longer be eligible for FSC or ETI benefits.

[Law at ¶5715 and ¶5720. CCH Explanation at ¶475.]

Act Sec. 415   ¶10,710

[¶ 10,720] Act Sec. 416. Modification of exceptions under subpart F for active financing

House Committee Report (H.R. REP. NO. 108-548, pt. 1)

[Code Sec. 954]

Present Law

Under the subpart F rules, U.S. shareholders with a 10-percent or greater interest in a controlled foreign corporation ("CFC") are subject to U.S. tax currently on certain income earned by the CFC, whether or not such income is distributed to the shareholders. The income subject to current inclusion under the subpart F rules includes, among other things, foreign personal holding company income and insurance income. In addition, 10-percent U.S. shareholders of a CFC are subject to current inclusion with respect to their shares of the CFC's foreign base company services income (i.e., income derived from services performed for a related person outside the country in which the CFC is organized).

Foreign personal holding company income generally consists of the following: (1) dividends, interest, royalties, rents, and annuities; (2) net gains from the sale or exchange of (a) property that gives rise to the preceding types of income, (b) property that does not give rise to income, and (c) interests in trusts, partnerships, and REMICs; (3) net gains from commodities transactions; (4) net gains from foreign currency transactions; (5) income that is equivalent to interest; (6) income from notional principal contracts; and (7) payments in lieu of dividends.

Insurance income subject to current inclusion under the subpart F rules includes any income of a CFC attributable to the issuing or reinsuring of any insurance or annuity contract in connection with risks located in a country other than the CFC's country of organization. Subpart F insurance income also includes income attributable to an insurance contract in connection with risks located within the CFC's country of organization, as the result of an arrangement under which another corporation receives a substantially equal amount of consideration for insurance of other country risks. Investment income of a CFC that is allocable to any insurance or annuity contract related to risks located outside the CFC's country of organization is taxable as subpart F insurance income (Treas. Reg. sec. 1.953-1(a)).

Temporary exceptions from foreign personal holding company income, foreign base company services income, and insurance income apply for subpart F purposes for certain income that is derived in the active conduct of a banking, financing, or similar business, or in the conduct of an insurance business (so-called "active financing income").[160]

With respect to income derived in the active conduct of a banking, financing, or similar business, a CFC is required to be predominantly engaged in such business and to conduct substantial activity with respect to such business in order to qualify for the exceptions. In addition, certain nexus requirements apply, which provide that income derived by a CFC or a qualified business unit ("QBU") of a CFC from transactions with customers is eligible for the exceptions if, among other things, substantially all of the activities in connection with such transactions are conducted directly by the CFC or QBU in its home country, and such income is treated as earned by the CFC or QBU in its home country for purposes of such country's tax laws. Moreover, the exceptions apply to income derived from certain cross border transactions, provided that certain requirements are met. Additional exceptions from foreign personal holding company income apply for certain income derived by a securities dealer within the meaning of section 475 and for gain from the sale of active financing assets.

In the case of insurance, in addition to temporary exceptions from insurance income and from foreign personal holding company income for certain income of a qualifying insurance company with respect to risks located within the CFC's country of creation or organization, temporary exceptions from insurance income and from foreign personal holding company income apply for certain income of a qualifying branch of a qualifying insurance company with respect to risks located within the home country of the branch, provided certain requirements are met under each of the exceptions. Further, additional temporary exceptions from insurance income and from foreign personal holding company income apply for certain income of certain CFCs or

---

[160] Temporary exceptions from the subpart F provisions for certain active financing income applied only for taxable years beginning in 1998. Those exceptions were modified and extended for one year, applicable only for taxable years beginning in 1999. The Tax Relief Extension Act of 1999 (Pub.L. No. 106-170) clarified and extended the temporary exceptions for two years, applicable only for taxable years beginning after 1999 and before 2002. The Job Creation and Worker Assistance Act of 2002 (Pub.L. No. 107-147) extended the temporary exceptions for five years, applicable only for taxable years beginning after 2001 and before 2007, with a modification relating to insurance reserves.

branches with respect to risks located in a country other than the United States, provided that the requirements for these exceptions are met.

Reasons for Change

The Committee believes that the rules for determining whether income earned by an eligible CFC or QBU is active financing income should be more consistent with the rules for determining whether a CFC or QBU is eligible to earn active financing income.

Explanation of Provision

The provision modifies the present-law temporary exceptions from subpart F foreign personal holding company income and foreign base company services income for income derived in the active conduct of a banking, financing, or similar business. For purposes of determining whether a CFC or QBU has conducted directly in its home country substantially all of the activities in connection with transactions with customers, the provision provides that an activity is treated as conducted directly by the CFC or QBU in its home country if the activity is performed by employees of a related person and: (1) the related person is itself an eligible CFC the home country of which is the same as that of the CFC or QBU; (2) the activity is performed in the home country of the related person; and (3) the related person is compensated on an arm's length basis for the performance of the activity by its employees and such compensation is treated as earned by such person in its home country for purposes of the tax laws of such country. For purposes of determining whether a CFC or QBU is eligible to earn active financing income, such activity may not be taken into account by any CFC or QBU (including the employer of the employees performing the activity) other than the CFC or QBU for which the activities are performed.

Effective Date

The provision is effective for taxable years of foreign corporations beginning after December 31, 2004, and taxable years of U.S. shareholders with or within which such taxable years of foreign corporations end.

Conference Committee Report (H.R. CONF. REP. NO. 108-755)

Senate Amendment

The Senate amendment is the same as the House bill.

[Law at ¶5720. CCH Explanation at ¶480.]

Conference Agreement

The conference agreement follows the House bill and the Senate amendment.

[¶10,730] Act Sec. 417. Ten-year foreign tax credit carryover; one-year foreign tax credit carryback

Senate Committee Report (S. REP. NO. 108-192)

[Code Secs. 904 and 907]

Present Law

U.S. persons may credit foreign taxes against U.S. tax on foreign-source income. The amount of foreign tax credits that may be claimed in a year is subject to a limitation that prevents taxpayers from using foreign tax credits to offset U.S. tax on U.S.-source income. The amount of foreign tax credits generally is limited to a portion of the taxpayer's U.S. tax which portion is calculated by multiplying the taxpayer's total U.S. tax by a fraction, the numerator of which is the taxpayer's foreign-source taxable income (i.e., foreign-source gross income less allocable expenses or deductions) and the denominator of which is the taxpayer's worldwide taxable income for the year.[15]

In addition, this limitation is calculated separately for various categories of income, generally referred to as "separate limitation categories." The total amount of the foreign tax credit used to offset the U.S. tax on income in each separate limitation category may not exceed the proportion of the taxpayer's U.S. tax which the taxpayer's foreign-source taxable income in that category bears to its worldwide taxable income.

The amount of creditable taxes paid or accrued (or deemed paid) in any taxable year which exceeds the foreign tax credit limitation is permitted to be carried back to the two immediately preceding taxable years (to the earliest year first) and carried forward five taxable years (in chronological order) and credited (not deducted)

---

[15] Section 904(a).

to the extent that the taxpayer otherwise has excess foreign tax credit limitation for those years. Excess credits that are carried back or forward are usable only to the extent that there is excess foreign tax credit limitation in such carryover or carryback year. Consequently, foreign tax credits arising in a taxable year are utilized before excess credits from another taxable year may be carried forward or backward. In addition, excess credits are carried forward or carried back on a separate limitation basis. Thus, if a taxpayer has excess foreign tax credits in one separate limitation category for a taxable year, those excess credits may be carried back and forward only as taxes allocable to that category, notwithstanding the fact that the taxpayer may have excess foreign tax credit limitation in another category for that year. If credits cannot be so utilized, they are permanently disallowed.

Reasons for Change

The Committee is concerned that excessive double taxation of foreign earnings may result

from the expiration of foreign tax credits under present law. The Committee believes that the purposes of the foreign tax credit would be better served by providing a larger window within which credits may be used, thereby reducing the likelihood that credits may expire.

Explanation of Provision

The provision extends the excess foreign tax credit carryforward period to twenty years and limits the carryback period to one year.

Effective Date

The extension of the carryforward period is effective for excess foreign tax credits that may be carried to any taxable years ending after the date of enactment of the provision; the limited carryback period is effective for excess foreign tax credits arising in taxable years beginning after the date of enactment of the provision.

Conference Committee Report (H.R. CONF. REP. NO. 108-755)

House Bill

No provision.

Conference Agreement

The conference agreement follows the Senate amendment, with the modification that the

foreign tax credit carryforward period is extended to 10 years.

[Law at ¶ 5655 and ¶ 5660. CCH Explanation at ¶ 415.]

[¶ 10,740] Act Sec. 418. Modify FIRPTA rules for real estate investment trusts

Senate Committee Report (S. REP. NO. 108-192)

[Code Secs. 857 and 897]

Present Law

A real estate investment trust ("REIT") is a U.S. entity that derives most of its income from passive real-estate-related investments. A REIT must satisfy a number of tests on an annual basis that relate to the entity's organizational structure, the source of its income, and the nature of its assets. If an electing entity meets the requirements for REIT status, the portion of its income that is distributed to its investors each year generally is treated as a dividend deductible by the REIT, and includible in income by its investors. In this manner, the distributed income of the REIT is not taxed at the entity level. The distributed income is taxed only at the investor level. A REIT generally is required to distribute 90 percent of its income to its investors before the end of its taxable year.

Special U.S.-tax rules apply to gains of foreign persons attributable to dispositions of inter-

ests in U.S.-real property, including certain transactions involving REITs. The rules governing the imposition and collection of tax on such dispositions are contained in a series of provisions that were enacted in 1980 and that are collectively referred to as the Foreign Investment in Real Property Tax Act ("FIRPTA").

In general, FIRPTA provides that gain or loss of a foreign person from the disposition of a U.S.-real property interest is taken into account for U.S.-tax purposes as if such gain or loss were effectively connected with a U.S. trade or business during the taxable year. Accordingly, foreign persons generally are subject to U.S. tax on any gain from a disposition of a U.S. real property interest at the same rates that apply to similar income received by U.S. persons. For these purposes, the receipt of a distribution from a REIT is treated as a disposition of a U.S.-real property interest by the recipient to the extent that it is attributable to a sale or exchange of a U.S.-real property interest by the REIT. These capital gains distributions from REITs generally are subject to withholding tax at a rate of 35 percent (or a lower treaty rate). In addition, the recipients of these capital gains distributions are required to file Federal income tax returns in the United States, since the recipients are treated as earning income effectively connected with a U.S. trade or business.

In addition, foreign corporations that have effectively connected income generally are subject to the branch profits tax at a 30-percent rate (or a lower treaty rate).

Reasons for Change

The Committee believes that it is appropriate to provide greater conformity in the tax consequences of REIT distributions and other corporate stock distributions.

Explanation of Provision

The provision removes from treatment as effectively connected income for a foreign investor a capital gain distribution from a REIT, provided that: (1) the distribution is received with respect to a class of stock that is regularly traded on an established securities market located in the United States; and (2) the foreign investor does not own more than 5 percent of the class of stock at any time during the taxable year within which the distribution is received.

Thus, a foreign investor is not required to file a U.S. Federal income tax return by reason of receiving such a distribution. The distribution is to be treated as a REIT dividend to that investor, taxed as a REIT dividend that is not a capital gain. Also, the branch profits tax no longer applies to such a distribution.

Effective Date

The provision applies to taxable years beginning after the date of enactment.

Conference Committee Report (H.R. Conf. Rep. No. 108-755)

House Bill

No provision.

[Law at ¶5555 and ¶5630. CCH Explanation at ¶540.]

Conference Agreement

The conference agreement follows the Senate amendment.

[¶10,750] Act Sec. 419. Exclusion of certain horse-racing and dog-racing gambling winnings from the income of nonresident alien individuals

Senate Committee Report (S. Rep. No. 108-192)

[Code Sec. 872]

Present Law

Under section 871, certain items of gross income received by a nonresident alien from sources within the United States are subject to a flat 30-percent withholding tax. Gambling winnings received by a nonresident alien from wagers placed in the United States are U.S.-source and thus generally are subject to this withholding tax, unless exempted by treaty. Currently, several U.S. income tax treaties exempt U.S.-source gambling winnings of residents of the other treaty country from U.S. withholding tax. In addition, no withholding tax is imposed under section 871 on the non-business gambling income of a nonresident alien from wagers on the following games (except to the extent that

the Secretary determines that collection of the tax would be administratively feasible): blackjack, baccarat, craps, roulette, and big-6 wheel. Various other (non-gambling-related) items of income of a nonresident alien are excluded from gross income under section 872(b) and are thereby exempt from the 30-percent withholding tax, without any authority for the Secretary to impose the tax by regulation. In cases in which a withholding tax on gambling winnings applies, section 1441(a) of the Code requires the party making the winning payout to withhold the appropriate amount and makes that party responsible for amounts not withheld.

With respect to gambling winnings of a nonresident alien resulting from a wager initiated outside the United States on a pari-mutuel[64]

---

[64] In pari-mutuel wagering (common in horse racing), odds and payouts are determined by the aggregate bets placed. The money wagered is placed into a pool, the party maintaining the pool takes a percentage of the total, and the

bettors effectively bet against each other. Pari-mutuel wagering may be contrasted with fixed-odds wagering (common in sports wagering), in which odds (or perhaps a point

event taking place within the United States, the source of the winnings, and thus the applicability of the 30-percent U.S. withholding tax, depends on the type of wagering pool from which the winnings are paid. If the payout is made from a separate foreign pool, maintained completely in a foreign jurisdiction (e.g., a pool maintained by a racetrack or off-track betting parlor that is showing in a foreign country a simulcast of a horse race taking place in the United States), then the winnings paid to a nonresident alien generally would not be subject to withholding tax, because the amounts received generally would not be from sources within the United States. However, if the payout is made from a "merged" or "commingled" pool, in which betting pools in the United States and the foreign country are combined for a particular event, then the portion of the payout attributable to wagers placed in the United States could be subject to withholding tax. The party making the payment, in this case a racetrack or off-track betting parlor in a foreign country, would be responsible for withholding the tax.

Reasons for Change

The Committee believes that nonresident aliens should be able to wager outside the United States in pari-mutuel pools on live horse or dog races taking place within the United States without any resulting winnings being subjected to U.S. income tax, regardless of whether the foreign pool is merged with a U.S. pool.

Explanation of Provision

The provision provides an exclusion from gross income under section 872(b) for winnings paid to a nonresident alien resulting from a legal wager initiated outside the United States in a pari-mutuel pool on a live horse or dog race in the United States, regardless of whether the pool is a separate foreign pool or a merged U.S.-foreign pool.

Effective Date

The provision is effective for wagers made after the date of enactment of the provision.

Conference Committee Report (H.R. CONF. REP. NO. 108-755)

House Bill

No provision.

Conference Agreement

The conference agreement follows the Senate amendment.

[Law at ¶ 5610 and ¶ 5625. CCH Explanation at ¶ 565.]

[¶ 10,760] Act Sec. 420. Limitation of withholding on U.S.-source dividends paid to Puerto Rico corporation

Senate Committee Report (S. REP. NO. 108-192)

[Code Secs. 881 and 1442]

Present Law

In general, dividends paid by corporations organized in the United States[65] to corporations organized outside of the United States and its possessions are subject to U.S. income tax withholding at the flat rate of 30-percent. The rate may be reduced or eliminated under a tax treaty. Dividends paid by U.S. corporations to corporations organized in certain U.S. possessions are subject to different rules.[66] Corporations organized in the U.S. possessions of the Virgin Islands, Guam, American Samoa or the Northern Mariana Islands are not subject to withholding tax on dividends from corporations organized in the United States, provided that certain local ownership and activity requirements are met. Each of those possessions have adopted local internal revenue codes that provide a zero rate of withholding tax on dividends paid by corporations organized in the possession to corporations organized in the United States.

Under the tax laws of Puerto Rico, which is also a U.S. possession, a 10-percent withholding tax is imposed on dividends paid by Puerto Rico

---

(Footnote Continued)

spread) are agreed to by the bettor and the party taking the bet and are not affected by the bets placed by other bettors.

[65] The team "United States" does not include its possessions. Sec. 7701(a)(9).

[66] The usual method of effecting a mitigation of the flat 30 percent rate—an income tax treaty providing for a lower rate—is not possible in the case of a possession. See S. Rep. No. 1707, 89th Cong., 2d Sess. 34 (1966).

corporations to non-Puerto Rico corporations.[67] Dividends paid by corporations organized in the United States to Puerto Rico corporations are subject to U.S. withholding tax at a 30-percent rate. Under Puerto Rico law, Puerto Rico corporations may elect to credit their U.S. income taxes against their Puerto Rico income taxes. Creditable income taxes include the 30-percent dividend withholding tax and the underlying U.S. corporate tax attributable to the dividends. However, a Puerto Rico corporation's tax credit for U.S. income taxes may be limited because the sum of the U.S. withholding tax and the underlying U.S. corporate tax generally exceeds the amount of Puerto Rico corporate income tax imposed on the dividend. Consequently, Puerto Rico corporations with subsidiaries organized in the United States may be subject to some degree of double taxation on their U.S. subsidiaries' earnings.

Reasons for Change

The 30-percent withholding tax rate on U.S.-source dividends to Puerto Rico corporations places such companies at an economic disadvantage relative to corporations organized in foreign countries with which the United States has a tax treaty, and relative to corporations organized in other possessions. The Committee believes that

creating and maintaining parity between U.S. and Puerto Rico dividend withholding tax rates would place Puerto Rico corporations on a more level playing field with corporations organized in treaty countries and other possessions.

Explanation of Provision

The provision lowers the withholding income tax rate on U.S. source dividends paid to a corporation created or organized in Puerto Rico from 30 percent to 10 percent, to create parity with the 10-percent withholding tax imposed by Puerto Rico on dividends paid to non-Puerto Rico corporations. The lower rate applies only if the same local ownership and activity requirements are met that are applicable to corporations organized in other possessions receiving dividends from corporations organized in the United States. The Committee believes that it is desirable that the U.S. and Puerto Rico corporate dividend withholding tax rates should remain in parity in the future. Accordingly, the Committee intends to revisit the U.S. dividend withholding tax rate should there be a change to the relevant Puerto Rico rate.

Effective Date

The provision is effective for dividends paid after date of enactment.

Conference Committee Report (H.R. CONF. REP. NO. 108-755)

House Bill

No provision.

Conference Agreement

The conference agreement follows the Senate amendment with modifications. Under the provision as modified, if the generally applicable

withholding tax rate imposed by Puerto Rico on dividends paid to U.S. corporations increases to greater than 10 percent, the U.S. withholding rate on dividends to Puerto Rico corporations reverts to 30 percent.

[Law at ¶ 5620 and ¶ 5930. CCH Explanation at ¶ 585.]

[¶ 10,770] Act Sec. 421. Alternative minimum tax relief: Repeal limitation on use of foreign tax credit

House Committee Report (H.R. REP. NO. 108-548, pt. 1)

[Code Secs. 53 and 59]

Present Law

In general

Under present law, taxpayers are subject to an alternative minimum tax ("AMT"), which is payable, in addition to all other tax liabilities, to the extent that it exceeds the taxpayer's regular income tax liability. The tax is imposed at a flat

rate of 20 percent, in the case of corporate taxpayers, on alternative minimum taxable income ("AMTI") in excess of a phased-out exemption amount. AMTI is the taxpayer's taxable income increased for certain tax preferences and adjusted by determining the tax treatment of certain items in a manner that limits the tax benefits resulting from the regular tax treatment of such items.

---

[67] The 10-percent withholding rate may be subject to exemption or elimination if the dividend is paid out of income that is subject to certain tax incentives offered by Puerto

Rico. These tax incentives may also reduce the rate of underlying Puerto Rico corporate tax to a flat rate of between two and seven percent.

Foreign tax credit

Taxpayers are permitted to reduce their AMT liability by an AMT foreign tax credit. The AMT foreign tax credit for a taxable year is determined under principles similar to those used in computing the regular tax foreign tax credit, except that (1) the numerator of the AMT foreign tax credit limitation fraction is foreign source AMTI and (2) the denominator of that fraction is total AMTI. Taxpayers may elect to use as their AMT foreign tax credit limitation fraction the ratio of foreign source regular taxable income to total AMTI.

The AMT foreign tax credit for any taxable year generally may not offset a taxpayer's entire pre-credit AMT. Rather, the AMT foreign tax credit is limited to 90 percent of AMT computed without any AMT net operating loss deduction and the AMT foreign tax credit. For example, assume that a corporation has $10 million of AMTI, has no AMT net operating loss deduction, and has no regular tax liability. In the absence of the AMT foreign tax credit, the corporation's tax liability would be $2 million. Accordingly, the AMT foreign tax credit cannot be applied to reduce the taxpayer's tax liability below $200,000. Any unused AMT foreign tax credit may be carried back two years and carried forward five years for use against AMT in those years under the principles of the foreign tax credit carryback and carryover rules set forth in section 904(c).

* * *

Reasons for Change

The Committee believes that the AMT is merely a prepayment of tax. The corporate AMT requires businesses to prepay their taxes when they can least afford it, during a business downturn. * * * The Committee also believes that taxpayers should be permitted full use of foreign tax credits in computing the AMT. * * *

Explanation of Provision

The provision repeals the 90-percent limitation on the utilization of the AMT foreign tax credit.

* * *

Effective Date

The provision relating to the foreign tax credit applies to taxable years beginning after December 31, 2004.

* * *

Conference Committee Report (H.R. CONF. REP. NO. 108-755)

Senate Amendment

Same as House bill.

Conference Agreement

The conference agreement includes the provision in the House bill and Senate amendment.

[Law at ¶5075 and ¶5090. CCH Explanation at ¶455.]

[¶ 10,780] Act Sec. 422. Incentives to reinvest foreign earnings in the United States

House Committee Report (H.R. REP. NO. 108-548, pt. 1)

[New Code Sec. 965]

Present Law

The United States employs a "worldwide" tax system, under which domestic corporations generally are taxed on all income, whether derived in the United States or abroad. Income earned by a domestic parent corporation from foreign operations conducted by foreign corporate subsidiaries generally is subject to U.S. tax when the income is distributed as a dividend to the domestic corporation. Until such repatriation, the U.S. tax on such income generally is deferred, and U.S. tax is imposed on such income when repatriated. However, under anti-deferral rules, the domestic parent corporation may be taxed on a current basis in the United States with respect to certain categories of passive or highly mobile income earned by its foreign subsidiaries, regardless of whether the income has been distributed as a dividend to the domestic parent corporation. The main anti-deferral provisions in this context are the controlled foreign corporation rules of subpart F[66] and the passive foreign investment company rules.[67] A foreign tax credit generally is available to offset, in whole or in part, the U.S. tax owed on foreign-source income, whether earned di-

---

[66] Secs. 951-964.

[67] Secs. 1291-1298.

rectly by the domestic corporation, repatriated as a dividend from a foreign subsidiary, or included in income under the anti-deferral rules.[68]

Reasons for Change

The Committee observes that the residual U.S. tax imposed on the repatriation of foreign earnings can serve as a disincentive to repatriate these earnings. The Committee believes that a temporary reduction in the U.S. tax on repatriated dividends will stimulate the U.S. domestic economy by triggering the repatriation of foreign earnings that otherwise would have remained abroad. The Committee emphasizes that this is a temporary economic stimulus measure.

Explanation of Provision

Under the provision, certain dividends received by a U.S. corporation from a controlled foreign corporation are eligible for an 85-percent dividends-received deduction. At the taxpayer's election, this deduction is available for dividends received either: (1) during the first six months of the taxpayer's first taxable year beginning on or after the date of enactment of the bill; or (2) during any six-month or shorter period after the date of enactment of the bill, during the taxpayer's last taxable year beginning before such date. Dividends received after the election period will be taxed in the normal manner under present law.

The deduction applies only to dividends and other amounts included in gross income as dividends (e.g., amounts described in section 1248(a)). The deduction does not apply to items that are not included in gross income as dividends, such as subpart F inclusions or deemed repatriations under section 956. Similarly, the deduction does not apply to distributions of earnings previously taxed under subpart F, except to the extent that the subpart F inclusions result from the payment of a dividend by one controlled foreign corporation to another controlled foreign corporation within a certain chain of ownership during the election period. This exception enables multinational corporate groups to qualify for the deduction in connection with the repatriation of earnings from lower-tier controlled foreign corporations.

The deduction is subject to a number of limitations. First, it applies only to repatriations in excess of the taxpayer's average repatriation level over three of the five most recent taxable years ending on or before March 31, 2003, determined by disregarding the highest-repatriation year and the lowest-repatriation year among such five years (the "base-period average"). In addition to actual dividends, deemed repatriations under section 956 and distributions of earnings previously taxed under subpart F are included in the base-period average.

Second, the amount of dividends eligible for the deduction is limited to the greatest of: (1) $500 million; (2) the amount of earnings shown as permanently invested outside the United States on the taxpayer's most recent audited financial statement which is certified on or before March 31, 2003; or (3) in the case of an applicable financial statement that fails to show a specific amount of such earnings, but that does show a specific amount of tax liability attributable to such earnings, the amount of such earnings determined in such manner as the Treasury Secretary may prescribe.

Third, dividends qualifying for the deduction must be invested in the United States pursuant to a plan approved by the senior management and board of directors of the corporation claiming the deduction.

No foreign tax credit (or deduction) is allowed for foreign taxes attributable to the deductible portion of any dividend received during the taxable year for which an election under the provision is in effect. For this purpose, the taxpayer may specifically identify which dividends are treated as carrying the deduction and which are not; in the absence of such identification, a pro rata amount of foreign tax credits will be disallowed with respect to every dividend received during the taxable year.

In addition, the income attributable to the nondeductible portion of a qualifying dividend may not be offset by net operating losses, and the tax attributable to such income generally may not be offset by credits (other than foreign tax credits and AMT credits) and may not reduce the alternative minimum tax otherwise owed by the taxpayer. No deduction under sections 243 or 245 is allowed for any dividend for which a deduction is allowed under the provision.

Conference Committee Report (H.R. CONF. REP. NO. 108-755)

The conference agreement follows the House bill, with modifications.

Under the conference agreement, certain dividends received by a U.S. corporation from controlled foreign corporations are eligible for an 85-percent dividends-received deduction. At the taxpayer's election, this deduction is available for dividends received either during the tax-

---

[68] Secs. 901, 902, 960, 1291(g).

payer's first taxable year beginning on or after the date of enactment of the bill, or during the taxpayer's last taxable year beginning before such date.[107] Dividends received after the election period will be taxed in the normal manner under present law. The conferees emphasize that this is a temporary economic stimulus measure, and that there is no intent to make this measure permanent, or to "extend" or enact it again in the future.

The deduction applies only to cash dividends and other cash amounts included in gross income as dividends, such as cash amounts treated as dividends under sections 302 or 304 (but not to amounts treated as dividends under Code sections 78, 367, or 1248).[108] The deduction does not apply to items that are not included in gross income as dividends, such as subpart F inclusions or deemed repatriations under section 956. Similarly, the deduction does not apply to distributions of earnings previously taxed under subpart F, except to the extent that the subpart F inclusions result from the payment of a dividend by one controlled foreign corporation to another controlled foreign corporation within a certain chain of ownership during the election period, with the result that cash travels through a chain of controlled foreign corporations to the taxpayer within the election period. The amount of dividends eligible for the deduction is reduced by any increase in related-party indebtedness on the part of a controlled foreign corporation between October 3, 2004 and the close of the taxable year for which the deduction is being claimed, determined by treating all controlled foreign corporations with respect to which the taxpayer is a U.S. shareholder as one controlled foreign corporation.[109] This rule is intended to prevent a deduction from being claimed in cases in which the U.S. shareholder directly or indirectly (e.g., through a related party) finances the payment of a dividend from a controlled foreign corporation. In such a case, there may be no net repatriation of funds, and thus it would be inappropriate to provide the deduction.

The deduction is subject to a number of general limitations. First, it applies only to repatriations in excess of the taxpayer's average repatriation level over three of the five most recent taxable years ending on or before June 30, 2003, determined by disregarding the highest-repatriation year and the lowest-repatriation year among such five years (the "base-period average"). If the taxpayer has fewer than five such years, then all taxable years ending on or before June 30, 2003 are included in the base period.[110] Repatriation levels are determined by reference to base-period tax returns as filed, including any amended returns that were filed on or before June 30, 2003. U.S. shareholders that file a consolidated tax return are treated as one U.S. shareholder for all purposes of this dividends-received deduction provision. Thus, all such shareholders are aggregated in determining the base-period average (as are all controlled foreign corporations). In addition to cash dividends, dividends of property, deemed repatriations under section 956, and distributions of earnings previously taxed under subpart F are included in the base-period average.

Second, the amount of dividends eligible for the deduction is limited to the greatest of: (1) $500 million; (2) the amount of earnings shown as permanently invested outside the United States on the taxpayer's most recent audited financial statement which is certified on or before June 30, 2003;[111] or (3) in the case of an applicable financial statement that does not show a specific amount of such earnings, but that does show a specific amount of tax liability attributable to such earnings, the amount of such earnings determined by grossing up the tax liability at a 35-percent rate. If there is no applicable financial statement, or if such statement does not show a specific earnings or tax liability amount, then the $500 million limit applies. This $500 million amount is divided among corporations that are members of a controlled group, using a 50-percent standard of common control. The two financial statement amounts described above are

---

[107] The election is to be made on a timely filed return (including extensions) for the taxable year with respect to which the deduction is claimed.

[108] However, to the extent that the taxpayer actually receives cash in an inbound liquidation that is described in Code section 332 and treated as a dividend under Code section 367(b), such amount is treated as a dividend for these purposes. The conferees note that a deemed liquidation effectuated by means of a "check the box" election under the entity classification regulations will not involve an actual receipt of cash that is reinvested in the United States as required for purposes of this provision.

[109] Thus, indebtedness between such controlled foreign corporations is disregarded for purposes of this determination.

[110] A corporation that was spun off from another corporation during the five-year period is treated for this purpose

as having been in existence for the same period that such other corporation has been in existence. The pre-spin-off dividend history of the two corporations is generally allocated between them on the basis of their interests in the dividend-paying controlled foreign corporations immediately after the spin-off. In other cases involving companies entering and exiting corporate groups, the principles of Code section 41(f)(3)(A) and (B) apply.

[111] This rule refers to elements of Accounting Principles Board Opinion 23 ("APB 23"), which provides an exception to the general rule of comprehensive recognition of deferred taxes for temporary book-tax differences. The exception is for temporary differences related to undistributed earnings of foreign subsidiaries and foreign corporate joint ventures that meet the indefinite reversal criterion in APB 23.

divided among the U.S. shareholders that are included on such statements.

Third, in order to qualify for the deduction, dividends must be described in a domestic reinvestment plan approved by the taxpayer's senior management and board of directors. This plan must provide for the reinvestment of the repatriated dividends in the United States, including as a source for the funding of worker hiring and training, infrastructure, research and development, capital investments, and the financial stabilization of the corporation for the purposes of job retention or creation. The conferees note that this list of permitted uses is not exclusive. The reinvestment plan cannot, however, designate repatriated funds for use as payment for executive compensation. Dividends with respect to which the deduction is not being claimed are not required to be included in any domestic reinvestment plan.

No foreign tax credit (or deduction) is allowed for foreign taxes attributable to the deductible portion of any dividend. For this purpose, the taxpayer may specifically identify which dividends are treated as carrying the deduction and which dividends are not.[112] In other words, the taxpayer is allowed to choose which of its dividends are treated as meeting the base-period repatriation level (and thus carry foreign tax credits, to the extent otherwise allowable), and which of its dividends are treated as comprising the excess eligible for the deduction (and thus entail proportional disallowance of any associated foreign tax credits). The deduction itself will have the effect of appropriately reducing the taxpayer's foreign tax credit limitation.

Deductions are disallowed for expenses that are properly allocated and apportioned to the deductible portion of any dividend.

The income attributable to the nondeductible portion of a qualifying dividend may not be offset by expenses, losses, or deductions, and the tax attributable to such income generally may not be offset by credits (other than foreign tax credits and AMT credits).[113] The tax on this amount also cannot reduce the alternative minimum tax that otherwise would be owed by the taxpayer. However, the deduction available under this provision is not treated as a preference item for purposes of computing the AMT. Thus, the deduction is allowed in computing alternative minimum taxable income notwithstanding the fact that it may not be deductible in computing earnings and profits. No deduction under sections 243 or 245 is allowed for any dividend for which a deduction is allowed under the provision.

Effective Date

The provision is effective only for a taxpayer's first taxable year beginning on or after the date of enactment of the bill, or the taxpayer's last taxable year beginning before such date, at the taxpayer's election. The deduction available under the provision is not allowed for dividends received in any taxable year beginning one year or more after the date of enactment.

[Law at ¶5085 and ¶5735. CCH Explanation at ¶535.]

[¶10,790] Act Sec. 423. Delay in effective date of final regulations governing exclusion of income from international operations of ships and aircraft

Conference Committee Report (H.R. CONF. REP. NO. 108-755)

[Act Sec. 423]

Present Law

Section 883 generally provides an exemption from gross income for earnings of a foreign corporation derived from the international operation of ships and aircraft if an equivalent exemption from tax is granted by the applicable foreign country to corporations organized in the United States.

Treasury has issued regulations implementing the rules of section 883 that are effective for

taxable years beginning 30 days or more after August 26, 2003. The regulations provide, in general, that a foreign corporation organized in a qualified foreign country and engaged in the international operation of ships or aircraft shall exclude qualified income from gross income for purposes of United States Federal income taxation, provided that the corporation can satisfy certain ownership and related documentation requirements. The proposed rules explain when a foreign country is a qualified foreign country

---

[112] In the absence of such a specification, a pro rata amount of foreign tax credits will be disallowed with respect to every dividend repatriated during the taxable year.

[113] These expenses, losses, and deductions may, however, have the effect of reducing other income of the taxpayer.

and what income is considered to be qualified income.

House Bill

No provision.

Senate Amendment

The provision delays the effective date for the Treasury regulations so that they apply to taxable years of foreign corporations seeking qualified foreign corporation status beginning after December 31, 2004.

Effective Date

The provision is effective after date of enactment.

Conference Agreement

The conference agreement follows the Senate amendment, except the regulations apply to taxable years of foreign corporations seeking qualified foreign corporation status beginning after September 24, 2004.

[Law at ¶7025. CCH Explanation at ¶552.]

[¶ 10,800] Act Sec. 424. Study of earnings stripping provisions

Conference Committee Report (H.R. CONF. REP. NO. 108-755)

[Act Sec. 424]

Present Law

Present law provides rules to limit the ability of U.S. corporations to reduce the U.S. tax on their U.S.-source income through certain earnings stripping transactions. These rules limit the deductibility of interest paid to certain related parties ("disqualified interest"), if the payor's debt-equity ratio exceeds 1.5 to 1 and the payor's net interest expense exceeds 50 percent of its "adjusted taxable income" (generally taxable income computed without regard to deductions for net interest expense, net operating losses, and depreciation, amortization, and depletion). Disqualified interest for these purposes also may include interest paid to unrelated parties in certain cases in which a related party guarantees the debt.

House Bill

No provision.

Senate Amendment

No provision.

Conference Agreement

The conference agreement requires the Treasury Department to conduct a study of the earnings stripping rules, including a study of the effectiveness of these rules in preventing the shifting of income outside the United States, whether any deficiencies in these rules have the effect of placing U.S.-based businesses at a competitive disadvantage relative to foreign-based businesses, the impact of earnings stripping activities on the U.S. tax base, whether laws of foreign countries facilitate the stripping of earnings out of the United States, and whether changes to the earnings stripping rules would affect jobs in the United States. This study is to include specific recommendations for improving these rules and is to be submitted to the Congress not later than June 30, 2005.

Effective Date

The provision is effective on the date of enactment.

[Law at ¶7030. CCH Explanation at ¶525.]

[¶ 10,810] Act Sec. 501. Deduction of state and local general sales taxes

House Committee Report (H.R. REP. NO. 108-548, pt. 1)

[Code Sec. 164]

Present Law

An itemized deduction is permitted for certain taxes paid, including individual income taxes, real property taxes, and personal property taxes. No itemized deduction is permitted for State or local general sales taxes.

Reasons for Change

The Committee recognizes that not all States rely on income taxes as a primary source of revenue, and that allowing a deduction for State and local income taxes, but not sales taxes, may create inequities across States and may also create bias in the types of taxes that States and localities choose to impose. The Committee believes that the provision of an itemized deduction for State and local general sales taxes in lieu of the deduction for State and local income taxes provides more equitable Federal tax treatment across States, and will cause the Federal tax laws to have a more neutral effect on the types of taxes that State and local governments utilize.

Explanation of Provision

The provision provides that, at the election of the taxpayer, an itemized deduction may be taken for State and local general sales taxes in lieu of the itemized deduction provided under present law for State and local income taxes.

The term "general sales tax" means a tax imposed at one rate with respect to the sale at retail of a broad range of classes of items. However, in the case of items of food, clothing, medical supplies, and motor vehicles, the fact that the tax does not apply with respect to some or all of such items is not taken into account in determining whether the tax applies with respect to a broad range of classes of items, and the fact that

the rate of tax applicable with respect to some or all of such items is lower than the general rate of tax is not taken into account in determining whether the tax is imposed at one rate. Except in the case of a lower rate of tax applicable with respect to food, clothing, medical supplies, or motor vehicles, no deduction is allowed for any general sales tax imposed with respect to an item at a rate other than the general rate of tax. However, in the case of motor vehicles, if the rate of tax exceeds the general rate, such excess shall be disregarded and the general rate is treated as the rate of tax.

A compensating use tax with respect to an item is treated as a general sales tax, provided such tax is complimentary to a general sales tax and a deduction for sales taxes is allowable with respect to items sold at retail in the taxing jurisdiction that are similar to such item.

Effective Date

The provision is effective for taxable years beginning after December 31, 2003, and prior to January 1, 2006.

Conference Committee Report (H.R. Conf. Rep. No. 108-755)

Senate Amendment

No provision.

Conference Agreement

The conference agreement follows the House bill with the following modification.

Rather than requiring that taxpayers use tables prescribed by the Secretary to determine their allowable sales tax deduction, taxpayers would instead have two options with respect to the determination of the sales tax deduction amount. Taxpayers would be able to deduct the total amount of general State and local sales taxes paid by accumulating receipts showing general sales taxes paid. Alternatively, taxpayers may use tables created by the Secretary of the Treasury. The tables are to be based on average consumption by taxpayers on a State-by-State basis taking into account filing status, number of dependents, adjusted gross income and rates of

State and local general sales taxation. Taxpayers who use the tables created by the Secretary may, in addition to the table amounts, deduct eligible general sales taxes paid with respect to the purchase of motor vehicles, boats and other items specified by the Secretary. Sales taxes for items that may be added to the tables would not be reflected in the tables themselves.

The IRS is currently in the process of finalizing tax forms for 2004. The Code has not contained an itemized deduction for State and local sales taxes for a number of years. Developing the tables required by the provision will in general require a significant amount of time and effort. The conferees anticipate that IRS will do the best they can to reasonably and accurately implement this statutory provision in order to effectuate the deduction for the 2005 filing season.

[Law at ¶ 5170. CCH Explanation at ¶ 1205.]

[¶ 10,830] Act Sec. 701. Brownfields demonstration program for qualified green building and sustainable design projects

Conference Committee Report (H.R. Conf. Rep. No. 108-755)

[Code Secs. 142 and 146]

Present Law

In general

Interest on debt incurred by States or local governments is excluded from income if the pro-

ceeds of the borrowing are used to carry out governmental functions of those entities or the debt is repaid with governmental funds. Interest on bonds that nominally are issued by States or local governments, but the proceeds of which are used (directly or indirectly) by a private person and payment of which is derived from funds of such a private person is taxable unless the purpose of the borrowing is approved specifically in the Code or in a non-Code provision of a revenue Act. These bonds are called "private activity bonds." The term "private person" includes the Federal Government and all other individuals and entities other than States or local governments.

Private activities eligible for financing with tax-exempt private activity bonds

Present law includes several exceptions permitting States or local governments to act as conduits providing tax-exempt financing for private activities. For example, interest on bonds issued to benefit section 501(c)(3) organizations is generally tax-exempt ("qualified 501(c)(3) bonds"). Both capital expenditures and limited working capital expenditures of section 501(c)(3) organizations may be financed with qualified 501(c)(3) bonds.

In addition, States or local governments may issue tax-exempt "exempt-facility bonds" to finance property for certain private businesses.[194] Business facilities eligible for this financing include transportation (airports, ports, local mass commuting, and high speed intercity rail facilities); privately owned and/or privately operated public works facilities (sewage, solid waste disposal, local district heating or cooling, hazardous waste disposal facilities, and public educational facilities); privately owned and/or operated low-income rental housing;[195] and certain private facilities for the local furnishing of electricity or gas. A further provision allows tax-exempt financing for "environmental enhancements of hydro-electric generating facilities." Tax-exempt financing also is authorized for capital expenditures for small manufacturing facilities and land and equipment for first-time farmers ("qualified small-issue bonds"), local redevelopment activities ("qualified redevelopment bonds"), and eligible empowerment zone and enterprise community businesses. Tax-exempt private activity bonds also may be issued to finance limited non-business purposes: certain student loans and mortgage loans for owner-occupied housing ("qualified mortgage bonds" and "qualified veterans' mortgage bonds").

Generally, tax-exempt private activity bonds are subject to restrictions that do not apply to other bonds issued by State or local governments. For example, most tax-exempt private activity bonds are subject to annual volume limits on the aggregate face amount of such bonds that may be issued.[196]

House Bill

No provision.

Senate Amendment

In general

The Senate amendment creates a new category of exempt-facility bond, the qualified green building and sustainable design project bond ("qualified green bond"). A qualified green bond is defined as any bond issued as part of an issue that finances a project designated by the Secretary, after consultation with the Administrator of the Environmental Protection Agency (the "Administrator") as a green building and sustainable design project that meets the following eligibility requirements: (1) at least 75 percent of the square footage of the commercial buildings that are part of the project is registered for the U.S. Green Building Council's LEED[197] certification and is reasonably expected (at the time of designation) to meet such certification; (2) the project includes a brownfield site;[198] (3) the project receives at least $5 million dollars in specific State or local resources; and (4) the project includes at least one million square feet of building or at least 20 acres of land.

Under the provision, qualified green bonds are not subject to the State bond volume limitations. Rather, there is a national limitation of $2 billion of qualified green bonds that the Secretary may allocate, in the aggregate, to qualified green building and sustainable design projects. Qualified green bonds may be currently refunded if certain conditions are met, but cannot be advance refunded. The authority to issue

---

[194] Secs. 141(e) and 142(a).

[195] Residential rental projects must satisfy low-income tenant occupancy requirements for a minimum period of 15 years.

[196] Sec. 146.

[197] The LEED ("Leadership in Energy and Environmental Design) Green Building Rating System is a voluntary, consensus-based national standard for developing high-performance sustainable buildings. Registration is the first step toward LEED certification. Actual certification requires that the applicant project satisfy a number of requirements. Commercial buildings, as defined by standard building

codes are eligible for certification. Commercial occupancies include, but are not limited to, offices, retail and service establishments, institutional buildings (e.g. libraries, schools, museums, churches, etc.), hotels, and residential buildings of four or more habitable stories.

[198] For this purpose, a brownfield site is defined by section 101(39) of the Comprehensive Environmental Response, Compensation, and Liability Act of 1980 (42 U.S.C. 9601), including a site described in subparagraph (D)(ii)(II)(aa) thereof (relating to a site that is contaminated by petroleum or a petroleum product excluded from the definition of 'hazardous substance' under section 101).

qualified green bonds terminates after September 30, 2009.

Application and designation process

The provision requires the submission of an application that meets certain requirements before a project may be designated for financing with qualified green bonds. In addition to the eligibility requirements listed above, each project application must demonstrate that the net benefit of the tax-exempt financing provided will be allocated for (i) the purchase, construction, integration or other use of energy efficiency, renewable energy and sustainable design features of the project, (ii) compliance with LEED certification standards, and/or (iii) the purchase, remediation, foundation construction, and preparation of the brownfield site. The application also must demonstrate that the project is expected, based on independent analysis, to provide the equivalent of at least 1,500 full-time permanent employees (150 full-time employees in rural States) when completed and the equivalent of at least 1,000 construction employees (100 full-time employees in rural States). In addition, each project application shall contain a description of: (1) the amount of electric consumption reduced as compared to conventional construction; (2) the amount of sulfur dioxide daily emissions reduced compared to coal generation; (3) the amount of gross installed capacity of the project's solar photovoltaic capacity measured in megawatts; and (4) the amount of the project's fuel cell energy generation, measured in megawatts.

Under the Senate Amendment, each project must be nominated by a State or local government within 180 days of enactment of this Act and such State or local government must provide written assurances that the project will satisfy certain eligibility requirements. Within 60 days after the end of the application period, the Secretary, after consultation with the Administrator, will designate the qualified green building and sustainable design projects eligible for financing with qualified green bonds. At least one of the projects must be in or within a ten-mile radius of an empowerment zone (as defined under section 1391 of the Code) and at least one project must be in a rural State.[199] No more than one project is permitted in a State. A project shall not be designated for financing with qualified green bonds if such project includes a stadium or arena for professional sports exhibitions or games.

The provision requires the Secretary, after consultation with the Administrator, to ensure that the projects designated shall, in the aggregate: (1) reduce electric consumption by more than 150 megawatts annually as compared to conventional construction; (2) reduce daily sulfur dioxide emissions by at least 10 tons compared to coal generation power; (3) expand by 75 percent the domestic solar photovoltaic market in the United States (measured in megawatts) as compared to the expansion of that market from 2001 to 2002; and (4) use at least 25 megawatts of fuel cell energy generation.

Each project must certify to the Secretary, no later than 30 days after the completion of the project, that the net benefit of the tax-exempt financing was used for the purposes described in the project application. In addition, no bond proceeds can be used to provide any facility the principal business of which is the sale of food or alcoholic beverages for consumption on the premises.

Special rules

The provision requires each issuer to maintain, on behalf of each project, an interest bearing reserve account equal to one percent of the net proceeds of any qualified green bond issued for such project. Not later than five years after the date of issuance, the Secretary, after consultation with the Administrator, shall determine whether the project financed with the proceeds of qualified green bonds has substantially complied with the requirements and goals described in the project application. If the Secretary, after such consultation, certifies that the project has substantially complied with the requirements and goals, amounts in the reserve account, including all interest, shall be released to the project. If the Secretary determines that the project has not substantially complied with such requirements and goals, amounts in the reserve account, including all interest, shall be paid to the United States Treasury.

Effective Date

The provision is effective for bonds issued after December 31, 2004, and before October 1, 2009.

Conference Agreement

The conference agreement follows the Senate amendment.

[**Law at ¶5145, ¶5155 and ¶7055. CCH Explanation at ¶745.**]

---

[199] The term "rural State" means any State that has (1) a population of less than 4.5 million according to the 2000 census; (2) a population density of less than 150 people per square mile according to the 2000 census; and (3) increased in population by less than half the rate of the national increase between the 1990 and 2000 censuses.

[¶ 10,840] Act Sec. 702. Exclusion of gain or loss on sale or exchange of certain brownfield sites from unrelated business taxable income

Conference Committee Report (H.R. CONF. REP. NO. 108-755)

[Code Secs. 512 and 514]

Present Law

In general, an organization that is otherwise exempt from Federal income tax is taxed on income from a trade or business regularly carried on that is not substantially related to the organization's exempt purposes. Gains or losses from the sale, exchange, or other disposition of property, other than stock in trade, inventory, or property held primarily for sale to customers in the ordinary course of a trade or business, generally are excluded from unrelated business taxable income. Gains or losses are treated as unrelated business taxable income, however, if derived from "debt-financed property." Debt-financed property generally means any property that is held to produce income and with respect to which there is acquisition indebtedness at any time during the taxable year.

In general, income of a tax-exempt organization that is produced by debt-financed property is treated as unrelated business income in proportion to the acquisition indebtedness on the income-producing property. Acquisition indebtedness generally means the amount of unpaid indebtedness incurred by an organization to acquire or improve the property and indebtedness that would not have been incurred but for the acquisition or improvement of the property. Acquisition indebtedness does not include: (1) certain indebtedness incurred in the performance or exercise of a purpose or function constituting the basis of the organization's exemption; (2) obligations to pay certain types of annuities; (3) an obligation, to the extent it is insured by the Federal Housing Administration, to finance the purchase, rehabilitation, or construction of housing for low and moderate income persons; or (4) indebtedness incurred by certain qualified organizations to acquire or improve real property.

Special rules apply in the case of an exempt organization that owns a partnership interest in a partnership that holds debt-financed property. An exempt organization's share of partnership income that is derived from debt-financed property generally is taxed as debt-financed income unless an exception provides otherwise.

House Bill

No provision.

Senate Amendment

In general

The Senate amendment provides an exclusion from unrelated business taxable income for the gain or loss from the qualified sale, exchange, or other disposition of a qualifying brownfield property by an eligible taxpayer. The exclusion from unrelated business taxable income generally is available to an exempt organization that acquires, remediates, and disposes of the qualifying brownfield property. In addition, the Senate amendment provides an exception from the debt-financed property rules for such properties.

In order to qualify for the exclusions from unrelated business income and the debt-financed property rules, the eligible taxpayer is required to: (a) acquire from an unrelated person real property that constitutes a qualifying brownfield property; (b) pay or incur a minimum level of eligible remediation expenditures with respect to the property; and (c) transfer the remediated site to an unrelated person in a transaction that constitutes a sale, exchange, or other disposition for purposes of Federal income tax law.[343]

Qualifying brownfield properties

Under the Senate amendment, the exclusion from unrelated business taxable income applies only to real property that constitutes a qualifying brownfield property. A qualifying brownfield property means real property that is certified, before the taxpayer incurs any eligible remediation expenditures (other than to obtain a Phase I environmental site assessment), by an appropriate State agency (within the meaning of section 198(c)(4)) in the State in which the property is located as a brownfield site within the meaning of section 101(39) of the Comprehensive Environmental Response, Compensation, and Liability Act of 1980 (CERCLA) (as in effect on the date of enactment of the proposal). The Senate amendment provision requires that the taxpayer's request for certification include a sworn

---

[343] For purposes of the provision, a person is related to another person if (1) such person bears a relationship to such other person that is described in section 267(b) (determined without regard to paragraph (9)), or section 707(b)(1), determined by substituting 25 percent for 50 percent each place it appears therein; or (2) if such other person is a nonprofit organization, if such person controls directly or indirectly more than 25 percent of the governing body of such organization.

statement of the taxpayer and supporting documentation of the presence of a hazardous substance, pollutant, or contaminant on the property that is complicating the expansion, redevelopment, or reuse of the property given the property's reasonably anticipated future land uses or capacity for uses of the property (including a Phase I environmental site assessment and, if applicable, evidence of the property's presence on a local, State, or Federal list of brownfields or contaminated property) and other environmental assessments prepared or obtained by the taxpayer.

Eligible taxpayer

An eligible taxpayer with respect to a qualifying brownfield property is an organization exempt from tax under section 501(a) that acquired such property from an unrelated person and paid or incurred a minimum amount of eligible remediation expenditures with respect to such property. The exempt organization (or the qualifying partnership of which it is a partner) is required to pay or incur eligible remediation expenditures with respect to a qualifying brownfield property in an amount that exceeds the greater of: (a) $550,000; or (b) 12 percent of the fair market value of the property at the time such property is acquired by the taxpayer, determined as if the property were not contaminated.

An eligible taxpayer does not include an organization that is: (1) potentially liable under section 107 of CERCLA with respect to the property; (2) affiliated with any other person that is potentially liable thereunder through any direct or indirect familial relationship or any contractual, corporate, or financial relationship (other than a contractual, corporate, or financial relationship that is created by the instruments by which title to a qualifying brownfield property is conveyed or financed by a contract of sale of goods or services); or (3) the result of a reorganization of a business entity which was so potentially liable.[344]

Qualified sale, exchange, or other disposition

Under the Senate amendment, a sale, exchange, or other disposition of a qualifying

brownfield property shall be considered as qualified if such property is transferred by the eligible taxpayer to an unrelated person, and within one year of such transfer the taxpayer has received a certification (a "remediation certification") from the Environmental Protection Agency or an appropriate State agency (within the meaning of section 198(c)(4)) in the State in which the property is located that, as a result of the taxpayer's remediation actions, such property would not be treated as a qualifying brownfield property in the hands of the transferee. A taxpayer's request for a remediation certification shall be made no later than the date of the transfer and shall include a sworn statement by the taxpayer certifying that: (1) remedial actions that comply with all applicable or relevant and appropriate requirements (consistent with section 121(d) of CERCLA) have been substantially completed, such that there are no hazardous substances, pollutants or contaminants that complicate the expansion, redevelopment, or reuse of the property given the property's reasonably anticipated future land uses or capacity for uses of the property; (2) the reasonably anticipated future land uses or capacity for uses of the property are more economically productive or environmentally beneficial than the uses of the property in existence on the date the property was certified as a qualifying brownfield property;[345] (3) a remediation plan has been implemented to bring the property in compliance with all applicable local, State, and Federal environmental laws, regulations, and standards and to ensure that remediation protects human health and the environment; (4) the remediation plan, including any physical improvements required to remediate the property, is either complete or substantially complete, and if substantially complete,[346] sufficient monitoring, funding, institutional controls, and financial assurances have been put in place to ensure the complete remediation of the site in accordance with the remediation plan as soon as is reasonably practicable after the disposition of the property by the taxpayer; and (5) public notice and the opportunity for comment on the request for certification (in the same form and manner as required for public participation required under section 117(a) of CERCLA (as in

---

[344] In general, a person is potentially liable under section 107 of CERCLA if: (1) it is the owner and operator of a vessel or a facility; (2) at the time of disposal of any hazardous substance it owned or operated any facility at which such hazardous substances were disposed of; (3) by contract, agreement, or otherwise it arranged for disposal or treatment, or arranged with a transporter for transport for disposal or treatment, of hazardous substances owned or possessed by such person, by any other party or entity, at any facility or incineration vessel owned or operated by another party or entity and containing such hazardous substances; or (4) it accepts or accepted any hazardous substances for transport to disposal or treatment facilities,

incineration vessels or sites selected by such person, from which there is a release, or a threatened release which causes the incurrence of response costs, of a hazardous substance. 42 U.S.C. sec. 9607(a) (2004).

[345] For this purpose, use of the property as a landfill or other hazardous waste facility shall not be considered more economically productive or environmentally beneficial.

[346] For these purposes, substantial completion means any necessary physical construction is complete, all immediate threats have been eliminated, and all long-term threats are under control.

effect on the date of enactment of the provision)) was completed before the date of such request. Public notice shall include, at a minimum, publication in a major local newspaper of general circulation.

A copy of each of the requests for certification that the property was a brownfield site, and that it would no longer be a qualifying brownfield property in the hands of the transferee, shall be included in the tax return of the eligible taxpayer (and, where applicable, of the qualifying partnership) for the taxable year during which the transfer occurs.

Eligible remediation expenditures

Under the Senate amendment, eligible remediation expenditures means, with respect to any qualifying brownfield property: (1) expenditures that are paid or incurred by the taxpayer to an unrelated person to obtain a Phase I environmental site assessment of the property; (2) amounts paid or incurred by the taxpayer after receipt of the certification that the property is a qualifying brownfield property for goods and services necessary to obtain the remediation certification; and (3) expenditures to obtain remediation cost-cap or stop-loss coverage, re-opener or regulatory action coverage, or similar coverage under environmental insurance policies,[347] or to obtain financial guarantees required to manage the remediation and monitoring of the property. Eligible remediation expenditures include expenditures to (1) manage, remove, control, contain, abate, or otherwise remediate a hazardous substance, pollutant, or contaminant on the property; (2) obtain a Phase II environmental site assessment of the property, including any expenditure to monitor, sample, study, assess, or otherwise evaluate the release, threat of release, or presence of a hazardous substance, pollutant, or contaminant on the property, or (3) obtain environmental regulatory certifications and approvals required to manage the remediation and monitoring of the hazardous substance,

pollutant, or contaminant on the property. Eligible remediation expenditures do not include (1) any portion of the purchase price paid or incurred by the eligible taxpayer to acquire the qualifying brownfield property; (2) environmental insurance costs paid or incurred to obtain legal defense coverage, owner/operator liability coverage, lender liability coverage, professional liability coverage, or similar types of coverage;[348] (3) any amount paid or incurred to the extent such amount is reimbursed, funded or otherwise subsidized by: (a) grants provided by the United States, a State, or a political subdivision of a State for use in connection with the property; (b) proceeds of an issue of State or local government obligations used to provide financing for the property, the interest of which is exempt from tax under section 103; or (c) subsidized financing provided (directly or indirectly) under a Federal, State, or local program in connection with the property; or (4) any expenditure paid or incurred before the date of enactment of the proposal.[349]

Qualified gain or loss

The Senate amendment generally excludes from unrelated business taxable income the exempt organization's gain or loss from the sale, exchange, or other disposition of a qualifying brownfield property. Income, gain, or loss from other transfers does not qualify under the provision.[350] The amount of gain or loss excluded from unrelated business taxable income is not limited to or based upon the increase or decrease in value of the property that is attributable to the taxpayer's expenditure of eligible remediation expenditures. Further, the exclusion does not apply to an amount treated as gain that is ordinary income with respect to section 1245 or section 1250 property, including any amount deducted as a section 198 expense that is subject to the recapture rules of section 198(e), if the taxpayer had deducted such amount in the computation of its unrelated business taxable income.[351]

---

[347] Cleanup cost-cap or stop-loss coverage is coverage that places an upper limit on the costs of cleanup that the insured may have to pay. Re-opener or regulatory action coverage is coverage for costs associated with any future government actions that require further site cleanup, including costs associated with the loss of use of site improvements.

[348] For this purpose, professional liability insurance is coverage for errors and omissions by public and private parties dealing with or managing contaminated land issues, and includes coverage under policies referred to as owner-controlled insurance. Owner/operator liability coverage is coverage for those parties that own the site or conduct business or engage in cleanup operations on the site. Legal defense coverage is coverage for lawsuits associated with liability claims against the insured made by enforcement agencies or third parties, including by private parties.

[349] The provision authorizes the Secretary of the Treasury to issue guidance regarding the treatment of government-provided funds for purposes of determining eligible remediation expenditures.

[350] For example, rent income from leasing the property does not qualify under the proposal.

[351] Depreciation or section 198 amounts that the taxpayer had not used to determine its unrelated business taxable income are not treated as gain that is ordinary income under sections 1245 or 1250 (secs. 1.1245-2(a)(8) and 1.1250-2(d)(6)), and are not recognized as gain or ordinary income upon the sale, exchange, or disposition of the property. Thus, an exempt organization would not be entitled to a double benefit resulting from a section 198 expense deduction and the proposed exclusion from gain with respect to any amounts it deducts under section 198.

Special rules for qualifying partnerships

In general

In the case of a tax-exempt organization that is a partner of a qualifying partnership that acquires, remediates, and disposes of a qualifying brownfield property, the Senate amendment provision applies to the tax-exempt partner's distributive share of the qualifying partnership's gain or loss from the disposition of the property.[352] A qualifying partnership is a partnership that (1) has a partnership agreement that satisfies the requirements of section 514(c)(9)(B)(vi) at all times beginning on the date of the first certification received by the partnership that one of its properties is a qualifying brownfield property; (2) satisfies the requirements of the proposal if such requirements are applied to the partnership (rather than to the eligible taxpayer that is a partner of the partnership); and (3) is not an organization that would be prevented from constituting an eligible taxpayer by reason of it or an affiliate being potentially liable under CERCLA with respect to the property.

The exclusion is available to a tax-exempt organization with respect to a particular property acquired, remediated, and disposed of by a qualifying partnership only if the exempt organization is a partner of the partnership at all times during the period beginning on the date of the first certification received by the partnership that one of its properties is a qualifying brownfield property, and ending on the date of the disposition of the property by the partnership.[353]

Under the Senate amendment, the Secretary shall prescribe such regulations as are necessary to prevent abuse of the requirements of the provision, including abuse through the use of special allocations of gains or losses, or changes in ownership of partnership interests held by eligible taxpayers.

Certifications and multiple property elections

If the property is acquired and remediated by a qualifying partnership of which the exempt organization is a partner, it is intended that the certification as to status as a qualified brownfield property and the remediation certification will be obtained by the qualifying partnership, rather than by the tax-exempt partner, and that both the eligible taxpayer and the qualifying partnership will be required to make available such copies of the certifications to the IRS. Any elec-

tions or revocations regarding the application of the eligible remediation expenditure rules to multiple properties (as described below) acquired, remediated, and disposed of by a qualifying partnership must be made by the partnership. A tax-exempt partner is bound by an election made by the qualifying partnership of which it is a partner.

Special rules for multiple properties

The eligible remediation expenditure determinations generally are made on a property-by-property basis. An exempt organization (or a qualifying partnership of which the exempt organization is a partner) that acquires, remediates, and disposes of multiple qualifying brownfield properties, however, may elect to make the eligible remediation expenditure determinations on a multiple-property basis. In the case of such an election, the taxpayer satisfies the eligible remediation expenditures test with respect to all qualifying brownfield properties acquired during the election period if the average of the eligible remediation expenditures for all such properties exceeds the greater of: (a) $550,000; or (b) 12 percent of the average of the fair market value of the properties, determined as of the dates they were acquired by the taxpayer and as if they were not contaminated. If the eligible taxpayer elects to make the eligible remediation expenditure determination on a multiple property basis, then the election shall apply to all qualifying sales, exchanges, or other dispositions of qualifying brownfield properties the acquisition and transfer of which occur during the period for which the election remains in effect.[354]

An acquiring taxpayer makes a multiple-property election with its timely filed tax return (including extensions) for the first taxable year for which it intends to have the election apply. A timely filed election is effective as of the first day of the taxable year of the return in which the election is included or a later day in such taxable year selected by the taxpayer. An election remains effective until the earliest of a date selected by the taxpayer, the date which is eight years after the effective date of the election, the effective date of a revocation of the election, or, in the case of a partnership, the date of the termination of the partnership.

A taxpayer may revoke a multiple-property election by filing a statement of revocation with

---

[352] The provision's exclusions do not apply to a tax-exempt partner's gain or loss from the tax-exempt partner's sale, exchange, or other disposition of its partnership interest. Such transactions continue to be governed by present-law.

[353] The provision subjects a tax-exempt partner to tax on gain previously excluded by the partner (plus interest) if a

property subsequently becomes ineligible for exclusion under the qualifying partnership's multiple-property election.

[354] If the taxpayer fails to satisfy the averaging test for the properties subject to the election, then the taxpayer may not apply the exclusion on a separate property basis with respect to any of such properties.

a timely filed tax return (including extensions). A revocation is effective as of the first day of the taxable year of the return in which the revocation is included or a later day in such taxable year selected by the eligible taxpayer or qualifying partnership. Once a taxpayer revokes the election, the taxpayer is ineligible to make another multiple-property election with respect to any qualifying brownfield property subject to the revoked election.[355]

Debt-financed property

The Senate amendment provides that debt-financed property, as defined by section 514(b), does not include any property the gain or loss from the sale, exchange, or other disposition of which is excluded by reason of the provisions of the proposal that exclude such gain or loss from computing the gross income of any unrelated trade or business of the taxpayer. Thus, gain or loss from the sale, exchange, or other disposition of a qualifying brownfield property that otherwise satisfies the requirements of the provision is not taxed as unrelated business taxable income merely because the taxpayer incurred debt to acquire or improve the site.

Conference Agreement

The conference agreement follows the Senate amendment, modified to provide a termina-

tion date of December 31, 2009. The conference agreement provision applies to gain or loss on the sale, exchange, or other disposition of property that is acquired by the eligible taxpayer or qualifying partnership during the period beginning January 1, 2005, and ending December 31, 2009. Property acquired during the five-year acquisition period need not be disposed of by the termination date in order to qualify for the exclusion. For purposes of the multiple property election, gain or loss on property acquired after December 31, 2009, is not eligible for the exclusion from unrelated business taxable income, although properties acquired after the termination date (but during the election period) are included for purposes of determining average eligible remediation expenditures.

Effective Date

The conference agreement provision applies to gain or loss on property that is acquired after December 31, 2004.

[Law at ¶ 5410, ¶ 5415 and ¶ 7060. CCH Explanation at ¶ 1330.]

[¶ 10,850] Act Sec. 703. Civil rights tax relief

Conference Committee Report (H.R. CONF. REP. NO. 108-755)

[Code Sec. 62]

Present Law

Under present law, gross income generally does not include the amount of any damages (other than punitive damages) received (whether by suit or agreement and whether as lump sums or as periodic payments) by individuals on account of personal physical injuries (including death) or physical sickness.[356] Expenses relating to recovering such damages are generally not deductible.[357]

Other damages are generally included in gross income. The related expenses to recover the damages, including attorneys' fees, are generally deductible as expenses for the production of income,[358] subject to the two-percent floor on itemized deductions.[359] Thus, such expenses are

deductible only to the extent the taxpayer's total miscellaneous itemized deductions exceed two percent of adjusted gross income. Any amount allowable as a deduction is subject to reduction under the overall limitation of itemized deductions if the taxpayer's adjusted gross income exceeds a threshold amount.[360] For purposes of the alternative minimum tax, no deduction is allowed for any miscellaneous itemized deduction.

In some cases, claimants will engage an attorney to represent them on a contingent fee basis. That is, if the claimant recovers damages, a prearranged percentage of the damages will be paid to the attorney; if no damages are recovered, the attorney is not paid a fee. The proper tax treatment of contingent fee arrangements with attorneys has been litigated in recent years.

---

[355] The provision subjects a taxpayer to tax on gain previously excluded (plus interest) in the event a site subsequently becomes ineligible for gain exclusion under the multiple-property election.

[356] Sec. 104(a)(2).

[357] Sec. 265(a)(1).
[358] Sec. 212.
[359] Sec. 67.
[360] Sec. 68.

Some courts[361] have held that the entire amount of damages is income and that the claimant is entitled to a miscellaneous itemized deduction subject to both the two-percent floor as an expense for the production of income for the portion paid to the attorney and to the overall limitation on itemized deductions. Other courts have held that the portion of the recovery that is paid directly to the attorney is not income to the claimant, holding that the claimant has no claim of right to that portion of the recovery.[362]

House Bill

No provision.

Senate Amendment

The Senate amendment provides an above-the-line deduction for attorneys' fees and costs paid by, or on behalf of, the taxpayer in connection with any action involving a claim of unlawful discrimination, certain claims against the Federal Government, or a private cause of action under the Medicare Secondary Payer statute. The amount that may be deducted above-the-line may not exceed the amount includible in the taxpayer's gross income for the taxable year on account of a judgment or settlement (whether by suit or agreement and whether as lump sum or periodic payments) resulting from such claim.

Under the proposal, "unlawful discrimination" means an act that is unlawful under certain provisions of any of the following: the Civil Rights Act of 1991; the Congressional Accountability Act of 1995; the National Labor Relations Act; the Fair Labor Standards Act of 1938; the Age Discrimination in Employment Act of 1967; the Rehabilitation Act of 1973; the Employee Retirement Income Security Act of 1974; the Education Amendments of 1972; the Employee Polygraph Protection Act of 1988; the Worker Adjustment and Retraining Notification Act; the Family and Medical Leave Act of 1993; chapter 43 of Title 38 of the United States Code; the Revised Statutes; the Civil Rights Act of 1964; the Fair Housing Act; the Americans with Disabilities Act of 1990; any provision of Federal law (popularly known as whistleblower protection provisions) prohibiting the discharge of an employee, discrimination against an employee, or any other form of retaliation or reprisal against an employee for asserting rights or taking other actions permitted under Federal law; or any provision of Federal, State or local law, or common law claims permitted under Federal, State, or local law providing for the enforcement of civil rights or regulating any aspect of the employment relationship, including claims for wages, compensation, or benefits, or prohibiting the discharge of an employee, discrimination against an employee, or any other form of retaliation or reprisal against an employee for asserting rights or taking other actions permitted by law.

Effective Date

The Senate amendment provision applies to fees and costs paid after December 31, 2002, with respect to any judgment or settlement occurring after such date.

Conference Agreement

The conference agreement follows the Senate amendment except for the effective date.

Effective Date

The conference agreement applies to fees and costs paid after the date of enactment with respect to any judgment or settlement occurring after such date.

[Law at ¶ 5095. CCH Explanation at ¶ 1215.]

[¶ 10,860] Act Sec. 704. 7-year recovery period for certain track facilities

Conference Committee Report (H.R. Conf. Rep. No. 108-755)

[Code Sec. 168]

Present Law

A taxpayer generally must capitalize the cost of property used in a trade or business and recover such cost over time through annual deductions for depreciation or amortization. Tangible property generally is depreciated under the modified accelerated cost recovery system ("MACRS"), which determines depreciation by applying specific recovery periods, placed-in-service conventions, and depreciation methods

---

[361] *Kenseth v. Commissioner*, 114 T.C. 399 (2000), *aff'd* 259 F.3d 881 (7th Cir. 2001); *Coady v. Commissioner*, 213 F.3d 1187 (9th Cir. 2000); *Benci-Woodward v. Commissioner*, 219 F.3d 941 (9th Cir. 2000); *Baylin v. United States*, 43 F.3d 1451 (Fed. Cir. 1995).

[362] *Cotnam v. Commissioner*, 263 F.2d 119 (5th Cir. 1959); *Estate of Arthur Clarks v. United States*, 202 F.3d 854 (6th Cir.

2000); *Srivastava v. Commissioner*, 220 F.3d 353 (5th Cir. 2000). In some of these cases, such as *Cotnam*, State law has been an important consideration in determining that the claimant has no claim of right to the recovery.

to the cost of various types of depreciable property (sec. 168). The cost of nonresidential real property is recovered using the straight-line method of depreciation and a recovery period of 39 years. Nonresidential real property is subject to the mid-month placed-in-service convention. Under the mid-month convention, the depreciation allowance for the first year property is placed in service is based on the number of months the property was in service, and property placed in service at any time during a month is treated as having been placed in service in the middle of the month. Land improvements (such as roads and fences) are recovered over 15 years. An exception exists for the theme and amusement park industry, whose assets are assigned a recovery period of seven years.

House Bill

No provision.

Senate Amendment

The Senate amendment provides a statutory 7-year recovery period for permanent motorsports racetrack complexes. For this purpose, motorsports racetrack complexes include land improvements and support facilities but do not include transportation equipment, warehouses, administrative buildings, hotels, or motels.

Effective Date

The Senate amendment is effective for property placed in service after date of enactment and before January 1, 2008. No inference is intended with respect to the treatment of expenses incurred prior to the effective date.

Conference Agreement

The conference agreement follows the Senate amendment with the following modification to the effective date provisions.

Effective Date

The conference agreement is effective for property placed in service after the date of enactment and before January 1, 2008. The conference agreement also excludes racetrack facilities placed in service after the date of enactment from the definition of theme and amusement facilities classified under Asset Class 80.0. The conferees do not intend for this provision to create any inference as to the treatment of property placed in service on or before the date of enactment. Accordingly, the conferees do not intend for the provision to affect the interpretation of the scope of Asset Class 80.0 for assets placed in service prior to the date of enactment. The conferees strongly urge the Secretary to resolve expeditiously any taxpayer disputes with respect to the scope of Class 80.0.

[Law at ¶5180. CCH Explanation at ¶340.]

[¶10,870] Act Sec. 705. Distributions to shareholders from policyholders surplus account of life insurance companies

Conference Committee Report (H.R. CONF. REP. NO. 108-755)

[Code Sec. 815]

Prior and Present Law

Under the law in effect from 1959 through 1983, a life insurance company was subject to a three-phase taxable income computation under Federal tax law. Under the three-phase system, a company was taxed on the lesser of its gain from operations or its taxable investment income (Phase I) and, if its gain from operations exceeded its taxable investment income, 50 percent of such excess (Phase II). Federal income tax on the other 50 percent of the gain from operations was deferred, and was accounted for as part of a policyholder's surplus account and, subject to certain limitations, taxed only when distributed to stockholders or upon corporate dissolution (Phase III). To determine whether amounts had been distributed, a company maintained a shareholders surplus account, which generally included the company's previously taxed income

that would be available for distribution to shareholders. Distributions to shareholders were treated as being first out of the shareholders surplus account, then out of the policyholders surplus account, and finally out of other accounts.

The Deficit Reduction Act of 1984 included provisions that, for 1984 and later years, eliminated further deferral of tax on amounts (described above) that previously would have been deferred under the three-phase system. Although for taxable years after 1983, life insurance companies may not enlarge their policyholders surplus account, the companies are not taxed on previously deferred amounts unless the amounts are treated as distributed to shareholders or subtracted from the policyholders surplus account (sec. 815).

Under present law, any direct or indirect distribution to shareholders from an existing policyholders surplus account of a stock life insurance company is subject to tax at the corporate rate in the taxable year of the distribution. Present law (like prior law) provides that any distribution to shareholders is treated as made (1) first out of the shareholders surplus account, to the extent thereof, (2) then out of the policyholders surplus account, to the extent thereof, and (3) finally, out of other accounts.

House Bill

No provision.

Senate Amendment

The Senate amendment provision suspends for a stock life insurance company's taxable years beginning after December 31, 2003, and before January 1, 2006, the application of the rules imposing income tax on distributions to shareholders from the policyholders surplus account of a life insurance company (sec. 815). The provision also reverses the order in which distributions reduce the various accounts, so that distributions would be treated as first made out of the policyholders surplus account, to the extent thereof, and then out of the shareholders surplus account, and lastly out of other accounts.

Effective Date

The Senate amendment provision is effective for taxable years beginning after December 31, 2003.

Conference Agreement

The conference agreement follows the Senate amendment, with a modification.

The conference agreement provision suspends for a stock life insurance company's taxable years beginning after December 31, 2004, and before January 1, 2007, the application of the rules imposing income tax on distributions to shareholders from the policyholders surplus account of a life insurance company (sec. 815). The conference agreement includes the Senate amendment provision reversing the order in which distributions reduce the various accounts, so that distributions would be treated as first made out of the policyholders surplus account, to the extent thereof, and then out of the shareholders surplus account, and lastly out of other accounts.

Effective Date

The conference agreement provision is effective for taxable years beginning after December 31, 2004.

[Law at ¶ 5535. CCH Explanation at ¶ 1125.]

[¶ 10,880] Act Sec. 706. Treat certain Alaska pipeline property as seven-year property

Conference Committee Report (H.R. CONF. REP. NO. 108-755)

[Code Sec. 168]

Present Law

The applicable recovery period for assets placed in service under the Modified Accelerated Cost Recovery System is based on the "class life of the property." The class lives of assets placed in service after 1986 are generally set forth in Revenue Procedure 87-56.[408] Asset class 46.0, describing assets used in the private, commercial, and contract carrying of petroleum, gas and other products by means of pipes and conveyors, are assigned a class life of 22 years and a recovery period of 15 years.

House Bill

No provision.

Senate Amendment

The Senate amendment establishes a statutory seven-year recovery period and a class life of 22 years for any Alaska natural gas pipeline. The term "Alaska natural gas pipeline" is defined as any natural gas pipeline system (including the pipe, trunk lines, related equipment, and appurtenances used to carry natural gas, but not any gas processing plant) located in the State of Alaska that has a capacity of more than 500 billion Btu of natural gas per day and is placed in service after December 31, 2012. A taxpayer who places an otherwise qualifying system in service before January 1, 2013 may elect to treat the system as placed in service on January 1,

---

[408] 1987-2 C.B. 674 (as clarified and modified by Rev. Proc. 88-22, 1988-1 C.B. 785).

2013, thus qualifying for the seven-year recovery period.

Conference Agreement

The conference agreement follows the Senate amendment with the following modification. In order to qualify for the seven-year recovery period, otherwise qualifying property must be placed in service after December 31, 2013. A taxpayer who places an otherwise qualifying system in service before January 1, 2014 may elect to treat the system as placed in service on January 1, 2014, thus qualifying for the seven-year recovery period.

Effective Date

The provision is effective for property placed in service after December 31, 2004.

[Law at ¶ 5180. CCH Explanation at ¶ 345.]

[¶ 10,890] Act Sec. 707. Enhanced oil recovery credit for certain gas processing facilities

Conference Committee Report (H.R. CONF. REP. NO. 108-755)

[Code Sec. 43(c)]

Present Law

The taxpayer may claim a credit equal to 15 percent of enhanced oil recovery costs. Qualified enhanced oil recovery costs include costs of depreciable tangible property that is part of an enhanced oil recovery project, intangible drilling and development costs with respect to an enhanced oil recovery project, and tertiary injectant expenses incurred with respect to an enhanced oil recovery project. The credit is phased out when oil prices exceed a threshold amount.

House Bill

No provision.

Senate Amendment

The Senate amendment provides that expenses in connection with the construction of any qualifying natural gas processing plant capable of processing two trillion British thermal units of Alaskan natural gas into a natural gas pipeline system on a daily basis are qualified enhanced oil recovery costs eligible for the enhanced oil recovery credit. A qualifying natural gas processing plant also must produce carbon dioxide for re-injection into a producing oil or gas field.

Effective Date

The provision is effective for costs paid or incurred in taxable years beginning after December 31, 2004.

Conference Agreement

The conference agreement follows the Senate amendment.

[Law at ¶ 5030. CCH Explanation at ¶ 865.]

[¶ 10,900] Act Sec. 708. Method of accounting for naval shipbuilders

Conference Committee Report (H.R. CONF. REP. NO. 108-755)

[Act Sec. 708]

Present Law

Generally, taxpayers must use the percentage-of-completion method to determine taxable income from long-term contracts.[364] Under sec. 10203(b)(2)(B) of the Revenue Act of 1987,[365] an exception exists for certain ship construction contracts, which may be accounted for using the 40/60 percentage-of-completion/capitalized cost method ("PCCM"). Under the 40/60 PCCM, 60 percent of a taxpayer's long-term contract income is exempt from the requirement to use the percentage-of-completion method while 40 percent remains subject to the requirement. The ex-

empt 60 percent of long-term contract income must be reported by consistently using the taxpayer's exempt contract method. Permissible exempt contract methods include the percentage of completion method, the exempt-contract percentage-of-completion method, and the completed contract method.[366]

House Bill

No provision.

Senate Amendment

The Senate amendment provides that qualified naval ship contracts may be accounted for using the 40/60 PCCM during the first five taxa-

---

[364] Sec. 460(a).
[365] Pub. Law No. 100-203 (1987).

[366] Treas. Reg. 1.460-4(c)(1).

ble years of the contract. The cumulative reduction in tax resulting from the provision over the five-year period is recaptured and included in the taxpayer's tax liability in the sixth year. Qualified naval ship contracts are defined as any contract or portion thereof that is for the construction in the United States of one ship or submarine for the Federal Government if the taxpayer reasonably expects the acceptance date will occur no later than nine years after the construction commencement date.

Effective Date

The Senate amendment is effective for contracts with respect to which the construction commencement date occurs after date of enactment.

Conference Agreement

The conference agreement follows the Senate amendment with the following modification. The provision specifies that the construction commencement date is the date on which the physical fabrication of any section or component of the ship or submarine begins in the taxpayer's shipyard.

Effective Date

The provision is effective for contracts with respect to which the construction commencement date occurs after date of enactment.

[Law at ¶7065. CCH Explanation at ¶395.]

[¶ 10,910] Act Sec. 709. Minimum cost requirement for excess asset transfers

Conference Committee Report (H.R. CONF. REP. NO. 108-755)

[Code Sec. 420]

Present Law

Defined benefit plan assets generally may not revert to an employer prior to termination of the plan and satisfaction of all plan liabilities. In addition, a reversion may occur only if the plan so provides. A reversion prior to plan termination may constitute a prohibited transaction and may result in plan disqualification. Any assets that revert to the employer upon plan termination are includible in the gross income of the employer and subject to an excise tax. The excise tax rate is 20 percent if the employer maintains a replacement plan or makes certain benefit increases in connection with the termination; if not, the excise tax rate is 50 percent. Upon plan termination, the accrued benefits of all plan participants are required to be 100-percent vested.

A pension plan may provide medical benefits to retired employees through a separate account that is part of such plan. A qualified transfer of excess assets of a defined benefit plan to such a separate account within the plan may be made in order to fund retiree health benefits.[384] A qualified transfer does not result in plan disqualification, is not a prohibited transaction, and is not treated as a reversion. Thus, transferred assets are not includible in the gross income of the employer and are not subject to

the excise tax on reversions. No more than one qualified transfer may be made in any taxable year. No qualified transfer may be made after December 31, 2013.

Excess assets generally means the excess, if any, of the value of the plan's assets[385] over the greater of (1) the accrued liability under the plan (including normal cost) or (2) 125 percent of the plan's current liability.[386] In addition, excess assets transferred in a qualified transfer may not exceed the amount reasonably estimated to be the amount that the employer will pay out of such account during the taxable year of the transfer for qualified current retiree health liabilities. No deduction is allowed to the employer for (1) a qualified transfer or (2) the payment of qualified current retiree health liabilities out of transferred funds (and any income thereon).

Transferred assets (and any income thereon) must be used to pay qualified current retiree health liabilities for the taxable year of the transfer. Transferred amounts generally must benefit pension plan participants, other than key employees, who are entitled upon retirement to receive retiree medical benefits through the separate account. Retiree health benefits of key employees may not be paid out of transferred assets.

---

[384] Sec. 420.

[385] The value of plan assets for this purpose is the lesser of fair market value or actuarial value.

[386] In the case of plan years beginning before January 1, 2004, excess assets generally means the excess, if any, of the value of the plan's assets over the greater of (1) the lesser of

(a) the accrued liability under the plan (including normal cost) or (b) 170 percent of the plan's current liability (for 2003), or (2) 125 percent of the plan's current liability. The current liability full funding limit was repealed for years beginning after 2003. Under the general sunset provision of EGTRRA, the limit is reinstated for years after 2010.

Amounts not used to pay qualified current retiree health liabilities for the taxable year of the transfer are to be returned to the general assets of the plan. These amounts are not includible in the gross income of the employer, but are treated as an employer reversion and are subject to a 20-percent excise tax.

In order for a transfer to be qualified, accrued retirement benefits under the pension plan generally must be 100-percent vested as if the plan terminated immediately before the transfer (or in the case of a participant who separated in the one-year period ending on the date of the transfer, immediately before the separation).

In order for a transfer to be qualified, the transfer must meet the minimum cost requirement. To satisfy the minimum cost requirement, an employer generally must maintain retiree health benefits at the same level for the taxable year of the transfer and the following four years (referred to as the cost maintance period). The applicable employer cost during the cost maintenance period cannot be less than the higher of the applicable employer costs for each of the two taxable years preceding the taxable year of the transfer. The applicable employer cost is generally determined by dividing the current retiree health liabilities by the number of individuals provided coverage for applicable health benefits during the year. The Secretary is directed to prescribe regulations as may be necessary to prevent an employer who significantly reduces retiree health coverage during the period from being treated as satisfying the minimum cost requirement.

Under Treasury regulations,[387] the minimum cost requirement is not satisfied if the employer significantly reduces retiree health coverage during the cost maintenance period. Under the regulations, an employer significantly reduces retiree health coverage for a year (beginning after 2001) during the cost maintenance period if either (1) the employer-initiated reduction percentage for that taxable year exceeds 10 percent, or (2) the sum of the employer-initiated

reduction percentages for that taxable year and all prior taxable years during the cost maintenance period exceeds 20 percent.[388] The employer-initiated reduction percentage is percentage of the number of individuals receiving coverage for applicable health benefits as of the day before the first day of the taxable year over the total number of such individuals whose coverage for applicable health benefits ended during the taxable year by reason of employer action.[389]

House Bill

No provision.

Senate Amendment

The Senate amendment provides that an eligible employer does not fail the minimum cost requirement if, in lieu of any reduction of health coverage permitted by Treasury regulations, the employer reduces applicable employer cost by an amount not in excess of the reduction in costs which would have occurred if the employer had made the maximum permissible reduction in retiree health coverage under such regulations. An employer is an eligible employer if, for the preceding taxable year, the qualified current retiree health liabilities of the employer were at least five percent of gross receipts.

In applying such regulations to any subsequent taxable year, any reduction in applicable employer cost under the proposal is treated as if it were an equivalent reduction in retiree health coverage.

Effective Date

The provision is effective for taxable years ending after the date of enactment.

Conference Agreement

The conference agreement follows the Senate amendment.

[Law at ¶5355 and ¶7070. CCH Explanation at ¶1420.]

[¶10,920] Act Sec. 710. Credit for electricity produced from certain sources

Conference Committee Report (H.R. CONF. REP. NO. 108-755)

[Code Sec. 45]

Present Law

An income tax credit is allowed for the production of electricity from either qualified wind

energy, qualified "closed-loop" biomass, or qualified poultry waste facilities (sec. 45). The amount of the credit is 1.5 cents per kilowatt-hour (indexed for inflation) of electricity produced. The amount of the credit is 1.8 cents per

---

[387] Treas. Reg. sec. 1.420-1(a).
[388] Treas. Reg. sec. 1.420-1(b)(1).

[389] Treas. Reg. sec. 1.420-1(b)(2).

kilowatt-hour for 2004. The credit is reduced for grants, tax-exempt bonds, subsidized energy financing, and other credits.

The credit applies to electricity produced by a wind energy facility placed in service after December 31, 1993, and before January 1, 2006, to electricity produced by a closed-loop biomass facility placed in service after December 31, 1992, and before January 1, 2006, and to a poultry waste facility placed in service after December 31, 1999, and before January 1, 2006. The credit is allowable for production during the 10-year period after a facility is originally placed in service. In order to claim the credit, a taxpayer must own the facility and sell the electricity produced by the facility to an unrelated party. In the case of a poultry waste facility, the taxpayer may claim the credit as a lessee/operator of a facility owned by a governmental unit.

House Bill

No provision.

Senate Amendment

Extension of placed in service date for existing facilities

The Senate amendment extends the placed in service date for wind facilities, closed-loop biomass facilities, and poultry waste facilities to facilities placed in service after December 31, 1993 (December 31, 1992, in the case of closed-loop biomass facilities and December 31, 1999, in the case of poultry waste facilities) and before January 1, 2007.

Modification of credit amount

The Senate amendment modifies the credit rate applicable to electricity produced from after December 31, 2004 from facilities placed in service after December 31, 2004 to be 1.8 cents per kilowatt hour and repeals the indexing of the credit amount.

Additional qualifying facilities

The Senate amendment also defines six new qualifying energy resources: open-loop biomass including agricultural livestock waste nutrients, geothermal energy, solar energy, municipal biosolids and sludge, small irrigation, and municipal solid waste.

Open-loop biomass is defined as any solid, nonhazardous, cellulosic waste material which is segregated from other waste materials and which is derived from any of forest-related resources, solid wood waste materials, or agricultural sources. Eligible forest-related resources are mill residues, other than spent chemicals from pulp manufacturing, precommercial thinnings, slash, and brush. Solid wood waste materials include waste pallets, crates, dunnage, manufac-

turing and construction wood wastes (other than pressure-treated, chemically-treated, or painted wood wastes), and landscape or right-of-way tree trimmings. Agricultural sources include orchard tree crops, vineyard, grain, legumes, sugar, and other crop by-products or residues. However, qualifying open-loop biomass does not include municipal solid waste (garbage), gas derived from biodegradation of solid waste, or paper that is commonly recycled. In addition, open-loop biomass does not include closed-loop biomass or any biomass burned in conjunction with fossil fuel (cofiring) beyond such fossil fuel required for start up and flame stabilization.

Agricultural livestock waste nutrients are defined as agricultural livestock manure and litter, including bedding material for the disposition of manure.

Geothermal energy is energy derived from a geothermal deposit which is a geothermal reservoir consisting of natural heat which is stored in rocks or in an aqueous liquid or vapor (whether or not under pressure).

Municipal biosolids and sludge are the residue or solids removed by a municipal wastewater treatment facility. Sludge is the recycled residue byproduct created in the treatment of commercial, industrial, municipal, or navigational wastewater, but not including residues from incineration.

A small irrigation power facility is a facility that generates electric power through an irrigation system canal or ditch without any dam or impoundment of water. The installed capacity of a qualified facility is less than five megawatts.

Qualifying open-loop biomass facilities, other than qualifying agricultural livestock waste nutrient facilities are facilities using open-loop biomass to produce electricity that are placed in service prior to January 1, 2005. Qualifying agricultural livestock waste nutrient facilities are facilities using agricultural livestock waste nutrients to produce electricity that are placed in service after December 31, 2004 and before January 1, 2007. Qualifying geothermal energy facilities are facilities using geothermal deposits to produce electricity that are placed in service after December 31, 2004 and before January 1, 2007. Qualifying solar energy facilities are facilities using solar energy to generate electricity that are placed in service December 31, 2004 and before January 1, 2007. Qualifying municipal biosolids and sludge facilities are facilities using municipal biosolids or sludge to generate electricity that are originally placed in service after December 31, 2004, and before January 1, 2007. Qualifying small irrigation power facilities are facilities using small irrigation power systems to generate electricity that are originally placed in service after December 31, 2004 and before January 1, 2007. Qualifying municipal solid waste facilities are facilities or units incinerating municipal solid waste placed in service after December 31, 2004 and before January 1, 2007.

In the case of qualifying open-loop biomass facilities placed in service prior to January 1, 2005, taxpayers may claim a credit of 1.2 cents per kilowatt hour, rather than 1.8 cents per kilowatt hour for the five-year period beginning on January 1, 2005. the otherwise allowable credit for a three-year period. For a facility placed in service after the date of enactment, the three-year period commences when the facility is placed in service.

In addition, the Senate amendment modifies present law to provide that qualifying closed-loop biomass facilities include any facility originally placed in service before December 31, 1992 and modified to use closed-loop biomass to co-fire with coal, with other biomass, or both, before January 1, 2007. The amount of credit the taxpayer may claim credit is adjusted for the thermal value of the qualifying closed-loop biomass relative to the thermal value of the closed-loop biomass and the coal. The ten-year credit period for such a qualifying facility commences no earlier than January 1, 2005.

Credit claimants and treatment of other subsidies

In the case of qualifying open-loop biomass facilities and qualifying closed-loop biomass facilities modified to use closed-loop biomass to co-fire with coal, the Senate amendment permits a lessee operator to claim the credit in lieu of the owner of the facilities.

The Senate amendment provides that certain persons (public utilities, electric cooperatives, rural electric cooperatives, and Indian tribes) may sell, trade, or assign to any taxpayer any credits that would otherwise be allowable to that person, if that person were a taxpayer, for production of electricity from a qualified facility owned by such person. However, any credit sold, traded, or assigned may only be sold, traded, or assigned once. Subsequent trades are not permitted. In addition, any credits that would otherwise be allowable to such person, to the extent provided by the Administrator of the Rural Electrification Administration, may be applied as a prepayment to certain loans or obligations undertaken by such person under the Rural Electrification Act of 1936.

The Senate amendment repeals the present-law reduction in allowable credit for facilities financed with tax-exempt bonds or with certain loans received under the Rural Electrification Act of 1936.

Conference Agreement

The conference agreement follows the Senate amendment with modifications.

Extension of placed in service date for existing facilities

The conference agreement does not include the provisions of the Senate amendment with respect to the extension of placed in service dates for qualifying wind, closed-loop, and poultry waste facilities.

Modification of placed in service date for existing facilities

The conference agreement includes the Senate amendment provision with respect to qualifying closed-loop biomass facilities modified to use closed-loop biomass to co-fire with coal, to co-fire with other biomass, or to co-fire with coal and other biomass, with the modification that the 10-year credit period begin no earlier than the date of enactment of the provision.

Additional qualifying resource and facilities

The conference agreement also defines five new qualifying resources for the production of electricity: open-loop biomass (including agricultural livestock waste nutrients), geothermal energy, solar energy, small irrigation power, and municipal solid waste. Two different qualifying facilities use municipal solid waste as a qualifying resource: landfill gas facilities and trash combustion facilities. In addition, the conference agreement defines refined coal as a qualifying resource.

Qualifying open-loop biomass facilities are facilities using biomass to produce electricity that are placed in service prior to January 1, 2006. Qualifying agricultural livestock waste nutrient facilities are facilities using agricultural livestock waste nutrients to produce electricity that are placed in service after the date of enactment and before January 1, 2006. The installed capacity of a qualified agricultural livestock waste nutrient facility is not less than 150 kilowatts.

Qualifying geothermal energy facilities are facilities using geothermal deposits to produce electricity that are placed in service after the date of enactment and before January 1, 2006. Qualifying solar energy facilities are facilities using solar energy to generate electricity that are placed in service after the date of enactment and before January 1, 2006. A qualifying geothermal energy facility or solar energy facility may not have claimed any credit under sec. 48 of the Code.[390]

A qualified small irrigation power facility is a facility originally placed in service after the date of enactment and before January 1, 2006. A small irrigation power facility is a facility that generates electric power through an irrigation system canal or ditch without any dam or impoundment of water. The installed capacity of a qualified facility is not less than 150 kilowatts and less than five megawatts.

Landfill gas is defined as methane gas derived from the biodegradation of municipal solid waste. Trash combustion facilities are facilities that burn municipal solid waste (garbage) to produce steam to drive a turbine for the production of electricity. Qualifying landfill gas facilities and qualifying trash combustion facilities include facilities used to produce electricity placed in service after the date of enactment and before January 1, 2006.

Refined coal is a qualifying liquid, gaseous, or solid synthetic fuel produced from coal (including lignite) or high-carbon fly ash, including such fuel used as a feedstock. A qualifying fuel is a fuel that when burned emits 20 percent less SO2 and nitrogen oxides than the burning of feedstock coal or comparable coal predominantly available in the marketplace as of January 1, 2003, and if the fuel sells at prices at least 50 percent greater than the prices of the feedstock coal or comparable coal. In addition, to be qualified refined coal the fuel must be sold by the taxpayer with the reasonable expectation that it will be used for the primary purpose of producing steam. A qualifying refined coal facility is a facility producing refined coal that is placed in service after the date of enactment and before January 1, 2009.

Credit period and credit rates

In general, as under present law, taxpayers may claim the credit at a rate of 1.5 cents per kilowatt-hour (indexed for inflation and currently 1.8 cents per kilowatt-hour) for 10 years of production commencing on the date the facility is placed in service. In the case of open-loop biomass facilities, (including agricultural livestock waste nutrients), geothermal energy, solar energy, small irrigation power, landfill gas facilities, and trash combustion facilities the 10-year credit period is reduced to five years commencing on the date the facility is placed in service. In general, for facilities placed in service prior to January 1, 2005, the credit period commences on January 1, 2005. In the case of a closed-loop biomass facilities modified to co-fire with coal, to

co-fire with other biomass, or to co-fire with coal and other biomass, the credit period shall begin no earlier than the date of enactment.

In the case of open-loop biomass facilities (including agricultural livestock waste nutrients), small irrigation power, landfill gas facilities, and trash combustion facilities, the otherwise allowable credit amount is reduced by one half.

An alternative credit applies for the production of refined coal. A qualified refined coal facility may claim credit at a rate of $4.375 per ton (indexed for inflation after 1992) of refined coal sold to a unrelated person. As is the case for facilities that produce electricity, the credit a taxpayer may claim for the production of refined coal is phased out as the market price of refined coal exceeds certain threshold levels. The threshold is defined by reference to the price of feedstock fuel used to produce refined coal. Thus if a producer of refined coal uses Powder River Basin coal as a feedstock, the threshold price is determined by reference to prices of Powder River Basin coal. If the producer uses Appalachian coal, the threshold price is determined by reference to prices of Appalachian coal.

Credit claimants and treatment of other subsidies

A lessee or operator may claim the credit in lieu of the owner of the qualifying facility in the case of qualifying open-loop biomass facilities originally placed in service on or before the date of enactment and in the case of a closed-loop biomass facilities modified to co-fire with coal, to co-fire with other biomass, or to co-fire with coal and other biomass.

In addition, for all qualifying facilities, other than closed-loop biomass facilities modified to co-fire with coal, to co-fire with other biomass, or to co-fire with coal and other biomass, any reduction in credit by reason of grants, tax-exempt bonds, subsidized energy financing, and other credits cannot exceed 50 percent. In the case of closed-loop biomass facilities modified to co-fire with coal, to co-fire with other biomass, or to co-fire with coal and other biomass, there is no reduction in credit by reason of grants, tax-exempt bonds, subsidized energy financing, and other credits.

The amendments made by the conference report do not apply with respect to any poultry waste facility placed in service prior to January 1, 2005. Such facilities placed in service after December 31, 2004 generally may qualify for

---

[390] If a geothermal facility or solar facility claims credit for any year under section 45 of the Code, the facility is precluded from claiming any investment credit under section 48 of the Code in the future.

credit as animal livestock waste nutrient facilities.

No facility that previously claimed or currently claims credit under section 29 of the Code is a qualifying facility for purposes of section 45.

Effective Date

The provision is effective for electricity produced and sold from qualifying facilities after the date of enactment in taxable years ending after the date of enactment. With respect to open-loop biomass facilities placed in service prior to January 1, 2005, the provisions are effective for electricity produced and sold after December 31, 2004.

[Law at ¶5035 and ¶5065. CCH Explanation at ¶870, ¶872 and ¶874.]

[¶ 10,924] Act Sec. 711. Increase tax limitation on use of business energy credits

Conference Committee Report (H.R. CONF. REP. NO. 108-755)

[Code Sec. 38]

Present Law

Generally, business tax credits may not exceed the excess of the taxpayer's income tax liability over the tentative minimum tax (or, if greater, 25 percent of the regular tax liability). Credits in excess of the limitation may be carried back one year and carried over for up to 20 years.

The tentative minimum tax is an amount equal to specified rates of tax imposed on the excess of the alternative minimum taxable income over an exemption amount. To the extent the tentative minimum tax exceeds the regular tax, a taxpayer is subject to the alternative minimum tax.

House Bill

No provision.

Senate Amendment

The Senate amendment treats the tentative minimum tax as being zero for purposes of de-

termining the tax liability limitation with respect to (1) the Alaska natural gas credit, (2) for taxable years beginning after December 31, 2004, the alcohol fuels credit determined under section 40; and (3) the section 45 credit for electricity produced from a facility (placed in service after the date of enactment) during the first four years of production beginning on the date the facility is placed in service.

Effective Date

The provision is effective for taxable years ending after the date of enactment of the Act.

Conference Agreement

The conference agreement includes the provision in the Senate amendment relating to the credits under sections 40 and 45.

[Law at ¶5010. CCH Explanation at ¶370.]

[¶ 10,930] Act Sec. 712. Inclusion of primary and secondary medical strategies for children and adults with sickle cell disease as medical assistance under the Medicaid program

Conference Committee Report (H.R. CONF. REP. NO. 108-755)

[Act Sec. 712]

Present Law

Medicaid programs are generally operated by the States, in part with funds received from the Federal government. Within broad Federal guidelines, States can design the scope and availability of Medicaid benefits. Medicaid law requires States to provide certain services including, for example, hospital and physician services. Federal funds are available for additional optional services if States choose to in-

clude them in their Medicaid plans. Within Federal guidelines, States may limit the amount, duration of any Medicaid service. Under present law, States may have covered some of the primary and secondary medical strategies, treatments, and services for Sickle Cell Disease, however such services are not specifically listed in the Medicaid statute as either mandatory or optional services.

The Federal government shares in States' Medicaid service costs by means of a statutory formula designed to provide a higher Federal matching rate to States with lower per capita incomes. The Federal share is referred to as the Federal Medical Assistance Percentage ("FMAP"). For some Medicaid services and activities, such as costs associated with program administration, the FMAP rate is set in statute. Because Medicaid is an individual entitlement, there is no annual ceiling on Federal expenditures; however, in order to continue receiving Federal payments, States must contribute their share of the matching funds.

House Bill

No provision.

Senate Amendment

The Senate amendment amends Title XIX of the Social Security Act to add primary and secondary medical strategies, treatment and services for individuals who have Sickle Cell Disease as a new optional medical assistance category under the Medicaid program. Such strategies, treatment, and services include: (1) chronic blood transfusion (with deferoxamine chelation) to prevent stroke in individuals with Sickle Cell Disease who have been identified as being at high risk for stroke; (2) genetic counseling, testing, and treatment for individuals with Sickle Cell Disease or the Sickle Cell trait; and (3) other treatment and services to prevent individuals who have Sickle Cell Disease and who have had a stroke having another stroke. The amendment sets the FMAP rate at 50 percent for costs attributable to providing: (1) services to identify and educate likely Medicaid enrollees who have or are carriers of Sickle Cell Disease; or (2) education regarding the risks of stroke and other complications, as well as the prevention of stroke and complications for likely Medicaid enrollees with Sickle Cell Disease.

The Senate amendment also authorizes an appropriation in the amount of $10,000,000 for each of fiscal years 2005 through 2009 for a demonstration program under which the Administrator of the Health Resources and Services Administration (through the Bureau of Primary Health Care and the Maternal Child Health Bureau) would make grants up to 40 eligible entities in each such fiscal year for the development and establishment of systemic mechanisms for the prevention and treatment of the Sickle Cell Disease. Eligible entities include Federallyqualified health centers as defined in the Medicaid statute; nonprofit hospitals or clinics, or university health centers that provide primary health care that: (1) have a collaborative agreement with a community-based Sickle Cell Disease organization or a nonprofit entity with experience in working with individuals who have the Sickle Cell Disease; and (2) demonstrate that they have at least five years of experience in working with individuals who have the Sickle Cell Disease. Systematic mechanisms for the prevention and treatment of the Sickle Cell Disease include: (1) coordination of service delivery for individuals with the disease; (2) genetic counseling and testing; (3) bundling of technical services related to the prevention and treatment of the disease; (4) training health professionals; and (5) identifying and establishing efforts related to the expansion and coordination of education, treatment, and continuity of care programs for individuals with the disease.

In awarding such grants to eligible entities, the Administrator of Health Resources and Services Administration is to take into consideration geographic diversity and to give priority to: (1) Federally-qualified health centers that have a partnership or other arrangement with a comprehensive Sickle Cell Disease treatment center and does not receive funds from the National Institutes of Health; or (2) Federally-qualified health centers that intend to develop a partnership or other arrangement with a comprehensive Sickle Cell Disease treatment center, and that does not receive funds from the National Institutes of Health. Eligible entities that are awarded grants are required to use the funds for the following activities: (1) to facilitate and coordinate the delivery of education, treatment, and continuity of care under: (a) the entity's collaborative agreement with a community-based Sickle Cell Disease organization or a nonprofit entity that works with individuals who have Sickle Cell Disease; (b) the Sickle Cell Disease newborn screening program for the State in which the entity is located; and (c) the Maternal and Child Health program for the State in which the entity is located; (2) to train nursing and other health staff who provide care for individuals with Sickle Cell Disease; (3) to enter into a partnership with adult or pediatric hematologists in the region and other regional experts in the Sickle Cell Disease at tertiary or academic health centers and State and county health offices; and (4) to identify and secure resources for ensuring reimbursement under the Medicaid program, State children's health insurance program, and other health programs for the prevention and treatment of Sickle Cell Disease.

The Senate amendment also requires the Administrator of Health Resources and Services Administration to enter into a contract with an entity and to serve as a National Coordinating Center for the demonstration program. The center is to: (1) collect, coordinate, monitor and distribute data, best practices, and findings regarding the activities funded under grants made to eligible entities under the demonstration program; (2) develop a model protocol for eligible

Act Sec. 712   ¶10,930

entities with respect to prevention and treatment of the disease; (3) develop educational materials regarding the prevention and treatment of the disease; and (4) submit a written report to Congress. The written report to Congress should include recommendations on the effectiveness of the demonstration program direct outcome measures, such as the number and type of health care resources utilized (such as emergency room visits, hospital visits, length of stay, and physician visits for individuals with Sickle Cell Disease) and the number of individuals that were tested and subsequently received genetic counseling for the sickle cell trait.

Effective Date

The Senate amendment is effective on the date of enactment.

Conference Agreement

The conference agreement follows the Senate amendment provision.

[Law at ¶ 7075. CCH Explanation at ¶ 1230.]

[¶ 10,940] Act Sec. 713. Suspension of duties on ceiling fans

House Committee Report (H.R. REP. NO. 108-548, pt. 1)

[Act Sec. 801]

Present Law

A 4.7-percent ad valorem customs duty is collected on imported ceiling fans from all sources.

Reasons for Change

The Committee observes that ceiling fans are an energy efficient method of cooling and heating residences and commercial buildings. However, because there is a lack of U.S. production of ceiling fans, the Committee notes that a tariff only serves to increase the cost of ceiling fans to the U.S. consumer. Reducing the tariff on imported ceiling fans is expected to reduce the costs to consumers and encourage energy conservation.

Explanation of Provision

The provision agreement suspends the present customs duty applicable to ceiling fans through December 31, 2006.

Effective Date

The provision is effective on the fifteenth day after the date of enactment.

Conference Committee Report (H.R. CONF. REP. NO. 108-755)

Senate Amendment

No provision.

Conference Agreement

The conference agreement includes the House bill provision.

[Law at ¶ 7080. CCH Explanation at ¶ 590.]

[¶ 10,950] Act Sec. 714. Suspension of duties on nuclear steam generators

House Committee Report (H.R. REP. NO. 108-548, pt. 1)

[Act Sec. 802(a)]

Present Law

Nuclear steam generators, as classified under heading 9902.84.02 of the Harmonized Tariff Schedule of the United States, enter the United States duty free until December 31, 2006. After December 31, 2006, the duty on nuclear steam generators returns to the column 1 rate of 5.2 percent under subheading 8402.11.00 of the Harmonized Tariff Schedule of the United States.

Reasons for Change

The Committee notes that nuclear steam generators are essential components to nuclear electricity plants, but at the present time, there is a lack of U.S. production of nuclear steam generators. Therefore the Committee concludes that a tariff only serves to increase the cost of these products to the U.S. purchasers. Reducing the tariff on imported nuclear steam generators is expected to encourage installation of more modern and energy efficient equipment and to reduce the costs to consumers of electricity.

Explanation of Provision

The provision extends the present-law suspension of customs duty applicable to nuclear steam generators through December 31, 2008.

Effective Date

The provision is effective on the date of enactment.

Conference Committee Report (H.R. CONF. REP. NO. 108-755)

Senate Amendment

No provision.

[Law at ¶ 7085. CCH Explanation at ¶ 595.]

Conference Agreement

The conference agreement includes the House bill provision.

[¶ 10,960] Act Sec. 714. Suspension of duties on nuclear reactor vessel heads

House Committee Report (H.R. REP. NO. 108-548, pt. 1)

[Act Sec. 802(b)]

Present Law

According to section 5202 of the Trade Act of 2002, nuclear reactor vessel heads are classified under subheading 8401.40.00 of the Harmonized Tariff Schedule of the United States and enter the United States with a column 1 duty rate of 3.3 percent.

Reasons for Change

The Committee notes that nuclear reactor vessel heads are essential components to nuclear electricity plants, but at the present time, there is a lack of U.S. production of nuclear reactor vessel heads. Therefore the Committee concludes that a tariff only serves to increase the cost of

these products to the U.S. purchasers. Reducing the tariff on imported nuclear reactor vessel heads is expected to encourage installation of more modern and energy efficient equipment and to reduce the costs to consumers of electricity.

Explanation of Provision

The provision temporarily suspends the present customs duty applicable to nuclear reactor vessel heads for column 1 countries through December 31, 2008.

Effective Date

The provision is effective on the fifteenth day after the date of enactment.

Conference Committee Report (H.R. CONF. REP. NO. 108-755)

Senate Amendment

No provision.

Conference Agreement

The conference agreement includes the House bill provision with a modification. The

conference agreement also temporarily suspends the customs duty applicable to nuclear reactor pressurizers.

[Law at ¶ 7085. CCH Explanation at ¶ 595.]

[¶ 10,970] Act Sec. 801. Tax treatment of expatriated entities and their foreign parents

House Committee Report (H.R. REP. NO. 108-548, pt. 1)

[New Code Sec. 7874]

Present Law

Determination of corporate residence

The U.S. tax treatment of a multinational corporate group depends significantly on whether the parent corporation of the group is domestic or foreign. For purposes of U.S. tax law, a corporation is treated as domestic if it is incorporated under the law of the United States or of any State. All other corporations (i.e., those incorporated under the laws of foreign countries) are treated as foreign.

U.S. taxation of domestic corporations

The United States employs a "worldwide" tax system, under which domestic corporations generally are taxed on all income, whether derived in the United States or abroad. In order to mitigate the double taxation that may arise from taxing the foreign-source income of a domestic corporation, a foreign tax credit for income taxes paid to foreign countries is provided to reduce or eliminate the U.S. tax owed on such income, subject to certain limitations.

Income earned by a domestic parent corporation from foreign operations conducted by foreign corporate subsidiaries generally is subject to U.S. tax when the income is distributed as a dividend to the domestic corporation. Until such repatriation, the U.S. tax on such income generally is deferred, and U.S. tax is imposed on such income when repatriated. However, certain anti-deferral regimes may cause the domestic parent corporation to be taxed on a current basis in the United States with respect to certain categories of passive or highly mobile income earned by its foreign subsidiaries, regardless of whether the income has been distributed as a dividend to the domestic parent corporation. The main anti-deferral regimes in this context are the controlled foreign corporation rules of subpart F (secs. 951-964) and the passive foreign investment company rules (secs. 1291-1298). A foreign tax credit is generally available to offset, in whole or in part, the U.S. tax owed on this foreign-source income, whether repatriated as an actual dividend or included under one of the anti-deferral regimes.

U.S. taxation of foreign corporations

The United States taxes foreign corporations only on income that has a sufficient nexus to the United States. Thus, a foreign corporation is generally subject to U.S. tax only on income that is "effectively connected" with the conduct of a trade or business in the United States. Such "effectively connected income" generally is taxed in the same manner and at the same rates as the income of a U.S. corporation. An applicable tax treaty may limit the imposition of U.S. tax on business operations of a foreign corporation to cases in which the business is conducted through a "permanent establishment" in the United States.

In addition, foreign corporations generally are subject to a gross-basis U.S. tax at a flat 30-percent rate on the receipt of interest, dividends, rents, royalties, and certain similar types of income derived from U.S. sources, subject to certain exceptions. The tax generally is collected by means of withholding by the person making the payment. This tax may be reduced or eliminated under an applicable tax treaty.

U.S. tax treatment of inversion transactions

Under present law, a U.S. corporation may reincorporate in a foreign jurisdiction and thereby replace the U.S. parent corporation of a multinational corporate group with a foreign parent corporation. These transactions are commonly referred to as inversion transactions. Inversion transactions may take many different forms, including stock inversions, asset inversions, and various combinations of and variations on the two. Most of the known transactions to date have been stock inversions. In one example of a stock inversion, a U.S. corporation forms a foreign corporation, which in turn forms a domestic merger subsidiary. The domestic merger subsidiary then merges into the U.S. corporation, with the U.S. corporation surviving, now as a subsidiary of the new foreign corporation. The U.S. corporation's shareholders receive shares of the foreign corporation and are treated as having exchanged their U.S. corporation shares for the foreign corporation shares. An asset inversion reaches a similar result, but through a direct merger of the top-tier U.S. corporation into a new foreign corporation, among other possible forms. An inversion transaction may be accompanied or followed by further restructuring of the corporate group. For example, in the case of a stock inversion, in order to remove income from foreign operations from the U.S. taxing jurisdiction, the U.S. corporation may transfer some or all of its foreign subsidiaries directly to the new foreign parent corporation or other related foreign corporations.

In addition to removing foreign operations from the U.S. taxing jurisdiction, the corporate group may derive further advantage from the inverted structure by reducing U.S. tax on U.S.-source income through various earnings stripping or other transactions. This may include earnings stripping through payment by a U.S. corporation of deductible amounts such as interest, royalties, rents, or management service fees to the new foreign parent or other foreign affiliates. In this respect, the post-inversion structure enables the group to employ the same tax-reduction strategies that are available to other multinational corporate groups with foreign parents and U.S. subsidiaries, subject to the same limitations (e.g., secs. 163(j) and 482).

Inversion transactions may give rise to immediate U.S. tax consequences at the shareholder and/or the corporate level, depending on the type of inversion. In stock inversions, the U.S. shareholders generally recognize gain (but not loss) under section 367(a), based on the difference between the fair market value of the foreign corporation shares received and the adjusted basis of the domestic corporation stock exchanged. To the extent that a corporation's share value has declined, and/or it has many foreign or tax-exempt shareholders, the impact of this section 367(a) "toll charge" is reduced. The transfer of foreign subsidiaries or other assets to the foreign parent corporation also may give rise to U.S. tax consequences at the corporate level (e.g., gain recognition and earnings and profits inclusions under secs. 1001, 311(b), 304, 367, 1248 or other provisions). The tax on any income recognized as a result of these restructurings may be reduced or eliminated through the use of net operating losses, foreign tax credits, and other tax attributes.

In asset inversions, the U.S. corporation generally recognizes gain (but not loss) under section 367(a) as though it had sold all of its assets, but the shareholders generally do not recognize gain or loss, assuming the transaction meets the requirements of a reorganization under section 368.

Reasons for Change

The Committee believes that corporate inversion transactions are a symptom of larger problems with our current uncompetitive system for taxing U.S.-based global businesses and are also indicative of the unfair advantages that our tax laws convey to foreign ownership. The bill addresses the underlying problems with the U.S. system of taxing U.S.-based global businesses and contains provisions to remove the incentives for entering into inversion transactions. Imposing full U.S. tax on gains of companies undertak-

ing an inversion transaction is one such provision that helps to remove the incentive to enter into an inversion transaction.

Explanation of Provision

The bill applies special tax rules to corporations that undertake certain defined inversion transactions. For this purpose, an inversion is a transaction in which, pursuant to a plan or a series of related transactions: (1) a U.S. corporation becomes a subsidiary of a foreign-incorporated entity or otherwise transfers substantially all of its properties to such an entity after March 4, 2003; (2) the former shareholders of the U.S. corporation hold (by reason of holding stock in the U.S. corporation) 60 percent or more (by vote or value) of the stock of the foreign-incorporated entity after the transaction; and (3) the foreign-incorporated entity, considered together with all companies connected to it by a chain of greater than 50-percent ownership (i.e., the "expanded affiliated group") does not conduct substantial business activities in the entity's country of incorporation compared to the total worldwide business activities of the expanded affiliated group.

In such a case, any applicable corporate-level "toll charges" for establishing the inverted structure are not offset by tax attributes such as net operating losses or foreign tax credits. Specifically, any applicable corporate-level income or gain required to be recognized under sections 304, 311(b), 367, 1001, 1248, or any other provision with respect to the transfer of controlled foreign corporation stock or the transfer or license of other assets by a U.S. corporation as part of the inversion transaction or after such transaction to a related foreign person is taxable, without offset by any tax attributes (e.g., net operating losses or foreign tax credits). This rule does not apply to certain transfers of inventory and similar property. These measures generally apply for a 10-year period following the inversion transaction.

In determining whether a transaction meets the definition of an inversion under the provision, stock held by members of the expanded affiliated group that includes the foreign incorporated entity is disregarded. For example, if the former top-tier U.S. corporation receives stock of the foreign incorporated entity (e.g., so-called "hook" stock), the stock would not be considered in determining whether the transaction meets the definition. Similarly, if a U.S. parent corporation converts an existing wholly owned U.S. subsidiary into a new wholly owned controlled foreign corporation, the stock of the new foreign corporation would be disregarded. Stock sold in a public offering related to the transaction also is disregarded for these purposes.

Act Sec. 801   ¶10,970

Transfers of properties or liabilities as part of a plan a principal purpose of which is to avoid the purposes of the provision are disregarded. In addition, the Treasury Secretary is granted authority to prevent the avoidance of the purposes of the provision, including avoidance through the use of related persons, pass-through or other noncorporate entities, or other intermediaries, and through transactions designed to qualify or disqualify a person as a related person or a member of an expanded affiliated group. Similarly, the Treasury Secretary is granted authority to treat certain non-stock instruments as stock, and certain stock as not stock, where necessary, to carry out the purposes of the provision.

Under the provision, inversion transactions include certain partnership transactions. Specifically, the provision applies to transactions in which a foreign-incorporated entity acquires substantially all of the properties constituting a trade or business of a domestic partnership, if after the acquisition at least 60 percent of the stock of the entity is held by former partners of the partnership (by reason of holding their partnership interests), provided that the other terms of the basic definition are met. For purposes of applying this test, all partnerships that are under common control within the meaning of section 482 are treated as one partnership, except as provided otherwise in regulations. In addition, the modified "toll charge" provisions apply at the partner level.

A transaction otherwise meeting the definition of an inversion transaction is not treated as an inversion transaction if, on or before March 4, 2003, the foreign-incorporated entity had acquired directly or indirectly more than half of the properties held directly or indirectly by the domestic corporation, or more than half of the properties constituting the partnership trade or business, as the case may be.

Effective Date

The provision applies to taxable years ending after March 4, 2003.

Conference Committee Report (H.R. CONF. REP. NO. 108-755)

Senate Amendment

In general

The provision defines two different types of corporate inversion transactions and establishes a different set of consequences for each type. Certain partnership transactions also are covered.

Transactions involving at least 80 percent identity of stock ownership

The first type of inversion is a transaction in which, pursuant to a plan or a series of related transactions: (1) a U.S. corporation becomes a subsidiary of a foreign-incorporated entity or otherwise transfers substantially all of its properties to such an entity;[429] (2) the former shareholders of the U.S. corporation hold (by reason of holding stock in the U.S. corporation) 80 percent or more (by vote or value) of the stock of the foreign-incorporated entity after the transaction; and (3) the foreign-incorporated entity, considered together with all companies connected to it by a chain of greater than 50 percent ownership (i.e., the "expanded affiliated group"), does not have substantial business activities in the entity's country of incorporation, compared to the total worldwide business activities of the expanded affiliated group. The provision denies the intended tax benefits of this type of inversion by deeming the top-tier foreign corporation to be a domestic corporation for all purposes of the Code.[430]

Except as otherwise provided in regulations, the provision does not apply to a direct or indirect acquisition of the properties of a U.S. corporation no class of the stock of which was traded on an established securities market at any time within the four-year period preceding the acquisition. In determining whether a transaction would meet the definition of an inversion under the provision, stock held by members of the expanded affiliated group that includes the foreign incorporated entity is disregarded. For example, if the former top-tier U.S. corporation receives stock of the foreign incorporated entity (e.g., so-called "hook" stock), the stock would not be considered in determining whether the transaction meets the definition. Stock sold in a public offering (whether initial or secondary) or private placement related to the transaction also is disregarded for these purposes. Acquisitions with respect to a domestic corporation or partnership are deemed to be "pursuant to a plan" if they occur within the four-year period beginning on the date which is two years before the ownership threshold under the provision is met with respect to such corporation or partnership.

---

[429] It is expected that the Treasury Secretary will issue regulations applying the term "substantially all" in this context and will not be bound in this regard by interpretations of the term in other contexts under the Code.

[430] Since the top-tier foreign corporation is treated for all purposes of the Code as domestic, the shareholder-level

"toll charge" of sec. 367(a) does not apply to these inversion transactions. However, with respect to inversion transactions completed before 2004, regulated investment companies and certain similar entities are allowed to elect to recognize gain as if sec. 367(a) did apply.

Transfers of properties or liabilities as part of a plan a principal purpose of which is to avoid the purposes of the provision are disregarded. In addition, the Treasury Secretary is granted authority to prevent the avoidance of the purposes of the provision, including avoidance through the use of related persons, pass-through or other noncorporate entities, or other intermediaries, and through transactions designed to qualify or disqualify a person as a related person, a member of an expanded affiliated group, or a publicly traded corporation. Similarly, the Treasury Secretary is granted authority to treat certain nonstock instruments as stock, and certain stock as not stock, where necessary to carry out the purposes of the provision.

Transactions involving greater than 50 percent but less than 80 percent identity of stock ownership

The second type of inversion is a transaction that would meet the definition of an inversion transaction described above, except that the 80-percent ownership threshold is not met. In such a case, if a greater-than-50-percent ownership threshold is met, then a second set of rules applies to the inversion. Under these rules, the inversion transaction is respected (i.e., the foreign corporation is treated as foreign), but: (1) any applicable corporate-level "toll charges" for establishing the inverted structure may not be offset by tax attributes such as net operating losses or foreign tax credits; (2) the accuracy-related penalty is increased; and (3) section 163(j), relating to "earnings stripping" through related-party debt, is strengthened. These measures generally apply for a 10-year period following the inversion transaction. In addition, inverting entities are required to provide information to shareholders or partners and the IRS with respect to the inversion transaction.

With respect to "toll charges," any applicable corporate-level income or gain required to be recognized under sections 304, 311(b), 367, 1001, 1248, or any other provision with respect to the transfer of controlled foreign corporation stock or other assets by a U.S. corporation as part of the inversion transaction or after such transaction to a related foreign person is taxable, without offset by any tax attributes (e.g., net operating losses or foreign tax credits). To the extent provided in regulations, this rule will not apply to certain transfers of inventory and similar transactions conducted in the ordinary course of the taxpayer's business.

The 20-percent penalty for negligence or disregard of rules or regulations, substantial understatement of income tax, and substantial valuation misstatement is increased to 30 percent with respect to taxpayers related to the inverted entity. In addition, the 40-percent penalty for gross valuation misstatement is increased to 50 percent with respect to such taxpayers.

The "earnings stripping" rules of section 163(j), which deny or defer deductions for certain interest paid to foreign related parties, are strengthened for inverted corporations. With respect to such corporations, the provision eliminates the debt-equity threshold generally applicable under section 163(j) and reduces the 50-percent thresholds for "excess interest expense" and "excess limitation" to 25 percent.

In cases in which a U.S. corporate group acquires subsidiaries or other assets from an unrelated inverted corporate group, the provisions described above generally do not apply to the acquiring U.S. corporate group or its related parties (including the newly acquired subsidiaries or assets) by reason of acquiring the subsidiaries or assets that were connected with the inversion transaction. The Treasury Secretary is given authority to issue regulations appropriate to carry out the purposes of this provision and to prevent its abuse.

Partnership transactions

Under the provision, both types of inversion transactions include certain partnership transactions. Specifically, both parts of the provision apply to transactions in which a foreign-incorporated entity acquires substantially all of the properties constituting a trade or business of a domestic partnership (whether or not publicly traded), if after the acquisition at least 80 percent (or more than 50 percent but less than 80 percent, as the case may be) of the stock of the entity is held by former partners of the partnership (by reason of holding their partnership interests), and the "substantial business activities" test is not met. For purposes of determining whether these tests are met, all partnerships that are under common control within the meaning of section 482 are treated as one partnership, except as provided otherwise in regulations. In addition, the modified "toll charge" provisions apply at the partner level.

Effective Date

The regime applicable to transactions involving at least 80 percent identity of ownership applies to inversion transactions completed after March 20, 2002. The rules for inversion transactions involving greater-than-50-percent identity of ownership apply to inversion transactions completed after 1996 that meet the 50-percent test and to inversion transactions completed after 1996 that would have met the 80-percent test but for the March 20, 2002 date.

Conference Agreement

The conference agreement follows the House bill and Senate amendment with modifications.

In general

The provision defines two different types of corporate inversion transactions and establishes a different set of consequences for each type. Certain partnership transactions also are covered.

Transactions involving at least 80 percent identity of stock ownership

The first type of inversion is a transaction in which, pursuant to a plan[431] or a series of related transactions: (1) a U.S. corporation becomes a subsidiary of a foreign-incorporated entity or otherwise transfers substantially all of its properties to such an entity in a transaction completed after March 4, 2003; (2) the former shareholders of the U.S. corporation hold (by reason of holding stock in the U.S. corporation) 80 percent or more (by vote or value) of the stock of the foreign-incorporated entity after the transaction; and (3) the foreign-incorporated entity, considered together with all companies connected to it by a chain of greater than 50 percent ownership (i.e., the "expanded affiliated group"), does not have substantial business activities in the entity's country of incorporation, compared to the total worldwide business activities of the expanded affiliated group. The provision denies the intended tax benefits of this type of inversion by deeming the top-tier foreign corporation to be a domestic corporation for all purposes of the Code.[432]

In determining whether a transaction meets the definition of an inversion under the proposal, stock held by members of the expanded affiliated group that includes the foreign incorporated entity is disregarded. For example, if the former top-tier U.S. corporation receives stock of the foreign incorporated entity (e.g., so-called "hook" stock), the stock would not be considered in determining whether the transaction meets the definition. Similarly, if a U.S. parent corporation converts an existing wholly owned U.S. subsidiary into a new wholly owned controlled foreign corporation, the stock of the new foreign corporation would be disregarded. Stock sold in a public offering related to the transaction also is disregarded for these purposes.

Transfers of properties or liabilities as part of a plan a principal purpose of which is to avoid the purposes of the proposal are disregarded. In addition, the Treasury Secretary is granted authority to prevent the avoidance of the purposes of the proposal, including avoidance through the use of related persons, pass-through or other noncorporate entities, or other intermediaries, and through transactions designed to qualify or disqualify a person as a related person or a member of an expanded affiliated group. Similarly, the Treasury Secretary is granted authority to treat certain non-stock instruments as stock, and certain stock as not stock, where necessary to carry out the purposes of the proposal.

Transactions involving at least 60 percent but less than 80 percent identity of stock ownership

The second type of inversion is a transaction that would meet the definition of an inversion transaction described above, except that the 80-percent ownership threshold is not met. In such a case, if at least a 60-percent ownership threshold is met, then a second set of rules applies to the inversion. Under these rules, the inversion transaction is respected (i.e., the foreign corporation is treated as foreign), but any applicable corporate-level "toll charges" for establishing the inverted structure are not offset by tax attributes such as net operating losses or foreign tax credits. Specifically, any applicable corporate-level income or gain required to be recognized under sections 304, 311(b), 367, 1001, 1248, or any other provision with respect to the transfer of controlled foreign corporation stock or the transfer or license of other assets by a U.S. corporation as part of the inversion transaction or after such transaction to a related foreign person is taxable, without offset by any tax attributes (e.g., net operating losses or foreign tax credits). This rule does not apply to certain transfers of inventory and similar property. These measures generally apply for a 10-year period following the inversion transaction.

Under the proposal, inversion transactions include certain partnership transactions. Specifically, the proposal applies to transactions in which a foreign-incorporated entity acquires substantially all of the properties constituting a trade or business of a domestic partnership, if after the acquisition at least 60 percent of the stock of the entity is held by former partners of

---

[431] Acquisitions with respect to a domestic corporation or partnership are deemed to be "pursuant to a plan" if they occur within the four-year period beginning on the date which is two years before the ownership threshold under the provision is met with respect to such corporation or partnership.

[432] Since the top-tier foreign corporation is treated for all purposes of the Code as domestic, the shareholder-level "toll charge" of sec. 367(a) does not apply to these inversion transactions.

the partnership (by reason of holding their partnership interests), provided that the other terms of the basic definition are met. For purposes of applying this test, all partnerships that are under common control within the meaning of section 482 are treated as one partnership, except as provided otherwise in regulations. In addition, the modified "toll charge" proposals apply at the partner level.

A transaction otherwise meeting the definition of an inversion transaction is not treated as an inversion transaction if, on or before March 4, 2003, the foreign-incorporated entity had acquired directly or indirectly more than half of the properties held directly or indirectly by the domestic corporation, or more than half of the properties constituting the partnership trade or business, as the case may be.

Effective Date

The provision applies to taxable years ending after March 4, 2003.

[Law at ¶ 6375. CCH Explanation at ¶ 506.]

[¶ 10,980] Act Sec. 802. Excise tax on stock compensation of insiders in expatriated corporations

House Committee Report (H.R. REP. NO. 108-548, pt. 1)

[Code Secs. 162(m), 275(a) and New Code Sec. 4985]

Present Law

The income taxation of a nonstatutory[204] compensatory stock option is determined under the rules that apply to property transferred in connection with the performance of services (sec. 83). If a nonstatutory stock option does not have a readily ascertainable fair market value at the time of grant, which is generally the case unless the option is actively traded on an established market, no amount is included in the gross income of the recipient with respect to the option until the recipient exercises the option.[205] Upon exercise of such an option, the excess of the fair market value of the stock purchased over the option price is generally included in the recipient's gross income as ordinary income in such taxable year.[206]

The tax treatment of other forms of stock-based compensation (e.g., restricted stock and stock appreciation rights) is also determined under section 83. The excess of the fair market value over the amount paid (if any) for such property is generally includable in gross income in the first taxable year in which the rights to the property are transferable or are not subject to substantial risk of forfeiture.

Shareholders are generally required to recognize gain upon stock inversion transactions. An inversion transaction is generally not a taxable event for holders of stock options and other stock-based compensation.

Reasons for Change

The Committee believes that certain inversion transactions are a means of avoiding U.S. tax and should be curtailed. The Committee is concerned that, while shareholders are generally required to recognize gain upon stock inversion transactions, executives holding stock options and certain stock-based compensation are not taxed upon such transactions. Since such executives are often instrumental in deciding whether to engage in inversion transactions, the Committee believes that, upon certain inversion transactions, it is appropriate to impose an excise tax on certain executives holding stock options and stock-based compensation. Because shareholders are taxed at the capital gains rate upon inversion transactions, the Committee believes that it is appropriate to impose the excise tax at an equivalent rate.

Explanation of Provision

Under the provision, specified holders of stock options and other stock-based compensation are subject to an excise tax upon certain inversion transactions. The provision imposes a 15-percent excise tax on the value of specified stock compensation held (directly or indirectly) by or for the benefit of a disqualified individual, or a member of such individual's family, at any time during the 12-month period beginning six

---

[204] Nonstatutory stock options refer to stock options other than incentive stock options and employee stock purchase plans, the taxation of which is determined under sections 421-424.

[205] If an individual receives a grant of a nonstatutory option that has a readily ascertainable fair market value at the time the option is granted, the excess of the fair market value of the option over the amount paid for the option is included in the recipient's gross income as ordinary income in the first taxable year in which the option is either transferable or not subject to a substantial risk of forfeiture.

[206] Under section 83, such amount is includable in gross income in the first taxable year in which the rights to the stock are transferable or are not subject to substantial risk of forfeiture.

months before the corporation's expatriation date. Specified stock compensation is treated as held for the benefit of a disqualified individual if such compensation is held by an entity, e.g., a partnership or trust, in which the individual, or a member of the individual's family, has an ownership interest.

A disqualified individual is any individual who, with respect to a corporation, is, at any time during the 12-month period beginning on the date which is six months before the expatriation date, subject to the requirements of section 16(a) of the Securities and Exchange Act of 1934 with respect to the corporation, or any member of the corporation's expanded affiliated group,[207] or would be subject to such requirements if the corporation (or member) were an issuer of equity securities referred to in section 16(a). Disqualified individuals generally include officers (as defined by section 16(a)),[208] directors, and 10-percent-or-greater owners of private and publicly-held corporations.

The excise tax is imposed on a disqualified individual of an expatriated corporation (as previously defined in the bill) only if gain (if any) is recognized in whole or part by any shareholder by reason of a corporate inversion transaction previously defined in the bill.

Specified stock compensation subject to the excise tax includes any payment[209] (or right to payment) granted by the expatriated corporation (or any member of the corporation's expanded affiliated group) to any person in connection with the performance of services by a disqualified individual for such corporation (or member of the corporation's expanded affiliated group) if the value of the payment or right is based on, or determined by reference to, the value or change in value of stock of such corporation (or any member of the corporation's expanded affiliated group). In determining whether such compensation exists and valuing such compensation, all restrictions, other than a non-lapse restriction, are ignored. Thus, the excise tax applies, and the value subject to the tax is determined, without regard to whether such specified stock compensation is subject to a substantial risk of forfeiture or is exercisable at the time of the inversion transaction. Specified stock compensation includes compensatory stock and restricted stock grants, compensatory stock options, and other forms of stock-based compensation, including stock appreciation rights, phantom stock, and phantom stock options. Specified stock compensation also includes nonqualified deferred compensation that is treated as though it were invested in stock or stock options of the expatriating corporation (or member). For example, the provision applies to a disqualified individual's deferred compensation if company stock is one of the actual or deemed investment options under the nonqualified deferred compensation plan.

Specified stock compensation includes a compensation arrangement that gives the disqualified individual an economic stake substantially similar to that of a corporate shareholder. Thus, the excise tax does not apply if a payment is simply triggered by a target value of the corporation's stock or where a payment depends on a performance measure other than the value of the corporation's stock. Similarly, the tax does not apply if the amount of the payment is not directly measured by the value of the stock or an increase in the value of the stock. For example, an arrangement under which a disqualified individual would be paid a cash bonus of $500,000 if the corporation's stock increased in value by 25 percent over two years or $1,000,000 if the stock increased by 33 percent over two years is not specified stock compensation, even though the amount of the bonus generally is keyed to an increase in the value of the stock. By contrast, an arrangement under which a disqualified individual would be paid a cash bonus equal to $10,000 for every $1 increase in the share price of the corporation's stock is subject to the provision because the direct connection between the compensation amount and the value of the corporation's stock gives the disqualified individual an economic stake substantially similar to that of a shareholder.

The excise tax applies to any such specified stock compensation previously granted to a disqualified individual but cancelled or cashed-out within the six-month period ending with the expatriation date, and to any specified stock compensation awarded in the six-month period beginning with the expatriation date. As a result, for example, if a corporation cancels outstanding options three months before the transaction and then reissues comparable options three months after the transaction, the tax applies both to the cancelled options and the newly granted op-

---

[207] An expanded affiliated group is an affiliated group (under section 1504) except that such group is determined without regard to the exceptions for certain corporations and is determined applying a greater than 50 percent threshold, in lieu of the 80 percent test.

[208] An officer is defined as the president, principal financial officer, principal accounting officer (or, if there is no such accounting officer, the controller), any vice-president in charge of a principal business unit, division or function (such as sales, administration or finance), any other officer who performs a policy-making function, or any other person who performs similar policymaking functions.

[209] Under the provision, any transfer of property is treated as a payment and any right to a transfer of property is treated as a right to a payment.

tions. It is intended that the Secretary issue guidance to avoid double counting with respect to specified stock compensation that is cancelled and then regranted during the applicable twelve-month period.

Specified stock compensation subject to the tax does not include a statutory stock option or any payment or right from a qualified retirement plan or annuity, tax-sheltered annuity, simplified employee pension, or SIMPLE. In addition, under the provision, the excise tax does not apply to any stock option that is exercised during the six-month period before the expatriation date or to any stock acquired pursuant to such exercise, if income is recognized under section 83 on or before the expatriation date with respect to the stock acquired pursuant to such exercise. The excise tax also does not apply to any specified stock compensation that is exercised, sold, exchanged, distributed, cashed-out, or otherwise paid during such period in a transaction in which income, gain, or loss is recognized in full.

For specified stock compensation held on the expatriation date, the amount of the tax is determined based on the value of the compensation on such date. The tax imposed on specified stock compensation cancelled during the six-month period before the expatriation date is determined based on the value of the compensation on the day before such cancellation, while specified stock compensation granted after the expatriation date is valued on the date granted. Under the provision, the cancellation of a non-lapse restriction is treated as a grant.

The value of the specified stock compensation on which the excise tax is imposed is the fair value in the case of stock options (including warrants or other similar rights to acquire stock) and stock appreciation rights and the fair market value for all other forms of compensation. For purposes of the tax, the fair value of an option (or a warrant or other similar right to acquire stock) or a stock appreciation right is determined using an appropriate option-pricing model, as specified or permitted by the Secretary, that takes into account the stock price at the valuation date; the exercise price under the option; the remaining term of the option; the volatility of the underlying stock and the expected dividends on it; and the risk-free interest rate over the remaining term of the option. Options that have no intrinsic value (or "spread") because the exercise price under the option equals or exceeds the fair market value of the stock at valuation nevertheless have a fair value and are subject to tax under the provision. The value of other forms of compensation, such as phantom stock or restricted stock, is the fair market value of the stock as of the date of the expatriation transaction. The value of any deferred compensation that can be valued by reference to stock is the amount that

the disqualified individual would receive if the plan were to distribute all such deferred compensation in a single sum on the date of the expatriation transaction (or the date of cancellation or grant, if applicable). It is expected that the Secretary issue guidance on valuation of specified stock compensation, including guidance similar to the revenue procedures issued under section 280G, except that the guidance would not permit the use of a term other than the full remaining term and would be modified as necessary or appropriate to carry out the purposes of the provision. Pending the issuance of guidance, it is intended that taxpayers can rely on the revenue procedure issued under section 280G (except that the full remaining term must be used and recalculation is not permitted).

The excise tax also applies to any payment by the expatriated corporation or any member of the expanded affiliated group made to an individual, directly or indirectly, in respect of the tax. Whether a payment is made in respect of the tax is determined under all of the facts and circumstances. Any payment made to keep the individual in the same after-tax position that the individual would have been in had the tax not applied is a payment made in respect of the tax. This includes direct payments of the tax and payments to reimburse the individual for payment of the tax. It is expected that the Secretary issue guidance on determining when a payment is made in respect of the tax and that such guidance include certain factors that give rise to a rebuttable presumption that a payment is made in respect of the tax, including a rebuttable presumption that if the payment is contingent on the inversion transaction, it is made in respect to the tax. Any payment made in respect of the tax is includible in the income of the individual, but is not deductible by the corporation.

To the extent that a disqualified individual is also a covered employee under section 162(m), the $1,000,000 limit on the deduction allowed for employee remuneration for such employee is reduced by the amount of any payment (including reimbursements) made in respect of the tax under the provision. As discussed above, this includes direct payments of the tax and payments to reimburse the individual for payment of the tax.

The payment of the excise tax has no effect on the subsequent tax treatment of any specified stock compensation. Thus, the payment of the tax has no effect on the individual's basis in any specified stock compensation and no effect on the tax treatment for the individual at the time of exercise of an option or payment of any specified stock compensation, or at the time of any lapse or forfeiture of such specified stock compensation. The payment of the tax is not deductible and has no effect on any deduction that might be allowed at the time of any future exercise or payment.

Under the provision, the Secretary is authorized to issue regulations as may be necessary or appropriate to carry out the purposes of the provision.

Effective Date

The provision is effective as of March 4, 2003, except that periods before March 4, 2003,

are not taken into account in applying the excise tax to specified stock compensation held or cancelled during the six-month period before the expatriation date.

Conference Committee Report (H.R. CONF. REP. NO. 108-755)

House Bill

* * *

Specified stock compensation

* * *

Specified stock compensation includes a compensation arrangement that gives the disqualified individual an economic stake substantially similar to that of a corporate shareholder. A payment directly tied to the value of the stock is specified stock compensation. The excise tax does not apply if a payment is simply triggered by a target value of the corporation's stock or where a payment depends on a performance measure other than the value of the corporation's stock. Similarly, the tax does not apply if the amount of the payment is not directly measured by the value of the stock or an increase in the value of the stock. For example, an arrangement under which a disqualified individual would be paid a cash bonus equal to $10,000 for every $1 increase in the share price of the corporation's stock is subject to the provision because the direct connection between the compensation

amount and the value of the corporation's stock gives the disqualified individual an economic stake substantially similar to that of a shareholder. By contrast, an arrangement under which a disqualified individual would be paid a cash bonus of $500,000 if the corporation's stock increased in value by 25 percent over two years or $1,000,000 if the stock increased by 33 percent over two years is not specified stock compensation, even though the amount of the bonus generally is keyed to an increase in the value of the stock.

* * *

Conference Agreement

The conference agreement follows the House bill except that the excise tax is imposed at a rate equal to the maximum rate of tax on the adjusted net capital gain of an individual (i.e., the rate of the excise tax would be 15 percent for 2005 through 2008 and 20 percent for taxable years beginning after December 31, 2008).

[Law at ¶5160, ¶5285, ¶5960 and ¶6105. CCH Explanation at ¶508.]

[¶10,990] Act Sec. 803. Reinsurance of U.S. risks in foreign jurisdictions

House Committee Report (H.R. REP. NO. 108-548, pt. 1)

[Code Sec. 845(a)]

Present Law

In the case of a reinsurance agreement between two or more related persons, present law provides the Treasury Secretary with authority to allocate among the parties or recharacterize income (whether investment income, premium or otherwise), deductions, assets, reserves, credits and any other items related to the reinsurance agreement, or make any other adjustment, in

order to reflect the proper source and character of the items for each party.[210] For this purpose, related persons are defined as in section 482. Thus, persons are related if they are organizations, trades or businesses (whether or not incorporated, whether or not organized in the United States, and whether or not affiliated) that are owned or controlled directly or indirectly by the same interests. The provision may apply to a contract even if one of the related parties is not a

---

[210] Sec. 845(a).

domestic company.[211] In addition, the provision also permits such allocation, recharacterization, or other adjustments in a case in which one of the parties to a reinsurance agreement is, with respect to any contract covered by the agreement, in effect an agent of another party to the agreement, or a conduit between related persons.

Reasons for Change

The Committee is concerned that reinsurance transactions are being used to allocate income, deductions, or other items inappropriately among U.S. and foreign related persons. The Committee is concerned that foreign related party reinsurance arrangements may be a technique for eroding the U.S. tax base. The Committee believes that the provision of present law permitting the Treasury Secretary to allocate or recharacterize items related to a reinsurance agreement should be applied to prevent misallocation, improper characterization, or to make any other adjustment in the case of such reinsurance transactions between U.S. and foreign related persons (or agents or conduits). The Committee also wishes to clarify that, in applying the authority with respect to reinsurance agreements, the amount, source or character of the items may be allocated, recharacterized or adjusted.

Explanation of Provision

The bill clarifies the rules of section 845, relating to authority for the Treasury Secretary to allocate items among the parties to a reinsurance agreement, recharacterize items, or make any other adjustment, in order to reflect the proper source and character of the items for each party. The bill authorizes such allocation, recharacterization, or other adjustment, in order to reflect the proper source, character or amount of the item. It is intended that this authority[212] be exercised in a manner similar to the authority under section 482 for the Treasury Secretary to make adjustments between related parties. It is intended that this authority be applied in situations in which the related persons (or agents or conduits) are engaged in cross-border transactions that require allocation, recharacterization, or other adjustments in order to reflect the proper source, character or amount of the item or items. No inference is intended that present law does not provide this authority with respect to reinsurance agreements.

No regulations have been issued under section 845(a). It is expected that the Treasury Secretary will issue regulations under section 845(a) to address effectively the allocation of income (whether investment income, premium or otherwise) and other items, the recharacterization of such items, or any other adjustment necessary to reflect the proper amount, source or character of the item.

Effective Date

The provision is effective for any risk reinsured after the date of enactment of the provision.

Conference Committee Report (H.R. CONF. REP. NO. 108-755)

Senate Amendment

[Law at ¶ 5540. CCH Explanation at ¶ 515.]

The Senate amendment is the same as the House bill.

Conference Agreement

The Conference agreement follows the House bill.

---

[211] See S. Rep. No. 97-494, 97th Cong., 2d Sess., 337 (1982) (describing provisions relating to the repeal of modified coinsurance provisions).

[212] The authority to allocate, recharacterize or make other adjustments was granted in connection with the repeal of provisions relating to modified coinsurance transactions.

[¶ 11,000] Act Sec. 804. Revision of tax rules on expatriation of individuals

House Committee Report (H.R. Rep. No. 108-548, pt. 1)

[Code Secs. 877, 2107, 2501, 6039G and 7701

Present Law

In general

U.S. citizens and residents generally are subject to U.S income taxation on their worldwide income. The U.S. tax may be reduced or offset by a credit allowed for foreign income taxes paid with respect to foreign source income. Nonresident aliens are taxed at a flat rate of 30 percent (or a lower treaty rate) on certain types of passive income derived from U.S. sources, and at regular graduated rates on net profits derived from a U.S. trade or business. The estates of nonresident aliens generally are subject to estate tax on U.S.-situated property (e.g., real estate and tangible property located within the United States and stock in a U.S. corporation). Nonresident aliens generally are subject to gift tax on transfers by gift of U.S.-situated property (e.g., real estate and tangible property located within the United States, but excluding intangibles, such as stock, regardless of where they are located).

Income tax rules with respect to expatriates

For the 10 taxable years after an individual relinquishes his or her U.S. citizenship or terminates his or her U.S. residency[213] with a principal purpose of avoiding U.S. taxes, the individual is subject to an alternative method of income taxation than that generally applicable to nonresident aliens (the "alternative tax regime"). Generally, the individual is subject to income tax only on U.S.-source income[214] at the rates applicable to U.S. citizens for the 10-year period.

An individual who relinquishes citizenship or terminates residency is treated as having done so with a principal purpose of tax avoidance and is generally subject to the alternative tax regime if: (1) the individual's average annual U.S. Federal income tax liability for the five taxable years preceding citizenship relinquishment or residency termination exceeds $100,000; or (2) the individual's net worth on the date of citizenship

relinquishment or residency termination equals or exceeds $500,000. These amounts are adjusted annually for inflation.[215] Certain categories of individuals (e.g., dual residents) may avoid being deemed to have a tax avoidance purpose for relinquishing citizenship or terminating residency by submitting a ruling request to the IRS regarding whether the individual relinquished citizenship or terminated residency principally for tax reasons.

Anti-abuse rules are provided to prevent the circumvention of the alternative tax regime.

Estate tax rules with respect to expatriates

Special estate tax rules apply to individuals who relinquish their citizenship or long-term residency within the 10 years prior to the date of death, unless he or she did not have a tax avoidance purpose (as determined under the test above). Under these special rules, certain closely-held foreign stock owned by the former citizen or former long-term resident is includible in his or her gross estate to the extent that the foreign corporation owns U.S.-situated assets.

Gift tax rules with respect to expatriates

Special gift tax rules apply to individuals who relinquish their citizenship or long-term residency within the 10 years prior to the date of death, unless he or she did not have a tax avoidance purpose (as determined under the rules above). The individual is subject to gift tax on gifts of U.S.-situated intangibles made during the 10 years following citizenship relinquishment or residency termination.

Information reporting

Under present law, U.S. citizens who relinquish citizenship and long-term residents who terminate residency generally are required to provide information about their assets held at the time of expatriation. However, this information is only required once.

Reasons for Change

The Committee believes there are several difficulties in administering the present-law al-

---

[213] Under present law, an individual's U.S. residency is considered terminated for U.S. Federal tax purposes when the individual ceases to be a lawful permanent resident under the immigration law (or is treated as a resident of another country under a tax treaty and does not waive the benefits of such treaty).

[214] For this purpose, however, U.S.-source income has a broader scope than it does typically in the Code.

[215] The income tax liability and net worth thresholds under section 877(a)(2) for 2004 are $124,000 and $622,000, respectively. See Rev. Proc. 2003-85, 2003-49 I.R.B. 1184.

ternative tax regime. One such difficulty is that the IRS is required to determine the subjective intent of taxpayers who relinquish citizenship or terminate residency. The present-law presumption of a tax-avoidance purpose in cases in which objective income tax liability or net worth thresholds are exceeded mitigates this problem to some extent. However, the present-law rules still require the IRS to make subjective determinations of intent in cases involving taxpayers who fall below these thresholds, as well for certain taxpayers who exceed these thresholds but are nevertheless allowed to seek a ruling from the IRS to the effect that they did not have a principal purpose of tax avoidance. The Committee believes that the replacement of the subjective determination of tax avoidance as a principal purpose for citizenship relinquishment or residency termination with objective rules will result in easier administration of the tax regime for individuals who relinquish their citizenship or terminate residency.

Similarly, present-law information-reporting and return-filing provisions do not provide the IRS with the information necessary to administer the alternative tax regime. Although individuals are required to file tax information statements upon the relinquishment of their citizenship or termination of their residency, difficulties have been encountered in enforcing this requirement. The Committee believes that the tax benefits of citizenship relinquishment or residency termination should be denied an individual until he or she provides the information necessary for the IRS to enforce the alternative tax regime. The Committee also believes an annual report requirement and a penalty for the failure to comply with such requirement are needed to provide the IRS with sufficient information to monitor the compliance of former U.S. citizens and long-term residents.

Individuals who relinquish citizenship or terminate residency for tax reasons often do not want to fully sever their ties with the United States; they hope to retain some of the benefits of citizenship or residency without being subject to the U.S. tax system as a U.S. citizen or resident. These individuals generally may continue to spend significant amounts of time in the United States following citizenship relinquishment or residency termination—approximately four months every year—without being treated as a U.S. resident. The Committee believes that provisions in the bill that impose full U.S. taxation if the individual is present in the United States for more than 30 days in a calendar year will substantially reduce the incentives to relinquish citi-

zenship or terminate residency for individuals who desire to maintain significant ties to the United States.

With respect to the estate and gift tax rules, the Committee is concerned that present-law does not adequately address opportunities for the avoidance of tax on the value of assets held by a foreign corporation whose stock the individual transfers. Thus, the provision imposes gift tax under the alternative tax regime in the case of gifts of certain stock of a closely held foreign corporation.

Explanation of Provision

In general

The bill provides: (1) objective standards for determining whether former citizens or former long-term residents are subject to the alternative tax regime; (2) tax-based (instead of immigration-based) rules for determining when an individual is no longer a U.S. citizen or long-term resident for U.S. Federal tax purposes; (3) the imposition of full U.S. taxation for individuals who are subject to the alternative tax regime and who return to the United States for extended periods; (4) imposition of U.S. gift tax on gifts of stock of certain closely-held foreign corporations that hold U.S.-situated property; and (5) an annual return-filing requirement for individuals who are subject to the alternative tax regime, for each of the 10 years following citizenship relinquishment or residency termination.[216]

Objective rules for the alternative tax regime

The bill replaces the subjective determination of tax avoidance as a principal purpose for citizenship relinquishment or residency termination under present law with objective rules. Under the bill, a former citizen or former long-term resident would be subject to the alternative tax regime for a 10-year period following citizenship relinquishment or residency termination, unless the former citizen or former long-term resident: (1) establishes that his or her average annual net income tax liability for the five preceding years does not exceed $124,000 (adjusted for inflation after 2004) and his or her net worth does not exceed $2 million, or alternatively satisfies limited, objective exceptions for dual citizens and minors who have had no substantial contact with the United States; and (2) certifies under penalties of perjury that he or she has complied with all U.S. Federal tax obligations for the preceding five years and provides such evidence of

---

[216] These provisions reflect recommendations contained in Joint Committee on Taxation, Review of the Present Law Tax and Immigration Treatment of Relinquishment of Citi-

zenship and Termination of Long-Term Residency, (JCS-2-03), February 2003.

compliance as the Secretary of the Treasury may require.

The monetary thresholds under the bill replace the present-law inquiry into the taxpayer's intent. In addition, the bill eliminates the present-law process of IRS ruling requests.

If a former citizen exceeds the monetary thresholds, that person is excluded from the alternative tax regime if he or she falls within the exceptions for certain dual citizens and minors (provided that the requirement of certification and proof of compliance with Federal tax obligations is met). These exceptions provide relief to individuals who have never had substantial connections with the United States, as measured by certain objective criteria, and eliminate IRS inquiries as to the subjective intent of such taxpayers.

In order to be excepted from the application of the alternative tax regime under the bill, whether by reason of falling below the net worth and income tax liability thresholds or qualifying for the dual-citizen or minor exceptions, the former citizen or former long-term resident also is required to certify, under penalties of perjury, that he or she has complied with all U.S. Federal tax obligations for the five years preceding the relinquishment of citizenship or termination of residency and to provide such documentation as the Secretary of the Treasury may require evidencing such compliance (*e.g.*, tax returns, proof of tax payments). Until such time, the individual remains subject to the alternative tax regime. It is intended that the IRS will continue to verify that the information submitted was accurate, and it is intended that the IRS will randomly audit such persons to assess compliance.

Termination of U.S. citizenship or long-term resident status for U.S. Federal income tax purposes

Under the bill, an individual continues to be treated as a U.S. citizen or long-term resident for U.S. Federal tax purposes, including for purposes of section 7701(b)(10), until the individual: (1) gives notice of an expatriating act or termination of residency (with the requisite intent to relinquish citizenship or terminate residency) to the Secretary of State or the Secretary of Home-

land Security, respectively; and (2) provides a statement in accordance with section 6039G.

Sanction for individuals subject to the individual tax regime who return to the United States for extended periods

The alternative tax regime does not apply to any individual for any taxable year during the 10-year period following citizenship relinquishment or residency termination if such individual is present in the United States for more than 30 days in the calendar year ending in such taxable year. Such individual is treated as a U.S. citizen or resident for such taxable year and therefore is taxed on his or her worldwide income.

Similarly, if an individual subject to the alternative tax regime is present in the United States for more than 30 days in any calendar year ending during the 10-year period following citizenship relinquishment or residency termination, and the individual dies during that year, he or she is treated as a U.S. resident, and the individual's worldwide estate is subject to U.S. estate tax. Likewise, if an individual subject to the alternative tax regime is present in the United States for more than 30 days in any year during the 10-year period following citizenship relinquishment or residency termination, the individual is subject to U.S. gift tax on any transfer of his or her worldwide assets by gift during that taxable year.

For purposes of these rules, an individual is treated as present in the United States on any day if such individual is physically present in the United States at any time during that day. The present-law exceptions from being treated as present in the United States for residency purposes[217] generally do not apply for this purpose. However, for individuals with certain ties to countries other than the United States[218] and individuals with minimal prior physical presence in the United States,[219] a day of physical presence in the United States is disregarded if the individual is performing services in the United States on such day for an unrelated employer (within the meaning of sections 267 and 707(b)), who meets the requirements the Secretary of the Treasury may prescribe in regulations.

---

[217] Secs. 7701(b)(3)(D), 7701(b)(5) and 7701(b)(7)(B)-(D).

[218] An individual has such a relationship to a foreign country if the individual becomes a citizen or resident of the country in which (1) the individual becomes fully liable for income tax or (2) the individual was born, such individual's spouse was born, or either of the individual's parents was born.

[219] An individual has a minimal prior physical presence in the United States if the individual was physically present for no more than 30 days during each year in the ten-year

period ending on the date of loss of United States citizenship or termination of residency. However, an individual is not treated as being present in the United States on a day if (1) the individual is a teacher or trainee, a student, a professional athlete in certain circumstances, or a foreign government-related individual or (2) the individual remained in the United States because of a medical condition that arose while the individual was in the United States. Sec. 7701(b)(3)(D)(ii).

No more than 30 days may be disregarded during any calendar year under this rule.

Imposition of gift tax with respect to stock of certain closely held foreign corporations

Gifts of stock of certain closely-held foreign corporations by a former citizen or former long-term resident who is subject to the alternative tax regime are subject to gift tax under this bill, if the gift is made within the 10-year period after citizenship relinquishment or residency termination. The gift tax rule applies if: (1) the former citizen or former long-term resident, before making the gift, directly or indirectly owns 10 percent or more of the total combined voting power of all classes of stock entitled to vote of the foreign corporation; and (2) directly or indirectly, is considered to own more than 50 percent of (a) the total combined voting power of all classes of stock entitled to vote in the foreign corporation, or (b) the total value of the stock of such corporation. If this stock ownership test is met, then taxable gifts of the former citizen or former long-term resident include that proportion of the fair market value of the foreign stock transferred by the individual, at the time of the gift, which the fair market value of any assets owned by such foreign corporation and situated in the United States (at the time of the gift) bears to the total fair market value of all assets owned by such foreign corporation (at the time of the gift).

This gift tax rule applies to a former citizen or former long-term resident who is subject to the alternative tax regime and who owns stock in a foreign corporation at the time of the gift, regardless of how such stock was acquired (e.g., whether issued originally to the donor, purchased, or received as a gift or bequest).

Annual return

The bill requires former citizens and former long-term residents to file an annual return for each year following citizenship relinquishment or residency termination in which they are subject to the alternative tax regime. The annual return is required even if no U.S. Federal income tax is due. The annual return requires certain information, including information on the permanent home of the individual, the individual's country of residence, the number of days the individual was present in the United States for the year, and detailed information about the individual's income and assets that are subject to the alternative tax regime. This requirement includes information relating to foreign stock potentially subject to the special estate tax rule of section 2107(b) and the gift tax rules of this bill.

If the individual fails to file the statement in a timely manner or fails correctly to include all the required information, the individual is required to pay a penalty of $5,000. The $5,000 penalty does not apply if it is shown that the failure is due to reasonable cause and not to willful neglect.

Effective Date

The provision applies to individuals who relinquish citizenship or terminate long-term residency after June 3, 2004.

Conference Committee Report (H.R. CONF. REP. NO. 108-755)

Conference Agreement

The conference agreement follows the House bill.

[Law at ¶ 5615, ¶ 5950, ¶ 5955, ¶ 6135 and ¶ 6355. CCH Explanation at ¶ 502 and ¶ 504.]

[¶ 11,010] Act Sec. 805. Reporting of taxable mergers and acquisitions

House Committee Report (H.R. REP. NO. 108-548, pt. 1)

[New Code Sec. 6043A]

Present Law

Under section 6045 and the regulations thereunder, brokers (defined to include stock transfer agents) are required to make information returns and to provide corresponding payee statements as to sales made on behalf of their customers, subject to the penalty provisions of sections 6721-6724. Under the regulations issued under section 6045, this requirement generally does not apply with respect to taxable transactions other than exchanges for cash (e.g., stock inversion transactions taxable to shareholders by reason of section 367(a)).[220]

---

[220] Recently issued temporary regulations under section 6043 (relating to information reporting with respect to liquidations, recapitalizations, and changes in control) impose information reporting requirements with respect to certain taxable inversion transactions, and proposed regulations would expand these requirements more generally to taxable transactions occurring after the proposed regulations are finalized.

Reasons for Change

The Committee believes that administration of the tax laws would be improved by greater information reporting with respect to taxable non-cash transactions, and that the Treasury Secretary's authority to require such enhanced reporting should be made explicit in the Code.

Explanation of Provision

Under the bill, if gain or loss is recognized in whole or in part by shareholders of a corporation by reason of a second corporation's acquisition of the stock or assets of the first corporation, then the acquiring corporation (or the acquired corporation, if so prescribed by the Treasury Secretary) is required to make a return containing:

(1) A description of the transaction;

(2) The name and address of each shareholder of the acquired corporation that recognizes gain as a result of the transaction (or would recognize gain, if there was a built-in gain on the shareholder's shares);

(3) The amount of money and the value of stock or other consideration paid to each shareholder described above; and

(4) Such other information as the Treasury Secretary may prescribe.

Alternatively, a stock transfer agent who records transfers of stock in such transaction may make the return described above in lieu of the second corporation.

In addition, every person required to make a return described above is required to furnish to each shareholder (or the shareholder's nominee[221]) whose name is required to be set forth in such return a written statement showing:

(1) The name, address, and phone number of the information contact of the person required to make such return;

(2) The information required to be shown on that return; and

(3) Such other information as the Treasury Secretary may prescribe.

This written statement is required to be furnished to the shareholder on or before January 31 of the year following the calendar year during which the transaction occurred.

The present-law penalties for failure to comply with information reporting requirements are extended to failures to comply with the requirements set forth under this bill.

Effective Date

The provision is effective for acquisitions after the date of enactment.

Conference Committee Report (H.R. CONF. REP. NO. 108-755)

Senate Amendment

Same as the House bill.

Conference Agreement

The conference agreement follows both the House bill and the Senate amendment.

[Law at ¶6145 and ¶6310. CCH Explanation at ¶510.]

[¶11,020] Act Sec. 806. Studies

House Committee Report (H.R. REP. NO. 108-548, pt. 1)

[Act Sec. 806]

Present Law

Due to the variation in tax rates and tax systems among countries, a multinational enterprise, whether U.S.-based or foreign-based, may have an incentive to shift income, deductions, or tax credits in order to arrive at a reduced overall tax burden. Such a shifting of items could be accomplished by establishing artificial, non-arm's-length prices for transactions between group members.

Under section 482, the Treasury Secretary is authorized to reallocate income, deductions, or credits between or among two or more organizations, trades, or businesses under common control if he determines that such a reallocation is necessary to prevent tax evasion or to clearly reflect income. Treasury regulations adopt the

---

[221] In the case of a nominee, the nominee must furnish the information to the shareholder in the manner prescribed by the Treasury Secretary.

arm's-length standard as the standard for determining whether such reallocations are appropriate. Thus, the regulations provide rules to identify the respective amounts of taxable income of the related parties that would have resulted if the parties had been uncontrolled parties dealing at arm's length. Transactions involving intangible property and certain services may present particular challenges to the administration of the arm's-length standard, because the nature of these transactions may make it difficult or impossible to compare them with third-party transactions.

In addition to the statutory rules governing the taxation of foreign income of U.S. persons and U.S. income of foreign persons, bilateral income tax treaties limit the amount of income tax that may be imposed by one treaty partner on residents of the other treaty partner. For example, treaties often reduce or eliminate withholding taxes imposed by a treaty country on certain types of income (e.g., dividends, interest and royalties) paid to residents of the other treaty country. Treaties also contain provisions governing the creditability of taxes imposed by the treaty country in which income was earned in computing the amount of tax owed to the other country by its residents with respect to such income. Treaties further provide procedures under which inconsistent positions taken by the treaty countries with respect to a single item of income or deduction may be mutually resolved by the two countries.

Reasons for Change

The Committee believes that it is important to evaluate the effectiveness of the current trans-

fer pricing rules and compliance efforts with respect to related-party transactions to ensure that income is not being shifted outside of the United States. The Committee also believes that it is necessary to review current U.S. income tax treaties to identify any inappropriate reductions in withholding tax rates that may create opportunities for shifting income outside the United States. In addition, the Committee believes that the impact of the provisions of this bill on inversion transactions should be studied.

Explanation of Provision

The bill requires the Treasury Secretary to conduct and submit to the Congress three studies. The first study will examine the effectiveness of the transfer pricing rules of section 482, with an emphasis on transactions involving intangible property. The second study will examine income tax treaties to which the United States is a party, with a view toward identifying any inappropriate reductions in withholding tax or opportunities for abuse that may exist. The third study will examine the impact of the provisions of this bill on inversion transactions.

Effective Date

The tax treaty study required under the provision is due no later than June 30, 2005. The transfer pricing study required under the provision is due no later than June 30, 2005. * * *

Conference Committee Report (H.R. CONF. REP. NO. 108-755)

Senate Amendment

No provision.

Conference Agreement

The conference agreement follows the House bill, except the inversions study required

under the provision is due no later than December 31, 2006.

[Law at ¶7090. CCH Explanation at ¶530.]

[¶11,030] Act Sec. 811. Penalty for failure to disclose reportable transactions

House Committee Report (H.R. REP. NO. 108-548, pt. 1)

[New Code Sec. 6707A]

Present Law

Regulations under section 6011 require a taxpayer to disclose with its tax return certain

information with respect to each "reportable transaction" in which the taxpayer participates.[222]

---

[222] On February 27, 2003, the Treasury Department and the IRS released final regulations regarding the disclosure of reportable transactions. In general, the regulations are effec-

tive for transactions entered into on or after February 28, 2003.

There are six categories of reportable transactions. The first category is any transaction that is the same as (or substantially similar to)[223] a transaction that is specified by the Treasury Department as a tax avoidance transaction whose tax benefits are subject to disallowance under present law (referred to as a "listed transaction").[224]

The second category is any transaction that is offered under conditions of confidentiality. In general, a transaction is considered to be offered to a taxpayer under conditions of confidentiality if the advisor who is paid a minimum fee places a limitation on disclosure by the taxpayer of the tax treatment or tax structure of the transaction and the limitation on disclosure protects the confidentiality of that advisor's tax strategies (irrespective if such terms are legally binding).[225]

The third category of reportable transactions is any transaction for which (1) the taxpayer has the right to a full or partial refund of fees if the intended tax consequences from the transaction are not sustained or, (2) the fees are contingent on the intended tax consequences from the transaction being sustained.[226]

The fourth category of reportable transactions relates to any transaction resulting in a taxpayer claiming a loss (under section 165) of at least (1) $10 million in any single year or $20 million in any combination of years by a corporate taxpayer or a partnership with only corporate partners; (2) $2 million in any single year or $4 million in any combination of years by all other partnerships, S corporations, trusts, and individuals; or (3) $50,000 in any single year for individuals or trusts if the loss arises with respect to foreign currency translation losses.[227]

The fifth category of reportable transactions refers to any transaction done by certain taxpayers[228] in which the tax treatment of the transaction differs (or is expected to differ) by more than $10 million from its treatment for book purposes (using generally accepted accounting principles) in any year.[229]

The final category of reportable transactions is any transaction that results in a tax credit exceeding $250,000 (including a foreign tax credit) if the taxpayer holds the underlying asset for less than 45 days.[230]

Under present law, there is no specific penalty for failing to disclose a reportable transaction; however, such a failure can jeopardize a taxpayer's ability to claim that any income tax understatement attributable to such undisclosed transaction is due to reasonable cause, and that the taxpayer acted in good faith.[231]

Reasons for Change

The Committee believes that the best way to combat tax shelters is to be aware of them. The Treasury Department, using the tools available, issued regulations requiring disclosure of certain transactions and requiring organizers and promoters of tax-engineered transactions to maintain customer lists and make these lists available to the IRS. Nevertheless, the Committee believes that additional legislation is needed to provide the Treasury Department with additional tools to assist its efforts to curtail abusive transactions. Moreover, the Committee believes that a penalty for failing to make the required disclosures, when the imposition of such penalty is not dependent on the tax treatment of the underlying transaction ultimately being sustained, will provide an additional incentive for taxpayers to satisfy their reporting obligations under the new disclosure provisions.

Explanation of Provision

In general

The provision creates a new penalty for any person who fails to include with any return or statement any required information with respect to a reportable transaction. The new penalty applies without regard to whether the transaction ultimately results in an understatement of tax, and applies in addition to any accuracy-related penalty that may be imposed.

(Footnote Continued)

The discussion of present law refers to the new regulations. The rules that apply with respect to transactions entered into on or before February 28, 2003, are contained in Treas. Reg. sec. 1.6011-4T in effect on the date the transaction was entered into.

[223] The regulations clarify that the term "substantially similar" includes any transaction that is expected to obtain the same or similar types of tax consequences and that is either factually similar or based on the same or similar tax strategy. Further, the term must be broadly construed in favor of disclosure. Treas. Reg. sec. 1.6011-4(c)(4).

[224] Treas. Reg. sec. 1.6011-4(b)(2).

[225] Treas. Reg. sec. 1.6011-4(b)(3).

[226] Treas. Reg. sec. 1.6011-4(b)(4).

[227] Treas. Reg. sec. 1.6011-4(b)(5). Rev. Proc. 2003-24, 2003-11 I.R.B. 599, exempts certain types of losses from this reportable transaction category.

[228] The significant book-tax category applies only to taxpayers that are reporting companies under the Securities Exchange Act of 1934 or business entities that have $250 million or more in gross assets.

[229] Treas. Reg. sec. 1.6011-4(b)(6). Rev. Proc. 2003-25, 2003-11 I.R.B. 601, exempts certain types of transactions from this reportable transaction category.

[230] Treas. Reg. sec. 1.6011-4(b)(7).

[231] Section 6664(c) provides that a taxpayer can avoid the imposition of a section 6662 accuracy-related penalty in cases where the taxpayer can demonstrate that there was reasonable cause for the underpayment and that the taxpayer acted in good faith. Regulations under sections 6662 and 6664 provide that a taxpayer's failure to disclose a reportable transaction is a strong indication that the taxpayer failed to act in good faith, which would bar relief under section 6664(c).

Transactions to be disclosed

The provision does not define the terms "listed transaction"[232] or "reportable transaction," nor does the provision explain the type of information that must be disclosed in order to avoid the imposition of a penalty. Rather, the provision authorizes the Treasury Department to define a "listed transaction" and a "reportable transaction" under section 6011.

Penalty rate

The penalty for failing to disclose a reportable transaction is $10,000 in the case of a natural person and $50,000 in any other case. The amount is increased to $100,000 and $200,000, respectively, if the failure is with respect to a listed transaction. The penalty cannot be waived with respect to a listed transaction. As to reportable transactions, the penalty can be rescinded (or abated) only if rescinding the penalty would promote compliance with the tax laws and effective tax administration. The authority to rescind the penalty can only be exercised by the IRS Commissioner personally. Thus, a revenue agent, an Appeals officer, or any other IRS personnel cannot rescind the penalty. The decision to rescind a penalty must be accompanied by a record describing the facts and reasons for the action and the amount rescinded. There will be no taxpayer right to appeal a refusal to rescind a penalty.[233] The IRS also is required to submit an annual report to Congress summarizing the application of the disclosure penalties and providing a description of each penalty rescinded under this provision and the reasons for the rescission.

Effective Date

The provision is effective for returns and statements the due date for which is after the date of enactment.

Conference Committee Report (H.R. Conf. Rep. No. 108-755)

The conference agreement follows the House bill, with the following modifications.

In determining whether to rescind (or abate) the penalty for failing to disclose a reportable transaction on the grounds that doing so would promote compliance with the tax laws and effective tax administration, the conferees intend that the IRS Commissioner take into account whether: (1) the person on whom the penalty is imposed has a history of complying with the tax laws; (2) the violation is due to an unintentional mistake of fact; and (3) imposing the penalty would be against equity and good conscience.

In addition, the conference agreement provides that a public entity that is required to pay a penalty for failing to disclose a listed transaction (or is subject to an understatement penalty attributable to a non-disclosed listed transaction or a non-disclosed reportable avoidance transaction) must disclose the imposition of the penalty in reports to the Securities and Exchange Commission for such period as the Secretary shall specify. This requirement applies without regard to whether the taxpayer determines the amount of the penalty to be material to the reports in which the penalty must appear, and treats any failure to disclose a transaction in such reports as a failure to disclose a listed transaction. A taxpayer must disclose a penalty in reports to the Securities and Exchange Commission once the taxpayer has exhausted its administrative and judicial remedies with respect to the penalty (or if earlier, when paid). However, the taxpayer is only required to report the penalty one time. The conference agreement further provides that this requirement also applies to a public entity that is subject to a gross valuation misstatement penalty under section 6662(h) attributable to a non-disclosed listed transaction or non-disclosed reportable avoidance transaction.

[Law at ¶6270 and ¶7095. CCH Explanation at ¶615.]

---

[232] The provision states that, except as provided in regulations, a listed transaction means a reportable transaction, which is the same as, or substantially similar to, a transaction specifically identified by the Secretary as a tax avoidance transaction for purposes of section 6011. For this purpose, it is expected that the definition of "substantially similar" will be the definition used in Treas. Reg. sec. 1.6011-4(c)(4). However, the Secretary may modify this definition (as well as the definitions of "listed transaction" and "reportable transactions") as appropriate.

[233] This does not limit the ability of a taxpayer to challenge whether a penalty is appropriate (e.g., a taxpayer may litigate the issue of whether a transaction is a reportable transaction (and thus subject to the penalty if not disclosed) or not a reportable transaction (and thus not subject to the penalty)).

[¶ 11,040] Act Sec. 812. Modifications to the accuracy-related penalties for listed transactions and reportable transactions having a significant tax avoidance purpose

House Committee Report (H.R. REP. NO. 108-548, pt. 1)

[New Code Sec. 6662A]

Present Law

The accuracy-related penalty applies to the portion of any underpayment that is attributable to (1) negligence, (2) any substantial understatement of income tax, (3) any substantial valuation misstatement, (4) any substantial overstatement of pension liabilities, or (5) any substantial estate or gift tax valuation understatement. If the correct income tax liability exceeds that reported by the taxpayer by the greater of 10 percent of the correct tax or $5,000 ($10,000 in the case of corporations), then a substantial understatement exists and a penalty may be imposed equal to 20 percent of the underpayment of tax attributable to the understatement.[234] The amount of any understatement generally is reduced by any portion attributable to an item if (1) the treatment of the item is or was supported by substantial authority, or (2) facts relevant to the tax treatment of the item were adequately disclosed and there was a reasonable basis for its tax treatment.[235]

Special rules apply with respect to tax shelters.[236] For understatements by non-corporate taxpayers attributable to tax shelters, the penalty may be avoided only if the taxpayer establishes that, in addition to having substantial authority for the position, the taxpayer reasonably believed that the treatment claimed was more likely than not the proper treatment of the item. This reduction in the penalty is unavailable to corporate tax shelters.

The understatement penalty generally is abated (even with respect to tax shelters) in cases in which the taxpayer can demonstrate that there was "reasonable cause" for the underpayment and that the taxpayer acted in good faith.[237] The relevant regulations provide that reasonable cause exists where the taxpayer "reasonably relies in good faith on an opinion based on a professional tax advisor's analysis of the pertinent facts and authorities [that] * * * unambigu-

ously concludes that there is a greater than 50-percent likelihood that the tax treatment of the item will be upheld if challenged" by the IRS.[238]

Reasons for Change

Because disclosure is so vital to combating abusive tax avoidance transactions, the Committee believes that taxpayers should be subject to a strict liability penalty on an understatement of tax that is attributable to non-disclosed listed transactions or non-disclosed reportable transactions that have a significant purpose of tax avoidance. Furthermore, in order to deter taxpayers from entering into tax avoidance transactions, the Committee believes that a more meaningful (but not a strict liability) accuracy-related penalty should apply to such transactions even when disclosed.

Explanation of Provision

In general

The provision modifies the present-law accuracy-related penalty by replacing the rules applicable to tax shelters with a new accuracy-related penalty that applies to listed transactions and reportable transactions with a significant tax avoidance purpose (hereinafter referred to as a "reportable avoidance transaction").[239] The penalty rate and defenses available to avoid the penalty vary depending on whether the transaction was adequately disclosed.

Disclosed transactions

In general, a 20-percent accuracy-related penalty is imposed on any understatement attributable to an adequately disclosed listed transaction or reportable avoidance transaction. The only exception to the penalty is if the taxpayer satisfies a more stringent reasonable cause and good faith exception (hereinafter referred to as the "strengthened reasonable cause exception"), which is described below. The strength-

---

[234] Sec. 6662.

[235] Sec. 6662(d)(2)(B).

[236] Sec. 6662(d)(2)(C).

[237] Sec. 6664(c).

[238] Treas. Reg. sec. 1.6662-4(g)(4)(i)(B); Treas. Reg. sec. 1.6664-4(c).

[239] The terms "reportable transaction" and "listed transaction" have the same meanings as used for purposes of the penalty for failing to disclose reportable transactions.

ened reasonable cause exception is available only if the relevant facts affecting the tax treatment are adequately disclosed, there is or was substantial authority for the claimed tax treatment, and the taxpayer reasonably believed that the claimed tax treatment was more likely than not the proper treatment.

Undisclosed transactions

If the taxpayer does not adequately disclose the transaction, the strengthened reasonable cause exception is not available (i.e., a strict-liability penalty applies), and the taxpayer is subject to an increased penalty rate equal to 30 percent of the understatement.

Determination of the understatement amount

The penalty is applied to the amount of any understatement attributable to the listed or reportable avoidance transaction without regard to other items on the tax return. For purposes of this provision, the amount of the understatement is determined as the sum of (1) the product of the highest corporate or individual tax rate (as appropriate) and the increase in taxable income resulting from the difference between the taxpayer's treatment of the item and the proper treatment of the item (without regard to other items on the tax return),[240] and (2) the amount of any decrease in the aggregate amount of credits which results from a difference between the taxpayer's treatment of an item and the proper tax treatment of such item.

Except as provided in regulations, a taxpayer's treatment of an item shall not take into account any amendment or supplement to a return if the amendment or supplement is filed after the earlier of when the taxpayer is first contacted regarding an examination of the return or such other date as specified by the Secretary.

Strengthened reasonable cause exception

A penalty is not imposed under the provision with respect to any portion of an understatement if it shown that there was reasonable cause for such portion and the taxpayer acted in good faith. Such a showing requires (1) adequate disclosure of the facts affecting the transaction in accordance with the regulations under section

6011,[241] (2) that there is or was substantial authority for such treatment, and (3) that the taxpayer reasonably believed that such treatment was more likely than not the proper treatment. For this purpose, a taxpayer will be treated as having a reasonable belief with respect to the tax treatment of an item only if such belief (1) is based on the facts and law that exist at the time the tax return (that includes the item) is filed, and (2) relates solely to the taxpayer's chances of success on the merits and does not take into account the possibility that (a) a return will not be audited, (b) the treatment will not be raised on audit, or (c) the treatment will be resolved through settlement if raised.

A taxpayer may (but is not required to) rely on an opinion of a tax advisor in establishing its reasonable belief with respect to the tax treatment of the item. However, a taxpayer may not rely on an opinion of a tax advisor for this purpose if the opinion (1) is provided by a "disqualified tax advisor," or (2) is a "disqualified opinion."

Disqualified tax advisor

A disqualified tax advisor is any advisor who (1) is a material advisor[242] and who participates in the organization, management, promotion or sale of the transaction or is related (within the meaning of section 267(b) or 707(b)(1)) to any person who so participates, (2) is compensated directly or indirectly[243] by a material advisor with respect to the transaction, (3) has a fee arrangement with respect to the transaction that is contingent on all or part of the intended tax benefits from the transaction being sustained, or (4) as determined under regulations prescribed by the Secretary, has a disqualifying financial interest with respect to the transaction.

Organization, management, promotion or sale of a transaction—A material advisor is considered as participating in the "organization" of a transaction if the advisor performs acts relating to the development of the transaction. This may include, for example, preparing documents (1) establishing a structure used in connection with the transaction (such as a partnership agreement), (2) describing the transaction (such as an

---

[240] For this purpose, any reduction in the excess of deductions allowed for the taxable year over gross income for such year, and any reduction in the amount of capital losses which would (without regard to section 1211) be allowed for such year, shall be treated as an increase in taxable income.

[241] See the previous discussion regarding the penalty for failing to disclose a reportable transaction.

[242] The term "material advisor" (defined below in connection with the new information filing requirements for material advisors) means any person who provides any material aid, assistance, or advice with respect to organiz-

ing, managing, promoting, selling, implementing, or carrying out any reportable transaction, and who derives gross income in excess of $50,000 in the case of a reportable transaction substantially all of the tax benefits from which are provided to natural persons ($250,000 in any other case).

[243] This situation could arise, for example, when an advisor has an arrangement or understanding (oral or written) with an organizer, manager, or promoter of a reportable transaction that such party will recommend or refer potential participants to the advisor for an opinion regarding the tax treatment of the transaction.

offering memorandum or other statement describing the transaction), or (3) relating to the registration of the transaction with any federal, state or local government body.[244] Participation in the "management" of a transaction means involvement in the decision-making process regarding any business activity with respect to the transaction. Participation in the "promotion or sale" of a transaction means involvement in the marketing or solicitation of the transaction to others. Thus, an advisor who provides information about the transaction to a potential participant is involved in the promotion or sale of a transaction, as is any advisor who recommends the transaction to a potential participant.

Disqualified opinion

An opinion may not be relied upon if the opinion (1) is based on unreasonable factual or legal assumptions (including assumptions as to future events), (2) unreasonably relies upon representations, statements, finding or agreements of the taxpayer or any other person, (3) does not

identify and consider all relevant facts, or (4) fails to meet any other requirement prescribed by the Secretary.

Coordination with other penalties

Any understatement upon which a penalty is imposed under this provision is not subject to the accuracy-related penalty under section 6662. However, such understatement is included for purposes of determining whether any understatement (as defined in sec. 6662(d)(2)) is a substantial understatement as defined under section 6662(d)(1).

The penalty imposed under this provision shall not apply to any portion of an understatement to which a fraud penalty is applied under section 6663.

Effective Date

The provision is effective for taxable years ending after the date of enactment.

Conference Committee Report (H.R. CONF. REP. NO. 108-755)

Conference Agreement

The conference agreement follows the House bill, except the conference agreement also provides that any understatement upon which a penalty is imposed under the conference agree-

ment is not subject to the valuation misstatement penalties under sections 6662(e) or 6662(h).

[**Law at ¶ 6235, ¶ 6240 and ¶ 6245. CCH Explanation at ¶ 620.**]

[¶ 11,050] Act Sec. 813. Tax shelter exception to confidentiality privileges relating to taxpayer communications

House Committee Report (H.R. REP. NO. 108-548, pt. 1)

[Code Sec. 7525]

Present Law

In general, a common law privilege of confidentiality exists for communications between an attorney and client with respect to the legal advice the attorney gives the client. The Code provides that, with respect to tax matters, the same common law protections of confidentiality that apply to a communication between a taxpayer and an attorney also apply to a communication between a taxpayer and a federally authorized tax practitioner to the extent the communication would be considered a privileged communication if it were between a taxpayer and an attorney. This rule is inapplicable to communications regarding corporate tax shelters.

Reasons for Change

The Committee believes that the rule currently applicable to corporate tax shelters should be applied to all tax shelters, regardless of whether or not the participant is a corporation.

Explanation of Provision

The provision modifies the rule relating to corporate tax shelters by making it applicable to all tax shelters, whether entered into by corporations, individuals, partnerships, tax-exempt entities, or any other entity. Accordingly, communications with respect to tax shelters are not subject to the confidentiality provision of the Code that otherwise applies to a communication

---

[244] An advisor should not be treated as participating in the organization of a transaction if the advisor's only involvement with respect to the organization of the transaction is the rendering of an opinion regarding the tax consequences of such transaction. However, such advisor may be a "disqualified tax advisor" with respect to the

transaction if the advisor participates in the management, promotion or sale of the transaction (or if the advisor is compensated by a material advisor, has a fee arrangement that is contingent on the tax benefits of the transaction, or as determined by the Secretary, has a continuing financial interest with respect to the transaction).

between a taxpayer and a federally authorized tax practitioner.

Effective Date

The provision is effective with respect to communications made on or after the date of enactment.

Conference Committee Report (H.R. CONF. REP. NO. 108-755)

Senate Amendment

The Senate amendment is the same as the House bill.

[Law at ¶ 6345. CCH Explanation at ¶ 665.]

Conference Agreement

The conference agreement follows the House bill and the Senate amendment.

[¶ 11,060] Act Sec. 814. Statute of limitations for unreported listed transactions

House Committee Report (H.R. REP. NO. 108-548, pt. 1)

[Code Sec. 6501]

Present Law

In general, the Code requires that taxes be assessed within three years[245] after the date a return is filed.[246] If there has been a substantial omission of items of gross income that totals more than 25 percent of the amount of gross income shown on the return, the period during which an assessment must be made is extended to six years.[247] If an assessment is not made within the required time periods, the tax generally cannot be assessed or collected at any future time. Tax may be assessed at any time if the taxpayer files a false or fraudulent return with the intent to evade tax or if the taxpayer does not file a tax return at all.[248]

Reasons for Change

The Committee has noted that some taxpayers and their advisors have been employing dilatory tactics and failing to cooperate with the IRS in an attempt to avoid liability because of the expiration of the statute of limitations. The Committee accordingly believes that it is appropriate to extend the statute of limitations for unreported listed transactions.

Explanation of Provision

The provision extends the statute of limitations with respect to a listed transaction if a taxpayer fails to include on any return or statement for any taxable year any information with respect to a listed transaction[249] which is required to be included (under section 6011) with such return or statement. The statute of limitations with respect to such a transaction will not expire before the date which is one year after the earlier of (1) the date on which the Secretary is furnished the information so required, or (2) the date that a material advisor (as defined in 6111) satisfies the list maintenance requirements (as defined by section 6112) with respect to a request by the Secretary. For example, if a taxpayer engaged in a transaction in 2005 that becomes a listed transaction in 2007 and the taxpayer fails to disclose such transaction in the manner required by Treasury regulations, then the transaction is subject to the extended statute of limitations.[250]

---

[245] Sec. 6501(a).

[246] For this purpose, a return that is filed before the date on which it is due is considered to be filed on the required due date (sec. 6501(b)(1)).

[247] Sec. 6501(e).

[248] Sec. 6501(c).

[249] The term "listed transaction" has the same meaning as described in a previous provision regarding the penalty for failure to disclose reportable transactions.

[250] If the Treasury Department lists a transaction in a year subsequent to the year in which a taxpayer entered into such transaction and the taxpayer's tax return for the year the transaction was entered into is closed by the statute of limitations prior to the date the transaction became a listed transaction, this provision does not re-open the statute of limitations with respect to such transaction for such year. However, if the purported tax benefits of the transaction are recognized over multiple tax years, the provision's extension of the statute of limitations shall apply to such tax benefits in any subsequent tax year in which the statute of limitations had not closed prior to the date the transaction became a listed transaction.

Effective Date

The provision is effective for taxable years with respect to which the period for assessing a

deficiency did not expire before the date of enactment.

Conference Committee Report (H.R. CONF. REP. NO. 108-755)

Senate Amendment

The Senate amendment is the same as the House bill.

Conference Agreement

The conference agreement follows the House bill and the Senate amendment.

[Law at ¶ 6225. CCH Explanation at ¶ 610.]

[¶ 11,070] Act Secs. 815 and 816. Disclosure of reportable transactions by material advisors

Senate Committee Report (S. REP. NO. 108-192)

[Code Secs. 6111, 6112, 6707 and 6708]

Present Law

Registration of tax shelter arrangements

An organizer of a tax shelter is required to register the shelter with the Secretary not later than the day on which the shelter is first offered for sale.[165] A "tax shelter" means any investment with respect to which the tax shelter ratio[166] for any investor as of the close of any of the first five years ending after the investment is offered for sale may be greater than two to one and which is: (1) required to be registered under Federal or State securities laws; (2) sold pursuant to an exemption from registration requiring the filing of a notice with a Federal or State securities agency; or (3) a substantial investment (greater than $250,000 and involving at least five investors).[167]

Other promoted arrangements are treated as tax shelters for purposes of the registration requirement if: (1) a significant purpose of the arrangement is the avoidance or evasion of Federal income tax by a corporate participant; (2) the arrangement is offered under conditions of confidentiality; and (3) the promoter may receive fees in excess of $100,000 in the aggregate.[168]

In general, a transaction has a "significant purpose of avoiding or evading Federal income tax" if the transaction: (1) is the same as or substantially similar to a "listed transaction",[169] or (2) is structured to produce tax benefits that constitute an important part of the intended results of the arrangement and the promoter reasonably expects to present the arrangement to more than one taxpayer.[170] Certain exceptions are provided with respect to the second category of transactions.[171]

An arrangement is offered under conditions of confidentiality if: (1) an offeree has an understanding or agreement to limit the disclosure of the transaction or any significant tax features of the transaction; or (2) the promoter knows, or has reason to know, that the offeree's use or disclosure of information relating to the transaction is limited in any other manner.[172]

Failure to register tax shelter

The penalty for failing to timely register a tax shelter (or for filing false or incomplete information with respect to the tax shelter registration) generally is the greater of one percent of the aggregate amount invested in the shelter or $500.[173] However, if the tax shelter involves an

---

[165] Sec. 6111(a).

[166] The tax shelter ratio is, with respect to any year, the ratio that the aggregate amount of the deductions and 350 percent of the credits, which are represented to be potentially allowable to any investor, bears to the investment base (money plus basis of assets contributed) as of the close of the tax year.

[167] Sec. 6111(c).

[168] Sec. 6111(d).

[169] Treas. Reg. sec. 301.6111-2(b)(2).

[170] Treas. Reg. sec. 301.6111-2(b)(3).

[171] Treas. Reg. sec. 301.6111-2(b)(4).

[172] The regulations provide that the determination of whether an arrangement is offered under conditions of confidentiality is based on all the facts and circumstances surrounding the offer. If an offeree's disclosure of the structure or tax aspects of the transaction are limited in any way by an express or implied understanding or agreement with or for the benefit of a tax shelter promoter, an offer is considered made under conditions of confidentiality, whether or not such understanding or agreement is legally binding. Treas. Reg. sec. 301.6111-2(c)(1).

[173] Sec. 6707.

arrangement offered to a corporation under conditions of confidentiality, the penalty is the greater of $10,000 or 50 percent of the fees payable to any promoter with respect to offerings prior to the date of late registration. Intentional disregard of the requirement to register increases the penalty to 75 percent of the applicable fees.

Section 6707 also imposes: (1) a $100 penalty on the promoter for each failure to furnish the investor with the required tax shelter identification number; and (2) a $250 penalty on the investor for each failure to include the tax shelter identification number on a return.

Reasons for Change

The Committee has been advised that the current promoter registration rules have not proven particularly helpful, because the rules are not appropriate for the kinds of abusive transactions now prevalent, and because the limitations regarding confidential corporate arrangements have proven easy to circumvent.

The Committee believes that providing a single, clear definition regarding the types of transactions that must be disclosed by taxpayers and material advisors, coupled with more meaningful penalties for failing to disclose such transactions, are necessary tools if the effort to curb the use of abusive tax avoidance transactions is to be effective.

Explanation of Provision

Disclosure of reportable transactions by material advisors

The provision repeals the present law rules with respect to registration of tax shelters. Instead, the provision requires each material advisor with respect to any reportable transaction (including any listed transaction)[174] to timely file an information return with the Secretary (in such form and manner as the Secretary may prescribe). The return must be filed on such date as specified by the Secretary.

The information return will include: (1) information identifying and describing the transaction; (2) information describing any potential tax benefits expected to result from the transaction; and (3) such other information as the Secretary may prescribe. It is expected that the Secretary may seek from the material advisor the same type of information that the Secretary may

request from a taxpayer in connection with a reportable transaction.[175]

A "material advisor" means any person: (1) who provides material aid, assistance, or advice with respect to organizing, promoting, selling, implementing, or carrying out any reportable transaction; and (2) who directly or indirectly derives gross income in excess of $250,000 ($50,000 in the case of a reportable transaction substantially all of the tax benefits from which are provided to natural persons) for such advice or assistance.

The Secretary may prescribe regulations which provide: (1) that only one material advisor has to file an information return in cases in which two or more material advisors would otherwise be required to file information returns with respect to a particular reportable transaction; (2) exemptions from the requirements of this section; and (3) other rules as may be necessary or appropriate to carry out the purposes of this section (including, for example, rules regarding the aggregation of fees in appropriate circumstances).

Penalty for failing to furnish information regarding reportable transactions

The provision repeals the present law penalty for failure to register tax shelters. Instead, the provision imposes a penalty on any material advisor who fails to file an information return, or who files a false or incomplete information return, with respect to a reportable transaction (including a listed transaction).[176] The amount of the penalty is $50,000. If the penalty is with respect to a listed transaction, the amount of the penalty is increased to the greater of: (1) $200,000; or (2) 50 percent of the gross income of such person with respect to aid, assistance, or advice which is provided with respect to the transaction before the date the information return that includes the transaction is filed. Intentional disregard by a material advisor of the requirement to disclose a listed transaction increases the penalty to 75 percent of the gross income.

The penalty cannot be waived with respect to a listed transaction. As to reportable transactions, the penalty can be rescinded (or abated) only in exceptional circumstances.[177] All or part of the penalty may be rescinded only if: (1) the

---

[174] The terms "reportable transaction" and "listed transaction" have the same meaning as previously described in connection with the taxpayer-related provisions.

[175] See the previous discussion regarding the disclosure requirements under new section 6707A.

[176] The terms "reportable transaction" and "listed transaction" have the same meaning as previously described in connection with the taxpayer-related provisions.

[177] The Secretary's present-law authority to postpone certain tax-related deadlines because of Presidentially-declared disasters (sec. 7508A) will also encompass the authority to postpone the reporting deadlines established by the provision.

material advisor on whom the penalty is imposed has a history of complying with the Federal tax laws; (2) it is shown that the violation is due to an unintentional mistake of fact; (3) imposing the penalty would be against equity and good conscience; and (4) rescinding the penalty would promote compliance with the tax laws and effective tax administration. The authority to rescind the penalty can only be exercised by the Commissioner personally or the head of the Office of Tax Shelter Analysis; this authority to rescind cannot otherwise be delegated by the Commissioner. Thus, a revenue agent, an Appeals officer, or other IRS personnel cannot rescind the penalty. The decision to rescind a penalty must be accompanied by a record describing the facts and reasons for the action and the amount rescinded. There will be no right to appeal a refusal to rescind a penalty. The IRS also is required to submit an annual report to Congress summarizing the application of the disclosure penalties and providing a description of each penalty rescinded under this provision and the reasons for the rescission.

Effective Date

The provision requiring disclosure of reportable transactions by material advisors applies to transactions with respect to which material aid, assistance or advice is provided after the date of enactment.

The provision imposing a penalty for failing to disclose reportable transactions applies to returns the due date for which is after the date of enactment.

Conference Committee Report (H.R. CONF. REP. NO. 108-755)

The conference agreement follows the Senate amendment.

[Law at ¶ 6165, ¶ 6170, ¶ 6265 and ¶ 6275. CCH Explanation at ¶ 605 and ¶ 630.]

[¶ 11,080] Act Sec. 817. Investor lists and modification of penalty for failure to maintain investor lists

House Committee Report (H.R. REP. NO. 108-548, pt. 1)

[Code Secs. 6112 and 6708]

Present Law

Investor lists

Any organizer or seller of a potentially abusive tax shelter must maintain a list identifying each person who was sold an interest in any such tax shelter with respect to which registration was required under section 6111 (even though the particular party may not have been subject to confidentiality restrictions).[264] Recently issued regulations under section 6112 contain rules regarding the list maintenance requirements.[265] In general, the regulations apply to transactions that are potentially abusive tax shelters entered into, or acquired after, February 28, 2003.[266]

The regulations provide that a person is an organizer or seller of a potentially abusive tax shelter if the person is a material advisor with respect to that transaction.[267] A material advisor is defined as any person who is required to register the transaction under section 6111, or

expects to receive a minimum fee of (1) $250,000 for a transaction that is a potentially abusive tax shelter if all participants are corporations, or (2) $50,000 for any other transaction that is a potentially abusive tax shelter.[268] For listed transactions (as defined in the regulations under section 6011), the minimum fees are reduced to $25,000 and $10,000, respectively.

A potentially abusive tax shelter is any transaction that (1) is required to be registered under section 6111, (2) is a listed transaction (as defined under the regulations under section 6011), or (3) any transaction that a potential material advisor, at the time the transaction is entered into, knows is or reasonably expects will become a reportable transaction (as defined under the new regulations under section 6011).[269]

The Secretary is required to prescribe regulations which provide that, in cases in which two or more persons are required to maintain the same list, only one person would be required to maintain the list.[270]

---

[264] Sec. 6112.

[265] Treas. Reg. sec. 301.6112-1.

[266] A special rule applies the list maintenance requirements to transactions entered into after February 28, 2000 if the transaction becomes a listed transaction (as defined in Treas. Reg. 1.6011-4) after February 28, 2003.

[267] Treas. Reg. sec. 301.6112-1(c)(1).

[268] Treas. Reg. sec. 301.6112-1(c)(2) and (3).

[269] Treas. Reg. sec. 301.6112-1(b).

[270] Sec. 6112(c)(2).

Penalty for failing to maintain investor lists

Under section 6708, the penalty for failing to maintain the list required under section 6112 is $50 for each name omitted from the list (with a maximum penalty of $100,000 per year).

Reasons for Change

The Committee has been advised that the present-law penalties for failure to maintain customer lists are not meaningful and that promoters often have refused to provide requested information to the IRS. The Committee believes that requiring material advisors to maintain a list of advisees with respect to each reportable transaction, coupled with more meaningful penalties for failing to maintain an investor list, are important tools in the ongoing efforts to curb the use of abusive tax avoidance transactions.

Explanation of Provision

Investor lists

Each material advisor[271] with respect to a reportable transaction (including a listed transaction)[272] is required to maintain a list that (1) identifies each person with respect to whom the advisor acted as a material advisor with respect to the reportable transaction, and (2) contains other information as may be required by the Secretary. In addition, the provision authorizes (but does not require) the Secretary to prescribe regulations which provide that, in cases in which two or more persons are required to maintain the same list, only one person would be required to maintain the list.

The provision also clarifies that, for purposes of section 6112, the identity of any person

is not privileged under the common law attorney-client privilege (or, consequently, the section 7525 federally authorized tax practitioner confidentiality provision).

Penalty for failing to maintain investor lists

The provision modifies the penalty for failing to maintain the required list by making it a time-sensitive penalty. Thus, a material advisor who is required to maintain an investor list and who fails to make the list available upon written request by the Secretary within 20 business days after the request will be subject to a $10,000 per day penalty. The penalty applies to a person who fails to maintain a list, maintains an incomplete list, or has in fact maintained a list but does not make the list available to the Secretary. The penalty can be waived if the failure to make the list available is due to reasonable cause.[273]

Effective Date

The provision requiring a material advisor to maintain an investor list applies to transactions with respect to which material aid, assistance or advice is provided after the date of enactment.

The provision imposing a penalty for failing to maintain investor lists applies to requests made after the date of enactment.

The provision clarifying that the identity of any person is not privileged for purposes of section 6112 is effective as if included in the amendments made by section 142 of the Deficit Reduction Act of 1984.

Conference Committee Report (H.R. Conf. Rep. No. 108-755)

Senate Amendment

The Senate amendment is the same as the House bill. In addition, the Senate amendment clarifies that, for purposes of section 6112, the identity of any person is not privileged under the common law attorney-client privilege (or, consequently, the section 7525 federally authorized tax practitioner confidentiality provision).

Effective Date

The Senate amendment provision clarifying that the identity of any person is not privileged

for purposes of section 6112 is effective as if included in the amendments made by section 142 of the Deficit Reduction Act of 1984.

Conference Agreement

The conference agreement follows the House bill.

[Law at ¶ 6275. CCH Explanation at ¶ 635.]

---

[271] The term "material advisor" has the same meaning as when used in connection with the requirement to file an information return under section 6111.

[272] The terms "reportable transaction" and "listed transaction" have the same meaning as previously described in connection with the taxpayer-related provisions.

[273] In no event will failure to maintain a list be considered reasonable cause for failing to make a list available to the Secretary.

[¶ 11,090] Act Sec. 818. Penalty on promoters of tax shelters

House Committee Report (H.R. REP. NO. 108-548, pt. 1)

[Code Sec. 6700]

Present Law

A penalty is imposed on any person who organizes, assists in the organization of, or participates in the sale of any interest in, a partnership or other entity, any investment plan or arrangement, or any other plan or arrangement, if in connection with such activity the person makes or furnishes a qualifying false or fraudulent statement or a gross valuation overstatement.[274] A qualified false or fraudulent statement is any statement with respect to the allowability of any deduction or credit, the excludability of any income, or the securing of any other tax benefit by reason of holding an interest in the entity or participating in the plan or arrangement which the person knows or has reason to know is false or fraudulent as to any material matter. A "gross valuation overstatement" means any statement as to the value of any property or services if the stated value exceeds 200 percent of the correct valuation, and the value is directly related to the amount of any allowable income tax deduction or credit.

The amount of the penalty is $1,000 (or, if the person establishes that it is less, 100 percent of the gross income derived or to be derived by the person from such activity). A penalty attribu-table to a gross valuation misstatement can be waived on a showing that there was a reasonable basis for the valuation and it was made in good faith.

Reasons for Change

The Committee believes that the present-law $1,000 penalty for tax shelter promoters is insufficient to deter tax shelter activities. The Committee believes that the increased penalties for tax shelter promoters are meaningful and will help deter the promotion of tax shelters.

Explanation of Provision

The provision modifies the penalty amount to equal 50 percent of the gross income derived by the person from the activity for which the penalty is imposed. The new penalty rate applies to any activity that involves a statement regarding the tax benefits of participating in a plan or arrangement if the person knows or has reason to know that such statement is false or fraudulent as to any material matter. The enhanced penalty does not apply to a gross valuation overstatement.

Effective Date

The provision is effective for activities after the date of enactment.

Conference Committee Report (H.R. CONF. REP. NO. 108-755)

Conference Agreement

The conference agreement follows the House bill.

[Law at ¶ 6260. CCH Explanation at ¶ 640.]

[¶ 11,100] Act Sec. 819. Modifications of substantial understatement penalty for nonreportable transactions

House Committee Report (H.R. REP. NO. 108-548, pt. 1)

[Code Sec. 6662

Present Law

An accuracy-related penalty equal to 20 percent applies to any substantial understatement of tax. A "substantial understatement" exists if the correct income tax liability for a taxable year exceeds that reported by the taxpayer by the greater of 10 percent of the correct tax or $5,000 ($10,000 in the case of most corporations).[275]

Reasons for Change

The Committee believes that the present-law definition of substantial understatement allows large corporate taxpayers to avoid the accuracy-related penalty on questionable transactions of a significant size. The Committee believes that an understatement of more than $10 million is substantial in and of itself, regardless of the propor-

---

[274] Sec. 6700.

[275] Sec. 6662(a) and (d)(1)(A).

tion it represents of the taxpayer's total tax liability.

Explanation of Provision

The provision modifies the definition of "substantial" for corporate taxpayers. Under the provision, a corporate taxpayer has a substantial understatement if the amount of the understate-

ment for the taxable year exceeds the lesser of (1) 10 percent of the tax required to be shown on the return for the taxable year (or, if greater, $10,000), or (2) $10 million.

Effective Date

The provision is effective for taxable years beginning after date of enactment.

Conference Committee Report (H.R. Conf. Rep. No. 108-755)

Conference Agreement

The conference agreement follows the House bill, except the conference agreement also modifies the requirement of the Secretary to pre-

scribe a list of positions that do not have substantial authority, and authorizes (but does not require) the Secretary to publish such list.

[Law at ¶ 6235. CCH Explanation at ¶ 645.]

[¶ 11,110] Act Sec. 820. Modification of actions to enjoin certain conduct related to tax shelters and reportable transactions

Senate Committee Report (S. Rep. No. 108-192)

[Code Sec. 7408]

Present Law

The Code authorizes civil actions to enjoin any person from promoting abusive tax shelters or aiding or abetting the understatement of tax liability.[188]

Reasons for Change

The Committee understands that some promoters are blatantly ignoring the rules regarding registration and list maintenance regardless of the penalties. An injunction would place these promoters in a public proceeding under court order. Thus, the Committee believes that the types of tax shelter activities with respect to which an injunction may be sought should be expanded.

Explanation of Provision

The provision expands this rule so that injunctions may also be sought with respect to the requirements relating to the reporting of reportable transactions[189] and the keeping of lists of investors by material advisors.[190] Thus, under the provision, an injunction may be sought against a material advisor to enjoin the advisor from (1) failing to file an information return with respect to a reportable transaction, or (2) failing to maintain, or to timely furnish upon written request by the Secretary, a list of investors with respect to each reportable transaction.

Effective Date

The provision is effective on the day after the date of enactment.

Conference Committee Report (H.R. Conf. Rep. No. 108-755)

Senate Amendment

The Senate amendment is the same as the House bill, except the Senate amendment also permits injunctions to be sought with respect to violations of any of the rules under Circular 230, which regulates the practice of representatives of persons before the Department of the Treasury.

Conference Agreement

The conference agreement follows the Senate amendment.

[Law at ¶ 6330. CCH Explanation at ¶ 650.]

---

[188] Sec. 7408.
[189] Sec. 6707, as amended by other provisions of this bill.

[190] Sec. 6708, as amended by other provisions of this bill.

[¶ 11,120] Act Sec. 821. Penalty on failure to report interests in foreign financial accounts

Senate Committee Report (S. REP. NO. 108-192)

[Act Sec. 412]

Present Law

The Secretary of the Treasury must require citizens, residents, or persons doing business in the United States to keep records and file reports when that person makes a transaction or maintains an account with a foreign financial entity.[191] In general, individuals must fulfill this requirement by answering questions regarding foreign accounts or foreign trusts that are contained in Part III of Schedule B of the IRS Form 1040. Taxpayers who answer "yes" in response to the question regarding foreign accounts must then file Treasury Department Form TD F 90-22.1. This form must be filed with the Department of the Treasury, and not as part of the tax return that is filed with the IRS.

The Secretary of the Treasury may impose a civil penalty on any person who willfully violates this reporting requirement. The civil penalty is the amount of the transaction or the value of the account, up to a maximum of $100,000; the minimum amount of the penalty is $25,000.[192] In addition, any person who willfully violates this reporting requirement is subject to a criminal penalty. The criminal penalty is a fine of not more than $250,000 or imprisonment for not more than five years (or both); if the violation is part of a pattern of illegal activity, the maximum amount of the fine is increased to $500,000 and the maximum length of imprisonment is increased to 10 years.[193]

On April 26, 2002, the Secretary of the Treasury submitted to the Congress a report on these reporting requirements.[194] This report, which was statutorily required,[195] studies methods for improving compliance with these reporting re-

quirements. It makes several administrative recommendations, but no legislative recommendations. A further report was required to be submitted by the Secretary of the Treasury to the Congress by October 26, 2002.

Reasons for Change

The Committee understands that the number of individuals involved in using offshore bank accounts to engage in abusive tax scams has grown significantly in recent years. For one scheme alone, the IRS estimates that there may be hundreds of thousands of taxpayers with offshore bank accounts attempting to conceal income from the IRS. The Committee is concerned about this activity and believes that improving compliance with this reporting requirement is vitally important to sound tax administration, to combating terrorism, and to preventing the use of abusive tax schemes and scams. Adding a new civil penalty that applies without regard to willfulness will improve compliance with this reporting requirement.

Explanation of Provision

The provision adds an additional civil penalty that may be imposed on any person who violates this reporting requirement (without regard to willfulness). This new civil penalty is up to $5,000. The penalty may be waived if any income from the account was properly reported on the income tax return and there was reasonable cause for the failure to report.

Effective Date

The provision is effective with respect to failures to report occurring on or after the date of enactment.

Conference Committee Report (H.R. CONF. REP. NO. 108-755)

Senate Amendment

The Senate amendment is the same as the House bill, except the maximum additional civil penalty for a non-willful act is up to $10,000. In addition, the Senate amendment increases the present-law penalty for willful behavior to the

greater of $100,000 or 50 percent of the amount of the transaction or account.

Conference Agreement

The conference agreement follows the Senate amendment.

[Law at ¶ 7100. CCH Explanation at ¶ 655.]

---

[191] 31 U.S.C. 5314.

[192] 31 U.S.C. 5321(a)(5).

[193] 31 U.S.C. 5322.

[194] A Report to Congress in Accordance with Sec. 361(b) of the Uniting and Strengthening America by Providing

Appropriate Tools Required to Intercept and Obstruct Terrorism Act of 2001, April 26, 2002.

[195] Sec. 361(b) of the USA PATRIOT Act of 2001 (Pub. L. 107-56).

[¶ 11,130] Act Sec. 822. Regulation of individuals practicing before the Department of the Treasury

Senate Committee Report (S. REP. NO. 108-192)

[Act Sec. 822]

Present Law

The Secretary of the Treasury is authorized to regulate the practice of representatives of persons before the Department of the Treasury.[197] The Secretary is also authorized to suspend or disbar from practice before the Department a representative who is incompetent, who is disreputable, who violates the rules regulating practice before the Department, or who (with intent to defraud) willfully and knowingly misleads or threatens the person being represented (or a person who may be represented). The rules promulgated by the Secretary pursuant to this provision are contained in Circular 230.

Reasons for Change

The Committee believes that it is critical that the Secretary have the authority to censure tax advisors as well as to impose monetary sanctions against tax advisors because of the important role of tax advisors in our tax system. Use of these sanctions is expected to curb the participation of tax advisors in both tax shelter activity and any other activity that is contrary to Circular 230 standards.

Explanation of Provision

The provision makes two modifications to expand the sanctions that the Secretary may im-

pose pursuant to these statutory provisions. First, the provision expressly permits censure as a sanction. Second, the provision permits the imposition of a monetary penalty as a sanction. If the representative is acting on behalf of an employer or other entity, the Secretary may impose a monetary penalty on the employer or other entity if it knew, or reasonably should have known, of the conduct. This monetary penalty on the employer or other entity may be imposed in addition to any monetary penalty imposed directly on the representative. These monetary penalties are not to exceed the gross income derived (or to be derived) from the conduct giving rise to the penalty. These monetary penalties may be in addition to, or in lieu of, any suspension, disbarment, or censure.

The provision also confirms the present-law authority of the Secretary to impose standards applicable to written advice with respect to an entity, plan, or arrangement that is of a type that the Secretary determines as having a potential for tax avoidance or evasion.

Effective Date

The modifications to expand the sanctions that the Secretary may impose are effective for actions taken after the date of enactment.

Conference Committee Report (H.R. CONF. REP. NO. 108-755)

The conference agreement follows the Senate amendment.

[Law at ¶ 7105. CCH Explanation at ¶ 660.]

[¶ 11,140] Act Sec. 831. Treatment of stripped bonds to apply to stripped interests in bond and preferred stock funds

House Committee Report (H.R. REP. NO. 108-548, pt. 1)

[Code Secs. 305 and 1286]

Present Law

Assignment of income in general

In general, an "income stripping" transaction involves a transaction in which the right to receive future income from income-producing property is separated from the property itself. In such transactions, it may be possible to generate

artificial losses from the disposition of certain property or to defer the recognition of taxable income associated with such property.

Common law has developed a rule (referred to as the "assignment of income" doctrine) whereby income that is transferred without an accompanying transfer of the underlying property is not respected. A leading judicial decision relating to the assignment of income doctrine

---

[197] 31 U.S.C. 330.

involved a case in which a taxpayer made a gift of detachable interest coupons before their due date while retaining the bearer bond. The U.S. Supreme Court ruled that the donor was taxable on the entire amount of interest when paid to the donee on the grounds that the transferor had "assigned" to the donee the right to receive the income.[285]

In addition to general common law assignment of income principles, specific statutory rules have been enacted to address certain specific types of stripping transactions, such as transactions involving stripped bonds and stripped preferred stock (which are discussed below).[286] However, there are no specific statutory rules that address stripping transactions with respect to common stock or other equity interests (other than preferred stock).[287]

Stripped bonds

Special rules are provided with respect to the purchaser and "stripper" of stripped bonds.[288] A "stripped bond" is defined as a debt instrument in which there has been a separation in ownership between the underlying debt instrument and any interest coupon that has not yet become payable.[289] In general, upon the disposition of either the stripped bond or the detached interest coupons each of the retained portion and the portion that is disposed is treated as a new bond that is purchased at a discount and is payable in a fixed amount on a future date. Accordingly, section 1286 treats both the stripped bond and the detached interest coupons as individual bonds that are newly issued with original issue discount ("OID") on the date of disposition. Consequently, section 1286 effectively subjects the stripped bond and the detached interest coupons to the general OID periodic income inclusion rules.

A taxpayer who purchases a stripped bond or one or more stripped coupons is treated as holding a new bond that is issued on the purchase date with OID in an amount that is equal to the excess of the stated redemption price at maturity (or in the case of a coupon, the amount payable on the due date) over the ratable share of the purchase price of the stripped bond or coupon, determined on the basis of the respective fair market values of the stripped bond and coupons on the purchase date.[290] The OID on the stripped bond or coupon is includible in gross income under the general OID periodic income inclusion rules.

A taxpayer who strips a bond and disposes of either the stripped bond or one or more stripped coupons must allocate his basis, immediately before the disposition, in the bond (with the coupons attached) between the retained and disposed items.[291] Special rules apply to require that interest or market discount accrued on the bond prior to such disposition must be included in the taxpayer's gross income (to the extent that it had not been previously included in income) at the time the stripping occurs, and the taxpayer increases his basis in the bond by the amount of such accrued interest or market discount. The adjusted basis (as increased by any accrued interest or market discount) is then allocated between the stripped bond and the stripped interest coupons in relation to their respective fair market values. Amounts realized from the sale of stripped coupons or bonds constitute income to the taxpayer only to the extent such amounts exceed the basis allocated to the stripped coupons or bond. With respect to retained items (either the detached coupons or stripped bond), to the extent that the price payable on maturity, or on the due date of the coupons, exceeds the portion of the taxpayer's basis allocable to such retained items, the difference is treated as OID that is required to be included under the general OID periodic income inclusion rules.[292]

Stripped preferred stock

"Stripped preferred stock" is defined as preferred stock in which there has been a separation in ownership between such stock and any dividend on such stock that has not become paya-

---

[285] *Helvering* v. *Horst*, 311 U.S. 112 (1940).

[286] Depending on the facts, the IRS also could determine that a variety of other Code-based and common law-based authorities could apply to income stripping transactions, including: (1) sections 165, 269, 382, 446(b), 482, 701, or 704 and the regulations thereunder; (2) authorities that recharacterize certain assignments or accelerations of future payments as financings; (3) business purpose, economic substance, and sham transaction doctrines; (4) the step transaction doctrine; and (5) the substance-over-form doctrine. See Notice 2003-55, 2003-34 I.R.B. 395, modifying and superseding Notice 95-53, 1995-2 C.B. 334 (accounting for lease strips and other stripping transactions).

[287] However, in *Estate of Stranahan* v. *Commissioner*, 472 F.2d 867 (6th Cir. 1973), the court held that where a taxpayer sold a carved-out interest of stock dividends, with no per-

sonal obligation to produce the income, the transaction was treated as a sale of an income interest.

[288] Sec. 1286.

[289] Sec. 1286(e).

[290] Sec. 1286(a).

[291] Sec. 1286(b). Similar rules apply in the case of any person whose basis in any bond or coupon is determined by reference to the basis in the hands of a person who strips the bond.

[292] Special rules are provided with respect to stripping transactions involving tax-exempt obligations that treat OID (computed under the stripping rules) in excess of OID computed on the basis of the bond's coupon rate (or higher rate if originally issued at a discount) as income from a non-tax-exempt debt instrument (sec. 1286(d)).

ble.[293] A taxpayer who purchases stripped preferred stock is required to include in gross income, as ordinary income, the amounts that would have been includible if the stripped preferred stock was a bond issued on the purchase date with OID equal to the excess of the redemption price of the stock over the purchase price.[294] This treatment is extended to any taxpayer whose basis in the stock is determined by reference to the basis in the hands of the purchaser. A taxpayer who strips and disposes the future dividends is treated as having purchased the stripped preferred stock on the date of such disposition for a purchase price equal to the taxpayer's adjusted basis in the stripped preferred stock.[295]

Reasons for Change

The Committee is concerned that taxpayers are entering into tax avoidance transactions to generate artificial losses, or defer the recognition of ordinary income and convert such income into capital gains, by selling or purchasing stripped interests that are not subject to the present-law rules relating to stripped bonds and preferred stock but that represent interests in bonds or preferred stock. Therefore, the Committee believes that it is appropriate to provide Treasury with regulatory authority to apply such rules to interests that do not constitute bonds or preferred stock but nevertheless derive their economic value and characteristics exclusively from underlying bonds or preferred stock.

Explanation of Provision

The provision authorizes the Treasury Department to promulgate regulations that, in appropriate cases, apply rules that are similar to the present-law rules for stripped bonds and stripped preferred stock to direct or indirect interests in an entity or account substantially all of the assets of which consist of bonds (as defined in section 1286(e)(1)), preferred stock (as defined in section 305(e)(5)(B)), or any combination thereof. The provision applies only to cases in which the present-law rules for stripped bonds and stripped preferred stock do not already apply to such interests.

For example, such Treasury regulations could apply to a transaction in which a person effectively strips future dividends from shares in a money market mutual fund (and disposes either the stripped shares or stripped future dividends) by contributing the shares (with the future dividends) to a custodial account through which another person purchases rights to either the stripped shares or the stripped future dividends. However, it is intended that Treasury regulations issued under this provision would not apply to certain transactions involving direct or indirect interests in an entity or account substantially all the assets of which consist of tax-exempt obligations (as defined in section 1275(a)(3)), such as an eligible tax-exempt bond partnership described in Rev. Proc. 2003-84,[296] modifying and superseding Rev. Proc. 2002-68[297] and Rev. Proc. 2002-16.[298]

No inference is intended as to the treatment under the present-law rules for stripped bonds and stripped preferred stock, or under any other provisions or doctrines of present law, of interests in an entity or account substantially all of the assets of which consist of bonds, preferred stock, or any combination thereof. The Treasury regulations, when issued, would be applied prospectively, except in cases to prevent abuse.

Effective Date

The provision is effective for purchases and dispositions occurring after the date of enactment.

Conference Committee Report (H.R. CONF. REP. NO. 108-755)

Senate Amendment

The Senate amendment is the same as the House bill.

Conference Agreement

The conference agreement follows the House bill and the Senate amendment.

[Law at ¶5295 and ¶5830. CCH Explanation at ¶725.]

---

[293] Sec. 305(e)(5).
[294] Sec. 305(e)(1).
[295] Sec. 305(e)(3).

[296] 2003-48 I.R.B. 1159.
[297] 2002-43 I.R.B. 753.
[298] 2002-9 I.R.B. 572.

[¶ 11,150] Act Sec. 832. Minimum holding period for foreign tax credit with respect to withholding taxes on income other than dividends

House Committee Report (H.R. REP. NO. 108-548, pt. 1)

[Code Sec. 901]

Present Law

In general, U.S. persons may credit foreign taxes against U.S. tax on foreign-source income. The amount of foreign tax credits that may be claimed in a year is subject to a limitation that prevents taxpayers from using foreign tax credits to offset U.S. tax on U.S.-source income. Separate limitations are applied to specific categories of income.

As a consequence of the foreign tax credit limitations of the Code, certain taxpayers are unable to utilize their creditable foreign taxes to reduce their U.S. tax liability. U.S. taxpayers that are tax-exempt receive no U.S. tax benefit for foreign taxes paid on income that they receive.

Present law denies a U.S. shareholder the foreign tax credits normally available with respect to a dividend from a corporation or a regulated investment company ("RIC") if the shareholder has not held the stock for more than 15 days (within a 30-day testing period) in the case of common stock or more than 45 days (within a 90-day testing period) in the case of preferred stock (sec. 901(k)). The disallowance applies both to foreign tax credits for foreign withholding taxes that are paid on the dividend where the dividend-paying stock is held for less than these holding periods, and to indirect foreign tax credits for taxes paid by a lower-tier foreign corporation or a RIC where any of the required stock in the chain of ownership is held for less than these holding periods. Periods during which a taxpayer is protected from risk of loss (e.g., by purchasing a put option or entering into a short sale with respect to the stock) generally are not counted toward the holding period requirement. In the case of a bona fide contract to sell stock, a special rule applies for purposes of indirect foreign tax credits. The disallowance does not apply to foreign tax credits with respect to certain dividends received by active dealers in securities. If a taxpayer is denied foreign tax credits because the applicable holding period is not satisfied, the taxpayer is entitled to a deduction for the foreign taxes for which the credit is disallowed.

Reasons for Change

The Committee believes that the present-law holding period requirement for claiming foreign tax credits with respect to dividends is too narrow in scope and, in general, should be extended to apply to items of income or gain other than dividends, such as interest.

Explanation of Provision

The provision expands the present-law disallowance of foreign tax credits to include credits for gross-basis foreign withholding taxes with respect to any item of income or gain from property if the taxpayer who receives the income or gain has not held the property for more than 15 days (within a 30-day testing period), exclusive of periods during which the taxpayer is protected from risk of loss. The provision does not apply to foreign tax credits that are subject to the present-law disallowance with respect to dividends. The provision also does not apply to certain income or gain that is received with respect to property held by active dealers. Rules similar to the present-law disallowance for foreign tax credits with respect to dividends apply to foreign tax credits that are subject to the provision. In addition, the provision authorizes the Treasury Department to issue regulations providing that the provision does not apply in appropriate cases.

Effective Date

The provision is effective for amounts that are paid or accrued more than 30 days after the date of enactment.

Conference Committee Report (H.R. CONF. REP. NO. 108-755)

Senate Amendment

The Senate amendment is the same as the House bill.

Conference Agreement

The conference agreement follows the House bill and the Senate amendment provision, except the 30-day testing period is changed to a 31-day testing period.

In addition, the conferees intend that the Secretary will prescribe regulations to adapt the holding period and hedging rules of section 901(k) to property other than stock. It is anticipated that such regulations will provide that credits are not disallowed merely because a taxpayer eliminates its risk of loss from interest rate or currency fluctuations. In addition, it is intended that such regulations might permit other hedging activities, such as hedging of credit risk, provided that the taxpayer does not hedge most of its risk of loss with respect to the property unless there has been a meaningful and unanticipated change in circumstances.

[Law at ¶ 5640. CCH Explanation at ¶ 440.]

[¶ 11,160] Act Sec. 833. Treatment of partnership loss transfers and partnership basis adjustments

House Committee Report (H.R. REP. NO. 108-548, pt. 1)

[Code Secs. 704, 734 and 743]

Present Law

Contributions of property

Under present law, if a partner contributes property to a partnership, generally no gain or loss is recognized to the contributing partner at the time of contribution.[299] The partnership takes the property at an adjusted basis equal to the contributing partner's adjusted basis in the property.[300] The contributing partner increases its basis in its partnership interest by the adjusted basis of the contributed property.[301] Any items of partnership income, gain, loss and deduction with respect to the contributed property are allocated among the partners to take into account any built-in gain or loss at the time of the contribution.[302] This rule is intended to prevent the transfer of built-in gain or loss from the contributing partner to the other partners by generally allocating items to the noncontributing partners based on the value of their contributions and by allocating to the contributing partner the remainder of each item.[303]

If the contributing partner transfers its partnership interest, the built-in gain or loss will be allocated to the transferee partner as it would have been allocated to the contributing partner.[304] If the contributing partner's interest is liquidated, there is no specific guidance preventing the allocation of the built-in loss to the remaining partners. Thus, it appears that losses can be "transferred" to other partners where the contributing partner no longer remains a partner.

Transfers of partnership interests

Under present law, a partnership does not adjust the basis of partnership property following the transfer of a partnership interest unless the partnership has made a one-time election under section 754 to make basis adjustments.[305] If an election is in effect, adjustments are made with respect to the transferee partner to account for the difference between the transferee partner's proportionate share of the adjusted basis of the partnership property and the transferee's basis in its partnership interest.[306] These adjustments are intended to adjust the basis of partnership property to approximate the result of a direct purchase of the property by the transferee partner. Under these rules, if a partner purchases an interest in a partnership with an existing built-in loss and no election under section 754 is in effect, the transferee partner may be allocated a share of the loss when the partnership disposes of the property (or depreciates the property).

Distributions of partnership property

With certain exceptions, partners may receive distributions of partnership property without recognition of gain or loss by either the partner or the partnership.[307] In the case of a distribution in liquidation of a partner's interest, the basis of the property distributed in the liquidation is equal to the partner's adjusted basis in its partnership interest (reduced by any money distributed in the transaction).[308] In a distribution other than in liquidation of a partner's interest, the distributee partner's basis in the distributed property is equal to the partnership's adjusted basis in the property immediately before the distribution, but not to exceed the partner's adjusted basis in the partnership interest (reduced by any money distributed in the same transaction).[309]

---

[299] Sec. 721.

[300] Sec. 723.

[301] Sec. 722.

[302] Sec. 704(c)(1)(A).

[303] If there is an insufficient amount of an item to allocate to the noncontributing partners, Treasury regulations allow for curative or remedial allocations to remedy this insufficiency. Treas. Reg. sec. 1.704-3(c) and (d).

[304] Treas. Reg. 1.704-3(a)(7).

[305] Sec. 743(a).

[306] Sec. 743(b).

[307] Sec. 731(a) and (b).

[308] Sec. 732(b).

[309] Sec. 732(a).

Adjustments to the basis of the partnership's undistributed properties are not required unless the partnership has made the election under section 754 to make basis adjustments.[310] If an election is in effect under section 754, adjustments are made by a partnership to increase or decrease the remaining partnership assets to reflect any increase or decrease in the adjusted basis of the distributed properties in the hands of the distributee partner (or gain or loss recognized by the distributee partner).[311] To the extent the adjusted basis of the distributed properties increases (or loss is recognized) the partnership's adjusted basis in its properties is decreased by a like amount; likewise, to the extent the adjusted basis of the distributed properties decrease (or gain is recognized), the partnership's adjusted basis in its properties is increased by a like amount. Under these rules, a partnership with no election in effect under section 754 may distribute property with an adjusted basis lower than the distributee partner's proportionate share of the adjusted basis of all partnership property and leave the remaining partners with a smaller net built-in gain or a larger net built-in loss than before the distribution.

Reasons for Change

The Committee believes that the partnership rules currently allow for the inappropriate transfer of losses among partners. This has allowed partnerships to be created and used to aid tax-shelter transactions. The bill limits the ability to transfer losses among partners, while preserving the simplification aspects of the current partnership rules for transactions involving smaller amounts. The Committee was made aware that certain types of investment partnerships would incur administrative difficulties in making partnership-level basis adjustments in the event of a transfer of a partnership interest, as evidenced by the present practice of a number of investment partnerships not to elect partnership basis adjustments even when the adjustments would be upward adjustments to the basis of partnership property. Accordingly, the bill provides a partner-level loss limitation as an alternative to the partnership basis adjustments otherwise required under the bill in the case of transfers of interests in certain investment partnerships that are engaged in investment activities rather than in any trade or business activity.

Explanation of Provision

Contributions of property

Under the provision, a built-in loss may be taken into account only by the contributing partner and not by other partners. Except as provided in regulations, in determining the amount of items allocated to partners other than the contributing partner, the basis of the contributed property is treated as the fair market value at the time of contribution. Thus, if the contributing partner's partnership interest is transferred or liquidated, the partnership's adjusted basis in the property is based on its fair market value at the time of contribution, and the built-in loss is eliminated.[312]

Transfers of partnership interests

The provision provides generally that the basis adjustment rules under section 743 are mandatory in the case of the transfer of a partnership interest with respect to which there is a substantial built-in loss (rather than being elective as under present law). For this purpose, a substantial built-in loss exists if the partnership's adjusted basis in its property exceeds by more than $250,000 the fair market value of the partnership property.

Thus, for example, assume that partner A sells his 25-percent partnership interest to B for its fair market value of $1 million. Also assume that, immediately after the transfer, the fair market value of partnership assets is $4 million and the partnership's adjusted basis in the partnership assets is $4.3 million. Under the bill, section 743(b) applies, so that an adjustment is required to the adjusted basis of the partnership assets with respect to B. As a result, B would recognize no gain or loss if the partnership immediately sold all its assets for their fair market value.

The bill provides that an electing investment partnership is not treated as having a substantial built-in loss, and thus is not required to make basis adjustments to partnership property, in the case of a transfer of a partnership interest. In lieu of the partnership basis adjustments, a partner-level loss limitation rule applies. Under this rule, the transferee partner's distributive share of losses (determined without regard to gains) from the sale or exchange of partnership property is

---

[310] Sec. 734(a).

[311] Sec. 734(b).

[312] It is intended that a corporation succeeding to attributes of the contributing corporate partner under section 381

shall be treated in the same manner as the contributing partner.

not allowed, except to the extent it is established that the partner's share of such losses exceeds the loss recognized by the transferor partner. In the event of successive transfers, the transferee partner's distributive share of such losses is not allowed, except to the extent that it is established that such losses exceed the loss recognized by the transferor (or any prior transferor to the extent not fully offset by a prior disallowance under this rule). Losses disallowed under this rule do not decrease the transferee partner's basis in its partnership interest. Thus, on subsequent disposition of its partnership interest, the partner's gain is reduced (or loss increased) because the basis of the partnership interest has not been reduced by such losses. The provision is applied without regard to any termination of a partnership under section 708(b)(1)(B). In the case of a basis reduction to property distributed to the transferee partner in a nonliquidating distribution, the amount of the transferor's loss taken into account under this rule is reduced by the amount of the basis reduction.

For this purpose, an electing investment partnership means a partnership that satisfies the following requirements: (1) it makes an election under the provision that is irrevocable except with the consent of the Secretary; (2) it would be an investment company under section 3(a)(1)(A) of the Investment Company Act of 1940[313] but for an exemption under paragraph (1) or (7) of section 3(c) of that Act; (3) it has never been engaged in a trade or business; (4) substantially all of its assets are held for investment; (5) at least 95 percent of the assets contributed to it consist of money; (6) no assets contributed to it had an adjusted basis in excess of fair market value at the time of contribution; (7) all partnership interests are issued by the partnership pursuant to a private offering and during the 24-month period beginning on the date of the first capital contribution to the partnership; (8) the partnership agreement has substantive restrictions on each partner's ability to cause a redemption of the partner's interest, and (9) the partnership agreement provides for a term that is not in excess of 15 years.

The provision requires an electing investment partnership to furnish to any transferee partner the information necessary to enable the partner to compute the amount of losses disallowed under this rule.

Distributions of partnership property

The provision provides that a basis adjustment under section 734(b) is required in the case of a distribution with respect to which there is a substantial basis reduction. A substantial basis reduction means a downward adjustment of more than $250,000 that would be made to the basis of partnership assets if a section 754 election were in effect.

Thus, for example, assume that A and B each contributed $2.5 million to a newly formed partnership and C contributed $5 million, and that the partnership purchased LMN stock for $3 million and XYZ stock for $7 million. Assume that the value of each stock declined to $1 million. Assume LMN stock is distributed to C in liquidation of its partnership interest. Under present law, the basis of LMN stock in C's hands is $5 million. Under present law, C would recognize a loss of $4 million if the LMN stock were sold for $1 million.

Under the provision, there is a substantial basis adjustment because the $2 million increase in the adjusted basis of LMN stock (described in section 734(b)(2)(B)) is greater than $250,000. Thus, the partnership is required to decrease the basis of XYZ stock (under section 734(b)(2)) by $2 million (the amount by which the basis of LMN stock was increased), leaving a basis of $5 million. If the XYZ stock were then sold by the partnership for $1 million, A and B would each recognize a loss of $2 million.

Effective Date

The provision applies to contributions, distributions and transfers (as the case may be) after the date of enactment.

In the case of an electing investment partnership in existence on June 4, 2004, the requirement that the partnership agreement have substantive restrictions on redemptions does not apply, and the requirement that the partnership agreement provide for a term not exceeding 15 years is modified to permit a term not exceeding 20 years.

Conference Committee Report (H.R. CONF. REP. NO. 108-755)

The conference agreement generally follows the House bill, with modifications.

The conference agreement modifies the qualification requirements for electing investment partnerships that are subject to a partner-level loss limitation rule in lieu of the requirement of partnership basis adjustments following certain transfers of partnership interests. Specifically, the conference agreement requires that all partnership interests be issued by such a part-

---

[313] Section 3(a)(1)(A) of the Act provides, "when used in this title, 'investment company' means any issuer which is or hold itself out as being engaged primarily, or proposes to engage primarily, in the business of investing, reinvesting, or trading in securities."

nership pursuant to a private offering prior to the date that is 24 months after the date of the first capital contribution to the partnership. The conferees intend that "dry" closings in which partnership interests are issued without the contribution of capital not start the running of the 24-month period.

It is intended that in applying the requirement (with respect electing investment partnerships) that the partnership agreement have substantive restrictions on each partner's ability to cause a redemption, the following are illustrative examples of substantive restrictions: a violation of Federal or State law (such as ERISA or the Bank Holding Company Act); and imposition of a Federal excise tax on, or a change in the Federal tax-exempt status of, a tax-exempt partner.

The conferees understand that electing investment partnerships will generally include venture capital funds, buyout funds, and funds of funds. These funds are formed to raise capital from investors pursuant to a private offering and to make investments during the limited term of the partnership with the intention of holding the investments for capital appreciation.

With respect to the requirement that an electing investment partnership furnish to any transferee partner the information necessary to enable the partner to compute the amount of losses disallowed under this rule, it is expected that in some cases the transferor of the partnership interest will furnish information relating to the amount of its loss to the transferee partner. It is intended that the requirement that the electing investment partnership furnish necessary information to the transferee partner be administered by the Treasury Secretary in a manner that (to the greatest extent feasible) minimizes the need for the partnership to furnish information to the transferee partner that the transferee partner has obtained from the transferor.

The conference agreement adds an exception for securitization partnerships to the rules requiring partnership basis adjustments in the case of transfers of partnership interests and distributions of property to a partner. The exceptions provide that a securitization partnership is not treated as having a substantial built-in loss in the case of a transfer of a partnership interest, or as having a substantial basis reduction in the case of a partnership distribution, and thus is not required to make basis adjustments to partner-

ship property. Partnership basis adjustments remain elective for such a partnership. Unlike in the case of an electing investment partnership, the partner-level loss limitation rule does not apply in the case of a securitization partnership. For this purpose, a securitization partnership is any partnership the sole business activity of which is to issue securities that provide for a fixed principal (or similar) amount and that are primarily serviced by the cash flows of a discrete pool (either fixed or revolving) of receivables or other financial assets that by their terms convert into cash in a finite period, but only if the sponsor of the pool reasonably believes that the receivables and other financial assets comprising the pool are not acquired so as to be disposed of. It is intended that rules similar to those applicable to sponsors of REMICs apply in determining whether the sponsor's belief is reasonable.[548] It is not intended that the rules requiring partnership basis adjustments on transfers or distributions be avoided through dispositions of pool assets.

It is intended that an electing investment partnership or securitization partnership that subsequently fails to meet the definition of an electing investment partnership or of a securitization partnership will be subject to the partnership basis adjustment rules of the provision with respect to the first transfer of a partnership interest (and, in the case of a securitization partnership, the first distribution) that occurs after the partnership ceases to meet the applicable definition and to each subsequent transfer (and distribution, in the case of a securitization partnership).

It is not intended that the rules of the conference agreement provisions be avoided through the use of tiered partnerships.

It is not intended that the provision relating to contributions of built-in loss property limit the ability of master-feeder structures to apply an aggregate method for making allocations under section 704(c) to the extent the aggregate method is permitted under present law.[549]

Effective Date

The conference agreement follows the House bill.

[Law at ¶5505, ¶5515, ¶5520 and ¶6125. CCH Explanation at ¶960.]

---

[548] See Treas. Reg. sec. 1.860G-2(a)(3), providing that a sponsor's belief is not reasonable if the sponsor actually knows or has reason to know that the requirement is not met, or if the requirement is later discovered not to have been met.

[549] See Rev. Proc. 2001-36, 2001-1 C.B. 1326. Definitional requirements of a master-feeder structure include that there is a portfolio of assets that is treated as a partnership for Federal tax purposes and that is registered as an investment

company under the Investment Company Act of 1940, each partner of which is a feeder fund that is a registered investment company (RIC) for Federal tax purposes, or is an investment advisor, principal underwriter, or manager of the portfolio. The conferees believe that these restrictions (and other applicable restrictions) serve to limit potential avoidance of the section 704(c) provision of the conference agreement through use of the aggregate method in the case of master-feeder structures.

[¶ 11,170] Act Sec. 834. No reduction of basis under section 734 in stock held by partnership in corporate partner

House Committee Report (H.R. REP. NO. 108-548, pt. 1)

[Code Sec. 755]

Present Law

In general

Generally, a partner and the partnership do not recognize gain or loss on a contribution of property to the partnership.[314] Similarly, a partner and the partnership generally do not recognize gain or loss on the distribution of partnership property.[315] This includes current distributions and distributions in liquidation of a partner's interest.

Basis of property distributed in liquidation

The basis of property distributed in liquidation of a partner's interest is equal to the partner's tax basis in its partnership interest (reduced by any money distributed in the same transaction).[316] Thus, the partnership's tax basis in the distributed property is adjusted (increased or decreased) to reflect the partner's tax basis in the partnership interest.

Election to adjust basis of partnership property

When a partnership distributes partnership property, the basis of partnership property generally is not adjusted to reflect the effects of the distribution or transfer. However, the partnership is permitted to make an election (referred to as a 754 election) to adjust the basis of partnership property in the case of a distribution of partnership property.[317] The effect of the 754 election is that the partnership adjusts the basis of its remaining property to reflect any change in basis of the distributed property in the hands of the distributee partner resulting from the distribution transaction. Such a change could be a basis increase due to gain recognition, or a basis decrease due to the partner's adjusted basis in its partnership interest exceeding the adjusted basis of the property received. If the 754 election is made, it applies to the taxable year with respect

to which such election was filed and all subsequent taxable years.

In the case of a distribution of partnership property to a partner with respect to which the 754 election is in effect, the partnership increases the basis of partnership property by (1) any gain recognized by the distributee partner and (2) the excess of the adjusted basis of the distributed property to the partnership immediately before its distribution over the basis of the property to the distributee partner, and decreases the basis of partnership property by (1) any loss recognized by the distributee partner and (2) the excess of the basis of the property to the distributee partner over the adjusted basis of the distributed property to the partnership immediately before the distribution.

The allocation of the increase or decrease in basis of partnership property is made in a manner that has the effect of reducing the difference between the fair market value and the adjusted basis of partnership properties.[318] In addition, the allocation rules require that any increase or decrease in basis be allocated to partnership property of a like character to the property distributed. For this purpose, the two categories of assets are (1) capital assets and depreciable and real property used in the trade or business held for more than one year, and (2) any other property.[319]

Reasons for Change

The Joint Committee on Taxation staff's investigative report of Enron Corporation[320] revealed that certain transactions were being undertaken that purported to use the interaction of the partnership basis adjustment rules and the rules protecting a corporation from recognizing gain on its stock to obtain unintended tax results. These transactions generally purported to increase the tax basis of depreciable assets and to decrease, by a corresponding amount, the tax basis of the stock of a partner. Because the tax rules protect a corporation from gain on the sale

---

[314] Sec. 721(a).
[315] Sec. 731(a) and (b).
[316] Sec. 732(b).
[317] Sec. 754.
[318] Sec. 755(a).

[319] Sec. 755(b).
[320] See Joint Committee on Taxation, Report of Investigation of Enron Corporation and Related Entities Regarding Federal Tax and Compensation Issues, and Policy Recommendations (JCS-3-03), February 2003.

of its stock (including through a partnership), the transactions enable taxpayers to duplicate tax deductions at no economic cost. The provision precludes the ability to reduce the basis of corporate stock of a partner (or related party) in certain transactions.

Explanation of Provision

The provision provides that in applying the basis allocation rules to a distribution in liquidation of a partner's interest, a partnership is precluded from decreasing the basis of corporate stock of a partner or a related person. Any decrease in basis that, absent the provision, would have been allocated to the stock is allocated to other partnership assets. If the decrease in basis exceeds the basis of the other partnership assets, then gain is recognized by the partnership in the amount of the excess.

Effective Date

The provision applies to distributions after the date of enactment.

Conference Committee Report (H.R. CONF. REP. NO. 108-755)

The conference agreement follows the House bill.

[Law at ¶ 5530. CCH Explanation at ¶ 965.]

[¶ 11,180] Act Sec. 835. Repeal of special rules for FASITs

House Committee Report (H.R. REP. NO. 108-548, pt. 1)

[Code Secs. 860H, 860I, 860J, 860K, and 860L]

Present Law

Financial asset securitization investment trusts

In 1996, Congress created a new type of statutory entity called a "financial asset securitization trust" ("FASIT") that facilitates the securitization of debt obligations such as credit card receivables, home equity loans, and auto loans.[321] A FASIT generally is not taxable. Instead, the FASIT's taxable income or net loss flows through to the owner of the FASIT.

The ownership interest of a FASIT generally is required to be held entirely by a single domestic C corporation. In addition, a FASIT generally may hold only qualified debt obligations, and certain other specified assets, and is subject to certain restrictions on its activities. An entity that qualifies as a FASIT can issue one or more classes of instruments that meet certain specified requirements and treat those instruments as debt for Federal income tax purposes.

Qualification as a FASIT

To qualify as a FASIT, an entity must: (1) make an election to be treated as a FASIT for the year of the election and all subsequent years;[322] (2) have assets substantially all of which (including assets that the FASIT is treated as owning

because they support regular interests) are specified types called "permitted assets;" (3) have non-ownership interests be certain specified types of debt instruments called "regular interests"; (4) have a single ownership interest which is held by an "eligible holder"; and (5) not qualify as a regulated investment company ("RIC"). Any entity, including a corporation, partnership, or trust may be treated as a FASIT. In addition, a segregated pool of assets may qualify as a FASIT.

An entity ceases qualifying as a FASIT if the entity's owner ceases being an eligible corporation. Loss of FASIT status is treated as if all of the regular interests of the FASIT were retired and then reissued without the application of the rule that deems regular interests of a FASIT to be debt.

Permitted assets

For an entity or arrangement to qualify as a FASIT, substantially all of its assets must consist of the following "permitted assets": (1) cash and cash equivalents; (2) certain permitted debt instruments; (3) certain foreclosure property; (4) certain instruments or contracts that represent a hedge or guarantee of debt held or issued by the FASIT; (5) contract rights to acquire permitted debt instruments or hedges; and (6) a regular interest in another FASIT. Permitted assets may be acquired at any time by a FASIT, including any time after its formation.

---

[321] Sections 860H-860L.

[322] Once an election to be a FASIT is made, the election applies from the date specified in the election and all subsequent years until the entity ceases to be a FASIT. If an election to be a FASIT is made after the initial year of an

entity, all of the assets in the entity at the time of the FASIT election are deemed contributed to the FASIT at that time and, accordingly, any gain (but not loss) on such assets will be recognized at that time.

"Regular interests" of a FASIT

"Regular interests" of a FASIT are treated as debt for Federal income tax purposes, regardless of whether instruments with similar terms issued by non-FASITs might be characterized as equity under general tax principles. To be treated as a "regular interest", an instrument generally must have fixed terms and must: (1) unconditionally entitle the holder to receive a specified principal amount; (2) pay interest that is based on (a) fixed rates, or (b) except as provided by regulations issued by the Secretary, variable rates permitted with respect to real estate mortgage investment conduit interests under section 860G(a)(1)(B)(i); (3) have a term to maturity of no more than 30 years, except as permitted by Treasury regulations; (4) be issued to the public with a premium of not more than 25 percent of its stated principal amount; and (5) have a yield to maturity determined on the date of issue of less than five percentage points above the applicable Federal rate ("AFR") for the calendar month in which the instrument is issued. Instruments that do not satisfy certain of these general requirements nevertheless may be treated as regular interests if they are held by a domestic taxable C corporation that is not a RIC, real estate investment trust ("REIT"), FASIT, or cooperative.

Transfers to FASITs

In general, gain (but not loss) is recognized immediately by the owner of the FASIT upon the transfer of assets to a FASIT. Where property is acquired by a FASIT from someone other than the FASIT's owner (or a person related to the FASIT's owner), the property is treated as being first acquired by the FASIT's owner for the FASIT's cost in acquiring the asset from the nonowner and then transferred by the owner to the FASIT.

Valuation rules

In general, except in the case of debt instruments, the value of FASIT assets is their fair market value. Similarly, in the case of debt instruments that are traded on an established securities market, the market price is used for purposes of determining the amount of gain realized upon contribution of such assets to a FASIT. However, in the case of debt instruments that are not traded on an established securities market, special valuation rules apply for purposes of computing gain on the transfer of such debt instruments to a FASIT. Under these rules, the value of such debt instruments is the sum of the present values of the reasonably expected cash flows from such obligations discounted over the weighted average life of such assets. The discount rate is 120 percent of the AFR, compounded semiannually, or such other rate that the Secretary shall prescribe by regulations.

Taxation of a FASIT

A FASIT generally is not subject to tax. Instead, all of the FASIT's assets and liabilities are treated as assets and liabilities of the FASIT's owner and any income, gain, deduction or loss of the FASIT is allocable directly to its owner. Accordingly, income tax rules applicable to a FASIT (e.g., related party rules, sec. 871(h), sec. 165(g)(2)) are to be applied in the same manner as they apply to the FASIT's owner. The taxable income of a FASIT is calculated using an accrual method of accounting. The constant yield method and principles that apply for purposes of determining original issue discount ("OID") accrual on debt obligations whose principal is subject to acceleration apply to all debt obligations held by a FASIT to calculate the FASIT's interest and discount income and premium deductions or adjustments.

Taxation of holders of FASIT regular interests

In general, a holder of a regular interest is taxed in the same manner as a holder of any other debt instrument, except that the regular interest holder is required to account for income relating to the interest on an accrual method of accounting, regardless of the method of accounting otherwise used by the holder.

Taxation of holders of FASIT ownership interests

Because all of the assets and liabilities of a FASIT are treated as assets and liabilities of the holder of a FASIT ownership interest, the ownership interest holder takes into account all of the FASIT's income, gain, deduction, or loss in computing its taxable income or net loss for the taxable year. The character of the income to the holder of an ownership interest is the same as its character to the FASIT, except tax-exempt interest is included in the income of the holder as ordinary income.

Although the recognition of losses on assets contributed to the FASIT is not allowed upon contribution of the assets, such losses may be allowed to the FASIT owner upon their disposition by the FASIT. Furthermore, the holder of a FASIT ownership interest is not permitted to offset taxable income from the FASIT ownership interest (including gain or loss from the sale of the ownership interest in the FASIT) with other losses of the holder. In addition, any net operating loss carryover of the FASIT owner shall be computed by disregarding any income arising by reason of a disallowed loss. Where the holder of a FASIT ownership interest is a member of a consolidated group, this rule applies to the consolidated group of corporations of which the holder is a member as if the group were a single taxpayer.

Act Sec. 835   ¶11,180

Real estate mortgage investment conduits

In general, a real estate mortgage investment conduit ("REMIC") is a self-liquidating entity that holds a fixed pool of mortgages and issues multiple classes of investor interests. A REMIC is not treated as a separate taxable entity. Rather, the income of the REMIC is allocated to, and taken into account by, the holders of the interests in the REMIC under detailed rules.[323] In order to qualify as a REMIC, substantially all of the assets of the entity must consist of qualified mortgages and permitted investments as of the close of the third month beginning after the startup day of the entity. A "qualified mortgage" generally includes any obligation which is principally secured by an interest in real property, and which is either transferred to the REMIC on the startup day of the REMIC in exchange for regular or residual interests in the REMIC or purchased by the REMIC within three months after the startup day pursuant to a fixed-price contract in effect on the startup day. A "permitted investment" generally includes any intangible property that is held for investment and is part of a reasonably required reserve to provide for full payment of certain expenses of the REMIC or amounts due on regular interests.

All of the interests in the REMIC must consist of one or more classes of regular interests and a single class of residual interests. A "regular interest" is an interest in a REMIC that is issued with a fixed term, designated as a regular interest, and unconditionally entitles the holder to receive a specified principal amount (or other similar amount) with interest payments that are either based on a fixed rate (or, to the extent provided in regulations, a variable rate) or consist of a specified portion of the interest payments on qualified mortgages that does not vary during the period such interest is outstanding. In general, a "residual interest" is any interest in the REMIC other than a regular interest, and which is so designated by the REMIC, provided that there is only one class of such interest and that all distributions (if any) with respect to such interests are pro rata. Holders of residual REMIC interests are subject to tax on the portion of the income of the REMIC that is not allocated to the regular interest holders.

Reasons for Change

The Joint Committee on Taxation staff's investigative report of Enron Corporation[324] de-

scribed two structured tax-motivated transactions—Projects Apache and Renegade—that Enron undertook in which the use of a FASIT was a key component in the structure of the transactions. The Committee is aware that FASITs are not being used widely in the manner envisioned by the Congress and, consequently, the FASIT rules have not served the purpose for which they originally were intended. Moreover, the Joint Committee staff's report and other information indicate that FASITs are particularly prone to abuse and likely are being used primarily to facilitate tax avoidance transactions.[325] Therefore, the Committee believes that the potential for abuse that is inherent in FASITs far outweighs any beneficial purpose that the FASIT rules may serve. Accordingly, the Committee believes that these rules should be repealed, with appropriate transition relief for existing FASITs and appropriate modifications to the present-law REMIC rules to permit the use of REMICs by taxpayers that have relied upon FASITs to securitize certain obligations secured by interests in real property.

Explanation of Provision

The provision repeals the special rules for FASITs. The provision provides a transition period for existing FASITs, pursuant to which the repeal of the FASIT rules generally does not apply to any FASIT in existence on the date of enactment to the extent that regular interests issued by the FASIT prior to such date continue to remain outstanding in accordance with their original terms.

For purposes of the REMIC rules, the provision also modifies the definitions of REMIC regular interests, qualified mortgages, and permitted investments so that certain types of real estate loans and loan pools can be transferred to, or purchased by, a REMIC. Specifically, the provision modifies the present-law definition of a REMIC "regular interest" to provide that an interest in a REMIC does not fail to qualify as a regular interest solely because the specified principal amount of such interest or the amount of interest accrued on such interest could be reduced as a result of the nonoccurrence of one or more contingent payments with respect to one or more reverse mortgages loans, as defined below, that are held by the REMIC, provided that on the startup day for the REMIC, the REMIC sponsor reasonably believes that all

---

[323] See sections 860A-860G.

[324] See Joint Committee on Taxation, Report of Investigation of Enron Corporation and Related Entities Regarding Federal Tax and Compensation Issues, and Policy Recommendations (JCS-3-03), February 2003.

[325] For example, the Committee is aware that FASITs also have been used to facilitate the issuance of certain tax-

advantaged cross-border hybrid instruments that are treated as indebtedness in the United States but equity in the foreign country of the holder of the instruments. Congress did not intend such use of FASITs when it enacted the FASIT rules.

principal and interest due under the interest will be paid at or prior to the liquidation of the REMIC. For this purpose, a reasonable belief concerning ultimate payment of all amounts due under an interest is presumed to exist if, as of the startup day, the interest receives an investment grade rating from at least one nationally recognized statistical rating agency.

In addition, the provision makes three modifications to the present-law definition of a "qualified mortgage." First, the provision modifies the definition to include an obligation principally secured by real property which represents an increase in the principal amount under the original terms of an obligation, provided such increase: (1) is attributable to an advance made to the obligor pursuant to the original terms of the obligation; (2) occurs after the REMIC startup day; and (3) is purchased by the REMIC pursuant to a fixed price contract in effect on the startup day. Second, the provision modifies the definition to generally include reverse mortgage loans and the periodic advances made to obligors on such loans. For this purpose, a "reverse mortgage loan" is defined as a loan that: (1) is secured by an interest in real property; (2) provides for one or more advances of principal to the obligor (each such advance giving rise to a "balance increase"), provided such advances are principally secured by an interest in the same real property as that which secures the loan; (3) may provide for a contingent payment at matur-

ity based upon the value or appreciation in value of the real property securing the loan; (4) provides for an amount due at maturity that cannot exceed the value, or a specified fraction of the value, of the real property securing the loan; (5) provides that all payments under the loan are due only upon the maturity of the loan; and (6) matures after a fixed term or at the time the obligor ceases to use as a personal residence the real property securing the loan. Third, the provision modifies the definition to provide that, if more than 50 percent of the obligations transferred to, or purchased by, the REMIC are (1) originated by the United States or any State (or any political subdivision, agency, or instrumentality of the United States or any State) and (2) principally secured by an interest in real property, then each obligation transferred to, or purchased by, the REMIC shall be treated as secured by an interest in real property.

In addition, the provision modifies the present-law definition of a "permitted investment" to include intangible investment property held as part of a reasonably required reserve to provide a source of funds for the purchase of obligations described above as part of the modified definition of a "qualified mortgage."

Effective Date

Except as provided by the transition period for existing FASITs, the provision is effective on January 1, 2005.

Conference Committee Report (H.R. CONF. REP. NO. 108-755)

Senate Amendment

The Senate amendment is the same as the House bill, except for the effective date.

[Law at ¶5085, ¶5345, ¶5490, ¶5550, ¶5565, ¶5570, ¶5575, ¶5580, ¶5585, ¶5590, ¶5780 and ¶6355. CCH Explanation at ¶1120.]

* * *

Conference Agreement

The conference agreement follows the House bill provision.

[¶ 11,190] Act Sec. 836. Limitation on transfer and importation of built-in losses

Senate Committee Report (S. REP. NO. 108-192)

[Code Secs. 334 and 362]

Present Law

Generally, no gain or loss is recognized when one or more persons transfer property to a corporation in exchange for stock and immediately after the exchange such person or persons

control the corporation.[241] The transferor's basis in the stock of the controlled corporation is the same as the basis of the property contributed to the controlled corporation, increased by the amount of any gain (or dividend) recognized by the transferor on the exchange, and reduced by the amount of any money or property received,

---

[241] Sec. 351.

and by the amount of any loss recognized by the transferor.[242]

The basis of property received by a corporation, whether from domestic or foreign transferors, in a tax-free incorporation, reorganization, or liquidation of a subsidiary corporation is the same as the adjusted basis in the hands of the transferor, adjusted for gain or loss recognized by the transferor.[243]

Reasons for Change

The Joint Committee on Taxation staff's investigative report of Enron Corporation[244] and other information reveal that taxpayers are engaging in various tax motivated transactions to duplicate a single economic loss and, subsequently, deduct such loss more than once. Congress has previously taken actions to limit the ability of taxpayers to engage in specific transactions that purport to duplicate a single economic loss. However, new schemes that purport to duplicate losses continue to proliferate. In furtherance of the overall tax policy objective of accurately measuring taxable income, the Committee believes that a single economic loss should not be deducted more than once. Thus, the Committee believes that it is generally appropriate to limit a corporation's basis in property acquired in a tax-free transfer to the fair market value of such property. In addition, the Committee believes that it is appropriate to prevent the importation of economic losses into the U.S. tax system if such losses arose prior to the assets becoming subject to the U.S. tax system.

Explanation of Provision

Importation of built-in losses

The provision provides that if a net built-in loss is imported into the U.S. in a tax-free organization or reorganization from persons not subject to U.S. tax, the basis of each property so transferred is its fair market value. A similar rule applies in the case of the tax-free liquidation by a domestic corporation of its foreign subsidiary.

Under the provision, a net built-in loss is treated as imported into the U.S. if the aggregate adjusted bases of property received by a transferee corporation exceeds the fair market value of the properties transferred. Thus, for example, if in a tax-free incorporation, some properties are received by a corporation from U.S. persons subject to tax, and some properties are received from foreign persons not subject to U.S. tax, this provision applies to limit the adjusted basis of each property received from the foreign persons to the fair market value of the property. In the case of a transfer by a partnership (either domestic or foreign), this provision applies as if each partner had transferred such partner's proportionate share of the property of such partnership.

Limitation on transfer of built-in-losses in section 351 transactions

The provision provides that if the aggregate adjusted bases of property contributed by a transferor (or by a control group of which the transferor is a member) to a corporation exceed the aggregate fair market value of the property transferred in a tax-free incorporation, the transferee's aggregate bases of the property is limited to the aggregate fair market value of the transferred property. Under the provision, any required basis reduction is allocated among the transferred properties in proportion to their built-in-loss immediately before the transaction. In the case of a transfer after which the transferor owns at least 80 percent of the vote and value of the stock of the transferee corporation, any basis reduction required by the provision is made to the stock received by the transferor and not to the assets transferred.

Effective Date

The provision applies to transactions after February 13, 2003.

Conference Committee Report (H.R. CONF. REP. NO. 108-755)

Senate Amendment

* * *

Effective Date

The Senate amendment provision applies to transactions after December 31, 2003.

Conference Agreement

The conference agreement follows the Senate amendment, with modifications to the limitation on transfer of built-in losses in section 351 transactions. The conference agreement eliminates the provision that requires a basis reduc-

---

[242] Sec. 358.

[243] Secs. 334(b) and 362(a) and (b).

[244] See Joint Committee on Taxation, Report of Investigation of Enron Corporation and Related Entities Regarding

Federal Tax and Compensation Issues, and Policy Recommendations (JCS-3-03), February 2003.

tion to be made to stock received by the transferor (rather than to the assets transferred) in the case of a transfer in which the transferor owns at least 80 percent of the vote and value of the stock of the transferee corporation. Thus, the provision that limits the transferee's aggregate basis in the transferred property to the aggregate fair market value of the transferred property generally applies, regardless of the ownership percentage of the transferor in the stock of the transferee corporation.

In addition, the conference agreement permits the transferor and transferee to elect to limit the basis in the stock received by the transferor to the aggregate fair market value of the transferred property, in lieu of limiting the basis in the assets transferred. Such election shall be included with the tax returns of the transferor and transferee for the taxable year in which the transaction occurs and, once made, shall be irrevocable.

[Law at ¶ 5310 and ¶ 5335. CCH Explanation at ¶ 520.]

[¶ 11,200] Act Sec. 837. Clarification of banking business for purposes of determining investment of earnings in U.S. property

Conference Committee Report (H.R. Conf. Rep. No. 108-755)

[Code Sec. 956]

Present Law

In general, the subpart F rules[562] require the U.S. 10-percent shareholders of a controlled foreign corporation to include in income currently their pro rata shares of certain income of the controlled foreign corporation (referred to as "subpart F income"), whether or not such earnings are distributed currently to the shareholders. In addition, the U.S. 10-percent shareholders of a controlled foreign corporation are subject to U.S. tax currently on their pro rata shares of the controlled foreign corporation's earnings to the extent invested by the controlled foreign corporation in certain U.S. property.[563]

A shareholder's current income inclusion with respect to a controlled foreign corporation's investment in U.S. property for a taxable year is based on the controlled foreign corporation's average investment in U.S. property for such year. For this purpose, the U.S. property held (directly or indirectly) by the controlled foreign corporation must be measured as of the close of each quarter in the taxable year.[564] The amount taken into account with respect to any property is the property's adjusted basis as determined for purposes of reporting the controlled foreign corporation's earnings and profits, reduced by any liability to which the property is subject. The amount determined for current inclusion is the shareholder's pro rata share of an amount equal to the lesser of: (1) the controlled foreign corporation's average investment in U.S. property as of the end of each quarter of such taxable year, to the extent that such investment exceeds the foreign corporation's earnings and profits that were previously taxed on that basis; or (2) the controlled foreign corporation's current or accumulated earnings and profits (but not including a deficit), reduced by distributions during the year and by earnings that have been taxed previously as earnings invested in U.S. property.[565] An income inclusion is required only to the extent that the amount so calculated exceeds the amount of the controlled foreign corporation's earnings that have been previously taxed as subpart F income.[566]

For purposes of section 956, U.S. property generally is defined to include tangible property located in the United States, stock of a U.S. corporation, an obligation of a U.S. person, and certain intangible assets including a patent or copyright, an invention, model or design, a secret formula or process or similar property right which is acquired or developed by the controlled foreign corporation for use in the United States.[567]

Specified exceptions from the definition of U.S. property are provided for: (1) obligations of the United States, money, or deposits with persons carrying on the banking business; (2) certain export property; (3) certain trade or business obligations; (4) aircraft, railroad rolling stock, vessels, motor vehicles or containers used in transportation in foreign commerce and used predominantly outside of the United States; (5) certain insurance company reserves and unearned premiums related to insurance of foreign risks; (6) stock or debt of certain unrelated U.S. corporations; (7) moveable property (other than a vessel or aircraft) used for the purpose of exploring, developing, or certain other activities in connection with the ocean waters of the U.S.

---

[562] Secs. 951-964.
[563] Sec. 951(a)(1)(B).
[564] Sec. 956(a).

[565] Secs. 956 and 959.
[566] Secs. 951(a)(1)(B) and 959.
[567] Sec. 956(c)(1).

Continental Shelf; (8) an amount of assets equal to the controlled foreign corporation's accumulated earnings and profits attributable to income effectively connected with a U.S. trade or business; (9) property (to the extent provided in regulations) held by a foreign sales corporation and related to its export activities; (10) certain deposits or receipts of collateral or margin by a securities or commodities dealer, if such deposit is made or received on commercial terms in the ordinary course of the dealer's business as a securities or commodities dealer; and (11) certain repurchase and reverse repurchase agreement transactions entered into by or with a dealer in securities or commodities in the ordinary course of its business as a securities or commodities dealer.[568]

With regard to the exception for deposits with persons carrying on the banking business, the U.S. Court of Appeals for the Sixth Circuit in *The Limited, Inc. v. Commissioner*[569] concluded that a U.S. subsidiary of a U.S. shareholder was "carrying on the banking business" even though its operations were limited to the administration of the private label credit card program of the U.S. shareholder. Therefore, the court held that a controlled foreign corporation of the U.S. shareholder could make deposits with the subsidiary (e.g., through the purchase of certificates of deposit) under this exception, and avoid taxation of the deposits under section 956 as an investment in U.S. property.

House Bill

The House bill provides that the exception from the definition of U.S. property under section 956 for deposits with persons carrying on the banking business is limited to deposits with persons at least 80 percent of the gross income of which is derived in the active conduct of a banking business from unrelated persons. For purposes of applying the House bill, the deposit recipient and all persons related to the deposit recipient are treated as one person in applying the 80-percent test.

No inference is intended as to the meaning of the phrase "carrying on the banking business" under present law.

Effective Date

The House bill provision is effective on the date of enactment.

Senate Amendment

The Senate amendment is the same as the House bill, except the Senate amendment applies the 80-percent test by reference to financial services income (as defined in section 904(d)(2)(C)(ii) rather than the active conduct of a banking business.

Effective Date

The Senate amendment provision is effective on the date of enactment.

Conference Agreement

The conference agreement provides that the exception from the definition of U.S. property under section 956 for deposits with persons carrying on the banking business is limited to deposits with: (1) any bank (as defined by section 2(c) of the Bank Holding Company Act of 1956 (12 U.S.C. 1841(c), without regard to paragraphs (C) and (G) of paragraph (2) of such section); or (2) any other corporation with respect to which a bank holding company (as defined by section 2(a) of such Act) or financial holding company (as defined by section 2(p) of such Act) owns directly or indirectly more than 80 percent by vote or value of the stock of such corporation.

No inference is intended as to the meaning of the phrase "carrying on the banking business" under present law.

Effective Date

The conference agreement provision is effective on the date of enactment.

[Law at ¶ 5725. CCH Explanation at ¶ 485.]

[¶ 11,210] Act Sec. 838. Denial of deduction for interest on underpayments attributable to nondisclosed reportable transactions

House Committee Report (H.R. REP. NO. 108-548, pt. 1)

[Code Sec. 163]

Present Law

In general, corporations may deduct interest paid or accrued within a taxable year on indebtedness.[339] Interest on indebtedness to the Federal government attributable to an underpayment of

tax generally may be deducted pursuant to this provision.

Reasons for Change

The Committee believes that it is inappropriate for corporations to deduct interest paid to

---

[568] Sec. 956(c)(2).
[569] 286 F.3d 324 (6th Cir. 2002), *rev'g* 113 T.C. 169 (1999).

[339] Sec. 163(a).

the Government with respect to certain tax shelter transactions.

Explanation of Provision

The provision disallows any deduction for interest paid or accrued within a taxable year on any portion of an underpayment of tax that is attributable to an understatement arising from an undisclosed listed transaction or from an undisclosed reportable avoidance transaction (other than a listed transaction).[340]

Effective Date

The provision is effective for underpayments attributable to transactions entered into in taxable years beginning after the date of enactment.

Conference Committee Report (H.R. CONF. REP. NO. 108-755)

The conference agreement follows the House bill.

[Law at ¶ 5165. CCH Explanation at ¶ 625.]

[¶ 11,220] Act Sec. 839. Clarification of rules for payment of estimated tax for certain deemed asset sales

House Committee Report (H.R. REP. NO. 108-548, pt. 1)

[Code Sec. 338]

Present Law

In certain circumstances, taxpayers can make an election under section 338(h)(10) to treat a qualifying purchase of 80 percent of the stock of a target corporation by a corporation from a corporation that is a member of an affiliated group (or a qualifying purchase of 80 percent of the stock of an S corporation by a corporation from S corporation shareholders) as a sale of the assets of the target corporation, rather than as a stock sale. The election must be made jointly by the buyer and seller of the stock and is due by the 15th day of the ninth month beginning after the month in which the acquisition date occurs. An agreement for the purchase and sale of stock often may contain an agreement of the parties to make a section 338(h)(10) election.

Section 338(a) also permits a unilateral election by a buyer corporation to treat a qualified stock purchase of a corporation as a deemed asset acquisition, whether or not the seller of the stock is a corporation (or an S corporation is the target). In such a case, the seller or sellers recognize gain or loss on the stock sale (including any estimated taxes with respect to the stock sale), and the target corporation recognizes gain or loss on the deemed asset sale.

Section 338(h)(13) provides that, for purposes of section 6655 (relating to additions to tax for failure by a corporation to pay estimated income tax), tax attributable to a deemed asset sale under section 338(a)(1) shall not be taken into account.

Reasons for Change

The Committee is concerned that some taxpayers may inappropriately be taking the position that estimated tax and the penalty (computed in the amount of an interest charge) under section 6655 applies neither to the stock sale nor to the asset sale in the case of a section 338(h)(10) election. The Committee believes that estimated tax should not be avoided merely because an election may be made under section 338(h)(10). Furthermore, the Committee understands that parties typically negotiate a sale with an understanding as to whether or not an election under section 338(h)(10) will be made. In the event there is a contingency in this regard, the parties may provide for adjustments to the price to reflect the effect of the election.

Explanation of Provision

The provision clarifies section 338(h)(13) to provide that the exception for estimated tax purposes with respect to tax attributable to a deemed asset sale does not apply with respect to a qualified stock purchase for which an election is made under section 338(h)(10).

Under the provision, if a qualified stock purchase transaction eligible for the election under section 338(h)(10) occurs, estimated tax would be determined based on the stock sale unless and until there is an agreement of the parties to make a section 338(h)(10) election.

If at the time of the sale there is an agreement of the parties to make a section 338(h)(10) election, then estimated tax is computed based

---

[340] The definitions of these transactions are the same as those previously described in connection with the provision elsewhere in this bill to modify the accuracy-related penalty for listed and certain reportable transactions.

on an asset sale, computed from the date of the sale.

If the agreement to make a section 338(h)(10) election is concluded after the stock sale, such that the original computation was based on the stock sale, estimated tax is recomputed based on the asset sale election.

No inference is intended as to present law.

Effective Date

The bill is effective for qualified stock purchase transactions that occur after the date of enactment.

Conference Committee Report (H.R. CONF. REP. NO. 108-755)

Senate Amendment

The Senate amendment is the same as the House bill.

Conference Agreement

The Conference agreement follows the House bill and the Senate amendment.

[Law at ¶5315. CCH Explanation at ¶1020.]

[¶11,230] Act Sec. 840. Exclusion of like-kind exchange property from nonrecognition treatment on the sale or exchange of a principal residence

House Committee Report (H.R. REP. NO. 108-548, pt. 1)

[Code Sec. 121]

Present Law

Under present law, a taxpayer may exclude up to $250,000 ($500,000 if married filing a joint return) of gain realized on the sale or exchange of a principal residence.[341] To be eligible for the exclusion, the taxpayer must have owned and used the residence as a principal residence for at least two of the five years prior to the sale or exchange. A taxpayer who fails to meet these requirements by reason of a change of place of employment, health, or, to the extent provided under regulations, unforeseen circumstances is able to exclude an amount equal to the fraction of the $250,000 ($500,000 if married filing a joint return) that is equal to the fraction of the two years that the ownership and use requirements are met. There are no special rules relating to the sale or exchange of a principal residence that was acquired in a like-kind exchange within the prior five years.

Reasons for Change

The Committee believes that the present-law exclusion of gain allowable upon the sale or exchange of principal residences serves an important role in encouraging home ownership. The Committee does not believe that this exclusion is appropriate for properties that were re-

cently acquired in like-kind exchanges. Under the like-kind exchange rules, a taxpayer that exchanges property that was held for productive use or investment for like-kind property may acquire the replacement property on a tax-free basis. Because the replacement property generally has a low carry-over tax basis, the taxpayer will have taxable gain upon the sale or exchange of the replacement property. However, when the taxpayer converts the replacement property into the taxpayer's principal residence, the taxpayer may shelter some or all of this gain from income taxation. The Committee believes that this provision balances the concerns associated with these provisions to reduce this tax shelter concern without unduly limiting the exclusion on sales or exchanges of principal residences.

Explanation of Provision

The bill provides that the exclusion for gain on the sale or exchange of a principal residence does not apply if the principal residence was acquired in a like-kind exchange in which any gain was not recognized within the prior five years.

Effective Date

The provision is effective for sales or exchanges of principal residences after the date of enactment.

---

[341] Sec. 121.

Conference Committee Report (H.R. CONF. REP. NO. 108-755)

Senate Amendment

[Law at ¶ 5130. CCH Explanation at ¶ 1210.]

The Senate amendment is the same as the House bill.

Conference Agreement

The conference agreement follows the House bill and the Senate amendment.

[¶ 11,240] Act Sec. 841. Prevention of mismatching of interest and original issue discount deductions and income inclusions in transactions with related foreign persons

House Committee Report (H.R. REP. NO. 108-548, pt. 1)

[Code Secs. 163 and 267]

Present Law

Income earned by a foreign corporation from its foreign operations generally is subject to U.S. tax only when such income is distributed to any U.S. person that holds stock in such corporation. Accordingly, a U.S. person that conducts foreign operations through a foreign corporation generally is subject to U.S. tax on the income from such operations when the income is repatriated to the United States through a dividend distribution to the U.S. person. The income is reported on the U.S. person's tax return for the year the distribution is received, and the United States imposes tax on such income at that time. However, certain anti-deferral regimes may cause the U.S. person to be taxed on a current basis in the United States with respect to certain categories of passive or highly mobile income earned by the foreign corporations in which the U.S. person holds stock. The main anti-deferral regimes are the controlled foreign corporation rules of subpart F (secs. 951-964), the passive foreign investment company rules (secs. 1291-1298), and the foreign personal holding company rules (secs. 551-558).

As a general rule, there is allowed as a deduction all interest paid or accrued within the taxable year with respect to indebtedness, including the aggregate daily portions of original issue discount ("OID") of the issuer for the days during such taxable year.[342] However, if a debt instrument is held by a related foreign person, any portion of such OID is not allowable as a deduction to the payor of such instrument until paid ("related-foreign-person rule"). This related-foreign-person rule does not apply to the

extent that the OID is effectively connected with the conduct by such foreign related person of a trade or business within the United States (unless such OID is exempt from taxation or is subject to a reduced rate of taxation under a treaty obligation).[343] Treasury regulations further modify the related-foreign-person rule by providing that in the case of a debt owed to a foreign personal holding company ("FPHC"), controlled foreign corporation ("CFC") or passive foreign investment company ("PFIC"), a deduction is allowed for OID as of the day on which the amount is includible in the income of the FPHC, CFC or PFIC, respectively.[344]

In the case of unpaid stated interest and expenses of related persons, where, by reason of a payee's method of accounting, an amount is not includible in the payee's gross income until it is paid but the unpaid amounts are deductible currently by the payor, the amount generally is allowable as a deduction when such amount is includible in the gross income of the payee.[345] With respect to stated interest and other expenses owed to related foreign corporations, Treasury regulations provide a general rule that requires a taxpayer to use the cash method of accounting with respect to the deduction of amounts owed to such related foreign persons (with an exception for income of a related foreign person that is effectively connected with the conduct of a U.S. trade or business and that is not exempt from taxation or subject to a reduced rate of taxation under a treaty obligation).[346] As in the case of OID, the Treasury regulations additionally provide that in the case of stated interest owed to a FPHC, CFC, or PFIC, a deduction is allowed as of the day on which the amount is

---

[342] Sec. 163(e)(1).

[343] Sec. 163(e)(3).

[344] Treas. Reg. sec. 1.163-12(b)(3). In the case of a PFIC, the regulations further require that the person owing the

amount at issue have in effect a qualified electing fund election pursuant to section 1295 with respect to the PFIC.

[345] Sec. 267(a)(2).

[346] Treas. Reg. sec. 1.267(a)-3(b)(1), -3(c).

includible in the income of the FPHC, CFC or PFIC.[347]

Reasons for Change

The special rules in the Treasury regulations for FPHCs, CFCs and PFICs are exceptions to the general rule that OID and unpaid interest owed to a related foreign person are deductible when paid (i.e., under the cash method). These special rules were deemed appropriate in the case of FPHCs, CFCs and PFICs because it was thought that there would be little material distortion in matching of income and deductions with respect to amounts owed to a related foreign corporation that is required to determine its taxable income and earnings and profits for U.S. tax purposes pursuant to the FPHC, subpart F or PFIC provisions. The Committee believes that this premise fails to take into account the situation where amounts owed to the related foreign corporation are included in the income of the related foreign corporation but are not currently included in the income of the related foreign corporation's U.S. shareholder. Consequently, under the Treasury regulations, both the U.S. payors and U.S.-owned foreign payors may be able to accrue deductions for amounts owed to related FPHCs, CFCs or PFICs without the U.S. owners of such related entities taking into account for U.S. tax purposes a corresponding amount of income. These deductions can be used to reduce U.S. income or, in the case of a U.S.-owned foreign payor, to reduce earnings and profits which could reduce a CFC's income that would be currently taxable to its U.S. shareholders under subpart F.

Explanation of Provision

The provision provides that deductions for amounts accrued but unpaid (whether by U.S. or foreign persons) to related FPHCs, CFCs, or PFICs are allowable only to the extent that the amounts accrued by the payor are, for U.S. tax purposes, currently includible in the income of the direct or indirect U.S. owners of the related foreign corporation under the relevant inclusion rules.[348] Deductions that have accrued but are not allowable under this provision are allowed when the amounts are paid.

For purposes of determining how much of the amount accrued, if any, is currently includible in the income of a U.S. person under the

relevant inclusion rules, properly allowable deductions of the related foreign corporation and qualified deficits under section 952(c)(1)(B) are taken into account. For this purpose, properly allowable deductions of the related foreign corporation are those expenses, losses, or other deductible amounts of the foreign corporation that are properly allocable, under the principles of section 954(b)(5), to the relevant income of the foreign corporation.

For example, assume the following facts. A U.S. parent corporation accrues an expense item of 100 to its 60-percent owned CFC. The item constitutes foreign base company income in the hands of the CFC. An unrelated foreign corporation owns the remaining 40 percent interest in the CFC. The item is the only potential subpart F income of the CFC and has not been paid by the end of the taxable year of the parent. Expenses of 60 are properly allocated or apportioned to the 100 of foreign base company income under the principles of section 954(b)(5). In addition, other income and expense items of the CFC net to a loss of 30, which, when taken together with the 40 (100 − 60) of net foreign base company income, results in current net income for the CFC of 10. Assuming further that the CFC has no current earnings and profits adjustments, the CFC's subpart F income in this case is limited to 10, six of which is includible in the gross income of the U.S. parent as its pro rata share of subpart F income. Under these facts, the U.S. parent is allowed a current deduction of 42 ((10 + 60) × 60%) under this provision. If the other income and expense items of the CFC net to a loss of 50 instead of 30, the U.S. parent would instead be allowed a current deduction of 30 ((40 − 50 + 60) ×60%).

The provision grants the Secretary regulatory authority to provide exceptions to these rules, including an exception for amounts accrued where payment of the amount accrued occurs within a short period after accrual, and the transaction giving rise to the payment is entered into by the payor in the ordinary course of a business in which the payor is predominantly engaged.

Effective Date

The provision is effective for payments accrued on or after date of enactment.

---

[347] Treas. Reg. sec. 1.267(a)-3(c)(4).

[348] Section 313 of the bill repeals the foreign personal holding company regime, effective for taxable years of for-

eign corporations beginning after December 31, 2004, and taxable years of U.S. shareholders with or within which such taxable years of foreign corporations end.

Conference Committee Report (H.R. CONF. REP. NO. 108-755)

Senate Amendment

The Senate amendment is the same as the House bill.

Conference Agreement

The conference agreement follows the House bill and the Senate amendment.

The following examples illustrate the operation of this provision. Assume the following facts. A U.S. parent corporation owns 60 percent of the stock of a CFC. An unrelated foreign corporation owns the remaining 40 percent interest in the CFC. The U.S. parent accrues an expense item of 100 to the CFC. The parent would be entitled to a current deduction of 100 for the accrued amount, before taking into account this provision. The item constitutes gross foreign base company income in the hands of the CFC. The item is the only gross income item of the CFC that has the potential to result in the CFC having subpart F income, and has not been paid by the end of the taxable year of the parent. The CFC has deductions of 60 that are properly allocated or apportioned to the 100 of gross foreign base company income under the principles of section 954(b)(5), resulting in 40 (100 − 60) of net foreign base company income. The CFC has earnings and profits for its taxable year in excess of 40, and has 40 of subpart F income. Under these facts, the U.S. parent is allowed a current deduction of 60 (100 × 60%) under the provision.

If, in the example above, the CFC has deductions of 100 (or more) properly allocated or apportioned to the sole item of 100 of gross foreign base company income under the princi-

ples of section 954(b)(5), and has no other income or deductions, the same deduction is allowed to the U.S. parent. Under these circumstances, the parent is allowed a deduction of 60, whether the CFC has positive earnings and profits for its taxable year or has a deficit in earnings and profits for such year.

If the CFC's item of net foreign base company income is positive, and the earnings and profits limitation of section 952(c)(1)(A) reduces what would otherwise be a U.S. shareholder's pro rata share of the CFC's subpart F income, then the deduction will also be reduced under the provision. For example, assume the facts in the first example above, in which the CFC has deductions of 60 that are properly allocated or apportioned to the item of 100 of gross foreign base company income under the principles of section 954(b)(5), resulting in 40 of net foreign base company income. Further assume that, due solely to other losses, the CFC's earnings and profits for its taxable year are 10 instead of 40. In that case, the CFC's subpart F income is limited to 10, and only six is includible in the gross income of the U.S. parent as its pro rata share of subpart F income. Under the provision, the U.S. parent is allowed a current deduction in that case of 42 ((10 + 60) × 60%). The conferees intend that, if as a result of such other losses, the CFC has no earnings and profits for its taxable year or has a deficit in earnings and profits for such year, the U.S. parent is instead allowed a current deduction of 36 ((0 + 60) × 60%).

[Law at ¶5165 and ¶5275. CCH Explanation at ¶705.]

[¶11,250] Act Sec. 842. Deposits made to suspend the running of interest on potential underpayments

House Committee Report (H.R. REP. NO. 108-548, pt. 1)

[New Code Sec. 6603]

Present Law

Generally, interest on underpayments and overpayments continues to accrue during the period that a taxpayer and the IRS dispute a liability. The accrual of interest on an underpayment is suspended if the IRS fails to notify an individual taxpayer in a timely manner, but interest will begin to accrue once the taxpayer is properly notified. No similar suspension is available for other taxpayers.

A taxpayer that wants to limit its exposure to underpayment interest has a limited number

of options. The taxpayer can continue to dispute the amount owed and risk paying a significant amount of interest. If the taxpayer continues to dispute the amount and ultimately loses, the taxpayer will be required to pay interest on the underpayment from the original due date of the return until the date of payment.

In order to avoid the accrual of underpayment interest, the taxpayer may choose to pay the disputed amount and immediately file a claim for refund. Payment of the disputed amount will prevent further interest from accruing if the taxpayer loses (since there is no longer any underpayment) and the taxpayer will earn interest on the resultant overpayment if the taxpayer wins. However, the taxpayer will generally lose access to the Tax Court if it follows this alternative. Amounts paid generally cannot be recovered by the taxpayer on demand, but must await final determination of the taxpayer's liability. Even if an overpayment is ultimately determined, overpaid amounts may not be refunded if they are eligible to be offset against other liabilities of the taxpayer.

The taxpayer may also make a deposit in the nature of a cash bond. The procedures for making a deposit in the nature of a cash bond are provided in Rev. Proc. 84-58.

A deposit in the nature of a cash bond will stop the running of interest on an amount of underpayment equal to the deposit, but the deposit does not itself earn interest. A deposit in the nature of a cash bond is not a payment of tax and is not subject to a claim for credit or refund. A deposit in the nature of a cash bond may be made for all or part of the disputed liability and generally may be recovered by the taxpayer prior to a final determination. However, a deposit in the nature of a cash bond need not be refunded to the extent the Secretary determines that the assessment or collection of the tax determined would be in jeopardy, or that the deposit should be applied against another liability of the taxpayer in the same manner as an overpayment of tax. If the taxpayer recovers the deposit prior to final determination and a deficiency is later determined, the taxpayer will not receive credit for the period in which the funds were held as a deposit. The taxable year to which the deposit in the nature of a cash bond relates must be designated, but the taxpayer may request that the deposit be applied to a different year under certain circumstances.

Reasons for Change

The Committee believes that taxpayers should be able to limit their underpayment interest exposure in a tax dispute. An improved deposit system will help taxpayers better manage their exposure to underpayment interest without requiring them to surrender access to their funds or requiring them to make a potentially indefinite-term investment in a non-interest bearing account. The Committee believes that an improved deposit system that allows for the payment of interest on amounts that are not ultimately needed to offset tax liability when the taxpayer's position is upheld, as well as allowing for the offset of tax liability when the taxpayer's position fails, will provide an effective way for taxpayers to manage their exposure to underpayment interest. However, the Committee believes that such an improved deposit system

should be reserved for the issues that are known to both parties, either through IRS examination or voluntary taxpayer disclosure.

Explanation of Provision

In general

The provision allows a taxpayer to deposit cash with the IRS that may subsequently be used to pay an underpayment of income, gift, estate, generation-skipping, or certain excise taxes. Interest will not be charged on the portion of the underpayment that is deposited for the period that the amount is on deposit. Generally, deposited amounts that have not been used to pay a tax may be withdrawn at any time if the taxpayer so requests in writing. The withdrawn amounts will earn interest at the applicable Federal rate to the extent they are attributable to a disputable tax.

The Secretary may issue rules relating to the making, use, and return of the deposits.

Use of a deposit to offset underpayments of tax

Any amount on deposit may be used to pay an underpayment of tax that is ultimately assessed. If an underpayment is paid in this manner, the taxpayer will not be charged underpayment interest on the portion of the underpayment that is so paid for the period the funds were on deposit.

For example, assume a calendar year individual taxpayer deposits $20,000 on May 15, 2005, with respect to a disputable item on its 2004 income tax return. On April 15, 2007, an examination of the taxpayer's year 2004 income tax return is completed, and the taxpayer and the IRS agree that the taxable year 2004 taxes were underpaid by $25,000. The $20,000 on deposit is used to pay $20,000 of the underpayment, and the taxpayer also pays the remaining $5,000. In this case, the taxpayer will owe underpayment interest from April 15, 2005 (the original due date of the return) to the date of payment (April 15, 2007) only with respect to the $5,000 of the underpayment that is not paid by the deposit. The taxpayer will owe underpayment interest on the remaining $20,000 of the underpayment only from April 15, 2005, to May 15, 2005, the date the $20,000 was deposited.

Withdrawal of amounts

A taxpayer may request the withdrawal of any amount of deposit at any time. The Secretary must comply with the withdrawal request unless the amount has already been used to pay tax or the Secretary properly determines that collection of tax is in jeopardy. Interest will be paid on deposited amounts that are withdrawn at a rate equal to the short-term applicable Federal rate for the period from the date of deposit to a date not more than 30 days preceding the date of the check paying the withdrawal. Interest is not payable to the extent the deposit was not attributable to a disputable tax.

For example, assume a calendar year individual taxpayer receives a 30-day letter showing a deficiency of $20,000 for taxable year 2004 and deposits $20,000 on May 15, 2006. On April 15, 2007, an administrative appeal is completed, and the taxpayer and the IRS agree that the 2004 taxes were underpaid by $15,000. $15,000 of the deposit is used to pay the underpayment. In this case, the taxpayer will owe underpayment interest from April 15, 2005 (the original due date of the return) to May 15, 2006, the date the $20,000 was deposited. Simultaneously with the use of the $15,000 to offset the underpayment, the taxpayer requests the return of the remaining amount of the deposit (after reduction for the underpayment interest owed by the taxpayer from April 15, 2005, to May 15, 2006). This amount must be returned to the taxpayer with interest determined at the short-term applicable Federal rate from the May 15, 2006, to a date not more than 30 days preceding the date of the check repaying the deposit to the taxpayer.

Limitation on amounts for which interest may be allowed

Interest on a deposit that is returned to a taxpayer shall be allowed for any period only to the extent attributable to a disputable item for that period. A disputable item is any item for which the taxpayer (1) has a reasonable basis for the treatment used on its return and (2) reasonably believes that the Secretary also has a reasonable basis for disallowing the taxpayer's treatment of such item.

All items included in a 30-day letter to a taxpayer are deemed disputable for this purpose. Thus, once a 30-day letter has been issued, the disputable amount cannot be less than the amount of the deficiency shown in the 30-day letter. A 30-day letter is the first letter of proposed deficiency that allows the taxpayer an opportunity for administrative review in the Internal Revenue Service Office of Appeals.

Deposits are not payments of tax

A deposit is not a payment of tax prior to the time the deposited amount is used to pay a tax. Similarly, withdrawal of a deposit will not establish a period for which interest was allowable at the short-term applicable Federal rate for the purpose of establishing a net zero interest rate on a similar amount of underpayment for the same period.

Effective Date

The provision applies to deposits made after the date of enactment. Amounts already on deposit as of the date of enactment are treated as deposited (for purposes of applying this provision) on the date the taxpayer identifies the amount as a deposit made pursuant to this provision.

Conference Committee Report (H.R. CONF. REP. NO. 108-755)

Senate Amendment

The Senate amendment is the same as the House bill.

Conference Agreement

The conference agreement follows the House bill and the Senate amendment.

[Law at ¶ 6230. CCH Explanation at ¶ 1615.]

[¶ 11,260] Act Sec. 843. Authorize IRS to enter into installment agreements that provide for partial payment

House Committee Report (H.R. Rep. No. 108-548, pt. 1)

[Code Sec. 6159]

Present Law

The Code authorizes the IRS to enter into written agreements with any taxpayer under which the taxpayer is allowed to pay taxes owed, as well as interest and penalties, in installment payments if the IRS determines that doing so will facilitate collection of the amounts owed (sec. 6159). An installment agreement does not reduce the amount of taxes, interest, or penalties owed. Generally, during the period installment payments are being made, other IRS enforcement actions (such as levies or seizures) with respect to the taxes included in that agreement are held in abeyance.

Prior to 1998, the IRS administratively entered into installment agreements that provided for partial payment (rather than full payment) of the total amount owed over the period of the agreement. In that year, the IRS Chief Counsel issued a memorandum concluding that partial payment installment agreements were not permitted.

Reasons for Change

According to the Department of the Treasury, at the end of fiscal year 2003, the IRS had not pursued 2.25 million cases totaling more than $16.5 billion in delinquent taxes. The Committee believes that clarifying that the IRS is authorized to enter into installment agreements with taxpayers that do not provide for full payment of the taxpayer's liability over the life of the agreement will improve effective tax administration.

The Committee recognizes that some taxpayers are unable or unwilling to enter into a realistic offer-in-compromise. The Committee believes that these taxpayers should be encouraged to make partial payments toward resolving their tax liability, and that providing for partial payment installment agreements will help facilitate this.

Explanation of Provision

The provision clarifies that the IRS is authorized to enter into installment agreements with taxpayers which do not provide for full payment of the taxpayer's liability over the life of the agreement. The provision also requires the IRS to review partial payment installment agreements at least every two years. The primary purpose of this review is to determine whether the financial condition of the taxpayer has significantly changed so as to warrant an increase in the value of the payments being made.

Effective Date

The provision is effective for installment agreements entered into on or after the date of enactment.

Conference Committee Report (H.R. Conf. Rep. No. 108-755)

Senate Amendment

The Senate amendment is the same as the House bill.

Conference Agreement

The conference agreement follows the House bill and the Senate amendment.

[Law at ¶ 6180. CCH Explanation at ¶ 1610.]

[¶ 11,270] Act Sec. 844. Affirmation of consolidated return regulation authority

House Committee Report (H.R. Rep. No. 108-548, pt. 1)

[Code Sec. 1502]

Present Law

An affiliated group of corporations may elect to file a consolidated return in lieu of separate returns. A condition of electing to file a consolidated return is that all corporations that are members of the consolidated group must consent to all the consolidated return regulations prescribed under section 1502 prior to the last day prescribed by law for filing such return.[349]

Section 1502 states:

The Secretary shall prescribe such regulations as he may deem necessary in order that the tax liability of any affiliated group of corporations making a consolidated return and of each corporation in the group, both during and after the period of affiliation, may be returned, determined, computed, assessed, collected, and adjusted, in such manner as clearly to reflect the income-tax liability and the various factors necessary for the determination of such liability, and in order to prevent the avoidance of such tax liability.[350]

Under this authority, the Treasury Department has issued extensive consolidated return regulations.[351]

In the recent case of *Rite Aid Corp.* v. *United States*,[352] the Federal Circuit Court of Appeals addressed the application of a particular provision of certain consolidated return loss disallowance regulations, and concluded that the provision was invalid.[353] The particular provision, known as the "duplicated loss" provision,[354] would have denied a loss on the sale of stock of a subsidiary by a parent corporation that had filed a consolidated return with the subsidiary, to the extent the subsidiary corporation had assets that had a built-in loss, or had a net operating loss, that could be recognized or used later.[355]

The Federal Circuit Court opinion contained language discussing the fact that the regulation produced a result different than the result that would have obtained if the corporations had

---

[349] Sec. 1501.

[350] Sec. 1502.

[351] Regulations issued under the authority of section 1502 are considered to be "legislative" regulations rather than "interpretative" regulations, and as such are usually given greater deference by courts in case of a taxpayer challenge to such a regulation. See, S. Rep. No. 960, 70th Cong., 1st Sess. at 15 (1928), describing the consolidated return regulations as "legislative in character". The Supreme Court has stated that ". . . legislative regulations are given controlling weight unless they are arbitrary, capricious, or manifestly contrary to the statute." *Chevron, U.S.A., Inc.* v. *Natural Resources Defense Council, Inc.,* 467 U.S. 837, 844 (1984) (involving an environmental protection regulation). For examples involving consolidated return regulations, see, e.g., *Wolter Construction Company* v. *Commissioner,* 634 F.2d 1029 (6th Cir. 1980); *Garvey, Inc.* v. *United States,* 1 Ct. Cl. 108 (1983), aff'd 726 F.2d 1569 (Fed. Cir. 1984), cert. denied, 469 U.S. 823 (1984). Compare, e.g., *Audrey J. Walton* v. *Commissioner,* 115 T.C. 589 (2000), describing different standards of review. The case did not involve a consolidated return regulation.

[352] 255 F.3d 1357 (Fed. Cir. 2001), reh'g denied, 2001 U.S. App. LEXIS 23207 (Fed. Cir. Oct. 3, 2001).

[353] Prior to this decision, there had been a few instances involving prior laws in which certain consolidated return regulations were held to be invalid. See, e.g., *American Standard, Inc.* v. *United States,* 602 F.2d 256 (Ct. Cl. 1979), discussed in the text infra. See also *Union Carbide Corp.* v. *United States,* 612 F.2d 558 (Ct. Cl. 1979), and *Allied Corporation* v. *United States,* 685 F. 2d 396 (Ct. Cl. 1982), all three cases involving the allocation of income and loss within a consolidated group for purposes of computation of a deduction allowed under prior law by the Code for Western Hemisphere Trading Corporations. See also *Joseph Weidenhoff* v. *Commissioner,* 32 T.C. 1222, 1242-1244 (1959), involving the application of certain regulations to the excess profits tax credit allowed under prior law, and concluding that the Commissioner had applied a particular regulation in an arbitrary manner inconsistent with the wording of the regulation and inconsistent with even a consolidated group computation. Cf. *Kanawha Gas & Utilities Co.* v. *Commissioner,* 214 F.2d 685 (1954), concluding that the substance of a transaction was an acquisition of assets rather than stock.

Thus, a regulation governing basis of the assets of consolidated subsidiaries did not apply to the case. See also *General Machinery Corporation* v. *Commissioner,* 33 B.T.A. 1215 (1936); *Lefcourt Realty Corporation,* 31 B.T.A. 978 (1935); *Helvering* v. *Morgans, Inc.,* 293 U.S. 121 (1934), interpreting the term "taxable year."

[354] Treas. Reg. sec. 1.1502-20(c)(1)(iii).

[355] Treasury Regulation section 1.1502-20, generally imposing certain "loss disallowance" rules on the disposition of subsidiary stock, contained other limitations besides the "duplicated loss" rule that could limit the loss available to the group on a disposition of a subsidiary's stock. Treasury Regulation section 1.1502-20 as a whole was promulgated in connection with regulations issued under section 337(d), principally in connection with the so-called *General Utilities* repeal of 1986 (referring to the case of *General Utilities & Operating Company* v. *Helvering,* 296 U.S. 200 (1935)). Such repeal generally required a liquidating corporation, or a corporation acquired in a stock acquisition treated as a sale of assets, to pay corporate level tax on the excess of the value of its assets over the basis. Treasury regulation section 1.1502-20 principally reflected an attempt to prevent corporations filing consolidated returns from offsetting income with a loss on the sale of subsidiary stock. Such a loss could result from the unique upward adjustment of a subsidiary's stock basis required under the consolidated return regulations for subsidiary income earned in consolidation, an adjustment intended to prevent taxation of both the subsidiary and the parent on the same income or gain. As one example, absent a denial of certain losses on a sale of subsidiary stock, a consolidated group could obtain a loss deduction with respect to subsidiary stock, the basis of which originally reflected the subsidiary's value at the time of the purchase of the stock, and that had then been adjusted upward on recognition of any built-in income or gain of the subsidiary reflected in that value. The regulations also contained the duplicated loss factor addressed by the court in *Rite Aid.* The preamble to the regulations stated: "it is not administratively feasible to differentiate between loss attributable to built-in gain and duplicated loss." T.D. 8364, 1991-2 C.B. 43, 46 (Sept. 13, 1991). The government also argued in the *Rite Aid* case that duplicated loss was a separate concern of the regulations. 255 F.3d at 1360.

filed separate returns rather than consolidated returns.[356]

The Federal Circuit Court opinion cited a 1928 Senate Finance Committee Report to legislation that authorized consolidated return regulations, which stated that "many difficult and complicated problems, . . . have arisen in the administration of the provisions permitting the filing of consolidated returns" and that the committee "found it necessary to delegate power to the commissioner to prescribe regulations legislative in character covering them."[357] The Court's opinion also cited a previous decision of the Court of Claims for the proposition, interpreting this legislative history, that section 1502 grants the Secretary "the power to conform the applicable income tax law of the Code to the special, myriad problems resulting from the filing of consolidated income tax returns;" but that section 1502 "does not authorize the Secretary to choose a method that imposes a tax on income that would not otherwise be taxed."[358]

The Federal Circuit Court construed these authorities and applied them to invalidate Treas. Reg. Sec. 1.1502-20(c)(1)(iii), stating that:

> The loss realized on the sale of a former subsidiary's assets after the consolidated group sells the subsidiary's stock is not a problem resulting from the filing of consolidated income tax returns. The scenario also arises where a corporate shareholder sells the stock of a non-consolidated subsidiary. The corporate shareholder could realize a loss under I.R.C. sec. 1001, and

deduct the loss under I.R.C. sec. 165. The subsidiary could then deduct any losses from a later sale of assets. The duplicated loss factor, therefore, addresses a situation that arises from the sale of stock regardless of whether corporations file separate or consolidated returns. With I.R.C. secs. 382 and 383, Congress has addressed this situation by limiting the subsidiary's potential future deduction, not the parent's loss on the sale of stock under I.R.C. sec. 165.[359]

The Treasury Department has announced that it will not continue to litigate the validity of the duplicated loss provision of the regulations, and has issued interim regulations that permit taxpayers for all years to elect a different treatment, though they may apply the provision for the past if they wish.[360]

Reasons for Change

The Committee is concerned that Treasury Department resources might be unnecessarily devoted to defending challenges to consolidated return regulations on the mere assertion by a taxpayer that the result under the consolidated return regulations is different than the result for separate taxpayers. The consolidated return regulations offer many benefits that are not available to separate taxpayers, including generally rules that tax income received by the group once and attempt to avoid a second tax on that same income when stock of a subsidiary is sold.

---

[356] For example, the court stated: "The duplicated loss factor . . . addresses a situation that arises from the sale of stock regardless of whether corporations file separate or consolidated returns. With I.R.C. secs. 382 and 383, Congress has addressed this situation by limiting the subsidiary's potential future deduction, not the parent's loss on the sale of stock under I.R.C. sec. 165." 255 F.3d 1357, 1360 (Fed. Cir. 2001).

[357] S. Rep. No. 960, 70th Cong., 1st Sess. 15 (1928). Though not quoted by the court in *Rite Aid*, the same Senate report also indicated that one purpose of the consolidated return authority was to permit treatment of the separate corporations as if they were a single unit, stating "The mere fact that by legal fiction several corporations owned by the same shareholders are separate entities should not obscure the fact that they are in reality one and the same business owned by the same individuals and operated as a unit." S. Rep. No. 960, 70th Cong., 1st Sess. 29 (1928).

[358] *American Standard, Inc.* v. *United States*, 602 F.2d 256, 261 (Ct. Cl. 1979). That case did not involve the question of separate returns as compared to a single return approach. It involved the computation of a Western Hemisphere Trade Corporation ("WHTC") deduction under prior law (which deduction would have been computed as a percentage of each WHTC's taxable income if the corporations had filed separate returns), in a case where a consolidated group included several WHTCs as well as other corporations. The question was how to apportion income and losses of the admittedly consolidated WHTCs and how to combine that computation with the rest of the group's consolidated in-

come or losses. The court noted that the new, changed regulations approach varied from the approach taken to a similar problem involving public utilities within a group and previously allowed for WHTCs. The court objected that the allocation method adopted by the regulation allowed non-WHTC losses to reduce WHTC income. However, the court did not disallow a method that would net WHTC income of one WHTC with losses of another WHTC, a result that would not have occurred under separate returns. Nor did the court expressly disallow a different fractional method that would net both income and losses of the WHTCs with those of other corporations in the consolidated group. The court also found that the regulation had been adopted without proper notice.

[359] *Rite Aid*, 255 F.3d at 1360.

[360] See Temp. Reg. Sec. 1.1502-20T(i)(2), Temp. Reg. Sec. 1.337(d)-2T, and Temp. Reg. Sec. 1.1502-35T. The Treasury Department has also indicated its intention to continue to study all the issues that the original loss disallowance regulations addressed (including issues of furthering single entity principles) and possibly issue different regulations (not including the particular approach of Treas. Reg. Sec. 1.1502-20(c)(1)(iii)) on the issues in the future. See Notice 2002-11, 2002-7 I.R.B. 526 (Feb. 19, 2002); T.D. 8984, 67 F.R. 11034 (March 12, 2002); REG-102740-02, 67 F.R. 11070 (March 12, 2002); see also Notice 2002-18, 2002-12 I.R.B. 644 (March 25, 2002); REG-131478-02, 67 F.R. 65060 (October 18, 2002); T.D. 9048, 68 F.R. 12287 (March 14, 2003); and T.D. 9118, REG-153172-03 (March 17, 2004).

Explanation of Provision

The provision confirms that, in exercising its authority under section 1502 to issue consolidated return regulations, the Treasury Department may provide rules treating corporations filing consolidated returns differently from corporations filing separate returns.

Thus, under the statutory authority of section 1502, the Treasury Department is authorized to issue consolidated return regulations utilizing either a single taxpayer or separate taxpayer approach or a combination of the two approaches, as Treasury deems necessary in order that the tax liability of any affiliated group of corporations making a consolidated return, and of each corporation in the group, both during and after the period of affiliation, may be determined and adjusted in such manner as clearly to reflect the income-tax liability and the various factors necessary for the determination of such liability, and in order to prevent avoidance of such liability.

Rite Aid is thus overruled to the extent it suggests that the Secretary is required to identify a problem created from the filing of consolidated returns in order to issue regulations that change the application of a Code provision. The Secretary may promulgate consolidated return regulations to change the application of a tax code provision to members of a consolidated group, provided that such regulations are necessary to clearly reflect the income tax liability of the group and each corporation in the group, both during and after the period of affiliation.

The provision nevertheless allows the result of the *Rite Aid* case to stand with respect to the type of factual situation presented in the case. That is, the bill provides for the override of the regulatory provision that took the approach of denying a loss on a deconsolidating disposition of stock of a consolidated subsidiary[361] to the extent the subsidiary had net operating losses or built in losses that could be used later outside the group.[362]

Retaining the result in the *Rite Aid* case with respect to the particular regulation section 1.1502-20(c)(1)(iii) as applied to the factual situation of the case does not in any way prevent or invalidate the various approaches Treasury has announced it will apply or that it intends to consider in lieu of the approach of that regulation, including, for example, the denial of a loss on a stock sale if inside losses of a subsidiary may also be used by the consolidated group, and the possible requirement that inside attributes be adjusted when a subsidiary leaves a group.[363]

Effective Date

The provision is effective for all years, whether beginning before, on, or after the date of enactment of the provision. No inference is intended that the results following from this provision are not the same as the results under present law.

Conference Committee Report (H.R. Conf. Rep. No. 108-755)

Senate Amendment

The Senate amendment is the same as the House bill.

Conference Agreement

The Conference agreement follows the House bill and the Senate Amendment.

[Law at ¶5935 and ¶7110. CCH Explanation at ¶1635.]

---

[361] Treas. Reg. sec. 1.1502-20(c)(1)(iii).

[362] The provision is not intended to overrule the current Treasury Department regulations, which allow taxpayers in certain circumstances for the past to follow Treasury Regulations Section 1.1502-20(c)(1)(iii), if they choose to do so. Temp. Reg. Sec. 1.1502-20T(i)(2).

[363] See, e.g., Notice 2002-11, 2002-7 I.R.B. 526 (Feb. 19, 2002); Temp. Reg. Sec. 1.337(d)-2T, (T.D. 8984, 67 F.R. 11034 (March 12, 2002) and T.D. 8998, 67 F.R. 37998 (May 31,

2002)); REG-102740-02, 67 F.R. 11070 (March 12, 2002); see also Notice 2002-18, 2002-12 I.R.B. 644 (March 25, 2002); REG-131478-02, 67 F.R. 65060 (October 18, 2002); Temp. Reg. Sec. 1.1502-35T (T.D. 9048, 68 F.R. 12287 (March 14, 2003)); and T.D. 9118, REG-153172-03 (March 17, 2004). In exercising its authority under section 1502, the Secretary is also authorized to prescribe rules that protect the purpose of *General Utilities* repeal using presumptions and other simplifying conventions.

Act Sec. 844 ¶11,270

[¶ 11,280] Act Sec. 845. Expanded disallowance of deduction for interest on convertible debt

Senate Committee Report (S. Rep. No. 108-192)

[Code Sec. 163]

Present Law

Whether an instrument qualifies for tax purposes as debt or equity is determined under all the facts and circumstances based on principles developed in case law. If an instrument qualifies as equity, the issuer generally does not receive a deduction for dividends paid and the holder generally includes such dividends in income (although corporate holders generally may obtain a dividends-received deduction of at least 70 percent of the amount of the dividend). If an instrument qualifies as debt, the issuer may receive a deduction for accrued interest and the holder generally includes interest in income, subject to certain limitations.

Original issue discount ("OID") on a debt instrument is the excess of the stated redemption price at maturity over the issue price of the instrument. An issuer of a debt instrument with OID generally accrues and deducts the discount as interest over the life of the instrument even though interest may not be paid until the instrument even though interest may not be paid until the instrument matures. The holder of such a debt instrument also generally includes the OID in income on an accrual basis.

Under present law, no deduction is allowed for interest or OID on a debt instrument issued by a corporation (or issued by a partnership to the extent of its corporate partners) that is payable in equity of the issuer or a related party (within the meaning of sections 267(b) and 707(b)), including a debt instrument a substantial portion of which is mandatorily convertible or convertible at the issuer's option into equity of the issuer or a related party.[257] In addition, a debt instrument is treated as payable in equity if a substantial portion of the principal or interest is required to be determined, or may be determined at the option of the issuer or related party, by reference to the value of equity of the issuer or related party.[258] A debt instrument also is treated as payable in equity if it is part of an arrangement that is designed to result in the payment of the debt instrument with or by reference to such equity, such as in the case of certain issuances of a forward contract in connection with the issuance of debt, nonrecourse debt that is secured principally by such equity, or certain debt instruments that are paid in, converted to, or determined with reference to the value of equity if it may be so required at the option of the holder or a related party and there is a substantial certainty that option will be exercised.[259]

Reasons for Change

The Joint Committee on Taxation staff's investigative report of Enron Corporation[260] described two structured financing transactions that Enron undertook in 1995 and 1999 involving what the report referred to as "investment unit securities." In substance, these securities featured principal repayment that was not unconditional in amount, as generally is required in order for debt characterization to be respected for tax purposes. Instead, principal on the securities was payable upon maturity in stock of an Enron affiliate (or in cash equivalent to the value of such stock).

The Committee believes that the financing activities undertaken by Enron in 1995 and 1999 using investment unit securities cast doubt upon the tax policy rationale for excluding stock ownership interests of 50 percent or less (by virtue of the present-law related party definition) from the application of the interest expense disallowance rules for certain convertible equity-linked debt instruments. With regard to the securities issued by Enron, the fact that Enron owned more than 50 percent of the affiliate stock at the time of the 1995 issuance but owned less than 50 percent of such stock at the time of the 1999 issuance (or shortly thereafter) had no discernible bearing on the intent or economic consequences of either transaction. In each instance, the transaction did not involve a borrowing by Enron in substance for which an interest deduction is appropriate. Rather, these transactions had the purpose and effect of carrying out a monetization of the affiliate stock. Nevertheless, the tax consequences of the 1995 issuance likely would have been different from those of the 1999 issuance if the present-law rules had been in effect at the time of both transactions, rather than only at the time of the 1999 transaction (to which the interest expense disallowance rules did not apply because

---

[257] Sec. 163(l), enacted in the Taxpayer Relief Act of 1997, Pub. L. No. 105-34, sec. 1005(a).

[258] Sec. 163(l)(3)(B).

[259] Sec. 163(l)(3)(C).

[260] See Joint Committee on Taxation, Report of Investigation of Enron Corporation and Related Entities Regarding Federal Tax and Compensation Issues, and Policy Recommendations (JCS-3-03), February 2003.

of the present-law 50-percent related party threshold). Therefore, the Committee believes that eliminating the related party threshold for the application of these rules furthers the tax policy objective of similar tax treatment of economically equivalent transactions. The Committee further believes that disallowed interest under this provision should increase the basis of the equity to which the equity is linked in a manner similar to that contemplated under currently proposed Treasury regulations.[261]

Explanation of Provision

The provision expands the present-law disallowance of interest deductions on certain corporate convertible or equity-linked debt that is payable in, or by reference to the value of, equity. Under the provision, the disallowance is expanded to include interest on corporate debt that is payable in, or by reference to the value of, any equity held by the issuer (or any related party) in any other person, without regard to

whether such equity represents more than a 50-percent ownership interest in such person. The basis of such equity is increased by the amount of interest deductions that is disallowed by the provision. The provision directs the Treasury Department to issue regulations that provide rules for determining the manner in which the basis of equity held by the issuer (or related party) is increased by the amount of interest deductions that is disallowed under the provision.

The provision does not apply to debt that is issued by an active dealer in securities (or a related party) if the debt is payable in, or by reference to the value of, equity that is held by the securities dealer in its capacity as a dealer in securities.

Effective Date

This provision applies to debt instruments that are issued after February 13, 2003.

Conference Committee Report (H.R. CONF. REP. NO. 108-755)

House Bill

No provision.

Conference Agreement

The conference agreement follows the Senate amendment, except the conference agree-

ment applies to debt instruments that are issued after October 3, 2004.

[Law at ¶ 5165. CCH Explanation at ¶ 715.]

[¶ 11,290] Act Secs. 847, 848 and 849. Reform of tax treatment of certain leasing arrangements and limitation on deductions allocable to property used by governments or other tax-exempt entities

House Committee Report (H.R. REP. NO. 108-548, pt. 1)

[Code Secs. 167, 168, 197 and New Code Sec. 470]

Present Law

Overview of depreciation

A taxpayer is allowed to recover, through annual depreciation deductions, the cost of certain property used in a trade or business or for the production of income. The amount of the depreciation deduction allowed with respect to tangible property for a taxable year is determined under the modified accelerated cost recovery system ("MACRS"). Under MACRS, different types of property generally are assigned applicable recovery periods and depreciation methods based on such property's class life. The recovery periods applicable to most tangible personal property (generally tangible property

other than residential rental property and nonresidential real property) range from 3 to 25 years and are significantly shorter than the property's class life, which is intended to approximate the economic useful life of the property. In addition, the depreciation methods generally applicable to tangible personal property are the 200-percent and 150-percent declining balance methods, switching to the straight-line method for the taxable year in which the depreciation deduction would be maximized.

Characterization of leases for tax purposes

In general, a taxpayer is treated as the tax owner and is entitled to depreciate property leased to another party if the taxpayer acquires and retains significant and genuine attributes of a traditional owner of the property, including

---

[261] Prop. Treas. reg. sec. 1.263(g)-4.

the benefits and burdens of ownership. No single factor is determinative of whether a lessor will be treated as the owner of the property. Rather, the determination is based on all the facts and circumstances surrounding the leasing transaction.

A sale-leaseback transaction is respected for Federal tax purposes if "there is a genuine multiple-party transaction with economic substance which is compelled or encouraged by business or regulatory realities, is imbued with tax-independent considerations, and is not shaped solely by tax-avoidance features that have meaningless labels attached."[364]

Recovery period for tax-exempt use property

Under present law, "tax-exempt use property" must be depreciated on a straight-line basis over a recovery period equal to the longer of the property's class life or 125 percent of the lease term.[365] For purposes of this rule, "tax-exempt use property" is tangible property that is leased (other than under a short-term lease) to a tax-exempt entity.[366] For this purpose, the term "tax-exempt entity" includes Federal, State and local governmental units, charities, and, foreign entities or persons.[367]

In determining the length of the lease term for purposes of the 125-percent calculation, several special rules apply. In addition to the stated term of the lease, the lease term includes options to renew the lease or other periods of time during which the lessee could be obligated to make rent payments or assume a risk of loss related to the leased property.

Tax-exempt use property does not include property that is used by a taxpayer to provide a service to a tax-exempt entity. So long as the relationship between the parties is a bona fide service contract, the taxpayer will be allowed to depreciate the property used in satisfying the contract under normal MACRS rules, rather than the rules applicable to tax-exempt use property.[368] In addition, property is not treated as tax-exempt use property merely by reason of a

short-term lease. In general, a short-term lease means any lease the term of which is less than three years and less than the greater of one year or 30 percent of the property's class life.[369]

Also, tax-exempt use property generally does not include qualified technological equipment that meets the exception for leases of high technology equipment to tax-exempt entities with lease terms of five years or less.[370] The recovery period for qualified technological equipment that is treated as tax-exempt use property, but is not subject to the high technology equipment exception, is five years.[371]

The term "qualified technological equipment" is defined as computers and related peripheral equipment, high technology telephone station equipment installed on a customer's premises, and high technology medical equipment.[372] In addition, tax-exempt use property does not include computer software because it is intangible property.

Reasons for Change

The special rules applicable to the depreciation of tax-exempt use property were enacted to prevent tax-exempt entities from using leasing arrangements to transfer the tax benefits of accelerated depreciation on property they used to a taxable entity. The Committee is concerned that some taxpayers are attempting to circumvent this policy through the creative use of service contracts with the tax-exempt entities.

More generally, the Committee believes that certain ongoing leasing activity with tax-exempt entities and foreign governments indicates that the present-law tax rules are not effective in curtailing the ability of a tax-exempt entity to transfer certain tax benefits to a taxable entity. The Committee is concerned about this activity and the continual development of new structures that purport to minimize or neutralize the effect of these rules. In addition, the Committee also is concerned by the increasing use of certain leasing structures involving property purported to be qualified technological equipment. Although the Committee recognizes that leasing plays an

---

[364] *Frank Lyon Co.* v. *United States*, 435 U.S. 561, 583-84 (1978).

[365] Sec. 168(g)(3)(A). Under present law, section 168(g)(3)(C) states that the recovery period of "qualified technological equipment" is five years.

[366] Sec. 168(h)(1).

[367] Sec. 168(h)(2).

[368] Sec. 7701(e) provides that a service contract will not be respected, and instead will be treated as a lease of property, if such contract is properly treated as a lease taking into account all relevant factors. The relevant factors include, among others, the service recipient controls the property, the service recipient is in physical possession of the property, the service provider does not bear significant risk of

diminished receipts or increased costs if there is nonperformance, the property is not used to concurrently provide services to other entities, and the contract price does not substantially exceed the rental value of the property.

[369] Sec. 168(h)(1)(C).

[370] Sec. 168(h)(3). However, the exception does not apply if part or all of the qualified technological equipment is financed by a tax-exempt obligation, is sold by the tax-exempt entity (or related party) and leased back to the tax-exempt entity (or related party), or the tax-exempt entity is the United States or any agency or instrumentality of the United States.

[371] Sec. 168(g)(3)(C).

[372] Sec. 168(i)(2).

important role in ensuring the availability of capital to businesses, it believes that certain transactions of which it recently has become aware do not serve this role. These transactions result in little or no accumulation of capital for financing or refinancing but, instead, essentially involve an accommodation fee paid by a U.S. taxpayer to a tax indifferent party.

In discussing the reasons for the enactment of rules in 1984 that were intended to limit the transfer of tax benefits to taxable entities with respect to property used by tax-exempt entities, Congress at the time stated that: (1) the Federal budget was in no condition to sustain substantial and growing revenue losses by making additional tax benefits (in excess of tax exemption itself) available to tax-exempt entities through leasing transactions; (2) there were concerns about possible problems of accountability of governments to their citizens, and of tax-exempt organizations to their clientele, if substantial amounts of their property came under the control of outside parties solely because the Federal tax system made leasing more favorable than owning; (3) the tax system should not encourage tax-exempt entities to dispose of assets they own or to forego control over the assets they use; (4) there were concerns about waste of Federal revenues because in some cases a substantial portion of the tax savings was retained by lawyers, investment bankers, lessors, and investors and, thus, the Federal revenue loss became more of a gain to financial entities than to tax-exempt entities; (5) providing aid to tax-exempt entities through direct appropriations was more efficient and appropriate than providing such aid through the Code; and (6) popular confidence in the tax system must be sustained by ensuring that the system generally is working correctly and fairly.[373]

The Committee believes that the reasons stated above for the enactment in 1984 of the present-law rules are as important today as they were in 1984. Unfortunately, the present-law rules have not adequately deterred taxpayers from engaging in transactions that attempt to circumvent the rules enacted in 1984. Therefore, the Committee believes that changes to present law are essential to ensure the attainment of the

aforementioned Congressional intentions, provided such changes do not inhibit legitimate commercial leasing transactions that involve a significant and genuine transfer of the benefits and burdens of tax ownership between the taxpayer and the tax-exempt lessee.

Explanation of Provision

Overview

The bill modifies the recovery period of certain property leased to a tax-exempt entity, alters the definition of lease term for all property leased to a tax-exempt entity, expands the short-term lease exception for qualified technological equipment, and establishes rules to limit deductions associated with leases to tax-exempt entities if the leases do not satisfy specified criteria.

Modify the recovery period of certain property leased to a tax-exempt entity

The bill modifies the recovery period for qualified technological equipment and computer software leased to a tax-exempt entity[374] to be the longer of the property's assigned class life (or assigned useful life in the case of computer software) or 125 percent of the lease term. The bill does not apply to short-term leases, as defined under present law with a modification described below for short-term leases of qualified technological equipment.

Modify definition of lease term

In determining the length of the lease term for purposes of the 125-percent calculation, the bill provides that the lease term includes all service contracts (whether or not treated as a lease under section 7701(e)) and other similar arrangements that follow a lease of property to a tax-exempt entity and that are part of the same transaction (or series of transactions) as the lease.[375]

Under the bill, service contracts and other similar arrangements include arrangements by which services are provided using the property in exchange for fees that provide a source of repayment of the capital investment in the property.[376]

---

[373] See H. Rep. 98-432, Pt. 2, pp. 1140-1141 (1984) and S. Prt. 98-169, Vol. I, pp. 125-127 (1984).

[374] The bill defines a tax-exempt entity as under present law. Thus, it includes Federal, State, local, and foreign governmental units, charities, foreign entities or persons.

[375] A service contract involving property that previously was leased to the tax-exempt entity is not part of the same transaction as the preceding leasing arrangement (and, thus, is not included in the lease term of such arrangement) if the service contract was not included in the terms and conditions, or contemplated at the inception, of the preceding leasing arrangement.

[376] For purposes of the bill, a service contract does not include an arrangement for the provision of services if the leased property or substantially similar property is not utilized to provide such services. For example, if at the conclusion of a lease term, a tax-exempt lessee purchases property from the taxpayer and enters into an agreement pursuant to which the taxpayer maintains the property, the maintenance agreement will not be included in the lease term for purposes of the 125-percent computation.

This requirement applies to all leases of property to a tax-exempt entity.

Expand short-term lease exception for qualified technological equipment

For purposes of determining whether a lease of qualified technological equipment to a tax-exempt entity satisfies the present-law 5-year short-term lease exception for leases of qualified technological equipment, the bill provides that the term of the lease does not include an option or options of the lessee to renew or extend the lease, provided the rents under the renewal or extension are based upon fair market value determined at the time of the renewal or extension. The aggregate period of such renewals or extensions not included in the lease term under this provision may not exceed 24 months. In addition, this provision does not apply to any period following the failure of a tax-exempt lessee to exercise a purchase option if the result of such failure is that the lease renews automatically at fair market value rents.

Limit deductions for certain leases of property to tax-exempt parties

The bill also provides that if a taxpayer leases property to a tax-exempt entity, the taxpayer may not claim deductions from the lease transaction in excess of the taxpayer's gross income from the lease for that taxable year. This provision does not apply to certain transactions involving property with respect to which the low-income housing credit or the rehabilitation credit is allowable.

This provision applies to deductions or losses related to a lease to a tax-exempt entity and the leased property.[377] Any disallowed deductions are carried forward and treated as deductions related to the lease in the following taxable year subject to the same limitations. Under rules similar to those applicable to passive activity losses (including the treatment of dispositions of property in which less than all of the gain or loss from the disposition is recognized),[378] a taxpayer generally is permitted to deduct previously disallowed deductions and losses when the taxpayer completely disposes of its interest in the property.

A lease of property to a tax-exempt party is not subject to the deduction limitations of this provision if the lease satisfies all of the following requirements:[379]

(1) Tax-exempt lessee does not monetize its lease obligations

In general, the tax-exempt lessee may not monetize its lease obligations (including any purchase option) in an amount that exceeds 20 percent of the taxpayer's adjusted basis[380] in the leased property at the time the lease is entered into.[381] Specifically, a lease does not satisfy this requirement if the tax-exempt lessee monetizes such excess amount pursuant to an arrangement, set-aside, or expected set-aside, that is to or for the benefit of the taxpayer or any lender, or is to or for the benefit of the tax-exempt lessee, in order to satisfy the lessee's obligations or options under the lease. This determination shall be made at all times during the lease term and shall include the amount of any interest or other income or gain earned on any amount set aside or subject to an arrangement described in this provision. For purposes of determining whether amounts have been set aside or are expected to be set aside, amounts are treated as set aside or expected to be set aside only if a reasonable person would conclude that the facts and circumstances indicate that such amounts are set aside or expected to be set aside.[382]

The Secretary may provide by regulations that this requirement is satisfied, even if a tax-exempt lessee monetizes its lease obligations or options in an amount that exceeds 20 percent of the taxpayer's adjusted basis in the leased prop-

---

[377] Deductions related to a lease of tax-exempt use property include any depreciation or amortization expense, maintenance expense, taxes or the cost of acquiring an interest in, or lease of, property. In addition, this provision applies to interest that is properly allocable to tax-exempt use property, including interest on any borrowing by a related person, the proceeds of which were used to acquire an interest in the property, whether or not the borrowing is secured by the leased property or any other property.

[378] See Sec. 469(g).

[379] Even if a transaction satisfies each of the following requirements, the taxpayer will be treated as the owner of the leased property only if the taxpayer acquires and retains significant and genuine attributes of an owner of the property under the present-law tax rules, including the benefits and burdens of ownership.

[380] For purposes of this requirement, the adjusted basis of property acquired by the taxpayer in a like-kind exchange or involuntary conversion to which section 1031 or section 1033 applies is equal to the lesser of (1) the fair market value of the property as of the beginning of the lease term, or (2) the amount that would be the taxpayer's adjusted basis if section 1031 or section 1033 did not apply to such acquisition.

[381] Arrangements to monetize lease obligations include defeasance arrangements, loans by the tax-exempt entity (or an affiliate) to the taxpayer (or an affiliate) or any lender, deposit agreements, letters of credit collateralized with cash or cash equivalents, payment undertaking agreements, prepaid rent (within the meaning of the regulations under section 467), sinking fund arrangements, guaranteed investment contracts, financial guaranty insurance, or any similar arrangements.

[382] It is anticipated that the customary and budgeted funding by tax-exempt entities of current obligations under a lease through unrestricted accounts or funds for general working capital needs will not be considered arrangements, set-asides, or expected set-asides under this requirement.

erty, in cases in which the creditworthiness of the tax-exempt lessee would not otherwise satisfy the taxpayer's customary underwriting standards. Such credit support would not be permitted to exceed 50 percent of the taxpayer's adjusted basis in the property. In addition, if the lease provides the tax-exempt lessee an option to purchase the property for a fixed purchase price (or for other than the fair market value of the property determined at the time of exercise of the option), such credit support at the time that such option may be exercised would not be permitted to exceed 50 percent of the purchase option price.

Certain lease arrangements that involve circular cash flows or insulation of the taxpayer's equity investment from the risk of loss fail this requirement without regard to the amount in which the tax-exempt lessee monetizes its lease obligations or options. Thus, a lease does not satisfy this requirement if the tax-exempt lessee enters into an arrangement to monetize in any amount its lease obligations or options if such arrangement involves (1) a loan (other than an amount treated as a loan under section 467 with respect to a section 467 rental agreement) from the tax-exempt lessee to the taxpayer or a lender, (2) a deposit that is received, a letter of credit that is issued, or a payment undertaking agreement that is entered into by a lender otherwise involved in the transaction, or (3) in the case of a transaction that involves a lender, any credit support made available to the taxpayer in which any such lender does not have a claim that is senior to the taxpayer.

(2) Taxpayer makes and maintains a substantial equity investment in the leased property

The taxpayer must make and maintain a substantial equity investment in the leased property. For this purpose, a taxpayer generally does not make or maintain a substantial equity investment unless (1) at the time the lease is entered into, the taxpayer initially makes an unconditional at-risk equity investment in the property of at least 20 percent of the taxpayer's adjusted basis[383] in the leased property at that time,[384] (2) the taxpayer maintains such equity investment throughout the lease term, and (3) at all times during the lease term, the fair market value of the property at the end of the lease term is reasonably expected to be equal to at least 20 percent of such basis.[385] For this purpose, the fair market value of the property at the end of the lease term is reduced to the extent that a person other than the taxpayer bears a risk of loss in the value of the property.

This requirement does not apply to leases with lease terms of 5 years or less.

(3) Tax-exempt lessee does not bear more than a minimal risk of loss

The tax-exempt lessee generally may not assume or retain more than a minimal risk of loss, other than the obligation to pay rent and insurance premiums, to maintain the property, or other similar conventional obligations of a net lease.[386] For this purpose, a tax-exempt lessee assumes or retains more than a minimal risk of loss if, as a result of obligations assumed or retained by, on behalf of, or pursuant to an agreement with the tax-exempt lessee, the taxpayer is protected from either (1) any portion of the loss that would occur if the fair market value of the leased property were 25 percent less than the leased property's reasonably expected fair market value at the time the lease is terminated, or (2) an aggregate loss that is greater than 50 percent of the loss that would occur if the fair market value of the leased property were zero at lease termination.[387] In addition, the Secretary may provide by regulations that this requirement is not satisfied where the tax-exempt lessee otherwise retains or assumes more than a minimal risk of loss. Such regulations shall be prospective only.

---

[383] For purposes of this requirement, the adjusted basis of property acquired by the taxpayer in a like-kind exchange or involuntary conversion to which section 1031 or section 1033 applies is equal to the lesser of (1) the fair market value of the property as of the beginning of the lease term, or (2) the amount that would be the taxpayer's adjusted basis if section 1031 or section 1033 did not apply to such acquisition.

[384] The taxpayer's at-risk equity investment shall include only consideration paid, and personal liability incurred, by the taxpayer to acquire the property. Cf. Rev. Proc. 2001-28, 2001-2 C.B. 1156.

[385] Cf. Rev. Proc. 2001-28, sec. 4.01(2), 2001-1 C.B. 1156. The fair market value of the property must be determined without regard to inflation or deflation during the lease term and after subtracting the cost of removing the property.

[386] Examples of arrangements by which a tax-exempt lessee might assume or retain a risk of loss include put

options, residual value guarantees, residual value insurance, and service contracts. However, leases do not fail to satisfy this requirement solely by reason of lease provisions that require the tax-exempt lessee to pay a contractually stipulated loss value to the taxpayer in the event of an early termination due to a casualty loss, a material default by the tax-exempt lessee (excluding the failure by the tax-exempt lessee to enter into an arrangement described above), or other similar extraordinary events that are not reasonably expected to occur at lease inception.

[387] For purposes of this requirement, residual value protection provided to the taxpayer by a manufacturer or dealer of the leased property is not treated as borne by the tax-exempt lessee if the manufacturer or dealer provides such residual value protection to customers in the ordinary course of its business.

This requirement does not apply to leases with lease terms of 5 years or less.

Coordination with like-kind exchange and involuntary conversion rules

Under this provision, neither the like-kind exchange rules (sec. 1031) nor the involuntary conversion rules (sec. 1033) apply if either (1) the exchanged or converted property is tax-exempt use property subject to a lease that was entered into prior to the effective date of this provision and the lease would not have satisfied the requirements of this provision had such requirements been in effect when the lease was entered into, or (2) the replacement property is tax-exempt use property subject to a lease that does not meet the requirements of this provision.

Other rules

This provision continues to apply throughout the lease term to property that initially was tax-exempt use property, even if the property ceases to be tax-exempt use property during the lease term.[388] In addition, this provision is applied before the application of the passive activity loss rules under section 469.

This provision does not alter the treatment of any Qualified Motor Vehicle Operating Agreement within the meaning of section 7701(h). In the case of any such agreement, the second and third requirements provided by this provision (relating to taxpayer equity investment and tax-exempt lessee risk of loss, respectively) shall be applied without regard to any terminal rental adjustment clause.

Conference Committee Report (H.R. CONF. REP. NO. 108-755)

The conference agreement follows the House bill, with the following modifications.

Definition of tax-exempt entity

The conference agreement expands the present-law definition of tax-exempt entity for this purpose to include certain Indian tribal governments in addition to Federal, State, local, and foreign governmental units, charities, foreign entities or persons.

Modify the recovery period of certain property leased to a tax-exempt entity

The conference agreement also modifies the recovery period for certain intangibles leased to a tax-exempt entity to be the no less than 125 percent of the lease term.[621] The conference agreement modification does not apply to short-term leases, as defined under present law with a modification described below for short-term leases of qualified technological equipment.

Limit deductions for leases of property to tax-exempt parties

The conference agreement provides an additional requirement that must be satisfied to avoid the deduction limitations for certain leases of property to tax-exempt parties. This requirement provides that the tax-exempt lessee may not have an option to purchase the leased property for any stated purchase price other than the fair market value of the property (as determined at the time of exercise of the option). This requirement does not apply to (1) property with a class life (as defined in section 168(i)(1)) of seven years or less, or (2) any fixed-wing aircraft or vessels (i.e., ships).

Effective Date

The conference agreement modifies the Federal Transit Administration approval deadline to January 1, 2006.

In addition, the conference agreement provides that the provisions relating to intangible assets and Indian tribal governments are effective for leases entered into after October 3, 2004.

[Law at ¶ 5175, ¶ 5180, ¶ 5225 and ¶ 5395. CCH Explanation at ¶ 670.]

---

[388] Conversely, however, a lease of property that is not tax-exempt use property does not become subject to this provision solely by reason of requisition or seizure by the Federal government in national emergency circumstances.

[621] In the case of computer software and intangible assets, this rule is applied by substituting useful life and amortization period, respectively, for class life.

[¶ 11,320] Act Secs. 851 and 852. Exemption from certain excise taxes for mobile machinery vehicles and modification of definition of offhighway vehicle

House Committee Report (H.R. REP. NO. 108-548, pt. 1)

[Code Secs. 4053, 4072, 4082, 4483, 6421, 6427, and 7701]

Present Law

Under present law, the definition of a "highway vehicle" affects the application of the retail tax on heavy vehicles, the heavy vehicle use tax, the tax on tires, and fuel taxes.[390] Section 4051 of the Code provides for a 12-percent retail sales tax on tractors, heavy trucks with a gross vehicle weight ("GVW") over 33,000 pounds, and trailers with a GVW over 26,000 pounds. Section 4071 provides for a tax on highway vehicle tires that weigh more than 40 pounds, with higher rates of tax for heavier tires. Section 4481 provides for an annual use tax on heavy vehicles with a GVW of 55,000 pounds or more, with higher rates of tax on heavier vehicles. All of these excise taxes are paid into the Highway Trust Fund.

Federal excise taxes are also levied on the motor fuels used in highway vehicles. Gasoline is subject to a tax of 18.4 cents per gallon, of which 18.3 cents per gallon is paid into the Highway Trust Fund and 0.1 cent per gallon is paid into the Leaking Underground Storage Tank ("LUST") Trust Fund. Highway diesel fuel is subject to a tax of 24.4 cents per gallon, of which 24.3 cents per gallon is paid into the Highway Trust Fund and 0.1 cent per gallon is paid into the LUST Trust Fund.

The Code does not define a "highway vehicle." For purposes of these taxes, Treasury regulations define a highway vehicle as any self-propelled vehicle or trailer or semitrailer designed to perform a function of transporting a load over the public highway, whether or not also designed to perform other functions. Excluded from the definition of highway vehicle are (1) certain specially designed mobile machinery vehicles for non-transportation functions (the "mobile machinery exception"); (2) certain vehicles specially designed for off-highway transportation for which the special design substantially limits or impairs the use of such vehicle to transport loads over the highway (the "off-highway transportation vehicle" exception); and (3) certain trailers and semi-trailers specially designed to function only as an enclosed stationary shelter for the performance of non-transportation functions off the public highways.[391]

The mobile machinery exception applies if three tests are met: (1) the vehicle consists of a chassis to which jobsite machinery (unrelated to transportation) has been permanently mounted; (2) the chassis has been specially designed to serve only as a mobile carriage and mount for the particular machinery; and (3) by reason of such special design, the chassis could not, without substantial structural modification, be used to transport a load other than the particular machinery. An example of a mobile machinery vehicle is a crane mounted on a truck chassis that meets the forgoing factors.

On June 6, 2002, the Treasury Department put forth proposed regulations that would eliminate the mobile machinery exception.[392] The other exceptions from the definition of highway vehicle would continue to apply with some modifications. Under the proposed regulations, the chassis of a mobile machinery vehicle would be subject to the retail sales tax on heavy vehicles unless the vehicle qualified under the off-highway transportation vehicle exception. Also, under the proposed regulations, mobile machinery vehicles may be subject to the heavy vehicle use tax. In addition, the tax credits, refunds, and exemptions from tax may not be available for the fuel used in these vehicles.

Reasons for Change

The Treasury Department has delayed issuance of final regulations regarding mobile machinery to allow Congressional action on a statutory definition of mobile machinery vehicle. The Highway Trust Fund is supported by taxes related to the use of vehicles on the public highways. The Committee understands that a mobile machinery exemption was created by Treasury regulation because the Treasury Department believed that mobile machinery used the public highways only incidentally to get from one job site to another. However, it has come to the Committee's attention that certain vehicles are taking advantage of the mobile machinery exemption even though they spend a significant amount of time on public highways and, therefore, cause wear and tear to such highways. Because the mobile machinery exemption is based on incidental use of the public highways, the Committee believes it is appropriate to add a use-based test to the design-based test that exists

---

[390] Secs. 4051, 4071, 4481, 4041 and 4081.

[391] See Treas. Reg. sec. 48.4061-1(d)).

[392] Prop. Treas. Reg. sec. 48.4051-1(a), 67 Fed. Reg. 38913, 38914-38915 (2002).

under current regulation. The Committee believes that a use-based test is practical to administer only for purposes of the fuel excise tax.

Explanation of Provision

The provision codifies the present-law mobile machinery exemption for purposes of three taxes: the retail tax on heavy vehicles, the heavy vehicle use tax, and the tax on tires. Thus, if a vehicle can satisfy the three-part test, it will not be treated as a highway vehicle and will be exempt from these taxes.

For purposes of the fuel excise tax, the three-part design test is codified and a use test is added by the provision. Specifically, in addition to the three-part design test, the vehicle must not have traveled more than 7,500 miles over public highways during the owner's taxable year. Refunds of fuel taxes are permitted on an annual basis only. For purposes of this rule, a person's taxable year is his taxable year for income tax purposes.

Conference Committee Report (H.R. CONF. REP. NO. 108-755)

Present Law

* * *

On June 6, 2002, the Treasury Department put forth proposed regulations that would modify the off-highway transportation vehicle exception.[693] Under the proposed regulations, a vehicle is not treated as a highway vehicle if it is specially designed for the primary function of transporting a particular type of load other than over the public highway and because of this special design its capability to transport a load over the public highway is substantially limited or impaired. A vehicle's design is determined solely on the basis of its physical characteristics. In determining whether substantial limitation or impairment exists, account may be taken of factors such as the size of the vehicle, whether it is subject to the licensing, safety, and other requirements applicable to highway vehicles, and whether it can transport a load at a sustained speed of at least 25 miles per hour. Under the proposed regulation, it is not material that a vehicle can transport a greater load off the public highway than it is permitted to transport over the public highway.

The proposed regulation provides an exception to the definition of a highway vehicle for nontransportation trailers and semitrailers.[694] Under the proposed regulation, a trailer or semitrailer is not treated as a highway vehicle if it is specially designed to function only as an enclosed stationary shelter for the carrying on of an offhighway function at an offhighway site. For example, a trailer that is capable only of functioning as an office for an offhighway construction operation is not a highway vehicle.

Conference Agreement

The conference agreement follows the House bill. Vehicles owned by an organization described in section 501(c), exempt from tax under section 501(a), need only satisfy the three-part design test to recover taxes paid with respect to such vehicles.

The conference agreement adopts the definition of an offhighway transportation vehicle and a nontransportation trailer and semitrailer described in Proposed Treasury Regulation section 48.4051-1(a)(2).

For example, as provided in the proposed regulations,[695] Vehicle C consists of a truck chassis on which an oversize body designed to transport and apply liquid agricultural chemicals on farms has been installed. It is capable of transporting a load over the public highway. It is 132 inches in width, which is considerably in excess of standard highway vehicle width. For travel on uneven and soft terrain, it is equipped with oversize wheels with high-flotation tires, and nonstandard axles, brakes, and transmission. It has a special fuel and carburetor air filtration system that enable it to perform efficiently in an environment of dirt and dust. It is not able to maintain a speed of 25 miles per hour for more than one mile while fully loaded. Because Vehicle C is a self-propelled vehicle capable of transporting a load over the public highway, it would meet the general definition of a highway vehicle. However, its considerable physical characteristics for transporting its load other than over the public highway, when compared with its physical characteristics for transporting the load over the public highway, establish that it is specially designed for the primary function of transporting its load other than over the public highway. Further, the physical characteristics for transporting its load other than over the public highway substantially limit its capability to transport a load over the public highway. Therefore, Vehicle C is an offhighway vehicle and is not treated as a highway vehicle.

Effective Date

Generally effective after the date of enactment. As to the fuel taxes, effective for taxable years beginning after the date of enactment.

[Law at ¶5990, ¶6000, ¶6015, ¶6085, ¶6210, ¶6220 and ¶6355. CCH Explanation at ¶1549 and ¶1551.]

---

[693] Prop. Treas. Reg. sec. 48.4051-1(a)(2)(i).
[694] Prop. Treas. Reg. sec. 48.4051-1(a)(2)(ii).

[695] Prop. Treas. Reg. sec. 48.4051-1(c), *Example* (3).

[¶ 11,340] Act Sec. 853. Taxation of aviation-grade kerosene

House Committee Report (H.R. REP. NO. 108-548, pt. 1)

[Code Secs. 4041, 4081, 4082, 4083, 4091,
4092, 4093,4101 and 6427]

Present Law

In general

Aviation fuel is kerosene and any liquid (other than any product taxable under section 4081) that is suitable for use as a fuel in an aircraft.[393] Unlike other fuels that generally are taxed upon removal from a terminal rack,[394] aviation fuel is taxed upon sale of the fuel by a producer or importer.[395] Sales by a registered producer to another registered producer are exempt from tax, with the result that, as a practical matter, aviation fuel is not taxed until the fuel is used at the airport (or sold to an unregistered person). Use of untaxed aviation fuel by a producer is treated as a taxable sale.[396] The producer or importer is liable for the tax. The rate of tax on aviation fuel is 21.9 cents per gallon.[397]

The tax on aviation fuel is reported by filing Form 720—Quarterly Federal Excise Tax Return. Generally, semi-monthly deposits are required using Form 8109B—Federal Tax Deposit Coupon or by depositing the tax by electronic funds transfer.

Partial exemptions

In general, aviation fuel sold for use or used in commercial aviation is taxed at a reduced rate of 4.4 cents per gallon.[398] Commercial aviation means any use of an aircraft in a business of transporting persons or property for compensation or hire by air (unless the use is allocable to any transportation exempt from certain excise taxes).[399]

In order to qualify for the 4.4 cents per gallon rate, the person engaged in commercial aviation must be registered with the Secretary[400] and provide the seller with a written exemption

certificate stating the airline's name, address, taxpayer identification number, registration number, and intended use of the fuel. A person that is registered as a buyer of aviation fuel for use in commercial aviation generally is assigned a registration number with a "Y" suffix (a "Y" registrant), which entitles the registrant to purchase aviation fuel at the 4.4 cents per gallon rate.

Large commercial airlines that also are producers of aviation fuel qualify for registration numbers with an "H" suffix. As producers of aviation fuel, "H" registrants may buy aviation fuel tax free pursuant to a full exemption that applies to sales of aviation fuel by a registered producer to a registered producer. If the "H" registrant ultimately uses such untaxed fuel in domestic commercial aviation, the H registrant is liable for the aviation fuel tax at the 4.4 cents per gallon rate.

Exemptions

Aviation fuel sold by a producer or importer for use by the buyer in a nontaxable use is exempt from the excise tax on sales of aviation fuel.[401] To qualify for the exemption, the buyer must provide the seller with a written exemption certificate stating the buyer's name, address, taxpayer identification number, registration number (if applicable), and intended use of the fuel.

Nontaxable uses include: (1) use other than as fuel in an aircraft (such as use in heating oil); (2) use on a farm for farming purposes; (3) use in a military aircraft owned by the United States or a foreign country; (4) use in a domestic air carrier engaged in foreign trade or trade between the United States and any of its possessions;[402] (5) use in a foreign air carrier engaged in foreign trade or trade between the United States and any of its possessions (but only if the foreign carrier's country of registration provides similar privi-

---

[393] Sec. 4093(a).

[394] A rack is a mechanism capable of delivering taxable fuel into a means of transport other than a pipeline or vessel. Treas. Reg. sec. 48.4081-1(b).

[395] Sec. 4091(a)(1).

[396] Sec. 4091(a)(2).

[397] Sec. 4091(b). This rate includes a 0.1 cent per gallon Leaking Underground Storage Tank ("LUST") Trust Fund tax. The LUST Trust Fund tax is set to expire after March 31, 2005, with the result that on April 1, 2005, the tax rate is scheduled to be 21.8 cents per gallon. Secs. 4091(b)(3)(B) and 4081(d)(3). Beginning on October 1, 2007, the rate of tax is reduced to 4.3 cents per gallon. Sec. 4091(b)(3)(A).

[398] Sec. 4092(b). The 4.4 cent rate includes 0.1 cent per gallon that is attributable to the LUST Trust Fund financing

rate. A full exemption, discussed below, applies to aviation fuel that is sold for use in commercial aviation as fuel supplies for vessels or aircraft, which includes use by certain foreign air carriers and for the international flights of domestic carriers. Secs. 4092(a), 4092(b), and 4221(d)(3).

[399] Secs. 4092(b) and 4041(c)(2).

[400] Notice 88-132, sec. III(D). See also, Form 637—Application for Registration (For Certain Excise Tax Activities). A bond may be required as a condition of registration.

[401] Sec. 4092(a).

[402] "Trade" includes the transportation of persons or property for hire. Treas. Reg. sec. 48.4221-4(b)(8).

leges to United States carriers); (6) exclusive use of a State or local government; (7) sales for export, or shipment to a United States possession; (8) exclusive use by a nonprofit educational organization; (9) use by an aircraft museum exclusively for the procurement, care, or exhibition of aircraft of the type used for combat or transport in World War II, and (10) use as a fuel in a helicopter or a fixed-wing aircraft for purposes of providing transportation with respect to which certain requirements are met.[403]

A producer that is registered with the Secretary may sell aviation fuel tax-free to another registered producer.[404] Producers include refiners, blenders, wholesale distributors of aviation fuel, dealers selling aviation fuel exclusively to producers of aviation fuel, the actual producer of the aviation fuel, and with respect to fuel purchased at a reduced rate, the purchaser of such fuel.

Refunds and credits

A claim for refund of taxed aviation fuel held by a registered aviation fuel producer is allowed[405] (without interest) if: (1) the aviation fuel tax was paid by an importer or producer (the "first producer") and the tax has not otherwise been credited or refunded; (2) the aviation fuel was acquired by a registered aviation fuel producer (the "second producer") after the tax was paid; (3) the second producer files a timely refund claim with the proper information; and (4) the first producer and any other person that owns the fuel after its sale by the first producer and before its purchase by the second producer have met certain reporting requirements.[406] Refund claims should contain the volume and type of aviation fuel, the date on which the second producer acquired the fuel, the amount of tax that the first producer paid, a statement by the claimant that the amount of tax was not collected nor included in the sales price of the fuel by the claimant when the fuel was sold to a subsequent purchaser, the name, address, and employer identification number of the first producer, and a copy of any required statement of a subsequent seller (subsequent to the first producer but prior to the second producer) that the second producer received. A claim for refund is filed on Form 8849, Claim for Refund of Excise Taxes, and may not be combined with any other refunds.[407]

A payment is allowable to the ultimate purchaser of taxed aviation fuel if the aviation fuel is used in a nontaxable use.[408] A claim for payment may be made on Form 8849 or on Form 720,

Schedule C. A claim made on Form 720, Schedule C, may be netted against the claimant's excise tax liability.[409] Claims for payment not so taken may be allowable as income tax credits[410] on Form 4136, Credit for Federal Tax Paid on Fuels.

Reasons for Change

The Committee believes that the present law rules for taxation of aviation fuel create opportunities for widespread abuse and evasion of fuels excise taxes. In general, aviation fuel is taxed on its sale, whereas other fuel generally is taxed on its removal from a refinery or terminal rack. Because the incidence of tax on aviation fuel is sale and not removal, under present law, aviation fuel may be removed from a refinery or terminal rack tax free if such fuel is intended for use in aviation purposes. The Committee is aware that unscrupulous persons are removing fuel tax free, purportedly for aviation use, but then selling the fuel for highway use, charging their customer the full rate of tax that would be owed on highway fuel, and keeping the amount of the tax.

In order to prevent such fraud, the Committee believes that it is appropriate to conform the tax treatment of all taxable fuels by shifting the incidence of taxation on aviation fuel from the sale of aviation fuel to the removal of such fuel from a refinery or terminal rack. In general, all removals of aviation fuel will be fully taxed at the time of removal, therefore minimizing the cost to the government of the fraudulent diversion of aviation fuel for non-aviation uses. If fuel is later used for an aviation use to which a reduced rate of tax applies, refunds are available. The Committee notes that when the incidence of tax for other fuels (for example, gasoline or diesel) was shifted to the rack, collection of the tax increased significantly indicating that fraud had been occurring.

The provision provides exceptions to the general rule in cases where the opportunities for fraud are insignificant. For example, if fuel is removed from an airport terminal directly into the wing of a commercial aircraft by a hydrant system, it is clear that the fuel will be used in commercial aviation and that the reduced rate of tax for commercial aviation should apply. In addition, if a terminal is located within an airport and, except in exigent circumstances, does not fuel highway vehicles, then the Committee believes it is appropriate to permit certain airline refueling vehicles to transport fuel from

---

[403] Secs. 4041(f)(2), 4041(g), 4041(h), 4041(l), and 4092.

[404] Sec. 4092(c).

[405] Sec. 4091(d).

[406] Treas. Reg. sec. 48.4091-3(b).

[407] Treas. Reg. sec. 48.4091-3(d)(1).

[408] Sec. 6427(l)(1).

[409] Treas. Reg. sec. 40.6302(c)-1(a)(3).

[410] Sec. 34.

the terminal rack directly to the wing of an aircraft and have the applicable rate of tax (reduced or otherwise) apply upon removal from the refueling vehicle.

Explanation of Provision

The provision changes the incidence of taxation of aviation fuel from the sale of aviation fuel to the removal of aviation fuel from a refinery or terminal, or the entry into the United States of aviation fuel. Sales of not previously taxed aviation fuel to an unregistered person also are subject to tax.

Under the provision, the full rate of tax— 21.9 cents per gallon—is imposed upon removal of aviation fuel from a refinery or terminal (or entry into the United States). Aviation fuel may be removed at a reduced rate—either 4.4 or zero cents per gallon—only if the aviation fuel is: (1) removed directly into the wing of an aircraft (i) that is registered with the Secretary as a buyer of aviation fuel for use in commercial aviation (e.g., a "Y" registrant under current law), (ii) that is a foreign airline entitled to the present law exemption for aviation fuel used in foreign trade, or (iii) for a tax-exempt use; or (2) removed or entered as part of an exempt bulk transfer.[411] An exempt bulk transfer is a removal or entry of aviation fuel transferred in bulk by pipeline or vessel to a terminal or refinery if the person removing or entering the aviation fuel, the operator of such pipeline or vessel, and the operator of such terminal or refinery are registered with the Secretary.

Under a special rule, the provision treats certain refueler trucks, tankers, and tank wagons as a terminal if certain requirements are met. For the special rule to apply, a qualifying truck, tanker, or tank wagon must be loaded with aviation fuel from a terminal: (1) that is located within an airport, and (2) from which no vehicle licensed for highway use is loaded with aviation fuel, except in exigent circumstances identified by the Secretary in regulations. The Committee intends that a terminal is located within an airport if the terminal is located in a secure facility on airport grounds. For example, if an access road runs between a terminal and an airport's runways, and the terminal, like the runways, is physically located on airport grounds and is part of a secure facility, the Committee intends that under the provision the terminal is located within the airport. The Committee intends that an exigent circumstance under which loading a vehicle registered for highway use with fuel would not disqualify a terminal under the special rule would include, for example, the unloading of fuel from bulk storage tanks into highway vehicles in order to repair the storage tanks.

In order to qualify for the special rule, a refueler truck, tanker, or tank wagon must: (1) deliver the aviation fuel directly into the wing of the aircraft at the airport where the terminal is located; (2) have storage tanks, hose, and coupling equipment designed and used for the purposes of fueling aircraft; (3) not be licensed for highway use; and (4) be operated by the terminal operator (who operates the terminal rack from which the fuel is unloaded) or by a person that makes a daily accounting to such terminal operator of each delivery of fuel from such truck, tanker, or tank wagon.[412]

The provision does not change the applicable rates of tax under present law, 21.9 cents per gallon for use in noncommercial aviation, 4.4 cents per gallon for use in commercial aviation, and zero cents per gallon for use by domestic airlines in an international flight, by foreign airlines, or other nontaxable use. The provision imposes liability for the tax on aviation fuel removed from a refinery or terminal directly into the wing of an aircraft for use in commercial aviation on the person receiving the fuel, in which case, such person self-assesses the tax on a return. The provision does not change present-law nontaxable uses of aviation fuel, or change the persons or the qualifications of persons who are entitled to purchase fuel at a reduced rate, except that a producer is not permitted to purchase aviation fuel at a reduced rate by reason of such persons' status as a producer.

Under the provision, a refund is allowable to the ultimate vendor of aviation fuel if such ultimate vendor purchases fuel tax paid and subsequently sells the fuel to a person qualified to purchase at a reduced rate and who waives the right to a refund. In such a case, the provision permits an ultimate vendor to net refund claims against any excise tax liability of the ultimate vendor, in a manner similar to the present law treatment of ultimate purchaser payment claims.

As under present law, if previously taxed aviation fuel is used for a nontaxable use, the ultimate purchaser may claim a refund for the tax previously paid. If previously taxed aviation fuel is used for a taxable non aircraft use, the fuel is subject to the tax imposed on kerosene (24.4 cents per gallon) and a refund of the previously paid aviation fuel tax is allowed. Claims by the ultimate vendor or the purchaser that are not taken as refund claims may be allowable as income tax credits.

---

[411] See sec. 4081(a)(1)(B).

[412] The provision requires that if such delivery of information is provided to a terminal operator (or if a terminal operator collects such information), that the terminal operator provide such information to the Secretary.

For example, for an airport that is not served by a pipeline, aviation fuel generally is removed from a terminal and transported to an airport storage facility for eventual use at the airport. In such a case, the aviation fuel will be taxed at 21.9 cents per gallon upon removal from the terminal. At the airport, if the fuel is purchased from a vendor by a person registered with the Secretary to use fuel in commercial aviation, the purchaser may buy the fuel at a reduced rate (generally, 4.4 cents per gallon for domestic flights and zero cents per gallon for international flights) and waive the right to a refund. The ultimate vendor generally may claim a refund for the difference between 21.9 cents per gallon of tax paid upon removal and the rate of tax paid to the vendor by the purchaser. To obtain a zero rate upon purchase, a registered domestic airline must certify to the vendor at the time of purchase that the fuel is for use in an international flight; otherwise, the airline must pay the 4.4 cents per gallon rate and file a claim for refund to the Secretary if the fuel is used for international aviation. If a zero rate is paid and the fuel subsequently is used in domestic and not international travel, the domestic airline is liable for tax at 4.4 cents per gallon. A foreign airline eligible under present law to purchase aviation fuel tax-free would continue to purchase such fuel tax-free.

As another example, for an airport that is served by a pipeline, aviation fuel generally is delivered to the wing of an aircraft either by a refueling truck or by a "hydrant" that runs directly from the pipeline to the airplane wing. If a refueling truck that is not licensed for highway use loads fuel from a terminal located within the airport (and the other requirements of the provision for such truck and terminal are met), and

delivers the fuel directly to the wing of an aircraft for use in commercial aviation, the aviation fuel is taxed at 4.4 cents per gallon upon delivery to the wing and the person receiving the fuel is liable for the tax, which such person would be able to self-assess on a return.[413] If fuel is loaded into a refueling truck that does not meet the requirements of the provision, then the fuel is treated as removed from the terminal into the refueling truck and tax of 21.9 cents per gallon is paid on such removal. The ultimate vendor is entitled to a refund of the difference between 21.9 cents per gallon paid on removal and the rate paid by a commercial airline purchaser (assuming the purchaser waived the refund right). If fuel is removed from a terminal directly to the wing of an aircraft registered to use fuel in commercial aviation by a hydrant or similar device, the person removing the aviation fuel is liable for a tax of 4.4 cents per gallon (or zero in the case of an international flight or qualified foreign airline) and may self-assess such tax on a return.

Under the provision, a floor stocks tax applies to aviation fuel held by a person (if title for such fuel has passed to such person) on October 1, 2004. The tax is equal to the amount of tax that would have been imposed before October 1, 2004, if the provision was in effect at all times before such date, reduced by the tax imposed by section 4091, as in effect on the day before the date of enactment. The Secretary shall determine the time and manner for payment of the tax, including the nonapplication of the tax on de minimis amounts of aviation fuel. Under the provision, 0.1 cents per gallon of such tax is transferred to the LUST Trust Fund. The remainder is transferred to the Airport and Airway Trust Fund.

Conference Committee Report (H.R. CONF. REP. NO. 108-755)

The conference agreement follows the House bill, with the following modifications. The rule that permits certain refueler trucks to be treated as a terminal for purposes of the provision is modified to require that, in addition to the requirements specified in the House bill, a

qualifying truck, tanker, or tank wagon must be loaded with aviation fuel from a terminal that is located within a secured area of an airport. The Secretary is required to publish, by December 15, 2004, and maintain a list of airports that include a secured area in which a terminal is located.[718]

---

[413] Alternatively, if the aviation fuel in the example is for use in noncommercial aviation, the fuel is taxed at 21.9 cents per gallon upon delivery into the wing. Self-assessment of the tax would not apply in such case.

[718] The conferees intend that the following airports, subject to verification by the Secretary, be included on the Secretary's initial list of airports that include a secured area in which a terminal is located. The airports are listed by airport name, and the terminal with respect to the airport is identified by terminal control number. In maintaining the list of qualified airports, the Secretary has the discretion to add or remove airports from the list. Ted Stevens International Airport, T-91-AK-4520; William B. Hartsfield Atlanta International Airport, T-58-GA-2512; William B. Hartsfield

Atlanta International Airport, T-58-GA-2513; William B. Hartsfield Atlanta International Airport, T-58-GA-2536; Bradley International Airport, T-06-CT-1271; Nashville Metropolitan Airport, T-62-TN-2222; Logan International Airport, T-04-MA-1171; Baltimore/Washington International Airport, T-52-MD-1569; Cleveland Hopkins International Airport, T-31-OH-3109; Charlotte/Douglas International Airport, T-56-NC-2032; Colorado Springs Airport, T-84-CO-4108; Cincinnati/Northern Kentucky International Airport, T-61-KY-3277; Dallas Love Field Airport, T-75-TX-2663; Ronald Reagan National Airport, T-54-VA-1686; Denver International Airport, T-84-CO-4111; Dallas Fort Worth International Airport, T-75-TX-2673; Wayne County Metropolitan Airport, T-38-MI-3018; Newark

In addition, the conference agreement modifes the requirement that in order to qualify for the special rule, a refueler truck, tanker, or tank wagon must deliver the aviation fuel directly into the wing of the aircraft at the airport where the terminal is located to a requirement that a refueler truck, tanker, or tank wagon be loaded with aviation fuel for delivery into aircraft at the airport where the terminal is located.

The conference agreement modifies the floor stocks tax. Under the conference agreement, a floor stocks tax applies to aviation fuel held by a person (if title for such fuel has passed to such person) on January 1, 2004. The tax is equal to the amount of tax that would have been imposed before January 1, 2004, if the proposal was in effect at all times before such date, reduced by (1) the tax imposed by section 4091, as in effect on the day before such date and, (2) in the case of kerosene held exclusively for the holder's own use, the amount which such holder would reasonably expect under the proposal to be paid as a refund for a nontaxable use with respect to the kerosene. The tax does not apply to kerosene

held in the fuel tank of an aircraft on January 1, 2004. The Secretary shall determine the time and manner for payment of the tax, including the nonapplication of the tax on de minimis amounts of aviation fuel. Under the conference agreement, 0.1 cents per gallon of such tax is transferred to the LUST Trust Fund. The remainder is transferred to the Airport and Airway Trust Fund.

The conferees expect the Secretary to delay the due date of the excise tax return with respect to aviation fuel for the quarter beginning on January 1, 2005. It is intended that the requirement of semi-monthly deposits of aviation fuel taxes continue unchanged.

Effective Date

Effective for aviation-grade kerosene removed, entered, or sold after December 31, 2004.

[Law at ¶5980, ¶6010, ¶6015, ¶6020, ¶6025, ¶6030, ¶6035, ¶6040, ¶6045, ¶6075, ¶6185, ¶6205, ¶6220, ¶6310, ¶6380, ¶6390 and ¶7115. CCH Explanation at ¶1507.]

[¶ 11,350] Act Secs. 854, 855, 856 and 857. Mechanical dye injection and related penalties

House Committee Report (H.R. REP. NO. 108-548, pt. 1)

[Code Secs. 4082, 6427 and 6715; New Code Sec. 6715A]

Present Law

Statutory rules

Gasoline, diesel fuel and kerosene are generally subject to excise tax upon removal from a refinery or terminal, upon importation into the

United States, and upon sale to unregistered persons unless there was a prior taxable removal or importation of such fuels.[414] However, a tax is not imposed upon diesel fuel or kerosene if all of the following are met: (1) the Secretary determines that the fuel is destined for a nontaxable use, (2) the fuel is indelibly dyed in accordance with regulations prescribed by the Secretary,[415] and (3) the fuel meets marking requirements

---

(Footnote Continued)

Liberty International Airport, T-22-NJ-1532; Fort Lauderdale/Hollywood International Airport, T-65-FL-2158; Piedmont Triad International Airport, T-56-NC-2038; Honolulu International Airport, T-91-HI-4570; Dulles International Airport, T-54-VA-1676; George Bush Intercontinental Airport, T-76-TX-2818; Mid Continent Airport, T-43-KS-3653; John F. Kennedy International Airport, T-11-NY-1334; McCarren International Airport, T-86-NV-4355; Kansas City International Airport, T-43-MO-3723; Orlando International Airport, T-59-FL-2111; Midway Airport, T-36-IL-3376; Memphis International Airport, T-62-TN-2212; General Mitchell International Airport, T-39-WI-3092; Minneapolis-St. Paul International Airport, T-41-MN-3419; Minneapolis-St. Paul International Airport, T-41-MN-3420; Minneapolis-St. Paul International Airport, T-41-MN-3421; Louis Armstrong New Orleans International Airport, T-72-LA-2356; Oakland International Airport, T-94-CA-4702; Eppley Airfield, T-47-NE-3608; Ontario International Airport, T-33-CA-4792; O'Hare International Airport, T-36-IL-3325; Portland International Airport, T-91-OR-4450; Philadelphia International Airport, T-23-PA-1770; Sky Harbor International Airport, T-86-AZ-4302; Pittsburgh International Airport, T-23-PA-1766; Raleigh/Durham International,

T-56-NC-2045; Reno Cannon International Airport, T-86-NV-4352; San Diego International Airport, T-33-CA-4788; San Antonio International Airport, pending; Seattle Tacoma International Airport, T-91-WA-4425; San Francisco International Airport, T-94-CA-4701; San Jose Municipal Airport, T-77-CA-4650; Salt Lake City International Airport, T-84-UT-4207; John Wayne Airport/Orange County, T-33-CA-4772; Lambert International Airport, T-43-MO-3722; Tampa/St. Petersburg International Airport, T-59-FL-2110.

[414] Sec. 4081(a)(1)(A). If such fuel is used for a nontaxable purpose, the purchaser is entitled to a refund of tax paid, or in some cases, an income tax credit. See sec. 6427.

[415] Dyeing is not a requirement, however, for certain fuels under certain conditions, i.e., diesel fuel or kerosene exempted from dyeing in certain States by the EPA under the Clean Air Act, aviation-grade kerosene as determined under regulations prescribed by the Secretary, kerosene received by pipeline or vessel and used by a registered recipient to produce substances (other than gasoline, diesel fuel or special fuels), kerosene removed or entered by a registrant to produce such substances or for resale, and (under regula-

prescribed by the Secretary.[416] A nontaxable use is defined as (1) any use that is exempt from the tax imposed by section 4041(a)(1) other than by reason of a prior imposition of tax, (2) any use in a train, or (3) certain uses in buses for public and school transportation, as described in section 6427(b)(1) (after application of section 6427(b)(3)).[417]

The Secretary is required to prescribe necessary regulations relating to dyeing, including specifically the labeling of retail diesel fuel and kerosene pumps.[418]

A person who sells dyed fuel (or holds dyed fuel for sale) for any use that such person knows (or has reason to know) is a taxable use, or who willfully alters or attempts to alter the dye in any dyed fuel, is subject to a penalty.[419] The penalty also applies to any person who uses dyed fuel for a taxable use (or holds dyed fuel for such a use) and who knows (or has reason to know) that the fuel is dyed.[420] The penalty is the greater of $1,000 per act or $10 per gallon of dyed fuel involved. In determining the amount of the penalty, the $1,000 is increased by the product of $1,000 and the number of prior penalties imposed upon such person (or a related person or predecessor of such person or related person).[421] The penalty may be imposed jointly and severally on any business entity, each officer, employee, or agent of such entity who willfully participated in any act giving rise to such penalty.[422] For purposes of the penalty, the term "dyed fuel" means any dyed diesel fuel or kerosene, whether or not the fuel was dyed pursuant to section 4082.[423]

Regulations

The Secretary has prescribed certain regulations under this provision, including regulations that specify the allowable types and concentration of dye, that the person claiming the exemption must be a taxable fuel registrant, that the terminal must be an approved terminal (in the case of a removal from a terminal rack), and the contents of the notice to be posted on diesel fuel and kerosene pumps.[424] However, the regulations do not prescribe the time or method of adding the dye to taxable fuel.[425] Diesel fuel is usually dyed at a terminal rack by either manual dyeing or mechanical injection.

Reasons for Change

The Federal government, State governments, and various segments of the petroleum industry have long been concerned with the problem of diesel fuel tax evasion. To address this problem, Congress changed the law to require that untaxed diesel fuel be indelibly dyed. The Committee is concerned, however, that tax can still be evaded through removals at a terminal of undyed fuel that has been designated as dyed.

Manual dyeing is inherently difficult to monitor. It occurs after diesel fuel has been withdrawn from a terminal storage tank, generally requires the work of several people, is imprecise, and does not automatically create a reliable record. The Committee believes that requiring that untaxed diesel fuel be dyed only by mechanical injection will significantly reduce the opportunities for diesel fuel tax evasion.

The Committee further believes that security of such mechanical dyeing systems will be enhanced by the establishment of standards for making such systems tamper resistant, and by the addition of new penalties for tampering with such mechanical dyeing systems and for failing to maintain the established security standards for such systems. In furtherance of the enforcement of these penalties in the case of business entities, it is appropriate to impose joint and several liability for such penalties upon natural persons who have willfully participated in any act giving rise to these penalties and upon the parent corporation of an affiliated group of which the business entity is a member.

Explanation of Provision

With respect to terminals that offer dyed fuel, the provision eliminates manual dyeing of fuel and requires dyeing by a mechanical system. Not later than 180 days after enactment of this provision, the Secretary of the Treasury is to prescribe regulations establishing standards for tamper resistant mechanical injector dyeing.

(Footnote Continued)

tions) kerosene sold by a registered distributor who sells kerosene exclusively to ultimate vendors that resell it (1) from a pump that is not suitable for fueling any diesel-powered highway vehicle or train, or (2) for blending with heating oil to be used during periods of extreme or unseasonable cold. Sec. 4082(c), (d).

[416] Sec. 4082(a).

[417] Sec. 4082(b).

[418] Sec. 4082(e).

[419] Sec. 6715(a).

[420] Sec. 6715(a).

[421] Sec. 6715(b).

[422] Sec. 6715(d).

[423] Sec. 6715(c)(1).

[424] Treas. Reg. secs. 48.4082-1, -2.

[425] In March 2000, the IRS withdrew its Notice of Proposed Rulemaking PS-6-95 (61 F.R. 10490 (1996)) relating to dye injection systems. Announcement 2000-42, 2000-1 C.B. 949. The proposed regulation established standards for mechanical dye injection equipment and required terminal operators to report nonconforming dyeing to the IRS. See also Treas. Reg. sec. 48.4082-1(c), (d).

Such standards shall be reasonable, cost-effective, and establish levels of security commensurate with the applicable facility.

The provision adds an additional set of penalties for violation of the new rules. A penalty, equal to the greater of $25,000 or $10 for each gallon of fuel involved, applies to each act of tampering with a mechanical dye injection system. The person committing the act is also responsible for any unpaid tax on removed undyed fuel. A penalty of $1,000 is imposed for each failure to maintain security for mechanical dye injection systems. An additional penalty of $1,000 is imposed for each day any such violation remains uncorrected after the first day such violation has been or reasonably should have been discovered. For purposes of the daily penalty, a violation may be corrected by shutting down the portion of the system causing the violation. If any of these penalties are imposed on any business entity, each officer, employee, or agent of such entity or other contracting party who willfully participated in any act giving rise to such penalty shall be jointly and severally liable with such entity for such penalty. If such business entity is part of an affiliated group, the parent corporation of such entity shall be jointly and severally liable with such entity for the penalty.

Effective Date

The provision is effective 180 days after the date that the Secretary issues the required regulations. The Secretary must issue such regulations no later than 180 days after enactment.

Conference Committee Report (H.R. CONF. REP. NO. 108-755)

Senate Amendment

The Senate amendment contains a mechanical dyeing provision similar to the provision in the House bill, except that the Secretary of the Treasury is to prescribe regulations establishing standards by June 30, 2004.

The Senate amendment also contains two additional provisions not in the House bill.

The Senate amendment denies administrative appeal or review for repeat offenders (more than two violations) of present law after a chemical analysis of the fuel, except in the case of a claim regarding fraud or mistake in the chemical analysis or error in the mathematical calculation of the amount of penalty.

The Senate amendment also extends present-law penalties to any person who knows that the strength or composition of any dye or marking in any dyed fuel has been altered, chemically or otherwise, and who sells (or holds for sale) such fuel for any use that the person knows or has reason to know is a taxable use of such fuel.

Conference Agreement

The conference agreement follows the House bill with respect to mechanical dye injection systems and related penalties. The conference agreement follows the Senate amendment with respect to denying administrative review to repeat offenders and extending present law penalties to any person who knows that the strength or composition of any dye or marking in any dyed fuel has been altered, chemically or otherwise, and who sells (or holds for sale) such fuel for any use that the person knows or has reason to know is a taxable use of such fuel.

[Law at ¶6015, ¶6220, ¶6280, ¶6285 and ¶7120. CCH Explanation at ¶1517, ¶1519, ¶1521 and ¶1523.]

[¶11,390] Act Sec. 858. Authority to inspect on-site records

House Committee Report (H.R. REP. NO. 108-548, pt. 1)

[Code Sec. 4083]

Present Law

The IRS is authorized to inspect any place where taxable fuel[426] is produced or stored (or may be stored). The inspection is authorized to: (1) examine the equipment used to determine the amount or composition of the taxable fuel and the equipment used to store the fuel; and (2) take and remove samples of taxable fuel. Places of inspection include, but are not limited to, terminals, fuel storage facilities, retail fuel facilities or any designated inspection site.[427]

In conducting the inspection, the IRS may detain any receptacle that contains or may contain any taxable fuel, or detain any vehicle or train to inspect its fuel tanks and storage tanks. The scope of the inspection includes the book and records kept at the place of inspection to

---

[426] "Taxable fuel" means gasoline, diesel fuel, and kerosene. Sec. 4083(a).

[427] Sec. 4083(c)(1)(A).

determine the excise tax liability under section 4081.[428]

Reasons for Change

The Committee believes it is appropriate to expand the authority of the IRS to make on-site inspections of books and records. The Committee believes that such expanded authority will aid in the detection of fuel tax evasion and the enforcement of Federal fuel taxes.

Explanation of Provision

The provision expands the scope of the inspection to include any books, records, or shipping papers pertaining to taxable fuel located in any authorized inspection location.

Effective Date

The provision effective on the date on enactment.

Conference Committee Report (H.R. CONF. REP. NO. 108-755)

Senate Amendment

The Senate amendment is the same as the House bill.

Conference Agreement

The conference agreement follows the House bill and Senate amendment.

[Law at ¶ 6020. CCH Explanation at ¶ 1539.]

[¶ 11,400] Act Sec. 859. Assessable penalty for refusal of entry

Conference Committee Report (H.R. CONF. REP. NO. 108-755)

[New Code Sec. 6717]

Present Law

The Internal Revenue Service is authorized to inspect any place where taxable fuel is produced or stored (or may be stored). As part of the inspection, the Internal Revenue Service is authorized to: (1) examine the equipment used to determine the amount or composition of the taxable fuel and the equipment used to store the fuel; and (2) take and remove samples of taxable fuel. Places of inspection, include, but are not limited to, terminals, fuel storage facilities, retail fuel facilities or any designated inspection site.[742]

In conducting the inspection, the Internal Revenue Service may detain any receptacle that contains or may contain any taxable fuel, or detain any vehicle or train to inspect its fuel tanks and storage tanks. The scope of the inspection includes the book and records kept to determine the excise tax liability under section 4081.[743] The Internal Revenue Service is authorized to establish inspection sites. A designated inspection site includes any State highway inspection station, weigh station, agricultural inspection station, mobile station or other location designated by the Internal Revenue Service.[744]

Any person that refuses to allow an inspection is subject to a penalty in the amount of $1,000 for each refusal.[745] The IRS is not able to assess this penalty in the same manner as it would a tax. It must first seek the assistance of the Department of Justice to obtain a judgment. Assessable penalties are payable upon notice and demand by the Secretary and are assessed and collected in the same manner as taxes.[746]

House Bill

No provision.

Senate Amendment

In addition to the $1,000 penalty under present law, the Senate amendment imposes an assessable penalty with respect to the refusal of entry. The assessable penalty is $1,000 for such refusal. The penalty will not apply if it is shown that such failure is due to reasonable cause. If the penalty is imposed on a business entity, the proposal provides for joint and several liability with respect to each officer, employee, or agent of such entity or other contracting party who willfully participated in the act giving rise to the penalty. If the business entity is part of an affiliated group, the parent corporation also will be jointly and severally liable for the penalty.

Effective Date

The provision is effective on October 1, 2004.

---

[428] Treas. Reg. sec. 48.4083-1(c)(1).

[742] Sec. 4083(c)(1)(A).

[743] Treas. Reg. sec. 48.4083-1(b)(2).

[744] Sec. 4083(c); Treas. Reg. sec. 48.4083-1(b)(1).

[745] Sec. 4083(c)(3) and 7342.

[746] Sec. 6671.

Conference Agreement

The conference agreement follows the Senate amendment, except for effective date.

Effective Date

The provision is effective on January 1, 2005.

[Law at ¶ 6020 and ¶ 6290. CCH Explanation at ¶ 1541.]

[¶ 11,410] Act Sec. 860. Registration of pipeline or vessel operators required for exemption of bulk transfers to registered terminals or refineries

House Committee Report (H.R. REP. NO. 108-548, pt. 1)

[Code Sec. 4081]

Present Law

In general, gasoline, diesel fuel, and kerosene ("taxable fuel") are taxed upon removal from a refinery or a terminal.[429] Tax also is imposed on the entry into the United States of any taxable fuel for consumption, use, or warehousing. The tax does not apply to any removal or entry of a taxable fuel transferred in bulk (a "bulk transfer") to a terminal or refinery if both the person removing or entering the taxable fuel and the operator of such terminal or refinery are registered with the Secretary.[430]

Present law does not require that the vessel or pipeline operator that transfers fuel as part of a bulk transfer be registered in order for the transfer to be exempt. For example, a registered refiner may transfer fuel to an unregistered vessel or pipeline operator who in turn transfers fuel to a registered terminal operator. The transfer is exempt despite the intermediate transfer to an unregistered person.

In general, the owner of the fuel is liable for payment of tax with respect to bulk transfers not received at an approved terminal or refinery.[431] The refiner is liable for payment of tax with respect to certain taxable removals from the refinery.[432]

Reasons for Change

The Committee is concerned that unregistered pipeline and vessel operators are receiving bulk transfers of taxable fuel, and then diverting the fuel to retailers or end users without the tax ever being paid. The Committee believes that requiring that a pipeline or vessel operator be registered with the IRS in order for a bulk transfer exemption to be valid, in combination with other provisions that impose penalties relating to registration, will help to ensure that transfers of fuel in bulk are delivered as intended to approved refineries and terminals and taxed appropriately.

Explanation of Provision

The provision requires that for a bulk transfer of a taxable fuel to be exempt from tax, any pipeline or vessel operator that is a party to the bulk transfer be registered with the Secretary. Transfer to an unregistered party will subject the transfer to tax.

The Secretary is required to publish periodically a list of all registered persons that are required to register.

Conference Committee Report (H.R. CONF. REP. NO. 108-755)

Conference Agreement

The conference agreement follows the House bill, modified to provide that the Secretary shall periodically publish a current list of persons required to register under the authority of section 6103(k)(7).

Effective Date

Effective on March 1, 2005, except that the Secretary is required to publish the list of persons required to register beginning on January 1, 2005.

[Law at ¶ 6010 and ¶ 7125. CCH Explanation at ¶ 1527.]

---

[429] Sec. 4081(a)(1)(A).

[430] Sec. 4081(a)(1)(B). The sale of a taxable fuel to an unregistered person prior to a taxable removal or entry of the fuel is subject to tax. Sec. 4081(a)(1)(A).

[431] Treas. Reg. sec. 48.4081-3(e)(2).

[432] Treas. Reg. sec. 48.4081-3(b).

[¶ 11,420] Act Sec. 861. Display of registration and penalties for failure to display registration and to register

House Committee Report (H.R. Rep. No. 108-548, pt. 1)

[Code Sec. 4101 and New Code Sec. 6718]

Present Law

Blenders, enterers, pipeline operators, position holders, refiners, terminal operators, and vessel operators are required to register with the Secretary with respect to fuels taxes imposed by sections 4041(a)(1) and 4081.[433] A non-assessable penalty for failure to register is $50.[434] A criminal penalty of $5,000, or imprisonment of not more than five years, or both, together with the costs of prosecution also applies to a failure to register and to certain false statements made in connection with a registration application.[435]

Reasons for Change

Registration with the Secretary is a critical component of enabling the Secretary to regulate the movement and use of taxable fuels and ensure that the appropriate excise taxes are being collected. The Committee believes that present law penalties are not severe enough to ensure that persons that are required to register in fact register. Accordingly, the Committee believes it is appropriate to increase present law penalties significantly and to add a new assessable penalty for failure to register. In addition, the Committee believes that persons that do business with vessel operators should be able easily to verify whether the vessel operator is registered. Thus, the Committee requires that vessel operators display proof of registration on their vessels and

imposes an attendant penalty for failure to display such proof.

Explanation of Provision

The provision requires that every operator of a vessel who is required to register with the Secretary display on each vessel used by the operator to transport fuel, proof of registration through an electronic identification device prescribed by the Secretary. A failure to display such proof of registration results in a penalty of $500 per month per vessel. The amount of the penalty is increased for multiple prior violations. No penalty is imposed upon a showing by the taxpayer of reasonable cause. The provision authorizes amounts equivalent to the penalties received to be appropriated to the Highway Trust Fund.

The provision imposes a new assessable penalty for failure to register of $10,000 for each initial failure, plus $1,000 per day that the failure continues. No penalty is imposed upon a showing by the taxpayer of reasonable cause. In addition, the provision increases the present-law non-assessable penalty for failure to register from $50 to $10,000 and the present law criminal penalty for failure to register from $5,000 to $10,000. The provision authorizes amounts equivalent to any of such penalties received to be appropriated to the Highway Trust Fund.

Conference Committee Report (H.R. Conf. Rep. No. 108-755)

Conference Agreement

The conference agreement follows the House bill except that the identification device is not required to be electronic.

Effective Date

The provision requiring display of registration is effective on January 1, 2005. The provision

relating to penalties is effective for penalties imposed after December 31, 2004.

[Law at ¶ 6040 and ¶ 6295. CCH Explanation at ¶ 1529.]

---

[433] Sec. 4101; Treas. Reg. sec. 48.4101-1(a) and (c)(1).
[434] Sec. 7272(a).

[435] Sec. 7232.

[¶ 11,430] Act Sec. 862. Registration of persons within foreign trade zones

Conference Committee Report (H.R. CONF. REP. NO. 108-755)

[Code Sec. 4101]

Present Law

Blenders, enterers, pipeline operators, position holders, refiners, terminal operators, and vessel operators are required to register with the Secretary with respect to fuels taxes imposed by sections 4041(a)(1) and 4081.[754]

House Bill

No provision.

Senate Amendment

The Secretary shall require registration by any person that operates a terminal or refinery within a foreign trade zone or within a customs bonded storage facility, or holds an inventory position with respect to a taxable fuel in such a terminal.

Conference Agreement

The conference agreement follows the Senate amendment. It is intended that the Secretary shall establish a date by which persons required to register under the provision must be registered.

Effective Date

Effective on January 1, 2005.

[Law at ¶ 6040 and ¶ 6295. CCH Explanation at ¶ 1535.]

[¶ 11,440] Act Sec. 863. Penalties for failure to report

House Committee Report (H.R. REP. NO. 108-548, pt. 1)

[Code Secs. 7232 and 7272 and New Code Secs. 6719 and 6725]

Present Law

A fuel information reporting program, the Excise Summary Terminal Activity Reporting System ("ExSTARS"), requires terminal operators and bulk transport carriers to report monthly on the movement of any liquid product into or out of an approved terminal.[436] Terminal operators file Form 720-TO—Terminal Operator Report, which shows the monthly receipts and disbursements of all liquid products to and from an approved terminal.[437] Bulk transport carriers (barges, vessels, and pipelines) that receive liquid product from an approved terminal or deliver liquid product to an approved terminal file Form 720-CS—Carrier Summary Report, which details such receipts and disbursements. In general, the penalty for failure to file a report or a failure to furnish all of the required information in a report is $50 per report.[438]

Reasons for Change

The Committee believes that the proper and timely reporting of the disbursements of taxable fuels under the ExSTARs system is essential to the Treasury Department's ability to monitor and enforce the excise fuels taxes. Accordingly, the Committee believes it is appropriate to provide for significant penalties if required information is not provided accurately, completely, and on a timely basis.

Explanation of Provision

The provision imposes a new assessable penalty for failure to file a report or to furnish information required in a report required by the ExSTARS system. The penalty is $10,000 per failure with respect to each vessel or facility (e.g., a terminal or other facility) for which information is required to be furnished. No penalty is imposed upon a showing by the taxpayer of reasonable cause. The provision authorizes amounts equivalent to the penalties received to be appropriated to the Highway Trust Fund.

---

[754] Sec. 4101; Treas. Reg. sec. 48.4101-1(a) & (c)(1).

[436] Sec. 4010(d); Treas. Reg. sec. 48.4101-2. The reports are required to be filed by the end of the month following the month to which the report relates.

[437] An approved terminal is a terminal that is operated by a taxable fuel registrant that is a terminal operator. Treas. Reg. sec. 48.4081-1(b).

[438] Sec. 6721(a).

Conference Committee Report (H.R. CONF. REP. NO. 108-755)

Senate Amendment

Similar to House bill, except for technical wording differences.

Conference Agreement

The conference agreement follows the House bill.

Effective Date

Effective for penalties imposed after December 31, 2004.

[Law at ¶6300, ¶6315, ¶6320 and ¶6325. CCH Explanation at ¶1533.]

[¶ 11,450] Act Sec. 864. Electronic filing of required information reports

Conference Committee Report (H.R. CONF. REP. NO. 108-755)

[Code Sec. 4101]

Present Law

A fuel information reporting program, the Excise Summary Terminal Activity Reporting System ("ExSTARS"), requires terminal operators and bulk transport carriers to report monthly on the movement of any liquid product into or out of an approved terminal.[758] Terminal operators file Form 720-TO - Terminal Operator Report, which shows the monthly receipts and disbursements of all liquid products to and from an approved terminal.[759] Bulk transport carriers (barges, vessels, and pipelines) that receive liquid product from an approved terminal or deliver liquid product to an approved terminal file Form 720-CS - Carrier Summary Report, which details such receipts and disbursements.

House Bill

No provision.

Senate Amendment

The Senate amendment requires information reporting with respect to taxable fuels removed,

entered, or transferred from any refinery, pipeline, or vessel that is registered. The proposal also requires that any person who must report under the ExSTARs systems and who has 25 or more reportable transactions in a month to report in electronic format.

Effective Date

Effective on October 1, 2005.

Conference Agreement

The conference agreement follows the Senate amendment except that the conference agreement does not adopt the information reporting requirement with respect to taxable fuels removed, entered, or transferred from any refinery, pipeline, or vessel that is registered.

Effective Date

Effective on January 1, 2006.

[Law at ¶6040. CCH Explanation at ¶1531.]

[¶ 11,460] Act Sec. 865. Taxable fuel refunds for certain ultimate vendors

House Committee Report (H.R. REP. NO. 108-548, pt. 1)

[Code Secs. 6416 and 6427]

Present Law

The Code provides that, in the case of gasoline on which tax has been paid and sold to a State or local government, to a nonprofit educational organization, for supplies for vessels or aircraft, for export, or for the production of spe-

cial fuels, a wholesale distributor that sells the gasoline for such exempt purposes is treated as the person who paid the tax and thereby is the proper claimant for a credit or refund of the tax paid. In the case of undyed diesel fuel or kerosene used on a farm for farming purposes or by a State or local government, a credit or payment

---

[758] Sec. 4101(d); Treas. Reg. sec. 48.4101-2. The reports are required to be filed by the end of the month following the month to which the report relates.

[759] An approved terminal is a terminal that is operated by a taxable fuel registrant that is a terminal operator. Treas. Reg. sec. 48.4081-1(b).

is allowable only to the ultimate, registered vendors ("ultimate vendors") of such fuels.

In general, refunds are paid without interest. However, in the case of overpayments of tax on gasoline, diesel fuel, or kerosene that is used to produce a qualified alcohol mixture and for refunds due ultimate vendors of diesel fuel or kerosene used on a farm for farming purposes or by a State or local government, the Secretary is required to pay interest on certain refunds. The Secretary must pay interest on refunds of $200 or more ($100 or more in the case of kerosene) due to the taxpayer arising from sales over any period of a week or more, if the Secretary does not make payment of the refund within 20 days.

Reasons for Change

The Committee observes that refund procedures for gasoline differ from those for diesel fuel and kerosene. The Committee believes that simplification of administration can be achieved for both taxpayers and the IRS by providing a more uniform refund procedure applicable to all taxed highway fuels. The Committee further believes that compliance can be increased and administration made less costly by increased use of electronic filing.

The Committee further observes that often State and local governments find it prudent to monitor and pay for fuel purchases by the use of a credit card, fleet buying card, or similar arrangement. In such a case the person extending the credit stands between the vendor of fuel and purchaser of fuel (the State or local government) in an exempt transaction, and the person extending the credit insures payment of the fuel bill thereby paying the amount of any tax owed that is embedded in the price of the fuel. In addition, because the person extending credit to the tax-exempt purchaser has a contractual relationship with the tax-exempt user, the person extending the credit should be best able to establish that the fuel should be sold at a tax-exempt price. The Committee believes that in such a situation it is appropriate to deem the person

extending the credit to hold ultimate vendor status, not withstanding that such a person is not actually a vendor of fuel. The Committee observes that the billing service provided by the person extending credit to the tax-exempt purchaser creates a "paper trail" that should facilitate compliance and aid in any necessary audits that the IRS may undertake.

Explanation of Provision

For sales of gasoline to a State or local government for the exclusive use of a State or local government or to a nonprofit educational organization for its exclusive use on which tax has been imposed, the provision conforms the payment of refunds to that procedure established under present law in the case of diesel fuel or kerosene. That is, the ultimate vendor claims for refund.

The provision modifies the payment of interest on refunds. Under the provision, in the case of overpayments of tax on gasoline, diesel fuel, or kerosene that is used to produce a qualified alcohol mixture and for refunds due ultimate vendors of diesel fuel or kerosene used on a farm for farming purposes or by a State or local government, all refunds unpaid after 45 days must be paid with interest. If the taxpayer has filed for his or her refund by electronic means, refunds unpaid after 20 days must be paid with interest.

Lastly, for claims for refund of tax paid on diesel fuel or kerosene sold to State and local governments or for sales of gasoline to a State or local government for the exclusive use of a State or local government or to a nonprofit educational organization for its exclusive use on which tax has been imposed and for which the ultimate purchaser utilized a credit card, the provision deems the person extending the credit to the ultimate purchaser to be the ultimate vendor. That is, the person extending credit via a credit card administers claims for refund, and is responsible for supplying all the appropriate documentation currently required from ultimate vendors.

Conference Committee Report (H.R. CONF. REP. No. 108-755)

Senate Amendment

The Senate amendment is the same as the House bill.

Conference Agreement

The conference agreement follows the House bill and Senate amendment, with modifications. For sales of gasoline to a State or local government for the exclusive use of a State or local government or to a nonprofit educational

organization for its exclusive use on which tax has been imposed, claims for credits or refund are made by the ultimate vendor.

The conference agreement provides that the rules for vendor refunds apply to claims made under this provision, except that the rules regarding electronic claims shall not apply unless the ultimate vendor has certified to the Secretary for the most recent quarter of the taxable year that all ultimate purchasers of the vendor are

State or local governments or to a nonprofit educational organizations.[771]

The conference agreement does not include the House bill or Senate amendment provisions that deem the person extending credit via a credit card to the ultimate purchaser to be the ultimate vendor for purposes of refund claims.

[¶11,470] Act Sec. 866. Two party exchanges

House Committee Report (H.R. REP. NO. 108-548, pt. 1)

[New Code Sec. 4105]

Present Law

Most fuel is taxed when it is removed from a registered terminal.[445] The party liable for payment of this tax is the "position holder." The position holder is the person reflected on the records of the terminal operator as holding the inventory position in the fuel.[446]

It is common industry practice for oil companies to serve customers of other oil companies under exchange agreements, e.g., where Company A's terminal is more conveniently located for wholesale or retail customers of Company B. In such cases, the exchange agreement party (Company B in the example) owns the fuel when the motor fuel is removed from the terminal and sold to B's customer.

Reasons for Change

The Committee believes it is appropriate to recognize industry practice under exchange agreements by relieving the original position holder of tax liability for the removal of a taxable fuel from a terminal if certain circumstances are met.

Explanation of Provision

The provision permits two registered parties to switch position holder status in fuel within a

registered terminal (thereby relieving the person originally owning the fuel[447] of tax liability as the position holder) if all of the following occur:

(1) The transaction includes a transfer from the original owner, i.e., the person who holds the original inventory position for taxable fuel in the terminal as reflected in the records of the terminal operator prior to the transaction.

(2) The exchange transaction occurs at the same time as completion of removal across the rack from the terminal by the receiving person or its customer.

(3) The terminal operator in its books and records treats the receiving person as the person that removes the product across a terminal rack for purposes of reporting the transaction to the Internal Revenue Service.

(4) The transaction is the subject of a written contract.

Effective Date

The provision is effective on the date of enactment.

Effective Date

The provision is effective on January 1, 2005.

[Law at ¶6205. CCH Explanation at ¶1511.]

Conference Committee Report (H.R. CONF. REP. NO. 108-755)

Senate Amendment

The Senate amendment is the same as the House bill.

Conference Agreement

The conference agreement follows the House bill and Senate amendment.

[Law at ¶6055. CCH Explanation at ¶1505.]

---

[771] Sec. 6416(b)(2)(C) or (D).

[445] A "terminal" is a storage and distribution facility that is supplied by pipeline or vessel, and from which fuel may be removed at a rack. A "rack" is a mechanism capable of delivering taxable fuel into a means of transport other than a pipeline or vessel.

[446] Such person has a contractual agreement with the terminal operator to store and provide services with respect

to the fuel. A "terminal operator" is any person who owns, operates, or otherwise controls a terminal. A terminal operator can also be a position holder if that person owns fuel in its terminal.

[447] In the provision, this person is referred to as the "delivering person."

[¶ 11,480] Act Sec. 867. Modification of the use tax on heavy highway vehicles

House Committee Report (H.R. REP. NO. 108-548, pt. 1)

[Code Secs. 4481, 4483 and 6165]

Present Law

An annual use tax is imposed on heavy highway vehicles, at the rates below.[441]

Under 55,000 pounds	. .	No tax.
55,000-75,000 pounds	. .	$100 plus $22 per 1,000 pounds over 55,000.
Over 75,000 pounds	. . .	$550.

The annual use tax is imposed for a taxable period of July 1 through June 30. Generally, the tax is paid by the person in whose name the vehicle is registered. In certain cases, taxpayers are allowed to pay the tax in installments.[442] State governments are required to receive proof of payment of the use tax as a condition of vehicle registration.

Exemptions and reduced rates are provided for certain "transit-type buses," trucks used for fewer than 5,000 miles on public highways (7,500 miles for agricultural vehicles), and logging trucks.[443] Any highway motor vehicle that is issued a base plate by Canada or Mexico and is operated on U.S. highways is subject to the highway use tax whether or not the vehicles are required to be registered in the United States. The tax rate for Canadian and Mexican vehicles is 75 percent of the rate that would otherwise be imposed.[444]

Reasons for Change

The Committee notes that in the case of taxpayers that elect quarterly installment payments, the IRS has no procedure for ensuring

that installments subsequent to the first one actually are paid. Thus, it is possible for taxpayers to receive State registrations when only the first quarterly installment is paid with the return. Similarly, it is possible for taxpayers repeatedly to pay the first quarterly installment and continue to receive State registrations because the IRS has no computerized system for checking past compliance when it issues certificates of payment for the current year. In the case of taxpayers owning only one or a few vehicles, it is not cost effective for the IRS to monitor and enforce compliance. Thus, the Committee believes it is appropriate to eliminate the ability of taxpayers to pay the use tax in installments. The Committee also believes that Canadian and Mexican vehicles operating on U.S. highways should be subject to the full amount of use tax, as such vehicles contribute to the wear and tear on U.S. highways.

Explanation of Provision

The provision eliminates the ability to pay the tax in installments. It also eliminates the reduced rates for Canadian and Mexican vehicles. The provision requires taxpayers with 25 or more vehicles for any taxable period to file their returns electronically. Finally, the provision permits proration of tax for vehicles sold during the taxable period.

Effective Date

The provision is effective for taxable periods beginning after the date of enactment.

Conference Committee Report (H.R. CONF. REP. NO. 108-755)

Conference Agreement

The conference agreement follows the House bill.

[Law at ¶ 6080, ¶ 6085 and ¶ 6175. CCH Explanation at ¶ 1547.]

---

[441] Sec. 4481.
[442] Sec. 6156.

[443] See generally, sec. 4483.
[444] Sec. 4483(f): Treas. Reg. sec. 41.4483-7(a).

[¶ 11,490] Act Sec. 868. Dedication of revenue from certain penalties to the Highway Trust Fund

House Committee Report (H.R. REP. NO. 108-548, pt. 1)

[Code Sec. 9503]

Present Law

Present law does not dedicate to the Highway Trust Fund any penalties assessed and collected by the Secretary.

Reasons for Change

The Committee believes it is appropriate to dedicate to the Highway Trust Fund penalties associated with the administration and enforcement of taxes supporting the Highway Trust Fund.

Explanation of Provision

The provision dedicates to the Highway Trust Fund amounts equivalent to the penalties paid under sections 6715 (relating to dyed fuel sold for use or used in taxable use), 6715A (penalty for tampering or failing to maintain security requirements for mechanical dye injection systems), 6717 (penalty for failing to display tax registration on vessels), 6718 (penalty for failing to register under section 4101), 6725 (penalty for failing to report information required by the Secretary), 7232 (penalty for failing to register and false representations of registration status), and 7272 (but only with regard to penalties related to failure to register under section 4101).

Conference Committee Report (H.R. CONF. REP. NO. 108-755)

Senate Amendment

The Senate amendment similarly dedicates certain penalties to the Highway Trust Fund.

Conference Agreement

The conference agreement generally follows the House bill and the Senate amendment by dedicating certain penalties to the Highway Trust Fund. The conference agreement dedicates to the Highway Trust Fund amounts equivalent to the penalties paid under sections 6715 (relating to dyed fuel sold for use or used in taxable use), 6715A (penalty for tampering with or failing to maintain security requirements for mechanical dye injection systems), 6717 (assessable penalty for refusal of entry), 6718 (penalty for failing to display tax registration on vessels), 6719 (assessable penalty for failure to register), 6725 (penalty for failing to report information required by the Secretary), 7232 (penalty for failing to register and false representations of registration status), and 7272 (but only with regard to penalties related to failure to register under section 4101).

Effective Date

The provision is effective for penalties assessed on or after the date of enactment.

[Law at ¶ 6385. CCH Explanation at ¶ 1573.]

[¶ 11,500] Act Sec. 869. Simplification of tax on tires

House Committee Report (H.R. REP. NO. 108-548, pt. 1)

[Code Secs. 4071, 4072 and 4073]

Present Law

A graduated excise tax is imposed on the sale by a manufacturer (or importer) of tires designed for use on highway vehicles (sec. 4071). The tire tax rates are as follows:

Tire weight	Tax rate
Not more than 40 lbs.	No tax.
More than 40 lbs., but not more than 70 lbs.	15 cents/lb. in excess of 40 lbs
More than 70 lbs., but not more than 90 lbs.	$4.50 plus 30 cents/lb. in excess of 70 lbs.
More than 90 lbs.	$10.50 plus 50 cents/lb. in excess of 90 lbs.

No tax is imposed on the recapping of a tire that previously has been subject to tax. Tires of extruded tiring with internal wire fastening also are exempt.

The tax expires after September 30, 2005.

Reasons for Change

Under present law, the tire excise tax is based on the weight of each tire. This forces tire manufacturers to weigh sample batches of every type of tire made and collect the tax based on that weight. This regime also makes it difficult for the IRS to measure and enforce compliance with the tax, as the IRS likewise must weigh sample batches of tires to ensure compliance. The Committee believes significant administrative simplification for both tire manufacturers and the IRS will be achieved if the tax were based on the weight carrying capacity of the tire, rather than the weight of the tire, because Department of Transportation requires the load rating to be stamped on the side of highway tires. Thus, both the manufacturer and the IRS will know immediately whether a tire is taxable and how much tax should be paid.

Explanation of Provision

The provision modifies the excise tax applicable to tires. The provision replaces the present-law tax rates based on the weight of the tire with a tax rate based on the load capacity of the tire. In general, the tax is 9.4 cents for each 10 pounds of tire load capacity in excess of 3,500 pounds. In the case of a biasply tire, the tax rate is 4.7 cents for each 10 pounds of tire load capacity in excess of 3,500 pounds.

The provision modifies the definition of tires for use on highway vehicles to include any tire marked for highway use pursuant to certain regulations promulgated by the Secretary of Transportation. The provision also exempts from tax any tire sold for the exclusive use of the United States Department of Defense or the United States Coast Guard.

Tire load capacity is the maximum load rating labeled on the tire pursuant to regulations promulgated by the Secretary of Transportation. A biasply tire is any tire manufactured primarily for use on piggyback trailers.

Effective Date

The provision is effective for sales in calendar years beginning more than 30 days after the date of enactment.

Conference Committee Report (H.R. CONF. REP. NO. 108-755)

Senate Amendment

No provision.

Conference Agreement

The conference agreement follows the House bill with the following modifications. The conference agreement modifies the rate of tax applicable to 9.45 cents for each 10 pounds of tire load capacity in excess of 3,500 pounds. In the case of a biasply tire, the conference agreement modifies the tax rate is 4.725 cents for each 10 pounds of tire load capacity in excess of 3,500 pounds. The conference agreement also imposes tax at a rate of is 4.725 cents for each 10 pounds of tire load capacity in excess of 3,500 pounds an any super single tire. A super single tire is a single tire greater than 13 inches in cross section width designed to replace two tires in a dual fitment. The conference agreement provides that a biasply tire means a pneumatic tire on which the ply cords that extend to the beads are laid at alternate angles substantially less than 90 degrees to the centerline of the tread.

Nothing in the amendments made by this section shall be construed to have any effect on subsection (d) of section 48.4701-1 of Title 26, Code of Federal Regulations (relating to recapped and retreaded tires). The conferees expect that the Secretary will prescribe regulations implementing the amendment to section 4071 but that such regulations will not affect subsection (d). The conferees believe no tax should be imposed on the recapping of a tire that previously has been subject to tax.

[Law at ¶ 5995, ¶ 6000 and ¶ 6005. CCH Explanation at ¶ 1553.]

[¶ 11,510] Act Secs. 870 and 871. Taxation of transmix and diesel fuel blend stocks and Treasury study on fuel tax compliance

Conference Committee Report (H.R. Conf. Rep. No. 108-755)

[Code Sec. 4083]

Present Law

Definition of taxable fuels

A "taxable fuel" is gasoline, diesel fuel (including any liquid, other than gasoline, which is suitable for use as a fuel in a diesel-powered highway vehicle or train), and kerosene.[784]

Under the regulations, "gasoline" includes all products commonly or commercially known or sold as gasoline and suited for use as a motor fuel, and that have an octane rating of 75 or more. Gasoline also includes, to the extent provided in regulations, gasoline blendstocks and products commonly used as additives in gasoline. The term "gasoline blendstocks" does not include any product that cannot be blended into gasoline without further processing or fractionation ("off-spec gasoline").[785]

Diesel fuel is any liquid (other than gasoline) that is suitable for use as a fuel in a diesel-powered highway vehicle or diesel-powered train.[786] By regulation, diesel fuel does not include kerosene, gasoline, No. 5 and No. 6 fuel oils (as described in ASTM Specification D 396), or F-76 (Fuel Naval Distillates MIL-F-16884) any liquid that contains less than four percent normal parafins, or any liquid that has a distillation range of 125 degrees Fahrenheit or less, sulfur content of 10 ppm or less and minimum color of +27 Saybolt (these are known as "excluded liquids").[787]

By regulation, kerosene is defined as the kerosene described in ASTM Specification D 3699 (No. 1-K and No. 2-K), ASTM Specification D 1655 (kerosene-type jet fuel), and military specifications MIL-DTL-5624T (Grade JP-5) and MIL-DTL-83133E (Grade JP-8). Kerosene does not include any liquid that is an excluded liquid.[788]

Taxable events and exemptions

An excise tax is imposed upon (1) the removal of any taxable fuel from a refinery or terminal, (2) the entry of any taxable fuel into the United States, or (3) the sale of any taxable fuel to any person who is not registered with the IRS to receive untaxed fuel, unless there was a prior taxable removal or entry.[789] The tax does not apply to any removal or entry of taxable fuel transferred in bulk to a terminal or refinery if the person removing or entering the taxable fuel and the operator of such terminal or refinery are registered with the Secretary.[790]

Gasoline exemptions

If certain conditions are met, the removal, entry, or sale of gasoline blendstocks is not taxable. Generally, the exemption from tax applies if a gasoline blendstock is not used to produce finished gasoline or is received at an approved terminal or refinery. No tax is imposed on nonbulk removals from a terminal or refinery, or nonbulk entries into the United States or on any gasoline blendstocks if the person liable for the tax is a gasoline registrant, has an unexpired notification certificate, knows of no false information in the certificate, and has verified the accuracy of the notification certificate. The sale of a gasoline blendstock that was not subject to tax on nonbulk removal or entry is taxable unless the seller has an unexpired certificate from the buyer and has no reason to believe that any information in the certificate is false. No tax is imposed on, or purchaser certification required for, off-spec gasoline.

Diesel fuel and kerosene exemptions

Diesel fuel and kerosene that is to be used for a nontaxable purpose will not be taxed upon removal from the terminal if it is dyed to indicate its nontaxable purpose. Undyed aviation-

---

[784] Sec. 4083(a).

[785] Treas. Reg. sec. 48.4081-1(c)(3)(ii). The term "gasoline blendstocks" means alkylate; butane; catalytically cracked gasoline; coker gasoline; ethyl tertiary butyl ether (ETBE); hexane; hydrocrackate; isomerate; methyl tertiary butyl ether (MTBE); mixed xylene (not including any separated isomer of xylene); natural gasoline; pentane; pentane mixture; polymer gasoline; raffinate; reformate; straight-run gasoline; straight-run naphtha; tertiary amyl methyl ether (TAME); tertiary butyl alcohol (gasoline grade) (TBA); ther-

mally cracked gasoline; toluene; and transmix containing gasoline. Treas. Reg. sec. 48.4081-1(c)(3)(i).

[786] Sec. 4083(a)(3).

[787] Treas. Reg. sec. 48.4081-1(c)(2)(ii).

[788] Treas. Reg. sec. 48.4081-1(b).

[789] Sec. 4081(a)(1).

[790] Sec. 4081(a)(1)(B).

grade kerosene also is exempt from tax at the rack if it is destined for use as a fuel in an aircraft. The tax does not apply to diesel fuel asserted to be "not suitable for use" or kerosene asserted to qualify as an excluded liquid.

Feedstock kerosene that a registered industrial user receives by pipeline or vessel also is exempt from the dyeing requirement. A kerosene feedstock user is defined as a person that receives kerosene by bulk transfer for its own use in the manufacture or production of any substance (other than gasoline, diesel fuel or special fuels subject to tax). Thus, for example, kerosene is used for a feedstock purpose when it is used as an ingredient in the production of paint and is not used for a feedstock purpose when it is used to power machinery at a factory where paint is produced. The person receiving the kerosene must be registered with the IRS and provide a certificate noting that the kerosene will be used for a feedstock purpose in order for the exemption to apply.

Information and tax return reporting

The IRS collects data under the ExSTARS reporting system that tracks all removals across the terminal rack regardless of whether or not the product is technically excluded from the definition of gasoline, diesel or blendstocks. ExSTARS reporting identifies the position holder at the time of removal. Below the rack, no information is gathered for exempt or excluded products or uses.

Taxpayers file quarterly excise tax returns showing only net taxable gallons.[791] Taxpayers do not account for gallons they claim to be exempt on such returns. Although the return is a quarterly return, the excise taxes are paid in semimonthly deposits.[792] If deposits are not made as required, a taxpayer may be required to file returns on a monthly or semimonthly basis instead of quarterly.[793]

House Bill

No provision.

Senate Amendment

The Senate amendment creates a new category of taxable liquids, "reportable liquids". A reportable liquid is any petroleum-based liquid other than a taxable fuel. For purposes of the imposition of tax, the provision treats "reportable liquids" in a manner similar to taxable fuels. Tax is imposed upon the removal, entry, or sale of such liquids, unless the removal, entry, or sale

is (1) to a registered person who certifies that such liquid will not be used as a fuel or in the production of a fuel, or (2) the sale is to the ultimate purchaser of such liquid. Under the provision, the current exclusions for distillates not suitable for use in a highway vehicle, excluded liquids, and gasoline blendstocks requiring further processing (off-spec gasoline) are eliminated. The provision also provides that dyed diesel (a taxable fuel) also is taxable unless removed by a taxable fuel registrant (a person registered with the Secretary under section 4101).

The provision authorizes the Secretary to pay (without interest) an amount equal to the tax imposed, if a person establishes that the ultimate use of a gasoline blendstock, or additive, was not to produce gasoline. Similarly, if tax is imposed on a reportable liquid and the person establishes that the liquid was not used to produce a taxable, fuel, the Secretary is authorized to pay (without interest) an amount equal to the tax imposed on such person with respect to the reportable liquid.

Taxpayers are to file a monthly fuel excise tax return. Not earlier than January 1, 2005, such filings shall be in electronic form as prescribed by the Secretary. In addition, under the provision, the Secretary is to require that all persons removing refined product, whether a taxable product or an untaxed product, over the terminal rack to report such products on an excise tax return. The return is to specifically identify the class of product and its quantity.[794]

Effective Date

The provision is effective for fuel sold or used after September 30, 2004.

Conference Agreement

The conference agreement adds two new categories to the definition of diesel fuel. Under the conference agreement, diesel fuel means: (1) any liquid (other than gasoline) which is suitable for use as a fuel in a diesel-powered highway vehicle, or a diesel-powered train; (2) transmix; and (3) diesel fuel blend stocks as identified by the Secretary. Transmix means a by-product of refined products pipeline operations created by the mixing of different specification products during pipeline transportation. Transmix generally results when one fuel, such as diesel fuel, is placed in a pipeline followed by another taxable fuel, such as kerosene. The mixture created between the two fuels when it is neither all diesel fuel nor all kerosene, is an example of a trans-

---

[791] Treas. Reg. sec. 406011(a)-1(a); Form 720, Quarterly Federal Excise Tax Return.

[792] Treas. Reg. 40.6302(c)-1(a).

[793] Treas. Reg. 40.6011(a)-1(b).

[794] Persons not liable for tax, will make their reports in the same manner as taxpayers who file fuel excise tax returns as described above.

mix. Under the conference agreement, all transmix is taxable as diesel fuel, regardless of whether it contains gasoline.

Under the conference agreement, it is intended that the re-refining of tax-paid transmix into gasoline, diesel fuel or kerosene qualify as a nontaxable off-highway business use of such transmix, for purposes of the refund and payment provisions relating to nontaxable uses of diesel fuel.

Not later than January 31, 2005, the Secretary shall submit to the Committee on Finance of the Senate and the Committee on Ways and Means of the House of Representatives a report regarding fuel tax compliance, which shall include information, and analysis as specified below, and recommendations to address the issues identified.

The Secretary is to identify chemical products that should be added to the list of blendstocks. The Secretary is to identify those chemical products, as identified by lab analysis of fuel samples taken by the IRS, that have been blended with taxable fuel but are not currently treated as a blendstock. The report should indicate, to the extent possible, any statistics as to the frequency in which such chemical product has

been discovered, and whether the samples contained above-normal concentrations of such chemical product. The report also shall include a discussion of IRS findings regarding the addition of waste products to taxable fuel and any recommendations to address the taxation of such products. The report shall include a discussion of IRS findings regarding sales of taxable fuel to entities claiming exempt status as a State or local government. Such discussion shall include the frequency of erroneous certifications as to exempt status determined on audit. The Secretary shall consult with representatives of State and local governments in providing recommendations to address this issue, including the feasibility of State maintained lists of their exempt governmental entities.

Effective Date

The provision regarding the taxation of transmix and diesel fuel blendstocks is effective for fuel removed, sold, or used after December 31, 2004. The requirement for a Treasury study is effective on the date of enactment.

[**Law at ¶ 6020, ¶ 6220 and ¶ 7130. CCH Explanation at ¶ 1509 and ¶ 1543.**]

[¶ 11,530] Act Sec. 881. Permit private sector debt collection companies to collect tax debts

House Committee Report (H.R. Rep. No. 108-548, pt. 1)

[Code Secs. 7809(a) and 7811(g) and New Code Secs. 6306 and 7433A]

Present Law

In fiscal years 1996 and 1997, the Congress earmarked $13 million for IRS to test the use of private debt collection companies. There were several constraints on this pilot project. First, because both IRS and OMB considered the collection of taxes to be an inherently governmental function, only government employees were permitted to collect the taxes.[460] The private debt collection companies were utilized to assist the IRS in locating and contacting taxpayers, reminding them of their outstanding tax liability, and suggesting payment options. If the taxpayer agreed at that point to make a payment, the taxpayer was transferred from the private debt collection company to the IRS. Second, the private debt collection companies were paid a flat fee for services rendered; the amount that was

ultimately collected by the IRS was not taken into account in the payment mechanism.

The pilot program was discontinued because of disappointing results. GAO reported[461] that IRS collected $3.1 million attributable to the private debt collection company efforts; expenses were also $3.1 million. In addition, there were lost opportunity costs of $17 million to the IRS because collection personnel were diverted from their usual collection responsibilities to work on the pilot. The pilot program results were disappointing because "IRS' efforts to design and implement the private debt collection pilot program were hindered by limitations that affected the program's results." The limitations included the scope of work permitted to the private debt collection companies, the number and type of cases referred to the private debt collection companies, and the ability of IRS'

---

[460] Sec. 7801(a).

[461] GAO/GGD-97-129R Issues Affecting IRS' Collection Pilot (July 18, 1997).

computer systems to identify, select, and transmit collection cases to the private debt collectors.

The IRS has in the last several years expressed renewed interest in the possible use of private debt collection companies; for example, IRS recently revised its extensive Request for Information concerning its possible use of private debt collection companies.[462] GAO recently reviewed IRS' planning and preparation for the use of private debt collection companies.[463] GAO identified five broad factors critical to the success of using private debt collection companies to collect taxes. GAO concluded: "If Congress does authorize PCA[464] use, IRS's planning and preparations to address the critical success factors for PCA contracting provide greater assurance that the PCA program is headed in the right direction to meet its goals and achieve desired results. Nevertheless, much work and many challenges remain in addressing the critical success factors and helping to maximize the likelihood that a PCA program would be successful."[465]

In general, Federal agencies are permitted to enter into contracts with private debt collection companies for collection services to recover indebtedness owed to the United States.[466] That provision does not apply to the collection of debts under the Internal Revenue Code.[467]

The President's fiscal year 2004 and 2005 budget proposals proposed the use of private debt collection companies to collect Federal tax debts.

Reasons for Change

The Committee believes that the use of private debt collection agencies will help facilitate the collection of taxes that are owed to the Government. The Committee also believes that the safeguards it has incorporated will protect taxpayers' rights and privacy.

Explanation of Provision

The bill permits the IRS to use private debt collection companies to locate and contact taxpayers owing outstanding tax liabilities of any type[468] and to arrange payment of those taxes by the taxpayers. There must be an assessment pursuant to section 6201 in order for there to be an outstanding tax liability. An assessment is the formal recording of the taxpayer's tax liability that fixes the amount payable. An assessment must be made before the IRS is permitted to commence enforcement actions to collect the amount payable. In general, an assessment is made at the conclusion of all examination and appeals processes within the IRS.[469]

Several steps are involved in the deployment of private debt collection companies. First, the private debt collection company contacts the taxpayer by letter.[470] If the taxpayer's last known address is incorrect, the private debt collection company searches for the correct address. Second, the private debt collection company telephones the taxpayer to request full payment.[471] If the taxpayer cannot pay in full immediately, the private debt collection company offers the taxpayer an installment agreement providing for full payment of the taxes over a period of as long as five years. If the taxpayer is unable to pay the outstanding tax liability in full over a five-year period, the private debt collection company obtains financial information from the taxpayer and will provide this information to the IRS for further processing and action by the IRS.

The bill specifies several procedural conditions under which the provision would operate. First, provisions of the Fair Debt Collection Practices Act apply to the private debt collection company. Second, taxpayer protections that are statutorily applicable to the IRS are also made statutorily applicable to the private sector debt

---

[462] TIRNO-03-H-0001 (February 14, 2003), at www.procurement.irs.treas.gov. The basic request for information is 104 pages, and there are 16 additional attachments.

[463] GAO-04-492 Tax Debt Collection: IRS Is Addressing Critical Success Factors for Contracting Out but Will Need to Study the Best Use of Resources (May 2004).

[464] Private collection agencies.

[465] Page 19 of the May 2004 GAO report.

[466] 31 U.S.C. sec. 3718.

[467] 31 U.S.C. sec. 3718(f).

[468] The provision generally applies to any type of tax imposed under the Internal Revenue Code. It is anticipated that the focus in implementing the provision will be: (a) taxpayers who have filed a return showing a balance due but who have failed to pay that balance in full; and (b) taxpayers who have been assessed additional tax by the IRS and who have made several voluntary payments toward satisfying their obligation but have not paid in full.

[469] An amount of tax reported as due on the taxpayer's tax return is considered to be self-assessed. If the IRS determines that the assessment or collection of tax will be jeopardized by delay, it has the authority to assess the amount immediately (sec. 6861), subject to several procedural safeguards.

[470] Several portions of the provision require that the IRS disclose confidential taxpayer information to the private debt collection company. Section 6103(n) permits disclosure for "the providing of other services . . . for purposes of tax administration." Accordingly, no amendment to section 6103 is necessary to implement the provision. It is intended, however, that the IRS vigorously protect the privacy of confidential taxpayer information by disclosing the least amount of information possible to contractors consistent with the effective operation of the provision.

[471] The private debt collection company is not permitted to accept payment directly. Payments are required to be processed by IRS employees.

collection companies. In addition, taxpayer protections that are statutorily applicable to IRS employees are also made statutorily applicable to employees of private sector debt collection companies. Third, subcontractors are prohibited from having contact with taxpayers, providing quality assurance services, and composing debt collection notices; any other service provided by a subcontractor must receive prior approval from the IRS. In addition, the Committee intends that the IRS require the private sector debt collection companies to inform every taxpayer they contact of the availability of assistance from the Taxpayer Advocate.

The bill creates a revolving fund from the amounts collected by the private debt collection companies. The private debt collection companies will be paid out of this fund. The bill prohibits the payment of fees for all services in excess of 25 percent of the amount collected under a tax collection contract.[472]

Effective Date

The provision is effective on the date of enactment.

Senate Committee Report (S. Rep. No. 108-192)

Present Law

* * *

On February 3, 2003, the President submitted to the Congress his fiscal year 2004 budget proposal,[407] which proposed the use of private debt collection companies to collect Federal tax debts.

Reasons for Change

The Committee believes that the use of private debt collection agencies will help facilitate

the collection of taxes that are owed to the Government. The Committee also believes that the safeguards it has incorporated will protect taxpayers' rights and privacy.

Explanation of Provision

* * *

* * * The bill prohibits the payment of fees for all services in excess of 25 percent of the amount collected under a tax collection contract.[412]

Conference Committee Report (H.R. Conf. Rep. No. 108-755)

Senate Amendment

The Senate amendment is the same as the House bill, except that it: (1) * * * (2) * * * (3) provides that up to 25 percent of amount collected may be used for IRS collection enforcement activities; (4) and requires Treasury to provide a biennial report to Congress.

Conference Agreement

The conference agreement follows the House bill, with the addition of two provisions from the Senate amendment: (1) the conference agreement provides that up to 25 percent of amount collected may be used for IRS collection enforcement activities; and (2) the conference agreement requires Treasury to provide a biennial report to Congress. The conferees expect that, consistent with best management practices

and sound tax administration principles, the Secretary will utilize this new debt collection provision to the maximum extent feasible.

The conferees expect that activities conducted by any person under a qualified tax collection contract will be in compliance with the Fair Debt Collection Practices Act, as required by new section 6306(e) of the Code. Accordingly, the conferees anticipate that the Secretary will not impose requirements that would violate this provision of the Code. The conferees believe that this new debt collection provision will protect both taxpayers' rights and the confidentiality of tax information.

[Law at ¶6190, ¶6340, ¶6365, ¶6370 and ¶7135. CCH Explanation at ¶1605.]

---

[472] It is assumed that there will be competitive bidding for these contracts by private sector tax collection agencies and that vigorous bidding will drive the overhead costs down.

[407] See Office of Management and Budget, Budget of the United States Government, Fiscal Year 2004 (H. Doc. 108-3, Vol. I), p. 274.

[412] It is assumed that there will be competitive bidding for these contracts by private sector tax collection agencies and that vigorous bidding will drive the overhead costs down.

[¶ 11,540] Act Sec. 882. Modify charitable contribution rules for donations of patents and other intellectual property

House Committee Report (H.R. REP. NO. 108-548, pt. 1)

[Code Secs. 170 and 6050L]

Present Law

In general, a deduction is permitted for charitable contributions, subject to certain limitations that depend on the type of taxpayer, the property contributed, and the donee organization.[473] In the case of non-cash contributions, the amount of the deduction generally equals the fair market value of the contributed property on the date of the contribution.

For certain contributions of property, the taxpayer is required to reduce the deduction amount by any gain, generally resulting in a deduction equal to the taxpayer's basis. This rule applies to contributions of: (1) Property that, at the time of contribution, would not have resulted in long-term capital gain if the property was sold by the taxpayer on the contribution date; (2) tangible personal property that is used by the donee in a manner unrelated to the donee's exempt (or governmental) purpose; and (3) property to or for the use of a private foundation (other than a foundation defined in section 170(b)(1)(E)).

Charitable contributions of capital gain property generally are deductible at fair market value. Capital gain property means any capital asset or property used in the taxpayer's trade or business the sale of which at its fair market value, at the time of contribution, would have resulted in gain that would have been long-term capital gain. Contributions of capital gain property are subject to different percentage limitations than other contributions of property. Under present law, certain copyrights are not considered capital assets, in which case the charitable deduction for such copyrights generally is limited to the taxpayer's basis.[474]

In general, a charitable contribution deduction is allowed only for contributions of the donor's entire interest in the contributed property, and not for contributions of a partial interest.[475] If a taxpayer sells property to a charitable organization for less than the property's fair market value, the amount of any charitable contribution deduction is determined in accordance with the bargain sale rules.[476] In general, if a donor receives a benefit or quid pro quo in return for a contribution, any charitable contribution deduction is reduced by the amount of the benefit received. For contributions of $250 or more, no charitable contribution deduction is allowed unless the donee organization provides a contemporaneous written acknowledgement of the contribution that describes and provides a good faith estimate of the value of any goods or services provided by the donee organization in exchange for the contribution.[477]

Taxpayers are required to obtain a qualified appraisal for donated property with a value of $5,000 or more, and to attach the appraisal to the tax return in certain cases.[478] Under Treasury regulations, a qualified appraisal means an appraisal document that, among other things, (1) relates to an appraisal that is made not earlier than 60 days prior to the date of contribution of the appraised property and not later than the due date (including extensions) of the return on which a deduction is first claimed under section 170;[479] (2) is prepared, signed, and dated by a qualified appraiser; (3) includes (a) a description of the property appraised; (b) the fair market value of such property on the date of contribution and the specific basis for the valuation; (c) a statement that such appraisal was prepared for income tax purposes; (d) the qualifications of the qualified appraiser; and (e) the signature and taxpayer identification number ("TIN") of such appraiser; and (4) does not involve an appraisal fee that violates certain prescribed rules.[480]

---

[473] Charitable deductions are provided for income, estate, and gift tax purposes. Secs. 170, 2055, and 2522, respectively.

[474] See sec. 1221(a)(3), 1231(b)(1)(C).

[475] Sec. 170(f)(3).

[476] Sec. 1011(b) and Treas. Reg. sec. 1.1011-2.

[477] Sec. 170(f)(8).

[478] Pub. L. No. 98-369, sec. 155(a)(1) through (6) (1984) (providing that not later than December 31, 1984, the Secretary shall prescribe regulations requiring an individual, a closely held corporation, or a personal service corporation claiming a charitable deduction for property (other than publicly traded securities) to obtain a qualified appraisal of the property contributed and attach an appraisal summary to the taxpayer's return if the claimed value of such property (plus the claimed value of all similar items of property

donated to one or more donees) exceeds $5,000). Under Pub. L. No. 98-369, a qualified appraisal means an appraisal prepared by a qualified appraiser that includes, among other things, (1) a description of the property appraised; (2) the fair market value of such property on the date of contribution and the specific basis for the valuation; (3) a statement that such appraisal was prepared for income tax purposes; (4) the qualifications of the qualified appraiser; (5) the signature and TIN of such appraiser; and (6) such additional information as the Secretary prescribes in such regulations.

[479] In the case of a deduction first claimed or reported on an amended return, the deadline is the date on which the amended return is filed.

[480] Treas. Reg. sec. 1.170A-13(c)(3).

Reasons for Change

The Committee believes that the value of certain intellectual property, such as patents, copyrights, trademarks, trade names, trade secrets, know-how, software, similar property, or applications or registrations of such property, that is contributed to a charity often is highly speculative. Some donated intellectual property may prove to be worthless, or the initial promise of worth may be diminished by future inventions, marketplace competition, or other factors. Although in theory, such intellectual property may promise significant monetary benefits, the benefits generally will not materialize if the charity does not make the appropriate investments, have the right personnel and equipment, or even have sufficient sustained interest to exploit the intellectual property. The Committee understands that valuation is made yet more difficult in the charitable contribution context because the transferee does not provide full, if any, consideration in exchange for the transferred property pursuant to arm's length negotiations, and there may not be a comparable sales market for such property to use as a benchmark for valuations.

The Committee is concerned that taxpayers with intellectual property are taking advantage of the inherent difficulties in valuing such property and are preparing or obtaining erroneous valuations. In such cases, the charity receives an asset of questionable value, while the taxpayer receives a significant tax benefit. The Committee believes that the excessive charitable contribution deductions enabled by inflated valuations is best addressed by ensuring that the amount of the deduction for charitable contributions of such property may not exceed the taxpayer's basis in the property. The Committee notes that for other types of charitable contributions for which valuation is especially problematic—charitable contributions of property created by the personal efforts of the taxpayer and charitable contributions to certain private foundations—a

basis deduction generally is the result under present law.

Although the Committee believes that a deduction of basis is appropriate in this context, the Committee recognizes that some contributions of intellectual property may prove to be of economic benefit to the charity and that donors may need an economic incentive to make such contributions. Accordingly, the Committee believes that it is appropriate to permit donors of intellectual property to receive certain additional charitable contribution deductions in the future but only if the contributed property generates qualified income for the charitable organization.

Explanation of Provision

The provision provides that if a taxpayer contributes a patent or other intellectual property (other than certain copyrights or inventory) to a charitable organization, the taxpayer's initial charitable deduction is limited to the lesser of the taxpayer's basis in the contributed property or the fair market value of the property. In addition, the taxpayer is permitted to deduct, as a charitable deduction, certain additional amounts in the year of contribution or in subsequent taxable years based on a specified percentage of the qualified donee income received or accrued by the charitable donee with respect to the contributed property. For this purpose, "qualified donee income" includes net income received or accrued by the donee that properly is allocable to the intellectual property itself (as opposed to the activity in which the intellectual property is used).

The amount of any additional charitable deduction is calculated as a sliding-scale percentage of qualified donee income received or accrued by the charitable donee that properly is allocable to the contributed property to the applicable taxable year of the donor, determined as follows:

Taxable year of donor	Deduction permitted for such taxable year
1st year ending on or after contribution	100 percent of qualified donee income.
2nd year ending on or after contribution	100 percent of qualified donee income.
3rd year ending on or after contribution	90 percent of qualified donee income.
4th year ending on or after contribution	80 percent of qualified donee income.
5th year ending on or after contribution	70 percent of qualified donee income.
6th year ending on or after contribution	60 percent of qualified donee income.
7th year ending on or after contribution	50 percent of qualified donee income.
8th year ending on or after contribution	40 percent of qualified donee income.
9th year ending on or after contribution	30 percent of qualified donee income.
10th year ending on or after contribution	20 percent of qualified donee income.
11th year ending on or after contribution	10 percent of qualified donee income.
12th year ending on or after contribution	10 percent of qualified donee income.
Taxable years thereafter	No deduction permitted.

An additional charitable deduction is allowed only to the extent that the aggregate of the amounts that are calculated pursuant to the sliding-scale exceed the amount of the deduction claimed upon the contribution of the patent or intellectual property.

No charitable deduction is permitted with respect to any revenues or income received or accrued by the charitable donee after the expiration of the legal life of the patent or intellectual property, or after the tenth anniversary of the date the contribution was made by the donor.

The taxpayer is required to inform the donee at the time of the contribution that the taxpayer intends to treat the contribution as a contribution subject to the additional charitable deduction provisions of the provision. In addition, the taxpayer must obtain written substantiation from the donee of the amount of any qualified donee income properly allocable to the contributed property during the charity's taxable year.[481] The donee is required to file an annual information return that reports the qualified do-nee income and other specified information relating to the contribution. In instances where the donor's taxable year differs from the donee's taxable year, the donor bases its additional charitable deduction on the qualified donee income of the charitable donee properly allocable to the donee's taxable year that ends within the donor's taxable year.

Under the provision, additional charitable deductions are not available for patents or other intellectual property contributed to a private foundation (other than a private operating foundation or certain other private foundations described in section 170(b)(1)(E)).

Under the provision, the Secretary may prescribe regulations or other guidance to carry out the purposes of the provision, including providing for the determination of amounts to be treated as qualified donee income in certain cases where the donee uses the donated property to further its exempt activities or functions, or as may be necessary or appropriate to prevent the avoidance of the purposes of the provision.

Conference Committee Report (H.R. CONF. REP. NO. 108-755)

Conference Agreement

The conference agreement follows the House bill.

[Law at ¶5185, ¶6150 and ¶7140. CCH Explanation at ¶1315.]

Effective Date

Effective for contributions made after June 3, 2004.

[¶11,550] Act Sec. 883. Require increased reporting for noncash charitable contributions

House Committee Report (H.R. REP. NO. 108-548, pt. 1)

[Code Sec. 170]

Present Law

In general, a deduction is permitted for charitable contributions, subject to certain limitations that depend on the type of taxpayer, the property contributed, and the donee organization.[482] In the case of non-cash contributions, the amount of the deduction generally equals the fair market value of the contributed property on the date of the contribution.

In general, if the total charitable deduction claimed for non-cash property exceeds $500, the taxpayer must file IRS Form 8283 (Noncash Charitable Contributions) with the IRS. C corporations (other than personal service corporations and closely-held corporations) are required to file Form 8283 only if the deduction claimed exceeds $5,000.

Taxpayers are required to obtain a qualified appraisal for donated property (other than money and publicly traded securities) with a value of more than $5,000.[483] Corporations (other than a closely-held corporation, a personal service corporation, or an S corporation) are not required to obtain a qualified appraisal. Taxpay-

---

[481] The net income taken into account by the taxpayer may not exceed the amount of qualified donee income reported by the donee to the taxpayer and the IRS under the provision's substantiation and reporting requirements.

[482] Charitable deductions are provided for income, estate, and gift tax purposes. Secs. 170, 2055, and 2522, respectively.

[483] Pub. L. No. 98-369, sec. 155(a)(1) through (6) (1984) (providing that not later than December 31, 1984, the Secretary shall prescribe regulations requiring an individual, a closely held corporation, or a personal service corporation claiming a charitable deduction for property (other than publicly traded securities) to obtain a qualified appraisal of

ers are not required to attach a qualified appraisal to the taxpayer's return, except in the case of contributed art-work valued at more than $20,000. Under Treasury regulations, a qualified appraisal means an appraisal document that, among other things, (1) relates to an appraisal that is made not earlier than 60 days prior to the date of contribution of the appraised property and not later than the due date (including extensions) of the return on which a deduction is first claimed under section 170;[484] (2) is prepared, signed, and dated by a qualified appraiser; (3) includes (a) a description of the property appraised; (b) the fair market value of such property on the date of contribution and the specific basis for the valuation; (c) a statement that such appraisal was prepared for income tax purposes; (d) the qualifications of the qualified appraiser; and (e) the signature and taxpayer identification number of such appraiser; and (4) does not involve an appraisal fee that violates certain prescribed rules.[485]

Reasons for Change

Under present law, an individual who contributes property to a charity and claims a deduction in excess of $5,000 must obtain a qualified appraisal, but a C corporation (other than a closely-held corporation or a personal services corporation) that donates property in excess of $5,000 is not required to obtain such an appraisal. Present law does not require that appraisals, even for large gifts, be attached to a taxpayer's return. The Committee believes that requiring C corporations to obtain a qualified appraisal for charitable contributions of certain property in excess of $5,000, and requiring that appraisals be attached to a taxpayer's return for large gifts, will reduce valuation abuses.

Explanation of Provision

The provision requires increased donor reporting for certain charitable contributions of property other than cash, inventory, or publicly traded securities. The provision extends to all C corporations the present law requirement, applicable to an individual, closely-held corporation, personal service corporation, partnership, or S corporation, that the donor must obtain a qualified appraisal of the property if the amount of the deduction claimed exceeds $5,000. The provision also provides that if the amount of the contribution of property other than cash, inventory, or publicly traded securities exceeds $500,000, then the donor (whether an individual, partnership, or corporation) must attach the qualified appraisal to the donor's tax return. For purposes of the dollar thresholds under the provision, property and all similar items of property donated to one or more donees are treated as one property.

The provision provides that a donor that fails to substantiate a charitable contribution of property, as required by the Secretary, is denied a charitable contribution deduction. If the donor is a partnership or S corporation, the deduction is denied at the partner or shareholder level. The denial of the deduction does not apply if it is shown that such failure is due to reasonable cause and not to willful neglect.

The provision provides that the Secretary may prescribe such regulations as may be necessary or appropriate to carry out the purposes of the provision, including regulations that may provide that some or all of the requirements of the provision do not apply in appropriate cases.

Conference Committee Report (H.R. CONF. REP. NO. 108-755)

Senate Amendment

No provision.

Conference Agreement

The conference agreement follows the House bill, except that appraisals are not required for charitable contributions of certain vehicles that are sold by the donee organization without a significant intervening use or material

improvement of the vehicle by such organization, and for which the organization provides an acknowledgement to the donor containing a certification that the vehicle was sold in an arm's length transaction between unrelated parties, and providing the gross sales proceeds from the sale, and a statement that the donor's deductible amount may not exceed the amount of such gross proceeds.

(Footnote Continued)

the property contributed and attach an appraisal summary to the taxpayer's return if the claimed value of such property (plus the claimed value of all similar items of property donated to one or more donees) exceeds $5,000). Under Pub. L. No. 98-369, a qualified appraisal means an appraisal prepared by a qualified appraiser that includes, among other things, (1) a description of the property appraised; (2) the fair market value of such property on the date of contribution and the specific basis for the valuation; (3) a statement that such appraisal was prepared for income tax

purposes; (4) the qualifications of the qualified appraiser; (5) the signature and taxpayer identification number of such appraiser; and (6) such additional information as the Secretary prescribes in such regulations.

[484] In the case of a deduction first claimed or reported on an amended return, the deadline is the date on which the amended return is filed.

[485] Treas. Reg. sec. 1.170A-13(c)(3).

Effective Date [Law at ¶ 5185. CCH Explanation at ¶ 1310.]

Effective for contributions made after June 3, 2004.

[¶ 11,560] Act Sec. 884. Limit deduction for charitable contributions of vehicles

Conference Committee Report (H.R. CONF. REP. NO. 108-755)

[Code Sec. 170 and New Code Sec. 6720]

Present Law

In general, a deduction is permitted for charitable contributions, subject to certain limitations that depend on the type of taxpayer, the property contributed, and the donee organization.[843] In the case of non-cash contributions, the amount of the deduction generally equals the fair market value of the contributed property on the date of the contribution.

For certain contributions of property, the taxpayer is required to determine the deductible amount by subtracting any gain from fair market value, generally resulting in a deduction equal to the taxpayer's basis. This rule applies to contributions of: (1) property that, at the time of contribution, would not have resulted in long-term capital gain if the property was sold by the taxpayer on the contribution date; (2) tangible personal property that is used by the donee in a manner unrelated to the donee's exempt (or governmental) purpose; and (3) property to or for the use of a private foundation (other than a foundation defined in section 170(b)(1)(E)).

Charitable contributions of capital gain property generally are deductible at fair market value. Capital gain property means any capital asset or property used in the taxpayer's trade or business the sale of which at its fair market value, at the time of contribution, would have resulted in gain that would have been long-term capital gain. Contributions of capital gain property are subject to different percentage limitations than other contributions of property.

A taxpayer who donates a used automobile to a charitable donee generally deducts the fair market value (rather than the taxpayer's basis) of the automobile. A taxpayer who donates a used automobile generally is permitted to use an established used car pricing guide to determine the fair market value of the automobile, but only if the guide lists a sales price for an automobile of the same make, model and year, sold in the same area, and in the same condition as the donated automobile. Similar rules apply to contributions of other types of vehicles and property, such as boats.

Charities are required to provide donors with written substantiation of donations of $250 or more. Taxpayers are required to report non-cash contributions totaling $500 or more and the method used for determining fair market value.

Taxpayers are required to obtain a qualified appraisal for donated property with a value of $5,000 or more, and to attach the appraisal to the tax return in certain cases.[844] Under Treasury regulations, a qualified appraisal means an appraisal document that, among other things, (1) relates to an appraisal that is made not earlier than 60 days prior to the date of contribution of the appraised property and not later than the due date (including extensions) of the return on which a deduction is first claimed under section 170;[845] (2) is prepared, signed, and dated by a qualified appraiser; (3) includes (a) a description of the property appraised; (b) the fair market value of such property on the date of contribution and the specific basis for the valuation; (c) a statement that such appraisal was prepared for income tax purposes; (d) the qualifications of the qualified appraiser; and (e) the signature and taxpayer identification number ("TIN") of such

---

[843] Charitable deductions are provided for income, estate, and gift tax purposes. Secs. 170, 2055, and 2522, respectively.

[844] Pub. L. No. 98-369, sec. 155(a)(1) through (6) (1984) (providing that not later than December 31, 1984, the Secretary shall prescribe regulations requiring an individual, a closely held corporation, or a personal service corporation claiming a charitable deduction for property (other than publicly traded securities) to obtain a qualified appraisal of the property contributed and attach an appraisal summary to the taxpayer's return if the claimed value of such property (plus the claimed value of all similar items of property donated to one or more donees) exceeds $5,000). Under Pub. L. No. 98-369, a qualified appraisal means an appraisal

prepared by a qualified appraiser that includes, among other things, (1) a description of the property appraised; (2) the fair market value of such property on the date of contribution and the specific basis for the valuation; (3) a statement that such appraisal was prepared for income tax purposes; (4) the qualifications of the qualified appraiser; (5) the signature and TIN of such appraiser; and (6) such additional information as the Secretary prescribes in such regulations.

[845] In the case of a deduction first claimed or reported on an amended return, the deadline is the date on which the amended return is filed.

appraiser; and (4) does not involve an appraisal fee that violates certain prescribed rules.[846]

Appraisal fees paid by an individual to determine the fair market value of donated property are deductible as miscellaneous expenses subject to the 2 percent of adjusted gross income limit.[847]

House Bill

The provision allows a charitable deduction for contributions of vehicles for which the taxpayer claims a deduction of more than $250 only if the taxpayer obtains a qualified appraisal of the vehicle. The provision applies to automobiles and other types of motor vehicles manufactured primarily for use on public streets, roads, and highways; boats; and aircraft. The provision does not affect contributions of inventory property. The definition of qualified appraisal generally follows the definition contained in present law, subject to additional regulations or guidance provided by the Secretary. The qualified appraisal of a donated vehicle must be obtained by the taxpayer by the time the contribution is made. Under the provision, the Secretary shall prescribe such regulations or other guidance as may be necessary to carry out the purposes of the provision.

Effective Date

Effective for contributions made after June 3, 2004.

Senate Amendment

Under the Senate amendment, the amount of deduction for charitable contributions of vehicles (generally including automobiles, boats, and airplanes for which the claimed value exceeds $500 and excluding inventory property) depends upon the use of the vehicle by the donee organization. If the donee organization sells the vehicle without any significant intervening use or material improvement of such vehicle by the organization, the amount of the deduction shall not exceed the gross proceeds received from the sale.

The proposal imposes new substantiation requirements for contributions of vehicles for which the claimed value exceeds $500 (excluding inventory). A deduction is not allowed unless the taxpayer substantiates the contribution by a contemporaneous written acknowledgement by the donee. The acknowledgement must contain the name and taxpayer identification number of the donor and the vehicle identification number (or similar number) of the vehicle. In addition, if the donee sells the vehicle without performing a significant intervening use or material improvement of such vehicle, the acknowledgement

must provide a certification that the vehicle was sold in an arm's length transaction between unrelated parties, and state the gross proceeds from the sale and that the deductible amount may not exceed such gross proceeds. In all other cases, the acknowledgement must contain a certification of the intended use or material improvement of the vehicle and the intended duration of such use, and a certification that the vehicle will not be transferred in exchange for money, other property, or services before completion of such use or improvement. The donee must notify the Secretary of the information contained in an acknowledgement, in a time and manner provided by the Secretary. An acknowledgement is considered contemporaneous if provided within 30 days of sale of a vehicle that is not significantly improved or materially used by the donee, or, in all other cases, within 30 days of the contribution.

A penalty applies if a donee organization knowingly furnishes a false or fraudulent acknowledgement, or knowingly fails to furnish an acknowledgement in the manner, at the time, and showing the required information. In the case of an acknowledgement provided within 30 days of sale of a vehicle which is not significantly used or materially improved by the donee, the penalty is the greater of the value of the tax benefit to the donor or the gross proceeds from the sale of the vehicle. For all other acknowledgements, the penalty is the greater of the value of the tax benefit to the donor or the claimed value of the vehicle or $5,000.

The Senate amendment provides that the Secretary shall prescribe such regulations or other guidance as may be necessary to carry out the purposes of the proposal.

Effective Date

Contributions after June 30, 2004.

Conference Agreement

The conference agreement follows the Senate amendment, except that the penalty on the donee organization for knowingly furnishing a false or fraudulent acknowledgement is determined differently. With respect to a qualified vehicle sold without a significant intervening use or material improvement, the penalty is the greater of the gross proceeds from the sale of the vehicle or the product of the highest rate of tax specified in section 1 and the sales price stated on the acknowledgement. For all other acknowledgements, the penalty is the greater of $5,000 or the product of the highest rate of tax specified in section 1 and the claimed value of the vehicle.

---

[846] Treas. Reg. sec. 1.170A-13(c)(3).

[847] Rev. Rul. 67-461, 1967-2 C.B. 125.

The conference agreement also provides that the Secretary may prescribe regulations or other guidance that exempts sales of vehicles that are in direct furtherance of the donee's charitable purposes from the requirement that the donor may not deduct an amount in excess of the gross proceeds from the sale, and the requirement that the donee certify that the vehicle will not be transferred in exchange for money, other property, or services before completion of a significant use or material improvement by the donee. The conferees intend that such guidance may be appropriate, for example, if an organization directly furthers its charitable purposes by selling automobiles to needy persons at a price significantly below fair market value.

The conferees intend that in providing guidance on the provision, the Secretary shall strictly construe the requirement of significant use or material improvement. To meet the significant use test, an organization must actually use the vehicle to substantially further the organization's regularly conducted activities and the use must be significant. A donee will not be considered to significantly use a qualified vehicle if, under the facts and circumstances, the use is incidental or not intended at the time of the contribution. Whether a use is significant also depends on the frequency and duration of use. With respect to the material improvement test, the conferees intend that a material improvement would include major repairs to a vehicle, or other improvements to the vehicle that improve the condition of the vehicle in a manner that significantly increases the vehicle's value. Cleaning the vehicle, minor repairs, and routine maintenance are not considered a material improvement.

Example 1. As part of its regularly conducted activities, an organization delivers meals to needy individuals. The use requirement would be met if the organization actually used a donated qualified vehicle to deliver food to the needy. Use of the vehicle to deliver meals substantially furthers a regularly conducted activity of the organization. However, the use also must be significant, which depends on the nature, extent, and frequency of the use. If the organization used the vehicle only once or a few times to deliver meals, the use would not be considered significant. If the organization used the vehicle to deliver meals every day for one year the use would be considered significant. If the organization drove the vehicle 10,000 miles while delivering meals, such use likely would be considered significant. However, use of a vehicle in such an activity for one week or for several hundreds of miles generally would not be considered a significant use.

Example 2. An organization uses a donated qualified vehicle to transport its volunteers. The use would not be significant merely because a volunteer used the vehicle over a brief period of time to drive to or from the organization's premises. On the other hand, if at the time the organization accepts the contribution of a qualified vehicle, the organization intends to use the vehicle as a regular and ongoing means of transport for volunteers of the organization, and such vehicle is so used, then the significant use test likely would be met.

Example 3. The following example is a general illustration of the provision. A taxpayer makes a charitable contribution of a used automobile in good running condition and that needs no immediate repairs to a charitable organization that operates an elder care facility. The donee organization accepts the vehicle and immediately provides the donor a written acknowledgment containing the name and TIN of the donor, the vehicle identification number, a certification that the donee intends to retain the vehicle for a year or longer to transport the facility's residents to community and social events and deliver meals to the needy, and a certification that the vehicle will not be transferred in exchange for money, other property, or services before completion of such use by the organization. A few days after receiving the vehicle, the donee organization commences to use the vehicle three times a week to transport some of its residents to various community events, and twice a week to deliver food to needy individuals. The organization continues to regularly use the vehicle for these purposes for approximately one year and then sells the vehicle. Under the provision, the donee's use of the vehicle constitutes a significant intervening use prior to the sale by the organization, and the donor's deduction is not limited to the gross proceeds received by the organization.

Effective Date

Effective for contributions made after December 31, 2004.

[Law at ¶5185 and ¶6305. CCH Explanation at ¶1305.]

[¶ 11,570] Act Sec. 885. Treatment of nonqualified deferred compensation plans

House Committee Report (H.R. REP. NO. 108-548, pt. 1)

[Code Secs. 3401, 6041 and 6051 and New Code Sec. 409A]

Present Law

In general

The determination of when amounts deferred under a nonqualified deferred compensation arrangement are includible in the gross income of the individual earning the compensation depends on the facts and circumstances of the arrangement. A variety of tax principles and Code provisions may be relevant in making this determination, including the doctrine of constructive receipt, the economic benefit doctrine,[448] the provisions of section 83 relating generally to transfers of property in connection with the performance of services, and provisions relating specifically to nonexempt employee trusts (sec. 402(b)) and nonqualified annuities (sec. 403(c)).

In general, the time for income inclusion of nonqualified deferred compensation depends on whether the arrangement is unfunded or funded. If the arrangement is unfunded, then the compensation is generally includible in income when it is actually or constructively received. If the arrangement is funded, then income is includible for the year in which the individual's rights are transferable or not subject to a substantial risk of forfeiture.

Nonqualified deferred compensation is generally subject to social security and Medicare taxes when the compensation is earned (i.e., when services are performed), unless the nonqualified deferred compensation is subject to a substantial risk of forfeiture. If nonqualified deferred compensation is subject to a substantial risk of forfeiture, it is subject to social security and Medicare tax when the risk of forfeiture is removed (i.e., when the right to the nonqualified deferred compensation vests). Amounts deferred under a nonaccount balance plan that are not reasonably ascertainable are not required to be taken into account as wages subject to social security and Medicare taxes until the first date

that such amounts are reasonably ascertainable. Social security and Medicare tax treatment is not affected by whether the arrangement is funded or unfunded, which is relevant in determining when amounts are includible in income (and subject to income tax withholding).

In general, an arrangement is considered funded if there has been a transfer of property under section 83. Under that section, a transfer of property occurs when a person acquires a beneficial ownership interest in such property. The term "property" is defined very broadly for purposes of section 83.[449] Property includes real and personal property other than money or an unfunded and unsecured promise to pay money in the future. Property also includes a beneficial interest in assets (including money) that are transferred or set aside from claims of the creditors of the transferor, for example, in a trust or escrow account. Accordingly, if, in connection with the performance of services, vested contributions are made to a trust on an individual's behalf and the trust assets may be used solely to provide future payments to the individual, the payment of the contributions to the trust constitutes a transfer of property to the individual that is taxable under section 83. On the other hand, deferred amounts are generally not includible in income if nonqualified deferred compensation is payable from general corporate funds that are subject to the claims of general creditors, as such amounts are treated as unfunded and unsecured promises to pay money or property in the future.

As discussed above, if the arrangement is unfunded, then the compensation is generally includible in income when it is actually or constructively received under section 451.[450] Income is constructively received when it is credited to an individual's account, set apart, or otherwise made available so that it may be drawn on at any time. Income is not constructively received if the taxpayer's control of its receipt is subject to substantial limitations or restrictions. A requirement to relinquish a valuable right in order to make withdrawals is generally treated as a substantial limitation or restriction.

---

[448] See, e.g., *Sproull* v. *Commissioner*, 16 T.C. 244 (1951), aff'd per curiam, 194 F.2d 541 (6th Cir. 1952); Rev. Rul. 60-31, 1960-1 C.B. 174.

[449] Treas. Reg. sec. 1.83-3(e). This definition in part reflects previous IRS rulings on nonqualified deferred compensation.

[450] Treas. Reg. secs. 1.451-1 and 1.451-2.

Rabbi trusts

Arrangements have developed in an effort to provide employees with security for nonqualified deferred compensation, while still allowing deferral of income inclusion. A "rabbi trust" is a trust or other fund established by the employer to hold assets from which nonqualified deferred compensation payments will be made. The trust or fund is generally irrevocable and does not permit the employer to use the assets for purposes other than to provide nonqualified deferred compensation, except that the terms of the trust or fund provide that the assets are subject to the claims of the employer's creditors in the case of insolvency or bankruptcy.

As discussed above, for purposes of section 83, property includes a beneficial interest in assets set aside from the claims of creditors, such as in a trust or fund, but does not include an unfunded and unsecured promise to pay money in the future. In the case of a rabbi trust, terms providing that the assets are subject to the claims of creditors of the employer in the case of insolvency or bankruptcy have been the basis for the conclusion that the creation of a rabbi trust does not cause the related nonqualified deferred compensation arrangement to be funded for income tax purposes.[451] As a result, no amount is included in income by reason of the rabbi trust; generally income inclusion occurs as payments are made from the trust.

The IRS has issued guidance setting forth model rabbi trust provisions.[452] Revenue Procedure 92-64 provides a safe harbor for taxpayers who adopt and maintain grantor trusts in connection with unfunded deferred compensation arrangements. The model trust language requires that the trust provide that all assets of the trust are subject to the claims of the general creditors of the company in the event of the company's insolvency or bankruptcy.

Since the concept of rabbi trusts was developed, arrangements have developed which attempt to protect the assets from creditors despite the terms of the trust. Arrangements also have developed which attempt to allow deferred amounts to be available to individuals, while still purporting to meet the safe harbor requirements set forth by the IRS.

Reasons for Change

The Committee is aware of the popular use of deferred compensation arrangements by executives to defer current taxation of substantial amounts of income. The Committee believes that many nonqualified deferred compensation arrangements have developed which allow improper deferral of income. Executives often use arrangements that allow deferral of income, but also provide security of future payment and control over amounts deferred. For example, nonqualified deferred compensation arrangements often contain provisions that allow participants to receive distributions upon request, subject to forfeiture of a minimal amount (i.e., a "haircut" provision).

The Committee is aware that since the concept of a rabbi trust was developed, techniques have been used that attempt to protect the assets from creditors despite the terms of the trust. For example, the trust or fund may be located in a foreign jurisdiction, making it difficult or impossible for creditors to reach the assets.

While the general tax principles governing deferred compensation are well established, the determination whether a particular arrangement effectively allows deferral of income is generally made on a facts and circumstances basis. There is limited specific guidance with respect to common deferral arrangements. The Committee believes that it is appropriate to provide specific rules regarding whether deferral of income inclusion should be permitted.

The Committee believes that certain arrangements that allow participants inappropriate levels of control or access to amounts deferred should not result in deferral of income inclusion. The Committee also believes that certain arrangements, such as offshore trusts, which effectively protect assets from creditors, should be treated as funded and not result in deferral of income inclusion.[453]

Explanation of Provision

Under the provision, all amounts deferred under a nonqualified deferred compensation plan[454] for all taxable years are currently includible in gross income to the extent not subject to a

---

[451] This conclusion was first provided in a 1980 private ruling issued by the IRS with respect to an arrangement covering a rabbi; hence the popular name "rabbi trust." Priv. Ltr. Rul. 8113107 (Dec. 31, 1980).

[452] Rev. Proc. 92-64, 1992-2 C.B. 422, modified in part by Notice 2000-56, 2000-2 C.B. 393.

[453] The staff of the Joint Committee on Taxation made recommendations similar to the new provision in the report on their investigation of Enron Corporation, which detailed

how executives deferred millions of dollars in Federal income taxes through nonqualified deferred compensation arrangements. See Joint Committee on Taxation, Report of Investigation of Enron Corporation and Related Entities Regarding Federal Tax and Compensation Issues, and Policy Recommendations (JCS-3-03), February 2003.

[454] A plan includes an agreement or arrangement, including an agreement or arrangement that includes one person.

Act Sec. 885   ¶11,570

substantial risk of forfeiture[455] and not previously included in gross income, unless certain requirements are satisfied. If the requirements of the provision are not satisfied, in addition to current income inclusion, interest at the underpayment rate plus one percentage point is imposed on the underpayments that would have occurred had the compensation been includible in income when first deferred, or if later, when not subject to a substantial risk of forfeiture. Actual or notional earnings on amounts deferred are also subject to the provision.

Under the provision, distributions from a nonqualified deferred compensation plan may be allowed only upon separation from service (as determined by the Secretary), death, a specified time (or pursuant to a fixed schedule), change in control in a corporation (to the extent provided by the Secretary), occurrence of an unforeseeable emergency, or if the participant becomes disabled. A nonqualified deferred compensation plan may not allow distributions other than upon the permissible distribution events and may not permit acceleration of a distribution, except as provided in regulations by the Secretary.

In the case of a specified employee, distributions upon separation from service may not be made earlier than six months after the date of the separation from service. Specified employees are key employees[456] of publicly-traded corporations.

Amounts payable at a specified time or pursuant to a fixed schedule must be specified under the plan at the time of deferral. Amounts payable upon the occurrence of an event are not treated as amounts payable at a specified time. For example, amounts payable when an individual attains age 65 are payable at a specified time, while amounts payable when an individual's child begins college are payable upon the occurrence of an event.

Distributions upon a change in the ownership or effective control of a corporation, or in the ownership of a substantial portion of the assets of a corporation, may only be made to the extent provided by the Secretary. It is intended that the Secretary use a similar, but more restrictive, definition of change in control as is used for purposes of the golden parachute provisions of section 280G consistent with the purposes of the provision. The provision requires the Secretary to issue guidance defining change of control within 90 days after the date of enactment.

An unforeseeable emergency is defined as a severe financial hardship to the participant resulting from a sudden and unexpected illness or accident of the participant, the participant's spouse, or a dependent (as defined in 152(a)) of the participant; loss of the participant's property due to casualty; or other similar extraordinary and unforeseeable circumstances arising as a result of events beyond the control of the participant. The amount of the distribution must be limited to the amount needed to satisfy the emergency plus taxes reasonably anticipated as a result of the distribution. Distributions may not be allowed to the extent that the hardship may be relieved through reimbursement or compensation by insurance or otherwise, or by liquidation of the participant's assets (to the extent such liquidation would not itself cause a severe financial hardship).

A participant is considered disabled if he or she (i) is unable to engage in any substantial gainful activity by reason of any medically determinable physical or mental impairment which can be expected to result in death or can be expected to last for a continuous period of not less than 12 months; or (ii) is, by reason on any medically determinable physical or mental impairment which can be expected to result in death or can be expected to last for a continuous period of not less than 12 months, receiving income replacement benefits for a period of not less than three months under an accident and health plan covering employees of the participant's employer.

As previously discussed, except as provided in regulations by the Secretary, no accelerations of distributions may be allowed. For example, changes in the form of a distribution from an annuity to a lump sum are not permitted. The provision provides the Secretary authority to provide, through regulations, limited exceptions to the general rule that no accelerations can be permitted. It is intended that exceptions be provided only in limited cases where the accelerated distribution is required for reasons beyond the control of the participant. For example, it is anticipated that an exception could be provided in order to comply with Federal conflict of interest requirements or court-approved settlements.

---

[455] As under section 83, the rights of a person to compensation are subject to a substantial risk of forfeiture if the person's rights to such compensation are conditioned upon the performance of substantial services by any individual.

[456] Key employees are defined in section 416(i) and generally include officers having annual compensation greater than $130,000 (adjusted for inflation and limited to 50 employees), five percent owners, and one percent owners having annual compensation from the employer greater than $150,000.

The provision requires that the plan must provide that compensation for services performed during a taxable year may be deferred at the participant's election only if the election to defer is made no later than the close of the preceding taxable year, or at such other time as provided in Treasury regulations. For example, it is expected that Treasury regulations provide that, in appropriate circumstances, elections to defer incentive bonuses earned over a period of several years may be made after the beginning of the service period, as long as such elections may in no event be made later than 12 months before the earliest date on which such incentive bonus is initially payable. The Secretary may consider other factors in determining the appropriate election period, such as when the amount of the bonus payment is determinable. It is expected that Treasury regulations will not permit any election to defer any bonus or other compensation if the timing of such election would be inconsistent with the purposes of the provision. Under the provision, in the first year that an employee becomes eligible for participation in a nonqualified deferred compensation plan, the election may be made within 30 days after the date that the employee is initially eligible.

The time and form of distributions must be specified at the time of initial deferral. A plan could specify the time and form of payments that are to be made as a result of a distribution event (e.g., a plan could specify that payments upon separation of service will be paid in lump sum within 30 days of separation from service) or could allow participants to elect the time and form of payment at the time of the initial deferral election. If a plan allows participants to elect the time and form of payment, such election is subject to the rules regarding initial deferral elections under the provision.

Under the provision, a plan may allow changes in the time and form of distributions subject to certain requirements. A nonqualified deferred compensation plan may allow a subsequent election to delay the timing or form of distributions only if: (1) the plan requires that such election cannot be effective for at least 12 months after the date on which the election is made; (2) except in the case of elections relating to distributions on account of death, disability or unforeseeable emergency, the plan requires that the additional deferral with respect to which such election is made is for a period of not less than five years from the date such payment would otherwise have been made; and (3) the plan requires that an election related to a distribution to be made upon a specified time may not be made less than 12 months prior to the date of the first scheduled payment. It is expected that in limited cases, the Secretary shall issue guidance, consistent with the purposes of the provi-sion, regarding to what extent elections to change a stream of payments are permissible.

If impermissible distributions or elections are made, or if the nonqualified deferred compensation plan allows impermissible distributions or elections, all amounts deferred under the plan (including amounts deferred in prior years) are currently includible in income to the extent not subject to a substantial risk of forfeiture and not previously included in income. In addition, interest at the underpayment rate plus one percentage point is imposed on the underpayments that would have occurred had the compensation been includible in income when first deferred, or if later, when not subject to a substantial risk of forfeiture.

Under the provision, in the case of assets set aside (directly or indirectly) in a trust (or other arrangement determined by the Secretary) for purposes of paying nonqualified deferred compensation, such assets are treated as property transferred in connection with the performance of services under section 83 (whether or not such assets are available to satisfy the claims of general creditors) at the time set aside if such assets are located outside of the United States or at the time transferred if such assets are subsequently transferred outside of the United States. Any subsequent increases in the value of, or any earnings with respect to, such assets are treated as additional transfers of property. Interest at the underpayment rate plus one percentage point is imposed on the underpayments that would have occurred had the amounts been includible in income for the taxable year in which first deferred or, if later, the first taxable year not subject to a substantial risk of forfeiture. It is expected that the Secretary shall provide rules for identifying the deferrals to which assets set aside are attributable, for situations in which assets equal to less than the full amount of deferrals are set aside. The Secretary has authority to exempt arrangements from the provision if the arrangements do not result in an improper deferral of U.S. tax and will not result in assets being effectively beyond the reach of creditors.

Under the provision, a transfer of property in connection with the performance of services under section 83 also occurs with respect to compensation deferred under a nonqualified deferred compensation plan if the plan provides that upon a change in the employer's financial health, assets will be restricted to the payment of nonqualified deferred compensation. The transfer of property occurs as of the earlier of when the assets are so restricted or when the plan provides that assets will be restricted. It is intended that the transfer of property occurs to the extent that assets are restricted or will be restricted with respect to such compensation. For example, in the case of a plan that provides that upon a change in the employer's financial health, a trust will become funded to the extent of all deferrals, all amounts deferred under the plan are treated as property transferred under section 83. If a plan provides that deferrals of certain individuals will be funded upon a change in financial health, the transfer of property would occur with respect to compensation deferred by such individuals. Any subsequent increases in the value of, or any earnings with respect to, such assets are treated as additional transfers of property. Interest at the underpayment rate plus one percentage point is imposed on the underpayments that would have occurred had the amounts been includible in income for the taxable year in which first deferred or, if later, the first taxable year not subject to a substantial risk of forfeiture.

A nonqualified deferred compensation plan is any plan that provides for the deferral of compensation other than a qualified employer plan or any bona fide vacation leave, sick leave, compensatory time, disability pay, or death benefit plan. A qualified employer plan means a qualified retirement plan, tax-deferred annuity, simplified employee pension, and SIMPLE.[457] A governmental eligible deferred compensation plan (sec. 457) is also a qualified employer plan under the provision.[458] Plans subject to section 457, other than governmental eligible deferred compensation plans, are subject to both the requirements of section 457 and the provision. For example, in addition to the requirements of the provision, an eligible deferred compensation plan of a tax-exempt employer would still be required to meet the applicable dollar limits under section 457.

Interest imposed under the provision is treated as interest on an underpayment of tax. Income (whether actual or notional) attributable to nonqualified deferred compensation is treated as additional deferred compensation and is subject to the provision. The provision is not intended to prevent the inclusion of amounts in gross income under any provision or rule of law earlier than the time provided in the provision. Any amount included in gross income under the provision shall not be required to be included in

gross income under any provision of law later than the time provided in the provision. The provision does not affect the rules regarding the timing of an employer's deduction for nonqualified deferred compensation.

The provision requires annual reporting to the Internal Revenue Service of amounts deferred. Such amounts are required to be reported on an individual's Form W-2 for the year deferred even if the amount is not currently includible in income for that taxable year. Under the provision, the Secretary is authorized, through regulations, to establish a minimum amount of deferrals below which the reporting requirement does not apply. The Secretary may also provide that the reporting requirement does not apply with respect to amounts of deferrals that are not reasonably ascertainable. It is intended that the exception for amounts not reasonable ascertainable only apply to nonaccount balance plans and that amounts be required to be reported when they first become reasonably ascertainable.[459]

The provision provides the Secretary authority to prescribe regulations as are necessary to carry out the purposes of provision, including regulations: (1) providing for the determination of amounts of deferral in the case of defined benefit plans; (2) relating to changes in the ownership and control of a corporation or assets of a corporation; (3) exempting from the provisions providing for transfers of property arrangements that will not result in an improper deferral of U.S. tax and will not result in assets being effectively beyond the reach of creditors; (4) defining financial health; and (5) disregarding a substantial risk of forfeiture.

It is intended that substantial risk of forfeitures may not be used to manipulate the timing of income inclusion. It is intended that substantial risks of forfeiture should be disregarded in cases in which they are illusory or are used inconsistent with the purposes of the provision. For example, if an executive is effectively able to control the acceleration of the lapse of a substantial risk of forfeiture, such risk of forfeiture should be disregarded and income inclusion should not be postponed on account of such restriction.

Conference Committee Report (H.R. Conf. Rep. No. 108-755)

In general

The conference agreement follows the House bill with the following modifications.

Under the conference agreement, all amounts deferred under a nonqualified deferred compensation plan[807] for all taxable years are currently

---

[457] A qualified employer plan also includes a section 501(c)(18) trust.

[458] A governmental deferred compensation plan that is not an eligible deferred compensation plan is not a qualified employer plan.

[459] It is intended that the exception be similar to that under Treas. Reg. sec. 31.3121(v)(2)-1(e)(4).

[807] A plan includes an agreement or arrangement, including an agreement or arrangement that includes one person. Amounts deferred also include actual or notional earnings.

includible in gross income to the extent not subject to a substantial risk of forfeiture[808] and not previously included in gross income, unless certain requirements are satisfied.[809] If the requirements of the provision are not satisfied, in addition to current income inclusion, interest at the underpayment rate plus one percentage point is imposed on the underpayments that would have occurred had the compensation been includible in income when first deferred, or if later, when not subject to a substantial risk of forfeiture. The amount required to be included in income is also subject to a 20-percent additional tax.[810]

Current income inclusion, interest, and the additional tax apply only with respect to the participants with respect to whom the requirements of the provision are not met. For example, suppose a plan covering all executives of an employer (including those subject to section 16(a) of the Securities and Exchange Act of 1934) allows distributions to individuals subject to section 16(a) upon a distribution event that is not permitted under the provision. The individuals subject to section 16(a), rather than all participants of the plan, would be required to include amounts deferred in income and would be subject to interest and the 20-percent additional tax.

Permissible distributions

In general

Under the provision, distributions from a nonqualified deferred compensation plan may be allowed only upon separation from service (as determined by the Secretary), death, a specified time (or pursuant to a fixed schedule), change in control of a corporation (to the extent provided by the Secretary), occurrence of an unforeseeable emergency, or if the participant becomes disabled. A nonqualified deferred compensation plan may not allow distributions other than upon the permissible distribution events and, except as provided in regulations by the Secretary, may not permit acceleration of a distribution.

Separation from service

In the case of a specified employee who separates from service, distributions may not be

made earlier than six months after the date of the separation from service or upon death. Specified employees are key employees[811] of publicly-traded corporations.

Specified time

Amounts payable at a specified time or pursuant to a fixed schedule must be specified under the plan at the time of deferral. Amounts payable upon the occurrence of an event are not treated as amounts payable at a specified time. For example, amounts payable when an individual attains age 65 are payable at a specified time, while amounts payable when an individual's child begins college are payable upon the occurrence of an event.

Change in control

Distributions upon a change in the ownership or effective control of a corporation, or in the ownership of a substantial portion of the assets of a corporation, may only be made to the extent provided by the Secretary. It is intended that the Secretary use a similar, but more restrictive, definition of change in control as is used for purposes of the golden parachute provisions of section 280G consistent with the purposes of the provision. The provision requires the Secretary to issue guidance defining change of control within 90 days after the date of enactment.

Unforeseeable emergency

An unforeseeable emergency is defined as a severe financial hardship to the participant: (1) resulting from an illness or accident of the participant, the participant's spouse, or a dependent (as defined in sec. 152(a)); (2) loss of the participant's property due to casualty; or (3) other similar extraordinary and unforeseeable circumstances arising as a result of events beyond the control of the participant. The amount of the distribution must be limited to the amount needed to satisfy the emergency plus taxes reasonably anticipated as a result of the distribution. Distributions may not be allowed to the extent that the hardship may be relieved through reimbursement or compensation by insurance or otherwise, or by liquidation of the participant's assets (to the extent such liquidation would not itself cause a severe financial hardship).

---

[808] As under section 83, the rights of a person to compensation are subject to a substantial risk of forfeiture if the person's rights to such compensation are conditioned upon the performance of substantial services by any individual.

[809] It is intended that Treasury regulations will provide guidance regarding when an amount is deferred. It is intended that timing of an election to defer is not determinative of when the deferral is made.

[810] These consequences apply under the provision to amounts deferred after the effective date of the provision.

[811] Key employees are defined in section 416(i) and generally include officers having annual compensation greater than $130,000 (adjusted for inflation and limited to 50 employees), five percent owners, and one percent owners having annual compensation from the employer greater than $150,000.

Disability

A participant is considered disabled if he or she (1) is unable to engage in any substantial gainful activity by reason of any medically determinable physical or mental impairment which can be expected to result in death or can be expected to last for a continuous period of not less than 12 months; or (2) is, by reason of any medically determinable physical or mental impairment which can be expected to result in death or can be expected to last for a continuous period of not less than 12 months, receiving income replacement benefits for a period of not less than three months under an accident and health plan covering employees of the participant's employer.

Prohibition on acceleration of distributions

As mentioned above, except as provided in regulations by the Secretary, no accelerations of distributions may be allowed. In general, changes in the form of distribution that accelerate payments are subject to the rule prohibiting acceleration of distributions. However, it is intended that the rule against accelerations is not violated merely because a plan provides a choice between cash and taxable property if the timing and amount of income inclusion is the same regardless of the medium of distribution. For example, the choice between a fully taxable annuity contract and a lump-sum payment may be permitted. It is also intended that the Secretary provide rules under which the choice between different forms of actuarially equivalent life annuity payments is permitted.

It is intended that the Secretary will provide other, limited, exceptions to the prohibition on accelerated distributions, such as when the accelerated distribution is required for reasons beyond the control of the participant and the distribution is not elective. For example, it is anticipated that an exception could be provided if a distribution is needed in order to comply with Federal conflict of interest requirements or a court-approved settlement incident to divorce. It is intended that Treasury regulations provide that a plan would not violate the prohibition on accelerations by providing that withholding of an employee's share of employment taxes will be made from the employee's interest in the nonqualified deferred compensation plan. It is also intended that Treasury regulations provide that a plan would not violate the prohibition on accelerations by providing for a distribution to a participant to pay income taxes due upon a vesting event subject to section 457(f), provided that such amount is not more than an amount equal to the income tax withholding that would have

been remitted by the employer if there had been a payment of wages equal to the income includible by the participant under section 457(f). It is also intended that Treasury regulations provide that a plan would not violate the prohibition on accelerations by providing for automatic distributions of minimal interests in a deferred compensation plan upon permissible distribution events for purposes of administrative convenience. For example, a plan could provide that upon separation from service of a participant, account balances less than $10,000 will be automatically distributed (except in the case of specified employees).

Requirements with respect to elections

The provision requires that a plan must provide that compensation for services performed during a taxable year may be deferred at the participant's election only if the election to defer is made no later than the close of the preceding taxable year, or at such other time as provided in Treasury regulations.[812] In the case of any performance-based compensation based on services performed over a period of at least 12 months, such election may be made no later than six months before the end of the service period. It is not intended that the provision override the constructive receipt doctrine, as constructive receipt rules continue to apply. It is intended that the term "performance-based compensation" will be defined by the Secretary to include compensation to the extent that an amount is: (1) variable and contingent on the satisfaction of preestablished organizational or individual performance criteria and (2) not readily ascertainable at the time of the election. For the purposes of the provision, it is intended that performance-based compensation may be required to meet certain requirements similar to those under section 162(m), but would not be required to meet all requirements under that section. For example, it is expected that the Secretary will provide that performance criteria would be considered preestablished if it is established in writing no later than 90 days after the commencement of the service period, but the requirement of determination by the compensation committee of the board of directors would not be required. It is expected that the Secretary will issue guidance providing coordination rules, as appropriate, regarding the timing of elections in the case when the fiscal year of the employer and the taxable year of the individual are different. It is expected that Treasury regulations will not permit any election to defer any bonus or other compensation if the timing of such election would be inconsistent with the purposes of the provision.

---

[812] Under the provision, in the first year that an employee becomes eligible for participation in a nonqualified deferred compensation plan, the election may be made within 30 days after the date that the employee is initially eligible.

The time and form of distributions must be specified at the time of initial deferral. A plan could specify the time and form of payments that are to be made as a result of a distribution event (e.g., a plan could specify that payments upon separation of service will be paid in lump sum within 30 days of separation from service) or could allow participants to elect the time and form of payment at the time of the initial deferral election. If a plan allows participants to elect the time and form of payment, such election is subject to the rules regarding initial deferral elections under the provision. It is intended that multiple payout events are permissible. For example, a participant could elect to receive 25 percent of their account balance at age 50 and the remaining 75 percent at age 60. A plan could also allow participants to elect different forms of payment for different permissible distribution events. For example, a participant could elect to receive a lump-sum distribution upon disability, but an annuity at age 65.

Under the provision, a plan may allow changes in the time and form of distributions subject to certain requirements. A nonqualified deferred compensation plan may allow a subsequent election to delay the timing or form of distributions only if: (1) the plan requires that such election cannot be effective for at least 12 months after the date on which the election is made; (2) except in the case of elections relating to distributions on account of death, disability or unforeseeable emergency, the plan requires that the additional deferral with respect to which such election is made is for a period of not less than five years from the date such payment would otherwise have been made; and (3) the plan requires that an election related to a distribution to be made upon a specified time may not be made less than 12 months prior to the date of the first scheduled payment. It is expected that in limited cases, the Secretary will issue guidance, consistent with the purposes of the provision, regarding to what extent elections to change a stream of payments are permissible. The Secretary may issue regulations regarding elections with respect to payments under nonelective, supplemental retirement plans.

Foreign trusts

Under the provision, in the case of assets set aside (directly or indirectly) in a trust (or other arrangement determined by the Secretary) for purposes of paying nonqualified deferred compensation, such assets are treated as property transferred in connection with the performance of services under section 83 (whether or not such assets are available to satisfy the claims of general creditors) at the time set aside if such assets (or trust or other arrangement) are located outside of the United States or at the time trans-

ferred if such assets (or trust or other arrangement) are subsequently transferred outside of the United States. Any subsequent increases in the value of, or any earnings with respect to, such assets are treated as additional transfers of property. Interest at the underpayment rate plus one percentage point is imposed on the underpayments that would have occurred had the amounts set aside been includible in income for the taxable year in which first deferred or, if later, the first taxable year not subject to a substantial risk of forfeiture. The amount required to be included in income is also subject to an additional 20-percent tax.

It is expected that the Secretary will provide rules for identifying the deferrals to which assets set aside are attributable, for situations in which assets equal to less than the full amount of deferrals are set aside. The provision does not apply to assets located in a foreign jurisdiction if substantially all of the services to which the nonqualified deferred compensation relates are performed in such foreign jurisdiction. The provision is specifically intended to apply to foreign trusts and arrangements that effectively shield from the claims of general creditors any assets intended to satisfy nonqualified deferred compensation arrangements. The Secretary has authority to exempt arrangements from the provision if the arrangements do not result in an improper deferral of U.S. tax and will not result in assets being effectively beyond the reach of creditors.

Triggers upon financial health

Under the provision, a transfer of property in connection with the performance of services under section 83 also occurs with respect to compensation deferred under a nonqualified deferred compensation plan if the plan provides that upon a change in the employer's financial health, assets will be restricted to the payment of nonqualified deferred compensation. An amount is treated as restricted even if the assets are available to satisfy the claims of general creditors. For example, the provision applies in the case of a plan that provides that upon a change in financial health, assets will be transferred to a rabbi trust.

The transfer of property occurs as of the earlier of when the assets are so restricted or when the plan provides that assets will be restricted. It is intended that the transfer of property occurs to the extent that assets are restricted or will be restricted with respect to such compensation. For example, in the case of a plan that provides that upon a change in the employer's financial health, a trust will become funded to the extent of all deferrals, all amounts deferred under the plan are treated as property transferred under section 83. If a plan provides that deferrals of certain individuals will be funded upon a change in financial health, the transfer of property would occur with respect to compensation deferred by such individuals. The provision is not intended to apply when assets are restricted for a reason other than change in financial health (e.g., upon a change in control) or if assets are periodically restricted under a structured schedule and scheduled restrictions happen to coincide with a change in financial status. Any subsequent increases in the value of, or any earnings with respect to, restricted assets are treated as additional transfers of property. Interest at the underpayment rate plus one percentage point is imposed on the underpayments that would have occurred had the amounts been includible in income for the taxable year in which first deferred or, if later, the first taxable year not subject to a substantial risk of forfeiture. The amount required to be included in income is also subject to an additional 20-percent tax.

Definition of nonqualified deferred compensation plan

A nonqualified deferred compensation plan is any plan that provides for the deferral of compensation other than a qualified employer plan or any bona fide vacation leave, sick leave, compensatory time, disability pay, or death benefit plan.[813] A qualified employer plan means a qualified retirement plan, tax-deferred annuity, simplified employee pension, and SIMPLE.[814] A qualified governmental excess benefit arrangement (sec. 415(m)) is a qualified employer plan. An eligible deferred compensation plan (sec. 457(b)) is also a qualified employer plan under the provision. A tax-exempt or governmental deferred compensation plan that is not an eligible deferred compensation plan is not a qualified employer plan. The application of the provision is not limited to arrangements between an employer and employee.

For purposes of the provision, it is not intended that the term "nonqualified deferred compensation plan" include an arrangement taxable under section 83 providing for the grant of an option on employer stock with an exercise price that is not less than the fair market value of the underlying stock on the date of grant if such arrangement does not include a deferral feature other than the feature that the option holder has the right to exercise the option in the future. The provision is not intended to change the tax treatment of incentive stock options meeting the re-

quirements of 422 or options granted under an employee stock purchase plan meeting the requirements of section 423.

It is intended that the provision does not apply to annual bonuses or other annual compensation amounts paid within 2 $1/2$ months after the close of the taxable year in which the relevant services required for payment have been performed.

Other rules

Interest imposed under the provision is treated as interest on an underpayment of tax. Income (whether actual or notional) attributable to nonqualified deferred compensation is treated as additional deferred compensation and is subject to the provision. The provision is not intended to prevent the inclusion of amounts in gross income under any provision or rule of law earlier than the time provided in the provision. Any amount included in gross income under the provision is not be required to be included in gross income under any provision of law later than the time provided in the provision. The provision does not affect the rules regarding the timing of an employer's deduction for nonqualified deferred compensation.

Treasury regulations

The provision provides the Secretary authority to prescribe regulations as are necessary to carry out the purposes of provision, including regulations: (1) providing for the determination of amounts of deferral in the case of defined benefit plans; (2) relating to changes in the ownership and control of a corporation or assets of a corporation; (3) exempting from the provisions providing for transfers of property arrangements that will not result in an improper deferral of U.S. tax and will not result in assets being effectively beyond the reach of creditors; (4) defining financial health; and (5) disregarding a substantial risk of forfeiture. It is intended that substantial risk of forfeitures may not be used to manipulate the timing of income inclusion. It is intended that substantial risks of forfeiture should be disregarded in cases in which they are illusory or are used in a manner inconsistent with the purposes of the provision. For example, if an executive is effectively able to control the acceleration of the lapse of a substantial risk of forfeiture, such risk of forfeiture should be disregarded and income inclusion should not be postponed on account of such restriction. The

---

[813] The provision does not apply to a plan meeting the requirements of section 457(e)(12) if the plan was in existence as of May 1, 2004, was providing nonelective deferred compensation described in section 457(e)(12) on such date, and is established or maintained by an organization incorporated on July 2, 1974. If the plan has a material change in

the class of individuals eligible to participate in the plan after May 1, 2004, the provision applies to compensation provided under the plan after the date of such change.

[814] A qualified employer plan also includes a section 501(c)(18) trust.

Secretary may also address in regulations issues relating to stock appreciation rights.

Aggregation rules

Under the provision, except as provided by the Secretary, employer aggregation rules apply. It is intended that the Secretary issue guidance providing aggregation rules as are necessary to carry out the purposes of the provision. For example, it is intended that aggregation rules would apply in the case of separation from service so that the separation from service from one entity within a controlled group, but continued service for another entity within the group, would not be a permissible distribution event. It is also intended that aggregation rules would not apply in the case of change in control so that the change in control of one member of a controlled group would not be a permissible distribution event for participants of a deferred compensation plan of another member of the group.

Reporting requirements

Amounts required to be included in income under the provision are subject to reporting and Federal income tax withholding requirements. Amounts required to be includible in income are required to be reported on an individual's Form W-2 (or Form 1099) for the year includible in income.

The provision also requires annual reporting to the Internal Revenue Service of amounts deferred. Such amounts are required to be reported on an individual's Form W-2 (or Form 1099) for the year deferred even if the amount is not currently includible in income for that taxable year. It is expected that annual reporting of annual amounts deferred will provide the IRS greater information regarding such arrangements for enforcement purposes. It is intended that the information reported would provide an indication of what arrangements should be examined and challenged. Under the provision, the Secretary is authorized, through regulations, to establish a minimum amount of deferrals below which the reporting requirement does not apply. The Secretary may also provide that the reporting requirement does not apply with respect to amounts of deferrals that are not reasonably ascertainable. It is intended that the exception for amounts not reasonable ascertainable only apply to nonaccount balance plans and that amounts be required to be reported when they first become reasonably ascertainable.[815]

Effective Date

The provision is effective for amounts deferred in taxable years beginning after December 31, 2004. Earnings on amounts deferred before the effective date are subject to the provision to the extent that such amounts deferred are subject to the provision.

Amounts deferred in taxable years beginning before January 1, 2005, are subject to the provision if the plan under which the deferral is made is materially modified after October 3, 2004. The addition of any benefit, right or feature is a material modification. The exercise or reduction of an existing benefit, right, or feature is not a material modification. For example, an amendment to a plan on November 1, 2004, to add a provision that distributions may be allowed upon request if participants are required to forfeit 10 percent of the amount of the distribution (i.e., a "haircut") would be a material modification to the plan so that the rules of the provision would apply to the plan. Similarly, accelerating vesting under a plan after October 3, 2004, would be a material modification. A change in the plan administrator would not be a material modification. As another example, amending a plan to remove a distribution provision (e.g., to remove a "haircut") would not be considered a material modification.

Operating under the terms of a deferred compensation arrangement that complies with current law and is not materially modified after October 3, 2004, with respect to amounts deferred before January 1, 2005, is permissible, as such amounts would not be subject to the requirements of the provision. For example, subsequent deferrals with respect to amounts deferred before January 1, 2005, under a plan that is not materially modified after October 3, 2004, would be subject to present law and would not be subject to the provision.[816] No inference is intended that all deferrals before the effective date are permissible under present law. It is expected that the IRS will challenge pre-effective date deferral arrangements that do not comply with present law.

For purposes of the effective date, an amount is considered deferred before January 1, 2005, if the amount is earned and vested before such date. To the extent there is no material modification after October 3, 2004, present law applies with respect to vested rights.

---

[815] It is intended that the exception be similar to that under Treas. Reg. sec. 31.3121(v)(2)-1(e)(4).

[816] There is no inference that all subsequent deferral elections under plans that are not materially modified are permissible under present law.

No later than 60 days after the date of enactment, the Secretary shall issue guidance providing a limited period of time during which a nonqualified deferred compensation plan adopted before December 31, 2004, may, without violating the requirements of the provision relating to distributions, accelerations, and elections be amended (1) to provide that a participant may terminate participation in the plan, or cancel an outstanding deferral election with respect to amounts deferred after December 31, 2004, if such amounts are includible in income of the participant as earned, or if later, when not subject to a substantial risk of forfeiture, and (2) to conform with the provision with respect to amounts deferred after December 31, 2004. It is expected that the Secretary may provide exceptions to certain requirements of the provision during the transition period (e.g., the rules regarding timing of elections) for plans coming into compliance with the provision. Moreover, it is expected that the Secretary will provide a reasonable time, during the transition period but after the issuance of guidance, for plans to be amended and approved by the appropriate parties in accordance with this provision.

[Law at ¶ 5350, ¶ 5975, ¶ 6140, ¶ 6155 and ¶ 7145. CCH Explanation at ¶ 1405.]

[¶ 11,580] Act Sec. 886. Extend the present-law intangible amortization provisions to acquisitions of sports franchises

House Committee Report (H.R. REP. NO. 108-548, pt. 1)

[Code Sec. 197]

Present Law

The purchase price allocated to intangible assets (including franchise rights) acquired in connection with the acquisition of a trade or business generally must be capitalized and amortized over a 15-year period.[491] These rules were enacted in 1993 to minimize disputes regarding the proper treatment of acquired intangible assets. The rules do not apply to a franchise to engage in professional sports and any intangible asset acquired in connection with such a franchise.[492] However, other special rules apply to certain of these intangible assets.

Under section 1056, when a franchise to conduct a sports enterprise is sold or exchanged, the basis of a player contract acquired as part of the transaction is generally limited to the adjusted basis of such contract in the hands of the transferor, increased by the amount of gain, if any, recognized by the transferor on the transfer of the contract. Moreover, not more than 50 percent of the consideration from the transaction may be allocated to player contracts unless the transferee establishes to the satisfaction of the Commissioner that a specific allocation in excess of 50 percent is proper. However, these basis rules may not apply if a sale or exchange of a franchise to conduct a sports enterprise is effected through a partnership.[493] Basis allocated to the franchise or to other valuable intangible assets acquired with the franchise may not be amortizable if these assets lack a determinable useful life.

In general, section 1245 provides that gain from the sale of certain property is treated as ordinary income to the extent depreciation or amortization was allowed on such property. Section 1245(a)(4) provides special rules for recapture of depreciation and deductions for losses taken with respect to player contracts. The special recapture rules apply in the case of the sale, exchange, or other disposition of a sports franchise. Under the special recapture rules, the amount recaptured as ordinary income is the amount of gain not to exceed the greater of (1) the sum of the depreciation taken plus any deductions taken for losses (i.e., abandonment losses) with respect to those player contracts which are initially acquired as a part of the original acquisition of the franchise or (2) the amount of depreciation taken with respect to those player contracts which are owned by the seller at the time of the sale of the sports franchise.

Reasons for Change

The present-law rules under section 197 were enacted to minimize disputes regarding the measurement of acquired intangible assets. Prior to the enactment of the rules, there were many disputes regarding the value and useful life of various intangible assets acquired together in a business acquisition. Furthermore, in the absence of a showing of a reasonably determinable useful life, an asset could not be amortized. Taxpayers tended to identify and allocate large amounts of purchase price to assets said to have short useful lives, while the IRS would allocate a large

---

[491] Sec. 197.
[492] Sec. 197(e)(6).

[493] *P.D.B. Sports, Ltd. v. Comm.,* 109 T.C. 423 (1997).

amount of value to intangible assets for which no determinable useful life could be shown (e.g., goodwill), and would deny amortization for that amount of purchase price.

The present-law rules for acquisitions of sports franchises do not eliminate the potential for disputes, because they address only player contracts, while a sports franchise acquisition can involve many intangibles other than player contracts. In addition, disputes may arise regarding the appropriate period for amortization of particular player contracts. The Committee believes expending taxpayer and government resources disputing these items is an unproductive use of economic resources. The Committee further believes that the section 197 rules should apply to all types of businesses regardless of the nature of their assets.

Explanation of Provision

The provision extends the 15-year recovery period for intangible assets to franchises to engage in professional sports and any intangible asset acquired in connection with the acquisition of such a franchise (including player contracts). Thus, the same rules for amortization of intangibles that apply to other acquisitions under present law will apply to acquisitions of sports franchises. The provision also repeals the special rules under section 1245(a)(4) and makes other conforming changes.

Effective Date

The provision is effective for property acquired after the date of enactment. The amendment to section 1245(a)(4) applies to franchises acquired after the date of enactment.

Conference Committee Report (H.R. CONF. REP. NO. 108-755)

Senate Amendment

The Senate amendment is the same as the House bill.

Conference Agreement

The conference agreement follows the House bill and the Senate amendment.

[Law at ¶5225, ¶5770, ¶5795 and ¶5815. CCH Explanation at ¶355.]

[¶ 11,590] Act Sec. 887. Increase continuous levy for certain federal payments

House Committee Report (H.R. REP. NO. 108-548, pt. 1)

[Code Sec. 6331]

Present Law

If any person is liable for any internal revenue tax and does not pay it within 10 days after notice and demand[494] by the IRS, the IRS may then collect the tax by levy upon all property and rights to property belonging to the person,[495] unless there is an explicit statutory restriction on doing so. A levy is the seizure of the person's property or rights to property. Property that is not cash is sold pursuant to statutory requirements.[496]

A continuous levy is applicable to specified Federal payments.[497] This includes any Federal payment for which eligibility is not based on the income and/or assets of a payee. Thus, a Federal payment to a vendor of goods or services to the government is subject to continuous levy. This continuous levy attaches up to 15 percent of any specified payment due the taxpayer.

Reasons for Change

There have recently been reports[498] of abuses of the Federal tax system by some Federal contractors. Consequently, the Committee believes that it is appropriate to increase the permissible percentage of Federal payments subject to levy.

Explanation of Provision

The provision permits a levy of up to 100 percent of a Federal payment to a vendor of goods or services to the Government.

Effective Date

The provision is effective on the date of enactment.

---

[494] Notice and demand is the notice given to a person liable for tax stating that the tax has been assessed and demanding that payment be made. The notice and demand must be mailed to the person's last known address or left at the person's dwelling or usual place of business (Code sec. 6303).

[495] Code sec. 6331.

[496] Code secs. 6335-6343.

[497] Code sec. 6331(h).

[498] Some DOD Contractors Abuse the Federal Tax System with Little Consequence, GAO-04-95, February 2004.

Conference Committee Report (H.R. CONF. REP. NO. 108-755)

Senate Amendment   [Law at ¶ 6195. CCH Explanation at ¶ 1625.]

The Senate amendment is the same as the House bill.

Conference Agreement

The conference agreement follows the House bill and the Senate amendment.

[¶ 11,600] Act Sec. 888. Modification of straddle rules

House Committee Report (H.R. REP. NO. 108-548, pt. 1)

[Code Sec. 1092]

Present Law

Straddle rules

In general

A "straddle" generally refers to offsetting positions (sometimes referred to as "legs" of the straddle) with respect to actively traded personal property. Positions are offsetting if there is a substantial diminution in the risk of loss from holding one position by reason of holding one or more other positions in personal property. A "position" is an interest (including a futures or forward contract or option) in personal property. When a taxpayer realizes a loss with respect to a position in a straddle, the taxpayer may recognize that loss for any taxable year only to the extent that the loss exceeds the unrecognized gain (if any) with respect to offsetting positions in the straddle.[499] Deferred losses are carried forward to the succeeding taxable year and are subject to the same limitation with respect to unrecognized gain in offsetting positions.

Positions in stock

The straddle rules generally do not apply to positions in stock. However, the straddle rules apply where one of the positions is stock and at least one of the offsetting positions is: (1) an option with respect to the stock, (2) a securities futures contract (as defined in section 1234B) with respect to the stock, or (3) a position with respect to substantially similar or related property (other than stock) as defined in Treasury regulations. In addition, the straddle rules apply to stock of a corporation formed or availed of to take positions in personal property that offset positions taken by any shareholder.

Although the straddle rules apply to offsetting positions that consist of stock and an option with respect to stock, the straddle rules generally do not apply if the option is a "qualified covered call option" written by the taxpayer.[500] In general, a qualified covered call option is defined as an exchange-listed option that is not deep-in-the-money and is written by a non-dealer more than 30 days before expiration of the option.

The stock exception from the straddle rules has been largely curtailed by statutory amendment and regulatory interpretation. Under proposed Treasury regulations, the application of the stock exception essentially would be limited to offsetting positions involving direct ownership of stock and short sales of stock.[501]

Unbalanced straddles

When one position with respect to personal property offsets only a portion of one or more other positions ("unbalanced straddles"), the Treasury Secretary is directed to prescribe by regulations the method for determining the portion of such other positions that is to be taken into account for purposes of the straddle rules.[502] To date, no such regulations have been promulgated.

Unbalanced straddles can be illustrated with the following example: Assume the taxpayer holds two shares of stock (i.e., is long) in XYZ stock corporation—share A with a $30 basis and share B with a $40 basis. When the value of the XYZ stock is $45, the taxpayer pays a $5 premium to purchase a put option on one share

---

[499] Sec. 1092.

[500] However, if the option written by the taxpayer is a qualified covered call option that is in-the-money, then (1) any loss with respect to such option is treated as long-term capital loss if, at the time such loss is realized, gain on the sale or exchange of the offsetting stock held by the taxpayer would be treated as long-term capital gain, and (2) the

holding period of such stock does not include any period during which the taxpayer is the grantor of the option (sec. 1092(f)).

[501] Prop. Treas. Reg. sec. 1.1092(d)-2(c).

[502] Sec. 1092(c)(2)(B).

of the XYZ stock with an exercise price of $40. The issue arises as to whether the purchase of the put option creates a straddle with respect to share A, share B, or both. Assume that, when the value of the XYZ stock is $100, the put option expires unexercised. Taxpayer incurs a loss of $5 on the expiration of the put option, and sells share B for a $60 gain. On a literal reading of the straddle rules, the $5 loss would be deferred because the loss ($5) does not exceed the unrecognized gain ($70) in share A, which is also an offsetting position to the put option—notwithstanding that the taxpayer recognized more gain than the loss through the sale of share B. This problem is exacerbated when the taxpayer has a large portfolio of actively traded personal property that may be offsetting the loss leg of the straddle.

Although Treasury has not issued regulations to address unbalanced straddles, the IRS issued a private letter ruling in 1999 that addressed an unbalanced straddle situation.[503] Under the facts of the ruling, a taxpayer entered into a costless collar with respect to a portion of the shares of a particular stock held by the taxpayer.[504] Other shares were held in an account as collateral for a loan and still other shares were held in excess of the shares used as collateral and the number of shares specified in the collar. The ruling concluded that the collar offset only a portion of the stock (i.e., the number of shares specified in the costless collar) because that number of shares determined the payoff under each option comprising the collar. The ruling further concluded that:

> In the absence of regulations under section 1092(c)(2)(B), we conclude that it is permissible for Taxpayer to identify which shares of Corporation stock are part of the straddles and which shares are used as collateral for the loans using appropriately modified versions of the methods of section 1.1012-1(c)(2) and (3) [providing rules for adequate identification of shares of stock sold or transferred by a taxpayer] or section 1.1092(b)-3T(d)(4) [providing requirements and methods for identification of positions that are part of a section 1092(b)(2) identified mixed straddle].

Holding period for dividends-received deduction

If an instrument issued by a U.S. corporation is classified for tax purposes as stock, a corporate holder of the instrument generally is entitled to a dividends-received deduction for dividends received on that instrument.[505] The dividends-received deduction is allowed to a corporate shareholder only if the shareholder satisfies a 46-day holding period for the dividend-paying stock (or a 91-day holding period for certain dividends on preferred stock).[506] The holding period must be satisfied for each dividend over a period that is immediately before and immediately after the taxpayer becomes entitled to receive the dividend. The 46- or 91-day holding period generally does not include any time during which the shareholder is protected (other than by writing a qualified covered call) from the risk of loss that is otherwise inherent in the ownership of any equity interest.[507]

Reasons for Change

The Committee believes that the straddle rules should be modified in several respects. While the present-law rules provide authority for the Secretary to issue guidance concerning unbalanced straddles, the Committee is of the view that such guidance is not forthcoming. Therefore, the Committee believes that it is necessary at this time to provide such guidance by statute. The Committee further believes that it is appropriate to repeal the exception from the straddle rules for positions in stock, particularly in light of statutory changes in the straddle rules and elsewhere in the Code that have significantly diminished the continuing utility of the exception. In addition, the Committee believes that the present-law treatment of physically settled positions under the straddle rules requires clarification.

Explanation of Provision

Straddle rules

The bill modifies the straddle rules in three respects: (1) permits taxpayers to identify offsetting positions of a straddle; (2) provides a special rule to clarify the present-law treatment of certain physically settled positions of a straddle;

---

[503] Priv. Ltr. Rul. 199925044 (Feb. 3, 1999).

[504] A costless collar generally is comprised of the purchase of a put option and the sale of a call option with the same trade dates and maturity dates and set such that the premium paid substantially equals the premium received. The collar can be considered as economically similar to a short position in the stock.

[505] Sec. 243. The amount of the deduction is 70 percent of dividends received if the recipient owns less than 20 percent

(by vote and value) of stock of the payor. If the recipient owns more than 20 percent of the stock, the deduction is increased to 80 percent. If the recipient owns more than 80 percent of the stock, the deduction is further increased to 100 percent for qualifying dividends.

[506] Sec. 246(c).

[507] Sec. 246(c)(4).

and (3) repeals the stock exception from the straddle rules.

Identified straddles

Under the bill, taxpayers generally are permitted to identify the offsetting positions that are components of a straddle at the time the taxpayer enters into a transaction that creates a straddle, including an unbalanced straddle.[508] If there is a loss with respect to any identified position that is part of an identified straddle, the general straddle loss deferral rules do not apply to such loss. Instead, the basis of each of the identified positions that offset the loss position in the identified straddle is increased by an amount that bears the same ratio to the loss as the unrecognized gain (if any) with respect to such offsetting position bears to the aggregate unrecognized gain with respect to all positions that offset the loss position in the identified straddle.[509] Any loss with respect to an identified position that is part of an identified straddle cannot otherwise be taken into account by the taxpayer or any other person to the extent that the loss increases the basis of any identified positions that offset the loss position in the identified straddle.

In addition, the provision provides authority to issue Treasury regulations that would specify (1) the proper methods for clearly identifying a straddle as an identified straddle (and identifying positions as positions in an identified straddle), (2) the application of the identified straddle rules for a taxpayer that fails to properly identify the positions of an identified straddle,[510] and (3) provide an ordering rule for dispositions of less than an entire position that is part of an identified straddle.

Physically settled straddle positions

The bill also clarifies the present-law straddle rules with respect to taxpayers that settle a position that is part of a straddle by delivering property to which the position relates. Specifically, the provision clarifies that the present-law straddle loss deferral rules treat as a two-step transaction the physical settlement of a straddle position that, if terminated, would result in the realization of a loss. With respect to the physical settlement of such a position, the taxpayer is treated as having terminated the position for its fair market value immediately before the settlement. The taxpayer then is treated as having sold at fair market value the property used to physically settle the position.

Stock exception repeal

The bill also eliminates the exception from the straddle rules for stock (other than the exception relating to qualified covered call options). Thus, offsetting positions comprised of actively traded stock and a position with respect to substantially similar or related property generally constitute a straddle.[511]

Dividends-received deduction holding period

The bill also modifies the required 46- or 91-day holding period for the dividends-received deduction by providing that the holding period does not include any time during which the shareholder is protected from the risk of loss otherwise inherent in the ownership of any equity interest if the shareholder obtains such protection by writing an in-the-money call option on the dividend-paying stock.

Effective Date

The provision is effective for positions established on or after the date of enactment that substantially diminish the risk of loss from holding offsetting positions (regardless of when such offsetting position was established).

Conference Committee Report (H.R. Conf. Rep. No. 108-755)

The conference agreement follows the House bill.

[Law at ¶ 5255, ¶ 5775 and ¶ 5820. CCH Explanation at ¶ 730.]

---

[508] However, to the extent provided by Treasury regulations, taxpayers are not permitted to identify offsetting positions of a straddle if the fair market value of the straddle position already held by the taxpayer at the creation of the straddle is less than its adjusted basis in the hands of the taxpayer.

[509] For this purpose, "unrecognized gain" is the excess of the fair market value of an identified position that is part of an identified straddle at the time the taxpayer incurs a loss with respect to another identified position in the identified straddle, over the fair market value of such position when the taxpayer identified the position as a position in the identified straddle.

[510] For example, although the provision does not require taxpayers to identify any positions of a straddle as an identi-

fied straddle, it may be necessary to provide rules requiring all balanced offsetting positions to be included in an identified straddle if a taxpayer elects to identify any of the offsetting positions as an identified straddle.

[511] It is intended that Treasury regulations defining substantially similar or related property for this purpose will continue to apply subsequent to repeal of the stock exception and generally will constitute the exclusive definition of a straddle with respect to offsetting positions involving stock. See Prop. Treas. Reg. sec. 1.1092(d)-2(b). However, the general straddles rules regarding substantial diminution in risk of loss will continue to apply to stock of corporations formed or availed of to take positions in personal property that offset positions taken by the shareholder.

[¶ 11,610] Act Sec. 889. Add vaccines against hepatitis A to the list of taxable vaccines

House Committee Report (H.R. REP. NO. 108-548, pt. 1)

[Code Sec. 4132]

Present Law

A manufacturer's excise tax is imposed at the rate of 75 cents per dose[512] on the following vaccines routinely recommended for administration to children: diphtheria, pertussis, tetanus, measles, mumps, rubella, polio, HIB (haemophilus influenza type B), hepatitis B, varicella (chicken pox), rotavirus gastroenteritis, and streptococcus pneumoniae. The tax applied to any vaccine that is a combination of vaccine components equals 75 cents times the number of components in the combined vaccine.

Amounts equal to net revenues from this excise tax are deposited in the Vaccine Injury Compensation Trust Fund to finance compensation awards under the Federal Vaccine Injury Compensation Program for individuals who suffer certain injuries following administration of the taxable vaccines. This program provides a substitute Federal, "no fault" insurance system for the State-law tort and private liability insurance systems otherwise applicable to vaccine manufacturers. All persons immunized after September 30, 1988, with covered vaccines must pursue compensation under this Federal program before bringing civil tort actions under State law.

Reasons for Change

The Committee is aware that the Centers for Disease Control and Prevention have recommended that children in 17 highly endemic States be inoculated with a hepatitis A vaccine. The population of children in the affected States exceeds 20 million. Several of the affected States mandate childhood vaccination against hepatitis A. The Committee is aware that the Advisory Commission on Childhood Vaccines has recommended that the vaccine excise tax be extended to cover vaccines against hepatitis A. For these reasons, the Committee believes it is appropriate to include vaccines against hepatitis A as part of the Vaccine Injury Compensation Program. Making the hepatitis A vaccine taxable is a first step.[513] In the unfortunate event of an injury related to this vaccine, families of injured children are eligible for the no-fault arbitration system established under the Vaccine Injury Compensation Program rather than going to Federal Court to seek compensatory redress.

Explanation of Provision

The provision adds any vaccine against hepatitis A to the list of taxable vaccines.

Effective Date

The provision is effective for vaccines sold beginning on the first day of the first month beginning more than four weeks after the date of enactment.

Conference Committee Report (H.R. CONF. REP. NO. 108-755)

The conference agreement includes the House bill provision.

[Law at ¶ 6060. CCH Explanation at ¶ 1565.]

[¶ 11,620] Act Sec. 890. Add vaccines against influenza to the list of taxable vaccines

House Committee Report (H.R. REP. NO. 108-548, pt. 1)

[Code Sec. 4132]

Present Law

A manufacturer's excise tax is imposed at the rate of 75 cents per dose[514] on the following vaccines routinely recommended for administration to children: diphtheria, pertussis, tetanus, measles, mumps, rubella, polio, HIB (haemophilus influenza type B), hepatitis B, varicella (chicken pox), rotavirus gastroenteritis, and

---

[512] Sec. 4131.

[513] The Committee recognizes that, to become covered under the Vaccine Injury Compensation Program, the Secre-

tary of Health and Human Services also must list the hepatitis A vaccine on the Vaccine Injury Table.

[514] Sec. 4131.

streptococcus pneumoniae. The tax applied to any vaccine that is a combination of vaccine components equals 75 cents times the number of components in the combined vaccine.

Amounts equal to net revenues from this excise tax are deposited in the Vaccine Injury Compensation Trust Fund to finance compensation awards under the Federal Vaccine Injury Compensation Program for individuals who suffer certain injuries following administration of the taxable vaccines. This program provides a substitute Federal, "no fault" insurance system for the State-law tort and private liability insurance systems otherwise applicable to vaccine manufacturers. All persons immunized after September 30, 1988, with covered vaccines must pursue compensation under this Federal program before bringing civil tort actions under State law.

Reasons for Change

The Committee understands that on October 15, 2003, the Advisory Committee on Immunization Practices of the Centers for Disease Control and Prevention issued a recommendation for the routine annual vaccination of infants six to 23 months of age with an inactivated influenza vaccine licensed by FDA. This is the first recommendation for "routine use" in children

although trivalent influenza vaccine products have long been available and approved for use in children of varying ages and these vaccines have long been recommended for use by seniors. For these reasons, the Committee believes it is appropriate to include trivalent vaccines against influenza as part of the Vaccine Injury Compensation Program. Making an influenza vaccine taxable is a first step.[515] In the unfortunate event of an injury related to these vaccines, an injured individual is eligible for the no-fault arbitration system established under the Vaccine Injury Compensation Program rather than going to Federal Court to seek compensatory redress.

Explanation of Provision

The provision adds any trivalent vaccine against influenza to the list of taxable vaccines.

Effective Date

The provision is effective for vaccines sold or used beginning on the later of the first day of the first month beginning more than four weeks after the date of enactment or the date on which the Secretary of Health and Human Services lists any such vaccine for purpose of compensation for any vaccine-related injury or death through the Vaccine Injury Compensation Trust Fund.

Conference Committee Report (H.R. CONF. REP. NO. 108-755)

Senate Amendment

The Senate amendment is identical to the House bill.

Conference Agreement

The conference agreement includes the provision of the House bill and the Senate amendment.

[Law at ¶6060. CCH Explanation at ¶1565.]

[¶11,630] Act Sec. 891. Extension of IRS user fees

House Committee Report (H.R. REP. NO. 108-548, pt. 1)

[Code Sec. 7528]

Present Law

The IRS provides written responses to questions of individuals, corporations, and organizations relating to their tax status or the effects of particular transactions for tax purposes. The IRS

generally charges a fee for requests for a letter ruling, determination letter, opinion letter, or other similar ruling or determination.[516] Public Law 108-89[517] extended the statutory authorization for these user fees through December 31, 2004, and moved the statutory authorization for these fees into the Code.[518]

---

[515] The Committee recognizes that, to become covered under the Vaccine Injury Compensation Program, the Secretary of Health and Human Services also must list each trivalent vaccine against influenza on the Vaccine Injury Table.

[516] These user fees were originally enacted in section 10511 of the Revenue Act of 1987 (Pub. Law No. 100-203, December 22, 1987). Public Law 104-117 (An Act to provide that members of the Armed Forces performing services for the peacekeeping efforts in Bosnia and Herzegovina, Croatia, and Macedonia shall be entitled to tax benefits in the

same manner as if such services were performed in a combat zone, and for other purposes (March 20, 1996)) extended the statutory authorization for these user fees through September 30, 2003.

[517] 117 Stat. 1131; H.R. 3146, signed by the President on October 1, 2003.

[518] That Public Law also moved into the Code the user fee provision relating to pension plans that was enacted in section 620 of the Economic Growth and Tax Relief Reconciliation Act of 2001 (Pub. L. 107-16, June 7, 2001).

Reasons for Change

The Committee believes that it is appropriate to provide a further extension of the applicability of these user fees.

Explanation of Provision

The provision extends the statutory authorization for these user fees through September 30, 2014.

Effective Date

The provision is effective for requests made after the date of enactment.

Conference Committee Report (H.R. CONF. REP. NO. 108-755)

Conference Agreement

[Law at ¶ 6350. CCH Explanation at ¶ 1630.]

The conference agreement follows the House bill.

[¶ 11,640] Act Sec. 892. Extension of Customs user fees

House Committee Report (H.R. REP. NO. 108-548, pt. 1)

[Act Sec. 892]

Present Law

Section 13031 of the Consolidated Omnibus Budget Reconciliation Act of 1985 (COBRA) (P.L. 99-272), authorized the Secretary of the Treasury to collect certain service fees. Section 412 (P.L 107-296) of the Homeland Security Act of 2002 authorized the Secretary of the Treasury to delegate such authority to the Secretary of Homeland Security. Provided for under 19 U.S.C. 58c, these fees include: processing fees for air and sea passengers, commercial trucks, rail cars, private aircraft and vessels, commercial vessels, dutiable mail packages, barges and bulk carriers, merchandise, and Customs broker permits. COBRA was amended on several occasions but most recently by P.L. 108-121 which extended authorization for the collection of these fees through March 1, 2005.[519]

Reasons for Change

The Committee believes it is important to extend these fees to cover the expenses of the services provided. However, the Committee also believes it is important that any fee imposed be a true user fee. That is, the Committee believes that when the Congress authorizes the executive branch to assess user fees, those fees must be determined to reflect only the cost of providing the service for which the fee is assessed.

Explanation of Provision

The provision extends the passenger and conveyance processing fees and the merchandise processing fees authorized under the Consolidated Omnibus Budget Reconciliation Act of 1985 through September 30, 2014. For fiscal years after September 30, 2005, the Secretary is to charge fees in amount that are reasonably related to the costs of providing customs services in connection with the activity or item for which the fee is charged.

The provision also includes a Sense of the Congress that the fees set forth in paragraphs (1) through (8) of subsection (a) of section 13031 of the Consolidated Omnibus Budget Reconciliation Act of 1985 have been reasonably related to the costs of providing customs services in connection with the activities or items for which the fees have been charged under such paragraphs. The Sense of Congress also states that the fees collected under such paragraphs have not exceeded, in the aggregate, the amounts paid for the costs described in subsection (f)(3)(A) incurred in providing customs services in connection with the activities or items for which the fees were charged under such paragraphs.

The provision further provides that the Secretary conduct a study of all the fees collected by the Department of Homeland Security, and shall submit to the Congress, not later than September 30, 2005, a report containing the recommendations of the Secretary on what fees should be eliminated, what the rate of fees retains should be, and any other recommendations with respect to the fees that the Secretary considers appropriate.

Effective Date

The provisions are effective upon the date of enactment.

---

[519] Sec. 201; 117 Stat. 1335.

Conference Committee Report (H.R. CONF. REP. NO. 108-755)

Conference Agreement   [Law at ¶7150. CCH Explanation at ¶597.]

The conference agreement follows the House bill provision.

[¶ 11,650] Act Sec. 893. Prohibition on nonrecognition of gain through complete liquidation of holding company

Senate Committee Report (S. REP. NO. 108-192)

[Code Sec. 332]

Present Law

A U.S. corporation owned by foreign persons is subject to U.S. income tax on its net income. In addition, the earnings of the U.S. corporation are subject to a second tax, when dividends are paid to the corporation's shareholders.

In general, dividends paid by a U.S. corporation to nonresident alien individuals and foreign corporations that are not effectively connected with a U.S. trade or business are subject to a U.S. withholding tax on the gross amount of such income at a rate of 30 percent. The 30-percent withholding tax may be reduced pursuant to an income tax treaty between the United States and the foreign country where the foreign person is resident.

In addition, the United States imposes a branch profits tax on U.S. earnings of a foreign corporation that are shifted out of a U.S. branch of the foreign corporation. The branch profits tax is comparable to the second-level taxes imposed on dividends paid by a U.S. corporation to foreign shareholders. The branch profits tax is 30 percent (subject to possible income tax treaty reduction) of a foreign corporation's dividend equivalent amount. The "dividend equivalent amount" generally is the earnings and profits of a U.S. branch of a foreign corporation attributable to its income effectively connected with a U.S. trade or business.

In general, U.S. withholding tax is not imposed with respect to a distribution of a U.S. corporation's earnings to a foreign corporation in complete liquidation of the subsidiary, because the distribution is treated as made in exchange for stock and not as a dividend. In addition, detailed rules apply for purposes of exempting foreign corporations from the branch profits tax for the year in which it completely terminates its U.S. business conducted in branch form. The exemption from the branch profits tax generally applies if, among other things, for three years after the termination of the U.S. branch, the foreign corporation has no income effectively connected with a U.S. trade or business, and the U.S. assets of the terminated branch are not used by the foreign corporation or a related corporation in a U.S. trade or business.

Regulations under section 367(e) provide that the Commissioner may require a domestic liquidating corporation to recognize gain on distributions in liquidation made to a foreign corporation if a principal purpose of the liquidation is the avoidance of U.S. tax. Avoidance of U.S. tax for this purpose includes, but is not limited to, the distribution of a liquidating corporation's earnings and profits with a principal purpose of avoiding U.S. tax.

Reasons for Change

The Committee is concerned that foreign corporations may establish a U.S. holding company to receive tax-free dividends from U.S. operating companies, liquidate the U.S. holding company to distribute the U.S. earnings free of U.S. withholding taxes, and then reestablish another U.S. holding company, with the intention of escaping U.S. withholding taxes. The Committee believes that instances of such withholding tax abuse will be significantly restricted by imposing U.S. withholding taxes on a liquidating distribution to foreign corporate shareholders of earnings and profits of a U.S. holding company created within five years of the liquidation.

Explanation of Provision

The provision treats as a dividend any distribution of earnings by a U.S. holding company to a foreign corporation in a complete liquidation, if the U.S. holding company was in existence for less than five years.

Effective Date

The provision is effective for distributions occurring on or after the date of enactment.

Conference Committee Report (H.R. Conf. Rep. No. 108-755)

| House Bill | [Law at ¶ 5305. CCH Explanation at ¶ 1010.] |

No provision.

Conference Agreement

The conference agreement follows the Senate amendment.

[¶ 11,660] Act Sec. 894. Effectively connected income to include certain foreign source income

Senate Committee Report (S. Rep. No. 108-192)

[Code Sec. 864]

Present Law

Nonresident alien individuals and foreign corporations (collectively, foreign persons) are subject to U.S. tax on income that is effectively connected with the conduct of a U.S. trade or business; the U.S. tax on such income is calculated in the same manner and at the same graduated rates as the tax on U.S. persons.[312] Foreign persons also are subject to a 30-percent gross-basis tax, collected by withholding, on certain U.S.-source income, such as interest, dividends and other fixed or determinable annual or periodical ("FDAP") income, that is not effectively connected with a U.S. trade or business. This 30-percent withholding tax may be reduced or eliminated pursuant to an applicable tax treaty. Foreign persons generally are not subject to U.S. tax on foreign-source income that is not effectively connected with a U.S. trade or business.

Detailed rules apply for purposes of determining whether income is treated as effectively connected with a U.S. trade or business (so-called "U.S.-effectively connected income").[313] The rules differ depending on whether the income at issue is U.S.-source or foreign-source income. Under these rules, U.S.-source FDAP income, such as U.S.-source interest and dividends, and U.S.-source capital gains are treated as U.S.-effectively connected income if such income is derived from assets used in or held for use in the active conduct of a U.S. trade or business, or from business activities conducted in the United States. All other types of U.S.-source income are treated as U.S.-effectively connected income (sometimes referred to as the "force of attraction rule").

In general, foreign-source income is not treated as U.S.-effectively connected income.[314]

However, foreign-source income, gain, deduction, or loss generally is considered to be effectively connected with a U.S. business only if the person has an office or other fixed place of business within the United States to which such income, gain, deduction, or loss is attributable and such income falls into one of three categories described below.[315] For these purposes, income generally is not considered attributable to an office or other fixed place of business within the United States unless such office or fixed place of business is a material factor in the production of the income, and such office or fixed place of business regularly carries on activities of the type that generate such income.[316]

The first category consists of rents or royalties for the use of patents, copyrights, secret processes, or formulas, good will, trademarks, trade brands, franchises, or other similar intangible properties derived in the active conduct of the U.S. trade or business.[317] The second category consists of interest or dividends derived in the active conduct of a banking, financing, or similar business within the United States, or received by a corporation whose principal business is trading in stocks or securities for its own account.[318] Notwithstanding the foregoing, foreign-source income consisting of dividends, interest, or royalties is not treated as effectively connected if the items are paid by a foreign corporation in which the recipient owns, directly, indirectly, or constructively, more than 50 percent of the total combined voting power of the stock.[319] The third category consists of income, gain, deduction, or loss derived from the sale or exchange of inventory or property held by the taxpayer primarily for sale to customers in the ordinary course of the trade or business where the property is sold or exchanged outside the United States through the foreign person's

---

[312] Sections 871(b) and 882.

[313] Section 864(c).

[314] Section 864(c)(4).

[315] Section 864(c)(4)(B).

[316] Section 864(c)(5).

[317] Section 864(c)(4)(B)(i).

[318] Section 864(c)(4)(B)(ii).

[319] Section 864(c)(4)(D)(i).

U.S. office or other fixed place of business.[320] Such amounts are not treated as effectively connected if the property is sold or exchanged for use, consumption, or disposition outside the United States and an office or other fixed place of business of the taxpayer in a foreign country materially participated in the sale or exchange.

The Code provides sourcing rules for enumerated types of income, including interest, dividends, rents, royalties, and personal services income.[321] For example, interest income generally is sourced based on the residence of the obligor. Dividend income generally is sourced based on the residence of the corporation paying the dividend. Thus, interest paid on obligations of foreign persons and dividends paid by foreign corporations generally are treated as foreign-source income.

Other types of income are not specifically covered by the Code's sourcing rules. For example, fees for accepting or confirming letters of credit have been sourced under principles analogous to the interest sourcing rules.[322] In addition, under regulations, payments in lieu of dividends and interest derived from securities lending transactions are sourced in the same manner as interest and dividends, including for purposes of determining whether such income is effectively connected with a U.S. trade or business.[323] Moreover, income from notional principal contracts (such as interest rate swaps) generally is sourced based on the residence of the recipient of the income, but is treated as U.S.-source effectively connected income if it arises from the conduct of a United States trade or business.[324]

Reasons for Change

The Committee believes that present law creates arbitrary distinctions between economically similar transactions that are equally related to a U.S. trade of business. The Committee believes that the rules for determining whether foreign-source income (e.g., interest and dividends) is U.S.-effectively connected income should be the same as the rules for determining whether income that is economically equivalent to such foreign-source income is U.S.-effectively connected income.

Explanation of Provision

Each category of foreign-source income that is treated as effectively connected with a U.S. trade or business is expanded to include economic equivalents of such income (i.e., economic equivalents of certain foreign-source: (1) rents and royalties; (2) dividends and interest; and (3) income on sales or exchanges of goods in the ordinary course of business). Thus, such economic equivalents are treated as U.S.-effectively connected income in the same circumstances that foreign-source rents, royalties, dividends, interest, or certain inventory sales are treated as U.S.-effectively connected income. For example, foreign-source interest and dividend equivalents are treated as U.S.-effectively connected income if the income is attributable to a U.S. office of the foreign person, and such income is derived by such foreign person in the active conduct of a banking, financing, or similar business within the United States, or the foreign person is a corporation whose principal business is trading in stocks or securities for its own account.

Effective Date

The provision is effective for taxable years beginning after the date of enactment.

Conference Committee Report (H.R. CONF. REP. NO. 108-755)

House Bill

[Law at ¶ 5600. CCH Explanation at ¶ 575.]

No provision.

Conference Agreement

The conference agreement follows the Senate amendment.

---

[320] Section 864(c)(4)(B)(iii).
[321] Sections 861 through 865.
[322] See *Bank of America* v. *United States*, 680 F.2d 142 (Ct. Cl. 1982).

[323] Treas. Reg. sec. 1.864-5(b)(2)(ii).
[324] Treas. Reg. sec. 1.863-7(b)(3).

[¶ 11,670] Act Sec. 895. Recapture of overall foreign losses on sale of controlled foreign corporation stock

Senate Committee Report (S. Rep. No. 108-192)

[Code Sec. 904]

Present Law

U.S. persons may credit foreign taxes against U.S. tax on foreign-source income. The amount of foreign tax credits that may be claimed in a year is subject to a limitation that prevents taxpayers from using foreign tax credits to offset U.S. tax on U.S.-source income. The amount of foreign tax credits generally is limited to a portion of the taxpayer's U.S. tax which portion is calculated by multiplying the taxpayer's total U.S. tax by a fraction, the numerator of which is the taxpayer's foreign-source taxable income (i.e., foreign-source gross income less allocable expenses or deductions) and the denominator of which is the taxpayer's worldwide taxable income for the year.[325] Separate limitations are applied to specific categories of income.

Special recapture rules apply in the case of foreign losses for purposes of applying the foreign tax credit limitation.[326] Under these rules, losses for any taxable year in a limitation category which exceed the aggregate amount of foreign income earned in other limitation categories (a so-called "overall foreign loss") are recaptured by resourcing foreign-source income earned in a subsequent year as U.S.-source income.[327] The amount resourced as U.S.-source income generally is limited to the lesser of the amount of the overall foreign losses not previously recaptured, or 50 percent of the taxpayer's foreign-source income in a given year (the "50-percent limit"). Taxpayers may elect to recapture a larger percentage of such losses.

A special recapture rule applies to ensure the recapture of an overall foreign loss where property which was used in a trade or business predominantly outside the United States is disposed of prior to the time the loss has been recaptured.[328] In this regard, dispositions of trade or business property used predominantly outside the United States are treated as resulting in the recognition of foreign-source income (regardless of whether gain would otherwise be recognized upon disposition of the assets), in an amount equal to the lesser of the excess of the fair market value of such property over its ad-justed basis, or the amount of unrecaptured overall foreign losses. Such foreign-source income is resourced as U.S.-source income without regard to the 50-percent limit. For example, if a U.S. corporation transfers its foreign branch business assets to a foreign corporation in a nontaxable section 351 transaction, the taxpayer would be treated for purposes of the recapture rules as having recognized foreign-source income in the year of the transfer in an amount equal to the excess of the fair market value of the property disposed over its adjusted basis (or the amount of unrecaptured foreign losses, if smaller). Such income would be recaptured as U.S.-source income to the extent of any prior unrecaptured overall foreign losses.[329]

Detailed rules apply in allocating and apportioning deductions and losses for foreign tax credit limitation purposes. In the case of interest expense, such amounts generally are apportioned to all gross income under an asset method, under which the taxpayer's assets are characterized as producing income in statutory or residual groupings (i.e., foreign-source income in the various limitation categories or U.S.-source income).[330] Interest expense is apportioned among these groupings based on the relative asset values in each. Taxpayers may elect to value assets based on either tax book value or fair market value.

Each corporation that is a member of an affiliated group is required to apportion its interest expense using apportionment fractions determined by reference to all assets of the affiliated group. For this purpose, an affiliated group generally is defined to include only domestic corporations. Stock in a foreign subsidiary, however, is treated as a foreign asset that may attract the allocation of U.S. interest expense for these purposes. If tax basis is used to value assets, the adjusted basis of the stock of certain 10-percent or greater owned foreign corporations or other non-affiliated corporations must be increased by the amount of earnings and profits of such corporation accumulated during the period the U.S. shareholder held the stock, for purposes of the interest apportionment.

---

[325] Section 904(a).

[326] Section 904(f).

[327] Section 904(f)(1).

[328] Section 904(f)(3).

[329] Coordination rules apply in the case of losses recaptured under the branch loss recapture rules. Section 367(a)(3)(C).

[330] Section 864(e) and Temp. Treas. Reg. sec. 1.861-9T.

Reasons for Change

The Committee believes that dispositions of corporate stock should be subject to the special recapture rules for overall foreign losses. Ownership of stock in a foreign subsidiary can lead to, or increase, an overall foreign loss as a result of interest expenses allocated against foreign-source income under the interest expense allocation rules. The recapture of overall foreign losses created by such interest expense allocations may be avoided if, for example, the stock of the foreign subsidiary subsequently were transferred to unaffiliated parties in non-taxable transactions.

The Committee believes that overall foreign losses should be recaptured when stock of a controlled foreign corporation is disposed of regardless of whether such stock is disposed of a non-taxable transaction.

Explanation of Provision

* * *

Effective Date

The provision applies to dispositions after the date of enactment.

Conference Committee Report (H.R. CONF. REP. NO. 108-755)

House Bill

No provision.

Senate Amendment

Under the provision, the special recapture rule for overall foreign losses that currently applies to dispositions of foreign trade or business assets applies to the disposition of stock in a controlled foreign corporation controlled by the taxpayer. Thus, a disposition of controlled foreign corporation stock by a controlling shareholder results in the recognition of foreign-source income in an amount equal to the lesser of the fair market value of the stock over its adjusted basis, or the amount of prior unrecaptured overall foreign losses. Such income is resourced as U.S.-source income for foreign tax credit limitation purposes without regard to the 50-percent limit.

Although the provision generally extends to all dispositions of such stock, regardless of whether gain or loss is recognized on the transfer, exceptions are made for certain internal restructurings. Contributions to corporations or partnerships under sections 351 and 721, respectively, and certain stock and asset reorganizations do not trigger recapture of overall foreign

losses, provided that the transferor's underlying indirect interest in the disposed controlled foreign corporation does not change. However, any gain recognized in connection with a transaction meeting any of these exceptions, such as boot, triggers recapture of overall foreign losses to the extent of such gain.

Effective Date

The provision applies to dispositions after the date of enactment.

Conference Agreement

The conference agreement follows the Senate amendment with modifications. Under the provision as modified, a disposition of controlled foreign corporation stock in a transaction in which the taxpayer or a member of its consolidated group acquires the assets of the controlled foreign corporation in a liquidation under section 332 or a reorganization does not trigger the recapture of overall foreign losses. Any gain recognized in connection with a transaction meeting this exception triggers recapture of overall foreign losses to the extent of such gain.

[Law at ¶ 5655. CCH Explanation at ¶ 425.]

[¶ 11,680] Act Sec. 896. Recognition of cancellation of indebtedness income realized on satisfaction of debt with partnership interest

Senate Committee Report (S. REP. NO. 108-192)

[Code Sec. 108]

Present Law

Under present law, a corporation that transfers shares of its stock in satisfaction of its debt must recognize cancellation of indebtedness income in the amount that would be realized if the

debt were satisfied with money equal to the fair market value of the stock.[350] Prior to enactment of this present-law provision in 1993, case law provided that a corporation did not recognize cancellation of indebtedness income when it transferred stock to a creditor in satisfaction of

---

[350] Sec. 108(e)(8).

debt (referred to as the "stock-for-debt exception").[351]

When cancellation of indebtedness income is realized by a partnership, it generally is allocated among the partners in accordance with the partnership agreement, provided the allocations under the agreement have substantial economic effect. A partner who is allocated cancellation of indebtedness income is entitled to exclude it if the partner qualifies for one of the various exceptions to recognition of such income, including the exception for insolvent taxpayers or that for qualified real property indebtedness of taxpayers other than subchapter C corporations.[352] The availability of each of these exceptions is determined at the partner, rather than the partnership, level.

In the case of a partnership that transfers to a creditor a capital or profits interest in the partnership in satisfaction of its debt, no Code provision expressly requires the partnership to realize cancellation of indebtedness income. Thus, it is unclear whether the partnership is required to recognize cancellation of indebtedness income under either the case law that established the stock-for-debt exception or the present-law statutory repeal of the stock-for-debt exception. It also is unclear whether any requirement to recognize cancellation of indebtedness income is affected if the cancelled debt is nonrecourse indebtedness.[353]

Reasons for Change

The Committee believes that further guidance is necessary with regard to the application of the stock-for-debt exception in the context of transfers of partnership interests in satisfaction of partnership debt. In particular, the Committee believes that it is necessary to clarify that the present-law treatment of corporate indebtedness that is satisfied with transfers of stock of the debtor corporation also applies to partnership indebtedness that is satisfied with transfers of capital or profits interests in the debtor partnership.

Explanation of Provision

The provision provides that when a partnership transfers a capital or profits interest in the partnership to a creditor in satisfaction of partnership debt, the partnership generally recognizes cancellation of indebtedness income in the amount that would be recognized if the debt were satisfied with money equal to the fair market value of the partnership interest. The provision applies without regard to whether the cancelled debt is recourse or nonrecourse indebtedness. Any cancellation of indebtedness income recognized under the provision is allocated solely among the partners who held interests in the partnership immediately prior to the satisfaction of the debt.

Under the provision, no inference is intended as to the treatment under present law of the transfer of a partnership interest in satisfaction of partnership debt.

Effective Date

This provision is effective for cancellations of indebtedness occurring on or after the date of enactment.

Conference Committee Report (H.R. Conf. Rep. No. 108-755)

House Bill

[Law at ¶5120. CCH Explanation at ¶720.]

No provision.

Conference Agreement

The conference agreement includes the Senate amendment.

---

[351] E.g., *Motor Mart Trust* v. *Commissioner*, 4 T.C. 931 (1945), aff'd, 156 F.2d 122 (1st Cir. 1946), acq. 1947-1 C.B. 3; *Capento Sec. Corp.* v. *Commissioner*, 47 B.T.A. 691 (1942), nonacq. 1943 C.B. 28, aff'd, 140 F.2d 382 (1st Cir. 1944); *Tower Bldg. Corp.* v. *Commissioner*, 6 T.C. 125 (1946), acq. 1947-1 C.B. 4; *Alcazar Hotel, Inc.* v. *Commissioner*, 1 T.C. 872 (1943), acq. 1943 C.B. 1.

[352] Sec. 108(a).

[353] See, e.g., *Fulton Gold Corp.* v. *Commissioner*, 31 B.T.A. 519 (1934); *American Seating Co.* v. *Commissioner*, 14 B.T.A. 328, aff'd in part and rev'd in part, 50 F.2d 681 (7th Cir. 1931); *Hiatt* v. *Commissioner*, 35 B.T.A. 292 (1937); *Hotel Astoria, Inc.* v. *Commissioner*, 42 B.T.A. 759 (1940); Rev. Rul. 91-31, 1991-1 C.B. 19.

[¶ 11,690] Act Sec. 897. Denial of installment sale treatment for all readily tradable debt

Senate Committee Report (S. REP. NO. 108-192)

[Code Sec. 453]

Present Law

Under present law, taxpayers are permitted to recognize as gain on a disposition of property only that proportion of payments received in a taxable year which is the same as the proportion that the gross profit bears to the total contract price (the "installment method").[362] However, the installment method is not available if the taxpayer sells property in exchange for a readily tradable evidence of indebtedness that is issued by a corporation or a government or political subdivision.[363]

No similar provision under present law prohibits the use of the installment method where the taxpayer sells property in exchange for readily tradable indebtedness issued by a partnership or an individual.

Reasons for Change

The Committee believes that the present-law exception from the installment method for dispositions of property in exchange for readily tradable debt is too narrow in scope and, in general, should be extended to apply to all dispositions in exchange for readily tradable debt, regardless of the nature of the issuer of such debt.

Explanation of Provision

The provision denies installment sale treatment with respect to all sales in which the taxpayer receives indebtedness that is readily tradable under present-law rules, regardless of the nature of the issuer. For example, if the taxpayer receives readily tradable debt of a partnership in a sale, the partnership debt is treated as payment on the installment note, and the installment method is unavailable to the taxpayer.

Effective Date

The provision is effective for sales occurring on or after date of enactment.

Conference Committee Report (H.R. CONF. REP. NO. 108-755)

House Bill

No provision.

[Law at ¶ 5380. CCH Explanation at ¶ 710.]

Conference Agreement

The conference agreement includes the Senate amendment.

[¶ 11,700] Act Sec. 898. Modify treatment of transfers to creditors in divisive reorganizations

Senate Committee Report (S. REP. NO. 108-192)

[Code Secs. 357 and 361]

Present Law

Section 355 of the Code permits a corporation ("distributing") to separate its businesses by distributing a controlled subsidiary ("controlled") tax-free, if certain conditions are met. In cases where the distributing corporation contributes property to the controlled corporation that is to be distributed, no gain or loss is recognized if the property is contributed solely in exchange for stock or securities of the controlled corporation (which are subsequently distributed to distributing's shareholders). The contribution of property to a controlled corporation that is followed by a distribution of its stock and securities may qualify as a reorganization described in section 368(a)(1)(D). That section also applies to certain transactions that do not involve a distribution under section 355 and that are considered "acquisitive" rather than "divisive" reorganizations.

---

[362] Sec. 453.

[363] Sec. 453(f)(3). Instead, the receipt of such indebtedness is treated as a receipt of payment.

The contribution in the course of a divisive section 368(a)(1)(D) reorganization is also subject to the rules of section 357(c). That section provides that the transferor corporation will recognize gain if the amount of liabilities assumed by controlled exceeds the basis of the property transferred to it.

Because the contribution transaction in connection with a section 355 distribution is a reorganization under section 368(a)(1)(D), it is also subject to certain rules applicable to both divisive and acquisitive reorganizations. One such rule, in section 361(b), states that a transferor corporation will not recognize gain if it receives money or other property and distributes that money or other property to its shareholders or creditors. The amount of property that may be distributed to creditors without gain recognition is unlimited under this provision.

Reasons for Change

The Committee is concerned that taxpayers engaged in section 355 transactions can effectively avoid the rules that require gain recognition if the controlled corporation assumes liabilities of the transferor that exceed the basis of the assets transferred to such corporation. This could occur because of the rules of section 361(b), which state that the transferor can receive money or other property from the transferee without gain recognition, so long as the money or property is distributed to creditors of the transferor. For example, a transferor corporation could receive money from the transferee corporation (e.g., money obtained from a borrowing by the transferee) and use that money to pay the transferor's creditors, without gain recognition. Such a transaction is economically similar to the actual assumption by the transferee of the transferor's liabilities, but is taxed differently under

present law because section 361(b) does not contain a limitation on the amount that can be distributed to creditors.

The Committee also believes that it is appropriate to liberalize the treatment of acquisitive reorganizations that are included under section 368(a)(1)(D). The Committee believes that in these cases, the transferor should be permitted to assume liabilities of the transferee without application of the rules of section 357(c). This is because in an acquisitive reorganization under section 368(a)(1)(D), the transferor must generally transfer substantially all its assets to the acquiring corporation and then go out of existence. Assumption of its liabilities by the acquiring corporation thus does not enrich the transferor corporation, which ceases to exist and whose liability was limited to its assets in any event, by corporate form. The Committee believes that it is appropriate to conform the treatment of acquisitive reorganizations under section 368(a)(1)(D) to that of other acquisitive reorganizations.

Explanation of Provision

The bill limits the amount of money plus the fair market value of other property that a distributing corporation can distribute to its creditors without gain recognition under section 361(b) to the amount of the basis of the assets contributed to a controlled corporation in a divisive reorganization. In addition, the bill provides that acquisitive reorganizations under section 368(a)(1)(D) are no longer subject to the liabilities assumption rules of section 357(c).

Effective Date

The bill is effective for transactions on or after the date of enactment.

Conference Committee Report (H.R. CONF. REP. NO. 108-755)

House Bill

No provision.

[Law at ¶5325 and ¶5330. CCH Explanation at ¶1015.]

Conference Agreement

The conference agreement follows the Senate amendment.

[¶11,710] Act Sec. 899. Clarify definition of nonqualified preferred stock

Senate Committee Report (S. REP. NO. 108-192)

[Code Sec. 351(g)]

Present Law

The Taxpayer Relief Act of 1997 amended sections 351, 354, 355, 356, and 1036 to treat

"nonqualified preferred stock" as boot in corporate transactions, subject to certain exceptions. For this purpose, preferred stock is defined as stock that is "limited and preferred as to dividends and does not participate in corporate growth to any significant extent." Nonqualified preferred stock is defined as any preferred stock if (1) the holder has the right to require the issuer or a related person to redeem or purchase the stock, (2) the issuer or a related person is required to redeem or purchase, (3) the issuer or a related person has the right to redeem or repurchase, and, as of the issue date, it is more likely than not that such right will be exercised, or (4) the dividend rate varies in whole or in part (directly or indirectly) with reference to interest rates, commodity prices, or similar indices, regardless of whether such varying rate is provided as an express term of the stock (as in the case of an adjustable rate stock) or as a practical result of other aspects of the stock (as in the case of auction stock). For this purpose, clauses (1), (2), and (3) apply if the right or obligation may be exercised within 20 years of the issue date and is not subject to a contingency which, as of the issue date, makes remote the likelihood of the redemption or purchase.

Reasons for Change

The Committee is concerned that taxpayers may attempt to avoid characterization of an instrument as nonqualified preferred stock by including illusory participation rights or including terms that taxpayers argue create an "unlimited" dividend.

Clarification is desirable to conserve IRS resources that otherwise might have to be devoted to this area.

Explanation of Provision

The provision clarifies the definition of nonqualified preferred stock to ensure that stock for which there is not a real and meaningful likelihood of actually participating in the earnings and profits of the corporation is not considered to be outside the definition of stock that is limited and preferred as to dividends and does not participate in corporate growth to any significant extent.

As one example, instruments that are preferred on liquidation and that are entitled to the same dividends as may be declared on common stock do not escape being nonqualified preferred stock by reason of that right if the corporation does not in fact pay dividends either to its common or preferred stockholders. As another example, stock that entitles the holder to a dividend that is the greater of 7 percent or the dividends common shareholders receive does not avoid being preferred stock if the common shareholders are not expected to receive dividends greater than 7 percent.

No inference is intended as to the characterization of stock under present law that has terms providing for unlimited dividends or participation rights but, based on all the facts and circumstances, is limited and preferred as to dividends and does not participate in corporate growth to any significant extent.

Effective Date

The provision is effective for transactions after May 14, 2003.

Conference Committee Report (H.R. Conf. Rep. No. 108-755)

House Bill

No provision.

Conference Agreement

The conference agreement follows the Senate amendment.

[Law at ¶ 5320. CCH Explanation at ¶ 1005.]

[¶ 11,720] Act Sec. 900. Modify definition of controlled group of corporations

Senate Committee Report (S. Rep. No. 108-192)

[Code Sec. 1563]

Present Law

Under present law, a tax is imposed on the taxable income of corporations. The rates are as follows:

TABLE 2.—MARGINAL FEDERAL CORPORATE INCOME TAX RATES

If taxable income is:	Then the income tax rate is:
$0-$50,000	15 percent of taxable income.
$50,001-$75,000	25 percent of taxable income.
$75,001-$10,000,000	34 percent of taxable income.
Over $10,000,000	35 percent of taxable income.

The first two graduated rates described above are phased out by a five-percent surcharge for corporations with taxable income between $100,000 and $335,000. Also, the application of the 34-percent rate is phased out by a three-percent surcharge for corporations with taxable income between $15 million and $18,333,333.

The component members of a controlled group of corporations are limited to one amount in each of the taxable income brackets shown above.[364] For this purpose, a controlled group of corporations means a parent-subsidiary controlled group and a brother-sister controlled group.

A brother-sister controlled group means two or more corporations if five or fewer persons who are individuals, estates or trusts own (or constructively own) stock possessing (1) at least 80 percent of the total combined voting power of all classes of stock entitled to vote and at least 80 percent of the total value of all stock, and (2) more than 50 percent of percent of the total combined voting power of all classes of stock entitled to vote or more than 50 percent of the total value of all stock, taking into account the stock ownership of each person only to the extent the stock ownership is identical with respect to each corporation.

Reasons for Change

The Committee is concerned that taxpayers may be able to obtain benefits, such as multiple lower-bracket corporate tax rates, through the use of corporations that are effectively under common control even though the 80-percent test of present law is not satisfied. The Committee believes it is appropriate to eliminate the 80-percent test for purposes of the currently effective provisions under section 1561 (corporate tax brackets, the accumulated earnings credit, and the minimum tax.)

Explanation of Provision

Under the provision, a brother-sister controlled group means two or more corporations if five or fewer persons who are individuals, estates or trusts own (or constructively own) stock possessing more than 50 percent of the total combined voting power of all classes of stock entitled to vote, or more than 50 percent of the total value of all stock, taking into account the stock ownership of each person only to the extent the stock ownership is identical with respect to each corporation.

The provision applies only for purposes of section 1561, currently relating to corporate tax brackets, the accumulated earnings credit, and the minimum tax. The provision does not affect other Code sections or other provisions that utilize or refer to the section 1563 brother-sister corporation controlled group test for other purposes.[365]

Effective Date

The provision applies to taxable years beginning after the date of enactment.

Conference Committee Report (H.R. CONF. REP. NO. 108-755)

House Bill

No provision.

[Law at ¶5940. CCH Explanation at ¶1025.]

Conference Agreement

The conference agreement follows the Senate amendment.

---

[364] Component members are also limited to one alternative minimum tax exemption and one accumulated earnings credit.

[365] As one example, the provision does not change the present law standards relating to deferred compensation,

contained in subchapter D of the Code, that refer to section 1563.

[¶ 11,730] Act Sec. 901. Establish specific class lives for utility grading costs

Senate Committee Report (S. REP. NO. 108-192)

[Code Sec. 168]

Present Law

A taxpayer is allowed a depreciation deduction for the exhaustion, wear and tear, and obsolescence of property that is used in a trade or business or held for the production of income. For most tangible property placed in service after 1986, the amount of the depreciation deduction is determined under the modified accelerated cost recovery system (MACRS) using a statutorily prescribed depreciation method, recovery period, and placed in service convention. For some assets, the recovery period for the asset is provided in section 168. In other cases, the recovery period of an asset is determined by reference to its class life. The class lives of assets placed in service after 1986 are generally set forth in Revenue Procedure 87-56.[382] If no class life is provided, the asset is allowed a 7-year recovery period under MACRS.

Assets that are used in the transmission and distribution of electricity for sale are included in asset class 49.14, with a class life of 30 years and a MACRS recovery period of 20 years. Assets class 00.3 provides a class life of 20 years and a MACRS recovery period of 15 years for land improvements. The cost of initially clearing and grading land improvements are specifically excluded from asset classes 00.3 and 49.14. Prior to the adoption of the accelerated cost recovery system, the IRS ruled that an average useful life of 84 years for the initial clearing and grading relating to electric transmission lines and 46 years for the initial clearing and grading relating to electric distribution lines, would be accepted. However, the result in this ruling was not incorporated in the asset classes included in Rev. Proc. 87-56 or its predecessors. Accordingly such costs are depreciated over a 7-year recovery period under MACRS as section 1245 real property for which no class life is provided.

A similar situation exists with regard to gas utility trunk pipelines and related storage facilities. Such assets are included in asset class 49.24, with a class life of 22 years and a MACRS recovery period of 15 years. Initial clearing and grade improvements are specifically excluded from this asset class as well as asset class 00.3, and no separate asset class is provided for such costs. Accordingly, such costs are depreciated over a 7-year recovery period under MACRS as section 1245 real property for which no class life is provided.

Reasons for Change

The Committee believes the clearing and grading costs in question are incurred for the purpose of installing the transmission lines or pipelines and are properly seen as part of the cost of installing such lines or pipelines and their cost should be recovered in the same manner. The clearing and grading costs are not expected to have a useful life other than the useful life of the transmission line or pipeline to which they relate.

Explanation of Provision

The provision assigns a class life to depreciable electric and gas utility clearing and grading costs incurred to locate transmission and distribution lines and pipelines. The provision includes these assets in the asset classes of the property to which the clearing and grading costs relate (generally, asset class 49.14 for electric utilities and asset class 49.24 for gas utilities, giving these assets a recovery period of 20 years and 15 years, respectively).

Effective Date

The provision is effective for property placed in service after the date of enactment.

Conference Committee Report (H.R. CONF. REP. NO. 108-755)

House Bill

No provision.

Conference Agreement

The conference agreement follows the Senate amendment.

[Law at ¶ 5180. CCH Explanation at ¶ 335.]

---

[382] 1987-2 C.B. 674 (as clarified and modified by Rev. Proc. 88-22, 1988-1 C.B. 785).

[¶ 11,740] Act Sec. 902. Provide consistent amortization period for intangibles

Senate Committee Report (S. Rep. No. 108-192)

[Code Secs. 195, 248, and 709]

Present Law

At the election of the taxpayer, start-up expenditures[387] and organizational expenditures[388] may be amortized over a period of not less than 60 months, beginning with the month in which the trade or business begins. Start-up expenditures are amounts that would have been deductible as trade or business expenses, had they not been paid or incurred before business began. Organizational expenditures are expenditures that are incident to the creation of a corporation (sec. 248) or the organization of a partnership (sec. 709), are chargeable to capital, and that would be eligible for amortization had they been paid or incurred in connection with the organization of a corporation or partnership with a limited or ascertainable life.

Treasury regulations[389] require that a taxpayer file an election to amortize start-up expenditures no later than the due date for the taxable year in which the trade or business begins. The election must describe the trade or business, indicate the period of amortization (not less than 60 months), describe each start-up expenditure incurred, and indicate the month in which the trade or business began. Similar requirements apply to the election to amortize organizational expenditures. A revised statement may be filed to include start-up and organizational expenditures that were not included on the original statement, but a taxpayer may not include as a start-up expenditure any amount that was previously claimed as a deduction.

Section 197 requires most acquired intangible assets (such as goodwill, trademarks, franchises, and patents) that are held in connection with the conduct of a trade or business or an activity for the production of income to be amortized over 15 years beginning with the month in which the intangible was acquired.

Reasons for Change

The Committee believes that allowing a fixed amount of start-up and organizational expenditures to be deductible, rather than requiring their amortization, may help encourage the formation of new businesses that do not require significant start-up or organizational costs to be incurred. In addition, the Committee believes a consistent amortization period for intangibles is appropriate.

Explanation of Provision

The provision modifies the treatment of start-up and organizational expenditures. A taxpayer would be allowed to elect to deduct up to $5,000 of start-up and $5,000 of organizational expenditures in the taxable year in which the trade or business begins. However, each $5,000 amount is reduced (but not below zero) by the amount by which the cumulative cost of start-up or organizational expenditures exceeds $50,000, respectively. Start-up and organizational expenditures that are not deductible in the year in which the trade or business begins would be amortized over a 15-year period consistent with the amortization period for section 197 intangibles.

Effective Date

The provision is effective for start-up and organizational expenditures incurred after the date of enactment. Start-up and organizational expenditures that are incurred on or before the date of enactment would continue to be eligible to be amortized over a period not to exceed 60 months. However, all start-up and organizational expenditures related to a particular trade or business, whether incurred before or after the date of enactment, would be considered in determining whether the cumulative cost of start-up or organizational expenditures exceeds $50,000.

Conference Committee Report (H.R. Conf. Rep. No. 108-755)

House Bill

No provision.

Conference Agreement

The conference agreement follows the Senate amendment.

[Law at ¶ 5215, ¶ 5260 and ¶ 5510. CCH Explanation at ¶ 350.]

---

[387] Sec. 195
[388] Secs. 248 and 709.

[389] Treas. Reg. sec. 1.195-1.

[¶ 11,750] Act Sec. 903. Freeze of provision regarding suspension of interest where Secretary fails to contact taxpayer

Conference Committee Report (H.R. CONF. REP. NO. 108-755)

[Code Sec. 6404(g)]

Present Law

In general, interest and penalties accrue during periods for which taxes were unpaid without regard to whether the taxpayer was aware that there was tax due. The Code suspends the accrual of certain penalties and interest after 1 year after the filing of the tax return[935] if the IRS has not sent the taxpayer a notice specifically stating the taxpayer's liability and the basis for the liability within the specified period.[936] With respect to taxable years beginning before January 1, 2004, the one-year period is increased to 18 months. Interest and penalties resume 21 days after the IRS sends the required notice to the taxpayer. The provision is applied separately with respect to each item or adjustment. The provision does not apply where a taxpayer has self-assessed the tax. The suspension only applies to taxpayers who file a timely tax return. The provision applies only to individuals and does not apply to the failure to pay penalty, in the case of fraud, or with respect to criminal penalties.

House Bill

No provision.

Senate Amendment

The Senate amendment makes the 18-month rule the permanent rule. The Senate amendment also adds gross misstatements[937] and listed and reportable transactions to the list of provisions to which the suspension of interest rules do not apply.

Effective Date

The Senate amendment is effective for taxable years beginning after December 31, 2003,[938] except that the addition of listed and reportable transactions applies to interest accruing after May 5, 2004.

Conference Agreement

The conference agreement follows the Senate amendment, except: (1) the provision relating to reportable transactions is made applicable only to reportable avoidance transactions;[939] and (2) that the addition of listed and reportable avoidance transactions applies to interest accruing after October 3, 2004.

[Law at ¶ 6200. CCH Explanation at ¶ 1620.]

[¶ 11,760] Act Sec. 904. Increase in withholding from supplemental wage payments in excess of $1 million

Conference Committee Report (H.R. CONF. REP. NO. 108-755)

[Act Sec. 904]

Present Law

An employer must withhold income taxes from wages paid to employees; there are several possible methods for determining the amount of income tax to be withheld. The IRS publishes tables (Publication 15, "Circular E") to be used in determining the amount of income tax to be withheld. The tables generally reflect the income tax rates under the Code so that withholding approximates the ultimate tax liability with respect to the wage payments. In some cases, "supplemental" wage payments (e.g., bonuses or commissions) may be subject to withholding at a

---

[935] If the return is filed before the due date, for this purpose it is considered to have been filed on the due date.

[936] Sec. 6404(g). This provision was added to the Code by sec. 3305 of the IRS Restructuring and Reform Act of 1998 (Pub. L. No. 105-206, July 22,1998).

[937] This includes any substantial omission of items to which the six-year statute of limitations applies (sec. 6051(e)), gross valuation misstatements (sec. 6662(h)), and similar provisions.

[938] It is intended that this provision apply retroactively to the period beginning January 1, 2004 and ending on the date

of enactment. The due date for returns for the taxable period beginning January 1, 2004 is generally April 15, 2005; April 15, 2005 is therefore the date from which the 12-month period that must pass under present-law prior to the commencement of suspension is calculated. Consequently, suspension of interest would generally not begin until April 15, 2006. Accordingly, the provision has no actual retroactive effect.

[939] A reportable avoidance transaction is a reportable transaction with a significant tax avoidance purpose.

flat rate,[940] based on the third lowest income tax rate under the Code (25 percent for 2005).[941]

House Bill

No provision.

Senate Amendment

Under the Senate amendment, once annual supplemental wage payments to an employee exceed $1 million, any additional supplemental wage payments to the employee in that year are subject to withholding at the highest income tax rate (35 percent for 2004 and 2005), regardless of any other withholding rules and regardless of the employee's Form W-4.

This rule applies only for purposes of wage withholding; other types of withholding (such as pension withholding and backup withholding) are not affected.

Effective Date

The provision is effective with respect to payments made after December 31, 2003.

Conference Agreement

The conference agreement follows the Senate amendment except that the conference agreement is effective for payments made after December 31, 2004.

[Law at ¶7155. CCH Explanation at ¶1430.]

[¶ 11,770] Act Sec. 905. Capital gain treatment on sale of stock acquired from exercise of statutory stock options to comply with conflict of interest requirements

Conference Committee Report (H.R. CONF. REP. NO. 108-755)

[Code Sec. 421]

Present Law

Statutory stock options

Generally, when an employee exercises a compensatory option on employer stock, the difference between the option price and the fair market value of the stock (i.e., the "spread") is includible in income as compensation. Upon such exercise, an employer is allowed a corresponding compensation deduction. In the case of an incentive stock option or an option to purchase stock under an employee stock purchase plan (collectively referred to as "statutory stock options"), the spread is not included in income at the time of exercise.[942]

If an employee disposes of stock acquired upon the exercise of a statutory option, the employee generally is taxed at capital gains rates with respect to the excess of the fair market value of the stock on the date of disposition over the option price, and no compensation expense deduction is allowable to the employer, unless the employee fails to meet a holding period requirement. The employee fails to meet this holding period requirement if the disposition occurs within two years after the date the option is granted or one year after the date the option is exercised. The gain upon a disposition that occurs prior to the expiration of the applicable holding period(s) (a "disqualifying disposition") does not qualify for capital gains treatment. In

the event of a disqualifying disposition, the income attributable to the disposition is treated by the employee as income received in the taxable year in which the disposition occurs, and a corresponding deduction is allowable to the employer for the taxable year in which the disposition occurs.

Sale of property to comply with conflict of interest requirements

The Code provides special rules for recognizing gain on sales of property which are required in order to comply with certain conflict of interest requirements imposed by the Federal Government.[943] Certain executive branch Federal employees (and their spouses and minor or dependent children) who are required to divest property in order to comply with conflict of interest requirements may elect to postpone recognition of resulting gains by investing in certain replacement property within a 60-day period. The basis of the replacement property is reduced by the amount of the gain not recognized. Permitted replacement property is limited to any obligation of the United States or any diversified investment fund approved by regulations issued by the Office of Government Ethics. The rule applies only to sales under certificates of divestiture issued by the President or the Director of the Office of Government Ethics.

House Bill

No provision.

---

[940] Sec. 13273 of the Revenue Reconciliation Act of 1993.

[941] Sec. 101(c)(11) of the Economic Growth and Tax Relief Reconciliation Act of 2001.

[942] Sec. 421.

[943] Sec. 1043.

Senate Amendment

Under the Senate amendment, an eligible person who, in order to comply with Federal conflict of interest requirements, is required to sell shares of stock acquired pursuant to the exercise of a statutory stock option is treated as satisfying the statutory holding period requirements, regardless of how long the stock was actually held. An eligible person generally includes an officer or employee of the executive branch of the Federal Government (and any spouse or minor or dependent children whose ownership in property is attributable to the officer or employee). Because the sale is not treated as a disqualifying disposition, the individual is afforded capital gain treatment on any resulting gains. Such gains are eligible for deferral treatment under section 1043.

The employer granting the option is not allowed a deduction upon the sale of the stock by the individual.

Effective Date

The Senate amendment is effective for sales after the date of enactment.

Conference Agreement

The conference agreement follows the Senate amendment.

[Law at ¶ 5360. CCH Explanation at ¶ 1415.]

[¶ 11,780] Act Sec. 906. Application of basis rules to nonresident aliens

Conference Committee Report (H.R. CONF. REP. NO. 108-755)

[Code Secs. 72 and 83]

Present Law

Distributions from retirement plans

Distributions from retirement plans are includible in gross income under the rules relating to annuities[944] and, thus, are generally includible in income, except to the extent the amount received represents investment in the contract (i.e., the participant's basis). The participant's basis includes amounts contributed by the participant on an after-tax basis, together with certain amounts contributed by the employer, minus the aggregate amount (if any) previously distributed to the extent that such amount was excludable from gross income. Amounts contributed by the employer are included in the calculation of the participant's basis only to the extent that such amounts were includible in the gross income of the participant, or to the extent that such amounts would have been excludable from the participant's gross income if they had been paid directly to the participant at the time they were contributed.[945]

Employer contributions to retirement plans and other payments for labor or personal services performed outside the United States by a nonresident alien generally are not treated as U.S. source income. Such contributions, therefore, generally would not be includible in the nonresident alien's gross income if they had been paid directly to the nonresident alien at the time they were contributed. Consequently, the amounts of such contributions generally are includible in the employee's basis and are not taxed by the United States if a distribution is made when the employee is a U.S. citizen or resident.[946]

Earnings on contributions are not included in basis unless previously includible in income. In general, in the case of a nonexempt trust, earnings are includible in income when distributed or made available.[947] In the case of highly compensated employees, the amount of the vested accrued benefit under the trust (other than the employee's investment in the contract) is generally required to be included in income annually (to the extent not previously includible). That is, earnings, as well as contributions, that are part of the vested accrued benefit are currently includible in income.[948]

Property transferred in connection with the performance of services

The Code contains rules governing the amount and timing of income and deductions attributable to transfers of property in connection with the performance of services. If, in connection with the performance of services, property is transferred to any person other than the person for whom such services are performed, in general, an amount is includible in the gross income of the person performing the services (the "service provider") for the taxable year in which the property is first vested (i.e., transferable or not subject to a substantial risk of forfeiture).[949] The amount includible in the service provider's income is the excess of the fair market value of the property over the amount (if any) paid for the property. Basis in such prop-

---

[944] Secs. 72 and 402.
[945] Sec. 72(f).
[946] Rev. Rul. 58-236, 1958-1 C.B. 37.

[947] Sec. 402(b)(2).
[948] Sec. 402(b)(4).
[949] Sec. 83(a).

erty includes any amount that is included in income as a result of the transfer.[950]

U.S. income tax treaties

Under the 1996 U.S. Model Income Tax Treaty ("U.S. Model") and some U.S. income tax treaties in force, retirement plan distributions beneficially owned by a resident of a treaty country in consideration for past employment generally are taxable only by the individual recipient's country of residence. Under the U.S. Model treaty and some U.S. income tax treaties, this exclusive residence-based taxation rule is limited to the taxation of amounts that were not previously included in taxable income in the other country. For example, if a treaty country had imposed tax on a resident individual with respect to some portion of a retirement plan's earnings, subsequent distributions to that person while a resident of the United States would not be taxable in the United States to the extent the distributions were attributable to such previously taxed amounts.

Compensation of employees of foreign governments or international organizations

Under section 893, wages, fees, and salaries of any employee of a foreign government or international organization (including a consular or other officer or a nondiplomatic representative) received as compensation for official services to the foreign government or international organization generally are excluded from gross income when (1) the employee is not a citizen of the United States, or is a citizen of the Republic of the Philippines (whether or not a citizen of the United States); (2) in the case of an employee of a foreign government, the services are of a character similar to those performed by employees of the United States in foreign countries; and (3) in the case of an employee of a foreign government, the foreign government grants an equivalent exemption to employees of the United States performing similar services in such foreign country. The Secretary of State certifies the names of the foreign countries which grant an equivalent exclusion to employees of the United States performing services in those countries, and the character of those services.

The exclusion does not apply to employees of controlled commercial entities or employees of foreign governments whose services are primarily in connection with commercial activity (whether within or outside the United States) of the foreign government.

House Bill

No provision.

Senate Amendment

The Senate amendment modifies the present-law rules under which certain contributions and earnings that have not been previously taxed are treated as basis (under sec. 72). Under the Senate amendment, employee or employer contributions are not included in basis if: (1) the employee was a nonresident alien at the time the services were performed with respect to which the contribution was made; (2) the contribution is with respect to compensation for labor or personal services from sources without the United States; and (3) the contribution was not subject to income tax under the laws of the United States or any foreign country.

The Senate amendment authorizes the Secretary of the Treasury to issue regulations to carry out the purposes of the Senate amendment, including regulations treating contributions as not subject to income tax under the laws of any foreign country under appropriate circumstances.

Conference Agreement

The conference agreement follows the Senate amendment with modifications.

Under the conference agreement, employee or employer contributions are not included in basis (under sec. 72) if: (1) the employee was a nonresident alien at the time the services were performed with respect to which the contribution was made; (2) the contribution is with respect to compensation for labor or personal services from sources without the United States; and (3) the contribution was not subject to income tax (and would have been subject to income tax if paid as cash compensation when the services were rendered) under the laws of the United States or any foreign country.

Additionally, earnings on employer or employee contributions are not included in basis if: (1) the earnings are paid or accrued with respect to any employer or employee contributions which were made with respect to compensation for labor or personal services; (2) the employee was a nonresident alien at the time the earnings were paid or accrued; and (3) the earnings were not subject to income tax under the laws of the United States or any foreign country.

The conference agreement does not change the rules applicable to calculation of basis with respect to contributions or earnings while an employee is a U.S. resident.

There is no inference that this conference agreement applies in any case to create tax jurisdiction with respect to wages, fees, and salaries otherwise exempt under section 893. Similarly,

---

[950] Treas. Reg. sec. 1.61-2(d)(i).

there is no inference that the conference agreement applies where contrary to an agreement of the United States that has been validly authorized by Congress (or in the case of a treaty, ratified by the Senate), and which provides an exemption for income.

Most U.S. tax treaties specifically address the taxation of pension distributions. The U.S. Model treaty provides for exclusive residence-based taxation of pension distributions to the extent such distributions were not previously included in taxable income in the other country. For purposes of the U.S. Model treaty, the United States treats any amount that has increased the recipient's basis (as defined in section 72) as having been previously included in taxable income. The following example illustrates how the conference agreement could affect the amount of a distribution that may be taxed by the United States pursuant to a tax treaty.

Assume the following facts. A, a nonresident alien individual, performs services outside the United States, in A's country of residence, country Z. A's employer makes contributions on behalf of A to a pension plan established in country Z. For U.S. tax purposes, no portion of the contributions or earnings are included in A's income (and would not be included in income if the amounts were paid as cash compensation when the services were performed) because such amounts relate to services performed without the United States.[951] Later in time, A retires and becomes a permanent resident of the United States.

Under the conference agreement, the employer contributions to the pension plan would not be taken into account in determining A's basis if A was not subject to income tax on the contributions by a foreign country and the contributions would have been subject to tax by a foreign country if the contributions had been paid to A as cash compensation when the services were performed. Thus, in those circumstances, A would be subject to U.S. tax on the distribution of all of the contributions, as such distributions are made. However, if the contributions would not have been subject to tax in the foreign country if they had been paid to A as cash compensation when the services were performed, under the conference agreement, the contributions would be included in A's basis. Earnings that accrued while A was a nonresident alien would not result in basis if not taxed under U.S. or foreign law. Earnings that accrued while A was a permanent resident of the United States would be subject to present-law rules. This result generally is consistent with the treatment of pension distributions under the U.S. Model treaty.

The conference agreement authorizes the Secretary of the Treasury to issue regulations to carry out the purposes of the conference agreement, including regulations treating contributions as not subject to income tax under the laws of any foreign country under appropriate circumstances. For example, Treasury could provide that foreign income tax that was merely nominal would not satisfy the "subject to income tax" requirement.

The conference agreement also changes the rules for determining basis in property received in connection for the performance of services in the case of an individual who was a nonresident alien at the time of the performance of services, if the property is treated as income from sources outside the United States. In that case, the individual's basis in the property does not include any amount that was not subject to income tax (and would have been subject to income tax if paid as cash compensation when the services were performed) under the laws of the United States or any foreign country.

Effective Date

The conference agreement is effective for distributions occurring on or after the date of enactment. No inference is intended that the earnings subject to the conference agreement are included in basis under present law.

[Law at ¶ 5100 and ¶ 5105. CCH Explanation at ¶ 1425.]

[¶ 11,790] Act Sec. 907. Deduction for personal use of company aircraft and other entertainment expenses

Conference Committee Report (H.R. Conf. Rep. No. 108-755)

[Code Sec. 274]

Present Law

Under present law, no deduction is allowed with respect to (1) an activity generally considered to be entertainment, amusement or recreation, unless the taxpayer establishes that the item was directly related to (or, in certain cases, associated with) the active conduct of the taxpayer's trade or business, or (2) a facility (e.g., an airplane) used in connection with such activity.[957] The Code includes a number of exceptions to the

---

[951] Sec. 872.

[957] Sec. 274(a).

general rule disallowing deductions of entertainment expenses. Under one exception, the deduction disallowance rule does not apply to expenses for goods, services, and facilities to the extent that the expenses are reported by the taxpayer as compensation and wages to an employee.[958] The deduction disallowance rule also does not apply to expenses paid or incurred by the taxpayer for goods, services, and facilities to the extent that the expenses are includible in the gross income of a recipient who is not an employee (e.g., a nonemployee director) as compensation for services rendered or as a prize or award.[959] The exceptions apply only to the extent that amounts are properly reported by the company as compensation and wages or otherwise includible in income. In no event can the amount of the deduction exceed the amount of the actual cost, even if a greater amount is includible in income.

Except as otherwise provided, gross income includes compensation for services, including fees, commissions, fringe benefits, and similar items. In general, an employee or other service provider must include in gross income the amount by which the fair value of a fringe benefit exceeds the amount paid by the individual. Treasury regulations provide rules regarding the valuation of fringe benefits, including flights on an employer-provided aircraft.[960] In general, the value of a non-commercial flight is determined under the base aircraft valuation formula, also known as the Standard Industry Fare Level formula or "SIFL".[961] If the SIFL valuation rules do not apply, the value of a flight on a company-provided aircraft is generally equal to the amount that an individual would have to pay in an arm's-length transaction to charter the same or a comparable aircraft for that period for the same or a comparable flight.[962]

In the context of an employer providing an aircraft to employees for nonbusiness (e.g., vacation) flights, the exception for expenses treated as compensation has been interpreted as not limiting the company's deduction for operation of the aircraft to the amount of compensation reportable to its employees,[963] which can result in a deduction multiple times larger than the amount required to be included in income. In many cases, the individual including amounts attributable to personal travel in income directly benefits from the enhanced deduction, resulting in a net deduction for the personal use of the company aircraft.

House Bill

No provision.

Senate Amendment

Under the Senate amendment, in the case of covered employees, the exceptions to the general entertainment expense disallowance rule for expenses treated as compensation or includible in income apply only to the extent of the amount of expenses treated as compensation or includible in income. Covered employees are defined as under section 162(m)(3) and include the chief executive officer (or individual acting in such capacity) and the four highest-compensated officers of publicly-traded corporations. No deduction is allowed with respect to expenses for (1) a nonbusiness activity generally considered to be entertainment, amusement or recreation, or (2) a facility (e.g., an airplane) used in connection with such activity to the extent that such expenses exceed the amount treated as compensation or includible in income to the covered employee. For example, a company's deduction attributable to aircraft operating costs for a covered employee's vacation use of a company aircraft is limited to the amount reported as compensation to the employee. As under present law, the amount of the deduction cannot exceed the actual cost.

The provision is intended to overturn *Sutherland Lumber-Southwest, Inc. v. Commissioner* with respect to covered employees. As under present law, the exceptions apply only if amounts are properly reported by the company as compensation and wages or otherwise includible in income.

Conference Agreement

The conference agreement follows the Senate amendment except that the provision applies with respect to individuals who, with respect to an employer or other service recipient, are subject to the requirements of section 16(a) of the Securities and Exchange Act of 1934, or would be subject to such requirements if the employer or service recipient were an issuer of equity securities referred to in section 16(a). Such individuals generally include officers (as defined by section 16(a)),[964] directors, and 10-percent-or-

---

[958] Sec. 274(e)(2).

[959] Sec. 274(e)(9).

[960] Treas. Reg. sec. 1.61-21.

[961] Treas. Reg. sec. 1.61-21(g).

[962] Treas. Reg. sec. 1.61-21(b)(6).

[963] *Sutherland Lumber-Southwest, Inc. v. Comm.*, 114 T.C. 197 (2000), *aff'd*, 255 F.3d 495 (8th Cir. 2001), *acq.*, AOD 2002-02 (Feb. 11, 2002).

[964] An officer is defined as the president, principal financial officer, principal accounting officer (or, if there is no such accounting officer, the controller), any vice-president in charge of a principal business unit, division or function (such as sales, administration or finance), any other officer who performs a policy-making function, or any other person who performs similar policy-making functions.

greater owners of private and publicly-held companies.

Effective Date

The conference agreement is effective for amounts deferred after the date of enactment.

[¶ 11,800] Act Sec. 908. Residence and source rules related to a United States possession

Conference Committee Report (H.R. CONF. REP. NO. 108-755)

[Law at ¶ 5280. CCH Explanation at ¶ 360.]

[New Code Sec. 937]

Present Law

In general

Generally, U.S. citizens are subject to U.S. income taxation on their worldwide income. Thus, all income earned by U.S. citizens is subject to U.S. income tax, regardless of its source.

The U.S. income taxation of alien individuals varies depending on whether they are resident or non-resident aliens. A resident alien is generally taxed in the same manner as a U.S. citizen.[952] In contrast, a nonresident alien is generally subject to U.S. tax only on certain gross U.S. source income at a flat 30 percent rate (unless such rate is eliminated or reduced by treaty) and on net income that has a sufficient nexus to the United States at the graduated rates applicable to U.S. citizens and residents under section 1.

An alien is considered a resident of the United States if the individual: (1) has entered the United States as a lawful permanent resident and is such a resident at any time during the calendar year, (2) is present in the United States for a substantial period of time (the so-called "substantial presence test"), or (3) makes an election to be treated as a resident of the United States (sec. 7701(b)). An alien who does not meet the definition of a "resident alien" is considered to be a non-resident alien for U.S. income tax purposes.

Under the substantial presence test, an alien individual is generally treated as a resident alien if he or she is present in the United States for 31 days during the taxable year and the sum of the number of days on which such individual was present in the United States (when multiplied by the applicable multiplier) during the current year and the preceding two calendar years equals or exceeds 183 days. The applicable multiplier for: the current year is one; the first preceding year is one-third; and the second preceding year is one-sixth.

An alien individual who meets the above test may nevertheless be a nonresident if he or she (1) is present in the United States for fewer than 183 days during the current year; (2) has a tax home in a foreign country during the year; and (3) has a closer connection to that country than to the United States.

For purposes of the substantial presence test, the United States includes the states and the District of Columbia, but does not include U.S. possessions. An individual is present in the United States for a particular day if he or she is physically present in the United States during any time during such day. However, in certain circumstances an individual's presence in the United States is ignored, including presence in the United States as a result of certain medical emergencies.

U.S. income taxation of residents of U.S. possessions

Generally, special U.S. income tax rules apply with respect to U.S. persons who are bona fide residents of certain U.S. possessions (i.e., Puerto Rico, Virgins Islands, Guam, Northern Mariana Islands and American Samoa) and who have possession source income or income effectively connected to the conduct of a trade or business within a possession.

Generally, a bona fide resident of a U.S. possession (regardless of whether the individual is a U.S. citizen or alien) is determined using the principles of a subjective, facts-and-circumstances test set forth in the regulations under section 871. Prior to the adoption of present-law section 7701(b), this subjective test was used to determine whether an alien individual was a resident of the United States. Under these rules, an individual is generally a resident of the United States if an individual (1) is actually present in the United States, and (2) is not a mere transient or sojourner.[953] Whether individuals are transients is determined by their intentions with regard to the length and nature of their

---

[952] Section 7701(a)(30) defines a citizen or resident of the United States as "U.S. persons."

[953] Treas. Reg. sec. 1.871-2(b).

stay. However, the regulations provide that section 7701(b) (discussed above) provides the basis for determining whether an alien individual is a resident of a U.S. possession with a mirror income tax code.[954]

Pursuant to regulations, the principles that generally apply for determining income from sources within and without the United States also generally apply in determining income from sources within and without a U.S. possession.[955] The Code and regulations do not indicate how to determine whether income is effectively connected with the conduct of a trade or business within a U.S. possession. However, section 864(c) provides rules for determining whether income is effectively connected to a trade or business conducted within the United States.

Information reporting

Section 7654(e) provides that Treasury may require information reporting with respect to individuals that may take advantage of certain special U.S. income tax rules with respect to U.S. possessions. Section 6688 provides that an individual may be subject to a $100 penalty if the individual fails to furnish the information required by regulations issued pursuant to section 7654(e).

House Bill

No provision.

Senate Amendment

The provision provides the term "bona fide resident" means a person who satisfies a test, determined by the Secretary, similar to the substantial presence test of section 7701(b)(3) with respect to Guam, American Samoa, the Northern Mariana Islands, Puerto Rico, or the Virgin Islands.

The provision also requires bona fide residents of the Virgin Islands to file an informational income tax return with the United States and imposes a penalty for the failure to file such a return.

Conference Agreement

The conference agreement follows the Senate amendment with modifications.

The conferees understand that certain U.S. citizens and residents are claiming that they are exempt from U.S. income tax on their worldwide income based on a position that they are bona fide residents of the Virgin Islands or another possession. However, these individuals often do not spend a significant amount of time in the

particular possession during a taxable year and, in some cases, continue to live and work in the United States. Under the Virgin Island's Economic Development Program, many of these same individuals secure a reduction of up to 90 percent of their Virgin Islands income tax liability on income they take the position is Virgin Islands source or effectively connected with the conduct of a Virgin Islands trade or business. The conferees are also aware that taxpayers are taking the position that income earned for services performed in the United States is Virgin Islands source or that their U.S. activities generate income effectively connected with the conduct of a Virgin Islands trade or business.

The conferees believe that the various exemptions from U.S. tax provided to residents of possessions should not be available to individuals who continue to live and work in the United States. The conferees also believe that the special U.S. income tax rules applicable to residents in a possession need to be rationalized. The conferees are further concerned that the general rules for determining whether income is effectively connected with the conduct of a trade or business in a possession present numerous opportunities for erosion of the U.S. tax base.

Generally, the provision provides that the term "bona fide resident" means a person who meets a two-part test with respect to Guam, American Samoa, the Northern Mariana Islands, Puerto Rico, or the Virgin Islands, as the case may be, for the taxable year. First, an individual must be present in the possession for at least 183 days in the taxable year. Second, an individual must (i) not have a tax home outside such possession during the taxable year and (ii) not have a closer connection to the United States or a foreign country during such year.

The provision also grants authority to Treasury to create exceptions to these general rules as appropriate. The conferees intend for such exceptions to cover, in particular, persons whose presence outside a possession for extended periods of time lacks a tax avoidance purpose, such as military personnel, workers in the fisheries trade, and retirees who travel outside the possession for certain personal reasons.

An individual is present in a possession for a particular day if he is physically present in such possession during any time during such day. In certain circumstances an individual's presence outside a possession is ignored (e.g., certain medical emergencies) as provided under the principles of section 7701(b).

---

[954] A U.S. possession with a mirror income tax code is "a United States possession . . . that administers income tax laws that are identical (except for the substitution of the name of the possession or territory for the term 'United

States' where appropriate) to those in the United States." Treas. Reg. sec. 7701(b)-1(d)(1).
[955] Treas. Reg. sec. 1.863-6.

The provision provides that a taxpayer must file a notice in the first taxable year they claim bona fide residence in a possession. The provision imposes a penalty of $1000 for the failure to file such notice or to comply with any filing required by regulation under section 7654(e).

The provision generally codifies the existing rules for determining when income is considered to be from sources within a possession by providing that, as a general rule, for all purposes of the Code, the principles for determining whether income is U.S. source are applicable for purposes of determining whether income is possession source. In addition, the provision provides that the principles for determining whether income is effectively connected with the conduct of a U.S. trade or business are applicable for purposes of determining whether income is effectively connected to the conduct of a possession trade or business. However, the provision further provides that except as provided in regulations any income treated as U.S. source income or as effectively connected with the conduct of a U.S. trade or business is not treated as income from within any possession or as effectively connected with a trade or business within any such possession.

The provision also grants authority to the Secretary of the Treasury to create exceptions to these general rules regarding possession source income and income effectively connected with a possession trade or business as appropriate. The conferees anticipate that this authority will be used to continue the existing treatment of income from the sale of goods manufactured in a possession. The conferees also intend for this authority to be used to prevent abuse, for example, to prevent U.S. persons from avoiding U.S. tax on appreciated property by acquiring residence in a possession prior to its disposition.

No inference is intended as to the present-law rules for determining (1) bona fide residence in a possession, (2) whether income is possession source, and (3) whether income is effectively connected with the conduct of a trade or business within a possession.

Effective Date

Generally, the provision is effective for taxable years ending after the date of enactment. The first prong of the two-part residency test (i.e., the 183-day test) is effective for taxable years beginning after date of enactment. The general effective date applies with respect to the second prong of such test. The rule providing that income treated as U.S. source income or as effectively connected with the conduct of a U.S. trade or business is not treated as income from within any possession or as effectively connected with the conduct of a trade or business within any such possession is effective for income earned after date of enactment.

[**Law at ¶ 5665, ¶ 5670, ¶ 5675, ¶ 5680, ¶ 5690, ¶ 5730 and ¶ 6255. CCH Explanation at ¶ 580.**]

[¶ 11,810] Act Sec. 909. Dispositions of transmission property to implement Federal Energy Regulatory Commission restructuring policy (no reinvestment obligation)

Conference Committee Report (H.R. Conf. Rep. No. 108-755)

[Code Sec. 451]

Present Law

Generally, a taxpayer recognizes gain to the extent the sales price (and any other consideration received) exceeds the seller's basis in the property. The recognized gain is subject to current income tax unless the gain is deferred or not recognized under a special tax provision.

House Bill

No provision.

Senate Amendment

The Senate amendment permits a taxpayer to elect to recognize gain from a qualifying electric transmission transaction ratably over an eight-year period beginning in the year of sale.

A qualifying electric transmission transaction is the sale or other disposition of property used by the taxpayer in the trade or business of providing electric transmission services, or any stock or partnership interest in a corporation or partnership whose principal trade or business consists of providing electrical services. In order to qualify, the transaction must occur before January 1, 2008 and the sale or disposition must be to an independent transmission company.

In general, an independent transmission company is defined as: (1) a regional transmission organization approved by the Federal Entergy [sic—CCH.]Regulatory Commission ("FERC"); (2) a person (i) who the FERC determines under section 203 of the Federal Power Act (or by declaratory order) is not a "market participant" and (ii) whose transmission facilities are placed under the operational control of a FERC-approved independent transmission provider before the close of the period specified in such authorization, but not later than January 1,

2008; or (3) in the case of facilities subject to the jurisdiction of the Public Utility Commission of Texas, a person which is approved by that Commission as consistent with Texas State law regarding an independent transmission organization.

An electing taxpayer is required to attach a statement to that effect in the tax return for the taxable year in which the transaction takes place in such manner as the Secretary shall prescribe. The election shall be binding for that taxable year and all subsequent taxable years. Finally, the provision provides that the installment sale rules shall not apply to any qualifying electric transmission transaction for which a taxpayer elects the application of this provision.

Conference Agreement

The conference agreement follows the Senate amendment with the following modifications. The provision permits taxpayers to elect to recognize gain from qualifying electric transmission transactions ratably over an eight-year period beginning in the year of sale if the amount realized from such sale is used to purchase exempt utility property within the applicable period[422] (the "reinvestment property"). If the amount realized exceeds the amount used to purchase reinvestment property, any realized gain shall be recognized to the extent of such excess in the year of the qualifying electric transmission transaction. Any remaining realized gain is recognized ratably over the eight-year period.

A qualifying electric transmission transaction is the sale or other disposition of property used by the taxpayer in the trade or business of providing electric transmission services, or an ownership interest in such an entity, to an independent transmission company prior to January 1, 2007. In general, an independent transmission company is defined as: (1) an independent transmission provider[423] approved by the FERC; (2) a person (i) who the FERC determines under section 203 of the Federal Power Act (or by declaratory order) is not a "market participant" and (ii) whose transmission facilities are placed under the operational control of a FERC-approved independent transmission provider before the

close of the period specified in such authorization, but not later than January 1, 2007; or (3) in the case of facilities subject to the jurisdiction of the Public Utility Commission of Texas, (i) a person which is approved by that Commission as consistent with Texas State law regarding an independent transmission organization, or (ii) a political subdivision, or affiliate thereof, whose transmission facilities are under the operational control of an organization described in (i).

Exempt utility property is defined as: (1) property used in the trade or business of generating, transmitting, distributing, or selling electricity or producing, transmitting, distributing, or selling natural gas, or (2) stock in a controlled corporation whose principal trade or business consists of the activities described in (1).

If a taxpayer is a member of an affiliated group of corporations filing a consolidated return, the proposal permits the reinvestment property to be purchased by any member of the affiliated group (in lieu of the taxpayer).

If a taxpayer elects the application of the provision, then the statutory period for the assessment of any deficiency, for any taxable year in which any part of the gain eligible for the provision is realized, attributable to such gain shall not expire prior to the expiration of three years from the date the Secretary of the Treasury is notified by the taxpayer of the reinvestment property or an intention not to reinvest.

An electing taxpayer is required to attach a statement to that effect in the tax return for the taxable year in which the transaction takes place in the manner as the Secretary shall prescribe. The election shall be binding for that taxable year and all subsequent taxable years.[424] In addition, an electing taxpayer is required to attach a statement that identifies the reinvestment property in the manner as the Secretary shall prescribe.

Effective Date

The provision is effective for transactions occurring after the date of enactment, in taxable years ending after such date.

[Law at ¶ 5375. CCH Explanation at ¶ 890.]

---

[422] The applicable period for a taxpayer to reinvest the proceeds is four years after the close of the taxable year in which the qualifying electric transmission transaction occurs.

[423] For example, a regional transmission organization, an independent system operator, or and independent transmission company.

[424] The provision also provides that the installment sale rules shall not apply to any qualifying electric transmission transaction for which a taxpayer elects the application of this provision.

[¶ 11,820] Act Sec. 910. Expansion of limitation on expensing of certain passenger automobiles

Senate Committee Report (S. REP. NO. 108-192)

[Code Sec. 179]

Present Law

A taxpayer is allowed to recover, through annual depreciation deductions, the cost of certain property used in a trade or business or for the production of income. The amount of the depreciation deduction allowed with respect to tangible property for a taxable year is determined under the modified accelerated cost recovery system ("MACRS"). Under MACRS, passenger automobiles generally are recovered over five years. However, section 280F limits the annual depreciation deduction with respect to certain passenger automobiles.[383]

For purposes of the depreciation limitation, passenger automobiles are defined broadly to include any 4-wheeled vehicles that are manufactured primarily for use on public streets, roads, and highways and which are rated at 6,000 pounds unloaded gross vehicle weight or less.[384] In the case of a truck or a van, the depreciation limitation applies to vehicles that are rated at 6,000 pounds gross vehicle weight or less. Sports utility vehicles are treated as a truck for the purpose of applying the section 280F limitation.

In lieu of depreciation, a taxpayer with a sufficiently small amount of annual investment may elect to expense such investment (sec. 179). The Jobs and Growth Tax Relief Reconciliation Act (JGTRRA) of 2003[385] increased the amount a taxpayer may deduct, for taxable years beginning in 2003 through 2005, to $100,000 of the cost of qualifying property placed in service for the taxable year.[386] In general, qualifying property is defined as depreciable tangible personal property that is purchased for use in the active conduct of a trade or business. The $100,000 amount is reduced (but not below zero) by the amount by which the cost of qualifying property placed in service during the taxable year exceeds

$400,000. Prior to the enactment of JGTRRA (and for taxable years beginning in 2006 and thereafter) a taxpayer with a sufficiently small amount of annual investment may elect to deduct up to $25,000 of the cost of qualifying property placed in service for the taxable year. The $25,000 amount is reduced (but not below zero) by the amount by which the cost of qualifying property placed in service during the taxable year exceeds $200,000. Passenger automobiles subject to section 280F are eligible for section 179 expensing only to the extent of the applicable limits contained in section 280F.

Reasons for Change

The Committee believes that section 179 expensing provides two important benefits for small business. First, it lowers the cost of capital for property used in a trade or business. With a lower cost of capital, the Committee believes small business will invest in more equipment and employ more workers. Second, it eliminates depreciation recordkeeping requirements with respect to expensed property. However, the Committee understands that some taxpayers are using section 179 to lower the cost of purchasing certain types of vehicles (1) that are not subject to the luxury automobile limitations imposed by Congress and (2) for which the specific features of such vehicle are not necessary for purposes of conducting the taxpayer's business. The Committee is concerned about such market distortions and does not believe that the United States taxpayers should subsidize a portion of such purchase. The Committee's provision places new restrictions on the ability of certain vehicles to qualify for the expensing provisions of section 179.

Explanation of Provision

The provision limits the ability of taxpayers to claim deductions under section 179 for certain

---

[383] The limitation is commonly referred to as the "luxury automobile depreciation limitation." For passenger automobiles (subject to such limitation) placed in service in 2002, the maximum amount of allowable depreciation is $7,660 for the year in which the vehicle was placed in service, $4,900 for the second year, $2,950 for the third year, and $1,775 for the fourth and later years. This limitation applies to the combined depreciation deduction provided under present law for depreciation, including section 179 expensing and the temporary 30 percent additional first year depreciation allowance. For luxury automobiles eligible for the 50% additional first depreciation allowance, the first year limitation is increased by an additional $3,050.

[384] Sec. 280F(d)(5). Exceptions are provided for any ambulance, hearse, or any vehicle used by the taxpayer directly in the trade or business of transporting persons or property for compensation or hire.

[385] Pub. Law No. 108-27, sec. 202 (2003).

[386] Additional section 179 incentives are provided with respect to a qualified property used by a business in the New York Liberty Zone (sec. 1400L(f)), an empowerment zone (sec. 1397A), or a renewal community (sec. 1400J).

vehicles not subject to section 280F to $25,000. The provision applies to sport utility vehicles rated at 14,000 pounds gross vehicle weight or less (in place of the present law 6,000 pound rating). For this purpose, a sport utility vehicle is defined to exclude any vehicle that: (1) does not have a primary load device or container attached; (2) has a seating capacity of more than 12 individuals; (3) is designed for more than nine individuals in seating rearward of the driver's seat; (4) is equipped with an open cargo area, or a covered box not readily accessible from the passenger compartment, of at least 72.0 inches in interior length; or (5) has an integral enclosure, fully enclosing the driver compartment and load carrying device, does not have seating rearward of the driver's seat, and has no body section protruding more than 30 inches ahead of the leading edge of the windshield.

The following example illustrates the operation of the provision.

Example.—Assume that during 2004, a calendar year taxpayer acquires and places in service a sport utility vehicle subject to the provision that costs $70,000. In addition, assume that the property otherwise qualifies for the expensing election under section 179. Under the provision, the taxpayer is first allowed a $25,000 deduction under section 179. The taxpayer is also allowed an additional first-year depreciation deduction (sec. 168(k)) of $22,500 based on $45,000 ($70,000 original cost less the section 179 deduction of $25,000) of adjusted basis. Finally, the remaining adjusted basis of $22,500 ($45,000 adjusted basis less $22,500 additional first-year depreciation) is eligible for an additional depreciation deduction of $4,500 under the general depreciation rules (automobiles are five-year recovery property). The remaining $18,000 of cost ($70,000 original cost less $52,000 deductible currently) would be recovered in 2005 and subsequent years pursuant to the general depreciation rules.

Effective Date

The proposal is effective for property placed in service after the date of enactment.

Conference Committee Report (H.R. CONF. REP. NO. 108-755)

House Bill

No provision.

Senate Amendment

The Senate amendment limits the ability of taxpayers to claim deductions under section 179 for certain vehicles not subject to section 280F to $25,000. The provision applies to sport utility vehicles rated at 14,000 pounds gross vehicle weight or less (in place of the present law 6,000 pound rating). For this purpose, a sport utility vehicle is defined to exclude any vehicle that: (1) is designed for more than nine individuals in seating rearward of the driver's seat; (2) is equipped with an open cargo area, or a covered box not readily accessible from the passenger compartment, of at least six feet in interior length; or (3) has an integral enclosure, fully enclosing the driver compartment and load carrying device, does not have seating rearward of the driver's seat, and has no body section protruding more than 30 inches ahead of the leading edge of the windshield.

The following example illustrates the operation of the provision.

Example.—Assume that during 2005, a calendar year taxpayer acquires and places in service a sport utility vehicle subject to the provision that costs $70,000. In addition, assume that the property otherwise qualifies for the expensing election under section 179. Under the provision, the taxpayer is first allowed a $25,000 deduction under section 179. The taxpayer is also allowed an additional first-year depreciation deduction (sec. 168(k)) of $22,500 based on $45,000 ($70,000 original cost less the section 179 deduction of $25,000) of adjusted basis. Finally, the remaining adjusted basis of $22,500 ($45,000 adjusted basis less $22,500 additional first-year depreciation) is eligible for an additional depreciation deduction of $4,500 under the general depreciation rules (automobiles are five-year recovery property). The remaining $18,000 of cost ($70,000 original cost less $52,000 deductible currently) would be recovered in 2006 and subsequent years pursuant to the general depreciation rules.

Conference Agreement

The conference agreement follows the Senate amendment.

[Law at ¶5195. CCH Explanation at ¶310.]

¶ 20,001

Effective Dates

American Jobs Creation Act of 2004

This CCH-prepared table presents the general effective dates for major law provisions added, amended or repealed by the American Jobs Creation Act of 2004. Entries are listed in Code Section order.

Code Sec.	Act Sec.	Act Provision Subject	Effective Date
1(h)(10)(F)-(H)	413(c)(1)(A)	Repeal of Foreign Personal Holding Company Rules and Foreign Investment Company Rules-Conforming Amendments	Tax years of foreign corporations beginning after December 31, 2004 and to tax years of United States shareholders with or within which such tax years of foreign corporations end
1(h)(11)(C)	413(c)(1)(B)	Repeal of Foreign Personal Holding Company Rules and Foreign Investment Company Rules-Conforming Amendments	Tax years of foreign corporations beginning after December 31, 2004 and to tax years of United States shareholders with or within which such tax years of foreign corporations end
38(b)(14)-(16)	245(c)(1)	Credit for Maintenance of Railroad Track-Limitation on Carryback	Tax years beginning after December 31, 2004
38(b)(15)-(17)	302(b)	Biodiesel Income Tax Credit-Credit Treated as Part of General Business Credit	Fuel produced, and sold or used, after December 31, 2004, in tax years ending after such date
38(b)(16)-(18)	339(b)	Credit For Production Of Low Sulphor Diesel Fuel-Credit Made Part Of General Business Credit	Expenses paid or incurred after December 31, 2002 in tax years ending after such date
38(b)(17)-(19)	341(b)	Oil And Gas From Marginal Wells-Credit Treated As Business Credit	Production in tax years beginning after December 31, 2004
38(c)(2)(A)	711(b)	Certain Business Related Credits Allowed Against Regular And Minimum Tax-Conforming Amendments	Tax years ending after date of enactment
38(c)(3)(A)	711(b)	Certain Business Related Credits Allowed Against Regular And Minimum Tax-Conforming Amendments	Tax years ending after date of enactment
38(c)(4)-(5)	711(a)	Certain Business Related Credits Allowed Against Regular And Minimum Tax	Tax years ending after date of enactment
39(a)(3)	341(c)	Oil And Gas From Marginal Wells-Carryback	Production in tax years beginning after December 31, 2004

Code Sec.	Act Sec.	Act Provision Subject	Effective Date
39(d)	245(b)(1)	Credit for Maintenance of Railroad Track-Limitation on Carryback	Tax years ending after December 31, 2003
40(c)	301(c)(1)	Alcohol and Biodiesel Excise Tax Credit And Extension of Alcohol Fuels Income Tax Credit-Additional Amendments	Fuel sold or used after December 31, 2004
40(d)(4)	301(c)(2)	Alcohol and Biodiesel Excise Tax Credit And Extension of Alcohol Fuels Income Tax Credit-Additional Amendments	Fuel sold or used after December 31, 2004
40(e)(1)	301(c)(3)(A)-(B)	Alcohol and Biodiesel Excise Tax Credit And Extension of Alcohol Fuels Income Tax Credit-Additional Amendments	Date of enactment
40(g)(6)	313(a)	Apportionment Of Small Ethanol Producer Credit	Tax years ending after date of enactment
40(h)(1)-(2)	301(c)(4)(A)-(B)	Alcohol and Biodiesel Excise Tax Credit And Extension of Alcohol Fuels Income Tax Credit-Additional Amendments	Date of enactment
40A	302(a)	Biodiesel Income Tax Credit	Fuel produced, and sold or used, after December 31, 2004, in tax years ending after such date
43(c)(1)(D)	707(a)	Extension Of Enhanced Oil Recovery Credit To Certain Alaska Facilities	Costs paid or incurred in tax years beginning after December 31, 2004
43(c)(5)	707(b)	Extension Of Enhanced Oil Recovery Credit To Certain Alaska Facilities-Alaska Natural Gas	Costs paid or incurred in tax years beginning after December 31, 2004
45	710(b)(3)(B)	Expansion Of Credit For Electricity Produced From Certain Renewable Resources-Expansion Of Qualified Facilities	Electricity produced and sold after date of enactment in tax years ending after such date, generally
45(b)(2)	710(b)(3)(C)	Expansion Of Credit For Electricity Produced From Certain Renewable Resources-Expansion Of Qualified Facilities	Electricity produced and sold after date of enactment in tax years ending after such date, generally
45(b)(3)	710(f)(1)-(2)	Expansion Of Credit For Electricity Produced From Certain Renewable Resources-Elimination Of Certain Credit Reductions	Electricity produced and sold after date of enactment in tax years ending after such date, generally
45(b)(4)	710(c)	Expansion Of Credit For Electricity Produced From Certain Renewable Resources-Special Credit Rate For Electricity Produced And Sold After Enactment Date	Electricity produced and sold after December 31, 2004, in tax years ending after such date

Code Sec.	Act Sec.	Act Provision Subject	Effective Date
45(c)	710(a)	Expansion Of Credit For Electricity Produced From Certain Renewable Resources-Expansion Of Qualified Energy Resources	Electricity produced and sold after date of enactment in tax years ending after such date, generally
45(d)-(e)	710(b)(1)	Expansion Of Credit For Electricity Produced From Certain Renewable Resources-Expansion Of Qualified Facilities	Electricity produced and sold after December 31, 2004, in tax years ending after such date
45(e)(7)(A)	710(b)(3)(A)	Expansion Of Credit For Electricity Produced From Certain Renewable Resources-Expansion Of Qualified Facilities	Electricity produced and sold after date of enactment in tax years ending after such date, generally
45(e)(8)	710(b)(2)	Expansion Of Credit For Electricity Produced From Certain Renewable Resources-Expansion Of Qualified Facilities	Refined coal produced and sold after the date of enactment
45(e)(9)	710(d)	Expansion Of Credit For Electricity Produced From Certain Renewable Resources-Coordination With Other Credits	Electricity produced and sold after date of enactment in tax years ending after such date, generally
45D(e)(2)	221(a)	Modification of Targeted Areas and Low-Income Communities for New Markets Tax Credit-Targeted Areas	Designations made after date of enactment
45D(e)(4)	221(b)	Modification of Targeted Areas and Low-Income Communities for New Markets Tax Credit-Tracts with Low Population	Investments made after date of enactment
45D(e)(5)	223(a)	Modification of Income Requirement for Census Tracts Within High Migration Rural Counties	Investments made after December 31, 2000
45G	245(a)	Credit for Maintenance of Railroad Track	Qualified railroad track maintenance expenditures paid or incurred during tax years beginning after December 31, 2004, and before January 1, 2008
45H	339(a)	Credit For Production Of Low Sulphor Diesel Fuel	Expenses paid or incurred after December 31, 2002 in tax years ending after such date
45I	341(a)	Oil And Gas From Marginal Wells	Production in tax years beginning after December 31, 2004
46(1)-(3)	322(d)(1)(A)-(C)	Expensing of Certain Reforestation Expenditures-Repeal Of Reforestation Credit	Expenditures paid or incurred after the date of enactment
48	322(d)(2)(B)	Expensing of Certain Reforestation Expenditures-Repeal Of Reforestation Credit	Expenditures paid or incurred after the date of enactment

Code Sec.	Act Sec.	Act Provision Subject	Effective Date
48(a)(3)	710(e)	Expansion Of Credit For Electricity Produced From Certain Renewable Resources-Coordination With Section 48	Electricity produced and sold after date of enactment in tax years ending after such date, generally
48(a)-(b)	322(d)(2)(A)	Expensing of Certain Reforestation Expenditures-Repeal Of Reforestation Credit	Expenditures paid or incurred after the date of enactment
50(c)(3)	322(d)(2)(D)	Expensing of Certain Reforestation Expenditures-Repeal Of Reforestation Credit	Expenditures paid or incurred after the date of enactment
53(d)(1)(B)	421(a)(2)	Foreign Tax Credit Under Alternative Minimum Tax	Tax years beginning after December 31, 2004
55(c)(2)-(3)	314(a)	Coordinate Farmers And Fisherman Income Averaging And The Alternative Minimum Tax	Tax years beginning after December 31, 2003
56(g)(4)(B)	101(b)(4)	Repeal of Exclusion for Extraterritorial Income-Conforming Amendments	Transactions after December 31, 2004
56(g)(4)(B)	248(b)(1)	Election to Determine Corporate Tax on Certain International Shipping Activities Using Per Ton Rate-Technical Amendments	Tax years beginning after date of enactment
56(g)(4)(C)	102(b)	Income Attributable to Domestic Production Activities-Minimum Tax	Tax years beginning after December 31, 2004
56(g)(4)(C)	422(b)	Incentives To Reinvest Foreign Earnings In United States-Alternative Minimum Tax	Tax years ending on or after date of enactment
56(g)(6)	835(b)(1)	Repeal Of Special Rules-Conforming Amendments	January 1, 2005, generally
59(a)(2)-(4)	421(a)(1)	Foreign Tax Credit Under Alternative Minimum Tax	Tax years beginning after December 31, 2004
62(a)(19)	703(a)	Civil Rights Tax Relief-Deduction Allowed Whether Or Not Taxpayer Itemizes Other Deductions	Fees and costs paid after date of enactment with respect to any judgment or settlement occurring after date
62(e)	703(b)	Civil Rights Tax Relief-Unlawful Discrimination Defined	Fees and costs paid after date of enactment with respect to any judgment or settlement occurring after date
72(w)-(x)	906(a)	Application Of Basis Rules To Nonresident Aliens	Distributions on or after date of enactment
83(c)(4)	906(b)	Application Of Basis Rules To Nonresident Aliens-Basis	Distributions on or after date of enactment
86(b)(2)(A)	102(d)(1)	Income Attributable to Domestic Production Activities-Technical Amendments	Tax years beginning after December 31, 2004
87	302(c)(1)(A)	Biodiesel Income Tax Credit-Conforming Amendments	Fuel produced, and sold or used, after December 31, 2004, in tax years ending after such date

Code Sec.	Act Sec.	Act Provision Subject	Effective Date
108(e)(8)	896(a)	Recognition Of Cancellation Of Indebtedness Income Realized On Satisfaction Of Debt With Partnership Interest	Cancellations of indebtedness occurring on or after date of enactment
108(f)(4)	320(a)	Exclusion For Payments To Individuals Under National Health Service Corps Loan Repayment Program And Certain State Loan Repayment Programs	Amounts received by an individual in tax years beginning after December 31, 2003
114	101(a)	Repeal of Exclusion for Extraterritorial Income	Transactions after December 31, 2004
121(d)(10)	840(a)	Recognition Of Gain From The Sale Of A Principal Residence Acquired In A Like-Kind Exchange Within 5 Years Of Sale	Sales or exchanges after the date of enactment
135(c)(4)(A)	102(d)(1)	Income Attributable to Domestic Production Activities-Technical Amendments	Tax years beginning after December 31, 2004
137(b)(3)(A)	102(d)(1)	Income Attributable to Domestic Production Activities-Technical Amendments	Tax years beginning after December 31, 2004
142(a)(12)-(14)	701(a)	Brownfields Demonstration Program For Qualified Green Building And Sustainable Design Projects-Treatment As Exempt Facility Bond	Bonds issued after December 31, 2004
142(l)	701(b)	Brownfields Demonstration Program For Qualified Green Building And Sustainable Design Projects-Qualified Green Building And Sustainable Design Projects	Bonds issued after December 31, 2004
144(a)(4)(F)	340(b)	Expansion Of Qualified Small-Issue Bond Program-Conforming Amendment	Date of enactment
144(a)(4)(G)	340(a)	Expansion Of Qualified Small-Issue Bond Program	Date of enactment
146(g)(3)	701(c)(1)-(2)	Brownfields Demonstration Program For Qualified Green Building And Sustainable Design Projects-Exemption From General State Volume Caps	Bonds issued after December 31, 2004
162(m)94)(G)	802(b)(2)	Stock Compensation Of Insiders In Expatriated Corporations-Denial Of Deduction-$1,000,000 Limit On Deductible Compensation Reduced By Payment Of Excise Tax On Specified Stock Compensation	March 4, 2003, generally
162(o)	318(b)	Certain Expenses of Rural Letter Carriers-Conforming Amendment	Tax years beginning after December 31, 2003
162(o)(2)-(3)	318(a)	Certain Expenses of Rural Letter Carriers	Tax years beginning after December 31, 2003
163(e)(3)(b)-(C)	841(a)	Prevention Of Mismatching Of Interest And Original Issue Discount Deductions And Income Inclusions In Transactions With Related Foreign Persons-Original Issue Discount	Payments accrued on or after date of enactment
163(l)(2)	845(a)	Expanded Disallowance Of Deduction For Interest On Convertible Debt	Debt instruments issued after October 3, 2004

Code Sec.	Act Sec.	Act Provision Subject	Effective Date
163(l)(3)	845(d)	Expanded Disallowance Of Deduction For Interest On Convertible Debt-Conforming Amendment	Debt instruments issued after October 3, 2004
163(l)(4)-(6)	845(b)	Expanded Disallowance Of Deduction For Interest On Convertible Debt-Capitalization Allowed With Respect To Equity Of Persons Other Than Issuer And Related Parties	Debt instruments issued after October 3, 2004
163(l)(5)-(7)	845(c)	Expanded Disallowance Of Deduction For Interest On Convertible Debt-Exception For Certain Instruments Issued By Dealers In Securities	Debt instruments issued after October 3, 2004
163(m)-(n)	838(a)	Denial Of Deduction For Interest On Underpayments Attributable To Non-disclosed Reportable Transactions	Transactions in tax years beginning after date of enactment
164(b)(5)	501(a)	Deduction Of State And Local General Sales Taxes In Lieu Of State And Local Income Taxes	Tax years beginning after December 31, 2003
167(f)(1)(C)	847(b)(1)	Reform Of Tax Treatment Of Certain Leasing Arrangements-Limitation ON Depreciation And Amortization Periods For Intangibles Leased To Tax-Exempt Entity	Date of enactment
167(f)(2)	847(b)(2)	Reform Of Tax Treatment Of Certain Leasing Arrangements-Limitation ON Depreciation And Amortization Periods For Intangibles Leased To Tax-Exempt Entity	Date of enactment
167(g)(5)(E)-(G)	242(b)	Modification of Application of Income Forecast Method of Depreciation-Determination of Income	Property placed in service after the date of enactment
167(g)(7)	242(a)	Modification of Application of Income Forecast Method of Depreciation	Property placed in service after the date of enactment
168(b)(2)(A)	211(d)(2)	Recovery Period for Depreciation of Certain Leasehold Improvements and Restaurant Properties-Requirement to Use Straight Line Method	Property placed in service after date of enactment
168(b)(3)(G)-(H)	211(d)(1)	Recovery Period for Depreciation of Certain Leasehold Improvements and Restaurant Properties-Requirement to Use Straight Line Method	Property placed in service after date of enactment
168(e)(3)(B)	211(e)	Recovery Period for Depreciation of Certain Leasehold Improvements and Restaurant Properties-Alternate System	Property placed in service after date of enactment
168(e)(3)(C)	704(a)	Modification Of Class Life For Certain Track Facilities-7-Year Property	Any property placed in service after date of enactment, generally
168(e)(3)(C)	706(a)	Certain Alaska Natural Gas Pipeline Property Treated As 7-Year Property	Property placed in service after December 31, 2004
168(e)(3)(E)	211(a)	Recovery Period for Depreciation of Certain Leasehold Improvements and Restaurant Properties-15-Year Recovery Period	Property placed in service after date of enactment

¶20,001

Code Sec.	Act Sec.	Act Provision Subject	Effective Date
168(e)(3)(E)	901(a)	Class Lives For Utility Grading Costs-Gas Utility Property	Property placed in service after date of enactment
168(e)(3)(F)	901(b)	Class Lives For Utility Grading Costs-Electric Utility Property	Property placed in service after date of enactment
168(e)(6)	211(b)	Recovery Period for Depreciation of Certain Leasehold Improvements and Restaurant Properties-Qualified Leasehold Improvement Property	Property placed in service after date of enactment
168(e)(7)	211(c)	Recovery Period for Depreciation of Certain Leasehold Improvements and Restaurant Properties-Qualified Restaurant Property	Property placed in service after date of enactment
168(g)(3)(A)	847(a)	Reform Of Tax Treatment Of Certain Leasing Arrangements-Clarification Of Recovery Period For Tax-Exempt Use Property Subject To Lease	Date of enactment
168(g)(3)(B)	706(c)	Certain Alaska Natural Gas Pipeline Property Treated As 7-Year Property-Alternative System	Property placed in service after December 31, 2004
168(g)(3)(B)	901(c)	Class Lives For Utility Grading Costs-Conforming Amendment	Property placed in service after date of enactment
168(h)(2)(A)	847(e)	Reform Of Tax Treatment Of Certain Leasing Arrangements-Treatment Of Certain Indian Tribal Governments As Tax-Exempt Entities	Date of enactment
168(h)(3)(A)	847(d)	Reform Of Tax Treatment Of Certain Leasing Arrangements-Expansion Of Short-Term Lease Exemption For Qualified Technological Equipment	Date of enactment
168(i)(15)	704(b)	Modification Of Class Life For Certain Track Facilities	Any property placed in service after date of enactment, generally
168(i)(16)	706(b)	Certain Alaska Natural Gas Pipeline Property Treated As 7-Year Property-Alaska Natural Gas Pipeline	Property placed in service after December 31, 2004
168(i)(3)(A)	847(c)	Reform Of Tax Treatment Of Certain Leasing Arrangements-Lease Term To Include Related Service Contracts	Date of enactment
168(k)(2)(A)	336(a)(2)	Modification Of Depreciation Allowance For Aircraft-Placed in Service Date	Property placed in service after September 10, 2001, in tax years ending after such date
168(k)(2)(B)	336(b)(1)	Modification Of Depreciation Allowance For Aircraft-Conforming Amendments	Property placed in service after September 10, 2001, in tax years ending after such date
168(k)(2)(C)-(G)	336(a)(1)	Modification Of Depreciation Allowance For Aircraft-Aircraft Treated As Qualified Property	Property placed in service after September 10, 2001, in tax years ending after such date

Code Sec.	Act Sec.	Act Provision Subject	Effective Date
168(k)(2)(E)	337(a)	Modification Of Placed In Service Rule For Bonus Depreciation Property	Property sold after June 4, 2004
168(k)(4)(A)	336(b)(2)	Modification Of Depreciation Allowance For Aircraft-Conforming Amendments	Property placed in service after September 10, 2001, in tax years ending after such date
168(k)(4)(B)	336(b)(3)	Modification Of Depreciation Allowance For Aircraft-Conforming Amendments	Property placed in service after September 10, 2001, in tax years ending after such date
168(k)(4)(C)	336(b)(4)	Modification Of Depreciation Allowance For Aircraft-Conforming Amendments	Property placed in service after September 10, 2001, in tax years ending after such date
168(k)(4)(D)	336(b)(5)	Modification Of Depreciation Allowance For Aircraft-Conforming Amendments	Property placed in service after September 10, 2001, in tax years ending after such date
170(e)(1)(B)	882(a)	Treatment Of Charitable Contributions Of Patents And Similar Property	Contributions made after June 3, 2004
170(f)(10)(A)	413(c)(30)	Repeal of Foreign Personal Holding Company Rules and Foreign Investment Company Rules-Conforming Amendments	Tax years of foreign corporations beginning after December 31, 2004 and to tax years of United States shareholders with or within which such tax years of foreign corporations end
170(f)(11)	883(a)	Increased Reporting For Noncash Contributions	Contributions made after June 3, 2004
170(f)(11)(A)	882(d)	Treatment Of Charitable Contributions Of Patents And Similar Property-Coordination With Appraisal Requirements	Contributions made after June 3, 2004
170(f)(12)	884(a)	Donations Of Motor Vehicles, Boats, And Airplanes	Contributions made after December 31, 2004
170(m)-(n)	882(b)	Treatment Of Charitable Contributions Of Patents And Similar Property-Certain Donee Income From Intellectual Property Treated As An Additional Charitable Contribution	Contributions made after June 3, 2004
170(n)-(o)	335(a)	Charitable Contribution Deduction For Certain Expenses Incurred In Support Of Native Alaskan Subsistence Whaling	Contributions Made After December 31, 2004

Code Sec.	Act Sec.	Act Provision Subject	Effective Date
171(c)(2)	413(c)(2)(A)-(B)	Repeal of Foreign Personal Holding Company Rules and Foreign Investment Company Rules-Conforming Amendments	Tax years of foreign corporations beginning after December 31, 2004 and to tax years of United States shareholders with or within which such tax years of foreign corporations end
179(b)(6)	910(a)	Expansion Of Limitation On Depreciation Of Certain Passenger Automobiles	Property placed in service after date of enactment
179(b)-(d)	201	2-Year Extension of Increased Expensing for Small Business	Date of enactment
179B	338(a)	Expensing Of Capital Costs Incurred IN Complying With Environmental Protection Agency Sulphur Regulations	Expenses paid or incurred after December 31, 2002 in tax years ending after such date
181	244(a)	Special Rules For Certain Film and Television Productions	Qualified film and television productions commencing after the date of enactment
194	322(c)(4)	Expensing of Certain Reforestation Expenditures-Conforming Amendments	Expenditures paid or incurred after the date of enactment
194(b)	322(a)	Expensing of Certain Reforestation Expenditures	Expenditures paid or incurred after the date of enactment
194(b)(2)	322(c)(2)	Expensing of Certain Reforestation Expenditures-Conforming Amendments	Expenditures paid or incurred after the date of enactment
194(b)(3)-(4)	322(c)(1)	Expensing of Certain Reforestation Expenditures-Conforming Amendments	Expenditures paid or incurred after the date of enactment
194(c)(2)	322(b)	Expensing of Certain Reforestation Expenditures-Net Amortizable Base	Expenditures paid or incurred after the date of enactment
194(c)(4)-(5)	322(c)(3)	Expensing of Certain Reforestation Expenditures-Conforming Amendments	Expenditures paid or incurred after the date of enactment
195(b)	902(a)(2)	Consistent Amortization Of Periods For Intangibles	Amounts paid or incurred after date of enactment
195(b)(1)	902(a)(1)	Consistent Amortization Of Periods For Intangibles-Start-Up Expenditures	Amounts paid or incurred after date of enactment
196(c)(10)-(12)	339(e)	Credit For Production Of Low Sulphor Diesel Fuel-Deduction For Certain Unused Business Credits	Expenses paid or incurred after December 31, 2002 in tax years ending after such date
197(e)(6)-(8)	886(a)	Extension Of Amortization Of Intangibles To Sports Franchises	Property acquired after date of enactment

Code Sec.	Act Sec.	Act Provision Subject	Effective Date
197(f)(10)	847(b)(3)	Reform Of Tax Treatment Of Certain Leasing Arrangements-Limitation On Depreciation And Amortization Periods For Intangibles Leased To Tax-Exempt Entity	Date of enactment
199	102(a)	Income Attributable to Domestic Production Activities-Allowance of the Deduction	Tax years beginning after December 31, 2004
219(g)(3)(A)	102(d)(1)	Income Attributable to Domestic Production Activities-Technical Amendments	Tax years beginning after December 31, 2004
221(b)(2)(C)	102(d)(2)	Income Attributable to Domestic Production Activities-Technical Amendments	Tax years beginning after December 31, 2004
222(b)(2)(C)	102(d)(3)	Income Attributable to Domestic Production Activities-Technical Amendments	Tax years beginning after December 31, 2004
245(a)(2)	413(c)(3)	Repeal of Foreign Personal Holding Company Rules and Foreign Investment Company Rules-Conforming Amendments	Tax years of foreign corporations beginning after December 31, 2004 and to tax years of United States shareholders with or within which such tax years of foreign corporations end
246(b)(1)	102(d)(4)	Income Attributable to Domestic Production Activities-Technical Amendments	Tax years beginning after December 31, 2004
246(c)	888(d)	Modification Of Straddle Rules-Holding Period For Dividend Exclusion	Positions established on or after date of enactment
248(a)	902(b)	Consistent Amortization Of Periods For Intangibles-Organizational Expenditures	Amounts paid or incurred after date of enactment
263(a)(1)(G)-(I)	338(b)(1)	Expensing Of Capital Costs Incurred IN Complying With Environmental Protection Agency Sulphur Regulations-Conforming Amendments	Expenses paid or incurred after December 31, 2002 in tax years ending after such date
263A(c)(3)	338(b)(2)	Expensing Of Capital Costs Incurred IN Complying With Environmental Protection Agency Sulphur Regulations-Conforming Amendments	Expenses paid or incurred after December 31, 2002 in tax years ending after such date
267(a)(3)	841(b)(1)-(2)	Prevention Of Mismatching Of Interest And Original Issue Discount Deductions And Income Inclusions In Transactions With Related Foreign Persons-Interest And Other Deductible Amounts	Payments accrued on or after date of enactment
274(e)(2)	907(a)	Limitation Of Employer Deduction For Certain Entertainment Expenses	Expenses incurred after date of enactment
275(a)	101(b)(5)(B)	Repeal of Exclusion for Extraterritorial Income-Conforming Amendments	Transactions after December 31, 2004

¶20,001

Code Sec.	Act Sec.	Act Provision Subject	Effective Date
275(a)(4)(A)-(C)	101(b)(5)(A)	Repeal of Exclusion for Extraterritorial Income-Conforming Amendments	Transactions after December 31, 2004
275(a)(6)	802(b)(1)	Stock Compensation Of Insiders In Expatriated Corporations-Denial Of Deduction	March 4, 2003, generally
280C(d)	339(c)	Credit For Production Of Low Sulphor Diesel Fuel-Denial Of Double Benefit	Expenses paid or incurred after December 31, 2002 in tax years ending after such date
305(e)(7)	831(b)	Treatment Of Stripped Interests In Bond And Preferred Stock Funds-Cross Reference	Purchases and dispositions after date of enactment
312(j)	413(c)(4)	Repeal of Foreign Personal Holding Company Rules and Foreign Investment Company Rules-Conforming Amendments	Tax years of foreign corporations beginning after December 31, 2004 and to tax years of United States shareholders with or within which such tax years of foreign corporations end
312(k)(3)(B)	338(b)(3)	Expensing Of Capital Costs Incurred In Complying With Environmental Protection Agency Sulphur Regulations-Conforming Amendments	Expenses paid or incurred after December 31, 2002 in tax years ending after such date
312(m)	413(c)(5)	Repeal of Foreign Personal Holding Company Rules and Foreign Investment Company Rules-Conforming Amendments	Tax years of foreign corporations beginning after December 31, 2004 and to tax years of United States shareholders with or within which such tax years of foreign corporations end
332(d)	893(a)	Prohibition On Nonrecognition Of Gain Through Complete Liquidation Of Holding Company	Distributions in complete liquidation occurring on or after date of enactment
334(b)(1)	836(b)	Limitation On Transfer Or Importation Of Built-In Losses-Comparable Treatment Where Liquidation	Liquidations after date of enactment
338(h)(13)	839(a)	Clarification Of Rules For Payment Of Estimated Tax For Certain Deemed Asset Sales	Transactions occurring after date of enactment
351(g)(3)(A)	899(a)	Clarification Of Definition Of Nonqualified Preferred Stock	Transactions after May 14, 2003
357(c)(1)(B)	898(b)	Modification Of Treatment Of Transfers To Creditors In Divisive Reorganizations-Liabiliities In Excess Of Basis	Transfers of money or other property, or liabilities assumed, in connection with a reorganization occurring on or after date of enactment

Code Sec.	Act Sec.	Act Provision Subject	Effective Date
361(b)(3)	898(a)	Modification Of Treatment Of Transfers To Creditors In Divisive Reorganizations	Transfers of money or other property, or liabilities assumed, in connection with a reorganization occurring on or after date of enactment
362(e)	836(a)	Limitation ON Transfer Or Importation Of Built-In Losses	Transactions after date of enactment
367(d)(2)(C)	406(a)	Clarification Of Treatment Of Certain Transfers Of Intangible Property	Amounts treated as received pursuant to Code Sec. 367(d)(2) on or after August 5, 1997
382(l)(4)(B)	835(b)(2)	Repeal Of Special Rules-Conforming Amendments	January 1, 2005, generally
409A	885(a)	Inclusion In Gross Income Of Deferred Compensation Under Nonqualified Compensation Plans-Rules Relating To Constructive Receipt	Amounts deferred after December 31, 2004; generally
420(c)(3)(E)	709(b)(1)	Modification Of Minimum Cost Requirement For Transfer Of Excess Pension Assets-Minimum Cost Requirements	Tax years ending after date of enactment
420(c)(3)(E)	709(b)(2)	Modification Of Minimum Cost Requirement For Transfer Of Excess Pension Assets-Minimum Cost Requirements	Tax years ending after date of enactment
421(b)	251(b)	Exclusion of Incentive Stock Options and Employee Stock Purchase Plan Stock Options From Wages-Wage Withholding Not Required On Disqualifying Dispositions	Stock acquired pursuant to options exercised after the date of enactment
421(d)	905(a)	Treatment Of Sale Of Stock Acquired Pursuant To Exercise Of Stock Options To Comply With Conflict-Of-Interest Requirements	Sales after date of enactment
423(c)	251(c)	Exclusion of Incentive Stock Options and Employee Stock Purchase Plan Stock Options From Wages-Wage Withholding Not Required On Compensation Where Option Price Is Between 85 Percent and 100 Percent of Value of Stock	Stock acquired pursuant to options exercised after the date of enactment
443(e)(3)-(5)	413(c)(6)	Repeal of Foreign Personal Holding Company Rules and Foreign Investment Company Rules-Conforming Amendments	Tax years of foreign corporations beginning after December 31, 2004 and to tax years of United States shareholders with or within which such tax years of foreign corporations end
451(e)(3)	311(c)	Special Rules For Livestock Sold On Account of Weather-Related Conditions-Income Inclusion Rules	Any tax year with respect to which the due date (without regard to extensions) for the return is after December 31, 2002

Code Sec.	Act Sec.	Act Provision Subject	Effective Date
451(i)	909(a)	Sales Or Dispositions To Implement Federal Energy Regulatory Commission Or State electric Restructuring Policy	Transactions occurring after date of enactment, in tax years ending after such date
453(f)(4)(B)	897(a)	Denial Of Installment Sale Treatment For All Readily Tradable Debt	Sales occurring or or after date of enactment
465(c)(7)(B)	413(c)(7)	Repeal of Foreign Personal Holding Company Rules and Foreign Investment Company Rules-Conforming Amendments	Tax years of foreign corporations beginning after December 31, 2004 and to tax years of United States shareholders with or within which such tax years of foreign corporations end
469(i)(3)(F)	102(d)(5)	Income Attributable to Domestic Production Activities-Technical Amendments	Tax years beginning after December 31, 2004
469(k)(4)	331(g)	Net Income From Publicly Traded Partnerships Treated As Qualifying Income Of Regulated Investment Companies-Application To Regulated Investment Companies	Tax years beginning after date of enactment
470	848(a)	Limitation On Deductions Allocable To Property Used By governments Or Other Tax-Exempt Entities	Date of enactment
501(c)(12)(C)	319(a)(1)	Treatment of Certain Income of Cooperatives-Income From Open Access And Nuclear Decommisioning Transactions	Tax year beginning after date of enactment
501(c)(12)(E)-(G)	319(a)(2)	Treatment of Certain Income of Cooperatives-Income From Open Access And Nuclear Decommissioning Transactions	Tax year beginning after date of enactment
501(c)(12)(H)	319(b)	Treatment of Certain Income of Cooperatives-Treatment Of Income From Load Loss Transactions, Etc.	Tax year beginning after date of enactment
508(d)	413(c)(30)	Repeal of Foreign Personal Holding Company Rules and Foreign Investment Company Rules-Conforming Amendments	Tax years of foreign corporations beginning after December 31, 2004 and to tax years of United States shareholders with or within which such tax years of foreign corporations end
512(b)(18)	319(c)	Treatment of Certain Income of Cooperatives-Exception From Unrelated Business Taxable Income	Tax year beginning after date of enactment
512(b)(18)	702(a)	Exclusion Of Gain Or Loss On Sale Or Exchange Of Certain Brownfield Sites From Unrelated Business Taxable Income	Gain or loss on sale, exchange, or other disposition of any property acquired by taxpayer after December 31, 2004

Code Sec.	Act Sec.	Act Provision Subject	Effective Date
512(e)(1)	233(d)	Expansion of Bank S Corporation Eligible Shareholders to Include IRAs-Conforming Amendment	Date of enactment
514(b)(1)(C)-(E)	702(b)	Exclusion Of Gain Or Loss On Sale Or Exchange Of Certain Brownfield Sites From Unrelated Business Taxable Income-Exclusion From Definition Of Debt Financed Property	Gain or loss on sale, exchange, or other disposition of any property acquired by taxpayer after December 31, 2004
514(c)(6)	247(a)	Modification of Unrelated Business Income Limitation on Investment in Certain Small Business Investment Companies	Indebtedness incurred after date of enactment by a small business investment company licensed after date of enactment
521(b)(7)	316(b)	Modification To Cooperative Marketing Rules To Include Value Added Processing Involving Animals-Conforming Amendment	Tax years beginning after date of enactment
535(d)(2)	402(b)(1)	Recharacterization of Overall Domestic Loss-Conforming Amendments	Losses for tax years beginning after December 31, 2006
542(c)(5)	413(b)(1)(A)	Repeal of Foreign Personal Holding Company Rules and Foreign Investment Company Rules-Exemption Of Foreign Corporations From Personal Holding Company Rules	Tax years of foreign corporations beginning after December 31, 2004 and to tax years of United States shareholders with or within which such tax years of foreign corporations end
542(c)(7)	413(b)(1)(C)	Repeal of Foreign Personal Holding Company Rules and Foreign Investment Company Rules-Exemption Of Foreign Corporations From Personal Holding Company Rules	Tax years of foreign corporations beginning after December 31, 2004 and to tax years of United States shareholders with or within which such tax years of foreign corporations end
542(c)(7)-(10)	413(b)(1)(B)	Repeal of Foreign Personal Holding Company Rules and Foreign Investment Company Rules-Exemption Of Foreign Corporations From Personal Holding Company Rules	Tax years of foreign corporations beginning after December 31, 2004 and to tax years of United States shareholders with or within which such tax years of foreign corporations end

Code Sec.	Act Sec.	Act Provision Subject	Effective Date
542(c)(8)	413(b)(1)(D)	Repeal of Foreign Personal Holding Company Rules and Foreign Investment Company Rules-Exemption Of Foreign Corporations From Personal Holding Company Rules	Tax years of foreign corporations beginning after December 31, 2004 and to tax years of United States shareholders with or within which such tax years of foreign corporations end
543(b)(1)(A)-(C)	413(c)(8)	Repeal of Foreign Personal Holding Company Rules and Foreign Investment Company Rules-Conforming Amendments	Tax years of foreign corporations beginning after December 31, 2004 and to tax years of United States shareholders with or within which such tax years of foreign corporations end
551	413(a)(1)	Repeal of Foreign Personal Holding Company Rules and Foreign Investment Company Rules-General Rule	Tax years of foreign corporations beginning after December 31, 2004 and to tax years of United States shareholders with or within which such tax years of foreign corporations end
552	413(a)(1)	Repeal of Foreign Personal Holding Company Rules and Foreign Investment Company Rules-General Rule	Tax years of foreign corporations beginning after December 31, 2004 and to tax years of United States shareholders with or within which such tax years of foreign corporations end
553	413(a)(1)	Repeal of Foreign Personal Holding Company Rules and Foreign Investment Company Rules-General Rule	Tax years of foreign corporations beginning after December 31, 2004 and to tax years of United States shareholders with or within which such tax years of foreign corporations end
554	413(a)(1)	Repeal of Foreign Personal Holding Company Rules and Foreign Investment Company Rules-General Rule	Tax years of foreign corporations beginning after December 31, 2004 and to tax years of United States shareholders with or within which such tax years of foreign corporations end

Code Sec.	Act Sec.	Act Provision Subject	Effective Date
555	413(a)(1)	Repeal of Foreign Personal Holding Company Rules and Foreign Investment Company Rules-General Rule	Tax years of foreign corporations beginning after December 31, 2004 and to tax years of United States shareholders with or within which such tax years of foreign corporations end
556	413(a)(1)	Repeal of Foreign Personal Holding Company Rules and Foreign Investment Company Rules-General Rule	Tax years of foreign corporations beginning after December 31, 2004 and to tax years of United States shareholders with or within which such tax years of foreign corporations end
557	413(a)(1)	Repeal of Foreign Personal Holding Company Rules and Foreign Investment Company Rules-General Rule	Tax years of foreign corporations beginning after December 31, 2004 and to tax years of United States shareholders with or within which such tax years of foreign corporations end
558	413(a)(1)	Repeal of Foreign Personal Holding Company Rules and Foreign Investment Company Rules-General Rule	Tax years of foreign corporations beginning after December 31, 2004 and to tax years of United States shareholders with or within which such tax years of foreign corporations end
562(b)(1)	413(c)(9)	Repeal of Foreign Personal Holding Company Rules and Foreign Investment Company Rules-Conforming Amendments	Tax years of foreign corporations beginning after December 31, 2004 and to tax years of United States shareholders with or within which such tax years of foreign corporations end
563(c)	413(c)(10)(A)	Repeal of Foreign Personal Holding Company Rules and Foreign Investment Company Rules-Conforming Amendments	Tax years of foreign corporations beginning after December 31, 2004 and to tax years of United States shareholders with or within which such tax years of foreign corporations end

Code Sec.	Act Sec.	Act Provision Subject	Effective Date
563(c)	413(c)(10)(C)	Repeal of Foreign Personal Holding Company Rules and Foreign Investment Company Rules-Conforming Amendments	Tax years of foreign corporations beginning after December 31, 2004 and to tax years of United States shareholders with or within which such tax years of foreign corporations end
563(c)-(d)	413(c)(10)(B)	Repeal of Foreign Personal Holding Company Rules and Foreign Investment Company Rules-Conforming Amendments	Tax years of foreign corporations beginning after December 31, 2004 and to tax years of United States shareholders with or within which such tax years of foreign corporations end
582(c)(1)	835(b)(3)	Repeal Of Special Rules-Conforming Amendments	January 1, 2005, generally
613(a)	102(d)(6)	Income Attributable to Domestic Production Activities-Technical Amendments	Tax years beginning after December 31, 2004
631(b)	315(a)	Capital Gain Treatment Under Section 631(b) To Apply To Outright Sales By Landowners	Sales after December 31, 2004
631(b)	315(b)(1)	Capital Gain Treatment Under Section 631(b) To Apply To Outright Sales By Landowners-Conforming Amendments	Sales after December 31, 2004
631(b)	315(b)(2)	Capital Gain Treatment Under Section 631(b) To Apply To Outright Sales By Landowners-Conforming Amendments	Sales after December 31, 2004
704(c)(1)(A)-(C)	833(a)	Disallowance Of Certain Partnership Loss Transfers-Treatment Of Contributed Property With Built-In Loss	Contributions made after date of enactment
709(b)	902(c)(2)	Consistent Amortization Of Periods For Intangibles-Conforming Amendment	Amounts paid or incurred after date of enactment
709(b)(1)-(3)	902(c)(1)	Consistent Amortization Of Periods For Intangibles-Conforming Amendment	Amounts paid or incurred after date of enactment
734(a)	833(c)(1)	Disallowance of Certain Partnership Loss Transfers-Adjustments To Basis Of Undistributed Partnership Property If There Is Substantial Basis Reduction	Distributions after date of enactment
734(b)	833(c)(2)	Disallowance of Certain Partnership Loss Transfers-Adjustments To Basis Of Undistributed Partnership Property If There Is Substantial Basis Reduction	Distributions after date of enactment

Code Sec.	Act Sec.	Act Provision Subject	Effective Date
734(d)	833(c)(3)	Disallowance of Certain Partnership Loss Transfers-Adjustments To Basis Of Undistributed Partnership Property If There Is Substantial Basis Reduction	Distributions after date of enactment
734(e)	833(c)(4)	Disallowance of Certain Partnership Loss Transfers-Adjustments To Basis Of Undistributed Partnership Property If There Is Substantial Basis Reduction	Distributions after date of enactment
734	833(c)(5)(A)	Disallowance of Certain Partnership Loss Transfers-Clerical Amendments	Distributions after date of enactment
743(a)	833(b)(1)	Disallowance Of Certain Partnership Loss Transfers-Special Rules For Transfers Of Partnership Interest If There Is Substantial Built-In Loss	Transfers after date of enactment, generally
743(b)	833(b)(2)	Disallowance Of Certain Partnership Loss Transfers-Special Rules For Transfers Of Partnership Interest If There Is Substantial Built-In Loss	Transfers after date of enactment, generally
743(d)	833(b)(3)	Disallowance Of Certain Partnership Loss Transfers-Special Rules For Transfers Of Partnership Interest If There Is Substantial Built-In Loss	Transfers after date of enactment, generally
743(e)	833(b)(4)(A)	Disallowance Of Certain Partnership Loss Transfers-Special Rules For Transfers Of Partnership Interest If There Is Substantial Built-In Loss	Transfers after date of enactment, generally
743(f)	833(b)(5)	Disallowance Of Certain Partnership Loss Transfers-Special Rules For Transfers Of Partnership Interest If There Is Substantial Built-In Loss	Transfers after date of enactment, generally
743	833(b)(6)(A)	Disallowance Of Certain Partnership Loss Transfers-Special Rules For Transfers Of Partnership Interest If There Is Substantial Built-In Loss-Clerical Amendment	Transfers after date of enactment, generally
751(d)(2)-(4)	413(c)(11)	Repeal of Foreign Personal Holding Company Rules and Foreign Investment Company Rules-Conforming Amendments	Tax years of foreign corporations beginning after December 31, 2004 and to tax years of United States shareholders with or within which such tax years of foreign corporations end
755(c)	834(a)	No Reduction Of Basis Under Section 734 In Stock Held By Partnership In Corporate Partner	Distributions after date of enactment
815(g)	705(a)	Suspension Of Policyholders Surplus Account Provisions-Distributions To Shareholders From Pre-1984 Policyholders Surplus Account	Tax years beginning after December 31, 2004
845(a)	803(a)	Reinsurance Of United States Risks In Foreign Jurisdictions	Any risk reinsured after date of enactment

¶20,001

Code Sec.	Act Sec.	Act Provision Subject	Effective Date
851(b)	331(b)	Net Income From Publicly Traded Partnerships Treated As Qualifying Income Of Regulated Investment Companies-Source Flow-Through Rule Not To Apply	Tax years beginning after date of enactment
851(b)(2)	331(a)	Net Income From Publicly Traded Partnerships Treated As Qualifying Income Of Regulated Investment Companies	Tax years beginning after date of enactment
851(b)(3)(B)	331(f)	Net Income From Publicly Traded Partnerships Treated As Qualifying Income Of Regulated Investment Companies-Limitation On Composition Of Assets	Tax years beginning after date of enactment
851(c)(5)-(6)	331(c)	Net Income From Publicly Traded Partnerships Treated As Qualifying Income Of Regulated Investment Companies-Limitation of Ownership	Tax years beginning after date of enactment
851(h)	331(d)	Net Income From Publicly Traded Partnerships Treated As Qualifying Income Of Regulated Investment Companies-Definition Of Publicly Traded Partnership	Tax years beginning after date of enactment
856(c)(5)(E)	835(b)(4)	Repeal Of Special Rules-Conforming Amendments	January 1, 2005, generally
856(c)(5)(G)	243(d)	Improvements Related To Real Estate Investment Trusts-Conformity With General Hedging Definition	Tax years beginning after date of enactment
856(c)(7)	243(a)(1)	Improvements Related To Real Estate Investment Trusts-Expansion of Straight Debt Harbor	Tax years beginning after December 31, 2000
856(c)(7)	243(f)(1)	Improvements Related To Real Estate Investment Trusts-Savings Provisions	Tax years beginning after date of enactment
856(c)(A)-(C)	243(f)(2)	Improvements Related To Real Estate Investment Trusts-Savings Provisions	Tax years beginning after date of enactment
856(d)(8)(A)	243(b)	Improvements Related To Real Estate Investment Trusts-Clarification of Application of Limited Rental Exception	Tax years beginning after December 31, 2000
856(g)(1)	243(f)(3)(A)	Improvements Related To Real Estate Investment Trusts-Savings Provisions	Tax years beginning after date of enactment
856(g)(5)	243(f)(3)(B)	Improvements Related To Real Estate Investment Trusts-Savings Provisions	Tax years beginning after date of enactment
856(m)	243(a)(2)	Improvements Related To Real Estate Investment Trusts-Expansion of Straight Debt Safe Harbor	Tax years beginning after December 31, 2000
857(b)(2)(E)	243(f)(4)	Improvements Related To Real Estate Investment Trusts-Savings Provisions	Tax years beginning after date of enactment
857(b)(3)(F)	418(b)	Modification Of The Treatment Of Certain REIT Distributions Attributable To Gain From Sales Or Exchanges OF United States Real Property Interests-Conforming Amendment	Tax years beginning after date of enactment
857(b)(5)(A)	243(e)	Improvements Related To Real Estate Investment Trusts-Conformity With Regulated Investment Company Rules	Tax years beginning after date of enactment

Code Sec.	Act Sec.	Act Provision Subject	Effective Date
57(b)(6)(D)-(F)	321(a)	Modification Of Safe Harbor Rules For Timber REITS-Expansion Of Prohibited Transaction Safe Harbor	Tax years beginning after date of enactment
57(b)(7)(B)	243(c)	Improvements Related To Real Estate Investment Trusts-Deletion of Customary Services Exception	Tax years beginning after date of enactment
60(e)(2)-(4)	243(f)(5)	Improvements Related To Real Estate Investment Trusts-Savings Provisions	Tax years beginning after date of enactment
60(H)-(L)	835(a)	Repeal Of Special Rules	January 1, 2005, generally
60G(a)(1)	835(b)(5)(A)	Repeal Of Special Rules-Conforming Amendments	January 1, 2005, generally
60G(a)(3)	835(b)(5)(B)	Repeal Of Special Rules-Conforming Amendments	January 1, 2005, generally
60G(a)(3)	835(b)(7)	Repeal Of Special Rules-Conforming Amendments	January 1, 2005, generally
60G(a)(3)(A)	835(b)(8)(A)	Repeal Of Special Rules-Conforming Amendments	January 1, 2005, generally
60G(a)(3)(B)-D)	835(b)(6)	Repeal Of Special Rules-Conforming Amendments	January 1, 2005, generally
60G(a)(7)(B)	835(b)(8)(B)	Repeal Of Special Rules-Conforming Amendments	January 1, 2005, generally
861(a)(1)(A)-(C)	410(a)	Equal Treatment Of Interest Paid By Foreign Partnerships And Foreign Corporations	Tax years beginning after December 31, 2003
864(c)(4)(B)	894(a)	Effectively Connected Income To Include Certain Foreign Source Income	Tax years beginning after date of enactment
864(d)(2)(A)-(C)	413(c)(12)	Repeal of Foreign Personal Holding Company Rules and Foreign Investment Company Rules-Conforming Amendments	Tax years of foreign corporations beginning after December 31, 2004 and to tax years of United States shareholders with or within which such tax years of foreign corporations end
864(d)(5)(A)	403(b)(6)	Look-Thru Rules To Apply To Dividends From Noncontrolled Section 902 Corporations-Conforming Amendments	Tax years beginning after December 31, 2002
864(e)(3)	101(b)(6)(A)-(B)	Repeal of Exclusion for Extraterritorial Income-Conforming Amendments	Transactions after December 31, 2004
864(e)(7)(B)	401(b)(1)	Interest Expense Allocation Rules-Expansion of Regulatory Authority	Tax years beginning after December 31, 2008
864(e)(7)(E)-(G)	401(b)(2)	Interest Expense Allocation Rules-Expansion of Regulatory Authority	Tax years beginning after December 31, 2008
864(f)-(g)	401(a)	Interest Expense Allocation Rules	Tax years beginning after December 31, 2008
871(i)(2)(D)	409(a)	Repeal Of Withholding Tax On Dividends From Certain Foreign Corporations	Payments made after December 31, 2004
871(k)-(l)	411(a)(1)	Treatment of Certain Dividends Of Regulated Investment Companies-Treatment of Certain Dividends	Dividends with respect to tax years of regulated investment companies beginning after December 31, 2004

Code Sec.	Act Sec.	Act Provision Subject	Effective Date
872(b)(5)-(8)	419(a)	Exclusion Of Income Derived From Certain Wagers On Horse Races And Dog Races From Gross Income Of Nonresident Alien Individuals	Wages made after date of enactment
877(a)	804(a)(1)	Revision of Tax Rules On Expatriation Of Individuals-Expatriation To Avoid Tax	Individuals Who Expatriate After June 3, 2004
877(c)	804(a)(2)	Revision of Tax Rules On Expatriation Of Individuals-Expatriation To Avoid Tax	Individuals Who Expatriate After June 3, 2004
877(g)	804(c)	Revision of Tax Rules On Expatriation Of Individuals-Physical Presence In The United States For More Than 30 Days	Individuals Who Expatriate After June 3, 2004
881(b)	420(c)(1)	Limitation Of Withholding Tax For Puerto Rico Corporations-Conforming Amendments	Dividends paid after date of enactment
881(b)(1)	420(c)(2)	Limitation Of Withholding Tax For Puerto Rico Corporations-Conforming Amendments	Dividends paid after date of enactment
881(b)(2)-(3)	420(a)	Limitation Of Withholding Tax For Puerto Rico Corporations	Dividends paid after date of enactment
881(e)-(f)	411(a)(2)	Treatment of Certain Dividends Of Regulated Investment Companies-Treatment of Certain Dividends	Dividends with respect to tax years of regulated investment companies beginning after December 31, 2004
883(a)(4)	419(b)	Exclusion Of Income Derived From Certain Wagers On Horse Races And Dog Races From Gross Income Of Nonresident Alien Individuals-Conforming Amendment	Wages made after the date of enactment
897(h)	411(c)(5)	Treatment of Certain Dividends Of Regulated Investment Companies-Treatment of Regulated Investment Companies Under Section 897	December 31, 2004
897(h)(1)	411(c)(1)	Treatment of Certain Dividends Of Regulated Investment Companies-Treatment of Regulated Investment Companies Under Section 897	Dividends with respect to tax years of regulated investment companies beginning after December 31, 2004
897(h)(1)	418(a)	Modification Of The Treatment Of Certain REIT Distributions Attributable To Gain From Sales Or Exchanges OF United States Real Property Interests	Tax years beginning after date of enactment
897(h)(2)-(3)	411(c)(2)	Treatment of Certain Dividends Of Regulated Investment Companies-Treatment of Regulated Investment Companies Under Section 897	December 31, 2004
897(h)(4)(A)-(B)	411(c)(3)	Treatment of Certain Dividends Of Regulated Investment Companies-Treatment of Regulated Investment Companies Under Section 897	December 31, 2004

¶20,001

Code Sec.	Act Sec.	Act Provision Subject	Effective Date
897(h)(4)(C)-(D)	411(c)(4)	Treatment of Certain Dividends Of Regulated Investment Companies-Treatment of Regulated Investment Companies Under Section 897	December 31, 2004
898(b)(1)(A)	413(c)(13)(A)	Repeal of Foreign Personal Holding Company Rules and Foreign Investment Company Rules-Conforming Amendments	Tax years of foreign corporations beginning after December 31, 2004 and to tax years of United States shareholders with or within which such tax years of foreign corporations end
898(b)(2)(B)	413(c)(13)(B)	Repeal of Foreign Personal Holding Company Rules and Foreign Investment Company Rules-Conforming Amendments	Tax years of foreign corporations beginning after December 31, 2004 and to tax years of United States shareholders with or within which such tax years of foreign corporations end
898(b)(3)	413(c)(13)(C)	Repeal of Foreign Personal Holding Company Rules and Foreign Investment Company Rules-Conforming Amendments	Tax years of foreign corporations beginning after December 31, 2004 and to tax years of United States shareholders with or within which such tax years of foreign corporations end
898(c)	413(c)(13)(D)	Repeal of Foreign Personal Holding Company Rules and Foreign Investment Company Rules-Conforming Amendments	Tax years of foreign corporations beginning after December 31, 2004 and to tax years of United States shareholders with or within which such tax years of foreign corporations end
901(b)(5)	405(b)	Attribution Of Stock Ownership Through Partnerships To Apply In Determining Section 902 And 960 Credits-Clarification of Comparable Attribution Under Section 901(b)(5)	Taxes of foreign corporations for tax years beginning after date of enactment
901(k)	832(b)	Minimum Holding Period For Foreign Tax Credit On Withholding Taxes On Income Other Than Dividends-Conforming Amendment	Amounts paid or accrued more than 30 days after date of enactment
901(l)-(m)	832(a)	Minimum Holding Period For Foreign Tax Credit On Withholding Taxes On Income Other Than Dividends	Amounts paid or accrued more than 30 days after date of enactment
902(c)(7)-(8)	405(a)	Attribution Of Stock Ownership Through Partnerships To Apply In Determining Section 902 And 960 Credits	Taxes of foreign corporations for tax years beginning after date of enactment

Code Sec.	Act Sec.	Act Provision Subject	Effective Date
903	101(b)(7)	Repeal of Exclusion for Extraterritorial Income-Conforming Amendments	Transactions after December 31, 2004
904(c)	417(a)(1)	10-Year Foreign Tax Credit Carryover; 1-Year Foreign Tax Credit Carryback	Excess foreign taxes which may be carried to any tax year ending after date of enactment
904(d)(1)	404(a)	Reduction to 2 Foreign Tax Credit Baskets	Tax years beginning after December 31, 2006
904(d)(1)(E)	403(b)(1)	Look-Thru Rules To Apply To Dividends From Noncontrolled Section 902 Corporations-Conforming Amendments	Tax years beginning after December 31, 2002
904(d)(2)(A)	413(c)(14)	Repeal of Foreign Personal Holding Company Rules and Foreign Investment Company Rules-Conforming Amendments	Tax years of foreign corporations beginning after December 31, 2004 and to tax years of United States shareholders with or within which such tax years of foreign corporations end
904(d)(2)(A)-(B)	404(b)	Reduction to 2 Foreign Tax Credit Baskets-Categories	Tax years beginning after December 31, 2006
904(d)(2)(B)	404(c)	Reduction to 2 Foreign Tax Credit Baskets-Specified Passive Category Income	Tax years beginning after December 31, 2006
904(d)(2)(B)	404(f)(1)	Reduction to 2 Foreign Tax Credit Baskets-Conforming Amendments	Tax years beginning after December 31, 2006
904(d)(2)(C)	403(b)(2)	Look-Thru Rules To Apply To Dividends From Noncontrolled Section 902 Corporations-Conforming Amendments	Tax years beginning after December 31, 2002
904(d)(2)(C)-(D)	404(d)	Reduction to 2 Foreign Tax Credit Baskets-Treatment Of Financial Services	Tax years beginning after December 31, 2006
904(d)(2)(D)	403(b)(3)	Look-Thru Rules To Apply To Dividends From Noncontrolled Section 902 Corporations-Conforming Amendments	Tax years beginning after December 31, 2002
904(d)(2)(D)	404(f)(2)	Reduction to 2 Foreign Tax Credit Baskets-Conforming Amendments	Tax years beginning after December 31, 2006
904(d)(2)(D)	404(f)(3)	Reduction to 2 Foreign Tax Credit Baskets-Conforming Amendments	Tax years beginning after December 31, 2006
904(d)(2)(E)	403(b)(4)(A)-(B)	Look-Thru Rules To Apply To Dividends From Noncontrolled Section 902 Corporations-Conforming Amendments	Tax years beginning after December 31, 2002
904(d)(2)(H)-(J)	404(e)	Reduction to 2 Foreign Tax Credit Baskets-Treatment Of Income Tax Base Differences	Tax years beginning after December 31, 2004
904(d)(2)(K)	404(f)(5)	Reduction to 2 Foreign Tax Credit Baskets-Conforming Amendments	Tax years beginning after December 31, 2006
904(d)(3)	404(f)(4)	Reduction to 2 Foreign Tax Credit Baskets-Conforming Amendments	Tax years beginning after December 31, 2006
904(d)(3)(F)	403(b)(5)	Look-Thru Rules To Apply To Dividends From Noncontrolled Section 902 Corporations-Conforming Amendments	Tax years beginning after December 31, 2002
904(d)(4)	403(a)	Look-Thru Rules To Apply To Dividends From Noncontrolled Section 902 Corporations-General Rule	Tax years beginning after December 31, 2002

Code Sec.	Act Sec.	Act Provision Subject	Effective Date
904(f)(3)(D)	895(a)	Recapture Of Overall Foreign Losses On Sale Of Controlled Foreign Corporation	Dispositions after date of enactment
904(g)-(l)	402(a)	Recharacterization of Overall Domestic Loss	Losses for tax years beginning after December 31, 2006
904(h)(1)(A)	413(c)(15)(A)	Repeal of Foreign Personal Holding Company Rules and Foreign Investment Company Rules-Conforming Amendments	Tax years of foreign corporations beginning after December 31, 2004 and to tax years of United States shareholders with or within which such tax years of foreign corporations end
904(h)(2)	413(c)(15)(B)	Repeal of Foreign Personal Holding Company Rules and Foreign Investment Company Rules-Conforming Amendments	Tax years of foreign corporations beginning after December 31, 2004 and to tax years of United States shareholders with or within which such tax years of foreign corporations end
904(j)(3)(A)	404(f)(6)	Reduction to 2 Foreign Tax Credit Baskets-Conforming Amendments	Tax years beginning after December 31, 2006
907(c)	417(a)(2)	10-Year Foreign Tax Credit Carryover; 1-Year Foreign Tax Credit Carryback	Excess foreign taxes which may be carried to any tax year ending after date of enactment
907(f)(1)	417(b)(1)	10-Year Foreign Tax Credit Carryover; 1-Year Foreign Tax Credit Carryback-Excess Extraction Taxes	Excess foreign taxes which may be carried to any tax year ending after date of enactment
907(f)(1)	417(b)(2)	10-Year Foreign Tax Credit Carryover; 1-Year Foreign Tax Credit Carryback-Excess Extraction Taxes	Excess foreign taxes which may be carried to any tax year ending after date of enactment
907(f)(1)	417(b)(3)	10-Year Foreign Tax Credit Carryover; 1-Year Foreign Tax Credit Carryback-Excess Extraction Taxes	Date of enactment
931(d)	908(c)(1)	Residence And Source Rules Relating To United States Possession-Conforming And Clerical Amendments	Tax years ending after date of enactment, generally
932	908(c)(2)	Residence And Source Rules Relating To United States Possession-Conforming And Clerical Amendments	Tax years ending after date of enactment, generally
934(b)(4)	908(c)(3)	Residence And Source Rules Relating To United States Possession-Conforming And Clerical Amendments	Tax years ending after date of enactment, generally
935(a)	908(c)(4)(A)	Residence And Source Rules Relating To United States Possession-Conforming And Clerical Amendments	Tax years ending after date of enactment, generally

¶20,001

Code Sec.	Act Sec.	Act Provision Subject	Effective Date
935(a)(1)	908(c)(4)(B)	Residence And Source Rules Relating To United States Possession-Conforming And Clerical Amendments	Tax years ending after date of enactment, generally
935(b)(1)(A)-(B)	908(c)(4)(C)	Residence And Source Rules Relating To United States Possession-Conforming And Clerical Amendments	Tax years ending after date of enactment, generally
935(b)(2)	908(c)(4)(D)	Residence And Source Rules Relating To United States Possession-Conforming And Clerical Amendments	Tax years ending after date of enactment, generally
936(a)(2)(A)	402(b)(2)	Recharacterization of Overall Domestic Loss-Conforming Amendments	Losses for tax years beginning after December 31, 2006
937	908(a)	Residence And Source Rules Relating To United States Possession-Bona Fide Resident	Tax years ending after date of enactment, generally
941	101(b)(1)	Repeal of Exclusion for Extraterritorial Income-Conforming Amendments	Transactions after December 31, 2004
942	101(b)(1)	Repeal of Exclusion for Extraterritorial Income-Conforming Amendments	Transactions after December 31, 2004
943	101(b)(1)	Repeal of Exclusion for Extraterritorial Income-Conforming Amendments	Transactions after December 31, 2004
951(c)-(f)	413(c)(16)	Repeal of Foreign Personal Holding Company Rules and Foreign Investment Company Rules-Conforming Amendments	Tax years of foreign corporations beginning after December 31, 2004 and to tax years of United States shareholders with or within which such tax years of foreign corporations end
952(c)(1)(B)	415(c)(1)	Modifications To Treatment Of Aircraft Leasing and Shipping Income-Conforming Amendments	Tax years of foreign corporations beginning after December 31, 2004 and to tax years of United States shareholders with or within which such tax years of foreign corporations end
954(a)(4)	415(a)(1)	Modifications To Treatment Of Aircraft Leasing and Shipping Income-Elimination Of Foreign Base Company Shipping Income	Tax years of foreign corporations beginning after December 31, 2004 and to tax years of United States shareholders with or within which such tax years of foreign corporations end
954(b)(5)-(8)	415(c)(2)(A)-(C)	Modifications To Treatment Of Aircraft Leasing and Shipping Income-Conforming Amendments	Tax years of foreign corporations beginning after December 31, 2004 and to tax years of United States shareholders with or within which such tax years of foreign corporations end

Code Sec.	Act Sec.	Act Provision Subject	Effective Date
954(c)(1)(C)	414(a)	Determination of Foreign Personal Holding Company Income With Respect To Transactions in Commodities	Transactions entered into after December 31, 2004
954(c)(1)(I)	413(b)(2)	Repeal of Foreign Personal Holding Company Rules and Foreign Investment Company Rules-Exemption Of Foreign Corporations From Personal Holding Company Rules	Tax years of foreign corporations beginning after December 31, 2004 and to tax years of United States shareholders with or within which such tax years of foreign corporations end
954(c)(2)(A)	415(b)	Modifications To Treatment Of Aircraft Leasing and Shipping Income-Safe Harbor For Certain Leasing Activities	Tax years of foreign corporations beginning after December 31, 2004 and to tax years of United States shareholders with or within which such tax years of foreign corporations end
954(c)(2)(C)	414(c)	Determination of Foreign Personal Holding Company Income With Respect To Transactions in Commodities-Modification of Exception For Dealers	Transactions entered into after December 31, 2004
954(c)(4)	412(a)	Look-Thru Treatment For Sales Of Partnership Interests	December 31, 2004
954(c)(5)	414(b)	Determination of Foreign Personal Holding Company Income With Respect To Transactions in Commodities-Definition and Special Rules	Transactions entered into after December 31, 2004
954(f)	415(a)(2)	Modifications To Treatment Of Aircraft Leasing and Shipping Income-Elimination Of Foreign Base Company Shipping Income	Tax years of foreign corporations beginning after December 31, 2004 and to tax years of United States shareholders with or within which such tax years of foreign corporations end
954(h)(3)(E)	416(a)	Modification Of Exceptions Under Subpart F For Active Financing	Tax years of foreign corporations beginning after December 31, 2004 and to tax years of United States shareholders with or within which such tax years of foreign corporations end

Code Sec.	Act Sec.	Act Provision Subject	Effective Date
956(c)(2)	407(b)	United States Property Not To Include Certain Assets of Controlled Foreign Corporation-Conforming Amendment	Tax years of foreign corporations beginning after December 31, 2004 and to tax years of United States shareholders with or within which such tax years of foreign corporations end
956(c)(2)(A)	837(a)	Clarification Of Banking Business For Purposes Of Determining Investment Of Earnings In United States Property	Date of enactment
956(c)(2)(J)-(M)	407(a)	United States Property Not To Include Certain Assets of Controlled Foreign Corporation	Tax years of foreign corporations beginning after December 31, 2004 and to tax years of United States shareholders with or within which such tax years of foreign corporations end
957(c)	908(c)(5)(B)	Residence And Source Rules Relating To United States Possession-Conforming And Clerical Amendments	Tax years ending after date of enactment, generally
957(c)(2)(B)	908(c)(5)(A)	Residence And Source Rules Relating To United States Possession-Conforming And Clerical Amendments	Tax years ending after date of enactment, generally
965	422(a)	Incentives To Reinvest Foreign Earnings In United States	Tax years ending on or after date of enactment
986(a)(1)(D)-(E)	408(a)	Translation of Foreign Taxes-Elective Exception For Taxes Paid Other Than In Functional Currency	Tax years beginning after December 31, 2004
986(a)(1)(E)-(F)	408(b)(1)	Translation of Foreign Taxes-Special Rule For Regulated Investment Companies	Tax years beginning after December 31, 2004
986(a)(2)	408(b)(2)	Translation of Foreign Taxes-Special Rule For Regulated Investment Companies-Conforming Amendment	Tax years beginning after December 31, 2004
989(b)(3)	413(c)(17)	Repeal of Foreign Personal Holding Company Rules and Foreign Investment Company Rules-Conforming Amendments	Tax years of foreign corporations beginning after December 31, 2004 and to tax years of United States shareholders with or within which such tax years of foreign corporations end
999(c)(1)	101(b)(8)	Repeal of Exclusion for Extraterritorial Income-Conforming Amendments	Transactions after December 31, 2004

Code Sec.	Act Sec.	Act Provision Subject	Effective Date
1014(b)(5)	413(c)(18)	Repeal of Foreign Personal Holding Company Rules and Foreign Investment Company Rules-Conforming Amendments	Tax years of foreign corporations beginning after December 31, 2004 and to tax years of United States shareholders with or within which such tax years of foreign corporations end
1016(a)(13)	413(c)(19)	Repeal of Foreign Personal Holding Company Rules and Foreign Investment Company Rules-Conforming Amendments	Tax years of foreign corporations beginning after December 31, 2004 and to tax years of United States shareholders with or within which such tax years of foreign corporations end
1016(a)(27)-(29)	245(c)(2)	Credit for Maintenance of Railroad Track-Conforming Amendments	Tax years beginning after December 31, 2004
1016(a)(28)-(30)	338(b)(4)	Expensing Of Capital Costs Incurred IN Complying With Environmental Protection Agency Sulphur Regulations-Conforming Amendments	Expenses paid or incurred after December 31, 2002 in tax years ending after such date
1016(a)(29)-(31)	339(d)	Credit For Production Of Low Sulphor Diesel Fuel-Basis Adjustment	Expenses paid or incurred after December 31, 2002 in tax years ending after such date
1033(e)	311(b)(1)-(2)	Special Rules For Livestock Sold On Account of Weather-Related Conditions-Extension of Replacement Period Of Involuntarily Converted Livestock	Any tax year with respect to which the due date (without regard to extensions) for the return is after December 31, 2002
1033(f)	311(a)(1)-(3)	Special Rules For Livestock Sold On Account of Weather-Related Conditions-Replacement of Livestock Sold On Account of Weather-Related Conditions	Any tax year with respect to which the due date (without regard to extensions) for the return is after December 31, 2002
1056	886(b)(1)(A)	Extension Of Amortization Of Intangibles To Sports Franchises-Conforming Amendments	Property acquired after date of enactment
1092(a)(2)(A)	888(a)(1)	Modification Of Straddle Rules	Positions established on or after date of enactment
1092(a)(2)(B)	888(a)(2)(A)-(B)	Modification Of Straddle Rules	Positions established on or after date of enactment
1092(a)(3)(B)-(C)	888(a)(3)	Modification Of Straddle Rules	Positions established on or after date of enactment
1092(c)(2)(B)-(C)	888(a)(4)	Modification Of Straddle Rules	Positions established on or after date of enactment

Code Sec.	Act Sec.	Act Provision Subject	Effective Date
1092(d)(3)	888(c)(1)	Modification Of Straddle Rules-Repeal Of Stock Exception	Positions established on or after date of enactment
1092(d)(8)	888(b)	Modification Of Straddle Rules-Physically Settled Positions	Positions established on or after date of enactment
1202(e)(4)(C)	835(b)(9)	Repeal Of Special Rules-Conforming Amendments	January 1, 2005, generally
1212(a)(3)	413(c)(20)(A)	Repeal of Foreign Personal Holding Company Rules and Foreign Investment Company Rules-Conforming Amendments	Tax years of foreign corporations beginning after December 31, 2004 and to tax years of United States shareholders with or within which such tax years of foreign corporations end
1223(10)-(17)	413(c)(21)	Repeal of Foreign Personal Holding Company Rules and Foreign Investment Company Rules-Conforming Amendments	Tax years of foreign corporations beginning after December 31, 2004 and to tax years of United States shareholders with or within which such tax years of foreign corporations end
1245(a)(2)(C)	338(b)(5)	Expensing Of Capital Costs Incurred IN Complying With Environmental Protection Agency Sulphur Regulations-Conforming Amendments	Expenses paid or incurred after December 31, 2002 in tax years ending after such date
1245(a)(3)(C)	338(b)(5)	Expensing Of Capital Costs Incurred IN Complying With Environmental Protection Agency Sulphur Regulations-Conforming Amendments	Expenses paid or incurred after December 31, 2002 in tax years ending after such date
1245(a)(4)	886(b)(2)	Extension Of Amortization Of Intangibles To Sports Franchises-Conforming Amendments	Franchises acquired after date of enactment
1246	413(a)(2)	Repeal of Foreign Personal Holding Company Rules and Foreign Investment Company Rules-General Rule	Tax years of foreign corporations beginning after December 31, 2004 and to tax years of United States shareholders with or within which such tax years of foreign corporations end
1247	413(a)(3)	Repeal of Foreign Personal Holding Company Rules and Foreign Investment Company Rules-General Rule	Tax years of foreign corporations beginning after December 31, 2004 and to tax years of United States shareholders with or within which such tax years of foreign corporations end

Code Sec.	Act Sec.	Act Provision Subject	Effective Date
1248(d)(5)-(7)	413(c)(22)	Repeal of Foreign Personal Holding Company Rules and Foreign Investment Company Rules-Conforming Amendments	Tax years of foreign corporations beginning after December 31, 2004 and to tax years of United States shareholders with or within which such tax years of foreign corporations end
1253(e)	886(b)(3)	Extension Of Amortization Of Intangibles To Sports Franchises-Conforming Amendments	Property acquired after date of enactment
1258(d)(1)	888(c)(2)	Modification Of Straddle Rules-Repeal Of Stock Exception	Positions established on or after date of enactment
1260(c)(2)(H)-(J)	413(c)(23)	Repeal of Foreign Personal Holding Company Rules and Foreign Investment Company Rules-Conforming Amendments	Tax years of foreign corporations beginning after December 31, 2004 and to tax years of United States shareholders with or within which such tax years of foreign corporations end
1286(f)-(g)	831(a)	Treatment Of Stripped Interests In Bond And Preferred Stock Funds	Purchases and dispositions after date of enactment
1291(b)(3)(F)	413(c)(24)(A)	Repeal of Foreign Personal Holding Company Rules and Foreign Investment Company Rules-Conforming Amendments	Tax years of foreign corporations beginning after December 31, 2004 and to tax years of United States shareholders with or within which such tax years of foreign corporations end
1291(e)	413(c)(24)(B)	Repeal of Foreign Personal Holding Company Rules and Foreign Investment Company Rules-Conforming Amendments	Tax years of foreign corporations beginning after December 31, 2004 and to tax years of United States shareholders with or within which such tax years of foreign corporations end
1294(a)(2)	413(c)(25)	Repeal of Foreign Personal Holding Company Rules and Foreign Investment Company Rules-Conforming Amendments	Tax years of foreign corporations beginning after December 31, 2004 and to tax years of United States shareholders with or within which such tax years of foreign corporations end

¶20,001

Code Sec.	Act Sec.	Act Provision Subject	Effective Date
1301(a)	314(b)(1)	Coordinate Farmers And Fisherman Income Averaging And The Alternative Minimum Tax-Allowing Income Averaging For Fisherman	Tax years beginning after December 31, 2003
1301(b)(1)(A)	314(b)(2)(A)	Coordinate Farmers And Fisherman Income Averaging And The Alternative Minimum Tax-Allowing Income Averaging For Fisherman	Tax years beginning after December 31, 2003
1301(b)(1)(B)	314(b)(2)(B)	Coordinate Farmers And Fisherman Income Averaging And The Alternative Minimum Tax-Allowing Income Averaging For Fisherman	Tax years beginning after December 31, 2003
1301(b)(4)	314(b)(3)	Coordinate Farmers And Fisherman Income Averaging And The Alternative Minimum Tax-Allowing Income Averaging For Fisherman	Tax years beginning after December 31, 2003
1352	248(a)	Election to Determine Corporate Tax on Certain International Shipping Activities Using Per Ton Rate	Tax years beginning after date of enactment
1353	248(a)	Election to Determine Corporate Tax on Certain International Shipping Activities Using Per Ton Rate	Tax years beginning after date of enactment
1354	248(a)	Election to Determine Corporate Tax on Certain International Shipping Activities Using Per Ton Rate	Tax years beginning after date of enactment
1355	248(a)	Election to Determine Corporate Tax on Certain International Shipping Activities Using Per Ton Rate	Tax years beginning after date of enactment
1356	248(a)	Election to Determine Corporate Tax on Certain International Shipping Activities Using Per Ton Rate	Tax years beginning after date of enactment
1357	248(a)	Election to Determine Corporate Tax on Certain International Shipping Activities Using Per Ton Rate	Tax years beginning after date of enactment
1358	248(a)	Election to Determine Corporate Tax on Certain International Shipping Activities Using Per Ton Rate	Tax years beginning after date of enactment
1359	248(a)	Election to Determine Corporate Tax on Certain International Shipping Activities Using Per Ton Rate	Tax years beginning after date of enactment
1361(b)(1)(A)	232(a)	Increase in Number of Eligible Shareholders to 100	Tax years beginning after December 31, 2004
1361(b)(3)(A)	239(a)	Information Returns for Qualified Subchapter S Subsidiaries	Tax years beginning after December 31, 2004
1361(c)(1)	231(a)	Members of Family Treated as 1 Shareholder	Tax years beginning after December 31, 2004
1361(c)(2)(A)	233(a)	Expansion of Bank S Corporation Eligible Shareholders to Include IRAs	Date of enactment
1361(c)(2)(B)	233(b)	Expansion of Bank S Corporation Eligible Shareholders to Include IRAs-Treatment of Shareholder	Date of enactment
1361(d)(1)(A)	236(a)(1)	Use of Passive Activity Loss and At-Risk Amounts By Qualified Subchapter S Trust Income Beneficiaries	Transfers made after December 31, 2004

Code Sec.	Act Sec.	Act Provision Subject	Effective Date
1361(d)(1)(B)	236(a)(2)	Use of Passive Activity Loss and At-Risk Amounts By Qualified Subchapter S Trust Income Beneficiaries	Transfers made after December 31, 2004
1361(d)(1)(C)	236(a)(3)	Use of Passive Activity Loss and At-Risk Amounts By Qualified Subchapter S Trust Income Beneficiaries	Transfers made after December 31, 2004
1361(e)(2)	234(a)(1)-(2)	Disregard of Unexercised Powers of Appointment in Determining Potential Current Beneficiaries of ESBT	Tax years beginning after December 31, 2004.
1362(d)(3)(F)	237(a)	Exclusion of Investment Securities Income from Passive Income Test for Bank S Corporations	Tax years beginning after December 31, 2004.
1362(f)(1)	231(b)(1)	Members of Family Treated as 1 Shareholder-Relief From Inadvertant Invalid Election or Termination	Elections and terminations made after December 31, 2004
1362(f)(1)	238(a)(1)	Relief From Inadvertantly Invalid Qualified Subchapter S Subsidiary Elections and Terminations	Elections made and terminations made beginning after December 31, 2004
1362(f)(1)(B)	231(b)(1)	Members of Family Treated as 1 Shareholder-Relief From Inadvertant Invalid Election or Termination	Elections and terminations made after December 31, 2004
1362(f)(1)(B)	238(a)(2)	Relief From Inadvertantly Invalid Qualified Subchapter S Subsidiary Elections and Terminations	Elections made and terminations made beginning after December 31, 2004
1362(f)(3)(A)	238(a)(3)	Relief From Inadvertantly Invalid Qualified Subchapter S Subsidiary Elections and Terminations	Elections made and terminations made beginning after December 31, 2004
1362(f)(4)	238(a)(4)	Relief From Inadvertantly Invalid Qualified Subchapter S Subsidiary Elections and Terminations	Elections made and terminations made beginning after December 31, 2004
1362(f)(4)	238(a)(5)	Relief From Inadvertantly Invalid Qualified Subchapter S Subsidiary Elections and Terminations	Elections made and terminations made beginning after December 31, 2004
1366(d)(2)	235(a)	Transfer of Suspended Losses Incident to Divorce, etc.	Tax years beginning after December 31, 2004.
1381(c)	319(d)	Treatment of Certain Income of Cooperatives-Exception From Unrelated Business Taxable Income	Tax year beginning after date of enactment
1388(a)	312(a)	Payment of Dividends On Stock Of Cooperatives Without Reducing Patronage Dividends	Distributions in tax years beginning after date of enactment
1388(k)	316(a)	Modification To Cooperative Marketing Rules To Include Value Added Processing Involving Animals	Tax years beginning after date of enactment
1400E(g)	222(a)	Expansion of Designated Renewal Community Area Based on 2000 Census Data	December 21, 2000
1402(a)(14)-(16)	102(d)(7)	Income Attributable to Domestic Production Activities-Technical Amendments	Tax years beginning after December 31, 2004

¶20,001

Code Sec.	Act Sec.	Act Provision Subject	Effective Date
1441(c)(12)	411(a)(3)(A)	Treatment of Certain Dividends Of Regulated Investment Companies-Treatment of Certain Dividends	Dividends with respect to tax years of regulated investment companies beginning after December 31, 2004
1442(a)	411(a)(3)(B)	Treatment of Certain Dividends Of Regulated Investment Companies-Treatment of Certain Dividends	Dividends with respect to tax years of regulated investment companies beginning after December 31, 2004
1442(c)	420(b)(1)-(2)	Limitation Of Withholding Tax For Puerto Rico Corporations-Withholding	Dividends paid after date of enactment
1502	844(a)	Affirmation Of Consolidated Return Regulation Authority	Tax years beginning before, on or after date of enactment
1563(a)(2)	900(a)	Modification Of Definition Of Controlled Group Of Corporations	Tax years beginning after date of enactment
1563(f)(5)	900(b)	Modification Of Definition Of Controlled Group Of Corporations-Application Of Existing Rules To Other Code Provisions	Tax years beginning after date of enactment
2105(d)	411(b)	Treatment of Certain Dividends Of Regulated Investment Companies-Estate Tax Treatment Of Interest In Certain Regulated Investment Companies	Estates of decedents dying after December 31, 2004
2107(a)	804(a)(3)	Revision of Tax Rules On Expatriation Of Individuals-Expatriation To Avoid Tax	Individuals Who Expatriate After June 3, 2004
2501(a)(3)-(5)	804(d)(1)	Revision of Tax Rules On Expatriation Of Individuals-Transfer Subject To Tax	Individuals Who Expatriate After June 3, 2004
2501(a)(5)	804(d)(2)	Revision of Tax Rules On Expatriation Of Individuals-Transfer Subject To Tax	Individuals Who Expatriate After June 3, 2004
3121(a)(20)	320(b)(1)	Exclusion For Payments To Individuals Under National Health Service Corps Loan Repayment Program And Certain State Loan Repayment Programs-Treatment For Purposes Of Employment Taxes	Amounts received by an individual in tax years beginning after December 31, 2003
3121(a)(20)-(22)	251(a)(1)(A)	Exclusion of Incentive Stock Options and Employee Stock Purchase Plan Stock Options From Wages-Exclusion From Employment Taxes	Stock acquired pursuant to options exercised after the date of enactment
3121(v)(2)(A)	802(c)(1)	Stock Compensation Of Insiders In Expatriated Corporations-Conforming Amendments	March 4, 2003, generally
3231(e)(12)	251(a)(2)	Exclusion of Incentive Stock Options and Employee Stock Purchase Plan Stock Options From Wages-Exclusion From Employment Taxes	Stock acquired pursuant to options exercised after the date of enactment
3231(e)(5)	320(b)(2)	Exclusion For Payments To Individuals Under National Health Service Corps Loan Repayment Program And Certain State Loan Repayment Programs-Treatment For Purposes Of Employment Taxes	Amounts received by an individual in tax years beginning after December 31, 2003

Code Sec.	Act Sec.	Act Provision Subject	Effective Date
3306(b)(16)	320(b)(3)	Exclusion For Payments To Individuals Under National Health Service Corps Loan Repayment Program And Certain State Loan Repayment Programs-Treatment For Purposes Of Employment Taxes	Amounts received by an individual in tax years beginning after December 31, 2003
3306(b)(17)-(19)	251(a)(3)	Exclusion of Incentive Stock Options and Employee Stock Purchase Plan Stock Options From Wages-Exclusion From Employment Taxes	Stock acquired pursuant to options exercised after the date of enactment
3401(a)	885(b)(2)	Inclusion In Gross Income Of Deferred Compensation Under Nonqualified Compensation Plans-Treatment Of Deferred Amounts	Amounts deferred after December 31, 2004; generally
3401(a)(19)	320(b)(4)	Exclusion For Payments To Individuals Under National Health Service Corps Loan Repayment Program And Certain State Loan Repayment Programs-Treatment For Purposes Of Employment Taxes	Amounts received by an individual in tax years beginning after December 31, 2003
4041(a)(1)	853(a)(6)(B)	Taxation Of Aviation-Grade Kerosene-Rate Of Tax	Aviation-grade kerosene removed, entered, or sold after December 31, 2004
4041(a)(1)(B)	853(a)(6)(A)	Taxation Of Aviation-Grade Kerosene-Rate Of Tax	Aviation-grade kerosene removed, entered, or sold after December 31, 2004
4041(a)(1)(C)	241(a)(1)	Phaseout of 4.3-Cent Motor Fuel Excise Taxes on Railroads and Inland Waterway Transportation Which Remain in General Fund-Taxes on Trains	January 1, 2005
4041(b)(2)(B)	301(c)(5)	Alcohol and Biodiesel Excise Tax Credit And Extension of Alcohol Fuels Income Tax Credit-Additional Amendments	Fuel sold or used after December 31, 2004
4041(c)	853(d)(2)(A)	Taxation Of Aviation-Grade Kerosene-Repeal Of Prior Taxation Of Aviation Fuel	Aviation-grade kerosene removed, entered, or sold after December 31, 2004
4041(d)(2)	853(d)(2)(B)	Taxation Of Aviation-Grade Kerosene-Rate Of Tax	Aviation-grade kerosene removed, entered, or sold after December 31, 2004
4041(d)(3)-(4)	241(a)(2)(A)	Phaseout of 4.3-Cent Motor Fuel Excist Taxes on Railroads and Inland Waterway Transportation Which Remain in General Fund-Taxes on Trains-Conforming Amendments	January 1, 2005
4041(e)	853(d)(2)(C)	Taxation Of Aviation-Grade Kerosene-Rate Of Tax	Aviation-grade kerosene removed, entered, or sold after December 31, 2004

¶20,001

Code Sec.	Act Sec.	Act Provision Subject	Effective Date
4041(i)	853(d)(2)(D)	Taxation Of Aviation-Grade Kerosene-Rate Of Tax	Aviation-grade kerosene removed, entered, or sold after December 31, 2004
4041(k)	301(c)(6)	Alcohol and Biodiesel Excise Tax Credit And Extension of Alcohol Fuels Income Tax Credit-Additional Amendments	Fuel sold or used after December 31, 2004
4041(m)(1)	853(d)(2)(E)	Taxation Of Aviation-Grade Kerosene-Rate Of Tax	Aviation-grade kerosene removed, entered, or sold after December 31, 2004
4042(b)(2)(C)	241(b)	Phaseout of 4.3-Cent Motor Fuel Excise Taxes on Railroads and Inland Waterway Transportation Which Remain in General Fund-Fuel Used on Inland Waterways	January 1, 2005
4053(8)	851(a)(1)	Exemption From Certain Excise Taxes For Middle Machinery-Exemption From Certain Excise Taxes For Mobile Machinery	Day after date of enactment
4071(a)	869(a)	Simplication Of Tax On Tires	Sales in calendar years beginning more than 30 days after date of enactment
4071(c)	869(d)[(e)](1)	Simplication Of Tax On Tires-Conforming Amendments	Sales in calendar years beginning more than 30 days after date of enactment
4071(e)	869(d)[(e)](1)	Simplication Of Tax On Tires-Conforming Amendments	Sales in calendar years beginning more than 30 days after date of enactment
4072(a)-(e)	869(b)[(c)]	Simplication Of Tax On Tires-Biasply and Super Single Tires	Sales in calendar years beginning more than 30 days after date of enactment
4072(b)(2)	851(c)(1)	Exemption From Certain Excise Taxes For Middle Machinery-Exemption From Tax On Tires	Day after date of enactment
4072(c)-(d)	869(b)	Simplication Of Tax On Tires-Biasply and Super Single Tires	Sales in calendar years beginning more than 30 days after date of enactment
4073	869(c)[(d)]	Simplication Of Tax On Tires-Exemption For Tires Sold To Department Of Defense	Sales in calendar years beginning more than 30 days after date of enactment
4081(a)(1)(B)	860(a)(1)-(2)	Registration Of Pipeline Or Vessle Operators Required For Exemption Of Bulk Transfers To Registered Terminals Or Refineries	March 1, 2005
4081(a)(2)(A)	853(a)(1)	Taxation Of Aviation-Grade Kerosene-Rate Of Tax	Aviation-grade kerosene removed, entered, or sold after December 31, 2004

Code Sec.	Act Sec.	Act Provision Subject	Effective Date
4081(a)(2)(C)	853(a)(2)	Taxation Of Aviation-Grade Kerosene-Rate Of Tax	Aviation-grade kerosene removed, entered, or sold after December 31, 2004
4081(a)(3)	853(a)(3)(A)	Taxation Of Aviation-Grade Kerosene-Rate Of Tax	Aviation-grade kerosene removed, entered, or sold after December 31, 2004
4081(a)(4)	853(a)(4)	Taxation Of Aviation-Grade Kerosene-Rate Of Tax	Aviation-grade kerosene removed, entered, or sold after December 31, 2004
4081(c)	301(c)(7)	Alcohol and Biodiesel Excise Tax Credit And Extension of Alcohol Fuels Income Tax Credit-Additional Amendments	Fuel sold or used after December 31, 2004
4082(a)(2)	854(a)	Dye Injection Equipment	180th day after date on which the Secretary issues the resolutions described in Act Sec. 854(b)
4082(b)	851(d)(2)	Exemption From Certain Excise Taxes For Middle Machinery-Refund of Fuel Taxes	Tax years beginning after date of enactment
4082(b)	853(a)(5)(B)(i)	Taxation Of Aviation-Grade Kerosene-Rate Of Tax	Aviation-grade kerosene removed, entered, or sold after December 31, 2004
4082(b)(3)	857(a)	Termination Of Dyed Diesel use By Inter-City Buses	Fuel sold after December 31, 2004
4082(d)(1)-(3)	853(a)(5)(B)(ii)	Taxation Of Aviation-Grade Kerosene-Rate Of Tax	Aviation-grade kerosene removed, entered, or sold after December 31, 2004
4082(e)-(g)	853(a)(5)(A)	Taxation Of Aviation-Grade Kerosene-Rate Of Tax	Aviation-grade kerosene removed, entered, or sold after December 31, 2004
4082(f)	241(a)(2)(B)	Phaseout of 4.3-Cent Motor Fuel Excise Taxes on Railroads and Inland Waterway Transportation Which Remain in General Fund-Taxes on Trains-Conforming Amendments	January 1, 2005
4083(a)(2)	301(c)(8)	Alcohol and Biodiesel Excise Tax Credit And Extension of Alcohol Fuels Income Tax Credit-Additional Amendments	Fuel sold or used after December 31, 2004
4083(a)(3)	870(a)	Transmix And Diesel Fuel Blend Stocks Treated As Taxable Fuel	Fuel removed, sold, or used after December 31, 2004
4083(b)-(d)	853(b)	Taxation Of Aviation-Grade Kerosene-Commercial Aviation	Aviation-grade kerosene removed, entered, or sold after December 31, 2004
4083(d)(1)(A)	858(a)	Authority To Inspect On-Site Records	Date of enactment

¶20,001

Code Sec.	Act Sec.	Act Provision Subject	Effective Date
4083(d)(3)	859(b)(1)(A)-(B)	Assessable Penalty For Refusal Of Entry-Conforming Amendments	January 1, 2005
4091-4093	853(d)(1)	Taxation Of Aviation-Grade Kerosene-Repeal Of Prior Taxation Of Aviation Fuel	Aviation-grade kerosene removed, entered, or sold after December 31, 2004
4101(a)	853(d)(2)(F)	Taxation Of Aviation-Grade Kerosene-Rate Of Tax	Aviation-grade kerosene removed, entered, or sold after December 31, 2004
4101(a)	861(a)(1)-(2)	Display of Registration	January 1, 2005
4101(a)(1)	301(b)	Alcohol and Biodiesel Excise Tax Credit And Extension of Alcohol Fuels Income Tax Credit-Registration Requirement	April 1, 2005
4101(a)(2)-(3)	862(a)	Registration Of Persons Within Foreign Trade Zones, Etc.	January 1, 2005
4101(d)	864(a)	Electronic Filing Of Required Information Reports	January 1, 2006
4103	853(d)(2)(F)	Taxation Of Aviation-Grade Kerosene-Rate Of Tax	Aviation-grade kerosene removed, entered, or sold after December 31, 2004
4104	303(a)	Information Reporting For Persons Claiming Certain Tax Benefits	January 1, 2005
4105	866(a)	Two-Party Exchanges	Date of enactment
4132(a)(1)(I)-(M)	889(a)	Addition Of Vaccines Against Hepatitis A To List of Taxable Vaccines	Sales and uses on or after first day of first month which begins more than 4 weeks after date of enactment
4132(a)(1)(N)	890(a)	Addition of Vaccines Against Influenza To List Of Taxable Vaccines	Sales and uses on or after first day of first month which begins more than 4 weeks after date of enactment, generally
4161(a)(3)-(4)	333(a)	Reduction Of Excise Tax On Fishing Tackle Boxes	Articles sold by manufacturer, producer, or importer after December 31, 2004
4161(b)(1)	332(a)	Simplification Of Excise Tax Imposed On Bows And Arrows-Bows	Articles sold by manufacturer, producer, or importer after date which is 30 days after date of enactment
4161(b)(2)	332(c)((1)-(2)	Simplification Of Excise Tax Imposed On Bows And Arrows-Conforming Amendments	Articles sold by manufacturer, producer, or importer after date which is 30 days after date of enactment

Code Sec.	Act Sec.	Act Provision Subject	Effective Date
4161(b)(3)-(4)	332(b)	Simplification Of Excise Tax Imposed On Bows And Arrows-Arrows	Articles sold by manufacturer, producer, or importer after date which is 30 days after date of enactment
4162(a)(8)-(10)	334(a)	Sonar Devices Suitable For Finding Fish-Not Treated As Sport Fishing Equipment	Articles sold by manufacturer, producer, or importer after December 31, 2004
4162(b)-(c)	334(b)	Sonar Devices Suitable For Finding Fish-Conforming Amendment	Articles sold by manufacturer, producer, or importer after December 31, 2004
4221(a)	853(d)(2)(F)	Taxation Of Aviation-Grade Kerosene-Rate Of Tax	Aviation-grade kerosene removed, entered, or sold after December 31, 2004
4481(c)(2)	867(a)(1)	Modifications Of Tax On Use Of Certain Vehicles-Proration Of Tax Where Vehicle Sold	Taxable periods after date of enactment
4481(c)(2)	867(a)(2)	Modifications Of Tax On Use Of Certain Vehicles-Proration Of Tax Where Vehicle Sold	Taxable periods after date of enactment
4481(e)-(f)	867(c)	Modifications Of Tax On Use Of Certain Vehicles-Electronic Filing	Taxable periods after date of enactment
4483(f)	867(d)	Modifications Of Tax On Use Of Certain Vehicles-Repeal Of Reduction In Tax For Certain Trucks	Taxable periods after date of enactment
4483(g)-(h)	851(b)(1)	Exemption From Certain Excise Taxes For Middle Machinery-Exemption From Tax On Use Of Certain Vehicles	Day after date of enactment
4947	413(c)(30)	Repeal of Foreign Personal Holding Company Rules and Foreign Investment Company Rules-Conforming Amendments	Tax years of foreign corporations beginning after December 31, 2004 and to tax years of United States shareholders with or within which such tax years of foreign corporations end
4948(c)(4)	413(c)(30)	Repeal of Foreign Personal Holding Company Rules and Foreign Investment Company Rules-Conforming Amendments	Tax years of foreign corporations beginning after December 31, 2004 and to tax years of United States shareholders with or within which such tax years of foreign corporations end
4975(d)(14)-(16)	233(c)	Expansion of Bank S Corporation Eligible Shareholders to Include IRAs-Sale of Bank Stock in IRA Relating to S Corporation Election Exempt From Prohibited Transaction Rules	Date of enactment

Code Sec.	Act Sec.	Act Provision Subject	Effective Date
4975(f)(7)	240(a)	Repayment of Loans for Qualifying Employer Securities	Distributions with respect to S corporation stock made after December 31, 1997
4985	802(a)	Stock Compensation Of Insiders In Expatriated Corporations	March 4, 2003, generally
5117(d)	246(b)	Suspension of Occupational Tax-Conforming Amendment	Date of enactment
5148	246(a)	Suspension of Occupational Tax	Date of enactment
6031(f)	833(b)(4)(B)	Disallowance Of Certain Partnership Loss Transfers-Special Rules For Transfers Of Partnership Interest If There Is Substantial Built-In Loss	Transfers after date of enactment, generally
6035	413(c)(26)	Repeal of Foreign Personal Holding Company Rules and Foreign Investment Company Rules-Conforming Amendments	Tax years of foreign corporations beginning after December 31, 2004 and to tax years of United States shareholders with or within which such tax years of foreign corporations end
6039G(a)	804(e)(1)	Revision of Tax Rules On Expatriation Of Individuals-Enhanced Information Reporting From Individuals Losing United States Citizenship	Individuals Who Expatriate After June 3, 2004
6039G(b)	804(e)(2)	Revision of Tax Rules On Expatriation Of Individuals-Enhanced Information Reporting From Individuals Losing United States Citizenship	Individuals Who Expatriate After June 3, 2004
6039G(c)-(g)	804(e)(4)	Revision of Tax Rules On Expatriation Of Individuals-Enhanced Information Reporting From Individuals Losing United States Citizenship	Individuals Who Expatriate After June 3, 2004
6039G(d)	804(e)(3)	Revision of Tax Rules On Expatriation Of Individuals-Enhanced Information Reporting From Individuals Losing United States Citizenship	Individuals Who Expatriate After June 3, 2004
6041(g)	885(b)(3)	Inclusion In Gross Income Of Deferred Compensation Under Nonqualified Compensation Plans-Treatment Of Deferred Amounts	Amounts deferred after December 31, 2004; generally
6043A	805(a)	Reporting Of Taxable Mergers And Acquisitions	Acquisitions after date of enactment
6050L	882(c)(1)	Treatment Of Charitable Contributions Of Patents And Similar Property-Reporting Requirements	Contributions made after June 3, 2004
6051(a)	885(b)(1)(B)	Inclusion In Gross Income Of Deferred Compensation Under Nonqualified Compensation Plans-Treatment Of Deferred Amounts	Amounts deferred after December 31, 2004; generally
6051(a)(11)-(13)	885(b)(1)(A)	Inclusion In Gross Income Of Deferred Compensation Under Nonqualified Compensation Plans-Treatment Of Deferred Amounts	Amounts deferred after December 31, 2004; generally

Code Sec.	Act Sec.	Act Provision Subject	Effective Date
6103(e)(1)(D)	413(c)(27)	Repeal of Foreign Personal Holding Company Rules and Foreign Investment Company Rules-Conforming Amendments	Disclosures of return or return information with respect to tax years beginning after December 31, 2004
6111	815(a)	Disclosure Of Reportable Transactions	Transactions with respect to which material aid, assistance, or advice provided after date of enactment
6112(b)(1)	815(b)(3)(B)	Disclosure Of Reportable Transactions-Conforming Amendments	Transactions with respect to which material aid, assistance, or advice provided after date of enactment
6112(b)(2)	815(b)(3)(C)	Disclosure Of Reportable Transactions-Conforming Amendments	Transactions with respect to which material aid, assistance, or advice provided after date of enactment
6112(b)-(c)	815(b)(3)(A)	Disclosure Of Reportable Transactions-Conforming Amendments	Transactions with respect to which material aid, assistance, or advice provided after date of enactment
6112	815(b)(2)	Disclosure Of Reportable Transactions-Conforming Amendments	Transactions with respect to which material aid, assistance, or advice provided after date of enactment
6156	867(b)(1)	Modifications Of Tax On Use Of Certain Vehicles-Conforming Amendment	Taxable periods after date of enactment
6159(a)	843(a)(1)(A)-(B)	Partial Payment Of Tax Liability In Installment Agreements	Agreements entered into on or after date of enactment
6159(c)	843(a)(2)	Partial Payment Of Tax Liability In Installment Agreements	Agreements entered into on or after date of enactment
6159(d)-(f)	843(b)	Partial Payment Of Tax Liability In Installment Agreements-Requirement To Review Partial Payment Agreements Every Two Years	Agreements entered into on or after date of enactment
6206	853(d)(2)(F)	Taxation Of Aviation-Grade Kerosene-Rate Of Tax	Aviation-grade kerosene removed, entered, or sold after December 31, 2004
6306	881(a)(1)	Qualified Tax Collection Contracts-Contract Requirements	Date of enactment
6331(h)(3)	887(a)	Modification Of Continuing Levy On Payments To Federal Venders	Date of enactment
6404(g)	903(a)	Freeze Of Provisions Regarding Suspension Of Interest Where Secretary Fails To Contact Payer	Tax years beginning after December 31, 2003
6404(g)(2)(C)-(E)	903(b)	Freeze Of Provisions Regarding Suspension Of Interest Where Secretary Fails To Contact Payer	Tax years beginning after December 31, 2003

Code Sec.	Act Sec.	Act Provision Subject	Effective Date
6404(g)(2)(D)-(F)	903(c)	Freeze Of Provisions Regarding Suspension Of Interest Where Secretary Fails To Contact Payer	Interest accruing after October 3, 2004
6416(a)(4)	865(a)	Taxable Fuel Refunds For Certain Ultimate Vendors	January 1, 2005
6416(b)(2)	853(d)(2)(G)	Taxation Of Aviation-Grade Kerosene-Rate Of Tax	Aviation-grade kerosene removed, entered, or sold after December 31, 2004
6416(b)(3)	853(d)(2)(H)	Taxation Of Aviation-Grade Kerosene-Rate Of Tax	Aviation-grade kerosene removed, entered, or sold after December 31, 2004
6416(d)	853(d)(2)(I)	Taxation Of Aviation-Grade Kerosene-Rate Of Tax	Aviation-grade kerosene removed, entered, or sold after December 31, 2004
6421(e)(2)(C)	851(d)(1)	Exemption From Certain Excise Taxes For Middle Machinery-Refund of Fuel Taxes	Tax years beginning after date of enactment
6421(f)(3)(B)	241(a)(2)(C)	Phaseout of 4.3-Cent Motor Fuel Excist Taxes on Railroads and Inland Waterway Transportation Which Remain in General Fund-Taxes on Trains-Conforming Amendments	January 1, 2005
6426	301(a)	Alcohol and Biodiesel Excise Tax Credit And Extension of Alcohol Fuels Income Tax Credit	Fuel sold or used after December 31, 2004
6427(b)(4)	857(b)	Termination Of Dyed Diesel use By Inter-City Buses-Ultimate Vendor Refund	Fuel sold after December 31, 2004
6427(e)	301(c)(9)	Alcohol and Biodiesel Excise Tax Credit And Extension of Alcohol Fuels Income Tax Credit-Additional Amendments	Fuel sold or used after December 31, 2004
6427(h)	870(b)	Transmix And Diesel Fuel Blend Stocks Treated As Taxable Fuel-Conforming Amendment	Fuel removed, sold, or used after December 31, 2004
6427(i)(2)(C)	851(d)(3)	Exemption From Certain Excise Taxes For Middle Machinery-Refund of Fuel Taxes	Tax years beginning after date of enactment
6427(i)(3)	301(c)(10)(F)	Alcohol and Biodiesel Excise Tax Credit And Extension of Alcohol Fuels Income Tax Credit-Additional Amendments	Fuel sold or used after December 31, 2004
6427(i)(3)(A)	301(c)(10)(A)-(C)	Alcohol and Biodiesel Excise Tax Credit And Extension of Alcohol Fuels Income Tax Credit-Additional Amendments	Fuel sold or used after December 31, 2004
6427(i)(3)(B)	301(c)(10)(D)-(E)	Alcohol and Biodiesel Excise Tax Credit And Extension of Alcohol Fuels Income Tax Credit-Additional Amendments	Fuel sold or used after December 31, 2004
6427(i)(4)(A)	853(c)(2)(A)-(B)	Taxation Of Aviation-Grade Kerosene-Refunds	Aviation-grade kerosene removed, entered, or sold after December 31, 2004

Code Sec.	Act Sec.	Act Provision Subject	Effective Date
6427(i)(4)(A)	857(c)	Termination Of Dyed Diesel use By Inter-City Buses-Payment Of Refunds	Fuel sold after December 31, 2004
6427(j)(1)	853(d)(2)(J)	Taxation Of Aviation-Grade Kerosene-Rate Of Tax	Aviation-grade kerosene removed, entered, or sold after December 31, 2004
6427(l)(1)	853(d)(2)(K)	Taxation Of Aviation-Grade Kerosene-Rate Of Tax	Aviation-grade kerosene removed, entered, or sold after December 31, 2004
6427(l)(2)(B)	853(c)(3)	Taxation Of Aviation-Grade Kerosene-Refunds	Aviation-grade kerosene removed, entered, or sold after December 31, 2004
6427(l)(3)(B)	241(a)(2)(D)	Phaseout of 4.3-Cent Motor Fuel Excist Taxes on Railroads and Inland Waterway Transportation Which Remain in General Fund-Taxes on Trains-Conforming Amendments	January 1, 2005
6427(l)(4)	853(c)(1)	Taxation Of Aviation-Grade Kerosene-Refunds	Aviation-grade kerosene removed, entered, or sold after December 31, 2004
6427(l)(5)(B)	853(d)(2)(K)	Taxation Of Aviation-Grade Kerosene-Rate Of Tax	Aviation-grade kerosene removed, entered, or sold after December 31, 2004
6501(c)(10)	814(a)	Statute Of Limitations For Taxaable Years For Which Required Listed Transactions Not Reported	Tax years with respect to which period for assessing a deficiency did not expire before date of enactment
6501(e)(1)(B)	413(c)(28)	Repeal of Foreign Personal Holding Company Rules and Foreign Investment Company Rules-Conforming Amendments	Tax years of foreign corporations beginning after December 31, 2004 and to tax years of United States shareholders with or within which such tax years of foreign corporations end
6603	842(a)	Deposits Made To Suspend Running Of Interest On Potential Underpayments	Deposits made after date of enactment
6662(d)(1)(B)	819(a)	Modifications Of Substantial Understatement Penalty For Nonreportable Transactions-Substantial Understatement Of Corporations	Tax years beginning after date of enactment
6662(d)(2)(A)	812(b)	Accuracy-Related Penalty For Listed Transactions, Other Reportable Transactions Having a Significant Tax Avoidance Purpose, Etc.-Determination Of Other Understatements	Tax years ending after date of enactment

Code Sec.	Act Sec.	Act Provision Subject	Effective Date
6662(d)(2)(C)	812(d)	Accuracy-Related Penalty For Listed Transactions, Other Reportable Transactions Having a Significant Tax Avoidance Purpose, Etc.-Reduction IN Penalty For Substantial Understatement Of Income Tax Not To Apply To Tax Shelters	Tax years ending after date of enactment
6662(d)(2)(D)	819(b)(2)	Modifications Of Substantial Understatement Penalty For Nonreportable Transactions-Secretarial List-Conforming Amendment	Tax years beginning after date of enactment
6662(d)(3)	819(b)(1)	Modifications Of Substantial Understatement Penalty For Nonreportable Transactions-Secretarial List	Tax years beginning after date of enactment
6662A	812(a)	Accuracy-Related Penalty For Listed Transactions, Other Reportable Transactions Having a Significant Tax Avoidance Purpose, Etc.	Tax years ending after date of enactment
6662	812(e)(1)	Accuracy-Related Penalty For Listed Transactions, Other Reportable Transactions Having a Significant Tax Avoidance Purpose, Etc.-Clerical Amendments	Tax years ending after date of enactment
6664(c)	812(c)(2)(B)	Accuracy-Related Penalty For Listed Transactions, Other Reportable Transactions Having a Significant Tax Avoidance Purpose, Etc.-Reasonable Cause Exception-Conforming Amendments	Tax years ending after date of enactment
6664(c)(1)	812(c)(2)(A)	Accuracy-Related Penalty For Listed Transactions, Other Reportable Transactions Having a Significant Tax Avoidance Purpose, Etc.-Reasonable Cause Exception-Conforming Amendments	Tax years ending after date of enactment
6664(d)	812(c)(1)	Accuracy-Related Penalty For Listed Transactions, Other Reportable Transactions Having a Significant Tax Avoidance Purpose, Etc.-Reasonable Cause Exception	Tax years ending after date of enactment
6679(a)(1)	413(c)(29)(A)	Repeal of Foreign Personal Holding Company Rules and Foreign Investment Company Rules-Conforming Amendments	Tax years of foreign corporations beginning after December 31, 2004 and to tax years of United States shareholders with or within which such tax years of foreign corporations end

Code Sec.	Act Sec.	Act Provision Subject	Effective Date
6679(a)(3)	413(c)(29)(B)	Repeal of Foreign Personal Holding Company Rules and Foreign Investment Company Rules-Conforming Amendments	Tax years of foreign corporations beginning after December 31, 2004 and to tax years of United States shareholders with or within which such tax years of foreign corporations end
6688	908(b)(1)-(2)	Residence And Source Rules Relating To United States Possession-Penalty	Tax years ending after date of enactment, generally
6700(a)	818(a)	Penalty On Promoters Of Tax Shelters	Activities after date of enactment
6707A	811(a)	Penalty For Failing To Disclose Reportable Transactions	Returns and statements the due date for which is after date of enactment
6707	816(a)	Failure To Furnish Information Regarding Reportable Transactions	Returns the due date for which is after date of enactment
6708	815(b)(5)(A)	Disclosure Of Reportable Transactions-Conforming Amendments	Transactions with respect to which material aid, assistance, or advice provided after date of enactment
6708(a)	817(a)	Modification Of Penalty For Failure To Maintain Lists Of Investors	Requests made after date of enactment
6715(a)(2)-(4)	856(a)	Penalty On Untaxed Chemically Altered Dyed Fuel Mixtures	Date of enactment
6715(a)(3)	856(b)	Penalty On Untaxed Chemically Altered Dyed Fuel Mixtures-Conforming Amendment	Date of enactment
6715(e)	855(a)	Elimination Of Administrative Review For Taxable Use Of Dyed Fuel	Penalties assessed after date of enactment
6715A	854(c)(1)	Dye Injection Equipment-Penalty For Tampering With Or Failing To Maintain Seciurty Requirements For Mechanical Dye Injection Systems	180 days after date of enactment
6717	859(a)	Assessable Penalty For Refusal Of Entry	January 1, 2005
6718	861(b)(1)	Display of Registration-Civil Penalty For Failure To Display Registration	Penalties imposed after December 31, 2004
6718(a)	862(b)	Registration Of Persons Within Foreign Trade Zones, Etc.-Technical Amendment	January 1, 2005
6719	863(c)(1)	Penalties For Failure To Register And Failure To Report-Assessable Penalty For Failure To Register	Penalties imposed after December 31, 2004
6720	884(b)(1)	Donations Of Motor Vehicles, Boats, And Airplanes-Penalty For Fraudulent Acknowledgments	Contributions made after December 31, 2004
6724(d)(1)(B)	853(d)(2)(L)	Taxation Of Aviation-Grade Kerosene-Rate Of Tax	Aviation-grade kerosene removed, entered, or sold after December 31, 2004

Code Sec.	Act Sec.	Act Provision Subject	Effective Date
6724(d)(1)(B)	805(b)(1)	Reporting Of Taxable Mergers And Acquisitions-Assessible Penalties	Acquisitions after date of enactment
6724(d)(2)(F)-(CC)	805(b)(2)	Reporting Of Taxable Mergers And Acquisitions-Assessible Penalties	Acquisitions after date of enactment
6724(d)(2)(X)-(AA)	853(d)(2)(M)	Taxation Of Aviation-Grade Kerosene-Rate Of Tax	Aviation-grade kerosene removed, entered, or sold after December 31, 2004
6725	863(d)(1)	Penalties For Failure To Register And Failure To Report-Assessable Penalty For Failure To Report	Penalties imposed after December 31, 2004
7232	863(b)	Penalties For Failure To Register And Failure To Report-Increased Criminal Penalty	Penalties imposed after December 31, 2004
7272(a)	863(a)	Penalties For Failure To Register And Failure To Report-Increased Penalty	Penalties imposed after December 31, 2004
7408	820(b)(1)	Modification Of Actions To Enjoin Certain Conduct Related To Tax Shelters And Reportable Transactions-Conforming Amendments	Day after date of enactment
7408(a)-(d)	820(a)	Modification Of Actions To Enjoin Certain Conduct Related To Tax Shelters And Reportable Transactions	Day after date of enactment
7428(a)(1)	317(a)	Extension of Declaratory Judgment Procedures To Farmers' Cooperative Organizations	Pleading filed after date of enactment
7433A	881(b)(1)	Qualified Tax Collection Contracts-Civil Damages For Certain Unauthorized Collection Actions By Persons Performing Services Under Qualified Tax Collection Contracts	Date of enactment
7525(b)	813(a)	Tax Shelter Exception To Confidentiality Privileges Relating To Taxpayer Communications	Communications made on or after date of enactment
7528(c)	891(a)	Extension Of User Fees	Requests after date of enactment
7701(a)(19)(C)	835(b)(10)(A)-(B)	Repeal Of Special Rules-Conforming Amendments	January 1, 2005, generally
7701(a)(48)	852(a)	Modification Of Definition Of Off-Highway Vehicle	Date of enactment, generally
7701(i)(2)(A)	835(b)(11)	Repeal Of Special Rules-Conforming Amendments	January 1, 2005, generally
7701(n)-(o)	804(b)	Revision of Tax Rules on Expatriation Of Individuals-Special Rules For Determining When An Individual Is No Longer a United States Citizen Or Long-Term Resident	Individuals Who Expatriate After June 3, 2004
7704(d)(4)	331(e)	Net Income From Publicly Traded Partnerships Treated As Qualifying Income Of Regulated Investment Companies-Definition Of Qualifying Income	Tax years beginning after date of enactment
7809(a)	881(a)(2)(A)	Qualified Tax Collection Contracts-Contract Requirements	Date of enactment

Code Sec.	Act Sec.	Act Provision Subject	Effective Date
7811(g)	881(c)	Qualified Tax Collection Contracts-Application Of Taxpayer Assistance Orders To Persons Performing Services Under A Qualified Tax Collection Contract	Date of enactment
7874	801(a)	Tax Treatment Of Expatriated Entities And Their Foreign Agents	Tax years ending after March 4, 2003
9502(b)	853(d)(2)(O)	Taxation Of Aviation-Grade Kerosene-Rate Of Tax	Aviation-grade kerosene removed, entered, or sold after December 31, 2004
9502(b)(1)(B)-(D)	853(d)(2)(N)	Taxation Of Aviation-Grade Kerosene-Rate Of Tax	Aviation-grade kerosene removed, entered, or sold after December 31, 2004
9503(b)	868(b)(1)	Dedication Of Revenues From Certain Penalties To The Highway Trust Fund-Conforming Amendments	Penalties Assessed On or After Date Of Enactment
9503(b)(1)	301(c)(11)	Alcohol and Biodiesel Excise Tax Credit And Extension of Alcohol Fuels Income Tax Credit-Additional Amendments	Fuel sold or used after December 31, 2004
9503(b)(1)	868(b)(2)	Dedication Of Revenues From Certain Penalties To The Highway Trust Fund-Conforming Amendments	Penalties Assessed On or After Date Of Enactment
9503(b)(4)(C)-(F)	301(c)(12)(A)-(C)	Alcohol and Biodiesel Excise Tax Credit And Extension of Alcohol Fuels Income Tax Credit-Additional Amendments	Fuel sold or used after September 30, 2004
9503(b)(5)-(6)	868(a)	Dedication Of Revenues From Certain Penalties To The Highway Trust Fund	Penalties Assessed On or After Date Of Enactment
9503(c)(2)(A)	301(c)(13)	Alcohol and Biodiesel Excise Tax Credit And Extension of Alcohol Fuels Income Tax Credit-Additional Amendments	Fuel sold or used after December 31, 2004
9508(b)(3)-(5)	853(d)(2)(P)	Taxation Of Aviation-Grade Kerosene-Rate Of Tax	Aviation-grade kerosene removed, entered, or sold after December 31, 2004
9508(c)(2)(A)	853(d)(2)(Q)	Taxation Of Aviation-Grade Kerosene-Rate Of Tax	Aviation-grade kerosene removed, entered, or sold after December 31, 2004
. . .	102(c)	Income Attributable to Domestic Production Activities-Special Rule Relating to Treat Cutting of Timber as a Sale or Exchange	Tax years beginning after December 31, 2004
. . .	245(d)	Credit for Maintenance of Railroad Track-Clerical Amendment	Tax years beginning after December 31, 2004
. . .	301(c)(14)	Alcohol and Biodiesel Excise Tax Credit And Extension of Alcohol Fuels Income Tax Credit-Additional Amendments	Date of enactment

Code Sec.	Act Sec.	Act Provision Subject	Effective Date
. . .	320(b)(5)	Exclusion For Payments To Individuals Under National Health Service Corps Loan Repayment Program And Certain State Loan Repayment Programs-Treatment For Purposes Of Employment Taxes	Amounts received by an individual in tax years beginning after December 31, 2003
. . .	422(c)	Incentives To Reinvest Foreign Earnings In United States-Aalternative Minimum Tax-Clerical Amendment	Tax years ending on or after date of enactment
. . .	611(a)	Termination Of Tobacco Quota Program And Related Provisions-Marketing Quotas	2005 and subsequent crops of each kind of tobacco
. . .	611(b)	Termination Of Tobacco Quota Program And Related Provisions-Tobacco Inspections	2005 and subsequent crops of each kind of tobacco
. . .	611(c)	Termination Of Tobacco Quota Program And Related Provisions-Tobacco Control	2005 and subsequent crops of each kind of tobacco
. . .	611(d)	Termination Of Tobacco Quota Program And Related Provisions-Processing Tax	2005 and subsequent crops of each kind of tobacco
. . .	611(e)	Termination Of Tobacco Quota Program And Related Provisions-Declaration Of Policy	2005 and subsequent crops of each kind of tobacco
. . .	611(f)	Termination Of Tobacco Quota Program And Related Provisions-Definitions	2005 and subsequent crops of each kind of tobacco
. . .	611(g)	Termination Of Tobacco Quota Program And Related Provisions-Parity Payments	2005 and subsequent crops of each kind of tobacco
. . .	611(h)	Termination Of Tobacco Quota Program And Related Provisions-Administrative Provisions	2005 and subsequent crops of each kind of tobacco
. . .	611(i)	Termination Of Tobacco Quota Program And Related Provisions-Adjustment Of Quotas	2005 and subsequent crops of each kind of tobacco
. . .	611(j)	Termination Of Tobacco Quota Program And Related Provisions-Reports And Records	2005 and subsequent crops of each kind of tobacco
. . .	611(k)	Termination Of Tobacco Quota Program And Related Provisions-Regulations	2005 and subsequent crops of each kind of tobacco
. . .	611(l)	Termination Of Tobacco Quota Program And Related Provisions-Eminent Domain	2005 and subsequent crops of each kind of tobacco
. . .	611(m)	Termination Of Tobacco Quota Program And Related Provisions-Burley Tobacco Farm Reconstitution	2005 and subsequent crops of each kind of tobacco
. . .	611(n)	Termination Of Tobacco Quota Program And Related Provisions-Acreage-Poundage Quotas	2005 and subsequent crops of each kind of tobacco
. . .	611(o)	Termination Of Tobacco Quota Program And Related Provisions-Burley Tobacco Acreage Allotments	2005 and subsequent crops of each kind of tobacco

Code Sec.	Act Sec.	Act Provision Subject	Effective Date
...	611(p)	Termination Of Tobacco Quota Program And Related Provisions-Transfer of Allotments	2005 and subsequent crops of each kind of tobacco
...	611(q)	Termination Of Tobacco Quota Program And Related Provisions-Advance Recourse Loans	2005 and subsequent crops of each kind of tobacco
...	611(r)	Termination Of Tobacco Quota Program And Related Provisions-Tobacco Field Measurement	2005 and subsequent crops of each kind of tobacco
...	611(s)	Termination Of Tobacco Quota Program and Related Provisions-Burley Tobacco Import Review	2005 and subsequent crops of each kind of tobacco
...	612(a)	Termination of Tobacco Price Support Program and Related Provision-Terminatin of Tobacco Price Support And No Net Cost Provisions	2005 and subsequent crops of each kind of tobacco
...	612(b)	Termination of Tobacco Price Support Program and Related Provision-Parity Price Support	2005 and subsequent crops of each kind of tobacco
...	612(c)	Termination of Tobacco Price Support Program and Related Provision-Definition Of Basic Agricultural Commodity	2005 and subsequent crops of each kind of tobacco
...	612(d)	Termination of Tobacco Price Support Program and Related Provision-Powers Of Commodity Credit Corporation	2005 and subsequent crops of each kind of tobacco
...	613	Conforming Amendments	2005 and subsequent crops of each kind of tobacco
...	614	Continuation Of Liability For 2004 And Earlier Crop Years	2005 and subsequent crops of each kind of tobacco
...	621	Definitions	2005 and subsequent crops of each kind of tobacco
...	622(a)	Contract Payments To Tobacco Quota Holders-Contract Offered	2005 and subsequent crops of each kind of tobacco
...	622(b)	Contract Payments To Tobacco Quota Holders-Eligibility	2005 and subsequent crops of each kind of tobacco
...	622(c)	Contract Payments To Tobacco Quota Holders-Base Quota Level	2005 and subsequent crops of each kind of tobacco
...	622(d)	Contract Payments To Tobacco Quota Holders-Treatment Of Certain Contracts And Agreements	2005 and subsequent crops of each kind of tobacco
...	622(e)	Contract Payments To Tobacco Quota Holders-Contract Payments	2005 and subsequent crops of each kind of tobacco
...	622(f)	Contract Payments To Tobacco Quota Holders-Death Of Tobacco Quota Holder	2005 and subsequent crops of each kind of tobacco

Code Sec.	Act Sec.	Act Provision Subject	Effective Date
. . .	623(a)	Contract Payments For Producers Of Quota Tobacco-Contract Offered	2005 and subsequent crops of each kind of tobacco
. . .	623(b)	Contract Payments For Producers Of Quota Tobacco-Eligibility	2005 and subsequent crops of each kind of tobacco
. . .	623(c)	Contract Payments For Producers Of Quota Tobacco-Base Quota Level	2005 and subsequent crops of each kind of tobacco
. . .	623(d)	Contract Payments For Producers Of Quota Tobacco-Contract Payments	2005 and subsequent crops of each kind of tobacco
. . .	623(e)	Contract Payments For Producers Of Quota Tobacco-Death Of Tobacco Producer	2005 and subsequent crops of each kind of tobacco
. . .	624(a)	Administration-Time For Payment Of Contract Payments	2005 and subsequent crops of each kind of tobacco
. . .	624(b)	Administration-Use Of County Committees To Resolve Disputes	2005 and subsequent crops of each kind of tobacco
. . .	624(c)	Administration-Role Of National Appeals Division	2005 and subsequent crops of each kind of tobacco
. . .	624(d)	Administration-Use Of Financial Institutions	2005 and subsequent crops of each kind of tobacco
. . .	624(e)	Administration-Payment To Financial Institutions	2005 and subsequent crops of each kind of tobacco
. . .	625(a)	Use Of Assessments As Source Of Funds For Payments-Definitions	2005 and subsequent crops of each kind of tobacco
. . .	625(b)	Use Of Assessments As Source Of Funds For Payments-Quarterly Assessments	2005 and subsequent crops of each kind of tobacco
. . .	625(c)	Use Of Assessments As Source Of Funds For Payments-Assessments For Classes Of Tobacco Products	2005 and subsequent crops of each kind of tobacco
. . .	625(d)	Use Of Assessments As Source Of Funds For Payments-Notification And Timing Of Assessments	2005 and subsequent crops of each kind of tobacco
. . .	625(e)	Use Of Assessments As Source Of Funds For Payments-Allocation Of Assessment Within Each Class Of Tobacco Product	2005 and subsequent crops of each kind of tobacco
. . .	625(f)	Use Of Assessments As Source Of Funds For Payments-Allocation Of Total Assessments By Market Share	2005 and subsequent crops of each kind of tobacco
. . .	625(g)	Use Of Assessments As Source Of Funds For Payments-Determination Of Volume Of Domestic Sales	2005 and subsequent crops of each kind of tobacco
. . .	625(h)	Use Of Assessments As Source Of Funds For Payments-Measurement Of Volume Of Domestic Sales	2005 and subsequent crops of each kind of tobacco

Code Sec.	Act Sec.	Act Provision Subject	Effective Date
. . .	625(i)	Use Of Assessments As Source Of Funds For Payments-Challenge To Assessment	2005 and subsequent crops of each kind of tobacco
. . .	625(j)	Use Of Assessments As Source Of Funds For Payments-Judicial Review	2005 and subsequent crops of each kind of tobacco
. . .	625(k)	Use Of Assessments As Source Of Funds For Payments-Termination Date	2005 and subsequent crops of each kind of tobacco
. . .	626(a)	Tobacco Trust Fund-Establishment	2005 and subsequent crops of each kind of tobacco
. . .	626(b)	Tobacco Trust Fund-Expenditures	2005 and subsequent crops of each kind of tobacco
. . .	626(c)	Tobacco Trust Fund-Investment Of Amounts	2005 and subsequent crops of each kind of tobacco
. . .	627	Limitation On Total Expenditures	2005 and subsequent crops of each kind of tobacco
. . .	641(a)	Treatment Of Tobacco Loan Pool Stocks And Outstanding Loan Costs-Disposal Of Stocks	2005 and subsequent crops of each kind of tobacco
. . .	641(b)	Treatment Of Tobacco Loan Pool Stocks And Outstanding Loan Costs-Disposal By Associations	2005 and subsequent crops of each kind of tobacco
. . .	641(c)	Treatment Of Tobacco Loan Pool Stocks And Outstanding Loan Costs-Disposal Of Remainder By Commodity Credit Corporation	2005 and subsequent crops of each kind of tobacco
. . .	641(d)	Treatment Of Tobacco Loan Pool Stocks And Outstanding Loan Costs-Transfer Of Remaining No Net Cost Funds	2005 and subsequent crops of each kind of tobacco
. . .	642(a)	Regulations	2005 and subsequent crops of each kind of tobacco
. . .	642(b)	Regulations-Procedure	2005 and subsequent crops of each kind of tobacco
. . .	642(c)	Regulations-Congressional Review Of Agency Rulemaking	2005 and subsequent crops of each kind of tobacco
. . .	701(d)	Brownsfields Demonstration Program For Qualified Green Building And Sustainable Design Projects-Accountability	Bonds issued after December 31, 2004
. . .	702(c)	Exclusion Of Gain Or Loss On Sale Or Exchange Of Certain Brownfield Sites From Unrelated Business Taxable Income-Savings Clause	Gain or loss on sale, exchange, or other disposition of any property acquired by taxpayer after December 31, 2004

Code Sec.	Act Sec.	Act Provision Subject	Effective Date
. . .	708(a)	Method Of Accounting For Naval Shipbuilders	Contracts for ships or submarines with respect to which construction commencement date occurs after date of enactment
. . .	708(b)	Method Of Accounting For Naval Shipbuilders-Recapture of Tax Benefit	Contracts for ships or submarines with respect to which construction commencement date occurs after date of enactment
. . .	708(c)	Method Of Accounting For Naval Shipbuilders-Qualified Naval Ship Contract	Contracts for ships or submarines with respect to which construction commencement date occurs after date of enactment
. . .	709(a)	Modification Of Minimum Cost Requirement For Transfer Of Excess Pension Assets-Amendments Of ERISA	Tax years ending after date of enactment
. . .	712(a)	Inclusion Of Primary And Secondary Medical Strategies For children And adults With Sickle Cell Disease As Medical Assistance Under The Medicaid Program-Optional Medical Assistance	Date of enactment, generally
. . .	712(b)	Inclusion Of Primary And Secondary Medical Strategies For children And adults With Sickle Cell Disease As Medical Assistance Under The Medicaid Program-Federal Reimbursement For Education And Other Services Related To Prevention And Treatment Of Sickle Cell Disease	Date of enactment, generally
. . .	712(c)	Inclusion Of Primary And Secondary Medical Strategies For children And adults With Sickle Cell Disease As Medical Assistance Under The Medicaid Program-Demonstration Program For Development And Establishment Of Systemic Mechanisms For Prevention And Treatment Of Sickle Cell Disease	Date of enactment
. . .	714(a)	Certain Steam Generators, and Certain Reactor Vessel Heads and Pressurizers, Used in Nuclear Facilities-Certain Steam Generators	Date of enactment
. . .	714(b)	Certain Steam Generators, and Certain Reactor Vessel Heads and Pressurizers, Used in Nuclear Facilities-Certain Reactor Vessel Heads and Pressurizers	Goods entered, or withdrawn from warehouse, for consumption on or after 15th day after date of enactment

Code Sec.	Act Sec.	Act Provision Subject	Effective Date
...	801(b)	Tax Treatment Of Expatriated Entities And Their Foreign Agents-Conforming Amendment	Tax years ending after March 4, 2003
...	802(c)(2)	Stock Compensation Of Insiders In Expatriated Corporations-Conforming Amendments	March 4, 2003, generally
...	805(c)	Reporting Of Taxable Mergers And Acquisitions-Clerical Amendment	Acquisitions after date of enactment
...	806(a)	Studies-Transfer Pricing Rules	Date of enactment
...	806(b)	Studies-Income Tax Treaties	Date of enactment
...	806(c)	Studies-Effectiveness Of Corporate Expatriation Provisions	Date of enactment
...	811(b)	Penalty For Failing To Disclose Reportable Transactions-Conforming Amendment	Date of enactment
...	812(e)(2)	Accuracy-Related Penalty For Listed Transactions, Other Reportable Transactions Having a Significant Tax Avoidance Purpose, Etc.-Clerical Amendments	Tax years ending after date of enactment
...	815(b)(1)	Disclosure Of Reportable Transactions-Conforming Amendments	Transactions with respect to which material aid, assistance, or advice provided after date of enactment
...	815(b)(4)	Disclosure Of Reportable Transactions-Conforming Amendments	Transactions with respect to which material aid, assistance, or advice provided after date of enactment
...	816(b)	Failure To Furnish Information Regarding Reportable Transactions-Clerical Amendment	Returns the due date for which is after date of enactment
...	820(b)(2)	Modification Of Actions To Enjoin Certain Conduct Related To Tax Shelters And Reportable Transactions-Conforming Amendments	Day after date of enactment
...	821(a)	Penalty On Failure To Report Interests In Foreign Financial Accounts	Violations occurring after date of enactment
...	822(a)	Regulation Of Individuals Practicing Before The Department Of Treasury-Censure; Imposition Of Penalty	Actions taken after date of enactment
...	833(b)(6)(B)	Disallowance Of Certain Partnership Loss Transfers-Special Rules For Transfers Of Partnership Interest If There Is Substantial Built-In Loss	Transfers after date of enactment, generally
...	833(c)(5)(B)	Disallowance of Certain Partnership Loss Transfers-Clerical Amendments	Distributions after date of enactment
...	835(b)(12)	Repeal Of Special Rules-Conforming Amendments	January 1, 2005, generally
...	842(b)	Deposits Made To Suspend Running Of Interest On Potential Underpayments-Clerical Amendment	Deposits made after date of enactment
...	844(b)	Affirmation Of Consolidated Return Regulation Authority-Result Not Overturned	Tax years beginning before, on or after date of enactment

Code Sec.	Act Sec.	Act Provision Subject	Effective Date
...	848(b)	Limitation On Deductions Allocable To Property Used By governments Or Other Tax-Exempt Entities-Conforming Amendments	Date of enactment
...	849(a)	Effective Date	Leases entered into after March 12, 2004, generally
...	849(b)	Effective Date-Exception	Leases entered into after March 12, 2004, generally
...	853(d)(2)(R)	Taxation Of Aviation-Grade Kerosene-Rate Of Tax	Aviation-grade kerosene removed, entered, or sold after December 31, 2004
...	853(d)(2)(S)	Taxation Of Aviation-Grade Kerosene-Rate Of Tax	Aviation-grade kerosene removed, entered, or sold after December 31, 2004
...	853(d)(2)(T)	Taxation Of Aviation-Grade Kerosene-Rate Of Tax	Aviation-grade kerosene removed, entered, or sold after December 31, 2004
...	854(b)	Dye Injection Equipment-Dye Injector Security	Date of enactment
...	854(c)(2)	Dye Injection Equipment-Penalty For Tampering With Or Failing To Maintain Secuirty Requirements For Mechanical Dye Injection Systems-Clerical Amendment	180 days after date of enactment
...	859(b)(2)	Assessable Penalty For Refusal Of Entry-Conforming Amendments	January 1, 2005
...	863(c)(2)	Penalties For Failure To Register And Failure To Report-Assessable Penalty For Failure To Register-Clerical Amendment	Penalties imposed after December 31, 2004
...	866(b)	Two-Party Exchanges-Conforming Amendment	Date of enactment
...	867(b)(2)	Modifications Of Tax On Use Of Certain Vehicles-Conforming Amendment	Taxable periods after date of enactment
...	869(d)(2)	Simplication Of Tax On Tires-Conforming Amendments	Sales in calendar years beginning more than 30 days after date of enactment
...	881(a)(2)(B)	Qualified Tax Collection Contracts-Contract Requirements	Date of enactment
...	881(b)(2)	Qualified Tax Collection Contracts-Civil Damages For Certain Unauthorized Collection Actions By Persons Performing Services Under Qualified Tax Collection Contracts	Date of enactment
...	881(d)	Qualified Tax Collection Contracts-Ineligibility Of Individuals Who Commit Misconduct To Perform Under Contract	Date of enactment
...	881(e)	Qualified Tax Collection Contracts-Biennial Report	Date of enactment

Code Sec.	Act Sec.	Act Provision Subject	Effective Date
. . .	882(c)(2)	Treatment Of Charitable Contributions Of Patents And Similar Property-Reporting Requirements	Contributions made after June 3, 2004
. . .	882(e)	Treatment Of Charitable Contributions Of Patents And Similar Property-Anti-Abuse Rules	Contributions made after June 3, 2004
. . .	885(c)	Inclusion In Gross Income Of Deferred Compensation Under Nonqualified Compensation Plans-Clerical Amendment	Amounts deferred after December 31, 2004; generally
. . .	886(b)(1)(B)	Extension Of Amortization Of Intangibles To Sports Franchises-Conforming Amendments	Property acquired after date of enactment
. . .	892(a)	COBRA Fees-Use of Merchandise Processing Fee	Date of enactment
. . .	892(b)	COBRA Fees-Reimbursement Of Appropriations From COBRA Fees	Date of enactment
. . .	892(c)	COBRA Fees-Sense Of Congress; Effective Period For Collecting Fees; Standard For Setting Fees	Date of enactment
. . .	892(d)	COBRA Fees-Clerical Amendments	Date of enactment
. . .	892(e)	COBRA Fees-Study Of All Fees Collected By Department Of Homeland Security	Date of enactment
. . .	904(a)	Increase In Withholding From Supplemental Wage Payments In Excess Of $1,000,000	Payments made after December 31, 2004
. . .	904(b)	Increase In Withholding From Supplemental Wage Payments In Excess Of $1,000,000-Special Rule For Large Payments	Payments made after December 31, 2004
. . .	904(c)	Increase In Withholding From Supplemental Wage Payments In Excess Of $1,000,000-Conforming Amendment	Payments made after December 31, 2004
. . .	908(c)(6)	Residence And Source Rules Relating To United States Possession-Conforming And Clerical Amendments	Tax years ending after date of enactment, generally

¶ 25,001

Code Section to Explanation Table

¶25,001

¶ 25,005

Code Sections Added, Amended or Repealed

The list below notes all the Code Sections or subsections of the Internal Revenue Code that were added, amended or repealed by the American Jobs Creation Act of 2004 (H.R. 4520). The first column indicates the Code Section added, amended or repealed and the second column indicates the Act Section.

American Jobs Creation Act of 2004

Code Sec.	Act Sec.	Code Sec.	Act Sec.
1(h)(10)(F)-(H)	413(c)(1)(A)	50(c)(3)	322(d)(2)(D)
1(h)(11)(C)(iii)	413(c)(1)(B)	53(d)(1)(B)(i)(II)	421(a)(2)
38(b)(14)-(16)	245(c)(1)	55(c)(2)-(3)	314(a)
38(b)(15)-(17)	302(b)	56(g)(4)(B)(i)	101(b)(4)
38(b)(16)-(18)	339(b)	56(g)(4)(B)(i)	248(b)(1)
38(b)(17)-(19)	341(b)	56(g)(4)(C)(v)	102(b)
38(c)(2)(A)(ii)(II)	711(b)	56(g)(4)(C)(vi)	422(b)
38(c)(3)(A)(ii)(II)	711(b)	56(g)(6)	835(b)(1)
38(c)(4)-(5)	711(a)	59(a)(2)-(4)	421(a)(1)
39(a)(3)	341(c)	62(a)(19)[(20)]	703(a)
39(d)	245(b)(1)	62(e)	703(b)
40(c)	301(c)(1)	72(w)-(x)	906(a)
40(d)(4)	301(c)(2)	83(c)(4)	906(b)
40(e)(1)	301(c)(3)(A)-(B)	86(b)(2)(A)	102(d)(1)
40(g)(6)	313(a)	87	302(c)(1)(A)
40(h)(1)-(2)	301(c)(4)(A)-(B)	108(e)(8)	896(a)
40A	302(a)	108(f)(4)	320(a)
43(c)(1)(D)	707(a)	114	101(a)
43(c)(5)	707(b)	121(d)(10)[(11)]	840(a)
45	710(b)(3)(B)	135(c)(4)(A)	102(d)(1)
45(b)(2)	710(b)(3)(C)	137(b)(3)(A)	102(d)(1)
45(b)(3)	710(f)(1)-(2)	142(a)(12)-(14)	701(a)
45(b)(4)	710(c)	142(l)	701(b)
45(c)	710(a)	144(a)(4)(F)	340(b)
45(d)-(e)	710(b)(1)	144(a)(4)(G)	340(a)
45(e)(7)(A)(i)	710(b)(3)(A)	146(g)(3)	701(c)(1)-(2)
45(e)(8)	710(b)(2)	162(m)(4)(G)	802(b)(2)
45(e)(9)	710(d)	162(o)	318(b)
45D(e)(2)	221(a)	162(o)(2)-(3)	318(a)
45D(e)(4)	221(b)	163(e)(3)(B)-(C)	841(a)
45D(e)(5)	223(a)	163(l)(2)	845(a)
45G	245(a)	163(l)(3)	845(d)
45H	339(a)	163(l)(4)-(6)	845(b)
45I	341(a)	163(l)(5)-(7)	845(c)
46(1)-(3)	322(d)(1)(A)-(C)	163(m)-(n)	838(a)
48	322(d)(2)(B)	164(b)(5)	501(a)
48(a)(3)	710(e)	167(f)(1)(C)	847(b)(1)
48(a)-(b)	322(d)(2)(A)(i)-(iii)	167(f)(2)	847(b)(2)

Code Sec.	Act Sec.	Code Sec.	Act Sec.
167(g)(5)(E)-(G)	242(b)	196(c)(10)-(12)	339(e)
167(g)(7)	242(a)	197(e)(6)-(8)	886(a)
168(b)(2)(A)	211(d)(2)	197(f)(10)	847(b)(3)
168(b)(3)(G)-(H)	211(d)(1)	199	102(a)
168(e)(3)(C)(ii)-(iii)	704(a)	219(g)(3)(A)(ii)	102(d)(1)
168(e)(3)(C)(ii)-(iv)	706(a)	221(b)(2)(C)(i)	102(d)(2)
168(e)(3)(E)(ii)-(v)	211(a)	222(b)(2)(C)(i)	102(d)(3)
168(e)(3)(E)(iv)-(vi)	901(a)	245(a)(2)	413(c)(3)
168(e)(3)(F)	901(b)	246(b)(1)	102(d)(4)
168(e)(6)	211(b)	246(c)	888(d)
168(e)(7)	211(c)	248(a)	902(b)
168(g)(3)(A)	847(a)	263(a)(1)(G)-(I)	338(b)(1)
168(g)(3)(B)	211(e)	263A(c)(3)	338(b)(2)
168(g)(3)(B)	706(c)	267(a)(3)	841(b)(1)-(2)
168(g)(3)(B)	901(c)	274(e)(2)	907(a)
168(h)(2)(A)	847(e)	275(a)	101(b)(5)(B)
168(h)(3)(A)	847(d)	275(a)(4)(A)-(C)	101(b)(5)(A)
168(i)(3)(A)(i)-(iii)	847(c)	275(a)(6)	802(b)(1)
168(i)(15)	704(b)	280C(d)	339(c)
168(i)(16)	706(b)	305(e)(7)	831(b)
168(k)(2)(A)(iv)	336(a)(2)	312(j)	413(c)(4)
168(k)(2)(B)(iv)	336(b)(1)	312(k)(3)(B)	338(b)(3)
168(k)(2)(C)-(G)	336(a)(1)	312(m)	413(c)(5)
168(k)(2)(E)(iii)(II)	337(a)	332(d)	893(a)
168(k)(4)(A)(ii)	336(b)(2)	334(b)(1)	836(b)
168(k)(4)(B)(iii)	336(b)(3)	338(h)(13)	839(a)
168(k)(4)(C)	336(b)(4)	351(g)(3)(A)	899(a)
168(k)(4)(D)	336(b)(5)	357(c)(1)(B)	898(b)
170(e)(1)(B)(i)-(iii)	882(a)	361(b)(3)	898(a)
170(f)(10)(A)	413(c)(30)	362(e)	836(a)
170(f)(11)	883(a)	367(d)(2)(C)	406(a)
170(f)(11)(A)(ii)(I)	882(d)	382(l)(4)(B)(ii)	835(b)(2)
170(f)(12)	884(a)	409A	885(a)
170(m)-(n)	882(b)	420(c)(3)(E)	709(b)(2)
170(n)-(o)	335(a)	420(c)(3)(E)(ii)	709(b)(1)
171(c)(2)	413(c)(2)(A)-(B)	421(b)	251(b)
179(b)-(d)	201	421(d)	905(a)
179(b)(6)	910(a)	423(c)	251(c)
179B	338(a)	443(e)(3)-(5)	413(c)(6)
181	244(a)	451(e)(3)	311(c)
194	322(c)(4)	451(i)	909(a)
194(b)	322(a)	453(f)(4)(B)	897(a)
194(b)(2)	322(c)(2)	465(c)(7)(B)(i)-(iii)	413(c)(7)
194(b)(3)-(4)	322(c)(1)	469(i)(3)(F)(iii)	102(d)(5)
194(c)(2)	322(b)	469(k)(4)	331(g)
194(c)(4)-(5)	322(c)(3)	470	848(a)
195(b)	902(a)(2)	501(c)(12)(C)	319(a)(1)
195(b)(1)	902(a)(1)	501(c)(12)(E)-(G)	319(a)(2)
196(c)(9)-(11)	302(c)(2)	501(c)(12)(H)	319(b)

¶25,005

Code Sec.	Act Sec.	Code Sec.	Act Sec.
508(d)	413(c)(30)	856(c)(7)	243(a)(1)
512(b)(18)	319(c)	856(c)(7)	243(f)(1)
512(b)(18)[(19)]	702(a)	856(d)(8)(A)	243(b)
512(e)(1)	233(d)	856(g)(1)	243(f)(3)(A)
514(b)(1)(C)-(E)	702(b)	856(g)(5)	243(f)(3)(B)
514(c)(6)	247(a)	856(m)	243(a)(2)
521(b)(7)	316(b)	857(b)(2)(E)	243(f)(4)
535(d)(2)	402(b)(1)	857(b)(3)(F)	418(b)
542(c)(5)	413(b)(1)(A)	857(b)(5)(A)(i)	243(e)
542(c)(7)	413(b)(1)(C)	857(b)(6)(D)-(F)	321(a)
542(c)(7)-(10)	413(b)(1)(B)	857(b)(7)(B)(ii)-(vii)	243(c)
542(c)(8)	413(b)(1)(D)	860(e)(2)-(4)	243(f)(5)
543(b)(1)(A)-(C)	413(c)(8)	860G(a)(1)	835(b)(5)(A)
551-558	413(a)(1)	860G(a)(3)	835(b)(5)(B)
562(b)(1)	413(c)(9)	860G(a)(3)	835(b)(7)
563(c)	413(c)(10)(A)	860G(a)(3)(A)(i)-(iii)	835(b)(8)(A)
563(c)	413(c)(10)(C)	860G(a)(3)(B)-(D)	835(b)(6)
563(c)-(d)	413(c)(10)(B)	860G(a)(7)(B)	835(b)(8)(B)
582(c)(1)	835(b)(3)	860H-860L	835(a)
613(a)	102(d)(6)	861(a)(1)(A)-(C)	410(a)
631(b)	315(a)	864(c)(4)(B)	894(a)
631(b)	315(b)(1)	864(d)(2)(A)-(C)	413(c)(12)
631(b)	315(b)(2)	864(d)(5)(A)(i)	403(b)(6)
704(c)(1)(A)-(C)	833(a)	864(e)(3)	101(b)(6)(A)-(B)
709(b)	902(c)(2)	864(e)(7)(B)	401(b)(1)
709(b)(1)-(3)	902(c)(1)	864(e)(7)(E)-(G)	401(b)(2)
734(a)	833(c)(1)	864(f)-(g)	401(a)
734(b)	833(c)(2)	871(i)(2)(D)	409(a)
734(d)	833(c)(3)	871(k)-(l)	411(a)(1)
734	833(c)(5)(A)	872(b)(5)-(8)	419(a)
734(e)	833(c)(4)	877(a)	804(a)(1)
743	833(b)(6)(A)	877(c)	804(a)(2)
743(a)	833(b)(1)	877(g)	804(c)
743(b)	833(b)(2)	881(b)	420(c)(1)
743(d)	833(b)(3)	881(b)(1)	420(c)(2)
743(e)	833(b)(4)(A)	881(b)(2)-(3)	420(a)
743(f)	833(b)(5)	881(e)-(f)	411(a)(2)
751(d)(2)-(4)	413(c)(11)	883(a)(4)	419(b)
755(c)	834(a)	897(h)	411(c)(5)
815(g)	705(a)	897(h)(1)	411(c)(1)
845(a)	803(a)	897(h)(1)	418(a)
851(b)	331(b)	897(h)(2)-(3)	411(c)(2)
851(b)(2)	331(a)	897(h)(4)(A)-(B)	411(c)(3)
851(b)(3)(B)	331(f)	897(h)(4)(C)-(D)	411(c)(4)
851(c)(5)-(6)	331(c)	898(b)(1)(A)	413(c)(13)(A)
851(h)	331(d)	898(b)(2)(B)	413(c)(13)(B)
856(c)(5)(E)	835(b)(4)	898(b)(3)	413(c)(13)(C)
856(c)(5)(G)	243(d)	898(c)	413(c)(13)(D)
856(c)(6)(A)-(C)	243(f)(2)	901(b)(5)	405(b)

Code Sec.	Act Sec.	Code Sec.	Act Sec.
901(k)	832(b)	954(f)	415(a)(2)
901(l)-(m)	832(a)	954(h)(3)(E)	416(a)
902(c)(7)-(8)	405(a)	956(c)(2)	407(b)
903	101(b)(7)	956(c)(2)(A)	837(a)
904(c)	417(a)(1)-(2)	956(c)(2)(J)-(M)	407(a)
904(d)(1)	404(a)	957(c)	908(c)(5)(B)
904(d)(1)(E)	403(b)(1)	957(c)(2)(B)	908(c)(5)(A)
904(d)(2)(A)-(B)	404(b)	965	422(a)
904(d)(2)(A)(ii)	413(c)(14)	986(a)(1)(D)-(E)	408(a)
904(d)(2)(B)(iii)(I)-(III)	404(f)(1)	986(a)(1)(E)-(F)	408(b)(1)
904(d)(2)(B)(v)	404(c)	986(a)(2)	408(b)(2)
904(d)(2)(C)-(D)	404(d)	989(b)(3)	413(c)(17)
904(d)(2)(C)(iii)(I)-(III)	403(b)(2)	999(c)(1)	101(b)(8)
904(d)(2)(D)	403(b)(3)	1014(b)(5)	413(c)(18)
904(d)(2)(D)(i)(I)-(III)	404(f)(2)	1016(a)(13)	413(c)(19)
904(d)(2)(D)(iii)	404(f)(3)	1016(a)(27)-(29)	245(c)(2)
904(d)(2)(E)(i)	403(b)(4)(A)	1016(a)(28)-(30)	338(b)(4)
904(d)(2)(E)(ii)-(iv)	403(b)(4)(B)	1016(a)(29)-(31)	339(d)
904(d)(2)(H)-(J)	404(e)	1033(e)	311(b)(1)-(2)
904(d)(2)(K)	404(f)(5)	1033(f)	311(a)(1)-(3)
904(d)(3)	404(f)(4)	1056	886(b)(1)(A)
904(d)(3)(F)	403(b)(5)	1092(a)(2)(A)	888(a)(1)
904(d)(4)	403(a)	1092(a)(2)(B)	888(a)(2)(B)
904(f)(3)(D)	895(a)	1092(a)(2)(B)(ii)	888(a)(2)(A)
904(g)-(l)	402(a)	1092(a)(3)(B)-(C)	888(a)(3)
904(h)(1)(A)(i)-(iii)	413(c)(15)(A)	1092(c)(2)(B)-(C)	888(a)(4)
904(h)(2)	413(c)(15)(B)	1092(d)(3)	888(c)(1)
904(j)(3)(A)(i)	404(f)(6)	1092(d)(8)	888(b)
907(f)(1)	417(b)(1)-(3)	1202(e)(4)(C)	835(b)(9)
931(d)	908(c)(1)	1212(a)(3)	413(c)(20)(A)
932	908(c)(2)	1223(10)-(17)	413(c)(21)
934(b)(4)	908(c)(3)	1245(a)(2)(C)	338(b)(5)
935(a)	908(c)(4)(A)	1245(a)(3)(C)	338(b)(5)
935(a)(1)	908(c)(4)(B)	1245(a)(4)	886(b)(2)
935(b)(1)(A)-(B)	908(c)(4)(C)(i)-(ii)	1246	413(a)(2)
935(b)(2)	908(c)(4)(D)	1247	413(a)(3)
936(a)(2)(A)	402(b)(2)	1248(d)(5)-(7)	413(c)(22)
937	908(a)	1253(e)	886(b)(3)
941-943	101(b)(1)	1258(d)(1)	888(c)(2)
951(c)-(f)	413(c)(16)	1260(c)(2)(H)-(J)	413(c)(23)
952(c)(1)(B)(iii)(I)-(VI)	415(c)(1)	1286(f)-(g)	831(a)
954(a)(4)	415(a)(1)	1291(b)(3)(F)	413(c)(24)(A)
954(b)(5)-(8)	415(c)(2)(A)-(C)	1291(e)	413(c)(24)(B)
954(c)(1)(C)(i)-(ii)	414(a)	1294(a)(2)	413(c)(25)
954(c)(1)(I)[(H)]	413(b)(2)	1301(a)	314(b)(1)
954(c)(2)(A)	415(b)	1301(b)(1)(A)(i)	314(b)(2)(A)
954(c)(2)(C)(i)	414(c)	1301(b)(1)(B)	314(b)(2)(B)
954(c)(4)	412(a)	1301(b)(4)	314(b)(3)
954(c)(5)	414(b)	1352-1359	248(a)

Code Sec.	Act Sec.	Code Sec.	Act Sec.
1361(b)(1)(A)	232(a)	4041(k)	301(c)(6)
1361(b)(3)(A)	239(a)	4041(m)(1)	853(d)(2)(E)
1361(c)(1)	231(a)	4042(b)(2)(C)	241(b)
1361(c)(2)(A)(vi)	233(a)	4053(8)	851(a)(1)
1361(c)(2)(B)(vi)	233(b)	4071(a)	869(a)
1361(d)(1)(A)-(C)	236(a)(1)-(3)	4071(c)	869(d)[(e)](1)
1361(e)(2)	234(a)(1)-(2)	4071(e)	869(d)[(e)](1)
1362(d)(3)(F)	237(a)	4072(a)-(e)	869(b)[(c)]
1362(f)	238(a)(5)	4072(b)(2)	851(c)(1)
1362(f)(1)	231(b)(1)	4072(c)-(d)	869(b)
1362(f)(1)	238(a)(1)	4073	869(c)[(d)]
1362(f)(1)(B)	231(b)(2)	4081(a)(1)(B)	860(a)(1)-(2)
1362(f)(1)(B)	238(a)(2)	4081(a)(2)(A)(ii)-(iv)	853(a)(1)
1362(f)(3)(A)	238(a)(3)	4081(a)(2)(C)	853(a)(2)
1362(f)(4)	238(a)(4)	4081(a)(3)	853(a)(3)(A)
1366(d)(2)	235(a)	4081(a)(4)	853(a)(4)
1381(c)	319(d)	4081(c)	301(c)(7)
1388(a)	312(a)	4082(a)(2)	854(a)
1388(k)	316(a)	4082(b)	851(d)(2)
1400E(g)	222(a)	4082(b)	853(a)(5)(B)(i)
1402(a)(14)-(16)	102(d)(7)	4082(b)(3)	857(a)
1441(c)(12)	411(a)(3)(A)	4082(d)(1)-(3)	853(a)(5)(B)(ii)
1442(a)	411(a)(3)(B)(i)-(ii)	4082(e)-(g)	853(a)(5)(A)
1442(c)	420(b)(1)-(2)	4082(f)	241(a)(2)(B)
1502	844(a)	4083(a)(2)	301(c)(8)
1563(a)(2)	900(a)	4083(a)(3)	870(a)
1563(f)(5)	900(b)	4083(b)-(d)	853(b)
2105(d)	411(b)	4083(d)(1)(A)(i)-(iii)	858(a)
2107(a)	804(a)(3)	4083(d)(3)	859(b)(1)(A)-(B)
2501(a)(3)-(5)	804(d)(1)	4091-4093	853(d)(1)
2501(a)(5)	804(d)(2)	4101(a)	853(d)(2)(F)
3121(a)(20)	320(b)(1)	4101(a)	861(a)(1)-(2)
3121(a)(20)-(22)	251(a)(1)(A)	4101(a)(1)	301(b)
3121(v)(2)(A)	802(c)(1)	4101(a)(2)-(3)	862(a)
3231(e)(5)	320(b)(2)	4101(d)	864(a)
3231(e)(12)	251(a)(2)	4103	853(d)(2)(F)
3306(b)(16)	320(b)(3)	4104	303(a)
3306(b)(17)-(19)	251(a)(3)	4105	866(a)
3401(a)	885(b)(2)	4132(a)(1)(I)-(M)	889(a)
3401(a)(19)	320(b)(4)	4132(a)(1)(N)	890(a)
4041(a)(1)	853(a)(6)(B)	4161(a)(3)-(4)	333(a)
4041(a)(1)(B)	853(a)(6)(A)	4161(b)(1)	332(a)
4041(a)(1)(C)(ii)(I)-(III)	241(a)(1)	4161(b)(2)	332(c)(1)-(2)
4041(b)(2)(B)	301(c)(5)	4161(b)(3)-(4)	332(b)
4041(c)	853(d)(2)(A)	4162(a)(8)-(10)	334(a)
4041(d)(2)	853(d)(2)(B)	4162(b)-(c)	334(b)
4041(d)(3)-(4)	241(a)(2)(A)	4221(a)	853(d)(2)(F)
4041(e)	853(d)(2)(C)	4481(c)(2)	867(a)(2)
4041(i)	853(d)(2)(D)	4481(c)(2)(A)	867(a)(1)

Code Sec.	Act Sec.	Code Sec.	Act Sec.
7408(a)-(d)	820(a)	7874	801(a)
7428(a)(1)	317(a)	9502(b)	853(d)(2)(O)
7433A	881(b)(1)	9502(b)(1)(B)-(D)	853(d)(2)(N)
7525(b)	813(a)	9503(b)	868(b)(1)
7528(c)	891(a)	9503(b)(1)	301(c)(11)
7701(a)(19)(C)(xi)	835(b)(10)(A)-(B)	9503(b)(1)	868(b)(2)
7701(a)(48)	852(a)	9503(b)(4)(C)-(F)	301(c)(12)(A)-(C)
7701(i)(2)(A)	835(b)(11)	9503(b)(5)-(6)	868(a)
7701(n)-(o)	804(b)	9503(c)(2)(A)	301(c)(13)
7704(d)(4)	331(e)	9508(b)(3)-(5)	853(d)(2)(P)
7809(a)	881(a)(2)(A)	9508(c)(2)(A)	853(d)(2)(Q)
7811(g)	881(c)		

¶ 25,010

Table of Amendments to Other Acts

American Jobs Creation Act of 2004

Amended Act Sec.	H.R. 4520 Sec.	Par. (¶)
IRS Restructuring and Reform Act of 1998 (P.L. 105-206)		
1203(e)	881(d)	7135
Revenue Reconciliation Act of 1993 (P.L. 103-66)		
13273	904(c)	7155
Consolidated Omnibus Budget Reconciliation Act of 1985 (P.L. 99-272)		
13031(a)(5)(B)	892(d)(1)	7150
13031(b)	892(d)(2)	7150
13031(e)(2)	892(d)(3)	7150
13031(f)(1)-(2)	892(a)(1)-(2)	7150
13031(f)(3)(E)	892(b)	7150
13031(j)(3)	892(c)(2)	7150
Employee Retirement Income Security Act of 1974 (P.L. 93-406)		
101(e)(3)	709(a)(1)	7070

Amended Act Sec.	H.R. 4520 Sec.	Par. (¶)
403(c)(1)	709(a)(2)	7070
408(b)(13)	709(a)(3)	7070
Social Security Act		
209(a)(17)	320(b)(5)	7021
209(a)(17)-(19)	251(a)(1)(B)	7018
1903(a)(3)(D)-(E)	712(b)(1)-(2)	7075
1905(a)(26)-(28)	712(a)(1)(A)	7075
1905(x)	712(a)(1)(B)	7075
Title 31 U.S.C.		
330(b)	822(a)(1)	7105
330(d)	822(b)	7105
5321(a)(5)	821(a)	7100
Harmonized Tariff Schedule of the U.S.		
9902.84.02	714(a)	7085
9902.84.03	714(b)	7085
9902.84.14	713(a)	7080

¶ 25,015

Table of Act Sections Not Amending Internal Revenue Code Sections

American Jobs Creation Act of 2004

¶ 25,020

Act Sections Amending Code Sections

American Jobs Creation Act of 2004

Act Sec.	Code Sec.	Act Sec.	Code Sec.
101(a)	114	238(a)(2)	1362(f)(1)(B)
101(b)(1)	941-943	238(a)(3)	1362(f)(3)(A)
101(b)(4)	56(g)(4)(B)(i)	238(a)(4)	1362(f)(4)
101(b)(5)(A)	275(a)(4)(A)-(C)	238(a)(5)	1362(f)
101(b)(5)(B)	275(a)	239(a)	1361(b)(3)(A)
101(b)(6)(A)-(B)	864(e)(3)	240(a)	4975(f)(7)
101(b)(7)	903	241(a)(1)	4041(a)(1)(C)(ii)(I)-(III)
101(b)(8)	999(c)(1)	241(a)(2)(A)	4041(d)(3)-(4)
102(a)	199	241(a)(2)(B)	4082(f)
102(b)	56(g)(4)(C)(v)	241(a)(2)(C)	6421(f)(3)(B)
102(d)(1)	86(b)(2)(A)	241(a)(2)(D)	6427(l)(3)(B)
102(d)(1)	135(c)(4)(A)	241(b)	4042(b)(2)(C)
102(d)(1)	137(b)(3)(A)	242(a)	167(g)(7)
102(d)(1)	219(g)(3)(A)(ii)	242(b)	167(g)(5)(E)-(G)
102(d)(2)	221(b)(2)(C)(i)	243(a)(1)	856(c)(7)
102(d)(3)	222(b)(2)(C)(i)	243(a)(2)	856(m)
102(d)(4)	246(b)(1)	243(b)	856(d)(8)(A)
102(d)(5)	469(i)(3)(F)(iii)	243(c)	857(b)(7)(B)(ii)-(vii)
102(d)(6)	613(a)	243(d)	856(c)(5)(G)
102(d)(7)	1402(a)(14)-(16)	243(e)	857(b)(5)(A)(i)
201	179(b)-(d)	243(f)(1)	856(c)(7)
211(a)	168(e)(3)(E)(ii)-(v)	243(f)(2)	856(c)(6)(A)-(C)
211(b)	168(e)(6)	243(f)(3)(A)	856(g)(1)
211(c)	168(e)(7)	243(f)(3)(B)	856(g)(5)
211(d)(1)	168(b)(3)(G)-(H)	243(f)(4)	857(b)(2)(E)
211(d)(2)	168(b)(2)(A)	243(f)(5)	860(e)(2)-(4)
211(e)	168(g)(3)(B)	244(a)	181
221(a)	45D(e)(2)	245(a)	45G
221(b)	45D(e)(4)	245(b)(1)	39(d)
222(a)	1400E(g)	245(c)(1)	38(b)(14)-(16)
223(a)	45D(e)(5)	245(c)(2)	1016(a)(27)-(29)
231(a)	1361(c)(1)	246(a)	5148-5149
231(b)(1)	1362(f)(1)	246(b)	5117(d)
231(b)(2)	1362(f)(1)(B)	247(a)	514(c)(6)
232(a)	1361(b)(1)(A)	248(a)	1352-1359
233(a)	1361(c)(2)(A)(vi)	248(b)(1)	56(g)(4)(B)(i)
233(b)	1361(c)(2)(B)(vi)	251(a)(1)(A)	3121(a)(20)-(22)
233(c)	4975(d)(14)-(16)	251(a)(2)	3231(e)(12)
233(d)	512(e)(1)	251(a)(3)	3306(b)(17)-(19)
234(a)(1)-(2)	1361(e)(2)	251(b)	421(b)
235(a)	1366(d)(2)	251(c)	423(c)
236(a)(1)-(3)	1361(d)(1)(A)-(C)	301(a)	6426
237(a)	1362(d)(3)(F)	301(b)	4101(a)(1)
238(a)(1)	1362(f)(1)	301(c)(1)	40(c)

Act Sec.	Code Sec.	Act Sec.	Code Sec.
415(a)(1)	954(a)(4)	711(b)	38(c)(2)(A)(ii)(II)
415(a)(2)	954(f)	711(b)	38(c)(3)(A)(ii)(II)
415(b)	954(c)(2)(A)	801(a)	7874
415(c)(1)	952(c)(1)(B)(iii)(I)-(VI)	802(a)	4985
415(c)(2)(A)-(C)	954(b)(5)-(8)	802(b)(1)	275(a)(6)
416(a)	954(h)(3)(E)	802(b)(2)	162(m)(4)(G)
417(a)(1)-(2)	904(c)	802(c)(1)	3121(v)(2)(A)
417(b)(1)-(3)	907(f)(1)	803(a)	845(a)
418(a)	897(h)(1)	804(a)(1)	877(a)
418(b)	857(b)(3)(F)	804(a)(2)	877(c)
419(a)	872(b)(5)-(8)	804(a)(3)	2107(a)
419(b)	883(a)(4)	804(b)	7701(n)-(o)
420(a)	881(b)(2)-(3)	804(c)	877(g)
420(b)(1)-(2)	1442(c)	804(d)(1)	2501(a)(3)-(5)
420(c)(1)	881(b)	804(d)(2)	2501(a)(5)
420(c)(2)	881(b)(1)	804(e)(1)	6039G(a)
421(a)(1)	59(a)(2)-(4)	804(e)(2)	6039G(b)
421(a)(2)	53(d)(1)(B)(i)(II)	804(e)(3)	6039G(d)
422(a)	965	804(e)(4)	6039G(c)-(g)
422(b)	56(g)(4)(C)(vi)	805(a)	6043A
501(a)	164(b)(5)	805(b)(1)	6724(d)(1)(B)(ii)-(xix)
701(a)	142(a)(12)-(14)	805(b)(2)	6724(d)(2)(F)-(CC)
701(b)	142(l)	811(a)	6707A
701(c)(1)-(2)	146(g)(3)	812(a)	6662A
702(a)	512(b)(18)[(19)]	812(b)	6662(d)(2)(A)
702(b)	514(b)(1)(C)-(E)	812(c)(1)	6664(d)
703(a)	62(a)(19)[(20)]	812(c)(2)(A)	6664(c)(1)
703(b)	62(e)	812(c)(2)(B)	6664(c)
704(a)	168(e)(3)(C)(ii)-(iii)	812(d)	6662(d)(2)(C)
704(b)	168(i)(15)	812(e)(1)	6662
705(a)	815(g)	813(a)	7525(b)
706(a)	168(e)(3)(C)(ii)-(iv)	814(a)	6501(c)(10)
706(b)	168(i)(16)	815(a)	6111
706(c)	168(g)(3)(B)	815(b)(2)	6112
707(a)	43(c)(1)(D)	815(b)(3)(A)	6112(b)-(c)
707(b)	43(c)(5)	815(b)(3)(B)	6112(b)(1)
709(b)(1)	420(c)(3)(E)(ii)	815(b)(3)(C)	6112(b)(2)
709(b)(2)	420(c)(3)(E)	815(b)(5)(A)	6708
710(a)	45(c)	816(a)	6707
710(b)(1)	45(d)-(e)	817(a)	6708(a)
710(b)(2)	45(e)(8)	818(a)	6700(a)
710(b)(3)(A)	45(e)(7)(A)(i)	819(a)	6662(d)(1)(B)
710(b)(3)(B)	45	819(b)(1)	6662(d)(3)
710(b)(3)(C)	45(b)(2)	819(b)(2)	6662(d)(2)(D)
710(c)	45(b)(4)	820(a)	7408(a)-(d)
710(d)	45(e)(9)	820(b)(1)	7408
710(e)	48(a)(3)	831(a)	1286(f)-(g)
710(f)(1)-(2)	45(b)(3)	831(b)	305(e)(7)
711(a)	38(c)(4)-(5)	832(a)	901(l)-(m)

Act Sec.	Code Sec.	Act Sec.	Code Sec.
832(b)	901(k)	847(b)(3)	197(f)(10)
833(a)	704(c)(1)(A)-(C)	847(c)	168(i)(3)(A)(i)-(iii)
833(b)(1)	743(a)	847(d)	168(h)(3)(A)
833(b)(2)	743(b)	847(e)	168(h)(2)(A)
833(b)(3)	743(d)	848(a)	470
833(b)(4)(A)	743(e)	851(a)(1)	4053(8)
833(b)(4)(B)	6031(f)	851(b)(1)	4483(g)-(h)
833(b)(5)	743(f)	851(c)(1)	4072(b)(2)
833(b)(6)(A)	743	851(d)(1)	6421(e)(2)(C)
833(c)(1)	734(a)	851(d)(2)	4082(b)
833(c)(2)	734(b)	851(d)(3)	6427(i)(2)(C)
833(c)(3)	734(d)	852(a)	7701(a)(48)
833(c)(4)	734(e)	853(a)(1)	4081(a)(2)(A)(ii)-(iv)
833(c)(5)(A)	734	853(a)(2)	4081(a)(2)(C)
834(a)	755(c)	853(a)(3)(A)	4081(a)(3)
835(a)	860H-860L	853(a)(4)	4081(a)(4)
835(b)(1)	56(g)(6)	853(a)(5)(A)	4082(e)-(g)
835(b)(2)	382(l)(4)(B)(ii)	853(a)(5)(B)(i)	4082(b)
835(b)(3)	582(c)(1)	853(a)(5)(B)(ii)	4082(d)(1)-(3)
835(b)(4)	856(c)(5)(E)	853(a)(6)(A)	4041(a)(1)(B)
835(b)(5)(A)	860G(a)(1)	853(a)(6)(B)	4041(a)(1)
835(b)(5)(B)	860G(a)(3)	853(b)	4083(b)-(d)
835(b)(6)	860G(a)(3)(B)-(D)	853(c)(1)	6427(l)(4)
835(b)(7)	860G(a)(3)	853(c)(2)(A)-(B)	6427(i)(4)(A)
835(b)(8)(A)	860G(a)(3)(A)(i)-(iii)	853(c)(3)	6427(l)(2)(B)
835(b)(8)(B)	860G(a)(7)(B)	853(d)(1)	4091-4093
835(b)(9)	1202(e)(4)(C)	853(d)(2)(A)	4041(c)
835(b)(10)(A)-(B)	7701(a)(19)(C)(xi)	853(d)(2)(B)	4041(d)(2)
835(b)(11)	7701(i)(2)(A)	853(d)(2)(C)	4041(e)
836(a)	362(e)	853(d)(2)(D)	4041(i)
836(b)	334(b)(1)	853(d)(2)(E)	4041(m)(1)
837(a)	956(c)(2)(A)	853(d)(2)(F)	4101(a)
838(a)	163(m)-(n)	853(d)(2)(F)	4103
839(a)	338(h)(13)	853(d)(2)(F)	4221(a)
840(a)	121(d)(10)[(11)]	853(d)(2)(F)	6206
841(a)	163(e)(3)(B)-(C)	853(d)(2)(G)	6416(b)(2)
841(b)(1)-(2)	267(a)(3)	853(d)(2)(H)	6416(b)(3)
842(a)	6603	853(d)(2)(I)	6416(d)
843(a)(1)(A)-(B)	6159(a)	853(d)(2)(J)	6427(j)(1)
843(a)(2)	6159(c)	853(d)(2)(K)(i)	6427(l)(1)
843(b)	6159(d)-(f)	853(d)(2)(K)(ii)	6427(l)(5)(B)
844(a)	1502	853(d)(2)(L)	6724(d)(1)(B)(xvi)-(xviii)
845(a)	163(l)(2)		
845(b)	163(l)(4)-(6)	853(d)(2)(M)	6724(d)(2)(X)-(BB)
845(c)	163(l)(5)-(7)	853(d)(2)(N)	9502(b)(1)(B)-(D)
845(d)	163(l)(3)	853(d)(2)(O)	9502(b)
847(a)	168(g)(3)(A)	853(d)(2)(P)	9508(b)(3)-(5)
847(b)(1)	167(f)(1)(C)	853(d)(2)(Q)	9508(c)(2)(A)
847(b)(2)	167(f)(2)	854(a)	4082(a)(2)

Act Sec.	Code Sec.	Act Sec.	Code Sec.
854(c)(1)	6715A	885(a)	409A
855(a)	6715(e)	885(b)(1)(A)	6051(a)(11)-(13)
856(a)	6715(a)(2)-(4)	885(b)(1)(B)	6051(a)
856(b)	6715(a)(3)	885(b)(2)	3401(a)
857(a)	4082(b)(3)	885(b)(3)	6041(g)
857(b)	6427(b)(4)	886(a)	197(e)(6)-(8)
857(c)	6427(i)(4)(A)	886(b)(1)(A)	1056
858(a)	4083(d)(1)(A)(i)-(iii)	886(b)(2)	1245(a)(4)
859(a)	6717	886(b)(3)	1253(e)
859(b)(1)(A)-(B)	4083(d)(3)	887(a)	6331(h)(3)
860(a)(1)-(2)	4081(a)(1)(B)	888(a)(1)	1092(a)(2)(A)
861(a)(1)-(2)	4101(a)	888(a)(2)(A)	1092(a)(2)(B)(ii)
861(b)(1)	6718	888(a)(2)(B)	1092(a)(2)(B)
862(a)	4101(a)(2)-(3)	888(a)(3)	1092(a)(3)(B)-(C)
862(b)	6718(a)	888(a)(4)	1092(c)(2)(B)-(C)
863(a)	7272(a)	888(b)	1092(d)(8)
863(b)	7232	888(c)(1)	1092(d)(3)
863(c)(1)	6719	888(c)(2)	1258(d)(1)
863(d)(1)	6725	888(d)	246(c)
864(a)	4101(d)	889(a)	4132(a)(1)(I)-(M)
865(a)	6416(a)(4)	890(a)	4132(a)(1)(N)
866(a)	4105	891(a)	7528(c)
867(a)(1)	4481(c)(2)(A)	893(a)	332(d)
867(a)(2)	4481(c)(2)	894(a)	864(c)(4)(B)
867(b)(1)	6156	895(a)	904(f)(3)(D)
867(c)	4481(e)-(f)	896(a)	108(e)(8)
867(d)	4483(f)	897(a)	453(f)(4)(B)
868(a)	9503(b)(5)-(6)	898(a)	361(b)(3)
868(b)(1)	9503(b)	898(b)	357(c)(1)(B)
868(b)(2)	9503(b)(1)	899(a)	351(g)(3)(A)
869(a)	4071(a)	900(a)	1563(a)(2)
869(b)	4072(c)-(d)	900(b)	1563(f)(5)
869(b)[(c)]	4072(a)-(e)	901(a)	168(e)(3)(E)(iv)-(vi)
869(c)[(d)]	4073	901(b)	168(e)(3)(F)
869(d)[(e)](1)	4071(c)	901(c)	168(g)(3)(B)
869(d)[(e)](1)	4071(e)	902(a)(1)	195(b)(1)
870(a)	4083(a)(3)	902(a)(2)	195(b)
870(b)	6427(h)	902(b)	248(a)
881(a)(1)	6306	902(c)(1)	709(b)(1)-(3)
881(a)(2)(A)	7809(a)	902(c)(2)	709(b)
881(b)(1)	7433A	903(a)	6404(g)
881(c)	7811(g)	903(b)	6404(g)(2)(C)-(E)
882(a)	170(e)(1)(B)(i)-(iii)	903(c)	6404(g)(2)(D)-(F)
882(b)	170(m)-(n)	905(a)	421(d)
882(c)(1)	6050L	906(a)	72(w)-(x)
882(d)	170(f)(11)(A)(ii)(I)	906(b)	83(c)(4)
883(a)	170(f)(11)	907(a)	274(e)(2)
884(a)	170(f)(12)	908(a)	937
884(b)(1)	6720	908(b)(1)-(2)	6688

Act Sec.	Code Sec.	Act Sec.	Code Sec.
908(c)(1)	931(d)	908(c)(4)(D)	935(b)(2)
908(c)(2)	932	908(c)(5)(A)	957(c)(2)(B)
908(c)(3)	934(b)(4)	908(c)(5)(B)	957(c)
908(c)(4)(A)	935(a)	909(a)	451(i)
908(c)(4)(B)	935(a)(1)	910(a)	179(b)(6)
908(c)(4)(C)(i)-(ii)	935(b)(1)(A)-(B)		

INDEX

References are to explanation paragraph (¶) numbers.

ECO

Get the most complete resources available

Order your copies TODAY!

BY PHONE:
Call 1 800 248 3248
Priority Code: GCY3148

BY FAX:
1 800 224 8299

ONLINE:
Tax.CCHGroup.com

For the latest news on tax legislation developments, please visit
Tax.CCHGroup.com/specialreport